"You have the most exhaustive textbook on the planet! I have read your PC repair books from the 6th edition to the present."

GENE FOWLER
Deputy Director
St. John's Recreation Center
Corona, NY

"This book is worth its weight in gold."

PAUL CULLEN
University of Texas at Austin
Graduate School of Business, MBA 2001

"Wow! Fantastic reference! I'm studying for the A+ exams and found Scott's book to be the most comprehensive and reliable source of info."

CRAIG WIGLEY, A+, MCP
Ann Arbor, MI

"I have been using Scott Mueller's *Upgrading and Repairing PCs* since the 4th edition (1994). The 12th edition simply carries on its tradition of excellence."

MICHAEL J. D'SILVA
Computer Service Technician and Consultant
DMD Technical Solutions P/L
Australia

"When this treasure trove is not in use (hardly) it occupies a place of honour on my shelves next to J.R.R. Tolkien's works. Technicians and geeks everywhere shall sing the praises."

ANDRÉ LEON PRETORIUS
Chief Support Technician
Dept. Water Affairs & Forestry
Pretoria, South Africa

"I am in the process of building my first of what I hope to be many computers and consider *Upgrading and Repairing PCs* to be my PC Bible."

WARREN LYSAGHT
Australia

"Your coverage, explanation and writing style are the best in the business. I have the 11th and 12th editions and would not part with them for twice the price I paid."

KEN DUGE, A+
Skidmore, Texas

UPGRADING AND REPAIRING PCS,

13th Edition

Scott Mueller

201 West 103rd Street,
Indianapolis, Indiana 46290

Contents at a Glance

Upgrading and Repairing PCs, 13th Edition

International Standard Book Number: 0-7897-2542-8

Library of Congress Catalog Card Number: 00-110466

Printed in the United States of America

First Printing: September 2001

03 02 01   4 3 2 1

Trademarks

Warning and Disclaimer

Associate Publisher
Greg Wiegand

Executive Editor
Rick Kughen

Acquisitions Editor
Rick Kughen

Development Editor
Todd Brakke

Managing Editor
Thomas F. Hayes

Project Editor
Tricia Sterling Liebig

Copy Editor
Megan Wade

Team Coordinator
Sharry Lee Gregory

Indexer
Erika Millen

Proofreader
Harvey Stanbrough

Technical Editors
Mark Soper
Mark Reddin
Karen Weinstein
Kent Easley
Jeff Sloan
Dan Rodemack

Software Development Specialist
Michael Hunter

Interior Designer
Anne Jones

Cover Designer
Anne Jones

Photography
John Freeland

Layout Technician
Mark Walchle

Reviewers
Jean F. Coppola
James F. Kelley
Josh Norem

Contents

4 Motherboards and Buses   193

10 Hard Disk Storage 569

11 Floppy Disk Storage 609

12 High-Capacity Removable Storage 635

13 Optical Storage   687

To Emerson:

"There's a difference between knowing the path…, and walking the path."
(Morpheus)

About the Author

Scott Mueller is president of Mueller Technical Research, an international research and corporate training firm. Since 1982, MTR has specialized in the industry's most in-depth, accurate, and effective corporate PC hardware and technical training seminars, maintaining a client list that includes Fortune 500 companies, the U.S. and foreign governments, major software and hardware corporations, as well as PC enthusiasts and entrepreneurs. His seminars have been presented to several thousands of PC support professionals throughout the world.

Scott has developed and presented training courses in all areas of PC hardware and software. He is an expert in PC hardware, operating systems, and data-recovery techniques. He currently spends about 20–25 weeks per year on the road teaching his seminars at several corporate clients. For more information about a custom PC hardware or data-recovery training seminar for your organization, contact Lynn at

Mueller Technical Research
21 Spring Lane
Barrington Hills, IL 60010-9009
(847) 854-6794
(847) 854-6795 Fax
Internet: scottmueller@compuserve.com
Web: http://www.upgradingandrepairingpcs.com
           http://www.m-tr.com

Scott has many popular books, articles, and course materials to his credit, including *Upgrading and Repairing PCs*, which has sold more than 2 million copies, making it by far the most popular PC hardware book on the market today.

If you have suggestions for the next version of the book, or any comments about the book in general, send them to Scott via email at scottmueller@compuserve.com or visit www.upgradingandrepairingpcs.com and click the Ask Scott button.

When he is not working on PC-related books or on the road teaching seminars, Scott can usually be found in the garage working on several projects. This year he continues to work on his customized '99 Harley FLHRCI Road King Classic with a 95ci Twin-Cam motor (see you in Sturgis <g>), as well as a modified 1998 5.9L Grand Cherokee (imagine a hotrod SUV).

Contributors and Technical Editors

Mark Edward Soper is president of Select Systems and Associates, Inc., a technical writing and training organization.

Mark has taught computer troubleshooting and other technical subjects to thousands of students from Maine to Hawaii since 1992. He is an A+ Certified hardware technician and a Microsoft Certified Professional. He has been writing technical documents since the mid-1980s and has contributed to several other Que books, including *Upgrading and Repairing PCs, 11th and 12th Editions; Upgrading and Repairing Networks, Second Edition; and Special Edition Using Microsoft Windows Millennium Edition*. Mark coauthored both the first and second editions of *Upgrading and Repairing PCs, Technician's Portable Reference* and *Upgrading and Repairing PCs: A+ Study Certification Guide, Second Edition*. He is the author of *The Complete Idiot's Guide to High-Speed Internet Connections* and coauthor of *TechTV's Upgrading Your PC*.

Mark has been writing for major computer magazines since 1990, with more than 125 articles in publications such as *SmartComputing, PCNovice, PCNovice Guides*, and the *PCNovice Learning Series*. His early work was published in *WordPerfect Magazine, The WordPerfectionist*, and *PCToday*. Many of Mark's articles are available in back issues or electronically via the World Wide Web at www.smartcomputing.com. Select Systems maintains a subject index of all Mark's articles at http://www.selectsystems.com.

Mark welcomes comments at mesoper@selectsystems.com.

Mark Reddin is president of Trinity Microsystems, Inc., a computer reseller and repair center in Indiana. He is a Microsoft Certified Systems Engineer (MCSE) and A+ Certified PC technician who has enjoyed using computers, as well as breaking and fixing them, since the days of the early Commodore and Atari machines. Mark still enjoys being involved with computers and networks at a hands-on level and can often be found in the trenches, configuring hardware and running cables. He has been involved with several Que publications, providing technical verification as well as development. You can reach him through the contacts page at www.trinitymicrosystems.com.

Jeff Sloan is the Dimension OEM BIOS development manager for Dell Computers. Prior to Dell, he worked at IBM PC Company for 15 years, the last 8 of which were spent in PS/2 BIOS development and the Problem Determination SWAT team. He has a bachelor of science degree in computer science from the University of Pittsburgh, 1979, and is currently working on a master of science degree in software engineering at Southwest Texas State. Jeff has tech edited numerous Que books.

Kent Easley is an assistant professor of computer information systems at Howard College in Big Spring, Texas. He teaches introductory computer science, networking, and programming. He is a Microsoft Certified Professional and supervises the Microsoft Authorized Academic Training Program (AATP) at Howard College. He has experience as a network administrator and as a systems librarian. Kent has tech edited numerous Que books. He can be reached by email at keasley@hc.cc.tx.us.

Karen Weinstein is an independent computer consultant living in North Potomac, Maryland. She has had more than a decade of experience in PC sales and support. Karen has a B.S. in business administration from the University of Maryland.

Acknowledgments

The 13th Edition continues the long tradition of making this the most accurate, in-depth, and up-to-date book of its kind on the market. Plus, by the title you can tell I'm not superstitious. <g> This new edition is the product of a great deal of additional research and development over the previous editions. Several people have helped me with both the research and production of this book. I would like to thank the following people:

First, a very special thanks to my wife and partner, Lynn. This book continues to be an incredible burden on both our business and family life, and apparently I can be slightly incorrigible after staying up all night writing. Who would've guessed?

I suppose it doesn't help that most of my all-night writing raves are fueled by a variety of possibly less than nutritious (but very tasty and loaded with temporary energy) food and beverage. In particular, this edition was fueled mainly by Starbucks coffee (by the 2lb. bag of course), Coke Classic (no Pepsi allowed—gotta have the burn!), and literally cases of Trolli Brite Crawler Eggs and Pearson's Salted NutRolls. Why, that covers the three major workaholic nerd/geek food groups right there: caffeine, sugar, and salt!

Thanks to Lisa Carlson of Mueller Technical Research for helping with product research and office management. She has fantastic organizational skills that have been a tremendous help in managing all of the information that comes into and goes out of this office.

I must give a special thanks to Rick Kughen at Que. Rick is the number one person responsible for taking what I submit and turning it into a finished book. His office is like a shrine to *Upgrading and Repairing PCs*, sporting a complete collection of every single edition since the first, along with enough PC parts, peripherals, and components to build several systems. His attention to detail is amazing, and he genuinely cares about both the book and my readers, often going far above and beyond the call of duty when it comes to customer service and support. Rick is also largely responsible for the excellent content we've included on the CD, especially the new video clips we shot for this edition. Rick, thanks so much for your dedication and hard work!

I'd also like to thank Todd Brakke as well as the numerous other editors, illustrators, designers, and technicians at Que who work so hard to complete the finished product and get this book out the door! They are a wonderful team that produces clearly the best computer books on the market. I am happy and proud to be associated with all the people at Que.

I would also like to say thanks to Mark Soper, who added expertise in areas that I might tend to neglect. Also thanks to all the technical editors who checked my work and questioned me at every turn, helping me to ensure the highest level of technical accuracy and coverage.

Thanks to all the readers who have emailed me with suggestions concerning this book; I welcome all your comments. A special thanks to Paul Reid, who has helped orchestrate online conferences on the Compuserve PC Hardware forum and who has been a long-time reader.

Finally, I would like to thank the thousands of people who have attended my seminars; you might not realize how much I learn from each of you and all your questions! Thanks also to those of you on the Internet and CompuServe forums with both questions and answers, from which I have also learned a great deal.

Tell Us What You Think!

As the reader of this book, *you* are our most important critic and commentator. We value your opinion and want to know what we're doing right, what we could do better, what areas you'd like to see us publish in, and any other words of wisdom you're willing to pass our way.

As an associate publisher for Que, I welcome your comments. You can fax, email, or write me directly to let me know what you did or didn't like about this book—as well as what we can do to make our books stronger.

Scott Mueller welcomes your technical questions. The best way to reach him with a question is via the "Ask Scott" section on the www.upgradingandrepairingpcs.com *Web site. Although he sometimes falls behind in getting to all the questions directly, he does his best to answer them all. Be sure to check the Frequently Asked Questions listed on the Web site before asking your question, as Scott might have already posted an answer.*

When you write, please be sure to include this book's title and author as well as your name and phone or fax number. I will carefully review your comments and share them with the author and editors who worked on the book.

Fax: 317-581-4666

Email: hardware@mcp.com

Mail: Greg Wiegand
Que Corporation
201 West 103rd Street
Indianapolis, IN 46290 USA

Editor's Note

Welcome to *Upgrading and Repairing PCs, 13th Edition*. The book you are holding isn't just another PC hardware book. It isn't a technical manual suited only for geeks with screwdrivers. This book is a way of life. Ask the buyers before you who have purchased more than two million copies of this book in its storied history. These readers have made this book far and away the most popular PC hardware book ever written and one of the best-selling computer books of all time. Those millions of readers will tell you that this book changed their lives, launched careers, resurrected dead PCs, and helped them achieve personal computing nirvana.

If you are new to the phenomenon that is *Upgrading and Repairing PCs*, it might be news to you that you are holding an industry classic. If you are a longtime reader of Scott's opus, this book is an old friend to you. Thank you for making this book the runaway success that it has become.

For every industry expert using this book, there are probably 10 teachers, students, auto mechanics, accountants, physicians, lawyers, and sales clerks who rely on this book to troubleshoot and upgrade their PCs. You don't have to be a computer guru to understand the material provided here. So long as you are armed with a desire to learn what goes on under the hood of your PC, this book will be your guide. I am living proof of this. I spent my collegiate and early professional years conjugating verbs, diagramming sentences, and arguing the merits of Shakespeare. Prior to editing this book for the first time, I didn't know the business end of a screwdriver from a torque wrench and most certainly had never ventured inside my PC, where there lived a rat's nest of cables and, and *things*. I learned PC repair and upgrading from Scott. Today, I'm as at home inside a PC as I am fixing sentences ending in prepositions and clipping participles that dangle.

Scott has taught thousands of people, just like you, in his live corporate seminars. This book is an extension of those classes and is used by Scott every day as he travels the country teaching PC hardware upgrading and repair. Every word, illustration, and photo has been painstakingly shaped and molded to help you and your PC coexist in harmony. Whether you are a corporate IT manager charged with maintaining hundreds of workstations or a sales clerk who would like to put a little spring back into your PC's step, this book is for you.

In this edition, you'll find hundreds of pages of new material covering the Intel Itanium and Pentium 4 processors, as well as AMD's Athlon and Duron. You'll find coverage of CD and DVD technology that will literally bring tears to your eyes. If you are an owner of a newer Dell PC, you'll learn about some things lurking in your PC that could spell disaster if you attempt to upgrade the motherboard. Speaking of disasters, Scott also has included a special troubleshooting index that points you to the sections in this mammoth book that can help you when you're sweating bullets trying to repair your beloved PC. Scott knows it's a little tough to dig through a book this size when fire is licking from the case vents or your PC looks as though it might sprout legs, skitter off the desk, and make a wild grab for the fireplace poker. When you're in trouble, this index will be just the ticket.

The CD contains 90 minutes of all-new video that was shot in a professional-grade studio in the Spring 2001. This video shows you how to build a PC from the ground up. Along the way, Scott tells you how each component works, and which tools you will need to do the job right. If you aren't one of the lucky few who get to attend one of Scott's seminars, think of the video as your way of learning from him in person.

Take a few minutes in whatever bookstore you are reading this and compare this book to Scott's competition. Get a cup of coffee and have a seat in the aisle. Flip through this book and see whether you come to the same conclusion that millions of readers before you have come to: *This is the book that could change my life.*

I'm betting that you will.

Rick Kughen
Executive Editor
Que

Introduction

Welcome to *Upgrading and Repairing PCs, 13th Edition*. More than just a minor revision, this new edition contains hundreds pages of new material, not to mention extensive updates to existing material. The PC industry is moving faster than ever, and this book is the most accurate, complete, in-depth, and up-to-date book of its type on the market today.

This book is for people who want to upgrade, repair, maintain, and troubleshoot computers or for those enthusiasts who want to know more about PC hardware. This book covers the full range of PC-compatible systems from the oldest 8-bit machines to the latest in high-end 64-bit Gigahertz-plus speed PC-based workstations. If you need to know about everything from the original PC to the latest in PC technology on the market today, this book and the accompanying information-packed CD is definitely for you.

This book covers state-of-the-art hardware and accessories that make the most modern personal computers easier, faster, and more productive to use. Hardware coverage includes all the Intel and Intel-compatible processors through the latest Itanium and Pentium 4 models, the Pentium III/Celeron, AMD Athlon and Duron CPU chips; new cache and main memory technology, such as RDRAM and DDR SDRAM; PCI and AGP local bus technology; CD-ROM/DVD drives, including recordable types; tape drives; sound boards; PC-card and Cardbus devices for laptops; IDE/ATA and SCSI interface devices; larger and faster hard drives; and new video adapter and display capabilities.

The comprehensive coverage of the Intel-compatible personal computer in this book has consistently won acclaim since debuting as the first book of its kind on the market in 1988. Now with the release of this 13th Edition, *Upgrading and Repairing PCs* continues its role as not only the best-selling book of its type, but also the most comprehensive and complete reference on even the most modern systems—those based on cutting-edge hardware and software. This book examines PCs in depth, outlines the differences among them, and presents options for configuring each system.

Sections of this book provide detailed information about each internal component of a personal computer system, from the processor to the keyboard and video display. This book examines the options available in modern, high-performance PC configurations and how to use them to your advantage; it focuses on much of the hardware and software available today, and specifies the optimum configurations for achieving maximum benefit for the time and money you spend.

New in the 13th Edition

Many of you who are reading this have purchased one or more of the previous editions. Based on your letters, emails, and other correspondence, I know that as much as you value each new edition, you want to know what new information I'm bringing you. So, here is a short list of the major improvements to this edition:

- This book contains hundreds of pages of deep and balanced coverage of new processors from Intel and AMD, including the long-awaited Pentium 4 and 64-bit Itanium processors. No other PC book on the shelf provides comprehensive coverage of the bevy of processors available from AMD and Intel—and no other PC book explains just exactly what you're up against when matching motherboards and RAM to these processors.

- Cutting-edge coverage of the Pentium 4—Intel's long-awaited Pentium 4 processor hit the shelves in 2000. I steer you through what promises to be the biggest—and most demanding—processor upgrade since the world shifted from 486 processors to the Pentium.

■ Own a Dell PC? Interested in not turning it into a charcoal briquette when installing a new power supply or motherboard? What you read here could prevent an untimely meltdown of your beloved PC!

■ Interested in turning your PC into a hot rod game machine? Want to rule the Internet Unreal community with an iron fist? Read my coverage of audio, video, and Internet connectivity for the lowdown on supercharging your PC.

■ Use the new troubleshooting index to track down pesky problems with everything from IRQ conflicts to audio quality. When your beloved PC is in trouble, head straight to this index for help—*fast.*

■ Many new, high-quality technical illustrations. I've really pushed the quality of the illustrations of this book. These new and revised illustrations provide more technical detail, helping you understand difficult topics or showing you exactly how to complete a task.

■ The CD contains 90 minutes of new, professional-grade video of me explaining the hands-on concepts discussed throughout the book, such as swapping out a motherboard, properly installing a processor, and installing hard drives. For somebody who has never opened up her system or disassembled a computer, these videos will be a lifesaver. These videos also will be extremely helpful for instructors who teach PC hardware upgrading and repair. I also show you how to identify your motherboard, processor, chipset, memory, connectors, and much more. Some of the latest hardware, including the Pentium 4, is featured. The videos, along with the new illustrations and photographs, will greatly enhance any classroom or seminar using this book.

■ Chapter 13, "Optical Storage," is completely rewritten to cover the latest in optical drive technology. Coverage of everything from the first CD-ROM drives to the latest DVD+RW (rewritable) drives has been added in great detail. This includes extensive coverage of the popular CD-RW format that seems to be replacing the floppy drive as the industry standard removable-media format. DVD coverage has been greatly extended, especially the new (and possibly confusing) DVD recordable and rewritable standards. The time for rewritable DVD is now, and with at least four different (and somewhat incompatible) recordable/rewritable DVD standards, you'll want to read this chapter thoroughly before making a purchase.

■ Chapter 7, "The IDE Interface," has extensive updates covering the latest breakthroughs in capacity and speed for ATA/IDE drives. There is coverage of the latest ATA-6 standard, as well as the new Serial-ATA, which is poised to dramatically change the connection between drives and motherboards.

■ Chapter 21, "Power Supply and Chassis/Case," has been extensively updated to cover the latest developments, including the new ATX12V standard for use with the new high-powered processors like the Pentium 4. Also included are several new figures and information on Power Factor Correction, which is included in many of the new supplies on the market. There is also a section detailing the problems with one very popular PC manufacturer and its use of nonstandard power supply wiring. You'll definitely want to read this before upgrading any of your systems.

■ More than 100 pages of new content covering the gamut of changes in the PC hardware industry, including:

  • Deep coverage of Intel and AMD processors, including Intel's Itanium and Pentium 4 processor as well as AMD's Athlon and Duron. I cover these critical changes in the CPU industry including 1GHz processors, new high speed 266MHz and 400MHz processor buses, and the evolution of 64-bit computing.

- RDRAM and SDRAM—A year ago, industry forecasters were betting the farm on RDRAM. Today, RDRAM still remains a somewhat expensive memory option that some say fails to significantly out-perform DDR SDRAM, which is far less expensive and is readily available. Both types are covered in detail.

- As the bevy of hot, new processors from Intel and AMD begin hitting the market, you'll need new, improved motherboards. I delve into these new motherboard architectures, including the 400MHz motherboard bus designed for the Pentium 4 processor, as well as the 266MHz bus used by the AMD Athlon. You'll also learn about new processor sockets, including Socket 423 for the Pentium 4.

- Want to supercharge your PC for hardcore game performance? I give you the inside scoop on today's hottest audio and 3D video cards that bring 3D gaming to a disturbing reality.

- High-speed Internet connectivity isn't just something you can have at the office anymore. I dig into the latest high-speed connectivity options—such as DSL, CATV (cable modems), ISDN, and DirecPC (satellite)—that will make your trusty 56Kbps modem pale in comparison.

Although these are the major changes to the core of the book, every chapter has seen substantial updates. If you thought the additions to the 12th Edition were incredible, you'll appreciate the further enhancements and additions to the new 13th Edition. It is the most comprehensive and complete edition since I wrote the first edition 13 years ago!

The 13th Edition includes more detailed troubleshooting advice that will help you track down problems with your memory, system resources, new drive installations, BIOS, I/O addresses, video and audio performance, modems, and much more.

I also focus on software problems, starting with the basics of how an operating system such as DOS or Windows works with your system hardware to start your system. You also learn how to troubleshoot and avoid problems involving system hardware, the operating system, and applications software.

This book is the result of years of research and development in the production of my PC hardware, operating system, and data recovery seminars. Since 1982, I have personally taught (and still teach) thousands of people about PC troubleshooting, upgrading, maintenance, repair, and data recovery. This book represents the culmination of many years of field experience and knowledge culled from the experiences of thousands of others. What originally started out as a simple course workbook has over the years grown into a complete reference on the subject. Now you can benefit from this experience and research.

Book Objectives

Upgrading and Repairing PCs focuses on several objectives. The primary objective is to help you learn how to maintain, upgrade, and repair your PC system. To that end, *Upgrading and Repairing PCs* helps you fully understand the family of computers that has grown from the original IBM PC, including all PC-compatible systems. This book discusses all areas of system improvement, such as motherboards, processors, memory, and even case and power-supply improvements. The book discusses proper system and component care, specifies the most failure-prone items in various PC systems, and tells you how to locate and identify a failing component. You'll learn about powerful diagnostics hardware and software that enable a system to help you determine the cause of a problem and how to repair it.

PCs are moving forward rapidly in power and capabilities. Processor performance increases with every new chip design. *Upgrading and Repairing PCs* helps you gain an understanding of all the processors used in PC-compatible computer systems.

This book covers the important differences between major system architectures from the original Industry Standard Architecture (ISA) to the latest in PCI and AGP systems. *Upgrading and Repairing PCs* covers each of these system architectures and their adapter boards to help you make decisions about which type of system you want to buy in the future, and to help you upgrade and troubleshoot such systems.

The amount of storage space available to modern PCs is increasing geometrically. *Upgrading and Repairing PCs* covers storage options ranging from larger, faster hard drives to state-of-the-art storage devices. In addition, it provides detailed information on upgrading and troubleshooting system RAM.

When you finish reading this book, you should have the knowledge to upgrade, troubleshoot, and repair almost all systems and components.

Is This Book for You?

Yes.

Upgrading and Repairing PCs is designed for people who want a thorough understanding of how their PC systems work. Each section fully explains common and not-so-common problems, what causes problems, and how to handle problems when they arise. You will gain an understanding of disk configuration and interfacing, for example, that can improve your diagnostics and troubleshooting skills. You'll develop a feel for what goes on in a system so you can rely on your own judgment and observations and not some table of canned troubleshooting steps.

Upgrading and Repairing PCs is written for people who will select, install, configure, maintain, and repair systems they or their companies use. To accomplish these tasks, you need a level of knowledge much higher than that of an average system user. You must know exactly which tool to use for a task and how to use the tool correctly. This book can help you achieve this level of knowledge.

Scott has taught millions of people to upgrade and build PCs. Some of his students are computer experts, and some are computer novices. But they all have one thing in common: They believe Scott's book changed their lives. Scott can teach anyone.

Chapter-by-Chapter Breakdown

This book is organized into chapters that cover the components of a PC system. A few chapters serve to introduce or expand in an area not specifically component related, but most parts in the PC have a dedicated chapter or section, which will aid you in finding the information you want. Also note that the index has been improved greatly over previous editions, which will further aid in finding information in a book of this size.

Chapters 1 and 2 of this book serve primarily as an introduction. Chapter 1, "Personal Computer Background," begins with an introduction to the development of the original IBM PC and PC-compatibles. This chapter incorporates some of the historical events that led to the development of the microprocessor and the PC. Chapter 2, "PC Components, Features, and System Design," provides information about the various types of systems you encounter and what separates one type of system from another, including the types of system buses that differentiate systems. Chapter 2 also provides an overview of the types of PC systems that help build a foundation of knowledge essential for the remainder of the book, and it offers some insight as to how the PC market is driven and where components and technologies are sourced.

Chapter 3, "Microprocessor Types and Specifications," includes detailed coverage of Itanium, Pentium 4, Pentium III, Pentium II, Celeron, Xeon, and earlier central processing unit (CPU) chips as well as Intel-compatible processors from AMD, including the Athlon, Duron, and K6 series; processors from Cyrix; and other vendors as well. The processor is one of the most important parts of a PC, and this book features more extensive and updated processor coverage than ever before. I dig deeply into the latest processor-upgrade socket and slot specifications, including expanded coverage of Socket 423 for the Pentium 4, Socket A for AMD Athlon and Duron processors, and Socket 370 (PGA370) for the FCPGA (Flip Chip Pin Grid Array) Pentium III and Celeron processors. Chapter 3 also includes new coverage of spotting overclocked processors. These are processors that have been modified by unscrupulous resellers to run faster than their rated speeds. These chips are then sold to the consumer as faster processors. I show you how to spot and avoid fakes.

Chapter 4, "Motherboards and Buses," covers the motherboard, chipsets, motherboard components, and system buses in detail. This chapter contains discussions of new motherboard designs, including the ATX, Micro-ATX, Flex-ATX, and NLX form factors. This new edition features the most accurate, detailed, and complete reference to PC motherboards that you will find anywhere. I also cover the latest chipsets for current processor families, including all new coverage of the Intel 800 series chipsets—such as the 810, 815, 820, 840, and 850—as well as complete coverage of the older 440 chipset family and the new chipsets from AMD, VIA, SiS, and ALI. This chapter also covers special bus architectures and devices, including high-speed Peripheral Component Interconnect (PCI), Accelerated Graphics Port (AGP), and the 266MHz and faster processor buses. A detailed reference comparing virtually all PC buses is included.

Chapter 5, "BIOS," has a detailed discussion of the system BIOS, including types, features, and upgrades. This has grown from a section of the book to a complete chapter, with more information on this subject than ever before. Also included is updated coverage of the BIOS, with detailed coverage of BIOS setup utilities, Flash upgradable BIOSes, and Plug and Play BIOS.

See the exhaustive list of BIOS codes and error messages included on the CD-ROM. They're all printable, so be sure to print the codes for your BIOS in case you need them later.

Chapter 6, "Memory," gives a detailed discussion of PC memory, including the latest in cache and main memory specifications. Next to the processor and motherboard, the system memory is one of the most important parts of a PC. Memory is also one of the most difficult things to understand because it is somewhat intangible and it's not always obvious how it works. This chapter has received extensive updates to make memory technology more understandable, as well as to cover the newest technologies on the market today. Coverage of cache memory has been updated to help you understand this difficult subject and know exactly how the various levels of cache in a modern PC function, interact, and affect system performance. In particular, new types of memory, including Double Data Rate SDRAM (DDR) and Rambus DRAM (RDRAM), are examined. Also discussed is increasing system memory capacity with SIMM, DIMM, DDR DIMM, and RIMM modules and increasing system reliability with ECC RAM.

Chapter 7, "The IDE Interface," provides a detailed discussion of ATA/IDE, including types and specifications. This covers the Ultra-ATA modes that allow 100MB/sec operation, as well as the new Serial ATA that is destined to replace the parallel ATA we have been using for the last 14 years.

Chapter 8, "The SCSI Interface," discusses SCSI, including the new higher-speed modes possible with SCSI-3. This chapter covers the new Low Voltage Differential signaling used by some of the higher-speed devices on the market, as well as the latest information on cables, terminators, and SCSI configurations. This chapter also includes the latest on UltraSCSI.

Chapter 9, "Magnetic Storage Principles," details the inner workings of magnetic storage devices such as disk and tape drives. Regardless of whether you understood electromagnetism in high school science, this chapter breaks down these difficult concepts and presents them in a way that will change the way you think about data and drives.

Chapter 10, "Hard Disk Storage," breaks down how data is stored to your drives and how it is retrieved when you double-click a file.

Chapter 11, "Floppy Disk Storage," takes an inside view of the venerable floppy disk drive. You learn how to properly connect these drives as well as how information is written to a floppy.

Chapter 12, "High-Capacity Removable Storage," covers removable storage drives, such as SuperDisk (LS-120), Iomega Zip, Jaz, and Click! drives, as well as provides all-new coverage of magnetic tape drives.

Chapter 13, "Optical Storage," covers optical drives and storage using CD and DVD technology, including CD recorders, rewritable CDs, and other optical technologies. This chapter includes detailed steps and advice for avoiding buffer underruns, creating bootable CDs, burning music CDs, and selecting the most reliable media. Extensive coverage of DVD has been added, including the new recordable and rewritable formats.

Chapter 14, "Physical Drive Installation and Configuration," covers how to install drives of all types in a PC system. You learn how to format and partition hard drives after they are installed.

Chapter 15, "Video Hardware," covers everything there is to know about video cards and displays. If you're a gamer or multimedia buff, you'll want to read about choosing the right 3D graphics accelerator. The leading technologies are compared, and I help you choose the right card. I also dig into flat-panel monitors and help you decide whether they're worth the investment.

Chapter 16, "Audio Hardware," covers sound and sound-related devices, including sound boards and speaker systems. I help you optimize your system's audio performance for gaming, listening to CDs, and recording and playing MP3 music files.

Chapter 17, "I/O Interfaces from Serial and Parallel to IEEE-1394 and USB," covers the standard serial and parallel ports still found in most systems, as well as newer technology such as USB and iLink (FireWire). I also cover USB 2.0, which is 40 times faster than the original USB specification!

Chapter 18, "Input Devices," covers keyboards, pointing devices, and game ports used to communicate with a PC. I also discuss wireless mice and keyboards.

Chapter 19, "Internet Connectivity," compares high-speed connectivity methods that have come to the home desktop, including DSL, CATV, and DirecPC.

Chapter 20, "Local Area Networking," has been heavily updated for this edition to cover setting up an Ethernet network in your home or small office. I show you how to install NICs, make your own Ethernet cables, and set up Windows networking services.

Chapter 21, "Power Supply and Chassis/Case," is a detailed investigation of the power supply, which still remains the primary cause for PC system problems and failures. Coverage of the new ATX12V standard has been added, as well as additional information on keeping your system cool.

Chapter 22, "Portable PCs," covers portable systems, including laptop and notebook systems. It also focuses on all the technology unique and peculiar to portable systems, such as mobile processors, display, battery, and other technologies.

Chapter 23, "Building or Upgrading Systems," is where I show you how to select the parts you'll need for your upgrade or to build a PC from scratch. Then, I walk you step by step through the process. This chapter is loaded with professional photos that help you follow along.

Chapter 24, "PC Diagnostics, Testing, and Maintenance," covers diagnostic and testing tools and procedures. This chapter also adds more information on general PC troubleshooting and problem determination. Here, I show you what the prepared PC technician has in his toolkit. I also show you a few tools you might have never seen or used before.

Chapter 25, "File Systems and Data Recovery," covers file systems and data recovery procedures. If you've ever wondered why you should upgrade from FAT16 to FAT32, you should read this chapter.

The 13th Edition CD-ROM

In addition to the sweeping changes in the printed book, I've also included a CD packed with useful video how-to and technical documentation that will make your job easier—whether you're upgrading your PC at home or managing a stable of PCs at the office:

■ **Scott Mueller on video!**—The video we made for the 12th Edition was so well received, he went back into the studio and taped 90 minutes of all-new video, showing you step-by-step upgrading and repairing procedures, such as memory and processor upgrades, motherboard swapping, and using the tools of the trade. I show you all the essentials skills you need to learn to build and maintain your own PCs. I cover the Pentium 4 extensively, showing the unique requirements for chassis and heatsinks the high-powered processors require. I also go through the steps in bringing a new system to life and troubleshooting one that seems dead.

■ **Hundreds of pages of legacy and technical documentation!**—Rather than eliminate outdated coverage, I've placed this valuable content (especially for PC repair technicians or support staff) in a printable PDF format. The Technical Reference section of the CD contains hundreds of pages of content from previous editions of the book.

■ **Searchable vendor database!**—This custom database contains hundreds of entries of contact information for the industry's leading manufacturers and vendors. It's like having my Rolodex on your computer. This database is fully searchable and printable.

■ **Searchable hard drive specifications!**—This custom database contains literally thousands of specs for nearly any hard drive in production and most any other drive you'll ever encounter. Need to know the number of cylinders or tracks for an antiquated Seagate drive? Chances are you'll find it here.

■ **Entire previous editions!**—Need to find a table from a previous edition? Looking for detailed coverage of legacy standards and system design? Look no further because I've also included four entire editions of the book on this CD—in printable format. See the CD for printable PDF versions of the 6th, 8th, 10th, 11th, and 12th editions.

■ **Printers and scanners coverage in printable PDF!**—This full-length chapter covers laser, ink jet, dye sublimation, thermal wax transfer, and dot matrix printers in detail, as well as scanners and PostScript technology.

Scott's Web Site— *upgradingandrepairingpcs.com*

Don't miss my book Web site at www.upgradingandrepairingpcs.com! Here, you'll find a cache of helpful material to go along with the book you're holding. I've loaded this site with tons of material, from video clips to monthly book updates. I use this spot to keep you updated throughout the year on major changes in the PC hardware industry. Each month, I write new articles covering new technologies released after this book was printed. These articles are archived so you can refer to them anytime.

I also use this site to post your reader questions and my answers. This Frequently Asked Questions (FAQ) is a tremendous resource because you benefit from the hundreds of reader emails I answer each month. Log on and post a question. I endeavor to answer each and every email personally.

You'll also find exclusive video clips available nowhere else!

I also use this site to tell you about some of the other fantastic *Upgrading and Repairing PCs* products I work on, including

- *Upgrading and Repairing PCs, A+ Certification Study Guide, Second Edition*
- *Upgrading and Repairing PCs, Technician's Portable Reference, Third Edition*
- *Upgrading and Repairing PCs, Academic Edition*
- *Upgrading and Repairing Networks, Third Edition*

Don't miss out on this valuable resource!

A Personal Note

When asked which was his favorite Corvette, Dave McLellan, former manager of the Corvette platform at General Motors, always said "Next year's model." Now with the new 13th Edition, next year's model has just become this year's model, until next year that is....

I believe this book is absolutely the best book of its kind on the market, and that is due in a large part to the extensive feedback I have received from both my seminar attendees and book readers. I am so grateful to everyone who has helped me with this book over the last 13 years as well as all the loyal readers who have been reading this book, many of you since the first edition came out. I have had personal contact with many thousands of you in the seminars I have been teaching since 1982, and I enjoy your comments and even your criticisms tremendously. Using this book in a teaching environment has been a major factor in its development. Some of you might be interested to know that I originally began writing this book in early 1985; back then it was self-published and used exclusively in my PC hardware seminars before being professionally published by Que in 1988. In one way or another, I have been writing and rewriting this book for more than 17 years! In the more than 13 years since it was professionally published, *Upgrading and Repairing PCs* has proven to be not only the first but also the most comprehensive and yet approachable and easy-to-understand book of its kind. With the new 13th Edition, it is even better than ever. Your comments, suggestions, and support have helped this book to become the best PC hardware book on the market. I look forward to hearing your comments after you see this exciting new edition.

Scott

CHAPTER 1

Personal Computer Background

Computer History—Before Personal Computers

Many discoveries and inventions have directly and indirectly contributed to the development of the personal computer as we know it today. Examining a few important developmental landmarks can help bring the entire picture into focus.

The first computers of any kind were simple calculators. Even these evolved from mechanical devices to electronic digital devices.

Timeline

The following is a timeline of some significant events in computer history. It is not meant to be complete, just a representation of some of the major landmarks in computer development:

1617   John Napier creates "Napier's Bones," wooden or ivory rods used for calculating.

1642   Blaise Pascal introduces the Pascaline digital adding machine.

1822   Charles Babbage conceives the Difference Engine and later the Analytical Engine, a true general-purpose computing machine.

1906   Lee De Forest patents the vacuum tube triode, used as an electronic switch in the first electronic computers.

1937   John V. Atanasoff begins work on the Atanasoff-Berry Computer (ABC), which would later be officially credited as the first electronic computer.

1943   Alan Turing develops the Colossus, a secret British code-breaking computer designed to decode German secret messages.

1945   John von Neumann writes "First Draft of a Report on the EDVAC," in which he outlines the architecture of the modern stored-program computer.

1946   ENIAC is introduced, an electronic computing machine built by John Mauchly and J. Presper Eckert.

1947   On December 23, William Shockley, Walter Brattain, and John Bardeen successfully test the point-contact transistor, setting off the semiconductor revolution.

1949   Maurice Wilkes assembles the EDSAC, the first practical stored-program computer, at Cambridge University.

1950   Engineering Research Associates of Minneapolis builds the ERA 1101, one of the first commercially produced computers.

1952   The UNIVAC I delivered to the U.S. Census Bureau is the first commercial computer to attract widespread public attention.

1953   IBM ships its first electronic computer, the 701.

1954   A silicon-based junction transistor, perfected by Gordon Teal of Texas Instruments, Inc., brings a tremendous reduction in costs.

1954   The IBM 650 magnetic drum calculator establishes itself as the first mass-produced computer, with the company selling 450 in one year.

1955   Bell Laboratories announces the first fully transistorized computer, TRADIC.

1956   MIT researchers build the TX-0, the first general-purpose, programmable computer built with transistors.

1956   The era of magnetic disk storage dawns with IBM's shipment of a 305 RAMAC to Zellerbach Paper in San Francisco.

1958   Jack Kilby creates the first integrated circuit at Texas Instruments to prove that resistors and capacitors could exist on the same piece of semiconductor material.

1959   IBM's 7000 series mainframes are the company's first transistorized computers.

1959   Robert Noyce's practical integrated circuit, invented at Fairchild Camera and Instrument Corp., allows printing of conducting channels directly on the silicon surface.

1960   Bell Labs designs its Dataphone, the first commercial modem, specifically for converting digital computer data to analog signals for transmission across its long-distance network.

1960   The precursor to the minicomputer, DEC's PDP-1, sells for $120,000.

1961   According to *Datamation* magazine, IBM has an 81.2-percent share of the computer market in 1961, the year in which it introduces the 1400 Series.

1964   CDC's 6600 supercomputer, designed by Seymour Cray, performs up to three million instructions per second—a processing speed three times faster than that of its closest competitor, the IBM Stretch.

1964   IBM announces System/360, a family of six mutually compatible computers and 40 peripherals that could work together.

1964   Online transaction processing makes its debut in IBM's SABRE reservation system, set up for American Airlines.

1965   Digital Equipment Corp. introduces the PDP-8, the first commercially successful minicomputer.

1966   Hewlett-Packard enters the general-purpose computer business with its HP-2115 for computation, offering a computational power formerly found only in much larger computers.

1970   Computer-to-computer communication expands when the Department of Defense establishes four nodes on the ARPAnet: two at University of California campuses (one at Santa Barbara and one at Los Angeles) and one each at SRI International and the University of Utah.

1971   A team at IBM's San Jose Laboratories invents the 8-inch floppy disk.

1971   The first advertisement for a microprocessor, the Intel 4004, appears in *Electronic News*.

1971   The Kenbak-1, one of the first personal computers, advertises for $750 in *Scientific American*.

1972   Hewlett-Packard announces the HP-35 as "a fast, extremely accurate electronic slide rule" with a solid-state memory similar to that of a computer.

1972   Intel's 8008 microprocessor makes its debut.

1972   Steve Wozniak builds his "blue box," a tone generator to make free phone calls.

1973   Robert Metcalfe devises the Ethernet method of network connection at the Xerox Palo Alto Research Center.

1973   The Micral is the earliest commercial, non-kit personal computer based on a microprocessor, the Intel 8008.

1973   The TV Typewriter, designed by Don Lancaster, provides the first display of alphanumeric information on an ordinary television set.

1974 Researchers at the Xerox Palo Alto Research Center design the Alto, the first work station with a built-in mouse for input.

1974 Scelbi advertises its 8H computer, the first commercially advertised U.S. computer based on a microprocessor, Intel's 8008.

1975 Telenet, the first commercial packet-switching network and civilian equivalent of ARPAnet, is born.

1975 The January edition of *Popular Electronics* features the Altair 8800, which is based on Intel's 8080 microprocessor, on its cover.

1975 The visual display module (VDM) prototype, designed by Lee Felsenstein, marks the first implementation of a memory-mapped alphanumeric video display for personal computers.

1976 Steve Wozniak designs the Apple I, a single-board computer.

1976 The 5 1/4-inch flexible disk drive and disk are introduced by Shugart Associates.

1976 The Cray I makes its name as the first commercially successful vector processor.

1977 Tandy Radio Shack introduces the TRS-80.

1977 Apple Computer introduces the Apple II.

1977 Commodore introduces the PET (Personal Electronic Transactor).

1978 The VAX 11/780 from Digital Equipment Corp. features the capability to address up to 4.3GB of virtual memory, providing hundreds of times the capacity of most minicomputers.

1979 Motorola introduces the 68000 microprocessor.

1980 John Shoch, at the Xerox Palo Alto Research Center, invents the computer "worm," a short program that searches a network for idle processors.

1980 Seagate Technology creates the first hard disk drive for microcomputers, the ST-506.

1980 The first optical data storage disk has 60 times the capacity of a 5 1/4-inch floppy disk.

1981 Xerox introduces the Star, the first personal computer with a graphical user interface (GUI).

1981 Adam Osborne completes the first portable computer, the Osborne I, which weighs 24 pounds and costs $1,795.

1981 IBM introduces its PC, igniting a fast growth of the personal computer market. The IBM PC is the grandfather of all modern PCs.

1981 Sony introduces and ships the first 3 1/2-inch floppy drives and disks.

1983 Apple introduces its Lisa, which incorporates a GUI very similar to that first introduced on the Xerox Star.

1983 Compaq Computer Corp. introduces its first PC clone that uses the same software as the IBM PC.

1984 Apple Computer launches the Macintosh, the first successful mouse-driven computer with a GUI, with a single $1.5 million commercial during the 1984 Super Bowl.

1984 IBM releases the PC-AT (PC Advanced Technology), three times faster than original PCs and based on the Intel 286 chip. The AT introduces the 16-bit ISA bus and is the computer all modern PCs are based on.

1985 Philips introduces the CD-ROM.

1986 Compaq announces the Deskpro 386, the first computer on the market to use what was then Intel's new 386 chip.

1987 IBM introduces its PS/2 machines, which make the 3 1/2-inch floppy disk drive and VGA video standard for PCs. The PS/2 also introduces the MicroChannel Architecture (MCA) bus, the first plug-and-play bus for PCs.

1988 Apple cofounder Steve Jobs, who left Apple to form his own company, unveils the NeXT.

1988 Compaq and other PC-clone makers develop Enhanced Industry Standard Architecture (EISA), which unlike MicroChannel retains backward-compatibility with the existing ISA bus.

1988 Robert Morris's worm floods the ARPAnet. The 23-year-old Morris, the son of a computer security expert for the National Security Agency, sends a nondestructive worm through the Internet, causing problems for about 6,000 of the 60,000 hosts linked to the network.

1989 Intel releases the 486 (P4) microprocessor, which contains more than one million transistors. Intel also introduces 486 motherboard chipsets.

1990 The World Wide Web (WWW) is born when Tim Berners-Lee, a researcher at CERN—the high-energy physics laboratory in Geneva—develops Hypertext Markup Language (HTML).

1993 Intel releases the Pentium (P5) processor. Intel shifts from numbers to names for its chips after it learns it's impossible to trademark a number. Intel also releases motherboard chipsets and for the first time complete motherboards as well.

1995 Intel releases the Pentium Pro processor, the first in the P6 processor family.

1995 Microsoft releases Windows 95, the first mainstream 32-bit operating system, in a huge rollout.

1997 Intel releases the Pentium II processor, essentially a Pentium Pro with MMX features added.

1997 AMD introduces the K6, which is compatible with the Intel P5 (Pentium).

1998 Microsoft releases Windows 98.

1998 Intel releases the Celeron, a low-cost version of the Pentium II processor with reduced L2 cache.

1999 Intel releases the Pentium III, essentially a Pentium II with SSE (Streaming SIMD Extensions) added.

1999 AMD introduces the Athlon.

2000 Microsoft releases Windows Me (Millennium Edition) and Windows 2000.

2000 Both Intel and AMD introduce processors running at 1GHz.

2000 AMD introduces the Duron, a low-cost Athlon with reduced L2 cache.

2000 Intel introduces the Pentium IV, the latest processor in the Intel Architecture 32-bit (IA-32) family.

2000 Intel releases the Itanium processor, their first 64-bit (IA-64) processor for PCs.

Mechanical Calculators

One of the earliest calculating devices on record is the abacus, which has been known and widely used for more than 2,000 years. The abacus is a simple wooden rack holding parallel rods on which beads are strung. When these beads are manipulated back and forth according to certain rules, several types of arithmetic operations can be performed.

Math with standard Arabic numbers found its way to Europe in the eighth and ninth centuries. In the early 1600s, a man named Charles Napier (the inventor of logarithms) developed a series of rods (later called Napier's Bones) that could be used to assist with numeric multiplication.

Blaise Pascal is normally credited with building the first digital calculating machine in 1642. It could perform the addition of numbers entered on dials and was intended to help his father, who was a tax collector. Then in 1671, Gottfried Wilhelm von Leibniz invented a calculator that was finally built in 1694. His calculating machine could not only add, but by successive adding and shifting, could also multiply.

In 1820, Charles Xavier Thomas developed the first commercially successful mechanical calculator that could not only add but also subtract, multiply, and divide. After that, a succession of ever improving mechanical calculators created by various other inventors followed.

The First Mechanical Computer

Charles Babbage, a mathematics professor in Cambridge, England, is considered by many to be the father of computers because of his two great inventions—each a different type of mechanical computing engine.

The Difference Engine, as he called it, was conceived in 1812 and solved polynomial equations by the method of differences. By 1822, he had built a small working model of his Difference Engine for demonstration purposes. With financial help from the British government, Babbage started construction of a full-scale model in 1823. It was intended to be steam-powered and fully automatic and would even print the resulting tables.

Babbage continued work on it for 10 years, but by 1833 he had lost interest because he now had an idea for an even better machine, something he described as a general-purpose, fully program-controlled, automatic mechanical digital computer. Babbage called his new machine an Analytical Engine. The plans for the Analytical Engine specified a parallel decimal computer operating on numbers (words) of 50 decimal digits and with a storage capacity (memory) of 1,000 such numbers. Built-in operations were to include everything that a modern general-purpose computer would need, even the all-important conditional function, which would allow instructions to be executed in an order depending on certain conditions, not just in numerical sequence. In modern computers, this conditional capability is manifested in the IF statement found in modern computer languages. The Analytical Engine was also intended to use punched cards, which would control or program the machine. The machine was to operate automatically by steam power and would require only one attendant.

The Analytical Engine is regarded as the first real predecessor to a modern computer because it had all the elements of what is considered a computer today. These included

- *An input device.* Using an idea similar to the looms used in textile mills at the time, a form of punched cards supplied the input.
- *A control unit.* A barrel-shaped section with many slats and studs was used to control or program the processor.
- *A processor (or calculator).* A computing engine containing hundreds of axles and thousands of gears about 10 feet tall.
- *Storage.* A unit containing more axles and gears that could hold 1,000 50-digit numbers.
- *An output device.* Plates designed to fit in a printing press, used to print the final results.

Alas, this potential first computer was never actually completed because of the problems in machining all the precision gears and mechanisms required. The tooling of the day was simply not good enough.

An interesting side note is that the punched card idea first proposed by Babbage finally came to fruition in 1890. That year a competition was held for a better method to tabulate the U.S. Census information, and Herman Hollerith—a Census Department employee—came up with the idea for punched cards. Without these cards, department employees had estimated the census data would take years to tabulate; with these cards they were able to finish in about six weeks. Hollerith went on to found the Tabulating Machine Company, which later became known as IBM.

IBM and other companies at the time developed a series of improved punch-card systems. These systems were constructed of electromechanical devices, such as relays and motors. Such systems included features to automatically feed in a specified number of cards from a "read-in" station; perform operations, such as addition, multiplication, and sorting; and feed out cards punched with results. These punched-card computing machines could process 50–250 cards per minute, with each card holding up to 80-digit numbers. The punched cards not only provided a means of input and output, but they also served as a form of memory storage. Punched-card machines did the bulk of the world's computing for more than 50 years and gave many of the early computer companies their starts.

Electronic Computers

A physicist named John V. Atanasoff (with associate Clifford Berry) is credited with creating the first true digital electronic computer during 1937–1942, while working at Iowa State University. The Atanasoff-Berry Computer (called the ABC) was the first to use modern digital switching techniques and vacuum tubes as switches, and it introduced the concepts of binary arithmetic and logic circuits. This was made legally official on October 19, 1973, when following a lengthy court trial, U.S. Federal Judge Earl R. Larson voided the ENIAC patent of Eckert and Mauchly and named Atanasoff as the inventor of the first electronic digital computer.

Military needs during World War II caused a great thrust forward in the evolution of computers. In 1943, Alan Turing completed a secret British code-breaking computer called Colossus, which was used to decode German secret messages. Unfortunately, Turing's work went largely uncredited because Colossus was kept secret until many years after the war.

Besides code-breaking, systems were needed to calculate weapons trajectory and other military functions. In 1946, John P. Eckert, John W. Mauchly, and their associates at the Moore School of Electrical Engineering at the University of Pennsylvania built the first large-scale electronic computer for the military. This machine became known as *ENIAC*, the *Electrical Numerical Integrator and Calculator*. It operated on 10-digit numbers and could multiply two such numbers at the rate of 300 products per second by finding the value of each product from a multiplication table stored in its memory. ENIAC was about 1,000 times faster than the previous generation of electromechanical relay computers.

ENIAC used about 18,000 vacuum tubes, occupied 1,800 square feet (167 square meters) of floor space, and consumed about 180,000 watts of electrical power. Punched cards served as the input and output; registers served as adders and also as quick-access read/write storage.

The executable instructions composing a given program were created via specified wiring and switches that controlled the flow of computations through the machine. As such, ENIAC had to be rewired and switched for each program to be run.

Although Eckert and Mauchly were originally given a patent for the electronic computer, it was later voided and the patent awarded to John Atanasoff for creating the Atanasoff-Berry Computer.

Earlier in 1945, the mathematician John von Neumann demonstrated that a computer could have a very simple, fixed physical structure and yet be capable of executing any kind of computation effectively by means of proper programmed control without the need for any changes in hardware. In other words, you could change the program without rewiring the system. The *stored-program technique*, as von Neumann's ideas are known, became fundamental for future generations of high-speed digital computers and has become universally adopted.

The first generation of modern programmed electronic computers to take advantage of these improvements appeared in 1947. This group of machines included EDVAC and UNIVAC, the first commercially available computers. These computers included, for the first time, the use of true random access memory (RAM) for storing parts of the program and data that is needed quickly. Typically, they were programmed directly in machine language, although by the mid-1950s progress had been made in several aspects of advanced programming. The standout of the era is the UNIVAC (Universal Automatic Computer), which was the first true general-purpose computer designed for both alphabetical and numerical uses. This made the UNIVAC a standard for business, not just science and the military.

Modern Computers

From UNIVAC to the present, computer evolution has moved very rapidly. The first-generation computers were known for using vacuum tubes in their construction. The generation to follow would use the much smaller and more efficient transistor.

From Tubes to Transistors

Any modern digital computer is largely a collection of electronic switches. These switches are used to represent and control the routing of data elements called *binary digits* (or *bits*). Because of the on or off nature of the binary information and signal routing used by the computer, an efficient electronic switch was required. The first electronic computers used vacuum tubes as switches, and although the tubes worked, they had many problems.

The type of tube used in early computers was called a *triode* and was invented by Lee De Forest in 1906. It consists of a cathode and a plate, separated by a control grid, suspended in a glass vacuum tube. The cathode is heated by a red-hot electric filament, which causes it to emit electrons that are attracted to the plate. The control grid in the middle can control this flow of electrons. By making it negative, the electrons are repelled back to the cathode; by making it positive, they are attracted toward the plate. Thus, by controlling the grid current, you can control the on/off output of the plate.

Unfortunately, the tube was inefficient as a switch. It consumed a great deal of electrical power and gave off enormous heat—a significant problem in the earlier systems. Primarily because of the heat they generated, tubes were notoriously unreliable—in larger systems, one failed every couple of hours or so.

The invention of the transistor, or semiconductor, was one of the most important developments leading to the personal computer revolution. The transistor was first invented in 1947, and announced in 1948, by Bell Laboratory engineers John Bardeen and Walter Brattain. Bell associate William Shockley invented the junction transistor a few months later, and all three jointly shared the Nobel Prize in Physics in 1956 for inventing the transistor. The transistor, which essentially functions as a solid-state electronic switch, replaced the less-suitable vacuum tube. Because the transistor was so much smaller and consumed significantly less power, a computer system built with transistors was also much smaller, faster, and more efficient than a computer system built with vacuum tubes.

Transistors are made primarily from the elements silicon and germanium, with certain impurities added. Depending on the impurities added—its electron content—the material becomes known as either N-Type (negative) or P-Type (positive). Both types are conductors, allowing electricity to flow in either direction. However, when the two types are joined, a barrier is formed where they meet that allows current to flow only in one direction when a voltage is present in the right polarity. This is why they are normally called semiconductors.

A transistor is made by placing two P-N junctions back to back. They are made by sandwiching a thin wafer of one type of semiconductor material between two wafers of the other type. If the wafer in between is made from P-type material, the transistor is designated a NPN. If the wafer in between is N-type, the transistor is designated PNP.

In an NPN transistor, the N-type semiconductor material on one side of the wafer is called the *emitter* and is normally connected to a negative current. The P-type material in the center is called the *base*. And the N-type material on the other side of the base is called the *collector*.

An NPN transistor compares to a triode tube such that the emitter is equivalent to the cathode, the base is equivalent to the grid, and the collector is equivalent to the plate. By controlling the current at the base, you can control the flow of current between the emitter and collector.

Compared to the tube, the transistor is much more efficient as a switch and can be miniaturized to microscopic scale. The latest Pentium II and III microprocessors consist of more than 27 million transistors on a single chip die!

The conversion from tubes to transistors began the trend toward miniaturization that continues to this day. Today's small laptop (or palmtop) PC systems, which run on batteries, have more computing power than many earlier systems that filled rooms and consumed huge amounts of electrical power.

Integrated Circuits

The third generation of modern computers is known for using integrated circuits instead of individual transistors. In 1959, engineers at Texas Instruments invented the *integrated circuit (IC)*, a semiconductor circuit that contains more than one transistor on the same base (or substrate material) and connects the transistors without wires. The first IC contained only six transistors. By comparison, the Intel Pentium Pro microprocessor used in many of today's high-end systems has more than 5.5 million transistors, and the integral cache built into some of these chips contains as many as an additional 32 million transistors! Today, many ICs have transistor counts in the multimillion range.

The First Microprocessor

In 1998, Intel celebrated its 30th anniversary. Intel was founded on July 18, 1968, by Robert Noyce, Gordon Moore, and Andrew Grove. They had a specific goal: to make semiconductor memory practical and affordable. This was not a given at the time, considering that silicon chip–based memory was at least 100 times more expensive than the magnetic core memory commonly used in those days. At the time, semiconductor memory was going for about a dollar a bit, whereas core memory was about a penny a bit. Noyce said, "All we had to do was reduce the cost by a factor of a hundred, then we'd have the market; and that's basically what we did."

By 1970, Intel was known as a successful memory chip company, having introduced a 1Kb memory chip much larger than anything else available at the time. (1Kb equals 1,024 bits, and a byte equals 8 bits. This chip, therefore, stored only 128 bytes—not much by today's standards.) Known as the 1103 dynamic random access memory (DRAM), it became the world's largest-selling semiconductor device by the end of the following year. By this time, Intel had also grown from the core founders and a handful of others to more than 100 employees.

Because of Intel's success in memory chip manufacturing and design, Japanese manufacturer Busicom asked Intel to design a set of chips for a family of high-performance programmable calculators. At the time, all logic chips were custom designed for each application or product. Because most chips had to be custom designed specific to a particular application, no one chip could have any widespread usage.

Busicom's original design for its calculator called for at least 12 custom chips. Intel engineer Ted Hoff rejected the unwieldy proposal and instead designed a single-chip, general-purpose logic device that retrieved its application instructions from semiconductor memory. As the core of a four-chip set, this central processing unit could be controlled by a program that could essentially tailor the function of the chip to the task at hand. The chip was generic in nature, meaning it could function in designs other than calculators. Previous designs were hard-wired for one purpose, with built-in instructions; this chip would read a variable set of instructions from memory, which would control the function of the chip. The idea was to design almost an entire computing device on a single chip that could perform various functions, depending on which instructions it was given.

There was one problem with the new chip: Busicom owned the rights to it. Hoff and others knew that the product had almost limitless application, bringing intelligence to a host of "dumb" machines. They urged Intel to repurchase the rights to the product. While Intel founders Gordon Moore and Robert Noyce championed the new chip, others within the company were concerned that the product would distract Intel from its main focus—making memory. They were finally convinced by the fact that every four-chip microcomputer set included two memory chips. As the director of marketing at the time recalled, "Originally, I think we saw it as a way to sell more memories, and we were willing to make the investment on that basis."

Intel offered to return Busicom's $60,000 investment in exchange for the rights to the product. Struggling with financial troubles, the Japanese company agreed. Nobody else in the industry at the time, even at Intel, realized the significance of this deal. Of course, it paved the way for Intel's future in processors. The result was the 1971 introduction of the 4-bit Intel 4004 microcomputer set (the term *microprocessor* was not coined until later). Smaller than a thumbnail and packing 2,300 transistors, the $200 chip delivered as much computing power as the first electronic computer, ENIAC. By comparison, ENIAC relied on 18,000 vacuum tubes packed into 3,000 cubic feet (85 cubic meters) when it was built in 1946. The 4004 executed 60,000 operations in one second, primitive by today's standards, but a major breakthrough at the time.

Intel introduced the 8008 microcomputer in 1972, which processed 8 bits of information at a time, twice as much as the original chip. By 1981, Intel's microprocessor family had grown to include the 16-bit 8086 and the 8-bit 8088 processors. These two chips garnered an unprecedented 2,500 design wins in a single year. Among those designs was a product from IBM that was to become the first PC.

In 1982, Intel introduced the 286 chip. With 134,000 transistors, it provided about three times the performance of other 16-bit processors of the time. Featuring on-chip memory management, the 286 was the first microprocessor that offered software compatibility with its predecessors. This revolutionary chip was first used in IBM's benchmark PC-AT.

In 1985 came the Intel386 processor. With a new 32-bit architecture and 275,000 transistors, the chip could perform more than 5 million instructions every second (MIPS). Compaq's DESKPRO 386 was the first PC based on the new microprocessor.

Next out of the block was the Intel486 processor in 1989. The 486 had 1.2 million transistors and the first built-in math coprocessor. It was some 50 times faster than the original 4004, equaling the performance of powerful mainframe computers.

Then, in 1993, Intel introduced the first Pentium processor, setting new performance standards with up to five times the performance of the Intel486 processor. The Pentium processor uses 3.1 million transistors to perform up to 90 MIPS—now up to about 1,500 times the speed of the original 4004.

The first processor in the P6 family, called the Pentium Pro processor, was introduced in 1995. With 5.5 million transistors, it was the first to be packaged with a second die containing high-speed memory cache to accelerate performance. Capable of performing up to 300 MIPS, the Pentium Pro continues to be a popular choice for multiprocessor servers and high-performance workstations.

Intel revised the original P6 (Pentium Pro) and introduced the Pentium II processor in May 1997. Pentium II processors had 7.5 million transistors packed into a cartridge rather than a conventional chip, allowing them to attach the L2 cache chips directly on the module. The Pentium II family was augmented in April 1998, with both the low-cost Celeron processor for basic PCs and the high-end

Pentium II Xeon processor for servers and workstations. Intel followed with the Pentium III in 1999, essentially a Pentium II with SSE (Streaming SIMD Extensions) added.

Around the time the Pentium was establishing its dominance, AMD acquired NexGen, who had been working on their Nx686 processor, and incorporated that design along with a Pentium interface into what would be called the AMD K6. The K6 was both hardware and software compatible with the Pentium, meaning it plugged into the same Socket 7 and could run the same programs. As Intel dropped their Pentium in favor of the Pentium II and III, AMD continued making faster versions of the K6 and made huge inroads in the low-end PC market.

AMD introduced the Athlon in 1999 to compete with Intel head to head in the high-end PC market. Athlon is very successful, and it seems for the first time Intel has real competition.

The year 2000 saw both companies introduce more new chips to the market. AMD premiered both their Athlon Thunderbird and Duron processors. The Duron is essentially an Athlon with a smaller L2 cache designed for lower-cost systems, whereas the Thunderbird uses a more integrated cache to ratchet up the Athlon's performance.

Intel introduced the Pentium IV in 2000, the latest processor in the Intel Architecture 32-bit (IA-32) family. They also announced the Itanium processor (code named Merced), which is the first IA-64 (Intel Architecture-64 bit) processor. Itanium is Intel's first processor with 64-bit instructions and will spawn a whole new category of operating systems and applications while still remaining backward-compatible with 32-bit software.

2000 also saw another significant milestone written into the history books when both Intel and AMD crossed the 1GHz barrier, a speed that many thought could never be accomplished.

▶▶ See "Itanium Processors," p. 187.

Personal Computer History

The fourth and current generation of the modern computer includes those that incorporate micro-processors in their designs. Of course, part of this fourth generation of computers is the personal computer, which itself was made possible by the advent of low-cost microprocessors and memory.

Birth of the Personal Computer

In 1973, some of the first microcomputer kits based on the 8008 chip were developed. These kits were little more than demonstration tools and didn't do much except blink lights. In late 1973, Intel introduced the 8080 microprocessor, which was 10 times faster than the earlier 8008 chip and addressed 64KB of memory. This was the breakthrough the personal computer industry had been waiting for.

A company called MITS introduced the Altair kit in a cover story in the January 1975 issue of *Popular Electronics*. The Altair kit, considered the first personal computer, included an 8080 processor, a power supply, a front panel with a large number of lights, and 256 bytes (not kilobytes) of memory. The kit sold for $395 and had to be assembled. Assembly back then meant you got out your soldering iron to actually finish the circuit boards, not like today where you can assemble a system of premade components with nothing more than a screwdriver.

The Altair included an open architecture system bus called the S-100 bus because it had 100 pins per slot. The open architecture meant that anybody could develop boards to fit in these slots and interface to the system. This prompted various add-ons and peripherals from numerous aftermarket companies. The new processor inspired software companies to write programs, including the CP/M (control program for microprocessors) operating system and the first version of the Microsoft BASIC (beginners all-purpose symbolic instruction code) programming language.

IBM introduced what can be called its first personal computer in 1975. The Model 5100 had 16KB of memory, a built-in 16-line–by–64-character display, a built-in BASIC language interpreter, and a built-in DC-300 cartridge tape drive for storage. The system's $9,000 price placed it out of the mainstream personal computer marketplace, which was dominated by experimenters (affectionately referred to as *hackers*) who built low-cost kits ($500 or so) as a hobby. Obviously, the IBM system was not in competition for this low-cost market and did not sell as well by comparison.

The Model 5100 was succeeded by the 5110 and 5120 before IBM introduced what we know as the IBM Personal Computer (Model 5150). Although the 5100 series preceded the IBM PC, the older systems and the 5150 IBM PC had nothing in common. The PC IBM turned out was more closely related to the IBM System/23 DataMaster, an office computer system introduced in 1980. In fact, many of the engineers who developed the IBM PC had originally worked on the DataMaster.

In 1976, a new company called Apple Computer introduced the Apple I, which originally sold for $666.66. The selling price was an arbitrary number selected by one of Apple's cofounders, Steve Jobs. This system consisted of a main circuit board screwed to a piece of plywood; a case and power supply were not included. Only a few of these computers were made, and they reportedly have sold to collectors for more than $20,000. The Apple II, introduced in 1977, helped set the standard for nearly all the important microcomputers to follow, including the IBM PC.

The microcomputer world was dominated in 1980 by two types of computer systems. One type, the Apple II, claimed a large following of loyal users and a gigantic software base that was growing at a fantastic rate. The other type, CP/M systems, consisted not of a single system but of all the many systems that evolved from the original MITS Altair. These systems were compatible with one another and were distinguished by their use of the CP/M operating system and expansion slots, which followed the S-100 standard. All these systems were built by a variety of companies and sold under various names. For the most part, however, these systems used the same software and plug-in hardware. It is interesting to note that none of these systems was PC compatible or Macintosh compatible, the two primary standards in place today.

A new competitor looming on the horizon was able to see that to be successful, a personal computer needed to have an open architecture, slots for expansion, a modular design, and healthy support from both hardware and software companies other than the original manufacturer of the system. This competitor turned out to be IBM, which was quite surprising at the time because IBM was not known for systems with these open-architecture attributes! IBM, in essence, became more like the early Apple, and Apple itself became like everybody expected IBM to be. The open architecture of the forthcoming IBM PC and the closed architecture of the forthcoming Macintosh caused a complete turnaround in the industry.

The IBM Personal Computer

At the end of 1980, IBM decided to truly compete in the rapidly growing low-cost personal computer market. The company established the Entry Systems Division, located in Boca Raton, Florida, to develop the new system. The division was located intentionally far away from IBM's main headquarters in New York, or any other IBM facilities, so that this new division would be able to operate independently as a separate unit. This small group consisted of 12 engineers and designers under the direction of Don Estridge, and was charged with developing IBM's first real PC. (IBM considered the previous 5100 system, developed in 1975, to be an intelligent programmable terminal rather than a genuine computer, even though it truly was a computer.) Nearly all these engineers had come to the new division from the System/23 DataMaster project, which was a small office computer system introduced in 1980 and was the direct predecessor of the IBM PC.

Much of the PC's design was influenced by the DataMaster design. In the DataMaster's single-piece design, the display and keyboard were integrated into the unit. Because these features were limiting, they became external units on the PC, although the PC keyboard layout and electrical designs were copied from the DataMaster.

Several other parts of the IBM PC system also were copied from the DataMaster, including the expansion bus (or input/output slots), which included not only the same physical 62-pin connector, but also almost identical pin specifications. This copying of the bus design was possible because the PC used the same interrupt controller as the DataMaster and a similar direct memory access (DMA) controller. Also, expansion cards already designed for the DataMaster could easily be redesigned to function in the PC.

The DataMaster used an Intel 8085 CPU, which had a 64KB address limit and an 8-bit internal and external data bus. This arrangement prompted the PC design team to use the Intel 8088 CPU, which offered a much larger (1MB) memory address limit and an internal 16-bit data bus, but only an 8-bit external data bus. The 8-bit external data bus and similar instruction set enabled the 8088 to be easily interfaced into the earlier DataMaster designs.

IBM brought its system from idea to delivery of functioning systems in one year by using existing designs and purchasing as many components as possible from outside vendors. The Entry Systems Division was granted autonomy from IBM's other divisions and could tap resources outside the company, rather than go through the bureaucratic procedures that required exclusive use of IBM resources. IBM contracted out the PC's languages and operating system to a small company named Microsoft. That decision was the major factor in establishing Microsoft as the dominant force in PC software today.

Note

It is interesting to note that IBM had originally contacted Digital Research (the company that created CP/M, then the most popular personal computer operating system) to have it develop an operating system for the new IBM PC. However, Digital was leery of working with IBM and especially balked at the nondisclosure agreement IBM wanted Digital to sign. Microsoft jumped on the opportunity left open by Digital Research and, consequently, has become one of the largest software companies in the world. IBM's use of outside vendors in developing the PC was an open invitation for the aftermarket to jump in and support the system—and it did.

On Wednesday, August 12, 1981, a new standard was established in the microcomputer industry with the debut of the IBM PC. Since then, hundreds of millions of PC-compatible systems have been sold, as the original PC has grown into an enormous family of computers and peripherals. More software has been written for this computer family than for any other system on the market.

The PC Industry 20 Years Later

In the more than 20 years since the original IBM PC was introduced, many changes have occurred. The IBM-compatible computer, for example, advanced from a 4.77MHz 8088-based system to 1.5GHz or faster Pentium IV-based systems—nearly 12,000 times faster than the original IBM PC (in actual processing speed, not just clock speed). The original PC had only one or two single-sided floppy drives that stored 160KB each using DOS 1.0, whereas modern systems easily can have 75GB (75 billion bytes) or more of hard disk storage.

A rule of thumb in the computer industry (called Moore's Law, originally set forth by Intel cofounder Gordon Moore) is that available processor performance and disk-storage capacity doubles every two years, give or take.

Since the beginning of the PC industry, this pattern has held steady, and if anything, it may be accelerating.

In addition to performance and storage capacity, another major change since the original IBM PC was introduced is that IBM is not the only manufacturer of PC-compatible systems. IBM originated the PC-compatible standard, of course, but today it no longer sets the standards for the system it originated. More often than not, new standards in the PC industry are developed by companies and organizations other than IBM. Today, it is Intel and Microsoft who are primarily responsible for developing and extending the PC hardware and software standards, respectively. Some have even taken to calling PCs "Wintel" systems, owing to the dominance of those two companies.

In more recent years, Intel and Microsoft have carried the evolution of the PC forward. The introduction of hardware standards such as the PCI (Peripheral Component Interconnect) bus, AGP (Accelerated Graphics Port) bus, ATX and NLX motherboard form factors, processor socket and slot interfaces, and numerous others show that Intel is really pushing PC hardware design these days. In a similar fashion, Microsoft is pushing the software side of things with the continual evolution of the Windows operating system as well as applications such as the Office suite.

Today literally hundreds of system manufacturers follow the collective PC standard and produce computers that are fully PC compatible. In addition, thousands of peripheral manufacturers produce components that expand and enhance PC-compatible systems.

PC-compatible systems have thrived not only because compatible hardware can be assembled easily, but also because the primary operating system was available not from IBM but from a third party (Microsoft). The core of the system software is the BIOS (basic input/output system), and this was also available from third-party companies, such as AMI, Award, Phoenix, and others. This situation enabled other manufacturers to license the operating system and BIOS software and to sell their own compatible systems. The fact that DOS borrowed the functionality and user interface from both CP/M and UNIX probably had a lot to do with the amount of software that became available. Later, with the success of Windows, even more reasons would exist for software developers to write programs for PC-compatible systems.

One reason Apple Macintosh systems never enjoyed the extreme success of PC systems is that Apple controls all the primary systems software (BIOS and OS) and has never licensed it to other companies for use in compatible systems.

At some point in its development, Apple seemed to recognize this flawed stance, and in the mid-1990s, licensed its software to third-party manufacturers such as Power Computing. After a short time, though, Apple cancelled its licensing agreements with other manufacturers. Because Apple remains essentially a closed system, other companies cannot develop compatible machines, meaning Apple-compatible systems are available from only one source: Apple. As such, it seems too late for Apple to effectively compete with the PC-compatible juggernaut. It is fortunate for the computing public as a whole that IBM created a more open and extendible standard, which today finds systems being offered by hundreds of companies in thousands of configurations. This kind of competition among manufacturers and vendors of PC-compatible systems is the reason such systems offer so much performance and so many capabilities for the money.

The PC continues to thrive and prosper, and new technology continues to be integrated into these systems, enabling them to grow with the times. These systems offer a high value for the money and have plenty of software available to run on them. It's a safe bet that PC-compatible systems will dominate the personal computer marketplace for the next 15 to 20 years.

Moore's Law

In 1965, Gordon Moore was preparing a speech about the growth trends in computer memory, and he made an interesting observation. When he began to graph the data, he realized a striking trend existed. Each new chip contained roughly twice as much capacity as its predecessor, and each chip was released within 18–24 months of the previous chip. If this trend continued, he reasoned, computing power would rise exponentially over relatively brief periods of time.

Moore's observation, now known as Moore's Law, described a trend that has continued to this day and is still remarkably accurate. It was found to not only describe memory chips, but also accurately describe the growth of processor power and disk-drive storage capacity. It has become the basis for many industry performance forecasts. In 28 years, the number of transistors on a chip has increased more than 12,000 times, from 2,300 on the 4004 in 1971 to more than 28.1 million on the Pentium III in 1999.

What does the future hold? For PCs, one thing is sure: They will continue to become faster, smaller, and cheaper. According to Gordon Moore, computing power continues to increase at a rate of about double the power every two years or less. This has held true not only for speed but for storage capacity as well. This means that computers you will purchase two years from now will be about twice as fast and store twice as much as what you can purchase today. The really amazing part is that this rapid pace of evolution shows no signs of letting up; in fact the pace might be increasing.

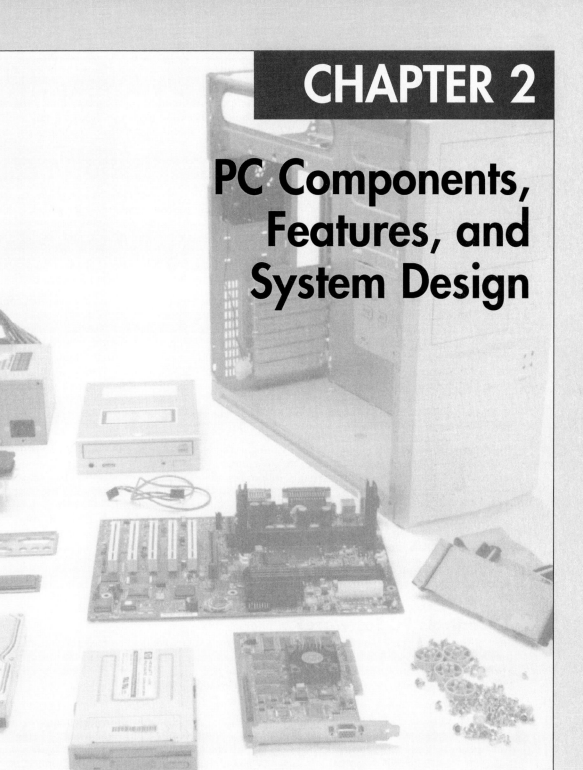

CHAPTER 2

PC Components, Features, and System Design

This chapter defines what a *PC* really is and continues by defining the types of PCs on the market. In addition, the chapter provides an overview of the components found in a modern PC. I'll also point you to sources (magazines, seminars, and online resources) that will help if you need to locate additional information. If you want to become A+ certified, you'll find the breakdown of test objectives at the end of this chapter to be a handy reference.

What Is a PC?

I normally ask the question, "What exactly is a PC?" when I begin one of my PC hardware seminars. Of course, most people immediately answer that PC stands for *personal computer*, which in fact it does. They might then continue by defining a personal computer as any small computer system purchased and used by an individual. Unfortunately, that definition is not nearly precise or accurate enough for our purposes. I agree that a PC is a personal computer, but not all personal computers are PCs. For example, an Apple Macintosh system is clearly a personal computer, but nobody I know would call a Mac a PC, least of all Mac users! For the true definition of what a PC is, you must look deeper.

Calling something a PC implies that it is something much more specific than just any personal computer. One thing it implies is a family relation to the first IBM PC from 1981. In fact, I'll go so far as to say that IBM literally *invented* the PC; that is, IBM designed and created the very first one, and IBM originally defined and set all the standards that made the PC distinctive from other personal computers. Note that it is very clear in my mind—as well as in the historical record—that IBM did *not* invent the personal computer. (Most recognize the historical origins of the personal computer in the MITS Altair, introduced in 1975.) IBM did not invent the personal computer, but it did invent the PC. Some people might take this definition a step further and define a PC as any personal computer that is "IBM compatible." In fact, many years back, PCs were called either IBM compatibles or IBM clones, in essence paying homage to the origins of the PC at IBM.

The reality today is that although IBM clearly designed and created the first PC in 1981 and controlled the development and evolution of the PC standard for several years thereafter, IBM is no longer in control of the PC standard; that is, it does not dictate what makes up a PC today. IBM lost control of the PC standard in 1987 when it introduced its PS/2 line of systems. Up until then, other companies that were producing PCs literally copied IBM's systems right down to the chips; connectors; and even the shapes (form factors) of the boards, cases, and power supplies. After 1987, IBM abandoned many of the standards it created in the first place. That's why for many years now I have refrained from using the designation "IBM compatible" when referring to PCs.

If a PC is no longer an IBM compatible, what is it? The real question seems to be, "Who is in control of the PC standard today?" That question is best broken down into two parts. First, who is in control of PC software? Second, who is in control of PC hardware?

Who Controls PC Software?

Most of the people in my seminars don't even hesitate for a split second when I ask this question; they immediately respond "Microsoft!" I don't think there is any argument with that answer. Microsoft clearly controls the operating systems used on PCs, which have migrated from the original MS-DOS to Windows 3.1/95/98/Me, Windows NT, and Windows 2000.

Microsoft has effectively used its control of the PC operating system as leverage to also control other types of PC software, such as utilities and applications. For example, many utility programs originally offered by independent companies, such as disk caching, disk compression, defragmentation, file structure repair, and even calculators and notepads, are now bundled in (included with) Windows. Microsoft has even bundled applications such as Web browsers, ensuring an automatic installed base for these applications—much to the dismay of companies who produce competing versions. Microsoft has also leveraged its control of the operating system to integrate its own networking software and applications suites more seamlessly into the operating system than others. That's why it now dominates most of the PC software universe, from operating systems to utilities, from word processors to spreadsheets.

In the early days of the PC, when IBM was clearly in control of the PC hardware standard, it hired Microsoft to provide most of the core software for the PC. IBM developed the hardware, wrote the BIOS (basic input/output system), and then hired Microsoft to develop the disk operating system (DOS), as well as several other programs and utilities for IBM. In what was later viewed as perhaps the most costly business mistake in history, IBM failed to secure exclusive rights to the DOS it had contracted from Microsoft, either by purchasing it outright or by an exclusive license agreement. Instead, IBM licensed it non-exclusively, which subsequently allowed Microsoft to sell the same MS-DOS code it developed for IBM to any other company that was interested. Early PC cloners such as Compaq eagerly licensed this same operating system code, and suddenly consumers could purchase the same basic MS-DOS operating system with several different company names on the box. In retrospect, that single contractual error made Microsoft into the dominant software company it is today, and subsequently caused IBM to lose control of the very PC standard it had created.

As a writer myself (of words, not software), I can appreciate what an incredible oversight this was. Imagine that a book publisher comes up with a great idea for a very popular book and then contracts with and subsequently pays an author to write it. Then, by virtue of a poorly written contract, the author discovers that the publisher can legally sell the very same book (perhaps with a different title) to all the competitors of the original publisher. Of course, no publisher I know would allow this to happen; yet that is exactly what IBM allowed Microsoft to do back in 1981. By virtue of its deal with Microsoft, IBM had essentially lost control of the software it commissioned for its new PC from day one.

It is interesting to note that in the PC business software enjoys copyright protection, whereas hardware can be protected only by patents, which are difficult, are time-consuming to get, and expire after 17 years. To patent something requires that it be a unique and substantially new design. This made it impossible to patent most aspects of the IBM PC because it was designed using previously existing parts that anybody could purchase off the shelf! In fact, most of the important parts for the original PC came from Intel, such as the 8088 processor, 8284 clock generator, 8253/54 timer, 8259 interrupt controller, 8237 DMA (direct memory access) controller, 8255 peripheral interface, and 8288 bus controller. These chips made up the heart and soul of the original PC.

Because the design of the original PC was not wholly patentable, anybody could duplicate the hardware of the IBM PC. All he or she had to do was purchase the same chips from the same manufacturers and suppliers IBM used and design a new motherboard with a similar circuit. Seemingly as if to aid in this, IBM even published complete schematic diagrams of its motherboards and all its adapter cards in very detailed and easily available technical reference manuals. I have several of these early IBM manuals and still refer to them from time to time for specific component-level PC design information. In fact, I still recommend these original manuals to anybody who wants to delve deeply into PC design.

The difficult part of copying the IBM PC was the software, which is protected by copyright law. Phoenix Software was among the first to develop a legal way around this problem, which enabled it to functionally duplicate (but not exactly copy) software such as the BIOS (basic input/output system). The *BIOS* is defined as the core set of control software, which drives the hardware devices in the system directly. These types of programs are normally called *device drivers*, so in essence, the BIOS is a collection of all the core device drivers used to operate and control the system hardware. What is called the *operating system* (such as DOS or Windows) uses the drivers in the BIOS to control and communicate with the various hardware and peripherals in the system.

▶▶ See Chapter 5, "BIOS," p. 345.

Phoenix's method for legally duplicating the BIOS was an ingenious form of reverse-engineering. It hired two teams of software engineers, the second of which had to be specially screened to consist only of people who had never seen or studied the IBM BIOS code. The first team did study the IBM BIOS and wrote as complete a description of what it did as possible. The second team read the description written by the first team and set out to write from scratch a new BIOS that did everything the first team described. The end result was a new BIOS written from scratch with code that, although not identical to IBM's, had exactly the same functionality.

Phoenix called this a "clean room" approach to reverse-engineering software, and it can escape any legal attack. Because IBM's original PC BIOS consisted of only 8KB of code and had limited functionality, duplicating it through the clean room approach was not very difficult nor time consuming. As the IBM BIOS evolved, Phoenix—as well as the other BIOS companies—found it relatively easy to keep up with any changes IBM made. Discounting the POST (power on self test) or BIOS Setup program (used for configuring the system) portion of the BIOS, most BIOSes—even today—have only about 32KB of active code. Today, Phoenix and others, such as AMI and Microid Research, are producing BIOS software for PC system manufacturers.

After the hardware and the BIOS of the IBM PC were duplicated, all that was needed to produce a fully IBM-compatible system was DOS. Reverse engineering DOS—even with the clean room approach—would have been a daunting task because DOS is much larger than the BIOS and consists of many more programs and functions. Also, the operating system has evolved and changed more often than the BIOS, which by comparison has remained relatively constant. This means that the only way to get DOS on an IBM compatible is to license it. This is where Microsoft comes in. Because IBM (who hired Microsoft to write DOS in the first place) did not ensure that Microsoft signed an exclusive license agreement, Microsoft was free to sell the same DOS to anybody. With a licensed copy of MS-DOS, the last piece was in place and the floodgates were open for IBM-compatible systems to be produced whether IBM liked it or not.

In retrospect, this is exactly why there are no clones or compatibles of the Apple Macintosh system. It is not that Mac systems cannot be duplicated; in fact, Mac hardware is fairly simple and easy to produce using off-the-shelf parts. The real problem is that Apple owns the Mac OS as well as the BIOS, and because Apple has seen fit not to license them, no other company can sell an Apple-compatible system. Also, note that the Mac BIOS and OS are very tightly integrated; the Mac BIOS is very large and complex, and it is essentially a part of the OS, unlike the much more simple and easily duplicated BIOS found on PCs. The greater complexity and integration has allowed both the Mac BIOS and OS to escape any clean-room duplication efforts. This means that without Apple's blessing (in the form of licensing), no Mac clones are likely ever to exist.

It might be interesting to note that during 1996–97, an effort was made by the more liberated thinkers at Apple to license its BIOS/OS combination, and several Mac-compatible machines were not only developed but also were produced and sold. Companies such as Sony, Power Computing, Radius, and even Motorola invested millions of dollars in developing these systems, but shortly after these first Mac clones were sold, Apple rudely canceled all licensing! This was apparently the result of an edict from Steve Jobs, who had been hired back to run the company and who was one of the original architects of the closed-box, proprietary-design Macintosh system in the first place. By canceling these licenses, Apple has virtually guaranteed that its systems will never be a mainstream success. Along with its smaller market share come much higher system costs, fewer available software applications, and fewer hardware upgrades as compared to PCs. The proprietary design also means that major repair or upgrade components, such as motherboards, power supplies, and cases, are available only from Apple at very high prices, and upgrades of these components are normally not cost effective.

I often think that if Apple had a different view and had licensed its OS and BIOS early on, this book might be called *Upgrading and Repairing Macs* instead!

Who Controls PC Hardware?

Although it is clear that Microsoft has always controlled PC software by virtue of its control over the PC operating system, what about the hardware? It is easy to see that IBM controlled the PC hardware standard up through 1987. After all, IBM invented the core PC motherboard design, expansion bus slot architecture (8/16-bit ISA bus), serial and parallel port design, video card design through VGA and XGA standards, floppy and hard disk interface and controller designs, power supply design, keyboard interface and design, mouse interface, and even the physical shapes (form factors) of everything from the motherboard to the expansion cards, power supplies, and system chassis. All these pre-1987 IBM PC, XT, and AT system design features are still influencing modern systems today.

But to me the real question is what company has been responsible for creating and inventing new and more recent PC hardware designs, interfaces, and standards? When I ask people that question, I normally see some hesitation in their responses—some people say Microsoft (but it controls the software, not the hardware), and some say Compaq or name a few other big-name system manufacturers. Only a few surmise the correct answer—Intel.

I can see why many people don't immediately realize this; I mean, how many people actually own an Intel-brand PC? No, not just one that says "Intel inside" on it (which refers only to the system having an Intel processor), but a system that was designed and built by, or even purchased through, Intel. Believe it or not, I think that many—if not most—people today do have Intel PCs!

Certainly this does not mean that consumers have purchased their systems from Intel because it is well known that Intel does not directly sell complete PCs to end users. You cannot currently order a system from Intel, nor can you purchase an Intel-brand system from somebody else. What I am talking about is the motherboard. In my opinion, the single most important part in a PC system is the motherboard, and I'd say that whoever made your motherboard should be considered the legitimate manufacturer of your system. Even back when IBM was the major supplier of PCs, it made only the motherboard and contracted the other components of the system (power supply, disk drives, and so on) out to others.

▶▶ See Chapter 4, "Motherboards and Buses," p. 193.

Most of the top-tier system manufacturers do make their own motherboards. According to *Computer Reseller News* magazine, the top desktop systems manufacturers for the last several years have consistently been Compaq, HP, and IBM. These companies, for the most part, do design and manufacture their own motherboards, as well as many other system components. In some cases, they even design their own chips and chipset components for their own boards. Although sales are high for these individual companies, a larger overall segment of the market can be called the second tier.

In this second tier are companies that do not really manufacture systems, but assemble them instead. That is, they purchase motherboards, cases, power supplies, disk drives, peripherals, and so on, and assemble and market the components together as complete systems. Dell, Gateway, and Micron are some of the larger system assemblers today, but hundreds more could be listed. In overall total volume, this ends up being the largest segment of the PC marketplace today. What is interesting about the second-tier systems is that, with very few exceptions, you and I can purchase the same motherboards and other components any of the second-tier manufacturers can (although we pay more than they do). We also can assemble a virtually identical system from scratch ourselves, but that is a story for Chapter 23, "Building or Upgrading Systems."

Note that some of these second-tier companies have incredible sales—for example, Dell is poised to take the top PC sales spot from Compaq, who has held it for many years. Gateway and the other system assemblers are not far behind.

The point of all this is, of course, that if Gateway, Dell, Micron, and others do not manufacture their own motherboards, who does? You guessed it—Intel. Not only do those specific companies use largely

Intel motherboards, if you check around, you'll find today that many of the systems on the market in the second tier come with Intel motherboards. The only place Intel doesn't dominate is the AMD-based systems using the Athlon or Duron.

Although this is an extreme case, one review of 10 systems in *Computer Shopper* magazine listed 8 out of the 10 systems evaluated as having Intel motherboards. In fact, those 8 used the exact same board. That means that those systems differed only in the cosmetics of the exterior case assemblies and by which peripheral components, such as video card, disk drives, keyboards, and so on, were selected. The funny thing was that many of the peripheral items were identical among the systems as well. Before you compare pre-assembled systems from different manufacturers, be sure to get a listing of which parts they are using; you might be surprised to see how similar the systems on the market today can be.

Although Intel still dominates motherboard sales, that dominance has faltered somewhat from a few years back. Because of Intel's focus on Rambus memory with many of its newer boards, many of the lower-cost system builders have been switching to alternative products. Also, Intel's boards are set up to make overclocking either impossible or extremely difficult, so "hotrod" system builders normally choose non-Intel boards.

▶▶   See "Chipsets," p. 225.

How did Intel come to dominate the interior of our PCs? Intel has been the dominant PC processor supplier since IBM chose the Intel 8088 CPU in the original IBM PC in 1981. By controlling the processor, Intel naturally controlled the chips needed to integrate its processors into system designs. This naturally led Intel into the chipset business. It started its chipset business in 1989 with the 82350 Extended Industry Standard Architecture (EISA) chipset, and by 1993 it had become—along with the debut of the Pentium processor—the largest-volume major motherboard chipset supplier. Now I imagine Intel sitting there, thinking that it makes the processor and all the other chips necessary to produce a motherboard, so why not just eliminate the middleman and make the entire motherboard, too? The answer to this, and a real turning point in the industry, came about in 1994 when Intel became the largest-volume motherboard manufacturer in the world. And Intel has remained solidly on top ever since. It doesn't just lead in this category by any small margin; in fact, during 1997, Intel made more motherboards than the next eight largest motherboard manufacturers combined, with sales of more than 30 million boards, worth more than $3.6 billion! Note that this figure does not include processors or chipsets—only the boards themselves. These boards end up in the various system assembler brand PCs you and I buy, meaning that most of us are now essentially purchasing Intel-manufactured systems, no matter who actually wielded the screwdriver.

Intel controls the PC hardware standard because it controls the PC motherboard. It not only makes the vast majority of motherboards being used in systems today, but it also supplies the vast majority of processors and motherboard chipsets to other motherboard manufacturers.

Intel also has had a hand in setting several recent PC hardware standards, such as the following:

- PCI (Peripheral Component Interconnect) local bus interface
- AGP (Accelerated Graphics Port) interface for high-performance video cards
- ATX motherboard, form factor that replaces the (somewhat long in the tooth) IBM-designed Baby-AT form factor that has been used since the early 1980s
- NLX motherboard form factor to replace the proprietary and limited LPX design used by many lower-cost systems, which finally brought motherboard upgradability to those systems
- DMI (Desktop Management Interface) for monitoring system hardware functions
- DPMA (Dynamic Power Management Architecture) and APM (Advanced Power Management) standards for managing power usage in the PC

Intel dominates not only the PC, but the entire semiconductor industry. According to the sales figures compiled by Cahners Research (shown in Figure 2.1), Intel has almost three times the sales of its closest competitor.

Figure 2.1   Top 25 companies ranked by 1999 semiconductor sales.

Whoever controls the operating system controls the software for the PC, and whoever controls the processor—and therefore the motherboard—controls the hardware. Because Microsoft and Intel together seem to control software and hardware in the PC today, it is no wonder the modern PC is often called a "Wintel" system.

PC 9x Specifications

Even though Intel fully controls PC hardware, Microsoft recognizes its power over the PC from the operating system perspective and has been releasing a series of documents called the "PC xx Design Guides" (where xx designates the year) as a set of standard specifications to guide both hardware and software developers who are creating products that work with Windows. The requirements in these guides are part of Microsoft's "Designed for Windows" logo requirement. In other words, if you produce either a hardware or software product and you want the official "Designed for Windows" logo to be on your box, your product must meet the PC xx minimum requirements.

Following are the documents that have been produced so far:

- "Hardware Design Guide for Microsoft Windows 95"
- "Hardware Design Guide Supplement for PC 95"
- "PC 97 Hardware Design Guide"
- "PC 98 System Design Guide"
- "PC 99 System Design Guide"
- "PC 2000 System Design Guide"

All these documents are available for download from Microsoft's Web site, and they also have been available as published books from Microsoft Press.

These system-design guides present information for engineers who build personal computers, expansion cards, and peripheral devices that are to be used with Windows 9x/Me, NT, and 2000 operating systems. The requirements and recommendations for PC design in these guides form the basis for the requirements of the "Designed for Windows" logo program for hardware Microsoft sponsors.

These guides include requirements for basic (desktop and mobile) systems, workstations, and even entertainment PCs. They also address Plug and Play device configuration and power management in PC systems; requirements for universal serial bus (USB) and IEEE 1394; and new devices supported under Windows, including new graphics and video device capabilities, DVD, scanners and digital cameras, and other devices.

Note

Note that these guides do not mean anything directly for the end user; instead, they are meant to be guides for PC manufacturers to build their systems. As such, they are only recommendations, and they do not have to be followed to the letter. In some ways, they are a market-control tool for Intel and Microsoft to further wield their influence over PC hardware and software. In reality, the market often dictates that some of these recommendations are disregarded, which is one reason why they continue to evolve with new versions year after year.

System Types

PCs can be broken down into many categories. I like to break them down in two ways—one by the type of software they can run, and the other by the motherboard host bus, or processor bus design and width. Because this book concentrates mainly on hardware, let's look at that first.

When a processor reads data, the data moves into the processor via the processor's external data bus connection. The processor's data bus is directly connected to the processor host bus on the motherboard. The processor data bus or host bus is also sometimes referred to as the *local bus* because it is local to the processor that is connected directly to it. Any other devices connected to the host bus essentially appear as if they are directly connected to the processor as well. If the processor has a 32-bit data bus, the motherboard must be wired to have a 32-bit processor host bus. This means the system can move 32 bits of data into or out of the processor in a single cycle.

▶▶ See "Data Bus," p. 58.

Different processors have different data bus widths, and the motherboards designed to accept them require a processor host bus with a matching width. Table 2.1 lists all the Intel processors and their data bus widths.

Table 2.1   Intel Processors and Their Data Bus Widths

Processor	Data Bus Width
8088	8-bit
8086	16-bit
286	16-bit
386SX	16-bit
386DX	32-bit
486/5x86	32-bit
Pentium (P5)/K6	64-bit

Table 2.1   Continued

Processor	Data Bus Width
Pentium Pro (P6)/Celeron/II/III	64-bit
AMD Duron/Athlon	64-bit
Pentium IV	64-bit

A common misconception arises in discussions of processor widths. Although the Pentium and newer processors all have 64-bit data bus widths, their internal registers are only 32 bits wide, and they process 32-bit commands and instructions. Thus, from a software point of view, all chips from the 386 to the Athlon/Duron and Pentium IV have 32-bit registers and execute 32-bit instructions. From the electronic or physical perspective, these 32-bit, software-capable processors have been available in physical forms with 16-bit (386SX), 32-bit (386DX and 486), and 64-bit (Pentium) data bus widths. The data bus width is the major factor in motherboard and memory system design because it dictates how many bits move in and out of the chip in one cycle.

▶▶ See "Internal Registers," p. 59.

The Itanium processor (code-named Merced) will have a new Intel architecture 64-bit (IA-64) instruction set, but it also will process the same 32-bit instructions as processors ranging from the 386 through the Pentium do, although we don't know how efficiently. It is not known whether Itanium will have a 64-bit data bus like the Pentium or will include a 128-bit data bus.

▶▶ See "Processor Specifications," p. 42.

Referring to Table 2.1, you can see that Pentium III systems have a 64-bit processor bus, which means any Pentium III motherboard has a 64-bit processor host bus. Pentium processors, whether they are the original Pentium, Pentium MMX, Pentium Pro, or even the Pentium II and III, all have 64-bit data busses.

As you can see from Table 2.1, systems can be broken down into the following hardware categories:

- 8-bit
- 16-bit
- 32-bit
- 64-bit

What is interesting is that besides the bus width, the 16- through 64-bit systems are remarkably similar in basic design and architecture. The older 8-bit systems are very different, however. This gives us two basic system types, or classes, of hardware:

- 8-bit (PC/XT-class) systems
- 16/32/64-bit (AT-class) systems

PC stands for personal computer; XT stands for an extended PC; and AT stands for an advanced technology PC. The terms *PC*, *XT*, and *AT*, as they are used here, are taken from the original IBM systems of those names. The XT was a PC system that included a hard disk for storage in addition to the floppy drives found in the basic PC system. These systems had an 8-bit 8088 processor and an 8-bit Industry Standard Architecture (ISA) bus for system expansion. The *bus* is the name given to expansion slots in which additional plug-in circuit boards can be installed. The 8-bit designation comes from the fact that the ISA bus found in the PC/XT class systems can send and receive only eight bits of data in a single cycle. The data in an 8-bit bus is sent along eight wires simultaneously, in parallel.

▶▶ See "The ISA Bus," p. 300.

16-bit and greater systems are said to be AT-class, which indicates that they follow certain standards and that they follow the basic design first set forth in the original IBM AT system. AT is the designation IBM applied to systems that first included more advanced 16-bit (and later, 32- and 64-bit) processors and expansion slots. AT-class systems must have a processor that is compatible with Intel 286 or higher processors (including the 386, 486, Pentium, Pentium Pro, Pentium II, and Pentium III processors), and they must have a 16-bit or greater system bus. The system bus architecture is central to the AT system design, along with the basic memory architecture, interrupt request (IRQ), direct memory access (DMA), and I/O port address design. All AT-class systems are similar in the way these resources are allocated and how they function.

The first AT-class systems had a 16-bit version of the ISA bus, which is an extension of the original 8-bit ISA bus found in the PC/XT-class systems. Eventually, several expansion slot or bus designs were developed for AT-class systems, including the following:

- 16-bit ISA bus
- 16/32-bit Extended ISA (EISA) bus
- 16/32-bit PS/2 Micro Channel Architecture (MCA) bus
- 16-bit PC-Card (PCMCIA) bus
- 32-bit Cardbus (PCMCIA) bus
- 32-bit VESA Local (VL) bus
- 32/64-bit Peripheral Component Interconnect (PCI) bus
- 32-bit Accelerated Graphics Port (AGP)

A system with any of these types of expansion slots is by definition an AT-class system, regardless of the actual Intel or Intel-compatible processor that is used. AT-type systems with 386 or higher processors have special capabilities not found in the first generation of 286-based ATs. These distinct capabilities are in the areas of memory addressing, memory management, and possible 32- or 64-bit wide access to data. Most systems with 386DX or higher chips also have 32-bit bus architectures to take full advantage of the 32-bit data transfer capabilities of the processor.

Most PC systems today incorporate 16-bit ISA slots for backward-compatibility and lower-function adapters, and PCI slots for truly high-performance adapters. In addition, most portable systems use PC-Card and Cardbus slots in the portable unit and ISA and PCI slots in optional docking stations.

Chapter 4, "Motherboards and Buses," contains in-depth information on these and other PC system buses, including technical information such as pinouts, performance specifications, and bus operation and theory.

Table 2.2 summarizes the primary differences between the older 8-bit (PC/XT) systems and modern AT systems. This information distinguishes between these systems and includes all IBM and compatible models.

Table 2.2 Differences Between PC/XT and AT Systems

System Attributes	(8-Bit) PC/XT Type	(16/32/64-Bit) AT Type
Supported processors	All x86 or x88	286 or higher
Processor modes	Real	Real/Protected/Virtual Real
Software supported	16-bit only	16- or 32-bit
Bus slot width	8-bit	16/32/64-bit

Table 2.2   Continued

System Attributes	(8-Bit) PC/XT Type	(16/32/64-Bit) AT Type
Slot type	ISA only	ISA, EISA, MCA, PC-Card, Cardbus, VL-Bus, and PCI
Hardware interrupts	8 (6 usable)	16 (11 usable)
DMA channels	4 (3 usable)	8 (7 usable)
Maximum RAM	1MB	16MB/4GB or more
Floppy controller speed	250Kbps	250/300/500/1,000Kbps
Standard boot drive	360KB or 720KB	1.2MB/1.44MB/2.88MB
Keyboard interface	Unidirectional	Bidirectional
CMOS memory/clock	None standard	MC146818-compatible
Serial-port UART	8250B	16450/16550A

The easiest way to identify a PC/XT (8-bit) system is by the 8-bit ISA expansion slots. No matter which processor or other features the system has, if all the slots are 8-bit ISA, the system is a PC/XT. AT (16-bit plus) systems can be similarly identified—they have 16-bit or greater slots of any type. These can be ISA, EISA, MCA, PC-Card (formerly PCMCIA), Cardbus, VL-Bus, or PCI. Using this information, you can properly categorize virtually any system as a PC/XT type or an AT type. No PC/XT type (8-bit) systems have been manufactured for many years. Unless you are in a computer museum, virtually every system you encounter today is based on the AT-type design.

System Components

A modern PC is both simple and complicated. It is simple in the sense that over the years, many of the components used to construct a system have become integrated with other components into fewer and fewer actual parts. It is complicated in the sense that each part in a modern system performs many more functions than did the same types of parts in older systems.

This section briefly examines all the components and peripherals in a modern PC system. Each item is discussed further in later chapters.

Here are the components and peripherals necessary to assemble a basic modern PC system:

- Motherboard
- Processor
- Memory (RAM)
- Case/chassis
- Power supply
- Floppy drive
- Hard disk
- CD-ROM, CD-R, or DVD-ROM drive
- Keyboard
- Mouse
- Video card
- Monitor (display)
- Sound card
- Speakers
- Modem

A breakdown of these items is shown in Table 2.3.

Table 2.3   **Basic PC Components**

Component	Description
Motherboard	The motherboard is the core of the system. It really is the PC; everything else is connected to it, and it controls everything in the system. Microprocessors are covered in detail in Chapter 3, "Microprocessor Types and Specifications."
Processor	The processor is often thought of as the "engine" of the computer. It's also called the CPU (central processing unit).
Memory (RAM)	The system memory is often called RAM (for random access memory). This is the primary memory, which holds all the programs and data the processor is using at a given time. Memory is covered in detail in Chapter 6, "Memory."
Case/chassis	The case is the frame or chassis that houses the motherboard, power supply, disk drives, adapter cards, and any other physical components in the system. The case is covered in detail in Chapter 21, "Power Supply and Chassis/Case."
Power supply	The power supply is what feeds electrical power to every single part in the PC. The power supply is covered in detail in Chapter 21.
Floppy drive	The floppy drive is a simple, inexpensive, low-capacity, removable-media, magnetic-storage device.
Hard drive	The hard disk is the primary archival storage memory for the system. Hard disk drives are also covered in detail in Chapter 10, "Hard Disk Storage."
CD-ROM/DVD-ROM	CD-ROM (compact disc read-only) and DVD-ROM (digital versatile disc read-only) drives are relatively high-capacity, removable media, optical drives. These drives are covered in detail in Chapter 13, "Optical Storage."
Keyboard	The keyboard is the primary device on a PC that is used by a human being to communicate with and control a system. Keyboards are covered in detail in Chapter 18, "Input Devices."
Mouse	Although many types of pointing devices are on the market today, the first and most popular device for this purpose is the mouse. The mouse and other pointing devices are covered in detail in Chapter 18.
Video card	The video card controls the information you see on the monitor. Video cards are covered in detail in Chapter 15, "Video Hardware."
Monitor	Monitors are covered in detail in Chapter 15.
Modem	Most prebuilt PCs ship with a modem (generally an internal modem). Modems and other Internet-connectivity devices and methods are covered in Chapter 19, "Internet Connectivity."

CHAPTER 3

Microprocessor Types and Specifications

Microprocessors

The brain or engine of the PC is the *processor* (sometimes called *microprocessor*), or *central processing unit (CPU)*. The CPU performs the system's calculating and processing. The processor is often the most expensive single component in the system; in higher-end systems it can cost up to four or more times more than the motherboard it plugs into. Intel is generally credited with creating the first micro-processor in 1971 with the introduction of a chip called the 4004. Today Intel still has control over the processor market, at least for PC systems. This means that all PC-compatible systems use either Intel processors or Intel-compatible processors from a handful of competitors (such as AMD or VIA/Cyrix).

Intel's dominance in the processor market hadn't always been assured. Although Intel is generally credited with inventing the processor and introducing the first one on the market, by the late 1970s the two most popular processors for PCs were *not* from Intel (although one was a clone of an Intel processor). Personal computers of that time primarily used the Z-80 by Zilog and the 6502 by MOS Technologies. The Z-80 was noted for being an improved and less expensive clone of the Intel 8080 processor, similar to the way companies today such as AMD, Cyrix, IDT, and Rise Technologies have cloned Intel's Pentium processors. In that case, though, the clone had become more popular than the original. Some might argue that AMD has achieved that type of status over the past year, but even though they have made significant gains, Intel still runs the PC processor show.

Back then I had a system containing both of those processors, consisting of a 1MHz (yes, that's *1*, as in 1MHz!) 6502-based Apple main system with a Microsoft Softcard (Z-80 card) plugged into one of the slots. The Softcard contained a 2MHz Z-80 processor. This enabled me to run software for both types of processors on the one system. The Z-80 was used in systems of the late 1970s and early 1980s that ran the CP/M operating system, whereas the 6502 was best known for its use in the early Apple computers (before the Mac).

The fate of both Intel and Microsoft was dramatically changed in 1981 when IBM introduced the IBM PC, which was based on a 4.77MHz Intel 8088 processor running the Microsoft Disk Operating System (MS-DOS) 1.0. Since that fateful decision was made, PC-compatible systems have used a string of Intel or Intel-compatible processors, with each new one capable of running the software of the processor before it—from the 8088 to the current Pentium 4/III/Celeron and Athlon/Duron. The fol-lowing sections cover the various types of processor chips that have been used in personal computers since the first PC was introduced almost two decades ago. These sections provide a great deal of tech-nical detail about these chips and explain why one type of CPU chip can do more work than another in a given period of time.

Pre-PC Microprocessor History

It is interesting to note that the microprocessor had existed for only 10 years prior to the creation of the PC! The microprocessor was invented by Intel in 1971; the PC was created by IBM in 1981. Now nearly 20 years later, we are still using systems based more or less on the design of that first PC. The processors powering our PCs today are still backward compatible in many ways with the 8088 selected by IBM in 1981.

The story of the development of the first microprocessor, the Intel 4004, can be read in Chapter 1, "Personal Computer Background." The 4004 processor was introduced on November 15, 1971, and originally ran at a clock speed of 108KHz (108,000 cycles per second, or just over one-tenth a mega-hertz). The 4004 contained 2,300 transistors and was built on a 10-micron process. This means that each line, trace, or transistor could be spaced about 10 microns (millionths of a meter) apart. Data was transferred 4 bits at a time, and the maximum addressable memory was only 640 bytes. The 4004 was designed for use in a calculator but proved to be useful for many other functions because of its inher-ent programmability.

In April 1972, Intel released the 8008 processor, which originally ran at a clock speed of 200KHz (0.2MHz). The 8008 processor contained 3,500 transistors and was built on the same 10-micron process as the previous processor. The big change in the 8008 was that it had an 8-bit data bus, which meant it could move data 8 bits at a time—twice as much as the previous chip. It could also address more memory, up to 16KB. This chip was primarily used in dumb terminals and general-purpose calculators.

The next chip in the lineup was the 8080, introduced in April 1974, running at a clock rate of 2MHz. Due mostly to the faster clock rate, the 8080 processor had 10 times the performance of the 8008. The 8080 chip contained 6,000 transistors and was built on a 6-micron process. Similar to the previous chip, the 8080 had an 8-bit data bus, so it could transfer 8 bits of data at a time. The 8080 could address up to 64KB of memory, significantly more than the previous chip.

It was the 8080 that helped start the PC revolution because this was the processor chip used in what is generally regarded as the first personal computer, the Altair 8800. The CP/M operating system was written for the 8080 chip, and Microsoft was founded and delivered its first product: Microsoft BASIC for the Altair. These initial tools provided the foundation for a revolution in software because thousands of programs were written to run on this platform.

In fact, the 8080 became so popular that it was cloned. A company called Zilog formed in late 1975, joined by several ex-Intel 8080 engineers. In July of 1976, it released the Z-80 processor, which was a vastly improved version of the 8080. It was not pin compatible but instead combined functions such as the memory interface and RAM refresh circuitry, which enabled cheaper and simpler systems to be designed. The Z-80 also incorporated a superset of 8080 instructions, meaning it could run all 8080 programs. It also included new instructions and new internal registers, so software designed for the Z-80 would not necessarily run on the older 8080. The Z-80 ran initially at 2.5MHz (later versions ran up to 10MHz) and contained 8,500 transistors. The Z-80 could access 64KB of memory.

Radio Shack selected the Z-80 for the TRS-80 Model 1, its first PC. The chip also was the first to be used by many pioneering systems, including the Osborne and Kaypro machines. Other companies followed, and soon the Z-80 was the standard processor for systems running the CP/M operating system and the popular software of the day.

Intel released the 8085, its followup to the 8080, in March of 1976. Even though it predated the Z-80 by several months, it never achieved the popularity of the Z-80 in personal computer systems. It was popular as an embedded controller, finding use in scales and other computerized equipment. The 8085 ran at 5MHz and contained 6,500 transistors. It was built on a 3-micron process and incorporated an 8-bit data bus.

Along different architectural lines, MOS Technologies introduced the 6502 in 1976. This chip was designed by several ex-Motorola engineers who had worked on Motorola's first processor, the 6800. The 6502 was an 8-bit processor like the 8080, but it sold for around $25, whereas the 8080 cost about $300 when it was introduced. The price appealed to Steve Wozniak, who placed the chip in his Apple I and Apple II designs. The chip was also used in systems by Commodore and other system manufacturers. The 6502 and its successors were also used in computer games, including the original Nintendo Entertainment System (NES) among others. Motorola went on to create the 68000 series, which became the basis for the Apple Macintosh line of computers. Today those systems use the PowerPC chip, also by Motorola and a successor to the 68000 series.

All these previous chips set the stage for the first PC chips. Intel introduced the 8086 in June 1978. The 8086 chip brought with it the original x86 instruction set that is still present on x86-compatible chips such as the Pentium 4. A dramatic improvement over the previous chips, the 8086 was a full 16-bit design with 16-bit internal registers and a 16-bit data bus. This meant that it could work on 16-bit numbers and data internally and also transfer 16 bits at a time in and out of the chip. The 8086 contained 29,000 transistors and initially ran at up to 5MHz. The chip also used 20-bit addressing, so it could directly address up to 1MB of memory. Although not directly backward compatible with the

8080, the 8086 instructions and language were very similar and enabled older programs to quickly be ported over to run. This later proved important to help jumpstart the PC software revolution with recycled CP/M (8080) software.

Although the 8086 was a great chip, it was expensive at the time and more importantly required an expensive 16-bit support chip and board design. To help bring costs down, in 1979, Intel released a crippled version of the 8086 called the 8088. The 8088 processor used the same internal core as the 8086, had the same 16-bit registers, and could address the same 1MB of memory, but the external data bus was reduced to 8 bits. This enabled support chips from the older 8-bit 8085 to be used, and far less expensive boards and systems could be made. It is for these reasons that IBM chose the crippled chip, the 8088, for the first PC.

This decision would affect history in several ways. The 8088 was fully software compatible with the 8086, so it could run 16-bit software. Also, because the instruction set was very similar to the previous 8085 and 8080, programs written for those older chips could be quickly and easily modified to run. This enabled a large library of programs to be quickly released for the IBM PC, thus helping it become a success. The overwhelming blockbuster success of the IBM PC left in its wake the legacy of requiring backward compatibility with it. To maintain the momentum, Intel has pretty much been forced to maintain backward compatibility with the 8088/8086 in most of the processors it has released since then.

In some ways the success of the PC, and the Intel architecture it contains, has limited the growth of the personal computer. In other ways, however, its success has caused a huge number of programs, peripherals, and accessories to be developed and the PC to become a de facto standard in the industry. The original 8088 processor used in the first PC contained close to 30,000 transistors and ran at less than 5MHz. Intel introduced one version of the Pentium III Xeon with 2MB of on-die cache that has a whopping 140 million transistors—the largest ever in a single processor chip. Intel has also released processors running at speeds of 2GHz and beyond, and AMD is not very far behind. And the progress doesn't stop there because, according to Moore's Law, processing speed and transistor counts are doubling every 1.5–2 years.

Processor Specifications

Many confusing specifications often are quoted in discussions of processors. The following sections discuss some of these specifications, including the data bus, address bus, and speed. The next section includes a table that lists the specifications of virtually all PC processors.

Processors can be identified by two main parameters: how wide they are and how fast they are. The speed of a processor is a fairly simple concept. Speed is counted in megahertz (MHz) and gigahertz (GHz), which means millions and billions, respectively, of cycles per second—and faster is better! The width of a processor is a little more complicated to discuss because three main specifications in a processor are expressed in width. They are

- Internal registers
- Data input and output bus
- Memory address bus

Systems below 16MHz usually had no cache memory at all. Starting with 16MHz systems, high-speed cache memory appeared on the motherboard because the main memory at the time could not run at 16MHz. Prior to the 486 processor, the cache on the motherboard was the only cache used in the system.

Starting with the 486 series, processors began including what was called Level 1 (L1) cache directly on the processor die. Therefore, the L1 cache always ran at the full speed of the chip, especially important when the later 486 chips began to run at speeds higher than the motherboards they were plugged into. During this time the cache on the motherboard was called the second level, or L2, cache and ran at the slower motherboard speed.

Starting with the Pentium Pro and Pentium II, Intel began including L2 cache memory chips directly within the same package as the main processor. Originally, this built-in L2 cache was implemented as physically separate chips contained within the processor package but not a part of the processor die. Because the speed of commercially available cache memory chips could not keep pace with the main processor, most of the L2 cache in these processors ran at one-half speed (Pentium II/III and AMD Athlon), whereas some ran the cache even slower—at two-fifths or even one-third the processor speed (AMD Athlon).

The original Pentium II, III, Celeron, and Athlon (Model 1 and 2) processors use 512KB of either one-half, two-fifths, or one-third speed L2 cache, as Table 3.1 shows.

Table 3.1   L2 Cache Speeds

Processor	Speed	L2 Size	L2 Type	L2 Speed
Pentium III	450–600MHz	512KB	External	1/2 core (225–300MHz)
Athlon	550–700MHz	512KB	External	1/2 core (275–350MHz)
Athlon	750–850MHz	512KB	External	2/5 core (300–340MHz)
Athlon	900–1000MHz	512KB	External	1/3 core (300–333MHz)

The Pentium Pro, Pentium II/III Xeon, newer Pentium III, Celeron, K6-3, Athlon (Model 4, code-named Thunderbird), and Duron processors include full-core speed L2, as shown in Table 3.2.

Table 3.2   Full-Core Speed Cache

Processor	Speed	L2 Size	L2 Type	L2 Speed
Pentium Pro	150–200MHz	256KB–1MB	External	Full core
K6-3	350–450MHz	256KB	On-die	Full core
Duron	550–700+MHz	64KB	On-die	Full core
Celeron	300–600+MHz	128KB	On-die	Full core
Pentium II Xeon	400–450MHz	512KB–2MB	External	Full core
Athlon	650–1000+MHz	256KB	On-die	Full core
Pentium III	500–1000+MHz	256KB	On-die	Full core
Pentium III Xeon	500–1000+MHz	256KB–2MB	On-die	Full core
Pentium 4	1.3–2.0+GHz	256KB	On-die	Full core
Xeon	1.4–2.0+GHz	256KB–1MB	On-die	Full core

The problem originally forcing the L2 cache to run at less than the processor core speed was simple: The cache chips available on the market simply couldn't keep up. Intel built its own high-speed cache memory chips for the earlier Xeon processors, but it also made them very expensive. A breakthrough occurred in the second-generation Celeron, in which Intel built both the L1 and L2 caches directly on the processor die, where they both ran at the full-core speed of the chip. This type of design was then quickly adopted by the second-generation Pentium III, as well as the AMD K6-3, Athlon, and Duron processors. In fact, virtually all future processors from Intel and AMD have adopted or will adopt on-die L2 cache because it is the only cost-effective way to include the L2 and increase the speed.

Table 3.3 lists the primary specifications for the Intel family of processors used in IBM and compatible PCs. Table 3.4 lists the Intel-compatible processors from AMD, Cyrix, NexGen, IDT, and Rise.

Table 3.3   Intel Processor Specifications

Processor	CPU Clock	Voltage	Internal Register Size	Data Bus Width	Max. Memory	Level 1 Cache
8088	1x	5v	16-bit	8-bit	1MB	—
8086	1x	5v	16-bit	16-bit	1MB	—
286	1x	5v	16-bit	16-bit	16MB	—
386SX	1x	5v	32-bit	16-bit	16MB	—
386SL	1x	3.3v	32-bit	16-bit	16MB	0KB[1]
386DX	1x	5v	32-bit	32-bit	4GB	—
486SX	1x	5v	32-bit	32-bit	4GB	8KB
486SX2	2x	5v	32-bit	32-bit	4GB	8KB
487SX	1x	5v	32-bit	32-bit	4GB	8KB
486DX	1x	5v	32-bit	32-bit	4GB	8KB
486SL[2]	1x	3.3v	32-bit	32-bit	4GB	8KB
486DX2	2x	5v	32-bit	32-bit	4GB	8KB
486DX4	2-3x	3.3v	32-bit	32-bit	4GB	16KB
486Pentium OD	2.5x	5v	32-bit	32-bit	4GB	2x16KB
Pentium 60/66	1x	5v	32-bit	64-bit	4GB	2x8KB
Pentium 75-200	1.5-3x	3.3-3.5v	32-bit	64-bit	4GB	2x8KB
Pentium MMX	1.5-4.5x	1.8-2.8v	32-bit	64-bit	4GB	2x16KB
Pentium Pro	2-3x	3.3v	32-bit	64-bit	64GB	2x8KB
Pentium II	3.5-4.5x	1.8-2.8v	32-bit	64-bit	64GB	2x16KB
Pentium II PE	3.5-6x	1.6v	32-bit	64-bit	64GB	2x16KB
Celeron	3.5-4.5x	1.8-2.8v	32-bit	64-bit	64GB	2x16KB
Celeron A	3.5-8x	1.5-2v	32-bit	64-bit	64GB	2x16KB
Celeron III	4.5-9x	1.3-1.6v	32-bit	64-bit	64GB	2x16KB
Pentium III	4-6x	1.8-2v	32-bit	64-bit	64GB	2x16KB
Pentium IIIE	4-9x	1.3-1.7v	32-bit	64-bit	64GB	2x16KB
Pentium II Xeon	4-4.5x	1.8-2.8v	32-bit	64-bit	64GB	2x16KB
Pentium III Xeon	5-6x	1.8-2.8v	32-bit	64-bit	64GB	2x16KB
Pentium IIIE Xeon	4.5-6.5x	1.65v	32-bit	64-bit	64GB	2x16KB
Pentium 4	3-5x	1.7v	32-bit	64-bit	64GB	12+8KB
Pentium 4 Xeon	3-5x	1.7v	32-bit	64-bit	64GB	12+8KB
Itanium	3-5x	1.6v	64-bit	64-bit	16TB	2x16KB

L1 Cache Type	Level 2 Cache	L2 Cache Speed	Integral FPU	Multimedia Instructions	No. of Transistors	Date Introduced
—	—	—	—	—	29,000	June '79
—	—	—	—	—	29,000	June '78
—	—	—	—	—	134,000	Feb. '82
—	—	Bus	—	—	275,000	June '88
WT	—	Bus	—	—	855,000	Oct. '90
—	—	Bus	—	—	275,000	Oct. '85
WT	—	Bus	—	—	1.185M	April '91
WT	—	Bus	—	—	1.185M	April '94
WT	—	Bus	Yes	—	1.2M	April '91
WT	—	Bus	Yes	—	1.2M	April '89
WT	—	Bus	Opt.	—	1.4M	Nov. '92
WT	—	Bus	Yes	—	1.2M	March '92
WT	—	Bus	Yes	—	1.6M	Feb. '94
WB	—	Bus	Yes	—	3.1M	Jan. '95
WB	—	Bus	Yes	—	3.1M	March '93
WB	—	Bus	Yes	—	3.3M	Oct. '94
WB	—	Bus	Yes	MMX	4.5M	Jan. '97
WB	256KB 512KB 1MB	Core	Yes	—	5.5M	Nov. '95
WB	512KB	_ Core	Yes	MMX	7.5M	May '97
WB	256KB	Core[3]	Yes	MMX	27.4M	Jan. '99
WB	0KB	—	Yes	MMX	7.5M	April '98
WB	128KB	Core[3]	Yes	MMX	19M	Aug. '98
WB	128KB	Core[3]	Yes	SSE	28.1M[4]	Feb. '00
WB	512KB	_ Core	Yes	SSE	9.5M	Feb. '99
WB	256KB	Core[3]	Yes	SSE	28.1M	Oct. '99
WB	512KB 1MB 2MB	Core	Yes	MMX	7.5M	April '98
WB	512KB 1MB 2MB	Core	Yes	SSE	9.5M	March '99
WB	256KB 1MB 2MB	Core[3]	Yes	SSE	28.1M 84M 140M	Oct. '99 May '00
WB	256KB	Core[3]	Yes	SSE2	42M	Nov. '00
WB	256KB	Core[3]	Yes	SSE2	42M	May '01
WB	96KB[5]	Core[3]	Yes	MMX	25M	May '01

Table 3.4   AMD, Cyrix, NexGen, IDT, and Rise Processors

Processor	CPU Clock	Voltage	Internal Register Size	Data Bus Width	Max. Memory	Level 1 Cache
AMD K5	1.5–1.75x	3.5v	32-bit	64-bit	4GB	16+8KB
AMD K6	2.5–4.5x	2.2–3.2v	32-bit	64-bit	4GB	2x32KB
AMD K6-2	2.5–6x	1.9–2.4v	32-bit	64-bit	4GB	2x32KB
AMD K6-3	3.5–4.5x	1.8–2.4v	32-bit	64-bit	4GB	2x32KB
AMD Athlon	5–10x	1.6–1.8v	32-bit	64-bit	8TB	2x64KB
AMD Duron	5–10x	1.5–1.8v	32-bit	64-bit	8TB	2x64KB
AMD Athlon 4	5–10x	1.5–1.8v	32-bit	64-bit	8TB	2x64KB
Cyrix 6x86	2x	2.5–3.5v	32-bit	64-bit	4GB	16KB
Cyrix 6x86MX/MII	2–3.5x	2.2–2.9v	32-bit	64-bit	4GB	64KB
Cyrix III	2.5–7x	2.2v	32-bit	64-bit	4GB	64KB
NexGen Nx586	2x	4v	32-bit	64-bit	4GB	2x16KB
IDT Winchip	3–4x	3.3–3.5v	32-bit	64-bit	4GB	2x32KB
IDT Winchip2/2A	2.33–4x	3.3–3.5v	32-bit	64-bit	4GB	2x32KB
Rise mP6	2–3.5x	2.8v	32-bit	64-bit	4GB	2x8KB

FPU = Floating-Point unit (internal math coprocessor)

WT = Write-Through cache (caches reads only)

WB = Write-Back cache (caches both reads and writes)

M = Millions

Bus = Processor external bus speed (motherboard speed)

Core = Processor internal core speed (CPU speed)

MMX = Multimedia extensions, 57 additional instructions for graphics and sound processing

3DNow = MMX plus 21 additional instructions for graphics and sound processing

Enh. 3DNow = 3DNow plus 24 additional instructions for graphics and sound processing

Note

Note in Table 3.3 that the Pentium Pro processor includes 256KB, 512KB, or 1MB of full-core speed L2 cache in a separate die within the chip. The Pentium II/III processors include 512KB of half-core speed L2 cache on the processor card. The Celeron, Pentium II PE, and Pentium IIIE processors include full-core speed L2 cache integrated directly within the processor die. The Celeron III uses the same die as the Pentium IIIE, but half of the on-die cache is disabled, leaving 128KB functional.

The transistor count figures do not include the external (off-die) 256KB, 512KB, 1MB, or 2MB L2 cache built into the Pentium Pro, Pentium II/III, Xeon, and AMD Athlon CPU packages, or the 2MB or 4MB of L3 cache in the Itanium. The external L2 cache in those processors contains an additional 15.5 (256KB), 31 (512KB), 62 million (1MB), or 124 million (2MB) transistors in separate chips, whereas the external 2MB or 4MB of L3 cache in the Itanium includes up to 300 million transistors!

Note in Table 3.4 that the Athlon includes either 512KB of L2 cache via separate chips, running at either one-half, two-fifths, or one-third the core speed, or 256KB of on-die L2 running at full-core speed, depending on which version you have.

L1 Cache Type	Level 2 Cache	L2 Cache Speed	Integral FPU	Multimedia Instructions	No. of Transistors	Date Introduced
WB	—	Bus	Yes	—	4.3M	March '96
WB	—	Bus	Yes	MMX	8.8M	April '97
WB	—	Bus	Yes	3DNow	9.3M	May '98
WB	256KB	Core[3]	Yes	3DNow	21.3M	Feb. '99
WB	512KB	1/2–1/3 core	Yes	Enh. 3DNow	22M	Jun. '99
WB	64KB	Core[3]	Yes	Enh. 3DNow	25M	June '00
WB	256KB	Core[3]	Yes	Enh. 3DNow	37M	June '00
WB	—	Bus	Yes	—	3M	Feb. '96
WB	—	Bus	Yes	MMX	6.5M	May '97
WB	256KB	Core[3]	Yes	3Dnow	22M	Feb. '00
WB	—	Bus	Yes	—	3.5M	March '94
WB	—	Bus	Yes	MMX	5.4M	Oct. '97
WB	—	Bus	Yes	3Dnow	5.9M	Sept. '98
WB	—	Bus	Yes	MMX	3.6M	Oct. '98

SSE = Streaming SIMD (single instruction multiple data) Extensions, MMX plus 70 additional instructions for graphics and sound processing

SSE2 = Streaming SIMD Extensions 2, SSE plus 144 additional instructions for graphics and sound processing

1. The 386SL contains an integral-cache controller, but the cache memory must be provided outside the chip.

2. Intel later marketed SL Enhanced versions of the SX, DX, and DX2 processors. These processors were available in both 5v and 3.3v versions and included power-management capabilities.

3. On-die integrated L2 cache—runs at full-core speed.

4. 128KB functional L2 cache (256KB total, 128KB disabled); uses same die as Pentium IIIE.

5. The Itanium also includes an additional 2MB (150M transistors) or 4MB (300M transistors) of integrated on-cartridge L3 cache running at full core speed.

Processor Speed Ratings

A common misunderstanding about processors is their different speed ratings. This section covers processor speed in general and then provides more specific information about Intel processors.

A computer system's clock speed is measured as a frequency, usually expressed as a number of cycles per second. A crystal oscillator controls clock speeds using a sliver of quartz sometimes contained in what looks like a small tin container. Newer systems include the oscillator circuitry in the mother-board chipset, so it might not be a visible separate component on newer boards. As voltage is applied to the quartz, it begins to vibrate (oscillate) at a harmonic rate dictated by the shape and size of the crystal (sliver). The oscillations emanate from the crystal in the form of a current that alternates at the harmonic rate of the crystal. This alternating current is the clock signal that forms the time base on which the computer operates. A typical computer system runs millions of these cycles per second, so speed is measured in megahertz. (One hertz is equal to one cycle per second.) An alternating current signal is like a sine wave, with the time between the peaks of each wave defining the frequency (see Figure 3.1).

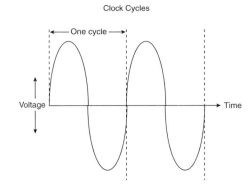

Figure 3.1 Alternating current signal showing clock cycle timing.

Note

The hertz was named for the German physicist Heinrich Rudolf Hertz. In 1885, Hertz confirmed the electromagnetic theory, which states that light is a form of electromagnetic radiation and is propagated as waves.

A single cycle is the smallest element of time for the processor. Every action requires at least one cycle and usually multiple cycles. To transfer data to and from memory, for example, a modern processor such as the Pentium III needs a minimum of three cycles to set up the first memory transfer and then only a single cycle per transfer for the next three to six consecutive transfers. The extra cycles on the first transfer typically are called *wait states*. A wait state is a clock tick in which nothing happens. This ensures that the processor isn't getting ahead of the rest of the computer.

▶▶ See "SIMMs, DIMMs, and RIMMs," p. 421.

The time required to execute instructions also varies:

- *8086 and 8088.* The original 8086 and 8088 processors take an average of 12 cycles to execute a single instruction.
- *286 and 386.* The 286 and 386 processors improve this rate to about 4.5 cycles per instruction.
- *486.* The 486 and most other fourth-generation Intel-compatible processors, such as the AMD 5x86, drop the rate further, to about 2 cycles per instruction.
- *Pentium, K6 series.* The Pentium architecture and other fifth-generation Intel-compatible processors, such as those from AMD and Cyrix, include twin instruction pipelines and other improvements that provide for operation at one or two instructions per cycle.
- *Pentium Pro, Pentium II/III/Celeron, and Athlon/Duron.* These P6 class processors, as well as other sixth-generation processors such as those from AMD and Cyrix, can execute as many as three or more instructions per cycle.

Different instruction execution times (in cycles) make comparing systems based purely on clock speed or number of cycles per second difficult. How can two processors that run at the same clock rate perform differently with one running "faster" than the other? The answer is simple: efficiency.

The main reason the 486 was considered fast relative to a 386 is that it executes twice as many instructions in the same number of cycles. The same thing is true for a Pentium; it executes about twice as many instructions in a given number of cycles as a 486. Therefore, given the same clock speed, a Pentium is twice as fast as a 486, and consequently a 133MHz 486 class processor (such as the AMD 5x86-133) is not even as fast as a 75MHz Pentium! That is because Pentium megahertz are "worth" about double what 486 megahertz are worth in terms of instructions completed per cycle. The Pentium II and III are about 50% faster than an equivalent Pentium at a given clock speed because they can execute about that many more instructions in the same number of cycles.

Comparing relative processor performance, you can see that a 1GHz Pentium III is about equal to a (theoretical) 1.5GHz Pentium, which is about equal to a 3GHz 486, which is about equal to a 6GHz 386 or 286, which is about equal to a 12GHz 8088. The original PC's 8088 ran at only 4.77MHz; today, we have systems that are comparatively at least 2,500 times faster! As you can see, you must be careful in comparing systems based on pure MHz alone because many other factors affect system performance.

Evaluating CPU performance can be tricky. CPUs with different internal architectures do things differently and can be relatively faster at certain things and slower at others. To fairly compare various CPUs at different clock speeds, Intel has devised a specific series of benchmarks called the *iCOMP (Intel Comparative Microprocessor Performance) index* that can be run against processors to produce a relative gauge of performance. The iCOMP index benchmark has been updated twice and released in original iCOMP, iCOMP 2.0, and now iCOMP 3.0 versions. More information on benchmarks, including iCOMP, can be found on Intel's site at http://developer.intel.com/procs/perf/resources/spectrum.htm.

Table 3.5 shows the relative power, or iCOMP 2.0 index, for several processors.

Note

Note that this reflects the most recent iCOMP index. Intel is designing new benchmarks that will show the power of the newer Pentium 4 and Itanium processor when running software optimized for their internal architectures.

Table 3.5 Intel iCOMP 2.0 Index Ratings

Processor	iCOMP 2.0 Index	Processor	iCOMP 2.0 Index
Pentium 75	67	Pentium Pro 200	220
Pentium 100	90	Celeron 300	226
Pentium 120	100	Pentium II 233	267
Pentium 133	111	Celeron 300A	296
Pentium 150	114	Pentium II 266	303
Pentium 166	127	Celeron 333	318
Pentium 200	142	Pentium II 300	332
Pentium-MMX 166	160	Pentium II Overdrive 300	351
Pentium Pro 150	168	Pentium II 333	366
Pentium-MMX 200	182	Pentium II 350	386
Pentium Pro 180	197	Pentium II Overdrive 333	387
Pentium-MMX 233	203	Pentium II 400	440
Celeron 266	213	Pentium II 450	483

The iCOMP 2.0 index is derived from several independent benchmarks and is a stable indication of relative processor performance. The benchmarks balance integer with floating-point and multimedia performance.

Recently, Intel discontinued the iCOMP 2.0 index and released the iCOMP 3.0 index. iCOMP 3.0 is an updated benchmark that incorporates an increasing use of 3D, multimedia, and Internet technology and software, as well as the increasing use of rich data streams and compute-intensive applications, including 3D, multimedia, and Internet technology. iCOMP 3.0 combines six benchmarks: WinTune 98 Advanced CPU Integer test, CPUmark 99, 3D WinBench 99-3D Lighting and Transformation Test, MultimediaMark 99, Jmark 2.0 Processor Test, and WinBench 99-FPU WinMark. These newer benchmarks take advantage of the SSE (Streaming SIMD Extensions), additional graphics and sound instructions built into the PIII. Without taking advantage of these new instructions, the PIII would benchmark at about the same speed as a PII at the same clock rate.

Table 3.6 shows the iCOMP Index 3.0 ratings for Pentium II and III processors.

Table 3.6   Intel iCOMP 3.0 Ratings

Processor	iCOMP 3.0 Index	Processor	iCOMP 3.0 Index
Pentium II 350	1000	Pentium III 650	2270
Pentium II 450	1240	Pentium III 700	2420
Pentium III 450	1500	Pentium III 750	2540
Pentium III 500	1650	Pentium III 800	2690
Pentium III 550	1780	Pentium III 866	2890
Pentium III 600	1930	Pentium III 1000	3280
Pentium III 600E	2110		

Considerations When Interpreting iCOMP Scores

Each processor's rating is calculated at the time the processor is introduced, using a particular, well-configured, commercially available system. Relative iCOMP index 3.0 scores and actual system performance might be affected by future changes in software design and configuration. Relative scores and actual system performance also can be affected by differences in components or characteristics of microprocessors, such as L2 cache, bus speed, extended multimedia or graphics instructions, or improvements in the microprocessor manufacturing process.

Differences in hardware components other than microprocessors used in the test systems also can affect how iCOMP scores relate to actual system performance. iCOMP 3.0 ratings cannot be compared with earlier versions of the iCOMP index because different benchmarks and weightings are used in calculating the result.

Processor Speeds and Markings Versus Motherboard Speed

Another confusing factor when comparing processor performance is that virtually all modern processors since the 486DX2 run at some multiple of the motherboard speed. For example, a Celeron 600 runs at a multiple of nine times the motherboard speed of 66MHz, whereas a Pentium III 1GHz runs at 7 1/2 times the motherboard speed of 133MHz. Up until early 1998, most motherboards ran at 66MHz or less because that is all Intel supported with its processors until then. Starting in April 1998, Intel released both processors and motherboard chipsets designed to run at 100MHz. Cyrix has a few processors designed to run on 75MHz motherboards, and many Pentium motherboards are capable of running that speed as well, although technically Intel never supported it. AMD also has versions of the K6-2 designed to run at motherboard speeds of 100MHz.

Starting in late 1999, chipsets and motherboards running at 133MHz became available to support the newer Pentium III processors. At that time, AMD Athlon motherboards and chipsets were introduced running at 100MHz but using a double transfer technique for an effective 200MHz data rate between the Athlon processor and the main chipset North Bridge chip.

In 2000 and 2001, processor bus speeds advanced further to 266MHz for the AMD Athlon and Intel Itanium and up to 400MHz for the Pentium 4.

Some might wonder why the more powerful Itanium processor uses a slower CPU bus than the Pentium 4. Actually, I wonder that as well! My guess is because they were designed by completely different teams with completely different agendas. The Itanium was designed in conjunction with HP, and from the get-go it was intended to use double-data rate (DDR) memory, which runs at 266MHz because that was favored by the server community. Because matching the CPU bus to the memory bus allows for the best performance, a system using DDR SDRAM works best if the CPU bus is also at 266MHz.

The P4, on the other hand, was designed to use RDRAM, hence the quad-pumped bus matching RDRAM in speed. Note that these bus speeds can easily be changed in the future, just as virtually every other processor that Intel has released can be. So, for example, I fully expect the Itanium to come out in a quad-pumped version using quad-data rate (QDR) memory when that technology becomes available. The bottom line is that nobody outside of the chip maker's inner circle really knows why some of these things come out the way they do!

Note

See Chapter 4, "Motherboards and Buses," for more information on chipsets and bus speeds.

Normally, you can set the motherboard speed and multiplier setting via jumpers or other configuration mechanism (such as BIOS setup) on the motherboard. Modern systems use a variable-frequency synthesizer circuit usually found in the main motherboard chipset to control the motherboard and CPU speed. Most Pentium motherboards have three or four speed settings. The processors used today are available in a variety of versions that run at different frequencies based on a given motherboard speed. For example, most of the Pentium chips run at a speed that is some multiple of the true motherboard speed. For example, Pentium processors and motherboards run at the speeds shown in Table 3.7.

Note

For information on specific AMD or Cyrix processors, see their respective sections later in this chapter.

Table 3.7   Intel Processor and Motherboard Speeds

CPU Type	CPU Speed (MHz/GHz)	CPU Clock Multiplier	Motherboard Speed (MHz)
Pentium	75	1.5x	50
Pentium	60	1x	60
Pentium	90	1.5x	60
Pentium	120	2x	60
Pentium	150	2.5x	60
Pentium/Pentium Pro	180	3x	60
Pentium	66	1x	66
Pentium	100	1.5x	66
Pentium	133	2x	66
Pentium/Pentium Pro	166	2.5x	66
Pentium/Pentium Pro	200	3x	66
Pentium/Pentium II	233	3.5x	66
Pentium(Mobile)/Pentium II/Celeron	266	4x	66

Table 3.7 Continued

CPU Type	CPU Speed (MHz/GHz)	CPU Clock Multiplier	Motherboard Speed (MHz)
Pentium II/Celeron	300	4.5x	66
Pentium II/Celeron	333	5x	66
Pentium II/Celeron	366	5.5x	66
Celeron	400	6x	66
Celeron	433	6.5x	66
Celeron	466	7x	66
Celeron	500	7.5x	66
Celeron	533	8x	66
Celeron	566	8.5x	66
Celeron	600	9x	66
Celeron	633	9.5x	66
Celeron	667	10x	66
Celeron	700	10.5x	66
Celeron	733	11x	66
Celeron	766	11.5x	66
Pentium II	350	3.5x	100
Pentium II	400	4x	100
Pentium II/III	450	4.5x	100
Pentium III	500	5x	100
Pentium III	550	5.5x	100
Pentium III	600	6x	100
Pentium III	650	6.5x	100
Pentium III	700	7x	100
Pentium III	750	7.5x	100
Pentium III/Celeron	800	8x	100
Pentium III/Celeron	850	8.5x	100
Pentium III	533	4x	133
Pentium III	600	4.5x	133
Pentium III	667	5x	133
Pentium III	733	5.5x	133
Pentium III	800	6x	133
Pentium III	866	6.5x	133
Pentium III	933	7x	133
Pentium III	1.0	7.5x	133
Pentium III	1.06	8x	133
Pentium III	1.13	8.5x	133
Pentium III	1.2	9x	133
Pentium III	1.26	9.5x	133
Pentium III	1.33	10x	133

Table 3.7   Continued

CPU Type	CPU Speed (MHz/GHz)	CPU Clock Multiplier	Motherboard Speed (MHz)
Pentium 4	1.3	3.25x	400
Pentium 4	1.4	3.5x	400
Pentium 4	1.5	3.75x	400
Pentium 4	1.6	4x	400
Pentium 4	1.7	4.25x	400
Pentium 4	1.8	4.5x	400
Pentium 4	1.9	4.75x	400
Pentium 4	2.0	5x	400
Pentium 4	2.1	5.25x	400
Itanium	733	2.75x	266
Itanium	800	3x	266

If all other variables are equal—including the type of processor, the number of wait states (empty cycles) added to different types of memory accesses, and the width of the data bus—you can compare two systems by their respective clock rates. However, the construction and design of the memory controller (contained in the motherboard chipset) as well as the type and amount of memory installed can have an enormous effect on a system's final execution speed.

In building a processor, a manufacturer tests it at various speeds, temperatures, and pressures. After the processor is tested, it receives a stamp indicating the maximum safe speed at which the unit will operate under the wide variation of temperatures and pressures encountered in normal operation. These ratings are clearly marked on the processor package.

Overclocking

In some systems, the processor speed can be set higher than the rating on the chip; this is called *over-clocking* the chip. In many cases, you can get away with a certain amount of overclocking because Intel, AMD, and others often build safety margins into their ratings. So, a chip rated for, say, 800MHz might in fact run at 900MHz or more but is instead down-rated to allow for a greater margin of reliability. By overclocking, you are using this margin and running the chip closer to its true maximum speed. I don't normally recommend overclocking for a novice, but if you are comfortable with playing with your system, and you can afford and are capable of dealing with any potential consequences, overclocking might enable you to get more performance from your system.

If you are intent on overclocking, there are several issues to consider. One is that most Intel processors since the Pentium II have been multiplier-locked before they are shipped out. Therefore, any changes to the multiplier setting on the motherboard simply are ignored by the chip. Both Intel and AMD lock the multipliers on most of their newer processors. Although originally done to prevent re-markers from fraudulently relabeling processors, this has impacted the computing performance enthusiast, leaving tweaking the motherboard bus speed as the only way to achieve a clock speed higher than standard.

You can run into problems increasing motherboard bus speed as well. Intel motherboards, for example, simply don't support clock speeds other than the standard 66MHz, 100MHz, and 133MHz settings. Also all their boards with speed settings done via software (BIOS Setup) read the proper settings from the installed processor and only allow those settings. In other words, you simply plug in the processor, and the Intel motherboard won't allow any other settings other than what that processor is designed for.

Even if you could fool the processor into accepting a different setting, the jump from 66MHz to 100MHz, or from 100 to 133MHz, is a large one, and many processors would not make that much of a jump reliably. For example, a Pentium III 800E runs at a 100MHz bus speed with an 8x multiplier. Bumping the motherboard speed to 133MHz would cause the processor to try to run at 8×133 or 1066MHz. It is highly unlikely that the chip would run reliably at that speed. Likewise, a Celeron 600E runs at 9×66MHz. Raising the bus speed to 100MHz would cause the chip to try and run at 9×100MHz or 900MHz, likely an unsuccessful change.

What is needed is a board that supports intermediate speed settings and that allows the settings to be changed in smaller increments. This is because a given chip is generally overclockable by a certain percentage. The smaller steps you can take when increasing speed, the more likely that you'll be able to come close to the actual maximum speed of the chip without going over. For example, the Asus P3V4X motherboard supports front-side bus speed settings of 66MHz, 75MHz, 83MHz, 90MHz, 95MHz, 100MHz, 103MHz, 105MHz, 110MHz, 112MHz, 115MHz, 120MHz, 124MHz, 133MHz, 140MHz, and 150MHz. By setting the 800MHz Pentium IIIE to increments above 100MHz, you'd have:

Multiplier (fixed)	Bus Speed	Processor Speed
8x	100MHz	800MHz
8x	103MHz	824MHz
8x	105MHz	840MHz
8x	110MHz	880MHz
8x	112MHz	896MHz
8x	115MHz	920MHz
8x	120MHz	960MHz
8x	124MHz	992MHz
8x	133MHz	1066MHz

Likewise, using this motherboard with a Celeron 600, you could try settings above the standard 66MHz bus speed as follows:

Multiplier (fixed)	Bus Speed	Processor Speed
9x	66MHz	600MHz
9x	75MHz	675MHz
9x	83MHz	747MHz
9x	90MHz	810MHz
9x	95MHz	855MHz
9x	100MHz	900MHz

Typically, a 10%–20% increase is successful, so with this motherboard, you are likely to get your processor running 100MHz or more faster than it was originally designed for.

Another trick used by overclockers is to play with the voltage settings for the CPU. All Slot 1, Slot A, Socket 8, Socket 370, and Socket A processors have automatic voltage detection, where the system will detect and set the correct voltage by reading certain pins on the processor. Some motherboards, such as those made by Intel, do not allow any changes to these settings manually. Other motherboards, such as the Asus P3V4X I mentioned earlier, allow you to tweak the voltage settings from the automatic setting up or down by tenths of a volt. Some experimenters have found that by either increasing or decreasing voltage slightly from the standard, a higher speed of overclock can be achieved with the system running stable.

My recommendation is to be careful when playing with voltages. You can damage the chip in this manner. Even without changing voltage, overclocking with an adjustable bus speed motherboard is very easy and fairly rewarding. I do recommend you make sure you are using a high-quality board, good memory, and especially a good system chassis with additional cooling fans and a heavy-duty power supply. See Chapter 21, "Power Supply and Chassis/Case," for more information on upgrading power supplies and chassis. Especially when overclocking, it is essential that the system components and especially the CPU remain properly cooled. Going a little bit overboard on the processor heatsink and adding extra cooling fans to the case never hurts and in many cases helps a great deal when hotrodding a system in this manner.

Note

One good source of online overclocking information is located at `http://www.tomshardware.com`. It includes, among other things, fairly thorough overclocking FAQs and an ongoing survey of users who have successfully (and sometimes unsuccessfully) overclocked their CPUs. Note that many of the newer Intel processors incorporate fixed bus multiplier ratios, which effectively prevent or certainly reduce the ability to overclock. Unfortunately, this can be overridden with a simple hardware fix, and many counterfeit processor vendors are selling re-marked (overclocked) chips.

The Processor Heatsink Might Hide the Rating

Most processors have heatsinks on top of them, which can prevent you from reading the rating printed on the chip.

A *heatsink* is a metal device that draws heat away from an electronic device. Most processors running at 50MHz and faster should have a heatsink installed to prevent the processor from overheating.

Fortunately, most CPU manufacturers are placing marks on the top and bottom of the processor. If the heatsink is difficult to remove from the chip, you can take the heatsink and chip out of the socket together and read the markings on the bottom of the processor to determine what you have.

Cyrix P-Ratings

Cyrix/IBM 6x86 processors use a PR (performance rating) scale that is not equal to the true clock speed in megahertz. For example, the Cyrix 6x86MX/MII-PR366 actually runs at only 250MHz (2.5 × 100MHz). This is a little misleading—you must set up the motherboard as if a 250MHz processor were being installed, not the 366MHz you might suspect. Unfortunately, this leads people to believe these systems are faster than they really are. Table 3.8 shows the relationship between the Cyrix 6x86, 6x86MX, and M-II P-Ratings versus the actual chip speeds in MHz.

Table 3.8 Cyrix P-Ratings Versus Actual Chip Speeds in MHz

CPU Type	P-Rating	Actual CPU Speed (MHz)	Clock Multiplier	Motherboard Speed (MHz)
6x86	PR90	80	2x	40
6x86	PR120	100	2x	50
6x86	PR133	110	2x	55
6x86	PR150	120	2x	60
6x86	PR166	133	2x	66
6x86	PR200	150	2x	75
6x86MX	PR133	100	2x	50

Table 3.8 Continued

CPU Type	P-Rating	Actual CPU Speed (MHz)	Clock Multiplier	Motherboard Speed (MHz)
6x86MX	PR133	110	2x	55
6x86MX	PR150	120	2x	60
6x86MX	PR150	125	2.5x	50
6x86MX	PR166	133	2x	66
6x86MX	PR166	137.5	2.5x	55
6x86MX	PR166	150	3x	50
6x86MX	PR166	150	2.5x	60
6x86MX	PR200	150	2x	75
6x86MX	PR200	165	3x	55
6x86MX	PR200	166	2.5x	66
6x86MX	PR200	180	3x	60
6x86MX	PR233	166	2x	83
6x86MX	PR233	187.5	2.5x	75
6x86MX	PR233	200	3x	66
6x86MX	PR266	207.5	2.5x	83
6x86MX	PR266	225	3x	75
6x86MX	PR266	233	3.5x	66
M-II	PR300	225	3x	75
M-II	PR300	233	3.5x	66
M-II	PR333	250	3x	83
M-II	PR366	250	2.5x	100
M-II	PR400	285	3x	95
M-II	PR433	300	3x	100
Cyrix III	PR433	350	3.5x	100
Cyrix III	PR466	366	3x	122
Cyrix III	PR500	400	3x	133
Cyrix III	PR533	433	3.5x	124
Cyrix III	PR533	450	4.5x	100

Note that a given P-Rating can mean several different actual CPU speeds—for example, a Cyrix 6x86MX-PR200 might actually be running at 150MHz, 165MHz, 166MHz, or 180MHz, but *not* at 200MHz.

This P-Rating is supposed to indicate speed in relation to an Intel Pentium processor, but the processor being compared to is the original non-MMX, small L1 cache version running on an older motherboard platform with an older chipset and slower technology memory. The P-Rating does not compare well against the Celeron, Pentium II, or Pentium III processors. In that case these chips are more comparative at their true speeds. In other words, the MII-PR366 really runs at only 250MHz and compares well against Intel processors running at closer to that speed. I consider calling a chip an MII-366 when it really runs at only 250MHz very misleading, to say the least.

AMD P-Ratings

Although both AMD and Cyrix concocted this misleading P-Rating system, AMD thankfully used it for only a short time and only on the older K5 processor. It still has the PR designation stamped on its newer chips, but all K6 and Athlon processors have PR numbers that match their actual CPU speeds in MHz. Table 3.9 shows the P-Rating and actual speeds of the AMD K5, K6, and Athlon processors.

Table 3.9   AMD P-Ratings Versus Actual Chip Speeds in MHz

CPU Type	P-Rating	Actual CPU Speed (MHz)	Clock Multiplier	Motherboard Speed (MHz)
K5	PR75	75	1.5x	50
K5	PR90	90	1.5x	60
K5	PR100	100	1.5x	66
K5	PR120	90	1.5x	60
K5	PR133	100	1.5x	66
K5	PR166	116.7	1.75x	66
K6	PR166	166	2.5x	66
K6	PR200	200	3x	66
K6	PR233	233	3.5x	66
K6	PR266	266	4x	66
K6	PR300	300	4.5x	66
K6-2	PR233	233	3.5x	66
K6-2	PR266	266	4x	66
K6-2	PR300	300	4.5x	66
K6-2	PR300	300	3x	100
K6-2	PR333	333	5x	66
K6-2	PR333	333	3.5x	95
K6-2	PR350	350	3.5x	100
K6-2	PR366	366	5.5x	66
K6-2	PR380	380	4x	95
K6-2	PR400	400	6x	66
K6-2	PR400	400	4x	100
K6-2	PR450	450	4.5x	100
K6-2	PR475	475	5x	95
K6-2	PR500	500	5x	100
K6-2	PR533	533	5.5x	97
K6-2	PR550	550	5.5x	100
K6-3	PR400	400	4x	100
K6-3	PR450	450	4.5x	100
Athlon	PR500	500	2.5x	200
Athlon	PR550	550	2.75x	200
Athlon/Duron	PR600	600	3x	200
Athlon/Duron	PR650	650	3.25x	200

Table 3.9   Continued

CPU Type	P-Rating	Actual CPU Speed (MHz)	Clock Multiplier	Motherboard Speed (MHz)
Athlon/Duron	PR700	700	3.5x	200
Athlon/Duron	PR750	750	3.75x	200
Athlon/Duron	PR800	800	4x	200
Athlon/Duron	PR850	850	4.25x	200
Athlon/Duron	PR900	900	4.5x	200
Athlon/Duron	PR950	950	4.75x	200
Athlon/Duron	PR1000	1.0	5x	200
Athlon	PR1100	1.1	5.5x	200
Athlon	PR1200	1.2	6x	200
Athlon	PR1300	1.3	6.5x	200
Athlon	PR1000	1.0	3.75x	266
Athlon	PR1133	1.13	4.25x	266
Athlon	PR1200	1.2	4.5x	266
Athlon	PR1333	1.33	5x	266

Note the Athlon to North Bridge processor bus actually runs at a double (2x) transfer speed, which is twice that of actual the motherboard clock speed.

Data Bus

Perhaps the most common way to describe a processor is by the speed at which it runs and the width of the processor's external data bus. This defines the number of data bits that can be moved into or out of the processor in one cycle. A *bus* is a series of connections that carry common signals. Imagine running a pair of wires from one end of a building to another. If you connect a 110v AC power generator to the two wires at any point and place outlets at convenient locations along the wires, you have constructed a power bus. No matter into which outlet you plug the wires, you have access to the same signal, which in this example is 110v AC power. Any transmission medium that has more than one outlet at each end can be called a bus. A typical computer system has several internal and external buses.

The processor bus discussed most often is the external data bus—the bundle of wires (or pins) used to send and receive data. The more signals that can be sent at the same time, the more data can be transmitted in a specified interval and, therefore, the faster (and wider) the bus. A wider data bus is like having a highway with more lanes, which enables greater throughput.

Data in a computer is sent as digital information consisting of a time interval in which a single wire carries 5v to signal a 1 data bit, or 0v to signal a 0 data bit. The more wires you have, the more individual bits you can send in the same time interval. A chip such as the 286 or 386SX, which has 16 wires for transmitting and receiving such data, has a 16-bit data bus. A 32-bit chip, such as the 386DX and 486, has twice as many wires dedicated to simultaneous data transmission as a 16-bit chip; a 32-bit chip can send twice as much information in the same time interval as a 16-bit chip. Modern processors such as the Pentium series have 64-bit external data buses. This means that all processors from the Pentium to the Athlon, Pentium 4, or Itanium can transfer 64 bits of data at a time to and from the system memory.

A good way to understand this flow of information is to consider a highway and the traffic it carries. If a highway has only one lane for each direction of travel, only one car at a time can move in a certain direction. If you want to increase traffic flow, you can add another lane so that twice as many cars pass in a specified time. You can think of an 8-bit chip as being a single-lane highway because 1 byte flows through at a time. (One byte equals 8 individual bits.) The 16-bit chip, with 2 bytes flowing at a time, resembles a two-lane highway. You might have four lanes in each direction to move a large number of automobiles; this structure corresponds to a 32-bit data bus, which has the capability to move 4 bytes of information at a time. Taking this further, a 64-bit data bus is like having an 8-lane highway moving data in and out of the chip!

Just as you can describe a highway by its lane width, you can describe a chip by the width of its data bus. When you read an advertisement that describes a 32-bit or 64-bit computer system, the ad usually refers to the CPU's data bus. This number provides a rough idea of the chip's performance potential (and, therefore, the system).

Perhaps the most important ramification of the data bus in a chip is that the width of the data bus also defines the size of a bank of memory. So, a 32-bit processor, such as the 486 class chips, reads and writes memory 32 bits at a time. Pentium-class processors, including the Pentium III and Celeron, read and write memory 64 bits at a time. Because standard 72-pin single inline memory modules (SIMMs) are only 32 bits wide, they must be installed one at a time in most 486 class systems; they're installed two at a time in most Pentium class systems. Newer dual inline memory modules (DIMMs) are 64 bits wide, so they are installed one at a time in Pentium class systems. Each DIMM is equal to a complete bank of memory in Pentium systems, which makes system configuration easy because they can then be installed or removed one at a time.

▶▶ See "Memory Banks," p. 438.

Internal Registers (Internal Data Bus)

The size of the internal registers indicate how much information the processor can operate on at one time and how it moves data around internally within the chip. This is sometimes also referred to as the *internal data bus*. The register size is essentially the same as the internal data bus size. A *register* is a holding cell within the processor; for example, the processor can add numbers in two different registers, storing the result in a third register. The register size determines the size of data on which the processor can operate. The register size also describes the type of software or commands and instructions a chip can run. That is, processors with 32-bit internal registers can run 32-bit instructions that are processing 32-bit chunks of data, but processors with 16-bit registers cannot. Most advanced processors today—chips from the 386 to the Pentium 4—use 32-bit internal registers and can therefore run the same 32-bit operating systems and software. The new Itanium processor has 64-bit internal registers, which require new operating systems and software to fully utilize.

Some processors have an internal data bus (made up of data paths and storage units called registers) that is larger than the external data bus. The 8088 and 386SX are examples of this structure. Each chip has an internal data bus twice the width of the external bus. These designs, which sometimes are called h*ybrid designs*, usually are low-cost versions of a "pure" chip. The 386SX, for example, can pass data around internally with a full 32-bit register size; for communications with the outside world, however, the chip is restricted to a 16-bit-wide data path. This design enables a systems designer to build a lower-cost motherboard with a 16-bit bus design and still maintain software and instruction set compatibility with the full 32-bit 386.

Internal registers often are larger than the data bus, which means the chip requires two cycles to fill a register before the register can be operated on. For example, both the 386SX and 386DX have internal 32-bit registers, but the 386SX must "inhale" twice (figuratively) to fill them, whereas the 386DX can do the job in one "breath." The same thing would happen when the data is passed from the registers back out to the system bus.

The Pentium is an example of this type of design. All Pentiums have a 64-bit data bus and 32-bit registers—a structure that might seem to be a problem until you understand that the Pentium has two internal 32-bit pipelines for processing information. In many ways, the Pentium is like two 32-bit chips in one. The 64-bit data bus provides for very efficient filling of these multiple registers. Multiple pipelines are called *superscalar* architecture, which was introduced with the Pentium processor.

▶▶ See "Pentium Processors," p. 129.

More advanced sixth-generation processors, such as the Pentium Pro and Pentium II/III, have as many as six internal pipelines for executing instructions. Although some of these internal pipes are dedicated to special functions, these processors can still execute as many as three instructions in one clock cycle. The newest Itanium processor uses 10-stage parallel pipelines, which enable it to execute as many as 20 operations per clock cycle.

Address Bus

The address bus is the set of wires that carries the addressing information used to describe the memory location to which the data is being sent or from which the data is being retrieved. As with the data bus, each wire in an address bus carries a single bit of information. This single bit is a single digit in the address. The more wires (digits) used in calculating these addresses, the greater the total number of address locations. The size (or width) of the address bus indicates the maximum amount of RAM that a chip can address.

The highway analogy can be used to show how the address bus fits in. If the data bus is the highway and the size of the data bus is equivalent to the number of lanes, the address bus relates to the house number or street address. The size of the address bus is equivalent to the number of digits in the house address number. For example, if you live on a street in which the address is limited to a two-digit (base 10) number, no more than 100 distinct addresses (00–99) can exist for that street (10^2). Add another digit, and the number of available addresses increases to 1,000 (000–999), or 10^3.

Computers use the binary (base 2) numbering system, so a two-digit number provides only four unique addresses (00, 01, 10, and 11), calculated as 2^2. A three-digit number provides only eight addresses (000–111), which is 2^3. For example, the 8086 and 8088 processors use a 20-bit address bus that calculates as a maximum of 2^{20} or 1,048,576 bytes (1MB) of address locations. Table 3.10 describes the memory-addressing capabilities of processors.

Table 3.10   Processor Memory-Addressing Capabilities

Processor Family	Address Bus	Bytes	Kilobytes (KB)	Megabytes (MB)	Giga-bytes (GB)	Tera-bytes (TB)
8088 8086	20-bit	1,048,576	1,024	1	—	—
286 386SX	24-bit	16,777,216	16,384	16	—	—
386DX 486 586	32-bit	4,294,967,296	4,194,304	4,096	4	—
686 786	36-bit	68,719,476,736	67,108,864	65,536	64	—
Itanium	44-bit	17,592,186,044,416	17,179,869,184	16,777,216	16,384	16

Note: The Pentium and AMD K6 are 586 (fifth-generation) processors. The Pentium Pro/II/III/Celeron and AMD Athlon/Duron are 686 (sixth-generation) processors, and the Pentium 4 is considered a 786 (seventh-generation) processor.

The data bus and address bus are independent, and chip designers can use whatever size they want for each. Usually, however, chips with larger data buses have larger address buses. The sizes of the buses can provide important information about a chip's relative power, measured in two important ways. The size of the data bus is an indication of the chip's information-moving capability, and the size of the address bus tells you how much memory the chip can handle.

Internal Level 1 Cache

All modern processors starting with the 486 family include an integrated L1 cache and controller. The integrated L1 cache size varies from processor to processor, starting at 8KB for the original 486DX and now up to 32KB, 64KB, or more in the latest processors.

Because L1 cache is always built into the processor die, it runs at the full-core speed of the processor internally. By full-core speed, I mean this cache runs at the higher clock multiplied internal processor speed rather than the external motherboard speed. This cache basically is an area of very fast memory built into the processor and is used to hold some of the current working set of code and data. Cache memory can be accessed with no wait states because it is running at the same speed as the processor core.

Using cache memory reduces a traditional system bottleneck because system RAM often is much slower than the CPU. This prevents the processor from having to wait for code and data from much slower main memory, therefore improving performance. Without the L1 cache, a processor frequently would be forced to wait until system memory caught up.

L1 cache is even more important in modern processors because it is often the only memory in the entire system that can truly keep up with the chip. Most modern processors are clock multiplied, which means they are running at a speed that is really a multiple of the motherboard into which they are plugged. The Pentium III 1GHz, for example, runs at a multiple of 7 1/2 times the true motherboard speed of 133MHz. Because the main memory is plugged into the motherboard, it can also run at only 133MHz maximum. The only 1GHz memory in such a system is the L1 and L2 caches built into the processor core. In this example, the Pentium III 1GHz processor has 32KB of integrated L1 cache in two separate 16KB blocks and 256KB of L2, all running at the full speed of the processor core.

▶▶   See "Memory Module Speed," p. 440.

If the data the processor wants is already in the internal cache, the CPU does not have to wait. If the data is not in the cache, the CPU must fetch it from the Level 2 cache or (in less sophisticated system designs) from the system bus, meaning main memory directly.

To understand the importance of cache, you need to know the relative speeds of processors and memory. The problem with this is that processor speed usually is expressed in MHz (millions of cycles per second), whereas memory speeds often are expressed in nanoseconds (billionths of a second per cycle).

Both are really time- or frequency-based measurements, and a chart comparing them can be found in Chapter 6, "Memory," Table 6.3. In this table, you will note that a 233MHz processor equates to 4.3 nanosecond cycling, which means you would need 4ns memory to keep pace with a 200MHz CPU. Also note that the motherboard of a 233MHz system typically runs at 66MHz, which corresponds to a speed of 15ns per cycle, and requires 15ns memory to keep pace. Finally note that 60ns main memory (common on many Pentium class systems) equates to a clock speed of approximately 16MHz. So in a typical Pentium 233 system, you have a processor running at 233MHz (4.3ns per cycle), a motherboard running at 66MHz (15ns per cycle), and main memory running at 16MHz (60ns per cycle).

How Cache Works

To learn how the L1 and L2 caches work, consider the following analogy.

This story involves a person (in this case you) eating food to act as the processor requesting and operating on data from memory. The kitchen where the food is prepared is the main memory (SIMM/DIMM) RAM. The cache controller is the waiter, and the L1 cache is the table at which you are seated. L2 cache is introduced as a food cart, which is positioned between your table and the kitchen.

Okay, here's the story. Say you start to eat at a particular restaurant every day at the same time. You come in, sit down, and order a hot dog. To keep this story proportionately accurate, let's say you normally eat at the rate of one bite (byte? <g>) every four seconds (233MHz = about 4ns cycling). It also takes 60 seconds for the kitchen to produce any given item that you order (60ns main memory).

So, when you first arrive, you sit down, order a hot dog, and you have to wait for 60 seconds for the food to be produced before you can begin eating. After the waiter brings the food, you start eating at your normal rate. Pretty quickly you finish the hot dog, so you call the waiter and order a hamburger. Again you wait 60 seconds while the hamburger is being produced. When it arrives, you again begin eating at full speed. After you finish the hamburger, you order a plate of fries. Again you wait, and after it is delivered 60 seconds later, you eat it at full speed. Finally, you decide to finish the meal and order cheesecake for dessert. After another 60-second wait, you can again eat dessert at full speed. Your overall eating experience consists of mostly a lot of waiting, followed by short bursts of actual eating at full speed.

After coming into the restaurant for two consecutive nights at exactly 6 p.m. and ordering the same items in the same order each time, on the third night the waiter begins to think; "I know this guy is going to be here at 6 p.m., order a hot dog, a hamburger, fries, and then cheesecake. Why don't I have these items prepared in advance and surprise him, maybe I'll get a big tip?" So you enter the restaurant and order a hot dog, and the waiter immediately puts it on your plate, with no waiting! You then proceed to finish the hot dog and right as you are about to request the hamburger, the waiter deposits one on your plate. The rest of the meal continues in the same fashion, and you eat the entire meal, taking a bite every four seconds, and never have to wait for the kitchen to prepare the food. Your overall eating experience this time consists of all eating, with no waiting for the food to be prepared, due primarily to the intelligence and thoughtfulness of your waiter.

This analogy exactly describes the function of the L1 cache in the processor. The L1 cache itself is the table that can contain one or more plates of food. Without a waiter, the space on the table is a simple food buffer. When stocked, you can eat until the buffer is empty, but nobody seems to be intelligently refilling it. The waiter is the cache controller who takes action and adds the intelligence to decide which dishes are to be placed on the table in advance of your needing them. Like the real cache controller, he uses his skills to literally guess which food you will require next, and if and when he guesses right, you never have to wait.

Let's now say on the fourth night you arrive exactly on time and start off with the usual hot dog. The waiter, by now really feeling confident, has the hot dog already prepared when you arrive, so there is no waiting.

Just as you finish the hot dog, and right as he is placing a hamburger on your plate, you say "Gee, I'd really like a bratwurst now; I didn't actually order this hamburger." The waiter guessed wrong, and the consequence is that this time you have to wait the full 60 seconds as the kitchen prepares your brat. This is known as a *cache miss*, in which the cache controller did not correctly fill the cache with the data the processor actually needed next. The result is waiting, or in the case of a sample 233MHz Pentium system, the system essentially throttles back to 16MHz (RAM speed) whenever a cache miss occurs. According to Intel, the L1 cache in most of its processors has approximately a 90% hit ratio.

This means that the cache has the correct data 90% of the time, and consequently the processor runs at full speed—233MHz in this example—90% of the time. However, 10% of the time the cache controller guesses wrong and the data has to be retrieved out of the significantly slower main memory, meaning the processor has to wait. This essentially throttles the system back to RAM speed, which in this example was 60ns or 16MHz.

In this analogy, the processor was 14 times faster than the main memory. Memory speeds have increased from 16MHz (60ns) to 266MHz (3.8ns), but processor speeds have also risen to 2GHz and beyond, so even in the latest systems, memory is still 7.5 or more times SLOWER than the processor. Cache is what makes up the difference.

The main feature of L1 cache is that it has always been integrated into the processor core, where it runs at the same speed as the core. This, combined with the hit ratio of 90% or greater, makes L1 cache very important for system performance.

Level 2 Cache

To mitigate the dramatic slowdown every time an L1 cache miss occurs, a secondary (L2) cache can be employed.

Using the restaurant analogy I used to explain L1 cache in the previous section, I'll equate the L2 cache to a cart of additional food items placed strategically such that the waiter can retrieve food from it in 15 seconds. In an actual Pentium class (Socket 7) system, the L2 cache is mounted on the motherboard, which means it runs at motherboard speed—66MHz, or 15ns in this example. Now, if you ask for an item the waiter did not bring in advance to your table, instead of making the long trek back to the kitchen to retrieve the food and bring it back to you 60 seconds later, he can first check the cart where he has placed additional items. If the requested item is there, he will return with it in only 15 seconds. The net effect in the real system is that instead of slowing down from 233MHz to 16MHz waiting for the data to come from the 60ns main memory, the data can instead be retrieved from the 15ns (66MHz) L2 cache. The effect is that the system slows down from 233MHz to 66MHz.

Just as with the L1 cache, most L2 caches have a hit ratio also in the 90% range; therefore, if you look at the system as a whole, 90% of the time it will be running at full speed (233MHz in this example) by retrieving data out of the L1 cache. Ten percent of the time it will slow down to retrieve the data from the L2 cache. Ninety percent of the time the processor goes to the L2 cache, the data will be in the L2, and 10% of that time it will have to go to the slow main memory to get the data because of an L2 cache miss. So, by combining both caches, our sample system runs at full processor speed 90% of the time (233MHz in this case), at motherboard speed 9% (90% of 10%) of the time (66MHz in this case), and at RAM speed about 1% (10% of 10%) of the time (16MHz in this case). You can clearly see the importance of both the L1 and L2 caches; without them the system uses main memory more often, which is significantly slower than the processor.

This brings up other interesting points. If you could spend money doubling the performance of either the main memory (RAM) or the L2 cache, which would you improve? Considering that main memory is used directly only about 1% of the time, if you doubled performance there, you would double the speed of your system only 1% of the time! That doesn't sound like enough of an improvement to justify much expense. On the other hand, if you doubled L2 cache performance, you would be doubling system performance 9% of the time, a much greater improvement overall. I'd much rather improve L2 than RAM performance.

The processor and system designers at Intel and AMD know this and have devised methods of improving the performance of L2 cache. In Pentium (P5) class systems, the L2 cache usually was found on the motherboard and had to therefore run at motherboard speed. Intel made the first dramatic improvement by migrating the L2 cache from the motherboard directly into the processor and initially running it at the same speed as the main processor. The cache chips were made by Intel and mounted next to the main processor die in a single chip housing. This proved too expensive, so with the Pentium II Intel began using cache chips from third-party suppliers such as Sony, Toshiba, NEC, Samsung, and others. Because these were supplied as complete packaged chips and not raw die, Intel mounted them on a circuit board alongside the processor. This is why the Pentium II was designed as a cartridge rather than what looked like a chip.

One problem was the speed of the available third-party cache chips. The fastest ones on the market were 3ns or higher, meaning 333MHz or less in speed. Because the processor was being driven in speed above that, in the Pentium II and initial Pentium III processors Intel had to run the L2 cache at half the processor speed because that is all the commercially available cache memory could handle. AMD followed suit with the Athlon processor, which had to drop L2 cache speed even further in some models to two-fifths or one-third the main CPU speed to keep the cache memory speed less than the 333MHz commercially available chips.

Then a breakthrough occurred, which first appeared in the Celeron processor 300A and above. These had 128KB of L2 cache, but no external chips were used. Instead, the L2 cache had been integrated directly into the processor core just like the L1. Consequently, both the L1 and L2 caches now would run at full processor speed, and more importantly scale up in speed as the processor speeds increased in the future. In the newer Pentium III, as well as all the Xeon and Celeron processors, the L2 cache runs at full processor core speed, which means there is no waiting or slowing down after an L1 cache miss. AMD also achieved full-core speed on-die cache in its later Athlon and Duron chips. Using on-die cache improves performance dramatically because the 9% of the time the system would be using the L2 it would now remain at full speed instead of slowing down to one-half or less the processor speed or, even worse, slow down to motherboard speed as in Socket 7 designs. Another benefit of on-die L2 cache is cost, which is less because now fewer parts are involved.

Let's revisit the restaurant analogy using a modern Pentium III 1GHz. You would now be taking a bite every one second (1GHz = 1ns cycling). The L1 cache would also be running at that speed, so you could eat anything on your table at that same rate (the table = L1 cache). The real jump in speed comes when you want something that isn't already on the table (L1 cache miss), in which case the waiter runs to the cart and returns nine out of ten times with the food you want in only one second (L2 speed = 1GHz or 1ns cycling). In this more modern system, you would run at 1GHz 99% of the time (L1 and L2 hit ratios combined) and slow down to RAM speed (wait for the kitchen) only 1% of the time as before. With faster memory running at 133MHz (7.5ns), you would have to wait only 7.5 seconds for the food to come from the kitchen. If only restaurant performance increased at the same rate processor performance has!

Cache Organization

The organization of the cache memory in the 486 and Pentium family is called a *four-way set associative cache*, which means that the cache memory is split into four blocks. Each block also is organized as 128 or 256 lines of 16 bytes each.

To understand how a four-way set associative cache works, consider a simple example. In the simplest cache design, the cache is set up as a single block into which you can load the contents of a corresponding block of main memory. This procedure is similar to using a bookmark to locate the current page of a book you are reading. If main memory equates to all the pages in the book, the bookmark indicates which pages are held in cache memory. This procedure works if the required data is located within the pages marked with the bookmark, but it does not work if you need to refer to a previously read page. In that case, the bookmark is of no use.

An alternative approach is to maintain multiple bookmarks to mark several parts of the book simultaneously. Additional hardware overhead is associated with having multiple bookmarks, and you also have to take time to check all the bookmarks to see which one marks the pages of data you need.

Each additional bookmark adds to the overhead but also increases your chance of finding the desired pages.

If you settle on marking four areas in the book, you have essentially constructed a four-way set associative cache. This technique splits the available cache memory into four blocks, each of which stores different lines of main memory. Multitasking environments, such as Windows, are good examples of environments in which the processor needs to operate on different areas of memory simultaneously and in which a four-way cache improves performance greatly.

The contents of the cache must always be in sync with the contents of main memory to ensure that the processor is working with current data. For this reason, the internal cache in the 486 family is a *write-through* cache. Write-through means that when the processor writes information out to the cache, that information is automatically written through to main memory as well.

By comparison, the Pentium and later chips have an internal write-back cache, which means that both reads and writes are cached, further improving performance. Even though the internal 486 cache is write-through, the system can employ an external write-back cache for increased performance. In addition, the 486 can buffer up to 4 bytes before actually storing the data in RAM, improving efficiency in case the memory bus is busy.

Another feature of improved cache designs is that they are nonblocking. This is a technique for reducing or hiding memory delays by exploiting the overlap of processor operations with data accesses. A *nonblocking* cache enables program execution to proceed concurrently with cache misses as long as certain dependency constraints are observed. In other words, the cache can handle a cache miss much better and enable the processor to continue doing something nondependent on the missing data.

The cache controller built into the processor also is responsible for watching the memory bus when alternative processors, known as *bus masters*, are in control of the system. This process of watching the bus is referred to as *bus snooping*. If a bus master device writes to an area of memory that also is stored in the processor cache currently, the cache contents and memory no longer agree. The cache controller then marks this data as invalid and reloads the cache during the next memory access, preserving the integrity of the system.

A secondary external L2 cache of extremely fast static RAM (SRAM) chips also is used in most systems. It further reduces the amount of time the CPU must spend waiting for data from system memory. The function of the secondary processor cache is similar to that of the onboard cache. The secondary processor cache holds information that is moving to the CPU, thereby reducing the time the CPU spends waiting and increasing the time the CPU spends performing calculations. Fetching information from the secondary processor cache rather than from system memory is much faster because of the SRAM chips' extremely fast speed—15 nanoseconds (ns) or less.

Pentium systems incorporate the secondary cache on the motherboard, whereas Pentium Pro and later systems have the secondary cache inside the processor package. By moving the L2 cache into the processor, systems are capable of running at speeds higher than the motherboard—up to as fast as the processor core.

As clock speeds increase, cycle time decreases. Most SIMM memory used in Pentium and earlier systems was 60ns, which works out to be only about 16MHz! Standard motherboard speeds are now 66MHz, 100MHz, or 133MHz, and processors are available at 600MHz or more. Newer systems don't use cache on the motherboard any longer because the faster SDRAM or RDRAM used in modern Pentium Celeron/II/III systems can keep up with the motherboard speed. The trend today is toward integrating the L2 cache into the processor die just like the L1 cache. This enables the L2 to run at full-core speed because it is now a part of the core. Cache speed is always more important than size. The rule is that a smaller but faster cache is always better than a slower but bigger cache. Table 3.11 illustrates the need for and function of L1 (internal) and L2 (external) caches in modern systems.

Table 3.11   CPU Speeds Relative to Cache, SIMM/DIMM, and Motherboard

CPU Type	Pentium	Pentium Pro	Pentium II	Pentium II
CPU speed	233MHz	200MHz	333MHz	450MHz
L1 cache speed	4.3ns (233MHz)	5.0ns (200MHz)	3.0ns (333MHz)	2.2ns (450MHz)
L2 cache speed	15ns (66MHz)	5ns (200MHz)	6ns (166MHz)	4.4ns (225MHz)
Motherboard speed	66MHz	66MHz	66MHz	100MHz
RAM type	FPM/EDO	FPM/EDO	SDRAM	SDRAM
RAM speed	60ns (16MHz)	60ns (16MHz)	15ns (66MHz)	10ns (100MHz)

CPU Type	AMD K6-2	AMD K6-3	Pentium III (Katmai)	AMD Athlon
CPU speed	550MHz	450MHz	600MHz	800MHz
L1 cache speed	1.8ns (550MHz)	2.2ns (450MHz)	1.6ns (600MHz)	1.3ns (800MHz)
L2 cache speed	10ns (100MHz)	2.2ns (450MHz)	3.3ns (300MHz)	3.1ns (320MHz)
Motherboard speed	100MHz	100MHz	100MHz	200MHz
RAM type	SDRAM	SDRAM	SDRAM	SDRAM
RAM speed	10ns (100MHz)	10ns (100MHz)	10ns (100MHz)	10ns (100MHz)

CPU Type	AMD Athlon	AMD Duron	AMD Athlon (Thunderbird)	Celeron
CPU speed	1000MHz	800MHz	1000MHz	800MHz
L1 cache speed	1ns (1000MHz)	1.3ns (800MHz)	1ns (1000MHz)	1.3ns (800MHz)
L2 cache speed	3ns (333MHz)	1.3ns (800MHz)	1ns (1000MHz)	1.3ns (800MHz)
Motherboard speed	200MHz	200MHz	266MHz	100MHz
RAM type	SDRAM	SDRAM	DDR	SDRAM
RAM speed	10ns (100MHz)	10ns (100MHz)	3.8ns (266MHz)	10ns (100MHz)

CPU Type	Pentium III (Coppermine)	Pentium 4	Itanium
CPU speed	1000MHz	1.7GHz	800MHz
L1 cache speed	1ns (1000MHz)	0.6ns (1.7GHz)	1.3ns (800MHz)
L2 cache speed	1ns (1000MHz)	0.6ns (1.7GHz)	1.3ns (800MHz)
Motherboard speed	133MHz	400MHz	266MHz
RAM type	SDRAM	RDRAM	DDR
RAM speed	7.5ns (133MHz)	2.5ns (800MHz)	3.8ns (266MHz)

Note: RDRAM technically runs at 800MHz, but the channel is only 16 bits wide, resulting in a bandwidth of 1.6GB/sec, which is equivalent to running 200MHz at the 64-bit width of the processor data bus.

The Celeron processors at 300MHz and faster as well as the Pentium III processors at 600MHz and faster have on-die L2 cache that runs at the full-core speed of the processor. Newer Athlon processors and all Duron processors have full-core speed on-die cache as well. The older Pentium II and III processors, as well as the older Athlons, use external L2 and run the cache at either one-half, two-fifths, or one-third of the core processor speed. As you can see, having two levels of cache between the very fast CPU and the much slower main memory helps minimize any wait states the processor might have to endure, especially those with the on-die L2. This enables the processor to keep working closer to its true speed.

Processor Modes

All Intel 32-bit and later processors, from the 386 on up, can run in several modes. Processor modes refer to the various operating environments and affect the instructions and capabilities of the chip. The processor mode controls how the processor sees and manages the system memory and the tasks that use it.

Three different modes of operation possible are

- Real mode (16-bit software)
- Protected mode (32-bit software)
- Virtual real mode (16-bit programs within a 32-bit environment)

Real Mode

The original IBM PC included an 8088 processor that could execute 16-bit instructions using 16-bit internal registers and could address only 1MB of memory using 20 address lines. All original PC software was created to work with this chip and was designed around the 16-bit instruction set and 1MB memory model. For example, DOS and all DOS software, Windows 1.x through 3.x, and all Windows 1.x through 3.x applications are written using 16-bit instructions. These 16-bit operating systems and applications are designed to run on an original 8088 processor.

◄◄ See "Internal Registers," p. 59.

◄◄ See "Address Bus," p. 60.

Later processors such as the 286 could also run the same 16-bit instructions as the original 8088, but much faster. In other words, the 286 was fully compatible with the original 8088 and could run all 16-bit software just the same as an 8088, but, of course, that software would run faster. The 16-bit instruction mode of the 8088 and 286 processors has become known as *real mode*. All software running in real mode must use only 16-bit instructions and live within the 20-bit (1MB) memory architecture it supports. Software of this type is usually single-tasking—only one program can run at a time. No built-in protection exists to keep one program from overwriting another program or even the operating system in memory, so if more than one program is running, one of them could bring the entire system to a crashing halt.

Protected (32-bit) Mode

Then came the 386, which was the PC industry's first 32-bit processor. This chip could run an entirely new 32-bit instruction set. To take full advantage of the 32-bit instruction set, a 32-bit operating system and a 32-bit application were required. This new 32-bit mode was referred to as *protected mode*, which alludes to the fact that software programs running in that mode are protected from overwriting one another in memory. Such protection helps make the system much more crash-proof because an errant program cannot very easily damage other programs or the operating system. In addition, a crashed program can be terminated, while the rest of the system continues to run unaffected.

Knowing that new operating systems and applications—which take advantage of the 32-bit protected mode—would take some time to develop, Intel wisely built a backward-compatible real mode into the 386. That enabled it to run unmodified 16-bit operating systems and applications. It ran them quite well—much more quickly than any previous chip. For most people, that was enough; they did not necessarily want any new 32-bit software—they just wanted their existing 16-bit software to run more quickly. Unfortunately, that meant the chip was never running in the 32-bit protected mode, and all the features of that capability were being ignored.

When a high-powered processor such as a Pentium III is running DOS (real mode), it acts like a "Turbo 8088." Turbo 8088 means that the processor has the advantage of speed in running any 16-bit programs; it otherwise can use only the 16-bit instructions and access memory within the same 1MB memory map of the original 8088. Therefore, if you have a 128MB Pentium III system running Windows 3.x or DOS, you are effectively using only the first megabyte of memory, leaving the other 127MB largely unused!

New operating systems and applications that ran in the 32-bit protected mode of the modern processors were needed. Being stubborn, we resisted all the initial attempts at getting switched over to a 32-bit environment. It seems that as a user community, we are very resistant to change and would be content with our older software running faster rather than adopting new software with new features. I'll be the first one to admit that I was one of those stubborn users myself!

Because of this resistance, 32-bit operating systems, such as Unix or variants (such as Linux), OS/2, and even Windows NT and Windows 2000, have had a very hard time getting any mainstream share in the PC marketplace. Out of those, Windows 2000 is the only one that will likely become a true mainstream product, and that is mainly because Microsoft has coerced us in that direction with Windows 95 through 98 and Me. Windows 3.x was the last full 16-bit operating system. In fact, it was not a complete operating system because it ran on top of DOS.

Microsoft realized how stubborn the installed base of PC users was so it developed Windows 95 through the current Windows Me as a bridge to a full 32-bit world. Windows 95, 98, and Me are mostly 32-bit operating systems but retain enough 16-bit capability to fully run old 16-bit applications. Windows 95 came out in August 1995, a full 10 years later than the introduction of the first 32-bit PC processor! It has taken us only 10 years to migrate to software that can fully use the processors we have in front of us.

The new Itanium processor adds 64-bit native capability to the table. It also runs all the existing 32-bit software, but to fully take advantage of the processor, a 64-bit OS and applications are required. Microsoft has released 64-bit versions of Windows XP, and several companies have released 64-bit applications for networking and workstation use.

Virtual Real Mode

The key to the backward compatibility of the Windows 32-bit environment is the third mode in the processor: virtual real mode. *Virtual real* is essentially a virtual real mode 16-bit environment that runs inside 32-bit protected mode. When you run a DOS prompt window inside Windows, you have created a virtual real mode session. Because protected mode enables true multitasking, you can actually have several real mode sessions running, each with its own software running on a virtual PC. This can all run simultaneously, even while other 32-bit applications are running.

Note that any program running in a virtual real mode window can access up to only 1MB of memory, which that program will believe is the first and only megabyte of memory in the system. In other words, if you run a DOS application in a virtual real window, it will have a 640KB limitation on memory usage. That is because there is only 1MB of total RAM in a 16-bit environment, and the upper 384KB is reserved for system use. The virtual real window fully emulates an 8088 environment, so that aside from speed, the software runs as if it were on an original real mode-only PC. Each virtual machine gets its own 1MB address space, an image of the real hardware BIOS routines, and emulation of all other registers and features found in real mode.

Virtual real mode is used when you use a DOS window to run a DOS or Windows 3.x 16-bit program. When you start a DOS application, Windows creates a virtual DOS machine under which it can run.

One interesting thing to note is that all Intel and Intel-compatible (such as AMD and Cyrix) processors power up in real mode. If you load a 32-bit operating system, it automatically switches the processor into 32-bit mode and takes control from there.

Some 16-bit (DOS and Windows 3.x) applications misbehave, which means they do things that even virtual real mode does not support. Diagnostics software is a perfect example of this. Such software does not run properly in a real-mode (virtual real) window under Windows. In that case, you can still run your Pentium III in the original no-frills real mode by either booting to a DOS floppy or, in the case of Windows 9x (excluding Me), interrupting the boot process and commanding the system to boot plain DOS. This is accomplished on Windows 9x systems by pressing the F8 key when you see the prompt Starting Windows... on the screen or immediately after the beep when the power on self test (POST) is completed. In the latter case, it helps to press the F8 key multiple times because getting the timing just right is difficult and Windows 9x looks for the key during only a short two-second time window. If successful, you will then see the Startup menu; you can select one of the command prompt choices, which tell the system to boot plain 16-bit real mode DOS. The choice of Safe Mode Command Prompt is best if you are going to run true hardware diagnostics, which do not normally run in protected mode and should be run with a minimum of drivers and other software loaded.

Note that even though Windows Me is based on Windows 98, Microsoft removed the Startup menu option in an attempt to further wean us from any 16-bit operation. Windows NT and 2000 also lack the capability to interrupt the startup in this manner. For these operating systems, you need a Startup Disk (floppy), which you can create and then use to boot the system in real mode. Normally, you would do this to perform certain maintenance procedures, especially such as running hardware diagnostics or doing direct disk sector editing.

Although real mode is used by 16-bit DOS and "standard" DOS applications, special programs were available that "extend" DOS and allow access to extended memory (over 1MB). These are sometimes called *DOS extenders* and usually are included as a part of any DOS or Windows 3.x software that uses them. The protocol that describes how to make DOS work in protected mode is called DOS protected mode interface (DPMI). DPMI was used by Windows 3.x to access extended memory for use with Windows 3.x applications. It allowed these programs to use more memory even though they were still 16-bit programs. DOS extenders are especially popular in DOS games because they enable them to access much more of the system memory than the standard 1MB most real mode programs can address. These DOS extenders work by switching the processor in and out of real mode. In the case of those that run under Windows, they use the DPMI interface built into Windows, enabling them to share a portion of the system's extended memory.

Another exception in real mode is that the first 64KB of extended memory is actually accessible to the PC in real mode, despite the fact that it's not supposed to be possible. This is the result of a bug in the original IBM AT with respect to the 21st memory address line, known as A20 (A0 is the first address line). By manipulating the A20 line, real-mode software can gain access to the first 64KB of extended memory—the first 64KB of memory past the first megabyte. This area of memory is called the *high memory area (HMA)*.

SMM (Power Management)

Spurred on primarily by the goal of putting faster and more powerful processors in laptop computers, Intel has created power-management circuitry. This circuitry enables processors to conserve energy use and lengthen battery life. This was introduced initially in the Intel 486SL processor, which is an enhanced version of the 486DX processor. Subsequently, the power-management features were universalized and incorporated into all Pentium and later processors. This feature set is called SMM, which stands for *system management mode*.

SMM circuitry is integrated into the physical chip but operates independently to control the processor's power use based on its activity level. It enables the user to specify time intervals after which the CPU will be partially or fully powered down. It also supports the Suspend/Resume feature that allows for instant power on and power off, used mostly with laptop PCs. These settings usually are controlled via system BIOS settings.

Superscalar Execution

The fifth-generation Pentium and newer processors feature multiple internal instruction execution pipelines, which enable them to execute multiple instructions at the same time. The 486 and all preceding chips can perform only a single instruction at a time. Intel calls the capability to execute more than one instruction at a time *superscalar* technology. This technology provides additional performance compared with the 486.

▶▶ See "Pentium Processors," p. 129.

Superscalar architecture usually is associated with high-output Reduced Instruction Set Computer (RISC) chips. A RISC chip has a less complicated instruction set with fewer and simpler instructions. Although each instruction accomplishes less, overall the clock speed can be higher, which can usually increase performance. The Pentium is one of the first Complex Instruction Set Computer (CISC) chips to be considered superscalar. A CISC chip uses a richer, fuller-featured instruction set, which has more complicated instructions. As an example, say you wanted to instruct a robot to screw in a light bulb. Using CISC instructions you would say

1. Pick up the bulb.
2. Insert it into the socket.
3. Rotate clockwise until tight.

Using RISC instructions, you would say something more along the lines of

1. Lower hand.
2. Grasp bulb.
3. Raise hand.
4. Insert bulb into socket.
5. Rotate clockwise one turn.
6. Is bulb tight? If not repeat step 5.
7. End.

Overall, many more RISC instructions are required to do the job because each instruction is simpler (reduced) and does less. The advantage is that there are fewer overall commands the robot (or processor) has to deal with, and it can execute the individual commands more quickly, and thus in many cases execute the complete task (or program) more quickly as well. The debate goes on whether RISC or CISC is really better, but in reality there is no such thing as a pure RISC or CISC chip—it is all just a matter of definition, and the lines are somewhat arbitrary.

Intel and compatible processors have generally been regarded as CISC chips, although the fifth- and sixth-generation versions have many RISC attributes and internally break CISC instructions down into RISC versions.

MMX Technology

MMX technology was originally named for multimedia extensions, or matrix math extensions, depending on whom you ask. Intel officially states that it is actually not an abbreviation and stands for nothing other than the letters MMX (not being an abbreviation was apparently required so that the letters could be trademarked); however, the internal origins are probably one of the preceding.

MMX technology was introduced in the later fifth-generation Pentium processors (see Figure 3.2) as a kind of add-on that improves video compression/decompression, image manipulation, encryption, and I/O processing—all of which are used in a variety of today's software.

Figure 3.2   An Intel Pentium MMX chip shown from the top and bottom (exposing the die). *Photograph used by permission of Intel Corporation.*

MMX consists of two main processor architectural improvements. The first is very basic; all MMX chips have a larger internal L1 cache than their non-MMX counterparts. This improves the performance of any and all software running on the chip, regardless of whether it actually uses the MMX-specific instructions.

The other part of MMX is that it extends the processor instruction set with 57 new commands or instructions, as well as a new instruction capability called single instruction, multiple data (SIMD).

Modern multimedia and communication applications often use repetitive loops that, while occupying 10% or less of the overall application code, can account for up to 90% of the execution time. SIMD enables one instruction to perform the same function on multiple pieces of data, similar to a teacher telling an entire class to "sit down," rather than addressing each student one at a time. SIMD enables the chip to reduce processor-intensive loops common with video, audio, graphics, and animation.

Intel also added 57 new instructions specifically designed to manipulate and process video, audio, and graphical data more efficiently. These instructions are oriented to the *highly parallel* and often repetitive sequences often found in multimedia operations. Highly parallel refers to the fact that the same processing is done on many data points, such as when modifying a graphic image. The main drawbacks to MMX were that it worked only on integer values and used the floating-point unit for processing, so time was lost when a shift to floating-point operations was necessary. These drawbacks were corrected in the additions to MMX from Intel and AMD.

Intel licensed the MMX capabilities to competitors such as AMD and Cyrix, who were then able to upgrade their own Intel-compatible processors with MMX technology.

SSE and SSE2

In February 1999, Intel introduced the Pentium III processor, and included in that processor was an update to MMX called Streaming SIMD Extensions (SSE). These were also called Katmai New Instructions (KNI) up until their debut because they were originally included on the Katmai processor, which was the codename for the Pentium III. The Celeron 533A and faster Celeron processors based on the Pentium III core also support SSE instructions. The earlier Pentium II and Celeron 533 and lower (based on the Pentium II core) do not support SSE.

SSE includes 70 new instructions for graphics and sound processing over what MMX provided. SSE is similar to MMX; in fact, besides being called KNI, SSE was also called MMX-2 by some before it was released. In addition to adding more MMX style instructions, the SSE instructions allow for floating-point calculations and now use a separate unit within the processor instead of sharing the standard floating-point unit as MMX did.

SSE2 was introduced in November 2000, along with the Pentium 4 processor, and adds 144 additional SIMD instructions. SSE2 also includes all the previous MMX and SSE instructions.

The Streaming SIMD Extensions consist of new instructions, including SIMD floating-point, additional SIMD integer, and cacheability control instructions. Some of the technologies that benefit from the Streaming SIMD Extensions include advanced imaging, 3D video, streaming audio and video (DVD playback), and speech-recognition applications. The benefits of SSE include the following:

- Higher resolution and higher quality image viewing and manipulation for graphics software
- High-quality audio, MPEG2 video, and simultaneous MPEG2 encoding and decoding for multimedia applications
- Reduced CPU utilization for speech recognition, as well as higher accuracy and faster response times when running speech-recognition software

The SSE and SSE2 instructions are particularly useful with MPEG2 decoding, which is the standard scheme used on DVD video discs. SSE-equipped processors should therefore be more capable of performing MPEG2 decoding in software at full speed without requiring an additional hardware MPEG2 decoder card. SSE-equipped processors are much better and faster than previous processors when it comes to speech recognition, as well.

One of the main benefits of SSE over plain MMX is that it supports single-precision floating-point SIMD operations, which have posed a bottleneck in the 3D graphics processing. Just as with plain MMX, SIMD enables multiple operations to be performed per processor instruction. Specifically, SSE supports up to four floating-point operations per cycle; that is, a single instruction can operate on four pieces of data simultaneously. SSE floating-point instructions can be mixed with MMX instructions with no performance penalties. SSE also supports data *prefetching*, which is a mechanism for reading data into the cache before it is actually called for.

Note that for any of the SSE instructions to be beneficial, they must be encoded in the software you are using, so SSE-aware applications must be used to see the benefits. Most software companies writing graphics- and sound-related software today have updated those applications to be SSE aware and use the features of SSE. For example, high-powered graphics applications such as Adobe Photoshop support SSE instructions for higher performance on processors equipped with SSE. Microsoft includes support for SSE in its DirectX 6.1 and later video and sound drivers, which are included with Windows 98 Second Edition, Windows Me, Windows NT 4.0 (with service pack 5 or later), and Windows 2000.

SSE is an extension to MMX, and SSE2 is an extension to SSE; therefore, processors that support SSE2 also support the SSE instructions, and processors that support SSE also support the original MMX instructions. This means that standard MMX-enabled applications run as they did on MMX-only processors.

3DNow and Enhanced 3DNow

3DNow technology is AMD's alternative to the SSE instructions in the Intel processors. Actually, 3DNow originally came out in the K6 series before Intel released SSE in the Pentium III, and then AMD added Enhanced 3DNow to the Athlon and Duron processors. AMD licensed MMX from Intel, and all its K6 series, Athlon, Duron, and later processors include full MMX instruction support. Not wanting to additionally license the SSE instructions being developed by Intel, AMD first came up with a different set of extensions beyond MMX called 3DNow. Introduced in May 1998 in the K6-2 processor and later enhanced when the Athlon was introduced in June 1999, 3DNow and Enhanced 3DNow are sets of instructions that extend the multimedia capabilities of the AMD chips beyond MMX. This enables greater performance for 3D graphics, multimedia, and other floating-point–intensive PC applications.

3DNow technology is a set of 21 instructions that uses SIMD techniques to operate on arrays of data rather than single elements. Enhanced 3DNow adds 24 more instructions to the original 21 for a total of 45 new instructions. Positioned as an extension to MMX technology, 3DNow is similar to the SSE found in the Pentium III and Celeron processors from Intel. According to AMD, 3DNow provides approximately the same level of improvement to MMX as did SSE, but in fewer instructions with less complexity. Although similar in capability, they are not compatible at the instruction level, so software specifically written to support SSE does not support 3DNow, and vice versa.

Just as with SSE, 3DNow also supports single precision floating-point SIMD operations and enables up to four floating-point operations per cycle. 3DNow floating-point instructions can be mixed with MMX instructions with no performance penalties. 3DNow also supports data prefetching.

Also like SSE, 3DNow is well supported by software, including Windows 9x, Windows NT 4.0, and all newer Microsoft operating systems. Application programming interfaces such as Microsoft's DirectX 6.x API and SGI's Open GL API have been optimized for 3DNow technology as have the drivers for many leading 3D graphic accelerator suppliers, including 3Dfx, ATI, Matrox, and nVidia. Although many games and video drivers support 3DNow, support is lacking from some of the major business graphics applications, such as Adobe Photoshop.

Dynamic Execution

First used in the P6 or sixth-generation processors, *dynamic execution* is an innovative combination of three processing techniques designed to help the processor manipulate data more efficiently. Those techniques are multiple branch prediction, data flow analysis, and speculative execution. Dynamic execution enables the processor to be more efficient by manipulating data in a more logically ordered fashion rather than simply processing a list of instructions, and it is one of the hallmarks of all sixth-generation processors.

The way software is written can dramatically influence a processor's performance. For example, performance is adversely affected if the processor is frequently required to stop what it is doing and jump or branch to a point elsewhere in the program. Delays also occur when the processor cannot process a new instruction until the current instruction is completed. Dynamic execution enables the processor to not only dynamically predict the order of instructions, but execute them out of order internally, if necessary, for an improvement in speed.

Multiple Branch Prediction

Multiple branch prediction predicts the flow of the program through several branches. Using a special algorithm, the processor can anticipate jumps or branches in the instruction flow. It uses this to predict where the next instructions can be found in memory with an accuracy of 90% or greater. This is possible because, while the processor is fetching instructions, it is also looking at instructions further ahead in the program.

Data Flow Analysis

Data flow analysis analyzes and schedules instructions to be executed in an optimal sequence, independent of the original program order. The processor looks at decoded software instructions and determines whether they are available for processing or are instead dependent on other instructions to be executed first. The processor then determines the optimal sequence for processing and executes the instructions in the most efficient manner.

Speculative Execution

Speculative execution increases performance by looking ahead of the program counter and executing instructions that are likely to be needed later. Because the software instructions being processed are based on predicted branches, the results are stored in a pool for later referral. If they are to be executed by the resultant program flow, the already completed instructions are retired and the results are committed to the processor's main registers in the original program execution order. This technique essentially enables the processor to complete instructions in advance and then grab the already completed results when necessary.

Dual Independent Bus Architecture

The Dual Independent Bus (DIB) architecture was first implemented in the sixth-generation processors from Intel and AMD. DIB was created to improve processor bus bandwidth and performance. Having two (dual) independent data I/O buses enables the processor to access data from either of its buses simultaneously and in parallel, rather than in a singular sequential manner (as in a single-bus system). The main (often called front-side) processor bus is the interface between the processor and the motherboard or chipset. The second (back-side) bus in a processor with DIB is used for the L2 cache, enabling it to run at much greater speeds than if it were to share the main processor bus.

Note

The DIB architecture is explained more fully in Chapter 4. For an example of the typical Pentium II/III system architecture, see Figure 4.34.

Two buses make up the DIB architecture: the L2 cache bus and the processor-to-main-memory, or system, bus. The P6 class processors from the Pentium Pro to the Celeron, Pentium II/III/4, and Athlon/Duron processors can use both buses simultaneously, eliminating a bottleneck there. The DIB architecture enables the L2 cache of the 1GHz Pentium III or Athlon, for example, to run 15 times faster than the L2 cache of older Pentium and K6 processors. Because the back-side, or L2 cache, bus is coupled to the speed of the processor core as the frequency of processors increases, so will the speed of the L2 cache increase.

The key to implementing DIB was to move the L2 cache memory off the motherboard and into the processor package. L1 cache always has been a direct part of the processor die, but L2 was larger and had to be external. By moving the L2 cache into the processor, the L2 cache could run at speeds more like the L1 cache, much faster than the motherboard or processor bus. To move the L2 cache into the processor initially, modifications had to be made to the CPU socket or slot. Two slot-based and five socket-based solutions fully support DIB: Slot 1 (Pentium II/III/Celeron), Slot A (Athlon), Socket 8 (Pentium Pro), Socket 370 (Pentium III/Celeron), Socket 423 (Pentium 4), Socket A (Athlon/Duron), and Socket 603 (Xeon).

DIB also enables the system bus to perform multiple simultaneous transactions (instead of singular sequential transactions), accelerating the flow of information within the system and boosting performance. Overall, DIB architecture offers up to three times the bandwidth performance over a single-bus architecture processor.

Processor Manufacturing

Processors are manufactured primarily from silicon, the second most common element on the planet (only the element oxygen is more common). Silicon is the primary ingredient in beach sand; however, in that form it isn't pure enough to be used in chips.

The manner in which silicon is formed into chips is a lengthy process that starts by growing pure silicon crystals via what is called the Czochralski method (named after the inventor of the process). In this method, electric arc furnaces transform the raw materials (primarily quartz rock that is mined) into metallurgical-grade silicon. Then to further weed out impurities, the silicon is converted to a liquid, distilled, and then redeposited in the form of semiconductor-grade rods, which are 99.999999% pure. These rods are then mechanically broken up into chunks and packed into quartz crucibles, which are loaded into electric crystal pulling ovens. There the silicon chunks are melted at more than 2,500° Fahrenheit. To prevent impurities, the ovens usually are mounted on very thick concrete cubes—often on a suspension to prevent any vibration, which would damage the crystal as it forms.

After the silicon is melted, a small seed crystal is inserted into the molten silicon and slowly rotated (see Figure 3.3). As the seed is pulled out of the molten silicon, some of the silicon sticks to the seed and hardens in the same crystal structure as the seed. By carefully controlling the pulling speed (10–40 millimeters per hour) and temperature (approximately 2,500° F), the crystal grows with a narrow neck that then widens into the full desired diameter. Depending on the chips being made, each ingot is approximately 8 or 12 inches in diameter and more than 5 feet long, weighing hundreds of pounds.

Seed

Single silicon crystal

Water-cooled chamber

Heat shield

Carbon heater

Graphite crucible

Crucible support

Spill tray

Electrode

Figure 3.3   Growing a pure silicon ingot in a high-pressure, high-temperature oven.

The ingot is then ground into a perfect 200mm- (8-inch) or 300mm-diameter cylinder, with a flat cut on one side for positioning accuracy and handling. Each ingot is then cut with a high-precision diamond saw into more than a thousand circular wafers, each less than a millimeter thick (see Figure 3.4). Each wafer is then polished to a mirror-smooth surface.

Figure 3.4   Slicing a silicon ingot into wafers with a diamond saw.

Chips are manufactured from the wafers using a process called *photolithography*. Through this photographic process, transistors and circuit and signal pathways are created in semiconductors by depositing different layers of various materials on the chip, one after the other. Where two specific circuits intersect, a transistor or switch can be formed.

The photolithographic process starts when an insulating layer of silicon dioxide is grown on the wafer through a vapor deposition process. Then a coating of photoresist material is applied, and an image of that layer of the chip is projected through a mask onto the now light-sensitive surface.

Doping is the term used to describe chemical impurities added to silicon (which is naturally a nonconductor), creating a material with semiconductor properties. The projector uses a specially created mask, which is essentially a negative of that layer of the chip etched in chrome on a quartz plate. The Pentium III currently uses 20 or more masks to create six layers of metal and semiconductor interconnects.

As the light passes through a mask, the light is focused on the wafer surface, imprinting it with the image of that layer of the chip. Each individual chip image is called a *die*. A device called a *stepper* then moves the wafer over a little bit, and the same mask is used to imprint another chip die immediately next to the previous one. After the entire wafer is imprinted with chips, a caustic solution washes away the areas where the light struck the photoresist, leaving the mask imprints of the individual chip vias (interconnections between layers) and circuit pathways. Then, another layer of semiconductor material is deposited on the wafer with more photoresist on top, and the next mask is used to produce the next layer of circuitry. Using this method, the layers and components of each chip are built one on top of the other until the chips are completed.

The final masks add the *metallization* layers, which are the metal interconnects used to tie all the individual transistors and other components together. Most chips use aluminum interconnects, although during 2002 many will be moving to copper. The first commercial PC processor chip to use copper is the 0.18 micron Athlon made in AMD's Dresden fab. Copper is a better conductor than aluminum and allows smaller interconnects with less resistance, meaning smaller and faster chips can be made. The reason copper hasn't been used up until recently is that there were difficult corrosion problems to overcome during the manufacturing process that were not as much of a problem with aluminum. Now that these problems have been solved, more and more chips will be fabricated with copper interconnects.

Note

The Pentium III and Celeron chips with the "coppermine" (codename for the 0.18 micron die used in those chips) die use aluminum and not copper metal interconnects as many people assume. The chip name had nothing to do with metal; it was instead named after the Coppermine River in the Northwest Territory of Canada. Intel has long had a fondness for using codenames based on rivers (and sometimes, other geological features), especially those in the northwest region of the North American continent. For example, the previous version of the Pentium III (0.25 micron die) was codenamed Katmai, after an Alaskan river. Current Intel code names read like the travel itinerary of a whitewater rafting enthusiast: Deerfield, Foster, Northwood, Tualatin, Gallatin, McKinley, and Madison are all rivers in Oregon, California, Alaska, Montana, and—in the case of Deerfield—Massachusetts and Vermont.

A completed circular wafer has as many chips imprinted on it as can possibly fit. Because each chip usually is square or rectangular, there are some unused portions at the edges of the wafer, but every attempt is made to use every square millimeter of surface.

The standard wafer size used in the industry today is 200mm in diameter, or just under 8 inches. This results in a wafer of about 31,416 square millimeters. The Pentium II 300MHz processor, for example, was made up of 7.5 million transistors using a 0.35 micron (millionth of a meter) process. This process results in a die of exactly 14.2mm on each side, which is 202 square millimeters of area. This means that about 150 total Pentium II 300MHz chips on the .35 micron process could be made from a single 200mm-diameter wafer.

The trend in the industry is to go to both larger wafers and a smaller chip die process. *Process* refers to the size of the individual circuits and transistors on the chip. For example, the Pentium II 333MHz through 450MHz processors were made on a newer and smaller .25 micron process, which reduced the total chip die size to only 10.2mm on each side, or a total chip area of 104 square millimeters. On the same 200mm (8-inch) wafer as before, Intel can make about 300 Pentium II chips using this process, or double the amount of the larger .35 micron process 300MHz version.

The Pentium III in the 600MHz and faster speeds is built on a .18 micron process and has a die size of only 104 square millimeters, which is about 10.2mm on each side. This is the same size as the older Pentium II, even though the newer PIII has 28.1 million transistors (including the on-die L2 cache) compared to only 7.5 million for the Pentium II. The Tualatin die version of the Pentium III uses a 0.13 micron process, as does the Northwood die version of the Pentium 4.

The industry is going through several transitions in chip manufacturing. The processes are moving from .18 micron to .13 micron, and wafers are moving from 200mm (8-inch) wafers to 300mm (12-inch) wafers. The larger 300mm wafers alone will enable more than double the number of chips to be made, compared to the 200mm mostly used today. The smaller 0.13-micron process will enable more transistors to be incorporated into the die while maintaining a reasonable die size allowing for sufficient yield. This means the trend for incorporating L2 cache within the die will continue, and transistor counts will rise up to 200 million per chip or more in the future. The current king of transistors is the Intel Pentium III Xeon introduced in May 2000 with 2MB of on-die cache and a whopping 140 million transistors in a single die.

The trend in wafers is to move from the current 200mm (8-inch) diameter to a bigger, 300mm (12-inch) diameter wafer. This will increase surface area dramatically over the smaller 200mm design and boost chip production to about 675 chips per wafer. Intel and other manufacturers expect to have 300mm wafer production in place during 2002. After that happens, chip prices should continue to drop dramatically as supply increases.

Note that not all the chips on each wafer will be good, especially as a new production line starts. As the manufacturing process for a given chip or production line is perfected, more and more of the chips will be good. The ratio of good to bad chips on a wafer is called the *yield*. Yields well under 50% are common when a new chip starts production; however, by the end of a given chip's life, the yields are normally in the 90% range. Most chip manufacturers guard their yield figures and are very secretive about them because knowledge of yield problems can give their competitors an edge. A low yield causes problems both in the cost per chip and in delivery delays to their customers. If a company has specific knowledge of competitors' improving yields, it can set prices or schedule production to get higher market share at a critical point. For example, AMD was plagued by low-yield problems during 1997 and 1998, which cost it significant market share. It has since solved the problems, and lately it seems Intel has had the harder time meeting production demands.

After a wafer is complete, a special fixture tests each of the chips on the wafer and marks the bad ones to be separated out later. The chips are then cut from the wafer using either a high-powered laser or diamond saw.

After being cut from the wafers, the individual dies are then retested, packaged, and retested again. The packaging process is also referred to as *bonding* because the die is placed into a chip housing in which a special machine bonds fine gold wires between the die and the pins on the chip. The package is the container for the chip die, and it essentially seals it from the environment.

After the chips are bonded and packaged, final testing is done to determine both proper function and rated speed. Different chips in the same batch often run at different speeds. Special test fixtures run each chip at different pressures, temperatures, and speeds, looking for the point at which the chip stops working. At this point, the maximum successful speed is noted and the final chips are sorted into bins with those that tested at a similar speed. For example, the Pentium III 750, 866, and 1000 are all exactly the same chip made using the same die. They were sorted at the end of the manufacturing cycle by speed.

One interesting thing about this is that as a manufacturer gains more experience and perfects a particular chip assembly line, the yield of the higher-speed versions goes way up. This means that out of a wafer of 150 total chips, perhaps more than 100 of them check out at 1000MHz, whereas only a few won't run at that speed. The paradox is that Intel often sells a lot more of the lower-priced 933 and 866MHz chips, so it will just dip into the bin of 1000MHz processors and label them as 933 or 866 chips and sell them that way. People began discovering that many of the lower-rated chips would actually run at speeds much higher than they were rated, and the business of overclocking was born.

An interesting problem then arose: Unscrupulous vendors began re-marking slower chips and reselling them as if they were faster. Often the price between the same chip at different speed grades can be substantial—in the hundreds of dollars—so by changing a few numbers on the chip, the potential profits can be huge. Because most of the Intel and AMD processors are produced with a generous safety margin—that is, they typically run well past their rated speeds—the re-marked chips would seem to work fine in most cases. Of course, in many cases they wouldn't work fine, and the system would end up crashing or locking up periodically.

At first the re-marked chips were just a case of rubbing off the original numbers and restamping with new official-looking numbers. These were easy to detect, though. Re-markers then resorted to manufacturing completely new processor housings, especially for the plastic-encased Slot 1 and Slot A processors from Intel and AMD. Although it might seem to be a huge bother to make a custom plastic case and swap it with the existing case, because the profits can be huge, criminals find it very lucrative. This type of re-marking is a form of organized crime and isn't just some kid in his basement with sandpaper and a rubber stamp.

Intel and AMD have seen fit to put a stop to some of the re-marking by building overclock protection in the form of a multiplier lock into most of its newer chips. This is usually done in the bonding or cartridge manufacturing process, where the chips are intentionally altered so they won't run at any speeds higher than they are rated. Usually this involves changing the bus frequency (BF) pins on the chip, which control the internal multipliers the chip uses. Even so, enterprising individuals have found ways to run their motherboards at bus speeds higher than normal, so even though the chip won't allow a higher multiplier, you can still run it at a speed higher than it was designed for.

Be Wary of PII and PIII Overclocking Fraud

Also note that unscrupulous individuals have devised a small logic circuit that bypasses the multiplier lock, enabling the chip to run at higher multipliers. This small circuit can be hidden in the PII or PIII cartridge, and then the chip can be re-marked or relabeled to falsely indicate it is a higher-speed version. This type of chip remarketing fraud is far more common in the industry than people want to believe. In fact, if you purchase your system or processor from a local computer flea market show, you have an excellent chance of getting a re-marked chip. I recommend purchasing processors only from more reputable direct distributors or dealers. You can contact Intel, AMD, or Cyrix for a list of them.

I recently installed a 200MHz Pentium processor in a system that is supposed to run at a 3x multiplier based off a 66MHz motherboard speed. I tried changing the multiplier to 3.5x, but the chip refused to go any faster; in fact, it ran at the same or lower speed than before. This is a sure sign of overclock protection inside, which is to say that the chip won't support any higher level of multiplier than it was designed for. Today, all Intel Pentium II and III processors are multiplier locked, which means the multiplier can no longer be controlled by the motherboard. So, overclocking can be accomplished only by running the motherboard at a higher bus speed than the processor was designed for. My motherboard at the time included a jumper setting for an unauthorized speed of 75MHz, which when multiplied by 3x resulted in an actual processor speed of 225MHz. This worked like a charm, and the system is now running fast and clean. Many new motherboards have BIOS or jumper settings that can be used to tweak the motherboard bus speeds a few MHz higher than normal, which is then internally multiplied by the processor to even higher speeds. Note that I am not necessarily recommending overclocking for everybody; in fact, I normally don't recommend it at all for any important systems. If you have a system you want to fool around with, it is interesting to try. Like my cars, I always seem to want to hotrod my computers.

The real problem with the overclock protection as implemented by Intel and AMD is that the professional counterfeiter can still override it by inserting some custom circuitry underneath the plastic case enclosing the processor. This again is particularly a problem with the slot-based processors because they use a case cover that can hide this circuitry. Socketed processors are much more immune to these re-marking attempts. To protect yourself from purchasing a fraudulent chip, verify the specification numbers and serial numbers with Intel and AMD before you purchase. Also beware where you buy your hardware. Purchasing over online auction sites can be extremely dangerous because defrauding the purchaser is so easy. Also, the traveling computer show/flea market arenas can be a hotbed of this type of activity.

Fraudulent computer components are not limited to processors. I have seen fake memory (SIMMs/DIMMs), fake mice, fake video cards, fake cache memory, counterfeit operating systems and applications, and even fake motherboards. The hardware that is faked usually works but is of inferior quality to the type it is purporting to be. For example, one of the most highly counterfeited pieces of hardware is the Microsoft mouse. They sell for $35 wholesale and yet I can purchase cheap mice from overseas manufacturers for as little as $2.32 each. It didn't take somebody long to realize that if they made the $2 mouse look like a $35 Microsoft mouse, they could sell it for $20 and people would think they were getting a genuine article for a bargain, while the thieves run off with a substantial profit.

PGA Chip Packaging

PGA packaging has been the most common chip package used until recently. It was used starting with the 286 processor in the 1980s and is still used today for Pentium and Pentium Pro processors. PGA takes its name from the fact that the chip has a grid-like array of pins on the bottom of the package. PGA chips are inserted into sockets, which are often of a ZIF (zero insertion force) design. A ZIF socket has a lever to allow for easy installation and removal of the chip.

Most Pentium processors use a variation on the regular PGA called staggered pin grid array (SPGA), in which the pins are staggered on the underside of the chip rather than in standard rows and columns. This was done to move the pins closer together and decrease the overall size of the chip when a large number of pins is required. Figure 3.5 shows a Pentium Pro that uses the dual-pattern SPGA (on the right) next to an older Pentium 66 that uses the regular PGA. Note that the right half of the Pentium Pro shown here has additional pins staggered among the other rows and columns.

Figure 3.5   PGA on Pentium 66 (left) and dual-pattern SPGA on Pentium Pro (right).

Single Edge Contact and Single Edge Processor Packaging

Abandoning the chip-in-a-socket approach used by virtually all processors until this point, the Pentium II/III chips are characterized by their single edge contact (SEC) cartridge design. The processor, along with several L2 cache chips, is mounted on a small circuit board (much like an oversized memory SIMM), which is then sealed in a metal and plastic cartridge. The cartridge is then plugged into the motherboard through an edge connector called Slot 1, which looks very similar to an adapter card slot.

By placing the processor and L2 cache as separate chips inside a cartridge, Intel now has a CPU module that is easier and less expensive to make than the Pentium Pro that preceded it. The SEC cartridge is an innovative—if a bit unwieldy—package design that incorporates the back-side bus and L2 cache internally. Using the SEC design, the core and L2 cache are fully enclosed in a plastic and metal cartridge. These subcomponents are surface mounted directly to a substrate (or base) inside the cartridge to enable high-frequency operation. The SEC cartridge technology enables the use of widely available, high-performance industry standard burst static RAMs (BSRAMs) for the dedicated L2 cache. This greatly reduces the cost compared to the proprietary cache chips used inside the CPU package in the Pentium Pro.

A less expensive version of the SEC is called the single edge processor (SEP) package. The SEP package is basically the same circuit board containing processor and (optional) cache as the Pentium II, but without the fancy plastic cover. The SEP package plugs directly into the same Slot 1 connector used by the standard Pentium II. Four holes on the board enable the heatsink to be installed.

Slot 1 is the connection to the motherboard and has 242 pins. The Slot 1 dimensions are shown in Figure 3.6. The SEC cartridge or SEP processor is plugged into Slot 1 and secured with a processor-retention mechanism, which is a bracket that holds it in place. There also might be a retention mechanism or support for the processor heatsink. Figure 3.7 shows the parts of the cover that make up the SEC package. Note the large thermal plate used to aid in dissipating the heat from this processor. The SEP package is shown in Figure 3.8.

Figure 3.6   Pentium II Processor Slot 1 dimensions (metric/English).

Figure 3.7   Pentium II Processor SEC package parts.

Figure 3.8 Celeron Processor SEP package front-side view.

With the Pentium III, Intel introduced a variation on the SEC packaging called SECC2 (single edge contact cartridge version 2). This new package covers only one side of the processor board and enables the heatsink to directly attach to the chip on the other side. This direct thermal interface allows for better cooling, and the overall lighter package is cheaper to manufacture. Note that a new Universal Retention System, consisting of a plastic upright stand, is required to hold the SECC2 package chip in place on the board. The Universal Retention System also works with the older SEC package as used on most Pentium II processors, as well as the SEP package used on the slot-based Celeron processors. This makes it the ideal retention mechanism for all Slot 1-based processors. Figure 3.9 shows the SECC2 package.

Figure 3.9 SECC2 packaging used in newer Pentium II and III processors.

The main reason for going to the SEC and SEP packages in the first place was to be able to move the L2 cache memory off the motherboard and onto the processor in an economical and scalable way. This has since been superceded in most processors by on-die cache, which eliminates the need for a cartridge.

Processor Sockets and Slots

Intel and AMD have created a set of socket and slot designs for their processors. Each socket or slot is designed to support a different range of original and upgrade processors. Table 3.12 shows the specifications of these sockets.

Table 3.12   CPU Socket and Slot Types and Specifications

Socket Number	Pins	Pin Layout	Voltage	Supported Processors
Socket 1	169	17x17 PGA	5v	486 SX/SX2, DX/DX2[1], DX4 OverDrive
Socket 2	238	19x19 PGA	5v	486 SX/SX2, DX/DX2[1], DX4 OverDrive, 486 Pentium OverDrive
Socket 3	237	19x19 PGA	5v/3.3v	486 SX/SX2, DX/DX2, DX4, 486 Pentium OverDrive, AMD 5x86
Socket 4	273	21x21 PGA	5v	Pentium 60/66, OverDrive
Socket 5	320	37x37 SPGA	3.3/3.5v	Pentium 75-133, OverDrive
Socket 6[2]	235	19x19 PGA	3.3v	486 DX4, 486 Pentium OverDrive
Socket 7	321	37x37 SPGA	VRM	Pentium 75–233+, MMX, OverDrive, AMD K5/K6, Cyrix M1/II
Socket 8	387	dual-pattern SPGA	Auto VRM	Pentium Pro, OverDrive
Socket 370	370	37x37 SPGA	Auto VRM	Celeron/Pentium III PPGA/FC-PGA
Socket PAC418	418	38x22 split SPGA	Auto VRM	Itanium
Socket 423	423	39x39 SPGA	Auto VRM	Pentium 4
Socket A (462)	462	37x37 SPGA	Auto VRM	AMD Athlon/Duron PGA
Socket 603	603	31x25 SPGA	Auto VRM	Xeon (P4)
Slot A	242	Slot	Auto VRM	AMD Athlon SECC
Slot 1 (SC242)	242	Slot	Auto VRM	Pentium II/III, Celeron SECC
Slot 2 (SC330)	330	Slot	Auto VRM	Pentium II/III Xeon SECC

1. Nonoverdrive DX4 or AMD 5x86 also can be supported with the addition of an aftermarket 3.3v voltage-regulator adapter.

2. Socket 6 was a paper standard only and was never actually implemented in any systems.

PGA = Pin grid array

PPGA = Plastic pin grid array

FC-PGA = Flip chip pin grid array

SPGA = Staggered pin grid array

SECC = Single edge contact cartridge

PAC = Pin array cartridge

VRM = Voltage regulator module

Sockets 1, 2, 3, and 6 are 486 processor sockets and are shown together in Figure 3.10 so you can see the overall size comparisons and pin arrangements between these sockets. Sockets 4, 5, 7, and 8 are Pentium and Pentium Pro processor sockets and are shown together in Figure 3.11 so you can see the overall size comparisons and pin arrangements between these sockets. More detailed drawings of each socket are included throughout the remainder of this section with the thorough descriptions of the sockets.

Socket 1

The original OverDrive socket, now officially called Socket 1, is a 169-pin PGA socket. Motherboards that have this socket can support any of the 486SX, DX, and DX2 processors and the DX2/OverDrive versions. This type of socket is found on most 486 systems that originally were designed for OverDrive upgrades. Figure 3.12 shows the pinout of Socket 1.

Figure 3.10 486 processor sockets.

Figure 3.11 Pentium and Pentium Pro processor sockets.

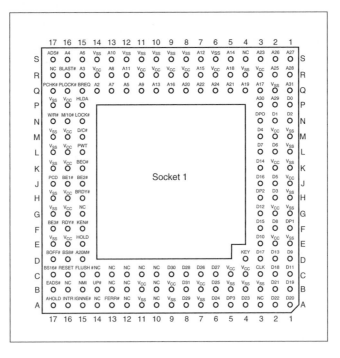

Figure 3.12 Intel Socket 1 pinout.

The original DX processor draws a maximum 0.9 amps of 5v power in 33MHz form (4.5 watts) and a maximum 1 amp in 50MHz form (5 watts). The DX2 processor, or OverDrive processor, draws a maximum 1.2 amps at 66MHz (6 watts). This minor increase in power requires only a passive heatsink consisting of aluminum fins that are glued to the processor with thermal transfer epoxy. Passive heatsinks don't have any mechanical components like fans. Heatsinks with fans or other devices that use power are called *active* heatsinks. OverDrive processors rated at 40MHz or less do not have heatsinks.

Socket 2

When the DX2 processor was released, Intel was already working on the new Pentium processor. The company wanted to offer a 32-bit, scaled-down version of the Pentium as an upgrade for systems that originally came with a DX2 processor. Rather than just increasing the clock rate, Intel created an all-new chip with enhanced capabilities derived from the Pentium.

The chip, called the Pentium OverDrive processor, plugs into a processor socket with the Socket 2 or Socket 3 design. These sockets hold any 486 SX, DX, or DX2 processor, as well as the Pentium OverDrive. Because this chip is essentially a 32-bit version of the (normally 64-bit) Pentium chip, many have taken to calling it a Pentium-SX. It was available in 25/63MHz and 33/83MHz versions. The first number indicates the base motherboard speed; the second number indicates the actual operating speed of the Pentium OverDrive chip. As you can see, it is a clock-multiplied chip that runs at 2.5 times the motherboard speed. Figure 3.13 shows the pinout configuration of the official Socket 2 design.

Figure 3.13   238-pin Intel Socket 2 configuration.

Notice that although the new chip for Socket 2 is called Pentium OverDrive, it is not a full-scale (64-bit) Pentium. Intel released the design of Socket 2 a little prematurely and found that the chip ran too hot for many systems. The company solved this problem by adding a special active heatsink to the Pentium OverDrive processor. This active heatsink is a combination of a standard heatsink and a built-in electric fan. Unlike the aftermarket glue-on or clip-on fans for processors that you might have seen, this one actually draws 5v power directly from the socket to drive the fan. No external connection to disk drive cables or the power supply is required. The fan/heatsink assembly clips and plugs directly into the processor and provides for easy replacement if the fan fails.

Another requirement of the active heatsink is additional clearance—no obstructions for an area about 1.4 inches off the base of the existing socket to allow for heatsink clearance. The Pentium OverDrive upgrade is difficult or impossible in systems that were not designed with this feature.

Another problem with this particular upgrade is power consumption. The 5v Pentium OverDrive processor draws up to 2.5 amps at 5v (including the fan) or 12.5 watts, which is more than double the 1.2 amps (6 watts) drawn by the DX2 66 processor.

Note

See Intel's Web site (`http://www.intel.com`) for a comprehensive list of certified OverDrive-compatible systems.

Socket 3

Because of problems with the original Socket 2 specification and the enormous heat the 5v version of the Pentium OverDrive processor generates, Intel came up with an improved design. The new processor is the same as the previous Pentium OverDrive processor, except that it runs on 3.3v and draws a maximum 3.0 amps of 3.3v (9.9 watts) and 0.2 amp of 5v (1 watt) to run the fan—a total of 10.9 watts. This configuration provides a slight margin over the 5v version of this processor. The fan is easy to remove from the OverDrive processor for replacement, should it ever fail.

Intel had to create a new socket to support both the DX4 processor, which runs on 3.3v, and the 3.3v Pentium OverDrive processor. In addition to the new 3.3v chips, this new socket supports the older 5v SX, DX, DX2, and even the 5v Pentium OverDrive chip. The design, called Socket 3, is the most flexible upgradable 486 design. Figure 3.14 shows the pinout specification of Socket 3.

Notice that Socket 3 has one additional pin and several others plugged in compared with Socket 2. Socket 3 provides for better keying, which prevents an end user from accidentally installing the processor in an improper orientation. However, one serious problem exists: This socket cannot automatically determine the type of voltage that is provided to it. You will likely find a jumper on the motherboard near the socket to enable selecting 5v or 3.3v operation.

Caution

Because this jumper must be manually set, however, a user could install a 3.3v processor in this socket when it is configured for 5v operation. This installation instantly destroys the chip when the system is powered on. So, it is up to the end user to ensure that this socket is properly configured for voltage, depending on which type of processor is installed. If the jumper is set in 3.3v configuration and a 5v processor is installed, no harm will occur, but the system will not operate properly unless the jumper is reset for 5v.

Socket 4

Socket 4 is a 273-pin socket designed for the original Pentium processors. The original Pentium 60MHz and 66MHz version processors had 273 pins and plugged into Socket 4—a 5v-only socket because all the original Pentium processors run on 5v. This socket accepts the original Pentium 60MHz or 66MHz processor and the OverDrive processor. Figure 3.15 shows the pinout specification of Socket 4.

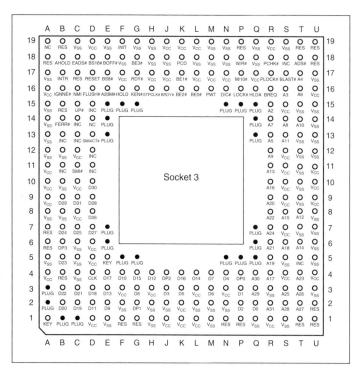

Figure 3.14   237-pin Intel Socket 3 configuration.

Somewhat amazingly, the original Pentium 66MHz processor consumes up to 3.2 amps of 5v power (16 watts), not including power for a standard active heatsink (fan). The 66MHz OverDrive processor that replaced it consumes a maximum 2.7 amps (13.5 watts), including about 1 watt to drive the fan. Even the original 60MHz Pentium processor consumes up to 2.91 amps at 5v (14.55 watts). It might seem strange that the replacement processor, which is twice as fast, consumes less power than the original, but this has to do with the manufacturing processes used for the original and OverDrive processors.

Although both processors run on 5v, the original Pentium processor was created with a circuit size of 0.8 micron, making that processor much more power-hungry than the 0.6 micron circuits used in the OverDrive and the other Pentium processors. Shrinking the circuit size is one of the best ways to decrease power consumption. Although the OverDrive processor for Pentium-based systems draws less power than the original processor, additional clearance might have to be allowed for the active heatsink assembly that is mounted on top. As in other OverDrive processors with built-in fans, the power to run the fan is drawn directly from the chip socket, so no separate power-supply connection is required. Also, the fan is easy to replace should it ever fail.

Socket 5

When Intel redesigned the Pentium processor to run at 75MHz, 90MHz, and 100MHz, the company went to a 0.6-micron manufacturing process and 3.3v operation. This change resulted in lower power consumption: only 3.25 amps at 3.3v (10.725 watts). Therefore, the 100MHz Pentium processor used far less power than even the original 60MHz version. This resulted in lower power consumption and enabled the extremely high clock rates without overheating.

Figure 3.15 273-pin Intel Socket 4 configuration.

The Pentium 75 and higher processors actually have 296 pins, although they plug into the official Intel Socket 5 design, which calls for a total of 320 pins. The additional pins are used by the Pentium OverDrive for Pentium processors. This socket has the 320 pins configured in a staggered PGA, in which the individual pins are staggered for tighter clearance.

Several OverDrive processors for existing Pentiums were available. These usually were later design chips with integral voltage regulators to enable operating on the higher voltages the older chips originally required. Intel no longer sells these; however, companies such as Evergreen and Kingston do still sell upgrade chips for older systems. Figure 3.16 shows the standard pinout for Socket 5.

The Pentium OverDrive for Pentium processors has an active heatsink (fan) assembly that draws power directly from the chip socket. The chip requires a maximum 4.33 amps of 3.3v to run the chip (14.289 watts) and 0.2 amp of 5v power to run the fan (one watt), which results in a total power consumption of 15.289 watts. This is less power than the original 66MHz Pentium processor requires, yet it runs a chip that is as much as four times faster!

Socket 6

The last 486 socket was designed for the 486 DX4 and the 486 Pentium OverDrive processor. Socket 6 was intended as a slightly redesigned version of Socket 3 and had an additional 2 pins plugged for proper chip keying. Socket 6 has 235 pins and accepts only 3.3v 486 or OverDrive processors. Although Intel went to the trouble of designing this socket, it never was built or implemented in any systems. Motherboard manufacturers instead stuck with Socket 3.

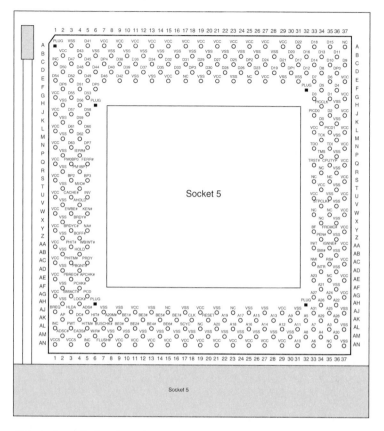

Figure 3.16 320-pin Intel Socket 5 configuration.

Socket 7 (and Super7)

Socket 7 is essentially the same as Socket 5 with one additional key pin in the opposite inside corner of the existing key pin. Socket 7, therefore, has 321 pins total in a 21×21 SPGA arrangement. The real difference with Socket 7 is not the socket but with the companion voltage regulator module (VRM) circuitry on the motherboard that must accompany it.

The VRM is either a small circuit board or a group of circuitry embedded in the motherboard that supplies the proper voltage level and regulation of power to the processor.

The main reason for the VRM is that Intel and AMD wanted to drop the voltages the processors would use from the 3.3V or 5V supplied to the motherboard by the power supply. Rather than require custom power supplies for different processors, the VRM converts the 3.3V or 5V to the proper voltage for the particular CPU you are using. Intel released different versions of the Pentium and Pentium-MMX processors that ran on 3.3v (called VR), 3.465v (called VRE), or 2.8v. Equivalent processors from AMD, Cyrix, and others used different variations of 3.3V, 3.2V, 2.9V, 2.4V, 2.3V, 2.2V, 2.1V, 2.0V, 1.9V, or 1.8V. Because of the variety of voltages that might be required to support different processors, most motherboard manufacturers started including VRM sockets or building adaptable VRMs into their Pentium motherboards.

Figure 3.17 shows the Socket 7 pinout.

Figure 3.17   Socket 7 (Pentium) pinout (top view).

AMD, along with Cyrix and several chipset manufacturers, pioneered an improvement or extension to the Intel Socket 7 design called Super Socket 7 (or Super7), taking it from 66MHz to 95MHz and 100MHz. This enables faster Socket 7–type systems to be made, which are nearly as fast as the newer Slot 1– and Socket 370–type systems using Intel processors. Super7 systems also have support for the AGP video bus, as well as Ultra DMA hard disk controllers and advanced power management.

New chipsets are required for Super7 boards. Major third-party chipset suppliers, including Acer Laboratories Inc. (ALi), VIA Technologies, and Silicon Integrated Systmes (SiS), all released chipsets for Super7 boards. Most of the major motherboard manufacturers made Super7 boards in both Baby-AT and ATX form factors.

Socket 8

Socket 8 is a special SPGA (socket featuring a whopping 387 pins! This was specifically designed for the Pentium Pro processor with the integrated L2 cache. The additional pins are to enable the chipset to control the L2 cache integrated in the same package as the processor. Figure 3.18 shows the Socket 8 pinout.

Socket 370 (PGA-370)

In January 1999, Intel introduced a new socket for P6 class processors. The new socket is called Socket 370 or PGA-370 because it has 370 pins and originally was designed for lower-cost PGA versions of the Celeron and Pentium III processors. Socket 370 is designed to directly compete in the lower-end system market along with the Super7 platform supported by AMD and Cyrix. Socket 370 brings the low cost of a socketed design, with less expensive processors, mounting systems, heatsinks, and so on to the high-performance P6 line of processors.

Figure 3.18 Socket 8 (Pentium Pro) pinout showing power pin locations.

Initially all the Celeron and Pentium III processors were made in SECC or SEPP format. These are essentially circuit boards containing the processor and separate L2 cache chips on a small board that plugs into the motherboard via Slot 1. This type of design was necessary when the L2 cache chips were made a part of the processor but were not directly integrated into the processor die. Intel did make a multidie chip package for the Pentium Pro, but this proved to be a very expensive way to package the chip, and a board with separate chips was cheaper, which is why the Pentium II looks different from the Pentium Pro.

Starting with the Celeron 300A processor introduced in August 1998, Intel began combining the L2 cache directly on the processor die; it was no longer in separate chips. With the cache fully integrated into the die, there was no longer a need for a board-mounted processor. Because it costs more to make a Slot 1 board or cartridge-type processor instead of a socketed type, Intel moved back to the socket design to reduce the manufacturing cost—especially with the Celeron, which competes on the low end with Socket 7 chips from AMD and Cyrix.

The Socket 370 (PGA-370) pinout is shown in Figure 3.19.

The Celeron is gradually being shifted over to PGA-370, although for a time both were available. All Celeron processors at 333MHz and lower were available only in the Slot 1 version. Celeron processors from 366MHz to 433MHz were available in both Slot 1 and Socket 370 versions; all Celeron processors from 466MHz and up are available only in the Socket 370 version.

Flip Chip Pin Grid Array

Starting in October 1999, Intel also introduced Pentium III processors with integrated cache that plug into Socket 370. These use a packaging called flip chip pin grid array (FC-PGA), which is a type of packaging in which the raw die is mounted on the substrate upside down. The slot version is more expensive and no longer necessary because of the on-die L2 cache.

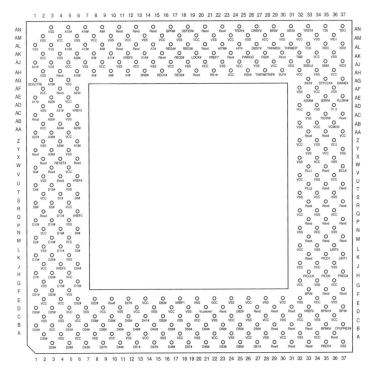

Figure 3.19 Socket 370 (PGA-370) Pentium III/Celeron pinout (top view).

Note that because of some voltage changes and one pin change, many original Socket 370 motherboards do not accept the later FC-PGA versions of the Pentium III and Celeron. Pentium III processors in the FC-PGA form have two RESET pins and require VRM 8.4 specifications. Prior motherboards designed only for the Celeron are referred to as *legacy motherboards*, and the newer motherboards supporting the second RESET pin and VRM 8.4 specification are referred to as *flexible motherboards*. Contact your motherboard or system manufacturer for information to see whether your socket is the flexible version. Some motherboards, such as the Intel CA810, do support the VRM 8.4 specifications and supply proper voltage, but without Vtt support the Pentium III processor in the FC-PGA package will be held in RESET#.

Installing a Pentium III processor in the FC-PGA package into an older motherboard is unlikely to damage the motherboard. However, the processor itself could be damaged. Pentium III processors in the 0.18 micron process operate on either 1.60 or 1.65 volts, whereas the Intel Celeron processors operate at 2.00 volts. The motherboard could possibly be damaged if the motherboard BIOS fails to recognize the voltage identification of the processor. Contact your PC or motherboard manufacturer before installation to ensure compatibility.

A motherboard with a Slot 1 can be designed to accept almost any Celeron, Pentium II, or Pentium III processor. To use the socketed Celerons and Pentium III processors, a low-cost slot-to-socket adapter sometimes called a *slot-ket* has been made available by several manufacturers. This is essentially a Slot 1 board containing only a Socket 370, which enables you to use a PGA processor in any Slot 1 board. A typical slot-ket adapter is shown in the "Celeron" section, later in this chapter.

▶▶ See "Celeron," p. 159.

Socket 423

Socket 423 is a ZIF-type socket introduced in November 2000 for the Pentium 4, codenamed Willamette. Figure 3.20 shows Socket 423.

Figure 3.20   Socket 423 (Pentium 4) showing pin 1 location.

Socket 423 supports a 400MHz processor bus, which connects the processor to the Memory Controller Hub (MCH), which is the main part of the motherboard chipset. Five voltage ID (VID) pins are used by the processor to signal the VRM built into the motherboard to deliver the correct voltage for the particular CPU you install. This makes the voltage selection completely automatic and foolproof. The initial Pentium 4 processors require 1.7 volts, but that might change for newer processors. A small triangular mark indicates the pin-1 corner for proper orientation of the chip.

Socket A (Socket 462)

AMD introduced Socket A, also called Socket 462, in June 2000 to support the PGA versions of the Athlon and Duron processors. It is designed as a replacement for Slot A used by the original Athlon processor. Because the Athlon has now moved to incorporate L2 cache on-die, and the new Duron is available only in an on-die cache version, there was no longer a need for the expensive cartridge packaging used by the original Athlon processors.

Socket A has 462 pins and 11 plugs oriented in an SPGA form (see Figure 3.21). Socket A has the same physical dimensions and layout as Socket 370; however, the location and placement of the plugs prevent Socket 370 processors from being inserted. Socket A supports 32 voltage levels from 1.100V to 1.850V in 0.025V increments, controlled by the VID0-VID4 pins on the processor. The automatic voltage regulator module circuitry typically is embedded on the motherboard.

Figure 3.21   Socket A (Socket 462) Athlon/Duron layout.

There are 11 total plugged holes, including 2 of the outside pin holes at A1 and AN1. These are used to allow for keying to force the proper orientation of the processor in the socket. The pinout of Socket A is shown in Figure 3.22.

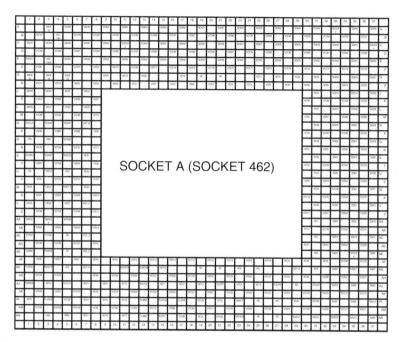

Figure 3.22   Socket A (Socket 462) Athlon/Duron pinout (top view).

AMD has indicated that all future Athlon and Duron processors, at least for the time being, will be made in Socket A form, and the Slot A versions of the Athlon will be phased out.

Zero Insertion Force Sockets

When the Socket 1 specification was created, manufacturers realized that if users were going to upgrade processors, they had to make the process easier. The socket manufacturers found that it typically takes 100 lbs. of insertion force to install a chip in a standard 169-pin screw Socket 1 motherboard. With this much force involved, you easily could damage either the chip or socket during removal or reinstallation. Because of this, some motherboard manufacturers began using low insertion force (LIF) sockets, which typically required only 60 lbs. of insertion force for a 169-pin chip. With the LIF or standard socket, I usually advise removing the motherboard—that way you can support the board from behind when you insert the chip. Pressing down on the motherboard with 60–100 lbs. of force can crack the board if it is not supported properly. A special tool is also required to remove a chip from one of these sockets. As you can imagine, even the low insertion force was relative, and a better solution was needed if the average person was going to ever replace his CPU.

Manufacturers began inserting special ZIF sockets in their later Socket 1 motherboard designs. Since then, virtually all processor sockets have been of the ZIF design. Note, however, that a given Socket X specification has nothing to do with whether it is ZIF, LIF, or standard; the socket specification covers only the pin arrangement. Since the 486 era, nearly all motherboard manufacturers have been using ZIF sockets. These sockets almost eliminate the risk involved in upgrading because no insertion force is necessary to install the chip and no tool is need to extract one. Most ZIF sockets are handle-actuated; you lift the handle, drop the chip into the socket, and then close the handle. This design makes replacing the original processor with the upgrade processor an easy task.

Processor Slots

After introducing the Pentium Pro with its integrated L2 cache, Intel discovered that the physical package it chose was very costly to produce. Intel was looking for a way to easily integrate cache and possibly other components into a processor package, and it came up with a cartridge or board design as the best way to do this. To accept its new cartridges, Intel designed two types of slots that could be used on motherboards.

Slot 1 is a 242-pin slot designed to accept Pentium II, Pentium III, and most Celeron processors. Slot 2, on the other hand, is a more sophisticated 330-pin slot designed for the Pentium II and III Xeon processors, which are primarily for workstations and servers. Besides the extra pins, the biggest difference between Slot 1 and Slot 2 is the fact that Slot 2 was designed to host up to four-way or more processing in a single board. Slot 1 allows only single or dual processing functionality.

Note that Slot 2 is also called SC330, which stands for slot connector with 330 pins.

Slot 1 (SC242)

Slot 1, also called SC242 (slot connector 242 pins), is used by the SEC design used with the cartridge-type Pentium II/III and Celeron processors (see Figure 3.23).

◄◄ See "Single Edge Contact and Single Edge Processor Packaging," p. 80.

Figure 3.23   Slot 1 connector dimensions and pin layout.

Slot 2 (SC330)

Slot 2, otherwise called SC330 (slot connector 330 pins) is used on high-end motherboards that support the Pentium II and III Xeon processors. Figure 3.24 shows the Slot 2 connector.

The Xeon processors are designed in a cartridge similar to, but larger than, that used for the standard Pentium II/III. Figure 3.25 shows the Xeon cartridge.

Motherboards featuring Slot 2 are found primarily in higher-end systems, such as workstations or servers, which use the Xeon processors. These are Intel's high-end chips, which differ from the standard Pentium II/III mainly by virtue of having full-core speed L2 cache, and in some versions more of it. The additional pins allow for additional signals needed by multiple processors.

Figure 3.24   Slot 2 (SC330) connector dimensions and pin layout.

Figure 3.25   Pentium II/III Xeon cartridge.

CPU Operating Voltages

One trend that is clear to anybody who has been following processor design is that the operating voltages have gotten lower and lower. The benefits of lower voltage are threefold. The most obvious is that with lower voltage comes lower overall power consumption. By consuming less power, the system is less expensive to run, but more importantly for portable or mobile systems, it runs much longer on existing battery technology. The emphasis on battery operation has driven many of the advances in lowering processor voltage because this has a great effect on battery life.

The second major benefit is that with less voltage and therefore less power consumption, less heat is produced. Processors that run cooler can be packed into systems more tightly and last longer. The third major benefit is that a processor running cooler on less power can be made to run faster. Lowering the voltage has been one of the key factors in enabling the clock rates of processors to go higher and higher.

Until the release of the mobile Pentium and both desktop and mobile Pentium MMX, most processors used a single voltage level to power both the core as well as run the input/output circuits. Originally, most processors ran both the core and I/O circuits at 5 volts, which was later was reduced to 3.5 or 3.3 volts to lower power consumption. When a single voltage is used for both the internal processor core power as well as the external processor bus and I/O signals, the processor is said to have a single or unified power plane design.

When originally designing a version of the Pentium processor for mobile or portable computers, Intel came up with a scheme to dramatically reduce the power consumption while still remaining compatible with the existing 3.3v chipsets, bus logic, memory, and other components. The result was a dual-plane or split-plane power design in which the processor core ran off a lower voltage while the I/O circuits remained at 3.3v. This originally was called voltage reduction technology (VRT) and first debuted in the Mobile Pentium processors released in 1996. Later, this dual-plane power design also appeared in desktop processors such as the Pentium MMX, which used 2.8v to power the core and 3.3v for the I/O circuits. Now most recent processors, whether for mobile or desktop use, feature a dual-plane power design. Some of the more recent Mobile Pentium II processors run on as little as 1.6v for the core while still maintaining compatibility with 3.3v components for I/O.

Knowing the processor voltage requirements is not a big issue with Socket 8, Socket 370, Socket A, Pentium Pro (Socket 8), or Pentium II (Slot 1 or Slot 2) processors because these sockets and slots have special VID pins the processor uses to signal to the motherboard the exact voltage requirements. This enables the voltage regulators built into the motherboard to be automatically set to the correct voltage levels by merely installing the processor.

Unfortunately, this automatic voltage setting feature is not available on Socket 7 and earlier motherboard and processor designs. Therefore, you usually must set jumpers or otherwise configure the motherboard according to the voltage requirements of the processor you are installing. Pentium (Socket 4, 5, or 7) processors have run on a number of voltages, but the latest MMX versions are all 2.8v—except for mobile Pentium processors, which are as low as 1.8v. Table 3.12 lists the voltage settings used by Intel Pentium (non-MMX) processors that use a single power plane. This means that both the CPU core and the I/O pins run at the same voltage.

Table 3.13 shows voltages used by Socket 7 processors.

Table 3.13   Socket 7 Single- and Dual-Plane Processor Voltages

Voltage Setting	Processor	Core Voltage	I/O Voltage	Voltage Planes
VRE (3.5v)	Intel Pentium	3.5v	3.5v	Single
STD (3.3v)	Intel Pentium	3.3v	3.3v	Single
MMX (2.8v)	Intel MMX Pentium	2.8v	3.3v	Dual
VRE (3.5v)	AMD K5	3.5v	3.5v	Single
3.2v	AMD-K6	3.2v	3.3v	Dual
2.9v	AMD-K6	2.9v	3.3v	Dual
2.4v	AMD-K6-2/K6-3	2.4v	3.3v	Dual
2.2v	AMD-K6/K6-2	2.2v	3.3v	Dual
VRE (3.5v)	Cyrix 6x86	3.5v	3.5v	Single
2.9v	Cyrix 6x86MX/M-II	2.9v	3.3v	Dual
MMX (2.8v)	Cyrix 6x86L	2.8v	3.3v	Dual
2.45v	Cyrix 6x86LV	2.45v	3.3v	Dual

Normally, the acceptable range is plus or minus 5% from the nominal intended setting.

Most Socket 7 and later Pentium motherboards supply several voltages (such as 2.5v, 2.7v, 2.8v, and 2.9v) for compatibility with future devices. A voltage regulator built into the motherboard converts the power supply voltage into the various levels required by the processor core. Check the documentation for your motherboard and processor to find the appropriate settings.

The Pentium Pro and Pentium II processors automatically determine their voltage settings by controlling the motherboard-based voltage regulator through built-in VID pins. Those are explained in more detail later in this chapter.

▶▶ See "Pentium Pro Processors," p. 143.

▶▶ See "Pentium II Processors," p. 147.

Note that on the STD or VRE settings, the core and I/O voltages are the same; these are single-plane voltage settings. Any time a voltage other than STD or VRE is set, the motherboard defaults to a dual-plane voltage setting where the core voltage can be specifically set, while the I/O voltage remains constant at 3.3v no matter what.

Socket 5 was designed to supply only STD or VRE settings, so any processor that can work at those settings can work in Socket 5 as well as Socket 7. Older Socket 4 designs can supply only 5v, plus they have a completely different pinout (fewer pins overall), so using a processor designed for Socket 7 or Socket 5 in Socket 4 is not possible.

Most Socket 7 and later Pentium motherboards supply several voltages (such as 2.2v, 2.4v, 2.5v, 2.7v, 2.8v, and 2.9v as well as the older STD or VRE settings) for compatibility with many processors. A voltage regulator built into the motherboard converts the power supply voltage into the various levels required by the processor core. Check the documentation for your motherboard and processor to find the appropriate settings.

The Pentium Pro, Celeron, and Pentium II/III processors automatically determine their voltage settings by controlling the motherboard-based voltage regulator. That's done through built-in VID pins.

For hotrodding purposes, many newer motherboards for these processors have override settings that allow for manual voltage adjustment if desired. Many people have found that when attempting to overclock a processor, increasing the voltage by a tenth of a volt or so often helps. Of course, this increases the heat output of the processor and must be accounted for with adequate heatsinking.

Heat and Cooling Problems

Heat can be a problem in any high-performance system. The higher-speed processors typically consume more power and therefore generate more heat. The processor is usually the single most power-hungry chip in a system, and in most situations, the fan inside your computer case might not be capable of handling the load without some help.

Heatsinks

To cool a system in which processor heat is a problem, you can buy (for less than $5, in most cases) a special attachment for the CPU chip called a *heatsink*, which draws heat away from the CPU chip. Several heatsink manufacturers are listed in the Vendor List on the CD.

A heatsink works like the radiator in your car, pulling heat away from the engine. In a similar fashion, the heatsink conducts heat away from the processor so it can be vented out of the system. It does this by using a thermal conductor (usually metal) to carry heat away from the processor into fins that expose a high amount of surface area to moving air. This enables the air to be heated, thus cooling the heatsink and the processor as well. Just like the radiator in your car, the heatsink depends on airflow. With no moving air, a heatsink is incapable of radiating the heat away. To keep the engine in your car from overheating when the car is not moving, auto engineers incorporate a fan. Likewise, there is always a fan somewhere inside your PC helping to move air across the heatsink and vent it out of the system. Sometimes the fan included in the power supply is enough; other times an additional fan must be added to the case, or even directly over the processor to provide the necessary levels of cooling.

The heatsink is clipped or glued to the processor. A variety of heatsinks and attachment methods exist. Figure 3.26 shows various passive heatsinks and attachment methods.

Figure 3.26 Passive heatsinks for socketed processors showing various attachment methods.

Tip

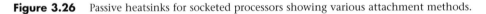

According to data from Intel, heatsink clips are the number-two destroyer of motherboards (screwdrivers are number one). When installing or removing a heatsink that is clipped on, be sure you don't scrape the surface of the motherboard. In most cases, the clips hook over protrusions in the socket, and when installing or removing the clips, scratching or scraping the surface of the board right below where the clip ends attach is very easy. I like to place a thin sheet of plastic underneath the edge of the clip while I work, especially if board traces that can be scratched are in the vicinity.

Heatsinks are rated for their cooling performances. Typically, the ratings are expressed as a resistance to heat transfer, in degrees centigrade per watt (°C/W), where lower is better. Note that the resistance varies according to the airflow across the heatsink. To ensure a constant flow of air and more consistent performance, many heatsinks incorporate fans so they don't have to rely on the airflow within the system. Heatsinks with fans are referred to as *active* heatsinks (see Figure 3.27). Active heatsinks have a power connection, often using a spare disk drive power connector, although most newer motherboards now have dedicated heatsink power connections right on the board.

Active heatsinks use a fan or other electric cooling device, which requires power to run. The fan type is most common but some use a peltier cooling device, which is basically a solid-state refrigerator. Active heatsinks require power and normally plug into a disk drive power connector or special 12v fan power connectors on the motherboard. If you do get a fan-type heatsink, be aware that some on the market are very poor quality. The bad ones have motors that use sleeve bearings, which freeze up after a very short life. I recommend only fans with ball-bearing motors, which last about 10 times longer than the sleeve-bearing types. Of course, they cost more—but only about twice as much, so you'll save money in the long run.

Figure 3.27 Active heatsinks for socketed processors.

Figure 3.28 shows an active heatsink arrangement on a Pentium II/III type processor. This is common on what Intel calls its "boxed processors," which are sold individually and through dealers.

Figure 3.28 An active (fan-powered) heatsink and supports used with Pentium II/III–type processors.

The passive heatsinks are 100% reliable because they have no mechanical components to fail. *Passive* heatsinks are basically aluminum-finned radiators that dissipate heat through convection (see Figure 3.29). Passive types don't work well unless there is some airflow across the fins, usually provided by the power supply fan or an extra fan in the case. If your case or power supply is properly designed, you can use a less-expensive passive heatsink instead of an active one.

Tip

To function effectively, a heatsink must be as directly attached to the processor as possible. To eliminate air gaps and ensure a good transfer of heat, in most cases, you should put a thin coating of thermal transfer grease on the surface of the processor where the heatsink attaches. This dramatically decreases the thermal resistance properties and is required for maximum performance.

Figure 3.29   A passive heatsink and supports used with Pentium II/III–type processors.

To have the best possible transfer of heat from the processor to the heatsink, most heatsink manufac-turers specify some type of thermal interface material to be placed between the processor and the heatsink. This normally consists of a zinc-based white grease (similar to what skiers put on their noses to block the sun) but can also be a special pad or even a type of double-stick tape. Using a thermal interface aid such as thermal grease can improve heatsink performance dramatically. Figure 3.30 shows the thermal interface pad or grease positioned between the processor and heatsink.

You can purchase thermal paste in small single-use tubes or larger versions that can service multiple processor installations.

Figure 3.30   Thermal interface material helps transfer heat from the processor die to the heatsink.

Most of the newer systems on the market use an improved motherboard form factor (shape) design called ATX. Systems made from this type of motherboard and case allow for improved cooling of the processor because of the processor being repositioned in the case near the power supply. Also, most of these cases now feature a secondary fan to further assist in cooling. The larger case-mounted fans typi-cally are more reliable than the smaller fans included in active heatsinks. A properly designed case can move sufficient air across the processor, enabling a more reliable and less-expensive passive (no fan) heatsink to be used.

▶▶ See "ATX Style," p. 1112.

▶▶ See "ATX," p. 204.

Math Coprocessors (Floating-Point Units)

Th is section covers the floating-point unit (FPU) contained in the processor, which was formerly a separate external math coprocessor in the 386 and older chips. Older central processing units designed by Intel (and cloned by other companies) used an external math coprocessor chip. However, when Intel introduced the 486DX, it included a built-in math coprocessor, and every processor built by Intel (and AMD and Cyrix, for that matter) since then includes a math coprocessor. Coprocessors provide hardware for floating-point math, which otherwise would create an excessive drain on the main CPU. Math chips speed your computer's operation only when you are running software designed to take advantage of the coprocessor. All the subsequent fifth- and sixth-generation Intel and compatible processors (such as those from AMD and Cyrix) have featured an integrated floating-point unit.

Math chips (as coprocessors sometimes are called) can perform high-level mathematical operations—long division, trigonometric functions, roots, and logarithms, for example—at 10–100 times the speed of the corresponding main processor. The operations performed by the math chip are all operations that make use of noninteger numbers (numbers that contain digits after the decimal point). The need to process numbers in which the decimal is not always the last character leads to the term *floating point* because the decimal (point) can move (float), depending on the operation. The integer units in the primary CPU work with integer numbers, so they perform addition, subtraction, and multiplication operations. The primary CPU is designed to handle such computations; these operations are not offloaded to the math chip.

The instruction set of the math chip is different from that of the primary CPU. A program must detect the existence of the coprocessor and then execute instructions written explicitly for that coprocessor; otherwise, the math coprocessor draws power and does nothing else. Fortunately, most modern programs that can benefit from the use of the coprocessor correctly detect and use the coprocessor. These programs usually are math intensive: spreadsheet programs, database applications, statistical programs, and graphics programs, such as computer-aided design (CAD) software. Word processing programs do not benefit from a math chip and therefore are not designed to use one. Table 3.14 summarizes the coprocessors available for the Intel family of processors.

Table 3.14   Math Coprocessor Summary

Processor	Coprocessor
8086	8087
8088	8087
286	287
386SX	387SX
386DX	387DX
486SX	487SX, DX2/OverDrive[1]
487SX[1]	Built-in FPU
486SX2	DX2/OverDrive[2]
486DX	Built-in FPU

Table 3.14   Continued

Processor	Coprocessor
486DX2	Built-in FPU
486DX4/5x86	Built-in FPU
Intel Pentium/Pentium MMX	Built-in FPU
Cyrix 6x86/MI/MII	Built-in FPU
AMD K5/K6/Athlon/Duron	Built-in FPU
Pentium II/III/Celeron/Xeon	Built-in FPU
Pentium 4	Built-in FPU
Itanium	Built-in FPU

FPU = Floating-point unit

1. The 487SX chip is a modified pinout 486DX chip with the math coprocessor enabled. When you plug in a 487SX chip, it disables the 486SX main processor and takes over all processing.

2. The DX2/OverDrive is equivalent to the SX2 with the addition of a functional FPU.

Although virtually all processors since the 486 series have built-in floating-point units, they vary in performance. Historically, the Intel processor FPUs have dramatically outperformed those from AMD and Cyrix, although AMD and Cyrix are achieving performance parity in their newer offerings.

Within each of the original 8087 group, the maximum speed of the math chips varies. A suffix digit after the main number, as shown in Table 3.15, indicates the maximum speed at which a system can run a math chip.

Table 3.15   Maximum Math Chip Speeds

Part	Speed	Part	Speed
8087	5MHz	287	6MHz
8087-3	5MHz	287-6	6MHz
8087-2	8MHz	287-8	8MHz
8087-1	10MHz	287-10	10MHz

The 387 math coprocessors and the 486 or 487 and Pentium processors always indicate their maximum speed ratings in MHz in the part number suffix. A 486DX2-66, for example, is rated to run at 66MHz. Some processors incorporate clock multiplication, which means they can run at different speeds compared with the rest of the system.

Tip

The performance increase in programs that use the math chip can be dramatic—usually, a geometric increase in speed occurs. If the primary applications you use can take advantage of a math coprocessor, you should upgrade your system to include one.

Most systems that use the 386 or earlier processors are socketed for a math coprocessor as an option, but they do not include a coprocessor as standard equipment. A few systems on the market at that time didn't even have a socket for the coprocessor because of cost and size considerations. These systems were usually low-cost or portable systems, such as older laptops, the IBM PS/1, and the PCjr. For more specific information about math coprocessors, see the discussions of the specific chips—8087, 287, 387, and 487SX—in the later sections. Table 3.16 shows the specifications of the various math coprocessors.

Table 3.16 Older Intel Math Coprocessor Specifications

Name	Power Consumption	Case Minimum Temperature	Case Maximum Temperature	No. of Transistors	Date Introduced
8087	3 watts	0°C, 32°F	85°C, 185°F	45,000	1980
287	3 watts	0°C, 32°F	85°C, 185°F	45,000	1982
287XL	1.5 watts	0°C, 32°F	85°C, 185°F	40,000	1990
387SX	1.5 watts	0°C, 32°F	85°C, 185°F	120,000	1988
387DX	1.5 watts	0°C, 32°F	85°C, 185°F	120,000	1987

Most often, you can learn which CPU and math coprocessor are installed in a particular system by checking the markings on the chip.

Processor Bugs

Processor manufacturers use specialized equipment to test their own processors, but you have to settle for a little less. The best processor-testing device to which you have access is a system that you know is functional; you then can use the diagnostics available from various utility software companies or your system manufacturer to test the motherboard and processor functions.

Companies such as Diagsoft, Symantec, Micro 2000, Trinitech, Data Depot, and others offer specialized diagnostics software that can test the system, including the processor. If you don't want to purchase this type of software, you can perform a quick-and-dirty processor evaluation by using the diagnostics program supplied with your system.

Perhaps the most infamous of these bugs is the floating-point division math bug in the early Pentium processors. This and a few other bugs are discussed in detail later in this chapter.

Because the processor is the brain of a system, most systems don't function with a defective processor. If a system seems to have a dead motherboard, try replacing the processor with one from a functioning motherboard that uses the same CPU chip. You might find that the processor in the original board is the culprit. If the system continues to play dead, however, the problem is elsewhere, most likely in the motherboard, memory, or power supply. See the chapters that cover those parts of the system for more information on troubleshooting those components. I must say that in all my years of troubleshooting and repairing PCs, I have rarely encountered defective processors.

A few system problems are built in at the factory, although these bugs or design defects are rare. By learning to recognize these problems, you can avoid unnecessary repairs or replacements. Each processor section describes several known defects in that generation of processors, such as the infamous floating-point error in the Pentium. For more information on these bugs and defects, see the following sections, and check with the processor manufacturer for updates.

Processor Update Feature

All processors can contain design defects or errors. Many times, the effects of any given bug can be avoided by implementing hardware or software workarounds. Intel documents these bugs and workarounds well for its processors in its processor Specification Update manual; this manual is available from Intel's Web site. Most of the other processor manufacturers also have bulletins or tips on their Web sites listing any problems or special fixes or patches for their chips.

Previously, the only way to fix a processor bug was to work around it or replace the chip with one that had the bug fixed. Now, a new feature built into the Intel P6 processors, including the Pentium Pro through Pentium III and Celeron, can allow many bugs to be fixed by altering the *microcode* in the processor. Microcode is essentially a set of instructions and tables in the processor that control how the processor operates. These processors incorporate a new feature called *reprogrammable microcode*, which enables certain types of bugs to be worked around via microcode updates. The microcode updates reside in the system ROM BIOS and are loaded into the processor by the system BIOS during the POST. Each time the system is rebooted, the fix code is reloaded, ensuring that it will have the bug fix installed anytime the processor is operating.

The easiest method for checking the microcode update is to use the processor update utility, which is developed and supplied by Intel. This utility can verify whether the correct update is present. The utility displays the processor *stepping* and version of the microcode update. A stepping is the processor hardware equivalent of a new version. In software, we refer to minor version changes as 1.0, 1.1, 1.2, and so on, whereas in processors we call these minor revisions steppings.

To install a new microcode update, however, the motherboard BIOS must contain the routines to support the microcode update, which virtually all Pentium Pro and Pentium II BIOSes do have. The Intel processor update utility determines whether the code is present in the BIOS, compares the processor stepping with the microcode update currently loaded, and installs the new update, if necessary. Use of this utility with motherboards containing the BIOS microcode update routine allows just the microcode update data to be changed; the rest of the BIOS is unchanged. A version of the update utility is provided with all Intel boxed processors. The term *boxed processors* refers to processors packaged for use by system integrators—that is, people who build systems. If you want the most current version of this utility, you must contact an Intel processor dealer to download it because Intel supplies it only to its dealers.

Note that if the BIOS in your motherboard does not include the processor microcode update routine, you should get a complete system BIOS upgrade from the motherboard vendor.

You can use the processor update utility to check that the system BIOS contains microcode updates specific to the particular silicon stepping of the processor you are installing. In other words, you must ensure that the update matches the processor stepping being used.

Table 3.17 contains the current microcode update revision for each processor stepping. These update revisions are contained in the microcode update database file that comes with the Pentium Pro processor and Pentium II processor update utility. Processor steppings are listed in the sections on the Pentium, Pentium Pro, and Pentium II processors later in this chapter.

Table 3.17   Processor Steppings (Revisions) and Microcode Update Revisions Supported by the Update Database File *PEP6.PDB*

Processor	Stepping	Stepping Signature	Microcode Update Revision Required
Pentium Pro	C0	0x612	0xC6
Pentium Pro	sA0	0x616	0xC6
Pentium Pro	sA1	0x617	0xC6
Pentium Pro	sB1	0x619	0xD1
Pentium II	C0	0x633	0x32
Pentium II	C1	0x634	0x33
Pentium II	dA0	0x650	0x15

Using the processor update utility (CHECKUP3.EXE) available from Intel, a system builder easily can verify that the correct microcode update is present in all systems based on the P6 (Pentium Pro, Celeron, Pentium II/III) processors. For example, if a system contains a processor with stepping C1 and stepping signature 0x634, the BIOS should contain the microcode update revision 0x33. The processor update utility identifies the processor stepping, signature, and microcode update revision that is currently in use.

If a new microcode update needs to be installed in the system BIOS, the system BIOS must contain the Intel-defined processor update routines so the processor update utility can permanently install the latest update. Otherwise, a complete system BIOS upgrade is required from the motherboard manufacturer. It is recommended that the processor update utility be run after upgrading a motherboard BIOS and before installing the operating system when building a system based on any P6 processor. The utility is easy to use and executes in just a few seconds. Because the update utility might need to load new code into your BIOS, ensure that any jumper settings on the motherboard are placed in the "enable flash upgrade" position. This enables writing to the flash memory.

After running the utility, turn off power to the system and reboot—do not warm boot—to ensure that the new update is correctly initialized in the processor. Also ensure that all jumpers, such as any flash upgrade jumpers, and so on, are returned to their normal positions.

Both Intel and AMD have a number of useful utilities available for downloading from their Web sites, utilities that can be very useful for somebody who is building a system. These include utilities that identify exactly which processor you have, the speed the processor is running at, in some cases whether it has been overclocked, and even useful information such as processor temperature, steppings, and more.

In addition to software utilities, both Intel and AMD have extensive technical documentation libraries online, all free for downloading. These documents range from the actual processor and chipset data books to motherboard schematics, design guides, and even information about cooling and thermal requirements.

Processor Codenames

Intel, AMD, and Cyrix have always used codenames when talking about future processors. The codenames usually are not supposed to become public, but often they do. They can often be found in magazine articles talking about future-generation processors. Sometimes, they even appear in motherboard manuals because the manuals are written before the processors are officially introduced. Table 3.18 lists processor codenames for reference purposes.

Table 3.18   Processors and Codenames

AMD Codename	AMD Processor
X5	5x86-133 [Socket 3]
SSA5	K5 (PR75-100) [Socket 5, 7]
5k86	K5 (PR120-200) [Socket 7]
K6	Original K6 core; killed after AMD acquired NexGen
NX686	NexGen core that became the K6 [Socket 7]
Little Foot	0.25µ K6 [Socket 7]
Chompers	K6-2 (formerly K6-3D) [Socket 7, Super 7]
Sharptooth	K6-3 (formerly K6 Plus-3D) [Super 7]
Argon	Original codename for K7

Table 3.18   Continued

AMD Codename	AMD Processor
K7	Athlon [Slot A]
K75	0.18μ Athlon [Slot A]
Spitfire	Duron [Socket A]
Thunderbird	Athlon [Slot A, Socket A]
Mustang	Athlon w/copper interconnects [Slot A, Socket A]
Corvette	Mobile Athlon [Socket A]
SledgeHammer	K8 (64-bit CPU)

Cyrix Codename	Cyrix Processor
M6	486DX [Socket 1, 2, 3]
M7	486DX2/DX4 [Socket 3]
M9	5x86 [Socket 3]
M1sc	5x86 [Socket 3]
Chili	5x86 project
M1	6x86 (3.3v or 3.52v version) [Socket 7]
M1L	6x86L (2.8v/3.3v split version) [Socket 7]
M1R	Switch from 3M SGS process to 5M IBM process for 6x86
M2	6x86MX/M-II [Socket 7, Super 7]
Cayenne	MXi and Gobi core
Jedi	Original codename for Joshua (before Gobi)
Gobi	Former codename for Joshua
Joshua	VIA/Cyrix-III [Socket 370]
Jalapeno	Former codename for Mojave
Mojave	Cyrix/VIA M3 [Socket 370]
Serrano	Cyrix/VIA M4
C5	Samuel core (Winchip-4 plus on-die L2 cache)
Samuel	Cyrix/VIA chip based on Winchip-4 [Socket 370]

Intel Codename	Intel Processor
P23	486SX [Socket 1, 2, 3]
P23S	486SX SL-enhanced [Socket 1, 2, 3]
P23N	487SX (coprocessor) [Socket 1]
P4	486DX [Socket 1, 2, 3]
P4S	486DX SL-enhanced [Socket 1, 2, 3]
P24	486DX2 [Socket 1, 2, 3]
P24S	486DX2 SL-enhanced [Socket 1, 2, 3]
P24D	486DX2 (write-back enhanced version) [Socket 3]
P24C	486DX4 [Socket 3]
P23T	486DXODP (486 OverDrive) [Socket 1, 2, 3]
P4T	486DXODPR (486 OverDrive) [Socket 1, 2, 3]

Table 3.18   Continued

Intel Codename	Intel Processor
P24T	PODP5V (Pentium OverDrive for 486) [Socket 2, 3]
P24CT	Pentium OverDrive for 486DX4 (3.3v core) [Socket 2, 3]
P5	Pentium (60/66MHz versions) [Socket 4]
P5T	Pentium OverDrive (120, 133) [Socket 4]
P54C	Pentium (75–120MHz versions) [Socket 5, 7]
P54CQS	Pentium (120–133MHz version) [Socket 5, 7]
P54CS	Pentium (120–200MHz versions) [Socket 7]
P54CTA	Pentium OverDrive (125, 150, 166) [Socket 5, 7]
P55C	Pentium MMX [Socket 7]
P54CTB	Pentium MMX OverDrive [Socket 5, 7]
Tillamook	Mobile Pentium MMX
P6	Pentium Pro [Socket 8]
P6T	Pentium II OverDrive [Socket 8]
Klamath	Pentium II [Slot 1]
Drake	Pentium II Xeon [Slot 2]
Deschutes	0.25µ Pentium II [Slot 1 & 2]
Tonga	Mobile Pentium II
Covington	Celeron (cacheless Deschutes) [Slot 1]
Mendocino	Celeron (128KB on-die L2) [Slot 1, Socket 370]
Dixon	Mobile Pentium II (256KB on-die L2)
Katmai	Pentium III [Slot 1]
Tanner	Pentium III Xeon [Slot 2]
Coppermine	0.18µ PIII w/256KB on-die L2 [Slot 1, Socket 370]
Tualatin	0.13µ PIII
Cascades	Coppermine Xeon (256KB on-die L2) [Slot 2]
Coppermine-128	Celeron III (128KB on-die L2) [Socket 370]
Timna	Celeron III w/integral chipset hub
P68	Former codename for Willamette
Willamette	Pentium 4 [Socket 423]
Foster	Pentium 4 Xeon [Socket 603]
Prestonia	Successor to P4 Xeon
Gallatin	0.13µ successor to Foster [Socket 603]
Northwood	0.13 Pentium 4
P7	Former codename for Merced
Merced	Itanium (IA64) [PAC418]
McKinley	Second-generation Itanium [PAC418]
Madison	0.13µ McKinley [PAC418]
Deerfield	Low-cost Madison [PAC418]

Note that the codenames and information listed in these tables is not officially released, so by the time many of these future processors come out, names or specifications might change. Most companies who actually get this information from Intel are required to sign nondisclosure agreements that prevent them from sharing this information. This information has been gathered from a number of contacts and sources.

Intel-Compatible Processors (AMD and Cyrix)

Several companies—mainly AMD and Cyrix—have developed processors that are compatible with Intel processors. These chips are fully Intel compatible, so they emulate every processor instruction in the Intel chips. Many of the chips are also pin compatible, which means that they can be used in any system designed to accept an Intel processor; others require a custom motherboard design. Any hardware or software that works on Intel-based PCs will work on PCs made with these third-party CPU chips. A number of companies currently offer Intel-compatible chips, and some of the most popular ones are discussed here.

AMD Processors

Advanced Micro Devices (AMD) has become a major player in the Pentium-compatible chip market with its own line of Intel-compatible processors. AMD ran into trouble with Intel several years ago because its 486-clone chips used actual Intel microcode. These differences have been settled, and AMD now has a five-year cross-license agreement with Intel. In 1996, AMD finalized a deal to absorb NexGen, another maker of Intel-compatible CPUs. NexGen had been working on a chip it called the Nx686, which was renamed the K6 and introduced by AMD. Since then, AMD has refined the design as the K6-2 and K6-3. Its newest chips, called the Athlon and Duron, are designed similarly to the Pentium II/III and Celeron and use a similar but not identical slot and now socket design. AMD currently offers a wide variety of CPUs, from 486 upgrades to the K6 series and the Athlon/Duron.

Table 3.19 lists the basic processors offered by AMD.

Table 3.19   AMD CPU Summary

CPU Type	P-Rating	Actual CPU Speed (MHz)	Clock Multiplier	Motherboard Speed (MHz)	CPU Socket or Slot
Am486DX4-100	n/a	100	3x	33	Socket 1,2,3
Am486DX4-120	n/a	120	3x	40	Socket 1,2,3
Am5x86-133	75	133	4x	33	Socket 1,2,3
K5	PR75	75	1.5x	50	Socket 5,7
K5	PR90	90	1.5x	60	Socket 5,7
K5	PR100	100	1.5x	66	Socket 5,7
K5	PR120	90	1.5x	60	Socket 5,7
K5	PR133	100	1.5x	66	Socket 5,7
K5	PR166	116.7	1.75x	66	Socket 5,7
K6	PR166	166	2.5x	66	Socket 7
K6	PR200	200	3x	66	Socket 7
K6	PR233	233	3.5x	66	Socket 7
K6	PR266	266	4x	66	Socket 7
K6	PR300	300	4.5x	66	Socket 7
K6-2	PR233	233	3.5x	66	Socket 7

Table 3.19   Continued

CPU Type	P-Rating	Actual CPU Speed (MHz)	Clock Multiplier	Motherboard Speed (MHz)	CPU Socket or Slot
K6-2	PR266	266	4x	66	Socket 7
K6-2	PR300	300	4.5x	66	Socket 7
K6-2	PR300	300	3x	100	Super7
K6-2	PR333	333	5x	66	Socket 7
K6-2	PR333	333	3.5x	95	Super7
K6-2	PR350	350	3.5x	100	Super7
K6-2	PR366	366	5.5x	66	Socket 7
K6-2	PR380	380	4x	95	Super7
K6-2	PR400	400	6x	66	Socket 7
K6-2	PR400	400	4x	100	Super7
K6-2	PR450	450	4.5x	100	Super7
K6-2	PR475	475	5x	95	Super7
K6-2	PR500	500	5x	100	Super7
K6-2	PR533	533	5.5x	97	Super7
K6-2	PR550	550	5.5x	100	Super7
K6-3	PR400	400	4x	100	Super7
K6-3	PR450	450	4.5x	100	Super7
Athlon	PR500	500	2.5x	200	Slot A
Athlon/Duron	PR550	550	2.75x	200	Slot A/Socket A
Athlon/Duron	PR600	600	3x	200	Slot A/Socket A
Athlon/Duron	PR650	650	3.25x	200	Slot A/Socket A
Athlon/Duron	PR700	700	3.5x	200	Slot A/Socket A
Athlon/Duron	PR750	750	3.75x	200	Slot A/Socket A
Athlon/Duron	PR800	800	4x	200	Slot A/Socket A
Athlon/Duron	PR850	850	4.25x	200	Slot A/Socket A
Athlon/Duron	PR900	900	4.5x	200	Slot A/Socket A
Athlon/Duron	PR950	950	4.75x	200	Slot A/Socket A
Athlon/Duron	PR1000	1.0	5x	200	Slot A/Socket A
Athlon	PR1100	1.1	5.5x	200	Socket A
Athlon	PR1200	1.2	6x	200	Socket A
Athlon	PR1300	1.3	6.5x	200	Socket A
Athlon	PR1000	1.0	3.75x	266	Socket A
Athlon	PR1133	1.13	4.25x	266	Socket A
Athlon	PR1200	1.2	4.5x	266	Socket A
Athlon	PR1333	1.33	5x	266	Socket A

Notice in the table that for the K5 PR120 through PR166, the model designation does not match the CPU clock speed. This is called a PR rating instead and is further described earlier in this chapter.

Starting with the K6, the P-Rating equals the true MHz clock speed.

Most of the newer AMD Athlon and all Duron processors are designed to use Socket A, also called Socket 462.

Cyrix

Cyrix was purchased by National Semiconductor in November 1997 and by VIA Technologies in 1999. Prior to that, it had been a fabless company, meaning it had no chip-manufacturing capability. All the Cyrix chips were manufactured for Cyrix first by Texas Instruments and then mainly by IBM up through the end of 1998. Starting in 1999, National Semiconductor took over manufacturing of the Cyrix processors. More recently, National has been purchased by VIA Technologies.

Similar to Intel, Cyrix has begun to limit its selection of available CPUs to only the latest technology. Cyrix is currently focusing on the Pentium market with the M1 (6x86) and M2 (6x86MX) processors. The 6x86 has dual internal pipelines and a single, unified 16KB internal cache. It offers speculative and out-of-order instruction execution, much like the Intel Pentium Pro processor. The 6x86MX adds MMX technology to the CPU. The chip is Socket 7 compatible, but some require modified chipsets and new motherboard designs. See Table 3.5 earlier in this chapter, which shows the Cyrix processors.

The 6x86MX features 64KB of unified L1 cache and more than double the performance of the previous 6x86 CPUs. The 6x86MX is offered in clock speeds ranging from 180 to 266MHz, and similar to the 6x86, it is Socket 7 compatible. When running at speeds of 300MHz and higher, the 686MX was renamed the MII. Besides the higher speeds, all other functions are virtually identical. All Cyrix chips were manufactured by other companies such as IBM, which also markets the 6x86 chips under its own name. National began manufacturing Cyrix processors during 1998, but now that Cyrix is selling them off, the future is unclear.

Note that later versions of the 6x86MX chip have been renamed the MII to deliberately invoke comparisons with the Pentium II, instead of the regular Pentium processor. The MII chips are not redesigned; they are, in fact, the same 6x86MX chips as before, only running at higher clock rates. The first renamed 6x86MX chip is the MII 300, which actually runs at only 233MHz on a 66MHz Socket 7 motherboard. There is also an MII 333, which will run at a 250MHz clock speed on newer 100MHz Super7 motherboards.

Cyrix also has made an attempt at capturing even more of the low-end market than it already has by introducing a processor called the MediaGX. This is a low-performance cross between a 486 and a Pentium combined with a custom motherboard chipset in a two-chip package. These two chips contain everything necessary for a motherboard, except the Super I/O chip, and make very low-cost PCs possible.

P1 (086) First-Generation Processors

The first generation of processors represents the series of chips from Intel that were found in the first PCs. IBM, as the architect of the PC at the time, chose Intel processors and support chips to build the PC motherboard, setting a standard that would hold for many subsequent processor generations to come.

8088 and 8086 Processors

Intel introduced a revolutionary new processor called the 8086 back in June 1978. The 8086 was one of the first 16-bit processor chips on the market; at the time, virtually all other processors were 8-bit designs. The 8086 had 16-bit internal registers and could run a new class of software using 16-bit instructions. It also had a 16-bit external data path, so it could transfer data to memory 16 bits at a time.

The address bus was 20 bits wide, which enabled the 8086 to address a full 1MB (2^{20}) of memory. This was in stark contrast to most other chips of that time that had 8-bit internal registers, an 8-bit external data bus, and a 16-bit address bus allowing a maximum of only 64KB of RAM (2^{16}).

Unfortunately, most of the personal computer world at the time was using 8-bit processors, which ran 8-bit CP/M (Control Program for Microprocessors) operating systems and software. The board and circuit designs at the time were largely 8-bit, as well. Building a full 16-bit motherboard and memory system was costly, pricing such a computer out of the market.

The cost was high because the 8086 needed a 16-bit data bus rather than a less expensive 8-bit bus. Systems available at that time were 8-bit, and slow sales of the 8086 indicated to Intel that people weren't willing to pay for the extra performance of the full 16-bit design. In response, Intel introduced a kind of crippled version of the 8086, called the 8088. The 8088 essentially deleted 8 of the 16 bits on the data bus, making the 8088 an 8-bit chip as far as data input and output were concerned. However, because it retained the full 16-bit internal registers and the 20-bit address bus, the 8088 ran 16-bit software and was capable of addressing a full 1MB of RAM.

For these reasons, IBM selected the 8-bit 8088 chip for the original IBM PC. Years later, IBM was criticized for using the 8-bit 8088 instead of the 16-bit 8086. In retrospect, it was a very wise decision. IBM even covered up the physical design in its ads, which at the time indicated its new PC had a "high-speed 16-bit microprocessor." IBM could say that because the 8088 still ran the same powerful 16-bit software the 8086 ran, just a little more slowly. In fact, programmers universally thought of the 8088 as a 16-bit chip because there was virtually no way a program could distinguish an 8088 from an 8086. This enabled IBM to deliver a PC capable of running a new generation of 16-bit software, while retaining a much less expensive 8-bit design for the hardware. Because of this, the IBM PC was actually priced less at its introduction than the most popular PC of the time, the Apple II. For the trivia buffs out there, the IBM PC listed for $1,265 and included only 16KB of RAM, whereas a similarly configured Apple II cost $1,355.

Even though the 8088 was introduced in June 1979, the original IBM PC that used the processor did not appear until August 1981. Back then, a significant lag time often occurred between the introduction of a new processor and systems that incorporated it. That is unlike today, when new processors and systems using them often are released on the same day.

The 8088 in the IBM PC ran at 4.77MHz; the average instruction on the 8088 took 12 cycles to complete.

Computer users sometimes wonder why a 640KB conventional-memory barrier exists if the 8088 chip can address 1MB of memory. The conventional-memory barrier exists because IBM reserved 384KB of the upper portion of the 1,024KB (1MB) address space of the 8088 for use by adapter cards and system BIOS. The lower 640KB is the conventional memory in which DOS and software applications execute.

80186 and 80188 Processors

After Intel produced the 8086 and 8088 chips, it turned its sights toward producing a more powerful chip with an increased instruction set. The company's first efforts along this line—the 80186 and 80188—were unsuccessful. But incorporating system components into the CPU chip was an important idea for Intel because it led to faster, better chips, such as the 286.

The relationship between the 80186 and 80188 is the same as that of the 8086 and 8088; one is a slightly more advanced version of the other. Compared CPU to CPU, the 80186 is almost the same as the 8088 and has a full 16-bit design. The 80188 (like the 8088) is a hybrid chip that compromises the 16-bit design with an 8-bit external communications interface. The advantage of the 80186 and 80188 is that they combine on a single chip 15–20 of the 8086–8088 series system components—a fact that can greatly reduce the number of components in a computer design. The 80186 and 80188 chips were used for highly intelligent peripheral adapter cards of that age, such as network adapters.

8087 Coprocessor

Intel introduced the 8086 processor in 1976. The math coprocessor that was paired with the chip—the 8087—often was called the numeric data processor (NDP), the math coprocessor, or simply the math chip. The 8087 is designed to perform high-level math operations at many times the speed of the main processor. The primary advantage of using this chip is the increased execution speed in number-crunching programs, such as spreadsheet applications.

P2 (286) Second-Generation Processors

The second generation of PC processors allowed for a great leap in system speed and processing efficiency. With these chips we went from moving 8 bits of data around to moving 16 bits at a time. The following section details the second-generation PC processor, the 286.

286 Processors

The Intel 80286 (normally abbreviated as 286) processor did not suffer from the compatibility problems that damned the 80186 and 80188. The 286 chip, first introduced in 1981, is the CPU behind the original IBM AT. Other computer makers manufactured what came to be known as IBM clones, with many of these manufacturers calling their systems AT-compatible or AT-class computers.

When IBM developed the AT, it selected the 286 as the basis for the new system because the chip provided compatibility with the 8088 used in the PC and the XT. Therefore, software written for those chips should run on the 286. The 286 chip is many times faster than the 8088 used in the XT, and it offered a major performance boost to PCs used in businesses. The processing speed, or throughput, of the original AT (which ran at 6MHz) was five times greater than that of the PC running at 4.77MHz. The die for the 286 is shown in Figure 3.31.

Figure 3.31   286 Processor die. *Photograph used by permission of Intel Corporation.*

286 systems are faster than their predecessors for several reasons. The main reason is that 286 processors are much more efficient in executing instructions. An average instruction takes 12 clock cycles on the 8086 or 8088, but takes an average of only 4.5 cycles on the 286 processor. Additionally, the 286 chip can handle up to 16 bits of data at a time through an external data bus twice the size of the 8088.

The 286 chip has two modes of operation: real mode and protected mode. The two modes are distinct enough to make the 286 resemble two chips in one. In real mode, a 286 acts essentially the same as an 8086 chip and is fully *object-code compatible* with the 8086 and 8088. (A processor with object-code compatibility can run programs written for another processor without modification and execute every system instruction in the same manner.)

In the protected mode of operation, the 286 was truly something new. In this mode, a program designed to take advantage of the chip's capabilities believes that it has access to 1GB of memory (including virtual memory). The 286 chip, however, can address only 16MB of hardware memory. A significant failing of the 286 chip is that it cannot switch from protected mode to real mode without a hardware reset (a warm reboot) of the system. (It can, however, switch from real mode to protected mode without a reset.) A major improvement of the 386 over the 286 is that software can switch the 386 from real mode to protected mode, and vice versa. See the section "Processor Modes," earlier in this chapter for more information.

Only a small amount of software that took advantage of the 286 chip was sold until Windows 3.0 offered standard mode for 286 compatibility; by that time, the hottest-selling chip was the 386. Still, the 286 was Intel's first attempt to produce a CPU chip that supported multitasking, in which multiple programs run at the same time. The 286 was designed so that if one program locked up or failed, the entire system didn't need a warm boot (reset) or cold boot (power off, then back on). Theoretically, what happened in one area of memory didn't affect other programs. Before multitasked programs could be "safe" from one another, however, the 286 chip (and subsequent chips) needed an operating system that worked cooperatively with the chip to provide such protection.

80287 Coprocessor

The 80287, internally, is the same math chip as the 8087, although the pins used to plug them into the motherboard are different. Both the 80287 and the 8087 operate as though they were identical.

In most systems, the 80286 internally divides the system clock by two to derive the processor clock. The 80287 internally divides the system-clock frequency by three. For this reason, most AT-type computers run the 80287 at one-third the system clock rate, which also is two-thirds the clock speed of the 80286. Because the 286 and 287 chips are asynchronous, the interface between the 286 and 287 chips is not as efficient as with the 8088 and 8087.

In summary, the 80287 and the 8087 chips perform about the same at equal clock rates. The original 80287 is not better than the 8087 in any real way—unlike the 80286, which is superior to the 8086 and 8088. In most AT systems, the performance gain that you realize by adding the coprocessor is much less substantial than the same type of upgrade for PC- or XT-type systems or for the 80386.

286 Processor Problems

After you remove a math coprocessor from an AT-type system, you must rerun your computer's Setup program. Some AT-compatible Setup programs do not properly unset the math coprocessor bit. If you receive a POST error message because the computer cannot find the math chip, you might have to unplug the battery from the system board temporarily. All Setup information will be lost, so be sure to write down the hard drive type, floppy drive type, and memory and video configurations before unplugging the battery. This information is critical in reconfiguring your computer correctly.

P3 (386) Third-Generation Processors

The third generation represents perhaps the most significant change in processors since the first PC. The big deal was the migration from processors that handled 16-bit operations to true 32-bit chips. The third-generation processors were so far ahead of their time, it took fully 10 years before 32-bit operating systems and software became mainstream, and by that time the third-generation chips had become a memory. The following section details the third-generation processors.

386 Processors

The Intel 80386 (normally abbreviated as 386) caused quite a stir in the PC industry because of the vastly improved performance it brought to the personal computer. Compared with 8088 and 286 systems, the 386 chip offered greater performance in almost all areas of operation.

The 386 is a full 32-bit processor optimized for high-speed operation and multitasking operating systems. Intel introduced the chip in 1985, but the 386 appeared in the first systems in late 1986 and early 1987. The Compaq Deskpro 386 and systems made by several other manufacturers introduced the chip; somewhat later, IBM used the chip in its PS/2 Model 80. The 386 chip rose in popularity for several years, which peaked around 1991. Obsolete 386 processor systems are mostly retired or scrapped, having been passed down the user chain. If they are in operating condition, they can be useful for running old DOS or Windows 3.x–based applications, which they can do quite nicely.

The 386 can execute the real-mode instructions of an 8086 or 8088, but in fewer clock cycles. The 386 was as efficient as the 286 in executing instructions—the average instruction took about 4.5 clock cycles. In raw performance, therefore, the 286 and 386 actually seemed to be at almost equal clock rates. Many 286 system manufacturers were touting their 16MHz and 20MHz 286 systems as being just as fast as 16MHz and 20MHz 386 systems, and they were right! The 386 offered greater performance in other ways, mainly because of additional software capability (modes) and a greatly enhanced memory management unit (MMU). The die for the 386 is shown in Figure 3.32.

The 386 can switch to and from protected mode under software control without a system reset—a capability that makes using protected mode more practical. In addition, the 386 has a new mode, called virtual real mode, which enables several real-mode sessions to run simultaneously under protected mode.

The protected mode of the 386 is fully compatible with the protected mode of the 286. The protected mode for both chips often is called their native mode of operation because these chips are designed for advanced operating systems such as OS/2 and Windows NT, which run only in protected mode. Intel extended the memory-addressing capabilities of 386 protected mode with a new MMU that provided advanced memory paging and program switching. These features were extensions of the 286 type of MMU, so the 386 remained fully compatible with the 286 at the system-code level.

The 386 chip's virtual real mode was new. In virtual real mode, the processor could run with hardware memory protection while simulating an 8086's real-mode operation. Multiple copies of DOS and other operating systems, therefore, could run simultaneously on this processor, each in a protected area of memory. If the programs in one segment crashed, the rest of the system was protected. Software commands could reboot the blown partition.

Numerous variations of the 386 chip exist, some of which are less powerful and some of which are less power hungry. The following sections cover the members of the 386-chip family and their differences.

Figure 3.32 386 processor die. *Photograph used by permission of Intel Corporation.*

386DX Processors

The 386DX chip was the first of the 386 family members that Intel introduced. The 386 is a full 32-bit processor with 32-bit internal registers, a 32-bit internal data bus, and a 32-bit external data bus. The 386 contains 275,000 transistors in a very large scale integration (VLSI) circuit. The chip comes in a 132-pin package and draws approximately 400 milliamperes (ma), which is less power than even the 8086 requires. The 386 has a smaller power requirement because it is made of Complementary Metal-Oxide Semiconductor (CMOS) materials. The CMOS design enables devices to consume extremely low levels of power.

The Intel 386 chip was available in clock speeds ranging from 16MHz–33MHz; other manufacturers, primarily AMD and Cyrix, offered comparable versions with speeds up to 40MHz.

The 386DX can address 4GB of physical memory. Its built-in virtual memory manager enables software designed to take advantage of enormous amounts of memory to act as though a system has 64TB of memory. (A terabyte, or TB, is 1,099,511,627,776 bytes of memory, or about 1,000GB.)

386SX Processors

The 386SX was designed for systems designers looking for 386 capabilities at 286 system prices. Similar to the 286, the 386SX is restricted to only 16 bits when communicating with other system components, such as memory. Internally, however, the 386SX is identical to the DX chip; the 386SX has 32-bit internal registers and can therefore run 32-bit software. The 386SX uses a 24-bit memory-addressing scheme like that of the 286, rather than the full 32-bit memory address bus of the standard

386. The 386SX, therefore, can address a maximum 16MB of physical memory rather than the 4GB of physical memory the 386DX can address. Before it was discontinued, the 386SX was available in clock speeds ranging from 16MHz to 33MHz.

The 386SX signaled the end of the 286 because of the 386SX chip's superior MMU and the addition of the virtual real mode. Under a software manager such as Windows or OS/2, the 386SX can run numerous DOS programs at the same time. The capability to run 386-specific software is another important advantage of the 386SX over any 286 or older design. For example, Windows 3.1 runs nearly as well on a 386SX as it does on a 386DX.

386SL Processors

The 386SL is another variation on the 386 chip. This low-power CPU had the same capabilities as the 386SX, but it was designed for laptop systems in which low power consumption was necessary. The SL chips offered special power-management features that were important to systems that ran on batteries. The SL chip also offered several sleep modes to conserve power.

The chip included an extended architecture that contained a System Management Interrupt (SMI), which provided access to the power-management features. Also included in the SL chip was special support for LIM (Lotus Intel Microsoft) expanded memory functions and a cache controller. The cache controller was designed to control a 16KB–64KB external processor cache.

These extra functions account for the higher transistor count in the SL chips (855,000) compared with even the 386DX processor (275,000). The 386SL was available in 25MHz clock speed.

Intel offered a companion to the 386SL chip for laptops called the 82360SL I/O subsystem. The 82360SL provided many common peripheral functions, such as serial and parallel ports, a direct memory access (DMA) controller, an interrupt controller, and power-management logic for the 386SL processor. This chip subsystem worked with the processor to provide an ideal solution for the small size and low power-consumption requirements of portable and laptop systems.

80387 Coprocessor

Although the 80387 chips ran asynchronously, 386 systems were designed so that the math chip runs at the same clock speed as the main CPU. Unlike the 80287 coprocessor, which was merely an 8087 with different pins to plug into the AT motherboard, the 80387 coprocessor was a high-performance math chip specifically designed to work with the 386.

All 387 chips used a low power-consumption CMOS design. The 387 coprocessor had two basic designs: the 387DX coprocessor, which was designed to work with the 386DX processor, and the 387SX coprocessor, which was designed to work with the 386SX, SL, or SLC processor.

Intel originally offered several speeds for the 387DX coprocessor. But when the company designed the 33MHz version, a smaller mask was required to reduce the lengths of the signal pathways in the chip. This increased the performance of the chip by roughly 20%.

Note

Because Intel lagged in developing the 387 coprocessor, some early 386 systems were designed with a socket for a 287 coprocessor. Performance levels associated with that union, however, leave much to be desired.

Installing a 387DX is easy, but you must be careful to orient the chip in its socket properly; otherwise, the chip will be destroyed. The most common cause of burned pins on the 387DX is incorrect installation. In many systems, the 387DX was oriented differently from other large chips. Follow the manufacturer's installation instructions carefully to avoid damaging the 387DX; Intel's warranty does not cover chips that are installed incorrectly.

Several manufacturers developed their own versions of the Intel 387 coprocessors, some of which were touted as being faster than the original Intel chips. The general compatibility record of these chips was very good.

Weitek Coprocessors

In 1981, several Intel engineers formed the Weitek Corporation. Weitek developed math coprocessors for several systems, including those based on Motorola processor designs. Intel originally contracted Weitek to develop a math coprocessor for the Intel 386 CPU because Intel was behind in its own development of the 387 math coprocessor. The result was the Weitek 1167, a custom math coprocessor that uses a proprietary Weitek instruction set that is incompatible with the Intel 387.

To use the Weitek coprocessor, your system must have the required additional socket, which is different from the standard Intel coprocessor sockets.

80386 Bugs

Some early 16MHz Intel 386DX processors had a small bug that appeared as a software problem. The bug, which apparently was in the chip's 32-bit multiply routine, manifested itself only when true 32-bit code was run in a program such as OS/2 2.x, Unix/386, or Windows in enhanced mode. Some specialized 386 memory-management software systems also might invoke this subtle bug, but 16-bit operating systems (such as DOS and OS/2 1.x) probably will not.

The bug usually causes the system to lock up. Diagnosing this problem can be difficult because the problem generally is intermittent and software related. Running tests to find the bug is difficult; only Intel, with proper test equipment, can determine whether a chip has a bug. Some programs can diagnose the problem and identify a defective chip, but they cannot identify all defective chips. If a program indicates a bad chip, you certainly have a defective one; however, if the program passes the chip, you still might have a defective one.

Intel requested that its 386 customers return possibly defective chips for screening, but many vendors did not return them. Intel tested returned chips and replaced defective ones. The defective chips later were sold to bargain liquidators or systems houses that wanted chips that would not run 32-bit code. The defective chips were stamped with a 16-bit SW Only logo, indicating they were authorized to run only 16-bit software.

Chips that passed the test, and all subsequent chips produced as bug-free, were marked with a double-sigma code (SS). 386DX chips not marked with either of these designations have not been tested by Intel and might be defective.

This problem was discovered and corrected before Intel officially added DX to the part number. So, if you have a chip labeled 80386DX or 386DX, it does not have this problem.

Another problem with the 386DX can be stated more specifically. When 386-based versions of XENIX or other Unix implementations are run on a computer that contains a 387DX math coprocessor, the computer locks up under certain conditions. The problem does not occur in the DOS environment, however. For the lockup to occur, all the following conditions must be in effect:

- Demand page virtual memory must be active.
- A 387DX must be installed and in use.
- DMA must occur.
- The 386 must be in a wait state.

When all these conditions are true at the same instant, the 386DX ends up waiting for the 387DX and vice versa. Both processors will continue to wait for each other indefinitely. The problem is in certain versions of the 386DX, not in the 387DX math coprocessor.

Intel published this problem (Errata 21) immediately after it was discovered to inform its OEM customers. At that point, it became the responsibility of each manufacturer to implement a fix in its hardware or software product. Some manufacturers, such as Compaq and IBM, responded by modifying their motherboards to prevent these lockups from occurring.

The Errata 21 problem occurs only in the B-stepping version of the 386DX and not in the later D-stepping version. You can identify the D-stepping version of the 386DX by the letters DX in the part number (for example, 386DX-20). If DX is part of the chip's part number, the chip does not have this problem.

P4 (486) Fourth-Generation Processors

The third generation had been a large change from the previous generations of processors. With the fourth generation, more refinement than complete redesign was accomplished. Even so, Intel, AMD, and others managed to literally double processor performance with their fourth-generation processors. The following section defines the fourth-generation processors from Intel, AMD, and others.

486 Processors

In the race for more speed, the Intel 80486 (normally abbreviated as 486) was another major leap forward. The additional power available in the 486 fueled tremendous growth in the software industry. Tens of millions of copies of Windows, and millions of copies of OS/2, have been sold largely because the 486 finally made the GUI of Windows and OS/2 a realistic option for people who work on their computers every day.

Four main features make a given 486 processor roughly twice as fast as an equivalent MHz 386 chip. These features are

- *Reduced instruction-execution time.* A single instruction in the 486 takes an average of only two clock cycles to complete, compared with an average of more than four cycles on the 386. Clock-multiplied versions, such as the DX2 and DX4, further reduced this to about two cycles per instruction.

- *Internal (Level 1) cache.* The built-in cache has a hit ratio of 90%–95%, which describes how often zero-wait-state read operations occur. External caches can improve this ratio further.

- *Burst-mode memory cycles.* A standard 32-bit (4-byte) memory transfer takes two clock cycles. After a standard 32-bit transfer, more data up to the next 12 bytes (or three transfers) can be transferred with only one cycle used for each 32-bit (4-byte) transfer. Thus, up to 16 bytes of contiguous, sequential memory data can be transferred in as little as five cycles instead of eight cycles or more. This effect can be even greater when the transfers are only 8 bits or 16 bits each.

▶▶ See "Burst EDO," p. 417.

- *Built-in (synchronous) enhanced math coprocessor (some versions).* The math coprocessor runs synchronously with the main processor and executes math instructions in fewer cycles than previous designs did. On average, the math coprocessor built into the DX-series chips provides two to three times greater math performance than an external 387 chip.

The 486 chip is about twice as fast as the 386, so a 386DX-40 is about as fast as a 486SX-20. This made the 486 a much more desirable option, primarily because it could more easily be upgraded to a DX2 or DX4 processor at a later time. You can see why the arrival of the 486 rapidly killed off the 386 in the marketplace.

Before the 486, many people avoided GUIs because they didn't have time to sit around waiting for the hourglass, which indicates that the system is performing behind-the-scenes operations the user cannot interrupt. The 486 changed that situation. Many people believe the 486 CPU chip spawned the widespread acceptance of GUIs.

With the release of its faster Pentium CPU chip, Intel began to cut the price of the 486 line to entice the industry to shift over to the 486 as the mainstream system. Intel later did the same thing with its Pentium chips, spelling the end of the 486 line. The 486 is now offered by Intel only for use in embedded microprocessor applications, used primarily in expansion cards.

Most of the 486 chips were offered in a variety of maximum speed ratings, varying from 16MHz up to 120MHz. Additionally, 486 processors have slight differences in overall pin configurations. The DX, DX2, and SX processors have a virtually identical 168-pin configuration, whereas the OverDrive chips have either the standard 168-pin configuration or a specially modified 169-pin OverDrive (sometimes also called 487SX) configuration. If your motherboard has two sockets, the primary one likely supports the standard 168-pin configuration, and the secondary (OverDrive) socket supports the 169-pin OverDrive configuration. Most newer motherboards with a single ZIF socket support any of the 486 processors except the DX4. The DX4 is different because it requires 3.3v to operate instead of 5v, like most other chips up to that time.

A processor rated for a given speed always functions at any of the lower speeds. A 100MHz-rated 486DX4 chip, for example, runs at 75MHz if it is plugged into a 25MHz motherboard. Note that the DX2/OverDrive processors operate internally at two times the motherboard clock rate, whereas the DX4 processors operate at two, two-and-one-half, or three times the motherboard clock rate. Table 3.20 shows the various speed combinations that can result from using the DX2 or DX4 processors with different motherboard clock speeds.

Table 3.20   Intel DX2 and DX4 Operating Speeds Versus Motherboard Clock Speeds

Processor Speed	DX2 (2× mode) Speed	DX4 (2.5× mode) Speed	DX4 (3× mode) Speed	DX4
16MHz Motherboard	32MHz	32MHz	40MHz	48MHz
40MHz Motherboard	80MHz	80MHz	100MHz	120MHz
20MHz Motherboard	40MHz	40MHz	50MHz	60MHz
50MHz Motherboard	n/a	100MHz	n/a	n/a
25MHz Motherboard	50MHz	50MHz	63MHz	75MHz
33MHz Motherboard	66MHz	66MHz	83MHz	100MHz

The internal core speed of the DX4 processor is controlled by the CLKMUL (clock multiplier) signal at pin R-17 (Socket 1) or S-18 (Socket 2, 3, or 6). The CLKMUL input is sampled only during a reset of the CPU and defines the ratio of the internal clock to the external bus frequency CLK signal at pin C-3 (Socket 1) or D-4 (Socket 2, 3, or 6). If CLKMUL is sampled low, the internal core speed is two times the external bus frequency. If driven high or left floating (most motherboards would leave it floating), triple speed mode is selected. If the CLKMUL signal is connected to the BREQ (bus request) output signal at pin Q-15 (Socket 1) or R-16 (Socket 2, 3, or 6), the CPU internal core speed is two and a half times the CLK speed. To summarize, here is how the socket must be wired for each DX4 speed selection:

CPU Speed	CLKMUL (Sampled Only at CPU Reset)
2x	Low
2.5x	Connected to BREQ
3x	High or floating

You must determine how your particular motherboard is wired and whether it can be changed to alter the CPU core speed in relation to the CLK signal. In most cases, one or two jumpers will be on the board near the processor socket. The motherboard documentation should cover these settings if they can be changed.

One interesting capability here is to run the DX4-100 chip in a doubled mode with a 50MHz motherboard speed. This gives you a very fast memory bus, along with the same 100MHz processor speed, as if you were running the chip in a 33/100MHz tripled mode.

Note

One caveat is that if your motherboard has VL-Bus slots, they must be slowed down to 33MHz or 40MHz to operate properly.

Many VL-Bus motherboards can run the VL-Bus slots in a buffered mode, add wait states, or even selectively change the clock only for the VL-Bus slots to keep them compatible. In most cases, they don't run properly at 50MHz. Consult your motherboard—or even better, your chipset documentation—to see how your board is set up.

Caution

When upgrading an existing system, you should be sure that your socket supports the chip you are installing. This was especially true when putting a DX4 processor in an older system. In that scenario, you needed some type of adapter to regulate the voltage down to 3.3v. Putting the DX4 in a 5v socket destroys the chip! See the earlier section on processor sockets for more information.

The 486-processor family is designed for greater performance than previous processors because it integrates formerly external devices, such as cache controllers, cache memory, and math coprocessors. Also, 486 systems were the first designed for true processor upgradability. Most 486 systems can be upgraded by simple processor additions or swaps that can effectively double the speed of the system.

486DX Processors

The original Intel 486DX processor was introduced on April 10, 1989, and systems using this chip first appeared during 1990. The first chips had a maximum speed rating of 25MHz; later versions of the 486DX were available in 33MHz- and 50MHz-rated versions. The 486DX originally was available only in a 5v, 168-pin PGA version, but now is also available in 5v, 196-pin plastic quad flat pack (PQFP) and 3.3v, 208-pin small quad flat pack (SQFP). These latter form factors are available in SL enhanced versions, which are intended primarily for portable or laptop applications in which saving power is important.

Two main features separate the 486 processor from its predecessors:

- The 486DX integrates functions such as the math coprocessor, cache controller, and cache memory into the chip.
- The 486 also was designed with upgradability in mind; double-speed OverDrive were upgrades available for most systems.

The 486DX processor is fabricated with low-power CMOS technology. The chip has a 32-bit internal register size, a 32-bit external data bus, and a 32-bit address bus. These dimensions are equal to those of the 386DX processor. The internal register size is where the "32-bit" designation used in advertisements comes from. The 486DX chip contains 1.2 million transistors on a piece of silicon no larger than your thumbnail. This figure is more than four times the number of components on 386 processors and should give you a good indication of the 486 chip's relative power. The die for the 486 is shown in Figure 3.33.

Figure 3.33 486 processor die. *Photograph used by permission of Intel Corporation.*

The standard 486DX contains a processing unit, floating-point unit (math coprocessor), memory-management unit, and cache controller with 8KB of internal-cache RAM. Due to the internal cache and a more efficient internal processing unit, the 486 family of processors can execute individual instructions in an average of only 2 processor cycles. Compare this figure with the 286 and 386 families, both of which execute an average 4.5 cycles per instruction. Compare it also with the original 8086 and 8088 processors, which execute an average 12 cycles per instruction. At a given clock rate (MHz), therefore, a 486 processor is roughly twice as efficient as a 386 processor; a 16MHz 486SX is roughly equal to a 33MHz 386DX system; and a 20MHz 486SX is equal to a 40MHz 386DX system. Any of the faster 486s are way beyond the 386 in performance.

The 486 is fully instruction-set–compatible with previous Intel processors, such as the 386, but offers several additional instructions (most of which have to do with controlling the internal cache).

Similar to the 386DX, the 486 can address 4GB of physical memory and manage as much as 64TB of virtual memory. The 486 fully supports the three operating modes introduced in the 386: real mode, protected mode, and virtual real mode:

- *In real mode*, the 486 (similar to the 386) runs unmodified 8086-type software.
- *In protected mode*, the 486 (similar to the 386) offers sophisticated memory paging and program switching.

■ *In virtual real mode*, the 486 (similar to the 386) can run multiple copies of DOS or other operating systems while simulating an 8086's real-mode operation. Under an operating system such as Windows or OS/2, therefore, both 16-bit and 32-bit programs can run simultaneously on this processor with hardware memory protection. If one program crashes, the rest of the system is protected, and you can reboot the blown portion through various means, depending on the operating software.

The 486DX series has a built-in math coprocessor that sometimes is called an MCP (math coprocessor) or FPU. This series is unlike previous Intel CPU chips, which required you to add a math coprocessor if you needed faster calculations for complex mathematics. The FPU in the 486DX series is 100% software-compatible with the external 387 math coprocessor used with the 386, but it delivers more than twice the performance. It runs in synchronization with the main processor and executes most instructions in half as many cycles as the 386.

486SL

The 486SL was a short-lived, standalone chip. The SL enhancements and features became available in virtually all the 486 processors (SX, DX, and DX2) in what are called SL enhanced versions. SL enhancement refers to a special design that incorporates special power-saving features.

The SL enhanced chips originally were designed to be installed in laptop or notebook systems that run on batteries, but they found their way into desktop systems, as well. The SL enhanced chips featured special power-management techniques, such as sleep mode and clock throttling, to reduce power consumption when necessary. These chips were available in 3.3v versions, as well.

Intel designed a power-management architecture called system management mode. This mode of operation is totally isolated and independent from other CPU hardware and software. SMM provides hardware resources such as timers, registers, and other I/O logic that can control and power down mobile-computer components without interfering with any of the other system resources. SMM executes in a dedicated memory space called system management memory, which is not visible and does not interfere with operating system and application software. SMM has an interrupt called system management interrupt (SMI), which services power-management events and is independent from— and higher priority than—any of the other interrupts.

SMM provides power management with flexibility and security that were not available previously. For example, an SMI occurs when an application program tries to access a peripheral device that is powered down for battery savings, which powers up the peripheral device and reexecutes the I/O instruction automatically.

Intel also designed a feature called Suspend/Resume in the SL processor. The system manufacturer can use this feature to provide the portable computer user with instant on-and-off capability. An SL system typically can resume (instant on) in one second from the suspend state (instant off) to exactly where it left off. You do not need to reboot, load the operating system, load the application program, and then load the application data. Simply push the Suspend/Resume button and the system is ready to go.

The SL CPU was designed to consume almost no power in the suspend state. This feature means that the system can stay in the suspend state possibly for weeks and yet start up instantly right where it left off. An SL system can keep working data in normal RAM memory safe for a long time while it is in the suspend state, but saving to a disk still is prudent.

486SX

The 486SX, introduced in April 1991, was designed to be sold as a lower-cost version of the 486. The 486SX is virtually identical to the full DX processor, but the chip does not incorporate the FPU or math coprocessor portion.

As you read earlier in this chapter, the 386SX was a scaled-down (some people would say crippled) 16-bit version of the full-blown 32-bit 386DX. The 386SX even had a completely different pinout and was not interchangeable with the more powerful DX version. The 486SX, however, is a different story. The 486SX is, in fact, a full-blown 32-bit 486 processor that is basically pin compatible with the DX. A few pin functions are different or rearranged, but each pin fits into the same socket.

The 486SX chip is more a marketing quirk than new technology. Early versions of the 486SX chip actually were DX chips that showed defects in the math-coprocessor section. Instead of being scrapped, the chips were packaged with the FPU section disabled and sold as SX chips. This arrangement lasted for only a short time; thereafter, SX chips got their own mask, which is different from the DX mask. (A *mask* is the photographic blueprint of the processor and is used to etch the intricate signal pathways into a silicon chip.) The transistor count dropped to 1.185 million (from 1.2 million) to reflect this new mask.

The 486SX chip is twice as fast as a 386DX with the same clock speed. Intel marketed the 486SX as being the ideal chip for new computer buyers because fewer entry-level programs of that day used math-coprocessor functions.

The 486SX was available in 16MHz-, 20MHz-, 25MHz-, and 33MHz-rated speeds, an a 486 SX/2 was also available that ran at up to 50MHz or 66MHz. The 486SX typically comes in a 168-pin version, although other surface-mount versions are available in SL-enhanced models.

Despite what Intel's marketing and sales information implies, no technical provision exists for adding a separate math coprocessor to a 486SX system; neither was a separate math coprocessor chip ever available to plug in. Instead, Intel wanted you to add a new 486 processor with a built-in math unit and disable the SX CPU that already was on the motherboard. If this situation sounds confusing, read on because this topic brings you to the most important aspect of 486 design: upgradability.

487SX

The 487SX math coprocessor, as Intel calls it, really is a complete 25MHz 486DX CPU with an extra pin added and some other pins rearranged. When the 487SX is installed in the extra socket provided in a 486SX CPU-based system, the 487SX turns off the existing 486SX via a new signal on one of the pins. The extra key pin actually carries no signal itself and exists only to prevent improper orientation when the chip is installed in a socket.

The 487SX takes over all CPU functions from the 486SX and also provides math coprocessor functionality in the system. At first glance, this setup seems rather strange and wasteful, so perhaps further explanation is in order. Fortunately, the 487SX turned out to be a stopgap measure while Intel prepared its real surprise: the OverDrive processor. The DX2/OverDrive speed-doubling chips, which are designed for the 487SX 169-pin socket, have the same pinout as the 487SX. These upgrade chips are installed in exactly the same way as the 487SX; therefore, any system that supports the 487SX also supports the DX2/OverDrive chips.

Although in most cases you can upgrade a system by removing the 486SX CPU and replacing it with a 487SX (or even a DX or DX2/OverDrive), Intel originally discouraged this procedure. Instead, Intel recommended that PC manufacturers include a dedicated upgrade (OverDrive) socket in their systems because several risks were involved in removing the original CPU from a standard socket. (The following section elaborates on those risks.) Now Intel recommends—or even insists on—the use of a single processor socket of a ZIF design, which makes upgrading an easy task physically.

◀◀   See "Zero Insertion Force Sockets," p. 95.

Very few early 486 systems had a socket for the Weitek 4167 coprocessor chip for 486 systems that existed in November 1989.

DX2/OverDrive and DX4 Processors

On March 3, 1992, Intel introduced the DX2 speed-doubling processors. On May 26, 1992, Intel announced that the DX2 processors also would be available in a retail version called OverDrive. Originally, the OverDrive versions of the DX2 were available only in 169-pin versions, which meant that they could be used only with 486SX systems that had sockets configured to support the rearranged pin configuration.

On September 14, 1992, Intel introduced 168-pin OverDrive versions for upgrading 486DX systems. These processors could be added to existing 486 (SX or DX) systems as an upgrade, even if those systems did not support the 169-pin configuration. When you use this processor as an upgrade, you install the new chip in your system, which subsequently runs twice as fast.

The DX2/OverDrive processors run internally at twice the clock rate of the host system. If the motherboard clock is 25MHz, for example, the DX2/OverDrive chip runs internally at 50MHz; likewise, if the motherboard is a 33MHz design, the DX2/OverDrive runs at 66MHz. The DX2/OverDrive speed doubling has no effect on the rest of the system; all components on the motherboard run the same as they do with a standard 486 processor. Therefore, you do not have to change other components (such as memory) to accommodate the double-speed chip. The DX2/OverDrive chips have been available in several speeds. Three speed-rated versions have been offered:

- 40MHz DX2/OverDrive for 16MHz or 20MHz systems
- 50MHz DX2/OverDrive for 25MHz systems
- 66MHz DX2/OverDrive for 33MHz systems

Notice that these ratings indicate the maximum speed at which the chip is capable of running. You could use a 66MHz-rated chip in place of the 50MHz- or 40MHz-rated parts with no problem, although the chip will run only at the slower speeds. The actual speed of the chip is double the motherboard clock frequency. When the 40MHz DX2/OverDrive chip is installed in a 16MHz 486SX system, for example, the chip functions only at 32MHz—exactly double the motherboard speed. Intel originally stated that no 100MHz DX2/OverDrive chip would be available for 50MHz systems—which technically has not been true because the DX4 could be set to run in a clock-doubled mode and used in a 50MHz motherboard (see the discussion of the DX4 processor in this section).

The only part of the DX2 chip that doesn't run at double speed is the bus interface unit, a region of the chip that handles I/O between the CPU and the outside world. By translating between the differing internal and external clock speeds, the bus interface unit makes speed doubling transparent to the rest of the system. The DX2 appears to the rest of the system to be a regular 486DX chip, but one that seems to execute instructions twice as fast.

DX2/OverDrive chips are based on the 0.8-micron circuit technology that was first used in the 50MHz 486DX. The DX2 contains 1.1 million transistors in a three-layer form. The internal 8KB cache, integer, and floating-point units all run at double speed. External communication with the PC runs at normal speed to maintain compatibility.

Besides upgrading existing systems, one of the best parts of the DX2 concept was the fact that system designers could introduce very fast systems by using cheaper motherboard designs, rather than the more costly designs that would support a straight high-speed clock. Therefore, a 50MHz 486DX2 system was much less expensive than a straight 50MHz 486DX system. The system board in a 486DX-50 system operates at a true 50MHz. The 486DX2 CPU in a 486DX2-50 system operates internally at 50MHz, but the motherboard operates at only 25MHz.

You might be thinking that a true 50MHz DX processor–based system still would be faster than a speed-doubled 25MHz system, and this generally is true. But, the differences in speed actually are very slight—a real testament to the integration of the 486 processor and especially to the cache design.

When the processor has to go to system memory for data or instructions, for example, it must do so at the slower motherboard operating frequency (such as 25MHz). Because the 8KB internal cache of the 486DX2 has a hit rate of 90%–95%, however, the CPU must access system memory only 5%–10% of the time for memory reads. Therefore, the performance of the DX2 system can come very close to that of a true 50MHz DX system and cost much less. Even though the motherboard runs at only 33.33MHz, a system with a DX2 66MHz processor ends up being faster than a true 50MHz DX system, especially if the DX2 system has a good L2 cache.

Many 486 motherboard designs also include a secondary cache that is external to the cache integrated into the 486 chip. This external cache allows for much faster access when the 486 chip calls for external-memory access. The size of this external cache can vary anywhere from 16KB to 512KB or more. When you add a DX2 processor, an external cache is even more important for achieving the greatest performance gain. This cache greatly reduces the wait states the processor must add when writing to system memory or when a read causes an internal cache miss. For this reason, some systems perform better with the DX2/OverDrive processors than others, usually depending on the size and efficiency of the external-memory cache system on the motherboard. Systems that have no external cache still enjoy a near-doubling of CPU performance, but operations that involve a great deal of memory access are slower.

This brings us to the DX4 processor. Although the standard DX4 technically was not sold as a retail part, it could be purchased from several vendors, along with the 3.3v voltage adapter needed to install the chip in a 5v socket. These adapters have jumpers that enable you to select the DX4 clock multiplier and set it to 2x, 2.5x, or 3x mode. In a 50MHz DX system, you could install a DX4/voltage-regulator combination set in 2x mode for a motherboard speed of 50MHz and a processor speed of 100MHz! Although you might not be able to take advantage of certain VL-Bus adapter cards, you will have one of the fastest 486-class PCs available.

Intel also sold a special DX4 OverDrive processor that included a built-in voltage regulator and heatsink that are specifically designed for the retail market. The DX4 OverDrive chip is essentially the same as the standard 3.3v DX4 with the main exception that it runs on 5v because it includes an on-chip regulator. Also, the DX4 OverDrive chip runs only in the tripled speed mode, and not the 2x or 2.5x modes of the standard DX4 processor.

Note

As of this writing, Intel has discontinued all 486 and DX2/DX4/OverDrive processors, including the so-called Pentium OverDrive processor.

Pentium OverDrive for 486SX2 and DX2 Systems

The Pentium OverDrive Processor became available in 1995. An OverDrive chip for 486DX4 systems had been planned, but poor marketplace performance of the SX2/DX2 chip resulted in it never seeing the light of day. One thing to keep in mind about the 486 Pentium OverDrive chip is that although it is intended primarily for SX2 and DX2 systems, it should work in any upgradable 486SX or DX system that has a Socket 2 or Socket 3. If in doubt, check Intel's online upgrade guide for compatibility.

The Pentium OverDrive processor is designed for systems that have a processor socket that follows the Intel Socket 2 specification. This processor also works in systems that have a Socket 3 design, although you should ensure that the voltage is set for 5v rather than 3.3v. The Pentium OverDrive chip includes a 32KB internal L1 cache and the same superscalar (multiple instruction path) architecture of the real Pentium chip. Besides a 32-bit Pentium core, these processors feature increased clock-speed operation due to internal clock multiplication and incorporate an internal write-back cache (standard with the Pentium). If the motherboard supports the write-back cache function, increased performance is realized. Unfortunately, most motherboards, especially older ones with the Socket 2 design, support only write-through cache.

Most tests of these OverDrive chips show them to be only slightly ahead of the DX4-100 and behind the DX4-120 and true Pentium 60, 66, or 75. Unfortunately, these are the only solutions still offered by Intel for upgrading the 486. Based on the relative affordability of low-end "real" Pentiums (in their day), it was hard not to justify making the step up to a Pentium system. At the time, I did not recommend the 486 Pentium OverDrive chips as a viable solution for the future.

AMD 486 (5x86)

AMD makes a line of 486-compatible chips that install into standard 486 motherboards. In fact, AMD makes the fastest 486 processor available, which it calls the Am5x86(TM)-P75. The name is a little misleading because the 5x86 part makes some people think that this is a fifth-generation Pentium-type processor. In reality, it is a fast clock-multiplied (4x clock) 486 that runs at four times the speed of the 33MHz 486 motherboard you plug it into.

The 5x85 offers high-performance features such as a unified 16KB write-back cache and 133MHz core clock speed; it is approximately comparable to a Pentium 75, which is why it is denoted with a P-75 in the part number. It is the ideal choice for cost-effective 486 upgrades, where changing the motherboard is difficult or impossible.

Not all motherboards support the 5x86. The best way to verify that your motherboard supports the chip is by checking with the documentation that came with the board. Look for keywords such as "Am5X86," "AMD-X5," "clock-quadrupled," "133MHz," or other similar wording. Another good way to determine whether your motherboard supports the AMD 5x86 is to look for it in the listed models on AMD's Web site.

There are a few things to note when installing a 5x86 processor into a 486 motherboard:

- *The operating voltage for the 5x86 is 3.45v +/- 0.15v.* Not all motherboards have this setting, but most that incorporate a Socket 3 design should. If your 486 motherboard is a Socket 1 or 2 design, you cannot use the 5x86 processor directly. The 3.45 volt processor will not operate in a 5-volt socket and can be damaged. To convert a 5-volt motherboard to 3.45 volts, processors with adapters can be purchased from several vendors, including Kingston and Evergreen. Both sell the 5x86 complete with a voltage regulator adapter attached in an easy-to-install package. These versions are ideal for older 486 motherboards that don't have a Socket 3 design.

- *It is generally better to purchase a new motherboard with Socket 3 than to buy one of these adapters.* However, 486 motherboards are hard to find these days, and your old board might be in a proprietary form factor for which finding a replacement is impossible. Buying a new motherboard is also better than using an adapter because the older BIOS might not understand the requirements of the processor as far as speed is concerned. BIOS updates often are required with older boards.

- *Most Socket 3 motherboards have jumpers, enabling you to set the voltage manually.* Some boards don't have jumpers, but have voltage autodetect instead. These systems check the VOLDET pin (pin S4) on the microprocessor when the system is powered on.

- *The VOLDET pin is tied to ground (Vss) internally to the microprocessor.* If you cannot find any jumpers for setting voltage, you can check the motherboard as follows: Switch the PC off, remove the microprocessor, connect pin S4 to a Vss pin on the ZIF socket, power on, and check any Vcc pin with a voltmeter. This should read 3.45 (± 0.15) volts. See the previous section on CPU sockets for the pinout.

- *The 5x86 requires a 33MHz motherboard speed, so be sure the board is set to that frequency.* The 5x86 operates at an internal speed of 133MHz. Therefore, the jumpers must be set for "clock-quadrupled" or "4x clock" mode. By setting the jumpers correctly on the motherboard, the CLKMUL pin (pin R17) on the processor will be connected to ground (Vss). If there is no 4x clock setting, the standard DX2 2x clock setting should work.

■ *Some motherboards have jumpers that configure the internal cache in either write-back (WB) or write-through (WT) mode.* They do this by pulling the WB/WT pin (pin B13) on the microprocessor to logic High (Vcc) for WB or to ground (Vss) for WT. For best performance, configure your system in WB mode; however, reset the cache to WT mode if problems running applications occur or the floppy drive doesn't work right (DMA conflicts).

■ *The 5x86 runs hot, so a heatsink is required.* It normally must have a fan.

In addition to the 5x86, the AMD-enhanced 486 product line includes 80MHz; 100MHz; and 1,20MHz CPUs. These are the A80486DX2-80SV8B (40MHz×2), A80486DX4-100SV8B (33MHz×3), and A80486DX4-120SV8B (40MHz×3).

Cyrix/TI 486

The Cyrix 486DX2/DX4 processors were available in 100MHz, 80MHz, 75MHz, 66MHz, and 50MHz versions. Similar to the AMD 486 chips, the Cyrix versions are fully compatible with Intel's 486 processors and work in most 486 motherboards.

The Cx486DX2/DX4 incorporates an 8KB write-back cache, an integrated floating-point unit, advanced power management, and SMM, and was available in 3.3v versions.

Note

TI originally made all the Cyrix-designed 486 processors, and under the agreement it also sold them under the TI name. They are essentially the same as the Cyrix chips.

P5 (586) Fifth-Generation Processors

After the fourth-generation chips such as the 486, Intel and other chip manufacturers went back to the drawing board to come up with new architectures and features that they incorporated into what they called fifth-generation chips. This section defines the fifth-generation processors from Intel, AMD, and others.

Pentium Processors

On October 19, 1992, Intel announced that the fifth generation of its compatible microprocessor line (codenamed P5) would be named the Pentium processor rather than the 586, as everybody had assumed. Calling the new chip the 586 would have been natural, but Intel discovered that it could not trademark a number designation, and the company wanted to prevent other manufacturers from using the same name for any clone chips they might develop. The actual Pentium chip shipped on March 22, 1993. Systems that use these chips were only a few months behind.

The Pentium is fully compatible with previous Intel processors, but it differs from them in many ways. At least one of these differences is revolutionary: The Pentium features twin data pipelines, which enable it to execute two instructions at the same time. The 486 and all preceding chips can perform only a single instruction at a time. Intel calls the capability to execute two instructions at the same time superscalar technology. This technology provides additional performance compared with the 486.

The standard 486 chip can execute a single instruction in an average of two clock cycles—cut to an average of one clock cycle with the advent of internal clock multiplication used in the DX2 and DX4 processors. With superscalar technology, the Pentium can execute many instructions at a rate of two instructions per cycle. Superscalar architecture usually is associated with high-output RISC chips. The Pentium is one of the first CISC chips to be considered superscalar. The Pentium is almost like having two 486 chips under the hood. Table 3.21 shows the Pentium processor specifications.

Table 3.21   Pentium Processor Specifications

Introduced	March 22, 1993 (first generation); March 7, 1994 (second generation)
Maximum rated speeds	60, 66, 75, 90, 100, 120, 133, 150, 166, 200MHz (second generation)
CPU clock multiplier	1x (first generation), 1.5x–3x (second generation)
Register size	32-bit
External data bus	64-bit
Memory address bus	32-bit
Maximum memory	4GB
Integral-cache size	8KB code, 8KB data
Integral-cache type	Two-way set associative, write-back data
Burst-mode transfers	Yes
Number of transistors	3.1 million
Circuit size	0.8 micron (60/66MHz), 0.6 micron (75MHz–100MHz), 0.35 micron (120MHz and up)
External package	273-pin PGA, 296-pin SPGA, tape carrier
Math coprocessor	Built-in FPU
Power management	SMM, enhanced in second generation
Operating voltage	5v (first generation); 3.465v, 3.3v, 3.1v, 2.9v (second generation)

PGA = Pin grid array
SPGA = Staggered pin grid array

The two instruction pipelines within the chip are called the u- and v-pipes. The *u-pipe*, which is the primary pipe, can execute all integer and floating-point instructions. The *v-pipe* is a secondary pipe that can execute only simple integer instructions and certain floating-point instructions. The process of operating on two instructions simultaneously in the different pipes is called *pairing*. Not all sequentially executing instructions can be paired, and when pairing is not possible, only the u-pipe is used. To optimize the Pentium's efficiency, you can recompile software to enable more instructions to be paired.

The Pentium processor has a branch target buffer (BTB), which employs a technique called branch prediction. It minimizes stalls in one or more of the pipes caused by delays in fetching instructions that branch to nonlinear memory locations. The BTB attempts to predict whether a program branch will be taken and then fetches the appropriate instructions. The use of branch prediction enables the Pentium to keep both pipelines operating at full speed. Figure 3.34 shows the internal architecture of the Pentium processor.

The Pentium has a 32-bit address bus width, giving it the same 4GB memory-addressing capabilities as the 386DX and 486 processors. But the Pentium expands the data bus to 64 bits, which means it can move twice as much data into or out of the CPU, compared with a 486 of the same clock speed. The 64-bit data bus requires that system memory be accessed 64 bits wide, so each bank of memory is 64 bits.

On most motherboards, memory is installed via SIMMs or DIMMs. SIMMs are available in 8-bit–wide and 32-bit–wide versions, whereas DIMMs are 64 bits wide. In addition, versions are available with additional bits for parity or error correcting code (ECC) data. Most Pentium systems use the 32-bit–wide SIMMs—two of these SIMMs per bank of memory. Most Pentium motherboards have at least four of these 32-bit SIMM sockets, providing for a total of two banks of memory. Later Pentium systems and most Pentium II systems today use DIMMs, which are 64 bits wide—just like the processor's external data bus, so only one DIMM is used per bank. This makes installing or upgrading memory much easier because DIMMs can go in one at a time and don't have to be matched up in pairs.

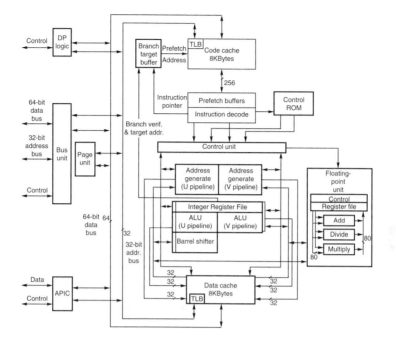

Figure 3.34   Pentium processor internal architecture.

▶▶   See "SIMMs, DIMMs, and RIMMs," p. 421, and "Memory Banks," p. 438.

Even though the Pentium has a 64-bit data bus that transfers information 64 bits at a time into and out of the processor, the Pentium has only 32-bit internal registers. As instructions are being processed internally, they are broken down into 32-bit instructions and data elements and processed in much the same way as in the 486. Some people thought that Intel was misleading them by calling the Pentium a 64-bit processor, but 64-bit transfers do indeed take place. Internally, however, the Pentium has 32-bit registers that are fully compatible with the 486.

The Pentium has two separate internal 8KB caches, compared with a single 8KB or 16KB cache in the 486. The cache-controller circuitry and the cache memory are embedded in the CPU chip. The cache mirrors the information in normal RAM by keeping a copy of the data and code from different memory locations. The Pentium cache also can hold information to be written to memory when the load on the CPU and other system components is less. (The 486 makes all memory writes immediately.)

The separate code and data caches are organized in a two-way set associative fashion, with each set split into lines of 32 bytes each. Each cache has a dedicated translation lookaside buffer (TLB) that translates linear addresses to physical addresses. You can configure the data cache as write-back or write-through on a line-by-line basis. When you use the write-back capability, the cache can store write operations and reads, further improving performance over read-only write-through mode. Using write-back mode results in less activity between the CPU and system memory—an important improvement because CPU access to system memory is a bottleneck on fast systems. The code cache is an inherently write-protected cache because it contains only execution instructions and not data, which is updated. Because burst cycles are used, the cache data can be read or written very quickly.

Systems based on the Pentium can benefit greatly from secondary processor caches (L2), which usually consist of up to 512KB or more of extremely fast (15ns or less) SRAM chips. When the CPU fetches data that is not already available in its internal processor (L1) cache, wait states slow the CPU. If the data already is in the secondary processor cache, however, the CPU can go ahead with its work without pausing for wait states.

The Pentium uses a Bipolar Complementary Metal-Oxide Semiconductor (BiCMOS) process and super-scalar architecture to achieve the high level of performance expected from the chip. BiCMOS adds about 10% to the complexity of the chip design, but adds about 30%–35% better performance without a size or power penalty.

All Pentium processors are SL enhanced—they incorporate the SMM to provide full control of power-management features, which helps reduce power consumption. The second-generation Pentium processors (75MHz and faster) incorporate a more advanced form of SMM that includes processor clock control. This enables you to throttle the processor up or down to control power use. You can even stop the clock with these more advanced Pentium processors, putting the processor in a state of suspension that requires very little power. The second-generation Pentium processors run on 3.3v power (instead of 5v), reducing power requirements and heat generation even further.

Many current motherboards supply either 3.465v or 3.3v. The 3.465v setting is called VRE (voltage reduced extended) by Intel and is required by some versions of the Pentium, particularly some of the 100MHz versions. The standard 3.3v setting is called STD (standard), which most of the second-generation Pentiums use. STD voltage means anything in a range from 3.135v to 3.465v with 3.3v nominal. Additionally, a special 3.3v setting called VR (voltage reduced) reduces the range from 3.300v to 3.465v with 3.38v nominal. Some of the processors require this narrower specification, which most motherboards provide. Here is a summary:

Voltage Specification	Nominal	Tolerance	Minimum	Maximum
STD (standard)	3.30v	±0.165	3.135v	3.465v
VR (voltage reduced)	3.38v	±0.083	3.300v	3.465v
VRE (VR extended)	3.50v	±0.100	3.400v	3.600v

For even lower power consumption, Intel introduced special Pentium processors with voltage reduction technology in the 75 to 266MHz family; the processors are intended for mobile computer applications. They do not use a conventional chip package and are instead mounted using a new format called tape carrier packaging (TCP). The tape carrier packaging does not encase the chip in ceramic or plastic as with a conventional chip package, but instead covers the actual processor die directly with a thin, protective plastic coating. The entire processor is less than 1mm thick, or about half the thickness of a dime, and weighs less than 1 gram. They are sold to system manufacturers in a roll that looks very much like a filmstrip. The TCP processor is directly affixed (soldered) to the motherboard by a special machine, resulting in a smaller package, lower height, better thermal transfer, and lower power consumption. Special solder plugs on the circuit board located directly under the processor draw heat away and provide better cooling in the tight confines of a typical notebook or laptop system—no cooling fans are required. For more information on mobile processors and systems, see Chapter 22, "Portable PCs."

The Pentium, like the 486, contains an internal math coprocessor or FPU. The FPU in the Pentium has been rewritten and performs significantly better than the FPU in the 486, yet it is fully compatible with the 486 and 387 math coprocessors. The Pentium FPU is estimated to be two to as much as ten times faster than the FPU in the 486. In addition, the two standard instruction pipelines in the Pentium provide two units to handle standard integer math. (The math coprocessor handles only more complex calculations.) Other processors, such as the 486, have only a single-standard execution pipe and one integer math unit. Interestingly, the Pentium FPU contains a flaw that received widespread publicity. See the discussion in the section "Pentium Defects," later in this chapter.

First-Generation Pentium Processor

The Pentium has been offered in three basic designs, each with several versions. The first-generation design, which is no longer available, came in 60MHz and 66MHz processor speeds. This design used a 273-pin PGA form factor and ran on 5v power. In this design, the processor ran at the same speed as the motherboard—in other words, a 1x clock was used.

The first-generation Pentium was created through an 0.8- micron BiCMOS process. Unfortunately, this process, combined with the 3.1 million transistor count, resulted in a die that was overly large and complicated to manufacture. As a result, reduced yields kept the chip in short supply; Intel could not make them fast enough. The 0.8-micron process was criticized by other manufacturers, including Motorola and IBM, which had been using 0.6-micron technology for their most advanced chips. The huge die and 5v operating voltage caused the 66MHz versions to consume up to an incredible 3.2 amps or 16 watts of power, resulting in a tremendous amount of heat and problems in some systems that did not employ conservative design techniques. Fortunately, adding a fan to the processor solved most cooling problems, as long as the fan kept running.

Much of the criticism leveled at Intel for the first-generation Pentium was justified. Some people realized that the first-generation design was just that; they knew that new Pentium versions, made in a more advanced manufacturing process, were coming. Many of those people advised against purchasing any Pentium system until the second-generation version became available.

Tip

A cardinal rule of computing is never buy the first generation of any processor. Although you can wait forever because something better always will be on the horizon, a little waiting is worthwhile in some cases.

Those who purchased first-generation Pentiums still had a way out, however. As with previous 486 systems, Intel released OverDrive upgrade chips that effectively doubled the processor speed of the Pentium 60 or 66. These are a single-chip upgrade, meaning they replace the existing CPU. Because subsequent Pentiums are incompatible with the Pentium 60/66 Socket 4 arrangement, these OverDrive chips were the only way to upgrade an existing first-generation Pentium without replacing the motherboard.

Generally, it was better to consider a complete motherboard replacement, which would accept a newer design processor that would potentially be many times faster, than to upgrade using just an OverDrive processor, that might only be twice as fast.

Second-Generation Pentium Processor

Intel announced the second-generation Pentium on March 7, 1994. This new processor was introduced in 90MHz and 100MHz versions, with a 75MHz version not far behind. Eventually, 120MHz, 133MHz, 150MHz, 166MHz, and 200MHz versions were also introduced. The second-generation Pentium uses 0.6-micron (75/90/100MHz) BiCMOS technology to shrink the die and reduce power consumption. The newer, faster 120MHz (and higher) second-generation versions incorporate an even smaller die built on a 0.35-micron BiCMOS process. These smaller dies are not changed from the 0.6-micron versions; they are basically a photographic reduction of the P54C die. The die for the Pentium is shown in Figure 3.35. Additionally, these new processors run on 3.3v power. The 100MHz version consumes a maximum of 3.25 amps of 3.3v power, which equals only 10.725 watts. Further up the scale, the 150MHz chip uses 3.5 amps of 3.3v power (11.6 watts); the 166MHz unit draws 4.4 amps (14.5 watts); and the 200MHz processor uses 4.7 amps (15.5 watts).

Figure 3.35 Pentium processor die. *Photograph used by permission of Intel Corporation.*

The second-generation Pentium processors come in a 296-pin SPGA form factor that is physically incompatible with the first-generation versions. The only way to upgrade from the first generation to the second is to replace the motherboard. The second-generation Pentium processors also have 3.3 million transistors—more than the earlier chips. The extra transistors exist because additional clock-control SL enhancements were added, along with an on-chip advanced programmable interrupt controller (APIC) and dual-processor interface.

The APIC and dual-processor interface are responsible for orchestrating dual-processor configurations in which two second-generation Pentium chips can process on the same motherboard simultaneously. Many of the Pentium motherboards designed for file servers come with dual Socket 7 specification sockets, which fully support the multiprocessing capability of the new chips. Software support for what usually is called symmetric multiprocessing (SMP) is being integrated into operating systems such as Windows NT and OS/2.

The second-generation Pentium processors use clock-multiplier circuitry to run the processor at speeds faster than the bus. The 150MHz Pentium processor, for example, can run at 2.5 times the bus frequency, which normally is 60MHz. The 200MHz Pentium processor can run at a 3x clock in a system using a 66MHz bus speed.

Virtually all Pentium motherboards have three speed settings: 50MHz, 60MHz, and 66MHz. Pentium chips are available with a variety of internal clock multipliers that cause the processor to operate at various multiples of these motherboard speeds. Refer to Table 3.7 for a list of the speeds of currently available Pentium processors and motherboards.

The core-to-bus frequency ratio or clock multiplier is controlled in a Pentium processor by two pins on the chip labeled BF1 and BF2. Table 3.22 shows how the state of the BFx pins affect the clock multiplication in the Pentium processor.

Table 3.22   Pentium BFx Pins and Clock Multipliers

BF1	BF2	Clock Multiplier	Bus Speed (MHz)	Core Speed (MHz)
0	1	3x	66	200
0	1	3x	60	180
0	1	3x	50	150
0	0	2.5x	66	166
0	0	2.5x	60	150
0	0	2.5x	50	125
1	0	2x/4x	66	133/266[1]
1	0	2x	60	120
1	0	2x	50	100
1	1	1.5x/3.5x	66	100/233[1]
1	1	1.5x	60	90
1	1	1.5x	50	75

1. The 233MHz and 266MHz processors have modified the 1.5x and 2x multipliers to 3.5x and 4x, respectively.

Not all chips support all the bus frequency (BF) pins or combinations of settings. In other words, some of the Pentium processors operate only at specific combinations of these settings or might even be fixed at one particular setting. Many of the later Pentium motherboards included jumpers or switches that enable you to control the BF pins and, therefore, alter the clock-multiplier ratio within the chip. In theory, you could run a 75MHz-rated Pentium chip at 133MHz by changing jumpers on the motherboard. This is called overclocking and is discussed in the section "Processor Speed Ratings," earlier in this chapter. What Intel has done to discourage overclockers in its most recent Pentiums is discussed near the end of the "Processor Manufacturing" section of this chapter.

A single-chip OverDrive upgrade currently is offered for second-generation Pentiums. These OverDrive chips are fixed at a 3x multiplier; they replace the existing Socket 5 or 7 CPU, increase processor speed up to 200MHz (with a 66MHz motherboard speed), and add MMX capability, as well. Simply stated, a Pentium 100, 133, or 166 system equipped with the OverDrive chip has a processor speed of 200MHz. Perhaps the best feature of these Pentium OverDrive chips is that they incorporate MMX technology. MMX provides greatly enhanced performance while running the multimedia applications that are so popular today.

If you have a Socket 7 motherboard, you might not need the special OverDrive versions of the Pentium processor that have built-in voltage regulators. Instead, you can purchase a standard Pentium or Pentium-compatible chip and replace the existing processor with it. You must be sure to set the multiplier and voltage settings so that they are correct for the new processor.

Pentium-MMX Processors

A third generation of Pentium processors (codenamed P55C) was released in January 1997, and incorporates what Intel calls MMX technology into the second-generation Pentium design (see Figure 3.36). These Pentium-MMX processors are available in clock rates of 66/166MHz, 66/200MHz, and

66/233MHz and in a mobile-only version, which is 66/266MHz. The MMX processors have a lot in common with other second-generation Pentiums, including superscalar architecture, multiprocessor support, on-chip local APIC controller, and power-management features. New features include a pipelined MMX unit, 16KB code, write-back cache (versus 8KB in earlier Pentiums), and 4.5 million transistors. Pentium-MMX chips are produced on an enhanced 0.35-micron CMOS silicon process that allows for a lower 2.8v voltage level. The newer mobile 233MHz and 266MHz processors are built on a 0.25-micron process and run on only 1.8 volts. With this newer technology, the 266 processor actually uses less power than the non-MMX 133.

Figure 3.36   Pentium MMX. The left side shows the underside of the chip with the cover plate removed exposing the processor die. *Photograph used by permission of Intel Corporation.*

To use the Pentium-MMX, the motherboard must be capable of supplying the lower (2.8v or less) voltage these processors use. To enable a more universal motherboard solution with respect to these changing voltages, Intel has come up with the Socket 7 with VRM. The VRM is a socketed module that plugs in next to the processor and supplies the correct voltage. Because the module is easily replaced, reconfiguring a motherboard to support any of the voltages required by the newer Pentium processors is easy.

Of course, lower voltage is nice, but MMX is what this chip is really all about. MMX technology was developed by Intel as a direct response to the growing importance and increasing demands of multi-media and communication applications. Many such applications run repetitive loops of instructions that take vast amounts of time to execute. As a result, MMX incorporates a process Intel calls single instruction multiple data (SIMD), which enables one instruction to perform the same function on many pieces of data. Furthermore, 57 new instructions designed specifically to handle video, audio, and graphics data have been added to the chip.

To add maximum upgradability to the MMX Pentiums, a Pentium motherboard needs 321-pin processor sockets that fully meet the Intel Socket 7 specification. These also would include the VRM socket. If you have dual sockets, you can add a second Pentium processor to take advantage of SMP support in operating systems that support this feature.

Pentium Defects

Probably the most famous processor bug in history is the now legendary flaw in the Pentium FPU. It has often been called the FDIV bug because it affects primarily the FDIV (floating-point divide) instruction, although several other instructions that use division are also affected. Intel officially refers to this problem as Errata No. 23, titled "Slight precision loss for floating-point divides on specific operand pairs." The bug has been fixed in the D1 or later steppings of the 60/66MHz Pentium processors, as well as the B5 and later steppings of the 75/90/100MHz processors. The 120MHz and higher processors are manufactured from later steppings, which do not include this problem. Tables listing all the variations of Pentium processors and steppings and how to identify them appear later in this chapter.

This bug caused a tremendous fervor when it first was reported on the Internet by a mathematician in October 1994. Within a few days, news of the defect had spread nationwide, and even people who did not have computers had heard about it. The Pentium incorrectly performed floating-point division calculations with certain number combinations, with errors anywhere from the third digit on up.

By the time the bug was publicly discovered outside of Intel, the company had already incorporated the fix into the next stepping of both the 60/66MHz and the 75/90/100MHz Pentium processor, along with the other corrections Intel had made.

After the bug was made public and Intel admitted to already knowing about it, a fury erupted. As people began checking their spreadsheets and other math calculations, many discovered they had also encountered this problem and did not know it. Others who had not encountered the problem had their faith in the core of their PCs very shaken. People had come to put so much trust in the PC that they had a hard time coming to terms with the fact that it might not even be capable of doing math correctly!

One interesting result of the fervor surrounding this defect is that people are less likely to implicitly trust their PCs and are therefore doing more testing and evaluating of important results. The bottom line is that if your information and calculations are important enough, you should implement some results tests. Several math programs were found to have problems. For example, a bug was discovered in the yield function of Excel 5.0 that some were attributing to the Pentium processor. In this case, the problem turned out to be the software, which has been corrected in later versions (5.0c and later).

Intel finally decided that in the best interest of the consumer and its public image, it would begin a lifetime replacement warranty on the affected processors. Therefore, if you ever encounter one of the Pentium processors with the Errata 23 floating-point bug, Intel will replace the processor with an equivalent one without this problem. Usually, all you have to do is call Intel and ask for the replacement. It will ship you a new part matching the ratings of the one you are replacing in an overnight shipping box. The replacement is free, including all shipping charges. You merely remove your old processor, replace it with the new one, and put the old one back in the box. Then you call the overnight service, who picks it up and sends it back. Intel will take a credit card number when you first call for the replacement only to ensure that the original defective chip is returned. As long as it gets the original CPU back within a specified amount of time, there will be no charges to you. Intel has indicated that these defective processors will be destroyed and will not be remarketed or resold in another form.

Testing for the FPU Bug

Testing a Pentium for this bug is relatively easy. All you have to do is execute one of the test division cases cited here and see whether your answer compares to the correct result.

The division calculation can be done in a spreadsheet (such as Lotus 1-2-3, Microsoft Excel, or any other), the Microsoft Windows built-in calculator, or any other calculating program that uses the FPU. Make sure that for the purposes of this test the FPU has not been disabled. That typically requires some special command or setting specific to the application and, of course, ensures that the test comes out correct, regardless of whether the chip is flawed.

The most severe Pentium floating-point errors occur as early as the third significant digit of the result. Here is an example of one of the more severe instances of the problem:

962,306,957,033 / 11,010,046 = 87,402.6282027341 (correct answer)

962,306,957,033 / 11,010,046 = 87,399.5805831329 (flawed Pentium)

Note

Note that your particular calculator program might not show the answer to the number of digits shown here. Most spreadsheet programs limit displayed results to 13 or 15 significant digits.

As you can see in the previous case, the error turns up in the third most significant digit of the result. In an examination of more than 5,000 integer pairs in the 5- to 15-digit range found to produce Pentium floating-point division errors, errors beginning in the sixth significant digit were the most likely to occur.

Here is another division problem that comes out incorrectly on a Pentium with this flaw:

4,195,835 / 3,145,727 = 1.33382044913624100 (correct answer)

4,195,835 / 3,145,727 = 1.33373906890203759 (flawed Pentium)

This one shows an error in the fifth significant digit. A variation on the previous calculation can be performed as follows:

x = 4,195,835

y = 3,145,727

z = x − (x/y)*y

4,195,835 − (4,195,835 / 3,145,727) × 3,145,727 = 0 (correct answer)

4,195,835 − (4,195,835 / 3,145,727) × 3,145,727 = 256 (flawed Pentium)

With an exact computation, the answer here should be 0. In fact, you will get 0 on most machines, including those using Intel 286, 386, and 486 chips. But, on the Pentium, the answer is 256!

Here is one more calculation you can try:

5,505,001 / 294,911 = 18.66665197 (correct answer)

5,505,001 / 294,911 = 18.66600093 (flawed Pentium)

This one represents an error in the sixth significant digit.

Several workarounds are available for this bug, but they extract a performance penalty. Because Intel has agreed to replace any Pentium processor with this flaw under a lifetime warranty replacement program, the best workaround is a free replacement!

Power Management Bugs

Starting with the second-generation Pentium processors, Intel added functions that enable these CPUs to be installed in energy-efficient systems. These are usually called *Energy Star systems* because they meet the specifications imposed by the EPA Energy Star program, but they are also unofficially called *green PCs* by many users.

Unfortunately, there have been several bugs with respect to these functions, causing them to either fail or be disabled. These bugs are in some of the functions in the power-management capabilities accessed through SMM. These problems are applicable only to the second-generation 75/90/100MHz processors because the first-generation 60/66MHz processors do not have SMM or power-management capabilities, and all higher-speed (120MHz and up) processors have the bugs fixed.

Most of the problems are related to the STPCLK# pin and the HALT instruction. If this condition is invoked by the chipset, the system will hang. For most systems, the only workaround for this problem is to disable the power-saving modes, such as suspend or sleep. Unfortunately, this means that your green PC won't be so green anymore! The best way to repair the problem is to replace the processor with a later stepping version that does not have the bug. These bugs affect the B1 stepping version of the 75/90/100MHz Pentiums, and they were fixed in the B3 and later stepping versions.

Pentium Processor Models and Steppings

We know that like software, no processor is truly ever perfect. From time to time, the manufacturers gather up what problems they have found and put into production a new stepping, which consists of a new set of masks that incorporate the corrections. Each subsequent stepping is better and more refined than the previous ones. Although no microprocessor is ever perfect, they come closer to perfection with each stepping. In the life of a typical microprocessor, a manufacturer might go through half a dozen or more such steppings.

See the previous editions of this book on the included CD-ROM for tables showing the Pentium processor steppings and revisions. This information is also available online from Intel via its Web site.

To determine the specifications of a given processor, you must look up the S-spec number in the table of processor specifications. To find your S-spec number, you have to read it off the chip directly. It can be found printed on both the top and bottom of the chip. If your heatsink is glued on, remove the chip and heatsink from the socket as a unit and read the numbers from the bottom of the chip. Then, you can look up the S-spec number in the Specification Guide Intel publishes (via its Web site); it tells you the specifications of that particular processor. Intel is introducing new chips all the time, so visit its Web site and search for the Pentium processor "Quick Reference Guide" in the developer portion of its site. There you will find a complete listing of all current processor specifications by S-spec number.

One interesting item to note is that several subtly different voltages are required by different Pentium processors. Table 3.23 summarizes the various processors and their required voltages.

Table 3.23   Pentium Processor Voltages

Model	Stepping	Voltage Spec.	Voltage Range
1	—	Std.	4.75–5.25v
1	—	5v1	4.90–5.25v
1	—	5v2	4.90–5.40v
1	—	5v3	5.15–5.40v
2+	B1-B5	Std.	3.135–3.465v
2+	C2+	Std.	3.135–3.600v
2+	—	VR	3.300–3.465v
2+	B1-B5	VRE	3.45–3.60v
2+	C2+	VRE	3.40–3.60v
4+	—	MMX	2.70–2.90v
4	3	Mobile	2.285–2.665v
4	3	Mobile	2.10–2.34v
8	1	Mobile	1.850–2.150v
8	1	Mobile	1.665–1.935v

Many of the newer Pentium motherboards have jumpers that allow for adjustments to the different voltage ranges. If you are having problems with a particular processor, it might not be matched correctly to your motherboard voltage output.

If you are purchasing an older, used Pentium system today, I recommend using only Model 2 (second-generation) or later version processors that are available in 75MHz or faster speeds. You should definitely get stepping C2 or later. Virtually all the important bugs and problems were fixed in the C2 and later releases. The newer Pentium processors have no serious bugs to worry about.

AMD-K5

The AMD-K5 is a Pentium-compatible processor developed by AMD and available as the PR75, PR90, PR100, PR120, PR133, and PR-166. Because it is designed to be physically and functionally compatible, any motherboard that properly supports the Intel Pentium should support the AMD-K5. However, a BIOS upgrade might be required to properly recognize the AMD-K5. AMD keeps a list of motherboards that have been tested for compatibility.

The K5 has the following features:

- 16KB instruction cache, 8KB write-back data cache
- Dynamic execution—branch prediction with speculative execution
- Five-stage, RISC-like pipeline with six parallel functional units
- High-performance floating-point unit
- Pin-selectable clock multiples of 1.5x and 2x

The K5 is sold under the P-Rating system, which means that the number on the chip does not indicate true clock speed, only apparent speed when running certain applications.

◄◄ See "AMD P-Ratings," p. 57.

Note that several of these processors do not run at their apparent rated speeds. For example, the PR-166 version actually runs at only 117 true MHz. Sometimes this can confuse the system BIOS, which might report the true speed rather than the P-Rating, which compares the chip against an Intel Pentium of that speed. AMD claims that because of architecture enhancements over the Pentium, they do not need to run the same clock frequency to achieve that same performance. Even with such improvements, AMD markets the K5 as a fifth-generation processor, just like the Pentium.

The AMD-K5 operates at 3.52 volts (VRE setting). Some older motherboards default to 3.3 volts, which is below specification for the K5 and could cause erratic operation.

Intel P6 (686) Sixth-Generation Processors

The P6 (686) processors represent a new generation with features not found in the previous generation units. The P6 processor family began when the Pentium Pro was released in November 1995. Since then, many other P6 chips have been released by Intel, all using the same basic P6 core processor as the Pentium Pro. Table 3.24 shows the variations in the P6 family of processors.

Table 3.24   Intel P6 Processor Variations

Pentium Pro	Original P6 processor, includes 256KB, 512KB, or 1MB of full-core speed L2 cache
Pentium II	P6 with 512KB of half-core speed L2 cache
Pentium II Xeon	P6 with 512KB, 1MB, or 2MB of full-core speed L2 cache
Celeron	P6 with no L2 cache
Celeron-A	P6 with 128KB of on-die full-core speed L2 cache
Pentium III	P6 with SSE (MMX2), 512KB of half-core speed L2 cache
Pentium IIPE	P6 with 256KB of full-core speed L2 cache

Table 3.24   Continued

Pentium IIIE	P6 with SSE (MMX2) plus 256KB of full-core speed L2 cache
Pentium III Xeon	P6 with SSE (MMX2), 512KB, 1MB, or 2MB of full-core speed L2 cache

Even more are expected in this family, including versions of the Pentium III with on-die full-core speed L2 cache, and faster versions of the Celeron.

The main new feature in the fifth-generation Pentium processors was the superscalar architecture, in which two instruction execution units could execute instructions simultaneously in parallel. Later fifth-generation chips also added MMX technology to the mix, as well. So then what did Intel add in the sixth-generation to justify calling it a whole new generation of chip? Besides many minor improvements, the real key features of all sixth-generation processors are Dynamic Execution and the Dual Independent Bus (DIB) architecture, plus a greatly improved superscalar design.

Dynamic Execution enables the processor to execute more instructions on parallel, so tasks are completed more quickly. This technology innovation is comprised of three main elements:

- *Multiple branch prediction.* Predict the flow of the program through several branches

- *Dataflow analysis.* Schedules instructions to be executed when ready, independent of their order in the original program

- *Speculative execution.* Increases the rate of execution by looking ahead of the program counter and executing instructions that are likely to be necessary

Branch prediction is a feature formerly found only in high-end mainframe processors. It enables the processor to keep the instruction pipeline full while running at a high rate of speed. A special fetch/decode unit in the processor uses a highly optimized branch prediction algorithm to predict the direction and outcome of the instructions being executed through multiple levels of branches, calls, and returns. It is like a chess player working out multiple strategies in advance of game play by predicting the opponent's strategy several moves into the future. By predicting the instruction outcome in advance, the instructions can be executed with no waiting.

Dataflow analysis studies the flow of data through the processor to detect any opportunities for out-of-order instruction execution. A special dispatch/execute unit in the processor monitors many instructions and can execute these instructions in an order that optimizes the use of the multiple superscalar execution units. The resulting out-of-order execution of instructions can keep the execution units busy even when cache misses and other data-dependent instructions might otherwise hold things up.

Speculative execution is the processor's capability to execute instructions in advance of the actual program counter. The processor's dispatch/execute unit uses dataflow analysis to execute all available instructions in the instruction pool and store the results in temporary registers. A retirement unit then searches the instruction pool for completed instructions that are no longer data dependent on other instructions to run, or which have unresolved branch predictions. If any such completed instructions are found, the results are committed to memory by the retirement unit or the appropriate standard Intel architecture in the order they were originally issued. They are then retired from the pool.

Dynamic Execution essentially removes the constraint and dependency on linear instruction sequencing. By promoting out-of-order instruction execution, it can keep the instruction units working rather than waiting for data from memory. Even though instructions can be predicted and executed out of order, the results are committed in the original order so as not to disrupt or change program flow. This enables the P6 to run existing Intel architecture software exactly as the P5 (Pentium) and previous processors did, just a whole lot more quickly!

The other main P6 architecture feature is known as the Dual Independent Bus. This refers to the fact that the processor has two data buses: one for the system (motherboard) and the other just for cache. This enables the cache memory to run at speeds previously not possible.

Previous P5 generation processors have only a single motherboard host processor bus, and all data, including cache transfers, must flow through it. The main problem with that is the cache memory was restricted to running at motherboard bus speed, which is 66MHz, 100MHz, or 133MHz. The solution was to essentially build in what is called a back-side bus to the processor, otherwise known as a dedicated cache bus. The L2 cache would then be connected to this bus and could run at any speed. The first implementation of this was in the Pentium Pro, where the L2 cache was built right into the processor package and ran at the full-core processor speed. Later, that proved to be too costly, so the L2 cache was moved outside the processor package and onto a cartridge module, which we now know as the Pentium II/III. With that design, the cache bus could run at any speed, with the first units running the cache at half-processor speed.

By having the cache on a back-side bus directly connected to the processor, the speed of the cache is scalable to the processor. In current PC architecture—66MHz Pentiums all the way through the 333MHz Pentium IIs—the motherboard runs at a speed of 66MHz. Faster Pentium II systems run a 100MHz motherboard bus and have clock speeds of 350MHz and higher. If the cache were restricted to the motherboard as is the case with Socket 7 (P5 processor) designs, the cache memory would have to remain at 66MHz, even though the processor was running as fast as 333MHz. With newer boards, the cache would be stuck at 100MHz, while the processor ran as fast as 500MHz or more. With the DIB design in the P6 processors, as the processor runs more quickly, at higher multiples of the motherboard speed, the cache increases by the same amount that the processor speed increases. The cache on the DIB is coupled to processor speed, so doubling the speed of the processor also doubles the speed of the cache.

The DIB architecture is necessary to have decent processor performance in the 300MHz and beyond range. Older Socket 7 (P5 processor) designs aren't capable of moving up to these higher speeds without suffering a tremendous performance penalty due to the slow motherboard-bound L2 cache. That is why Intel did not develop any Pentium (P5 class) processors beyond 266MHz; however, the P6 processors are available in speeds of up to 1000MHz or more.

Finally, the P6 architecture upgrades the superscalar architecture of the P5 processors by adding more instruction execution units and by breaking down the instructions into special micro-ops. This is where the CISC instructions are broken down into more RISC commands. The RISC-level commands are smaller and easier for the parallel instruction units to execute more efficiently. With this design, Intel has brought the benefits of a RISC processor—high-speed dedicated instruction execution—to the CISC world. Note that the P5 had only two instruction units, whereas the P6 has at least six separate dedicated instruction units. It is said to be three-way superscalar because the multiple instruction units can execute up to three instructions in one cycle.

Other improvements in efficiency also are included in the P6 architecture: built-in multiprocessor support, enhanced error detection and correction circuitry, and optimization for 32-bit software.

Rather than just being a faster Pentium, the Pentium Pro, Pentium II/III, and other sixth-generation processors have many feature and architectural improvements. The core of the chip is very RISC-like, whereas the external instruction interface is classic Intel CISC. By breaking down the CISC instructions into several RISC instructions and running them down parallel execution pipelines, the overall performance is increased.

Compared to a Pentium at the same clock speed, the P6 processors are faster—as long as you're running 32-bit software. The P6 Dynamic Execution is optimized for performance primarily when running 32-bit software, such as Windows NT. If you are using 16-bit software, such as Windows 95 or 98 (which still operate part time in a 16-bit environment) and most older applications, the P6 does not provide as marked a performance improvement over similarly speed-rated Pentium and Pentium-MMX processors. That's because the Dynamic Execution capability is not fully exploited. Because of this, Windows NT/2000 often are regarded as the most desirable operating systems for use with Pentium Pro/II/III/Celeron processors. Although this is not exactly true (a Pentium Pro/II/III/Celeron runs fine under Windows 95/98), Windows NT/2000 does take better advantage of the P6's capabilities. Note that it is really not so much the operating system but which applications you use. Software developers can take steps to gain the full advantages of the sixth-generation processors. This includes using modern compilers that can improve performance for all current Intel processors, writing 32-bit code where possible, and making code as predictable as possible to take advantage of the processor's Dynamic Execution multiple branch prediction capabilities.

Pentium Pro Processors

Intel's successor to the Pentium is called the Pentium Pro. The Pentium Pro was the first chip in the P6 or sixth-generation processor family. It was introduced in November 1995 and became widely available in 1996. The chip is a 387-pin unit that resides in Socket 8, so it is not pin compatible with earlier Pentiums. The new chip is unique among processors because it is constructed in a multichip module (MCM) physical format, which Intel calls a dual cavity PGA package. Inside the 387-pin chip carrier are two dies. One contains the actual Pentium Pro processor (shown in Figure 3.37), and the other contains a 256KB (the Pentium Pro with 256KB cache is shown in Figure 3.38), 512KB, or 1MB L2 cache. The processor die contains 5.5 million transistors, the 256KB cache die contains 15.5 million transistors, and the 512KB cache die(s) have 31 million transistors each—for a potential total of nearly 68 million transistors in a Pentium Pro with 1MB of internal cache! A Pentium Pro with 1MB cache has two 512KB cache die and a standard P6 processor die (see Figure 3.39).

Figure 3.37   Pentium Pro processor die. *Photograph used by permission of Intel Corporation.*

Figure 3.38 Pentium Pro processor with 256KB L2 cache (the cache is on the left side of the processor die). *Photograph used by permission of Intel Corporation.*

Figure 3.39 Pentium Pro processor with 1MB L2 cache (the cache is in the center and right portions of the die). *Photograph used by permission of Intel Corporation.*

The main processor die includes a 16KB split L1 cache with an 8KB two-way set associative cache for primary instructions and an 8KB four-way set associative cache for data.

Another sixth-generation processor feature found in the Pentium Pro is the DIB architecture, which addresses the memory bandwidth limitations of previous-generation processor architectures. Two buses make up the DIB architecture: the L2 cache bus (contained entirely within the processor package) and the processor-to-main memory system bus. The speed of the dedicated L2 cache bus on the Pentium Pro is equal to the full-core speed of the processor. This was accomplished by embedding the cache chips directly into the Pentium Pro package. The DIB processor bus architecture addresses processor-to-memory bus bandwidth limitations. It offers up to three times the performance bandwidth of the single-bus, "Socket 7" generation processors, such as the Pentium.

Table 3.25 shows Pentium Pro processor specifications. Table 3.26 shows the specifications for each model within the Pentium Pro family because many variations exist from model to model.

Table 3.25 Pentium Pro Family Processor Specifications

Introduced	November 1995
Maximum rated speeds	150MHz, 166MHz, 180MHz, 200MHz
CPU	2.5x, 3x
Internal registers	32-bit
External data bus	64-bit
Memory address bus	36-bit
Addressable memory	64GB
Virtual memory	64TB
Integral L1 cache size	8KB code, 8KB data (16KB total)
Integrated L2 cache bus	64-bit, full-core speed
Socket/Slot	Socket 8
Physical package	387-pin dual cavity PGA
Package dimensions	2.46 (6.25cm) × 2.66 (6.76cm)
Math coprocessor	Built-in FPU
Power management	SMM
Operating voltage	3.1v or 3.3v

Table 3.26   **Pentium Pro Processor Specifications by Processor Model**

Pentium Pro Processor (200MHz) with 1MB Integrated Level 2 Cache

Introduction date	August 18, 1997
Clock speeds	200MHz (66MHz × 3)
Number of transistors	5.5 million (0.35 micron process), plus 62 million in 1MB L2 cache (0.35 micron)
Cache memory	8Kx2 (16KB) L1, 1MB core-speed L2
Die size	0.552 (14.0mm)

Pentium Pro Processor (200MHz)

Introduction date	November 1, 1995
Clock speeds	200MHz (66MHz × 3)
iCOMP Index 2.0 rating	220
Number of transistors	5.5 million (0.35 micron process), plus 15.5 million in 256KB L2 cache (0.6 micron), or 31 million in 512KB L2 cache (0.35 micron)
Cache memory	8Kx2 (16KB) L1, 256KB or 512KB core-speed L2
Die size	0.552 inches per side (14.0mm)

Pentium Pro Processor (180MHz)

Introduction date	November 1, 1995
Clock speeds	180MHz (60MHz × 3)
iCOMP Index 2.0 rating	197
Number of transistors	5.5 million (0.35 micron process), plus 15.5 million in 256KB L2 cache (0.6 micron)
Cache memory	8Kx2 (16KB) L1, 256KB core-speed L2
Die size	0.552 inches per side (14.0mm)

Pentium Pro Processor (166MHz)

Introduction date	November 1, 1995
Clock speeds	166MHz (66MHz × 2.5)
Number of transistors	5.5 million (0.35 micron process), plus 31 million in 512KB L2 cache (0.35 micron)
Cache memory	8Kx2 L1, 512KB core-speed L2
Die size	0.552 inches per side (14.0mm)

Pentium Pro Processor (150MHz)

Introduction date	November 1, 1995
Clock speeds	150MHz (60MHz × 2.5)
Number of transistors	5.5 million (0.6 micron process), plus 15.5 million in 256KB L2 cache (0.6 micron)
Cache memory	8Kx2 speed L2
Die size	0.691 inches per side (17.6mm)

As you saw in Table 3.5, performance comparisons on the iCOMP 2.0 Index rate a classic Pentium 200MHz at 142, whereas a Pentium Pro 200MHz scores an impressive 220. Just for comparison, note that a Pentium MMX 200MHz falls right about in the middle in regards to performance at 182. Keep in mind that using a Pentium Pro with any 16-bit software applications nullifies much of the performance gain shown by the iCOMP 2.0 rating.

Similar to the Pentium before it, the Pentium Pro runs clock multiplied on a 66MHz motherboard. The following table lists speeds for Pentium Pro processors and motherboards.

CPU Type/Speed	CPU Clock	Motherboard Speed
Pentium Pro 150	2.5x	60
Pentium Pro 166	2.5x	66
Pentium Pro 180	3x	60
Pentium Pro 200	3x	66

The integrated L2 cache is one of the really outstanding features of the Pentium Pro. By building the L2 cache into the CPU and getting it off the motherboard, the Pentium Pro can now run the cache at full processor speed rather than the slower 60MHz or 66MHz motherboard bus speed. In fact, the L2 cache features its own internal 64-bit back-side bus, which does not share time with the external 64-bit front-side bus used by the CPU. The internal registers and data paths are still 32-bit, as with the Pentium. By building the L2 cache into the system, motherboards can be cheaper because they no longer require separate cache memory. Some boards might still try to include cache memory in their designs, but the general consensus is that L3 cache (as it would be called) would offer less improvement with the Pentium Pro than with the Pentium.

One of the features of the built-in L2 cache is that multiprocessing is greatly improved. Rather than just SMP, as with the Pentium, the Pentium Pro supports a new type of multiprocessor configuration called the Multiprocessor Specification (MPS 1.1). The Pentium Pro with MPS enables configurations of up to four processors running together. Unlike other multiprocessor configurations, the Pentium Pro avoids cache coherency problems because each chip maintains a separate L1 and L2 cache internally.

Pentium Pro–based motherboards are pretty much exclusively PCI and ISA bus-based, and Intel is producing its own chipsets for these motherboards. The first chipset was the 450KX/GX (codenamed Orion), whereas the most recent chipset for use with the Pentium Pro is the 440LX (Natoma). Because of the greater cooling and space requirements, Intel designed the new ATX motherboard form factor to better support the Pentium Pro and other future processors, such as the Pentium II/III/4. Even so, the Pentium Pro can be found in all types of motherboard designs; ATX is not mandatory.

▶▶ See "Motherboard Form Factors," p. 194, and "Sixth-Generation and Seventh-Generation Chipsets," p. 246.

Some Pentium Pro system manufacturers were tempted to stick with the Baby-AT form factor. The big problem with the standard Baby-AT form factor is keeping the CPU properly cooled. The massive Pentium Pro processor consumes more than 25 watts and generates an appreciable amount of heat.

Four special VID pins are on the Pentium Pro processor. These pins can be used to support automatic selection of power supply voltage. Therefore, a Pentium Pro motherboard does not have voltage regulator jumper settings like most Pentium boards, which greatly eases the setup and integration of a Pentium Pro system. These pins are not actually signals, but are either an open circuit in the package or a short circuit to voltage. The sequence of opens and shorts define the voltage required by the processor. In addition to allowing for automatic voltage settings, this feature has been designed to support voltage specification variations on future Pentium Pro processors. The VID pins are named VID0 through VID3, and the definition of these pins is shown in Table 3.27. A 1 in this table refers to an open pin, and 0 refers to a short to ground. The voltage regulators on the motherboard should supply the voltage that is requested or disable itself.

Table 3.27   Pentium Pro Voltage Identification Definition

VID[3:0]	Voltage Setting	VID[3:0]	Voltage Setting
0000	3.5	1000	2.7
0001	3.4	1001	2.6
0010	3.3	1010	2.5
0011	3.2	1011	2.4
0100	3.1	1100	2.3
0101	3.0	1101	2.2
0110	2.9	1110	2.1
0111	2.8	1111	No CPU present

Most Pentium Pro processors run at 3.3v, but a few run at 3.1v. Although those are the only versions available now, support for a wider range of VID settings will benefit the system in meeting the power requirements of future Pentium Pro processors. Note that the 1111 (or all opens) ID can be used to detect the absence of a processor in a given socket.

The Pentium Pro never did become very popular on the desktop, but it did find a niche in file-server applications primarily because of the full-core speed high-capacity internal L2 cache.

Pentium II Processors

Intel revealed the Pentium II in May 1997. Prior to its official unveiling, the Pentium II processor was popularly referred to by its codename, Klamath, and was surrounded by much speculation throughout the industry. The Pentium II is essentially the same sixth-generation processor as the Pentium Pro, with MMX technology added (which included double the L1 cache and 57 new MMX instructions); however, there are a few twists to the design. The Pentium II processor die is shown in Figure 3.40.

From a physical standpoint, it is truly something new. Abandoning the chip in a socket approach used by virtually all processors up until this point, the Pentium II chip is characterized by its SEC cartridge design. The processor, along with several L2 cache chips, is mounted on a small circuit board (much like an oversized-memory SIMM) as shown in Figure 3.41, and the circuit board is then sealed in a metal and plastic cartridge. The cartridge is then plugged into the motherboard through an edge connector called Slot 1, which looks very much like an adapter card slot.

The two variations on these cartridges are called SECC (single edge contact cartridge) and SECC2. Figure 3.42 shows a diagram of the SECC package; Figure 3.43 shows the SECC2 package.

As you can see from these figures, the SECC2 version is cheaper to make because it uses fewer overall parts. It also allows for a more direct heatsink attachment to the processor for better cooling. Intel transitioned from SECC to SECC2 in the beginning of 1999; all later PII chips, and the Slot 1 PIII chips that followed, use the improved SECC2 design.

By using separate chips mounted on a circuit board, Intel can build the Pentium II much less expensively than the multiple die within a package used in the Pentium Pro. Intel can also use cache chips from other manufacturers and more easily vary the amount of cache in future processors compared to the Pentium Pro design.

Figure 3.40   Pentium II Processor die. *Photograph used by permission of Intel Corporation.*

Figure 3.41   Pentium II processor board (inside SEC cartridge). *Photograph used by permission of Intel Corporation.*

Figure 3.42 SECC components showing an enclosed processor board.

Figure 3.43 Two SECC, rev. 2 components showing a half-enclosed processor board.

Intel has offered Pentium II processors with the following speeds:

CPU Type/Speed	CPU Clock	Motherboard Speed
Pentium II 233MHz	3.5x	66MHz
Pentium II 266MHz	4x	66MHz
Pentium II 300MHz	4.5x	66MHz
Pentium II 333MHz	5x	66MHz
Pentium II 350MHz	3.5x	100MHz
Pentium II 400MHz	4x	100MHz
Pentium II 450MHz	4.5x	100MHz

The Pentium II processor core has 7.5 million transistors and is based on Intel's advanced P6 architecture. The Pentium II started out using .35 micron process technology, although the 333MHz and faster Pentium IIs are based on 0.25-micron technology. This enables a smaller die, allowing increased core frequencies and reduced power consumption. At 333MHz, the Pentium II processor delivers a 75%–150% performance boost, compared to the 233MHz Pentium processor with MMX technology, and approximately 50% more performance on multimedia benchmarks. As shown earlier in Table 3.3, the iCOMP 2.0 Index rating for the Pentium II 266MHz chip is more than twice as fast as a classic Pentium 200MHz.

Aside from speed, the best way to think of the Pentium II is as a Pentium Pro with MMX technology instructions and a slightly modified cache design. It has the same multiprocessor scalability as the Pentium Pro, as well as the integrated L2 cache. The 57 new multimedia-related instructions carried over from the MMX processors and the capability to process repetitive loop commands more efficiently are included as well. Also included as a part of the MMX upgrade is double the internal L1 cache from the Pentium Pro (from 16KB total to 32KB total in the Pentium II).

Maximum power usage for the Pentium II is shown in the following table:

Core Speed	Power Draw	Process	Voltage
450MHz	27.1w	0.25 micron	2.0v
400MHz	24.3w	0.25 micron	2.0v
350MHz	21.5w	0.25 micron	2.0v
333MHz	23.7w	0.25 micron	2.0v
300MHz	43.0w	0.35 micron	2.8v
266MHz	38.2w	0.35 micron	2.8v
233MHz	34.8w	0.35 micron	2.8v

You can see that the highest speed 450MHz version of the Pentium II actually uses less power than the slowest original 233MHz version! This was accomplished by using the smaller 0.25-micron process and running the processor on a lower voltage of only 2.0v. Future Pentium III processors will use the 0.25- and 0.18-micron processes and even lower voltages to continue this trend.

The Pentium II includes Dynamic Execution, which describes unique performance-enhancing developments by Intel and was first introduced in the Pentium Pro processor. Major features of Dynamic Execution include multiple branch prediction, which speeds execution by predicting the flow of the program through several branches; dataflow analysis, which analyzes and modifies the program order to execute instructions when ready; and speculative execution, which looks ahead of the program counter and executes instruction that are likely to be needed. The Pentium II processor expands on these capabilities in sophisticated and powerful new ways to deliver even greater performance gains.

Similar to the Pentium Pro, the Pentium II also includes DIB architecture. The term *Dual Independent Bus* comes from the existence of two independent buses on the Pentium II processor—the L2 cache bus and the processor–to–main-memory system bus. The Pentium II processor can use both buses simultaneously, thus getting as much as twice as much data in and out of the Pentium II processor than a single-bus architecture processor. The DIB architecture enables the L2 cache of the 333MHz Pentium II processor to run 2 1/2 times as fast as the L2 cache of Pentium processors. As the frequency of future Pentium II processors increases, so will the speed of the L2 cache. Also, the pipelined system bus enables simultaneous parallel transactions instead of singular sequential transactions. Together, these DIB architecture improvements offer up to three times the bandwidth performance over a single-bus architecture as with the regular Pentium.

Table 3.28 shows the general Pentium II processor specifications. Table 3.29 shows the specifications that vary by model for the models that have been introduced to date.

Table 3.28   Pentium II General Processor Specifications

Bus Speeds	66MHz, 100MHz
CPU clock multiplier	3.5x, 4x, 4.5x, 5x
CPU speeds	233MHz, 266MHz, 300MHz, 333MHz, 350MHz, 400MHz, 450MHz
Cache memory	16Kx2 (32KB) L1, 512KB 1/2-speed L2
Internal registers	32-bit
External data bus	64-bit system bus w/ ECC; 64-bit cache bus w/ optional ECC
Memory address bus	36-bit
Addressable memory	64GB
Virtual memory	64TB
Physical package	Single edge contact cartridge (S.E), 242 pins
Package dimensions	5.505 in. (12.82cm)×2.473 inches (6.28cm)×0.647 in. (1.64cm)
Math coprocessor	Built-in FPU
Power management	SMM

Table 3.29   Pentium II Specifications by Model

Pentium II MMX Processor (350MHz, 400MHz, and 450MHz)	
Introduction date	April 15, 1998
Clock speeds	350MHz (100MHz×3.5), 400MHz (100MHz ×4), and 450MHz (100MHz×4.5)
iCOMP Index 2.0 rating	386 (350MHz), 440 (400MHz), and 483 (450MHz)
Number of transistors	7.5 million (0.25-micron process), plus 31 million in 512KB L2 cache
Cacheable RAM	4GB
Operating voltage	2.0v
Slot	Slot 2
Die size	0.400 inches per side (10.2mm)
Mobile Pentium II Processor (266MHz, 300MHz, 333MHz, and 366MHz)	
Introduction date	January 25, 1999
Clock speeds	266MHz, 300MHz, 333MHz, and 366MHz
Number of transistors	27.4 million (0.25-micron process), 256KB on-die L2 cache
Ball grid array (BGA)	Number of balls = 615
Dimensions	Width = 31mm; length = 35mm
Core voltage	1.6 volts
Thermal design power ranges by frequency	366MHz = 9.5 watts; 333MHz = 8.6 watts; 300MHz = 7.7 watts; 266MHz = 7.0 watts

Table 3.29 Continued

Pentium II MMX Processor (333MHz)

Introduction date	January 26, 1998
Clock speed	333MHz (66MHz×5)
iCOMP Index 2.0 rating	366
Number of transistors	7.5 million (0.25-micron process), plus 31 million in 512KB L2 cache
Cacheable RAM	512MB
Operating voltage	2.0v
Slot	Slot 1
Die size	0.400 inches per side (10.2mm)

Pentium II MMX Processor (300MHz)

Introduction date	May 7, 1997
Clock speed	300MHz (66MHz×4.5)
iCOMP Index 2.0 rating	332
Number of transistors	7.5 million (0.35-micron process), plus 31 million in 512KB L2 cache
Cacheable RAM	512MB
Die size	0.560 inches per side (14.2mm)

Pentium II MMX Processor (266MHz)

Introduction date	May 7, 1997
Clock speed	266MHz (66MHz×4)
iCOMP Index 2.0 rating	303
Number of transistors	7.5 million (0.35-micron process), plus 31 million in 512KB L2 cache
Cacheable RAM	512MB
Slot	Slot 1
Die size	0.560 inches per side (14.2mm)

Pentium II MMX Processor (233MHz)

Introduction date	May 7, 1997
Clock speed	233MHz (66MHz×3.5)
iCOMP Index 2.0 rating	267
Number of transistors	7.5 million (0.35-micron process), plus 31 million in 512KB L2 cache
Cacheable RAM	512MB
Slot	Slot 1
Die size	0.560 inches per side (14.2mm)

As you can see from Table 3.30, the Pentium II can handle up to 64GB of physical memory. Similar to the Pentium Pro, the CPU incorporates DIB architecture. Therefore, chip has two independent buses: one for accessing the L2 cache and the other for accessing main memory. These dual buses can operate simultaneously, greatly accelerating the flow of data within the system. The L1 cache always runs at full-core speeds because it is mounted directly on the processor die. The L2 cache in the Pentium II normally runs at half-core speed, which saves money and allows for less expensive cache chips to be used. For example, in a 333MHz Pentium II, the L1 cache runs at a full 333MHz, whereas the L2 cache runs at 167MHz. Even though the L2 cache is not at full-core speed as it was with the Pentium Pro, this is still far superior to having cache memory on the motherboard running at the 66MHz motherboard speed of most Socket 7 Pentium designs. Intel claims that the DIB architecture in the Pentium II enables up to three times the bandwidth of normal single-bus processors, such as the original Pentium.

By removing the cache from the processor's internal package and using external chips mounted on a substrate and encased in the cartridge design, Intel can now use more cost-effective cache chips and more easily scale the processor up to higher speeds. The Pentium Pro was limited in speed to 200MHz, largely due to the inability to find affordable cache memory that runs any faster. By running the cache memory at half-core speed, the Pentium II can run up to 400MHz while still using 200MHz-rated cache chips. To offset the half-core speed cache used in the Pentium II, Intel doubled the basic amount of integrated L2 cache from 256KB standard in the Pro to 512KB standard in the Pentium II.

Note that the tag RAM included in the L2 cache enables up to 512MB of main memory to be cacheable in PII processors from 233MHz to 333MHz. The 350MHz, 400MHz, and faster versions include an enhanced tag-RAM that allows up to 4GB of main memory to be cacheable. This is very important if you ever plan on adding more than 512MB of memory. In that case, you would definitely want the 350MHz or faster version; otherwise, memory performance would suffer.

The system bus of the Pentium II provides "glueless" support for up to two processors. This enables low-cost, two-way multiprocessing on the L2 cache bus. These system buses are designed especially for servers or other mission-critical system use where reliability and data integrity are important. All Pentium IIs also include parity-protected address/request and response system bus signals with a retry mechanism for high data integrity and reliability.

To install the Pentium II in a system, a special processor-retention mechanism is required. This consists of a mechanical support that attaches to the motherboard and secures the Pentium II processor in Slot 1 to prevent shock and vibration damage. Retention mechanisms should be provided by the motherboard manufacturer. (For example, the Intel Boxed AL440FX and DK440LX motherboards include a retention mechanism, plus other important system integration components.)

The Pentium II can generate a significant amount of heat that must be dissipated. This is accomplished by installing a heatsink on the processor. Many of the Pentium II processors use an active heatsink that incorporates a fan. Unlike heatsink fans for previous Intel boxed processors, the Pentium II fans draw power from a three-pin power header on the motherboard. Most motherboards provide several fan connectors to supply this power.

Special heatsink supports are necessary to furnish mechanical support between the fan heatsink and support holes on the motherboard. Normally, a plastic support is inserted into the heatsink holes in the motherboard next to the CPU, before installing the CPU/heatsink package. Most fan heatsinks have two components: a fan in a plastic shroud and a metal heatsink. The heatsink is attached to the processor's thermal plate and should not be removed. The fan can be removed and replaced if necessary—for example, if it has failed. Figure 3.44 shows the SEC assembly with fan, power connectors, mechanical supports, and the slot and support holes on the motherboard.

The following tables show the specifications unique to certain versions of the Pentium II processor.

To identify exactly which Pentium II processor you have and what its capabilities are, look at the specification number printed on the SEC cartridge. You will find the specification number in the dynamic mark area on the top of the processor module. See Figure 3.45 to locate these markings.

After you have located the specification number (actually, it is an alphanumeric code), you can look it up in Table 3.30 to see exactly which processor you have.

Figure 3.44 Pentium II/III processor and heatsink assembly.

Figure 3.45 Pentium II/III SECC.

For example, a specification number of SL2KA identifies the processor as a Pentium II 333MHz running on a 66MHz system bus, with an ECC L2 cache—and indicates that this processor runs on only 2.0 volts. The stepping is also identified, and by looking in the Pentium II Specification Update Manual published by Intel, you could figure out exactly which bugs were fixed in that revision.

Table 3.30   Basic Pentium II Processor Identification Information

S-spec	Core Stepping	CPUID	Core/Bus Speed (MHz)	L2 Cache Size (MB)	L2 Cache Type	CPU Package	Notes (see footnotes)
SL264	C0	0633h	233/66	512	non-ECC	SECC 3.00	5
SL265	C0	0633h	266/66	512	non-ECC	SECC 3.00	5
SL268	C0	0633h	233/66	512	ECC	SECC 3.00	5
SL269	C0	0633h	266/66	512	ECC	SECC 3.00	5
SL28K	C0	0633h	233/66	512	non-ECC	SECC 3.00	1, 3, 5
SL28L	C0	0633h	266/66	512	non-ECC	SECC 3.00	1, 3, 5
SL28R	C0	0633h	300/66	512	ECC	SECC 3.00	5
SL2MZ	C0	0633h	300/66	512	ECC	SECC 3.00	1, 5
SL2HA	C1	0634h	300/66	512	ECC	SECC 3.00	5
SL2HC	C1	0634h	266/66	512	non-ECC	SECC 3.00	5
SL2HD	C1	0634h	233/66	512	non-ECC	SECC 3.00	5
SL2HE	C1	0634h	266/66	512	ECC	SECC 3.00	5
SL2HF	C1	0634h	233/66	512	ECC	SECC 3.00	5
SL2QA	C1	0634h	233/66	512	non-ECC	SECC 3.00	1, 3, 5
SL2QB	C1	0634h	266/66	512	non-ECC	SECC 3.00	1, 3, 5
SL2QC	C1	0634h	300/66	512	ECC	SECC 3.00	1, 5
SL2KA	dA0	0650h	333/66	512	ECC	SECC 3.00	5
SL2QF	dA0	0650h	333/66	512	ECC	SECC 3.00	1
SL2K9	dA0	0650h	266/66	512	ECC	SECC 3.00	
SL35V	dA1	0651h	300/66	512	ECC	SECC 3.00	1, 2
SL2QH	dA1	0651h	333/66	512	ECC	SECC 3.00	1, 2
SL2S5	dA1	0651h	333/66	512	ECC	SECC 3.00	2, 5
SL2ZP	dA1	0651h	333/66	512	ECC	SECC 3.00	2, 5
SL2ZQ	dA1	0651h	350/100	512	ECC	SECC 3.00	2, 5
SL2S6	dA1	0651h	350/100	512	ECC	SECC 3.00	2, 5
SL2S7	dA1	0651h	400/100	512	ECC	SECC 3.00	2, 5
SL2SF	dA1	0651h	350/100	512	ECC	SECC 3.00	1, 2
SL2SH	dA1	0651h	400/100	512	ECC	SECC 3.00	1, 2
SL2VY	dA1	0651h	300/66	512	ECC	SECC 3.00	1, 2
SL33D	dB0	0652h	266/66	512	ECC	SECC 3.00	1, 2, 5
SL2YK	dB0	0652h	300/66	512	ECC	SECC 3.00	1, 2, 5
SL2WZ	dB0	0652h	350/100	512	ECC	SECC 3.00	1, 2, 5
SL2YM	dB0	0652h	400/100	512	ECC	SECC 3.00	1, 2, 5
SL37G	dB0	0652h	400/100	512	ECC	SECC2 OLGA	1, 2, 4

Table 3.30   Continued

S-spec	Core Stepping	CPUID	Core/Bus Speed (MHz)	L2 Cache Size (MB)	L2 Cache Type	CPU Package	Notes (see footnotes)
SL2WB	dB0	0652h	450/100	512	ECC	SECC 3.00	1, 2, 5
SL37H	dB0	0652h	450/100	512	ECC	SECC2 OLGA	1, 2
SL2KE	TdB0	1632h	333/66	512	ECC	PGA	2, 4
SL2W7	dB0	0652h	266/66	512	ECC	SECC 2.00	2, 5
SL2W8	dB0	0652h	300/66	512	ECC	SECC 3.00	2, 5
SL2TV	dB0	0652h	333/66	512	ECC	SECC 3.00	2, 5
SL2U3	dB0	0652h	350/100	512	ECC	SECC 3.00	2, 5
SL2U4	dB0	0652h	350/100	512	ECC	SECC 3.00	2, 5
SL2U5	dB0	0652h	400/100	512	ECC	SECC 3.00	2, 5
SL2U6	dB0	0652h	400/100	512	ECC	SECC 3.00	2, 5
SL2U7	dB0	0652h	450/100	512	ECC	SECC 3.00	2, 5
SL356	dB0	0652h	350/100	512	ECC	SECC2 PLGA	2, 5
SL357	dB0	0652h	400/100	512	ECC	SECC2 OLGA	2, 5
SL358	dB0	0652h	450/100	512	ECC	SECC2 OLGA	2, 5
SL37F	dB0	0652h	350/100	512	ECC	SECC2 PLGA	1, 2, 5
SL3FN	dB0	0652h	350/100	512	ECC	SECC2 OLGA	2, 5
SL3EE	dB0	0652h	400/100	512	ECC	SECC2 PLGA	2, 5
SL3F9	dB0	0652h	400/100	512	ECC	SECC2 PLGA	1, 2
SL38M	dB1	0653h	350/100	512	ECC	SECC 3.00	1, 2, 5
SL38N	dB1	0653h	400/100	512	ECC	SECC 3.00	1, 2, 5
SL36U	dB1	0653h	350/100	512	ECC	SECC 3.00	2, 5
SL38Z	dB1	0653h	400/100	512	ECC	SECC 3.00	2, 5
SL3D5	dB1	0653h	400/100	512	ECC	SECC2 OLGA	1, 2

SECC = Single edge contact cartridge

SECC2 = Single edge contact cartridge revision 2

PLGA = Plastic land grid array

OLGA = Organic land grid array

CPUID = The internal ID returned by the CPUID instruction

ECC = Error correcting code

1. This is a boxed Pentium II processor with an attached fan heatsink.

2. These processors have an enhanced L2 cache, which can cache up to 4GB of main memory. Other standard PII processors can cache only up to 512MB of main memory.

3. These boxed processors might have packaging that incorrectly indicates ECC support in the L2 cache.

4. This is a boxed Pentium II OverDrive processor with an attached fan heatsink, designed for upgrading Pentium Pro (Socket 8) systems.

5. These parts operate at only the specified clock multiplier frequency ratio at which they were manufactured. They can be overclocked only by increasing bus speed.

The two variations of the SECC2 cartridge vary by the type of processor core package on the board. The plastic land grid array (PLGA) is the older type of packaging used in previous SECC cartridges as well and is being phased out. Taking its place is the newer organic land grid array (OLGA), which is a processor core package that is smaller and easier to manufacture. It also enables better thermal transfer between the processor die and the heatsink, which is attached directly to the top of the OLGA chip package. Figure 3.46 shows the open back side (where the heatsink would be attached) of SECC2 processors with PLGA and OLGA cores.

Figure 3.46   SECC2 processors with PLGA and OLGA cores.

Pentium II motherboards have an onboard voltage regulator circuit designed to power the CPU. Currently, some Pentium II processors run at several different voltages, so the regulator must be set to supply the correct voltage for the specific processor you are installing. As with the Pentium Pro and unlike the older Pentium, no jumpers or switches must be set; the voltage setting is handled completely automatically through the VID pins on the processor cartridge. Table 3.31 shows the relationship between the pins and the selected voltage.

Table 3.31   Slot 1 and Socket 370 Voltage ID Pin Definitions

VID4	VID3	VID2	VID1	VID0	Voltage
0	1	1	1	1	1.30
0	1	1	1	0	1.35
0	1	1	0	1	1.40
0	1	1	0	0	1.45
0	1	0	1	1	1.50
0	1	0	1	0	1.55
0	1	0	0	1	1.60

Table 3.31   Continued

VID4	VID3	VID2	VID1	VID0	Voltage
0	1	0	0	0	1.65
0	0	1	1	1	1.70
0	0	1	1	0	1.75
0	0	1	0	1	**1.80**
0	0	1	0	0	**1.85**
0	0	0	1	1	**1.90**
0	0	0	1	0	**1.95**
0	0	0	0	1	**2.00**
0	0	0	0	0	**2.05**
1	1	1	1	1	**No Core**
1	1	1	1	0	**2.1**
1	1	1	0	1	**2.2**
1	1	1	0	0	**2.3**
1	1	0	1	1	**2.4**
1	1	0	1	0	**2.5**
1	1	0	0	1	**2.6**
1	1	0	0	0	**2.7**
1	0	1	1	1	**2.8**
1	0	1	1	0	2.9
1	0	1	0	1	3.0
1	0	1	0	0	3.1
1	0	0	1	1	3.2
1	0	0	1	0	3.3
1	0	0	0	1	3.4
1	0	0	0	0	3.5

0 = Processor pin connected to Vss
1 = Open on processor
VID0–VID3 used on Socket 370
Socket 370 supports 1.30–2.05V settings only.
VID0-VID4 used on Slot 1
Slot 1 supports 1.30–3.5V settings.

To ensure the system is ready for all Pentium II processor variations, the values in **bold** must be supported. Most Pentium II processors run at 2.8v, with some newer ones at 2.0v.

The Pentium II Mobile Module is a Pentium II for notebooks that includes the North Bridge of the high-performance 440BX chipset. This is the first chipset on the market that allows 100MHz processor bus operation, although that is currently not supported in the mobile versions. The 440BX chipset was released at the same time as the 350MHz and 400MHz versions of the Pentium II; it is the recommended minimum chipset for any new Pentium II motherboard purchases.

Newer variations on the Pentium II include the Pentium IIPE, which is a mobile version that includes 256KB of L2 cache directly integrated into the die. Therefore, it runs at full-core speed, making it faster than the desktop Pentium II because the desktop chips use half-speed L2 cache.

Celeron

The Celeron processor is a P6 with the same processor core as the Pentium II in the original two versions and now the same core as the PIII in the latest version. It is mainly designed for lower-cost PCs in the $600 or less price category. The best "feature" is that although the cost is low, the performance is not. In fact, because of the superior integrated cache design of all but the first units, the Celeron outperforms the Pentium II at the same speed and at a lower cost.

Most of the features for the Celeron are the same as the Pentium II and III because it uses the same internal processor core. The main differences are in packaging and L2 cache design.

Up until recently, all Celeron processors were available in a package called the single edge processor package (SEPP or SEP package). The SEP package is basically the same Slot 1 design as the SECC used in the Pentium II/III, with the exception of the fancy plastic cartridge cover. This cover is deleted in the Celeron, making it cheaper to produce and sell. Essentially, the Celeron uses the same circuit board as is inside the Pentium II package.

◄◄ See "Single Edge Contact and Single Edge Processor Packaging," p. 80.

Even without the plastic covers, the Slot 1 packaging was more expensive than it should have been. This was largely due to the processor retention mechanisms (stands) required to secure the processor into Slot 1 on the motherboard, as well as the larger and more complicated heatsinks required. This, plus competition from the lower-end Socket 7 systems using primarily AMD processors, led Intel to introduce the Celeron in a socketed form. The socket is called PGA-370 or Socket 370 because it has 370 pins. The processor package designed for this socket is called the plastic pin grid array (PPGA) package (see Figure 3.47) or flip chip PGA (FC-PGA). Both the PPGA and FC-PGA packages plug into the 370 pin socket and allow for lower-cost, lower-profile, and smaller systems because of the less expensive processor retention and cooling requirements of the socketed processor.

◄◄ See "Socket 370 (PGA-370)," p. 90.

All Celeron processors at 433MHz and lower have been available in the SEPP that plugs into the 242-contact slot connector. The 300MHz and higher versions also are available in the PPGA package. This means that the 300MHz to 433MHz have been available in both packages, whereas the 466MHz and higher-speed versions are available only in the PPGA.

Motherboards that include Socket 370 can accept the PGA versions of both the Celeron and Pentium III in most cases. If you want to use a Socket 370 version of the Celeron in a Slot 1 motherboard, slot-to-socket adapters (usually called slot-kets) are available for about $10–$20 that plug into Slot 1 and incorporate a Socket 370 on the card. Figure 3.48 shows a typical slot-ket adapter.

Highlights of the Celeron include

- Available at 300MHz (300A) and higher core frequencies with 128KB on-die L2 cache; 300MHz and 266MHz core frequencies without L2 cache
- L2 cache supports up to 4GB RAM address range and ECC
- Uses same P6 core processor as the Pentium II (266MHz through 533MHz) and now the Pentium III (533A MHz and higher)
- Dynamic execution microarchitecture
- Operates on a 66MHz CPU bus (future versions will likely also use the 100MHz bus)
- Specifically designed for lower-cost value PC systems

- Includes MMX technology; Celeron 533A and higher include SSE
- More cost-effective packaging technology, including SEP, PPGA, or FC-PGA packages
- Integrated 32KB L1 cache, implemented as separate 16KB instruction and 16KB data caches
- Integrated thermal diode for temperature monitoring

Figure 3.47   Celeron processors in the FC-PGA, PPGA, and SEP packages.

Figure 3.48   Slot-ket adapter for installing PPGA processors in Slot 1 motherboards.

The Intel Celeron processors from the 300A and higher include integrated 128KB L2 cache. The core for the 300A through 533MHz versions that are based on the Pentium II core include 19 million transistors because of the addition of the integrated 128KB L2 cache. The 533A and faster versions are based on the Pentium III core and incorporate 28.1 million transistors. The Pentium III–based versions actually have 256KB of L2 cache on the die; however, 128KB is disabled, leaving 128KB of functional L2 cache. This was done because it was cheaper for Intel to simply make the Pentium III and Celeron using the same die and just disable part of the cache on the Celeron versions, rather than coming up with a unique die for the newer Celerons. The Pentium III–based Celeron processors also support the SSE in addition to MMX instructions. The older Celerons based on the Pentium II core support only MMX.

All the Celerons in SEPP and PPGA form are manufactured using the 0.25-micron process, whereas those in FC-PGA form are made using an even better 0.18-micron process. The smaller process reduces processor heat and enables higher speeds. Table 3.35 shows the power consumed by the various Celeron processors.

Figure 3.49 shows the Intel Celeron processor identification information. Figure 3.50 shows the Celeron's PPGA processor markings, which can be used to identify the chip and prevent being duped by a re-marked chip.

Figure 3.49   Celeron SEPP processor markings.

Note

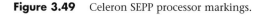

The markings on the processor identify the following information:

    SYYYY = S-spec. number

    FFFFFFFF = FPO # (test lot traceability #)

    COA = Country of assembly

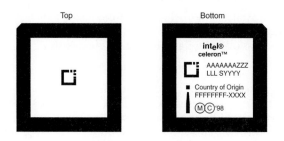

Figure 3.50   Celeron PPGA processor markings.

Note

The PPGA processor markings identify the following information:

AAAAAAA = Product code

ZZZ = Processor speed (MHz)

LLL = Integrated L2 cache size (in kilobytes)

SYYYY = S-spec. number

FFFFFFFF-XXXX = Assembly lot tracking number

Table 3.32 shows all the available variations of the Celeron, indicated by the S-specification number.

Pentium III

The Pentium III processor, shown in Figure 3.51, was first released in February 1999 and introduced several new features to the P6 family. The most important advancements are the streaming SSE and the integrated on-die L2 cache in the later versions. SSE consists of 70 new instructions that dramatically enhance the performance and possibilities of advanced imaging, 3D, streaming audio, video, and speech-recognition applications.

Figure 3.51   Pentium III processor in SECC2 (Slot 1) and FC-PGA (Socket 370) packages.

Originally based on Intel's advanced 0.25-micron CMOS process technology, the PIII core started out with more than 9.5 million transistors. In late 1999, Intel shifted to a 0.18- micron process die (code-named Coppermine) and added 256KB of on-die L2 cache, which brought the transistor count to a whopping 28.1 million! The Pentium III is available in speeds from 450MHz through 1000MHz and beyond, as well as server versions with larger or faster cache called Xeon. The Pentium III also incorporates advanced features such as a 32KB L1 cache and either half-core speed 512KB L2 cache or full-core speed on-die 256KB L2 with cacheability for up to 4GB of addressable memory space. The PIII also can be used in dual-processing systems with up to 64GB of physical memory. A self-reportable processor serial number gives security, authentication, and system management applications a powerful new tool for identifying individual systems.

Pentium III processors are available in Intel's SECC2 form factor, which is replacing the more expensive older SEC packaging. The SECC2 package covers only one side of the chip and allows for better heatsink attachment and less overall weight. It is also less expensive.

Architectural features of the Pentium III processor include

- *Streaming SIMD Extensions.* Seventy new instructions for dramatically faster processing and improved imaging, 3D streaming audio and video, Web access, speech recognition, new user interfaces, and other graphics and sound-rich applications.

■ *Intel processor serial number.* The processor serial number, the first of Intel's planned building blocks for PC security, serves as an electronic serial number for the processor and, by extension, its system or user. This enables the system/user to be identified by networks and applications. The processor serial number will be used in applications that benefit from stronger forms of system and user identification, such as the following:

- *Applications using security capabilities.* Managed access to new Internet content and services; electronic document exchange.

- *Manageability applications.* Asset management; remote system load and configuration.

- *Intel MMX technology.*

- *Dynamic Execution technology.*

- *Those incorporating an on-die diode.* This can be used to monitor the die temperature for thermal management purposes.

Most of the Pentium III processors will be made in the improved SECC2 packaging or, even better, the FC-PGA package, which is much less expensive to produce and enables a more direct attachment of the heatsink to the processor core for better cooling. The FC-PGA version plugs into Socket 370 but can be used in Slot 1 with a slot-ket adapter.

All Pentium III processors have either 512KB or 256KB of L2 cache, which runs at either half-core or full-core speed. Xeon versions have 512KB, 1MB, or 2MB of L2 cache that runs at full-core speed. These are more expensive versions designed for servers and workstations.

All PIII processor L2 caches can cache up to 4GB of addressable memory space and include ECC capability.

Pentium III processors can be identified by their markings, which are found on the top edge of the processor cartridge. Figure 3.52 shows the format and meaning of the markings.

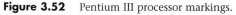

Figure 3.52 Pentium III processor markings.

Table 3.33 shows the available variations of the Pentium III, indicated by the S-specification number.

Table 3.32   Intel Celeron Variations and Specifications

Speed (MHz)	Bus Speed (MHz)	Multiplier	Boxed CPU S-spec	OEM CPU S-spec	Stepping	CPUID	L2 Cache
266	66	4x	SL2YN	SL2SY	dA0	0650	none
266	66	4x	SL2QG	SL2TR	dA1	0651	none
300	66	4.5x	SL2Z7	SL2YP	dA0	0650	none
300	66	4.5x	SL2Y2	SL2X8	dA1	0651	none
300A	66	4.5x	SL32A	SL2WM	mA0	0660	128KB
300A	66	4.5x	SL2WM	SL2WM	mA0	0660	128KB
300A	66	4.5x	SL35Q	SL36A	mB0	0665	128KB
333	66	5x	SL32B	SL2WN	mA0	0660	128KB
333	66	5x	SL2WN	SL2WN	mA0	0660	128KB
333	66	5x	SL35R	SL36B	mB0	0665	128KB
366	66	5.5x	SL37Q	SL376	mA0	0660	128KB
366	66	5.5x	SL35S	SL36C	mB0	0665	128KB
400	66	6x	SL37V	SL39Z	mA0	0660	128KB
400	66	6x	SL37X	SL3A2	mB0	0665	128KB
433	66	6.5x	SL3BS	SL3BA	mB0	0665	128KB
466	66	7x	SL3FL	SL3EH	mB0	0665	128KB
500	66	7.5x	SL3LQ	SL3FY	mB0	0665	128KB
533	66	8x	SL3PZ	SL3FZ	mB0	0665	128KB
533A	66	8x	SL3W6	SL46S	cBO	0683	128KB
566	66	8.5x	SL3W7	SL46T	cB0	0683	128KB
566	66	8.5x	SL4NW	SL4PC	cC0	0686	128KB
600	66	9x	SL3W8	SL46U	cBO	0683	128KB
600	66	9x	SL4NX	SL4PB	cC0	0686	128KB
633	66	9.5x	SL3W9	SL3VS	cBO	0683	128KB
633	66	9.5x	SL4NY	SL4PA	cC0	0686	128KB
667	66	10x	SL4AB	SL48E	cBO	0683	128KB
667	66	10x	SL4NZ	SL4P9	cC0	0686	128KB
700	66	10.5x	SL4E6	SL48F	cBO	0683	128KB
700	66	10.5x	SL4P2	SL4P8	cC0	0686	128KB
733	66	11x	SL4P3	SL4P7	cC0	0686	128KB
766	66	11.5x	SL4QF	SL4P6	cC0	0686	128KB
800	100	8x	SL55R	SL4TF	cC0	0686	128KB
850	100	8.5x	SL5GB	SL5GA	cC0	0686	128KB

SEPP = Single edge processor package (card)

PPGA = Plastic pin grid array

FC-PGA = Flip chip pin grid array

MMX = Multimedia extensions

Graphics Extensions	Max. Temp. (C)	Voltage	Max. Power (W)	Process (Microns)	Transistors	Package
MMX	85	2.0V	16.59	0.25	7.5M	SEPP
MMX	85	2.0V	16.59	0.25	7.5M	SEPP
MMX	85	2.0V	18.48	0.25	7.5M	SEPP
MMX	85	2.0V	18.48	0.25	7.5M	SEPP
MMX	85	2.0V	19.05	0.25	19M	SEPP
MMX	85	2.0V	19.05	0.25	19M	SEPP
MMX	85	2.0V	19.05	0.25	19M	PPGA
MMX	85	2.0V	20.94	0.25	19M	SEPP
MMX	85	2.0V	20.94	0.25	19M	SEPP
MMX	85	2.0V	20.94	0.25	19M	PPGA
MMX	85	2.0V	21.70	0.25	19M	SEPP
MMX	85	2.0V	21.70	0.25	19M	PPGA
MMX	85	2.0V	23.70	0.25	19M	SEPP
MMX	85	2.0V	23.70	0.25	19M	PPGA
MMX	85	2.0V	24.1	0.25	19M	PPGA
MMX	70	2.0V	25.7	0.25	19M	PPGA
MMX	70	2.0V	27.2	0.25	19M	PPGA
MMX	70	2.0V	28.3	0.25	19M	PPGA
SSE	90	1.5V	11.2	0.18	28.1M	FC-PGA
SSE	90	1.5V	11.9	0.18	28.1M	FC-PGA
SSE	90	1.7V	11.9	0.18	28.1M	FC-PGA
SSE	90	1.5V	12.6	0.18	28.1M	FC-PGA
SSE	90	1.7V	12.6	0.18	28.1M	FC-PGA
SSE	82	1.65V	16.5	0.18	28.1M	FC-PGA
SSE	82	1.7V	16.5	0.18	28.1M	FC-PGA
SSE	82	1.65V	17.5	0.18	28.1M	FC-PGA
SSE	82	1.7V	17.5	0.18	28.1M	FC-PGA
SSE	80	1.65V	18.3	0.18	28.1M	FC-PGA
SSE	80	1.7V	18.3	0.18	28.1M	FC-PGA
SSE	80	1.7V	19.1	0.18	28.1M	FC-PGA
SSE	80	1.7V	20.0	0.18	28.1M	FC-PGA
SSE	80	1.7V	20.8	0.18	28.1M	FC-PGA
SSE	80	1.7V	22.5	0.18	28.1M	FC-PGA

SSE = MMX plus Streaming SIMD extensions

Boxed processors include a heatsink with fan.

266MHz through 533MHz are based on 0.25-micron Pentium II core.

533A MHz and higher are based on 0.18-micron Pentium III core.

Table 3.33 Intel Pentium III Processor Variations

Speed (MHz)	Bus Speed (MHz)	Multiplier	Boxed CPU S-spec	OEM CPU S-spec	Stepping	CPUID	L2 Cache
450	100	4.5x	SL3CC	SL364	kB0	0672	512K
450	100	4.5x	SL37C	SL35D	kC0	0673	512K
500	100	5x	SL3CD	SL365	kB0	0672	512K
500	100	5x	SL365	SL365	kB0	0672	512K
500	100	5x	SL37D	SL35E	kC0	0673	512K
500E	100	5x	SL3R2	SL3Q9	cA2	0681	256K
500E	100	5x	SL45R	SL444	cB0	0683	256K
533B	133	4x	SL3E9	SL3BN	kC0	0673	512K
533EB	133	4x	SL3SX	SL3N6	cA2	0681	256K
533EB	133	4x	SL3VA	SL3VF	cA2	0681	256K
533EB	133	4x	SL44W	SL3XG	cB0	0683	256K
533EB	133	4x	SL45S	SL3XS	cB0	0683	256K
550	100	5.5x	SL3FJ	SL3F7	kC0	0673	512K
550E	100	5.5x	SL3R3	SL3QA	cA2	0681	256K
550E	100	5.5x	SL3V5	SL3N7	cA2	0681	256K
550E	100	5.5x	SL44X	SL3XH	cB0	0683	256K
550E	100	5.5x	SL45T	N/A	cB0	0683	256K
600	100	6x	SL3JT	SL3JM	kC0	0673	512K
600E	100	6x	SL3NA	SL3H6	cA2	0681	256K
600E	100	6x	SL3NL	SL3VH	cA2	0681	256K
600E	100	6x	SL44Y	SL43E	cB0	0683	256K
600E	100	6x	SL45U	SL3XU	cB0	0683	256K
600E	100	6x	n/a	SL4CM	cC0	0686	256K
600E	100	6x	n/a	SL4C7	cC0	0686	256K
600B	133	4.5x	SL3JU	SL3JP	kC0	0673	512K
600EB	133	4.5x	SL3NB	SL3H7	cA2	0681	256K
600EB	133	4.5x	SL3VB	SL3VG	cA2	0681	256K
600EB	133	4.5x	SL44Z	SL3XJ	cB0	0683	256K
600EB	133	4.5x	SL45V	SL3XT	cB0	0683	256K
600EB	133	4.5x	SL4CL	SL4CL	cC0	0686	256K
600EB	133	4.5x	n/a	SL46C	cC0	0686	256K
650	100	6.5x	SL3NR	SL3KV	cA2	0681	256K
650	100	6.5x	SL3NM	SL3VJ	cA20	681	256K
650	100	6.5x	SL452	SL3XK	cB0	0683	256K
650	100	6.5x	SL45W	SL3XV	cB0	0683	256K
650	100	6.5x	n/a	SL4CK	cC0	0686	256K
650	100	6.5x	n/a	SL4C5	cC0	0686	256K
667	133	5x	SL3ND	SL3KW	cA2	0681	256K
667	133	5x	SL3T2	SL3VK	cA2	0681	256K

L2 Speed	Max. Temp. (C)	Voltage	Max. Power (W)	Process (Microns)	Transistors	Package
225	90	2.00	25.3	0.25	9.5M	SECC2
225	90	2.00	25.3	0.25	9.5M	SECC2
250	90	2.00	28.0	0.25	9.5M	SECC2
250	90	2.00	28.0	0.25	9.5M	SECC2
250	90	2.00	28.0	0.25	9.5M	SECC2
500	85	1.60	13.2	0.18	28.1M	FC-PGA
500	85	1.60	13.2	0.18	28.1M	FC-PGA
267	90	2.05	29.7	0.25	9.5M	SECC2
533	85	1.65	14.0	0.18	28.1M	SECC2
533	85	1.65	14.0	0.18	28.1M	FC-PGA
533	85	1.65	14.0	0.18	28.1M	SECC2
533	85	1.65	14.0	0.18	28.1M	FC-PGA
275	80	2.00	30.8	0.25	9.5M	SECC2
550	85	1.60	14.5	0.18	28.1M	FC-PGA
550	85	1.60	14.5	0.18	28.1M	SECC2
550	85	1.60	14.5	0.18	28.1M	SECC2
550	85	1.60	14.5	0.18	28.1M	FC-PGA
300	85	2.00	34.5	0.25	9.5M	SECC2
600	82	1.65	15.8	0.18	28.1M	SECC2
600	82	1.65	15.8	0.18	28.1M	FC-PGA
600	82	1.65	15.8	0.18	28.1M	SECC2
600	82	1.65	15.8	0.18	28.1M	FC-PGA
600	82	1.7	15.8	0.18	28.1M	FC-PGA
600	82	1.7	15.8	0.18	28.1M	SECC2
300	85	2.05	34.5	0.25	9.5M	SECC2
600	82	1.65	15.8	0.18	28.1M	SECC2
600	82	1.65	15.8	0.18	28.1M	FC-PGA
600	82	1.65	15.8	0.18	28.1M	SECC2
600	82	1.65	15.8	0.18	28.1M	FC-PGA
600	82	1.7	15.8	0.18	28.1M	FC-PGA
600	82	1.7	15.8	0.18	28.1M	SECC2
650	82	1.65	17.0	0.18	28.1M	SECC2
650	82	1.65	17.0	0.18	28.1M	FC-PGA
650	82	1.65	17.0	0.18	28.1M	SECC2
650	82	1.65	17.0	0.18	28.1M	FC-PGA
650	82	1.7	17.0	0.18	28.1M	FC-PGA
650	82	1.7	17.0	0.18	28.1M	SECC2
667	82	1.65	17.5	0.18	28.1M	SECC2
667	82	1.65	17.5	0.18	28.1M	FC-PGA

Table 3.33 Continued

Speed (MHz)	Bus Speed (MHz)	Multiplier	Boxed CPU S-spec	OEM CPU S-spec	Stepping	CPUID	L2 Cache
667	133	5x	SL453	SL3XL	cB0	0683	256K
667	133	5x	SL45X	SL3XW	cB0	0683	256K
667	133	5x	n/a	SL4CJ	cC0	0686	256K
667	133	5x	n/a	SL4C4	cC0	0686	256K
700	100	7x	SL3SY	SL3S9	cA2	0681	256K
700	100	7x	SL3T3	SL3VL	cA2	0681	256K
700	100	7x	SL454	SL453	cB0	0683	256K
700	100	7x	SL45Y	SL3XX	cB0	0683	256K
700	100	7x	SL4M7	SL4CH	cC0	0686	256K
700	100	7x	n/a	SL4C3	cC0	0686	256K
733	133	5.5x	SL3SZ	SL3SB	cA2	0681	256K
733	133	5.5x	SL3T4	SL3VM	cA2	0681	256K
733	133	5.5x	SL455	SL3XN	cB0	0683	256K
733	133	5.5x	SL45Z	SL3XY	cB0	0683	256K
733	133	5.5x	SL4M8	SL4CG	cC0	0686	256K
733	133	5.5x	SL4KD	SL4C2	cC0	0686	256K
733	133	5.5x	SL4FQ	SL4CX	cC0	0686	256K
750	100	7.5x	SL3V6	SL3WC	cA2	0681	256K
750	100	7.5x	SL3VC	SL3VN	cA2	0681	256K
750	100	7.5x	SL456	SL3XP	cB0	0683	256K
750	100	7.5x	SL462	SL3XZ	cB0	0683	256K
750	100	7.5x	SL4M9	SL4CF	cC0	0686	256K
750	100	7.5x	SL4KE	SL4BZ	cC0	0686	256K
800	100	8x	SL457	SL3XR	cB0	0683	256K
800	100	8x	SL463	SL3Y3	cB0	0683	256K
800	100	8x	SL4MA	SL4CE	cC0	0686	256K
800	100	8x	SL4KF	SL4BY	cC0	0686	256K
800EB	133	6x	SL458	SL3XQ	cB0	0683	256K
800EB	133	6x	SL464	SL3Y2	cB0	0683	256K
800EB	133	6x	SL4MB	SL4CD	cC0	0686	256K
800EB	133	6x	SL4G7	SL4XQ	cC0	0686	256K
800EB	133	6x	SL4KG	SL4BX	cC0	0686	256K
850	100	8.5x	SL47M	SL43F	cB0	0683	256K
850	100	8.5x	SL49G	SL43H	cB0	0683	256K
850	100	8.5x	SL4MC	SL4CC	cC0	0686	256K
850	100	8.5x	SL4KH	SL4BW	cC0	0686	256K
866	133	6.5x	SL47N	SL43G	cB0	0683	256K
866	133	6.5x	SL49H	SL43J	cB0	0683	256K

L2 Speed	Max. Temp. (C)	Voltage	Max. Power (W)	Process (Microns)	Transistors	Package
667	82	1.65	17.5	0.18	28.1M	SECC2
667	82	1.65	17.5	0.18	28.1M	FC-PGA
667	82	1.7	17.5	0.18	28.1M	FC-PGA
667	82	1.7	17.5	0.18	28.1M	SECC2
700	80	1.65	18.3	0.18	28.1M	SECC2
700	80	1.65	18.3	0.18	28.1M	FC-PGA
700	80	1.65	18.3	0.18	28.1M	SECC2
700	80	1.65	18.3	0.18	28.1M	FC-PGA
700	80	1.7	18.3	0.18	28.1M	FC-PGA
700	80	1.7	18.3	0.18	28.1M	SECC2
733	80	1.65	19.1	0.18	28.1M	SECC2
733	80	1.65	19.1	0.18	28.1M	FC-PGA
733	80	1.65	19.1	0.18	28.1M	SECC2
733	80	1.65	19.1	0.18	28.1M	FC-PGA
733	80	1.7	19.1	0.18	28.1M	FC-PGA
733	80	1.7	19.1	0.18	28.1M	SECC2
733	80	1.7	19.1	0.18	28.1M	SECC2
750	80	1.65	19.5	0.18	28.1M	SECC2
750	80	1.65	19.5	0.18	28.1M	FC-PGA
750	80	1.65	19.5	0.18	28.1M	SECC2
750	80	1.65	19.5	0.18	28.1M	FC-PGA
750	80	1.7	19.5	0.18	28.1M	FC-PGA
750	80	1.7	19.5	0.18	28.1M	SECC2
800	80	1.65	20.8	0.18	28.1M	SECC2
800	80	1.65	20.8	0.18	28.1M	FC-PGA
800	80	1.7	20.8	0.18	28.1M	FC-PGA
800	80	1.7	20.8	0.18	28.1M	SECC2
800	80	1.65	20.8	0.18	28.1M	SECC2
800	80	1.65	20.8	0.18	28.1M	FC-PGA
800	80	1.7	20.8	0.18	28.1M	FC-PGA
800	80	1.7	20.8	0.18	28.1M	SECC2
800	80	1.7	20.8	0.18	28.1M	SECC2
850	80	1.65	22.5	0.18	28.1M	SECC2
850	80	1.65	22.5	0.18	28.1M	FC-PGA
850	80	1.7	22.5	0.18	28.1M	FC-PGA
850	80	1.7	22.5	0.18	28.1M	SECC2
866	80	1.65	22.9	0.18	28.1M	SECC2
866	80	1.65	22.9	0.18	28.1M	FC-PGA

Table 3.33 Continued

Speed (MHz)	Bus Speed (MHz)	Multiplier	Boxed CPU S-spec	OEM CPU S-spec	Stepping	CPUID	L2 Cache
866	133	6.5x	SL4MD	SL4CB	cC0	0686	256K
866	133	6.5x	SL4KJ	SL4BV	cC0	0686	256K
866	133	6.5x	SL5B5	SL5QE	cD0	068A	256K
900	100	9x	n/a	SL4SD	cC0	0686	256K
933	133	7x	SL47Q	SL448	cB0	0683	256K
933	133	7x	SL49J	SL44J	cB0	0683	256K
933	133	7x	SL4ME	SL4C9	cC0	0686	256K
933	133	7x	SL4KK	SL4BT	cC0	0686	256K
933	133	7x	n/a	SL5QF	cD0	068A	256K
1000B	133	7.5x	SL4FP	SL48S	cB0	0683	256K
1000B	133	7.5x	SL4MF	SL4C8	cB0	0683	256K
1000	100	10x	SL4KL	SL4BR	cC0	0686	256K
1000B	133	7.5x	n/a	SL4BS	cC0	0686	256K
1000B	133	7.5x	n/a	SL5QK	cD0	068A	256K
1000B	133	7.5x	n/a	SL5QJ	cD0	068A	256K
1000B	133	7.5x	n/a	SL5B2	cD0	068A	256K
1000B	133	7.5x	n/a	SL4YV	cD0	068A	256K

SECC = Single edge contact cartridge
SECC2 = Single edge contact cartridge revision 2

Pentium III processors are all clock multiplier locked. This is a means to prevent processor fraud and overclocking by making the processor work only at a given clock multiplier. Unfortunately, this feature can be bypassed by making modifications to the processor under the cartridge cover, and unscrupulous individuals have been selling lower-speed processors re-marked as higher speeds. It pays to purchase your systems or processors from direct Intel distributors or high-end dealers who do not engage in these practices.

Pentium II/III Xeon

The Pentium II and III processors are available in special high-end versions called Xeon processors. Originally introduced in June 1998 in Pentium II versions, later Pentium III versions were introduced in March 1999. These differ from the standard Pentium II and III in three ways: packaging, cache size, and cache speed.

Xeon processors use a larger SEC cartridge than the standard PII/III processors, mainly to house a larger internal board with more cache memory. The Xeon processor is shown in Figure 3.53; the Xeon's SEC is shown in Figure 3.54.

Besides the larger package, the Xeon processors also include more L2 cache. They are available in three variations, with 512KB, 1MB, or 2MB of L2 cache. This cache is costly; the list price of the 2MB version is more than $2,000!

L2 Speed	Max. Temp. (C)	Voltage	Max. Power (W)	Process (Microns)	Transistors	Package
866	80	1.7	22.5	0.18	28.1M	FC-PGA
866	80	1.7	22.5	0.18	28.1M	SECC2
866	80	1.75	26.1	0.18	28.1M	FC-PGA
900	75	1.7	23.2	0.18	28.1M	FC-PGA
933	75	1.7	25.5	0.18	28.1M	SECC2
933	75	1.7	24.5	0.18	28.1M	FC-PGA
933	75	1.7	24.5	0.18	28.1M	FC-PGA
933	75	1.7	25.5	0.18	28.1M	SECC2
933	77	1.75	27.3	0.18	28.1M	FC-PGA
1000	70	1.7	26.1	0.18	28.1M	SECC2
1000	70	1.7	26.1	0.18	28.1M	FC-PGA
1000	70	1.7	26.1	0.18	28.1M	SECC2
1000	70	1.7	26.1	0.18	28.1M	SECC2
1000	64	1.75	29.0	0.18	28.1M	FC-PGA
1000	64	1.75	29.0	0.18	28.1M	FC-PGA
1000	75	1.75	29.0	0.18	28.1M	FC-PGA
1000	75	1.75	29.0	0.18	28.1M	FC-PGA

CPUID = The internal ID returned by the CPUID instruction

ECC = Error correcting code

Figure 3.53   Pentium III Xeon processor. *Photograph used by permission of Intel Corporation.*

Figure 3.54 Xeon processor internal components.

Even more significant than the size of the cache is its speed. All the cache in the Xeon processors run at the full-core speed. This is difficult to do considering that the cache chips are separate chips on the board; up until recently they were not integrated into the processor die. The original Pentium II Xeon processors had 7.5 million transistors in the main processor die, whereas the later Pentium III Xeon came with 9.5 million. When the Pentium III versions with on-die cache were released, the transistor count went up to 28.1 million transistors in the 256KB cache version, 84 million transistors in the 1MB cache version, and a whopping 140 million transistors in the latest 2MB cache version, setting an industry record. The high transistor counts are due to the on-die L2 cache, which is very transistor intensive. The L2 cache in all Xeon processors has a full 64GB RAM address range and supports ECC.

Note that the Slot 2 Xeon processors do not replace the Slot 1 processors. Xeon processors for Slot 2 are targeted at the mid-range to high-end server and workstation market segments, offering larger, full-speed L2 caches and four-way multiprocessor support. Pentium III processors for Slot 1 will continue to be the processor used in the business and home desktop market segments, and for entry-level servers and workstations (single- and dual-processor systems).

Other Sixth-Generation Processors

Besides Intel, many other manufacturers are now making P6-type processors, but often with a difference. Most of them are designed to interface with P5 class motherboards and for the lower-end markets. AMD has recently offered up the Athlon and Duron processors, which are true sixth-generation designs using their own proprietary connections to the system.

This section examines the various sixth-generation processors from manufacturers other than Intel.

NexGen Nx586

NexGen was founded by Thampy Thomas, who hired some of the people formerly involved with the 486 and Pentium processors at Intel. At NexGen, developers created the Nx586, a processor that was functionally the same as the Pentium but not pin compatible. As such, it was always supplied with a motherboard; in fact, it was usually soldered in. NexGen did not manufacture the chips or the motherboards they came in; for that it hired IBM Microelectronics. Later NexGen was bought by AMD, right before it was ready to introduce the Nx686—a greatly improved design done by Greg Favor and a true competitor for the Pentium. AMD took the Nx686 design and combined it with a Pentium electrical interface to create a drop-in Pentium-compatible chip called the K6, which actually outperformed the original from Intel.

The Nx586 had all the standard fifth-generation processor features, such as superscalar execution with two internal pipelines and a high-performance integral L1 cache with separate code and data caches. One advantage is that the Nx586 includes separate 16KB instruction and 16KB data caches compared to 8KB each for the Pentium. These caches keep key instruction and data close to the processing engines to increase overall system performance.

The Nx586 also includes branch prediction capabilities, which are one of the hallmarks of a sixth-generation processor. Branch prediction means the processor has internal functions to predict program flow to optimize the instruction execution.

The Nx586 processor also featured a RISC core. A translation unit dynamically translates x86 instructions into RISC86 instructions. These RISC86 instructions were designed specifically with direct support for the x86 architecture while obeying RISC performance principles. They are thus simpler and easier to execute than the complex x86 instructions. This type of capability is another feature normally found only in P6 class processors.

The Nx586 was discontinued after the merger with AMD, which then took the design for the successor Nx686 and released it as the AMD-K6.

AMD-K6 Series

The AMD-K6 processor is a high-performance sixth-generation processor that is physically installable in a P5 (Pentium) motherboard. It essentially was designed for AMD by NexGen and was first known as the Nx686. The NexGen version never appeared because it was purchased by AMD before the chip was due to be released. The AMD-K6 delivers performance levels somewhere between the Pentium and Pentium II processor as a result of its unique hybrid design. Because it is designed to install in Socket 7, which is a fifth-generation processor socket and motherboard design, it can't quite perform as a true sixth-generation chip because the Socket 7 architecture severely limits cache and memory performance. However, with this processor, AMD gave Intel a lot of competition in the low- to mid-range market, where the Pentium was still popular.

The K6 processor contains an industry-standard, high-performance implementation of the new multimedia instruction set, enabling a high level of multimedia performance. The K6-2 introduced an upgrade to MMX that AMD calls 3DNow, which adds even more graphics and sound instructions. AMD designed the K6 processor to fit the low-cost, high-volume Socket 7 infrastructure. This enables PC manufacturers and resellers to speed time to market and deliver systems with an easy upgrade path for the future. AMD's state-of-the-art manufacturing facility in Austin, Texas (Fab 25) makes the AMD-K6 series processors. Initially, it used AMD's 0.35-micron, five-metal layer process technology; newer variations use the 0.25-micron processor to increase production quantities because of reduced die size, as well as to decrease power consumption.

AMD-K6 processor technical features include

- Sixth-generation internal design, fifth-generation external interface
- Internal RISC core, translates x86 to RISC instructions
- Superscalar parallel execution units (seven)

- Dynamic execution

- Branch prediction

- Speculative execution

- Large 64KB L1 cache (32KB instruction cache plus 32KB write-back dual-ported data cache)

- Built-in floating-point unit

- Industry-standard MMX instruction support

- System Management Mode

- Ceramic pin grid array (CPGA) Socket 7 design

- Manufactured using a 0.35-micron and a 0.25-micron, five-layer design

The K6-2 adds

- Higher clock speeds

- Higher bus speeds of up to 100MHz (Super7 motherboards)

- 3DNow; 21 new graphics and sound processing instructions

The K6-3 adds

- 256KB of on-die full-core speed L2 cache

The addition of the full-speed L2 cache in the K6-3 is significant. It brings the K6 series to a level where it can fully compete with the Intel Celeron and Pentium II processors. The 3DNow capability added in the K6-2/3 is also being exploited by newer graphics programs, making these processors ideal for lower-cost gaming systems.

The AMD-K6 processor architecture is fully x86 binary code compatible, which means it runs all Intel software, including MMX instructions. To make up for the lower L2 cache performance of the Socket 7 design, AMD has beefed up the internal L1 cache to 64KB total, twice the size of the Pentium II or III. This, plus the dynamic execution capability, enables the K6 to outperform the Pentium and come close to the Pentium II in performance for a given clock rate. The K6-3 is even better with the addition of full-core speed L2 cache.

Both the AMD-K5 and AMD-K6 processors are Socket 7 bus compatible. However, certain modifications might be necessary for proper voltage setting and BIOS revisions. To ensure reliable operation of the AMD-K6 processor, the motherboard must meet specific voltage requirements.

The AMD processors have specific voltage requirements. Most older split-voltage motherboards default to 2.8v Core/3.3v I/O, which is below specification for the AMD-K6 and could cause erratic operation. To work properly, the motherboard must have Socket 7 with a dual-plane voltage regulator supplying 2.9v or 3.2v (233MHz) to the CPU core voltage (Vcc2) and 3.3v for the I/O (Vcc3). The voltage regulator must be capable of supplying up to 7.5A (9.5A for the 233MHz) to the processor. When used with a 200MHz or slower processor, the voltage regulator must maintain the core voltage within 145 mV of nominal (2.9v+/-145 mV). When used with a 233MHz processor, the voltage regulator must maintain the core voltage within 100 mV of nominal (3.2v+/-100 mV).

If the motherboard has a poorly designed voltage regulator that cannot maintain this performance, unreliable operation can result. If the CPU voltage exceeds the absolute maximum voltage range, the processor can be permanently damaged. Also note that the K6 can run hot. Make sure your heatsink is securely fitted to the processor and that the thermally conductive grease or pad is properly applied.

The motherboard must have an AMD-K6 processor-ready BIOS with support for the K6 built in. Award has that support in its March 1, 1997 or later BIOS; AMI had K6 support in any of its BIOS with CPU Module 3.31 or later; and Phoenix supports the K6 in version 4.0, release 6.0, or release 5.1 with build dates of 4/7/97 or later.

Because these specifications can be fairly complicated, AMD keeps a list of motherboards that have been verified to work with the AMD-K6 processor on its Web site. All the motherboards on that list have been tested to work properly with the AMD-K6. So, unless these requirements can be verified elsewhere, it is recommended that you use only a motherboard from that list with the AMD-K6 processor.

The multiplier, bus speed, and voltage settings for the K6 are shown in Table 3.34. You can identify which AMD-K6 you have by looking at the markings on this chip, as shown in Figure 3.55.

Table 3.34   AMD-K6 Processor Speeds and Voltages

Processor	Core Speed	Clock Multiplier	Bus Speed	Core Voltage	I/O Voltage
K6-3	450MHz	4.5x	100MHz	2.4v	3.3v
K6-3	400MHz	4x	100MHz	2.4v	3.3v
K6-2	475MHz	5x	95MHz	2.4v	3.3v
K6-2	450MHz	4.5x	100MHz	2.4v	3.3v
K6-2	400MHz	4x	100MHz	2.2v	3.3v
K6-2	380MHz	4x	95MHz	2.2v	3.3v
K6-2	366MHz	5.5x	66MHz	2.2v	3.3v
K6-2	350MHz	3.5x	100MHz	2.2v	3.3v
K6-2	333MHz	3.5x	95MHz	2.2v	3.3v
K6-2	333MHz	5.0x	66MHz	2.2v	3.3v
K6-2	300MHz	3x	100MHz	2.2v	3.3v
K6-2	300MHz	4.5x	66MHz	2.2v	3.3v
K6-2	266MHz	4x	66MHz	2.2v	3.3v
K6	300MHz	4.5x	66MHz	2.2v	3.45v
K6	266MHz	4x	66MHz	2.2v	3.3v
K6	233MHz	3.5x	66MHz	3.2v	3.3v
K6	200MHz	3x	66MHz	2.9v	3.3v
K6	166MHz	2.5x	66MHz	2.9v	3.3v

Figure 3.55   AMD-K6 processor markings.

Older motherboards achieve the 3.5x setting by setting jumpers for 1.5x. The 1.5x setting for older motherboards equates to a 3.5x setting for the AMD-K6 and newer Intel parts. To get the 4x and higher setting requires a motherboard that controls three BF pins, including BF2. Older motherboards can control only two BF pins. The settings for the multipliers are shown in Table 3.35.

Table 3.35   AMD-K6 Multiplier Settings

Multiplier Setting	BF0	BF1	BF2
2.5x	Low	Low	High
3x	High	Low	High
3.5x	High	High	High
4x	Low	High	Low
4.5x	Low	Low	Low
5x	High	Low	Low
5.5x	High	High	Low

These settings usually are controlled by jumpers on the motherboard. Consult your motherboard documentation to see where they are and how to set them for the proper multiplier and bus speed settings.

Unlike Cyrix and some of the other Intel competitors, AMD is a manufacturer and a designer. Therefore, it designs and builds its chips in its own fabs. Similar to Intel, AMD has migrated to 0.25-micron process technology and beyond. The original K6 has 8.8 million transistors and is built on a 0.35-micron, five-layer process. The die is 12.7mm on each side, or about 162 square mm. The K6-3 uses a 0.25-micron process and now incorporates 21.3 million transistors on a die only 10.9mm on each side, or about 118 square mm. Further process improvements will enable even more transistors, smaller die, higher yields, and greater numbers of processors. AMD has recently won contracts with several high-end system suppliers, which gives it an edge on the other Intel competitors.

Because of its performance and compatibility with the Socket 7 interface, the K6 series is often looked at as an excellent processor upgrade for motherboards currently using older Pentium or Pentium MMX processors. Although they do work in Socket 7, the AMD-K6 processors have different voltage and bus speed requirements from the Intel processors. Before attempting any upgrades, you should check the board documentation or contact the manufacturer to see whether your board meets the necessary requirements. In some cases, a BIOS upgrade also is necessary.

AMD Athlon

The Athlon is AMD's successor to the K6 series (refer to Figure 3.55). The Athlon is a whole new chip from the ground up and does not interface via the Socket 7 or Super7 sockets like its previous chips. In the initial Athlon versions, AMD used a cartridge design, called Slot A, almost exactly like that of the Intel Pentium II and III. This was due to the fact that the original Athlons used 512KB of external L2 cache, which was mounted on the processor cartridge board. The external cache ran at one-half core, two-fifths core, or one-third core depending on which speed processor you had. In June 2000, AMD introduced a revised version of the Athlon (codenamed Thunderbird) that incorporates 256KB of L2 cache directly on the processor die. This on-die cache runs at full-core speed and eliminates a bottleneck in the original Athlon systems. Along with the change to on-die L2 cache, the Athlon was also introduced in a PGA or chip Socket A version, which is replacing the Slot A cartridge version.

Although the Slot A cartridge looks a lot like the Intel Slot 1, and the Socket A looks like Intel's Socket 370, the pinouts are completely different, and the AMD chips do not work in the same motherboards as the Intel chips. This was by design because AMD was looking for ways to improve its chip architecture and distance itself from Intel. Special blocked pins in either socket or slot design prevent accidentally installing the chip in the wrong orientation or wrong slot. Figure 3.56 shows the Athlon in the Slot A cartridge. Figure 3.57 shows the Athlon in the PGA package (Socket A).

Figure 3.56 AMD Athlon processor for Slot A (cartridge form factor).

Figure 3.57 AMD Athlon processor for Socket A (PGA form factor).

The Athlon is available in speeds from 550MHz up to 1GHz and beyond and uses a 200MHz or 266MHz processor (front-side) bus called the EV6 to connect to the motherboard North Bridge chip as well as other processors. Licensed from Digital Equipment, the EV6 bus is the same as that used for the Alpha 21264 processor, now owned by Compaq. The EV6 bus uses a clock speed of 100MHz or 133MHz but double-clocks the data, transferring data twice per cycle, for a cycling speed of 200MHz or 266MHz. Because the bus is 8 bytes (64 bits) wide, this results in a throughput of 8 bytes times

200MHz/266MHz, which amounts to 1.6GB/sec or 2.1GB/sec. This bus is ideal for supporting PC1600 or PC2100 DDR memory, which also runs at those speeds. The AMD bus design eliminates a potential bottleneck between the chipset and processor and enables more efficient transfers compared to other processors. The use of the EV6 bus is one of the primary reasons the Athlon and Duron chips perform so well.

The Athlon has a very large 128KB of L1 cache on the processor die and one-half, two-fifths, or one-third core speed 512KB L2 cache in the cartridge in the older versions, or 256KB of full-core speed cache in the later ones. All PGA socket A versions have the full-speed cache. The Athlon also has support for MMX and the Enhanced 3DNow instructions, which are 45 new instructions designed to support graphics and sound processing. 3DNow is very similar to Intel's SSE in design and intent, but the

Table 3.36   AMD Athlon Slot A Cartridge Processor Information

Part Number	Model	Speed (MHz)	Bus Speed (MHz)	Multiplier	L2 Cache
AMD-K7500MTR51B	Model 1	500	100x2	5x	512KB
AMD-K7550MTR51B	Model 1	550	100x2	5.5x	512KB
AMD-K7600MTR51B	Model 1	600	100x2	6x	512KB
AMD-K7650MTR51B	Model 1	650	100x2	6.5x	512KB
AMD-K7700MTR51B	Model 1	700	100x2	7x	512KB
AMD-K7550MTR51B	Model 2	550	100x2	5.5x	512KB
AMD-K7600MTR51B	Model 2	600	100x2	6x	512KB
AMD-K7650MTR51B	Model 2	650	100x2	6.5x	512KB
AMD-K7700MTR51B	Model 2	700	100x2	7x	512KB
AMD-K7750MTR52B	Model 2	750	100x2	7.5x	512KB
AMD-K7800MPR52B	Model 2	800	100x2	8x	512KB
AMD-K7850MPR52B	Model 2	850	100x2	8.5x	512KB
AMD-K7900MNR53B	Model 2	900	100x2	9x	512KB
AMD-K7950MNR53B	Model 2	950	100x2	9.5x	512KB
AMD-K7100MNR53B	Model 2	1000	100x2	10x	512KB
AMD-A0650MPR24B	Model 4	650	100x2	6.5x	256KB
AMD-A0700MPR24B	Model 4	700	100x2	7x	256KB
AMD-A0750MPR24B	Model 4	750	100x2	7.5x	256KB
AMD-A0800MPR24B	Model 4	800	100x2	8x	256KB
AMD-A0850MPR24B	Model 4	850	100x2	8.5x	256KB
AMD-A0900MMR24B	Model 4	900	100x2	9x	256KB
AMD-A0950MMR24B	Model 4	950	100x2	9.5x	256KB
AMD-A1000MMR24B	Model 4	1000	100x2	10x	256KB

specific instructions are different and require software support. Fortunately, most companies producing graphics software have decided to support the 3DNow instructions along with the Intel SSE instructions, with only a few exceptions.

The initial production of the Athlon used 0.25-micron technology, with newer and faster versions being made on a 0.18-micron process. The latest versions are even built using copper metal technology, a first in the PC processor business. Eventually all other processors will follow because copper connects allow for lower power consumption and faster operation.

Table 3.36 shows detailed information on the Slot A version of the Athlon processor.

Table 3.37 shows information on the PGA or Socket A version of the AMD Athlon processor.

L2 Speed (MHz)	Voltage	Max. Current (A)	Max. Power (W)	Process (Microns)	Transistors	Introduced
250	1.60V	25A	42W	0.25	22M	Jun. 1999
275	1.60V	30A	46W	0.25	22M	Jun. 1999
300	1.60V	33A	50W	0.25	22M	Jun. 1999
325	1.60V	36A	54W	0.25	22M	Aug. 1999
350	1.60V	33A	50W	0.25	22M	Oct. 1999
275	1.60V	20A	31W	0.18	22M	Nov. 1999
300	1.60V	21A	34W	0.18	22M	Nov. 1999
325	1.60V	22A	36W	0.18	22M	Nov. 1999
350	1.60V	24A	39W	0.18	22M	Nov. 1999
300	1.60V	25A	40W	0.18	22M	Nov. 1999
320	1.70V	29A	48W	0.18	22M	Jan. 2000
340	1.70V	30A	50W	0.18	22M	Feb. 2000
300	1.80V	34A	60W	0.18	22M	Mar. 2000
317	1.80V	35A	62W	0.18	22M	Mar. 2000
333	1.80V	37A	65W	0.18	22M	Mar. 2000
650	1.70V	23.8A	36.1W	0.18	37M	Jun. 2000
700	1.70V	25.2A	38.3W	0.18	37M	Jun. 2000
750	1.70V	26.6A	40.4W	0.18	37M	Jun. 2000
800	1.70V	28.0A	42.6W	0.18	37M	Jun. 2000
850	1.70V	29.4A	44.8W	0.18	37M	Jun. 2000
900	1.75V	31.7A	49.7W	0.18	37M	Jun. 2000
950	1.75V	33.2A	52.0W	0.18	37M	Jun. 2000
1000	1.75V	34.6A	54.3W	0.18	37M	Jun. 2000

Table 3.37 AMD Athlon PGA Processor Information

Speed (MHz)	Bus Speed (MHz)	Multiplier	L2 Cache	L2 Speed (MHz)
650	200	3.25x	256KB	650
700	200	3.5x	256KB	700
750	200	3.25x	256KB	750
800	200	4x	256KB	800
850	200	4.25x	256KB	850
900	200	4.5x	256KB	900
950	200	4.75x	256KB	950
1000	200	5x	256KB	1000
1000	266	3.75x	256KB	1000
1100	200	5.5x	256KB	1100
1133	266	4.25x	256KB	1133
1200	200	6x	256KB	1200
1200	266	4.5x	256KB	1200
1300	200	6.5x	256KB	1300
1333	266	5x	256KB	1333

AMD is taking on Intel full force in the high-end market with the Athlon. It beat Intel to the 1GHz mark by introducing its 1GHz Athlon two days before Intel introduced the 1GHz Pentium III, and in most benchmarks the AMD Athlon compares as equal if not superior to the Intel Pentium III.

AMD Duron

The AMD Duron processor (codenamed Spitfire) was announced in June 2000 and is a derivative of the AMD Athlon processor in the same fashion as the Celeron is a derivative of the Pentium II and III (see Figure 3.58). Basically, the Duron is an Athlon with less L2 cache; all other capabilities are essentially the same. It is designed to be a lower-cost version with less cache but only slightly less performance. In keeping with the low-cost theme, Duron contains 64KB on-die L2 cache and is designed for Socket A, a socket version of the Athlon Slot A. With the high-value design the Duron processor is expected to compete in the sub $600 PC market against the Celeron, just as the Athlon is designed to compete in the higher-end Pentium III market.

Because the Duron processor is derived from the Athlon core, it includes the Athlon 200MHz front-side system bus (interface to the chipset) as well as enhanced 3DNow instructions.

Table 3.38 shows information on the PGA or Socket A version of the AMD Athlon processor.

Voltage	Max. Current (A)	Max. Power (W)	Process (Microns)	Transistors
1.75V	22A	38.5W	0.18	37M
1.75V	23A	40.3W	0.18	37M
1.75V	25A	43.8W	0.18	37M
1.75V	26A	45.5W	0.18	37M
1.75V	27A	47.3W	0.18	37M
1.75V	29A	50.8W	0.18	37M
1.75V	30A	52.5W	0.18	37M
1.75V	31A	54.3W	0.18	37M
1.75V	31A	54.3W	0.18	37M
1.75V	34A	59.5W	0.18	37M
1.75V	36A	63.0W	0.18	37M
1.75V	38A	66.5W	0.18	37M
1.75V	38A	66.5W	0.18	37M
1.75V	39A	68.3W	0.18	37M
1.75V	40A	70.0W	0.18	37M

Figure 3.58   AMD Duron processor.

Table 3.38   AMD Duron Processor Information

Speed (MHz)	Bus Speed (MHz)	Multiplier	L2 Cache	L2 Speed (MHz)
550	200	2.75X	64KB	550
600	200	3x	64KB	600
650	200	3.25x	64KB	650
700	200	3.5x	64KB	700
750	200	3.75x	64KB	750
800	200	4x	64KB	800
850	200	4.25x	64KB	850
900	200	4.5x	64KB	900

Cyrix/IBM 6x86 (M1) and 6x86MX (MII)

The Cyrix 6x86 processor family consists of the now-discontinued 6x86 and the newer 6x86MX processors. They are similar to the AMD-K5 and K6 in that they offer sixth-generation internal designs in a fifth-generation P5 Pentium-compatible Socket 7 exterior.

The Cyrix 6x86 and 6x86MX (renamed MII) processors incorporate two optimized superpipelined integer units and an on-chip floating-point unit. These processors include the dynamic execution capability that is the hallmark of a sixth-generation CPU design. This includes branch prediction and speculative execution.

The 6x86MX/MII processor is compatible with MMX technology to run MMX games and multimedia software. With its enhanced memory-management unit, a 64KB internal cache, and other advanced architectural features, the 6x86MX processor achieves higher performance and offers better value than competitive processors.

Features and benefits of the 6x86 processors include

- *Superscalar architecture.* Two pipelines to execute multiple instructions in parallel
- *Branch prediction.* Predicts with high accuracy the next instructions needed
- *Speculative execution.* Enables the pipelines to continuously execute instructions following a branch without stalling the pipelines
- *Out-of-order completion.* Lets the faster instruction exit the pipeline out of order, saving processing time without disrupting program flow

The 6x86 incorporates two caches: a 16KB dual-ported unified cache and a 256-byte instruction line cache. The unified cache is supplemented with a small quarter-K–size high-speed, fully associative instruction line cache. The improved 6x86MX design quadruples the internal cache size to 64KB, which significantly improves performance.

The 6x86MX also includes the 57 MMX instructions that speed up the processing of certain computing-intensive loops found in multimedia and communication applications.

All 6x86 processors feature support for SMM. This provides an interrupt that can be used for system power management or software transparent emulation of I/O peripherals. Additionally, the 6x86 supports a hardware interface that enables the CPU to be placed into a low-power suspend mode.

Voltage	Max. Current (A)	Max. Power (W)	Process (Microns)	Transistors
1.6V	15.8A	25.3W	0.18	25M
1.6V	17.1A	27.4W	0.18	25M
1.6V	18.4A	29.4W	0.18	25M
1.6V	19.6A	31.4W	0.18	25M
1.6V	20.9A	33.4W	0.18	25M
1.6V	22.1A	35.4W	0.18	25M
1.6V	23.4A	37.4W	0.18	25M
1.6V	24.7A	39.5W	0.18	25M

The 6x86 is compatible with x86 software and all popular x86 operating systems, including Windows 95/98/Me, Windows NT/2000, OS/2, DOS, Solaris, and Unix. Additionally, the 6x86 processor has been certified Windows 95 compatible by Microsoft.

As with the AMD-K6, there are some unique motherboard requirements for the 6x86 processors. Cyrix maintains a list of recommended motherboards on its Web site that should be consulted if you are considering installing one of these chips in a board.

When installing or configuring a system with the 6x86 processors, you have to set the correct motherboard bus speed and multiplier settings. The Cyrix processors are numbered based on a P-Rating scale, which is not the same as the true megahertz clock speed of the processor.

See the section "Cyrix P-Ratings," earlier in this chapter, for the correct and true speed settings for the Cyrix 6x86 processors.

Note that because of the use of the P-Rating system, the actual speed of the chip is not the same number at which it is advertised. For example, the 6x86MX-PR300 is not a 300MHz chip; it actually runs at only 263MHz or 266MHz, depending on exactly how the motherboard bus speed and CPU clock multipliers are set. Cyrix says it runs as fast as a 300MHz Pentium, hence the P-Rating. Personally, I wish it would label the chip at the correct speed and then say that it runs faster than a Pentium at the same speed.

To install the 6x86 processors in a motherboard, you also must set the correct voltage. Normally, the markings on top of the chip indicate which voltage setting is appropriate. Various versions of the 6x86 run at 3.52v (use VRE setting), 3.3v (VR setting), or 2.8v (MMX) settings. The MMX versions use the standard split-plane 2.8v core 3.3v I/O settings.

Intel Pentium 4 (Seventh-Generation) Processors

The Pentium 4 was introduced in November 2000 and represents a new generation in processors (see Figure 3.59). If this one had a number instead of a name, it might be called the 786 because it represents a generation beyond the previous 686 class processors. The processor die is shown in Figure 3.60.

Figure 3.59   Pentium 4 processor.

The main technical details for the Pentium 4 include

- Speeds range from 1.3GHz to 1.7GHz and beyond.
- 42 million transistors, 0.18-micron process.
- Software compatible with previous Intel 32-bit processors.
- Processor (front-side) bus runs at 400MHz.
- Arithmetic logic units (ALUs) run at twice the processor core frequency.
- Hyper-pipelined (20-stage) technology.
- Very deep out-of-order instruction execution.
- Enhanced branch prediction.
- 20KB L1 cache (12KB L1 execution trace cache plus 8KB L1 data cache).
- 256KB on-die, full-core speed 128-bit L2 cache with eight-way associativity.
- L2 cache can handle up to 4GB RAM and supports ECC.
- SSE2—144 new SSE2 instructions.
- Enhanced floating-point unit.
- Multiple low-power states.

Figure 3.60 Pentium 4 die (0.18-micron process, 42 million transistors). *Photograph used by permission of Intel Corporation.*

Intel has abandoned roman numerals for a standard Arabic numeral 4 designation. Internally, the Pentium 4 introduces a new architecture Intel calls NetBurst microarchitecture, which includes hyper-pipelined technology, a rapid execution engine, a 400MHz system bus, and an execution trace cache. The hyper-pipelined technology doubles the instruction pipeline depth as compared to the Pentium III, meaning more and smaller steps are required to execute instructions. However, it also enables much higher clock speeds to be more easily attained. The rapid execution engine enables the two integer arithmetic logic units (ALUs) to run at twice the processor core frequency, which means instructions can execute in 1/2 a clock cycle. The 400MHz system bus is a quad-pumped bus running off a 100MHz system clock transferring data four times per clock cycle. The execution trace cache is a high-performance Level 1 cache that stores approximately 12k decoded micro-operations. This removes the instruction decoder from the main execution pipeline, increasing performance.

Of these the high-speed processor bus is most notable. Technically speaking, the processor bus is a 100MHz quad-pumped bus that transfers four times per cycle (4x), for a 400MHz effective rate. Because the bus is 64 bits (8 bytes) wide, this results in a throughput rate of 3,200MB/sec. This matches the speed of the dual-channel RDRAM, which is 1,600MB/sec per channel, or 3,200MB/sec total. The use of dual-channel RDRAM means that RIMMs must be added in matched pairs. Dual banks of PC1600 DDR would also match this bandwidth, and that might be an option in the future as new chipsets arrive.

In the new 20-stage pipelined internal architecture, individual instructions are broken down into many more sub-stages, making this almost like a RISC processor. Unfortunately, this can add to the number of cycles taken to execute instructions if they are not optimized for this processor. Early benchmarks running existing software showed that existing Pentium III or AMD Athlon processors could easily keep pace with or even exceed the Pentium 4 in specific tasks; however, this is changing now that applications are being recompiled to work smoothly with the Pentium 4's deep pipelined architecture.

The Intel Pentium 4 also introduces a new CPU socket, more stringent memory configuration, and even new power supply and case requirements.

The Pentium 4 is the first Intel CPU to use Socket 423, which has 423 pins in a 39x39 SPGA arrangement. Voltage selection is made via an automatic voltage regulator module installed on the motherboard and wired to the socket.

Memory Requirements

Although current Pentium 4–based motherboards use the same Rambus RDRAM RIMM modules introduced for use with some of the chipsets used in Pentium III motherboards, the dual RDRAM channels the Pentium 4 uses require you to install pairs of identical modules (called RIMMs). If your Pentium III motherboard uses SDRAM, you must get entirely new RDRAM memory for any P4 upgrade. If your Pentium III board uses RIMMs, but is not using two identical (same speed/same size) RIMM modules, you must buy additional RIMMs to match the modules you're currently using to make identical pairs to use on your new Pentium 4 motherboard. What if you're using three RIMM modules on your current motherboard? If two are identical, you can use them on your new motherboard; if you want to use the third one, you must buy a matching module because you must populate your Pentium 4 motherboard with either one or two pairs of RIMMs. Both pairs of memory must be the same speed, but need not be the same size.

Whereas most initial Pentium 4 motherboard chipsets supported only RDRAM memory, newer chipsets are either available or becoming available that support more standard memory, such as DDR SDRAM.

Power Supply Issues

The Pentium 4 requires a lot of electrical power, and because of this, most Pentium 4 motherboards use a new design voltage regulator module that is powered from 12v instead of 3.3v or 5v, as with previous designs. By using the 12v power, more 3.3v and 5v power is available to run the rest of the system, and the overall current draw is greatly reduced with the higher voltage as a source. PC power supplies generate a more than adequate supply of 12v power, but the ATX motherboard and power supply design originally allotted only one pin for 12v power (each pin is rated for only 6 amps), so additional 12v lines were necessary to carry this power to the motherboard.

The fix appears in the form of a third power connector, called the ATX12V connector. This new connector is used in addition to the standard 20-pin ATX power supply connector and 6-pin auxiliary (3.3/5v) connector. Fortunately, the power supply itself won't need a redesign; there is more than enough 12v power available from the drive connectors. To utilize this, companies such as PC Power and Cooling sell an inexpensive ($8) adapter that converts a standard Molex-type drive power connector to the ATX12V connector. Normally, a 300-watt (the minimum recommended) or larger power supply has more than adequate levels of 12v power for both the drives and the ATX12V connector.

If your power supply is less than the 300-watt minimum recommended, you need to purchase a replacement; some vendors now sell an off-the-shelf ATX12V ready model or one that uses the adapter mentioned previously.

The various Pentium 4 versions, including thermal and power specifications, are shown in Table 3.39.

Table 3.39   Pentium 4 Processor Information

Speed (GHz)	Boxed CPU S-spec	OEM CPU S-spec	Stepping	CPUID	L2 Cache Size	Thermal Spec (°C)	Nominal Power (W)
1.3	SL4QD	SL4SF	B2	0F07h	256K	69	48.9
1.3	SL5GC	SL5FW	C1	0F0Ah	256K	70	51.6
1.4	SL4SG	SL4SG	B2	0F07h	256K	70	51.8
1.4	SL4SC	SL4SG	B2	0F07h	256K	70	51.8
1.4	SL4X2	SL4WS	C1	0F0Ah	256K	72	54.7

Table 3.39   Continued

Speed (GHz)	Boxed CPU S-spec	OEM CPU S-spec	Stepping	CPUID	L2 Cache Size	Thermal Spec (°C)	Nominal Power (W)
1.5	SL4SH	SL4SH	B2	0F07h	256K	72	54.7
1.5	SL4TY	SL4SH	B2	0F07h	256K	72	54.7
1.5	SL4X3	SL4WT	C1	0F0Ah	256K	73	54.7
1.7	SL57V	SL57W	C1	0F0Ah	256K	70	64.0

Cooling a high wattage unit such as the Pentium 4 requires a large active heatsink. These heavy (sometimes more than 1 lb.) heatsinks can damage a CPU or destroy a motherboard when subjected to vibration or shock, especially during shipping. To prevent this, Intel's specifications for the Pentium 4 add four standoffs to the ATX chassis design flanking the Socket 423 to support the heatsink retention brackets. These standoffs enable the chassis to support the weight of the heatsink instead of depending on the motherboard, as with older designs.

The heatsink retention mechanism consists of two brackets screwed to new chassis standoffs through the motherboard, and then two clips that attach the heatsink to the brackets. The brackets and clips are to be included with the motherboard, and the standoffs with screws are to be included with the chassis. For compatibility between chassis and motherboards, Intel is recommending that all Pentium 4 motherboards use the same location for the CPU: near the right edge of the motherboard. This enables case designers to supply a single modified ATX case design for all Pentium 4 motherboards. Even so, vendors can also use other means to reinforce the CPU location without requiring a direct chassis attachment. For example, Asus' P4T motherboard ships with a metal reinforcing plate to enable off-the-shelf ATX cases to work with the motherboard.

A future version of the Pentium 4 (codenamed Northwood) will be built using a 0.13-micron process and will use a different socket (called Socket 478) from the initial Pentium 4. This would be similar to how Intel changed the original Pentium sockets early in their lifecycles. An upgrade to this newer version will require a new motherboard with Socket 478.

Itanium (Eighth-Generation) Processors

Introduced in May 2001, the Itanium is currently the highest-end processor from Intel, designed mainly for the server market. If Intel was still using numbers to designate its processors, Itanium might be called the 886 because it is the eighth-generation processor in the Intel family, and it represents the most significant processor architecture advancement since the 386.

Itanium is the first processor in Intel's IA-64 (Intel Architecture 64-bit) product family and incorporates innovative performance-enhancing architecture techniques, such as prediction and speculation.

Itanium

Intel's IA-64 product family is designed to expand the capabilities of the Intel architecture to address the high-performance server and workstation market segments.

As with previous new processor introductions, the Itanium is not designed to replace the Pentium 4 or III, at least not at first. It features an all-new design that is initially expensive and is found only in the highest-end systems such as file servers or workstations. Intel is already developing an even more advanced Itanium class processor, due to ship in 2002, which will be significantly faster than Itanium.

The Itanium technical details are as follows:

- Introduced at 733MHz and 800MHz speeds.
- Three levels of integrated cache:
  - 2MB or 4MB unified on-cartridge L3 cache running at full-core speed on an integrated 128-bit L3 cache bus
  - 96KB unified on-die L2 cache running at full-core speed
  - 32KB segmented (16KB instruction/16KB data) L1 cache
- 266MHz, 64-bit wide (plus 8 bits for ECC) CPU front-side bus with 2.1GB/sec bandwidth.
- 25 million transistors, with up to 300 million additional in the L3 cache.
- 16TB (terabytes) physical memory addressing (44-bit address bus).
- Full 32-bit instruction compatibility in hardware.
- EPIC (explicitly parallel instruction computing) technology, which enables up to 20 operations per cycle.
- Two integer and two memory units that can execute four instructions per clock.
- Two FMAC (floating-point multiply accumulate) units with 82-bit operands.
- Each FMAC unit is capable of executing two floating-point operations per clock.
- Two additional MMX units are capable of executing two single-precision FP operations each.
- A total of eight single-precision FP operations can be executed every cycle.
- 128 integer registers, 128 floating-point registers, 8 branch registers, 64 predicate registers.
- 3-inch×5-inch cartridge includes processor and 2MB or 4MB L3 cache.
- Dedicated cartridge power connector improves signal integrity.

Intel and Hewlett-Packard began jointly working on the Itanium processor in 1994. In October 1997, more than three years after they first disclosed their plan to work together on a new microprocessor architecture, Intel and HP officially announced some of the new processor's technical details.

Itanium is the first microprocessor based on the Intel architecture-64 (IA-64) specification. IA-64 is a completely different processor design, which will use Very Long Instruction Words (VLIW), instruction prediction, branch elimination, speculative loading, and other advanced processes for enhancing parallelism from program code. The new chip features elements of both CISC and RISC design.

Itanium incorporates a new architecture Intel calls explicitly parallel instruction computing (EPIC), which enables the processor to execute *parallel instructions*—several instructions at the same time. In the Itanium, three instructions can be encoded in one 128-bit word, so that each instruction has a few more bits than today's 32-bit instructions. The extra bits let the chip address more registers and tells the processor which instructions to execute in parallel. This approach simplifies the design of processors with many parallel-execution units and should let them run at higher clock rates. In other words, besides being capable of executing several instructions in parallel within the chip, the Itanium can be linked to other Itanium chips in a parallel processing environment.

Besides having new features and running a completely new 64-bit instruction set, Itanium features full backward compatibility with the current 32-bit Intel x86 software. In this way, Itanium supports 64-bit instructions while retaining full compatibility with today's 32-bit applications. Full backward compatibility means it will run all existing applications as well as any new 64-bit applications.

To use the IA-64 instructions, programs must be recompiled for the new instruction set. This is similar to what happened in 1985, when Intel introduced the 386, the first 32-bit PC processor. The 386 gave us a platform for an advanced 32-bit operating system that tapped this new power. To ensure immediate acceptance, the 386 and future 32-bit processors still ran 16-bit code. To take advantage of the 32-bit capability first found in the 386, new software would have to be written. Unfortunately, software evolves much more slowly than hardware. It took Microsoft a full 10 years after the 386 debuted to release Windows 95, the first mainstream 32-bit operating system for Intel processors.

That won't happen with the Itanium, which already has support from four operating systems, including Microsoft Windows (XP 64-bit Edition and 64-bit Windows Advanced Server Limited Edition 2002), Linux (from four distributor companies: Red Hat, SuSE, Caldera, and Turbo Linux), and two Unix versions (Hewlett-Packard's HP-UX 11i v 1.5 and IBM's AIX-5L).

Despite the immediate OS support, it will likely take several years before the mainstream software market shifts to 64-bit operating systems and software. The installed base of 32-bit processors is simply too great, and the backward-compatible 32-bit mode of the Itanium will enable it to run 32-bit software very well because 32-bit instructions are handled directly in the hardware rather than through software emulation.

Itanium is initially based on 0.18-micron technology; however, later versions will move to 0.13 micron, allowing for higher speeds and larger caches.

Itanium comes in a new package called the pin array cartridge (PAC). This cartridge includes L3 cache and plugs into a PAC418 (418-pin) socket on the motherboard and not a slot. The package is about the size of a standard index card, weighs about 6oz. (170g), and has an alloy metal on its base to dissipate the heat (see Figure 3.61). Itanium has clips on its sides, enabling four to be hung from a motherboard, both below and above.

Itanium Cartridge Features

Figure 3.61 Itanium processor.

Itanium incorporates three levels of cache. The L1 cache is closely tied to the execution unit, and it is backed by on-die L2 cache. Finally, a 2MB or 4MB L3 cache is housed in separate chips contained within the cartridge.

Itanium will be followed in 2002 by a second IA-64 processor codenamed McKinley. McKinley will have larger on-die L2 cache and target clock speeds of more than 1.5GHz, offering more than twice the performance of Itanium. Following McKinley will be Madison, based on 0.13-micron technology. Both Itanium and McKinley are based on 0.18-micron technology.

Processor Upgrades

Since the 486, processor upgrades have been relatively easy for most systems. With the 486 and later processors, Intel designed in the capability to upgrade by designing standard sockets that would take a variety of processors. Thus, if you have a motherboard with Socket 3, you can put virtually any 486 processor in it; if you have a Socket 7 motherboard, it should be capable of accepting virtually any Pentium processor.

To maximize your motherboard, you can almost always upgrade to the fastest processor your particular board will support. Because of the varieties of processor sockets and slots—not to mention voltages, speeds, and other potential areas of incompatibility—you should consult with your motherboard manufacturer to see whether a higher-speed processor will work in your board. Usually, that can be determined by the type of socket or slot on the motherboard, but other things such as the voltage regulator and BIOS can be deciding factors as well.

For example, if your motherboard has a Pentium Socket 5, you can install a Pentium MMX 233MHz processor with a 2.8v voltage regulator adapter, or optionally an AMD-K6, also with a voltage regulator adapter. If you have Socket 7, your motherboard should be capable of supporting the lower-voltage Pentium MMX or AMD-K6 series directly without any adapters. The K6-2 and K6-3 are the fastest and best processors for Socket 7 motherboards.

Rather than purchasing processors and adapters separately, I usually recommend you purchase them together in a module from companies such as Kingston or Evergreen (see the Vendor List on the CD).

Upgrading the processor can, in some cases, double the performance of a system, such as if you were going from a Pentium 100 to an MMX 233. However, if you already have a Pentium 233, you already have the fastest processor that goes in that socket. In that case, you really should look into a complete motherboard change, which would let you upgrade to a Pentium III processor at the same time. If your chassis design is not proprietary and your system uses an industry-standard Baby-AT or ATX motherboard design, I normally recommend changing the motherboard and processor rather than trying to find an upgrade processor that will work with your existing board.

OverDrive Processors

Intel at one time offered special OverDrive processors for upgrading systems. Often these were repackaged versions of the standard processors, sometimes including necessary voltage regulators and fans. Unfortunately, they frequently were overpriced, even when compared against purchasing a complete new motherboard and processor. They have all been withdrawn, and Intel has not announced any new versions. I don't recommend the OverDrive processors unless the deal is too good to pass up.

Processor Benchmarks

People love to know how fast (or slow) their computers are. We have always been interested in speed; it is human nature. To help us with this quest, various benchmark test programs can be used to measure different aspects of processor and system performance. Although no single numerical measurement can completely describe the performance of a complex device such as a processor or a complete PC, benchmarks can be useful tools for comparing different components and systems.

However, the only truly accurate way to measure your system's performance is to test the system using the actual software applications you use. Although you think you might be testing one component of a system, often other parts of the system can have an effect. It is inaccurate to compare systems with different processors, for example, if they also have different amounts or types of memory, different hard disks, video cards, and so on. All these things and more will skew the test results.

Benchmarks can typically be divided into two types: component or system tests. *Component* benchmarks measure the performance of specific parts of a computer system, such as a processor, hard disk, video card, or CD-ROM drive, whereas *system* benchmarks typically measure the performance of the entire computer system running a given application or test suite.

Benchmarks are, at most, only one kind of information you can use during the upgrading or purchasing process. You are best served by testing the system using your own set of software operating systems and applications and in the configuration you will be running.

Several companies specialize in benchmark tests and software. The following table lists the company and the benchmarks they are known for. You can contact these companies via the information in the Vendor List on the CD.

Company	Benchmarks Published	Benchmark Type
Intel	iCOMP index 3.0	Processor/System
Business Applications	SYSmark	System
Performance Corporation	(BAPCo)	
Standard Performance	SPECint,	Processor Integer
Evaluation Corporation	SPECfp	Processor Floating
PointZiff-Davis		
Benchmark	CPUmark	Processor
Ziff-Davis Benchmark	Winstone	System
Ziff-Davis Benchmark	WinBench	System
Symantec Corporation	Norton SI32	Processor
Symantec Corporation	Norton SI32,	System

Processor Troubleshooting Techniques

Processors are normally very reliable. Most PC problems are with other devices, but if you suspect the processor, there are some steps you can take to troubleshoot it. The easiest thing to do is to replace the microprocessor with a known-good spare. If the problem goes away, the original processor is defective. If the problem persists, the problem is likely elsewhere.

Table 3.40 provides a general troubleshooting checklist for processor-related PC problems.

Table 3.40   Troubleshooting Processor-Related Problems

Problem Identification	Possible Cause	Resolution
System is dead, no cursor, no beeps, no fan.	Power cord failure.	Plug in or replace power cord. Power cords can fail even though they look fine.
	Power supply failure.	Replace the power supply. Use a known-good spare for testing.
	Motherboard failure.	Replace motherboard. Use a known-good spare for testing.
	Memory failure.	Remove all memory except 1 bank and retest. If the system still won't boot replace bank 1.

Table 3.40   Continued

Problem Identification	Possible Cause	Resolution
System is dead, no beeps, or locks up before POST begins.	All components either not installed or incorrectly installed.	Check all peripherals, especially memory and graphics adapter. Reseat all boards and socketed components.
System beeps on startup, fan is running, no cursor on screen.	Improperly seated or failing graphics adapter.	Reseat or replace graphics adapter. Use known-good spare for testing.
Locks up during or shortly after POST.	Poor heat dissipation.	Check CPU heatsink/fan; replace if necessary, use one with higher capacity.
	Improper voltage settings.	Set motherboard for proper core processor voltage.
	Wrong motherboard bus speed.	Set motherboard for proper speed.
	Wrong CPU clock multiplier.	Jumper motherboard for proper clock multiplier.
Improper CPU identification during POST.	Old BIOS.	Update BIOS from manufacturer.
	Board not configured properly.	Check manual and jumper board accordingly to proper bus and multiplier settings.
Operating system will not boot.	Poor heat dissipation.	Check CPU fan; replace if necessary, might need higher-capacity heatsink.
	Improper voltage settings.	Jumper motherboard for proper core voltage.
	Wrong motherboard bus speed.	Jumper motherboard for proper speed.
	Wrong CPU clock multiplier.	Jumper motherboard for proper clock multiplier.
	Applications will not install or run.	Improper drivers or incompatible hardware; update drivers and check for compatibility issues.
System appears to work, but no video is displayed.	Monitor turned off or failed.	Check monitor and power to monitor. Replace with known-good spare for testing.

If during the POST the processor is not identified correctly, your motherboard settings might be incorrect or your BIOS might need to be updated. Check that the motherboard is jumpered or configured correctly for the processor that you have, and make sure you have the latest BIOS for your motherboard.

If the system seems to run erratically after it warms up, try setting the processor to a lower speed setting. If the problem goes away, the processor might be defective or overclocked.

Many hardware problems are really software problems in disguise. Be sure you have the latest BIOS for your motherboard, as well as the latest drivers for all your peripherals. Also, it helps to use the latest version of your given operating system because there usually will be fewer problems.

CHAPTER 4

Motherboards and Buses

Motherboard Form Factors

Without a doubt, the most important component in a PC system is the main board or motherboard. Some companies refer to the motherboard as a system board or planar. The terms *motherboard*, *main board*, *system board*, and *planar* are interchangeable. This chapter examines the various types of motherboards available and those components usually contained on the motherboard and motherboard interface connectors.

Several common form factors are used for PC motherboards. The *form factor* refers to the physical dimensions and size of the board and dictates what type of case the board will fit into. Some are true standards (meaning that all boards with that form factor are interchangeable), whereas others are not standardized enough to allow for true interchangeability. Unfortunately, these nonstandard form factors preclude any easy upgrade, which generally means they should be avoided. The more commonly known PC motherboard form factors include the following:

Obsolete Form Factors

- Baby-AT
- Full-size AT
- LPX (semiproprietary)

Modern Form Factors

- ATX
- Micro-ATX
- Flex-ATX
- NLX
- WTX (no longer in production)

All Others

- Proprietary Designs (certain Compaq, Packard Bell, Hewlett-Packard, notebook/portable systems, and so on)

Motherboards have evolved over the years from the original Baby-AT form factor boards used in the original IBM PC and XT to the current ATX and NLX boards used in most full-size desktop and tower systems. ATX has a number of variants, including Micro-ATX (which is a smaller version of the ATX form factor used in the smaller systems) and Flex-ATX (an even smaller version for the lowest-cost home PCs). NLX is designed for corporate desktop–type systems; WTX was designed for workstations and medium-duty servers, but never became popular. Table 4.1 shows the modern industry-standard form factors and their recommended uses.

Table 4.1   Industry-Standard Motherboard Form Factors

Form Factor	Use
ATX	Standard desktop, mini-tower, and full-tower systems; most common form factor today; most flexible design for power users, enthusiasts, low-end servers/workstations, higher-end home systems; ATX boards support up to seven expansion slots
Mini-ATX	A slightly smaller version of ATX that fits into the same case as ATX. Many so-called ATX motherboards are actually Mini-ATX motherboards; Mini-ATX boards support up to six expansion slots
Micro-ATX	Midrange desktop or mini-tower systems
Flex-ATX	Least expensive or low-end small desktop or mini-tower systems, entertainment or appliance systems
NLX	Corporate desktop or mini-tower systems; fast and easy serviceability
WTX	Mid- to high-end workstations, servers (withdrawn)

Although the Baby-AT, Full-size AT, and LPX boards were once popular, they have all but been replaced by more modern and interchangeable form factors. The modern form factors are true standards, which guarantees improved interchangeability within each type. This means that ATX boards will interchange with other ATX boards, NLX with other NLX, and so on. The additional features found on these boards as compared to the obsolete form factors, combined with true interchangeability, has made the migration to these newer form factors quick and easy. Today I recommend purchasing only systems with one of the modern industry-standard form factors.

Anything that does not fit into one of the industry-standard form factors is considered proprietary. Unless there are special circumstances, I do not recommend purchasing systems with proprietary board designs. They will be virtually impossible to upgrade and very expensive to repair later because the motherboard, case, and often power supply will not be interchangeable with other models. I call proprietary form factor systems "disposable" PCs because that's what you must normally do with them when they are too slow or need repair out of warranty.

Caution

"Disposable" PCs might be more common than ever. Some estimate that as much as 60% of all PCs sold today are disposable models, not so much because of the motherboards used (Flex or Micro-ATX motherboards are frequently used today instead of the semiproprietary LPX models previously favored) but because of the tiny SFX power supplies and cramped micro-tower cases that are favored on most retail-market PCs today. Although low-cost PCs using small chassis and power supplies are theoretically more upgradable than past disposable type systems, you'll still hit the wall over time if you need more than three expansion slots or want to use more than two or three internal drives. Because mini-tower systems are so cramped and limited, I consider them to be almost as disposable as the LPX systems they have largely replaced.

You also need to watch out for systems that only appear to meet industry standards, such as Dell computer models built from September 1998 to the present. These computers use a rewired version of the ATX power supply and motherboard power connectors, which makes both components completely incompatible with standard motherboards and power supplies. If you want to upgrade the power supply, you must use a special Dell-compatible power supply. And if you want to upgrade the motherboard, you must buy a standard power supply to match.

If you want to have a truly upgradable system, insist on a system that uses Micro-ATX or full-ATX motherboards in a mid-tower or larger case with at least five drive bays.

The following sections detail each of the standard form factors.

Baby-AT

The first popular PC motherboard was, of course, the original IBM PC released in 1981. Figure 4.1 shows how this board looked. IBM followed the PC with the XT motherboard in 1983, which had the same basic shape as the PC board but had eight slots instead of five. Also, the slots were spaced 0.8 inch apart instead of 1 inch apart as in the PC (see Figure 4.2). The XT also eliminated the weird cassette port in the back, which was supposed to be used to save BASIC programs on cassette tape instead of the much more expensive (at the time) floppy drive.

Figure 4.1 IBM PC motherboard (circa 1981).

The minor differences in the slot positions and the now-lonesome keyboard connector on the back required a minor redesign of the case. This motherboard became very popular, and many other PC motherboard manufacturers of the day copied IBM's XT design and produced similar boards. By the time most of these clones or compatible systems came out, IBM had released its AT system, which initially used a larger form factor motherboard. Due to the advances in circuit miniaturization, these companies found they could fit all the additional circuits found on the 16-bit AT motherboard into the XT motherboard form factor. Rather than call these boards XT-sized, which might have made people think they were 8-bit designs, these companies referred to them as Baby-AT, which ended up meaning an XT-sized board with AT motherboard design features (16-bit or greater).

Note

The CD accompanying this book contains detailed information on the PC (5150) and XT (5160). See the Technical Reference section of the CD. All the information there is printable.

Figure 4.2 IBM PC-XT motherboard (circa 1983).

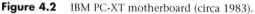

Thus, the Baby-AT form factor is essentially the same as the original IBM XT motherboard. The only difference is a slight modification in one of the screw hole positions to fit into an AT-style case. These motherboards also have specific placement of the keyboard and slot connectors to match the holes in the case. Note that virtually all full-size AT and Baby-AT motherboards use the standard 5-pin DIN type connector for the keyboard. Baby-AT motherboards can be used to replace full-sized AT motherboards and will fit into a number of case designs. Because of their flexibility, from 1983 into early 1996 the Baby-AT form factor was the most popular motherboard type. Starting in mid-1996, Baby-AT was replaced by the superior ATX motherboard design, which is not directly interchangeable. Most systems sold since 1996 have used the improved ATX, Micro-ATX, or NLX design, and Baby-AT is getting harder and harder to come by. Figure 4.3 shows the onboard features and layout of a late-model Baby-AT motherboard. Older Baby-AT motherboards have the same general layout but lack advanced features, such as USB connectors, DIMM memory sockets, and the AGP slot.

Any case that accepts a full-sized AT motherboard will also accept a Baby-AT design. Since its debut in the IBM XT motherboard in 1983 and lasting well into 1996, the Baby-AT motherboard form factor was, for that time, the most popular design. PC motherboards using the Baby-AT design have been manufactured to use virtually any processor from the original 8088 to the Pentium III or Athlon, although the pickings are slim where the newer processors are concerned. As such, systems with Baby-AT motherboards were the original upgradable systems. Because any Baby-AT motherboard can be replaced with any other Baby-AT motherboard, this is an interchangeable design. Even though the Baby-AT design (shown in Figure 4.3) is now obsolete, ATX carries on its philosophy of interchange-ability. Figure 4.4 shows a more modern Baby-AT motherboard, which includes USB compatibility, SIMM and DIMM sockets, and even a supplemental ATX power supply connection.

Figure 4.3   Baby-AT motherboard form factor dimensions.

The easiest way to identify a Baby-AT form factor system without opening it is to look at the rear of the case. In a Baby-AT motherboard, the cards plug directly into the board at a 90° angle; in other words, the slots in the case for the cards are perpendicular to the motherboard. Also, the Baby-AT motherboard has only one visible connector directly attached to the board, which is the keyboard connector. Typically, this connector is the full-sized 5-pin DIN type connector, although some Baby-AT systems use the smaller 6-pin mini-DIN connector (sometimes called a PS/2 type connector) and might even have a mouse connector. All other connectors are mounted on the case or on card edge brackets and attached to the motherboard via cables. The keyboard connector is visible through an appropriately placed hole in the case.

▶▶   See "Keyboard/Mouse Interface Connectors," p. 969.

Baby-AT boards all conform to specific width, screw hole, slot, and keyboard connector locations, but one thing that can vary is the length of the board. Versions have been built that are shorter than the full 13-inch length; these are often called Mini-AT, Micro-AT, or even things such as 2/3-Baby or 1/2-Baby. Even though they might not have the full length, they still bolt directly into the same case as a standard Baby-AT board and can be used as a direct replacement for one.

1) LPX (12-pin) power supply connector
2) 5-pin DIN keyboard connector
3) PS/2 mouse port header cable connector
4) IDE host adapter cable connectors (2)
5) 32-bit PCI expansion slots (3)
6) BIOS chip
7) Combo PCI/ISA expansion slot
8) USB port header cable connector
9) COM (serial) ports header cable connectors (2)
10) LPT (parallel) port header cable connector
11) Floppy controller cable connector
12) ATX (20-pin) power supply connector
13) CPU fan power connector
14) 72-pin SIMM sockets (2)

15) 168-pin DIMM sockets (3)
16) AGP video card slot
17) VIA Apollo MVP 3 chipset (2 chips)
18) L2 cache memory (1MB total from 2 chips)
19) Super Socket 7 CPU socket
20) Connectors for case speaker, reset button, and other front panel devices
21) Case fan power connector
22) ISA expansion slots (3)
23) CR2032 battery for maintaining CMOS (RTC/NVRAM) contents
24) Voltage regulator assembly
25) CPU temperature sensor
26) CPU fan power connector

Figure 4.4 A late-model Baby-AT motherboard, the Tyan Trinity 100AT (S1590). *Photo courtesy of Tyan Computer Corporation.*

Full-Size AT

The full-size AT motherboard matches the original IBM AT motherboard design. This allows for a very large board of up to 12 inches wide by 13.8 inches deep. When the full-size AT board debuted in 1984, IBM needed more room for additional circuits when it migrated from the 8-bit architecture of the PC/XT to the 16-bit architecture of the AT. So, IBM started with an XT board and extended it in two directions (see Figure 4.5).

Figure 4.5   IBM AT motherboard (circa 1984).

The board was redesigned to make it slightly smaller a little over a year after being introduced. Then, as discussed previously, it was redesigned again as IBM shrank the board down to XT-size in a system it called the XT-286. The XT-286 board size was virtually identical to the original XT and was adopted by most PC-compatible manufacturers when it became known as Baby-AT.

Note

The enclosed CD contains detailed coverage of the AT and the XT Model 286. See the Technical Reference section of the CD for this legacy coverage.

The keyboard connector and slot connectors in the full-size AT boards still conformed to the same specific placement requirements to fit the holes in the XT cases already in use, but a larger case was still required to fit the larger board. Because of the larger size of the board, a full-size AT motherboard only fits into full-size AT desktop or tower cases. Because these motherboards do not fit into the smaller Baby-AT or mini-tower cases, and because of advances in component miniaturization, they are no longer being produced by most motherboard manufacturers—except in some cases for dual processor server applications.

Note that you can always replace a full-size AT motherboard with a Baby-AT board, but the opposite is not true unless the case is large enough to accommodate the full-size AT design.

LPX

The LPX and Mini-LPX form factor boards are a semiproprietary design originally developed by Western Digital in 1987 for some of its motherboards. The LP in LPX stands for Low Profile, which is so named because these boards incorporated slots that were parallel to the main board, enabling the expansion cards to install sideways. This allowed for a slim or low-profile case design and overall a smaller system than the Baby-AT.

Although Western Digital no longer produces PC motherboards, the form factor lives on, and many other motherboard manufacturers have duplicated the design. Unfortunately, because the specifications were never laid out in exact detail—especially with regard to the bus riser card portion of the design—these boards are termed semiproprietary and are not interchangeable between manufacturers. Some vendors, such as IBM and HP, for example, have built LPX systems that use a T-shaped riser card that allows expansion cards to be mounted at the normal 90° angle to the motherboard but still above the motherboard. This lack of standardization means that if you have a system with an LPX board, in most cases you will not be able to replace the motherboard with a different LPX board later. You essentially have a system you can't upgrade or repair by replacing the motherboard with something better. In other words, you have what I call a disposable PC, something I would not normally recommend that anybody purchase.

Most people were not aware of the semiproprietary nature of the design of these boards, and they were extremely popular in what I call "retail store" PCs from the late 1980s through the late 1990s. This would include primarily Compaq and Packard Bell systems, as well as many others who used this form factor in their lower-cost systems. These boards were most often used in low-profile or Slimline case systems but were also found in tower cases, too. These were often lower-cost systems such as those sold at retail electronics superstores. Although scarce even in retail chains today, because of their proprietary nature, I recommend staying away from any system that uses an LPX motherboard.

Tip

Normally, I would never recommend upgrading an LPX system—they simply aren't worth the expense. However, a few vendors do sell LPX motherboards, so if it's absolutely necessary, an upgrade might be possible. The problem is the riser card, which is typically sold separately from the motherboard itself. It is up to you to figure out which riser card will work in your existing case, and often, if you choose the wrong riser card, you're stuck with it.

If you must locate LPX-compatible products, try these Web sites and vendors:

■ Unicorn Computers (Taiwan): `www.unicorn-computer.com.tw`

■ Hong Faith America (Taiwan): `www.america.hongfaith.com`

■ FriendTech's LPX Zone (`www.friendtech.com/LPX_Zone/LPX_Zone.htm`) has links to other vendors and is developing a comprehensive knowledge base of LPX-related information and possible upgrades.

LPX boards are characterized by several distinctive features (see Figure 4.6). The most noticeable is that the expansion slots are mounted on a bus riser card that plugs into the motherboard. In most designs, expansion cards plug sideways into the riser card. This sideways placement allows for the low-profile case design. Slots are located on one or both sides of the riser card depending on the system and case design. Vendors who use LPX-type motherboards in tower cases sometimes use a T-shaped riser card instead, which puts the expansion slots at the normal right angle to the motherboard but on a raised shelf above the motherboard itself.

Figure 4.6 Typical LPX system chassis and motherboard.

Another distinguishing feature of the LPX design is the standard placement of connectors on the back of the board. An LPX board has a row of connectors for video (VGA 15-pin), parallel (25-pin), two serial ports (9-pin each), and mini-DIN PS/2 style mouse and keyboard connectors. All these connectors are mounted across the rear of the motherboard and protrude through a slot in the case. Some LPX motherboards might have additional connectors for other internal ports, such as network or SCSI adapters. Because LPX systems use a high degree of motherboard port integration, many vendors of LPX motherboards, cases, and systems often refer to LPX products as having an "all-in-one" design.

The standard form factor used for LPX and Mini-LPX motherboards used in many typical low-cost systems is shown in Figure 4.7.

I am often asked, "How can I tell whether a system has an LPX board without opening the cover?" Because of the many variations in riser card design, and because newer motherboards such as NLX also use riser cards, the most reliable way to distinguish an LPX motherboard from other systems is to look at the connector signature (the layout and pattern of connectors on the back of the board). As you can see in Figure 4.8, all LPX motherboards—regardless of variations in riser card shape, size, or location—place all external ports along the rear of the motherboard. By contrast, Baby-AT motherboards use case-mounted or expansion slot–mounted connectors for serial, parallel, PS/2 mouse, and USB ports, whereas ATX-family motherboards group all external ports together to the left side of the expansion slots.

Figure 4.7 LPX motherboard dimensions.

On an LPX board, the riser is placed in the middle of the motherboard, whereas NLX boards have the riser to the side (the motherboard actually plugs into the riser in NLX).

Figure 4.8 shows two typical examples of the connectors on the back of LPX boards. Note that not all LPX boards have the built-in audio, so those connectors might be missing. Other ports (such as USB) might be missing from what is shown in these diagrams, depending on exactly what options are included on a specific board; however, the general layout will be the same.

The connectors along the rear of the board would interfere with locating bus slots directly on the motherboard, which accounts for why riser cards are used for adding expansion boards.

Although the built-in connectors on the LPX boards were a good idea, unfortunately the LPX design was semiproprietary (not a fully interchangeable standard) and thus, not a good choice. Newer motherboard form factors such as ATX, Micro-ATX, and NLX have both built-in connectors and use a standard board design. The riser card design of LPX allowed system designers to create a low-profile desktop system, a feature now carried by the much more standardized NLX form factor. In fact, NLX was developed as the modern replacement for LPX.

Figure 4.8 LPX motherboard back panel connectors.

ATX

The ATX form factor was the first of a dramatic evolution in motherboard form factors. ATX is a combination of the best features of the Baby-AT and LPX motherboard designs, with many new enhancements and features thrown in. The ATX form factor is essentially a Baby-AT motherboard turned sideways in the chassis, along with a modified power supply location and connector. The most important thing to know initially about the ATX form factor is that it is physically incompatible with either the previous Baby-AT or LPX design. In other words, a different case and power supply are required to match the ATX motherboard. These case and power supply designs have become common and are found in most new systems.

The official ATX specification was initially released by Intel in July 1995 and was written as an open specification for the industry. ATX boards didn't hit the market in force until mid-1996, when they rapidly began replacing Baby-AT boards in new systems. The ATX specification was updated to version 2.01 in February 1997, and has had several minor revisions since. The latest revision is ATX version 2.03 (with Engineering Change Revision P1), released in May 2000. Intel has published detailed specifications so other manufacturers can use the ATX design in their systems. The current specifications for ATX and other current motherboard types are available online from the Desktop Form Factors site, www.formfactors.org. Currently, ATX is the most popular motherboard form factor for new systems, and it is the one I recommend most people get in their systems today. An ATX system will be upgradable for many years to come, exactly like Baby-AT was in the past.

ATX improved on the Baby-AT and LPX motherboard designs in several major areas:

■ *Built-in double high external I/O connector panel.* The rear portion of the motherboard includes a stacked I/O connector area that is 6 1/4-inches wide by 1 3/4-inches tall. This enables external connectors to be located directly on the board and negates the need for cables running from internal connectors to the back of the case as with Baby-AT designs.

■ *Single main keyed internal power supply connector.* This is a boon for the average end user who always had to worry about interchanging the Baby-AT power supply connectors and subsequently blowing the motherboard! The ATX specification includes a keyed and shrouded main power connector that is easy to plug in and can't be installed incorrectly. This connector also features pins for supplying 3.3v to the motherboard, so ATX motherboards do not require built-in voltage regulators that are susceptible to failure. The ATX specification was extended to include two additional optional keyed power connectors called the Auxiliary Power connector (3.3V and 5V) and the ATX12V connector for systems that require more power than the original specification would allow.

▶▶   See "AT Power Supply Connectors," p. 1117.

■ *Relocated CPU and memory.* The CPU and memory modules are relocated so they can't interfere with any bus expansion cards and can easily be accessed for upgrade without removing any of the installed bus adapters. The CPU and memory are relocated next to the power supply, which is where the primary system fan is located. The improved airflow concentrated over the processor, in some cases, eliminates the need for extra-cost CPU cooling fans (lower power configurations only). There is room for a CPU and heatsink of up to 2.8 inches in height, as well as more than adequate side clearance provided in that area.

Note

Note that most systems still require additional processor cooling, either from a case-mounted fan or an active heatsink with an integral fan. Intel and AMD supply processors with attached high-quality (ball bearing) fans for CPUs sold to smaller vendors. These are so-called "boxed" processors because they are sold in single-unit box quantities instead of cases of 100 or more like the raw CPUs sold to the larger vendors. The included fan heatsink is a form of thermal insurance because most smaller vendors and system self-assemblers lack the engineering knowledge necessary to perform thermal analysis, temperature measurements, and the testing required to select the properly sized passive heatsinks. The only thermal requirement spelled out for the boxed processors is that the temperature of the air entering the active heatsink (usually the same as the system interior ambient temperature) is kept to 45°C (113°F) or less in Pentium III or earlier models, or 40°C (104°F) or less in the Pentium 4 or later processors. By putting a high-quality fan on these "boxed" processors, Intel and AMD can put a warranty on the boxed processors that is independent of the system warranty. Larger vendors have the engineering talent to select the proper passive heatsink, thus reducing the cost of the system as well as increasing reliability. With an OEM non-boxed processor, the warranty is with the system vendor and not the processor manufacturer directly. Heatsink mounting instructions usually are included with a motherboard if non-boxed processors are used.

■ *Relocated internal I/O connectors.* The internal I/O connectors for the floppy and hard disk drives are relocated to be near the drive bays and out from under the expansion board slot and drive bay areas. This means that internal cables to the drives can be much shorter, and accessing the connectors does not require card or drive removal.

■ *Improved cooling.* The CPU and main memory are designed and positioned to improve overall system cooling. This can decrease—but not necessarily eliminate—the need for separate case or CPU cooling fans. Most higher-speed systems still need additional cooling fans for the CPU and chassis. Note that the ATX specification originally specified that the ATX power supply fan blows into the system chassis instead of outward. This reverse flow, or positive pressure design, pressurizes the case, which minimizes dust and dirt intrusion. More recently, the ATX specification was revised to allow the more normal standard flow, which negatively pressurizes the case by having the fan blow outward. Because the specification technically allows either type of airflow, and because some overall cooling efficiency is lost with the reverse flow design, most power supply manufacturers provide ATX power supplies with fans that exhaust air from the system, otherwise called a negative pressure design. See Chapter 21, "Power Supply and Chassis/Case," for more detailed information.

■ *Lower cost to manufacture.* The ATX specification eliminates the need for the rat's nest of cables to external port connectors found on Baby-AT motherboards, additional CPU or chassis cooling fans, or onboard 3.3v voltage regulators. Instead, ATX allows for shorter internal drive cables and no cables for standard external serial or parallel ports. These all conspire to greatly reduce the cost of the motherboard and the cost of a complete system—including the case and power supply.

Figure 4.9 shows the new ATX system layout and chassis features, as you would see them looking in with the lid off on a desktop, or sideways in a tower with the side panel removed. Notice how virtually the entire motherboard is clear of the drive bays and how the devices such as CPU, memory, and internal drive connectors are easy to access and do not interfere with the bus slots. Also notice how the processor is positioned near the power supply.

Figure 4.9   When mounted inside the case, the ATX motherboard is oriented so that the CPU socket is near the power supply fan and case fan (if your case includes one).

The ATX motherboard shape is basically a Baby-AT design rotated sideways 90°. The expansion slots are now parallel to the shorter side dimension and do not interfere with the CPU, memory, or I/O connector sockets (see Figure 4.10). There are actually two basic sizes of standard ATX boards. In addition to a full-size ATX layout, Intel also has specified a mini-ATX design, which is a fully compatible subset in size and will fit into the same case:

- A full-size ATX board is 12" wide × 9.6" deep (305mm×244mm).
- The mini-ATX board is 11.2" × 8.2" (284mm×208mm).

In addition, two smaller variations of ATX exist, called Micro-ATX and Flex-ATX. They are discussed in the following sections in this chapter.

Although the case holes are similar to the Baby-AT case, cases for the two formats are generally not compatible. The power supplies require a connector adapter to be interchangeable, but the basic ATX power supply design is similar to the standard Slimline power supply.

Clearly, the advantages of the ATX form factor make it the best choice for new systems. For backward compatibility, you can still find Baby-AT boards for use in upgrading older systems, but the choices are becoming slimmer every day. I would never recommend building or purchasing a new system with a Baby-AT motherboard because you will severely limit your future upgrade possibilities. In fact, I have been recommending only ATX systems for new system purchases since late 1996 and will probably continue to do so for the next several years.

The best way to tell whether your system has an ATX-board design without removing the lid is to look at the back of the system. Two distinguishing features identify ATX. One is that the expansion boards plug directly into the motherboard. There is usually no riser card as with LPX or NLX, so the slots are perpendicular to the plane of the motherboard. Also, ATX boards have a unique double-high connector area for all the built-in connectors on the motherboard (see Figure 4.11). This is found just to the side of the bus slot area and can be used to easily identify an ATX board.

Note

Although Figure 4.11 shows typical ATX rear-panel connectors, many variations are already available, and more are coming in the future. For example, systems with integrated video will have a VGA 15-pin connector in addition to those shown, whereas systems that use a separate sound card will omit the MIDI/game port and audio jacks.

In the future, you can expect to see more and more so-called "legacy-free" systems that omit the serial and parallel ports, and at some point in the future, even the PS/2 mouse and keyboard ports might be dropped because USB devices can be used for all the functions currently performed by these ports.

The specification and related information about the ATX, mini-ATX, micro-ATX, flex-ATX, or NLX form factor specifications are available from the Form Factors (formerly Platform Developer) Web site at http://www.formfactors.org. The Form Factors site provides form factor specifications and design guides, as well as design considerations for new technologies, information on initiative supporters, vendor products, and a form factor discussion forum.

Micro-ATX

Micro-ATX is a motherboard form factor originally introduced by Intel in December of 1997 as an evolution of the ATX form factor for smaller and lower-cost systems. The reduced size as compared to standard ATX allows for a smaller chassis, motherboard, and power supply, reducing the cost of entire system. The micro-ATX form factor is also backward compatible with the ATX form factor and can be used in full-size ATX cases. Of course, a micro-ATX case doesn't take a full-size ATX board. During early 1999, this form factor began to really catch on in the low-cost, sub-$1,000 PC market. Currently, mini-tower chassis systems dominate the low-cost PC market, although their small sizes and cramped interiors severely limit future upgradability.

Figure 4.10 *ATX specification version 2.03, showing ATX and mini-ATX dimensions.*

The main differences between micro-ATX and standard or mini-ATX are as follows:

- Reduced width motherboard (9.6" [244mm] instead of 12" [305mm] or 11.2" [284mm])
- Fewer I/O bus expansion slots (four maximum, although most boards feature only three)
- Smaller power supply optional(SFX form factor)

The micro-ATX motherboard maximum size is only 9.6" × 9.6" (244mm×244mm) as compared to the full-size ATX size of 12" × 9.6" (305mm×244mm) or the mini-ATX size of 11.2" × 8.2" (284mm×208mm). Even smaller boards can be designed as long as they conform to the location of the mounting holes, connector positions, and so on, as defined by the standard. Fewer slots aren't a problem for typical home or small-business PC users because more components such as sound and video are usually integrated on the motherboard and therefore don't require separate slots. This higher integration reduces motherboard and system costs. External buses, such as USB, 10/100 Ethernet, and optionally SCSI or 1394 (FireWire), can provide additional expansion out of the box. The specifications for micro-ATX motherboard dimensions are shown in Figure 4.12.

A PS/2 keyboard or mouse   G Serial Port B
B PS/2 keyboard or mouse   H MIDI/game Port (optional)
C USB Port 1   I Audio Line Out (optional)
D USB Port 0   J Audio Line In (optional)
E Serial Port A   K Audio Mic In (optional)
F Parallel Port

Figure 4.11   Typical ATX motherboard rear panel connectors.

A new, small form factor (called SFX) power supply has been defined for optional use with micro-ATX systems, although the standard ATX supply also works fine because the connectors are the same. The smaller size of the SFX power supply encourages flexibility in choosing mounting locations within the chassis and allows for smaller systems that consume less power overall. Although the smaller SFX power supply can be used, it lacks sufficient power output for faster or fully configured systems. Because of the high power demands of most modern systems, most micro-ATX chassis are designed to accept standard ATX power supplies.

▶▶ See "SFX Style," p. 1114.

The micro-ATX form factor is similar to ATX for compatibility. The similarities include the following:

- Standard ATX 20-pin power connector
- Standard ATX I/O panel
- Mounting holes are a subset of ATX

Figure 4.12 Micro-ATX specification 1.0 motherboard dimensions.

These similarities ensure that a micro-ATX motherboard will easily work in a standard ATX chassis with a standard ATX power supply, as well as the smaller micro-ATX chassis and SFX power supply.

The overall system size for a micro-ATX is very small. A typical case is only 12" to 14" tall, about 7" wide, and 12" deep. This results in a kind of micro-tower or desktop size. A typical micro-ATX motherboard is shown in Figure 4.13.

As with ATX, micro-ATX was released to the public domain by Intel to facilitate adoption as a de facto standard. The specification and related information on micro-ATX are available through the Desktop Form Factors site (www.formfactors.org).

Flex-ATX

In March of 1999, Intel released the flex-ATX addendum to the micro-ATX specification. This added a new and even smaller variation of the ATX form factor to the motherboard scene. Flex-ATX's smaller design is intended to allow a variety of new PC designs, especially extremely inexpensive, smaller, consumer-oriented, appliance-type systems.

Flex-ATX defines a board that is only 9.0" × 7.5" (229mm×191mm) in size, which is the smallest of the ATX family boards. Besides the smaller size, the other biggest difference between the flex-ATX form factor and the micro-ATX is that flex-ATX supports only socketed processors. Therefore, a flex-ATX board does not have a Slot 1, Slot 2, or Slot A–type connector for the cartridge versions of the Pentium II/III and Athlon processors. However, it can have Socket 7 or Socket A for AMD processors, Socket 370 for the PPGA (Plastic Pin Grid Array), FCPGA (Flip Chip PGA) versions of the Intel Celeron and Pentium III, or the newer Socket 423 for the Pentium 4. Because both Intel and AMD use socketed processors for their newest designs, the loss of compatibility with slot-based processors is no great sacrifice.

Rear panel connectors

Motherboard power connector

CPU socket

Memory slots

Hard drive and floppy drive connectors

AGP slot

PCI slots

Figure 4.13 A typical micro-ATX motherboard's dimensions are 9.6"×9.6".

Besides the smaller size and socketed processor–only requirement, the rest of flex-ATX is backward compatible with standard ATX, using a subset of the mounting holes and the same I/O and power supply connector specifications (see Figure 4.14).

Most flex-ATX systems likely use the SFX (small form factor) type power supplies (introduced in the micro-ATX specification), although if the chassis allows it, a standard ATX power supply can also be used.

Note

Some motherboards, especially those used in server systems, come in nonstandard ATX variations collectively called *extended ATX*. This is a term applied to any board larger than the ATX standard. Note that because no official "extended ATX" standard exists, any board claiming this is unique in shape or size and might not fit in your existing chassis. If purchasing any so-called extended ATX board, be sure that it will fit in the chassis you intend to use. Dual Xeon processors fit in a standard ATX-size board, so choose a standard ATX-size board for maximum compatibility with the existing ATX chassis.

With the addition of flex-ATX, the family of ATX boards has now grown to include four definitions of size, as shown in Table 4.2.

Figure 4.14 Size and mounting hole comparison between ATX, micro-ATX, and flex-ATX motherboards.

Form Factor	Mounting Hole Locations	Notes
• FlexATX	B, C, F, H, J, S	
• Micro-ATX	B, C, F, H, J, L, M, R, S	Holes R and S were added for micro-ATX form factor. Hole B was defined in full-AT format.
• ATX	A, C, F, G, H, J, K, L, M	Hole F must be implemented in all ATX 2.03–compliant chassis assemblies. The hole was optional in the ATX 1.1 specification.

Table 4.2   ATX Motherboard Form Factors

Form Factor	Max. Width	Max. Depth
ATX	12.0" (305mm)	9.6" (244mm)
Mini-ATX	11.2" (284mm)	8.2" (208mm)
Micro-ATX	9.6" (244mm)	9.6" (244mm)
Flex-ATX	9.0" (229mm)	7.5" (191mm)

Note that these dimensions are the maximum the board can be. Making a board smaller is always possible as long as it conforms to the mounting hole and connector placement requirements detailed in the respective specifications. Each board has the same basic screw hole and connector placement requirements, so if you have a case that fits a full-size ATX board, you could also mount a mini-, micro-, or flex-ATX board in that same case. Obviously, if you have a smaller case designed for micro-ATX or flex-ATX, you won't be able to put the larger mini-ATX or full-size ATX boards in that case.

ATX Riser

In December 1999, Intel introduced a riser card design modification for ATX motherboards. The design includes the addition of a 22-pin (2×11) connector to one of the PCI slots on the motherboard, along with a two- or three-slot riser card that plugs in. The riser enables two or three PCI cards to be installed. Note that the riser does not support AGP.

ATX motherboards typically are found in vertically oriented tower-type cases, but often a horizontal desktop system is desired for a particular application. When ATX boards are installed in desktop cases, PCI cards can be as tall as 4.2 inches, thus requiring a case that is at least 6–7 inches tall. For Slimline desktop systems, most manufacturers now use the NLX format, but the more complex design and lower popularity of NLX makes that a more expensive alternative. What was needed was a low-cost way to use an industry-standard ATX form factor board in a Slimline desktop case. The best long-term solution to this problem is the eventual adoption of a lower-profile PCI card design that is shorter than the current 4.2 inches. The PCI Low-Profile specification was released for engineering review by the Peripheral Component Interconnect Special Interest Group (PCI SIG) on February 14, 2000, and some PCI card products are now being produced in this shorter (2.5-inch) form factor. Until Low-Profile PCI becomes widespread, Intel has suggested a riser card approach to enable standard-height PCI cards to be used in Slimline and rack-mount systems.

By adding a small 22-pin extension connector to one of the PCI slots on a motherboard, the necessary additional signals for riser card support could be implemented. The current design allows for the use of a two- or three-slot riser that is either 2 inches or 2.8 inches tall, respectively. To this riser, you can attach full-length cards sideways in the system. The motherboard can be used with or without the riser. The only caveat is that if a riser card is installed, the remaining PCI slots on the motherboard can't be used. You can have expansion cards plugged into only the riser or the motherboard, but not both. The riser card supports only PCI cards, not AGP or ISA cards. An sample ATX board with riser installed is shown in Figure 4.15.

Up to three standard PCI cards

Three-slot ATX riser

Standard PCI connector

22-pin riser extension connector

Processor with passive heatsink

RAM

Figure 4.15   Three-slot ATX riser implementation on a micro-ATX motherboard.

The 22-pin extension connector usually is installed in line with PCI slot 6, which is the second one from the right—the slots are normally numbered from right to left (facing the board) starting with 7 as the one closest to the processor. Some boards number the slots from right to left starting with 1; in that case, the extension connector is on PCI slot 2. The pinout of the ATX 22-pin riser extension connector is shown in Figure 4.16.

Signal	Pin	Pin	Signal
Ground	B1	A1	PCI_GNT1#
PCI_ CLK1	B2	A2	Ground
Ground	B3	A3	PCI_GNT2#
PCI_REQ1#	A4	B4	Ground
Ground	A5	B5	PCI_CLK3
PCI_CLK2	A6	B6	RISER_ID1
Ground	A7	B7	Reserved
PCI_REQ2#	A8	B8	RISER_ID2
Ground	A9	B9	NOGO
PC/PCI_DREQ#	A10	B10	+12V
PC/PCI_DGNT#	A11	B11	SER_IRQ

Figure 4.16   ATX 22-pin riser extension connector pinout.

The PCI connector that is in line with the riser extension connector is just a standard PCI slot; none of the signals are changed.

Systems that use the riser generally are low-profile designs. Therefore, they don't fit normal PCI or AGP cards in the remaining (nonriser-bound) slots. Although the ATX riser standard originally was developed for use with low-end boards, which have integrated video, sound, and network support, many rack-mounted servers are also using the ATX riser because these boards also have most of their required components already integrated. In fact, the ATX riser appears to be more popular for rack-mounted servers than for the originally intended target market of Slimline desktop systems.

ATX riser cards, compatible cases, and compatible motherboards are available from a variety of vendors, though, allowing you to build your own Slimline ATX system.

NLX

NLX is a low-profile form factor designed to replace the nonstandard LPX design used in previous low-profile systems. First introduced in November of 1996 by Intel, NLX has become the form factor of choice for Slimline corporate desktop systems. NLX is similar in initial appearance to LPX, but with numerous improvements designed to enable full integration of the latest technologies. NLX is basically an improved version of the proprietary LPX design, but, unlike LPX, NLX is fully standardized, which means you should be able to replace one NLX board with another from a different manufacturer—something that was not possible with LPX.

Another limitation of LPX boards is the difficulty in handling the larger physical size of the newer processors and their larger heatsinks, as well as newer bus structures such as AGP for video. The NLX form factor has been designed specifically to address these problems (see Figure 4.17). In fact, NLX provides enough room for some vendors to support dual Slot 1 Pentium III processors in this form factor.

The main characteristic of an NLX system is that the motherboard plugs into the riser, unlike LPX where the riser plugs into the motherboard. This means the motherboard can be removed from the system without disturbing the riser or any of the expansion cards plugged into it. In addition, the motherboard in a typical NLX system literally has no internal cables or connectors attached to it! All devices that normally plug into the motherboard—such as drive cables, the power supply, the front panel light, switch connectors, and so on—plug into the riser instead (see Figure 4.18). By using the riser card as a connector concentration point, you can remove the lid on an NLX system and literally slide the motherboard out the left side of the system without unplugging a single cable or connector on the inside. This allows for unbelievably quick motherboard changes; in fact, I have swapped motherboards in less than 30 seconds on NLX systems!

Figure 4.17   NLX motherboard and riser combination.

As Figure 4.18 shows, by using different sizes and types of riser cards, a system designer can customize the features of a given NLX system.

Such a design is a boon for the corporate market, where ease and swiftness of servicing is a major feature. Not only can components be replaced with lightning speed, but because of the industry-standard design, motherboards, power supplies, and other components are interchangeable even among different systems.

Specific advantages of the NLX form factor include

- *Support for all desktop system processor technologies.* This is especially important in the later processors that are not only larger but also require larger heatsinks to cool them.

- *Flexibility in the face of rapidly changing processor technologies.* Backplane-like flexibility has been built into the form by allowing a new motherboard to be easily and quickly installed without tearing your entire system to pieces. But unlike traditional backplane systems, many industry leaders, such as Compaq, Toshiba, and HP, are selling NLX-based systems.

- *Support for newer technologies.* This includes Accelerated Graphics Port (AGP) high-performance graphic solutions, Universal Serial Bus (USB), and memory modules in DIMM or RIMM form.

- *Ease and speed of servicing and repair.* Compared to other industry-standard interchangeable form factors, NLX systems are by far the easiest to work on and allow component swaps or other servicing in the shortest amount of time.

Furthermore, with the importance of multimedia applications, connectivity support for such things as video playback, enhanced graphics, and extended audio has been built into the motherboard. This should represent a good cost savings over expensive daughterboard arrangements that have been necessary for many advanced multimedia uses in the past. Although ATX also has this support, LPX and Baby-AT don't have the room for these additional connectors.

Figure 4.18   Typical NLX riser cards. Although most NLX systems use a low-profile riser card similar to the top riser card, others use a taller riser card to provide more slots for add-on cards.

Figure 4.19 shows the basic NLX system layout. Notice that, similar to ATX, the motherboard is clear of the drive bays and other chassis-mounted components. Also, the motherboard and I/O cards (which, like the LPX form factor, are mounted parallel to the motherboard) can easily be slid in and out of the side of the chassis, leaving the riser card and other cards in place. The processor can be easily accessed and enjoys greater cooling than in a more closed-in layout.

Note the position of the optional AGP slot shown previously in Figure 4.16. It is mounted on the motherboard itself, not on the riser card as with PCI or ISA slots. This location was necessary because AGP was developed well after the NLX form factor was introduced. Most NLX motherboards use chipset-integrated or motherboard-based video instead of a separate AGP card, but you must remove an AGP card installed in an NLX system before you can remove the motherboard for servicing. Also, the AGP card used in an NLX system must have a different form factor to enable it to clear the rear connector shield at the back of the NLX motherboard (see Figure 4.20).

Figure 4.19 NLX system chassis layout and cooling airflow.

Figure 4.20 Elsa's Erazor III Pro is a high-performance AGP card that can be installed in either a standard ATX/Baby-AT system or an NLX system. This is because of the PCB design, which leaves room between the AGP port connector and the card's circuits for the NLX motherboard's rear connector shield. *Photo courtesy Elsa AG.*

The NLX motherboard is specified in three lengths, front to back: 13.6", 11.2", or 10" total (see Figure 4.21). With proper bracketry, the shorter boards can go into a case designed for a longer board.

Figure 4.21 NLX form factor. This shows a 13.6" long NLX board. The NLX specification also allows shorter 11.2" and 10" versions.

As with most of the form factors, you can identify NLX via the unique I/O shield or connector area at the back of the board (see Figure 4.22). You only need a quick look at the rear of any given system to determine which type of board is contained within. Figure 4.22 shows the unique stepped design of the NLX I/O connector area. This allows for a row of connectors all along the bottom and has room for double-stacked connectors on one side.

As you can see, the NLX form factor has been designed for maximum flexibility and space efficiency. Even extremely long I/O cards will fit easily, without getting in the way of other system components—a problem with Baby-AT form factor systems.

The specification and related information about the NLX form factor are available through the Desktop Form Factor site located at http://formfactors.org. ATX, mini-ATX, micro-ATX, flex-ATX, and NLX form factors will be the predominant form factors used in virtually all future systems. Because these are well-defined standards that have achieved acceptance in the marketplace, I would avoid the older, obsolete standards, such as Baby-AT. I recommend avoiding LPX or other proprietary systems if upgradability is a factor because not only is locating a new motherboard that will fit difficult, but LPX systems are also limited in expansion slots and drive bays. Overall, ATX is still the best choice for most new systems where expandability, upgradability, low cost, and ease of service are of prime importance.

WTX

WTX was a board and system form factor developed for the mid-range workstation market; however, it didn't seem to catch on. WTX went beyond ATX and defined the size and shape of the board and the interface between the board and chassis, as well as required chassis features.

Figure 4.22   Typical NLX motherboard rear connector layout.

WTX was first released in September 1998 (1.0) and updated in February of 1999 (1.1). The specification and other information on WTX were available at the following Web site: http://www.wtx.org; however, they have been withdrawn and the site taken down. I am unsure whether it will be reintroduced later or whether something else will take its place in the future.

The very few WTX form factor systems that have been introduced were designed as servers. Figure 4.23 shows a typical WTX system with the cover removed. Note that easy access is provided to internal components via pull-out drawers and swinging side panels.

WTX motherboards have a maximum width of 14 inches (356mm) and a maximum length of 16.75 inches (425mm), which is significantly larger than ATX. There are no minimum dimensions, so board designers are free to design smaller boards as long as they meet the mounting criteria.

The WTX specification offers flexibility by leaving motherboard mounting features and locations undefined. Instead of defining exact screw hole positions, WTX motherboards must mount to a standard mounting adapter plate, which must be supplied with the board. The WTX chassis is designed to accept the mounting plate with attached motherboard and not just a bare board alone.

Note

For more information about WTX, see *Upgrading and Repairing PCs, 12th Edition,* available as a PDF on the CD-ROM included with this book.

Figure 4.23 Typical WTX system chassis showing internal layout and ease of access.

Proprietary Designs

Motherboards that are *not* one of the standard form factors, such as full-size or Baby-AT, ATX, mini-ATX, micro-ATX, flex-ATX, or NLX, are deemed *proprietary*. LPX systems fall into this category. Most people purchasing PCs should avoid proprietary designs because they do not allow for a future motherboard, power supply, or case upgrade, which limits future use and serviceability of the system. To me, proprietary systems are disposable PCs because you can neither upgrade them nor easily repair them. The problem is that the proprietary parts can come only from the original system manufacturer, and they usually cost many times more than nonproprietary parts. Therefore, after your proprietary system goes out of warranty, not only is it not upgradable, but it is also essentially no longer worth repairing. If the motherboard or any component on it goes bad, you will be better off purchasing a completely new standard system than paying five times the normal price for a new proprietary motherboard. In addition, a new motherboard in a standard form factor system would be one or more generations newer and faster than the one you would be replacing. In a proprietary system, the replacement board would not only cost way too much, but it would be the same as the one that failed.

Note that you might be able to perform limited upgrades to older systems with proprietary motherboards, in the form of custom (non-OEM) processor replacements with attached voltage regulators, usually called "overdrive" or "turbo" chips. Unfortunately, these often don't perform up to the standards of a less expensive new processor and motherboard combination. Of course, I usually recommend upgrading the motherboard and processor together—but that is something that can't be done with a proprietary system.

The popular LPX motherboard design is at the heart of most proprietary systems. These systems are, or were, sold primarily in the retail store channel. This class of system has traditionally been dominated by Compaq (although some of the recent systems are now using industry-standard form factors), Hewlett- Packard (Vectra line), and formerly Packard Bell (no longer in business). As such, virtually all their systems have the problems inherent with their proprietary designs.

If the motherboard in your current ATX form factor system (and any system using a Baby-AT motherboard and case) dies, you can find any number of replacement boards that will bolt directly in—with your choice of processors and clock speeds—at great prices. If the motherboard dies in a proprietary form factor system, you'll pay for a replacement available only from the original manufacturer, and you have little or no opportunity to select a board with a faster or better processor than the one that failed. In other words, upgrading or repairing one of these systems via a motherboard replacement is difficult and usually not cost-effective.

Systems sold by the leading mail-order suppliers, such as Gateway, Micron, Dell, and others, are available in industry-standard form factors such as ATX, micro-ATX, and NLX. This allows for easy upgrading and system expansion in the future. These standard factors allow you to replace your own motherboards, power supplies, and other components easily and select components from any number of suppliers other than where you originally bought the system.

Backplane Systems

One type of proprietary design is the *backplane system*. These systems do not have a motherboard in the true sense of the word. In a backplane system, the components normally found on a motherboard are located instead on an expansion adapter card plugged into a slot.

In these systems, the board with the slots is called a backplane, rather than a motherboard. Systems using this type of construction are called backplane systems.

Backplane systems come in two main types—passive and active. A *passive* backplane means the main backplane board does not contain any circuitry at all except for the bus connectors and maybe some buffer and driver circuits. All the circuitry found on a conventional motherboard is contained on one or more expansion cards installed in slots on the backplane. Some backplane systems use a passive design that incorporates the entire system circuitry into a single mothercard. The mothercard is essentially a complete motherboard designed to plug into a slot in the passive backplane. The passive backplane/mothercard concept enables the entire system to be easily upgraded by changing one or more cards. Because of the expense of the high-function mothercard, this type of system design is rarely found in standard PC systems today, although it was once favored by a few early 286/386 vendors such as Zenith Data Systems. The passive backplane design does enjoy popularity in industrial systems, which are often rack-mounted. Some high-end fileservers also feature this design. Figure 4.24 shows a typical Pentium II single-board computer used in passive backplane systems. Figure 4.25 shows a rack-mount chassis with a passive backplane.

Passive backplane systems with mothercards (often called single-board computers) are by far the most popular backplane design. They are used in industrial or laboratory-type systems and are normally rack-mountable. They usually have a large number of slots and extremely heavy-duty power supplies; they also feature high-capacity, reverse flow cooling designed to pressurize the chassis with cool, filtered air. Many passive backplane systems, such as the one pictured in Figure 4.25, adhere to the PCI/ISA passive backplane and CompactPCI form factor standards set forth by the PCI Industrial Computer Manufacturers Group (PICMG). You can get more information about these standards from PICMG's Web site at www.picmg.org.

An *active* backplane means the main backplane board contains bus control and usually other circuitry as well. Most active backplane systems contain all the circuitry found on a typical motherboard except for what is then called the *processor complex*. The processor complex is the name of the circuit board that contains the main system processor and any other circuitry directly related to it, such as clock control, cache, and so forth. The processor complex design enables the user to easily upgrade the system later to a new processor type by changing one card. In effect, it amounts to a modular motherboard with a replaceable processor section.

Figure 4.24   A typical Pentium IIPICMG single-board computer (top) and its major components (bottom). This single card provides PCI and ISA interfacing, AGP video, two Ethernet network interfaces, and a 68-pin Wide SCSI interface, as well as normal parallel, serial, IDE, and floppy interfaces.

Many large PC manufacturers have built systems with an active backplane/processor complex. Both IBM and Compaq, for example, have used this type of design in some of their high-end (server class) systems. ALR once made a series of desktop and server PCs that also featured this design. This allows an easier and generally more affordable upgrade than the passive backplane/mothercard design because the processor complex board is usually much cheaper than a mothercard. Unfortunately, because no standards exist for the processor complex interface to the system, these boards are proprietary and can be purchased only from the system manufacturer. This limited market and availability causes the prices of these boards to be higher than most complete motherboards from other manufacturers.

The motherboard system design and the backplane system design have advantages and disadvantages. Most original PCs were designed as backplanes in the late 1970s. Apple and IBM shifted the market to the now traditional motherboard with a slot-type design because this kind of system generally is cheaper to mass-produce than one with the backplane design. The theoretical advantage of a backplane system, however, is that you can upgrade it easily to a new processor and level of performance by changing a single card. For example, you can upgrade a system's processor just by changing the card. In a motherboard-design system, you often must change the motherboard, a seemingly more formidable task. Unfortunately, the reality of the situation is that a backplane design is often much more expensive to upgrade. For example, because the bus remains fixed on the backplane, the backplane design precludes more comprehensive upgrades that involve adding local bus slots.

Another nail in the coffin of backplane designs is the upgradable processor. Starting with the 486, Intel and AMD began standardizing the sockets or slots in which processors were to be installed, allowing a single motherboard to support a wider variety of processors and system speeds. Because board designs could be made more flexible, changing only the processor chip for a faster standard OEM type (not one of the kludgy "overdrive" chips) is the easiest and most cost-effective way to upgrade without changing the entire motherboard.

Figure 4.25   A rack-mount chassis with passive backplane.

Because of the limited availability of the processor-complex boards or mothercards, they usually end up being more expensive than a complete new motherboard that uses an industry-standard form factor. The bottom line is that unless you have a requirement for a large capacity industrial or laboratory-type system, especially one that would be rack-mounted, you are better off sticking with standard ATX form factor PCs. They will certainly be far less expensive.

Note

Some companies offer plug-in processor cards that essentially turn your existing motherboard into an active backplane, shutting down the main CPU and memory and having the card's processor and memory essentially take over. These are unfortunately much more expensive than a new motherboard and processor alone, normally use the more expensive SO-DIMM memory, don't provide AGP video, and are generally not recommended.

Motherboard Components

A modern motherboard has several components built in, including various sockets, slots, connectors, chips, and so on. This section examines the components found on a typical motherboard.

Most modern motherboards have at least the following major components on them:

- Processor socket/slot
- Chipset (North/South Bridge or memory and I/O controller hubs)
- Super I/O chip

- ROM BIOS (Flash ROM/firmware hub)
- SIMM/DIMM/RIMM (RAM memory) sockets
- ISA/PCI/AGP bus slots
- CPU voltage regulator
- Battery

Some motherboards also include integrated video, audio, networking, SCSI, Audio Modem Riser (AMR), Communications and Networking Riser (CNR) connectors, or other optional interfaces, depending on the individual board.

These standard components are discussed in the following sections.

Processor Sockets/Slots

The CPU is installed in either a socket or a slot, depending on the type of chip.

Starting with the 486 processors, Intel designed the processor to be a user-installable and replaceable part and developed standards for CPU sockets and slots that would allow different models of the same basic processor to plug in. These specifications were given a designation that is usually imprinted or embossed on the connector or board. After you know the type of socket or slot on your motherboard, you essentially know which type of processors are designed to plug in.

◄◄ See "Processor Sockets and Slots," 82.

Sockets for processors prior to the 486 were not designated, and interchangeability was limited. Table 4.3 shows the designations for the various processor sockets/slots and lists the chips designed to plug into them.

Table 4.3   CPU Socket Specifications

Number Socket	Pin	Pin Layout	Voltage	Supported Processors
Socket 1	169	17×17 PGA	5V	486 SX/SX2, DX/DX2[1], DX4 OD
Socket 2	238	19×19 PGA	5V	486 SX/SX2, DX/DX2[1], DX4 OD, 486 Pentium OD
Socket 3	237	19×19 PGA	5V/3.3V	486 SX/SX2, DX/DX2, DX4, 486 Pentium OD, 5x86
Socket 4	273	21×21 PGA	5V	Pentium 60/66, OD
Socket 5	320	37×37 SPGA	3.3V/3.5V	Pentium 75-133, OD
Socket 6[2]	235	19×19 PGA	3.3V	486 DX4, 486 Pentium OD
Socket 7	321	37×37 SPGA	VRM	Pentium 75-266+, MMX, OD, 6x86, K6
Socket 8	387	Dual-pattern SPGA	Auto VRM	Pentium Pro
Socket 370 (PGA370)	370	37×37 SPGA	Auto VRM	PIII/Celeron PPGA/FCPGA
Socket PAC418	418	38×22 split SPGA	Auto VRM	Itanium PAC
Socket 423 (PGA423)	423	39×39 SPGA	Auto VRM	Pentium 4
Socket A (PGA462)	462	37×37 SPGA	Auto VRM	Athlon/Duron PGA
Socket 603	603	31×25 SPGA	Auto VRM	Xeon (P4)

Table 4.3   Continued

Number Socket	Pin	Pin Layout	Voltage	Supported Processors
Slot 1 (SC242)	242	Keyed Slot	Auto VRM	PII, PIII/Celeron SECC
Slot A	242	Keyed Slot	Auto VRM	Athlon SECC
Slot 2 (SC330)	330	Keyed Slot	Auto VRM	PII Xeon, PIII Xeon

1. *Non-OverDrive DX4 also can be supported with the addition of an aftermarket 3.3v voltage regulator adapter.*

2. *Socket 6 was a proposed standard only and was never actually implemented in any systems.*

OD = OverDrive (retail upgrade processors).

PGA = Pin grid array.

SPGA = Staggered pin grid array.

PPGA = Plastic pin grid array.

FCPGA = Flip-Chip pppin grid array.

PAC = Pin array cartridge.

VRM = Voltage regulator module with variable voltage output determined by module or manual jumpers.

Auto-VRM = Voltage regulator module with automatic voltage selection determined by processor VID pins.

SECC = Single edge contact cartridge.

SC242 = Slot connector, 242 pins.

SC330 = Slot connector, 330 pins.

Originally, all processors were mounted in sockets (or soldered directly to the motherboard). With the advent of the Pentium II and original Athlon processors, both Intel and AMD shifted to a slot-based approach for their processors because the processors now incorporated built-in L2 cache, purchased as separate chips from third-party Static RAM (SRAM) memory chip manufacturers. Therefore, the processor then consisted not of one but of several chips, all mounted on a daughterboard that was then plugged into a slot in the motherboard. This worked well, but there were additional expenses in the extra cache chips, the daughterboard itself, the slot, optional casings or packaging, and the support mechanisms and physical stands and latches for the processor and heatsink. All in all, slot-based processors were expensive to produce compared to the previous socketed versions.

With the advent of the second-generation Celeron, Intel integrated the L2 cache directly into the processor die, meaning within the main CPU chip circuits, with no extra chips required. The second-generation (codenamed Coppermine) Pentium III also received on-die L2 cache, as did the K6-3, Duron (codenamed Spitfire), and second-generation Athlon (codenamed Thunderbird) processors from AMD (some early Thunderbird Athlon CPUs were also made in the Slot A configuration). With on-die L2, the processor was back to being a single chip again, which also meant that mounting it on a separate board plugged into a slot was expensive and unnecessary. Because of on-die integrated L2 cache, the trend for processor packaging has shifted back to sockets and will likely continue that way for the foreseeable future. All modern processors now use the socket form. Besides allowing a return to socketed packaging, the on-die L2 cache runs at full processor speed, instead of the one-half or one-third speed of the previous integrated (but not on-die) L2 cache.

The Itanium features a cartridge design that includes L3 cache, and yet plugs into a socket rather than a slot.

Chipsets

We cannot talk about modern motherboards without discussing chipsets. The chipset *is* the motherboard; therefore, any two boards with the same chipsets are functionally identical. The chipset contains the processor bus interface (called front-side bus, or FSB), memory controllers, bus controllers, I/O controllers, and more. All the circuits of the motherboard are contained within the chipset. If the processor in your PC is like the engine in your car, the chipset represents the chassis. It is the framework in which the engine rests and its connection to the outside world. The chipset is the frame, suspension, steering, wheels and tires, transmission, driveshaft, differential, and brakes. The chassis in your car is what gets the power to the ground, allowing the vehicle to start, stop, and corner. In the PC, the chipset represents the connection between the processor and everything else. The processor cannot talk to the memory, adapter boards, devices, and so on without going through the chipset. The chipset is the main hub and central nervous system of the PC. If you think of the processor as the brain, the chipset is the spine and central nervous system.

Because the chipset controls the interface or connections between the processor and everything else, the chipset ends up dictating which type of processor you have; how fast it will run; how fast the buses will run; the speed, type, and amount of memory you can use; and more. In fact, the chipset might be the single most important component in your system, possibly even more important than the processor. I've seen systems with faster processors be outperformed by systems with slower processor but a better chipset, much like how a car with less power might win a race through better cornering and braking. When deciding on a system, I start by choosing the chipset first because the chipset decision then dictates the processor, memory, I/O, and expansion capabilities.

Chipset Evolution

When IBM created the first PC motherboards, it used several discrete (separate) chips to complete the design. Besides the processor and optional math coprocessor, many other components were required to complete the system. These other components included items such as the clock generator, bus controller, system timer, interrupt and DMA controllers, CMOS RAM and clock, and keyboard controller. Additionally, a number of other simple logic chips were used to complete the entire motherboard circuit, plus, of course, things such as the actual processor, math coprocessor (floating-point unit), memory, and other parts. Table 4.4 lists all the primary chip components used on the original PC/XT and AT motherboards.

Table 4.4   Primary Chip Components on PC/XT and AT Motherboards

Chip Function	PC/XT Version	AT Version
Processor	8088	80286
Math Coprocessor (Floating-Point Unit	8087	80287
Clock Generator	8284	82284
Bus Controller	8288	82288
System Timer	8253	8254
Low-order Interrupt Controller	8259	8259
High-order Interrupt Controller	—	8259
Low-order DMA Controller	8237	8237
High-order DMA Controller	—	8237
CMOS RAM/Real-Time Clock	—	MC146818
Keyboard Controller	8255	8042

In addition to the processor/coprocessor, a six-chip set was used to implement the primary mother-board circuit in the original PC and XT systems. IBM later upgraded this to a nine-chip design in the AT and later systems, mainly by adding additional interrupt and DMA controller chips and the non-volatile CMOS RAM/Real-time Clock chip. All these motherboard chip components came from Intel or an Intel-licensed manufacturer, except the CMOS/Clock chip, which came from Motorola. To build a clone or copy of one of these IBM systems required all these chips plus many smaller discrete logic chips to glue the design together, totaling 100 or more individual chips. This kept the price of a motherboard high and left little room on the board to integrate other functions.

In 1986, a company called Chips and Technologies introduced a revolutionary component called the 82C206—the main part of the first PC motherboard chipset. This was a single chip that integrated into it all the functions of the main motherboard chips in an AT-compatible system. This chip included the functions of the 82284 Clock Generator, 82288 Bus Controller, 8254 System Timer, dual 8259 Interrupt Controllers, dual 8237 DMA Controllers, and even the MC146818 CMOS/Clock chip. Besides the processor, virtually all the major chip components on a PC motherboard could now be replaced by a single chip. Four other chips augmented the 82C206 acting as buffers and memory con-trollers, thus completing virtually the entire motherboard circuit with five total chips. This first chipset was called the CS8220 chipset by Chips and Technologies. Needless to say, this was a revolu-tionary concept in PC motherboard manufacturing. Not only did it greatly reduce the cost of building a PC motherboard, but it also made designing a motherboard much easier. The reduced component count meant the boards had more room for integrating other items formerly found on expansion cards. Later, the four chips augmenting the 82C206 were replaced by a new set of only three chips, and the entire set was called the New Enhanced AT (NEAT) CS8221 chipset. This was later followed by the 82C836 Single Chip AT (SCAT) chipset, which finally condensed all the chips in the set down to a single chip.

The chipset idea was rapidly copied by other chip manufacturers. Companies such as Acer, Erso, Opti, Suntac, Symphony, UMC, and VLSI each gained an important share of this market. Unfortunately, for many of them, the chipset market has been a volatile one, and many of them have long since gone out of business. In 1993, VLSI had become the dominant force in the chipset market and had the vast majority of the market share; by the next year, VLSI (which later was merged into Philips Semiconductors), along with virtually everybody else in the chipset market, were fighting to stay alive. This is because a new chipset manufacturer had come on the scene, and within a year or so of getting serious, it was totally dominating the chipset market. That company was Intel, and after 1994 it had a virtual lock on the chipset market. If you have a motherboard built since 1994 that uses or accepts an Intel processor, chances are good that it has an Intel chipset on it as well.

More recently, Intel has struggled somewhat with chipsets because of its reliance on RDRAM memory. Intel signed a contract with Rambus back in 1996 declaring it would support this memory as its pri-mary focus for desktop PC chipsets through 2001. I suspect this has turned out to be something Intel regrets. RDRAM memory has a significantly higher price than SDRAM memory and doesn't seem to have any significant performance advantages. In fact, it is slower than the double data rate (DDR) SDRAM the mainstream has decided to support. Consequently, Intel is developing a DDR SDRAM chipset codenamed Brookdale for release in late 2001 or early 2002.

A few chipset manufacturers have carved out a niche supporting AMD processors. Today, that would include primarily Acer Laboratories, Inc. (ALi), VIA Technologies, and Silicon integrated Systems (SiS). Along with AMD's own chipsets, these companies have products that support the AMD Athlon and Duron processors, and previously the AMD K6 as well. Currently, VIA and AMD seem to dominate the Athlon/Duron chipset market.

It is interesting to note that Chips and Technologies survived by changing course to design and man-ufacture video chips and found a niche in that market specifically for laptop and notebook video chipsets. Chips and Technologies was subsequently bought out by Intel in 1998 as a part of Intel's video strategy.

Intel Chipsets

You cannot talk about chipsets today without discussing Intel because it currently owns the vast majority of the chipset market. It is interesting to note that we probably have Compaq to thank for forcing Intel into the chipset business in the first place!

The thing that really started it all was the introduction of the EISA bus designed by Compaq in 1989. At that time, it had shared the bus with other manufacturers in an attempt to make it a market standard. However, it refused to share its EISA bus chipset—a set of custom chips necessary to implement this bus on a motherboard.

Enter Intel, who decided to fill the chipset void for the rest of the PC manufacturers wanting to build EISA bus motherboards. As is well known today, the EISA bus failed to become a market success except for a short-term niche server business, but Intel now had a taste of the chipset business and this it apparently wouldn't forget. With the introduction of the 286 and 386 processors, Intel became impatient with how long it took the other chipset companies to create chipsets around its new processor designs; this delayed the introduction of motherboards that supported the new processors. For example, it took more than two years after the 286 processor was introduced for the first 286 motherboards to appear and just over a year for the first 386 motherboards to appear after the 386 had been introduced. Intel couldn't sell its processors in volume until other manufacturers made motherboards that would support them, so it thought that by developing motherboard chipsets for a new processor in parallel with the new processor, it could jumpstart the motherboard business by providing ready-made chipsets for the motherboard manufacturers to use.

Intel tested this by introducing the 420 series chipsets along with its 486 processor in April of 1989. This enabled the motherboard companies to get busy right away, and it was only a few months before the first 486 motherboards appeared. Of course, the other chipset manufacturers weren't happy; now they had Intel as a competitor, and Intel would always have chipsets for new processors on the market first!

Intel then realized that it now made both processors *and* chipsets, which were 90% of the components on a typical motherboard. What better way to ensure that motherboards were available for its Pentium processor when it was introduced than by making its own motherboards as well and having these boards ready on the new processor's introduction date. When the first Pentium processor debuted in 1993, Intel also debuted the 430LX chipset and a fully finished motherboard as well. Now, not only were the chipset companies upset, but the motherboard companies weren't too happy either. Intel was not only the major supplier of parts needed to build finished boards (processors and chipsets), but Intel was now building and selling the finished boards as well. By 1994, Intel had not only dominated the processor and chipset markets, but it had cornered the motherboard market as well.

Now as Intel develops new processors, it develops chipsets and motherboards simultaneously, which means they can be announced and shipped in unison. This eliminates the delay between introducing new processors and waiting for motherboards and systems capable of using them, which was common in the industry's early days. For the consumer, this means no waiting for new systems. Since the original Pentium processor in 1993, we have been able to purchase ready-made systems on the same day a new processor is released.

In my seminars, I ask how many people in the class have Intel brand PCs. Of course, Intel does not sell or market a PC under its own name, so nobody thinks they have an "Intel brand" PC. But, if your motherboard was made by Intel, for all intents and purposes you sure seem to have an Intel brand PC, at least as far as the components are concerned. Does it really matter whether Dell, Gateway, or Micron put that same Intel motherboard into a slightly different looking case with their name on it?

If you look under the covers, you'll find that many, if not most, of the systems from the major manufacturers are really the same because they use basically the same parts. Although more and more major manufacturers are offering AMD Athlon- and Duron-based systems as alternatives to Intel's, no manufacturer dominates AMD motherboard sales the way Intel has dominated OEM sales to major system manufacturers.

To hold down pricing, many low-cost retail systems based on micro-ATX motherboards use non-Intel motherboards. But, even though many companies make Intel-compatible motherboards for aftermarket upgrades or local computer assemblers, Intel still dominates the major vendor OEM market for midrange and high-end systems.

Intel Chipset Model Numbers

Intel started a pattern of numbering its chipsets as follows:

Chipset Number	Processor Family
420xx	P4 (486)
430xx	P5 (Pentium)
440xx	P6 (Pentium Pro/PII/PIII)
8xx	P6 (PII/PIII/P4) with hub architecture
450xx	P6 Server (Pentium Pro/PII/PIII Xeon)

The chipset numbers listed here are an abbreviation of the actual chipset numbers stamped on the individual chips. For example, one of the popular Pentium II/III chipsets is the Intel 440BX chipset, which really consists of two components, the 82443BX North Bridge and the 82371EX South Bridge. Likewise, the 850 chipset supports the Pentium 4 and consists of two main parts, including the 82850 Memory Controller Hub (MCH) and an 82801BA I/O Controller Hub (ICH2). By reading the logo (Intel or others) as well as the part number and letter combinations on the larger chips on your motherboard, you can quickly identify the chipset your motherboard uses.

Intel has used two distinct chipset architectures: a North/South Bridge architecture and a newer hub architecture. All its more recent 800 series chipsets use the hub architecture.

AMD Athlon/Duron Chipsets

AMD took a gamble with its Athlon and Duron processors. With these processors, AMD decided for the first time to create a chip that was Intel-compatible with regards to software but not directly hardware or pin compatible. Whereas the K6 series would plug into the same Socket 7 that Intel designed for the Pentium processor line, the AMD Athlon and Duron would not be pin compatible with the Pentium II/III and Celeron chips. This also meant that AMD could not take advantage of the previously existing chipsets and motherboards when the Athlon and Duron were introduced; instead, AMD would have to either create its own chipsets and motherboards or find other companies who would.

The gamble seems to have paid off. AMD bootstrapped the market by introducing its own chipset, referred to as the AMD-750 chipset and codenamed Irongate. The AMD 750 chipset consists of the 751 System Controller (North Bridge) and the 756 Peripheral Bus Controller (South Bridge). More recently, AMD introduced the AMD-760 chipset for the Athlon/Duron processors, which is the first major chipset on the market supporting DDR SDRAM for memory. It consists of two chips—the AMD-761 System Bus Controller (North Bridge) and the AMD-766 Peripheral Bus Controller (South Bridge). Other companies, such as VIA Technologies and SiS, have also introduced chipsets specifically designed for the Socket/Slot A processors from AMD. This enabled the motherboard companies to make a variety of boards supporting these chips and the Athlon and Duron processors to take a fair amount of market share away from Intel in the process.

North/South Bridge Architecture

Most of Intel's earlier chipsets (and virtually all non-Intel chipsets) are broken into a multi-tiered architecture incorporating what are referred to as North and South Bridge components, as well as a Super I/O chip:

- *The North Bridge.* So named because it is the connection between the high-speed processor bus (400/266/200/133/100/66MHz) and the slower AGP (533/266/133/66MHz) and PCI (33MHz) buses. The North Bridge is what the chipset is named after, meaning that, for example, what we call the 440BX chipset is actually derived from the fact that the actual North Bridge chip part number for that set is 82443BX.

- *The South Bridge.* So named because it is the bridge between the PCI bus (66/33MHz) and the even slower ISA bus (8MHz).

- *The Super I/O chip.* It's a separate chip attached to the ISA bus that is not really considered part of the chipset and often comes from a third party, such as National Semiconductor or Standard MicroSystems Corp. (SMSC). The Super I/O chip contains commonly used peripheral items all combined into a single chip.

▶▶ See "Super I/O Chips," p. 283.

Chipsets have evolved over the years to support various processors, bus speeds, peripheral connections, and features.

Figure 4.26 shows a typical AMD Socket A motherboard using North/South Bridge architecture with the locations of all chips and components.

The North Bridge is sometimes referred to as the PAC (PCI/AGP Controller). It is essentially the main component of the motherboard and is the only motherboard circuit besides the processor that normally runs at full motherboard (processor bus) speed. Most modern chipsets use a single-chip North Bridge; however, some of the older ones actually consisted of up to three individual chips to make up the complete North Bridge circuit.

The South Bridge is the lower-speed component in the chipset and has always been a single individual chip. The South Bridge is a somewhat interchangeable component in that different chipsets (North Bridge chips) often are designed to use the same South Bridge component. This modular design of the chipset allows for lower cost and greater flexibility for motherboard manufacturers. The South Bridge connects to the 33MHz PCI bus and contains the interface or bridge to the 8MHz ISA bus. It also normally contains dual IDE hard disk controller interfaces, one or two USB interfaces, and in later designs even the CMOS RAM and real-time clock functions. The South Bridge contains all the components that make up the ISA bus, including the interrupt and DMA controllers.

The third motherboard component, the Super I/O chip, is connected to the 8MHz ISA bus and contains all the standard peripherals that are built in to a motherboard. For example, most Super I/O chips contain the serial ports, parallel port, floppy controller, and keyboard/mouse interface. Optionally, they also might contain the CMOS RAM/Clock, IDE controllers, and game port interface as well. Systems that integrate IEEE-1394 and SCSI ports use separate chips for these port types.

AC '97 Audio Codec chip
(for built-in audio)

AGP Pro
slot

MIDI/Joystick
port

Parallel port

USB ports

Modem In
connector

Video/Audio
In connector

Audio/Modem
Riser (AMR)
connector

PCI slots (5)

USB header
cable connector
(for front-mounted
USB ports)

PS/2 mouse
and keyboard
ports

Socket A
(Socket 462)
for AMD Athlon/Duron
processors

VIA Apollo
KT-133 chipset
(2 pcs)

ATX power
supply (20-pin)
connector

DIMM slots

Flash BIOS and
socket for optional
second flash BIOS
chip

Battery

IDE connectors

Floppy connector

Figure 4.26   A typical Socket A (AMD Athlon/Duron) motherboard showing component locations.

Hub Architecture

The newer 800 series chips use a hub architecture in which the former North Bridge chip is now called a Memory Controller Hub (MCH), and the former South Bridge is called an I/O Controller Hub (ICH). Rather than connect them through the PCI bus as in a standard North/South Bridge design, they are connected via a dedicated hub interface that is twice as fast as PCI. The hub design offers several advantages over the conventional North/South Bridge design:

- *It's faster.* The hub interface is a 4X (quad-clocked) 66MHz 8-bit ($4 \times 66MHz \times 1$ Byte = 266MB/sec) interface, which has twice the throughput of PCI ($33MHz \times 32$-bit = 133MB/sec).

- *Reduced PCI loading.* The hub interface is independent of PCI and doesn't share or steal PCI bus bandwidth for chipset or Super I/O traffic. This improves performance of all other PCI bus connected devices because the PCI bus is not involved in these transactions.

- *Reduced board wiring.* Although twice as fast as PCI, the hub interface is only 8 bits wide and requires only 15 signals to be routed on the motherboard. By comparison, PCI requires no less than 64 signals be routed on the board, causing increased electro-magnetic interference (EMI) generation, greater susceptibility to signal degradation and noise, and increased board manufacturing costs.

This hub interface design allows for a much greater throughput for PCI devices because there is no South Bridge chip (also carrying traffic from the Super I/O chip) hogging the PCI bus. Due to bypassing PCI, hub architecture also enables greater throughput for devices directly connected to the I/O Controller Hub (formerly the South Bridge), such as the new higher-speed ATA-100 and USB 2.0 interfaces.

The hub interface design is also very economical, being only 8 bits wide. Although this seems too narrow to be useful, there is a reason for the design. By making the interface only 8 bits wide, it uses only 15 signals, compared to the 64 signals required by the 32-bit-wide PCI bus interface used by North/South Bridge chip designs. The lower pin count means less circuit routing exists on the board, less signal noise and jitter occur, and the chips themselves have many fewer pins, making them smaller and more economical to produce.

Although it transfers only 8 bits at a time, the hub interface does four transfers per cycle and cycles at 66MHz. This gives it an effective throughput of $4 \times 66\text{MHz} \times 1$ byte = 266MB/second. This is twice the bandwidth of PCI, which is 32 bits wide but runs only one transfer per 33MHz cycles for a total bandwidth of 133MB/second. So by virtue of a very narrow—but very fast—design, the hub interface achieves high performance with less cost and more signal integrity than with the previous North/South Bridge design.

The MCH interfaces between the high-speed processor bus (400/133/100/66MHz) and the hub interface (66MHz) and AGP bus (533/266/133/66MHz), whereas the ICH interfaces between the hub interface (66MHz) and the ATA(IDE) ports (66/100MHz) and PCI bus (33MHz).

The ICH also includes a new low-pin-count (LPC) bus, consisting basically of a stripped 4-bit wide version of PCI designed primarily to support the motherboard ROM BIOS and Super I/O chips. By using the same four signals for data, address, and command functions, only nine other signals are necessary to implement the bus, for a total of only thirteen signals. This dramatically reduces the number of traces connecting the ROM BIOS chip and Super I/O chips in a system as compared to the ninety-six ISA bus signals necessary for older North/South Bridge chipsets that used ISA as the interface to those devices. The LPC bus has a maximum bandwidth of 6.67MB/sec, which is close to ISA and more than enough to support devices such as ROM BIOS and Super I/O chips.

Figure 4.27 shows a typical Intel motherboard that uses bus architecture—the Intel DB850GB, which supports the Intel Pentium 4 processor. Unlike some of Intel's less-expensive hub-based motherboards, the DB850GB's Intel 850 chipset doesn't incorporate video.

Let's examine the popular chipsets, starting with those used in 486 motherboards and working all the way through to the latest Pentium III/Celeron, Athlon/Duron, and VIA chipsets.

Intel's Early 386/486 Chipsets

Intel's first real PC motherboard chipset was the 82350 chipset for the 386DX and 486 processors. This chipset was not very successful, mainly because the EISA bus was not very popular and many other manufacturers were making standard 386 and 486 motherboard chipsets at the time. The market changed very quickly, and Intel dropped the EISA bus support and introduced follow-up 486 chipsets that were much more successful.

Table 4.5 shows the Intel 486 chipsets.

The 420 series chipsets were the first to introduce the North/South Bridge design that is still used in many chipsets today.

A   AD1881/AD1885 audio codec (optional)
B   AGP connector (AGP Pro 1.5V connector optional)
C   Intel 82850 Memory Controller Hub (MCH)
D   Back panel connectors
E   +12V power connector (ATX 12V)
F   Pentium 4 Processor socket
G   Hardware monitor
H   RAMBUS Bank 0 (RIMM1 and RIMM2)
I   RAMBUS Bank 1 (RIMM3 and RIMM4)
J   Power connector
K   Auxiliary power connector

L   Diskette drive connector
M   IDE connectors
N   Intel 82801BA I/O Controller Hub (ICH2)
O   SMSC LPC47M102 I/O Controller
P   Front panel connector
Q   Enhanced thermal monitor and fan control device
R   Battery
S   SST 49LF004A 4Mbit Firmware Hub (FWH)
T   Speaker
U   PCI bus add-in card connectors
V   Communication and Networking Riser (CNR) connector (optional)

Figure 4.27   Intel DB850GB motherboard showing component locations. *Illustration used by permission of Intel Corporation.*

Table 4.5   Intel 486 Motherboard Chipsets

Chipset	420TX	420EX	420ZX
Codename	Saturn	Aries	Saturn II
Date introduced	Nov. 1992	March 1994	March 1994
Processor	5v 486	5v/3.3v 486	5v/3.3v 486
Bus speed	up to 33MHz	up to 50MHz	up to 333MHz
SMP (dual CPUs)	No	No	No
Memory types	FPM	FPM	FPM
Parity/ECC	Parity	Parity	Parity
Max. memory	128MB	128MB	160MB
L2 cache type	Async	Async	Async
PCI support	2.0	2.0	2.1
AGP support	No	No	No

SMP = Symmetric multiprocessing (dual processors).
FPM = Fast page mode.
PCI = Peripheral component interconnect.

AGP = Accelerated graphics port.
Note: PCI 2.1 supports concurrent PCI operations.

Fifth-Generation (P5 Pentium Class) Chipsets

With the advent of the Pentium processor in March of 1993, Intel also introduced its first Pentium chipset, the 430LX chipset (codenamed Mercury). This was the first Pentium chipset on the market and set the stage as Intel took this lead and ran with it. Other manufacturers took months to a year or more to get their Pentium chipsets out the door. Since the debut of its Pentium chipsets, Intel has dominated the chipset market. Table 4.6 shows the Intel Pentium motherboard chipsets. Note that none of these chipsets support AGP; Intel supports AGP only in its chipsets for the Pentium II/Celeron and later processors.

Table 4.6   Intel Pentium Motherboard Chipsets (North Bridge)

Chipset	430LX	430NX	430FX	430MX	430HX	430VX	430TX
Codename	Mercury	Neptune	Triton	Mobile Triton	Triton II	Triton III	n/a
Date introduced	March 1993	March 1994	Jan. 1995	Oct. 1995	Feb. 1996	Feb. 1996	Feb. 1997
CPU bus speed	66MHz	66MHz	66MHz	66MHz	66MHz	66MHz	66MHz
CPUs supported	P60/66	P75+	P75+	P75+	P75+	P75+	P75+
SMP (dual CPUs)	No	Yes	No	No	Yes	No	No
Memory types	FPM	FPM	FPM/EDO	FPM/EDO	FPM/EDO	FPM/ EDO/ SDRAM	FPM/ EDO/ SDRAM
Parity/ECC	Parity	Parity	Neither	Neither	Both	Neither	Neither
Max. memory	192MB	512MB	128MB	128MB	512MB	128MB	256MB
Max. cacheable	192MB	512MB	64MB	64MB	512MB	64MB	64MB
L2 cache type	Async	Async	Async/ Pburst	Async/ Pburst	Async/ Pburst	Async/ Pburst	Async/ Pburst
PCI support	2.0	2.0	2.0	2.0	2.1	2.1	2.1
AGP support	No	No	No	No	No	No	No
South Bridge	SIO	SIO	PIIX	MPIIX	PIIX3	PIIX3	PIIX4

SMP = Symmetric multiprocessing (dual processors)   SDRAM = Synchronous dynamic RAM
FPM = Fast page mode   SIO = System I/O
EDO = Extended data out   PIIX = PCI ISA IDE Xcelerator

Note

PCI 2.1 supports concurrent PCI operations, enabling multiple PCI cards to perform transactions at the same time for greater speed.Bridge

Table 4.7 shows all the applicable Intel South Bridge chips, which are the second part of the modern Intel motherboard chipsets.

Table 4.7   Intel South Bridge Chips

Chip Name	SIO	PIIX	PIIX3	PIIX4	PIIX4E	ICH0	ICH
Part number	82378IB/ZB	82371FB	82371SB	82371AB	82371EB	82801AB	82801AA
IDE support	None	BMIDE	BMIDE	UDMA-33	UDMA-33	UDMA-33	UDMA-66
USB support	None	None	Yes	Yes	Yes	Yes	Yes
CMOS/clock	No	No	No	Yes	Yes	Yes	Yes
Power management	SMM	SMM	SMM	SMM	SMM/ ACPI	SMM/ ACPI	SMM/ ACPI

SIO = System I/O
PIIX = PCI ISA IDE Xcelerator
ICH = I/O Controller Hub
USB = Universal serial bus
IDE = Integrated Drive Electronics (AT attachment)

BMIDE = Bus master IDE
UDMA = Ultra-DMA IDE
SMM = System management mode
ACPI = Advanced configuration and power interface

The following sections detail all the Pentium motherboard chipsets and their specifications.

Intel 430LX (Mercury)

The 430LX was introduced in March of 1993, concurrent with the introduction of the first Pentium processors. This chipset was used only with the original Pentiums, which came in 60MHz and 66MHz versions. These were 5v chips and were used on motherboards with Socket 4 processor sockets.

◄◄   See "Processor Sockets and Slots," p. 82.

◄◄   See "First-Generation Pentium Processor," p. 133.

The 430LX chipset consisted of three total chips for the North Bridge portion. The main chip was the 82434LX system controller. This chip contained the processor-to-memory interface, cache controller, and PCI bus controller. There was also a pair of PCI bus interface accelerator chips, which were identical 82433LX chips.

The 430LX chipset was noted for the following:

- Single processor
- Support for up to 512KB of L2 cache
- Support for up to 192MB of standard DRAM

This chipset died off along with the 5v 60/66MHz Pentium processors.

Intel 430NX (Neptune)

Introduced in March 1994, the 430NX was the first chipset designed to run the new 3.3v second-generation Pentium processor. These were noted by having Socket 5 processor sockets and an onboard 3.3v/3.5v voltage regulator for both the processor and chipset. This chipset was designed primarily for Pentiums with speeds from 75MHz to 133MHz, although it was used mostly with 75MHz–100MHz systems. Along with the lower voltage processor, this chipset ran faster, cooler, and more reliably than the first-generation Pentium processor and the corresponding 5v chipsets.

◄◄   See "CPU Operating Voltages," p. 97.

◄◄   See "Second-Generation Pentium Processor," p. 133.

The 430NX chipset consisted of three chips for the North Bridge component. The primary chip was the 82434NX, which included the cache and main memory (DRAM) controller and the control interface to the PCI bus. The actual PCI data was managed by a pair of 82433NX chips called local bus accelerators. Together, these two chips, plus the main 82434NX chip, constituted the North Bridge.

The South Bridge used with the 430NX chipset was the 82378ZB System I/O (SIO) chip. This component connected to the PCI bus and generated the lower-speed ISA bus.

The 430NX chipset introduced the following improvements over the Mercury (430LX) chipset:

- Dual processor support
- Support for 512MB of system memory (up from 192MB for the LX Mercury chipset)

This chipset rapidly became the most popular chipset for the early 75MHz–100MHz systems, overshadowing the older 60MHz and 66MHz systems that used the 430LX chipset.

Intel 430FX (Triton)

The 430FX (Triton) chipset rapidly became popular after it was introduced in January 1995. This chipset is noted for being the first to support extended data out (EDO) memory, which subsequently became very popular. EDO was about 21% faster than the standard fast page mode (FPM) memory that had been used up until that time but cost no more than the slower FPM. Unfortunately, while being known for faster memory support, the Triton chipset was also known as the first Pentium chipset without support for parity checking for memory. This was somewhat of a blow to PC reliability and fault tolerance, although many did not know it at the time.

▶▶ See "Extended Data Out RAM," p. 416.

▶▶ See "Parity and ECC," p. 443.

The Triton chipset lacked not only parity support from the previous 430NX chipset, but it also would support only a single CPU. The 430FX was designed as a low-end chipset for home or non–mission-critical systems. As such, it did not replace the 430NX, which carried on in higher-end network fileservers and other more mission-critical systems.

The 430FX consisted of a three-chip North Bridge. The main chip was the 82437FX system controller that included the memory and cache controllers, CPU interface, and PCI bus controller, along with dual 82438FX data path chips for the PCI bus. The South Bridge was the first PIIX (PCI ISA IDE Xcelerator) chip that was the 82371FB. This chip acted not only as the bridge between the 33MHz PCI bus and the slower 8MHz ISA bus, but also incorporated for the first time a dual-channel IDE interface. By moving the IDE interface off the ISA bus and into the PIIX chip, it was now effectively connected to the PCI bus, enabling much faster Bus Master IDE transfers. This was key in supporting the ATA-2 or Enhanced IDE interface for better hard disk performance.

The major points on the 430FX are

- Support for EDO memory
- Support for higher speed—pipelined burst L2 cache
- PIIX South Bridge with high-speed Bus Master IDE
- Lack of support for parity-checked memory
- Only single CPU support
- Supported only 128MB of RAM, of which only 64MB could be cached

That last issue is one that many people are not aware of. The 430FX chipset can cache only up to 64MB of main memory. So, if you install more than 64MB of RAM in your system, performance suffers greatly. At the time, many didn't think this would be that much of a problem—after all, they didn't usually run enough software to load past the first 64MB anyway. That is another misunderstanding because Windows 9x and NT/2000 (as well as all other protected-mode operating systems including Linux and so on) load from the top down. So, for example, if you install 96MB of RAM (one 64MB and one 32MB bank), virtually all your software, including the main operating system, will be loading into the noncached region above 64MB. Needless to say, performance would suffer greatly. Try disabling the L2 cache via your CMOS Setup to see how slow your system runs without it. That is the performance you can expect if you install more than 64MB of RAM in a 430FX-based system.

Intel 430HX (Triton II)

Intel created the Triton II 430HX chipset as a true replacement for the powerful 430NX chip. It added some of the high-speed memory features from the low-end 430FX, such as support for EDO memory and pipeline burst L2 cache. It also retained dual-processor support. In addition to supporting parity checking to detect memory errors, it also added support for error correcting code (ECC) memory to detect and correct single bit errors on-the-fly. And the great thing was that this was implemented using plain parity memory.

The HX chipset's primary advantages over the FX are

- Symmetric multiprocessor (dual processor) support.
- Support for ECC and parity memory.
- 512MB maximum RAM support (versus 128MB).
- L2 cache functions over 512MB RAM versus 64MB (providing optional cache tag RAM is installed).
- Memory transfers in fewer cycles overall.
- PCI Level 2.1 compliance that allows concurrent PCI operations.
- PIIX3 supports different IDE/ATA transfer speed settings on a single channel.
- PIIX3 South Bridge component supports USB.

The memory problems with caching in the 430FX were corrected in the 430HX. This chipset allowed for the possibility of caching the full 512MB of possible RAM as long as the correct amount of cache *tag* was installed. Tag is a small cache memory chip used to store the index to the data in the cache. Most 430HX systems shipped with a tag chip that could manage only 64MB of cached main memory, although you could optionally upgrade it to a larger capacity tag chip that would allow for caching the full 512MB of RAM.

The 430HX chipset was a true one-chip North Bridge. It was also one of the first chips out in a ball-grid array (BGA) package, in which the chip leads are configured as balls on the bottom of the chip. This made possible a smaller chip package than the previous plastic quad flat pack (PQFP) packaging used on the older chips, and, because only one chip existed for the North Bridge, a very compact motherboard was possible. The South Bridge was the PIIX3 (82371SB) chip, which enabled independent timing of the dual IDE channels. Therefore, you could install two different speed devices on the same channel and configure their transfer speeds independently. Previous PIIX chips allowed both devices to work at the lowest common denominator speed supported by both. The PIIX3 also incorporated the USB for the first time on a PC motherboard. Unfortunately at the time, there were no devices available to attach to USB, nor was there any operating systems or driver support for the bus. USB ports were a curiosity at the time, and nobody had a use for them.

▶▶ See "Universal Serial Bus," p. 940.

The 430HX supports the newer PCI 2.1 standard, which allowed for concurrent PCI operations and greater performance. Combined with the support for EDO and pipelined burst cache, this was perhaps the best Pentium chipset for the power user's system. It offered not only excellent performance, but with ECC memory it offered a truly reliable and stable system design.

The 430HX was the only modern Intel Pentium-class chipset to offer parity and error-corrected memory support. This made it the recommended Intel chipset at the time for mission-critical applications, such as fileservers, database servers, business systems, and so on.

Intel 430VX (Triton III)

The 430VX was designed to be a replacement for the low-end 430FX chipset. It was not a replacement for the higher-powered 430HX chipset. As such, the VX has only one significant technical advantage over the HX, but in almost all other respects it is more like the 430FX than the HX.

The VX has the following features:

- Support for 66MHz SDRAM
- No parity or ECC memory support
- Single processor only
- Supports only 128MB RAM
- Supports caching for only 64MB RAM

Most notable was the support for SDRAM, which was about 27% faster than the more popular EDO memory used at the time. Although the support for SDRAM was a nice bonus, the actual improvement in system speed derived from such memory was somewhat limited. This was because with a normal L1/L2 cache combination, the processor read from the caches 99% of the time. A combined miss (both L1 and L2 missing) only happened about 1% of the time while reading/writing memory. Thus with SDRAM, the system would be up to 27% faster, but only about 1% of the time. Therefore, the cache performance was actually far more important than main memory performance. See the section "How Cache Works" in Chapter 3, "Microprocessor Types and Specifications," for more information.

As with the 430FX, the VX has the limitation of being capable of caching only 64MB of main memory. This means that installing more than 64MB of memory actually slows down the system dramatically because none of the memory past that point can be cached. Because Windows loads from the top of memory down, installing any amount of memory greater than 64MB in a system using this chipset dramatically decreases performance.

The 430VX chipset was rapidly made obsolete in the market by the 430TX chipset that followed.

Intel 430TX

The 430TX was Intel's final Pentium chipset. It was designed not only to be used in desktop systems, but to replace the 430MX mobile Pentium chipset for laptop and notebook systems.

The 430TX has some refinements over the 430VX, but, unfortunately, it still lacks support for parity or ECC memory and retains the 64MB cacheable RAM limitation of the older FX and VX chipsets. The 430TX was not designed to replace the more powerful 430HX chipset, which still remained the chipset of choice for Pentium class mission-critical systems.

The TX chipset features include the following:

- 66MHz SDRAM support
- Cacheable memory still limited to 64MB

- Support for Ultra-ATA, or Ultra-DMA 33 (UDMA) IDE transfers
- Lower power consumption for mobile use
- No parity or ECC memory support
- Single processor only

▶▶ See "ATA/ATAPI-4 (AT Attachment with Packet Interface Extension-4)," p. 483.

Third-Party (Non-Intel) P5 Pentium Class Chipsets

The development of non-Intel Pentium-class chipsets was spurred by AMD's development of its own equivalents to the Pentium processor—the K5 and K6 processor families. Although the K5 was not a successful processor, the K6 family, on the other hand, has been very successful in the low-cost (under-$1,000) market and as an upgrade for Pentium systems. AMD's own chipsets aren't used as often as other third-party chipsets, but AMD's capability to support its own processors with timely chipset deliveries has helped make the K6 and its successors—the Athlon and Duron—into credible rivals for Intel's Pentium MMX and Pentium II/III/Celeron families and has spurred other vendors, such as VIA, Acer Laboratories, and SiS, to support AMD's processors.

AMD 640

The AMD-640 chipset was designed by AMD for its K5 and K6 series processors. The AMD-640 chipset consists of the AMD-640 system controller in a 328-pin BGA package and the AMD-645 peripheral bus controller in a 208-pin PQFP package. The system controller includes a 64-bit Socket 7 interface, integrated writeback cache controller, system memory controller, and PCI bus controller.

Key features of the 640 chipset are

- Supports all 64-bit AMD-K5 processors and AMD-K6 processors
- Operates at processor bus speeds up to 66MHz
- Low voltage 3.3V processor interface
- Integrated L2 cache controller
- Supports pipelined burst synchronous SRAM (PBSRAM) cache
- Supports 256KB, 512KB, 1MB, and 2MB cache sizes
- Supports FPM, EDO, and SDRAM
- Maximum of 768MB of RAM; 512MB cacheable
- Supports parity and ECC memory options
- Supports PCI 2.1

Because the AMD-640 did not support bus speeds over 66MHz, it was not used with the later K6-2 and K6-III processors. These processors were supported by chipsets made by VIA Technologies and Acer Laboratories.

VIA Technologies

VIA Technologies, Inc. was founded in 1987 and has become a major designer of PC motherboard chipsets. VIA employs state-of-the-art manufacturing capability through foundry relationships with leading silicon manufacturers, such as Toshiba and Taiwan Semiconductor Manufacturing Corporation.

Apollo VP-1

The VT82C580VP Apollo VP-1 is a four-chip set released in October of 1995 and used in older Socket 5 and Socket 7 systems. The Apollo VP-1 is an equivalent alternative to the Intel 430VX chipset and features support for SDRAM, EDO, or FPM memory as well as pipeline-burst SRAM cache. The VP-1 consists of the VT82C585VP 208-pin PQFP, two VT82C587VP 100-pin PQFP chips acting as the North Bridge, and the VT82C586 208-pin PQFP South Bridge chip.

Apollo VP2

The two-chip Apollo VP2 chipset was released in May of 1996. The VP2 is a high-performance Socket 7 chipset including several features over the previous VP-1 chipset. The VP2 adds support for ECC memory over the VPX. The VP2 has also been licensed by AMD as its AMD 640 chipset. Motherboards using the Apollo VP2 can support P5 class processors, including the Intel Pentium and Pentium MMX, AMD K5 and K6, and Cyrix/IBM 6x86 and 6x86MX (MII) processors.

The VP2 chipset consists of the VT82C595 328 pin BGA package North Bridge chip, which supports up to 2MB of L2 cache and up to 512MB DRAM. Additional performance-related features include a fast DRAM controller with support for SDRAM, EDO, BEDO, and FPM DRAM types in mixed combinations with 32/64-bit data bus widths and row and column addressing; a deeper buffer with enhanced performance; and an intelligent PCI bus controller with Concurrent PCI master/CPU/IDE (PCI 2.1) operations. For data integrity and server use, the VP2/97 incorporates support for ECC or parity memory.

The Apollo VP2 features the VIA VT82C586B PCI-IDE South Bridge controller chip, which complies with the Microsoft PC97 industry specification by supporting ACPI/OnNow, Ultra DMA/33, and USB technologies.

Apollo VPX

The VT82C580VPX Apollo VPX is a four-chip set for Socket 7 motherboards released in December of 1996. The Apollo VPX is functionally equivalent to the Intel 430TX chipset but also has specific performance enhancements relative to the 430TX. The VPX was designed as a replacement for the VP-1 chipset and is an upgrade of that set designed to add support for the newer AMD and Cyrix P5 processors.

The Apollo VPX consists of the VT82C585VPX North Bridge and VT82C586B South Bridge chips. There are also two 208-pin PQFP frame buffers that go with the North Bridge memory interface. The Apollo VPX/97 features the VIA VT82C586B PCI-IDE South Bridge controller chip that complies with the Microsoft PC97 industry standard by supporting ACPI/OnNow, Ultra-DMA/33, and USB technologies. VIA also offers a non-PC97 version of the Apollo VPX that includes the older VT82C586A South Bridge and which was used in more entry-level PC designs.

Motherboards using the Apollo VPX can support P5 class processors, including the Intel Pentium and Pentium MMX, AMD K5 and K6, and Cyrix/IBM 6x86 and 6x86MX (MII) processors. To enable proper implementation of the Cyrix/IBM 6x86 200+ processor, the chipset features an asynchronous CPU bus that operates at either 66MHz or 75MHz speed. The Apollo VPX is an upgrade over the Apollo VP-1 with the additional feature of Concurrent PCI master/CPU/IDE operations (PCI 2.1). The VPX also supports up to 2MB of L2 cache and up to 512MB DRAM.

Apollo VP3

The Apollo VP3 is one of the first P5 class chipsets to implement the Intel AGP specification. Intel offers that interface with its Pentium II (P6) class chipsets. This enables a higher-performance Socket 7 motherboard to be built that can accept the faster AGP video cards. The Socket 7 interface allows P5 class processors, such as the Intel Pentium and Pentium MMX, AMD K5 and K6, and Cyrix/IBM 6x86 and 6x86MX (MII), to be used.

The Apollo VP3 chipset consists of the VT82C597 North Bridge system controller (472-pin BGA) and the VT82C586B South Bridge (208-pin PQFP). The VT82C597 North Bridge provides superior performance between the CPU; optional synchronous cache; DRAM; AGP bus; and the PCI bus with pipelined, burst, and concurrent operation. The VT82C597 complies with the Accelerated Graphics Port Specification 1.0 and features a 66MHz master system bus.

Apollo MVP3

The Apollo MVP3 adds to the VP3 chip by supporting the Super-7 100MHz Socket-7 specification. This allows the higher-speed P5 processors, such as the AMD K6-2, K6-III, and Cyrix/IBM MII processors, to be supported. The Apollo MVP3 chipset is a two-chip chipset that consists of the VT82C598AT North Bridge system controller and the VT82C586B South Bridge. The VT82C598AT chip is a 476-pin BGA package, and the VT82C586B chip is a 208-pin PQFP package.

The VT82C598AT North Bridge chip includes the CPU-to-PCI bridge, L2 cache and buffer controller, DRAM controller, AGP interface, and PCI IDE controller. The VT82C598AT North Bridge provides superior performance between the CPU; optional synchronous cache; DRAM; AGP bus; and the PCI bus with pipelined, burst, and concurrent operation. The DRAM controller supports standard FPM, EDO, and SDRAM, although most boards most likely are configured to use SDRAM only. The VT82C598AT complies with the Accelerated Graphics Port Specification 1.0 and features support for 66/75/83/100MHz CPU bus frequencies and the 66MHz AGP bus frequency.

The VT82C586B South Bridge includes the PCI-to-ISA bridge, ACPI support, SMBus, the USB host/hub interface, the Ultra-33 IDE Master controller, the PS/2 Keyboard/Mouse controller, and the I/O controller. The chip also contains the keyboard and PS/2 mouse controller.

This chipset is closest to the Intel 430TX in that it supports Socket 7 chips (Pentium and P5-compatible processors) and SDRAM DIMM memory and is physically a two-chip set. It differs mainly in that it allows operation at speeds up to 100MHz and supports AGP. The South Bridge is compatible with the newer Intel PIIX4e in that it includes UDMA IDE, USB, CMOS RAM, and ACPI 1.0 power management.

One big benefit over the Intel 430TX is that support for ECC memory or parity checking can be selected on a bank-by-bank basis, which allows mixing of parity and ECC modules. The 430TX from Intel doesn't support any ECC or parity functions at all. Memory timing for FPM is X-3-3-3, whereas EDO is X-2-2-2, and SDRAM is X-1-1-1, which is similar to the Intel 430TX.

Another benefit over the 430TX is in memory cacheability. The 430TX allowed caching up to only 64MB of main memory, a significant limitation. The maximum cacheable range is determined by a combination of cache memory size and the number of cache tag bits used. The most common L2 cache sizes are 512KB or 1MB of L2 cache on the motherboard, allowing either 128MB or 256MB of main memory to be cached. The maximum configuration of 2MB of L2 cache allows up to 512MB of main memory to be cacheable.

The MVP3 seems to be the chipset of choice in the higher-end Socket 7 motherboards from DFI, FIC, Tyan, Acer, and others.

Apollo MVP4

The Apollo MVP4 is a high-end Super Socket 7 chipset designed to support the highest-speed AMD-K6-2, K6-III, and VIA Cyrix MII processors. The VIA Apollo MVP4 chipset consists basically of the MVP3 chipset combined with a built-in AGP2x Trident Blade3D graphics engine. This is designed for low-cost systems with integrated video.

Features of the MVP4 include

- Integrated AGP2x bus
- Integrated Trident Blade3D AGP graphics engine
- 66/75/83/95/100MHz processor bus speed settings
- Support for AMD-K6, AMD-K6-2, AMD-K6-III, and VIA Cyrix MII processors running at speeds of up to 533MHz
- PC-100 memory bus
- Support for up to 768MB PC100 SDRAM
- Integrated AC97 audio, Super I/O, USB, advanced power management, and hardware-monitoring capabilities
- Support for ATA-66
- Support for four USB ports

The VIA Apollo MVP4 chipset is a two-chip set consisting of the VT8501 North Bridge Controller paired with the VT82C686A South Bridge Controller for full-featured systems or the VT82C596B Mobile South Bridge Controller for mobile systems.

Acer Laboratories, Inc.

Acer Laboratories, Inc. (ALi) originally was founded in 1987 as an independent research and development center for the Acer Group. In 1993, ALi separated financially and legally from Acer Inc., and became a member company of the Acer Group. ALi has rapidly claimed a prominent position among PC chipset manufacturers.

Aladdin IV (Aladdin 4)

The Aladdin IV from Acer Labs is a two-chip set for P5 class processors consisting of the M1531 North Bridge and either an M1533 or M1543 South Bridge chip. The Aladdin IV supports all Intel, AMD, Cyrix/IBM, and other P5-class CPUs including the Intel Pentium and Pentium MMX, AMD K5 and K6, and Cyrix/IBM 6x86 and 6x86MX (MII) processors. The Aladdin IV is equivalent to the Intel 430TX chipset, with the addition of error-correcting memory support and higher-speed 75MHz and 83.3MHz operation. Also, when using the M1543 South Bridge, an additional Super I/O chip is not necessary because those functions are included in the M1543 South Bridge.

The M1531 North Bridge is a 328-pin BGA chip that supports CPU bus speeds of 83.3MHz, 75MHz, 66MHz, 60MHz, and 50MHz. The M1531 also supports pipelined-burst SRAM cache in sizes of up to 1MB, allowing either 64MB (with 8-bit tag SRAM) or up to 512MB (with 11-bit tag SRAM) of cacheable main memory. FPM, EDO, or SDRAM main memory modules are supported for a total capacity of 1GB in up to four total banks. Memory timing is 6-3-3-3 for back-to-back FPM reads, 5-2-2-2 for back-to-back EDO reads, and 6-1-1-1 for back-to-back SDRAM reads. For reliability and integrity in mission-critical or server applications, ECC or parity is supported. PCI spec. 2.1 is also supported, allowing concurrent PCI operations.

The M1533 South Bridge integrates ACPI support, two-channel Ultra-DMA 33 IDE master controller, two-port USB controller, and a standard keyboard/mouse controller. A more full-function M1543 South Bridge is also available that has everything in the M1533 South Bridge plus all the functions of a normally separate Super I/O controller. The M1543 integrates ACPI support, two-channel Ultra-DMA 33 IDE controller, two-port USB controller, and a standard keyboard/mouse controller. Also included is an integrated Super I/O including a 2.88MB floppy disk controller, two high-performance serial ports, and a multimode parallel port. The serial ports incorporate 16550-compatible universal asynchronous receiver transmitters (UARTs) with 16-byte first in first out (FIFO) buffers and SIR (serial infrared) capability. The multimode parallel port includes support for Standard Parallel Port (SPP) mode, PS/2 Bidirectional mode, Enhanced Parallel Port (EPP) mode, and the Microsoft and Hewlett-Packard Extended Capabilities Port (ECP) mode.

Aladdin V (Aladdin 5)

The Acer Labs Aladdin V Chipset is a two-chip set that consists of the M1541 North Bridge chip and the M1533 (see "Aladdin IV" for details) or M1543C/M1453 South Bridge/Super I/O controller combo chip. The M1541 North Bridge is a 456-pin BGA package chip, whereas the M1543C South Bridge is a 330-pin- BGA package chip (the now-discontinued M1543 South Bridge was a 328-pin BGA package chip). The M1541 chipset is similar to the previous M1532 chipset with the addition of higher-speed (up to 100MHz) operation and AGP support.

The M1541 North Bridge includes the CPU-to-PCI bridge, L2 cache and buffer controller, DRAM controller, AGP interface, and PCI controller. The M1541 supports the Super-7 high-speed 100MHz Socket 7 processor interface used by some of the newer AMD and Cyrix/IBM P5 processors. It also runs the processor bus at 83.3MHz, 75MHz, 66MHz, 60MHz, and 50MHz for backward compatibility. When running the CPU bus at 75MHz, the PCI bus runs only at 30MHz; however, when the CPU bus is running at 83.3MHz or 100MHz, the PCI bus runs at full 33MHz PCI standard speed.

The M1541 also integrates enough cache tag RAM (16KB×10) internally to support 512KB of L2 cache, simplifying the L2 cache design and further reducing the number of chips on the motherboard. Cacheable memory is up to 512MB of RAM when using 512KB L2 cache and 1GB of RAM when using 1MB of L2 cache. FPM, EDO, or SDRAM memory is supported, in up to four banks and up to 1GB total RAM. ECC/Parity is also supported for mission-critical or fileserver applications to improve reliability. Memory timing is 6-3-3-3-3-3-3-3 for back-to-back FPM reads, 5-2-2-2-2-2-2-2 for back-to-back EDO reads, and 6-1-1-1-2-1-1-1 for back-to-back SDRAM reads. For more information on memory timing, see Chapter 6, "Memory."

Finally, AGP Interface specification V1.0 is supported in 1x and 2x modes.

The M1543 South Bridge and Super I/O combo chip includes ACPI support, the USB host/hub interface, the dual-channel Ultra-DMA/33 IDE host interface, the keyboard and mouse controller, and the Super I/O controller. The built-in Super I/O consists of an integrated floppy disk controller, two serial ports with infrared support, and a multimode parallel port. This South Bridge has been replaced by the M1543C, which has similar features but supports Ultra-DMA/66 IDE hard disk instead of the UDMA/33 supported by the M1543; it also adds support for IrDA infrared serial ports and ACPI power management. The M1543C South Bridge can also be used with Pentium II-family processors.

The Aladdin V can also be used with the M1533 South Bridge, which must be used with a separate Super I/O chip. See the description of the Aladdin IV for details about the M1533 South Bridge.

Aladdin 7

The Acer Labs Aladdin 7 chipset consists of the M1561 North Bridge and either the M1535D or M1543C South Bridge chip. The M1561 North Bridge is a 492-pin thermally enhanced BGA (T 2 BGA) package chip, whereas the M1535D South Bridge is a 352-pin BGA package chip.

Aladdin 7's M1561 North Bridge integrates 3D graphics, 2D acceleration, VGA video, the SDRAM memory controller, and the PCI bus interface into its North Bridge chip. It supports unified memory architecture (UMA), which enables low-cost systems to share system memory with the video subsystem. It supports the CPU-to-PCI bridge, L2 cache and buffer controller, DRAM controller, and PCI controller (supporting PCI version 2.2). The M1561 supports Super 7 processors and up to 1GB of RAM at 66MHz, 100MHz, and 133MHZ FSB speeds. Its 128-bit memory pipeline is designed to run faster than other integrated-video chipsets, with a memory bandwidth up to 2.1GBps when used with two matched DIMM modules.

M1561's onboard 3D video is provided by ArtX (which is also providing graphics logic for Nintendo's new system) and features hardware-accelerated transform and lighting (T&L), standard 3D features, a setup engine, parallel rendering, and high-speed 8x AGP-equivalent performance. Its display controller supports 1,600×1,200 onscreen resolution, motion-compensated 30fps DVD playback, and 32-bit full-color support.

Unfortunately, this chipset doesn't support Level 2 cache because it was designed for the discontinued AMD K6-III CPU (which featured 256KB of L2 cache onboard). Thus, it provides very poor performance with AMD's K6-2 processor, which lacks its own L2 cache. However, it is a good match for the K6-2 Plus, which has 128KB of Level 2 cache onboard.

Silicon Integrated Systems

Silicon Integrated Systems (SiS) was formerly known as Symphony Labs and is one of the three largest non-Intel PC motherboard chipset manufacturers.

SiS540

The SiS540 chipset is a single chipset that combines North/South Bridge functions as well as video and networking all into a single chip. The SiS540 is a super Socket 7 chipset supporting AMD K6-2/K6-III and VIA Cyrix processors.

The integrated video is based on a 128-bit graphic display interface with AGP 2x performance. In addition to providing a standard analog interface for CRT monitors, the SiS540 provides the Digital Flat Panel Port (DFP) for a digital flat panel monitor. An optional SiS301 Video Bridge supports NTSC/PAL TV output.

The SiS540 also includes integrated 10/100Mb Fast Ethernet as well as an AC97-compliant interface that comprises digital audio engine with 3D-hardware accelerator, on-chip sample rate converter, and professional wavetable along with separate modem DMA controller. SiS540 also incorporates the Low Pin Count (LPC) interface for attaching newer Super I/O chips and a dual USB host controller with four USB ports.

Features of the SiS540 include

- Supports Intel/AMD/Cyrix/IDT Pentium CPU processor bus at 66/83/90/95/100MHz
- Integrated 2MB Level 2 cache controller
- Supports PC133 SDRAM
- Meets PC99 requirements
- Is PCI 2.2 compliant
- Supports Ultra DMA66/33
- Integrated AGP 2x 2D/3D Video/Graphics Accelerator
- Supports digital flat panel
- Built-in secondary CRT controller for independent secondary CRT, LCD, or TV digital output
- Low Pin Count Interface
- Advanced PCI H/W Audio and S/W Modem
- Meets ACPI 1.0 requirements
- PCI Bus Power Management Interface Spec. 1.0
- Integrated keyboard/mouse controller
- Dual USB controller with four USB ports
- Integrated 10/100Mb/sec Ethernet controller

SiS 530/5595

The SiS530/5595 chipset is a two-chip chipset that includes the SiS530 North Bridge and the 5595 South Bridge and integrates 3D video. The SiS530/5595 is a Super Socket 7 chipset supporting AMD K6-2/K6-III and VIA Cyrix processors.

The integrated video is based on a 64-bit graphic display interface with AGP performance. In addition to providing a standard analog interface for CRT monitors, the SiS530/5595 provides the DFP for a digital flat panel monitor. It also supports UMA memory up to 8MB.

The 5595 South Bridge also includes an integrated Super I/O interface including USB host controller with two USB ports.

Features of the SiS540 include

- Supports Intel/AMD/Cyrix/IDT Pentium CPU processor bus at 66/83/90/95/100MHz
- Integrated 2MB Level 2 cache controller
- Caches up to 256MB SDRAM
- Supports PC100 SDRAM
- Meets PC99 requirements
- Is PCI 2.2 compliant
- Supports Ultra DMA66/33
- Integrated AGP 2D/3D Video/Graphics Accelerator
- Supports digital flat panel
- Built-in secondary CRT controller for independent secondary CRT, LCD, or TV digital output
- Meets ACPI 1.0 requirements
- PCI Bus Power Management Interface Spec. 1.0
- Integrated keyboard/mouse controller
- USB controller with two USB ports

SiS598

The Sis5598 chip is a 553-pin BGA package single-chip set incorporating both North and South Bridge functions. The 5598 consists of both North and South Bridge functions, including PCI-to-ISA bridge function, PCI IDE function, USB host/hub function, integrated RTC, integrated keyboard controller, and onboard PCI VGA. These chips support CPU bus speeds of 50MHz, 55MHz, 60MHz, 66MHz, and 75MHz.

A maximum of 512KB of L2 cache is supported, with a maximum cacheable range of 128MB of main memory. ECC or parity functions are not supported. Main memory timing is 5-3-3-3 for FPM, EDO timing is 5-2-2-2, and SDRAM timing is 6-1-1-1.

The 5598 chip also includes Advanced Configuration and Power Interface (ACPI) power management, a dual-channel Ultra-DMA/33 IDE interface, a USB controller, and even the CMOS RAM and Real Time Clock (RTC). PCI v2.1 is supported that allows concurrent PCI operation; however, AGP is not supported in this chipset.

5581, 5582, and 5571

The SiS5581 and 5582 chips are both 553-pin BGA package single-chip sets incorporating both North and South Bridge functions. The SiS5582 is targeted for AT/ATX form factor motherboards, whereas the SiS5581 is intended to be used on LPX/NLX form factor boards. In all other ways, the two North

Bridge chips are identical. The SiS 5581/5582 is a single-chip set designed to be a high-performance, low-cost alternative that is functionally equivalent to Intel's 430TX chipset. By having everything in a single chip, a low-cost motherboard can be produced.

The 5581/5582 consists of both North and South Bridge functions, including PCI-to-ISA bridge function, PCI IDE function, USB host/hub function, integrated RTC, and the integrated keyboard controller. These chips support CPU bus speeds of 50MHz, 55MHz, 60MHz, 66MHz, and 75MHz.

A maximum of 512KB of L2 cache is supported, with a maximum cacheable range of 128MB of main memory. The maximum cacheable range is determined by a combination of cache memory size and the number of tag bits used. The most common cache size that allows caching of up to 128MB of RAM is 512KB, although up to 384MB of RAM can technically be installed in up to three total banks. Because this is designed for low-cost systems, ECC or parity functions are not supported. Main memory timing is x-3-3-3 for FPM, EDO timing is x-2-2-2, and SDRAM timing is x-1-1-1.

The 5581/5582 chipset also includes ACPI power management, a dual-channel Ultra-DMA/33 IDE interface, a USB controller, and even the CMOS RAM and RTC. PCI v2.1 is supported that allows concurrent PCI operation; however, AGP is not supported in this chipset.

The 5571 is an older version of this single-chip set, lacks support for bus speeds above 66MHz, supports only the older APM power management standard, and supports only PIO modes for hard disk access. The 5571 uses a 480-pin BGA package.

5591 and 5592

The SiS 5591/5592 is a two-chip set consisting of either a 5591 or 5592 North Bridge chip along with a SiS5595 South Bridge. The 5591/5592 North Bridge chips are both 3.3v 553-pin BGA package chips, whereas the 5595 South Bridge chip is a 5v 208-pin PQFP package chip. The SiS5591 North Bridge is targeted for ATX form factor motherboards, and the SiS5592 version is intended to be used on the NLX form factor. In all other ways, the two North Bridge chips are identical.

The 5591/5592 North Bridge chips include the host-to-PCI bridge, L2 cache controller, DRAM controller, AGP interface, and PCI IDE controller. The SiS5595 South Bridge includes the PCI-to-ISA bridge; ACPI/APM power management unit; USB host/hub interface; and ISA bus interface, which contains the ISA bus controller, DMA controllers, interrupt controllers, and timers. It also integrates the keyboard controller and RTC.

The 5591/5592 North Bridge chips support CPU bus speeds of up to 75MHz. They also support up to 1MB of L2 cache, allowing up to 256MB of main memory to be cacheable. The maximum cacheable main memory amount is determined by a combination of cache memory size and the number of tag bits used. Most common cache sizes are 512KB and 1MB. The 512KB cache with 7 tag bits allow only 64M of memory to be cached, whereas 8 tag bits allow caching of up to 128MB. With 1MB of cache onboard, the cacheable range is doubled to a maximum of 256MB.

A maximum of 256MB of total RAM is allowed in up to three banks. Both ECC and parity are supported for mission-critical or fileserver applications. Main memory timing for FPM memory is x-3-3-3, EDO timing is x-2-2-2, and SDRAM is x-1-1-1.

PCI specification 2.1 is supported at up to 33MHz, and AGP specification 1.0 is supported in both 1x and 2x modes. The separate 5595 South Bridge includes a dual-channel Ultra-DMA/33 interface and support for USB.

Sixth-Generation (P6 Pentium Pro/II/III Class) and Seventh-Generation (Pentium 4) Chipsets

Just as Intel clearly dominated the Pentium chipset world, it is also the leading vendor for chipsets supporting its P6, P7, and later processor families. As discussed earlier, the biggest reason for this is that, since the Pentium first came out in 1993, Intel has been introducing new chipsets (and even complete ready-to-go motherboards) simultaneously with its new processors. This makes it hard for anybody else to catch up. Another problem for other chipset manufacturers is that Intel had been reluctant until recently to license the Slot 1, Socket 370, and now Socket 423 interfaces used by the newer processors, although the Socket 7 interface used by the original Pentium has been freely available for some time. Still, some licenses have been granted, and other chipmakers, such as VIA Technologies, ,ALi, and SiS, have developed a wide range of Slot 1 and Socket 370 chipsets. The first license agreements for Socket 423, used by the Pentium 4, were inked early in 2001, paving the way for non-Intel chipsets for its newest processor in the future.

Note that because the Pentium Pro, Celeron, and Pentium II/III are essentially the same processor with different cache designs and minor internal revisions, the same chipset can be used for Socket 8 (Pentium Pro), Socket 370 (Celeron/Pentium III), and Slot 1 (Celeron/Pentium II/III) designs. Of course, the newer P6-class chipsets are optimized for the Socket 370 architecture and nobody is making any new designs for Socket 8 or Slot 1.

Table 4.8 shows the chipsets used on Pentium Pro motherboards.

Table 4.8   Pentium Pro Motherboard Chipsets (North Bridge)

Chipset	450KX	450GX	440FX
Codename	Orion	Orion Server	Natoma
Workstation date introduced	Nov. 1995	Nov. 1995	May 1996
Bus speed	66MHz	66MHz	66MHz
SMP (dual CPUs)	Yes	Yes (four CPUs)	Yes
Memory types	FPM	FPM	FPM/EDO/BEDO
Parity/ECC	Both	Both	Both
Maximum memory	8GB	1GB	1GB
L2 cache type	In CPU	In CPU	In CPU
Maximum cacheable	1GB	1GB	1GB
PCI support	2.0	2.0	2.1
AGP support	No	No	No
AGP speed	n/a	n/a	n/a
South Bridge	Various	Various	PIIX3

SMP = Symmetric multiprocessing (dual processors)   Pburst = Pipeline burst (synchronous)
FPM = Fast page mode   PCI = Peripheral component interconnect
EDO = Extended data out   AGP = Accelerated graphics port
BEDO = Burst EDO   SIO = System I/O
SDRAM = Synchronous dynamic RAM   PIIX = PCI ISA IDE Xcelerator

Note

PCI 2.1 supports concurrent PCI operations.

For the Celeron and Pentium II/III motherboards, Intel offers the chipsets in Table 4.9. 4xx series chipsets incorporate a North/South Bridge architecture, whereas 8xx series chipsets support the newer and faster hub architecture. P6/P7 (Pentium III/Celeron, Pentium 4, and Xeon) processor chipsets using hub architecture are shown in Table 4.10.

Table 4.9 P6 Processor Chipsets Using North/South Bridge Architecture

Chipset	440FX	440LX	440EX	440BX	440GX
Codename	Natoma	None	None	None	None
Date introduced	May 1996	Aug. 1997	April 1998	April 1998	June 1998
Part numbers	82441FX, 82442FX	82443LX	82443EX	82443BX	82443GX
Bus speed	66MHz	66MHz	66MHz	66/ 100MHz	100MHz
Supported processors	Pentium II	Pentium II	Celeron	Pentium II/III, Celeron	Pentium II/III, Xeon
SMP (dual CPUs)	Yes	Yes	No	Yes	Yes
Memory types	FPM/EDO/ BEDO	FPM/EDO/ SDRAM	EDO/SDRAM	SDRAM	SDRAM
Parity/ECC	Both	Both	Neither	Both	Both
Maximum memory	1GB	1GB EDO/ 512MB SDRAM	256MB	1GB	2GB
Memory banks	4	4	2	4	4
PCI support	2.1	2.1	2.1	2.1	2.1
AGP support	No	AGP 2x	AGP 2x	AGP 2x	AGP 2x
South Bridge	82371SB (PIIX3)	82371AB (PIIX4)	82371EB (PIIX4E)	82371EB (PIIX4E)	82371EB (PIIX4E)

Table 4.10 P6/P7 (Pentium III/Celeron, Pentium 4, and Xeon) Processor Chipsets Using Hub Architecture

Chipset	810	810E	8154	815E4	815EP
Codename	Whitney	Whitney	Solano	Solano	Solano
Date introduced	April 1999	Sept. 1999	June 2000	June 2000	Nov. 2000
Part number	82810	82810E	82815	82815	82815EP
Bus speed	66/100MHz	66/100/ 133MHz	66/100/ 133MHz	66/100/ 133MHz	66/100/ 133MHz
Supported processors	Celeron, Pentium II/III	Celeron, Pentium II/III	Celeron, Pentium II/III	Celeron, Pentium II/III	Celeron, Pentium II/III
SMP (dual CPUs)	No	No	No	No	No
Memory types	SDRAM (PC100), EDO	SDRAM (PC100)	SDRAM (PC133)	SDRAM (PC133)	SDRAM (PC133)
Parity/ECC	Neither	Neither	Neither	Neither	Neither
Maximum memory	512MB	512MB	512MB	512MB	512MB
Memory banks	2	2	3	3	3
PCI support	2.2	2.2	2.2	2.2	2.2

450NX	440ZX
None	None
June 1998	Nov. 1998
82451NX, 82452NX, 82453NX, 82454NX	82443ZX
100MHz	66/ 100MHz[1]
Pentium II/III, Xeon	Celeron, Pentium II/III
Yes, up to four	No
FPM/EDO	SDRAM
Both	Neither
8GB	256MB
4	2
2.1	2.1
No	AGP 2x
82371EB (PIIX4E)	82371EB (PIIX4E)

820	820E	840	850	860
Camino	Camino	Carmel	Tehama	Colusa
Nov. 1999	June 2000	Oct. 1999	Nov. 2000	May 2001
82820	82820	82840	82850	82860
66/100/ 133MHz	66/100/ 133MHz	66/100/ 133MHz	400MHz	400MHz
Pentium II/III, Celeron	Pentium II/III, Celeron	Pentium III, Xeon	Pentium 4	Xeon for DP (Socket 603)
Yes	Yes	Yes	Yes	Yes
RDRAM (PC800)	RDRAM (PC800)	RDRAM (PC800) Dual-Channel	RDRAM (PC800) Dual-Channel	RDRAM (PC800) Dual-Channel
Both	Both	Both	Both	Both
1GB	1GB	4GB	2GB	4GB with 2 memory repeaters
2	2	3x2	2	4 with optional memory repeaters
2.2	2.2	2.2	2.2	2.2

Table 4.10   **Continued**

Chipset	810	810E	8154	815E4	815EP
PCI speed/ width	33MHz/32-bit	33MHz/32-bit	33MHz/32-bit	33MHz/32-bit	33MHz/32-bit
AGP slot	No	No	AGP 4x	AGP 4x	AGP 4x
Integrated Video	AGP 2x[2]	AGP 2x[2]	AGP 2x[3]	AGP 2x[3]	No
South Bridge (Hub)	82801AA/ AB (ICH/ ICH0)	82801AA (ICH)	82801AA (ICH)	82801BA (ICH2)	82801BA (ICH2)

1. Note the 440ZX is available in a cheaper 440ZX-66 version, which runs only at 66MHz.

2. Note the 810 chipsets have integral AGP 2x 3D video, which is NOT upgradable via an external AGP adapter.

3. Note the 815/815E chipsets have integral AGP 2x 3D video, which IS upgradable via an APG 4x slot.

4. Note the only difference between the 815 and 815E is in which I/O controller hub (South Bridge) is used.

SMP = Symmetric multiprocessing (dual processors).

Note

Pentium Pro, Celeron, and Pentium II/III CPUs have their secondary caches integrated into the CPU package. Therefore, cache characteristics for these machines are not dependent on the chipset but are quite dependent on the processor instead.

Most Intel chipsets are designed as a two-part system, using a North Bridge and a South Bridge component. Often the same South Bridge component can be used with several different North Bridge chipsets. Table 4.11 shows a list of all the current Intel South Bridge components and their capabilities.

Table 4.11   **Intel South Bridge—I/O Controller Hub Chips**

Chip Name	SIO	PIIX	PIIX3	PIIX4	PIIX4E	ICH0	ICH	ICH2
Part number	82378IB/ZB	82371FB	82371SB	82371AB	82371EB	82801AB	82801AA	82801BA
IDE support	None	BMIDE	BMIDE	UDMA-33	UDMA-33	UDMA-33	UDMA-66	UDMA-100
USB support	None	None	1C/2P	1C/2P	1C/2P	1C/2P	1C/2P	2C/4P
CMOS/clock	No	No	No	Yes	Yes	Yes	Yes	Yes
ISA support	Yes	Yes	Yes	Yes	Yes	No	No	No
LPC support	No	No	No	No	No	Yes	Yes	Yes
Power management	SMM	SMM	SMM	SMM	SMM/ ACPI	SMM/ ACPI	SMM/ ACPI	SMM/ ACPI

SIO = System I/O   *USB = Universal serial bus*   *BMIDE = Bus Master IDE*

PIIX = PCI ISA IDE Xcelerator   *1C/2P = 1 controller, 2 ports*   *UDMA = Ultra-DMA IDE*

ICH = I/O controller hub   *2C/4P = 2 controllers, 4 ports*   *LPC = Low pin count bus*

IDE = Integrated Drive Electronics (AT attachment)   *ISA = Industry standard architecture bus*

ACPI = Advanced configuration and power interface   *SMM = System management mode*

820	820E	840	850	860
33MHz/32-bit	33MHz/32-bit	66MHz/64-bit	33MHz/32-bit	33MHz/32-bit, 33-66MHz/64-bit with optional PCI controller hub chip
AGP 4x	AGP 4x	AGP 4x	AGP 4x (1.5v)	AGP 4x (1.5v)
No	No	No	No	No
82801AA (ICH)	82801BA (ICH2)	82801AA (ICH)	82801BA (ICH2)	82801BA (ICH2)

FPM = Fast page mode.

EDO = Extended data out.

BEDO = Burst EDO.

SDRAM = Synchronous dynamic RAM.

Pburst = Pipeline burst (synchronous).

PCI = Peripheral component interconnect.

AGP = Accelerated graphics port.

SIO = System I/O.

PIIX = PCI ISA IDE Xcelerator.

ICH = I/O controller hub.

The following sections examine the chipsets for P6 processors up through the Celeron and Pentium III.

Intel 450KX/GX (Orion Workstation/Server)

The first chipsets to support the Pentium Pro were the 450KX and GX, both codenamed Orion. The 450KX was designed for networked or standalone workstations; the more powerful 450GX was designed for fileservers. The GX server chipset was particularly suited to the server role because it supports up to four Pentium Pro processors for symmetric multiprocessing (SMP) servers, up to 8GB of four-way interleaved memory with ECC or parity, and two bridged PCI buses. The 450KX is the workstation or standalone user version of Orion and as such it supports fewer processors (one or two) and less memory (1GB) than the GX. The 450GX and 450KX both have full support for ECC memory—a requirement for server and workstation use.

The 450GX and 450KX North Bridge comprises four individual chip components—an 82454KX/GX PCI bridge, an 82452KX/GX data path (DP), an 82453KX/GX data controller (DC), and an 82451KX/GX memory interface controller (MIC). Options for QFP or BGA packaging were available on the PCI Bridge and the DP. BGA uses less space on a board.

The 450's high reliability is obtained through ECC from the Pentium Pro processor data bus to memory. Reliability is also enhanced by parity protection on the processor bus, control bus, and all PCI signals. In addition, single-bit error correction is provided, thereby avoiding server downtime because of spurious memory errors caused by cosmic rays.

Until the introduction of the following 440FX chipset, these were used almost exclusively in fileservers. After the debut of the 440FX, the expensive Orion chips all but disappeared due to their complexity and high cost.

Intel 440FX (Natoma)

The first popular mainstream P6 (Pentium Pro or Pentium II) motherboard chipset was the 440FX, which was codenamed Natoma. The 440FX was designed by Intel to be a lower-cost and somewhat higher-performance replacement for the 450KX workstation chipset. It offered better memory performance through support of EDO memory, which the prior 450KX lacked.

The 440FX uses half the number of components than the previous Intel chipset. It offers additional features, such as support for the PCI 2.1 (concurrent PCI) standard, support for USB, and reliability through ECC.

The concurrent PCI processing architecture maximizes system performance with simultaneous activity on the CPU, PCI, and ISA buses. Concurrent PCI provides increased bandwidth to better support 2D/3D graphics, video and audio, and processing for host-based applications. ECC memory support delivers improved reliability to business system users.

The main features of this chipset include

- Support for up to 1GB of EDO memory
- Full 1GB cacheability (based on the processor because the L2 cache and tag are in the CPU)
- Support for USB
- Support for Bus Master IDE
- Support for full parity/ECC

The 440FX consists of a two-chip North Bridge. The main component is the 82441FX PCI Bridge and Memory controller, along with the 82442FX Data Bus accelerator for the PCI bus. This chipset uses the PIIX3 82371SB South Bridge chip that supports high-speed Bus Master DMA IDE interfaces and USB, and it acts as the bridge between the PCI and ISA buses.

Note that this was the first P6 chipset to support EDO memory, but it lacked support for the faster SDRAM. Also, the PIIX3 used with this chipset does not support the faster Ultra DMA IDE hard drives.

The 440FX was the chipset used on the first Pentium II motherboards, which have the same basic architecture as the Pentium Pro. The Pentium II was released several months before the chipset that was supposedly designed for it was ready, so early PII motherboards used the older 440FX chipset. This chipset was never designed with the Pentium II in mind, whereas the newer 440LX was optimized specifically to take advantage of the Pentium II architecture. For that reason, I normally recommended that people stay away from the original 440FX-based PII motherboards and wait for Pentium II systems that used the forthcoming 440LX chipset. When the new chipset was introduced, the 440FX was quickly superseded by the improved 440LX design.

Intel 440LX

The 440LX quickly took over in the marketplace after it debuted in August of 1997. This was the first chipset to really take full advantage of the Pentium II processor. Compared to the 440FX, the 440LX chipset offers several improvements:

- Support for the new AGP video card bus
- Support for 66MHz SDRAM memory
- Support for the Ultra DMA IDE interface
- Support for USB

The 440LX rapidly became the most popular chip for all new Pentium II systems from the end of 1997 through the beginning of 1998.

Intel 440EX

The 440EX was designed to be a low-cost, lower-performance alternative to the 440LX chipset. It was introduced in April 1998, along with the Intel Celeron processor. The 440EX lacks several features in the more powerful 440LX, including dual processor and ECC or parity memory support. This chipset is basically designed for low-end 66MHz bus-based systems that use the Celeron processor. Note that boards with the 440EX also fully support a Pentium II but lack some of the features of the more powerful 440LX or 440BX chipsets.

The main things to note about the 440EX are listed here:

- Designed with a feature set tuned for the low-end PC market
- Primarily for the Intel Celeron processor
- Supports AGP
- Does not support ECC or parity memory
- Single processor support only

The 440EX consists of an 82443EX PCI AGP Controller (PAC) North Bridge component and the new 82371EB (PIIX4E) South Bridge chip.

Note

The original 266MHz and 300MHz Celeron processors used with the 440EX chipset provided very low performance because these processors lacked any onboard Level 2 cache memory. Starting with the 300MHz Celeron 300A, Celeron added 128KB of Level 2 cache to its SEP packaging; all Socket 370 Celerons also include Level 2 cache. You should consider upgrading to a faster Celeron CPU with Level 2 cache if your 440EX-based system uses one of the original Celeron processors.

Intel 440BX

The Intel 440BX chipset was introduced in April of 1998 and was the first chipset to run the processor host bus (often called the front-side bus, or FSB) at 100MHz. The 440BX was designed specifically to support the faster Pentium II/III processors at 350MHz and higher. A mobile version of this chipset is the first Pentium II/III chipset for notebook or laptop systems.

The main change from the previous 440LX to the BX is that the 440BX chipset improves performance by increasing the bandwidth of the system bus from 66MHz to 100MHz. Because the chipset can run at either 66MHz or 100MHz, it allows one basic motherboard design to support all Pentium II/III processor speeds based on either the 66MHz or 100MHz processor bus.

Here are the Intel 440BX highlights:

- Support for 100MHz SDRAM (PC100); the now-common PC133 RAM can also be installed, but it will still run at just 100MHz
- Support for both 100MHz and 66MHz system and memory bus designs
- Support for up to 1GB of memory in up to four banks (four DIMMs)
- Support for ECC memory
- Support for ACPI
- The first chipset to support the Mobile Intel Pentium II processor

▶▶ See "Mobile Pentium II and III," p. 1175.

The Intel 440BX consists of a single North Bridge chip called the 82443BX Host Bridge/Controller, which is paired with a new 82371EB PCI-ISA/IDE Xcelerator (PIIX4E) South Bridge chip. The new South Bridge adds support for the ACPI specification version 1.0. Figure 4.28 shows a typical system block diagram using the 440BX.

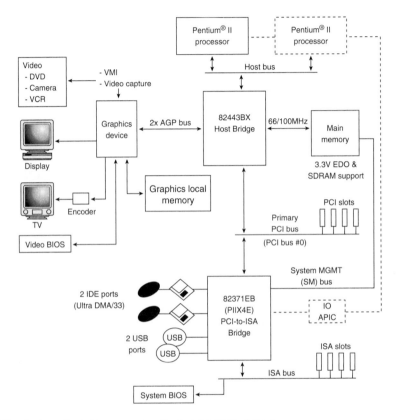

Figure 4.28   System block diagram using the Intel 440BX chipset.

The 440BX was a popular chipset during 1998 and into 1999. It offered superior performance and high reliability through the use of ECC, SDRAM, and DIMMs.

Intel 440ZX and 440ZX-66

The 440ZX was designed to be a low-cost version of the 440BX. The 440ZX brings 66MHz or 100MHz performance to entry-level Celerons (with or without Level 2 cache) and low-end Pentium II/III systems. The 440ZX is pin compatible with the more expensive 440BX, meaning existing 440BX motherboards can be easily redesigned to use this lower-cost chipset.

Note that two versions of the 440ZX are available: The standard one runs at 100MHz or 66MHz, and the 440ZX-66 runs only at the slower 66MHz.

The features of the 440ZX include the following:

■ Support for Celeron and Pentium II/III processors at up to 100MHz bus speeds

■ These main differences from the 440BX:

  • No parity or ECC memory support

  • Only two banks of memory (two DIMMs) supported

  • Maximum memory only 256MB

The 440ZX is not a replacement for the 440BX; instead, it was designed to be used in less expensive systems (such as those based on the micro-ATX form factor), in which the greater memory capabilities, performance, and data integrity functions (ECC memory) of the 440BX are not necessary.

Intel 440GX

The Intel 440GX AGP set is the first chipset optimized for high-volume midrange workstations and lower-cost servers. The 440GX is essentially a version of the 440BX that has been upgraded to support the Slot 2 (also called SC330) processor slot for the Pentium II/III Xeon processor. The 440GX can still be used in Slot 1 designs, as well. It also supports up to 2GB of memory, twice that of the 440BX. Other than these items, the 440GX is essentially the same as the 440BX. Because the 440GX is core compatible with the 440BX, motherboard manufacturers could quickly and easily modify their existing Slot 1 440BX board designs into Slot 1 or 2 440GX designs.

The main features of the 440GX include

■ Support for Slot 1 and Slot 2

■ Support for 100MHz system bus

■ Support for up to 2GB of SDRAM memory

This chipset allows for lower-cost, high-performance workstations and servers using the Slot 2–based Xeon processors.

Intel 450NX

The 450NX chipset is designed for multiprocessor systems and standard high-volume servers based on the Pentium II/III Xeon processor. The Intel 450NX chipset consists of four components: the 82454NX PCI Expander Bridge (PXB), 82451NX Memory and I/O Bridge Controller (MIOC), 82452NX RAS/CAS Generator (RCG), and 82453NX Data Path Multiplexor (MUX).

The 450NX supports up to four Pentium II/III Xeon processors at 100MHz. Two dedicated PCI Expander Bridges can be connected via the Expander Bus. Each PXB provides two independent 32-bit, 33MHz PCI buses, with an option to link the two buses into a single 64-bit, 33MHz bus.

Figure 4.29 shows a typical high-end server block diagram using the 450NX chipset.

The 450NX supports one or two memory cards. Each card incorporates an RCG chip and two MUX chips, in addition to the memory DIMMs. Up to 8GB of memory is supported in total.

The primary features of the 450NX include the following:

■ Slot 2 (SC330) processor bus interface at 100MHz

■ Support for up to four-way processing

■ Support for two dedicated PCI Expander Bridges

■ Up to four 32-bit PCI buses or two 64-bit PCI buses

The 450NX chipset does not support AGP because high-end video is not an issue in network file-servers.

Figure 4.29   High-end server block diagram using the Intel 440NX chipset.

Intel 810, 810E, and 810E2

Introduced in April of 1999, the Intel 810 chipset (codenamed Whitney) represents a major change in chipset design from the standard North and South Bridges that have been used since the 486 days. The 810 chipset allows for improvements in system performance, all for less cost and system complexity. The 810 (which supports 66MHz and 100MHz processor buses) was later revised as the 810E with support for the 133MHz processor bus.

Note

The 810E2 uses the same 82810E GMCH as the 810E but pairs it with the 82801BA I/O Controller Hub (ICH2) used by the Intel 815E. For information about the 82801BA ICH2 chip, see the section "Intel 815, 815E, and 815EP," later in this chapter.

The major features of the 810E chipset include

■ 66/100/133MHz system bus

■ Integrated AGP2x Intel 3D graphics

■ Efficient use of system memory for graphics performance

- Optional 4MB of dedicated display cache video memory
- Digital Video Out port compatible with DVI specification for flat panel displays
- Software MPEG-2 DVD playback with hardware motion compensation
- 266MB/sec hub interface
- Support for ATA-66
- Integrated Audio-Codec 97 (AC97) controller
- Support for low-power sleep modes
- Random number generator (RNG)
- Integrated USB controller
- LPC bus for Super I/O and Firmware Hub (ROM BIOS) connection
- Elimination of ISA bus

The 810E chipset consists of three major components (see Figure 4.30):

- *82810E Graphics Memory Controller Hub (GMCH).* 421 BGA package (the original 810 chipset used the 82810 GMCH)
- *82801 Integrated Controller Hub (ICH).* 241 BGA package
- *82802 Firmware Hub (FWH).* In either 32-pin plastic leaded chip carrier (PLCC) or 40-pin thin small outline package (TSOP) packages; although a functional part of the chipset, this component is actually sold separately by Intel to motherboard developers

Figure 4.30 Intel 810E chipset showing the 82810E (GMCH), 82801 (ICH), and 82802 (FWH) chips. *Photograph used by permission of Intel Corporation.*

Compared to the previous North/South Bridge designs, there are some fairly significant changes in the 810 chipset. The previous system designs had the North Bridge acting as the memory controller, talking to the South Bridge chip via the PCI bus. This new design has the GMCH taking the place of the North Bridge, which talks to the ICH via a 66MHz dedicated interface called the accelerated hub architecture (AHA) bus instead of the previously used PCI bus. In particular, implementing a direct connection between the North and South Bridges in this manner was key in implementing the new UDMA-66 high-speed IDE interface for hard disks, DVD drives, and other IDE devices.

Figure 4.31 shows a system block diagram for the 810E chipset. With the 810 chipset family, ISA is finally dead.

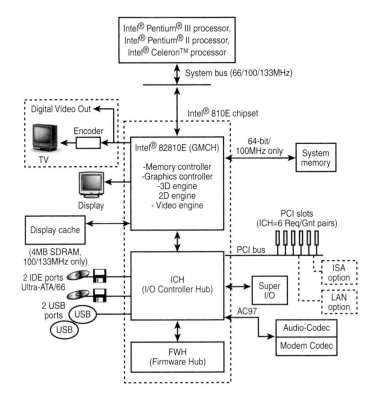

Figure 4.31 Intel 810E chipset system block diagram.

The 82810E GMCH uses an internal Direct AGP (integrated AGP) interface to create 2D and 3D effects and images. The video capability integrated into the 82810E chip features hardware motion compensation to improve software DVD video quality; it also features both analog and direct digital video out ports, which enable connections to either traditional TVs (via an external converter module) or the new direct digital flat panel displays. The GMCH chip also incorporates the System Manageability Bus, which enables networking equipment to monitor the 810 chipset platform. Using ACPI specifications, the system manageability function enables low-power sleep mode and conserves energy when the system is idle.

The 82801 I/O Controller Hub employs AHA for a direct connection from the GMCH chip. This is twice as fast (266MB/sec) as the previous North/South Bridge connections that used the PCI bus, and it uses far fewer pins for reduced electrical noise. Plus, the AHA bus is dedicated, meaning that no other devices will be on it. The AHA bus also incorporates optimized arbitration rules allowing more functions to run concurrently, enabling better video and audio performance.

The ICH also integrates dual IDE controllers, which run up to either 33MB/sec (UDMA-33 or Ultra-ATA/33) or 66MB/sec (UDMA-66 or Ultra-ATA/66). Note that two versions of the ICH chip exist. The 82801AA (ICH) incorporates the 66MB/sec-capable ATA/IDE and supports up to six PCI slots, whereas the 82801AB (ICH0) supports only 33MB/sec ATA/IDE maximum and supports up to four PCI slots.

The ICH also integrates an interface to an Audio-Codec 97 (AC97) controller, dual USB ports, and the PCI bus with up to four or six slots. The Integrated Audio-Codec 97 controller enables software audio and modem by using the processor to run sound and modem software via very simple digital-to-analog conversion circuits. By reusing existing system resources, this lowers the system cost by eliminating components.

The 82802 Firmware Hub (FWH) incorporates the system BIOS and video BIOS, eliminating a redundant nonvolatile memory component. The BIOS within the FWH is flash-type memory, so it can be field-updated at any time. In addition, the 82802 contains a hardware RNG. The RNG provides truly random numbers to enable fundamental security building blocks supporting stronger encryption, digital signing, and security protocols. Two versions of the FWH are available, called the 82802AB and 82802ACy. The AB version incorporates 512KB (4Mbit) of Flash BIOS memory, and the AC version incorporates a full 1MB (8Mbit) of BIOS ROM.

With the Intel 810 and 810E chipsets, Intel has done something that many in the industry were afraid of: It has integrated the video and graphics controller directly into the motherboard chipset with no means of upgrade. This means systems using the 810 chipset won't have an AGP slot and won't be capable of using conventional AGP video cards. For the low-end market for which this chipset is designed, lacking an AGP slot shouldn't be too much of a drawback. Higher-end systems, on the other hand, use the 815 or other chipsets that do support AGP slots. Intel calls the integrated interface Direct AGP, and it describes the direct connection between the memory and processor controllers with the video controller all within the same chip.

This probably dictates the future of mainstream PCs, which means the video card, as we know it, will be reserved only for midrange and higher-end systems, as well as gaming-oriented systems. With the 810 chipset, Intel has let it be known in a big way that it has entered the PC video business.

In fact, the theme with the 810 chipset is one of integration. The integrated video means no video cards are required; the integrated AC97 interface means that conventional modems and sound cards are not required. Plus, there is an integrated CMOS/Clock chip (in the ICH), and even the BIOS is integrated in the FWH chip. All in all, the 810 should be taken as a sign for things to come in the PC industry, which means more integration, better overall performance for low-end and mainstream systems, and less overall cost.

Intel Random Number Generator

The 8xx chipset series features the Intel RNG. The RNG is built into the 82802 FWH, which is the ROM BIOS component used on 8xx-based motherboards. The RNG provides software with true nondeterministic random numbers.

Most security routines, especially those providing authentication or encryption services, require random numbers for purposes such as key code generation. One method of cracking these types of codes is to predict the random numbers being used to generate the keys. Current methods that use system and user input as a seed to a conventional pseudorandom number generator have proven vulnerable to this type of attack. The Intel RNG uses thermal noise across a resistor contained in the FWH (that is, ROM BIOS in 8xx-based boards) to generate true nondeterministic, unpredictable random numbers. Therefore, "random" numbers generated by 8xx-series chipsets really are random.

Intel 815, 815E, and 815EP

Introduced in June 2000, the 815 and 815E chipsets are mainstream PC chipsets with integral video that is also upgradable via an AGP 4x slot. An 815EP version was introduced a few months later that lacks the integrated video for lower cost. The 815 chipsets are designed for Slot-1 or Socket-370 processors, such as the Celeron or Pentium III. These are the first chipsets from Intel designed to directly support PC133 SDRAM memory, allowing for a more affordable solution than other chipsets using RDRAM memory. Similar to the other 8xx series chipsets from Intel, the 815 uses hub architecture that provides a 266MB/sec connection between the main chipset components and does not share the PCI bus like the prior North/South Bridge designs.

Although three variations on the 815 chipset are available—including the regular 815, 815E, and 815EP—the only differences between them are in which I/O Controller Hub is used (ICH or ICH2) and whether the main chip includes integrated graphics. When the 82815 GMCH is combined with the 82801AA ICH, the result is called the 815 chipset. When the same GMCH is combined with the 82801BA ICH2, the result is called the 815E (see Figure 4.32).

Figure 4.32 Intel 815E chipset showing the 82815 (GMCH) and 82801BA (ICH2) chips. *Photograph used by permission of Intel Corporation.*

When the 82815EP Memory Controller Hub (MCH, which lacks the integrated graphics) is combined with the ICH2, you have the 815EP chipset. The ICH2 provides an additional USB controller, dual Ultra ATA/100 controllers and support for a LAN/Modem/Sound card via the integrated Communications and Networking Riser (CNR) interface. All 815 chipsets support the following features:

- 66/100/133MHz system bus
- 266MB/sec hub interface
- ATA-100 (815E/EP) or ATA-66 (815)
- PC100 or PC133 CL-2 SDRAM
- Up to 512MB RAM
- Integrated Audio-Codec 97 (AC97) controller
- Low-power sleep modes
- RNG for stronger security products
- One (815) or two (815E/EP) integrated USB controllers with either two or four ports, respectively
- LPC bus for Super I/O and Firmware Hub (ROM BIOS) connection
- Elimination of ISA Bus

The 815 and 815E also support

- Integrated Intel AGP2x 3D graphics
- Efficient use of system memory for graphics performance
- Optional 4MB of dedicated display cache video memory
- Digital Video Out port compatible with DVI specification for flat panel displays
- Software MPEG-2 DVD playback with hardware motion compensation

The 815E/EP uses the ICH2, which is most notable for providing ATA-100 support, allowing 100MB/sec drive performance. Of course, few drives can really take advantage of this much throughput, but in any case, there won't be a bottleneck there. The other notable feature is having two USB controllers and four ports on board. This allows double the USB performance by splitting up devices over the two ports and can allow up to four connections before a hub is required.

Another important feature of the 815 is the integration of a fast Ethernet controller directly into the chipset. The integrated LAN controller works with one of three new physical layer components from Intel and enables three distinct solutions for computer manufacturers. These include

- Enhanced 10/100Mbps Ethernet with Alert on LAN technology
- Basic 10/100Mbps Ethernet
- 1Mbps home networking

These physical layer components can be placed directly on the PC motherboard (additional chips) or installed via an adapter that plugs into the CNR slot. The CNR slot and cards enable PC assemblers to build network-ready systems for several markets.

Although the 815/815E features essentially the same built-in AGP 2x 3D video that comes with the 810 chipset, the difference is upgradability. The video can be easily upgraded by adding a graphics performance accelerator (GPA) card (see Figure 4.33) or an AGP 4x card for maximum 3D graphics and video performance. The GPA card (also called the AGP Inline Memory Module, or AIMM) is essentially a high-performance video memory card that works in the AGP 4x slot and which improves the performance of the integrated video by up to 30%. For even more performance, you can install a full 4x AGP card in the AGP 4x slot, which disables the integrated video. By having the video integrated, very low-cost systems with reasonable video performance can be assembled. By later installing either the GPA or a full 4x AGP card, you can improve video performance up to 100% or more.

AGP 4x slot connector

Figure 4.33   A typical 4MB GPA/AIMM module, which attaches to the AGP slot of a motherboard using the 815 or 815E chipset.

PC133 Memory Support

Another important feature of the 815 chipset is the support of PC133 memory. The 815 also uses PC100 memory if the higher-performance type is not available. With the PC133 support, Intel has also officially set a standard for PC133 memory that is higher than some of the PC133 memory currently on the market. This will no doubt create some confusion. To meet the Intel PC133 specification, the memory must support what is called 2-2-2 timing, sometimes also known as CAS-2 (column address strobe) or CL-2 timing. The numbers refer to the number of clock cycles for the following functions to complete:

- *Precharge command to Active command.* Charges the memory's storage capacitors to prepare them for data

- *Active command to Read command.* Selects rows and columns in memory array for reading

- *Read command to Data Out.* Reads data from selected rows and columns for transmission

Most PC133 memory on the market takes three cycles for each of these functions and would therefore be termed PC133 3-3-3, CAS-3, or CL-3 memory. Note that the faster PC133 CL-2 can be used in place of the slower CL-3 variety, but not the other way around.

As a result of the tighter cycling timing, PC133 CL-2 offers a lead-off latency of only 30ns, instead of the 45ns required by PC133 CL-3. This results in a 34% improvement in initial access due to the decreased latency.

With the improvements in the 815 chipset, it will likely be a popular chipset for the mainstream PC market that doesn't want to pay the higher prices for RDRAM memory. The 815 is essentially designed to replace the venerable 440BX chipset.

Intel 820 and 820E

The Intel 820 chipsets use the newer hub-based architecture like all the 800 series chips and were designed to support slot 1 or socket 370 processors, such as the Pentium III and Celeron (see Figure 4.34). The 820 chipset supports RDRAM memory technology, 133MHz system bus, and 4x AGP.

Figure 4.34 Intel 820 chipset showing the 82820 (MCH), 82801 (ICH), and 82802 (FWH) chips. *Photograph used by permission of Intel Corporation.*

The 82820 MCH provides the processor, memory, and AGP interfaces. Two versions are available: One supports a single processor (82820), whereas the other supports two processors (82820DP). Either is designed to work with the same 82801 ICH as used with the other 800 series chipsets, such as the 810 and 840. The 820 chipset also uses the 82802 FWH for BIOS storage and for the Intel RNG.

The connection between the MCH and ICH uses what is called the Intel Hub Architecture bus instead of the PCI bus as with prior North/South Bridge chipsets. The hub architecture bus provides twice the bandwidth of PCI at 266MB per second, enabling twice as much data to flow between them. The hub architecture bus also has optimized arbitration rules, allowing more functions run concurrently, as well as far fewer signal pins, reducing the likelihood of encountering or generating noise and signal errors.

The 820 chipset is designed to use RDRAM memory, which has a maximum throughput of up to 1.6GB/sec. The 820 supports PC600, PC700, and PC800 RDRAM, delivering up to 1.6GB/sec of theoretical memory bandwidth in the PC800 version. PC800 RDRAM is a 400MHz bus running double-clocked and transferring 16 bits (2 bytes) at a time ($2 \times 400MHz \times 2$ bytes = 1.6GB/sec). This compares to 800MB/sec for PC100 SDRAM, 1GB/sec for PC133 SDRAM, and 2.1GB/sec for DDR SDRAM. Two RIMM sockets are available to support up to 1GB of total system memory.

The AGP interface in the 820 enables graphics controllers to access main memory at AGP 4x speed, which is about 1GB per second—twice that of previous AGP 2x platforms. Figure 4.35 shows the 820 chipset architecture. Because the 820 was designed for midrange to higher-end systems, it does not include integrated graphics, relying instead on the AGP4x slot to contain a graphics card.

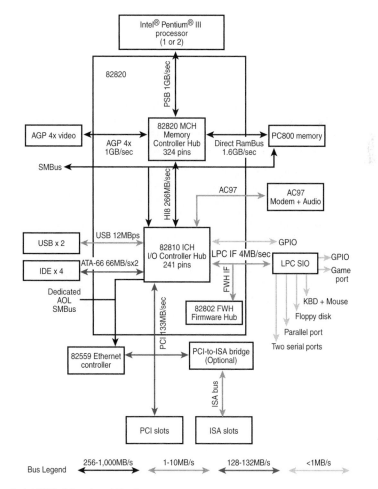

Figure 4.35   Intel 820 chipset architecture.

820 Chipset features include

- 100/133MHz processor bus
- Intel 266MB/sec hub interface
- PC800 RDRAM RIMM memory support
- AGP 4x support
- ATA-100 (820E) or ATA-66 interface
- Intel RNG
- LPC interface
- AC97 controller
- One (820) or two (820E) USB buses with either two or four ports, respectively

The 820 chipset consists of three main components with a few optional extras. The main component is the 82820 (single-processor) or 82820DP (dual-processor) MCH, which is a 324 BGA chip. That is paired with an 82801 ICH, which is a 241 BGA chip, and finally it has the 82802 FWH, which is really just a fancy Flash ROM BIOS chip. Optionally, there can be an 82380AB PCI-ISA bridge that is used only if the board is equipped with ISA slots.

The newer 820E version uses an updated 82801BA ICH2, which supports ATA-100 and incorporates dual USB controllers with two ports each, for a total of four USB ports.

820 Chipset MTH Bug

The 820 chipset is designed to support RDRAM memory directly. However, because the market still demanded lower-cost SDRAM, Intel created an RDRAM-to-SDRAM translator chip called the Memory Translator Hub (MTH). This enabled them to produce 820 chipset motherboards that supported SDRAM instead of the more expensive RDRAM.

Because the design of the MTH was proven defective, the chip (and any board using it) was simply discontinued. On May 10, 2000, Intel officially announced that it would replace any motherboards using the MTH with a new board lacking the component. The MTH translates signals from SDRAM memory to the Intel 820 chipset and is used only with motherboards utilizing SDRAM and the Intel 820 chipset; boards using RDRAM don't have an MTH and were not affected. Intel found electrical noise issues with the MTH that can cause some systems to intermittently reset, reboot, or hang. In addition, the noise issue can, under extreme conditions, potentially cause data corruption.

The MTH bug forced Intel to recall and replace more than a million motherboards in mid-2000, with new versions lacking the MTH and thus supporting only RDRAM memory. The final bill for this recall was reported at about $253 million, making this perhaps the most costly recall of computer components since the infamous Pentium math bug in 1994. I found it interesting that, due to the fact that Intel did more than $24.4 billion in sales the previous year, at least one article classified the cost of this recall as "chump change" to the chip giant!

Intel has an MTH I.D. Utility at www.intel.com/support/mth, which will tell you whether you have that component and whether your board is eligible for replacement, including a 128MB RDRAM RIMM. Again, note that the 820 chipset was really designed to support RDRAM as the native type of memory, and RDRAM-based systems are not affected because they don't use the memory translator hub component.

Intel 840

The Intel 840 is a high-end chipset designed for use in high-performance multiprocessor systems using slot 1, slot 2 (Xeon processor), or Socket 370 processors. The 840 chipset uses the same hub architecture and modular design as the rest of the 800 family chipsets, with some additional components enabling more performance. See Figure 4.36 for a photo of the Intel 840 chipset.

As with the other 800 series chipsets, the 840 has three main components:

- *82840 Memory Controller Hub.* Provides graphics support for AGP 2x/4x, dual RDRAM memory channels, and multiple PCI bus segments for high-performance I/O.

- *82801 I/O Controller Hub.* Equivalent to the South Bridge in older chipset designs, except it connects directly to the MCH component via the high-speed Intel Hub Architecture bus. The ICH supports 32-bit PCI, IDE controllers, and dual USB ports.

- *82802 Firmware Hub.* Basically an enhanced Flash ROM chip that stores system BIOS and video BIOS, as well as an Intel RNG. The RNG provides truly random numbers to enable stronger encryption, digital signing, and security protocols.

Figure 4.36   Intel 840 chipset showing the 82840 (MCH), 82801 (ICH), 82802 (FWH), 82803 (MRH-R), 82804 (MRH-S), and 82806 (P64H) chips. *Photograph used by permission of Intel Corporation.*

In addition to the core components, parts are available for scaling up to a more powerful design. Three additional components can be added:

■ *82806 64-bit PCI Controller Hub (P64H).* Supports 64-bit PCI slots at speeds of either 33MHz or 66MHz. The P64H connects directly to the MCH using Intel Hub Architecture, providing a dedicated path for high-performance I/O. This is the first implementation of the 66MHz 66-bit PCI on a PC motherboard chipset, allowing for a PCI bus four times faster than the standard 32-bit 33MHz version.

■ *82803 RDRAM-based Memory Repeater Hub (MRH-R).* Converts each memory channel into two memory channels for expanded memory capacity.

■ *82804 SDRAM-based Memory Repeater Hub (MRH-S).* Translates the RDRAM protocol into SDRAM-based signals for system memory flexibility. This would be used only in 840 systems that supported SDRAM.

Figure 4.37 shows the 840 chipset architecture.

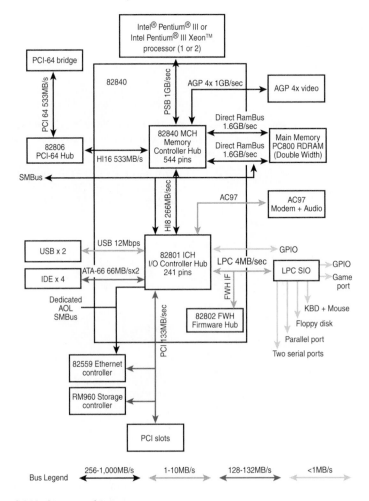

Figure 4.37   Intel 840 chipset architecture.

840 chipset features include

- 100/133MHz processor bus.
- Dual RDRAM memory channels, operating simultaneously, providing up to 3.2GB/sec memory bandwidth.
- 16-bit wide implementation of Intel Hub Architecture (HI16), which enables high-performance concurrent PCI I/O with the optional P64H component.
- AGP 4x.
- Prefetch cache, unique to the 840 chipset, enables highly efficient data flow and helps maximize system concurrency.
- Intel RNG (see the section "Intel Random Number Generator," earlier in this chapter).
- USB support.

Optionally, network interface and RAID controller interface chips can be added as well.

Intel 850

The Intel 850 is the first chipset for the Intel Pentium 4 processor and thus is also the first chipset to support the NetBurst microarchitecture. The 850 is designed for high-performance desktop computers and workstations and uses the same hub architecture and modular design as the rest of Intel's 8xx family of chipsets. See Figure 4.38 for a photo of the Intel 850 chipset.

The 850 has two main components, down from three in earlier 800-series chipsets:

- *82850 Memory Controller Hub.* Provides support for dual 400MHz RDRAM memory channels with a 3.2GBps bandwidth and a 100MHz system bus. The 82850 MCH also supports 1.5V AGP 4x video cards at a bandwidth exceeding 1GBps.
- *82801BA I/O Controller Hub 2.* The ICH2 (an enhanced version of the 82801 used by other 800-series chipsets) supports 32-bit PCI rev. 2.2, dual UDMA 33/66/100 IDE host adapters, four USB ports, an integrated LAN controller, six-channel AC-97 audio/modem codec, FWH interface support, SMBus support, and Alert on LAN and Alert on LAN 2 support.

Figure 4.38 The Intel 850 chipset. *Photo used by permission of Intel Corporation.*

Optionally, the Intel 82562ET/82562EM Platform LAN communication chips can be added to the 850 chipset to provide support for 10BASE-T and Fast Ethernet networking, building on the LAN features in the 82801BA ICH2 chip.

The 850 chipset, like most recent Intel and non-Intel chipsets, also supports the CNR card for integrated audio, modem, and network capabilities. See Figure 4.39 for a diagram of the 850's chipset architecture.

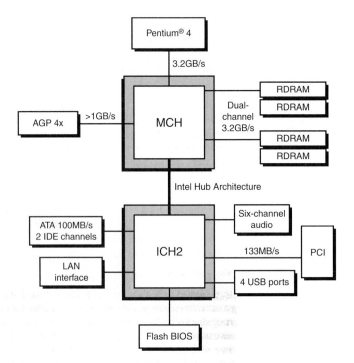

Figure 4.39 Architecture of the Intel 850 chipset.

Intel 860

The Intel 860 is a high-performance chipset designed for the newest Socket 602 Xeon processors for DP workstations. The 860 uses the same ICH2 as the Intel 850 but uses a different MCH—the 82860, which supports one or two Socket 602 ("Foster") Xeon processors. The other major features of the 82860 are similar to those of the 82850, including support for dual 400MHz RDRAM memory channels with a 3.2GBps bandwidth and a 100MHz system bus. The 82860 MCH also supports 1.5V AGP 4x video cards at a bandwidth exceeding 1GBps.

The 860 chipset uses a modular design, in which its two core chips can be supplemented by the 82860AA (P64H) 66MHz PCI Controller Hub and the 82803AA MRHR. The 82860AA supports 64-bit PCI slots at either 33MHz or 66MHz, and the 82803AA converts each RDRAM memory channel into two, which doubles memory capacity.

Third-Party (Non-Intel) P6-Class Chipsets

Several companies produce chipsets designed to support P6-class processors, including ALi, VIA Technologies, and SiS. The following sections discuss the offerings from these companies.

Acer Laboratories, Inc.

ALi has a variety of chipsets for the P6-class processors. They are discussed in the following sections.

Aladdin Pro II

The Acer Labs Aladdin Pro II M1621 is a two-chip set for P6 (Pentium Pro and Pentium II) Slot 1 processors consisting of two BGA package chips, the 456-pin BGA package M1621 North Bridge, and either the M1533 or M1543 South Bridge. The M1621 North Bridge includes an AGP, memory, and I/O controller and a data path with multiport buffers for data acceleration. It can support multiple Pentium II processors with bus speeds of 60MHz, 66MHz, and 100MHz. This chipset is equivalent to the 440BX chipset from Intel.

The integrated memory controller supports FPM, EDO, and SDRAM with a total capacity of up to 1GB (SDRAM) or 2GB (EDO). ECC memory is supported, enabling use in mission-critical or fileserver applications. Memory timing is x-1-1-1-1-1-1-1 in back-to-back SDRAM reads or x-2-2-2-2-2-2-2 in back-to-back EDO reads.

The M1621 supports AGP v1.0, in both 1x and 2x modes, and is fully compliant with PCI rev. 2.1, enabling concurrent PCI operations. The M1621 can be used with either the M1533 South Bridge or M1543 South Bridge/Super I/O combo chip.

The M1533 South Bridge includes the following features:

- PCI-to-ISA bridge
- Built-in keyboard/mouse controller
- Enhanced Power Management, featuring ACPI
- Two-port USB interface
- Dual-channel Ultra-DMA/33 IDE host adapter
- 328-pin BGA package

M1543 includes all features in the 1533 plus fully integrated Super I/O, including a floppy disk controller, two high-speed serial ports, and one multimode parallel port.

Aladdin Pro 4

The Acer Labs Aladdin Pro 4 for P6 (Pentium II/III/Celeron) Slot 1 or Socket 370 processor is a two-chip set consisting of two chips: the 508-pin BGA M1641 or M1641B North Bridge and the M1535D or M1535D+ South Bridge.

The M1641 North Bridge supports processor bus speeds of 66MHz, 100MHz, or 133MHz. The M1641B is a double–data-rate version supporting DDR SDRAM at speeds up to 266MHz.

The M1641/M1641B's integrated memory controller supports EDO, SDRAM, or VC-SDRAM with a total capacity of 1.5GB. ECC memory is supported, enabling this chipset to be used in file-server or mission-critical applications. Memory timing is x-1-1-1-1-1-1-1 in back-to-back SDRAM reads.

The M1641/M1641B supports AGP 4x video, PCI 2.2, and up to six PCI masters beyond the North Bridge and PCI bridge. They also support Dark Green power management, including Power On Suspend, Suspend to RAM, PCI Bus CLKRUN, and Dynamic Clock Stop.

The M1535D South Bridge includes the following features:

- Built-in keyboard/mouse controller
- Enhanced Power Management, featuring ACPI and PCI Power Management
- Four-port USB interface
- Dual-channel Ultra-DMA/66 IDE host adapter

- Integrated Super I/O including a floppy disk controller, two high-speed serial ports, one multi-mode parallel port, and an IrDA serial port
- Built-in Wavetable audio with Sound Blaster 16 compliance
- 'AC 97 soft modem compatible
- 352-pin BGA package

Aladdin TnT2

The Acer Labs Aladdin TnT2 for P6 (Pentium II/III/Celeron) Slot 1 or Socket 370 processor is a two-chip set consisting of two chips: the 556-pin BGA M1631 North Bridge and either the M1543C or M1535D South Bridge.

The M1631 North Bridge integrates nVidia's popular TnT2 3D graphics engine with the Aladdin Pro 4 chipset. It supports processor bus speeds of 66MHz, 100MHz, or 133MHz.

The integrated memory controller supports EDO, SDRAM, or VC-SDRAM with a total capacity of 1.5GB. ECC memory is supported, allowing this chipset to be used in file-server or mission-critical applications. Memory timing is x-1-1-1-1-1-1-1 in back-to-back SDRAM reads.

The M1641 supports PCI 2.2 and up to six PCI masters beyond the North Bridge and PCI-to-ISA bridge; it also supports Dark Green power management, including Power On Suspend, Suspend to RAM, PCI Bus CLKRUN, and Dynamic Clock Stop.

The integrated TnT2 3D graphics engine features a 128-bit graphic pipeline, DirectX-compatible 3D acceleration, 32-bit 3D True-Color rendering, multitextured bump maps, environment maps, and the other features of the nVidia TnT2 chipset. Motherboards using this chipset can use UMA shared memory or can provide 4MB, 8MB, or 16MB of SDRAM or SGRAM for the exclusive use of the graphics engine. The M1641 supports digital flat panel, TV-out, and video capture.

The M1543C South Bridge includes the following features:

- PCI-to-ISA bridge
- Built-in keyboard/mouse controller
- Enhanced Power Management, featuring ACPI and PCI Power Management
- Three-port USB interface
- Dual-channel Ultra-DMA/66 IDE host adapter
- Integrated Super I/O including a floppy disk controller, two high-speed serial ports, one multi-mode parallel port, and an IrDA serial port
- 330-pin BGA package

Aladdin Pro 5 and Pro 5T

The Acer Labs Aladdin Pro 5 for P6 (Pentium II/III/Celeron) Slot 1 or Socket 370 processor is a two-chip set consisting of two chips: the 528-pin BGA M1651 North Bridge and the M1535D+ or M1535D South Bridge. The Aladdin Pro 5M is a mobile version for notebook computers that uses the M1535 or M1535+ South Bridge.

The M1651 North Bridge supports SDRAM and processor bus speeds of 66MHz, 100MHz, 133MHz as well as DDR SDRAM at speeds of 200MHz or 266MHz. It supports up to 3GB of RAM but does not support ECC. Memory timing is x-1-1-1-1-1-1-1 in back-to-back SDRAM reads. Because the M1651 supports both conventional and DDR SDRAM, it enables system manufacturers to use the same chipset for both memory types.

The M1651 supports AGP 4x video, PCI 2.2, up to six PCI masters beyond the North Bridge and PCI bridge, and ACPI and Legacy green power management. In addition, it supports PCI Mobile CLKRUN# and AGP Mobile BUSY#/STOP#.

The Aladdin Pro 5T uses the M1651T North Bridge, which has been redesigned to comply with the requirements of the new .13 micron Pentium III Tualatin processors released in May 2001. Otherwise, it supports the same features as the regular M1651 North Bridge.

The M1535D+ South Bridge includes the following features:

- Built-in keyboard/mouse controller
- Enhanced Power Management, featuring ACPI and PCI Power Management with support for power management states G0–G3
- Six-port USB interface with support for USB keyboard and mouse
- Dual-channel Ultra-DMA/100 IDE host adapter
- Integrated Super I/O including a floppy disk controller, two high-speed serial ports, one multi-mode parallel port, and an IrDA serial port
- Built-in PCI audio with DirectSound 3D, MIDI, and Sound Blaster 16 compliance; SPDIF interface for digital audio
- Software modem compliance
- 352-pin BGA package

VIA Technologies

VIA Technologies has a variety of chipsets for the P6 processors. They are discussed in the following sections.

Apollo Pro266

The VIA Apollo Pro 266 is a high-performance North/South Bridge chipset designed to support Socket 370 processors, including the Pentium III, Celeron, and VIA's own C3. The Apollo Pro 266 is a development of the Apollo Pro 133A with provisions for both DDR200/266MHz RAM, as well as PC100/133 SDRAM and VC-SDRAM.

Features of the Apollo Pro266 include

- AGP 2x/4x graphics bus support
- 133/100/66MHz processor bus support
- PC-100/133 SDRAM and PC200/266 DDR SDRAM memory interface
- ATA-100 IDE interface
- Support for six USB ports
- Integrated AC97 six-channel audio
- Integrated MC97 modem
- Integrated 10/100 BASE-T Ethernet and 1/10MHz Home PNA networking
- Hardware monitoring
- ACPI/On Now! Power management

The VIA Apollo Pro266 chipset is a two-chip set consisting of the 552-pin BGA VT8633 North Bridge Controller and the 352-pin BGA VT82C686B South Bridge Controller.

Apollo Pro133A

The VIA Apollo Pro133A chipset is a North/South Bridge chipset designed to support Slot 1 and Socket 370 processors such as the Intel Pentium III, Intel Celeron, and VIA Cyrix III. The Apollo Pro133A is based on the previous Pro133 with even more high-end features added.

Features of the Apollo Pro133A include

- AGP 4x graphics bus support
- Support for one or two processors
- 133/100/66MHz processor bus support
- PC-133 SDRAM memory interface
- ATA-66 interface
- Support for four USB ports
- AC97 link for audio and modem
- Hardware monitoring
- Power management

The VIA Apollo Pro133A chipset is a two-chip set consisting of the VT82C694X North Bridge Controller and a choice of VT82C596B or VT82C686A South Bridge Controllers.

ProSavage PM133

The VIA ProSavage PM133 integrates S3 Graphics' S3 Savage 4 and S3 Savage 2000 3D and 2D graphics engines with the Apollo Pro 133A chipset. The major features of the chipset are the same as for the Apollo Pro 133A, with the following additions:

- 2MB to 32MB shared memory architecture integrated with Savage 4 3D and Savage 2000 2D video
- Z-buffering, 32-bit true-color rendering, massive 2K by 2K textures, single-pass multiple textures, sprite antialiasing, and other 3D features
- Support for DVD playback, DVI LCD displays, and TV-out
- PCI 2.2 compliance

An optional AGP 4x interface allows the integrated AGP 4x video to be upgraded with an add-on card if desired. This two-chip set consists of the VT8605 North Bridge and VT8231 South Bridge.

The VT8231 South Bridge integrates the Super I/O and supports the LPC interface.

Apollo Pro133

The VIA Apollo Pro133 was the first chipset on the market designed to support PC-133 SDRAM memory. This chipset supports Slot 1 and Socket 370 processors, such as the Intel Pentium III, Intel Celeron, and VIA Cyrix III processors.

Key features include the following:

- Support for AGP 2x graphics bus
- Support for 133/100/66MHz processor bus
- PC-133 SDRAM memory interface
- Support for 1.5GB of RAM

- ATA-66 interface
- Support for four USB ports
- AC97 link for audio and modem
- Hardware monitoring
- Power management

The VIA Apollo Pro133 is a two-chip set consisting of the VT82C693A North Bridge Controller and a choice of VT82C596B or VT82C686A South Bridge Controllers.

Apollo KLE133

The VIA Apollo KLE133 (previously known as the PM601) chipset is a highly integrated chipset platform designed for the value PC and Internet appliance market. As such, this chipset has a built-in Trident Blade3D graphics engine and 10/100 Ethernet. The KLE133 is designed for Slot 1 and Socket 370 processors, such as the Pentium III, Celeron, and VIA C3.

Key features include the following:

- Support for AGP 2x
- Integrated Trident Blade3D AGP graphics engine
- 66/100/133MHz processor bus
- Support for PC-133 SDRAM memory
- Integrated 10/100 Ethernet
- Support for AC97 audio, MC97 modem, Super I/O, and hardware monitoring
- Four USB ports
- Support for ATA-66
- Advanced power management

The VIA Apollo KLE133 is a two-chip set consisting of the VT8601 North Bridge Controller and the VT82C686A South Bridge Controller.

Apollo Pro

The Apollo Pro is a high-performance chipset for Slot 1 mobile and desktop PC systems; it can also support the Socket 8 Pentium Pro processor. The Apollo Pro includes support for advanced system power management capability for both desktop and mobile PC applications, PC100 SDRAM, AGP 2x mode, and multiple CPU/DRAM timing configurations. The Apollo Pro chipset is comparable in features to the 440BX and PIIX4e chipsets from Intel and represents one of the first non-Intel chipsets to support the Socket 1 architecture.

The VIA Apollo Pro consists of two devices—the VT82C691 North Bridge chip and the VT82C596, a BGA-packaged South Bridge with a full set of mobile, power-management features. For cost-effective desktop designs, the VT82C691 can also be configured with the VT82C586B South Bridge.

The VT82C691 Apollo Pro North Bridge supports all Slot 1 (Intel Pentium II) and Socket 8 (Intel Pentium Pro) processors. The Apollo Pro also supports the 66MHz external bus speed and the newer 100MHz CPU external bus speed required by the 350MHz and faster Pentium II processors. AGP v1.0 and PCI 2.1 are also supported, as are FPM, EDO, and SDRAM. Various DRAM types can be used in mixed combinations in up to eight banks and up to 1GB of DRAM. EDO memory timing is 5-2-2-2-2-2-2-2 for back-to-back accesses, and SDRAM timing is 6-1-1-1-2-1-1-1 for back-to-back accesses.

The VT82C596 South Bridge supports both ACPI and APM and includes an integrated USB controller and dual Ultra DMA-66 EIDE ports.

Apollo Pro Plus

The VIA Apollo Pro Plus is a high-performance chipset for Slot 1/Socket 370 mobile and desktop PC systems.

Features include

- 66/100MHz CPU bus
- AGP 1x
- PCI 2.1 compliant
- Support for eight banks up to 1GB PC-100 SDRAM
- Support for both ACPI and legacy (APM) power management
- Integrated USB controller
- Ultra DMA-33 controller

The Apollo Pro consists of two chips: a VT82C693 North Bridge paired with either the VT82C596A mobile South Bridge or the VT82C686A Super South Bridge.

Silicon Integrated Systems Chipsets for P6 Processors

Silicon Integrated Systems has a variety of chipsets for the P6-class processors. They are discussed in the following sections.

SiS633/635 Family

The SiS633/635 family is a series of high-performance single-chip chipsets that support the Pentium III and Celeron Socket 370 processors. T-series chipsets also support the new .13 micron Pentium III Tualatin processors released in May 2001.

The SiS633 and SiS633T chipsets support PC133 SDRAM, whereas the SiS635 and SiS635T chipsets support PC133 SDRAM, DDR266 DDR SDRAM, or a mixture of PC133 and DDR266 SDRAM. All chipsets in the family support the following features:

- Integrated 4x AGP
- Up to six PCI masters
- UDMA/100 IDE host adapters
- 1.5GB RAM
- Six USB ports
- AC97 audio and AMR support

SiS635/635T also support ACR or CNR riser technology and integrate 10/100 BASE-T Ethernet and 1/10MHz Home PNA networking.

These chips use a 677-pin BGA package.

SiS630 Family

The SiS630 is a high-performance, low-cost single-chip set with integrated 2D/3D graphics and support for Slot 1 and Socket 370 processors such as the Pentium III, Celeron, and Cyrix III.

The integrated video is based on a 128-bit graphic display interface with AGP 4x performance. In addition to providing a standard analog interface for CRT monitors, the SiS630 also provides the digital flat panel port (DFP) for a digital flat panel monitor. An optional SiS301 Video Bridge supports NTSC/PAL TV output.

The SiS630 also includes integrated 10/100Mb Fast Ethernet, as well as an AC97-compliant interface that comprises a digital audio engine with 3D-hardware accelerator, on-chip sample rate converter, and professional wavetable along with separate modem DMA controller. SiS630 also incorporates the LPC interface for attaching newer Super I/O chips and a dual USB host controller with four USB ports.

Features of the SiS630 include

- Support for Intel/AMD/Cyrix/IDT Pentium CPU processor bus at 66/83/90/95/100MHz
- Integrated 2MB Level 2 cache controller
- PC133 SDRAM support
- Meets PC99 requirements
- PCI 2.2 compliant
- Ultra DMA66/33 support
- Integrated AGP 2x 2D/3D Video/Graphics Accelerator
- Support for digital flat panel
- Hardware DVD decoding
- Built-in secondary CRT controller for independent secondary CRT, LCD, or TV digital output
- Low Pin Count interface
- Advanced PCI H/W Audio and S/W Modem
- Meets ACPI 1.0 requirements
- PCI Bus Power Management Interface Spec. 1.0
- Integrated keyboard/mouse controller
- Dual USB controller with five USB ports
- Integrated 10/100Mb/sec Ethernet controller

The SiS630E chip is almost identical in its feature set but doesn't support the secondary CRT controller (also called the video bridge). The SiS630S chip adds support for an AGP slot and the new Advanced Communication Riser to the basic SiS630 features. What's really amazing about the SiS630 family is that all these features are combined into a single chip that's not much larger than the North Bridge used by other chipsets.

SiS620/5595

The SiS620/5595 is a North/South Bridge chipset with integrated video that supports Slot 1 or Socket 370 processors.

Features include

- 66/100MHz processor bus
- Support for PC-100 SDRAM memory
- Support for Ultra DMA 33/66
- PCI 2.2 compliant

- Integrated AGP 3D graphics accelerator
- Support for digital flat panel port for LCD panel

SiS600/5595 and 5600/5595

The SiS600/SiS5595 is a slot-1 North/South Bridge chipset designed for lower-cost systems.

Features include

- 66/100MHz processor bus
- PC-100 SDRAM with ECC
- AGP 2x
- Ultra DMA/33
- Two USB ports
- Advanced Configuration and Power Interface revision 1.0

Athlon/Duron Chipsets

The Athlon and Duron are Slot A and Socket A chips made by AMD. Although similar to the Pentium III and Celeron, the AMD chips use a different interface and require different chipsets. AMD was originally the only supplier for Athlon chipsets, but VIA Technology, Acer Labs, and SiS are now providing a large number of chipsets with a wide range of features. These chipsets are covered in the following sections.

AMD Chipsets for Athlon/Duron Processors

AMD makes two chipsets for Athlon and Duron processors: the AMD-750 and AMD-760. The major features of these chipsets are compared in Table 4.12 and described in greater detail in the following sections.

Table 4.12   AMD Athlon/Duron Processor Chipsets Using North/South Bridge Architecture

Chipset	AMD-750	AMD-760
Codename	Irongate	None
Date introduced	Aug. 1999	Oct. 2000
Part numbers	AMD-751	AMD-761
Bus speed	200MHz	200/266MHz
Supported processors	Athlon/Duron	Athlon/Duron
SMP (dual CPUs)	No	Yes
Memory types	SDRAM	DDR SDRAM
Memory speed	PC100	PC1600/PC2100
Parity/ECC	Both	Both
Maximum memory	768MB	2GB buffered, 4GB registered
PCI support	2.2	2.2
AGP support	AGP 2x	AGP 4x
South Bridge	AMD-756	AMD-766
ATA/IDE support	ATA-66	ATA-100

Table 4.12   Continued

Chipset	AMD-750	AMD-760
USB support	1C/4P	1C/4P
CMOS/clock	Yes	Yes
ISA support	Yes	No
LPC support	No	Yes
Power management	SMM/ACPI	SMM/ACPI

SMP = Symmetric multiprocessing (dual processors)
SDRAM = Synchronous dynamic RAM
DDR-SDRAM = Double data rate SDRAM
ECC = Error correcting code
PCI = Peripheral component interconnect

AGP = Accelerated graphics port
ATA = AT attachment (IDE) interface
USB = Universal serial bus
ISA = Industry Standard Architecture
LPC = Low pin count bus

AMD 750

AMD's first chipset for its own Slot A and Socket A processors, called the AMD-750, is a traditional North/South Bridge design specifically for the Athlon and Duron processors. The AMD-750 chipset consists of the AMD-751 North Bridge and the AMD-756 South Bridge.

The AMD-751 system controller connects between the AMD Athlon processor bus to the processor and also features the memory controller, AGP 2x controller, and PCI bus controller. The AMD-756 South Bridge includes a PCI-to-ISA bridge, USB controller interface, and ATA 33/66 controller.

The AMD-750 chipset includes the following features:

- AMD Athlon 200MHz processor bus
- PCI 2.2 bus with up to six masters
- AGP 2x
- PC-100 SDRAM with ECC
- Up to 768MB of memory
- ACPI power management
- ATA-33/66 support
- USB controller
- ISA bus support
- Integrated 256-byte CMOS RAM with clock
- Integrated keyboard/mouse controller

AMD 760

The AMD-760 chipset was introduced in October 2000 and is notable as the first chipset supporting DDR SDRAM memory. The AMD-760 chipset consists of the AMD-761 system controller (North Bridge) in a 569-pin plastic ball-grid array package and the AMD-766 peripheral bus controller (South Bridge) in a 272-pin PBGA package. See Figure 4.40 for details of the 760's block diagram.

The AMD-761 North Bridge features the AMD Athlon system bus, DDR-SDRAM system memory controller with support for either PC1600 or PC2100 memory, AGP 4x controller, and PCI bus controller. The 761 allows for 200MHz or 266MHz processor bus operation and supports the newer Athlon chips that use the 266MHz processor (also called front-side) bus.

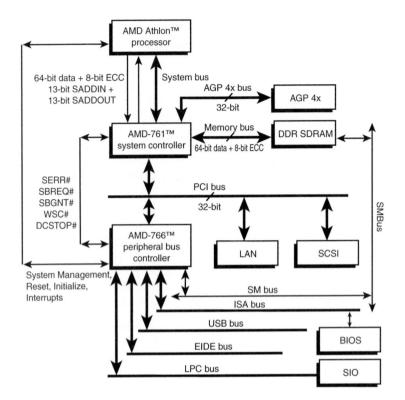

Figure 4.40 AMD 760 chipset block diagram.

The AMD-766 South Bridge includes a USB controller, dual UDMA/100 ATA/IDE interfaces, and the LPC bus for interfacing newer Super I/O and ROM BIOS components.

The AMD-760 chipset includes the following features:

- AMD Athlon 200/266MHz processor bus
- Dual processor support
- PCI 2.2 bus with up to six masters
- AGP 2.0 interface that supports 4x mode
- PC1600 or PC2100 DDR SDRAM with ECC
- Support for a maximum of 2GB buffered or 4GB registered DDR SDRAM
- ACPI power management
- ATA-100 support
- USB controller
- LPC bus for Super I/O support

VIA Chipsets

VIA Technologies, Inc., is the largest chipset and processor supplier outside of Intel and AMD. Originally founded in 1987, VIA is based in Taipei, Taiwan, and is the largest integrated circuit design firm on the island. VIA is a fabless company, which means they farm out the manufacturing to other companies with chip foundry capability. Although they are best known for their chipsets, in 1999 VIA purchased the Cyrix processor division from National Semiconductor and the Centaur processor division from IDT, respectively, thereby becoming a supplier of processors in addition to chipsets. VIA has also formed a joint venture with SonicBLUE (formerly S3) as a means of integrating graphics capabilities into various chipset products. This joint venture is known as S3 Graphics, Inc.

VIA makes chipsets for Intel, AMD, and Cyrix (VIA) processors. Table 4.13 lists the Athlon/Duron chipsets offered by VIA. These chipsets are discussed in the following sections.

Table 4.13   VIA Athlon/Duron Processor Chipsets Using North/South Bridge Architecture

Chipset	Apollo KX133	Apollo KT133	Apollo KT133A	Apollo KT266	Apollo KLE133
Introduced	Aug. 1999	Jun. 2000	Dec. 2000	January 2001	March 2001
North Bridge	VT8371	VT8363	VT8363A	VT8363	VT 8361
Processor support	Athlon	Athlon/Duron	Athlon/Duron	Athlon/Duron	Duron
CPU interface	Slot-A	Socket-A (462)	Socket-A (462)	Socket-A (462)	Socket-A (462)
CPU FSB	200MHz	200MHz	200/266MHz	200/266MHz	200/266MHz
AGP	4x	4x	4x	4x	Integrated AGP 2x
PCI	2.2	2.2	2.2	2.2	2.2
Memory type	SDRAM	SDRAM	SDRAM	SDRAM, DDR SDRAM	SDRAM
Memory speed	PC133	PC133	PC100/133	PC100/133, DDR200/266	PC100/133
Maximum memory	2GB	2GB	2GB	4GB	2GB
South Bridge	VT82C686A	VT82C686A	VT82C686B	VT8233	VT82C686B
ATA/IDE	ATA-66	ATA-66	ATA-100	ATA-100	ATA-100
USB ports	1C4P	1C4P	1C4P	2C6P	1C4P
Power management	SMM/ACPI	SMM/ACPI	SMM/ACPI	SMM/ACPI	SMM/ACPI
Super I/O	Yes	Yes	Yes	Yes	Yes
CMOS/Clock	Yes	Yes	Yes	Yes	Yes

VIA Technologies Apollo KX133

The VIA Apollo KX133 chipset brings AGP 4x, PC133, a 200MHz FSB, and ATA-66 technologies to the AMD Athlon processor platform, exceeding the performance of AMD's own 750 chipset. It was the first chipset to support AGP 4x.

Key features include the following:

- 200MHz processor bus
- AGP 4x graphics bus
- PC133 SDRAM memory
- 2GB maximum RAM
- ATA-66 support
- Four USB ports
- AC97 link for audio and modem
- Hardware monitoring
- Power management

The VIA Apollo KX133 is a two-chip set consisting of the VT8371 North Bridge controller and the VT82C686A South Bridge controller.

VIA Technologies Apollo KT133 and KT133A

The VIA Apollo KT133/A chipsets are designed to support the AMD Athlon and Duron processors in Socket-A (462) form. Based on the prior KX133 chipset, the KT133/A differ mainly in their support for Socket-A (462) over the previous Slot-A processor interface.

The VIA Apollo KT133 and KT133A are both two-chip sets consisting of the VT8363 North Bridge and the VT82C686A South Bridge (KT133) or the VT8363A North Bridge and the VT82C686B South Bridge (KT133A).

Both the KT133 and KT133A support the following standard features:

- Athlon/Duron Socket-A (462) processors
- 200MHz CPU (front-side) bus
- AGP 4x
- 2GB RAM maximum
- PC100/PC133MHz SDRAM
- PCI 2.2
- ATA-66
- USB support
- AC-97 audio
- Integrated Super I/O
- Integrated hardware monitoring
- ACPI power management

The KT133A (VT8363A North Bridge with VT82C686B South Bridge) adds the following exclusive features:

- 266MHz CPU (front-side) bus
- ATA-100

ProSavage PM133

The VIA ProSavage PM133 integrates S3 Graphics' S3 Savage 4 and S3 Savage 2000 3D and 2D graphics engines with the Apollo Pro KT133 chipset. The major features of the chipset are the same as for the Apollo Pro KT133, with the following additions:

- 2MB–32MB shared memory architecture integrated with Savage 4 3D and Savage 2000 2D video
- Z-buffering, 32-bit true-color rendering, massive 2K by 2K textures, single-pass multiple textures, sprite antialiasing, and other 3D features
- Support for DVD playback, DVI LCD displays, and TV-out
- PCI 2.2 compliance

An optional AGP 4x interface enables the integrated AGP 4x video to be upgraded with an add-on card if desired. This two-chip chipset consists of the VT8365 North Bridge and VT8231 South Bridge.

The VT8231 South Bridge integrates the Super I/O and supports the LPC interface.

Silicon Integrated Systems Chipsets for AMD Athlon/Duron Processors

SiS has a variety of chipsets for the Athlon and Duron processors. They are discussed in the following sections.

SiS733 and SiS735

The SiS733 and SiS735 are high-performance single-chip sets that support the AMD Athlon and Duron Socket A processors. Similar to other SiS single-chip sets, the SiS733 and SiS735 incorporate the features of a traditional North Bridge, South Bridge, and Super I/O chip into a single chip.

The SiS733 supports PC133 SDRAM and uses a 682-pin BGA package. The SiS735 supports either PC133 or DDR266 SDRAM and also integrates 10/100 Fast Ethernet and HomePNA 1Mbps/10Mbps Home Network interfaces. The SiS735 also uses a 682-pin BGA package.

The SiS733 and SiS735 share the following features:

- Support for 4x AGP
- Up to six PCI masters
- Dual UDMA/100 IDE host adapters
- 1.5GB RAM maximum
- Six USB ports
- AC-97 audio and AMR support
- Integrated RTC
- Low Pin Count interface for support of MIDI, joystick, and legacy BIOS devices
- PC2001 compliant

Figure 4.41 illustrates the SiS733's block diagram.

SiS730S

The SiS730S is a high-performance, low-cost, single-chip chipset with integrated 2D/3D graphics and support for Socket A versions of the AMD Athlon and Duron.

Figure 4.41   The SiS733 provides a single control interface for all major motherboard functions.

The integrated video is based on a 128-bit graphic display interface with AGP 4x performance. In addition to providing a standard analog interface for CRT monitors, the SiS730S also provides the DFP for a digital flat panel monitor. An optional SiS301 Video Bridge supports NTSC/PAL TV output. The SiS730S supports an AGP 4x slot, enabling users to upgrade to a separate AGP card in the future.

The SiS730S also includes integrated 10/100Mb Fast Ethernet as well as an AC-97–compliant interface that comprises a digital audio engine with 3D-hardware accelerator, on-chip sample rate converter, and professional wavetable along with separate modem DMA controller. SiS730S also incorporates the LPC interface for attaching newer Super I/O chips and a dual USB host controller with six USB ports. The SiS730S can also be used with ISA slots if an optional LPC/ISA bridge chip is used.

Features of the SiS730S include

- Support for AMD Athlon/Duron processors with 200MHz system bus
- Support for PC133 SDRAM
- Meet PC99 requirements
- PCI 2.2 compliant
- Four PCI masters
- Support for Ultra DMA100
- Integrated AGP 2x 2D/3D Video/Graphics Accelerator
- Support for digital flat panel
- Hardware DVD decoding
- Built-in secondary CRT controller for independent secondary CRT, LCD, or TV digital output
- LPC interface

- Advanced PCI H/W Audio (Sound Blaster 16 and DirectSound 3D compliant) and Modem
- Meets ACPI 1.0, APM 1.2 requirements
- PCI Bus Power Management Interface Spec. 1.0
- Integrated keyboard/mouse controller
- Dual USB controller with six USB ports
- Integrated 10/100Mb/sec Ethernet controller

Acer Labs Chipsets for AMD Athlon/Duron Systems

Acer Labs is a relative newcomer to the Athlon/Duron chipset business. Its Athlon/Duron chipset is described in detail in the following section.

ALiMagik1

The Acer Labs ALiMagik1 is a two-chip chipset that uses the M1647 Super North Bridge and the M1535D+ South Bridge (which is also used by its Pentium III/Celeron chipsets). The M1647 Super North Bridge is a 528-pin BGA chip.

The M1647 Super North Bridge supports SDRAM as well as DDR SDRAM at speeds of 200MHz or 266MHz. It supports up to 3GB of RAM but does not support ECC. Memory timing is x-1-1-1-1-1-1-1 in back-to-back SDRAM reads. Because the M1647 supports both conventional and DDR SDRAM, it enables system manufacturers to use the same chipset for both memory types.

The M1647 supports AGP 4x video, PCI 2.2, up to six PCI masters beyond the North Bridge and PCI bridge, ACPI and Legacy green power management, as well as PCI Mobile CLKRUN# and AGP Mobile BUSY#/STOP#.

When combined with an M1535+ South Bridge chip, the chipset is called the MobileMagiK1 and can be used on Athlon- or Duron-based portable systems.

Super I/O Chips

The third major chip seen on many PC motherboards is called the Super I/O chip. This is a chip that normally integrates devices formerly found on separate expansion cards in older systems.

Most Super I/O chips contain, at a minimum, the following components:

- Floppy controller
- Dual serial port controllers
- Parallel port controller

The floppy controllers on most Super I/O chips handle two drives, but some of them can handle only one. Older systems often required a separate floppy controller card.

The dual serial port is another item that was formerly on one or more cards. Most of the better Super I/O chips implement a buffered serial port design known as a universal asynchronous receiver transmitter (UART), one for each port. Most mimic the standalone NS16550A high-speed UART, which was created by National Semiconductor. By putting the functions of two of these chips into the Super I/O chip, we essentially have these ports built-in to the motherboard.

Virtually all Super I/O chips also include a high-speed multimode parallel port. The better ones allow three modes: standard (bidirectional), Enhanced Parallel Port (EPP), and the Enhanced Capabilities Port (ECP) modes. The ECP mode is the fastest and most powerful, but selecting it also means your port will use an ISA bus 8-bit DMA channel—usually DMA channel 3. As long as you account for this and don't set anything else to that channel (such as a sound card and so on), the EPC mode parallel port should work fine. Some of the newer printers and scanners that connect to the system via the parallel port use ECP mode, which was invented by Hewlett-Packard.

The Super I/O chip can contain other components, as well. For example, the Intel VC820 ATX motherboard uses an SMC (Standard Microsystems Corp.) LPC47M102 Super I/O chip. This chip incorporates the following functions:

- Floppy drive interface
- Two high-speed serial ports
- One ECP/EPP multimode parallel port
- 8042-style keyboard and mouse controller

Only the keyboard and mouse controller are surprising here; all the other components are in most Super I/O chips. The integrated keyboard and mouse controller saves the need to have this chip as a separate part on the board.

One thing I've noticed over the years is that the role of the Super I/O chip has decreased more and more in the newer motherboards. This is primarily due to Intel and other chipset manufacturers moving Super I/O functions, such as IDE, directly into the chipset South Bridge or ICH component, where these devices can attach to the PCI bus (North/South Bridge architecture) or to the high-speed hub interface (hub architecture) rather than the ISA bus. One of the shortcomings of the Super I/O chip is that originally it was interfaced to the system via the ISA bus and shared all the speed and performance limitations of that 8MHz bus. Moving the IDE over to the PCI bus allowed higher-speed IDE drives to be developed that could transfer at the faster 33MHz PCI bus speed.

Newer Super I/O chips interface to the system via the LPC bus, an interface designed by Intel to offer a low-speed connection (up to about 6.67MB/sec) using only 13 signals. Although technically slower than ISA, it is much more efficient, and nothing in the Super I/O chip needs any greater bandwidth anyway.

As the chipset manufacturers combine more and more functions into the main chipset, and as USB-based peripherals replace standard serial, parallel, and floppy controller–based devices, we will probably see the Super I/O chip continue to fade away in motherboard designs. More and more current chipsets are combining the South Bridge and Super I/O chips into a single component to save space and reduce parts count on the motherboard. Several of the SiS chipsets even integrate all three chips (North Bridge, South Bridge, and Super I/O) into a single chip.

Motherboard CMOS RAM Addresses

In the original AT system, a Motorola 146818 chip was used as the RTC and Complementary Metal-Oxide Semiconductor (CMOS) RAM chip. This is a special chip that had a simple digital clock, which used 10 bytes of RAM and an additional 54 more bytes of leftover RAM in which you could store anything you wanted. The designers of the IBM AT used these extra 54 bytes to store the system configuration.

Modern PC systems don't use the Motorola chip; instead, they incorporate the functions of this chip into the motherboard chipset (South Bridge) or Super I/O chip, or they use a special battery and NVRAM module from companies such as Dallas or Benchmarq.

For more detail on the CMOS RAM addresses, see the section "Motherboard CMOS RAM Addresses" in Chapter 5, "BIOS."

Motherboard Interface Connectors

There are a variety of connectors on a modern motherboard. Figure 4.42 shows the locations of these connectors on a typical motherboard (using the Intel SE440BX model as the example). Several of these connectors, such as power supply connectors, serial and parallel ports, and keyboard/mouse connectors, are covered in other chapters. Tables 4.14–4.18 contain the pinouts of most of the other different interface and I/O connectors you will find.

▶▶ See "AT Power Supply Connectors," p. 1117.

▶▶ See "Serial Ports," p. 924, and "Parallel Ports," p. 933.

▶▶ See "Keyboard/Mouse Interface Connectors," p. 969.

▶▶ See "Universal Serial Bus," p. 940.

▶▶ See "ATA I/O Connector," p. 486.

A	Communications and Network Riser (CNR)	N Auxiliary Front Panel LED
B	Optional auxiliary line in, ATAPI style (for audio)	O Front Panel USB
C	Optional ATAPI CD-ROM (for audio)	P Front Panel
D	Optional CD-ROM legacy style, 2mm (for audio)	Q IDE (top: primary; bottom: secondary)
E	Optional AGP Pro slot extension	R Floppy disk drive
F	ATX 12V power connector	S Auxiliary power
G	32-bit PCI expansion slots	T Main power
H	AGP slot	U RIMM fan (Fan 2)
I	PC/PCI	V Processor voltage regulator (Fan 4)
J	SCSI LED	W Socket 423 (for Pentium 4 processor)
K	Chassis fan (Fan 1)	X Processor fan (Fan 3)
L	Wake on LAN technology	Y RIMM sockets
M	Wake on ring	

Figure 4.42   Typical motherboard connectors (Intel DB850GB shown).

Table 4.14   Infrared Data (IrDA) Pin-Header Connector

Pin	Signal	Pin	Signal
1	+5 V	4	Ground
2	Key	5	IrTX
3	IrRX	6	CONIR (Consumer IR)

Table 4.15   Battery Connector

Pin	Signal	Pin	Signal
1	Gnd	3	KEY
2	Unused	4	+6v

Table 4.16   LED and Keylock Connector

Pin	Signal	Pin	Signal
1	LED Power (+5v)	4	Keyboard Inhibit
2	KEY	5	Gnd
3	Gnd		

Table 4.17   Speaker Connector

Pin	Signal	Pin	Signal
1	Ground	3	Board-Mounted Speaker
2	KEY	4	Speaker Output

Table 4.18   Microprocessor Fan Power Connector

Pin	Signal Name
1	Ground
2	+12V
3	Sense tachometer

Caution

Do not place a jumper on this connector; serious board damage will result if the 12v is shorted to ground.

Note that some boards have a board-mounted piezo speaker. It is enabled by placing a jumper over pins 3 and 4, which routes the speaker output to the board-mounted speaker. Removing the jumper enables a conventional speaker to be plugged in.

Some other connectors that you might find on some newer motherboards are listed in Tables 4.19–4.24.

Table 4.19   Chassis Intrusion (Security) Pin-Header

Pin	Signal Name
1	Ground
2	CHS_SEC

Table 4.20   Wake on LAN Pin-Header

Pin	Signal Name
1	+5 VSB
2	Ground
3	WOL

Table 4.21   CD Audio Connector

Pin	Signal Name	Pin	Signal Name
1	CD_IN-Left	3	Ground
2	Ground	4	CD_IN-Right

Table 4.22   Telephony Connector

Pin	Signal Name	Pin	Signal Name
1	Audio Out (monaural)	3	Ground
2	Ground	4	Audio In (monaural)

Table 4.23   ATAPI-Style Line In Connector

Pin	Signal Name	Pin	Signal Name
1	Left Line In	3	Ground
2	Ground	4	Right Line In (monaural)

Table 4.24   Wake on Ring Pin-Header

Pin	Signal Name
1	Ground
2	RINGA

Intel and several other motherboard manufacturers like to place all the front-panel motherboard connectors in a single row, as shown in Figure 4.43.

```
27 26 25 24 23 22 21 20 19 18 17 16 15 14 13 12 11 10 9 8 7 6 5 4 3 2 1

 *  *  ●  *  *  *  ●  *  ●  *  ●  *  *  ●  *  ●  *  *  *  *  ●  *  ●  *  *  *  *

Speaker      Reset     PowerLED   HDLED   Infrared Data        SleepPower
```

Figure 4.43   Typical ATX motherboard front panel connectors (Intel motherboard shown).

Table 4.25 shows the designations for the front-panel motherboard connectors commonly used on Intel ATX motherboards.

Table 4.25   ATX Motherboard Front Panel Connectors

Connector	Pin	Signal Name	Connector	Pin	Signal Name
Speaker	27	SPKR_HDR	none	12	No connect
	26	PIEZO_IN	IrDA	11	CONIR (Consumer IR)
	25	Key		10	IrTX
	24	Ground		9	Ground
Reset	23	SW_RST		8	IrRX
	22	Ground		7	Key
none	21	No connect/Key		6	+5V
Sleep/Power LED	20	PWR_LED	none	5	No connect
	19	Key	Sleep/Resume	4	SLEEP_PU (pullup)
	18	Ground		3	SLEEP
none	17	No connect/Key	Power On	2	Ground
Hard Drive LED	16	HD_PWR		1	SW_ON#
	15	HD Active#			
	14	Key			
	13	HD_PWR +5 V			

System Bus Types, Functions, and Features

The heart of any motherboard are the various buses that carry signals between the components. A *bus* is a common pathway across which data can travel within a computer. This pathway is used for communication and can be established between two or more computer elements.

The PC has a hierarchy of different buses. Most modern PCs have at least three buses; some have four or more. They are hierarchical because each slower bus is connected to the faster one above it. Each device in the system is connected to one of the buses, and some devices (primarily the chipset) act as bridges between the various buses.

The main buses in a modern system are as follows:

■ *Processor bus.* Also called the front-side bus (FSB), this is the highest-speed bus in the system and is at the core of the chipset and motherboard. This bus is used primarily by the processor to pass information to and from cache or main memory and the North Bridge of the chipset. The processor bus in a modern system runs at 66MHz, 100MHz, 133MHz, or 200MHz and is normally 64 bits (8 bytes) wide.

- *AGP bus.* This is a high-speed 32-bit bus specifically for a video card. It runs at 66MHz (AGP 1x), 133MHz (AGP 2x), 266MHz (AGP 4x), or 533MHz (AGP 8x), which allows for a bandwidth of up to 2,133MB/second. It is connected to the North Bridge or Memory Controller Hub of the chipset and is manifested as a single AGP slot in systems that support it.

- *PCI bus.* This is normally a 33MHz 32-bit bus found in virtually all newer 486 systems and Pentium and higher processor systems. Some newer systems include an optional 66MHz 64-bit version—mostly workstations or server-class systems. This bus is generated by either the chipset North Bridge in North/South Bridge chipsets or the I/O Controller Hub in chipsets using hub architecture. This bus is manifested in the system as a collection of 32-bit slots, normally white in color and numbering from four to six on most motherboards. High-speed peripherals, such as SCSI adapters, network cards, video cards, and more, can be plugged into PCI bus slots.

- *ISA bus.* This is an 8MHz, 16-bit bus that still remains in a few systems today after first appearing in the original PC in 8-bit, 5MHz form and in the 1984 IBM AT in full 16-bit 8MHz form. It is a very slow-speed bus but was ideal for certain slow-speed or older peripherals. Most newer PC motherboard designs no longer include this bus. It has been used in the past for plug-in modems, sound cards, and various other low-speed peripherals. The ISA bus is generated by the South Bridge part of the motherboard chipset, which acts as the ISA bus controller and the interface between the ISA bus and the faster PCI bus above it. The Super I/O chip usually was connected to the ISA bus on systems that included ISA slots.

Some newer motherboards feature a special connector called an Audio Modem Riser (AMR) or a Communications and Networking Riser (CNR). These are dedicated connectors for cards that are specific to the motherboard design to offer communications and networking options. They are *not* designed to be general-purpose bus interfaces, and few cards for these connectors will be offered on the open market. Usually, they're offered only as an option with a given motherboard. They are designed such that a motherboard manufacturer can easily offer its boards in versions with and without communications options, without having to reserve space on the board for optional chips. Normal network and modem options offered publicly will still be PCI based for the most part because the AMR/CNR connection is somewhat motherboard specific.

Several hidden buses exist on modern motherboards, buses that don't manifest themselves in visible slots or connectors. I'm talking about buses designed to interface chipset components, such as the Hub Interface and the LPC bus. The Hub Interface is a quad-clocked (4x) 66MHz 8-bit bus that carries data between the MCH and ICH in hub architecture chipsets. It operates at a bandwidth of 266MB/sec and was designed as a chipset component connection that is faster than PCI and yet uses fewer signals for a lower-cost design.

In a similar fashion, the LPC bus is a 4-bit bus that has a maximum bandwidth of 6.67MB/sec; it was designed as an economical onboard replacement for the ISA bus. In systems that use LPC, it typically is used to connect Super I/O chip or motherboard ROM BIOS components to the main chipset. LPC is nearly as fast as ISA and yet uses far fewer pins and enables ISA to be eliminated from the board entirely.

The system chipset is the conductor that controls the orchestra of system components, enabling each to have its turn on its respective buses. Table 4.26 shows the widths, speeds, data cycles, and overall bandwidth of virtually all PC buses.

Table 4.26   **Bandwidth (in MB/sec) and Detail Comparison of Most PC Buses and Interfaces**

Bus Type	Bus Width (bits)	Bus Speed (MHz)	Data Cycles per Clock	Bandwidth (MB/sec)
8-bit ISA (PC/XT)	8	4.77	1/2	2.39
8-bit ISA (AT)	8	8.33	1/2	4.17
LPC bus	4	33	~1/3	6.67
16-bit ISA (AT-Bus)	16	8.33	1/2	8.33
DD Floppy Interface	1	0.25	1	0.03125
HD Floppy Interface	1	0.5	1	0.0625
ED Floppy Interface	1	1	1	0.125
EISA Bus	32	8.33	1	33
VL-Bus	32	33	1	133
MCA-16	16	5	1	10
MCA-32	32	5	1	20
MCA-16 Streaming	16	10	1	20
MCA-32 Streaming	32	10	1	40
MCA-64 Streaming	64	10	1	80
MCA-64 Streaming	64	20	1	160
PC-Card (PCMCIA)	16	10	1	20
CardBus	32	33	1	133
Hub Interface (chipset)	8	66	4	266
PCI	32	33	1	133
PCI 66MHz	32	66	1	266
PCI 64-bit	64	33	1	266
PCI 66MHz/64-bit	64	66	1	533
PCI-X	64	133	1	1,066
AGP	32	66	1	266
AGP 2x	32	66	2	533
AGP 4X	32	66	4	1,066
AGP 8x	32	66	8	2,133
RS-232 Serial	1	0.1152	1/10	0.01152
RS-232 Serial HS	1	0.2304	1/10	0.02304
IEEE-1284 Parallel	8	8.33	1/6	1.38
IEEE-1284 EPP/ECP	8	8.33	1/3	2.77
USB 1.1	1	12	1	1.5
USB 2.0	1	480	1	60

Table 4.26   Continued

Bus Type	Bus Width (bits)	Bus Speed (MHz)	Data Cycles per Clock	Bandwidth (MB/sec)
IEEE-1394a S100	1	100	1	12.5
IEEE-1394a S200	1	200	1	25
IEEE-1394a S400	1	400	1	50
IEEE-1394b S800	1	800	1	100
IEEE-1394b S1600	1	1600	1	200
ATA PIO-4	16	8.33	1	16.67
ATA-UDMA/33	16	8.33	2	33
ATA-UDMA/66	16	16.67	2	66
ATA-UDMA/100	16	25	2	100
SATA-150	1	1500	1	150
SATA-300	1	3000	1	300
SATA-600	1	6000	1	600
SCSI	8	5	1	5
SCSI Wide	16	5	1	10
SCSI Fast	8	10	1	10
SCSI Fast/Wide	16	10	1	20
SCSI Ultra	8	20	1	20
SCSI Ultra/Wide	16	20	1	40
SCSI Ultra2	8	40	1	40
SCSI Ultra2/Wide	16	40	1	80
SCSI Ultra3 (Ultra160)	16	40	2	160
SCSI Ultra4 (Ultra320)	16	80	2	320
FPM DRAM	64	22	1	177
EDO DRAM	64	33	1	266
PC66 SDRAM	64	66	1	533
PC100 SDRAM	64	100	1	800
PC133 SDRAM	64	133	1	1,066
PC600 RDRAM	16	300	2	1,200
PC700 RDRAM	16	350	2	1,400
PC800 RDRAM	16	400	2	1,600
PC800 RDRAM Dual	32	400	2	3,200
PC1600 DDR SDRAM	64	100	2	1,600
PC2100 DDR SDRAM	64	133	2	2,133
33MHz 486 CPU FSB	32	33	1	133

Table 4.26   Continued

Bus Type	Bus Width (bits)	Bus Speed (MHz)	Data Cycles per Clock	Bandwidth (MB/sec)
66MHz 64-bit CPU FSB	64	66	1	533
100MHz 64-bit CPU FSB	64	100	1	800
133MHz 64-bit CPU FSB	64	133	1	1,066
200MHz 64-bit CPU FSB	64	100	2	1,600
266MHz 64-bit CPU FSB	64	133	2	2,133
400MHz 64-bit CPU FSB	64	100	4	3,200

Note: ISA, EISA, VL-Bus, and MCA are no longer used in current motherboard designs.

MB/sec = Megabytes per second.

ISA = Industry Standard Architecture, also known as the PC/XT (8-bit) or AT-Bus (16-bit).

LPC = Low pin count bus.

DD Floppy = Double-Density (360/720KB) Floppy.

HD Floppy = High-Density (1.2/1.44MB) Floppy.

ED Floppy = Extra-high Density (2.88MB) Floppy.

EISA = Extended Industry Standard Architecture (32-bit ISA).

VL-Bus = VESA (Video Electronics Standards Association) Local Bus (ISA extension).

MCA = Microchannel architecture (IBM PS/2 systems).

PC-Card = 16-bit PCMCIA (Personal Computer Memory Card International Association) interface.

CardBus = 32-bit PC-Card.

Hub Interface = Intel 8xx chipset bus.

PCI = Peripheral component interconnect.

AGP = Accelerated graphics port.

RS-232 = Standard serial port, 115.2Kbps.

RS-232 HS = High-speed serial port, 230.4Kbps.

IEEE-1284 Parallel = Standard bidirectional parallel port.

IEEE-1284 EPP/ECP = Enhanced parallel port/extended capabilities port.

USB = Universal serial bus.

IEEE-1394 = FireWire, also called i.Link.

ATA PIO = AT Attachment (also known as IDE) programmed I/O.

ATA-UDMA = AT Attachment Ultra DMA.

SCSI = Small computer system interface.

FPM = Fast page mode, based on X-3-3-3 (1/3 max) burst mode timing on a 66MHz bus.

EDO = Extended data out, based on X-2-2-2 (1/2 max) burst mode timing on a 66MHz bus.

SDRAM = Synchronous dynamic RAM.

RDRAM = Rambus dynamic RAM.

RDRAM Dual = Dual-channel RDRAM (operating simultaneously).

DDR-SDRAM = Double-data rate SDRAM.

CPU FSB = Processor front-side bus.

Note that many of the buses use multiple data cycles (transfers) per clock cycle to achieve greater performance. This means the data transfer rate is higher than it would seem for a given clock rate. This allows for an easy way to take an existing bus and make it go faster in a backward-compatible way.

The following sections discuss the processor and other subset buses in the system and the main I/O buses mentioned in the previous table.

The Processor Bus (Front-Side Bus)

The processor bus (also called the Front-side bus or FSB) is the communication pathway between the CPU and motherboard chipset, more specifically the North Bridge or Memory Controller Hub. This bus runs at the full motherboard speed—normally between 66MHz and 400MHz in modern systems, depending on the particular board and chipset design. This same bus also transfers data between the CPU and an external (L2) memory cache on Socket-7 (Pentium class) systems. Figure 4.44 shows how this bus fits into a typical Socket-7 PC system.

Figure 4.44 also shows where and how the other main buses, such as the PCI and ISA buses, fit into the system. As you can see, there is clearly a three-tier architecture with the fastest CPU bus on top, the PCI bus next, and the ISA bus at the bottom. Various components in the system are connected to one of these three main buses.

Figure 4.44   Typical Socket-7 (Pentium class) system architecture.

Socket-7 systems have an external (L2) cache for the CPU; the L2 cache is mounted on the motherboard and connected to the main processor bus that runs at the motherboard speed (normally between 66MHz and 100MHz). Thus, as the Socket-7 processors became available in faster and faster versions (through increasing the clock multiplier in the chip), the L2 cache unfortunately remained stuck on the motherboard running at the relatively slow (by comparison) motherboard speed. For example, the fastest Intel Socket-7 systems ran the CPU at 233MHz, which was 3.5X the CPU bus speed of 66MHz. Therefore, the L2 cache ran at only 66MHz. The fastest Socket-7 systems used the AMD K6-2 550 processor, which ran at 550MHz—5.5X a CPU bus speed of 100MHz. In those systems, the L2 cache ran at only 100MHz.

The problem of the slow L2 cache was first solved in the P6 class processors, such as the Pentium Pro, Pentium II, Celeron, Pentium III, and AMD Athlon and Duron. These processors used either Socket 8, Slot 1, Slot 2, Slot A, Socket A, or Socket 370. They moved the L2 cache off the motherboard and directly onto the CPU and connected it to the CPU via an on-chip back-side bus. Because the L2 cache bus was called the back-side bus, some in the industry began calling the main CPU bus the front-side bus. I still usually refer to it simply as the CPU bus.

By incorporating the L2 cache into the CPU, it can run at speeds up to the same speed as the processor itself. Most processors now incorporate the L2 cache directly on the CPU die, so the L2 cache runs at the same speed as the rest of the CPU. Others (mostly older versions) used separate die for the cache integrated into the CPU package, which ran the L2 cache at some lower multiple (1/2, 2/5, or 1/3) of the main CPU. Even if the L2 ran at 1/2 or 1/3 of the processor speed, it still was significantly faster than the motherboard-bound cache on the Socket-7 systems.

Figure 4.45 shows a typical Slot-1 type system, in which the L2 cache is built into the CPU but running at only half the processor speed. This would also be the same for systems using Slot-A. The CPU bus speed increased from 66MHz (used primarily in Socket-7 systems) to 100MHz, enabling a bandwidth of 800MB/sec. Note that most of these systems included AGP support. Basic AGP was 66MHz (twice the speed of PCI), but most of these systems incorporated AGP 2x, which operated at twice the speed of standard AGP, enabling a bandwidth of 533 MB/sec. These systems also typically used PC-100 SDRAM DIMMs, which have a bandwidth of 800MB/sec, matching the processor bus bandwidth for the best performance.

Slot-1 was dropped in favor of Socket 370 for the Pentium III and Celeron systems. This was mainly because these newer processors incorporated the L2 cache directly into the CPU die (running at the full core speed of the processor), and an expensive cartridge with multiple chips was no longer necessary. At the same time, processor bus speeds increased to 133MHz, which enabled a throughput of 1,066MB/sec. Figure 4.46 shows a typical Socket-370 system design. AGP speed was also increased to AGP 4x, with a bandwidth of 1,066MB/sec.

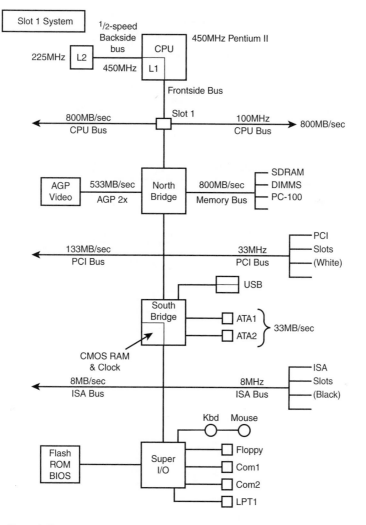

Figure 4.45   Typical Slot-1 (Pentium II class) system architecture.

Figure 4.46 Typical Socket-370 (Pentium III/Celeron class) system architecture.

Note the use of what Intel calls "hub architecture" instead of the older North/South Bridge design. This moves the main connection between the chipset components to a separate 266MB/sec hub inter-face (which has twice the throughput of PCI) and enables PCI devices to use the full bandwidth of PCI without fighting for bandwidth with a South Bridge. Also note that the flash ROM BIOS chip is now referred to as a Firmware Hub and is connected to the system via the LPC bus instead of via the Super I/O chip as in older North/South Bridge designs. The ISA bus is no longer used in most of these systems, and the Super I/O is connected via the LPC bus instead of ISA. The Super I/O chip also can be easily eliminated in these designs. This is commonly referred to as a *legacy-free* system because the ports supplied by the Super I/O chip are now known as *legacy* ports. Devices that would have used legacy ports must then be connected to the system via USB instead, and such systems would normally feature two USB controllers, with up to four total ports (more can be added by attaching USB hubs).

AMD processor systems adopted a Socket-A design, which is similar to Socket-370 except it uses faster processor and memory buses and yet also retains the older North/South Bridge design. Figure 4.47 shows a typical Socket-A system design. Note the high-speed CPU bus running up to 266MHz (2,133MB/sec throughput) and the use of DDR SDRAM DIMM modules that support a matching bandwidth of 2,133MB/sec. It is always best for performance when the bandwidth of memory matches that of the processor. Finally note how most of the South Bridge components include functions otherwise found in Super I/O chips; when these functions are included the chip is called a Super South Bridge.

Figure 4.47   Typical Socket-A (Athlon/Duron) system architecture.

The Pentium 4 uses a Socket-423 design with hub architecture (see Figure 4.48). This design is most notable for including a 400MHz CPU bus with a bandwidth of 3,200MB/sec, currently faster than anything else on the market. Also note the use of dual-channel PC-800 RDRAM RIMMs, which have a 3,200MB/sec bandwidth, matching that of the processor bus exactly for the best performance.

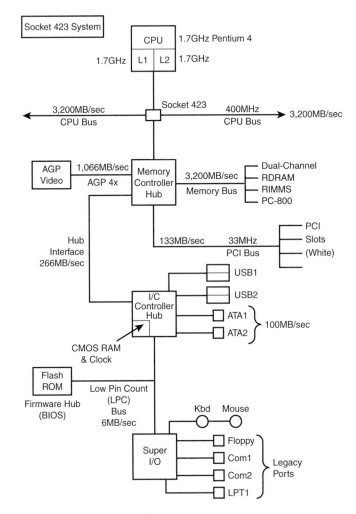

Figure 4.48 Typical Socket-423 (Pentium 4) system architecture.

Because the purpose of the processor bus is to get information to and from the CPU at the fastest possible speed, this bus typically operates at a faster rate than any other bus in your system. The bus consists of electrical circuits for data, addresses (the address bus, which is discussed in the following section), and control purposes. Most processors since the original Pentium have a 64-bit data bus, which means they transfer 64 bits (8 bytes) at a time over the CPU bus.

The processor bus operates at the same base clock rate as the CPU does externally. This can be misleading because most CPUs these days run internally at a higher clock rate than they do externally. For example, a Celeron 766 system has a processor running at 766MHz internally, but only 66MHz externally, whereas a Pentium III 1GHz runs at 1GHz internally but only 133MHz externally. In most newer systems, the actual processor speed is some multiple (2x, 2.5x, 3x, and higher) of the processor bus.

◄◄ See "Processor Speed Ratings," p. 47.

The processor bus is tied to the external processor pin connections and can transfer 1 bit of data per data line every cycle. Most modern processors transfer 64 bits (8 bytes) of data at a time.

To determine the transfer rate for the processor bus, you multiply the data width (64 bits for a Celeron/Pentium III/4 or Athlon/Duron) by the clock speed of the bus (the same as the base or unmultiplied clock speed of the CPU).

For example, if you are using a Pentium III 1.13GHz that runs at a 133MHz motherboard speed, you have a maximum instantaneous transfer rate of roughly 1,066MB/sec. You get this result by using the following formula:

133.33MHz × 8 bytes (64 bits) = 1,066MB/sec

With Socket A (Athlon) you get

266.66MHz × 8 bytes (64 bits) = 2,133MB/sec

With Socket 423 (Pentium 4) you get

400MHz × 8 bytes (64 bits) = 3,200MB/sec

This transfer rate, often called the *bandwidth* of the processor bus, represents the maximum speed at which data can move. Refer to Table 4.26 for a more complete list of various processor bus bandwidths.

The Memory Bus

The memory bus is used to transfer information between the CPU and main memory—the RAM in your system. This bus is connected to the motherboard chipset North Bridge or Memory Controller Hub chip. Depending on the type of memory your chipset (and therefore motherboard) is designed to handle, the North Bridge runs the memory bus at various speeds. The best solution is if the memory bus runs at the same speed as the processor bus. Systems that use PC133 SDRAM have a memory bandwidth of 1,066MB/sec, which is the same as the 133MHz CPU bus. In another example, Athlon and Pentium III systems running a 266MHz processor bus also run PC2100 DDR-SDRAM, which has a bandwidth of 2,133MB/sec—exactly the same as the processor bus in those systems. Also, systems running a Pentium 4 with its 400MHz processor bus also use dual-channel RDRAM memory, which runs 1,600MB/sec for each channel, or a combined bandwidth (both memory channels run simultaneously) of 3,200MB/sec, which is exactly the same as the Pentium 4 CPU bus.

Running memory at the same speed as the processor bus negates the need for having cache memory on the motherboard. That is why when the L2 cache moved into the processor, nobody added an L3 cache to the motherboard. Figure 4.40 and Figure 4.41, previously in this chapter, show how the memory bus fits into your PC.

Note

Notice that the main memory bus is always the same width as the processor bus. This defines the size of what is called a *bank* of memory, at least when dealing with anything but RDRAM. Memory banks and their widths relative to processor buses are discussed in the section "Memory Banks" in Chapter 6.

The Need for Expansion Slots

The I/O bus or expansion slots are what enables your CPU to communicate with peripheral devices. The bus and its associated expansion slots are needed because basic systems cannot possibly satisfy all the needs of all the people who buy them. The I/O bus enables you to add devices to your computer to expand its capabilities. The most basic computer components, such as sound cards and video cards, can be plugged into expansion slots; you also can plug in more specialized devices, such as network interface cards, SCSI host adapters, and others.

Note

In most modern PC systems, a variety of basic peripheral devices are built into the motherboard. Most systems today have at least dual (primary and secondary) IDE interfaces, dual USB ports, a floppy controller, two serial ports, a parallel port, keyboard, and mouse controller built directly into the motherboard. These devices are normally distributed between the motherboard chipset South Bridge and the Super I/O chip. (Super I/O chips are discussed earlier in this chapter.)

Many add even more items, such as a built-in sound card, video adapter, SCSI host adapter, or network interface, that also are built into the motherboard. Those items, however, are not built into the motherboard chipset or Super I/O chip, but are configured as additional chips installed on the board. Nevertheless, these built-in controllers and ports still use the I/O bus to communicate with the CPU. In essence, even though they are built in, they act as if there were cards plugged into the system's bus slots, including using system resources in the same manner.

Types of I/O Buses

Since the introduction of the first PC, many I/O buses have been introduced. The reason is simple: Faster I/O speeds are necessary for better system performance. This need for higher performance involves three main areas:

- Faster CPUs
- Increasing software demands
- Greater multimedia requirements

Each of these areas requires the I/O bus to be as fast as possible.

One of the primary reasons new I/O-bus structures have been slow in coming is compatibility—that old catch-22 that anchors much of the PC industry to the past. One of the hallmarks of the PC's success is its standardization. This standardization spawned thousands of third-party I/O cards, each originally built for the early bus specifications of the PC. If a new high-performance bus system was introduced, it often had to be compatible with the older bus systems so the older I/O cards would not be obsolete. Therefore, bus technologies seem to evolve rather than make quantum leaps forward.

You can identify different types of I/O buses by their architectures. The main types of I/O buses are detailed earlier in this chapter.

The main differences among buses consist primarily of the amounts of data they can transfer at one time and the speeds at which they can do it. The following sections describe the various types of PC buses.

The ISA Bus

ISA, which is an abbreviation for Industry Standard Architecture, is the bus architecture that was introduced as an 8-bit bus with the original IBM PC in 1981; it was later expanded to 16 bits with the IBM PC/AT in 1984. ISA is the basis of the modern personal computer and the primary architecture used in the vast majority of PC systems on the market today. It might seem amazing that such a presumably antiquated architecture is used in today's high-performance systems, but this is true for reasons of reliability, affordability, and compatibility, plus this old bus is still faster than many of the peripherals we connect to it!

Note

The ISA bus is vanishing from most of the latest systems, and few companies make or sell ISA cards anymore.

Two versions of the ISA bus exist, based on the number of data bits that can be transferred on the bus at a time. The older version is an 8-bit bus; the newer version is a 16-bit bus. The original 8-bit version ran at 4.77MHz in the PC and XT. The 16-bit version used in the AT ran at 6MHz and then 8MHz. Later, the industry as a whole agreed on an 8.33MHz maximum standard speed for 8/16-bit versions of the ISA bus for backward compatibility. Some systems have the capability to run the ISA bus faster than this, but some adapter cards will not function properly at higher speeds. ISA data transfers require anywhere from two to eight cycles. Therefore, the theoretical maximum data rate of the ISA bus is about 8MB/sec, as the following formula shows:

$$8.33\text{MHz} \times 2 \text{ bytes (16 bits)} \div 2 \text{ cycles per transfer} = 8.33\text{MB/sec}$$

The bandwidth of the 8-bit bus would be half this figure (4.17MB/sec). Remember, however, that these figures are theoretical maximums; because of I/O bus protocols, the effective bandwidth is much lower—typically by almost half. Even so, at about 8MB/sec, the ISA bus is still faster than many of the peripherals connected to it, such as serial ports, parallel ports, floppy controllers, keyboard controllers, and so on.

The 8-Bit ISA Bus

This bus architecture is used in the original IBM PC computers and was retained for a number of years in later systems. Although virtually nonexistent in new systems today, this architecture still exists in hundreds of thousands of PC systems in the field.

Physically, the 8-bit ISA expansion slot resembles the tongue-and-groove system furniture makers once used to hold two pieces of wood together. It is specifically called a *card/edge connector*. An adapter card with 62 contacts on its bottom edge plugs into a slot on the motherboard that has 62 matching contacts. Electronically, this slot provides 8 data lines and 20 addressing lines, enabling the slot to handle 1MB of memory.

Figure 4.49 describes the pinouts for the 8-bit ISA bus; Figure 4.50 shows how these pins are oriented in the expansion slot.

Although the design of the bus is simple, IBM waited until 1987 to publish full specifications for the timings of the data and address lines, so in the early days of PC compatibles, manufacturers had to do their best to figure out how to make adapter boards. This problem was solved, however, as PC-compatible personal computers became more widely accepted as the industry standard and manufacturers had more time and incentive to build adapter boards that worked correctly with the bus.

The dimensions of 8-bit ISA adapter cards are as follows:

> 4.2 inches (106.68mm) high
>
> 13.13 inches (333.5mm) long
>
> 0.5 inch (12.7mm) wide

The 16-Bit ISA Bus

IBM threw a bombshell on the PC world when it introduced the AT with the 286 processor in 1984. This processor had a 16-bit data bus, which meant communications between the processor and the motherboard as well as memory would now be 16 bits wide instead of only 8. Although this processor could have been installed on a motherboard with only an 8-bit I/O bus, that would have meant a huge sacrifice in the performance of any adapter cards or other devices installed on the bus.

Signal	Pin		Pin	Signal
Ground	B1		A1	-I/O CH CHK
RESET DRV	B2		A2	Data Bit 7
+5 Vdc	B3		A3	Data Bit 6
IRQ 2	B4		A4	Data Bit 5
-5 Vdc	B5		A5	Data Bit 4
DRQ 2	B6		A6	Data Bit 3
-12 Vdc	B7		A7	Data Bit 2
-CARD SLCTD	B8		A8	Data Bit 1
+12 Vdc	B9		A9	Data Bit 0
Ground	B10		A10	-I/O CH RDY
-SMEMW	B11		A11	AEN
-SMEMR	B12		A12	Address 19
-IOW	B13		A13	Address 18
-IOR	B14		A14	Address 17
-DACK 3	B15		A15	Address 16
DRQ 3	B16		A16	Address 15
-DACK 1	B17		A17	Address 14
DRQ 1	B18		A18	Address 13
-Refresh	B19		A19	Address 12
CLK(4.77MHz)	B20		A20	Address 11
IRQ 7	B21		A21	Address 10
IRQ 6	B22		A22	Address 9
IRQ 5	B23		A23	Address 8
IRQ 4	B24		A24	Address 7
IRQ 3	B25		A25	Address 6
-DACK 2	B26		A26	Address 5
T/C	B27		A27	Address 4
BALE	B28		A28	Address 3
+5 Vdc	B29		A29	Address 2
OSC(14.3MHz)	B30		A30	Address 1
Ground	B31		A31	Address 0

Figure 4.49   Pinouts for the 8-bit ISA bus.

Figure 4.50   The 8-bit ISA bus connector.

Rather than create a new I/O bus, at that time IBM instead came up with a system that could support both 8- and 16-bit cards by retaining the same basic 8-bit connector layout but adding an optional 16-bit extension connector. This first debuted on the PC/AT in August 1984, which is why we also refer to the ISA bus as the *AT-bus*.

The extension connector in each 16-bit expansion slot adds 36 connector pins (for a total of 96 signals) to carry the extra signals necessary to implement the wider data path. In addition, two of the pins in the 8-bit portion of the connector were changed. These two minor changes did not alter the function of 8-bit cards.

Figure 4.51 describes the pinouts for the full 16-bit ISA expansion slot, and Figure 4.52 shows how the additional pins are oriented in the expansion slot.

Because of physical interference with some ancient 8-bit card designs, IBM left 16-bit extension connectors off two of the slots in the AT. This was not a problem in newer systems, so any system with ISA slots would have all of them as full 16-bit versions.

The dimensions of a typical AT expansion board are as follows:

> 4.8 inches (121.92mm) high
>
> 13.13 inches (333.5mm) long
>
> 0.5 inch (12.7mm) wide

Signal	Pin	Pin	Signal
Ground	B1	A1	-I/O CH CHK
RESET DRV	B2	A2	Data Bit 7
+5 Vdc	B3	A3	Data Bit 6
IRQ 9	B4	A4	Data Bit 5
-5 Vdc	B5	A5	Data Bit 4
DRQ 2	B6	A6	Data Bit 3
-12 Vdc	B7	A7	Data Bit 2
-0 WAIT	B8	A8	Data Bit 1
+12 Vdc	B9	A9	Data Bit 0
Ground	B10	A10	-I/O CH RDY
-SMEMW	B11	A11	AEN
-SMEMR	B12	A12	Address 19
-IOW	B13	A13	Address 18
-IOR	B14	A14	Address 17
-DACK 3	B15	A15	Address 16
DRQ 3	B16	A16	Address 15
-DACK 1	B17	A17	Address 14
DRQ 1	B18	A18	Address 13
-Refresh	B19	A19	Address 12
CLK(8.33MHz)	B20	A20	Address 11
IRQ 7	B21	A21	Address 10
IRQ 6	B22	A22	Address 9
IRQ 5	B23	A23	Address 8
IRQ 4	B24	A24	Address 7
IRQ 3	B25	A25	Address 6
-DACK 2	B26	A26	Address 5
T/C	B27	A27	Address 4
BALE	B28	A28	Address 3
+5 Vdc	B29	A29	Address 2
OSC(14.3MHz)	B30	A30	Address 1
Ground	B31	A31	Address 0

Signal	Pin	Pin	Signal
-MEM CS16	D1	C1	-SBHE
-I/O CS16	D2	C2	Latch Address 23
IRQ 10	D3	C3	Latch Address 22
IRQ 11	D4	C4	Latch Address 21
IRQ 12	D5	C5	Latch Address 20
IRQ 15	D6	C6	Latch Address 19
IRQ 14	D7	C7	Latch Address 18
-DACK 0	D8	C8	Latch Address 17
DRQ 0	D9	C9	-MEMR
-DACK 5	D10	C10	-MEMW
DRQ5	D11	C11	Data Bit 8
-DACK 6	D12	C12	Data Bit 9
DRQ 6	D13	C13	Data Bit 10
-DACK 7	D14	C14	Data Bit 11
DRQ 7	D15	C15	Data Bit 12
+5 Vdc	D16	C16	Data Bit 13
-Master	D17	C17	Data Bit 14
Ground	D18	C18	Data Bit 15

Figure 4.51   Pinouts for the 16-bit ISA bus.

Figure 4.52   The ISA 16-bit bus connector.

Two heights actually are available for cards commonly used in AT systems: 4.8 inches and 4.2 inches (the height of older PC-XT cards). The shorter cards became an issue when IBM introduced the XT Model 286. Because this model has an AT motherboard in an XT case, it needs AT-type boards with the 4.2-inch maximum height. Most board makers trimmed the height of their boards; most manufacturers who still make ISA cards now make only 4.2-inch tall (or less) boards so they will work in systems with either profile.

32-Bit Buses

After 32-bit CPUs became available, it was some time before 32-bit bus standards became available. Before MCA and EISA specs were released, some vendors began creating their own proprietary 32-bit buses, which were extensions of the ISA bus. Although the proprietary buses were few and far between, they do still exist.

The expanded portions of the bus typically are used for proprietary memory expansion or video cards. Because the systems are proprietary (meaning that they are nonstandard), pinouts and specifications are not available.

The Micro Channel Bus

The introduction of 32-bit chips meant that the ISA bus could not handle the power of another new generation of CPUs. The 386DX chips could transfer 32 bits of data at a time, but the ISA bus can handle a maximum of only 16 bits. Rather than extend the ISA bus again, IBM decided to build a new bus; the result was the MCA bus. *MCA* (an abbreviation for microchannel architecture) is completely different from the ISA bus and was technically superior in every way.

IBM wanted not only to replace the old ISA standard, but also to require vendors to license certain parts of the technology. Many owed for licenses on the ISA-bus technology that IBM also created, but because IBM had not been aggressive in its licensing of ISA, many got away without any license. Problems with licensing and control led to the development of the competing EISA bus (see the next section on the EISA bus) and hindered acceptance of the MCA bus.

MCA systems produced a new level of ease of use; they were plug-and-play before the official Plug and Play specification even existed. An MCA system had no jumpers and switches—neither on the motherboard nor on any expansion adapter. Instead you used a special Reference disk, which went with the particular system, and Option disks, which went with each of the cards installed in the system. After a card was installed, you loaded the Option disks files onto the Reference disk; after that, you didn't need the Option disks anymore. The Reference disk contained the special BIOS and system setup program necessary for an MCA system, and the system couldn't be configured without it. To support older PS/2 systems, IBM maintains a library of all its Reference and Options disks at ftp://ftp.pc.ibm.com/pub/pccbbs. Check this site if you are supporting any old MCA-based systems and need any of these files.

For more information on the MCA bus, see the previous editions of this book on the included CD-ROM.

The EISA Bus

EISA is an abbreviation for Extended Industry Standard Architecture. This standard was announced in September 1988 as a response to IBM's introduction of the MCA bus—more specifically, to the way that IBM wanted to handle licensing of the MCA bus. Vendors did not feel obligated to pay retroactive royalties on the ISA bus, so they turned their backs on IBM and created their own buses.

The EISA standard was developed primarily by Compaq and was intended to be its way of taking over future development of the PC bus from IBM. Compaq knew that nobody would clone its bus if it was the only company that had it, so it essentially gave the design away to other leading manufacturers. Compaq formed the EISA committee, a nonprofit organization designed specifically to control development of the EISA bus. Very few EISA adapters were ever developed. Those that were developed centered mainly around disk array controllers and server-type network cards.

The EISA bus was essentially a 32-bit version of ISA. Unlike the MCA bus from IBM, you could still use older 8-bit or 16-bit ISA cards in 32-bit EISA slots, providing for full backward compatibility. As with MCA, EISA also allowed for automatic configuration of EISA cards via software.

The EISA bus added 90 new connections (55 new signals plus grounds) without increasing the physical connector size of the 16-bit ISA bus. At first glance, the 32-bit EISA slot looks a lot like the 16-bit ISA slot. The EISA adapter, however, has two rows of stacked contacts. The first row is the same type used in 16-bit ISA cards; the other, thinner row extends from the 16-bit connectors. Therefore, ISA cards can still be used in EISA bus slots. Although this compatibility was not enough to ensure the popularity of EISA buses, it is a feature that was carried over into the VL-Bus standard that followed. The physical specifications of an EISA card are as follows:

- 5 inches (127mm) high
- 13.13 inches (333.5mm) long
- 0.5 inches (12.7mm) wide

The EISA bus can handle up to 32 bits of data at an 8.33MHz cycle rate. Most data transfers require a minimum of two cycles, although faster cycle rates are possible if an adapter card provides tight timing specifications. The maximum bandwidth on the bus is 33MB/sec, as the following formula shows:

- 8.33MHz × 4 bytes (32 bits) = 33MB/sec

Figure 4.53 describes the pinouts for the EISA bus. Figure 4.54 shows the locations of the pins; note how some pins are offset to allow the EISA slot to accept ISA cards. Figure 4.55 shows the card connector for the EISA expansion slot.

Local Buses

The I/O buses discussed so far (ISA, MCA, and EISA) have one thing in common: relatively slow speed. The next three bus types that are discussed in the following few sections all use the *local bus* concept explained in this section to address the speed issue. The three main local buses found in PC systems are

- VL-Bus (VESA local bus)
- PCI
- AGP

The speed limitation of ISA, MCA, and EISA is a carryover from the days of the original PC, when the I/O bus operated at the same speed as the processor bus. As the speed of the processor bus increased, the I/O bus realized only nominal speed improvements, primarily from an increase in the bandwidth of the bus. The I/O bus had to remain at a slower speed because the huge installed base of adapter cards could operate only at slower speeds.

Lower Signal	Upper Signal	Pin	Pin	Upper Signal	Lower Signal
Ground	Ground	B1	A1	-I/O CH CHK	-CMD
+5 Vdc	RESET DRV	B2	A2	Data Bit 7	-START
+5 Vdc	+5 Vdc	B3	A3	Data Bit 6	EXRDY
Reserved	IRQ 9	B4	A4	Data Bit 5	-EX32
Reserved	-5 Vdc	B5	A5	Data Bit 4	Ground
KEY	DRQ 2	B6	A6	Data Bit 3	KEY
Reserved	-12 Vdc	B7	A7	Data Bit 2	-EX16
Reserved	-0 WAIT	B8	A8	Data Bit 1	-SLBURST
+12 Vdc	+12 Vdc	B9	A9	Data Bit 0	-MSBURST
M-IO	Ground	B10	A10	-I/O CH RDY	W-R
-LOCK	-SMEMW	B11	A11	AEN	Ground
Reserved	-SMEMR	B12	A12	Address 19	Reserved
Ground	-IOW	B13	A13	Address 18	Reserved
Reserved	-IOR	B14	A14	Address 17	Reserved
-BE 3	-DACK 3	B15	A15	Address 16	Ground
KEY	DRQ 3	B16	A16	Address 15	KEY
-BE 2	-DACK 1	B17	A17	Address 14	-BE 1
-BE 0	DRQ 1	B18	A18	Address 13	Latch Address 31
Ground	-Refresh	B19	A19	Address 12	Ground
+5 Vdc	CLK(8.33MHz)	B20	A20	Address 11	-Latch Address 30
Latch Address 29	IRQ 7	B21	A21	Address 10	-Latch Address 28
Ground	IRQ 6	B22	A22	Address 9	-Latch Address 27
Latch Address 26	IRQ 5	B23	A23	Address 8	-Latch Address 25
Latch Address 24	IRQ 4	B24	A24	Address 7	Ground
KEY	IRQ 3	B25	A25	Address 6	KEY
Latch Address 16	-DACK 2	B26	A26	Address 5	Latch Address 15
Latch Address 14	T/C	B27	A27	Address 4	Latch Address 13
+5 Vdc	BALE	B28	A28	Address 3	Latch Address 12
+5 Vdc	+5 Vdc	B29	A29	Address 2	Latch Address 11
Ground	OSC(14.3MHz)	B30	A30	Address 1	Ground
Latch Address 10	Ground	B31	A31	Address 0	Latch Address 9

Lower Signal	Upper Signal	Pin	Pin	Upper Signal	Lower Signal
Latch Address 8	-MEM CS16	D1	C1	-SBHE	Latch Address 7
Latch Address 6	-I/O CS16	D2	C2	Latch Address 23	Ground
Latch Address 5	IRQ 10	D3	C3	Latch Address 22	Latch Address 4
+5 Vdc	IRQ 11	D4	C4	Latch Address 21	Latch Address 3
Latch Address 4	IRQ 12	D5	C5	Latch Address 20	Ground
KEY	IRQ 15	D6	C6	Latch Address 19	KEY
Data Bit 16	IRQ 14	D7	C7	Latch Address 18	Data Bit 17
Data Bit 18	-DACK 0	D8	C8	Latch Address 17	Data Bit 19
Ground	DRQ 0	D9	C9	-MEMR	Data Bit 20
Data Bit 21	-DACK 5	D10	C10	-MEMW	Data Bit 22
Data Bit 23	DRQ5	D11	C11	Data Bit 8	Ground
Data Bit 24	-DACK 6	D12	C12	Data Bit 9	Data Bit 25
Ground	DRQ 6	D13	C13	Data Bit 10	Data Bit 26
Data Bit 27	-DACK 7	D14	C14	Data Bit 11	Data Bit 28
KEY	DRQ 7	D15	C15	Data Bit 12	KEY
Data Bit 29	+5 Vdc	D16	C16	Data Bit 13	Ground
+5 Vdc	-Master	D17	C17	Data Bit 14	Data Bit 30
+5 Vdc	Ground	D18	C18	Data Bit 15	Data Bit 31
-MAKx		D19	C19		-MREQx

Figure 4.53   Pinouts for the EISA bus.

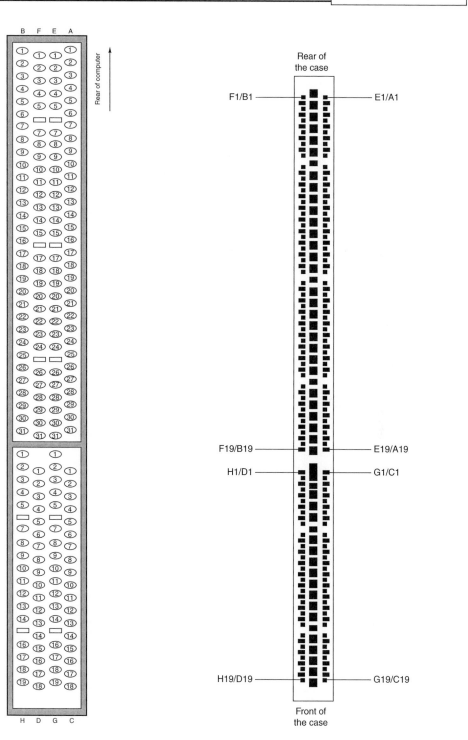

Figure 4.54 Pin locations inside the EISA bus connector.

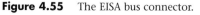

Figure 4.55 The EISA bus connector.

Figure 4.56 shows a conceptual block diagram of the buses in a computer system.

Figure 4.56   Bus layout in a traditional PC.

The thought of a computer system running more slowly than it could is very bothersome to some computer users. Even so, the slow speed of the I/O bus is nothing more than a nuisance in most cases. You don't need blazing speed to communicate with a keyboard or mouse—you gain nothing in performance. The real problem occurs in subsystems in which you need the speed, such as video and disk controllers.

The speed problem became acute when graphical user interfaces (such as Windows) became prevalent. These systems require the processing of so much video data that the I/O bus became a literal bottleneck for the entire computer system. In other words, it did little good to have a processor that was capable of 66MHz–450MHz or faster if you could put data through the I/O bus at a rate of only 8MHz.

An obvious solution to this problem is to move some of the slotted I/O to an area where it could access the faster speeds of the processor bus—much the same way as the external cache. Figure 4.57 shows this arrangement.

This arrangement became known as *local bus* because external devices (adapter cards) now could access the part of the bus that was local to the CPU—the processor bus. Physically, the slots provided to tap this new configuration would need to be different from existing bus slots to prevent adapter cards designed for slower buses from being plugged into the higher bus speeds, which this design made accessible.

It is interesting to note that the very first 8-bit and 16-bit ISA buses were a form of local bus architecture. These systems had the processor bus as the main bus, and everything ran at full processor speeds. When ISA systems ran faster than 8MHz, the main ISA bus had to be decoupled from the processor bus because expansion cards, memory, and so on could not keep up. In 1992, an extension to the ISA bus called the VESA local bus (VL-Bus) started showing up on PC systems, indicating a return to local bus architecture. Since then, the peripheral component interconnect local bus has supplanted VL-Bus, and the AGP bus has been introduced to complement PCI.

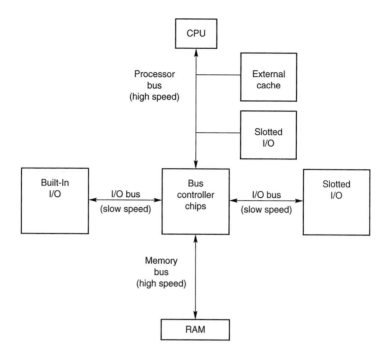

Figure 4.57   How a local bus works.

Note

A system does not have to have a local bus expansion slot to incorporate local bus technology; instead, the local bus device can be built directly into the motherboard. (In such a case, the local bus–slotted I/O shown in Figure 4.53 would in fact be built-in I/O.) This built-in approach to local bus is the way the first local bus systems were designed.

Local bus solutions do not replace earlier standards, such as ISA; they are designed into the system as a bus that is closer to the processor in the system architecture. Older buses such as ISA have been kept around for backward compatibility with slower types of adapters that don't need any faster connection to the system (such as modems). Therefore, a typical system might have AGP, PCI, and ISA slots. Older cards still are compatible with the system, but high-speed adapter cards can take advantage of the AGP and PCI local bus slots as well.

The performance of graphical user interfaces such as Windows and OS/2 have been tremendously improved by moving the video cards off the slow ISA bus and onto faster PCI and now AGP local buses.

VESA Local Bus

The Video Electronics Standards Association (VESA) local bus was the most popular local bus design from its debut in August 1992 through 1994. It was created by the VESA committee, a nonprofit organization originally founded by NEC to further develop video display and bus standards. In a similar fashion to how EISA evolved, NEC had done most of the work on the VL-Bus (as it would be called) and, after founding the nonprofit VESA committee, NEC turned over future development to VESA. At first, the local bus slot seemed primarily designed to be used for video cards. Improving video performance was a top priority at NEC to help sell its high-end displays as well as its own PC systems. By 1991, video performance had become a real bottleneck in most PC systems.

The VL-Bus can move data 32 bits at a time, enabling data to flow between the CPU and a compatible video subsystem or hard drive at the full 32-bit data width of the 486 chip. The maximum rated throughput of the VL-Bus is 133MB/sec. In other words, local bus went a long way toward removing the major bottlenecks that existed in earlier bus configurations.

Unfortunately, the VL-Bus did not seem to be a long-lived concept. The design was simple indeed—just take the pins from the 486 processor and run them out to a card connector socket. So, the VL-Bus is essentially the raw 486 processor bus. This allowed a very inexpensive design because no additional chipsets or interface chips were required. A motherboard designer could add VL-Bus slots to its 486 motherboards very easily and at a very low cost. This is why these slots appeared on virtually all 486 system designs overnight.

Problems arose with timing glitches caused by the capacitance introduced into the circuit by different cards. Because the VL-Bus ran at the same speed as the processor bus, different processor speeds meant different bus speeds, and full compatibility was difficult to achieve. Although the VL-Bus could be adapted to other processors—including the 386 or even the Pentium—it was designed for the 486 and worked best as a 486 solution only. Despite the low cost, after a new bus called PCI appeared, VL-Bus fell into disfavor very quickly. It never did catch on with Pentium systems, and there was little or no further development of the VL-Bus in the PC industry.

Physically, the VL-Bus slot was an extension of the slots used for whatever type of base system you have. If you have an ISA system, the VL-Bus is positioned as an extension of your existing 16-bit ISA slots. Figure 4.58 shows how the VL-Bus slots are oriented on a typical ISA/VL-Bus motherboard. The VESA extension has 112 contacts and uses the same physical connector as the MCA bus.

Figure 4.58 An example of a typical motherboard (albeit ancient) with VL-Bus slots.

The PCI Bus

In early 1992, Intel spearheaded the creation of another industry group. It was formed with the same goals as the VESA group in relation to the PC bus. Recognizing the need to overcome weaknesses in the ISA and EISA buses, the PCI Special Interest Group was formed.

The PCI bus specification was released in June 1992 as version 1.0 and since then has undergone several upgrades. Table 4.27 shows the various releases of PCI.

Table 4.27   PCI Specifications

PCI Specification	Released	Major Change
PCI 1.0	June 1992	Original 32/64-bit specification
PCI 2.0	April 1993	Defined connectors and expansion boards
PCI 2.1	June 1995	66MHz operation, transaction ordering, latency changes
PCI 2.2	Jan. 1999	Power management, mechanical clarifications
PCI-X	Sept. 1999	133MHz operation, addendum to 2.2
Mini-PCI	Nov. 1999	Small form factor boards, addendum to 2.2

PCI redesigned the traditional PC bus by inserting another bus between the CPU and the native I/O bus by means of bridges. Rather than tap directly into the processor bus, with its delicate electrical timing (as was done in the VL-Bus), a new set of controller chips was developed to extend the bus, as shown in Figure 4.59.

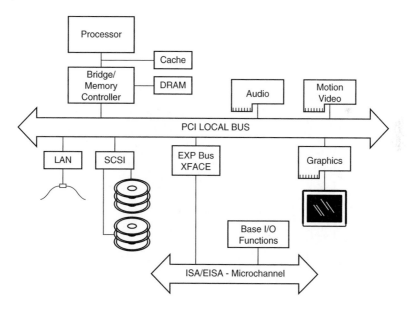

Figure 4.59   Conceptual diagram of the PCI bus.

The PCI bus often is called a *mezzanine bus* because it adds another layer to the traditional bus configuration. PCI bypasses the standard I/O bus; it uses the system bus to increase the bus clock speed and take full advantage of the CPU's data path. Systems that integrate the PCI bus became available in mid 1993 and have since become a mainstay in the PC.

Information typically is transferred across the PCI bus at 33MHz and 32 bits at a time. The bandwidth is 133MB per second, as the following formula shows:

$$33.33\text{MHz} \times 4 \text{ bytes (32 bits)} = 133\text{MB/sec}$$

Although 32-bit 33MHz PCI is the standard found in most PCs, there are now several variations on PCI as shown in Table 4.28.

Table 4.28   PCI Bus Types

PCI Bus Type	Bus Width (bits)	Bus Speed (MHz)	Data Cycles per Clock	Bandwidth (MB/sec)
PCI	32	33	1	133
PCI 66MHz	32	66	1	266
PCI 64-bit	64	33	1	266
PCI 66MHz/64-bit	64	66	1	533
PCI-X	64	133	1	1,066

Currently, the 64-bit or 66MHz and 133MHz variations are used only on server- or workstation-type boards and systems. Aiding performance is the fact that the PCI bus can operate concurrently with the processor bus; it does not supplant it. The CPU can be processing data in an external cache while the PCI bus is busy transferring information between other parts of the system—a major design benefit of the PCI bus.

A PCI adapter card uses its own unique connector. This connector can be identified within a computer system because it typically is offset from the normal ISA, MCA, or EISA connectors. See Figure 4.60 for an example. The size of a PCI card can be the same as that of the cards used in the system's normal I/O bus.

Figure 4.60   Typical configuration of 32-bit 33MHz PCI slots in relation to ISA or EISA and AGP slots.

The PCI specification identifies three board configurations, each designed for a specific type of system with specific power requirements; each specification has a 32-bit version and a longer 64-bit version. The 5v specification is for stationary computer systems, the 3.3v specification is for portable systems, and the universal specification is for motherboards and cards that work in either type of system. 64-bit versions of the 5v and universal PCI slots are found primarily on server motherboards.

Note

The pinouts for the 5v, 3.3v, and universal PCI slots can be found on the CD-ROM in the Technical Reference Section.

Figure 4.61 compares the 32-bit and 64-bit versions of the standard 5v PCI slot to a 64-bit universal PCI slot. Figure 4.62 shows how the connector on a 64-bit universal PCI card compares to the 64-bit universal PCI slot.

Notice that the universal PCI board specifications effectively combine the 5v and 3.3v specifications. For pins for which the voltage is different, the universal specification labels the pin simply V I/O. This type of pin represents a special power pin for defining and driving the PCI signaling rail.

Another important feature of PCI is the fact that it was the model for the Intel PnP specification. Therefore, PCI cards do not have jumpers and switches and are instead configured through software. True PnP systems are capable of automatically configuring the adapters, whereas non-PnP systems with ISA slots must configure the adapters through a program that is usually a part of the system CMOS configuration. Starting in late 1995, most PC-compatible systems have included a PnP BIOS that allows the automatic PnP configuration.

Accelerated Graphics Port

The AGP was created by Intel as a new bus specifically designed for high-performance graphics and video support. AGP is based on PCI, but it contains a number of additions and enhancements and is physically, electrically, and logically independent of PCI. For example, the AGP connector is similar to PCI, although it has additional signals and is positioned differently in the system. Unlike PCI, which is a true bus with multiple connectors (slots), AGP is more of a point-to-point high-performance connection designed specifically for a video card in a system because only one AGP slot is allowed for a single video card. The AGP specification 1.0 originally was released by Intel in July of 1996 and defined a 66MHz clock rate with 1x or 2x signaling using 3.3 volts. AGP version 2.0 was released in May 1998 and added 4x signaling as well as a lower 1.5v operating capability.

Caution

Some AGP 4x-compatible motherboards require you to use 1.5v AGP 4x cards only; be sure to check compatibility between the motherboard and the AGP card you want to buy to avoid problems. Some AGP 4x-compatible slots use the card retention mechanism shown in Figure 4.60. Note that AGP 1x/2x slots have a visible divider not present on the newer AGP 4x slot.

Additionally, a newer specification was introduced as AGP Pro 1.0 in August 1998 and revised in April 1999 as AGP Pro 1.1a. It defines a slightly longer slot with additional power pins at each end to drive bigger and faster AGP cards that consume more than 25 watts of power, up to a maximum of 110 watts. AGP Pro cards would likely be used for high-end graphics workstations and are not likely to be found in any normal PCs. However, AGP Pro slots are backward compatible, meaning standard AGP card will plug in, and a number of motherboard vendors are using AGP Pro slots rather than AGP 4x slots in their latest products. Because AGP Pro slots are longer, an AGP 1x/2x card can be incorrectly inserted into the slot, which could damage it, so some vendors supply a cover for the AGP Pro extension at the rear of the slot. This cover should be removed only if you want to install an AGP Pro card.

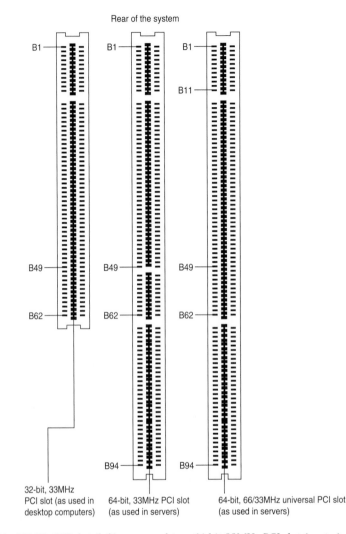

Figure 4.61 A 32-bit, 33MHz PCI slot (left) compared to a 64-bit 33MHz PCI slot (center) and a 64-bit universal PCI slot that runs at 66MHz (right).

Figure 4.62 A 64-bit universal PCI card (top) compared to the 64-bit universal PCI slot (bottom).

The standard AGP 1x/2x, AGP 4x, and AGP Pro slots are compared to each other in Figure 4.63. The latest revision to the AGP specification for PCs is AGP 8x, which was announced in August 2000; it defines a faster 8x transfer mode for even greater performance than before.

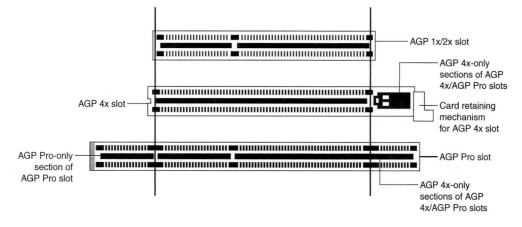

Figure 4.63   AGP standard (1x/2x), AGP 4x, and AGP Pro slots compared to each other. AGP 4x and AGP Pro can accept AGP 1x, 2x, and 4x cards.

AGP is a high-speed connection and runs at a base frequency of 66MHz (actually 66.66MHz), which is double that of standard PCI. In the basic AGP mode, called 1x, a single transfer is done every cycle. Because the AGP bus is 32 bits (4 bytes) wide, at 66 million times per second it would be capable of transferring data at a rate of about 266MB/sec! The original AGP specification also defines a 2x mode, in which two transfers are performed every cycle, resulting in 533MB/sec. Using an analogy in which every cycle is equivalent to the back-and-forth swing of a pendulum, the 1x mode is thought of as transferring information at the start of each swing. In 2x mode, an additional transfer would occur every time the pendulum completed half a swing, thereby doubling performance while technically maintaining the same clock rate, or in this case, the same number of swings per second. Although the earliest AGP cards supported only the AGP 1x mode, most vendors quickly shifted to the AGP 2x mode. The newer AGP 2.0 specification adds the capability for 4x transfers, in which data is transferred four times per cycle and equals a data transfer rate of 1,066MB/sec. Most newer AGP cards now have support for the 4x standard as a minimum. Table 4.29 shows the differences in clock rates and data transfer speeds (bandwidth) for the various AGP modes.

Table 4.29   AGP Modes Showing Clock Speeds and Bandwidth

AGP Bus Type	Bus Width (bits)	Bus Speed (MHz)	Data Cycles per Clock	Bandwidth (MB/sec)
AGP	32	66	1	266
AGP 2x	32	66	2	533
AGP 4x	32	66	4	1,066
AGP 8x	32	66	8	2,133

Because AGP is independent of PCI, using an AGP video card frees up the PCI bus for more traditional input and output, such as for IDE/ATA or SCSI controllers, USB controllers, sound cards, and so on.

Besides faster video performance, one of the main reasons Intel designed AGP was to allow the video card to have a high-speed connection directly to the system RAM, which would enable a reasonably fast and powerful video solution to be integrated at a lower cost. AGP allows a video card to have direct access to the system RAM, either enabling lower-cost video solutions to be directly built into a motherboard without having to include additional video RAM or enabling an AGP card to share the main system memory. High-performance cards will likely continue the trend of having more and more memory directly on the video card, which is especially important when running high-performance 3D video applications.

AGP allows the speed of the video card to pace the requirements for high-speed 3D graphics rendering as well as full motion video on the PC.

System Resources

System resources are the communications channels, addresses, and other signals used by hardware devices to communicate on the bus. At their lowest level, these resources typically include the following:

- Memory addresses
- IRQ (interrupt request) channels
- DMA (direct memory access) channels
- I/O port addresses

I have listed these roughly in the order you would experience problems with them. Memory conflicts are perhaps the most troublesome of these and certainly the most difficult to fully explain and overcome. These are discussed in Chapter 6, which focuses on the others listed here in the order you will likely have problems with them.

IRQs cause more problems than DMA because they are in much higher demand; virtually all cards use IRQ channels. Fewer problems exist with DMA channels because fewer cards use them, and there are usually more than enough channels to go around. I/O ports are used by all hardware devices on the bus, but there are technically 64KB of them, which means there are plenty to go around. With all these resources, you have to ensure that a unique card or hardware function uses each resource; in most cases they cannot or should not be shared.

These resources are required and used by many components of your system. Adapter cards need these resources to communicate with your system and accomplish their purposes. Not all adapter cards have the same resource requirements. A serial communications port, for example, needs an IRQ channel and I/O port address, whereas a sound card needs these resources and normally at least one DMA channel as well. Most network cards use an IRQ channel and an I/O port address, and some might also use a 16KB block of memory addresses.

As your system increases in complexity, the chance for resource conflicts increases. Modern systems with a number of additional devices can really push the envelope and become a configuration nightmare for the uninitiated. Sometimes under these situations the automatic configuration capability of Plug and Play can get confused or fail to optimally configure resources so that everything will work. Most adapter cards enable you to modify resource assignments by using the Plug and Play software that comes with the card or the Device Manager in Windows 9x and later, thus you can sometimes improve on a default configuration by making some changes. Even if the automatic configuration gets confused (which happens more often than it should), fortunately, in almost all cases a logical way to configure the system exists—once you know the rules.

Interrupts

Interrupt request channels, or hardware interrupts, are used by various hardware devices to signal the motherboard that a request must be fulfilled. This procedure is the same as a student raising his hand to indicate that he needs attention.

These interrupt channels are represented by wires on the motherboard and in the slot connectors. When a particular interrupt is invoked, a special routine takes over the system, which first saves all the CPU register contents in a stack and then directs the system to the interrupt vector table. This vector table contains a list of memory addresses that correspond to the interrupt channels. Depending on which interrupt was invoked, the program corresponding to that channel is run.

The pointers in the vector table point to the address of whatever software driver is used to service the card that generated the interrupt. For a network card, for example, the vector might point to the address of the network drivers that have been loaded to operate the card; for a hard disk controller, the vector might point to the BIOS code that operates the controller.

After the particular software routine finishes performing whatever function the card needed, the interrupt-control software returns the stack contents to the CPU registers, and the system then resumes whatever it was doing before the interrupt occurred.

Through the use of interrupts, your system can respond to external events in a timely fashion. Each time a serial port presents a byte to your system, an interrupt is generated to ensure that the system reads that byte before another comes in. Keep in mind that in some cases a port device—in particular, a modem with a 16550 or higher UART chip—might incorporate a byte buffer that allows multiple characters to be stored before an interrupt is generated.

Hardware interrupts are generally prioritized by their numbers; with some exceptions, the highest-priority interrupts have the lowest numbers. Higher-priority interrupts take precedence over lower-priority interrupts by interrupting them. As a result, several interrupts can occur in your system concurrently, each interrupt nesting within another.

If you overload the system—in this case, by running out of stack resources (too many interrupts were generated too quickly)—an internal stack overflow error occurs and your system halts. The message usually appears as Internal stack overflow - system halted at a DOS prompt. If you experience this type of system error and run DOS, you can compensate for it by using the STACKS parameter in your CONFIG.SYS file to increase the available stack resources. Most people will not see this error in Windows 9x/Me or Windows NT/2000/XP.

The ISA bus uses *edge-triggered* interrupt sensing, in which an interrupt is sensed by a changing signal sent on a particular wire located in the slot connector. A different wire corresponds to each possible hardware interrupt. Because the motherboard cannot recognize which slot contains the card that used an interrupt line and therefore generated the interrupt, confusion would result if more than one card were set to use a particular interrupt. Each interrupt, therefore, usually is designated for a single hardware device. Most of the time, interrupts cannot be shared.

Originally, IBM developed ways to share interrupts on the ISA bus, but few devices followed the necessary rules to make this a reality. The PCI bus inherently allows interrupt sharing; in fact, virtually all PCI cards are set to PCI interrupt A and share that interrupt on the PCI bus. The real problem is that there are technically two sets of hardware interrupts in the system: PCI interrupts and ISA interrupts. For PCI cards to work in a PC, the PCI interrupts are first mapped to ISA interrupts, which are then configured as nonshareable. Therefore, in many cases you must assign a nonconflicting interrupt for each card, even PCI cards. The conflict between assigning ISA IRQs for PCI interrupts caused many configuration problems for early users of PCI motherboards and continued to cause problems even after the development of Windows 95 and its Plug and Play technology.

The solution to the interrupt sharing problem for PCI cards was something called *PCI IRQ Steering*, which is supported in the more recent operating systems (starting with Windows 95 OSR 2.x) and BIOS. PCI IRQ Steering allows a plug-and-play operating system such as Windows to dynamically map or "steer" PCI cards (which almost all use PCI INTA#) to standard PC interrupts and allows several PCI cards to be mapped to the same interrupt. More information on PCI IRQ Steering is found in the section called "PCI Interrupts," later in this chapter.

Hardware interrupts are sometimes referred to as *maskable interrupts*, which means the interrupts can be masked or turned off for a short time while the CPU is used for other critical operations. It is up to the system BIOS and programs to manage interrupts properly and efficiently for the best system performance.

Because interrupts usually cannot be shared in an ISA bus system, you often run into conflicts and can even run out of interrupts when you are adding boards to a system. If two boards use the same IRQ to signal the system, the resulting conflict prevents either board from operating properly. The following sections discuss the IRQs that any standard devices use, as well as what might be free in your system.

8-Bit ISA Bus Interrupts

The PC and XT (the systems based on the 8-bit 8086 CPU) provide for eight different external hardware interrupts. Table 4.30 shows the typical uses for these interrupts, which are numbered 0–7.

Table 4.30   8-Bit ISA Bus Default Interrupt Assignments

IRQ	Function	Bus Slot
0	System Timer	No
1	Keyboard Controller	No
2	Available	Yes (8-bit)
3	Serial Port 2 (COM2:)	Yes (8-bit)
4	Serial Port 1 (COM1:)	Yes (8-bit)
5	Hard Disk Controller	Yes (8-bit)
6	Floppy Disk Controller	Yes (8-bit)
7	Parallel Port 1 (LPT1:)	Yes (8-bit)

If you have a system that has one of the original 8-bit ISA buses, you will find that the IRQ resources provided by the system present a severe limitation. Installing several devices that need the services of system IRQs in a PC/XT-type system can be a study in frustration because the only way to resolve the interrupt-shortage problem is to remove the adapter board that you need the least.

16-Bit ISA, EISA, and MCA Bus Interrupts

The introduction of the AT, based on the 286 processor, was accompanied by an increase in the number of external hardware interrupts the bus would support. The number of interrupts was doubled to 16 by using two Intel 8259 interrupt controllers, piping the interrupts generated by the second one through the unused IRQ 2 in the first controller. This arrangement effectively makes only 15 IRQ assignments available, and IRQ 2 effectively became inaccessible.

By routing all the interrupts from the second IRQ controller through IRQ 2 on the first, all these new interrupts are assigned a nested priority level between IRQ 1 and IRQ 3. Thus, IRQ 15 ends up having a higher priority than IRQ 3. Figure 4.64 shows how the two 8259 chips were wired to create the cascade through IRQ 2 on the first chip.

Figure 4.64   Interrupt controller cascade wiring.

To prevent problems with boards set to use IRQ 2, the AT system designers routed one of the new interrupts (IRQ 9) to fill the slot position left open after removing IRQ 2. This means that any card you install in a modern system that claims to use IRQ 2 is really using IRQ 9 instead. Some cards now label this selection as IRQ 2/9, whereas others might only call it IRQ 2 or IRQ 9. No matter what the labeling says, you must never set two cards to use that interrupt!

Table 4.31 shows the typical uses for interrupts in the 16-bit ISA and 32-bit PCI/AGP buses and lists them in priority order from highest to lowest. The obsolete EISA and MCA buses used a similar IRQ map.

Table 4.31   16/32-Bit ISA/PCI/AGP Default Interrupt Assignments

IRQ	Standard Function	Bus Slot	Card Type	Recommended Use
0	System Timer	No	-	-
1	Keyboard Controller	No	-	-
2	2nd IRQ Controller Cascade	No	-	-
8	Real-Time Clock	No	-	-
9	Avail. (as IRQ2 or IRQ9)	Yes	8/16-bit	Network Card
10	Available	Yes	16-bit	USB
11	Available	Yes	16-bit	SCSI Host Adapter
12	Mouse Port/Available	Yes	16-bit	Mouse Port
13	Math Coprocessor	No	—	—
14	Primary IDE	Yes	16-bit	Primary IDE (hard disks)
15	Secondary IDE	Yes	16-bit	2nd IDE (CD-ROM/Tape)
3	Serial 2 (COM2:)	Yes	8/16-bit	COM2:/Internal Modem
4	Serial 1 (COM1:)	Yes	8/16-bit	COM1:
5	Sound/Parallel 2 (LPT2:)	Yes	8/16-bit	Sound Card
6	Floppy Controller	Yes	8/16-bit	Floppy Controller
7	Parallel 1 (LPT1:)	Yes	8/16-bit	LPT1:

Notice that interrupts 0, 1, 2, 8, and 13 are not on the bus connectors and are not accessible to adapter cards. Interrupts 8, 10, 11, 12, 13, 14, and 15 are from the second interrupt controller and are accessible only by boards that use the 16-bit extension connector because this is where these wires are located. IRQ 9 is rewired to the 8-bit slot connector in place of IRQ 2, so IRQ 9 replaces IRQ 2 and, therefore, is available to 8-bit cards, which treat it as though it were IRQ 2.

Note

Although the 16-bit ISA bus has twice as many interrupts as systems that have the 8-bit ISA bus, you still might run out of available interrupts because only 16-bit adapters can use most of the newly available interrupts. Any 32-bit PCI adapter can be mapped to any ISA IRQs.

The extra IRQ lines in a 16-bit ISA system are of little help unless the adapter boards you plan to use enable you to configure them for one of the unused IRQs. Some devices are hard-wired so that they can use only a particular IRQ. If you have a device that already uses that IRQ, you must resolve the conflict before installing the second adapter. If neither adapter enables you to reconfigure its IRQ use, chances are that you cannot use the two devices in the same system.

PCI Interrupts

The PCI bus supports hardware interrupts (IRQs) that can be used by PCI devices to signal to the bus that they need attention. The four PCI interrupts are called INTA#, INTB#, INTC#, and INTD#. These INTx# interrupts are *level-sensitive*, which means that the electrical signaling enables them to be shared among PCI cards. In fact, all single device or single function PCI chips or cards that use only one interrupt must use INTA#. This is one of the rules in the PCI specification. If additional devices are within a chip or onboard a card, the additional devices can use INTB# through INTD#. Because there are very few multifunction PCI chips or boards, practically all the devices on a given PCI bus will be sharing INTA#.

For the PCI bus to function in a PC, the PCI interrupts must be mapped to ISA interrupts. Because ISA interrupts cannot be shared, in most cases each PCI card using INTA# on the PCI bus must be mapped to a different nonshareable ISA interrupt. For example, you could have a system with four PCI slots and four PCI cards installed, each using PCI interrupt INTA#. These cards would be each mapped to a different available ISA interrupt request, such as IRQ9, IRQ10, IRQ11, or IRQ5 in most cases.

Finding unique IRQs for each device on both the ISA and PCI buses has always been a problem; there simply aren't enough free ones to go around. Setting two ISA devices to the same IRQ has never been possible, but on most newer systems sharing IRQs between multiple PCI devices might be possible. Newer system BIOS as well as plug-and-play operating systems, such as Windows 95B (OSR 2) or later, Windows 98, and Windows 2000, all support a function known as PCI IRQ Steering. For this to work, both your system BIOS and operating system must support IRQ Steering. Older system BIOS and Windows 95 or 95A do not have support for PCI IRQ Steering.

Normally, the BIOS assigns unique IRQs to PCI devices. If your system supports PCI IRQ Steering and it is enabled, Windows assigns IRQs to PCI devices. Even when IRQ Steering is enabled, the BIOS still initially assigns IRQs to PCI devices. Although Windows has the capability to change these settings, it generally does not do so automatically, except where necessary to eliminate conflicts. If there are insufficient free IRQs to go around, IRQ Steering allows Windows to assign multiple PCI devices to a single IRQ, thus enabling all the devices in the system to function properly. Without IRQ Steering, Windows begins to disable devices after it runs out of free IRQs to assign.

To determine whether your system is using IRQ Steering, you can follow these steps:

1. Click Start, Settings, Control Panel, and then double-click System.

2. Click the Device Manager tab.

3. Double-click the System Devices branch.

4. Double-click PCI Bus, and then click the IRQ Steering tab. There will be a check that displays IRQ Steering as either Enabled or Disabled. If enabled, it also specifies where the IRQ table has been read from.

IRQ Steering is controlled by one of four routing tables Windows attempts to read. Windows searches for the tables in order and uses the first one it finds. You cannot control the order in which Windows searches for these tables, but by selecting or deselecting the Get IRQ Table Using check boxes, you can control which table Windows finds first by disabling the search for specific tables. Windows searches for the following tables:

- ACPI BIOS table
- MS Specification table
- Protected Mode PCIBIOS 2.1 table
- Real Mode PCIBIOS 2.1 table

Windows first tries to use the ACPI BIOS table to program IRQ Steering, followed by the MS Specification table, the Protected Mode PCIBIOS 2.1 table, and the Real Mode PCIBIOS 2.1 table. Windows 95 OSR2 and later versions only offer a choice for selecting the PCIBIOS 2.1 tables via a single check box, which is disabled by default. Under Windows 98, all IRQ table choices are selected by default, except the third one, which is the Protected Mode PCIBIOS 2.1 table.

If you are having a problem with a PCI device related to IRQ settings under Windows 95, try selecting the PCIBIOS 2.1 table and restarting. Under Windows 98, try clearing the ACPI BIOS table selection and restarting. If the problem persists, try selecting the Protected Mode PCIBIOS 2.1 table and restarting. You should select Get IRQ Table from Protected Mode PCIBIOS 2.1 Call only if a PCI device is not working properly. To access these settings in the Windows 98 Device Manager, do the following:

1. Click Start, Settings, Control Panel.

2. Open the System properties sheet.

3. Click the Device Manager tab.

4. Scroll down to the System Devices category, and double-click to open it.

5. Select PCI Bus and click Properties.

6. Click the IRQ Steering tab to see or change the current settings.

If IRQ Steering is shown as disabled in Device Manager, make sure the Use IRQ Steering check box is selected. After selecting this and restarting, if IRQ Steering is still showing as disabled, the IRQ routing table that must be provided by the BIOS to the operating system might be missing or contain errors. Check your BIOS setup to ensure PCI IRQ Steering is enabled. If there is still no success, you might have to select the Get IRQ Table from Protected Mode PCIBIOS 2.1 Call check box, or your BIOS might not support PCI bus IRQ Steering. Contact the manufacturer of your motherboard or BIOS to see whether your board or BIOS supports IRQ Steering.

On systems that have support for IRQ Steering, an IRQ Holder for PCI Steering might be displayed when you view the System Devices branch of Device Manager. This indicates that an IRQ has been mapped to PCI and is unavailable for ISA devices, even if no PCI devices are currently using the IRQ. To view IRQs programmed for PCI-mode, follow these steps:

1. Click Start, Settings, Control Panel, and then double-click System.

2. Click the Device Manager tab.

3. Double-click the System Devices branch.

4. Double-click the IRQ Holder for PCI Steering you want to view, and then click the Resources tab.

I have found this interrupt steering or mapping to be the source of a great deal of confusion. Even though PCI interrupts (INTx#) can be (and are by default) shared, each card or device that might be sharing a PCI interrupt must be mapped or steered to a unique ISA IRQ, which in turn cannot normally be shared. You can have several PCI devices mapped to the same ISA IRQ only if

■ No ISA devices are using the IRQ.

■ The BIOS and operating system support PCI IRQ Steering.

■ PCI IRQ Steering is enabled.

Without PCI IRQ Steering support, the sharing capabilities of the PCI interrupts are of little benefit because all PCI-to-ISA IRQ assignments must then be unique. Without PCI IRQ Steering, you can easily run out of available ISA interrupts. If IRQ Steering is supported and enabled, multiple PCI devices will be capable of sharing a single IRQ, allowing for more system expansion without running out of available IRQs. Better support for IRQ Steering is one of the best reasons for upgrading to Windows 98, especially if you are using the original OSR1 release of 95.

Another source of confusion is that the interrupt listing shown in the Windows Device Manager might show the PCI to ISA interrupt mapping as multiple entries for a given ISA interrupt. One entry would be for the device actually mapped to the interrupt—for example, a built-in USB controller—whereas the other entry for the same IRQ would say `IRQ Holder for PCI Steering`. This latter entry, even though claiming to use the same IRQ, does not indicate a resource conflict; instead it represents the chipset circuitry putting a reservation on that interrupt for mapping purposes. This is part of the plug-and-play capabilities of PCI and the modern motherboard chipsets.

Note that you can have internal devices on the PCI bus even though all the PCI slots are free. For example, most systems today have two IDE controllers and a USB controller as devices on the PCI bus. Normally, the PCI IDE controllers are mapped to ISA interrupts 14 (primary IDE) and 15 (secondary IDE), whereas the USB controller can be mapped to the normally available ISA interrupts 9, 10, 11, and 5.

▶▶ See "Universal Serial Bus," p. 940.

The PCI bus enables two types of devices to exist, called *bus masters* (initiators) or *slaves* (targets). A bus master is a device that can take control of the bus and initiate a transfer. The target device is the intended destination of the transfer. Most PCI devices can act as both masters and targets, and to be compliant with the PC 97 and newer system design guides, all PCI slots must support bus master cards.

The PCI bus is an arbitrated bus: A central arbiter (part of the PCI bus controller in the motherboard chipset) governs all bus transfers, giving fair and controlled access to all the devices on the bus. Before a master can use the bus, it must first request control from the central arbiter, and then it is granted control for only a specified maximum number of cycles. This arbitration allows equal and fair access to all the bus master devices, prevents a single device from hogging the bus, and also prevents deadlocks because of simultaneous multiple device access. In this manner, the PCI bus acts much like a local area network (LAN), albeit one that is contained entirely within the system and runs at a much higher speed than conventional external networks between PCs.

IRQ Conflicts

Perhaps the most common IRQ conflict is the one between the integrated COM2: port found in most modern motherboards and an internal (card-based) modem. The problem stems from the fact that true PC card–based modems (not the so-called WinModems, which are software based) incorporate a serial port as part of the card's circuitry. This serial port is set as COM2: by default. Your PC sees this as having two COM2: ports, each using the same IRQ and I/O port address resources.

The solution to this problem is easy: Enter the system BIOS Setup and disable the built-in COM2: port in the system. While you are there, you might think about disabling the COM1: port also because you are unlikely to use it. Disabling unused COMx: ports is one of the best ways to free up a couple of IRQs for other devices to use.

Another common IRQ conflict involves serial (COM) ports. You might have noticed in the preceding two sections that two IRQs are set aside for two COM ports. IRQ 3 is used for COM2:, and IRQ 4 is used for COM1:. The problem occurs when you have more than two serial ports in a system. When people add COM3: and COM4: ports, they often don't set them to nonconflicting interrupts, which results in a conflict and the ports not working.

Contributing to the problem are poorly designed COM port boards that do not allow IRQ settings other than 3 or 4. What happens is that they end up setting COM3: to IRQ 4 (sharing it with COM1:), and COM4: to IRQ 3 (sharing it with COM2:). This is not acceptable because it prevents you from using the two COM ports on any one of the interrupt channels simultaneously. This was somewhat acceptable under plain DOS because single-tasking (running only one program at a time) was the order of the day, but it is totally unacceptable with Windows and OS/2. If you must share IRQs, you can usually get away with sharing devices on the same IRQ as long as they use different COM ports. For instance, a scanner and an internal modem could share an IRQ, although if the two devices are used simultaneously, a conflict results.

The best solution is to purchase a multiport serial I/O card that allows nonconflicting interrupt settings or an intelligent card with its own processor that can handle the multiple ports onboard and use only one interrupt in the system.

▶▶   See "Serial Ports," p. 924.

If a device listed in the table is not present, such as the motherboard mouse port (IRQ 12) or parallel port 2 (IRQ 5), you can consider those interrupts as available. For example, a second parallel port is a rarity, and most systems have a sound card installed and set for IRQ 5. Also, on most systems IRQ 15 is assigned to a secondary IDE controller. If you do not have a second IDE hard drive, you could disable the secondary IDE controller to free up that IRQ for another device.

Note that an easy way to check your interrupt settings is to use the Device Manager in Windows 95/98, NT, or Windows 2000. By double-clicking the Computer Properties icon in the Device Manager, you can get concise lists of all used system resources. Microsoft has also included a program called HWDIAG on Windows 95B; Windows 98 and above feature the System Information program. HWDIAG and System Information do an excellent job of reporting system resource usage, as well as details about device drivers and Windows Registry entries for each hardware component.

DMA Channels

Direct Memory Access (DMA) channels are used by high-speed communications devices that must send and receive information at high speed. A serial or parallel port does not use a DMA channel, but a sound card or SCSI adapter often does. DMA channels sometimes can be shared if the devices are not the type that would need them simultaneously. For example, you can have a network adapter and a tape backup adapter sharing DMA channel 1, but you cannot back up while the network is running. To back up during network operation, you must ensure that each adapter uses a unique DMA channel.

Note

There are several types of DMA in a modern PC. The DMA channels referred to in this section involve the ISA bus. Other buses, such as the ATA/IDE bus used by hard drives, have different DMA use. The DMA channels explained here don't involve your ATA/IDE drives, even if they are set to use DMA or Ultra DMA transfers.

8-Bit ISA Bus DMA Channels

In the 8-bit ISA bus, four DMA channels support high-speed data transfers between I/O devices and memory. Three of the channels are available to the expansion slots. Table 4.32 shows the typical uses of these DMA channels.

Table 4.32   8-Bit ISA Default DMA-Channel Assignments

DMA	Standard Function	Bus Slot
0	Dynamic RAM Refresh	No
1	Available	Yes (8-bit)
2	Floppy disk controller	Yes (8-bit)
3	Hard disk controller	Yes (8-bit)

Because most systems typically have both a floppy and hard disk drive, only one DMA channel is available in 8-bit ISA systems.

16-Bit ISA DMA Channels

Since the introduction of the 286 CPU, the ISA bus has supported eight DMA channels, with seven channels available to the expansion slots. Similar to the expanded IRQ lines described earlier in this chapter, the added DMA channels were created by cascading a second DMA controller to the first one. DMA channel 4 is used to cascade channels 0–3 to the microprocessor. Channels 0–3 are available for 8-bit transfers, and channels 5–7 are for 16-bit transfers only. Table 4.33 shows the typical uses for the DMA channels.

Table 4.33   16-Bit ISA Default DMA-Channel Assignments

DMA	Standard Function	Bus Slot	Card Type	Transfer	Recommended Use
0	Available	Yes	16-bit	8-bit	Sound
1	Available	Yes	8/16-bit	8-bit	Sound
2	Floppy Disk Controller	Yes	8/16-bit	8-bit	Floppy Controller
3	Available	Yes	8/16-bit	8-bit	LPT1: in ECP Mode
4	1st DMA Controller Cascade	No	—	16-bit	—
5	Available	Yes	16-bit	16-bit	Sound
6	Available	Yes	16-bit	16-bit	Available
7	Available	Yes	16-bit	16-bit	Available

Note that PCI adapters don't use these ISA DMA channels; these are only for ISA cards. However, some PCI cards emulate the use of these DMA channels (such as sound cards) to work with older software.

The only standard DMA channel used in all systems is DMA 2, which is universally used by the floppy controller. DMA 4 is not usable and does not appear in the bus slots. DMA channels 1 and 5 are most commonly used by ISA sound cards, such as the Sound Blaster 16, or by newer PCI sound cards that emulate an older one for backwards compatibility. These cards use both an 8- and a 16-bit DMA channel for high-speed transfers.

Note

Although DMA channel 0 appears in a 16-bit slot connector extension and therefore can be used by only a 16-bit card, it performs only 8-bit transfers! Because of this, you generally don't see DMA 0 as a choice on 16-bit cards. Most 16-bit cards (such as SCSI host adapters) that use DMA channels have their choices limited to DMA 5–7.

I/O Port Addresses

Your computer's I/O ports enable communications between devices and software in your system. They are equivalent to two-way radio channels. If you want to talk to your serial port, you need to know on which I/O port (radio channel) it is listening. Similarly, if you want to receive data from the serial port, you need to listen on the same channel it is transmitting on.

Unlike IRQs and DMA channels, our systems have an abundance of I/O ports. There are 65,535 ports to be exact—numbered from 0000h to FFFFh—and this is an artifact of the Intel processor design more than anything else. Even though most devices use up to 8 ports for themselves, with that many to spare, you won't run out anytime soon. The biggest problem you have to worry about is setting two devices to use the same port.

Most modern plug-and-play systems resolve any port conflicts and select alternative ports for one of the conflicting devices.

One confusing issue is that I/O ports are designated by hexadecimal addresses similar to memory addresses. They are not memory; they are ports. The difference is that when you send data to memory address 1000h, it gets stored in your SIMM or DIMM memory. If you send data to I/O port address 1000h, it gets sent out on the bus on that "channel," and anybody listening in would then "hear" it. If nobody was listening to that port address, the data would reach the end of the bus and be absorbed by the bus terminating resistors.

Driver programs are primarily what interact with devices at the various port addresses. The driver must know which ports the device is using to work with it, and vice versa. That is not usually a problem because the driver and device both come from the same company.

Motherboard and chipset devices usually are set to use I/O port addresses from 0h to FFh, and all other devices use from 100h to FFFFh. Table 4.34 shows the commonly used motherboard and chipset-based I/O port usage.

Table 4.34 Motherboard and Chipset-Based Device Port Addresses

Address (hex)	Size	Description
0000–000F	16 bytes	Chipset - 8237 DMA 1
0020–0021	2 bytes	Chipset - 8259 interrupt controller 1
002E–002F	2 bytes	Super I/O controller configuration registers
0040–0043	4 bytes	Chipset - Counter/Timer 1
0048–004B	4 bytes	Chipset - Counter/Timer 2

Table 4.34   Continued

Address (hex)	Size	Description
0060	1 byte	Keyboard/Mouse controller byte - reset IRQ
0061	1 byte	Chipset - NMI, speaker control
0064	1 byte	Keyboard/Mouse controller, CMD/STAT byte
0070, bit 7	1 bit	Chipset - Enable NMI
0070, bits 6:0	7 bits	MC146818 - Real-time clock, address
0071	1 byte	MC146818 - Real-time clock, data
0078	1 byte	Reserved - Board configuration
0079	1 byte	Reserved - Board configuration
0080–008F	16 bytes	Chipset - DMA page registers
00A0–00A1	2 bytes	Chipset - 8259 interrupt controller 2
00B2	1 byte	APM control port
00B3	1 byte	APM status port
00C0–00DE	31 bytes	Chipset - 8237 DMA 2
00F0	1 byte	Math Coprocessor Reset Numeric Error

To find out exactly which port addresses are being used on your motherboard, consult the board documentation or look up these settings in the Windows Device Manager.

Bus-based devices typically use the addresses from 100h on up. Table 4.35 lists the commonly used bus-based device addresses and some common adapter cards and their settings.

Table 4.35   Bus-Based Device Port Addresses

Address (hex)	Size	Description
0130–0133	4 bytes	Adaptec SCSI adapter (alternate)
0134–0137	4 bytes	Adaptec SCSI adapter (alternate)
0168–016F	8 bytes	Fourth IDE interface
0170–0177	8 bytes	Secondary IDE interface
01E8–01EF	8 bytes	Third IDE interface
01F0–01F7	8 bytes	Primary IDE / AT (16-bit) hard disk controller
0200–0207	8 bytes	Gameport or joystick adapter
0210–0217	8 bytes	IBM XT expansion chassis
0220–0233	20 bytes	Creative Labs Sound Blaster 16 audio (default)
0230–0233	4 bytes	Adaptec SCSI adapter (alternate)
0234–0237	4 bytes	Adaptec SCSI adapter (alternate)
0238–023B	4 bytes	MS bus mouse (alternate)
023C–023F	4 bytes	MS bus mouse (default)
0240–024F	16 bytes	SMC Ethernet adapter (default)
0240–0253	20 bytes	Creative Labs Sound Blaster 16 audio (alternate)
0258–025F	8 bytes	Intel above board
0260–026F	16 bytes	SMC Ethernet adapter (alternate)

Table 4.35   Continued

Address (hex)	Size	Description
0260–0273	20 bytes	Creative Labs Sound Blaster 16 audio (alternate)
0270–0273	4 bytes	Plug and Play I/O read ports
0278–027F	8 bytes	Parallel port 2 (LPT2)
0280–028F	16 bytes	SMC Ethernet adapter (alternate)
0280–0293	20 bytes	Creative Labs Sound Blaster 16 audio (alternate)
02A0–02AF	16 bytes	SMC Ethernet adapter (alternate)
02C0–02CF	16 bytes	SMC Ethernet adapter (alternate)
02E0–02EF	16 bytes	SMC Ethernet adapter (alternate)
02E8–02EF	8 bytes	Serial port 4 (COM4)
02EC–02EF	4 bytes	Video, 8514, or ATI standard ports
02F8–02FF	8 bytes	Serial port 2 (COM2)
0300–0301	2 bytes	MPU-401 MIDI port (secondary)
0300–030F	16 bytes	SMC Ethernet adapter (alternate)
0320–0323	4 bytes	XT (8-bit) hard disk controller
0320–032F	16 bytes	SMC Ethernet adapter (alternate)
0330–0331	2 bytes	MPU-401 MIDI port (default)
0330–0333	4 bytes	Adaptec SCSI adapter (default)
0334–0337	4 bytes	Adaptec SCSI adapter (alternate)
0340–034F	16 bytes	SMC Ethernet adapter (alternate)
0360–036F	16 bytes	SMC Ethernet adapter (alternate)
0366	1 byte	Fourth IDE command port
0367, bits 6:0	7 bits	Fourth IDE status port
0370–0375	6 bytes	Secondary floppy controller
0376	1 byte	Secondary IDE command port
0377, bit 7	1 bit	Secondary floppy controller disk change
0377, bits 6:0	7 bits	Secondary IDE status port
0378–037F	8 bytes	Parallel Port 1 (LPT1)
0380–038F	16 bytes	SMC Ethernet adapter (alternate)
0388–038B	4 bytes	Audio - FM synthesizer
03B0–03BB	12 bytes	Video, Mono/EGA/VGA standard ports
03BC–03BF	4 bytes	Parallel port 1 (LPT1) in some systems
03BC–03BF	4 bytes	Parallel port 3 (LPT3)
03C0–03CF	16 bytes	Video, EGA/VGA standard ports
03D0–03DF	16 bytes	Video, CGA/EGA/VGA standard ports
03E6	1 byte	Third IDE command port
03E7, bits 6:0	7 bits	Third IDE status port
03E8–03EF	8 bytes	Serial port 3 (COM3)
03F0–03F5	6 bytes	Primary floppy controller
03F6	1 byte	Primary IDE command port
03F7, bit 7	1 bit	Primary floppy controller disk change

Table 4.35   Continued

Address (hex)	Size	Description
03F7, bits 6:0	7 bits	Primary IDE status port
03F8–03FF	8 bytes	Serial port 1 (COM1)
04D0–04D1	2 bytes	Edge/level triggered PCI interrupt controller
0530–0537	8 bytes	Windows sound system (default)
0604–060B	8 bytes	Windows sound system (alternate)
0678–067F	8 bytes	LPT2 in ECP mode
0778–077F	8 bytes	LPT1 in ECP mode
0A20–0A23	4 bytes	IBM Token-Ring adapter (default)
0A24–0A27	4 bytes	IBM Token-Ring adapter (alternate)
0CF8–0CFB	4 bytes	PCI configuration address registers
0CF9	1 byte	Turbo and reset control register
0CFC–0CFF	4 bytes	PCI configuration data registers
FF00–FF07	8 bytes	IDE bus master registers
FF80–FF9F	32 bytes	Universal serial bus
FFA0–FFA7	8 bytes	Primary bus master IDE registers
FFA8–FFAF	8 bytes	Secondary bus master IDE registers

To find out exactly what your devices are using, again I recommend consulting the documentation for the device or looking up the device in the Windows Device Manager. Note that the documentation for some devices might list only the starting address instead of the full range of I/O port addresses used.

Virtually all devices on your system buses use I/O port addresses. Most of these are fairly standardized, meaning you won't often have conflicts or problems with these settings. In the next section, you learn more about working with I/O addresses.

Resolving Resource Conflicts

The resources in a system are limited. Unfortunately, the demands on those resources seem to be unlimited. As you add more and more adapter cards to your system, you will find that the potential for resource conflicts increases. If your system is fully PnP-compatible, potential conflicts should be resolved automatically, but often are not.

How do you know whether you have a resource conflict? Typically, one of the devices in your system stops working. Resource conflicts can exhibit themselves in other ways, though. Any of the following events could be diagnosed as a resource conflict:

- A device transfers data inaccurately.
- Your system frequently locks up.
- Your sound card doesn't sound quite right.
- Your mouse doesn't work.
- Garbage appears on your video screen for no apparent reason.
- Your printer prints gibberish.
- You cannot format a floppy disk.
- The PC starts in Safe mode (Windows 9x).

Windows 9x/Me and Windows 2000/XP also show conflicts by highlighting a device in yellow or red in the Device Manager representation. By using the Windows Device Manager, you can usually spot the conflicts quickly.

In the following sections, you learn some of the steps you can take to head off resource conflicts or track them down when they occur.

Caution

Be careful in diagnosing resource conflicts; a problem might not be a resource conflict at all, but a computer virus. Many computer viruses are designed to exhibit themselves as glitches or periodic problems. If you suspect a resource conflict, it might be worthwhile to run a virus check first to ensure that the system is clean. This procedure could save you hours of work and frustration.

One way to resolve conflicts is to help prevent them in the first place. Especially if you are building up a new system, you can take several steps to avoid problems. One is to avoid using older ISA devices. By definition, they cannot share IRQs, and that is the resource most in demand. PCI (and AGP) cards can share IRQs with IRQ Steering and as such are a much better choice.

Another way you can help is to install cards in a particular sequence, and not all at once. Modifying the installation sequence often helps because many cards can use only one or two out of a predefined selection of IRQs that is specific to each brand or model of card. By installing the cards in a controlled sequence, the plug-and-play software can more easily work around IRQ conflicts caused by the default configurations of different cards.

The first time you start up a new system you have assembled or done major upgrades on, the first thing you should check is the BIOS Setup. If you have a setting for PnP Operating System in your BIOS, be sure it is enabled if you are running an operating system with plug-and-play support, such as Windows 9x/Me/2000. Otherwise, make sure it's disabled if you are running an OS that is not plug-and-play, such as Windows NT.

On initial startup I recommend a minimum configuration with only the graphics card, memory, and storage drives (floppy, hard disk, CD-ROM, and DVD). This allows for the least possibility of system conflicts in the initial configuration. If your motherboard came with a CD including drivers specific to the chipset or other built-in features of the board, now is the time to load or install them. Complete the configuration of all built-in devices before installing any other cards or external devices.

After the basic system has been configured (and after you have successfully loaded your operating system and any updates or patches), you can then begin adding one device at a time in a specific order. So, you will power down, install the new device, power up, and proceed to install any necessary drivers and configure the device. You'll probably have to restart your system after you are done to fully complete the configuration.

Tip

I sometimes recommend that between installing devices you enter the Device Manager in Windows and print out the resource settings as they are configured at the time. This way you have a record of how the configuration changes during the entire device installation and configuration process.

Here's the loading sequence for additional cards:

1. Sound card

2. Internal or external modem

3. Network card

4. Auxiliary video devices, such as MPEG decoders, 3D accelerators, and so on

5. SCSI adapter

6. Anything else

Normally, using this controlled sequence of configuring or building up your system results in easier integration with less conflicts and configuration hassles.

Resolving Conflicts Manually

In the past, the only way to resolve conflicts manually was to take the cover off your system and start changing switches or jumper settings on the adapter cards. Fortunately, this is a bit easier with plug-and-play because all the configuration is done via the Device Manager software included in the operating system. Although some early plug-and-play cards also had jumper switches or setup options to enable them to be configured manually, this feature was found primarily on ISA PnP-compatible cards.

Be sure you write down or print out your current system settings before you start making changes. That way, you will know where you began and can go back to the original configuration (if necessary).

Finally, dig out the manuals for all your adapter boards; you might need them. Additionally, you could look for more current information online at the manufacturers' Web sites.

Now you are ready to begin your detective work. As you try various resource settings, keep the following questions in mind; the answers will help you narrow down the conflict areas:

- *When did the conflict first become apparent?* If the conflict occurred after you installed a new adapter card, that new card probably is causing the conflict. If the conflict occurred after you started using new software, the software probably uses a device that is taxing your system's resources in a new way.

- *Are two similar devices in your system that do not work?* For example, if your modem, integrated serial ports, or mouse—devices that use a COM port—do not work, chances are good that these devices are conflicting with each other.

- *Have other people had the same problem, and if so, how did they resolve it?* Public forums—such as those on CompuServe, Internet newsgroups, and America Online—are great places to find other users who might be able to help you solve the conflict.

Whenever you make changes in your system, reboot and see whether the problem persists. When you believe that you have solved the problem, be sure to test all your software. Fixing one problem often seems to cause another to crop up. The only way to ensure that all problems are resolved is to test everything in your system.

One of the best pieces of advice I can give you is to try changing one thing at a time, and then retest. That is the most methodical and simplest way to isolate a problem quickly and efficiently.

As you attempt to resolve your resource conflicts, you should work with and update a system-configuration template, as discussed in the following section.

Using a System-Configuration Template

A *system-configuration template* is helpful because remembering something that is written down is easier than keeping it in your head. To create a configuration template, you need to start writing down which resources are used by which parts of your system. Then, when you need to make a change or add an adapter, you can quickly determine where conflicts might arise. You can also use the Windows 9x/Me/2000 Device Manager to list and print this information.

I like to use a worksheet split into three main areas—one for interrupts, another for DMA channels, and a middle area for devices that do not use interrupts. Each section lists the IRQ or DMA channel on the left and the I/O port device range on the right. This way, I get the clearest picture of which resources are used and which ones are available in a given system.

Page 332 shows the system-configuration template I have developed over the years and still use almost daily.

This type of configuration sheet is resource based instead of component based. Each row in the template represents a different resource and lists the component using the resource as well as the resources used. The chart has pre-entered all the fixed items in a modern PC for which the configuration cannot be changed.

To fill out this type of chart, you would perform the following steps:

1. Enter the default resources used by standard components, such as serial and parallel ports, disk controllers, and video. You can use the filled-out example I have provided to see how most standard devices are configured.

2. Enter the default resources used by additional add-on components, such as sound cards, SCSI cards, network cards, proprietary cards, and so on.

3. Change any configuration items that are in conflict. Try to leave built-in devices at their default settings, as well as sound cards. Other installed adapters might have their settings changed, but be sure to document the changes.

Of course, a template such as this is best used when first installing components, not after. After you have it completely filled out to match your system, you can label it and keep it with the system. When you add any more devices, the template will be your guide as to how any new devices should be configured.

Note

Thanks to plug-and-play configuration, the days of fixed IRQ and other hardware resources are receding into the past. Don't be surprised if your system has assigned different IRQ, I/O port address, or DMA settings after you install a new card. That's why I recommend recording information both before and after you add a new device to your system.

You also might want to track which PCI slot is used by a particular card because some systems convert PCI IRQs to different ISA IRQs depending on which slot is used for a card. Also, some systems pair PCI slots, assigning cards installed in both paired slots to the same ISA IRQ.

The example on page 333 is the same template filled out for a typical modern PC system.

System Resource Map

PC Make and Model: _____

Serial Number: _____

Date: _____

Interrupts (IRQs):	**I/O Port Addresses:**
0 - Timer Circuits _____	040–04B _____
1 - Keyboard/Mouse Controller _____	060 & 064 _____
2 - 2nd 8259 IRQ Controller _____	0A0–0A1 _____
8 - Real-time Clock/CMOS RAM_____	070–071_____
9 - _____	_____
10 - _____	_____
11 - _____	_____
12 - _____	_____
13 - Math Coprocesso_____	0F0 _____
14 - _____	_____
15 - _____	_____
3 - _____	_____
4 - _____	_____
5 - _____	_____
6 - _____	_____
7 - _____	_____

Devices Not Using Interrupts:	**I/O Port Addresses:**
Mono/EGA/VGA Standard Ports _____	3B0–3BB _____
EGA/VGA Standard Ports _____	3C0–3CF _____
CGA/EGA/VGA Standard Ports _____	3D0–3DF _____
_____	_____
_____	_____
_____	_____
_____	_____
_____	_____

DMA Channels:

0 - _____

1 - _____

2 - _____

3 - _____

4 - DMA Channel 0–3 Cascade _____

5 - _____

6 - _____

7 - _____

System Resource Map

PC Make and Model: Intel SE440BX-2

Serial Number: 100000

Date: 06/09/99

Interrupts (IRQs):	I/O Port Addresses:
0 - Timer Circuits	040–04B
1 - Keyboard/Mouse Controller	060 & 064
2 - 2nd 8259 IRQ Controller	0A0–0A1
8 - Real-time Clock/CMOS RAM	070–071
9 - SMC EtherEZ Ethernet card	340–35F
10 -	
11 - Adaptec 1542CF SCSI Adapter (scanner)	334–337[1]
12 - Motherboard Mouse Port	060 and 064
13 - Math Coprocessor	0F0
14 - Primary IDE (hard disk 1 and 2)	1F0–1F7, 3F6
15 - Secondary IDE (CD-ROM/tape)	170–177, 376
3 - Serial Port 2 (Modem)	3F8–3FF
4 - Serial Port 1 (COM1)	2F8–2FF
5 - Sound Blaster 16 Audio	220–233
6 - Floppy Controller	3F0–3F5
7 - Parallel Port 1 (Printer)	378–37F

Devices Not Using Interrupts:	I/O Port Addresses:
Mono/EGA/VGA Standard Ports	3B0–3BB
EGA/VGA Standard Ports	3C0–3CF
CGA/EGA/VGA Standard Ports	3D0–3DF
ATI Mach 64 video card additional ports	102, 1CE–1CF, 2EC–2EF
Sound Blaster 16 MIDI port	330–331
Sound Blaster 16 Game port (joystick)	200–207
Sound Blaster 16 FM synthesizer (music)	388–38B

DMA Channels:

0 -

1 - Sound Blaster 16 (8-bit DMA)

2 - Floppy Controller

3 - Parallel Port 1 (in ECP mode)

4 - DMA Channel 0-3 Cascade

5 - Sound Blaster 16 (16-bit DMA)

6 - Adaptec 1542CF SCSI adapter[1]

7 -

1. Represents a resource setting that had to be changed to resolve a conflict

As you can see from this template, only one IRQ and two DMA channels remain available, and that would be *no* IRQs if I enabled the USB on the motherboard! As you can see, interrupt shortages are a big problem in modern systems. In that case, I would probably find a way to recover one of the other interrupts; for example, I am not really using COM1, so I could disable that port and gain back IRQ 4. In this sample configuration, the primary and secondary IDE connectors were built into the motherboard:

- Floppy controller
- Two serial ports
- One parallel port

Whether these devices are built into the motherboard or on a separate card makes no difference because the resource allocations are the same in either case. All default settings usually are used for these devices and are indicated in the completed configuration. Next, the accessory cards were configured. In this example, the following cards were installed:

- SVGA video card (ATI Mach 64)
- Sound card (Creative Labs Sound Blaster 16)
- SCSI host adapter (Adaptec AHA-1542CF)
- Network interface card (SMC EtherEZ)

It helps to install the cards in this order. Start with the video card; next, add the sound card. Because of problems with software that must be configured to the sound card, it is best to install it early and ensure that only default settings are used. It is better to change settings on other cards than the sound card.

After the sound card, the SCSI adapter was installed; however, the default I/O port addresses (330–331) and DMA channel (DMA 5) used were in conflict with other cards (mainly the sound card). These settings were changed to their next logical settings that did not cause a conflict.

Finally, the network card was installed, which also had default settings that conflicted with other cards. In this case, the Ethernet card came preconfigured to IRQ 3, which was already in use by COM2:. The solution was to change the setting, and IRQ 9 was the next logical choice in the card's configuration settings.

Even though this is a fully loaded configuration, only three individual items among all the cards had to be changed to achieve an optimum system configuration. As you can see, using a configuration template such as the one shown can make what would otherwise be a jumble of settings lay out in an easy-to-follow manner. The only real problems you will run into after you work with these templates are cards that do not allow for enough adjustment in their settings or cards that are lacking in documentation. As you can imagine, you will need the documentation for each adapter card, as well as the motherboard, to accurately complete a configuration table such as the one shown.

Tip

Do not rely too much on third-party DOS-based software diagnostics, such as MSD.EXE, which claim to be capable of showing hardware settings such as IRQ and I/O port settings. Even though they can be helpful in certain situations, they are often wrong with respect to at least some of the information they display about your system. One or two items shown incorrectly can be very troublesome if you believe the incorrect information and configure your system based on it!

A much better utility to view these settings is the Device Manager built into Windows 9x/Me/2000. With plug-and-play hardware, it not only reports settings, but it allows you to change them. On older legacy hardware, you can view the settings but not change them. To change the settings of legacy (non–plug-and-play) hardware, you must manually move jumpers or switches and run the special configuration software that came with the card. Consult the card manufacturer or documentation for more information.

Heading Off Problems: Special Boards

A number of devices that you might want to install in a computer system require IRQ lines or DMA channels, which means that a world of conflict could be waiting in the box the device comes in. As mentioned in the preceding section, you can save yourself problems if you use a system-configuration template to keep track of the way your system is configured.

You also can save yourself trouble by carefully reading the documentation for a new adapter board before you attempt to install it. The documentation details the IRQ lines the board can use as well as its DMA-channel requirements. In addition, the documentation details the adapter's upper-memory needs for ROM and adapter.

The following sections describe some of the conflicts you might encounter when you install today's most popular adapter boards. Although the list of adapter boards covered in these sections is far from comprehensive, the sections serve as a guide to installing complex hardware with minimum hassle. Included are tips on soundboards, SCSI host adapters, and network adapters.

Sound Cards

Sound cards are probably the biggest single resource hog in your system. They typically use at least one IRQ, two DMA channels, and multiple I/O port address ranges. This is because a sound card is actually several different pieces of hardware all on one board. Most sound cards, including PCI-based models, emulate the Sound Blaster 16 from Creative Labs.

Table 4.36 shows the default resources used by a typical PCI sound card, the Creative Labs SB512. Because sound cards are multifunction devices, each function is listed separately as it appears in the Windows Device Manager.

Table 4.36   Default Resources Used by Creative Labs SB512

Device	IRQ	I/O Port Address	16-bit DMA Channel	8-bit DMA Channel
Sound Blaster 16 emulation	5	0220–022F 0330–0331[1] 0388–038B[2]	5	1
Creative Multimedia Interface	N/A	D400–D407	N/A	N/A
Creative Gameport Joystick	N/A	0200–0207	N/A	N/A
Creative SB512	9[3]	C860–C87F	N/A	N/A

1. *Used for MIDI interface*
2. *Used for FM Synthesis*
3. *Varies with system and PCI expansion slot used*

Although other brands of sound cards might use a slightly different configuration, the pattern is the same; Sound Blaster emulation requires a large number of resources. Even if SB emulation isn't used (you might be able to disable it if you no longer play DOS games), the card still uses a single IRQ and several I/O port address ranges. If you take the time to read your soundboard's documentation and determine its communications-channel needs, compare those needs to the IRQ lines and DMA channels that already are in use in your system, and then change the settings of the other adapters to avoid conflicts with the sound card, your installation will go quickly and smoothly. Unfortunately, many vendors no longer provide detailed information on their plug-and-play–compatible cards. That's why you need to install the sound card **first** and use the system resource map to record which settings the card uses before you install other cards.

Tip

The best advice I can give you for installing a sound card is to put the sound card in before all other cards—except for video. In other words, let the sound card retain all its default settings if you can. Try to change the settings of other adapters when a conflict with the sound card arises. The problem here is that many older programs that use sound are very poorly written with respect to supporting alternative resource settings on sound cards. Save yourself some grief, and let the sound card have its way!

Even the latest sound cards can have problems if they're installed after other cards. I know a user who had to remove all his plug-and-play cards before his system would recognize his plug-and-play sound card.

One example of a potential soundboard conflict is the combination of a Sound Blaster 16 and an Adaptec SCSI adapter, as I noted earlier in this chapter. The Sound and SCSI adapters conflict on DMA 5 as well as on I/O ports 330–331. Rather than changing the settings of the sound card, it is best to alter the SCSI adapter to the next available settings that will not conflict with the sound card or anything else. The final settings are shown in the previous configuration template.

The cards in question (Sound Blaster 16 and AHA-1542CF) are not singled out here because there is something wrong with them, but instead because they happen to be very popular cards of their respective types and, as such, often are paired together.

Most people would be using PCI versions of these cards today, but they still require the same types of resource settings with the only exception being DMA channels. Unfortunately, it wasn't DMA channels that we were really running out of! The interrupt shortage continues even with PCI cards because they must be mapped to ISA IRQs. The real solution to the ISA IRQ battle is now arriving, as most new systems are shipping with motherboards that lack ISA slots and break ties with that bus forever. When that happens, we will be free of the interrupt restrictions we have been under for so many years.

Tip

The newer PCI sound cards are largely incompatible with older DOS-based software because they don't use DMA channels like their ISA counterparts. If you don't update your software to 32-bit Windows versions, you won't be able to use these newer PCI bus sound cards. Most of the newer PCI cards do include an emulation program that allows the card to work with older DMA-dependent software, but the results are often problematic.

For the best results, use the PC/PCI connector found on some motherboards to connect a patch cable to a PC/PCI-compatible sound card. The PC/PCI connector enables the sound card to use ISA-style DMA channels without clumsy emulation software.

SCSI Adapter Boards

SCSI adapter boards use more resources than just about any other type of add-in device except perhaps a sound card. They often use resources that are in conflict with sound cards or network cards, especially if the card has an onboard BIOS for handling bootable drives. A typical ISA SCSI host adapter with onboard BIOS requires an IRQ line, a DMA channel, a range of I/O port addresses, plus a

16KB range of unused upper memory for its ROM and possible scratch-pad RAM use. Even a simple SCSI host adapter designed for use with scanners still requires an IRQ and a range of I/O port addresses. Fortunately, the typical SCSI adapter is also easy to reconfigure, and changing any of these settings should not affect performance or software operation. PCI-based SCSI host adapters require all of the above, except for the DMA channel.

Before installing a SCSI adapter, be sure to read the documentation for the card, and ensure that any IRQ lines, DMA channels, I/O ports, and upper memory the card needs are available. If the system resources the card needs are already in use, use your system-configuration template to determine how you can alter the settings on the SCSI card or other cards to prevent any resource conflicts before you attempt to plug in the adapter card.

Network Interface Cards

Networks are becoming more and more popular all the time, thanks to the rise of easy-to-configure small office/home office networks and the use of network cards to connect to broadband Internet devices such as cable and DSL modems. A typical network adapter does not require as many resources as some of the other cards discussed here, but it requires at least a range of I/O port addresses and an interrupt. Most network interface cards (NICs) also require a 16KB range of free upper memory to be used for the RAM transfer buffer on the network card. As with any other cards, be sure that all these resources are unique to the card and are not shared with any other devices.

Multiple-COM-Port Adapters

A serial port adapter usually has two or more ports onboard. These COM ports require an interrupt and a range of I/O ports each. There aren't too many problems with the I/O port addresses because the ranges used by up to four COM ports in a system are fairly well defined. The real problem is with the interrupts. Most older installations of more than two serial ports have any additional ones sharing the same interrupts as the first two. This is incorrect and causes nothing but problems with software that runs under Windows or OS/2. With these older boards, ensure that each serial port in your system has a unique I/O port address range and, more importantly, a unique interrupt setting.

Many newer multiport adapter cards—such as those offered by Byte Runner Technologies—allow "intelligent" interrupt sharing among ports. In some cases, you can have up to 12 COM port settings without conflict problems. Check with your adapter card's manufacturer to determine whether it allows for automatic or "intelligent" interrupt sharing.

Although most people have problems incorrectly trying to share interrupts when installing more than two serial ports in a system, a fairly common problem exists with the I/O port addressing that should be mentioned. Many of the high-performance video chipsets, such as those from S3 Inc., and ATI, use some additional I/O port addresses that conflicts with the standard I/O port addresses used by COM4:.

In the sample system configuration just covered, you can see that the ATI video card uses some additional I/O port addresses, specifically 2EC–2EF. This is a problem because COM4: usually is configured as 2E8–2EF, which overlaps with the video card. The video cards that use these addresses are not normally adjustable for this setting, so you either must change the address of COM4: to a nonstandard setting or disable COM4: and restrict yourself to using only three serial ports in the system. If you do have a serial adapter that supports nonstandard I/O address settings for the serial ports, you must ensure that those settings are not used by other cards, and you must inform any software or drivers, such as those in Windows, of your nonstandard settings.

Universal Serial Bus

USB ports are now found on most motherboards, and Windows 98, Windows Me, Windows 2000, and Windows XP provide you with a wide range of operating systems that support them properly. One potential problem is that USB takes another interrupt from your system, and many computers either don't have any free or are down to their last one. If your system supports PCI IRQ Steering, this shouldn't be much of a problem because the IRQ used by your USB controller should be sharable with other PCI devices. If you are out of interrupts, you should look at what other devices you can disable (such as COM or LPT ports) to gain back a necessary interrupt for other devices.

The big advantage of USB from an IRQ or a resource perspective is that the USB bus uses only one IRQ no matter how many devices (up to 127) are attached. Therefore, you can freely add or remove devices from the USB without worrying about running out of resources or having resource conflicts.

If you aren't using any USB devices, you should turn off the port using your motherboard CMOS Setup so that the IRQ it was using will be freed. As we continue move to USB-based keyboards, mice, modems, printers, and so on, the IRQ shortage will be less of a problem. As we have already seen, the elimination of the ISA bus in our systems will also go a long way toward solving this problem as well.

Miscellaneous Boards

Some video cards ship with advanced software that allows special video features, such as oversized desktops, custom monitors, switch modes on-the-fly, and so on. Unfortunately, this software requires that the card be configured to use an IRQ. If your video card doesn't require an IRQ, I suggest you dispense with this unnecessary software and configure the card to free up the interrupt for other devices. However, keep in mind that many of the latest 3D accelerators must use an IRQ to enable their bus-mastering feature to work correctly. See your video card's manual for details.

Also related to video is the use of an MPEG decoder add-on card that works in addition to your normal graphics adapter. These are used more in specialized video production and editing and in playing DVD movies; however, they do use additional system resources that must be available. If your CPU runs at speeds above 300MHz and you have an AGP video card, you can probably use your video card for DVD playback and remove the MPEG decoder card. You will need a DVD player program, which might be supplied with your video card. See your video card's manual for details.

Plug-and-Play Systems

Plug and Play (PnP) represents a major revolution in recent interface technology. PnP first came on the market in 1995, and most motherboards and adapter cards since 1996 take advantage of it. Prior to that, PC users were forced to muddle through a nightmare of DIP switches and jumpers every time they wanted to add new devices to their systems. The results, all too often, were system resource conflicts and nonfunctioning cards.

PnP was not an entirely new concept. It was a key design feature of MCA and EISA interfaces that preceded it by almost 10 years, but the limited appeal of MCA and EISA meant that they never became true de facto industry standards. Therefore, mainstream PC users still had to worry about I/O addresses, DMA channels, and IRQ settings. Early PCI-based systems also used a form of PnP configuration, but because there was no provision for managing conflicts between PCI and ISA cards, many users still had configuration problems. But now that PnP has become prevalent, worry-free hardware setup is available to all computer buyers.

For PnP to work, the following components are desired:

- PnP hardware
- PnP BIOS
- PnP operating system

Each of these components needs to be PnP-compatible, meaning that it complies with the PnP specifications.

The Hardware Component

The *hardware component* refers to both computer systems and adapter cards. The term does not mean, however, that you cannot use your older ISA adapter cards (referred to as *legacy cards*) in a PnP system. You can use these cards; in fact, your PnP BIOS automatically reassigns PnP-compatible cards around existing legacy components. Also, many late-model ISA cards can be switched into PnP-compatible mode.

PnP adapter cards communicate with the system BIOS and the operating system to convey information about which system resources are necessary. The BIOS and operating system, in turn, resolve conflicts (wherever possible) and inform the adapter cards which specific resources it should use. The adapter card then can modify its configuration to use the specified resources.

The BIOS Component

The BIOS component means that most users of pre-1996 PCs need to update their BIOSes or purchase new machines that have PnP BIOSes. For a BIOS to be compatible, it must support 13 additional system function calls, which can be used by the OS component of a PnP system. The PnP BIOS specification was developed jointly by Compaq, Intel, and Phoenix Technologies.

The PnP features of the BIOS are implemented through an expanded POST. The BIOS is responsible for identification, isolation, and possible configuration of PnP adapter cards. The BIOS accomplishes these tasks by performing the following steps:

1. Disables any configurable devices on the motherboard or on adapter cards
2. Identifies any PnP PCI or ISA devices
3. Compiles an initial resource-allocation map for ports, IRQs, DMAs, and memory
4. Enables I/O devices
5. Scans the ROMs of ISA devices
6. Configures initial program-load (IPL) devices, which are used later to boot the system
7. Enables configurable devices by informing them which resources have been assigned to them
8. Starts the bootstrap loader
9. Transfers control to the operating system

The Operating System Component

The operating system component is found in most modern operating systems, such as Windows 9x/Me/2000/XP. In some cases system manufacturers have provided extensions to the operating system for their specific hardware. Such is especially true for notebook systems, for example. Be sure you load these extensions if they are required by your system.

It is the responsibility of the operating system to inform users of conflicts that cannot be resolved by the BIOS. Depending on the sophistication of the operating system, the user then could configure the offending cards manually (onscreen) or turn off the system and set switches on the physical cards. When the system is restarted, the system is checked for remaining (or new) conflicts, any of which are brought to the user's attention. Through this repetitive process, all system conflicts are resolved.

Note

Because of revisions in some of the Plug and Play specifications, especially including the ACPI specification, it can help to ensure you are running the latest BIOS and drivers for your system. With the Flash ROM used in most PnP systems, you can download the new BIOS image from the system vendor or manufacturer and run the supplied BIOS update program.

Knowing What to Look For (Selection Criteria)

I am often asked to make a recommendation for purchases. Without guidance, many individuals don't have any rhyme or reason to their selections and instead base their choices solely on magazine reviews or, even worse, on some personal bias. To help eliminate this haphazard selection process, I have developed a simple checklist that will help you select a system. This list takes into consideration several important system aspects overlooked by most checklists. The goal is to ensure that the selected system truly is compatible and has a long life of service and upgrades ahead.

It helps to think like an engineer when you make your selection. Consider every aspect and detail of the motherboards in question. For instance, you should consider any future uses and upgrades. Technical support at a professional (as opposed to a user) level is extremely important. What support will be provided? Is there documentation, and does it cover everything else?

In short, a checklist is a good idea. Here is one for you to use in evaluating any PC-compatible system. A system might not have to meet every one of these criteria for you to consider purchasing it, but if it misses more than a few, consider staying away from that system. The items at the top of the list are the most important, and the items at the bottom are perhaps of lesser importance (although I think each item is important). The rest of this chapter discusses in detail the criteria in this checklist:

- *Processor.* A modern system should use a socket-based processor with on-die L2 cache. Evaluate the processor choices you have, and try to get the one with the highest speed CPU bus (front-side bus). Don't get too hung up on L2 cache size; a little cache goes a long way. It is more important that the cache run at full core speed (which it will if it is on-die). Processors such as the later Celeron/Pentium III, Duron/Athlon, and Pentium 4 all meet this criteria.

- *Processor sockets.* For maximum upgradability and performance, you should stick with a system that uses a socket for the CPU. The main sockets in use today are Socket 370 for the Celeron/Pentium III, Socket A (Socket 462) for the Duron/Athlon, and Socket 423 for the Pentium 4. As long as your motherboard has one of these sockets, you should be in good shape.

- *Motherboard speed.* The motherboard typically offers a choice of speeds, including anywhere from 66MHz to 266MHz for Celeron/Pentium III–based boards, 200MHZ–266MHz for the Duron/Athlon-based boards, or 400MHz for the Pentium 4–based boards. Check to ensure the board you are buying runs at the speeds necessary to support the processors you want to install.

- *Cache memory.* All modern systems use processors with integral cache, most of them now having the cache directly on the processor die for maximum speed. As such, there won't be any cache memory on the motherboard in a modern system. The tip is to make sure you are using a processor with full core speed on-die L2 cache because this offers the maximum in performance. All the modern processors now incorporate on-die L2 cache.

- *SIMM/DIMM/RIMM memory.* SIMMs are obsolete by today's standards, so stay away from any boards that use them. Your board should support either standard or DDR DIMMs or RIMMs that contain SDRAM, DDR SDRAM, or RDRAM, respectively. What you use depends mainly on your motherboard chipset, so choose the chipset and board that accepts the memory type you want to use. Currently, DDR SDRAM and RDRAM are the fastest types of memory available, with RDRAM being by far the most costly.

Mission-critical systems should use ECC memory and ensure that the motherboard fully supports ECC operation. Note that many of the low-end chipsets, such as the Intel 810/815 series, do not support ECC and should not be used for mission-critical applications. This is something you should know before purchasing the system.

Finally, note that most motherboards support either three or four DIMM sockets, or two or three RIMM sockets. Be sure that you populate them wisely so you don't have to resort to removing memory later to add more, which is not very cost-effective.

■ *Bus type.* Most motherboards no longer incorporate ISA bus slots, so if you have any ISA cards, you'll likely have to discard them. Instead you should find anywhere from one to five or more PCI local bus slots. Be sure the PCI slots conform to the PCI 2.1 or later revision (primarily based on the chipset). Take a look at the layout of the slots to ensure that cards inserted in them will not block access to memory sockets or be blocked by other components in the case. Systems without onboard video should also feature one AGP 4x slot for a high-performance AGP video card.

■ *BIOS.* The motherboard should use an industry-standard BIOS, such as those from AMI, Phoenix, or Award. The BIOS should be of a Flash ROM or EEPROM design for easy updating. Look for a BIOS Recover jumper or mode setting, as well as possibly a Flash ROM write-protect jumper on some systems.

■ *Form factor.* For maximum flexibility, performance, reliability, and ease-of-use, the ATX form factor (including micro-ATX and flex-ATX) cannot be beat. ATX has several distinct performance and functional advantages over Baby-AT and is vastly superior to any proprietary designs, such as LPX. Additionally, the new NLX form factor might be a consideration for low-profile or low-cost desktop systems.

■ *Built-in interfaces.* Ideally, a motherboard should contain as many built-in standard controllers and interfaces as possible (except perhaps video). There is a trend toward legacy-free PCs that lack the conventional Super I/O component and therefore have only USB for external expansion. Legacy-free PCs lack the conventional keyboard and mouse ports, serial and parallel ports, and possibly even the internal floppy controller. Systems that use an integrated Super I/O component have these interfaces.

Built-in 10/100 Ethernet network adapters are also handy, especially if you are using a cable modem or DSL connection to the Internet. A built-in sound card is a great feature, usually offering full Sound Blaster compatibility and functions, and possibly offering additional features as well. If your sound needs are more demanding, you might find the built-in solutions less desirable, and you might want to have a separate sound card in your system. Built-in video adapters are also a bonus in some situations, but because there are many video chipset and adapter designs from which to choose, generally you'll find better choices in external local bus video adapters. This is especially true if you need the highest performance video available.

Built-in devices usually can be disabled to allow future add-ons, but problems can result.

■ *Onboard IDE interfaces.* All motherboards on the market have included onboard IDE interfaces for some time now, but not all IDE interfaces are equal. Your motherboard should support at least UDMA/33 (ATA-33) speeds, which matches the best real-world performance currently available from IDE drives. UDMA/66 and UDMA/100 actually exceed the real-world performance of current drives using these standards and thus provide you with headroom for future drives. For even greater speed, consider motherboards with onboard IDE RAID controllers. These motherboards can be configured to perform data striping for extra speed or data mirroring for extra reliability when two or more identical IDE drives are used. These motherboards are based on a variety of standard chipsets with RAID functions added by RAID chipsets from AMI, HighPoint, or Promise.

Tip

With a never-ending stream of motherboards coming onto the market, finding motherboards with the features you want can be difficult. Motherboard Homeworld's Mobot search engine helps you find motherboards based on your choice of form factor, platform, chipset, CPU type, processor, manufacturer, memory type, slot types, built-on ports, and more. Check it out at

`<http://iceberg.pchomeworld.com/cgi-win/mobotGen/mobot.asp>`

- ■ *Power management.* The motherboard should fully support the latest standard for power management, which is ACPI. An Energy Star–compliant system is also a bonus because it uses less than 30 watts of electrical energy when in sleep mode, saving energy as well as your electric bill.

- ■ *Motherboard chipset.* Motherboards should use a high-performance chipset that supports standard or DDR SDRAM DIMMs or RDRAM RIMMs—preferably one that allows ECC memory as well, if you are concerned about catching possible memory errors before they corrupt your data. Also look for AGP 4x or faster video support and ATA-100 hard drive support.

- ■ *Documentation.* Good technical documentation is a requirement. Documents should include information on any and all jumpers and switches found on the board, connector pinouts for all connectors, specifications for other plug-in components, and any other applicable technical information. I would also acquire separate documentation from the BIOS manufacturer covering the specific BIOS used in the system, as well as the data books covering the specific chipset used in the motherboard. Additional data books for any other controller or I/O chips onboard are a bonus and can be acquired from the respective chip manufacturers.

  Another nice thing to have is available online support and documentation updates, although this should not be accepted in place of good hardcopy manuals. Remember that many vendors provide their "hardcopy" manuals as Adobe Acrobat files, which can be viewed and printed with the Adobe Acrobat Reader program.

You might notice that these selection criteria seem fairly strict and might disqualify many motherboards on the market, including what you already have in your system! These criteria will, however, guarantee you the highest-quality motherboard offering the latest in PC technology that will be upgradable, be expandable, and provide good service for many years.

Most of the time I recommend purchasing boards from better-known motherboard manufacturers such as Intel, Acer, ABIT, AsusTek, SuperMicro, Tyan, and others. These boards might cost a little more, but there is some safety in the more well-known brands. That is, the more boards they sell, the more likely that any problems will have been discovered by others and solved long before you get yours. Also, if service or support is necessary, the larger vendors are more likely to be around in the long run.

Documentation

As mentioned, extensive documentation is an important factor to consider when you're planning to purchase a motherboard. Most motherboard manufacturers design their boards around a particular chipset, which actually counts as the bulk of the motherboard circuitry. A number of manufacturers offer chipsets, such as Intel, VIA, ALi, SiS, and others. I recommend obtaining the data book or other technical documentation on the chipset directly from the chipset manufacturer.

One of the more common questions I hear about a system relates to the BIOS Setup program. People want to know what the "Advanced Chipset Setup" features mean and what the effects of changing them will be. Often they go to the BIOS manufacturer thinking that the BIOS documentation will offer help. Usually, however, people find that there is no real coverage of what the chipset setup features are in the BIOS documentation. You will find this information in the data book provided by the chipset manufacturer. Although these books are meant to be read by the engineers who design the boards, they contain all the detailed information about the chipset's features, especially those that might be adjustable. With the chipset data book, you will have an explanation of all the controls in the Advanced Chipset Setup section of the BIOS Setup program.

Besides the main chipset data books, I also recommend collecting any data books on the other major chips in the system. This would include any floppy or IDE controller chips, Super I/O chips, and of course the main processor. You will find an incredible amount of information on these components in the data books.

Caution

Most chipset manufacturers make a particular chip for only a short time, rapidly superseding it with an improved or changed version. The data books are available only during the time the chip is being manufactured, so if you wait too long, you will find that such documents might no longer be available. The time to collect documentation on your motherboard is *now*!

Using Correct Speed-Rated Parts

Some vendors use substandard parts in their systems to save money. Because the CPU is one of the most expensive components on the motherboard, and motherboards are sold to system assemblers without the CPU installed, it is tempting for the assembler to install a CPU rated for less than the actual operating speed. A system could be sold as a900MHz system, for example, but when you look under the hood, you might find a CPU rated for only 600MHz. This is called *overclocking*, and many vendors have practiced this over the last few years. Some even go so far as to re-mark the CPUs, so that even if you look, the part appears to have the correct rating. The best way to stop that is to purchase systems from known, reliable vendors and purchase processors from distributors that are closely connected with the manufacturer. Overclocking is fine if you want to do it yourself and understand the risks, but when I purchase a new system, I expect that all the parts included be rated to run at the speed they are set to.

◀◀ See "Processor Speed Ratings," p. 47.

When a chip is run at a speed higher than it is rated for, it runs hotter than it would normally. This can cause the chip to overheat occasionally, which would appear as random lockups, glitches, and frustration. I highly recommend that you check to ensure you are getting the right speed-rated parts you are paying for.

Also be sure you use the recommended heatsink compound (thermal grease). This can improve the efficiency of your heatsink by up to 30%.

This practice is easy to fall into because the faster-rated chips cost more money. Intel and other chip manufacturers usually rate their chips very conservatively. Over the years, I have overclocked many processors, running them sometimes well beyond their rated speeds. Although I might purchase a Pentium III 800 and run it at 1066MHz, if I were to experience lockups or glitches in operation, I would immediately return it to the original speed and retest. If I purchase a 1GHz system from a vendor, I fully expect it to have a 1GHz part, not slower parts running past their rated speeds!

Overclocking has been made more difficult by Intel and AMD, who have both started locking the bus multipliers in their chips to prevent easy overclocking by changing the multiplier setting on the motherboard. This is done mainly to combat re-marking CPUs and deceiving customers, although unfortunately it also can prevent those who want to from hotrodding their chips. Still, you can overclock most chips by increasing the CPU bus (front-side bus) speed within certain tolerances. Many of the motherboards on the market have tweakable CPU bus speeds specifically designed to allow overclocking. Check with your motherboard manual, or download the documentation from the manufacturer's Web site. You might find that your board is capable of things you didn't realize.

If you purchase a processor or a system, verify that the markings are the original Intel or AMD markings and that the speed rating on the chip is what you really paid for.

The bottom line: If the price is too good to be true, ask before you buy. Are the parts really manufacturer-rated for the system speed?

To determine the rated speed of a CPU chip, look at the writing on the chip. See Chapter 3 for details on how to interpret the marks to see what the real rating on the chip actually is.

Caution

Be careful when running software to detect processor speed. Most programs can only estimate what speed the chip is currently running at, not what the true original rating is. One exception to this is the Intel Processor Frequency ID Utility, which can determine whether an Intel processor is operating at the correct and rated frequency intended. Although it gives only basic information about any Intel processor, it can uniquely identify the original speed ratings of the Pentium III, third-generation Celeron (Coppermine-based), and any newer processors, accurately determining whether they have been overclocked. You can download the Intel Processor Frequency ID Utility from `http://developer.intel.com/support/processors/tools/frequencyid/download.htm`.

Older system chassis with speed markings or even indicator lights are usually no indication of the actual or rated speed of the processor inside. Those displays can literally be set via jumpers to read any speed you desire! They have no true relation to actual system speed.

Most of the better diagnostics on the market, such as the Norton Utilities from Symantec, read the processor ID and stepping information, as well as show current operating (but not rated) speed. You can consult the processor manufacturer or Chapter 3 for tables listing the various processor steppings to see exactly how yours stacks up.

BIOS Basics

It is often difficult for people to understand the difference between hardware and software in a PC system. The differences can be difficult because they are both very much intertwined in the system design, construction, and operation. Understanding these differences is essential to understanding the role of the BIOS in the system.

BIOS is a term that stands for *basic input/output system*. BIOS is really the link between hardware and software in a system. Most people know the term BIOS by another name—*device drivers*, or just *drivers*.

BIOS is a single term that describes all the drivers in a system working together to act as an interface between the hardware and the operating system software. What can be confusing is that some of the BIOS is burned or flashed into a ROM chip that is both nonvolatile (it doesn't get erased when the power is turned off) and read-only. This is a core part of the BIOS, but not all of it. The BIOS also includes ROM chips installed on adapter cards, as well as all the additional drivers loaded when your system boots up.

The combination of the motherboard BIOS, the adapter card BIOS, and the device drivers loaded from disk contribute to the BIOS as a whole. The portion of the BIOS contained in ROM chips both on the motherboard and in some adapter cards is sometimes called *firmware*, which is a name given to software stored in chips rather than on disk. This causes some people to incorrectly think of the BIOS as a hardware component.

A PC system can be described as a series of layers—some hardware and some software—that interface with each other. In the most basic sense, you can break a PC down into four primary layers, each of which can be broken down further into subsets. Figure 5.1 shows the four layers in a typical PC.

Figure 5.1 PC system layers.

The purpose of the layered design is to enable a given operating system and applications to run on different hardware. Figure 5.1 shows how two different machines with different hardware can each use a custom BIOS to interface the unique hardware to a common operating system and applications. Thus, two machines with different processors, storage media, video display units, and so on can run the same software.

In this layered architecture, the application programs talk to the operating system via what is called an Application Program Interface (API). The API varies according to the operating system you are using and consists of the various commands and functions the operating system can perform for an application. For example, an application can call on the operating system to load or save a file. This prevents the application itself from having to know how to read the disk, send data to a printer, or perform any other of the many functions the operating system can provide. Because the application is completely insulated from the hardware, you can essentially run the same applications on different systems; the application is designed to talk to the operating system rather than the hardware.

The operating system then interfaces with or talks to the BIOS layer. The BIOS consists of all the individual driver programs that operate between the operating system and the actual hardware. As such, the operating system never talks to the hardware directly; instead, it must always go through the appropriate driver. This provides a consistent way to talk to the hardware. It is usually the responsibility of the hardware manufacturer to provide drivers for its hardware. Because the drivers must act between both the hardware and the operating system, the drivers typically are operating system specific. Thus, the hardware manufacturer must offer different drivers so that its hardware works under DOS, Windows 9x, Windows NT, Windows 2000, OS/2, Linux, and so on.

Because the BIOS layer looks the same to the operating system no matter what hardware is above it (or underneath, depending on your point of view), you can have the same operating system running on a variety of PCs. For example, you can run Windows 98 on two systems with different processors, hard disks, video adapters, and so on, yet Windows 98 will look and feel pretty much the same on both of them. This is because the drivers provide the same basic functions no matter which specific hardware is used.

As you can see from Figure 5.1, the application and operating systems layers can be identical from system to system, but the hardware can differ radically. Because the BIOS consists of software drivers that act to interface the hardware to the software, the BIOS layer adapts to the unique hardware on one end but looks consistently the same to the operating system at the other end.

The hardware layer is where most differences lie between various systems. It is up to the BIOS to mask the differences between unique hardware so that the given operating system (and subsequently the application) can be run. This chapter focuses on the BIOS layer of the PC.

BIOS Hardware/Software

The BIOS itself is software running in memory that consists of all the various drivers that interface the hardware to the operating system. The BIOS is unique compared to normal software in that it doesn't all load from disk; some of it is preloaded into memory chips (read-only memory, or ROM) installed in the system or on adapter cards.

The BIOS in a PC comes from three possible sources:

- Motherboard ROM
- Adapter card ROM (such as that found on a video card)
- Loaded into RAM from disk (device drivers)

The motherboard ROM BIOS is most often associated with hardware rather than software. This is because the BIOS on the motherboard is contained in a ROM chip on the board, which contains the initial software drivers needed to get the system running. Years ago, when running only DOS on basic PCs, this was enough so that no other drivers were needed; the motherboard BIOS had everything that was necessary. The motherboard BIOS usually includes drivers for all the basic system components, including the keyboard, floppy drive, hard drive, serial and parallel ports, and more. As systems became more complex, new hardware was added for which no motherboard BIOS drivers existed. These included devices such as newer video adapters, CD-ROM drives, SCSI hard disks, USB ports, and so on.

Rather than requiring a new motherboard BIOS that would specifically support the new devices, it was far simpler and more practical to copy any new drivers that were necessary onto the system hard disk and configure the operating system to load them at boot time. This is how most CD-ROM drives, sound cards, scanners, printers, PC-card (PCMCIA) devices, and so on are supported. Because these devices don't need to be active during boot time, the system can boot up from the hard disk and wait to load the drivers during the initial operating system load.

Some drivers, however, must be active during boot time. For example, how could you boot from a hard disk if the drivers necessary to make the disk interface work must be loaded from that disk? Obviously, the hard disk drivers must be preloaded into ROM either on the motherboard or on an adapter card.

How will you be able to see anything onscreen if your video card doesn't have a set of drivers in a ROM? The solution to this could be to provide a motherboard ROM with the appropriate video drivers built in; however, this is impractical because of the variety of cards, each needing its own drivers. You would end up with hundreds of different motherboard ROMs, depending on which video card you had. Instead, when IBM designed the original PC, it created a better solution. It designed the PC's motherboard ROM to scan the slots looking for adapter cards with ROMs on them. If a card was found with a ROM on it, the ROM was executed during the initial system startup phase, before the system began loading the operating system from the hard disk.

By putting the ROM-based drivers right on the card, you didn't have to change your motherboard ROM to have built-in support for new devices, especially those that needed to be active during boot time. A few cards (adapter boards) almost always have a ROM onboard, including the following:

- *Video cards*. All have an onboard BIOS.

- *SCSI adapters*. Those that support booting from SCSI hard drives or CD-ROMs have an onboard BIOS. Note that, in most cases, the SCSI BIOS does not support any SCSI devices other than a hard disk; if you use a SCSI CD-ROM, scanner, Zip drive, and so on, you still need to load the appropriate drivers for those devices from your hard disk. Most newer SCSI adapters support booting from a SCSI CD-ROM, but CD-ROM drivers are still necessary to access the CD-ROM when booting from another drive or device.

- *Network cards*. Those that support booting directly from a file server have what is usually called a boot ROM or IPL (initial program load) ROM onboard. This enables PCs to be configured on a LAN as diskless workstations—also called Net PCs, NCs (network computers), or even smart terminals.

- *IDE or floppy upgrade boards*. Boards that enable you to attach more or different types of drives than what is normally supported by the motherboard alone. These cards require an onboard BIOS to enable these drives to be bootable.

- *Y2K boards*. Boards that incorporate BIOS fixes to update the century byte in the CMOS RAM. These boards have a small driver contained in a BIOS, which monitors the year byte for a change from 99 to 00. When this is detected, the driver updates the century byte from 19 to 20, correcting a flaw in some older motherboard BIOSes. Although it might seem strange to list Y2K boards, these will still be in use until the systems using them are retired.

BIOS and CMOS RAM

Some people confuse BIOS with the CMOS RAM in a system. This confusion is aided by the fact that the Setup program in the BIOS is used to set and store the configuration settings in the CMOS RAM. They are, in fact, two totally separate components.

The BIOS on the motherboard is stored in a fixed ROM chip. Also on the motherboard is a chip called the RTC/NVRAM chip, which stands for real-time clock/nonvolatile memory. This is actually a digital clock chip with a few extra bytes of memory thrown in.

The first one ever used in a PC was the Motorola MC146818 chip, which had 64 bytes of storage, of which 10 bytes were dedicated to the clock function. Although it is called nonvolatile, it is actually volatile, meaning that without power, the time/date settings and the data in the RAM portion will, in fact, be erased. It is called nonvolatile because it is designed using complementary metal-oxide semiconductor (CMOS) technology, which results in a chip that runs on very little power. A battery in the system, rather than the AC wall current, provides that power. This is also why most people incorrectly call this chip the CMOS RAM chip; although not technically accurate, that is easier to say than the RTC/NVRAM chip. Most RTC/NVRAM chips run on as little as one microamp (millionth of an amp), so they use very little battery power to run. Most last five years before the lithium battery runs out and the information stored gets erased. Some systems use a Dallas Semiconductor RTC/NVRAM chip (such as the DS12885 and DS12887) that also contain the battery.

When you enter your BIOS Setup, configure your hard disk parameters or other BIOS Setup settings and save them, these settings are written to the storage area in the RTC/NVRAM (otherwise called CMOS RAM) chip. Every time your system boots up, it reads the parameters stored in the CMOS RAM chip to determine how the system should be configured. A relationship exists between the BIOS and CMOS RAM, but they are two distinctly different parts of the system.

Motherboard BIOS

All motherboards must have a special chip containing software called the ROM BIOS. This ROM chip contains the startup programs and drivers used to get the system running and act as the interface to the basic hardware in the system. When you turn on a system, the power on self test (POST) in the BIOS also tests the major components in the system. Additionally, you can run a setup program to store system configuration data in the CMOS memory, which is powered by a battery on the motherboard. This CMOS RAM is often called NVRAM (nonvolatile RAM) because it runs on about one millionth of an amp of electrical current and can store data for years when powered by a tiny lithium battery.

▶▶ See "ROM Hardware," p. 350.

The BIOS is a collection of programs embedded in one or more chips, depending on the design of your computer. That collection of programs is the first thing loaded when you start your computer, even before the operating system. Simply put, the BIOS in most PCs has four main functions:

- *POST (power on self test).* The POST tests your computer's processor, memory, chipset, video adapter, disk controllers, disk drives, keyboard, and other crucial components.

- *Setup.* System configuration and setup program. This is usually a menu-driven program activated by pressing a special key during the POST, which enables you to configure the motherboard and chipset settings along with the date and time, passwords, disk drives, and other basic system settings. You also can control the power-management settings and boot-drive sequence from the BIOS Setup, and on some systems, you can also configure CPU timing and clock-multiplier settings. Some older 286 and 386 systems did not have the Setup program in ROM and required that you boot from a special setup disk.

- *Bootstrap loader.* A routine that reads the disk drives looking for a valid master boot sector. If one meeting certain minimum criteria (ending in the signature bytes 55AAh) is found, the code within is executed. This master boot sector program then continues the boot process by loading an operating system boot sector, which then loads the operating system core files.

- *BIOS (basic input/output system).* This refers to the collection of actual drivers used to act as a basic interface between the operating system and your hardware when the system is booted and running. When running DOS or Windows in safe mode, you are running almost solely on ROM-based BIOS drivers because none are loaded from disk.

ROM Hardware

Read-only memory (ROM) is a type of memory that can permanently or semipermanently hold data. It is called read-only because it is either impossible or difficult to write to. ROM is also often called non-volatile memory because any data stored in ROM remains even if the power is turned off. As such, ROM is an ideal place to put the PC's startup instructions—that is, the software that boots the system (the BIOS).

Note that ROM and RAM are not opposites, as some people seem to believe. In fact, ROM is technically a subset of the system's RAM. In other words, a portion of the system's random access memory address space is mapped into one or more ROM chips. This is necessary to contain the software that enables the PC to boot up; otherwise, the processor would have no program in memory to execute when it is powered on.

For example, when a PC is turned on, the processor automatically jumps to address FFFF0h, expecting to find instructions to tell the processor what to do. This location is exactly 16 bytes from the end of the first megabyte of RAM space, as well as the end of the ROM itself. If this location were mapped into regular RAM chips, any data stored there would have disappeared when the power was previously turned off, and the processor would subsequently find no instructions to run the next time the power was turned on. By placing a ROM chip at this address, a system startup program can be permanently loaded into the ROM and will be available every time the system is turned on.

▶▶ For more information about Dynamic RAM, see "DRAM," p. 407.

Normally, the system ROM starts at address E0000h or F0000h, which is 128KB or 64KB prior to the end of the first megabyte. Because the ROM chip usually is up to 128KB in size, the ROM programs are allowed to occupy the entire last 128KB of the first megabyte, including the critical FFFF0h startup instruction address, which is located 16 bytes from the end of the BIOS space. Some motherboard ROM chips are larger, up to 256KB or 512KB in size. The additional code in these is configured to act as a video card ROM (addresses C0000h–C7FFFh) on motherboards with built-in video and might even contain additional ROM drivers configured anywhere from C8000h to DFFFFh to support additional onboard devices, such as SCSI or network adapters.

Figure 5.2 shows a map of the first megabyte of memory in a PC, showing the upper memory areas reserved for adapter card and motherboard ROM BIOS at the end of the first megabyte.

Some think it is strange that the PC would start executing BIOS instructions 16 bytes from the end of the ROM, but this design was intentional. All the ROM programmer has to do is place a JMP (jump) instruction at that address that instructs the processor to jump to the actual beginning of the ROM—in most cases, close to F0000h—which is about 64KB earlier in the memory map. It's like deciding to read every book starting 16 pages from the end and then having all book publishers agree to place an instruction there to jump back the necessary number of pages to get to page 1. By setting the startup location in this way, Intel enabled the ROM to grow to be any size, all the while keeping it at the upper end of addresses in the first megabyte of the memory address space.

The main ROM BIOS is contained in a ROM chip on the motherboard, but adapter cards with ROMs contain auxiliary BIOS routines and drivers needed by the particular card, especially for those cards that must be active early in the boot process, such as video cards. Cards that don't need drivers active during boot (such as sound cards) typically don't have a ROM because those drivers can be loaded from the hard disk later in the boot process.

Because the BIOS is the main portion of the code stored in ROM, we often call the ROM the ROM BIOS. In older PCs, the motherboard ROM BIOS could consist of up to five or six total chips, but most PCs have required only a single chip for many years now.

```
    . = RAM
    G = Graphics Mode Video RAM
    M = Monochrome Text Mode Video RAM
    C = Color Text Mode Video RAM
    V = Video adapter ROM BIOS
    a = Reserved for other adapter board ROM
    r = Additional Motherboard ROM BIOS in some systems
    R = Motherboard ROM BIOS

    Conventional (Base) Memory

           : 0---1---2---3---4---5---6---7---8---9---A---B---C---D---E---F---
    000000: ................................................................
    010000: ................................................................
    020000: ................................................................
    030000: ................................................................
    040000: ................................................................
    050000: ................................................................
    060000: ................................................................
    070000: ................................................................
    080000: ................................................................
    090000: ................................................................

    Upper Memory Area (UMA)

           : 0---1---2---3---4---5---6---7---8---9---A---B---C---D---E---F---
    0A0000: GGGGGGGGGGGGGGGGGGGGGGGGGGGGGGGGGGGGGGGGGGGGGGGGGGGGGGGGGGGGGGGG
    0B0000: MMMMMMMMMMMMMMMMMMMMMMMMMMMMMMMMMCCCCCCCCCCCCCCCCCCCCCCCCCCCCCCCC
           : 0---1---2---3---4---5---6---7---8---9---A---B---C---D---E---F---
    0C0000: VVVVVVVVVVVVVVVVVVVVVVVVVVVVVVVVVaaaaaaaaaaaaaaaaaaaaaaaaaaaaaaaa
    0D0000: aaaaaaaaaaaaaaaaaaaaaaaaaaaaaaaaaaaaaaaaaaaaaaaaaaaaaaaaaaaaaaaa
           : 0---1---2---3---4---5---6---7---8---9---A---B---C---D---E---F---
    0E0000: rrrrrrrrrrrrrrrrrrrrrrrrrrrrrrrrrrrrrrrrrrrrrrrrrrrrrrrrrrrrrrrr
    0F0000: RRRRRRRRRRRRRRRRRRRRRRRRRRRRRRRRRRRRRRRRRRRRRRRRRRRRRRRRRRRRRRRR
```

Figure 5.2   PC memory map showing ROM BIOS.

Adapter card ROMs, such as those used for video, SCSI, add-on IDE cards, and network cards for diskless workstations, are automatically scanned and read by the motherboard ROM during the early part of the boot process, during the POST. The motherboard ROM scans a special area of RAM reserved for adapter ROMs (addresses C0000–DFFFFh) looking for a 55AAh signature byte pair that indicates the start of a ROM.

All adapter ROMs must start with 55AAh; otherwise, the motherboard won't recognize them. The third byte indicates the size of the ROM in 512-byte units called *paragraphs,* and the fourth byte is the actual start of the driver programs. The size byte is used by the motherboard ROM for testing purposes. The motherboard ROM adds all the bytes in the ROM and divides the sum by the number of bytes. The result should produce a remainder of 100h. Thus, when creating a ROM for an adapter, the programmer normally uses a "fill" byte at the end to get the checksum to come out right. Using this checksum the motherboard tests each adapter ROM during the POST and flags any that appear to have been corrupted.

The motherboard BIOS automatically runs the programs in any adapter ROMs it finds during the scan. You see this in most systems when you turn on your system, and during the POST you see the video card BIOS initialize and announce its presence.

ROM Shadowing

ROM chips by their natures are very slow, with access times of 150ns (nanoseconds, or billionths of a second), compared to DRAM access times of less than 10ns on the newest systems. Because of this, in virtually all systems the ROMs are *shadowed*, which means they are copied into DRAM chips at startup to allow faster access during normal operation. The shadowing procedure copies the ROM into RAM and then assigns that RAM the same address as the ROM originally used, disabling the actual ROM in the process. This makes the system seem as though it has ROM running at the same speed as RAM.

The performance gain from shadowing is often very slight, and it can cause problems if not set up properly. Therefore, in most cases, it is wise to shadow only the motherboard and maybe the video card BIOS and leave the others alone.

Mostly, shadowing is useful only if you are running 16-bit operating systems, such as DOS or Windows 3.x. If you are running a 32-bit operating system, such as Windows 9x, Windows Me, Windows 2000, Windows NT, or Windows XP, shadowing is virtually useless because those operating systems do not use the 16-bit ROM code while running. Instead, those operating systems load 32-bit drivers into RAM, which replace the 16-bit BIOS code used only during system startup.

Shadowing controls are found in the CMOS Setup program in the motherboard ROM, which is covered in more detail later in this chapter.

The four types of ROM chips are as follows:

- *ROM.* Read-only memory
- *PROM.* Programmable ROM
- *EPROM.* Erasable PROM
- *EEPROM.* Electrically erasable PROM, also called flash ROM

No matter which type of ROM your system uses, the data stored in a ROM chip is nonvolatile and remains indefinitely unless intentionally erased or overwritten (in those cases where that is possible).

Table 5.1 lists the identifying part numbers typically used for each type of ROM chip, along with any other identifying information.

Table 5.1   ROM Chip Part Numbers

ROM Type	Part Number	Other
ROM	No longer in use	
PROM	27nnnn	
EPROM	27nnnn	Quartz Window
EEPROM	28xxxx or 29xxxx	

ROM (True or Mask ROM)

Originally, most ROMs were manufactured with the binary data (0s and 1s) already "cast in" or integrated into the die. The die represents the actual silicon chip itself. These are called Mask ROMs because the data is formed into the mask from which the ROM die is photolithographically produced. This type of manufacturing method is economical if you are making hundreds of thousands of ROMs with the same information. If you must change a single bit, however, you must remake the mask, which is an expensive proposition. Because of costs and inflexibility, nobody uses Mask ROMs anymore.

Mask ROMs are exactly analogous to prerecorded CD-ROMs. Some people think a CD-ROM is first manufactured as a blank and then the data is written to it by laser, but that is not true. A CD-ROM is literally a piece of plastic that is stamped in a press, and the data is directly molded in, not written. The only actual recording is done with the master disc from which the molds or stamps are made.

PROM

PROMs are a type of ROM that is blank when new and that must be programmed with whatever data you want. The PROM was invented in the late 1970s by Texas Instruments and has been available in sizes from 1KB (8Kb) to 2MB (16Mb) or more. They can be identified by their part numbers, which usually are 27nnnn—where the 27 indicates the TI type PROM, and the nnnn indicates the size of the chip in kilobits (not bytes). For example, most PCs that used PROMs came with 27512 or 271000 chips, which indicate 512Kb (64KB) or 1Mb (128KB).

Note

Since 1981, all cars sold in the U.S. have used onboard computers with some form of ROM containing the control software. My 1989 Pontiac Turbo Trans Am came with an onboard computer containing a 2732 PROM, which was a 32Kb (4KB) chip in the ECM (electronic control module or vehicle computer) under the dash. This chip contained a portion of the vehicle operating software as well as all the data tables describing spark advance, fuel delivery, and other engine and vehicle operating parameters. Many devices with integrated computers use PROMs to store their operating programs.

Although we say these chips are blank when new, they are technically preloaded with binary 1s. In other words, a 1Mb ROM chip used in a modern PC would come with one million (actually 1,048,576) bit locations, each containing a binary 1. A blank PROM can then be programmed, which is the act of writing to it. This usually requires a special machine called a device programmer, a ROM programmer, or a ROM burner (see Figure 5.3).

Figure 5.3 Typical gang (multisocket) device programmer (PROM burner).

Programming the ROM is sometimes referred to as *burning* it because that is technically an apt description of the process. Each binary 1 bit can be thought of as a fuse, which is intact. Most chips run on 5 volts, but when a PROM is programmed, a higher voltage (normally 12 volts) is placed at the various addresses within the chip. This higher voltage actually blows or burns the fuses at the desired locations, thus turning any given 1 into a 0. Although you can turn a 1 into a 0, you should note that the process is irreversible; that is, you can't turn a 0 back into a 1.

The device programmer examines the program you want to write into the chip and then selectively changes only the 1s to 0s where necessary in the chip.

PROM chips are often referred to as OTP (one-time programmable) chips for this reason. They can be programmed once and never erased. Most PROMs are very inexpensive—about $3 for a typical PC motherboard PROM—so if you want to change the program in a PROM, you discard it and program a fresh one with the new data.

The act of programming a PROM takes anywhere from a few seconds to a few minutes, depending on the size of the chip and the algorithm used by the programming device. Figure 5.3 shows an illustration of a typical PROM programmer that has multiple sockets. This is called a *gang programmer* and can program several chips at once, saving time if you have several chips to write with the same data. Less expensive programmers are available with only one socket, which is fine for most individual use.

I use and recommend a very inexpensive programmer from a company called Andromeda Research (see the vendor list on the CD). Besides being economical, its unit has the advantage of connecting to a PC via the parallel port for fast and easy data transfer of files between the PC and the programming unit. The unit is also portable and comes built into a convenient carrying case. It is operated by an included menu-driven program you install on the connected PC. The program contains several features, including a function that enables you to read the data from a chip and save it in a file on your system, as well as to write a chip from a data file, verify that a chip matches a file, and verify that a chip is blank before programming begins. A low-cost BIOS backup option makes backing up the flash BIOS chip in your system easy (if it is removable) as a safeguard against disaster.

Chapter 4, "Motherboards and Buses," shows how I used my PROM programmer to modify the BIOS in some of my older PCs. With today's systems primarily using flash ROMs, this capability is somewhat limited, but I include the information because I think it is interesting.

Note

I even used my PROM programmer to reprogram the PROM in my 1989 Turbo Trans Am, changing the factory preset speed and rpm limiters, turbocharger boost, torque converter lockup points, spark advance, fuel delivery, idle speed, and much more! I also incorporated a switch box under the dash that enables me to switch among four different chips, even while the vehicle is running. One chip I created I call the "valet chip," which, when engaged, cuts off the fuel injectors at a preset speed of 36 miles per hour and restarts them when the vehicle coasts down to 35mph. I imagine this type of modification would be useful for those with teenage drivers because you could set the mph or engine rpm limit to whatever you want! Another chip I created cuts off fuel to the engine altogether, which I engage for security purposes when the vehicle is parked. No matter how clever, a thief will not be able to steal this car unless he tows it away. If you are interested in such a chip-switching device or custom chips for your Turbo Trans Am or Buick Grand National, contact Casper's Electronics (see the Vendor List on the CD-ROM accompanying this book). For other vehicles with replaceable PROMs, companies such as Superchips, Hypertech, or Evergreen offer custom PROMs for improved performance (see the Vendor List on the CD). I installed a Superchips chip in a Ford Explorer I had, and it made a dramatic improvement in engine operation and vehicle performance.

EPROM

One variation of the PROM that has been very popular is the EPROM. An *EPROM* is a PROM that is erasable. An EPROM chip can be easily recognized by the clear quartz crystal window set in the chip package directly over the die (see Figure 5.4). You can actually see the die through the window! EPROMs have the same 27xxxx part-numbering scheme as the standard PROM, and they are functionally and physically identical except for the clear quartz window above the die.

The purpose of the window is to allow ultraviolet light to reach the chip die because the EPROM is erased by exposure to intense UV light. The window is quartz crystal because regular glass blocks UV light. You can't get a suntan through a glass window!

Figure 5.4   An EPROM showing the quartz window for ultraviolet erasing.

Note

The quartz window makes the EPROMs more expensive than the OTP PROMs. This extra expense is needless if erasability is not important.

The UV light erases the chip by causing a chemical reaction, which essentially melts the fuses back together! Thus, any binary 0s in the chip become 1s, and the chip is restored to a new condition with binary 1s in all locations. To work, the UV exposure must be at a specific wavelength (2,537 angstroms), at a fairly high intensity (12,000 uw/cm^2), in close proximity (2cm–3cm, or about 1 inch), and last for between 5 and 15 minutes duration. An EPROM eraser (see Figure 5.5) is a device that contains a UV light source (usually a sunlamp-type bulb) above a sealed compartment drawer in which you place the chip or chips.

Figure 5.5   A professional EPROM eraser.

Figure 5.5 shows a professional-type EPROM eraser that can handle up to 50 chips at a time. I use a much smaller and less expensive one called the DataRase by Walling Co. This device erases up to four chips at a time and is both economical and portable. The current version is called DataRase II; the DataRase II and similar products are sold by many vendors of EPROM programming equipment.

The quartz crystal window on an EPROM typically is covered by tape, which prevents accidental exposure to UV light. UV light is present in sunlight, of course, and even in standard room lighting, so that over time a chip exposed to the light can begin to degrade. For this reason, after a chip is programmed, you should put a sticker over the window to protect it.

EEPROM/Flash ROM

A newer type of ROM is the *EEPROM*, which stands for electrically erasable PROM. These chips are also called flash ROMs and are characterized by their capability to be erased and reprogrammed directly in the circuit board they are installed in, with no special equipment required. By using an EEPROM, or flash ROM, you can erase and reprogram the motherboard ROM in a PC without removing the chip from the system or even opening up the system chassis!

With a flash ROM or EEPROM, you don't need a UV eraser or device programmer to program or erase chips. Not only do virtually all PC motherboards built since 1994 use flash ROMs or EEPROMs, most automobiles built since then also use them as well. For example, my 1994 Chevy Impala SS has a PCM (powertrain control module) with an integral flash ROM.

The EEPROM or flash ROM can be identified by a 28xxxx or 29xxxx part number, as well as by the absence of a window on the chip. Having an EEPROM or a flash ROM in your PC motherboard means you now can easily upgrade the motherboard ROM without having to swap chips. In most cases, you download the updated ROM from the motherboard manufacturer's Web site and then run a special program it provides to update the ROM. This procedure is described in more detail later in this chapter.

I recommend that you periodically check with your motherboard manufacturer to see whether an updated BIOS is available for your system. An updated BIOS might contain bug fixes or enable new features not originally found in your system. You might find fixes for IDE hard drive support over 8.4GB or new drivers to support booting from LS-120 (120MB floppy) drives.

Note

For the auto enthusiasts out there, you might want to do the same for your car; that is, check to see whether ROM upgrades are available for your vehicle's computer. Now that updates are so easy and inexpensive, vehicle manufacturers are releasing bug-fix ROM upgrades that correct operational problems or improve vehicle performance. In most cases, you must check with your dealer to see whether any new vehicle ROMs are available. If you have a GM car, GM has a Web site where you can get information about the BIOS revisions available for your car, which it calls Vehicle Calibrations. The GM Vehicle Calibration Information site address is `http://calid.gm.com/vci/`.

When you enter your VIN (vehicle identification number), this page displays the calibration history for the vehicle, which is a list of all the different flash ROM upgrades (calibrations) developed since the vehicle was new. For example, when I entered the VIN on my 1994 Impala, I found that five flash ROM calibrations had been released over the years, and my car had only the second revision installed originally, meaning there had been three newer ROMs than the one I had! The fixes in the various calibration updates are also listed. A trip to the dealer with this information enabled them to use their diagnostic computer to connect to my car and reflash the PCM with the latest software, which, in my case, fixed several problems, including engine surging under specific conditions, shift clunks, erroneous "check engine" light warnings, and several other minor problems.

With the flash ROM capability, I began experimenting with running calibrations originally intended for other vehicles, and I now run a modified Camaro calibration loaded into the flash ROM in my Impala. The spark-advance curve and fuel delivery parameters are much more aggressive in the Camaro calibration, as are the transmission shift points and other features. If you are interested in having a custom program installed in your flash ROM equipped vehicle, I recommend you contact Fastchip at `http://www.fastchip.com` or Superchips at `http://www.superchips.com` (see the Vendor List on the CD for more information). If you want to write and program your own vehicle calibrations, see `http://www.diy-efi.org` for more information.

These days, many objects with embedded computers controlling them are using flash ROMs. Pretty soon you'll be taking your toaster in for flash ROM upgrades as well!

Note

The method for locating and updating your PC motherboard flash ROMs is shown in Chapter 4.

Other devices might have flash ROMs as well; for example, I have updated the flash ROMs in my 3Com ISDN terminal adapter as well as in my Kodak digital camera. Both these items had minor quirks that were fixed by updating their internal ROM code, which was as easy as downloading a file from their respective Web sites and running the update program included in the file.

Flash ROMs are also frequently used to add new capabilities to peripherals or to update peripherals, such as modems, to the latest standards; for example, updating a modem from X2 or K56Flex to V.90 or V.92.

ROM BIOS Manufacturers

A number of popular BIOS manufacturers in the market today supply the majority of motherboard and system manufacturers with the code for their ROMs. This section discusses the various versions available.

Several companies have specialized in the development of a compatible ROM BIOS product. The three major companies that come to mind in discussing ROM BIOS software are American Megatrends, Inc. (AMI), Phoenix Technologies, and Award Software (now owned by Phoenix Technologies). Each company licenses its ROM BIOS to motherboard manufacturers so those manufacturers can worry about the hardware rather than the software. To obtain one of these ROMs for a motherboard, the original equipment manufacturer (OEM) must answer many questions about the design of the system so that the proper BIOS can be either developed or selected from those already designed. Combining a ROM BIOS and a motherboard is not a haphazard task. No single, generic, compatible ROM exists, either. AMI, Award, Microid Research (MR BIOS), and Phoenix ship many variations of their BIOS code to different board manufacturers, each one custom tailored to that specific motherboard.

Recently, some major changes have occurred in the BIOS industry. Intel, the largest BIOS customer, has gone from using mostly Phoenix, to AMI, back to Phoenix, and now back to AMI for most of its motherboards. Intel originally used the Phoenix BIOS core in its motherboards up through 1995, when it changed to an AMI core. It then used AMI until 1997, when it switched back to Phoenix. More recently in 1999 Intel switched again, this time back to AMI. In all these cases Intel, takes the core BIOS from Phoenix or AMI and highly customizes it for its particular motherboards. It is always a big deal which BIOS Intel uses because Intel sells about 80% or more of all PC motherboards. What that basically means is that if you purchase a PC today, you will probably get an Intel-made motherboard with the new AMI BIOS.

Another development is that in late 1998, Phoenix bought Award. While Phoenix continues to sell the Award BIOS as a separate product line, the big-three BIOS developers are now reduced to the big two—Phoenix and AMI. Many of the offshore motherboard manufacturers use the AMI or Award BIOS. Phoenix not only develops the BIOS for many systems, but is also the primary BIOS developer responsible for new BIOS development and new BIOS standards.

OEMs

Many OEMs have developed their own compatible ROMs independently. Companies such as Compaq, AT&T, and Acer have developed their own BIOS products that are comparable to those offered by AMI, Phoenix, Award, and others. These companies also offer upgrades to newer versions that often can provide more features and improvements or fix problems with the older versions. If you use a system with a proprietary ROM, ensure that it is from a larger company with a track record and one that will provide updates and fixes as necessary. Ideally, upgrades should be available for download from the Internet.

Most OEMs have their BIOS written for them by a third-party company. For example, Hewlett-Packard contracts with Phoenix to develop the motherboard BIOSes used in all the HP Vectra PCs. Note that even though Phoenix might have done the development, you still must get upgrades or fixes from Hewlett-Packard. This is really true for all systems because all motherboard manufacturers customize the BIOS for their boards.

AMI

Although AMI customizes the ROM code for a particular system, it does not sell the ROM source code to the OEM. An OEM must obtain each new release as it becomes available. Because many OEMs don't need or want every new version developed, they might skip several version changes before licensing a new one. The AMI BIOS is currently the most popular BIOS in PC systems. Newer versions of the AMI BIOS are called Hi-Flex because of the high flexibility found in the BIOS configuration program. The AMI Hi-Flex BIOS is used in Intel, AMI, and many other manufacturers' motherboards. One special AMI feature is that it is the only third-party BIOS manufacturer to make its own motherboard.

During powerup, the BIOS ID string is displayed on the lower-left part of the screen. This string tells you valuable information about which BIOS version you have and about certain settings that are determined by the built-in setup program.

Tip

A good trick to help you view the BIOS ID string is to shut down and either unplug your keyboard or hold down a key as you power back on. This causes a keyboard error, and the string remains displayed.

You also can download the AMI Motherboard ID Utility program (AMIMBID) from AMI's Web site and run it to determine the contents of ID String 1.

The primary BIOS Identification string (ID String 1) is displayed by any AMI BIOS during the POST at the bottom-left corner of the screen, below the copyright message. Two additional BIOS ID strings (ID Strings 2 and 3) can be displayed by the AMI Hi-Flex BIOS by pressing the Insert key during POST. These additional ID strings display the options installed in the BIOS.

The general BIOS ID String 1 format for older AMI BIOS versions is shown in Table 5.2.

Table 5.2   ABBB-NNNN-mmddyy-KK

Position	Description
A	BIOS Options: D = Diagnostics built in S = Setup built in E = Extended Setup built in

Table 5.2 Continued

Position	Description
BBB	Chipset or Motherboard Identifier: C&T = Chips & Technologies chipset NET = C&T NEAT 286 chipset 286 = Standard 286 motherboard SUN = Suntac chipset PAQ = Compaq motherboard INT = Intel motherboard AMI = AMI motherboard G23 = G2 chipset 386 motherboard
NNNN	The manufacturer license code reference number
mmddyy	The BIOS release date, mm/dd/yy
KK	The AMI keyboard BIOS version number

The BIOS ID String 1 format for AMI Hi-Flex BIOS versions is shown in Table 5.3.

Table 5.3 AB-CCcc-DDDDDD-EFGHIJKL-mmddyy-MMMMMMMM-N

Position	Description
A	Processor Type: 0 = 8086 or 8088 2 = 286 3 = 386 4 = 486 5 = Pentium 6 = Pentium Pro/II/III/Celeron/Athlon/Duron
B	Size of BIOS: 0 = 64KB BIOS 1 = 128KB BIOS 2 = 256KB BIOS
CCcc	Major and minor BIOS version number
DDDDDD	Manufacturer license code reference number 0036xx = AMI 386 motherboard, xx = Series # 0046xx = AMI 486 motherboard, xx = Series # 0056xx = AMI Pentium motherboard, xx = Series # 0066xx = AMI Pentium Pro motherboard, xx = Series #
E	1 = Halt on POST Error
F	1 = Initialize CMOS every boot
G	1 = Block pins 22 and 23 of the keyboard controller
H	1 = Mouse support in BIOS/keyboard controller
I	1 = Wait for <F1> key on POST errors
J	1 = Display floppy error during POST
K	1 = Display video error during POST
L	1 = Display keyboard error during POST
mmddyy	BIOS Date, mm/dd/yy
MMMMMMMM	Chipset identifier or BIOS name
N	Keyboard controller version number

AMI Hi-Flex BIOS ID String 2 is shown in Table 5.4.

Table 5.4   AAB-C-DDDD-EE-FF-GGGG-HH-II-JJJ

Position	Description
AA	Keyboard controller pin number for clock switching.
B	Keyboard controller clock switching pin function: H = High signal switches clock to high speed. L = High signal switches clock to low speed.
C	Clock switching through chipset registers: 0 = Disable. 1 = Enable.
DDDD	Port address to switch clock high.
EE	Data value to switch clock high.
FF	Mask value to switch clock high.
GGGG	Port address to switch clock low.
HH	Data value to switch clock low.
II	Mask value to switch clock low.
JJJ	Pin number for Turbo Switch Input.

AMI Hi-Flex BIOS ID String 3 is shown in Table 5.5.

Table 5.5   AAB-C-DDD-EE-FF-GGGG-HH-II-JJ-K-L

Position	Description
AA	Keyboard controller pin number for cache control.
B	Keyboard controller cache control pin function: H = High signal enables the cache. L = High signal disables the cache.
C	1 = High signal is used on the keyboard controller pin.
DDD	Cache control through chipset registers: 0 = Cache control off. 1 = Cache control on.
EE	Port address to enable cache.
FF	Data value to enable cache.
GGGG	Mask value to enable cache.
HH	Port address to disable cache.
II	Data value to disable cache.
JJ	Mask value to disable cache.
K	Pin number for resetting the 82335 memory controller.
L	BIOS Modification Flag: 0 = The BIOS has not been modified. 1–9, A–Z = Number of times the BIOS has been modified.

The AMI BIOS has many features, including a built-in setup program activated by pressing the Delete or Esc key in the first few seconds of booting up your computer. The BIOS prompts you briefly as to which key to press and when to press it. The AMI BIOS offers user-definable hard disk types, essential for optimal use of many IDE or ESDI drives. The 1995 and newer BIOS versions also support enhanced IDE drives and autoconfigure the drive parameters.

A unique feature of some of the AMI BIOS versions was that in addition to the setup, they had a built-in, menu-driven diagnostics package, essentially a very limited version of the standalone AMIDIAG product. The internal diagnostics are not a replacement for more comprehensive disk-based programs, but they can help in a pinch. The menu-driven diagnostics do not do extensive memory testing, for example, and the hard disk low-level formatter works only at the BIOS level rather than at the controller register level. These limitations often have prevented it from being capable of formatting severely damaged disks. Most newer AMI BIOS versions no longer include the full diagnostics.

AMI doesn't produce BIOS documentation; it leaves that up to the motherboard manufacturers who include their BIOS on the motherboard. However, AMI has published a detailed version of its documentation called the *Programmer's Guide to the AMIBIOS: Includes Descriptions of PCI, APM, and Socket Services BIOS Functions*, published by Windcrest/McGraw-Hill, ISBN 0-07-001561-9. This book, written by AMI engineers, describes all the BIOS functions, features, error codes, and more. Unfortunately, this book is out of print. If you can locate it, I recommend this book for users with an AMI BIOS in their systems because this provides a complete version of the documentation for which they might have been looking.

The AMI BIOS is sold through distributors, a list of which is available at its Web site. However, keep in mind that you can't buy upgrades and replacements directly from AMI, and AMI produces upgrades only for its own motherboards. If you have a non-AMI motherboard with a customized AMI BIOS, you must contact the motherboard manufacturer for an upgrade.

Award

Just as Award Software did before its merger with Phoenix, Phoenix continues to sell the Award BIOS code to the OEM and allows the OEM to customize the BIOS. Of course, the BIOS no longer is Award BIOS then, but rather a highly customized version. This permits the OEM to have total control over the BIOS code without having to write it from scratch.

By contrast, neither the Phoenix BIOS nor the AMI BIOS source code is sold to OEM customers. Phoenix and AMI customize their BIOS code for each customer's needs, but they retain control of it. Some OEMs that seem to have developed their own ROM code started with a base of source code licensed to them by Award or some other company.

The Award BIOS has all the features you expect, including a built-in setup program activated by pressing Ctrl+Alt+Esc or a particular key on startup (usually prompted on the screen). This setup offers user-definable drive types, required to fully use IDE or ESDI hard disks. The POST is good, although the few beep codes supported means that a POST card is necessary if you want to diagnose most power-on problems. Phoenix provides technical support on its Web site at http://www.phoenix.com. Phoenix purchased Award in late 1998 but continues to release Award BIOS products for the OEM market. eSupport.com (formerly Unicore Software) provides Award BIOS upgrades for end users.

Phoenix

The Phoenix BIOS for many years has been a standard of compatibility by which others are judged. It was one of the first third-party companies to legally reverse-engineer the IBM BIOS using a *clean-room* approach. In this approach, a group of engineers studied the IBM BIOS and wrote a specification for how that BIOS should work and what features should be incorporated. This information then was passed to a second group of engineers who had never seen the IBM BIOS. They could then legally write a new BIOS to the specifications set forth by the first group. This work was then unique and not a copy of IBM's BIOS; however, it functioned the same way.

The Phoenix BIOS excels in two areas that put it high on my list of recommendations. One is that the POST is excellent. The BIOS outputs an extensive set of beep codes that can be used to diagnose severe motherboard problems that would prevent normal operation of the system. In fact, with beep codes alone, this POST can isolate memory failures in Bank 0 right down to the individual SIMM or DIMM module. The Phoenix BIOS also has an excellent setup program free from unnecessary frills, but one that offers all the features the user would expect, such as user-definable drive types and so on. The built-in setup is activated by pressing Ctrl+Alt+S, Ctrl+Alt+Esc, or a particular key on startup, such as F1 or F2 on most newer systems, depending on the version of BIOS you have.

The second area in which Phoenix excels is the documentation. Not only are the manuals you get with the system detailed, but Phoenix has also written a set of BIOS technical-reference manuals that are a standard in the industry. The original set consists of three books, titled *System BIOS for IBM PC/XT/AT Computers and Compatibles*, *CBIOS for IBM PS/2 Computers and Compatibles*, and *ABIOS for IBM PS/2 Computers and Compatibles*; an updated version is called *System BIOS for IBM PCs, Compatibles, and EISA Computers: The Complete Guide to ROM-Based System Software*. In addition to being an excellent reference for the Phoenix BIOS, these books serve as an outstanding overall reference to the BIOS in general. These are out of print but might be available through bookfinder services.

Phoenix has extensive technical support and documentation on its Web site at http://www.phoenix.com, as does its largest nationwide distributor, Micro Firmware, Inc., at http://www.firmware.com, or check the phone numbers listed in the Vendor List on the CD. Micro Firmware offers upgrades to some older systems with a Phoenix BIOS, including many Packard Bell, Gateway (with Micronics motherboards), Micron Technologies, and other systems. For most systems, especially newer ones, you need to get any BIOS updates from the system or motherboard manufacturer.

These companies' products are established as ROM BIOS standards in the industry, and frequent updates and improvements ensure that a system containing these ROMs will have a long life of upgrades and service.

Microid Research (MR) BIOS

Microid Research is an interesting BIOS supplier. It primarily markets upgrade BIOSes for older Pentium and 486 motherboards that were abandoned by their original manufacturers. As such, it is an excellent upgrade for adding new features and performance to an older system. Microid Research BIOS upgrades are sold through eSupport.com (Unicore Software).

Tip

If you support several BIOS types, consider adding Phil Croucher's *The BIOS Companion* to your bookshelf or PDF file collection. This book provides detailed BIOS options and configuration information for today's leading BIOSes. You can purchase various editions from Amazon.com and other bookstores, but for the most up-to-date (and least expensive) edition, I suggest ordering the PDF (Adobe Acrobat) version of *The BIOS Companion - Engineer's Edition* from Electrocution.com.

Upgrading the BIOS

In this section, you learn how ROM BIOS upgrades can improve a system in many ways. You also learn why upgrades can be difficult and can require much more than plugging in a generic set of ROM chips.

The ROM BIOS provides the crude brains that get your computer's components working together. A simple BIOS upgrade can often give your computer better performance and more features.

The BIOS is the reason various operating systems can operate on virtually any PC-compatible system despite hardware differences. Because the BIOS communicates with the hardware, the BIOS must be specific to the hardware and match it completely. As discussed earlier, instead of creating their own BIOSes, many computer makers buy a BIOS from specialists such as American Megatrends, Inc. (AMI), Microid Research, or Phoenix Technologies Ltd. (for Phoenix and AwardBIOS). A motherboard manufacturer that wants to license a BIOS must undergo a lengthy process of working with the BIOS company to tailor the BIOS code to the hardware. This process is what makes upgrading a BIOS somewhat problematic; the BIOS usually resides on ROM chips on the motherboard and is specific to that motherboard model or revision. In other words, you must get your BIOS upgrades from your motherboard manufacturer or from a BIOS upgrade company that supports the motherboard you have, rather than directly from the BIOS developer.

Often, in older systems, you must upgrade the BIOS to take advantage of some other upgrade. To install some of the larger and faster IDE (Integrated Drive Electronics) hard drives and LS-120 (120MB) floppy drives in older machines, for example, you might need a BIOS upgrade. Some of the machines you have might be equipped with older BIOSes that do not support hard drives larger than 8GB, for example.

The following list shows the primary functions of a ROM BIOS upgrade:

- Adding LS-120 (120MB) floppy drive support (also known as a SuperDisk)
- Adding support for hard drives greater than 8GB
- Adding support for Ultra-DMA/33, UDMA/66, or UDMA/100 IDE hard drives
- Adding support for bootable ATAPI CD-ROM drives (called the El Torito specification)
- Adding or improving Plug and Play (PnP) support and compatibility
- Correcting calendar-related and leap-year bugs
- Correcting known bugs or compatibility problems with certain hardware and application or operating system software
- Adding support for newer-type and -speed processors
- Adding support for ACPI power management

If you install newer hardware or software and follow all the instructions properly, but you can't get it to work, specific problems might exist with the BIOS that an upgrade can fix. This is especially true for newer operating systems. Many systems need to have a BIOS update to properly work with the Plug and Play features of Windows 9x, Me, XP, and 2000. Because these problems are random and vary from board to board, it pays to periodically check the board manufacturer's Web site to see whether any updates are posted and what problems they fix.

You can use the BIOS Wizard utility available from eSupport.com (formerly Unicore) to test your BIOS for compatibility with popular BIOS features, such as Zip/LS-120 booting, ACPI power management, PCI IRQ routing, and more. Download it from `http://www.esupport.com/techsupport/award/awardutils.htm`.

Where to Get Your BIOS Update

For most BIOS upgrades, you must contact the motherboard manufacturer by phone or download the upgrade from its Web site. The BIOS manufacturers do not offer BIOS upgrades because the BIOS in your motherboard did not actually come from them. In other words, although you think you have a

Phoenix, AMI, or Award BIOS, you really don't! Instead, you have a custom version of one of these BIOSes, which was licensed by your motherboard manufacturer and uniquely customized for its board. As such, you must get any BIOS upgrades from the motherboard manufacturer because they must be customized for your board as well.

In the case of Phoenix or Award, another option might exist. A company called Unicore specializes in providing Award BIOS upgrades. Unicore might be able to help you out if you can't find your motherboard manufacturer or if it is out of business. Phoenix has a similar deal with Micro Firmware, a company it has licensed to provide various BIOS upgrades. If you have a Phoenix or an Award BIOS and your motherboard manufacturer can't help you, contact one of these companies for a possible solution. Microid Research (sold through Unicore) is another source of BIOS upgrades for a variety of older and otherwise obsolete boards. These upgrades are available for boards that originally came with AMI, Award, or Phoenix BIOSes, and they add new features to older boards that have been abandoned by their original manufacturers. Contact Microid or Unicore for more information.

Determining Your BIOS Version

When seeking a BIOS upgrade for a particular motherboard (or system), you need to know the following information:

- The make and model of the motherboard (or system)
- The version of the existing BIOS
- The type of CPU (for example, Pentium MMX, AMD K6, Cyrix/IBM 6x86MX, MII, Pentium II, Pentium III and later, AMD Athlon, and so on)

You usually can identify the BIOS you have by watching the screen when the system is first powered up. It helps to turn on the monitor first because some take a few seconds to warm up, and often the BIOS information is displayed for only a few seconds.

Note

Many newer PCs now do not display the typical POST screen. Instead, many show a logo for the motherboard or PC manufacturer, which is usually referred to as a *splash screen*. To enter BIOS Setup, you must press a key or keys (specific to the BIOS manufacturer). See the section "Running or Accessing the CMOS Setup Program," later in this chapter, for more information. You might hear some in the industry refer to displaying a manufacturer's logo instead of the default POST screen as a *quiet boot*. Often you can change these BIOS splash screens to your own liking, even including your own company logo or graphic of choice. Intel has free software at `http://developer.intel.com/design/motherbd/gen_indx.htm` that enables you to change or restore the splash screen on Intel motherboards.

Tip

Look for any copyright notices or part number information. Sometimes you can press the Pause key on the keyboard to freeze the POST, allowing you to take your time to write down the information. Pressing any other key then causes the POST to resume.

In addition, you often can find the BIOS ID information in the BIOS Setup screens. eSupport.com/Unicore Software also offers a downloadable BIOS Agent that can be used to determine this information, as well as the motherboard chipset and Super I/O chip used by your motherboard. After you have this information, you should be able to contact the motherboard manufacturer to see whether a new BIOS is available for your system. If you go to the Web site, check to see whether a version exists that is newer than the one you have. If so, you can download it and install it in your system.

Most BIOSes display version information onscreen when the system is first powered up. In some cases, the monitor takes too long to warm up, and you might miss this information because it is displayed for only a few seconds. Try turning on your monitor first, and then your system, which makes this information easier to see. You usually can press the Pause key on the keyboard when the BIOS ID information is being displayed; this freezes it so you can record the information. Pressing any other key allows the system startup to resume.

Part of the PC 2001 standard published by Intel and Microsoft requires something called Fast POST to be supported. Fast POST means that the time it takes from turning on the power until the system starts booting from disk must be 12 seconds or less (for systems not using SCSI as the primary storage connection). This time limit includes the initialization of the keyboard, video card, and ATA bus. For systems containing adapters with onboard ROMs, an additional 4 seconds are allowed per ROM. Intel calls this feature Rapid Bios Boot (RBB), and it is supported in all their motherboards from 2001 and beyond—some of which can begin booting from power-on in as little as 6 seconds.

Backing Up Your BIOS's CMOS Settings

A motherboard BIOS upgrade usually wipes out the BIOS Setup settings in the CMOS RAM. Therefore, you should record these settings, especially the important ones such as hard disk parameters. Some software programs, such as the Norton Utilities, can save and restore CMOS settings, but unfortunately, these types of programs are often useless in a BIOS upgrade situation. This is because sometimes the new BIOS offers new settings or changes the positions of the stored data in the CMOS RAM, which means you don't want to do an exact restore. Also, with the variety of BIOSes available, I have yet to find a CMOS RAM backup and restore program that works on more than just a few specific systems.

You are better off manually recording your BIOS Setup parameters, or possibly connecting a printer to your system and using the Shift+Prtsc (Print Screen) function to print out each of the setup screens. Some shareware programs could print or even save and restore the BIOS Setup settings stored in the CMOS RAM, but these were BIOS version specific and would not work on any other system. Most of these programs were useful during the 286/386 era, but most systems released since—especially those with Plug and Play capabilities—have rendered most of these older programs useless.

Keyboard-Controller Chips

In addition to the main system ROM, older AT-class (286 and later) computers also have a keyboard controller or keyboard ROM, which is a keyboard-controller microprocessor with its own built-in ROM. This often is found in the Super I/O or South Bridge chips on most newer boards. The keyboard controller was originally an Intel 8042 microcontroller, which incorporates a microprocessor, RAM, ROM, and I/O ports. This was a 40-pin chip that often had a copyright notice identifying the BIOS code programmed into the chip. Modern motherboards have this function integrated into the chipset, specifically the Super I/O or South Bridge chips, so you won't see the old 8042 chip anymore.

The keyboard controller controls the reset and A20 lines and also deciphers the keyboard scan codes. The A20 line is used in extended memory and other protected-mode operations. In many systems, one of the unused ports is used to select the CPU clock speed. Because of the tie-in with the keyboard controller and protected-mode operation, many problems with keyboard controllers became evident on these older systems when upgrading from DOS to Windows 95/98, NT, or Windows 2000.

Problems with the keyboard controller were solved in most systems in the early 1990s, so you shouldn't have to deal with this issue in systems newer than that. With older systems, when you upgraded the BIOS in the system, the BIOS vendor often included a new keyboard controller.

Using a Flash BIOS

Virtually all PCs built since 1996 include a flash ROM to store the BIOS. A flash ROM is a type of EEP-ROM chip you can erase and reprogram directly in the system without special equipment. Older

EPROMs required a special ultraviolet light source and an EPROM programmer device to erase and reprogram them, whereas flash ROMs can be erased and rewritten without even removing them from the system.

Using flash ROM enables you to download ROM upgrades from a Web site or to receive them on disk; you then can load the upgrade into the flash ROM chip on the motherboard without removing and replacing the chip. Normally, these upgrades are downloaded from the manufacturer's Web site, and then an included utility is used to create a bootable floppy with the new BIOS image and the update program. It is important to run this procedure from a boot floppy so that no other software or drivers are in the way that might interfere with the update. This method saves time and money for both the system manufacturer and end user.

Sometimes the flash ROM in a system is write-protected, and you must disable the protection before performing an update—usually by means of a jumper or switch that controls the lock on the ROM update. Without the lock, any program that knows the correct instructions can rewrite the ROM in your system—not a comforting thought. Without the write-protection, virus programs could be written that copy themselves directly into the ROM BIOS code in your system. Even without a physical write-protect lock, modern flash ROM BIOSes have a security algorithm that helps prevent unauthorized updates. This is the technique Intel uses on its motherboards.

Note that motherboard manufacturers will not notify you when they upgrade the BIOS for a particular board. You must periodically log in to their Web sites to check for updates. Usually, any flash updates are free.

Before proceeding with a BIOS upgrade, you first must locate and download the updated BIOS from your motherboard manufacturer. Consult the Vendor List on the CD to find the Web site address or other contact information for your motherboard manufacturer. Log in to its Web site, and follow the menus to the BIOS updates page; then select and download the new BIOS for your motherboard.

The BIOS upgrade utility is contained in a self-extracting archive file that can initially be downloaded to your hard drive, but it must be extracted and copied to a floppy before the upgrade can proceed. Different motherboard manufacturers have slightly different procedures and programs to accomplish a flash ROM upgrade, so you should read the directions included with the update. I include instructions here for Intel motherboards because they are by far the most common.

Intel and other typical flash BIOS upgrades fit on a bootable floppy disk. Older Intel and some other flash BIOS upgrades also provide the capability to save and verify the current BIOS version before replacing it with the new version and also provide the capability to install alternative languages for BIOS messages and the BIOS setup utility.

The first step in the upgrade after downloading the new BIOS file is to enter the CMOS Setup and write down your existing CMOS settings because they will be erased during the upgrade. Then, you create a DOS boot floppy and uncompress or extract the BIOS upgrade files to the floppy from the file you downloaded. Next, you reboot on the newly created upgrade disk and follow the menus for the actual reflash procedure.

The iFlash procedure covered in this section is similar to the BIOS update process used by most non-Intel motherboards and must be used for systems running Windows 95, MS-DOS, or non-Windows operating systems such as Linux. Intel's Express BIOS update (for Windows 98, Windows NT 4, and current Windows versions) uses the InstallShield loader program familiar to Windows users to install BIOS upgrades within the Windows GUI. Here is a step-by-step procedure for the process using Intel's iFlash (DOS-based) BIOS update:

1. Save your CMOS RAM setup configuration. You can do so by pressing the appropriate key during boot to start the BIOS setup program (usually F1 with an AMI BIOS and F2 with a Phoenix BIOS) and writing down all your current CMOS settings. You also might be able to print the

screens if you have a printer connected, using the PrtScr key on the keyboard. You must reset these settings after you have upgraded to the latest BIOS. Write down all settings that are unique to the system. These settings will be needed later to reconfigure the system. Pay special attention to any hard drive settings for geometry (Cylinder/Head/Sectors per track) and translation (LBA, Large, CHS); these are very important. If you fail to restore these properly, you might not be able to boot from the drive or access the data on it.

2. Exit the BIOS Setup and restart the system. Allow the system to fully start Windows and bring up a DOS prompt window or boot directly to a DOS prompt via the Windows Start menu (for example, press F8 when you see Starting Windows, and select Command Prompt).

3. Place a formatted blank floppy disk in the A: floppy drive. If the disk contains data, format the floppy using the normal format command:

```
C:\>FORMAT A:
```

You also can use Windows Explorer to format the floppy disk.

4. The file you originally downloaded from the Intel Web site is a self-extracting compressed archive that includes other files that need to be extracted. Put the file in a temporary directory, and then from within this directory, double-click the BIOS file you downloaded or type the file-name of the file and press Enter. This causes the file to self-extract. For example, if the file you downloaded is called CB-P06.EXE (for the Intel D810E2CB motherboard), you would enter the following command:

```
C:\TEMP>CB-P06 <enter>
```

5. The extracted files are stored in the same temporary folder as the downloaded BIOS. Recent Intel flash BIOS upgrades contain the following files: Desc.txt, License.txt, Readme.txt, Run.bat (which is run to create the bootable floppy), and SW.EXE (which contains the BIOS code).

6. To create the bootable floppy disk, open Run.bat, which extracts files from SW.EXEs and transfer the necessary files to the blank disk in Drive A:.

7. Now you can restart the system with the bootable floppy in drive A: containing the new BIOS files you just extracted. Upon booting from this disk, the iFLASH program automatically starts and updates the BIOS boot block and the main BIOS area.

8. When you're told that the BIOS has been successfully loaded, remove the bootable floppy from the drive and press Enter to reboot the system.

9. Press F1 or F2 to enter Setup. On the first screen within Setup, check the BIOS version to ensure that it is the new version.

10. In Setup, load the default values. If you have an AMI BIOS, press the F5 key. With a Phoenix BIOS, go to the Exit submenu and highlight Load Setup Defaults, and then press Enter.

Caution

If you do not set the values back to default, the system might function erratically.

11. If the system had unique settings, reenter those settings now. Press F10 to save the values, exit Setup, and restart the system. Your system should now be fully functional with the new BIOS.

Note

If you encounter a CMOS checksum error or other problems after rebooting, try rebooting the system again. CMOS checksum errors require that you enter Setup, check and save your settings, and exit Setup a second time.

Note

The procedure for older Intel BIOS upgrades differs from that described previously. If your BIOS upgrade contains the **BIOS.EXE** program, see the BIOS upgrade description contained in *Upgrading and Repairing PCs, 12th Edition*, included in electronic form on the CD-ROM packaged with this book.

Flash BIOS Recovery

When you performed the flash reprogramming, you should have seen a warning message onscreen similar to the following:

```
The BIOS is currently being updated. DO NOT REBOOT OR POWER DOWN until the update
➥is completed (typically within three minutes)...
```

If you fail to heed this warning or something interrupts the update procedure, you will be left with a system that has a corrupted BIOS. This means you will not be able to restart the system and redo the procedure, at least not easily. Depending on the motherboard, you might have to replace the flash ROM chip with one that was preprogrammed by the motherboard manufacturer. This is an unfortunate necessity because your board will be nonfunctional until a noncorrupted ROM is present. This is why I still keep my trusty ROM burner around; it is very useful for those motherboards with socketed flash ROM chips. In minutes, I can use the ROM burner to reprogram the chip and reinstall it in the board. If you need a ROM programmer, I recommend Andromeda Research (see the Vendor List on the CD).

In many of the latest systems, the flash ROM is soldered into the motherboard so it can't be replaced, rendering the reprogramming idea moot. However, this doesn't mean the only way out is a complete motherboard replacement. Most motherboards with soldered-in flash ROMs have a special BIOS Recovery procedure that can be performed. This hinges on a special nonerasable part of the flash ROM that is reserved for this purpose.

In the unlikely event that a flash upgrade is interrupted catastrophically, the BIOS might be left in an unusable state. Recovering from this condition requires the following steps. A minimum of a power supply, a speaker, and a floppy drive configured as drive A: should be attached to the motherboard for this procedure to work:

1. Change the Flash Recovery jumper to the recovery mode position. Virtually all Intel motherboards and many third-party motherboards have a jumper or switch for BIOS recovery, which in most cases is labeled "Recover/Normal." Figure 5.6 shows this jumper on the Intel SE440BX, a typical motherboard.

2. Install the bootable BIOS upgrade disk you previously created to do the flash upgrade into drive A: and reboot the system.

   Because of the small amount of code available in the nonerasable flash boot block area, no video prompts are available to direct the procedure. So, you will see nothing onscreen. In fact, it is not even necessary for a video card to be connected for this procedure to work. The procedure can be monitored by listening to the speaker and looking at the floppy drive LED. When the system beeps and the floppy drive LED is lit, the system is copying the BIOS recovery code into the flash device.

3. As soon as the drive LED goes off and the system beeps (normally twice), the recovery should be complete. Sometimes there might be pauses where the drive stops reading during the recovery process; however, the process might not be complete. Be sure to wait for a minute or so to ensure a complete recovery before turning off the system. When you are sure the recovery is complete and there is no further activity, power off the system.

4. Change the flash recovery jumper back to the default position for normal operation.

Figure 5.6   Typical Intel motherboard BIOS recovery jumper.

When you power the system back on, the new BIOS should be installed and functional. However, you might want to leave the BIOS upgrade floppy in drive A: and check to see that the proper BIOS version was installed.

Note

Note that this BIOS recovery procedure is often the fastest way to update a large number of machines, especially if you are performing other upgrades at the same time. This is how it is normally done in a system assembly or production environment.

Using IML System Partition BIOS

IBM and Compaq used a scheme similar to a flash ROM, called Initial Microcode Load (IML), in some of their older Pentium and 486 systems. IML is a technique in which the BIOS code is installed on the hard disk in a special hidden-system partition and is loaded every time the system is powered up. Of course, the system still has a core BIOS on the motherboard, but all that BIOS does is locate and load updated BIOS code from the system partition. This technique enabled Compaq and IBM to distribute ROM updates on disk for installation in the system partition. The IML BIOS is loaded every time the system is reset or powered on.

Along with the system BIOS code, the system partition contains a complete copy of the Setup and Diagnostics or Reference Disk, which provides the option of running the setup and system-configuration software at any time during a reboot operation. This option eliminates the need to boot from this disk to reconfigure the system and gives the impression that the entire Setup and Diagnostics or Reference Disk is contained in ROM.

One drawback to this technique is that the BIOS code is installed on the hard disk; the system can't function properly without the correctly set-up hard disk connected. You always can boot from the

Reference Disk floppy should the hard disk fail or become disconnected, but you can't boot from a standard floppy disk.

Caution

This scheme makes hard drive updates problematic and causes all kinds of support nightmares. I recommend avoiding any system with an IML BIOS, especially if you are buying it used, because support for these types of configurations is hard to come by and not many people know how to deal with them.

Motherboard CMOS RAM Addresses

In the original IBM AT system, a Motorola 146818 chip was used as the RTC (real-time clock) and CMOS (complementary metal-oxide semiconductor) RAM chip. This special chip had a simple digital clock that used 10 bytes of RAM and an additional 54 more bytes of leftover RAM in which you could store anything you wanted. The designers of the IBM AT used these extra 54 bytes to store the system configuration.

Modern PC systems don't use the Motorola chip; instead, they incorporate the functions of this chip into the motherboard chipset (South Bridge) or Super I/O chip, or they use a special battery and NVRAM (nonvolatile RAM) module from companies such as Dallas or Benchmarq.

Table 5.6 shows the standard format of the information stored in the 64-byte standard CMOS RAM module. This information controls the configuration of the system and is read and written by the system setup program.

Table 5.6   CMOS RAM Addresses

Offset (hex)	Offset (dec)	Field Size	Function
00h	0	1 byte	Current second in BCD (00–59)
01h	1	1 byte	Alarm second in BCD
02h	2	1 byte	Current minute in BCD (00–59)
03h	3	1 byte	Alarm minute in BCD
04h	4	1 byte	Current hour in BCD (00–23)
05h	5	1 byte	Alarm hour in BCD
06h	6	1 byte	Current day of week in BCD (00–06)
07h	7	1 byte	Current day of month in BCD (00–31)
08h	8	1 byte	Current month in BCD (00–12)
09h	9	1 byte	Current year in BCD (00–99)
0Ah	10	1 byte	Status register A
0Bh	11	1 byte	Status register B
0Ch	12	1 byte	Status register C
0Dh	13	1 byte	Status register D
0Eh	14	1 byte	Diagnostic status
0Fh	15	1 byte	Shutdown code
10h	16	1 byte	Floppy drive types
11h	17	1 byte	Advanced BIOS Setup options
12h	18	1 byte	Hard disk 0/1 types (0–15)

Table 5.6   Continued

Offset (hex)	Offset (dec)	Field Size	Function
13h	19	1 byte	Keyboard typematic rate and delay
14h	20	1 byte	Installed equipment
15h	21	1 byte	Base memory in 1K multiples, LSB
16h	22	1 byte	Base memory in 1K multiples, MSB
17h	23	1 byte	Extended memory in 1K multiples, LSB
18h	24	1 byte	Extended memory in 1K multiples, MSB
19h	25	1 byte	Hard Disk 0 Extended Type (0–255)
1Ah	26	1 byte	Hard Disk 1 Extended Type (0–255)
1Bh	27	8 bytes	Hard Disk 0 user-defined type information
24h	36	8 bytes	Hard Disk 1 user-defined type information
2Dh	45	1 byte	Advanced BIOS Setup options
2Eh	46	1 byte	CMOS checksum MSB
2Fh	47	1 byte	CMOS checksum LSB
30h	48	1 byte	POST reported extended memory LSB
31h	49	1 byte	POST reported extended memory MSB
32h	50	1 byte	Date century in BCD (00–99)
33h	51	1 byte	POST information flag
34h	52	2 bytes	Advanced BIOS Setup options
36h	54	1 byte	Chipset-specific BIOS Setup options
37h	55	7 bytes	Power-On Password (usually encrypted)
3Eh	62	1 byte	Extended CMOS checksum MSB
3Fh	63	1 byte	Extended CMOS checksum LSB

BCD = Binary-coded decimal
LSB = Least significant byte
MSB = Most significant byte
POST = Power on self test

Note that many newer systems have extended CMOS RAM with 2KB, 4KB, or more. The extra room is used to store the Plug and Play information detailing the configuration of adapter cards and other options in the system. As such, no 100% compatible standard exists for how CMOS information is stored in all systems. You should consult the BIOS manufacturer for more information if you want the full details of how CMOS is stored because the CMOS configuration and Setup program typically are part of the BIOS. This is another example of how close the relationship is between the BIOS and the motherboard hardware.

Backup programs and utilities are available in the public domain for CMOS RAM information, which can be useful for saving and later restoring a configuration. Unfortunately, these programs are BIOS specific and function only on a BIOS for which they are designed. As such, I don't normally rely on these programs because they are too motherboard and BIOS specific and will not work on all my systems seamlessly.

Table 5.7 shows the values that might be stored by your system BIOS in a special CMOS byte called the diagnostics status byte. By examining this location with a diagnostics program, you can determine whether your system has set trouble codes, which indicate that a problem previously has occurred.

Table 5.7   CMOS RAM Diagnostic Status Byte Codes

Bit Number 7	6	5	4	3	2	1	0	Hex	Function
1	•	•	•	•	•	•	•	80	Real-time clock (RTC) chip lost power.
•	1	•	•	•	•	•	•	40	CMOS RAM checksum is bad.
•	•	1	•	•	•	•	•	20	Invalid configuration information found at POST.
•	•	•	1	•	•	•	•	10	Memory size compare error at POST.
•	•	•	•	1	•	•	•	08	Fixed disk or adapter failed initialization.
•	•	•	•	•	1	•	•	04	Real-time clock (RTC) time found invalid.
•	•	•	•	•	•	1	•	02	Adapters do not match configuration.
•	•	•	•	•	•	•	1	01	Time-out reading an adapter ID.
•	•	•	•	•	•	•	•	00	No errors found (Normal).

If the diagnostic status byte is any value other than 0, you typically get a CMOS configuration error on bootup. These types of errors can be cleared by rerunning the setup program.

Replacing a BIOS ROM

Systems dating from 1995 or earlier usually don't have a flash ROM and instead use an EPROM. To upgrade the BIOS in one of these systems, you replace the EPROM chip with a new one preloaded with the new BIOS. As with a flash ROM upgrade, you must get this from your motherboard manufacturer. There is usually a fee for this because the manufacturer must custom-burn a chip just for you and mail it out. Most boards older than 1995 are probably not worth upgrading the BIOS on, so weigh this option carefully! It doesn't make sense to spend $50 on a new BIOS for an ancient board when a new Pentium or Pentium II board can be had for $75, and that new board will include a flash BIOS and many other new features.

The procedure for replacing the BIOS chip is also useful if you have made a backup copy of your socketed system BIOS chip and need to replace a damaged original with the backup copy.

To replace the BIOS chip, follow these steps:

1. Back up the CMOS RAM settings.
2. Power down the system and unplug the power cord.
3. Remove the cover and any other components in the way of the BIOS EPROM chip. Remember to use caution with respect to static discharges; you should wear an antistatic wrist strap for this procedure or ground yourself to the chassis before touching any internal components.
4. Using a chip puller or a thin flat-blade screwdriver, gently pry the chip out of its socket.
5. Remove the new EPROM from the antistatic packing material in which it came.
6. Install the new EPROM chip into the socket.
7. Reinstall anything you removed to gain access to the chip.
8. Put the cover back on, plug in the system, and power on.
9. Enter the BIOS setup information you saved earlier.
10. Reboot and enjoy the new BIOS!

As you can see, things are much easier with a modern motherboard with a flash ROM because you usually don't even have to remove the lid.

CMOS Setting Specifications

The CMOS RAM must be configured with information about your system's drives and user-selected options before you can use your computer. The Setup program provided with your system is used to select the options you want to use to start your computer.

Running or Accessing the CMOS Setup Program

If you want to run the BIOS Setup program, you usually have to reboot and press a particular key or key combination during the POST. The major vendors have standardized the following keystrokes to enter the BIOS Setup:

- *AMI BIOS.* Press Delete during POST.
- *Phoenix BIOS.* Press F2 during POST.
- *Award BIOS.* Press Delete or Ctrl+Alt+Esc during POST.
- *Microid Research BIOS.* Press Esc during POST.

If your system will not respond to one of these common keystroke settings, you might have to contact the manufacturer or read the system documentation to find the correct keystrokes.

Some unique ones are as follows:

- *IBM Aptiva/Valuepoint.* Press F1 during POST.
- *Older Phoenix BIOS.* Boot to a safe mode DOS command prompt, and then press Ctrl+Alt+Esc or Ctrl+Alt+S.
- *Compaq.* Press F10 during POST.

After you are at the BIOS Setup main screen, you'll usually find a main menu allowing access to other menus and submenus of different sections or screens. Using the Intel DB815EEA motherboard as an example (one of Intel's newer motherboards), let's go through all the menus and submenus of this typical motherboard. Although other motherboards might feature slightly different settings, most are very similar.

BIOS Setup Menus

Most modern BIOSes offer a menu bar at the top of the screen when you're in the BIOS Setup that controls navigation through the various primary menus. A typical menu bar offers the choices shown in Table 5.8.

Note

Because most common BIOSes use similar settings, I've chosen the Setup used by modern Intel motherboards to use as an example in the following tables. Because the BIOS is customized by the motherboard manufacturer, even the same BIOS might offer different options for different boards. The settings covered here will help you get a general idea of the type of settings to expect and how the BIOS Setup settings affect your computer.

Table 5.8   Typical BIOS Setup Menus*

Setup Menu Screen	Description
Maintenance	Specifies the processor speed and clears the setup passwords. This menu is available only in Configure mode, set by a jumper on the board.
Main	Allocates resources for hardware components.

Table 5.8   Continued

Setup Menu Screen	Description
Advanced	Specifies advanced features available through the chipset.
Security	Specifies passwords and security features.
Power	Specifies power management features.
Boot	Specifies boot options and power supply controls.
Exit	Saves or discards changes to the setup program options.

*Based on the BIOS used by the Intel DB815EEA motherboard. Used by permission of Intel Corporation.

Choosing each of these selections takes you to another menu with more choices. The following sections examine all the choices available in a typical motherboard, such as the Intel DB815EEA.

Maintenance Menu

The Maintenance menu is a special menu for setting the processor speed and clearing the setup passwords. Older motherboards used jumpers to configure the processor bus speed (motherboard speed) and processor multiplier. Most newer boards from Intel and others now offer this control via the BIOS Setup rather than moving jumpers. In the case of Intel, one jumper still remains on the board called the configuration jumper, which must be set to Configure mode for the Maintenance menu to be available.

Setup displays this menu only if the system is set in Configure mode. To set Configure mode, power off the system and move the configuration jumper on the motherboard from *Normal* to *Configure* (see Figure 5.6, earlier in this chapter). Because this is the only jumper on a modern Intel board, it is pretty easy to find. When the system is powered back on, the BIOS Setup automatically runs, and you will be able to select the Maintenance menu shown in Table 5.9. After making changes and saving, power off the system and reset the jumper to Normal mode for normal operation.

Table 5.9   Typical Maintenance Menu Settings*

Feature	Options	Description
Processor Speed	MHz	Specifies the processor speed in megahertz. This setup screen shows only speeds up to and including the maximum speed of the processor installed on the motherboard.
Clear All Passwords	No options	Clears the user and supervisor passwords.
Clear BiS	No options	Clears the Wired for Management Boot Integrity Service (BiS) credentials.
Extended Configuration	User-defined options	Displays Extended Configuration Submenu.
CPU Information	No options	Displays CPU information.
CPU Microcode Update Revision	No options	Displays CPU's microcode update revision.
CPU Stepping Signature	No options	Displays CPU's stepping revision.

*Based on the BIOS used by the Intel DB815EEA motherboard. Used by permission of Intel Corporation.

Note that most newer Intel processors are designed to allow operation only at or below their rated speeds (a feature called *speed locking*), whereas others allow higher-than-rated speeds to be selected.

If a user forgets his password, all he has to do is set the configuration jumper, enter the Maintenance menu in BIOS Setup, and use the option provided to clear the password. This function doesn't tell the user what the password was; it simply clears it, allowing a new one to be set if desired. This means the security is only as good as the lock on the system case because anybody who can get to the configuration jumper can clear the password and access the system. This is why most better cases come equipped with locks.

Extended Configuration Submenu

The Extended Configuration submenu on some Intel motherboards has memory setup options similar to those found in the section "Additional Advanced Features," later in this chapter. See this section for details.

Main Menu

The standard CMOS Setup menu dates back to the 286 days, when the complete BIOS Setup consisted of only one menu. In the standard menu, you can set the system clock and record hard disk and floppy drive parameters and the basic video type. Newer BIOSes have more complicated setups with more menus and submenus, so the main menu often is fairly sparse compared to older systems.

The main menu in a modern system reports system information such as the BIOS version, the processor type and speed, the amount of memory, and whether the memory or cache is configured for ECC functionality. The main menu also can be used to set the system date and time.

Table 5.10 shows a typical main menu.

Table 5.10   Typical Main Menu Settings*

Feature	Options	Description
BIOS Version	No options	Displays the version of the BIOS
Processor Type	No options	Displays the processor type
Processor Speed	No options	Displays the processor speed
System Bus Frequency	No options	Displays the system bus frequency
Cache RAM	No options	Displays the size of second-level (L2) cache and whether it is ECC capable
Total Memory	No options	Displays the total amount of RAM on the motherboard
Memory Bank 0 Memory Bank 1 Memory Bank 2	No options	Displays size and type of DIMM installed in each memory bank
Language	English (default) Deutch Espanol	Selects the default language used by the BIOS
Processor Serial Number	Disabled (default), enabled	Enables/disables processor serial number (present only when a Pentium III CPU is installed)
System Time	Hour, minute, second	Specifies the current time
System Date	Month, day, year	Specifies the current date

Based on the BIOS used by the Intel D815EEA motherboard. Used by permission of Intel Corporation.

Some motherboards might also offer the options shown in Table 5.11.

Table 5.11   Additional Main Menu Memory Settings

Feature	Options	Description
ECC Configuration	Non-ECC (default) ECC	Specifies ECC memory operation.
L2 cache ECC Support	Disabled (default) Enabled	Enabled allows error checking to occur on data accessed from L2 cache. This option does not appear when using processors that have L2 cache ECC permanently enabled.

ECC stands for error correcting code, which is the use of extra bits on the memory modules to detect and even correct memory errors on-the-fly. For ECC to be enabled, more expensive ECC DIMMs would have to be installed in the system. Note that all DIMMs would need to be ECC versions for this to work; if only one is non-ECC, ECC can't be enabled. I highly recommend purchasing ECC memory and enabling this function because it makes the system much more fault tolerant and prevents corrupted data due to soft errors in memory. Random memory errors occur at the rate of 1 bit error per month for every 64–256 megabytes installed. ECC ensures that these errors don't creep into your data files, corrupt the system, or cause it to crash.

▶▶   See "Error Correcting Code," p. 449.

Be sure to check and see whether your motherboard supports ECC memory before making a purchase. You can install ECC memory in a non-ECC capable board, but the ECC functions will not work. Also make sure you are aware of the memory requirements for your board. Don't try to install more memory than the board supports, and be sure the modules you use meet the specifications required by the board. See the documentation for the motherboard for more information on the type and amount of memory that can be installed.

Most older BIOSes report memory as base and extended memory instead of as a single value. Base memory is typically 640KB and sometimes is called *conventional* memory. Extended memory is that which is beyond the first megabyte in the system.

You can't change any values in the memory fields; they are only for your information because they are automatically counted up by the system. If the memory count doesn't match what you have installed, a problem has likely occurred with some of the memory: It is defective, not fully seated or properly installed, or it is a type that is incompatible with your system.

Advanced Menu

The Advanced menu is for setting advanced features that are available through the motherboard chipset. This part of your BIOS setup is specific to the particular chipset the motherboard uses. Many chipsets are available on the market today, and each has unique features. The chipset setup is designed to enable the user to customize these features and control some of the chipset settings. Right now, one of the most popular chipsets is the Intel 815E chipset. Table 5.12 shows the typical BIOS chipset settings for a board with a 815E chipset.

Table 5.12   Typical Advanced Menu Settings*

Feature	Options	Description
Extended Configuration	No options	If Used is displayed, User-defined has been selected in the Extended Configuration under the Maintenance menu.
PCI Configuration	No options	Configures the IRQ priority of individual PCI slots. When selected, displays the PCI Configuration submenu.

Table 5.12   Continued

Feature	Options	Description
Boot Settings Configuration	No options	Configures Numlock and Plug and Play, and resets configuration data. When selected, displays the Boot Configuration submenu.
Peripheral Configuration	No options	Configures peripheral ports and devices. When selected, displays the Peripheral Configuration submenu.
IDE Configuration	No options	Specifies type of connected IDE device.
Diskette Configuration	No options	When selected, displays the Diskette Configuration submenu.
Event Log	No options	Configures Event Logging. When selected, displays the Event Log Configuration submenu.
Video Configuration	No options	Configures video features. When selected, displays the Video Configuration submenu.

Based on the BIOS used by the Intel DB815EEA motherboard. Used by permission of Intel Corporation.

Motherboards based on the 440BX chipset also offer options such as those listed in Table 5.13.

Table 5.13   Additional Advanced Menu Settings*

Feature	Options	Description
Plug and Play O/S	No (default), Yes	Specifies whether a Plug and Play operating system is being used. No—lets the BIOS configure all devices. Yes—lets the operating system configure Plug and Play devices. Not required with a Plug and Play operating system.
Reset Configuration Data	No (default), Yes	Clears the Plug and Play BIOS configuration data on the next boot.
Numlock	Auto (default), On, Off	Specifies the power-on state of the Num Lock feature on the numeric keypad of the keyboard.
Resource Configuration	No options	Configures memory blocks and IRQs for legacy ISA devices. When selected, displays the Resource Configuration submenu.

Based on the BIOS used by the Intel SE440BX-2 motherboard. Used by permission of Intel Corporation.

The Plug and Play OS setting is important mainly if you are not using a plug-and-play operating system, such as Windows NT. In that case, you should set that function to No, which enables the Plug and Play BIOS to configure the devices.

Even if this function were set to No, if a plug-and-play operating system, such as Windows 95/98 or Windows 2000, were used, the operating system would override and reconfigure any settings configured by the BIOS. To speed system boot time, if a plug-and-play operating system is being used, you can set this function to Yes, which eliminates the BIOS configuration step.

The Reset Configuration Data setting is a one-time setting that causes the ESCD (enhanced system configuration data) plug-and-play data stored in CMOS RAM to be wiped out at the next boot time. The setting defaults back to No after the next boot. This is useful if the settings in CMOS don't match those stored in the cards themselves, which can happen, for example, if a previously configured card is moved from one system to another or even from one slot to another in the same system. This can cause the Plug and Play BIOS to become confused; resetting the plug-and-play data in CMOS helps clear up this type of problem.

PCI Configuration Submenu

The PCI Configuration submenu is used to select the IRQ priority of add-on cards plugged into the PCI slots. Auto (the default) should be used to allow the BIOS and operating system to assign IRQs to each slot unless specific PCI cards require unique IRQs. See Table 5.14 for a typical example.

Table 5.14   Typical PCI Configuration Submenu Settings*

Feature	Options	Description
PCI Slot 1 IRQ Priority	Auto (default), 9, 10, 11	Allows selection of IRQ priority.
PCI Slot 2 IRQ Priority	Auto (default), 9, 10, 11	Allows selection of IRQ priority.
PCI Slot 3 IRQ Priority	Auto (default), 9, 10, 11	Allows selection of IRQ priority. IRQ priority selections for PCI slot 3 and PCI slot 5 are linked; the options selected for PCI slot 3 are repeated for PCI slot 5.
PCI Slot 4 IRQ Priority	Auto (default), 9, 10, 11	Allows selection of IRQ priority.
PCI Slot 5 IRQ Priority	No options	Always set to Auto (matches settings for PC slot #3).

Based on the BIOS used by the Intel DB815EEA motherboard. Used by permission of Intel Corporation.

Boot Configuration Submenu

The options in Table 5.15 configure the system's PnP and keyboard configuration during initial boot.

Table 5.15   Typical Boot Configuration Submenu Settings*

Feature	Options	Description
Plug and Play O/S	No (default), Yes	Specifies whether a plug-and-play operating system is being used. No—Lets the BIOS configure all devices.
		Appropriate when using a PnP operating system.
		Yes—Lets the operating system configure Plug and Play devices.
Reset Config Data	No (default), Yes	Yes clears the PnP/PCI BIOS configuration data stored in flash memory on the next boot.
Numlock	On (default), Off	Specifies the power-on state of the Num Lock feature on the numeric keypad of the keyboard.

Based on the BIOS used by the Intel DB815EEA motherboard. Used by permission of Intel Corporation.

Additional Advanced Features

Many boards differ in the advanced chipset menus. In most cases, unless you know exactly which chipset and what type of memory and other items are found in your system, it is best to leave these settings on Auto. In that case, the modern boards use the configuration ROM found on the DIMM or RIMM memory modules to properly configure the memory settings. In fact, many newer boards no longer allow these settings to be manually adjusted because, in most cases, all that does is lead to trouble in the form of an unstable or a failing system. If you do want to play with these settings, I recommend first finding out exactly which memory modules and chipset you have and contacting the manufacturers of them to get their databooks. The databooks have all the technical information related to those devices.

Table 5.16 lists some additional settings you might find on some boards. Options found on the Intel DB815EEA motherboard's Extended Configuration submenu are marked with an * in Table 5.16.

Table 5.16   Additional Advanced Features Settings

Setting	Description
Auto Configuration*	Selects predetermined optimal values of chipset parameters. When Disabled, chipset parameters revert to setup information stored in CMOS. Many fields in this screen are not available when Auto Configuration is Enabled.
EDO DRAM Speed Selection	The value in this field must correspond to the speed of the EDO DRAM installed in your system. This value is access speed, so a lower value means a faster system.
SDRAM RAS-to-CAS Delay*	This field lets you control the number of cycles between a row activate command and a read or write command.
SDRAM RAS Precharge Time*	The precharge time is the number of cycles it takes for the RAS to accumulate its charge before DRAM refresh. If insufficient time is allowed, refresh might be incomplete, and the DRAM might fail to retain data.
SDRAM CAS Latency Time*	When synchronous DRAM is installed, you can control the number of cycles between when the SDRAMs sample a read command and when the controller samples read data from the SDRAMs.
SDRAM Precharge Control	When Enabled, all CPU cycles to SDRAM result in an All Banks Precharge command on the SDRAM interface.
DRAM Data Integrity Mode	Select Non-ECC or ECC (error correcting code) according to the type of installed DRAM. ECC allows for single-bit error correction and multibit error detection at a slight speed penalty to the system.
System BIOS Cacheable	Allows caching of the system BIOS ROM at F0000h–FFFFFh, resulting in better system performance. If any program writes to this memory area, a system error can result.
Video BIOS Cacheable	Allows caching of the video BIOS ROM at C0000h–C7FFFh, resulting in better video performance. If any program writes to this memory area, a system error can result.
Video RAM Cacheable* (Video Memory Cache Mode)	Selecting Enabled allows caching of the video memory (RAM) at A0000h–AFFFFh, resulting in better video performance. If any program writes to this memory area, a memory access error can result. Uncacheable Speculative Write-Combining (USWC) mode is the same as Enabled on some systems.
8/16 Bit I/O Recovery Time	The I/O recovery mechanism adds bus clock cycles between PCI-originated I/O cycles to the ISA bus. This delay takes place because the PCI bus is so much faster than the ISA bus.
Memory Hole at 15M–16M	Places a 1MB empty RAM area between 15MB and 16MB. Older software sometimes would not run with 16MB or more memory in the system; enabling this provides a workaround. This is normally not used.
Passive Release	When Enabled, CPU-to-PCI bus accesses are allowed during passive release. Otherwise, the arbiter accepts only another PCI master access to local DRAM.
Delayed Transaction	The chipset has an embedded 32-bit posted write buffer to support delay transactions cycles. Select Enabled to support compliance with PCI specification version 2.1.
AGP Aperture Size (MB)	Select the size of the accelerated graphics port (AGP) aperture. The aperture is a portion of the PCI memory address range dedicated for graphics memory address space. Host cycles that hit the aperture range are forwarded to the AGP without any translation.

Table 5.16   Continued

Setting	Description
CPU Warning Temperature	Select the combination of lower and upper limits for the CPU temperature if your computer contains an environmental monitoring system. If the CPU temperature extends beyond either limit, any warning mechanism programmed into your system is activated.
Current CPU Temperature	This field displays the current CPU temperature if your computer contains an environmental monitoring system.
Shutdown Temperature	Select the combination of lower and upper limits for the system shutdown temperature if your computer contains an environmental monitoring system. If the temperature extends beyond either limit, the system shuts down.
CPUFAN Turn On IN Win98	If you are running Windows 98, which supports ACPI, selecting Enabled gives the user a cooling choice at runtime. The user can run with the CPU fan turned on or off, depending on deciding factors such as CPU activity, battery power consumption, and noise tolerance.
Current System Temperature	This field displays the current system temperature if your computer contains a monitoring system.
Current CPUFAN 1/2/3 Speed	These fields display the current speed of up to three CPU fans if your computer contains a monitoring system.
IN0-IN6(V)	These fields display the current voltage of up to seven voltage input lines if your computer contains a monitoring system.
Spread Spectrum	When the system clock generator pulses, the extreme values of the pulse generate excess EMI. Enabling pulse spectrum spread modulation changes the extreme values from spikes to flat curves, thus reducing EMI. This benefit in some cases might be outweighed by problems with timing-critical devices, such as a clock-sensitive SCSI device.

Peripheral Configuration

The Peripheral Configuration menu is used to configure the devices built into the motherboard, such as serial ports, parallel ports, and built-in audio and USB ports.

Table 5.17 shows a typical Peripheral Configuration menu and choices.

Table 5.17   Typical Peripheral Configuration Menu*

Feature	Options	Description
Serial port A	Disabled Enabled Auto (default)	Configures serial port A. Auto-assigns the first free COM port (normally COM 1), the address 3F8h, and the interrupt IRQ4. An asterisk (*) displayed next to an address indicates a conflict with another device.
Base I/O address	3F8 (default) 2F8 3E8 2E8	Specifies the base I/O address for serial port A.
Interrupt	IRQ 3 IRQ 4 (default)	Specifies the interrupt for serial port A.

Table 5.17   Continued

Feature	Options	Description
Serial port B	Disabled Enabled Auto (default)	Configures serial port B. Auto-assigns the first free COM port (normally COM 2), the address 2F8h, and the interrupt IRQ3. An asterisk (*) displayed next to an address indicates a conflict with another device. If either serial port address is set, that address will not appear in the list of options for the other serial port.
Mode	Normal (default) IrDA-SIR ASK_IR	Specifies the mode for serial port B for normal (COM 2) or infrared applications.
Base I/O address	2F8 (default) 3E8 2E8	Specifies the base I/O address for serial port B.
Interrupt	IRQ 3 (default) IRQ 4	Specifies the interrupt for serial port B.
Parallel port	Disabled Enabled Auto (default)	Configures the parallel port. Auto-assigns LPT1 the address 378h and the interrupt IRQ7. An asterisk (*) displayed next to an address indicates a conflict with another device.
Mode	Output Only Bidirectional (default) EPP, ECP	Selects the mode for the parallel port. Output Only operates in AT-compatible mode. Bidirectional operates in bidirectional PS/2-compatible mode. EPP is Extended Parallel Port mode, a high-speed bidirectional mode. ECP is Enhanced Capabilities Port mode, a high-speed bidirectional mode. (EPP and ECP are IEEE-1284–compliant modes and require the use of an IEEE-1284–compliant printer cable.)
Base I/O address	378 (default) 278	Specifies the base I/O address for the parallel port.
Interrupt	IRQ 5 IRQ 7 (default)	Specifies the interrupt for the parallel port.
DMA Channel	DMA 1 DMA 3 (default)	Specifies DMA channel for parallel port (available only when ECP mode is selected).
Audio	Disabled Enabled (default)	Enables or disables the onboard audio subsystem.
LAN	Disabled Enabled (default)	Enables or disables the onboard LAN (network card) device.
Legacy USB Support	Disabled Enabled Auto (default)	Enables or disables USB legacy support. USB legacy support enables support for USB keyboards and mice even though no operating system drivers have been loaded.

Based on the BIOS used by the Intel DB815EEA motherboard. Used by permission of Intel Corporation.

I recommend disabling serial and parallel ports if they are not being used because this frees up those resources (especially interrupts that are in high demand) for other devices.

Legacy USB support means support for USB keyboards and mice. If you are using USB keyboards and mice, you will find that the keyboard is not functional until a USB-aware operating system is loaded. This can be a problem when running DOS, diagnostics software, or other applications that run outside of USB-aware operating systems, such as Windows 98, Windows Me, Windows XP, and Windows 2000. In that case, you should enable the USB legacy support via this menu.

Even with legacy support disabled, the system still recognizes a USB keyboard and enables it to work during the POST and BIOS Setup. With USB legacy support in the default (disabled) mode, the system operates as follows:

1. When you power up the computer, USB legacy support is disabled.

2. POST begins.

3. USB legacy support is temporarily enabled by the BIOS. This enables you to use a USB keyboard to enter the setup program or the Maintenance mode.

4. POST completes and disables USB legacy support (unless it was set to Enabled while in Setup).

5. The operating system loads. While the operating system is loading, USB keyboards and mice are not recognized. After the operating system loads the USB drivers, the USB devices are recognized.

To install an operating system that supports USB, enable USB legacy support in BIOS Setup and follow the operating system's installation instructions. After the operating system is installed and the USB drivers are configured, USB legacy support is no longer used, and the operating system USB drivers take over. However, I recommend that you leave legacy support enabled so the USB keyboard functions in DOS while running self-booting or DOS-based diagnostics, or when running other non–USB-aware operating systems.

Note that if USB legacy support is enabled, you shouldn't mix USB and PS/2 port keyboards and mice. For example, don't use a PS/2 keyboard with a USB mouse or a USB keyboard and a PS/2 mouse. Also remember that this legacy support is for keyboards and mice only; it won't work for USB hubs or other USB devices. For devices other than keyboards or mice to work, you need a USB-aware operating system with the appropriate USB drivers.

IDE Configuration Submenu

The IDE Configuration submenu is for configuring IDE devices, such as hard drives, CD-ROM drives, LS-120 (SuperDisk) drives, tape drives, and so on. Table 5.18 shows the IDE Configuration menu and options for a typical modern motherboard.

Table 5.18   Typical IDE Configuration Menu Settings*

Feature	Options	Description
IDE Controller	Disabled Primary Secondary Both (default)	Specifies the integrated IDE controller. Primary enables only the Primary IDE controller. Secondary enables only the Secondary IDE controller. Both enables both IDE controllers.
Hard Disk Pre-Delay	Disabled (default) 3 Seconds 6 Seconds 9 Seconds 12 Seconds 15 Seconds 21 Seconds 30 Seconds	Specifies the hard disk drive pre-delay.

Table 5.18   Continued

Feature	Options	Description
Primary IDE Master	No options	Reports type of connected IDE device. When selected, displays the Primary IDE Master submenu.
Primary IDE Slave	No options	Reports type of connected IDE device. When selected, displays the Primary IDE Slave submenu.
Secondary IDE Master	No options	Reports type of connected IDE device. When selected, displays the Secondary IDE Master submenu.
Secondary IDE Slave	No options	Reports type of connected IDE device. When selected, displays the Secondary IDE Slave submenu.

*Based on the BIOS used by the Intel DB815EEAmotherboard. Used by permission of Intel Corporation.

The hard disk pre-delay function is to delay accessing drives that are slow to spin up. Some drives aren't ready when the system begins to look for them during boot, causing the system to display Fixed Disk Failure messages and fail to boot. Setting this delay allows time for the drive to become ready before continuing the boot. Of course, this slows down the boot process, so if your drives don't need this delay, it should be disabled.

IDE Configuration Submenus

These submenus are for configuring each IDE device, including primary and secondary masters and slaves.

Of all the BIOS Setup menus, the hard disk settings are by far the most important. In fact, they are the most important of all the BIOS settings. Most modern motherboards incorporate two IDE controllers that support up to four drives. Most modern BIOSes have an autodetect feature that enables automatic configuration of the drives. If this is available, in most cases you should use it because it will prevent confusion in the future. With the Auto setting, the BIOS sends a special Identify Drive command to the drive, which responds with information about the correct settings. From this, the BIOS can automatically detect the specifications and optimal operating mode of almost all IDE hard drives. When you select type Auto for a hard drive, the BIOS redetects the drive specifications during POST, every time the system boots. You could swap drives with the power off, and the system would automatically detect the new drive the next time it was turned on.

In addition to the Auto setting, most older BIOSes offered a standard table of up to 47 drive types with specifically prerecorded parameters. Each defined drive type has a specified number of cylinders, number of heads, write precompensation factor, landing zone, and number of sectors. This often was used many years ago, but it is rarely used today because virtually no drives conform to the parameters on these drive type lists.

Another option is to select a setting called User or User Defined, which is where you can enter the specific drive CHS (Cylinder, Head, and Sector) parameters into the proper fields. These parameters are saved in the CMOS RAM and reloaded every time the system is powered up.

Most BIOSes today offer control over the drive translation settings if the type is set to User and not Auto. Usually, two translation settings are available, called Standard and LBA. Standard or LBA-disabled is used only for drives of 528MB or less, where the maximum number of cylinders, heads, and sectors are 1,024, 16, and 63, respectively. Because most drives today are larger, this setting is rarely used.

LBA (logical block addressing) is used for virtually all drives that are larger than 528MB. Note that systems dating from 1997 and earlier usually are limited to a maximum drive size of 8.4GB unless they have a BIOS upgrade. Systems from 1998 and later usually support drives up to 136.9GB. During drive accesses, the IDE controller transforms the data address described by sector, head, and cylinder number into a physical block address, significantly improving data transfer rates.

Table 5.19 shows the IDE drive settings found in a typical modern motherboard BIOS.

Table 5.19   Typical IDE Drive Settings*

Feature	Options	Description
Type	None ATAPI Removable Other ATAPI CD-ROM User IDE Removable Auto (default)	Specifies the IDE Configuration mode for IDE devices. Auto automatically fills in the transfer mode values. Other options are device dependent.
Maximum Capacity	No options	Reports the maximum capacity for the hard disk.
LBA Mode Control	Disabled Enabled	Enables or disables the LBA mode control.
Multi-Sector Transfers	Disabled 2 Sectors 4 Sectors 8 Sectors 16 Sectors (default)	Specifies number of sectors per block for transfers from the hard drive to memory. Check the hard drive's specifications for optimum setting.
PIO Mode	Auto (default) 0 1 2 3 4	Specifies the PIO mode for moving data to and from the drive.
Ultra DMA Mode	Disabled (default) 0 1 2 3 4 5	Specifies the Ultra DMA mode for moving data to and from the drive.
Cable Detected	No options	Displays the type of cable connected to the IDE interface: 40-conductor or 80-conductor (for Ultra ATA-66/100 devices).

Based on the BIOS used by the Intel DB815EEA motherboard. Used by permission of Intel Corporation.

Setting the drive type to Auto causes the other values to be automatically configured correctly. I recommend this for virtually all standard system configurations. When set to Auto, the BIOS sends an Identify command to the drive, causing it to report back all the options and features found on that drive. Using this information, the BIOS then automatically configures all the settings on this menu for maximum performance with that drive, including selecting the fastest possible transfer modes and other features.

For hard drives, the only option available other than Auto is User. When set to User, the other choices are made available and are not automatically set. This can be useful for somebody who wants to "play" with these settings, but in most cases, all you will get by doing so is lower performance and possibly even trouble in the form of corrupted data or a nonfunctional drive.

Diskette Configuration Submenu

The Diskette Configuration submenu is for configuring the floppy drive and interface. Table 5.20 shows the options in a typical BIOS Setup.

Table 5.20   Typical Diskette Configuration Settings*

Feature	Options	Description
Diskette Controller	Disabled Enabled (default)	Disables or enables the integrated diskette controller
Diskette A:	Disabled 360KB, 5 1/4-inch 1.2MB, 5 1/4-inch 720KB, 3 1/2-inch 1.44MB, 3 1/2-inch (default) 2.88MB, 3 1/2-inch	Specifies the capacity and physical size of floppy disk drive A:
Floppy Write Protect	Disabled (default) Enabled	Disables or enables write protect for floppy disk drive A:

*Based on the BIOS used by the Intel DB815EEA motherboard. Used by permission of Intel Corporation.

By enabling the write-protect feature, you can disallow writing to floppy disks. This can help prevent the theft of data as well as helping to prevent infecting disks with viruses should they be on the system.

Event Logging

The Event Logging menu is for configuring the System Management (SMBIOS) event logging features. SMBIOS is a DMI-compliant method for managing computers on a managed network. DMI stands for Desktop Management Interface, a special protocol software can use to communicate with the motherboard.

Using SMBIOS, a system administrator can remotely obtain information about a system. Applications such as the Intel LANDesk Client Manager can use SMBIOS to report the following DMI information:

- BIOS data, such as the BIOS revision level
- System data, such as installed peripherals, serial numbers, and asset tags
- Resource data, such as memory size, cache size, and processor speed
- Dynamic data, such as event detection including event detection and error logging

Table 5.21 shows a typical Event Logging menu in BIOS Setup.

Table 5.21   Typical Event Logging Menu*

Feature	Options	Description
Event log	No options	Indicates whether space is available in the event log
Event log validity	No options	Indicates whether contents of the event log are valid
View event log	Press [Enter]	Enables viewing of event log
Clear all event logs	No (default) Yes	Clears the event log after rebooting

Table 5.21 Continued

Feature	Options	Description
Event Logging	Disabled, Enabled (default)	Enables logging of events
Mark events as read	Press [Enter]	Marks all events as read.

Based on the BIOS used by the Intel DB815EEA motherboard. Used by permission of Intel Corporation.

Some motherboards with ECC memory support also log ECC events. I find event logging particularly useful for tracking errors such as ECC errors. Using the View Log feature, you can see whether any errors have been detected (and corrected) by the system.

Video Configuration

The Video Configuration menu is for configuring video features. Table 5.22 shows the functions of this menu in a typical modern motherboard BIOS.

Table 5.22 Typical Video Configuration Menu*

Feature	Options	Description
Default Primary Video Adapter	AGP (default) PCI	Selects the type of video card used for the boot display device

Based on the BIOS used by the Intel DB815-EEA motherboard. Used by permission of Intel Corporation.

Other motherboards might also include features such as those shown in Table 5.23.

Table 5.23 Additional Video Configuration Menu Options

Feature	Options	Description
Palette Snooping	Disabled (default) Enabled	Controls the capability of a primary PCI graphics controller to share a common palette with an ISA add-in video card
AGP Aperture Size	64MB (default) 256MB	Specifies the aperture size for the AGP video controller
AGP Hardware Detected	No options	Indicates whether AGP 1x, 2x, or 4x AGP card is installed; disables onboard graphics subsystem

The most common use of this menu is to change the primary video device. This is useful under Windows 98 and Windows 2000, which support dual-monitor configurations. Using this feature, you can set either the AGP or PCI video card to be the primary boot device.

Resource Configuration

The Resource Configuration menu is used for configuring the memory and interrupt usage of non–plug-and-play (legacy) ISA bus-based devices on motherboards that have one or more ISA slots. Table 5.24 shows the functions and options found in a typical modern BIOS.

Table 5.24   Typical Resource Configuration Menu*

Feature	Options	Description
Memory Reservation	C800 CBFF Available (default)	Reserved CC00 CFFF Available (default)	Reserved D000 D3FF Available (default)	Reserved D400 D7FF Available (default)	Reserved D800 DBFF Available (default)	Reserved DC00 DFFF Available (default)	Reserved	Reserves specific upper memory blocks for use by legacy ISA devices.
IRQ Reservation	IRQ3 Available (default)	Reserved IRQ4 Available (default)	Reserved IRQ5 Available (default)	Reserved IRQ7 Available (default)	Reserved IRQ10 Available (default)	Reserved IRQ11 Available (default)	Reserved	Reserves specific IRQs for use by legacy ISA devices. An asterisk (*) displayed next to an IRQ indicates an IRQ conflict.

Based on the BIOS used by the Intel SE440BX-2 motherboard. Used by permission of Intel Corporation.

Note that these settings are only for legacy (non–plug-and-play) ISA devices. For all Plug and Play ISA devices as well as PCI devices (which are Plug and Play by default), these resources are instead configured by the operating system or by software that comes with the cards.

Setting these resources here does not actually control the legacy ISA device; that usually must be done by moving jumpers on the card. By setting the resource as reserved here, you are telling the Plug and Play operating system that the reserved resources are off-limits, so it won't accidentally set a Plug and Play device to use the same resource as a legacy ISA device. Reserving resources in this manner is sometimes required because the Plug and Play software can't detect all legacy ISA devices and therefore won't know which settings the device might be using.

In a system with no legacy devices, you don't need to reserve any resources via this menu.

Some boards have additional configuration options for the Plug and Play (PnP) BIOS features as well as the PCI bus. These features are largely chipset dependent, but some common examples are shown in Table 5.25.

Table 5.25   Typical PnP and PCI Options*

DMA n Assigned to	When resources are controlled manually, assign each system DMA channel as one of the following types, depending on the type of device using the interrupt:
	■ Legacy ISA devices compliant with the original PC AT bus specification, requiring a specific DMA channel
	■ PCI/ISA PnP devices compliant with the Plug and Play standard, whether designed for PCI or ISA bus architecture

Table 5.25   Continued

PCI IRQ Activated by	Leave the IRQ trigger set at Level unless the PCI device assigned to the interrupt specifies edge-triggered interrupts.
PCI IDE IRQ Map to	This field enables you to select PCI IDE IRQ mapping or PC AT (ISA) interrupts. If your system does not have one or two PCI IDE connectors on the system board, select values according to the type of IDE interface(s) installed in your system (PCI or ISA). Standard ISA interrupts for IDE channels are IRQ14 for primary and IRQ15 for secondary.
Primary/Secondary IDE INT#	Each PCI peripheral connection is capable of activating up to four interrupts: INT# A, INT# B, INT# C, and INT# D. By default, a PCI connection is assigned INT# A. Assigning INT# B has no meaning unless the peripheral device requires two interrupt services rather than just one. Because the PCI IDE interface in the chipset has two channels, it requires two interrupt services. The primary and secondary IDE INT# fields default to values appropriate for two PCI IDE channels, with the primary PCI IDE channel having a lower interrupt than the secondary.
	Note that all single-function PCI cards normally use INT# A, and each of these must be assigned to a different and unique ISA interrupt request.
Used Mem base addr	Select a base address for the memory area used by any peripheral that requires high memory.
Used Mem Length	Select a length for the memory area specified in the previous field. This field does not appear if no base address is specified.
Assign IRQ for USB	Select Enabled if your system has a USB controller and you have one or more USB devices connected. If you are not using your system's USB controller, select Disabled to free the IRQ resource.

Based on the BIOS used by the Intel SE440BX-2 motherboard. Used by permission of Intel Corporation.

Security Menu

Most BIOSes include two passwords for security, called the supervisor and user passwords. These passwords help control who is allowed to access the BIOS Setup program and who is allowed to boot the computer. The supervisor password is also called a setup password because it controls access to the setup program. The user password is also called a system password because it controls access to the entire system.

If a supervisor password is set, a password prompt is displayed when an attempt is made to enter the BIOS Setup menus. When entered correctly, the supervisor password gives unrestricted access to view and change all the Setup options in the Setup program. If the supervisor password is not entered or is entered incorrectly, access to view and change Setup options in the Setup program is restricted.

If the user password is set, the password prompt is displayed before the computer boots up. The password must be entered correctly before the system is allowed to boot. Note that if only the supervisor password is set, the computer boots without asking for a password because the supervisor password controls access only to the BIOS Setup menus. If both passwords are set, the password prompt is displayed at boot time, and either the user or the supervisor password can be entered to boot the computer. In most systems, the password can be up to seven or eight characters long.

If you forget the password, most systems have a jumper on the board that allows all passwords to be cleared. This means that for most systems, the password security also requires that the system case be locked to prevent users from opening the cover and accessing the password-clear jumper. This jumper is often not labeled on the board for security reasons, but it can be found in the motherboard or system documentation.

Provided you know the password and can get into the BIOS Setup, a password can also be cleared by entering the BIOS Setup and selecting the Clear Password function. If no Clear function is available, you can still clear the password by selecting the Set Password function and pressing Enter (for no password) at the prompts.

Table 5.26 shows the security functions in a typical BIOS Setup.

Table 5.26   Typical Security Settings*

Feature	Options	Description
User Password Is	No options.	Reports whether a user password is set.
Supervisor Password Is	No options.	Reports whether a supervisor password is set.
Set User Password	Password can be up to seven alphanumeric characters.	Specifies the user password.
Set Supervisor Password	Password can be up to seven alphanumeric characters.	Specifies the supervisor password.
Clear User Password	No options.	Clears the user password.
User Setup Access	None View Only Limited Access Full Access (default).	Controls the user's capability to run the BIOS Setup program.
Unattended Start	Disabled (default) Enabled.	Enables the unattended start feature. When enabled, the computer boots, but the keyboard is locked. The user must enter a password to unlock the computer or boot from a disk.

Based on the BIOS used by the Intel DB815EEA motherboard. Used by permission of Intel Corporation.

To clear passwords if the password is forgotten, most motherboards have a password-clear jumper or switch. Intel motherboards require that you set the configuration jumper, enter the Maintenance menu in BIOS Setup, and select the Clear Password feature. If you can't find the documentation for your board and aren't sure how to clear the passwords, you can try removing the battery for 15 minutes or so, which clears the CMOS RAM. It can take that long for the CMOS RAM to clear on some systems because they have capacitors in the circuit that retain a charge. Note that this also erases all other BIOS settings, including the hard disk settings, so they should be recorded beforehand.

Power Management Menu

Power management is defined as the capability of the system to automatically enter power-conserving modes during periods of inactivity. Two main classes of power management exist; the original standard was called Advanced Power Management (APM) and was supported by most systems since the 386 and 486 processors. More recently, a new type of power management called Advanced Configuration and Power Interface (ACPI) has been developed and began appearing in systems during 1998. Most systems sold in 1998 or later support the more advanced ACPI type of power management. In APM, the hardware does the actual power management, and the operating system or other software had little control. With ACPI, the power management is now done by the operating system and BIOS, and not the hardware. This makes the control more centralized and easier to access and enables applications to work with the power management.

Table 5.27 shows the typical power settings found in most motherboard BIOSes.

Table 5.27   Typical Power Settings*

Feature	Options	Description
Power Management	Disabled Enabled (default)	Enables or disables the BIOS power-management feature.
Inactivity Timer	Off 1 Minute 5 Minutes 10 Minutes 20 Minutes (default) 30 Minutes 60 Minutes 120 Minutes	Specifies the amount of time before the computer enters Standby mode.
Hard Drive	Disabled Enabled (default)	Enables power management for hard disks during Standby and Suspend modes.
ACPI Suspend State	S1 (default) S3	Specifies the ACPI suspend state. S3 is Suspend to RAM; S1 is the default because it is compatible with USB devices that aren't ACPI compliant.
Video Repost Enable	Disable (default)	Allows video BIOS to be initialized coming out of the S3 state; required by some video controllers. This option is listed only if ACPI suspend state is set as S3.

Based on the BIOS used by the Intel DB815EEA motherboard. Used by permission of Intel Corporation.

When in Standby mode, the BIOS reduces power consumption by spinning down hard drives and reducing power to or turning off monitors that comply with Video Electronics Standards Organization (VESA) and Display Power Management Signaling (DPMS). While in Standby mode, the system can still respond to external interrupts, such as those from keyboards, mice, fax/modems, or network adapters. For example, any keyboard or mouse activity brings the system out of Standby mode and immediately restores power to the monitor.

In most systems, the operating system takes over most of the power management settings, and in some cases, it can even override the BIOS settings. This is definitely true if the operating system and motherboard both support ACPI.

Some systems feature additional power management settings in their BIOSes. Some of the more common ones are shown in Table 5.28.

Table 5.28   Typical Power Management Settings*

ACPI Function	Select Enabled only if your computer's operating system supports the ACPI specification. Windows 98 and all later versions support ACPI.
Power Management	This option enables you to select the type (or degree) of power saving for Doze, Standby, and Suspend modes. Following are the individual mode settings: Max Saving—Maximum power savings. Inactivity period is one minute in each mode. User Define—Set each mode individually. Select timeout periods in the section for each mode. Min Saving—Minimum power savings. Inactivity period is one hour in each mode (except the hard drive).

Table 5.28 **Continued**

PM Control by APM	If Advanced Power Management (APM) is installed on your system, selecting Yes gives better power savings.
Video Off Method	Determines the manner in which the monitor is blanked.
V/H SYNC+Blank	System turns off vertical and horizontal synchronization ports and writes blanks to the video buffer.
DPMS Support	Select this option if your monitor supports the DPMS standard of VESA. Use the software supplied for your video subsystem to select video power management values.
Blank Screen	System writes only blanks to the video buffer.
Video Off After	As the system moves from lesser to greater power-saving modes, select the mode in which you want the monitor to blank.
MODEM Use IRQ	Name the IRQ line assigned to the modem (if any) on your system. Activity of the selected IRQ always awakens the system.
Doze Mode	After the selected period of system inactivity, the CPU clock throttles to a small percentage of its duty cycle: between 10% and 25% for most chipsets. All other devices still operate at full speed.
Standby Mode	After the selected period of system inactivity, the CPU clock stops, the hard drive enters an idle state, and the L2 cache enters a power-save mode. All other devices still operate at full speed.
Suspend Mode	After the selected period of system inactivity, the chipset enters a hardware suspend mode, stopping the CPU clock and possibly causing other system devices to enter power-management modes.
HDD Power Down	After the selected period of drive inactivity, any system IDE devices compatible with the ATA-2 specification or later power manage themselves, putting themselves into an idle state after the specified timeout and then waking themselves up when accessed.
Throttle Duty Cycle	When the system enters Doze mode, the CPU clock runs only part of the time. You can select the percentage of time the clock runs.
VGA Active Monitor	When enabled, any video activity restarts the global timer for Standby mode.
Soft-Off by PWR-BTTN	When you select Instant Off or Delay 4 Sec., turning off the system with the On/Off button places the system in a very low power-usage state, either immediately or after 4 seconds, with only enough circuitry receiving power to detect power button activity or Resume by Ring activity.
CPUFAN Off in Suspend	When enabled, the CPU fan turns off during Suspend mode.
Resume by Ring	When enabled, an input signal on the serial Ring Indicator (RI) line (in other words, an incoming call on the modem) awakens the system from a soft off state.
Resume by Alarm	When enabled, you can set the date and time at which the RTC (real-time clock) alarm awakens the system from Suspend mode.
Date (of Month) Alarm	Select a date in the month when you want the alarm to go off.
Time (hh:mm:ss) Alarm	Set the time you want the alarm to go off.
Wake Up On LAN	When enabled, an input signal from a local area network (LAN) awakens the system from a soft off state.
IRQ8 Break [Event From] Suspend	You can select Enabled or Disabled for monitoring of IRQ8 (the real-time clock) so it does not awaken the system from Suspend mode.

Table 5.28   Continued

Reload Global Timer Events	When enabled, an event occurring on each device listed below restarts the global timer for Standby mode:
	IRQ3-7, 9-15, NMI Primary IDE 0 Primary IDE 1 Secondary IDE 0 Secondary IDE 1 Floppy Disk Serial Port Parallel Port

Based on the BIOS used by the Intel SE440BX-2 motherboard. Used by permission of Intel Corporation.

Boot Menu (Boot Sequence, Order)

The Boot menu is used for setting the boot features and the boot sequence. If your operating system includes a bootable CD—Windows 2000, for example—use this menu to change the boot drive order to check your CD before your hard drive. Table 5.29 shows the functions and settings available on a typical motherboard.

Table 5.29   Typical Boot Menu Settings*

Feature	Options	Description
Quiet Boot	Disabled Enabled (default)	Disabled displays normal POST messages; Enabled displays OEM graphic instead.
Intel Rapid BIOS Boot	Disabled Enabled (default)	Enables the computer to boot without running certain POST tests.
Scan User Flash Area	Disabled (default) Enabled	Enables the BIOS to scan the flash memory for user binary files that are executed at boot time.
After Power Failure	Power On Stay Off Last State (default)	Specifies the mode of operation if an AC/Power loss occurs. Power On restores power to the computer. Stay Off keeps the power off until the power button is pressed. Last State restores the previous power state before the power loss occurred.
On Modem Ring	Stay Off Power On (default)	In APM mode only, specifies how the computer responds to an incoming call on an installed modem when the power is off.
On LAN	Stay Off Power On (default)	In APM mode only. Specifies how the computer responds to a LAN wakeup event.
On PME	Stay Off (default) Power On	In APM mode only. Specifies how the computer responds to a PCI power management event.
On ACPI S5	Stay Off (default) Power On	In ACPI mode only. Specifies the action of the system when a LAN wakeup event occurs.

First Boot Device
Second Boot Device
Third Boot Device
Fourth Boot Device
	Floppy
	ARMD-FDD
	ARMD-HDD
	IDE-HDD
	ATAPI CD-ROM
	Intel UNDi, PXE 2.0
	Disabled
		Specifies the boot sequence from the available devices. To specify boot sequence, do this:
		   1. Select the boot device with up or down arrow keys.
		   2. Press Enter to set the selection as the intended boot device.
		The operating system assigns a drive letter to each boot device in the order listed. Changing the order of the devices changes the drive lettering.

Table 5.29   Continued

Feature	Options	Description
		The defaults for the first through fifth devices include: ■ Floppy ■ IDE-HDD ■ ATAPI CD-ROM ■ Intel UNDi, PXE 2.0 ■ Disabled
		ARMD-HDD is an ATAPI removable device hard disk drive.
		ARMD-FDD is an ATAPI removable devices floppy disk drive (such as an LS-120 SuperDisk or Zip drive).
		Intel UNDi, PXE 2.0 is available only if the onboard LAN subsystem is present.
IDE Drive Configuration	No options	Configures IDE drives. When selected, displays the IDE Drive Configuration submenu.

Based on the BIOS used by the Intel DB815EEA motherboard. Used by permission of Intel Corporation.

Using this menu, you can configure which devices your system boots from and in which order the devices are sequenced. From this menu, you also can access Hard Drive and Removable Devices submenus, which enable you to configure the ordering of these devices in the boot sequence. For example, you can set hard drives to be the first boot choice, and then in the hard drive submenu, decide to boot from the secondary drive first and the primary drive second. Normally, the default with two drives would be the other way around.

Some recent systems also enable you to boot from external USB drives, such as Zip or LS-120 SuperDisk drives.

IDE Drive Configuration Submenu

The IDE Drive Configuration submenu enables you to select the boot order for the IDE drives in your computer. This BIOS option enables you to install more than one bootable hard disk in your computer and select which one you want to boot from at a BIOS level, rather than by using a boot manager program. If you need to work with multiple operating systems, this menu can be very useful. Table 5.30 is an example of a typical IDE Drive Configuration menu.

Table 5.30   IDE Drive Configuration Submenu*

Feature	Options	Description
Primary Master IDE	1st IDE (default) 1–4	Allows you to select the order in which the Primary Master IDE drive boots
Primary Slave IDE	2nd IDE (default) 1–4	Allows you to select the order in which the Primary Slave IDE drive boots
Secondary Master IDE	3rd IDE (default) 1–4	Allows you to select the order in which the Secondary Master IDE drive boots
Secondary Slave IDE	4th IDE (default) 1–4	Allows you to select the order in which the Secondary Slave IDE drive boots

Based on the BIOS used by the Intel DB815EEA motherboard. Used by permission of Intel Corporation.

Exit Menu

The Exit menu is for exiting the Setup program, saving changes, and loading and saving defaults. Table 5.31 shows the typical selections found in most motherboard BIOSes.

Table 5.31   Typical Exit Menu Settings*

Feature	Description
Exit Saving Changes	Exits and saves the changes in CMOS RAM.
Exit Discarding Changes	Exits without saving any changes made in Setup.
Load Setup Defaults	Loads the factory default values for all the Setup options.
Load Custom Defaults	Loads the custom defaults for Setup options.
Save Custom Defaults	Saves the current values as custom defaults. Normally, the BIOS reads the Setup values from flash memory. If this memory is corrupted, the BIOS reads the custom defaults. If no custom defaults are set, the BIOS reads the factory defaults.
Discard Changes	Discards changes without exiting Setup. The option values present when the computer was turned on are used.

*Based on the BIOS used by the Intel DB815-EEA motherboard. Used by permission of Intel Corporation.

After you have selected an optimum set of BIOS Setup settings, you can save them using the Save Custom Defaults option. This enables you to quickly restore your settings if they are corrupted or lost. All BIOS settings are stored in the CMOS RAM memory, which is powered by a battery attached to the motherboard.

Additional BIOS Setup Features

Some systems have additional features in their BIOS Setup screens, which might not be found in all BIOSes. Some of the more common features you might see are shown in Table 5.32.

Table 5.32   Additional BIOS Setup Features

Virus Warning	When enabled, you receive a warning message if a program attempts to write to the boot sector or the partition table of the hard disk drive. If you get this warning during normal operation, you should run an antivirus program to see whether an infection has occurred. This feature protects only the master boot sector, not the entire hard drive. Note that programs which usually write to the master boot sector, such as FDISK, can trigger the virus warning message.
CPU Internal Cache/ External Cache	This allows you to disable the L1 (internal) and L2 (external) CPU caches. This is often used when testing memory, in which case you don't want the cache functioning. For normal operation, both caches should be enabled.
Quick Power On Self Test	When enabled, this reduces the amount of time required to run the POST. A quick POST skips certain steps, such as the memory test. If you trust your system, you can enable the quick POST, but in most cases I recommend leaving it disabled so you get the full-length POST version.
Swap Floppy Drive	This field is functional only in systems with two floppy drives. Selecting Enabled assigns physical drive B: to logical drive A: and physical drive A: to logical drive B:.
Boot Up Floppy Seek	When enabled, the BIOS tests (seeks) floppy drives to determine whether they have 40 or 80 tracks. Only 360KB floppy drives have 40 tracks; drives with 720KB, 1.2MB, and 1.44MB capacity all have 80 tracks. Because very few modern PCs have 40-track floppy drives, you can disable this function to save time.

Table 5.32 **Continued**

Boot Up System Speed	Select High to boot at the default CPU speed; select Low to boot at a simulated 8MHz speed. The 8MHz option often was used in the past with certain copy-protected programs, which would fail the protection scheme if booted at full speed. This option is not used today.
Gate A20 Option	Gate A20 refers to the way the system addresses memory above 1MB (extended memory). When set to Fast, the system chipset controls Gate A20. When set to Normal, a pin in the keyboard controller controls Gate A20. Setting Gate A20 to Fast improves system speed, particularly with protected-mode operating systems such as Windows 9x and Windows 2000.
Typematic Rate Setting	When disabled, the following two items (Typematic Rate and Typematic Delay) are irrelevant. Keystrokes repeat at a rate determined by the keyboard controller in your system. When enabled, you can select a typematic rate and typematic delay.
Typematic Rate (Chars/Sec)	When the typematic rate setting is enabled, you can select a typematic rate (the rate at which characters repeat when you hold down a key) of 6, 8, 10, 12, 15, 20, 24, or 30 characters per second.
Typematic Delay (Msec)	When the typematic rate setting is enabled, you can select a typematic delay (the delay before key strokes begin to repeat) of 250, 500, 750, or 1,000 milliseconds.
Security Option	If you have set a password, select whether the password is required every time the system boots or only when you enter Setup.
PS/2 Mouse Function Control	If your system has a PS/2 (motherboard) mouse port and you install a serial or USB pointing device, select Disabled.
PCI/VGA Palette Snoop	Allows multimedia boards to read data from video RAM. Normally set to Disabled unless specifically instructed when installing a multimedia board.
HDD S.M.A.R.T. Capability	S.M.A.R.T. is an acronym for Self-Monitoring Analysis and Reporting Technology system. S.M.A.R.T. is a hard drive self-diagnostic feature available on some IDE hard drives. Enabling this option is recommended if you use diagnostic software that can monitor S.M.A.R.T.-compatible drives to warn you of impending failures.
Report No FDD For WIN 95	Select Yes to release IRQ6 when the system contains no floppy drive, for compatibility with Windows 95 logo certification. In the Integrated Peripherals screen, select Disabled for the Onboard FDC Controller field.
ROM Shadowing	ROM chips typically are very slow, around 150ns (nanoseconds), and operate only 8 bits at a time, whereas RAM runs 60ns or even 10ns or less and is either 32 bits or 64 bits wide in most systems. Shadowing is the copying of BIOS code from ROM into RAM, where the CPU can read the BIOS drivers at the higher speed of RAM.
Operating Frequency	Some motherboards enable you to select the FSB (front-side bus) and CPU clock multiplier speeds within the BIOS rather than through the normal motherboard-based DIP switches or jumper blocks. Select this option to enable customized settings for the CPU Clock Multiplier and CPU Frequency options.
CPU Frequency	This option enables you to vary the CPU FSB frequency from the default 66MHz, 100MHz, or 133MHz to higher values, enabling you to overclock your system.
CPU Clock Multiplier	This option enables you to vary the CPU clock multiplier from its default values to higher values **if** the CPU is not multiplier-locked. Recent and current Intel CPUs ignore nonstandard CPU clock multiplier settings, but AMD Athlon and Duron CPUs can be overclocked with this option.
CPU Vcore Setting	This option enables you to vary the core voltage of the CPU to improve the stability of your system during overclocking or to install CPUs not specifically supported by the default Automatic voltage settings.

Year 2000 BIOS Issues

All systems now in use should be compliant with twenty-first century dates, either through BIOS updates or through software or hardware patches. However, if you are returning stored systems built before 1999 to service, you might want to test them for Year 2000 compliance. For details, see *Upgrading and Repairing PCs, 12th Edition*, available in electronic form on the CD-ROM packaged with this book.

Plug and Play BIOS

Traditionally, installing and configuring devices in PCs has been a difficult process. During installation, the user is faced with the task of configuring the new card by selecting the IRQ, I/O ports, and DMA channel. In the past, users were required to move jumpers or set switches on the add-in cards to control these settings. They needed to know exactly which resources were already in use so they could find a set of resources that did not conflict with the devices already in the system. If a conflict exists, the system might not boot and the device might fail or cause the conflicting hardware to fail.

PnP is technology designed to prevent configuration problems and provide users with the capability to easily expand a PC. With PnP, the user simply plugs in the new card and the system configures it automatically for proper operation.

PnP is composed of three principal components:

- Plug and Play BIOS
- Extended System Configuration Data (ESCD)
- Plug and Play operating system

The PnP BIOS initiates the configuration of the PnP cards during the boot-up process. If the cards previously were installed, the BIOS reads the information from ESCD and initializes the cards and boots the system. During the installation of new PnP cards, the BIOS consults the ESCD to determine which system resources are available and needed for the add-in card. If the BIOS is capable of finding sufficient available resources, it configures the card. However, if the BIOS is incapable of locating sufficient available resources, the Plug and Play routines in the operating system complete the configuration process. During the configuration process, the configuration registers (in flash BIOS) on the card and the ESCD are updated with the new configuration data.

PnP Device IDs

All Plug and Play devices must contain a Plug and Play device ID to enable the operating system to uniquely recognize the device so it can load the appropriate driver software. Each device manufacturer is responsible for assigning the Plug and Play ID for each product and storing it in the hardware.

Each manufacturer of Plug and Play devices must be assigned an industry-unique, three-character vendor ID. Then, the device manufacturer is responsible for assigning a unique product ID to each individual product model. After an ID is assigned to a product model, it must not be assigned to any other product model manufactured by the same company (that is, one that uses the same vendor ID).

Note

For a comprehensive, printable list of PnP device IDs, see "PnP Device IDs" in the Technical Reference section of the CD accompanying this book.

ACPI

ACPI stands for Advanced Configuration and Power Interface, which defines a standard method for integrating power management as well as system configuration features throughout a PC, including the hardware, operating system, and application software. ACPI goes far beyond the previous standard, called Advanced Power Management (APM), which consisted mainly of processor, hard disk, and display control. ACPI not only controls power, but also all the Plug and Play hardware configuration throughout the system. With ACPI, system configuration (Plug and Play) as well as power management configuration is no longer controlled via the BIOS Setup; it is controlled entirely within the operating system instead.

ACPI enables the system to automatically turn peripherals on and off (such as CD-ROMs, network cards, hard disk drives, and printers), as well as external devices connected to the PC (such as VCRs, televisions, telephones, and stereos). ACPI technology also enables peripherals to turn on or activate the PC. For example, inserting a tape into a VCR can turn on the PC, which could then activate a large-screen television and high-fidelity sound system.

ACPI enables system designers to implement a range of power management features with various hardware designs while using the same operating system driver. ACPI also uses the Plug and Play BIOS data structures and takes control over the Plug and Play interface, providing an operating-system–independent interface for configuration and control. ACPI is supported in Windows 98/Me, Windows 2000, XP, and later versions.

During the system setup and boot process, Windows versions supporting ACPI perform a series of checks and tests to see whether the system hardware and BIOS supports ACPI. If support for ACPI is either not detected or found to be faulty, the system typically reverts to standard Advanced Power Management control, but problems can also cause a lockup with either a red or blue screen with an ACPI error code.

Red screens indicate that the problem is probably related to hardware or the BIOS. Blue screens indicate that the problem is probably related to software or is an obscure problem. The ACPI error codes are described in Table 5.33.

Table 5.33   ACPI Error Codes

Error Code	Description
1xxx -	Indicates an error during initialization phase of the ACPI driver and usually means the driver can't read one or more of the ACPI tables
2xxx -	Indicates an ACPI machine language (AML) interpreter error
3xxx -	Indicates an error within the ACPI driver event handler
4xxx -	Indicates thermal management errors
5xxx -	Indicates device power management errors

Virtually all these errors are the result of partial or incomplete ACPI implementations or incompatibilities in either the BIOS or device drivers. If you encounter any of these errors, contact your motherboard manufacturer for an updated BIOS or the device manufacturers for updated drivers.

Initializing a PnP Device

One responsibility of a Plug and Play BIOS during POST is to isolate and initialize all Plug and Play cards and assign them with a valid Card Select Number (CSN). After a CSN is assigned, the system BIOS can then designate resources to the cards. The BIOS is responsible only for the configuration of boot devices; all the remaining Plug and Play devices can be configured dynamically by the operating system software.

The following steps outline a typical flow of a Plug and Play BIOS during the POST:

1. Disable all configurable devices.

2. Identify all Plug and Play devices.

3. Construct a resource map of resources that are statically allocated to devices in the system.

4. Enable input and output devices.

5. Perform ISA ROM scan.

6. Configure the boot device.

7. Enable Plug and Play ISA and other configurable devices.

8. Start the bootstrap loader.

If the loaded operating system is Plug and Play compliant, it takes over management of the system resources. Any unconfigured Plug and Play devices are configured by the appropriate system software or the Plug and Play operating system.

At this point, the operating system is loaded and takes control over Plug and Play system resources. Using the Device Manager in the operating system such as Windows, the user can now control any Plug and Play devices.

BIOS Error Messages

When a PC system is first powered on, the system runs a POST. If errors are encountered during the POST, you usually see a text error message displayed onscreen. Errors that occur very early in the POST might happen before the video card is initialized. These types of errors can't be displayed, so the system uses two other alternatives for communicating the error message. One is beeping—the system beeps the speaker in a specific pattern that indicates which error has occurred.

The other alternative is to send a hexadecimal error code to I/O port address 80h, which can be read by a special card in one of the bus slots. When the ROM BIOS is performing the POST, in most systems the results of these tests are continuously sent to I/O Port 80h so they can be monitored by special diagnostics cards called POST cards (see Figure 5.7). These tests sometimes are called *manufacturing tests* because they were designed into the system for testing systems on the assembly line without a video display attached.

Figure 5.7   A typical POST card with two-digit hexadecimal code display (left) and a POST card in operation (right).

The POST cards have a two-digit hexadecimal display used to report the number of the currently executing test routine. Before executing each test, a hexadecimal numeric code is sent to the port, and then the test is run. If the test fails and locks up the machine, the hexadecimal code of the last test being executed remains on the card's display.

Many tests are executed in a system before the video display card is enabled, especially if the display is EGA or VGA. Therefore, many errors can occur that would lock up the system before the system could possibly display an error code through the video system. Because not all these errors generate beep codes, to most normal troubleshooting procedures, a system with this type of problem (such as a memory failure in Bank 0) would appear completely "dead." By using one of the commercially available POST cards, however, you can often diagnose the problem.

These codes are completely BIOS dependent because the card does nothing but display the codes sent to it. Some BIOSes have more detailed POST procedures and therefore send more informative codes. POST cards can be purchased from JDR Microdevices or other sources and are available in both ISA and PCI bus versions.

For simple but otherwise fatal errors that can't be displayed onscreen, most of the BIOS versions also send audio codes that can be used to help diagnose such problems. The audio codes are similar to POST codes, but they are read by listening to the speaker beep rather than by using a special card.

The following sections detail the text, beep, and I/O port 80h error codes for all the popular BIOS versions.

Note

The CD accompanying this book contains an exhaustive listing of BIOS error codes, error messages, and beep codes for BIOSes from Phoenix, AMI, Award, Microid Research, and IBM.

General BIOS Boot Text Error Messages

The ROM maps of most PCs are similar to the original IBM systems with which they are compatible—with the exception of the Cassette BASIC portion (also called ROM BASIC). It might come as a surprise to some PC users, but the original IBM PC actually had a jack on the rear of the system for connecting a cassette tape recorder. This was to be used for loading programs and data to or from a cassette tape. Tapes were used at the time because floppy drives were very costly, and hard disks were not even an option yet. Floppy drives came down in price quickly at the time, and the cassette port never appeared on any subsequent IBM systems. The cassette port also never appeared on any compatible systems.

The original PC came standard with only 16KB of memory in the base configuration. No floppy drives were included, so you could not load or save files from disks. Most computer users at the time would either write their own programs in the BASIC (beginner's all-purpose symbolic instruction code) language or run programs written by others. A BASIC language interpreter was built into the ROM BIOS of these early IBMs and was designed to access the cassette port on the back of the system.

What is really strange is that IBM kept this ROM BASIC relationship all the way into the early 1990s! I liken this to humans having an appendix. The ROM BASIC in those IBM systems is a sort of vestigial organ—a leftover that had some use in prehistoric ancestors but that has no function today.

You can catch a glimpse of this ROM BASIC on older IBM systems that have it by disabling all the disk drives in the system. In that case, with nothing to boot from, most IBM systems unceremoniously dump you into the strange (vintage 1981) ROM BASIC screen. When this occurs, the message looks like this:

```
The IBM Personal Computer Basic
Version C1.10 Copyright IBM Corp 1981
62940 Bytes free
Ok
```

Many people used to dread seeing this because it usually meant that your hard disk had failed to be recognized! Because no compatible systems ever had the Cassette BASIC interpreter in ROM, they had to come up with different messages to display for the same situations in which an IBM system would invoke this BASIC. Compatibles that have an AMI BIOS in fact display a confusing message, as follows:

```
NO ROM BASIC - SYSTEM HALTED
```

This message is a BIOS error message that is displayed by the AMI BIOS when the same situations occur that would cause an IBM system to dump into Cassette BASIC, which, of course, is not present in an AMI BIOS (or any other compatible BIOS, for that matter). Other BIOS versions display different messages. For example, under the same circumstances, a Compaq BIOS displays the following:

```
Non-System disk or disk error
replace and strike any key when ready
```

This is somewhat confusing on Compaq's part because this very same (or similar) error message is contained in the DOS Boot Sector and would normally be displayed if the system files were missing or corrupted.

In the same situations in which you would see Cassette BASIC on an IBM system, a system with an Award BIOS would display the following:

```
DISK BOOT FAILURE, INSERT SYSTEM DISK AND PRESS ENTER
```

Phoenix BIOS systems display either

```
No boot device available -
strike F1 to retry boot, F2 for setup utility
```

or

```
No boot sector on fixed disk -
strike F1 to retry boot, F2 for setup utility
```

The first or second Phoenix message displays depending on which error actually occurred.

Although the message displayed varies from BIOS to BIOS, the cause is the same for all of them. Two things can generally cause any of these messages to be displayed, and they both relate to specific bytes in the Master Boot Record, which is the first sector of a hard disk at the physical location Cylinder 0, Head 0, Sector 1.

The first problem relates to a disk that has either never been partitioned or that has had the Master Boot Sector corrupted. During the boot process, the BIOS checks the last two bytes in the Master Boot Record (the first sector of the drive) for a "signature" value of 55AAh. If the last two bytes are not 55AAh, an Interrupt 18h is invoked. This calls the subroutine that displays the message you received, and the others indicated, or on an IBM system invokes Cassette (ROM) BASIC.

The Master Boot Sector (including the signature bytes) is written to the hard disk by the DOS FDISK program. Immediately after you low-level format a hard disk, all the sectors are initialized with a pattern of bytes, and the first sector does not contain the 55AAh signature. In other words, these ROM error messages are exactly what you see if you attempt to boot from a hard disk that has been low-level formatted but has not yet been partitioned.

Now consider the second situation that can cause these messages. If the signature bytes are correct, the BIOS executes the Master Partition Boot Record code, which performs a test of the Boot Indicator Bytes in each of the four partition table entries. These bytes are at offset 446 (1BEh), 462 (1CEh), 478 (1DEh), and 494 (1EEh), respectively. They are used to indicate which of the four possible partition table entries contains an active (bootable) partition. A value of 80h in any of these byte offsets indicates that table contains the active partition, whereas all other values must be 00h. If more than one of these bytes is 80h (indicating multiple active partitions), or any of the byte values is anything other than 80h or 00h, you see the following error message:

```
Invalid partition table
```

If all these four Boot Indicator Bytes are 00h, indicating no active (bootable) partitions, you also see Cassette BASIC on an IBM system or the other messages indicated earlier, depending on which BIOS you have. This is exactly what occurs if you were to remove the existing partitions from a drive using FDISK but had not created new partitions on the drive, or had failed to make one of the partitions Active (bootable) with FDISK before rebooting your system.

Unfortunately, no easy way exists to clear out the partition table on a system where it is damaged. You can try to use FDISK to remove damaged partitions, but FDISK doesn't always allow it. In that case, you must resort to something more powerful, such as the DISKEDIT command found in the Norton Utilities package by Symantec.

The third cause for these errors is tampering with the LBA mode translation in the system BIOS. LBA mode translates the actual disk geometry of the drive into a format that enables the entire disk to be used by DOS and Windows. If a drive is prepared with LBA mode enabled, and LBA mode is then disabled, the BIOS's boot loader will not be capable of locating the Master Boot Record and will display an error similar to those listed previously. Thus, if you see such errors on a system with a hard drive larger than 504MB (or 528 million bytes), be sure to check the LBA mode settings for the drive. On some of the older AMI BIOS Hi-Flex and WinBIOS (graphical) versions, the LBA mode setting is not on the same screen as the hard disk setup but is buried in the Advanced or Built-in Peripherals setup screens where it can be turned off by autoconfiguring BIOS setup options.

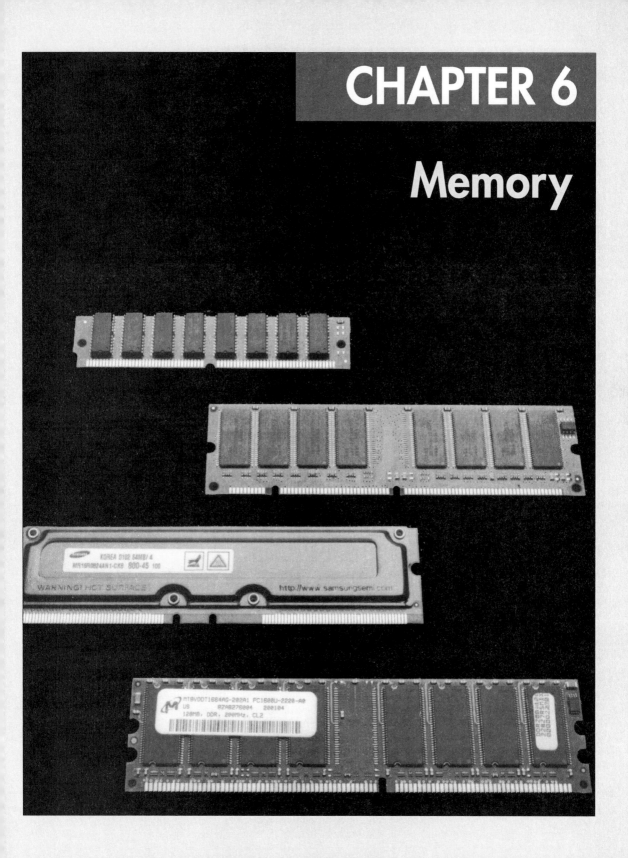

CHAPTER 6

Memory

Memory Basics

This chapter looks at memory from both a physical and logical point of view. First, you will look at what memory is, where it fits into the PC architecture, and how it works. Then I'll discuss the various types of memory, speeds, and packaging of the chips and memory modules you can buy and install.

This chapter also covers the logical layout of memory, defining the various areas and their uses from the system's point of view. Because the logical layout and uses are within the "mind" of the processor, memory mapping and logical layout remain perhaps the most difficult subjects to grasp in the PC universe. This chapter contains useful information that removes the mysteries associated with memory and enables you to get the most out of your system.

Memory is the workspace for the computer's processor. It is a temporary storage area where the programs and data being operated on by the processor must reside. Memory storage is considered temporary because the data and programs remain there only as long as the computer has electrical power or is not reset. Before being shut down or reset, any data that has been changed should be saved to a more permanent storage device of some type (usually a hard disk) so it can be reloaded into memory again in the future.

MMemory often is called *RAM*, for *random access memory*. Main memory is called RAM because you can randomly (as opposed to sequentially) access any location in memory. This designation is somewhat misleading and often misinterpreted. Read-only memory (ROM), for example, is also randomly accessible, yet usually is differentiated from the system RAM because it maintains data without power and can't normally be written to. Also, disk memory is randomly accessible, too, but we don't consider that RAM either.

Over the years, the definition of RAM has changed from a simple acronym to become something that means the primary memory workspace used by the processor to run programs, which usually is constructed of a type of chip called Dynamic RAM (DRAM). One of the characteristics of DRAM chips (and therefore RAM in general) is that they store data dynamically, which really has two meanings. One meaning is that the information can be written to RAM over and over again at any time. The other has to do with the fact that DRAM requires the data to be refreshed (essentially rewritten) every 15ms (milliseconds) or so. A type of RAM called Static RAM (SRAM) does not require the periodic refreshing. An important characteristic of RAM in general is that data is stored only as long as the memory has electrical power.

When we talk about a computer's memory, we usually mean the RAM or physical memory in the system, which is primarily the memory chips or modules used by the processor to store primary active programs and data. This often is confused with the term *storage*, which should be used when referring to things such as disk and tape drives (although they can be used as a form of RAM called virtual memory).

RAM can refer to both the physical chips that make up the memory in the system and the logical mapping and layout of that memory. *Logical mapping* and *layout* refer to how the memory addresses are mapped to actual chips and what address locations contain which types of system information.

People new to computers often confuse main memory (RAM) with disk storage because both have capacities that are expressed in similar megabyte or gigabyte terms. The best analogy to explain the relationship between memory and disk storage I've found is to think of an office with a desk and a file cabinet.

In this popular analogy, the file cabinet represents the system's hard disk, where both programs and data are stored for long-term safekeeping. The desk represents the system's main memory, which allows the person working at the desk (acting as the processor) direct access to any files placed on it. Files represent the programs and documents you can "load" into the memory. To work on a particular file, it must first be retrieved from the cabinet and placed on the desk. If the desk is large enough, you might be able to have several files open on it at one time; likewise, if your system has more memory, you can run more or larger programs and work on more or larger documents.

Adding hard disk space to a system is like putting a bigger file cabinet in the office; more files can be permanently stored. Adding more memory to a system is like getting a bigger desk; you can work on more programs and data at the same time.

One difference between this analogy and the way things really work in a computer is that when a file is loaded into memory, it is a copy of the file that is actually loaded; the original still resides on the hard disk. Note that because of the temporary nature of memory, any files that have been changed after being loaded into memory must then be saved back to the hard disk before the system is powered off and the memory subsequently cleared. If the changed file is not saved, the original copy of the file on the hard disk remains unaltered. This is like saying that any changes made to files left on the desktop are discarded when the office is closed, although the original files themselves are still in the cabinet.

Memory temporarily stores programs when they are running, along with the data being used by those programs. RAM chips are sometimes termed *volatile storage* because when you turn off your computer or an electrical outage occurs, whatever is stored in RAM is lost unless you saved it to your hard drive. Because of the volatile nature of RAM, many computer users make it a habit to save their work frequently. (Some software applications can do timed backups automatically.)

Launching a computer program brings files into RAM, and as long as they are running, computer programs reside in RAM. The CPU executes programmed instructions in RAM and also stores results in RAM. RAM stores your keystrokes when you use a word processor and also stores numbers used in calculations. Telling a program to save your data instructs the program to store RAM contents on your hard drive as a file.

Physically, the *main memory* in a system is a collection of chips or modules containing chips that are usually plugged into the motherboard. These chips or modules vary in their electrical and physical designs and must be compatible with the system into which they are being installed to function properly. In this chapter, I discuss the various types of chips and modules that can be installed in different systems.

Next to the processor, memory can be one of the more expensive components in a modern PC, although the total amount spent on memory for a typical system has declined over the past few years. Even after the price drops, you should still be spending more on the memory for your system than for your motherboard—in fact, up to twice as much. Before the memory price crash in mid-1996, memory had maintained a fairly consistent price for many years of about $40 per megabyte. A typical configuration back then of 16MB cost more than $600. In fact, memory was so expensive at that time that it was worth more than its weight in gold. These high prices caught the attention of criminals as memory module manufacturers were robbed at gunpoint in several large heists. These robberies were partially induced by the fact that memory was so valuable, the demand was high, and stolen chips or modules were virtually impossible to trace. After the rash of armed robberies and other thefts, memory module manufacturers began posting armed guards and implementing beefed-up security procedures.

By the end of 1996, memory prices had cooled considerably to about $4 per megabyte—a tenfold price drop in less than a year. Prices continued to fall after the major crash until they were at or below 50 cents per megabyte in 1997. All seemed well, until events in 1998 conspired to create a spike in memory prices, increasing them by four times their previous levels. The main culprits were Intel and Rambus, who had driven the industry to support a then-new type of memory called rambus DRAM (RDRAM) and then failed to deliver the supporting components on time. The industry was caught by shifting production to a memory type that nobody could use yet, and this created a shortage of the popular SDRAM memory. An earthquake in Taiwan that year served as the icing on the cake, furthering the spike in prices.

Since then, things have cooled somewhat, and even though prices haven't dropped to their lowest levels ever, they have come down to well below a dollar per megabyte.

Memory costs less now than a few years ago, but its useful life has become much shorter. New types of memory are being adopted more quickly than before, and any new systems you purchase now most likely will not accept the same memory as your existing ones. In an upgrade or a repair situation, that means you often have to change the memory if you change the motherboard. The chance that you can reuse the memory in an existing motherboard when upgrading to a new one is slim.

Because of this, you should understand all the various types of memory on the market today, so you can best determine which types are required by which systems, and thus more easily plan for future upgrades and repairs.

To better understand physical memory in a system, you should see where and how it fits into the system. Three main types of physical memory are used in modern PCs:

- *ROM.* Read-only memory
- *DRAM.* Dynamic random access memory
- *SRAM.* Static RAM

ROM

Read-only memory, or ROM, is a type of memory that can permanently or semipermanently hold data. It is called read-only because it is either impossible or difficult to write to. ROM also is often referred to as *nonvolatile memory* because any data stored in ROM remains there, even if the power is turned off. As such, ROM is an ideal place to put the PC's startup instructions—that is, the software that boots the system.

Note that ROM and RAM are not opposites, as some people seem to believe. Both are simply types of memory. In fact, ROM could be classified as technically a subset of the system's RAM. In other words, a portion of the system's random access memory address space is mapped into one or more ROM chips. This is necessary to contain the software that enables the PC to boot up; otherwise, the processor would have no program in memory to execute when it was powered on.

◀◀   For more information on ROM, see "Motherboard BIOS," p. 349.

The main ROM BIOS is contained in a ROM chip on the motherboard, but there are also adapter cards with ROMs on them as well. ROMs on adapter cards contain auxiliary BIOS routines and drivers needed by the particular card, especially for those cards that must be active early in the boot process, such as video cards. Cards that don't need drivers active at boot time typically don't have a ROM because those drivers can be loaded from the hard disk later in the boot process.

Most systems today use a type of ROM called electrically erasable programmable ROM (EEPROM), which is a form of Flash memory. Flash is a truly nonvolatile memory that is rewritable, enabling users to easily update the ROM or firmware in their motherboards or any other components (video cards, SCSI cards, peripherals, and so on).

DRAM

Dynamic RAM (DRAM) is the type of memory chip used for most of the main memory in a modern PC. The main advantages of DRAM are that it is very dense, meaning you can pack a lot of bits into a very small chip, and it is inexpensive, which makes purchasing large amounts of memory affordable.

The memory cells in a DRAM chip are tiny capacitors that retain a charge to indicate a bit. The problem with DRAM is that it is dynamic. Also, because of the design, it must be constantly refreshed; otherwise, the electrical charges in the individual memory capacitors will drain and the data will be lost. Refresh occurs when the system memory controller takes a tiny break and accesses all the rows of data in the memory chips. Most systems have a memory controller (normally built into the North Bridge portion of the motherboard chipset), which is set for an industry-standard refresh rate of 15μs (microseconds). This means that every 15μsec, all the rows in the memory are read to refresh the data.

◀◀ See "Chipsets," p. 225.

Refreshing the memory unfortunately takes processor time away from other tasks because each refresh cycle takes several CPU cycles to complete. In older systems, the refresh cycling could take up to 10% or more of the total CPU time, but with modern systems running in the hundreds of megahertz, refresh overhead is now on the order of a fraction of a percent or less of the total CPU time. Some systems allow you to alter the refresh timing parameters via the CMOS Setup, but be aware that increasing the time between refresh cycles to speed up your system can allow some of the memory cells to begin draining, which can cause random soft memory errors to appear. A *soft error* is a data error errors to appear. A soft error that is not caused by a defective chip. It is usually safer to stick with the recommended or default refresh timing. Because refresh consumes less than 1% of modern system overall bandwidth, altering the refresh rate has little effect on performance.

DRAMs use only one transistor and capacitor pair per bit, which makes them very dense, offering more memory capacity per chip than other types of memory. Currently, DRAM chips are available with densities of up to 256Mbits or more. This means that DRAM chips are available with 256 million or more transistors! Compare this to a Pentium 4, which has 42 million transistors, and it makes the processor look wimpy by comparison. The difference is that in a memory chip, the transistors and capacitors are all consistently arranged in a (normally square) grid of simple repetitive structures, unlike the processor, which is a much more complex circuit of different structures and elements interconnected in a highly irregular fashion. At least one manufacturer is working on chips, intended for the 2001–2002 timeframe, with 256-gigabit densities using circuit line widths of 0.05 micron, indicating that memory densities will continue to rise as they have for years.

The transistor for each DRAM bit cell reads the charge state of the adjacent capacitor. If the capacitor is charged, the cell is read to contain a 1; no charge indicates a 0. The charge in the tiny capacitors is constantly draining, which is why the memory must be refreshed constantly. Even a momentary power interruption, or anything that interferes with the refresh cycles, can cause a DRAM memory cell to lose the charge and therefore the data.

DRAM is used in PC systems because it is inexpensive and the chips can be densely packed, so a lot of memory capacity can fit in a small space. Unfortunately, DRAM is also slow, normally much slower than the processor. For this reason, many types of DRAM architectures have been developed to improve performance.

Cache Memory: SRAM

Another distinctly different type of memory exists that is significantly faster than most types of DRAM. SRAM stands for Static RAM, which is so named because it does not need the periodic refresh rates like DRAM. Because of SRAM's design, not only are refresh rates unnecessary, but SRAM is much faster than DRAM and fully capable of keeping pace with modern processors.

SRAM memory is available in access times of 2ns or less, so it can keep pace with processors running 500MHz or faster! This is because of the SRAM design, which calls for a cluster of six transistors for each bit of storage. The use of transistors but no capacitors means that refresh rates are not necessary because there are no capacitors to lose their charges over time. As long as there is power, SRAM remembers what is stored. With these attributes, why don't we use SRAM for all system memory? The answers are simple:

Type	Speed	Density	Cost
DRAM	Slow	High	Low
SRAM	Fast	Low	High

Compared to DRAM, SRAM is much faster but also much lower in density and much more expensive. The lower density means that SRAM chips are physically larger and store many fewer bits overall. The high number of transistors and the clustered design mean that SRAM chips are both physically larger and much more expensive to produce than DRAM chips. For example, a DRAM module might contain 64MB of RAM or more, whereas SRAM modules of the same approximate physical size would have room for only 2MB or so of data and would cost the same as the 64MB DRAM module. Basically, SRAM is up to 30 times larger physically and up to 30 times more expensive than DRAM. The high cost and physical constraints have prevented SRAM from being used as the main memory for PC systems.

Even though SRAM is too expensive for PC use as main memory, PC designers have found a way to use SRAM to dramatically improve PC performance. Rather than spend the money for all RAM to be SRAM memory, which can run fast enough to match the CPU, designing in a small amount of high-speed SRAM memory, called cache memory, is much more cost-effective. The cache runs at speeds close to or even equal to the processor and is the memory from which the processor usually directly reads from and writes to. During read operations, the data in the high-speed cache memory is resupplied from the lower-speed main memory or DRAM in advance. Up until recently, DRAM was limited to about 60ns (16MHz) in speed. To convert access time in nanoseconds to MHz, use the following formula:

1 / nanoseconds × 1000 = MHz

Likewise, to convert from MHz to nanoseconds, use the following inverse formula:

1 / MHz × 1000 = nanoseconds

When PC systems were running 16MHz and less, the DRAM could fully keep pace with the motherboard and system processor, and there was no need for cache. However, as soon as processors crossed the 16MHz barrier, DRAM could no longer keep pace, and that is exactly when SRAM began to enter PC system designs. This occurred back in 1986 and 1987 with the debut of systems with the 386 processor running at 16MHz and 20MHz. These were among the first PC systems to employ what's called *cache memory*, a high-speed buffer made up of SRAM that directly feeds the processor. Because the cache can run at the speed of the processor, the system is designed so that the cache controller anticipates the processor's memory needs and preloads the high-speed cache memory with that data. Then, as the processor calls for a memory address, the data can be retrieved from the high-speed cache rather than the much lower-speed main memory.

Cache effectiveness is expressed as a hit ratio. This is the ratio of cache hits to total memory accesses. A *hit* occurs when the data the processor needs has been preloaded into the cache from the main memory, meaning that the processor can read it from the cache. A *cache miss* is when the cache controller did not anticipate the the cache. A cache miss is when the cache controller did not anticipate theneed for a specific address; the desired data was not preloaded into the cache. Therefore, the processor must retrieve the data from the slower main memory, instead of the faster cache. Anytime the processor reads data from main memory, the processor must wait because the main memory cycles at a much slower rate than the processor. If the processor is running at 1000MHz, it is cycling at 1ns, whereas the main memory might be 7.5ns, which means it is running at only 133MHz. Therefore, every time the processor reads from main memory, it would effectively slow down to 133MHz! The slowdown is accomplished by having the processor execute what are called *wait states*, which are cycles in which nothing is done; the processor essentially cools its heels while waiting for the slower main memory to return the desired data. Obviously, you don't want your processors slowing down, so cache function and design become important as system speeds increase.

To minimize the processor being forced to read data from the slow main memory, two stages of cache usually exist in a modern system, called Level 1 (L1) and Level 2 (L2). The L1 cache is also called *integral* or *internal cache* because it is directly built into the processor and is actually a part of the processor die (raw chip). Because of this, L1 cache always runs at the full speed of the processor core and is the fastest cache in any system. All 486 and higher processors incorporate integral L1 cache, making them significantly faster than their predecessors. L2 cache is also called *external cache* because it is external to the processor chip. Originally, this meant it was installed on the motherboard, as was the case with all 386, 486, and Pentium systems. In those systems, the L2 cache runs at motherboard speed because it is installed on the motherboard. You typically can find the L2 cache directly next to the processor socket in Pentium and earlier systems.

◀◀ See "How Cache Works," p. 62.

In the interest of improved performance, later processor designs from Intel and AMD have included the L2 cache as a part of the processor. In all the processors since late 1999 (and some earlier models), the L2 cache was directly incorporated as a part of the processor die just like the L1 cache. In chips with on-die L2, the cache runs at the full core speed of the processor and is much more efficient. By contrast, most processors from 1999 and earlier had L2 cache in separate chips that were external to the main processor core. The L2 cache in many of these older chips ran at only half or one-third the processor core speed. Prior to the inclusion of L2 cache in the processor, the L2 was on the motherboard, where it ran even more slowly. Cache speed is very important, so systems having L2 cache on the motherboard were the slowest. Including L2 inside the processor made it faster, and including it directly on the processor die (rather than as chips external to the die) is the fastest yet. Any chip that has on-die full core speed L2 cache has a distinct performance advantage over any chip that doesn't.

Processors with built-in L2 cache, whether it's on-die or not, still run the cache more quickly than any fo*und on the motherboard. Thus, most motherboards designed for processors with built-in cache don't have any cache on the board; all the cache is contained in the processor module instead.

The new Itanium processor from Intel has three levels of cache within the processor module for even greater performance. More cache and more levels of cache help mitigate the speed differential between the fast processor core and the relatively slow motherboard and main memory.

The key to understanding both cache and main memory is to see where they fit in the overall system architecture.

Figure 6.1 shows the system architecture for a typical Pentium system with an Intel chipset.

Figure 6.1 System architecture: Pentium system with an Intel chipset.

See Chapter 4, "Motherboards and Buses," for a diagram showing a typical Pentium III system with integrated L2 cache.

Table 6.1 illustrates the need for and function of L1 (internal) and L2 (external) cache in modern systems.

Cache designs were originallyCache designs originally were *asynchronous*, meaning they ran at a clock speed that was not identical or in sync with the processor bus. Starting with the 430FX chipset released in early 1995, a new type of synchronous cache design was supported. It required that the chips now run in sync or at the same identical clock timing as the processor bus, further improving speed and performance. Also added at that time was a feature called *pipeline burst mode*, which reduces overall cache latency (wait states) by allowing single-cycle accesses for multiple transfers after the first one. Because both synchronous and pipeline burst capability came at the same time in new modules, specifying one usually implies the other. Synchronous pipeline burst cache allowed for about a 20% improvement in overall system performance, which was a significant jump.

The cache controller for a modern system is contained in either the North Bridge of the chipset, as with Pentium and lesser systems, or within the processor, as with the Pentium Pro/II and newer systems. The capabilities of the cache controller dictate the cache's performance and capabilities. One important thing to note is that most cache controllers have a limitation on the amount of memory that can be cached. Often, this limit can be quite low, as with the 430TX chipset-based Pentium systems. The 430TX chipset can cache data only within the first 64MB of system RAM. If you have more memory than that, you will see a noticeable slowdown in system performance because all data outside the first 64MB is never cached and is always accessed with all the wait states required by the slower DRAM. Depending on what software you use and where data is stored in memory, this can be significant. For example, 32-bit operating systems, such as Windows 9x and NT, load from the top down, so if you had 96MB of RAM, the operating system and applications would load directly into the upper 32MB (past 64MB), which is not cached. This results in a dramatic slowdown in overall system use. Removing the additional memory to bring the system total down to the cacheable limit of 64MB is the solution. In short, it is unwise to install more main RAM memory than your system (chipset) can cache. Consult your system documentation or the chipset section in Chapter 4 for more information.

Table 6.1   The Relationship Between L1 (Internal) and L2 (External) Cache in Modern Systems

CPU Type	486 DX4	Pentium	Pentium Pro	Pentium II	Pentium II	AMD K6-2	AMD K6-3
CPU speed	100MHz	233MHz	200MHz	333MHz	450MHz	550MHz	450MHz
L1 cache speed	10ns (100MHz)	4.3ns (233MHz)	5.0ns (200MHz)	3.0ns (333MHz)	2.2ns (450MHz)	1.8ns (550MHz)	2.2ns (450MHz)
L1 cache size	16K	16K	32K	32K	32K	64K	64K
L2 cache location	Motherboard	Motherboard	Chip	Chip	Chip	Motherboard	On-die
L2 core/ cache ratio	-	-	1/1	1/2	1/2	-	1/1
L2 cache speed	30ns (33MHz)	15ns (66MHz)	5ns (200MHz)	6ns (166MHz)	4.4ns (225MHz)	10ns (100MHz)	2.2ns (450MHz)
L2 cache size	varies[1]	varies[1]	256K[2]	512K	512K	varies[1]	256K
Motherboard speed	33MHz	66MHz	66MHz	66MHz	100MHz	100MHz	100MHz
SIMM/DIMM speed	60ns (16MHz)	60ns (16MHz)	60ns (16MHz)	15ns (66MHz)	10ns (100MHz)	10ns (100MHz)	10ns (100MHz)

1. *The L2 cache is on the motherboard, and the amount depends on which board is chosen and how much is installed.*

2. *The Pentium Pro also was available with 512KB and 1024KB L2 cache.*

3. *The Athlon uses a 200MHz bus between the CPU and North Bridge; however, the board and main memory still run at 100MHz.*

RAM Memory Types

The speed and performance issue with memory is confusing to some because memory speed is usually expressed in ns (nanoseconds), and processor speed has always been expressed in MHz (megahertz). Recently, however, some newer and faster types of memory have speeds expressed in MHz, adding to the confusion. Let's see if we can come up with a way to translate one to the other.

A *nanosecond* is defined as one billionth of a second—a very short time indeed. To put some perspective on that, the speed of light is 186,282 miles (299,792 kilometers) per second in a vacuum. In one billionth of a second, a beam of light travels a mere 11.80 inches or 29.98 centimeters—less than the length of a typical ruler!

Chip and system speed has been expressed in megahertz (MHz), which is millions of cycles per second. Some systems today have processors running up to and beyond 2000MHz (2GHz or two billion cycles per second), and we should see processors approaching 3GHz or 4GHz by next year.

Because it is confusing to speak in these different terms for speeds, I thought it would be interesting to see how they compare. Table 6.2 shows the relationship between nanoseconds (ns) and megahertz (MHz) for the speeds associated with PCs from yesterday to today and tomorrow.

Pentium III	AMD Athlon	AMD Athlon	AMD Duron	AMD Athlon (Thunderbird)	Celeron	Pentium III (Coppermine)	Pentium 4
600MHz	800MHz	1,000MHz	800MHz	1,000MHz	800MHz	1,000MHz	1.7GHz
1.6ns (600MHz)	1.3ns (800MHz)	1ns (1,000MHz)	1.3ns (800MHz)	1ns (1,000MHz)	1.3ns (800MHz)	1ns (1,000MHz)	0.6ns (1.7GHz)
32K	128K	128K	128K	128K	32K	32K	20K
Chip	Chip	Chip	on-die	On-die	On-die	On-die	On-die
1/2	2/5	1/3	1/1	1/1	1/1	1/1	1/1
3.3ns (300MHz)	3.1ns (320MHz)	3ns (333MHz)	1.3ns (800MHz)	1ns (1,000MHz)	1.3ns (800MHz)	1ns (1,000MHz)	0.6ns (1.7GHz)
512K	512K	512K	64K	256K	128K	256K	256K
100MHz	100MHz[3]	100MHz[3]	100MHz[3]	266MHz	100MHz	133MHz	400MHz
10ns (100MHz)	10ns (100MHz)	10ns (100MHz)	10ns (100MHz)	3.8ns (266MHz)	10ns (100MHz)	7.5ns (133MHz)4	2.5ns (400MHz)

4. These systems also can support PC800 RDRAM RIMM memory, which has about twice the bandwidth of PC100 and 1.5 times that of PC133.

5. Katmai is the codename for the first-generation Pentium III.

6. Coppermine is the codename for the second-generation Pentium III (0.18 micron, on-die L2 cache).

7. Thunderbird is the codename for the third-generation (Model 4) Athlon (0.18 micron, on-die L2 cache).

Table 6.2   The Relationship Between Megahertz (MHz) and Cycle Times in Nanoseconds (ns)

Clock Speed	Cycle Time	Clock Speed	Cycle Time	Clock Speed	Cycle Time
4.77MHz	210ns	225MHz	4.4ns	750MHz	1.33ns
6MHz	167ns	233MHz	4.3ns	766MHz	1.31ns
8MHz	125ns	250MHz	4.0ns	800MHz	1.25ns
10MHz	100ns	266MHz	3.8ns	833MHz	1.20ns
12MHz	83ns	300MHz	3.3ns	850MHz	1.18ns
16MHz	63ns	333MHz	3.0ns	866MHz	1.15ns
20MHz	50ns	350MHz	2.9ns	900MHz	1.11ns
25MHz	40ns	366MHz	2.7ns	933MHz	1.07ns
33MHz	30ns	400MHz	2.5ns	950MHz	1.05ns
40MHz	25ns	433MHz	2.3ns	966MHz	1.04ns
50MHz	20ns	450MHz	2.2ns	1,000MHz	1.00ns

Table 6.2   Continued

Clock Speed	Cycle Time	Clock Speed	Cycle Time	Clock Speed	Cycle Time
60MHz	17ns	466MHz	2.1ns	1,100MHz	0.91ns
66MHz	15ns	500MHz	2.0ns	1,133MHz	0.88ns
75MHz	13ns	533MHz	1.88ns	1,200MHz	0.83ns
80MHz	13ns	550MHz	1.82ns	1,300MHz	0.77ns
100MHz	10ns	566MHz	1.77ns	1,400MHz	0.71ns
120MHz	8.3ns	600MHz	1.67ns	1,500MHz	0.67ns
133MHz	7.5ns	633MHz	1.58ns	1,600MHz	0.63ns
150MHz	6.7ns	650MHz	1.54ns	1,700MHz	0.59ns
166MHz	6.0ns	666MHz	1.50ns	1,800MHz	0.56ns
180MHz	5.6ns	700MHz	1.43ns	1,900MHz	0.53ns
200MHz	5.0ns	733MHz	1.36ns	2,000MHz	0.50ns

As you can see from this table, as clock speeds increase, cycle time decreases proportionately.

If you examine Table 6.2, you can clearly see that the 60ns DRAM memory used in the typical PC for many years is totally inadequate when compared to processor speeds of 400MHz and higher. Up until 1998, most DRAM memory used in PCs had been rated at an access time of 60ns or higher, which works out to be 16.7MHz or slower! This super-slow 16MHz memory had been installed in systems running up to 300MHz or faster, and you can see what a mismatch has existed between processor and main memory performance. The dominant standard in 2000 was to have 100MHz and even 133MHz memory, called PC100 and PC133, respectively. Starting in early 2001, double data rate (DDR) memory of 200MHz and 266MHz become popular, along with 800MHz RDRAM.

System memory timing is a little more involved than simply converting nanoseconds to megahertz. The transistors for each bit in a memory chip are most efficiently arranged in a grid, using a row and column scheme to access each transistor. All memory accesses involve selecting a row address and then a column address, and then transferring the data. The initial setup for a memory transfer where the row and column addresses are selected is a necessary overhead normally referred to as *latency*. The access time for memory is the cycle time plus latency for selecting the row and column addresses. For example, SDRAM memory rated at 133MHz (7.5ns) typically takes five cycles to set up and complete the first transfer (5 × 7.5ns = 37.5ns) and then perform three additional transfers with no additional setup. Thus, four transfers take a total eight cycles, or an average of about two cycles per transfer.

What happens when a 1GHz processor is trying to read multiple bytes of data from 133MHz memory? A lot of wait states! A wait state is an additional "do nothing" cycle that the processor must execute while waiting for the data to become ready. With memory cycling every 7.5ns (133MHz) and a processor cycling every 1ns (1GHz), the processor must execute approximately six wait states before the data is ready on the seventh cycle. Adding wait states in this fashion effectively slows the processing speed to that of the memory, or 133MHz in this example. To reduce the number of wait states required, several types of faster memory and cache are available, all of which are discussed in this chapter.

Over the development life of the PC, memory has had a difficult time keeping up with the processor, requiring several levels of high-speed cache memory to intercept processor requests for the slower main memory. Table 6.3 shows the progress and relationship between system board (motherboard) speeds in PCs and the various types and speeds of main memory or RAM used and how these changes have affected total bandwidth.

Table 6.3   Memory Bus Bandwidth

Memory Bus Type	Memory Bus Width (bytes)	Memory Bus Speed (MHz)	Data Cycles per Clock	Bandwidth (MB/sec)
FPM DRAM	8	22	1	177
EDO DRAM	8	33	1	266
PC66 SDRAM	8	66	1	533
PC100 SDRAM	8	100	1	800
PC133 SDRAM	8	133	1	1,066
PC1600 DDR-SDRAM	8	100	2	1,600
PC2100 DDR-SDRAM	8	133	2	2,133
PC600 RDRAM	2	300	2	1,200
PC700 RDRAM	2	350	2	1,400
PC800 RDRAM	2	400	2	1,600
PC800 RDRAM Dual Channel	4	400	2	3,200

Generally, things work best when the throughput of the memory bus matches the throughput of the processor bus. Compare the memory bus speeds to the speeds of the processor bus (in Table 6.4), and you'll see that some of the memory bus speeds match that of some of the processor bus speeds. In most cases the type of memory that matches the CPU bus throughput is the best type of memory for systems with that type of processor.

Table 6.4 shows the relative speeds of the various processor buses according to bandwidth.

Table 6.4   Processor Bus Bandwidth

CPU Bus Type	CPU Bus Width (bytes)	CPU Bus Speed (MHz)	Data Cycles per Clock	Bandwidth (MB/sec)
33MHz 486 CPU FSB	32	33	1	133
66MHz 64-bit CPU FSB	64	66	1	533
100MHz 64-bit CPU FSB	64	100	1	800
133MHz 64-bit CPU FSB	64	133	1	1,066
200MHz 64-bit CPU FSB	64	100	2	1,600
266MHz 64-bit CPU FSB	64	133	2	2,133
400MHz 64-bit CPU FSB	64	100	4	3,200

FSB = Front Side Bus

Because the processor is fairly well insulated from directly dealing with main memory by the L1 and L2 cache, memory performance has often lagged behind the performance of the processor bus. More recently, however, systems using SDRAM, DDR SDRAM, and RDRAM have memory bus performance equaling that of the processor bus. When the speed of the memory bus equals the speed of the processor bus, memory performance is optimum for that system.

Fast Page Mode DRAM

Standard DRAM is accessed through a technique called *paging*. Normal memory access requires that a row and column address be selected, which takes time. Paging enables faster access to all the data within a given row of memory by keeping the row address the same and changing only the column.

Memory that uses this technique is called *Page Mode* or *Fast Page Mode* memory. Other variations on Page Mode were called *Static Column* or *Nibble Mode* memory.

Paged memory is a simple scheme for improving memory performance that divides memory into pages ranging from 512 bytes to a few kilobytes long. The paging circuitry then enables memory locations in a page to be accessed with fewer wait states. If the desired memory location is outside the current page, one or more wait states are added while the system selects the new page.

To improve further on memory access speeds, systems have evolved to enable faster access to DRAM. One important change was the implementation of burst mode access in the 486 and later processors. Burst mode cycling takes advantage of the consecutive nature of most memory accesses. After setting up the row and column addresses for a given access, using burst mode, you can then access the next three adjacent addresses with no additional latency or wait states. A burst access usually is limited to four total accesses. To describe this, we often refer to the timing in the number of cycles for each access. A typical burst mode access of standard DRAM is expressed as x-y-y-y; *x* is the time for the first access (latency plus cycle time), and *y* represents the number of cycles required for each consecutive access.

Standard 60ns DRAM normally runs 5-3-3-3 burst mode timing. This means the first access takes a total of five cycles (on a 66MHz system bus, this is about 75ns total or 5×15ns cycles), and the consecutive cycles take three cycles each (3×15ns = 45ns). As you can see, the actual system timing is somewhat less than the memory is technically rated for. Without the bursting technique, memory access would be 5-5-5-5 because the full latency is necessary for each memory transfer.

DRAM memory that supports paging and this bursting technique is called *Fast Page Mode (FPM)* memory. The term comes from the capability of memory accesses to data on the same page to be done with less latency. Most 486 and Pentium systems from 1995 and earlier use FPM memory.

Another technique for speeding up FPM memory was a technique called *interleaving*. In this design, two separate banks of memory are used together, alternating access from one to the other as even and odd bytes. While one is being accessed, the other is being precharged, when the row and column addresses are being selected. Then, by the time the first bank in the pair is finished returning data, the second bank in the pair is finished with the latency part of the cycle and is now ready to return data. While the second bank is returning data, the first bank is being precharged, selecting the row and column address of the next access. This overlapping of accesses in two banks reduces the effect of the latency or precharge cycles and allows for faster overall data retrieval. The only problem is that to use interleaving, you must install identical pairs of banks together, doubling the amount of SIMMs or DIMMs required. This method was popular on 32-bit wide memory systems on 486 processors but fell out of favor on Pentiums because of their 64-bit wide memory widths. To perform interleaving on a Pentium machine, you would need to install memory 128 bits at a time, meaning four 72-pin SIMMs or two DIMMs at a time.

Extended Data Out RAM

In 1995, aA newer type of memory called extended data out (EDO) RAM became available for Pentium systems. EDO, a modified form of FPM memory, is sometimes referred to as *Hyper Page mode*. EDO was invented and patented by Micron Technology, although Micron licensed production to many other memory manufacturers. EDO memory consists of specially manufactured chips that allow a timing overlap between successive accesses. The name *extended data out* refers specifically to the fact that unlike FPM, the data output drivers on the chip are not turned off when the memory controller removes the column address to begin the next cycle. This enables the next cycle to overlap the previous one, saving approximately 10ns per cycle.

The effect of EDO is that cycle times are improved by enabling the memory controller to begin a new column address instruction while it is reading data at the current address. This is almost identical to what was achieved in older systems by interleaving banks of memory, but unlike interleaving, with EDO you didn't need to install two identical banks of memory in the system at a time.

EDO RAM allows for burst mode cycling of 5-2-2-2, compared to the 5-3-3-3 of standard fast page mode memory. To do four memory transfers, then, EDO would require 11 total system cycles, compared to 14 total cycles for FPM. This is a 22% improvement in overall cycling time, but in actual testing, EDO typically increases overall system benchmark speed by about 5%. Even though the overall system improvement might seem small, the important thing about EDO was that it used the same basic DRAM chip design as FPM, meaning that there was practically no additional cost over FPM. In fact, in its heyday, EDO cost less than FPM and yet offered higher performance.

EDO RAM generally comes in 72-pin SIMM form. Figure 6.4 (later in this chapter) shows the physical characteristics of these SIMMs.

To actually use EDO memory, your motherboard chipset must support it. Most motherboard chipsets—starting in 1995 with the Intel 430FX (Triton) and through 1997—offered support for EDO. Because EDO memory chips cost the same to manufacture as standard chips, combined with Intel's support of EDO in all its chipsets, the PC market jumped on the EDO bandwagon full force.

◀◀ See "Fifth-Generation (P5 Pentium Class) Chipsets," p. 234, and "Sixth-Generation (P6 Pentium Pro/Pentium II/III Class) Chipsets," p. 246.

EDO RAM is ideal for systems with bus speeds of up to 66MHz, which fit perfectly with the PC market up through 1997. However, since 1998, the market for EDO has rapidly declined as the newer and faster SDRAM architecture has become the standard for new PC system memory.

Burst EDO

A variation of EDO is burst extended data out dynamic random access memory (BEDO DRAM). *BEDO* is basically EDO memory with special burst features for even speedier data transfers than standard EDO. Unfortunately, only one chipset (Intel 440FX Natoma) ever supported it, and it was quickly overshadowed by SDRAM, which seemed to be favored among PC system chipset and system designers. As such, BEDO never really saw the light of production, and to my knowledge no systems ever really used it.

SDRAM

Synchronous DRAM (SDRAM) is for Synchronous DRAM, a type of DRAM that runs in synchronization with the memory bus. SDRAM delivers information in very high-speed bursts using a high-speed, clocked interface. SDRAM removes most of the latency involved in asynchronous DRAM because the signals are already in synchronization with the motherboard clock.

Like EDO RAM, your chipset must support this type of memory for it to be usable in your system. Starting in 1997 with the 430VX and 430TX, most of Intel's chipsets began to support SDRAM, making it the most popular type of memory for new systems through 2000 and even into 2001.

SDRAM's performance is dramatically improved over FPM or EDO RAM. Because SDRAM is still a type of DRAM, the initial latency is the same, but overall cycle times are much faster than with FPM or EDO. SDRAM timing for a burst access would be 5-1-1-1, meaning that four memory reads would complete in only eight system bus cycles, compared to eleven cycles for EDO and fourteen cycles for FPM. This makes SDRAM almost 20% faster than EDO.

Besides being capable of working in fewer cycles, SDRAM is also capable of supporting up to 133MHz (7.5ns) system bus cycling. As such, most new PC systems sold in 1998, and through 2000, have included SDRAM memory.

SDRAM is sold in DIMM form and often is rated by megahertz speed rather than nanosecond cycling time, which can be kind of confusing. Figure 6.5 (later in this chapter) shows the physical characteristics of DIMMs.

To meet the stringent timing demands of its chipsets, Intel created specifications for SDRAM called PC66, PC100, and PC133. To meet the PC100 specification, 8ns chips usually are required. Normally, you would think 10ns would be considered the proper rating for 100MHz operation, but the PC100 specification calls for faster memory to ensure all timing parameters are met.

In May of 1999, the Joint Electron Device Engineering Council (JEDEC), an organization that creates most of the memory specifications used in the industry, created the PC133. They achieved this 33MHz speed increase by taking the PC100 specification and tightening up the timing and capacitance parameters. The faster PC133 quickly caught on as the most popular version of SDRAM for any systems running a 133MHz processor bus.

Table 6.5 shows the timing, actual speed, and rated speed for various SDRAM DIMMs.

Table 6.5   SDRAM Timing, Actual Speed, and Rated Speed

Timing	Actual Speed	Rated Speed
15ns	66MHz	PC66
10ns	100MHz	PC66
8ns	125MHz	PC100
7.5ns	133MHz	PC133

▶▶   See "SIMMs, DIMMs, and RIMMs," p. 421.

DDR SDRAM

Double data rate (DDR) SDRAM memory is an evolutionary design of standard SDRAM in which data is transferred twice as quickly. Instead of doubling the actual clock rate, DDR memory achieves the doubling in performance by transferring twice per transfer cycle: once at the leading (falling) edge and once at the trailing (rising) edge of the cycle (see Figure 6.2). This is similar to the way RDRAM operates and effectively doubles the transfer rate, even though the same overall clock and timing signals are used.

DDR, which found most of its initial support in the graphics card market, is also supported in many of the newest motherboard chipsets, including those for server use. It seems the server market is more comfortable with DDR SDRAM—which is almost identical to previous SDRAM, except for the double clocking—than it is with the more radical RDRAM. As such, DDR SDRAM is supported by processor companies, including Intel, AMD, and Cyrix, and chipset manufacturers, including Intel, VIA Technologies, ALi (Acer Labs, Inc.), and SiS (Silicon Integrated Systems). The DDR Consortium, an industry panel consisting of Fujitsu, Ltd.; Hitachi, Ltd.; Hyundai Electronics Industries Co.; Mitsubishi Electric Corp.; NEC Corp.; Samsung Electronics Co.; Texas Instruments, Inc.; and Toshiba Corp. undertook official standardization of DDR.

DDR SDRAM came to market during 2000, but it didn't really catch on until the advent of mainstream motherboards and chipsets supporting it during 2001.

DDR SDRAM uses a new DIMM module design with 184 pins. Figure 6.6 (later in this chapter) shows the DDR SDRAM DIMM.

DDR DIMMs are rated for either PC1600 (200MHz × 8) or PC2100 (266MHz × 8) operation and normally run on 2.5 volts. They are basically an extension of the PC100 and PC133 DIMMs redesigned to support double clocking, where data is sent on each clock transition (twice per cycle) rather than once per cycle as with standard SDRAM.

RDRAM

Rambus DRAM (RDRAM) is a fairly radical memory design found in high-end PC systems starting in late 1999. Intel signed a contract with Rambus in 1996 ensuring they would support RDRAM into 2001.

Rambus developed what is essentially a chip-to-chip memory bus, with specialized devices that communicate at very high rates of speed. What might be interesting to some is that this technology was first developed for game systems and first made popular by the Nintendo 64 game system and subsequently was used in the Sony Playstation 2.

Conventional memory systems that use FPM/EDO or SDRAM are known as *wide-channel systems*. They have memory channels as wide as the processor's data bus, which for the Pentium and up is 64 bits. The dual inline memory module (DIMM) is a 64-bit wide device, meaning data can be transferred to it 64 bits (or 8 bytes) at a time.

RDRAMs, on the other hand, are narrow-channel devices. They transfer data only 16 bits (2 bytes) at a time (plus 2 optional parity bits), but at much faster speeds.

RIMMs typically run 800MHz, so the overall throughput is 800 × 2, or 1.6GB per second for a single channel—the same as PC1600 DDR SDRAM. The RDRAM design features less latency between transfers because they all run synchronously in a looped system and in only one direction. For further increases in speed, you can use two or four RDRAM channels simultaneously, increasing memory throughput to 3.2GB/sec or 6.4GB/sec if necessary. Currently, motherboards exist that use dual-channel RDRAM designs. Dual-channel PC800 RDRAM is also currently the fastest type of PC memory, followed by PC2100 DDR SDRAM. Whether your board supports (requires) dual-channel RDRAM is dictated by the motherboard chipset; currently, the Intel 840 and 850 chipsets support dual-channel RDRAM.

A single Rambus memory channel can support up to 32 individual RDRAM devices (the RDRAM chips), more if buffers are used. Each individual chip is serially connected to the next on a package called a Rambus inline memory module (RIMM), but all memory transfers are done between the memory controller and a single device, not between devices. The individual RDRAM chips are contained on RIMMs, and a single channel normally has three RIMM sockets. The RDRAM memory bus is a continuous path through each device and module on the bus, with each module having input and output pins on opposite ends. Therefore, any RIMM sockets not containing a RIMM must then be filled with a continuity module to ensure that the path is completed. The signals that reach the end of the bus are terminated on the motherboard.

Each RDRAM on a RIMM essentially operates as a standalone module sitting on the 16-bit data bus. Internally, each RDRAM chip has a core that operates on a 128-bit wide bus split into eight 16-bit banks running at 100MHz. In other words, every 10ns (100MHz), each RDRAM chip can transfer 16 bytes to and from the core. This internally wide, yet externally narrow, high-speed interface is the key to RDRAM.

Other improvements to the design include separating control and data signals on the bus. There are independent control and address buses split into two groups of pins for row and column commands, while data is transferred across the 2-byte wide data bus. The actual memory bus clock runs at

400MHz; however, data is transferred on both the falling and rising edges of the clock signal, or twice per clock pulse. The falling edge is called an *even cycle*, and the rising edge is called an *odd cycle*. Complete memory bus synchronization is achieved by sending packets of data beginning on an even cycle interval. The overall wait before a memory transfer can begin (latency) is only one cycle, or 2.5ns maximum.

Figure 6.2 shows the relationship between clock and data cycles; you can see five total clock cycles (each with a falling and a rising edge) and 10 data cycles in the same time. An RDRAM data packet always begins on an even (falling) transition for synchronization purposes.

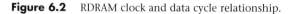

Figure 6.2   RDRAM clock and data cycle relationship.

The architecture also supports multiple, simultaneous interleaved transactions in multiple separate time domains. Therefore, before a transfer has even completed, another can begin.

Another important feature of RDRAM is that it is a low-power memory system. The RIMMs themselves as well as the RDRAM devices run on only 2.5 volts and use low-voltage signal swings from 1.0v to 1.8v, a swing of only 0.8v total. RDRAMs also have four power-down modes and can automatically transition into standby mode at the end of a transaction, which offers further power savings.

As discussed, RDRAM chips are installed in modules called RIMMs. A RIMM (shown in Figure 6.3, later in this chapter) is similar in size and physical form to current DIMMs, but they are not interchangeable. RIMMs are available in 64MB, 128MB, and 256MB capacities. They can be added to a system one at a time because each individual RIMM technically represents multiple banks to a system.

An RDRAM memory controller with a single Rambus channel supports up to three RIMM modules according to the design. However, most motherboards implement only two modules per channel to avoid problems with signal noise.

With Intel throwing its weight behind the Rambus memory, it seemed to be a sure thing for success. Unfortunately, delays in the chipsets due to technical difficulties with RDRAM memory designs have caused the RIMM modules to be priced three or more times that of a comparatively sized DIMM. Although the performance of RDRAM seems good, DDR SDRAM actually performs better in most systems and at significantly less cost. Unfortunately for the memory chip manufacturers, it seems that Rambus has claimed patents that cover both standard and DDR SDRAM designs, so regardless of whether these companies manufacture SDRAM, DDR, or RDRAM, they must pay royalties to Rambus. Several court cases are ongoing with companies challenging these patents, and a lot is riding on the outcome.

Memory Modules

The CPU and motherboard architecture (chipset) dictates a particular computer's physical memory capacity and the types and forms of memory that can be installed. Over the years, two main changes have occurred in computer memory—it has gradually become faster and wider. The CPU and the memory controller circuitry indicate the speed and width requirements. The memory controller in a modern PC resides in the motherboard chipset. Even though a system might physically support a given amount of memory, the type of software you run could dictate whether all the memory can be used.

The 8088 and 8086, with 20 address lines, can use as much as 1MB (1,024KB) of RAM. The 286 and 386SX CPUs have 24 address lines and can keep track of as much as 16MB of memory. The 386DX, 486, Pentium, Pentium-MMX, and Pentium Pro CPUs have a full set of 32 address lines, so they can keep track of 4GB of memory; the Pentium II/III and 4, as well as the AMD Athlon and Duron, have 36 address lines and can manage an impressive 64GB. The new Itanium processor, on the other hand, has 44-bit addressing, which allows for up to 16TB (terabytes) of physical RAM!

◄◄ See "Processor Specifications," p. 42.

When the 286 and higher chips emulate the 8088 chip (as they do when running 16-bit software, such as DOS or Windows 3.x), they implement a hardware operating mode called *real mode*. Real mode is the only mode available on the 8086 and 8088 chips used in PC and XT systems. In real mode, all Intel processors—even the mighty Pentium—are restricted to using only 1MB of memory, just as their 8086 and 8088 ancestors were, and the system design reserves 384KB of that amount. Only in protected mode can the 286 or better chips use their maximum potentials for memory addressing.

◄◄ See "Processor Modes," p. 67.

P5 class systems can address as much as 4GB of memory, and P6/P7 class systems can address up to 64GB. To put these memory-addressing capabilities into perspective, 64GB (65,536MB) of memory would cost about $70,000! Even if you could afford all this memory, some of the largest memory modules available today are 1GB DIMMs. To install 64GB of RAM would require 64 of the largest 1GB DIMMs available, and most systems today support up to only four DIMM sockets.

Most motherboards have a maximum of only three to six DIMM sockets, which allows a maximum of .75GB–1.5GB if all the sockets are filled. These limitations are from the chipset, not the processor. Although some processors can address 64GB, there isn't a chipset on the market that will allow that! Most of the chipsets today are limited to 1GB of memory, although some handle up to 4GB or more.

Some systems have even more limitations. P5 class systems have been available since 1993, but only those built in 1997 or later use a motherboard chipset that supports SDRAM DIMMs. Even those using the most recent P5 class chipset from Intel, such as the 430TX, do not support more than 256MB of total memory and should not have more than 64MB actually installed because of memory-caching limitations. Don't install more than 64MB of RAM in one of these systems unless you are sure the motherboard and chipset will allow the L2 cache to function with the additional memory.

Note

See the "Chipsets" section in Chapter 4 for the maximum cacheable limits on all the Intel and other motherboard chipsets.

SIMMs, DIMMs, and RIMMs

Originally, systems had memory installed via individual chips. They are often referred to as *dual inline package (DIP)* chips because of their designs. The original IBM XT and AT had 36 sockets on the motherboard for these individual chips, and then more of them were installed on the memory cards plugged into the bus slots. I remember spending hours populating boards with these chips, which was a tedious job.

Besides being a time-consuming and labor-intensive way to deal with memory, DIP chips had one notorious problem—they crept out of their sockets over time as the system went through thermal cycles. Every day, when you powered the system on and off, the system heated and cooled, and the chips gradually walked their way out of the sockets. Eventually, good contact was lost and memory errors resulted. Fortunately, reseating all the chips back in their sockets usually rectified the problem, but that method was labor intensive if you had a lot of systems to support.

The alternative to this at the time was to have the memory soldered into either the motherboard or an expansion card. This prevented the chips from creeping and made the connections more permanent, but that caused another problem. If a chip did go bad, you had to attempt desoldering the old one and resoldering a new one or resort to scrapping the motherboard or memory card on which the chip was installed. This was expensive and made memory troubleshooting difficult.

What was necessary was a chip that was both soldered and removable, and that is exactly what was found in the module called a *SIMM*. For memory storage, most modern systems have adopted the single inline memory module (SIMM), dual inline memory module (DIMM), or RIMM as an alternative to individual memory chips. These small boards plug into special connectors on a motherboard or memory card. The individual memory chips are soldered to the module, so removing and replacing them is impossible. Instead, you must replace the entire module if any part of it fails. The module is treated as though it were one large memory chip.

There are two main types of SIMMs, two main types of DIMMs, and so far one type of RIMM used in desktop systems. The various types are often described by their pin count, memory row width, or memory type.

SIMMs, for example, were available in two main physical types—30-pin (8 bits plus an option for 1 additional parity bit) and 72-pin (32 bits plus an option for 4 additional parity bits)—with various capacities and other specifications. The 30-pin SIMMs are physically smaller than the 72-pin versions, and either version can have chips on one or both sides.

DIMMs are also available in two types. DIMMs usually hold standard SDRAM or DDR SDRAM chips, and they are distinguished by different physical characteristics. Standard DIMMs have 168 pins, one notch on either side, and two notches along the contact area. DDR DIMMs, on the other hand, have 184 pins, two notches on each side, and only one notch along the contact area. All DIMMs are either 64-bits (nonparity) or 72-bits (parity or error correcting code [ECC]) wide (data paths). The main physical difference between SIMMs and DIMMs is that DIMMs have different signal pins on each side of the module. That is why they are called *dual* inline memory modules, and why with only an inch of additional length, they have many more pins than a SIMM.

RIMMs are also double-sided. Only one type of RIMM is available, which has 184 pins, one notch on either side, and two notches centrally located in the contact area. All RIMMs are either 16-bits wide or 18-bits wide (data path) for non-ECC and ECC versions, respectively.

Figures 6.3–6.7 show a typical 30-pin (8-bit) SIMM, 72-pin (32-bit) SIMM, 168-pin SDRAM DIMM, 184-pin DDR SDRAM (64-bit) DIMM, and 184-pin RIMM, respectively. The pins are numbered from left to right and are connected through to both sides of the module on the SIMMs. The pins on the DIMM are different on each side, but on a SIMM, each side is the same as the other and the connections carry through. Note that all dimensions are in both inches and millimeters (in parentheses).

Figure 6.3   A typical 30-pin SIMM. The one shown here is 9-bit, although the dimensions would be the same for 8-bit.

Figure 6.4   A typical 72-pin SIMM. The version shown here is 36-bit, although the dimensions would be the same for 32-bit.

Figure 6.5   A typical 168-pin SDRAM DIMM. The one shown here is 72-bit, although the dimensions would be the same for 64-bit.

Figure 6.6 A typical 184-pin DDR DIMM. The one shown here is 72-bit, although the dimensions would be the same for 64-bit.

Figure 6.7 A typical 184-pin RIMM. The one shown here is 18-bit, although the dimensions would be the same for 16-bit.

These memory modules are extremely compact, considering the amount of memory they hold, and are available in several capacities and speeds. Table 6.6 lists the various capacities available for SIMMs, DIMMs, and RIMMs.

Table 6.6 SIMM, DIMM, and RIMM Capacities

30-Pin SIMM Capacities		
Capacity	**Parity SIMM**	**Nonparity SIMM**
256KB	256KB×9	256KB×8
1MB	1MB×9	1MB×8
4MB	4MB×9	4MB×8
16MB	16MB×9	16MB×8
72-Pin SIMM Capacities		
Capacity	**Parity/ECC SIMM**	**Nonparity SIMM**
1MB	256KB×36	256KB×32
2MB	512KB×36	512KB×32
4MB	1MB×36	1MB×32

Table 6.6   Continued

72-Pin SIMM Capacities		
Capacity	**Parity/ECC SIMM**	**Nonparity SIMM**
8MB	2MB×36	2MB×32
16MB	4MB×36	4MB×32
32MB	8MB×36	8MB×32
64MB	16MB×36	16MB×32
128MB	32MB×36	32MB×32

168/184-Pin DIMM/DDR DIMM Capacities		
Capacity	**Parity/ECC DIMM**	**Nonparity DIMM**
8MB	1MB×72	1MB×64
16MB	2MB×72	2MB×64
32MB	4MB×72	4MB×64
64MB	8MB×72	8MB×64
128MB	16MB×72	16MB×64
256MB	32MB×72	32MB×64
512MB	64MB×72	64MB×64
1024MB	128MB×72	128MB×64

184-Pin RIMM Capacities		
Capacity	**Parity/ECC RIMM**	**Nonparity RIMM**
64MB	32MB×18	32MB×16
128MB	64MB×18	64MB×16
256MB	128MB×18	128MB×16

DRAM SIMMs, DIMMs, and RIMMs of each type and capacity are available in various speed ratings. SIMMs have been available in many speed ratings, ranging from 120ns for some of the slowest to 50ns for some of the fastest available. DIMMs are available in speeds of PC66 (66MHz), PC100 (100MHz), and PC133 (133MHz), whereas the DDR DIMMs are available in PC1600 (1,600MB/sec) and PC2100 (2,100MB/sec) versions.

If a system requires a specific speed, you can almost always substitute faster speeds if the one specified is not available. Generally, no problems occur in mixing module speeds, as long as you use modules equal to or faster than what the system requires. Because there's little price difference between the various speed versions, I often buy faster modules than are necessary for a particular application. This might make them more usable in a future system that could require the faster speed.

Because DIMMs and RIMMs have an onboard ROM that reports their speed and timing parameters to the system, most systems run the memory controller and memory bus at the speed matching the slowest DIMM/RIMM installed. Most DIMMs are SDRAM memory, which means they deliver data in very high-speed bursts using a clocked interface. DDR DIMMs are also SDRAM, but they transfer data two times per clock cycle and thus are twice as fast. SDRAM supports bus speeds of up to 133MHz, whereas DDR DIMMs support speeds of up to 266MHz.

Note

A *bank* is the smallest amount of memory needed to form a single row of memory addressable by the processor. It is the minimum amount of physical memory that is read or written by the processor at one time and usually corresponds to the data bus width of the processor. If a processor has a 64-bit data bus, a bank of memory also is 64-bits wide. If the memory is interleaved or runs dual-channel, a virtual bank is formed that is twice the absolute data bus width of the processor.

You can't always replace a module with a higher capacity unit and expect it to work. Systems might have specific design limitations for the maximum capacity of module they can take. A larger-capacity module works only if the motherboard is designed to accept it in the first place. Consult your system documentation to determine the correct capacity and speed to use.

SIMM Pinouts

Table 6.7 shows the interface connector pinouts for standard 72-pin SIMMs. They also include a special presence detect table that shows the configuration of the presence detect pins on various 72-pin SIMMs. The presence detect pins are used by the motherboard to detect exactly what size and speed SIMM is installed. Industry-standard 30-pin SIMMs do not have a presence detect feature, but IBM did add this capability to its modified 30-pin configuration. Note that all SIMMs have the same pins on both sides of the module.

Table 6.7 Standard 72-Pin SIMM Pinout

Pin	SIMM Signal Name	Pin	SIMM Signal Name	Pin	SIMM Signal Name	Pin	SIMM Signal Name
1	Ground	19	Address Bit 10	37	Parity Data Bit 1	55	Data Bit 11
2	Data Bit 0	20	Data Bit 4	38	Parity Data Bit 3	56	Data Bit 27
3	Data Bit 16	21	Data Bit 20	39	Ground	57	Data Bit 12
4	Data Bit 1	22	Data Bit 5	40	Column Address Strobe 0	58	Data Bit 28
5	Data Bit 17	23	Data Bit 21	41	Column Address Strobe 2	59	+5 Vdc
6	Data Bit 2	24	Data Bit 6	42	Column Address Strobe 3	60	Data Bit 29
7	Data Bit 18	25	Data Bit 22	43	Column Address Strobe 1	61	Data Bit 13
8	Data Bit 3	26	Data Bit 7	44	Row Address Strobe 0	62	Data Bit 30
9	Data Bit 19	27	Data Bit 23	45	Row Address Strobe 1	63	Data Bit 14
10	+5 Vdc	28	Address Bit 7	46	Reserved	64	Data Bit 31
11	Presence Detect 5	29	Address Bit 11	47	Write Enable	65	Data Bit 15
12	Address Bit 0	30	+5 Vdc	48	ECC Optimized	66	EDO
13	Address Bit 1	31	Address Bit 8	49	Data Bit 8	67	Presence Detect 1
14	Address Bit 2	32	Address Bit 9	50	Data Bit 24	68	Presence Detect 2
15	Address Bit 3	33	Address Bit 12	51	Data Bit 9	69	Presence Detect 3
16	Address Bit 4	34	Address Bit 13	52	Data Bit 25	70	Presence Detect 4
17	Address Bit 5	35	Parity Data Bit 2	53	Data Bit 10	71	Reserved
18	Address Bit 6	36	Parity Data Bit 0	54	Data Bit 26	72	Ground

Notice that the 72-pin SIMMs use a set of four or five pins to indicate the type of SIMM to the motherboard. These presence detect pins are either grounded or not connected to indicate the type of SIMM to the motherboard. Presence detect outputs must be tied to the ground through a zero-ohm resistor or jumper on the SIMM—to generate a high logic level when the pin is open or a low logic level when the pin is grounded by the motherboard. This produces signals that can be decoded by the memory interface logic. If the motherboard uses presence detect signals, a POST (power on self test) procedure can determine the size and speed of the installed SIMMs and adjust control and addressing signals automatically. This enables the memory size and speed to be autodetected.

Note

In many ways, the presence detect pin function is similar to the industry-standard DX coding used on modern 35mm film rolls to indicate the ASA (speed) rating of the film to the camera. When you drop the film into the camera, electrical contacts can read the film's speed rating via an industry-standard configuration.

Table 6.8 shows the Joint Electronic Devices Engineering Council (JEDEC) industry-standard presence detect configuration listing for the 72-pin SIMM family. JEDEC is an organization of U.S. semiconductor manufacturers and users that sets package outline dimension and other standards for chip and module packages.

Table 6.8   Presence Detect Pin Configurations for 72-Pin SIMMs

Size	Speed	Pin 67	Pin 68	Pin 69	Pin 70	Pin 11
1MB	100ns	Gnd	—	Gnd	Gnd	—
1MB	80ns	Gnd	—	—	Gnd	—
1MB	70ns	Gnd	—	Gnd	—	—
1MB	60ns	Gnd	—	—	—	—
2MB	100ns	—	Gnd	Gnd	Gnd	—
2MB	80ns	—	Gnd	—	Gnd	—
2MB	70ns	—	Gnd	Gnd	—	—
2MB	60ns	—	Gnd	—	—	—
4MB	100ns	Gnd	Gnd	Gnd	Gnd	—
4MB	80ns	Gnd	Gnd	—	Gnd	—
4MB	70ns	Gnd	Gnd	Gnd	—	—
4MB	60ns	Gnd	Gnd	—	—	—
8MB	100ns	—	—	Gnd	Gnd	—
8MB	80ns	—	—	—	Gnd	—
8MB	70ns	—	—	Gnd	—	—
8MB	60ns	—	—	—	—	—
16MB	80ns	Gnd	—	—	Gnd	Gnd
16MB	70ns	Gnd	—	Gnd	—	Gnd
16MB	60ns	Gnd	—	—	—	Gnd
16MB	50ns	Gnd	—	Gnd	Gnd	Gnd
32MB	80ns	—	Gnd	—	Gnd	Gnd

Table 6.8   Continued

Size	Speed	Pin 67	Pin 68	Pin 69	Pin 70	Pin 11
32MB	70ns	—	Gnd	Gnd	—	Gnd
32MB	60ns	—	Gnd	—	—	Gnd
32MB	50ns	—	Gnd	Gnd	Gnd	Gnd

— = No connection (open)   *Pin 69 = Presence detect 3*
Gnd = Ground   *Pin 70 = Presence detect 4*
Pin 67 = Presence detect 1   *Pin 11 = Presence detect 5*
Pin 68 = Presence detect 2

Unfortunately, unlike the film industry, not everybody in the computer industry follows established standards. As such, presence detect signaling is not a standard throughout the PC industry. Different system manufacturers sometimes use different configurations for what is expected on these four pins. Compaq, IBM (mainly PS/2 systems), and Hewlett-Packard are notorious for this type of behavior. Many of the systems from these vendors require special SIMMs that are basically the same as standard 72-pin SIMMs, except for special presence detect requirements. Table 6.9 shows how IBM defines these pins.

Table 6.9   72-Pin SIMM Presence Detect Pins

67	68	69	70	SIMM Type	IBM Part Number
—	—	—	—	Not a valid SIMM	n/a
Gnd	—	—	—	1MB 120ns	n/a
—	Gnd	—	—	2MB 120ns	n/a
Gnd	Gnd	—	—	2MB 70ns	92F0102
—	—	Gnd	—	8MB 70ns	64F3606
Gnd	—	Gnd	—	Reserved	n/a
—	Gnd	Gnd	—	2MB 80ns	92F0103
Gnd	Gnd	Gnd	—	8MB 80ns	64F3607
—	—	—	Gnd	Reserved	n/a
Gnd	—	—	Gnd	1MB 85ns	90X8624
—	Gnd	—	Gnd	2MB 85ns	92F0104
Gnd	Gnd	—	Gnd	4MB 70ns	92F0105
—	—	Gnd	Gnd	4MB 85ns	79F1003 (square notch) L40-SX
Gnd	—	Gnd	Gnd	1MB 100ns	n/a
Gnd	—	Gnd	Gnd	8MB 80ns	79F1004 (square notch) L40-SX
—	Gnd	Gnd	Gnd	2MB 100ns	n/a
Gnd	Gnd	Gnd	Gnd	4MB 80ns	87F9980
Gnd	Gnd	Gnd	Gnd	2MB 85ns	79F1003 (square notch) L40SX

— = No connection (open)   *Pin 68 = Presence detect 2*
Gnd = Ground   *Pin 69 = Presence detect 3*
Pin 67 = Presence detect 1   *Pin 70 = Presence detect 4*

Because these pins can have custom variations, you often must specify IBM, Compaq, HP, or generic SIMMs when you order memory.

DIMM Pinouts

Table 6.10 shows the pinout configuration of a 168-pin standard unbuffered SDRAM DIMM. Note again that the pins on each side of the DIMM are different.

Table 6.10   168-Pin SDRAM DIMM Pinouts

Pin	Signal	Pin	Signal	Pin	Signal	Pin	Signal
1	GND	43	GND	85	GND	127	GND
2	Data Bit 0	44	Do Not Use	86	Data Bit 32	128	Clock Enable 0
3	Data Bit 1	45	Chip Select 2#	87	Data Bit 33	129	Chip Select 3#
4	Data Bit 2	46	I/O Mask 2	88	Data Bit 34	130	I/O Mask 6
5	Data Bit 3	47	I/O Mask 3	89	Data Bit 35	131	I/O Mask 7
6	+3.3 V	48	Do Not Use	90	+3.3 V	132	Reserved
7	Data Bit 4	49	+3.3 V	91	Data Bit 36	133	+3.3 V
8	Data Bit 5	50	NC	92	Data Bit 37	134	NC
9	Data Bit 6	51	NC	93	Data Bit 38	135	NC
10	Data Bit 7	52	Parity Bit 2	94	Data Bit 39	136	Parity Bit 6
11	Data Bit 8	53	Parity Bit 3	95	Data Bit 40	137	Parity Bit 7
12	GND	54	GND	96	GND	138	GND
13	Data Bit 9	55	Data Bit 16	97	Data Bit 41	139	Data Bit 48
14	Data Bit 10	56	Data Bit 17	98	Data Bit 42	140	Data Bit 49
15	Data Bit 11	57	Data Bit 18	99	Data Bit 43	141	Data Bit 50
16	Data Bit 12	58	Data Bit 19	100	Data Bit 44	142	Data Bit 51
17	Data Bit 13	59	+3.3 V	101	Data Bit 45	143	+3.3 V
18	+3.3 V	60	Data Bit 20	102	+3.3 V	144	Data Bit 52
19	Data Bit 14	61	NC	103	Data Bit 46	145	NC
20	Data Bit 15	62	NC	104	Data Bit 47	146	NC
21	Parity Bit 0	63	Clock Enable 1	105	Parity Bit 4	147	NC
22	Parity Bit 1	64	GND	106	Parity Bit 5	148	GND
23	GND	65	Data Bit 21	107	GND	149	Data Bit 53
24	NC	66	Data Bit 22	108	NC	150	Data Bit 54
25	NC	67	Data Bit 23	109	NC	151	Data Bit 55
26	+3.3 V	68	GND	110	+3.3 V	152	GND
27	WE#	69	Data Bit 24	111	CAS#	153	Data Bit 56
28	I/O Mask 0	70	Data Bit 25	112	I/O Mask 4	154	Data Bit 57
29	I/O Mask 1	71	Data Bit 26	113	I/O Mask 5	155	Data Bit 58
30	Chip Select 0#	72	Data Bit 27	114	Chip Select 1#	156	Data Bit 59
31	Do Not Use	73	+3.3 V	115	RAS#	157	+3.3 V
32	GND	74	Data Bit 28	116	GND	158	Data Bit 60
33	Address Bit 0	75	Data Bit 29	117	Address Bit 1	59	Data Bit 61

Table 6.10 Continued

Pin	Signal	Pin	Signal	Pin	Signal	Pin	Signal
34	Address Bit 2	76	Data Bit 30	118	Address Bit 3	160	Data Bit 62
35	Address Bit 4	77	Data Bit 31	119	Address Bit 5	161	Data Bit 63
36	Address Bit 6	78	GND	120	Address Bit 7	162	GND
37	Address Bit 8	79	Clock 2	121	Address Bit 9	163	Clock 3
38	Address Bit 10	80	NC	122	Bank Address 0	164	NC
39	Bank Address 1	81	SPD Write Protect	123	Address Bit 11	165	SPD Address 0
40	+3.3 V	82	SPD Data	124	+3.3 V	166	SPD Address 1
41	+3.3 V	83	SPD Clock	125	Clock 1	167	SPD Address 2
42	Clock 0	84	+3.3 V	126	Reserved	168	+3.3 V

Gnd = Ground   *SPD = Serial presence detect*   *NC = No connection*

The DIMM uses a completely different type of presence detect called *serial presence detect (SPD)*. It consists of a small EEPROM or Flash memory chip on the DIMM that contains specially formatted data indicating the DIMM's features. This serial data can be read via the serial data pins on the DIMM, and it enables the motherboard to autoconfigure to the exact type of DIMM installed.

DIMMs can come in several varieties, including unbuffered or buffered and 3.3V or 5V. Buffered DIMMs have additional buffer chips on them to interface to the motherboard. Unfortunately, these buffer chips slow down the DIMM and are not effective at higher speeds. For this reason, all PC systems use unbuffered DIMMs. The voltage is simple—DIMM designs for PCs are almost universally 3.3V. If you install a 5V DIMM in a 3.3V socket, it would be damaged, but fortunately, keying in the socket and on the DIMM prevents that.

Modern PC systems use only unbuffered 3.3V DIMMs. Apple and other nonPC systems can use the buffered 5V versions. Fortunately, the key notches along the connector edge of a DIMM are spaced differently for buffered/unbuffered or 3.3V/5V DIMMs, as shown in Figure 6.8. This prevents inserting a DIMM of the wrong type into a given socket.

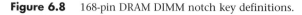

Figure 6.8   168-pin DRAM DIMM notch key definitions.

DDR DIMM Pinouts

Table 6.11 shows the pinout configuration of a 184-pin DDR SDRAM DIMM. Note again that the pins on each side of the DIMM are different.

Table 6.11   184-Pin DDR DIMM Pinouts

Pin	Symbol	Pin	Symbol	Pin	Symbol	Pin	Symbol
1	Reference +1.25 V	47	Data Strobe 8	93	GND	139	GND
2	Data Bit 0	48	Address Bit 0	94	Data Bit 4	140	Data Strobe 17
3	GND	49	Parity Bit 2	95	Data Bit 5	141	Address Bit 10
4	Data Bit 1	50	GND	96	I/O +2.5 V	142	Parity Bit 6
5	Data Strobe 0	51	Parity Bit 3	97	Data Strobe 9	143	I/O +2.5 V
6	Data Bit 2	52	Bank Address 1	98	Data Bit 6	144	Parity Bit 7
7	+2.5 V	53	Data Bit 32	99	Data Bit 7	145	GND
8	Data Bit 3	54	I/O +2.5 V	100	GND	146	Data Bit 36
9	NC	55	Data Bit 33	101	NC	147	Data Bit 37
10	NC	56	Data Strobe 4	102	NC	148	+2.5 V
11	GND	57	Data Bit 34	103	Address Bit 13	149	Data Strobe 13
12	Data Bit 8	58	GND	104	I/O +2.5 V	150	Data Bit 38
13	Data Bit 9	59	Bank Address 0	105	Data Bit 12	151	Data Bit 39
14	Data Strobe 1	60	Data Bit 35	106	Data Bit 13	152	GND
15	I/O +2.5 V	61	Data Bit 40	107	Data Strobe 10	153	Data Bit 44
16	Clock 1	62	I/O +2.5 V	108	+2.5 V	154	RAS#
17	Clock 1#	63	WE#	109	Data Bit 14	155	Data Bit 45
18	GND	64	Data Bit 41	110	Data Bit 15	156	I/O +2.5 V
19	Data Bit 10	65	CAS#	111	Clock Enable 1	157	S0#
20	Data Bit 11	66	GND	112	I/O +2.5 V	158	S1#
21	Clock Enable 0	67	Data Strobe 5	113	Bank Address 2	159	Data Strobe 14
22	I/O +2.5 V	68	Data Bit 42	114	Data Bit 20	160	GND
23	Data Bit 16	69	Data Bit 43	115	Address Bit 12	161	Data Bit 46
24	Data Bit 17	70	+2.5 V	116	GND	162	Data Bit 47
25	Data Strobe 2	71	S2#	117	Data Bit 21	163	S3#
26	GND	72	Data Bit 48	118	Address Bit 11	164	I/O +2.5 V
27	Address Bit 9	73	Data Bit 49	119	Data Strobe 11	165	Data Bit 52
28	Data Bit 18	74	GND	120	+2.5 V	166	Data Bit 53
29	Address Bit 7	75	Clock 2#	121	Data Bit 22	167	FETEN
30	I/O +2.5 V	76	Clock 2	122	Address Bit 8	168	+2.5 V
31	Data Bit 19	77	I/O +2.5 V	123	Data Bit 23	169	Data Strobe 15
32	Address Bit 5	78	Data Strobe 6	124	GND	170	Data Bit 54
33	Data Bit 24	79	Data Bit 50	125	Address Bit 6	171	Data Bit 55
34	GND	80	Data Bit 51	126	Data Bit 28	172	I/O +2.5 V
35	Data Bit 25	81	GND	127	Data Bit 29	173	NC
36	Data Strobe 3	82	+2.5 VID	128	I/O +2.5 V	174	Data Bit 60
37	Address Bit 4	83	Data Bit 56	129	Data Strobe 12	175	Data Bit 61
38	+2.5 V	84	Data Bit 57	130	Address Bit 3	176	GND
39	Data Bit 26	85	+2.5 V	131	Data Bit 30	177	Data Strobe 16

Table 6.11   Continued

Pin	Symbol	Pin	Symbol	Pin	Symbol	Pin	Symbol
40	Data Bit 27	86	Data Strobe 7	132	GND	178	Data Bit 62
41	Address Bit 2	87	Data Bit 58	133	Data Bit 31	179	Data Bit 63
42	GND	88	Data Bit 59	134	Parity Bit 4	180	I/O +2.5 V
43	Address Bit 1	89	GND	135	Parity Bit 5	181	SPD Address 0
44	Parity Bit 0	90	SPD Write Protect	136	I/O +2.5 V	182	SPD Address 1
45	Parity Bit 1	91	SPD Data	137	Clock 0	183	SPD Address 2
46	+2.5 V	92	SPD Clock	138	Clock 0#	184	SPD +2.5 V

Gnd = Ground   *SPD = Serial presence detect*   *NC = No connection*

DDR DIMMs use a single key notch to indicate voltage, as shown in Figure 6.9.

Figure 6.9   184-pin DDR SDRAM DIMM keying.

184-pin DDR DIMMs use two notches on each side to enable compatibility with both low- and high-profile latched sockets. Note that the key position is offset with respect to the center of the DIMM to prevent inserting it backward in the socket. The key notch is positioned to the left, centered, or to the right of the area between pins 52 and 53. This is used to indicate the I/O voltage for the DDR DIMM and to prevent installing the wrong type into a socket that might damage the DIMM.

RIMM Pinouts

RIMM modules and sockets are gold-plated and designed for 25 insertion/removal cycles. Each RIMM has 184 pins, split into two groups of 92 pins on opposite ends and sides of the module. The pinout of the RIMM is shown in Table 6.12.

Table 6.12   RIMM Pinout

Pin	Signal	Pin	Signal	Pin	Signal	Pin	Signal
A1	GND	B1	GND	A47	NC	B47	NC
A2	LData Bit A8	B2	LData Bit A7	A48	NC	B48	NC
A3	GND	B3	GND	A49	NC	B49	NC
A4	LData Bit A6	B4	LData Bit A5	A50	NC	B50	NC
A5	GND	B5	GND	A51	VREF	B51	VREF
A6	LData Bit A4	B6	LData Bit A3	A52	GND	B52	GND

Table 6.12   Continued

Pin	Signal	Pin	Signal	Pin	Signal	Pin	Signal
A7	GND	B7	GND	A53	SPD Clock	B53	SPD Address 0
A8	LData Bit A2	B8	LData Bit A1	A54	+2.5 V	B54	+2.5 V
A9	GND	B9	GND	A55	SDA	B55	SPD Address 1
A10	LData Bit A0	B10	Interface Clock+	A56	SVDD	B56	SVDD
A11	GND	B11	GND	A57	SPD Write Protect	B57	SPD Address 2
A12	LCTMN	B12	Interface Clock-	A58	+2.5 V	B58	+2.5 V
A13	GND	B13	GND	A59	RSCK	B59	RCMD
A14	LCTM	B14	NC	A60	GND	B60	GND
A15	GND	B15	GND	A61	Rdata Bit B7	B61	RData Bit B8
A16	NC	B16	LROW2	A62	GND	B62	GND
A17	GND	B17	GND	A63	Rdata Bit B5	B63	RData Bit B6
A18	LROW1	B18	LROW0	A64	GND	B64	GND
A19	GND	B19	GND	A65	Rdata Bit B3	B65	RData Bit B4
A20	LCOL4	B20	LCOL3	A66	GND	B66	GND
A21	GND	B21	GND	A67	Rdata Bit B1	B67	RData Bit B2
A22	LCOL2	B22	LCOL1	A68	GND	B68	GND
A23	GND	B23	GND	A69	RCOL0	B69	RData Bit B0
A24	LCOL0	B24	LData Bit B0	A70	GND	B70	GND
A25	GND	B25	GND	A71	RCOL2	B71	RCOL1
A26	LData Bit B1	B26	LData Bit B2	A72	GND	B72	GND
A27	GND	B27	GND	A73	RCOL4	B73	RCOL3
A28	LData Bit B3	B28	LData Bit B4	A74	GND	B74	GND
A29	GND	B29	GND	A75	RROW1	B75	RROW0
A30	LData Bit B5	B30	LData Bit B6	A76	GND	B76	GND
A31	GND	B31	GND	A77	NC	B77	RROW2
A32	LData Bit B7	B32	LData Bit B8	A78	GND	B78	GND
A33	GND	B33	GND	A79	RCTM	B79	NC
A34	LSCK	B34	LCMD	A80	GND	B80	GND
A35	VCMOS	B35	VCMOS	A81	RCTMN	B81	RCFMN
A36	SOUT	B36	SIN	A82	GND	B82	GND
A37	VCMOS	B37	VCMOS	A83	Rdata Bit A0	B83	RCFM
A38	NC	B38	NC	A84	GND	B84	GND
A39	GND	B39	GND	A85	Rdata Bit A2	B85	RData Bit A1
A40	NC	B40	NC	A86	GND	B86	GND
A41	+2.5 V	B41	+2.5 V	A87	Rdata Bit A4	B87	RData Bit A3
A42	+2.5 V	B42	+2.5 V	A88	GND	B88	GND
A43	NC	B43	NC	A89	Rdata Bit A6	B89	RData Bit A5
A44	NC	B44	NC	A90	GND	B90	GND
A45	NC	B45	NC	A91	Rdata Bit A8	B91	RData Bit A7
A46	NC	B46	NC	A92	GND	B92	GND

Note

RIMMs are designed for only 25 insertion and removal cycles, so if you are installing and removing them more times than that, you can compromise the gold plating on the module or connector. It is not likely that anybody would install or remove memory that many times, but it is worth noting.

RIMMs are keyed with two notches in the center. This prevents a backward insertion and prevents the wrong type (voltage) RIMM from being used in a system. Currently, all RIMMs run on 2.5V, but future versions might run on less. To allow for these new types of RIMMs, three keying options are possible in the design (see Figure 6.10). The left key (indicated as "DATUM A" in Figure 6.8) is fixed in position, but the center key can be in three different positions spaced 1mm or 2mm to the right, indicating different types of RIMMs. The current default is option A, as shown in Figure 6.10 and Table 6.13, which corresponds to 2.5V operation.

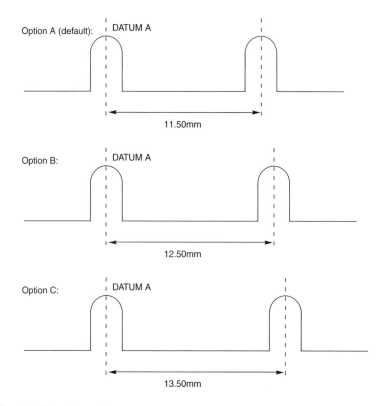

Figure 6.10 RIMM keying options.

Table 6.13   Possible Keying Options for RIMMs

Option	Notch Separation	Description
A	11.5mm	2.5V RIMM
B	12.5mm	Reserved
C	13.5mm	Reserved

RIMMs incorporate an SPD device, which is essentially a Flash ROM onboard. This ROM contains information about the RIMM's size and type, including detailed timing information for the memory controller. The memory controller automatically reads the data from the SPD ROM to configure the system to match the RIMMs installed.

Figure 6.11 shows a typical PC RIMM installation. The RDRAM controller and clock generator are typically in the motherboard chipset North Bridge component. As you can see, the Rambus memory channel flows from the memory controller through each of up to three RIMM modules in series. Each module contains 4, 8, 16, or more RDRAM devices (chips), also wired in series, with an onboard SPD ROM for system configuration. Any RIMM sockets without a RIMM installed must have a continuity module, shown in the last socket in Figure 6.11. This enables the memory bus to remain continuous from the controller through each module (and, therefore, each RDRAM device on the module) until the bus finally terminates on the motherboard. Note how the bus loops from one module to another. For timing purposes, the first RIMM socket must be 6 inches or less from the memory controller, and the entire length of the bus must not be more than it would take for a signal to go from one end to another in four data clocks, or about 5ns.

Figure 6.11   Typical RDRAM bus layout showing a RIMM and one continuity module.

Interestingly, Rambus does not manufacture the RDRAM devices (the chips) or the RIMMs; that is left to other companies. Rambus is merely a design company, and it has no chip fabs or manufacturing facilities of its own. It licenses its technology to other companies who then manufacture the devices and modules.

Physical RAM Capacity and Organization

Several types of memory chips have been used in PC system motherboards. Most of these chips are single-bit–wide chips, available in several capacities.

Note that chip capacity normally goes up by factors of four because the dies that make up the chips are square. When they increase capacity, this normally results in four times more transistors and four times more capacity. Most modern SIMMs and DIMMs use 16Mbit–256Mbit chips onboard.

Figure 6.12 shows the markings on a typical memory chip from Micron Technologies, one of the most popular chip and module manufacturers. Many memory manufacturers use similar schemes for numbering their chips; however, if you are really trying to identify a particular chip, it is best to consult the manufacturer catalog for more information.

The -75 marking corresponds to the chip speed in nanoseconds, in this case a 7.5 nanosecond or 133MHz designation.

The part number usually contains a clue about the chip's type and capacity. The chip here is MT48LC8M8A2TG-75L. This decodes as

> MT = Micron Technologies
>
> 48 = SDRAM
>
> LC = 3.3V CMOS
>
> 8M8 = 8 million rows deep × 8 bits wide
>
> A2 = Device version
>
> TG = TSOP (thin small outline package)
>
> -75 = 7.5 ns (133MHz) rating
>
> L = Low power

Note

Markings vary from manufacturer to manufacturer. The example shown here is for illustrative purposes only.

Because this chip is 8 bits wide, I'd expect to see either 8 or 16 of them on a DIMM to make up the 64 bits of width for the complete DIMM. If 16 chips were used, this would be known as a *double-sided* DIMM, and the chips would be arranged in a logically stacked form where the two banks of 8MB×8 chips work together as if they were a single bank of 16MB×8 chips. If 8 of these chips were on a DIMM, it would be 8MB×64 bits, which is the same as saying 8MB×8 bytes, which is the same as calling it a 64MB DIMM. If there were 16 of these chips, it would be a 128MB double-sided DIMM, and if there were either 9 or 18 of these chips, it would be a 72-bit wide DIMM with parity/ECC support.

Most chips also feature a four-digit number separate from the part number, which indicates the date of manufacture by week and day. For example, 0021 indicates the chip was made in the 21st week of 2000. To further decode the chip, contact the manufacturer or chip vendor for its catalog information.

SIMMs and DIMMs also have part numbers that can be difficult to decode. Unfortunately, no industry standard exists for numbering these modules, so you must contact the manufacturer if you want to decode the numbers.

Sometimes you can't find any writing on the SIMM or DIMM that tells you the capacity or other information. In that case, just look up the chip part numbers on the chip manufacturer's Web site, and from there you should be able to figure out what it is (see Figure 6.13).

MT48LC8M8A2TG-75L ES

Micron Technology

Product Family
4 = DRAM
46 = DDR SDRAM
48 = SDRAM
6 = Rambus®

Process Technology
C = 5V Vcc CMOS
LC = 3.3V VDD CMOS
V = 2.5V VDD CMOS

Device Number
Depth, Width
No Letter = Bits
K = Kilobits
M = Megabits
G = Gigabits

Device Versions
Alphanumeric character(s) specified by individual data sheet.

Package Codes
DJ = SOJ
DW = SOJ (Wide)
F = FBGA (54-pin, 4 row depop)
FB = FBGA (60-pin, 8x16)
FC = FBGA (60-pin, 11x13)
FP = Flip Chip in Package
FQ = Flip Chip in Sealed Package
F1 = FBGA (54-pin, 2 row depop)
F2 = FBGA (64-pin, 2 row depop)
LG = TQFP
R = FBGA (54-pin, 4 row depop, mirrored pins)
R1 = FBGA (54-pin, 2 row depop, mirrored pins)
R2 = FBGA (64-pin, 2 row depop, mirrored pins)
TG = TSOP(Type II)
U = μBGA®

Special Processing
ES = Engineering Sample
MS = Mechanical Sample

Operating Temperatures
Commerical (0°C to + 70°C) = Blank
Industrial (-40°C to + 85°C) = IT
Refresh Options
(Multiple processing codes are separated by a space and are listed in hierachical order.)
L = Low Power
S = Self Refresh

Access/Cycle Time

DRAM (Access Time)	SDRAM x32 DDR SDRAM (Clock Rate@ CL = 3)	DDR SDRAM (x4, x8, x16) (Clock Rate@ CL = 2.5)
-4 = 40ns		-8 = 125MHz
-5 = 50ns		-75 = 133MHz
-6 = 60ns	-15 = 66MHz	-7 = 143MHz
-7 = 70ns	-12 = 83MHz	
	-10 = 100MHz	**Rambus**
All DRAM	-8x = 125MHz	*(Clock Rate)*
-0 = Untested	-75 = 133MHz	-4D = 400MHz, 40ns
	-7x = 143MHz	-4C = 400MHz, 45ns
	-65 = 150MHz	-4B = 400MHz, 50ns
	-6 = 167MHz	-3C = 356MHz, 45ns
	-55 = 183MHz	-3B = 356MHz, 50ns
	-5 = 200MHz	-3M = 300MHz, 53ns

Figure 6.12 The markings on a typical memory chip (Micron shown).

The fact that I can't decipher the information on the stickers about the DIMM is not a problem, as long as I can read the chip part numbers.

The chips carry the Hyundai (HY) logo, with a part number of HY57V651620-TC10. I found the data sheet for these chips at the Hyundai Memory Web site. I can't tell who made the actual DIMM; at first I suspected Hyundai might have made it because of the HY-3U1606 number on the left side, but I can't find any corresponding information in the Hyundai catalog that matches this designation. No matter; I can still deduce all the information I need about this module by looking at the chip information.

Figure 6.13 DIMM front/rear view with indecipherable markings indicating part number, capacity, or speed.

According to the data sheet for the chips on this DIMM, these are 10ns chips, which, although technically rated 100MHz, would classify this as a 66MHz SDRAM DIMM (PC66). If they were 8ns (125MHz) chips, this would be a PC100 DIMM, and if 7.5ns, this would be a PC133 DIMM. These are 64Mbit chips, organized as 4MB×16 (rows by columns). There are four chips on one side, resulting in a full 64-bit wide bank of 4MB×64 bits (4MB×8 bytes or 32MB total). The other side contains the same number of chips, which would be electronically or logically "stacked" to double the depth (number of rows). This is because DIMMs can be only 64 bits wide, resulting in a total of 8MB×64 bits, which is 8MB×8 bytes, which is 64MB total. The additional tiny Atmel brand chip on the right side is the serial EPROM, which contains the data about this DIMM that can be read by the motherboard to configure the chipset memory controllers. Because there are no additional memory chips, this DIMM lacks the additional 8 bits of width to make it a 72-bit wide ECC DIMM.

So, by deciphering the chip part numbers and adding things up, I have figured out that this is a 64MB, double-sided, non-ECC, PC66 SDRAM DIMM.

Memory Banks

Memory chips (DIPs, SIMMs, SIPPs, and DIMMs) are organized in banks on motherboards and memory cards. You should know the memory bank layout and position on the motherboard and memory cards.

You need to know the bank layout when adding memory to the system. In addition, memory diagnostics report error locations by byte and bit addresses, and you must use these numbers to locate which bank in your system contains the problem.

The banks usually correspond to the data bus capacity of the system's microprocessor. Table 6.14 shows the widths of individual banks based on the type of PC.

Table 6.14   Memory Bank Widths on Various Systems

Processor	Data Bus	Memory Bank Size (No Parity)	Memory Bank Size (Parity)	30-Pin SIMMs per Bank	72-Pin SIMMs per Bank	168-Pin DIMMs per Bank
8088	8-bit	8 bits	9 bits	1	n/a	n/a
8086	16-bit	16 bits	18 bits	2	n/a	n/a
286	16-bit	16 bits	18 bits	2	n/a	n/a
386SX, SL, SLC	16-bit	16 bits	18 bits	2	n/a	n/a
486SLC, SLC2	16-bit	16 bits	18 bits	2	n/a	n/a
386DX	32-bit	32 bits	36 bits	4	1	n/a
486SX, DX, DX2, DX4, 5x86	32-bit	32 bits	36 bits	4	1	n/a
Pentium, K6 series	64-bit	64 bits	72 bits	8	2	1
PPro, PII, Celeron, PIII, P4, Athlon/Duron	64-bit	64 bits	72 bits	8	2	1

The number of bits for each bank can be made up of single chips, SIMMs, or DIMMs. Modern systems don't use individual chips; instead, they use only SIMMs or DIMMs. If the system has a 16-bit processor, such as a 386SX, it probably uses 30-pin SIMMs and has two SIMMs per bank. All the SIMMs in a single bank must be the same size and type.

A 486 system requires four 30-pin SIMMs or one 72-pin SIMM to make up a bank. A single 72-pin SIMM is 32 bits wide, or 36 bits wide if it supports parity. You can often tell whether a SIMM supports parity by counting its chips. To make a 32-bit SIMM, you could use 32 individual 1-bit–wide chips, or you could use eight individual 4-bit–wide chips to make up the data bits. If the system uses parity, four extra bits are required (36 bits total), so you would see one more 4-bit–wide or four individual 1-bit–wide chips added to the bank for the parity bits.

As you might imagine, 30-pin SIMMs are less than ideal for 32-bit or 64-bit systems (that is, 486 or Pentium) because you must use them in increments of four or eight per bank! Because these SIMMs are available in 1MB, 4MB, and 16MB capacities today, this means that a single bank of 30-pin SIMMs in a 486 system would be 4MB, 16MB, or 64MB; for a Pentium system, this would be 8MB, 32MB, or 128MB of memory, with no in-between amounts. Using 30-pin SIMMs in 32- and 64-bit systems artificially constrains memory configurations, and such systems are not recommended. If a 32-bit system (such as any PC with a 486 processor) uses 72-pin SIMMs, each SIMM represents a separate bank, and the SIMMs can be added or removed on an individual basis rather than in groups of four, as would be required with 30-pin SIMMs. This makes memory configuration much easier and more flexible. In modern 64-bit systems that use SIMMs, two 72-pin SIMMs are required per bank.

DIMMs are ideal for Pentium and higher systems because the 64-bit width of the DIMM exactly matches the 64-bit width of the Pentium processor data bus. This means that each DIMM represents an individual bank, and they can be added or removed one at a time.

The physical orientation and numbering of the SIMMs or DIMMs used on a motherboard is arbitrary and determined by the board's designers, so documentation covering your system or card comes in handy. You can determine the layout of a motherboard or an adapter card through testing, but that takes time and might be difficult, particularly after you have a problem with a system.

Memory Module Speed

When you replace a failed memory module or install a new module as an upgrade, you typically must install a module of the same type and speed as the others in the system. You can substitute a module with a different (faster) speed but only if the replacement module's speed is equal to or faster than that of the other modules in the system.

Some people have had problems when "mixing" modules of different speeds. With the wide variety of motherboards, chipsets, and memory types, few ironclad rules exist. When in doubt as to which speed module to install in your system, consult the motherboard documentation for more information.

Substituting faster memory of the same type doesn't result in improved performance if the system still operates the memory at the same speed. Systems that use DIMMs or RIMMs can read the speed and timing features of the module from a special SPD ROM installed on the module and then set chipset (memory controller) timing accordingly. In these systems, you might see an increase in performance by installing faster modules, to the limit of what the chipset will support.

To place more emphasis on timing and reliability, there are Intel and JEDEC standards governing memory types that require certain levels of performance. Intel, for example, has created the PC66, PC100, and PC133 standards supported by many newer chipsets. These are standards for certifying that memory modules perform within Intel's timing and performance guidelines. At 100MHz or higher, there is not much "forgiveness" or slop allowed in memory timing.

The same common symptoms result when the system memory has failed or is simply not fast enough for the system's timing. The usual symptoms are frequent parity check errors or a system that does not operate at all. The POST might report errors, too. If you're unsure of which chips to buy for your system, contact the system manufacturer or a reputable chip supplier.

▶▶ See "Parity Checking," p. 445.

Gold Versus Tin

Many people don't understand the importance of the memory module electrical contacts in a computer system. Modules (SIMMs, DIMMs, and RIMMs) are available in gold- or tin-plated contact form. I initially thought that gold contact modules were the best way to go for reliability in all situations, but that is not true. To have the most reliable system, you must install modules with gold-plated contacts into gold-plated sockets and modules with tin-plated contacts into only tin-plated sockets.

If you don't heed this warning and install memory with gold-plated contacts into tin sockets or vice versa, you will have problems with memory errors and reliability in the long run. In my experiences, they occur six months to one year after installation. I have encountered this problem several times in my own systems and in several systems I have serviced. I have even been asked to assist one customer in a lawsuit as an expert witness. The customer had bought several hundred machines from a vendor, and severe memory failures began appearing in most of the machines approximately a year after delivery. The cause was traced to dissimilar metals between the memory modules and sockets (gold-plated contact SIMMs in tin-plated contact sockets, in this case). The vendor refused to replace the SIMMs with tin-plated versions, hence the lawsuit.

Most systems using 72-pin SIMMs have tin-plated sockets, so they must have tin-plated SIMM memory installed. Studies done by the connector manufacturers, such as AMP, show that a type of corrosion called *fretting* occurs when tin comes in pressure contact with gold or any other metal. With fretting corrosion, tin oxide transfers to the harder gold surface, eventually causing a high-resistance connection. This happens whenever gold comes into contact with tin, no matter how thick or thin the gold coating is. Over time, depending on the environment, fretting corrosion can and will cause high resistance at the contact point and thus cause memory errors.

You might think tin makes a poor connector material because it readily oxidizes. Even so, electrical contact is easily made between two tin surfaces under pressure because the oxides on the softer tin surfaces bend and break, ensuring contact. In most memory modules, the contacts are under fairly high pressure when the modules are installed.

When tin and gold come into contact, because one surface is hard, the oxidation builds up and does not break easily under pressure. Increased contact resistance ultimately results in memory failures.

The connector manufacturer AMP has published several documents from the AMP Contact Physics Research Department that discuss this issue, but two are the most applicable. One is titled "Golden Rules: Guidelines for the Use of Gold on Connector Contacts," and the other is called "The Tin Commandments: Guidelines for the Use of Tin on Connector Contacts." Both can be downloaded in PDF form from the AMP Web site. Commandment Number Seven from the Tin Commandments specifically states "7. Mating of tin-coated contacts to gold-coated contacts is not recommended." For further technical details, you can contact Intel or AMP.

Certainly, the best type of arrangement is having gold-plated modules installed in gold-plated sockets. Most systems using DIMMs or RIMMs are designed this way.

If you have mixed metals in your memory now, the correct solution is to replace the memory modules with the appropriate contact type to match the socket. Another much less desirable solution is to wait until problems appear (about six months to a year, in my experience), and then remove the modules, clean the contacts, reinstall, and repeat the cycle. This is probably fine if you are an individual with one or two systems, but it is not fine if you are maintaining hundreds of systems. If your system does not feature parity or ECC memory (most systems sold today do not), when the problems do occur, you might not be able to immediately identify them as memory related (General Protection Faults, crashes, file and data corruption, and so on).

One problem with cleaning is that the hard tin oxide deposits that form on the gold surface are difficult to remove and often require abrasive cleaning (by using an eraser or a crocus cloth, for example). This should never be done dry because it generates static discharges that can damage the chips. Instead, use a contact cleaner to lubricate the contacts; wet contacts minimize the potential for static discharge damage when rubbing the eraser or other abrasive on the surface.

To further prevent this problem from occurring, I highly recommend using a liquid contact enhancer and lubricant called Stabilant 22 from D.W. Electrochemicals when installing SIMMs or DIMMs. Its Web site has a detailed application note on this subject if you are interested in more technical details; see the Vendor List on the CD-ROM.

Some people have accused me of being too picky by insisting that the memory match the socket. On several occasions, I have returned either memory or motherboards because the vendor putting them together did not have a clue that this is a problem. When I tell some people about it, they tell me they have a lot of PCs with mixed metal contacts that run fine and have been doing so for many years.

Of course, that is certainly a poor argument against sound engineering practices. Many people are running SCSI buses that are way too long, with improper termination, and they say it runs "fine." Parallel port cables are by the spec limited to 10 feet, yet I see many have longer cables, which they claim work "fine." The IDE cable limit is 18 inches; that spec is violated and people get away with it, saying their drive runs just "fine." I see cheap, crummy power supplies that put out noise, ripple, and loosely regulated voltages, and I have even measured up to 69 volts AC of ground leakage, and yet the systems appeared to be running "fine." I have encountered numerous systems without proper CPU heatsinks, or in which the active heatsink (fan) was seized, and the system ran "fine." This reminds me of when Johnny Carson would interview 100-year-old people and often got them to admit that they drank heavily and smoked cigarettes every day, as if those are good practices that ensure longevity!

The truth is I am often amazed at how poorly designed or implemented some systems are, and yet they do seem to work…for the most part. The occasional lockup or crash is just written off by the user as "that's they way they all are." All except my systems, of course. In my systems, I adhere to proper design and engineering practices. In fact, I am often guilty of engineering or specifying overkill into things. Although it adds to the cost, they do seem to run better because of it.

In other words, what one individual can "get away" with does not change the laws of physics. It does not change the fact that for those supporting many systems or selling systems where the maximum in reliability and service life is desired, the gold/tin issue does matter.

Another issue that was brought to my attention was the thickness of the gold on the contacts; people are afraid that it is so thin, it will wear off after one or two insertions. Certainly, the choice of gold coating thickness depends on the durability required by the application; because of gold's high cost, it is prudent to keep the gold coating thickness as low as is appropriate for the durability requirements.

To improve durability, a small amount of cobalt or nickel added to the gold usually hardens the gold coatings. Such coatings are defined as "hard gold" and produce coatings with a low coefficient of friction and excellent durability characteristics. Hard gold-coated contacts can generally withstand hundreds to thousands of durability cycles without failing. Using an underlayer with a hardness value greater than that of gold alone that provides additional mechanical support can enhance the durability of hard gold coatings. Nickel is generally recommended as an underlayer for this purpose. Special electronic contact lubricants or enhancers, such as Stabilant 22 from D.W. Electrochemicals, are also effective at increasing the durability of gold coatings. Generally, lubrication can increase the durability of a gold contact by an order of magnitude. These and other chemicals are discussed in more detail in Chapter 24, "PC Diagnostics, Testing, and Maintenance."

Increasing the thickness of a hard gold coating increases durability. The following laboratory results were obtained by AMP for the wear-through of a hard gold coating to the 1.3 micron (50 microinch) thick nickel underplate. The following data is for a 0.635cm. (0.250 in.) diameter ball wiped a distance of 1.27cm. (0.500 in.) under a normal force of 100 grams for each cycle.

Thickness Microns	Thickness Microinch	Cycles to Failure
0.4	15	200
0.8	30	1000
1.3	50	2000

As you can see from this table, an 0.8 micron (30 microinches) coating of hard gold results in durability that is more than adequate for most connector applications because it allows 1,000 insertion and removal cycles before wearing through. I studied the specification sheets for DIMM and SIMM sockets produced by AMP and found that its gold-plated sockets come mostly as .000030 (30 microinches) thick gold over .000050 (50 microinches) thick nickel in the contact area. As far as I can determine, the coating on virtually all memory module contacts would be similar in thickness, allowing for the same durability.

AMP also has a few gold-plated sockets with specifications of .001020-thick (1,020 microinches) gold over .001270-thick (1,270 microinches) nickel. I'd guess that the latter sockets were for devices such as SIMM testers, in which many insertions were expected over the life of the equipment. They could also be used in high-vibration or high-humidity environments.

For reference, all its tin-contact SIMM and DIMM sockets have the following connector plating specifications: .000030 (30 microinches) minimum thick tin on mating edge over .000050 (50 microinches) minimum thick nickel on entire contact.

The bottom line is that the thickness of the coating in current module sockets and modules is not an issue for the expected use of these devices. The thickness of the plating used is also not relevant to the tin versus gold matability issue. The only drawback to a thinner gold plating is that it will wear after fewer insertion/removal cycles, exposing the nickel underneath and allowing the onset of fretting corrosion.

In my opinion, this tin/gold issue is even more important for those using DIMMs and RIMMs, for two reasons. With SIMMs, you really have two connections for each pin (one on each side of the module), so if one of them goes high resistance, it will not matter; there is a built-in redundancy. With DIMMs and RIMMs, you have many, many more connections (168 or 184 versus 72) and no redundant connections. The chance for failure is much greater. Also, DIMMs and RIMMs run much faster, at speeds of up to 800MHz, where the timing is down in the single-digit nanosecond range. At these speeds, the slightest additional resistance in the connection causes problems.

Bottom line: Definitely don't mix metal types, but for the utmost in reliability for systems using DIMMs or RIMMs, be sure both the motherboard sockets as well as the modules themselves have gold-plated contacts. You usually can tell easily because tin is silver-colored, whereas gold is, well, gold-colored.

Parity and ECC

Part of the nature of memory is that it inevitably fails. These failures are usually classified as two basic types: hard fails and soft errors.

The best understood are *hard fails*, in which the chip is working and then, because of some flaw, physical damage, or other event, becomes damaged and experiences a permanent failure. Fixing this type of failure normally requires replacing some part of the memory hardware, such as the chip, SIMM, or DIMM. Hard error rates are known as *HERs*.

The other more insidious type of failure is the *soft error*, which is a nonpermanent failure that might never recur or could occur only at infrequent intervals. (Soft fails are effectively "fixed" by powering the system off and back on.) Soft error rates are known as *SERs*.

About 20 years ago, Intel made a discovery about soft errors that shook the memory industry. It found that alpha particles were causing an unacceptably high rate of soft errors or single event upsets (SEUs, as they are sometimes called) in the 16KB DRAMs that were available at the time. Because alpha particles are low-energy particles that can be stopped by something as thin and light as a sheet of paper, it became clear that for alpha particles to cause a DRAM soft error, they would have to be coming from within the semiconductor material. Testing showed trace elements of thorium and uranium in the plastic and ceramic chip packaging materials used at the time. This discovery forced all the memory manufacturers to evaluate their manufacturing process to produce materials free from contamination.

Today, memory manufacturers have all but totally eliminated the alpha-particle source of soft errors. Many people believed that was justification for the industry trend to drop parity checking. The argument is that, for example, a 16MB memory subsystem built with 4MB technology would experience a soft error caused by alpha particles only about once every 16 years! The real problem with this thinking is that it is seriously flawed, and many system manufacturers and vendors were coddled into removing parity and other memory fault-tolerant techniques from their systems even though soft errors continue to be an ongoing problem. More recent discoveries prove that alpha particles are now only a small fraction of the cause of DRAM soft errors!

As it turns out, the biggest cause of soft errors today are cosmic rays. IBM researchers began investigating the potential of terrestrial cosmic rays in causing soft errors similar to alpha particles. The difference is that cosmic rays are very high-energy particles and can't be stopped by sheets of paper or other more powerful types of shielding. The leader in this line of investigation was Dr. J.F. Ziegler of the IBM Watson Research Center in Yorktown Heights, New York. He has produced landmark research into understanding cosmic rays and their influence on soft errors in memory.

One example of the magnitude of the cosmic ray soft-error phenomenon demonstrated that with a certain sample of non-IBM DRAMs, the SER at sea level was measured at 5950 FIT (failures in time, which is measured at one billion hours) per chip. This was measured under real-life conditions with the benefit of millions of device hours of testing. In an average system, this would result in a soft error occurring every six months or less. In power-user or server systems with a larger amount of memory, it could mean one or more errors per month! When the exact same test setup and DRAMs were moved to an underground vault shielded by more than 50 feet of rock, thus eliminating all cosmic rays, absolutely no soft errors were recorded. This not only demonstrates how troublesome cosmic rays can be, but it also proves that the packaging contamination and alpha-particle problem has indeed been solved.

Cosmic-ray–induced errors are even more of a problem in SRAMs than DRAMS because the amount of charge required to flip a bit in an SRAM cell is less than is required to flip a DRAM cell capacitor. Cosmic rays are also more of a problem for higher-density memory. As chip density increases, it becomes easier for a stray particle to flip a bit. It has been predicted by some that the soft error rate of a 64MB DRAM will be double that of a 16MB chip, and a 256MB DRAM will have a rate four times higher.

Unfortunately, the PC industry has largely failed to recognize this cause of memory errors. Electrostatic discharge, power surges, or unstable software can much more easily explain away the random and intermittent nature of a soft error, especially right after a new release of an operating system or major application.

Studies have shown that the soft error rate for ECC systems is on the order of 30 times greater than the hard error rate. This is not surprising to those familiar with the full effects of cosmic ray–generated soft errors. There is now data suggesting that some 16MB DRAM chip designs will actually experience soft errors numbering in the 24,000 FIT range. This would result in a soft error about once a month for most systems today!

Although cosmic rays and other radiation events are the biggest cause of soft errors, others can be caused by the following:

- *Power glitches or noise on the line.* This can be caused by a defective power supply in the system or by defective power at the outlet.

- *Incorrect type or speed rating.* The memory must be the correct type for the chipset and match the system access speed.

- *RF (radio frequency) interference.* Caused by radio transmitters in close proximity to the system, which can generate electrical signals in system wiring and circuits.

- *Static discharges.* Causes momentary power spikes, which alter data.

- *Timing glitches.* Data doesn't arrive at the proper place at the proper time, causing errors. Often caused by improper settings in the BIOS Setup, by memory that is rated slower than the system requires, or by overclocked processors and other system components.

Most of these problems don't cause chips to permanently fail (although bad power or static can damage chips permanently), but they can cause momentary problems with data.

How can you deal with these errors? Just ignoring them is certainly not the best way to deal with them, but unfortunately that is what many system manufacturers and vendors are doing today. The best way to deal with this problem is to increase the system's fault tolerance. This means implementing ways of detecting and possibly correcting errors in PC systems. Three basic levels and techniques are used for fault tolerance in modern PCs:

- Nonparity
- Parity
- ECC

Nonparity systems have no fault tolerance at all. The only reason they are used is because they have the lowest inherent cost. No additional memory is necessary, as is the case with parity or ECC techniques. Because a parity-type data byte has 9 bits versus 8 for nonparity, memory cost is 12.5% higher. Also, the nonparity memory controller is simplified because it does not need the logic gates to calculate parity or ECC check bits. Portable systems that place a premium on minimizing power might benefit from the reduction in memory power resulting from fewer DRAM chips. Finally, the memory system data bus is narrower, which reduces the amount of data buffers. The statistical probability of memory failures in a modern office desktop computer is now estimated at about one error every few months. Errors will be more or less frequent depending on how much memory you have.

This error rate might be tolerable for low-end systems that are not used for mission-critical applications. In this case, their extreme market cost sensitivity probably can't justify the extra cost of parity or ECC memory, and such errors then must be tolerated.

At any rate, having no fault tolerance in a system is simply gambling that memory errors are unlikely. You further gamble that if they do occur, memory errors will result in an inherent cost less than the additional hardware necessary for error detection. However, the risk is that these memory errors can lead to serious problems. A memory error in a calculation could cause the wrong value to go into a bank check. In a server, a memory error could force a system to hang and bring down all LAN-resident client systems with subsequent loss of productivity. Finally, with a nonparity or non-ECC memory system, tracing the problem is difficult, which is not the case with parity or ECC. These techniques at least isolate a memory source as the culprit, thus reducing both the time and cost of resolving the problem.

Parity Checking

One standard IBM set for the industry is that the memory chips in a bank of nine each handle 1 bit of data: 8 bits per character plus 1 extra bit called the *parity bit*. The parity bit enables memory-control circuitry to keep tabs on the other 8 bits—a built-in cross-check for the integrity of each byte in the system. If the circuitry detects an error, the computer stops and displays a message informing you of the malfunction. If you are running a GUI operating system, such as Windows or OS/2, a parity error generally manifests itself as a locked system. When you reboot, the BIOS should detect the error and display the appropriate error message.

SIMMs and DIMMs are available both with and without parity bits. Originally, all PC systems used parity-checked memory to ensure accuracy. Starting in 1994, a disturbing trend developed in the PC-compatible marketplace. Most vendors began shipping systems without parity checking or any other means of detecting or correcting errors! These systems can use cheaper nonparity SIMMs, which saves about 10%–15% on memory costs for a system. Parity memory results in increased initial system cost, primarily because of the additional memory bits involved. Parity can't correct system errors, but because parity can detect errors, it can make the user aware of memory errors when they happen. This has two basic benefits:

- Parity guards against the consequences of faulty calculations based on incorrect data.
- Parity pinpoints the source of errors, which helps with problem resolution, thus improving system serviceability.

PC systems can easily be designed to function using either parity or nonparity memory. The cost of implementing parity as an option on a motherboard is virtually nothing; the only cost is in actually purchasing the parity SIMMs or DIMMs, which are about 10%–15% more expensive than nonparity versions. This enables a system manufacturer to offer its system purchasers the choice of parity if the purchasers feel the additional cost is justified for their particular applications.

Unfortunately, several of the big names began selling systems without parity to reduce their prices, and they did not make it well known that the lower cost meant parity memory was no longer included as standard. This began happening mostly in 1994 and 1995, and has continued until recently, with few people understanding the full implications. After one or two major vendors did this, most of the others were forced to follow to remain price-competitive.

Because nobody wanted to announce this information, it remained sort of a dirty little secret within the industry. Originally, when this happened, you could still specify parity memory when you ordered a system, even though the default configurations no longer included it. There was a 10%–15% surcharge on the memory, but those who wanted reliable, trustworthy systems could at least get them, provided they knew to ask, of course. Then a major bomb hit the industry, in the form of the Intel Triton 430FX Pentium chipset, which was the first major chipset on the market that did not support parity checking at all! It also became the most popular chipset of its time and was found in practically all Pentium motherboards sold in the 1995 timeframe. This set a disturbing trend for the next few years. All but one of Intel's Pentium processor chipsets after the 430FX did not support parity-checked memory; the only one that did was the 430HX Triton II.

Since then, Intel and other chipset manufacturers have put support for parity and ECC memory in most of their chipsets (especially so in their higher-end models). The low-end chipsets, however, typically do lack support for either parity or ECC. If more reliability is important to you, make sure the systems you purchase have this support.

Let's look at how parity checking works, and then examine in more detail the successor to parity checking, called ECC, which can not only detect but correct memory errors on-the-fly.

IBM originally established the odd parity standard for error checking. The following explanation might help you understand what is meant by odd parity. As the 8 individual bits in a byte are stored in memory, a parity generator/checker, which is either part of the CPU or located in a special chip on the motherboard, evaluates the data bits by adding up the number of 1s in the byte. If an even number of 1s is found, the parity generator/checker then creates a 1 and stores it as the ninth bit (parity bit) in the parity memory chip. That makes the sum for all 9 bits (including the parity bit) an odd number. If the original sum of the 8 data bits is an odd number, the parity bit created would be a 0, keeping the sum for all 9 bits an odd number. The basic rule is that the value of the parity bit is always chosen so that the sum of all 9 bits (8 data bits plus 1 parity bit) is stored as an odd number. If the system used even parity, the example would be the same except the parity bit would be created to ensure an even sum. It doesn't matter whether even or odd parity is used; the system uses one or the other, and it is completely transparent to the memory chips involved. Remember that the 8 data bits in a byte are numbered 0 1 2 3 4 5 6 7. The following examples might make it easier to understand:

```
Data bit number:    0 1 2 3 4 5 6 7     Parity bit
Data bit value:     1 0 1 1 0 0 1 1     0
```

In this example, because the total number of data bits with a value of 1 is an odd number (5), the parity bit must have a value of 0 to ensure an odd sum for all 9 bits.

Here is another example:

```
Data bit number:    0 1 2 3 4 5 6 7     Parity bit
Data bit value:     1 1 1 1 0 0 1 1     1
```

In this example, because the total number of data bits with a value of 1 is an even number (6), the parity bit must have a value of 1 to create an odd sum for all 9 bits.

When the system reads memory back from storage, it checks the parity information. If a (9-bit) byte has an even number of bits with a parity bit value of 1, that byte must have an error. The system can't tell which bit has changed or whether only a single bit has changed. If 3 bits changed, for example, the byte still flags a parity-check error; if 2 bits changed, however, the bad byte could pass unnoticed. Because multiple bit errors (in a single byte) are rare, this scheme gives you a reasonable and inexpensive ongoing indication that memory is good or bad.

The following examples show parity-check messages for three types of older systems:

```
For the IBM PC:                  PARITY CHECK x
For the IBM XT:                  PARITY CHECK x    yyyyy (z)
For the IBM AT and late model XT: PARITY CHECK x   yyyyy
```

Where x is 1 or 2:

> 1 = Error occurred on the motherboard

> 2 = Error occurred in an expansion slot

In this example, *yyyyy* represents a number from 00000 through FFFFF that indicates, in hexadecimal notation, the byte in which the error has occurred.

Where (z) is (S) or (E):

> (S) = Parity error occurred in the system unit

> (E) = Parity error occurred in an optional expansion chassis

Note

An expansion chassis was an option IBM sold for the original PC and XT systems to add more expansion slots. This unit consisted of a backplane motherboard with eight slots; one slot contained a special extender/receiver card cabled to a similar extender/receiver card placed in the main system. Because of the extender/receiver cards in the main system and the expansion chassis, the net gain was six slots. Although the IBM version has long since been discontinued, other companies have since produced 8-bit and 16-bit ISA expansion chassis, enabling more ISA slots to be added to a system.

When a parity-check error is detected, the motherboard parity-checking circuits generate a *nonmaskable interrupt (NMI)*, which halts processing and diverts the system's attention to the error. The NMI causes a routine in the ROM to be executed. The routine clears the screen and then displays a message in the screen's upper-left corner. The message differs depending on the type of computer system. On some older IBM systems, the ROM parity-check routine halts the CPU. In such a case, the system locks up, and you must perform a hardware reset or a power-off/power-on cycle to restart the system. Unfortunately, all unsaved work is lost in the process.

Most systems do not halt the CPU when a parity error is detected; instead, they offer you the choice of rebooting the system or continuing as though nothing happened. Additionally, these systems might display the parity error message in a different format from IBM, although the information presented is basically the same. For example, most systems with a Phoenix BIOS display one of these messages:

```
Memory parity interrupt at xxxx:xxxx
Type (S)hut off NMI, Type (R)eboot, other keys to continue
```

or

```
I/O card parity interrupt at xxxx:xxxx
Type (S)hut off NMI, Type (R)eboot, other keys to continue
```

The first of these two messages indicates a motherboard parity error (Parity Check 1), and the second indicates an expansion-slot parity error (Parity Check 2). Notice that the address given in the form *xxxx:xxxx* for the memory error is in a segment:offset form rather than a straight linear address, such as with IBM's error messages. The segment:offset address form still gives you the location of the error to a resolution of a single byte.

You have three ways to proceed after viewing this error message:

- You can press S, which shuts off parity checking and resumes system operation at the point where the parity check first occurred.

- You can press R to force the system to reboot, losing any unsaved work.

- You can press any other key to cause the system to resume operation with parity checking still enabled.

If the problem occurs, it is likely to cause another parity-check interruption. It's usually prudent to press S, which disables the parity checking so you can then save your work. In this case, it's best to save your work to a floppy disk to prevent the possible corruption of the hard disk. You should also avoid overwriting any previous (still good) versions of whatever file you are saving because you could be saving a bad file caused by the memory corruption. Because parity checking is now disabled, your save operations will not be interrupted. Then, you should power the system off, restart it, and run whatever memory diagnostics software you have to try to track down the error. In some cases, the POST finds the error on the next restart, but you usually need to run a more sophisticated diagnostics program—perhaps in a continuous mode—to locate the error.

Systems with an AMI BIOS display the parity error messages in the following forms:

```
ON BOARD PARITY ERROR ADDR (HEX) = (xxxxx)
```

or

```
OFF BOARD PARITY ERROR ADDR (HEX) = (xxxxx)
```

These messages indicate that an error in memory has occurred during the POST, and the failure is located at the address indicated. The first one indicates that the error occurred on the motherboard, and the second message indicates an error in an expansion slot adapter card. The AMI BIOS can also display memory errors in the following manners:

```
Memory Parity Error at xxxxx
```

or

```
I/O Card Parity Error at xxxxx
```

These messages indicate that an error in memory has occurred at the indicated address during normal operation. The first one indicates a motherboard memory error, and the second indicates an expansion slot adapter memory error.

Although many systems enable you to continue processing after a parity error and even allow disabling further parity checking, continuing to use your system after a parity error is detected can be dangerous. The idea behind letting you continue using either method is to give you time to save any unsaved work before you diagnose and service the computer, but be careful how you do this.

Note that these messages can vary depending not only on the ROM BIOS but also on your operating system. Protected mode operating systems, such as most versions of Windows, trap these errors and run their own handler program that displays a message different from what the ROM would have displayed. The message might be associated with a blue screen or might be a trap error, but it usually indicates that it is memory or parity related. For example, Windows 98 displays a message indicating `Memory parity error detected. System halted.` when such an error has occurred.

Caution

When you are notified of a memory parity error, remember the parity check is telling you that memory has been corrupted. Do you want to save potentially corrupted data over the good file from the last time you saved? Definitely not! Be sure you save your work with a different filename. In addition, after a parity error, save only to a floppy disk if possible and avoid writing to the hard disk; there is a slight chance that the hard drive could become corrupted if you save the contents of corrupted memory.

After saving your work, determine the cause of the parity error and repair the system. You might be tempted to use an option to shut off further parity checking and simply continue using the system as though nothing were wrong. Doing so is like unscrewing the oil pressure warning indicator bulb on a car with an oil leak so the oil pressure light won't bother you anymore!

A few years ago, when memory was more expensive, a few companies were marketing SIMMs with bogus parity chips. Instead of actually having the extra memory chips needed to store the parity bits, these "logic parity" or parity "emulation" SIMMs used an onboard parity generator chip. This chip ignored any parity the system was trying to store on the SIMM, but when data was retrieved, it always ensured that the correct parity was returned, thus making the system believe all was well even though there might be a problem.

These bogus parity modules were used because memory was much more expensive, and a company could offer a "parity" SIMM for only a few dollars more with the fake chip. Unfortunately, identifying them can be difficult. The bogus parity generator doesn't look like a memory chip, and has different markings from the other memory chips on the SIMM. Most of them had a "GSM" logo, which indicated the original manufacturer of the parity logic device, not necessarily the SIMM itself.

One way to positively identify these bogus fake parity SIMMs is by using a hardware SIMM test machine, such as those by Darkhorse Systems or Aristo. Of course, I don't recommend using bogus parity SIMMs. Fortunately, the problem has mostly subsided because honest-to-gosh memory is much cheaper these days.

Error Correcting Code

ECC goes a big step beyond simple parity-error detection. Instead of just detecting an error, ECC allows a single bit error to be corrected, which means the system can continue without interruption and without corrupting data. ECC, as implemented in most PCs, can only detect, not correct, double-bit errors. Because studies have indicated that approximately 98% of memory errors are the single-bit variety, the most commonly used type of ECC is one in which the attendant memory controller detects and corrects single-bit errors in an accessed data word (double-bit errors can be detected, but not corrected). This type of ECC is known as *single-bit error-correction double-bit error detection (SEC-DED)* and requires an additional 7 check bits over 32 bits in a 4-byte system and an additional 8 check bits over 64 bits in an 8-byte system. ECC in a 4-byte (32-bit, such as a 486) system obviously costs more than non-parity or parity, but in an 8-byte wide bus (64-bit, such as Pentium/Athlon) system, ECC and parity costs are equal because the same number of extra bits (8) is required for either parity or ECC. Because of this, you can purchase parity SIMMs (36-bit), DIMMs (72-bit), or RIMMs

(18-bit) for 32-bit systems and use them in an ECC mode if the chipset supports ECC functionality. If the system uses SIMMs, two 36-bit (parity) SIMMs are added for each bank (for a total of 72-bits), and ECC is done at the bank level. If the system uses DIMMs, a single parity/ECC 72-bit DIMM is used as a bank and provides the additional bits. RIMMs are installed in singles or pairs, depending on the chipset and motherboard. They must be 18-bit versions if parity/ECC is desired.

ECC entails the memory controller calculating the check bits on a memory-write operation, performing a compare between the read and calculated check-bits on a read operation, and, if necessary, correcting bad bits. The additional ECC logic in the memory controller is not very significant in this age of inexpensive, high-performance VLSI logic, but ECC actually affects memory performance on writes. This is because the operation must be timed to wait for the calculation of check bits and, when the system waits for corrected data, reads. On a partial-word write, the entire word must first be read, the affected byte(s) rewritten, and then new check bits calculated. This turns partial-word write operations into slower read-modify writes. Fortunately, this performance hit is very small, on the order of a few percent at maximum, so the tradeoff for increased reliability is a good one.

Most memory errors are of a single-bit nature, which can be corrected by ECC. Incorporating this fault-tolerant technique provides high system reliability and attendant availability. An ECC-based system is a good choice for servers, workstations, or mission-critical applications in which the cost of a potential memory error outweighs the additional memory and system cost to correct it, along with ensuring that it does not detract from system reliability. If you value your data and use your system for important (to you) tasks, you'll want ECC memory. No self-respecting manager would build or run a network server, even a lower-end one, without ECC memory.

By designing a system that allows the user to make the choice of ECC, parity, or nonparity, users can choose the level of fault tolerance desired, as well as how much they want to gamble with their data.

Installing RAM Upgrades

Adding memory to a system is one of the most useful upgrades you can perform, and also one of the least expensive—especially when you consider the increased capabilities of Windows 9x, Windows NT, Windows 2000, and OS/2 when you give them access to more memory. In some cases, doubling the memory can practically double the speed of a computer.

The following sections discuss adding memory, including selecting memory chips, installing memory chips, and testing the installation.

Upgrade Options and Strategies

Adding memory can be an inexpensive solution; at this writing, the cost of memory has fallen to about $1 per megabyte or less. A small dose can give your computer's performance a big boost.

How do you add memory to your PC? You have two options, listed in order of convenience and cost:

- Adding memory in vacant slots on your motherboard
- Replacing your current motherboard's memory with higher-capacity memory

If you decide to upgrade to a more powerful computer system or motherboard, you normally can't salvage the memory from your previous system. Most of the time it is best to plan on equipping a new board with the optimum type of memory that it supports.

Be sure to carefully weigh your future needs for computing speed and a multitasking operating system (OS/2, Windows 9x, Windows NT, Windows 2000, or Linux, for example) against the amount of money you spend to upgrade current equipment.

Before you add RAM to a system (or replace defective RAM chips), you must determine the memory chips required for your system. Your system documentation has this information.

If you need to replace a defective memory module and do not have the system documentation, you can determine the correct module for your system by inspecting the ones that are already installed. Each module has markings that indicate the module's capacity and speed. RAM capacity and speed are discussed in detail earlier in this chapter.

If you do not have the documentation for your system and the manufacturer does not offer technical support, open your system case and carefully write down the markings that appear on your memory chips. Then contact a local computer store or module vendor, such as Kingston, Micron (Crucial), PNY, or others, for help in determining the proper RAM chips for your system. Adding the wrong modules to a system can make it as unreliable as leaving a defective module installed and trying to use the system in that condition.

Note

Before upgrading an older Pentium (P5 class) system beyond 64MB of RAM, be sure that your chipset supports caching more than 64MB. Adding RAM beyond the amount supported by your L2 cache slows performance rather than increases it. See the section "Cache Memory: SRAM," earlier in this chapter, and the discussion of chipsets in Chapter 4 for a more complete explanation of this common system limitation. This limitation was mostly with Pentium (P5) class chipsets. Pentium II and later processors, including the AMD Athlon and Duron, have the L2 cache controller integrated in the processor (not the chipset), which supports caching up to 1GB, or 4GB on most newer models.

Selecting and Installing Memory

If you are upgrading a motherboard by adding memory, follow the manufacturer's guidelines on which memory chips or modules to buy. As you learned earlier, memory comes in various form factors, including SIMMs, DIMMs, and RIMMs.

No matter which type of memory modules you have, the chips are installed in memory banks. A *memory bank* is a collection of memory chips that make up a complete row of memory. Your processor reads each row of memory in one pass. A memory bank does not work unless the entire row is filled with memory chips. (Banks are discussed in more detail earlier in this chapter in the section "Memory Banks.")

Installing extra memory on your motherboard is an easy way to add memory to your computer. Most systems have at least one vacant memory bank where you can install extra memory at a later time and speed up your computer.

Replacing Modules with Higher-Capacity Versions

If all the memory module slots on your motherboard are occupied, your best option is to remove an existing bank of memory and replace it with higher-capacity modules. For example, if you have a motherboard that supports two DIMM modules (each representing one bank on a processor with a 64-bit data bus), you could remove one of them and replace it with a higher-capacity version. For example, if you have two 64MB modules giving a total of 128MB, you could remove one of the 64MB modules and replace it with a 128MB unit, in which case you'd then have a total of 192MB of RAM.

However, just because higher-capacity modules are available that are the correct pin count to plug into your motherboard, don't automatically assume the higher-capacity memory will work. Your system's chipset and BIOS set limits on the capacity of the memory you can use. Check your system or motherboard documentation to see which size modules work with it before purchasing the new RAM. You should make sure you have the latest BIOS when installing new memory.

Installing Memory

This section discusses installing memory—specifically, new SIMM or DIMM modules. It also covers the problems you are most likely to encounter and how to avoid them. You also get information on configuring your system to use new memory.

When you install or remove memory, you are most likely to encounter the following problems:

- Electrostatic discharge
- Improperly seated modules
- Incorrect memory configuration settings in the BIOS Setup

To prevent electrostatic discharge (ESD) when you install sensitive memory chips or boards, do not wear synthetic-fiber clothing or leather-soled shoes. Remove any static charge you are carrying by touching the system chassis before you begin, or better yet, wear a good commercial grounding strap on your wrist. You can order one from an electronics parts store or mail-order house. A grounding strap consists of a conductive wristband grounded at the other end by a wire clipped to the system chassis. Leave the system unit plugged in—but turned off—to keep it grounded.

Caution

Be sure to use a properly designed commercial grounding strap; do not make one yourself. Commercial units have a one-meg ohm resistor that serves as protection if you accidentally touch live power. The resistor ensures that you do not become the path of least resistance to the ground and therefore become electrocuted. An improperly designed strap can cause the power to conduct through you to the ground, possibly killing you.

Each memory chip or module must be installed in a specific orientation. Interference fit notches and tangs are designed to prevent improper installation of the module into the socket. As long as you are observant and don't try to force anything, the proper orientation should be fairly easy to figure out. As you insert the module, be sure the notches align with the appropriate tangs on the socket.

I would hope it goes without saying, but before installing memory, be sure the system power is off! You should make sure the system is unplugged just to be sure. If you were to install memory while the power was on (even if the system was in a sleep mode), you would probably fry not only the memory but possibly the entire motherboard as well.

You remove SIMMs and DIMMs by releasing the locking tabs and either pulling or rolling them out of their sockets. The installation is exactly the opposite.

After adding the memory and putting the system back together, you might have to run the BIOS Setup and resave with the new amount of memory being reported. Most newer systems automatically detect the new amount of memory and reconfigure the BIOS Setup settings for you. Most newer systems also don't require setting any jumpers or switches on the motherboard to configure them for your new memory.

Note

Information on installing memory on older memory expansion cards can be found in Chapter 7 of *Upgrading and Repairing PCs, 6th Edition*, which is included in its entirety on the CD accompanying this book.

After configuring your system to work properly with the additional memory, you might want to run a memory-diagnostics program to ensure that the new memory works properly. Some are run automatically for you. At least two and sometimes three memory-diagnostic programs are available for all systems. In order of accuracy, these programs are as follows:

- POST (power on self test)
- Disk-based advanced diagnostics software

The POST is used every time you power up the system.

Many additional diagnostics programs are available from aftermarket utility software companies. More information on aftermarket testing facilities can be found in Chapter 24.

Installing SIMMs

SIMM memory is oriented by a notch on one side of the module that is not present on the other side, as shown in Figure 6.14. The socket has a protrusion that must fit into this notched area on one side of the module. This protrusion makes installing a SIMM backward impossible unless you break the connector or the module. Figure 6.15 details the notch and the locking clip.

Figure 6.14   The notch on this SIMM is shown on the left side. Insert the SIMM at a 45° angle and then tilt it forward until the locking clips snap into place.

Installing DIMMs and RIMMs

Similarly, DIMMs and RIMMs are keyed by notches along the bottom connector edge that are offset from the center so they can be inserted in only one direction, as shown in Figure 6.16.

The DIMM/RIMM ejector tab locks into place in the notch on the side of the DIMM when it is fully inserted. Some DIMM sockets have ejector tabs on both ends. Take care not to force the module into the socket. If the module does not slip easily into the slot and then snap into place, there is a good chance the module is not oriented or aligned correctly. Forcing the module could break the module or the socket. If the retaining clips on the socket break, the memory isn't held firmly in place, and you likely will get random memory errors because the module can't make consistent electrical contact if it is loose.

Figure 6.15 This figure shows the SIMM inserted in the socket with the notch aligned, the locking clip locked, and the hole in the SIMM aligned with the tab in the socket.

Figure 6.16 DIMM keys match the protrusions in the DIMM sockets. DDR DIMM and RIMM keys are similar but not exactly the same.

Installing RIMMs

RIMMs install in exactly the same manner as DIMMs, although in different sockets. The ejector tabs on the sides are similar, and they go in at a straight 90° angle just like DIMMs. The key notches on the RIMM prevent backwards installation and aid alignment when inserting them.

You'll also need to fill any empty RIMM sockets with a continuity module. Refer to Figure 6.11 for details on adding this module.

Troubleshooting Memory

Memory problems can be difficult to troubleshoot. For one thing, computer memory is still mysterious to people because it is a kind of "virtual" thing that can be hard to grasp. The other difficulty is that memory problems can be intermittent and often look like problems with other areas of the system, even software. This section shows simple troubleshooting steps you can perform if you suspect you are having a memory problem.

To troubleshoot memory, you first need some memory-diagnostics testing programs. You already have several, and might not know it! Every motherboard BIOS has a memory diagnostic in the POST that runs when you first turn on the system. In most cases, you also received a memory diagnostic on a utility disk that came with your system. Finally, a commercial program called Check-It is included on the CD-ROM with this book. Many other commercial diagnostics programs are on the market, and almost all of them include memory tests.

When the POST runs, it not only tests memory, but also counts it. The count is compared to the amount counted the last time BIOS Setup was run; if it is different, an error message is issued. As the POST runs, it writes a pattern of data to all the memory locations in the system and reads that pattern back to verify that the memory works. If any failure is detected, you see or hear a message. Audio messages (beeping) are used for critical or "fatal" errors that occur in areas important for the system's operation. If the system can access enough memory to at least allow video to function, you see error messages instead of hearing beep codes.

See the CD accompanying this book for detailed listings of the BIOS beep and other error codes, which are specific to the type of BIOS you have. These BIOS codes are found in the Technical Reference section of the CD in printable PDF format for your convenience. For example, most Intel motherboards use the Phoenix BIOS. Several beep codes are used in that BIOS to indicate fatal memory errors.

If your system makes it through the POST with no memory error indications, there might not be a hardware memory problem, or the POST might not be able to detect the problem. Intermittent memory errors are often not detected during the POST, and other subtle hardware defects can be hard for the POST to catch. The POST is designed to run quickly, so the testing is not nearly as thorough as it could be. That is why you often have to boot from a DOS or diagnostic disk and run a true hardware diagnostic to do more extensive memory testing. These types of tests can be run continuously, and left running for days if necessary to hunt down an elusive intermittent defect.

Still, even these programs do only pass/fail type testing; that is, all they can do is write patterns to memory and read them back. They can't determine how close the memory is to failing—only that it worked or not. For the highest level of testing, the best thing to have is a dedicated memory test machine, usually called a *SIMM/DIMM tester*. These devices enable you to insert a module and test it thoroughly at a variety of speeds, voltages, and timings to let you know for certain whether the memory is good or bad. I have defective SIMMs, for example, that work in some systems (slower ones) but not others. What I mean is that the *same* memory test program fails the SIMM in one machine but passes it in another. In the SIMM tester, it is always identified as bad right down to the individual bit, and it even tells me the actual speed of the device, not just its rating. Several companies that offer SIMM/DIMM testers are included in the Vendor List, including Darkhorse Systems and Aristo. They can be expensive, but for a professional in the PC repair business, using one of these SIMM/DIMM testers is the only way to go.

After your operating system is running, memory errors can still occur, typically identified by error messages you might receive. These are the most common:

- *Parity errors*. Indicates that the parity-checking circuitry on the motherboard has detected a change in memory since the data was originally stored. (See the "Parity Checking" section earlier in this chapter.)

- *General or global protection faults*. A general-purpose error indicating that a program has been corrupted in memory, usually resulting in immediate termination of the application. This can also be caused by buggy or faulty programs.

- *Fatal exception errors*. Error codes returned by a program when an illegal instruction has been encountered, invalid data or code has been accessed, or the privilege level of an operation is invalid.

- *Divide error*. A general-purpose error indicating that a division by 0 was attempted or the result of an operation does not fit in the destination register.

If you are encountering these errors, they could be caused by defective or improperly configured memory, but they can also be caused by software bugs (especially drivers), bad power supplies, static discharges, close proximity radio transmitters, timing problems, and more.

If you suspect the problems are caused by memory, there are ways to test the memory to determine whether that is the problem. Most of this testing involves running one or more memory test programs.

I am amazed that most people make a critical mistake when they run memory test software. The biggest problem I see is that people run memory tests with the system caches enabled. This effectively invalidates memory testing because most systems have what is called a *write-back cache*. This means that data written to main memory is first written to the cache. Because a memory test program first writes data and then immediately reads it back, the data is read back from the cache, not the main memory. It makes the memory test program run very quickly, but all you tested was the cache. The bottom line is that if you test memory with the cache enabled, you aren't really writing to the SIMM/DIMMs, but only to the cache. Before you run any memory test programs, be sure your cache is disabled. The system will run very slowly when you do this, and the memory test will take much longer to complete, but you will be testing your actual RAM, not the cache.

The following steps enable you to effectively test and troubleshoot your system RAM. Figure 6.17 provides a boiled-down procedure to help you step through the process quickly.

First, let's cover the memory testing and troubleshooting procedures.

1. Power up the system and observe the POST. If the POST completes with no errors, basic memory functionality has been tested. If errors are encountered, go to the defect isolation procedures.

2. Restart the system, and enter your BIOS (or CMOS) Setup. In most systems, this is done by pressing the F2 key during the POST but before the boot process begins. Once in BIOS Setup, verify that the memory count is equal to the amount that has been installed. If the count does not match what has been installed, go to the defect isolation procedures.

3. Find the BIOS Setup options for cache, and set all cache options to disabled. Save the settings and reboot to a DOS-formatted system disk (floppy) containing the diagnostics program of your choice. If your system came with a diagnostics disk, you can use that, or you can use one of the many commercial PC diagnostics programs on the market, such as PC-Technician by Windsor Technologies (which comes in self-booting form), the Norton Utilities by Symantec, or others.

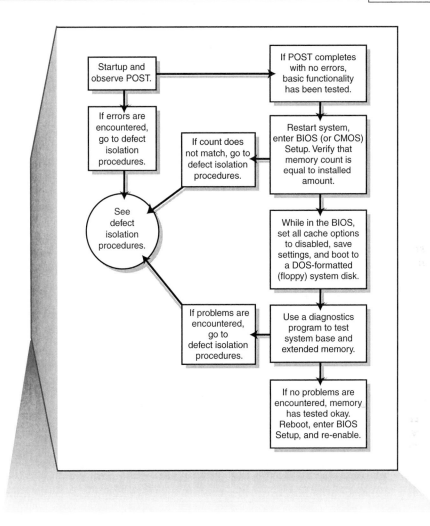

Figure 6.17   Testing and troubleshooting memory.

4. Follow the instructions that came with your diagnostic program to have it test the system base and extended memory. Most programs have a mode that enables them to loop the test—that is, to run it continuously, which is great for finding intermittent problems. If the program encounters a memory error, proceed to the defect isolation procedures.

5. If no errors are encountered in the POST or in the more comprehensive memory diagnostic, your memory has tested okay in hardware. Be sure at this point to reboot the system, enter the BIOS Setup, and reenable the cache. The system will run very slowly until the cache is turned back on.

6. If you are having memory problems yet the memory still tests okay, you might have a problem undetectable by simple pass/fail testing, or your problems could be caused by software or one of many other defects or problems in your system. You might want to bring the memory to a SIMM/DIMM tester for a more accurate analysis. Most PC repair shops have such a tester. I would also check the software (especially drivers, which might need updating), power supply, and system environment for problems such as static, radio transmitters, and so forth.

Memory Defect Isolation Procedures

To use these steps, I am assuming you have identified an actual memory problem that is being reported by the POST or disk-based memory diagnostics. If this is the case, see the following steps and Figure 6.18 for the steps to identify or isolate which SIMM or DIMM in the system is causing the problem.

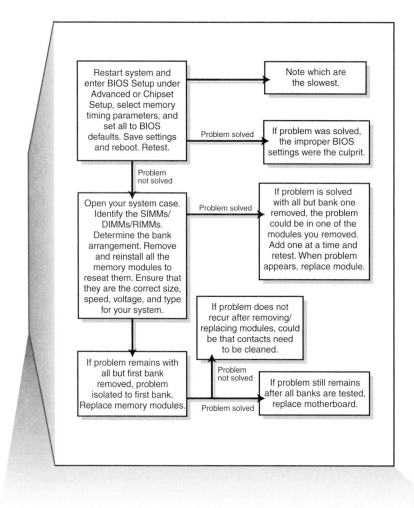

Figure 6.18   Follow these steps if you are still encountering memory errors after completing the steps in Figure 6.17.

1. Restart the system and enter the BIOS Setup. Under a menu usually called Advanced or Chipset Setup might be memory timing parameters. Select BIOS or Setup defaults, which are usually the slowest settings. Save the settings, reboot, and retest using the testing and troubleshooting procedures listed earlier. If the problem has been solved, improper BIOS settings were the problem. If the problem remains, you likely do have defective memory, so continue to the next step.

2. Open the system for physical access to the SIMM/DIMMs on the motherboard. Identify the bank arrangement in the system. For example, Pentium systems use 64-bit banks, which means two 72-pin SIMMs or one 168-pin DIMM per bank. Using the manual or the legend silk-screened on the motherboard, identify which SIMMs or DIMM correspond to which bank. Most Pentium boards that use SIMMs have four, six, or eight total SIMMs installed in two, three, or four banks. Most boards using DIMMs have two, three, or four total DIMMs, each of which represents a single bank.

3. Remove all the memory except the first bank, and retest using the troubleshooting and testing procedures listed earlier. If the problem remains with all but the first bank removed, the problem has been isolated to the first bank, which must be replaced.

4. Replace the memory in the first bank, preferably with known good spare modules, but you can also swap in others that you have removed and retest. If the problem *still* remains after testing all the memory banks (and finding them all to be working properly), it is likely the motherboard itself is bad (probably one of the memory sockets). Replace the motherboard and retest.

5. At this point, the first (or previous) bank has tested good, so the problem must be in the remaining modules that have been temporarily removed. Install the next bank of memory and retest. If the problem resurfaces now, the memory in that bank is defective. Continue testing each bank until you find the defective module.

6. Repeat the preceding step until all remaining banks of memory are installed and have been tested. If the problem has not resurfaced after removing and reinstalling all the memory, the problem was likely intermittent or caused by poor conduction on the memory contacts. Often simply removing and replacing memory can resolve problems because of the self-cleaning action between the SIMM/DIMM and the socket during removal and reinstallation.

The System Logical Memory Layout

The original PC had a total of 1MB of addressable memory, and the top 384KB of that was reserved for use by the system. Placing this reserved space at the top (between 640KB and 1024KB instead of at the bottom, between 0KB and 640KB) led to what is often called the *conventional memory barrier*. The constant pressures on system and peripheral manufacturers to maintain compatibility by never breaking from the original memory scheme of the first PC has resulted in a system memory structure that is (to put it kindly) a mess. Almost two decades after the first PC was introduced, even the newest Pentium 4–based systems are limited in many important ways by the memory map of the first PCs.

What we end up with is a PC with a split personality. There are two primary modes of operation that are very different from each other. The original PC used an Intel 8088 processor that could run only 16-bit instructions or code, which ran in what was called the real mode of the processor. These early processors had only enough address lines to access up to 1MB of memory, and the last 384KB of that was reserved for use by the video card as video RAM, other adapters (for on-card ROM BIOS), and finally the motherboard ROM BIOS.

The 286 processor brought more address lines, enough to allow up to 16MB of RAM to be used, and a new mode called *protected mode* that you had to be in to use it. Unfortunately, all the operating systems software at the time was designed to run only within the first 1MB, so extender programs were added and other tricks performed to eventually allow DOS and Windows 3.x access up to the first 16MB. One area of confusion was that RAM was now noncontiguous; that is, the operating system could use the first 640KB and the last 15MB, but not the 384KB of system reserved area that sat in between.

When the first 32-bit processor was released by Intel in 1985 (the 386DX), the memory architecture of the system changed dramatically. There were now enough address lines for the processor to use 4GB of memory, but this was accessible only in a new 32-bit *protected mode* in which only 32-bit instructions or code could run. This mode was designed for newer, more advanced operating systems, such as Windows 9x, NT, 2000, OS/2, Linux, Unix, and so forth. With the 386 came a whole new memory architecture in which this new 32-bit software could run. Unfortunately, it took 10 years for the mainstream user to upgrade to 32-bit operating systems and applications, which shows how stubborn we are! From a software instruction perspective, all the 32-bit processors since the 386 are really just faster versions of the same. Other than the more recent additions of MMX and SSE (or AMD's 3DNow) instructions to the processor, for all intents and purposes, a Pentium 4 or Athlon is just a "turbo" 386.

The real problem now is that the 32-bit processors have two distinctly different modes, with different memory architectures in each. For backward compatibility, you could still run the 32-bit processors in real mode, but only 16-bit software could run in that mode, and such software could access only the first 1MB or 16MB, depending on how it was written. For example, 16-bit drivers could load into and access only the first 1MB. Also, it is worth noting that the system ROM BIOS, including the POST, BIOS configuration, boot code, and all the internal drivers, is virtually all 16-bit software. This is because all Intel-compatible PC processors begin operation in 16-bit real mode when they are powered on. When a 32-bit operating system loads, it is that operating system code that instructs the processor to switch into 32-bit protected mode.

When an operating system such as Windows is loaded, the processor is switched into 32-bit protected mode early in the loading sequence. Then, 32-bit drivers for all the hardware can be loaded, and then the rest of the operating system can load. In 32-bit protected mode, the operating systems and applications can access all the memory in the system, up to the maximum limit of the processor (64TB for most of the Pentium II and later chips).

Unfortunately, one problem with protected mode is just that: It is protected. The name comes from the fact that only driver programs are allowed to talk directly to the hardware in this mode; programs loaded by the operating system, such as by clicking an icon in Windows, are not allowed to access memory or other hardware directly. This protection is provided so that a single program can't crash the machine by doing something illegal. You might have seen the error message in Windows indicating this, and that the program will be shut down.

Diagnostics software by nature must talk to the hardware directly. This means that little intensive diagnostics testing can be done while a protected mode operating system such as Windows 9x, NT, 2000, Linux, and so forth is running. For system testing, you usually have to boot from a DOS floppy or interrupt the loading of Windows (press the F8 key when "Starting Windows" appears during the boot process) and select Command Prompt Only, which boots you into DOS. In Windows 9x (but not Me), you can execute a shutdown and select Restart the Computer in MS-DOS Mode. Many of the higher-end hardware diagnostics programs include their own special limited 16-bit operating systems so they can more easily access memory areas even DOS would use.

For example, when you boot from a Windows 9x startup disk, you are running 16-bit DOS, and if you want to access your CD-ROM drive to install Windows, you must load a 16-bit CD-ROM driver program from that disk as well. In this mode, you can do things such as partition and format your hard disk, install Windows, or test the system completely.

The point of all this is that although you might not be running DOS very much these days, at least for system configuration and installation, as well as for high-level hardware diagnostics testing, data recovery, and so forth, you still must boot a 16-bit OS occasionally. When you are in that mode, the system's architecture changes, less memory is accessible, and some of the software you are running (16-bit drivers and most application code) must fight over the first 1MB or even 640KB for space.

The system memory areas discussed in this chapter, including the 384KB at the top of the first megabyte, which is used for video, adapter BIOS, and motherboard BIOS, as well as the remaining extended memory, are all part of the PC hardware design. They exist whether you are running 16-bit or 32-bit software; however, the limitations on their use in 16-bit (real) mode are much more severe. Because most people run 32-bit operating systems, such as Windows 9x, 2000, Linux, and so on, these operating systems automatically manage the use of RAM, meaning you don't have to interact with and manage this memory yourself as you often did with the 16-bit operating systems.

The following sections are intended to give you an understanding of the PC hardware memory layout, which is consistent no matter which operating system you use. The only things that change are how your operating system uses these areas and how they are managed by the OS.

The following sections detail the various types of memory installed on a modern PC. The kinds of memory covered in the following sections include

- Conventional (base) memory
- Upper memory area (UMA)
- High memory area (HMA)
- Extended memory (XMS)
- Expanded memory (obsolete)
- Video RAM memory (part of UMA)
- Adapter ROM and special-purpose RAM (part of UMA)
- Motherboard ROM BIOS (part of UMA)

Figure 6.19 shows the logical address locations for a 16-bit or higher system. If the processor is running in real mode, only the first megabyte is accessible. If the processor is in protected mode, the full 16MB, 4,096MB, or 65,536MB are accessible. Each symbol is equal to 1KB of memory, and each line or segment is 64KB. This map shows the first two megabytes of system memory.

◀◀ See "Processor Modes," p. 67.

Note

To save space, this map stops after the end of the second megabyte. In reality, this map continues to the maximum of addressable memory.

Conventional (Base) Memory

The original PC/XT-type system was designed to use 1MB of RAM. This 1MB of RAM is divided into several sections, some of which have special uses. DOS can read and write to the entire megabyte but can manage the loading of programs only in the portion of RAM space called *conventional memory*, which was 512KB at the time the first PC was introduced. The other 512KB was reserved for use by the system, including the motherboard and adapter boards plugged into the system slots.

After introducing the system, IBM decided that only 384KB was needed for these reserved uses, and the company began marketing PCs with 640KB of user memory. Therefore, 640KB became the standard for memory that can be used by DOS for running programs and often is termed the 640KB memory barrier. The remaining memory after 640KB was reserved for use by the graphics boards, other adapters, and the motherboard ROM BIOS.

```
. = Program-accessible memory (standard RAM)
G = Graphics Mode Video RAM
M = Monochrome Text Mode Video RAM
C = Color Text Mode Video RAM
V = Video ROM BIOS (would be "a" in PS/2)
a = Adapter board ROM and special-purpose RAM (free UMA space)
r = Additional PS/2 Motherboard ROM BIOS (free UMA in non-PS/2 systems)
R = Motherboard ROM BIOS
b = IBM Cassette BASIC ROM (would be "R" in IBM compatibles)
h = High Memory Area (HMA), if HIMEM.SYS is loaded.

Conventional (Base) Memory:

        : 0---1---2---3---4---5---6---7---8---9---A---B---C---D---E---F---
000000: ................................................................
010000: ................................................................
020000: ................................................................
030000: ................................................................
040000: ................................................................
050000: ................................................................
060000: ................................................................
070000: ................................................................
080000: ................................................................
090000: ................................................................

Upper Memory Area (UMA):

        : 0---1---2---3---4---5---6---7---8---9---A---B---C---D---E---F---
0A0000: GGGGGGGGGGGGGGGGGGGGGGGGGGGGGGGGGGGGGGGGGGGGGGGGGGGGGGGGGGGGGGGGG
0B0000: MMMMMMMMMMMMMMMMMMMMMMMMMMMMMMMMCCCCCCCCCCCCCCCCCCCCCCCCCCCCCCCCCC
        : 0---1---2---3---4---5---6---7---8---9---A---B---C---D---E---F---
0C0000: VVVVVVVVVVVVVVVVVVVVVVVVVVVVVVVVVaaaaaaaaaaaaaaaaaaaaaaaaaaaaaaaaa
0D0000: aaaaaaaaaaaaaaaaaaaaaaaaaaaaaaaaaaaaaaaaaaaaaaaaaaaaaaaaaaaaaaaaa
        : 0---1---2---3---4---5---6---7---8---9---A---B---C---D---E---F---
0E0000: rrrrrrrrrrrrrrrrrrrrrrrrrrrrrrrrrrrrrrrrrrrrrrrrrrrrrrrrrrrrrrrrrr
0F0000: RRRRRRRRRRRRRRRRRRRRRRRRRRRRRbbbbbbbbbbbbbbbbbbbbbbbbbbbbbRRRRRRRR

Extended Memory:

        : 0---1---2---3---4---5---6---7---8---9---A---B---C---D---E---F---
100000: hhhhhhhhhhhhhhhhhhhhhhhhhhhhhhhhhhhhhhhhhhhhhhhhhhhhhhhhhhhhhhhhhh

Extended Memory Specification (XMS) Memory:

110000: ................................................................
120000: ................................................................
130000: ................................................................
140000: ................................................................
150000: ................................................................
160000: ................................................................
170000: ................................................................
180000: ................................................................
190000: ................................................................
1A0000: ................................................................
1B0000: ................................................................
1C0000: ................................................................
1D0000: ................................................................
1E0000: ................................................................
1F0000: ................................................................
```

Figure 6.19   The logical memory map of the first 2MB.

This barrier largely affects 16-bit software, such as DOS and Windows 3.1, and is much less of a factor with 32-bit software and operating systems, such as Windows 9x, NT/2000, and so on.

Upper Memory Area

The term *Upper Memory Area (UMA)* describes the reserved 384KB at the top of the first megabyte of system memory on a PC/XT and the first megabyte on an AT-type system. This memory has the addresses from A0000 through FFFFF. The way the 384KB of upper memory is used breaks down as follows:

- *The first 128KB after conventional memory is called video RAM.* It is reserved for use by video adapters. When text and graphics are displayed onscreen, the data bits that make up those images reside in this space. Video RAM is allotted the address range A0000–BFFFF.

- *The next 128KB is reserved for the adapter BIOS that resides in read-only memory chips on some adapter boards plugged into the bus slots.* Most VGA-compatible video adapters use the first 32KB of this area for their onboard BIOSes. Any other adapters installed can use the rest. Many network adapters also use this area for special-purpose RAM called *shared memory*. Adapter ROM and special-purpose RAM is allotted the address range C0000–DFFFF.

- *The last 128KB of memory is reserved for motherboard BIOS (the basic input/output system, which is stored in read-only RAM chips or ROM).* The POST and bootstrap loader, which handles your system at boot-up until the operating system takes over, also reside in this space. Most systems use only the last 64KB (or less) of this space, leaving the first 64KB or more free for remapping with memory managers. Some systems also include the CMOS Setup program in this area. The motherboard BIOS is allotted the address range E0000–FFFFF.

Not all the 384KB of reserved memory is fully used on most 16-bit and higher systems. For example, according to the PC standard, reserved video RAM begins at address A0000, which is right at the 640KB boundary. Normally, it is used for VGA graphics modes, whereas the monochrome and color text modes use B0000–B7FFF and B8000–BFFFF, respectively. Older non-VGA adapters used memory only in the B0000 segment. Different video adapters use varying amounts of RAM for their operations, depending mainly on the mode they are in. To the processor, however, it always appears as the same 128KB area, no matter how much RAM is really on the video card. This is managed by bank switching areas of memory on the card in and out of the A0000–BFFFF segments.

Although the top 384KB of the first megabyte was originally termed *reserved memory*, it is possible to use previously unused regions of this memory to load 16-bit device drivers (such as the ANSI.SYS screen driver that comes with DOS) and memory-resident programs (such as MOUSE.COM, the DOS mouse driver), which frees up the conventional memory they would otherwise require. Note that this does not affect 32-bit device drivers such as those used with Windows 9x, NT/2000, and so forth because they load into extended memory with no restrictions. The amount of free UMA space varies from system to system, depending mostly on the adapter cards installed on the system. For example, most video adapters, SCSI adapters, and some network adapters require some of this area for built-in ROMs or special-purpose RAM use.

Segment Addresses and Linear Addresses

See the Technical Reference section of the CD accompanying this book for a discussion of segment and linear addressing.

Video RAM Memory

A video adapter installed in your system uses a portion of your system's first megabyte of memory to hold graphics or character information for display, but this typically is used or active only when in basic VGA mode.

Note that even though a modern video card can have 64MB or more of onboard memory, only 128KB of this memory appears available to the system in the video RAM area. The rest of the memory is accessible only by the video processor (on the video card) directly, or by your system processor via a memory aperture positioned near the 4GB top of the system address space. Because this aperture can be configured differently by various cards, you should consult the technical documentation for your card or video chipset for more information.

When in basic VGA mode, such as when at a DOS prompt or when running in Windows safe mode, your processor can directly access up to 128KB of the video RAM from address A0000–BFFFFh. All modern video cards also have onboard BIOS normally addressed at C0000–C7FFFh, which is part of the memory space reserved for adapter card BIOS. Generally, the higher the resolution and color capabilities of the video adapter, the more system memory the video adapter uses, but again, that additional memory (past 128KB) is not usually accessible by the processor. Instead, the system tells the video chip what should be displayed, and the video chip generates the picture by putting data directly into the video RAM on the card.

In the standard system-memory map, a total of 128KB is reserved for use by the video card to store currently displayed information when in basic VGA modes. The reserved video memory is located in segments A000 and B000. The video adapter ROM uses additional upper memory space in segment C000. Even with the new multiple monitor feature in Windows 98, only one video card (the primary video card) is in the memory map; all others use no low system memory.

Note

The location of video adapter RAM is responsible for the infamous 640KB DOS conventional memory barrier. DOS can use all available contiguous memory in the first megabyte of memory up to the point where the video adapter RAM is encountered. The use of ancient video adapters, such as the MDA and CGA, can enable DOS access to more than 640KB of system memory. For more information, see Chapter 5 of *Upgrading and Repairing PCs, 10th Anniversary Edition*, included on the CD.

To learn how the older video adapters use the system's memory, see "Obsolete Video Adapter Types," also in Chapter 5 of the *10th Edition*.

Video Graphics Array Memory

All VGA-compatible cards, including those running in PCI or AGP slots, use all 128KB of the system allocated video RAM from A0000–BFFFF, but not all at once. This video RAM area is used depending on the mode the card is in. Figure 6.20 shows the VGA adapter memory map.

You can see that the typical VGA card uses a full 32KB of space for the onboard ROM containing driver code. Some VGA cards might use slightly less, but this is rare. The video RAM areas are active only when the adapter is in the particular mode designated. In other words, when a VGA adapter is in graphics mode, only segment A000 is used; when it is in color text mode, only the last half of segment B000 is used. Because the VGA adapter is almost never run in monochrome text mode, the first half of segment B000 remains unused (B0000–B7FFF). Figure 6.20 shows the standard motherboard ROM BIOS so that you can get an idea of how the entire UMA is laid out with this adapter.

```
        . = Empty Addresses
        G = Video Graphics Array (VGA) Adapter Graphics Mode Video RAM
        M = VGA Monochrome Text Mode Video RAM
        C = VGA Color Text Mode Video RAM
        V = Standard VGA Video ROM BIOS
        R = Standard Motherboard ROM BIOS


        : 0---1---2---3---4---5---6---7---8---9---A---B---C---D---E---F---
0A0000: GGGGGGGGGGGGGGGGGGGGGGGGGGGGGGGGGGGGGGGGGGGGGGGGGGGGGGGGGGGGGGGGG
0B0000: MMMMMMMMMMMMMMMMMMMMMMMMMMMMMMMMCCCCCCCCCCCCCCCCCCCCCCCCCCCCCCCCC
        : 0---1---2---3---4---5---6---7---8---9---A---B---C---D---E---F---
0C0000: VVVVVVVVVVVVVVVVVVVVVVVVVVVVVVVVV...............................
0D0000: ................................................................
        : 0---1---2---3---4---5---6---7---8---9---A---B---C---D---E---F---
0E0000: ................................................................
0F0000: RRRRRRRRRRRRRRRRRRRRRRRRRRRRRRRRRRRRRRRRRRRRRRRRRRRRRRRRRRRRRRRRR
```

Figure 6.20   The VGA adapter memory map.

Some systems incorporate the video adapter into the motherboard or even directly in the motherboard chipset. In these systems, even though the video BIOS and motherboard BIOS might be from the same manufacturer, they are always set up to emulate a standard VGA-type adapter card. In other words, the video BIOS appears in the first 32KB of segment C000 just as though a standalone VGA-type card were plugged into a slot. The built-in video circuit in these systems can be easily disabled with a switch or jumper, which then enables a conventional VGA-type card to be plugged in. By having the built-in VGA act exactly as though it were a separate card, disabling it allows a new adapter to be installed with no compatibility problems that might arise if the video drivers had been incorporated into the motherboard BIOS.

Adapter ROM and Special-Purpose RAM Memory

The second 128KB of upper memory beginning at segment C000 is reserved for the software programs, or BIOS, on the adapter boards plugged into the system slots. These BIOS programs are stored on special chips known as ROM. Most adapters today use EEPROM or Flash ROM, which can be erased and reprogrammed right in the system without removing the chip or card. Updating the Flash ROM is as simple as running the update program you get from the manufacturer and following the directions onscreen. It pays to check periodically with your card manufacturers to see whether they have Flash ROM updates for their cards.

ROM is useful for semipermanent programs that must always be present while the system is running, and especially for booting. Graphics boards, hard disk controllers, communications boards, and expanded memory boards, for example, are adapter boards that might have adapter ROM. These adapter ROMs are in an area of memory separate from the VGA video RAM and motherboard ROM areas.

On systems based on the 386 CPU chip or higher, memory managers that are included with DOS 6 or third-party programs can load device drivers and memory-resident programs into unused regions in the UMA.

To actually move the RAM usage on any given adapter requires that you consult the documentation for the card. Most older cards require that specific switches or jumpers be changed, and the settings will probably not be obvious without the manual. Most newer cards, especially those that are Plug and Play, enable these settings to be changed by software that comes with the card or the Device Manager program that goes with some of the newer operating systems, such as Windows 9x or Windows 2000 and newer.

Video Adapter BIOS

The video adapter ROM BIOS controls the video card during the boot sequence and anytime the system is in basic VGA modes (such as when running DOS). You also are using the video ROM BIOS code whenever you are running Windows in safe mode. All modern video adapters (even AGP cards) use 32KB for their onboard BIOS, from addresses C0000–C7FFF.

Depending on the basic VGA mode selected (color text, monochrome text, or VGA graphics), the video card uses some or all of the 128KB of upper memory beginning at segment C000. In addition, graphics cards can contain up to 64MB or more of onboard memory for use in their native high-resolution modes in which to store currently displayed data and more quickly fetch new screen data for display.

Hard Disk Controller and SCSI Host Adapter BIOS

The upper memory addresses C0000–DFFFF are also used for the built-in BIOS contained on many hard drive and SCSI controllers. Table 6.15 lists the amount of memory and the addresses commonly used by the BIOS contained on hard drive adapter cards.

Table 6.15   Memory Addresses Used by Various Hard Drive Adapter Cards

Disk Adapter Type	Onboard BIOS Size	BIOS Address Range
Most XT-compatible controllers	8KB	C8000–C9FFF
Most AT controllers	None	Drivers in motherboard BIOS
Most standard IDE adapters	None	Drivers in motherboard BIOS
Most enhanced IDE adapters	16KB	C8000–CBFFF
Some SCSI host adapters	16KB	C8000–CBFFF
Some SCSI host adapters	16KB	DC000–DFFFF

The hard drive or SCSI adapter card used on a particular system might use a different amount of memory, but it is most likely to use the memory segment beginning at C800 because this address is considered part of the IBM standard for personal computers. Virtually all the disk controller or SCSI adapters today that have an onboard BIOS allow the BIOS starting address to be easily moved in the C000 and D000 segments. The locations listed in Table 6.15 are only the default addresses that most of these cards use. If the default address is already in use by another card, you have to consult the documentation for the new card to see how to change the BIOS starting address to avoid any conflicts.

Figure 6.21 shows a sample memory map for an Adaptec AHA-2940 SCSI adapter.

```
        . = Empty Addresses
        G = Video Graphics Array (VGA) Adapter Graphics Mode Video RAM
        M = VGA Monochrome Text Mode Video RAM
        C = VGA Color Text Mode Video RAM
        V = Standard VGA Video ROM BIOS
        S = SCSI Host Adapter ROM BIOS
        R = Standard Motherboard ROM BIOS

         : 0---1---2---3---4---5---6---7---8---9---A---B---C---D---E---F---
0A0000:  GGGGGGGGGGGGGGGGGGGGGGGGGGGGGGGGGGGGGGGGGGGGGGGGGGGGGGGGGGGGGGGGG
0B0000:  MMMMMMMMMMMMMMMMMMMMMMMMMMMMMMMMCCCCCCCCCCCCCCCCCCCCCCCCCCCCCCCCC
         : 0---1---2---3---4---5---6---7---8---9---A---B---C---D---E---F---
0C0000:  VVVVVVVVVVVVVVVVVVVVVVVVVVVVVVV..................................
0D0000:  ...........................................SSSSSSSSSSSSSSSSS
         : 0---1---2---3---4---5---6---7---8---9---A---B---C---D---E---F---
0E0000:  ................................................................
0F0000:  RRRRRRRRRRRRRRRRRRRRRRRRRRRRRRRRRRRRRRRRRRRRRRRRRRRRRRRRRRRRRRRRR
```

Figure 6.21   Adaptec AHA-2940U SCSI adapter default memory use.

Network Adapters

Network adapter cards can also use upper memory in segments C000 and D000. The exact amount of memory used and the starting address for each network card vary with the card's type and manufacturer. Some network cards do not use any memory at all. A network card might have two primary uses for memory. They are as follows:

- IPL (Initial Program Load or Boot) ROM
- Shared memory (RAM)

An IPL ROM is usually an 8KB ROM that contains a bootstrap loader program that enables the system to boot directly from a file server on the network. This enables the removal of all disk drives from the PC, creating a diskless workstation. Because no floppy or hard disk is in the system to boot from, the

IPL ROM gives the system the instructions necessary to locate an image of the operating system on the file server and load it as though it were on an internal drive. If you are not using your system as a diskless workstation, it is beneficial to disable any IPL ROM or IPL ROM socket on the adapter card. Note that many network adapters do not allow this socket to be disabled, which means that you lose the 8KB of address space for other hardware, even if the ROM chip is removed from the socket!

Shared memory refers to a small portion of RAM contained on the network card that is mapped into the PC's upper memory area. This region is used as a memory window onto the network and offers rapid data transfer from the network card to the system. IBM pioneered the use of shared memory for its first Token-Ring network adapters, and now shared memory is commonly used in other companies' network adapters. Shared memory first was devised by IBM because it found that transfers using the DMA channels were not fast enough in most systems. This mainly had to do with some quirks in the DMA controller and bus design, which especially affected 16-bit ISA bus systems. Network adapters that do not use shared memory use DMA or Programmed I/O (PIO) transfers to move data to and from the network adapter.

Although shared memory is faster than either DMA or PIO for ISA systems, it does require 16KB of UMA space to work. Most standard performance network adapters use PIO because it makes them easier to configure, and they require no free UMA space. However, most high-performance adapters use shared memory. The shared memory region on most network adapters that use one is usually 16KB in size and can be located at any user-selected 4KB increment of memory in segments C000 or D000.

Figure 6.22 shows the default memory addresses for the IPL ROM and shared memory of an IBM Token-Ring network adapter, although many other network adapters, such as Ethernet adapters, are similar. One thing to note is that most Ethernet adapters use either a DMA channel or standard PIO commands to send data to and from the network and don't use shared memory, as many Token-Ring cards do.

```
          . = Empty Addresses
          G = Video Graphics Array (VGA) Adapter Graphics Mode Video RAM
          M = VGA Monochrome Text Mode Video RAM
          C = VGA Color Text Mode Video RAM
          V = Standard VGA Video ROM BIOS
          I = Token Ring Network Adapter IPL ROM
          N = Token Ring Network Adapter Shared RAM
          R = Standard Motherboard ROM BIOS


            : 0---1---2---3---4---5---6---7---8---9---A---B---C---D---E---F---
    0A0000: GGGGGGGGGGGGGGGGGGGGGGGGGGGGGGGGGGGGGGGGGGGGGGGGGGGGGGGGGGGGGGGGG
    0B0000: MMMMMMMMMMMMMMMMMMMMMMMMMMMMMMMMMCCCCCCCCCCCCCCCCCCCCCCCCCCCCCCCC
            : 0---1---2---3---4---5---6---7---8---9---A---B---C---D---E---F---
    0C0000: VVVVVVVVVVVVVVVVVVVVVVVVVVVVVVVV................IIIIIIII........
    0D0000: ...........................NNNNNNNNNNNNNNNN................
            : 0---1---2---3---4---5---6---7---8---9---A---B---C---D---E---F---
    0E0000: ................................................................
    0F0000: RRRRRRRRRRRRRRRRRRRRRRRRRRRRRRRRRRRRRRRRRRRRRRRRRRRRRRRRRRRRRRRRR
```

Figure 6.22   Network adapter default memory map.

I have also included the standard VGA video BIOS in Figure 6.22 because nearly every system would have a VGA-type video adapter as well. Note that these default addresses for the IPL ROM and the shared memory can easily be changed by reconfiguring the adapter. Most other network adapters are similar in that they also have an IPL ROM and a shared memory address, although the sizes of these areas and the default addresses might be different. Most network adapters that incorporate an IPL ROM option can disable the ROM and socket so that those addresses are not needed at all. This helps conserve UMA space and prevent possible future conflicts if you are never going to use the function.

Note that the Plug and Play feature in Win9x, Me, and Windows 2000 does not attempt to optimize memory use, only to resolve conflicts. Of course, with 32-bit drivers, the locations and sizes of free upper memory blocks don't really matter because 32-bit drivers are loaded into extended memory. If you are still occasionally running DOS-based programs, such as games, you could manually optimize the upper memory area configuration for maximum memory and performance, but for the most part it isn't worth the effort.

Motherboard BIOS Memory

The last 128KB of reserved memory is used by the motherboard BIOS. The BIOS programs in ROM control the system during the boot-up procedure and remain as drivers for various hardware in the system during normal operation. Because these programs must be available immediately, they can't be loaded from a device such as a disk drive.

◀◀ See Chapter 5, "BIOS," p. 345.

Both segments E000 and F000 in the memory map are considered reserved for the motherboard BIOS, but only some systems actually use this entire area. Older 8-bit systems require only segment F000 and enable adapter card ROM or RAM to use segment E000. Most 16-bit or greater systems use all F000 for the BIOS and might decode but not use any of segment E000. By decoding an area, the motherboard essentially grabs control of the addresses, which precludes installing any other hardware in this region. In other words, configuring adapter cards to use this area isn't possible. That is why you will find that most adapters that use memory simply do not allow any choices for memory use in segment E000. Although this might seem like a waste of 64KB of memory space, any 386 or higher system can use the powerful MMU in the processor to map RAM from extended memory into segment E000 as an upper memory block. The system can subsequently load 16-bit driver software in this UMB if necessary. This is a nice solution to what otherwise would be wasted memory, although it is not important if you use 32-bit drivers.

Figure 6.23 shows the motherboard ROM BIOS memory use of most 16-bit or greater systems.

```
. = Empty Addresses
R = Standard Motherboard ROM BIOS

        : 0---1---2---3---4---5---6---7---8---9---A---B---C---D---E---F---
0E0000: ................................................................
0F0000: RRRRRRRRRRRRRRRRRRRRRRRRRRRRRRRRRRRRRRRRRRRRRRRRRRRRRRRRRRRRRRRRRR
```

Figure 6.23   Motherboard ROM BIOS memory use of most systems.

Note that the standard system BIOS uses only segment F000 (64KB). In almost every case, the remainder of the BIOS area (segment E000) is completely free and can be used as UMA block space.

Extended Memory

As mentioned previously in this chapter, the memory map on a system based on the 286 or higher processor can extend beyond the 1MB boundary that exists when the processor is in real mode. On a 286 or 386SX system, the extended memory limit is 16MB (16-bit addressing); on a 386DX, 486, Pentium, Pentium MMX, or Pentium Pro system, the extended memory limit is 4GB (4,096MB, using 32-bit addressing). Systems based on the Pentium II and newer processors have a limit of 64GB (65,536MB, using 36-bit addressing).

For a system to address memory beyond the first megabyte, the processor must be in protected mode—the native mode of 286 and higher processors. On a 286, only programs designed to run in protected mode can take advantage of extended memory; 386 and higher processors offer another mode, called virtual real mode, which enables extended memory to be, in effect, chopped into 1MB pieces (each its own real-mode session). Virtual real mode also enables several of these sessions to be running simultaneously in protected areas of memory. They can be seen as DOS prompt sessions or windows within Windows 9x, NT, or OS/2. Although several DOS programs can be running at once, each is still limited to a maximum of 640KB of memory because each session simulates a real-mode environment, right down to the BIOS and Upper Memory Area. Running several programs at once in virtual real mode, called *multitasking*, requires software that can manage each program and keep them from crashing into one another. OS/2, Windows 9x, and Windows NT all do this.

The 286 and higher CPU chips also run in what is termed *real mode*, which enables full compatibility with the 8088 CPU chip installed on the PC/XT-type computer. Real mode enables you to run DOS programs one at a time on an AT-type system just as you would on a PC/XT. However, an AT-type system running in real mode, particularly a system based on the 386 through Pentium III or Athlon, is really functioning as little more than a turbo PC. In real mode, these processors can emulate the 8086 or 8088, but they can't operate in protected mode at the same time. For that reason, the 386 and above also provide a virtual real mode that operates under protected mode. This enables real-mode programs to execute under the control of a protected-mode operating system, such as Win9x/Me or NT/2000.

Note

Extended memory is basically all memory past the first megabyte, which can be accessed only while the processor is in protected mode.

XMS Memory

Microsoft, Intel, AST Corp., and Lotus Development developed the extended memory specification (XMS) in 1987 to specify how programs would use extended memory. The XMS specification functions on systems based on the 286 or higher and enables real-mode programs (those designed to run in DOS) to use extended memory and another block of memory usually out of the reach of DOS.

Before XMS, there was no way to ensure cooperation between programs that switched the processor into protected mode and used extended memory. There was also no way for one program to know what another had been doing with the extended memory because none of them could see that memory while in real mode. HIMEM.SYS becomes an arbitrator of sorts that first grabs all the extended memory for itself and then doles it out to programs that know the XMS protocols. In this manner, several programs that use XMS memory can operate together under DOS on the same system, switching the processor into and out of protected mode to access the memory. XMS rules prevent one program from accessing memory that another has in use. Because Windows 3.x is a program manager that switches the system to and from protected mode in running several programs at once, it has been set up to require XMS memory to function. Windows 95 operates mostly in protected mode, but still calls on real mode for access to many system components. Windows NT and Windows 2000 are true protected-mode operating systems, as is OS/2.

Extended memory can be made to conform to the XMS specification by installing a device driver in the CONFIG.SYS file. The most common XMS driver is HIMEM.SYS, which is included with Windows 3.x and later versions of DOS, starting with 4.0 and up. Windows 9x and NT automatically allow XMS functions in DOS prompt sessions, and you can configure full-blown DOS-mode sessions to allow XMS functions as well.

Note

To learn more about the high memory area and expanded memory, see Chapter 5 of *Upgrading and Repairing PCs, 10th Anniversary Edition*, on the CD.

Preventing ROM BIOS Memory Conflicts and Overlap

As explained previously, C000 and D000 are reserved for use by adapter-board ROM and RAM. If two adapters have overlapping ROM or RAM addresses, usually neither board operates properly. Each board functions if you remove or disable the other one, but they do not work together.

With many adapter boards, you can change the actual memory locations to be used with jumpers, switches, or driver software, which might be necessary to allow two boards to coexist in one system. This type of conflict can cause problems for troubleshooters. You must read the documentation for each adapter to find out which memory addresses the adapter uses and how to change the addresses to allow coexistence with another adapter. Most of the time, you can work around these problems by reconfiguring the board or by changing jumpers, switch settings, or software-driver parameters. This change enables the two boards to coexist and stay out of each other's way.

Additionally, you must ensure that adapter boards do not use the same IRQ, DMA channel, or I/O port address. You can easily avoid adapter board memory, IRQ, DMA channel, and I/O port conflicts by creating a chart or template to mock up the system configuration by penciling on the template the resources already used by each installed adapter. You end up with a picture of the system resources and the relationship of each adapter to the others.

If you are running a Plug and Play operating system, such as Windows 9x/Me or 2000, you can use the Device Manager to view and optionally print all the device settings. I highly recommend you use this to print out all the settings in your system before and after you make modifications to see what has been changed. This will help you anticipate conflicts and ensures that you configure each adapter board correctly the first time. The template also becomes important documentation when you consider new adapter purchases. New adapters must be configurable to use the available resources in your system.

◀◀ See "System Resources," p. 316.

If your system has Plug and Play capabilities, and you use PnP adapters, it can resolve conflicts between the adapters by moving the memory usage on any conflict. Unfortunately, this routine is not intelligent and still requires human intervention—that is, manual specification of addresses to achieve the most optimum location for the adapter memory.

ROM Shadowing

Virtually all 386 and higher systems enable you to use what is termed *shadow memory* for the motherboard and possibly some adapter ROMs as well. Shadowing essentially moves the programming code from slow ROM chips into fast 32-bit system memory. Shadowing slower ROMs by copying their contents into RAM can greatly speed up these BIOS routines—sometimes making them four to five times faster.

Note that shadowing ROMs is not very important when running a 32-bit operating system, such as Win9x/Me or NT/2000. This is because those operating systems use the 16-bit BIOS driver code only during booting; then they load 32-bit replacement drivers into faster extended memory and use them. Therefore, shadowing normally affects only DOS or other 16-bit software and operating systems. Because of this, some people are tempted to turn off the Video BIOS shadowing feature in the BIOS setup. Unfortunately, it won't gain you any memory back (you've lost it anyway) and will make the system slightly slower to boot up and somewhat slower when in Windows safe mode. The 16-bit BIOS video driver code is used at those times.

Note

To learn more about ROM shadowing, see Chapter 5 of *Upgrading and Repairing PCs, 10th Anniversary Edition*, on the CD accompanying this book.

Total Installed Memory Versus Total Usable Memory

Most people don't realize that not all the RAM you purchase and install in a system is available. Because of some quirks in system design, the system usually has to "throw away" up to 384KB of RAM to make way for the Upper Memory Area.

For example, most systems with 16MB of RAM (which is 16,384KB) installed show a total of only 16,000KB installed during the POST or when running Setup. This indicates that 16,384KB–16,000KB = 384KB of missing memory! Some systems might show 16,256KB with the same 16MB installed, which works out to 16,384KB–16,256KB = 128KB missing.

If you run your Setup program and check out your base and extended memory values, you will find more information than just the single figure for the total shown during the POST. In most systems with 4,096KB (4MB), you have 640KB base and 3,072KB extended. In some systems, Setup reports 640KB base and 3,328KB extended memory, which is a bonus. In other words, most systems come up 384KB short, but some come up only 128KB short.

This shortfall is not easy to explain, but it is consistent from system to system. Say that you have a 486 system with two installed 72-pin (32-bit) 16MB SIMMs. This results in a total installed memory of 32MB in two separate banks because the processor has a 32-bit data bus. Each SIMM is a single bank in this system. The first bank (or SIMM, in this case) starts at address 0000000h (the start of the first megabyte), and the second starts at 1000000 (the start of the seventeenth megabyte).

One of the cardinal rules of memory is that you absolutely cannot have two hardware devices wired to the same address. This means that 384KB of the first memory bank in this system would be in direct conflict with the video RAM (segments A000 and B000), any adapter card ROMs (segments C000 and D000), and of course the motherboard ROM (segments E000 and F000). That means all SIMM RAM that occupies these addresses must be shut off; otherwise, the system will not function! Actually, a motherboard designer can do three things with the SIMM memory that would overlap from A0000–FFFFF:

- Use the faster RAM to hold a copy of any slow ROMs (shadowing), disabling the ROM in the process
- Turn off any RAM not used for shadowing, eliminating any UMA conflicts
- Remap any RAM not used for shadowing, adding to the stack of currently installed extended memory

Most systems shadow the motherboard ROM (usually 64KB) and the video ROM (32KB) and simply turn off the rest. Some motherboard ROMs allow additional shadowing to be selected between C8000 and DFFFF, usually in 16KB increments.

Note

You can shadow only ROM, never RAM, so if any card (such as a network card) has a RAM buffer in the C8000–DFFFF area, you must not shadow the RAM buffer addresses; otherwise, the card will not function. For the same reason, you can't shadow the A0000–BFFFF area because it is the video adapter RAM buffer.

Most motherboards do not do any remapping, which means that any of the 384KB not shadowed is simply turned off. That is why enabling shadowing does not seem to use any memory. The memory used for shadowing would otherwise be discarded in most systems. These systems would appear to be short by 384KB compared to what is physically installed in the system. For example, in a system with 32MB, no remapping would result in 640KB of base memory and 31,744KB of extended memory, for a total of 32,384KB of usable RAM—384KB short of the total (32,768KB–384KB).

Systems that show 384KB of "missing" memory do not do remapping. If you want to determine whether your system has any missing memory, all you need to know are three things. One is the total physical memory actually installed. Running your Setup program can discover the other two items. You want to know the total base and extended memory numbers recognized by the system. Then simply subtract the base and extended memory from the total installed to determine the missing memory. You usually will find that your system is missing 384KB, but you could be lucky and have a system that remaps 256KB of what is missing and thus shows only 128KB of memory missing.

Virtually all systems use some of the missing memory for shadowing ROMs, especially the motherboard and video BIOS, so what is missing is not completely wasted. Systems missing 128KB will find that it is being used to shadow your motherboard BIOS (64KB from F0000 to FFFFF) and video BIOS (32KB from C0000 to C8000). The remainder of segment C0000 (32KB from C8000 to CFFFF) is simply being turned off. All other segments (128KB from A0000 to BFFFF and 128KB from D0000 to EFFFF) are being remapped to the start of the fifth megabyte (400000–43FFFF). Most systems simply disable these remaining segments rather than take the trouble to remap them.

Adapter Memory Configuration and Optimization

Adapter boards use upper memory for their BIOS and as working RAM. If two boards attempt to use the same BIOS area or RAM area of upper memory, a conflict occurs that can keep your system from booting. In most cases, the plug-and-play software in the operating system ensures that such cards are automatically reconfigured so that they are not in conflict; however, sometimes problems can occur and you must step in and manually resolve a conflict. The following sections cover ways to avoid these potential unresolved conflicts and how to troubleshoot if they do occur. In addition, these sections discuss moving adapter memory to resolve conflicts and provide some ideas on optimizing adapter memory use.

How to Determine What Adapters Occupy the UMA

You can determine which adapters are using space in upper memory in the following two ways:

- Study the documentation for each adapter on your system to determine the memory addresses they use.

- Use a software utility or the Device Manager in your operating system to determine which upper memory areas your adapters are using.

The simplest way (although by no means always the most foolproof) is to use a software utility to determine the upper memory areas used by the adapters installed on your system. One such utility, Microsoft Diagnostics (MSD), comes with Windows 3.x and DOS 6 or higher versions. The Device Manager under System in the Windows 9x/Me and 2000 Control Panel also supplies this information, as does the new System Information utility that comes with Windows 98/Me. These utilities examine your system configuration and determine not only the upper memory used by your adapters, but also the IRQs used by each of these adapters.

True plug-and-play systems also shut down one of the cards involved in a conflict to prevent a total system lockup. This could cause Windows to boot in safe mode.

After you run MSD, Device Manager, or another utility to determine your system's upper memory configuration, make a printout of the memory addresses used. Thereafter, you can quickly refer to the printout when you are adding a new adapter to ensure that the new board does not conflict with any devices already installed on your system.

Moving Adapter Memory to Resolve Conflicts

After you identify a conflict or potential conflict using one of the two methods discussed in the previous section, you might have to reconfigure one or more of your adapters to move the upper memory space used by a problem adapter.

Most adapter boards make moving adapter memory a somewhat simple process, enabling you to change a few jumpers or switches to reconfigure the board. With plug-and-play cards, use the configuration program that comes with the board or the Windows Device Manager to make the changes. The following steps help you resolve most problems that arise because adapter boards conflict with one another:

1. Determine the upper memory addresses currently used by your adapter boards and write them down.

2. Determine whether any of these addresses are overlapping, which results in a conflict.

3. Consult the documentation for your adapter boards to determine which boards can be reconfigured so that all adapters have access to unique memory addresses.

4. Configure the affected adapter boards so that no conflict in memory addresses occurs.

For example, if one adapter uses the upper memory range C8000–CBFFF and another adapter uses the range CA000–CCFFF, you have a potential address conflict. One of them must be changed. Note that plug-and-play cards allow these changes to be made directly from the Windows Device Manager.

CHAPTER 7

The IDE Interface

An Overview of the IDE Interface

The primary interface used to connect a hard disk drive to a modern PC is typically called IDE (Integrated Drive Electronics). An interesting fact is that the true name of the interface is called ATA (AT Attachment), which refers to the fact that this interface originally was designed to connect a combined drive and controller directly to the bus of the 1984 vintage IBM AT computer, otherwise known as the ISA (Industry Standard Architecture) bus. *IDE* is a term originated by the marketing departments of some drive manufacturers to describe the drive/controller combination used in drives with the ATA interface. Integrated Drive Electronics refers to the fact that the interface electronics or controller is built into the drive and is not a separate board, as with earlier drive interfaces. Although technically the correct name for the interface is ATA, many persist in using the IDE designation today. Throughout this book, I will use both designations because they are essentially interchangeable. If you are being picky, you could say that *IDE* refers generically to any drive interface in which the controller is built into the drive, whereas *ATA* refers to the specific implementation of IDE that is used in PCs.

Today, ATA is used to connect not only hard disks, but also CD-ROM and CD-RW drives, DVD drives, high-capacity SuperDisk floppy drives, and tape drives. Even so, ATA is still thought of primarily as a hard disk interface, and it evolved directly from the separate controller and hard drive interfaces that were used prior to ATA. This chapter covers the ATA interface in detail, as well as the original interfaces from which ATA evolved. Because the ATA interface is directly integrated into virtually all motherboard chipsets, ATA is the primary storage interface used by most PCs.

Note

Even Apple has recognized the value of ATA and has incorporated it into virtually all modern Macintosh systems.

▶▶ See "LS-120 (120MB) SuperDisk Drives," p. 647.

Precursors to IDE

A variety of hard disk interfaces have been available for PC hard disks over the years. As time has passed, the number of choices has increased, and many older designs are no longer viable in newer systems.

The primary job of the hard disk controller or interface is to transmit and receive data to and from the drive. The various interface types limit how fast data can be moved from the drive to the system and offer different features as well as levels of performance. If you are putting together a system in which performance is a primary concern, you need to know how these various interfaces affect performance and what you can expect from them. Many statistics that appear in technical literature are not indicative of the real performance figures you will see in practice. I will separate the myths presented by some of these overly optimistic figures from the reality of what you will actually see.

Several types of hard disk interfaces have been used in PC systems over the years, as shown here:

Interface	When Used
ST-506/412	1978–1989
ESDI	1983–1991
SCSI	1986–Present
ATA (IDE)	1986–Present
Serial ATA	2001–Present

Of these interfaces, only ST-506/412 and ESDI are what you could call true disk-controller–to–drive interfaces, and they are obsolete. SCSI and ATA are system-level interfaces that usually incorporate a chipset-based controller interface internally. For example, most SCSI and ATA drives incorporate the same basic internal controller circuitry. The SCSI interface adds another layer of interface that attaches the controller to the system bus, whereas ATA is a more direct bus-attachment interface. Virtually all modern disk drives use either ATA or SCSI interfaces to connect to a system.

The IDE Interface

As discussed earlier, IDE (now officially referred to as ATA) is a generic term that applies to any drive with a built-in disk controller. It is an ANSI standard, or more accurately an evolving standard with various published standard versions. The term IDE can roughly apply to any disk drive with a built-in controller, whereas ATA denotes a specific interface. Referring to the original parallel version of the interface, what we call ATA originally referred to a hard disk drive that plugged directly into a version of the AT-bus, more commonly known as the 16-bit ISA bus.

ATA is a 16-bit parallel interface, meaning that 16 bits are transmitted simultaneously down the interface cable. A new interface called Serial ATA was officially introduced in late 2000 and is being adopted in systems starting in 2001. Serial ATA (SATA) sends 1 bit down the cable at a time, enabling thinner and smaller cables to be used, as well as providing higher performance due to the higher cycling speeds allowed. SATA is a completely new and updated physical interface design, while remaining compatible on the software level with parallel ATA. Throughout this book, *ATA* refers to the parallel version, whereas Serial ATA is explicitly referenced as SATA.

The first drives with integrated ISA bus (otherwise known as AT-bus) controllers were called *hardcards*; they consisted of a hard disk bolted directly to an ISA bus controller card and plugged into a slot as a single unit. Today, any drive with an integrated controller is called an IDE drive, although normally when we say *IDE*, we really mean the specific version of IDE called ATA. No matter what you call it, combining the drive and controller greatly simplifies installation because there are no separate power or signal cables from the controller to the drive. Also, when the controller and drive are assembled as a unit, the number of total components is reduced, signal paths are shorter, and the electrical connections are more noise-resistant. This results in a more reliable design than is possible when a separate controller, connected to the drive by cables, is used.

Placing the controller, including the digital-to-analog encoder/decoder (endec) on the drive offers an inherent reliability advantage over interfaces with separate controllers. Reliability is increased because the data encoding, from digital to analog, is performed directly on the drive in a tight noise-free environment. The timing-sensitive analog information does not have to travel along crude ribbon cables that are likely to pick up noise and insert propagation delays into the signals. The integrated configuration enables increases in the clock rate of the encoder and the storage density of the drive.

Integrating the controller and drive also frees the controller and drive engineers from having to adhere to the strict guidelines imposed by the earlier interface standards. Engineers can design what essentially are custom drive and controller implementations because no other controller will ever have to be connected to the drive. The resulting drive and controller combinations can offer higher performance than earlier standalone controller and drive setups. IDE drives sometimes are called drives with embedded controllers.

The ATA connector on motherboards in many systems started out as nothing more than a stripped-down ISA bus (AT-bus) slot. These connectors contain what started out as a 40-pin subset of the 98 pins that would make up a standard 16-bit ISA bus slot. Note that smaller 2 1/2-inch ATA drives use a superset 44-pin connection, which includes additional pins for power. The pins from the original ISA bus used in ATA are the only signal pins required by a standard-type AT hard disk controller. For example, because a primary AT-style disk controller uses only interrupt request (IRQ) line 14, the primary motherboard ATA IDE connector supplies only that IRQ line; no other IRQ lines are necessary. The obsolete 8-bit XT IDE motherboard connector supplied interrupt line 5 because that is what an XT controller used. Note that even if your ATA interface is integrated within the motherboard chipset South Bridge or I/O Controller Hub chip (as it would be in newer systems) and runs at higher bus speeds, the pinout and functions of the pins are still the same as the original design taken right off the ISA bus.

◀◀   See "Motherboard Interface Connectors," p. 285.

◀◀   See "The ISA Bus," p. 300.

Note

Many people who use systems with ATA connectors on the motherboard believe that a hard disk controller is built into their motherboards, but in a technical sense the controller is actually in the drive. Although the integrated ATA ports on a motherboard often are referred to as *controllers*, they are more accurately called *host adapters* (although you'll rarely hear this term). A host adapter can be thought of as a device that connects a controller to a bus.

When IDE drives are discussed, the ATA variety usually is the only kind mentioned because it is by far the most popular—and pretty much the only type in use in modern PCs. But other forms of IDE drives existed, based on other buses. For example, several PS/2 systems came with Micro-Channel (MCA)–based IDE drives that plugged directly into a Micro-Channel bus slot (through an interposer card). An 8-bit ISA form of IDE also existed but was never very popular. Most PCs use AT-Bus (16-bit)–based IDE drives, officially known as ATA drives. Many new systems are built using the Serial ATA interface as well. The ATA/IDE interfaces are by far the most popular type of drive interfaces available.

Note

IDE is a generic name that could be given to any interface in which the controller portion of the circuit is on the drive; ATA and Serial ATA refer to specific types of IDE interfaces. Because the popular form of IDE interface is ATA, the terms often are used interchangeably, even though on a technical level that is not correct. What most people call IDE is more properly called ATA.

The primary advantage of ATA drives over the older separate controller–based interfaces and newer host bus interface alternatives, such as SCSI and IEEE-1394 (iLink or FireWire), is cost. Because the separate controller or host adapter is eliminated and the cable connections are simplified, ATA drives cost much less than a standard controller and drive combination.

▶▶   See "Small Computer System Interface," p. 514.

▶▶   See "USB and IEEE-1394 (i.Link or FireWire)—Serial and Parallel Port Replacements," p. 940.

Another advantage is performance. ATA drives are some of the highest performance drives available—but they also are among the lowest performance drives. This apparent contradiction is a result of the fact that all ATA drives are different. You cannot make a blanket statement about the performance of ATA drives because each drive is unique. The high-end models, however, offer performance equal or superior to that of any other type of drive on the market for a single-user, single-tasking operating system.

IDE Origins

The earliest IDE drives were called hardcards and were nothing more than hard disks and controllers bolted directly together and plugged into a slot as a single unit. Companies such as the Plus

Development Division of Quantum took small 3 1/2-inch drives (either ST-506/412 or ESDI) and attached them directly to a standard controller. The assembly then was plugged into an ISA bus slot as though it were a normal disk controller. Unfortunately, the mounting of a heavy, vibrating hard disk in an expansion slot with nothing but a single screw to hold it in place left a lot to be desired—not to mention the possible interference with adjacent cards because many of these units were much thicker than a controller card alone.

Several companies got the idea to redesign the controller to replace the logic-board assembly on a standard hard disk and then mount it in a standard drive bay just like any other drive. Because the built-in controller in these drives still needed to plug directly into the expansion bus just like any other controller, a cable was run between the drive and one of the slots.

These connection problems were solved in various ways. Compaq was the first to incorporate a special bus adapter in its system to adapt the 98-pin AT (ISA) bus edge connector on the motherboard to a smaller 40-pin header style connector the drive would plug into. The 40-pin connectors were all that was necessary because it was known that a disk controller never would need more than 40 of the ISA bus lines.

In 1987, IBM developed its own MCA IDE drives and connected them to the bus through a bus adapter device called an *interposer card*. These bus adapters (sometimes called *paddle boards* or *angle boards*) needed only a few buffer chips and did not require any real circuitry because the drive-based controller was designed to plug directly into the bus. The paddle board nickname came from the fact that they resembled game paddle or joystick adapters, which do not have much circuitry on them. Another 8-bit variation of IDE appeared in 8-bit ISA systems, such as the PS/2 Model 30. The XT IDE interface uses a 40-pin connector similar to, but not compatible with, the 16-bit version.

IDE Bus Versions

There have been four main types of IDE interfaces based on three bus standards:

- Serial AT Attachment (SATA)
- Parallel AT Attachment (ATA) IDE (based on 16-bit ISA)
- XT IDE (based on 8-bit ISA)
- MCA IDE (based on 16-bit Micro Channel)

Of these, only the ATA versions are used today. ATA and Serial ATA have evolved with newer, faster, and more powerful versions. The improved versions of parallel ATA are referred to as ATA-2 and higher. They are also sometimes called EIDE (Enhanced IDE), Fast-ATA, Ultra-ATA, or Ultra-DMA. Even though ATA appears to have hit the end of the road with ATA-6, Serial ATA picks up where ATA leaves off and offers greater performance plus an established roadmap for future upgrades.

Note

Many people are confused about 16- versus 32-bit bus connections and 16- versus 32-bit hard drive connections. A PCI bus connection allows for a 32-bit (and possibly 64-bit in the future) connection between the bus and the IDE host interface, which is normally in the motherboard chipset South Bridge or I/O Controller Hub (ICH) chip. However, the actual parallel ATA interface between the host connector on the motherboard and the drive (or drives) itself is only a 16-bit interface. Thus, in a parallel ATA drive configuration, you are still getting only 16-bit transfers between the drive and the motherboard-based host interface. Even so, the clock speeds of the ATA interface are high enough that one or two hard drives normally cannot supply the controller enough data to saturate even a 16-bit channel. The same is true with Serial ATA, which—although it transmits only 1 bit at a time—does so at extremely high speeds.

The obsolete XT and current parallel ATA versions have standardized on 40-pin connectors and cables, but the connectors have slightly different pinouts, rendering them incompatible with one another. MCA IDE is also obsolete, uses a completely different 72-pin connector, and is designed for MCA bus systems only.

In most modern systems you will find two ATA connectors on the motherboard. If your motherboard does not have one of these connectors and you want to attach an ATA drive to your system, you can purchase an adapter card that adds an ATA interface (or two) to a system via the ISA or PCI bus slots. Some of the cards offer additional features, such as an onboard ROM BIOS or cache memory.

Because the ATA variety of IDE is the primary one in use today, that is what most of this chapter discusses.

ATA IDE

Control Data Corporation (CDC), Western Digital, and Compaq actually created what could be called the first ATA-IDE interface drive and were the first to establish the 40-pin ATA connector pinout. The first ATA IDE drives were 5 1/4-inch half-height CDC 40MB units with integrated WD controllers sold in the first Compaq 386 systems in 1986.

Eventually, the 40-pin ATA connector and drive interface design was placed before one of the ANSI standards committees that, in conjunction with drive manufacturers, ironed out some deficiencies, tied up some loose ends, and then published what was known as the CAM ATA (Common Access Method AT Attachment) interface. The CAM Committee was formed in October 1988, and the first working document of the AT Attachment interface was introduced in March 1989. Before the CAM ATA standard, many companies that followed CDC, such as Conner Peripherals, made proprietary changes to what had been done by CDC. As a result, many older ATA drives from the late 1980s are very difficult to integrate into a dual-drive setup that has newer drives. By the early 1990s, most drive manufacturers brought their drives into full compliance with the official standard, which eliminated many of these compatibility problems.

Some areas of the ATA standard have been left open for vendor-specific commands and functions. These vendor-specific commands and functions are the main reason it is so difficult to low-level format ATA drives. To work to full capability, the formatter you are using usually must know the specific vendor-unique commands for rewriting sector headers and remapping defects. Unfortunately, these and other specific drive commands differ from OEM to OEM, clouding the "standard" somewhat. Most ATA drive manufacturers have formatting software available on their Web sites.

Note

It is important to note that only the ATA IDE interface has been standardized by the industry. The XT IDE and MCA IDE never were adopted as industry-wide standards and never became very popular. These interfaces no longer are in production, and no new systems of which I am aware come with these nonstandard IDE interfaces.

ATA Standards

Today what we call the ATA interface is controlled by an independent group of representatives from major PC, drive, and component manufacturers. This group is called Technical Committee T13 and is responsible for all interface standards relating to the parallel AT Attachment storage interface. T13 is a part of the National Committee on Information Technology Standards (NCITS), which operates under rules approved by the American National Standards Institute (ANSI), a governing body that sets rules which control nonproprietary standards in the computer industry as well as many other industries. A second group called the Serial ATA Workgroup has formed to create the Serial ATA standards that will also come under ANSI control. Although these are different groups, many of the same people are in both groups. It seems as if little further development will be done on parallel ATA past the ATA-6 (ATA/100) specification. The further evolution of ATA will be in the Serial ATA form (discussed later in this chapter).

The rules these committees operate under are designed to ensure that voluntary industry standards are developed by the consensus of people and organizations in the affected industry. NCITS specifically develops Information Processing System standards, whereas ANSI approves the process under which they are developed and publishes them. Because T13 is essentially a public organization, all the working drafts, discussions, and meetings of T13 are open for all to see.

The parallel ATA interface has evolved into several successive standard versions, introduced as follows:

- ATA-1 (1986–1994)
- ATA-2 (1996; also called Fast-ATA, Fast-ATA-2, or EIDE)
- ATA-3 (1997)
- ATA-4 (1998; also called Ultra-ATA/33)
- ATA-5 (1999–present; also called Ultra-ATA/66)
- ATA-6 (2000–present; also called Ultra-ATA/100)

Each version of ATA is backward compatible with the previous versions. In other words, older ATA-1 or ATA-2 devices work fine on ATA-4, ATA-5, and ATA-6 interfaces. In cases in which the device version and interface version don't match, they work together at the capabilities of the lesser of the two. Newer versions of ATA are built on older versions and with few exceptions can be thought of as extensions of the previous versions. This means that ATA-6, for example, is generally considered equal to ATA-5 with the addition of some features.

Table 7.1 breaks down the various ATA standards. The following sections describe all the ATA versions in more detail.

Table 7.1 ATA Standards

Standard	Timeframe	PIO Modes	DMA Modes	Ultra-DMA Modes	Speed[1]	Features
ATA-1	1986–1994	0–2	0	—	8.33	Drive support up to 136.9GB BIOS issues not addressed
ATA-2	1995–1996	0–4	0–2	—	16.67	Faster PIO modes; CHS/LBA BIOS translation defined up to 8.4GB; PC Card
ATA-3	1997	0–4	0–2	—	16.67	SMART[2]; improved signal integrity; LBA support mandatory; eliminated single-word DMA modes
ATA-4	1998	0–4	0–2	0–2	33.33	Ultra-DMA modes; BIOS support up to 136.9GB
ATA-5	1999–2000	0–4	0–2	0–4	66.67	Faster UDMA modes; 80-pin cable with autodetection

Table 7.1   Continued

Standard	Timeframe	PIO Modes	DMA Modes	Ultra-DMA Modes	Speed[1]	Features
ATA-6	2001– present	0– 4	0– 2	0–5	100.00	100MB/sec UDMA mode; extended drive and BIOS support up to 144PB[3]

1. *Speed is MB/sec*
2. *SMART = Self-Monitoring, Analysis, and Reporting Technology*
3. *PB = Petabyte; 1PB is equal to 1 quadrillion bytes*
MB = Millions of bytes

GB = Billions of bytes
CHS = Cylinder head sector
LBA = Logical block address
UDMA = Ultra DMA (Direct Memory Access)

ATA-1 (AT Attachment Interface for Disk Drives)

Although ATA-1 had been used since 1986 before being published as a standard, and although it was first published in 1988 in draft form, ATA-1 wasn't officially approved as a standard until 1994 (committees often work slowly). ATA-1 defined the original AT Attachment interface, which was an integrated bus interface between disk drives and host systems based on the ISA (AT) bus. The major features that were introduced and documented in the ATA-1 specification are

- 40/44-pin connectors and cabling
- Master/slave or cable select drive configuration options
- Signal timing for basic PIO (Programmed I/O) and DMA (Direct Memory Access) modes
- CHS (cylinder head sector) and LBA (logical block address) drive parameter translations supporting drive capacities up to 2^{28}–2^{20} (267,386,880) sectors, or 136.9GB

ATA-1 was officially published as ANSI X3.221-1994, AT Attachment Interface for Disk Drives, and was officially withdrawn on August 6, 1999. ATA-2 and later are considered backward-compatible replacements.

Although ATA-1 supported theoretical drive capacities up to 136.9GB (2^{28}–2^{20} = 267,386,880 sectors), it did not address BIOS limitations that stopped at 528MB (1024×16×63 = 1,032,192 sectors). The BIOS limitations would be addressed in subsequent ATA versions because, at the time, no drives larger than 528MB had existed.

ATA-2 (AT Attachment Interface with Extensions-2)

Approved in 1996, ATA-2 was a major upgrade to the original ATA standard. Perhaps the biggest change was almost a philosophical one. ATA-2 was updated to define an interface between host systems and storage devices in general and not only disk drives. The major features added to ATA-2 as compared to the original ATA standard include

- Faster PIO and DMA transfer modes
- Support for power management
- Support for removable devices
- PCMCIA (PC card) device support
- Identify Drive command reports more information
- Defined standard CHS/LBA translation methods for drives up to 8.4GB in capacity

The most important additions in ATA-2 were the support for faster PIO and DMA modes, as well as methods to enable BIOS support up to 8.4GB. The BIOS support was necessary because, although even ATA-1 was designed to support drives of up to 136.9GB in capacity, the PC BIOS could originally handle drives of up to 528MB. Adding parameter-translation capability now allowed the BIOS to handle drives up to 8.4GB. This is discussed in more detail later in this chapter.

ATA-2 also featured improvements in the Identify Drive command that enabled a drive to tell the software exactly what its characteristics are; this is essential for both Plug and Play (PnP) and compatibility with future revisions of the standard.

ATA-2 was also known by unofficial marketing terms such as fast-ATA or fast-ATA-2 (Seagate/Quantum) and EIDE (Enhanced IDE, Western Digital). ATA-2 was officially published as ANSI X3.279-1996 AT Attachment Interface with Extensions.

ATA-3 (AT Attachment Interface-3)

First published in 1997, ATA-3 was a comparatively minor revision to the ATA-2 standard that preceded it. It consisted of a general cleanup of the specification and had mostly minor clarifications and revisions. The most major changes included the following:

- Eliminated single-word (8-bit) DMA transfer protocols.
- Added S.M.A.R.T. (Self-Monitoring, Analysis, and Reporting Technology) support for prediction of device performance degradation.
- LBA mode support was made mandatory (previously it had been optional).
- Added security mode, allowing password protection for device access.
- Recommendations for source and receiver bus termination to solve noise issues at higher transfer speeds.

ATA-3 has been officially published as ANSI X3.298-1997, AT Attachment 3 Interface.

ATA-3, which builds on ATA-2, adds improved reliability, especially of the faster PIO mode 4 transfers; however, ATA-3 does not define any faster modes. ATA-3 also adds a simple password-based security scheme, more sophisticated power management, and S.M.A.R.T. This enables a drive to keep track of problems that might result in a failure and therefore avoid data loss. S.M.A.R.T. is a reliability prediction technology that was initially developed by IBM.

ATA/ATAPI-4 (AT Attachment with Packet Interface Extension-4)

First published in 1998, ATA-4 included several important additions to the standard. It included the Packet Command feature known as the AT Attachment Packet Interface (ATAPI), which allowed devices such as CD-ROM and CD-RW drives, LS-120 SuperDisk floppy drives, tape drives, and other types of storage devices to be attached through a common interface. Until ATA-4 came out, ATAPI was a separately published standard. ATA-4 also added the 33MB/sec transfer mode known as Ultra-DMA or Ultra-ATA. ATA-4 is backward compatible with ATA-3 and earlier definitions of the ATAPI. The major revisions added in ATA-4 were as follows:

- Ultra-DMA (UDMA) transfer modes up to Mode 2, which is 33MB/sec (called UDMA/33 or Ultra-ATA/33)
- Integral ATAPI support
- Advanced power management support
- Defined an optional 80-conductor, 40-pin cable for improved noise resistance

- Compact Flash Adapter (CFA) support
- Introduced enhanced BIOS support for drives over 9.4ZB (zettabytes or trillion gigabytes) in size (even though ATA was still limited to 136.9GB)

ATA-4 was published as ANSI NCITS 317-1998, ATA-4 with Packet Interface Extension.

The speed and level of ATA support in your system is mainly dictated by your motherboard chipset. Most motherboard chipsets come with a component called either a South Bridge or an I/O Controller Hub that provides the ATA interface (as well as other functions) in the system. Check the specifications for your motherboard or chipset to see whether yours supports the faster ATA/33, ATA/66, or ATA/100 mode. One indication is to enter the BIOS Setup, put the hard disk on manual parameter settings (user defined), and see which if any Ultra-DMA modes are listed. Most boards built during 1998 support ATA/33; in 2000 they began to support ATA/66; and by late 2000 most started supporting ATA/100.

◀◀   See "Chipsets," p. 225.

ATA-4 made ATAPI support a full part of the ATA standard, and thus ATAPI was no longer an auxiliary interface to ATA but merged completely within. This promoted ATA for use as an interface for many other types of devices. ATA-4 also added support for new Ultra-DMA modes (also called Ultra-ATA) for even faster data transfer. The highest-performance mode, called UDMA/33, had 33MB/second bandwidth—twice that of the fastest programmed I/O mode or DMA mode previously supported. In addition to the higher transfer rate, because UDMA modes relieve the load on the processor, further performance gains were realized.

An optional 80-conductor cable (with cable select) is defined for UDMA/33 transfers. Although this cable was originally defined as optional, it would later be required for the faster ATA/66 and ATA/100 modes in ATA-5 and later.

Also included was support for queuing commands, which is similar to that provided in SCSI-2. This enabled better multitasking as multiple programs make requests for IDE transfers.

▶▶   See "SCSI Versus IDE," p. 540.

ATA/ATAPI-5 (AT Attachment with Packet Interface-5)

This version of the ATA standard was approved in early 2000 and builds on ATA-4. The major additions in the standard include the following:

- Ultra-DMA (UDMA) transfer modes up to Mode 4, which is 66MB/sec (called UDMA/66 or Ultra-ATA/66).
- 80-conductor cable now mandatory for UDMA/66 operation.
- Added automatic detection of 40- or 80-conductor cables.
- UDMA modes faster than UDMA/33 are enabled only if an 80-conductor cable is detected.

Another standard recently approved by the T13 committee is an IEEE-1394 (iLink or FireWire) extension to the ATA interface protocol. This specifies a bridge protocol between the iLink/FireWire bus and ATA, allowing ATA drives to be adapted to this newer interface.

▶▶   See "IEEE-1394," p. 948.

Copies of any of the published standards can be purchased from ANSI or Global Engineering Documents (see the Vendor List on the CD).

ATA-5 includes Ultra-ATA/66 (also called Ultra-DMA or UDMA/66), which doubles the Ultra-ATA burst transfer rate by reducing setup times and increasing the clock rate. The faster clock rate increases interference, which causes problems with the standard 40-pin cable used by ATA and Ultra-ATA. To eliminate noise and interference, the new 40-pin, 80-conductor cable has now been made mandatory for drives running in UDMA/66 or faster modes. This cable was first announced in ATA-4 but is now mandatory in ATA-5 to support the Ultra-ATA/66 mode. This cable adds 40 additional ground lines between each of the original 40 ground and signal lines, which help shield the signals from interference. Note that this cable works with older non–Ultra-ATA devices as well because it still has the same 40-pin connectors.

The 40-pin, 80-conductor cables will support the cable select feature and have color-coded connectors. The blue (end) connector should be connected to the ATA host interface (usually the motherboard). The black (opposite end) connector is known as the *master position*, which is where the primary drive plugs in. The gray (middle) connector is for slave devices.

To use either the UDMA/33 or UDMA/66 mode, your ATA interface, drive, BIOS, and cable must be capable of supporting the mode you want to use. The operating system also must be capable of handling Direct Memory Access. Windows 95 OSR2 or later, Windows 98/Me, and Windows 2000/XP are ready out of the box, but older versions of Windows 95 and NT (prior to Service Pack 3) require additional or updated drivers to fully exploit these faster modes.

For reliability, Ultra-DMA modes incorporate an error-detection mechanism known as *cyclical redundancy checking (CRC)*. CRC is an algorithm that calculates a checksum used to detect errors in a stream of data. Both the host (controller) and the drive calculate a CRC value for each Ultra-DMA transfer. After the data is sent, the drive calculates a CRC value, and this is compared to the original host CRC value. If a difference is reported, the host might be required to select a slower transfer mode and retry the original request for data.

ATA/ATAPI-6 (AT Attachment with Packet Interface-6)

This final version of the ATA standard was under development during 2001 and builds on ATA-5. The major additions in the standard include the following:

- Ultra-DMA (UDMA) transfer modes up to Mode 5, which is 100MB/sec (called UDMA/100, Ultra-ATA/100, or just ATA/100)
- LBA addressing extended to 2^{48} (281,474,976,710,656) sectors supporting drives up to 144.12PB (petabytes = quadrillion bytes)

ATA-6 includes Ultra-ATA/100 (also called Ultra-DMA or UDMA/100), which increases the Ultra-ATA burst transfer rate by reducing setup times and increasing the clock rate. As with ATA-5, the faster modes require the improved 80-conductor cable. Using the new ATA/100 mode requires both a drive and motherboard interface that supports that mode.

Besides adding the 100MB/sec UDMA Mode 5 transfer rate, ATA-6 also extends drive capacity greatly, and just in time. ATA-5 and earlier standards supported drives of up to only 136.9GB in capacity, which was becoming a limitation as larger drives are becoming available. At least one company has introduced 3 1/2-inch drives that are larger than that, but originally they could be released only in SCSI versions because SCSI didn't share the same limitation problems of ATA. With ATA-6, the drive limit has been expanded from (2^{28}–2^{20}) sectors to (2^{48}) sectors. What this means is that Logical Block Addressing used to use a 28-bit number, but with ATA-6 it now uses a 48-bit number instead. With 512 bytes per sector, this raises maximum supported drive capacity to 144.12PB. That is equal to more than 144.12 quadrillion bytes!

As a historical note, ATA-6 will likely be the last revision of the venerable parallel ATA standard. The future of ATA is called Serial ATA, and it is covered later in this chapter.

ATA Features

The ATA standards have gone a long way toward eliminating incompatibilities and problems with interfacing IDE drives to ISA/PCI bus systems. The ATA specifications define the signals on the 40-pin connector, the functions and timings of these signals, cable specifications, and so on. The following section lists some of the elements and functions defined by the ATA specification.

ATA I/O Connector

The ATA interface connector is normally a 40-pin header-type connector with pins spaced 0.1 inches (2.54mm) apart and generally is keyed to prevent the possibility of installing it upside down (see Figures 7.1 and 7.2). To create a keyed connector, the manufacturer generally removes pin 20 from the male connector and blocks pin 20 on the female cable connector, which prevents the user from installing the cable backward. Some cables also incorporate a protrusion on the top of the female cable connector, which fits into a notch in the shroud surrounding the mating male connector on the device. The use of keyed connectors and cables is highly recommended; plugging in an IDE cable backward normally won't cause any permanent damage. However, it can lock up the system and prevent it from running at all.

Figure 7.1 Typical ATA (IDE) hard drive connectors.

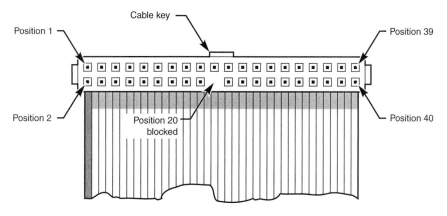

Figure 7.2   ATA (IDE) 40-pin interface connector detail.

Table 7.2 shows the standard 40-pin ATA-IDE interface connector pinout.

Table 7.2   40-Pin ATA Connector

Signal Name	Pin	Pin	Signal Name
-RESET	1	2	GROUND
Data Bit 7	3	4	Data Bit 8
Data Bit 6	5	6	Data Bit 9
Data Bit 5	7	8	Data Bit 10
Data Bit 4	9	10	Data Bit 11
Data Bit 3	11	12	Data Bit 12
Data Bit 2	13	14	Data Bit 13
Data Bit 1	15	16	Data Bit 14
Data Bit 0	17	18	Data Bit 15
GROUND	19	20	KEY (pin missing)
DRQ 3	21	22	GROUND
-IOW	23	24	GROUND
-IOR	25	26	GROUND
I/O CH RDY	27	28	CSEL:SPSYNC[1]
-DACK 3	29	30	GROUND
IRQ 14	31	32	Reserved[2]
Address Bit 1	33	34	-PDIAG
Address Bit 0	35	36	Address Bit 2
-CS1FX	37	38	-CS3FX
-DA/SP	39	40	GROUND
+5V (Logic)	41	42	+5V (Motor)
GROUND	43	44	Reserved

1. Pin 28 is normally cable select, but some older drives could use it for spindle synchronization.

2. Pin 32 was defined as -IOCS16 in ATA-2 but is no longer used.

Notebook-size, 2 1/2-inch drives normally use a smaller unitized 50-pin header connector with pins spaced only 2.0mm (0.079 inches) apart. The main 40-pin part of the connector is the same as the standard ATA connector (except for the physical pin spacing), but there are added pins for power and jumpering. Normally, the cable that plugs into this connector has 44 pins, carrying power as well as the standard ATA signals. The jumper pins normally have a jumper on them (the jumper position controls cable select, master, or slave settings). Figure 7.3 shows the unitized 50-pin connector used on 2 1/2-inch ATA drives.

Figure 7.3   50-pin unitized ATA connector detail (used on 2 1/2-inch ATA drives).

Note the jumper pins at positions A–D and that the pins at positions E and F are removed. A jumper usually is placed between positions B and D to set the drive for cable select operation. On this connector pin 41 provides +5V power to the drive logic (circuit board), pin 42 provides +5V power to the motor (2 1/2-inch drives use 5V motors, unlike larger drives that normally use 12V motors), and pin 43 provides a power ground. The last pin (44) is reserved and not used.

Table 7.3 shows the 50-pin unitized ATA interface connector pinout as used on most 2 1/2-inch (laptop or notebook computer) drives.

Table 7.3   50-Pin Unitized ATA Connector Pinout

Signal Name	Pin	Pin	Signal Name
Jumper pin	A	B	Jumper pin
Jumper pin	C	D	Jumper pin
KEY (pin missing)	E	F	KEY (pin missing)
-RESET	1	2	GROUND
Data Bit 7	3	4	Data Bit 8
Data Bit 6	5	6	Data Bit 9
Data Bit 5	7	8	Data Bit 10
Data Bit 4	9	10	Data Bit 11
Data Bit 3	11	12	Data Bit 12
Data Bit 2	13	14	Data Bit 13
Data Bit 1	15	16	Data Bit 14
Data Bit 0	17	18	Data Bit 15
GROUND	19	20	KEY (pin missing)
DRQ 3	21	22	GROUND
-IOW	23	24	GROUND

Table 7.3   Continued

Signal Name	Pin	Pin	Signal Name
-IOR	25	26	GROUND
I/O CH RDY	27	28	CSEL
-DACK 3	29	30	GROUND
IRQ 14	31	32	Reserved
Address Bit 1	33	34	-PDIAG
Address Bit 0	35	36	Address Bit 2
-CS1FX	37	38	-CS3FX
-DA/SP	39	40	GROUND
+5V (Logic)	41	42	+5V (Motor)
GROUND	43	44	Reserved

Not All Cables and Connectors Are Keyed

Note that many lower-cost board and cable manufacturers leave out the keying. Cheaper motherboards often won't have pin 20 removed on their IDE connectors, and consequently they won't supply a cable with pin 20 blocked. If they don't use a shrouded connector with a notch and a corresponding protrusion on the cable connector, no keying exists and the cables can be inserted backward. Fortunately, the only consequence of this in most cases is that the device won't work until the cable is attached with the correct orientation.

In rare situations in which you are mixing and matching items, you might encounter a cable with pin 20 blocked (as it should be) and a board with pin 20 still present. In that case, you can break off pin 20 from the board, or for the more squeamish, remove the block from the cable. Some cables have the block permanently installed as a part of the connector housing, in which case you must break off pin 20 on the board or device end or use a different cable.

The simple rule of thumb is that pin 1 should be oriented toward the power connector on the device, which normally corresponds to the stripe on the cable.

ATA I/O Cable

A 40-conductor ribbon cable is specified to carry signals between the bus adapter circuits and the drive (controller). To maximize signal integrity and eliminate potential timing and noise problems, the cable should not be longer than 18 inches (0.46 meters).

Note that ATA drives supporting the higher-speed transfer modes, such as PIO Mode 4 or any of the Ultra-DMA (UDMA) modes, are especially susceptible to cable integrity problems and cables that are too long. If the cable is too long, you can experience data corruption and other errors that can be maddening. This will be manifested in any type of problem reading from or writing to the drive. In addition, any drive using UDMA Mode 4 (66MB/sec transfer rate) or Mode 5 (100MB/sec transfer rate) must use a special higher-quality 80-conductor cable (the extra conductors are grounds to reduce noise). I also recommend this type of cable if your drive is running at UDMA Mode 2 (33MB/sec) or slower because it can't hurt and can only help. I always keep a high-quality 80-conductor IDE cable in my toolbox for testing drives where I suspect cable integrity or cable length problems. Figure 7.4 shows the typical ATA cable layout and dimensions.

Figure 7.4   ATA (IDE) cable, with 40-pin connectors and either 40- or 80-conductor cables (additional wires are grounded in 80-conductor versions).

Note

Most 40-conductor cables do not color-code the connectors, whereas all 80-conductor cables do color-code the connectors.

Two primary variations of IDE cables are used today: one with 40 conductors and the other with 80 conductors. Both use 40-pin connectors, and the additional wires in the 80-conductor version are simply wired to ground. The additional conductors are designed to reduce noise and interference and are required when setting the interface to run at 66MB/sec (ATA/66) or faster. The drive and host adapter are designed to disable the higher-speed ATA/66 or ATA/100 modes if an 80-conductor cable is not detected. The 80-conductor cable can also be used at lower speeds; although this is unnecessary, it improves the signal integrity. Therefore, it is the recommended version no matter which drive you use.

Note the keying on the cable that is designed to prevent backward installation.

ATA Signals

This section describes some of the most important signals in more detail.

Pin 20 is used as a key pin for cable orientation and is not connected to the interface. This pin should be missing from any ATA connectors, and the cable should have the pin-20 hole in the connector plugged off to prevent the cable from being plugged in backward.

Pin 39 carries the drive active/slave present (DASP) signal, which is a dual-purpose, time-multiplexed signal. During power-on initialization, this signal indicates whether a slave drive is present on the interface. After that, each drive asserts the signal to indicate that it is active. Early drives could not multiplex these functions and required special jumper settings to work with other drives. Standardizing this function to allow for compatible dual-drive installations is one of the features of the ATA standard. This is why some drives require a slave present (SP) jumper, whereas others do not.

Pin 28 carries the cable select signal (CSEL). In some older drives, it could also carry a spindle synchronization signal (SPSYNC), but that is not commonly found on newer drives. The CSEL function is the most widely used and is designed to control the designation of a drive as master (drive 0) or slave (drive 1) without requiring jumper settings on the drives. If a drive sees the CSEL as being grounded, the drive is a master; if CSEL is open, the drive is a slave.

You can install special cabling to ground CSEL selectively. This installation usually is accomplished through a Y-cable arrangement, with the IDE bus connector in the middle and each drive at opposite ends of the cable. One leg of the Y has the CSEL line connected through, indicating a master drive; the other leg has the CSEL line open (conductor interrupted or removed), making the drive at that end the slave.

Dual-Drive Configurations

Dual-drive ATA installations can be problematic because each drive has its own controller and both controllers must function while being connected to the same bus. There has to be a way to ensure that only one of the two controllers will respond to a command at a time.

The ATA standard provides the option of operating on the AT bus with two drives in a daisy-chained configuration. The primary drive (drive 0) is called the master, and the secondary drive (drive 1) is called the slave. You designate a drive as being master or slave by setting a jumper or switch on the drive or by using a special line in the interface called the cable select pin and setting the CS jumper on the drive.

When only one drive is installed, the controller responds to all commands from the system. When two drives (and, therefore, two controllers) are installed, both controllers receive all commands from the system. Each controller then must be set up to respond only to commands for itself. In this situation, one controller must be designated as the master and the other as the slave. When the system sends a command for a specific drive, the controller on the other drive must remain silent while the selected controller and drive are functioning. Setting the jumper to master or slave enables discrimination between the two controllers by setting a special bit (the DRV bit) in the Drive/Head Register of a command block.

Configuring IDE drives can be simple, as is the case with most single-drive installations, or troublesome, especially when it comes to mixing two drives from different manufacturers on a single cable.

Most IDE drives can be configured with four possible settings:

- Master (single-drive)
- Master (dual-drive)
- Slave (dual-drive)
- Cable select

Some drives simplify this to three settings: master, slave, and cable select. Because each IDE drive has its own controller, you must specifically tell one drive to be the master and the other to be the slave. No functional difference exists between the two, except that the drive that's specified as the slave will assert a signal called DASP after a system reset informs the master that a slave drive is present in the system. The master drive then pays attention to the drive select line, which it otherwise ignores. Telling a drive that it's the slave also usually causes it to delay its spinup for several seconds to allow the master to get going and thus to lessen the load on the system's power supply.

Until the ATA IDE specification, no common implementation for drive configuration was in use. Some drive companies even used different master/slave methods for different models of drives. Because of these incompatibilities, some drives work together only in a specific master/slave or slave/master order. This situation mostly affects older IDE drives introduced before the ATA specification.

Most drives that fully follow the ATA specification now need only one jumper (master/slave) for configuration. A few also need a slave present jumper, as well. Table 7.4 shows the jumper settings required by most ATA IDE drives.

Table 7.4   Jumper Settings for Most ATA IDE-Compatible Drives on Standard (Non–Cable Select) Cables

Jumper Name	Single-Drive	Dual-Drive Master	Dual-Drive Slave
Master (M/S)	On	On	Off
Slave Present (SP)	Off	On	Off
Cable Select (CS)	Off	Off	Off

Note

If a cable select cable is used, the CS jumper should be set On and all others should be Off. The cable connector then determines which drive will be master or slave.

Figure 7.5 shows the jumpers on a typical ATA drive.

The master jumper indicates that the drive is a master or a slave. Some drives also require a slave present jumper, which is used only in a dual-drive setup and then installed only on the master drive—which is somewhat confusing. This jumper tells the master that a slave drive is attached. With many ATA IDE drives, the master jumper is optional and can be left off. Installing this jumper doesn't hurt in these cases and can eliminate confusion; I recommend that you install the jumpers listed here.

Note

Note that some drives have these jumpers on the drive circuit board, and as such they might not be visible on the rear.

To eliminate confusion over master/slave settings, most newer systems now use the cable select option. This involves two things. The first is having a special IDE cable that has all the wires except pin 28 running from the motherboard connector to both drive connectors. Pin 28 is used for cable select and is connected to one of the drive connectors (labeled master) and not to the other (labeled slave). Both drives are then configured in cable select mode via the CS jumper on each drive.

With cable select, the drive that receives signals on pin 28 automatically becomes the master, and the other becomes the slave. Most cables implement this by removing the metal insulation displacement bit from the pin-28 hole, which can be difficult to see at a glance. Other cables have a section of pin 28 visibly cut from the cable somewhere along the ribbon. Because this is such a minor modification to the cable and can be difficult to see, cable select cables normally have the connectors labeled master, slave, and system, indicating that the cable controls these options rather than the drive. All 80-conductor UltraATA cables are designed to use cable select.

With cable select, you simply set the CS jumper on all drives and then plug the drive you want to be the master into the connector labeled master on the cable and the drive you want to be the slave into the connector labeled slave.

Figure 7.5 ATA (IDE) drive jumpers for most drives. Note that the drive is shown upside down in this figure, whereas previous figures in this chapter depict drives as they appear right side up.

ATA Commands

One of the best features of the ATA IDE interface is the enhanced command set. The ATA IDE interface was modeled after the WD1003 controller IBM used in the original AT system. All ATA IDE drives must support the original WD command set (eight commands) with no exceptions, which is why IDE drives are so easy to install in systems today. All IBM-compatible systems have built-in ROM BIOS support for the WD1003, so they essentially support ATA IDE as well.

In addition to supporting all the WD1003 commands, the ATA specification added numerous other commands to enhance performance and capabilities. These commands are an optional part of the ATA interface, but several of them are used in most drives available today and are very important to the performance and use of ATA drives in general.

Perhaps the most important is the Identify Drive command. This command causes the drive to transmit a 512-byte block of data that provides all details about the drive. Through this command, any program (including the system BIOS) can find out exactly which type of drive is connected, including the drive manufacturer, model number, operating parameters, and even the serial number of the drive. Many modern BIOSes use this information to automatically receive and enter the drive's parameters into CMOS memory, eliminating the need for the user to enter these parameters manually during system configuration. This arrangement helps prevent mistakes that can later lead to data loss when the user no longer remembers what parameters he used during setup.

The Identify Drive data can tell you many things about your drive, including the following:

- Number of cylinders in the recommended (default) translation mode
- Number of heads in the recommended (default) translation mode
- Number of sectors per track in the recommended (default) translation mode
- Number of cylinders in the current translation mode
- Number of heads in the current translation mode
- Number of sectors per track in the current translation mode
- Manufacturer and model number
- Firmware revision
- Serial number
- Buffer type, indicating sector buffering or caching capabilities

Several public-domain programs can execute this command to the drive and report the information onscreen. I use the IDEINFO (available at `http://www.dc.ee/Files/Utils/IDEINFO.ARJ`) or IDEDIAG (available from many of the popular shareware sites) program. I find these programs especially useful when I am trying to install IDE drives and need to know the correct parameters for a user-definable BIOS type. These programs get the information directly from the drive.

Two other important commands are the Read Multiple and Write Multiple commands. These commands permit multiple-sector data transfers and, when combined with block-mode PIO capabilities in the system, can result in incredible data-transfer rates many times faster than single-sector PIO transfers.

MMMany other enhanced commands are available, including room for a given drive manufacturer to implement what are called vendor-unique commands. These commands often are used by a particular vendor for features unique to that vendor. Often, features such as low-level formatting and defect management are controlled by vendor-unique commands. This is why low-level format programs can be so specific to a particular manufacturer's IDE drives and why many manufacturers make their own LLF programs available.

ATA Upgrades

Since ATA-1, newer versions of the ATA interface and complementary BIOS support larger and faster drives, as well as different types of devices other than hard disks. This section details these areas of improvement.

ATA-2 through ATA-6 have improved the original ATA/IDE interface in four main areas:

- Secondary two-device channel
- Increased maximum drive capacity
- Faster data transfer
- ATAPI (ATA Program Interface)

The following sections describe these improvements.

Secondary ATA Channel

Although even ATA-1 was never limited to a single channel, systems at that time normally had only a primary channel built into the motherboard. Starting when the ATA-2 standard was published, most systems began including a second ATA interface, called the secondary channel. Because each channel could support two drives, this allowed for up to four devices to be installed.

If more than four ATA devices are needed, you can install additional ATA ports via add-on cards, which normally plug into PCI slots. These additional ports are not supported directly by the motherboard BIOS, but the card can have an adapter BIOS that will be recognized at boot time. Even without an onboard BIOS, devices attached to the card can be supported by drivers—the only feature lacking without ROM-based support is that the capability to be directly bootable.

Companies such as Promise Technologies, MicroFirmware, GSI, and others make add-on ATA adapters that allow using more than the two ports that come built into most motherboards.

Drive Capacity Limitations

ATA interface versions up through ATA-5 suffered from a drive capacity limitation of 136.9GB (billion bytes). Depending on the BIOS used, this limitation can be further reduced to 8.4GB, or even as low as 528MB (million bytes). This is due to limitations in both the BIOS and the ATA interface, which when combined create even further limitations. To understand these limits, you have to look at the BIOS and ATA interface.

The pertinent limitations are those of the ATA interface itself as well as the BIOS (drivers) used to talk to the interface. A summary of the limitations are shown in Table 7.5.

Table 7.5   ATA/IDE Drive Capacity Limitations

Specification	Maximum Sectors	Capacity[1]	Maximum Capacity
ATA-5 interface	267,386,880	136,902,082,560	136.9GB
Standard CHS BIOS	1,032,192	528,482,304	528.5MB
CHS BIOS with translation	16,515,072	8,455,716,864	8.4GB
Enhanced (EDD BIOS)	18,446,744,073,709,551,600	9,444,732,965,739,290,430,000	9.4ZB

1. Maximum capacity in bytes
ATA = AT Attachment
CHS = cylinder head sector
EDD = enhanced disk drive

MB = million bytes
GB = billion bytes
ZB = zettabytes, one ZB equals one billion trillion bytes

This section explores these limitations in more detail.

The BIOS-based driver for hard disks is accessed via software interrupt 13h (13 hex), which offers functions for reading and writing drives at the sector level. INT13h requires that the particular sector be addressed by its cylinder, head, and sector location, otherwise known as *CHS addressing*. This interface is used by the operating system and low-level disk utilities to access the drive. The INT13h interface originally was written by IBM for the BIOS on the PC XT hard disk controller in 1983 and then incorporated into the AT motherboard BIOS in 1984. This interface used numbers to define the particular cylinder, head, and sector being addressed. Table 7.6, which shows the standard INT13h BIOS CHS parameter limits, includes the maximum values for these numbers.

Table 7.6   INT13h BIOS CHS Parameter Limits

Field	Field Size	Maximum Value	Range	Total Usable
Cylinder	10 bits	1,024	0–1023	1,024
Head	8 bits	256	0–255	256
Sector	6 bits	64	1–63	63

The concept is simple: If you had a hotel with two-digit decimal numbers, you could have only 100 rooms, numbered 0–99. CHS numbers used by the BIOS INT13h interface are binary, and with a 10-bit number being used for cylinders, you can have only 1,024 maximum, numbered 0–1023. Because the head you want to access is identified by an 8-bit number, the maximum number of heads the BIOS could handle is 256, numbered 0–255. Finally, with sectors there is a minor difference. Sectors on a track are identified by a 6-bit number, which would normally allow a maximum of 64; because sectors are numbered starting with 1 (instead of 0), however, the range is limited to 1–63, which means a total of 63 sectors per track is the maximum the BIOS can handle.

These BIOS limitations are true for all BIOS versions or programs that rely on standard CHS addressing, using the INT13h BIOS interface. Using the maximum numbers possible for CHS, a drive with 1,024 cylinders, 256 heads, and 63 sectors per track is possible. Because each sector is 512 bytes, the math works out as follows:

```
            Max. Values
      ---------------------------
      Cylinders          1,024
         Heads            256
```

```
Sectors/Track              63
============================
Total Sectors     16,515,072
----------------------------
Total Bytes   8,455,716,864
Megabytes (MB)         8,456
Mebibytes (MiB)        8,064
Gigabytes (GB)           8.4
Gibibytes (GiB)          7.8
```

From these calculations, you can see that the maximum size drive addressable via the BIOS INT13h interface is about 8.4GB (where GB equals roughly one billion bytes), or 7.8GiB (where GiB means *gigabinarybytes*).

Note that the Gi (gigabinary) designation is a standard designed to eliminate confusion between decimal- and binary-based multiples, especially in computer systems. In December 1998, the International Electrotechnical Commission (IEC) approved as an international standard the prefix names and symbols for binary multiples used in data processing and transmission. The prefixes are shown in Table 7.7.

Table 7.7   Standard Prefix Names and Symbols for Binary Multiples

Factor	Symbol	Name	Value	
Decimal Prefixes				
10^3	K	Kilo	1,000	
10^6	M	Mega	1,000,000	
10^9	G	Giga	1,000,000,000	
10^{12}	T	Tera	1,000,000,000,000	
10^{15}	P	Peta	1,000,000,000,000,000	
Binary Prefixes				
Factor	Symbol	Name	Derivation	Value
2^{10}	Ki	Kibi	Kilobinary	1,024
2^{20}	Mi	Mebi	Megabinary	1,048,576
2^{30}	Gi	Gibi	Gigabinary	1,073,741,824
2^{40}	Ti	Tebi	Terabinary	1,099,511,627,776
2^{50}	Pi	Pebi	Petabinary	1,125,899,906,842,624

Note

Under this standard terminology, an MB (megabyte) would be 1,000,000 bytes, whereas an MiB (mebibyte) would be 1,048,576 bytes.

Another way of looking at this is that each sector can be addressed using a single 24-bit number (10 bits plus 8 bits plus 6 bits). Because the 6-bit portion cannot be all 0s, the total number of sectors addressable would be defined as $2^{24} - 2^{18}$, or $16,777,216 - 262,144 = 16,515,072$ sectors. Because each sector is 512 bytes, the maximum capacity supported by the BIOS is 8.4GB.

Unfortunately for ATA, the BIOS limits are not the only limitations that apply. Limits also exist in the ATA interface itself. The ATA limits are shown in Table 7.8.

Table 7.8   Standard ATA Parameter Limitations

Field	Field Size	Maximum Value	Range	Total Usable
Cylinder	16 bits	65536	0–65535	65536
Head	4 bits	16	0–15	16
Sector	8 bits	256	1–255	255

As you can see, the ATA limits are higher than the BIOS limits for cylinders and sectors but lower than the BIOS limits for heads. The total limits for capacity according to the ATA specifications are as follows:

```
                    Max. Values
- - - - - - - - - - - - - - - - - - - - - - - - -
       Cylinders        65,536
           Heads            16
  Sectors/Track           255
===============================
  Total Sectors    267,386,880
- - - - - - - - - - - - - - - - - - - - - - - - -
  Total Bytes   136,902,082,560
  Megabytes (MB)        136,902
  Mebibytes (MiB)       130,560
  Gigabytes (GB)          136.9
  Gibibytes (GiB)         127.5
```

Note that the ATA limitations also can be expressed as a single 28-bit number—the 16-bit cylinder number plus the 4-bit head number plus the 8-bit sector number. To maintain compatibility between LBA and CHS modes in which the sector number must start from 1 instead of 0, the maximum capacity is $2^{28} - 2^{20}$, or 268,435,456 – 1,048,576 = 267,386,880 sectors. Because each sector is 512 bytes, the maximum capacity supported by ATA through ATA-5 is 136.9GB.

ATA-6 increases this limit substantially by going to an LBA interface that uses 48-bit sector addressing. This means that maximum capacity is increased to 2^{48} sectors. This is equal to 281,474,976,710,656 total sectors. Because each sector stores 512 bytes, this results in a maximum drive capacity of

```
                        Max. Values
- - - - - - - - - - - - - - - - - - - - - - - - - - - - - -
  Total Sectors      281,474,976,710,656
- - - - - - - - - - - - - - - - - - - - - - - - - - - - - -
  Total Bytes   144,115,188,075,855,888
  Megabytes (MB)     144,115,188,076
  Mebibytes (MiB)    137,438,953,472
  Gigabytes (GB)         144,115,188
  Gibibytes (GiB)        134,217,728
  Terabytes (TB)             144,115
  Tebibytes (TiB)            131,072
  Petabytes (PB)                 144
  Pebibytes (PiB)                128
```

This allows a capacity of just over 144PB (petabytes = quadrillion bytes)! It should be awhile before you have to worry about that barrier being broken.

When you combine the limitations of the BIOS and ATA interface, you end up with the situation as shown in Table 7.9.

Table 7.9   Combined CHS BIOS and ATA Parameter Limits

Field	CHS BIOS Parameter Limits	ATA Parameter Limits	Combined Limits
Cylinder	1,024	65,536	1,024
Head	256	16	16
Sector	63	255	63
Total Sectors	16,515,072	267,386,880	1,032,192
Maximum Capacity	8.4GB	136.9GB	528MB

As you can see, combining these limits results in maximum usable parameters of 1,024 cylinders, 16 heads, and 63 sectors, which results in a maximum drive capacity of 528MB.

Starting in 1993–94, most BIOSes began implementing a fix for these problems, which enabled drives up to the BIOS limit of 8.4GB to be used. This fix involved what is termed *parameter translation* at the BIOS Setup level, which adapted or translated the cylinder, head, and sector numbers to fit within the allowable BIOS parameters. There are two types of translation: One works mathematically off the reported CHS parameters (called Large or Extended CHS in the BIOS Setup); the other is derived from the total number of sectors (called Logical Block Address or LBA in the BIOS Setup). Both translation schemes result in the same thing; they just use two different mathematical algorithms to get there. Due to some limitations with the CHS translations, you usually should select LBA translation if that is an option in your BIOS setup.

Virtually all PC BIOSes since 1994 have translation capability in the BIOS Setup, and virtually all offer both CHS translation as well as LBA translation modes. If both translation modes are offered, you should choose the LBA method of translation because it is the more efficient of the two. Both normally result in the same translated CHS parameters; however, depending on the specific drive parameters reported, the geometries can vary depending on the translation method selected. If you were to set up and format a drive using CHS translation and then change to LBA translation, the interpreted geometry could change and the drive could then become unreadable. Bottom line: After you select a translation method, don't plan on changing it unless you have your data securely backed up.

With translation, the parameters reported by the drive are translated. The physical parameters reported by the drive are modified into parameters that are acceptable to the BIOS. Here is an example:

```
                      Physical      Logical
                          CHS          CHS
                   Parameters   Parameters
          -----------------------------------------
        Cylinders      12,000          750
            Heads          16          256
     Sectors/Track          63           63
          =========================================
    Total Sectors   12,096,000   12,096,000
     Capacity (MB)       6,193        6,193
    Capacity (Meg)       5,906        5,906
```

This example shows a drive with 12,000 cylinders and 16 heads. The physical cylinder count is way above the BIOS limit of 1,024, so in translating the BIOS Setup divides the cylinder count by 2, 4, 8, or 16 to bring it down below 1,024. In this case it was necessary to divide by 16, which results in a new cylinder count of 750—well below the 1,024 maximum. Because the cylinder count was divided by 16, the head count is then multiplied by the same number, resulting in 256 heads, which is right at the limit the BIOS can handle. So, although the drive physically has 12,000 cylinders and 16 heads, the BIOS and all software (including the operating system) instead see the drive as having 750 cylinders and 256 heads. Note that the 63 sector count is simply carried over without change. The result is that by using the new parameters the BIOS can see the entire 6GB drive and won't be limited to just the first 528MB.

When you install a drive, you don't have to do the translation math; the BIOS Setup does that for you behind the scenes. All you have to do is either allow the BIOS to autodetect the drive physical parameters and enable ECHS (large) or LBA translation. The BIOS Setup does the rest of the work for you.

You usually can tell whether your BIOS supports translation by the capability to specify more than 1,024 cylinders in the BIOS Setup, although this can be misleading. The best clue is to look for the translation setting parameters in the IDE drive setup page in the BIOS Setup. See Chapter 5, "BIOS," for more information on how to enter the BIOS Setup on your system. If you see drive-related settings, such as LBA or ECHS (sometimes called Large or Extended), these are telltale signs of a BIOS with translation support. Most BIOSes with a date of 1994 or later include this capability. If your system currently does not support parameter translation, you might be able to get an upgrade from your motherboard manufacturer or install a BIOS upgrade card with this capability such as the ATA Pro Flash by MicroFirmware (see the Vendor List on the CD included with this book).

Table 7.10 shows the four ways today's BIOSes can handle addressing sectors on the drive: Standard CHS (no translation), Extended CHS translation, LBA translation, and pure LBA addressing. They are summarized in the following table.

Table 7.10   Drive Sector Addressing Methods

BIOS Mode	Operating System to BIOS	BIOS to Drive
Standard (normal) No translation	Physical CHS Parameters	Physical CHS Parameters
Extended CHS (large) Translation	Logical CHS Parameters	Physical CHS Parameters
LBA Translation	Logical CHS Parameters	LBA Parameters
Pure LBA (EDD BIOS)	LBA Parameters	LBA Parameters

In Standard CHS, there is only one possible translation step internal to the drive. The drive's actual physical geometry is completely invisible from the outside with all zoned recorded ATA drives today. The cylinders, heads, and sectors printed on the label for use in the BIOS setup are purely logical geometry and do not represent the actual physical parameters. Standard CHS addressing is limited to 16 heads and 1,024 cylinders, which provides a limit of 504MB.

This is often called "Normal" in the BIOS setup and causes the BIOS to behave like an old-fashioned one without translation. Use this setting if your drive has fewer than 1,024 cylinders or if you want to use the drive with a non-DOS operating system that doesn't understand translation.

In Extended CHS, a translated logical geometry is used to communicate between the drive and the BIOS, whereas a different translated geometry is used to communicate between the BIOS and everything else. In other words, normally two translation steps exist. The drive still translates internally but has logical parameters that exceed the 1,024-cylinder limitation of the standard BIOS. In this case, the drive's cylinder count is usually divided by 2, and the head count is multiplied by 2 to get the translated values from those actually stored in the CMOS Setup. This type of setting breaks the 504MB/528MB barrier.

This often is called "Large" or "ECHS" in the BIOS setup and tells the BIOS to use Extended CHS translation. It uses a different geometry (cylinders/heads/sectors) when talking to the drive than when talking to the BIOS. This type of translation should be used with drives that have more than 1,024 cylinders but that do not support LBA. Note that the geometry entered in your BIOS Setup is the logical geometry, not the translated one.

LBA is a means of linearly addressing sector addresses, beginning at Cylinder 0, Head 0, Sector 1 as LBA 0, and proceeding on to the last physical sector on the drive. This is new in ATA-2 but has always been the one-and-only addressing mode in SCSI.

With LBA, each sector on the drive is numbered starting from 0. The number is a 28-bit binary number internally, which translates to a sector number from 0 to 267,386,879. Because each sector represents 512 bytes, this results in a maximum drive capacity of exactly 136.9GB. Unfortunately, the operating system still needs to see a translated CHS, so the BIOS determines how many sectors there are and comes up with Translated CHS to match. The BIOS CHS limits are 1,024 cylinders, 256 heads, and 63 sectors per track, which limits total drive capacity to 8.4GB.

In other words, this scheme breaks the 528MB barrier in essentially the same way as Extended CHS does. Because it is somewhat simpler to use a single linear number to address a sector on the hard disk compared to a CHS type address, LBA translation is the preferred method if the drive supports it.

Caution

A word of warning with these BIOS translation settings: If you switch between Standard CHS, Extended CHS, or LBA, the BIOS can change the (translated) geometry. This usually occurs only if the number of sectors reported by the Identify Drive command is fewer than 63 because LBA translations result in 63 sectors per track. The same thing can happen if you transfer a disk that has been formatted on an old, non-LBA computer to a new one that uses LBA. This causes the logical CHS geometry seen by the operating system to change and the data to appear in the wrong locations from where it actually is! This can cause you to lose access to your data if you are not careful. I always recommend recording the CMOS Setup screens associated with the hard disk configuration so you can properly match the setup of a drive to the settings to which it was originally set.

Breaking the 8.4GB Barrier

Systems using ATA drives have been plagued by size limitations because of ATA interface and BIOS issues. The first two limits were mostly BIOS related; the first was at 528MB and the second at 8.4GB using parameter translation.

Unfortunately, translating parameters works only within the limitations of the BIOS, which means that, although translation breaks the 528MB barrier, it runs into another barrier at 8.4GB. Therefore, translation is still limited by the BIOS maximum of 8.4GB support.

Supporting drives larger than that requires a whole new addressing scheme, which no longer uses the clumsy CHS numbers and instead uses only the LBA or sector number directly. Phoenix Technologies recognized this problem early on and, beginning in 1994, began publishing a document titled "BIOS Enhanced Disk Drive Specification," which addressed this problem with an elegant solution. Their idea in publishing was to get the other BIOS manufacturers to follow their lead so all the BIOSes would be compatible with each other.

To ensure further development and compatibility, after several revisions in 1996, Phoenix turned this document over to the National Committee on Information Technology Standards (NCITS) for further enhancement and certification as a standard called the "BIOS Enhanced Disk Drive Specification (EDD)." Starting in 1998, most of the other BIOS manufacturers began installing EDD support in their BIOSes, finally enabling support for ATA drives larger than 8.4GB. Coincidentally (or not), this support arrived just in time because ATA drives of that size and larger became available that year.

The EDD document describes new services provided by the BIOS to support storage devices of up to 2^{64} sectors, which results in a capacity of more than 9.44ZB (a zettabyte equals a trillion GB: 9.44×10^{21} or, to be more precise, 9,444,732,965,739,290,430,000 bytes!). Older BIOS services have a compatibility limit of 528MB and a theoretical limit of 8.4GB. Starting in mid-1998, most systems incorporated the enhanced BIOS services. Note that even though the BIOS can handle drives with up to 2^{64} sectors, an ATA drive is still currently limited in size to 2^{48} sectors, or 144,115,188GB (144PB) maximum.

According to this EDD specification, drives are accessed by the pure LBA number without any CHS translation, while still preserving limited backward compatibility with CHS for the first 8.4GB of the drive. EDD has support for up to 2^{64} total sectors. This works out to a drive capacity as shown in the following calculations:

$2^{64} = 1.84467440737095516 \times 10^{19}$ sectors

$\quad = 9.44473296573929043 \times 10^{21}$ bytes

$\quad = 9.4$ giga-tera (billion trillion) bytes!

Phoenix originally claimed that the EDD specification would hold us for another 15 years. However, at the rate of growth where drive capacity doubles every 1.5–2 years (Moore's Law), considering that 180GB ATA drives were available in 2001, this standard should take us at least through the year 2055, and possibly as far as the year 2073 before we need a new address scheme with more bits.

If your system BIOS dates to 1998 or later, you most likely have EDD support, which means support for drives as large as 136.9GB.

With the ATA-6 specification in 2001, a new 48-bit address scheme has been designed that extends the limits to 2^{48} sectors, which is 144.12PB (petabytes). Because the BIOS services allow up to 2^{64} sectors, the 144 petabyte limitation will be the lower of the two that will apply. Still, that should hold us for some time to come.

Note that if you use older software including utilities, applications, or even operating systems that rely exclusively on CHS parameters, they will see all drives over 8.4GB as 8.4GB only. You will need not only a newer BIOS, but also newer software designed to handle the direct LBA addressing to work with drives over 8.4GB.

Operating systems limitations with respect to drives over 8.4GB are shown in Table 7.11.

Table 7.11   Operating Systems Limitations

Operating System	Limitations for Hard Drive Size
DOS/Windows 3x	DOS 6.22 or lower cannot support drives greater than 8.4GB. DOS 7.0 or higher (included with Windows 95 or later) is required to recognize a drive over 8.4GB.
Windows 9X/Me	Windows 95a (original version) does support the INT13h extensions, which means it does support drives over 8.4GB; however, due to limitations of the FAT16 file system, the maximum individual partition size is limited to 2GB. Windows 95B / OSR2 or later (including Windows 98/Me) supports the INT13h extensions, which allows drives over 8.4GB, and also supports FAT32, which allows partition sizes up to the maximum capacity of the drive.

Table 7.11   Continued

Operating System	Limitations for Hard Drive Size
Windows NT	Windows NT 3.5x does not support drives greater than 8.4GB. Windows NT 4.0 does support drivers greater than 8.4GB; however, when a drive larger than 8.4GB is being used as the primary bootable device, Windows NT will not recognize more than 8.4GB. Microsoft has released Service Pack 4, which corrects this problem.
Windows 2000/XP	Windows 2000/XP supports drives greater than 8.4GB.
OS/2 Warp	Some versions of OS/2 are limited to a boot partition size of 3.1GB or 4.3GB. IBM has a Device Driver Pack upgrade that enables the boot partition to be as large as 8.4GB. The HPFS file system in OS/2 will support drives up to 64GB.
Novell	NetWare 5.0 or later supports drives greater than 8.4GB.

Faster Data Transfer

ATA-2/EIDE and ATA-3 define several high-performance modes for transferring data to and from the drive. These faster modes are the main part of the new specifications and were the main reason they were initially developed. The following section discusses these modes.

The PIO mode determines how fast data is transferred to and from the drive. In the slowest possible mode—PIO mode 0—the data cycle time cannot exceed 600 nanoseconds (ns). In a single cycle, 16 bits are transferred into or out of the drive, making the theoretical transfer rate of PIO Mode 0 (600ns cycle time) 3.3MB/sec. Most of the high-performance ATA-2 (EIDE) drives today support PIO Mode 4, which offers a 16.6MB/sec transfer rate.

Table 7.12 shows the PIO modes, with their respective transfer rates.

Table 7.12   PIO (Programmed I/O) Modes and Transfer Rates

PIO Mode	Bus Width (bits)	Cycle Speed (ns)	Bus Speed (MHz)	Cycles per Clock	Transfer Rate (MB/sec)	ATA Specification
0	16	600	1.67	1	3.33	ATA-1
1	16	383	2.61	1	5.22	ATA-1
2	16	240	4.17	1	8.33	ATA-1
3	16	180	5.56	1	11.11	ATA-2
4	16	120	8.33	1	16.67	ATA-2

ATA-2 was also referred to as EIDE (Enhanced IDE) or Fast-ATA

ns = nanoseconds (billionths of a second)

MB = million bytes

To run in Mode 3 or 4 requires that the IDE port on the system be a local bus port. This means that it must operate through either a VL-Bus or PCI bus connection. Most motherboards with ATA-2/EIDE support have dual IDE connectors on the motherboard, and most of them now allow full throughput. Most of the motherboard chipsets include the ATA interface in their South Bridge components, which in modern systems is tied into the PCI bus.

Older 486 and some early Pentium boards have only the primary connector running through the system's PCI local bus. The secondary connector on those boards usually runs through the ISA bus and therefore supports up to Mode 2 operation only.

When interrogated with an Identify Drive command, a hard disk returns, among other things, information about the PIO and DMA modes it is capable of using. Most enhanced BIOSes automatically set the correct mode to match the capabilities of the drive. If you set a mode faster than the drive can handle, data corruption results.

ATA-2 and newer drives also perform Block Mode PIO, which means they use the Read/Write Multiple commands that greatly reduce the number of interrupts sent to the host processor. This lowers the overhead, and the resulting transfers are even faster.

DMA Transfer Modes

ATA drives also support *Direct Memory Access (DMA)* transfers. DMA means that the data is transferred directly between drive and memory without using the CPU as an intermediary, as opposed to PIO. This has the effect of offloading much of the work of transferring data from the processor, in effect allowing the processor to do other things while the transfer is taking place.

There are two distinct types of direct memory access: singleword (8-bit) and multiword (16-bit) DMA. Singleword DMA modes were removed from the ATA-3 and later specifications and are obsolete. DMA modes are also sometimes called *busmaster* ATA modes because they use a host adapter that supports busmastering. Ordinary DMA relies on the legacy DMA controller on the motherboard to perform the complex task of arbitration, grabbing the system bus and transferring the data. In the case of busmastering DMA, all this is done by a higher-speed logic chip in the host adapter interface (which is also on the motherboard).

Systems using the Intel PIIX (PCI IDE ISA eXcelerator) and later South Bridge chips have the capability of supporting busmaster IDE. The singleword and doubleword busmaster IDE modes and transfer rates are shown in Tables 7.13 and 7.14.

Table 7.13   Singleword (8-bit) DMA Modes and Transfer Rates

8-bit DMA Mode	Bus Width (bits)	Cycle Speed (ns)	Bus Speed (MHz)	Cycles per Clock	Transfer Rate (MB/sec)	ATA Specification
0	16	960	1.04	1	2.08	ATA-1[1]
1	16	480	2.08	1	4.17	ATA-1[1]
2	16	240	4.17	1	8.33	ATA-1[1]

1. Singleword (8-bit) DMA modes were removed from the ATA-3 and later specifications.

Table 7.14   Multiword (16-bit) DMA Modes and Transfer Rates

16-bit DMA Mode	Bus Width (bits)	Cycle Speed (ns)	Bus Speed (MHz)	Cycles per Clock	Transfer Rate (MB/sec)	ATA Specification
0	16	480	2.08	1	4.17	ATA-1
1	16	150	6.67	1	13.33	ATA-2
2	16	120	8.33	1	16.67	ATA-2

ATA-2 was also referred to as EIDE (Enhanced IDE) or Fast-ATA.

Note that doubleword DMA modes are also called busmaster DMA modes by some manufacturers. Unfortunately, even the fastest doubleword DMA Mode 2 results in the same 16.67MB/sec transfer speed as PIO Mode 4, so DMA modes have never really caught on as being desirable. However, even though the transfer speed is the same as PIO because DMA offloads much of the work from the processor, overall system performance would be higher. Even so, multiword DMA modes were never very popular and have been superseded by the newer Ultra-DMA modes supported in ATA-4–compatible devices.

Table 7.15 shows the Ultra-DMA modes now supported in the ATA-4 and ATA-5 specifications.

Table 7.15   Ultra-DMA Support in ATA-4 and ATA-5

Ultra DMA Mode	Bus Width (bits)	Cycle Speed (ns)	Bus Speed (MHz)	Cycles per Clock	Transfer Rate (MB/sec)	ATA Specification
0	16	240	4.17	2	16.67	ATA-4
1	16	160	6.25	2	25.00	ATA-4
2	16	120	8.33	2	33.33	ATA-4
3	16	90	11.11	2	44.44	ATA-5
4	16	60	16.67	2	66.67	ATA-5
5	16	40	25.00	2	100.00	ATA-6

ATA-4 UDMA Mode 2 is sometimes called Ultra-ATA/33 or ATA-33.

ATA-5 UDMA Mode 4 is sometimes called Ultra-ATA/66 or ATA-66.

ATA-6 UDMA Mode 5 is sometimes called Ultra-ATA/100 or ATA-100.

ATAPI (ATA Packet Interface)

ATAPI is a standard designed to provide the commands needed for devices such as CD-ROMs and tape drives that plug into an ordinary ATA (IDE) connector. The principal advantage of ATAPI hardware is that it's cheap and works on your current adapter. For CD-ROMs, it has a somewhat lower CPU usage compared to proprietary adapters, but there's no performance gain otherwise. For tape drives, ATAPI has potential for superior performance and reliability compared to the popular floppy controller attached tape devices. ATAPI is also used to run other removable storage devices, such as the LS-120 superdisk drives and internal Iomega Zip and Jaz drives.

Although ATAPI CD-ROMs use the hard disk interface, this does not mean they look like ordinary hard disks; to the contrary, from a software point of view, they are a completely different kind of animal. They actually most closely resemble a SCSI device. All modern IDE CD-ROMs support the ATAPI protocols, and generally the terms are synonymous. In other words, an ATAPI CD-ROM is an IDE CD-ROM and vice versa.

Caution

ATAPI support is not found directly in the BIOS of many systems. Systems without ATAPI support in the BIOS cannot boot from an ATAPI CD-ROM, and you still must load a driver to use ATAPI under DOS or Windows. Windows 95 and later (including 98 and Me) and Windows NT (including Windows 2000 and XP) have native ATAPI support, and newer systems with ATAPI-aware BIOSes are now available, which allow booting from an ATAPI CD-ROM. Some versions of the Windows 98, NT, 2000, and XP CD-ROMs are directly bootable on those systems, greatly easing installation.

I normally recommend keeping different types of IDE devices on separate channels. Some older chipsets cannot support setting different transfer rates for different devices, which means the channel must be set to the speed of the slowest device. Because most CD-ROM and tape drives run at lower IDE mode speeds, this forces your hard disk to run more slowly if they share a single cable. Even if the chipset you have supports separate speed settings for devices on the same channel (cable), I still recommend keeping them separate because IDE does not normally support overlapping access, such as SCSI. So, when one drive is running, the other cannot be accessed. By keeping the CD-ROM and hard disk on separate channels, you can more effectively overlap accessing between them.

Serial ATA

With the introduction of ATA-6, it seems that the parallel ATA standard that has been in use for more than 10 years is running out of steam. Sending data at rates faster than 100MB/sec down a parallel ribbon cable is fraught with all kinds of problems because of signal timing, electromagnetic interference (EMI), and other integrity problems. The solution is in a new ATA interface called serial ATA, which is an evolutionary backward-compatible replacement for the parallel ATA physical storage interface. Serial ATA is backward compatible in that it is compatible with existing software, which will run on the new architecture without any changes. In other words, the existing BIOS, operating systems, and utilities that work on parallel ATA will also work on serial ATA. This means Serial ATA supports all existing ATA and ATAPI devices, including CD-ROM and CD-RW drives, DVD drives, tape devices, SuperDisk drives, and any other storage device currently supported by parallel ATA.

Of course, they do differ physically—that is, you won't be able to plug parallel ATA drives into serial ATA host adapters and vice versa. The physical changes are all for the better because serial ATA uses much thinner cables with only 7 pins that are easier to route inside the PC and easier to plug in with smaller redesigned cable connectors. The interface chip designs also are improved with fewer pins and lower voltages. These improvements are all designed to eliminate the design problems inherent in parallel ATA.

Serial ATA (SATA) won't be integrated into PCs overnight; however, it is clear to me that it will eventually replace parallel ATA as the de facto standard internal storage device interface found in PCs. The transition from ATA to SATA is a gradual one, and during this transition parallel ATA capabilities will continue to be available. I would also expect that with more than a 10-year history, parallel ATA devices will continue to be available even after most PCs have gone to SATA.

Development for Serial ATA started when the Serial ATA Working Group effort was announced at the Intel Developer Forum in February 2000. The initial members of the Serial ATA Working Group included APT Technologies, Dell, IBM, Intel, Maxtor, Quantum, and Seagate. The first serial ATA specification 1.0 was completed in November 2000, and can be downloaded from the Serial ATA Working Group Web site at http://www.serialata.org. Since forming, the group has added more than 60 Contributor and Adopter companies to the membership from all areas of industry. It is expected that by the beginning of 2002, serial ATA will be shipping in many new systems.

The performance of SATA is impressive. Currently, three versions of the standard are available, which all use the same cables and connectors; they differ only in transfer rate performance. Initially, only the first version will be available, but the roadmap to doubling and quadrupling performance from there has been clearly established. Table 7.15 shows the specifications for each of the three SATA versions.

Table 7.16   SATA Standards Specifications

Serial ATA Type	Bus Width (bits)	Bus Speed (MHz)	Data Cycles per Clock	Bandwidth (MB/sec)
SATA-150	1	1500	1	150
SATA-300	1	3000	1	300
SATA-600	1	6000	1	600

From the table, you can see that serial ATA sends data only a single bit at a time. The cable used has only 7 wires and is a very thin design, with keyed connectors only 14mm (0.55 inches) wide on each end. This eliminates problems with airflow around the wider parallel ATA ribbon cables. Each cable has connectors only at each end and connects the device directly to the host adapter (normally on the motherboard). There are no master/slave settings because each cable supports only a single device. The cable ends are interchangeable—the connector on the motherboard is the same as on the device, and both cable ends are identical. Maximum SATA cable length is 1 meter (39.37 inches), which is considerably longer than the 18-inch maximum for parallel ATA. Even with this thinner, longer, and less expensive cable, transfer rates initially of 150MB/sec (one and a half times greater than parallel ATA/100) and in the future up to 300MB/sec and even 600MB/sec are possible.

Serial ATA uses a special encoding scheme called 8B/10B to encode and decode data sent along the cable. The 8B/10B transmission code originally was developed (and patented) by IBM in the early 1980s for use in high-speed data communications. This encoding scheme is now used by many high-speed data transmission standards, including Gigabit Ethernet, Fibre Channel, FireWire, and others. The main purpose of the 8B/10B encoding scheme is to guarantee that there are never more than four 0s (or 1s) transmitted consecutively. This is a form of Run Length Limited (RLL) encoding called RLL 0,4 in which the 0 represents the minimum and the 4 represents the maximum number of consecutive 0s in each encoded character.

8B/10B encoding also ensures that there are never more than six or less than four 0s (or 1s) in a single encoded 10-bit character. Because 1s and 0s are sent as voltage changes on a wire, this ensures that the spacing between the voltage transitions sent by the transmitter will be fairly balanced, with a more regular and steady stream of pulses. This presents a more steady load on the circuits, increasing reliability. The conversion from 8-bit data to 10-bit encoded characters for transmission leaves a number of 10-bit patterns unused. Several of these additional patterns are used to provide flow control, delimit packets of data, perform error checking, or perform other special needs.

The physical transmission scheme for SATA uses what is called differential NRZ (Non-Return to Zero). This uses a balanced pair of wires, each carrying plus or minus 0.25V (one quarter-volt). The signals are sent differentially: If one wire in the pair is carrying +0.25V, the other wire is carrying -0.25V, where the differential voltage between the two wires is always 0.5V (a half-volt). This means that for a given voltage waveform, the opposite voltage waveform is sent along the adjacent wire. Differential transmission minimizes electromagnetic radiation and makes the signals easier to read on the receiving end.

A 15-pin power cable and power connector is optional with SATA, providing 3.3V power in addition to the 5V and 12V provided via the industry-standard 4-pin device power connectors. Although it has 15 pins, this new power connector design is only 24mm (0.945 inches). With 3 pins designated for each of the 3.3V, 5V, and 12V power levels, enough capacity exists for up to 4.5 amps of current at each voltage, which is ample for even the most power-hungry drives. For compatibility with existing power supplies, SATA drives can be made with either the original, standard 4-pin device power connector or the new 15-pin SATA power connector, or both.

Figure 7.6 shows what the new SATA signal and power connectors look like.

Figure 7.6   SATA (Serial ATA) signal and power connectors.

The pinouts for the Serial ATA data and optional power connectors are shown in Tables 7.17 and 7.18.

Table 7.17   Serial ATA (SATA) Data Connector Pinout

Signal Pin	Signal	Description
S1	Gnd	First mate
S2	A+	Host Transmit +
S3	A-	Host Transmit -
S4	Gnd	First mate
S5	B-	Host Receive -
S6	B+	Host Receive +
S7	Gnd	First mate

All pins are in a single row spaced 1.27mm (.050") apart.
All ground pins are longer so they will make contact before the signal/power pins to allow hot plugging.

Table 7.18   Serial ATA (SATA) Optional Power Connector Pinout

Power Pin	Signal	Description
P1	+3.3V	3.3V power
P2	+3.3V	3.3V power
P3	+3.3V	3.3V power

Table 7.18   Continued

Power Pin	Signal	Description
P4	Gnd	First mate
P5	Gnd	First mate
P6	Gnd	First mate
P7	+5V	5V power
P8	+5V	5V power
P9	+5V	5V power
P10	Gnd	First mate
P11	Gnd	First mate
P12	Gnd	First mate
P13	+12V	12V power
P14	+12V	12V power
P15	+12V	12V power

All pins are in a single row spaced 1.27mm (.050") apart.

All ground pins are longer so they will make contact before the signal/power pins to allow hot plugging.

Three power pins are used to carry 4.5 A maximum current for each voltage.

Configuration of serial ATA devices is also much simpler because the master/slave or cable select jumper settings used with parallel ATA are no longer necessary.

As with parallel ATA, serial ATA was designed to be the primary storage interface used inside a PC and was not designed to be used as an external interface. As such, SATA is not designed to compete with high-speed external device interfaces, such as SCSI, USB 2.0, or IEEE-1394 (FireWire). Therefore, I expect it to replace parallel ATA in systems over the next few years.

ATA RAID

RAID is an acronym for Redundant Array of Independent (or Inexpensive) Disks and was designed to improve the fault tolerance and performance of computer storage systems. RAID was first developed at the University of California at Berkeley in 1987, and was designed so that a group of smaller, less expensive drives could be interconnected with special hardware and software to make them appear as a single larger drive to the system. By using multiple drives to act as one drive, increases in fault tolerance and performance could be realized.

Initially, RAID was conceived to simply have all the individual drives in the array work together as a single larger drive with the combined storage space of all the individual drives added up. However, this actually reduced reliability and didn't do much for performance, either. For example, if you had four drives connected in an array acting as one drive, you would be four times as likely to experience a drive failure than if you used just a single larger drive. To improve on the reliability and performance, the Berkeley scientists proposed six levels (corresponding to different methods) of RAID. These levels provide varying emphasis on either fault tolerance (reliability), storage capacity, performance, or a combination of the three.

An organization called the RAID Advisory Board (RAB) was formed in July of 1992 to standardize, classify, and educate on the subject of RAID. They can be reached on the Web at http://www.raid-advisory.com. The RAB has developed specifications for RAID, a conformance program for the various RAID levels, and a classification program for RAID hardware.

Currently, seven standard RAID levels are defined by the RAID Advisory Board, called RAID 0 through 6. RAID normally is implemented by a RAID controller board, although software-only implementations are possible (but not recommended). The levels are as follows:

- *RAID Level 0—Striping.* File data is written simultaneously to multiple drives in the array, which act as a single larger drive. Offers high read/write performance but very low reliability. Requires a minimum of two drives to implement.

- *RAID Level 1—Mirroring.* Data written to one drive is duplicated on another, providing excellent fault tolerance (if one drive fails, the other will be used and no data lost), but no real increase in performance as compared to a single drive. Requires a minimum of two drives to implement (same capacity as one drive).

- *RAID Level 2—Bit-level ECC.* Data is split one bit at a time across multiple drives, and Error Correction Codes are written to other drives. Intended for storage devices that do not incorporate ECC internally (all SCSI and ATA drives have internal ECC). Provides high data rates with good fault tolerance, but large numbers of drives are required, and no commercial RAID 2 controllers or drives without ECC are available on the market that I am aware of.

- *RAID Level 3—Striped with parity.* Combines RAID Level 0 striping with an additional drive used for parity information. This RAID level is really an adaptation of RAID Level 0 that sacrifices some capacity, for the same number of drives. However, it also achieves a high level of data integrity or fault tolerance because data usually can be rebuilt if one drive fails. Requires a minimum of three drives to implement (two or more for data and one for parity).

- *RAID Level 4—Blocked data with parity.* Similar to RAID 3 except data is written in larger blocks to the independent drives, offering faster read performance with larger files. Requires a minimum of three drives to implement (two or more for data and one for parity).

- *RAID Level 5—Blocked data with distributed parity.* Similar to RAID 4 but offers improved performance by distributing the parity stripes over a series of hard drives. Requires a minimum of three drives to implement (two or more for data and one for parity).

- *RAID Level 6—Blocked data with double distributed parity.* Similar to RAID 5 except parity information is written twice using two different parity schemes to provide even better fault tolerance in case of multiple drive failures. Requires a minimum of four drives to implement (two or more for data and two for parity).

Additional RAID levels exist that are not supported by the RAID Advisory Board but which are instead custom implementations by specific companies. Note that the higher the number doesn't necessarily mean increased performance or fault tolerance; the numbered order of the RAID levels was entirely arbitrary.

Until recently, virtually all RAID controllers were SCSI based, meaning they used SCSI drives. For a professional setup, SCSI RAID is definitely the way to go because it combines the advantages of RAID with the advantages of SCSI—an interface that already was designed to support multiple drives. Now, however, ATA RAID controllers are available, allowing for even less expensive RAID implementations. These ATA RAID controllers usually are used in single-user systems for performance rather than reliability increases.

Most ATA RAID implementations are much simpler than the professional SCSI RAID adapters used on network file servers. ATA RAID is designed more for the individual who is seeking performance or simple drive mirroring for redundancy. When set up for performance, ATA RAID adapters run RAID Level 0, which incorporates data striping. Unfortunately, RAID 0 also sacrifices reliability such that if one drive fails, all data is lost. With RAID 0, performance scales up with the number of drives you add in the array. If you use four drives, you won't necessarily have four times the performance of a single drive, but it can be close to that for sustained transfers. Some overhead is still involved in the controller performing the striping and issues still exist with latency—that is, how long it takes to find the data—but performance will be higher than any single drive can normally achieve.

When set up for reliability, ATA RAID adapters generally run RAID Level 1, which is simple drive mirroring. All data written to one drive is written to the other. If one drive fails, the system can continue to work on the other drive. Unfortunately, this does not increase performance at all, and it also means you get to use only half of the available drive capacity. In other words, you must install two drives, but you get to use only one (the other is the mirror).

Combining performance with fault tolerance requires using one of the other RAID levels, such as 3 or 5. For example, virtually all professional RAID controllers used in network file servers are designed to use RAID Level 5. Controllers that implement RAID Level 5 are more expensive, and at least three drives must be connected. To improve reliability, but at a lower cost, many of the ATA RAID controllers enable combinations of the RAID levels—such as 0 and 1 combined. This usually requires four drives, two of which are striped together in a RAID Level 0 arrangement, which is then redundantly written to a second set of two drives in a RAID Level 1 arrangement. This enables you to have approximately double the performance of a single drive, and you have a backup set should one of the primary set fail.

Today, you can get IDE RAID controllers from companies such as Arco Computer Products, Iwill, Promise Technology, and more. A typical example of an ATA RAID controller is the Promise FastTrak 100/TX4. This controller enables up to four drives to be attached, and you can run them in RAID Level 0, 1, or 0+1 mode. This card also uses separate ATA data channels (cables) for each drive, allowing maximum performance. Promise Technology also has a less expensive ATA RAID card called the FastTrak 100/TX2, which has only two channels. You can still attach up to four drives, but because they share two ATA cables, performance isn't as good as if they were on separate cables. This is because only one drive can transfer on the cable at a time, which cuts performance in half.

If you are looking for an ATA RAID controller, things to look for include

- RAID levels supported (most support 0, 1, and 0+1 combined)
- Two or four channels
- Support for ATA/100 speeds
- Support for 33MHz or 66MHz PCI slots

If you want to experiment with RAID inexpensively, you can implement RAID without a custom controller when using certain higher-end (often server-based) operating systems. For example, Windows NT/2000 and XP Server operating systems provide a software implementation for RAID using both striping and mirroring. In these operating systems, the Disk Administrator tool is used to set up and control the RAID functions, as well as to reconstruct the volume when a failure has occurred. Normally, though, if you are building a server in which the ultimate in performance and reliability are desired, you should look for ATA or SCSI RAID controllers that support RAID Level 3 or 5.

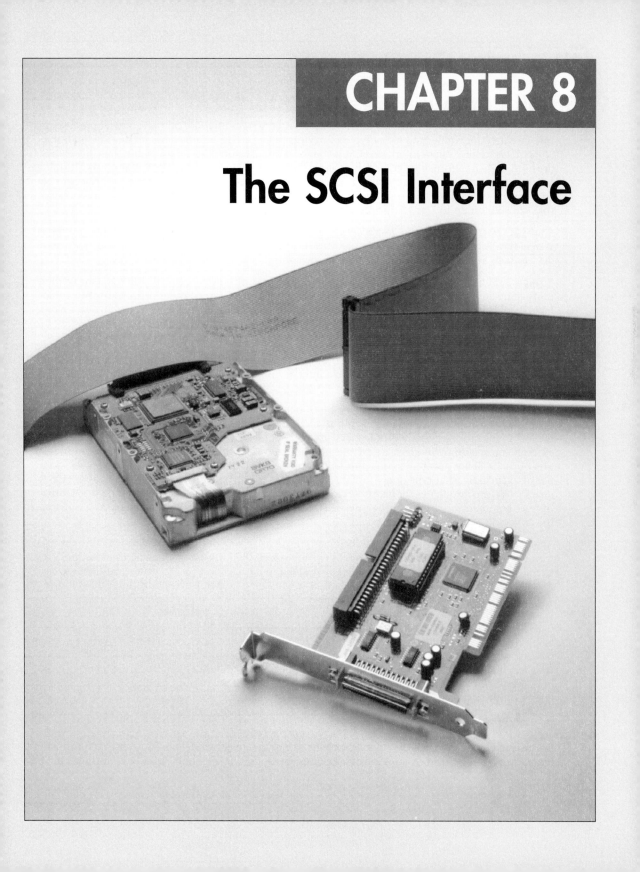

CHAPTER 8

The SCSI Interface

Small Computer System Interface

SCSI (pronounced "scuzzy") stands for Small Computer System Interface and is a general-purpose interface used for connecting many types of devices to a PC. This interface has its roots in SASI, the Shugart Associates System Interface. SCSI is the most popular interface for attaching high-speed disk drives to higher-performance PCs, such as workstations or network servers. SCSI is also very flexible; it is not only a disk interface, but is also a systems-level interface allowing many types of devices to be connected. SCSI is a bus that supports as many as 7 or 15 total devices. Multichannel adapters exist that can support up to 7 or 15 devices per channel.

The SCSI controller, called the *host adapter*, functions as the gateway between the SCSI bus and the PC system bus. Each device on the bus has a controller built in. The SCSI bus does not talk directly with devices such as hard disks; instead, it talks to the controller that is built into the drive.

A single SCSI bus can support as many as 8 or 16 physical units, usually called SCSI *IDs*. One of these units is the SCSI host adapter card in your PC; the other 7 or 15 can be other peripherals. You could have hard disks, tape drives, CD-ROM drives, a graphics scanner, or other devices attached to a single SCSI host adapter. Most systems can support up to four host adapters, each with up to 15 devices, for a total of 60 devices! There are even dual channel adapters that could double that figure.

SCSI is a fast interface, generally suited to high-performance workstations, servers, or anywhere the ultimate in performance for a storage system interface is needed. The latest Ultra4 (Ultra320) SCSI version supports transfer speeds of up to 320MB/sec!

When you purchase a SCSI device such as a SCSI hard disk, you usually are purchasing the device, controller, and SCSI adapter in one circuit; as such the device is ready to connect directly to the SCSI bus. This type of drive usually is called an *embedded* SCSI device—the SCSI interface is built in. For example, most SCSI hard drives are technically the same as their IDE counterparts except for the addition of the SCSI bus adapter circuits (normally a single chip) added to the controller board. You do not need to know what type of controller is inside the SCSI drive because your system cannot talk directly to the controller as though it were plugged into the system bus, like on a standard IDE drive. Instead, communications go through the SCSI host adapter installed in the system bus. You can access the drive only with the SCSI protocols.

Apple originally rallied around SCSI as being an inexpensive way out of the bind in which it put itself with the Macintosh. When the engineers at Apple realized their mistake in making the Macintosh a closed system (with no expansion slots), they decided that the easiest way to gain expandability was to build a SCSI port into the system, which is how external peripherals were originally added to the slotless Macs. Of course, in keeping with Apple tradition, they used a nonstandard SCSI connector. Now that Apple is designing systems with expansion slots, Universal Serial Bus (USB), and FireWire (iLINK or IEEE-1394), SCSI has been dropped from most Macs as a built-in option. Because PC systems always have been expandable, the push toward SCSI has not been as urgent. With up to eight or more bus slots supporting various devices and controllers in PC-compatible systems, it seemed as though SCSI was not as necessary for system expansion. In fact, with modern PCs sporting inexpensive built-in USB ports for external expansion, in most cases SCSI devices are necessary only when top performance is a critical issue.

SCSI has become popular in the PC-based workstation market because of the performance and expandability it offers. One block that stalled acceptance of SCSI in the early PC marketplace was the lack of a real standard; the SCSI standard originally was designed by one company and then turned into a committee-controlled public standard. Since then, no single manufacturer has controlled it.

Note

Most SCSI host adapters bundled with hardware, such as graphics scanners or SCSI CD-ROM, CD-R, or CD-RW drives, will not include all the features needed to support multiple SCSI devices or bootable SCSI hard drives. This has nothing to do with any limitations in the SCSI specification. The situation is simply that the manufacturer has included the most stripped-down version of a SCSI adapter available to save money. It has all the functionality necessary to support the device it came with, but nothing else. Fortunately, with the right adapter and drivers, one SCSI card could support all the SCSI devices in a system from hard drives to optical drives, scanners, tape drives, and more.

In the beginning, SCSI adapters lacked the capability to boot from hard disks on the SCSI bus. Booting from these drives and using a variety of operating systems was a problem that resulted from the lack of a software interface standard. The standard BIOS software in PC systems is designed to talk to ST-506/412, ESDI, or ATA (IDE) hard disks and devices. SCSI is so different from ATA/IDE that a new set of ROM BIOS routines is necessary to support the system so it can self-boot. Also, this BIOS support is unique to the SCSI host adapter you are using; so, unless the host adapter is built into your motherboard, this support won't be found in your motherboard BIOS. Instead, SCSI host adapters are available with BIOS support for SCSI hard disk drives right on the SCSI host adapter itself.

Note

For more information about the ST-506/412 Interface and the ESDI Interface, see "ST-506/412 Interface" and "ESDI Interface," respectively, in the Technical Reference section of the CD accompanying this book. An expanded discussion of both technologies can be found in *Upgrading and Repairing PCs, 6th Edition*, which is included in its entirety in PDF format on the CD with this book.

Because of the lead taken by Apple in developing systems software (operating systems and ROM) support for SCSI, peripherals connect to Apple systems in fairly standard ways. Until recently, this kind of standard-setting leadership was lacking for SCSI in the PC world. This situation changed dramatically with Windows 95 and later versions, which include drivers for most popular SCSI adapters and peripherals on the market. These days, Windows 98/Me and Windows 2000 include even more drivers and support for SCSI adapters and devices built in.

Many PC manufacturers have standardized SCSI for high-end systems. In these systems, a SCSI host adapter card is placed in one of the slots, or the system has a SCSI host adapter built into the motherboard. This arrangement is similar in appearance to the IDE interface because a single cable runs from the motherboard to the SCSI drive. SCSI supports as many as 7 or 15 additional devices per bus (some of which might not be hard disks), whereas IDE supports only 4 devices (2 per controller). Additionally, SCSI supports more types of devices other than hard disks than IDE supports. IDE devices must be a hard disk, an IDE-type CD-ROM drive, a tape drive, an LS-120 SuperDisk drive, a Zip drive, and so on. Systems with SCSI drives are easy to upgrade because virtually any third-party SCSI drive will plug in and function.

ANSI SCSI Standards

The SCSI standard defines the physical and electrical parameters of a parallel I/O bus used to connect computers and peripheral devices in daisy-chain fashion. The standard supports devices such as disk drives, tape drives, and CD-ROM drives. The original SCSI standard (ANSI X3.131-1986) was approved in 1986, SCSI-2 was approved in January 1994, and the first portions of SCSI-3 were approved in 1995. Note that SCSI-3 has evolved into an enormous standard with numerous sections and is an evolving, growing standard still very much under development. Because it has been broken down into multiple standards, there really is no single SCSI-3 standard.

The SCSI interface is defined as a standard by ANSI (American National Standards Institute), specifically by a committee currently known as T10. T10 is a technical committee of the National Committee on Information Technology Standards (NCITS, pronounced "insights"). NCITS is accredited by ANSI and operates under rules approved by ANSI. These rules are designed to ensure that voluntary standards are developed by the consensus of industry groups. NCITS develops information-processing system standards, whereas ANSI approves the process under which they are developed and publishes them. Working draft copies of all SCSI-related standards can be downloaded from the T10 Technical Committee site at `http://www.t10.org`.

One problem with the original SCSI-1 document was that many of the commands and features were optional, and there was little or no guarantee that a particular peripheral would support the expected commands. This problem caused the industry as a whole to define a set of 18 basic SCSI commands called the Common Command Set (CCS) to become the minimum set of commands supported by all peripherals. CCS became the basis for what is now the SCSI-2 specification.

Along with formal support for CCS, SCSI-2 provided additional definitions for commands to access CD-ROM drives (and their sound capabilities), tape drives, removable drives, optical drives, and several other peripherals. In addition, an optional higher speed called Fast SCSI-2 and a 16-bit version called Wide SCSI-2 were defined. Another feature of SCSI-2 is *command queuing*, which enables a device to accept multiple commands and execute them in the order that the device deems to be most efficient. This feature is most beneficial when you are using a multitasking operating system that could be sending several requests on the SCSI bus at the same time.

The X3T9 group approved the SCSI-2 standard as X3.131-1990 in August 1990, but the document was recalled in December 1990 for changes before final ANSI publication. Final approval for the SCSI-2 document was finally made in January 1994, although it has changed little from the original 1990 release. The SCSI-2 document is now called ANSI X3.131-1994. The official document is available from Global Engineering Documents or the ANSI committee—both are listed in the Vendor List on the CD. You can also download working drafts of these documents from the T10 Technical Committee home page as listed previously.

Most companies indicate that their host adapters follow both the ANSI X3.131-1986 (SCSI-1) and the X3.131-1994 (SCSI-2) standards. Note that because virtually all parts of SCSI-1 are supported in SCSI-2, virtually any SCSI-1 device is also considered SCSI-2 by default. Many manufacturers advertise that their devices are SCSI-2, but this does not mean they support any of the additional optional features that were incorporated in the SCSI-2 revision.

For example, an optional part of the SCSI-2 specification includes a fast synchronous mode that doubles the standard synchronous transfer rate from 5MB/sec to 10MB/sec. This Fast SCSI transfer mode can be combined with 16-bit Wide SCSI for transfer rates of up to 20MB/sec. An optional 32-bit version was defined in SCSI-2, but component manufacturers have shunned this as too expensive. In essence, 32-bit SCSI was a stillborn specification, as it was withdrawn from the SCSI-3 standard. Most SCSI implementations are 8-bit standard SCSI or 16-bit Fast/Wide SCSI. Even devices that support none of the Fast or Wide modes can still be considered SCSI-2.

SCSI-3 is broken down into a number of standards. The SCSI Parallel Interface (SPI) standard controls the parallel interconnection between SCSI devices, which is mostly what we are talking about here. So far several versions of SPI have existed, including SPI, SPI-2, SPI-3, and SPI-4. Versions through SPI-3 have been published, whereas SPI-4 is still in draft form.

What can be confusing is that several terms can be used to describe the newer SPI standards, as shown in Table 8.1.

Table 8.1   SPI (SCSI Parallel Interface) Standards

SCSI-3 Standard	Also Known As	Speed	Throughput
SPI	Ultra SCSI	Fast-20	20/40MB/sec
SPI-2	Ultra2 SCSI	Fast-40	40/80MB/sec
SPI-3	Ultra3 SCSI	Fast-80DT	160MB/sec
SPI-4	Ultra4 SCSI	Fast-160DT	320MB/sec

To add to the confusion, SPI-3 or Ultra3 SCSI is also called Ultra160 or Ultra160+, and SPI-4 or Ultra4 SCSI is also called Ultra320 or Ultra320+ by some companies. The Ultra160/320 designation refers to any device that includes the first three of the five main features from the Ultra3/4 SCSI specification. Ultra160/320+ refers to any device that supports all five main features of Ultra3/4 SCSI.

Table 8.2 shows the maximum transfer rates for the SCSI bus at various speeds and widths and the cable type required for the specific transfer widths.

Note

The A cable is the standard 50-pin SCSI cable, whereas the P cable is a 68-pin cable designed for 16-bit transfers. High Voltage Differential (HVD) signaling was never popular and is now considered obsolete. LVD (Low Voltage Differential) signaling is used in the Ultra2 and Ultra3 modes to increase performance and cabling lengths. Pinouts for the cable connections are listed in this chapter in Tables 8.3–8.6.

SCSI is both forward and backward compatible, meaning one can run faster devices on buses with slower host adapters or vice versa. In each case, the entire bus will run at the lowest common denominator speed. In fact, as was stated earlier, virtually any SCSI-1 device can also legitimately be called SCSI-2 (or even SCSI-3) because most of the improvements in the later versions are optional. Of course, you can't take advantage of the faster modes on an older, slower host adapter. By the same token, you can purchase an Ultra3 capable SCSI host adapter and still run older standard SCSI devices. You can even mix standard 8-bit and wide 16-bit devices on the same bus using cable adapters.

SCSI-1

SCSI-1 was the first implementation of SCSI. It was officially known as ANSI X3.131-1986. The major features of SCSI-1 were

- 8-bit parallel bus
- 5MHz asynchronous or synchronous operation
- 4MB/sec (asynchronous) or 5MB/sec (synchronous) throughput
- 50-pin cables with low-density pin-header internal and Centronics-style external connectors
- Single-ended (SE) unbalanced transmission
- Passive termination
- Optional bus parity

SCSI-1 is now considered obsolete; in fact, the standard has been withdrawn by ANSI and replaced by SCSI-2.

Table 8.2   SCSI Types, Data-Transfer Rates, and Cables

SCSI Standard	SCSI Technology	Marketing Term	Clock Speed (MHz)	Transfer Width
SCSI-1	Async	Asynchronous	5	8-bit
SCSI-1	Fast-5	Synchronous	5	8-bit
SCSI-2	Fast-5/Wide	Wide	5	16-bit
SCSI-2	Fast-10	Fast	10	8-bit
SCSI-2	Fast-10/Wide	Fast/Wide	10	16-bit
SPI (SCSI-3)	Fast-20	Ultra	20	8-bit
SPI (SCSI-3)	Fast-20/Wide	Ultra/Wide	20	16-bit
SPI-2 (SCSI-3)	Fast-40	Ultra2	40	8-bit
SPI-2 (SCSI-3)	Fast-40/Wide	Ultra2/Wide	40	16-bit
SPI-3 (SCSI-3)	Fast-80DT	Ultra3 (Ultra160)	40[3]	16-bit
SPI-4 (SCSI-3)	Fast-160DT	Ultra4 (Ultra320)	80[3]	16-bit

Not including the host adapter.

Cable Lengths are in meters: 25M = 80ft., 12M = 40ft., 6M = 20ft., 3M = 10ft., 1.5M = 5ft.

SE = Single-ended signaling;

HVD = High Voltage Differential signaling, obsolete

LVD = Low Voltage Differential signaling

SPI = SCSI Parallel Interface, part of SCSI-3

SCSI-2

SCSI-2 is officially known as ANSI X3.131-1994. The SCSI-2 specification is essentially an improved version of SCSI-1 with some parts of the specification tightened and several new features and options added. Normally, SCSI-1 and SCSI-2 devices are compatible, but SCSI-1 devices ignore the additional features in SCSI-2.

Some of the changes in SCSI-2 are very minor. For example, SCSI-1 allowed SCSI bus parity to be optional, whereas parity must be implemented in SCSI-2. Parity is an extra bit that is sent as a verification bit to ensure that the data is not corrupted. Another requirement is that initiator devices, such as host adapters, provide terminator power to the interface; most devices already did so.

SCSI-2 also added several optional features:

■ Fast SCSI (10MHz)

■ Wide SCSI (16-bit transfers)

■ Command queuing

■ New commands

■ High-density, 50-pin cable connectors

■ Active (Alternative 2) termination for improved single-ended (SE) transmission

■ High Voltage Differential (HVD) transmission (incompatible with SE on the same bus) for longer bus lengths

Transfer Speed (MB/s)	Max. No. of Devices*	Cable Type	Max. Length (SE)	Max. Length (HVD)	Max. Length (LVD)
4	7	A (50-pin)	6M	25M	-
5	7	A (50-pin)	6M	25M	-
10	15	P (68-pin)	6M	25M	-
10	7	A (50-pin)	3M	25M	-
20	15	P (68-pin)	3M	25M	-
20	7	A (50-pin)	3/1.5M[1]	25M	-
40	7	P (68-pin)	3/1.5M[1]	25M	-
40	7	A (50-pin)	-	-	12M[2]
80	15	P (68-pin)	-	-	12M[2]
160	15	P (68-pin)	-	-	12M[2]
320	15	P (68-pin)	-	-	12M[2]

DT = Double transition, or two transfers per clock cycle, 16-bit only

1 = Ultra SCSI cable total length is restricted to 1.5M if more than 3 devices exist on the bus (not including the host adapter). A maximum of 7 devices is allowed.

2 = A 25M cable may be used if only one device exists (point-to-point interconnect).

3 = Ultra3 (Ultra160) and Ultra4 (Ultra320) SCSI transfer twice per clock cycle and are 16-bit only.

Wide SCSI enables parallel data transfer at a bus width of 16 bits. The wider connection requires a new cable design. The standard 50-conductor, 8-bit cable is called the A cable. SCSI-2 originally defined a special 68-conductor B cable that was supposed to be used in conjunction with the A cable for 32-bit wide transfers. However, because of a lack of industry support and the added expenses involved, 32-bit SCSI was never actually implemented and was finally removed as a part of the SCSI-3 specifications. Therefore, two different types of SCSI cables are now available, called the A cable and the P cable. A cables are any SCSI cables with 50-pin connectors, whereas P cables are any SCSI cables with 68-pin connectors. You need a P cable if you are connecting a Wide SCSI device and want it to work in 16-bit mode. The P cable was not officially included in the standard until SCSI-3.

Fast SCSI refers to high-speed synchronous transfer capability. Fast SCSI achieves a 10MB/sec transfer rate on the standard 8-bit SCSI cabling. When combined with a 16-bit Wide SCSI interface, this configuration results in data-transfer rates of 20MB/sec (called Fast/Wide).

The high-density connectors enable smaller, more efficient connector and cable designs.

In SCSI-1, an initiator device, such as a host adapter, was limited to sending one command per device. In SCSI-2, the host adapter can send as many as 256 commands to a single device, which will store and process those commands internally before responding on the SCSI bus. The target device even can resequence the commands to allow for the most efficient execution or performance possible. This is especially useful in multitasking environments, such as OS/2 and Windows NT, which can take advantage of this feature.

SCSI-2 took the Common Command Set that was being used throughout the industry and made it an official part of the standard. The CCS was designed mainly for disk drives and did not include specific commands designed for other types of devices. In SCSI-2, many of the old commands are reworked, and several new commands have been added. New command sets have been added for CD-ROMs, optical drives, scanners, communications devices, and media changers (jukeboxes).

The single-ended SCSI bus depends on very tight termination tolerances to function reliably. Unfortunately, the original 132-ohm passive termination defined in the SCSI-1 document was not designed for use at the higher synchronous speeds now possible. These passive terminators can cause signal reflections to generate errors when transfer rates increase or when more devices are added to the bus. SCSI-2 defines an active (voltage-regulated) terminator that lowers termination impedance to 110 ohms and improves system integrity. Note that LVD SCSI requires special LVD terminators. If you use SE terminators on a bus with LVD devices, they either won't work or, if they are multimode devices, will default to SE operation.

These features are not required; they are optional under the SCSI-2 specification. If you connect a standard SCSI host adapter to a Fast SCSI drive, for example, the interface will work, but only at standard SCSI speeds.

SCSI-3

SCSI-3 is a term used to describe a set of standards currently being developed. Simply put, it is the next generation of documents a product conforms to. Unlike SCSI-1 and SCSI-2, SCSI-3 is not one document that covers all the layers and interfaces of SCSI, but is instead a collection of documents that covers the primary commands, specific command sets, and electrical interfaces and protocols. The command sets include hard disk interface commands, commands for tape drives, controller commands for RAID (Redundant Array of Inexpensive Drives), and other commands as well. There is also an overall SCSI Architectural Model (SAM) for the physical and electrical interfaces, as well as a SCSI Parallel Interface standard that controls the form of SCSI most commonly used. Each document within the standard is now a separate publication with its own revision level—for example, within SCSI-3 three different versions of the SCSI Parallel Interface have been published. Normally we don't refer to SCSI-3 anymore as a specific interface and instead refer to the specific subsets of SCSI-3, such as SPI-3 (Ultra3 SCSI).

The main additions to SCSI-3 include

- Ultra2 (Fast-40) SCSI
- Ultra3 (Fast-80DT) SCSI
- Ultra4 (Fast-160DT) SCSI
- New Low Voltage Differential signaling
- Elimination of High Voltage Differential signaling

Breaking up SCSI-3 into many smaller individual standards has enabled the standard as a whole to develop more quickly. The individual substandards can now be published rather than waiting for the entire standard to be approved.

Figure 8.1 shows the main parts of SCSI-3.

The primary changes being seen in the marketplace from SCSI-3 are the new Fast-40 (Ultra2) and Fast-80DT (Ultra3) high-speed drives and adapters. These have taken the performance of SCSI up to 160MB/sec. Also new is the LVD electrical standard, which allows for greater cable lengths. The older High Voltage Differential signaling has been removed from the standard.

A number of people are confused over the speed variations in SCSI. Part of the problem is that speeds are quoted as either clock speeds (MHz) or transfer speeds. With 8-bit transfers, you get one byte per transfer, so if the clock is 40MHz (Fast-40 or Ultra2 SCSI), the transfer speed is 40MB/sec. On the other hand, if you are using a Wide (16-bit) interface, the transfer speed doubles to 80MB/sec, even though the clock speed remains at 40MHz. With Fast-80DT, the bus speed technically remains at 40MHz; however, two transfers are made per cycle, resulting in a throughput speed of 160MB/sec. The same is true for Ultra4 SCSI, which runs at 80MHz and transfers 2 bytes at a time and two transfers per cycle. Ultra4 is also called Ultra320 and is the fastest form of parallel SCSI today.

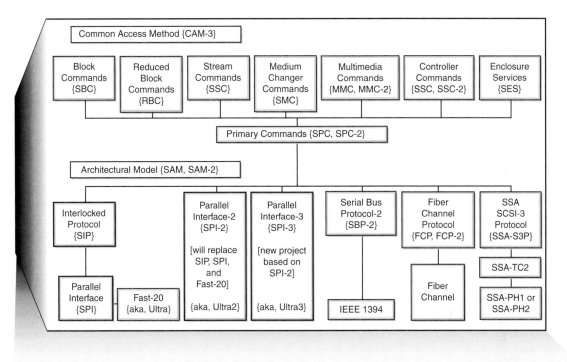

Figure 8.1 The SCSI-3 architecture.

Finally, confusion exists because SCSI speeds or modes are often discussed using either the official terms, such as Fast-10, Fast-20, Fast-40, and Fast-80DT, or the equivalent marketing terms, such as Fast, Ultra, Ultra2, and Ultra3 (also called Ultra160). Refer to Table 8.2 for a complete breakdown of SCSI official terms, marketing terms, and speeds.

The further evolution of the most commonly used form of SCSI is defined under the SPI standards within SCSI-3. The SPI standards are detailed in the following sections.

SPI or Ultra SCSI

The SCSI Parallel Interface standard was the first SCSI standard that fell under the SCSI-3 designation and is officially known as ANSI X3.253-1995. SPI is also called Ultra SCSI by most marketing departments and defines the parallel bus electrical connections and signals. A separate document called the SCSI Interlock Protocol (SIP) defines the parallel command set. SIP was included in the later SPI-2 and SPI-3 revisions and is no longer carried as a separate document. The main features added in SPI or Ultra SCSI are

- Fast-20 (Ultra) speeds (20MB/sec or 40MB/sec)
- 68-pin P-cable and connectors defined for Wide SCSI

SPI initially included speeds up to Fast SCSI (10MHz), which enables transfer speeds up to 20MB/sec using a 16-bit wide bus. Later, Fast-20 (20MHz), commonly known as Ultra SCSI, was added through an addendum document (ANSI X3.277-1996), allowing a throughput of 40MB/sec on a 16-bit wide bus (commonly called Ultra/Wide).

SPI-2 or Ultra2 SCSI

SPI-2 is also called Ultra2 SCSI, officially published as ANSI X3.302-1998, and adds several features to the prior versions:

- Fast-40 (Ultra2) speeds (40MB/sec or 80MB/sec)
- Low Voltage Differential signaling
- Single Connector Attachment (SCA-2) connectors
- 68-pin Very High Density Connector (VHDC)

The most notable of these is a higher speed called Fast-40, which is commonly called Ultra2 SCSI and runs at 40MHz. On a narrow (8-bit) bus, this results in 40MB/sec throughput, whereas on a wide bus (16-bit), this results in 80MB/sec throughput and is commonly referred to as Ultra2/Wide.

To achieve these speeds, a new electrical interface called LVD must be used. The slower single-ended electrical interface is only good for speeds up to Fast-20. Fast-40 mode requires LVD operation. The LVD signaling also enables longer cable lengths up to 12 meters with multiple devices or 25 meters with only one device. LVD and SE devices can share the same cable, but in that case the bus will run in SE mode and be restricted in length to as little as 1.5 meters in Fast-20 mode. LVD operation requires special LVD-only or LVD/SE multimode terminators. If multimode terminators are used, the same terminators will work on either SE or LVD buses.

The SPI-2 standard also includes SIP (SCSI Interlink Protocol) and defines the Single Connector Attachment (SCA-2) 80-pin connector for hot-swappable drive arrays. There is also a new 68-pin Very High Density Connector (VHDC), which is smaller than the previous types.

SCSI Signaling

"Normal," or standard, SCSI uses a signaling technique called single-ended signaling. SE signaling is a low-cost technique, but it also has performance and noise problems.

Single-ended signaling is also called unbalanced signaling. Each signal is carried on a pair of wires, normally twisted to help reduce noise. With SE one of the pair is grounded, often to a common ground for all signals, and the other carries the actual voltage transitions. It is up to a receiver at the other end of the cable to detect the voltage transitions, which are really just changes in voltage.

Unfortunately, this type of unbalanced signaling is very prone to problems with noise, electromagnetic interference, and ground leakage; these problems get worse the longer the cable is. This is the reason Ultra SCSI was limited to such short maximum bus lengths—as little as 1 1/2 meters or 5 feet.

When SCSI was first developed, a signaling technique called High Voltage Differential signaling was also introduced into the standard. Differential signaling, also known as *balanced signaling*, is still done with a pair of wires. In fact, the first in the pair carries the same type of signal that single-ended SCSI carries. The second in the pair, however, carries the logical inversion of that signal. The receiving device detects the difference between the pair (hence the name differential). By using the wires in a balanced pair, the receiver no longer needs to detect voltage magnitude, only the differential between voltage in two wires. This is much easier for circuits to do reliably, which makes them less susceptible to noise and enables greater cable length. Because of this, differential SCSI can be used with cable lengths of up to 25 meters, whereas single-ended SCSI is good only for 6 meters maximum, or as little as 1 1/2 meters in the faster modes.

Figure 8.2 shows the circuit differences between balanced (differential) and unbalanced (single-ended) transmission lines.

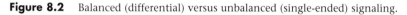

Figure 8.2   Balanced (differential) versus unbalanced (single-ended) signaling.

Unfortunately, the original standard for HVD signaling called for high voltage differentials between the two wires. This means that small, low-power, single-chip interfaces using HVD signaling could not be developed. Instead, circuits using several chips were required. This works at both ends, meaning both the host adapter and device circuitry had to be larger and more expensive.

Another problem with HVD SCSI is that although the cables and connectors look (and are) exactly the same as for SE SCSI, both types of devices cannot be mixed on the same bus. If they are, the high voltage from the HVD device will burn out the receiver circuits on all SE devices attached to the bus. In other words, the result will be smoked hardware—not a pretty sight.

Because SE SCSI worked well enough for the speeds that were necessary up until recently, HVD SCSI signaling never really caught on. It was used only in minicomputers and very rarely, if at all, in PCs. Because of this, the extra cost of this interface, and the fact that it is electrically incompatible with standard SE SCSI devices, HVD signaling was removed from the SCSI specification in the latest SCSI-3 documents. So, as far as we are concerned, it is obsolete.

Still, a need existed for a more reliable signaling technique that would allow for longer cable lengths. The answer came in the form of LVD signaling. By designing a new version of the differential interface, it can be made to work with inexpensive and low-power SCSI chips. Another advantage of LVD is that because it uses low voltage, if you plug an LVD device into an SE SCSI bus, nothing will be damaged. In fact, as an optional part of the LVD standard, the LVD device can be designed as a multimode device, which means it works on both SE and LVD buses. In the case of installing a multimode LVD device into an SE bus, the device detects that it is installed in an SE bus and defaults to SE mode.

This means that all multimode LVD/SE SCSI devices can be used on either LVD or SE SCSI buses. However, when on a bus with even one other SE device, all the LVD devices on the bus run only in SE mode. Because SE mode supports only SCSI speeds of up to 20MHz (Fast-20 or UltraSCSI) and cable lengths of up to 1 1/2 or 3 meters, the devices also work only at that speed or lower; you also might have problems with longer cables. Although you can purchase an Ultra3 SCSI multimode LVD/SE drive and install it on a SCSI bus along with single-ended devices, you will certainly be wasting the capabilities of the faster device.

Note that all Ultra2 and Ultra3 devices support LVD signaling because that is the only way they can be run at the Ultra2 (40MHz) or Ultra3 (80MHz) speeds. Ultra SCSI (20MHz) or slower devices can support LVD signaling, but in most cases LVD is synonymous with Ultra2 or Ultra3 only.

Table 8.2, shown earlier, lists all the SCSI speeds and maximum lengths for each speed using the supported signaling techniques for that speed.

Because the connectors are the same for SE, HVD, LVD, or multimode SE/LVD devices, and because putting an HVD device on any bus with SE or LVD devices causes damage, it would be nice to be able to tell them apart. One way is to look for a special symbol on the unit; the industry has adopted different universal symbols for single-ended and differential SCSI. Figure 8.3 shows these symbols.

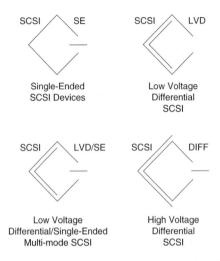

Figure 8.3   Universal symbol icons identifying SE, LVD, multimode LVD/SE, and HVD devices.

If you do not see such symbols, you can tell whether you have a High Voltage Differential device by using an ohmmeter to check the resistance between pins 21 and 22 on the device connector:

- On a single-ended or Low Voltage Differential device, the pins should be tied together and also tied to the ground.

- On a High Voltage Differential device, the pins should be open or have significant resistance between them.

Although you will blow up stuff if you plug HVD devices into LVD or SE buses, this generally should not be a problem because virtually all devices used in the PC environment are SE, LVD, or LVD/SE. HVD has essentially been rendered obsolete because it has been removed from the SCSI standard with Ultra3 SCSI (SPI-3).

SPI-3 or Ultra3 SCSI (Ultra160)

SPI-3, also known as Ultra3 or Ultra160 SCSI, builds on the previous standard and doubles the speed again to Fast-80DT (double transition). This results in a maximum throughput of 160MB/sec. The main features added to SPI-3 (Ultra3) are

- DT (double transition) clocking

- CRC (Cyclic Redundancy Check)

- Domain validation

- Packetization

- Quick Arbitrate and Select (QAS)

Double transition clocking sends data on both the rising and falling edges of the REQ/ACK clock. This enables Ultra3 SCSI to transfer data at 160MB/sec, while still running at a bus clock rate of 40MHz. This mode is defined for 16-bit wide bus use only.

Cyclic Redundancy Checking (CRC) is a form of error checking incorporated into Ultra3 SCSI. Previous versions of SCSI used simple parity checking to detect transmission errors. CRC is a much more robust form of error-detection capability that is far superior for operation at higher speeds.

Domain validation allows better negotiation of SCSI transfer speeds and modes. With prior SCSI versions, when the bus is initialized, the host adapter sends an INQUIRY command at the lowest 5MHz speed to each device to determine which data-transfer rate the device can use. The problem is that even though both the host adapter and device might support a given speed, there is no guarantee that the interconnection between the devices will reliably work at that speed. If a problem occurs, the device becomes inaccessible. With domain validation, after a maximum transfer speed is negotiated between the host and the device, it is then tested at that rate. If errors are detected, the rate is stepped down until the connection tests error-free. This is similar to how modems negotiate transmission speeds before communicating and will go a long way toward improve the flexibility and perceived reliability of SCSI.

Packetization is a protocol that enables information to be transferred between SCSI devices in a much more efficient manner. Traditional parallel SCSI uses multiple bus phases to communicate different types of information between SCSI devices: one for command information, two for messages, one for status, and two for data. In contrast, packetized SCSI communicates all this information by using only two phases: one for each direction. This dramatically reduces the command and protocol overhead, especially as higher and higher speeds are used.

Packetized SCSI is fully compatible with traditional parallel SCSI, which means packetized SCSI devices can reside on the same bus as traditional SCSI devices. As long as the host adapter supports the packetization, it can communicate with one device using packets and another using traditional protocol. Not all Ultra3 or Ultra160 SCSI devices include packetization support. Ultra3 devices that support packetization normally are referred to as Ultra160+ SCSI.

Quick Arbitrate and Select (QAS) is a feature in Ultra3 SCSI that reduces arbitration time by eliminating bus free time. QAS enables a device to transfer control of the bus to another device without an intervening BUS FREE phase. SCSI devices that support QAS report that capability in the INQUIRY command.

Ultra160 and Ultra160+

Because the five main new features of Ultra3 SCSI are optional, drives could claim Ultra3 capability and not have a consistent level of functionality. To ensure truth in advertising and a minimum level of performance, a group of manufacturers got together and created a substandard within Ultra3 SCSI that requires a minimum set of features. These are called Ultra160 and Ultra160+ because both indicate 160MB/sec throughput. These new substandards are not an official part of SCSI—they are not an official part of the standard. Even so, they do guarantee that certain specifications will be met and certain performance levels will be attained.

Ultra160 is a specific implementation of Ultra3 (SPI-3) SCSI that includes the first three additional features of Ultra3 SCSI:

- Fast-80DT clocking for 160MB/sec operation
- CRC
- Domain validation

Ultra160 SCSI runs in LVD mode and is backward compatible with all Ultra2 SCSI (LVD) devices. The only caveat is that no SE devices must be on the bus. When Ultra2 and Ultra160 (Ultra3) devices are mixed, each device can operate at its full-rated speed independent of the other. The bus will dynamically switch from single- to double-transition mode to support the differences in speeds.

Ultra160+ adds the other two features, ensuring a full implementation of Ultra3:

■ Packetization

■ Quick Arbitrate and Select

With Ultra160 and Ultra160+, you have a known level of functionality to ensure that a minimum level of performance will be met. Ultra160+ SCSI is the highest-performance PC-level storage interface and is best suited for high-traffic environments, such as high-end network servers or workstations. The adaptability and scalability of the interface enables high performance with high reliability.

SPI-4 or Ultra4 SCSI (Ultra320)

SPI-4, also known as Ultra4 or Ultra320 SCSI, is basically an update on the previous Ultra3 (Ultra160) SCSI. It has all the same features, except it doubles the speed again to Fast-160DT. This results in a maximum throughput of 320MB/sec, the current fastest form of parallel SCSI.

The SPI-4 standard is still in development, although products running at Ultra320 speeds will likely be available before the standard is officially published.

Fiber Channel SCSI

Fiber Channel SCSI is a specification for a serial interface using a fiber channel physical and protocol characteristic, with a SCSI command set. It can achieve 100MB/sec over either fiber or coaxial cable of several kilometers in length. Fiber Channel is designed for long-distance connectivity (such as several kilometers) and connecting multiple systems. Standard parallel SCSI will continue to be the I/O choice for inside the box or external close proximity connectivity for some time to come. Due to compatibility problems between various manufacturers' Fiber Channel devices and the fact that Ultra3 (Ultra160) and Ultra4 (Ultra320) SCSI are significantly faster, Fiber Channel is unlikely to become popular in the PC environment. Ultra160/320 SCSI is also far less expensive to implement and remains backward compatible with Ultra2 SCSI devices.

SCSI Cables and Connectors

The SCSI standards are very specific when it comes to cables and connectors. The most common connectors specified in this standard are the 50-position unshielded pin header connector for internal SCSI connections and the 50-position shielded Centronics latch-style connectors for external connections. The shielded Centronics-style connector also is called Alternative 2 in the official specification. Passive or Active termination (Active is preferred) is specified for both single-ended and differential buses. The 50-conductor bus configuration is defined in the SCSI-2 standard as the A cable.

Older narrow (8-bit) SCSI adapters and external devices use a full-size Centronics-type connector that normally has wire latches on each side to secure the cable connector. Figure 8.4 shows what the low-density, 50-pin SCSI connector looks like.

Figure 8.4   Low-density, 50-pin SCSI connector.

The SCSI-2 revision added a high-density, 50-position, D-shell connector option for the A-cable connectors. This connector now is called Alternative 1. Figure 8.5 shows the 50-pin, high-density SCSI connector.

Figure 8.5   High-density, 50-pin SCSI connector.

The Alternative 2 Centronics latch-style connector remains unchanged from SCSI-1. A 68-conductor B-cable specification was added to the SCSI-2 standard to provide for 16- and 32-bit data transfers; the connector, however, had to be used in parallel with an A cable. The industry did not widely accept the B-cable option, which has been dropped from the SCSI-3 standard.

To replace the ill-fated B cable, a new 68-conductor P cable was developed as part of the SCSI-3 specification. Shielded and unshielded high-density D-shell connectors are specified for both the A and P cables. The shielded high-density connectors use a squeeze-to-release latch rather than the wire latch used on the Centronics-style connectors. Active termination for single-ended buses is specified, providing a high level of signal integrity. Figure 8.6 shows the 68-pin, high-density SCSI connector.

Figure 8.6   High-density, 68-pin SCSI connector.

Drive arrays normally use special SCSI drives with what is called an 80-pin Alternative-4 connector, which is capable of Wide SCSI and also includes power signals. Drives with the 80-pin connector are normally *hot-swappable*—they can be removed and installed with the power on—in drive arrays. The 80-pin Alt-4 connector is shown in Figure 8.7.

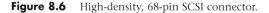

Figure 8.7   80-pin Alt-4 SCSI connector.

Apple and some other nonstandard implementations from other vendors used a 25-pin cable and connector for SCSI devices. They did this by eliminating most of the grounds from the cable, which unfortunately results in a noisy, error-prone connection. I don't recommend using 25-pin cables and connectors; you should avoid them if possible. The connector used in these cases was a standard female DB-25 connector, which looks exactly like a PC parallel port (printer) connector.

Unfortunately, you can damage equipment by plugging printers into DB-25 SCSI connectors or by plugging SCSI devices into DB-25 printer connectors. So, if you use this type of SCSI connection, be sure it is marked well because there is no way to tell DB-25 SCSI from DB-25 parallel printer connectors by looking at them. The DB-25 connector is shown in Figure 8.8.

Again, I recommend you avoid making SCSI connections using this type of cable or connector.

Figure 8.8 DB-25 SCSI connector.

SCSI Cable and Connector Pinouts

The following section details the pinouts of the various SCSI cables and connectors. Two electrically different versions of SCSI exist: single-ended and differential. These two versions are electrically incompatible and must not be interconnected; otherwise, damage will result. Fortunately, very few differential SCSI applications are available in the PC industry, so you will rarely (if ever) encounter one. Within each electrical type (single-ended or differential), there are basically two SCSI cable types:

- A cable (Standard 8-bit SCSI)
- P cable (16-bit Wide SCSI)

The 50-pin A-cable is used in most SCSI-1 and SCSI-2 installations and is the most common cable you will encounter. SCSI-2 Wide (16-bit) applications use a P cable instead, which has 68 pins. You can intermix standard and Wide SCSI devices on a single SCSI bus by interconnecting A and P cables with special adapters. SCSI-3 applications that are 32-bit wide would have used an additional Q cable, but this was finally dropped from the SCSI-3 standard after it was never implemented in actual products.

SCSI cables are specially shielded with the most important high-speed signals carried in the center of the cable and less important, slower ones in two additional layers around the perimeter. A typical SCSI cable is constructed as shown in Figure 8.9.

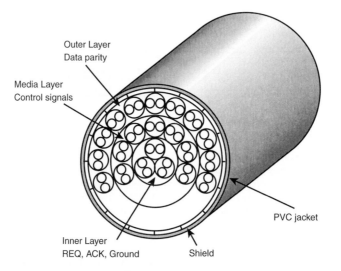

Figure 8.9 Cross section of a typical SCSI cable.

This specialized construction is what makes SCSI cables so expensive, as well as thicker than other types of cables. Note this specialized construction is necessary only for external SCSI cables. Cables used to connect devices inside a shielded enclosure (such as inside a PC) can use much less expensive ribbon cables.

The A cables can have pin-header–type (internal) connectors or external shielded connectors, each with a different pinout. The P cables feature the same connector pinout on either internal or external cable connections.

Single-Ended SCSI Cables and Connectors

The single-ended electrical interface is the most popular type for PC systems. Tables 8.3 and 8.4 show all the possible single-ended cable and connector pinouts. The A cable is available in both internal unshielded and external shielded configurations. A hyphen preceding a signal name indicates the signal is Active Low. The RESERVED lines have continuity from one end of the SCSI bus to the other. In an A cable bus, the RESERVED lines should be left open in SCSI devices (but may be connected to ground) and are connected to ground in the bus terminator assemblies. In the P and Q cables, the RESERVED lines are left open in SCSI devices and in the bus terminator assemblies.

Table 8.3   A-Cable (Single-Ended) Internal Unshielded Header Connector

Signal	Pin	Pin	Signal
GROUND	1	2	-DB(0)
GROUND	3	4	-DB(1)
GROUND	5	6	-DB(2)
GROUND	7	8	-DB(3)
GROUND	9	10	-DB(4)
GROUND	11	12	-DB(5)
GROUND	13	14	-DB(6)
GROUND	15	16	-DB(7)
GROUND	17	18	-DB(Parity)
GROUND	19	20	GROUND
GROUND	21	22	GROUND
RESERVED	23	24	RESERVED
Open	25	26	TERMPWR
RESERVED	27	28	RESERVED
GROUND	29	30	GROUND
GROUND	31	32	-ATN
GROUND	33	34	GROUND
GROUND	35	36	-BSY
GROUND	37	38	-ACK
GROUND	39	40	-RST
GROUND	41	42	-MSG
GROUND	43	44	-SEL
GROUND	45	46	-C/D
GROUND	47	48	-REQ
GROUND	49	50	-I/O

Table 8.4   A-Cable (Single-Ended) External Shielded Connector

Signal	Pin	Pin	Signal
GROUND	1	26	-DB(0)
GROUND	2	27	-DB(1)
GROUND	3	28	-DB(2)
GROUND	4	29	-DB(3)
GROUND	5	30	-DB(4)
GROUND	6	31	-DB(5)
GROUND	7	32	-DB(6)
GROUND	8	33	-DB(7)
GROUND	9	34	-DB(Parity)
GROUND	10	35	GROUND
GROUND	11	36	GROUND
RESERVED	12	37	RESERVED
Open	13	38	TERMPWR
RESERVED	14	39	RESERVED
GROUND	15	40	GROUND
GROUND	16	41	-ATN
GROUND	17	42	GROUND
GROUND	18	43	-BSY
GROUND	19	44	-ACK
GROUND	20	45	-RST
GROUND	21	46	-MSG
GROUND	22	47	-SEL
GROUND	23	48	-C/D
GROUND	24	49	-REQ
GROUND	25	50	-I/O

IBM used the SCSI interface in virtually all PS/2 systems introduced after 1990. These systems use a Micro-Channel SCSI adapter or have the SCSI Host Adapter built into the motherboard. In either case, IBM's SCSI interface uses a special 60-pin, mini-Centronics–type external shielded connector that is unique in the industry. A special IBM cable is required to adapt this connector to the standard 50-pin

Centronics-style connector used on most external SCSI devices. The pinout of the IBM 60-pin, mini-Centronics–style external shielded connector is shown in Table 8.5. Notice that although the pin arrangement is unique, the pin-number–to–signal designations correspond with the standard unshielded internal pin header type of SCSI connector. IBM has discontinued this design in all its systems because after the PS/2 series, all have used conventional SCSI connectors.

The P cable (single-ended) and connectors are used in 16-bit Wide SCSI-2 applications (see Table 8.6 for the pinout).

Table 8.5   IBM PS/2 SCSI External

Signal Name	Pin	Pin	Signal Name
GROUND	1	60	Not Connected
-DB(0)	2	59	Not Connected
GROUND	3	58	Not Connected
-DB(1)	4	57	Not Connected
GROUND	5	56	Not Connected
-DB(2)	6	55	Not Connected
GROUND	7	54	Not Connected
-DB(3)	8	53	Not Connected
GROUND	9	52	Not Connected
-DB(4)	10	51	GROUND
GROUND	11	50	-I/O
-DB(5)	12	49	GROUND
GROUND	13	48	-REQ
-DB(6)	14	47	GROUND
GROUND	15	46	-C/D
-DB(7)	16	45	GROUND
GROUND	17	44	-SEL
-DB(Parity)	18	43	GROUND
GROUND	19	42	-MSG
GROUND	20	41	GROUND
GROUND	21	40	-RST
GROUND	22	39	GROUND
RESERVED	23	38	-ACK
RESERVED	24	37	GROUND
Open	25	36	-BSY
TERMPWR	26	35	GROUND
RESERVED	27	34	GROUND
RESERVED	28	33	GROUND
GROUND	29	32	-ATN
GROUND	30	31	GROUND

Table 8.6   P-Cable (Single-Ended) Internal or External Shielded Connector

Signal Name	Pin	Pin	Signal Name
GROUND	1	35	-DB(12)
GROUND	2	36	-DB(13)
GROUND	3	37	-DB(14)
GROUND	4	38	-DB(15)
GROUND	5	39	-DB(Parity 1)
GROUND	6	40	-DB(0)
GROUND	7	41	-DB(1)
GROUND	8	42	-DB(2)
GROUND	9	43	-DB(3)
GROUND	10	44	-DB(4)
GROUND	11	45	-DB(5)
GROUND	12	46	-DB(6)
GROUND	13	47	-DB(7)
GROUND	14	48	-DB(Parity 0)
GROUND	15	49	GROUND
GROUND	16	50	GROUND
TERMPWR	17	51	TERMPWR
TERMPWR	18	52	TERMPWR
RESERVED	19	53	RESERVED
GROUND	20	54	GROUND
GROUND	21	55	-ATN
GROUND	22	56	GROUND
GROUND	23	57	-BSY
GROUND	24	58	-ACK
GROUND	25	59	-RST
GROUND	26	60	-MSG
GROUND	27	61	-SEL
GROUND	28	62	-C/D
GROUND	29	63	-REQ
GROUND	30	64	-I/O
GROUND	31	65	-DB(8)
GROUND	32	66	-DB(9)
GROUND	33	67	-DB(10)
GROUND	34	68	-DB(11)

High Voltage Differential SCSI Signals

High Voltage Differential SCSI is not normally used in a PC environment but is very popular with minicomputer installations because of the very long bus lengths that are allowed. This has changed with the introduction of Low Voltage Differential signaling for SCSI, bringing the benefits of differential signaling to lower-end and more mainstream SCSI products.

Differential signaling uses drivers on both the initiator and target ends of the bus and makes each signal work in a push/pull arrangement, rather than a signal/ground arrangement as with standard single-ended SCSI. This enables much greater cable lengths and eliminates some of the problems with termination.

Almost all PC peripherals produced since the beginning of SCSI have been SE types. These are incompatible with HVD devices, although HVD devices can be used on an SE bus with appropriate (and expensive) adapters. The LVD devices, on the other hand, can be used on an SE bus if they are multimode devices, in which case they switch into SE mode. If all devices—including the host adapter—support LVD mode, all the devices switch into that mode and much longer cable lengths and higher speeds can be used. The normal limit for an SE SCSI bus is 1.53 meters maximum (about 5–10 feet) and up to 20MHz. If run in LVD mode, the maximum bus length goes up to 12 meters (about 40 feet) and speeds can go up to 80MHz. HVD SCSI supports bus lengths of up to 25 meters (about 80 feet).

Note that almost all modern SCSI hard disks are Ultra2 or Ultra3 devices, which means by default they are also LVD or multimode LVD/SE devices.

Expanders

SCSI expanders separate a SCSI bus into more than one physical segment, each of which can have the full SCSI cable length for that type of signaling. They provide a complete regeneration of the SCSI bus signals, allowing greater cable lengths and incompatible devices to essentially share the same bus. An expander also can be used to separate incompatible parts of a SCSI bus—for example, to keep SE and HVD SCSI devices in separate domains.

Expanders are transparent to the software and firmware on the bus, and they don't take up a device ID. They are normally capable of providing termination if located at the end of a bus segment, or they can have termination disabled if they are in the middle of a bus segment.

Because of their expense, expanders are not normally used except in extreme situations in which no other alternative remains. In most cases it is better to stick within the recommended cable and bus length requirements and keep incompatible devices, such as HVD devices, off a standard SE or LVD bus.

Termination

Because a SCSI bus carries high-speed electrical signals, it can be affected by electrical reflections that might occur within any transmission line system. A terminator is designed to minimize the potential for reflections or noise on the bus, as well as to create the proper load for the bus transmitter circuits. Terminators are placed at each end of the bus to minimize these problems.

Despite the simple rules that only two terminators must be on the bus and they must be at each end, I still see improper termination as the most common cause of problems in SCSI installations.

Several kinds of SCSI terminators are available, dependent on the bus signaling and speed requirements:

- Passive
- Active (also called Alternative 2)
- Forced Perfect Termination (FPT): FPT-3, FPT-18, and FPT-27

- HVD termination
- LVD termination

The first three are used on single-ended SCSI buses only. Passive terminators use a passive network of 220ohm and 330ohm resistors to control bus termination. They should be used only in narrow (8-bit) SCSI buses running at 5MHz. Passive terminators allow signal fluctuations in relation to the terminator power signal on the bus. Usually, passive terminating resistors suffice over short distances, such as 2 or 3 feet, but for longer distances or higher speeds, active termination is a real advantage. Active termination is required with Fast SCSI.

Figure 8.10 shows the schematic of a typical passive terminator.

Figure 8.10   Passive SCSI terminator schematic.

Active terminators use built-in voltage regulator ICs combined with 110ohm resistors. An active terminator actually has one or more voltage regulators to produce the termination voltage, rather than resistor voltage dividers alone. This arrangement helps ensure that the SCSI signals always are terminated to the correct voltage level. Active terminators often have some sort of LED indicating the termination activity. The SCSI-2 specification recommends active termination on both ends of the bus and requires active termination whenever Fast or Wide SCSI devices are used. Most high-performance host adapters have an "auto-termination" feature, so if it is the end of a chain, it terminates itself. Figure 8.11 shows a typical active terminator.

A variation on active termination is available for single-ended buses: *forced perfect termination (FPT)*. Forced perfect termination is an even better form of active termination, in which diode clamps are added to eliminate signal overshoot and undershoot. The trick is that instead of clamping to +5 and ground, these terminators clamp to the output of two regulated voltages. This arrangement enables the clamping diodes to eliminate signal overshoot and undershoot, especially at higher signaling speeds and over longer distances. Forced perfect termination is technically not found in the SCSI specifications but is the superior type of termination for single-ended applications that experience high levels of electrical noise. Figure 8.12 shows the schematic of a typical FPT-18 type terminator (18 lines forced perfect, designed for 50-pin connections).

FPT terminators are available in several versions. FPT-3 and FPT-18 versions are available for 8-bit standard SCSI, whereas the FPT-27 is available for 16-bit (Wide) SCSI. The FPT-3 version forces perfect the three most highly active SCSI signals on the 8-bit SCSI bus, whereas the FPT-18 forces perfect all the SCSI signals on the 8-bit bus except grounds. FPT-27 also forces perfect all the 16-bit Wide SCSI signals except grounds.

HVD buses require HVD terminators, constructed using a passive network of 330ohm/150ohm/330ohm resistors. The only choice there is that the terminator matches your cable or device connection.

Figure 8.11   Active SCSI terminator schematic.

Figure 8.12   FPT SCSI terminator schematic.

The same is true for Low Voltage Differential buses. They require LVD terminators for the bus to function properly. One twist is that special LVD/SE (active) multimode terminators are available. These function as LVD types on an LVD bus and as active types on an SE bus. Note that if any SE devices are on the bus, it functions in SE mode and never uses LVD mode, severely limiting bus length and performance. If any SE-only terminators or SE devices are on the bus, the bus defaults into SE mode.

▶▶ See the next section, "SCSI Drive Configuration," p. 534.

Note

Several companies make high-quality terminators for the SCSI bus, including Aeronics and the Data Mate division of Methode. Both companies make a variety of terminators. Aeronics is well noted for some unique FPT versions that are especially suited to problem configurations that require longer cable runs or higher signal integrity. One of the best investments you can make in any SCSI installation is in high-quality cables and terminators. Contact information for both of these companies is in the Vendor List on the CD.

Special terminators also are required for LVD and HVD SCSI, so if you are using those interfaces, make sure your terminators are compatible.

With LVD or HVD buses, you don't have much choice in terminator types, but for single-ended (SE) buses, you have at least three choices.

Tip

My recommendation is to *never* use passive terminators; instead, use only active or FPT. If you want the best in reliability and integrity, choose FPT. The best rule for terminators as well as for cables is to get the best you can.

SCSI Drive Configuration

SCSI drives are not too difficult to configure, but they are more complicated than IDE drives. The SCSI standard controls the way the drives must be set up. You need to set up two or three items when you configure a SCSI drive:

- SCSI ID setting (0–7 or 0–15)
- Terminating resistors

The SCSI ID setting is very simple. Up to 7 SCSI devices can be used on a single narrow SCSI bus or up to 15 devices on a wide SCSI bus, and each device must have a unique SCSI ID address. There are 8 or 16 addresses respectively, and the host adapter takes 1 address, so the rest are free for up to 7 or 15 SCSI peripherals. Most SCSI host adapters are factory-set to ID 7 or 15, which is the highest priority ID. All other devices must have unique IDs that do not conflict with one another. Some host adapters boot only from a hard disk set to a specific ID. Older Adaptec host adapters required the boot hard disk to be ID 0; newer ones can boot from any ID.

Setting the ID usually involves changing jumpers on the drive. If the drive is installed in an external chassis, the chassis might have an ID selector switch that is accessible at the rear. This selector makes ID selection a simple matter of pressing a button or rotating a wheel until the desired ID number appears. If no external selector is present, you must open the external device chassis and set the ID via the jumpers on the drive.

Three jumpers are required to set the SCSI ID; the particular ID selected actually is derived from the binary representation of the jumpers themselves. One example is setting all three ID jumpers off results in a binary number of 000b, which translates to an ID of 0. A binary setting of 001b equals ID 1; 010b equals 2; 011b equals 3; and so on. (Notice that as I list these values, I append a lowercase b to indicate binary numbers.)

Unfortunately, the jumpers can appear either forward or backward on the drive, depending on how the manufacturer set them up. To keep things simple, I have recorded all the various ID jumper settings in the following tables. Table 8.7 shows the settings for drives that order the jumpers with the most significant bit (MSB) to the left; Table 8.8 shows the settings for drives that have the jumpers ordered so that the MSB is to the right.

Table 8.7   SCSI ID Jumper Settings with the Most Significant Bit to the Left

SCSI	ID	Jumper	Settings
0	0	0	0
1	0	0	1
2	0	1	0
3	0	1	1
4	1	0	0
5	1	0	1
6	1	1	0
7	1	1	1

1 = Jumper On; 0 = Jumper Off

Table 8.8   SCSI ID Jumper Settings with the Most Significant Bit to the Right

SCSI	ID	Jumper	Settings
0	0	0	0
1	1	0	0
2	0	1	0
3	1	1	0
4	0	0	1
5	1	0	1
6	0	1	1
7	1	1	1

1 = Jumper On; 0 = Jumper Off

SCSI termination is very simple. Termination is required at both ends of the bus; there are no exceptions. If the host adapter is at one end of the bus, it must have termination enabled. If the host adapter is in the middle of the bus, and if both internal and external bus links are present, the host adapter must have its termination disabled, and the devices at each end of the bus must have terminators installed. Unfortunately, the majority of problems I see with SCSI installations are the result of improper termination.

Figure 8.13 shows a representation of a SCSI bus with several devices attached. In this case, the host adapter is at one end of the bus and a CD-ROM drive is at the other. For the bus to work properly, those devices must be terminated, whereas the others do not.

When installing an external SCSI device, you usually will find the device in a storage enclosure with both input and output SCSI connectors, so you can use the device in a daisy-chain. If the enclosure is at the end of the SCSI bus, an external terminator module most likely will have to be plugged into the second (outgoing) SCSI port to provide proper termination at that end of the bus (see Figure 8.14).

External terminator modules are available in a variety of connector configurations, including pass-through designs, which are necessary if only one port is available. Pass-through terminators also are commonly used in internal installations in which the device does not have built-in terminating resistors. Many hard drives use pass-through terminators for internal installations to save space on the logic-board assembly (see Figure 8.15).

The pass-through models are required when a device is at the end of the bus and only one SCSI connector is available.

Figure 8.13 SCSI bus daisy-chain connections; the first and last devices must be terminated.

Figure 8.14 External SCSI device terminator.

Figure 8.15 Internal pin-header connector pass-through SCSI terminator.

Other configuration items on a SCSI drive can be set via jumpers. Following are several of the most common additional settings that you will find:

- Start on Command (delayed start)
- SCSI Parity
- Terminator Power
- Synchronous Negotiation

These configuration items are described in the following sections.

Start on Command (Delayed Start)

If you have multiple drives installed in a system, it is wise to set them up so that not all the drives start to spin immediately when the system is powered on. A hard disk drive can consume three or four times more power during the first few seconds after power-on than during normal operation. The motor requires this additional power to get the platters spinning quickly. If several drives are drawing all this power at the same time, the power supply can be overloaded, which can cause the system to hang or have intermittent startup problems.

Nearly all SCSI drives provide a way to delay drive spinning so this problem does not occur. When most SCSI host adapters initialize the SCSI bus, they send out a command called Start Unit to each of the ID addresses in succession. By setting a jumper on the hard disk, you can prevent the disk from spinning until it receives the Start Unit command from the host adapter. Because the host adapter sends this command to all the ID addresses in succession, from the highest priority address (ID 7) to the lowest (ID 0), the higher priority drives can be made to start first, with each lower priority drive spinning up sequentially. Because some host adapters do not send the Start Unit command, some drives might simply delay spin-up for a fixed number of seconds rather than wait for a command that never will arrive.

If drives are installed in external chassis with separate power supplies, you need not implement the delayed-start function. This function is best applied to internal drives that must be run from the same power supply that runs the system. For internal installations, I recommend setting Start on Command (delayed start) even if you have only one SCSI drive; this setting eases the load on the power supply by spinning the drive up after the rest of the system has full power. This method is especially good for portable systems and other systems in which the power supply is limited.

SCSI Parity

SCSI Parity is a limited form of error checking that helps ensure that all data transfers are reliable. Virtually all host adapters support SCSI parity checking, so this option should be enabled on every device. The only reason it exists as an option is that some older host adapters do not work with SCSI parity, so the parity must be turned off.

Terminator Power

The terminators at each end of the SCSI bus require power from at least one device on the bus. In most cases, the host adapter supplies this terminator power; in some cases, however, it does not. For example, parallel port SCSI host adapters typically do not supply terminator power. It is not a problem if more than one device supplies terminator power because each source is diode-protected. For simplicity's sake, many people often configure all devices to supply terminator power. If no device supplies terminator power, the bus is not terminated correctly and will not function properly.

SCSI Synchronous Negotiation

The SCSI bus can run in two modes: asynchronous (the default) and synchronous. The bus actually switches modes during transfers through a protocol called *synchronous negotiation*. Before data is transferred across the SCSI bus, the sending device (called the *initiator*) and the receiving device (called the *target*) negotiate how the transfer will take place. If both devices support synchronous transfers, they will discover this fact through the negotiation, and the transfer will take place at the faster synchronous rate.

Unfortunately, some older devices do not respond to a request for synchronous transfer and can actually be disabled when such a request is made. For this reason, both host adapters and devices that support synchronous negotiation often have a jumper that can be used to disable this negotiation so it can work with older devices. By default, all devices today should support synchronous negotiation, and this function should be enabled.

Plug-and-Play SCSI

Plug-and-Play (PnP) SCSI was originally released in April 1994. This specification enables SCSI device manufacturers to build PnP peripherals that are automatically configured when used with a PnP operating system. This enables you to easily connect or reconfigure external peripherals, such as hard disk drives, backup tapes, and CD-ROMs.

To connect SCSI peripherals to the host PC, the specification requires a PnP SCSI host adapter, such as PnP ISA or PCI. PnP add-in cards enable a PnP operating system to automatically configure software device drivers and system resources for the host bus interface.

The PnP SCSI specification version 1.0 includes these technical highlights:

- A single cable connector configuration
- Automatic termination of the SCSI bus
- SCAM (SCSI Configured AutoMagically*) automatic ID assignment
- Full backward compatibility of PnP SCSI devices with the installed base of SCSI systems

Note

"AutoMagically" is not a misspelling. The word is actually used in the official name for the specification, which the X3T9.2 committee designated X3T9.2/93-109r5.

This should go a long way in making SCSI easier to use for the normal user.

Each SCSI peripheral you add to your SCSI bus (other than hard disk drives) requires an external driver to make the device work. Hard disks are the exception; driver support for them normally is provided as part of the SCSI host adapter BIOS. These external drivers are specific not only to a particular device, but also to the host adapter.

Recently, two types of standard host adapter interface drivers have become popular, greatly reducing this problem. By having a standard host adapter driver to write to, peripheral makers can more quickly create new drivers that support their devices and then talk to the universal host adapter driver. This arrangement eliminates dependence on one particular type of host adapter. These primary or universal drivers link the host adapter and operating system.

The Advanced SCSI Programming Interface (ASPI) currently is the most popular universal driver, with most peripheral makers writing their drivers to talk to ASPI. The *A* in ASPI used to stand for Adaptec, the company that introduced it, but other SCSI device vendors have licensed the right to use ASPI with their products. DOS does not support ASPI directly, but it does when the ASPI driver is loaded. Windows 9x/Me, Windows NT/2000, and OS/2 2.1 and later versions provide automatic ASPI support for several SCSI host adapters.

Future Domain and NCR have created another interface driver called the Common Access Method (CAM). CAM is an ANSI-approved protocol that enables a single driver to control several host adapters. In addition to ASPI, OS/2 2.1 and later versions currently offer support for CAM. Future Domain also provides a CAM-to-ASPI converter in the utilities that go with its host adapters.

SCSI Configuration Troubleshooting

When you are installing a chain of devices on a single SCSI bus, the installation can get complicated very quickly. If you have a problem during installation, check these items first:

■ Make sure you are using the latest BIOS from your motherboard manufacturer. Some have had problems with their PCI bus slots not working properly.

■ Make sure that all SCSI devices attached to the bus are powered on.

■ Make sure all SCSI cables and power cables are properly connected. Try removing and reseating all the connectors to be sure.

■ Check that the host adapter and each device on each SCSI bus channel have a unique SCSI ID setting.

■ Make sure the SCSI bus is terminated properly. Remember there should be only two terminators on the bus, one at each end. All other termination should be removed or disabled.

■ If your system BIOS setup has settings for controlling PCI bus configuration, make sure the PCI slot containing the SCSI adapter is configured for an available interrupt. If your system is Plug and Play, use the Windows Device Manager to check and possibly change the resource configuration.

■ Make sure the host adapter is installed in a PCI slot that supports bus mastering. Some older motherboards did not allow bus mastering to work in all PCI slots. Check your motherboard documentation and try moving the SCSI host adapter to a different PCI slot.

■ If you have a SCSI hard disk installed and your system will not boot from the SCSI drive, there can be several causes for this problem. Note that if both SCSI and non-SCSI disk drives are installed in your computer, in almost all cases the non-SCSI drive will be the boot device. If you want to boot from a SCSI drive, check the boot sequence configuration in your BIOS. If your system allows it, change the boot sequence to allow SCSI devices to boot first. If not, try removing the non-SCSI drives from your system.

If the system has only SCSI disk drives and it still won't boot, check the following items:

■ Make sure your computer's BIOS Setup drive configuration is set to "No Drives Installed." The PC BIOS supports only ATA (IDE) drives; by setting this to no drives, the system will then try to boot from another device, such as SCSI.

■ Make sure the drive is partitioned and that a primary partition exists. Use FDISK from DOS or Windows to check.

■ Make sure the boot partition of the boot hard disk is set to active. This can be checked or changed with the FDISK program.

■ Finally as a last resort, you can try backing up all data on the SCSI hard disk, and then perform a low-level format with the Format utility built into or included with the host adapter.

Here are some tips for getting your setup to function quickly and efficiently:

- *Start by adding one device at a time.* Rather than plugging numerous peripherals into a single SCSI card and then trying to configure them at the same time, start by installing the host adapter and a single hard disk. Then, you can continue installing devices one at a time, checking to make sure that everything works before moving on.

- *Keep good documentation.* When you add a SCSI peripheral, write down the SCSI ID address and any other switch and jumper settings, such as SCSI Parity, Terminator Power, and Delayed or Remote Start. For the host adapter, record the BIOS addresses, Interrupt, DMA channel, and I/O Port addresses used by the adapter, and any other jumper or configuration settings (such as termination) that might be important to know later.

- *Use proper termination.* Each end of the bus must be terminated, preferably with active or Forced Perfect terminators. If you are using any Fast SCSI-2 device, you must use active terminators rather than the cheaper passive types. Even with standard (slow) SCSI devices, active termination is highly recommended. If you have only internal or external devices on the bus, the host adapter and last device on the chain should be terminated. If you have external and internal devices on the chain, you generally will terminate the first and last of these devices but not the SCSI host adapter (which is in the middle of the bus).

- *Use high-quality shielded SCSI cables.* Make sure your cable connectors match your devices. Use high-quality shielded cables, and observe the SCSI bus-length limitations. Use cables designed for SCSI use, and, if possible, stick to the same brand of cable throughout a single SCSI bus. Different brands of cables have different impedance values; this situation sometimes causes problems, especially in long or high-speed SCSI implementations.

Following these simple tips will help minimize problems and leave you with a trouble-free SCSI installation.

SCSI Versus IDE

When you compare the performance and capabilities of IDE and SCSI interfaced drives, you need to consider several factors. These two types of drives are the most popular drives used in PC systems today, and a single manufacturer might make identical drives in both interfaces. Deciding which drive type is best for your system is a difficult decision that depends on many factors.

In most cases, you will find that an IDE drive using the same head-disk assembly as a SCSI drive from the same manufacturer will perform about the same or outperform the equivalent SCSI drive at a given task or benchmark. This is mainly true when using a single disk drive with a single-user operating system, such as Windows 9x/Me. More powerful operating systems, such as Windows NT or Windows 2000, can more effectively use the command queuing and other features of SCSI, thus improving performance over IDE—especially when supporting multiple drives.

It is interesting to see that SCSI really evolved from IDE, or you could say that both evolved from the ST-506/412 and ESDI interfaces that were once used.

SCSI Hard Disk Evolution and Construction

SCSI is not a disk interface, but a bus that supports SCSI bus interface adapters connected to disk and other device controllers. The first SCSI drives for PCs were standard ST-506/412 or ESDI drives with a separate SCSI bus interface adapter (sometimes called a bridge controller) that converted the ST-506/412 or ESDI interfaces to SCSI. This interface originally was in the form of a secondary logic board, and the entire assembly often was mounted in an external case.

The next step was to build the SCSI bus interface "converter" board directly into the drive's own logic board. Today, we call these drives embedded SCSI drives because the SCSI interface is built in.

At that point, there was no need to conform to the absolute specifications of ST-506/412 or ESDI on the internal disk interface because the only other device the interface ever would have to talk to was built in as well. Thus, the disk-interface and controller-chipset manufacturers began to develop more customized chipsets that were based on the ST-506/412 or ESDI chipsets already available but offered more features and higher performance.

Today, if you look at a typical SCSI drive, you often can identify the chip or chipset that serves as the disk controller on the drive as being exactly the same kind that would be used on an ST-506/412 or ESDI controller, or as some evolutionary customized variation thereof.

Consider some examples. An ATA IDE drive must fully emulate the system-level disk-controller interface introduced with the Western Digital WD1003 controller series IBM used in the AT. These drives must act as though they have a built-in ST-506/412 or ESDI controller; in fact, they actually do. Most of these built-in controllers have more capabilities than the original WD1003 series (usually in the form of additional commands), but they must at least respond to all the original commands that were used with the WD1003.

If you follow the hard-drive market, you usually will see that drive manufacturers offer most of their newer drives in both ATA-IDE and SCSI versions. In other words, if a manufacturer makes a particular 20GB IDE drive, you invariably see that the company also makes a SCSI model with the same capacity and specifications, which uses the same head disk assembly (HDA) and even looks the same as the IDE version. If you study these virtually identical drives, the only major difference you will find is the additional chip on the logic board of the SCSI version, called a SCSI Bus Adapter Chip (SBIC).

Figures 8.16 and 8.17 show the logic-block diagrams of an ATA/IDE and a SCSI drive from the same manufacturer. These drives use the same HDA; they differ only in their logic boards, and even the logic boards are the same except for the addition of an SBIC on the SCSI drive's logic board.

Notice that even the circuit designs of these two drives are almost identical. Both drives use an LSI (large scale integrated circuit) chip called the WD42C22 Disk Controller and Buffer Manager chip. In the ATA drive, this chip is connected through a DMA control chip directly to the AT bus. In the SCSI version, a WD33C93 SCSI bus interface controller chip is added to interface the disk-controller logic to the SCSI bus. In fact, the logic diagrams of these two drives differ only in the fact that the SCSI version has a complete subset of the ATA drive, with the SCSI bus interface controller logic added. This essentially is a very condensed version of the separate drive and bridge controller setups that were used in the early days of PC SCSI.

◄◄   See "DMA Transfer Modes," p. 504.

To top off this example, study the logic diagram in Figure 8.18 for the WD 1006V-MM1, which is an ST-506/412 controller.

You can clearly see that the main LSI chip onboard is the same WD42C22 disk controller chip used in the IDE and SCSI drives. Here is what the technical reference literature says about that chip:

> The WD42C22 integrates a high performance, low cost Winchester controller's architecture. The WD42C22 integrates the central elements of a Winchester controller subsystem such as the host interface, buffer manager, disk formatter/controller, encoder/decoder, CRC/ECC (Cyclic Redundancy Check/Error Correction Code) generator/checker, and drive interface into a single 84-pin PQFP (Plastic Quad Flat Pack) device.

Figure 8.16   Typical ATA-IDE drive logic-board block diagram.

Figure 8.17   Typical SCSI drive logic board block diagram.

The virtually identical design of ATA-IDE and SCSI drives is not unique to Western Digital. Most drive manufacturers design their ATA-IDE and SCSI drives the same way, often using these very same WD chips, and disk controller and SCSI bus interface chips from other manufacturers. You now should be able to understand that most SCSI drives are "regular" ATA-IDE drives with SCSI bus logic added. This fact will come up again later in this chapter in the section "SCSI Versus IDE: Advantages and Limitations," which discusses performance and other issues differentiating these interfaces.

For another example, I have several old IBM 320MB and 400MB embedded SCSI-2 hard disks; each of these drives has onboard a WD-10C00 Programmable Disk Controller in the form of a 68-pin Plastic Leaded Chip Carrier (PLCC) chip. The technical literature states:

> This chip supports ST412, ESDI, SMD and Optical interfaces. It has 27Mbit/sec maximum transfer rate and an internal, fully programmable 48- or 32-bit ECC, 16-bit CRC-CCITT or external user defined ECC polynomial, fully programmable sector sizes, and 1.25 micron low power CMOS design.

In addition, these particular embedded SCSI drives include the 33C93 SCSI Bus Interface Controller chip, which also is used in the other SCSI drive I mentioned. Again, there is a distinctly separate disk controller, and the SCSI interface is added on.

So again, most embedded SCSI drives have a built-in disk controller (usually based on previous ST-506/412 or ESDI designs) and additional logic to interface that controller to the SCSI bus (a built-in bridge controller, if you like). Now think about this from a performance standpoint. If virtually all SCSI drives really are ATA-IDE drives with a SCSI Bus Interface Controller chip added, what conclusions can you draw?

Figure 8.18   Western Digital WD1006V-MM1 ST-506/412 Disk Controller block diagram.

First, no drive can perform sustained data transfers faster than the data can actually be read from the disk platters. In other words, the HDA limits performance to whatever it is capable of achieving. Drives can transmit data in short bursts at very high speeds because they often have built-in cache or read-ahead buffers that store data. Many of the newer high-performance SCSI and ATA-IDE drives have 1MB or more of cache memory onboard. No matter how big or intelligent the cache is, however, sustained data transfer is still limited by the HDA.

◀◀   See "ATA IDE," p. 480.

Data from the HDA must pass through the disk controller circuits, which, as you have seen, are virtually identical between similar SCSI and ATA-IDE drives. In the ATA-IDE drive, this data then is presented directly to the system bus. In the SCSI drive, however, the data must pass through a SCSI bus interface adapter on the drive, travel through the SCSI bus, and then pass through another SCSI bus interface controller in the SCSI host adapter card in your system. The longer route a SCSI transfer must take makes this type of transfer slower than the much more direct ATA-IDE transfer.

The conventional wisdom has been that SCSI always is much faster than IDE; unfortunately, this wisdom is usually wrong. This incorrect conclusion was derived by looking at the raw SCSI and ISA bus performance capabilities. A 16-bit Ultra3 SCSI drive can transfer data at a claimed 160MB/sec, whereas an Ultra-ATA/66 IDE drive can transfer data at 66MB/sec. Based on these raw transfer rates, SCSI seems to be faster, but the raw transfer rate of the bus is not the limiting factor. As discussed previously, the actual HDA and disk-controller circuitry place limits on this performance. The key figure to check is what is reported as the internal transfer rate for the drive. For example, here are the specs on two similar drives (one IDE and one SCSI):

IDE Drive	
Drive	IBM Deskstar 18GXP ATA
Interface	Ultra-ATA/66
Platters	5
Data heads	10
Capacity	18.0GB
Recording density	218.6KB/inch
Rotational speed	7,200rpm
Internal cache buffer	2MB
Interface transfer rate	up to 66.7MB/sec
Media transfer rate	27.9MB/sec max.
Sustained data transfer rate	10.7–17.9MB/sec max.
Average sustained transfer rate	14.3MB/sec

SCSI Drive	
Drive	IBM Ultrastar 18ES SCSI
Interface	Ultra2/Wide SCSI
Platters	5
Data heads	10
Capacity	18.2GB
Recording density	220KB/inch
Rotational speed	7,200rpm
Internal cache buffer	2MB
Interface transfer rate	up to 80MB/sec
Media transfer rate	30.5MB/sec maximum
Sustained data transfer rate	12.7–20.2MB/sec
Average sustained transfer rate	16.45MB/sec

Note that although the SCSI drive can claim a much higher external transfer rate of 80MB/sec as compared to the ATA drive's 66.7MB/sec, in actuality these drives are almost identical performers. The real specs to look at are in the last two lines of the tables, which detail how fast data can actually be read from the drive. In particular, the sustained transfer rates are the true transfer rates for reading data from these drives; as you can see, they are very close indeed. The true transfer rate of a drive is mainly influenced by the rotational speed, track density, and things such as internal buffers or caches.

Then you have to factor in that the SCSI drive listed earlier would cost 50%–100% more than the IDE counterpart. Not to mention the cost of springing for an Ultra2/Wide host adapter to plug the drive into. Decent SCSI adapters, especially Wide SCSI versions, can easily run $300 or more. When you consider that the UltraATA interface is built into most modern motherboards for free, you can see that, depending on your needs, spending a ton of extra cash for SCSI can be a significant waste of money.

Now to present the counterpoint: Although these two drives are basically equivalent, the ATA version was one of the top ATA drives offered by IBM at the time, whereas the SCSI drive listed earlier was only a middle-of-the-pack performer. IBM and others make SCSI drives that have rotational speeds of 10,000rpm, increased track density, and larger buffers. Of course, these drives cost even more. So the bottom line is that if you must have the absolute best performing drives, by all means get the top-of-the-line SCSI drives and Ultra SCSI Wide adapters. However, if you want something that is literally 1/3 to 1/4 the cost and 3/4 or more the performance, stick with IDE.

Performance

ATA IDE drives currently are used in most PC configurations on the market because the cost of an IDE-drive implementation is low and the performance capabilities are high. In comparing any given IDE and SCSI drive for performance, you have to look at the capabilities of the HDAs that are involved.

To minimize the variables in this type of comparison, it is easiest to compare IDE and SCSI drives from the same manufacturer that also use the identical HDA. You will find that in most cases, a drive manufacturer makes a given drive available in both IDE and SCSI forms. For example, most hard drive companies make similar SCSI and IDE drives that use identical HDAs and that differ only in the logic board. The IDE version has a logic board with a built-in disk controller and a direct AT bus interface. The SCSI version has the same built-in disk controller and bus interface circuits and also a SBIC chip. The SBIC chip is a SCSI adapter that places the drive on the SCSI bus. What you will find, in essence, is that virtually all SCSI drives actually are IDE drives with the SBIC chip added.

The HDAs in these sample drives are capable of transferring data at a sustained rate of up to 8MB/sec or more. Because the SCSI version always has the additional overhead of the SCSI bus to go through, in almost all cases the directly attached IDE version performs slightly faster.

SCSI Versus IDE: Advantages and Limitations

Modern operating systems are multitasking, and SCSI devices (with all their additional controller circuitry) function independently of one another, unlike IDE. Therefore, data can be read and written to any of the SCSI devices simultaneously. This enables smoother multitasking and increased overall data throughput. The most advanced operating systems, such as Windows NT/2000, even allow drive striping. A *striped drive set* is two or more drives that appear to the user as one drive. Data is split between the drives equally, again increasing overall throughput. Increased fault tolerance and performance are readily implemented and supported in SCSI drive arrays.

The new Ultra3 (Ultra160) SCSI drives offer even more advantages when compared with IDE. Ultra160 SCSI is 240% faster than UDMA/66 (Ultra DMA) IDE, which has a maximum data rate of 66MB/sec. Ultra160 SCSI also fully supports multitasking and can significantly improve system performance in workstations and servers running Windows NT or 2000. IDE limits cable lengths to 18 inches, effectively eliminating the ability to connect remote or external devices, whereas Ultra3 (Ultra160) SCSI allows external connections of up to 12 meters or more in length. Also note that IDE allows only 2 devices per cable, whereas Ultra160 SCSI can connect up to 15 devices. Finally, the domain validation feature of Ultra160 SCSI enables noise and other problems on the bus to be handled properly, whereas with IDE, if a problem occurs with the connection (and that is more common at the UDMA/66 speeds), the IDE drives simply fail.

IDE drives have much less command overhead for a given sector transfer than do SCSI drives. In addition to the drive-to-controller command overhead that both IDE and SCSI must perform, a SCSI transfer involves negotiating for the SCSI bus; selecting the target drive; requesting data; terminating the transfer over the bus; and finally converting the logical data addresses to the required cylinder, head, and sector addresses. This arrangement gives IDE an advantage in sequential transfers handled by a single-tasking operating system. In a multitasking system that can take advantage of the extra intelligence of the SCSI bus, SCSI can have the performance advantage.

SCSI drives offer significant architectural advantages over IDE and other drives. Because each SCSI drive has its own embedded disk controller that can function independently from the system CPU, the computer can issue simultaneous commands to every drive in the system. Each drive can store these commands in a queue and then perform the commands simultaneously with other drives in the system. The data could be fully buffered on the drive and transferred at high speed over the shared SCSI bus when a time slot was available.

Although IDE drives also have their own controllers, they do not operate simultaneously, and command queuing is not supported. In effect, the dual controllers in a dual-drive IDE installation work one at a time so as not to step on each other.

IDE does not support overlapped, multitasked I/O, which enables a device to take on multiple commands and work on them independently and in an order different from which they were received, releasing the bus for other devices to use. The ATA bus instead waits for each command to be completed before the next one can be sent.

As you can see, SCSI has some advantages over IDE, especially where expansion is concerned, and also with regard to support for multitasking operating systems. Unfortunately, it also costs more to implement.

One final advantage of SCSI is in the portability of external devices. It is easy to take an external SCSI CD-ROM, tape drive, scanner, or even a hard disk and quickly move it to another system. This allows moving peripherals more freely between systems and can be a bonus if you have several systems with which you might want to share a number of peripherals. Installing a new external SCSI device on a system is easier because you normally will not need to open it up.

Recommended SCSI Host Adapters

For SCSI host adapters, I normally recommend Adaptec. Its adapters work well and come with the necessary formatting and operating software. Windows 9x, Windows 2000, and even OS/2 have built-in support for Adaptec SCSI adapters. This support is a consideration in many cases because it frees you from having to deal with additional drivers.

Standard or Fast SCSI is adequately supported by the ISA bus, but if you are going to install a Wide SCSI bus—or especially an Ultra, Ultra2, or Ultra160 bus—you should consider some form of local bus SCSI adapter, normally PCI. This is because ISA supports a maximum transfer speed of only about 8MB/sec, whereas a Fast-Wide SCSI bus runs up to 20MB/sec, and an Ultra3 (Ultra160) SCSI bus runs up to a blazing 160MB/sec! In most cases, a local bus SCSI adapter would be a PCI bus version, which is supported in most current PC systems.

◄◄   See "The ISA Bus," p. 300.

◄◄   See "The PCI Bus," p. 310.

Like all modern PCI adapters, plug-and-play is supported, meaning virtually all functions on the card can be configured and set through software. No more digging through manuals or looking for interrupt, DMA, I/O port, and other jumper settings—everything is controlled by software and saved in a flash memory module on the card. Following are some features found on the latest SCSI cards:

- Complete configuration utility built into the adapter's ROM
- Software-configurable IRQ, ROM addresses, DMA, I/O port addresses, SCSI parity, SCSI ID, and other settings
- Software-selectable automatic termination (no resistors to pull out!)
- Enhanced BIOS support for up to 15 drives
- No drivers required for more than two hard disks
- Drive spin-up on a per-drive basis available
- Boots from any SCSI ID

Adaptec has full PnP support on all its SCSI adapters. These adapters either are automatically configured in any PC that supports the PnP specification or can be configured manually through supplied software in non-PnP systems. The PnP SCSI adapters are highly recommended because they can be configured without opening up the PC! All functions are set by software, and there are no jumpers or switches to attend to. Most peripheral manufacturers write drivers for Adaptec's cards first, so you will not have many compatibility or driver-support problems with any Adaptec card.

CHAPTER 9

Magnetic Storage Principles

Magnetic Storage

Permanent or semipermanent computer data storage works by either optical or magnetic principles or, in some cases, a combination of the two. In the case of magnetic storage, a stream of binary computer data bits (0s and 1s) is stored by magnetizing tiny pieces of metal embedded on the surface of a disk or tape in a pattern that represents the data. Later this magnetic pattern can be read and converted back into the exact same stream of bits you started with. This is the principle of magnetic storage and the subject of this chapter.

Magnetic storage is often difficult for people to understand because magnetic fields cannot be seen by the human eye. This chapter explains the principles, concepts, and techniques behind modern computer magnetic storage, enabling you to understand what is happening behind the scenes. This information is designed for those who have an insatiable curiosity about how these things work; it is not absolutely necessary to know this to use a PC or perform routine troubleshooting, maintenance, or upgrades. Because the data I store on my hard drives, tape drives, floppy drives, and other magnetic storage devices happens to be far more important to me than the devices themselves, knowing how my data is handled makes me feel much more comfortable with the system in general. Having an understanding of the underlying technology does help when it comes to dealing with problems that might arise.

This chapter covers magnetic storage principles and technology and can be considered an introduction to several other chapters in the book, including the following:

- Chapter 10, "Hard Disk Storage"
- Chapter 11, "Floppy Disk Storage"
- Chapter 12, "High-Capacity Removable Storage"
- Chapter 13, "Optical Storage"
- Chapter 14, "Physical Drive Installation and Configuration"

Consult these chapters for more specific information on various types of magnetic and optical storage, as well as drive installation and configuration.

History of Magnetic Storage

Before there was magnetic storage for computers, the primary storage medium was punched cards. What amazes me is that I missed contact with punched cards by about a year; the college I went to discontinued using them during my freshman year, before I was able to take any computer-related courses. I have to believe that this was more a reflection on their budget and lack of focus on current technology at the time (in 1979, there really weren't many punch-card readers being used in the field) than it is on my age!

The history of magnetic storage dates back to June 1949, when a group of IBM engineers and scientists began working on a new storage device. What they were working on was the first magnetic storage device for computers, and it revolutionized the industry. On May 21, 1952, IBM announced the IBM 726 Tape Unit with the IBM 701 Defense Calculator, marking the transition from punched-card calculators to electronic computers.

Four years later, on September 13, 1956, a small team of IBM engineers in San Jose, California, introduced the first computer disk storage system as part of the 305 RAMAC (Random Access Method of Accounting and Control) computer.

The 305 RAMAC drive could store five million characters (that's right, only 5MB!) of data on 50 disks, each a whopping 24 inches in diameter. Unlike tape drives, RAMAC's recording heads could go directly to any location on a disk surface without reading all the information in between. This random accessibility had a profound effect on computer performance at the time, enabling data to be stored and retrieved significantly faster than if it was on tape.

From these beginnings, the magnetic storage industry has progressed such that today you can store 75GB or more on tiny 3.5-inch drives that fit into a single computer drive bay.

IBM's contributions to the history and development of magnetic storage are incredible; in fact, most have either come directly from IBM or as a result of IBM research. Not only did IBM invent computer magnetic tape storage as well as the hard disk drive, but it also invented the floppy drive. The same San Jose facility where the hard drive was created introduced the first floppy drive, then using eight-inch diameter floppy disks, in 1971. The team that developed the drive was led by Alan Shugart, a now legendary figure in computer storage.

Since then, IBM has pioneered advanced magnetic data encoding schemes, such as Modified Frequency Modulation (MFM) and Run Length Limited (RLL); drive head designs, such as Thin Film, magneto-resistive (MR), and Giant magneto-resistive (GMR) heads; and drive technologies, such as Partial Response Maximum Likelihood (PRML), No-ID recording, and Self-Monitoring Analysis and Reporting Technology (S.M.A.R.T.). Today, IBM is arguably the leader in developing and implementing new drive technology and is second in sales only to Seagate Technology in PC hard drives.

How Magnetic Fields Are Used to Store Data

All magnetic storage devices, such as floppy disk drives and hard disk drives, read and write data by using electromagnetism. This basic principle of physics states that as an electric current flows through a conductor (wire), a magnetic field is generated around the conductor (see Figure 9.1). Note that electrons actually flow from negative to positive as shown in the figure, although we normally think of current flowing in the other direction.

Figure 9.1   A magnetic field is generated around a wire when current is passed through it.

Electromagnetism was discovered in 1819 by Danish physicist Hans Christian Oersted, when he found that a compass needle would deflect away from pointing north when brought near a wire conducting an electric current. When the current was shut off, the compass needle resumed its alignment with the Earth's magnetic field and again pointed north.

The magnetic field generated by a wire conductor can exert an influence on magnetic material in the field. When the direction of the flow of electric current or polarity is reversed, the magnetic field's polarity also is reversed. For example, an electric motor uses electromagnetism to exert pushing and pulling forces on magnets attached to a rotating shaft.

Another effect of electromagnetism was discovered by Michael Faraday in 1831. He found that if a conductor is passed through a moving magnetic field, an electrical current is generated. As the polarity of the magnetic field changes, so does the direction of the electric current's flow (see Figure 9.2).

Figure 9.2   Current is induced in a wire when passed through a magnetic field.

For example, an alternator, which is a type of electrical generator used in automobiles, operates by rotating electromagnets on a shaft past coils of stationary wire conductors, which consequently generates large amounts of electrical current in those conductors. Because electromagnetism works two ways, a motor can become a generator and vice versa. When applied to magnetic storage devices, this two-way operation of electromagnetism makes recording data on a disk and reading that data back later possible. When recording, the head changes electrical impulses to magnetic fields, and when reading, the head changes magnetic fields back into electrical impulses.

The read/write heads in a magnetic storage device are U-shaped pieces of conductive material, with the ends of the U situated directly above (or next to) the surface of the actual data storage medium. The U-shaped head is wrapped with coils or windings of conductive wire, through which an electric current can flow (see Figure 9.3). When the drive logic passes a current through these coils, it generates a magnetic field in the drive head. Reversing the polarity of the electric current causes the polarity of the generated field to change also. In essence, the heads are electromagnets whose voltage can be switched in polarity very quickly.

The disk or tape that constitutes the actual storage medium consists of some form of substrate material (such as Mylar for floppy disks or aluminum or glass for hard disks) on which a layer of magnetizable material has been deposited. This material usually is a form of iron oxide with various other elements added. Each of the individual magnetic particles on the storage medium has its own magnetic field. When the medium is blank, the polarities of those magnetic fields are normally in a state of random disarray. Because the fields of the individual particles point in random directions, each tiny magnetic field is canceled out by one that points in the opposite direction; the cumulative effect of this is a surface with no observable field polarity. With many randomly oriented fields, the net effect is no observable unified field or polarity.

Figure 9.3   A magnetic read/write head.

When a drive's read/write head generates a magnetic field, the field jumps the gap between the ends of the U shape. Because a magnetic field passes through a conductor much more easily than through the air, the field bends outward from the gap in the head and actually uses the adjacent storage medium as the path of least resistance to the other side of the gap. As the field passes through the medium directly under the gap, it polarizes the magnetic particles it passes through so they are aligned with the field. The field's polarity or direction—and, therefore, the polarity or direction of the field induced in the magnetic medium—is based on the direction of the flow of electric current through the coils. A change in the direction of the current flow produces a change in the direction of the magnetic field. During the development of magnetic storage, the distance between the read/write head and the media has decreased dramatically. This enables the gap to be smaller and also makes the size of the recorded magnetic domain smaller. The smaller the recorded magnetic domain, the higher the density of data that can be stored on the drive.

When the magnetic field passes through the medium, the particles in the area below the head gap are aligned in the same direction as the field emanating from the gap. When the individual magnetic domains of the particles are in alignment, they no longer cancel one another out, and an observable magnetic field exists in that region of the medium. This local field is generated by the many magnetic particles that now are operating as a team to produce a detectable cumulative field with a unified direction.

The term *flux* describes a magnetic field that has a specific direction or polarity. As the surface of the medium moves under the drive head, the head can generate what is called a *magnetic flux* of a given polarity over a specific region of the medium. When the flow of electric current through the coils in the head is reversed, so is the magnetic field polarity or flux in the head gap. This flux reversal in the head causes the polarity of the magnetized particles on the disk medium to reverse.

The flux reversal or flux transition is a change in the polarity of the aligned magnetic particles on the surface of the storage medium. A drive head creates flux reversals on the medium to record data. For each data bit (or bits) that a drive writes, it creates a pattern of positive-to-negative and negative-to-positive flux reversals on the medium in specific areas known as *bit cells* or *transition cells*. A bit cell or transition cell is a specific area of the medium—controlled by the time and speed at which the medium travels—in which the drive head creates flux reversals. The particular pattern of flux reversals within the transition cells used to store a given data bit (or bits) is called the *encoding method*. The drive logic or controller takes the data to be stored and encodes it as a series of flux reversals over a period of time, according to the pattern dictated by the encoding method it uses.

Note

The two most popular encoding methods for magnetic media are Modified Frequency Modulation (MFM) and Run Length Limited (RLL). All floppy disk drives and some older hard disk drives use the MFM scheme. Today's hard disk drives use one of several variations on the RLL encoding method. These encoding methods are described in more detail later in this chapter in the section "Data Encoding Schemes."

During the write process, voltage is applied to the head. As the polarity of this voltage changes, the polarity of the magnetic field being recorded also changes. The flux transitions are written precisely at the points where the recording polarity changes. Strange as it might seem, during the read process, a head does not generate exactly the same signal that was written. Instead, the head generates a voltage pulse or spike only when it crosses a flux transition. When the transition changes from positive to negative, the pulse that the head detects is a negative voltage. When the transition changes from negative to positive, the pulse is a positive voltage spike. This effect occurs because current is generated in a conductor only when passing through lines of magnetic force at an angle. Because the head moves parallel to the magnetic fields it created on the media, the only time the head generates voltage when reading is when passing through a polarity or flux transition (flux reversal).

In essence, while reading from the medium, the head becomes a flux transition detector, emitting voltage pulses whenever it crosses a transition. Areas of no transition generate no pulse. Figure 9.4 shows the relationship between the read and write waveforms and the flux transitions recorded on a storage medium.

Figure 9.4   Magnetic write and read processes.

You can think of the write pattern as being a square waveform that is at a positive or negative voltage level. When the voltage is positive, a field is generated in the head, which polarizes the magnetic media in one direction. When the voltage changes to negative, the magnetic field induced in the media also changes direction. Where the waveform actually transitions from positive to negative voltage, or vice versa, the magnetic flux on the disk also changes polarity. During a read, the head senses these flux transitions and generates a pulsed positive or negative waveform, rather than the continuously positive or negative waveform used during the original recording. In other words, the signal when reading is 0 volts unless the head detects a magnetic flux transition, in which case it generates a positive or negative pulse accordingly. Pulses appear only when the head is passing over flux transitions on the medium. By knowing the clock timing the drive uses, the controller circuitry can determine whether a pulse (and therefore a flux transition) falls within a given transition cell time period.

The electrical pulse currents generated in the head while it is passing over the storage medium in read mode are very weak and can contain significant noise. Sensitive electronics in the drive and controller assembly amplify the signal above the noise level and decode the train of weak pulse currents back into binary data that is (theoretically) identical to the data originally recorded.

As you can see, hard disk drives and other storage devices read and write data by means of basic electromagnetic principles. A drive writes data by passing electrical currents through an electromagnet (the drive head), generating a magnetic field that is stored on the medium. The drive reads data by passing the head back over the surface of the medium. As the head encounters changes in the stored magnetic field, it generates a weak electrical current that indicates the presence or absence of flux transitions in the signal as it was originally written.

Read/Write Head Designs

As disk drive technology has evolved, so has the design of the read/write head. The earliest heads were simple iron cores with coil windings (electromagnets). By today's standards, the original head designs were enormous in physical size and operated at very low recording densities. Over the years, head designs have evolved from the first simple ferrite core designs into the several types and technologies available today. This section discusses the various types of heads found in PC hard disk drives, including the applications and relative strengths and weaknesses of each.

Five main types of heads have been used in hard disk drives over the years:

- Ferrite
- Thin-Film (TF)
- Metal-In-Gap (MIG)
- Magneto-resistive (MR)
- Giant Magneto-resistive (GMR)

Ferrite

Ferrite heads, the traditional type of magnetic-head design, evolved from the original IBM 30-30 Winchester drive. These heads have an iron-oxide core wrapped with electromagnetic coils. The drive produces a magnetic field by energizing the coils or by passing a magnetic field near them. This gives the heads full read/write capability. Ferrite heads are larger and heavier than thin-film heads and therefore require a larger floating height to prevent contact with the disk while it is spinning.

Manufacturers have made many refinements to the original (monolithic) ferrite head design. One type of ferrite head, called a composite ferrite head, has a smaller ferrite core bonded with glass in a ceramic housing. This design permits a smaller head gap, which enables higher track densities. These heads are less susceptible to stray magnetic fields than the older monolithic design heads.

During the 1980s, composite ferrite heads were popular in many low-end drives, such as the Seagate ST-225. As density demands grew, the competing MIG and thin-film head designs came to be used in place of ferrite heads, which are virtually obsolete today. Ferrite heads cannot write to the higher coercivity media necessary for high-density disk designs and have poor frequency response with higher noise levels. The main advantage of ferrite heads is that they are the cheapest type available.

Metal-In-Gap

Metal-In-Gap heads are a specially enhanced version of the composite ferrite design. In MIG heads, a metal substance is applied to the head's recording gap. Two versions of MIG heads are available: single-sided and double-sided. Single-sided MIG heads are designed with a layer of magnetic alloy placed along the trailing edge of the gap. Double-sided MIG designs apply the layer to both sides of the gap. The metal alloy is applied through a vacuum-deposition process called sputtering.

This magnetic alloy has twice the magnetization capability of raw ferrite and enables the head to write to the higher coercivity thin-film media needed at the higher densities. MIG heads also produce a sharper gradient in the magnetic field for a better-defined magnetic pulse. Double-sided MIG heads offer even higher coercivity capability than the single-sided designs.

Because of these increases in capabilities through improved designs, MIG heads were for a time the most popular head design and were used in many hard disk drives in the late '80s and early '90s. They are still used today in LS-120 (SuperDisk) drives.

Thin Film

Thin-film heads are manufactured much the same way as a semiconductor chip—through a photolithographic process. This process creates many thousands of heads on a single circular wafer and produces a very small, high-quality product.

TF heads have an extremely narrow and controlled head gap that is created by sputtering a hard aluminum material. Because this material completely encloses the gap, the area is very well protected, minimizing the chance of damage from contact with the spinning disk. The core is a combination of iron and nickel alloy that has two to four times more magnetic power than a ferrite head core.

TF heads produce a sharply defined magnetic pulse that enables them to write at extremely high densities. Because they do not have a conventional coil, TF heads are more immune to variations in coil impedance. These small, lightweight heads can float at a much lower height than the ferrite and MIG heads; in some designs, the floating height is two micro-inches or less. Because the reduced height enables the heads to pick up and transmit a much stronger signal from the platters, the signal-to-noise ratio increases, improving accuracy. At the high track and linear densities of some drives, a standard ferrite head would not be capable of picking out the data signal from the background noise. Another advantage of TF heads is that their small size enables the platters to be stacked closer together, enabling more platters to fit into the same space.

Until the past few years, TF heads were relatively expensive compared with older technologies, such as ferrite and MIG. Better manufacturing techniques and the need for higher densities, however, have driven the market to TF heads. The widespread use of these heads has also made them cost-competitive with, if not cheaper than, MIG heads.

Many of the drives in the 100MB to 2GB range used TF heads, especially in the smaller form factors. TF heads displaced MIG heads as the most popular head design, but they have now themselves been displaced by newer magneto-resistive heads.

Magneto-Resistive Heads

A more recent development in magnetic recording, or more specifically, the read phase of magnetic recording, is the magneto-resistive head, sometimes also referred to as the anisotropic magneto-resistant (AMR) head. In the last few years, virtually all modern hard disk designs have shifted to using MR heads. MR heads are capable of increasing density four times or greater as compared to the previous inductive-only heads. IBM introduced the first commercially available drive with MR heads in 1991, in a 1GB 3.5-inch model.

All heads are detectors; that is, they are designed to detect the flux transitions in the media and convert them back to an electrical signal that can be interpreted as data. One problem with magnetic recording is the ever increasing desire for more and more density, which is putting more information (flux transitions) in a smaller and smaller space. As the magnetic domains on the disk get smaller, the signal from the heads during reading operations becomes weaker; distinguishing the true signal from the random noise or stray fields present becomes difficult. What is needed is a more efficient read head, which is a more efficient way to detect these transitions on the disk.

Another magnetic effect that is well known today is being used in modern drives. When a wire is passed through a magnetic field, not only does the wire generate a small current, but the resistance of the wire also changes. Standard read heads use the head as a tiny generator, relying on the fact that the heads will generate a pulsed current when passed over magnetic flux transitions. A newer type of head design pioneered by IBM instead relies on the fact that the resistance in the head wires will also change.

Rather than use the head to generate tiny currents, which must then be filtered, amplified, and decoded, a magneto-resistive head uses the head as a resistor. A circuit passes a voltage through the head and watches for the voltage to change, which will occur when the resistance of the head changes as it passes through the flux reversals on the media. This mechanism for using the head results in a much stronger and clearer signal of what was on the media and enables the density to be increased.

MR heads rely on the fact that the resistance of a conductor changes slightly when an external magnetic field is present. Rather than put out a voltage by passing through a magnetic-field flux reversal—as a normal head would—the MR head senses the flux reversal and changes resistance. A small current flows through the heads, and this sense current measures the change in resistance. This design provides an output that is three or more times more powerful than a TF head during a read. In effect, MR heads are power-read heads, acting more like sensors than generators.

MR heads are more costly and complex to manufacture than other types of heads because several special features or steps must be added:

- Additional wires must be run to and from the head to carry the sense current.
- Four to six more masking steps are required.
- Because MR heads are so sensitive, they are very susceptible to stray magnetic fields and must be shielded.

Because the MR principle can only read data and is not used for writing, MR heads are really two heads in one. The assembly includes a standard inductive TF head for writing data and an MR head for reading. Because two separate heads are built into one assembly, each head can be optimized for its task. Ferrite, MIG, and TF heads are known as single-gap heads because the same gap is used for both reading and writing, whereas the MR head uses a separate gap for each operation.

The problem with single-gap heads is that the gap length is always a compromise between what is best for reading and what is best for writing. The read function needs a thin gap for higher resolution; the write function needs a thicker gap for deeper flux penetration to switch the medium. In a dual-gap MR head, the read and write gaps can be optimized for both functions independently. The write (TF) gap writes a wider track than the read (MR) gap reads. Thus, the read head is less likely to pick up stray magnetic information from adjacent tracks.

A typical IBM-designed MR head is shown in Figure 9.5. This figure first shows the complete MR head-and-slider assembly on the end of an actuator arm. This is the part you would see if you opened up a drive. The slider is the block device on the end of the triangular-shaped arm that carries the head. The actual head is the tiny piece shown magnified at the end of the slider, and then the MR read sensor in the head is shown further magnified.

The read element, which is the actual magneto-resistive sensor, consists of a nickel-ferrite (NiFe) film separated by a spacer from a magnetically soft layer. The NiFe film layer changes resistance in the presence of a magnetic field. Layers of shielding protect the MR sensor read element from being corrupted by adjacent or stray magnetic fields. In many designs, the second shield also functions as one pole of the write element, resulting in what is called a *merged* MR head. The write element is not of MR design but is instead a traditional thin film inductive head.

IBM's MR head design employs a Soft Adjacent Layer (SAL) structure, consisting of the MR NiFe film, as well as a magnetically soft alloy layer separated by a film with high electrical resistance. In this design a resistance change occurs in the NiFe layer as the MR sensor passes through a magnetic field.

Figure 9.5   Cross section of a magneto-resistive head.

As areal densities have increased, heads have been designed with narrower and thinner MR elements. The newest heads have reduced the film width between the side contacts to as little as half a micron or less.

Giant Magneto-Resistive Heads

In the quest for even more density, IBM introduced a new type of MR head in 1997. Called giant magneto-resistive (GMR) heads, they are physically smaller than standard MR heads but are so named for the GMR effect on which they are based. The design is very similar; however, additional layers replace the single NiFe layer in a conventional MR design. In MR heads, a single NiFe film changes resistance in response to a flux reversal on the disk. In GMR heads, two films (separated by a very thin copper conducting layer) perform this function.

The GMR effect was first discovered in 1988 in crystal samples exposed to high-powered magnetic fields (1,000 times the fields used in HDDs). It was discovered that large resistance changes were occurring in materials comprised of alternating very thin layers of various metallic elements. The key structure in GMR materials is a spacer layer of a nonmagnetic metal between two layers of magnetic metals. One of the magnetic layers is *pinned*, which means it has a forced magnetic orientation. The other magnetic layer is *free*, which means it is free to change orientation or alignment. Magnetic materials tend to align themselves in the same direction. So if the spacer layer is thin enough, the free layer takes on the same orientation as the pinned layer. What was discovered was that the magnetic alignment of the free magnetic layer would periodically swing back and forth from being aligned in the same magnetic direction as the pinned layer to being aligned in opposite magnetic directions. The overall resistance is relatively low when the layers were in the same alignment and relatively high when in opposite magnetic alignment.

Figure 9.6 shows a GMR read element.

Figure 9.6   Cross section of a giant magneto-resistive head.

When a weak magnetic field, such as that from a bit on a hard disk, passes beneath a GMR head, the magnetic orientation of the free magnetic layer rotates relative to that of the other, generating a significant change in electrical resistance due to the GMR effect. Because the physical nature of the resistance change was determined to be caused by the relative spin of the electrons in the different layers, GMR heads are often referred to as *spin-valve heads*.

IBM announced the first commercially available drive using GMR heads (a 16.8GB 3.5-inch drive) in December 1997. Since then, GMR heads have become the standard in most drives of 20GB and beyond. The latest GMR drives have data densities exceeding 20GB per platter, enabling drives as large as 80GB to be produced in the standard 3.5-inch wide, 1-inch high form factor.

Head Sliders

The term *slider* is used to describe the body of material that supports the actual drive head itself. The slider is what actually floats or slides over the surface of the disk, carrying the head at the correct distance from the medium for reading and writing. Most sliders resemble a trimaran, with two outboard pods that float along the surface of the disk media and a central "hull" portion that actually carries the head and the read/write gap. Figure 9.7 shows a typical slider. Note the actual head, with the read/write gap, is on the trailing end of the slider.

The trend toward smaller and smaller form factor drives has forced sliders to become smaller and smaller as well. The typical mini-Winchester slider design is about .160×.126×.034 inches in size. Most head manufacturers have now shifted to 50% smaller nanosliders, or 70% smaller picosliders. A nanoslider has dimensions of about .08×.063×.017 inches, whereas the smaller picoslider is .049×.039×.012 inches. Picosliders are assembled by using flex interconnect cable (FIC) and chip on ceramic (COC) technology that enables the process to be completely automated.

Figure 9.7   The underside of a typical head slider.

Smaller sliders reduce the mass carried at the end of the head actuator arms, providing increased acceleration and deceleration, leading to faster seek times. The smaller sliders also require less area for a landing zone, thus increasing the usable area of the disk platters. Further, the smaller slider contact area reduces the slight wear on the platter surface that occurs during normal startup and spindown of the drive platters.

The newer nanoslider and picoslider designs also have specially modified surface patterns that are designed to maintain the same floating height above the disk surface, whether the slider is positioned above the inner or outer cylinders. Conventional sliders increase or decrease their floating heights considerably, according to the velocity of the disk surface traveling beneath them. Above the outer cylinders, the velocity and floating height are higher. This arrangement is undesirable in newer drives that use zoned bit recording, in which the bit density is the same on all the cylinders. When the bit density is uniform throughout the drive, the head floating height should be relatively constant as well for maximum performance. Special textured surface patterns and manufacturing techniques enable the sliders to float at a much more consistent height, making them ideal for zoned bit recording drives. For more information on zoned recording, see the section "Disk Formatting" in Chapter 10.

Data Encoding Schemes

Magnetic storage is essentially an analog medium. The data a PC stores on it, however, is digital information—that is, 1s and 0s. When the drive sends digital information to a magnetic recording head, the head creates magnetic domains on the storage medium with specific polarities corresponding to the positive and negative voltages the drive applies to the head. It is the flux reversals that form the boundaries between the areas of positive and negative polarity that the drive controller uses to encode the digital data onto the analog medium. During a read operation, each flux reversal the drive detects generates a positive or negative pulse that the device uses to reconstruct the original binary data.

To optimize the placement of flux transitions during magnetic storage, the drive passes the raw digital input data through a device called an encoder/decoder (endec), which converts the raw binary information to a waveform designed to optimally place the flux transitions (pulses) on the media. During a read operation, the endec reverses the process and decodes the pulse train back into the original binary data. Over the years, several schemes for encoding data in this manner have been developed; some are better or more efficient than others, which you see later in this section.

Other descriptions of the data encoding process might be much simpler, but they omit the facts that make some of the issues related to hard drive reliability so critical—namely, timing. Engineers and designers are constantly pushing the envelope to stuff more and more bits of information into the limited quantity of magnetic flux reversals per inch. What they've came up with, essentially, is a design in which the bits of information are not only decoded from the presence or absence of flux reversals, but from the timing between them. The more accurately they can time the reversals, the more information that can be encoded (and subsequently decoded) from that timing information.

In any form of binary signaling, the use of timing is significant. When interpreting a read or write waveform, the timing of each voltage transition event is critical. Timing is what defines a particular bit or transition cell—that is, the time window within which the drive is either writing or reading a transition. If the timing is off, a given voltage transition might be recognized at the wrong time as being in a different cell, which would throw the conversion or encoding off, resulting in bits being missed, added, or misinterpreted. To ensure that the timing is precise, the transmitting and receiving devices must be in perfect synchronization. For example, if recording a zero is done by placing no transition on the disk for a given time period or cell, imagine recording 10 zero bits in a row—you would have a long period of 10 time periods or cells with no transitions.

Imagine now that the clock on the encoder was slightly off time while reading data as compared to when it was originally written. If it were fast, the encoder might think that during this long stretch of 10 cells with no transitions, only nine cells had actually elapsed. Or if it were slow, it might think that 11 cells had elapsed instead. In either case, this would result in a read error, meaning the bits that were originally written would not be read as being the same. To prevent timing errors in drive encoding/decoding, perfect synchronization is necessary between the reading and writing processes. This synchronization often is accomplished by adding a separate timing signal, called a *clock signal*, to the transmission between the two devices. The clock and data signals also can be combined and transmitted as a single signal. Most magnetic data encoding schemes use this type of combination of clock and data signals.

Adding a clock signal to the data ensures that the communicating devices can accurately interpret the individual bit cells. Each bit cell is bounded by two other cells containing the clock transitions. By sending clock information along with the data, the clocks remain in sync, even if the medium contains a long string of identical zero bits. Unfortunately, the transition cells used solely for timing take up space on the medium that could otherwise be used for data.

Because the number of flux transitions a drive can record in a given space on a particular medium is limited by the physical nature or density of the medium and the head technology, drive engineers have developed various ways of encoding the data by using a minimum number of flux reversals (taking into consideration the fact that some flux reversals used solely for clocking are required). Signal encoding enables the system to make the maximum use of a given drive hardware technology.

Although various encoding schemes have been tried, only a few are popular today. Over the years, these three basic types have been the most popular:

- Frequency Modulation
- Modified Frequency Modulation
- Run Length Limited

The following sections examine these codes, how they work, where they are used, and any advantages or disadvantages that apply to them. It will help to refer to Figure 9.8 (later in the chapter) as you read the descriptions of each of these encoding schemes because this figure depicts how each of these schemes would store an "X" on the same media.

FM Encoding

One of the earliest techniques for encoding data for magnetic storage is called Frequency Modulation encoding. This encoding scheme—sometimes called Single-Density encoding—was used in the earliest floppy disk drives installed in PC systems. The original Osborne portable computer, for example, used these Single-Density floppy disk drives, which stored about 80KB of data on a single disk. Although it was popular until the late 1970s, FM encoding is no longer used.

MFM Encoding

Modified Frequency Modulation encoding was devised to reduce the number of flux reversals used in the original FM encoding scheme and, therefore, to pack more data onto the disk. MFM encoding minimizes the use of clock transitions, leaving more room for the data. MFM records clock transitions only when a stored zero bit is preceded by another zero bit; in all other cases, a clock transition is not required. Because MFM minimizes the use of clock transitions, it can double the clock frequency used by FM encoding, enabling it to store twice as many data bits in the same number of flux transitions.

Because MFM encoding writes twice as many data bits by using the same number of flux reversals as FM, the clock speed of the data is doubled, so the drive actually sees the same number of total flux reversals as with FM. This means a drive using MFM encoding reads and writes data at twice the speed of FM, even though the drive sees the flux reversals arriving at the same frequency as in FM.

Because it is twice as efficient as FM encoding, MFM encoding also has been called Double-Density recording. MFM is used in virtually all PC floppy disk drives today and was used in nearly all PC hard disks for a number of years. Today, virtually all hard disks use variations of RLL encoding, which provides even greater efficiency than MFM.

Table 9.1 shows the data bit to flux reversal translation in MFM encoding.

Table 9.1   MFM Data to Flux Transition Encoding

Data Bit Value	Flux Encoding
1	NT
0 preceded by 0	TN
0 preceded by 1	NN

T = Flux transition

N = No flux transition

RLL Encoding

Today's most popular encoding scheme for hard disks, called Run Length Limited, packs up to twice the information on a given disk than MFM does and three times as much information as FM. In RLL encoding, the drive combines groups of bits into a unit to generate specific patterns of flux reversals. By combining the clock and data signals in these patterns, the clock rate can be further increased while maintaining the same basic distance between the flux transitions on the storage medium.

IBM invented RLL encoding and first used the method in many of its mainframe disk drives. During the late 1980s, the PC hard disk industry began using RLL encoding schemes to increase the storage capabilities of PC hard disks. Today, virtually every drive on the market uses some form of RLL encoding.

Instead of encoding a single bit, RLL normally encodes a group of data bits at a time. The term *Run Length Limited* is derived from the two primary specifications of these codes, which are the minimum number (the run length) and maximum number (the run limit) of transition cells allowed between two actual flux transitions. Several variations of the scheme are achieved by changing the length and limit parameters, but only two have achieved any real popularity: RLL 2,7 and RLL 1,7.

You can even express FM and MFM encoding as a form of RLL. FM can be called RLL 0,1, because as few as zero and as many as one transition cells separate two flux transitions. MFM can be called RLL 1,3, because as few as one and as many as three transition cells separate two flux transitions. (Although these codes can be expressed as variations of RLL form, it is not common to do so.)

RLL 2,7 was initially the most popular RLL variation because it offers a high-density ratio with a transition detection window that is the same relative size as that in MFM. This method provides high storage density and fairly good reliability. In very high-capacity drives, however, RLL 2,7 did not prove to be reliable enough. Most of today's highest capacity drives use RLL 1,7 encoding, which offers a density ratio 1.27 times that of MFM and a larger transition detection window relative to MFM. Because of the larger relative timing window or cell size within which a transition can be detected, RLL 1,7 is a more forgiving and more reliable code, which is important when media and head technology are being pushed to their limits.

Another little-used RLL variation called RLL 3,9—sometimes called Advanced RLL (ARLL)—allows an even higher density ratio than RLL 2,7. Unfortunately, reliability suffered too greatly under the RLL 3,9 scheme; the method was used by only a few now-obsolete controllers and has all but disappeared.

Understanding how RLL codes work is difficult without looking at an example. Within a given RLL variation such as RLL 2,7 or 1,7, you can construct many flux transition encoding tables to demonstrate how particular groups of bits are encoded into flux transitions.

In the conversion table shown in Table 9.2, specific groups of data bits two, three, and four bits long are translated into strings of flux transitions 4, 6, and 8 transition cells long, respectively. The selected transitions for a particular bit sequence are designed to ensure that flux transitions do not occur too close together or too far apart.

Limiting how close two flux transitions can be is necessary because of the fixed resolution capabilities of the head and the storage medium. Limiting how far apart two flux transitions can be ensures that the clocks in the devices remain in sync.

Table 9.2   RLL 2,7 Data to Flux Transition Encoding

Data Bit Values	Flux Encoding
10	NTNN
11	TNNN
000	NNNTNN
010	TNNTNN
011	NNTNNN
0010	NNTNNTNN
0011	NNNNTNNN

T = Flux transition

N = No flux transition

In studying this table, you might think that encoding a byte value such as 00000001b would be impossible because no combinations of data bit groups fit this byte. Encoding this type of byte is not a problem, however, because the controller does not transmit individual bytes; instead, the controller sends whole sectors, making encoding such a byte possible by including some of the bits in the following byte. The only real problem occurs in the last byte of a sector, if additional bits are necessary to complete the final group sequence. In these cases, the endec in the controller adds excess bits to the end of the last byte. These excess bits are truncated during any reads so the controller always decodes the last byte correctly.

Encoding Scheme Comparisons

Figure 9.8 shows an example of the waveform written to store the ASCII character X on a hard disk drive by using three different encoding schemes.

In each of these encoding scheme examples, the top line shows the individual data bits (01011000b, for example) in their bit cells separated in time by the clock signal, which is shown as a period (.). Below that line is the actual write waveform, showing the positive and negative voltages as well as head voltage transitions that result in the recording of flux transitions. The bottom line shows the transition cells, with T representing a transition cell that contains a flux transition and N representing a transition cell that is empty.

The FM encoding example shown in Figure 9.8 is easy to explain. Each bit cell has two transition cells: one for the clock information and one for the data itself. All the clock transition cells contain flux transitions, and the data transition cells contain a flux transition only if the data is a one bit. No transition is present when the data is a zero bit. Starting from the left, the first data bit is 0, which decodes as a flux transition pattern of TN. The next bit is a 1, which decodes as TT. The next bit is 0, which decodes as TN, and so on.

Figure 9.8 ASCII character "X" write waveforms using FM, MFM, and RLL 2,7 encoding.

The MFM encoding scheme also has clock and data transition cells for each data bit to be recorded. As you can see, however, the clock transition cells carry a flux transition only when a zero bit is stored after another zero bit. Starting from the left, the first bit is a 0, and the preceding bit is unknown (assume 0), so the flux transition pattern is TN for that bit. The next bit is a 1, which always decodes to a transition-cell pattern of NT. The next bit is 0, which was preceded by 1, so the pattern stored is NN. By using Table 9.1 (shown earlier), you easily can trace the MFM encoding pattern to the end of the byte. You can see that the minimum and maximum number of transition cells between any two flux transitions are one and three, respectively, which explains why MFM encoding can also be called RLL 1,3.

The RLL 2,7 pattern is more difficult to see because it encodes groups of bits rather than individual bits. Starting from the left, the first group that matches the groups listed in Table 9.2 is the first three bits, 010. These bits are translated into a flux transition pattern of TNNTNN. The next two bits, 11, are translated as a group to TNNN; and the final group, 000 bits, is translated to NNNTNN to complete the byte. As you can see in this example, no additional bits were needed to finish the last group.

Notice that the minimum and maximum number of empty transition cells between any two flux transitions in this example are 2 and 6, although a different example could show a maximum of seven empty transition cells. This is where the RLL 2,7 designation comes from. Because even fewer transitions are recorded than in MFM, the clock rate can be increased to three times that of FM or 1.5 times that of MFM, thus storing more data in the same space. Notice, however, that the resulting write waveform itself looks exactly like a typical FM or MFM waveform in terms of the number and separation of the flux transitions for a given physical portion of the disk. In other words, the physical minimum and maximum distances between any two flux transitions remain the same in all three of these encoding scheme examples.

Partial-Response, Maximum-Likelihood Decoders

Another feature often used in modern hard disk drives involves the disk read circuitry. Read channel circuits using Partial-Response, Maximum-Likelihood (PRML) technology enable disk drive manufacturers to increase the amount of data stored on a disk platter by up to 40%. PRML replaces the standard "detect one peak at a time" approach of traditional analog peak-detect, read/write channels with digital signal processing.

As the data density of hard drives increases, the drive must necessarily record the flux reversals closer together on the medium. This makes reading the data on the disk more difficult because the adjacent magnetic peaks can begin to interfere with each other. PRML modifies the way the drive reads the data from the disk. The controller analyzes the analog data stream it receives from the heads by using digital signal sampling, processing, and detection algorithms (this is the partial response element) and predicts the sequence of bits the data stream is most likely to represent (the maximum likelihood element). PRML technology can take an analog waveform, which might be filled with noise and stray signals, and produce an accurate reading from it.

This might not sound like a very precise method of reading data that must be bit-perfect to be usable, but the aggregate effect of the digital signal processing filters out the noise efficiently enough to enable the drive to place the flux change pulses much closer together on the platter, thus achieving greater densities. Most drives with capacities of 2GB or above use PRML technology in their endec circuits.

Capacity Measurements

In December 1998, the International Electrotechnical Commission (IEC)—the leading international organization for worldwide standardization in electrotechnology—approved as an IEC International Standard names and symbols for prefixes for binary multiples for use in the fields of data processing and data transmission. Prior to this there had been a lot of confusion as to whether a megabyte stood for 1 million bytes (10^6) or 1,048,576 bytes (2^{20}). Even so, these new prefixes have yet to be widely adopted and confusion still reigns. The industry-standard abbreviations for the units used to measure the capacity of magnetic (and other) drives are shown in Table 9.3.

Table 9.3   Standard Abbreviations and Meanings

Abbreviation	Description	Power	Value
K	Kilo	10^3	1,000
Ki	Kibi	2^{10}	1,024
M	Mega	10^6	1,000,000
Mi	Mebi	2^{20}	1,048,576
G	Giga	10^9	1,000,000,000
Gi	Gibi	2^{30}	1,073,741,824
T	Tera	10^{12}	1,000,000,000,000
Ti	Tebi	2^{40}	1,099,511,627,776
P	Peta	10^{15}	1,000,000,000,000,000
Pi	Pebi	2^{50}	1,125,899,906,842,624

According to the new prefix standard, one mebibyte (1 MiB = 2^{20} B = 1,048,576 B), and one megabyte (1 MB = 10^6 B = 1,000,000 B). Because the new prefixes are not in widespread use (and they might never be) M in most cases can indicate both decimal *millions of bytes* and binary *megabytes*. Similarly, G is often used to refer to decimal *billions of bytes* and binary *gigabytes*. In general, memory values are expressed by using the binary values, although disk capacities can go either way. This often leads to confusion in reporting disk capacities because many manufacturers tend to use whichever value makes their products look better. For example, drive capacities are often rated in decimal billions (G - Giga), whereas most BIOS chips and operating system utilities, such as Windows' FDISK, rate the same drive in binary gigabytes (Gi -Gibi). Note also that when bits and bytes are used as part of some other measurement, the difference between bits and bytes is often distinguished by the use of a lower- or uppercase *B*. For example, megabits are typically abbreviated with a lowercase *b*, resulting in the abbreviation *Mbps* for *megabits per second*, whereas *MBps* indicates *megabytes per second*.

Areal Density

Areal density is often used as a technology growth-rate indicator for the hard disk drive industry. *Areal density* is defined as the product of the linear bits per inch (BPI), measured along the length of the tracks around the disk, multiplied by the number of tracks per inch (TPI), measured radially on the disk (see Figure 9.9). The results are expressed in units of megabits or gigabits per square inch (Mbit/sq.-inch or Gbit/sq.-inch) and are used as a measure of efficiency in drive recording technology. Current high-end 3.5-inch drives record at areal densities of 10Gbit/sq.-inch–20Gbit/sq.-inch. Prototype drives with densities as high as 40Gbit/sq.-inch now exist, which will allow 3.5-inch drives with capacities of 400GB or more in the next few years.

Drives record data in tracks, which are circular bands of data on the disk. Each track is divided into sectors. Figure 9.10 shows an actual floppy disk sprayed with magnetic developer (powdered iron) such that an image of the actual tracks and sectors can be clearly seen. The disk shown is a 5 1/4-inch 360KB floppy, which has 40 tracks per side, and each track is divided into 9 sectors. Note that each sector is delineated by gaps in the recording, which precede and postcede the track and sector headers (where ID and address information resides). You can clearly see the triple gap preceding the first sector, which includes the track and sector headers. Then following in a counterclockwise direction, you see each subsequent sector, preceded by gaps delineating the header for that sector. The area between the headers is where the sector data is written.

Tracks Per Inch (TPI)

Bits Per Inch (BPI)

Lower Areal Density

Track bits

Tracks Per Inch (TPI)

Bits Per Inch (BPI)

Higher Areal Density

Figure 9.9 Areal density, combining tracks per inch and bits per inch.

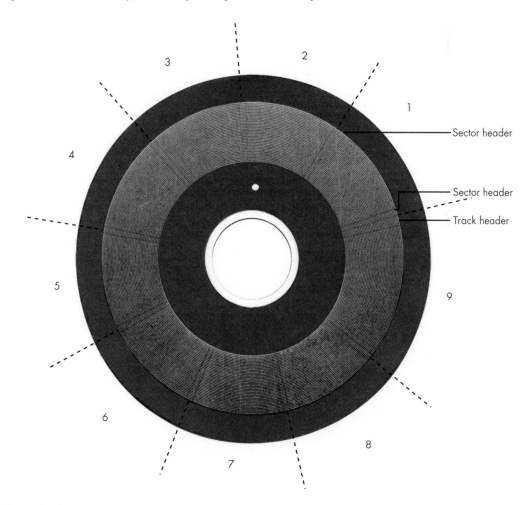

3 2 1

4

5

6 7 8 9

Sector header

Sector header

Track header

Figure 9.10 360KB floppy disk media sprayed with magnetic developer (powdered iron) showing the actual track and sector images.

Notice that sector 9 is longer than the rest; this is to enable rotational speed differences between drives, so that all the data can be written before running into the start of the track. Also notice that a good portion of the disk surface isn't used because it is simply impractical to have the heads travel in and out that far, and the difference in length between the sectors on the inner and outer tracks becomes more of a problem.

Areal density has been rising steadily since the first magnetic storage drive (IBM RAMAC) was introduced in 1956, initially at a growth rate of about 25% per year (doubling every four years), and since the early 1990s at a growth rate of about 60% per year (doubling every 1.5 years). The development and introduction of magneto-resistive in 1991 and giant magneto-resistive heads in 1997 propelled the increase in the areal density growth rate. In the 44+ years since the RAMAC drive was introduced, the areal density of magnetic storage has increased more than five million fold.

At the current growth rate, within the next five years or so, drive manufacturers will achieve areal densities of approximately 100Gbit/sq.-inch, which is considered near the point at which the superparamagnetic effect takes place. This is an effect in which the magnetic domains become so small that they are intrinsically unstable at room temperature. Techniques such as extremely high coercivity media and vertical polarity recording are projected to enable magnetic storage densities of 200Gbit/sq.-inch or more, but beyond that, scientists and engineers will have to look toward other technologies. One such technology being considered for the future is holographic storage, in which a laser writes data three-dimensionally in a crystal plate or cube.

Figure 9.11 shows how areal density has increased from when magnetic storage was first developed (1956 RAMAC) through the present time.

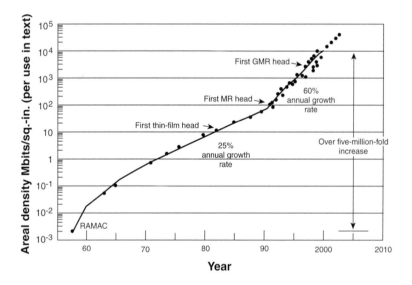

Figure 9.11   Evolution of areal density in magnetic disk storage.

To increase areal density while maintaining the same external drive form factors, drive manufacturers have developed media and head technologies to support these higher areal densities, such as ceramic/glass platters, GMR heads, pseudo-contact recording, and PRML electronics, as discussed earlier in this chapter. The primary challenge in achieving higher densities is manufacturing drive heads and disks to operate at closer tolerances. Improvements in tolerances and the use of more platters in a given form factor continue to fuel improvements in drive capacity, but drive makers continue to seek even greater capacity increases, both by improving current technologies and by developing new ones.

To fit more data on a platter of a given size, the tracks must be placed closer together, and the heads must be capable of achieving greater precision in their placements over the tracks. This also means that as hard disk capacities increase, heads must float ever closer to the disk surface during operation. The gap between the head and disk is as close as 10 nanometers (0.01 microns) in some drives, which is approximately the thickness of a cell membrane. By comparison, a human hair is typically 80 microns in diameter, which is 8,000 times thicker than the gap between the head and disk in some drives. The prospect of actual contact or near contact recording is being considered for future drives to further increase density.

CHAPTER 10

Hard Disk Storage

Definition of a Hard Disk

To many users, the hard disk drive is the most important and yet the most mysterious part of a computer system. A *hard disk drive* is a sealed unit that a PC uses for nonvolatile data storage. *Nonvolatile*, or semi-permanent, storage means that the storage device retains the data even when no power is supplied to the computer. Because the hard disk drive is expected to retain data until deliberately erased or overwritten, the hard drive is used to store crucial programming and data. As a result, when the hard disk fails, the consequences are usually very serious. To maintain, service, and upgrade a PC system properly, you must understand how the hard disk functions.

A hard disk drive contains rigid, disk-shaped platters, usually constructed of aluminum or glass (see Figure 10.1). Unlike floppy disks, the platters cannot bend or flex—hence the term *hard disk*. In most hard disk drives, you cannot remove the platters, which is why they are sometimes called *fixed* disk drives. Removable hard disk drives are also available. Sometimes this term refers to a device in which the entire drive unit (that is, the disk and the drive) is removable, but it is more commonly used to refer to cartridge drives, where the platters are contained in a removable cartridge.

Figure 10.1   Hard disk heads and platters.

Note

Hard disk drives are sometimes referred to as *Winchester drives*. This term dates back to 1973, when IBM introduced the model 3340 drive, which had 30MB of fixed platter and 30MB of removable platter storage on separate spindles. The drive was codenamed Winchester by project leader Ken Haughton, because the original capacity designation (30-30) sounded like the popular .30-30 (caliber-grains of charge) cartridge used by the Winchester 94 rifle introduced in 1895. The original 3340 "Winchester" drive was the first to use a sealed head/disk assembly, and the name has since been applied to all subsequent drives with similar technology.

Hard Drive Advancements

In the almost 20 years that hard disks have commonly been used in PC systems, they have undergone tremendous changes. To give you an idea of how far hard drives have come in that time, I've outlined some of the more profound changes in PC hard disk storage:

- Maximum storage capacities have increased from the 5MB and 10MB 5 1/4-inch full-height drives available in 1982 to 180GB or more for even smaller 3 1/2-inch half-height drives (Seagate Barracuda 180), and 32GB or more for notebook system 2 1/2-inch drives (IBM

Travelstar 32GH) that are 12.5mm (or less) in height. Hard drives smaller than 10GB are rare in today's desktop personal computers.

- Data transfer rates from the media (sustained transfer rates) have increased from 85KB to 102KB/sec for the original IBM XT in 1983 to an average of 51.15MB/sec or more for the fastest drives today (Seagate Cheetah 73LP).

- Average seek times (how long it takes to move the heads to a particular cylinder) have decreased from more than 85ms (milliseconds) for the 10MB XT hard disk in 1983 to 4.2ms or less for some of the fastest drives today (Seagate Cheetah X15).

- In 1982, a 10MB drive cost more than $1,500 ($150 per megabyte). Today, the cost of hard drives has dropped to one-half cent per megabyte or less!

Hard Disk Drive Operation

The basic physical construction of a hard disk drive consists of spinning disks with heads that move over the disks and store data in tracks and sectors. The heads read and write data in concentric rings called *tracks*, which are divided into segments called *sectors*, which normally store 512 bytes each (see Figure 10.2).

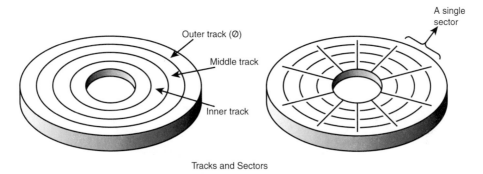

Figure 10.2   The tracks and sectors on a disk.

Hard disk drives usually have multiple disks, called *platters*, that are stacked on top of each other and spin in unison, each with two sides on which the drive stores data. Most drives have two or three platters, resulting in four or six sides, but some PC hard disks have up to 12 platters and 24 sides with 24 heads to read them (Seagate Barracuda 180). The identically aligned tracks on each side of every platter together make up a cylinder (see Figure 10.3). A hard disk drive normally has one head per platter side, with all the heads mounted on a common carrier device or rack. The heads move radially across the disk in unison; they cannot move independently because they are mounted on the same carrier or rack, called an *actuator*.

Originally, most hard disks spun at 3,600rpm—approximately 10 times faster than a floppy disk drive. For many years, 3,600rpm was pretty much a constant among hard drives. Now, however, most drives spin the disks even faster. While speeds can vary, most modern drives spin the platters at 4,200; 5,400; 7,200; 10,000; or 15,000rpm. High rotational speeds combined with a fast head-positioning mechanism and more sectors per track are what make one hard disk faster than another.

The heads in most hard disk drives do not (and should not!) touch the platters during normal operation. When the heads are powered off, however, in most drives they land on the platters as they stop spinning. While the drive is running, a very thin cushion of air keeps each head suspended a short distance above or below the platter. If the air cushion is disturbed by a particle of dust or a shock, the head can come into contact with the platter while it is spinning at full speed. When contact with the spinning platters is forceful enough to do damage, the event is called a *head crash*. The result of a head crash can be anything from a few lost bytes of data to a completely ruined drive. Most drives have special lubricants on the platters and hardened surfaces that can withstand the daily "takeoffs and landings" as well as more severe abuse.

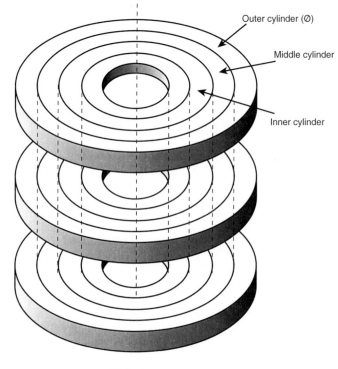

Cylinders

Figure 10.3   Hard disk cylinders.

Because the platter assemblies are sealed and nonremovable, the track densities on the disk can be very high. Hard drives today have up to 38,000 or more TPI (tracks per inch) recorded on the media (IBM Travelstar 30GT). Head Disk Assemblies (HDAs), which contain the platters, are assembled and sealed in clean rooms under absolutely sanitary conditions. Because few companies repair HDAs, repair or replacement of the parts inside a sealed HDA can be expensive. Every hard disk ever made eventually fails. The only questions are when the failure will occur and whether your data is backed up.

Caution

It is strongly recommended that you do not even attempt to open a hard disk drive's HDA unless you have the equipment and the expertise to make repairs inside. Most manufacturers deliberately make the HDA difficult to open, to discourage the intrepid do-it-yourselfer. Opening the HDA almost certainly voids the drive's warranty.

Many PC users think that hard disks are fragile, and comparatively speaking, they are one of the more fragile components in your PC. In many of my PC Hardware and Troubleshooting or Data Recovery seminars, however, I have run various hard disks with the covers removed, and have even removed and installed the covers while the drives were operating! Those drives continue to store data perfectly to this day with their lids either on or off. Of course, I do not recommend that you try this with your own drives.

The Ultimate Hard Disk Drive Analogy

There is an old analogy that compares the interaction of the heads and the medium in a typical hard disk drive as being similar in scale to a 747 flying a few feet off the ground at cruising speed (500+ mph). I have heard this analogy used over and over again for years, and I've even used it in my seminars many times without checking to see whether the analogy is technically accurate with respect to modern hard drives. It isn't.

One highly inaccurate aspect of the 747 analogy has always bothered me—the use of an airplane of any type to describe the head-and-platter interaction. This analogy implies that the heads fly very low over the surface of the disk, but technically, this is not true. The heads do not fly at all in the traditional aerodynamic sense; instead, they float on a cushion of air that is being dragged around by the platters.

A much better analogy would use a hovercraft instead of an airplane; the action of a hovercraft much more closely emulates the action of the heads in a hard disk drive. Like a hovercraft, the drive heads rely somewhat on the shape of the bottom of the head to capture and control the cushion of air that keeps them floating over the disk. By nature, the cushion of air on which the heads float forms only in very close proximity to the platter, and is often called an *air bearing* by the disk drive industry.

I thought it was time to come up with a new analogy that more correctly describes the dimensions and speeds at which a hard disk drive operates today. I looked up the specifications on a specific hard disk drive, and then magnified and rescaled all the dimensions involved to make the head floating height equal to one inch. For my example, I used an IBM Deskstar 75GXP drive, which is a 75GB (formatted capacity), 3 1/2-inch ATA (AT Attachment interface) drive. The head sliders (called pico sliders) in this drive are about 0.049 inches long, 0.039 inches wide, and 0.012 inches high. They float on a cushion of air about 15 nanometers (nm or billionths of a meter) over the surface of the disk while traveling at an average speed of 53.55 miles per hour (figuring an average track diameter of about 2.5 inches). These heads read and write individual bits spaced only 2.56 micro-inches (millionths of an inch) apart, along tracks separated by only 35.27 micro-inches. The heads can move from one track to another in 8.5 milliseconds during an average seek.

To create my analogy, I magnified the scale to make the head floating height equal to 5 millimeters (about 0.2 inches). Because 5 millimeters is about 333,333 times greater than 15 nanometers (nm), I scaled up everything else by the same amount.

Magnified to such a scale, the heads in this typical hard disk would be about 1,361 feet long, 1,083 feet wide, and 333 feet high (the length and height are about equal to the Sears Tower if it were toppled over sideways). These skyscraper-sized heads would float on a cushion of air which to scale would be only 5mm thick (about 0.2 inches) while travelling at a speed of 17.8 million miles per hour (4,958 miles per second), all while reading data bits spaced a mere 0.85 inches apart on tracks separated by only 0.98 feet!

The forward scale speed of this imaginary head is difficult to comprehend, so I'll elaborate. The diameter of the Earth at the equator is 7,926 miles, which means a circumference of about 24,900 miles. At 4,958 miles per second, this imaginary skyscraper-sized head would circle the earth once every five seconds (at only two-tenths of an inch over the surface)! It would also read 231.33MB in one lap around this equatorial track.

There is also sideways velocity to consider. Because the average seek time of 8.5 milliseconds is defined as the time it takes to move the heads over one-third of the total tracks (about 9,241 tracks in this case), the heads could move sideways within a scale distance of 1.71 miles in that short time. This results in a scale seek velocity of more than 726,321mph, or 202 miles per second!

This analogy should give you a new appreciation of the technological marvel that the modern hard disk drive actually represents. It makes the old 747 analogy look rather pathetic (not to mention inaccurate), doesn't it?

Tracks and Sectors

A *track* is a single ring of data on one side of a disk. A disk track is too large to manage data effectively as a single storage unit. Many disk tracks can store 100,000 or more bytes of data, which would be very inefficient for storing small files. For that reason, tracks are divided into several numbered divisions known as sectors. These sectors represent arc-shaped pieces of the track.

Various types of disk drives split their disk tracks into different numbers of sectors, depending on the density of the tracks. For example, floppy disk formats use 8–36 sectors per track, although hard disks usually store data at a higher density and today can have 900 or more sectors per track physically. The sectors created by the standard formatting procedure on a PC system have a capacity of 512 bytes, which has been one constant throughout the history of the PC. One interesting phenomenon of the PC standard is that to be compatible with most older BIOS and drivers, drives will usually perform an internal translation to a logical 63 sectors per track.

The sectors on a track are numbered starting with 1, unlike the heads or cylinders that are numbered starting with 0. For example, a 1.44MB floppy disk contains 80 cylinders numbered 0–79 and two heads numbered 0 and 1, whereas each track on each cylinder has 18 sectors numbered 1–18.

When a disk is formatted, the formatting program creates ID areas before and after each sector's data that the disk controller uses for sector numbering and for identifying the start and end of each sector. These areas precede and follow each sector's data area and consume some of the disk's total storage capacity. This accounts for the difference between a disk's unformatted and formatted capacities. Note that most modern hard drives are sold preformatted and only advertise the formatted capacity. The unformatted capacity is usually not mentioned anymore. Another interesting development is that IBM and others now make drives with ID-less recording, which means that the sectors are recorded without ID marks before and after each sector. This means that more of the disk can be used for actual data.

Each sector on a disk normally has a prefix portion, or header, that identifies the start of the sector and contains the sector number, as well as a suffix portion, or trailer, that contains a checksum (which helps ensure the integrity of the data contents). Many newer drives omit this header and have what is called a No-ID recording, allowing more space for data.

Each sector contains 512 bytes of data. The low-level formatting process normally fills the data bytes with some specific value, such as F6h (hex), or some other repeating test pattern used by the drive manufacturer. Some patterns are more difficult for the drive to encode/decode, so these patterns normally are used when the manufacturer is testing the drive during initial formatting. A special test pattern might cause errors to surface that a normal data pattern would not show. This way, the manufacturer can more accurately identify marginal sectors during testing.

Note

The type of disk formatting discussed here is a physical or low-level format, not the high-level format you perform when you use the Windows 9x/Me/2000 Explorer or the DOS FORMAT program on a disk. See the section "Disk Formatting" later in this chapter to learn about the difference between these two types of formatting.

The sector headers and trailers are independent of the operating system, the file system, and the files stored on the drive. In addition to the headers and trailers, gaps exist within the sectors, between the sectors on each track, and also between tracks, but none of these gaps contain usable data space. The gaps are created during the low-level format process when the recording is turned off momentarily. They serve the same function as having gaps of no sound between the songs recorded on a cassette tape. The prefix, suffix, and gaps account for the lost space between the unformatted capacity of a disk and the formatted capacity. For example, a 4MB (unformatted) floppy disk (3 1/2-inch) has a capacity of 2.88MB when it is formatted, a 2MB (unformatted) floppy has a formatted capacity of 1.44MB, and an older 38MB unformatted capacity (for instance, Seagate ST-4038) hard disk has a capacity of only 32MB when it is formatted. Because the ATA/IDE and SCSI hard drives you purchase today are low-level formatted at the factory, the manufacturers now advertise only the formatted capacity. Even so, nearly all drives use some reserved space for managing the data that will be stored on the drive.

Thus, while I stated earlier that each disk sector is 512 bytes in size, this statement is technically not true. Each sector does allow for the storage of 512 bytes of data, but the data area is only a portion of the sector. Each sector on a disk typically occupies 571 bytes of the disk, of which only 512 bytes are available for the storage of user data. The actual number of bytes required for the sector header and trailer can vary from drive to drive, but this figure is typical. As mentioned earlier, though, many modern drives now use a No-ID recording scheme that virtually eliminates the storage overhead of the sector header information. You might find it helpful to think of each disk sector as being a page in a book. In a book, each page contains text, but the entire page is not filled with text; rather, each page has top, bottom, left, and right margins. Information such as chapter titles (track and cylinder numbers) and page numbers (sector numbers) is placed in the margins. The "margin" areas of a sector are created and written to during the low-level formatting process. Formatting also fills the data area of each sector with dummy values. After you perform a high-level format on the disk, the PC's file system can write to the data area of each sector, but the sector header and trailer information cannot be altered during normal write operations unless the disk is low-level formatted again.

Table 10.1 shows the format for each track and sector on a typical hard disk drive with 17 sectors per track.

Table 10.1   Typical Disk Track/Sector Format Using ID Marks

Bytes	Name	Description
16	POST INDEX GAP	All 4Eh, at the track beginning after the Index mark.

The following sector data (shown between the lines in this table) is repeated as many times as there are sectors on the track.

Bytes	Name	Description
13	ID VFO LOCK	All 00h; synchronizes the VFO for the sector ID.
1	SYNC BYTE	A1h; notifies the controller that data follows.
1	ADDRESS MARK	FEh; defines that ID field data follows.
2	CYLINDER NUMBER	A value that defines the head actuator position.
1	HEAD NUMBER	A value that defines the particular head selected.
1	SECTOR NUMBER	A value that defines the sector.
2	CRC	Cyclic Redundancy Check to verify ID data.
3	WRITE TURN-ON GAP	00h written by format to isolate the ID from DATA.
13	DATA SYNC VFO LOCK	All 00h; synchronizes the VFO for the DATA.
1	SYNC BYTE	A1h; notifies the controller that data follows.
1	ADDRESS MARK	F8h; defines that user DATA field follows.

Table 10.1 Continued

Bytes	Name	Description
512	DATA	The area for user DATA.
2	CRC	Cyclic Redundancy Check to verify DATA.
3	WRITE TURN-OFF GAP	00h; written by DATA update to isolate DATA.
15	INTER-RECORD GAP	All 00h; a buffer for spindle speed variation.
693	PRE-INDEX GAP	All 4Eh, at track end before Index mark.

571 = Total bytes per sector; 512 = Data (usable) bytes per sector

Note: "All XXh" indicates that field will be filled with XXh bytes.

As you can see, the usable space for data on each track is about 15% less than its total unformatted capacity. This is true for most disks, although the percentage can vary slightly, depending on how many sectors exist per track. The following paragraphs detail each piece of the sector data listed in Table 10.1.

The POST INDEX GAP provides a head-switching recovery period, so when switching from one track to another, the heads can read sequential sectors without waiting for an additional revolution of the disk. Because the disk is continuously spinning and the heads take some small amount of time to move radially from track to track, reading consecutive sectors on two different tracks, one right after the other, is not possible. By the time the head moves to the new track, the beginning of the second sector has already spun past it. Leaving a gap between sectors provides the heads with time to move to another track.

In some drives, this gap does not provide sufficient time for the heads to move. When this is the case, a drive can gain additional time by skewing the sectors on different tracks so the arrival of the first sector is delayed. In other words, the low-level formatting process offsets the sector numbering, so instead of the same numbered sectors on each track being adjacent to each other, Sector 9 on one track might be next to Sector 8 of the next track, which is next to Sector 7 on the next, and so forth. The optimum skew value is based on the rotational speed of the disk as compared to the lateral speed of the heads.

Note

At one time, the head skew was a parameter you could set yourself while low-level formatting a drive. Today's ATA/IDE and SCSI drives are low-level formatted at the factory with the optimum skew values.

The Sector ID data consists of the Cylinder, Head, and Sector Number fields, as well as a CRC field used to verify the ID data. Most controllers use bit 7 of the Head Number field to mark a sector as bad during a low-level format or surface analysis. This convention is not absolute, however. Some controllers use other methods to mark a bad sector, but usually the mark involves one of the ID fields.

The WRITE TURN-ON GAP follows the ID field's CRC bytes and provides a pad to ensure a proper recording of the user data area that follows, as well as to enable full recovery of the ID CRC.

The user DATA field consists of all 512 bytes of data stored in the sector. This field is followed by a CRC field to verify the data. Although many controllers use two bytes of CRC here, the controller might implement a longer Error Correction Code (ECC) that requires more than two CRC bytes to store. The ECC data stored here provides the possibility of correcting errors in the DATA field as well as detecting them. The correction/detection capabilities depend on the ECC code the drive uses and its implementation by the controller. The WRITE TURN-OFF GAP is a pad that enables the ECC (CRC) bytes to be fully recovered.

The INTER-RECORD GAP provides a means to accommodate variances in drive spindle speeds. A track might have been formatted while the disk was running slightly more slowly than normal and then written to while the disk was running slightly more quickly than normal. In such cases, this gap prevents the accidental overwriting of any information in the next sector. The actual size of this padding varies, depending on the speed of the DATA disk's rotation when the track was formatted and each time the DATA field is updated.

The PRE-INDEX GAP enables speed tolerance over the entire track. This gap varies in size, depending on the variances in disk rotation speed and write-frequency tolerance at the time of formatting.

This sector prefix information is extremely important because it contains the numbering information that defines the cylinder, head, and sector. So this information—except the DATA field, DATA CRC bytes, and WRITE TURN-OFF GAP—is written only during a low-level format.

Disk Formatting

Two formatting procedures are required before you can write user data to a disk:

- Physical, or low-level formatting
- Logical, or high-level formatting

When you format a blank floppy disk, the Windows 9x/Me/2000 Explorer or the DOS FORMAT command performs both types of formats simultaneously. If the floppy was already formatted, DOS and Windows will default to doing only a high-level format.

A hard disk, however, requires two separate formatting operations. Moreover, a hard disk requires a third step, between the two formatting procedures, to write the partitioning information to the disk. Partitioning is required because a hard disk is designed to be used with more than one operating system. Using multiple operating systems on one hard drive is possible by separating the physical formatting in a procedure that is always the same, regardless of the operating system used and the high-level format (which is different for each operating system). Partitioning enables a single hard disk drive to run more than one type of operating system, or it can enable a single operating system to use the disk as several volumes or logical drives. A *volume* or *logical drive* is any section of the disk to which the operating system assigns a drive letter or name.

Consequently, preparing a hard disk drive for data storage involves three steps:

1. Low-level formatting (LLF)

2. Partitioning

3. High-level formatting (HLF)

Low-Level Formatting

During a low-level format, the formatting program divides the disk's tracks into a specific number of sectors, creating the intersector and intertrack gaps and recording the sector header and trailer information. The program also fills each sector's data area with a dummy byte value or a pattern of test values. For floppy disks, the number of sectors recorded on each track depends on the type of disk and drive. For hard disks, the number of sectors per track depends on the drive and the controller interface.

Originally, PC hard disk drives used a separate controller that took the form of an expansion card or was integrated into the motherboard. Because the controller could be used with various disk drives and might even have been made by a different manufacturer, some uniformity had to exist in the communications between the controller and the drive. For this reason, the number of sectors written to a track tended to be relatively consistent.

The original ST-506/412 MFM controllers always placed 17 sectors per track on a disk, although ST-506/412 controllers with RLL encoding increased the number of sectors to 25 or 26 per track; ESDI drives had 32 or more sectors per track. The ATA/IDE and SCSI drives found in PCs today can have anywhere from 17 to 900 or more sectors per track.

Virtually all ATA and SCSI drives use a technique called *zoned-bit recording*, which writes a variable number of sectors per track. Without zoned-bit recording, the number of sectors, and therefore bits, on each track is a constant. This means the actual number of bits per inch will vary. More bits per inch will exist on the inner tracks, and fewer will exist on the outer. The data rate and rotational speed will remain constant, as will the number of bits per track. Figure 10.4 shows a drive recorded with the same number of sectors per track.

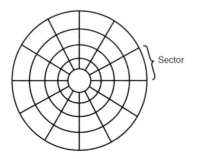

Figure 10.4   Standard recording, where the same number of sectors comprise every track.

A standard recording wastes capacity on the outer tracks, because it is longer and yet holds the same amount of data (more loosely spaced) as the inner tracks. One way to increase the capacity of a hard drive during the low-level format is to create more sectors on the disks' outer cylinders than on the inner ones. Because they have a larger circumference, the outer cylinders can hold more data. Drives without zoned-bit recording store the same amount of data on every cylinder, even though the tracks of the outer cylinders might be twice as long as those of the inner cylinders. The result is wasted storage capacity because the disk medium must be capable of storing data reliably at the same density as on the inner cylinders. When the number of sectors per track is fixed, as in older controllers, the drive capacity is limited by the density of the innermost (shortest) track.

Drives that use zoned-bit recording split the cylinders into groups called *zones*, with each successive zone having more sectors per track as you move outward from the center of the disk. All the cylinders in a particular zone have the same number of sectors per track. The number of zones varies with specific drives, but most drives have 10 or more zones.

Figure 10.5 shows a drive with zoned-bit recording.

Another effect of zoned-bit recording is that transfer speeds vary depending on which zone the heads are in. A drive with zoned-bit recording still spins at a constant speed; because more sectors exist per track in the outer zones, however, data transfer is fastest there. Consequently, data transfer is slowest when reading or writing to the inner zones. That is why virtually all drives today report minimum and maximum sustained transfer rates, which depend on where on the drive you are reading from or writing to.

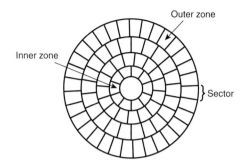

Figure 10.5   Zoned-bit recording, where the number of sectors per track increases within each zone, moving out from the center.

As an example, see Table 10.2, which shows the zones defined for an IBM Travelstar 32GH 2 1/2-inch notebook drive, the sectors per track for each zone, and the resulting data transfer rate.

Table 10.2   Zoned Bit Recording Information for the IBM Travelstar 32GH 32GB 2 1/2-inch Hard Disk Drive

Zone	Sectors per Track	Data Transfer Rate (MB/sec)	Bytes per Track	Sectors per Zone
0	617	28.49	315,904	835,418
1	598	27.60	306,005	809,241
2	578	26.70	296,107	783,063
3	559	25.81	286,208	756,886
4	540	24.92	276,309	730,709
5	520	24.03	266,411	704,531
6	501	23.13	256,512	678,354
7	482	22.24	246,613	652,177
8	462	21.35	236,715	625,999
9	443	20.46	226,816	599,822
10	424	19.56	216,917	573,645
11	404	18.67	207,019	547,467
12	385	17.78	197,120	521,290
13	366	16.88	187,221	495,113
14	346	15.99	177,323	468,935
15	327	15.10	167,424	442,758

21,664 Total Tracks; 16 Zones; 1,354 Tracks per Zone
512 Bytes per Sector; 5,411 rpm; 10,225,408 Total Sectors per Side

This drive has a total of 21,664 tracks on each platter surface and, as you can see, the tracks are divided into 16 zones of 1,354 tracks each. It is not essential for all the zones to be the same size; this is simply how this drive is arranged. Zone 0 consists of the outermost 1,354 tracks, which are the longest and contain the most sectors: 617. Because each sector is 512 bytes, each track in this zone can therefore provide about 315,904 bytes of user data storage, although the 327 sector tracks in zone 15 can hold only 167,424 bytes.

Thus, with zoned-bit recording, each platter surface in this disk drive contains 10,225,408 sectors, for a storage capacity of 5,235MB per side. Without zoned-bit recording, the number of sectors per track would be limited to 327 over the entire surface of each platter, for a total of 7,084,128 sectors, storing 3,627MB. Zoned-bit recording, therefore, provides a 44% increase in the storage capacity of this particular drive.

Notice also the difference in the data transfer rates for each of the zones. The tracks in the outermost zone (0) yield a transfer rate of 28.49MB/sec, which is 89% higher than the 15.10MB/sec of the innermost zone (15). This is one reason you might notice huge discrepancies in the results produced by disk drive benchmark programs. A test that reads or writes files on the outer tracks of the disk naturally yields far better results than one conducted on the inner tracks. It might appear as though your drive is running more slowly, when the problem is actually that the test results you are comparing stem from disk activity on different zones.

Another thing to note is that this drive conforms to the ATA-5 specification and is capable of running in Ultra-ATA/66 mode (also called UDMA-66), which implies a transfer speed of 66MB/sec. As you can see, that is entirely theoretical because the true *media transfer speed* of this drive varies between about 15MB/sec and 28MB/sec, averaging about 21.8MB/sec overall. The interface transfer rate is just that: what the interface is capable of. It has little bearing on the actual capabilities of the drive.

Drives with separate controllers used in the past could not handle zoned-bit recording because no standard way existed to communicate information about the zones from the drive to the controller.

With SCSI and ATA disks, however, formatting individual tracks with different numbers of sectors became possible because these drives have the disk controller built in. The built-in controllers on these drives are fully aware of the zoning algorithm and can translate the physical Cylinder, Head, and Sector numbers to logical Cylinder, Head, and Sector numbers so the drive appears to have the same number of sectors on each track. Because the PC BIOS is designed to handle only a single number of sectors per track throughout the entire drive, a zoned drive must run by using a sector translation scheme.

The use of zoned-bit recording enables drive manufacturers to increase the capacity of their hard drives by 20%–50% compared with a fixed–sector-per-track arrangement. All modern ATA (IDE) and SCSI drives today use zoned-bit recording.

Partitioning

Creating a partition on a hard disk drive enables it to support separate file systems, each in its own partition.

Each file system can then use its own method to allocate file space in logical units called *clusters* or *allocation units*. Every hard disk drive must have at least one partition on it and can have up to four partitions, each of which can support the same or different type file systems. Three common file systems are used by PC operating systems today:

- *FAT (File Allocation Table)*. The standard file system supported by DOS, Windows 9x/Me/2000, and Windows NT. FAT partitions support filenames of 11 characters maximum (8 characters+ 3-character extension) under DOS, and 255 characters under Windows 9x/Me/2000 or Windows NT 4.0 (or later). The standard FAT file system uses 12- or 16-bit numbers to identify clusters, resulting in a maximum volume size of 2GB.

  Using FDISK, you can create only two physical FAT partitions on a hard disk drive—primary and extended—but you can subdivide the extended partition into as many as 25 logical volumes. Alternative partitioning programs, such as Partition Magic, can create up to four primary partitions or three primary and one extended.

■ *FAT32 (File Allocation Table, 32-bit).* An optional file system supported by Windows 95 OSR2 (OEM Service Release 2), Windows 98, Windows Me, and Windows 2000.

FAT32 uses 32-bit numbers to identify clusters, resulting in a maximum single volume size of 2TB or 2,048GB.

■ *NTFS (Windows NT File System).* The native file system for Windows NT/2000 that supports file-names up to 256 characters long and partitions up to (a theoretical) 16 exabytes. NTFS also pro-vides extended attributes and file system security features that do not exist in the FAT file system. Of these three file systems, the FAT file system still is by far the most popular and is accessible by nearly every operating system, which makes it the most compatible as well. FAT32 and NTFS provide additional features but are not universally accessible by other operating sys-tems.

▶▶ See "FAT Disk Structures," p. 1316 and "FAT32," p. 1334.

Partitioning normally is accomplished by running the FDISK program that comes with your operating system. FDISK enables you to select the amount of space on the drive to use for a partition, from a single megabyte or 1% of the drive up to the entire capacity of the drive, or as much as the particular file system will allow. Normally, it is recommended to have as few partitions as possible, and many people (myself included) try to stick with only one or two at the most. This was more difficult before FAT32 because the maximum partition size for a FAT16 partition was only 2GB. With FAT32, the max-imum partition size can be up to 2,048GB.

Caution

FDISK cannot be used to change the size of a partition; all it can do is remove or create partitions. The act of removing or creating a partition destroys any data that was contained in the partition or was on that part of the disk. To manipulate partitions without destroying data, you can use third-party utility programs, such as Partition Magic from PowerQuest or Partition Commander from V Communications.

After a drive is partitioned, each partition must then be high-level formatted by the operating system that will use it.

High-Level Formatting

During the high-level format, the operating system (such as Windows 9x/Me/2000, Windows NT, or DOS) writes the structures necessary for managing files and data on the disk. FAT partitions have a Volume Boot Sector (VBS), two copies of a file allocation table (FAT), and a root directory on each for-matted logical drive. These data structures enable the operating system to manage the space on the disk, keep track of files, and even manage defective areas so they do not cause problems.

High-level formatting is not really a physical formatting of the drive, but rather the creation of a table of contents for the disk. In low-level formatting, which is the real physical formatting process, tracks and sectors are written on the disk. As mentioned, the DOS FORMAT command can perform both low-level and high-level format operations on a floppy disk, but it performs only the high-level format for a hard disk. Low-level formats of ATA and SCSI hard disk drives are performed by the manufacturer and should almost never be performed by the end user. The only time I low-level format ATA or SCSI drives is when I am attempting to repair a format that has become damaged (parts of the disk become unreadable), or in some cases when I want to wipe away all data on the drive.

Basic Hard Disk Drive Components

Many types of hard disk drives are on the market, but nearly all share the same basic physical compo-nents. Some differences might exist in the implementation of these components (and in the quality of the materials used to make them), but the operational characteristics of most drives are similar. The basic components of a typical hard disk drive are as follows (see Figure 10.6):

- Disk platters
- Read/write heads
- Head actuator mechanism
- Spindle motor (inside platter hub)
- Logic board (controller or Printed Circuit Board)
- Cables and connectors
- Configuration items (such as jumpers or switches)

Figure 10.6 Typical hard disk drive components.

The platters, spindle motor, heads, and head actuator mechanisms usually are contained in a sealed chamber called the Head Disk Assembly (HDA). The HDA is usually treated as a single component; it is rarely opened. Other parts external to the drive's HDA, such as the logic boards, bezel, and other configuration or mounting hardware, can be disassembled from the drive.

Hard Disk Platters (Disks)

A hard disk drive has one or more platters, or disks. Hard disks for PC systems have been available in a number of form factors over the years. Normally, the physical size of a drive is expressed as the size of the platters. Following are the platter sizes that have been associated with PC hard disk drives:

- 5 1/4-inch (actually 130mm, or 5.12 inches)
- 3 1/2-inch (actually 95mm, or 3.74 inches)
- 2 1/2-inch (actually 65mm, or 2.56 inches)
- 1-inch (actually 34mm, or 1.33 inches)

Larger hard disk drives that have 8-inch, 14-inch, or even larger platters are available, but these drives are not used with PC systems. Currently, the 3 1/2-inch drives are the most popular for desktop and some portable systems, whereas the 2 1/2-inch and smaller drives are very popular in portable or notebook systems.

During 1998, IBM introduced a drive called the MicroDrive, which currently can store up to 1GB or more on a single platter about the size of a quarter! This type of drive can be used in information appliances, digital cameras, and anywhere else flash memory cards have been used.

Most hard disk drives have two or more platters, although some of the smaller drives used in portable systems have only one. The number of platters a drive can have is limited by the drive's vertical physical size. The maximum number of platters I have seen in any 3 1/2-inch drive is 12; however, most drives have 6 or fewer.

Platters have traditionally been made from an aluminum/magnesium alloy, which provides both strength and light weight. However, manufacturers' desire for higher and higher densities and smaller drives has led to the use of platters made of glass (or, more technically, a glass-ceramic composite). One such material, produced by the Dow Corning Corporation, is called MemCor. MemCor is composed of glass with ceramic implants, enabling it to resist cracking better than pure glass. Glass platters offer greater rigidity than metal (because metal can be bent and glass cannot) and can therefore be machined to one-half the thickness of conventional aluminum disks—sometimes less. Glass platters are also much more thermally stable than aluminum platters, which means they do not expand or contract very much with changes in temperature. Several hard disk drives made by companies such as IBM, Seagate, Toshiba, Areal Technology, and Maxtor currently use glass or glass-ceramic platters. For most manufacturers, glass disks will probably replace the standard aluminum/magnesium substrate over the next few years, especially in high-performance 2 1/2- and 3 1/2-inch drives.

Recording Media

No matter which substrate is used, the platters are covered with a thin layer of a magnetically retentive substance, called the *medium*, on which magnetic information is stored. Two popular types of magnetic media are used on hard disk platters:

- Oxide medium
- Thin-film medium

The oxide medium is made of various compounds, containing iron oxide as the active ingredient. The magnetic layer is created on the disk by coating the aluminum platter with a syrup containing iron-oxide particles. This syrup is spread across the disk by spinning the platters at high speed; centrifugal force causes the material to flow from the center of the platter to the outside, creating an even coating of the material on the platter. The surface is then cured and polished. Finally, a layer of material that protects and lubricates the surface is added and burnished smooth. The oxide coating is normally about 30 millionths of an inch thick. If you could peer into a drive with oxide-coated platters, you would see that the platters are brownish or amber.

As drive density increases, the magnetic medium needs to be thinner and more perfectly formed. The capabilities of oxide coatings have been exceeded by most higher-capacity drives. Because the oxide medium is very soft, disks that use it are subject to head-crash damage if the drive is jolted during operation. Most older drives, especially those sold as low-end models, use oxide media on the drive platters. Oxide media, which have been used since 1955, remained popular because of their relatively low cost and ease of application. Today, however, very few drives use oxide media.

The thin-film medium is thinner, harder, and more perfectly formed than oxide medium. Thin film was developed as a high-performance medium that enabled a new generation of drives to have lower head-floating heights, which in turn made increases in drive density possible. Originally, thin-film media were used only in higher-capacity or higher-quality drive systems, but today, virtually all drives use thin-film media.

The thin-film medium is aptly named. The coating is much thinner than can be achieved by the oxide-coating method. Thin-film media are also known as plated, or sputtered, media because of the various processes used to deposit the thin film on the platters.

Thin-film plated media are manufactured by depositing the magnetic medium on the disk with an electroplating mechanism, in much the same way that chrome plating is deposited on the bumper of a car. The aluminum/magnesium or glass platter is immersed in a series of chemical baths that coat the platter with several layers of metallic film. The magnetic medium layer itself is a cobalt alloy about 1 μ-inch thick.

Thin-film sputtered media are created by first coating the aluminum platters with a layer of nickel phosphorus and then applying the cobalt-alloy magnetic material in a continuous vacuum-deposition process called *sputtering*. This process deposits magnetic layers as thin as 1 μ-inch or less on the disk, in a fashion similar to the way that silicon wafers are coated with metallic films in the semiconductor industry. The same sputtering technique is then used again to lay down an extremely hard, 1 μ-inch protective carbon coating. The need for a near-perfect vacuum makes sputtering the most expensive of the processes described here.

The surface of a sputtered platter contains magnetic layers as thin as 1 μ-inch. Because this surface also is very smooth, the head can float more closely to the disk surface than was possible previously. Floating heights as small as 15nm (nanometers, or about 0.6 μ-inch) above the surface are possible. When the head is closer to the platter, the density of the magnetic flux transitions can be increased to provide greater storage capacity. Additionally, the increased intensity of the magnetic field during a closer-proximity read provides the higher signal amplitudes needed for good signal-to-noise performance.

Both the sputtering and plating processes result in a very thin, hard film of magnetic medium on the platters. Because the thin-film medium is so hard, it has a better chance of surviving contact with the heads at high speed. In fact, modern thin-film media are virtually uncrashable. If you could open a drive to peek at the platters, you would see that platters coated with the thin-film medium look like mirrors.

Read/Write Heads

A hard disk drive usually has one read/write head for each platter surface (meaning that each platter has two sets of read/write heads—one for the top side and one for the bottom side). These heads are connected, or ganged, on a single movement mechanism. The heads, therefore, move across the platters in unison.

Mechanically, read/write heads are simple. Each head is on an actuator arm that is spring-loaded to force the head into contact with a platter. Few people realize that each platter actually is "squeezed" by the heads above and below it. If you could open a drive safely and lift the top head with your finger, the head would snap back down into the platter when you released it. If you could pull down on one of the heads below a platter, the spring tension would cause it to snap back up into the platter when you released it.

Figure 10.7 shows a typical hard disk head-actuator assembly from a voice coil drive.

When the drive is at rest, the heads are forced into direct contact with the platters by spring tension, but when the drive is spinning at full speed, air pressure develops below the heads and lifts them off the surface of the platter. On a drive spinning at full speed, the distance between the heads and the platter can be anywhere from 0.5 to 5 μ-inch or more in a modern drive.

Figure 10.7 Read/write heads and rotary voice coil actuator assembly.

In the early 1960s, hard disk drive recording heads operated at floating heights as large as 200–300 μ-inch; today's drive heads are designed to float as low as 10nm (nanometers) or 0.4 μ-inch above the surface of the disk. To support higher densities in future drives, the physical separation between the head and disk is expected to drop even further, such that on some drives there will even be contact with the platter surface. New media and head designs will make full or partial contact recording possible.

Caution

The small size of the gap between the platters and the heads is why you should never open the disk drive's HDA except in a clean-room environment. Any particle of dust or dirt that gets into this mechanism could cause the heads to read improperly or possibly even to strike the platters while the drive is running at full speed. The latter event could scratch the platter or the head.

To ensure the cleanliness of the interior of the drive, the HDA is assembled in a class-100 or better clean room. This specification means that a cubic foot of air cannot contain more than 100 particles that measure up to 0.5 microns (19.7 μ-inch). A single person breathing while standing motionless spews out 500 such particles in a single minute! These rooms contain special air-filtration systems that continuously evacuate and refresh the air. A drive's HDA should not be opened unless it is inside such a room.

Although maintaining a clean-room environment might seem to be expensive, many companies manufacture tabletop or bench-size clean rooms that sell for only a few thousand dollars. Some of these devices operate like a glove box; the operator first inserts the drive and any tools required, and then closes the box and turns on the filtration system. Inside the box, a clean-room environment is maintained, and a technician can use the built-in gloves to work on the drive.

In other clean-room variations, the operator stands at a bench where a forced-air curtain maintains a clean environment on the bench top. The technician can walk in and out of the clean-room field by walking through the air curtain. This air curtain is very similar to the curtain of air used in some stores and warehouses to prevent heat from escaping in the winter while leaving a passage wide open.

Because the clean environment is expensive to produce, few companies, except those that manufacture the drives, are properly equipped to service hard disk drives.

Read/Write Head Designs

As disk drive technology has evolved, so has the design of the read/write head. The earliest heads were simple iron cores with coil windings (electromagnets). By today's standards, the original head designs were enormous in physical size and operated at very low recording densities. Over the years, head designs have evolved from the first simple Ferrite Core designs into the Magneto-Resistive and Giant Magneto-Resistive types available today.

For more information on the various head designs, see Chapter 9, "Magnetic Storage Principles."

Head Actuator Mechanisms

Possibly more important than the heads themselves is the mechanical system that moves them: the head actuator. This mechanism moves the heads across the disk and positions them accurately above the desired cylinder. Many variations on head actuator mechanisms are in use, but all fall into one of two basic categories:

- Stepper motor actuators
- Voice coil actuators

The use of one or the other type of actuator has profound effects on a drive's performance and reliability. The effects are not limited to speed; they also include accuracy, sensitivity to temperature, position, vibration, and overall reliability. The head actuator is the single most important specification in the drive, and the type of head actuator mechanism in a drive tells you a great deal about the drive's performance and reliability characteristics. Table 10.3 shows the two types of hard disk drive head actuators and the affected performance characteristics.

Table 10.3   Characteristics of Stepper Motor Versus Voice Coil Drives

Characteristic	Stepper Motor	Voice Coil
Relative access speed	Slow	Fast
Temperature sensitive	Yes (very)	No
Positionally sensitive	Yes	No
Automatic head parking	Not usually	Yes
Preventive maintenance	Periodic reformat	None required
Relative reliability	Poor	Excellent

Generally, a stepper motor drive has a slower average access rating, is temperature sensitive during read and write operations, is sensitive to physical orientation during read and write operations, does not automatically park its heads above a save zone during power-down, and usually requires annual or biannual reformats to realign the sector data with the sector header information due to mistracking. To put it bluntly, a drive equipped with a stepper motor actuator is much less reliable (by a large margin) than a drive equipped with a voice coil actuator.

Floppy disk drives position their heads by using a stepper motor actuator. The accuracy of the stepper mechanism is suited to a floppy disk drive because the track densities usually are nowhere near those of a hard disk. The track density of a 1.44MB floppy disk is 135 tracks per inch, whereas hard disk drives have densities of more than 5,000 tracks per inch. Virtually all the hard disk drives being manufactured today use voice coil actuators because stepper motors cannot achieve the degree of accuracy necessary.

Stepper Motor Actuators

A stepper motor is an electrical motor that can "step," or move from position to position, with mechanical detents or click-stop positions. If you were to grip the spindle of one of these motors and spin it manually, you would hear a clicking or buzzing sound as the motor passed each detent position with a soft click.

Stepper motors cannot position themselves between step positions; they can stop only at the predetermined detent positions. The motors are small (between 1 and 3 inches) and can be square, cylindrical, or flat. Stepper motors are outside the sealed HDA, although the spindle of the motor penetrates the HDA through a sealed hole.

Stepper motor mechanisms are affected by a variety of problems; the greatest problem is temperature. As the drive platters heat and cool, they expand and contract, and the tracks on the platters move in relation to a predetermined track position. The stepper mechanism cannot move in increments of less than a single track to correct for these temperature-induced errors. The drive positions the heads to a particular cylinder according to a predetermined number of steps from the stepper motor, with no room for nuance.

Figure 10.8 shows a common stepper motor design, where a split metal band is used to transfer the movement from the rotating motor shaft to the head actuator itself.

Figure 10.8 A stepper motor actuator.

Voice Coil Actuators

The voice coil actuators used in virtually all hard disk drives made today—unlike stepper motor actuators—use a feedback signal from the drive to accurately determine the head positions and adjust them, if necessary. This arrangement provides significantly greater performance, accuracy, and reliability than traditional stepper motor actuator designs.

A voice coil actuator works by pure electromagnetic force. The construction of the mechanism is similar to that of a typical audio speaker, from which the term *voice coil* is derived. An audio speaker uses a stationary magnet surrounded by a voice coil, which is connected to the speaker's paper cone. Energizing the coil causes it to move relative to the stationary magnet, which produces sound from the cone. In a typical hard disk drive's voice coil system, the electromagnetic coil is attached to the end of the head rack and placed near a stationary magnet. No physical contact occurs between the coil and the magnet; instead, the coil moves by pure magnetic force. As the electromagnetic coils are energized, they attract or repulse the stationary magnet and move the head rack. Systems like these are extremely quick and efficient and usually much quieter than systems driven by stepper motors.

Unlike a stepper motor, a voice coil actuator has no click-stops, or detent positions; rather, a special guidance system stops the head rack above a particular cylinder. Because it has no detents, the voice coil actuator can slide the heads in and out smoothly to any position desired. Voice coil actuators use a guidance mechanism called a *servo* to tell the actuator where the heads are in relation to the cylinders and to place the heads accurately at the desired positions. This positioning system often is called a *closed loop feedback mechanism*. It works by sending the index (or servo) signal to the positioning electronics, which return a feedback signal that is used to position the heads accurately. The system also is called *servo-controlled*, which refers to the index or servo information that is used to dictate or control head-positioning accuracy.

A voice coil actuator with servo control is not affected by temperature changes, as a stepper motor is. When temperature changes cause the disk platters to expand or contract, the voice coil system compensates automatically because it never positions the heads in predetermined track positions. Rather, the voice coil system searches for the specific track, guided by the prewritten servo information, and then positions the head rack precisely above the desired track, wherever it happens to be. Because of the continuous feedback of servo information, the heads adjust to the current position of the track at all times. For example, as a drive warms up and the platters expand, the servo information enables the heads to "follow" the track. As a result, a voice coil actuator is sometimes called a *track following system*.

The two main types of voice-coil positioner mechanisms are

- Linear voice-coil actuators
- Rotary voice-coil actuators

The two types differ only in the physical arrangement of the magnets and coils.

A linear actuator (see Figure 10.9) moves the heads in and out over the platters in a straight line. The coil moves in and out on a track surrounded by the stationary magnets. The primary advantage of the linear design is that it eliminates the head *azimuth* variations that occur with rotary positioning systems. (Azimuth refers to the angular measurement of the head position relative to the tangent of a given cylinder.) A linear actuator does not rotate the head as it moves from one cylinder to another, thus eliminating this problem.

Although the linear actuator seems to be a good design, it has one fatal flaw: The devices are much too heavy. As drive performance has increased, the desire for lightweight actuator mechanisms has become very important. The lighter the mechanism, the faster it can accelerate and decelerate from one cylinder to another. Because they are much heavier than rotary actuators, linear actuators were popular only for a short time; they are virtually nonexistent in drives manufactured today.

Rotary actuators also use stationary magnets and a movable coil, but the coil is attached to the end of an actuator arm. As the coil moves relative to the stationary magnet, it swings the head arms in and out over the surface of the disk. The primary advantage of this mechanism is its light weight, which means that the heads can accelerate and decelerate very quickly, resulting in very fast average seek times. Because of the lever effect on the head arm, the heads move faster than the actuator, which also helps to improve access times. (Refer to Figure 10.7, which shows a rotary voice coil actuator.)

Servo head

Head travel

Read/write heads

Magnets

Coils

Figure 10.9   A linear voice coil actuator.

The disadvantage of a rotary system is that as the heads move from the outer to the inner cylinders, they rotate slightly with respect to the tangent of the cylinders. This rotation results in an azimuth error and is one reason why the area of the platter in which the cylinders are located is somewhat limited. By limiting the total motion of the actuator, the azimuth error is contained to within reasonable specifications. Virtually all voice coil drives today use rotary actuator systems.

Servo Mechanisms

Three servo mechanism designs have been used to control voice coil positioners over the years:

- Wedge servo
- Embedded servo
- Dedicated servo

The three designs are slightly different, but they accomplish the same basic task: They enable the head positioner to adjust continuously so it is precisely positioned above a given cylinder on the disk. The main difference between these servo designs is where the gray code information is actually written on the drive.

All servo mechanisms rely on special information that is written to the disk when it is manufactured. This information is usually in the form of a special code called a *gray code*. A gray code is a special binary notational system in which any two adjacent numbers are represented by a code that differs in only one bit place or column position. This system makes it easy for the head to read the information and quickly determine its precise position.

At the time of manufacture, a special machine called a servowriter writes the servo gray code on the disk. The servowriter is basically a jig that mechanically moves the heads to a given reference position and then writes the servo information at that position. Many servowriters are themselves guided by a laser-beam reference that calculates its own position by calculating distances in wavelengths of light. Because the servowriter must be capable of moving the heads mechanically, the process requires either that the lid of the drive be removed or that access be available through special access ports in the HDA. After the servowriting is complete, these ports are usually covered with sealing tape. You often see these tape-covered holes on the HDA, usually accompanied by warnings that you will void the warranty if you remove the tape. Because servowriting exposes the interior of the HDA, it requires a clean-room environment.

A servowriter is an expensive piece of machinery, costing up to $50,000 or more, and often must be custom-made for a particular make or model of drive. Some drive-repair companies have servowriting capability, which means they can rewrite the servo information on a drive if it becomes damaged. If a servowriter is not available, a drive with servo-code damage must be sent back to the drive manufacturer for the servo information to be rewritten.

Fortunately, damaging the servo information through disk read and write processes is impossible. Drives are designed so the heads cannot overwrite the servo information, even during a low-level format. One myth that has been circulating (especially with respect to ATA drives) is that you can damage the servo information by improper low-level formatting. This is not true. An improper low-level format can compromise the performance of the drive, but the servo information is totally protected and cannot be overwritten. Even so, the servo information on some drives can be damaged by a strong adjacent magnetic field or by jarring the drive while it is writing, causing the heads to move off track.

The track-following capabilities of a servo-controlled voice coil actuator eliminate the positioning errors that occur over time with stepper motor drives. Voice coil drives are not affected by conditions such as thermal expansion and contraction of the platters. In fact, many voice coil drives today perform a special thermal-recalibration procedure at predetermined intervals while they run. This procedure usually involves seeking the heads from cylinder 0 to some other cylinder one time for every head on the drive. As this sequence occurs, the control circuitry in the drive monitors how much the track positions have moved since the last time the sequence was performed, and a thermal-recalibration adjustment is calculated and stored in the drive's memory. This information is then used every time the drive positions the heads to ensure the most accurate positioning possible.

Most drives perform the thermal-recalibration sequence every 5 minutes for the first 30 minutes that the drive is powered on and then once every 25 minutes after that. With some drives, this thermal-recalibration sequence is very noticeable; the drive essentially stops what it is doing, and you hear rapid ticking for a second or so. Some people think this is an indication that their drive is having a problem reading something and perhaps is conducting a read retry, but this is not true. Most drives today (ATA and SCSI) employ this thermal-recalibration procedure to maintain positioning accuracy.

As multimedia applications grew in popularity, thermal recalibration became a problem with some manufacturers' drives. The thermal-recalibration sequence sometimes interrupted the transfer of a large data file, such as an audio or a video file, which resulted in audio or video playback jitter. Some companies released special A/V (audio visual) drives that hide the thermal-recalibration sequences so they never interrupt a file transfer. Most of the newer ATA and SCSI drives are A/V capable, which means that the thermal-recalibration sequences will not interrupt a transfer such as a video playback.

While we are on the subject of automatic drive functions, most of the drives that perform thermal-recalibration sequences also automatically perform a function called a *disk sweep*. Also called *wear leveling* by some manufacturers, this procedure is an automatic head seek that occurs after the drive has been idle for a period of time. The disk-sweep function moves the heads to a cylinder in the outer portion of the platters, which is where the head float-height is highest (because the head-to-platter velocity is highest). Then, if the drive continues to remain idle for another period, the heads move to another cylinder in this area, and the process continues indefinitely as long as the drive is powered on.

The disk-sweep function is designed to prevent the head from remaining stationary above one cylinder in the drive for too long, where friction between the head and platter eventually would dig a trench in the medium. Although the heads are not in direct contact with the medium, they are so close that the constant air pressure from the head floating above a single cylinder could cause friction and excessive wear. Figure 10.10 shows both a wedge and an embedded servo.

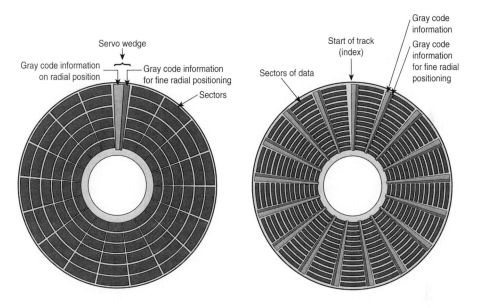

Figure 10.10   A wedge and an embedded servo.

Wedge Servo

Early servo-controlled drives used a technique called a *wedge servo*. In these drives, the gray-code guidance information is contained in a "wedge" slice of the drive in each cylinder immediately preceding the index mark. The index mark indicates the beginning of each track, so the wedge-servo information was written in the PRE-INDEX GAP, which is at the end of each track. This area is provided for speed tolerance and normally is not used by the controller.

Some controllers had to be notified that the drive was using a wedge servo so they could shorten the sector timing to allow for the wedge-servo area. If they were not correctly configured, these controllers would not work properly with the drive.

Another problem was that the servo information appears only one time every revolution, which means that the drive often needed several revolutions before it could accurately determine and adjust the head position. Because of these problems, the wedge servo never was a popular design; it no longer is used in drives.

Embedded Servo

An embedded servo is an enhancement of the wedge servo. Instead of placing the servo code before the beginning of each cylinder, an embedded servo design writes the servo information before the start of each sector. This arrangement enables the positioner circuits to receive feedback many times in a single revolution, making the head positioning much faster and more precise. Another advantage is that every track on the drive has its own positioning information, so each head can quickly and efficiently adjust position to compensate for any changes in the platter or head dimensions, especially for changes due to thermal expansion or physical stress.

Most drives today use an embedded servo to control the positioning system. As in the wedge servo design, the embedded servo information is protected by the drive circuits, and any write operations are blocked whenever the heads are above the servo information. Thus, it is impossible to overwrite the servo information with a low-level format, as some people incorrectly believe.

Although the embedded servo works much better than the wedge servo because the servo feedback information is made available several times in a single disk revolution, a system that offered continuous servo feedback information would be better.

Dedicated Servo

A dedicated servo is a design in which the servo information is written continuously throughout the entire track, rather than just once per track or at the beginning of each sector. Unfortunately, if this procedure were used on the entire drive, no room would be left for data. For this reason, a *dedicated servo* uses one side of one of the platters exclusively for the servo-positioning information. The term "dedicated" comes from the fact that this platter side is completely dedicated to the servo information and cannot contain any data.

When building a dedicated servo drive, the manufacturer deducts one side of one platter from normal read/write usage and records a special set of gray-code data there that indicates the proper track positions. Because the head that rests above this surface cannot be used for normal reading and writing, the gray code can never be erased, and the servo information is protected—as in the other servo designs. No low-level format or other procedure can possibly overwrite the servo information. Figure 10.11 shows a dedicated servo mechanism. Normally, the head on top or one in the center is dedicated for servo use.

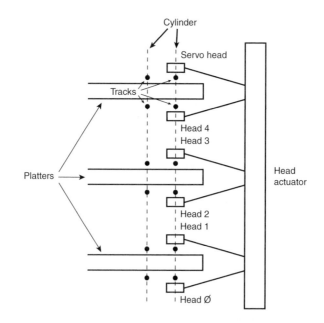

Figure 10.11   A dedicated servo, showing one entire head/side used for servo reading.

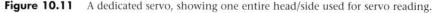

When the drive moves the heads to a specific cylinder, the internal drive electronics use the signals received by the servo head to determine the position of the read/write heads. As the heads move, the track counters are read from the dedicated servo surface. When the servo head detects the requested track, the actuator stops. The servo electronics then fine-tune the position so the heads are positioned precisely above the desired cylinder before any writing is permitted. Although only one head is used for servo tracking, the other heads are attached to the same rack so if one head is above the desired cylinder, all the others will be as well.

One way of telling whether a drive uses a dedicated servo platter is if it has an odd number of heads. For example, the Toshiba MK-538FB 1.2GB drive that I used to have in one of my systems had eight platters, but only 15 read/write heads. That drive uses a dedicated servo positioning system, and the 16th head is the servo head. The advantage of the dedicated servo concept is that the servo information is continuously available to the drive, making the head positioning process faster and more precise.

The drawback to a dedicated servo is that dedicating an entire platter surface for servo information is wasteful. Virtually all drives today use a variation on the embedded servo technique instead. Some drives combined a dedicated servo with an embedded servo, but this type of hybrid design is rare. Regardless of whether the servo mechanism is dedicated or embedded, it is far more accurate than the stepper motor mechanisms of the past.

Of course, as mentioned earlier, today's ATA and SCSI drives have head, track, and sector-per-track parameters that are translated from the actual physical numbers. Therefore, you usually can't tell from the published numbers exactly how many heads or platters are contained within a drive.

Automatic Head Parking

When you power off a hard disk drive, the spring tension in each head arm pulls the heads into contact with the platters. The drive is designed to sustain thousands of takeoffs and landings, but it is wise to ensure that the landing occurs at a spot on the platter that contains no data. Older drives required manual head parking; you had to run a program that positioned the drive heads to a landing zone, usually the innermost cylinder, before turning the system off. Modern drives automatically park the heads, so park programs are no longer necessary.

Some amount of abrasion occurs during the landing and takeoff process, removing just a "micro puff" from the magnetic medium—but if the drive is jarred during the landing or takeoff process, real damage can occur.

One benefit of using a voice coil actuator is automatic head parking. In a drive that has a voice coil actuator, the heads are positioned and held by magnetic force. When the power to the drive is removed, the magnetic field that holds the heads stationary over a particular cylinder dissipates, enabling the head rack to skitter across the drive surface and potentially cause damage. In the voice coil design, the head rack is attached to a weak spring at one end and a head stop at the other end. When the system is powered on, the spring is overcome by the magnetic force of the positioner. When the drive is powered off, however, the spring gently drags the head rack to a park-and-lock position before the drive slows down and the heads land. On some drives, you can actually hear the "ting...ting...ting...ting" sound as the heads literally bounce-park themselves, driven by this spring.

On a drive with a voice coil actuator, you activate the parking mechanism by turning off the computer; you do not need to run a program to park or retract the heads. In the event of a power outage, the heads park themselves automatically. (The drives unpark automatically when the system is powered on.)

Air Filters

Nearly all hard disk drives have two air filters. One is called the recirculating filter, and the other is called either a barometric or breather filter. These filters are permanently sealed inside the drive and are designed never to be changed for the life of the drive, unlike many older mainframe hard disks that had changeable filters.

A hard disk on a PC system does not circulate air from inside to outside the HDA or vice versa. The recirculating filter permanently installed inside the HDA is designed to filter only the small particles scraped off the platters during head takeoffs and landings (and possibly any other small particles dislodged inside the drive). Because PC hard disk drives are permanently sealed and do not circulate outside air, they can run in extremely dirty environments (see Figure 10.12).

Figure 10.12   Air circulation in a hard disk.

The HDA in a hard disk drive is sealed but not airtight. The HDA is vented through a barometric or breather filter element that enables pressure equalization (breathing) between the inside and outside of the drive. For this reason, most hard drives are rated by the drive's manufacturer to run in a specific range of altitudes, usually from 1,000 feet below to 10,000 feet above sea level. In fact, some hard drives are not rated to exceed 7,000 feet while operating because the air pressure would be too low inside the drive to float the heads properly. As the environmental air pressure changes, air bleeds into or out of the drive so internal and external pressures are identical. Although air does bleed through a vent, contamination usually is not a concern because the barometric filter on this vent is designed to filter out all particles larger than 0.3 microns (about 12 μ-inch) to meet the specifications for cleanliness inside the drive. You can see the vent holes on most drives, which are covered internally by this breather filter. Some drives use even finer grade filter elements to keep out even smaller particles.

I conducted a seminar in Hawaii several years ago, and several of the students were from one of the astronomical observatories atop Mauna Kea. They indicated that virtually all the hard disk drives they had tried to use at the observatory site had failed very quickly, if they worked at all. This was no surprise because the observatories are at the 13,796-foot peak of the mountain, and at that altitude, even people don't function very well! At the time, they had to resort to solid-state (RAM) disks, tape drives, or even floppy disk drives as their primary storage medium. Since then, IBM's Adstar division (which produces all IBM hard drives) has introduced a line of rugged 3 1/2-inch drives that are hermetically sealed (airtight), although they do have air inside the HDA. Because they carry their own internal air under pressure, these drives can operate at any altitude and can also withstand extremes of shock and temperature. The drives are designed for military and industrial applications, such as systems used aboard aircraft and in extremely harsh environments. They are, of course, more expensive than typical hard drives that operate under ambient pressures.

Hard Disk Temperature Acclimation

Because hard drives have a filtered port to bleed air into or out of the HDA, moisture can enter the drive, and after some period of time, it must be assumed that the humidity inside any hard disk is similar to that outside the drive. Humidity can become a serious problem if it is allowed to condense—and especially if you power up the drive while this condensation is present. Most hard disk manufacturers have specified procedures for acclimating a hard drive to a new environment with different temperature and humidity ranges, and especially for bringing a drive into a warmer environment in which condensation can form. This situation should be of special concern to users of laptop or portable systems. If you leave a portable system in an automobile trunk during the winter, for example, it could be catastrophic to bring the machine inside and power it up without allowing it to acclimate to the temperature indoors.

The following text and Table 10.4 are taken from the factory packaging that Control Data Corporation (later Imprimis and eventually Seagate) used to ship with its hard drives:

> If you have just received or removed this unit from a climate with temperatures at or below 50°F (10°C) do not open this container until the following conditions are met, otherwise condensation could occur and damage to the device and/or media may result. Place this package in the operating environment for the time duration according to the temperature chart.

Table 10.4   Hard Disk Drive Environmental Acclimation Table

Previous Climate Temperature	Acclimation Time	Previous Climate Temperature	Acclimation Time
+40°F (+4°C)	13 hours	-10°F (-23°C)	20 hours
+30°F (-1°C)	15 hours	-20°F (-29°C)	22 hours
+20°F (-7°C)	16 hours	-30°F (-34°C) or less	27 hours
+10°F (-12°C)	17 hours		
0°F (-18°C)	18 hours		

As you can see from this table, you must place a hard disk drive that has been stored in a colder-than-normal environment into its normal operating environment for a specified amount of time to allow it to acclimate before you power it on.

Spindle Motors

The motor that spins the platters is called the spindle motor because it is connected to the spindle around which the platters revolve. Spindle motors in hard disk drives are always connected directly; no belts or gears are involved. The motor must be free of noise and vibration; otherwise, it can transmit a rumble to the platters, which can disrupt reading and writing operations.

The spindle motor also must be precisely controlled for speed. The platters in hard disk drives revolve at speeds ranging from 3,600rpm to 15,000rpm (60–250 revolutions per second) or more, and the motor has a control circuit with a feedback loop to monitor and control this speed precisely. Because the speed control must be automatic, hard drives do not have a motor-speed adjustment. Some diagnostics programs claim to measure hard drive rotation speed, but all these programs do is estimate the rotational speed by the timing at which sectors pass under the heads.

There is actually no way for a program to measure the hard disk drive's rotational speed; this measurement can be made only with sophisticated test equipment. Don't be alarmed if some diagnostics program tells you that your drive is spinning at an incorrect speed; most likely, the program is wrong, not the drive. Platter rotation and timing information is not provided through the hard disk controller interface. In the past, software could give approximate rotational speed estimates by performing multiple sector read requests and timing them, but this was valid only when all drives had the same number of sectors per track and spun at the same speed. Zoned-bit recording—combined with the many various rotational speeds used by modern drives, not to mention built-in buffers and caches—means that these calculation estimates cannot be performed accurately by software.

On most drives, the spindle motor is on the bottom of the drive, just below the sealed HDA. Many drives today, however, have the spindle motor built directly into the platter hub inside the HDA. By using an internal hub spindle motor, the manufacturer can stack more platters in the drive because the spindle motor takes up no vertical space.

Note

Spindle motors, particularly on the larger form-factor drives, can consume a great deal of 12-volt power. Most drives require two to three times the normal operating power when the motor first spins the platters. This heavy draw lasts only a few seconds or until the drive platters reach operating speed. If you have more than one drive, you should try to sequence the start of the spindle motors so the power supply does not have to provide such a large load to all the drives at the same time. Most SCSI and some ATA drives have a delayed spindle-motor start feature.

Logic Boards

All hard disk drives have one or more logic boards mounted on them. The logic boards contain the electronics that control the drive's spindle and head actuator systems and present data to the controller in some agreed-upon form. On ATA drives, the boards include the controller itself, whereas SCSI drives include the controller and the SCSI bus adapter circuit.

Many disk drive failures occur in the logic board, not in the mechanical assembly. (This statement does not seem logical, but it is true.) Therefore, you sometimes can repair a failed drive by replacing the logic board rather than the entire drive. Replacing the logic board, moreover, enables you to regain access to the data on the drive—something that replacing the entire drive does not provide.

In many cases, logic boards plug into the drive and are easily replaceable. These boards are usually mounted with standard screw hardware. If a drive is failing and you have a spare, you might be able to verify a logic-board failure by taking the board off the known good drive and mounting it on the bad one. If your suspicions are confirmed, you can order a new logic board from the drive manufacturer, but unless you have data on the drive you need to recover, it might make more sense to buy a new drive, considering today's low disk drive costs.

To reduce costs further, many third-party vendors can also supply replacement logic-board assemblies. These companies often charge much less than the drive manufacturers for the same components. (See the Vendor List on the CD for vendors of drive components, including logic boards.)

Cables and Connectors

Hard disk drives typically have several connectors for interfacing to the computer, receiving power, and sometimes grounding to the system chassis. Most drives have at least these three types of connectors:

- Interface connector(s)
- Power connector
- Optional ground connector (tab)

Of these, the interface connectors are the most important because they carry the data and command signals between the system and the drive. In most cases, the drive interface cables can be connected in a daisy-chain or bus-type configuration. Most interfaces support at least two devices, and SCSI (Small Computer System Interface) can support up to seven (Wide SCSI can support up to 15) devices in the chain, in addition to the host adapter. Older interfaces, such as ST-506/412 or ESDI (Enhanced Small Device Interface), used separate cables for data and control signals, but today's SCSI and ATA (AT Attachment) drives have a single connector.

◀◀ See "ATA I/O Connector," p. 486, and "SCSI Cables and Connectors," p. 526.

The power connector is usually the same four-pin type that is used in floppy disk drives, and the same power-supply connector plugs into it. Most hard disk drives use both 5- and 12-volt power, although some of the smaller drives designed for portable applications use only 5-volt power. In most cases, the 12-volt power runs the spindle motor and head actuator, and the 5-volt power runs the circuitry. Make sure your power supply can supply adequate power for the hard disk drives installed in your system.

The 12-volt power consumption of a drive usually varies with the physical size of the unit. The larger the drive is, the faster it spins. In addition, the more platters there are to spin, the more power it requires. For example, most of the 3 1/2-inch drives on the market today use roughly one-half to one-fourth the power (in watts) of the older 5 1/4-inch drives. Some of the very small (2 1/2- or 1.8-inch) hard disks barely sip electrical power and actually use 1 watt or less!

A grounding tab provides an optional ground connection between the drive and the system's chassis. In most computers, the hard disk drive is mounted directly to the chassis using screws, or the drive is grounded via the ground wires in the power connector, so an extra ground wire is unnecessary.

Configuration Items

To configure a hard disk drive for installation in a system, you usually must set several jumpers (and, possibly, terminating resistors) properly. These items vary from interface to interface and often from drive to drive, as well.

The Faceplate or Bezel

Many hard disk drives offer as an option a front faceplate, or bezel (see Figure 10.13). A bezel usually is supplied as an option for the drive rather than as a standard item. In most cases today, the bezel is a part of the case and not the drive itself.

Older systems had the drive installed so it was visible outside the system case. To cover the hole in the case, you would use an optional bezel or faceplate. Bezels often come in several sizes and colors to match various PC systems. Many faceplate configurations for 3 1/2-inch drives are available, including bezels that fit 3 1/2-inch drive bays as well as 5 1/4-inch drive bays. You even have a choice of colors (usually black, cream, or white).

Figure 10.13   Typical 5 1/4- and 3 1/2-inch hard drives bezel shown from the front (as seen on the outside of the PC case) (top) and from the back (bottom—the inside mounting and LED wiring).

Some bezels feature a light-emitting diode (LED) that flickers when your hard disk is in use. The LED is mounted in the bezel; the wire hanging off the back of the LED plugs into the drive. In some drives, the LED is permanently mounted on the drive, and the bezel has a clear or colored window so you can see the LED flicker while the drive is being accessed.

In systems in which the hard disk is hidden by the unit's cover, a bezel is not needed. In fact, using a bezel can prevent the cover from resting on the chassis properly, in which case the bezel will have to be removed. If you are installing a drive that does not have a proper bezel, frame, or rails to attach to the system, check the Vendor List on the CD; several listed vendors offer these accessories for a variety of drives.

Hard Disk Features

To make the best decision in purchasing a hard disk for your system or to understand what distinguishes one brand of hard disk from another, you must consider many features. This section examines some of the issues you should consider when you evaluate drives:

- Reliability
- Performance
- Cost

Reliability

When you shop for a drive, you might notice a statistic called the Mean Time Between Failures (MTBF) described in the drive specifications. MTBF figures usually range from 300,000 to 1,000,000 hours or more. I usually ignore these figures because they are derived theoretically.

In understanding the MTBF claims, you must understand how the manufacturers arrive at them and what they mean. Most manufacturers have a long history of building drives, and their drives have seen millions of hours of cumulative use. They can look at the failure rate for previous drive models with the same components and calculate a failure rate for a new drive based on the components used to build the drive assembly. For the electronic circuit board, they also can use industry standard techniques for predicting the failure of the integrated electronics. This enables them to calculate the predicted failure rate for the entire drive unit.

To understand what these numbers mean, you must know that the MTBF claims apply to a population of drives, not an individual drive. This means that if a drive claims to have an MTBF of 500,000 hours, you can expect a failure in that population of drives in 500,000 hours of total running time. If 1,000,000 drives of this model are in service and all 1,000,000 are running at once, you can expect one failure out of this entire population every half-hour. MTBF statistics are not useful for predicting the failure of any individual drive or a small sample of drives.

You also need to understand the meaning of the word *failure*. In this sense, a failure is a fault that requires the drive to be returned to the manufacturer for repair, not an occasional failure to read or write a file correctly.

Finally, as some drive manufacturers point out, this measure of MTBF should really be called mean time to first failure. "Between failures" implies that the drive fails, is returned for repair, and then at some point fails again. The interval between repair and the second failure here would be the MTBF. Because in most cases, a failed hard drive that would need manufacturer repair is replaced rather than repaired, the whole MTBF concept is misnamed.

The bottom line is that I do not really place much emphasis on MTBF figures. For an individual drive, they are not accurate predictors of reliability. However, if you are an information systems manager considering the purchase of thousands of PCs or drives per year, or a system vendor building and supporting thousands of systems, it is worth your while to examine these numbers and study the methods used to calculate them by each vendor. If you can understand the vendor's calculations and compare the actual reliability of a large sample of drives, you can purchase more reliable drives and save time and money in service and support.

S.M.A.R.T.

S.M.A.R.T. (Self-Monitoring, Analysis, and Reporting Technology) is an industry standard providing failure prediction for disk drives. When S.M.A.R.T. is enabled for a given drive, the drive monitors predetermined attributes that are susceptible to or indicative of drive degradation. Based on changes in the monitored attributes, a failure prediction can be made. If a failure is deemed likely to occur, S.M.A.R.T. makes a status report available so the system BIOS or driver software can notify the user of the impending problems, perhaps enabling the user to back up the data on the drive before any real problems occur.

Predictable failures are the types of failures S.M.A.R.T. attempts to detect. These failures result from the gradual degradation of the drive's performance. According to Seagate, 60% of drive failures are mechanical, which is exactly the type of failures S.M.A.R.T. is designed to predict.

Of course, not all failures are predictable, and S.M.A.R.T. cannot help with unpredictable failures that occur without any advance warning. These can be caused by static electricity; improper handling or sudden shock; or circuit failure, such as thermal-related solder problems or component failure.

S.M.A.R.T. was originally created by IBM in 1992. That year IBM began shipping 3 1/2-inch hard disk drives equipped with Predictive Failure Analysis (PFA), an IBM-developed technology that periodically measures selected drive attributes and sends a warning message when a predefined threshold is exceeded. IBM turned this technology over to the ANSI organization, and it subsequently became the ANSI-standard S.M.A.R.T. protocol for SCSI drives, as defined in the ANSI-SCSI Informational Exception Control (IEC) document X3T10/94-190.

Interest in extending this technology to IDE/ATA drives led to the creation of the S.M.A.R.T. Working Group in 1995. Besides IBM, other companies represented in the original group were Seagate Technology, Conner Peripherals (now a part of Seagate), Fujitsu, Hewlett-Packard, Maxtor, Quantum, and Western Digital. The S.M.A.R.T. specification produced by this group and placed in the public domain covers both IDE/ATA and SCSI hard disk drives and can be found in most of the more recently produced drives on the market.

The S.M.A.R.T. design of attributes and thresholds is similar in IDE/ATA and SCSI environments, but the reporting of information differs.

In an IDE/ATA environment, driver software on the system interprets the alarm signal from the drive generated by the S.M.A.R.T. "report status" command. The driver polls the drive on a regular basis to check the status of this command and, if it signals imminent failure, sends an alarm to the operating system where it will be passed on via an error message to the end user. This structure also enables future enhancements, which might allow reporting of information other than drive failure conditions. The system can read and evaluate the attributes and alarms reported in addition to the basic "report status" command.

SCSI drives with S.M.A.R.T. communicate a reliability condition only as either good or failing. In a SCSI environment, the failure decision occurs at the disk drive, and the host notifies the user for action. The SCSI specification provides for a sense bit to be flagged if the drive determines that a reliability issue exists. The system then alerts the end user via a message.

The basic requirements for S.M.A.R.T. to function in a system are simple. All you need are a S.M.A.R.T.-capable hard disk drive and a S.M.A.R.T.-aware BIOS or hard disk driver for your particular operating system. If your BIOS does not support S.M.A.R.T., utility programs are available that can support S.M.A.R.T. on a given system. These include Norton Disk Doctor from Symantec, EZ Drive from StorageSoft, and Data Advisor from Ontrack Data International.

Note that traditional disk diagnostics, such as Scandisk and Norton Disk Doctor, work only on the data sectors of the disk surface and do not monitor all the drive functions that are monitored by S.M.A.R.T. Most modern disk drives keep spare sectors available to use as substitutes for sectors that have errors. When one of these spares is reallocated, the drive reports the activity to the S.M.A.R.T. counter but still looks completely defect-free to a surface analysis utility, such as Scandisk.

Drives with S.M.A.R.T. monitor a variety of attributes that vary from one manufacturer to another. Attributes are selected by the device manufacturer based on their capability to contribute to the prediction of degrading or fault conditions for that particular drive. Most drive manufacturers consider the specific set of attributes being used and the identity of those attributes as vendor specific and proprietary.

Some drives monitor the floating height of the head above the magnetic media. If this height changes from a nominal figure, the drive could fail. Other drives can monitor different attributes, such as ECC (error correcting code) circuitry that indicates whether soft errors are occurring when reading or writing data. Some of the attributes monitored on various drives include the following:

- Head floating height
- Data throughput performance
- Spin-up time
- Reallocated (spared) sector count
- Seek error rate
- Seek time performance

- Drive spin-up retry count
- Drive calibration retry count

Each attribute has a threshold limit that is used to determine the existence of a degrading or fault condition. These thresholds are set by the drive manufacturer and cannot be changed.

When sufficient changes occur in the monitored attributes to trigger a S.M.A.R.T. alert, the drive sends an alert message via an IDE/ATA or a SCSI command (depending on the type of hard disk drive you have) to the hard disk driver in the system BIOS, which then forwards the message to the operating system. The operating system then displays a warning message as follows:

Immediately back up your data and replace your hard disk drive. A failure may be imminent.

The message might contain additional information, such as which physical device initiated the alert; a list of the logical drives (partitions) that correspond to the physical device; and even the type, manufacturer, and serial number of the device.

The first thing to do when you receive such an alert is to heed the warning and back up all the data on the drive. It also is wise to back up to new media and not overwrite any previous good backups you might have, just in case the drive fails before the backup is complete.

After backing up your data, what should you do? S.M.A.R.T. warnings can be caused by an external source and might not actually indicate that the drive itself is going to fail. For example, environmental changes, such as high or low ambient temperatures, can trigger a S.M.A.R.T. alert, as can excessive vibration in the drive caused by an external source. Additionally, electrical interference from motors or other devices on the same circuit as your PC can induce these alerts.

If the alert was not caused by an external source, a drive replacement might be indicated. If the drive is under warranty, contact the vendor and ask them whether they will replace it. If no further alerts occur, the problem might have been an anomaly, and you might not need to replace the drive. If you receive further alerts, replacing the drive is recommended. If you can connect both the new and existing (failing) drive to the same system, you might be able to copy the entire contents of the existing drive to the new one, saving you from having to install or reload all the applications and data from your backup.

Performance

When you select a hard disk drive, one of the important features you should consider is the performance (speed) of the drive. Hard drives can have a wide range of performance capabilities. As is true of many things, one of the best indicators of a drive's relative performance is its price. An old saying from the automobile-racing industry is appropriate here: "Speed costs money. How fast do you want to go?"

You can measure the speed of a disk drive in two ways:

- Average seek time
- Transfer rate

Average seek time, normally measured in milliseconds (ms), is the average amount of time it takes to move the heads from one cylinder to another a random distance away. One way to measure this specification is to run many random track-seek operations and then divide the timed results by the number of seeks performed. This method provides an average time for a single seek.

The standard method used by many drive manufacturers to measure the average seek time involves measuring the time it takes the heads to move across one-third of the total cylinders. Average seek time depends only on the drive itself; the type of interface or controller has little effect on this specification. The rating is a gauge of the capabilities of the head actuator.

Note

Be wary of benchmarks that claim to measure drive seek performance. Most ATA/IDE and SCSI drives use a scheme called sector translation, so any commands the drive receives to move the heads to a specific cylinder might not actually result in the intended physical movement. This situation renders some benchmarks meaningless for those types of drives. SCSI drives also require an additional step because the commands first must be sent to the drive over the SCSI bus. These drives might seem to have the fastest access times because the command overhead is not factored in by most benchmarks. However, when this overhead is factored in by benchmark programs, these drives receive poor performance figures.

Average Access Time

A slightly different measurement, called average access time, involves another element called *latency*. Latency is the average time (in milliseconds) it takes for a sector to be available after the heads have reached a track. On average, this figure is half the time it takes for the disk to rotate once. A drive that spins twice as fast would have half the latency. A measurement of a drive's average access time is the sum of its average seek time and latency. This number provides the average amount of time required before the drive can access a randomly requested sector.

Latency

Latency is a factor in disk read and write performance. Decreasing the latency increases the speed of access to data or files and is accomplished only by spinning the drive platters more quickly. Latency figures for most popular drive rotational speeds are shown in Table 10.5.

Table 10.5   Hard Disk Rotation Speeds and Their Latencies

Revs/Minute	Revs/Second	Latency
3,600	60	8.33
4,200	70	7.14
5,400	90	5.56
7,200	120	4.17
10,000	167	3.00
15,000	250	2.00

Many drives today spin at 7,200rpm, resulting in a latency time of only 4.17ms, whereas others spin at 10,000rpm or even 15,000rpm, resulting in incredible 3.00ms or 2.00ms latency figures. In addition to increasing performance where real-world access to data is concerned, spinning the platters more quickly also increases the data-transfer rate after the heads arrive at the desired sectors.

Transfer Rate

The transfer rate is probably more important to overall system performance than any other statistic, but it is also one of the most misunderstood specifications. The problem stems from the fact that now several transfer rates can be specified for a given drive.

Most drive manufacturers now report up to five transfer rates. One is the interface transfer rate, which for most newer ATA drives is 100MB/sec. The other (FAR more important) transfer rate specifications are the media transfer rates, which can be expressed as a raw maximum, a raw minimum, a formatted maximum, or a formatted minimum. Few report the average, but that can be easily calculated.

The media transfer rate is far more important than the interface transfer rate because the media transfer rate is the true rate at which data can be read from the disk, which is how fast data can be read from the drive platters (media). It is the maximum rate that any sustained transfer can hope to achieve.

Drive makers report a minimum and maximum media transfer rate because drives today have a zoned recording with various numbers of sectors per track. Typically, a drive is divided into 16 zones, and the inner zone has about half the sectors (and therefore about half the transfer rate) of the outer zone. Because the drive spins at a constant rate, data is read more quickly from the outer cylinders (with more sectors per track) than from the inner cylinders.

Another issue is the raw transfer rate versus the formatted transfer rate. The *raw* rate refers to how fast bits can be read off the media. Because not all bits represent data (some are intersector or ID bits), and because some time is lost when the heads have to move from track to track, the *formatted* transfer rate represents the true rate at which data can be read from or written to the drive.

Note that some manufacturers report only raw transfer rates, but you usually can figure that the formatted rates are about two-thirds of the raw rates. Likewise, some manufacturers report only maximum transfer rates (either raw, formatted, or both); in that case you can generally assume the minimum transfer rate is one-half of the maximum and that the average transfer rate is three-fourths of the maximum.

Let's look at a specific drive as an example. The IBM Deskstar 60GXP is one of the fastest ATA/IDE drives on the market, spins at 7,200rpm, and fully supports the ATA/100 interface transfer rate (100MB/sec from the controller to the motherboard). As with all current drives, the actual transfer rate is much less.

Table 10.6 shows the specifications for the 7,200rpm Ultra-ATA/100 IBM Deskstar 60GXP drive.

Table 10.6   Transfer Rate Specifications for the IBM Deskstar 60GXP Drive

Transfer Rates	Megabits/Sec	Megabytes/Sec
Interface Transfer Rate	800Mb/sec	100.0MB/sec
Raw Media Transfer Rate (Min)	253Mb/sec	31.6MB/sec
Raw Media Transfer Rate (Max)	494Mb/sec	61.8MB/sec
Formatted Media Transfer Rate (Min)	167Mb/sec	20.9MB/sec
Formatted Media Transfer Rate (Max)	326Mb/sec	40.8MB/sec
Formatted Media Transfer Rate (Avg)	247Mb/sec	30.8MB/sec

MB/sec = Million bytes per second; Mb/sec = Million bits per second

As you can see, the TRUE media transfer rate for this drive is between 20.9MB/sec and 40.8MB/sec, or an average of about 30.8MB/sec, or less than one-third of the interface transfer rate. Of course, if this were your drive you shouldn't be dissapointed becuase 30.8MB/sec is excellent performance—in fact, this is one of the fastest ATA drives on the market. Many, if not most other, ATA/IDE drives would have equal or slower performance.

A common question I get is about upgrading the ATA interface in a system. Many people are using older motherboards that support only ATA/33 or ATA/66 modes and not the faster ATA/100 specification. After studying the true formatted media transfer rates of most drives, you can see why I generally do not recommend installing a separate ATA/100 controller for those systems. Those who perform such an upgrade will see little if any increase in performance. This is because in almost all cases, the drives they are using will be on average slower than even ATA/33—and often significantly slower than the ATA/66 or ATA/100 interface speeds.

Two primary factors contribute to transfer rate performance: rotational speed and the linear recording density or sector-per-track figures. When comparing two drives with the same number of sectors per track, the drive that spins more quickly will transfer data more quickly. Likewise, when comparing two drives with identical rotational speeds, the drive with the higher recording density (more sectors per track) will be faster. A higher-density drive can be faster than one that spins faster—both factors have to be taken into account.

Let's look at another example. One of the fastest rotating drives today is the Seagate Cheetah X15, which spins at 15,000rpm.

Table 10.7 shows the specifications for the 15,000rpm Ultra3-SCSI/160 Seagate Cheetah X15 drive.

Table 10.7   Transfer Rate Specifications for the Seagate Cheetah X15 Drive

Transfer Rates	Megabits/Sec	Megabytes/Sec
Interface Transfer Rate	1,280Mb/sec	160.0MB/sec
Raw Media Transfer Rate (Min)	385Mb/sec	48.1MB/sec
Raw Media Transfer Rate (Max)	508Mb/sec	63.5MB/sec
Formatted Media Transfer Rate (Min)	299Mb/sec	37.4MB/sec
Formatted Media Transfer Rate (Max)	391Mb/sec	48.9MB/sec
Formatted Media Transfer Rate (Avg)	345Mb/sec	43.2MB/sec

As a comparison, Table 10.8 contains the specifications for the 10,000rpm Ultra3-SCSI/160 Seagate Cheetah 73LP drive.

Table 10.8   Transfer Rates for the Seagate Cheetah 73LP Drive

Transfer Rates	Megabits/Sec	Megabytes/Sec
Interface Transfer Rate	1,280Mb/sec	160.0MB/sec
Raw Media Transfer Rate (Min)	399Mb/sec	49.9MB/sec
Raw Media Transfer Rate (Max)	671Mb/sec	83.9MB/sec
Formatted Media Transfer Rate (Min)	307Mb/sec	38.4MB/sec
Formatted Media Transfer Rate (Max)	511Mb/sec	63.9MB/sec
Formatted Media Transfer Rate (Avg)	409Mb/sec	51.2MB/sec

As you can see, in this case the 10,000rpm Cheetah 73LP is significantly faster than the 15,000rpm Cheetah X15. Neither of these drives, however, is close to the Ultra3 SCSI (160MB/sec) bandwidth that the interface would allow. With a comparison such as this, you can see that you need to be careful. Don't just compare one specification, such as rotational speed, because in some cases (like this one), the drive that spins twice as quickly is actually slower in transfer performance. This is a good reminder why you need to be careful with simplistic comparisons. With hard drives, the bottom line is that the media transfer rate is probably the most important specification you can know about a drive, and faster is better.

With older drives the manufacturers often reported minimum and maximum sector per track specifications, which—combined with the rotational speed—can be used to calculate true formatted media performance. Also, be aware that many drives (especially zoned-bit recording drives) are configured with sector translation, so the number of sectors per track reported by the BIOS has little to do with the actual physical characteristics of the drive. You must know the drive's true physical parameters, rather than the values the BIOS uses.

When you know these figures, you can use the following formula to determine the true media data transfer rate in millions of bytes per second (MBps):

Media Transfer Rate (MBps) = SPT×512 bytes×rpm/60 seconds/1,000,000 bytes

For example, the IBM Travelstar 32GH 32GB 2 1/2-inch drive spins at 5,411rpm and has an average of 472 sectors per track. The average media transfer rate for this drive is figured as follows:

472×512×(5,411/60)/1,000,000 = 21.8MBps

Using this formula, you can calculate the media transfer rate of any drive, if you know the rotational speed and average sectors per track.

Some drives report their transfer speeds as a maximum sustainable formatted rate. For example, the IBM Deskstar 60GXP drive detailed earlier has minimum and maximum formatted transfer rates of 20.9MB/sec and 40.8MB/sec, respectively (to or from the media), and spins at 7,200rpm, which works out to be:

20.9×1,000,000/(7200/60)/512 = 340 sectors per track maximum

40.8×1,000,000/(7200/60)/512 = 664 sectors per track maximum

Averaging these figures results in a 30.8MB/sec average transfer rate and 502 sectors per track average.

Note that these are the true numbers of sectors per track (with differing values across 18 zones in this case) even though the drive would report only 63 sectors per track if queried with the ATA Identify command, such as in a BIOS Setup with autodetect. Don't be confused because the numbers reported by the drive are different from what is actually inside. For example, this drive has 6 actual heads even though it would report 16, and it has about 34,000 actual cylinders even though it would report 16,384 to the BIOS setup.

Cache Programs and Caching Controllers

At the software level, disk cache programs, such as SMARTDRV (in DOS) and VCACHE (in Windows 9x, Windows NT, and Windows 2000), can have a major effect on disk drive performance. These cache programs hook into the BIOS hard drive interrupt and intercept the read and write calls to the disk BIOS from application programs and device drivers.

When an application program wants to read data from a hard drive, the cache program intercepts the read request, passes the read request to the hard drive controller in the usual way, saves the data read from the disk in its cache memory buffer, and then passes the data back to the application program. Depending on the size of the cache buffer, data from numerous sectors can be read into and saved in the buffer.

When the application wants to read more data, the cache program again intercepts the request and examines its buffers to see whether the requested data is still in the cache. If so, the program passes the data back from the cache to the application immediately, without another hard drive operation. Because the cached data is stored in memory, this method speeds access tremendously and can greatly affect disk drive performance measurements.

Most controllers now have some form of built-in hardware buffer or cache that doesn't intercept or use any BIOS interrupts. Instead, the drive caches data at the hardware level, which is invisible to normal performance-measurement software. Manufacturers originally included track read-ahead buffers in controllers to permit 1:1 interleave performance. Some manufacturers now increase the size of these read-ahead buffers in the controller, whereas others add intelligence by using a cache instead of a simple buffer.

Many ATA and SCSI drives have cache memory built directly into the drive's onboard controller. Most newer ATA drives have between 512KB and 2MB of built-in cache, whereas many SCSI drives have up to 16MB. I remember when 640KB was a lot of memory for an entire system. Now, tiny 3 1/2-inch hard disk drives can have 16MB built right in! These integrated caches are part of the reason many ATA (IDE) and SCSI drives perform so well.

Although software and hardware caches can make a drive faster for routine transfer operations, a cache will not affect the true maximum transfer rate the drive can sustain.

Interleave Selection

In a discussion of disk performance, the issue of interleave often comes up. Although traditionally this was more a controller performance issue than a drive issue, modern ATA/IDE and SCSI hard disk drives with built-in controllers are fully capable of processing the data as fast as the drive can send it. In other words, all modern ATA and SCSI drives are formatted with no interleave (sometimes expressed as a 1:1 interleave ratio). On older hard drive types, such as MFM and ESDI, you could modify the interleave during a low-level format to optimize the drive's performance. Today, drives are low-level formatted at the factory and interleave adjustments are a moot topic.

Note

For more information on interleaving and cylinder skewing as used on older drives, see Chapter 10 of *Upgrading and Repairing PCs, 12th Edition*, included in its entirety on the CD included with this book.

Cost

The cost of hard disk storage is continually falling. You can now purchase a 30GB ATA drive for around $150, which is about half a cent per megabyte.

A drive I bought in 1983 had a maximum capacity of 10MB and cost $1,800. At current pricing (0.5 cents per megabyte), that drive is worth about 5 cents!

Of course, the cost of drives continues to fall, and eventually, even half a cent per megabyte will seem expensive. Because of the low costs of disk storage today, not many 3-1/2 inch drives with capacities of less than 10GB are even being manufactured.

Capacity

Four figures are commonly used in advertising drive capacity:

- Unformatted capacity, in millions of bytes
- Formatted capacity, in millions of bytes
- Unformatted capacity, in megabytes
- Formatted capacity, in megabytes

The term *formatted*, in these figures, refers to the low-level (or physical) formatting of the drive. Most manufacturers of ATA/IDE and SCSI drives now report only the formatted capacities because these drives are delivered preformatted. Usually, advertisements and specifications refer to the unformatted or formatted capacity in millions of bytes because these figures are larger than the same capacity expressed in megabytes. This situation generates a great deal of confusion when the user runs FDISK (which reports total drive capacity in megabytes) and wonders where the missing space is. This question can seem troubling. Fortunately, the answer is easy; it only involves a little math to figure it out.

Perhaps the most common questions I get are concerning "missing" drive capacity. Consider the following example: I just installed a new Seagate ST330630A drive in a system, which is advertised as having 30.6GB capacity. After entering the drive parameters in the BIOS Setup (I used the autodetect feature to automate the process), when I went to partition the drive using FDISK, the capacity was reported by FDISK as only 203MB! "What happened to the other 29.8GB?"

The answer is only a few calculations away. By multiplying the drive specification parameters, you get this result:

Total sectors:	59,777,640
Bytes per sector:	512
Total bytes (in decimal megabytes):	30,606
Total bytes (in decimal gigabytes):	30.6
Total bytes (in binary megabytes):	29,188
Total bytes (in binary gigabytes):	28.5
As reported by FDISK:	29,188

All the numbers in the table above are correct. Drive manufacturers usually report drive capacity in decimal megabytes (millions of bytes) because they result in larger, more impressive sounding numbers, although your BIOS and especially the FDISK drive partitioning software report the capacity in binary megabytes. One decimal megabyte equals one million bytes, whereas one binary megabyte equals 1,048,576 bytes (or 1,024KB, in which each kilobyte is 1,024 bytes). So the bottom line is that, because the same abbreviations are often used for both millions of bytes and megabytes, this 30.6GB drive could also be called a 28.5GB drive, depending on how you look at it!

Specific Recommendations

If you are going to add a hard disk to a system today, I can give you a few recommendations. For the drive interface, there really are only two types to consider:

- ATA (AT Attachment, also called IDE)
- SCSI (Small Computer System Interface)

These interfaces are covered more completely in Chapters 7, "The IDE Interface," and 8, "The SCSI Interface." SCSI offers great expandability, cross-platform compatibility, high capacity, performance, and flexibility. ATA is less expensive than SCSI and also offers a very high-performance solution, but expansion, compatibility, capacity, and flexibility are more limited when compared with SCSI. I usually recommend ATA for most people for two reasons. First, the interface is already integrated into virtually every motherboard and BIOS sold today. Second, most users will not need more capacity than the four devices supported by the standard primary and secondary ATA interfaces found in most systems. SCSI offers additional performance potential with a multithreaded operating system, such as Windows NT/2000, as well as support for more devices, but it also requires the purchase of a separate host adapter card, which is in addition to the higher cost for the drive itself.

Note

Note that the current fastest ATA standard is UltraDMA/100 or UltraATA/100, which runs at 100MB/sec raw interface transfer rate. Serial ATA is coming out with a 150MB/sec transfer rate. The current fastest SCSI standard is Ultra4 (also called Ultra/320)-SCSI, which runs a raw interface transfer rate of 320MB/sec. Both interfaces have improvements slated that should double their respective transfer rates in the future.

CHAPTER 11

Floppy Disk Storage

This chapter examines the standard types of floppy disk drives and disks that have been used in PCs since the beginning. It explores the various types of drives and disks, how they function, and how to properly install and service them. The newer high-capacity floppy drives, such as the SuperDisk (LS-120), are covered separately in Chapter 12, "High-Capacity Removable Storage." Magnetic storage in general—that is, how data is actually stored on the disk media—is covered in Chapter 9, "Magnetic Storage Principles."

Floppy Disk Drives

Although no longer used for primary storage, the floppy is still necessary in most systems as a system installation and configuration device, and also especially when troubleshooting. When building up a system or installing one from scratch, the floppy is often used to load software necessary for partitioning and formatting the hard disk, as well as to run diagnostics in case of problems.

Another interesting use is in the transfer of data from some digital cameras. A device called the *FlashPath adapter* enables your PC to read SmartMedia flash memory storage chips via the floppy drive. These are covered in more detail in Chapter 12, although I think they are worth mentioning here.

Even though higher-capacity storage devices are available and most modern systems can boot directly from CD-ROMs, the ubiquitous floppy drive will likely remain as a staple in systems for several more years to come.

History of the Floppy

Alan Shugart is generally credited with inventing the floppy disk drive in 1967 while working for IBM. One of Shugart's senior engineers, David Noble, actually proposed the flexible medium (then 8 inches in diameter) and the protective jacket with the fabric lining. Shugart left IBM in 1969, and in 1976 his company, Shugart Associates, introduced the minifloppy (5 1/4-inch) disk drive. It, of course, became the standard eventually used by personal computers, rapidly replacing the 8-inch drives. He also helped create the Shugart Associates System Interface (SASI), which was later renamed SCSI (small computer system interface) when approved as an ANSI standard.

Sony introduced the first 3 1/2-inch microfloppy drives and disks in 1983. The first significant company to adopt the 3 1/2-inch floppy for general use was Hewlett-Packard in 1984 with its partially PC-compatible HP-150 system. The industry adoption of the 3 1/2-inch drive was furthered when Apple used it in the first Macintosh systems in 1984, and IBM put the drive into its entire PC product line starting in 1986.

Note that all PC floppy disk drives are still based on (and mostly compatible with) the original Shugart designs, including the electrical and command interfaces. Compared to other parts of the PC, the floppy disk drive has undergone relatively few changes over the years.

Drive Components

All floppy disk drives, regardless of type, consist of several basic common components. To properly install and service a disk drive, you must be able to identify these components and understand their functions (see Figure 11.1).

Figure 11.1 A typical floppy disk drive.

Read/Write Heads

A floppy disk drive normally has two read/write heads, one for each side of the disk, with both heads being used for reading and writing on their respective disk sides (see Figure 11.2). At one time, single-sided drives were available for PC systems (the original PC had such drives), but today single-sided drives are a fading memory.

Read/write head
(Side 1)

Read/write head
(Side 0)

Head carriage assembly
(double-sided)

Figure 11.2   A double-sided drive head assembly.

Note

Many people do not realize that Head 0, or the first head on a floppy disk drive, is the bottom one. Single-sided drives, in fact, used only the bottom head; the top head has been replaced by a felt pressure pad. Another bit of disk trivia is that the top head (Head 1) is not positioned directly over the bottom head (Head 0). The top head is instead offset by either four or eight tracks inward from the bottom head, depending on the drive type.

The head mechanism is moved by a motor called a *head actuator*. The heads can move in and out over the surface of the disk in a straight line to position themselves over various tracks. On a floppy drive, the heads move in and out tangentially to the tracks they record on the disk. This is different from hard disks, where the heads move on a rotating arm similar to the tone-arm of a record player. Because the top and bottom heads are mounted on the same rack, or mechanism, they move in unison and cannot move independently of each other. The upper and lower heads each define tracks on their respective sides of the disk medium, whereas at any given head position, the tracks under the top and bottom head simultaneously are called a *cylinder*. Most floppy disks are recorded with 80 tracks on each side (160 tracks total), which is 80 cylinders.

The heads themselves are made of soft ferrous (iron) compounds with electromagnetic coils. Each head is a composite design, with a read/write head centered within two tunnel-erase heads in the same physical assembly (see Figure 11.3).

Floppy disk drives use a recording method called *tunnel erasure*. As the drive writes to a track, the trailing tunnel-erase heads erase the outer bands of the track, trimming it cleanly on the disk. The heads force the data into a specified narrow "tunnel" on each track. This process prevents the signal from one track from being confused with the signals from adjacent tracks, which would happen if the signal were allowed to naturally "taper off" to each side. *Alignment* is the placement of the heads with respect to the tracks they must read and write. Head alignment can be checked against only some sort of reference-standard disk recorded by a perfectly aligned machine. These types of disks are available, and you can use one to check your drive's alignment. However, this is usually not practical for the end user because one calibrated analog alignment disk can cost more than a new drive.

The floppy disk drive's two heads are spring-loaded and physically grip the disk with a small amount of pressure, which means they are in direct contact with the disk surface while reading and writing to the disk. Because floppy disk drives spin at only 300rpm or 360rpm, this pressure does not present an excessive friction problem. Some newer disks are specially coated with Teflon or other compounds to further reduce friction and enable the disk to slide more easily under the heads. Because of the contact between the heads and disk, a buildup of the magnetic material from the disk eventually forms on the heads. The buildup should periodically be cleaned off the heads as part of a preventive maintenance or normal service program. Most manufacturers recommend cleaning the heads after every 40 hours of drive operation, which, considering how many people use these drives today, could be a lifetime.

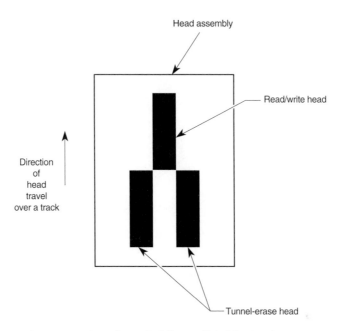

Figure 11.3 Composite construction of a typical floppy disk drive head.

To read and write to the disk properly, the heads must be in direct contact with the magnetic medium. Very small particles of loose oxide, dust, dirt, smoke, fingerprints, or hair can cause problems with reading and writing the disk. Disk and drive manufacturers' tests have found that a spacing as little as .000032 inch (32 millionths of an inch) between the heads and medium can cause read/write errors. You now can understand why it is important to handle disks carefully and avoid touching or contaminating the surface of the disk medium in any way. The rigid jacket and protective shutter for the head access aperture on 3 1/2-inch disks is excellent for preventing problems caused by contamination. Disks that are 5 1/4-inch do not have the same protective elements, which is perhaps one reason why they have fallen into disuse. If you still use 5 1/4-inch floppy disks, you should exercise extra care in their handling.

The Head Actuator

The *head actuator* for a floppy disk drive is what moves the heads across the disk and is driven by a special kind of motor, called a *stepper motor* (see Figure 11.4). This type of motor does not spin around continuously; rather, the motor turns a precise specified distance and stops. Stepper motors are not infinitely variable in their positioning; they move in fixed increments—or *detents*—and must stop at a particular detent position. This is ideal for disk drives because the location of each track on the disk can then be defined by moving one or more increments of the motor's motion. The disk controller can instruct the motor to position itself any number of steps within the range of its travel. To position the heads at cylinder 25, for example, the controller instructs the motor to go to the 25th detent position or step from Cylinder 0.

Figure 11.4 An expanded view of a stepper motor and head actuator.

The stepper motor can be linked to the head rack in one of two ways. In the first, the link is a coiled, split-steel band. The band winds and unwinds around the spindle of the stepper motor, translating the rotary motion into linear motion. Some drives, however, use a worm-gear arrangement rather than a band. In this type of drive, the head assembly rests on a worm gear driven directly off the stepper motor shaft. Because this arrangement is more compact, you normally find worm-gear actuators on the smaller 3 1/2-inch drives.

Most stepper motors used in floppy disk drives can step in specific increments that relate to the track spacing on the disk. Older 48-track-per-inch (TPI) drives have a motor that steps in increments of 3.6 degrees. This means that each 3.6 degrees of stepper motor rotation moves the heads from one track to the next. Most 96 or 135 TPI drives have a stepper motor that moves in 1.8-degree increments, which is exactly half of what the 48 TPI drives use. Sometimes you see this information actually printed or stamped right on the stepper motor itself, which is useful if you are trying to figure out which type of drive you have. 5 1/4-inch 360KB drives are the only 48 TPI drives that use the 3.6 degree increment stepper motor. All other drive types normally use the 1.8-degree stepper motor. On most drives, the stepper motor is a small cylindrical object near one corner of the drive.

A stepper motor usually has a full travel time of about 1/5 of a second—about 200ms. On average, a half-stroke is 100ms, and a one-third stroke is 66ms. The timing of a one-half or one-third stroke of the head-actuator mechanism is often used to determine the reported average access time for a disk drive. Average access time is the normal amount of time the heads spend moving at random from one track to another.

The Spindle Motor

The *spindle motor* is what spins the disk. The normal speed of rotation is either 300rpm or 360rpm, depending on the type of drive. The 5 1/4-inch high-density (HD) drive is the only drive that spins at 360rpm. All others, including the 5 1/4-inch double-density (DD), 3 1/2-inch DD, 3 1/2-inch HD, and 3 1/2-inch extra-high density (ED) drives, spin at 300rpm. This is a slow speed when compared to a hard disk drive, which helps explain why floppy disk drives have much lower data transfer rates. However, this slow speed also enables the drive heads to be in physical contact with the disk while it is spinning, without causing friction damage.

Many earlier drives used a mechanism by which the spindle motor physically turned the disk spindle with a belt, but all modern drives use a direct-drive system with no belts. The direct-drive systems are more reliable and less expensive to manufacture, as well as smaller in size. The earlier belt-driven systems did have more rotational torque available to turn a sticky disk because of the torque multiplication factor of the belt system. Most newer direct-drive systems, on the other hand, use an automatic torque-compensation capability that sets the disk-rotation speed to a fixed 300rpm or 360rpm and compensates with additional torque for high-friction disks or less torque for more slippery ones. Besides compensating for varying amounts of friction, this arrangement eliminates the need to adjust the rotational speed of the drive, something that was frequently required on older drives.

Circuit Boards

A disk drive always incorporates one or more *logic boards*, which are circuit boards that contain the circuitry used to control the head actuator, read/write heads, spindle motor, disk sensors, and other components on the drive. The logic board implements the drive's interface to the controller board in the system unit.

The standard interface used by all PC floppy disk drives is termed the Shugart Associates SA-400 interface, which was invented in the 1970s and is based on the NEC 765 controller chip. All modern floppy controllers contain circuits that are compatible with the original NEC 765 chip. This industry-standard interface is why you can purchase drives from almost any manufacturer and they will all be compatible.

The Controller

At one time, the controller for a computer's floppy disk drives took the form of a dedicated expansion card installed in an Industry Standard Architecture (ISA) bus slot. Later implementations used a multi-function card that provided the IDE/ATA, parallel, and serial port interfaces in addition to the floppy disk drive controller. Today's PCs have the floppy controller integrated into the motherboard, usually in the form of a Super I/O chip that also includes the serial and parallel interfaces, among other things. Even though the floppy controller can be found in the Super I/O chip on the motherboard, it is still interfaced to the system via the ISA bus and functions exactly as if it were a card installed in an ISA slot. These built-in controllers are normally configured via the system BIOS Setup routines and can be disabled if an actual floppy controller card is going to be installed.

Whether it is built in or not, each primary floppy controller uses a standard set of system resources:

- IRQ 6 (Interrupt Request)
- DMA 2 (Direct Memory Address)
- I/O ports 3F0–3F5, 3F7 (input/output)

These system resources are standardized and generally not changeable. This normally does not present a problem because no other devices will try to use these resources (which would result in a conflict).

◄◄ See "System Resources," p. 316.

Unlike the IDE interface, the floppy disk controller has not changed much over the years. Virtually the only thing that has changed is the controller's maximum speed. As the data density of floppy disks (and their capacity) has increased over the years, the controller speed has had to increase, as well. Nearly all floppy disk controllers in computers today support speeds of up to 1Mbit/sec, which supports all the standard floppy disk drives. 500Kbit/sec controllers can support all floppy disk drives except for the 2.88MB extra high-density models. Older computers used 250Kbit/sec controllers that could support only 360KB 5 1/4-inch and 720KB 3 1/2-inch drives. To install a standard 1.44MB 3 1/2-inch drive in an older machine you might have to replace the floppy controller with a faster model.

Tip

The best way to determine the speed of the floppy disk drive controller in your computer is to examine the floppy disk drive options provided by the system BIOS.

◀◀ See Chapter 5, "BIOS," p. 345.

Even if you do not intend to use a 2.88MB floppy disk drive, you still might want to ensure that your computer has the fastest possible controller. Some of the tape drives on the market use the floppy disk interface to connect to the system, and in this case, the controller has a profound effect on the overall throughput of the tape drive.

The Faceplate

The *faceplate*, or *bezel*, is the plastic piece that comprises the front of the drive. This piece, usually removable, comes in various colors and configurations.

Most floppy drive manufacturers offer drives with matching faceplates in gray, beige, or black and with a choice of red, green, or yellow activity LEDs as well. This enables a system builder to better match the drive to the aesthetics of the case for a seamless, integrated, and more professional look.

Connectors

Nearly all floppy disk drives have two connectors—one for power to run the drive and the other to carry the control and data signals to and from the drive. These connectors are fairly standardized in the computer industry. A 4-pin in-line connector (called Mate-N-Lock by AMP) in both large and small styles is used for power (see Figure 11.5), and a 34-pin connector in both edge and pin header designs is used for the data and control signals. Normally, 5 1/4-inch drives use the large style power connector and the 34-pin edge-type connector, whereas most 3 1/2-inch drives use the smaller version of the power connector and the 34-pin header-type logic connector. The drive controller and logic connectors and pinouts are detailed later in this chapter, as well as on the Vendor List on this book's CD-ROM.

Both the large and small power connectors from the power supply are female plugs. They plug into the male portion, which is attached to the drive itself. One common problem with upgrading an older system with 3 1/2-inch drives is that your power supply has only the large-style connectors, whereas the drive has the small style. An adapter cable is available, from Radio Shack (cat. no. 278-765) and other sources, which converts the large-style power connector to the proper small style used on most 3 1/2-inch drives.

Most standard PCs use 3 1/2-inch drives with a 34-pin signal connector and a separate small-style power connector. For older systems, many drive manufacturers also sell 3 1/2-inch drives installed in a 5 1/4-inch frame assembly with a special adapter built in that enables you to use the larger power connector and older edge-type signal connectors.

Figure 11.5   Large (5.25″ drive) and small (3.5″ drive) disk drive female power supply cable connectors.

The Floppy Disk Drive Cable

The 34-pin connector on a floppy disk drive takes the form of either an edge connector (on 5 1/4-inch drives) or a pin connector (on 3 1/2-inch drives). The pinouts for the connector are shown in Table 11.1.

Table 11.1   Pinouts for the Standard Floppy Disk Drive Connector

Pin	Signal	Pin	Signal
1	Ground	2	Density Select
3	Ground	4	Reserved (Unused)
5	Ground	6	Reserved (Unused)
7	Ground	8	Index
9	Ground	10	Motor Enable A
11	Ground	12	Drive Select B
13	Ground	14	Drive Select A
15	Ground	16	Motor Enable B
17	Ground	18	Direction (Stepper motor)
19	Ground	20	Step Pulse
21	Ground	22	Write Data
23	Ground	24	Write Enable
25	Ground	26	Track 0
27	Ground	28	Write Protect
29	Ground	30	Read Data
31	Ground	32	Head Select
33	Ground	34	Disk Change

The cable used to connect the floppy disk drive(s) to the controller on the motherboard is quite strange. To support various drive configurations, the cable typically has five connectors on it—two edge connectors and two pin connectors to attach to the drives and one pin connector to connect to the controller. The cable has redundant connectors for each of the two drives (A and B) supported by the standard floppy disk drive controller, so you can install any combination of 5 1/4-inch and 3 1/2-inch drives (see Figure 11.6).

Figure 11.6 Standard five-connector floppy interface cable.

In addition to the connectors, the cable on most systems has a special twist that inverts the signals of wires 10–16. These are the wires carrying the Drive Select (DS) and Motor Enable signals for each of the two drives. Floppy disk drives have DS jumpers designed to enable you to select whether a given drive should be recognized as A or B.

You might not even know that these jumpers exist because the twist in the cable prevents you from having to adjust them. When installing two floppy disk drives in one system (admittedly a rarity nowadays), the cable electrically changes the DS configuration of the drive that is plugged in after the twist. Thus, the twist causes a drive physically set to the second DS position (B) to appear to the controller to be set to the first DS position (A) and vice versa. The adoption of this cable has enabled the use of a standard jumper configuration for all floppy disk drives, regardless of whether you install one or two drives in a computer.

If you install only a single floppy disk drive, you use the connector after the twist, which causes the drive to be recognized as drive A.

Disk Physical Specifications and Operation

Most PCs sold today are equipped with a 3 1/2-inch 1.44MB floppy disk drive. You might run into an older system that has a 5 1/4-inch 1.2MB drive instead of, or in addition to, the 3 1/2-inch drive. In addition, some PC systems have a 2.88MB 3 1/2-inch drive that can also read and write 1.44MB disks. The older drive types—5 1/4-inch 360KB and 3 1/2-inch 720KB—are obsolete and rarely found anymore.

The physical operation of a disk drive is fairly simple to describe. The disk rotates in the drive at either 300rpm or 360rpm. Most drives spin at 300rpm; only the 5 1/4-inch 1.2MB drives spin at 360rpm. With the disk spinning, the heads can move in and out approximately one inch and write 80 tracks. The tracks are written on both sides of the disk and are therefore sometimes called *cylinders*. A single cylinder comprises the tracks on the top and bottom of the disk. The heads record by using a tunnel-erase procedure that writes a track to a specified width, and then erases the edges of the track to prevent interference with any adjacent tracks.

Different drives record tracks at different widths. Table 11.2 shows the track widths in both millimeters and inches for the various types of floppy disk drives found in modern PC systems.

Table 11.2   Floppy Disk Drive Track-Width Specifications

Drive Type	No. of Tracks	Track Width	
5 1/4-in. 360KB	40 per side	0.300mm	0.0118 in.
5 1/4-in. 1.2MB	80 per side	0.155mm	0.0061 in.
3 1/2-in. 720KB	80 per side	0.115mm	0.0045 in.
3 1/2-in. 1.44MB	80 per side	0.115mm	0.0045 in.
3 1/2-in. 2.88MB	80 per side	0.115mm	0.0045 in.

How the Operating System Uses a Disk

To the operating system, data on your PC disks is organized in tracks and sectors, just as on a hard disk drive. *Tracks* are narrow, concentric circles on a disk. *Sectors* are pie-shaped slices of the individual tracks.

Table 11.3 summarizes the standard disk formats for PC floppy disk drives.

Table 11.3   5 1/4-Inch and 3 1/2-Inch Floppy Disk Drive Formats

5 1/4-Inch Floppy Disks	Double-Density 360KB (DD)	High-Density 1.2MB (HD)
Bytes per sector	512	512
Sectors per track	9	15
Tracks per side	40	80
Sides	2	2
Capacity (kilobytes)	360	1,200
Capacity (megabytes)	0.352	1.172
Capacity (million bytes)	0.369	1.229

Table 11.3 Continued

3 1/2-Inch Floppy Disks	Double-Density 720KB (DD)	High-Density 1.44MB (HD)	Extra High-Density 2.88MB (ED)
Bytes per sector	512	512	512
Sectors per track	9	18	36
Tracks per side	80	80	80
Sides	2	2	2
Capacity (kilobytes)	720	1,440	2,880
Capacity (megabytes)	0.703	1.406	2.813
Capacity (million bytes)	0.737	1.475	2.949

You can calculate the capacity differences between various formats by multiplying the sectors per track by the number of tracks per side together with the constants of two sides and 512 bytes per sector.

Note that the floppy disk's capacity can actually be expressed in various ways. The traditional method is to refer to the capacity of a floppy by the number of kilobytes (1,024 bytes equals 1KB). This works fine for the old-style 360KB and 720KB disks but is strange when applied to the 1.44MB and 2.88MB disks. As you can see, a 1.44MB disk is really 1,440KB and not actually 1.44 megabytes. Because a megabyte is 1,024KB, what we call a 1.44MB disk actually has a capacity of 1.406MB.

Another way of expressing disk capacity is in millions of bytes. In that case, the 1.44MB disk has 1.475 million bytes of capacity.

Note

Again, as with hard disk drives, both megabyte and millions of bytes are abbreviated as MB or M, often resulting in a great deal of confusion.

Like blank sheets of paper, new, unformatted disks contain no information. Formatting a disk is similar to adding lines to the paper so you can write straight across. Formatting the disk writes the information the operating system needs to maintain a directory and file table of contents. On a floppy disk, no distinction exists between a high-level and low-level format, nor do you have to create any partitions. When you format a floppy disk with Windows 9x Explorer or the DOS FORMAT.COM program, both the high- and low-level formats are performed at the same time.

When you format a floppy disk, the operating system reserves the track nearest to the outside edge of a disk (track 0) almost entirely for its purposes. Track 0, Side 0, Sector 1 contains the DOS Boot Record (DBR), or Boot Sector, that the system needs to begin operation. The next few sectors contain the file allocation tables (FATs), which keep records of which clusters or allocation units on the disk contain file information and which are empty. Finally, the next few sectors contain the root directory, in which the operating system stores information about the names and starting locations of the files on the disk.

Note that most floppies today are sold preformatted. This saves time because the formatting can take a minute or more per disk. Even if disks come preformatted, they can always be reformatted later.

Cylinders

The cylinder number is usually used in place of the track number because all floppy drives today are double-sided. A cylinder on a floppy disk includes two tracks: the one on the bottom of the disk above Head 0, and the one on the top of the disk below Head 1. Because a disk cannot have more than two sides and the drive has two heads, there are always two tracks per cylinder for floppy disks. Hard disk drives, on the other hand, can have multiple disk platters—each with two heads—resulting in many tracks per single cylinder. The simple rule is that there are as many tracks per cylinder as there are heads on the drive.

Cylinders are discussed in more detail in Chapter 10, "Hard Disk Storage," and Chapter 25, "File Systems and Data Recovery."

Clusters or Allocation Units

A *cluster* also is called an *allocation unit* in DOS version 4.0 and higher. The term is appropriate because a single cluster is the smallest unit of the disk that DOS can allocate when it writes a file. A cluster or allocation unit consists of one or more sectors—usually a power of two (1, 2, 4, 8, and so on). Having more than one sector per cluster reduces the FAT size and enables DOS to run more quickly because it has fewer individual clusters to manage. The tradeoff is in some wasted disk space. Because DOS can manage space only in the cluster size unit, every file consumes space on the disk in increments of one cluster.

For more information on allocation units, see Chapter 25.

Table 11.4 lists the default cluster sizes used by DOS and Windows for various floppy disk formats.

Table 11.4   Default Cluster and Allocation Unit Sizes

Floppy Disk Capacity	Cluster/Allocation Unit Size	FAT Type	
5 1/4-in., 360KB	2 sectors	1,024 bytes	12-bit
5 1/4-in., 1.2MB	1 sector	512 bytes	12-bit
3 1/2-in., 720KB	2 sectors	1,024 bytes	12-bit
3 1/2-in., 1.44MB	1 sector	512 bytes	12-bit
3 1/2-in., 2.88MB	2 sectors	1,024 bytes	12-bit

KB = 1,024 bytes
MB = 1,048,576 bytes

Disk Change

The standard PC floppy controller and drive use a special signal on pin 34 called *Disk Change* to determine whether the disk has been changed—or more accurately, to determine whether the same disk loaded during the previous disk access is still in the drive. Disk Change is a pulsed signal that changes a status register in the controller to let the system know that a disk has been either inserted or ejected. This register is set to indicate that a disk has been inserted or removed (changed) by default.

The register is cleared when the controller sends a step pulse to the drive and the drive responds, acknowledging that the heads have moved. At this point, the system knows that a specific disk is in the drive. If the Disk Change signal is not received before the next access, the system can assume that the same disk is still in the drive. Any information read into memory during the previous access can therefore be reused without rereading the disk.

Because of this process, systems can buffer or cache the contents of the FAT or directory structure of a disk in the system's memory. By eliminating unnecessary rereads of these areas of the disk, the apparent speed of the drive is increased. If you move the door lever or eject button on a drive that supports the Disk Change signal, the DC pulse is sent to the controller, thus resetting the register and indicating that the disk has been changed. This procedure causes the system to purge buffered or cached data that had been read from the disk because the system then cannot be sure that the same disk is still in the drive.

One interesting problem can occur when certain drives are installed in a 16-bit or greater system. As mentioned, some drives use pin 34 for a "Ready" (RDY) signal. The RDY signal is sent whenever a disk is installed and rotating in the drive. If you install a drive that has pin 34 set to send RDY, the system "thinks" it is continuously receiving a Disk Change signal, which causes problems. Usually, the drive fails with a Drive Not Ready error and is inoperable. The only reason the RDY signal exists on some drives is that it happens to be a part of the standard Shugart SA-400 disk interface; however, it has never been used in PC systems.

The biggest problem occurs if the drive should be sending the DC signal on pin 34 but isn't. If a system is told (through CMOS setup) that the drive is any type other than a 360KB (which cannot ever send the DC signal), the system expects the drive to send DC whenever a disk has been ejected. If the drive is not configured properly to send the signal, the system never recognizes that a disk has been changed. Therefore, even if you do change the disk, the system still acts as though the first disk is in the drive and holds the first disk's directory and FAT information in RAM. This can be dangerous because the FAT and directory information from the first disk can be partially written to any subsequent disks written to in the drive.

Caution

If you ever have seen a system with a floppy disk drive that shows "phantom directories" of the previously installed disk, even after you have changed or removed it, you have experienced this problem firsthand. The negative side effect is that all disks after the first one you place in this system are in extreme danger. You likely will overwrite the directories and FATs of many disks with information from the first disk.

If it's even possible at all, data recovery from such a catastrophe can require quite a bit of work with utility programs, such as Norton Utilities. These problems with Disk Change most often are traced to an incorrectly configured drive.

If the drive you are installing is a 5 1/4-inch 1.2MB or 3 1/2-inch 720KB, 1.44MB, or 2.88MB drive, be sure to set pin 34 to send the Disk Change (DC) signal. Most drives come permanently preset this way, but some have used a jumper (usually labeled DC) to set this option.

Types of Floppy Disk Drives

The characteristics of the floppy disk drives you might encounter in PC-compatible systems are summarized in Table 11.5. As you can see, the different disk capacities are determined by several parameters, some of which seem to remain constant on all drives, although others change from drive to drive. For example, all drives use 512-byte physical sectors, which is true for hard disks as well.

Table 11.5   Floppy Disk Logical Formatted Parameters

	Current Formats					Obsolete Formats		
Disk Size (Inches)	**3 1/2**	**3 1/2**	**3 1/2**	**5 1/4**	**5 1/4**	**5 1/4**	**5 1/4**	**5 1/4**
Disk Capacity (KB)	**2,880**	**1,440**	**720**	**1,200**	**360**	**320**	**180**	**160**
Media descriptor byte	F0h	F0h	F9h	F9h	FDh	FFh	FCh	FEh
Sides (heads)	2	2	2	2	2	2	1	1
Tracks per side	80	80	80	80	40	40	40	40
Sectors per track	36	18	9	15	9	8	9	8
Bytes per sector	512	512	512	512	512	512	512	512
Sectors per cluster	2	1	2	1	2	2	1	1
FAT length (sectors)	9	9	3	7	2	1	2	1
Number of FATs	2	2	2	2	2	2	2	2
Root dir. length (sectors)	15	14	7	14	7	7	4	4
Maximum root entries	240	224	112	224	112	112	64	64
Total sectors per disk	5,760	2,880	1,440	2,400	720	640	360	320
Total available sectors	5,726	2,847	1,426	2,371	708	630	351	313
Total available clusters	2,863	2,847	713	2,371	354	315	351	313

The 1.44MB 3 1/2-Inch Drive

The 3 1/2-inch, 1.44MB, high-density (HD) drives first appeared from IBM in the PS/2 product line introduced in 1987. Most other computer vendors started offering the drives as an option in their systems immediately afterward. This type of floppy drive is still the most popular in systems today.

The drive records 80 cylinders consisting of 2 tracks each with 18 sectors per track, resulting in a formatted capacity of 1.44MB. Some disk manufacturers label these disks as 2.0MB, and the difference between this unformatted capacity and the formatted usable result is lost during the format. Note that the 1,440KB of total formatted capacity does not account for the areas the FAT file system reserves for file management, leaving only 1,423.5KB of actual file-storage area.

The drive spins at 300rpm, and in fact must spin at that speed to operate properly with existing high- and low-density controllers. To use the 500KHz data rate (the maximum from most standard high- and low-density floppy controllers), these drives must spin at a maximum of 300rpm. If the drives were to spin at the faster 360rpm rate of the 5 1/4-inch drives, they would have to reduce the total number of sectors per track to 15; otherwise, the controller could not keep up. In short, the 1.44MB 3 1/2-inch drives store 1.2 times the data of the 5 1/4-inch 1.2MB drives, and the 1.2MB drives spin exactly 1.2 times faster than the 1.44MB drives. The data rates used by both of these HD drives are identical and compatible with the same controllers. In fact, because these 3 1/2-inch HD drives can run at the 500KHz data rate, a controller that can support a 1.2MB 5 1/4-inch drive can also support the 1.44MB drives.

The 2.88MB 3 1/2-Inch Drive

The 3 1/2-inch, 2.88MB drive was developed by Toshiba Corporation in the 1980s and was officially announced in 1987. Toshiba began production manufacturing of the drives and disks in 1989, and several vendors began selling the drives as upgrades for their systems. IBM officially adopted these drives in its PS/2 systems in 1991, and a number of manufacturers began making them, including Toshiba, Mitsubishi, Sony, and Panasonic. Because a 2.88MB drive can fully read and write 1.44MB disks, the change is an easy one. Unfortunately, due to high media costs and a relatively low increase in data capacity, these drives never caught on widely, although virtually all systems today have built-in support for them. DOS version 5.0 or later is required to support the 2.88MB drives.

The 2.88MB extra high-density (ED) drive uses a technique called *vertical recording* to achieve its great linear density of 36 sectors per track. This technique increases density by magnetizing the domains perpendicular to the recording surface. By essentially placing the magnetic domains on their ends and stacking them side by side, the disk density increases enormously.

The technology for producing heads that can perform a vertical or perpendicular recording has been around for some time. But it is not the heads or even the drive that represent the major breakthrough in technology; rather, it is the medium that is special. Standard disks have magnetic particles shaped like tiny needles that lie on the surface of the disk. Orienting these acicular particles in a perpendicular manner to enable vertical recording is very difficult. The particles on a barium-ferrite floppy disk are shaped like tiny, flat, hexagonal platelets that can more easily be arranged to have their axes of magnetization perpendicular to the plane of recording.

Toshiba perfected a glass-crystallization process for manufacturing the ultra-fine platelets used in coating the barium-ferrite disks. This technology, patented by Toshiba, is being licensed to a number of disk manufacturers, all of whom are producing barium-ferrite disks using Toshiba's process. Toshiba also made certain modifications to the design of standard disk drive heads to enable them to read and write the new barium-ferrite disks, as well as standard cobalt or ferrite disks. This technology is being used not only in floppy disk drives, but also in a variety of tape drive formats.

The disks are called 4MB disks in reference to their unformatted capacity. The actual formatted capacity is 2,880KB, or 2.88MB. Because of space lost in the formatting process—as well as space occupied by the volume boot sector, FATs, and root directory—the total usable storage space is 2,863KB.

To support the 2.88MB drive, modifications to the disk controller circuitry were required because these drives spin at the same 300rpm but have an astonishing 36 sectors per track. Because all floppy disks are formatted with consecutively numbered sectors (1:1 interleave), the drive must read and write 36 sectors in the same time it takes a 1.44MB drive to read and write 18 sectors. This requires that the controller support a much higher data transmission rate of 1MHz (1 million bps). Most older floppy controllers support only the maximum data rate of 500KHz used by the 1.44MB drives. To upgrade to a 2.88MB drive, the controller must be changed to one that supports the higher 1MHz data rate.

An additional support issue is the ROM BIOS. The BIOS must have support for the controller and the capability to specify and accept the 2.88MB drive as a CMOS setting.

Virtually all modern PCs have built-in floppy controllers and ROM BIOS software that fully support the 2.88MB drives. Adding or upgrading to a 2.88MB drive in these systems is as easy as plugging in the drive and running the CMOS Setup program. For systems that do not have this built-in support, the upgrade process is much more difficult. Several companies offer new controllers and BIOS upgrades as well as the 2.88MB drives specifically for upgrading older systems.

The 720KB 3 1/2-Inch Drive

The 720KB, 3 1/2-inch, DD drives first appeared in an IBM system with the IBM Convertible laptop system introduced in 1986. In fact, all IBM systems introduced since that time have 3 1/2-inch drives as the standard supplied drives.

Note

Outside the PC-compatible world, other computer-system vendors (Apple, Hewlett-Packard, and so on) offered 3 1/2-inch drives for their systems two years before the PC-compatible world "caught on."

The 720KB, 3 1/2-inch, DD drive normally records 80 cylinders of 2 tracks each, with 9 sectors per track, resulting in the formatted capacity of 720KB.

PC-compatible systems have used 720KB, 3 1/2-inch DD drives primarily in XT-class systems because the drives operate from any low-density controller. The drives spin at 300rpm, and therefore require only a 250KHz data rate from the controller to operate properly. This data rate is the same as the 360KB disk drives, which means any controller that supports a 360KB drive also supports the 720KB drives.

An IBM system with a ROM BIOS date of 06/10/85 or later has built-in support for 720KB drives and requires no driver to use them. If your system has an earlier ROM BIOS date, the DRIVER.SYS program from DOS V3.2 or later—as well as the CONFIG.SYS DRIVPARM command in some OEM DOS versions— is all you need to provide the necessary software support to operate these drives.

The 1.2MB 5 1/4-Inch Drive

The 1.2MB high-density floppy disk drive first appeared in the IBM AT system introduced in August 1984. The drive required the use of a new type of disk to achieve the 1.2MB format capacity, but it still could read and write (although not always reliably) the lower-density 360KB disks.

The 1.2MB 5 1/4-inch drive normally recorded 80 cylinders of 2 tracks each, starting with cylinder 0 at the outside of the disk. This situation differs from the low-density 5 1/4-inch drive in its capability to record twice as many cylinders in approximately the same space on the disk. This capability alone suggests that the recording capacity for a disk would double, but that is not all. Each track normally is recorded with 15 sectors of 512 bytes each, increasing the storage capacity even more. In fact, these drives store nearly four times the data of the 360KB disks. The density increase for each track required the use of special disks with a modified medium designed to handle this type of recording. Because these disks initially were expensive and difficult to obtain, many users attempted incorrectly to use the low-density disks in the 1.2MB 5 1/4-inch drives and format them to the higher 1.2MB- density format, which resulted in data loss and unnecessary data-recovery operations.

A compatibility problem with the 360KB drives stems from the 1.2MB drive's capability to write twice as many cylinders in the same space as the 360KB drives. The 1.2MB drives position their heads over the same 40 cylinder positions used by the 360KB drives through *double stepping*, a procedure in which the heads are moved every 2 cylinders to arrive at the correct positions for reading and writing the 40 cylinders on the 360KB disks. The problem is that because the 1.2MB drive normally must write 80 cylinders in the same space in which the 360KB drive writes 40, the heads of the 1.2MB units had to be made dimensionally smaller. These narrow heads can have problems overwriting tracks pro- duced by a 360KB drive that has a wider head because the narrower heads on the 1.2MB drive cannot "cover" the entire track area written by the 360KB drive.

The 1.2MB 5 1/4-inch drives spin at 360rpm, or six revolutions per second, or 166.67ms per revolu- tion. The drives spin at this rate no matter what type of disk is inserted—either low- or high-density.

To send or receive 15 sectors (plus required overhead) six times per second, a controller must use a data transmission rate of 500,000bps (500KHz). All standard high- and low-density controllers support this data rate and, therefore, these drives.

This support also depends on proper ROM BIOS support of the controller in this mode of operation. When a standard 360KB disk is running in an HD drive, it also is spinning at 360rpm. A data rate of 300,000bps (300KHz), therefore, is required to work properly. All standard AT-style low- and high-density controllers support the 250KHz, 300KHz, and 500KHz data rates. The 300KHz rate, however, is used only for HD 5 1/4-inch drives reading or writing to low-density 5 1/4-inch disks.

The 360KB 5 1/4-Inch Drive

The 5 1/4-inch double-density drive is designed to create a standard-format disk with 360KB capacity. The term "double-density" arose from the use of the term "single-density" to indicate a type of drive that used frequency modulation (FM) encoding to store approximately 90KB on a disk. This type of obsolete drive never was used in any PC-compatible systems, but was used in some older systems, such as the original Osborne-1 portable computer. When drive manufacturers changed the drives to use modified frequency modulation (MFM) encoding, they began using the term double-density to indicate it, as well as the (approximately doubled) increase in recording capacity realized from this encoding method.

The 360KB 5 1/4-inch drives spin at 300rpm, which equals exactly five revolutions per second, or 200ms per revolution. All standard floppy controllers support a 1:1 interleave, in which each sector on a specific track is numbered (and read) consecutively. To read and write to a disk at full speed, a controller sends data at a rate of 250,000bps.

Analyzing Floppy Disk Construction

The 5 1/4-inch and 3 1/2-inch disks each have unique construction and physical properties. The flexible (or floppy) disk is contained within a plastic jacket. The 3 1/2-inch disks are covered by a more rigid jacket than are the 5 1/4-inch disks. The disks within the jackets, however, are virtually identical except, of course, for size.

When you look at a typical 5 1/4-inch floppy disk, you see several things (see Figure 11.7). Most prominent is the large, round hole in the center. When you close the disk drive's "door," a cone-shaped clamp grabs and centers the disk through the center hole. Many disks come with *hub-ring reinforcements*—thin, plastic rings that help the disk withstand the mechanical forces of the clamping mechanism. The HD disks usually lack these reinforcements because the difficulty in accurately placing them on the disk means they can cause alignment problems.

On the right side, just below the center of the hub hole, is a smaller round hole called the *index hole*. If you carefully turn the disk within its protective jacket, you can see a small hole in the disk itself. The drive uses the index hole as the starting point for all the sectors on the disk—sort of the "prime meridian" for the disk sectors. A disk with a single index hole is a soft-sectored disk; the software (operating system) decides the actual number of sectors on the disk. Some older equipment, such as Wang word processors, use hard-sectored disks, which have an index hole to demarcate individual sectors. Do not use hard-sectored disks in a PC.

Below the hub hole is a slot shaped somewhat like a long racetrack through which you can see the disk surface. The disk drive heads read and write data to the disk surface through this media-access hole.

On the right side, about one inch from the top, is a rectangular punch from the side of the disk cover. If this write-enable notch is present, writing to the disk has been enabled. Disks without this notch (or with the notch taped over) are write-protected disks. The notch might not be present on all disks, particularly those purchased with programs on them.

Courtesy of IBM Corporation

Figure 11.7   Construction of a 5 1/4-inch floppy disk.

On the rear of the disk jacket at the bottom, two very small oval notches flank the head slot. These notches relieve stress on the disk and help prevent it from warping. The drive might also use these notches to assist in keeping the disk in the proper position in the drive.

Because the 3 1/2-inch disks use a much more rigid plastic case, which helps stabilize the magnetic medium inside, these disks can record at track and data densities greater than the 5 1/4-inch disks (see Figure 11.8). A metal shutter protects the media-access hole. The drive manipulates the shutter, leaving it closed whenever the disk is not in a drive. The medium is then completely insulated from the environment and from your fingers. The shutter also obviates the need for a disk jacket.

Because the shutter is not necessary for the disk to work, you can remove it from the plastic case if it becomes bent or damaged. Pry it off the disk case; it will pop off with a snap. You also should remove the spring that pushes it closed. Additionally, after removing the damaged shutter, you should copy the data from the damaged disk to a new one.

Rather than an index hole in the disk, the 3 1/2-inch disks use a metal center hub with an alignment hole. The drive "grasps" the metal hub, and the hole in the hub enables the drive to position the disk properly.

On the lower-left part of the disk is a hole with a plastic slider—the write-protect/enable hole. When the slider is positioned so the hole is visible, the disk is *write-protected*—the drive is prevented from recording on the disk. When the slider is positioned to cover the hole, writing is enabled, and you can save data to the disk. For more permanent write-protection, some commercial software programs are supplied on disks with the slider removed so you cannot easily enable recording on the disk. This is exactly opposite of a 5 1/4-inch floppy, in which covered means write-protected, not write-enabled.

On the other (right) side of the disk from the write-protect hole, usually is another hole called the media-density-selector hole. If this hole is present, the disk is constructed of a special medium and is therefore an HD or ED disk. If the media-sensor hole is exactly opposite the write-protect hole, it indicates a 1.44MB HD disk. If the media-sensor hole is located more toward the top of the disk (the metal shutter is at the top of the disk), it indicates an ED disk. No hole on the right side means that the disk is a low-density disk. Most 3 1/2-inch drives have a media sensor that controls recording capability based on the absence or presence of these holes.

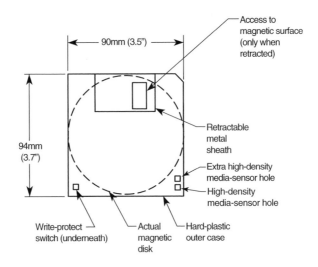

Figure 11.8   Construction of a 3 1/2-inch floppy disk.

The actual magnetic medium in both the 3 1/2-inch and 5 1/4-inch disks is constructed of the same basic materials. They use a plastic base (usually Mylar) coated with a magnetic compound. High-density disks use a cobalt-ferric compound; extended-density disks use a barium-ferric media compound. The rigid jacket material on the 3 1/2-inch disks often causes people to believe incorrectly that these disks are some sort of "hard disk" and not really a floppy disk. The disk cookie inside the 3 1/2-inch case is just as floppy as the 5 1/4-inch variety.

Floppy Disk Media Types and Specifications

This section examines the types of disks that have been available to PC owners over the years. Especially interesting are the technical specifications that can separate one type of disk from another, as Table 11.6 shows. The following sections define all the specifications used to describe a typical disk.

Table 11.6   Floppy Disk Media Specifications

Media Parameters	5 1/4-Inch			3 1/2-Inch		
	Double-Density (DD)	Quad-Density (QD)	High-Density (HD)	Double-Density (DD)	High-Density (HD)	Extra High-Density (ED)
Tracks per inch (TPI)	48	96	96	135	135	135
Bits per inch (BPI)	5,876	5,876	9,646	8,717	17,434	34,868
Media formulation	Ferrite	Ferrite	Cobalt	Cobalt	Cobalt	Barium
Coercivity (oersteds)	300	300	600	600	720	750
Thickness (micro-in.)	100	100	50	70	40	100
Recording polarity	Horiz.	Horiz.	Horiz.	Horiz.	Horiz.	Vert.

Density

Density, in simplest terms, is a measure of the amount of information that can be reliably packed into a specific area of a recording surface. The keyword here is *reliably*.

Disks have two types of densities: longitudinal density and linear density. *Longitudinal density* is indicated by how many tracks can be recorded on the disk and is often expressed as a number of tracks per inch (TPI). *Linear density* is the capability of an individual track to store data and is often indicated as a number of bits per inch (BPI). Unfortunately, these types of densities are often confused when discussing different disks and drives.

Media Coercivity and Thickness

The *coercivity* specification of a disk refers to the magnetic-field strength required to make a proper recording. Coercivity, measured in oersteds, is a value indicating magnetic strength. A disk with a higher coercivity rating requires a stronger magnetic field to make a recording on that disk. With lower ratings, the disk can be recorded with a weaker magnetic field. In other words, the lower the coercivity rating, the more sensitive the disk.

HD media demands higher coercivity ratings so the adjacent magnetic domains don't interfere with each other. For this reason, HD media is actually less sensitive and requires a stronger recording signal strength.

Another factor is the thickness of the disk. The thinner the disk, the less influence a region of the disk has on another adjacent region. The thinner disks, therefore, can accept many more bits per inch without eventually degrading the recording.

Caring for and Handling Floppy Disks and Drives

Most computer users know the basics of disk care. Disks can be damaged or destroyed easily by the following:

- Touching the recording surface with your fingers or anything else
- Writing on a disk label (which has been affixed to a disk) with a ball-point pen or pencil
- Bending the disk
- Spilling coffee or other substances on the disk
- Overheating a disk (leaving it in the hot sun or near a radiator, for example)
- Exposing a disk to stray magnetic fields

Despite all these cautions, disks are rather hardy storage devices; I can't say that I have ever destroyed one by just writing on it with a pen, because I do so all the time. I am careful, however, not to press too hard, so I don't put a crease in the disk. Also, touching a disk does not necessarily ruin a disk, but rather makes the disk and your drive head dirty with oil and dust. The real danger to your disks comes from magnetic fields that, because they are unseen, can sometimes be found in places you never imagined.

For example, all color monitors (and color TV sets) have a degaussing coil around the face of the tube that demagnetizes the shadow mask when you turn the monitor on. If you keep your disks anywhere near (within one foot of) the front of the color monitor, you expose them to a strong magnetic field every time you turn on the monitor. Keeping disks in this area is not a good idea because the field is designed to demagnetize objects, and indeed works well for demagnetizing disks. The effect is cumulative and irreversible.

Another source of powerful magnetic fields is an electric motor found in vacuum cleaners, heaters, air conditioners, fans, electric pencil sharpeners, and so on. Do not place these devices near areas where you store disks. Audio speakers also contain magnets, but most of the speakers sold for use with PCs are shielded to minimize disk corruption.

Store 3 1/2-inch disks between 40° and 127° Fahrenheit, and store 5 1/4-inch disks between 40° and 140° Fahrenheit. In both cases, humidity should not exceed 90%.

Airport X-Ray Machines and Metal Detectors

One of my favorite myths to dispel is that the airport X-ray machine somehow damages disks. I have a great deal of experience in this area from having traveled around the country for the past 20 years or so with disks and portable computers in hand. I fly about 150,000 miles per year, and my portable computer equipment and disks have been through X-ray machines hundreds of times.

X-rays are essentially just a form of light, and disks and computers are not affected by X-rays at anywhere near the levels found in these machines.

What could potentially damage your magnetic media is the metal detector. Metal detectors work by monitoring disruptions in a weak magnetic field. A metal object inserted in the field area causes the field's shape to change, which the detector observes. This principle, which is the reason the detectors are sensitive to metal objects, can be dangerous to your disks; the X-ray machine, however, is the safest area through which to pass either your disk or your computer.

The X-ray machine is not dangerous to magnetic media because it merely exposes the media to electromagnetic radiation at a particular (very high) frequency. Blue light is an example of electromagnetic radiation of a different frequency. The only difference between X-rays and blue light is in the frequency, or wavelength, of the emission.

Some people worry about the effect of X-ray radiation on their system's EPROM (erasable programmable read-only memory) chips. This concern might actually be more valid than worrying about disk damage because EPROMs are erased by certain forms of electromagnetic radiation. In reality, however, you do not need to worry about this effect either. EPROMs are erased by direct exposure to very intense ultraviolet light. Specifically, to be erased, an EPROM must be exposed to a 12,000 uw/cm^2 UV light source with a wavelength of 2,537 angstroms for 15–20 minutes, and at a distance of 1 inch. Increasing the power of the light source or decreasing the distance from the source can shorten the erasure time to a few minutes.

The airport X-ray machine is different by a factor of 10,000 in wavelength. The field strength, duration, and distance from the emitter source are nowhere near what is necessary for EPROM erasure. Many circuit-board manufacturers even use X-ray inspection on circuit boards (with components including EPROMs installed) to test and check quality control during manufacture.

Now, you might not want to take my word for it, but scientific research has been published that corroborates what I have stated. A few years ago, a study was published by two scientists—one of whom actually designs X-ray tubes for a major manufacturer. Their study was titled "Airport X-rays and Floppy Disks: No Cause for Concern" and was published in 1993 in the journal *Computer Methods and Programs in Biomedicine*. According to the abstract,

> A controlled study was done to test the possible effects of X-rays on the integrity of data stored on common sizes of floppy disks. Disks were exposed to doses of X-rays up to seven times that to be expected during airport examination of baggage. The readability of nearly 14 megabytes of data was unaltered by X-irradiation, indicating that floppy disks need not be given special handling during X-ray inspection of baggage.

In fact, the disks were retested after two years of storage, and there still has been no measurable degradation since the exposure.

Drive-Installation Procedures

In most cases, installing a floppy disk drive is a matter of physically attaching the drive to the computer chassis or case and then plugging the power and signal cables into the drive. Some types of brackets and screws are normally required to attach the drive to the chassis. These are normally included with the chassis or case itself. Several companies listed in the Vendor List on the CD-ROM specialize in cases, cables, brackets, screw hardware, and other items useful in assembling systems or installing drives.

Note

Because floppy disk drives are generally installed into the same half-height bays as hard disk drives, the physical mounting of the drive in the computer case is the same for both units. See the section "Hard Disk Installation Procedures" in Chapter 14, "Physical Drive Installation and Configuration," for more information on the process.

Troubleshooting Floppy Drives

Because of their very low cost, floppy drives have become a fairly disposable item these days. Also, their connection to the system has become simpler over the years as drives today come preconfigured with no jumpers or switches to set. The cables are fairly standardized as well. What all this means is that if the drive or cable is suspected of being defective, it should be replaced rather than repaired. This section discusses some of the most common problems floppy drives can have and how to troubleshoot them.

Problem

Dead drive—The drive does not spin and the LED never comes on.

Cause/Solution

The drive or controller is not properly configured in the BIOS setup. Check the BIOS setup for proper drive type and make sure the controller is enabled if it's built in to the motherboard.

Other causes for a dead drive include

- *Bad power supply or power cable.* Measure the power at the cable with a voltmeter, and ensure that 12v and 5v are available to the drive.
- *Bad data cable.* Replace the cable and retest.
- *Defective drive.* Replace the drive and retest.
- *Defective controller.* Replace the controller and retest. If the controller is built in to the motherboard, disable it via the BIOS setup, install a card-based controller, and retest, or replace the entire motherboard and retest.

Problem

Drive LED remains on continuously.

Cause/Solution

Data cable is on backward at either the drive or controller connection. Reinstall the cable properly and retest.

Also, the data cable could be offset on the connector by one or more pins. Reinstall the cable properly and retest. If this does not solve the problem, it could be a defective cable. Replace the cable and retest.

Problem

Phantom directories—You have exchanged disks in the drive, but the system still believes the previous disk is inserted, and even shows directories of the previous disk.

Cause/Solution

Several causes and solutions are possible:

- *Defective cable (pin 34).* Replace the cable and retest.

- *Improper drive configuration.* If the drive is an older model and has a DC jumper, it must be set to enabled. You also should ensure the BIOS Setup has the proper drive type entered.

- *Defective drive.* Replace the drive and retest.

Common Floppy Drive Error Messages—Causes and Solutions

Error Message

Invalid Media or Track Zero Bad, Disk Unusable

Cause/Solution

You are formatting the disk and the disk media type does not match the format parameters. Make sure you are using the correct type of disk for your drive and formatting the disk to its correct capacity. Other causes and solutions are

- *Defective or damaged disk.* Replace the disk and retest.

- *Dirty heads.* Clean the drive heads and retest.

Error Message

CRC Error or Disk Error 23

Cause/Solution

The data read from the disk does not match the data that was originally written. (CRC stands for cyclic redundancy check.) Replace the disk and retest, or possibly, clean the drive heads. Use the Norton Utilities for possible data recovery from the disk.

Error Message

General Failure Reading Drive A, Abort, Retry, Fail or Disk Error 31

Cause/Solution

The disk is not formatted or has been formatted for a different operating system (Macintosh, for example). Reformat the disk and retest. Another cause could be that damaged areas exist on the disk medium. Replace the disk and retest. Use the Norton Utilities for possible data recovery from the disk.

Error Message

Access Denied

Cause/Solution

You are trying to write to a write-protected disk or file. Move the write-protect switch to allow writing on the disk, or remove the read-only file attribute from the files. File attributes can be changed with the ATTRIB command.

Error Message

Insufficient Disk Space or Disk Full

Cause/Solution

The disk is filled, or the root directory is filled. Check to see whether sufficient free space is available on the disk for your intended operation.

Error Message

Bytes in Bad Sectors

Cause/Solution

This is displayed after formatting or running the CHKDSK command and shows that the disk has several allocation units that are marked bad. This is not a problem in itself because when the allocation units are marked in this fashion, the operating system will not use them for file storage. Even so, I normally don't recommend using disks with bad sectors.

Error Message

Disk Type or Drive Type Incompatible or Bad

Cause/Solution

You are attempting to DISKCOPY between two incompatible drive or disk types. Disks can be copied only between drives using the same disk density and size.

CHAPTER 12

High-Capacity Removable Storage

Why Use Removable-Media Drives?

As operating systems and applications continue to grow in size and features, more and more storage space is needed for these programs as well as for the data they create.

A typical installation of Windows 2000 Professional can occupy close to 600MB, for example. Windows 98 or Windows Me can use more than 200MB of disk space, and the various versions of Windows require 1GB of disk space or more. And even if you install your Windows applications on a different drive, your \WINNT or \WINDOWS folder is likely to grow in size as time passes. Why? The reason is simple: Nearly all Windows applications place shared program or support files in one of the Windows directories (such as \WINDOWS\SYSTEM). These files include those with extensions such as DLL, 386, VBX, DRV, TTF, and many others. Even non-Windows operating systems, such as OS/2 and Linux, can also consume large amounts of space.

Operating systems aren't the only program types that are growing. Applications whose MS-DOS versions once fit on a few floppy disks have now mutated into "everything but the kitchen sink" do-it-all behemoths that can take 100MB–500MB of disk space. The multimedia revolution—fueled by powerful, low-cost digital cameras, scanners, and video recorders—enables you to capture and store images that easily can consume hundreds of megabytes of space, and the MP3 craze is filling countless gigabytes of storage on individual users' systems with digitized musical hits and classics.

Whether you're looking for additional storage you can access as an additional drive letter or as a means of backup, if you're a typical user, you need more storage today than ever before.

This section focuses on some of the more advanced data storage options on the market: high-capacity removable-media storage, including disk drives, tape drives, and flash-memory cards. This chapter focuses on magnetic, floptical, flash storage, and magneto-optical devices. Pure optical storage—such as CD-R, CD-RW, DVD-RAM, DVD+RW, DVD-RW, and others—is covered in Chapter 13, "Optical Storage."

Some removable-media drives use media as small as a 3 1/2-inch floppy disk or a type II PC Card, whereas others use larger media up to 5 1/4-inches. Most popular removable-storage drives today have capacities that range from 100MB to 70GB or more. These drives offer fairly speedy performance and the capability to store anything from a few data files or less frequently used programs to complete hard disk images on a removable disk or tape. Besides backup, this provides the capability to easily transport huge data files—computer-aided drawing (CAD) files and graphics files, for example—from one computer to another. Or, you can use a removable cartridge to take sensitive data away from your office so you can lock it safely away from prying eyes. Some types of removable-media storage feature archival durability, whereas others are designed for the "shoot it today, delete it tomorrow" world of digital photography.

Backing Up Your Data

Any computer book worth reading warns repeatedly that you should back up your system regularly. Backups are necessary because at any time a major problem, or even some minor ones, can corrupt the important information and programs stored on your computer's hard disk drive, rendering this information useless. A wide range of problems can damage the data on your hard drive. Here is a list of some of these data-damaging problems:

- *Sudden fluctuations in the electricity that powers your computer (power spikes), resulting in data damage or corruption.*
- *Overwriting a file by mistake.*
- *Mistakenly formatting your hard disk when you meant to format a floppy.*

- *Hard drive failure resulting in loss of data that has not been backed up.* Not only do you have to install a new drive, but, because you have no backup, you also must reinstall all your software.

- *Catastrophic damage to your computer (storm, flood, lightning strike, fire, theft, and so on).* A single lightning strike near your office or home can destroy the circuitry of your computer, including your hard drive. Theft of your computer, of course, is equally devastating. A recent, complete backup greatly simplifies the process of setting up a replacement computer.

- *Loss of valuable data due to a computer-related virus.* One single download or floppy disk can contain a virus that can damage valuable files and even your entire hard disk. With several hundred new viruses appearing each month, no antivirus software program can keep you entirely safe. A recent backup of uninfected, critical files can help repair even the worst damage.

Backups are also the cure for such common headaches as a full hard drive and the need to transfer data between computers. By backing up data you rarely use and deleting the original data from your hard drive, you free up space once occupied by that data. If you later need a particular data file, you can retrieve that file from your backup. You also can more easily share large amounts of data between computers—when you send data from one city to another, for example—by backing up the data to a tape or other media and sending the media.

Regardless of how important regular backups are, many people avoid making them. A major reason for this lapse is that for many people, backing up their systems is tedious work when they have to use floppy disks or other low-capacity media. When you use these media, you might have to insert and remove many disks to back up all the important programs and data.

Optical storage, high-capacity magnetic media, and tape backups are all useful devices for making backups. Historically, tape backups have been regarded as the most powerful of these technologies because tape backups are among the few backup devices capable of recording the contents of today's multi-gigabyte drives to a single cartridge for restoration.

Comparing Disk, Tape, and Flash Memory Technologies

Several types of removable-media disk drives are commonly used. The most common varieties use magnetic media, but some use one of two combinations of magnetic and optical storage: floptical or magneto-optical. Magnetic media drives use technology similar to that of a floppy or hard disk drive to encode data for storage. Floptical and magneto-optical media drives encode information on disk by using different combinations of laser and magnetic technologies.

Flash memory devices emulate disk drives and are also discussed in this chapter. Some tape drives are also capable of emulating disk drives by providing drive letter access to a portion of the media but are used primarily to perform streaming backups of large disk drives and network drive arrays.

▶▶ See "Flash Card and Digital 'Film,'" p. 662.

Magnetic Disk Media

Whether you are looking at "pure" magnetic media, floptical media, or magneto-optical drives, all types of magnetic disk media share similar characteristics. Disk media is more expensive per megabyte or gigabyte than tape, usually has a lower capacity, and is more easily used on a file-by-file basis as compared to tape. Disk media uses random access, which enables you to find, use, modify, or delete any file or group of files on a disk without disturbing the rest of the disk's contents. Disk media is faster for copying a few files but normally slower for copying large numbers of files or entire drives.

Magnetic Tape Media

Tape media has much less expensive costs overall per megabyte or gigabyte than disk media, has a higher total capacity, and is more easily used on an image or a multiple-file basis. Tape drives use sequential access, meaning that the contents of a tape must be read from the beginning and that individual files must be retrieved in the order found on the tape. Also, individual files usually can't be modified on the tape or removed from the tape; the contents of the entire cartridge must be deleted and rewritten. Thus, tape drives are more suited for complete backups of entire hard disks including all applications and data. Because it is suited for mass backup, tape can be difficult to use for copying single files.

Note

Removable-media disk drives can be used as system backup devices similar to tape. However, the higher price of the medium itself (disks or cartridges) and the generally slower speed at which they perform can make this use somewhat prohibitive on a large scale. For file-by-file backups, disk media is ideal; if, however, you're completely backing up entire drives or systems, tape is faster and more economical.

Flash Memory Media

The newest type of removable storage is not magnetically based but uses flash memory—a special type of solid-state memory chip that requires no power to maintain its contents. Flash memory cards can easily be moved from digital cameras to notebook or desktop computers and can even be connected directly to photo printers or self-contained display units. Flash memory can be used to store any type of computer data, but its primary application is digital photography.

Tip

Literally dozens of removable storage devices are currently on the market. Be sure to compare your chosen solution against the competition before making a final purchase. Be especially wary of missing statistics in press releases and product packaging—manufacturers are apt to omit a specification if their drives don't measure up to the competition.

Comparing Removable Media Types

Table 12.1 summarizes the major features of the removable-media drives that are covered in this chapter. Because optical storage can be more suitable for some uses, the major types of optical storage are also listed for comparison.

Table 12.1 Quick Reference to Storage Devices[1]

Media Type	Media Brands	Mfrs.	Capacity	Interface Type	Best Use
Flash memory	SmartMedia; ATA Data Flash; Compact Flash; Memory Stick	Various	2MB–512MB, depending on brand and model	Proprietary; PC Card or floppy via adapters; PC Card Type II	Digital camera "film;" storage for PDAs; portable devices

Table 12.1   Continued

Media Type	Media Brands	Mfrs.	Capacity	Interface Type	Best Use
Flexible magnetic disk	Zip; LS-120 SuperDisk; PocketZip (formerly Clik!)	Various	40MB–250MB, depending on brand and model	Parallel; IDE; SCSI; USB; PC Card (PCMCIA); IEEE-1394	Data and program backups; storage for direct access
Hard disk	MicroDrive	IBM	170MB; 340MB; 512MB; 1GB	CF+ Type II; PC Card Type II via adapter	Digital camera "film;" program and data storage for notebook computers
	DataPak Type II	Kingston	260MB; 2GB	PC Card	
High-performance flexible magnetic disk	Jaz	Iomega	1GB; 2GB	SCSI	Program storage; data and program backups
High-performance hard disk cartridge	Orb	Castlewood	2.2GB	IDE; SCSI; USB; Parallel	Program storage; data and program backups
.315" magnetic tape cartridge	Travan and Travan NS	Various	Up to 10GB[2], depending on brand and model	IDE; SCSI; Parallel; USB	Data and program backups; full drive backup
ADR magnetic tape cartridge	ADR 30GB and 50GB	OnStream Data	15GB[2]; 25GB[2]	IDE; SCSI; Parallel; USB; IEEE-1394	Data and program backups; full drive backup; works-in-progress storage and playback
DAT; Exabyte 8MM; AIT DDS magnetic tape cartridge	Various	Various	Up to 50GB[2]	SCSI	Data and program backups; full drive backup

1. In order by capacity.

2. Uncompressed capacity: Tape drives are usually rated at 2:1 compression; multiply uncompressed capacity by actual compression ratio obtained to determine your nominal working capacity.

Interfaces for Removable-Media Drives

In addition, several connection options are available for the leading removable drives. The most common interface (and one of the fastest) for internally mounted drives is the same Enhanced IDE (EIDE) interface used for most hard drives. SCSI interfacing is as fast or even faster for use with either internal or external drives but requires adding an interface card to most systems. Most high-end tape backups require a SCSI interface.

The most common external interface is now the USB port, which is replacing the venerable parallel port for printing as well as interfacing low-cost external drives and other types of I/O devices. The USB port is available on virtually all recent PCs (both desktop and notebook models); can be hot-swapped; and is supported by Windows 98, Windows Me, Windows 2000, and Windows XP. Older interfaces, such as the parallel port and PC Card (for notebook computers), are still used on some devices but have limited performance. These are recommended only for systems that don't support USB (such as those still running most releases of Windows 95 or any release of Windows NT 4). Some external removable-media drives allow you to interchange interfaces to enable a single drive to work with a variety of systems.

Note

Although late versions of Windows 95 ("Win95C" or OSR2.1 and above) also have USB drivers, many developers of USB devices do not support their use with Windows 95. For reliable results and manufacturer support, use Windows 98, Windows Me, Windows 2000, or above.

As you will see in the following sections, most removable-media drives are available in two or more of these interface types, allowing you to choose the best interface option for your needs.

Note

Connecting or installing removable-media drives is similar to connecting and installing other internal and external peripherals.

The external USB, IEEE-1394, or parallel port drives are the simplest of the available interfaces, requiring only a special cable that comes with the drive and installation of special software drivers. See the instructions that come with each drive for the specifics of its installation.

See Chapter 7, "The IDE Interface"; Chapter 8, "The SCSI Interface"; and Chapter 16, "Audio Hardware," for details on how IDE, SCSI, USB, IEEE-1394, and parallel interfaces operate.

Overview of Removable Magnetic Storage Devices

A small group of companies dominates the market for magnetic removable-media drives. 3M's spin-off company Imation, Iomega, and Castlewood are the leading names in removable magnetic media drives.

Removable magnetic media drives are usually floppy or hard disk based. For example, the popular Zip drive is a 3 1/2-inch version of the original Bernoulli flexible disk drive made by Iomega. The Imation SuperDisk LS-120 drive is a floppy-based drive that stores 120MB on a disk that looks almost exactly like a 1.44MB floppy! The former SyQuest SparQ, current Iomega Jaz and Castlewood Orb drives, and the new Iomega Peerless drive system are all based on hard-disk technology.

From the standpoint of widespread industry adoption and multiple sources of media, both the Iomega LS-120 SuperDisk and Iomega Zip drives can be considered some type of industry standard. Most computer vendors offer models with either drive already installed; various models can be purchased as upgrades for existing computers; and third-party media vendors, such as Maxell, Verbatim, Sony, and Fujifilm, sell Zip and LS-120 media.

The LS-120, as you'll read shortly, can be used as a direct replacement for the 3 1/2-inch 1.44MB floppy drive, whereas the Iomega Zip drives work with only Zip media. However, because both models are so popular, the wisest choice for near-universal compatibility might be to have both drives on hand.

The following sections provide information about all types of magnetic media, including floptical and magneto-optical drive types.

Iomega Zip and PocketZip

Unlike the LS-120 SuperDisk, the Iomega Zip drive can't use standard 3 1/2-inch floppy disks. At first glance, this might make these drives a more risky choice, but what really matters is how widely the drive has been adopted. With millions sold and media available at stores ranging from drug stores to computer superstores, the Iomega Zip is among the most popular drives ever created. The Iomega Zip is a descendent of a long line of removable-media drives from Iomega that go back to the first Bernoulli cartridge drives released in the early 1980s. The Iomega PocketZip, despite the similarity in name, is actually a much smaller removable-media drive oriented toward digital cameras, MP3 music players, and data transfer between devices and computers. Both Zip and PocketZip are technologies based on flexible media and have capacities up to 250MB. Iomega's other removable-media drives—the Jaz and new Peerless drive system—offer capacities starting at 1GB and are based on hard-disk technology.

Early Iomega Bernoulli Drives

Back in the early 1980s, Iomega introduced the Bernoulli drive. The disk used in the original 10MB "Alpha" Bernoulli drive was a thick, rigid plastic cartridge roughly the same width as an 8-inch floppy disk. The 20MB "Beta" and later models used a 5 1/4-inch disk cartridge. A large shutter, similar to the shutter on a 3 1/2-inch floppy disk, easily distinguished both types of Bernoulli disks from standard floppy disks. The 5 1/4-inch Bernoulli drives were manufactured in capacities ranging from 20MB up to 230MB.

Bernoulli disks originally were known as the most durable of the removable-media drive types because the media is well protected inside the cartridge. When it rotates in the drive, the Bernoulli disk media is pulled by air pressure toward the drive heads. As the disk spins, the airflow generated by the disk movement encounters what is called a Bernoulli *plate*, which is a stationary plate designed to control the airflow so the disk is pulled toward the read/write head. At full speed, the head touches the disk, which causes wear. Bernoulli drives have built-in random seek functions that prevent any single track on the disk from wearing excessively during periods of inactivity. Bernoulli disk cartridges should be replaced periodically because they can wear out.

Note

These drives are basically obsolete, but drives, parts, service, and media for many models are still available from Comet Enterprises, LLC (`http://www.gocomet.com`, 88 North Fort Lane, Layton, UT 84041, 801-444-3600, fax 801-444-3606) and other sources.

Zip Drives

The current form of Bernoulli-technology drive from Iomega is the popular Zip drive. This device is available as an internal SCSI or IDE unit, or as an external SCSI, parallel port, or USB device. In addition, low-power PC Card or internal drive bay versions are available from various aftermarket vendors designed for use in notebook computers. Iomega also offers a USB to IEEE-1394 port adapter for the USB version of the Zip 250, enabling this model to work with IEEE-1394 ports. For a brief period, Iomega also produced a "plus" version that featured both SCSI and parallel interfaces, but this product has been discontinued.

Zip 100 drives can store up to 100MB of data on a small removable magnetic cartridge that resembles a 3 1/2-inch floppy disk. The newer Zip 250 drives store up to 250MB of data on the same size cartridge and can read and write to the Zip 100 cartridges. The latest Zip 250 cartridges have a U-shaped case and use media containing titanium particles for greater durability.

Zip drives use a proprietary 3 1/2-inch disk made by Iomega and also sold by other major media vendors, such as Maxell, Verbatim, and Fuji. It is about twice as thick as a standard 3 1/2-inch floppy disk or SuperDisk (see Figure 12.1).

2MB floppy disk

120MB Imation SuperDisk   100MB Iomega Zip disk

Figure 12.1 The Zip 100MB disk (right) compared to the standard 3 1/2-inch 1.44MB disk (middle) and the LS-120 SuperDisk (left). The Zip disk is thicker, has a tapered top, and has a much narrower shutter than either the LS-120 or 1.44MB disk.

The Zip drives do not accept standard 1.44MB or 720KB floppy disks, making them unlikely candidates for a floppy disk drive replacement. Internal Zip drives have become popular options in new PCs, and the external models are an effective solution for exchanging data between systems.

Tip

Recent systems support the Zip drive in their BIOS setup programs, which enables you to use the IDE version as a boot drive.

Zip drives also have suffered from reliability problems, such as the so-called "click of death," which occurs when the drive begins a rhythmic ticking sound. At this point, the data on the disk can be corrupted and both the drive and the media must be replaced.

▶▶   See "Zip Drive 'Click of Death,'" p. 644.

Table 12.2 lists the Zip 100 and Zip 250 specifications. SCSI versions of the Iomega Zip drive can be used with standard SCSI host adapters or with the Iomega Zip Zoom, a low-cost SCSI host adapter designed especially for the Zip drive.

Table 12.2   Zip 100 and Zip 250 Specifications

	Formatted Capacity	100MB			
Model (Interface)	**EIDE**	**USB**	**PC Card**	**Parallel**	**SCSI**
Sustained transfer rate min.	N/A	N/A	N/A	790KB/sec	790KB/sec
Sustained transfer rate max.	1.4MB/sec	1.2MB/sec	1.4MB/sec	1.4MB/sec	1.4MB/sec
Typical throughput	N/A	N/A	N/A	25MB/min	60MB/min
Average seek time	29ms	29ms	29ms	29ms	29ms
	Formatted Capacity	250MB			
Model (Interface)	**EIDE**	**USB**	**PC Card**	**Parallel**	**SCSI**
Sustained transfer rate max.	2.4MB/sec	900KB/sec[1]	440KB/sec	800KB/sec	2.4MB/sec
Typical throughput	N/A	55MB/min	N/A	N/A	N/A
Average seek time	29ms	<50ms	70ms	29ms	29ms

1. *The USB version of the Zip 250 drive can now be connected to the Zip 250 USB FireWire (IEEE-1394) adapter made by Iomega. This device more than doubles the sustained transfer rate of the drive (from 900KB/sec to 2.0MB/sec).*

Note that although the SCSI and Parallel port versions of the Zip 100 claim the same sustained transfer rate, the throughput of the SCSI drive is more than twice as fast—a fact that owners of both models can attest to. If you have a SCSI card with an external port, use the SCSI Zip drives; they're fast!

Media for the Zip 100 drive is about $9–$10 per disk in quantities. Media for the Zip 250 drive is about $17 per disk in quantities.

Figure 12.2 shows the interior of a Zip drive, listing the various components within.

The interior assembly forms a tray that is mounted on a sliding track. This allows the entire tray to move with the disk.

Iomega FotoShow

The most unusual version of the Zip drive is the FotoShow Digital Image Center, which combines the features of the Zip 250 USB drive with flash memory card and TV compatibility and a remote control.

FotoShow contains two flash memory card-reader slots, one for CompactFlash and one for SmartMedia, enabling it to read files created with most digital cameras. FotoShow copies the contents of either type of flash memory card to a Zip 100 or Zip 250 disk when you click the Copy button. You can also transfer pictures from your computer because FotoShow acts as a normal Zip 250 USB drive.

Figure 12.2 Iomega Zip drive internal view.

After you've loaded photos into a Zip disk, attach FotoShow to any NTSC (North American Broadcast Standard) TV through composite, S-Video, or RF-coaxial connectors. Use the remote control to create a slideshow from the pictures. You can also crop, rotate, and even remove red-eye from photos while they're displayed onscreen. FotoShow is compatible with the most common types of JPEG photos, including files ending in .jpg, .jpe, and .jpeg.

Zip Drive "Click of Death"

Iomega has acknowledged that as many as 100,000 users of Zip drives have suffered what is called the "click of death." The name refers to a sharp clicking sound that is heard from the drive as the heads are continually loaded and unloaded as they try to read a disk. This unfortunately means at a minimum that the disk, and possibly the drive, is likely trashed.

In fact, many users have found that the disk cartridge can be damaged in such a way that if you attempt to read it on another Zip drive, that drive will be damaged as well. The only solution is to get a new disk and drive, and to not try to read damaged disks in new drives.

If you think your drive or disk has been damaged, call Iomega technical support (see the vendor list); they should replace the defective disk and possibly the drive as well.

Iomega lists these precautions to help prevent damaged disks and drives:

- *Eject disks prior to transporting any Iomega drive.* This allows the drive heads (which read and write to the disks) to park in a natural position.

- *Avoid dropping your drive.* It can damage internal structures.

- *Be especially careful to transport and store Zip disks only in the Zip disk cases.*

Note

Iomega offers utility diagnostics software that tests the integrity of the Zip heads and Zip media. You can download this from its Web site.

Another company, Gibson Research, has developed a unique program for diagnosing problems with Zip and Jaz drives. It is called Trouble In Paradise (TIP) and can be downloaded free from the Gibson Research site. Gibson is well known as the manufacturer of the Spinrite program for hard disks. The Gibson Research Web site has a lot of additional information on the click of death and other Zip drive issues. See the vendor list for its URL and address.

Because of the high frequency of this problem, many data recovery companies have had a large business in recovering data from damaged Zip cartridges. In fact, the problem has even prompted a class action lawsuit. The law firm of Dodge, Fazio, Anderson, and Jones, P.C. announced that a nationwide class action (known as the Rinaldi lawsuit for Jason Rinaldi, the first-named member of the class) was commenced on September 10, 1998, in the Superior Court of New Castle County in Delaware on behalf of all owners of the Iomega Zip drive. The complaint contains claims for breach of warranty, negligence in manufacturing and design, consumer fraud, and failure to warn.

Investigation has shown that the click of death has three main causes:

- Magnetic particles corrupt the read/write mechanism of the drive, as well as any disk it is attempting to read.
- Lubricant on the disk decomposes, forming a solid material, which accumulates on the heads of the drive. This prevents the heads from reading the disk and subsequently corrupts it.
- The drive heads come in contact with the edge of the spinning disk, which can dislodge the drive heads or tear the storage media and render the disk useless.

This latter point is especially troublesome because if damaged media is inserted into a new drive, it can damage the new drive as well, in some cases tearing the heads off their mounts.

Tip

Before you insert a previously used Iomega Zip disk into a drive, you can check the media for damage by **carefully** sliding open the shutter on the disk and rotating the media using the spindle at the bottom of the disk. If you see roughness or damage, contact Iomega or the media vendor for replacement.

Note also that if you purchase brand-new media in bulk from a store that uses magnetic antitheft strips that must be demagnetized before you leave the store, the Zip media can be demagnetized as well. Return such media to the store for replacement.

Data recovery from a damaged Zip disk can cost $400 or more, so I suggest you keep backups of any important data you store on these disks, and if your drive starts clicking, don't use media with any data already onboard to test it.

A proposed settlement for the Rinaldi lawsuit was announced on March 21, 2001; offers rebates to **all** Zip drive owners who purchased drives between January 1, 1995 and March 19, 2001. The proposed settlement offers rebates on future purchases of Zip and Pocket Zip drives and media. Users who certify that their drives were affected by the click of death will receive higher amounts for their rebates.

If you have not received information on the settlement, you can read the details of the settlement and receive a copy of the notice by going to the Iomega Web site (www.iomega.com), following the Rinaldi Class Action Settlement link and downloading the notice form.

As mentioned before, the new U250 cartridges from Iomega have been redesigned to use titanium particles in the media. This improvement in media design should significantly improve operations of the drives. The U250 cartridge is also self-cleaning to improve reliability of the cartridge and the Zip 250 drive.

Click of death problems can still occur with Zip drives and, to a lesser extent, with Jaz drives as well. Users of these drives should regularly test their drives and media with Iomega's diagnostics supplied with the drives and the Gibson Research TIP program to avoid problems.

Iomega PocketZip

One of the newer products in Iomega's current line of removable-media drives is now called the PocketZip drive, although you might have first heard of this drive when it was called the Clik! drive. Despite the name, this product doesn't use the same mechanism or cartridges as the Zip. Its tiny dimensions (2"×2") and capacity (40MB) position it as a product intended primarily for digital cameras and notebook computers. A new version of the PocketZip drive featuring 100MB storage is scheduled to be introduced during the fourth quarter of 2001.

The PocketZip drive, unlike other magnetic removable-media drives discussed earlier, is not built directly into a computer. It is designed to act as a bridge between flash memory devices and computers, using the PocketZip Card Dock. The USB-based Card Dock also uses CompactFlash and IBM MicroDrive media, enabling you to transfer data from these media types to a PocketZip disk, and then from PocketZip to your computer. Iomega also offers a PocketZip PC Card drive, enabling you to transfer data via a notebook's Type II PC Card slots. PocketZip also works with Iomega's HipZip portable audio player.

Using PocketZip

PocketZip can be used to share information between notebook computers by inserting the PocketZip Card into the PocketZip PC Card drive, which fits into a standard Type II PC Card (PCMCIA) slot. The PocketZip USB drive can accept PocketZip cartridges and connects with any PC or Mac with a USB port. The PocketZip PC Card Dock enables USB-equipped PCs and Macs to read PocketZip PC Card drives. The PocketZip drive is also available in a customized version for the Compaq iPAQ Pocket PC.

The PocketZip drive is also built into some noncomputer devices, such as Agfa's ePhoto CL30 Clik! Digital camera, which uses the PocketZip disk instead of flash memory cards for its digital film, and Iomega's HipZip portable music player.

PocketZip Drive Performance and Size

The PocketZip PC Card drive has a maximum data transfer rate of 620KB/second, and the cartridges are approximately 2" square and about 3/4" thick, making PocketZip media very portable. Each PocketZip disk weighs about 1/3 of an ounce and costs about $10 per disk in quantity.

The high cost per MB and low capacity of the Iomega PocketZip media make, at first glance, a very poor comparison to other removable-media drives. But, no other removable-media drive is as compact, fitting into a Type II PC Card slot. The extremely small size of PocketZip and its capability to provide storage for a wide variety of computers and devices can balance off the high cost per MB of the media and drives for some users.

High-Capacity Floptical Drives

One of the first removable-media drives to break the 20MB barrier and maintain backward compatibility with standard 3 1/2-inch media was a drive made by a company called Insite Peripherals in the early 1990s. Their patented floptical technology used optical tracking to precisely align the magnetic read/write heads of the drive, which could store a then-amazing 21MB in the same form factor used by a 1.44MB 3 1/2-inch drive.

Although the Insite drive never became popular because of a combination of high drive and media cost and lack of BIOS support, it started several trends in high-capacity drive development, including backward compatibility with existing media, faster performance than ordinary floppy drives, and the combination of optical positioning and magnetic storage.

The performance specifications of the drive (average access time of 65ms, transfer rate of 1.6MB/sec, and rotational speed of 720rpm) are similar to those used by higher-capacity drives today. The Insite Peripherals floptical is a direct ancestor of the Imation LS-120 SuperDisk, which uses an advanced version of the same head-positioning techniques. Both the now-obsolete Insite floptical and the current Imation LS-120 are able to read, write, and format standard 3 1/2-inch 720KB and 1.44MB floppy disks, but the relatively unpopular 2.88MB floppy is not supported. The Imation LS-120 has survived challenges from other high-capacity, floppy-compatible products made by Sony (HiFD) and Caleb (UHD144/it) to be the only high-capacity drive that can also read and write standard 3 1/2-inch floppy media.

Floptical Drive Operation

The read/write heads of a floptical drive use magnetic recording technology—similar to that of floppy disk drives—and the floptical disk itself is composed of the same ferrite materials common to floppy and hard disks. Floptical drives are capable of such increased capacity because many more tracks are packed on each disk, compared with a standard 1.44MB floppy. Obviously, to fit so many tracks on the floptical disk, the tracks must be much narrower than those on a floppy disk.

That's where optical technology comes into play. Flopticals use a special optical mechanism to properly position the drive read/write heads over the data tracks on the disk. Servo information, which specifically defines the location of each track, is embedded in the disk during the manufacturing process. Each track of servo information is actually etched or stamped on the disk and is never disturbed during the recording process. Each time the floptical drive writes to the disk, the recording mechanism (including the read/write heads) is guided by a laser beam precisely into place by this servo information. When the floptical drive reads the encoded data, the laser uses this servo information again to guide the read/write heads precisely into place. The use of servo information is not unique to flopticals; hard drives have used servo tracks for years, but the use of a laser beam to read the servo tracks is what makes floptical drives unique.

LS-120 (120MB) SuperDisk Drives

The LS-120 drive (also called a SuperDisk drive) was designed to become the new standard floppy disk drive in the PC industry, replacing the venerable 3 1/2-inch 1.44MB floppy drive. LS-120 technology stores 120MB of data—or about 83 times more data than current 1.44MB floppy disks—and was developed by Imation; Compaq; Matsushita-Kotobuki Industries, Ltd. (MKE); and O.R. Technology. In addition to storing more, the newest models of drives read at up to 27 times the speed of standard floppy disk drives and write data up to 20 times faster than standard floppy disk drives when LS-120/ SuperDisk media is used. Figure 12.3 shows the media types that are compatible with the LS-120 drive.

Note

SuperDisk drives can use either SuperDisks or standard 3 1/2-inch floppies. Because the media sense hole and write-protect/enable slider are on opposite sides of the media, the SuperDisk is protected from damage if it is inserted into an ordinary floppy drive by mistake.

Media shutter on
1.44MB floppy

Media shutter
on SuperDisk

Write-protect/enable
slider on 1.44MB floppy

Media sense hole
on 1.44MB floppy

Write-protect/enable
slider on SuperDisk

Media sense hole
on SuperDisk

Figure 12.3   A standard 1.44MB 3 1/2-inch floppy disk (left) compared to LS-120 SuperDisk media (right).

The LS-120 floppy disk drive can act as the PC's bootable A: drive (in newer systems that support ATAPI removable devices; a few of the newest systems even support booting from USB drives) and is fully compatible with Windows NT, Windows 2000, and Windows 9x/Me. Windows XP supports the USB and ATAPI versions of the drive; check with vendors of PC Card and parallel-port versions for support and drivers. Macintoshes can also use USB-based SuperDisk drives, so data (and the drive itself) can be shared between PCs and Macs.

In addition to its own 120MB floppy disks, the LS-120 drive accepts standard 720KB and 1.44MB floppy disks and actually reads and writes those disks up to three times faster than standard floppy disk drives. By contrast, the rival Iomega Zip drives can't use existing floppy disks.

The most popular version of the LS-120 SuperDisk uses the standard IDE interface, which is available as an option for many new systems or can be added later. The most popular OEM supplier for the SuperDisk is Panasonic. USB and parallel versions also are available for an easy external connection, and PC Card (PCMCIA) and interchangeable drive-bay versions are available for notebook computers. The LS-120 provides a solution that not only replaces the existing floppy, but can even replace the floppy disk drive internally for virtually all purposes.

Note

The SmartDisk Corporation FlashPath flash-card adapters (covered later in this chapter) for 3 1/2-inch disk drives will not work in drives such as the LS-120 or PC Card-connected floppy drives; they are designed to work with standard 1.44MB 3 1/2-inch drives connected via a standard floppy controller only.

Having one of these high-capacity drives in a portable PC enables the use of relatively inexpensive 120MB removable disks while on the road. They are perfect for utility programs or databases and spreadsheets and can be removed and secured when the portable system is not in use.

LS-120 specifications are compared to standard 1.44MB floppy disks in Table 12.3; the following specifications reflect the revised versions of the LS-120 drive.

Note

In mid-1999, Imation redesigned the LS-120 drives to provide faster performance than the original version. Most models have now been upgraded, but Imation's PC Card model still uses the original mechanism, as seen in Table 12.3.

Table 12.3   Imation LS-120 Specifications Versus 1.44MB Floppy[1]

Drive type	LS-120	LS-120	LS-120	LS-120	3 1/2-inch floppy
Formatted capacity	120MB	120MB	120MB	120MB	1.44MB
Model (interface)	EIDE	USB	PC Card	Parallel	floppy cable
Maximum data transfer rate	1100KB/sec	750KB/sec	440KB/sec	750KB/sec	45KB/sec
Buffer size	10KB	10KB	8KB	10KB	none
Average seek time	60ms	60ms	70ms	60ms	84ms
Disk rotational speed	1440rpm	1440rpm	720rpm	1440rpm	300rpm
Track density	2,490tpi	2,490tpi	2,490tpi	2,490tpi	135tpi
Number of tracks	1,736× 2 sides	1,736× 2 sides	1,736× 2 sides	1,736× 2 sides	80× 2 sides

1. Third-party LS-120 drives might vary.

LS-120 SuperDisk Media

The LS-120 disk has the same shape and size as a standard 1.44MB 3 1/2-inch floppy disk; however, it uses a combination of magnetic and optical technology to enable greater capacity and performance. Named after the laser servo (LS) mechanism it employs, LS-120 technology places optical reference tracks on the disk that are read by a laser system. The optical sensor in the drive enables the read/write head to be precisely positioned over the magnetic data tracks, enabling track densities of 2,490tpi versus 135tpi for a 1.44MB floppy disk. Unlike phase-change, magneto-optical, or CD-R/CD-RW drives, the laser in the LS-120 drive is used strictly for positioning purposes.

Tip

For security-minded users, the LS-120 SuperDisk drives can use special LS-120 Secure Encryption media, which comes with software that enables data stored on the disks to be encrypted with the Blowfish algorithm, a powerful 64-bit block cipher first developed in 1993. Secure Encryption media costs about $16 each in quantities.

The LS-120 SuperDisk also can be used in the interchangeable drive bays of many high-end notebook computers. A pair of Panasonic digital cameras, the 1.3 megapixel PV-SD4090, and the 3.3 megapixel PV-SD5000 use SuperDisk media to store digital photos.

Many PC manufacturers provide the option of using an LS-120 drive in their products as standard equipment in place of the floppy drive. Besides coming in new systems, these drives also are available separately at a cost of about $75 or less in internal or external versions for upgrading older systems. The 120MB floppy disks are available for around $8.50–$10 per disk.

Other High-Capacity "Beyond Floppy" Drive Options

The LS-120 is the overwhelming favorite of users who want more than 100MB capacity and backward compatibility with ordinary 3 1/2-inch media. However, other drives have achieved the same capabilities. Sony's 200MB HiFD drive (also sold by IBM in an internal IDE/ATA form factor) and Caleb Technology's 144MB drive (which has been sold under the UHD144, it, and Monster Disk names) are capable of using standard 3 1/2-inch media as well as their proprietary high-capacity media. However, neither of these products is widely available and Caleb Technology (`www.calebstor.com`) went into Chapter 11 bankruptcy in May 2000. Because of the lack of available products and difficulties in obtaining media for existing drives, neither of these drives is recommended as a floppy replacement.

For more information about these drives, see *Upgrading and Repairing PCs, 12th Edition*, which is included in its entirety on the CD accompanying this book.

Hard-Disk–Sized Removable-Media Drives

The following drives have capacities of 1GB or larger and are fast enough to be considered removable-media hard drives. You can install an entire operating system and a major application on these cartridges and boot from it to completely customize your system's operation.

Jaz Drives

The Jaz drive from Iomega is a true removable-cartridge hard disk, available in 1GB and 2GB internal and external models. Unfortunately, the cartridges themselves cost $90–$100 each in quantity, making them much more expensive per GB than DAT or Travan backup tapes. The high cost of the media makes the Jaz drive unsuitable for backup when compared to traditional tape media, but it is possibly useful as an add-on external SCSI hard disk drive for either data or program files.

Figure 12.4 shows the 2GB external SCSI version of the Jaz drive. Jaz media is thicker and has a different shape from the media made for the lower-capacity Zip drives also produced by Iomega.

Figure 12.4 A 2GB external Jaz drive and media. *Photo courtesy of Iomega Corporation.*

Jaz drives are available in SCSI interface versions only; the 2GB model is backward compatible with 1GB media. Table 12.4 lists the specifications for Jaz drives.

Table 12.4   Jaz Specifications

Model	1GB	2GB
Formatted capacity	1070 million bytes	2000 million bytes
Transfer rate:		
Maximum	6.62MB/sec	8.7MB/sec
Average	5.4MB/sec	7.35MB/sec
Minimum	3.41MB/sec	3.41MB/sec
Burst	10MB/sec	20MB/sec
Average seek time read	10ms	10ms
Average seek time write	12ms	12ms
Access time	15.5ms–17.5ms	15.5ms–17.5ms
Disk rotational speed	5,400rpm	5,394rpm
Buffer size	256KB	512KB
Interface	Fast SCSI II	Ultra SCSI

Note

Some users of Jaz drives have also reported click-of-death problems similar to those experienced by Zip drive users. For more information, testing software, and solutions, see the Gibson Research Web site.

Castlewood Orb

The Castlewood Orb (see Figure 12.5) uses the same magneto-resistive (MR) technology used by many hard drives and achieves hard drive–like performance and capacity at a relative low cost per GB (2.2GB per cartridge at a cost of less than $30 per cartridge).

Figure 12.5   The external SCSI version of the Castlewood Orb drive comes with an HD-50 SCSI cable, an AC power pack, driver files on CD-ROM, one Orb disk with case, and a manual. As is typical with most SCSI drives, the SCSI host adapter is not included. *Photo courtesy of Castlewood Systems, Inc.*

The Orb is available in models supporting all leading interfaces, including EIDE, internal and external SCSI, parallel, and USB. Third-party vendors also have introduced IEEE-1394 versions of the Orb. Table 12.5 lists specifications for the various models made by Castlewood.

Table 12.5   Orb Specifications

Formatted capacity	2.2GB				
Average seek time read	11ms				
Average seek time write	12ms				
Disk rotational speed	5,400rpm				
Transfer rate by model:	EIDE	USB	Ext. SCSI[1]	Int. SCSI[2]	Parallel[3]
Maximum	12.2MB/sec	1.0MB/sec[3]	12.2MB/sec	12.2MB/sec	2MB/sec
Burst	16.6MB/sec	16.6MB/sec	20MB/sec	40MB/sec	40MB/sec

1. *Ultra SCSI*

2. *Ultra Wide SCSI*

3. *Runs at maximum speed of interface; varies with device bus speed or number of drives on the USB port*

Helping Your Orb Drive Run More Reliably

The price and performance of Orb drives and media makes them a promising alternative to other removable-media drives, but a large number of early adopters of the Orb have had problems. Some of the causes include

- Clashes between older Iomega and Orb drivers
- Not allowing the drive to initialize completely before using the drive

These problems led to a large number of drive and media failures when the drives were first released.

For more reliable operation, I recommend that you do the following:

- *Remove all Iomega drivers (Zip/Jaz tools, Guest, and so on) before installing the Orb and its drivers.* If you are using Iomega drives as well as the Orb, download the newest Iomega driver software and install it **after** you install the latest Orb software.

- *Download and install the latest Orb drivers for your operating system and firmware for your Orb drive model.* Check Castlewood's Web site (http://www.castlewood.com) for the latest information.

- *Allow the drive to spin up completely before using Windows Explorer or any other utility that views the drive's contents.*

Comparing Orb and Jaz Drives

Orb drives transfer data much more quickly than Jaz and are available in a wider variety of interfaces, including the easy-to-install and low-cost IDE internal model. Orb's cost per GB is 60% less than Jaz's.

Neither Orb nor Jaz media are produced by third-party vendors, so the drive manufacturer is the only source for media.

Note

In July 1999, Iomega sued Castlewood Systems for patent infringement; the lawsuit continues as of this writing. While none of Iomega's current product line uses a drive mechanism similar to the Orb's MR technology, Iomega also owns the intellectual property of the old SyQuest company. In addition, Castlewood was founded by a former SyQuest executive.

Iomega Peerless

The Iomega Peerless removable hard disk system was introduced at the January 2001 Consumer Electronics Show (CES) and MacWorld and should have hit store shelves in mid-2001.

Peerless features 10GB and 20GB removable hard disks, which integrate the read/write heads into a sealed case. This should eliminate head contamination, a frequent cause of removable-media drive failures in the past. The Peerless base station is a vertical mount enclosure about 4 inches wide and 5 inches tall and uses interchangeable interface modules. The first interface modules to be made available include the IEEE-1394 (FireWire) and USB 1.1 interface modules; USB 2.0 and SCSI versions will be introduced later. The base station contains the electronics for the drive system, which enables disks to be sold at very low costs.

The estimated transfer rate of the Peerless drive (when attached to the IEEE-1394 interface) is 15MBps.

"Orphan" Removable-Media Drives

Several recent removable-media drives have become "orphans" because of the closing of their manufacturers. This section discusses where you can get support for your "orphan" drives.

SyQuest Drives

Over the years, SyQuest has offered a wide variety of removable-media drives in capacities ranging from 44MB up to 1.5GB. They were very popular in the Macintosh world, but most SyQuest models were also made in PC versions. The last SyQuest models produced were the EzFlyer 230MB drive, the SparQ 1GB drive, and the SyJet 1.5GB drive. Parallel-port, IDE, and SCSI interface versions were produced, but the USB and IEEE-1394 interfaces were never supported.

From SyQuest to SYQT, Inc.

SyQuest filed a Chapter 11 petition with the United States Bankruptcy Court in Oakland, California on November 17, 1998. On January 13, 1999, SyQuest announced that it had entered into an agreement with Iomega Corporation to sell certain assets, including all its intellectual property, its U.S. inventory, and its U.S. fixed assets. Iomega *did not* take over support of SyQuest products.

SyQuest successor SYQT, Inc., offers limited sales and support operations. This includes online technical support via the World Wide Web, warranty returns, and product service operations. This means you can still purchase blank cartridges, buy drives, download drivers, and get repairs for most recent SyQuest products, but there will be no further development of the SyQuest "family" of products.

Even though SYQT, Inc. continues to sell and support SyQuest-brand drive products and media through the SYQT Web site, http://www.syqt.com. SyQuest products still qualify as "orphans" because there is no ongoing development of products. However, the Web site does now offer drivers for use with Windows 98, Windows Me, and Windows 2000, as well as drivers for older versions of Windows and MS-DOS on PC models from the old 44MB on up to the last models produced.

The SyQuest drives and media shown in Table 12.6 are supported by SYQT, Inc., and can be purchased from its Web site.

Table 12.6   Available SyQuest Drives and Media Quick Reference

Drive	Capacity	Media	Interface
SparQ	1GB	SparQ 1GB cartridge	Parallel; IDE
SyJet	1.5GB	SyJet 1.5GB cartridge	Parallel; IDE; SCSI (PC and Mac)
EzFlyer	230MB	EzFlyer 230MB cartridge; EZ135 135MB cartridge	IDE; SCSI (PC and Mac); Parallel

SYQT, Inc., provides driver and other technical support for these drives when used with Windows 95/98, Windows NT, Windows 2000, MS-DOS and Windows 3.1, and OS/2. SCSI drives are also supported on the Macintosh platform.

The SyQuest disks, like the Bernoulli cartridges, are easily distinguished from floppy disks. The 5 1/4-inch 44MB, 88MB, and 200MB cartridges used in some SyDOS drives are encased in clear plastic and are still available from SYQT, Inc.'s Web site. By contrast, the 3 1/2-inch SyJet 1.5GB and SparQ 1GB cartridges (also available from SYQT, Inc.) are an opaque black color.

The disks for the SyQuest and SyDOS drives are composed of a rigid platter inside a plastic cartridge but are not as well-protected as the disk in a Bernoulli cartridge. Some people consider these disks fragile. If the SyQuest and SyDOS cartridges are not severely jostled or dropped, they can be transported safely. However, these cartridges must be carefully protected when you mail or ship them.

According to SYQT technical support, most SyQuest and SyDOS cartridges can be left in the drive when powered down. However, SYQT recommends that cartridges for the 44MB and 88MB drives be removed before powering down the drive. With all drives, cartridges should be removed before transporting the drive.

Non-SYQT Support Sites

A third-party volunteer-staffed Web site you can also consult for technical support is http://www.syquestsupport.com; windrivers.com also has SyQuest drivers.

Avatar Shark Parts and Drivers

The Avatar Shark 250MB drive was a small removable-media drive that connected to the parallel port or PC Card slot of a PC. The Shark was built by Avatar Peripherals, which is now out of business.

Replacement cartridges, accessories, and drives can be purchased from Weymouth Technologies (http://www.weymouthtech.com), 119 Winthrop Lane, Holden, MA, 508-735-3513. Drivers and documentation for Windows 95/98, Windows NT, IBM OS/2, and MS-DOS can be downloaded from the Dead Boards link at http://www.windrivers.com/company.htm. A discussion forum is also available at this Web site.

Management Strategies for "Orphan" or Out-of-Production Drives

Because "orphan" drives have very small capacities, limited performance, and limited or no support by current and forthcoming operating systems, I recommend that you follow the strategy outlined here to help you move away from their use and toward up-to-date drives. Continuing to depend on an "orphan" can leave you stranded in the case of a drive or media failure. The following strategy is designed to help you protect your data (the most important part of any computer system!):

- Transfer all data on "orphan" drives to a current removable-media or optical-technology drive.
- Stop using the "orphan" drives for normal operations.

- Maintain a small inventory of the "orphan" drives in good working order if you provide services or perform data interchange with other users of these drives.

- Encourage suppliers and clients to start using currently available removable-media drives for data interchange.

- Determine which current drive or drives these other companies are using.

- Replace the "orphans" with drives that are compatible with the most popular media types used by your clients or business partners.

Removable Drive Letter Assignments

One problem people have when installing new drives is confusion with drive letter assignments. This becomes especially true when adding a new drive moves the assignments of previous drives, something that most people don't expect. Some simple rules govern drive letter assignments in Windows and DOS, which is discussed here.

All versions of Windows (as well as MS-DOS) treat floppy drives the same way, but major differences exist in the management of hard drives, CD-ROM/optical drives, and removable-media drives with Windows 9x/Me on the one hand and Windows NT 4.0, Windows 2000, and Windows XP on the other hand.

Floppy Drive Disk Assignments

With any version of MS-DOS or Windows, the system assigns the drive letter A to the first physical floppy drive. If a second physical floppy drive is present, it is assigned drive letter B. If no second floppy drive exists, the system automatically reserves B: as a logical drive representation of the same physical drive A:. This allows files to be copied from one disk to another by specifying COPY file.ext A: B:.

MS-DOS and Windows 9x/Me Disk Management

The basic rule with these operating systems is that devices supported by ROM BIOS–based drivers come first, and those assigned by disk-loaded drivers come second. Because floppy drives and hard drives are normally ROM BIOS–supported, these come first, before any other removable drives. After assigning A: and B: to floppy drives, the system then checks for installed hard drives and begins by assigning C: to the master partition on the first drive. **If you have only one hard disk,** any extended partitions on that drive are read, and any volumes in them are assigned consecutive letters after C:. For example, if you have a hard disk with a primary partition as C: and an extended partition divided into two logical volumes, they will be assigned D: and E:.

After the hard drive partitions and logical volumes are assigned, the system begins assigning letters to devices that are driver controlled, such as CD-ROM drives, PCMCIA attached devices, parallel port devices, SCSI devices, and so on. Here is how it works with only one hard drive split into three volumes, and a CD-ROM drive:

One drive primary partition	C:
One drive extended partition 1st volume	D:
One drive extended partition 2nd volume	E:
CD-ROM drive	F:

When a removable drive is added to the system proposed in the previous scenario, it is assigned either F: or G:, depending on the driver and when it is loaded. If the CD-ROM driver is loaded first, the removable drive is G:. If the removable drive driver is loaded first, it becomes F: and the CD-ROM drive is bumped to G:. In DOS, you control the driver load order by rearranging the DEVICE= statements in the CONFIG.SYS file. This doesn't work in Windows because Windows 9x, Me, NT, and 2000 use 32-bit drivers, which aren't loaded via CONFIG.SYS. You can exert control over the drive letters in Windows by manually assigning drive letters to the CD-ROM or removable drives. You do this as follows with Windows 9x and Windows Me:

1. Right-click My Computer, and select Properties.

2. Select the Device Manager tab.

3. Click the + next to the CD-ROM drive icon. Right-click the CD-ROM drive, select Properties, and select the Settings tab.

4. Select and change the Start Drive Letter.

5. Select the same letter for End Drive Letter.

6. Click OK, and allow your system to reboot for changes to take effect.

7. Repeat the previous steps by clicking the + next to Disk Drives, and assign a different drive letter to your removable drive.

Using these steps, you can interchange the removable drive with the CD-ROM drive, but you can't set either type to a drive letter below any of your existing floppy or hard drives.

So far, this seems just as everybody would expect, but from here forward is where it can get strange. The rule is that the system always assigns a drive letter to all primary partitions first and all logical volumes in extended partitions second. This means that if you have a second hard disk, it also can have primary and extended partitions, the extended partition can have two logical volumes, and the primary partition on the second drive could become D:, with the extended partition logical volumes becoming G: and H:.

Here is how it works with two hard drives, each split into three volumes, and a CD-ROM drive:

First drive primary partition	C:
Second drive primary partition	D:
First drive extended partition 1st volume	E:
First drive extended partition 2nd volume	F:
Second drive extended partition 1st volume	G:
Second drive extended partition 2nd volume	H:
CD-ROM drive	I:

In this example, if a removable drive were added, it would become either I: or J:. Using the same procedure outlined previously, you could swap I: or J: or assign them higher (but not lower) letters as well. Some factory-installed removable drives that use the IDE interface (such as some versions of the Zip 100 IDE) act like a second hard disk, rather than an add-on removable drive.

The utility software provided with the Iomega Zip and Jaz drives also can be used to assign the drive to any available drive letter.

To avoid scrambling existing hard drive letters when you install additional drives, prepare additional drives with extended partitions only. Drive letters in the extended partition on the second drive will follow the drive letters in the first drive's extended partitions and so forth if you install a third or even more hard drives. Here's what the result would be when you have two hard drives, with the first drive split up as a primary disk partition with two drives in an extended partition, and the second drive having no primary partition, but three logical drives in its extended partition:

First drive primary partition	C:
First drive extended partition 1st volume	D:
First drive extended partition 2nd volume	E:
Second drive extended partition 1st volume	F:
Second drive extended partition 2nd volume	G:
Second drive extended partition 3rd volume	H:

Drive Remapping Utilities

Although some utilities are available for remapping drive letters under Windows, I normally don't recommend them. This is because if you boot under DOS or via a floppy, these remappings are no longer in place and the standard BIOS mapping prevails. Because you might often boot to DOS to perform setup, diagnostics, configuration, or formatting/partitioning, confusion about which drive letters are what can lead to mistakes and lost data!

If you reset your CD-ROM or other removable-media drive to a different drive letter in Windows, be sure to set the drive to the same letter when you run the computer in command-prompt or MS-DOS mode. This is typically done through command-line options you can add to the **AUTOEXEC.BAT** statement for the drive. See your drive's instruction manual for details.

Windows NT 4.0, Windows 2000, and Windows XP Disk Management

Disk management for NT-based versions of Windows, including Windows NT 4.0, Windows 2000, and Windows XP (including XP Home Edition), offers many more options than in MS-DOS and Windows 9x/Me. The Disk Administrator tool is launched from the Drive properties Tools menu in Windows NT 4.0. The similar Disk Management tool is started from the Computer Management (Microsoft Management Console) utility in Windows 2000 and Windows XP. Both Disk Administrator and Disk Management can be used to control drive letters. To change a drive letter with either tool, right-click the drive and select Change Drive Letter and Path.

Although C: drive is assigned to the first hard drive by default in these versions of Windows, you can assign the drive letters you prefer to both CD-ROM/removable-media drives and to logical drives on a hard disk. By default, when additional hard-disk–based logical drives are added to a system, existing CD-ROM or other removable-media drive letters are not disturbed. Therefore, programs that depend on CD-ROM or removable-media drive paths continue to work.

You also can change the default boot drive letter from C: to another drive letter, but this is not recommended because it prevents your system from booting until manual Registry changes are made to correct the problem.

Comparing Price and Performance of Removable-Media Drives

Tables 12.7 and 12.8 compare the performance and price per MB of the best-performing (SCSI or EIDE) versions of the drives discussed in detail earlier in this chapter. The price per MB is calculated from the lowest cost per cartridge purchased in a multipack. Typical CD-R/CD-RW drives have been added to this comparison because many individuals might find these products a better choice for removable-media storage.

The tables are ranked in order by performance or cost per MB, from fastest/least expensive to slowest/most expensive.

Table 12.7 High-Capacity Removable-Media Magnetic Storage Drives Ranked by Performance and Compared with CD-R/CD-RW Drives

Drive	Capacity	Interface	Maximum Sustained Speed
Iomega Peerless	10GB	IEEE-1394	15MB/sec
Castlewood Orb	2.2GB	SCSI or EIDE	12.2MB/sec
Iomega Jaz 2GB	2GB	SCSI	8.7MB/sec
Typical 40x	700MB	SCSI or EIDE	6.0MB/sec
CD-ROM Drive			
Typical 24x CD-ROM/CD-R/ CD-RW drive in playback mode	700MB	SCSI or EIDE	3.6MB/sec read
Typical 16X	700MB	SCSI or EIDE	2.4MB/sec
CD-R Drive			
Iomega Zip 250	250MB	SCSI or EIDE	2.4MB/sec
Typical 12x CD-R drive	700MB	SCSI	1.8MB/sec write
Iomega Zip 100	100MB	EIDE	1.4MB/sec
Imation LS-120 SuperDisk	120MB	EIDE	1.1MB/sec
Typical 6x CD-R	650MB	EIDE	900KB/sec write
Iomega PocketZip	40MB	PC Card (n/a in EIDE)	620KB/sec
Typical 4x CD-RW (rewriteable) optical drive	Up to 650MB	EIDE	600KB/sec write

Figure 12.6 and Table 12.8 compare high-capacity SCSI-based drives with Zip, LS-120, and similar drives.

Table 12.8 High-Capacity Removable-Media Magnetic Storage Drives Ranked by Media Cost per MB and Compared with CD-R/CD-RW Drives

Drive	Capacity	Typical Media Cost in Quantities	Cost per MB
CD-R media (12x or faster speed)	700MB	$.40	Under 1 cent
CD-RW media (1x–4x speed)	650MB	$1.10	Under 1 cent
Castlewood Orb	2.2GB	$30	1.5 cents
Iomega Jaz 2GB	2GB	$80	3 cents
Iomega Peerless	20GB	$200	1 cent
Iomega Zip 250	250MB	$16	6.4 cents
Imation LS-120 SuperDisk	120MB	$10	8.3 cents
Iomega Zip 100	100MB	$9	9 cents
Iomega PocketZip	40MB	$10	23.8 cents

Figure 12.6 High-capacity SCSI or IEEE-1394–based drives, such as the Castlewood Orb, Iomega Jaz, and new Iomega Peerless, are as much as eight times faster than Zip, LS-120, or similar "large floppy" drives.

Figure 12.7 compares the cost per MB of CD-R/CD-RW media to the per MB cost of magnetic media.

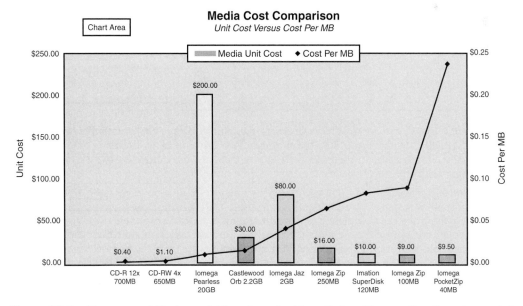

Figure 12.7 The cost per MB of recordable and rewriteable optical media, as well as the unit cost, is far lower than for magnetic media. The Iomega Peerless is the best value in magnetic media in cost per MB, whereas the Castlewood Orb is the best value in unit cost for greater than 1GB removable media. The least expensive media is the Iomega Zip 100, but it has the second-highest cost per MB.

As you can see from the previous comparisons, optical storage is substantially cheaper per MB than most magnetic removable-media drives, but the optical drive's write performance is substantially lower than many magnetic drives. For many users, the best strategy is to use magnetic storage for short-term use and projects in process and optical storage for near-archival storage and sending out finished information to other users.

When shopping for a removable drive, keep the following in mind:

- *Price per megabyte of storage.* Take the cost of the drive's cartridge or disk and divide it by the storage capacity to see how much you are paying per megabyte of storage. This difference in price becomes quite apparent as you buy more cartridges or disks for the drive. (Don't forget to factor in the cost of the drive itself if you are trying to decide which removable-media drive to buy!)

- *Access time versus need of access.* The access and data transfer speeds are important only if you need to access the data frequently or quickly. If your primary use is archiving data, a slower drive might be fine. However, if you plan to run programs off the drive, choose a faster drive instead.

- *Compatibility and portability.* Opt for an external SCSI, IEEE-1394, USB, or parallel port solution if you need to move the drive between various computers. USB is the lowest-cost and friendliest solution because it's built into recent systems and supports hot-swapping. Also verify that drivers are available for each type of machine and operating system you want to use with the drive, and consider whether you need to exchange disks with other users. The Iomega Zip disk and Imation LS-120 SuperDisk drives have become standards for removable-cartridge media. For some users, this might be the most important factor in choosing a drive.

- *Storage capacity.* For maximum safety and ease of use, the capacity of your storage device should be the largest available that meets your other requirements. Digital camera users, for example, will want the largest possible flash or disk storage supported by their cameras to allow more photos or higher-quality photos to be stored. Desktop and notebook computer users will want the largest drives possible for data backup or program storage.

Note

For one-time use, the CD-R drive is the best choice for two reasons: low media cost (well under $1 each in quantity) and near-universal compatibility (virtually all systems sold since the mid-1990s can read CD-R media in ordinary CD-ROM drives).

- *Internal versus external.* Most users find external parallel port or USB drives the easiest to install; additionally, they give you the option of using the drive on several systems. Internal drives are usually faster because of their IDE or SCSI interfaces and are more cleanly integrated into the system from a physical perspective.

- *Bootable or not.* The ATAPI/IDE version of the Imation LS-120 SuperDisk is BIOS supported in almost all new systems, and it is fully compatible with existing floppy drives. Therefore, the SuperDisk drive can completely replace the floppy, a decided advantage over Zip and the others. Although many recent systems can use the IDE Zip drive as a bootable drive, Zip drives are not compatible with standard 3 1/2-inch diskettes.

Magneto-Optical Drives

One of the most neglected types of removable-drive technologies is the magneto-optical (MO) drive. Introduced commercially in 1985, magneto-optical drives are now available in capacities exceeding 5GB, beating the size of the largest removable magnetic storage drives by a factor of about 2.5:1.

Two sizes of magneto-optical media and drives are available: 3 1/2-inch and 5 1/4-inch. The 3 1/2-inch drives have capacities up to 1.3GB, and the 5 1/4-inch drives have capacities that exceed 5GB. Originally, magneto-optical drives were strictly WORM (write-once, read many) drives that produced media that could be added to, but not erased. WORM drives are still on the market, but for desktop computer users, read/write MO drives are preferable.

Magneto-Optical Technology

At normal temperatures, the magnetic surface of an MO disk is very stable, with archival ratings of up to 30 years.

One surface of an MO disk faces a variable-power laser, whereas the other surface of the disk faces a magnet. Both the laser beam and the magnet are used to change the data on an MO disk. Figure 12.8 illustrates the magneto-optical writing and reading process.

The "optical" portion of an MO drive is the laser beam, which is used at high power during the erasing process to heat the destination area of the MO drive to a temperature of about 200° Celsius (the Curie point, at which a normally magnetic surface ceases to be magnetic). This enables any existing information in that area to be erased by a uniform magnetic field, which doesn't affect the other portions of the disk that are at normal temperature.

Next, the laser beam and magnetic field are used together to write information to the location by applying high power to the laser and applying a controlled magnetic signal to the media to change it to either a binary 0 or 1.

During the read process, the laser is used at low power to send neutrally polarized light to the surface of the MO disk. The areas of the MO disk that store binary 0s reflect light at a polarization angle different from those that store binary 1s. This difference of one degree is called the *Kerr effect*.

Figure 12.8   Magneto-optical drives use the laser at high power to heat the magnetic surface to enable its contents to be magnetically changed during the write cycle (left) and use the laser at low power to determine the angle of polarization (the Kerr effect) during the read cycle (right).

In older MO drives, the erase and write process involved two separate operations, but most recent MO drives starting with the Plasmon DW260 of 1997 use the LIMDOW method (light intensity modulated direct overwrite) for a single-pass operation with some media types. LIMDOW drives use magnets built into the disk itself, rather than separate magnets as in older MO drives. LIMDOW drives are fast enough to store MPEG-2 streaming video and make achieving higher capacities easier.

MO drives are available from many manufacturers at a variety of price points. The models listed in Table 12.9 are readily available from major computer retailers.

Table 12.9   Typical Magneto-Optical Drives and Media

Size	Example Drive and Interface	Max. Capacity and Other Usable Media	Performance	Approximate Drive Cost	Approximate Media Cost
3 1/2 inch	Fujitsu DynaMO 1300FE External IEEE-1394	1.3GB; can use 640MB, 540MB 230MB, and 128MB	5.9MB/sec maximum with 1/3GB (lower with smaller media)	around $400	around $35
5 1/4 inch	Sony SMO-F551/S Magneto-Optical Drive Internal SCSI	5.2GB; can use 4.8GB, 4.1GB, 2.6GB, and 2.3GB	5.07MB/sec read, 2.48MB/sec write (5.2GB media)	around $1,700	around $60

5 1/4-inch media MO drives are also available in external SCSI versions at slightly higher prices. ATAPI/IDE models are sold by some vendors, but aren't as easy to find.

Comparing MO to "Pure" Magnetic Media

Compared to most high-capacity removable-media drives, MO drive hardware is more expensive (especially in the 5 1/4 inch-media size), but media costs are far less per MB, durability is far better, and performance is as good or better than the 200MB-or-under class drives. The use of SCSI interfaces for most models was a drawback when MS-DOS/Windows 3.1 were the leading operating systems, but Windows 9x/Me/NT/2000/XP have much easier SCSI installation processes, and SCSI interfaces have dropped in price (and are included with some internal drives). If you can afford the high initial cost of the 5 1/4-inch–media MO drives, you'll have a fairly fast, durable, long-term storage solution that's also a good storage area for works in process.

Flash Card and Digital "Film"

The newest "hot" storage technology, flash memory, has really been around for several years as a main or an auxiliary storage medium for notebook computers. However, the rise of devices such as digital cameras and MP3 players has transformed this technology from a niche product into a mainstream must-have accessory.

How Flash Memory Works

Flash memory is a type of nonvolatile memory that is divided into blocks, rather than bytes as with normal RAM memory modules. Flash memory, which also is used in most recent computers for BIOS chips, is changed by a process known as Fowler-Nordheim tunneling. This process removes the charge from the floating gate associated with each memory cell. Flash memory then must be erased before it can be charged with new data.

The speed, low reprogramming current requirements, and compact size of recent flash memory devices have made flash memory a perfect counterpart for portable devices such as notebook computers and digital cameras, which often refer to flash memory devices as so-called "digital film." Unlike real film, digital film can be erased and reshot.

Types of Flash Memory Devices

Several types of flash memory devices are in common use today, and it's important to know which ones your digital camera is designed to use. The major types include

- CompactFlash
- SmartMedia
- ATA PC Cards (PCMCIA)
- MultiMediaCards
- Memory Stick

CompactFlash

CompactFlash was developed by SanDisk Corporation in 1994 and uses ATA architecture to emulate a disk drive; a CompactFlash device attached to a computer has a disk drive letter just like your other drives.

The original size was Type I (3.3mm thick); a newer Type II size (5mm thick) accommodates higher-capacity devices. Both CompactFlash cards are 1.433 inches wide by 1.685 inches long, and adapters allow them to be inserted into notebook computer PC Card slots. The CompactFlash Association (http://www.compactflash.org) is the organization that oversees development of the standard.

SmartMedia

Ironically, SmartMedia (originally known as SSFDC for solid state floppy disk card) is the simplest of any flash memory device; SmartMedia cards contain only flash memory on a card without any control circuits. This simplicity means that compatibility with different generations of SmartMedia cards can require manufacturer upgrades of SmartMedia-using devices. The Solid State Floppy Disk Forum (http://www.ssfdc.or.jp/english) oversees development of the SmartMedia standard.

MultiMediaCard

The MultiMediaCard (MMC) is the newest and smallest flash memory storage device designed for use in digital cameras and a wide variety of other devices, including smart phones, MP3 players, and digital camcorders. MMC was co-developed by SanDisk and Infineon Technologies AG (formerly Siemens AG) in November 1997. The MMC uses a simple 7-pin serial interface to devices and contains low-voltage flash memory. A proposed Secure MultiMediaCard might be developed to provide flash memory storage for copyrighted digital music. The MultiMediaCard Association (www.mmca.org) was founded in 1998 to promote the MMC standard and aid development of new products.

Sony Memory Stick

Sony, which is heavily involved in both notebook computers and a wide variety of digital cameras and camcorder products, has its own version of flash memory, known as the Sony Memory Stick. These devices feature the unique erase-protection switch, which prevents accidental erasure of your photographs. Sony has also licensed Memory Stick technology to other companies, such as Lexar Media.

ATA-Compliant PC Card

Although the PC Card (PCMCIA) form factor is now used for everything from game adapters to modems, from SCSI interfacing to network cards, its original use was computer memory, as the old PCMCIA (Personal Computer Memory Card International Association) acronym indicated.

Unlike normal RAM modules, PC Card memory acts like a disk drive, using the PCMCIA ATA (AT Attachment) standard. PC Cards come in three thicknesses (Type I is 3.3mm, Type II is 5mm, and Type III is 10.5mm), but all are 3.3 inches long by 2.13 inches wide. Type I and Type II cards are used for ATA-compliant flash memory and the newest ATA-compliant hard disks. Type III cards are used for older ATA-compliant hard disks; a Type III slot also can be used as two Type II slots.

Comparing Flash Memory Devices

As with any storage issue, you must compare each product's features to your needs. You should check the following issues before purchasing flash memory devices:

■ *Which flash memory products does your camera or other device support?* Although adapters allow some interchange of the various types of flash memory devices, for best results, you should stick with the flash memory type your device was designed to use.

■ *Which capacities does your device support?* Flash memory devices are available in ever-increasing capacities, but not every device can handle the higher-capacity devices. Check the device and flash memory card's Web sites for compatibility information.

■ *Are some flash memory devices better than others?* Some manufacturers have added improvements to the basic requirements for the flash memory device. For example, Lexar, maker of CompactFlash+, makes two series of faster-than-normal cards (the 4x and 8x series) and also produces some models that can be attached to USB ports for fast data transfer using a simple USB cable rather than an expensive and bulky card reader.

Table 12.10 compares the major types of flash memory devices. Devices are listed in alphabetical order.

Table 12.10 Major Flash Memory Devices Compared

Flash Memory Device	Maximum Capacity	Interface
ATA DataFlash	2GB	PC Card Type II
CompactFlash	160MB	Proprietary
Memory Stick	64MB	Proprietary
MultiMediaCard	128MB	Proprietary
SmartMedia	128MB	Proprietary

Only the ATA DataFlash cards can be attached directly to a notebook computer's PC Card slots. All other devices need some type of adapter to transfer data. Figure 12.9 shows how CompactFlash, Memory Stick, MultiMediaCards, and SmartMedia compare in size to each other.

Moving Flash Memory Devices from Camera to Computer

Several types of devices can be purchased to enable the data on flash memory cards to be moved from digital cameras and other devices to a computer. Although some digital cameras come with an RS-232 serial cable for data downloading, this is a painfully slow method, even for low-end cameras with less than a megapixel (1,000 pixel horizontal width) resolution.

Figure 12.9   SmartMedia, CompactFlash, Memory Stick, and MultiMediaCard flash memory devices.

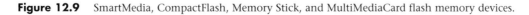

Card Readers

The major companies who produce flash card products sell card readers that can be used to transfer data from proprietary flash memory cards to PCs. These card readers typically plug into the computer's USB ports (some older versions might use the parallel port) for fast access to the data on the card.

In addition to providing fast data transfer, card readers enable the reuse of expensive digital film after the photos are copied from the camera.

The major benefit to external card readers is that they can be used with either notebook or desktop computers. Figure 12.10 shows a typical card reader with a CompactFlash memory card inserted.

Type II PC Card Adapters

For use in the field, you might prefer to adapt flash memory cards to the Type II PC Card slot. You insert the flash memory into the adapter; then, you slide the adapter into the notebook computer's

Type II PC Card slot. Figure 12.11 shows how a CompactFlash card Type II PC Card adapter works. As with card readers, check with the major companies who produce your type of flash memory device for the models available.

Figure 12.10   A SanDisk CompactFlash card reader. *Photo courtesy of SanDisk.*

CompactFlash media   ATA Data Flash card

Typical Type II PC Card adapter

Figure 12.11   A typical Type II PC Card adapter for CompactFlash media (left) compared to an ATA DataFlash card (right).

Floppy Adapters

If you have a standard 3 1/2-inch floppy drive connected to a standard floppy controller, you have a third alternative for reading the contents of flash memory cards: SmartDisk (http://www. smartdisk.com) makes the FlashPath line of flash memory card adapters that fit in place of a 3 1/2-inch floppy disk. Separate models are available for SmartMedia, Sony Memory Stick, and CompactFlash cards. As shown in Figure 12.12, the flash memory devices are inserted into the FlashPath adapter. Then, the FlashPath adapter is inserted into a 3 1/2-inch floppy drive.

Assembly is inserted into a
standard 3.5-inch floppy disk drive

Compact Flash module is
inserted into the FlashPath adapter

Figure 12.12 A CompactFlash module is inserted into the FlashPath adapter; the assembly is then inserted into a standard 3 1/2-inch floppy drive. *Photo courtesy of SanDisk.*

Microdrive Technology

If you prefer magnetic storage for digital camera data storage, consider the IBM Microdrive, which is sold by IBM and various other companies under OEM agreements.

The IBM Microdrive comes in four capacities (170MB, 340MB, 512MB, and 1GB) and can be used with several digital cameras, many notebook computers, and other devices. The Microdrive is a true hard drive at 1" wide and works in CompactFlash+ Type II slots, enabling it to be a direct replacement for standard CompactFlash memory cards on compatible equipment. IBM also offers the Microdrive as part of a Travel Kit containing a PC Card adapter, and the drive is compatible with many standard CompactFlash card readers. See the www.storage.ibm.com Web site for more information about Microdrive products, a compatibility matrix, and other information. Figure 12.13 shows how a Microdrive's mechanism compares in size to a standard U.S. quarter (25-cent piece).

Figure 12.13 A U.S. quarter (left) is just slightly smaller than the IBM Microdrive (right). *Courtesy of International Business Machines Corporation. Unauthorized use not permitted.*

Now that the IBM Microdrive is being sold by Iomega as part of its big push into CompactFlash-compatible storage devices, this amazing drive might become better known and more popular than ever. Iomega's version of the Microdrive includes a PC Card adapter for use with notebook computers and QuickSync 2 backup software, Adobe ActiveShare photo album software, and the Music Match JukeBox Plus digital music player.

Tape Drives

The data backup and archive needs of a personal computer can be overwhelming. People with large hard drives and numerous applications installed and those who generate a large amount of data might need to back up their computers on a weekly or even a daily basis.

In addition, a critical need on today's PCs is data storage space. Sometimes it seems as though the storage requirements of a PC can never be satisfied. On nearly any PC used for business, study, or even fun, the amount of software installed can quickly overwhelm even a large hard drive. To save space on the primary storage devices, you can archive infrequently used data to another storage medium.

Historically, a popular method for backing up full hard disks or modified files has been a tape backup drive. This section focuses on current tape backup drive technologies to help you determine whether this type of storage technology is right for you.

Tape backup drives are the most simple and efficient device for creating a full backup of your hard disk if the tape is large enough. With a tape backup drive installed in your computer, you insert a tape into the drive, start your backup software, and select the drive and files you want to back up. The backup software copies your selected files onto the tape while you attend to other business. Later, when you need to retrieve some or all of the files on the backup tape, you insert the tape in the drive, start your backup program, and select the files you want to restore. The tape backup drive takes care of the rest of the job.

This section examines the various types of tape backup drives on the market, describing the capacities of different drives as well as the system requirements for installation and use of a tape drive. The following topics are covered in this section:

- Hard-disk–based alternatives to tape backup
- Advantages and disadvantages to tape backup
- Common standards for tape backup drives
- Common backup tape capacities
- Newer higher-capacity tape drives
- Common tape drive interfaces
- Portable tape drives
- Tape backup software

Hard-Disk–Based Alternatives to Tape Backup

Before you decide to adopt a tape backup as your backup strategy, keep the following alternatives in mind.

The high capacity and low cost per MB of the new Iomega Peerless drive system might make this appealing for both primary and backup storage. Conventional hard disks also can be used for backups if both the original drive and an identical drive are connected to a mirroring RAID (redundant array of inexpensive drives) array. RAID arrays were once strictly for SCSI drives on networks because of their high cost. However, recent developments in high-performance, low-cost RAID-compatible IDE/ATA host adapters on motherboards and incorporated into add-on cards make this another useful backup strategy to consider.

Disadvantages of Tape Backup Drives

Many computer users who once used tape backups for data backup purposes have turned to other technologies for the following reasons:

- *Creating a tape backup copy of files or of a drive requires the use of a special backup program in almost all cases.* A few tape drives allow drive letter access to at least part of the tape capacity, but this feature is far from universal.

- *Retrieving data from most tape backup drives requires that the data files be restored to the hard disk.* Other types of backup storage can be treated as a drive letter for direct use from the media.

- *Tape backups store and retrieve data sequentially.* The last file backed up can't be accessed until the rest of the tape is read; other types of backup storage use random access, which enables any file on the device to be located and used in mere seconds.

- *Tape backups can be cantankerous.* The magnetic tape used can be easily erased or can stretch out of shape, destroying the data onboard; other types of backup storage are more durable.

- *Low-cost tape backups using QIC (Quarter Inch Committee), QIC-Wide, or Travan technology once had little problem keeping up with increases in hard disk capacity and once sold for prices comparable to or less than the hard disks they protected.* Today's hard disks have capacities of 20 to 40GB and are far less expensive than most comparably sized tape backups.

- *Newer backup and restore techniques, such as drive imaging/ghosting, rival the ease of use of tape backups and permit data restoration with lower-cost optical storage devices such as CD-R drives.*

For these reasons, the once-unassailable position of a tape backup drive as being the must-have data protection accessory is no longer a secure one; plenty of rivals to tape backups are on the market. However, if you can afford a high-quality DDS or AIT tape drive, you can get a high-performance and high-reliability solution because these same drives are used in the demanding roles of network backup.

Advantages to Tape Backup Drives

Although tape backup drives are no longer the one-size-fits-all panacea for all types of bigger-than-floppy storage problems, they have their place in keeping your data safe. Following are several good reasons for using tape backup drives:

- *Tape backups are a true one-cartridge backup process for individual client PCs, standalone computers, or network servers when high-capacity tape drives and cartridges are used.*

- *If you or your company has made previous backup tapes, you must keep a tape drive to access that data or to perform a restore from it.* Tape backup drives are needed if you need to restore from previously made backup tapes.

- *If you want an easy media rotation method for preserving multiple full-system backups, tape backup drives are a good choice.*

Common Tape Backup Standards

Several tape backup standards exist for individual client PC and small server tape backup drives:

- *QIC, QIC-Wide, and Travan.* These are three branches of a large and diverse family of low-cost, entry-level tape backup drives that can handle data up to 20GB at 2:1 compression.

- *DAT (Digital Audio Tape).* This is a newer technology than QIC and its offshoots, using Digital Data Storage (DDS) technology to store data up to 40GB at 2:1 compression. DAT drives are often referred to as DDS drives for this reason.

- *AIT (Advanced Intelligent Tape).* This is becoming the successor to DAT/DDS because it can handle higher capacities than DAT.

- *OnStream's ADR (Advanced Digital Recording).* This features a capacity up to 50GB at 2:1 compression and a choice of SCSI, IDE, and popular external interfaces in its 30GB (2:1 compression) version for desktop computers.

- *Ecrix's VXA drives.* These offer a capacity of 66GB at 2:1 compression and a variety of high-speed SCSI and IEEE-1394 interface options. The VXA-1 format has been approved by the ECMA, an important international organization that establishes standards for information and communication systems.

Other tape backup standards, such as DLT (Digital Linear Tape) and 8mm, are used primarily with larger network file servers and are beyond the scope of this book.

QIC and Its Variants (QIC-Wide and Travan)

The first quarter-inch tape drive was introduced in 1972 by 3M, and it used a cartridge size of 6×4×5/8 inches. This pioneering cartridge established the so-called "DC" data cartridge standard that was used with the first true QIC-standard drive—the 60MB QIC-02, introduced in 1983–84. The QIC-02–compatible drives were sold for several years and, like many early tape backup drives, used a dedicated host adapter board. QIC-02's small capacity began to be a problem in the mid-1980s, and many other QIC standards were created for larger drives.

The QIC (http://www.qic.org) has introduced more than 120 standards over the years in both the older DC and newer minicartridge (MC) forms. This huge number of standards has actually led to a fragmented marketplace that makes it increasingly difficult to determine the backward compatibility and cross-compatibility factors that QIC, ironically, was established to provide.

This section focuses on the recent and current versions of the minicartridge versions of QIC and related technologies, such as QIC-Wide and Travan.

Note

For more information on older QIC standards, see Chapter 12 of *Upgrading and Repairing PCs, 11th Edition*, and Chapter 12 of *Upgrading and Repairing PCs, 12th Edition*, found in their entirety on the CD-ROM accompanying this book.

QIC Tapes and Head Recording Technologies

QIC-standard backup tapes are magnetic media, primarily ferric oxide, and are recorded in a manner similar to the way data is encoded on your hard drive, using either Modified Frequency Modulation (MFM) or Run-Length Limited (RLL) technology.

QIC and related technologies use a simple linear recording head mechanism, similar to the way that cassette tapes are recorded and erased. Different QIC standards use different types of tape and record different numbers of tracks to reach specified capacities.

The most common QIC MC standards used in recent years are listed in Table 12.11. Although new drives no longer use QIC cartridges as their primary backup technology, backward compatibility with popular sizes you might have used in the past is an important consideration when you purchase a new tape drive. For economy, some drives allow you to use less expensive QIC media for day-to-day backups of changed files only and larger QIC-Wide or Travan cartridges for full backups. Generally, recent tape drives maintain read compatibility with several older tape standards but support a very limited number of tape standards for write compatibility.

Internal versions of the QIC MC tape backup drives in Table 12.11 were connected to the floppy controller, either in place of the B: drive or by using a special piggyback cable that enables two floppy drives plus the tape backup to function on a single floppy controller. External versions could connect to the parallel port.

The QIC-40 and QIC-80 cartridges must be formatted before use; some tape vendors have sold both formatted and unformatted versions of these cartridges. Because formatting even a short tape can take more than an hour, you should buy preformatted tapes. Later QIC cartridge versions always are preformatted at the factory.

Table 12.11   Popular QIC MC Standards

Standard/Cartridge	Size/2:1 Compression	Interface
QIC-40/DC-2000	40MB/80MB	Floppy
QIC-40/DC-2060	60MB/120MB	Floppy
QIC-80/MC-2120	125MB/250MB	Floppy, parallel port
QIC-80XL/MC-2120XL	170MB/340MB	Floppy, parallel port
QIC-3020XL/MC-3020XL	680MB/1.36GB	Floppy, parallel port, IDE

As you can see from Table 12.11, QIC drives have fallen behind the hard drive developments of the late 1990s. Because the safest and best way to back up a hard disk with tape is to use a single tape, a solution to the QIC storage "crisis" was necessary.

Increased QIC and Travan Performance

Because of the fragmented nature of the QIC MC standards and the need to increase storage capacity as drive size increased, several approaches have been used to help QIC grow to meet the needs of larger, faster hard disks and systems:

- Longer data cartridges
- QIC-Wide tapes and drives
- Travan tapes and drives

Longer Data Cartridges

The tape length in normal QIC-80 (MC-2120) cartridges is 300 feet, allowing only 125MB of uncompressed data to be stored on a single tape using drives such as the HP/Colorado Jumbo 250. The MC-2120XL extended the tape length to 425 feet, enabling up to 170MB of uncompressed data to be stored.

This same approach has been taken to its logical conclusion by Verbatim, which offers its QIC Xtra EX-series cartridges for a variety of popular QIC standards, as seen in Table 12.12.

Table 12.12   Standard and QIC Xtra Tape Cartridges and Capacities

Standard/Cartridge	Capacity/ 2:1 Compression	QIC Xtra Replacement	Capacity/ 2:1 Compression
QIC-80/MC2120	125MB/250MB	DC 2120Extra	400MB/800MB
QIC-3020XL/MC3020XL	680MB/1.36GB	MC 3020Extra	1.6GB/3.2GB

Verbatim also makes EX-series cartridges compatible with some of the Travan series drives. A major advantage of the Verbatim EX series is that QIC, QIC-Wide, and Travan drives can all use the same tape (depending on model), enabling a single cartridge to be used for several tape drives. If you are unable to replace your older tape drives with higher-capacity models, the Verbatim Xtra series can provide your existing units with significantly higher capacity.

Figure 12.14 compares a normal QIC minicartridge to the Verbatim Xtra series.

Figure 12.14   A Verbatim DC2120-EX (QIC-80) tape cartridge (left) holds 1,000 feet of tape, compared to the standard DC-2120 tape cartridge's 307 feet of tape (right), and provides more than three times the storage per cartridge in this size. The Verbatim Xtra cartridge also uses internal stabilizers for the larger tape spool, not shown in this photo.

QIC-Wide Drives and Media

Sony developed its proprietary QIC-Wide drives and media to provide a growth path for QIC MC tape drive users. The name, QIC-Wide, is amusing because a QIC-Wide tape isn't a quarter-inch wide; the tape contained in a QIC-Wide cartridge is 8mm, or .315 inches wide. The "wider than QIC" tape allows QIC-Wide cartridges to hold more data per foot than the QIC standard on which each cartridge is based. Although Sony's QIC-Wide drives are no longer on the market, the wider tape and backward compatibility with QIC standards have provided the inspiration for Travan drives—many of which can use QIC-Wide cartridges as an alternative to their native Travan media.

Table 12.13 lists common QIC-Wide cartridges and their capacities, along with the QIC MC standard the cartridge is based on for backward compatibility.

Table 12.13   QIC-Wide Cartridges and Capacities

QIC-Wide Cartridge	Capacity/2:1 Compression	Based on QIC Standard
QW5122F	208MB/410MB	QIC-80
QW3000XL	1GB/2GB	QIC-3000
QW3010XLF	450MB/900MB	QIC-3010
QW3020XLF	849MB/1.6GB	QIC-3020
QW2GB[1]	1GB/2GB	N/A
QW3080XLF	2GB/4GB	QIC-3080
QW3095XLF	2GB/4GB	QIC-3095
QW3210XLF	2.3GB/4.6GB	QIC-3210

1. This is the same cartridge used by the Iomega Ditto 2GB drive.

Travan Cartridge Tape

The successor to both QIC-MC and QIC-Wide drives was created in 1994 by 3M (now Imation). Travan drives maintain backward compatibility with various QIC standards and provide backup capabilities up to 10GB uncompressed and 20GB at 2:1 compression.

The Travan platform features a unique drive/minicartridge interface patented by Imation. The Travan platform fits in a 3 1/2-inch form factor, enabling easy installation in a variety of systems and enclosures. Travan drives can accept current QIC, QIC-Wide, and Travan minicartridges—a critical need for users, given the installed base of more than 200 million QIC-compatible minicartridges worldwide.

Currently, several levels of Travan cartridges and drives are available, each based on a particular QIC standard. Table 12.14 lists the currently available Travan cartridges and capacities. All Travan cartridges use .315 inch (8mm) wide tape.

Table 12.14   Travan Family Cartridges and Capacities

Travan Cartridge (Previous Name)	Capacity/ 2:1 Compression	Read/Write Compatible with	Read Compatible with
Travan-1 (TR-1)	400MB/800MB	QIC-80, QW5122	QIC-40
Travan-3 (TR-3)	1.6GB/3.2GB	TR-2, QIC-3020, QIC-3010, QW-3020XLW, QW-3010XLW	QIC-80, QW-5122, TR-1

Table 12.14   Continued

Travan Cartridge (Previous Name)	Capacity/ 2:1 Compression	Read/Write Compatible with	Read Compatible with
Travan 8GB (Travan 4/TR-4)	4GB/8GB	QIC-3095	QIC-3020, QIC-3010, QIC-80, QW-5122, TR-3, TR-1
Travan NS-8[1]	4GB/8GB		QIC-3020, QIC-3010, QIC-80
Travan NS-20	10GB/20GB		Travan 8GB, QIC-3095

1. *This cartridge can be used in place of the Travan 8GB (TR-4); the same cartridge can be used on either NS8 or TR-4 drives.*

Note

Backward compatibility can vary with drive; consult the manufacturer before purchasing any drive to verify backward-compatibility issues.

Most Travan drives on the market today use the Network Series (NS) technology described in the following section. At one time, an NS-36 standard (36GB compressed) was planned, but it appears that the NS-20 is the end of the line for the Travan technology.

The Travan NS

Drives that support Travan NS technology are designed to solve two problems that have plagued tape backup users for many years: data compression and data verification.

On QIC-40 and above, QIC-Wide, and standard Travan drives, data compression is performed by the backup software used by the drive. This could cause the following problems:

- Drives might have difficulty reading data if different backup software were used to make the backup and perform the restoration.
- The speed of the computer had a major impact on how fast backups could be performed; a typical backup program (such as Iomega's Ditto Tools) would offer three settings: no compression, compress to save time, and compress to save space, forcing the user to choose between maximum data storage and maximum speed.

On the same drives, backup software supports a verification step, which compares the data written to the tape with the data on the drive. Unfortunately, this requires that the tape be rewound to the beginning of the current backup and be read to the end while the hard disk is also read. The result? A backup that took 45 minutes without verification would take more than 90 minutes with verification enabled. This inefficient write-rewind-reread process has discouraged many users from relying on this safer backup method. Also, errors caused by changes in the state of a Windows 9x computer (such as screensavers being enabled or swapfiles changing in size) during the time passage between backup and verify tended to create the erroneous notion that the backup wasn't accurate.

Travan NS–compatible drives use a dual-head design (see Figure 12.15) that enables data to be verified as soon as it is written (read-while-write). They also feature hardware data compression, which allows a higher data capacity (up to 20GB at 2:1 compression). The result is faster and more reliable backups. The Travan NS20 cartridges also use a different metal media formula for greater data density than older Travan drives do.

Currently, Travan NS8 and NS20-based drives are sold primarily by Seagate Technologies, Tecmar Technologies, and Tandberg Data.

Write heads ──────┐↑↑┌────── Write heads
Read (Verify) heads

Figure 12.15 Travan NS tape drives use separate read and write heads to enable data to be verified as soon as it is written, saving the time-consuming rewind and verify operation used with QIC, QIC-Wide, and earlier Travan drives.

Proprietary Versions of Travan Technology

Ironically, because Travan technology was designed to bring an end to the QIC MC—QIC-Wide tape "wars," some drives use proprietary versions of the Travan standard. Nonstandard sizes include

- 5GB Tecmar/Iomega DittoMax
- 5GB HP/Colorado
- 6.6GB AIWA Bolt
- 7GB Tecmar/Iomega DittoMax
- 10GB Tecmar DittoMax
- 14GB HP/Colorado

The drive manufacturer is the principal supplier of media for some of these drives, whereas others are also supported with third-party media. Consult the drive manufacturers' Web sites for details.

OnStream ADR Technology

OnStream was founded in February 1998 as a spin-off from Philips Electronics, and its CEO, William T. Beierwaltes, had previously founded low-cost backup leader Colorado Memory Systems (now the HP/Colorado division of Hewlett-Packard).

Although the future of OnStream was uncertain after the liquidation of OnStream's U.S. operations (OnStream, Inc.) in March 2001, a new company—OnStream Data B.V.—based in the Netherlands, immediately took over sales, support, and development of OnStream drives and technology. The U.S. operations of the new OnStream Data company are located in Austin, TX. OnStream-compatible ADR tape cartridges are available from Verbatim in both 30GB and 50GB capacities, as well as from OnStream Data.

Introduced in 1999, OnStream's ADR (advanced digital recording) technology tape drives are designed to answer many of the limitations and complaints that users have had about traditional tape backup solutions.

◀◀ See "Disadvantages of Tape Backup Drives," p. 669.

Features of ADR

ADR uses a multiple-track linear recording system that reads and writes eight tracks at once, enabling read-while-write verify for speed and reliability and a relatively low tape travel speed to minimize wear (and noise!). ADR also uses several other techniques to foster additional reliability:

- Embedded servo information keeps the read/write heads aligned with the tracks at all times.

- ECC (error correction code) recording applied over all eight tracks (spatially distributed) allows reliable data recovery even if an entire track is destroyed.

- Continuously variable tape-travel speeds enable the drive to adjust to the different speeds of data flow from the hard drive without slowing down the entire tape backup process; as the data transfer rate increases, the drive runs faster, and the drive slows down as the data-transfer rate decreases.

- Single-pass media defect mapping allows reliable recording without rewinding the tape for a separate verify pass.

User Benefits of ADR

Several benefits to ADR are as follows:

- *ADR drives can be treated as a drive letter when used with the included Echo software.* This includes drag-and-drop file transfer and direct use of the tape's contents without a restore step (including viewing full-motion video and listening to MP3s).

- *Quiet backups.* These result from the multiple-track recording feature and variable-speed motor.

- *Background "set it and forget it" backup operation at reduced speed or fast dedicated backup of large hard drives in just an hour or two.*

- *Low cost per MB for both drives and media.*

- *Reliable data backup and online storage in a single device.* The claimed reliability for ADR-technology media exceeds the reliability of both other tape-backup systems and hard drives.

ADR Technical Specifications

Table 12.15 lists the technical specifications for OnStream's line of ADR drives, available in IDE, various flavors of SCSI, parallel, and USB interfaces. Drives for Macintosh only and drives bundled with third-party backup programs are also available but are not listed. All drives listed are supplied with OnStream's Echo software.

Media retail is $40 for the 30GB cartridge in a single pack and $60 for the 50GB cartridge in a single pack. Multiple-cartridges packs are available at a reduced price.

OnStream is the only producer of ADR drives at this writing. The ADR recording process is illustrated in Figure 12.16 (as compared to the DAT helical recording process).

Table 12.15   OnStream ADR Family Specifications for Windows PCs

Drive Model	Interface	Performance	Retail	Media Used
DI30	IDE ATAPI	1–2MB/sec	$299	ADR 30GB
DP30	Parallel	.7–1.4MB/sec	$399	ADR 30GB
USB30	USB	.85–1.7MB/sec	$399	ADR 30GB
SC30	SCSI internal	2–4MB/sec	$499	ADR 30GB
SC30	SCSI external	2–4MB/sec	$599	ADR 30GB
SC50	SCSI internal	2–4MB/sec	$699	ADR 50GB or 30GB
ADR50 Int	LVD SCSI internal	4–8MB/sec	$799	ADR 50GB or 30GB
ADR50 Ext	LVD SCSI external	4–8MB/sec	$949	ADR 50GB or 30GB

Figure 12.16   ADR drives use a multitrack linear recording mechanism (left), whereas DAT drives use a helical scan recording head that resembles the mechanism in a VCR (right). Both methods greatly increase data density compared to QIC-family drives, but helical scan recording exposes more of the tape to potential contamination.

OnStream Data also makes an external IEEE-1394 version of its 30GB (2:1 compression) drive but offers it for only the Macintosh platform.

DAT/DDS, AIT, and Other High-Capacity Tape Drive Standards

With the abandonment of Travan capacities beyond 20GB compressed, users of today's high-capacity hard drives must turn to larger tape backup standards. In addition to the OnStream ADR, the same tape backup standards long supported by workstation and large network servers can also be used with today's versions of Windows for both individual desktop computers and small network servers. Additionally, new high-capacity technologies are available to support today's larger drives.

4mm digital audio tape (DAT/DSS), 8mm videotape, 8mm AIT, digital linear tape, scalable linear recording (SLR), and Ecrix VXA are the major choices available for users who need higher-capacity backups. An emerging choice for very high-capacity (100GB and up) drives is the Ultrium version of the LTO Technology standard. All these technologies are available in autoloading tape libraries suitable for large networks, as well as single-cartridge drives intended for small network servers or desktop use.

Proprietary Versus Open Standards

If you want a wider variety of choices in drives, media, and pricing, you might prefer to purchase a high-performance drive type that is made by several companies. However, some of the most advanced technologies are controlled by a single vendor.

Drive technologies available from multiple vendors include

- *DAT/DDS.* Introduced and licensed by Sony to numerous manufacturers
- *AIT.* Introduced and licensed by Sony to numerous manufacturers
- *DLT.* Originally developed by Digital Equipment Corporation, but was purchased by Quantum in 1994
- *LTO (Linear Tape-Open).* Developed by HP, IBM, and Seagate

The following drive technologies are sold by a single vendor:

- *SLR.* Tandberg Data
- *VXA.* Ecrix

However, third-party vendors might sell tape cartridges compatible with even so-called "proprietary" standards.

DAT/DDS Tape Drives

Of the many high-performance tape drives on the market, this author's favorite is the DAT/DDS tape drive family because of its combination of performance, capacity, reliability, and reasonable price. Four levels of DAT/DDS drive capacity are available:

- *DDS-1.* This entry-level member of the family (2GB/4GB at 2:1 compression) is now obsolete.
- *DDS-2.* Has the same capacity as drives based on Travan NS8 (4GB/8GB at 2:1 compression).
- *DDS-3.* Has a slightly larger capacity (12GB/24GB at 2:1 compression) than Travan NS20.
- *DDS-4.* The largest member of the DAT/DDS family, it has a 20GB/40GB at 2:1 compression capacity, which is double the capacity of Travan NS20.

Even though DAT/DDS drives are more expensive than Travan drives with similar capacities, the media cost is much lower because of the drive's design. For example, you will pay about three times as much for a Travan NS20 cartridge as for a slightly higher-capacity DDS-3 cartridge. A DDS-4 cartridge, which offers double the capacity of Travan NS20, still sells for about 30% less. DDS drives are more reliable than Travan or earlier QIC-based drives, which is a vital consideration because the most important reason to use a tape backup is to perform a restore. The enhanced reliability of DDS drives is aided by the inclusion of automatic head-cleaning features built into most DDS drives and media.

Helical Scan Recording on DAT, 8mm, and AIT Drives

Exabyte 8mm, Sony DAT/DDS, and Sony AIT use helical scan recording. The read/write heads used in helical scan recording are mounted on a drum and write data at a slight angle to the tape, using a mechanism highly reminiscent of that in a VCR (refer to Figure 12.16). The entire surface of the tape is used to store data, enabling more data to be placed in a given length of tape than with the linear recording techniques used by the QIC family of drives.

AIT Unique Features

Sony's AIT has several unique features designed to make backup and restoration faster and more reliable. An optional Memory In Cassette (MIC) chip allows the cartridge to remember which of the 256 on-tape partitions were used for the data you want to restore, so the correct starting point can be located in seconds. AIT drives also have a servo tracking system called Auto Tracking Following (ATF), which is used for accurate data-track writing, and Advanced Lossless Data Compression (ALDC), a mainframe-style compression method that can compress data to a greater extent than other methods. The drives also feature built-in head cleaning that is activated when soft (correctable) errors reach a preset limit, metal-evaporated tape media that avoids head contamination, and a 3 1/2-inch form factor.

DLT Unique Features

DLT segments the tape into parallel horizontal tracks and records data by streaming the tape across a single stationary head at 100–150 inches/sec during read/write operations. This is a dramatic contrast to traditional helical-scan technology, in which the data is recorded in diagonal stripes with a rotating drumhead while a much slower tape motor draws the media past the recording head.

The result is a very durable drive and a robust medium. DLT drive heads have a minimum life expectancy of 15,000 hours under worst-case temperature and humidity conditions, and the tapes have a life expectancy of 500,000 passes.

SLR Unique Features

Tandberg's SLR drives use a linear recording method; the tape used by the SLR 40, SLR 60, and SLR 100 is divided into 192 tracks. Twenty-four prewritten servo tracks are used to adjust the position of the read/write head as necessary. This feature is designed to ensure compatibility of SLR tapes between drives, enabling a tape written by one drive unit to be readable by another unit. Six tracks are written at the same time. The entry-level SLR7 uses a simplified recording method that uses two tracks. Both tape types have fault tolerance features that enable the drive to switch to another track for data recording if the original track fails.

Ecrix VXA Unique Features

The Ecrix VXA drives combine a special recording and special playback method. The recording method used somewhat resembles a normal helical scan, but the tape is guided past the magnetic drum with a completely different type of mechanism and the data is recorded at variable speeds that change according to how fast the host can transmit data. This eliminates the need to wind tape backward because of data underruns (back-hitching). Data is recorded in 64-byte groups of 387 data packets rather than in linear blocks. VXA drives use a special read feature called overscan operation (OSO). OSO performs redundant reads of each group of data packets, enabling data to be retrievable even from damaged tapes. The packetizing of data works the same way as on the Internet: Data can be read in any order and reassembled into its original form when all packets are received. In tests, Ecrix has boiled, frozen, and even poured hot coffee over VXA tapes and been able to retrieve 100% of the stored data.

LTO Technology Unique Features

Linear Tape-Open, better known as LTO, is a very high-performance tape backup technology that offers two distinct types of mechanisms:

- *Ultrium.* This implementation of LTO is optimized for very high capacity. For example, Ultrium drives have an uncompressed capacity of 100GB (200GB at 2:1 compression). They also have special features such as dynamic powerdown (protects tapes from damage during a power interruption), intelligent data compression, intelligent media analysis to avoid suspect tape areas, and variable tape speed to minimize back-hitching (moving the tape backward because of a data underrun). Ultrium drives are popular in both single-drive and tape-library formats, although they are quite expensive: Basic single-cartridge units start at just under $5,000.

- *Accelis.* This implementation of LTO is optimized for very high speed, using a dual-reel cartridge that enables tape to be loaded from the mid-point instead of the beginning. It has a native capacity of 25GB (50GB at 2:1 compression). Accelis also features cartridge memory (used to retrieve data about the cartridge's previous use to make locating data faster) and throughput of 20MB–40MB per second. Accelis appears to be an on-paper variation at this point, with no drives on the market using this variation on LTO.

Comparing High-Performance Tape Backup Technologies

As the preceding sections indicate, you have many choices in large, high-performance tape backup. All the drive technologies discussed in this section use various SCSI interface versions and can be purchased as internal or external drives. Even though they are more expensive than Travan or OnStream ADR drives, they offer the capacities needed by today's larger hard drives.

Unlike the confusing backward-compatibility picture for QIC-family drives, the more advanced drives in each family are backward compatible with smaller drives.

Table 12.16 summarizes the performance and other characteristics of these tape technologies and compares them to Travan NS8 and NS20 drives and OnStream ADR. The price of the tape drives varies tremendously depending on which version of SCSI is selected, whether the drive is internal or external, and whether a single-tape or tape-library drive is selected. The standards shown in Table 12.17 are listed in order by native capacity. All drive interfaces are SCSI, except as noted. Maximum prices listed are for the most expensive single-drive SCSI interface model except as noted; most models of a given drive will be cheaper, depending on the SCSI version supported, whether the drive is sold bare or as a kit, and whether it is internal (less expensive) or external.

Table 12.16   High-Performance Tape Backup Standards Compared

Drive Type	Capacity/2:1 Compressed	Backup Speed (Native/Compressed)	Drive Price Range	Media Cost
DAT DDS-2	4GB/8GB	.5–1.1MB/sec	under $1,000	under $10
Travan NS8	4GB/8GB	.6–1.2MB/sec	under $500	under $35
SLR5	4GB/8GB	.38–.56MB/sec	under $600	around $40
Exabyte 8mm (Eliant 820)	7GB/14GB	1–2MB/sec	under $1,600	around $10
Travan NS20	10GB/20GB	1–2MB/sec	under $500	under $40
DAT DDS-3	12GB/24GB	1.1–2.2MB/sec	under $1,000	around $15
Exabyte 8mm (Mammoth-LT)	14GB/28GB	2–4MB/sec	under $1,600	around $40
ADR 30GB	15GB/30GB	1–2MB/sec IDE 2–4MB/sec SCSI	under $300 under $600	around $40
SCSIDAT DDS-4	20GB/40GB	2–4.8MB/sec	under $1,500	under $40
Exabyte 8mm (Mammoth)	20GB/40GB	3–6MB/sec	under $2,700	around $60
SLR7	20GB/40GB	3–6MB/sec	under $1,000	around $50
DLT 4000	20GB/40GB	1.5–3MB/sec	under $2,000	around $70
SLR50	25GB/50GB	2–4MB/sec	around $2,300	around $90
VXA-1	33GB/66GB	3–6MB/sec	under $1,200	around $80 (33/66GB); around $50 (20/40GB); around $30 (12/24GB)
AIT-1	25GB/50GB or 35GB/70GB	3–6MB/sec	under $2,600	around $70
DLT 7000	35GB/70GB	5–10MB/sec	under $4,300	around $80
ADR 50GB	25GB/50GB	2–4MB/sec SCSI 4–8MB/sec LVD SCSI	under $950	$60
AIT-2 SLR	50GB/100GB	6–12MB/sec	under $3,900	around $100

From Table 12.16, you can see that the Travan NS8 and NS20 drives are among the least expensive SCSI-based drives to purchase, but the cost per MB for media is much lower with DAT/DDS drives. The performance is higher with all 20GB and up drives of other types. For an individual computer or small network server, the ADR50, DDS-3, DDS-4, SLR7, and VXA-1 drive families represent the best balance of initial cost, performance, and media cost per MB. DLT, Exabyte 8mm, and AIT drives are better choices for larger network server backup, especially if purchased in their more expensive tape-library forms (not listed).

Note

To learn more about DAT, DLT, and Exabyte 8mm tape drives, see *Upgrading and Repairing PCs, 11th Edition,* which is included in printable PDF format on the CD accompanying this book.

Choosing a Tape Backup Drive

Choosing a tape backup drive can be a simple job if you need to back up a single standalone system with a relatively small hard drive. The decision becomes more complex if the system has a larger hard drive or if you must back up not only a desktop system but also a laptop. Choosing a tape backup drive type can be an even more complex program if you must back up a network server's hard drives and perhaps even back up the workstations from the server. As you ponder which backup tape drive type you should select, consider the following factors:

■ The amount of data you must back up

■ The interfaces your equipment supports

■ The data throughput you need

■ The tape standard that is best for your needs

■ The cost of the drive and tapes

■ The capabilities and compatibility of the included driver and backup software

By balancing the considerations of price, capacity, throughput, compatibility, and tape standard, you can find a tape drive that best meets your needs.

Note

When purchasing a tape backup drive, take the time to look through magazines in which dealers or distributors advertise. Several publications specialize in PCs and carry advertising from many hardware and software distributors. I recommend publications such as the *Computer Reseller News* and *Computer Shopper. Computer Shopper's* online shopping service can help you locate multiple sources for both popular and rare items quickly.

These publications cater to people or companies willing to go around the middlemen and buy direct. By reading such publications, you can get an excellent idea of the drives available and the price you can expect to pay.

While reading about drive capabilities and prices, don't neglect to read reviews of the software included with each drive. Verify that the software capabilities match your expectations and needs. This is especially important if you intend to use the drive on a non–Windows 9x system because most backup software today is tailored for Windows 9x.

Capacity

The first rule for selecting a tape backup drive is to buy a drive with a capacity large enough for your needs, both now and for the foreseeable future. The ideal is to buy a drive with enough capacity so you can start your backup software, insert a blank tape in the drive, walk away from the system, and find the backup completed when you return. Because tape backups are generally rated by their maximum (2:1 compression) capacities—which is seldom reached in practice—you should calculate the "true" size of a tape backup drive by multiplying the native (noncompressed) capacity of a drive by 1.5 (equal to rating the drive as 1.5:1 compression). Thus, a so-called "20GB" tape backup might be better described as having a "15GB" capacity (10GB uncompressed times 1.5).

You should always ensure that your tape backup medium supports a capacity larger than your largest single drive or partition. This makes automated backups possible because you won't have to change a tape in the middle of a backup. And, even if you don't mind replacing tapes in the middle of a backup, a single-tape backup is safer. If the first tape of a multiple-tape backup is damaged or lost, the entire backup is unusable with most backup systems!

Tape Standards and Compatibility

The next most important consideration, after adequate capacity, is choosing a drive whose tapes meet a standard that is useful to you. If you have existing tapes you want to restore, or you receive tapes from other users that you must read, you need a drive that can work with those tapes. Use the backward-compatibility information listed earlier to help you decide on a drive to purchase if this feature is important to you.

If your ability to work with older tape media is only an occasional issue, you might prefer to buy a high-performance drive for current backups and maintain an older drive that matches the older standard. Most Travan-type and QIC-Wide drives can read QIC-80 tape cartridges, for example.

Tip

It is important that you make a choice you can live with. If you manage a large installation of computers, mixing QIC, Travan, DAT, and 8mm drives among systems is seldom a good idea.

Software Compatibility

Equally important to your consideration is the software required to operate each drive. Currently, most parallel port and IDE drives come with software that runs under the Windows 9x operating system. SCSI tape drives usually also support Windows NT, Windows 2000/XP, or Unix. USB-based drives are primarily designed for Windows 98/Me/2000/XP, although Windows 2000/XP might not support as many devices as Windows 9x/Me does. Check the manufacturers' Web sites for operating-system compliance if your office's computers use more than one operating system.

Most operating systems have their own software for backing up data to a tape drive. If you intend to use this software, you should verify that the drive you purchase is supported by each piece of software on each system you intend to use with the drive. Third-party programs usually offer more features, but you might need to buy separate programs for the various operating systems your office uses.

Data Throughput

Any of the IDE or SCSI interface drives covered earlier should provide adequate performance (1MB/sec or above when backing up compressed data), but performance suffers if you opt for the convenience of USB or parallel port drives.

Floppy-interface QIC, QIC-Wide, and Travan drives should be considered obsolete for large-drive backups because of the limitations of the floppy interface and their small capacities.

Cost

You can figure the cost per MB for a drive in two ways: media cost only (which is valid for users with an existing drive) or drive plus media costs (which is a better method for new purchasers). Regardless of your favorite choice(s) in removable storage, be sure to look at the total picture, taking into account the savings from multipack data and the benefits of the extra speed of SCSI and IDE.

Tip

One point worth remembering when you evaluate whether to buy a tape drive is that the cost of the tapes and drive, taken as a whole, is nowhere near as high as the costs (in terms of frustration and lost productivity) of a single data-damaging hard drive problem. Considering that most people are more likely to back up a system if they have a tape drive installed than if they must use another medium for the backup, the cost of a drive and tapes is quite small, even on a standalone PC used mostly for fun.

Tape Drive Installation

Because most tape drives today use the same IDE, SCSI, USB, or parallel-port connection options that are used by other types of storage devices, you should see the appropriate sections of this book for more details about these devices:

- Chapter 14, "Physical Drive Installation and Configuration," provides detailed instructions for installing hard drives, floppy drives, and CD drives.
- Chapter 7 provides exhaustive coverage of the IDE interface.
- Chapter 8 provides detailed coverage of the SCSI interface.
- Chapter 16 provides information on USB and serial interfaces.

Note

For more details about installing the older floppy-interface tape backup drives, see *Upgrading and Repairing PCs, 11th Edition*, available in printable PDF format on the CD included with this book.

Tape Drive Backup Software

The most important decision you can make after you choose the tape standard and capacity of your backup tape drive is the backup software you will use with it.

The three sources for tape backup software are

- Software bundled with the drive
- Software bundled with the operating system
- Software obtainable from third parties

Use the following checklist to evaluate the software you plan to use with your tape backup drive:

- *Device support.* You might prefer to use tape for most backups, but can you change your mind and use high-capacity removable magnetic or optical storage if you need to? Some backup software bundled with a particular drive will work only with that drive; check whether a full version with more options is available.
- *Compatibility with existing backups.* If you have replaced an older tape drive with a new one, can the backup software as well as the tape drive read your old data?
- *Adjustable compression options.* If you are using a drive without hardware data compression, you should be able to adjust the compression methods used, or even turn them off to make sending the tape to the user of another drive easier.
- *Data safety options.* In addition to verify, good tape software should also include some form of ECC error correction to make recovering the data in case of media damage easier.

- *Disaster recovery.* Many bundled or operating system–standard backup programs require you to reinstall the operating system before you can restore the contents of a crashed drive. Insist on a disaster recovery feature that will allow you to restore a drive from bootable disks and the tape backup without taking the time to reinstall the operating system first.

Other useful features to look for include

- *Unattended backup scheduling.* Enables you to schedule a backup for a time when you won't need to use your computer
- *Macro capability.* Use when selecting options and the files to back up
- *A quick tape-erase capability.* Use when erasing the entire contents of a tape
- *Partial tape-erase capability.* Use when erasing only part of a tape
- *Tape unerase capability.* Use when recovering erased data
- *Password-protect capability.* Enables you to protect backup data from access by unauthorized persons

Read reviews, check compatibility, look for trial versions, and be sure to test the backup and restore features as you look for the best tape backup program for your needs.

Tip

Backup software vendor Novastor (`www.novastor.com`) has a unique solution for a major problem caused by moving from an older backup system to a new one: What to do with the data on the older tapes? Its Tape Copy software enables you to move data archives from your outmoded SCSI or IDE tape backup to a new SCSI- or IDE-based backup system. If you have extensive backup data and don't want to retain your old tape backup drive, Tape Copy might be the answer.

Tape Drive Troubleshooting

Tape drives can be troublesome to install and operate. Any type of removable media is more susceptible to problems or damage, and tape is no exception. This section lists some common problems and resolutions. After each problem or symptom is a list of troubleshooting steps.

Can't Detect the Drive

- For parallel port drives, use the tape backup as the only device on the drive and check the IEEE-1284 (EPP or ECP) mode required by the drive against the parallel port configuration.
- For USB drives, be sure you're using Windows 98 or higher and that the USB port is enabled in the BIOS; many systems originally shipped with Windows 95 have this port disabled.
- For IDE drives, ensure that the master/slave jumpers on both drives are set properly.
- For SCSI drives, check termination and Device ID numbers.
- For external drives of any type, ensure that the drive is turned on a few seconds before starting the system. If not, you might be able to use the Windows 9x Device Manager to Refresh the list of devices, but if this doesn't work, you must restart the computer.

Backup or Restore Operation Failure

If your tape drive suffers a backup or restore operation failure, follow these steps:

1. Make sure you are using the correct type of tape cartridge.
2. Remove and replace the cartridge.

3. Restart the system.

4. Retension the tape.

5. Try a new tape.

6. Clean the tape heads.

7. Make sure all cables are securely connected.

8. Rerun the confidence test that checks data-transfer speed with a blank tape (this test overwrites any data already on the tape).

Bad Block or Other Tape Media Errors

To troubleshoot bad block or other types of media errors, follow these steps:

1. Retension the tape.

2. Clean the heads.

3. Try a new tape.

4. Restart the system.

5. Try initializing the tape.

6. Perform a secure erase on the tape (previous data will no longer be retrievable from the tape).

Caution

Note that most minicartridge tapes are preformatted and can't be reformatted by your drive. Do not attempt to bulk-erase preformatted tape because this renders the tapes unusable.

System Lockup or System Freezing When Running a Tape Backup

If your system locks up or freezes while running a tape backup, follow these steps:

1. Ensure that your system meets at least the minimum requirements for both the tape drive and the backup software.

2. Check for driver or resource (IRQ, DMA, or I/O port address) conflicts with your tape drive controller card or interface; using the floppy drive while making a floppy or parallel port tape backup is a major cause of DMA conflicts.

3. Set the CD-ROM to master and the tape drive to slave if both are using the same IDE port.

4. Check the BIOS boot sequence; ensure that it is not set to ATAPI (tape/CD-ROM) devices if the tape drive is configured as a master device or as a slave with no master.

5. Make sure the hard drive has sufficient free space; most backup programs temporarily use hard drive space as a buffer for data transfer.

6. Hard drive problems can cause the backup software to lock up. Check your hard disk for errors with SCANDISK or a comparable utility.

7. Check for viruses.

8. Check for previous tape drive installations; ensure that any drivers from previous installations are removed.

9. Temporarily disable the current VGA driver and test with the standard 640×480×16 VGA driver supplied by Microsoft. If the problem does not recur, contact your graphics board manufacturer for an updated video driver.

10. Empty the Recycle Bin before attempting a backup. Files in some third-party Recycle Bins can cause backup software to lock up.

11. Disable antivirus programs and Advanced Power Management.

12. Try the tape drive on another computer system and different operating system, or try swapping the drive, card, and cable with known-good, working equipment.

Other Tape Drive Problems

Other issues that might cause problems in general with tape backups include

- Corrupted data or ID information on the tape.

- Incorrect BIOS (CMOS) settings.

- Networking problems (outdated network drivers, and so on).

- A tape that was recorded by another tape drive. If the other drive can still read the tape, this might indicate a head-alignment problem or incompatible environment.

Tape Retensioning

Retensioning a tape is the process of fast-forwarding and then rewinding the tape to ensure that there is even tension on the tape and rollers throughout the entire tape travel. Retensioning is recommended as a preventive maintenance operation when using a new tape or after an existing tape has been exposed to temperature changes or shock (for example, dropping the tape). Retensioning restores the proper tension to the media and removes unwanted tight spots that can develop.

Some general rules for retensioning include the following:

- Retension any tapes that have not been used for more than a month or two.

- Retension tapes if you have errors reading them.

- Retension any tapes that have been dropped.

- In some cases, you might need to perform the retension operation several times to achieve the proper effect. Most tape drive or backup software includes a Retension feature as a menu selection.

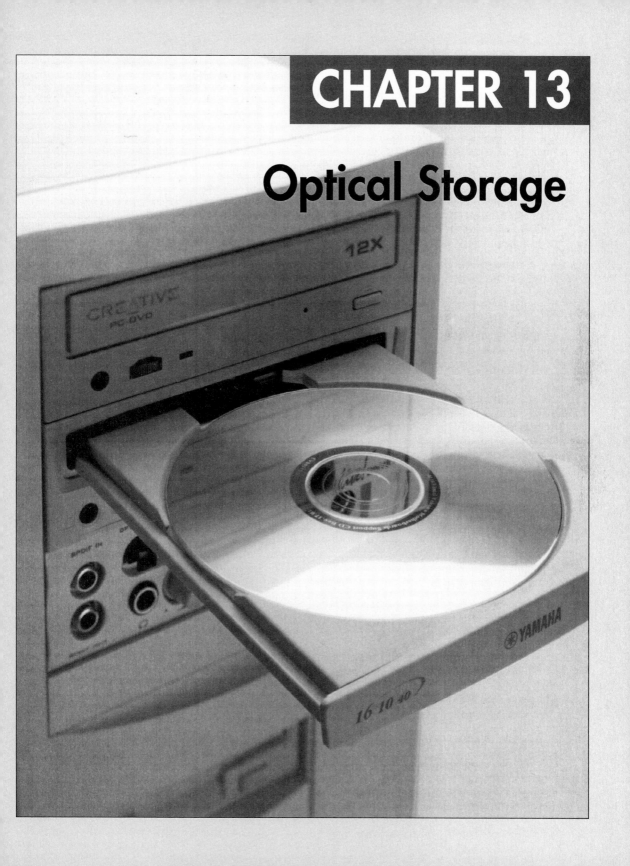

CHAPTER 13

Optical Storage

There are basically two types of disk storage for computers: magnetic and optical. *Magnetic* storage is represented by the standard floppy and hard disks that are installed in most PC systems, where the data is recorded magnetically on rotating disks. *Optical* disc storage is similar to magnetic disk storage in basic operation, but it reads and records using light (optically) instead of magnetism. Although most magnetic disk storage is fully read- and write-capable many times over, many optical storage media are either read-only or write-once. Note the convention in which we refer to magnetic as *disk* and optical as *disc*. This is not a law or rule but seems to be followed by most in the industry.

Some media combine magnetic and optical techniques, using either an optical guidance system (called a laser servo) to position a magnetic read/write head (as in the LS-120 or SuperDisk floppy drive) or a laser to heat the disk so it can be written magnetically thus polarizing areas of the track, which can then be read by a lower-powered laser, as in magneto-optical (MO) drives.

At one time, it was thought that optical storage would replace magnetic as the primary online storage medium. However, optical storage has proven to be much slower and far less dense than magnetic storage and is much more adaptable to removable-media designs. As such, optical storage is more often used for backup or archival storage purposes, and as a mechanism by which programs or data can be loaded onto magnetic drives. Magnetic storage, being significantly faster and capable of holding much more information than optical media in the same amount of space, is more suited for direct online storage and most likely won't be replaced in that role by optical storage anytime soon.

The most promising development in the optical area is that in the near future CD-RW (compact disc-rewritable) or DVD+RW (DVD+rewritable) will likely replace the venerable floppy disk as the de facto standard interchangeable, transportable drive and media of choice for PCs. In fact, some would say that has already happened. Most new systems today include a CD-RW drive, and even though a floppy drive is also included with most systems, it is rarely used except for running tests; running diagnostics; or doing basic system maintenance, disk formatting, preparation for OS installation, or configuration.

This chapter investigates the popular and standard forms of optical storage found in modern PCs.

What Is a CD-ROM?

CD-ROM, or *compact disc read-only memory*, is an optical read-only storage medium based on the original CD-DA (digital audio) format first developed for audio CDs. Other formats, such as CD-R (CD-recordable) and CD-RW (CD-rewritable), are expanding the compact disc's capabilities by making it writable. Additionally, new technologies such as DVD (digital versatile disc) are making it possible to store more data than ever on the same size disc.

CD-ROM drives have been considered standard equipment on most PCs for many years now. The primary exceptions to this rule are *thin clients*—PCs intended for use only on networks and which normally lack drives of any type.

CD-ROM is a read-only optical storage medium capable of holding up to 74 or 80 minutes of high-fidelity audio (depending on the disc used), or up to 682MB (74-minute disc) or 737MB (80-minute disc) of data, or some combination of the two, on one side (only the bottom is used) of a 120mm (4.72-inch) diameter, 1.2mm (0.047 inches) thick plastic disc. CD-ROM has exactly the same form factor (physical shape and layout) of the familiar CD-DA audio compact disc and can, in fact, be inserted in a normal audio player. It usually isn't playable, though, because the player reads the subcode information for the track, which indicates that it is data and not audio. If it could be played, the result would be noise—unless audio tracks precede the data on the CD-ROM (see the section "Blue Book— CD EXTRA," later in this chapter). Accessing data from a CD-ROM using a computer is quite a bit faster than from a floppy disk but slower than a modern hard drive. The term *CD-ROM* refers to both the discs themselves and the drive that reads them.

Although only a few dozen CD-ROM discs, or titles, were published by 1988, currently hundreds of thousands of individual titles exist, containing data and programs ranging from worldwide agricultural statistics to preschool learning games. Individual businesses, local and federal government offices, and large corporations also publish thousands of their own limited-use titles. As one example, the storage space and expense that so many business offices once dedicated to the maintenance of a telephone book library can now be replaced by two discs containing the telephone listings for the entire United States.

CDs: A Brief History

In 1979, the Philips and Sony corporations joined forces to co-produce the CD-DA (Compact Disc-Digital Audio) standard. Philips had already developed commercial laserdisc players, and Sony had a decade of digital recording research under its belt. The two companies were poised for a battle—the introduction of potentially incompatible audio laser disc formats—when instead they came to terms on an agreement to formulate a single industry-standard digital audio technology.

Philips contributed most of the physical design, which was similar to the laserdisc format it had created with regards to using pits and lands on the disk that are read by a laser. Sony contributed the digital-to-analog circuitry, and especially the digital encoding and error-correction code designs.

In 1980, the companies announced the CD-DA standard, which has since been referred to as the Red Book format (so named because the cover of the published document was red). The Red Book included the specifications for recording, sampling, and—above all—the 120mm (4.72-inch) diameter physical format you live with today. This size was chosen, legend has it, because it could contain all of Beethoven's approximately 70-minute Ninth Symphony without interruption.

After the specification was set, both manufacturers were in a race to introduce the first commercially available CD audio drive. Because of its greater experience with digital electronics, Sony won that race and beat Philips to market by one month, when on October 1, 1982 Sony introduced the CDP-101 player and the world's first CD recording—Billy Joel's *52nd Street* album. The player was first introduced in Japan and then Europe; it wasn't available in the U.S. until early 1983. In 1984, Sony also introduced the first automobile and portable CD players.

Sony and Philips continued to collaborate on CD standards throughout the decade, and in 1984 they jointly released the Yellow Book CD-ROM standard. It turned the CD from a digital audio storage medium to one that could now store read-only data for use with a computer. The Yellow Book used the same physical format as audio CDs but modified the decoding electronics to allow data to be stored reliably. In fact, all subsequent CD standards (usually referred to by their colored book binders) have referred back to the original Red Book standard for the physical parameters of the disc. With the advent of the Yellow Book standard (CD-ROM), what originally was designed to hold a symphony could now be used to hold practically any type of information or software.

CD-ROM Technology

Although identical in appearance to CD-DAs, CD-ROMs store data instead of (or in addition to) audio. The CD-ROM drives in PCs that read the data discs are almost identical to audio CD players, with the main changes in the circuitry to provide additional error detection and correction. This is to ensure data is read without errors because what would be a minor—if not unnoticeable—glitch in a song would be unacceptable as missing data in a file.

A CD is made of a polycarbonate wafer, 120mm in diameter and 1.2mm thick, with a 15mm hole in the center. This wafer base is stamped or molded with a single physical track in a spiral configuration starting from the inside of the disc and spiraling outward. The track has a pitch, or spiral separation, of 1.6 microns (millionths of a meter, or thousandths of a millimeter). By comparison, an LP record has a physical track pitch of about 125 microns. When viewed from the reading side (the bottom), the disc rotates counterclockwise. If you examined the spiral track under a microscope, you would see that along the track are raised bumps, called *pits*, and flat areas between the pits, called *lands*. It seems strange to call a raised bump a *pit*, but that is because when the discs are pressed, the stamper works from the top side. So, from that perspective, the pits are actually depressions made in the plastic.

The laser used to read the disc would pass right through the clear plastic, so the stamped surface is coated with a reflective layer of metal (usually aluminum) to make it reflective. Then, the aluminum is coated with a thin protective layer of acrylic lacquer, and finally a label or printing is added.

Note

CD-ROM media should be handled with the same care as a photographic negative. The CD-ROM is an optical device and degrades as its optical surface becomes dirty or scratched. Also it is important to note that, although discs are read from the bottom, the layer containing the track is actually much closer to the top of the disc. Writing on the top surface of a disc with a ballpoint pen, for example, easily damages the recording underneath. You need to be careful even when using a marker to write on the disc. The inks and solvents used in some markers can damage the print and lacquer over-coat on the top of the disc, and subsequently the information layer right below. Use only markers designed for writing on CDs. The important thing is to treat both sides of the disc carefully, especially the top (label) side.

Mass-Producing CD-ROMs

Commercial mass-produced CDs are stamped or pressed and not burned by a laser as many people believe (see Figure 13.1). Although a laser is used to etch data onto a glass master disc that has been coated with a photosensitive material, using a laser to directly burn copies would be impractical for the reproduction of hundreds or thousands of copies.

The steps in manufacturing CDs are as follows (use Figure 13.1 as a visual):

1. *Photoresist Coating.* A circular 240mm diameter piece of polished glass 6mm thick is spin-coated with a photoresist layer about 150 microns thick and then hardened by baking at 80°C (176°F) for 30 minutes.

2. *Laser Recording.* A Laser beam recorder (LBR) fires pulses of blue/violet laser light to expose and soften portions of the photoresist layer on the glass master.

3. *Master Development.* A sodium hydroxide solution is spun over the exposed glass master, which then dissolves the areas exposed to the laser, thus etching pits in the photoresist.

4. *Electroforming.* The developed master is then coated with a layer of nickel alloy through a process called *electroforming.* This creates a metal master called a *father.*

5. *Master Separation.* The metal master father is then separated from the glass master. The father is a metal master that can be used to stamp discs, and for short runs, it can in fact be used that way. However, because the glass master is damaged when the father is separated, and because a stamper can produce only a limited number of discs before it wears out, the father often is electroformed to create several reverse image *mothers.* These mothers are then subsequently electroformed to create the actual stampers. This enables many more discs to be stamped without ever having to go through the glass mastering process again.

6. *Disc Stamping Operation.* A metal stamper is used in an injection molding machine to press the data image (pits and lands) into approximately 18 grams of molten (350°C or 662°F) polycarbonate plastic with a force of about 20,000psi. Normally, one disc can be pressed every 3 seconds in a modern stamping machine.

7. *Metalization.* The clear stamped disc base is then sputter-coated with a thin (0.05–0.1 micron) layer of aluminum to make the surface reflective.

8. *Protective Coating.* The metalized disc is then spin-coated with a thin (6–7 micron) layer of acrylic lacquer, which is then cured with UV (ultraviolet) light to protect the aluminum from oxidation.

9. *Finished Product.* Finally, a label or printing is screen-printed on the disc and also cured with UV light.

This manufacturing process is identical for both data CD-ROMs and audio CDs.

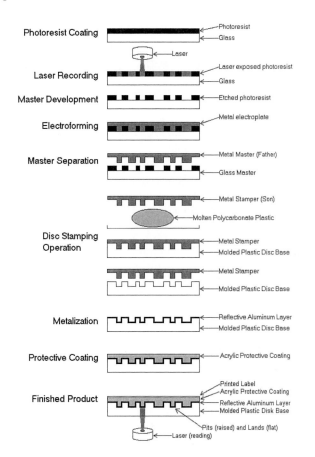

Figure 13.1 CD manufacturing process.

Pits and Lands

Reading the information back is a matter of bouncing a low-powered laser beam off the reflective layer in the disc. The laser shines a focused beam on the underside of the disc, and a photosensitive receptor detects when the light is reflected back. When the light hits a land (flat spot) on the track, the light is reflected back; however, when the light hits a pit (raised bump), no light is reflected back.

As the disc rotates over the laser and receptor, the laser shines continuously while the receptor sees what is essentially a pattern of flashing light as the laser passes over pits and lands. Each time the laser passes over the edge of a pit, the light seen by the receptor changes in state from being reflected to not reflected or vice versa. Each change in state of reflection caused by crossing the edge of a pit is translated into a 1 bit digitally. Microprocessors in the drive translate the light/dark and dark/light (pit edge) transitions into 1 bits, translate areas with no transitions into 0 bits, and then translate the bit patterns into actual data or sound.

The individual pits on a CD are 0.125 microns deep and 0.6 microns wide (1 micron equals one-millionth of a meter). Both the pits and lands vary in length from about 0.9 microns at their shortest to about 3.3 microns at their longest (see Figure 13.2).

Figure 13.2 Pit and land geometry on a CD.

The pit height above the land is especially critical as it relates to the wavelength of the laser light used when reading the disc. The pit (bump) height is exactly 1/4 of the wavelength of the laser light used to read the disc. Therefore, the light striking a land travels 1/4 + 1/4 = 1/2 of a wavelength further than light striking the top of a pit. This means the light reflected from a pit is 1/2 wavelength out of phase with the rest of the light being reflected from the disc. The out-of-phase waves cancel each other out, dramatically reducing the light that is reflected back and making the pit appear dark even though it is coated with the same reflective aluminum as the lands.

The read laser in a CD drive is a 780nm (nanometer) wavelength laser of about 1 milliwatt in power. The polycarbonate plastic used in the disc has a refractive index of 1.55, so light travels through the plastic 1.55 times more slowly than through the air around it. Because the frequency of the light passing through the plastic remains the same, this has the effect of shortening the wavelength inside the plastic by the same factor. Therefore, the 780nm light waves are now compressed to 780/1.55 = 500nm. One quarter of 500nm is 125nm, which is 0.125 microns—the specified height of the pit.

Drive Mechanical Operation

CD-ROM drives operate in the following manner (see Figure 13.3):

1. The laser diode emits a low-energy infrared beam toward a reflecting mirror.

2. The servo motor, on command from the microprocessor, positions the beam onto the correct track on the CD-ROM by moving the reflecting mirror.

3. When the beam hits the disc, its refracted light is gathered and focused through the first lens beneath the platter, bounced off the mirror, and sent toward the beam splitter.

4. The beam splitter directs the returning laser light toward another focusing lens.

5. The last lens directs the light beam to a photo detector that converts the light into electric impulses.

6. These incoming impulses are decoded by the microprocessor and sent along to the host computer as data.

Figure 13.3 Typical components inside a CD-ROM drive.

When first introduced, CD-ROM drives were too expensive for widespread adoption. In addition, drive manufacturers were slow in adopting standards, causing a lag time for the production of CD-ROM titles. Without a wide base of software to drive the industry, acceptance was slow.

After the production costs of both drives and discs began to drop, however, CD-ROMs were rapidly assimilated into the PC world. This was particularly due to the ever-expanding size of PC applications. Virtually all software is now supplied on CD-ROM, even if the disc doesn't contain data representing a tenth of its potential capacity. As the industry stands now, if a software product requires more than one or two floppy disks, it is more economical to put it on a CD-ROM.

For large programs, the advantage is obvious. The Windows 98SE operating system would require more than 75 floppy disks, an amount certainly nobody would want to deal with.

Track and Sectors

The pits are stamped into a single spiral track with a spacing of 1.6 microns between turns, corresponding to a track density of 625 turns per millimeter, or 15,875 turns per inch. This equates to a total of 22,188 turns for a normal 74-minute (650MiB) disc. The disc is divided into six main areas (discussed here and shown in Figure 13.4):

- *Hub clamping area.* The Hub clamp area is just that: a part of the disc where the hub mechanism in the drive can grip the disc. No data or information is stored in that area.

- *Power calibration area (PCA).* This is found only on writable (CD-R/RW) discs and is used only by recordable drives to determine the laser power necessary to perform an optimum burn. A single CD-R or CD-RW disc can be tested this way up to 99 times.

- *Program memory area (PCA).* This is found only on writable (CD-R/RW) discs and is the area where the TOC (table of contents) is temporarily written until a recording session is closed. After the session is closed, the TOC information is written to the ILead-in area.

- *Lead-in.* The lead-in area contains the disc (or session) TOC in the Q subcode channel. The TOC contains the start addresses and lengths of all tracks (songs or data), the total length of the program (data) area, and information about the individual recorded sessions. A single lead-in area exists on a disc recorded all at once (Disc At Once or DAO mode), or a lead-in area starts each session on a multisession disc. The lead-in takes up 4,500 sectors on the disc (1 minute if measured in time, or about 9.2MB worth of data). The lead-in also indicates whether the disc is multisession and what the next writable address on the disc is (if the disc isn't closed).

- *Program (data) area.* This area of the disc starts at a radius of 25mm from the center.
- *Lead-out.* The lead-out marks the end of the program (data) area or the end of the recording session on a multisession disc. No actual data is written in the lead-out; it is simply a marker. The first lead-out on a disc (or the only one if it is a single session or Disk At Once recording) is 6,750 sectors long (1.5 minutes if measured in time, or about 13.8MB worth of data). If the disc is a multisession disc, any subsequent lead-outs are 2,250 sectors long (0.5 minutes in time, or about 4.6MB worth of data

The hub clamp, lead-in, program, and lead-out areas are found on all CDs, whereas only recordable CDs (such as CD-Rs and CD-RWs) have the additional power calibration area and program memory area at the start of the disc.

The center hole in a CD is 15mm in diameter, which means it has a radius of 7.5mm from the center of the disc. From the edge of the center hole to a point at a radius of 20.5mm is the HCA. That is followed by the PCA, which starts at a radius of 20.5mm from the center. The PCA is followed by the PMA, which starts at a radius of 22.35mm, and then the lead-in area, which starts at a radius of 23mm from the center of the disc. The program (data) area of the disc starts at a radius of 25mm from the center, and that is followed by the lead-out area at 58mm. The disc track officially ends at 58.5mm, which is followed by a 1.5mm buffer to the edge of the disc. Figure 13.4 shows these areas in actual relative scale as they appear on a disc.

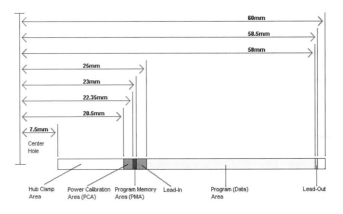

Figure 13.4 Areas on a CD (side view).

Officially, the spiral track of a standard CD-DA or CD-ROM disc starts with this lead-in area and ends at the finish of the lead-out area, which is 58.5mm from the center of the disc, or 1.5mm from the outer edge. This single spiral track is about 5.77 kilometers or 3.59 miles long. An interesting fact is that in a 56x CAV (constant angular velocity) drive, when reading the outer part of the track, the data moves at an actual speed of 162.8 miles per hour (262km/h) past the laser. What is more amazing is that even when the data is traveling at that speed, the laser pickup can accurately read bits (pit/land transitions) spaced as little as only 0.9 microns or 35.4 millionths of an inch apart!

Table 13.1 shows some of the basic information about the two main CD capacities, which are 74- and 80-minute. The CD standard originally was created around the 74-minute disc; the 80-minute versions were added later and basically stretch the standard by tightening up the track spacing a little bit.

Table 13.1   CD-ROM Technical Parameters

Advertised CD length (minutes)	74	80
Advertised CD capacity (MiB)	650	700
1x read speed (m/sec)	1.3	1.3
Track (turn) spacing (um)	1.6	1.48
Turns per mm	625	676
Turns per inch	15,875	17,162
Total track Length (m)	5,772	6,240
Total track length (feet)	18,937	20,472
Total track length (miles)	3.59	3.88
Pit width (um)	0.6	0.6
Pit depth (um)	0.125	0.125
Min. nominal pit length (um)	0.90	0.90
Max. nominal pit length (um)	3.31	3.31
Lead-in inner radius (mm)	23	23
Data inner radius (mm)	25	25
Data outer radius (mm)	58	58
Lead-out outer radius (mm)	58.5	58.5
Data area width (mm)	33	33
Total track area width (mm)	35.5	35.5
Max. rotating speed 1x CLV (rpm)	540	540
Min. rotating speed 1x CLV (rpm)	212	212
Track revolutions (data area)	20,625	22,297
Track revolutions (total)	22,188	23,986

B = Byte (8 bits)	m = meters
KB = Kilobyte (1,000 bytes)	mm = millimeters (thousandths of a meter)
KiB = Kibibyte (1,024 bytes)	um = micrometers = microns (millionths of a meter)
MB = Megabyte (1,000,000 bytes)	CLV = Constant linear velocity
MiB = Mebibyte (1,048,576 bytes)	rpm = revolutions per minute

The spiral track is divided into sectors that are stored at the rate of 75 sectors per second. On a disc that can hold a total of 74 minutes of information, that results in a maximum of 333,000 sectors. Each sector is then divided into 98 individual frames of information. Each frame contains 33 bytes, of which 24 bytes are audio data, 1 byte contains subcode information, and 8 bytes are used for parity/ECC (error correction code) information. Table 13.2 shows the sector, frame, and audio data calculations.

Table 13.2   CD-ROM Sector, Frame, and Audio Data Information

Advertised CD length (minutes)	74	80
Sectors/second	75	75
Frames/sector	98	98

Table 13.2   Continued

Number of sectors	333,000	360,000	
Sector length (mm)	17.33	17.33	
Byte length (um)	5.36	5.36	
Bit length (um)	0.67	0.67	

Each Frame:

Subcode bytes	1	1	
Data bytes	24	24	
Q+P parity bytes	8	8	
Total bytes/frame	33	33	

Audio Data:

Audio sampling rate (Hz)	44,100	44,100	
Samples per Hz (stereo)	2	2	
Sample size (bytes)	2	2	
Audio bytes per second	176,400	176,400	
Sectors per second	75	75	
Audio bytes per sector	2,352	2,352	

Each Audio Sector (98 Frames):

Q+P parity bytes	784	784	
Subcode bytes	98	98	
Audio data bytes	2,352	2,352	
Bytes/sector RAW (unencoded)	3,234	3,234	

Hz = Hertz (cycles per second)   *um = micrometers = microns (millionths of a meter)*
mm = millimeters (thousandths of a meter)

Sampling

When music is recorded on a CD, it is sampled at a rate of 44,100 times per second (Hz). Each music sample has a separate left and right channel (stereo) component, and each channel component is digitally converted into a 16-bit number. This allows for a resolution of 65,536 possible values, which represents the amplitude of the sound wave for that channel at that moment.

The sampling rate determines the range of audio frequencies that can be represented in the digital recording. The more samples of a wave that are taken per second, the closer the sampled result will be to the original. The Nyquist theorem (originally published by American physicist Harry Nyquist in 1928) states that the sampling rate must be at least twice the highest frequency present in the sample to reconstruct the original signal accurately. That explains why the 44,100Hz sampling rate intentionally was chosen by Philips and Sony when developing the CD—that rate could be used to accurately reproduce sounds of up to 20,000Hz, which is the upper limit of human hearing.

So, you can see that audio sectors combine 98 frames of 33 bytes each, which results in a total of 3,234 bytes per sector, of which only 2,352 bytes are actual audio data. Besides the 98 subcode bytes per frame, the other 784 bytes are used for parity and error correction.

Subcodes

The subcode bytes enable the drive to find songs (which are confusingly also called *tracks*) along the spiral track and convey additional information about the disc. The subcode bytes are stored as 1 byte per frame, which gives 98 subcode bytes for each sector. Two of these bytes are used as start block and end block markers, leaving 96 bytes of subcode information. These are then divided into eight 12-byte subcode blocks, each of which is assigned a letter designation P–W. Each subcode channel can hold about 31.97MB of data across the disc, which is about 4% of the capacity of an audio disc. The interesting thing about the subcodes is that the data is woven continuously throughout the disc; in other words, subcode data is contained piecemeal in every sector on the disc.

The P and Q subcode blocks are used on all discs, and the R–W subcodes are used only on CD+G (graphics) or CD TEXT–type discs.

The P subcode is used to identify the start of the tracks on the CD. The Q subcode contains a multitude of information, including

- *Whether the sector data is audio (CD-DA) or data (CD-ROM).* This prevents most players from trying to "play" CD-ROM data discs, which might damage speakers due to the resulting noise that would occur.
- *Whether the audio data is two or four channel.* Four channel is rarely if ever used.
- *Whether digital copying is permitted.* CD-R and RW drives ignore this; it was instituted to prevent copying to DAT (digital audio tape) drives.
- *Whether the music is recorded with pre-emphasis.* This is a hiss or noise reduction technique.
- *The track (song) layout on the disc.*
- *The track (song) number.*
- *The minutes, seconds, and frame number from the start of the track (song).*
- *A countdown during an intertrack (intersong) pause.*
- *The minutes, seconds, and frame from the start of the first track (song).*
- *The barcode of the CD.*
- *The ISRC (International Standard Recording Code).* This is unique to each track (song) on the disc.

The R-W subcodes are used on CD+G (graphics) discs to contain graphics and text. This enables a limited amount of graphics and text to be displayed while the music is being played. These same subcodes are used on CD TEXT discs to store disc- and track-related information that is added to standard audio CDs for playback on compatible CD audio players. The CD TEXT information is stored as ASCII characters in the R–W channels in the lead-in and program areas of a CD. On a CD TEXT disc, the lead-in area subcodes contain text information about the entire disc, such as the album, track (song) titles, and artist names. The program area subcodes, on the other hand, contain text information for the current track (song), including track title, composer, performers, and so on. The CD TEXT data is repeated throughout each track to reduce the delay in retrieving the data.

CD TEXT–compatible players typically have a text display to show this information, ranging from a simple one- or two-line, 20-character display such as on many newer RBDS (radio broadcast data system) automobile radio/CD players up to 21 lines of 40-color, alphanumeric or graphics characters on home- or computer-based players. The specification also allows for future additional data, such as Joint Photographics Expert Group (JPEG) images. Interactive menus also can be used for the selection of text for display.

Handling Errors

Handling errors was a big part of the original Red Book CD standard. CDs use parity and interleaving techniques called *cross-interleave Reed-Solomon code (CIRC)* to minimize the effects of errors on the disk. This works at the frame level. When being stored, the 24 data bytes in each frame are first run through a Reed-Solomon encoder to produce a 4-byte parity code called "Q" parity, which then is added to the 24 data bytes. The resulting 28 bytes are then run though another encoder that uses a different scheme to produce an additional 4-byte partity value called "P" parity. These are added to the 28 bytes from the previous encoding, resulting in 32 bytes (24 of the original data plus the Q and P parity bytes). An additional byte of subcode (tracking) information is then added, resulting in 33 bytes total for each frame. Note that the P and Q parity bytes are not related to the P and Q subcodes mentioned earlier.

To minimize the effects of a scratch or physical defect that would damage adjacent frames, several interleaves are added before the frames are actually written. Parts of 109 frames are cross-interleaved (stored in different frames and sectors) using delay lines. This scrambling decreases the likelihood of a scratch or defect affecting adjacent data because the data is actually written out of sequence.

With audio CDs and CD-ROMs, the CIRC scheme can correct errors up to 3,874 bits long (which would be 2.6mm in track length). In addition, for audio CDs, only the CIRC can also conceal (through interpolation) errors up to 13,282 bits long (8.9mm in track length). Interpolation is the process in which the data is estimated or averaged to restore what is missing. That would of course be unacceptable on a CD-ROM data disc, so this applies only to audio discs. The Red Book CD standard defines the *block error rate (BLER)* as the number of frames (98 per sector) per second that have any bad bits (averaged over 10 seconds) and requires that this be less than 220. This allows a maximum of up to about 3% of the frames to have errors, and yet the disc will still be functional.

An additional layer of error detection and correction circuitry is the key difference between audio CD players and CD-ROM drives. Audio CDs convert the digital information stored on the disc into analog signals for a stereo amplifier to process. In this scheme, some imprecision is acceptable because it would be virtually impossible to hear in the music. CD-ROMs, however, can't tolerate any imprecision. Each bit of data must be read accurately. For this reason, CD-ROM discs have a great deal of additional ECC information written to the disc along with the actual stored information. The ECC can detect and correct most minor errors, improving the reliability and precision to levels that are acceptable for data storage.

In the case of an audio CD, missing data can be interpolated—that is, the information follows a predictable pattern that enables the drive to guess the missing values. For example, if three values are stored on an audio disc, say 10, 13, and 20 appearing in a series, and the middle value is missing—because of damage or dirt on the CD's surface—you could interpolate a middle value of 15, which is midway between 10 and 20. Although this might not be exactly correct, in the case of audio recording, it will not be noticeable to the listener. If those same three values appear on a CD-ROM in an executable program, there is no way to guess at the correct value for the middle sample. Interpolation can't work because executable program instructions or data must be exact; otherwise, the program will crash or improperly read data needed for a calculation. Using the previous example with a CD-ROM running an executable program, to guess 15 is not merely slightly off, it is completely wrong.

In a CD-ROM on which data is stored instead of audio information, additional information is added to each sector to detect and correct errors as well as to identify the location of data sectors more accurately. To accomplish this, 304 bytes are taken from the 2,352 that originally were used for audio data and are instead used for sync (synchronizing bits), ID (identification bits), ECC, and EDC information. This leaves 2,048 bytes for actual user data in each sector. Just as when reading an audio CD, on a 1x (standard speed) CD-ROM, sectors are read at a constant speed of 75 per second. This results in a standard CD-ROM transfer rate of $2,048 \times 75 = 153,600$ bytes per second, which is expressed as either 153.6KB/sec or 150KiB/sec.

CD Capacity

Because a typical disc can hold a maximum of 74 minutes of data, and each second contains 75 blocks of 2,048 bytes each, you can calculate the absolute maximum storage capacity of a CD-ROM at 681,984,000 bytes—rounded as 682MB (megabytes) or 650MiB (mebibytes). Table 13.3 shows the structure and layout of each sector on a CD-ROM on which data is stored.

Table 13.3   CD-ROM Sector Information and Capacity

Each Data Sector (Mode 1):	74-minute	80-minute
Q+P parity bytes	784	784
Subcode bytes	98	98
Sync bytes	12	12
Header bytes	8	8
ECC/EDC bytes	284	284
Data bytes	2,048	2,048
Bytes/sector RAW (unencoded)	3,234	3,234
Actual CD-ROM Data Capacity:		
B	681,984,000	737,280,000
KiB	666,000	720,000
KB	681,984	737,280
MiB	650.39	703.13
MB	681.98	737.28

B = Byte (8 bits)

KB = Kilobyte (1,000 bytes)

KiB = Kibibyte (1,024 bytes)

MB = Megabyte (1,000,000 bytes)

MiB = Mebibyte (1,048,576 bytes)

ECC = Error correction code

EDC = Error detection code

This information assumes the data is stored in Mode 1 format, which is used on virtually all data discs. You can learn more about the Mode 1/Mode 2 formats in the section on the Yellow Book and XA standards later in this chapter.

With data sectors, you can see that out of 3,234 actual bytes per sector, only 2,048 are actual CD-ROM user data. Most of the 1,186 other bytes are used for the intensive error detection and correction schemes to ensure error-free performance.

Data Encoding on the Disc

The final part of how data is actually written to the CD is very interesting. After all 98 frames are composed for a sector (whether audio or data), the information is then run through a final encoding process called EFM (eight to fourteen modulation). This scheme takes each byte (8 bits) and converts it into a 14-bit value for storage. The 14-bit conversion codes are designed so that there are never less than 2 or more than 10 adjacent 0 bits. This is a form of Run Length Limited (RLL) encoding called RLL 2,10 (RLL x,y where x = the minimum and y = the maximum run of 0s). This is designed to prevent long strings of 0s, which could more easily be misread, as well as to limit the minimum and maximum frequency of transitions actually placed on the recording media. With as few as 2 or as many as 10 0 bits separating 1 bits in the recording, the minimum distance between 1s is three bit time intervals (usually refered to as 3T) and the maximum spacing between 1s is 11 time intervals (11T).

Because some of the EFM codes start and end with a 1 or more than five 0s, three additional bits called *merge bits* are added between each 14-bit EFM value written to the disc. The merge bits usually are 0s but might contain a 1 if necessary to break a long string of adjacent 0s formed by the adjacent 14-bit EFM values. In addition to the now 17-bits created for each byte (EFM plus merge bits), a 24-bit sync word (plus 3 more merge bits) is added to the beginning of each frame. This results in a total of 588 bits (73.5 bytes) actually being stored on the disc for each frame. Multiply this for 98 frames per sector and you have 7,203 bytes actually being stored on the disc to represent each sector. A 74-minute disc, therefore, really has something like 2.4GB of actual data being written, which after being fully decoded and stripped of error correcting codes and other information, results in about 682MB (650MiB) of actual user data.

The calculations for EFM encoded frames and sectors are shown in Table 13.4.

Table 13.4   EFM Encoded Data Calculations

EFM-Encoded Frames:	74-minute	80-minute
Sync word bits	24	24
Subcode bits	14	14
Data bits	336	336
Q+P parity bits	112	112
Merge bits	102	102
EFM bits per frame	588	588
EFM Encoded Sectors:		
EFM bits per sector	57,624	57,624
EFM bytes per sector	7,203	7,203
Total EFM data on disc (MB)	2,399	2,593

B = Byte (8 bits)

KB = Kilobyte (1,000 bytes)

KiB = Kibibyte (1,024 bytes)

MB = Megabyte (1,000,000 bytes)

MiB = Mebibyte (1,048,576 bytes)

EFM = Eight to fourteen modulation

To put this into perspective, see Table 13.5 for an example of what familar data would actually look like when written to a CD. As an example, I'll use the letters "N" and "O" as they would be written on the disk. Here are the computer representations of these letters.

Table 13.5   How Data Is Written to a CD

Character	"N"	"O"
ASCII decimal code	78	79
ASCII hexadecimal code	4E	4F
ASCII binary code	01001110	01001111
EFM code	00010001000100	00100001000100

ASCII = American Standard Code for Information Interchange

EFM = Eight to fourteen modulation

Figure 13.5 shows how this data would look when actually written to a CD.

Figure 13.5   EFM data encoding on a CD.

The edges of the pits are translated into the binary 1 bits. As you can see, each 14-bit grouping is used to represent a byte of actual EFM encoded data on the disc, and each 14-bit EFM code is separated by three merge bits (all 0s in this example). The three pits produced by this example are 4T (4 transitions), 8T, and 4T long. The string of 1s and 0s on the top of the figure represent how the actual data would be read; note that a 1 is read wherever a pit-to-land transition occurs. It is interesting to note that this drawing is actually to scale, meaning the pits (raised bumps) would be about that long and wide relative to each other. If you could use a microscope to view the disc, this is what the word "NO" would look like as actually recorded.

CD Drive Speed

When a drive seeks out a specific data sector or musical track on the disc, it looks up the address of the data from a table of contents contained in the lead-in area and positions itself near the beginning of this data across the spiral, waiting for the right string of bits to flow past the laser beam.

Because CDs originally were designed to record audio, the speed at which the drive reads the data had to be constant. To maintain this constant flow, CD-ROM data is recorded using a technique called *constant linear velocity (CLV)*. This means that the track (and thus the data) is always moving past the read laser at the same speed, which originally was defined as 1.3 meters per second. Because the track is a spiral that is wound more tightly near the center of the disc, the disc must spin at various rates to maintain the same track linear speed. In other words, to maintain a CLV, the disk must spin more quickly when reading the inner track area and more slowly when reading the outer track area. The speed of rotation in a 1x drive (1.3 meters per second is considered 1x speed) varies from 540rpm when reading the start (inner part) of the track down to 212rpm when reading the end (outer part) of the track.

In the quest for greater performance, drive manufacturers began increasing the speeds of their drives by making them spin more quickly. A drive that spins twice as fast was called a 2x drive, one that spins four times faster was called 4x, and so on. This was fine until about the 12x point, where drives were spinning discs at rates from 2,568rpm to 5,959rpm to maintain a constant data rate. At higher speeds than this, it became difficult to build motors that could change speeds (spin up or down) as quickly as necessary when data was read from different parts of the disc. Because of this, most drives rated faster than 12x spin the disc at a fixed rotational, rather than linear speed. This is termed *constant angular velocity (CAV)* because the angular velocity (or rotational speed) is what remains a constant.

CAV drives are also generally quieter than CLV drives because the motors don't have to try to accelerate or decelerate as quickly. A drive (such as most rewritables) that combines CLV and CAV technologies is referred to as *Partial-CAV* or *P-CAV*. Most writable drives, for example, function in CLV mode when burning the disc and in CAV mode when reading. Table 13.6 compares CLV and CAV.

Table 13.6 CLV Versus CAV Technology Quick Reference

	CLV (Constant Linear Velocity)	CAV (Constant Angular Velocity)
Speed of CD rotation:	Varies with data position on CD— faster on inner tracks than on outer tracks	Constant
Data transfer rate:	Constant	Varies with data position on CD— faster on outer tracks than on inner tracks
Noise level:	Higher	Lower

CD-ROM drives have been available in speeds from 1x up to 56x and beyond. Most nonrewritable drives up to 12x were CLV; most drives from 16x and up are CAV. With CAV drives, the track data is moving past the read laser at various speeds, depending on where the data is physically located on the CD (near the inner or outer part of the track). This also means that CAV drives read the data at the edge of the disk more quickly than data near the center. This allowed for some misleading

Table 13.7 CD-ROM Drive Speeds and Transfer Rates

Column 1	Column 2	Column 3	Column 4	Column 5	Column 6
Advertised CD-ROM Speed (Max. if CAV)	Time to Read 74-minute CD if CLV	Time to Read 80-minute CD if CLV	Transfer Rate (Bytes/sec) (Max. if CAV)	Actual CD-ROM Speed Minimum if CAV	Minimum Transfer Rate if CAV (Bytes/sec)
1x	74.0	80.0	153,600	0.4x	61,440
2x	37.0	40.0	307,200	0.9x	138,240
4x	18.5	20.0	614,400	1.7x	261,120
6x	12.3	13.3	921,600	2.6x	399,360
8x	9.3	10.0	1,228,800	3.4x	522,240
10x	7.4	8.0	1,536,000	4.3x	660,480
12x	6.2	6.7	1,843,200	5.2x	798,720
16x	4.6	5.0	2,457,600	6.9x	1,059,840
20x	3.7	4.0	3,072,000	8.6x	1,320,960
24x	3.1	3.3	3,686,400	10.3x	1,582,080
32x	2.3	2.5	4,915,200	13.8x	2,119,680
40x	1.9	2.0	6,144,000	17.2x	2,641,920
48x	1.5	1.7	7,372,800	20.7x	3,179,520
50x	1.5	1.6	7,680,000	21.6x	3,317,760
52x	1.4	1.5	7,987,200	22.4x	3,440,640
56x	1.3	1.4	8,601,600	24.1x	3,701,760

advertising when these drives first came out. For example, a 12x CLV drive reads data at 1.84MB/sec no matter where that data is on the disc. On the other hand, a 16x CAV drive reads data at speeds up to 16x (2.46MB/sec) on the outer part of the disc, but it also reads at a much lower speed of only 6.9x (1.06MB/sec) when reading the inner part of the disc. On average, this would be only 11.5x, or about 1.76MB/sec. The average is actually overly optimistic because discs are read from the inside (slower part) out, and an average would relate only to reading completely full discs. The real-world average could be much less than that.

What this all means is that the 12x CLV drive would be noticeably faster than the 16x drive, and faster than even a 20x drive! Remember that all advertised speeds on CAV drives are only the maximum transfer speed the drive can achieve, and it can achieve that only when reading the very end part of the disc.

Table 13.7 contains data showing CD-ROM drive speeds along with transfer rates and other interesting data.

Column 7	Column 8	Column 9	Column 10	Column 11	Column 12
Average CD-ROM Speed if CAV	Average Transfer Rate if CAV (Bytes/sec)	Maximum Linear Speed (m/sec)	Maximum Linear Speed (mph)	Speed Min. if CLV Max. if CAV (rpm)	Rotational Speed Max. if CLV (rpm)
0.7x	107,520	1.3	2.9	214	497
1.5x	222,720	2.6	5.8	428	993
2.9x	437,760	5.2	11.6	856	1,986
4.3x	660,480	7.8	17.4	1,284	2,979
5.7x	875,520	10.4	23.3	1,712	3,973
7.2x	1,098,240	13.0	29.1	2,140	4,966
8.6x	1,320,960	15.6	34.9	2,568	5,959
11.5x	1,758,720	20.8	46.5	3,425	7,945
14.3x	2,196,480	26.0	58.2	4,281	9,931
17.2x	2,634,240	31.2	69.8	5,137	11,918
22.9x	3,517,440	41.6	93.1	6,849	15,890
28.6x	4,392,960	52.0	116.3	8,561	19,863
34.4x	5,276,160	62.4	139.6	10,274	23,835
35.8x	5,498,880	65.0	145.4	10,702	24,828
37.2x	5,713,920	67.6	151.2	11,130	25,821
40.1x	6,151,680	72.8	162.8	11,986	27,808

Each of the columns in Table 13.7 contains interesting information, explained here:

- *Column 1.* Indicates the advertised drive speed. This is a constant speed if the drive is CLV (most 12x and lower) or a maximum speed only if CAV.

- *Columns 2 and 3.* Indicate how long it would take to read a full disc if the drive was CLV. For CAV drives, those figures would be longer because the average read speed is less than the advertised speed. The fourth column indicates the data transfer rate, which for CAV drives would be a maximum figure only when reading the end of a disc.

- *Columns 3–6.* Indicate the actual minimum "x" speed for CAV drives, along with the minimum transfer speed (when reading the start of any disc) and an optimistic average speed (true only when reading a full disc; otherwise, it would be even lower) in both "x" and byte-per-second formats.

- *Columns 7–8.* Indicate the maximum linear speeds the drive will attain, in both meters per second and miles per hour. CLV drives maintain those speeds everywhere on the disc, whereas CAV drives reach those speeds only on the outer part of a disc.

- *Columns 9–12.* Indicate the rotational speeds of a drive. The first of those shows how fast the disc spins when reading the start of a disc; this would apply to either CAV or CLV drives. For CAV drives, that figure is constant no matter where on the disc it is reading. The last column shows the maximum rotational speed if the drive were a CLV type. Because most drives over 12x are CAV, those figures are mostly theoretical for the 16x and faster drives.

Vibration problems can cause high-speed drives to drop to lower speeds to enable reliable reading of CD-ROMs. Your CD-ROM can become unbalanced, for example, if you apply a small paper label to its surface to identify the CD or affix its serial number or code for easy reinstallation. For this reason, many of the faster CD and DVD drives come with autobalancing or vibration-control mechanisms to overcome these problems. The only drawback is that if they detect a vibration, they slow down the disc, thereby reducing the transfer rate performance. .

TrueX Technology

Drives that are 16x or faster are usually CAV drives. Even with CAV, at these speeds the rotational speed of the disc is nearly 12,000rpm and the data is moving at nearly 163 miles per hour past the laser on the outer part of the track! Rather than try to spin discs even faster for higher speeds, a company called Zen Research has developed a technology they call TrueX, (also called Multibeam), which uses multiple laser beams to achieve constant high transfer rates without the limitations of CAV. Currently, this technology is licensed by several companies, although Kenwood has been the primary promotor and manufacturer of TrueX drives and has released drives in 42x, 52x, 62x, and 72x models, which have benchmarked as the fastest CD-ROM drives available.

TrueX drives use a diffraction grating to split a single beam into seven beams reading seven tracks simultaneously to improve the transfer rate while maintaining a slower rotational speed that reduces noise and vibration. Drives with TrueX technology are the fastest CD-ROM drives on the market, capable of sustaining near-CLV performance at high speeds consistently no matter where they are reading on the disc.

The net effect is that the reading speed is consistently higher than equivelant speed CAV drives, and yet the TrueX drives spin at a slower speed. For example, a 52x CAV drive performs from about 22x at the start of a disk to 52x at the end, whereas a 52x TrueX drive performs at about 45x at the start of a disc to 52x at the end. This results in a much higher average performance that is nearly consistent with CLV drives.

One drawback is that this technology is useful only for reading (and not writing). This means that for reading information, TrueX CD-ROM drives are the fastest CD-ROM drives on the market.

Compact Disc and Drive Formats

After Philips and Sony had created the Red Book CD-DA format discussed earlier in the chapter, they began work on other format standards that would allow CDs to store computer files, data, and even video and photos. These standards control how the data is formatted so that the drive can read it, and additional file format standards can then control how the software and drivers on your PC can be designed to understand and interpret the data properly. Note that the physical format and storage of data on the disc as defined in the Red Book was adopted by all subsequent CD standards. This refers to the encoding and basic levels of error correction provided by CD-DA discs. What the other "books" specify is primarily how the 2,352 bytes in each sector are to be handled, what type of data can be stored, how it should be formatted, and more.

All the official CD standard books and related documents can be purchased from Philips for $100–$150 each. See the Philips licensing site at `http://www.licensing.philips.com` for more information.

Table 13.8 describes the various standard CD formats.

Table 13.8   Compact Disc Formats

Format	Name	Introduced	Notes
Red Book	CD-DA (compact disc digital audio)	1980 - by Philips and Sony	The original CD audio standard on which all subsequent CD standards are based.
Yellow Book	CD-ROM (compact disc read-only memory)	1983 - by Philips and Sony	Specifies additional ECC and EDC for data in several sector formats, including Mode 1 and Mode 2.
Green Book	CD-i (compact disc-interactive)	1986 - by Philips and Sony	Specifies an interactive audio/video standard for nonPC-dedicated player hardware (now mostly obsolete) and discs used for interactive presentations. Defines Mode 2, Form 1 and Mode 2, Form 2 sector formats along with interleaved MPEG-1 video and ADPCM audio.
CD-ROM XA	CD-ROM XA (extended architecture)	1989 - by Philips, Sony, and Microsoft	Combines Yellow Book and CD-i to bring CD-i audio and video capabilities to PCs.
Orange Book	CD-R (recordable) and CD-RW (rewritable)	1989 - by Philips and Sony (Part I/II); 1996 - by Philips and Sony (Part III)	Defines single session, multisession, and packet writing on recordable discs. Part I—CD-MO (magneto-optical, withdrawn). Part II—CD-R (recordable). Part III—CD-RW (rewritable).
Photo-CD	CD-P	1990 - by Philips and Kodak	Combines CD-ROM XA with CD-R multisession capability in a standard for photo storage on CD-R discs.

Table 13.8 **Continued**

Format	Name	Introduced	Notes
White Book	Video CD	1993 - by Philips, JVC, Matsushita, and Sony	Based on CD-i and CD-ROM XA. It stores up to 74 minutes of MPEG-1 video and ADPCM digital audio data.
Blue Book	CD EXTRA (formerly CD-Plus or enhanced music)	1995 - by Philips and Sony	Multisession format for stamped discs; used by musical artists to incorporate videos, liner notes, and other information on audio CDs.

Red Book—CD-DA

The Red Book introduced by Philips and Sony in 1980 is the father of all compact-disc specifications because all other "books" or formats are based on the original CD-DA Red Book format. For more information on the Red Book format, see the section "CDs: A Brief History" at the beginning of this chapter.

The Red Book specification includes the main parameters, audio specification, disc specification, optical stylus, modulation system, error correction system, and the control and display system. The latest revision of the Red Book is dated May 1999.

Yellow Book—CD-ROM

The Yellow Book was first published by Philips, Sony, and Microsoft in 1983 and has been revised and amended several times since. The Yellow Book standard took the physical format of the original CD-DA, or Red Book, standard and added another layer of error detection and correction to enable data to be stored reliably. It also added additional synchronization and header information to enable sectors to be more accurately located. Yellow Book specifies two types of sectoring—called Mode 1 (with error correction) and Mode 2—which offer different levels of error detection and correction schemes. Some data (computer files, for example) can't tolerate errors. However, other data, such as a video image or sound, can tolerate minor errors. By using a mode with less error correction information, more data can be stored, but with the possibility of uncorrected errors.

In 1989, the Yellow Book was issued as an international standard by the ISO as *ISO/IEC 10149, Data Interchange on Read-Only 120mm Optical Discs (CD-ROM)*. The latest version of the Yellow Book is dated May 1999.

Green Book—CD-i

The Green Book was published by Philips and Sony in 1986. CD-i is much more than just a disc format; instead it is a complete specification for an entire interactive system consisting of custom hardware (players) designed to be connected to a television, software designed to deliver video and audio together with user interactivity in real time, and the media and format. A CD-i player is actually a dedicated computer usually running a variant on the Motorola 68000 processor line, as well as a customized version of the Microware OS/9 Real Time Operating System.

CD-i enables both audio and video to share a disc and enables the information to be interleaved so as to maintain syncronization between the pictures and sounds. To fit both audio and video in the same space originally designed for just audio, compression was performed. The video was compressed using the Moving Picture Experts Group-1 (MPEG-1) compression standard, whereas the audio was compressed with adaptive differential pulse code modulation (ADPCM). ADPCM is an audio encoding algorithm that takes about half the space for the same quality of standard PCM, and even less if quality is reduced by lowering the sampling rate or bits per sample. Using ADPCM, up to 8 hours of stereo or 16 hours of mono sound can fit on one CD. The "differential" part of ADPCM refers to the fact that it records the differences between one signal and the next (using only 4-bit numbers), which reduces the total amount of data involved. ADPCM audio can be interleaved with video in CD-i (and CD-ROM XA) applications.

The Yellow Book defines two CD-ROM sector structures, called Mode 1 and Mode 2. The Green Book (CD-i) refines the Mode 2 sector definition by adding two forms, called Mode 2, Form 1 and Mode 2, Form 2. The Mode 2, Form 1 sector definition uses ECC and allows for 2,048 bytes of data storage like the Yellow Book Mode 1 sectors, but it rearranged things slightly to use the 8 formerly unused (blank or 0) bytes as a subheader containing additional information about the sector. The Mode 2, Form 2 definition drops the ECC and allows 2,324 bytes for data. Without the ECC, only video or audio information should be stored in Form 2 sectors because that type of information can tolerate minor errors.

Media or titles available for CD-i include all manner of educational and training applications, games, encyclopedias, karaoke, and movies. Note that CD-i discs can't be "played" on PCs. In fact, because the files are in an OS/9 file format, your PC won't even be capable of seeing the files on the disc! Even so, drivers have been written that can be installed and will enable viewing the files, and one enterprising individual has even written a CD-i emulator called CD-iCE that emulates a CD-i player thus enabling CD-i applications to be run. You can find out more about the CD-iCE emulator at `http://www.emuhq.com/cdi`.

Today. the CD-i format is largely obsolete. The last revision of the standard was produced in May 1994. Philips sold off its entire consumer CD-i catalogue to Infogrames Multimedia in 1998, which now owns the rights for virtually all consumer CD-i titles ever produced. Philips made a final run of CD-i players in 1999, and it is doubtful any new ones will ever be produced. The legacy of CD-i lives on in the other formats that use specifications originally devised for CD-i, such as the Mode 2, Form 1 and Form 2 sector structures later used in CD-XA and the MPEG-1 video format later used in the White Book (CD-Video).

CD-ROM XA

CD-ROM XA originally was defined in 1989 by Philips, Sony, and Microsoft as a supplement to the Yellow Book. CD-ROM XA brings some of the features originally defined in the Green Book (CD-i) to the Yellow Book (CD-ROM) standard, especially for multimedia use. CD-ROM XA adds three main features to the Yellow Book standard. The first consists of the CD-i–enhanced sector definitions (called forms) for the Mode 2 sectors, and the second is a capability called interleaving (mixing audio and video information). The third is ADPCM for compressed audio. The latest version of the CD-ROM XA standard was released in May 1991.

Interleaving

CD-ROM XA drives can employ a technique known as interleaving. The specification calls for the capability to encode on disc whether the data directly following an identification mark is graphics, sound, or text. Graphics can include standard graphics pictures, animation, or full-motion video. In addition, these blocks can be interleaved, or interspersed, with each other. For example, a frame of video can start a track followed by a segment of audio, which would accompany the video, followed by yet another frame of video. The drive picks up the audio and video sequentially, buffering the information in memory and then sending it along to the PC for synchronization.

In short, the data is read off the disc in alternating pieces and then synchronized at playback so that the result is a simultaneous presentation of the data. Without interleaving, the drive would have to read and buffer the entire video track before it could read the audio track and synchronize the two for playback.

Sector Modes and Forms

Mode 1 is the standard Yellow Book CD sector format with ECC and EDC to enable error-free operation. Each Mode 1 sector is broken down as shown in Tables 13.9 and 13.10.

Table 13.9   Yellow Book Mode 1 Sector Format Breakdown

Yellow Book (CD-ROM) Sectors (Mode 1):

Q+P parity bytes	784
Subcode bytes	98
Sync bytes	12
Header bytes	4
Data bytes	2,048
EDC bytes	4
Blank (0) bytes	8
ECC bytes	276
Bytes/sector RAW (unencoded)	3,234

Table 13.10   Yellow Book (CD-ROM) Mode 1 Sector Format

Sync	Header	User Data	EDC	Blank	ECC
12	4	2,048	4	8	276

Mode 2 was defined as a sector without any ECC or EDC in the original Yellow Book. Unfortunately, Mode 1 (which had ECC and EDC) couldn't be mixed with Mode 2 sectors on the same track (program or song). To enable data with and without error detection and correction in a single track, new sector format subsets for Mode 2 sectors were added in the Green Book (CD-i) and subsequently adopted in the CD-ROM XA extensions. This enabled information that would not tolerate errors (such as programs or computer data) to be interleaved or mixed within the same track with information that would tolerate errors (such as audio or video data). These variations on Mode 2 include Form 1 and Form 2 sectors. Each Mode 2, Form 1 sector is broken down as shown in Tables 13.11, 13.12, 13.13, and 13.14.

Table 13.11   Green Book Mode 1 Sector Format Breakdown

Green Book/CD-ROM XA Sectors (Mode 2, Form 1):

Q+P parity bytes	784
Subcode bytes	98
Sync bytes	12
Header bytes	4
Subheader bytes	8
Data bytes	2,048
EDC bytes	4
ECC bytes	276
Bytes/sector RAW (unencoded)	3,234

Table 13.12   Green Book/CD-ROM XA (Yellow Book Extensions) Mode 2, Form 1 Sector Format

Sync	Header	Subheader	User Data	EDC	ECC
12	4	8	2,048 bytes	4	276

Table 13.13   Green Book Mode 2 Sector Format Breakdown

Green Book/CD-ROM XA Sectors (Mode 2, Form 2):

Q+P parity bytes	784
Subcode bytes	98
Sync bytes	12
Header bytes	4
Subheader bytes	8
Data bytes	2,324
EDC bytes	4
Bytes/sector RAW (unencoded)	3,234

Table 13.14   Green Book/CD-ROM XA (Yellow Book Extensions) Mode 2, Form 2 Sector Format

Sync	Header	Subheader	User Data	EDC
12	4	8	2,324 bytes	4

Both Mode 2 sector formats add a subheader field that identifies the type of information (such as audio or video) carried in the user data field. The Form 2 sector lacks the ECC of the Form 1 sector and increases the size of the user data field instead. This type of sector is for storing audio or video data that can tolerate errors.

Because they don't use any third-level error correction, CD-ROMs that use the Mode 2, Form 2 sector format (such as MPEG video CDs) can hold more user information than other CD-ROM types in the same number of sectors, and as a result also have a higher data transfer rate of 174.3KB/sec instead of the standard 153.6KB/sec. Note that Form 2 sectors are never used to store data or program files because errors can't be tolerated in that type of information. In that case, the Mode 2, Form 1 sector format would be used.

For a drive to be truly XA compatible, the audio data written in Form 2 sectors on the disc as audio must be ADPCM audio—specially compressed and encoded audio. This requires that the drive or the SCSI controller have a signal processor chip that can decompress the audio during the synchronization process.

Some earlier drives were called XA-ready, which meant they were capable of Mode 2, Form 1 and Form 2 reading but did not incorporate the ADPCM chip. This is not a signficant shortcoming, however, because only certain multimedia titles use the ADPM encoding (with interleaved audio and video). The main benefit XA brought to the table was the additional sector modes and forms taken from the Green Book.

Orange Book

The Orange Book defines the standards for recordable CDs and originally was announced in 1989 by Philips and Sony. The Orange Book comes in three parts: Part I describes a format called CD-MO (magneto-optical), which was to be a rewritable format but was withdrawn before any products really came to market; Part II (1989) describes CD-R; and Part III (1996) describes CD-RW. Note that originally, CD-R was refered to as CD-WO (write-once), and CD-RW originally was called CD-E (erasable).

The Orange Book Part II CD-R design is known as a WORM (write once read mostly) format. After a portion of a CD-R disc is recorded, it can't be overwritten or reused. Recorded CD-R discs are Red Book and Yellow Book compatible, which means they are readable on conventional CD-DA or CD-ROM drives. The CD-R definition in the Orange Book Part II is divided into two volumes. Volume 1 defines recording speeds of 1x, 2x, and 4x the standard CD speed; the last revision, dated December 1998, is 3.1. Volume 2 defines recording speeds up to 16x the standard CD speed, and the last version released, 0.9, is dated December 2000.

The Orange Book Part III describes CD-RW. As the name implies, CD-RW enables you to erase and overwrite information in addition to reading and writing. The Orange Book Part III CD-RW definition was broken into two volumes. Volume 1 defines recording speeds of 1x, 2x, and 4x times the standard CD speed; the latest version, 2.0, is dated August 1998. Volume 2 defines recording speeds from 4x to 10x standard CD speed, and is sometimes refered to as high-speed CD-RW; the latest version, 1.0, is dated May 2000.

Besides the capability to record on CDs, the most important features instituted in the Orange Book specification is the capability to do multisession recording.

Multisession Recording

Before the Orange Book specification, CDs had to be written as a single session. A *session* is defined as a lead-in, followed by one or more tracks of data (or audio), followed by a lead-out. The lead-in takes up 4,500 sectors on the disc (1 minute if measured in time or about 9.2MB worth of data). The lead-in also indicates whether the disc is multisession, and what the next writable address on the disc is (if the disc isn't closed). The first lead-out on a disc (or the only one if it is a single session or Disk At Once recording) is 6,750 sectors long (1.5 minutes if measured in time or about 13.8MB worth of data). If the disc is a multisession disc, any subsequent lead-outs are 2,250 sectors long (0.5 minutes in time or about 4.6MB worth of data).

A multisession CD has multiple sessions, with each individual session complete from lead-in to lead-out. The mandatory lead-in and lead-out for each session does waste space on the disc. In fact, 48 sessions would literally use up all of a 74-minute disc even with no data recorded in each session! Therefore, the practical limit for the number of sessions you can record on a disc would be much less than that.

CD-DA and older CD-ROM drives couldn't read more than one session on a disc, so that is the way most pressed CDs are recorded. The Orange Book allows multiple sessions on a single disc. To allow this, the Orange Book defines three main methods or modes of recording:

- Disk-at-Once (DAO)
- Track-at-Once (TAO)
- Packet writing

Disc-at-Once

Disc-at-Once means pretty much what it says: It is a single- session method of writing CDs in which the lead-in, data tracks, and lead-out are written in a single operation without ever turning off the writing laser, and the disc is closed. A disc is considered closed when the last (or only) lead-in is fully written and the next usable address on the disc is not recorded in that lead-in. In that case, the CD recorder is incapable of writing any further data on the disc. Note that it is not necessary to close a disc to read it in a normal CD-ROM drive, although if you were submitting a disc to a CD duplicating company for replication, most require that it be closed.

Track-at-Once

Multisession discs can be recorded in either Track-at-Once (TAO) or Packet writing mode. In Track-at-Once recording, each track can be individually written (laser turned on and off) within a session, until the session is closed. Closing a session is the act of writing the lead-out for that session, which means no more tracks can be added to that session. If the disc is closed at the same time, no further sessions can be added either.

The tracks recorded in TAO mode are divided by gaps of normally 2 seconds. Each track written has 150 sectors of overhead for run-in, run-out, pre-gap, and linking. A CD-R/RW drive can read the tracks even if the session is not closed, but to read them in a CD-DA or CD-ROM drive, the session must be closed. If you intend to write more sessions to the disc, you can close the session and not close the disc. At that point, you could start another session of recording to add more tracks to the disc. The main thing to remember is that each session must be closed (lead-out written) before another session can be written or before a normal CD-DA or CD-ROM drive can read the tracks in the session.

Packet Writing

Packetwriting is a method whereby multiple writes are allowed within a track, thus reducing the overhead and wasted space on a disc. Each packet uses 4 sectors for run-in, 2 for run-out, and 1 for linking. Packets can be of fixed or variable length, but most drives and packet-writing software uses a fixed length because it is much easier and more efficient to deal with file systems that way.

With packet writing, you normally use the Universal Disk Format (UDF) file system, which enables the CD to be treated essentially like a big floppy drive. That is, you can literally drag and drop files to it, use the copy command to copy files onto the disc, and so on. The packet-writing software and UDF file system manage everything. If the disc you are using for packet writing is a CD-R, every time a file is overwritten or deleted, the file seems to dissapear, but you don't get the space back on the disc. Instead the file system simply forgets about the file. If the disc is a CD-RW, the space is indeed reclaimed and the disc won't be full until you literally have more than the limit of active files stored there.

Unfortunately, Windows versions up through Windows 2000 don't support packet writing or the UDF file system directly, so drivers must be loaded. Fortunately, though, these typically are included with CD-R/RW drives. One of the most popular packet-writing programs is DirectCD from Roxio (Adaptec).

When you remove a packet-written disc from the drive, the packet-writing software first asks whether you want the files to be visible to normal CD-ROM drives. If you do then the session must be closed. Even if the session is closed, you can still write more to the disc later, but there is an overhead of wasted space every time you close a session. If you are going to read the disc in a CD-R/RW drive, you don't have to close the session because they will be capable of reading the files even if the session isn't closed.

PhotoCD

First announced back in 1990 but not available until 1992, PhotoCD is a standard for CD-R discs and drives to store photos. You simply drop off a roll of film at a participating Kodak developer, and they digitize and store the photos on a specially formatted CD-R disc called a PhotoCD, which you can then read on virtually any CD-ROM drive connected to a PC running the appropriate software. Originally, Kodak sold PhotoCD "players" designed to display the photos to a connected TV, but these have since been dropped in favor of simply using a PC with software to decode and display the photos.

Perhaps the main benefit PhotoCD has brought to the table is that it was the first CD format to use the Orange Book Part II (CD-R) specification with multisession recordings. Additionally, the data is recorded in CD-ROM XA Mode 2, Form 2 sectors so more photo information could be stored on the disc.

Using the PhotoCD software, you can view your photographs at any one of several resolutions and manipulate them using standard graphics software packages.

When you drop off your roll of film, the Kodak developers produce prints as they normally do. After prints are made, they scan the prints with ultra–high-resolution scanners. To give you an idea of the amount of information each scan carries, one color photograph can take 15MB–20MB of storage. The compressed, stored images are then encoded onto special writable CDs. The finished product is packaged and shipped back to your local developer for pickup. Some developers can do the scanning on-site.

PhotoCD Disc Types

The images on the disc are compressed and stored using Kodak's own PhotoYCC encoding format, which includes up to six resolutions for each image, as shown in Table 13.15. Kodak has defined several types of PhotoCD discs to accommodate the needs of various types of users. The PhotoCD Master disc is the standard consumer format and contains up to 100 photos in all the resolutions shown in the table except for base x64.

Table 13.15   PhotoCD Resolutions

Base	Resolution (pixels)	Description
/16	128×192	Thumbnail
/4	256×384	Thumbnail
x1	512×768	TV resolution
x4	1,024×1,536	HDTV resolution
x16	2,048×3,072	Print size
x64	4,096×6,144	Pro PhotoCD master only

The various resolutions supply you with images appropriate for various applications. If, for example, you want to include a PhotoCD image on a Web page, you would choose a low-resolution image. A professional photographer shooting photos for a print ad would want to use the highest resolution possible.

The Pro PhotoCD Master disc is intended for professional photographers using larger film formats, such as 70mm, 120mm, or 4×5 inch. This type of disc adds an even higher-resolution image (4,096×6,144 pixels) to those already furnished on the PhotoCD Master disc. Because of this added high-resolution image, this type of disc can hold anywhere from 25 to 100 images, depending on the film format.

The PhotoCD Portfolio disc is designed for interactive presentations that include sound and other multimedia content. The high-resolution images that take up the most space are not necessary here, so this type of disc can contain up to 700 images, depending on how much other content is included.

Multisession Photo CDs

One breakthrough of the PhotoCD concept is that each of the disc types is capable of containing multiple sessions. Because the average consumer wouldn't usually have enough film processed to fill an entire disc, you can bring back your partially filled CDs each time you have more film to develop. A new session is then added to your existing CD until the entire disc is filled. You pay less for the processing because a new CD is not necessary, and all your images are stored on a smaller number of discs.

Any XA-compliant or XA-ready CD-ROM drive can read the multiple sessions on a PhotoCD disc, and even if your drive is not multisession capable, it can still read the first session on the disc. If this is the case, you must purchase a new disc for each batch of film you process, but you can still take advantage of PhotoCD technology.

Kodak provides software that enables you to view the PhotoCD images on your PC and licenses a PhotoCD import filter to the manufacturers of many desktop publishing, image-editing, and paint programs. Therefore, you can modify your PhotoCD images using a program such as Adobe Photoshop and integrate them into documents for printing or electronic publication with a page layout program such as Adobe PageMaker.

Picture CD

Although Kodak still offers PhotoCD services, the high cost has led to limited popularity. Kodak now offers the simpler Picture CD and Picture Disk services. Unlike PhotoCD, these services use the industry-standard JPEG file format. Picture CD uses a CD-R, with images stored at a single medium-resolution scan of 1,024×1,536 pixels. This resolution is adequate for 4"×6" and 5"×7" prints. The less-expensive Picture Disk service stores images on a 1.44MB floppy disk at a resolution of 400×600, suitable for screensavers and slide shows.

The software provided with Picture CD enables the user to manipulate images with various automatic or semiautomatic operations, but unlike PhotoCD, the standard JPEG (JPG) file format used for storage enables any popular image-editing program to work with the images without conversion. Although the image quality of Picture CD isn't as high as with PhotoCD, the much lower price of the service should make it far more popular with amateur photographers.

White Book—Video CD

The White Book was introduced in 1993 by Philips, JVC, Matsushita, and Sony. It is based on the Green Book (CD-i) and CD-ROM XA standards and allows for storing up to 74 minutes of MPEG-1 video and ADPCM digital audio data on a single disc. The latest version was released in April 1995.

You can think of video CDs as a sort of poor man's DVD format, although the picture and sound quality is actually quite good—certainly better than VHS or most other videotape formats. You can play video CDs on virtually any PC with a CD-ROM drive using the free Windows Media Player (other media player applications can be used as well). They also can be played on most DVD players and even some game consoles, such as the Playstation (with the right options). Video CDs are an especially big hit with people who travel with laptop computers, and the prerecorded discs are much cheaper than DVD—many as little as $5.

Blue Book—CD EXTRA

Manufacturers of CD-DA media were looking for a standard method to combine both music and data on a single CD. The intention was for a user to be able to play only the audio tracks in a standard audio CD player while remaining unaware of the data track. However, a user with a PC or a dedicated combination audio/data player could access both the audio and data tracks on the same disc.

The fundamental problem with nonstandard mixed-mode CDs is that if or when an audio player tries to play the data track, the result is static that could conceivably damage speakers and possibly hearing if the volume level has been turned up. Various manufacturers originally addressed this problem in different ways, resulting in a number of confusing methods for creating these types of discs, some of which still allowed the data tracks to be accidentally "played" on an audio player.

In 1995, Philips and Sony developed the CD EXTRA specification, as defined in the Blue Book standard. CDs conforming to this specification usually are refered to as CD EXTRA (formerly called CD Plus or CD Enhanced Music) discs and use the multisession technology defined in the CD-ROM XA standard to separate the audio and data tracks. These are a form of stamped multisession disc. The audio portion of the disc can consist of up to 98 standard Red Book audio tracks, whereas the data track typically is composed of XA Mode 2 sectors and can contain video, song lyrics, still images, or other multimedia content. Such discs can be identified by the CD EXTRA logo, which is the standard CD-DA logo with a plus sign to the right. Often the logo or markings on the disc package are overlooked or somewhat obscure, and you might not know that an audio CD contains this extra data until you play it in a CD-ROM drive.

A CD EXTRA disc normally contains two sessions. Because audio CD players are only single-session capable, they play only the audio session and ignore the additional session containing the data. A CD-ROM drive in a PC, however, can see both sessions on the disc and access both the audio and data tracks.

Note

Many artists have released audio CDs in the CD EXTRA format that include things such as lyrics, video, artist bio, photos, and so on in data files on the disc. *Tidal* by Fiona Apple (released in 1996) was one of the first CD EXTRA discs from Sony Music. There have been many CD EXTRA releases since then. For examples of other CD EXTRA discs, including current releases, see `http://www.cdextra.com`.

CD-ROM File Systems

Manufacturers of early CD-ROM discs required their own custom software to read the discs. This is because the Yellow Book specification for CD-ROM details only how data sectors—rather than audio sectors—can be stored on a disc, and did not cover the file systems or deal with how data should be stored in files and how these should be formatted for use by PCs with different operating systems. Obviously, noninterchangeable file formats presented an obstacle to the industrywide compatiblity for CD-ROM applications.

In 1985–1986, several companies got together and published the High Sierra file format specification, which finally enabled CD-ROMs for PCs to be universally readable. That was the first industry-standard CD-ROM file system that made CD-ROMs universally usable in PCs. Today several file systems are used on CDs, including

- High Sierra
- ISO 9660 (based on High Sierra)
- Joliet
- UDF (Universal Disk Format)
- Mac HFS (Hierarchical File Format)
- Rock Ridge

Not all CD file system formats can be read by all operating systems. Table 13.17 shows the primary file systems used and which operating systems support them.

Table 13.16   CD File System Formats

CD File System	DOS/Win 3.1	Win 9x/Me	Win NT/2000	Mac OS
High Sierra	Yes	Yes	Yes	Yes
ISO 9660	Yes	Yes	Yes	Yes
Joliet	Yes[1]	Yes	Yes	Yes[1]
UDF	No	Yes[2]	Yes[2]	Yes[2]

1. *A short name, such as (SHORTN~1.TXT), is shown.*
2. *Only if a UDF driver is installed.*

Note

The Mac HFS and Rock Ridge file systems are not supported by PC operating systems such as DOS or Windows and therefore are not covered in depth here.

High Sierra

To make CD-ROM discs readable on all systems without having to develop custom file systems and drivers, it was in the best interests of all PC hardware and software manufacturers to resolve the CD-ROM file format standardization issue. In 1985, representatives from TMS, DEC, Microsoft, Hitachi, LaserData, Sony, Apple, Philips, 3M, Video Tools, Reference Technology, and Xebec met at what was then called the High Sierra Hotel and Casino in Lake Tahoe, Nevada, to create a common logical format and file structure for CD-ROMs. In 1986, they jointly published this standard as the "Working Paper for Information Processing: Volume and File Structure of CD-ROM Optical Discs for Information Exchange (1986)." This standard was subsequently referred to as the High Sierra format.

This agreement enabled all drives using the appropriate driver (such as MSCDEX.EXE supplied by Microsoft with DOS) to read all High Sierra format discs, opening the way for the mass production and acceptance of CD-ROM software publishing. Adoption of this standard also enabled disc publishers to provide cross-platform support for their software, easily manufacturing discs for DOS, Unix, and other operating system formats. Without this agreement, the maturation of the CD-ROM marketplace would have taken years longer and the production of CD-ROM–based information would have been stifled.

The High Sierra format was submitted to the International Organization for Standardization (ISO), and two years later (in 1988) and with several enhancements and changes it was republished as the ISO 9660 standard. ISO 9660 was not exactly the same as High Sierra, but all the drivers that would read High Sierra–formatted discs were quickly updated to handle both ISO 9660 and the original High Sierra format on which it was based.

For example, Microsoft wrote the MSCDEX.EXE (Microsoft CD-ROM extensions) driver in 1988 and licensed it to CD-ROM hardware and software vendors to include with their products. It wasn't until 1993 when MS-DOS 6.0 was released that MSCDEX was included with DOS as a standard feature. MSCDEX enables DOS to read ISO 9660–formatted (and High Sierra–formatted) discs. This driver works with the AT Attachment Packet Interface (ATAPI) or Advanced SCSI Programming Interface (ASPI) hardware-level device driver that comes with the drive. Microsoft built ISO 9660 and Joliet file system support directly into Windows 95 and later, with no additional drivers necessary.

ISO 9660

The ISO 9660 standard enabled full cross compatibility among different computer and operating systems. ISO 9660 was released in 1988 and was based on the work done by the High Sierra group.

Although based on High Sierra, ISO 9660 does have some differences and refinements. But any drivers that can read ISO 9660 also can read discs formatted in High Sierra. ISO 9660 has three levels of inter-change that dictate the features that can be used to ensure compatibility with different systems.

ISO 9660 Level 1 is the lowest common denominator of all CD file systems and is capable of being read by almost every computer platform, including Unix and Macintosh. The downside of this file system is that it is very limited with respect to filenames and directories. Level 1 interchange restric-tions include

- Only uppercase characters A–Z, numbers 0–9, and the underscore (_) are allowed in filenames.
- 8.3 characters maximum for the name.extension (based on DOS limits).
- Directory names are eight characters maximum (no extension allowed).
- Directories are limited to eight levels deep.
- Files must be contiguous.

Level 2 interchange rules have the same limitations as Level 1, except that the filename and extension can be up to 30 characters long (both added together, not including the . separator). Finally, Level 3 interchange rules are the same as Level 2 except that files don't have to be contiguous.

Note that Windows 95 and later versions enable you to use file and folder names up to 255 characters long, which can include spaces as well lowercase and many other characters not allowed in ISO 9660. To maintain backward compatiblity with DOS, Win95 and later associate a short 8.3 format filename as an alias for each file that has a longer name. These alias short names are created automatically by Windows and can be viewed in the Properties for each file or by using the DIR command at a comm-mand prompt. To create these alias names, Windows truncates the name to six (or fewer) characters followed by a tilde (~) and a number starting with 1 and truncates the extension to three characters. Other numbers are used in the first part if other files that would have the same alias when truncated already exist. For example, the filename This is a.test gets THISIS~1.TES as an alias.

This filename alias creation is independent of your CD drive, but it is important to know that if you create or write to a CD using the ISO 9660 format using Level 1 restrictions, the alias short names are used when recording files to the disc, meaning any long filenames will be lost in the process. In fact, even the alias short name will be modified because ISO 9660 Level 1 restrictions don't allow a tilde— that character is converted to an underscore in the names written to the CD.

The ISO 9660 data starts at 2 seconds and 16 sectors into the disc, which is also known as *logical sector 16 of track one*. For a multisession disc, the ISO 9660 data is present in the first data track of each ses-sion containing CD-ROM tracks. This data identifies the location of the volume area—where the actual data is stored. The system area also lists the directories in this volume as the volume table of contents (VTOC), with pointers or addresses to various named areas, as illustrated in Figure 13.6. A significant difference between the CD directory structure and that of a normal hard disk is that the CD's system area also contains direct addresses of the files within the subdirectories, allowing the CD to seek specific sector locations on the spiral data track. Because the CD data is all on one long spiral track, when speaking of tracks in the context of a CD, we're actually talking about sectors or segments of data along that spiral.

To put the ISO 9660 format in perspective, the disc layout is roughly analogous to that of a floppy disk. A floppy disk has a system track that not only identifies itself as a floppy disk and reveals its density and operating system, but also tells the computer how it's organized—into directories, which are made up of files.

Figure 13.6 A diagram of basic ISO 9660 file organizational format.

Joliet

Joliet is an extension of the ISO 9660 standard developed by Microsoft for use with Windows 95 and later. Joliet enables CDs to be recorded using filenames up to 64 characters long, including spaces and other characters from the Unicode international character set. Joliet also preserves an 8.3 alias for those programs that can't use the longer filenames.

In general, Joliet features the followig specifications:

- File or directory names can be up to 64 Unicode characters (128 bytes) in length.
- Directory names can have extensions.
- Directories can be deeper than eight levels.
- Multisession recording is inherently supported.

Due to backward-compatibility provisions, systems that don't support the Joliet extensions (such as older DOS systems) should still be capable of reading the disc. However, it will be interpreted as an ISO 9660 format using the short names instead.

Note

A bit of trivia: "Chicago" was the code name used by Microsoft for Windows 95. Joliet is the town outside of Chicago where Jake was locked up in the movie *The Blues Brothers*.

Universal Disk Format

UDF is a relatively new file system created by the Optical Storage Technology Association (OSTA) as an industry-standard format for use on optical media such as CD-ROM and DVD. UDF has several advantages over the ISO 9660 file system used by standard CD-ROMs but is most noted because it is designed to work with packet writing, a technique for writing small amounts of data to a CD-R/RW disc, treating it much like a standard magnetic drive.

The UDF file system allows long filenames up to 255 characters per name. There have been several versions of UDF, with most packet-writing software using UDF 1.5 or later. Packet-writing software such as DirectCD from Roxio writes in the UDF file system. Standard CD-ROM drives, drivers, or operating systems such as DOS can't read UDF formatted discs. Recordable drives can read them, but regular CD-ROM drives must conform to the MultiRead specification (see the section "MultiRead Specifications," later in this chapter) to be capable of reading UDF discs.

After you are sure that your drive can read UDF, you must check the OS. Most operating systems can't read UDF natively—the support has to be added via a driver. DOS can't read UDF at all; however, with Windows 95 and later, UDF-formatted discs can be read by installing a UDF driver. Normally such a driver is included with the software that is included with most CD-RW drives. If you don't have a UDF driver, you can download one for free from Roxio at http://www.roxio.com. The Roxio UDF Reader is included with DirectCD 3.0 and later. After the UDF driver is installed, you do not need to take any special steps to read a UDF-formatted disc. The driver will be in the background waiting for you to insert a UDF-formatted disc.

You can close a DirectCD for Windows disc to make it readable in a normal CD-ROM drive, which will convert the filenames to Joliet format, causing them to be truncated to 64 characters.

Macintosh HFS

HFS is the file system used by the Macintosh OS. HFS can also be used on CD-ROMs; however if that is done, they will not be readable on a PC. A hybrid disc can be produced with both Joliet and HFS or ISO 9660 and HFS file systems, and the disc would then be readable on both PCs and Macs. In that case, the system will see only the disc that is compatible, which is ISO 9660 or Joliet in the case of PCs.

Rock Ridge

The Rock Ridge Interchange Protocol (RRIP) was developed by an industry consortium called the Rock Ridge group. It was officially released in 1994 by the IEEE CD-ROM File System Format Working Group and specifies an extension to the ISO 9660 standard for CD-ROM that enables the recording of additional information to support Unix/POSIX file system features. Rock Ridge is not supported by DOS or Windows. However, because it is based on ISO 9660, the files are still readable on a PC and the RRIP extensions are simply ignored.

Note

An interesting bit of trivia is that the Rock Ridge name was taken from the fictional Western town in the movie *Blazing Saddles.*

DVD

DVD stands for digital versatile disc and in simplest terms is a high-capacity CD. In fact, every DVD-ROM drive *is* a CD-ROM drive; that is, they can read CDs as well as DVDs (discs). DVD uses the same optical technology as CD, with the main difference being higher density. The DVD standard dramatically increases the storage capacity of, and therefore the useful applications for, CD-ROM–sized discs. A CD-ROM can hold a maximum of about 737MB (80-minute disc) of data, which might sound like a lot but is simply not enough for many up-and-coming applications, especially where the use of video is concerned. DVD discs, on the other hand, can hold up to 4.7GB (single layer) or 8.5GB (dual layer) on a single side of the disc, which is more than 11 1/2 times greater than a CD. Double-sided DVD discs can hold up to twice that amount; although currently you must manually flip the disc over to read the other side.

Up to two layers of information can be recorded to DVD discs, with an initial storage capacity of 4.7GB of digital information on a single-sided, single-layer disc—a disk that is the same overall diameter and thickness of a current CD-ROM. With Moving Picture Experts Group–standard 2 (MPEG-2) compression, that's enough to contain approximately 133 minutes of video, which is enough for a full-length, full-screen, full-motion feature film—including three channels of CD-quality audio and four channels of subtitles. Using both layers, a single-sided disc could easily hold 240 minutes of video or more. This initial capacity is no coincidence; the creation of DVD was driven by the film industry, which has long sought a storage medium cheaper and more durable than videotape.

Note

It is important to know the difference between the DVD-Video and DVD-ROM standards. DVD-Video discs contain only video programs and are intended to be played in a DVD player, connected to a television and possibly an audio system. DVD-ROM is a data storage medium intended for use by PCs and other types of computers. The distinction is similar to that between an audio CD and a CD-ROM. Computers might be capable of playing audio CDs as well as CD-ROMs, but dedicated audio CD players can't use a CD-ROM's data tracks. Likewise, computer DVD drives can play DVD-video discs (with MPEG-2 decoding in either hardware or software), but DVD video players can't access data on a DVD-ROM.

The initial application for DVDs was as an upgrade for CDs as well as a replacement for prerecorded videotapes. DVDs can be rented or purchased like prerecorded VCR tapes, but they offer much higher resolution and quality with greater content. As with CDs, which initially were designed only for music, DVDs have since developed into a wider range of uses, including computer data storage.

DVD History

DVD had a somewhat rocky start. During 1995, two competing standards for high-capacity CD-ROM drives were being developed to compete with each other for future market share. One standard, called Multimedia CD, was introduced and backed by Philips and Sony, whereas a competing standard, called the Super Density (SD) disk, was introduced and backed by Toshiba, Time Warner, and several other companies. If both standards had hit the market as is, consumers as well as entertainment and software producers would have been in a quandary over which one to choose.

Fearing a repeat of the Beta/VHS situation that occured in the videotape market, several organizations, including the Hollywood Video Disc Advisory Group and the Computer Industry Technical Working Group, banded together to form a consortium to develop and control the DVD standard. The consortium insisted on a single format for the industry and refused to endorse either competing proposal. With this incentive, both groups worked out an agreement on a single, new, high-capacity CD type disc in September of 1995. The new standard combined elements of both previously proposed standards and was called DVD, which originally stood for digital video disc, but has since been changed to digital versatile disc. The single DVD standard has avoided a confusing replay of the VHS versus Beta tape fiasco and has given the software, hardware, and movie industries a single, unified standard to support.

After agreeing on copy protection and other items, the DVD-ROM and DVD-Video standards were officially announced in late 1996. Players, drives, and discs were announced in January 1997 at the Consumer Electronics Show (CES) in Las Vegas, and the players and discs became available in March of 1997. The initial players were about $1,000 each. Only 36 movies were released in the first wave, and they were available only in seven cities nationwide (Chicago, Dallas, Los Angeles, New York, San Francisco, Seattle, and Washington, D.C.) until August 1997 when the full release began. After a somewhat rocky start (much had to do with agreements on copy protection to get the movie companies to go along, and there was a lack of titles available in the beginning), DVD has become an incredible success. It will likely continue to grow after the rewritable +RW format becomes available in 2001 and changes DVD from a read-only to a fully rewritable consumer as well as computer device.

The organization that controls the DVD standard is called the DVD Forum and was founded by 10 companies, including Hitachi, Matsushita, Mitsubishi, Victor, Pioneer, Sony, Toshiba, Philips, Thomson, and Time Warner. Since its founding in 1995, more than 230 companies have joined the forum. Because it is a public forum, anybody can join and attend the meetings; the site for the DVD forum is http://www.dvdforum.org.

DVD Technology

DVD technology is similar to CD technology. Both use the same size (120mm diameter, 1.2mm thick, with a 15mm hole in the center) discs with pits and lands stamped in a polycarbonate base. Unlike a CD, though, DVDs can have two layers of recordings on a side and be double-sided as well. Each layer is separately stamped, and they are all bonded together to make the final 1.2mm-thick disc. The manufacturing process is largely the same, with the exception that each layer on each side is stamped from a separate piece of polycarbonate plastic and are then bonded together to form the completed disc. The main difference between CD and DVD is that DVD is a higher-density recording read by a laser with a shorter wavelength, which enables more information to be stored. Also, whereas CDs are single-sided and have only one layer of stamped pits and lands, DVDs can have up to two layers per side and can have information on both sides.

As with CDs, each layer is stamped or molded with a single physical track in a spiral configuration starting from the inside of the disc and spiraling outward. The disc rotates counterclockwise (as viewed from the bottom), and each spiral track contains pits (bumps) and lands (flat portions) just as on a CD. Each recorded layer is coated with a thin film of metal to reflect the laser light. The outer layer has a thinner coating to allow the light to pass through to read the inner layer. If the disc is single-sided, a label can be placed on top; otherwise, if it's double-sided, only a small ring near the center provides room for labeling.

Reading the information back is a matter of bouncing a low-powered laser beam off one of the reflective layers in the disc. The laser shines a focused beam on the underside of the disc, and a photosensitive receptor detects when the light is reflected back. When the light hits a land (flat spot) on the track, the light is reflected back; when the light hits a pit (raised bump), no light is reflected back.

As the disc rotates over the laser and receptor, the laser shines continuously while the receptor sees what is essentially a pattern of flashing light as the laser passes over pits and lands. Each time the laser passes over the edge of a pit the light seen by the receptor changes in state from being reflected to not reflected or vice versa. Each change in state of reflection caused by crossing the edge of a pit is translated into a 1 bit digitally. Microprocessors in the drive translate the light/dark and dark/light (pit edge) transitions into 1 bits, translate areas where there are no transitions into 0 bits, and then translate the bit patterns into actual data or sound.

The individual pits on a DVD are 0.105 microns deep and 0.4 microns wide. Both the pits and lands vary in length from about 0.4 microns at their shortest to about 1.9 microns at their longest (on single-layer discs).

See the section "CD-ROM Technology" earlier in this chapter for more information on how the pits and lands are read and converted into actual data, as well as how the drives physically and mechanically work.

DVD uses the same optical laser read pit and land storage that CDs do. The greater capacity is made possible by several factors, including the following:

- A 2.25 times smaller pit length (0.9–0.4 microns)
- A 2.16 times reduced track pitch (1.6–0.74 microns)
- A slightly larger data area on the disc (8,605–8,759 square millimeters)
- About 1.06 times more efficient channel bit modulation
- About 1.32 times more efficient error correction code
- About 1.06 times less sector overhead (2,048/2,352–2,048/2,064 bytes)

The DVD disc's pits and lands are much smaller and closer together than those on a CD, allowing the same physical-sized platter to hold much more information. Figure 13.7 shows how the grooved tracks with pits and lands are just over four times as dense on a DVD as compared to a CD.

DVD   CD

Figure 13.7   DVD data markings (pits and lands) versus those of a standard CD.

DVD drives use a shorter wavelength laser to read these smaller pits and lands. DVD can have nearly double the initial capacity by using two separate layers on one side of a disc and double it again by using both sides of the disc. The second data layer is written to a separate substrate below the first layer, which is then made semireflective to enable the laser to penetrate to the substrate beneath it. By focusing the laser on one of the two layers, the drive can read roughly twice the amount of data from the same surface area.

DVD Tracks and Sectors

The pits are stamped into a single spiral track (per layer) with a spacing of 0.74 microns between turns, corresponding to a track density of 1,351 turns per millimeter or 34,324 turns per inch. This equates to a total of 49,324 turns and a total track length of 11.8km or 7.35 miles in length. The track is comprised of sectors, with each sector containing 2,048 bytes of data. The disc is divided into four main areas:

- *Hub clamping area.* The hub clamp area is just that, a part of the disc where the hub mechanism in the drive can grip the disc. No data or information is stored in that area.

- *Lead-in zone.* The lead-in zone contains buffer zones, reference code, and mainly a control data zone with information about the disc. The control data zone consists of 16 sectors of information repeated 192 times for a total of 3,072 sectors. Contained in the 16 (repeated) sectors is information about the disc, including disc category and version number, disc size and maximum transfer rate, disc structure, recording density, and data zone allocation. The entire lead-in zone takes up to 196,607 (2FFFFh) sectors on the disc. Unlike CDs, the basic structure of all sectors on a DVD are the same. The buffer zone sectors in the lead-in zone have all 00h (zero hex) recorded for data.

- *Data zone.* The data zone contains the video, audio, or other data on the disc and starts at sector number 196,608 (30000h). The total number of sectors in the data zone can be up to 2,292,897 per layer for single layer discs.

- *Lead-out (or middle) zone.* The lead-out zone marks the end of the data zone. The sectors in the lead-out zone all contain zero (00h) for data. This is called the middle zone if the disc is dual layer and is recorded in opposite track path (OPT) mode, in which the second layer starts from the outside of the disc and is read in the opposite direction from the first layer.

The center hole in a DVD is 15mm in diameter, so it has a radius of 7.5mm from the center of the disc. From the edge of the center hole to a point at a radius of 16.5mm is the hub clamp area. The lead-in zone starts at a radius of 22mm from the center of the disc. The data zone starts at a radius of 24mm from the center and is followed by the lead-out (or middle) zone at 58mm. The disc track officially ends at 58.5mm, which is followed by a 1.5mm blank area to the edge of the disc. Figure 13.8 shows these zones in actual relative scale as they appear on a DVD.

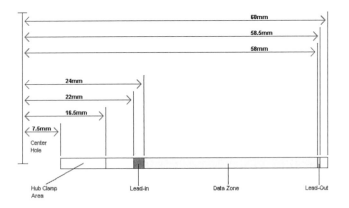

Figure 13.8 Areas on a DVD (side view).

Officially, the spiral track of a standard DVD starts with the lead-in zone and ends at the finish of the lead-out zone. This single spiral track is about 11.84 kilometers or 7.35 miles long. An interesting fact is that in a 20x CAV drive, when reading the outer part of the track, the data moves at an actual speed of 156 miles per hour (251km/h) past the laser. What is more amazing is that even when the data is traveling at that speed, the laser pickup can accurately read bits (pit/land transitions) spaced as little as only 0.4 microns or 15.75 millionths of an inch apart!

DVDs come in both single- and dual-layer as well as single- and double-sided versions. The double-sided discs are essentially the same as two single-sided discs glued together back to back, but subtle differences do exist between the single- and dual-layer discs. Table 13.17 shows some of the basic information about DVD technology, including single- and dual-layer DVDs. The dual-layer versions are recorded with slightly longer pits, resulting in slightly less information being stored in each layer.

Table 13.17   DVD Technical Parameters

DVD Type:	Single-Layer	Dual-Layer
1x read speed (m/sec)	3.49	3.84
Laser wavelength (nm)	650	650
Media refractive index	1.55	1.55
Track (turn) spacing (um)	0.74	0.74
Turns per mm	1,351	1,351
Turns per inch	34,324	34,324
Total track length (m)	11,836	11,836
Total track length (feet)	38,832	38,832
Total track length (miles)	7.35	7.35

Table 13.17 Continued

Media bit cell length (nm)	133.3	146.7
Media byte length (um)	1.07	1.17
Media sector length (mm)	5.16	5.68
Pit width (um)	0.40	0.40
Pit depth (um)	0.105	0.105
Min. nominal pit length (um)	0.40	0.44
Max. nominal pit length (um)	1.87	2.05
Lead-in inner radius (mm)	22	22
Data zone inner radius (mm)	24	24
Data zone outer radius (mm)	58	58
Lead-out outer radius (mm)	58.5	58.5
Data zone width (mm)	34	34
Data zone area (mm2)	8,759	8,759
Total track area width (mm)	36.5	36.5
Max. rotating speed 1x CLV (rpm)	1,515	1,667
Min. rotating speed 1x CLV (rpm)	570	627
Track revolutions (data zone)	45,946	45,946
Track revolutions (total)	49,324	49,324
Data zone sectors per layer per side	2,292,897	2,083,909
Sectors per second	676	676
Media data rate (mbits/sec)	26.15625	26.15625
Media bits per sector	38,688	38,688
Media bytes per sector	4,836	4,836
Interface data Rate (mbits/sec)	11.08	11.08
Interface data bits per sector	16,384	16,384
Interface data bytes per sector	2,048	2,048
Track time per layer (minutes)	56.52	51.37
Track time per side (minutes)	56.52	102.74
MPEG-2 video per layer (minutes)	133	121
MPEG-2 video per side (minutes)	133	242

B = Byte (8 bits)

KB = Kilobyte (1,000 bytes)

KiB = Kibibyte (1,024 bytes)

MB = Megabyte (1,000,000 bytes)

MiB = Mebibyte (1,048,576 bytes)

GB = Gigabyte (1,000,000,000 bytes)

GiB = Gibibyte (1,073,741,824 bytes)

m = meters

mm = millimeters (thousandths of a meter)

mm2 = square millimeters

um = micrometers = microns (millionths of a meter)

nm = nanometers (billionths of a meter)

rpm = revolutions per minute

ECC = Error correction code

EDC = Error detection code

CLV = Constant linear velocity

CAV = Constant angular velocity

As you can see from the information in Table 13.17, the spiral track is divided into sectors that are stored at the rate of 676 sectors per second. Each sector contains 2,048 bytes of data.

When being written, the sectors are first formatted into data frames of 2,064 bytes, of which 2,048 are data, 4 bytes contain ID information, 2 bytes contain ID error detection (IED) codes, 6 bytes contain copyright information, and 4 bytes contain EDC for the frame.

The data frames then have ECC information added to convert them into ECC frames. Each ECC frame contains the 2,064-byte data frame plus 182 parity outer (PO) bytes and 120 parity inner (PI) bytes, for a total of 2,366 bytes for each ECC frame.

Finally, the ECC frames are converted into physical sectors on the disc. This is done by taking 91 bytes at a time from the ECC frame and converting them into recorded bits via 8 to 16 modulation. This is where each byte (8 bits) is converted into a special 16-bit value, which is selected from a table. These values are designed using an RLL 2,10 scheme, which is designed so that the encoded information never has a run of less than 2 or more than 10 0 bits in a row. After each group of 91 bytes is converted via the 8 to 16 modulation, 320 bits (4 bytes) of synchronization information is added. After the entire ECC frame is converted into a physical sector, 4,836 total bytes are stored.

Table 13.18 shows the sector, frame, and audio data calculations.

Table 13.18   DVD Data Frame, ECC Frame, and Physical Sector Layout and Information

DVD Data Frame:	
Identification data (ID) bytes	4
ID Error detection code (IED) bytes	2
Copyright Info (CI) bytes	6
Data bytes	2,048
Error detection code (EDC)	4
Data frame total bytes	2,064
DVD ECC Frame:	
Data frame total bytes	2,064
Parity outer (PO) bytes	182
Parity inner (PI) bytes	120
ECC Frame total bytes	2,366
DVD Media Physical Sectors:	
ECC frame bytes	2,366
8 to 16 modulation bits	37,856
Syncronization bits	832
Total encoded media bits/sector	38,688
Total encoded media bytes/sector	4,836
Original data bits/sector	16,384
Original data bytes/sector	2,048
Ratio of original to media data	2.36

Unlike CDs, DVDs do not use subcodes and instead use the ID bytes in each data frame to store the sector number and information about the sectors.

Handling Errors

DVDs use more powerful error correcting codes than were first devised for CDs. Unlike CDs, which have different levels of error correction depending on whether audio/video or data is being stored, DVDs treat all information equally and apply the full error correction to all sectors.

The main error correcting in DVDs takes place in the ECC frame. Parity outer (column) and parity inner (row) bits are added to detect and correct errors. The scheme is simple and yet very effective. The information from the data frames is first broken up into 192 rows of 172 bytes each. Then, a polynomial equation is used to calculate and add 10 PI bytes to each row, making the rows now 182 bytes each. Finally, another polynomial equation is used to calculate 16 PO (Parity Outer) bytes for each column, resulting in 16 bytes (rows) being added to each column. What started out as 192 rows of 172 bytes becomes 208 rows of 182 bytes with the PI and PO information added.

The function of the PI and PO bytes can be explained with a simple example using simple parity. In this example, 2 bytes are stored (01001110 = N, 01001111 = O). To add the error correcting information, they are organized in rows, as shown in the following:

```
           Data bits
           1 2 3 4 5 6 7 8
-------------------------------------
Byte 1     0 1 0 0 1 1 1 0
Byte 2     0 1 0 0 1 1 1 1
-------------------------------------
```

Then, 1 PI bit is added for each row, using odd parity. This means you count up the 1 bits: In the first row there are 4, so the parity bit is created as a 1, making the sum an odd number. In the second row, the parity bit is a 0 because the sum of the 1s was already an odd number. The result is as follows:

```
           Data bits        |
           1 2 3 4 5 6 7 8   |   PI
------------------------------|---------
Byte 1     0 1 0 0 1 1 1 0   |   1
Byte 2     0 1 0 0 1 1 1 1   |   0
------------------------------|---------
```

Next, the parity bits for each column are added and calculated the same as before. In other words, the parity bit will be such that the sum of the 1s in each column is an odd number. The result is as follows:

```
           Data bits        |
           1 2 3 4 5 6 7 8   |   PI
------------------------------|---------
Byte 1     0 1 0 0 1 1 1 0   |   1
Byte 2     0 1 0 0 1 1 1 1   |   0
------------------------------|---------
   PO      1 1 1 1 1 1 1 0   |   1
```

Now the code is complete, and the extra bits are stored along with the data. So, instead of just the 2 bytes being stored, 11 addition bits are stored for error correction. When the data is read back, the error correction bit calculations are repeated and they're checked to see whether they are the same as before. To see how it works, let's change one of the data bits (due to a read error) and recalculate the error correcting bits as follows:

```
            Data bits      |
            1 2 3 4 5 6 7 8 |   PI
------------------------------------|---------
Byte 1      0 1 0 0 1 0 1 0 |   0
Byte 2      0 1 0 0 1 1 1 1 |   0
------------------------------------|---------
    PO      1 1 1 1 1 0 1 0 |   1
```

Now, when you compare the PI and PO bits you calculated after reading the data to what was originally stored, you see a change in the PI bit for byte (row) 1 and in the PO bit for bit (column) 6. This identifies the precise row and column where the error was, which is at byte 1 (row 1), bit 6 (column 6). That bit was read as a 0, and you now know it is wrong, so it must have been a 1. The error correction circuitry then simply changes it back to a 1 before passing it back to the system. As you can see, with some extra information added to each row and column, error correction codes can indeed detect and correct errors on-the-fly.

Besides the ECC frames, DVDs also scramble the data in the frames using a bit-shift technique and also interleave parts of the ECC frames when they are actually recorded on the disc. These schemes serve to store the data somewhat out of sequence, preventing a scratch from corrupting consecutive pieces of data.

DVD Capacity (Sides and Layers)

Four main types of DVD discs are available, categorized by whether they are single- or double-sided, and single- or dual-layered. They are designated as follows:

■ *DVD-5 - 4.7GB Single-Side, Single-Layer.* A DVD-5 is constructed from two substrates bonded together with adhesive. One is stamped with a recorded layer (called Layer 0), and the other is blank. An aluminum coating typically is applied to the single recorded layer.

■ *DVD-9 - 8.5GB Single-Side, Dual-Layer.* A DVD-9 is constructed of two stamped substrates bonded together to form two recorded layers for one side of the disc, along with a blank substrate for the other side. The outer stamped layer (0) is coated with a semitransparent gold coating to both reflect light if the laser is focused on it and pass light if the laser is focused on the layer below. A single laser is used to read both layers; only the focus of the laser is changed.

■ *DVD-10 - 9.4GB Double-Side, Single-Layer.* A DVD-10 is constructed of two stamped substrates bonded together back to back. The recorded layer (Layer 0 on each side) usually is coated with aluminum. Note that these discs are double-sided; however, drives have a read laser only on the bottom, which means the disc must be removed and flipped to read the other side.

■ *DVD-18 - 17.1GBDouble-Side, Dual-Layer.* A DVD-18 combines both double layers and double sides. Two stamped layers form each side, and the substrate pairs are bonded back to back. The outer layers (Layer 0 on each side) are coated with semitransparent gold, whereas the inner layers (Layer 1 on each side) are coated with aluminum. The reflectivity of a single-layer disc is 45%–85%, and for a dual-layer disc the reflectivity is 18%–30%. The automatic gain control (AGC) circuitry in the drive compensates for the different reflective properties.

Figure 13.9 shows the construction of each of the DVD disc types.

Note that although Figure 13.9 shows two lasers reading the bottom of the dual-layer discs, in actual practice only one laser is used. Only the focus is changed to read the different layers.

Dual-layer discs can have the layers recorded in two ways: either OTP or parallel track path (PTP). OTP minimizes the time needed to switch from one layer to the other when reading the disc. When reaching the inside of the disc (end of Layer 0), the laser pickup remains in the same location—it merely moves towards the disc slightly to focus on Layer 1. When written in OTP mode, the lead-out zone toward the outer part of the disc is called a middle zone instead.

Figure 13.9 DVD disk types and construction.

Discs written in PTP have both spiral layers written (and read) from the inside out. When changing from Layer 0 to Layer 1, PTP discs require the laser pickup to move from the outside (end of the first layer) back to the inside (start of the second layer), as well as for the focus of the laser to change. Virtually all discs are written in OTP mode to make the layer change quicker.

To allow the layers to be read more easily even though they are on top of one another, discs written in PTP mode have the spiral direction changed from one layer to the other. Layer 0 has a spiral winding clockwise (which is read counterclockwise), whereas Layer 1 has a spiral winding counterclockwise. This typically requires that the drive spin the disc in the opposite direction to read that layer, but with OTP the spiral is read from the outside in on the second layer. So Layer 0 spirals from the inside out, and Layer 1 spirals from the outside in.

Figure 13.10 shows the differences between PTP and OTP on a DVD:

DVDs store up to 4.7GB–17.1 GB, depending on the type. Table 13.19 shows the precise capacities of the various types of DVDs.

Figure 13.10 PTP versus OTP.

Table 13.19   DVD Capacity

	Single-Layer	Dual-Layer
DVD Designation	DVD-5	DVD-9
B	4,695,853,056	8,535,691,264
KiB	4,585,794	8,335,636
KB	4,695,853	8,535,691
MiB	4,586	8,336
MB	4,696	8,536
GiB	4.6	8.3
GB	4.7	8.5
MPEG-2 video (approx. minutes)	133	242
MPEG-2 video (hours:minutes)	2:13	4:02
	Single Layer Double Sided	Dual Layer Double Sided
DVD Designation	DVD-10	DVD-18
B	9,391,706,112	17,071,382,528
KiB	9,171,588	16,671,272
KB	9,391,706	17,071,383
MiB	9,172	16,671
MB	9,392	17,071
GiB	9.2	16.7
GB	9.4	17.1

Table 13.19   Continued

MPEG-2 video (approx. minutes)	266	484
MPEG-2 video (hours:minutes)	4:26	8:04

B = Byte (8 bits)

KB = Kilobyte (1,000 bytes)

KiB = Kibibyte (1,024 bytes)

MB = Megabyte (1,000,000 bytes)

MiB = Mebibyte (1,048,576 bytes)

GB = Gigabyte (1,000,000,000 bytes)

GiB = Mebibyte (1,073,741,824 bytes)

As you might notice, the capacity of dual-layer discs is slightly less than twice of single-layer discs, even though the layers take up the same space on the discs (the spiral tracks are the same length). This was done intentionally to improve the readability of both layers in a dual-layer configuration. To do this, the bit cell spacing was slightly increased, which increases the length of each pit and land. When reading a dual-layer disc, the drive spins slightly faster to compensate, resulting in the same data rate. However, because the distance on the track is covered more quickly, less overall data can be stored.

Besides the standard four capacities listed here, a double-sided disc with one layer on one side and two layers on the other can also be produced. This would be called a DVD-14 and have a capacity of 13.2GB, or about 6 hours and 15 minutes of MPEG-2 video. Additionally, 80mm discs, which store less data in each configuration than the standard 120mm discs, can be produced.

Because of the manufacturing difficulties and the extra expense of double-sided discs—and the fact that they must be ejected and flipped to play both sides—most DVDs are configured as either a DVD-5 (single-sided, single-layer) or a DVD-9 (single-sided, dual-layer), which allows up to 8.5GB of data or 242 minutes of uninterrupted MPEG-2 video to be played. The 133-minute capacity of DVD-5 video discs accomodates 95% or more of the movies ever made.

Data Encoding on the Disc

As with CDs, the pits and lands themselves do not determine the bits; instead, the transitions (changes in reflectivity) from pit to land and land to pit are what determines the actual bits on the disc. The disc track is divided into bit cells or time intervals (T), and a pit or land used to represent data is required to be a minimum of 3T or a maximum of 11T intervals (cells) long. A 3T-long pit or land represents a 1001, and a 11T long pit or land represents a 100000000001.

Data is stored using 8 to 16 modulation, which is a modified version of the 8 to 14 modulation (EFM) used on CDs. Because of this, 8 to 16 modulation is sometimes called EFM+. This modulation takes each byte (8 bits) and converts it into a 16-bit value for storage. The 16-bit conversion codes are designed so that there are never less than 2 or more than 10 adjacent 0 bits (resulting in no less than 3 or no more than 11 time intervals between 1s). EFM+ is a form of RLL encoding called RLL 2,10 (RLL x,y where x = the minimum and y = the maximum run of 0s). This is designed to prevent long strings of 0s, which could more easily be misread due to clocks becoming out of sync, as well as to limit the minimum and maximum frequency of transitions actually placed on the recording media. Unlike CDs, no merge bits exist between codes. The 16-bit modulation codes are designed so that they will not violate the RLL 2,10 form without needing merge bits. Because the EFM used on CDs really requires more than 17 bits for each byte (because of the added merge and sync bits), EFM+ is slightly more efficient since only slightly more than 16 bits are generated for each byte encoded.

Note that although no more than 10 0s are allowed in the modulation generated by EFM+, the sync bits added when physical sectors are written can have up to 13 0s, meaning a time period of up to 14T between 1s written on the disc and pits or lands up to 14T intervals or bit cells in length.

DVD Drive Speed

As with CDs, DVDs rotate counterclockwise (as viewed from the reading laser) and typically are recorded at a constant data ratecalled CLV. This means that the track (and thus the data) is always moving past the read laser at the same speed, which originally was defined as 3.49 meters per second (or 3.84m/sec on dual-layer discs). Because the track is a spiral that is wound more tightly near the center of the disc, the disc must spin at varying rates to maintain the same track linear speed. In other words, to maintain a CLV, the disk must spin more quickly when reading the inner track area and more slowly when reading the outer track area. The speed of rotation in a 1x drive (3.49 meters per second is considered 1x speed) varies from 1,515rpm when reading the start (inner part) of the track down to 570rpm when reading the end (outer part) of the track.

Single-speed (1x) DVD-ROM drives provide a data transfer rate of 1.385MB/second, which means the data transfer rate from a DVD-ROM at 1x speed is roughly equivalent to a 9x CD-ROM (1x CD-ROM data transfer rate is 153.6KB/s, or 0.1536MB/s). This does not mean, however, that a 1x DVD drive can read CDs at 9x rates: DVD drives actually spin at a rate that is just under three times faster than a CD-ROM drive of the same speed. So, a 1x DVD drive spins at about the same rotational speed as a

Table 13.20   DVD Speeds and Transfer Rates

Column 1	Column 2	Column 3	Column 4	Column 5	Column 6	Column 7
Advertised DVD-ROM Speed (Max. if CAV)	Time to Read Single Layer DVD if CLV	Time to Read Dual Layer DVD if CLV	Transfer Rate (Bytes/sec) (Max. if CAV)	Actual DVD Speed Minimum if CAV	Minimum Transfer Rate if CAV (Bytes/sec)	Average DVD Speed if CAV
1x	56.5	51.4	1,384,615	0.4x	553,846	0.7x
2x	28.3	25.7	2,769,231	0.8x	1,107,692	1.4x
4x	14.1	12.8	5,538,462	1.7x	2,353,846	2.9x
6x	9.4	8.6	8,307,692	2.5x	3,461,538	4.3x
8x	7.1	6.4	11,076,923	3.3x	4,569,231	5.7x
10x	5.7	5.1	13,846,154	4.1x	5,676,923	7.1x
12x	4.7	4.3	16,615,385	5.0x	6,923,077	8.5x
16x	3.5	3.2	22,153,846	6.6x	9,138,462	11.3
20x	2.8	2.6	27,692,308	8.3x	11,492,308	14.2
24x	2.4	2.1	33,230,769	9.9x	13,707,692	17.0
32x	1.8	1.6	44,307,692	13.2x	18,276,923	22.6
40x	1.4	1.3	55,384,615	16.6x	22,984,615	28.3
48x	1.2	1.1	66,461,538	19.9x	27,553,846	34.0
50x	1.1	1.0	69,230,769	20.7x	28,661,538	35.4

2.7x CD drive. Many DVD drives list two speeds, one for reading DVD discs and another for reading CD discs. For example, a DVD-ROM drive listed as a 16x/40x would indicate the performance when reading DVD/CD discs, respectively.

As with CDs, drive manufacturers began increasing the speeds of their drives by making them spin more quickly. A drive that spins twice as fast was called a 2x drive, drive that spins four times faster was 4x, and so on. At higher speeds, it became difficult to build motors that could change speeds (spin up or down) as quickly as needed when data was read from different parts of the disc. Because of this, most faster DVD drives spin the disc at a fixed rotational, rather than linear speed. This istermed *constant angular velocity (CAV)* because the angular velocity (or rotational speed) is what remains a constant.

The faster drives are useful primarily for data, not video. Having a faster drive can reduce or eliminate the pause during layer changes when playing a DVD video disc, but having a faster drive has no effect on video quality.

DVD-ROM drives have been available in speeds up to 20x or more, but because virtually all are CAV, they actually achieve the rated transfer speed only when reading the outer part of a disc. Table 13.20 shows the data rates for DVD drives reading DVD discs and how that rate compares to a CD-ROM drive.

Column 8	Column 9	Column 10	Column 11	Column 12	Column 13
Average Transfer Rate if CAV (Bytes/sec)	Maximum Linear Speed (m/sec)	Maximum Linear Speed (mph)	Single Layer Rot. Speed Min. if CLV Max. if CAV (rpm)	Single Layer Rot. Speed Max. if CLV (rpm)	Usual Transfer Rate When Reading CD-ROMs
969,231	3.5	7.8	570	1,515	2.7x
1,938,462	7.0	15.6	1,139	3,030	5.4x
3,946,154	14.0	31.2	2,279	6,059	11x
5,884,615	20.9	46.8	3,418	9,089	16x
7,823,077	27.9	62.5	4,558	12,119	21x
9,761,538	34.9	78.1	5,697	15,149	27x
11,769,231	41.9	93.7	6,836	18,178	32x
15,646,154	55.8	124.9	9,115	24,238	43x
19,592,308	69.8	156.1	11,394	30,297	54x
23,469,231	83.8	187.4	13,673	36,357	64x
31,292,308	111.7	249.8	18,230	48,476	86x
39,184,615	139.6	312.3	22,788	60,595	107x
47,007,692	167.5	374.7	27,345	72,714	129x
48,946,154	174.5	390.3	28,485	75,743	134x

- *Column 1.* Indicates the advertised drive speed. This is a constant speed if the drive is CLV or a maximum speed only if CAV (most DVD-ROM drives are CAV).

- *Columns 2 and 3.* Indicate how long it would take to read a full disc (single- or dual-layer) if the drive were CLV. For CAV drives, those figures are longer because the average read speed is less than the advertised speed. The fourth column indicates the data transfer rate, which for CAV drives is a maximum figure seen only when reading the end of a disc.

- *Columns 4–8.* Indicate the actual minimum "x" speed for CAV drives, along with the minimum transfer speed (when reading the start of any disc) and an optimistic average speed (true only when reading a full disc; otherwise, it's even lower) in both "x" and byte-per-second formats.

- *Columns 9 and 10.* Indicate the maximum linear speeds the drive attains, in both meters per second and miles per hour. CLV drives maintain those speeds everywhere on the disc, whereas CAV drives reach those speeds only on the outer part of a disc.

- *Columns 11 and 12.* Indicate the rotational speeds of a drive. The first of those shows how quickly the disc spins when reading the start of a disc. This applies to either CAV or CLV drives. For CAV drives, that figure is constant no matter where on the disc is being read. The second of those two colums shows the maximum rotational speed if the drive were a CLV type. Because most faster drives are CAV, those figures are mostly theoretical for the faster drives.

- *Column 13.* Shows the speed the drive would be rated if it were a CD-ROM drive. This is based on the rotational speed, not the transfer rate. In other words, a 12x DVD drive would perform as a 32x CD-ROM drive when reading CDs. Most DVD drives list their speeds when reading CDs in the specifications. Due to the use of PCAV (Partial CAV) designs, some might have higher CD performances than the table indicates.

DVD Formats and Standards

As with the CD standards, the DVD standards are published in reference books produced mainly by the DVD forum, but also by other companies.

The DVD-Video and DVD-ROM standards are pretty well established, but recordable DVD technology is still evolving. The standards situation for recordable DVD is more confusing than usual, especially because there are at least four different (and somewhat incompatible) recording formats! It remains to be seen which will have the best support and become the most popular, but so far the DVD+RW format looks to be the most promising.

The current standard DVD formats are shown in Table 13.21.

Table 13.21   Standard DVD Formats and Capacities

Format	Disc Size	Sides	Layers	Data Capacity	Video Capacity
DVD-ROM Formats and Capacities					
DVD-5	120mm	Single	Single	4.7GB	2.2 hours
DVD-9	120mm	Single	Double	8.5GB	4.0 hours
DVD-10	120mm	Double	Single	9.4GB	4.4 hours
DVD-14	120mm	Double	Both	13.2GB	6.3 hours
DVD-18	120mm	Double	Double	17.1GB	8.1 hours
DVD-1	80mm	Single	Single	1.5GB	0.7 hours
DVD-2	80mm	Single	Double	2.7GB	1.3 hours

Table 13.21 Continued

Format	Disc Size	Sides	Layers	Data Capacity	Video Capacity
DVD-3	80mm	Double	Single	2.9GB	1.4 hours
DVD-4	80mm	Double	Double	5.3GB	2.5 hours
Recordable DVD Formats and Capacities					
DVD-R 1.0	120mm	Single	Single	3.95GB	N/A
DVD-R 2.0	120mm	Single	Single	4.7GB	N/A
DVD-RAM 1.0	120mm	Single	Single	2.58GB	N/A
DVD-RAM 1.0	120mm	Double	Single	5.16GB	N/A
DVD-RAM 2.0	120mm	Single	Single	4.7GB	N/A
DVD-RAM 2.0	120mm	Double	Single	9.4GB	N/A
DVD-RAM 2.0	80mm	Single	Single	1.46GB	N/A
DVD-RAM 2.0	80mm	Double	Single	2.65GB	N/A
DVD-RW 2.0	120mm	Single	Single	4.7GB	N/A
DVD+RW 2.0	120mm	Single	Single	4.7GB	N/A
DVD+RW 2.0	120mm	Double	Single	9.4GB	N/A
CD-ROM Formats and Capacities (for comparison)					
CD-ROM/R/RW	120mm	Single	Single	0.737GB	N/A
CD-ROM/R/RW	80mm	Single	Single	0.194GB	N/A

With advancements coming in blue-light lasers, this capacity will be increased several-fold in the future with a HD-DVD format that can store up to 20GB per layer. Prototype players have already been shown by major manufacturers, although you shouldn't expect to see HD-DVD on the market for several years yet.

DVD drives are fully backward compatible, and as such, are capable of playing today's CD-ROMs as well as audio CDs. When playing existing CDs, the performance of current models is equivalent to a 40x or faster CD-ROM drive. As such, users who currently own slower CD-ROM drives might want to consider a DVD drive instead of upgrading to a faster CD-ROM drive. Several manufacturers have announced plans to phase out their CD-ROM drive products in favor of DVD. DVD is rapidly making CD-ROMs obsolete, in the same way that audio CDs displaced vinyl records in the 1980s. The only thing keeping the CD-ROM format alive is the battle between competing DVD recordable standards and the fact that CD-R and CD-RW are rapidly becoming the de facto replacement for the floppy drive.

The current crop of DVD drives feature several improvements over the first-generation models of 1997. Those units were expensive, slow, and incompatible with either CD-R or CD-RW media. Many early units asked your overworked video card to try to double as an MPEG decoder to display DVD movies, with mediocre results in speed and image quality. As is often the case with "leading-edge" devices, their deficiencies make them eminently avoidable.

Many PC vendors have integrated DVD-ROM drives into their new high-end computers, usually as an option. Originally, most of these installations included an MPEG-2 decoder board for processing the compressed video on DVD discs. This offloads the intensive MPEG calculations from the system processor and enables the display of full-screen, full-motion video on a PC. After processors crossed 400MHz in speed, performing MPEG-2 decoding reliably in software became possible, so any systems faster than that usually doesn't include a hardware decoder card.

Some manufacturers of video display adapters have begun to include MPEG decoder hardware on their products. These adapters are called "DVD MPEG-2 accelerated" and call for some of the MPEG decoding tasks to be performed by software. Any software decoding involved in an MPEG solution places a greater burden on the main system processor and can therefore yield less satisfactory results on slower systems.

DIVX (Discontinued Standard)

DIVX (Digital Video Express) was a short-lived proprietary and incompatible DVD format developed by Digital Video Express (a Hollywood law firm) and Circuit City. It was discontinued on June 16, 1999, less than a year after it was released.

Note

More detailed coverage of DIVX is included in the 11th and 12th editions of this book, both of which are included in their entirety on the CD accompanying this book.

DVD Drive Compatibility

When DVD drives first appeared on the market, they were touted to be fully backward compatible with CD-ROM drives. Although that might be the case when reading commercially pressed CD-ROM discs, that was not necessarily true when reading CD-R or CD-RW media. Fortunately, the industry has responded with standards that let you to know in advance how compatible your DVD drive will be. These standards are called *MultiRead* for computer-based drives and *MultiPlay* for consumer stand-alone devices, such as DVD-Video or CD-DA players. See the section "MultiRead Specifications," later in this chapter.

DVD Copy Protection

DVD video discs employ several levels of protection, which are mainly controlled by the DVD Copy Control Association (DVD CCA) and a third-party company called Macrovision. This protection typically applies only to DVD-Video discs, not DVD-ROM software. So, for example, copy protection might affect your ability to make backup copies of *The Matrix*, but it won't affect a DVD encyclopedia or other software application distributed on DVD-ROM discs.

Note that every one of these protection systems has been broken, which means that with a little extra expense or the correct software, the protection can be defeated and you can make copies of your DVDs either to other digital media (hard drive, DVD+RW, CD-R/RW, and so on) or to analog media (such as a VHS or other tape format).

A lot of time and money are wasted on these protection schemes, which can't really foil the professional bootleggers willing to spend the time and money to work around them. But they can make it difficult for the average person to legitimately back up her expensive media.

The three main protection systems used with DVD-Video discs are

- Regional Playback Control (RPC)
- Content Scrambling System (CSS)
- Analog Protection System (APS)

Regional Playback Control

Regional playback was designed to allow discs sold in specific geographical regions of the world to play only on players sold in those same regions. The idea was to allow a movie to be released at different times in different parts of the world, and to prevent people from ordering discs from regions in which the movie had not been released yet.

Eight regions are defined in the RPC standard. Discs (and players) usually are identified by a small logo or label showing the region number superimposed on a world globe. Multiregion discs are possible, as are discs that are not region locked. If a disc plays in more than one region, it will have more than one number on the globe. The regions are

- United States, Canada, U.S. Territories
- Japan, Europe, South Africa, and the Middle East
- Southeast Asia and East Asia
- Australia, New Zealand, Pacific Islands, Central America, Mexico, South America, and the Caribbean
- Eastern Europe, Indian subcontinent, Africa, North Korea, and Mongolia
- China
- Reserved
- Special international or mobile venues, such as airplanes, cruise ships, and so on

The region code is embedded in the hardware of DVD video players. Most players are preset for a specific region and can't be changed. Some companies who sell the players modify them to play discs from all regions; these are called *region-free* or *code-free* players. Some newer discs have an added region code enhancement (RCE) function that checks to see whether the player is configured for multiple or all regions and then refuses to play. Most newer region-free modified players know how to query the disc first to circumvent this check as well.

DVD-ROM drives used in PCs originally did not have RPC in the hardware, placing that responsibility instead on the software used to play DVD video discs on the PC. The player software would normally lock the region code to the first disc that was played and then from that point on, play only discs from that region. Reinstalling the software enabled the region code to be reset, and numerous patches were posted on Web sites to enable resetting the region code even without reinstalling the software. Because of the relative ease of defeating the region-coding restrictions with DVD-ROM drives, starting on January 1, 2000, all DVD-ROM drives were required to have RPC-II, which embeds the region coding directly into the drive.

RPC-II (or RPC-2) places the region lock in the drive, and not in the playing or MPEG-2 decoding software. You can set the region code in RPC-II drives up to five times total, which basically means you can change it up to four times after the initial setting. Usually, the change can be made using the player software you are using, or you can download region change software from the drive manufacturer. Upon making the fourth change (which is the fifth setting), the drive is locked on the last region set.

Content Scramble System

The Content Scramble System (CSS) provides the main protection for DVD-Video discs. It wasn't until this protection was implemented that the Motion Picture Association of America (MPAA) would agree to release movies in the DVD format, which is the main reason the rollout of DVD had been significantly delayed.

CSS originally was developed by Matsushita (Panasonic) and is used to digitally scramble and encrypt the audio and video data on a DVD-Video disc. Descrambling requires a pair of 40-bit (5-byte) keys (numeric codes). One of the keys is unique to the disc, whereas the other is unique to the video title set (VTS file) being descrambled. The disc and title keys are stored in the lead-in area of the disc in an encrypted form. The CSS scrambling and key writing are carried out during the glass mastering procedure, which is part of the disc manufacturing process.

You can see this encryption in action if you put a DVD disc into a DVD-ROM drive on a PC, copy the files to your hard drive, and then try to view the files. The files are usually called VTS_xx_yy.VOB (video object), where the xx represents the title number and the yy represents the section number. Usually, all the files for a given movie have the same title number, and the movie is spread out among several 1GB or smaller files with different section numbers. These .VOB files contain both the encrypted video and audio streams for the movie interleaved together. Other files with an .IFO extention contain information used by the DVD player to decode the video and audio streams in the .VOB files. If you copy the .VOB and .IFO files onto your hard drive and try to click or play the .VOB files directly, you either see and hear scrambled video and audio or receive an error message about playing copy protected files.

This encryption is not a problem if you use a CSS-licensed player (either hardware or software) and play the files directly from the DVD disc. All DVD players, whether they are consumer standalone units or software players on your PC, have their own unique CSS unlock key assigned to them. Every DVD video disc has 400 of these 5-byte keys stamped onto the disc in the lead-in area (which is not usually accessible by programs) on the DVD in encrypted form. The decryption routine in the player uses its unique code to retrieve and unencrypt the disc key, which is then used to retrieve and unencrypt the title keys. CSS is essentially a three-level encryption that originally was thought to be very secure, but has proven otherwise.

In October 1999, a 16-year-old Norwegian programmer was able to extract the first key from one of the commercial PC-based players, which allowed him to very easily decrypt disc and title keys. A now famous program called DeCSS was then written that can break the CSS protection on any DVD video title and save unencrypted .VOB files to a hard disk that can be played by any MPEG-2 decoder program. Needless to say, this utility (and others based on it) has been the cause of much concern in the movie industry and has caused many legal battles over the distribution and even links to this code on the Web. Do a search on DeCSS for some interesting legal reading.

As if that wasn't enough, in March 2001, two MIT students published an incredibly short (only seven lines long!) and simple program that can unscramble CSS so quickly that a movie can essentially be unscrambled in real-time while it is playing. They wrote and demonstrated the code as part of a two-day seminar they conducted on the controversial Digital Millenium Copyright Act, illustrating how trivial the CSS protection really is.

Because of the failure of CSS, the DVD forum is now actively looking into other means of protection, especially including digital watermarks, which consists essentially of digital noise buried into the data stream, which is supposed to be invisible to normal viewing. Unfortunately, when similar technology was applied to DIVX (the discontinued proprietary DVD standard), these watermarks caused slight impairment of the image—a raindrop or bullet-hole effect could be seen by some in the picture. Watermarks also might require new equipment to play the discs.

Analog Protection System

APS (also called CopyGuard by Macrovision) is an analog protection system developed by Macrovision and is designed to prevent making VCR tapes of DVD-Video discs. APS requires codes to be added to the disc, as well as special modifications in the player. APS starts with the creation or mastering of a DVD, where APS is enabled by setting predefined control codes in the recording.

During playback in an APS-enabled (Macrovision-enabled) player, the digital-to-analog converter (DAC) chip inside the player adds the APS signals to the analog output signal being sent to the screen. These additions to the signal are designed so that they are invisible when viewed on a television or monitor but cause copies made on most VCRs to appear distorted. Unfortunately, some TVs or other displays can react to the distortions added to creat a less-than-optimum picture.

APS uses two signal modifications called automatic gain control and colorstripe. The automatic gain control process consists of pulses placed in the vertical scan interval of the video signal, which TVs can't detect but which cause dim and noisy pictures, loss of color, loss of video, tearing, and so on on a VCR. This process has been used since 1985 on many prerecorded video tapes to prevent copying. The colorstripe process modifies colorburst information that is also transparent on television displays but produces lines across the picture when recorded on a VCR.

Note that many older players don't have the licensed Macrovision circuits and simply ignore the code to turn on the APS signal modifications. Also, various image stabilizer, enhancer, or copyguard decoder units are available that can plug in between the player and VCR to remove the APS copyguard signal and allow a perfect recording to be made.

Adding a DVD Drive to Your System

A DVD drive installs in a manner similar to that of a CD-ROM or any other type of drive. See Chapter 14, "Physical Drive Installation and Configuration," to learn how to install a 5 1/4-inch DVD drive.

Following are some basic principles to keep in mind when installing a DVD drive:

- *Most DVD drives are ATAPI devices.* So, you have the issue of master/slave setups on the dual-connector 40-pin ATA cable. If you're replacing an old CD-ROM drive, simply note its master/slave configuration when you remove it from your system, set the new DVD drive the same way, attach it to the data cable, connect the power, and you're finished.

- *Many current DVD drives require that you connect them to a busmastering ATA interface.* If your drive requires a busmastering interface, check out the tips later in this chapter.

- *If you want to play DVD movies using your drive, you need an MPEG-2 decoder.* This can be either a card (hardware decoder) or a program (software decoder). If you are using a hardware decoder, it requires an open PCI expansion slot, as well as an IRQ (interrupt request) resource from your system. Also, to view the movies on your PC's display, you must somehow connect the decoder card to your existing video card. This can be accomplished via an internal connection to the card, or it can use a loop through connection to the monitor port on the back of the card. Some video cards include MPEG-2 decoders (players) built in. Table 13.22 compares MPEG decoder cards to video cards with built-in MPEG players.

Table 13.22   MPEG Decoder Cards Versus Video Cards with MPEG Players

Consideration	MPEG Decoder	MPEG Player
PCI slot usage	One for decoder; one for VGA	One slot only
Movie image quality	High	Varies
Playback speed	High	Varies
MPEG game compatibility	Yes	No

Note that as processors have become more powerful, many DVD drives now ship with MPEG-2 software decoders. These eliminate the need for an MPEG-2 decoder card, and if your processor is fast enough, it allows for adequate performance when playing DVD video discs. Most of the decoders recommend a minimum of a 400MHz processor, and of course, even faster would be better. Although the software decoders can work well, in most cases if you really plan on using your PC to watch DVD movies, it is worth the extra cost for a hardware MPEG-2 decoder card.

Another performance issue is related to data transfer. Most ATAPI DVD drives support Ultra-DMA transfers. Be sure you enable DMA transfers in your BIOS setup and in the DVD driver installed in your operating system. Most installation programs automatically enable DMA support in the driver, but it's a good idea to check anyway. Enabling DMA dramatically reduces the load on your processor and greatly enhances system performance when playing or reading DVDs.

CD/DVD Drives and Specifications

When purchasing a CD or DVD drive for your PC, you should consider three distinct sets of criteria, as follows:

- The drive's performance specifications
- The interface the drive requires for connection to your PC
- The physical disc-handling system the drive uses

Performance Specifications

Typical performance figures published by manufacturers are the data transfer rate, the access time, the internal cache or buffers (if any), and the interface the drive uses.

Data Transfer Rate

The data transfer rate tells you how quickly the drive can read from the disc and transfer to the host computer. Normally, transfer rates indicate the drive's capability for reading large, sequential streams of data.

Transfer speed is measured two ways. The one most commonly quoted with CD/DVD drives is the "x" speed, which is defined as a multiple of the particular standard base rate. For example, CD-ROM drives transfer at 153.6KB/sec according to the original standard. Drives that transfer twice that are 2x, 40 times that are 40x, and so on. DVD drives transfer at 1,385KB/sec at the base rate, whereas drives that are 20 times faster than that are listed as 20x. Note that because almost all faster drives feature CAV, the "x" speed is usually indicated is a maximum that is seen only when reading data near the outside (end) of a disc. The speed near the beginning of the disc might be as little as half that, and of course, average speeds are somewhere in the middle.

With recordable CD drives, the speed is reported for various modes. CD-R drives have two speeds listed (one for writing, the other for reading), and CD-RW drives have three. On a CD-RW drive, the speeds are in the form A/B/C, where A is the speed when writing CD-Rs, B is the speed when writing CD-RWs, and C is the speed when reading. The first CD-RW drive on the market was 2/2/6, with versions up to 20/10/40 available today.

See the previous sections "CD Drive Speed" and "DVD Drive Speed," earlier in this chapter, for more information about speeds and transfer rates.

Access Time

The access time for a CD or DVD drive is measured the same way as for PC hard disk drives. In other words, the access time is the delay between the drive receiving the command to read and its actual first reading of a bit of data. The time is recorded in milliseconds; a typical manufacturer's rating would be listed as 95ms. This is an average access rate; the true access rate depends entirely on where the data is located on the disc. When the read mechanism is positioned to a portion of the disc nearer to the narrower center, the access rate is faster than when it is positioned at the wider outer perimeter. Access rates quoted by many manufacturers are an average taken by calculating a series of random reads from a disc.

Obviously, a faster (that is, a lower) average access rate is desirable, especially when you rely on the drive to locate and pull up data quickly. Access times for CD and DVD drives have been steadily improving, and the advancements are discussed later in this chapter. Note that these average times are significantly slower than PC hard drives, ranging from 200ms to below 100ms, compared to the 8ms access time of a typical hard disk drive. Most of the speed difference lies in the construction of the drive itself. Hard drives have multiple-read heads that range over a smaller surface area of the medium; CD/DVD drives have only one laser pickup, and it must be capable of accessing the entire range of the disc. In addition, the data on a CD is organized in a single long spiral. When the drive positions its head to read a track, it must estimate the distance into the disc and skip forward or backward to the appropriate point in the spiral. Reading off the outer edge requires a longer access time than the inner segments, unless you have a CAV drive, which spins at a constant rate so the access time to the outer tracks is equal to that of the inner tracks.

Access times have fallen a great deal since the original single-speed drives came out. However, recently a plateau seems to have been reached with most CD/DVD drives hovering right around the 100ms area, with some as low as 80ms. With each increase in data transfer speed, you usually see an improvement in access time as well. But as you can see in Table 13.23, these improvements are much less significant because of the physical limitation of the drive's single-read mechanism design.

Table 13.23   Typical CD-ROM Drive Access Times

Drive Speed	Access Time (ms)
1x	400
2x	300
3x	200
4x	150
6x	150
8x–12x	100
16x–24x	90
32x–52x or greater	85 or less

The times listed here are typical examples for good drives; within each speed category some drives are faster and some are slower. Because of the additional positioning accuracy required and the overall longer track, DVD drives usually report two access speeds—one when reading DVDs and the other when reading CDs. The DVD access times run usually 10ms–20ms slower than when readingCDs.

Buffer/Cache

Most CD/DVD drivesinclude internal buffers or caches of memory installed onboard. These buffers are actual memory chips installed on the drive's circuit board that enable it to stage or store data in larger segments before sending it to the PC. A typical buffer for a CD/DVD drive is 128KB, although drives are available that have either more or less (more is usually better). Recordable CD or DVD drives typically have much larger buffers of 2MB–4MB or more to prevent buffer underrun problems and to smooth writing operations. Generally, faster drives come with more buffer memory to handle the higher transfer rates.

Having buffer or cache memory for the CD/DVD drive offers a number of advantages. Buffers can ensure that the PC receives data at a constant rate; when an application requests data from the drive, the data can be found in files scattered across different segments of the disc. Because the drive has a relatively slow access time, the pauses between data reads can cause a drive to send data to the PC sporadically. You might not notice this in typical text applications, but on a drive with a slower access rate coupled with no data buffering, it is very noticeable—and even irritating—during the display of video or some audio segments. In addition, a drive's buffer, when under the control of sophisticated software, can read and have ready the disc's table of contents, speeding up the first request for data. A minimum size of 128KB for a built-in buffer or cache is recommended and is standard on many 24x and faster drives. For greater performance, look for drives with 256KB or larger buffers.

CPU Utilization

A once-neglected but very real issue in calculating computer performance is the impact that any piece of hardware or software has on the central processing unit (CPU). This "CPU utilization" factor refers to how much attention the CPU (such as Pentium III/4, Athlon, and so on) must provide to the hardware or software to help it work. A low CPU utilization percentage score is desirable because the less time a CPU spends on any given hardware or software process, the more time it has for other tasks, and thus the greater the performance for your system. On CD-ROM drives, three factors influence CPU utilization: drive speed, drive buffer size, and interface type.

Drive buffer size can influence CPU utilization. For CD-ROM drives with similar performance ratings, the drive with a larger buffer is likely to require less CPU time (lower CPU utilization percentage) than the one with a smaller buffer.

Because drive speed and buffer size are more of a given, the most important factor influencing CPU utilization is the interface type. Traditionally, SCSI-interface CD-ROM drives have had far lower CPU utilization rates than ATAPI drives of similar ratings. One review of 12x drives done several years ago rated CPU utilization for ATAPI CD-ROM drives at 65%–80%, whereas SCSI CD-ROM drives checked in at less than 11%. By using DMA or Ultra-DMA modes with an ATA interface drive, near-SCSI levels of low CPU utilization can be realized. Using DMA or Ultra-DMA modes can cut CPU utilization down to the 10% or lower range, leaving the CPU free to run applications and other functions.

Direct Memory Access and Ultra-DMA

Busmastering ATA controllers use Direct Memory Access (DMA) or Ultra-DMA transfers to improve performance and reduce CPU utilization. Virtually all modern ATA drives support Ultra-DMA. With busmastering, CPU utilization for ATA/ATAPI and SCSI CD-ROM drives is about equal at around 11%. Thus, it's to your benefit to enable DMA access for your CD-ROM drives (and your ATA hard drives, too) if your system permits it.

Most recent ATAATAPI CD-ROM drives (12x and above) support DMA or Ultra-DMA transfers, as does Windows 95B and above and most recent Pentium-class motherboards. To determine whether your Win9x or Me system has this feature enabled, check the System Properties' Device Manager tab and click the + mark next to Hard Disk Controllers. A drive interface capable of handling DMA transfers lists "Bus Master" in the name. Next, check the hard drive and CD-ROM information for your system. You can use the properties sheet for your system's CD-ROM drives under Windows 9x/Me and Windows 2000/XP to find this information; you might need to open the system to determine your hard drive brand and model. Hard disk drives and CD-ROM drives that support MultiWord DMA Mode 2 (16.6MB/sec), UltraDMA Mode 2 (33MB/sec), UltraDMA Mode 4 (66MB/sec), or faster can use DMA transfers. Check your product literature or the manufacturer's Web sites for information.

To enable DMA transfers if your motherboard and drives support it, open the System Properties sheet in Windows 9x or later, click the Device Manager tab, and open the Properties sheet for your hard drive. Click the Settings tab, and place a check mark in the box labeled DMA.

Repeat the same steps to enable DMA transfers for any additional hard drives and ATAPI CD-ROM drives in your computer. Restart your computer after making these changes.

Note

I strongly recommend that you back up your drives and your Windows 9x Registry before you enable DMA support or before you install and enable the driver to allow DMA support. If your system hangs after you enable this feature, you must restart the system in Safe mode and uncheck the DMA box. In some cases, if you can't access safe mode, you might have to replace the Registry with the pre-DMA–enabled copy you saved. Otherwise, you'll be faced with editing Registry keys by hand to start your system again. Because DMA transfers bypass the CPU to achieve greater speed, DMA problems could result in data loss. Make backups first, instead of wishing you had later.

Also, if your drive supports any of the Ultra-DMA (also called Ultra-ATA) modes, you should upgrade your ATA cables to the 80-conductor style. Using these cables prevents noise and signal distortion that will occur if you try to use a standard 40-conductor cable with the Ultra-DMA modes. Most drives and motherboards refuse to enable Ultra-DMA modes faster than 33MB/sec if an 80-conductor cable is not detected.

Drive interfaces that don't mention busmastering can't perform this speedup or need to have the correct driver installed. In some cases, depending on your Windows version and when your motherbaord chipset was made, you must install chipset drivers to enable Windows to properly recognize the chipset and enable DMA modes. A good Web site for both Intel and non-Intel chipset support of this important feature is www.bmdrivers.com. Follow the links at this site to the motherboard chipset vendors, their technical notes (to determine whether your chipset supports busmastering), and the drivers you need to download. Virtually all motherboard chipsets produced since 1995 provide busmaster ATA support. Most of those produced since 1997 also provide UltraDMA support, for up to 33MHz (Ultra-ATA/33) or 66MHz (Ultra-ATA/66) speed operation. Still, you should make sure that DMA is enabled to ensure you are benefiting from the performance it offers. Enabling DMA can dramatically improve DVD performance, for example.

Interface

The drive's interface is the physical connection of the drive to the PC's expansion bus. The interface is the data pipeline from the drive to the computer, and its importance shouldn't be minimized. Five types of interfaces are available for attaching a CD-ROM, CD-R, or CD-RW drive to your system:

- SCSI/ASPI (Small Computer System Interface/Advanced SCSI Programming Interface)
- ATA/ATAPI (AT Attachment/AT Attachment Packet Interface)
- Parallel port
- USB port
- FireWire (IEEE 1394)

The following sections examine these interface choices.

SCSI/ASPI

SCSI (pronounced *scuzzy*), or the Small Computer System Interface, is a name given to a special interface bus that allows many types of peripherals to communicate.

A standard software interface called ASPI (Advanced SCSI Programming Interface) enables CD-ROM drives (and other SCSI peripherals) to communicate with the SCSI host adapter installed in the computer. SCSI offers the greatest flexibility and performance of the interfaces available for CD-ROM drives and can be used to connect many other types of peripherals to your system as well.

The SCSI bus enables computer users to string a group of devices along a chain from one SCSI host adapter, avoiding the complication of installing a separate adapter card into the PC bus slots for each new hardware device, such as a tape unit or additional CD-ROM drive added to the system. These traits make the SCSI interface preferable for connecting a peripheral such as a CD-ROM to your PC.

Not all SCSI adapters are created equal, however. Although they might share a common command set, they can implement these commands differently, depending on how the adapter's manufacturer designed the hardware. ASPI was created to eliminate these incompatibilities. ASPI was originally developed by Adaptec, Inc., a leader in the development of SCSI controller cards and adapters who originally named it the Adaptec SCSI Programming Interface before it became a de facto standard. ASPI consists of two main parts. The primary part is an ASPI-Manager program, which is a driver that functions between the operating system and the specific SCSI host adapter. The ASPI-Manager sets up the ASPI interface to the SCSI bus.

The second part of an ASPI system is the individual ASPI device drivers. For example, you would get an ASPI driver for your SCSI CD-ROM drive. You can also get ASPI drivers for your other SCSI peripherals, such as tape drives and scanners. The ASPI driver for the peripheral talks to the ASPI-Manager for the host adapter. This is what enables the devices to communicate together on the SCSI bus.

The bottom line is that if you are getting a SCSI interface CD-ROM, be sure it includes an ASPI driver that runs under your particular operating system. Also, be sure that your SCSI host adapter has the corresponding ASPI-Manager driver as well. There are substantial differences between SCSI adapters because SCSI can be used for a wide variety of peripherals. Low-cost, SCSI-3–compliant ISA or PCI adapters can be used for CD-ROM interfacing. In contrast, higher-performance PCI adapters that support more advanced SCSI standards, such as Wide, Ultra, UltraWide, Ultra2Wide, and so on, can be used with both CD-ROM drives and other devices, such as CD-R/CD-RW drives, hard drives, scanners, tape backups, and so forth. To help you choose the appropriate SCSI adapter for both your CD-ROM drive and any other SCSI-based peripheral you're considering, visit Adaptec's Web site.

The SCSI interface offers the most powerful and flexible connection for CD-ROMs and other devices. It provides better performance, and seven or more drives can be connected to a single host adapter. The drawback is cost. If you do not need SCSI for other peripherals and intend on connecting only one CD-ROM drive to the system, you will be spending a lot of money on unused potential. In that case, an ATAPI interface CD-ROM drive would be a more cost-effective choice.

◄◄   See "Small Computer System Interface," p. 514.

ATA/ATAPI

The ATA/ATAPI (AT Attachment/AT Attachment Packet Interface) is an extension of the same ATA (AT Attachment) interface most computers use to connect to their hard disk drives. ATA is sometimes also refered to as IDE (Integrated Drive Electronics). ATAPI is an industry-standard ATA ATA/ATAPI is an extension of the same ATA interface most computers use to connect to their hard disk drives. ATA is sometimes also refered to as IDE (Integrated Drive Electronics). ATAPI is an industry-standard ATA interface used for CD/DVD and other drives. ATAPI is a software interface that adapts the SCSI/ASPI commands to the ATA interface. This enables drive manufacturers to take their high-end CD/DVD drive products and quickly adapt them to the ATA interface. This also enables the ATA drives to remain compatible with the MSCDEX (Microsoft CD-ROM Extensions) that provide a software interface with DOS. With Windows 9x and later, the CD-ROM extensions are contained in the CD file system (CDFS) VxD (virtual device) driver.

ATA/ATAPI drives are sometimes also called enhanced IDE (EIDE) drives because this is an extension of the original IDE (technically the ATA) interface. In most cases, an ATA drive connects to the system via a second ATA interface connector and channel, leaving the primary one for hard disk drives only.

This is preferable because ATA does not share the single channel well and would cause a hard disk drive to wait for CD/DVD commands to complete and vice versa. SCSI does not have this problem because a SCSI host adapter can send commands to different devices without having to wait for each previous command to complete.

The ATA interface represents the most cost-effective and high-performance interface for CD-ROM drives. Most new systems that include a CD and/or DVD drive have it connected through ATA. You can connect up to two drives to the secondary ATA connector; for more than that, SCSI is your only choice and provides better performance as well.

Many systems on the market today can use the ATA/ATAPI CD/DVD drive as a bootable device, which allows the vendor to supply a recovery CD that can restore the computer's software to its factory-shipped condition. Later, you'll see how bootable CDs differ from ordinary CDs and how you can use low-cost CD-R/CD-RW drives, along with mastering and imaging software to make your own bootable CDs with your own preferred configuration.

◀◀ See "An Overview of the IDE Interface," p. 476.

▶▶ See "Creating a Bootable Floppy with CD-ROM Support," p. 772.

Parallel Port

Rather than opening the case to insert a SCSI adapter or connect an internal drive, you can install some CD-ROM drives simply by connecting a cable to the PC's parallel port and loading the appropriate software. Although parallel port drives have been available for some time now, USB has for the most part replaced the parallel port for this type of use.

Obviously, the advantages of CD-ROMs that use the parallel port interface are their ease of installation and their portability. In an office environment where the primary function of CD-ROMs is to install software, you can easily move one parallel port drive from machine to machine, rather than purchase a drive for each system. If you use an operating system that supports Plug and Play (PnP), such as Windows 9x, simply plugging a PnP drive into the parallel port causes the OS to detect the new hardware and load the appropriate driver for you automatically.

For best performance, it's recommended that you set your printer port to use IEEE-1284 standards, such as ECP/EPP or ECP, before connecting your parallel-port CD-ROM. These are bidirectional, high-speed extensions to the standard Centronics parallel port standard and provide better performance for virtually any recent parallel device. These devices include printers, tape backups, and Zip and LS-120 drives (also known as SuperDrives), as well as CD-ROM, CD-R, and CD-RW drives.

Using the IEEE-1284 enhanced settings can make a tremendous difference in parallel-port CD-ROM performance. For example, bidirectional (PS/2 style) can achieve data transfer rates of 100KB/sec–530KB/second, whereas EPP can achieve rates of about 1,200KB/second—12 times that of standard (unidirectional).

▶▶ See "IEEE 1284 Parallel Port Standard," p. 934.

Note

Parallel port CD-ROM drives nearly always include a cable with a pass-through connector. This connector plugs into the parallel port and, if necessary, a printer cable can plug into the connector. This enables you to continue using the port to connect to your printer while sharing the interface with the CD-ROM drive. Note there might be performance problems when trying to print and read from the drive at the same time.

I generally do not recommend that you purchase parallel port drives because internal drives are much faster and generally more compatible. And if you need an external portable drive, more universal interfaces, such as USB or FireWire, offer greater performance, compatability, and ease of use.

USB Interface

USB (Universal Serial Bus) has proven to be extremely flexible and has been used for everything from keyboards and joysticks to CD/DVD drives from several vendors.

USB 1.1 and earlier drives provide read and write transfer rates that match the fastest rates possible with IEEE-1284 parallel ports, with read rates on typical 6x models ranging from 1,145KB/sec to 1,200KB/sec. USB 2.0 provides a transfer rate up to 60MB/sec, which is 40 times faster than USB 1.1 and yet fully backward compatible.

USB also provides benefits that no parallel port drive can match: for example, hot-swappability, the capability to be plugged in or unplugged without removing the power or rebooting the system. Additionally, USB devices are fully Plug and Play (PnP), allowing the device to be automatically recognized by the system and the drivers automatically installed.

For Windows 98/Me or Windows 2000/XP systems with USB ports, USB-based CD-RW drives are an excellent solution for backup and archiving of data onto low-cost, durable optical media. Although Windows 95 OSR 2.1 and above also support USB, at least in theory, USB device support with Windows 95 is chancy at best. It usually is recommended to run Windows 98 or later to properly support USB on your system.

FireWire

More recently, external CD/DVD drives have come on the market with a FireWire (also called IEEE-1394 or iLink) interface. FireWire is a high-performance external interface designed mainly for video use. Because very few systems include FireWire ports as a standard item, I normally recommend the more universally recognized USB for external CD/DVD drives instead. Also, USB 2.0 (also known as Hi-Speed USB) is faster and more generally available than the current FireWire implementations.

▶▶ See "USB and IEEE-1394 (i.Link or FireWire)—Serial and Parallel Port Replacements," p. 940.

Loading Mechanism

Three distinctly different mechanisms exist for loading a disc into a CD/DVD drive: the tray, caddy, and slot. Each one offers some benefits and features. Which type you select has a major impact on your use of the drive because you interact with this mechanism every time you load a disc.

Some drives on the market allow you to insert more than one disc at a time. Some of these use a special cartridge that you fill with discs, much like multidisc CD-changers used in automobiles. Newer models are slot-loading, allowing you to push a button to select which internal cartridge slot you want to load with a CD/DVD. The drive's door opens and you slide in the CD, which the drive mechanism grabs and pulls into place. Typical capacities range from 3 to 6 discs or more, and these are available in both SCSI and ATA interfaces.

Tray

Most current SCSI and ATAPI CD/DVD drives use a tray-loading mechanism. This is similar to the mechanism used with a stereo system. Because you don't need to put each disc into a separate caddy, this mechanism is much less expensive overall. However, it also means that you must handle each disc every time you insert or remove it.

Tray loading is more convenient and less expensive than a caddy system (see the section, "Caddy," later in this chapter) because you don't need a caddy. However, this can make it much more difficult for young children or those who work in harsh environments to use the discs without smudging or damaging them due to excess handling.

The tray loader itself is also subject to damage. The trays can easily break if bumped or if something is dropped on them while they are extended. Also, any contamination you place on the tray or disc is brought right into the drive when the tray is retracted. Tray-loaded drives should not be used in a harsh environment, such as a commercial or an industrial application. Make sure both the tray and the data surface of the disc are clean whenever you use a tray-loading drive.

The tray mechanism also does not hold the disc as securely as the caddy. If you don't have the disc placed in the tray properly when it retracts, the disc or tray can be damaged. Even a slight misalignment can prevent the drive from reading the disc properly, forcing you to open the tray and reset the disc.

Some tray drives can't operate in a vertical (sideways) position because gravity prevents proper loading and operation. Check to see whether the drive tray has retaining clips, which grab the hub of the disc. If so, you can run the drive in either horizontal or vertical position.

Some drives equipped with retaining clips still aren't capable of running reliably in the vertical position. If this is a critical feature for you, be sure to test a unit before you install it in a system, or make sure you can return it if it doesn't work properly.

Apart from the convenience, the other advantage of the tray mechanism over the caddy system is in cost, and that is a big factor. If you do not have young children and plan to use the drive in a clean environment where careful handling and cleanliness can be assured, the tray mechanism is recommended because of its significantly lower cost.

Caddy

At one time, the caddy system was used on most high-end CD-ROM drives as well as the early CD-R and DVD-RAM drives. It has since declined in popularity because of the convenience of the tray. The caddy system requires that you place the disc itself into a special caddy, which is a sealed container with a metal shutter. The caddy has a hinged lid that you open to insert the disc, but after that the lid remains shut. When you insert the caddy containing the disc into the drive, the drive opens a metal shutter on the bottom of the caddy, allowing access to the disc by the laser.

The caddy is not the most convenient loading mechanism, although if all your discs are in their own caddies, all you have to do is grab the caddy containing the disc you want and insert it into the drive. This makes the drive operate similar to a 3 1/2-inch disk. You can handle the caddy without worrying about touching or contaminating the disc or the drive, making this the most accurate and durable mechanism as well. Young children can easily handle the caddies and don't have to touch the compact discs themselves.

Because the caddy is sealed, the discs are protected from damage caused by handling. The only time you actually handle the disc is when you first put it into the caddy. The caddy loading system also ensures that the disc is properly located when inside the drive. This allows for more accurate laser-head positioning mechanisms, and caddy drives generally have faster access times, as well.

The drawbacks to the caddy system are the expense and the inconvenience. You only get one caddy with the drive, so if you want to store your discs in their own caddies, you must buy many more. Additional caddies can cost $4–$10 each, which can lead to a significant expense if you have a large number of discs.

The best application for caddy drives is in severe environments such as machine shops, repair shops, factories, or anywhere somebody with dirty hands or gloves on will have to change discs.

When DVD-RAM was first introduced, the disc had to remain in a caddy because the recordable surface is delicate. Since then, DVD-RAM drives have been made caddy-less, but especially with double-sided discs the information is at risk every time you handle the disc. Because of this fragility, as well as the general incompatibility of DVD-RAM with DVD-ROM, I recommend DVD+RW as the best solution for recordable DVD. No caddy is required with DVD+RW, and the format is fully two-way compatible with DVD-Video and DVD-ROM.

Slot

Some drives now use a slot-loading mechanism, identical to that used in most automotive CD players. This is very convenient, because you just slip the disc into the slot, where the mechanism grabs it and draws it inside. There are drives that can load several CDs at a time this way, holding them internally inside the drive and switching discs as access is required.

The primary drawback to this type of mechanism is that if a jam occurs, it can be much more difficult to repair because you might have to remove the drive to free the disc. Another drawback is that slot-loading drives normally can't handle the smaller 80mm discs, card-shaped discs, or other modified disc physical formats or shapes.

Other Drive Features

Although drive specifications are of the utmost importance, you should also consider other factors and features when evaluating CD-ROM drives. Besides quality of construction, the following criteria bear scrutiny when making a purchasing decision:

- Drive sealing
- Self-cleaning lenses
- Internal versus external drive

Drive Sealing

Dirt is your CD/DVD drive's biggest enemy. Dust or dirt, when it collects on the lens portion of the mechanism, can cause read errors or severe performance loss. Many manufacturers seal off the lens and internal components from the drive bay in airtight enclosures. Other drives, although not sealed, have double dust doors—one external and one internal—to keep dust from the inside of the drive. All these features help prolong the life of your drive.

Some drives are sealed, which means that no air flows through the chamber in which the laser and lens reside. Always look for sealed drives in harsh industrial or commercial environments. In a standard office or home environment, it is probably not worth the extra expense.

Self-Cleaning Lenses

If the laser lens gets dirty, so does your data. The drive will spend a great deal of time seeking and reseeking or will finally give up. Lens-cleaning discs are available, but built-in cleaning mechanisms are now included on virtually all good-quality drives. This might be a feature you'll want to consider, particularly if you work in a less-than-pristine work environment or have trouble keeping your desk clean, let alone your drive laser lens. You can clean the lens manually, but it is generally a delicate operation requiring that you partially disassemble the drive. Also, damaging the lens mechanism by using too much force is pretty easy to do. Because of the risks involved, in most cases I do not recommend the average person dissasemble and try to manually clean the laser lens.

Internal Versus External Drives

When deciding whether you want an internal or external drive, think about where and how you're going to use your drive. What about the future expansion of your system? Both types of drives have advantages and disadvantages, such as the following:

- *External enclosure.* These tend to be rugged, portable, and large—in comparison to their internal versions. External drives are ideal for sharing a drive with multiple systems or especially with laptops or notebook portable systems. Parallel port drives are very portable and supported on a broad range of machines, but USB drives are a better choice for Windows 98 or later systems that have USB ports.

  SCSI drives are also ideal for external configurations because performance is even better than with internal ATA drives. If each PC has its own SCSI adapter with an external connection, all you need to do is unplug the drive from one adapter and plug it in to the other. I use SCSI drives extensively, and with SCSI I can get the same level of performance when the drive is connected to my laptop as when it is connected to a desktop system.

- *Internal enclosure.* Internal drives won't take up any space on your desk. Buy an internal drive if you have a free drive bay and a sufficient power supply and you plan to keep the drive exclusively on one machine. The internal drives are also nice because you can connect the audio connector to your sound card and leave the external audio connectors free for other inputs. Internal drives can be ATA or SCSI.

Writable CDs

Although the CD originally was concieved as a read-only device, these daysyou easily can create your own data and audio CDs. By purchasing CD-R or CD-RW discs and drives, you can record (or burn) your own CDs. This enables you to store large amounts of data at a cost that is lower than most other removable, random-access mediums.

It might surprise newcomers to the world of PCs to see just how far recordable CD technology, performance, and pricing has come. Today you can buy recorders that operate at up to 20x speeds and cost as little as $100. You can even purchase slimline CD drives for laptops. This is compared to the first CD-R recording system on the market in 1988, which cost more than $50,000 (back then, they used a $35,000 Yamaha audio recording drive along with thousands of dollars of additional error correction and other circuitry for CD-ROM use), operated at 1x speed only, and was part of a subsystem that was the size of a washing machine! The blank discs also cost about $100 each—a far cry from the 25 cents or less they cost today (if you purchase in bulk and are willing to supply your own jewel cases). With prices that high, the main purpose for CD recording was to produce prototype CDs that could then be replicated via the standard stamping process.

In 1991, Philips introduced the first 2x recorder (the CDD 521), which was about the size of a stereo receiver and cost about $12,000. Sony in 1992 and then JVC in 1993 followed with their 2x recorders, and the JVC was the first drive that had the half-height 5 1/4-inch form factor that most desktop system drives still use today. In 1995, Yamaha released the first 4x recorder (the CDR100), which sold for $5,000. A breakthrough in pricing came in late 1995 when Hewlett-Packard released a 2x recorder (the 4020i, which was actually made for them by Philips) for under $1,000. This proved to be exactly what the market was waiting for. With a surge in popularity after that, prices rapidly fell to below $500, and then down to $200 or less. In 1996, Ricoh introduced the first CD-RW drive.

Compared with either tape or other removable media, using a CD burner is a very cost-effective and easy method for transporting large files or making archival copies. Another benefit of the CD for archiving data is that CDs have a much longer shelf life than tapes or other removable media.

Two main types of recordable CD drives and discs are available, called CD-R (recordable) and CD-RW (rewritable). Because all CD-RW drives can also function as CD-R drives, and the prices of CD-R and RW drives are similar, virtually all drives sold today are CD-RW. Those drives can work with either CD-R or CD-RW discs. In addition, because the CD-RW discs are 1.5–4 times more expensive than CD-R discs, only half as fast (or less) as CD-R discs, and won't work in all CD audio or CD-ROM drives, people usually write to CD-R media in their CD-RW drives.

Note

Because of differences in reflectivity of the media, older CD and DVD drives can't read CD-RW media. Most newer CD or DVD-ROM drives conform to the MultiRead specification and as such can read CD-RWs. But many older drives are still out there that do not conform. As such, if you are recording something that many people or systems will need to read, CD-R is your best choice for overall compatibility.

CD-R media is WORM, meaning that after you fill a CD-R with data, it is permanently stored and can't be erased. The write-once limitation makes this type of disc less than ideal for system backups or other purposes in which it would be preferable to reuse the same media over and over. However, because of the low cost of CD-R media, you might find that making permanent backups to essentially disposable CD-R discs is as economically feasible as tape or other media.

CD-RW discs can be reused up to 1,000 times, making them suitable for almost any type of data storage task. When first introduced, there were many CD-R–only drives; however, today most recordable CD drives are both CD-R and CD-RW in one. The following sections examine these two standards and how you can use them for your own data storage needs.

CD-R

Once recorded, CD-R discs can be played back or read in any standard CD-ROM drive. CD-R discs are useful for archival storage and creating master CDs, which can be duplicated for distribution within a company.

CD-Rs function using the same principle as standard CD-ROMs, by bouncing laser light off the disc and tracking the changes in reflectivity when pit/land and land/pit boundaries are encountered. The main difference is that instead of being stamped or embossed into plastic as on regular CDs, CD-Rs have images of pits burned onto a raised groove instead. Therefore, the pits are not really raised bumps like on a standard CD, but instead are rendered as dark (burned) areas on the groove that reflect less light. Because the overall reflectivity of pit and land areas remains the same as on a stamped disc, normal CD-ROM or CD audio drives can read CD-Rs exactly as if they were stamped discs.

Part of the recording process with CD-Rs starts before you even insert the disc into the drive. CD-R media is manufactured much like a standard CD—a stamper is used to mold a base of polycarbonate plastic. However, instead of stamping pits and lands, the stamper imprints a spiral groove (called a *pre-groove*), into the disc. From the perspective of the reading (and writing) laser underneath the disc, this groove is seen as a raised spiral ridge and not a depression.

The pre-groove (or ridge) is not perfectly straight; instead it has a slight wobble. The amplitude of the wobble is generally very small compared to the track pitch (spacing). The groove separation is 1.6 microns, but it wobbles only 0.030 microns from side to side. The wobble of a CD-R groove is modulated to carry supplemental information read by the drive. The signal contained in the wobble is called absolute time in pre-groove (ATIP) because it is modulated with time code and other data. The time code is the same minutes:seconds:frame format that will eventually be found in the Q-subcode of the frames after they are written to the disc. The ATIP enables the drive to locate positions on the disc before the frames are actually written. Technically, the wobble signal is frequency shift keyed with a carrier frequency of 22.05KHz and a deviation of 1KHz. The wobble uses changes in frequency to carry information.

To complete the CD-R disc, an organic dye is evenly applied across the disc by a spin-coating process. Next, a gold reflective layer is then applied, followed by a protective coat of UV-cured lacquer to protect the gold and dye layers. Gold is used in CD-R discs to get the reflectivity as high as possible, and it was found that the organic dye tends to oxidize aluminum. Then, silk-screen printing is applied on top of the lacquer for identification and further protection. When seen from the underside, the laser used to read (or write) the disc first passes through the clear polycarbonate and the dye layer, hits the gold layer where it is reflected back through the dye layer and the plastic, and finally is picked up by the optical pickup sensor in the drive.

The dye and reflective layer together have the same reflective properties as a *virgin* CD. In other words, a CD reader would read the groove of an unrecorded CD-R disc as one long land. To record on a CD-R disc, a laser beam of the same wavelength (780nm) as is normally used to read the disc, but with 10 times the power, is used to heat up the dye. The laser is fired in a pulsed fashion at the top of the ridge (groove), heating the layer of organic dye to between 482° and 572°F (250°–300°C). This temperature literally burns the organic dye, causing it to become opaque. When read, this prevents the light from passing through the dye layer to the gold and reflecting back, having the same effect of cancelling the laser reflection that an actual raised pit would on a normal stamped CD.

Figure 13.11 shows the CD-R media layers, along with the pre-groove (raised ridge from the laser perspective) with burned pits.

Figure 13.11 CD-R media layers.

The drive reading the disc is fooled into thinking a pit exists, but no actual pit exists—there's simply a spot of less-reflective material on the ridge. This use of heat to create the pits in the disc is why the recording process is often referred to as *burning* a CD. When burned, the dye changes from a reflective to a nonreflective state. This change of state is permanent and can't be undone, which is why CD-R is considered a write-once medium.

CD-R Capacity

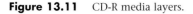

All CD-R drives can work with the standard 650MiB (682MB) CD-R media (equal to 74 minutes of recorded music), as well as the higher-capacity 700MiB (737MB) CD-R blanks(equal to 80 minutes of recorded music). The 80-minute discs cost only about 2 cents more than the 74-minute discs, so most would figure why not purchase only the higher-capacity media? Although the extra 55MB of storage can be useful and the cost difference is neglegible, the 80-minute discs can actually be harder to read on older CD-ROM and CD-DA drives, especially car audio units. This is because to get the extra 55MB/6 minutes of capacity, the spiral track is wound a little more tightly, making them a bit more difficult read. If you'll be using the discs for audio or interchange purposes and might be dealing with older equipment, you might want to stick with the 74-minute discs instead. If not, the 80-minute media will be just fine.

Some drives and burning software are capable of overburning, whereby they write data partially into the lead-out area and essentially extend the data track. This is definitely risky as far as compatibility is concerned. Many drives, especially older ones, fail when reading near the end of an overburned disc. It's best to consider this form of overclocking CDs somewhat experimental. It might be useful for your own purposes if it works with your drives and software, but interchangeability will be problematic.

CD-R Media Color

There's been some controversy over the years about which colors of CD-R media provide the best performance. Table 13.24 shows the most common color combinations, along with which brands use them and some technical information.

Some brands are listed with more than one color combination, due to production changes or different product lines. You should check color combinations whenever you purchase a new batch of CD-R media if you've found that particular color combinations work better for you in your applications.

Table 13.24   CD-R Media Color and Its Effect on Recording

Media Color (first color is reflective layer; second is die layer)	Brands	Technical Notes
Gold-gold	Mitsui, Kodak, Maxell, Ricoh	Phthalocyanine dye
		Less tolerance for power variations
		Might be less likely to work in a wide variety of drives
		Invented by Mitsui Toatsu Chemicals
		Works best in drives that use a Long Write Strategy (longer laser pulse) to mark media
Gold-green	Imation (nee 3M), Memorex, Kodak, BASF, TDK	Cyanine dye; more forgiving of disc-write and disc-read variations
		Has a rated life span of 10 years
		Color combination developed by Taiyo Yuden
		Used in the development of the original CD-R standards
		De facto standard for CD-R industry and was the original color combination used during the development of CD-R technology
		Works best in drives that use a Short Write Strategy (shorter laser pulse) to mark media
Silver-blue	Verbatim, DataLifePlus, HiVal, Maxell, TDK	Process developed by Verbatim
		Azo dye
		Similar performance to green media plus rated to last up to 100 years
		A good choice for long-term archiving

Ultimately, although the various color combinations have their advantages, the best way to choose a media type is to try a major brand of media in your CD-R/CD-RW drive with both full-disc and small-disc recording jobs and then try the completed CD-R in as wide a range of CD-ROM drive brands and speeds as you can.

The perfect media for you will be the ones that offer you

- High reliability in writing
- No dye or reflective surface dropouts (areas where the media won't record properly)
- Durability through normal handling (scratch-resistant coating on media surface)
- Compatibility across the widest range of CD-ROM drives
- Lowest unit cost

Choosing the Best Media

After you determine which media works the best for you and your target drives, you might still be faced with a wide variety of choices, including conventional surface, printable surface, unbranded, jewel case, and bulk on spindle. The following list discusses these options:

- *Conventional surface.* Choose this type of media if you want to use a marker to label the CD rather than adding a paper label. This type of CD often has elaborate labeling, including areas to indicate CD title, date created, and other information as well as prominent brand identification. Because of the surface marking, it's not suitable for relabeling unless you use very opaque labels. It's a good choice for internal backups and data storage, though, where labeling is less important.
- *Printable surface.* Choose this type of media if you have a CD printer (a special type of inkjet printer that can print directly onto the face of the CD). Because the brand markings are usually low-contrast or even nonexistent (to allow overprinting), this type also works well with labeling kits such as NEATO and others.
- *Unbranded.* Usually sold in bulk on spindle, these are good choices for economy or use with labeling kits.
- *Jewel case.* Any of the preceding versions can be sold with jewel cases (the same type of case used for CD-ROM software and music CDs). This is a good choice if you plan to distribute the media in a jewel case, but it raises your costs if you plan to distribute or store the media in paper, Tyvek, or plastic sleeves. Hint: Use extra jewel cases to replace your broken jewel cases in your CD software or music collection!
- *Bulk on spindle.* This media generally comes with no sleeves and no cases. It is usually the lowest-priced packaging within any brand of media. This is an excellent choice for mass duplication, or for those who don't use jewel cases for distribution.

CD-R Media Recording Speed Rating

With CD-R mastering speeds ranging from 1x (now-discontinued first-generation units) up through fast 12x and state-of-the-art 20x rates, it's important to check the speed rating (x-rating) of your CD-R media.

Most branded media on the market today is rated to work successfully at up to 16x recording speeds. Some brands indicate this specifically on their packaging, whereas you must check the Web sites for others to get this information.

If speed ratings are unavailable, you might want to restrict your burning to 8x or lower. Media that is 16x or higher rated is now the most popular, but speed ratings higher than that might be more difficult to find.

CD-RW

Beginning in early 1996, an industry consortium that included Ricoh, Philips, Sony, Yamaha, Hewlett-Packard, and Mitsubishi Chemical Corporation announced the CD-RW format. The design was largely led by Ricoh, and they were the first manufacturer to introduce a CD-RW drive in May of 1996. It was the MP6200S, which was a 2/2/6 (2x record, 2x rewrite, 6x read) rated unit. At the same time, the Orange Book Part III was published, which officially defined the CD-RW standard.

Since that time, CD-RW drives have pretty much replaced CD-R–only drives in the market today, mainly because CD-RW drives are fully backward compatible with CD-R drives and can read and write the same CD-R media with the same capabilities. So, a CD-RW drive can also function as a CD-R drive. CD-RW discs can be burned or written to just like CD-Rs; the main difference is that they can be erased and reburned again and again. They are very useful for prototyping a disc that will then be duplicated in less expensive CD-R or even stamped CDs for distribution. They can be rewritten at least 1,000 times or more. Additionally, with packet-writing software, they can even be treated like a giant floppy disk, where you can simply drag and drop or copy and delete files at will. Although CD-RW discs are about twice as expensive as CD-R media, CD-RWs are still far cheaper than optical cartridges and other removable formats. This makes CD-RW a viable technology for system backups, file archiving, and virtually any other data storage task.

Note

The CD-RW format originally was referred to as CD-Erasable, or CD-E.

Four main differences exist between CD-RW and CD-R media. In a nutshell, CD-RW discs are

- Rewritable
- More expensive
- Slower when writing
- Less reflective

Besides the CD-RW media being rewritable and costing a bit more, they also are writable at about half (or less) the speed of CD-R discs. This is because the laser needs more time to operate on a particular spot on the disk when writing. They also have a lower reflectivity, which limits readability in older drives. Many standard CD-ROM and CD-R drives can't read CD-RWs. However, MultiRead capability is now found in virtually all CD-ROM drives of 24x speed or above, enabling them to read CD-RWs without problems. In general, CD-DA drives—especially the car audio players—seem to have the most difficulty reading CD-RWs. So, for music recording or compatibility with older drives, you should probably stick to CD-R media. Look for the MultiRead logo on a CD-ROM drive, indicates the capability to read CD-RW.

CD-RW drives and media use a phase change process to create the illusion of pits on the disc. As with CD-R media, the disc starts out with the same polycarbonate base with a wobbled pre-groove molded in, which contains ATIP information. Then, on top of the base a special dielectric (insulating) layer is spin-coated, followed by the phase change recording layer, another dielectric layer, an aluminum reflective layer, and finally a UV-cured lacquer protective layer (and optional screen printing). The dielectric layers above and below the recording layer are designed to insulate the polycarbonate and reflective layers from the intense heat used during the phase-change process.

Figure 13.12 shows the CD-RW media layers, along with the pre-groove (raised ridge from the laser perspective) with burned pits in the phase change layer.

Figure 13.12   CD-RW media layers.

Instead of burning an organic dye as with CD-R, the recording layer in a CD-RW disc is made up of a phase-change alloy consisting of silver, indium, antimony, and tellurium (Ag-In-Sb-Te). The reflective part of the recording layer is an aluminum alloy, the same as used in normal stamped discs. The read/write laser works from the underside of the disk, where the groove again appears like a ridge, and the recording is made in the phase-change layer on top of this ridge.

The recording layer of Ag-In-Sb-Te alloy normally has a polycrystalline structure that is about 20% reflective. When data is written to a CD-RW disc, the laser in the drive alternates between two power settings, called P-write and P-erase. The higher power setting (P-write) is used to heat the material in the recording layer to a temperature between 500° and 700°C (932°–1292°F), causing it to melt. In a liquid state the molecules of the material flow freely, losing their polycrystalline structure and taking what is called an *amorphous* (random) state. When the material then solidifies in this amorphous state, it is only about 5% reflective. When being read, these areas lower in reflectivity simulate the pits on a stamped CD-ROM disc.

That would be all to the story if CD-RW discs were read-only, but because they can be rewritten, there must be a way to bring the material back to a polycrystalline state. This is done by setting the laser to the lower-power P-erase mode. This heats the active material to approximately 200°C (392°F), which is well below the liquid melting point but high enough to soften the material. When the material is softened and allowed to cool more slowly, the molecules realign from a 5% reflective amorphous state back to a 20% reflective polycrystalline state. These higher reflective areas simulate the lands on a stamped CD-ROM disc.

Note that despite the name of the P-erase laser power setting, the disc is not ever explicitly "erased." Instead, CD-RW uses a recording technique called *direct overwrite*, in which a spot doesn't have to be erased to be rewritten; it is simply rewritten. In other words, when data is recorded the laser remains on and pulses between the P-write and P-erase power levels to create amorphous and polycrystalline areas of low and high reflectivity, regardless of which state the areas were in prior. It is similar in many ways to writing data on a magnetic disk that also uses direct overwrite. Every sector already has data patterns, so when you write data, all you are really doing is writing new patterns. Sectors are never really erased; they are merely overwritten. The media in CD-RW discs is designed to be written and rewritten up to 1,000 times.

CD-RW Speeds

The original Orange Book Part III Volume 1 (CD-RW specification) allowed for CD-RW writing at up to 4x speeds. New developments in the media and drives were required to support speeds higher than that, so in May 2000, Part III Volume 2 was published, defining CD-RW recording at speeds from 4x to 10x. This new revision of the CD-RW standard is called High-Speed Rewritable, and both the discs and drives capable of CD-RW speeds higher than 4x will indicate this via the logos printed on them.

Because of the differences required in the High-Speed media (discs), they can be used only in High-Speed CD-RW drives. If you try to write on the High-Speed media in a 2x or 4x CD-RW drive, the recording will fail and you will possibly see several error messages. Note that you can use the slower 4x or less rated media in the High-Speed drives, providing you write at only the 4x or lower speed for which the media is rated.

Mount Rainier

Mountainier is a new standard being promoted by Philips, Sony, Microsoft, and Compaq; it enables native operating system support for data storage on CD-RW. This makes the technology much easier to use (no special drivers or packet-writing software is necessary) and enables CD-RW drives to become a fully integrated storage solution. The main features of Mount Rainier are

- Integral defect management
- Direct addressing at the 2KB sector level
- Background formatting
- Standardized command set
- Standardized physical layout

This standard requires support directly in the operating system, BIOS, and requires drives with modified firmware and design. If it catches on, it might change the way CD-RW drives are used in 2002 and later.

MultiRead Specifications

The original red and yellow bookThe original Red and Yellow Book CD standards specified that on a CD the landsshould have a minimum reflectance value of about 70%, and the pits should have a maximum reflectance of about 28%. This means that the area of a disc that represents a land should reflect back no less than 70% of the laser light directed at it, whereas the pits should reflect no more than 28%. In the early 1980s when these standards were developed, the photodetector diodes used in the drives were relatively insensitive, and these minimim and maximum reflectance requirements were deliberately designed to create enough brightness and contrast between pits and lands to accommodate them.

On a CD-RW disc, the reflectance of a land is approximately 20% (plus or minus 5%), and the reflectivity of a pit is only 5%, obviously well below the original requirements. Fortunately, it was found that by the addition of a relatively simple AGC circuit, the ratio of amplification in the detector circuitry can be changed dynamically to allow for reading the lower-reflective CD-RW discs. Thus, although CD-ROM drives were not initially capable of reading CD-RW discs, modifying the existing designs to enable them to do so wasn't difficult. Where you might encounter problems reading CD-RW discs is with CD audio drives, especially older ones. Because CD-RW first came out in 1996 (and took a year or more to become popular), most CD-ROM drives manufactured in 1997 or earlier have problems reading CD-RW discs. Reflectivity is also a problem on DVD-Video and DVD-ROM drives—because they use a different frequency laser, they actually have more trouble reading CD-R discs than CD-RWs.

DVDs also have some compatibility problems. With DVD, the problem isn't just simple reflectivity as it is an inherent incompatibility with the laser wavelength used for DVD versus CD-R and RW. The problem in this case stems from the dyes used in the recording layer of CD-R and RW discs, which are very sensitive to the wavelength of light used to read them. At the proper CD laser wavelength of 780nm, they are very reflective, but at other wavelengths, the reflectivity falls off markedly. Normally, CD-ROM drives use a 780nm (infrared) laser to read the data, whereas DVD drives use a shorter wavelength 650nm (red) laser. Although the shorter wavelength laser works well for reading commercial CD-ROM discs because the aluminum reflective layer they use is equally reflective at the shorter DVD laser wavelength, it doesn't work well at all for reading CD-R or RW discs.

Fortunately, a solution was first introduced by Sony and then similarly by all the other DVD drive manufacturers. This solution consists of a dual-laser pickup that incorporates both a 650nm (DVD) and 780nm (CD) laser. Some of these used two discrete pickup units with separate optics mounted to the same assembly, but they eventually changed to dual-laser units that use the same optics for both, making the pickup smaller and less expensive. Because most manufacturers wanted to make a variety of drives—including cheaper ones without the dual-laser pickup—a standard needed to be created so that someone purchasing a drive would know the drive's capabilities.

So, how can you tell whether your drive is compatible with CD-R and RW discs? To demonstrate the compatibility of a particular drive, OSTA created industry standard tests and logos that would guarantee specific levels of compatibility. These are called the MultiRead specifications. Currently there are two levels, as follows:

- *MultiRead.* For CD-ROM drives
- *MultiRead2.* For DVD-ROM drives

In addition, a similar MultiPlay standard exists that is for consumer DVD-Video and CD-DA devices.

Table 13.25 shows the two levels of MultiRead capability that can be assigned to drives and the types of media guaranteed to be readable in such drives.

Table 13.25   MultiRead and MultiRead2 Compatibility Standards for CD/DVD Drives

Media	MultiRead	MultiRead2
CD-DA	X	X
CD-ROM	X	X
CD-R	X	X
CD-RW	X	X
DVD-ROM	-	X
DVD-Video	-	X
DVD-Audio	-	X
DVD-RAM	-	X

X = Compatible; drive will read this media   *- = Incompatible; drive won't read*

Note that MultiRead also indicates that the drive is capabile of reading discs written in packet writing mode because this mode is now being used more commonly with both CD-R and RW media.

To determine whether your drive meets either of these standards, merely look for the MultiRead or MultiRead2 logo on the drive. These logos are shown in Figure 13.13.

The presence of these logos guarantees that particular level of compatibility. If you are purchasing a CD-ROM or DVD drive and want to be able to read recordable or rewritable discs, be sure to look for the MultiRead or MultiRead2 logo on your drive. Especially in the case of DVD drives, MultiRead2 versions generally are more expensive because of the extra cost of the dual-mode laser pickup required. Virtually all DVD-ROM drives for computers have the dual pickup mechanism, enabling them to properly read CD-R or CD-RW discs. However, most DVD video players used in entertainment systems do not have the dual pickups.

Figure 13.13   MultiRead and MultiRead2 logos.

How to Reliably Record CDs

With typical burn times for full CD-Rs ranging from under 4 minutes (20x) to as long as 80 minutes (1x), it is frustrating when a buffer underrun or some other problem forces you to rewrite your CD-RW disc, or worse yet, turn your CD-R media to a coaster—an unusable disc that must be discarded.

Five major factors influence your ability to create a working CD-R: interface type, drive buffer size, the location and condition of the data you want to record to CD-R, the recording speed, and whether the computer is performing other tasks while trying to create the CD-R.

To improve the odds of getting reliable CD-R/RW creation, look for drives with

- *A large data buffer (2MB or larger), or better yet some form of buffer underrun protection.* The data buffer in the drive holds information read from the original data source, so that if a pause in data reading occurs, there's less of a possibility of a buffer underrun until the on-drive buffer runs empty. A larger buffer minimizes the chance of "running out of data." Newer drives with buffer underrun protection virtually eliminate this problem, no matter what size buffer is in the drive.

- *Support for UDMA operating modes.* As you've already seen, UDMA modes transfer data more quickly and with less CPU intervention than earlier versions of ATA. To use this feature, you'll also need a motherboard with a busmastering UDMA interface with the appropriate drivers installed.

Tip

Also, if you have problems with reliable CD-R creation at the drive's maximum speed, try using a lower speed (4x instead of 8x, for example). Your mastering job will take twice as long, but it's better to create a working CD-R slowly than ruin a blank quickly.

An alternative approach is to use packet-writing software to create your CD-R. All late-model CD-R/CD-RW drives support packet writing, which allows drag-and-drop copying of individual files to the CD-R/RW rather than transferring all the files at once as with normal mastering software. This "a little at a time" approach means that less data must be handled in each write and can make the difference between success and failure. If your drive supports this feature, it probably includes packet-writing software in the package. Note that although packet-written CDs can be read with Windows 9x, Me, NT, and 2000, they can't be read with Windows 3.1 and MS-DOS because these operating systems don't have drivers available that support packet-written CDs.

If your CD-R/RW drive is SCSI-based, be sure you have the correct type of SCSI interface card and cables. Although many drive vendors take the uncertainty out of this issue by supplying an appropriate card and cables, others don't.

If you must buy your own SCSI card for your recorder, follow these tips:

■ *Forget about ISA cards.* Many new motherboards no longer include ISA slots, and even if they do, the performance of the ISA bus presents a bottleneck that will seriously inhibit drive performance.

■ *PCI or Cardbus SCSI works well.* As discussed in Chapter 17, "I/O Interfaces from Serial and Parallel to IEEE-1394 and USB," PCI's 32-bit data bus and 33MHz typical performance is far faster than ISA's 16-bit data bus and 8.33MHz typical performance. Cardbus is PCI for notebooks, so the same benefits apply there as well.

Tip

A number of CD-R manufacturers offer high-performance PCI SCSI cards, including Adaptec, Amedia, Promise Tech, SIIG, Tekram, DTC, and Advansys.

Buffer Underruns

Whenever a drive writes data to a CD-R/RW disc in either Disk at Once or Track at Once mode, it writes to the spiral track on the CD, alternating on and off to etch the pattern into the raw media. Because the drive can't easily realign where it starts and stops writing like a hard drive can, after it starts writing it must continue until it's finished with the track or disc. Otherwise, the recording (and disc if it is a CD-R) will be ruined. This means that the CD recording software, in combination with your system hardware, must be capable of delivering a consistent stream of data to the drive while it's writing. To aid in this effort, the software uses a buffer that it creates on your hard disk to temporarily store the data as it is being sent to the drive.

If the system is incapable of delivering data at a rate sufficient to keep the drive happy, you receive a buffer underrun message and the recording attempt fails. The buffer underrun message indicates that the drive had to abort recording because it ran out of data in its buffer to write to the CD. For many years, this was the biggest problem people had when recording to CD-R/RW media.

And for many years, the best way to prevent buffer underruns was to either slow down the writing speeds or have a large buffer in the recording drive, as well as to use the fastest interface and reading drive as possible. Nobody wants to write at lower speeds (otherwise, why buy a fast drive?), so buffer sizes grew as did the interface speeds. Still, it was possible to get a buffer underrun if, for example, you tried browsing Web pages or doing other work while burning a disc.

Buffer Underrun Protection

Sanyo was the first to develop a technology that eliminates buffer underruns once and for all. They call the technology Burn (buffer underrun) Proof, which sounds a little confusing (some people thought it prevented any writing on discs), but in practice it has proven to be excellent.

After Sanyo, several other companies have developed similar and compatible technology with various names. The most common you'll see are

■ BURN-Proof, from Sanyo

■ JustLink, from Ricoh

■ Waste-Proof, from Yamaha

Buffer underrun protection technology involves having a special chipset in the drive, which monitors the drive buffer. When it anticipates that a buffer underrun might occur (the buffer is running low on data), it temporarily suspends the recording until more data fills the buffer. When the buffer is sufficiently restocked, the drive then locates exactly where the recording left off earlier and restarts recording again immediately after that position.

According to the Orange Book specification, gaps between data in a CD recording must not be more than 100 milliseconds in length. The buffer underrun technology can restart the recording with a gap of 40–45 milliseconds or less from where it left off, which is well within the specification. These small gaps are easily compensated for by the error correction built into the recording, so no data is lost.

Note that it is important that the drive incorporate buffer underrun technology, but the recording software must support it as well for everything to work properly. Fortunately, all the popular CD recording programs on the market now support this technology.

If your drive incorporates buffer underrun protection, you can multitask—do other things while burning CDs—without fear of producing a bad recording.

Producing Error-Free Recordings

If you have an older drive that doesn't feature buffer underrun protection, follow these recommendations to help ensure error-free recordings and prevent buffer underruns:

- *Whenever possible, move all data you want to put onto a CD-R to a fast local hard drive.* If you can't do this, avoid using the following sources for data: floppy drives, parallel port–connected storage drives, and slower CD-ROM drives (especially 8x or slower). These locations for data usually can't feed data quickly enough to maintain data flow to the recording drive.

- *Before you master the CD-R, check your hard disk or data source for errors (the scandisk program can often be used for this).* Also try defragmenting the drive. This ensures that disk errors or file fragmentation, both of which slow down disk access, won't be a factor in program or data search and retrieval.

- *Avoid trying to burn from active files or zero-byte files (often used for temporary storage).* If you must burn these files to make an archival copy of your current system configuration, use a program such as Norton Ghost or PowerQuest Drive Image. These programs create a single compressed file from your drive's contents. Then, burn the disc using the resulting compressed file.

- *Turn off power management for your hard disk and other peripherals.* You can normally do this through the Power icon in Windows 9x.

- *Make sure your temporary drive has at least twice the empty space of your finished CD.* Your CD's estimated space requirements are shown during the mastering process with programs such as Roxio Easy CD-Creator or NERO Burning ROM. Thus, if you're creating a CD with 500MB of data, your temporary drive should have at least 1GB of empty space.

- *With Windows 9x, you'll improve disk caching by adjusting the typical role of the computer from workstation to server in the Performance tab of the System Properties dialog box.* Note that this change works correctly with Windows 95B and 95C (OSR 2.x) and Windows 98/Me, but the Registry keys are incorrect in Windows 95 original retail and OSR1 (95A) versions. Check Microsoft's Web site for the correct Registry key settings for Windows 95/95A, back up and edit the Registry, and restart the computer before making this change with those versions.

- *If your original data is coming from a variety of sources, consider using the Create Disk Image option found in most CD mastering software.* This feature creates an image file on your hard drive that contains all the files you want to put onto a CD. Then, use Create CD from Disk Image to actually master the CD from that information.

- *If you're uncertain of success, why waste a CD-R blank?* Use a CD-RW instead, which usually is written at a slower speed, or use the "test-then-create" option found in most recording software that does a simulated burn of the CD before the actual creation. After the simulation, you're warned of any problems before the actual process begins. This is not always foolproof, but it can help.

- *Small files are harder to use in mastering a CD than large ones because of the excessive drive tracking necessary to find them and load them.* You might want to use the packet writing mode instead if your drive and software support it.

- *Keep your drives clean and free from dust.* Use a cleaning CD if necessary. Dirty drives cause data-read errors or data-write errors if your recording drive is the dirty one.

- *Don't multitask.* If you run another program during the mastering process, the computer is forced to perform time-slicing, which causes it to start a process, switch away from it to start the next process, switch back to the first process, and so forth. This switching process could cause the recording drive to run out of data because it isn't receiving data in a steady stream. Forget about surfing the Internet, playing Solitaire, or creating a label for your new CD during the burning process if you want reliable mastering on a drive that doesn't feature buffer underrun protection.

If you're still having buffer underrun problems despite taking all the precautions listed here, try dropping down a speed. Go to the next lower speed and see how you do. Using a lower speed than the drive is rated for can be frustrating, but it's preferable to wasting time creating unusable discs.

Recording Software

Another difficulty with CD-R/RW devices is that they require special software to write them. Although most cartridge drives and other removable media mount as standard devices in the system and can be accessed exactly like a hard drive, the CD-R/RW drive uses special CD-ROM burning software to write to the disc. This software handles the differences between how data is stored on a CD and how it is stored on a hard drive. As you learned earlier, there are several CD-ROM standards for storing information. The CD-ROM–burning software arranges the data into one of these formats so a CD-ROM reader can read the CD later.

At one time, CD recording technology required that you have what amounted to a replica of the CD on a local hard drive. In fact, some software packages even required a separate, dedicated disk partition for this purpose. You would copy all the files to the appropriate place on the hard drive, creating the directory structure for the CD, and then the software would create an exact replica of every sector for the proposed CD-ROM—including every file, all the directory information, and the volume information—and copy it to the CD-R drive. The result was that you had to have about 1.5GB of storage to burn a single CD (650MB/CD × 2 = 1.3GB + overhead = 1.5GB). This is no longer a requirement because most software supports virtual images. You select the files and directories you want to write to the CD from your hard drive and create a virtual directory structure for the CD-ROM in the software. This means you can select files from different directories on different hard drives, or even files from network or other CD-ROM drives, and combine them any way you want on the CD-R. This works well provided the drives have adequate speed and your drive has a large buffer or features buffer underrun protection. If you have problems, follow the advice given earlier to overcome slow data sources.

The software assembles the directory information, burns it onto the CD, opens each file on the CD, and copies the data directly from the original source. This generally works well, but you must be aware of the access times for the media you select as data sources. If, for example, you select directories from a slow hard drive or from a busy network, the software might not be capable of reading the data quickly enough to maintain a consistent stream to the recorder. This causes the write to fail, resulting in a wasted disc.

Don't Forget the Software!

If you have persistent problems with making CDs, your recording software might be to blame. Check the vendor's Web site for tips and software updates. Be sure that your software is up-to-date and compatible with your drive and your drive's firmware revision. Some drives offer software-upgradable firmware similar to the motherboard's flash BIOS; if so, be sure your drive has the latest firmware available.

Each of the major CD-R/CD-RW drive vendors provides extensive technical notes to help you achieve reliable recordings. You can also find helpful information on SCSI adapter vendors' Web sites and the Web sites of the media vendors.

Creating Music CDs

Newer CD-R, CD-RW, and CD-ROM drives are enabling people to create customized archives of their favorite prerecorded music. Roxio's Easy CD-Creator, for example, features the SpinDoctor utility to build music CDs and even removes pops, hiss, and other problems from old analog cassette tapes and vinyl LPs.

Digital audio extraction allows the digital tracks on commercial CDs to be transformed into WAV files by compatible mastering programs. Those WAV files, exactly like the ones created from older music sources via your sound card, can then create a CD-R, which can be played back in any popular CD stereo system.

Many users can take advantage of this type of software to burn greatest hits collections and holiday CDs from their purchased cassette and music CD collections.

This exciting technology is not intended to give you a way to create a free music library. Instead, use it to give the music recordings you've paid for an extra dimension of usefulness, and of course, to make legal backups of the discs you have purchased.

Digital Audio Extraction

All CD-ROM drives can *play* Red Book–formatted CD-DA discs, but not all CD-ROM drives can *read* CD-DA discs. The difference sounds subtle, but it is actually quite dramatic. If you enjoy music and want to use your PC to manage your music collection, the ability to read the audio data digitally is an important function for your CD (and DVD) drives because it enables you to much more easily and accurately store, manipulate, and eventually write back out audio tracks.

CD-ROM drives installed in PCs can play audio discs. The playing function is simple: Using a CD player application (such as the one included with Windows 95 and later), you can insert a CD-DA disc into a CD-ROM drive and play it just as you could with a standard audio CD player. While playing, the analog sound waveform is sent over a thin stereo cable (usually refered to as the CD audio cable) connected between your CD-ROM drive and the sound card in your PC. The same analog waveform usually is also sent to the headphone jack on the front of the drive (or sound card). Your sound card then amplifies the analog signal so you can hear it through the speakers plugged into your sound card or via headphones plugged into the front of the drive (or the sound card).

That is just fine if all you want to do is play discs, but if you ever want to record one of the songs on your hard disk, you will run into some problems. To transfer the song to your hard drive, you would have to play the song as you did normally and simultaneously use a sound recorder application, such as the Sound Recorder supplied with Windows 95 and later (similar recording software is also typically supplied with your sound card), to redigitize the audio waveform for storage as a .WAV file on the PC. This means the sound goes from digital as originally stored on the disc to analog in the CD-ROM drive and back to digital in your sound card, with the resulting digital file being only an approxima-tion of the original digital data. Another drawback is that this procedure runs only at 1x speed—hardly an ideal situation!

It would be much better if you could read the original digital data directly off the disc. That was not possible with older CD-ROM drives, but newer drives can do what is called *digital audio extraction (DAE)*. This is a process in which they read the digital audio sectors directly and, rather than decode them into analog signals, pass each 2,352-byte sector of raw (error-corrected) digital audio data directly to the PC's processor via the (ATA, SCSI, USB, or FireWire) drive interface cable. Therefore, no digital-to-analog conversion (and back) occurs, and you essentially get the audio data exactly as it was originally recorded on the CD (within the limits of the CD-DA error-correction standards). You would have essentially extracted the exact digital audio data from the disc onto your PC.

Another term for digital audio extraction is *ripping*, so named because you can "rip" the raw audio data from the drive at full drive read speed, rather than the normal 1x speed at which you listen to audio discs. Actually, most drives can't do DAE at their full rated speeds. Although some are faster (or slower) than others, most perform DAE at speeds from about one-quarter to about one-half of their rated read speed. So, you might be able to extract audio data at speeds only up to 20x on a 40x rated drive. However, that is still quite a bit better than at 1x as it would be on drives that can't do DAE (not to mention skipping the conversion to analog and back to digital with the resultant loss of information).

Virtually all newer CD/DVD drives can perform digital audio extraction on music discs. How fast or accurately they do this can vary from model to model. One might think any extraction (digital copy) of a given track (song) should be the same because it is a digital copy of the original; however, that is not always the case. The CD-DA format was designed to play music, not to transfer data with 100% accuracy. Errors beyond the capability of the CIRC in the CD-DA format cause the firmware in the drive to interpolate or approximate the data. In addition, time-based problems due to clock inaccuracies can occur in the drive, causing it to get slightly out of step when reading the frames in the sector (this is refered to as *jitter*). Differences in the internal software (firmware) in the drive and differences in the drivers used are other problems that can occur.

Positioning can also be a problem because the CD-DA format was designed to stream (play continuously) and not to read individual sectors. CD-ROM sectors are 2,352 bytes long,and these bytes are further divided into 2,048 bytes of data plus 304 bytes of syncronization, header, and additional ECC information to control positioning and allow for error-free reads. No such syncronization, header, or extra ECC information exists for audio sectors; instead, all 2,352 bytes are used for pure audio data. To address an audio sector, the Q subcode information is used instead (see the section "Subcodes," earlier in this chapter). Most audio players position to within only 75 sectors (1 second) using the Q subcode information. CD-ROM drives that can perform digital audio extraction are usually much more accurate than that, but because of how the subcode works (as well as the cross-interleaved way audio data is stored), designing a drive that can position every time to the precise audio sector that starts the track can be difficult.

All of this conspires to cause inaccuracies or slight differences in multiple extractions of the same track (song). Perfect extractions are possible, but making perfect extractions is difficult to achieve for a lot of reasons. For example, even a slight amount of dirt or scratches on the disc has a great effect on the quality of your extractions, so be sure the discs are clean. As a test of your drive's capability to perform DAE, try extracting the same track (song) multiple times from a new, clean, scratch-free disc, using a different filename for each extraction. Then, bring up a command prompt and use the FC (file compare) command to compare the different files to each other. If they compare exactly, you have a combination of hardware and software that can do perfect or near-perfect extractions.

If you intend to do a lot of extracting, you should ask around to see what hardware and software others are using for this purpose. As a general rule, SCSI drives work better than ATA, but some ATA drives are just as good as the better SCSI drives. Plextor is well known for drives that are excellent when it comes to digital audio extraction, and I've always had good luck with Toshiba drives, too.

The bottom line is that DAE enables you to extract audio data tracks directly to your PC as .WAV files. Once on the PC, you can play the WAV files as is or convert them to other (usually more compressed) formats, such as MP3 (MPEG-1/2 Layer III) for use with the MP3 audio players on the market.

Note

Because the WAV files extracted match the high 44.1KHz sampling rate used on the CD, you have 176,400 bytes per second of sound information, which means 1 minute of music consumes nearly 10.6MB worth of space on your hard drive! MP3 compression can reduce that by a factor of 6 or more, with little to no perceptible loss in quality.

You can also use a CD-R/RW drive that can perform DAE to make copies of audio CDs (for backup purposes only) or to compile several songs into your own greatest hits collections that you can use to burn your own custom audio CDs.

Serial Copy Management System

Because of the possiblity of the illegal duplication of commercial audio CDs, the recording industry is not in favor of DAE, and some drive manufacturers don't like to tout how well (or not so well) their drives perform this function.

The Recording Industry Association of America (RIAA) and others involved in the creation and distribution of prerecorded music were concerned about digital recording because no loss occurs in digital copies—a digital copy is just as good as the original. This also means that copies of copies are just as good, too. They feared that unless digital copying were somehow limited, it would easily allow the pirating of master-quality recordings.

The first digital recording technology accessible to consumers (before CD-R and CD-RW) was digital audio tape (DAT), which debuted to consumers in 1987. Because the DAT drive manufacturers could not reach an agreement with the RIAA on how to control copying, most record labels did not release any prerecorded software on DAT tapes. What followed instead was several years of controversy over digital copying, which finally culminated in an agreement in July 1989 mandating the inclusion of Serial Copy Management System (SCMS) in digital recorders.

SCMS originally was developed by Philips and is designed to allow digital copies only from original source material. SCMS recognizes a "copyright" bit encoded on a prerecorded digital original (such as a CD, where it is contained in the Q subcode channel) indicating that this is an original and writes a modified bit indicating that this is now a copy into the subcode of digital copies (such as when copying to a CD-R/RW (or DAT tape). The presence of the copy flag prevents any SCMS-compliant recorder from digitally copying the copy. SCMS lets you digitally copy originals as many times as you want, but you can't digitally copy any of the copies.

For many reasons, including the delay in agreeing on SCMS, a lack of prerecorded material in DAT form, and no support from the auto manufacturers (who continued to install either cassette tape or CD players in automobiles), DAT for audio use has remained a niche format used by a selective few. On the other hand, for computer use as a tape backup device, DAT has been used for many years and is still one of the more popular tape formats.

In the early 1990s, several other digital recording formats became available, most of which included SCMS. Philips introduced a tape format called DCC (digital compact cassette), whereas Sony introduced its MiniDisc format, which uses magneto-optical recording and playback from a small 64mm disc. DCC has all but dissapeared, and MiniDisc has achieved a modicum of popularity. Consumer-level MiniDisc players accept only analog signals (which they digitize and record digitally), so straight digital copies of information is possible only with professional (read expensive) units. The early 1990s also saw the introduction of CD-R and RW, which include SCMS only when sold in consumer (and not computer) versions. The drive manufacturers didn't have to include SCMS in the drives for computers according to the Audio Home Recording Act (AHRA), even though the record companies didn't agree with this.

Audio Home Recording Act

What started as an agreement between the recording industry and drive manufacturers in 1989 was translated into law in the U.S. with the passage of the Audio Home Recording Act of 1992. The AHRA was passed by Congress to protect artists and recording companies from losing royalties from unauthorized copying of compact discs, but it was also passed to guarantee the consumers' right to engage in home audio recording, eliminating the fear of copyright suits when making copies for private, noncommercial, personal use.

The AHRA calls for the mandatory inclusion of serial copying technology in devices and media but applies only to devices or media designed or marketed for the "primary purpose" of making digital audio recordings. Therefore, standalone home audio CD writers (and the media they use) must include SCMS, but general-purpose computer devices such as CD-R/RW drives and media don't. Additionally, the AHRA has also been found to exclude MP3 players as well, much to the dismay of the RIAA. Sensing that the AHRA did not provide as much legal protection as the recording industry desired, a new group called the Secure Digital Music Initiative (SDMI) has been formed to develop voluntary, open standards for digital music.

"For Music Use Only" CD-R/RW Discs

According to the Audio Home Recording Act, consumer CD recordable drives *and media* sold specifically for recording music are required to have specific safeguards against copying discs, mainly SCMS. That means these recorders can make digital copies only from original prerecorded discs. You can copy a copy, but in that case, the data being recorded goes from digital to analog and back to digital on the second copy, resulting in a generational loss of quality.

The media for these recorders must be special as well. They work only with special discs labeled "For Music Use" or "For Consumer" discs. These carry the standard Compact Disk Digital Audio Recordable logo that most are familiar with, but below that, as part of the logo, is an added line that says "For Consumer." These discs feature a special track prerecorded onto the disc, which the consumer music recorders look for. Built into the price of the AHRA-compliant media is a royalty for the music industry that this track protects. The media costs about six times what regular CD-R/RW media costs. If you try to use standard non–AHRA-compliant CD-R/RW discs in these drives, the drive refuses to recognize the disc. These music devices also refuse to copy CD-ROM or data discs.

Note that this does not apply to the CD-R/RW drive you have installed or attached to your PC. It does not have to be AHRA compliant, nor does it need to use AHRA-compliant "For Music Use" media, even if you are copying or recording music discs. Additionally, you can make digital copies of copies— the SCMS does not apply, either. The bottom line is that you do not have to purchase AHRA-compliant discs for the CD-R/RW drives in your PC. If you do purchase such discs, despite the "For Music Use Only" designation, AHRA-compliant discs can be used in your CD-R/RW drives just as regular CD-R/RW discs and can be used for storing data. The extra information indicating AHRA compliance is simply ignored.

Recordable DVD Standards

The history of recordable DVD drives dates back to April 1997, when the companies comprising the DVD Forum announced the finalization of specifications for rewritable DVD, DVD-RAM, and a write-once DVD, DVD-R.

In a war that brings back unhappy memories of the VHS/Beta struggle of the 1980s, even with the DVD Forum attempting to create unified standards, the computer and movie industries are locked in a struggle to see which enhancements to the basic DVD standard will win out. Table 13.26 compares the competing recordable DVD standards, and Table 13.27 breaks down the compatibilities between the drives and media.

Table 13.26   Recordable DVD Standards

Format	Type	Capacity	Compatibility
DVD-R	Recordable	Up to 4.7GB/side	Most existing DVD drives can read
DVD-RAM	Rewritable	Up to 4.7GB/side	Incompatible with existing DVD drives unless they support the MultiRead2 standard
DVD-RW	Rewritable	4.7GB/side	Most existing DVD drives can read
DVD+RW	Rewritable	4.7GB/side	The most compatible for video and data recording

Table 13.27   DVD Drive and Media Compatibility

Drives	CD-ROM	CD-R	CD-RW	DVD-Video	DVD-ROM	DVD-R	DVD-RAM	DVD-RW	DVD+RW
DVD-Video Player	R	?	?	R	—	R	?	R	R
DVD-ROM Drive	R	R	R	R	R	R	?	R	R
DVD-R Drive	R	R/W	R/W	R	R	R/W	—		R
DVD-RAM Drive	R	R	R	R	R	R	R/W	R	R
DVD-RW Drive	R	R/W	R/W	R	R	R/W	—	R/W	R
DVD+RW Drive	R	R/W	R/W	R	R	R	R	R	R/W

R = Read   — = Will not read or write

W = Write   ? = MultiRead/MultiPlay drives will read

DVD-R and DVD-RAM have been available the longest, but DVD-R is not rewritable, and DVD-RAM is not fully compatible with existing DVD-ROM drives. DVD+RW looks to be the standard that will win out in the industry among all of these because it is among the least expensive, easiest to use, and the most compatible with existing formats.

DVD-RAM

DVD-RAM is the rewritable DVD standard endorsed by Panasonic, Hitachi, and Toshiba. DVD-RAM uses a phase-change technology similar to that of CD-RW. Unfortunately, DVD-RAM discs can't be read by most standard DVD-ROM drives because of differences in both reflectivity of the media and the data format. (DVD-R, by comparison, is backward compatible with DVD-ROM.) DVD-ROM drives that can read DVD-RAM discs began to come on the market in early 1999 and follow the MultiRead2 specification. DVD-ROM drives and DVD-Video players labeled as MultiRead2 compliant are capable of reading DVD-RAM discs. See the section "MultiRead Specifications," earlier in this chapter, for more information.

The first DVD-RAM drives were introduced in Spring 1998 and had a capacity of 2.6GB (single-sided) or 5.2GB (double-sided). DVD-RAM Version 2 discs with 4.7GB arrived in late 1999, and double-sided 9.4GB discs arrived in 2000. DVD-RAM drives typically read DVD-Video, DVD-ROM, and CD media. The current installed base of DVD-ROM drives and DVD-Video players can't read DVD-RAM media.

DVD-RAM uses what is called the wobbled land and groove recording method, which records signals on both the lands (the areas between grooves) and inside the grooves that are preformed on the disc. The tracks wobble, which provides clock data for the drive. Special sector header pits are prepressed into the disc during the manufacturing process as well. See Figure 13.14, which shows the wobbled tracks (lands and grooves) with data recorded both on the lands and in the grooves. This is unlike CD-R or CD-RW, in which data is recorded on the groove only.

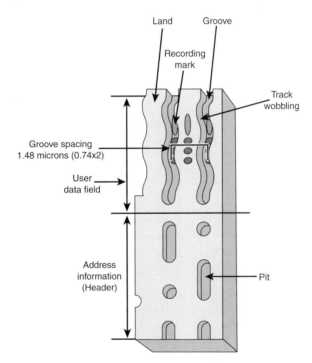

Figure 13.14   DVD-RAM wobbled land and groove recording.

The disc is recorded using phase-change recording, in which data is written by selectively heating spots in the grooves or on the lands with a high-powered laser. The DVD-RAM drive write laser transforms the film from a crystalline to an amorphous state by heating a spot, which is then rendered less reflective than the remaining crystalline portions. The signal is read as the difference of the laser reflection rate between the crystalline and amorphous states. The modulation and error correction codes are the same as for DVD-Video and DVD-ROM, ensuring compatibility with other DVD formats. For rewriting, a lower-powered laser reheats the spot to a lower temperature, where it recrystallizes.

Disc cartridges or caddies originally were required for both single- and double-sided discs but have now been made optional for single-sided discs. Double-sided discs must remain inside the caddy at all times for protection; however, single-sided discs can be taken out of the cartridge if necessary.

DVD-RAM specifications are shown in Table 13.28.

Table 13.28   DVD-RAM Specifications

Storage capacity	2.6GB single-sided; 5.2GB double sided
Disc diameter	80mm–120mm
Disc thickness	1.2mm (0.6mm×2: bonded structure)
Recording method	Phase change
Laser wavelength	650nm
Data bit length	0.41–0.43 microns
Recording track pitch	0.74 microns
Track format	Wobbled land and groove

DVD-R

DVD-R is a write-once medium very similar to CD-R. As such, it is ideal for recording archival data or distribution discs. DVD-R discs can be played on standard DVD-ROM drives.

DVD-R has a single-sided storage capacity of 3.95GB—about six times that of a CD-R—and double that for a double-sided disc. These discs use an organic dye recording layer that allows for a low material cost, similar to CD-R.

To enable positioning accuracy, DVD-R uses a wobbled groove recording, in which special grooved tracks are pre-engraved on the disc during the manufacturing process. Data is recorded within the grooves only. The grooved tracks wobble slightly right and left, and the frequency of the wobble contains clock data for the drive to read, as well as clock data for the drive. The grooves are spaced more closely together than with DVD-RAM, but data is recorded only in the grooves and not on the lands (see Figure 13.15).

Figure 13.15   DVD-R wobbled groove recording.

Table 13.29 has the basic specifications for DVD-R drives.

Table 13.29   DVD-R Specifications

Storage capacity	3.95GB single-sided; 7.9GB double-sided
Disc diameter	80mm–120mm
Disc thickness	1.2mm (0.6mm×2: bonded structure)
Recording method	Organic dye layer recording method
Laser wavelength	635nm (recording); 635/650nm (playback)
Data bit length	0.293 microns
Recording track pitch	0.80 microns
Track format	Wobbled groove

DVD-RW

The DVD Forum introduced DVD-RW in March 1998. Created mainly by Pioneer, DVD-RW also uses a phase-change technology and is somewhat more compatible with standard DVD-ROM drives than DVD-RAM. Drives based on this technology began shipping in late 1999. Although newer DVD-type drives have become more compatible with the CD-R/CD-RW standards, a major problem still exists in harmonizing the many types of writable DVD formats. As with the old Beta-versus-VHS battle, even the introduction of a superior specification complicates the process of accepting a single specification as an industry standard.

DVD+RW

DVD+RW, also called DVD Phase Change Rewritable, is destined to be the premier DVD recordable standard because it is the least expensive, easiest to use, and most compatible with existing formats. It was developed and is supported by Philips, Sony, Hewlett-Packard, Mitsubishi Chemical, Ricoh, Yamaha, Verbatim, and Thompson, who are all part of an industry standard group called the DVD+RW Alliance (http://www.dvdrw.com). In addition, companies such as Ahead Software (Nero Burning ROM software) and Roxio (CD Creator and DirectCD software) have announced they are developing support software for DVD+RW. In fact, more than 19 independent software vendors and equipment manufacturers pledged their support for DVD+RW and announced software availability, making DVD+RW the most well supported of all the DVD rewritable formats.

DVD+RW is the only rewritable format that provides full compatibility with existing DVD-Video players and DVD-ROM drives for both real-time video recording and random data recording across PC and entertainment applications. DVD+RW is designed to not only be useful for PC data storage, but to also directly record video in the DVD-Video format. This is the breakthrough the recordable DVD industry has been waiting for, and as such, DVD+RW is destined to replace the VCR in consumer-level home recorders.

Some of the features of DVD+RW includes are as follows:

- Single-sided discs (4.7GB).
- Double-sided discs (9.4GB).
- Up to 4 hours video recording (single-sided discs).
- Up to 8 hours video recording (double-sided discs).
- Bare discs—no caddy required.
- 650nm laser (same as DVD-Video).
- Constant linear data density.

- CLV and CAV recording.

- Write speeds 1x–2.4x and higher.

- DVD-Video data rates.

- UDF (Universal Disc Format) file system.

- Defect management integral to the drive.

- Quick formatting.

- Uses same 8 to 16 Modulation and error correcting codes as DVD-ROM.

- Sequential and random recording.

- Lossless linking (multiple recording sessions don't waste space).

- Spiral groove with radial wobble.

- After recording, all physical parameters comply with the DVD-ROM specification.

As consumer and PC applications for DVD continue to develop, DVD+RW provides the only recordable DVD format that seamlessly integrates into both the consumer DVD-Video market as well as PC DVD-ROM market, offering the best of both worlds. DVD+RW technology is very similar to CD-RW, and DVD+RW drives can read DVD-ROMs and all CD formats, including CD-R and CD-RW.

With DVD+RW, the writing process can be suspended and continued without a loss of space linking the recording sessions together. This increases efficiency in random writing and video applications. This "lossless linking" also enables the selective replacing of any individual 32KB block of data (the minimum recording unit) with a new block, accurately positioning with a space of 1 micron. To enable this high accuracy for placement of data on the track, the pre-groove is wobbled at a higher frequency. The timing and addressing information read from the groove is very accurate.

The quick formatting feature means you can pop a DVD+RW blank into the drive and almost instantly begin writing to it. The actual formatting is carried out in the background ahead of where any writing will occur.

Out of the three DVD rewritable formats that have been released, it seems that DVD+RW is poised to become the format that brings recordable DVD to the masses in both standalone home consumer units as well as integrated into newer PCs.

CD/DVD Software and Drivers

After you've physically installed the drive, you're ready for the last step—installing the drivers and other CD-ROM/DVD-ROM software. As usual, this process can be simple with a PnP operating system such as Windows 9x or later. The optical drive needs the following three software components for it to operate on a PC:

- *A SCSI adapter driver (not needed for ATAPI CD-ROM drives).* Most popular SCSI adapter drivers are built in to Windows 9x.

- *A SCSI driver for the specific CD-ROM drive you've installed.* An ASPI driver is built into Windows 9x, as is an ATAPI CD-ROM driver.

- *MSCDEX.* Microsoft CD Extensions for DOS, which is built into Windows 9x as the CDFS VxD.

If you are using DOS, you can have the first two drivers—the SCSI adapter driver and CD-ROM driver—load into your system at startup by placing command lines in your CONFIG.SYS file. The MSCDEX, or DOS extension, is an executable file added into your system through your AUTOEXEC.BAT file. This is not required in Windows 9x or later; the operating system autodetects the drive on startup and prompts you to install the correct drivers if it can't find them in its standard arsenal of device drivers.

Using Windows 9x along with a CD-ROM or DVD-ROM drive that conforms to the ATAPI specification does not require you to do anything. All the driver support for these drives is built into Windows 9x, including the ATAPI driver and the CDFS VxD driver.

If you are running a SCSI CD-ROM drive under Windows 9x, you still need the ASPI driver that goes with your drive. The ASPI driver for your drive usually comes from the drive manufacturer and is included with the drive in most cases. However, by arrangement with hardware manufacturers, Windows 9x usually includes the ASPI driver for most SCSI host adapters and also automatically runs the CDFS VxD virtual device driver. In some rare cases, you might have to install an updated driver that you have obtained from the manufacturer.

When you install a PnP SCSI host adapter in a Windows 9x system, simply booting the computer should cause the operating system to detect, identify, and install drivers for the new device. When the driver for the host adapter is active, the system should detect the SCSI devices connected to the adapter and again load the appropriate drivers automatically.

The only problem you might encounter is if you are installing a new device, such as a DVD-ROM drive, on an older version of Windows. Windows 98 includes drivers for most of the DVD-ROM drives on the market, but Windows 95 was released before these devices existed. In this case, you will probably have to supply a device driver on floppy disk, in response to a request from the OS, during the installation process.

DOS SCSI Adapter Driver

For DOS users, of course, the installation process is not so easy. Each SCSI adapter model has a specific driver that enables communication between the PC and the SCSI interface. Normally, these drivers conform to the the SCSI interface. Normally, these drivers conform to the ASPI. The ASPI driver for the drive connects with the ASPI driver for the SCSI host adapter; this is how the adapter and the drive communicate. An ASPI driver should be provided both with your SCSI drive and with the host adapter. Documentation should also have been included that walks you through the installation of the software.

Most SCSI adapters come with an installation program that automates the process of installing the appropriate ASPI drivers, both for the adapter and for the devices connected to the SCSI bus. However, you can manually add the SCSI device driver to your CONFIG.SYS file. In the CONFIG.SYS file, add the name and path of the appropriate driver with the DEVICE= command (replace C:\DRIVERS with the actual location of your files and MYSCSI.SYS with the actual name of your SCSI driver):

```
DEVICE=C:\DRIVERS\MYSCSI.SYS
```

C:\DRIVERS is the subdirectory into which you copied the SCSI ASPI device drivers. Some drivers have option switches or added commands that, for example, enable you to view the progress of the driver being loaded.

DOS ATAPI CD-ROM Device Driver

This driver should be a part of your basic installation kit as well. If not, contact the drive's manufacturer for the proper device driver for your SCSI card.

The device driver should come with an installation program that prompts you for the memory I/O address for the SCSI adapter to which you've connected the CD-ROM drive. This device driver enables the adapter to communicate with the drive through the SCSI bus. Installation programs add a line similar to the following to your CONFIG.SYS file (replace MYCDROM.SYS with the actual name of your CD-ROM driver file and C:\DRIVERS with the actual location of your files):

DEVICE=C:\DRIVERS\MYCDROM.SYS /D:mscd001

C:\DRIVERS is the subdirectory that contains the driver MYCDROM.SYS, the driver for your specific CD-ROM drive.

Note the /D:mscd001 option after the preceding statement. This designation, called the device signature, identifies this CD-ROM driver as controlling the first (001), and only, CD-ROM drive on the system. This portion of the device driver statement is for the Microsoft DOS Extensions driver, which designates CD-ROM drives in this fashion. In fact, you could use any designation here, as long as the MSCDEX command line uses the same one.

MSCDEX: Adding CDs to DOS/Win3.x

The Microsoft CD Extensions for DOS enable the DOS operating system (and by extension, Windows 3.x) to identify and use data from CD-ROMs attached to the system. The original DOS operating system had no provisions for this technology, so "hooks" or handling of this unique media are not part of the basic operating environment. Using these extensions is convenient for all involved, however. As CD-ROM technology changes, the MSCDEX can be changed, independently of DOS. For example, most PhotoCD, multiple-session CD-ROM drives require MSCDEX.EXE version 2.21 or higher, which has been modified from earlier versions to accommodate the newer CD-ROM format.

MSCDEX.EXE should be in your software kit with your drive. If not, you can obtain the latest copy directly from Microsoft. If you are a registered user of DOS or Windows 3.1, MSCDEX.EXE is free. Read the licensing agreement that appears on the disc or in your manual concerning the proper licensing of the MSCDEX files.

Your installation software should add a line similar to the following to your AUTOEXEC.BAT file:

```
C:\WINDOWS\COMMAND\MSCDEX.EXE /d:mscd001
```

C:\WINDOWS\COMMAND is the directory in which the MSCDEX.EXE file is located by default with Windows 9x and later; with MS-DOS and Windows 3.1, it could be located in the \DOS directory or in the directory containing the CD-ROM drivers. The /d:mscd001 portion of the command line supplies the MSCDEX extension with the device signature defined in the CD-ROM device driver of your CONFIG.SYS file.

Note

The MSCDEX and CD-ROM device signatures must match. The defaults that most installations provide are used in this example. As long as the two names are the same, the drivers can find one another.

As long as you have these three drivers—the SCSI adapter driver, the CD-ROM driver, and the DOS CD extensions—loaded properly in your system, the CD-ROM drive will operate as transparently as any other drive in your system.

Table 13.30 lists the options you can add to the MSCDEX.EXE command line.

Table 13.30   MSCDEX Command-Line Options

Switch	Function
/V	Called Verbose; when this option is added to the command line, it displays information about memory allocation, buffers, drive letter assignments, and device driver names on your screen at boot time.

Table 13.30   Continued

Switch	Function
/L:<letter>	Designates which DOS drive letter you want to assign to the drive. For example, /L:G assigns the drive letter G: to your CD-ROM drive. Two conditions apply: First, you must not have another drive assigned to that letter; second, your lastdrive= statement in your CONFIG.SYS file must be equal to or greater than the drive letter you're assigning. LASTDRIVE=G would be fine; LASTDRIVE=F would cause an error if you attempt to assign the CD-ROM drive to the G: drive with the /L: switch.
/M:<buffers>	Enables you to buffer the data from the CD-ROM drive. This is useful if you want faster initial access to the drive's directory. Buffers of 10 to 15 are more than enough for most uses. Any more is overkill. Each buffer, however, is equal to 2KB of memory. So a /M:10 buffer argument, for example, would take 20KB of memory. Note that this does not significantly increase the overall performance of the drive, just DOS's initial access to the drive and the access of large data blocks when the drive is reading live-motion video files, for example. You can't turn a 400ms drive into a speed demon by adding a 200KB buffer. With no /M: argument added, MSCDEX adds six buffers as a default. That may be fine for most PCs and CD-ROM drives.
/E	Loads the aforementioned buffers into DOS high memory, freeing up space in the conventional 640KB. Early versions of MSCDEX—anything below version 2.1—do not load into extended memory. You must have DOS 5.0 for this option to load.
/K	Provides Kanji (Japanese) language support.
/S	Enables you to share your CD-ROM drive on a peer-to-peer network, such as Windows for Workgroups.

Note that Windows 9x uses a built-in CDFS driver that takes the place of MSCDEX. It is configured through the Windows 9x Registry and requires no AUTOEXEC.BAT command. USB-based CD-ROM/CD-R/CD-RW drives are also configured through the Windows 9x Registry and use no CONFIG.SYS or AUTOEXEC.BAT commands.

CD-ROM Support in Windows 9x and Windows NT 4.0

As stated earlier, Windows 9x/Me and Windows NT/2000 include virtually all the drivers you will need to run your optical drive, making the software installation automatic. Windows automatically recognizes most ATAPIIDE earlier, Windows 9x/Me and Windows NT/2000 include virtually all the drivers you will need to run your optical drive, making the software installation automatic. Windows automatically recognizes most ATAPI drives, and with the addition of the appropriate drive-specific ASPI driver, most SCSI drives as well.

There are several new capabilities with CDs and DVDs in Windows 9x/NT. The most dramatic is the Autoplay feature, which is available on Windows 95/98 and some versions of Windows NT 4.0.

Autoplay is a feature integrated into Windows 9x that enables you to simply insert a disc into the drive, and Windows will automatically run it without any user intervention. It also detects whether that particular disc has already been installed on your system, and if not, automatically starts the install program. If the disc has already been installed, it starts the application program on the disc.

The Autoplay feature is simple. When you insert a disc, Windows 9x automatically spins it and looks for a file called AUTORUN.INF. If this file exists, Windows 9x opens it and follows the instructions contained within. As you can see, this Autoplay feature works only on discs that have this file. Most software companies are now shipping CD-ROM and DVD-ROM titles that incorporate the Autoplay feature.

Tip

You can disable the Autoplay feature for all CD-ROMs by opening the Windows 9x System control panel to the Device Manager page, highlighting your CD-ROM drive, and clicking the Properties button. The Properties dialog box for the drive has a Settings page that contains an Auto Insert Notification check box. Clearing this box prevents the operating system from processing the AUTORUN.INF file.

If you want to use Autoplay for some CDs, but not others, hold down the Shift key when inserting a CD you don't want to Autoplay.

Windows 9x/NT includes a new version of the Media Player found in Windows 3.x called the CD Player. This application enables you to play audio CDs in your drive while you work at the computer. The CD Player features graphical controls that look like a standard audio CD-ROM drive and even has advanced features found in audio drives, such as random play, programmable playback order, and the capability to save play list programs.

MS-DOS Drivers and Windows 9x

Many users have discovered that their CD-ROM drives didn't come with MS-DOS drivers at a very unfortunate time: when their Windows 9x system wouldn't start up. All too often, the "cure" for a "dead" Windows 9x system is a complete reinstallation from the Windows 9x CD, to replace defective files and settings with new copies. Of course, if Windows isn't working, its 32-bit CD-ROM device drivers aren't working either. And, if you don't have your CONFIG.SYS and AUTOEXEC.BAT files and the files listed earlier either, you can't reload Windows! You should have a bootable disk ready that has the appropriate drivers included to enable you to rebuild your Windows 9x installation in case of emergencies.

If you have Windows 98 or later, the Emergency Startup disk you create during installation or later already has the appropriate drivers, AUTOEXEC.BAT, and CONFIG.SYS included to run most popular SCSI and ATAPI-based CD-ROMs. However, a Windows 95 bootable disk doesn't include the AUTOEXEC.BAT, CONFIG.SYS, or drivers; you must add these yourself (see the next section).

Note

If you can't find any references to the MS-DOS drivers needed for your CD-ROM drive on your Windows 9x computer, check for an installation disk that might have been shipped with the drive. To install the CD-ROM device driver files you need, use that disk to perform an MS-DOS/Windows 3.1 installation, which adds the appropriate lines to your CONFIG.SYS and AUTOEXEC.BAT files and copies the drivers to your system.

Creating a Bootable Floppy with CD-ROM Support

If your system BIOS is a version from 1998 or later, most likely it has "El Torito" support, which means it supports booting from a bootable CD. The El Torito name comes from the Phoenix Software/IBM standard that apparently was discussed at an El Torito restaurant near the Phoenix Software offices. What El Torito means is that you can boot from CDs, which opens up several new possibilities, including creating bootable CD rescue discs, booting from newer OS discs when installing to new systems, creating bootable diagnostics and test CDs, and more.

To create a bootable CD, you need a bootable floppy that contains the drivers to support your CD drive in DOS mode (sometimes called real-mode drivers).

Tip

Optionally, you can use a Windows 98/Me startup floppy because these have the DOS-level CD-ROM support already configured and installed. You can even use a Windows 98/Me startup disk to boot a Windows 95 system, so getting a disk from a 98/Me system is definitely the easiest way to proceed. If that is not an option, you can add the CD-ROM support to the Windows 95 or any DOS startup disk.

Test your boot floppy (with CD-ROM drivers) by first booting to the floppy. Then, with a CD containing files in the CD-ROM drive, see whether you can change to the CD-ROM drive and read a directory of the files (try the DIR command). The CD usually is the next drive letter after your last hard drive letter. For example, if your last hard drive letter is C:, the CD-ROM will be D:.

If you can display a directory listing of the CD after booting from the floppy, your CD-ROM drivers are properly loaded.

Creating a Rescue CD

A number of programs on the market today allow you to make a compressed image file of the contents of any drive. These programs, such as the Ghost program sold by Symantec or PowerQuest's Drive Image, enable you to lock in the condition of any drive as of a particular time.

This enables you to create an image file of your system when it's working and use the image-restore feature to reset your system when it fails.

The perfect place to store a compressed image file is on a CD-R. At a minimum, your rescue disc should contain the compressed image file (a 737MB, 80-minute CD-R/RW could contain the equivalent of a nearly 1.5GB drive's normal contents if maximum compression option is used). It's also desirable to place a copy of the image-restore program on the CD. Mastering this type of rescue CD is done exactly the same as a conventional CD mastering process. To use the rescue CD, you must boot your system with drivers that allow the CD-ROM drive to work, run the restore program to read the data from the CD, and overwrite the drive's existing contents.

If you're looking for a single-CD solution to rescuing your system, one that won't require you to lug around a bootable floppy disk, you can burn a rescue CD that is bootable all by itself.

Making a Bootable CD for Emergencies

A little-known capability to PC users is that they can create their own versions of what is standard with more and more new computers: a bootable CD that can be used to start up a system and restore it to a previously saved state.

Files Needed for a Bootable CD

The minimum requirements for a bootable CD include

- A system in which the CD/DVD can be designated as a boot drive

Note

Check your BIOS under Advanced Setup or similar options. Recent and current BIOS code supplied by AMI, Award Software, and Phoenix Technologies typically support the CD as a bootable device.

- A CD-R or CD-RW drive and either CD-R or CD-RW media
- Recording software that allows creation of a bootable CD

Note

Most modern CD recording software, such as NERO Burning ROM or Roxio CD Creator, support creating bootable CDs. If your current CD-recording software lacks this option, you must upgrade to something that does.

■ A floppy disk containing your operating system boot files

ATAPI Drives Are Bootable

Most ATAPI drives connected to a motherboard ATA interface can be used as a bootable device if the BIOS permits it. If your CD-ROM is connected to a sound card, this procedure won't work. If your CD-ROM is connected to a SCSI interface, you'll need a SCSI interface with a BIOS chip that permits booting as well as a bootable CD.

Check your BIOS Setup for a page on which boot devices are listed to see whether yours supports a CD-ROM drive as a bootable device.

The basic procedure for creating a bootable CD is as follows:

1. Create a bootable floppy for the operating system you want to install on the CD.

2. Get a blank CD-R, and place it into your CD-R/CD-RW drive.

3. Start your mastering software.

4. Under disc layout, ensure that ISO 9660 is selected. This CD format doesn't permit long filenames, so be sure that any additional files you add to the CD have no more than eight characters plus up to three characters for the filename extension.

5. Make sure the bootable option is enabled in the disc layout.

6. When prompted, insert the floppy disk containing boot files into A: drive.

7. These files are copied to your CD layout. Note that the names of these files are not the same as the normal operating system boot files. The files are called BOOTCAT.BIN and BOOTIMG.BIN.

8. Add any additional files (image files, operating system install files, and so on) you want to the layout.

9. Start the CD creation process.

10. When the process is completed, view the contents of the finished CD-R.

11. Close your mastering program, saving the layout if you desire.

12. Insert the bootable CD you just created into your CD-ROM drive.

13. Restart the computer and see whether your system boots from the CD.

If you follow these directions, you will discover that the CD-ROM disc appears as both drive A: and another letter. A: is the floppy image you copied during the creation process, whereas all the other files show up on the main CD drive letter.

Caring for Optical Media

Some peoplepeople believe that optical discs and drives are indestructible when compared to their magnetic counterparts. Actually, modern optical drives are far less reliable than modern hard disk drives. Reliability is the bane of any removable media, and CD-ROMs and DVD-ROMs are no exception.

By far the most common causes of problems with optical discs and drives are scratches, dirt, and other contamination. Small scratches or fingerprints on the bottom of the disc should not affect performance because the laser focuses on a point inside the actual disc, but dirt or deep scratches can interfere with reading a disc.

To remedy this type of problem, you can clean the bottom surface of the CD with a soft cloth, but be careful not to scratch the surface in the process. The best technique is to wipe the disc in a radial fashion, using strokes that start from the center of the disc and emanate toward the outer edge. This way, any scratches will be perpendicular to the tracks rather than parallel to them, minimizing the interference they might cause. You can use any type of solution on the cloth to clean the disc, so long as it will not damage plastic. Most window cleaners are excellent at removing fingerprints and other dirt from the disc and don't damage the plastic surface.

If your disc has deep scratches, they can often be buffed or polished out. A commercial plastic cleaner such as that sold in auto parts stores for cleaning plastic instrument cluster and tail-lamp lenses is very good for removing these types of scratches. This type of plastic polish or cleaner has a very mild abrasive that polishes scratches out of a plastic surface. Products labeled as cleaners usually are designed for more serious scratches, whereas those labeled as polishes are usually milder and work well as a final buff after using the cleaner. Polishes can be used alone if the surface is not scratched very deeply.

Most people are careful about the bottom of the disc because that is where the laser reads, but the top is actually more fragile! This is because the lacquer coating on top of the disc is very thin, normally only 6–7 microns (0.24–0.28 thousandths of an inch). If you write on a disc with a ball point pen, for example, you will press through the lacquer layer and damage the reflective layer underneath, ruining the disc. Also, certain types of markers have solvents that can eat through the lacquer and damage the disc as well. You should write on discs only with felt tip pens that have compatible inks, such as the Sharpie or Staedtler Lumocolor brand, or other markers specifically sold for writing on CDs. In any case, remember that scratches or dents on the top of the disc are more fatal than those on the bottom.

Read errors can also occur when dust accumulates on the read lens of your CD-ROM drive. You can try to clean out the drive and lens with a blast of "canned air" or by using a drive cleaner (which can be purchased at most music stores that sell audio CDs).

If your discs and your drive are clean, but you still can't read a particular disc, your trouble might be due to disc capacity. Many older CD-ROM drives are unreliable when they try to read the outermost tracks of newer discs where the last bits of data are stored. You're more likely to run into this problem with a CD that has lots of data—including some multimedia titles. If you have this problem, you might be able to solve it with a firmware or driver upgrade for your CD-ROM drive, but the only solution might be to replace the drive.

Sometimes too little data on the disc can be problematic as well. Some older CD-ROM drives use an arbitrary point on the disc's surface to calibrate their read mechanism, and if there happens to be no data at that point on the disc, the drive will have problems calibrating successfully. Fortunately, this problem usually can be corrected by a firmware or driver upgrade for your drive.

Many older drives have had problems working under Windows 9x. If you are having problems, contact your drive manufacturer to see whether a firmware or software-driver upgrade is available that might take care of your problem. With new high-speed drives available for well under $100, it might not make sense to spend any time messing with an older drive that is having problems. It might be more cost-effective to upgrade to a new drive instead.

If you are having problems with only one particular disc and not the drive in general, you might find that your difficulties are in fact caused by a defective disc. See whether you can exchange the disc for another to determine whether that is indeed the cause.

Troubleshooting Optical Drives

Failure Reading a CD

If your CD fails to read a CD, try the following solutions:

- Check for scratches on the CD data surface.
- Check the drive for dust and dirt; use a cleaning CD.
- Make sure the drive shows up as a working device in System Properties.
- Try a CD that you know to work.
- Restart the computer (the magic cure-all).
- Remove the drive from Device Manager in Windows 9x, allow the system to redetect the drive, and then reinstall the drivers (if PnP-based system).

Failure to Read CD-R, CD-RW Discs in CD-ROM or DVD Drive

If your CD-ROM or DVD drive fails to read CD-R and CD-RW discs, try the following solutions:

- Check compatibility; some very old 1x CD-ROM drives can't read CD-R media. Replace the drive with a newer, faster, cheaper model.
- Many early-model DVD drives can't read CD-R, CD-RW media; check compatibility.
- The CD-ROM drive must be MultiRead compatible to read CD-RW because of the lower reflectivity of the media; replace the drive.
- If some CD-Rs but not others can be read, check the media color combination to see whether some color combinations work better than others; change the brand of media.
- Packet-written CD-Rs (from Adaptec DirectCD and backup programs) can't be read on MS-DOS/Windows 3.1 CD-ROM drives because of the limitations of the operating system.

ATAPI CD-ROM Drive Runs Slowly

If your IDE/ATAPI CD-If your ATAPI CD-ROM drive performs poorly, check the following items:

- Check the cache size in the Performance tab of the System Properties control panel. Select the quad-speed setting (largest cache size).
- Check to see whether the CD-ROM drive is set as the slave to your hard disk; move the CD-ROM to the secondary controller if possible.
- Your PIO (Programmed I/O) or UDMA mode might not be set correctly for your drive in the BIOS; check the drive specs and use autodetect in BIOS for the best results (see Chapter 5, "BIOS").
- Check that you are using busmastering drivers on compatible systems; install the appropriate drivers for the motherboard's chipset and the operating system in use. See the section "DMA (Direct Memory Access)," earlier in this chapter.

■ Check to see whether you are using the CD-ROM interface on your sound card instead of ATA connection on motherboard. Move the drive connection to the ATA interface on the motherboard and disable the sound card ATA if possible to free up IRQ and I/O port address ranges.

■ Open the System Properties control panel and select the Performance tab to see whether the system is using MS-DOS Compatibility Mode for CD-ROM drive. If all ATA drives are running in this mode, see www.microsoft.com and query on "MS-DOS Compatibility Mode" for a troubleshooter. If only the CD-ROM drive is in this mode, see whether you're using CD-ROM drivers in CONFIG.SYS and AUTOEXEC.BAT. Remove the lines containing references to the CD-ROM drivers (don't actually delete the lines—REM them), reboot the system, and verify that your CD-ROM drive still works and that it's running in 32-bit mode. Some older drives require at least the CONFIG.SYS driver to operate.

Poor Results When Writing to CD-R Media

If you are having problems successfully writing data to a CD, see "How to Reliably Record CDs," earlier in this chapter.

Trouble Reading CD-RW Discs on CD-ROM

If you can't read CD-RW discs in your CD-ROM, check the vendor specifications to see whether your drive is MultiRead compliant. Some drives are not compliant.

If your drive is MultiRead compliant, try the CD-RW disc on a known-compliant CD-ROM drive (a drive with the MultiRead feature).

Trouble Reading CD-R Discs on DVD Drive

If your DVD drive can't read a CD-R disc, check to see that the drive is MultiRead2 compliant—non-compliant DVDs can't read CD-R media. Newer DVD drives generally support reading CD-R media.

Trouble Making Bootable CDs

If you are having problems creating a bootable CD, try these possible solutions:

■ Check the contents of bootable floppy disk from which you copied the boot image. To access the entire contents of a CD, a bootable disk must contain CD-ROM drivers, AUTOEXEC.BAT, and CONFIG.SYS.

■ Use the ISO 9660 format. Don't use the Joliet format because it is for long-filename CDs and can't boot.

■ Check your system's BIOS for boot compliance and boot order; the CD-ROM should be listed first.

■ SCSI CD-ROMs need a SCSI card with BIOS and bootable capability as well as special motherboard BIOS settings.

Physical Drive Installation and Configuration

This chapter covers the actual installation of hard drives, optical drives (CD/DVD), floppy drives, and tape drives. This includes everything from preparing the components to setting jumpers to installing the actual cabling and physical installation. I also dig into some initial system software configuration issues as well, right up to the point of installing the operating system. From that point on, the steps you take depend on which operating system you are installing.

For more information on drive interfaces, magnetic storage, drive operation, and operating system issues, see the following chapters:

- Chapter 7, "The IDE Interface"
- Chapter 8, "The SCSI Interface"
- Chapter 9, "Magnetic Storage Principles"
- Chapter 10, "Hard Disk Storage"
- Chapter 11, "Floppy Disk Storage"
- Chapter 12, "High-Capacity Removable Storage"
- Chapter 13, "Optical Storage"
- Chapter 17, "I/O Interfaces from Serial and Parallel to IEEE-1394 and USB"

Although most of the drives you would install in a PC are covered here, the primary emphasis is on hard disks. For USB devices, see Chapter 17.

Hard Disk Installation Procedures

This section describes the hard disk drive installation process, particularly the configuration, physical installation, and formatting of a hard disk drive.

To install a hard drive in a PC, you must perform some or all of the following procedures:

- Configure the drive.
- Configure the host adapter (if used).
- Physically install the drive.
- Configure the system to recognize the drive.
- Partition the drive (FDISK).
- High-level format the drive (FORMAT).

As you perform the setup procedure, you might need to know various details about the hard disk drive, host adapter (if used), and system ROM BIOS, as well as many of the other devices in the system. This information usually appears in the various manuals or reference sheets that come with these devices. When you purchase these items make sure the vendor includes any documentation that came with the original components. (Many do not include the manuals unless you ask for them.) For most equipment sold today, you will get enough documentation from the vendor to enable you to proceed.

If you are like me, however, and want all the technical documentation on the device, you should contact the original manufacturer of the device and order the technical specification manual. For example, if you purchase a system that comes with an IBM brand ATA (IDE) hard disk, the seller probably will give you some limited information on the drive, but not nearly the amount that the actual IBM technical manual for the drive provides. To get this documentation, you normally download it from the drive manufacturer's Web site. The same rule applies for any of the other components in most of the systems sold today. I find the OEM technical manuals essential in providing the highest level of technical support possible.

For reference, you can look up the hard disk manufacturer names in the Vendor List on the CD-ROM, and you will find numbers to call for technical support, as well as URLs for their Web sites.

Note

You also will find a drive specification database on the CD. This database contains an exhaustive list of drive specs for thousands of drives. If you don't have ready access to your drive specs, check out this searchable database.

Drive Configuration

Before you physically install a hard disk drive in the computer, you must ensure that it is properly configured. For an ATA/IDE drive, this generally means designating the drive as a master/slave or using the Cable Select (CS) feature and a special cable to determine the relationship. For SCSI drives, you must set the device's SCSI ID and possibly its SCSI bus termination state.

◀◀ These procedures are covered in "The IDE Interface," p. 475, and "The SCSI Interface," p. 513.

Host Adapter Configuration

Older hard disk drive types used separate disk controller cards you had to install in a bus slot. The IDE and SCSI hard disk drives used in today's PCs, however, have the disk controller integrated into the drive assembly. For IDE drives, the I/O interface is nearly always integrated into the system's motherboard, and you configure the interface through the system BIOS. No separate host adapter exists; therefore, if you have an IDE drive, you can proceed to the section "Physical Installation" later in this chapter. Some systems might use ATA/IDE adapters in lieu of the built-in interface. This is because some of the motherboard-integrated ATA interfaces might not support the faster modes (such as Ultra-ATA/33 through Ultra-ATA/100) most newer drives use. In most cases, I would recommend upgrading the motherboard rather than getting an IDE host adapter because a new motherboard has other benefits and the cost isn't much higher.

SCSI drives, however, usually require a host adapter card you must install in a bus slot like any other card. A few motherboards have integrated SCSI adapters, but these are rare. Configuring a SCSI host adapter card involves setting the various system resources the adapter requires. As with most expansion cards, a SCSI host adapter requires some combination of the following system resources:

- Boot ROM address (optional)
- Interrupt request (IRQ)
- Direct Memory Access (DMA) channel
- I/O port address

Not all adapters use every one of these resources, but some might use them all. In most cases with modern plug-and-play adapters and systems, the BIOS and your operating system automatically configure these resources. The computer sets the required hardware resource settings to values that do not conflict with other devices in the computer.

◀◀ See "Plug and Play BIOS," p. 396.

Note

A detailed list of PnP device IDs is included in the Technical Reference section of the CD included with this book.

If your hardware or operating system does not support Plug and Play, you must manually configure the adapter to use the appropriate resources. Some adapters provide software that enables you to reconfigure or change the hardware resources, whereas others might use jumpers or DIP switches on the adapter card.

◄◄ See "System Resources," p. 316.

The IDE interface driver is part of the standard PC BIOS, which enables booting from an IDE drive. The BIOS provides the device driver functionality the system needs to access the drive before any files can be loaded from disk. However, a SCSI interface driver is not part of the standard PC BIOS, so most SCSI host adapters have their own onboard ROM BIOS that enables SCSI drives to function as bootable devices.

Note

Although standard IDE/ATA drivers are provided with Windows, this interface is normally built into the motherboard chipset South Bridge or I/O Controller Hub (ICH) component, and it usually requires that specific chipset drivers be loaded. If you are using a motherboard that is newer than your operating system version (for example, a new board purchased in 2001 with Windows Me, 2000, or 9x), be sure you install the chipset drivers that came with your motherboard immediately after installing Windows.

Use of the SCSI BIOS is usually optional. If you are not booting from a SCSI drive, you can leave the BIOS on the card disabled and merely install the appropriate device driver to access the SCSI devices. Most host adapters have switches, jumpers, or configuration software you can use to enable or disable SCSI BIOS support.

In addition to providing boot functionality, the SCSI BIOS can provide many other functions, including any or all of the following:

- Low-level formatting
- Drive-type (parameter) control
- Host adapter configuration
- SCSI diagnostics
- Support for nonstandard I/O port addresses and interrupts

If the adapter's onboard BIOS is enabled, it uses specific memory address space in the upper memory area (UMA). The UMA is the top 384KB in the first megabyte of system memory. It is divided into three areas of two 64KB segments each, with the first and last areas being used by the video adapter circuits and the motherboard BIOS, respectively. Segments C000h and D000h are reserved for use by adapter ROMs, such as those found on disk controllers or SCSI host adapters.

Note

You must ensure that any adapters using space in these segments of the UMA (upper memory area) do not overlap with another adapter that uses this space. No two adapters can share this memory space. Most adapters have software, jumpers, or switches that can adjust the configuration of the board and change the addresses it uses to prevent conflict.

Physical Installation

The procedure for the physical installation of a hard disk drive is much the same as that for installing any other type of drive. You must have the correct screws, brackets, and faceplates for the specific drive and system before you can install the drive.

Some computer cases require plastic or metal rails that are secured to the sides of a hard disk drive so it can slide into the proper place in the system (see Figure 14.1). Other case designs have drive bays that directly accept the drive via screws through the side supports and no other hardware is necessary, whereas others use a cage arrangement where you first install the drives into a cage, and then slide the cage into the case (see Figure 14.2). If your case uses rails or a cage, these are normally included with the case. With the proper mounting mechanism supplied via the case, all you need is the bare drive to install.

Because cables can vary for both IDE and SCSI interfaces, be sure you have the proper cable for both your drive and controller. For example, to run the newer Ultra-ATA/66 or Ultra-ATA/100 mode, you need a special 80-conductor cable that supports the CS feature. This cable is also recommended if you are running Ultra-ATA/33; it works for all slower modes as well. To determine whether your cable has 40 or 80 conductors, simply count the ridges on the ribbon cable—each ridge contains a conductor (wire). Another indication is that the 80-conductor cable normally has the motherboard connector color-coded blue, and the master and slave drive connectors colored-coded black and gray, respectively.

Screw holes

Disk drive mounting rail

Figure 14.1 A typical 3 1/2-inch hard disk with mounting rails for a 3 1/2-inch drive bay.

If you need additional drive-mounting hardware not included with either your case or the drive, several companies that specialize in drive-mounting brackets, cables, and other hardware accessories are listed in the Vendor List (on the CD). If you intend to install a 3 1/2-inch hard drive in a 5 1/4-inch drive bay, you need yet another type of mounting bracket (as shown in Figure 14.3). Many 3 1/2-inch hard drives come with these brackets, or one might be supplied with your case or chassis.

Note

You should also note the length of the drive cable itself when you plan to add a hard disk drive. It can be very annoying to assemble everything you think you'll need to install a drive, and then find that the drive cable is not long enough to reach the new drive location. You can try to reposition the drive to a location closer to the interface connector on the host adapter or motherboard, or just get a longer cable. ATA/IDE cables are limited to 18 inches in overall length; if they are shorter, that is all the better. This is most important if your drive is going to use the faster ATA/33 through ATA/100 modes. Using a cable that is too long causes timing errors and signal degradation, possibly corrupting the data on your drive. I see many 24-inch cable assemblies being sold or used in systems; you are asking for trouble if you violate the 18-inch maximum-length specification.

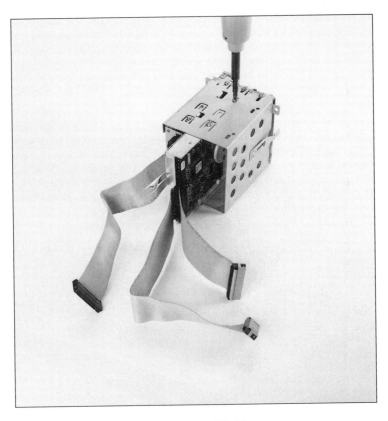

Figure 14.2 A typical hard disk mounted in a removable drive cage.

Figure 14.3 A typical bracket used to mount a 3 1/2-inch drive in a 5 1/4-inch drive bay. The bracket is screwed to the drive and then mounted in the bay by using screws or rails, as determined by the case.

Different faceplate, or bezel, options are also available. Make sure you have the correct bezel for your application. Some systems, for example, do not need a bezel; if a bezel exists on the drive, you must remove it.

Caution

Be sure you use only the screws that come with your new drive. Many drives come with special short-length screws that may have the same size thread as other screws you might use in your system, but that should not be interchanged. If you use screws that are too long, they might protrude too far into the drive casing and cause problems.

Hard Drive Physical Installation—Step by Step

The step-by-step procedures for installing a hard drive are as follows:

Note

Be sure to see the more visual step-by-step instructions and photos for installing a hard drive in Chapter 23, "Building or Upgrading Systems."

1. Check your computer for an unused ATA/IDE connector. Typical Pentium-class and newer PCs have two ATA/IDE connectors, allowing for up to four ATA/IDE devices.

Tip

Normally it is best for performance to keep hard drives on the primary IDE cable and other types of drives (CD-ROM, DVD, tape, SuperDisk, and so on) on the secondary.

You might need an additional cable if both master and slave connectors are used on the primary and you are adding a third device.

2. Double-check the pin configuration and cable type. The colored (normally red or red-flecked) stripe on one edge of the cable goes to pin 1 of the hard drive's data connector. Most cables and drive connectors are keyed to prevent improper (backward) installation, but many are not. Keying can be done via missing and plugged pins, a ridge on one side of the connector, or both. One tip to note is that pin 1 on the drive connector is almost always oriented nearest to the power connector.

Tip

Newer ATA drives that operate in Ultra-DMA modes require a special 80-conductor cable, whereas lesser drives can use a 40-conductor cable. Note that you can always use the superior 80-conductor cable for slower drives, so normally that is all I recommend purchasing. SCSI drives use either 50-pin or 68-pin (wide) cables.

3. Configure the drive jumpers. If the drive is ATA/IDE and you are using a cable that supports CS, you must set the CS jumper on any drives connected to that cable. Otherwise, you must set the drives on the cable as either master or slave. Note that some older drives also required a slave-present jumper be set if the drive was configured as a master with a slave drive on the same cable. You'll find more detail on the drive configuration procedures later in this chapter.

4. Slide the drive carefully into a drive bay of the correct size. Most hard drives—except for a few very high-capacity SCSI drives meant for servers and the Quantum Bigfoot series—are 3 1/2-inch wide and one-inch high. If you have no 3 1/2-inch drive bays left for your hard disk, attach a drive-adapter kit to the sides of the drive to make it wide enough to fit into a 5 1/4-inch wide drive bay (refer to Figure 14.3). Some case designs require you to attach rails to the side of the hard drive. If so, attach them to the drive using the screws supplied with either the case or the drive. Be sure the screws aren't too long; if you bottom the screws in the drive, you can damage it. Then, slide the drive into the bay in the case until the rails latch into place.

5. Attach the data cable connector to the back of the drive, unless you are adding the drive and cable at the same time. In that case, attach the cable to the drive before you slide it into the drive bay and fasten it into place (step 2).

6. Attach the appropriate power connector to the drive. Most hard drives use the larger, or "Molex," four-wire power connector. If necessary, purchase a Y-splitter cable (see Figure 14.4) to create two power connectors from one (many computers have fewer power connectors than drive bays).

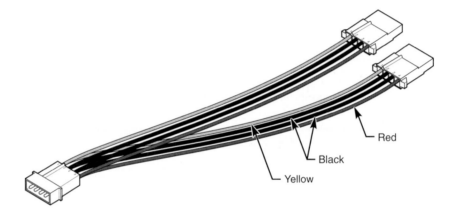

Red

Black

Yellow

Figure 14.4   Power cord splitter and connector.

7. Turn on the computer and listen for the new hard disk to spin up. Even though today's drives are very quiet compared to early hard disks, you should still hear a faint rattling or clicking as the new hard disk starts to run. If you don't hear anything from the drive, double-check the data and power cables.

8. Restart the computer and access the BIOS setup screens to configure the new hard disk. At a minimum, you'll need to detect (or set) the following parameters: cylinders, heads, sectors per track (called CHS parameters), and write precompensation. If your BIOS has an autodetect or auto type setting, I recommend you use it because it will configure most parameters automatically. For IDE hard drives above 528MB (504 megabytes), you also must set logical block address (LBA) translation to access the drive's full capacity. If autodetect was selected, LBA translation should already be set correctly. Many systems have a Peripherals Configuration screen, which also enables you to set transfer speeds for maximum drive performance, but again these should be configured automatically if you enabled autodetect. If your BIOS cannot autodetect your drive, see the documentation that came with the drive for the correct settings. Most drives have the CHS parameters as well as jumper setting information displayed on a sticker attached to the drive, and all modern BIOSes support autodetect, as well. Save the BIOS configuration and exit the BIOS Setup screen to continue. The following section has more information on this step, as it can be complicated.

9. Restart the computer and prepare to run FDISK to prepare the hard drive for formatting and use. Or, you can use drive partitioning software, such as PowerQuest's PartitionMagic, to automatically create and manage disk partitions. Normally, FDISK can be found on the operating system start disk, such as the Windows startup disk. Simply insert the startup disk in the floppy drive, boot from it, and type the FDISK command at the A: prompt.

◀◀   See "The IDE Interface," p. 475, and "The SCSI Interface," p. 513.

System Configuration

After your drive is physically installed, you must provide the computer with basic information about the drive so the system can access and boot from it. How you set and store this information depends on the type of drive and system you have. Standard (IDE) setup procedures apply for most hard disks except SCSI drives. SCSI drives normally follow a custom setup procedure that varies depending on the host adapter you are using. If you have a SCSI drive, follow the instructions included with the host adapter to configure the drive.

Automatic Drive Detection

For IDE drives, virtually all new BIOS versions in today's PCs have automatic parameter detection (autodetect). The BIOS sends a special Identify Drive command to all the devices connected to the IDE interface during the system startup sequence; the drives are intelligent enough to respond with the correct parameters. The BIOS then automatically enters the parameter information returned by the drive. This procedure eliminates errors or confusion in parameter selection. However, even with autodetect, some BIOSes alert you that you need to enter the system Setup program and configure the drive. In these situations, just enter the system BIOS configuration utility and save the settings the BIOS has detected for the drive. You don't need to enter any settings yourself.

If your system supports autodetect but no drive information appears onscreen, first check to see that autodetect is selected or enabled. Other possible problems include forgetting to attach the power cable to the drive, or reversing the IDE interface cable at either the motherboard or the hard drive connections. The red stripe on the 40-pin IDE cable is supposed to be aligned with pin 1 at both ends. Without power or proper data connection, the drive doesn't spin up and, therefore, cannot be detected.

Even though most new BIOSes support automatic drive detection at startup, performing this task within the BIOS configuration screen has a couple of benefits:

■ In the event that you need to move the drive to another system, you'll know the drive geometry and translation scheme (such as LBA) that was used to access the drive. If the drive is moved to another computer, the identical drive geometry (cylinder, head, sectors per track) and translation scheme must be used in the other computer; otherwise, the data on the drive will not be accessible and can be lost. Because many systems with autoconfiguration don't display these settings during the startup process, performing the drive-typing operation yourself might be the only way to get this information.

■ Even if you never expect to move the drive, you'll gain several seconds on every startup by detecting the drive in the BIOS configuration screens and saving the setting there. You also can save time by setting unused drive interfaces to Not Installed. Otherwise, the computer will try to detect devices on all four IDE ports (primary master, primary slave, secondary master, and secondary slave) each time you start the computer.

Manual Drive Parameters

If you are dealing with a motherboard that does not support autodetect, you must enter the appropriate drive information in the system BIOS manually. The BIOS has a selection of preconfigured drive types, but these are woefully outdated in most cases, providing support for only drives holding a few hundred megabytes or less. In nearly every case, you must select the user-defined drive type and provide values for the following settings:

- Cylinders
- Heads
- Sectors per track

The values you use for these settings should be provided in the documentation for the hard disk drive, but they also might be printed on the drive itself. It's a good idea to check for these settings and write them down because they might not be visible after you've installed the drive. You also should maintain a copy of these settings in case your system BIOS loses its data due to a battery failure. One of the best places to store this information is inside the computer itself. Taping a note with vital settings such as these to the inside of the case can be a lifesaver.

In the event that you are unable to determine the correct settings for your hard drive from either the drive case or the Technical Reference, utility programs are available on the Internet that can query the drive for this information. Western Digital's TBLCHK.EXE has been updated to handle LBA-mode hard drives—unlike many older utilities—and can be obtained from Western Digital's Web site.

Note

The setup parameters for more than 1,000 popular drive models are included in the Technical Reference on the CD.

Depending on the maker and version of your system BIOS, you might have to configure other settings as well, such as which transfer mode to use and whether the BIOS should use logical block addressing.

◄◄ See "Drive Capacity Limitations," p. 495.

Formatting

Proper setup and formatting are critical to a drive's performance and reliability. This section describes the procedures used to format a hard disk drive correctly. Use these procedures when you install a new drive in a system or immediately after you recover data from a hard disk that has been exhibiting problems.

The three major steps in the formatting process for a hard disk drive subsystem are as follows:

1. Low-level formatting
2. Partitioning
3. High-level formatting

Low-Level Formatting

All new hard disk drives are low-level formatted by the manufacturer, and you do not have to perform another LLF before you install the drive. In fact, under normal circumstances, you should not ever have to perform a low-level format on an IDE or SCSI drive. Most manufacturers no longer recommend that you low-level format any IDE type drive.

This recommendation has been the source of some myths about IDE. Many people say, for example, that you cannot perform a low-level format on an IDE drive, and that if you do, you will destroy the drive. This statement is untrue! What can happen with some of the earliest IDE drives is that you might lose the optimal head and cylinder skew factors that were set by the manufacturer for the drive, as well as the map of drive defects. This can have a negative effect on the drive's performance, but you still can reliably use the drive. Note that all drives that internally use a zoned recording (where there is a variable number of sectors per track internally) are immune to any problems due to low-level formatting because the actual sector marks can't be rewritten. This includes pretty much all modern IDE drives made in the last 10 years.

However, sometimes you must perform a low-level format on an IDE or a SCSI drive. The following sections discuss the software you can use to do this.

SCSI Low-Level Format Software

If you are using a SCSI drive, you must use the LLF program provided by the manufacturer of the SCSI host adapter. The designs of these devices vary enough that a register-level program can work only if it is tailored to the individual controller. Fortunately, all SCSI host adapters include low-level format software, either in the host adapter's BIOS or in a separate disk-based program.

The interface to the SCSI drive is through the host adapter. SCSI is a standard, but no true standards exist for what a host adapter is supposed to look like. This means that any formatting or configuration software is specific to a particular host adapter.

Note

Notice that SCSI format and configuration software is keyed to the host adapter and is not specific in any way to the particular SCSI hard disk drive you are using.

IDE Low-Level Format Software

IDE drive manufacturers have defined extensions to the standard WD1002/1003 AT interface, which was further standardized for IDE drives as the ATA (AT Attachment) interface. The ATA specification provides for vendor-unique commands, which are manufacturer proprietary extensions to the standard. To prevent improper low-level formatting, many of these IDE drives have special codes that must be sent to the drive to unlock the format routines. These codes vary among manufacturers. If possible, you should obtain LLF and defect management software from the drive manufacturer; this software usually is specific to that manufacturer's products and often is model specific. Check the brand and model number of your hard disk to determine the utility program you need.

Most ATA IDE drives are protected from any alteration to the skew factors or defect map erasure because they are always in a translated mode internally. Zoned bit recording drives are always under translation and are fully protected. Most ATA drives have a custom command set that must be used in the format process; the standard format commands defined by the ATA specification usually do not work, especially with intelligent or zoned bit recording IDE drives. Without the proper manufacturer-specific format commands, you can't perform the defect management by the manufacturer-specified method, in which bad sectors often can be spared.

Most manufacturers supply low-level format programs for their drives. Here are a few examples:

- *Seagate.* ftp://ftp.seagate.com/techsuppt/seagate_utils/sgatfmt4.zip
- *IBM.* http://www.storage.ibm.com/techsup/hddtech/welcome.htm
- *Quantum.* http://www.quantum.com/support/csr/software/csr_software.htm
- *Western Digital.* http://www.wdc.com/service/ftp/wddiag/wd_diag.exe
- *Maxtor.* http://www.maxtor.com/SoftwareDownload/utilities.html

You should try the manufacturer-specific format programs first. They are free and can often work at a lower level and handle defects in ways that the more generic ones can't. If formatting software is not available from your drive's manufacturer, I recommend Disk Manager by Ontrack and the MicroScope program by Micro 2000. Another excellent, inexpensive, general-purpose PC hardware diagnostic that includes low-level format capability is #1 TuffTEST Pro from #1-PC Diagnostics. These programs can format many IDE drives because they know the manufacturer-specific IDE format commands and routines. They also can perform defect-mapping and surface-analysis procedures.

Note

Although Ontrack Disk Manager can be purchased in a "generic" version that works with any manufacturer's hard drives, brand-specific OEM versions are often available free of charge on the utility disks or CD-ROMs shipped with new retail-packaged hard disk drives. You should also check your drive maker's Web site for updated versions of Disk Manager. These OEM versions are designed to check for a particular brand's drive firmware and do not work on any brand other than the one for which they are modified.

Nondestructive Formatters

General-purpose, BIOS-level, nondestructive formatters, such as Calibrate and SpinRite, are not recommended in most situations in which a real LLF is required. These programs have several limitations and problems that limit their effectiveness; in some cases, they can even cause problems with the way defects are handled on a drive. These programs attempt to perform a track-by-track LLF by using BIOS functions, while backing up and restoring the track data as they go. These programs do not actually perform a complete LLF because they do not even try to low-level format the first track (Cylinder 0, Head 0) due to problems with some controller types that store hidden information on the first track.

These programs also do not perform defect mapping in the way standard LLF programs do, and they even can remove the carefully applied sector header defect marks during a proper LLF. This situation potentially enables data to be stored in sectors that originally were marked defective and might actually void the manufacturer's warranty on some drives. Another problem is that these programs work only on drives that have already been formatted and can format only drives that are formattable through BIOS functions.

Note

SpinRite is useful for recovering data found on drives with read errors because of its thorough method of repeatedly rereading the errors and analyzing the results to reconstruct the missing data.

A true LLF program bypasses the system BIOS and sends commands directly to the disk controller hardware. For this reason, many LLF programs are specific to the disk controller hardware for which they are designed. Having a single format program that will run on all types of controllers is virtually impossible. Many hard drives have been incorrectly diagnosed as being defective because the wrong format program was used and the program did not operate properly.

Drive Partitioning with FDISK

Partitioning a hard disk is the act of defining areas of the disk for an operating system to use as a volume.

When you partition a disk, the partitioning software writes a master partition boot sector at Cylinder 0, Head 0, Sector 1—the first sector on the hard disk. This sector contains data that describes the partitions by their starting and ending cylinder, head, and sector locations. The partition table also indicates to the ROM BIOS which of the partitions is bootable and, therefore, where to look for an operating system to load.

▶▶ See "File Systems and Data Recovery," p. 1315.

The FDISK program is the accepted standard for partitioning hard disk drives for use with all operating systems. The program is included with your operating system, and although it has the same name and basic functions with any OS, you should normally use the one that specifically came with your OS. Partitioning prepares the boot sector of the disk in such a way that the FORMAT.COM program or the Windows GUI format utility can operate correctly. FDISK also makes it possible for various operating systems to coexist on a single hard disk. No matter which operating system you use, it should come with an FDISK program that can be used to partition the drive.

Note

Because FDISK depends on BIOS information about the hard disk to determine the size and drive geometry of the hard disk, having correct BIOS settings saved in the BIOS Setup is vital to the correct operation of FDISK. If a 10GB hard drive is defined in the BIOS as a 10MB hard drive, for example, all that FDISK will prepare for use—and all that FORMAT will ultimately prepare—is 10MB.

With any version of Windows, as with MS-DOS, FDISK enables you to create two types of disk partitions: primary and extended. A primary partition can be bootable but an extended partition cannot. If you have only a single hard disk in your system, at least part of the drive must be prepared as a primary partition if you want to start your computer from the hard disk (and who doesn't?). A primary partition is seen as a single volume or drive letter (C: on one-drive systems), whereas an extended partition acts as a sort of logical container for additional volumes (drive letters D: and beyond). A single extended partition can contain a single volume (also referred to by FDISK as a *logical DOS drive*) or several volumes (logical DOS drives) of various sizes.

Don't get hung up on the fact that FDISK calls partitions "DOS" partitions or "DOS" drives. This is true even though the operating system you are installing is Windows 95, 98, Me, NT, 2000, Linux, and so on.

Depending on the version of Windows in use (and with any version of MS-DOS), you might need to subdivide a hard drive through the use of FDISK. The original release of Windows 95 and MS-DOS supports a file system known as FAT16, which allows no more than 65,536 files per drive and a single drive letter or volume size of no more than 2.1GB in size. Thus, a 10.1GB hard disk prepared with MS-DOS or the original Windows 95 (or 95A) must have a minimum of five drive letters, and could have more (see Figure 14.5).

Another reason for subdividing a single drive into multiple volumes is for increased data security. For example, PowerQuest (the creator of PartitionMagic) suggests a three-volume partitioning scheme that looks like this:

C: for the operating system and utilities

D: for applications

E: and above for data

In this example, primary and extended partitions would be assigned as shown here:

C: the primary partition

D: and E: in the extended partition as logical DOS drives (volumes)

If a catastrophic failure to the disk structure wipes out C: or D:, drive E:—which contains the data—will normally still be intact. This method also makes backing up the data easier; just set the backup program to back up all of E:, or all the changed files on E:.

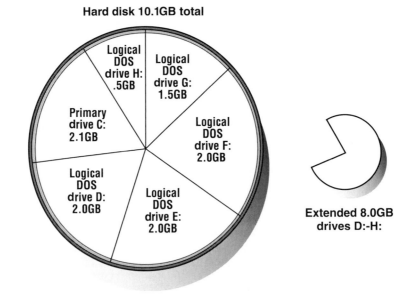

Figure 14.5   Adding a hard drive above 2.1GB in size to an MS-DOS or original Windows 95A computer forces the user to create multiple drive letters to use the entire drive capacity. The logical DOS drives are referenced like any other drive, although they are portions of a single physical hard disk.

Large Hard Disk Support

If you use the Windows 95B or above (Win95 OSR 2.x), Windows 98, Windows Me, or Windows 2000 versions of FDISK with a hard drive greater than 512MB, FDISK offers to enable large disk support.

Choosing to enable large disk support provides several benefits:

■ *You can use a large hard disk (greater than 2.1GB) as a single drive letter.* In fact, your drive can be as large as 2TB and still be identified by a single drive letter. This is because of the FAT32 file system, which allows for many more files per drive than FAT16.

▶▶   See "FAT32," p. 1334.

■ *Because of the more efficient storage methods of FAT-32, your files will use less hard disk space overall.*

However, keep in mind that all disk operations must be performed through an operating system with FAT32 support (Windows 95B or later, Windows 98, Windows Me, or Windows 2000). If you have old MS-DOS games or applications that are bootable, you won't be able to access a FAT32 volume unless you replace the DOS version on the disk with the DOS included on Win95B or Windows 98. This normally can be done by using the SYS A: command from the \Windows\Command folder. Another option is to use the Windows Startup menu in Win95B or Win98 (press F8 as Windows starts to load) and select Command Prompt to get to a FAT32 capable DOS. On the other hand, you can select Start, Shutdown, Restart the Computer in MS-DOS Mode from the Windows desktop.

A drive prepared with the large hard disk support (FAT32) option enabled can still be partitioned into primary and secondary partitions with FDISK, as with FAT16 for the data-security reasons listed earlier.

Another type of file system is NTFS, which is supported by only Windows NT and Windows 2000. This is a high-performance file system with additional security and networking features. NTFS was revised to NTFS5 in Windows NT 4.0 with Service Pack 4 and later, as well as Windows 2000. It is discussed in more detail in Chapter 25, "File Systems and Data Recovery." Note that Windows 9x cannot read NTFS partitions, and Windows NT cannot read FAT32 partitions. Windows 2000, however, can handle both FAT32 and NTFS.

Assigning Drive Letters with FDISK

FDISKcan be used in many ways, depending on the number of hard drives you have in your system and the number of drive letters you want to create.

With a single drive, creating a primary partition (C:) and an extended partition with two logical DOS drives within it results in the following drive letters:

Partition Type	Drive letter(s)
Primary	C:
Extended	D: and E:

Most people think that a second physical drive added to this system should have drive letters that follow the E: drive.

However, you must understand how drive letters are allocated by the system to know how to use FDISK correctly in this situation. Table 14.1 shows how FDISK assigns drive letters by drive and partition type.

Table 14.1   Drive Letter Allocations by Drive and Partition Type

Drive	Partition	Order	Drive Letter
1st	Primary	1st	C:
1st	Extended	3rd	E:
2nd	Primary	2nd	D:
2nd	Extended	4th	F:

How does this affect you when you add another hard drive? If you prepare the second hard drive with a primary partition and your first hard drive has an extended partition on it, the second hard drive takes the primary partition's D: drive letter. This moves all the drive letters in the first hard drive's extended partition up one drive letter.

In the first example, a drive is listed with C: (primary partition), D:, and E: (extended partition volumes) as the drive letters (D: and E: were in the extended partition). Table 14.2 indicates what happens if a second drive is added with a primary partition and an extended partition with two volumes (same setup as the first drive).

Table 14.2   Drive Letter Changes Caused by Addition of Second Drive with Primary Partition

Drive	Partition Type	Order	Original Drive Letters (First Drive Only)	New Drive Letters After Adding Second Drive
1st	Primary	1st	C:	C:
1st	Extended	3rd	D:, E:	E:, F:
2nd	Primary	2nd		D:
2nd	Extended	4th		G:, H:

After adding the second drive, the original drive letters D: and E: have now become E: and F:. The primary partition on the new drive has become D:, and the extended partition volumes on the second drive are G: and H:. Confused? Well, you better not be or you'll find yourself deleting or copying data to or from the wrong drive.

This principle extends to third and fourth physical drives as well: The primary partitions on each drive get their drive letters first, followed by logical DOS drives in the extended partitions.

One way to affect this is to partition additional drives with only extended partitions—in other words, do not create primary partitions on them. That enables the new drive's partitions to be seen only as additional letters, and the letters used by the first drive's partitions to remain unchanged.

If you're *adding* a drive to your system, you should now understand why preparing that second, third, or fourth drive with a primary partition is a bad idea. If you're installing an additional hard drive (not a replacement), remember that it can't be a bootable drive. And if it can't be bootable, there's no reason to make it a primary partition. FDISK allows you to create an extended partition using 100% of the space on any drive. Table 14.3 shows the same example used in Table 14.2 with the second drive installed as an extended partition.

Table 14.3   Drive Letter Allocations After Addition of Second Drive with Extended Partition Only

Drive	Partition Type	Order	Original Drive Letters (First Drive Only)	New Drive Letters After Adding Second Drive
1st	Primary	1st	C:	C:
1st	Extended	3rd	D:, E:	D:, E:
2nd	Primary	2nd	—	—
2nd	Extended	4th		F:

When a new drive is added with only extended partition volumes, you can see that the original drive letters remain undisturbed. This arrangement is much easier to understand, and it prevents accidents with data because of drive letters changing. This operating-system behavior also explains why some of the first computers with IDE-based (ATAPI) Iomega Zip drives had the Zip drive as D:, with a single hard disk identified as C: and E:. The Zip drive was treated as the second hard drive with a primary partition. Subsequently Iomega changed the Zip drive format and driver so that the Zip disk is recognized as an extended partition at the end of the drive letter chain.

Running FDISK

When you run newer versions of FDISK, the first thing that happens is you are prompted with the following:

```
Do you wish to enable large disk support (Y/N)...........? [Y]
```

If you answer Yes to this question, FDISK creates FAT32 volumes for all volumes created that are larger than 512MB. Answering No to this question forces FDISK to create only FAT16 volumes, which are limited to a 2GB maximum size and waste more space on the disk due to larger cluster sizes.

Normally, in a modern system you would answer Yes, allowing the use of FAT32. After answering the question, FDISK shows a menu similar to the following:

```
Current fixed disk drive: 1

    Choose one of the following:
```

```
1. Create DOS partition or Logical DOS Drive
2. Set active partition
3. Delete partition or Logical DOS Drive
4. Display partition information
5. Change current fixed disk drive

Enter choice: [1]
```

Option 5 is shown only if FDISK detects more than one drive on your system (if more than one is entered via your BIOS Setup). In that case, FDISK defaults to the first drive, and via option 5 you can cause FDISK to work with any of the other hard disks on the system.

To create partitions, you select option 1. If the drive is already partitioned, however, you can use option 4 to display the current layout of the drive.

After selecting option 1, the menu changes to enable you to create primary or extended partitions on a drive as follows:

```
Create DOS Partition or Logical DOS Drive

    Current fixed disk drive: 1

    Choose one of the following:

    1. Create Primary DOS Partition
    2. Create Extended DOS Partition
    3. Create Logical DOS Drive(s) in the Extended DOS Partition

    Enter choice: [1]
```

The rules require you to create a primary partition first on the boot drive, but on a secondary or non-boot drive, you can create just an extended partition if you choose. So, if you are partitioning the first drive in a system and it will be bootable, you would choose option 1.

At this point, you are prompted to decide whether you want to use the maximum available size for a Primary DOS Partition. If you say Yes and you're using FAT32, the primary partition uses the entire drive. Conversely, if you say Yes and you did not enable large drive support (meaning you are using FAT16), the partition uses the entire drive or 2GB, whichever is smaller.

If you decide to create a primary partition that is not the full drive, you should go back through the menus and create an extended partition using the rest of the drive, and then further divide it into logical drives. Normally, I recommend making the primary partition the full size of the drive, keeping all of the drive as one letter. But there are various reasons you might want to split the drive into multiple partitions, such as for different operating systems, different file systems, applications, and so on.

After all the partitions are created, the final operation is to make one of them active (bootable), which is option 2 from the main FDISK menu. Normally, the only one that can be active is the primary partition. After that is done, all FDISK operations are complete, and you can exit the program.

When exiting FDISK after making partition changes, the system must be rebooted before these changes will be recognized. After rebooting, you must then high-level format each of the volumes with the operating system FORMAT command, which then allows the operating system to store files on them.

The C: volume must normally be formatted with the system files, although when you install Windows via the Windows Setup command, it detects whether the system files are present and offers to install them for you.

Drive Partitioning with PartitionMagic

PowerQuest's PartitionMagic (6.0 and later) enables you to take an existing hard drive and perform the following changes to it without loss of data:

- Create, resize, split, move, and merge partitions on the fly without losing data.

- Convert between file systems without losing data—conversions include FAT to FAT32 and NTFS; FAT32 to FAT; NTFS to FAT and FAT32; primary to logical and vice versa; and FAT32 to NTFS under Windows 2000 Professional. It also includes support for ext2 and Linux SWAP file systems.

- Move applications between partitions and automatically update the drive-letter references after partitioning with their DriveMapper utility.

- Undelete FAT, FAT32, Linux ext2, and NTFS partitions that have been deleted. You can restore partitions that have been deleted on disk as long as the space has not been reallocated or written over.

- Copy or move a partition to another partition or drive.

- Switch between multiple operating systems using the included BootMagic utility.

Note

I still recommend FDISK be used for initial partitioning and setup of any drive, but PartitionMagic can be very useful for reconfiguring a system that is already partitioned.

Although the program recommends a full backup before starting, I've used PartitionMagic many times to turn a single "big drive" into two or more drive letters in less than 10 minutes. Performing the same task with backup software and FDISK/FORMAT can take several hours.

High-Level (Operating System) Formatting

The final step in the installation of a hard disk drive is the high-level format. Similar to the partitioning process, the high-level format is specific to the file system you've chosen to use on the drive. On Windows 9x and DOS systems, the primary function of the high-level format is to create a FAT and a directory system on the disk so the operating system can manage files. You must run FDISK before formatting a drive. Each drive letter created by FDISK must be formatted before it can be used for data storage.

Usually, you perform the high-level format with the FORMAT.COM program or the formatting utility in Windows 9x Explorer. FORMAT.COM uses the following syntax:

```
FORMAT C: /S /V
```

This command high-level formats drive C:, writes the hidden operating system files in the first part of the partition, and prompts for the entry of a volume label to be stored on the disk at the completion of the process.

The FAT high-level format program performs the following functions and procedures:

1. Scans the disk (read-only) for tracks and sectors marked as bad during the LLF, and notes these tracks as being unreadable.

2. Returns the drive heads to the first cylinder of the partition, and at that cylinder (Head 1, Sector 1) writes a DOS volume boot sector.

3. Writes a FAT at Head 1, Sector 2. Immediately after this FAT, it writes a second copy of the FAT. These FATs are essentially blank except for bad-cluster marks noting areas of the disk that were found to be unreadable during the marked-defect scan.

4. Writes a blank root directory.

5. If the /S parameter is specified, copies the system files, IO.SYS and MSDOS.SYS (or IBMBIO.COM and IBMDOS.COM, depending on which DOS you run), and COMMAND.COM to the disk (in that order).

6. If the /V parameter is specified, prompts the user for a volume label, which is written as the fourth file entry in the root directory.

Now, the operating system can use the disk for storing and retrieving files, and the disk is a bootable disk.

During the first phase of the high-level format, the program performs a marked defect scan. Defects marked by the LLF operation show up during this scan as being unreadable tracks or sectors. When the high-level format encounters one of these areas, it automatically performs up to five retries to read these tracks or sectors. If the unreadable area was marked by the LLF, the read fails on all attempts.

After five retries, the DOS FORMAT program gives up on this track or sector and moves to the next one. If an area remains unreadable after the initial read and five retries, it is marked in the FAT as a bad cluster.

Note

Because the high-level format doesn't overwrite data areas beyond the root directory of the hard disk, using programs such as Norton Utilities to unformat the hard disk that contains data from previous operations is possible, provided no programs or data has been copied to the drive after high-level formatting. Unformatting can be performed because the data from the drive's previous use is still present.

If you create an extended partition, the logical DOS drive letters found there need a simpler FORMAT command because system files aren't necessary—for example, FORMAT D:/V for drive D:, FORMAT E:/V for drive E:, and so on.

FDISK and FORMAT Limitations

The biggest problem with FDISK is that it is destructive. If you change your mind about disk structure, you must back up your system and start over again. That alone is cause for using FDISK with care, but here are other limitations you should keep in mind:

■ FDISK doesn't provide any help with issues of drive letter changes.

■ FDISK requires FORMAT before the drive is ready for use.

■ FORMAT must check the entire drive before making it ready for use. Its error management is rudimentary and can waste a lot of disk space with older drives that have disk errors.

■ FDISK and FORMAT are designed for a single operating system environment, with no provision for multiboot options (Windows 9x and NT or Windows 9x and Linux, for example).

■ FDISK and FORMAT offer no procedure for migrating data to a new drive, and the XCOPY command is tricky to use.

■ FDISK and FORMAT might cause conflicts with existing CD-ROM drives, which often use the next available drive letter after the existing hard drive.

For these reasons, many drive vendors offer some sort of automatic disk installation software with their hard drives. These routines can make the task of disk migration a fast, easy, reliable operation.

Typical features of automatic disk installation programs include the following:

- *Replacement for FDISK and FORMAT.* A single program performs both functions more quickly than FDISK and FORMAT separately.

- *Database of drive jumpers for major brands and models.*

- *Drive copy function.* Copies contents of old MS-DOS or Windows 9x drive to new drive, retaining long filenames, file attributes, and so on.

- *CD-ROM drive letter relocation utility.* Moves CD-ROM to new drive letter (to make room for new hard drive letters) and resets Windows Registry and INI file references to new drive letter so CD-ROM software works without reinstallation.

- *Menu-driven or wizard-driven process for installing new hard drive.*

- *Optional override of BIOS limitations for installation of large hard drives (>504MB, 2.1GB, 8.4GB, and so on).*

The two major vendors in the automated disk-utility business are Ontrack Data International, Inc., and StorageSoft. These companies sell their disk-installation products to OEM hard drive vendors for use with particular brands of drives. They also sell to the public "generic" versions that can be purchased for use with any brand or model of hard disk. Table 14.4 provides a basic overview of the most popular disk-installation programs.

Table 14.4   Overview of Automatic Disk-Installation Programs

Vendor	Software	Current Version	OEM	Retail
Ontrack	Disk Manager	9.xx	Yes	Yes
	Disk Manager DiskGo!	2.5x	Yes	Yes
StorageSoft	EZ Drive	9x	Yes	Yes
	DrivePro	3.x	No	Yes
Seagate[1]	DiscWizard	2.4x	Yes	No
Maxtor[2]	MaxBlast!	9.x	Yes	No

1. *Seagate's DiscWizard was co-developed with Ontrack and contains Ontrack Disk Manager v9.x.*

2. *Maxtor's MaxBlast! Software v9.x is a customized version of EZ-Drive. Versions 7.x and 8.x of MaxBlast! are customized versions of Ontrack Disk Manager.*

Disk Manager and EZ-Drive are DOS-based utility programs, whereas DiscWizard and Disk Manager DiskGo! offer a Windows-like interface. Seagate's DiscWizard actually analyzes the system, asks the user questions about the intended installation, and prepares a customized procedure based on the user's responses.

OEM versions of disk-installation programs are available from the drive makers' Web sites; retail versions usable with any combination of drives can be purchased from retail stores or at the vendors' online stores.

Replacing an Existing Drive

Previous sections discuss installing a single hard drive or adding a new hard drive to a system. Although formatting and partitioning a new hard disk can be challenging, replacing an existing drive and moving your programs and files to it can be a lot more challenging.

Drive Migration for MS-DOS Users

When MS-DOS 6.x was dominant, many users used this straightforward method to transfer the contents of their old hard drive to their new hard drive:

1. The user creates a bootable disk containing FDISK, FORMAT, and XCOPY.

2. The new hard drive is prepared with a primary partition (and possibly an extended partition, depending on the user's desires).

3. The new hard drive is formatted with system files, although the operating system identifies it as D:.

4. The XCOPY command is used to transfer all non-hidden files from C:\ (the old hard drive) to D:\, thus:

```
XCOPY C:\ D:\ /S /E
```

The XCOPY command also is used as necessary to transfer files from any remaining drive letters on the old hard drive to the corresponding drive letters on the new drive.

Because the only hidden files such a system would have were probably the operating system boot files (already installed) and the Windows 3.1 permanent swap file (which could be re-created after restarting Windows), this "free" data transfer routine worked well for many people.

After the original drive was removed from the system, the new drive would be jumpered as master and assigned C:. The user then would need to run FDISK from a floppy and set the primary partition on the new C: drive as Active. Then, the user would exit FDISK and the drive would boot.

Drive Migration for Windows 9x/Me Users

Windows 9x/Me have complicated the once-simple act of data transfer to a new system by their frequent use of hidden files and folders (such as \Windows\Inf, where Windows 9x hardware drivers are stored). The extensive use of hidden files was a major reason for a greatly enhanced version of XCOPY to be included in Windows 9x/Me.

Note

XCOPY32 is automatically used in place of XCOPY when XCOPY is started within a DOS session under Windows.

XCOPY32 for Windows 9x Data Transfer

Compared to "classic" XCOPY, XCOPY32 can copy hidden files; can preserve file attributes such as system, hidden, read-only, and archive; can automatically create folders; and is compatible with long filenames. Thus, using it to duplicate an existing drive is possible, but with these cautions:

■ The XCOPY32 command is much more complex.

■ Errors might occur during the copy process because of Windows's use of temporary files during normal operation, but XCOPY32 can be forced to continue.

This command line calls XCOPY32 and transfers all files and folders with their original attributes intact from the original drive (C:) to the new drive (D:). This command, however, must be run from an MS-DOS prompt window (and not MS-DOS Mode) under Windows 9x/Me, as follows:

```
xcopy32 c:\. d:\ /e/c/h/r/k
```

The command switches are explained here:

- /e. Copies folders, even if empty; also copies all folders beneath the starting folder.
- /c. Continues to copy after errors. The Windows swap file can't be copied due to being in use.
- /h. Copies hidden and system files.
- /r. Overwrites read-only files.
- /k. Preserves file attributes.

Repeat the command with appropriate drive-letter changes for any additional drive letters on your old drive.

After the original drive is removed from the system, the new drive must be jumpered as master (or single), and the operating system assigns it C:. You next need to run FDISK from a floppy and set the primary partition on the new C: drive as Active. Then, exit FDISK, and the drive will boot.

Note that although the XCOPY method has worked for me, some people have problems with it. A much more automated and easy approach to cloning drives is to use commercial software designed for that purpose, such as Drive Copy by PowerQuest or Norton Ghost by Symantec.

Even though many users have prepared new hard drives for use with nothing but FDISK and FORMAT, today's more complex systems are presenting increasingly good reasons for looking at alternatives.

Interfacing to Disk Drives

DOS uses a combination of disk management components to make files accessible. These components differ slightly between floppies and hard disks and among disks of varying sizes. They determine how a disk appears to DOS and applications. Each component used to describe the disk system fits as a layer into the complete system. Each layer communicates with the layer above and below it. When all the components work together, an application can access the disk to find and store data.

Four primary interface layers exist between an application program running on a system and the disk drives attached to the system. They consist of software routines that can perform various functions, usually to communicate with the adjacent layers. These layers are as follows:

- DOS Interrupt 21h (Int 21h) routines
- DOS Interrupt 25/26h (Int 25/26h) routines
- ROM BIOS Disk Interrupt 13h (Int 13h) routines
- Disk controller I/O port commands

Each layer accepts various commands, performs different functions, and generates results. These interfaces are available for both floppy disk drives and hard disks, although the floppy disk and hard disk Int 13h routines differ widely. The floppy disk controllers and hard disk controllers are very different as well, but all the layers perform the same functions for both floppy disks and hard disks.

Interrupt 21h

The DOS Int 21h routines exist at the highest level and provide the most functionality with the least amount of work. For example, if an application program needs to create a subdirectory on a disk, it can call Int 21h, Function 39h. This function performs all the operations necessary to create the subdirectory, including updating the appropriate directory and FAT sectors. The only information this function needs is the name of the subdirectory to create. DOS Int 21h would do much more work by using one of the lower-level access methods to create a subdirectory. Most applications access the disk through this level of interface.

Interrupt 25h and 26h

The DOS Int 25h and Int 26h routines provide much lower level access to the disk than the Int 21h routines. Int 25h reads only specified sectors from a disk, and Int 26h writes only specified sectors to a disk. If you were to write a program that used these functions to create a subdirectory on a disk, the amount of work would be much greater than that required by the Int 21h method. For example, your program would have to perform all these tasks:

- Calculate exactly which directory and FAT sectors need to be updated.
- Use Int 25h to read these sectors.
- Modify the sectors appropriately to add the new subdirectory information.
- Use Int 26h to write the sectors back to the disk.

The number of steps is even greater when you factor in the difficulty in determining exactly which sectors must be modified. According to Int 25/26h, the entire DOS-addressable area of the disk consists of sectors numbered sequentially from 0. A program designed to access the disk using Int 25h and Int 26h must know the correct disk locations by sector number. A program designed this way might have to be modified to handle disks with different numbers of sectors or different directory and FAT sizes and locations. Because of all the overhead required to get the job done, most programmers do not choose to access the disk in this manner and instead use the higher-level Int 21h, which does all the work automatically.

Typically, only disk- and sector-editing programs access disk drives at the Int 25h and Int 26h level. Programs that work at this level of access can edit only areas of a disk that have been defined to DOS as a logical volume (drive letter). For example, the DOS DEBUG program can read sectors from and write sectors to disks with this level of access.

Interrupt 13h

The next lower level of communications with drives, the ROM BIOS Int 13h routines, usually are found in ROM chips on the motherboard or on an adapter card in an expansion slot. However, an Int 13h handler also can be implemented by using a device driver loaded at boot time. Because DOS requires Int 13h access to boot from a drive (and a device driver cannot be loaded until after bootup), only drives with ROM BIOS–based Int 13h support can be bootable. Int 13h routines communicate directly with the controller using the I/O ports on the controller.

Note

The CD accompanying this book contains a list of functions available at the Interrupt 13h BIOS interface, as well as the error codes that might be returned by the BIOS INT 13h routines. See the Technical Reference section of the CD.

Few high-powered disk utility programs, other than some basic disk-formatting applications, can talk to the disk at the Int 13h level. The DOS FDISK program communicates at the Int 13h level, as does the Norton Utilities' DISKEDIT program when it is in its absolute sector mode; these are some of the few disk-repair utilities that can do so. These programs are important because you can use them for the worst data recovery situations in which the partition tables have been corrupted. Because the partition tables, and any non-DOS partitions, exist outside the area of a disk that is defined by DOS, only programs that work at the Int 13h level can access them. Most utility programs for data recovery work at only the DOS Int 25/26h level, which makes them useless for accessing areas of a disk outside DOS's domain.

Disk Controller I/O Port Commands

At the lowest interface level, programs communicate directly with the disk controller in the controller's own specific native language. To do this, a program must send controller commands through the I/O ports to which the controller responds.

◄◄   See "IDE Origins," p. 478.

Most applications work through the Int 21h interface. This interface passes commands to the ROM BIOS as Int 13h commands; the ROM BIOS then converts these commands into direct controller commands. The controller executes the commands and returns the results through the layers until the desired information reaches the application. This process enables developers to write applications without worrying about such low-level system details, leaving them instead up to DOS and the ROM BIOS. This also enables applications to run on widely varying types of hardware—as long as the correct ROM BIOS and DOS support is in place.

Any software can bypass any level of interface and communicate with the level below it, but doing so requires much more work. The lowest level of interface available is direct communication with the controller using I/O port commands. Each type of controller has different I/O port locations. With different controllers also come differences among the commands presented at the ports. Only the controller can talk directly to the disk drive.

If not for the ROM BIOS Int 13h interface, a unique DOS would have to be written for each available type of hard and floppy disk drive. Instead, DOS communicates with the ROM BIOS using standard Int 13h function calls translated by the Int 13h interface into commands for the specific hardware. Because of the standard ROM BIOS interface, DOS is relatively independent from the disk hardware and can support many types of drives and controllers.

Hard Disk Drive Troubleshooting and Repair

If a hard drive has a mechanical problem inside the sealed head disk assembly (HDA), repairing the drive is usually unfeasible. It might be doable, but purchasing a new drive will be far less expensive. If the failure is in the logic board, that board can be replaced with one from a donor drive. Normally, this is done only for the purposes of reading the information on the failed drive because you must purchase a complete second drive to cannibalize for the logic board. None of the drive manufacturers normally sell spare parts for their drives anymore.

Most hard disk drive problems are not mechanical hardware problems; instead, they are "soft" problems that can be solved by a new LLF and defect-mapping session. Soft problems are characterized by a drive that sounds normal but produces various read and write errors.

Hard problems are mechanical, such as when the drive sounds as though it contains loose marbles. Constant scraping and grinding noises from the drive, with no reading or writing capability, also qualify as hard errors. In these cases, an LLF is unlikely to put the drive back into service. If a hardware problem is indicated, first replace the logic-board assembly. You can make this repair yourself and, if successful, you can recover the data from the drive.

If replacing the logic assembly does not solve the problem, contact the manufacturer or a specialized repair shop that has clean-room facilities for hard disk repair. (See the Vendor's List on the CD for a list of drive manufacturers and companies that specialize in hard disk drive repair.) Because of the costs, simply purchasing a new drive is probably more economical.

Testing a Drive

When accessing a drive, determining whether the drive has been partitioned and formatted properly is easy. A simple test can tell you whether a stored drive is in its "raw" condition or has been partitioned and formatted properly. These tests work best if you have a boot disk available and if the spare hard drive is the only hard drive attached.

First, attach the drive to your system. If you can attach power and data cables to it, you need not install it into a drive bay unless you are planning to use it immediately. If the drive will be run loose, I recommend placing it on a nonconductive foam pad or other soft surface. This insulates the drive from potential shocks and other hazards. After detecting the drive in the BIOS and saving the changes, start your operating system from the boot disk.

Then, from the A: prompt, enter the following command:

DIR C:

This produces one of the following responses:

- *Invalid drive specification.* This indicates the drive does not have a valid partition (created by FDISK) or that the existing Master Boot Sector or partition tables have been damaged. No matter what, the drive must be partitioned and FORMATted before use. You also get this warning on a FAT32 or NTFS partitioned drive if you use a Windows 95 (original version) or MS-DOS boot disk when checking. Use a Windows 95B, Windows 98/Me, or Windows 2000 boot disk to avoid this false message from FAT32 partitions. Or, use a Windows NT or Windows 2000 boot disk to detect NTFS partitions.

- *Invalid media type.* This drive has been partitioned but not FORMATted, or the format has been corrupted. You should use FDISK's #4 option to examine the drive's existing partitions, and either delete them and create new ones or keep the existing partitions and run FORMAT on each drive letter.

- *Directory of C:.* The contents of C: drive are listed, indicating the drive was stored with a valid FDISK and FORMAT structure and data.

Installing an Optical Drive

Installation of a CD-ROM, CD-R, CD-RW, or DVD-ROM drive can be as difficult or as easy as you make it. If you plan ahead, the installation should go smoothly.

This section walks you through the installation of a typical internal (SCSI or IDE) and external (SCSI only) optical drive, with tips that often aren't included in the manufacturer's installation manuals. After you install the hardware, your job might be finished if you are running Windows 9x and using a Plug and Play drive, or you might have to manually load the software necessary to access the drive.

Note

CD-ROM and DVD-ROM drives use the same IDE and SCSI system interfaces and can be installed using the same basic procedures. Some DVD-ROM drives come with an MPEG-2 decoder board or MPEG decoder software that enables you to view DVD movies and video on your PC. If a board is included, it normally installs in a PCI bus slot like any other expansion card and performs the video decoding process that would otherwise fall to the system processor. Software decoding does not require a board and instead uses your processor to do the decoding work. Software decoding normally requires a fast processor (see the software manufacturer's recommendations for how fast); otherwise, the video appears jumpy, jerky, or unsynchronized with the sound. Premium DVD setups almost always include hardware decoding for this reason.

Note that usually a separate analog or digital audio connection exists between the drive and the sound card as well, used primarily for playing audio CDs.

Avoiding Conflict: Get Your Cards in Order

Regardless of the type of installation—internal or external drive—you must have a functioning IDE or SCSI host adapter before the drive can function. In most cases, you will be connecting the optical drive to an existing IDE or SCSI adapter. If so, the adapter should already be configured not to conflict with other devices in your system. All you have to do is connect the drive with the appropriate cable and proceed from there.

Most computers today have an IDE adapter integrated into the motherboard. However, if you are adding SCSI to your system for the first time, you must install a SCSI host adapter into an expansion slot and ensure it is configured to use the appropriate hardware resources, such as the following:

- IRQ
- DMA channel
- I/O port address

As always, Windows 9x/Me/2000 and PnP hardware can completely automate this process; however, if you're using another operating system, you might have to configure the adapter manually.

Drive Configuration

Configuration of your new optical drive is paramount to its proper functioning. Examine your new drive (see Figure 14.6) and locate any jumpers. For an IDE drive, here are the typical ways to jumper the drive:

- As the primary (master) drive on the secondary IDE connection
- As the secondary (slave) drive to a current hard disk drive
- Using Cable Select (CS), where the cable connector determines which drive is master or slave automatically

Figure 14.6 The rear connection interfaces of a typical IDE internal CD-ROM drive.

If the drive is to be the only device on your secondary EIDE interface, the factory settings are usually correct. Consult the manual to make sure this is so.

When you use the CD-ROM or DVD-ROM as a secondary drive—that is, the second drive on the same ribbon cable with another device—make sure it is jumpered as the slave drive, and configure the other device so it is the master drive (see Figure 14.7). In most cases, the drive shows up as the next logical drive, or the D: drive.

Caution

Whenever possible, you should not connect a CD-ROM or DVD-ROM drive to the same channel as a hard disk drive because sharing the channel can slow down both devices. If your computer has the two IDE channels standard in systems today, you should connect the optical drive to the secondary channel, even if you have only one hard disk drive on the primary.

Figure 14.7   An embedded EIDE interface with primary and secondary IDE connections (the pen is pointing to the primary IDE connector).

◄◄   These procedures are covered in "The IDE Interface," p. 475, and "The SCSI Interface," p. 513.

Depending on how you look at it, SCSI drives can be a bit easier to configure because you need only to select the proper SCSI ID for the drive. By convention, the boot disk (the C: drive) in a SCSI system is normally set as ID0, and the host adapter has the ID of 7. You are free to choose any ID in between that is not being used by another device. Most SCSI devices use some sort of rotating or pushbutton selector to cycle between the SCSI IDs, but some might use jumpers.

SCSI devices are cabled together in a bus configuration. If your new SCSI drive falls at the end of the SCSI bus, you also must terminate the drive. Note that the SCSI bus refers to the physical arrangement of the devices, and not the SCSI IDs selected for each one.

Note

IDE/EIDE discs and SCSI optical drives easily can coexist in the same system. However, the optical drive must be connected to a SCSI host adapter separate from the IDE subsystem. In addition, some audio adapters have a SCSI interface built in.

External (SCSI) Drive Hookup

Unpack the drive carefully. With the purchase of an external drive, you should receive the following items:

- CD-ROM or DVD-ROM drive
- SCSI adapter cable

With the exception of the SCSI host adapter, this is the bare minimum you need to get the drive up and running. You'll probably also find a CD caddy, documentation for the drive, driver software, a SCSI terminator plug, and possibly a sampling of CDs to get you started. SCSI drives almost never come with the SCSI host adapter necessary to connect them to the system. Because SCSI is designed to support up to seven devices on the same system (or up to fifteen devices for Ultra2 SCSI), including a host adapter with every peripheral is impractical. Although a few computers have SCSI interfaces integrated into the motherboard, in most cases you have to purchase a SCSI adapter as a separate expansion card.

To begin the installation, take a look at your work area and the SCSI cable that came with the drive. Where will the drive find a new home? You're limited by the length of the cable. Find a spot for the drive, and insert the power cable into the back of the unit. Make sure you have an outlet or, preferably, a free socket in a surge-suppressing power strip to plug in the new drive.

SCSI devices generally use one of two cable types. Some older drives use a 50-pin Centronics cable, referred to as an A-cable. On the other hand, most drives today use a 68-pin cable called a P-cable. Plug one end of the supplied cable into the connector socket of the drive and one into the SCSI connector on the adapter card. Most external drives have two connectors on the back—either connector can be hooked to the PC (see Figure 14.8). You use the other connector to attach another SCSI device or, if the drive is at the end of the bus, to connect a terminator plug. Secure the cable with the guide hooks on both the drive and adapter connectors, if provided.

Note

A SCSI device should include some means of terminating the bus, when necessary. The terminator might take the form of a cableless plug you connect to the second SCSI connector on the drive, or the drive might be self-terminating, in which case there should be a jumper or a switch you can set to activate termination.

External CD SCSI connectors

Figure 14.8   External drive with dual SCSI connectors.

Finally, your external drive should have a SCSI ID select switch on the back. This switch sets the identification number the host adapter uses to distinguish the drive from the other devices on the bus. The host adapter, by most manufacturers' defaults, should be set for SCSI ID 7, and some (but not all) manufacturers reserve the IDs 0 and 1 for use by hard disk drives. Be sure you set the SCSI ID for the CD-ROM or DVD-ROM drive to any other number—6, 5, or 4, for example. The only rule to follow is to be sure you do not set the drive for an ID that is already occupied—by either the adapter or any other SCSI peripheral on the bus.

Internal Drive Installation

Unpack your internal drive kit. You should have the following pieces:

- The drive
- Internal CD-audio cable
- Floppy disks/CD-ROM with device driver software and manual
- Drive rails and mounting screws

Your manufacturer also might have provided a power cable splitter—a bundle of wires with plastic connectors on each of three ends. A disc caddy and owner's manual might also be included. If you do not already have one in the computer, you also will need a SCSI host adapter to connect SCSI peripherals.

Make sure the PC is turned off, and remove the cover from the case. Before installing a SCSI adapter into the PC's expansion bus, connect the SCSI ribbon cable to the adapter card (see Figure 14.9).

Figure 14.9   Connecting a ribbon cable to a SCSI adapter.

Ribbon Cable and Card Edge Connector

The ribbon cable should be identical on both ends. You'll find a red stripe or dotted line down one side of the outermost edge of the cable. This stripe indicates a pin-1 designation and ensures that the SCSI cable is connected properly to the card and drive. If you're lucky, the manufacturer has supplied a cable with notches or keys along one edge of the connector. With such a key, you can insert the cable into the card and drive in only one way. Unkeyed cables must be hooked up according to the pin-1 designation.

Along one edge of your SCSI adapter is a double row of 50 brass-colored pins. This is the card edge connector. In small print along the base of this row of pins you should find at least two numbers next to the pins—1 and 50. Aligning the ribbon cable's marked edge over pin 1, carefully and evenly insert the ribbon cable connector.

Next, insert the adapter card into a free bus slot in the computer, leaving the drive end of the cable loose for the time being.

Choose a bay in the front of your computer's case for your internal drive. Make sure it's easily accessible from the outside and not blocked by other items on your desk. You'll be inserting the CDs or DVDs here, and you'll need the elbow room.

Remove the drive bay cover from the computer case. You might have to loosen some screws to do this, or the cover might just pop off. Inside the drive bay, you should find a metal enclosure with screw holes for mounting the drive. If the drive has mounting holes along its side and fits snugly into the enclosure, you won't need mounting rails. If it's a loose fit, however, mount the rails along the sides of the drive with the rail screws, and then slide the drive into the bay. Secure the drive into the bay with four screws—two on each side. If the rails or drive don't line up evenly with four mounting holes, be sure you use at least two screws—one mounting screw on each side. Because you'll be inserting and ejecting many discs over the years, mounting the drive securely is a must.

Once again, find the striped side of the ribbon cable and align it with pin 1 on the drive's edge connector. Either a diagram in your owner's manual or a designation on the connector itself tells you which is pin 1.

The back of the drive has a four-pin power connector outlet. Inside the case of your PC, at the back of your floppy or hard disk, are power cords—bundled red and yellow wires with plastic connectors on them. You might already have an open power connector lying open in the case. Take the open connector and plug it into the back of the power socket on the CD-ROM or DVD-ROM drive. These connectors can go in only one way. If you do not have an open connector, use a drive power splitter (refer to Figure 14.4). Disconnect an existing drive power cord from the device that uses the least power. Next, attach the splitter to the detached power cord. Plug one of the free ends back into the drive you removed the power from and the other into the CD-ROM or DVD-ROM drive.

Note

It's preferable to "borrow" power from the drive that consumes the least power so you don't overload the connection. Check the specification sheets for your drives to determine their power consumption. In general, devices that are physically smaller or that spin more slowly draw less power. If you have no choice—if the splitter and ribbon cable won't reach, for example—you can split off any power cord that hasn't already been split. Check the power cable to ensure that you have a line not already overloaded with another splitter.

Do not replace the PC cover yet—you need to make sure that everything is running perfectly before you seal the case. You're now ready to turn on the computer. If everything runs normally, it's time to put that cover back on.

SCSI Chains: Internal, External, or Both

Remember, one of the primary reasons for using the SCSI interface for your CD-ROM or DVD-ROM drive is the capability to connect a string of peripherals from one adapter, thus saving card slots inside the PC and limiting the nightmare of tracking IRQs, DMAs, and I/O memory addresses.

You can add hard drives, scanners, tape backup units, and other SCSI peripherals to this chain (see Figure 14.10). You must keep a few things in mind, however, and chief among them is SCSI termination.

◄◄ See "Termination," p. 531.

Figure 14.10   A SCSI chain of devices on one adapter card.

Example One: All External SCSI Devices. Say that you installed your CD-ROM or DVD-ROM drive and added a tape device to the SCSI bus with the extra connector on the back of the optical drive. The first device in this SCSI bus is the adapter card itself. Most modern host adapters are *autoterminating*, meaning they will terminate themselves without your intervention if they are at the end of the bus.

From the card, you ran an external cable to the optical drive, and from the optical drive, you added another cable to the back of the tape unit. You must now terminate the tape unit as well. Most external units are terminated with a SCSI cap—a small connector that plugs into the unused external SCSI connector. These external drive connectors come in two varieties: a SCSI cap and a pass-through terminator. The cap is just that; it plugs over the open connector and covers it. The pass-through terminator, however, plugs into the connector and has an open end into which you can plug the SCSI cable. This type of connector is essential if your external drive has only one SCSI connector; you can plug the drive in and make sure it's terminated—all with one connector.

Example Two: Internal Chain and Termination. On an internal SCSI bus, the same rules apply: All the internal devices must have unique SCSI ID numbers, and the first and last devices must be terminated. In the case of internal devices, however, you must check for termination. Internal devices typically have DIP switches or terminator packs similar to those on your adapter card. If you install a tape unit as the last device on the chain, it must have some means of terminating the bus. If you place your optical drive in the middle of the bus, you must deactivate its termination. The host adapter at the end of the chain must still be terminated.

Note

Most internal SCSI devices ship with terminating resistors or DIP switches onboard, usually the latter. Check your user's manuals for their locations. Any given device can have one, two, or even three such resistors.

Example Three: Internal and External SCSI Devices. If you mix and match external as well as internal devices, follow the same rules. The bottom example shown in Figure 14.11 has an internal CD-ROM drive, terminated and set for SCSI ID 6; the external hard drive also is terminated, and it is using SCSI ID 5. The SCSI adapter itself is set for ID 7 and, most importantly, its termination has been disabled because it is no longer at the end of the bus.

Note

As with any adapter card, be careful when handling the card itself. Be sure to ground yourself first.

Figure 14.11 Examples of various SCSI termination scenarios.

To help you determine whether your SCSI interface card and devices are functioning properly, Adaptec supplies a utility program called SCSI Interrogator. Use it to determine which logical unit numbers (LUNs) are available for new devices.

If you don't see any devices listed, you might have a termination problem. Shut down your system and your devices. Then, check terminator plugs, switches, or resistor packs. If they appear correct, turn on the external devices about five seconds before you start the system. A multiswitch power director with high-quality surge protection works well for this because it allows you to turn on individual devices. If the devices fail to show up after you restart the system, you might have a problem with the SCSI BIOS or device driver software. Check the documentation for your particular card and device to ensure you have installed the proper drivers.

One peculiarity of the Adaptec SCSI Interrogator is that it lists a "host adapter #1" that's actually your IDE interface! If your SCSI card isn't working, both "host adapter #0" and "host adapter #1" are actually IDE. You can tell whether this is happening with Windows 9x because it will list "ESDI_506" as the driver version.

Floppy Drive Installation Procedures

A floppy drive is one of the simplest types of drives to install. In most cases, installing a floppy disk drive is a matter of attaching the drive to the computer chassis or case and then plugging the power and signal cables into the drive. Some type of brackets and screws are normally required to attach the drive to the chassis; however, some chassis are designed to accept the drive with no brackets at all. Any brackets, if necessary, are normally included with the chassis or case itself. Several companies listed in the Vendor List on the CD specialize in cases, cables, brackets, screw hardware, and other items useful in assembling systems or installing drives.

Note

Because floppy disk drives are generally installed into the same half-height bays as hard disk drives, the physical mounting of the drive in the computer case is the same for both units. See the section "Hard Disk Installation Procedures," earlier in this chapter, for more information on the process.

When you connect the drive, make sure the power cable is installed properly. The cable is normally keyed so you cannot plug it in backward, but the keying can be defeated by somebody forcing the connection. If that is done, the drive will be fried the instant the power is turned on.

Next install the interface cable. A floppy interface cable is a 34-pin cable that normally has a twist in it. What I mean is that pins 10–16 are twisted around before they reach the last (A:) drive connector. Normally, the A: drive must be plugged in after this twist; any drive plugged in to a connector before the twist is seen by the system as drive B:. The twist reverses the drive select and motor enable signals, enabling A: and B: drives to coexist without rejumpering. This is similar to the way Cable Select works for ATA/IDE drives. Because of this, all floppy drives are jumpered the same way, in the second Drive Select (DS) position.

Older drives used to require various jumpers to be set to enable the drive to work properly. The two most common jumpers were the Drive Select jumper and the Disk Change (DC) jumper. If you encounter an older drive with these jumpers, you should follow a few simple rules. The DS jumper normally has two positions, labeled 0 and 1—or in some cases, 1 and 2. In all PC installations, the DS jumper should be set on the second position, no matter what it is numbered. This enables the drive on the cable before the twist to function as drive B: and the drive at the end of the cable after the twist to function as drive A:. The DC jumper setting is normally an on or off setting. For PC use, if the drive has a DC jumper, it must be set on or enabled. This enables the PC to detect when you have changed disks in the drive. For more information on floppy drives and interfacing, see Chapter 11.

The interface cable is normally keyed to prevent backward installation. If no key exists in this cable, use the colored wire in the cable as a guide to the position of pin 1. Normally, pin 1 is oriented closest to the power connector, which is the same as other drives. If the drive LED stays on continuously when you power up the system or when the system is running, that is a sure sign you have the floppy cable on backward either at the drive end or at the controller (motherboard) end.

CHAPTER 15

Video Hardware

Video Display Technologies

As much as the mouse and keyboard, the video display is a vital part of the user interface of any computer. The video display is actually a latecomer to computing; before CRT monitors came into general use, the teletypewriter was the standard computer interface—a large, loud device that printed the input and output characters on a roll of paper. The first CRT displays were primitive by today's standards; they displayed only text in a single color (usually green), but to users at the time they were a great improvement, allowing real-time display of input and output data.

Today, PC video displays are much more sophisticated, but you must be careful when selecting video hardware for your computer. Working with even the fastest and most-powerful PC can be a chore when the video adapter slows the system down, causes eyestrain, or is unsuitable for the tasks you want to accomplish.

The video subsystem of a PC consists of two main components:

- *Monitor (or video display)*. The monitor can be either a CRT or an LCD panel.
- *Video adapter (also called the video card or graphics adapter)*. On many recent low-cost systems, video might be built into the motherboard or included as part of this motherboard's chipset.

This chapter explores the range of PC video adapters on the market today and the displays that work with them.

Note

The term *video*, as it is used in this context, does not necessarily imply the existence of a moving image, such as on a television screen. All adapters that feed signals to a monitor or other display are video adapters, regardless of whether they are used with applications that display moving images, such as multimedia or video-conferencing software.

How CRT Display Technology Works

A monitor can use one of several display technologies. The most popular continues to be cathode ray tube (CRT) technology, the same technology used in television sets. CRTs consist of a vacuum tube enclosed in glass. One end of the tube contains an electron gun assembly that projects three electron beams, one each for the red, green, and blue phosphors used to create the colors you see onscreen; the other end contains a screen with a phosphorous coating.

When heated, the electron gun emits a stream of high-speed electrons that are attracted to the other end of the tube. Along the way, a focus control and deflection coil steer the beam to a specific point on the phosphorous screen. When struck by the beam, the phosphor glows. This light is what you see when you watch TV or your computer screen. Three layers of phosphors are used: red, green, and blue. A metal plate called a *shadow mask* is used to align the electron beams; it has slots or holes that divide the red, green, and blue phosphors into groups of three (one of each color). Various types of shadow masks affect picture quality, and the distance between each group of three (the *dot pitch*) affects picture sharpness.

▶▶ See "Dot Pitch," p. 826.

Figure 15.1 illustrates the interior of a typical CRT.

The phosphor chemical has a quality called *persistence*, which indicates how long this glow remains onscreen. Persistence is what causes a faint image to remain on your TV screen for a few seconds after you turn the set off. The scanning frequency of the display specifies how often the image is refreshed. You should have a good match between persistence and scanning frequency so the image has less flicker (which occurs when the persistence is too low) and no ghost images (which occurs when the persistence is too high).

Electron gun
assembly

Shadow
mask

Glass
panel

Internal
magnetic
shield

Red, green,
and blue
phosphors

Figure 15.1   A typical CRT monitor is a large vacuum tube. It contains three electron guns (red, green, and blue) that project the picture toward the front glass of the monitor. High voltage is used to produce the magnetism that controls the electron beams that create the picture displayed on the front of the CRT.

The electron beam moves very quickly, sweeping the screen from left to right in lines from top to bottom, in a pattern called a *raster*. The horizontal scan rate refers to the speed at which the electron beam moves laterally across the screen.

During its sweep, the beam strikes the phosphor wherever an image should appear onscreen. The beam also varies in intensity to produce different levels of brightness. Because the glow begins to fade almost immediately, the electron beam must continue to sweep the screen to maintain an image—a practice called redrawing or refreshing the screen.

Most current CRT displays have an ideal refresh rate (also called the vertical scan frequency) of about 85 hertz (Hz), which means the screen is refreshed 85 times per second. Refresh rates that are too low cause the screen to flicker, contributing to eyestrain. The higher the refresh rate, the better for your eyes. Low-cost monitors often have flicker-free refresh rates available only at 640×480 and 800×600 resolutions; you should insist on high refresh rates at resolutions such as 1,024×768 or higher.

It is important that the refresh rates expected by your monitor match those produced by your video card. If you have mismatched rates, you will not see an image and can actually damage your monitor.

Multiple Frequency Monitors

Although a few very old monitors had fixed refresh rates, most monitors support a range of frequencies. This support provides built-in compatibility with a wide range of current and future video standards (described in the "Video Display Adapters" section later in this chapter). A monitor that supports many video standards is called a *multiple-frequency monitor*. Virtually all monitors sold today are multiple frequency, which means they support operation with a variety of popular video signal standards. Different vendors call their multiple-frequency monitors by different trade names, including multisync, multifrequency, multiscan, autosynchronous, and autotracking.

Curved Versus Flat Picture Tubes

Phosphor-based screens come in two styles: curved and flat. Until recently, the typical display screen has been curved; it bulges outward from the middle of the screen. This design is consistent with the vast majority of CRT designs (the same as the tube in most television sets).

The traditional screen is curved both vertically and horizontally. Some monitor models use the Sony Trinitron CRT, some versions of which are curved only horizontally and flat vertically; these are referred to as *flat square tube (FST)* designs.

Many manufacturers are now selling monitors featuring CRTs that are flat both horizontally and vertically. Sony's FD Trinitron, NEC-Mitsubishi's DiamondTron NF, and ViewSonic's PerfectFlat are some of the more popular flat CRT designs, the first such screens for PCs since the short-lived Zenith FTM monitors of the late 1980s. Many people prefer this type of flatter screen because these picture tubes show less glare and provide a higher-quality, more-accurate image. Although flat-screen CRTs are slightly more expensive than conventional curved CRTs, they are only one-third to one-half the price of comparably sized flat-panel LCD displays.

Figure 15.2 compares the cross-section of typical curved and flat CRT picture tubes.

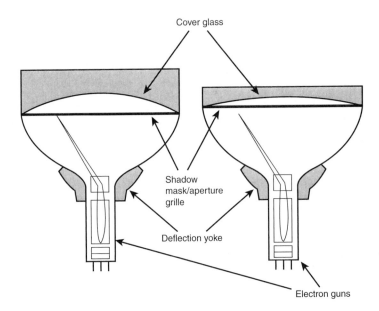

Figure 15.2 A typical curved-tube CRT (left) compared to a Sony Trinitron FD flat tube (right).

DVI—Digital Signals for CRT Monitors

The latest trend in CRT monitor design is the use of digital input signals using the same DVI (Digital Video Interface) standard used for LCD flat-panel displays. Although several major monitor vendors announced support for DVI-I interfaces for their CRT monitors in 1999, most CRT monitors except for a few 19-inch or larger high-end monitors continue to use the conventional 15-pin analog VGA connector. CRT monitors that use the DVI-I connector—unlike the TTL digital displays of the 1980s that supported only a few colors—support the same unlimited color spectrum as analog CRTs. Users benefit from digital displays because these displays can feature better picture quality, better signal reception, and precise auto setup.

Because most video cards still feature only analog (DB-15) VGA connectors, many of these monitors feature both analog and 20-pin DVI interfaces. However, as all-digital LCD display panels that also use the DVI interface increase in popularity, analog VGA eventually might be replaced by DVI-based CRT and LCD displays.

▶▶ See "Flat-Panel LCD Displays," p. 820.

Video Adapter Types

A monitor requires a source of input. The signals that run to your monitor come from a video adapter inside or plugged into your computer.

The three ways computer systems connect to either CRT or LCD displays are as follows:

- *Add-on video cards.* This method requires the use of an AGP or a PCI expansion slot but provides the highest possible level of performance and the greatest versatility in memory size and features.
- *Video-only chipset on motherboard.* Performance is less than with add-on video cards, and memory is seldom upgradeable.
- *Motherboard chipset with integrated video.* Lowest cost of any video solution, but performance is also very low, especially for 3D gaming or other graphics-intensive applications. Resolution and color-depth options are also more limited than those available with add-on video cards.

Most systems that use Baby-AT or ATX motherboards typically use add-on video cards, whereas older LPX, NLX, and Micro-ATX motherboards typically use video chipsets on the motherboard. Many of the most recent low-cost computers built on the Micro-ATX, Flex-ATX, or NLX form factors use motherboard chipsets that integrate video, such as the Intel 810 series. Systems with integrated video (either with video chipsets or motherboard chipsets that include video) usually can be upgraded with an add-on video card, but most do not include an AGP slot, which is best suited for high-speed video today.

▶▶ See "Integrated Video/Motherboard Chipsets," p. 843.

▶▶ See "3D Chipsets," p. 869.

The term *video adapter* applies to either integrated or separate video circuitry.

LCD Displays

Borrowing technology from laptop manufacturers, most major monitor makers sell monitors with liquid crystal displays (LCDs). LCDs have low-glare, completely flat screens and low power requirements (five watts versus nearly 100 watts for an ordinary monitor). The color quality of an active-matrix LCD panel actually exceeds that of most CRT displays.

At this point, however, LCD screens usually are more limited in resolution than typical CRTs and are more expensive; for example, a 15-inch LCD screen can cost more than $600—more than twice the cost of a high-quality 17-inch CRT monitor. However, it is important to consider that an LCD screen provides a larger viewable image than a CRT monitor of the same size. See Figure 15.3 for an example of a typical desktop LCD display panel.

Three basic LCD choices are available today on notebook computers: passive-matrix color, active-matrix analog color, and the latest—active-matrix digital. Monochrome LCD displays are obsolete for PCs, although they remain popular for Palm and similar organizer devices and are sometimes used for industrial display panels. Virtually all passive-matrix designs sold today use dual-scan technology, with the dimmer single-scan versions again being relegated to handheld organizers. The passive-matrix color panels are primarily found in low-cost notebook computer displays or in industrial-use desktop display panels because of their relatively low cost and enhanced durability compared to active-matrix models. Desktop LCD panels are analog or digital active-matrix units.

Figure 15.3 A typical example of a 15-inch LCD display panel. Note the small footprint, which makes LCD panels ideal for use in cramped quarters.

Note

The most common type of passive-matrix display uses a supertwist numatic design, so these panels are often referred to as STNs. Active-matrix panels usually use a thin-film transistor design and are thus referred to as TFTs.

In an LCD, a polarizing filter creates two separate light waves. The polarizing filter allows light waves that are aligned only with the filter to pass through. After passing through the polarizing filter, the remaining light waves are all aligned in the same direction. By aligning a second polarizing filter at a right angle to the first, all those waves are blocked. By changing the angle of the second polarizing filter, the amount of light allowed to pass can be changed. It is the role of the liquid crystal cell to change the angle of polarization and control the amount of light that passes. In a color LCD, an additional filter has three cells for each pixel—one each for displaying red, green, and blue.

The light wave passes through a liquid-crystal cell, with each color segment having its own cell. The liquid crystals are rod-shaped molecules that flow like a liquid. They enable light to pass straight through, but an electrical charge alters their orientations and the orientation of light passing through them. Although monochrome LCDs do not have color filters, they can have multiple cells per pixel for controlling shades of gray.

In a passive-matrix LCD, each cell is controlled by the electrical charges of two transistors, determined by the cell's row and column positions on the display. The number of transistors along the screen's horizontal and vertical edges determines the resolution of the screen. For example, a screen with a 1024×768 resolution has 1024 transistors on its horizontal edge and 768 on the vertical, for a total of 2,000. As the cell reacts to the pulsing charge from its two transistors, it twists the light wave, with stronger charges twisting the light wave more. *Supertwist* refers to the orientation of the liquid crystals, comparing on mode to off mode—the greater the twist, the higher the contrast.

Charges in passive-matrix LCDs are pulsed; therefore, the displays lack the brilliance of active-matrix, which provides a constant charge to each cell. To increase the brilliance, virtually all vendors have turned to a technique called double-scan LCD, which splits passive-matrix screens into a top half and bottom half, reducing the time between each pulse. In addition to increasing the brightness, dual-scan designs also increase the response time and therefore the perceptible speed of the display, making this type more usable for full-motion video or other applications in which the displayed information changes rapidly.

In an active-matrix LCD, each cell has its own dedicated transistor behind the panel to charge it and twist the light wave. Thus, a 1024×768 active-matrix display has 786,432 transistors. This provides a brighter image than passive-matrix displays because the cell can maintain a constant, rather than a momentary, charge. However, active-matrix technology uses more energy than passive-matrix, leading to shorter battery life on portable systems. With a dedicated transistor for every cell, active-matrix displays are more difficult and expensive to produce, but in return they offer a faster display that can be used in outdoor as well as indoor conditions and at wider viewing angles than dual-scan displays.

Note

Because an LCD display requires a specified number of transistors to support each cell, there are no multiple frequency displays of this type. All the pixels on an LCD screen are of a fixed size, although CRT pixels are variable. Thus, LCD displays are designed to be operated at a specific resolution; however, most recent notebook and desktop display panels offer onboard scaling. Before purchasing this type of display, be sure your video adapter supports the same resolution as the screen and that the resolution is sufficient for your needs throughout the life of the monitor.

▶▶   See "Flat-Panel LCD Displays," p. 820.

In both active- and passive-matrix LCDs, the second polarizing filter controls how much light passes through each cell. Cells twist the wavelength of light to closely match the filter's allowable wavelength. The more light that passes through the filter at each cell, the brighter the pixel.

Monochrome LCDs used in hand-held organizers and industrial LCD panels achieve grayscales (up to 64) by varying the brightness of a cell or dithering cells in an on-and-off pattern. Color LCDs, on the other hand, dither the three-color cells and control their brilliance to achieve different colors on the screen. Double-scan passive-matrix LCDs (also known as DSTN) have recently gained in popularity because they approach the quality of active-matrix displays but do not cost much more to produce than other passive-matrix displays. Although DSTN panels offer better on-axis (straight-ahead) viewing quality than straight passive-matrix panels, their off-axis (viewing at an angle) performance is still poor when compared to active-matrix (TFT) panels.

Note

An alternative to LCD screens is gas-plasma technology, typically known for its black and orange screens in some of the older Toshiba notebook computers. Some companies are incorporating full-color gas-plasma technology for desktop screens and color high-definition television (HDTV) flat-panel screens, such as the Philips Flat TV.

Historically, the big problem with active-matrix LCDs has been that the manufacturing yields are lower than for passive-matrix LCDs, forcing higher prices. This means many of the panels produced have more than a certain maximum number of failed transistors. The resulting low yields limit the production capacity and incurs somewhat higher prices. However, as with any technology as it matures, as the yield improves and production increases, prices drop. As a result, prices have dropped below $600 for some of the newest 15-inch desktop LCD display panels and to the use of active-matrix LCDs in all but the lowest-cost notebook computers now on the market.

In the past, several hot, miniature CRTs were needed to light an LCD screen, but portable computer manufacturers now use a single tube the size of a cigarette. Fiber-optic technology evenly spreads light emitted from the tube across an entire display.

Thanks to supertwist and triple-supertwist LCDs, today's screens enable you to see the screen clearly from more angles with better contrast and lighting. To improve readability, especially in dim light, virtually all laptops include backlighting or edgelighting (also called sidelighting). Backlit screens provide light from a panel behind the LCD. Edgelit screens get their light from small fluorescent tubes mounted along the sides of the screen. Some older laptops excluded such lighting systems to lengthen battery life. Power-management features incorporated into notebook computers enable you to run the backlight at a reduced power setting that dims the display but that allows for longer battery life.

Flat-Panel LCD Displays

LCD desktop monitors, once seen mainly on the office sets of futuristic TV shows, are now becoming an increasingly reasonable choice for use in today's office computing environment.

LCD desktop monitors offer the following benefits over conventional CRT "glass tube" monitors:

- Virtually 100% of LCD size is viewable area, compared to a loss of 1 to 1 1/2-inches of viewable area versus the diagonal tube measurement on CRT monitors. Thus, a 15-inch LCD provides a viewable area roughly equal to a typical 17-inch CRT monitor.

- Small front-to-back dimensions free up desk space.

- Removable bases on some models enable the screen to be mounted on a wall or stand

- Direct addressing of display (each pixel in the picture corresponds with a transistor) and always perfect alignment provide a high-precision image that lacks CRT's problems with pincushion or barrel distortion or convergence errors (halos around the edges of onscreen objects).

- Low power consumption and less heat buildup make LCD units less expensive to operate.

- Because LCD units lack a CRT, no concerns exist about electromagnetic VLF or ELF emissions.

- A number of LCD panels offer a pivoting feature, enabling the unit to swivel 90°, allowing a choice of the traditional landscape horizontal mode for Web surfing and the portrait vertical mode for word processing and page-layout programs.

■ LCD panels weigh substantially less than comparably sized CRTs. For example, the ViewSonic VA 550, a 15-inch LCD display, weighs only 10.1 lbs., compared to the 35 lbs.–50 lbs. weight of typical 17-inch CRTs.

There are two major proposals for digital LCD display panel standards:

■ *The Digital Flat Panel (DFP) standard approved by the Video Electronic Standards Association (VESA) in February 1999.* DFP was previously known as PanelLink.

■ *The Digital Visual Interface (DVI) standard proposed by the Digital Display Working Group (DDWG) in April 1999.* DVI is much more popular with hardware vendors and has become a de facto standard.

Figure 15.4 shows how DFP and DVI connectors found on some video cards and digital LCD displays compare to the standard VGA connector used on conventional video cards, CRTs, and analog-compatible LCD displays.

Figure 15.4 Conventional VGA cards, CRTs, and analog-compatible LCD displays use the standard VGA connector (top). Early digital LCDs and their matching video cards often used the DFP connector (second from top). Most recent digital LCD panels use the DVI-D connector (third from top), whereas video cards used with both analog and digital displays use the DVI-I connector (bottom).

Before you rush to the store to purchase an LCD desktop monitor, you should consider several potential drawbacks:

■ *If you routinely switch display resolutions (as Web developers do to preview their work), LCD monitors must take one of two approaches to change resolutions.* They must either reduce the onscreen image to occupy only the pixels of the new resolution, thus using only a portion of a typical 1024×768 LCD panel to display a 640×480 image, or scale the image to occupy the entire screen. Scaling is becoming more common because the Digital Display Work Group standard for LCD desktop displays specifies that the scaling must take place in the display panel, the graphics controller, or both places. Look at the quality of a scaled image if using different resolutions is important to you.

■ *If you choose an analog LCD panel, you'll usually save money and be able to use your existing video card.* However, image quality for both text and graphics can suffer because of the conversion of the computer's digital signal to analog (at the video card) and back to digital again (inside the LCD panel). The conversion can lead to pixel jitter or pixel swim, in which adjacent LCD cells are turned on and off by the display's incapability to determine which cells should stay on and stay off. Most panels come with adjustment software to reduce this display-quality problem, but you might not be able to eliminate it entirely.

■ *Digital LCD panels avoid conversion problems when attached to a digital-compatible display card.* However, most off-the-shelf display cards don't support digital signals yet. Some digital LCD panels bundle a matching display card with the unit, raising its cost.

Note

Video card and chipset makers, such as nVidia, S3-Via, Matrox, ATI, and others, are rapidly adding support for digital and analog display panels to their newest 3D chipsets and video cards.

■ *High-quality LCD display panels of either digital or analog type are great for displaying sharp text and graphics.* But they often can't display as wide a range of very light and very dark colors as CRTs can.

■ *LCD displays don't react as quickly as CRTs.* This can cause full-motion video, full-screen 3D games, and animation to look smeared onscreen.

Thanks to price decreases, larger panel sizes, and more support for DVI digital connectors on current systems and video cards, this is the best time ever to consider buying an LCD panel for your desktop PC.

Be sure that you use the following criteria when you consider purchasing an LCD monitor:

■ *Evaluate the panel both at its native resolution and at any other resolutions you plan to use.*

■ *If you're considering an analog LCD panel, try it with the video cards you plan to use and be sure to check the panel maker's list of suggested video cards for each model.*

■ *If you're considering a digital LCD panel, determine whether either your existing or the bundled video card (if any) supports the features you need.* Features you might find necessary include OpenGL and high-speed 3D support (for gaming), VGA-to-TV support (for video producers), and DVD playback software (for watching DVD movies). If you opt for a panel with a bundled video card, be sure that the panel also supports standards such as DVI, so you can change to another card in the future.

■ *Make sure your system has a suitable expansion slot for the recommended or bundled video-card type.* Many low-cost systems today feature onboard AGP video but no AGP slot, which can't be upgraded unless the user opts for the obsolescent (for video) PCI slot. As the move to LCD panels continues, more of these systems should feature built-in support for LCD displays, but this could be a problem for some time to come.

■ *Evaluate the panel and card combo's performance on video clips and animation if you work with full-motion video or animated presentation programs.*

■ *Because most video cards aren't optimized for the pivoting feature found in many LCD panels, the portrait mode's performance is often as much as 10%–45% slower than the default landscape mode.*

■ *Although active-matrix (analog) and digital LCD monitors have much wider viewing areas than do passive-matrix and dual-scan LCD panels used in low-cost notebook computers, their viewing angles are still usually much less than CRTs.* This is an important consideration if you're planning to use your LCD monitor for group presentations. In a test of 14 different 15-inch LCD panels in *PC Magazine's* May 23, 2000 issue, horizontal viewing angles without noticeable color shift ranged from as little as 50° to as much as 125° (higher is better). The average viewing angle of models tested just 78°, a very narrow viewing angle compared to CRTs. A typical CRT monitor enables viewing up to 120° without noticeable color shift.

■ *A high-contrast ratio (luminance difference between white and black) makes for sharper text and vivid colors.* A typical CRT has a contrast ratio of about 245:1. LCD panels in the May 23, 2000 *PC Magazine* test had contrast ratios ranging from a low of 186:1 to a high of 370:1, with the average score of 264:1 exceeding the 245:1 contrast ratio of typical CRTs. Panels could be viewed at an average horizontal angle of as much as 129° without loss of contrast.

■ *Features such as integrated speakers and Universal Serial Bus (USB) hubs are pleasant additions, but your eyes should make the final decision about which panel is best for you.*

Monitor Selection Criteria

Stores offer a dizzying variety of monitor choices, from the low-cost units bundled with computers to large-screen tubes that cost more than many systems. Because a monitor can account for a large part of the price of your computer system, you need to know what to look for when you shop for a monitor.

The Right Size

CRT-based monitors come in various sizes ranging from 15-inch to 42-inch diagonal measure. The larger the monitor, the higher the price tag—after you get beyond 19-inch displays, the prices skyrocket. The most common CRT monitor sizes are 15, 17, 19, and 21 inches. These diagonal measurements, unfortunately, often represent not the size of the actual image the screen displays, but the size of the tube.

As a result, comparing one company's 17-inch monitor to that of another might be unfair unless you actually measure the active screen area. The active screen area refers to the diagonal measure of the lighted area on the screen. In other words, if you are running Windows, the viewing area is the actual diagonal measure of the desktop.

This area can vary widely from monitor to monitor, so one company's 17-inch monitor can display a 15-inch image, and another company's 17-inch monitor can present a 15 1/2-inch image.

Table 15.1 shows the monitor's advertised diagonal screen size, along with the approximate diagonal measure of the actual active viewing area for the most common display sizes. Use the following chart as a guideline; most monitor packaging and advertising provide precise information for a given model.

Table 15.1   Advertised Screen Size Versus Actual Viewing Area

Monitor CRT Size (in Inches)	Actual Viewing Area (in Inches)
12	10 1/2
14	12 1/2
15	13 1/2
16	14 1/2
17	15 1/2
18	16 1/2
19	17 1/2
20	18 1/2
21	19 1/2

Note

Most CRTs currently on the market are 15 inches in size or larger; 17 inches is becoming the current standard.

The size of the actual viewable area varies from manufacturer to manufacturer but tends to be approximately 1 1/2-inches less than the actual screen size. However, you can adjust many better-quality monitors to display a high-quality image that completely fills the tube from edge to edge. Less-expensive monitors can fill the screen also, but some of them do so only by pushing the monitor beyond its comfortable limits. The result is a distorted image that is worse than the monitor's smaller, properly adjusted picture.

In most cases, the 17-inch monitor is currently the best bargain in the industry. A 17-inch monitor is recommended for new systems, especially when running Windows, and is not much more expensive than a 15-inch display. I recommend a 17-inch monitor as the minimum you should consider for most normal applications. Low-end applications can still get away with a 15-inch display, but you will be limited in the screen resolutions you can view comfortably. Displays of 18–21 inches or larger are recommended for high-end systems, especially where graphics applications are the major focus.

Larger monitors are particularly handy for applications such as CAD and desktop publishing, in which the smallest details must be clearly visible. With a 17-inch or larger display, you can see nearly an entire 8 1/2×11-inch print page in 100% view; in other words, what you see onscreen virtually matches the page that will be printed. Being able to see the entire page at its actual size can save you the trouble of printing several drafts of a document or project to get it right.

With the popularity of the Internet, monitor size and resolution become even more of an issue. Many Web pages are being designed for 800×600 or higher resolutions. Whereas a 15-inch monitor can handle 800×600 fairly well, a 17-inch monitor set to 1,024×768 resolution enables you to comfortably view any Web site without eyestrain or excessive scrolling.

Note

Although many monitors smaller than 17 inches are physically capable of running at 1,024×768 and even higher resolutions, most people have trouble reading print at that size.

If you have Windows 98/Me or 2000, a partial solution is to enable the larger icons by opening the Display control panel, clicking the Settings tab, clicking Advanced, and selecting Large Icons. With either Windows 95 or 98, you can also use Large Fonts, but many programs have problems with font sizes larger than the default Small Fonts setting.

Monitor Resolution

Resolution is the amount of detail a monitor can render. This quantity is expressed in the number of horizontal and vertical picture elements, or *pixels*, contained in the screen. The greater the number of pixels, the more detailed the images. The resolution required depends on the application. Character-based applications (such as DOS command-line programs) require little resolution, whereas graphics-intensive applications (such as desktop publishing and Windows software) require a great deal.

It's important to realize that CRTs are designed to handle a range of resolutions natively, but LCD panels (both desktop and notebook) are built to run a single native resolution and must scale to other choices.

As PC video technology developed, the screen resolutions supported by video adapters grew at a steady pace. The following list shows standard resolutions used in PC video adapters and the terms commonly used to describe them:

Resolution	Abbreviation	Standard Designation
640×480	VGA	Video Graphics Array
800×600	SVGA	Super VGA
1,024×768	XGA	eXtended Graphics Array
1,280×1,024	UVGA	Ultra VGA
1,600×1,200	(none)	(none)

Today, the term *VGA* is still in common use as a reference to the standard 640×480 16-color display that the Windows operating systems use as their default. The 15-pin connector to which you connect the CRT monitor on most video adapters is also often called a VGA plug. A 20-pin connector is used for DFP-compatible LCD display panels. A larger 24-pin connector is used on DVI-D displays, and a 29-pin version of the DVI-D connector is used by DVI-I displays.

However, the terms SVGA, XGA, and UVGA have fallen into disuse. The industry now describes screen resolutions simply by citing the number of pixels. Nearly all the video adapters sold today support the 640×480, 800×600, and 1,024×768 pixel resolutions at several color depths, and most support 1,280×1,024 and higher as well.

Because all CRT and most new and upcoming LCD displays can handle various resolutions, you have a choice. As you'll see later in this chapter, the combinations of resolution and color depth (number of colors onscreen) that you can choose may be limited by how much RAM your graphics adapter has onboard. If you switch to a larger display and you can't set the color depth you want to use, a new video card with more RAM is a desirable upgrade.

What resolution do you want for your display? Generally, the higher the resolution, the larger the display you will want. Why? Because Windows icons and text use a constant number of pixels, higher display resolutions make these screen elements a smaller part of the desktop onscreen. By using a larger display (17-inch or larger), you can use higher resolution settings and still have text and icons that are readable.

To understand this issue, you might want to try various resolutions on your system. As you change from 640×480 to 800×600 and 1,024×768, you'll notice several changes to the appearance of your screen.

At 640×480, text and onscreen icons are very large. Because the screen elements used for the Windows 9x/2000/Me desktop and software menus are at a fixed pixel width and height, you'll notice that they shrink in size onscreen as you change to the higher resolutions. You'll be able to see more of your document or Web page onscreen at the higher resolutions because each object requires less of the screen.

If you are operating at 640×480 resolution, for example, you should find a 15-inch monitor to be comfortable. At 1,024×768, you probably will find that the display of a 15-inch monitor is too small; therefore, you will prefer to use a larger one, such as a 17-inch monitor. The following list shows the minimum-size monitors I recommend to properly display the resolutions users typically select:

Resolution	Minimum Recommended Monitor
640×480	14-inch
800×600	15-inch
1,024×768	17-inch
1,280×1,024 or higher	21-inch

Although these are not necessarily the limits of a given monitors' capabilities, they are what I recommend. On small monitors set to high resolutions, characters, icons, and other information are too small for most users and can cause eyestrain.

One exception to this rule is with the LCD displays used in portable systems and a few desktop monitors. LCD-type displays are always crisp and perfectly focused by nature. Also, the dimensions advertised for the LCD screens represent the exact size of the viewable image, unlike most conventional CRT-based monitors. So, the 13.3-inch LCD panels found on many notebook systems today actually have a viewable area with a 13.3-inch diagonal measurement. This measurement is comparable to a 15-inch CRT display in most cases. In addition, the LCD is so crisp that screens of a given size can easily handle resolutions that are higher than what would otherwise be acceptable on a CRT.

For example, many of the high-end notebook systems now use 14-inch or 15-inch LCD panels that feature 1,024×768 resolution. Although this resolution would be unacceptable on a 14-inch or 15-inch CRT display, it works well on the 14-inch or 15-inch LCD panel because of the crystal-clear image.

Dot Pitch

Another important specification that denotes the quality of a given CRT monitor is its dot pitch, which is controlled by the design of the shadow mask or aperture grille inside the CRT. A shadow mask is a metal plate built into the front area of the CRT, next to the phosphor layers. It has thousands of holes that are used to help focus the beam from each electron gun so that it illuminates only one correctly colored phosphor dot at a time. Because of the immense speed of screen rewriting (60–85 times per second), all dots appear to be illuminated at the same time. The mask prevents the electron gun from illuminating the wrong dots.

In a monochrome monitor, the picture element is a screen phosphor, but in a color monitor, the picture element is a phosphor triad—which is a group of three phosphor dots (red, green, and blue). Dot pitch, which applies only to color monitors, is the distance (in millimeters) between phosphor triads, measured from the center of a phosphor dot in a given triad to the same color phosphor dot in the next triad. Screens with a small dot pitch have a smaller space between the phosphor triads. As a result, the picture elements are closer together, producing a sharper picture onscreen. Conversely, screens with a large dot pitch tend to produce images that are less clear. Figure 15.5 illustrates dot pitch.

Note

Dot pitch is not an issue with LCD portable or desktop display panels because of their designs, which use transistors rather than phosphor triads.

Figure 15.5   Dot pitch is the distance between each group (triad) of red, green, and blue (RGB) phosphors. A smaller dot pitch helps produce sharper, clearer images.

The original IBM PC color monitor had a dot pitch of 0.43mm, which is considered to be poor by almost any standard. Smaller pitch values indicate sharper images. Most monitors have a dot pitch between 0.25 and 0.30mm, with state-of-the-art monitors at the lower end of the scale. To avoid grainy images, look for a dot pitch of 0.26mm or smaller. Be wary of monitors with anything larger than a 0.28mm dot pitch; they lack clarity for fine text and graphics. Although you can save money by buying monitors with smaller tubes or a higher dot pitch, the trade-off isn't worth it.

Monitors based on Sony's Trinitron picture tubes and Mitsubishi's DiamondTron picture tubes use an aperture grille, which uses vertical strips to separate red, green, and blue phosphors, rather than a shadow mask. This produces a brighter picture, although the stabilizing wires shown in Figure 15.6 are visible on close examination. Monitors using an aperture grille–type picture tube use a stripe pitch measurement instead of dot pitch. An aperture grille monitor stripe pitch of .25mm is comparable to a .27mm dot pitch on a conventional monitor.

Figure 15.6   Aperture-grille picture tubes have their phosphors arranged in vertical stripes with one or two reinforcing wires, depending on CRT size.

NEC's monitors use a variation on aperture grille called the slotted mask, which is brighter than standard shadow-mask monitors and more mechanically stable than aperture grille–based monitors (see Figure 15.7).

Figure 15.7   NEC's slotted mask picture tube design provides many of the benefits of both shadow-mask and aperture-grille designs.

The dot pitch or stripe pitch measurement is one of the most important specifications of any monitor, but it is not the only specification. You might find the image on a monitor with a slightly higher dot pitch superior to that of a monitor with a lower dot pitch. There is no substitute for actually looking at images and text on the monitors you're considering purchasing.

Image Brightness and Contrast (LCD Panels)

As previously mentioned, dot pitch is not a factor in deciding which LCD panel to purchase. Although it's a consideration that applies to both LCDs and CRTs, the brightness of a display is especially important in judging the quality of an LCD display.

Although a dim CRT display is almost certainly a sign of either improper brightness control or a dying monitor, brightness in LCD displays can vary a great deal from one model to another. Brightness for LCD panels is measured in candelas per square meter, which for some reason is referred to as a *nit*. Typical ratings for analog and digital display panels range from under 100 to as much as 250 nits. A good combination is a high nit rating (150 or above) and a high contrast rating.

Interlaced Versus Noninterlaced

Monitors and video adapters can support interlaced or noninterlaced resolution. In *noninterlaced* (conventional) mode, the electron beam sweeps the screen in lines from top to bottom, one line after the other, completing the screen in one pass. In *interlaced* mode, the electron beam also sweeps the screen from top to bottom, but it does so in two passes—sweeping the odd lines first and the even lines second. Each pass takes half the time of a full pass in noninterlaced mode. Early high-resolution monitors, such as the IBM 8514/A, used interlacing to reach their maximum resolutions, but all recent and current high-resolution (1,024×768 and higher) monitors are noninterlaced, avoiding the slow screen response and flicker caused by interlacing.

For more information about interlaced displays, see *Upgrading and Repairing PCs, 12th Edition*, included in electronic form on the CD-ROM accompanying this book.

Energy and Safety

Monitors, like virtually all power-consuming computer devices, have been designed to save energy for a number of years. Virtually all monitors sold in recent years have earned the Environmental Protection Agency's Energy Star logo by reducing their current draw to 30 watts or less when idle. Power-management features in the monitor, as well as controls provided in the system BIOS and in the latest versions of Windows, help both monitors and other types of computing devices use less power.

Power Management

One of the first energy-saving standards for monitors was VESA's Display Power-Management Signaling (DPMS) spec, which defines the signals a computer sends to a monitor to indicate idle times. The computer or video card decides when to send these signals.

In Windows 9x/Me or 2000, you must enable this feature if you want to use it because it's turned off by default. To enable it, open the Display properties in the Control Panel, switch to the Screen Saver tab, and make sure the Energy Star low-power settings and Monitor Shutdown settings are checked. You can adjust how long the system remains idle before the monitor picture is blanked or the monitor shuts down completely. Use the Power icon in Windows 2000 to set power management for the monitor and other peripherals.

Intel and Microsoft jointly developed the Advanced Power Management (APM) specification, which defines a BIOS-based interface between hardware that is capable of power-management functions and an operating system that implements power-management policies. In short, this means you can configure an OS such as Windows 9x to switch your monitor into a low-power mode after an interval of nonuse and even to shut it off entirely. For these actions to occur, however, the monitor, system BIOS, and operating system must all support the APM standard.

With Windows 98, Windows Me, Windows 2000, and Windows XP, Microsoft introduced a more comprehensive power-management method called Advanced Configuration and Power Interface (ACPI). ACPI also works with displays, hard drives, and other devices supported by APM and allows the computer to automatically turn peripherals on and off, such as CD-ROMs, network cards, hard disk drives, printers, as well as consumer devices connected to the PC such as VCRs, televisions, telephones, and stereos.

Although APM compatibility has been standard in common BIOSes for several years, a number of recent-model computers from major manufacturers required BIOS upgrades to add ACPI support when Windows 98 was introduced.

Note

ACPI support is installed on Windows 98, Windows Me, Windows 2000, and Windows XP computers **only** if an ACPI-compliant BIOS is present when either version of Windows is first installed. If an ACPI-compliant BIOS is installed after the initial Windows installation, it will be ignored. Fortunately, both versions of Windows still support APM as well. See Microsoft's FAQ for ACPI on the Microsoft Web site.

Use Table 15.2 to select the most appropriate DPMS power-management setting(s) for your needs. Most recent systems enable you to select separate values for standby (which saves minimal amounts of power) and for monitor power-down (which saves more power but requires the user to wait several seconds for the monitor to power back up).

Note

For more information about power management, see Chapter 21, "Power Supply and Chassis/Case."

Table 15.2 Display Power Management Signaling

State	Horizontal	Vertical	Video	Power Savings	Recovery Time
On	Pulses	Pulses	Active	None	n/a
Stand-By	No Pulses	Pulses	Blanked	Minimal	Short
Suspend	Pulses	No Pulses	Blanked	Substantial	Longer
Off	No Pulses	No Pulses	Blanked	Maximum	System Dependent

Emissions

Another trend in green monitor design is to minimize the user's exposure to potentially harmful electromagnetic fields. Several medical studies indicate that these electromagnetic emissions can cause health problems, such as miscarriages, birth defects, and cancer. The risk might be low, but if you spend a third of your day (or more) in front of a computer monitor, that risk is increased.

The concern is that VLF (very low frequency) and ELF (extremely low frequency) emissions might affect the body. These two emissions come in two forms: electric and magnetic. Some research indicates that ELF magnetic emissions are more threatening than VLF emissions because they interact with the natural electric activity of body cells. Monitors are not the only culprits; significant ELF emissions also come from electric blankets and power lines.

Note

ELF and VLF are a form of electromagnetic radiation; they consist of radio frequencies below those used for normal radio broadcasting.

The standards shown in Table 15.3 have been established to regulate emissions and other aspects of monitor operations. Even though these standards originated with Swedish organizations, they are recognized and supported throughout the world.

Table 15.3 Monitor Emissions Standards

Standard Name	Established By	Date Established	Regulates	Notes
MPR I	SWEDAC[1]	1987	Monitor emissions	Replaced by MPR II.
MPR II	SWEDAC[1]	1990	Monitor emissions	Added maximums for ELF and VLF; minimum standard in recent monitors.
TCO[2]	TCO[2]	1992	Tighter monitor emissions limits than MPR II; power management	TCO 95 and TCO 99 add other classes of devices to the TCO standard.

1. The Swedish Board for Accreditation and Conformity Assessment

2. Swedish abbreviation for the Swedish Confederation of Professional Employees

Today, virtually all monitors on the market support TCO standards.

If you aren't using a low-emission monitor yet, you can take other steps to protect yourself. The most important is to stay at arm's length (about 28 inches) from the front of your monitor. When you move a couple of feet away, ELF magnetic emission levels usually drop to those of a typical office with fluorescent lights. Likewise, monitor emissions are weakest at the front of a monitor, so stay at least three feet from the sides and backs of nearby monitors and five feet from any photocopiers, which are also strong sources of ELF.

Electromagnetic emissions should not be your only concern; you also should be concerned about screen glare. In fact, some of the antiglare panels that fit in front of a monitor screen not only reduce eyestrain, but also cut ELF and VLF emissions.

Frequencies

One essential buying decision is to choose a monitor that works with your selected video adapter. Today, virtually all monitors are multiple-frequency (also called multiscanning and multifrequency) units that accommodate a range of standards, including those that are not yet standardized. However, big differences exist in how well various monitors cope with various video adapters.

Tip

High-quality monitors retain their value longer than most other computer components. Although it's common for a newer, faster processor to come out right after you have purchased your computer, or to find the same model with a bigger hard disk for the same money, a good quality monitor should outlast your computer. If you purchase a unit with the expectation that your own personal requirements will grow over the years, you might be able to save money on your next system by reusing your old monitor.

Some useful features include

- Front-mounted digital controls that can memorize screen settings
- Onscreen programmability to enable you to precisely set desired values for screen size and position
- Self-test mode, which displays a picture even when your monitor is not receiving a signal from the computer

With multiple-frequency monitors, you must match the range of horizontal and vertical frequencies the monitor accepts with those generated by your video adapter. The wider the range of signals, the more expensive—and more versatile—the monitor. Your video adapter's vertical and horizontal frequencies must fall within the ranges supported by your monitor. The vertical frequency (or refresh/frame rate) determines the stability of your image (the higher the vertical frequency, the better). Typical vertical frequencies range from 50Hz to 160Hz, but multiple-frequency monitors support different vertical frequencies at different resolutions. You might find that a bargain monitor has a respectable 100Hz vertical frequency at 640×480 but drops to a less desirable 60Hz at 1,024×768. The horizontal frequency (or line rate) typically ranges from 31.5KHz to 90KHz or more.

Refresh Rates

The *refresh rate* (also called the vertical scan frequency) is the rate at which the screen display is rewritten. This is measured in hertz (Hz). A refresh rate of 72Hz means that the screen is refreshed 72 times per second. A refresh rate that is too low causes the screen to flicker, contributing to eyestrain. The higher the refresh rate, the better for your eyes and your comfort during long sessions at the computer.

A *flicker-free refresh rate* is a refresh rate high enough to prevent you from seeing any flicker. The flicker-free refresh rate varies with the resolution of your monitor setting (higher resolutions require a higher refresh rate) and must be matched by both your monitor and display card. Because a refresh rate that is too high can slow down your video display, use the lowest refresh rate that is comfortable for you.

One factor that is important to consider when you purchase a monitor is the refresh rate, especially if you are planning to use the monitor at 1,024×768 or higher resolutions. Low-cost monitors sometimes have refresh rates that are too low to achieve flicker-free performance for most users, and thus can lead to eyestrain.

Table 15.4 compares two typical 17-inch CRT monitors and a typical mid-range graphics card.

Note the differences in the refresh rates supported by the Creative 3D Blaster Annihilator (based on the popular nVidia GeForce 2 MX graphics chip) and two 17-inch CRT monitors from MAG InnoVision, the 770V and the 796FD.

The 770V is a typical, under-$230 monitor, and the 796FD sells for about $380. Note the 796FD offers flicker-free refresh rates at higher resolutions than the less-expensive 770V.

Although the 3D Blaster Annihilator video card supports higher refresh rates than either monitor, these rates can't be used safely. Use of video adapter refresh rates in excess of the monitor's maximum refresh rate can damage the monitor!

Table 15.4   Refresh Rates Comparison

Resolution	3D Blaster Annihilator Video Card Vertical Refresh	770V (17") Monitor Vertical Refresh (Maximum)	796FD (17") Monitor Vertical Refresh (Maximum)
1,024×768	60–240[1]	85Hz[1]	85Hz[1]
1,280×1,024	60–170Hz[1]	60Hz	85Hz[1]
1,600×1,200	60–120Hz[1]	Not supported	85Hz[1]

1. *Rates above 72Hz will be flicker-free for many users; VESA standard for flicker-free refresh is 85Hz or above.*

To determine a monitor's refresh rates for the resolutions you're planning to use, check out the monitor manufacturer's Web site.

During installation, Windows 2000, Windows 98, Windows 95B (OSR 2.x), Windows Me, and Windows XP support Plug and Play (PnP) monitor configuration if both the monitor and the video adapter support the Data Display Channel (DDC) feature. When DDC communication is available, the monitor can send signals to the operating system that indicate which refresh rates it supports, as well as other display information, and this data is reflected by the Display Properties sheet for that monitor.

Monitors that don't support PnP configuration via DDC can be configured with an .INF (information) file, just as with other Windows-compatible devices. This might be supplied with a setup disk or can be downloaded from the monitor vendor's Web site.

Note

Because monitors are redrawing the screen many times per second, the change in a noninterlaced screen display is virtually invisible to the naked eye, but it is very obvious when computer screens are photographed, filmed, or videotaped. Because these cameras aren't synchronized to the monitor's refresh cycle, it's inevitable that the photo, film, or videotape will show the refresh in progress as a line across the picture.

In my experience, a 60Hz vertical scan frequency (frame rate) is the minimum anybody should use, and even at this frequency, most people notice a flicker. Especially on a larger display, onscreen flicker can cause eyestrain and fatigue. If you can select a frame rate (vertical scan frequency) of 72Hz or higher, most people are not able to discern any flicker. Most modern mid-range or better displays easily handle vertical frequencies up to 85Hz or more at resolutions up to 1,024×768. This greatly reduces the flicker a user sees. However, note that increasing the frame rate, although improving the quality of the image, can also slow down the video hardware because it now needs to display each image more times per second. In general, I recommend that you set the lowest frame rate you find comfortable. To adjust the video card's refresh rate with Windows 9x/Me/2000/XP, use the Display icon in Control Panel.

Depending on your flavor of Windows, the refresh rates supported by the video card will appear on one of the Display tabs. Optimal is the default setting, but this really is a "safe" setting for any monitor. Select a refresh rate of at least 72Hz or higher to reduce or eliminate flicker. Click Apply for the new setting to take effect. If you choose a refresh rate other than Optimal, you'll see a warning about possible monitor damage. This is a warning you should take seriously, especially if you don't have detailed information about your monitor available. You can literally smoke a monitor if you try to use a refresh rate higher than the monitor is designed to accept. Before you try using a custom refresh rate, do the following:

- Make sure Windows has correctly identified your monitor as either a Plug and Play monitor or by brand and model.

- Check the manual supplied with the monitor (or download the stats) to determine which refresh rates are supported at a given resolution. As in the example listed earlier, low-cost monitors often don't support high refresh rates at higher resolutions.

Click OK to try the new setting. The screen changes to show the new refresh rate. If the screen display looks scrambled, wait a few moments and the screen will be restored to the previous value; you'll see a dialog box asking whether you want to keep the new setting. If the display was acceptable, click Yes; otherwise, click No to restore your display. If the screen is scrambled and you can't see your mouse pointer, just press the Enter key on your keyboard because No is the default answer. With some older video drivers, this refresh rate dialog box is not available. Get an updated video driver, or check with the video card vendor for a separate utility program that sets the refresh rate for you.

If you have a scrambled display with a high refresh rate, but you think the monitor should be able to handle the refresh rate you chose, you might not have the correct monitor selected. To check your Windows 9x/Me/2000/XP monitor selection, check the Display Properties dialog box. If your monitor is listed as Super VGA, Windows is using a generic driver that will work with a wide variety of monitors. However, this generic driver doesn't support refresh rates above 75Hz because some monitors could be damaged by excessive refresh rates.

In some cases, you might need to manually select the correct monitor brand and model in the Windows Display Properties dialog box. If you don't find your brand and model of monitor listed, check with your monitor vendor for a driver specific for your model. After you install it, see whether your monitor will safely support a higher refresh rate.

Horizontal Frequency

When you shop for a VGA monitor, be sure the monitor supports a horizontal frequency of at least 31.5KHz—the minimum a VGA card needs to paint a 640×480 screen. The 800×600 resolution requires a vertical frequency of at least 72Hz and a horizontal frequency of at least 48KHz. The 1,024×768 image requires a vertical frequency of 60Hz and a horizontal frequency of 58KHz, and the 1,280×1,024 resolution requires a vertical frequency of 60Hz and a horizontal frequency of 64KHz. If the vertical frequency increases to 75Hz at 1,280×1,024, the horizontal frequency must be 80KHz. For a super-crisp display, look for available vertical frequencies of 75Hz or higher and horizontal frequencies of up to 90KHz or more. My favorite 17-inch NEC monitor supports vertical resolutions of up to 75Hz at 1,600×1,200 pixels, 117Hz at 1,024×768, and 160Hz at 640×480!

Virtually all the analog monitors on the market today are, to one extent or another, multiple frequency. Because literally hundreds of manufacturers produce thousands of monitor models, it is impractical to discuss the technical aspects of each monitor model in detail. Suffice it to say that before investing in a monitor, you should check the technical specifications to ensure that the monitor meets your needs. If you are looking for a place to start, check out some of the magazines that periodically feature reviews of monitors. If you can't wait for a magazine review, investigate monitors at the Web sites run by any of the following vendors: IBM, Sony, NEC-Mitsubishi, and ViewSonic. Each of these manufacturers creates monitors that set the standards by which other monitors can be judged. Although you typically pay a bit more for these manufacturers' monitors, they offer a known, high level of quality and compatibility, as well as service and support.

Controls

Most of the newer monitors now use digital controls instead of analog controls. This has nothing to do with the signals the monitor receives from the computer, but only the controls (or lack of them) on the front panel that enable you to adjust the display. Monitors with digital controls have a built-in menu system that enables you to set parameters such as brightness, contrast, screen size, vertical and horizontal shifts, and even focus. A button brings the menu up on the screen, and you use controls to make menu selections and vary the settings. When you complete your adjustments, the monitor saves the settings in NVRAM (nonvolatile RAM) located inside the monitor. This type of memory provides permanent storage for the settings with no battery or other power source. You can unplug the monitor without losing your settings, and you can alter them at any time in the future. Digital controls provide a much higher level of control over the monitor and are highly recommended.

Digital controls make adjusting monitors suffering from any of the geometry errors shown in Figure 15.8 easy. Before making these adjustments, make sure the vertical and horizontal size and position are correct.

Tip

Get a monitor with positioning and image controls that are easy to reach, preferably on the front of the case. Look for more than just basic contrast and brightness controls; a good monitor should enable you to adjust the width and height of your screen images and the placement of the image on the screen. The monitor should also be equipped with a tilt-swivel stand so you can adjust the monitor to the best angle for your use.

Environment

One factor you might not consider when shopping for a monitor is the size and strength of the desk on which you intend to put it. Although many 17-inch monitors use less desk space than before, reducing the 18–24-inch depth used by older models to a more reasonable 17-inch depth, these monitors are still relatively heavy at around 40 pounds. 21-inch and larger monitors can be truly huge, weighing in at over 65 pounds! Some of the rickety computer stands and mechanical arms used to keep monitors off the desktop might not be capable of safely holding or supporting a large unit. Check the weight rating of the computer stand or support arm you're planning to use before you put a monitor on it. It's tragic to save a few dollars on these accessories, only to watch them crumple under the weight of a large monitor and wipe out your monitor investment.

Tip

If you are using a relatively narrow computer table, look for a monitor that uses the so-called short-neck or short-depth CRTs. These short-neck CRTs are used in many recent 17-inch and 19-inch models and allow the monitor to take up less space front to back; this often is referred to as a smaller footprint. Some 17-inch short-neck models use no more front-to-back space than typical 15-inch models and weigh less. ViewSonic's GS773 short-depth 17" monitor is only 15.2 inches deep and weighs only 35 pounds.

Figure 15.8 Typical geometry errors in monitors; these can be corrected on most models that have digital picture controls.

Another important consideration is the lighting in the room in which you will use the monitor. The appearance of a CRT display in the fluorescent lighting of an office is markedly different from that in your home. The presence or absence of sunlight in the room also makes a big difference. Office lighting and sunlight can produce glare that becomes incredibly annoying when you are forced to stare at it for hours on end. You can reduce onscreen glare by choosing monitors equipped with flat-square or other flat CRT technologies or LCD panels and antiglare coatings. You can retrofit aftermarket filters to monitors that lack these features to help reduce glare.

Tip

If you are extremely short of space or have relatively light-duty computer furniture, consider the newest 15-inch LCD display panels, which weigh only 10 pounds or so and feature a much narrower front-to-back footprint than 17-inch CRTs.

Testing a Display

Unlike most of the other peripherals you can connect to your computer, you can't really tell whether a monitor suits you by examining its technical specifications. Price might not be a reliable indicator either. Testing monitors is a highly subjective process, and it is best to "kick the tires" of a few at a dealer showroom or in the privacy of your home or office (if the dealer has a liberal return policy).

Testing should also not be simply a matter of looking at whatever happens to be displayed on the monitor at the time. Many computer stores display movies, scenic photos, or other flashy graphics that are all but useless for a serious evaluation and comparison. If possible, you should look at the same images on each monitor you try and compare the manner in which they perform a specific series of tasks.

Before running the tests listed here, set your display to the highest resolution and refresh rate allowed by your combination of display and graphics card.

One good series of tasks is as follows:

■ *Draw a perfect circle with a graphics program.* If the displayed result is an oval, not a circle, this monitor will not serve you well with graphics or design software.

■ *Using a word processor, type some words in 8- or 10-point type (1 point equals 1/72 inch).* If the words are fuzzy, or if the black characters are fringed with color, select another monitor.

■ *Turn the brightness up and down while examining the corner of the screen's image.* If the image blooms or swells, it is likely to lose focus at high brightness levels.

■ *Display a screen with as much white space as possible and look for areas of color variance.* This can indicate a problem with only that individual unit or its location, but if you see it on more than one monitor of the same make, it might indicate a manufacturing problem; or it could indicate problems with the signal coming from the graphics card. Move the monitor to another system equipped with a different graphics card model and retry this test to see for certain whether it's the monitor or the video card.

■ *Display the Microsoft Windows desktop to check for uniform focus.* Are the corner icons as sharp as the rest of the screen? Are the lines in the title bar curved or wavy? Monitors usually are sharply focused at the center, but seriously blurred corners indicate a poor design. Bowed lines can be the result of a poor video adapter, so don't dismiss a monitor that shows those lines without using another adapter to double-check the effect. You can also use diagnostics that come with the graphics card or third-party system diagnostics programs to perform these tests.

■ *With LCD displays in particular, change to a lower resolution from the panel's native resolution using the Microsoft Windows Display properties settings.* Because LCD panels have only one native resolution, the display must use scaling to handle other resolutions full-screen. If you are a Web designer, are a gamer, or must capture screens at a particular resolution, this test will show you whether the LCD panel produces acceptable display quality at resolutions other than normal. You can also use this test on a CRT, but CRTs, unlike LCD panels, are designed to handle a wide variety of resolutions.

■ *Create a large, solid black box with a paint program and evaluate the quality of the box.* Low-quality monitors often display a mottled black, which can be very distracting when you view DVD movies or work with a black background such as those used by some of the high-contrast desktop display options in Windows.

■ *A good monitor is calibrated so that rays of red, green, and blue light hit their targets (individual phosphor dots) precisely.* If they don't, you have bad convergence. This is apparent when edges of lines appear to illuminate with a specific color. If you have good convergence, the colors are crisp, clear, and true, provided there isn't a predominant tint in the phosphor.

■ *If the monitor has built-in diagnostics (a recommended feature), try them as well to test the display independent of the graphics card and system to which it's attached.*

Caring for Your Monitor

Because a good 17-inch or larger monitor can be used for several years on more than one computer, proper care is essential to extend its life to the fullest extent.

Use the following guidelines for proper care of your monitors:

■ *Although phosphor burn (in which an image left onscreen eventually leaves a permanent shadow onscreen) is next-to-impossible with VGA-type displays, unlike the old TTL displays, screensavers are still useful for casual security.* You can password-protect your system with both the standard Windows screensaver and third-party programs (although a determined snoop can easily thwart screensaver password protection). Windows includes several screensavers that can be enabled via the Display Control Panel. A bevy of free and inexpensive screensavers is available for download from the Internet. Keep in mind, though, that add-on screensavers can cause crashes and lockups if poorly written or out-of-date.

■ *To prevent premature failure of the monitor's power supply, use the power-management feature of the Display Properties sheet to put the monitor into a low-power standby mode after a reasonable period of inactivity (10–15 minutes) and to turn it off after about 60 minutes.* Using the power management feature is far better than using the on/off switch when you are away from the computer for brief periods. Turn off the monitor only at the end of your computing "day."

How can you tell whether the monitor is really off or in standby mode? Look at the power LCD on the front of the monitor. A monitor that's in standby mode usually has a blinking green or solid amber LCD in place of the solid green LCD displayed when it's running in normal mode. Because monitors in standby mode still consume some power, they should be shut off at the end of the computing day.

If the monitor will not go into standby when the PC isn't sending signals to it, make sure the monitor is properly defined in Windows' Display Properties sheet. In addition, the Energy Star check box should be selected for any monitor that supports power management, unless the monitor should be left on at all times (such as when used in a retail kiosk or self-standing display).

■ *Make sure the monitor has adequate ventilation along the sides, rear, and top.* Because monitors use passive cooling, a lack of adequate airflow caused by piling keyboards, folders, books, or other office debris on top of the monitor will cause it to overheat and considerably shorten its life. If you're looking at a monitor with a partly melted grille on the top of the case, you're looking at a victim of poor cooling.

■ *The monitor screen and case should be kept clean.* Turn off the power, spray a cleaner such as Endust for Electronics onto a soft cloth (never directly onto the monitor!), and wipe the screen and the case gently.

■ *If your monitor has a degaussing button or feature, use it periodically to remove stray magnetic signals.* Keep in mind that CRTs have powerful magnets around the picture tube, so keep magnetic media away from them.

Video Display Adapters

A video adapter provides the interface between your computer and your monitor and transmits the signals that appear as images on the display. Throughout the history of the PC, there have been a succession of standards for video display characteristics that represent a steady increase in screen resolution and color depth. The following list of standards can serve as an abbreviated history of PC video-display technology:

MDA (Monochrome Display Adapter)

HGC (Hercules Graphics Card)

CGA (Color Graphics Adapter)

EGA (Enhanced Graphics Adapter)

VGA (Video Graphics Array)

SVGA (Super VGA)

XGA (Extended Graphics Array)

UVGA (Ultra VGA)

IBM pioneered most of these standards, but other manufacturers of compatible PCs adopted them as well. Today, IBM is no longer the industry leader it once was (and hasn't been for some time), and many of these standards are obsolete. Those that aren't obsolete seldom are referred to by these names anymore. The sole exception to this is *VGA*, which is a term that is still used to refer to a baseline graphics display capability supported by virtually every video adapter on the market today.

When you shop for a video adapter today, you are more likely to see specific references to the screen resolutions and color depths that the device supports than a list of standards such as VGA, SVGA, XGA, and UVGA. However, reading about these standards gives you a good idea of how video-display technology developed over the years and prepares you for any close encounters you might have with legacy equipment from the dark ages.

Today's VGA and later video adapters can also display most older color graphics software written for CGA, EGA, and most other obsolete graphics standards. This enables you to use older graphics software (such as games and educational programs) on your current system. Although not a concern for most users, some older programs wrote directly to hardware registers that are no longer found on current video cards.

Obsolete Display Adapters

Although many types of display systems were at one time considered to be industry standards, few of these are viable standards for today's hardware and software.

Note

If you are interested in reading more about MDA, HGC, CGA, EGA, or MCGA display adapters, see Chapter 8 of *Upgrading and Repairing PCs, 10th Anniversary Edition*, included on the CD with this book.

VGA Adapters and Displays

When IBM introduced the PS/2 systems on April 2, 1987, it also introduced the Video Graphics Array (VGA) display. On that day, in fact, IBM also introduced the lower-resolution Multicolor Graphics Array (MCGA) and higher-resolution 8514 adapters. The MCGA and 8514 adapters did not become popular standards like the VGA became, and both were discontinued.

Digital Versus Analog Signals

Unlike earlier video standards, which are digital, the VGA is an analog system. Why have displays gone from digital to analog when most other electronic systems have gone digital? Compact disc players (digital) have replaced most turntables (analog), and newer VCRs and camcorders have digital picture storage for smooth slow-motion and freeze-frame capability. With a digital television set, you can watch several channels on a single screen by splitting the screen or placing a picture within another picture.

Most personal computer displays introduced before the PS/2 are digital. This type of display generates different colors by firing the RGB electron beams in on-or-off mode, which allows for the display of up to eight colors (2^3). In the IBM displays and adapters, another signal doubles the number of color combinations from 8 to 16 by displaying each color at one of two intensity levels. This digital display is easy to manufacture and offers simplicity with consistent color combinations from system to system. The real drawback of the older digital displays such as CGA and EGA is the limited number of possible colors.

In the PS/2 systems, IBM went to an analog display circuit. Analog displays work like the digital displays that use RGB electron beams to construct various colors, but each color in the analog display system can be displayed at varying levels of intensity—64 levels, in the case of the VGA. This versatility provides 262,144 possible colors (64^3), of which 256 could be simultaneously displayed. For realistic computer graphics, color depth is often more important than high resolution because the human eye perceives a picture that has more colors as being more realistic. IBM moved to analog graphics to enhance the color capabilities of its systems.

Video Graphics Array

PS/2 systems incorporated the primary display adapter circuitry onto the motherboard, and both IBM and third-party companies introduced separate VGA cards to enable other types of systems to enjoy the advantages of VGA.

Although the IBM MicroChannel (MCA) computers, such as the PS/2 Model 50 and above, introduced VGA, it's impossible today to find a brand-new replacement for VGA that fits in the obsolete MCA-bus systems. However, surplus and used third-party cards might be available if you look hard enough.

The VGA BIOS (basic input/output system) is the control software residing in the system ROM for controlling VGA circuits. With the BIOS, software can initiate commands and functions without having to manipulate the VGA directly. Programs become somewhat hardware independent and can call a consistent set of commands and functions built into the system's ROM-control software.

◀◀ See "Video Adapter BIOS," p. 465.

Other implementations of the VGA differ in their hardware but respond to the same BIOS calls and functions. New features are added as a superset of the existing functions, and VGA remains compatible with the graphics and text BIOS functions built into the PC systems from the beginning. The VGA can run almost any software that originally was written for the CGA or EGA, unless it was written to directly access the hardware registers of these cards.

A standard VGA card displays up to 256 colors onscreen, from a palette of 262,144 (256KB) colors; when used in the 640×480 graphics or 720×400 text mode, 16 colors at a time can be displayed. Because the VGA outputs an analog signal, you must have a monitor that accepts an analog input.

VGA displays originally came not only in color, but also in monochrome VGA models, which use color summing. With color summing, 64 gray shades are displayed instead of colors. The summing routine is initiated if the BIOS detects a monochrome display when the system boots. This routine uses an algorithm that takes the desired color and rewrites the formula to involve all three color guns, producing varying intensities of gray. Users who preferred a monochrome display, therefore, could execute color-based applications.

Note

For a listing of the VGA display modes supported by the original IBM VGA card (and thus all subsequent VGA-type cards), see *Upgrading and Repairing PCs, 12th Edition*, available in electronic form on the CD-ROM supplied with this book.

Even the least-expensive video adapters on the market today can work with modes beyond the VGA standard. VGA, at its 16-color, 640×480 resolution, has come to be the baseline for PC graphical display configurations. VGA is accepted as the least common denominator for all Windows systems and must be supported by the video adapters in all systems running Windows. The installation programs of all Windows versions use these VGA settings as their default video configuration. In addition to VGA, most adapters support a range of higher screen resolutions and color depths, depending on the capabilities of the hardware. If a Windows 9x/Me or Windows 2000 system must be started in Safe Mode because of a startup problem, the system defaults to VGA in the 640×480, 16-color mode. Windows 2000 also offers a VGA Mode startup that also uses this mode but doesn't slow down the rest of the computer the way Safe Mode (which replaces 32-bit drivers with BIOS services) does.

IBM introduced higher-resolution versions of VGA called XGA and XGA-2 in the early 1990s, but most of the development of VGA standards has come from the third-party video card industry and its trade group, the Video Electronic Standards Association (VESA).

Note

If you are interested in reading more about the XGA and XGA-2 display adapters, see Chapter 8 of *Upgrading and Repairing PCs, 10th Anniversary Edition*, included on the CD with this book.

Super VGA

When IBM's XGA and 8514/A video cards were introduced, competing manufacturers chose not to attempt to clone these incremental improvements on their VGA products. Instead, they began producing lower-cost adapters that offered even higher resolutions. These video cards fall into a category loosely known as Super VGA (SVGA).

SVGA provides capabilities that surpass those offered by the VGA adapter. Unlike the display adapters discussed so far, SVGA refers not to an adapter that meets a particular specification, but to a group of adapters that have different capabilities.

For example, one card might offer several resolutions (such as 800×600 and 1,024×768) that are greater than those achieved with a regular VGA, whereas another card might offer the same or even greater resolutions but also provide more color choices at each resolution. These cards have different capabilities; nonetheless, both are classified as SVGA.

The SVGA cards look much like their VGA counterparts. They have the same connectors, but because the technical specifications from different SVGA vendors vary tremendously, it is impossible to provide a definitive technical overview in this book. The connector is shown in Figure 15.9; the pinouts are shown in Table 15.5.

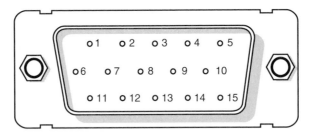

Figure 15.9 SVGA connector.

Table 15.5 Standard 15-Pin VGA Connector Pinout

Pin	Function	Direction	Pin	Function	Direction
1	Red Video	Out	2	Green Video	Out
3	Blue Video	Out	4	Monitor ID 2	In
5	TTL Ground (monitor self-test)	-_	6	Red Analog Ground	-_
7	Green Analog Ground	-_	8	Blue Analog Ground	-_
9	Key (Plugged Hole)	-_	10	Sync Ground	-_
11	Monitor ID 0	In	12	Monitor ID 1	In
13	Horizontal Sync	Out	14	Vertical Sync	Out
15	Monitor ID 3	In			

On the VGA cable connector that plugs into your video adapter, pin 9 is often pinless. Pin 5 is used only for testing purposes, and pin 15 is rarely used; these are often pinless as well. To identify the type of monitor connected to the system, some manufacturers use the presence or absence of the monitor ID pins in various combinations.

VESA SVGA Standards

The Video Electronics Standards Association includes members from various companies associated with PC and computer video products. In October 1989, VESA, recognizing that programming applications to support the many SVGA cards on the market was virtually impossible, proposed a standard for a uniform programmer's interface for SVGA cards known as the VESA BIOS extension (VBE). VBE support might be provided through a memory-resident driver (used by older cards) or through additional code added to the VGA BIOS chip itself (the more common solution). The benefit of the VESA BIOS extension is that a programmer needs to worry about only one routine or driver to support SVGA. Various cards from various manufacturers are accessible through the common VESA interface. Today, VBE support is a concern primarily for real-mode DOS applications, usually older games, and for non-Microsoft operating systems that need to access higher resolutions and color depths. VBE supports resolutions up to 1,280×1,024 and color depths up to 24-bit (16.8 million colors), depending on the mode selected and the memory on the video card. VESA compliance is of virtually no consequence to Windows versions 95 and up. These operating systems use custom video drivers for their graphics cards.

Note

For a listing of VESA BIOS modes by resolution, color depth, and scan frequency, see *Upgrading and Repairing PCs, 12th Edition*, available in electronic form on the CD-ROM accompanying this book.

Video Adapter Components

All video display adapters contain certain basic components, such as the following:

- Video BIOS
- Video processor
- Video memory
- Digital-to-analog converter (DAC)
- Bus connector
- Video driver

Figure 15.10 indicates the locations of many of these components on a typical video card.

Virtually all video adapters on the market today include 3D acceleration features. The following sections examine these components and features in greater detail.

The Video BIOS

Video adapters include a BIOS that is similar in construction but completely separate from the main system BIOS. (Other devices in your system, such as SCSI adapters, might also include their own BIOS.) If you turn on your monitor first and look quickly, you might see an identification banner for your adapter's video BIOS at the very beginning of the system startup process.

Similar to the system BIOS, the video adapter's BIOS takes the form of a ROM (read-only memory) chip containing basic instructions that provide an interface between the video adapter hardware and the software running on your system. The software that makes calls to the video BIOS can be a stand-alone application, an operating system, or the main system BIOS. The programming in the BIOS chip enables your system to display information on the monitor during the system POST and boot sequences, before any other software drivers have been loaded from disk.

◀◀ See "BIOS Basics," p. 346.

Figure 15.10 The Hercules 3D Prophet II GTS Pro is a typical example of a mid-range video card optimized for gaming. Like most recent graphics cards, it uses a nonremovable flash BIOS.

The video BIOS also can be upgraded, just like a system BIOS, in one of two ways. The BIOS uses a rewritable chip called an EEPROM (electrically erasable programmable read-only memory) that you can upgrade with a utility the adapter manufacturer provides. Alternatively, you might be able to completely replace the chip with a new one—again, if supplied by the manufacturer and if the manufacturer did not hard solder the BIOS to the printed circuit board. A BIOS you can upgrade using software is referred to as a *flash* BIOS, and most current-model video cards that offer BIOS upgrades use this method.

Video BIOS upgrades are sometimes necessary to use an existing adapter with a new operating system, or when the manufacturer encounters a significant bug in the original programming. As a general rule, the video BIOS is a component that falls into the "if it ain't broke, don't fix it" category. Try not to let yourself be tempted to upgrade just because you've discovered that a new BIOS revision is available. Check the documentation for the upgrade, and unless you are experiencing a problem the upgrade addresses, leave it alone.

◀◀ See "Video Adapter BIOS," p. 465.

The Video Processor

The video processor, or chipset, is the heart of any video adapter and essentially defines the card's functions and performance levels. Two video adapters built using the same chipset often have many of the same capabilities and deliver comparable performance. Also, the software drivers that operating systems and applications use to address the video adapter hardware are written primarily with the chipset in mind. You often can use a driver intended for an adapter with a particular chipset on any other adapter using the same chipset. Of course, cards built using the same chipset can differ in the amount and type of memory installed, so performance can vary.

Several main types of processors are used in video adapters:

- Frame buffer controllers
- Coprocessors
- Accelerators
- 3D graphics processors

Table 15.6 compares these technologies.

Table 15.6   Video Processor Technologies

Processor Type	Where Video Processing Takes Place	Relative Speed	Relative Cost	How Used Today
Frame-buffer	Computer's CPU	Very slow	Very low	Obsolete; mostly ISA video cards
Graphics coprocessor	Video card's own processor	Very fast	Very high	CAD and engineering workstations
Graphics accelerator	Video chip draws lines, circles, shapes; CPU sends commands to draw them	Fast	Low to moderate	All mainstream viedo cards
3D graphics processor	Video cards 3D graphics processing unit (in accelerator chipset) renders polygons, adds lighting and shading effects as needed	Fast 2D and 3D display	Most price ranges depending on chipset, memory, and RAMDAC speed	All gaming optimized video cards and most mainstream video cards

Integrated Video/Motherboard Chipsets

Although built-in video has been a staple of low-cost computing for a number of years, until recently most motherboard-based video simply moved the standard video components discussed earlier in this chapter to the motherboard. Many low-cost systems—especially those using the semiproprietary LPX motherboard form factor—have incorporated standard VGA-type video circuits on the motherboard. The performance and features of the built-in video differed only slightly from add-on cards using the same or similar chipsets, and in most cases the built-in video could be replaced by adding a video card. Some motherboard-based video also had provisions for memory upgrades.

◄◄ See "LPX," p. 201.

However, in recent years the move toward increasing integration on the motherboard has led to the development of chipsets that include 3D accelerated video and audio support as part of the chipset design. In effect, the motherboard chipset takes the place of most of the video-card components listed earlier and uses a portion of main system memory as video memory. The use of main system memory for video memory is often referred to as *Unified Memory Architecture (UMA)*, and although this memory-sharing method was also used by some built-in video that used its own chipset, it has become much more common with the rise of integrated motherboard chipsets.

The pioneer of integrated chipsets containing video (and audio) features was Cyrix. While Cyrix was owned by National Semiconductor, it developed a two-chip product called MediaGX. MediaGX incorporated the functions of a CPU, memory controller, sound, and video, making very low-cost computers possible (although with performance significantly slower than that of Pentium-class systems with similar clock speeds). The MediaGX was retained by National Semiconductor after it sold Cyrix to VIA Technologies, and National Semiconductor has developed improved versions of the MediaGX, called the Geode GX1, for use in thin clients, interactive set-top boxes, and other embedded devices.

Intel became the next major player to develop integrated chipsets, with its 810 chipset (codenamed "Whitney" before its official release) heralding the beginning of widespread industry support for this design. The following Intel chipsets support integrated video:

- Intel 810 family (all)
- Intel 815 and 815E

The 810 chipset family supports relatively low-performance (PCI-equivalent) integrated graphics, whereas the 815 and 815E chipsets support AGP-equivalent integrated 3D graphics with i740-class performance. Motherboards with the 815 and 815E chipset can also be equipped with an optional AGP slot for video card upgrades. Both chipsets are designed to support recent and current Intel processors, such as the Pentium III and Celeron, in their Socket 370 form factors. Both the 810 family and 815 family chipsets are two-piece sets: One chip contains the Graphics Memory Controller Hub, which replaces the traditional North Bridge chip and adds integrated video, and the other chip contains the I/O Controller Hub, which replaces the traditional South Bridge.

◀◀ See "Intel 810, 810E, and 810E2," p. 256, and "Intel 815, 815E, and 815EP," p. 259.

Intel is not alone in its support for integrated chipsets; other major chipset vendors also have developed similar integrated chipsets for use in low-cost computers and motherboards using both Intel and AMD CPUs, as shown in Table 15.7.

Table 15.7   Major Non-Intel Integrated Chipsets

Vendor	Chipset	Processors Supported	Number of Chips in Chipset	Notes
VIA Technology	VIA Apollo PM601	Pentium III/Celeron/ VIA Cyrix III (Socket 370)	2	Incorporates Trident Blade3D graphics
VIA Technology	VIA Apollo PLE133	Pentium III/Celeron/ VIA Cyrix III (Socket 370)	2	Incorporates Trident Blade3D graphics
VIA Technology	VIA Apollo MVP4	Super Socket 7 (AMD K6 family, Cyrix MII, Intel Pentium MMX)	2	Incorporates Trident Blade3D graphics
Silicon Integrated Systems (SiS)	SiS 530/ 5595	Super Socket 7 (AMD K6 family, Cyrix MII, Intel Pentium MMX)	2	Incorporates SiS6320 3D graphics
Silicon Integrated Systems (SiS)	SiS 620/ 5595	Pentium II/III/Celeron (Slot 1 or Socket 370)	2	Incorporates SiS6320 3D graphics

Table 15.7   Continued

Vendor	Chipset	Processors Supported	Number of Chips in Chipset	Notes
Silicon Integrated Systems (SiS)	SiS 630	Pentium III/ Celeron (Socket 370)	1	Incorporates SiS300 3D graphics; compatible with SiS Video Bridge
Silicon Integrated Systems (SiS)	SiS 630E	Pentium III/ Celeron (Socket 370)	1	Incorporates SiS300 3D graphics
Silicon Integrated Systems (SiS)	SiS 630S	Pentium III/ Celeron (Socket 370)	1	Incorporates SiS300 3D graphics; also supports external AGP card for upgrades
Silicon Integrated Systems (SiS)	SiS 730S	AMD Athlon/ Duron (Socket A)	1	Incorporates 3D graphics; also supports external AGP card for upgrades
S3 Graphics, Inc.	ProSavage PM133	Pentium III/ Celeron (Socket 370)	2	Based on VIA Apollo Pro 133A motherboard and S3 Savage 4 3D chipsets
S3 Graphics, Inc.	ProSavage KM133	AMD Athlon/ Duron (Socket A)	2	Based on VIA Apollo Pro KT133A motherboard and S3 Savage 4 3D chipsets
Acer Labs	Aladdin TNT2	Pentium II/III/Celeron (Slot A and Socket A)	2	Based on nVidia's RIVA TNT2 3D video chipset

Although a serious 3D gamer will not be satisfied with the performance of any integrated chipset, business, home/office, and casual gamers will find that integrated chipset-based video, particularly those that support advanced AGP 2x and faster 3D functions, are satisfactory in performance and provide cost savings compared with separate video cards.

Identifying the Video and System Chipsets

Before you purchase a system or a video card, you should find out which chipset the video card or video circuit uses, or, for systems with integrated chipset video, which integrated chipset the system uses. This allows you to have

- Better comparisons of card or system to others
- Access to technical specifications
- Access to reviews and opinions
- Better buying decisions
- Choice of card manufacturer or chipset manufacturer support and drivers

Because video card performance and features are critical to enjoyment and productivity, find out as much as you can before you buy the system or video card by using the chipset or video card manufacturer's Web site and third-party reviews.

The Vendor List on the CD has information on most of the popular video chipset manufacturers, including how to contact them.

The Video RAM

Most video adapters rely on their own onboard memory that they use to store video images while processing them; although some AGP video cards can use system memory for 3D textures, this feature is not universally supported. Many low-cost systems with onboard video use the Unified Memory Architecture feature to share the main system memory. In any case, the memory on the video card or borrowed from the system performs the same tasks.

The amount of memory on the adapter or used by integrated video determines the maximum screen resolution and color depth the device can support. You often can select how much memory you want on a particular video adapter; for example, 4MB, 8MB, 16MB, or even 32MB are common choices today. Most cards today come with at least 8MB, and many have 16MB or more. Although adding more memory is not guaranteed to speed up your video adapter, it can increase the speed if it enables a wider bus (from 64 bits wide to 128 bits wide) or provides nondisplay memory as a cache for commonly displayed objects. It also enables the card to generate more colors and higher resolutions and, for AGP cards (see the following) allows 3D textures to be stored and processed on the card, rather than in slower main memory.

Many types of memory have been used with video adapters. These memory types are summarized in Table 15.8 and are examined more fully in upcoming sections.

Table 15.8   Memory Types Used in Video Display Adapters

Memory Type	Definition	Relative Speed	Usage
FPM DRAM	Fast Page-Mode RAM	Slow	Low-end ISA cards; obsolete
VRAM[1]	Video RAM	Very fast	Expensive; obsolete
WRAM[1]	Window RAM	Very fast	Expensive; obsolete
EDO DRAM	Extended Data Out DRAM	Moderate	Low-end PCI-bus
SDRAM	Synchronous DRAM	Fast	Mid-range PCI/AGP
MDRAM	Multibank DRAM	Fast	Little used; obsolete
SGRAM	Synchronous Graphics DRAM	Very fast	High-end PCI/AGP
DDR SDRAM	Double-Data Rate SDRAM	Very fast	High-end AGP

1. *VRAM and WRAM are dual-ported memory types that can read from one port and write data through the other port. This improves performance by reducing wait times for accessing the video RAM compared to FPM DRAM and EDO DRAM.*

RAM Calculations

The amount of memory a video adapter needs to display a particular resolution and color depth is based on a mathematical equation. A location must be present in the adapter's memory array to display every pixel on the screen, and the resolution determines the number of total pixels. For example, a screen resolution of 1,024×768 requires a total of 786,432 pixels.

If you were to display that resolution with only two colors, you would need only one bit of memory space to represent each pixel. If the bit has a value of 0, the dot is black, and if its value is 1, the dot is white. If you use 24 bits of memory space to control each pixel, you can display more than 16.7 million colors because 16,777,216 combinations are possible with a 4-digit binary number (2^{24}=16,777,216). If you multiply the number of pixels necessary for the screen resolution by the number of bits required to represent each pixel, you have the amount of memory the adapter needs to display that resolution. Here is how the calculation works:

$$1{,}024 \times 768 = 786{,}432 \text{ pixels} \times 24 \text{ bits per pixel}$$
$$= 18{,}874{,}368 \text{ bits}$$
$$= 2{,}359{,}296 \text{ bytes}$$
$$= 2.25\text{MB}$$

As you can see, displaying 24-bit color (16,777,216 colors) at 1,024×768 resolution requires exactly 2.25MB of RAM on the video adapter. Because most adapters support memory amounts of only 256KB, 512KB, 1MB, 2MB, or 4MB, you would need to use a video adapter with at least 4MB of RAM onboard to run your system using that resolution and color depth.

To use the higher-resolution modes and greater numbers of colors common today, you would need much more memory on your video adapter than the 256KB found on the original IBM VGA. Table 15.9 shows the memory requirements for some of the most common screen resolutions and color depths used for 2D graphics operations, such as photo editing, presentation graphics, desktop publishing, and Web page design.

Table 15.9   Video Display Adapter Minimum Memory Requirements for 2D Operations

Resolution	Color Depth	No. Colors	Onboard Video RAM	Actual Memory Required
640×480	8-bit	256	512KB	307,200 bytes
640×480	16-bit	65,536	1MB	614,400 bytes
640×480	24-bit	16,777,216	1MB	921,600 bytes
800×600	8-bit	256	512KB	480,000 bytes
800×600	16-bit	65,536	1MB	960,000 bytes
800×600	24-bit	16,777,216	2MB	1,440,000 bytes
1,024×768	16-bit	65,536	2MB	1,572,864 bytes
1,024×768	24-bit	16,777,216	4MB	2,359,296 bytes
1,280×1,024	16-bit	65,536	4MB	2,621,440 bytes
1,280×1,024	24-bit	16,777,216	4MB	3,932,160 bytes

From this table, you can see that a video adapter with 2MB can display 65,536 colors in 1,024×768 resolution mode, but for a true color (16.8 million colors) display, you would need to upgrade to 4MB.

3D video cards require more memory for a given resolution and color depth because the video memory must be used for three buffers: the front buffer, back buffer, and Z-buffer. The amount of video memory required for a particular operation varies according to the settings used for the color depth and Z-buffer. Triple buffering allocates more memory for 3D textures than double-buffering but can slow down performance of some games. The buffering mode used by a given 3D video card usually can be adjusted through its properties sheet.

Table 15.10 lists the memory requirements for 3D cards in selected modes. For memory sizes used by other combinations of color depth and Z-buffer depth, see the ZD Labs' Memory Requirements for 3D Applications page at the following address:

http://www.zdnet.com/etestinglabs/stories/benchmarks/0,8829,2392081,00.html

Table 15.10   Video Display Adapter Memory Requirements for 3D Operations

Resolution	Color Depth	Z-Buffer Depth	Buffer Mode	Actual Memory Used	Onboard Video Memory Size Required
640×480	16-bit	16-bit	Double	1.76MB	2MB
			Triple	2.34MB	4MB
	24-bit	24-bit	Double	2.64MB	4MB
			Triple	3.52MB	4MB
	32-bit	32-bit	Double	3.52MB	4MB
			Triple	4.69MB	8MB
800×600	16-bit	16-bit	Double	2.75MB	4MB
			Triple	3.66MB	4MB
	24-bit	24-bit	Double	4.12MB	8MB
			Triple	5.49MB	8MB
	32-bit	32-bit	Double	5.49MB	8MB
			Triple	7.32MB	8MB
1,024×768	16-bit	16-bit	Double	4.12MB	8MB
			Triple	5.49MB	8MB
	24-bit	24-bit	Double	6.75MB	8MB
			Triple	9.00MB	16MB
	32-bit[1]	32-bit	Double	9.00MB	16MB
			Triple	12.00MB	16MB
1,280×1,024	16-bit	16-bit	Double	7.50MB	8MB
			Triple	10.00MB	16MB
	24-bit	24-bit	Double	11.25MB	16MB
			Triple	15.00MB	16MB
	32-bit	32-bit	Double	15.00MB	16MB
			Triple	20.00MB	32MB
1,600×1,280	16-bit	16-bit	Double	10.99MB	16MB
			Triple	14.65MB	16MB
	24-bit	24-bit	Double	16.48MB	32MB
			Triple	21.97MB	32MB
	32-bit	32-bit	Double	21.97MB	32MB
			Triple	29.30MB	32MB

Note

Although 3D adapters typically operate in a 32-bit mode (refer to Table 15.10), this does not necessarily mean they can produce more than the 16,277,216 colors of a 24-bit true color display. Many video processors and video memory buses are optimized to move data in 32-bit words, and they actually display 24-bit color while operating in a 32-bit mode, instead of the 4,294,967,296 colors you would expect from a true 32-bit color depth.

If you spend a lot of time working with graphics and want to enjoy 3D games, you might want to invest in a 24-bit (2D) or 32-bit (3D) video card with at least 32MB or more of RAM. Although 2D operations can be performed with as little as 4MB of RAM, 32-bit color depths for realistic 3D operation with large Z-buffers use most of the RAM available on a 16MB card at 1,024×768 resolution; higher resolutions use more than 16MB of RAM at higher color depths. Today's video cards provide more RAM and more 2D/3D performance for less money than ever before. Note that recent and current-model video cards don't use socketed memory anymore, so you must be sure to buy a video card with all the memory you might need now and in the future. Otherwise, you must replace a card with inadequate memory.

Windows Can't Display More Than 256 Colors

If you have a video card with 1MB or more of video memory, but the Windows 9x Display Settings properties sheet won't allow you to select a color depth greater than 256 colors, Windows 9x might have misidentified the video card during installation (this is a common problem with Trident 9680-series video cards, for example).

To see which video card Windows 9x recognizes, click the Advanced Properties button, and then click the Adapter tab if necessary. Your adapter type is listed near the middle of the dialog box. It might be listed either by the video card's brand name and model or by the video card's chipset maker and chipset model.

If the card model or chipset appears to be incorrect or not specific enough, click Change and see what other drivers your system lists that appear to be compatible. Many video card and chipset makers offer a free utility that you can download from their Web sites that identifies the card model, memory size, and other important information. Use such a utility program to determine which card you have, and then manually install the driver you need.

Video Bus Width

Another issue with respect to the memory on the video adapter is the width of the bus connecting the graphics chipset and memory on the adapter. The chipset is usually a single large chip on the card that contains virtually all the adapter's functions. It is wired directly to the memory on the adapter through a local bus on the card. Most of the high-end adapters use an internal memory bus that is 64 bits or even 128 bits wide. This jargon can be confusing because video adapters that take the form of separate expansion cards also plug into the main system bus, which has its own speed rating. When you read about a 64-bit or 128-bit video adapter, you must understand that this refers to the local video bus, and that the bus connecting the adapter to the system is actually the 32- or 64-bit PCI or AGP bus on the system's motherboard.

◀◀ See "System Bus Types, Functions, and Features," p. 288.

DRAM

Until recently, most video adapters have used regular dynamic RAM (DRAM) for this purpose. This type of RAM, although inexpensive, is extremely slow. The slowness can be attributed to the need to constantly refresh the information contained within the RAM and the fact that DRAM can't be read at the same time it is being written.

Modern PC graphics adapters need extremely high data transfer rates to and from the video memory. At a resolution of 1,024×768 and a standard refresh rate of 72Hz, the digital-to-analog converter (DAC) on the card must read the contents of the video memory frame buffer 72 times per second. In true color (24 bits per pixel) mode, this means the DAC must be capable of reading from the video memory at a rate of about 170MB/sec, which is just about the maximum available from a conventional DRAM design. Because of the high bandwidth required for higher refresh rates, resolutions, and color depths, a number of competing memory technologies have emerged over the past several years to meet the needs of high-performance video memory. Today, virtually no adapters rely on ordinary DRAM.

◀◀ See "DRAM," p. 407.

EDO DRAM

One of the first memory designs to be used as a replacement for DRAM on low-cost video adapters was Extended Data Out (EDO) DRAM. EDO provides a wider effective bandwidth by offloading memory precharging to separate circuits, which means the next access can begin before the last access has finished. As a result, EDO offers a 10% speed boost over DRAM, at a similar cost. Micron Technologies introduced EDO DRAM, which originally was designed for use in a PC's main RAM array, but also became common for video adapter memory in low-cost PCI-bus video cards. EDO chips are constructed using the same dies as conventional DRAM chips, and they differ from DRAMs only in how they are wired in final production. This method enabled manufacturers to make EDO chips on the same production lines and at the same relative costs as DRAM.

◄◄   See "Extended Data Out RAM," p. 416.

High-Speed Video RAM Solutions—Older Types

Over the years, several methods have been used for increasing video RAM speed above the slow DRAM and the only slightly faster EDO RAM. Several, including VRAM, WRAM, and MDRAM, were popular for brief periods of time, but SDRAM, SGRAM, and DRR SDRAM have almost completely replaced them.

VRAM

Video RAM (VRAM) is designed to be dual-ported, splitting the memory into two sections that can be accessed for reading and writing much more quickly than single-ported DRAM or EDO memory. This provides much greater performance than standard DRAM or even EDO, but it comes at a higher price.

WRAM

WRAM, or Windows RAM, is a modified VRAM-type, dual-ported memory technology developed by Samsung and is aimed specifically at graphics adapters. WRAM offers marginally better performance than standard VRAM at a lower cost.

MDRAM

Multibank DRAM (MDRAM) is a memory type also explicitly aimed at graphics and video applications. Developed by MoSys Inc., MDRAMs consist of a large number of small (32KB) banks.

MDRAM permits a video card with 2.5MB of RAM to be built, for example—enough to surpass the RAM requirements for 24-bit color at 1,024×768 resolution. Normally, 4MB of video RAM would be required. MDRAM was also designed to be accessed more quickly than even VRAM or WRAM. However, very few video card models ever featured this memory type.

Current High-Speed Video RAM Solutions

SGRAM, SDRAM, and DDR SDRAM have all but replaced VRAM, WRAM, and MDRAM as high-speed video RAM solutions. Similar to DRAM and SDRAM, SGRAM, SDRAM, and DDR SDRAM are derived from popular motherboard memory technologies. Their high speeds and low production costs have enabled even inexpensive video cards to have 16MB or more of high-speed RAM onboard.

SDRAM

Synchronous DRAM (SDRAM) is the same type of RAM used on Pentium II, Pentium III, Athlon, and other systems that use DIMMs (Dual Inline Memory Modules). The SDRAMs found on video cards are usually surface-mounted; on a few early models, they might be plugged into a proprietary connector. This memory is designed to work with bus speeds up to 200MHz and provides performance just slightly slower than SGRAM. SDRAM can be found in a number of AGP and PCI video cards from vendors who use SGRAM or DDR SDRAM for their top-line models.

SGRAM

Synchronous Graphics RAM (SGRAM) is a high-end solution for very fast video adapter designs. Similar to the SDRAM used in motherboard memory arrays, SGRAM can synchronize itself with the speed of the bus, up to 200MHz. This type of memory can be up to four times as fast as conventional DRAM and can operate at speeds up to 133MHz or faster; it is used frequently in many of the highest quality PCI and AGP adapters. SGRAM is one of the most expensive memory technologies used in video adapters, but it offers superior performance for graphics-intensive applications. The key difference between SGRAM and SDRAM is the inclusion of circuitry to perform block writes that can significantly increase the speed of graphics fill or 3D Z-buffer operations.

DDR SDRAM

Double Data Rate SDRAM (also called DDR SDRAM or SDRAM II) is one of the newest video RAM technologies. It is designed to transfer data at speeds twice that of conventional SDRAM by transferring data on both the rising and falling parts of the processing clock cycle. It is fast enough to work with the newest 133MHz-bus motherboards from Intel and other vendors and is designed so that current users of conventional SDRAM easily can adopt it by modifying their card designs. Several video card vendors, such as ATI and those making cards based on nVidia's popular GeForce 2 chipset, have already adopted DDR SDRAM. In comparing nVidia's original GeForce chipset, which came in both SDRAM and DDR SDRAM version, testers have found that at high resolutions, such as 1024×768 and above, there are game performance boosts of 20% or more for some functions over the same chipset with standard SDRAM.

Unless you dig deeply into the technical details for a particular 3D graphics card, determining whether a particular card uses SDRAM, DDR SDRAM, or SGRAM can be difficult. Because none of today's 3D accelerators feature upgradeable memory, I recommend that you look at the performance of a given card and choose the card with the performance, features, and price that's right for you.

The Digital-to-Analog Converter

The digital-to-analog converter on a video adapter (commonly called a RAMDAC) does exactly what its name describes. The RAMDAC is responsible for converting the digital images your computer generates into analog signals the monitor can display. The speed of the RAMDAC is measured in MHz; the faster the conversion process, the higher the adapter's vertical refresh rate. The speeds of the RAMDACs used in today's high-performance video adapters range from 300MHz to 350MHz.

The benefits of increasing the RAMDAC speed include higher vertical refresh rates, which allows higher resolutions with flicker-free refresh rates (72Hz–85Hz or above). Typically, cards with RAMDAC speeds of 300MHz or above display flicker-free (75Hz or above) at all resolutions up to 1,920×1,200. Of course, as discussed earlier in this chapter, you must ensure that any resolution you want to use is supported by both your monitor and video card.

The Bus

You've learned in this chapter that certain video adapters were designed for use with certain system buses. Earlier bus standards, such as the IBM MCA, ISA, EISA, and VL-Bus, have all been used for VGA and other video standards. Because of their slow performances, all are now obsolete; current video cards are made exclusively for either the PCI or AGP bus standard.

In July 1992, Intel Corporation introduced Peripheral Component Interconnect (PCI) as a blueprint for directly connecting microprocessors and support circuitry. It then extended the design to a full expansion bus with Release 2 in 1993; the current standard is Release 2.1. Popularly termed a mezzanine bus, PCI combines the speed of a local bus with microprocessor independence. PCI video adapters, similar to VL-Bus adapters, can dramatically increase video performance when compared with ISA adapters. PCI video adapters, by their design, are meant to be Plug and Play (PnP), which means they require little configuration. The PCI standard virtually replaced the older VL-Bus standard overnight and has dominated Pentium-class video until recently. Although the PCI bus remains the best general-purpose standard for expansion cards, the current king of high-speed video is AGP.

◀◀   See "Accelerated Graphics Port," p. 313.

◀◀   See "The PCI Bus," p. 310.

The most recent system bus innovation is the Accelerated Graphics Port (AGP), an Intel-designed dedicated video bus that delivers a maximum bandwidth up to 16 times larger than that of a comparable PCI bus. AGP is essentially an enhancement to the existing PCI bus, intended for use with only video adapters and providing them with high-speed access to the main system memory array. This enables the adapter to process certain 3D video elements, such as texture maps, directly from system memory rather than having to copy the data to the adapter memory before the processing can begin. This saves time and eliminates the need to upgrade the video adapter memory to better support 3D functions.

Note

Although the earliest AGP cards had relatively small amounts of onboard RAM, most recent and all current implementations of card-based AGP use large amounts of on-card memory and use a memory aperture (a dedicated memory address space above the area used for physical memory) to transfer data more quickly to and from the video card's own memory. Integrated chipsets featuring built-in AGP do use system memory for all operations, including texture maps.

Ironically, the memory aperture used by AGP cards can actually cause out-of-memory errors with Windows 9x and Windows Me on systems with more than 512MB of RAM. See Microsoft Knowledge Base document #Q253912 for details.

Although it was designed with the Pentium II in mind, AGP is not processor dependent. However, it does require support from the motherboard chipset, and AGP cards require a special expansion slot, which means you can't upgrade an existing non-AGP system to use AGP without replacing the motherboard.

Most recent motherboard chipsets from Intel, ALi, VIA Technologies, and SiS support at least AGP 2x.

◀◀   See "Socket 7 (and Super7)," p. 89.

Even with the proper chipset, however, you can't take full advantage of AGP's capabilities without the proper operating system support. AGP's Direct Memory Execute (DIME) feature uses main memory instead of the video adapter's memory for certain tasks, to lessen the traffic to and from the adapter. Windows 98/Me and Windows 2000/XP support this feature, but Windows 95 and Windows NT 4 donot.

AGP Speeds

AGP support currently is available in three speeds: AGP 1X, AGP 2X, and AGP 4X. AGP 1x and 2x are part of the original AGP Specification 1.0; AGP 4X is part of the AGP Specification 2.0. AGP 1X is the original version of AGP, running at 66MHz clock speed and a maximum transfer rate of 266MB/second (twice the speed of 32-bit PCI video cards). AGP 2X, which runs at 133MHz and offers transfer rates up to 533MB/second, has replaced it. The latest version of AGP supports 4X mode, which offers maximum transfer rates in excess of 1GB/second; AGP 4x also can be used with AGP 2x-compatible motherboards (although its performance then is limited to 2x). Intel's AGP 8x mode 1.0 specification, which doubles performance to above 2GB/second, was released in mid-2001, although products that will use 8x mode are not expected until later. 8x mode will be compatible with AGP 4x-compatible motherboards, but not with the earlier AGP 2x or 1x motherboards.

Which should you buy? Microsoft states that Windows 98 and Windows 2000 require that a system support AGP 2X or faster to be considered compatible with these operating systems. Because most AGP cards now on the market meet the AGP 2X or 4X standard, meeting this requirement is easy.

Some vendors have sold AGP 2x cards using chipsets that are really optimized for 2D operation. For best results, buy only AGP cards equipped with true 3D chipsets (refer ahead to Table 15.22). Should you buy an AGP 4x card? Yes, if you want the very fastest rendering rate for 3D games as well as faster performance for other graphics-intensive applications. These cards achieve their blazing transfer speeds through the use of two data channels that can operate simultaneously. AGP 4x cards are more expensive than their 2x siblings, but they are definitely faster. AGP 4x cards require that the motherboard be AGP version 2.0 compliant and will run at 2x on AGP 1.0–compliant motherboards.

Caution

Should you check motherboard-video card compatibility before you buy? Yes, because early AGP cards (especially those based on Intel's i740 chipset) were designed strictly for the original AGP Pentium II-based motherboards. Some AGP users have Super Socket 7 motherboards instead, and some early AGP cards don't work with these motherboards. Check with both the video card and motherboard vendors before you make your purchase.

◄◄ See "Socket 7 (and Super7)," p. 89.

The high end of the video card market has now shifted almost completely to AGP 2x or 4x; PCI video cards are being relegated to replacements for older systems. Ironically, because of the high popularity of AGP today, you might pay more for a slower PCI video card than for an AGP card with similar features.

Note

Many low-cost systems implement AGP video on the motherboard without providing an AGP expansion slot for future upgrades. This prevents you from changing to a faster or higher memory AGP video card in the future, although you might be able to use slower PCI video cards. For maximum flexibility, get your AGP video on a card.

VL-Bus, PCI, and AGP have some important differences, as Table 15.11 shows.

Table 15.11   Local Bus Specifications

Feature	VL-Bus	PCI	AGP
Theoretical maximum	132MB/sec	132MB/sec[1]	533MB/sec throughput (2x) 1.06GB/sec throughput (4x) 2.12GB/sec throughput (8x)[2]
Slots[2]	3 (typical)	4/5 (typical)	1
Plug and Play support	No	Yes	Yes
Cost	Inexpensive	Slightly higher	Similar to PCI
Ideal use	Low-cost 486	High-end 486, Pentium, P6	Pentium II/III/Celeron/4, K6, Athlon, Duron
Status	Obsolete	Current	Current

1. At the 66MHz bus speed and 32 bits. Throughput is higher on the 100MHz system bus.

2. Projected speed per standard; AGP 8x products are not expected until late 2001 or beyond.

The Video Driver

The software driver is an essential, and often a problematic, element of a video display subsystem. The driver enables your software to communicate with the video adapter. You can have a video adapter with the fastest processor and the most efficient memory on the market, but still have poor video performance because of a badly written driver.

DOS applications address the video display hardware directly and typically include their own drivers for various types of video adapters; most recent DOS-based games can use VESA BIOS extension modes to achieve higher resolutions and color depths. All versions of Windows, however, use a driver that is installed in the operating system. Applications then can use operating system function calls to access the video hardware.

Video drivers generally are designed to support the processor on the video adapter. All video adapters come equipped with drivers the card manufacturer supplies, but often you can use a driver the chipset maker created as well. Sometimes you might find that one of the two provides better performance than the other or resolves a particular problem you are experiencing.

Most manufacturers of video adapters and chipsets maintain Web sites from which you can obtain the latest drivers; drivers for chipset-integrated video are supplied by the system board or system vendor. A driver from the chipset manufacturer can be a useful alternative, but you should always try the adapter manufacturer's driver first. Before purchasing a video adapter, you should check out the manufacturer's site and see whether you can determine how up-to-date the available drivers are. At one time, frequent driver revisions were felt to indicate problems with the hardware, but the greater complexity of today's systems means that driver revisions are a necessity. Even if you are installing a brand-new model of a video adapter, be sure to check for updated drivers on the manufacturer's Web site for best results.

The video driver also provides the interface you can use to configure the display your adapter produces. On a Windows 9x/Me/2000/XP system, the Display Control Panel identifies the monitor and video adapter installed on your system and enables you to select the color depth and screen resolution you prefer. The driver controls the options that are available for these settings, so you can't choose parameters the hardware doesn't support. For example, the controls would not allow you to select a 1,024×768 resolution with 24-bit color if the adapter had only 1MB of memory.

When you click the Advanced button on the Settings page, you see the Properties dialog box for your particular video display adapter. The contents of this dialog box can vary, depending on the driver and the capabilities of the hardware. Typically, on the General page of this dialog box, you can select the size of the fonts (large or small) to use with the resolution you've chosen. Windows 98/Me/2000 also adds a control to activate a convenient feature. The Show Settings Icon on Task Bar check box activates a tray icon that enables you to quickly and easily change resolutions and color depths without having to open the Control Panel. This feature is often called QuickRes.

The Adapter page displays detailed information about your adapter and the drivers installed on the system, and it enables you to set the Refresh Rate for your display. If your adapter includes a graphics accelerator, the Performance page contains a Hardware Acceleration slider you can use to control the degree of graphic display assistance provided by your adapter hardware.

Setting the Hardware Acceleration slider to the Full position activates all the adapter's hardware acceleration features.

Moving the slider one notch to the left addresses mouse display problems by disabling the hardware's cursor support in the display driver. This is the equivalent of adding the `SWCursor=1` directive to the `[Display]` section of the `System.ini` file.

Moving the slider another notch (to the second notch from the right) prevents the adapter from performing certain bit-block transfers. With some drivers, this setting also disables memory-mapped I/O. This is the equivalent of adding the `Mmio=0` directive to the `[Display]` section of `System.ini` and the `SafeMode=1` directive to the `[Windows]` section of `Win.ini` (and the `SWCursor` directive mentioned previously).

Moving the slider to the None setting (the far left) adds the `SafeMode=2` directive to the `[Windows]` section of the `Win.ini` file. This disables all hardware acceleration support and forces the operating system to use only the device-independent bitmap (DIB) engine to display images, rather than bit-block transfers. Use this setting when you experience frequent screen lockups or receive invalid page fault error messages.

Note

If you need to disable any of the video hardware features listed earlier, this often indicates a buggy video or mouse driver. If you download and install updated video and mouse drivers, you should be able to revert to full acceleration.

Video cards with advanced 3D acceleration features often have additional properties; these are discussed later in this chapter.

Video Cards for Multimedia

Multimedia—including live full-motion video feeds, video conferencing, and animations—has become an important element of the personal computing industry and is helping to blur the once-solid lines between computer and broadcast media. As the demand for multimedia content increases, so do the capabilities of the hardware and software used to produce the content. Video is just one, albeit important, element of the multimedia experience, and the graphics adapters on the market today reflect the demand for these increased capabilities. Producing state-of-the-art multimedia content today often requires that the PC be capable of interfacing with other devices, such as cameras, VCRs, and television sets, and many video adapters are now equipped with this capability.

Other multimedia technologies, such as 3D animation, place an enormous burden on a system's processing and data-handling capabilities, and many manufacturers of video adapters are redesigning their products to shoulder this burden more efficiently.

The following sections examine some of the video adapter components that make these technologies possible and practical—including VFC, VAFC, VMC, and VESA VIP.

Because none of these specifications for internal video feature connectors have become true industry standards, some manufacturers of auxiliary video products—such as dedicated 3D accelerator boards and MPEG decoders—have taken an alternative route through the standard VGA connector.

Video Feature Connectors

To extend the capabilities of the VGA standard beyond direct connections to a monitor, several auxiliary connector standards have been devised, first by individual card makers and later by VESA.

Two early attempts to create a common connector were the Video Feature Connector (VFC) that IBM devised in 1987, the VESA Advanced Feature Connector (VAFC), and the VESA Media Channel (VMC). These connector designs were not widely used.

Note

If you are interested in reading more about VFC, VAFC, and VMC, see Chapter 8 of *Upgrading and Repairing PCs, 10th Anniversary Edition*, included on the CD with this book.

VESA Video Interface Port

The most recent attempt at a standard interface between video cards and other video devices today is the VESA Video Interface Port (VESA VIP), originally introduced in 1997. Version 2, the latest version of this standard, was introduced in October 1998.

The VESA VIP provides a dedicated connection designed to allow video cards to connect with one or more third-party hardware devices, such as MPEG-2 or HDTV decoders, video digitizers, video encoders, and so on. A dedicated connection prevents competition with other data movement on the PCI bus.

VIP is more widely supported than previous standards, but it exists in two versions (1.1 and 2.0) and is implemented in various ways by card vendors. For example, some versions of certain ATI video cards, such as the Xpert 99, Xpert 128, and Rage Magnum, use a 40-pin proprietary connector called the AMC connector, which also works as a 26-pin VIP connector. To avoid VESA VIP-compatibility problems, check the compatibility list for both the video card and the device you want to connect. You might need to purchase an adapter cable to connect the device to your card. Some very high-performance 3D gaming cards do not support either VESA VIP connector type.

Video Output Devices

When video technology first was introduced, it was based on television. However, a difference exists between the signals used by a television and the signals used by a computer. In the United States, the National Television System Committee (NTSC) established color TV standards in 1953. Some other countries, such as Japan, followed this standard. Many countries in Europe, though, developed more sophisticated standards, including Phase Alternate Line (PAL) and Sequential Couleur Avec Mémoire (SECAM). Table 15.12 shows the differences among these standards.

Table 15.12   Television Versus Computer Monitors

Standard	Year Est.	Country	Lines	Rate
		Television		
NTSC	1953 (color), 1941 (b&w)	U.S., Japan	525	60 fields/sec
PAL	1941	Europe[1]	625	50 fields/sec
SECAM	1962	France	625	25 fields/sec
		Computer		
VGA	1987	U.S.	640×480[2]	72Hz

Field = 1/2 (.5 frame)

1. England, Holland, and West Germany.

2. VGA is based on more lines and uses pixels (480) versus lines; genlocking is used to lock pixels into lines and synchronize computers with TV standards.

A video-output (or VGA-to-NTSC) adapter enables you to display computer screens on a TV set or record them onto videotape for easy distribution. These products fall into two categories: those with genlocking (which enables the board to synchronize signals from multiple video sources or video with PC graphics) and those without. Genlocking provides the signal stability necessary to obtain adequate results when recording to tape, but it is not necessary for using a television as a video display.

VGA-to-NTSC converters are available both as internal expansion boards and external boxes that are portable enough to use with a laptop for presentations on the road. Indeed, many laptop and notebook systems these days come equipped with a built-in VGA-to-NTSC converter.

The converter does not replace your existing video adapter but instead connects to the adapter using an external cable. In addition to VGA input and output ports, a video output board has a video output interface for S-Video and composite video.

Most VGA-to-TV converters support the standard NTSC television format and might also support the European PAL format. The resolution these devices display on a TV set or record on videotape often is limited to straight VGA at 640×480 pixels. The converter also might contain an antiflicker circuit to help stabilize the picture because VGA-to-TV products, as well as TV-to-VGA solutions, often suffer from a case of the jitters.

Still-Image Video Capture Cards

You can install a board into your PC that enables you to capture individual screen images for later editing and playback. There are also external devices that plug into a PC's parallel port. These units capture still images from NTSC video sources, such as camcorders and VCRs. Although image quality is limited by the input signal, the results are still good enough for presentations and desktop publishing applications. These devices work with 8-, 16-, and 24-bit VGA cards and usually accept video input from VHS, Super VHS, and Hi-8 devices. As you might expect, however, Super VHS and Hi-8 video sources give better results, as do configurations using more than 256 colors. For the best results, use DV camcorders equipped with IEEE-1394 (i.Link/FireWire) connectors; these can output high-quality digital video direct to your computer without the need to perform an analog-to-digital conversion.

Multiple Monitors

Windows 98/Me and Windows 2000 include a video display feature that Macintosh systems have had for years: the capability to use multiple monitors on one system. Windows 98/Me support up to nine monitors (and video adapters), each of which can provide a different view of the desktop. Windows 2000 supports up to 10 monitors and video adapters. Windows XP Professional will also support multiple monitors with its DualView feature, but Windows XP Home Edition will not. When you configure a Windows 98/Me or Windows 2000 system to use multiple monitors, the operating system creates a virtual desktop—that is, a display that exists in video memory that can be larger than the image actually displayed on a single monitor. You use the multiple monitors to display various portions of the virtual desktop, enabling you to place the windows for different applications on separate monitors and move them around at will.

Unless you use multiple-head video cards, each monitor you connect to the system requires its own video adapter. So, unless you have nine bus slots free, the prospects of seeing a nine-screen Windows display are slim, for now. However, even two monitors can be a boon to computing productivity.

On a multimonitor Windows 98/Me system, one display is always considered to be the primary display. The primary display can use any PCI or AGP VGA video adapter that uses a Windows 98/Me minidriver with a linear frame buffer and a packed (nonplanar) format, meaning that most of the brand-name adapters sold today are eligible. Additional monitors are called secondaries and are much more limited in their hardware support. To install support for multiple monitors, make sure you have only one adapter installed first; then reboot the system, and install each additional adapter one at a time. For more information about multiple monitor support for Windows 98/Me, including a list of supported adapters, see the Microsoft Knowledge Base article #Q182708.

It's important that the computer correctly identifies which one of the video adapters is the primary one. This is a function of the system BIOS, and if the BIOS on your computer does not let you select which device should be the primary VGA display, it decides based on the order of the PCI slots in the machine. You should, therefore, install the primary adapter in the highest-priority PCI slot. In some cases, an AGP adapter might be considered secondary to a PCI adapter.

◀◀   See "The PCI Bus," p. 310.

After the hardware is in place, you can configure the display for each monitor from the Display control panel's Settings page. The primary display is always fixed in the upper-left corner of the virtual desktop, but you can move the secondary displays to view any area of the desktop you like. You can also set the screen resolution and color depth for each display individually. For more information about configuring multiple monitor support in Windows 98, see Microsoft Knowledge Base article #Q179602.

Windows 2000 also provides multiple monitor support but with some differences from Windows 98/Me, as seen in Table 15.13.

Table 15.13   Comparing Windows 98/Me and Windows 2000 Multiple Monitor Support

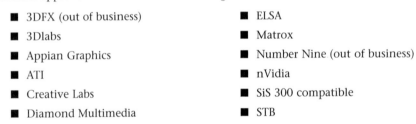

Windows Version	Number of Adapters/ Monitors Supported	How Compatible Cards Are Listed	Finding Compatible Cards
98/Me	9	By chipset	On Microsoft Web site
2000	10	By brand and model	HCL listing on CD-ROM

As of the initial release of Windows 2000, some of the major brands with products on the multiple-monitor approved list included the following:

- 3DFX (out of business)
- 3Dlabs
- Appian Graphics
- ATI
- Creative Labs
- Diamond Multimedia
- ELSA
- Matrox
- Number Nine (out of business)
- nVidia
- SiS 300 compatible
- STB

Windows 2000's Hardware Compatibility List is by graphics card brand and model, rather than by chipset (check the Windows 2000 CD-ROM Hardware Compatibility List for details). This list is likely to change as Windows 2000 support becomes more widespread, but unfortunately the online version of the Windows 2000 HCL doesn't provide an updated list of cards that support multiple-monitor configurations. You should check with your video card or chipset maker for the latest information on Windows 2000 and multiple-monitor support issues. For more information on troubleshooting Windows 2000 multiple-monitor configuration, see Microsoft Knowledge Base article #Q238886.

Because new chipsets and combinations of display adapters are a continuous issue for multiple-monitor support, I recommend the following online resources:

- http://www.realtime.com/ultramon. Home of the UltraMon multiple-monitor support enhancement program ($24.95) and an extensive database of user-supplied multiple-monitor configurations
- http://www.digitalroom.net/techpub/multimon.html. Excellent tips on multiple-monitor setups and links to other resources

Multiple monitor support can be enabled through either of the following:

- Installation of a separate AGP or PCI graphics card for each monitor you want to use
- Installation of a single AGP or PCI graphics card that can support two or more monitors

A card that supports multiple monitors (also called a multiple-head or dual-head card) saves slots inside your system.

Depending on the card in question, you can use the multiple-monitor feature in a variety of ways. For example, the ATI Radeon VE features a 15-pin analog VGA connector (for CRTs) and a DVI-I digital/analog connector for digital LCD panels. Thus, you can connect any of the following to the card:

■ One analog LCD or CRT display **and** one digital LCD display

■ Two analog LCD or CRT displays (when the DVI-I–to–VGA adapter is used)

Some of the major multiple-head cards on the market are listed in Table 15.14.

Table 15.14   Major Multiple-Head Video Cards

Brand	Model	Bus Type(s)	Number of Monitors Supported	Accelerator Chip(s)	Notes
Appian Graphics	Jeronimo Pro	PCI	2 or 4	3D Labs Permedia 2 3D (2 or 4)	Supports analog CRTs and LCD displays
Appian Graphics	Jeronimo 2000	AGP, PCI	2	3D Labs Permedia 3 (2)	Supports analog CRTs and LCD displays
ATI	Radeon VE	AGP	2	ATI Radeon 3D (1)	Supports analog CRTs and LCD displays; supports digital flat panel (DVI)
Gainward	CARDEXpert GeForce2 MX Twin View	AGP	2	NVidia GeForce2 (1)	Supports analog CRTs and LCD displays; supports TV-out option
LeadTek	WinFast GeForce2 MX DH Pro	AGP	2	NVidia GeForce2 (1)	Supports analog CRTs and LCD displays; supports TV-out option
Matrox	Millennium G450	AGP, PCI	2	Matrox G450 3D (1)	Supports analog CRT and LCD displays; supports TV-out; supports digital flat panel (DVI)[1]
Matrox	Millennium G200 MMS	PCI	2 or 4	MGA-G200 3D (2 or 4)	Supports analog CRT and digital flat panel (DVI PanelLink); supports TV-out

1. Optional adapter required

Desktop Video Boards

You can also capture NTSC (television) signals to your computer system for display or editing. In other words, you can literally watch TV in a window on your computer. When capturing video, you should think in terms of digital versus analog. The biggest convenience of an analog TV signal is efficiency; it is a compact way to transmit video information through a low-bandwidth pipeline. The disadvantage is that although you can control how the video is displayed, you can't edit it.

Actually capturing and recording video from external sources and saving the files onto your PC requires special technology. To do this, you need a device called a video capture board, also called a TV tuner, a video digitizer, or a video grabber.

Note

In this context, the technical nomenclature again becomes confusing because the term *video* here has its usual connotation; that is, it refers to the display of full-motion photography on the PC monitor. When evaluating video hardware, be sure to distinguish between devices that capture still images from a video source and those that capture full-motion video pstreams.

Today, video sources come in two forms:

- Analog
- Digital

Analog video can be captured from traditional sources such as broadcast or cable TV, VCRs, and camcorders using VHS or similar tape standards. This process is much more demanding of storage space and system performance than still images are. Here's why.television

The typical computer screen was designed to display mainly static images. The storing and retrieving of these images requires managing huge files. Consider this: A single, full-screen color image in an uncompressed format can require as much as 2MB of disk space; a one-second video would therefore require 45MB. Likewise, any video transmission you want to capture for use on your PC must be converted from an analog NTSC signal to a digital signal your computer can use. On top of that, the video signal must be moved inside your computer at 10 times the speed of the conventional ISA bus structure. You need not only a superior video card and monitor but also an excellent expansion bus, such as PCI or AGP.

Considering that full-motion video can consume massive quantities of disk space, it becomes apparent that data compression is all but essential. Compression and decompression applies to both video and audio. Not only does a compressed file take up less space, it also performs better; there is simply less data to process. When you are ready to replay the video/audio, the application decompresses the file during playback. In any case, if you are going to work with video, be sure that your hard drive is large enough and fast enough to handle the huge files that can result.

Compression/decompression programs and devices are called *codecs*. Two types of codecs exist: hardware-dependent codecs and software (or hardware-independent) codecs. Hardware codecs typically perform better; however, they require additional hardware—either an add-on card or a high-end video card with hardware codecs built in. Software codes do not require hardware for compression or playback, but they typically do not deliver the same quality or compression ratio. Two of the major codec algorithms are

- *JPEG (Joint Photographic Experts Group)*. Originally developed for still images, JPEG can compress and decompress at rates acceptable for nearly full-motion video (30fps). JPEG still uses a series of still images, which makes editing easier. JPEG is typically lossy (meaning that a small amount of the data is lost during the compression process, slightly diminishing the quality of the image), but it can also be lossless. JPEG compression functions by eliminating redundant data for each individual image (intraframe). Compression efficiency is approximately 30:1 (20:1–40:1).

- *MPEG (Motion Pictures Experts Group)*. MPEG by itself compresses video at approximately a 30:1 ratio, but with precompression through oversampling, the ratio can climb to 100:1 and higher, while retaining high quality. Thus, MPEG compression results in better, faster videos that require less storage space. MPEG is an interframe compressor. Because MPEG stores only incremental changes, it is not used during editing phases.

If you will be capturing or compressing video on your computer, you'll need software based on standards such as Microsoft's DirectShow (the successor to Video for Windows and ActiveMovie), Real Network's Real Producer series, or Apple's QuickTime Pro. Players for files produced with these technologies can be downloaded free from the vendors' Web sites.

To play or record video on your multimedia PC (MPC), you need some extra hardware and software:

- Video system software, such as Apple's QuickTime for Windows or Microsoft's Windows Media Player.
- A compression/digitization video adapter that enables you to digitize and play large video files.
- An NTSC-to-VGA adapter that combines TV signals with computer video signals for output to a VCR. Video can come from a variety of sources: TV, VCR, video camera, laserdisc player, or DVD player. When you record an animation file, you can save it in a variety of file formats: AVI (Audio Video Interleave), MOV (Apple QuickTime format), or MPG (MPEG format).

Depending on the video-capture product you use, you have several choices for capturing analog video. The best option is to use component video. Component video uses three RCA-type jacks to carry the luminance (Y) and two chrominance (PR and PB) signals; this type of connector commonly is found on DVD players and high-end conventional and HDTV television sets. However, home-market video capture devices usually don't support component video. A typical professional capture device designed for component video, such as Pinnacle Systems' miroVideo DC50, retails for about $1,300.

The next best choice, and one that is supported by many home-market video-capture devices, is the S-Video (S-VHS) connector. This cable transmits separate signals for color (chroma) and brightness (luma). Otherwise, you must use composite video, which mixes luma and chroma. This results in a lower-quality signal. The better your signal, the better your video quality will be.

You also can purchase devices that display only NTSC (TV) signals on your computer. The built-in digital movie editing features found in Windows Me, the increasing popularity of computer/TV solutions, and broadband Internet connections make onscreen full-motion video an increasingly common part of the computing experience. Because of the growing importance of onscreen full-motion video, more and more recent CPUs have added features to enhance playback—including MMX and SSE instructions found in the Pentium II, Pentium III, Celeron, AMD Athlon, and Duron and the instruction set found in the Intel Pentium 4's NetBurst microarchitecture and SSE2.

Table 15.15 provides a breakdown of some common video cards and capture devices supporting key features. This table is not inclusive and is meant to serve only as a reference example.

Table 15.15 Video Capture Devices

Device Type	Example
Built-in TV tuner and capture	ATI Radeon All-in-Wonder, All-in-Wonder 128
TV-tuner and capture	ATI-TV Wonder
Parallel port	Snappy Video Snapshot (still images)
USB port video capture	Dazzle Digital Video Creator
PCI video capture card	Broadway Pro
IEEE-1394 (FireWire)	AVerMedia AverDV

Figure 15.11 shows a typical video adapter incorporating TV tuner and video-in and video-out features: the ATI All-in-Wonder 128.

CD in

A/V In (connects to breakout box with composite, S-Video, and audio connectors)

Line out

75-ohm CATV/antenna connector

A/V Out (connects to output adapter)

VGA 15-pin monitor connector

RAGE 128 Pro accelerator chip

AGP 2x/4x bus connector

RAM

Figure 15.11 ATI's All-in-Wonder 128 Pro is a typical video accelerator with integrated TV tuner and video-capture features.

Each type of device has advantages and potential drawbacks. Table 15.16 provides a summary that will help you decide which solution is best for you.

Table 15.16 Multimedia Device Comparison

Device Type	Pros	Cons
Graphics card with built-in TV tuner and capture	Convenience, single-slot solution	Upgrading requires card replacement.
TV-tuner attachment	Allows upgrade to existing graphics cards; might be movable to newer models	Can't be used with all graphics cards.
Parallel-port attachment	Universal usage on desktop or notebook computer; inexpensive	Frame rate limited by speed of port.
USB-port attachment	Easy installation on late-model USB-equipped computers with Windows 98/Me and Windows 2000	Might not work on Windows 95B OSR 2.x with USB; requires active USB port; not all devices might be compatible with Windows 2000; low bandwidth; not suitable for high-res or full-motion applications.
Dedicated PCI interface card	Fast frame rate for realistic video; works with any graphics card	High resource requirements (IRQ and so on) on some models; requires internal installation.

Table 15.16 Continued

Device Type	Pros	Cons
IEEE-1394 (FireWire) connection to digital video	No conversion from analog to digital needed; all-digital image is very high quality without compression artifacts (blocky areas) in video; fast throughput	Requires IEEE-1394 interface card, IEEE-1394 digital video source; card requires internal installation; some cards don't include capture/editing software; verify that editing software purchased separately works with card.

Troubleshooting Video Capture Devices

Table 15.17 provides some advice for troubleshooting problems with video capture devices.

Table 15.17 Troubleshooting Video Capture Devices

Device Type	Problem	Solutions
Parallel-port attachment	Can't detect device, but printers work okay.	Check port settings; device might require IEEE-1284 settings (EPP and ECP); change in BIOS; ensure device is connected directly to port; avoid daisy-chaining devices unless device specifically allows it; check Windows Device Manager for IRQ conflicts.
TV tuners (built-in graphics card or add-on)	No picture.	Check cabling; set signal source correctly in software.
All devices	Video capture is jerky.	Frame rate is too low. Increasing it might require capturing video in a smaller window; use fastest parallel-port setting you can; use faster CPU and increase RAM to improve results.
All devices	Video playback has pauses, dropped frames.	Hard disk might be pausing for thermal recalibration; use AV-rated SCSI hard drives or UDMA EIDE drives; install correct bus-mastering EIDE drivers for motherboard chipset to improve speed.
USB devices	Device can't be detected or doesn't work properly.	Use Windows 98/Me/2000; late versions of Windows 95 have USB drivers, but they often don't work; if you use a USB hub, be sure it's powered.
Interface cards (all types)	Card can't be detected or doesn't work.	Check for IRQ conflicts in Windows Device Manager; consider setting card manually if possible.
IEEE-1394 cards	Card can't be detected or doesn't work.	Make sure power connector is attached to card if card has 4-pin Molex jack.
All devices	Capture or installation problems.	Use the newest drivers available; check manufacturers' Web site for updates, FAQs, and so on.

3D Graphics Accelerators

The latest trend in PC graphic-display technology is the expanded use of 3D full-motion graphics in gameplaying. Although 3D effects for graphs and charts have been common in business software for years and a limited amount of pseudo-3D imagery has been used in gameplay in programs such as flight simulators and racing games, these programs used low graphics resolutions and did not use 3D lighting, perspective, texture, and shading effects. Onscreen displays made with these programs were always very obviously computer-generated.

Today, the situation is different. The combination of higher screen resolutions, 24-bit or 32-bit color, and dedicated 3D graphics processors has led to games that provide incredibly realistic detail. The latest 3D sports games provide lighting and camera angles so realistic that a casual observer could almost mistake the computer-generated game for an actual broadcast.

Although early 3D sequences were stored on disk for playback, such "canned" 3D sequences are no longer sufficient for today's hardcore PC gamers. Facing stiff competition from high-performance dedicated game machines, such as Sony's PlayStation 2 and Nintendo's GameCube (as well as the PC-based Microsoft Xbox), PCs need the capability to render realistic 3D animations in real time to satisfy hard-core gameplayers. 3D accelerator chips provide that capability.

To construct an animated 3D sequence, a computer can mathematically animate the sequences between keyframes. A keyframe identifies specific points. A bouncing ball, for example, can have three keyframes: up, down, and up. Using these frames as a reference point, the computer can create all the interim images between the top and bottom. This creates the effect of a smooth-bouncing ball.

After it has created the basic sequence, the system can then refine the appearance of the images by filling them in with color. The most primitive and least effective fill method is called *flat shading*, in which a shape is simply filled with a solid color. *Gouraud shading*, a slightly more effective technique, involves the assignment of colors to specific points on a shape. The points are then joined using a smooth gradient between the colors.

A more processor-intensive, and much more effective type of fill, is called *texture mapping*. The 3D application includes patterns—or textures—in the form of small bitmaps that it tiles onto the shapes in the image, just as you can tile a small bitmap to form the wallpaper for your Windows desktop. The primary difference is that the 3D application can modify the appearance of each tile by applying perspective and shading to achieve 3D effects. When lighting effects to simulate fog, glare, directional shadows, and others are added, the 3D animation comes very close indeed to matching reality.

Until the late 1990s, 3D applications had to rely on support from software routines to convert these abstractions into live images. This placed a heavy burden on the system processor in the PC, which has a significant impact on the performance not only of the visual display, but also of any other applications the computer might be running. Starting in the period from 1996 to 1997, chipsets on most video adapters began to take on many of the tasks involved in rendering 3D images, greatly lessening the load on the system processor and boosting overall system performance.

Because there have now been several generations of 3D accelerators, and more and more memory is standard to enable high-resolution 3D animations, most high-quality 3D accelerator cards cost at least $200, and some models packed with 64MB of DDR SDRAM and the best accelerator technology can sell for as much as $400. Both video games and 3D animation programs are taking advantage of their capability to render smooth, photorealistic images at high speeds and in real time.

Fortunately, users with less-demanding 3D performance requirements often can purchase low-end products based on the previous generation of 3D accelerator chips for about $100. These cards typically provide more-than-adequate performance for 2D business applications.

3D technology has added an entirely new vocabulary to the world of video display adapters. Before purchasing a 3D accelerator adapter, you should familiarize yourself with the some of the terms and concepts involved in the 3D image generation process.

The basic function of 3D software is to convert image abstractions into the fully realized images that are then displayed on the monitor. The image abstractions typically consist of the following elements:

■ *Vertices*. Locations of objects in three-dimensional space, described in terms of their X, Y, and Z coordinates on three axes representing height, width, and depth.

- *Primitives.* The simple geometric objects the application uses to create more complex constructions, described in terms of the relative locations of their vertices. This serves not only to specify the location of the object in the 2D image, but also provides perspective because the three axes can define any location in three-dimensional space.

- *Textures.* Two-dimensional bitmap images or surfaces designed to be mapped onto primitives. The software enhances the 3D effect by modifying the appearance of the textures, depending on the location and attitude of the primitive. This process is called *perspective correction.* Some applications use another process, called *MIP mapping,* which uses different versions of the same texture that contain varying amounts of detail, depending on how close the object is to the viewer in the three-dimensional space. Another technique, called *depth cueing,* reduces the color and intensity of an object's fill as the object moves farther away from the viewer.

Using these elements, the abstract image descriptions must then be rendered, meaning they are converted to visible form. Rendering depends on two standardized functions that convert the abstractions into the completed image that is displayed onscreen. The standard functions performed in rendering are

- *Geometry.* The sizing, orienting, and moving of primitives in space and the calculation of the effects produced by the virtual light sources that illuminate the image

- *Rasterization.* The converting of primitives into pixels on the video display by filling the shapes with properly illuminated shading, textures, or a combination of the two

A modern video adapter that includes a chipset capable of 3D video acceleration has special built-in hardware that can perform the rasterization process much more quickly than if it were done by software (using the system processor) alone. Most chipsets with 3D acceleration perform the following rasterization functions right on the adapter:

- *Scan conversion.* The determination of which onscreen pixels fall into the space delineated by each primitive

- *Shading.* The process of filling pixels with smoothly flowing color using the flat or Gouraud shading technique

- *Texture mapping.* The process of filling pixels with images derived from a 2D sample picture or surface image

- *Visible surface determination.* The identification of which pixels in a scene are obscured by other objects closer to the viewer in three-dimensional space

- *Animation.* The process of switching rapidly and cleanly to successive frames of motion sequences

- *Antialiasing.* The process of adjusting color boundaries to smooth edges on rendered objects

Common 3D Techniques

Virtually all 3D cards use the following techniques:

- *Fogging.* Fogging simulates haze or fog in the background of a game screen and helps conceal the sudden appearance of newly rendered objects (buildings, enemies, and so on).

- *Gouraud shading.* Interpolates colors to make circles and spheres look more rounded and smooth.

- *Alpha blending.* One of the first 3D techniques, alpha blending creates translucent objects onscreen, making it a perfect choice for rendering explosions, smoke, water, and glass. Alpha blending also can be used to simulate textures, but it is less realistic than environment-based bump mapping (see "Environment-Based Bump Mapping," later in this chapter.)

Because they are so common, data sheets for advanced cards frequently don't mention them, although these features are present.

Advanced 3D Techniques

The following are some of the latest techniques that leading 3D accelerator cards use. Not every card uses every technique.

Stencil Buffering

Stencil buffering is a technique useful for games such as flight simulators, in which a static graphic element—such as a cockpit windshield frame, known as a HUD (heads up display), used by real-life fighter pilots—is placed in front of dynamically changing graphics (such as scenery, other aircraft, sky detail, and so on). In this example, the area of the screen occupied by the cockpit windshield frame is not rerendered. Only the area seen through the "glass" is rerendered, saving time and improving frame rates for animation.

Z-Buffering

A closely related technique is *Z-buffering*, which originally was devised for CAD (computer-aided drafting) applications. The Z-buffer portion of video memory holds depth information about the pixels in a scene. As the scene is rendered, the Z-values (depth information) for new pixels are compared to the values stored in the Z-buffer to determine which pixels are in "front" of others and should be rendered. Pixels that are "behind" other pixels are not rendered. This method increases speed and can be used along with stencil buffering to create volumetric shadows and other complex 3D objects.

Environment-Based Bump Mapping

This technique introduces special lighting and texturing effects to simulate the rough texture of rippling water, bricks, and other complex surfaces. It combines three separate texture maps (for colors, for height and depth, and for environment—including lighting, fog, and cloud effects). This creates enhanced realism for scenery in games and could also be used to enhance terrain and planetary mapping, architecture, and landscape-design applications. This represents a significant step beyond alpha blending.

Texture Mapping Filtering Enhancements

To improve the quality of texture maps, several filtering techniques have been developed, including MIP mapping, bilinear filtering, trilinear filtering, and anisotropic filtering:

- *Bilinear filtering*. Improves the image quality of small textures placed on large polygons. The stretching of the texture that takes place can create blockiness, but bilinear filtering applies a blur to conceal this visual defect.

- *MIP mapping*. Improves the image quality of polygons that appear to recede into the distance by mixing low-res and high-res versions of the same texture; a form of antialiasing.

- *Trilinear filtering*. Combines bilinear filtering and MIP mapping, calculating the most realistic colors necessary for the pixels in each polygon by comparing the values in two MIP maps. This method is superior to either MIP mapping or bilinear filtering alone.

Note

Bilinear and trilinear filtering work well for surfaces viewed straight-on but might not work so well for oblique angles (such as a wall receding into the distance).

- *Anisotropic filtering.* Some video card makers use another method, called anisotropic filtering, for more realistically rendering oblique-angle surfaces containing text. This technique is used when a texture is mapped to a surface that changes in two of three spatial domains, such as text found on a wall down a roadway (for example, advertising banners at a raceway). The extra calculations used take time, and for that reason, this method is used only by a few video card makers on their fastest video card models.

- *T-buffer.* This technology eliminates aliasing (errors in onscreen images due to an undersampled original) in computer graphics, such as the "jaggies" seen in onscreen diagonal lines; motion stuttering; and inaccurate rendition of shadows, reflections, and object blur. The T-buffer replaces the normal frame buffer with a buffer that accumulates multiple renderings before displaying the image. Unlike some other 3D techniques, T-buffer technology doesn't require rewriting or optimization of 3D software to use this enhancement. The goal of T-buffer technology is to provide a movie-like realism to 3D rendered animations. The downside of enabling antialiasing using a card with T-buffer support is that it can dramatically impact the performance of an application. This technique originally was developed by now-defunct 3dfx.

- *Integrated transform and lighting.* The 3D display process includes transforming an object from one frame to the next and handling the lighting changes that result from those changes. Many 3D cards put the CPU in charge of these functions, but some graphics accelerators—such as the nVidia GeForce 2 GTS and ATI RADEON—integrate separate transform and lighting engines into the accelerator chip for faster 3D rendering, regardless of CPU speed. For more information, see the nVidia and ATI Web sites.

- *Full-Screen antialiasing.* This technology reduces the jaggies visible at any resolution by adjusting color boundaries to provide gradual, rather than abrupt, color changes. Whereas early 3D products used antialiasing for certain objects only, the latest accelerators from nVidia and ATI use this technology for the entire display.

- *Virtual texture.* This technology uses a logical address space for texture memory that is mapped to physical memory addresses on the graphics accelerator chip, on the graphics card, and in main system memory. The small 4KB logical pages allows texture data used with recent 3D games to be fetched on an as-needed basis and rendered immediately as soon as a small amount of texture data is retrieved, preventing slowdowns in graphics rendering caused by the normal practice of retrieving the entire texture before rendering begins. For more information, see the 3Dlabs Web site.

- *Vertex skinning.* Also referred to as vertex blending, this technique blends the connection between two angles, such as the joints in an animated character's arms or legs. NVidia's GeForce series cards use a software technique to perform blending at two matrices, whereas the ATI RADEON chip uses a more realistic hardware-based technique called 4-matrix skinning.

- *Keyframe interpolation.* Also referred to as vertex morphing, this technique animates the transitions between two facial expressions, allowing realistic expressions when skeletal animation can't be used or isn't practical. See the ATI Web site for details.

- *Programmable vertex and pixel shading.* The nVidia GeForce3's nfiniteFX technology enables software developers to customize effects such as vertex morphing and pixel shading (an enhanced form of bump mapping for irregular surfaces), rather than applying a narrow range of predefined effects.

Single- Versus Multiple-Pass Rendering

Various video card makers handle application of these advanced rendering techniques differently. The current trend is toward applying the filters and the basic rendering in a single pass rather than multiple passes. Video cards with single-pass rendering and filtering normally provide higher frame-rate performance in 3D-animated applications and avoid the problems of visible artifacts caused by errors in multiple floating-point calculations during the rendering process.

Hardware Acceleration Versus Software Acceleration

Compared to software-only rendering, hardware-accelerated rendering provides faster animation. Although most software rendering would create more accurate and better-looking images, software rendering is too slow. Using special drivers, these 3D adapters can take over the intensive calculations needed to render a 3D image that software running on the system processor formerly performed. This is particularly useful if you are creating your own 3D images and animation, but it is also a great enhancement to the many modern games that rely extensively on 3D effects. Note that motherboard-integrated video solutions, such as Intel's 810 and 815 series, typically have significantly lower 3D performance because they use the CPU for more of the 3D rendering than 3D video adapter chipsets do.

To achieve greater performance, many of the latest 3D accelerators run their accelerator chips at very high speeds, and some even allow overclocking of the default RAMDAC frequencies. Just as CPUs at high speeds produce a lot of heat, so do high-speed video accelerators. Additionally, just as CPUs now use auxiliary fans for cooling, so do many of the fastest accelerator cards today, such as the new ELSA Gladiac 920, based on the GeForce3 graphics processing unit, as shown in Figure 15.12.

64MB DDR SDRAM with passive heatsinks

Cooling fan over nVidia GeForce3 graphics processor

15-pin analog VGA Out connector

TV/Video Out connector

Power connector for cooling fan

4x AGP slot connector

Figure 15.12 The ELSA Gladiac 920 features a cooling fan to keep its high-speed nVidia GeForce3 accelerator chip cool and also features TV-out. *Photo courtesy ELSA AG.*

Software Optimization

It's important to realize that the presence of an advanced 3D-rendering feature on any given video card is meaningless unless game and application software designers optimize their software to take advantage of the feature. Although various 3D standards exist (OpenGL, Glide, and Direct 3D), video card makers provide drivers that make their games play with the leading standards. Because some cards do play better with certain games, you should read the reviews in publications such as *Maximum PC* to see how your favorite graphics card performs with them.

Some video cards allow you to perform additional optimization by adjusting settings for OpenGL, Direct 3D, RAMDAC and bus clock speeds, and other options.

Note

If you want to enjoy the features of your newest 3D card right away, be sure you purchase the individual retail-packaged version of the card from a hardware vendor. These packages typically come with a sampling of games (full and demo versions) designed or compiled to take advantage of the card with which they're sold. The lower-cost OEM or "white box" versions of video cards are sold without bundled software, come only with driver software, and might differ in other ways from the retail advertised product. Some even use modified drivers, use slower memory or RAMDAC components, or lack special TV-out or other features. Some 3D card makers use different names for their OEM versions to minimize confusion, but others don't. Also, some card makers sell their cards in bulk packs, which are intended for upgrading a large organization with its own support staff. These cards might lack individual documentation or driver CDs and also might lack some of the advanced hardware features found on individual retail-pack video cards.

Application Programming Interfaces

Application programming interfaces (APIs) provide hardware and software vendors a means to create drivers and programs that can work quickly and reliably across a wide variety of platforms. When APIs exist, drivers can be written to interface with the API rather than directly with the operating system and its underlying hardware.

Leading game APIs include SGI's OpenGL, 3Dfx's Glide, and Microsoft's Direct 3D. Glide, an enhanced version of OpenGL, is restricted to graphics cards that use 3Dfx chipsets, whereas OpenGL and Direct 3D (part of DirectX) are available for virtually all leading graphics cards. Thus, virtually all recent video cards provide support for OpenGL and Direct 3D.

Although the video card maker must provide OpenGL support, Microsoft provides support for Direct3D as part of a much larger API called DirectX.

The latest version of DirectX is DirectX 8.0a, which enhances 3D video support and provides other advanced gaming features. For more information about DirectX or to download the latest version, see Microsoft's DirectX Web site at www.microsoft.com/directx.

3D Chipsets

Virtually every mainstream video adapter in current production features a 3D acceleration-compatible chipset. With several generations of 3D adapters on the market from the major vendors, keeping track of the latest products can be difficult. Table 15.18 lists the major 3D chipset manufacturers, the various chipsets they make, and the video adapters that use them.

Note

Chipsets marked (3D only) in this table are used on boards that must be connected to and used with an existing 2D or 2D/3D graphics board in your computer. The rest of these chipsets support both 2D and 3D functions and thus are used to replace existing boards in your computer.

In each manufacturer's section, the following symbols are used to provide a ranking within that manufacturer's chipsets only: NEW—RECENT—OLD. Generally, NEW chipsets provide the fastest 3D performance and advanced 3D rendering features. RECENT chipsets, although lacking some of the speed or features of NEW chipsets, are also worthwhile, especially for those on a budget. OLD are generally superseded by RECENT and NEW chipsets and therefore not recommended. OLD chipsets are listed by chipset only, whereas NEW and RECENT chipsets list selected video cards using those chipsets. Be sure to use this information in conjunction with application-specific and game-specific tests to help you choose the best card/chipset solution for your needs.

For more information about older chipsets, see *Upgrading and Repairing PCs, 12th Edition*, which is available in electronic format on the CD packaged with this book.

Table 15.18   3D Video Chipset Manufacturers

Manufacturer	Chipset	Available Boards
3Dfx Interactive[1]	Voodoo Graphics (3D only OLD)	
	Voodoo Rush (OLD)	
	Voodoo Banshee (OLD)	
	Voodoo2 (3D only OLD)[2]	
	Voodoo3 (RECENT)	3Dfx Voodoo3 2000 AGP, 3Dfx Voodoo3 2000 PCI, 3Dfx Voodoo3 3000 AGP, 3Dfx Voodoo3 3500 AGP
	VSA-100 (RECENT)	3Dfx Voodoo4 4500 AGP, 3Dfx Voodoo4 4500 PCI, 3Dfx Voodoo5 5500 AGP, 3Dfx Voodoo5 5000 PCI
3D labs[4]	Permedia (OLD)	
	Permedia 2(OLD)	
	Permedia 3 (OLD)	
ATI	RAGE I (OLD)	
	RAGE II+ (OLD)	
	RAGE IIC (OLD)	
	3D RAGE II+DVD (OLD)	
	RAGE PRO (OLD)	
	RAGE 128 (RECENT)	ATI ALL-IN-WONDER 128, ATI RAGE FURY, ATI RAGE MAGNUM, ATI XPERT 128, ATI XPERT 99
	Rage 128 Pro (RECENT)	ATI ALL-IN-WONDER 128 PRO, RAGE FURY MAXX, RAGE FURY PRO, XPERT 2000 PRO
	RADEON (NEW)	ALL-IN-WONDER RADEON, RADEON 64MB DDR version, RADEON 32MB DDR version, RADEON 32MB SDRAM version
	RADEON VE (NEW)	RADEON VE
Intel	740 (OLD)	
Matrox	MGA-200 (OLD)	Matrox Millennium G200
	MGA-400 (OLD)	Matrox Millennium G400 series
	MGA-450 (NEW)	Matrox Millennium G450
NVIDIA	RIVA 128(2D/3D OLD)	
	RIVA 128ZX (OLD)	
	RIVA TNT (OLD)	

Table 15.18   Continued

Manufacturer	Chipset	Available Boards
	RIVA TNT2 (RECENT)	Aopen PA3010-A, Aopen PA3010-N, ASUSTeK AGP-V3800 series, Canopus Spectra 5400 series, Creative 3D Blaster RIVA TNT2, Creative 3D Blaster RIVA TNT2 Ultra, Diamond Viper V770, Diamond Viper V770Ultra, ELSA Erazor III, ELSA Synergy II, Guillemot Maxi Gamer Xentor, Guillemot Maxi Xentor 32 Ultra, Hercules Dynamite TNT2, Hercules Dynamite TNT2 Ultra, Leadtek Winfast 3D S320 II series, Micro-Star MS8802, Micro-Star MS8806, Yuan AGP-520T
	VANTA (2D/3D RECENT)	Guillemot Maxi Gamer Phoenix 2, GigaByte GA-620, Leadtek WinFast S320 V-series, Micro-Star MS-8807, Prolink PixelView TNTLite, Yuan AGP-320V, Yuan TUN-320V
	GeForce 256 and 256DDR (RECENT)	Asus AGP V6600 GeForce 256, Asus AGP V6800 Pure/Deluxe, Creative Labs 3D Blaster Annihilator, Creative Labs 3D Blaster Annihilator Pro, ELSA Erazor X2, ELSA Erazor X, Guillemot 3D Prophet, Guillemot 3D Prophet DDR-DVI, LeadTek WinFast GeForce 256
	GeForce 2 series (NEW)	Creative Labs 3D Blaster Annihilator 2 series
	(GTS/Pro/Ultra/MX)	Hercules 3D Prophet II series, Elsa Gladiac series (for Gladiac 920, see GeForce 3), LeadTek WinFast GeForce 2 series, VisionTek GeForce2 series, Asus AGP-7700 and AGP-7100
	GeForce 3 (NEW)	Elsa Gladiac 920, Hercules 3D Prophet III, VisionTek GeForce 3
Micron[5]	v2000 (OLD)	
	v1000 (2D/3D OLD)	
S3[6]	ViRGE (OLD)	
	Savage3D (OLD)	
	Trio3D (OLD)	
	Savage4 (RECENT)	Creative Technology 3D Blaster Savage 4, Diamond SpeedStar A200, Diamond Stealth III S540 series, ELSA Winner II
	Savage 2000 (RECENT)	Diamond Viper II
SiS	6326[7] (OLD)	
	SiS300 (NEW)	Aopen PA300 VR
	SiS305 (NEW)	Aopen PA305, DCS WS305, Pine Technologies SiS305, Chaintech AGP SI40

Table 15.18   Continued

Manufacturer	Chipset	Available Boards
ST Microelectronics	KYRO Power VR Series 3 (NEW)[8]	VideoLogic Vivid!, InnoVISION Inno3D KYRO 2000
VideoLogic[9]	PowerVR PCX2(3D OLD)	Matrox m3D, VideoLogic 3Dx, VideoLogic 5D, VideoLogic 5D Sonic
	PowerVR 250 (OLD)	VideoLogic Neon 250

1. *3Dfx closed in early 2001 after its technology (but not product line) was purchased by nVidia. Although drivers might still be available, all 3Dfx-branded products should be considered orphans without ongoing support.*

2. *Although the Voodoo2 chipset is a 3D-only product with cards that must be connected to a 2D video card to operate, it has the advantage of implementing support for scan line interleaving (SLI). By connecting two identical Voodoo2-chipset PCI cards from the same vendor with a special SLI ribbon cable, each card can be used to render alternate lines (card 1 renders lines 1, 3, 5, and so on; card 2 renders lines 2, 4, 6, and so on). This almost doubles fill rates and makes the combination of two Voodoo2 cards the equivalent of many of the cards that came after it (including the Voodoo3).*

3. *3Dfx acquired video board maker STB in 1999 and began to sell video cards under the 3Dfx name. 3Dfx supplied Voodoo2 and Voodoo Banshee chipsets to other video card makers.*

4. *3Dlabs now concentrates on workstation products based on their Oxygen and Wildcat chipsets.*

5. *Micron, which owns Rendition, supplies legacy graphics drivers for these chipsets but is no longer developing drivers or products in this market.*

6. *S3 Graphics, Inc. (a joint venture between SonicBLUE [formerly S3, Inc.] and VIA Technologies) provides driver support for legacy S3 3D and 2D chipsets. For Diamond Multimedia-branded cards, see Diamond Multimedia's Web site. S3 Graphics, Inc. lists the Savage 2000, Savage 4, and Trio 3D, originally developed by the former S3 company, as current chipset products.*

7. *The SiS 6326 has relatively weak 3D performance but is a popular choice for built-in video on motherboards using an SiS chipset.*

8. *Based on PowerVR technology developed by Imagination Technologies.*

9. *Division of Imagination Technologies; for current PowerVR-based products, see ST Microelectronics' KYRO Power VR Series 3 listing.*

Upgrading or Replacing Your Video Card

With current developments in rock-bottom video card pricing, improvements in 3D display technology, and massive amounts of high-speed memory available on new video cards (up to 64MB!), it makes little sense today to add most upgrades to an existing video card. The component-level upgrades that can be added include

- 3D-only cards, such as the cards based on the original 3Dfx Voodoo and Voodoo2 chipsets, which connect to your existing video card with a pass-through cable

- Memory upgrades to permit higher color depths at a specified screen resolution

- TV tuners, permitting you to watch cable or broadcast TV on your monitor

- Video capture devices, allowing you to capture still or moving video to a file

A few 3D-only cards might still be available from some dealers, but their major benefit (adding 3D support to 2D-only cards) has been superseded by improvements in standard video cards and by the lack of ongoing driver development for current and future Windows versions. Almost any current-model video card offers better and faster 3D, including advanced rendering features that were not available when 3D-only cards were developed.

Note

If you want to learn more about 3D add-on cards and SLI, see Chapter 15 of *Upgrading and Repairing PCs, 11th Edition*, available in electronic form on the CD-ROM included with this book.

Video Card Memory Upgrades

Historically, most video cards have had provisions for some sort of memory upgrade, either with individual Dual Inline Pin (DIP) chips or with proprietary modules. Usually, video cards came in two versions: a low-priced variant with built-in memory and a connection for a memory upgrade, and a top-end variant with its memory fully expanded out of the box.

Starting about 1997, video card vendors began to abandon the idea of user-upgradeable video card memory, probably for the following reasons:

- Most user-upgradeable video cards were never upgraded, but were replaced.

- Recent memory trends have made designing memory upgrades that would work on more than one or two models difficult.

- Increased use of surface-mount technology, high-capacity memory modules, and similar low-cost, high-reliability production techniques mean that a video card with user-upgradeable memory is more expensive to make than a card loaded with 16MB or more of video memory.

- With the massive amounts of video memory available today on video cards (major-brand 32MB AGP-bus video cards retail for less than $200), along with the improvements in 2D and 3D technology, it just makes sense to replace your aging 1MB, 2MB, or 4MB video card with an up-to-date card. When you compare the price of adding 2MB or 4MB of proprietary memory (assuming you can still get it) to your existing video card to the price of a new card with 16MB–32MB or more of memory and better features, you'll find the new cards a much better value.

TV Tuner and Video Capture Upgrades

Most video cards don't have TV tuner and video capture upgrade features built in. New cards with these features tend to be either in the middle to high range of their manufacturers' price structures or less expensive but of poor quality.

These features are exciting if you are already into video editing, want to add video to your Web site, or are trying to create CD-R/CD-RW archives of your home video. If you have an up-to-date video card with acceptable 2D and 3D performance and at least 16MB of video RAM, compare the price of the add-ons to the price of a new card with these features. You'll probably find the add-ons to be less expensive. If your card has 8MB of video RAM or less, I'd recommend replacing it with a new card with these features. Look at sample video captures before making your decision because all video capture solutions require image compression with at least some loss of quality. If you have a digital camcorder with IEEE-1394 (a.k.a. FireWire and i.Link) ports, you should purchase an IEEE-1394 interface board instead to use high-quality pure digital video that needs no conversion.

Note

If you're planning to upgrade to a new video card in the next year or two, find out whether the TV or video add-on you want to buy for your present video card will work with the new model. If it's a TV tuner, you might need to consider other cards from the same vendor your current video card came from. If you're unsure of future compatibility, hold off on your purchase or consider buying a card with the desired features included.

Warranty and Support

Because a video card can go through several driver changes during its effective lifetime (about three years or two operating-system revisions), buying a video card from a major manufacturer usually assures you of better support during the card's lifetime. If you buy a card that uses widely available chipsets (such as nVidia's), you might be able to try a different vendor's version of drivers or use the chipset vendor's "generic" drivers if you don't get satisfactory support from your card vendor.

Keep in mind that using generic drivers (chipset level) or a different brand of drivers can cause problems if your original card's design was tweaked from the chipset maker's reference design. Look at the vendor's technical support forums or third-party discussions on newsgroups, computer information Web sites such as ZDNet, or magazine Web sites to get a feel for the stability, reliability, and usefulness of a vendor's support and driver services. These sources generally also provide alternatives in case of difficulties with a specific brand or chipset.

Comparing Video Cards with the Same Chipset

Many manufacturers create a line of video cards with the same chipset to sell at different pricing points. Why not save some dollars and get the cheapest model? Why not say "price is no object" and get the most expensive one? When you're faced with various cards in the "chipsetX" family, look for differences such as those shown in Table 15.19.

Table 15.19   Comparing Video Cards with the Same Features

Feature	Effect on You
RAMDAC speed	Most current 3D accelerator cards use a 300MHz or faster RAMDAC, which provides flicker-free resolutions beyond 1,024×768. However, less-expensive cards in older designs often used a slower RAMDAC, which reduces maximum and flicker-free resolutions. If you use a 17-inch or larger monitor, this could be an eye-straining problem.
Amount of RAM	Although AGP video cards can use AGP memory (a section of main memory borrowed for texturing), performing as much work as possible on the card's own memory is still faster. PCI cards must perform all functions within their own memory. Less expensive cards in a chipset family often have lower amounts of memory onboard, and most current-model cards aren't expandable. Buy a card with enough memory for your games or applications—today and tomorrow; at least 8MB or more for business and 32MB or more for gaming or 3D graphics and video-related work.
Memory type	Virtually all video cards on the market today use SDRAM or its faster variants (SGRAM or DDR SDRAM). Any of these provides you with high performance in business applications, although DDR SDRAM is preferable when running high-resolution, high-quality 3D games faster.
	The once-popular EDO (Extended Data Out) RAM is obsolete for both main memory and video memory applications.
Core clock speed	Many suppliers adjust the recommended speed of graphics controllers in an effort to provide users with maximum performance. Sometimes the supplier can choose to exceed the rated specification of the graphics chip. Be cautious. Current controller chips are large and can overheat. An overclocked device in an open system with great airflow might work, or it might fail in a period of months from overstress of the circuitry. If you have questions about the rated speed of a controller, check the chip supplier's Web site. Many reputable companies do use overclocked parts, but the best vendors supply large heatsinks or powered fans to avoid overheating. Some vendors even provide on-card temperature monitoring.

Table 15.19   Continued

Feature	Effect on You
RAM Speed (ns rating)	Just as faster system RAM improves overall computer performance, faster video card RAM improves video card performance. Some high-performance 3D video cards now use DDR SDRAM memory chips with a 4ns access time.
TV-out	You can save some money by having it built in, but it's not as important as the other issues listed earlier unless you plan to do video capture. Some of the latest models have hardware-based MPEG-2 compression for higher video quality in less disk space.

Adapter and Display Troubleshooting

Solving most graphics adapter and monitor problems is fairly simple, although costly, because replacing the adapter or display is the usual procedure. However, before you take this step, be sure that you have exhausted all your other options. One embarrassingly obvious fix to monitor display problems that is often overlooked by many users is to adjust the controls on the monitor, such as the contrast and brightness. Although most monitors today have a control panel on the front of the unit, other adjustments might be possible as well.

Some NEC monitors, for example, have a focus adjustment screw on the left side of the unit. Because the screw is deep inside the case, the only evidence of its existence is a hole in the plastic grillwork on top of it. To adjust the monitor's focus, you must stick a long-shanked screwdriver about two inches into the hole and feel around for the screw head. This type of adjustment can save you both an expensive repair bill and the humiliation of being ridiculed by the repair technician. Always examine the monitor case, the documentation, and the manufacturer's Web site or other online services for the locations of adjustment controls.

A defective or dysfunctional adapter or display usually is replaced as a single unit rather than being repaired. Except for specialized CAD or graphics workstation–oriented adapters, virtually all today's adapters cost more to service than to replace, and the documentation required to service the hardware properly is not always available. You usually can't get schematic diagrams, parts lists, wiring diagrams, and other documents for most adapters or monitors. Also, virtually all adapters now are constructed with surface-mount technology that requires a substantial investment in a rework station before you can remove and replace these components by hand. You can't use a $25 pencil-type soldering iron on these boards!

Servicing monitors is a slightly different proposition. Although a display often is replaced as a whole unit, some displays—particularly 20-inch or larger CRTs or most LCD panels—might be cheaper to repair than to replace. If you decide to repair the monitor, your best bet is to either contact the company from which you purchased the display or contact one of the companies that specializes in monitor depot repair. If your monitor has a 15" diagonal measurement or less, consider replacing it with a unit that is 17" or larger because repair costs on small monitors come close to replacement costs, and large monitors aren't much more expensive these days.

Depot repair means that you send in your display to repair specialists who either fix your particular unit or return an identical unit they have already repaired. This usually is accomplished for a flat-rate fee; in other words, the price is the same no matter what they have done to repair your actual unit.

Because you usually get a different (but identical) unit in return, they can ship out your repaired display immediately on receiving the one you sent in, or even in advance in some cases. This way, you have the least amount of downtime and can receive the repaired display as quickly as possible. In some cases, if your particular monitor is unique or one they don't have in stock, you must wait while they repair your specific unit.

Troubleshooting a failed monitor is relatively simple. If your display goes out, for example, a swap with another monitor can confirm that the display is the problem. If the problem disappears when you change the display, the problem is almost certainly in the original display or the cable; if the problem remains, it is likely in the video adapter or PC itself.

Many of the better quality, late-model monitors have built-in self-diagnostic circuitry. Check your monitor's manual for details. Using this feature, if available, can help you determine whether the problem is really in the monitor, in a cable, or somewhere else in the system. If self diagnostics produce an image onscreen, look to other parts of the video subsystem for your problem.

The monitor cable can sometimes be the source of display problems. A bent pin in the DB-15 connector that plugs into the video adapter can prevent the monitor from displaying images, or it can cause color shifts. Most of the time, you can repair the connector by carefully straightening the bent pin with sharp-nosed pliers.

If the pin breaks off or if the connector is otherwise damaged, you can sometimes replace the monitor cable. Some monitor manufacturers use cables that disconnect from the monitor and the video adapter, whereas others are permanently connected. Depending on the type of connector the device uses at the monitor end, you might have to contact the manufacturer for a replacement.

If you narrow down the problem to the display, consult the documentation that came with the monitor or call the manufacturer for the location of the nearest factory repair depot. Third-party depot repair service companies are also available that can repair most displays (if they are no longer covered by a warranty); their prices often are much lower than factory service. Check the Vendor List on the CD for several companies that do depot repair of computer monitors and displays.

Caution

You should never attempt to repair a CRT monitor yourself. Touching the wrong component can be fatal. The display circuits can hold extremely high voltages for hours, days, or even weeks after the power is shut off. A qualified service person should discharge the cathode ray tube and power capacitors before proceeding.

For most displays, you are limited to making simple adjustments. For color displays, the adjustments can be quite formidable if you lack experience. Even factory service technicians often lack proper documentation and service information for newer models; they usually exchange your unit for another and repair the defective one later. Never buy a display for which no local factory repair depot is available.

If you have a problem with a display or an adapter, it pays to call the manufacturer, who might know about the problem and make repairs available. Sometimes, when manufacturers encounter numerous problems with a product, they might offer free repair, replacements, or another generous offer that you would never know about if you did not call.

Remember, also, that many of the problems you might encounter with modern video adapters and displays are related to the drivers that control these devices rather than to the hardware. Be sure you have the latest and proper drivers before you attempt to have the hardware repaired; a solution might already be available.

Troubleshooting Monitors

Problem

No picture.

Solution

If the LED on the front of the monitor is yellow or flashing green, the monitor is in power-saving mode. Move the mouse or press Alt+Tab on the keyboard and wait up to one minute to wake up the system if the system is turned on.

If the LED on the front of the monitor is green, the monitor is in normal mode (receiving a signal), but the brightness and contrast are set incorrectly; adjust them.

If no lights are lit on the monitor, check the power and the power switch. Check the surge protector or power director to ensure that power is going to the monitor. Replace the power cord with a known-working spare if necessary. Retest. Replace the monitor with a known-working spare to ensure that the monitor is the problem.

Check data cables at the monitor and video card end.

Problem

Jittery picture quality.

Solution

LCD monitors. Use display-adjustment software to reduce or eliminate pixel jitter and pixel swim.

All monitors. Check cables for tightness at the video card and the monitor (if removable):

- Remove the extender cable and retest with the monitor plugged directly into the video card. If the extended cable is bad, replace it.

- Check the cables for damage; replace as needed.

- If problems are intermittent, check for interference. (Microwave ovens near monitors can cause severe picture distortion when turned on.)

CRT monitors. Check refresh-rate settings; reduce them until acceptable picture quality is achieved:

- Use onscreen picture adjustments until an acceptable picture quality is achieved.

- If problems are intermittent and can be "fixed" by waiting or by gently tapping the side of the monitor, the monitor power supply is probably bad or has loose connections internally. Service or replace the monitor.

Troubleshooting Video Cards and Drivers

Problem

Display works in DOS, but not in Windows.

Solution

If you have an acceptable picture quality in MS-DOS mode (system boot) but no picture in Windows, most likely you have an incorrect or a corrupted video driver installed in Windows. Boot Windows 9x/Me in Safe Mode (which uses a VGA driver), boot Windows 2000 in Enable VGA mode, or install the VGA driver and restart Windows. If Safe Mode or VGA works, get the correct driver for the video card and reinstall.

If you have overclocked your card with a manufacturer-supplied or third-party utility, you might have set the speed too high. Restart the system in Safe Mode, and reset the card to run at its default speed.

Problem

Can't replace built-in video card with add-on PCI video card.

Solution

Check with the video card and system vendor for a list of acceptable replacement video cards. Try another video card with a different chipset. Check the BIOS or motherboard for jumper or configuration settings to disable built-in video. Place the add-on card in a different PCI slot.

Problem

Can't select desired color depth and resolution combination.

Solution

Verify that the card is properly identified in Windows and that the card's memory is working properly. Use diagnostic software provided by the video card or chipset maker to test the card's memory. If the hardware is working properly, check for new drivers.

Problem

Can't select desired refresh rate.

Solution

Verify that the card and monitor are properly identified in Windows. Obtain updated drivers for the card and monitor.

DisplayMate

DisplayMate is a unique diagnostic and testing program designed to thoroughly test your video adapter and display. It is somewhat unique in that most conventional PC hardware diagnostics programs do not emphasize video testing the way this program does.

I find it useful not only in testing whether a video adapter is functioning properly, but also in examining video displays. You easily can test the image quality of a display, which allows you to make focus, centering, brightness and contrast, color level, and other adjustments much more accurately than before. If you are purchasing a new monitor, you can use the program to evaluate the sharpness and linearity of the display and to provide a consistent way of checking each monitor you are considering. If you use projection systems for presentations—as I do in my PC hardware seminars—you will find it invaluable for setting up and adjusting the projector.

DisplayMate also can test a video adapter thoroughly. It sets the video circuits into each possible video mode so you can test all its capabilities. It also helps you determine the performance level of your card, both with respect to resolution and colors as well as speed. You can then use the program to benchmark the performance of the display, which enables you to compare one type of video adapter system to another.

See the Vendor List on the CD for more information on DisplayMate (formerly Sonera) Technologies, the manufacturer and distributor of DisplayMate.

Some video-card vendors supply a special version of DisplayMate for use in diagnostics testing.

CHAPTER 16

Audio Hardware

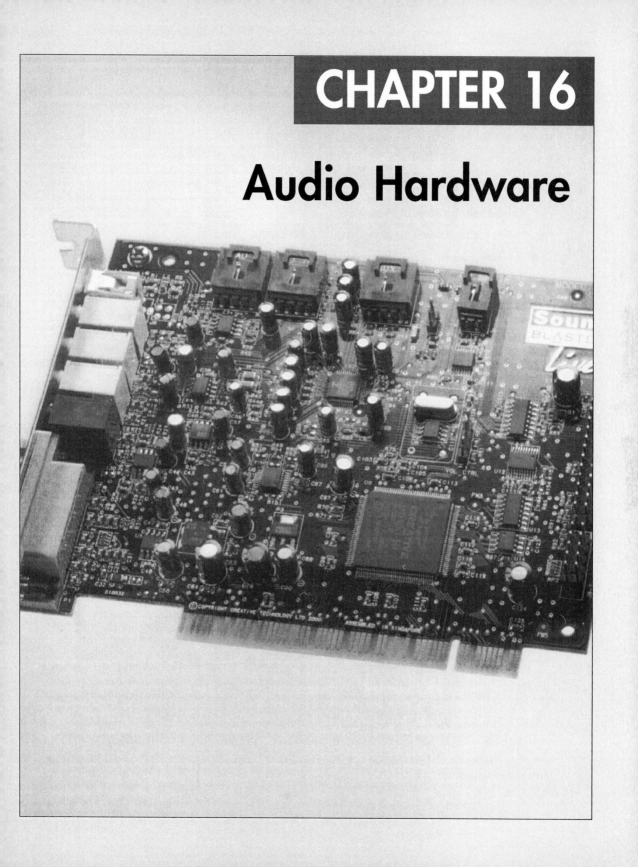

Since the first edition of this book was published in 1988, a lot has happened to audio hardware. Although the Macintosh, first introduced in 1984, included high-quality audio capabilities in its built-in hardware, PCs were still limited to the same rudimentary beeps that had been developed for the original IBM PC in 1981. Computers used beeps for little other than to signal problems such as a full keyboard buffer or errors during the POST (power on self test) sequence.

Since 1988, audio capabilities have come to the PC in a big way, and from the competition among many competitors have come de facto hardware and software standards for audio, which are widely supported. Audio hardware has gone from being an expensive, exotic add-on to being an assumed part of virtually any system configuration.

Today's PC audio hardware might take one of the following forms:

- An audio adapter on a PCI or an ISA expansion card that you install into a bus slot into the computer
- A sound chip on the motherboard from companies such as Crystal, Analog Devices, Sigmatel, ESS, or others
- Integrated into the motherboard's main chipset, as with some of Intel, SiS, and VIA Technologies's most recent chipsets for low-cost computers

Regardless of their location, the audio features use jacks for speakers and a microphone. In addition, almost all of them also provide dedicated jacks for analog joysticks and MIDI hardware, although some of the latest models rely on USB port connections for joysticks. On the software side, the audio adapter requires the support of a driver that you install either directly from an application or in your computer's operating system. This chapter focuses on the audio products found in today's PCs, their uses, and how you install and operate them.

Early PC Audio Adapters

At first, consumer audio adapters were used only for games. Several companies, including AdLiB, Roland, and Creative Labs, released products by the late 1980s. In 1989, Creative Labs introduced the Game Blaster, which provided FM-synthesized sound to a handful of computer games. The question for many buyers was, "Why spend $100 for a card that adds sound to a $50 game?" More importantly, because no sound standards existed at the time, the sound card you selected might turn out to be useless with some games if they chose not to specifically support it.

Note

About the same time as the release of the Game Blaster, hardware supporting the Musical Instrument Digital Interface (MIDI) became available for the PC. At this time, however, such hardware was used only in very specialized recording applications. As MIDI support became a more common feature in musical instruments, though, it also became a more affordable PC add-on.

The Game Blaster was soon replaced by the Sound Blaster, which was compatible with the AdLiB sound card and the Creative Labs Game Blaster card. The Sound Blaster included a built-in microphone jack, stereo output, and a MIDI port for connecting the PC to a synthesizer or other electronic musical instrument. Finally, the audio adapter had the potential for uses other than games. The follow-up Sound Blaster Pro featured improved sound when compared to the original Sound Blaster.

Although the Sound Blaster was just one of a number of audio adapters on the market in the early days of the technology, it eventually became a de facto standard in its Sound Blaster Pro and subsequent versions. Unlike de jure standards such as the IEEE-1394 port, which is an official standard of the IEEE organization, de facto standards are those that develop informally due to the widespread acceptance of the market leader's products in a particular segment of the marketplace.

Limitations of Sound Blaster Pro Compatibility

As long as MS-DOS was the standard, a sound card needed to be Sound Blaster Pro compatible to be popular in the marketplace. Ideally, a Sound Blaster Pro–compatible card would be capable of using the same IRQ, DMA, and I/O port addresses as a Sound Blaster Pro card from Creative Labs and would be used by an application program in the same way as an actual Sound Blaster Pro.

This was the goal of compatibility, but many third-party sound cards fell short in a variety of ways. Some cards required two separate sets of hardware resources, using one set of IRQ, DMA, and I/O port addresses for native mode and a second set for Sound Blaster Pro compatibility. Others worked well within Windows or within an MS-DOS session running with Windows in the background but required the user to install a DOS-based Terminate and Stay Resident (TSR) driver program to work in MS-DOS itself. As a result, most MS-DOS game developers had to develop configurations for each of the leading sound cards, frustrating users whose sound cards might not be listed or forcing users to select a lower-quality emulation setting instead of running the card with its native features.

The replacement of MS-DOS by 32-bit Windows versions starting with Windows 95 has made life easier for game and other multimedia developers because of a Microsoft innovation called DirectX, which was first introduced in December of 1995.

DirectX and Audio Adapters

Microsoft's DirectX is a series of Application Program Interfaces (APIs) that sit between multimedia applications and hardware. Unlike MS-DOS applications that required developers to develop direct hardware support for numerous models and brands of audio cards, video cards, and game controllers, Windows uses DirectX to "talk" to hardware in a more direct manner than normal Windows drivers do. This improves program performance and frees the software developer from the need to change the program to work with different devices. Instead, a game developer must work with only the DirectX sound engine, DirectX 3D renderer, and DirectX modem or network interface routines.

Note

For more information about DirectX and sound hardware, see "3D Audio," page 909, later in this chapter.

Thanks to DirectX, sound card and chipset developers are assured that their products will work with recent and current versions of Windows. However, if you still enjoy playing MS-DOS–based games, current audio adapters, chipsets, and integrated audio solutions still might present a compatibility challenge to you because of fundamental hardware differences between the ISA expansion slots used by classic Creative Labs and other sound cards and PCI slots, chipsets, and integrated audio.

Note

For more information about using PCI sound hardware with MS-DOS games, see "Legacy (MS-DOS) Game Support Issues," page 892, later in this chapter.

PC Multimedia History

Virtually every computer on the market today is equipped with some type of audio adapter and a CD-ROM or CD-ROM–compatible drive. Computers equipped with an audio adapter and a CD-ROM–compatible drive are often referred to as *Multimedia* PCs after the old MPC-1, MPC-2, and

MPC-3 standards that were used to rate early multimedia computers; MPC-1 was introduced in 1990. The last MPC standard, MPC-3, was introduced in June 1995 and specified the following hardware and software:

- CPU—75MHz Pentium CPU
- RAM—8MB
- Hard disk—540MB
- Floppy disk—1.44MB (3 1/2-inch high-density)
- CD-ROM drive—Quad-speed (4X)
- Audio sampling rate—16-bit
- VGA video resolution—640×480
- Color depth—65,536 colors (16-bit color)
- I/O devices—Serial, Parallel, MIDI, Game port
- Minimum operating system—Windows 3.1

All computers built from 1996 on exceed the MPC Level 3 specification by a substantial margin in every area if they have an audio adapter and a CD-ROM–compatible drive installed.

Note

For more information about the MPC series of multimedia standards, see Chapter 20 of *Upgrading and Repairing PCs, 11th Edition*, available in electronic form on the CD-ROM accompanying this book.

Suggested Multimedia Minimums

The following list of specifications gives you a comfortable multimedia experience today; in fact, even the lowest-cost computer currently available at retail will usually meet or exceed these specifications:

- CPU—600MHz Pentium III, Celeron, Athlon, Duron, or other Pentium-class processor
- RAM—64MB
- Hard disk—2GB
- Floppy disk—1.44MB (3 1/2-inch high-density)
- CD-ROM drive—24X
- Audio sampling rate—16-bit
- VGA video resolution—1024×768
- Color depth—16.8 million colors (24-bit color)
- I/O devices—Serial, Parallel, MIDI, Game port, USB
- Minimum operating system—Windows 98 or Windows Me

Note that although speakers or headphones are technically not a part of the MPC specification or the updated list, they are certainly required for sound reproduction. Additionally, sound input for voice recording or voice control also requires a microphone. Although low-cost powered or unpowered speakers typically are included with sound card–equipped systems, you will normally want to replace them with speakers or headphones that provide the mixture of size, frequency response, and overall sound quality you need.

Beyond MPC Standards—PC Design Standards

Because the MPC specifications reflect multimedia's past, users who want to know what comes next need somewhere else to turn for guidance. Microsoft and Intel jointly manage the PC Design Guide Web site at www.pcdesguide.com, where the older PC99 and current PC2001 specifications and addenda can be read and reviewed. These standards are widely followed by the industry and point the way to many other enhancements for audio hardware and software in the Windows environment.

Although virtually every computer is a "Multimedia PC" today, the features of the audio adapter in your system will help determine how satisfied you will be with the wide range of specialized uses for multimedia-equipped systems today.

Later in this chapter, you learn more about the features you need to specify to ensure your audio adapter—regardless of type—is ready to work for you.

Putting Basic Multimedia to Work

With any multimedia PC equipped with speakers and a microphone, you can

- Run sound-enabled multimedia game and educational software
- Add prerecorded or custom sound effects to business presentations and training software
- Create music by using MIDI hardware and software
- Add voice notes to files
- Use audio/video conferencing and network telephony software, such as Microsoft NetMeeting and Net2Phone
- Add sound effects to operating system events by using the Windows Control Panel Sounds icon
- Enable PC use by handicapped individuals by using text-to-speech software and HTML screen readers
- Play audio CDs and other popular music sources, such as MP3s

However, if you demand higher levels of system performance, want superior 3D audio, or want other specialized uses, you need to go beyond basic multimedia features. In the following section, you learn more about the features available in typical audio adapters today, as well as advanced features you might need to look for to accomplish certain tasks.

Audio Adapter Features

To make an intelligent purchasing decision, you should be aware of some audio adapter basic components and the features they provide, as well as the advanced features you can get on better audio adapters. The following sections discuss the features you should consider while evaluating audio adapters for your PC.

Basic Connectors

Most audio adapters have the same basic connectors. These 1/8-inch minijack connectors provide the means of passing sound signals from the adapter to speakers, headphones, and stereo systems, and of receiving sound from a microphone, CD player, tape player, or stereo. The four types of connectors your audio adapter should have at a minimum are shown in Figure 16.1. The colors listed for each jack are those specified in the PC99 Design Guide and might vary on some audio adapters:

Figure 16.1 The basic input and output connectors that most audio adapters have in common.

- *Stereo line, or audio, out connector (lime green).* The line-out connector is used to send sound signals from the audio adapter to a device outside the computer. You can hook up the cables from the line-out connector to stereo speakers, a headphone set, or your stereo system. If you hook up the PC to your stereo system, you can have amplified sound.

- *Stereo line, or audio, in connector (light blue).* With the line-in connector, you can record or mix sound signals from an external source, such as a stereo system or VCR, to the computer's hard disk.

- *Rear out or speaker/headphone connector (no standard color).* Older sound cards often provided an amplified jack supplying up to four watts of power for use with unpowered speakers or headphones along with the line-out connector. Today, you are more likely to find this jack being used for rear speakers in four-speaker setups. The rear out jack often is disabled by default; check your audio adapter properties or setup program to see whether you need to enable this port when you connect rear speakers.

Note

If you have only a single speaker/line-out connector, you must carefully adjust your mixer volume control and the volume control on your amplified speakers to find the best-quality sound. Don't use powered speakers with an already-amplified sound if you can avoid it.

- *Microphone, or mono, in connector (pink).* The mono-in connector is used to connect a microphone for recording your voice or other sounds to disk. This microphone jack records in mono, not in stereo, and is therefore not suitable for high-quality music recordings. Many audio adapters cards use Automatic Gain Control (AGC) to improve recordings. This feature adjusts the recording levels on-the-fly. A 600ohm–10,000ohm dynamic or condenser microphone works best with this jack. Some inexpensive audio adapters use the line-in connector instead of a separate microphone jack.

■ *Joystick connector (gold).* The joystick connector is a 15-pin, D-shaped connector that can connect to any standard joystick or game controller. Sometimes the joystick port can accommodate two joysticks if you purchase an optional Y-adapter. Many computers already contain a joystick port as part of a multifunction I/O circuit on the motherboard or an expansion card. If this is the case, you must note which port your operating system or application is configured to use when connecting the game controller.

■ *MIDI connector (gold).* Audio adapters typically use the same joystick port as their MIDI connector. Two of the pins in the connector are designed to carry signals to and from a MIDI device, such as an electronic keyboard. In most cases, you must purchase a separate MIDI connector from the audio adapter manufacturer that plugs into the joystick port and contains the two round, 5-pin DIN connectors used by MIDI devices, plus a connector for a joystick. Because their signals use separate pins, you can connect the joystick and a MIDI device at the same time. You need this connector only if you plan to connect your PC to external MIDI devices. You can still play the MIDI files found on many Web sites by using the audio adapter's internal synthesizer.

Note

Some recent systems with onboard audio lack the joystick/MIDI connector, but you can use digital game controllers that feature a game port or USB connector to attach your game controllers to the USB port. And, as mentioned earlier, you can also attach MIDI devices through the same USB connector with a suitable interface box.

■ *Internal CD-audio connector.* Most audio adapters have an internal 4-pin connector you can use to plug an internal CD-ROM drive directly into the adapter, using a small round cable. This connection enables you to channel audio signals from the CD-ROM directly to the audio adapter, so you can play the sound through the computer's speakers. Note that this connector is different from the CD-ROM controller connector found on some audio adapters. This connector does not carry data from the CD-ROM to the system bus; it provides the CD-ROM drive only with direct audio access to the speakers. If you install a new CD-ROM, CD-RW, or DVD drive or a new sound card, be sure you attach this CD-audio cable between the card and the drive; otherwise, you will not be able to play music CDs or hear some game audio.

Tip

The line-in, line-out, and speaker connectors on an audio adapter all use the same 1/8-inch minijack socket. The three jacks are usually labeled, but when setting up a computer on or under a desk, these labels on the back of the PC can be difficult to read. One of the most common reasons a PC fails to produce any sound is that the speakers are plugged into the wrong socket.

To avoid this problem, many consumer-oriented systems color-code microphone and speaker cables and the corresponding connections on the sound card. If you replace the color-coded OEM sound product, add labels if the replacements are not color-coded or use a color-code different from the original product's.

Before the PC99 design guide color standards were introduced, red was used for Mic, green for Line-Out, blue for Line-In, and black for Amplified (Speaker)-Out by most vendors who color-coded their audio connectors. To see the PC99 Design Guide color-coding, which primarily uses pastel colors, go to **www.pcdesguide.com/documents/pc99icons.htm**.

Connectors for Advanced Features

Many of the newest sound cards are designed for advanced gaming, DVD audio playback, and sound production uses and have additional connectors to support these uses, such as

- *MIDI in and MIDI out.* Some advanced sound cards don't require you to convert the game port (joystick port) to MIDI interfacing by offering these ports on a separate external connector. This permits you to use a joystick and have an external MIDI device connected at the same time. Typical location: external device.

- *SPDIF (also called SP/DIF) in and SPDIF out.* The Sony/Philips Digital Interface receives digital audio signals directly from compatible devices without converting them to analog format first. Typical location: external device. SPDIF interfaces are also referred to by some vendors as "Dolby Digital" interfaces.

Note

SPDIF connectors use cables with the standard RCA jack connector but are designed to work specifically at an impedance of 75ohms—the same as composite video cables. Thus, you can use RCA-jack composite video cables with your SPDIF connectors. Although audio cables are also equipped with RCA jacks, their impedance is different, making them a less desirable choice.

- *CD SPDIF.* Connects compatible CD-ROM drives with SPDIF interfacing to the digital input of the sound card. Typical location: side of audio card.

- *TAD in.* Connects internal modems with Telephone Answering Device support to the sound card for sound processing of voice messages. Typical location: side of audio card.

- *Digital DIN out.* This supports multispeaker digital speaker systems, such as those produced by Cambridge for use with the SoundBlaster Live! series. Typical location: external device.

- *Aux in.* Provides input for other sound sources, such as a TV tuner card. Typical location: side of audio card.

- *I2S in.* This enables the sound card to accept digital audio input from an external source, such as two-channel decoded AC-3 from DVD decoders and MPEG-2 Zoom Video. Typical location: side of audio card.

Sometimes, these additional connectors are found on the card itself, or sometimes they are attached to an external breakout box or daughtercard. For example, the Sound Blaster Live! Platinum 5.1 is a two-piece unit. The audio adapter itself plugs into a PCI slot, but some additional connectors are routed to a breakout box called the LiveDrive IR, which fits into an unused drive bay, as seen in Figure 16.2.

Figure 16.3 shows a Voyetra Turtle Beach's Santa Cruz audio adapter card with the internal connectors common on today's 3D sound cards.

Volume Control

Some older audio adapters include a thumbwheel volume control next to the input/output jacks, although sophisticated sound cards have no room for it. This control is usually redundant because the operating system or the software included with the adapter typically provides a combination of keys or a visual slider control you can use to adjust the volume. In fact, the volume wheel can be troublesome; if you aren't aware of its existence and it is turned all the way down, you might be puzzled by the adapter's failure to produce sufficient sound.

Figure 16.2   The Sound Blaster Live! Platinum 5.1 comes with the LiveDrive IR to support its many features.

Figure 16.3   Voyetra Turtle Beach's Santa Cruz is a typical example of an advanced 3D sound card.

If the PC speakers are amplified, remember to check that the power is on and the volume control on the speakers is turned up.

MIDI Support Features

At one time, when evaluating audio adapters, you had to decide whether to buy a monophonic or stereophonic card. Today, virtually all audio adapters are stereophonic and can play music using the MIDI standard, which plays scores using either synthesized instruments or digital samples stored on the audio adapter or in RAM.

Stereophonic cards produce many voices concurrently and from two sources. A voice is a single sound produced by the adapter. A string quartet uses four voices, one for each instrument. On the other hand, a polyphonic instrument, such as a piano, requires one voice for each note of a chord. Thus, to fully reproduce the capabilities of a pianist requires 10 voices—one for each finger. The more voices an audio adapter is capable of producing, the better the sound fidelity. The best audio adapters on the market today can produce up to 1,024 simultaneous voices.

Early audio adapters used FM synthesis for MIDI support; the Yamaha OPL2 (YM3812) featured 11 voices, whereas the OPL3 (YMF262) featured 20 voices and stereophonic sound. However, virtually all audio adapters today use recorded samples for MIDI support; audio adapters using this feature are referred to as *wavetable* adapters.

Wavetable MIDI

Wavetable audio adapters use digital recordings of real instruments and sound effects instead of imitations generated by an FM chip; when you hear a trumpet in a MIDI score played on a wavetable sound card, you hear the sound of an actual trumpet, not a synthetic imitation of a trumpet. The first cards featuring wavetable support stored 1MB of sound clips embedded in ROM chips on the card. However, with the widespread use of the high-speed PCI bus for sound cards and large amounts of RAM in computers, most soundcards now use a so-called "soft wavetable" approach, loading 2MB–8MB of sampled musical instruments into the computer's RAM.

Note

Some vendors, such as Creative Labs, Voyetra Turtle Beach, and Yamaha, have produced daughtercards to add wavetable support to FM-synthesis or soft-wavetable sound cards. Most of these products have been discontinued due to the popularity and high quality of PCI audio adapters with large sample sets of soft wavetable sounds.

Altlhough most games up to this point have not used MIDI sound, the improvements in Direct X 8 will make MIDI sound far more prevalent for game soundtracks. Whether you play the latest games or like music, good MIDI performance is likely to be important to you.

If your sound card is one of the low-priced PCI models that offers only 32 voices, check with your vendor for a software upgrade to a higher number for better MIDI reproduction. All Ensoniq-based 32-voice sound cards from any OEM vendor can be upgraded to 64 voices through software available at Ensoniq's Web site: www.ensoniq.com/audiopci.html. You should also consider replacing your sound card with a newer model because many models now on the market support more than 500 simultaneous voices and can be purchased for under $100.

Data Compression

Virtually all audio adapters on the market today can easily produce CD-quality audio, which is sampled at 44.1KHz. At this rate, recorded files (even of your own voice) can consume more than 10MB for every minute of recording. To counter this demand for disk space, many audio adapters include their own data-compression capability. For example, the Sound Blaster ASP 16 includes on-the-fly compression of sound files in ratios of 2:1, 3:1, or 4:1.

Most manufacturers of audio adapters use an algorithm called Adaptive Differential Pulse Code Modulation (ADPCM) compression to reduce file size by more than 50%. However, a simple fact of audio technology is that when you use such compression, you lose sound quality.

Because it degrades sound quality, no standard exists for the use of ADPCM. Creative Labs uses a proprietary hardware approach, whereas Microsoft is promoting the Business Audio ADPCM design, developed with Compaq. When you install an audio adapter, several codecs (programs that perform compression and decompression) are installed. Typically, some form of ADPCM is installed along with many others. To see which codecs are available on your system, open the Windows Control Panel and open the Multimedia icon (Windows 9x) or the Sounds and Multimedia icon (Windows 2000). With Windows 9x, click the Devices tab followed by the plus sign next to Audio Compression to see the installed codecs. With Windows 2000, click the Hardware tab, followed by audio codecs and properties. If you create your own recorded audio for use on another computer, both computers must use the same codec. You can select which codec you want to use for recording sounds with most programs, including the Windows Sound Recorder.

The most popular compression standard is the Motion Pictures Experts Group (MPEG) standard, which works with both audio and video compression and is gaining support in the non-PC world from products such as the new crop of DVD players now hitting the market. MPEG by itself provides a potential compression ratio of 30:1, and largely because of this, full-motion–video MPEG DVD and CD-ROM titles are now available. The popular MP3 sound compression scheme is an MPEG format, and it can be played back on the latest versions of the Windows 9x Media Player, as well as by MP3-only player programs and devices.

Multipurpose Digital Signal Processors

Many audio adapters use digital signal processors (DSPs) to add intelligence to the adapter, freeing the system processor from work-intensive tasks, such as filtering noise from recordings or compressing audio on-the-fly.

The Sound Blaster Live!'s EMU10K1 programmable DSP, for example, supports hardware sound acceleration needed by the latest version of Microsoft DirectX/DirectSound 3D, which enables multiple sounds to be played at the same time to synchronize with the onscreen action in a video game. The DSP can be upgraded with software downloads to accommodate more simultaneous audio streams. The widespread use of DSPs in better-quality audio adapters enables you to upgrade them through software instead of the time-consuming, expensive process of physical replacement. For additional examples of DSPs, see "Who's Who in Audio," page 906, later in this chapter.

CD-ROM Connectors

A few older audio adapters doubled as a CD-ROM controller, or interface, card. Before the EIDE interface made the CD-ROM a ubiquitous PC component, connecting the drive to the audio adapter was an inexpensive means of adding multimedia capabilities to a system. Although some adapters provide a SCSI port that you can theoretically use to connect any SCSI device, others used a proprietary connection that accommodates only a select few CD-ROM drives that support the same interface. The proprietary connectors once used by early Creative Labs Sound Blaster multimedia upgrade kits have long been obsolete and cannot be used with today's standard IDE and SCSI-interface CD-ROM drives. Although a few more recent ISA sound cards featured an IDE connector, this connector is far slower than the modern EIDE host adapter found on the motherboard. The IDE or SCSI CD-ROM interface has disappeared from PCI-based audio adapters; if you need to attach a CD-ROM drive, use the normal IDE interface on your motherboard or a SCSI host adapter.

◄◄ For more information on adding a CD-ROM drive to your system, see Chapter 13, "Optical Storage," p. 687.

Sound Drivers

As with many PC components, a software driver provides a vital link between an audio adapter and the application or operating system that uses it. Operating systems such as Windows 9x, Windows 2000, and Windows NT include a large library of drivers for most of the audio adapters on the market. In most cases, these drivers are written by the manufacturer of the audio adapter and only distributed by Microsoft. You might find that the drivers that ship with the adapter are more recent than those included with the operating system. As always, the best place to find the most recent drivers for a piece of hardware is the manufacturer's own Web site or other online service.

DOS applications do not usually include as wide a range of driver support as an operating system, but you should find that most games and other programs support the Sound Blaster adapters. If you are careful to buy an adapter that is compatible with Sound Blaster, you should have no trouble finding driver support for all your applications. It's preferable to have this support through hardware rather than software. If your game program locks up when you try to detect the sound card during configuration, set the card type and settings manually. This is often a symptom of inadequate emulation for Sound Blaster by a third-party card. If you have problems, check the game developer's or audio adapter's Web site for patches or workarounds. Remember that with many recent audio adapters, you might need to load a Sound Blaster emulation program into RAM before you start the game.

Choosing the Best Audio Adapter for Your Needs

Although sound features in computers have become commonplace, the demand for sophisticated uses for sound hardware have grown and demanded more and more powerful hardware. If your idea of a perfect multimedia PC includes any of the following, the plain-vanilla multimedia hardware found in many of today's PCs won't be sufficient:

■ Realistic 3D and 360° sound for games

■ Theater-quality audio for DVD movies

■ Voice dictation and voice command

■ Creating and recording MIDI, MP3, CD-Audio, and WAV audio files

Table 16.1 summarizes the additional hardware features and software you'll need to achieve the results you want with your high-performance audio adapter. The following sections examine these advanced uses and the features you'll need for each in detail.

Table 16.1   Audio Adapter Intended Uses and Features Comparison

Intended Use	Features You Need	Additional Hardware	Additional Software
Gaming	Game port; 3D sound; audio acceleration	Gaming controller; rear speakers	Games
DVD movies	Dolby 5.1 decoding	Dolby 5.1 speakers compatible with audio adapter	MPEG decoding program
Voice dictation and voice command	Audio adapter on program's compatibility list or equal to SB16 in quality	Voice-recognition microphone	Voice-dictation software
Creating MIDI files	MIDI In adapter	MIDI-compatible musical keyboard	MIDI composing program

Table 16.1   Continued

Intended Use	Features You Need	Additional Hardware	Additional Software
Creating MP3 files	Digital audio extraction	CD-R or CD-RW drive	MP3 ripper
Creating WAV files	Microphone	CD-R or CD-RW drive	Sound recording program
Creating CD audio files	External sound source	CD-R or CD-RW drive	WAV or MP3 to CD audio conversion program

The following sections discuss many of these special uses in detail.

Gaming

Thanks to the widespread availability of audio adapters, game playing has taken on a new dimension. Support for 3D and surround digitized sound and realistic MIDI music in current games has added a level of realism that would otherwise be impossible even with today's sophisticated graphics hardware. Mere stereo playback isn't good enough for hardcore gamers who want to be able to hear monsters behind them or feel the impact of a car crash. These users should choose sound cards with support for four or more speakers and some form of directional sound, such as Creative Labs's EAX technology used in Sound Blaster Live! or Sensaura's MultiDrive used by ESS, VideoLogic, and others. Many sound cards feature support for these standards, either through direct hardware support or through software emulation and conversion. As with 3D video cards (see Chapter 15, "Video Hardware"), most cards today merely need to work with the audio APIs in the current revision of Microsoft's DirectX technology.

Any audio adapter built in the last few years will still work with today's games, thanks in large part to the Hardware Emulation Layer (HEL) built into DirectX. HEL emulates the features of newer hardware, such as 3D sound, on older hardware. However, as you can imagine, the task of emulating advanced performance on older hardware can slow down gameplay and doesn't produce sounds as realistic as those available with today's best audio adapters.

Sound Card Minimums for Gameplay

The replacement of the old ISA Sound Blaster Pro standard by PCI sound card standards has helped improve performance a great deal, but for the best gameplay with current and forthcoming titles, you need to look at sound cards with the following features:

- *3D audio support in the chipset. 3D audio* means you'll be able to hear sounds appear to move toward you, away from you, and at various angles corresponding to what's happening onscreen. Microsoft's DirectX 8.0 includes support for 3D audio, but you'll have faster 3D audio performance if you use an audio adapter with 3D support built in (see "Who's Who in Audio," page 906, later in this chapter).

  DirectX 8.0 works along with proprietary 3D audio APIs, such as Creative's EAX, Sensaura's 3D Positional Audio, and the A3D technology from now-defunct Aureal.

- *3D sound acceleration.* Sound cards using chipsets with this feature require very little CPU utilization, which speeds up overall gameplay. For best results, use a chipset that can accelerate a large number of 3D streams; otherwise, the CPU will be bogged down with managing 3D audio, which slows down gameplay.

- *Game ports with support for force-feedback game controllers.* If your games don't work properly with USB controllers, or your force-feedback game controllers use the game port only, check the game port features to make sure you'll feel as well as hear and see the action.

Features such as these don't necessarily cost a ton of money; many of the mid-range audio adapters on the market ($50–$100 at retail) support at least the first two features. With new 3D audio chipsets available from a number of vendors, it might be time for you to consider an upgrade if you're heavily into 3D gaming.

Legacy (MS-DOS) Game Support Issues

Support for the classic Sound Blaster Pro standard was once the primary requirement for a good gaming audio adapter, but with the rise of great Windows-based games and the development of DirectX, this is no longer the case for many users.

If you want to play both MS-DOS and Windows games on the same computer, you need to understand the implications of the changes in the newer audio adapters. Emulating the Sound Blaster with a PCI-based sound card is difficult because today's PCI audio adapters and motherboard-based audio solutions don't use separate DMA channels the way that ISA cards and motherboard resources do. DMA support is vital to achieve a high degree of compatibility with software written for the older Sound Blaster Pro or Sound Blaster 16 cards.

There are four methods used by PCI-based sound cards to emulate Sound Blaster at the DMA hardware level demanded by older DOS and some early Windows games:

- DDMA (Distributed DMA, developed by Compaq
- TDMA (Transparent DMA), developed by ESS Technology
- PC/PCI interface, developed by Intel
- TSR (memory-resident) utility programs

Distributed DMA and Transparent DMA are similar; both convert calls to the 8237 DMA controller (no longer present on PCI-based motherboards) into calls to a "master DMA central resource," which converts the signals into a form compatible with the way PCI-based systems handle DMA transfers. No external connector is required for these features; just enable the Sound Blaster compatibility feature in your audio adapter's setup to activate these features. This is the easiest way for you to achieve Sound Blaster compatibility if you still need it.

Some recent motherboards support the 6-pin PC/PCI interface (also called the SB-Link), which uses a narrow ribbon cable between the sound card and the motherboard (see Figure 16.4). This feature was introduced on the Intel TX series chipsets for Pentium computers and is also supported on some newer motherboards using Intel chipsets. Even though this requires an extra step during installation, the PC/PCI interface is also a good way to achieve Sound Blaster compatibility if the motherboard or audio adapter manufacturer includes the cable or makes ordering the cable easy.

Current Intel motherboards that offer this feature include

- D850GB for the Pentium 4
- D820LP for the Pentium III
- SE440BX-2 for the Pentium II/III/Celeron

Other vendors who use the Intel 440BX chipset have also produced motherboards using this feature.

All these methods require that the feature be built into both the motherboard and the sound card. Many recent PCI-based sound cards support all three of these options, easing the issue of finding a match between your motherboard and your sound card's method of emulating the Sound Blaster.

Figure 16.4   A six-wire ribbon cable is used to connect the PC/PCI interface on a PCI-based audio adapter to a compatible motherboard. Audio adapters supporting this feature might require you to select this type of DMA access in the card's properties.

The least desirable method was primarily used by early PCI-based sound cards and has fallen from fashion: requiring the user to load a TSR (Terminate and Stay Resident) program into RAM before starting the DOS-based game or educational program. This might require you to create a batch file to start the emulation program before you start your game and can also cause problems with sound card detection by your game and compatibility problems with some games.

For these reasons, if you have an older sound card that works well with your DOS-based games, you might want to keep it installed if you can spare the hardware resources it uses, and if you bought an early PCI-based sound card, consider upgrading to a model that uses a hardware-based method of emulating the Sound Blaster Pro.

DOS and Windows Games

The ideal audio adapter for a DOS and Windows gamer is one that supports Sound Blaster Pro or 16 without TSR drivers and is supported by DirectX and at least one of the third-party 3D game APIs or engines, such as Creative's EAX or Sensaura's Virtual Ear. Most games are now being written for the Windows 9x or Me operating system, which eliminates the problem of audio adapter compatibility. In Windows 9x/Me, you install the driver in the operating system, and any application can take advantage of it. As long as you have a Windows 9x/Me driver for your adapter, you can run any game designed for the OS, although some games will provide enhanced sound if the card also supports 3D audio APIs.

Note

Using Windows 9x/Me software also means that the hardware settings used by your sound card (see the following section) no longer need to match the traditional Sound Blaster defaults when running a game in a DOS box and under Windows. Legacy applications that run in real-mode DOS will still need to use the legacy defaults. Overall, Windows makes configuring today's crowded systems much easier than it was in the past.

Avoiding Game Port Conflicts

On older systems that use multi-I/O type cards to provide serial and parallel ports, the game port could be a potential area of conflict because these cards sometimes also include a game port. You must disable one of the game interfaces if you have duplicate game ports. To learn how to disable a duplicate game port, see "Resolving Resource Conflicts" later in this chapter.

Game Ports and USB Ports

In many cases, you might not need to use the game port/MIDI port for gaming controllers. Many current game controllers often offer both USB and the traditional game port connectors, allowing you to use the control with either type of connector, although some features might work only when the USB port is used.

The game port is still useful for older games that might not recognize a USB-attached game controller. If you have invested in a high-performance game port, such as the Thrustmaster ACM Game card (www.thrustmaster.com) designed for fast PCs, and sophisticated controllers, such as driving wheels, force-feedback joysticks, and so on, you should disable the sound card's game port and use the separate one you installed. If you have a plain-vanilla standard game port, remove it or disable it and use the game adapter port on your audio adapter, especially if you plan to use the MIDI port.

DVD Movies on Your Desktop

You don't need a dedicated DVD player in your office to enjoy the clarity, control, extra features, and excitement of DVD movies. DVD-ROM drives help bring DVD movie excitement to your PC, but having a DVD-ROM and a DVD movie player program is only part of what you need to bring the big screen to your desktop.

To get the most out of your desktop DVD experience, you need the following:

- *DVD playback software that supports Dolby Digital 5.1 output.* One of the best choices is Cyberlink's PowerDVD 3.x, available from www.gocyberlink.com.

- *An audio adapter that supports Dolby Digital input from the DVD drive and will output to Dolby Digital 5.1-compatible audio hardware.* Some will remix Dolby 5.1 to work on four-speaker setups if you don't have Dolby 5.1 hardware or will accept S/PDIF AC3 (Dolby Surround) input designed for a four-speaker system; some can also pass through Dolby Digital audio to speakers that can perform the Dolby Digital 5.1 decoding.

- *Dolby Digital 5.1-compatible stereo receiver and speakers.* Most high-end sound cards with Dolby Digital 5.1 support connect to analog-input Dolby Digital 5.1 receivers, but some, such as the Creative Labs Sound Blaster Live! Platinum series, also support digital-input speaker systems by adding an optional Digital DIN connector to the card. Depending on which types of speakers you are using and how they are attached, you might need to switch your mixer settings in Windows from analog to digital to hear sounds from your applications (movies, games, and so on).

To learn more about speaker terminology and how to ensure your speaker configuration is correct, see "Speakers," page 919, later in this chapter.

Voice Dictation and Control

Some audio adapters are equipped with software capable of voice recognition that can be used to control some of your computer's operations. You also can get voice recognition for your current adapter in the form of add-on software. Voice recognition, as the name implies, is when your computer is "taught" to recognize spoken word forms and react to them. Voice recognition products generally take two forms: those that are designed to provide a simple voice interface to basic computer functions and those that can accept vocal dictation and insert the spoken text into an application, such as a word processor. The minimum standard for most voice-recognition software is a Sound Blaster 16 or equivalent sound card.

Voice Command Software

The voice interface application is clearly the simpler of the two because the software has to recognize only a limited vocabulary of words. With this type of software, you can sit in front of your computer and say the words "file open" to access the menu in your active Windows application.

For the average user, this type of application is of dubious value. For a time, Compaq was shipping computers to corporate clients with a microphone and an application of this type at little or no additional cost. The phenomenon of dozens of users in an office talking to their computers was interesting, to say the least. The experiment resulted in virtually no increased productivity, a lot of wasted time as users experimented with the software, and noisier offices.

However, for users with physical handicaps that limit their ability to use a keyboard, this type of software can represent a whole new avenue of communication. For this reason alone, continued development of voice-recognition technology is essential.

Note

Voice-recognition applications, by necessity, have to be somewhat limited in their scope. For example, it quickly becomes a standard office joke for someone to stick his head into another person's cubicle and call out "Format C!" as though this command would erase the user's hard drive. Obviously, the software must be incapable of damaging a user's system because of a misinterpreted voice command.

Voice Dictation Software

The other type of voice-recognition software is far more complex. Converting standard speech into text is an extraordinarily difficult task, given the wide variation in human speech patterns. For this reason, nearly all software of this type (and some of the basic voice command applications, as well) must be "trained" to understand a particular user's voice. You do this training by reading prepared text samples supplied with the software to the computer. Because the software knows what you're supposed to be saying beforehand, it can associate certain words with the manner in which you speak them.

Users' results with this sort of application vary widely, probably due in no small part to their individual speech patterns. I've heard people rave about being able to dictate pages of text without touching the keyboard, whereas others claim that correcting the many typographical errors is more trouble than typing the text manually.

Many variables can account for such variances in the quality of voice dictation, including

- *Discrete speech versus continuous speech programs.* Continuous speech, which allows a more natural "conversation" with the computer, is standard today but is harder to achieve with acceptable accuracy.
- *Training versus no-training-needed programs.* Training a program to recognize your voice produces better results, even for programs that allow you to skip this step.
- *Larger active and total vocabularies.* Programs with a larger active vocabulary can react more quickly to dictation, and programs with a larger total vocabulary allow you to store more unique vocabulary.

- *More powerful computer hardware.* Faster CPUs and more RAM enable programs to work more quickly and accurately, and allow developers to add more features to the newest versions of their programs.

- *High-quality sound card and voice-recognition microphone.* Use high-quality hardware recommended by the vendor to achieve the best results; voice-recognition headsets are designed especially for speaking voice rather than for sound effect or music recording.

Note

For more information about voice-recognition, see the CD-ROM accompanying this book.

Sound Producers

Producers are people who intend to create their own sound files. These can range from casual business users recording low-fidelity voice annotations to professional musicians and MIDI maniacs. These users need an adapter that can perform as much of the audio processing as possible itself, so as not to place an additional burden on the system processor. Adapters that use DSPs to perform compression and other tasks are highly recommended in this case. Musicians will certainly want an adapter with as many voices as possible and a wavetable synthesizer. Adapters with expandable memory arrays and the capability to create and modify custom wavetables are also preferable. Many of the best sound cards for "hardcore gamer" also are suitable for sound producers by adding the appropriate sound-editing programs, such as Sound Forge, and by equipping the card with the appropriate connectors for SPDIF digital audio and MIDI interfaces. The Sound Blaster Live! Platinum Edition features a drive bay–mounted external interface for these features called the Live Drive. This accessory can also be purchased separately and retrofitted to most other Sound Blaster Live! models.

Most other audio cards designed for sound production features add jacks to the traditional trio of connectors on the rear card bracket.

Playing and Creating Digitized Sound Files

You can use two basic types of files to store audio on your PC. One type is generically called a sound file and uses formats such as WAV, VOC, AU, and AIFF. Sound files contain waveform data, which means they are analog audio recordings that have been digitized for storage on a computer. Just as you can store graphic images at different resolutions, you can have sound files that use various resolutions, trading off sound quality for file size. The three default sound resolution levels used in Windows 9x and Windows Me are shown in Table 16.2.

Table 16.2   Windows 9x and Windows Me Sound File Resolutions

Resolution	Frequency	Bandwidth	File Size
Telephone quality	11,025Hz	8-bit mono	11KB/sec
Radio quality	22,050Hz	8-bit mono	22KB/sec
CD quality	44,100Hz	16-bit stereo	172KB/sec

Windows Me also supports additional resolution (48,000Hz, 16-bit stereo, 188KB/sec), although you must select it manually.

This additional resolution offered by Windows Me supports the 48KHz (48,000Hz) standard used by many new sound cards to support the requirements of DVD audio playback and Dolby Digital AC-3 (Dolby Digital 5.1) audio compression technologies. As you can see, the difference in file sizes between the highest and lowest audio resolution levels is substantial. CD-quality sound files can occupy enormous amounts of disk space. At this rate, just 60 seconds of audio would require more than 10MB of storage. For applications that don't require or benefit from such high resolution, such as voice annotation, telephone-quality audio is sufficient and generates much smaller files.

To achieve a balance between high quality and smaller file sizes, you can also convert conventional WAV files into compressed formats, such as MP3 audio files. See the following sections for details.

In addition to these standard quality designations, you can create your own combinations of frequency and bandwidth with virtually any audio recording program, including the Sound Recorder applet supplied with Windows.

Audio Compression for the Web and Music

Audio compression has two major uses:

- Enabling audio clips to be used on Web sites
- Enabling storage of hiqh-quality music in less space

By using audio-editing software, such as Real's RealProducer or Microsoft Windows Media Encoder 7, you can compress high-quality sound for use on Web sites with a minimal loss of quality but a large reduction in file size.

Note

RealProducer outputs Real Audio files; Windows Media Encoder 7 outputs Windows Media Audio (.WMA) files. Most commercial sites that offer streaming or downloadable media clips support both standards, and I recommend that you do so as well so that virtually anyone can hear your audio.

The latest example of a sound format being popularized by the Web is the popular MP3 file type, a digital sound-only flavor of MPEG that has become an overwhelmingly popular downloadable sound format on the World Wide Web. MP3 files can have near-CD quality, depending on the sampling rate used to create them, but are far smaller than normal CD-quality WAV files.

MP3 enables both downloading of these compact, quality music files and transformation of the CDs you now own into individual MP3 tracks. Although MP3-creation programs (also called rippers) can work at different sampling rates, a typical rate for pop music is 128Kb/second encoding, providing a balance between reasonable sound quality and amazingly small file size. A five-minute song that rips to a CD-quality 50MB WAV file would convert to an MP3 file that is less than 4MB.

Note

Thomson Multimedia, which is co-holder of the patent rights on the MP3 format, is developing an improved version of the MP3 format called MP3Pro. MP3Pro is designed to improve the efficiency of the current MP3 compression technology by reducing the file size by half over what can be achieved with normal MP3 encoding. MP3Pro is designed to counter Microsoft's Windows Media Audio (.WMA) format, which at 64Kbps sampling rate sounds as good as current MP3s sampled at 128Kbps. MP3Pro-format files will be playable by current MP3 players and devices.

Thanks to MP3, many PCs around the country are doubling as jukeboxes without the need to flip CDs and with the capability to construct custom music play lists. MP3 provides music lovers with the capability to store just the songs they want and to create customized CDs for personal use. MP3 files are being distributed legally by musicians wanting to build an audience or gain publicity for a new CD, an album, or an upcoming tour. Unfortunately, many MP3 Web sites are stuffed full of unauthorized MP3 tracks. Despite the problems of pirated MP3 files on the Web, MP3 has become the leading edge of a consumer-friendly music revolution: helping you get just the songs you want in the play-back form you want, whether it's portable player (such as Diamond Multimedia's RIO), computer storage, or music CD.

Note

Many recent CD-RW drives come with MP3 ripping software and instructions for creating your own music mix CDs. For more information on creating MP3s, see *Upgrading and Repairing PCs, 12th Edition*, Chapter 20 on the CD included with this book.

Caution

Although MP3 is an exciting method used legally by many artists to attract new audiences, be careful about what you download. Distributing MP3 sound files from copyrighted artists without permission is both unethical and illegal. If you find MP3 files on the Web and are unsure about their legitimacy, don't download them.

MIDI Files

Another popular type of audio file is a MIDI file, which is as different from a WAV, MP3, or WMA file as a vector graphic is from a bitmap. MIDI files, which use MID or RMI extensions, are wholly digital files that do not contain recordings of sound; instead, they contain the instructions the audio hardware uses to create the sound. Just as 3D video adapters use instructions and textures to create images for the computer to display, MIDI-capable audio adapters use MIDI files as instructions to guide the synthesis of music.

MIDI is a powerful programming language developed in the 1980s to permit electronic musical instruments to communicate. MIDI was the breakthrough standard in the electronic music industry, an industry that to this day shuns nearly all attempts at hardware standardization in favor of proprietary systems. With MIDI you can create, store, edit, and play back music files on your computer either in tandem with a MIDI-compatible electronic musical instrument (typically a keyboard synthesizer) or with just the computer.

Unlike the other types of sound files, MIDI messages require relatively little storage space. An hour of stereo music stored in MIDI format requires less than 500KB. Many games use MIDI sounds instead of recorded ones to supply large amounts of music while conserving disk space. Because they are not recordings, the use of various resolutions does not apply to MIDI files.

A MIDI file is actually a digital representation of a musical score. It is composed of a collection of separate channels, each of which represents a different musical instrument or type of sound. Each channel specifies the frequencies and duration of the notes to be "played" by that instrument, just as a piece of sheet music does. Thus, a MIDI file of a string quartet contains four channels representing two violins, a viola, and a cello.

Note

MIDI files are not intended to be a replacement for sound files such as WAVs; they should be considered a complementary technology. The biggest drawback of MIDI is that the playback technology is limited to sounds that can be readily synthesized. The most obvious shortcoming is that MIDI files are incapable of producing voices (except for synthesized choir effects). Therefore, when you download a MIDI file of your favorite song from the Internet, you'll have to do the singing.

A more significant limitation of MIDI also stems from its synthetic nature; the quality of your sound card directly influences what MIDI sounds like when you play it back. Because MIDI files can be played back with FM synthesis or wavetable synthesis, older low-cost sound cards without wavetable features will produce MIDI music that sounds like an orchestra of kazoos. Unfortunately, even with a high-quality wavetable sound card, some MIDI files still sound bad because they were produced for playback on FM-synthesis sound cards. Even though most sound cards sold today feature some form of wavetable synthesis, the number of instruments and the quality of the patch sets (the digital samples) can vary widely from card to card. Inexpensive wavetable cards might support only 32 voices, whereas better cards can support 256 or more.

Check the MIDI files you want to play back to see how many voices are needed to fully support the file before you decide you need a "better" MIDI-compatible sound card with more voices. Most readily available sound cards require no more than 20 voices.

All three MPC specifications as well as the PC9x specifications call for all audio adapters to support MIDI. The general MIDI standard used by most of the audio adapters on the market provide for up to 16 channels in a single MIDI file, but this does not necessarily limit you to 16 instruments. A single channel can represent the sound of a group of instruments, such as a violin section, enabling you to synthesize an entire orchestra.

Because MIDI files consist of digital instructions, you can edit them much more easily than you can a sound file, such as a WAV file. With the appropriate software, you can select any channel of a MIDI file and change the notes, the instrument used to play them, and many other attributes that affect the sound the PC produces.

Some software packages can even produce a manuscript of the music in a MIDI file by using standard musical notation. A composer can write a piece of music directly on the computer, edit it as needed, and then print out sheet music for live musicians to read. This is an enormous benefit for professional musicians, who historically have had to either employ music copyists or publishers or spend long hours copying music by hand.

Playing MIDI Files

When you play a MIDI file on your PC, you are not playing back a recording. Your system is actually creating music from scratch. To do this, the computer requires a synthesizer, and every MIDI-capable audio adapter has one. As the system reads the MIDI file, the synthesizer generates the appropriate sound for each channel, using the instructions in the file to create the proper pitches and note lengths and using a predefined patch to simulate the sound of a specific musical instrument. A patch is a set of instructions that the synthesizer uses to create sound similar to a particular instrument. You can control the speed at which the music plays and its volume in real-time with the MIDI player software.

The synthesizer on an audio adapter is similar electronically to those found in actual electronic keyboard instruments, but it is usually not as capable. The MPC specifications call for audio adapters to contain FM synthesizer chips that are capable of playing at least six melodic notes and two percussive notes simultaneously.

FM Synthesis

Until the mid-1990s, most low-cost sound boards generated sounds by using FM (frequency modulation) synthesis, a technology first pioneered in 1976. By using one sine wave operator to modify another, FM synthesis creates an artificial sound that mimics an instrument. The MIDI standard supported by the adapter specifies an array of preprogrammed sounds containing most of the instruments used by pop bands and orchestras.

Over the years, the technology has progressed (some FM synthesizers now use four operators) to a point where FM synthesis can sound moderately good, but it is still noticeably artificial. The trumpet sound, for example, is vaguely similar to that of a trumpet, but it would never be confused with the real thing. Today, virtually all new sound cards use more realistic wavetable sound (see the following section), although many still offer FM synthesis as an option.

Wavetable Synthesis

Today, few sound cards use FM synthesis for their sole method of playing MIDI files because even at its best, the sound it produces is not a realistic simulation of a musical instrument. More realistic, inexpensive sound was pioneered by Ensoniq Corp., the makers of professional music keyboards, in 1984.

Using a technology that was theorized at about the same time as FM synthesis, Ensoniq developed a method of sampling any instrument—including pianos, violins, guitars, flutes, trumpets, and drums—and storing the digitized sound in a wavetable. Stored either in ROM chips or on disk, the wavetable supplies an actual digitized sound of an instrument that the audio adapter can manipulate as needed. Soon after Ensoniq's discovery, other keyboard makers replaced their FM synthesizers with wavetable synthesis, paralleling how audio adapters would later move in the same direction. Early wavetable features for audio adapters were added with daughtercards, but almost all audio adapters in use today have wavetable features built in.

Today, Ensoniq is owned by Creative Labs, makers of the de facto industry-standard Sound Blaster line of sound cards. Ensoniq continues to create professional keyboards while also supplying OEM sound hardware to many computer vendors. Ensoniq technology has also been added to the Sound Blaster sound-card product line.

A number of low-cost, high-quality, PCI-based sound cards using Ensoniq or other chipsets supporting wavetable output are also available from various vendors.

A wavetable synthesizer can take a sample of an instrument playing a single note and modify its frequency to play any note on the scale. Some adapters produce better sound by using several samples of the same instrument. The highest note on a piano differs from the lowest note in more than just pitch, and the closer the pitch of the sample is to the note being synthesized, the more realistic the sound is.

Thus, the size of the wavetable has a powerful effect on the quality and variety of sounds the synthesizer can produce. The best-quality wavetable adapters on the market usually have several megabytes of memory on the card for storing samples. Some support optional daughtercards for the installation of additional memory and enable you to customize the samples in the wavetable to your own specifications.

To save money without compromising quality, most current PCI-based wavetable sound cards use so-called "soft wavetable" techniques, which borrow up to 4MB or more from main computer memory for storage of wavetable samples, which are also called "patch sets." The SoundBlaster Live! series from Creative Labs can use as much as 32MB of RAM for its samples, which are referred to as Sound Fonts. With most soft wavetable audio adapters, you can adjust the amount of RAM your samples will use; smaller sample sizes save RAM but might not provide you with all the instruments you want for certain music tracks.

Tip

If your system has both a "soft wavetable" sound card and integrated AGP graphics, your usable RAM is reduced by the memory sharing performed by both devices. A 4MB MIDI patch set and AGP graphics set for 8MB of RAM will reduce a 64MB system to 52MB of usable RAM. Because memory sharing like this is common, a memory upgrade from 64MB total to 128MB total will actually more than double your usable system RAM.

MIDI Connectivity

The advantages of MIDI go beyond the internal functions of your computer. You can also use your audio adapter's MIDI interface to connect an electronic keyboard, a sound generator, a drum machine, or other MIDI device to your computer. You can then play MIDI files by using the synthesizer in the keyboard instead of the one on your adapter or create your own MIDI files by playing notes on the keyboard. With the right software, you can compose an entire symphony by playing the notes of each instrument separately into its own channel and then playing back all the channels together. Many professional musicians and composers use MIDI to create music directly on computers, bypassing traditional instruments altogether.

Some manufacturers even offer high-end MIDI cards that can operate in full-duplex mode, meaning you can play back prerecorded audio tracks as you record a new track into the same MIDI file. This is technology that only a few years ago required the services of a professional recording studio with equipment costing hundreds of thousands of dollars.

To connect a MIDI device to your PC, you need an audio adapter that has the MIDI ports defined by the MIDI specification. MIDI uses two round, five-pin DIN ports (see Figure 16.5) for separate input (MIDI-IN) and output (MIDI-OUT). Many devices also have a MIDI-THRU port that passes the input from a device directly to output, but audio adapters generally do not have this. Interestingly, MIDI sends data through only pins 1 and 3 of the connector. Pin 2 is shielded, and pins 4 and 5 are unused.

Figure 16.5   The MIDI specification calls for the use of two or three five-pin DIN connectors on the MIDI device.

The primary function of the audio adapter's MIDI interface is to convert the parallel data bytes used on a computer's system bus into the serial MIDI data format. MIDI uses asynchronous serial ports that run at 31.25Kbaud. MIDI communications use 8 data bits, with 1 start bit and 1 stop bit, for a speed of 320 microseconds per serial byte.

Note

You can obtain the most recent specifications for the MIDI standard for a modest fee from the MIDI Manufacturers Association's sales-fulfillment address: MMA, PO Box 3173, La Habra, CA 90632-3173 USA.

The MIDI Manufacturers Association also has a Web site at www.midi.org.

MIDI runs over special unshielded twisted-pair cables that can have a maximum length of up to 50 feet (although most of the cables sold are 10 or 20 feet long). You can also daisy-chain multiple MIDI devices together to combine their capabilities. The total length of the MIDI chain is not limited as long as each individual cable is less than 50 feet.

Many audio adapters do not have MIDI ports directly on the adapter card. Instead, they use a separate connector that plugs into the adapter's game port and provides the MIDI ports. Unfortunately, this connector is rarely included in the box with the adapter. You have to purchase it separately from the audio-card manufacturer.

If you are using a "legacy-free" PC that doesn't include a MIDI/gameport connector, you can attach MIDI interfaces via your USB ports. For a selection of various USB-compatible MIDI devices, go to www.usbstuff.com/midi.html.

MIDI Software

Windows 9x, Me, and 2000 all include basic software that enables you to play MIDI files in the form of the Media Player application, and these versions of Windows also include a selection of MIDI music files. For full MIDI capabilities, however, you'll need sequencing software to either manipulate the tempo of MIDI files and the sounds used to play them or cut and paste together various prerecorded music sequences.

Many audio adapters come with a selection of software products that provide some MIDI capabilities, and shareware and freeware tools are available on the Internet, but the truly powerful software that enables you to create, edit, and manipulate MIDI files must be purchased separately.

Recording

Virtually all audio adapters have an audio input jack. With a microphone, you can record your voice. Using the Sound Recorder application included with all versions of Microsoft Windows, you can play, edit, or record a sound file in the WAV format.

The WAV files you create can be used in many ways, including

- Assigning specific WAV files to certain Windows events with the Sounds option in the Windows Control Panel
- Voice annotations that can be attached to various types of documents through Windows OLE and ActiveX controls
- Narration for presentations using PowerPoint, Freelance Graphics, Corel Presentations, or other products

WAV files can be converted into MP3 or WMA files to save space and for use on the Web.

Note

For more information on using WAV files and your audio card for tasks such as these, see *Upgrading and Repairing PCs, 12th Edition*, Chapter 20, on this book's CD.

Audio CDs

One convenient and entertaining use of a CD-ROM drive is to play audio CDs while you are working on something else. Virtually all CD-ROM drives support audio CDs. The music can be piped not only through a pair of speakers (and even a subwoofer) connected to the audio adapter, but some also support audio through headphones plugged into the front-mounted external jack provided on many CD-ROM drives. Most sound cards include a CD-player utility, as do Windows 9x/Me/2000, and free versions are available for download on the Internet. These programs usually present a visual display to simulate the control panel of an audio CD player. You operate the controls with a mouse or the keyboard and can listen to audio CDs as you work on other things.

If you want to hear CDs through your system's speakers, make sure your CD audio cable is attached to both the rear of the CD-ROM drive and your sound card. Some new systems feature digital speakers attached to the USB connection. These can provide excellent sound, but if used with older or cheaper CD-ROM drives, they might produce no sound at all. USB-based speakers *must* be used with CD-ROM drives that support a feature called digital audio extraction (DAE) if you want CD-based music to play through them. Check your CD-ROM drive's spec sheet for information about this feature.

Note

If you have a CD-R/CD-RW drive as well as an IDE-based CD-ROM, don't forget to check the recordable drive. Many of these do feature digital audio extraction, enabling you to play your music in that drive and use your (normally faster) CD-ROM for program loading and data access.

If your system is equipped with a DVD drive, make sure your audio CD player software is DVD-compatible. Many vendors of software DVD playback programs provide a program that can be launched at system startup to allow you to play back music CDs with your DVD drive.

◄◄ See Chapter 13, p. 687, to learn more about CD audio.

Sound Mixer

On a multimedia PC, it is often possible for two or more sound sources to require the services of the audio adapter at the same time. Any time you have multiple sound sources that you want to play through a single set of speakers, a mixer is necessary.

Most audio adapters include a mixer that enables all the different audio sources, MIDI, WAV, line in, and the CD to use the single line-out jack. Although a separate recording mixer was often used with Windows 3.1x systems, newer versions of Windows use a single mixer for both recording and play-back features. Normally, the adapter ships with software that displays visual sliders like you would see on an actual audio mixer in a recording studio. With these controls, you can set the relative volume of each of the sound sources.

Audio Adapter Concepts and Terms

To fully understand audio adapters and their functions, you need to understand various concepts and terms. Terms such as 16-bit, CD quality, and MIDI port are just a few. Concepts such as sampling and digital-to-audio conversion (DAC) are often sprinkled throughout stories about new sound products. You've already learned about some of these terms and concepts; the following sections describe many others.

The Nature of Sound

To understand an audio adapter, you must understand the nature of sound. Every sound is produced by vibrations that compress air or other substances. These sound waves travel in all directions, expanding in balloon-like fashion from the source of the sound. When these waves reach your ear, they cause vibrations that you perceive as sound.

Two of the basic properties of any sound are its pitch and its intensity.

Pitch is the rate at which vibrations are produced. It is measured in the number of hertz (Hz), or cycles per second. One cycle is a complete vibration back and forth. The number of Hz is the frequency of the tone; the higher the frequency, the higher the pitch.

Humans cannot hear all possible frequencies. Very few people can hear sounds with frequencies less than 16Hz or greater than about 20KHz (kilohertz; 1KHz equals 1,000Hz). In fact, the lowest note on a piano has a frequency of 27Hz, and the highest note a little more than 4KHz. Frequency-modulation (FM) radio stations can broadcast notes with frequencies as high as 15KHz.

The amazing compression ratios possible with MP3 files, compared to regular CD-quality WAV files, is due in part to the discarding of sound frequencies that are higher or lower than normal hearing range during the ripping process.

The intensity of a sound is called its *amplitude*. This intensity determines the sound's volume and depends on the strength of the vibrations producing the sound. A piano string, for example, vibrates gently when the key is struck softly. The string swings back and forth in a narrow arc, and the tone it sends out is soft. If the key is struck more forcefully, however, the string swings back and forth in a wider arc, producing a greater amplitude and a greater volume. The loudness of sounds is measured in decibels (db). The rustle of leaves is rated at 20db, average street noise at 70db, and nearby thunder at 120db.

Evaluating the Quality of Your Audio Adapter

The quality of an audio adapter is often measured by three criteria: frequency response (or range), total harmonic distortion, and signal-to-noise ratio.

The *frequency response* of an audio adapter is the range in which an audio system can record or play at a constant and audible amplitude level. Many cards support 30Hz–20KHz. The wider the spread, the better the adapter.

The *total harmonic distortion* measures an audio adapter's linearity and the straightness of a frequency response curve. In layman's terms, the harmonic distortion is a measure of accurate sound reproduction. Any nonlinear elements cause distortion in the form of harmonics. The smaller the percentage of distortion, the better. This harmonic distortion factor might make the difference between cards that use the same audio chipset. Cards with cheaper components might have greater distortion, making them produce poorer-quality sound.

The *signal-to-noise ratio (S/N or SNR)* measures the strength of the sound signal relative to background noise (hiss). The higher the number (measured in decibels), the better the sound quality.

These factors affect all types of audio adapter use, from WAV file playback to speech recognition. Keep in mind that low-quality microphones and speakers can degrade the performance of a high-quality sound card.

Sampling

With an audio adapter, a PC can record waveform audio. Waveform audio (also known as sampled or digitized sound) uses the PC as a recording device (like a tape recorder). Small computer chips built into the adapter, called analog-to-digital converters (ADCs), convert analog sound waves into digital bits that the computer can understand. Likewise, digital-to-analog converters (DACs) convert the recorded sounds to an audible analog format.

Sampling is the process of turning the original analog sound waves (see Figure 16.6) into digital (binary) signals that the computer can save and later replay. The system samples the sound by taking snapshots of its frequency and amplitude at regular intervals. For example, at time X the sound might be measured with an amplitude of Y. The higher (or more frequent) the sample rate, the more accurate the digital sound replicates its real-life source is and the larger the amount of disk space needed to store it is.

8-Bit Versus 16-Bit

The original MPC specifications required audio adapters to provide 8-bit sound. This doesn't mean the audio adapter must fit into an 8-bit instead of a 16-bit expansion slot. Rather, 8-bit audio means that the adapter uses eight bits to digitize each sound sample. This translates into 256 (2^8) possible digital values to which the sample can be pegged (less quality than the 65,536 values possible with a 16-bit sound card). Generally, 8-bit audio is adequate for recorded speech, whereas 16-bit sound is best for the demands of music. Figure 16.7 shows the difference between 8- and 16-bit sound.

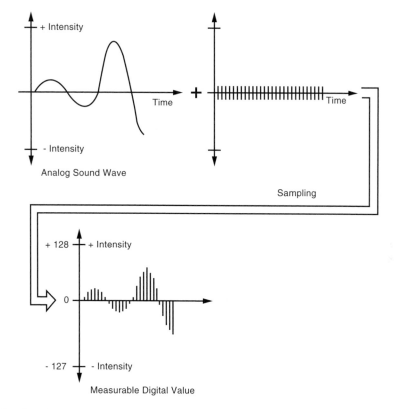

Figure 16.6   Sampling turns a changing sound wave into measurable digital values.

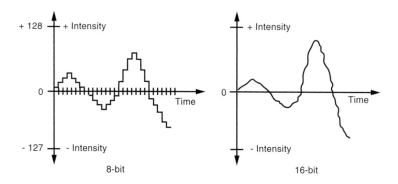

Figure 16.7   16-bit resolution provides more accurate sound reproduction than 8-bit resolution.

Many of the older audio adapters did only 8-bit sound reproduction. Today, all sound cards offer 16-bit reproduction, which provides very high resolution.

Besides resolution, the sampling rate or frequency determines how often the audio adapter measures the level of the sound being recorded or played back. Basically, you have to sample at about two times the highest frequency you want to produce, plus an extra 10% to keep out unwanted signals. Humans can hear up to 20,000 cycles per second, or 20KHz. If you double this number and add 10%, you get a 44.1KHz sampling rate, the same sampling rate used by high-fidelity audio CDs.

Sound recorded at the telephone-quality rate of 11KHz (capturing 11,000 samples per second) is fuzzier than sound sampled at the radio-quality rate of 22KHz. A sound sampled in 16-bit stereo (two channel) at 44KHz (CD-audio quality) requires as much as 10.5MB per minute of disk space. The same sound sample in 8-bit mono (single channel) at 11KHz takes 1/16th the space.

Remember that for best use of your disk space (and to improve Web download times for online sounds), you should match the sound quality to the type of sound you're recording.

You can experiment with the effects of various sampling rates by recording sound with the Windows Sound Recorder or a third-party application set to CD-quality sound. Save the sound and play it back at that highest quality setting. Then convert the file to a lower-quality setting. Save the sound file again with a different name. Play back the various versions, and determine the lowest quality (and smallest file size) you can use without serious degradation to sound quality.

Who's Who in Audio

Because audio adapters have become common features in systems, many vendors have produced audio adapters, audio chips, and integrated motherboard chipsets with audio features. This section examines some of these companies and their products.

As you've learned in other chapters, I believe it is very important to get all the technical information you can about your computer and its components. By knowing who makes the audio chip your computer depends on, you can find out what the hardware can do and be better able to find upgrades to the software drivers you need to get the most out of your audio hardware.

Chipset Makers Who Make Their Own Audio Adapters

Just as graphics card vendors are divided into two camps, chipset makers are divided into these two categories:

- Card makers who produce their own chipsets
- Card makers who use chipsets from other vendors

Audio adapter vendors fall into the same categories. One of the pioneers of the audio adapter business, Creative Labs, has also been among the leaders in developing audio chips. Creative Labs develops audio chips primarily for its own Sound Blaster–branded products, but it has sold some of its older Sound Blaster 16 products into OEM markets.

Creative's major audio chips have included the following:

- *Vibra-16.* This was used in the later Sound Blaster 16 cards; it doesn't support wavetable or 3D effects.
- *Ensoniq ES1370 series (ES1370/71/73).* These were used in the Sound Blaster PCI64 and PCI 128 series as well as the Ensoniq Audio PCI and Vibra PCI series; they support soft wavetable features, four speakers on some models and Microsoft Direct 3D, but no 3D acceleration or EAX positional audio.
- *EMU-8000.* This audio chip is used by the AWE32/64 series and features 32-voice wave table synthesis; the AWE64 used software to generate 32 additional voices for a total of 64 voices.
- *EMU10K1.* This is the audio chip at the heart of the current Live! and Live 5.1 series sound cards as well as the PCI 512; it features 3D acceleration, EAX positional audio, a reprogrammable DSP, and soft wavetable support.

Another major player is Philips, which bought chipset maker VLSI and integrated it into its Philips Semiconductor operation in mid-1999. Philips introduced its line of audio adapters in the fall of 2000, using the ThunderBird chipsets it jointly developed with Qsound Labs, Inc. These include

- *ThunderBird Q3D.* Features 3D audio acceleration of up to 64 3D streams in hardware, positional 3D audio supporting EAX and Qsound standards, quadraphonic speaker support with virtual surround sound, wavetable, and DOS Sound Blaster emulation; it is used by the Philips Rhythmic Edge and Seismic Edge audio adapters.

- *ThunderBird Avenger.* Features 3D audio acceleration of up to 96 3D streams in hardware, positional 3D audio supporting EAX and Qsound standards, support for Dolby Digital 5.1, wavetable, and DOS Sound Blaster emulation; it is used by the Philips Acoustic Edge audio adapters.

These chipsets, which have received high praise for performance, also can be used by other brands of audio adapters in the future because Philips offers these chipsets as OEM products as well as in their own brand of audio adapters.

Discontinued and Orphan Sound Card Makers

Other companies that have produced their own sound chips, but no longer produce sound cards include

- *Aureal.* Their A3D technology was regarded by many as superior to Creative Labs's EAX 3D positional audio, but they were absorbed by Creative Labs in mid-2000; no further development is anticipated.

- *Yamaha.* Their OPL2 and OPL3 chips were among the best FM-synthesis chips used on older sound cards, and their MIDI performance in later models was outstanding, but their emphasis is now on MIDI daughtercards and professional sound-recording cards; some of their retail and OEM products might still be available.

Should you panic if your favorite audio adapter is an "orphan"? Not necessarily. If the audio adapter vendor provides good technical support and up-to-date drivers, you're OK for now. But, the next time an operating system update or new audio API shows up, you probably won't be able to take advantage of it unless you replace your audio adapter.

Major Sound Chip Makers

Most companies other than Creative Labs and Philips depend on third parties to make their audio chips. Some of the major vendors include

- *Cirrus Logic/Crystal Semiconductors.* The top-of-the-line Sound Fusion CS4630 also features 3D acceleration, support for both EAX and Sensaura positional audio, unlimited-voice wavetable synthesis, and S/PDIF support for AC3 and Dolby 5.1 input and output. The CS4630 is used in the popular and highly rated Voyetra Turtle Beach Santa Cruz and similar Video Logic Sonic Fury audio adapters.

  Other Sound Fusion series chips include the CS4614 and CS4624, both of which feature support for 3D Direct Sound positional audio, DOS Sound Blaster emulation, and wavetable synthesis.

- *ESS Technology.* The Canyon3D-2, introduced at Fall 2000 Comdex is ESS Technology's flagship audio chip, featuring four-channel analog output, support for Dolby and THX digital sound, SPDIF input and output, and Sensaura 3D positional audio, and it is optimized for use with DirectX 8.0.

The Maestro-2 series features wavetable, positional 3D from Sensaura, and 3D audio acceleration; the Maestro 2E and 2EM also support S/PDIF output for DVD movie support. The Maestro series chips are optimized for notebook computers, and Maestro chips are used in recent models of Dell, Toshiba, Gateway, Compaq, and HP portables. ESS's AudioDrive series was popular with many notebook computers and second-tier sound card makers in the mid-1990s.

- *C-Media Electronics.* The CMI 8738 features 4.1 and 5.1 speaker support for quadraphonic and Dolby Digital output, Direct Sound 3D and A3D positional audio, and wavetable and is available for desktop or notebook computers. It is used by Guillemot's MUSE and Leadtek's WinFast 4x Sound, both of which have received favorable ratings in recent reviews.

- *ForteMedia, Inc.* The FM-801 is the first audio chip to feature Dolby Digital 5.1 output to analog speakers for both DVD movies and games. The FM-801 also features Qsound's Q3D 2.0 3D API and optional support for SPDIF input/output. The FM-801 is used by many smaller sound card makers. For a review of the sound chip and a feature comparison of sound cards using this chip, see http://www.3dsoundsurge.com/reviews/FM801/FM801.html.

Discontinued and Orphan Sound Chips and Sound Card Producers

The following sound chips are no longer being sold, and ongoing support is limited or no longer available. If you use an audio adapter based on one of these products, you might need to upgrade if you cannot get drivers for new and forthcoming operating systems.

Discontinued products include

- *Oak Technology OTI-601 series.* Oak left the audio chipset business in early 1998.

- *Trident 4DWave-NX series.* This 3D audio chipset is still available on cards from smaller audio adapter vendors, such as Aztech, Jaton, and Hoontech.

Diamond Multimedia, which used sound chips from several vendors, no longer produces sound cards since its parent company, S3, relaunched itself in the fall of 2000 as an Internet appliance and MP3 audio-focused company. SonicBlue still offers limited support for Diamond-brand audio cards, but ongoing driver support is not likely.

Motherboard Chipsets with Integrated Audio

The Intel 810 chipset was the first mainstream chipset for a major CPU to integrate audio; it works with Celeron CPUs. Its inspiration might have been the Cyrix/National Semiconductor Media GX series, which used a trio of chips to substitute for the CPU, VGA video, onboard audio, memory, and I/O tasks.

Other popular chipsets that integrate audio include Intel's 820, 850, and 815; some require the use of a CMR riser card (a small card that plugs into a dedicated expansion slot on some recent motherboards) to make audio available. Typically, chipsets with integrated audio have fairly low performance and aren't always easy to disable if you want something better. However, the SiS630S from Taiwan's Silicon Integrated Systems provides 3D support in hardware and six-channel sound and compares well to its Intel rivals.

Other motherboards that have Audio Modem Riser (AMR) support are available from many vendors; this is intended for a low-cost sound card or modem that will use the CPU and operating system for its intelligence. However, **no** official specification exists for the use of this tiny 2-part slot found on many recent motherboards, and thus this option is useless.

3D audio performance on any system with integrated audio chipsets such as the ones listed previously is likely to be lacking. Because DirectX 8 supports 3D audio better than previous versions, you should use it for the best results with your audio card (be sure to obtain drivers compatible with your product).

3D Audio

One of the biggest issues for serious game players when audio adapters are considered is how well they perform 3D audio tasks. This has been complicated by several factors, including

- Differing standards for positional audio
- Hardware versus software processing of 3D audio
- DirectX support issues

Positional Audio

The underlying issue common to all 3D sound cards is that of positional audio, which refers to adjusting features such as reverberation, balance, and apparent sound "location" to produce the illusion of sound coming from in front of, beside, or even behind the user. One very important element in positional audio is HRTF (Head Related Transfer Function), which refers to how the shape of the ear and the angle of the listener's head changes the perception of sound. Because HRTF factors mean that a "realistic" sound at one listener's head angle might sound artificial when the listener turns to one side or the other, the addition of multiple speakers that "surround" the user, as well as sophisticated sound algorithms that add controlled reverberation to the mix, are making computer-based sound more and more real.

Rival Standards for Positional APIs

One of the most frustrating problems for PC game players has been the continued rivalry between various APIs designed to perform essentially the same task. Game developers have been plagued by the issue of whether to support Glide or Open GL for graphics, and audio designers have wondered which 3D audio standard to support. The original version of Microsoft's Direct3D for DirectX didn't support third-party 3D software, but recent and current versions do, enabling 3D audio adapters to improve the normal positional audio available with Direct3D.

During 1999 and the first part of 2000, the major rivals for the most popular gaming 3D standard were Aureal's A3D and Creative Labs's EAX (Environmental Audio Extensions) technology. A3D, especially in version 2.0, was frequently regarded as superior to its Creative Labs rival. However, most developer support went to EAX. When Aureal closed in mid-2000 and was later absorbed by Creative, this spelled the end for A3D as a viable game API.

Virtually all new sound cards on the market support Creative's EAX. However, many audio adapter vendors are enhancing the effects of EAX by adopting Sensaura's Virtual Ear engine. Virtual Ear enables the user to adjust the apparent position of sound by adjusting the size and shape of the "ear" used to listen to sound. Virtual Ear is currently available on audio adapters from Aopen, Labway, Yamaha, Voyetra Turtle Beach, Guillemot, and others. Virtual Ear can be purchased as an upgrade for existing audio adapters that use the ADI SoundMax 2 and Yamaha YMF 724 and 744 chips.

3D Audio Processing

A second important issue for game players is how the sound cards produce 3D audio. As with 3D video, there are two major methods:

- Host-based processing (which uses the CPU to process 3D, which can slow down overall system operation)
- Processing on the audio adapter (referred to as 3D acceleration)

Some 3D audio cards perform some or all of the processing necessary for 3D using the host's CPU, whereas others use a powerful DSP which performs the processing on the audio adapter itself. Cards which use host-based processing for 3D can cause major drops in frame rate (frames per second of animation displayed onscreen by a 3D game) when 3D sound is enabled, whereas cards with their own 3D audio processors onboard have little change in frame rate whether 3D sound is enabled or disabled. Many of the latest chips from major audio adapter and chipset vendors support 3D acceleration, but the number of 3D audio streams supported varies greatly by chip—and can sometimes be limited by problems with software drivers.

A good rule of thumb for realistic gaming is to have an overall average frame rate of 30fps (frames per second). With fast CPUs, such as the Pentium III 800MHz, this is easy to achieve with any recent 3D card, but gamers using slower CPUs, such as the Celeron 300A (running at 300MHz), will find that cards using the host CPU for some of the 3D processing will have frame rates that fall below the desired average of 30fps, making for clumsy gameplay. To see the effect of enabling 3D sound on the speed of popular games, you can use the built-in frame-rate tracking feature found in many games or check online game-oriented hardware review sources, such as www.anandtech.com. Frame rates are closely related to CPU utilization; the more CPU attention your 3D audio card requires, the slower the frame rate will be.

As with 3D video, the main users of 3D sound are game developers, but business uses for ultra-realistic sound will no doubt follow.

DirectX Support Issues

The latest version of DirectX, DirectX 8, is designed to give all sound cards with 3D support major boosts in performance. Previous versions of DirectX supported 3D with DirectSound3D, but the performance of DirectSound3D was limited; game programmers needed to test the audio adapter to see whether it supported DirectSound3D acceleration and then would either enable or disable 3D sounds based on the host hardware. Starting with DirectX 5.0, DirectSound3D works with third-party 3D acceleration features.

Audio Adapter Installation (Overview)

Installing an audio adapter is no more intimidating than installing an internal modem or a video adapter, especially if you are using Windows 9x and the adapter conforms to the Plug-and-Play specification, as most do. Typically, you follow these steps:

1. Open your computer.
2. Configure your sound card (if it's a legacy card that isn't Plug-and-Play).
3. Insert the audio adapter into a bus slot and attach the CD-ROM drive to the CD Audio In connector, if present.
4. Close your computer.
5. Boot the system, causing Windows 9x, Me, or 2000 to locate and install the driver for the adapter (or install the sound card software for non–Plug-and-Play devices).
6. Attach your speakers and other sound accessories.

Tip

When Windows (9x/Me/2000) detects new hardware, it might ask you to reboot after finding a single new item. Because most sound cards today contain multiple features (Sound Blaster compatibility, MPU-401 MIDI compatibility, FM synthesis, digital signal processor, and so on), *don't* reboot when directed to after the drivers for the first item are loaded. Click No, and you'll often see the system find additional hardware items. Why? A single add-on card might contain multiple hardware components. Reboot manually, using Start, Shutdown, Restart, only after the Windows desktop has been displayed.

Installing the Sound Card (Detailed Procedure)

After your computer is open, you can install the audio adapter. I recommend you avoid installing 16-bit ISA cards unless they're necessary to meet a particular need. Unlike PCI-based audio adapters, ISA audio cards are resource hogs, can't share IRQs, and require a large percentage of CPU utilization to operate.

PCI audio adapters use fewer hardware resources, feature a lower CPU-utilization rate, and provide better support for advanced 3D gaming APIs. If you still want to use an ISA-bus audio card, make sure there's an open slot for it. Most recent systems have only one or two ISA slots, and many have dumped the ISA bus altogether.

If you have several empty bus slots from which to choose, install the audio adapter in the slot that is as far away as possible from the other cards in the computer. This reduces any possible electromagnetic interference; that is, it reduces stray radio signals from one card that might affect the sound card. The analog components on audio adapters are highly susceptible to interference, and even though they are shielded, they should be protected as well as possible. Next, you must remove the screw that holds the metal cover over the empty expansion slot you've chosen. Remove your audio adapter from its protective packaging. When you open the bag, carefully grab the card by its metal bracket and edges. Do not touch any of the components on the card. Any static electricity you might transmit can damage the card. Also, do not touch the gold-edge connectors. You might want to invest in a grounding wrist strap, which continually drains you of static build-up as you work on your computer.

Before you make your final decision about which slot to use for your audio adapter, take a careful look at the external cables you must attach to the card. Front and rear speakers, microphone, game controller, line in, S/PDIF, and other cables that attach to your system can interfere with (or be interfered by) existing cables already attached to your system. It's usually best to choose a slot that allows you to route the audio cables away from other cables.

If your adapter is not Plug-and-Play, you might have to set jumpers or DIP switches to configure the adapter to use the appropriate hardware resources in your computer. For example, you might have to adjust an IRQ or a DMA setting or turn off the adapter's joystick port because your joystick is already connected to your PC elsewhere. See the instructions that came with your audio adapter. Use the Windows 9x/Me/2000 Device Manager to see existing hardware settings, and compare them to the sound card's default settings. Use the default settings if possible. If you're installing a Plug-and-Play sound card into an older system that doesn't have a Plug-and-Play BIOS, you'll also install a program called an "enumerator" that runs early in the startup process to set the card.

◄◄ See "Plug and Play BIOS," p. 396.

If your system has an internal CD-ROM drive with an analog audio cable, connect the audio cable to the adapter's CD Audio In connector. This connector is a four-pin connector and is keyed so that you can't insert it improperly. Note that no true standard exists for this audio cable, so be sure you get the correct one that matches your drive and adapter. If you need to purchase one, you can find cables with multiple connectors designed for various brands of CD-ROM drives. This will allow you to play music CDs through the sound card's speakers and to use analog ripping if you want to create MP3 files from your CDs.

Many recent CD-ROM and DVD drives also have a digital audio connector, which supports a two-wire connector. Attach one end of the digital audio cable to the rear of the drive and the other end to the CD SPDIF or CD Digital Audio connector on the sound card. This enables you to perform digital ripping if you want to create MP3 files from your CDs.

Next, insert the adapter's edge connector in the bus slot, but first touch a metal object, such as the inside of the computer's cover, to drain yourself of static electricity. When the card is firmly in place, attach the screw to hold the expansion card and then reassemble your computer.

After the adapter card is installed, you can connect small speakers to the external speaker jack(s). Typically, sound cards provide four watts of power per channel to drive bookshelf speakers. If you are using speakers rated for less than four watts, do not turn up the volume on your sound card to the maximum; your speakers might burn out from the overload. You'll get better results if you plug your sound card into powered speakers—that is, speakers with built-in amplifiers. If your sound card supports a four-speaker system, check the documentation to see which jack is used for the front speakers and which for the rear speakers. To use the rear speakers for 3D audio, you might need to run a utility program supplied with the sound card.

Tip

If you have powered speakers but don't have batteries in them or have them connected to an AC adapter, don't turn on the speakers! Turning on the speakers without power will prevent you from hearing anything at all. Leave the speakers turned off and use the volume control built into your sound card's mixer software instead. Powered speakers sound better, but most small models can run without power in an emergency.

Some computer power supplies feature small jacks to provide power for computer speakers.

When the sound card installation is finished, you should have a speaker icon in the Windows 9x System Tray. If the speaker icon (indicating the Volume Control) isn't visible, you can install it through the Control Panel's Add/Remove Programs icon. Choose the Windows Setup tab and open the Multimedia section. Put a check mark next to Volume Control and insert the Windows 9x or 2000 CD-ROM or diskette if requested to complete the installation.

Use the Volume Control to ensure your speakers are receiving a sound signal. The mixer sometimes defaults to Mute. You can usually adjust volume separately for wave (WAV) files, MIDI, microphone, and other components.

Using Your Stereo Instead of Speakers

Another alternative is to patch your sound card into your stereo system for greatly amplified sound and for support of advanced Dolby Digital sound for DVD playback. Check the plugs and jacks at both ends of the connection. Most stereos use pin plugs—also called RCA or phono plugs—for input. Although pin plugs are standard on some sound cards, most use miniature 1/8-inch phono plugs, which require an adapter when connecting to your stereo system. From Radio Shack, for example, you can purchase an audio cable that provides a stereo 1/8-inch miniplug on one end and phono plugs on the other (Cat. No. 42-2481A).

Make sure that you get stereo—not mono—plugs, unless your sound card supports only mono. To ensure that you have enough cable to reach from the back of your PC to your stereo system, get a six-foot long cable.

Hooking up your stereo to an audio adapter is a matter of sliding the plugs into the proper jacks. If your audio adapter gives you a choice of outputs—speaker/headphone and stereo line-out—choose the stereo line-out jack for the connection. This will give you the best sound quality because the signals from the stereo line-out jack are not amplified. The amplification is best left to your stereo system. In some cases, you'll attach a special DIN plug to your audio adapter that has multiple connections to your stereo system.

Connect this cable output from your audio adapter to the auxiliary input of your stereo receiver, pre-amp, or integrated amplifier. If your stereo doesn't have an auxiliary input, other input options include—in order of preference—tuner, CD, or Tape 2. (Do not use phono inputs, however, because the level of the signals will be uneven.) You can connect the cable's single stereo miniplug to the sound card's stereo line-out jack, for example, and then connect the two RCA phono plugs to the stereo's Tape/VCR 2 Playback jacks.

The first time you use your audio adapter with a stereo system, turn down the volume on your receiver to prevent blown speakers. Barely turn up the volume control and then select the proper input (such as Tape/VCR 2) on your stereo receiver. Finally, start your PC. Never increase the volume to more than three-fourths of the way up. Any higher and the sound might become distorted.

Note

If your stereo speakers are not magnetically shielded, you might hear a lot of crackling if they are placed close to your computer. Try moving them away from the computer, or use magnetically shielded speakers.

Tricks for Using the Tape Monitor Circuit of Your Stereo

Your receiver might be equipped with something called a tape monitor. This outputs the sound coming from the tuner, tape, or CD to the tape-out port on the back, and it then expects the sound to come back in on the tape-in port. These ports, in conjunction with the line-in and line-out ports on your audio adapter, enable you to play computer sound and the radio through the same set of speakers.

Here's how you do it:

1. Turn off the tape monitor circuit on your receiver.
2. Turn down all the controls on the sound card's mixer application.
3. Connect the receiver's tape-out ports to the audio adapter's line-in port.
4. Connect the audio adapter's line-out port to the receiver's tape-in ports.
5. Turn on the receiver, select some music, and set the volume to a medium level.
6. Turn on the tape monitor circuit.
7. Slowly adjust the line-in and main-out sliders in the audio adapter's mixer application until the sound level is about the same as before.
8. Disengage and re-engage the tape monitor circuit while adjusting the output of the audio adapter so that the sound level is the same regardless of whether the tape monitor circuit is engaged.
9. Start playing a WAV file.
10. Slowly adjust up the volume slider for the WAV file in the audio adapter's mixer application until it plays at a level (slightly above or below the receiver) that is comfortable.

Now you can get sounds from your computer and the radio through the receiver's speakers.

Different connectors might be needed if you have digital surround speakers and newer PCI-based sound cards. Check your speakers and sound card before you start this project.

Troubleshooting Sound Card Problems

To operate, an audio adapter needs hardware resources, such as IRQ numbers, a base I/O address, and DMA channels that don't conflict with other devices. Most adapters come preconfigured to use the standard Sound Blaster resources that have come to be associated with audio adapters. However, problems occasionally arise even with Plug-and-Play adapters. Troubleshooting might mean that you have to change board jumpers or switches or even reconfigure the other devices in your computer. No one said life was fair.

Hardware (Resource) Conflicts

The most common problem for audio adapters is that they conflict with other devices installed in your PC. You might notice that your audio adapter simply doesn't work (no sound effects or music), repeats the same sounds over and over, or causes your PC to freeze. This situation is called a device, or hardware, conflict. What are they fighting over? Mainly the same bus signal lines or channels (called resources) used for talking to your PC. The sources of conflict in audio adapter installations are generally threefold:

■ *Interrupt Requests (IRQs).* Hardware devices use IRQs to "interrupt" your PC's CPU and get its attention.

■ *Direct Memory Access (DMA) channels.* DMA channels move information directly to your PC's memory, bypassing the system processor. DMA channels enable sound to play while your PC is doing other work. ISA sound cards and PCI sound cards emulating the Sound Blaster standard require DMA settings; PCI sound cards running in native mode don't use DMA channels.

■ *Input/output (I/O) port addresses.* Your PC uses I/O port addresses to channel information between the hardware devices on your audio adapter and your PC. The addresses usually mentioned in a sound card manual are the starting or base addresses. An audio adapter has several devices on it, and each one uses a range of addresses starting with a particular base address.

Most audio adapters include installation software that analyzes your PC and attempts to notify you should any of the standard settings be in use by other devices. The Windows 9x/Me/2000 or 2000 Device Manager (accessed from the System Control Panel) can also help you to resolve conflicts. Although these detection routines can be fairly reliable, unless a device is operating during the analysis, it might not always be detectable.

Some of the newer PCI-based sound cards and Intel-chipset motherboards might not properly support ISA-type I/O addresses used by Sound Blaster-compatible software to communicate with the card. If you have problems getting older games to work with your system, see the tips listed earlier for emulation methods, check with your sound card and system board/computer supplier for help, and check with the game developer for possible patches and workarounds.

Table 16.3 shows the default resources used by the components on a typical Sound Blaster 16 card, which uses a 16-bit ISA slot.

Table 16.3   Default Sound Blaster Resource Assignments

Device	Interrupt	I/O Ports	16-Bit DMA	8-Bit DMA
Audio	IRQ 5	220h-233h	DMA 5	DMA 1
MIDI Port	—	330h-331h	—	—
FM Synthesizer	—	388h-38Bh	—	—
Game Port	—	200h-207h	—	—

All these resources are used by a single sound card in your system. No wonder many people have conflicts and problems with audio adapter installations! In reality, working out these conflicts is not all that hard, as you shall see. You can change most of the resources that audio adapters use to alternative settings, should there be conflicts with other devices; even better, you can change the settings of the other device to eliminate the conflict. Note that some devices on the audio adapter, such as the MIDI Port, FM Synthesizer, and Game Port, do not use resources such as IRQs or DMA channels.

Compare the resource settings used by a traditional ISA sound card (in Table 16.3) to those used by a typical PCI-based sound card (in Table 16.4).

Table 16.4   Default Ensoniq PCI Resource Assignments

Device	Interrupt	I/O Ports	16-Bit DMA	8-Bit DMA
Audio	IRQ 5	DC80-DCBF	—	—
MIDI Port	(included in above configuration)			
FM Synthesizer	(included in above configuration)			
Game Port	—	200h-207h	—	—

If you don't need MS-DOS game support, the PCI card uses far fewer resources than the ISA card. However, if you are using MS-DOS games, you will need to set up a number of "virtual" IRQ, I/O port, and DMA port settings for use with those games only, as in the following figure:

When using a typical PCI-based sound card's Sound Blaster Legacy settings, you will need to verify that MS-DOS software using the Sound Blaster is set for the appropriate configuration (see Figure 16.8).

Figure 16.8   One advantage of PCI cards is visible here, even in emulation mode: All emulations can use the same IRQ, rather than up to three different IRQs, as would be the case with most third-party ISA cards that emulate the Sound Blaster.

It is always best to install an audio adapter (or a notebook computer's built-in sound adapter circuits) by using the default settings whenever possible. This is mainly because of poorly written software that cannot work properly with alternative settings, even if they do not cause conflicts. In other words, if you are having a conflict with another type of adapter, modify the settings of the other device, rather than those of the audio adapter. Take this from experience; otherwise, you will have to explain to your five-year-old why the new Dinosaur program you just installed does not make any sounds! This problem is primarily associated with DOS-based game programs, but some older Windows-based programs have also been unable to work with alternative hardware settings.

Note

Some of the recent chipsets for "legacy-free" systems, such as the Intel 810 and 820 chipsets, don't decode addresses below 1000h to the PCI bus. All the Sound Blaster I/O port addresses are well below 1000h, and thus sound card manufacturers will need to adjust driver software or use TSR programs to reroute calls to these I/O port addresses by software to the correct I/O port addresses. This design choice will not be a problem for typical Windows software that uses sound, but it can cause legacy (DOS-based) applications to fail.

Resolving Resource Conflicts

Resource conflicts are quite rare with current PCI-based audio adapters, thanks to their support of Windows Plug-and-Play technology and the PCI IRQ sharing/steering feature supported by Windows 95 OSR 2.x and above and recent chipsets.

However, if you are using the original version of Windows 95 or still use an ISA-based audio adapter (including some motherboard-based chipsets on older systems), you can have significant problems because of IRQ and DMA conflicts with other devices.

◀◀ See *Upgrading and Repairing PCs, 12th Edition* on the CD-ROM for details.

Other Sound Card Problems

Like the common cold, audio adapter problems have common symptoms. Use the following sections to diagnose your problem.

No Sound

If you don't hear anything from your audio adapter, consider these solutions:

- Make sure the audio adapter is set to use all default resources and that all other devices using these resources have been either reconfigured or removed.

- Are the speakers connected? Check that the speakers are plugged into the sound card's stereo line-out or speaker jack (not the line-in or microphone jack).

- Are the speakers receiving power? Check that the power "brick" or power cord is plugged in securely.

- Are the speakers stereo? Check that the plug inserted into the jack is a stereo plug, not mono.

- Are the mixer settings correct? Many audio adapters include a sound mixer application. The mixer controls the volume settings for various sound devices, such as the microphone or the CD player. There might be separate controls for both recording and playback. Increase the master volume or speaker volume when you are in the play mode.

  If the Mute option is selected in your sound mixer software, you won't hear anything. Depending on the speaker type and sound source type, you might need to switch from analog to digital sound for some types of sound output.

- Use your audio adapter's setup or diagnostic software to test and adjust the volume of the adapter. Such software usually includes sample sounds used to test the adapter.

- Turn off your computer for one minute and then turn it back on. A hard reset (as opposed to pressing the Reset button or pressing Ctrl+Alt+Delete) might clear the problem.

- If your computer game lacks sound, check that it is designed to work with your audio adapter. For example, some legacy and early Windows games might require the exact settings of IRQ 7 (or IRQ 5), DMA 1, and I/O address 220 to be Sound Blaster compatible.

One-Sided Sound

If you hear sound coming from only one speaker, check out these possible causes:

- Are you using a mono plug in the stereo jack? A common mistake is to use a mono plug into the sound card's speaker or stereo-out jacks. Seen from the side, a stereo connector has two darker stripes. A mono connector has only one stripe.

- If you're using amplified speakers, are they powered on? Check the strength of the batteries or the AC adapter's connection to the electrical outlet. If each speaker is powered separately, be sure that both have working batteries.

- Are the speakers wired correctly? When possible, use keyed and color-coded connectors to avoid mistakes, such as those found on the Altec Lansing ACS-340 and others.

- Is the audio adapter driver loaded? Some sound cards provide only left-channel sound if the driver is not loaded correctly. Rerun your adapter's setup software or reinstall it in the operating system.

- Are both speakers set to the same volume? Some speakers use separate volume controls on each speaker. Balance them for best results. Separate speaker volume controls can be an advantage if one speaker must be further away from the user than the other.

- Is the speaker jack loose? If you find that plugging your speaker into the jack properly doesn't produce sound, but pulling the plug half-way out or "jimmying" it around in its hole can temporarily correct the problem, you're on the road to a speaker jack failure. There's no easy solution; buy a new adapter or whip out your soldering iron and spend a lot more time on the test bench than most audio adapters are worth. To avoid damage to the speaker jack, be sure you insert the plug straight in, not at an angle.

Volume Is Low

If you can barely hear your sound card, try these solutions:

- Are the speakers plugged into the proper jack? Speakers require a higher level of drive signal than headphones. Again, adjust the volume level in your mixer application.

- Are the mixer settings too low? Again, adjust the volume level in your mixer application.

- Is the initial volume too low? If your audio adapter has an external thumbwheel volume control located on the card bracket, check to ensure that it is not turned down too low.

- Are the speakers too weak? Some speakers might need more power than your audio adapter can produce. Try other speakers or put a stereo amplifier between your sound card and speakers.

Scratchy Sound

Scratchy or static-filled sound can be caused by several problems. Improving the sound might be as simple as rearranging your hardware components. The following list suggests possible solutions to the problem of scratchy sound:

- Is your audio adapter near other expansion cards? The adapter might be picking up electrical interference from other expansion cards inside the PC. Move the audio card to an expansion slot as far away as possible from other cards.

- An ISA-based audio adapter requires a lot of CPU attention. Frequent hard disk access can cause dropouts due to the CPUs switching between managing the sound card and the hard drive.

- Are your speakers too close to your monitor? The speakers might pick up electrical noise from your monitor. Move them farther away. Subwoofers should *never* be placed near the monitor because their powerful magnets might interfere with the picture. They should be on the floor to maximize low-frequency transmission.

■ Are you using a cheaper audio adapter with an FM synthesizer? Some of the adapters that use FM synthesis instead of wavetable sound generation have very poor-quality output. Many people have been fooled into thinking they had a defective sound card, when in reality it was just a poor-quality FM synthesis card that simply does not sound good. You can test this by comparing the sound of a MIDI file (which uses the FM synthesizer) with that of a sound file such as a WAV (which doesn't). If the problem is the synthesizer, I recommend upgrading to an adapter that does wavetable synthesis so you can get the full benefit of high-quality sound.

Your Computer Won't Start

If your computer won't start at all, you might not have inserted the audio adapter completely into its slot. Turn off the PC and then press firmly on the card until it is seated correctly.

If you install an Ensoniq-based PCI sound card and get an IOS error after restarting Windows 95, the installation software should include an IOS fix-up program. You can start Windows 95 in command-prompt mode to get access to the CD-ROM to install this if needed, or it might be on one of the installation disks. Check the sound card's Readme file for more information.

You can use the Windows "bootlog" feature to record every event during startup; this file records which hardware drivers are loaded during startup and indicates whether the file loaded successfully, didn't load successfully, or froze the computer. See the documentation for your version of Windows for details on how to create a bootlog when needed.

Parity Errors or Other Lockups

Your computer might display a memory parity error message or simply crash. This is normally caused by resource conflicts in one of the following areas:

■ IRQ (Interrupt Request)

■ DMA (Direct Memory Access)

■ I/O (Input/Output) ports

If other devices in your system are using the same resources as your audio adapter, crashes, lockups, or parity errors can result. You must ensure that multiple devices in your system do not share these resources.

Game Controller Troubleshooting

If your game controller won't work, consider the following list of cures:

■ Are you using two game ports? If you already have a game port installed in your PC, the game or joystick port provided on your audio adapter might conflict with it. Usually, you should disable any other game ports and use the one on the audio adapter. Many of the multi-I/O or Super-I/O adapters that come in PC-compatible systems feature game ports that you should disable when you install an audio adapter.

■ Is your computer too fast? Some fast computers get confused by the inexpensive game ports. During the heat of virtual combat, for example, you might find yourself flying upside down or spiraling out of control. This is one sign that your game port is inadequate. Most of the game adapters built into audio adapters work better than the ones on the multi-I/O adapters. In addition, dedicated game cards are available that can work with faster computers. These game cards include software to calibrate your joystick and dual ports so you can enjoy a game with a friend. Another solution is to run your computer at a slower speed, which on some systems is as easy as pressing some type of "deturbo" button on the case.

Advanced Features

If you are having problems playing DVD audio, playing MP3 files, or using SPDIF connections, make sure that

- You have enabled the hardware resources on the sound card.
- You are using the correct playback program.
- Your mixer has the correct volume control setting for the device.
- Your cabling is correct for the device.

Other Problems

Sometimes sound problems can be difficult to solve. Due to quirks and problems with the way DMA is implemented in some motherboard chipsets, problems interacting with certain cards or drivers can occur. Sometimes altering the Chipset Setup options in your CMOS settings can resolve problems. These kinds of problems can take a lot of trial and error to solve.

The PC "standard" is based loosely on the cooperation among a handful of companies. Something as simple as one vendor's BIOS or motherboard design can make the standard nonstandard.

A good way to solve problems of all types with Plug-and-Play (PnP) cards, a PnP BIOS, and a PnP operating system (Windows 9x/Me/2000) is to use the Device Manager to remove the sound card, restart the system, and allow the card's components to be redetected. This installs a "fresh" copy of the software and reinserts Registry entries.

Speakers

Successful business presentations, multimedia applications, and MIDI work demand external high-fidelity stereo speakers. Although you can use standard stereo speakers, they are often too big to fit on or near your desk. Smaller bookshelf speakers are better.

Sound cards offer little or none of the amplification needed to drive external speakers. Although some sound cards have small four-watt amplifiers, they are not powerful enough to drive quality speakers. Also, conventional speakers sitting near your display might create magnetic interference, which can distort colors and objects onscreen or jumble the data recorded on nearby floppy disks or other magnetic media.

To solve these problems, computer speakers need to be small, efficient, and self-powered. Also, they should be provided with magnetic shielding, either in the form of added layers of insulation in the speaker cabinet or electronic cancellation of the magnetic distortion.

Caution

Although most computer speakers are magnetically shielded, do not leave recorded tapes, watches, credit cards, or floppy disks in front of the speakers for long periods of time.

Quality sound depends on quality speakers. A 16-bit audio adapter might provide better sound to computer speakers, but even an 8-bit adapter sounds good from a good speaker. Conversely, an inexpensive speaker makes both 8-bit and 16-bit adapter cards sound tinny.

Now dozens of models of PC speakers are on the market, ranging from inexpensive minispeakers from Sony, Koss, and LabTech to larger self-powered models from prestigious audio companies such as Bose and Altec Lansing. Many of the medium- to higher-end speaker systems even include subwoofers to provide additional bass response. To evaluate speakers, it helps to know the jargon. Speakers are measured by three criteria:

- *Frequency response.* A measurement of the range of high and low sounds a speaker can reproduce. The ideal range is from 20Hz to 20KHz, the range of human hearing. No speaker system reproduces this range perfectly. In fact, few people hear sounds above 18KHz. An exceptional speaker might cover a range of 30Hz–23,000Hz. Lesser models might cover only 100Hz–20,000Hz. Frequency response is the most deceptive specification because identically rated speakers can sound completely different.

- *Total Harmonic Distortion (THD).* An expression of the amount of distortion or noise created by amplifying the signal. Simply put, distortion is the difference between the sound sent to the speaker and the sound you hear. The amount of distortion is measured in percentages. An acceptable level of distortion is less than .1% (one-tenth of one percent). For some CD-quality recording equipment, a common standard is .05%. Some speakers have a distortion of 10% or more. Headphones often have a distortion of about 2% or less.

- *Watts.* Usually stated as watts per channel, this is the amount of amplification available to drive the speakers. Check that the company means "per channel" (or RMS) and not total power. Many audio adapters have built-in amplifiers, providing up to eight watts per channel (most provide four watts). This wattage is not enough to provide rich sound, however, which is why many speakers have built-in amplifiers. With the flick of a switch or the press of a button, these speakers amplify the signals they receive from the audio adapter. If you do not want to amplify the sound, you typically leave the speaker switch set to "direct." In most cases, you'll want to amplify the signal.

Inexpensive PC speakers often use batteries to power the amplifiers. Because these speakers require so much power, you might want to invest in an AC adapter or purchase speakers that use AC power. With an AC adapter, you won't have to buy new batteries every few weeks. If your speakers didn't come with an AC adapter, you can pick one up from your local Radio Shack or hardware store. Be sure that the adapter you purchase matches your speakers in voltage and polarity; most third-party adapters are multiple voltage, featuring interchangeable tips and reversible polarity.

You can control the volume and other sound attributes of your speakers in various ways, depending on their complexity and cost. Typically, each speaker has a volume knob, although some share a single volume control. If one speaker is farther away than the other, you might want to adjust the volume accordingly. Many computer speakers include a dynamic bass boost (DBB) switch. This button provides a more powerful bass and clearer treble, regardless of the volume setting. Other speakers have separate bass and treble boost switches or a three-band equalizer to control low, middle, and high frequencies. When you rely on your audio adapter's power rather than your speakers' built-in amplifier, the volume and dynamic bass boost controls have no effect. Your speakers are at the mercy of the adapter's power.

For best audio quality, adjust the master volume on the sound card near the high end, and use the volume control on powered speakers to adjust the volume. Otherwise, your speakers will try to amplify any distortions coming from the low-power input from the PC's audio adapter.

An 1/8-inch stereo minijack connects from the audio adapter's output jack to one of the speakers. The speaker then splits the signal and feeds through a separate cable from the first speaker to the second one (often referred to as the "satellite speaker").

Before purchasing a set of speakers, check that the cables between the speakers are long enough for your computer setup. For example, a tower case sitting alongside your desk might require longer speaker wires than a desktop computer.

Beware of speakers that have a tardy built-in sleep feature. Such speakers, which save electricity by turning themselves off when they are not in use, might have the annoying habit of clipping the first part of a sound after a period of inactivity.

Speakers that are USB-based will not be able to play CD music unless the CD-ROM drive can perform digital audio extraction. Check your drive's specifications for information.

Headphones are an option when you can't afford a premium set of speakers. Headphones also provide privacy and enable you to play your PC audio as loud as you like.

For best results with newer sound cards that support four speakers or more, check the properties sheet for the audio adapter and set whether you're using headphones, stereo speakers, or a larger number of speakers.

Make sure that speakers are placed properly. If you use a subwoofer, put it on the floor for better bass sound and to reduce EMI interference with other devices.

How can you tell whether wireless satellite speakers are causing interference? Watch your monitor; frequencies as high as 2KHz can interfere with your video display. Move the speakers away from the monitor and check the display again.

Theater and Surround Sound Considerations

If you're a serious gamer or DVD movie lover, you won't be content with ordinary stereophonic sound. Most audio adapters now support front and rear speakers, and many of the best audio adapters also support Dolby-compatible 4.1 and 5.1 speaker setups.

To ensure you get the sound you expect from four or more speakers, check the following:

- *Use the properties sheet for your audio adapter to properly describe your speaker setup.* This includes selecting the number of speakers you are using, setting options for 3D environmental audio and positional sound such as reverb, and setting up your subwoofer if present.

- *Make sure you use the correct cabling between your speakers and your audio adapter.* If you are planning to use AC3/Dolby speaker setups, such as 4.1 or 5.1, be sure you use the correct S/PDIF connection and configuration. This varies from audio adapter to audio adapter; check the vendor's Web site for details.

- *Make sure you have placed your speakers correctly.* In some cases you can adjust the audio adapter's properties to improve sound quality, but sometimes you might need to move the speakers themselves.

- *Make sure you have connected your speakers to the proper jacks.* Mixing up left and right or front and rear will cause poor sound quality.

Typical Speaker Setups

The simplest audio configuration available today is stereo, which uses two speakers placed to overlap sound.

Most audio adapters now support at least four speakers, but depending on the audio adapter, settings, and sound output options in the program, the rear speakers might simply mirror the front speakers' output, or you might have four distinct sound streams.

4-point Surround sound uses four speakers plus a subwoofer to surround you with music and gaming sound effects; the four speakers are placed around the listener, and the subwoofer is normally placed near a wall or in the corner to amplify its low-frequency sound. The subwoofer in such setups is not on a separate circuit but is controlled by the same signals sent to the other speakers.

5.1 Surround sound, also referred to as Dolby Digital or DTS Surround sound, uses five speakers plus a subwoofer. The fifth speaker is placed between the front two speakers to fill in any missing sound caused by incorrect speaker placement. The subwoofer is independently controlled. This is the preferred sound system for use with DVD movies. Most lower-cost audio adapters lack support for 5.1 Surround sound.

7.1 Surround sound is not generally supported by audio adapters at this time but will be in the future. Its configuration resembles the 5.1 Surround setup but adds left-middle and right-middle speakers that flank the listener, along with a subwoofer.

Microphones

Some audio adapters come complete with a microphone, but most do not. You'll need one to record your voice to a WAV file. Selecting a microphone is quite simple. You need one that has an 1/8-inch minijack to plug into your audio adapter's microphone, or audio in, jack. Most microphones have an on/off switch.

Like speakers, microphones are measured by their frequency range. This is not an important buying factor, however, because the human voice has a limited range. If you are recording only voices, consider an inexpensive microphone that covers a limited range of frequencies. An expensive microphone's recording capabilities extend to frequencies outside the voice's range. Why pay for something you won't be needing?

If you are recording music, invest in an expensive microphone, but make sure that your audio adapter can do justice to the signal produced by the microphone. A high-quality microphone can produce mediocre results when paired with a cheap 8-bit audio adapter.

Your biggest decision is to select a microphone that suits your recording style. If you work in a noisy office, you might want an unidirectional microphone that will prevent extraneous noises from being recorded. An omnidirectional microphone is best for recording a group conversation.

Most higher-priced audio adapters include a microphone of some type. This can be a small lapel microphone, a handheld microphone, or one with a desktop stand. If you want to keep your hands free, you might want to shun the traditional handheld microphone for a lapel or desktop model. If your audio adapter does not come with a microphone, see your local stereo or electronics parts store. Be sure that any microphone you purchase has the correct impedance to match the audio adapter's input.

If you're using software such as L & H's Voice Express series, Dragon Naturally Speaking, IBM Via Voice, Philips FreeSpeech, or other voice-recognition software, use the microphone supplied with the software or choose from alternative models the software vendor recommends. Run the microphone setup program again if your software has trouble recognizing your voice. Some newer models feature a battery pack to boost sound quality; be sure to check the batteries and replace them to keep recognition quality high.

If you're talking but your voice-recognition or recording software isn't responding, check the following:

- Incorrect jack; it's easy to plug the microphone into the wrong jack. Try using a magic marker to color-code the microphone wire and jack to make matching up easier.

- Check the recording volume in the mixer control. This usually defaults to Mute to avoid spurious noise.

- Make sure the microphone is on in the voice-recognition or recording software. You must click the Record button in recording software, and many voice-recognition programs let you "pick up" the microphone for use or "put it down" when you need to answer the phone. Look for an onscreen microphone icon in the Windows System Tray for fast toggling between modes.

CHAPTER 17

I/O Interfaces from Serial and Parallel to IEEE-1394 and USB

Introduction to Input/Output Ports

This chapter covers the primary peripheral input/output ports on a modern PC system. This includes a discussion of both the so-called "legacy" serial and parallel ports that have been standard on PCs since the beginning, as well as a discussion of the more current Universal Serial Bus (USB), which is replacing both serial and parallel ports, and IEEE-1394 (i.Link or FireWire) interfaces. (IEEE stands for the Institute of Electrical and Electronic Engineers.) Although SCSI and IDE are also I/O interfaces, they are important enough to warrant their own chapters for more specific and detailed coverage.

Traditionally, the most basic communications ports in any PC system have been the serial and parallel ports, and these ports continue to be important.

Serial ports (also known as *communication* or *COM* ports) were originally used for devices that had to communicate bidirectionally with the system. Such devices include modems, mice, scanners, digitizers, and any other devices that "talk to" and receive information from the PC. Newer parallel port standards now allow the parallel port to perform high-speed bidirectional communications.

Several companies manufacture communications programs that perform high-speed transfers between PC systems using serial or parallel ports. Versions of these file transfer programs have been included with DOS 6.0 and higher (Interlink) and with Windows 95 and newer versions (DCC—Direct Cable Connection). Currently, numerous products are on the market that make nontraditional use of the parallel port. For example, you can purchase network adapters, high-capacity floppy disk drives, CD-ROM drives, scanners, and tape backup units that attach to the parallel port.

The tasks traditionally performed by both serial and parallel ports are increasingly being performed by newer port types, such as USB and IEEE-1394, but, for some time to come, both legacy and newer port types will both be important I/O interface types.

Serial Ports

The asynchronous serial interface was designed as a system-to-system communications port. *Asynchronous* means that no synchronization or clocking signal is present, so characters can be sent with any arbitrary time spacing.

Each character that is sent over a serial connection is framed by a standard start-and-stop signal. A single 0 bit, called the *start bit*, precedes each character to tell the receiving system that the next eight bits constitute a byte of data. One or two stop bits follow the character to signal that the character has been sent. At the receiving end of the communication, characters are recognized by the start-and-stop signals instead of by the timing of their arrival. The asynchronous interface is character oriented and has about a 20% overhead for the extra information that is needed to identify each character.

Serial refers to data that is sent over a single wire, with each bit lining up in a series as the bits are sent. This type of communication is used over the phone system because it provides one wire for data in each direction.

Typical Locations for Serial Ports

Typical systems include one or two serial ports, usually located at the rear of the system. Some recent consumer-oriented computers label a front-mounted serial port the "digital camera port." This name comes from the use of serial ports for data transfer from low-end digital cameras. These built-in serial ports are controlled by either a Super I/O chip on the motherboard or a highly integrated South Bridge chip in the latest motherboard designs.

If you need more serial ports than your system has as standard, you can purchase single- or multi-port serial port cards or so-called *multi-I/O* cards that feature one or two serial ports and one or two parallel ports. Older systems based on the ISA or VL-Bus standard often have the serial ports attached to a multifunction card that also has IDE hard disk and floppy disk interfaces.

Note that card-based modems also incorporate a built-in serial port on the card as part of the modem circuitry. Figure 17.1 shows the standard 9-pin connector used with most modern external serial ports. Figure 17.2 shows the original standard 25-pin version.

Figure 17.1   AT-style 9-pin serial-port connector specifications.

Serial ports can connect to a variety of devices, such as modems, plotters, printers, other computers, bar code readers, scales, and device control circuits.

The official specification recommends a maximum cable length of 50 feet. The limiting factor is the total load capacitance of cable and input circuits of the interface. The maximum capacitance is specified as 2500pF (picofarads). Special low-capacitance cables can effectively increase the maximum cable length greatly, to as much as 500 feet or more. Also available are line drivers (amplifier/repeaters) that can extend cable length even further.

Tables 17.1, 17.2, and 17.3 show the pinouts of the 9-pin (AT-style), 25-pin, and 9-pin-to-25-pin serial connectors, respectively.

Description	Pin
NC	1
Transmitted Data	2
Received Data	3
Request to Send	4
Clear to Send	5
Data Set Ready	6
Signal Ground	7
Received Line Signal Detector	8
+ Transmit Current Loop Data	9
NC	10
- Transmit Current Loop Data	11
NC	12
NC	13
NC	14
NC	15
NC	16
NC	17
+ Receive Current Loop Data	18
NC	19
Data Terminal Ready	20
NC	21
Ring Indicator	22
NC	23
NC	24
- Receive Current Loop Return	25

External Device

Asynchronous Communications Adapter (RS-232C)

Figure 17.2 Standard 25-pin serial-port connector specifications.

Table 17.1   9-Pin (AT) Serial Port Connector

Pin	Signal	Description	I/O
1	CD	Carrier detect	In
2	RD	Receive data	In
3	TD	Transmit data	Out
4	DTR	Data terminal ready	Out
5	SG	Signal ground	—
6	DSR	Data set ready	In
7	RTS	Request to send	Out
8	CTS	Clear to send	In
9	RI	Ring indicator	In

Table 17.2   25-Pin (PC, XT, and PS/2) Serial Port Connector

Pin	Signal	Description	I/O
1	—	Chassis ground	—
2	TD	Transmit data	Out
3	RD	Receive data	In
4	RTS	Request to send	Out
5	CTS	Clear to send	In
6	DSR	Data set ready	In
7	SG	Signal ground	—
8	CD	Carrier detect	In
9	—	+Transmit current loop return	Out
11	—	-Transmit current loop data	Out
18	—	+Receive current loop data	In
20	DTR	Data terminal ready	Out
22	RI	Ring indicator	In
25	—	-Receive current loop return	In

Table 17.3   9-Pin to 25-Pin Serial Cable Adapter Connections

9-Pin	25-Pin	Signal	Description
1	8	CD	Carrier detect
2	3	RD	Receive data
3	2	TD	Transmit data
4	20	DTR	Data terminal ready
5	7	SG	Signal ground
6	6	DSR	Data set ready
7	4	RTS	Request to send
8	5	CTS	Clear to send
9	22	RI	Ring indicator

Note

Macintosh systems use a similar serial interface, defined as RS-422. Most external modems in use today can interface with either RS-232 or RS-422, but it is safest to make sure that the external modem you get for your PC is designed for a PC, not a Macintosh.

UARTs

The heart of any serial port is the Universal Asynchronous Receiver/Transmitter (UART) chip. This chip completely controls the process of breaking the native parallel data within the PC into serial format and later converting serial data back into the parallel format.

Several types of UART chips have been available on the market. The original PC and XT used the 8250 UART, which was used for many years in low-priced serial cards. Starting with the first 16-bit systems, the 16450 UART usually was used. The only difference between these chips is their suitability for high-speed communications. The 16450 is better suited for high-speed communications than is the 8250; otherwise, both chips appear identical to most software. The 16550 UART was the first serial chip used in the IBM PS/2 line. Other 386 and higher systems rapidly adopted it.The 16550 functioned as the earlier 16450 and 8250 chips, but it also included a 16-byte buffer that aided in faster communications. This is sometimes referred to as a *FIFO (First In First Out)* buffer. Unfortunately, the early 16550 chips had a few bugs, particularly in the buffer area. These bugs were corrected with the release of the 16550A. The most current version of the chip is the 16550D, released in 1995, which is produced by National Semiconductor.

Even though virtually all Pentium-class and newer systems have 16550-equivalent UART functionality in their serial ports, any search for a socketed 16550 chip on most of these systems would be done in vain. Instead, the functionality of the 16550, parallel port, and other ports is included as part of the Super I/O chip or, on the newest systems, the South Bridge chip.

Tip

The high-speed buffered 16550A (or newer) UART chip is pin for pin compatible with the 16450 UART. If your 16450 UART is socketed, a cheap and easy way to improve serial performance is to install a 16550 UART chip in the socket.

Because the 16550 is a faster, more reliable chip than its predecessors, it is best to ensure that your serial ports have either that chip or an equivalent. If you are in doubt about which type of UART you have in your system, you can use the Microsoft MSD program (provided with MS-DOS 6.x and Windows 9x/Me/2000) to determine the type of UART you have. Note that MSD often reports a 16450 UART as an 8250.

Note

Another way to tell whether you have a 16650 UART in Windows 9x/Me/2000 is to click the Start menu and then select Settings, Control Panel. Next, double-click Modems, and then click the Diagnostics tab. The Diagnostics tab shows a list of all COM ports in the system, even if they don't have a modem attached to them. Select the port you want to check in the list and click More Info. Windows 9x/Me/2000 communicates with the port to determine the UART type, and that information is listed in the Port Information portion of the More Info box. If a modem is attached, additional information about the modem is displayed.

The original designer of these UARTs is National Semiconductor (NS). So many other manufacturers are producing clones of these UARTs that you probably don't have an actual NS brand part in your system. Even so, the part you have is compatible with one of the NS parts, hopefully the 16550. In other words, check to see that whatever UART chip you have does indeed feature the 16-byte FIFO buffer, as found in the NS 16550 part.

◄◄   See "Super I/O Chips," p. 283.

8250

IBM used this original chip in the PC serial port card. This chip had no transmit/receive buffer, so it was very slow. The chip also had several bugs, none of which were serious. The PC and XT ROM BIOSes were written to anticipate at least one of the bugs. The 8250B replaced this chip.

8250A

Do not use the second version of the 8250 in any system. This upgraded chip fixes several bugs in the 8250, including one in the interrupt enable register, but because the PC and XT ROM BIOSes expect the bug, this chip does not work properly with those systems. The 8250A works in an AT system that does not expect the bug, but it does not work adequately at 9600bps.

8250B

The last version of the 8250 fixes bugs from the previous two versions. The interrupt enable bug in the original 8250, which is expected by the PC and XT ROM BIOS software, has been put back into this chip, making the 8250B the most desirable chip for any non-AT serial port application. The 8250B chip might work in an AT under DOS, but it does not run properly at 9600bps because, like all 8250s, it has no transmit/receive buffer.

16450

IBM selected the higher-speed version of the 8250 for the AT. The higher performance mainly comes from a 1-byte transmit/receive buffer contained within the chip. Because this chip has fixed the afore-mentioned interrupt enable bug, the 16450 does not operate properly in many PC or XT systems because they expect this bug to be present. OS/2 requires this chip as a minimum; otherwise, the serial ports do not function properly. It also adds a scratch-pad register as the highest register. The 16450 is used primarily in AT systems because of its increase in throughput over the 8250B.

16550 Series

This chip is pin compatible with the 16450 but is much faster due to a built-in 16-character transmit/receive FIFO buffer. It also allows multiple DMA channel access. The original version of this chip did not allow the buffer to work, but all 16550A or later revisions have the bug fixed. The last version produced by National Semiconductor was called the 16550D. Use a version of this UART in your serial port if you do any communications at 9600bps or higher. If your communications program uses the FIFO—and all of them do today—it can greatly increase communications speed and eliminate lost characters and data at the higher speeds. Virtually all Super I/O chips contain the equivalent of dual 16550A or later chips. Most 16550 UARTs have a maximum communications speed of 115Kbps (bits per second).

16650, 16750, and 16850

Several companies have produced versions of the 16550 with larger buffers:

■ The 16550 has a 32-byte buffer.
■ The 16750 has a 64-byte buffer.
■ The 16850 has a 128-byte buffer.

These chips are not from National Semiconductor, and the designations only imply that they are compatible with the 16550 but have a larger buffer. These larger-buffered versions allow speeds of 230Kbps (16650), 460Kbps (16750), and 920Kbps (16850) and are recommended when running a high-speed external communications link, such as an ISDN terminal adapter or external 56Kbps modem. These are discussed more in the following section.

High-Speed Serial Port Cards

If you are using external RS-232 devices designed to run at speeds higher than 115Kbps (the maximum speed of the 16550 series UARTs and equivalents), you can't achieve maximum performance unless you replace your existing serial ports with add-on cards using one of the 16650, 16650, or 16750 UARTs discussed earlier. Most cards allow raw port speed settings of 230Kbps, 460Kbps, or even higher, which is valuable when connecting a PC to a high-speed external component that is connected to a serial port, such as an ISDN terminal adapter. You can't really get the full-speed benefit of an external ISDN modem (terminal adapter) unless your serial port can go at least 230Kbps. Lava Computer Mfg. and SIIG are two of the companies that offer a complete line of high-speed serial and parallel port cards (see the Vendor List on the accompanying CD).

Multiport Serial Cards

Although most users find that one or two serial ports are adequate, some users with specialized needs require many more ports. Multiport serial port cards can provide the additional ports necessary for remote access services (RAS), multiuser computer systems using terminals, ISP modem pools, data acquisition, and so forth.

If just one or two additional serial ports are required, standard dual serial or multi-I/O (dual serial plus parallel) cards can be used. However, if four to eight ports are required, special multiport cards are available. These cards have a single proprietary connector at the rear bracket of the card that connects to a multipart fan-out cable; each arm of the cable has the standard DB9F RS-232 cable connection. The UART used by multiport cables can be the 16550 or a faster version.

Onboard Serial Ports

Starting with late-model 486-based systems in the mid-1990s, a component on the motherboard called a *Super I/O* chip began to replace separate UART chips. This normally has two serial port UARTs as well as a multimode parallel port, floppy controller, keyboard controller, and sometimes the CMOS memory, all built into a single tiny chip. Still, this chip acts as if all these separate devices were installed: That is, from a software point of view, both the operating system and applications still act as if separate UART chips were installed on serial port adapter cards. The most recent systems integrate the functions of a Super I/O chip into the South Bridge chip. As with the Super I/O chip, South Bridge chips with integrated I/O are transparent to software. Super I/O and South Bridge chips are discussed throughout this chapter and in Chapter 4, "Motherboards and Buses."

Serial Port Configuration

Each time a character is received by a serial port, it has to get the attention of the computer by raising an Interrupt Request Line (IRQ). Eight-bit ISA bus systems have eight of these lines, and systems with a 16-bit ISA bus have 16 lines. The 8259 interrupt controller chip or equivalent usually handles these requests for attention. In a standard configuration, COM 1 uses IRQ4, and COM 2 uses IRQ3. Even on the latest systems, the default COM port assignments remain the same for compatibility with older software and hardware.

When a serial port is installed in a system, it must be configured to use specific I/O addresses (called ports), and interrupts (called IRQs). The best plan is to follow the existing standards for how these devices are to be set up. For configuring serial ports, use the addresses and interrupts indicated in Table 17.4.

Table 17.4   Standard Serial I/O Port Addresses and Interrupts

COM x	I/O Ports	IRQ
COM 1	3F8-3FFh	IRQ4
COM 2	2F8-2FFh	IRQ3
COM 3	3E8-3EFh	IRQ4[1]
COM 4	2E8-2EFh	IRQ3[1]

1. Note that although many serial ports can be set up to share IRQ 3 and 4 with COM 1 and COM 2, it is not recommended. The best recommendation is setting COM 3 to IRQ 10 and COM4 to IRQ 11 (if available). If ports above COM 3 are required, it is recommended that you purchase a special multiport serial board, preferably a PCI-based board that supports IRQ sharing without conflicts.

Be sure that if you are adding more than the standard COM 1 and COM 2 serial ports, they use unique and nonconflicting interrupts. If you purchase a serial port adapter card and intend to use it to supply ports beyond the standard COM1 and COM2, be sure it can use interrupts other than IRQ3 and IRQ4; the latest PCI-based serial port boards take advantage of IRQ sharing features to allow COM 3 and above to use a single IRQ without conflicts.

Note that BIOS manufacturers never built support for COM 3 and COM 4 into the BIOS. Therefore, DOS cannot work with serial ports above COM 2 because DOS gets its I/O information from the BIOS. The BIOS finds out what is installed in your system, and where it is installed, during the POST (power on self test). The POST checks only for the first two installed ports. This is not a problem under Windows because Windows 9x/Me/2000 and NT have built-in support for up to 128 ports.

With support for up to 128 serial ports in Windows, using multiport boards in the system is much easier. Multiport boards give your system the capability to collect or share data with multiple devices while using only one slot and one interrupt.

Caution

Sharing interrupts between COM ports—or any devices—can function properly sometimes and not others. It is recommended that you never share interrupts between multiple ISA-based serial ports, such as the COM ports built into your motherboard or found on an ISA modem. Trying to track down drivers, patches, and updates to allow this to work successfully—if it's even possible at all in your system—can cause you hours of frustration.

◄◄   See "Resolving Resource Conflicts," p. 328.

Testing Serial Ports

You can perform several tests on serial and parallel ports. The two most common types of tests are those that involve software only and those that involve both hardware and software. The software-only tests are done with diagnostic programs, such as Microsoft's MSD or the Modem diagnostics built into Windows 9x/Me/2000, whereas the hardware and software tests involve using a wrap plug to perform loopback testing.

▶▶   See "Testing Parallel Ports," p. 939.

▶▶   See "Advanced Diagnostics Using Loopback Testing," p. 933.

Microsoft Diagnostics

Microsoft Diagnostics (MSD) is a diagnostic program supplied with MS-DOS 6.x, Windows 3.x, and Windows 9x/Me/2000. Note that with Windows 95 this program can be found on the CD-ROM in the \other\msd directory. In Windows 98/Me/2000, you can find it on the CD-ROM in the \tools\ oldmsdos directory. MSD is not automatically installed when you install the operating system. To use it, you must run it from the CD-ROM directly or copy the program from the CD-ROM to your hard disk.

For the most accurate results, many diagnostics programs, such as MSD, are best run in a DOS-only environment. Because of this, you need to restart the machine in DOS mode before using them. Then, to use MSD, switch to the directory in which it is located. This is not necessary, of course, if the directory that contains the program is in your search path—which is often the case with the DOS 6.x or Windows-provided versions of MSD. Then, simply type **MSD** at the DOS prompt and press Enter. Soon you see the MSD screen.

Select the Serial Ports option. Notice that you are given information about which type of serial chip you have in your system, as well as information about which ports are available. If any of the ports are in use (with a mouse, for example), that information is provided as well.

MSD is helpful in at least determining whether your serial ports are responding. If MSD cannot determine the existence of a port, it does not provide the report that indicates that the port exists. This sort of "look-and-see" test is the first action I usually take to determine why a port is not responding.

Troubleshooting I/O Ports in Windows

Windows 9x/Me can tell you whether your ports are functioning. First, you must verify that the required communications files are present to support the serial ports in your system:

1. Verify the file sizes and dates of both COMM.DRV (16-bit serial driver) and SERIAL.VXD (32-bit serial driver) in the SYSTEM directory, compared to the original versions of these files from the Windows 9x/Me CD-ROM.

2. Confirm that the following lines are present in SYSTEM.INI:

```
[boot]
comm.drv=comm.drv
[386enh]
device=*vcd
```

The SERIAL.VXD driver is not loaded in SYSTEM.INI; instead, it is loaded through the Registry.

Windows 2000 uses the SERIAL.SYS and SERENUM.SYS drivers for handling RS-232 devices. You can compare the file sizes and dates for these files to those on the Windows 2000 CD-ROM.

If both drivers are present and accounted for, you can determine whether a particular serial port's I/O address and IRQ settings are properly defined by following these steps for Windows 9x/Me/2000:

1. Right-click the My Computer icon on the desktop and select Properties, or double-click the System icon in the Control Panel. Click the Device Manager tab, click Ports, and then select a specific port (such as COM 1).

2. Click the Properties button, and then click the Resources tab to display the current resource settings (IRQ, I/O) for that port.

3. Check the Conflicting Devices List to see whether the port is using resources that conflict with other devices. If the port is in conflict with other devices, click the Change Setting button, and then select a configuration that does not cause resource conflicts. You might need to experiment with these settings until you find the correct one.

4. If the resource settings cannot be changed, most likely they must be changed via the BIOS Setup. Shut down and restart the system, enter the BIOS setup, and change the port configurations there.

◄◄   See "Resolving Resource Conflicts," p. 328.

A common problem with non-Plug and Play modems can occur when people try to use a modem on COM 3 with a serial mouse or other device on COM 1. Normally, COM 1 and COM 3 ports use the same IRQ, meaning that they cannot be used simultaneously. The COM 2 and COM 4 ports have the same problem sharing IRQs. If possible, change the COM 3 or COM 4 port to an IRQ setting that is not in conflict with COM1 or COM 2. Note also that some video adapters have an automatic address conflict with COM 4.

Advanced Diagnostics Using Loopback Testing

One of the most useful types of diagnostic test is the loopback test, which can be used to ensure the correct function of the serial port and any attached cables. Loopback tests are basically internal (digital) or external (analog). You can run internal tests by simply unplugging any cables from the port and executing the test via a diagnostics program.

The external loopback test is more effective. This test requires that a special loopback connector or wrap plug be attached to the port in question. When the test is run, the port is used to send data out to the loopback plug, which simply routes the data back into the port's receive pins so the port is transmitting and receiving at the same time. A loopback or wrap plug is nothing more than a cable that is doubled back on itself. Most diagnostics programs that run this type of test include the loopback plug, and if not, these types of plugs easily can be purchased or even built.

If you want to build your own loopback plugs, see the 12th edition of *Upgrading and Repairing PCs*, available in electronic form on the CD-ROM packaged with this book.

In most cases, purchasing a set of loopback connectors that are premade is less expensive than making them yourself. Most companies that sell diagnostics software can also sell you a set of loopback plugs. Some hardware diagnostic programs, such as Smith Micro's CheckIt Suite, include loopback plugs with the software.

One advantage of using loopback connectors is that you can plug them into the ends of a cable that is included in the test. This can verify that both the cable and the port are working properly.

If you need to test serial ports further, see Chapter 24, "PC Diagnostics, Testing, and Maintenance," which describes third-party testing software.

Parallel Ports

Parallel ports normally are used for connecting printers to a PC. Even though that was their sole original intention, parallel ports have become much more useful over the years as a more general-purpose, relatively high-speed interface between devices (when compared to serial ports). Today, USB 1.1-compliant ports are almost as fast as parallel ports, and IEEE-1394 ports are significantly faster. Originally, parallel ports were one way only; however, modern parallel ports can send and receive data when properly configured.

Parallel ports are so named because they have eight lines for sending all the bits that comprise 1 byte of data simultaneously across eight wires. This interface is fast and traditionally has been used for printers. However, programs that transfer data between systems always have used the parallel port as an option for transmitting data because it can do so 4 bits at a time rather than 1 bit at a time as with a serial interface.

The following section looks at how these programs transfer data between parallel ports. The only problem with parallel ports is that their cables cannot be extended for any great length without amplifying the signal; otherwise, errors occur in the data. Table 17.5 shows the pinout for a standard PC parallel port.

Table 17.5   25-Pin PC-Compatible Parallel Port Connector

Pin	Description	I/O		Pin	Description	I/O
1	-Strobe	Out		14	-Auto Feed	Out
2	+Data Bit 0	Out		15	-Error	In
3	+Data Bit 1	Out		16	-Initialize Printer	Out
4	+Data Bit 2	Out		17	-Select Input	Out
5	+Data Bit 3	Out		18	-Data Bit 0 Return (GND)	In
6	+Data Bit 4	Out		19	-Data Bit 1 Return (GND)	In
7	+Data Bit 5	Out		20	-Data Bit 2 Return (GND)	In
8	+Data Bit 6	Out		21	-Data Bit 3 Return (GND)	In
9	+Data Bit 7	Out		22	-Data Bit 4 Return (GND)	In
10	-Acknowledge	In		23	-Data Bit 5 Return (GND)	In
11	+Busy	In		24	-Data Bit 6 Return (GND)	In
12	+Paper End	In		25	-Data Bit 7 Return (GND)	In
13	+Select	In				

IEEE 1284 Parallel Port Standard

The IEEE 1284 standard, called Standard Signaling Method for a Bidirectional Parallel Peripheral Interface for Personal Computers, was approved for final release in March 1994. This standard defines the physical characteristics of the parallel port, including data-transfer modes and physical and electrical specifications. IEEE 1284 defines the electrical signaling behavior external to the PC for a multi-modal parallel port that can support 4-bit modes of operation. Not all modes are required by the 1284 specification, and the standard makes some provision for additional modes.

The IEEE 1284 specification is targeted at standardizing the behavior between a PC and an attached device, specifically attached printers. However, the specification is of interest to vendors of parallel port peripherals (removable-media drives, scanners, and so on).

IEEE 1284 pertains only to hardware and line control and does not define how software is to talk to the port. An offshoot of the original 1284 standard has been created to define the software interface. The IEEE 1284.3 committee was formed to develop a standard for software that is used with IEEE 1284-compliant hardware. This standard, designed to address the disparity among providers of parallel port chips, contains a specification for supporting EPP (the Enhanced Parallel Port) mode via the PC's system BIOS.

IEEE 1284 enables much higher throughput in a connection between a computer and a printer or two computers. The result is that the printer cable is no longer the standard printer cable. The IEEE-1284 printer cable uses twisted-pair technology, which results in a much more reliable and error-free connection.

The IEEE 1284 standard also defines the parallel port connectors, including the two preexisting types (called Type A and Type B), as well as an additional high-density Type C connector. Type A refers to the standard DB25 connector used on most PC systems for parallel port connections, whereas Type B refers to the standard 36-pin Centronics-style connector found on most printers. Type C is a new high-density 36-pin connector that can be found on some of the newer printers on the market, such as those from HP. The three connectors are shown in Figure 17.3.

Figure 17.3   The three different types of IEEE-1284 parallel port connectors.

The IEEE 1284 parallel port standard defines five port-operating modes, emphasizing the higher-speed EPP and ECP modes. Some of the modes are input only, whereas others are output only. These five modes combine to create four types of ports, as shown in Table 17.6.

Table 17.6   Types of IEEE-1284 Ports

Parallel Port Type	Input Mode	Output Mode	Comments
SPP (Standard Parallel Port)	Nibble	Compatible	4-bit input, 8-bit output
Bidirectional	Byte	Compatible	8-bit I/O
EPP (Enhanced Parallel Port)	EPP	EPP	8-bit I/O
ECP (Enhanced Capabilities Port)	ECP	ECP	8-bit I/O, uses DMA

The 1284-defined parallel port modes are shown in Table 17.7, which also shows the approximate transfer speeds.

Table 17.7   IEEE 1284 Parallel Port Modes

Parallel Port Mode	Direction	Transfer Rate
Nibble (4-bit)	Input only	50KB/sec
Byte (8-bit)	Input only	150KB/sec
Compatible	Output only	150KB/sec
EPP (Enhanced Parallel Port)	Input/Output	500KB–2MB/sec
ECP (Enhanced Capabilities Port)	Input/Output	500KB–2MB/sec

Each of the port types and modes is discussed in the following sections.

Standard Parallel Ports

Older PCs did not have different types of parallel ports available. The only available port was the parallel port that was used to send information from the computer to a device such as a printer. The unidirectional nature of the original PC parallel port is consistent with its primary use—that is, sending data to a printer. There were times, however, when it was desirable to have a bidirectional port—for example, when it was necessary to receive feedback from a printer, which was common with PostScript printers. This could not be done easily with the original unidirectional ports.

Although it was never intended to be used for input, a clever scheme was devised in which four of the signal lines can be used as a 4-bit input connection. Thus, these ports can do 8-bit (byte) output (called compatible mode) and 4-bit input (called nibble mode). This is still very common on low-end desktop systems. Systems built after 1993 are likely to have more capable parallel ports, such as bidirectional, EPP, or ECP.

Standard parallel ports are capable of effective transfer rates of about 150KB/sec output and about 50KB/sec input.

Bidirectional (8-bit) Parallel Ports

With the introduction of the PS/2 series of machines in 1987, IBM introduced the bidirectional parallel port. These are commonly found in PC-compatible systems today and can be designated "bidirectional," "PS/2 type," or "extended" parallel ports. This port design opened the way for true communication between the computer and the peripheral across the parallel port. This was done by defining a few of the previously unused pins in the parallel connector, and by defining a status bit to indicate in which direction information was traveling across the channel. This allows for a true 8-bit (called byte mode) input.

These ports can do both 8-bit input and output using the standard eight data lines and are considerably faster than the 4-bit ports when used with external devices. Bidirectional ports are capable of approximately 150KB/sec transfer rates on both output and input. Some newer systems use this as their "standard" mode.

Enhanced Parallel Port

EPP is a newer specification, sometimes referred to as the Fast Mode parallel port. Intel, Xircom, and Zenith Data Systems developed and announced, in October 1991, the EPP. The first products to offer EPP were Zenith Data Systems laptops, Xircom Pocket LAN adapters, and the Intel 82360 SL I/O chip. Currently, almost all systems include a multimode parallel port, usually built into the Super I/O chip on the motherboard, that supports EPP mode.

EPP operates at almost ISA bus speed and offers a tenfold increase in the raw throughput capability over a conventional parallel port. EPP is especially designed for parallel port peripherals, such as LAN adapters, disk drives, and tape backups. EPP has been included in the new IEEE 1284 Parallel Port standard. Transfer rates of up to 2MB/sec are possible with EPP.

Since the original Intel 82360 SL I/O chip in 1992, other major chip vendors (such as National Semiconductor, SMC, Western Digital, and VLSI) have also produced I/O chipsets that offer some form of EPP capability. One problem is that the procedure for enabling EPP across the various chips differs widely from vendor to vendor, and many vendors offer more than one I/O chip.

EPP version 1.7 (March 1992) identifies the first popular version of the hardware specification. With minor changes, this has since been abandoned and folded into the IEEE 1284 standard. Some technical reference materials have erroneously made reference to "EPP specification version 1.9," causing confusion about the EPP standard. Note that "EPP version 1.9" technically does not exist, and any EPP specification after the original version 1.7 is more accurately referred to as a part of the IEEE 1284 specification.

Unfortunately, this has resulted in two somewhat incompatible standards for EPP parallel ports: the original EPP Standards Committee version 1.7 standard and the IEEE 1284 Committee standard, normally called EPP version 1.9. The two standards are similar enough that new peripherals can be designed to support both, but older EPP 1.7 peripherals might not operate with EPP 1284 (EPP 1.9) ports. For this reason, many multimode ports allow configuration in either EPP 1.7 or 1.9 modes, normally selected via the BIOS Setup.

EPP ports are now supported in virtually all Super I/O chips that are used on modern motherboards and in South Bridge chips that integrate I/O functions. Because the EPP port is defined in the IEEE 1284 standard, it also has gained software and driver support, including support in Windows NT.

Enhanced Capabilities Port

In 1992, Microsoft and Hewlett-Packard announced another type of high-speed parallel port, the Enhanced Capabilities Port (ECP). Similar to EPP, ECP offers improved performance for the parallel port and requires special hardware logic.

Since the original announcement, ECP is included in IEEE 1284—just like EPP. Unlike EPP, however, ECP is not tailored to support portable PCs' parallel port peripherals; its purpose is to support an inexpensive attachment to a very high-performance printer or scanner. Furthermore, ECP mode requires the use of a DMA channel, which EPP did not define and which can cause troublesome conflicts with other devices that use DMA. Most PCs with newer Super I/O chips can support either EPP or ECP mode.

Most new systems are being delivered with ECP ports that support high throughput communications. In most cases, the ECP ports can be turned into EPP or standard parallel ports via BIOS. However, it's recommended that the port be placed in ECP mode for the best throughput.

Depending on the motherboard, the DMA channel assignment used for ECP mode on a built-in parallel might be performed through the BIOS setup program or through moving a jumper block on the motherboard itself.

Upgrading to EPP/ECP Parallel Ports

Virtually every new or recent system today supports both the EPP and ECP modes of the IEEE 1284 parallel port standard. However, if you are working with an older system that might not have these capabilities built into the BIOS or are dealing with an add-on parallel port card, you might not know which modes the port can support. If you want to test the parallel ports in a system, especially to determine which type they are, I highly recommend a utility called Parallel. This is a handy parallel port information utility that examines your system's parallel ports and reports the port type, I/O address, IRQ level, BIOS name, and an assortment of informative notes and warnings in a compact and easy-to-read display. The output can be redirected to a file for tech support purposes. Parallel uses very sophisticated techniques for port and IRQ detection, and it is aware of a broad range of quirky port features. You can get it from Parallel Technologies (see the Vendor's List on the CD-ROM).

If you have an older system that does not include an EPP/ECP port and you want to upgrade, several companies now offer boards with the correct Super I/O chips to implement these features. I recommend that you check with Parallel Technologies, Byterunner Technologies, Lava Computer Mfg., or SIIG; they are listed in the Vendor List on the CD accompanying this book.

High-speed parallel ports such as EPP and ECP often are used for supporting external peripherals, such as Zip drives, CD-ROM drives, scanners, tape drives, and even hard disks. Most of these devices attach to the parallel port using a pass-through connection. This means that your local printer can still work through the port, along with the device. The device will have its own drivers that mediate both the communications with the device and the printer pass-through. Using EPP or ECP mode, communications speeds that are as high as 2MB/sec can be achieved. This can enable a relatively high-speed device to function almost as if it were connected to the system bus internally.

Parallel Port Configuration

The configuration of parallel ports is not as complicated as it is for serial ports. Even the original IBM PC had BIOS support for three LPT ports. Table 17.8 shows the standard I/O address and interrupt settings for parallel port use.

Table 17.8   Parallel Interface I/O Port Addresses and Interrupts

Standard LPTx	Alternate LPTx	I/O Ports	IRQ
LPT1	—	3BC-3BFh	IRQ7
LPT1	LPT2	378-37Ah	IRQ5
LPT2	LPT3	278h-27Ah	IRQ5

Because the BIOS and DOS have always provided three definitions for parallel ports, problems with older systems are infrequent. Problems can arise, however, from the lack of available interrupt-driven ports for ISA/PCI bus systems. Normally, an interrupt-driven port is not absolutely required for printing operations; in fact, many programs do not use the interrupt-driven capability. However, some programs do use the interrupt, such as network print programs and other types of background or spooler-type printer programs.

Also, high-speed laser-printer utility programs often use the interrupt capabilities to enable printing. If you use these types of applications on a port that is not interrupt driven, you see the printing slow to a crawl—if it works at all. The only solution is to use an interrupt-driven port. MS-DOS and Windows 9x/Me/2000 now support up to 128 parallel ports.

To configure parallel ports in ISA/PCI bus systems, you normally use the BIOS Setup program for ports that are built into the motherboard, or you might need to set jumpers and switches or use a setup program for adapter-card–based ports. Because each board on the market is different, you always should consult the OEM manual for that particular card if you need to know how the card should be configured.

◄◄   See "BIOS Hardware/Software," p. 347.

Linking Systems with Parallel Ports

The original IBM PC designers envisioned that the parallel port would be used only for communicating with a printer. Over the years, the number of devices that can be used with a parallel port has increased tremendously. You can find everything from tape backup units to LAN adapters to CD-ROMs and scanners that connect through your parallel port. Many of these same devices can also be connected via the USB port, and some devices offer both types of connection for maximum flexibility.

Perhaps one of the most common uses of bidirectional parallel ports is to transfer data between your system and another, such as a laptop computer. If both systems use an EPP/ECP port, you can actually communicate at rates of up to 2MB/sec, which is far faster than the speeds achievable with serial port or infrared (IR) data transfers. A number of commercial programs support parallel-port file transfers, including Laplink.com's LapLink, SmithMicro's CheckIt Fast Move, Symantec's PC Anywhere, and others. MS-DOS 6.x, Windows 9x, Windows Me, and Windows 2000 also feature built-in support for parallel-port file transfers.

Connecting two computers with standard unidirectional parallel ports requires a special cable known as a *parallel null modem cable*. Most programs sell or provide these cables with their software. If you want to make one yourself, see *Upgrading and Repairing PCs, 12th Edition*, included in electronic form on the CD packaged with this book.

Tip

Even though cables usually are provided for data-transfer programs, notebook users might want to look for an adapter that makes the appropriate changes to a standard parallel cable. This can make traveling lighter by preventing the need for additional cables. Most of the time, these adapters attach to the Centronics end of the cable and provide a standard DB25 connection on the other end. They're sold under a variety of names; however, parallel null modem cable, Laplink adapter, Laplink converter, and Interlink cable are the most common names.

Although the prebuilt parallel cables referred to in the previous tip work for connecting two machines with ECP/EPP ports, they can't take advantage of the advanced transfer rates of these ports. Special cables are needed to communicate between ECP/EPP ports. Parallel Technologies is a company that sells ECP/EPP cables for connecting to other ECP/EPP computers, as well as a universal cable for connecting any two parallel ports to use the highest speed.

Windows 95 and newer versions include a special program called Direct Cable Connection (DCC), which enables two systems to be networked together via a null modem/Laplink cable. Windows 2000 calls this feature the Direct Parallel Connection, although it is compatible with the Windows 9x/Me DCC software. Consult the Windows documentation for information on how to establish a DCC connection. Parallel Technologies has been contracted by Microsoft to supply the special DCC cables used to connect the systems. Parallel has one special type of cable that uses active electronics to ensure a reliable high-speed interconnection.

Parallel to SCSI Converters

Parallel ports can also be used to connect SCSI peripherals to a PC. With a parallel-to-SCSI converter, you can connect any type of SCSI device—such as hard disks, CD-ROM drives, tape drives, Zip drives, or scanners—to your PC, all via the parallel port. To connect to a SCSI device and also continue to be able to print, most parallel-to-SCSI converters include a pass-through connection for a printer.

This means that at one end of the converter is a connection to your parallel port, and at the other end is both SCSI and parallel-port connections. Thus, you can plug in a single SCSI device and still connect your printer as well. The drivers for the parallel-to-SCSI converter automatically pass through any information to the printer, so the printer works normally.

Adaptec is the major supplier of such converters, but they are available from other companies as well. Note that these converters are designed to handle a single SCSI device; you should buy a SCSI host adapter if you need to support two or more devices. Also note that even an EPP/ECP parallel port runs at only a fraction of the speed (2MBps) of even the slowest SCSI device (10MBps and up).

Testing Parallel Ports

Testing parallel ports is, in most cases, simpler than testing serial ports. The procedures are effectively the same as those used for serial ports, except that when you use the diagnostics software, you, obviously, select choices for parallel ports rather than serial ports.

Even though the software tests are similar, the hardware tests require the proper plugs for the loopback tests on the parallel port. Several loopback plugs are required, depending on what software you are using. Most use the IBM-style loopback, but some use the style that originated in the Norton Utilities diagnostics.

You can purchase loopback plugs or build them yourself. To see the pinouts for parallel loopback plugs, see *Upgrading and Repairing PCs, 12th Edition*, included in electronic form on the CD-ROM packaged with this book.

USB and IEEE-1394 (i.Link or FireWire)—Serial and Parallel Port Replacements

The two most recently introduced high-speed serial-bus architectures for desktop and portable PCs are Universal Serial Bus (USB) and IEEE-1394, which is also called i.Link or FireWire. These are high-speed communications ports that far outstrip the capabilities of standard serial and parallel ports. They can be used as an alternative to SCSI for high-speed peripheral connections. In addition to performance, these newer ports offer I/O device consolidation, which means that all types of external peripherals can connect to these ports.

The recent trend in high-performance peripheral bus design is to use a serial architecture, in which 1 bit at a time is sent down a wire. Because parallel architecture uses 8, 16, or more wires to send bits simultaneously, the parallel bus is actually much faster at the same clock speed. However, increasing the clock speed of a serial connection is much easier than increasing that of a parallel connection.

Parallel connections suffer from several problems, the biggest being signal skew and jitter. Skew and jitter are the reasons high-speed parallel buses such as SCSI are limited to short distances of 3 meters or less. The problem is that, although the 8 or 16 bits of data are fired from the transmitter at the same time, by the time they reach the receiver, propagation delays have conspired to allow some bits to arrive before the others. The longer the cable, the longer the time between the arrival of the first and last bits at the other end! This *signal skew*, as it is called, prevents you from running a high-speed transfer rate or a longer cable—or both. *Jitter* is the tendency for the signal to reach its target voltage and float above and below for a short period of time.

With a serial bus, the data is sent 1 bit at a time. Because there is no worry about when each bit will arrive, the clocking rate can be increased dramatically. For example, the top transfer rate possible with EPP/ECP parallel ports is 2MBps, whereas IEEE-1394 ports (which use high-speed serial technology) support transfer rates as high as 400Mbps (about 50MBps)—25 times faster than parallel ports. USB 2.0 supports transfer rates of 480Mbps (about 60MBps)!

With a high clock rate, parallel signals tend to interfere with each other. Serial again has an advantage because, with only one or two signal wires, crosstalk and interference between the wires in the cable are negligible.

In general, parallel cabling is more expensive than serial cabling. In addition to the many additional wires needed to carry the multiple bits in parallel, the cable also must be specially constructed to prevent crosstalk and interference between adjacent data lines. This is one reason external SCSI cables are so expensive. Serial cabling, by comparison, is very inexpensive. For one thing, it has significantly fewer wires. Furthermore, the shielding requirements are far simpler, even at very high speeds. Because of this, transmitting serial data reliably over longer distances is also easier, which is why parallel interfaces have shorter recommended cable lengths than do serial interfaces.

For these reasons—in addition to the need for new Plug and Play external peripheral interfaces and the elimination of the physical port crowding on portable computers—these high-performance serial buses were developed. USB is a standard feature on virtually all PCs today and is used for general-purpose external interfacing. In addition, IEEE 1394, although originally developed for certain niche markets—such as connecting DV (digital video) camcorders—is also spreading into other high-bandwidth uses, such as high-resolution scanners and external hard drives.

Universal Serial Bus

Universal Serial Bus (USB) is an external peripheral bus standard designed to bring Plug and Play capability for attaching peripherals externally to the PC. USB eliminates the need for special-purpose ports, reduces the need to use special-purpose I/O cards, (thus reducing the need to reconfigure the system with each new device added), and saves important system resources such as interrupts (IRQs); regardless of the number of devices attached to a system's USB ports, only one IRQ is required. PCs equipped with USB enable peripherals to be automatically recognized and configured as soon as they are physically attached, without the need to reboot or run setup. USB allows up to 127 devices to run simultaneously on a computer, with peripherals such as monitors and keyboards acting as additional plug-in sites, or hubs. USB cables, connectors, hubs, and peripherals can be identified by an icon, as shown in Figure 17.4.

Figure 17.4   This icon is used to identify USB cables, connectors, hubs, and peripherals.

Intel has been the primary proponent of USB, and all its PC chipsets starting with the PIIX3 South Bridge chipset component (introduced in February 1996) have included USB support as standard. Other chipset vendors have followed suit, making USB as standard a feature of today's desktop and notebook PCs as the serial and parallel ports.

Six other companies initially worked with Intel in co-developing the USB, including Compaq, Digital, IBM, Microsoft, NEC, and Northern Telecom. Together, these companies have established the USB Implementers Forum (USB-IF) to develop, support, and promote USB architecture.

◀◀ See "Chipsets," p. 225.

The USB-IF formally released USB 1.0 in January 1996, and USB 1.1 in September of 1998. The 1.1 revision was mostly a clarification of some issues related to hubs and other areas of the specification. Most devices and hubs should be 1.1 compliant, even if they were manufactured before the release of the 1.1 specification. More recently the USB-IF released USB 2.0, which is 40 times faster than the original USB and yet fully backward compatible. USB ports can be retrofitted to older computers that lack built-in USB connectors through the use of either an add-on PCI card (for desktop computers) or a PC Card on Cardbus-compatible notebook computers. Most add-on cards are made for USB 1.1, but some add-on cards also support the emerging USB 2.0 standard.

USB Technical Details

USB 1.1 is defined to run at 12Mbit/sec (1.5MB/sec) over a simple four-wire connection. The bus supports up to 127 devices and uses a tiered-star topology, built on expansion hubs that can reside in the PC, any USB peripheral, or even standalone hub boxes. Note that although the standard allows up to 127 devices to be attached, they all must share the 1.5MB/sec bandwidth, meaning that for every active device you add, the bus will slow down some. In practical reality, few people will have more than 8 devices attached at any one time.

For low-speed peripherals, such as pointing devices and keyboards, the USB also has a slower 1.5Mbit/sec subchannel. The subchannel connection is used for slower interface devices, such as keyboards and mice.

USB employs what is called Non Return to Zero Invert (NRZI) data encoding. NRZI is a method of encoding serial data in which 1s and 0s are represented by opposite and alternating high and low voltages where there is no return to a zero (or reference) voltage between the encoded bits. In NRZI encoding, a 1 is represented by no change in signal level, and a 0 is represented by a change in level. A string of 0s causes the NRZI data to toggle each bit time. A string of 1s causes long periods with no transitions in the data. This is an efficient transfer encoding scheme because it eliminates the need for additional clock pulses that would otherwise waste time and bandwidth.

USB devices are considered either *hubs* or *functions*, or both. Functions are the individual devices that attach to the USB, such as a keyboard, mouse, camera, printer, telephone, and so on. Hubs provide additional attachment points to the USB, enabling the attachment of additional hubs or functions. The initial ports in the PC system unit are called the *root hub*, and they are the starting point for the USB. Most motherboards have two, three, or four USB ports, any of which can be connected to functions or additional hubs. Some systems place one or two of the USB ports in the front of the computer, which is very convenient for devices you use only occasionally, such as digital cameras or flash memory card readers.

Hubs are essentially wiring concentrators, and through a star-type topology they allow the attachment of multiple devices. Each attachment point is referred to as a *port*. Most hubs have either four or eight ports, but more are possible. For more expandability, you can connect additional hubs to the ports on an existing hub. The hub controls both the connection and distribution of power to each of the connected functions. A typical hub is shown in Figure 17.5.

Figure 17.5   A typical USB hub with four ports.

Besides providing additional sockets for connecting USB peripherals, a hub provides power to any attached peripherals. A hub recognizes the dynamic attachment of a peripheral and provides at least 0.5W of power per peripheral during initialization. Under control of the host PC driver software, the hub can provide more device power, up to a maximum of 2.5W, for peripheral operation.

Tip

For the most reliable operation, I recommend that you use self-powered hubs, which plug into an AC adapter. Bus-powered hubs pull power from the PC's USB root hub connector and aren't always capable of providing adequate power for high-power requirement devices, such as optical mice.

A newly attached hub is assigned a unique address, and hubs can be cascaded up to five levels deep (see Figure 17.6). A hub operates as a bidirectional repeater and repeats USB signals as required both upstream (toward the PC) and downstream (toward the device). A hub also monitors these signals and handles transactions addressed to itself. All other transactions are repeated to attached devices. A USB 1.1 hub supports both 12Mbit/sec (full-speed) and 1.5Mbit/sec (low-speed) peripherals.

Figure 17.6   A typical PC with USB devices can use multiple USB hubs to support a variety of peripherals, connected to whichever hub is most convenient.

Maximum cable length between two full-speed (12Mbit/sec) devices or a device and a hub is 5 meters using twisted-pair shielded cable with 20-gauge wire. Maximum cable length for low speed (1.5Mbit/sec) devices using non–twisted-pair wire is 3 meters. These distance limits are shorter if smaller-gauge wire is used (see Table 17.9).

Table 17.9   Maximum Cable Lengths Versus Wire Gauge

Gauge	Resistance (in Ohms/meter Ω/m)	Length (Max.)
28	0.232 Ω/m	0.81m
26	0.145 Ω/m	1.31m
24	0.091 Ω/m	2.08m
22	0.057 Ω/m	3.33m
20	0.036 Ω/m	5.00m

Although USB 1.1 is not as fast at data transfer as FireWire or SCSI, it is still more than adequate for the types of peripherals for which it is designed. USB 2.0 operates a surprising 40 times faster than USB 1.1 and allows transfer speeds of 480Mbit/sec or 60MB/sec. USB 2.0 does not yet enjoy widespread support, unfortunately; very few systems or devices are USB 2.0 compliant at present. However, if you are planning to purchase a USB add-on card for a system that has no USB ports, I suggest you purchase a USB 2.0-compliant card even if you have no USB 2.0-compliant devices. One of the additional benefits of USB 2.0 is the capability to handle concurrent transfers, which enables your USB 1.1 devices to transfer data at the same time without tying up the USB bus.

USB 2.0 drivers will not be provided with the initial launch of Windows XP but will be made available through downloads or as a service pack as soon as sufficient testing of USB 2.0 peripherals with Windows XP has taken place.

USB Connectors

Two connectors are specified for USB, called Series A and Series B. The Series A connector is designed for devices in which the cable remains permanently attached, such as hubs, keyboards, and mice. The USB ports on most motherboards are also normally a Series A connector. Series B connectors are designed for devices that require detachable cables, such as printers, scanners, modems, telephones, and speakers. The physical USB plugs are small and, unlike a typical serial or parallel cable, the plug is not attached by screws or thumbscrews. There are no pins to bend or break, making USB devices very user friendly to install and remove. The USB plug shown in Figure 17.7 snaps into place on the USB connector. Table 17.10 shows the pinout for the USB four-wire connector and cable. Most systems with USB connectors feature a pair of Series B connectors on the rear of the system, and some also feature one or two on the front of the system for use with digital cameras, card readers, keyboards, or pointing devices.

Figure 17.7   USB Series A and Series B plugs and receptacles.

Table 17.10   USB Connector Pinout

Pin	Signal Name	Wire Color	Comment
1	VCC	Red	Cable power
2	- Data	White	Data transfer
3	+ Data	Green	Data transfer
4	Ground	Black	Cable ground
Shell	Shield	—	Drain wire

USB conforms to Intel's Plug and Play (PnP) specification, including hot plugging, which means that devices can be plugged in dynamically without powering down or rebooting the system. Simply plug in the device, and the USB controller in the PC detects the device and automatically determines and allocates the required resources and drivers. Microsoft has developed USB drivers and included them automatically in Windows 95C/98/Me/2000.

Note that the Windows 95B release or later is required for USB support; the necessary drivers are not present in the original Windows 95 or 95A. Note also that many USB devices will not work with **any** Windows 95 release, including those that have the USB support files included. Windows 98 includes full USB support, as does Windows 2000 and Windows Me. With Windows 95B, the USB drivers are not automatically included; they are provided separately, although a late release of Windows 95— Windows 95C—includes USB support. USB support is also required in the BIOS. This is included in newer systems with USB ports built in. Aftermarket PCI and PC Card boards also are available for adding USB to systems that don't include it as standard on the motherboard. USB peripherals include printers, CD-ROMs, modems, scanners, telephones, joysticks, keyboards, and pointing devices such as mice and trackballs.

One interesting feature of USB is that all attached devices are powered by the USB bus. The PnP aspects of USB enable the system to query the attached peripherals as to their power requirements and issue a warning if available power levels are being exceeded. This is important for USB when it is used in portable systems because the battery power that is allocated to run the external peripherals might be limited. To avoid running out of power when connecting USB devices, use a self-powered hub.

Another of the benefits of the USB specification is the self-identifying peripheral, a feature that greatly eases installation because you don't have to set unique IDs or identifiers for each peripheral—the USB handles that automatically. Also, USB devices can be "hot" plugged or unplugged, meaning that you do not have to turn off your computer or reboot every time you want to connect or disconnect a peripheral.

Enabling USB Support

Many systems shipped before Windows 98 was introduced in mid-1998 have onboard USB ports that were disabled at the factory. In some cases, especially with Baby-AT motherboards, there is no way to tell from the outside which systems have USB support built in. This is because many of these same systems were not shipped with the USB header cables necessary to bring the USB root hub connectors from the motherboard to the rear of the system.

If USB support is disabled in the system BIOS, restart your system and locate the BIOS setup screen that refers to the USB ports. Enable the USB feature. If you see a separate entry for USB IRQ, enable this as well. After you restart the computer with a USB-aware operating system, your "new" USB root hub will be detected and the drivers will be installed if you are using Windows 98 or newer; you might need to manually install drivers with late releases of Windows 95.

If your system has USB connectors present, you also will be able to use the "new" USB ports as soon as the system is rebooted after the USB drivers are installed. However, if your motherboard vendor didn't provide USB connectors, you must buy USB header cables. Before you order them, check the configuration of your motherboard's USB header pins. The standard is two rows of five pins each. Companies such as Belkin, CyberGuys, and Cables To Go sell header cables that are compatible with standard USB header pins if your motherboard supplier doesn't have the header cable in stock. Figure 17.8 shows a typical USB header cable set.

Figure 17.8 A typical USB header cable set; plug it into your Baby-AT or early ATX motherboard to connect devices to the onboard USB ports (if present).

One of the biggest advantages of an interface such as USB is that it requires only a single interrupt (IRQ) from the PC. Therefore, you can connect up to 127 devices and they will not use separate interrupts as they might if each were connected over a separate interface. This is a major benefit of the USB interface.

Some unique USB devices are available, including USB-to-serial, USB-to-parallel, USB-to-Ethernet, USB-to-SCSI, USB-to-PS/2 (standard keyboard and mouse port), and even direct-connect USB bridges (which allow two systems to be connected together via USB for data transfers using Direct Cable Connection or similar programs). USB-to-serial or USB-to-parallel converters provide an easy way to connect legacy RS232 or Centronics parallel interface peripherals, such as modems and printers, to a USB port. USB-to-Ethernet adapters provide a LAN connection through a USB port. Drivers supplied with these devices enable them to fully emulate standard devices.

USB 2.0

USB 2.0 is a backward-compatible extension of the USB 1.1 specification that uses the same cables, connectors, and software interfaces, but that runs 40 times faster than the original 1.0 and 1.1 versions. The higher speed enables higher-performance peripherals, such as higher-resolution Web/videoconferencing cameras, scanners, and faster printers, to be connected externally with the same easy plug-and-play installation of current USB peripherals. From the end-user point of view, USB 2.0 works exactly the same as 1.1—only faster and with more interesting, higher-performance devices available. All existing USB 1.1 devices work in a USB 2.0 bus because USB 2.0 supports all the slower-speed connections. USB data rates are shown in Table 17.11.

Table 17.11   USB Data Rates

Interface	Megabits per Second	Megabytes per Second
USB 1.1 low speed	1.5Mbit/sec	0.1875MB/sec
USB 1.1 high speed	12Mbit/sec	1.5MB/sec
USB 2.0	480Mbit/sec	60MB/sec

The support of higher-speed USB 2.0 peripherals requires using a USB 2.0 hub. You can still use older USB 1.1 hubs on a 2.0 bus, but any peripherals or additional hubs connected downstream from a 1.1 hub will operate at the slower 1.5MB/sec USB 1.1 maximum speed. Devices connected to USB 2.0 hubs will operate at the maximum speed of the device, up to the full USB 2.0 speed of 60MB/sec. The higher transmission speeds through a 2.0 hub are negotiated on a device-by-device basis, and if the higher speed is not supported by a peripheral, the link operates at a lower USB 1.1 speed.

As such, a USB 2.0 hub accepts high-speed transactions at the faster USB 2.0 frame rate and must deliver them to high-speed USB 2.0 peripherals as well as USB 1.1 peripherals. This data rate matching responsibility requires increased complexity and buffering of the incoming high-speed data. When communicating with an attached USB 2.0 peripheral, the 2.0 hub simply repeats the high-speed signals; however, when communicating with USB 1.1 peripherals, a USB 2.0 hub will buffer and manage the transition from the high speed of the USB 2.0 host controller (in the PC) to the lower speed of a USB 1.1 device. This feature of USB 2.0 hubs means that USB 1.1 devices can operate along with USB 2.0 devices and not consume any additional bandwidth. USB 2.0 devices and root hubs are not yet widely available, but they are slowly being introduced by manufacturers. USB 2.0 devices, unlike USB 1.1 devices, might be located inside your system. Some manufacturers of add-on USB 2.0 cards are equipping the cards with both external and internal USB 2.0 ports.

How can you tell which devices are designed to support USB 1.1 and which support the emerging USB 2.0 standard? The USB Implementer's Forum (USB-IF), which owns and controls the USB standard, introduced new logos in late 2000 for products that have passed its certification tests. The new logos are shown in Figure 17.9.

Figure 17.9   The new USB-IF USB 1.1-compliant logo (left) compared to the new USB-IF USB 2.0-compliant logo (right).

As you can see from Figure 17.9, USB 1.1 will be called simply "USB," and USB 2.0 will now be called "Hi-Speed USB."

USB Adapters

If you still have a variety of older peripherals and yet you want to take advantage of the USB connector on your motherboard, a number of signal converters or adapters are available. Companies such as Belkin and others currently have adapters in the following types:

- USB-to-parallel (printer)
- USB-to-serial

- USB-to-SCSI
- USB-to-Ethernet
- USB-to-keyboard/mouse
- USB-to-TV/video

These adapters normally look just like a cable, with a USB connector at one end (which you plug into your USB port) and various other interface connectors at the other end. There is more to these devices than just a cable: Active electronics are hidden in a module along the cable or are sometimes packed into one of the cable ends. The electronics is powered by the USB bus and converts the signals to the appropriate other interface. Some drawbacks do exist to these adapters. One is cost—they normally cost $50–$100 or more. It can be tough to spend $70 on a USB-to-parallel adapter to drive a printer that barely cost twice that amount. In addition, other limitations might apply. For example, USB-to-parallel converters work only with printers and not other parallel-connected devices, such as scanners, cameras, external drives, and so on. Before purchasing one of these adapters, ensure that it will work with the device or devices you have in mind. If you need to use more than one non-USB device with your system, consider special USB hubs that also contain various combinations of other port types. These special hubs are more expensive than USB-only hubs but are less expensive than the combined cost of a comparable USB hub and two or more USB adapters.

Another type of adapter available is a direct-connect cable, which enables you to connect two USB-equipped PCs directly together using USB as a network. These are popular for people playing two-player games, with each player on his own system. Another use is for transferring files because this connection usually works as well or better than the direct parallel connection that otherwise might be used. Also available are USB switchboxes that enable one peripheral to be shared among two or more USB buses. Note that both the direct connect cables and USB switchboxes are technically not allowed as a part of the USB specification, although they do exist.

Legacy-Free PCs

USB adapters might find more use in the future as more and more legacy-free PCs are shipped. A *legacy-free PC* is one that lacks any components that were connected to or a part of the traditional ISA bus. This especially includes the otherwise standard Super I/O chip, which integrated serial, parallel, keyboard, mouse, floppy, and other connections. A legacy-free motherboard will therefore not have the standard serial, parallel, and keyboard/mouse connectors on the back and also will lack an integrated floppy controller. The devices previously connected to those ports must instead be connected via USB, ATA/IDE, PCI, and other interfaces.

Legacy-free systems primarily will be found on the low-end, consumer-oriented systems. For those systems, USB will likely be one of the only external connections provided. To compensate for the loss of the other external interfaces, most legacy-free motherboards will feature four or more integrated USB connectors on one or two buses.

IEEE-1394

The *Institute of Electrical and Electronic Engineers* Standards Board introduced IEEE-1394 (or just 1394 for short) in late 1995. The number comes from the fact that this happened to be the 1,394th standard they published. It is the result of the large data-moving demands of today's audio and video multimedia devices. The key advantage of 1394 is that it's extremely fast; the current standard supports data transfer rates up to an incredible 400Mbit/sec.

Current and Proposed 1394 Standards

The current version of the 1394 standard is actually referred to as 1394a, or sometimes as 1394a-2000 for the year it was adopted. The 1394a standard was introduced to solve interoperability and compatibility issues in the original 1394 standard; it uses the same connectors and supports the same speeds as the original 1394 standard.

The proposed 1394b standard is expected to support transfer rates of 1,600Mbps; future versions of the standard might reach speeds of up to 3,200Mbps. 1394b will be capable of reaching much higher speeds than the current 1394/1394a standard because it will also support network technologies such as glass and plastic fiber-optic cable and Category 5 UTP cable, increased distances when Category 5 cabling is used between devices, and improvements in signaling. 1394b will be fully backward compatible with 1394a devices.1394 is also known by two other common names: i.Link and FireWire. *i.Link* is an IEEE-1394 designation initiated by Sony in an effort to put a more user-friendly name on IEEE-1394 technology. Most companies that produce 1394 products for PCs have endorsed this new name initiative. The term *FireWire* is an Apple-specific trademark. Companies that want to include the FireWire name in a 1394 product first must sign a licensing agreement with Apple, something not all companies producing PC products have done.

1394 Technical Details

The IEEE-1394a standard currently exists with three signaling rates—100Mbit/sec, 200Mbit/sec, and 400Mbit/sec (12.5MB/sec, 25MB/sec, and 50MB/sec). Most PC adapter cards support the 200Mbit/sec rate, even though current devices generally operate at only 100Mbit/sec. A maximum of 63 devices can be connected to a single IEEE-1394 adapter card by way of daisy-chaining or branching. 1394 devices, unlike USB devices, can be used in a daisy-chain without using a hub, although hubs are recommended for devices that will be hot-swapped. Cables for IEEE-1394 devices use Nintendo GameBoy–derived connectors and consist of six conductors: Four wires transmit data, and two wires conduct power. Connection with the motherboard is made either by a dedicated IEEE-1394 interface or by a PCI adapter card. Figure 17.10 shows the 1394 cable, socket, and connector.

IEEE-1394
six-pin port

IEEE-1394
standard six-pin
cable

IEEE-1394 four-pin cable
used on DV camcorders

Figure 17.10 IEEE-1394 port, 6-pin cable, and 4-pin cable.

The 1394 bus was derived from the FireWire bus originally developed by Apple and Texas Instruments, and it is also a part of the new Serial SCSI standard discussed later in this chapter.

1394 uses a simple six-wire cable with two differential pairs of clock and data lines, plus two power lines; the four-wire cable shown in Figure 17.10 is used with self-powered devices, such as DV camcorders. Just as with USB, 1394 is fully PnP, including the capability for hot-plugging (insertion and removal of components without powering down). Unlike the much more complicated parallel SCSI bus, 1394 does not require complicated termination, and devices connected to the bus can draw up to 1.5 amps of electrical power. 1394 offers equal or greater performance compared to ultra-wide SCSI, with a much less expensive and less complicated connection.

1394 is built on a daisy-chained and branched topology, and it allows up to 63 nodes, with a chain of up to 16 devices on each node. If this is not enough, the standard also calls for up to 1,023 bridged buses, which can interconnect more than 64,000 nodes! Additionally, as with SCSI, 1394 can support devices with various data rates on the same bus. Most 1394 adapters have three nodes, each of which can support 16 devices in a daisy-chain arrangement. Some 1394 adapters also support internal 1394 devices.

The types of devices that can be connected to the PC via 1394 include all forms of disk drives, including hard disk, optical, floppy, CD-ROM, and DVD-ROM drives. Also, digital cameras, tape drives, high-resolution scanners, and many other high-speed peripherals that feature 1394 have interfaces built in. The 1394 bus is beginning to appear in both desktop and portable computers as a replacement for other external high-speed buses, such as SCSI.

Chipsets and PCI adapters for the 1394 bus are available from a number of manufacturers, including some models that support both 1394 and other port types in a single slot. Microsoft has developed drivers to support 1394 in Windows 9x/Me/2000 and Windows NT and will have 1394 support in the initial shipments of Windows XP. The most popular devices that conform to the IEEE 1394 standard primarily are camcorders and VCRs with digital video capability. Sony was among the first to release such devices, under the i.Link name. In typical Sony fashion, however, its products have a unique four-wire connector that requires an adapter cord to be used with IEEE-1394 PC cards, and Sony doesn't even call it IEEE-1394 or FireWire—it created its own designation (i.Link) instead. DV products using 1394 also are available from Panasonic, Sharp, Matsushita, and others. Non-computer IEEE-1394 applications include DV conferencing devices, satellite audio and video data streams, audio synthesizers, DVD, and other high-speed disc drives.

Because of the current DV emphasis for IEEE-1394 peripherals, most PC cards currently offered are bundled with DV capturing and editing software. With a DV camera or recording equipment, these items provide substantial video editing and dubbing capabilities on your PC. Of course, you need IEEE-1394 I/O connectivity, which is a growing, but still rare, feature on current motherboards.

Comparing IEEE-1394a and USB 1.1/2.0

Because of the similarity in both the form and function of USB and 1394, there has been some confusion about the two. Table 17.12 summarizes the differences between the two technologies.

Table 17.12   IEEE-1394a and USB Comparison

	IEEE-1394a (a.k.a. i.Link; FireWire)	USB 1.1	USB 2.0
PC-host required	No	Yes	Yes
Maximum number of devices	63	127	127
Hot-swappable?	Yes	Yes	Yes
Maximum cable length between devices	4.5 meters	5 meters	5 meters
Transfer rate	200Mbps (25MB/sec)	12Mbps (1.5MB/sec)	480Mbps (60MB/sec)

Table 17.12   Continued

	IEEE-1394a (a.k.a. i.Link; FireWire)	**USB 1.1**	**USB 2.0**
Proposed future transfer rates	400Mbps (50MB/sec) 800Mbps (100MB/sec) 1Gbps+ (125MB/sec+)	None	None
Typical devices	DV camcorders; high-res digital cameras; HDTV; set-top boxes; high-speed drives; high-res scanners; electronic musical instruments	keyboards; mice; joysticks; low-res digital cameras; low-speed drives; modems; printers; low-res scanners	All USB 1.1 devices, plus DV camcorders; high-res digital cameras; HDTV; set-top boxes; high-speed drives; high-res scanners

The main differences are popularity, PC- or non–PC-centricity, and speed. USB is by far the most popular external interface, eclipsing all others by comparison.

Although practically all PCs sold today include USB 1.1 as standard, 1394 is still primarily an aftermarket update; only a small number of current systems and motherboards feature integrated 1394 ports.

Even with the overwhelming popularity of USB, a market for 1394 still exists. Perhaps the main reason 1394 will survive in comparisons with the USB 2.0 interface is that USB is PC-centric, whereas 1394 is not. USB requires a PC as the host, but an important benefit of 1394 is that a PC host connection is not required. As such, 1394 can be used to directly connect a DV camcorder to a DV-VCR for dubbing tapes or editing. This is one reason it will remain popular in the digital video environment, even with the advent of USB 2.0.

As for speed, that is a constantly changing parameter. 1394 offers a data transfer rate more than 16 times faster than that of USB 1.1, but that is less than half as fast as USB 2.0. This speed differential will change again in the future as higher-speed versions of 1394 debut (such as the proposed 1394b with its 1.6Mbps initial speed rating). USB 1.1 is clearly designed for low-speed peripherals, such as keyboards, mice, modems, and printers, whereas USB 2.0 is designed to connect most high-speed external devices. 1394 is being used to connect both high-performance digital video electronics products and high-bandwidth computer products.

In general, IEEE-1394 offers unprecedented multimedia capabilities to current and future PC users. Current peripherals—particularly DV devices—are still fairly expensive, but as with any emerging technology, prices should come down in the future, opening the door wide for new PC uses in both the home and office. A great number of people will gain the capability to do advanced audio and video editing. If you anticipate having multimedia needs on your PC in the future, IEEE-1394 will likely be the interface of choice, with USB 2.0 providing connectivity for the peripherals that currently use legacy ports, such as the keyboard, PS/2 mouse, and serial and parallel ports.

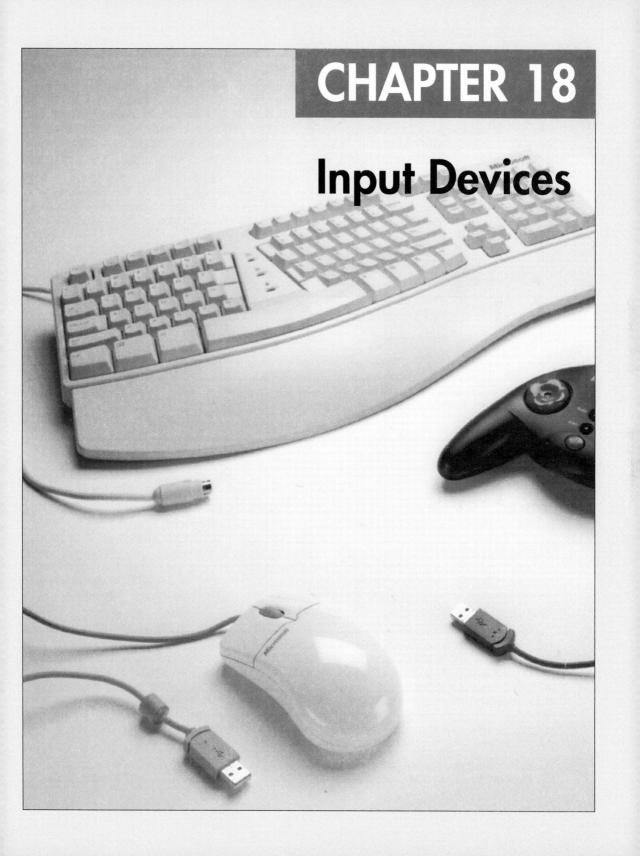

CHAPTER 18

Input Devices

Keyboards

One of the most basic system components is the keyboard, which is the primary input device. It is used for entering commands and data into the system. This section looks at the keyboards available for PC-compatible systems, examining the various types of keyboards, how the keyboard functions, the keyboard-to-system interface, and keyboard troubleshooting and repair.

In the years since the introduction of the original IBM PC, IBM has created three keyboard designs for PC systems; Microsoft has augmented one of them. These designs have become de facto standards in the industry and are shared by virtually all PC manufacturers. With the introduction of Windows 95, a modified version of the standard 101-key design (created by Microsoft) appeared, called the 104-key Windows keyboard.

The primary keyboard types are as follows:

- 101-key Enhanced keyboard
- 104-key Windows keyboard
- 83-key PC and XT keyboard (obsolete)
- 84-key AT keyboard (obsolete)

This section discusses the 101-key Enhanced keyboard and the 104-key Windows keyboard, showing the layout and physical appearance of both. Although you can still find old systems that use the 83-key and 84-key designs, these are rare today. Because all new systems today use the 101- or 104-key keyboard design, these versions are covered here.

Note

If you need to learn more about the 83-key PC and XT keyboard or the 84-key AT keyboard, see Chapter 7 of *Upgrading and Repairing PCs, 10th Anniversary Edition*, on the CD included with this book.

Enhanced 101-Key (or 102-Key) Keyboard

In 1986, IBM introduced the "corporate" Enhanced 101-key keyboard for the newer XT and AT models. I use the word "corporate" because this unit first appeared in IBM's RT PC, which was a RISC (Reduced Instruction Set Computer) system designed for scientific and engineering applications. Keyboards with this design were soon supplied with virtually every type of system and terminal that IBM sold. Other companies quickly copied this design, which became the standard on Intel-based PC systems until the introduction of the 104-key Windows keyboard in 1995 (discussed later in this chapter).

The layout of this universal keyboard was improved over that of the 84-key unit, with perhaps the exception of the Enter key, which reverted to a smaller size. The 101-key Enhanced keyboard was designed to conform to international regulations and specifications for keyboards. In fact, other companies, such as Digital Equipment Corporation (DEC) and Texas Instruments (TI), had already been using designs similar to the IBM 101-key unit. The IBM 101-key units originally came in versions with and without the status-indicator LEDs, depending on whether the unit was sold with an XT or AT system. Now there are many other variations from which to choose, including some with integrated pointing devices, such as the IBM TrackPoint II pointing stick, trackballs and touch pads, and programmable keys useful for automating routine tasks.

The Enhanced keyboard is available in several variations, but all are basically the same electrically and all can be interchanged. IBM—with its Lexmark keyboard and printer spinoff—and Unicomp (which now produces these keyboards) have produced a number of keyboard models, including versions with built-in pointing devices and new ergonomic layouts. With the replacement of the Baby-AT mother-board and its five-pin DIN (an acronym for Deutsche Industrie Norm) keyboard connector by ATX motherboards, which use the six-pin mini-DIN keyboard connector, virtually all keyboards on the market today come with cables for the six-pin mini-DIN connector introduced on the IBM PS/2s. Although the connectors might be physically different, the keyboards are not, and you can either interchange the cables or use a cable adapter to plug one type into the other; some keyboards you can buy at retail include the adapter in the package. See the section "Keyboard/Mouse Interface Connectors" (page 969) and Figure 18.7 later in this chapter for the physical and electronic details of these connectors. Some keyboards now connect to the Universal Serial Bus (USB) connector, but these keyboards are not compatible with either the original DIN or the mini-DIN keyboard standards unless the keyboard is supplied with an adapter. See the section "USB Keyboards" (page 957) later in this chapter for details.

The 101-key keyboard layout can be divided into the following four sections:

- Typing area
- Numeric keypad
- Cursor and screen controls
- Function keys

The 101-key arrangement is similar to the Selectric keyboard layout, with the exception of the Enter key. The Tab, Caps Lock, Shift, and Backspace keys have a larger striking area and are located in the familiar Selectric locations. Ctrl and Alt keys are on each side of the spacebar. The typing area and numeric keypad have home-row identifiers for touch typing.

The cursor- and screen-control keys have been separated from the numeric keypad, which is reserved for numeric input. (As with other PC keyboards, you can use the numeric keypad for cursor and screen control when the keyboard is not in Num Lock mode.) A division-sign key (/) and an additional Enter key have been added to the numeric keypad.

The cursor-control keys are arranged in the inverted T format that is now expected on all computer keyboards. The Insert, Delete, Home, End, Page Up, and Page Down keys, located above the dedicated cursor-control keys, are separate from the numeric keypad. The function keys, spaced in groups of four, are located across the top of the keyboard. The keyboard also has two additional function keys: F11 and F12. The Esc key is isolated in the upper-left corner of the keyboard. Dedicated Print Screen/Sys Req, Scroll Lock, and Pause/Break keys are provided for commonly used functions.

Foreign-language versions of the Enhanced keyboard include 102 keys and a slightly different layout from the 101-key U.S. versions.

One of the many useful features of the IBM/Lexmark enhanced keyboard (now manufactured by Unicomp) is removable keycaps. This permits the replacement of broken keys and provides access for easier cleaning. Also, with clear keycaps and paper inserts, you can customize the keyboard. Keyboard templates are also available to provide specific operator instructions.

104-Key (Windows 9x/Me/2000) Keyboard

If you are a touch typist as I am, you probably really hate to take your hands off the keyboard to use a mouse. Windows 9x and newer versions make this even more of a problem because they use both the right and left mouse buttons (the right button is used to open shortcut menus). Many new keyboards, especially those in portable computers, include a variation of the IBM TrackPoint or the Cirque GlidePoint pointing devices (discussed later in this chapter), which enable touch typists to keep their hands on the keyboard even while moving the pointer. However, another alternative is available that can help. When Microsoft released Windows 95, it also introduced the Microsoft Natural Keyboard, which implemented a revised keyboard specification that added three new Windows-specific keys to the keyboard.

The Microsoft Windows keyboard specification, which has since become a de facto industry standard for keyboard layouts, outlines a set of additional keys and key combinations. The 104-key layout includes left and right Windows keys and an Application key. These keys are used for operating-system and application-level keyboard combinations, similar to the existing Ctrl and Alt combinations. You don't need the new keys to use Windows 9x/Me/NT/2000, but software vendors are adding specific functions to their Windows products that use the new Application key (which provides the same functionality as clicking the right mouse button). The recommended Windows keyboard layout calls for the Left and Right Windows keys (called WIN keys) to flank the Alt keys on each side of the spacebar, as well as an Application key on the right of the Right Windows key. Note that the exact placement of these keys is up to the keyboard designer, so you will see variations from keyboard to keyboard.

The WIN keys open the Windows Start menu, which you can then navigate with the cursor keys. The Application key simulates the right mouse button; in most applications, it brings up a context-sensitive pop-up menu. Several WIN key combinations offer preset macro commands as well. For example, you press WIN+E to launch the Windows Explorer application. Table 18.1 shows a list of all the Windows 9x/Me/2000 key combinations used with the 104-key keyboard.

Table 18.1   Windows 9x/Me/2000 Key Combinations

Key Combination	Resulting Action
WIN+R	Runs dialog box
WIN+M	Minimize All
Shift+WIN+M	Undo Minimize All
WIN+D	Minimize All or Undo Minimize All
WIN+F1	Help
WIN+E	Starts Windows Explorer
WIN+F	Find Files or Folders
Ctrl+WIN+F	Find Computer
WIN+Tab	Cycles through taskbar buttons
WIN+Break	Displays System Properties dialog box
Application key	Displays a context menu for the selected item

The preceding keystroke combinations work with any manufacturer's 104-key keyboard, but users of certain Microsoft 104-key keyboards can enhance their keyboard use by installing the IntelliType Pro software supplied with the Microsoft keyboard.

IntelliType Pro enables the user to customize keyboard, Internet, and multimedia hot keys and settings. After you install IntelliType Pro with a supported Microsoft keyboard, you can use the key combinations listed in Table 18.2. Updates to IntelliType Pro software are available from Microsoft's Web site.

Table 18.2   IntelliType Pro Key Combinations

Key Combination	Resulting Action
WIN+L	Logs off Windows
WIN+P	Opens Print Manager
WIN+C	Opens the Control Panel
WIN+V	Opens the Clipboard
WIN+K	Opens the Keyboard Properties dialog box
WIN+I	Opens the Mouse Properties dialog box
WIN+A	Opens the Accessibility Options (if installed)
WIN+spacebar	Displays the list of IntelliType hotkeys
WIN+S	Toggles the Caps Lock key on and off

The Windows keyboard specification requires that keyboard makers increase the number of trilograms in their keyboard designs. A *trilogram* is a combination of three rapidly pressed keys that perform a special function, such as Ctrl+Alt+Delete. Designing a keyboard so that the switch matrix will correctly register the additional trilograms plus the additional Windows keys adds somewhat to the cost of these keyboards compared to the previous 101-key standard models.

Virtually all keyboard manufacturers have standardized on 104-key keyboards that include these Windows-specific keys.

The Windows keys are not mandatory when running Windows. In fact, preexisting standard key combinations perform the same functions as these newer keys. I also have noticed that few people who have these extra keys on their keyboards actually use them. Some manufacturers have added browser control or other keys that, although not standard, can make them easier to use for viewing Web pages.

USB Keyboards

The latest innovation in keyboard interfacing is connecting the keyboard to the PC via a USB port instead of the standard keyboard port. Because USB is a universal bus that uses a hub to enable multiple devices to connect to a single port, a single USB port in a system can replace the standard serial and parallel ports as well as the keyboard and mouse ports. Most current systems still include both USB and the standard ports, but some so-called "legacy-free" systems have only USB ports for interfacing all input/output devices.

Several keyboard manufacturers are marketing USB keyboards, including Microsoft with the Natural Keyboard Elite and Pro series keyboards. The Natural Keyboard Elite is virtually unique among USB keyboards because it is designed to work with standard keyboard ports and also comes with an adapter that enables it to connect to the USB port on systems using Windows 98/Me/2000.

Note

Note that the internal electronics of this keyboard are different from other models, and the USB adapter included with the Natural Keyboard Elite will not work on other standard keyboards, such as the original Microsoft Natural Keyboard version 1.0.

Not all systems accept USB keyboards, even those with USB ports, because the standard PC BIOS has a keyboard driver that expects a standard keyboard port interface keyboard to be present. When a USB keyboard is installed, the system can't use it because no driver exists in the BIOS to make it work. In fact, some systems see the lack of a standard keyboard as an error and halt the boot process until one is installed.

To use a keyboard connected via the USB port, you must meet three requirements:

- Have a USB port in the system
- Run Microsoft Windows 98, Windows Me, or Windows 2000 (all of which include USB keyboard drivers)
- Have a system chipset and BIOS that features USB Legacy support

USB Legacy support means your motherboard has a chipset and ROM BIOS drivers that enable a USB keyboard to be used outside the Windows GUI environment. When a system has USB Legacy support enabled, a USB keyboard can be used with MS-DOS, for configuring the system BIOS, when using a command prompt within Windows or when installing Windows on the system for the first time. If USB Legacy support is not enabled on the system, a USB keyboard will function only when Windows is running.

Most recent systems include USB Legacy support, although it is disabled by default in the system BIOS.

Also, if the Windows installation fails and requires manipulation outside of Windows, the USB keyboard will not function unless it is supported by the chipset and the BIOS. Almost all 1998 and newer systems with USB ports include a chipset and BIOS with USB Legacy (meaning USB Keyboard) support.

Even though USB Legacy support enables you to use a USB keyboard in almost all situations, don't scrap your standard-port keyboards just yet. Some Windows-related bugs and glitches reported by some users include the following:

- *Can't log on to Windows 98/Me/2000 the first time after installing a USB keyboard.* The solution is to click Cancel when you are asked to log on; then allow the system to detect the keyboard and install drivers. The logon should work normally thereafter.

- *Some USB keyboards won't work when the Windows 98/Me/2000 Emergency Boot Disk (EBD) is used to start the system.* The solution is to turn off the system, connect a standard keyboard, and restart the system.

- *Some users of Windows 98 and Windows 98 SE have reported conflicts between Windows and the BIOS when USB Legacy support is enabled on some systems.* This conflict can result in an incapability to detect the USB keyboard if you use the Windows 9x shutdown menu and choose to Restart the computer in MS-DOS mode. Check with the system or BIOS vendor for an updated BIOS or a patch to solve this conflict.

If you have problems with Legacy USB support, look at these possible solutions:

- Microsoft's Knowledge Base might address your specific combination of hardware.
- Your keyboard vendor might offer new drivers.
- Your system or motherboard vendor might have a BIOS upgrade you can install.

For more information on USB, see Chapter 17, "I/O Interfaces from Serial and Parallel to IEEE-1394 and USB."

Portable Keyboards

One of the biggest influences on keyboard design in recent years has been the proliferation of laptop and notebook systems. Because of size limitations, it is obviously impossible to use the standard keyboard layout for a portable computer. Manufacturers have come up with many solutions. Unfortunately, none of these solutions has become an industry standard, as is the 101-key layout. Because of the variations in design, and because a portable system keyboard is not as easily replaceable as that of a desktop system, the keyboard arrangement should be an important part of your purchasing decision.

Early laptop systems often used smaller-than-normal keys to minimize the size of the keyboard, which resulted in many complaints from users. Today, the keytops on portable systems are usually comparable in size to that of a desktop keyboard, although some systems include half-sized keytops for the function keys and other less frequently used keyboard elements. In addition, consumer demand has caused most manufacturers to retain the inverted-T design for the cursor keys after a few abortive attempts at changing their arrangement.

Of course, the most obvious difference in a portable system keyboard is the sacrifice of the numeric keypad. Most systems now embed the keypad into the standard alphabetical part of the keyboard, as shown in Figure 18.1. To switch the keys from their standard values to their keypad values, you typically must press a key combination involving a proprietary function key, often labeled Fn.

Figure 18.1   Most portable systems today embed the numeric keypad into an oddly shaped block of keys on the alphabetical part of the keyboard.

This is an extremely inconvenient solution, and many users abandon their use of the keypad entirely on portable systems. Unfortunately, some activities—such as the entry of ASCII codes using the Alt key—require the use of the keypad numbers, which can be quite frustrating on systems using this arrangement.

To alleviate this problem, many portable system manufacturers sell external numeric keypads that plug into the external keyboard port, a serial port, or a USB port. This is a great feature for somebody performing a lot of numeric data entry.

In addition to keypad control, the Fn key often is used to trigger other proprietary features in portable systems, such as toggling between an internal and external display and controlling screen brightness and sound volume.

Some portable system manufacturers have gone to great lengths to provide users with adequate keyboards. For a short time, IBM marketed systems with a keyboard that used a "butterfly" design. The keyboard was split into two halves that rested on top of one another when the system was closed. When you opened the lid, the two halves separated to rest side by side, forming a keyboard that was actually larger than the computer case.

Ironically, the trend toward larger-sized displays in portable systems has made this sort of arrangement unnecessary. Many manufacturers have increased the footprint of their notebook computers to accommodate 12- and even 15-inch display panels, leaving more than adequate room for a keyboard with full-size keys. However, even on the newest systems, there still isn't enough room for a separate numeric keypad.

▶▶   See "Keyboards," p. 1202.

Num Lock

On IBM systems that support the Enhanced keyboard, when the system detects the keyboard on powerup, it enables the Num Lock feature and the light goes on. If the system detects an older 84-key AT-type keyboard, it does not enable the Num Lock function because these keyboards do not have cursor keys separate from the numeric keypad. When the Enhanced keyboards first appeared in 1986, many users (including me) were irritated to find that the numeric keypad was automatically enabled every time the system booted. Most system manufacturers subsequently began integrating a function into the BIOS setup that enabled you to specify the Num Lock status imposed during the boot process.

Some users thought that the automatic enabling of Num Lock was a function of the Enhanced keyboard because none of the earlier keyboards seemed to operate in this way. Remember that this function is not really a keyboard function but instead a function of the motherboard ROM BIOS, which identifies an Enhanced 101-key unit and turns on the Num Lock as a "favor." In systems with a BIOS that cannot control the status of the numeric keypad, you can use the DOS 6.0 or higher version NUMLOCK= parameter in CONFIG.SYS to turn Num Lock on or off, as desired. Windows NT 4.0 and Windows 2000 disable the Num Lock by default.

Keyboard Technology

The technology that makes up a typical PC keyboard is very interesting. This section focuses on all the aspects of keyboard technology and design, including the keyswitches, the interface between the keyboard and the system, the scan codes, and the keyboard connectors.

Keyswitch Design

Today's keyboards use any one of several switch types to create the action for each key. Most keyboards use a variation of the mechanical keyswitch. A mechanical keyswitch relies on a mechanical momentary contact type switch to make the electrical contact that forms a circuit. Some high-end keyboards use a totally different nonmechanical design that relies on capacitive switches. This section discusses these switches and the highlights of each design.

The most common type of keyswitch is the mechanical type, available in the following variations:

- Pure mechanical
- Foam element
- Rubber dome
- Membrane

Pure Mechanical Switches

The pure mechanical type is just that—a simple mechanical switch that features metal contacts in a momentary contact arrangement. The switch often includes a tactile feedback mechanism, consisting of a clip and spring arrangement designed to give a "clicky" feel to the keyboard and offer some resistance to the keypress. See Figure 18.2.

Keytop

Contacts

Figure 18.2 A typical mechanical switch used in NMB keyboards. As the key is pressed, the switch pushes down on the contacts to make the connection.

Mechanical switches are very durable, usually have self-cleaning contacts, and are normally rated for 20 million keystrokes, which is second only to the capacitive switch in longevity. They also offer excellent tactile feedback.

Despite the tactile feedback and durability provided by mechanical keyswitch keyboards, they have become much less popular than membrane keyboards (discussed later in this chapter), and many companies that produce keyboards that use mechanical keyswitches use them for only a few of their high-priced models. With the price of keyboards nosediving along with other traditional devices, such as mice and drives, the pressure on keyboard makers to cut costs has led many of them to abandon or deemphasize mechanical-keyswitch designs in favor of the less expensive membrane keyswitch.

The Alps Electric mechanical keyswitch is used by many of the vendors who produce mechanical-switch keyboards, including Alps Electric itself. Other vendors who use mechanical keyswitches for some of their keyboard models include Adesso, Inc. (www.adessoinc.com), NMB Technologies (www.nmbtech.com), Chicony, Cherry (which uses its own 50-million keystroke switches for its G80-series keyboards; www.cherrycorp.com), Avant Prime and Stellar (revivals of the classic Northgate keyboards and available from Ergonomic Resources; www.ergo-2000.com), Kinesis (www.kinesis-ergo.com), SIIG (www.siig.com), and Focus (www.focustaipei.com). Many of these vendors sell through the OEM market, so you must look carefully at the detailed specifications for the keyboard to see whether it is a mechanical keyswitch model.

Foam Element Switches

Foam element mechanical switches were a very popular design in some older keyboards. Most of the older PC keyboards, including models made by Key Tronic and many others, used this technology. These switches are characterized by a foam element with an electrical contact on the bottom. This foam element is mounted on the bottom of a plunger that is attached to the key (see Figure 18.3).

Figure 18.3 Typical foam element mechanical keyswitch.

When the switch is pressed, a foil conductor on the bottom of the foam element closes a circuit on the printed circuit board below. A return spring pushes the key back up when the pressure is released. The foam dampens the contact, helping to prevent bounce, but unfortunately it gives these keyboards a "mushy" feel. The big problem with this type of keyswitch design is that often, little tactile feedback exists. These types of keyboards send a clicking sound to the system speaker to signify that contact has been made. Preferences in keyboard feel are somewhat subjective; I personally do not favor the foam element switch design.

Another problem with this type of design is that it is more subject to corrosion on the foil conductor and the circuit board traces below. When this happens, the key strikes can become intermittent, which can be frustrating. Fortunately, these keyboards are among the easiest to clean. By disassembling the keyboard completely, you usually can remove the circuit board portion—without removing each foam pad separately—and expose the bottoms of all the pads. Then, you easily can wipe the corrosion and dirt off the bottom of the foam pads and the circuit board, thus restoring the keyboard to a "like-new" condition. Unfortunately, over time, the corrosion problem will occur again. I recommend using some Stabilant 22a from D.W. Electrochemicals to improve the switch contact action and prevent future corrosion. Because of such problems, the foam element design is not used much anymore and has been superseded in popularity by the rubber dome design.

Key Tronic, the most well-known user of this technology, now uses a center-bearing membrane switch technology in its mid-range and high-end keyboards, so you are likely to encounter foam-switch keyboards only on older systems.

Rubber Dome Switches

Rubber dome switches are mechanical switches similar to the foam element type but are improved in many ways. Instead of a spring, these switches use a rubber dome that has a carbon button contact on the underside. As you press a key, the key plunger presses on the rubber dome, causing it to resist and then collapse all at once, much like the top of an oil can. As the rubber dome collapses, the user feels the tactile feedback, and the carbon button makes contact between the circuit board traces below. When the key is released, the rubber dome re-forms and pushes the key back up.

The rubber eliminates the need for a spring and provides a reasonable amount of tactile feedback without any special clips or other parts. Rubber dome switches use a carbon button because it resists corrosion and because it has a self-cleaning action on the metal contacts below. The rubber domes themselves are formed into a sheet that completely protects the contacts below from dirt, dust, and even minor spills. This type of switch design is the simplest, and it uses the fewest parts. This made the rubber dome keyswitch very reliable for several years. However, its relatively poor tactile feedback has led most keyboard manufacturers to switch to the membrane switch design covered in the next section.

Membrane Switches

The membrane keyswitch is a variation on the rubber dome type, using a flat, flexible circuit board to receive input and transmit it to the keyboard microcontroller. Industrial versions of membrane boards use a single sheet for keys that sits on the rubber dome sheet for protection against harsh environments. This arrangement severely limits key travel. For this reason, flat-surface membrane keyboards are not considered usable for normal touch typing. However, they are ideal for use in extremely harsh environments. Because the sheets can be bonded together and sealed from the elements, membrane keyboards can be used in situations in which no other type could survive. Many industrial applications use membrane keyboards for terminals that do not require extensive data entry but are used instead to operate equipment, such as cash registers and point-of-sale terminals in restaurants.

Membrane keyswitches are no longer relegated to fast food or industrial uses, though. Over the last few years, the membrane keyswitch used with conventional keyboard keytops has replaced the rubber dome keyswitch to become the most popular keyswitch used in low-cost to mid-range keyboards. Inexpensive to make, membrane switches have become the overwhelming favorite of low-cost Pacific Rim OEM suppliers and are found in most of the keyboards you'll see at your local computer store or find inside the box of your next complete PC. Although low-end membrane keyswitches have a limited life of only 5–10 million keystrokes, some of the better models are rated to handle up to 20 million keystrokes, putting them in the range of pure mechanical switches for durability (see Figure 18.4).

Figure 18.4 A typical membrane keyswitch used in NMB keyboards.

Membrane keyboards provide a firmer touch than rubber dome keyboards or the old foam-element keyboards, but they are still no match for mechanical or capacitive keyswitch models in their feel. One interesting exception is the line of keyboards made by Key Tronic using its center-bearing version of membrane keyswitches. Several of their keyboards feature Ergo Technology, which features five levels of force from 35 grams to 80 grams, depending on the relative strength of the fingers used to type various keys. As little as 35 grams of force is required for keys that are used by the little finger, such as Q, Z, and A, and greater levels of force are required for keys used by the other fingers. The space bar requires the most force: 80 grams. This compares to the standard force level of 55 grams for all keys on normal keyboards (see Figure 18.5). For more information about keyboards with Ergo Technology, visit Key Tronic's Web site (www.keytronic.com).

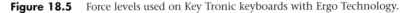

Figure 18.5   Force levels used on Key Tronic keyboards with Ergo Technology.

To find the best membrane keyboards from the vast numbers on the market, look at the lifespan rating of the keyswitches. Longer-lasting keyswitches make the keyboard cost more but will lead to a better experience over the life of the keyboard.

Capacitive Switches

Capacitive switches are the only nonmechanical types of keyswitch in use today (see Figure 18.6). The capacitive switch is the Cadillac of keyswitches. It is much more expensive than the more common mechanical membrane switch, but it is more resistant to dirt and corrosion and offers the highest-quality tactile feedback of any type of switch. This type of keyboard is sometimes referred to as a *buckling spring* keyboard because of the coiled spring used to provide feedback.

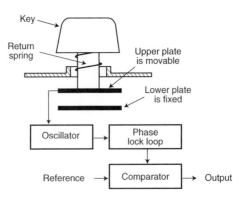

Figure 18.6   A capacitive keyswitch.

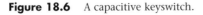

A capacitive switch does not work by making contact between conductors. Instead, two plates usually made of plastic are connected in a switch matrix designed to detect changes in the capacitance of the circuit.

When the key is pressed, the plunger moves the top plate in relation to the fixed bottom plate. Usually, a mechanism provides for a distinct over-center tactile feedback with a resounding "click." As the top plate moves, the capacitance between the two plates changes. The comparator circuitry in the keyboard detects this change.

Because this type of switch does not rely on metal contacts, it is nearly immune to corrosion and dirt. These switches are very resistant to the key bounce problems that result in multiple characters appearing from a single strike. They are also the most durable in the industry—rated for 25 million or more keystrokes, as opposed to 10–20 million for other designs. The tactile feedback is unsurpassed because the switch provides a relatively loud click and a strong over-center feel. The only drawback to the design is the cost. Capacitive switch keyboards are among the most expensive designs. The quality of the feel and their durability make them worth the price, however.

Originally, the only vendor of capacitive keyswitch keyboards was IBM. Although some of IBM's keyboards still feature capacitive keyswitches, most current IBM keyboards use rubber-dome or other lower-cost keyswitches. After IBM spun off printer maker Lexmark, Lexmark continued to make these keyboards for several years. Now, keyboards that use this high-quality keyswitch technology are produced and sold by Unicomp (`www.pckeyboard.com`), which bought the IBM keyboard technology in 1996 from Lexmark.

Unicomp sells its own branded capacitive-switch keyboards in a wide variety of models and still has an extensive inventory of new Lexmark-brand and IBM-brand keyboards that use capacitive technology. I'm using a Lexmark-brand keyboard made by Unicomp that incorporates the IBM TrackPoint pointing device. I never need to move my hands off the keyboard, and the feel and durability are outstanding.

The Keyboard Interface

A keyboard consists of a set of switches mounted in a grid or an array called the *key matrix*. When a switch is pressed, a processor in the keyboard identifies which key is pressed by determining which grid location in the matrix shows continuity. The keyboard processor, which also interprets how long the key is pressed, can even handle multiple keypresses at the same time. A 16-byte hardware buffer in the keyboard can handle rapid or multiple keypresses, passing each one to the system in succession.

When you press a key, the contact bounces slightly in most cases, meaning that several rapid on/off cycles occur just as the switch makes contact. This is called *bounce*. The processor in the keyboard is designed to filter this, or debounce the keystroke. The keyboard processor must distinguish bounce from a double key strike the keyboard operator intends to make. This is fairly easy, though, because the bouncing is much more rapid than a person could simulate by striking a key quickly several times.

The keyboard in a PC is actually a computer itself. It communicates with the main system in one of two ways:

- Through a special serial data link if a standard keyboard connector is used
- Through the USB port

The serial data link used by conventional keyboards transmits and receives data in 11-bit packets of information, consisting of 8 data bits, plus framing and control bits. Although it is indeed a serial link (in that the data flows on one wire), the keyboard interface is incompatible with the standard RS-232 serial port commonly used to connect modems.

The processor in the original PC keyboard was an Intel 8048 microcontroller chip. Newer keyboards often use an 8049 version that has built-in ROM or other microcontroller chips compatible with the 8048 or 8049. For example, in its Enhanced keyboards, IBM has always used a custom version of the Motorola 6805 processor, which is compatible with the Intel chips. The keyboard's built-in processor reads the key matrix, debounces the keypress signals, converts the keypress to the appropriate scan code, and transmits the code to the motherboard. The processors built into the keyboard contain their own RAM, possibly some ROM, and a built-in serial interface.

In the original PC/XT design, the keyboard serial interface is connected to an 8255 Programmable Peripheral Interface (PPI) chip on the motherboard of the PC/XT. This chip is connected to the inter-rupt controller IRQ1 line, which is used to signal to the system that keyboard data is available. The data is sent from the 8255 to the processor via I/O port address 60h. The IRQ1 signal causes the main system processor to run a subroutine (INT 9h) that interprets the keyboard scan code data and decides what to do.

In an AT-type keyboard design, the keyboard serial interface is connected to a special keyboard con-troller on the motherboard. This controller was an Intel 8042 Universal Peripheral Interface (UPI) slave microcontroller chip in the original AT design. This microcontroller is essentially another processor that has its own 2KB of ROM and 128 bytes of RAM. An 8742 version that uses Erasable Programmable Read Only Memory (EPROM) can be erased and reprogrammed. In the past, when you purchased a motherboard ROM upgrade from a motherboard manufacturer for an older system, the upgrade included a new keyboard controller chip as well because it had somewhat dependent and updated ROM code in it. Some older systems might use the 8041 or 8741 chips, which differ only in the amount of built-in ROM or RAM. However, recent systems incorporate the keyboard controller into the main system chipset.

In an AT system, the (8048-type) microcontroller in the keyboard sends data to the (8042-type) key-board controller on the motherboard. The motherboard-based controller also can send data back to the keyboard. When the keyboard controller on the motherboard receives data from the keyboard, it signals the motherboard with an IRQ1 and sends the data to the main motherboard processor via I/O port address 60h, just as in the PC/XT. Acting as an agent between the keyboard and the main system processor, the 8042-type keyboard controller can translate scan codes and perform several other func-tions as well. The system also can send data to the 8042 keyboard controller via port 60h, which then passes it on to the keyboard. Additionally, when the system needs to send commands to or read the status of the keyboard controller on the motherboard, it reads or writes through I/O port 64h. These commands usually are followed by data sent back and forth via port 60h.

In older systems, the 8042 keyboard controller is also used by the system to control the A20 memory address line, which provides access to system memory greater than 1MB. More modern motherboards usually incorporate this functionality directly into the motherboard chipset.

Keyboards connected to the USB port work in a surprisingly similar fashion to those connected to conventional DIN or mini-DIN ports after the data reaches the system. Inside the keyboard, a variety of custom controller chips are used by various keyboard manufacturers to receive and interpret key-board data before sending it to the system via the USB port. Some of these chips contain USB hub logic to enable the keyboard to act as a USB hub. After the keyboard data reaches the USB port on the system, the USB port routes the data to the 8042-compatible keyboard controller, where the data is treated as any other keyboard information.

This process works very well after a system has booted into Windows. But what about users who need to use the keyboard at a command prompt or within the BIOS configuration routine? As discussed earlier in this chapter, USB Legacy support must be enabled in the BIOS. A BIOS with USB Legacy support is capable of performing the following tasks:

- Configure the host controller
- Enable a USB keyboard and mouse
- Set up the host controller scheduler
- Route USB keyboard and mouse input to the 8042 Keyboard Controller

Systems with USB Legacy support enabled use the BIOS to control the USB keyboard until a supported operating system (Windows 98/Me/2000) is loaded. At that point, the USB host controller driver in the operating system takes control of the keyboard by sending a command called StopBIOS to the BIOS routine that was managing the keyboard. When Windows shuts down to MS-DOS, the USB host controller sends a command called StartBIOS to restart the BIOS routine that manages the keyboard.

When the BIOS controls the keyboard, after the signals reach the 8042 Keyboard Controller, the USB keyboard is treated just like a conventional keyboard if the BIOS is correctly designed to work with USB keyboards. As discussed previously in this chapter, a BIOS upgrade might be necessary in some cases to provide proper support of USB keyboards on some systems. The system chipset also must support USB Legacy features.

Typematic Functions

If a key on the keyboard is held down, it becomes *typematic*, which means the keyboard repeatedly sends the keypress code to the motherboard. In the AT-style keyboards, the typematic rate is adjusted by sending the appropriate commands to the keyboard processor. This is impossible for the earlier PC/XT keyboard types because the keyboard interface for these types is not bidirectional.

AT-style keyboards have programmable typematic repeat rate and delay parameters. You can adjust the typematic repeat rate and delay parameters with settings in your system BIOS (although not all BIOS chips can control all functions) or in your operating system. In Windows you use the Keyboard icon in the Control Panel. In DOS, you use the MODE command. The next section describes how to adjust the keyboard parameters in Windows because this is more convenient than the other methods and enables the user to make further adjustments at any time without restarting the system.

Adjusting Keyboard Parameters in Windows

You can modify the default values for the typematic repeat rate and delay parameters in any version of Windows using the Keyboard icon in the Control Panel. The Repeat Delay slider controls the number of times a key must be pressed before the character begins to repeat, and the Repeat Rate slider controls how fast the character repeats after the delay has elapsed.

Note

The increments on the Repeat Delay and Repeat Rate sliders in Keyboard Properties in the Control Panel correspond to the timings given for the MODE command's RATE and DELAY values. Each mark in the Repeat Delay slider adds about 0.25 seconds to the delay, and the marks in the Repeat Rate slider are worth about one character per second each.

The dialog box also contains a text box you can use to test the settings you have chosen before committing them to your system. When you click in the box and press a key, the keyboard reacts using the settings currently specified by the sliders, even if you have not yet applied the changes to the Windows environment.

To learn how to adjust keyboard parameters in DOS, see *Upgrading and Repairing PCs, 11th Edition*, available in electronic form on the CD-ROM included with this book.

Keyboard Key Numbers and Scan Codes

When you press a key on the keyboard, the processor built into the keyboard (8048- or 6805-type) reads the keyswitch location in the keyboard matrix. The processor then sends to the motherboard a serial packet of data containing the scan code for the key that was pressed.

This is called the *Make code*. When the key is released, a corresponding *Break code* is sent, indicating to the motherboard that the key has been released. The Break code is equivalent to the Make scan code plus 80h. For example, if the Make scan code for the "A" key is 1Eh, the Break code would be 9Eh. By using both Make and Break scan codes, the system can determine whether a particular key has been held down and determine whether multiple keys are being pressed.

In AT-type motherboards that use an 8042-type keyboard controller, the 8042 chip translates the actual keyboard scan codes into one of up to three sets of system scan codes, which are sent to the main processor. It can be useful in some cases to know what these scan codes are, especially when troubleshooting keyboard problems or when reading the keyboard or system scan codes directly in software.

When a keyswitch on the keyboard sticks or otherwise fails, the Make scan code of the failed keyswitch usually is reported by diagnostics software, including the POST (power on self test), as well as conventional disk-based diagnostics. That means you must identify the malfunctioning key by its scan code. See the Technical Reference section of the CD included with this book for a comprehensive listing of keyboard key numbers and scan codes for both the 101/102-key (Enhanced) keyboard and 104-key Windows keyboard. By looking up the reported scan code on these charts, you can determine which keyswitch is defective or needs to be cleaned.

Note

The 101-key Enhanced keyboards are capable of three scan code sets. Set 1 is the default. Some systems, including some of the IBM PS/2 machines, use one of the other scan code sets during the POST. For example, my IBM P75 uses Scan Code Set 2 during the POST, but switches to Set 1 during normal operation. This is rare, and it really threw me off in diagnosing a stuck key problem one time. It is useful to know whether you are having difficulty interpreting the scan code number, however.

IBM also assigns each key a unique key number to distinguish it from the others. This is important when you are trying to identify keys on foreign keyboards, which might use symbols or characters different from what the U.S. models do. In the Enhanced keyboard, most foreign models are missing one of the keys (key 29) found on the U.S. version and have two additional keys (keys 42 and 45). This accounts for the 102-key total instead of the 101 keys found on the U.S. version.

Note

See the Technical Reference section of the CD included with this book for a comprehensive listing of keyboard key numbers and scan codes for both the 101/102-key (Enhanced) keyboard and 104-key Windows keyboard, including HID and hotkey scancodes used on the latest USB and hotkey keyboards.

Knowing these key number figures and scan codes can be useful when you are troubleshooting stuck or failed keys on a keyboard. Diagnostics can report the defective keyswitch by the scan code, which varies from keyboard to keyboard on the character it represents and its location.

Many enhanced and USB keyboards now feature hotkeys that either have fixed uses—such as opening the default Web browser, sending the system into standby mode, and adjusting the speaker volume—or are programmable for user-defined functions. Each of these keys also has scan codes. USB keyboards use a special series of codes called Human Interface Device (HID), which are translated into PS/2 scan codes.

International Keyboard Layouts

After the keyboard controller in the system receives the scan codes generated by the keyboard and passes them to the main processor, the operating system converts the codes into the appropriate alphanumeric characters. In the United States, these characters are the letters, numbers, and symbols found on the standard American keyboard.

However, no matter which characters you see on the keytops, adjusting the scan code conversion process to map different characters to the keys is relatively simple. Windows 9x/Me/2000 and Windows NT take advantage of this capability by enabling you to install multiple keyboard layouts to support various languages.

Open the Keyboard icon in the Control Panel and select the Language page. The Language box should display the keyboard layout you selected when you installed the operating system. By clicking the Add button, you can select any one of several additional keyboard layouts supporting other languages.

These keyboard layouts map various characters to certain keys on the standard keyboard. The standard French layout provides easy access to the accented characters commonly used in that language. For example, pressing the 2 key produces the é character. To type the numeral 2, you press the Shift+2 key combination. Other French-speaking countries have different keyboard conventions for the same characters, so Windows includes support for several keyboard layout variations for some languages, based on nationality.

Note

It is important to understand that this feature is not the same as installing the operating system in a different language. These keyboard layouts do not modify the text already displayed onscreen; they only alter the characters generated when you press certain keys.

The alternative keyboard layouts also do not provide support for non-Roman alphabets, such as Russian and Chinese. The accented characters and other symbols used in languages such as French and German are part of the standard ASCII character set. They are always accessible to English-language users through the Windows Character Map utility or through the use of Alt+keypad combinations. An alternative keyboard layout simply gives you an easier way to access the characters used in certain languages.

If you work on documents using more than one language, you can install as many keyboard layouts as necessary and switch between them at will. When you click the Enable Indicator on Taskbar check box on the Language page of the Keyboard control panel, a selector appears in the taskbar's tray area that enables you to switch languages easily. On the same page, you can enable a key combination that switches between the installed keyboard layouts.

Keyboard/Mouse Interface Connectors

Keyboards have a cable with one of two primary types of connectors at the system end. On most aftermarket keyboards, the cable is connected inside the keyboard case on the keyboard end, requiring you to open the keyboard case to disconnect or test it; different vendors use different connections, making cable interchange between brands of keyboards unlikely. When IBM manufactured its own enhanced keyboards, it used a unique cable assembly that plugged into both the keyboard and the system unit to make cable replacement or interchange easy. Current IBM keyboards, unfortunately, no longer use either the SDL (Shielded Data Link) connector inside the keyboard or the telephone cable-style removable plug-in external keyboard connector used on some more recent models.

Although the method of connecting the keyboard cable to the keyboard can vary, all PC keyboards (except those using the USB port) use either one of the following two connectors to attach to the computer:

- *5-pin DIN connector*. Used on most PC systems with Baby-AT form factor motherboards.

- *6-pin mini-DIN connector*. Used on PS/2 systems and most PCs with LPX, ATX, and NLX motherboards.

Figure 18.7 and Table 18.3 show the physical layout and pinouts of all the respective keyboard connector plugs and sockets; although the 6-pin SDL connector is not used in this form by most keyboard vendors, most non-IBM keyboards use a somewhat similar connector to attach the keyboard cable to the inside of the keyboard. You can use the pinouts listed in Table 18.3 to test the continuity of each wire in the keyboard connector.

Figure 18.7   Keyboard and mouse connectors.

Table 18.3   Keyboard Connector Signals

Signal Name	5-Pin DIN	6-Pin Mini-DIN	6-Pin SDL
Keyboard Data	2	1	B
Ground	4	3	C
+5v	5	4	E
Keyboard Clock	1	5	D
Not Connected	—	2	A
Not Connected	—	6	F
Not Connected	3	—	—

DIN = Deutsche Industrie Norm, a committee that sets German dimensional standards.

SDL = Shielded Data Link, a type of shielded connector created by AMP and used by IBM and others for keyboard cables.

Motherboard mouse connectors also use the 6-pin mini-DIN connector and have the same pinout and signal descriptions as the keyboard connector; however, the data packets are incompatible. That means you can easily plug a motherboard mouse (PS/2 style) into a mini-DIN keyboard connector or plug the mini-DIN keyboard connector into a motherboard mouse port; however, neither one will work properly in this situation.

Caution

I have also seen PCs with external power supplies that used the same standard DIN connectors to attach the keyboard and the power supply. Although cross-connecting the mini-DIN connectors of a mouse and a keyboard is a harmless annoyance, connecting a power supply to a keyboard socket can be disastrous.

USB keyboards use the Series A USB connector to attach to the USB port built into recent computers. For more information on USB, see Chapter 17.

Keyboards with Special Features

A number of keyboards on the market have special features not found in standard designs. These additional features range from simple things, such as built-in calculators, clocks, and volume control, to more complicated features, such as integrated pointing devices, special character layouts, shapes, and even programmable keys.

Note

In 1936, August Dvorak patented a simplified character layout called the Dvorak Simplified Keyboard (DSK). The Dvorak keyboard was designed to replace the common QWERTY layout used on nearly all keyboards available today. The Dvorak keyboard was approved as an ANSI standard in 1982 but has seen limited use. For a comparison between the Dvorak keyboard and the common QWERTY keyboard you most likely use, see "The Dvorak Keyboard" in the Technical Reference section of the CD accompanying this book.

Ergonomic Keyboards

A trend that began in the late 1990s is to change the shape of the keyboard instead of altering the character layout. This trend has resulted in a number of so-called ergonomic designs. The goal is to shape the keyboard to better fit the human hand. The most common of these designs splits the keyboard in the center, bending the sides outward. Some designs allow the angle between the sides to be adjusted, such as the now-discontinued Lexmark Select-Ease, the Goldtouch keyboard designed by Mark Goldstein (who also designed the Select-Ease), and the Kenisis Maxim split keyboards. Others, such as the Microsoft Natural keyboard series, PC Concepts Wave, and Cirque Smooth Cat, are fixed. These split or bent designs more easily conform to the hands' natural angle while typing than the standard keyboard. They can improve productivity and typing speed and help prevent repetitive strain injuries (RSI), such as carpal tunnel syndrome (tendon inflammation). Even more radical keyboard designs are available from some vendors, including models such as the 3-part Comfort and ErgoMagic keyboards, the Kinisis concave contoured keyboard, and others. A good source for highly ergonomic keyboards, pointing devices, and furniture is Ergonomic Resources (www.ergo-2000.com).

One of the most popular ergonomic keyboards, the Microsoft Natural Keyboard Elite, is manufactured for Microsoft by Key Tronic. It uses the inexpensive soft-touch rubber dome keyswitches that Key Tronic is known for. If you're looking for a more rugged keyboard with a firmer touch, try the Kinisis Maxim.

Because of their novelty and their trendy appeal, some ergonomic keyboards can be considerably more expensive than traditional designs, but for users with medical problems caused or exacerbated by improper positioning of the wrists at the keyboard, they can be an important remedy to a serious problem. General users, however, are highly resistant to change, and these designs have yet to significantly displace the standard keyboard layout. If you don't want to spend big bucks on the more radical ergonomic keyboards but want to give yourself at least limited protection from RSI, consider keyboards with a built-in wrist rest, or add a gel-based wrist rest to your current keyboard. These provide hand support without making you learn a modified or brand-new keyboard layout.

USB Keyboards with Hubs

Many of the latest USB keyboards feature a built-in USB hub designed to add two or more USB ports to your system. Even though this sounds like a good idea, keep in mind that a keyboard-based hub won't provide additional power to the USB connectors. Powered hubs work better with a wider variety of devices than unpowered hubs do. I wouldn't choose a particular model based solely on this feature, although if your keyboard has it and your devices work well when plugged into it, that's great. I'd recommend that you use this type of keyboard with your USB mouse or other devices that don't require much power.

Multimedia and Web-Enabled Keyboards

As I discussed earlier in this chapter, many keyboards sold at retail and bundled with systems today feature fixed-purpose or programmable hotkeys that can launch Web browsers, run the Microsoft Media Player, adjust the volume on the speakers, change tracks on the CD player, and so forth. You need Windows 98 or better to use these hot keys; Windows Me and Windows 2000 add additional support for these keyboards.

Keyboard Troubleshooting and Repair

Keyboard errors are usually caused by two simple problems. Other more difficult, intermittent problems can arise, but they are much less common. The most frequent problems are as follows:

- Defective cables
- Stuck keys

Defective cables are easy to spot if the failure is not intermittent. If the keyboard stops working altogether or every keystroke results in an error or incorrect character, the cable is likely the culprit. Troubleshooting is simple, especially if you have a spare cable on hand. Simply replace the suspected cable with one from a known, working keyboard to verify whether the problem still exists. If it does, the problem must be elsewhere.

If you remove the cable from the keyboard, you can test it for continuity with a Digital Multi-Meter (DMM). DMMs that have an audible continuity tester built in make this procedure much easier to perform. To test each wire of the cable, insert the DMM's red pin into the keyboard connector and touch the DMM's black pin to the corresponding wire that attaches to the keyboard's circuit board. Wiggle the ends of the cable as you check each wire to make sure no intermittent connections exist. If you discover a problem with the continuity in one of the wires, replace the cable or the entire keyboard, whichever is cheaper. Because replacement keyboards are so inexpensive, it's almost always cheaper to replace the entire unit than to get a new cable, unless the keyboard is a deluxe model.

For more information about using digital multimeters (DMMs) for testing hardware, see Chapter 24, "PC Diagnostics, Testing, and Maintenance."

Many times you first discover a problem with a keyboard because the system has an error during the POST. Many systems use error codes in a 3xx numeric format to distinguish the keyboard. If you have any such errors during the POST, write them down. Some BIOS versions do not use cryptic numeric error codes; they simply state something such as the following:

```
Keyboard stuck key failure
```

This message is normally displayed by a system with a Phoenix BIOS if a key is stuck. Unfortunately, the message does not identify which key it is!

If your system displays a 3xx (keyboard) error preceded by a two-digit hexadecimal number, the number is the scan code of a failing or stuck keyswitch. Look up the scan code in the tables provided in this section to determine which keyswitch is the culprit. By removing the keycap of the offending key and cleaning the switch, you often can solve the problem.

For a simple test of the motherboard keyboard connector, you can check voltages on some of the pins. Using Figure 18.7 as a guide, measure the voltages on various pins of the keyboard connector. To prevent possible damage to the system or keyboard, turn off the power before disconnecting the keyboard. Then, unplug the keyboard and turn the power back on. Make measurements between the ground pin and the other pins according to Table 18.4. If the voltages are within these specifications, the motherboard keyboard circuitry is probably okay.

Table 18.4   Keyboard Connector Specifications

DIN Connector Pin	Mini-DIN Connector Pin	Signal	Voltage
1	5	Keyboard Clock	+2.0v to +5.5v
2	1	Keyboard Data	+4.8v to +5.5v
3	-	Reserved	—
4	3	Ground	—
5	4	+5v Power	+2.0v to +5.5v

If your measurements do not match these voltages, the motherboard might be defective. Otherwise, the keyboard cable or keyboard might be defective. If you suspect that the cable is the problem, the easiest thing to do is replace the keyboard cable with a known good one. If the system still does not work normally, you might have to replace the entire keyboard or the motherboard.

In many newer systems, the motherboard's keyboard and mouse connectors are protected by a fuse that can be replaced. Look for any type of fuse on the motherboard in the vicinity of the keyboard or mouse connectors. Other systems might have a socketed keyboard controller chip (8042-type). In that case, you might be able to repair the motherboard keyboard circuit by replacing this chip. Because these chips have ROM code in them, you should get the replacement from the motherboard or BIOS manufacturer. If the motherboard uses a soldered keyboard controller chip or a chipset that integrates the keyboard controller with other I/O chips, you'll need to replace the motherboard.

See the CD-ROM included with this book for a listing of the standard POST and diagnostic keyboard error codes used by some systems.

Keyboard Disassembly

Although disassembling a keyboard is possible, most likely you won't need or want to do that given the reasonable prices of keyboards. If you do want to disassemble your keyboard, see "Keyboard Disassembly" in the Technical Reference section of the CD accompanying this book.

Cleaning a Keyboard

One of the best ways to keep a keyboard in top condition is periodic cleaning. As preventive maintenance, you should vacuum the keyboard weekly, or at least monthly. When vacuuming, you should use a soft brush attachment; this will help dislodge the dust. Also note that many keyboards have key caps that can come off easily; be careful or you'll have to dig them out of the vacuum cleaner.

You also can use canned compressed air to blow the dust and dirt out instead of using a vacuum. Before you dust a keyboard with the compressed air, turn the keyboard upside down so that the particles of dirt and dust collected inside can fall out.

On all keyboards, each keycap is removable, which can be handy if a key sticks or acts erratically. For example, a common problem is a key that does not work every time you press it. This problem usually results from dirt collecting under the key. An excellent tool for removing keycaps on almost any keyboard is the U-shaped chip-puller included in many computer tool kits. Simply slip the hooked ends of the tool under the keycap, squeeze the ends together to grip the underside of the keycap, and lift up. IBM sells a tool designed specifically for removing keycaps from its keyboards, but the chip puller works even better. After removing the cap, spray some compressed air into the space under the cap to dislodge the dirt. Then replace the cap and check the action of the key.

Caution

When you remove the keycaps, be careful not to remove the spacebar on the original 83-key PC and the 84-key AT-type keyboards. This bar is difficult to reinstall. The newer 101-key units use a different wire support that can be removed and replaced much more easily.

When you remove the keycap on some keyboards, you are actually detaching the entire key from the keyswitch. Be careful during the removal or reassembly of the keyboard; otherwise, you'll break the switch. The classic IBM/Lexmark-type keyboards (now made by Unicomp) use a removable keycap that leaves the actual key in place, enabling you to clean under the keycap without the risk of breaking the switches.

Spills can be a problem, too. If you spill a soft drink or cup of coffee into a keyboard, you do not necessarily have a disaster. Many keyboards that use membrane switches are spill resistant. However, you should immediately (or as soon as possible) disconnect the keyboard and flush it out with distilled water. Partially disassemble the keyboard and use the water to wash the components. (See "Keyboard Disassembly" in the Technical Reference section of the CD accompanying this book for disassembly instructions.) If the spilled liquid has dried, soak the keyboard in some of the water for a while. When you are sure the keyboard is clean, pour another gallon or so of distilled water over it and through the keyswitches to wash away any residual dirt. After the unit dries completely, it should be perfectly functional. You might be surprised to know that drenching your keyboard with water does not harm the components. Just make sure you use distilled water, which is free from residue or mineral content (bottled water is **not** distilled; the distinct taste of many bottled waters comes from the trace minerals they contain!). Also, make sure the keyboard is fully dry before you try to use it; otherwise, some of the components might short out.

Tip

If spills or excessive dust or dirt are expected because of the environment or conditions in which the PC is used, several companies make thin membrane skins that mold over the top of the keyboard, protecting it from liquids, dust, and other contaminants. These skins are generally thin enough so that they don't interfere too much with the typing or action of the keys.

Keyboard Recommendations

In most cases, replacing a keyboard is cheaper or more cost effective than repairing it. This is especially true if the keyboard has an internal malfunction or if one of the keyswitches is defective.

Replacement parts for keyboards are almost impossible to procure, and installing any repair part is usually difficult. In addition, many of the keyboards supplied with lower-cost PCs leave much to be desired. They often have a mushy feel, with little or no tactile feedback. A poor keyboard can make using a system a frustrating experience, especially if you are a touch typist. For all these reasons, it is often a good idea to replace an existing keyboard with something better.

Perhaps the highest quality keyboards in the entire computer industry are those made by IBM, or, more accurately, Unicomp. Unicomp maintains an extensive selection of more than 1,400 Lexmark and IBM keyboard models and continues to develop and sell a wide variety of traditional and customized models, including keyboards that match the school colors of several universities.

Note

See Chapter 17 of *Upgrading and Repairing PCs, 11th Edition* on this book's CD for a listing of IBM keyboard and cable part numbers.

Some of the classic-design IBM keyboards are available in the retail market under either the IBM or IBM Options brand names. Items under the IBM Options program are sold through normal retail channels, such as CompUSA and Computer Discount Warehouse (CDW). These items are also priced much cheaper than items purchased as spare parts. They include a full warranty and are sold as complete packages, including cables. Table 18.5 lists some of the IBM Options keyboards and part numbers. Models marked with a * are also available from Unicomp.

Table 18.5   IBM Options Keyboards (Sold Retail)

Description	Part Number
IBM Enhanced keyboard (cable w/ DIN plug)	92G7454*
IBM Enhanced keyboard (cable w/ mini-DIN plug)	92G7453*
IBM Enhanced keyboard, built-in Trackball (cable w/ DIN plug)	92G7456*
IBM Enhanced keyboard, built-in Trackball (cable w/ mini-DIN plug)	92G7455*
IBM Enhanced keyboard, integrated TrackPoint II (cables w/ mini-DIN plugs)	92G7461*
IBM TrackPoint IV keyboard, Black	01K1260
IBM TrackPoint IV keyboard, White	01K1259

Keep in mind, though, that because IBM spun off its keyboard business some years ago, many recent and current IBM-labeled keyboards no longer have the distinct feel, quality, or durability found in the older models. Ironically, one of the best ways to get an "IBM" keyboard is to buy the model with the features you want from Unicomp, most of whose keyboards still use the capacitive buckling spring technology that IBM originally made famous.

The extremely positive tactile feedback of the IBM/Lexmark/Unicomp design is also a benchmark for the rest of the industry. Although keyboard feel is an issue of personal preference, I have never used a keyboard that feels better than the IBM/Lexmark/Unicomp designs. I now equip every system I use with a Unicomp keyboard, including the many non-IBM systems I use. You can purchase these keyboards directly from Unicomp at very reasonable prices.

Many models are available, including some with a built-in trackball or even the revolutionary TrackPoint pointing device. (TrackPoint refers to a small stick mounted between the G, H, and B keys.) This device was first featured on the IBM ThinkPad laptop systems, although the keyboards are now sold for use on other manufacturers' PCs. The technology is being licensed to many other manufacturers, including Toshiba. Other manufacturers of high-quality keyboards that are similar in feel to the IBM/Lexmark/Unicomp units are Alps, Lite-On, NMB Technologies, and the revived Northgate designs sold under the Avant Prime and Avant Stellar names. These keyboards have excellent tactile feedback, with a positive click sound. They are my second choice, after a Unicomp unit.

Pointing Devices

The mouse was invented in 1964 by Douglas Englebart, who at the time was working at the Stanford Research Institute (SRI), a think tank sponsored by Stanford University. The mouse was officially called an X-Y Position Indicator for a Display System. Xerox later applied the mouse to its revolutionary Alto computer system in 1973. At the time, unfortunately, these systems were experimental and used purely for research.

In 1979, several people from Apple—including Steve Jobs—were invited to see the Alto and the software that ran the system. Steve Jobs was blown away by what he saw as the future of computing, which included the use of the mouse as a pointing device and the GUI (graphical user interface) it operated. Apple promptly incorporated these features into what was to become the Lisa computer and lured away 15–20 Xerox scientists to work on the Apple system.

Although Xerox released the Star 8010 computer that used this technology in 1981, it was expensive, poorly marketed, and perhaps way ahead of its time. Apple released the Lisa computer, its first system that used the mouse, in 1983. It was not a runaway success, largely because of its $10,000 list price, but by then Jobs already had Apple working on the low-cost successor to the Lisa, the Macintosh. The Apple Macintosh was introduced in 1984. Although it was not an immediate hit, the Macintosh has grown in popularity since that time.

Many credit the Macintosh with inventing the mouse and GUI, but as you can see, this technology was actually borrowed from others, including SRI and Xerox. Certainly the Macintosh, and now Microsoft Windows and OS/2, have gone on to popularize this interface and bring it to the legion of Intel-based PC systems.

Although the mouse did not catch on quickly in the PC marketplace, today the GUIs for PC systems, such as Windows, practically demand the use of a mouse. Therefore, virtually every new system sold at retail comes with a mouse. And, because the mice packaged with retail systems are seldom high-quality or up-to-date designs, sooner or later most users are in the market for a better mouse or compatible pointing device.

Mice come in many shapes and sizes from many manufacturers. Some have taken the standard mouse design and turned it upside down, creating the trackball. In the trackball devices, you move the ball with your hand directly rather than moving the unit itself. Trackballs were originally found on video games in arcades, such as Missile Command, but have become popular with users who have limited desk space. In most cases, the dedicated trackballs have a much larger ball than would be found on a standard mouse. Other than the orientation and perhaps the size of the ball, a trackball is identical to a mouse in design, basic function, and electrical interface. And, like many recent mice, trackballs often come in ergonomic designs, and the latest models even use the same optical tracking mechanisms used by the latest Microsoft and Logitech mice.

The largest manufacturers of mice are Microsoft and Logitech; these two companies provide designs that inspire the rest of the industry and each other and are popular OEM choices as well as retail brands. Even though mice can come in different varieties, their actual use and care differ very little. The standard mouse consists of several components:

- A housing that you hold in your hand and move around on your desktop
- A method of transmitting movement to the system: either ball/roller or optical sensors
- Buttons (two or more, and often a wheel or toggle swich) for making selections

■ An interface for connecting the mouse to the system; conventional mice use a wire and connector, whereas wireless mice use a radio-frequency or infrared transceiver in both the mouse and a separate unit connected to the computer to interface the mouse to the computer

The housing, which is made of plastic, consists of very few moving parts. On top of the housing, where your fingers normally rest, are buttons. There might be any number of buttons, but in the PC world, typically only two exist. If additional buttons or a wheel are on your mouse, specialized driver software provided by the mouse vendor is required for them to operate to their full potential. Although the latest versions of Windows, Windows Me, and Windows 2000 support scrolling mice, other features supported by the vendor still require installing the vendor's own mouse driver software.

The bottom of the mouse housing is where the detection mechanisms or electronics are located. On traditional mice, the bottom of the housing contains a small rubber ball that rolls as you move the mouse across the tabletop. The movements of this rubber ball are translated into electrical signals transmitted to the computer across the cable.

The other major method of motion detection is optical. Some of the early mice made by Mouse Systems and a few other vendors used a sensor that required a special grid-marked pad. Although these mice were very accurate, the need to use them with a pad caused them to fall out of favor.

Microsoft's IntelliMouse Explorer pioneered the return of optical mice, but with a difference. Like the old-style optical mice, the IntelliMouse Explorer uses optical technology to detect movement, and it has no moving parts itself (except for the scroll wheel and buttons on top). The Explorer mouse needs no pad; it can work on virtually any surface. This is done by upgrading the optical sensor from the simple type used in older optical mice to a more advanced CCD (charge coupled device). This essentially is a crude version of a video camera sensor that detects movement by seeing the surface move under the mouse. An LED is used to provide light for the sensor.

The IntelliMouse Explorer is just the first of a growing family of optical mice made by Microsoft (the IntelliMouse Optical and WheelMouse Optical are less expensive versions), and Microsoft also offers an optical-technology trackball. Not to be outdone, Logitech also offers optical mice and optical trackballs using similar technology. In addition, other vendors, such as Kingston and Targus, are now offering optical mice as well (see Figure 18.8).

Figure 18.8   The bottom of the Logitech iFeel optical mouse.

Their versatility and low maintenance (not to mention that neat red glow out the sides!) make optical mice an attractive choice, and the variety of models available from both vendors means you can have the latest optical technology for about the price of a good ball-type mouse.

The cable can be any length, but it is typically between 4 and 6 feet long. Mice are also available in a cordless design, which uses either infrared or RF transceivers to replace the cable. A receiver is plugged into the mouse port, while the mouse contains a compatible transmitter.

Tip

If you have a choice on the length of cable to buy, go for a longer one. This allows easier placement of the mouse in relation to your computer. Extension cables can be used if necessary.

After the mouse is connected to your computer, it communicates with your system through the use of a device driver, which can be loaded explicitly or built into the operating system software. For example, no separate drivers are necessary to use a mouse with Windows or OS/2, but using the mouse with most DOS-based programs requires a separate driver to be loaded from the CONFIG.SYS or AUTOEXEC.BAT file. Regardless of whether it is built in, the driver translates the electrical signals sent from the mouse into positional information and indicates the status of the buttons.

The standard mouse drivers in Windows are designed for the traditional two-button mouse or scroll mouse (in Windows Me/2000), but increasing numbers of mice feature additional buttons, toggles, or wheels to make the mouse more useful. These additional features require special mouse driver software supplied by the manufacturer.

Internally, a ball-driven mouse is very simple, too. The ball usually rests against two rollers: one for translating the X-axis movement and the other for translating the Y-axis movement. These rollers are usually connected to small disks with shutters that alternately block and allow the passage of light. Small optical sensors detect movement of the wheels by watching an internal infrared light blink on and off as the shutter wheel rotates and "chops" the light. These blinks are translated into movement along the axes. This type of setup, called an *opto-mechanical mechanism*, is by far the most popular in use today (see Figure 18.9). Figure 18.10 shows a PS/2 mouse connector.

As the mouse is dragged, the mouse ball rolls in the same direction as your hand.

Your computer receives signals via the mouse cable which are translated by your operating system into the distance, direction, and speed of your movements.

The mouse buttons send signals to your computer, which in turn, sends those signals to the software.

As the ball rolls, it turns a pair of internal rollers that touch the ball at 90-degree angles. One roller controls vertical movement, while the other controls horizontal movement.

The pair of rollers are connected to an encoder wheel, which is turned as the rollers turn.

Metal contact points along the edge of each encoder make contact with two pairs of contact bars, creating an electrical signal. The number of signals corresponds to the speed and distance you have moved the mouse horizontally or vertically.

Figure 18.9   Typical opto-mechanical mouse mechanism.

Figure 18.10   Typical PS/2-type mouse connector.

Pointing Device Interface Types

The connector used to attach your mouse to the system depends on the type of interface you are using. Three main interfaces are used for mouse connections, with a fourth option you also occasionally might encounter. Mice are most commonly connected to your computer through the following three interfaces:

- Serial interface
- Dedicated motherboard (PS/2) mouse port
- USB port

Serial

A popular method of connecting a mouse to older PCs is through the standard serial interface. As with other serial devices, the connector on the end of the mouse cable is typically a 9-pin male connector; some very old mice used a 25-pin male connector. Only a couple of pins in the DB-9 or DB-25 connector are used for communications between the mouse and the device driver, but the mouse connector typically has all 9 or 25 pins present.

Because most PCs come with two serial ports, a serial mouse can be plugged into either COM1 or COM2. The device driver, when initializing, searches the ports to determine to which one the mouse is connected. Some mouse drivers cannot function if the serial port is set to COM3 or COM4, but most newer drivers can work with any COM port 1–4.

Because a serial mouse does not connect to the system directly, it does not use system resources by itself. Instead, the resources used are those used by the serial port to which it is connected. For example, if you have a mouse connected to COM2, and if COM2 is using the default IRQ and I/O port address range, both the serial port and the mouse connected to it use IRQ3 and I/O port addresses 2F8h–2FFh.

◄◄   See "Serial Ports," p. 924.

Motherboard Mouse Port (PS/2)

Most newer computers now come with a dedicated mouse port built into the motherboard. This practice was introduced by IBM with the PS/2 systems in 1987, so this interface is often referred to as a *PS/2 mouse interface*. This term does not imply that such a mouse can work only with a PS/2; instead, it means the mouse can connect to any system that has a dedicated mouse port on the motherboard.

From a hardware perspective, a motherboard mouse connector is usually exactly the same as the mini-DIN connector used for newer keyboards. In fact, the motherboard mouse port is connected to the 8042-type keyboard controller found on the motherboard. All the PS/2 computers include mini-DIN keyboard and mouse port connectors on the back. Most computers based on the semiproprietary LPX motherboards and all ATX-series motherboards use these same connectors for space reasons. Most Baby-AT motherboards have a pin-header type connector for the mouse port because most standard cases do not have a provision for the mini-DIN mouse connector. If that is the case, an adapter cable is usually supplied with the system. This cable adapts the pin-header connector on the motherboard to the standard mini-DIN type connector used for the motherboard mouse.

Caution

As mentioned in the "Keyboard/Mouse Interface Connectors" section earlier in this chapter, the mini-DIN sockets used for both keyboard and mouse connections on many systems are physically and electrically interchangeable, but the data packets they carry are not. Be sure to plug each device into the correct socket, or neither will function correctly. Don't panic if you mix them up, though. They are electrically identical to each other, so you can't damage the ports or the devices.

Caution

Connecting a mouse to the built-in mouse port is the best method of connection on systems that don't have USB ports because you do not sacrifice any of the system's interface slots or any serial ports, and the performance is not limited by the serial port circuitry. The standard resource usage for a motherboard (or PS/2) mouse port is IRQ12, as well as I/O port addresses 60h and 64h. Because the motherboard mouse port uses the 8042-type keyboard controller chip, the port addresses are those of this chip. IRQ12 is an interrupt that is usually free on most systems, and it, of course, must remain free on any ISA bus systems that have a motherboard mouse port because interrupt sharing is not allowed with the ISA bus.

Hybrid Mice

Hybrid mice are those designed to plug into two types of ports. Most of the low-cost mice sold at retail are designed to plug into either the serial port or the PS/2 port; more expensive mice often plug into either the PS/2 port or the USB port. These combination mice are more flexible than the mice usually bundled with systems, which are designed to work only with the PS/2 or USB port to which they attach.

Circuitry in a hybrid mouse automatically detects the type of port to which it is connected and configures the mouse automatically. Serial-PS/2 hybrid mice usually come with a mini-DIN connector on the end of their cable and an adapter that converts the mini-DIN to a 9- or 25-pin serial port connector, although the reverse is sometimes true on early examples of these mice. PS/2-USB mice usually come with the mini-DIN connector on the end of their cable and a USB adapter.

Sometimes people use adapters to try to connect a serial mouse to a motherboard mouse port or a motherboard mouse to a serial port. If this does not work, it is not the fault of the adapter. If the mouse does not explicitly state that it is both a serial and a PS/2-type mouse, it works only on the single interface for which it was designed. Most of the time, you find the designation for which type of mouse you have printed on its underside. A safe rule of thumb to follow is if the mouse didn't come with an adapter, or came bundled with a system, it probably won't work with an adapter.

USB

The extremely flexible USB port is increasingly being used for mice as well as keyboards and other I/O devices. Compared to the other interfaces, USB mice (and other USB pointing devices such as track-balls) have the following advantages:

- *Mice with the most advanced features are sometimes made especially for the USB port.* One example is the Logitech iFeel mouse, the first mouse with an optical sensor plus force feedback. It vibrates gently as you move the mouse over clickable buttons on Web pages, software menus, and the Windows desktop, and it's made especially for USB.

- *USB mice and pointing devices, similar to all other USB devices, are hot-swappable.* If you like to use a trackball, and your computing partners prefer mice, you can just lean over and unplug the other users' pointing device and plug in your own, or move it from PC to PC. You can't do that with the other port types.

- *USB mice can be attached to a USB hub, such as the hubs contained in some USB keyboards, as well as standalone hubs.* Using a hub makes attaching and removing your mouse easy without crawling around on the floor to reach the back of the computer.

Although the early USB mice were decidedly on the premium end of the price scale, you can buy decent USB mice for about the same cost as good-quality hybrid serial-PS/2 mice these days.

If you want to use a USB mouse at an MS-DOS prompt or within a graphical setup program, make sure that USB Legacy mode is enabled, as discussed earlier in this chapter.

A fourth type of connection, the bus mouse (referred to by Microsoft as the Inport mouse), used a dedicated adapter card and is now obsolete. For more information about the bus mouse, see Chapter 17 of *Upgrading and Repairing PCs, 11th Edition*, which is included on the CD-ROM supplied with this book.

Mouse Troubleshooting

If you are experiencing problems with your mouse, you need to look in only two general places—hardware or software. Because mice are basically simple devices, looking at the hardware takes very little time. Detecting and correcting software problems can take a bit longer, however. To troubleshoot wireless mice, see "Troubleshooting Wireless Input Devices," later in this chapter.

Cleaning Your Mouse

If you notice that the mouse pointer moves across the screen in a jerky fashion, it might be time to clean your mouse. This jerkiness is caused when dirt and dust become trapped around the mouse's ball-and-roller assembly, thereby restricting its free movement.

From a hardware perspective, the mouse is a simple device, so cleaning it is easy. The first step is to turn the mouse housing over so that you can see the ball on the bottom. Notice that surrounding the ball is an access panel you can open. Sometimes instructions indicate how the panel is to be opened. (Some off-brand mice might require you to remove some screws to get at the roller ball.) Remove the panel to see more of the roller ball and the socket in which it rests.

If you turn the mouse back over, the rubber roller ball should fall into your hand. Take a look at the ball. It might be gray or black, but it should have no visible dirt or other contamination. If it does, wash it in soapy water or a mild solvent, such as contact lens cleaner solution or alcohol, and dry it off.

Now take a look at the socket in which the roller ball normally rests. You will see two or three small wheels or bars against which the ball normally rolls. If you see dust or dirt on or around these wheels or bars, you need to clean them. The best way is to use a compressed air duster, which can blow out any dust or dirt. You also can use some electrical contact cleaner to clean the rollers. Remember, any remaining dirt or dust impedes the movement of the roller ball and results in the mouse not working as it should.

Put the mouse back together by inserting the roller ball into the socket and then securely attaching the cover panel. The mouse should look just as it did before you removed the panel, except that it will be noticeably cleaner.

One of the major advantages of the new breed of optical mice from Microsoft and Logitech is the lack of moving parts. Just wipe away dust from the optical sensor, and that's all the cleaning an optical mouse needs.

Interrupt Conflicts

Interrupts are internal signals used by your computer to indicate when something needs to happen. With a mouse, an interrupt is used whenever the mouse has information to send to the mouse driver. If a conflict occurs and the same interrupt used by the mouse is used by a different device, the mouse will not work properly—if at all.

Interrupt conflicts do not normally occur if your system uses a mouse port, but they can occur with the other types of mouse interfaces. Mouse ports built into modern motherboards are almost always set to IRQ12. If your system has a motherboard mouse port, be sure you don't set any other adapter cards to IRQ12; otherwise, a conflict will result.

When you are using a serial mouse, interrupt conflicts typically occur if you add third and fourth serial ports, using either an expansion card or an internal serial device, such as a modem. This happens because in ISA bus systems, the odd-numbered serial ports (1 and 3) usually are configured to use the same interrupts as the even-numbered ports (2 and 4) are; IRQ4 is shared by default between COM1 and COM3, and IRQ 2 is shared by default between COM2 and COM4. Therefore, if your mouse is connected to COM2 and an internal modem uses COM4, they both might use the same interrupt, and you cannot use them at the same time.

Because the mouse generates interrupts only when it is moved, you might find that the modem functions properly until you touch the mouse, at which point the modem is disconnected. Another example is when your system will run properly until you try to go online with your modem; then the conflict usually locks up the system. You might be able to use the mouse and modem at the same time by moving one of them to a different serial port. For instance, if your mouse uses COM1 and the modem still uses COM4, you can use them both at once because odd and even ports use different interrupts.

The best way around these interrupt conflicts is to make sure no two devices use the same interrupt. Serial port adapters are available for adding COM3 and COM4 serial ports that do not share the interrupts used by COM1 and COM2. These boards enable the new COM ports to use other normally available interrupts, such as IRQs 10, 11, 12, 15, and 5. I never recommend configuring a system with shared ISA interrupts; it is a sure way to run into problems later. However, interrupts used by PCI boards can be shared if you use Windows 95 OSR 2.x, Windows 98, Windows Me, or Windows 2000 with recent chipsets that support a feature called IRQ steering.

◀◀ See "PCI Interrupts," p. 320.

If you suspect an interrupt problem with a bus-type mouse, you can use the Device Manager built into Windows 9x/Me/2000 (which is accessible from the System control panel).

▶▶ See "Operating System Diagnostics," p. 1272.

The Device Manager in Windows 9x/Me/2000 is part of the Plug-and-Play (PnP) software for the system, and it is usually 100% accurate on PnP hardware. Although some of these interrupt-reporting programs can have problems, most can easily identify the mouse IRQ if the mouse driver has been loaded. After the IRQ is identified, you might need to change the IRQ setting of the bus mouse adapter or one or more other devices in your system so that everything works together properly.

If your driver refuses to recognize the mouse at all, regardless of its type, try using a different mouse that you know works. Replacing a defective mouse with a known good one might be the only way to know whether the problem is indeed caused by a bad mouse.

I have had problems in which a bad mouse caused the system to lock right as the driver loaded or when third-party diagnostics were being run on the system. If you use a DOS-based diagnostic, such as Norton Diagnostics, Microsoft MSD, or AMIDIAG, and the system locks up during the mouse test, you have found a problem with either the mouse or the mouse port. Try replacing the mouse to see whether that helps. If it does not, you might need to replace the serial port or bus mouse adapter. If a motherboard-based mouse port goes bad, you can replace the entire motherboard—which is usually expensive—or you can just disable the motherboard mouse port via jumpers or the system BIOS setup program and install a serial mouse instead. This method enables you to continue using the system without having to replace the motherboard. On systems with Windows 98/Me/2000, you also can switch to a USB mouse, using USB ports on your motherboard or by installing a PCI-based USB card—provided your system has a USB port.

Note

To learn more about using the Microsoft MSD diagnostic program to test for mouse or mouse-port problems, see Chapter 17 of *Upgrading and Repairing PCs, 11th Edition,* which is included on the CD-ROM packaged with this book.

Driver Software

To function properly, the mouse requires the installation of a device driver. In DOS, you must load the driver manually through your CONFIG.SYS or AUTOEXEC.BAT file, but the driver is automatically loaded in all versions of Windows. For maximum utility in both Windows and command-prompt sessions run under Windows, use the latest version of the manufacturer's mouse driver for the version of Windows you are using. You need to use a driver such as MOUSE.COM only if you are using a DOS application you run by booting the system directly to a DOS prompt in Windows 9x. Windows 9x/Me/2000 drivers support the use of the mouse in DOS applications running under Windows by default.

If you need to use a mouse driver when you boot to a command prompt in Windows 9x/Me/2000, the easiest way to enable the driver is to add it to your CONFIG.SYS or AUTOEXEC.BAT file; I recommend adding the driver that runs from a command prompt (often called MOUSE.COM) to your AUTOEXEC.BAT file. For example, if the mouse driver is installed in a folder called \MOUSE on your C: drive, add this line to your AUTOEXEC.BAT file:

```
C:\MOUSE\MOUSE.COM
```

This loads the DOS mouse driver into RAM when you boot the computer. One long-time problem with mouse drivers has been the amount of conventional memory (memory below 640KB) used by the mouse driver.

One of the biggest problems with the separate mouse driver is getting it loaded into an Upper Memory Block (UMB) to free up conventional memory. The older Microsoft mouse drivers—versions 9.0 and earlier—require a large block of 40KB–56KB UMB to load; upon loading, they shrink down to less than 20KB. Even though they take only 20KB or less after loading, you still need a very large area to get them "in the door."

The best tip I can give you for these separate drivers is to use the newest drivers available from Microsoft or Logitech because they use less conventional memory than earlier versions. If you need just the MS-DOS mouse drivers, you can download version 11.00 or above from the Microsoft Web site. The IntelliPoint driver for 32-bit versions of Windows also includes MS-DOS driver support.

Logitech's MOUSE.EXE MS-DOS mouse driver also can be loaded into UMBs, and all current versions of MouseWare (6.43 and above) also include the CLOAKING.EXE device driver to enable the Logitech mouse driver to be loaded into extended memory to save even more conventional/UMB space. See the `Readme.txt` file included in the Windows 3.1 folder of the MouseWare CD-ROM for details.

Keep in mind that you can use only serial or PS/2 port mice with MS-DOS; USB mice will not work. And, all mice are treated as two-button mice by the MS-DOS drivers unless you install Logitech menu software to activate the middle button.

After placing the proper driver load command in your `CONFIG.SYS` or `AUTOEXEC.BAT` file, reboot the system with the mouse connected and make sure the driver loads properly. If the proper command is in place and the driver is not loading, watch your video screen as your system boots. At some point, you should see a message from the mouse driver indicating that it is loaded. If you see a message indicating that the driver failed to load, you must determine why. For example, the driver might not be capable of loading because not enough memory is available. After you determine why the driver is not loading, you need to rectify the situation and make sure the driver loads.

DOS Application Software

If your mouse does not work with a specific piece of DOS application software, check the setup information or configuration section of the program. Make sure you indicated to the program (if necessary) that you are using a mouse. If it still does not work and the mouse works with other software you are using, contact the technical support department of the application software company.

Microsoft IntelliMouse/IBM Scrollpoint

Late in 1996, Microsoft introduced a new variation of its popular mouse, called the IntelliMouse. This device looks exactly like the standard Microsoft mouse except for a miniature gray wheel rising up between the two buttons. Since Microsoft introduced the first IntelliMouse, Logitech and most other vendors have introduced their own versions of scrolling mice. Even low-cost systems often bundle some form of scrolling mouse today to make Web site navigation and document scrolling easier.

The wheel has two main functions. The primary function is to act as a scrolling device, enabling you to scroll through documents or Web pages by manipulating the wheel with your index finger. The wheel also functions as a third mouse button when you press it.

Although three-button mice have been available for years from vendors such as Logitech, the scrolling function provided a real breakthrough. No longer do you have to move the mouse pointer to click the scrollbar on the right side of your screen or take your hand off the mouse to use the arrow keys on the keyboard. You just push or pull on the wheel. This is a major convenience, especially when browsing Web pages or working with word processing documents or spreadsheets. Also, unlike three-button mice from other vendors, the IntelliMouse's wheel-button doesn't seem to get in the way and you are less likely to click it by mistake. Although it took a while for software vendors to support the wheel, improvements in application software and Windows support allow today's wheel mice to be fully useful with almost any recent or current Windows program.

Each vendor's mouse driver software offers unique features to enhance the basic operation of the mouse. For example, Logitech's MouseWare 9.2 driver enables you to select many uses for all three mouse buttons (the scroll wheel is treated as a third mouse button), as well as provides various options for how to scroll with each wheel click (three lines, six lines, or one screen). Microsoft's IntelliMouse driver offers a feature called ClickLock, which allows you to drag items without holding down the primary mouse button. In addition, it offers a Universal Scroll feature that adds scrolling mouse support to applications that lack such support. To get the most from whatever scrolling or other advanced-feature mouse you have, be sure you periodically download and install new mouse drivers.

Instead of the wheel used by Microsoft and Logitech, IBM and other mouse vendors frequently use various types of buttons for scrolling. Some inexpensive mice use a rocker switch, but the most elegant of the non-wheel alternatives is IBM's ScrollPoint Pro, which uses a pressure-sensitive scroll stick similar to the TrackPoint pointing device used on IBM's notebook computer and some PC keyboards made by IBM and Unicomp. The scrollpointer in the center of the mouse enables you to smoothly scroll through documents without having to lift your finger to roll the wheel, as you do on the Microsoft version, which makes it much easier and more convenient to use. Because no moving parts exist, the ScrollPoint is also more reliable.

TrackPoint II/III/IV

On October 20, 1992, IBM introduced a revolutionary new pointing device called TrackPoint II as an integrated feature of its new ThinkPad 700 and 700C computers. Often referred to as a *pointing stick device*, TrackPoint II and its successors consists primarily of a small rubber cap that appears on the keyboard right above the B key, between the G and H keys. This was the first significant new pointing device since the mouse had been invented nearly 30 years earlier!

This device occupies no space on a desk, does not have to be adjusted for left-handed or right-handed use, has no moving parts to fail or become dirty, and—most importantly—does not require you to move your hands from the home row to use it. This is an absolute boon for touch typists.

I was fortunate enough to meet the actual creator and designer of this device in early 1992 at the spring Comdex/Windows World in Chicago. He was in a small corner of the IBM booth showing off his custom-made keyboards with a small silicone rubber nub in the middle. In fact, the devices he had were hand-built prototypes installed in standard desktop keyboards, and he was there trying to get public reaction and feedback on his invention.I was invited to play with one of the keyboards, which was connected to a demonstration system. By pressing on the stick with my index finger, I could move the mouse pointer on the screen. The stick itself did not move, so it was not a joystick. Instead, it had a silicone rubber cap that was connected to pressure transducers that measured the amount of force my finger was applying and the direction of the force and moved the mouse pointer accordingly. The harder I pressed, the faster the pointer moved. After playing around with it for just a few minutes, the movements became automatic—almost as though I could just think about where I wanted the pointer to go.

The gentleman at the booth turned out to be Ted Selker, the primary inventor of the device. He and Joseph Rutledge created this integrated pointing device at the IBM T.J. Watson Research Center. When I asked him when such keyboards would become available, he could not answer. At the time, there were apparently no plans for production, and he was only trying to test user reaction to the device.

Just over six months later, IBM announced the ThinkPad 700, which included this revolutionary device—then called the TrackPoint II Integrated Pointing Device. Since the original version came out, enhanced versions with greater control and sensitivity, called the TrackPoint III and IV, have become available.

Note

The reason the device was called TrackPoint II is that IBM had previously been selling a convertible mouse/trackball device called the TrackPoint. No relationship exists between the original TrackPoint mouse/trackball, which has since been discontinued, and the TrackPoint II integrated device. Since the original TrackPoint II came out, improved versions known as TrackPoint III and TrackPoint IV have become available. In the interest of simplicity, I will refer to all the TrackPoint II, III, and successive devices as just *TrackPoint*.

In its final production form, the TrackPoint consists of a small red silicone rubber knob nestled between the G, H, and B keys on the keyboard. The primary and secondary mouse buttons are placed below the spacebar where you can easily reach them with your thumbs without taking your hands off the keyboard.

IBM studies conducted by Selker found that the act of removing your hand from the keyboard to reach for a mouse and replacing the hand on the keyboard takes approximately 1.75 seconds. If you type 60wpm, that can equal nearly two lost words per minute, not including the time lost while you regain your train of thought. Almost all this time can be saved each time you use TrackPoint to move the pointer or make a selection (click or double-click). The combination of the buttons and the positioning knob also enable you to perform drag-and-drop functions easily.

IBM's research also found that people can get up to 20% more work accomplished using the TrackPoint instead of a mouse, especially when the application involves a mix of typing and pointing activities, such as with word processing, spreadsheets, and other typical office applications. In usability tests with the TrackPoint III, IBM gave a group of desktop computer users a TrackPoint and a traditional mouse. After two weeks, 80% of the users had unplugged their mice and switched solely to the TrackPoint device. Selker is convinced (as am I) that the TrackPoint is the best pointing solution for both laptop and desktop systems.

Another feature of the TrackPoint is that a standard mouse can be connected to the system at the same time to enable dual-pointer use. This setup not only enables a single person to use both devices, but also enables two people to use the TrackPoint and the mouse simultaneously to move the pointer on the screen. The first pointing device that moves (thus issuing a system interrupt) takes precedence and retains control over the mouse pointer on the screen until it completes its movement action. The second pointing device is automatically locked out until the primary device is stationary. This enables the use of both devices and prevents each one from interfering with the other.

IBM has added various versions of the TrackPoint to its notebook computers, as well as to high-end keyboards sold under the IBM, Lexmark, and Unicomp names. Notebook computer makers, such as HP and Toshiba, also have licensed the TrackPoint device (Toshiba calls it Accupoint).

I have compared the TrackPoint device to other pointing devices for notebooks, such as the trackballs and even the capacitive touch pads, but nothing compares in terms of accuracy and control—and, of course, you don't have to take your hands off the keyboard!

Some notebook computer makers copied the TrackPoint instead of licensing it, but with poor results that include sluggish response to input and poor accuracy. One way of telling whether the TrackPoint device is licensed from IBM and uses the IBM technology is if it accepts IBM TrackPoint II/III/IV rubber caps. They have a square hole in them and will properly lock on to any of the licensed versions, such as those found in Toshiba systems.

IBM has upgraded its pointing stick to the TrackPoint III and the current TrackPoint IV. Two main differences exist in the III/IV system, but the most obvious one is in the rubber cap. The IBM TrackPoint II and Toshiba Accupoint caps are made from silicone rubber, which is grippy and works well in most situations. However, if the user has greasy fingers, the textured surface of the rubber can absorb some of the grease and become slippery. Cleaning the cap (and the user's hands) solves the problem, but it can be annoying at times. The TrackPoint III/IV caps are made from a different type of rubber, which Selker calls "plastic sandpaper." This type of cap is much more grippy and does not require cleaning except for cosmetic purposes. I have used both types of caps and can say for certain that the TrackPoint III/IV cap is superior.

Note

Because the Accupoint device used in the Toshiba notebooks is licensed from IBM, it uses the same hardware (a pressure transducer called a *strain gauge*) and takes the same physical caps. I ordered a set of the new TrackPoint III caps and installed them on my Toshiba portable systems, which dramatically improved the grip. You can get these caps by ordering them from IBM Parts directly or from others who sell IBM parts, such as DakTech, under IBM part number 84G6536. The cost is approximately $5 for a set of two "plastic sandpaper" red caps.

Replacing the cap is easy—grab the existing cap with your fingers and pull straight up; it pops right off. Then, push on the new red IBM TrackPoint III/IV cap in its place. You will thank me when you feel how you can grip the new IBM cap much more easily than you can grip the designs used by others.

The other difference between the TrackPoint II and III/IV from IBM is in the control software. IBM added routines that implement a subtle technique Selker calls "negative inertia," which is marketed under the label *QuickStop response*. This software not only takes into account how far you push the pointer in any direction, but also how quickly you push or release it. Selker found that this improved software (and the sandpaper cap) enables people to make selections up to 8% faster.

TrackPoint IV includes an extra scroll button, as well as the ability to press the TrackPoint nub to select as if using the left mouse button. These new features make the TrackPoint even better to use.

The bottom line is that anyone who touch types should strongly consider only portable systems that include an IBM-licensed TrackPoint device (such as Toshiba). TrackPoints are far superior to other pointing devices, such as the touch pads, because the TrackPoint is faster to use (you don't have to take your hands off the keyboard's home row), easier to adapt to (especially for speedy touch typists), and far more precise. It takes some getting accustomed to, but the benefits are worth it.

The benefits of the TrackPoint are not limited to portable systems, however. If you use a notebook computer with TrackPoint like I do, you can have the same features on your desktop keyboard. For desktop systems, I use a Lexmark keyboard with the IBM-licensed TrackPoint device built in. This makes for a more consistent interface between desktop and notebook use because I can use the same pointing device in both environments. You also can buy these keyboards directly from Unicomp; IBM also offers TrackPoint IV in some of its high-end keyboards available at retail.

Mouse and Pointing Stick Alternatives

Because of Windows, many users spend at least as much time moving pointers around the screen as they do in typing, making pointing device choices very important. In addition to the mouse and the pointing stick choices discussed earlier in this chapter, several other popular pointing devices are available, including

- Track pads, such as the Cirque GlidePoint
- Trackballs from many vendors
- Upright mice, such as the 3M Renaissance Mouse

All these devices are treated as mice by the operating system, but offer radically different options for the user in terms of comfort. If you're not satisfied with a regular mouse and don't want to use an integrated pointing stick such as the TrackPoint II/III/IV, look into these options.

GlidePoint/Touch Pad

Cirque originated the touch pad (also called a *track pad*) pointing device in 1994. Cirque refers to its technology as the GlidePoint and has licensed the technology to other vendors, such as Alps Electric which also uses the term Glidepoint for its touch pads. The GlidePoint uses a flat, square pad that senses finger position through body capacitance. This is similar to the capacitance-sensitive elevator button controls you sometimes encounter in office buildings or hotels.

When it is used on a portable computer's keyboard, the touch pad is mounted below the spacebar, and it detects pressure applied by your thumbs or fingers. Transducers under the pad convert finger movement into pointer movement. Several laptop and notebook manufacturers have licensed this technology from Cirque and have incorporated it into their portable systems. Touch pads are also integrated into a number of mid-range to high-end keyboards from many vendors. When used on a desktop keyboard, touch pads are often offset to the right side of the keyboard's typing area.

Touch pads feature mouse buttons, although the user also can tap or double-tap on the touch pad's surface to activate an onscreen button located under the touch pad's cursor. Dragging and dropping is accomplished without touching the touch pad's buttons; just move the cursor to the object to be dragged, press down on the pad, hold while moving the cursor to the drop point, and raise the finger to drop the object. Some recent models also feature additional hot buttons with functions similar to those on hot-button keyboards.

The primary use for touch pads has been for notebook computer– and desktop keyboard–integrated pointing devices, although Cirque and Alps have both sold standalone versions of the touch pad for use as a mouse alternative on desktop systems. Cirque's touch pads are now available at retail under the Fellowes brand name, as well as direct from the Cirque Web site.

Although it has gained wide acceptance, especially on portable computers, touch pad technology can have a number of drawbacks for some users. Operation of the device can be erratic, depending on skin resistance and moisture content. The biggest drawback is that to operate the touch pad, users must remove their hands from the home row on the keyboard, which dramatically slows their progress. In addition, the operation of the touch pad can be imprecise, depending on how pointy your finger or thumb is! On the other hand, if you're not a touch typist, removing your hands from the keyboard to operate the touch pad might be easier than using a TrackPoint. Even with their drawbacks, touch pad pointing devices are still vastly preferable to using a trackball or a cumbersome external mouse with portable systems.

Unless you want to use a "real" mouse with a portable system, I recommend you sit down with portable computers that have both touch pad and TrackPoint pointing devices. Try them yourself for typing, file management, and simple graphics and see which type of integrated pointing device you prefer. I know what I like, but you might have different tastes.

Trackballs

The first trackball I ever saw outside of an arcade was the Wico trackball, a perfect match for mid-1980s video games and computer games, such as Missile Command and others. It emulated the eight-position Atari 2600 analog joystick, but was capable of much more flexibility.

Unlike the mid-80s trackballs, today's trackballs are used primarily for business instead of gaming. Most trackballs use a mouse-style positioning mechanism—the differences being that the trackball is on the top or side of the case and is much larger than a mouse ball. The user moves the trackball rather than the input device case, but rollers or wheels inside most models translate the trackball's motion and move a cursor onscreen the same way that mouse rollers or wheels convert the mouse ball's motion into cursor movement.

Trackballs come in a variety of forms, including ergonomic models shaped to fit the (right) hand, ambidextrous models suitable for both leftys and right-handers, optical models that use the same optical sensors found in the latest mice in place of wheels and rollers, and multibutton monsters that look as if they're the product of a meeting with a remote control.

Because they are larger than mice, trackballs lend themselves well to the extra electronics and battery power needed for wireless use. Logitech offers several wireless trackball models that use radio-frequency transceivers; for details of how this technology works, see the section "Wireless Input Devices," later in this chapter.

Trackballs use the same drivers and connectors as conventional mice. For basic operations, the operating-system–supplied drivers will work, but you should use the latest version of the vendor-supplied drivers to achieve maximum performance with recent models.

Cleaning and Troubleshooting Trackballs

Trackball troubleshooting is similar to mouse troubleshooting. For issues other than cleaning the trackball, see the section "Mouse Troubleshooting," earlier in this chapter.

Because trackballs are moved by the user's hand rather than by rolling against a tabletop or desktop, they don't need to be cleaned as often as mouse mechanisms do. However, occasional cleaning is recommended, especially with trackballs that use roller movement-detection mechanisms. If the trackball pointer won't move, skips, or drags when you move the trackball, try cleaning the trackball mechanism.

Trackballs can be held into place by a retaining ring, an ejection tab, or simply by gravity. Check the vendor's Web site for detailed cleaning instructions if your trackball didn't come with such instructions. Swabs and isopropyl alcohol are typically used to clean the trackball and rollers or bearings; see the trackball's instructions for details.

3M's Renaissance Mouse/Upright Mouse

Many PC users who grew up using joysticks on the older video games experienced some "interface shock" when they turned in their joysticks for mice. And even long-time mouse users nursing sore arms and elbows have wondered whether the mouse was really as "ergonomic" as it is sometimes claims to be.

3M's solution, developed late in 2000, is to keep the traditional ball-type mouse positioning mechanism but change the user interface away from the hockey puck/soap bar design used for many years to a slanted handle that resembles a joystick (see Figure 18.11). 3M's Renaissance Mouse is available in two hand sizes and attaches to either the PS/2 port or USB port (serial ports are not supported). The single button on the top of the handle is a rocker switch; push on the left side to left-click and on the right side to right-click. The front handgrip provides scrolling support when the special Renaissance Mouse driver software is installed.

The Renaissance Mouse enables the user to hold the pointing device with a "handshake"-style hand and arm position. 3M's Web site provides detailed ergonomic information to encourage the proper use of the Renaissance Mouse, which comes with software to support scrolling and other advanced functions. Because the Renaissance Mouse is a major departure from traditional mouse designs, it features both a 30-day money-back return policy as well as a two-year warranty.

Figure 18.11   The 3M Renaissance Mouse combines an ergonomic shape with a standard mouse-movement mechanism.

Pointing Devices for Gaming

Originally, game players on the PC used the arrow keys or letter keys on the keyboard to play all types of games; I remember putting Larry Bird and Dr. J through their paces in the original version of Electronic Arts One-on-One basketball with an 84-key keyboard! As you can imagine, this limited the number and type of games that could be played on the PC.

Analog Joysticks and the Game Port

As video standards improved, making games more realistic, input devices made especially for game play also became more and more popular. The first joysticks made for the IBM PC were similar to joysticks made for its early rival, the Apple II series. Both the IBM and Apple II joysticks were analog devices that lacked much of the positive feedback gameplayers were accustomed to from the Atari 2600, Commodore 64, or arcade joysticks. These joysticks also required frequent recalibration to work properly and were far from satisfactory to hardcore game players. Also, these devices required their own connector, the 15-pin game port. The game port found its way onto many sound cards as well as onto multi-I/O cards made for ISA and VL-Bus systems.

Even though joysticks began to add better features, including spring action, video game-style gamepads, and flight control options, the analog nature and slow speed of the gameport began to restrict performance as CPU speeds climbed above 200MHz and high-speed AGP and PCI video cards made ultra-realistic flying, driving, and fighting simulators possible.

A better gaming controller connector was badly needed, and USB again came to the rescue.

USB Ports for Gaming

The very versatile USB port has become the preferred connector for all types of gaming controllers, including joysticks, gamepads, and steering wheels. Instead of making a single inadequate joystick work for all types of games, users can now interchange controllers using the hot-swap benefits of USB and use the best controller for each type of game.

Although low-end game controllers now on the market can connect to either the venerable game port or the USB port, serious gamers will want USB because of its higher speed, better support for force feedback (which shakes the game controller realistically to match the action onscreen), and tilting (tilt the gamepad and the onscreen action responds).

As with USB mice, your USB-connected gaming controllers are only as good as their software drivers. Be sure to install the latest software available to keep up with the latest games.

Compatibility Concerns

If you play a lot of older games designed in the heyday of the 15-pin gameport, consider keeping around a gameport-type controller. Even though the vendors of USB game controllers strive to make the USB port emulate a game port for use with older games, some older games can't be fooled. If you have problems using a USB game controller with a specific game, check the game's Web site for patches, as well as your game controller's Web site for tips and workarounds.

Programmable Game Controllers

Some of the latest controllers are programmable, enabling you to develop profiles that provide you with features such as one-button operation of keyboard shortcuts or other game commands and adjustments to range of motion. To use these profiles, make sure you install the driver software supplied with your game controller, and be sure to change to the profile you have customized for a particular program whenever you start that program.

Choosing the Best Game Controller

If you're a serious gamer who likes various types of games, you might need about as many game controllers as a golfer needs clubs. An increasing number of specialized controllers are on the market, and even familiar favorites like joysticks and steering wheels are available in new variations.

Table 18.6 provides a quick reference to the many types of game controllers available today for PCs.

Table 18.6   Game Controller Overview

Controller Types	Suitable For	Desirable Features	Example Products
Joystick	Action games, including flight and shooting	Force feedback, programmable actions, rudder panels	Microsoft Sidewinder 2; Logitech WingMan Extreme Digital 3D; Thrustmaster Top Gun AfterBurner Joystick
Steering wheel	Driving games	Force feedback, programmable actions, foot pedals	Microsoft Precision Racing Wheel; Logitech WingMan Formula Force GP; Thrustmaster Force Feedback Racing Wheel-PC
Game pad	Driving and sports games	Force feedback, motion sensing, programmable buttons, mouse and keyboard emulation	Microsoft Sidewinder Freestyle Pro; Thrustmaster FireStorm Dual Power Gamepad; Logitech WingMan Gamepad Extreme
Voice chat and control	Most multiplayer games	Voice communication with other players in a game (such as conferences with members of your team or taunting an opponent)	Microsoft Game Voice

Table 18.6   Continued

Controller Types	Suitable For	Desirable Features	Example Products
Strategy controller	Strategy games	Programmable buttons, shortcuts, record actions as you play; can control camera movement in many 3D strategy titles	Microsoft Sidewinder Strategic Commander

The :CueCat—Beyond Bar Codes

Bar-code readers traditionally have been relegated to the retail/industrial side of computing. These devices convert those mysterious black-and-white stripes on packages, library books, and other items into alphanumeric data. Bar-code readers typically attach to the keyboard through a so-called *keyboard wedge* connection, a passthrough device that fastens between the keyboard connector and the keyboard. The keyboard wedge enables bar-code readers to send data through the keyboard interface described earlier in this chapter.

The :CueCat bar-code reading device developed by Digital :Convergence has brought bar-code reading to the desktops of ordinary computers, but with a twist. For example, instead of scanning a can of peas into a database, when the :CueCat scans a can of peas, its :CRQ software locates the pea packer's Web site and brings you the latest information about early June peas, peas with onions, and other developments in canned peas.

The :CueCat's :CRQ software automatically takes you to Web sites for companies of all sizes, including those you'd never know existed and those that have incredibly difficult URLs to type in. Both UPC and ISBN barcodes, as well as special printed cues, can be read by the :CueCat.

The :CueCat attaches to the keyboard port, reads bar codes to deliver product-specific information to your Web browser, and is free at Radio Shack stores. The :CRQ software included with the :CueCat reader also works with Internet Enhanced TV programs when you attach your TV's audio connection to your computer's sound card using the optional, low-cost convergence cable available at Radio Shack. When your computer is connected to your TV and you run the :CRQ software, it collects cues buried in the sound track of programs and commercials. You can customize which cues your computer responds to and use the :CRQ software in a special collect mode to store cues when you're offline until you review them and decide which cues you want to use to retrieve Web content.

:CueCat and :CRQ provide a level of consumer information that would have been regarded as science fiction just a few year ago. So, why are so many people concerned about this bar code reader for the masses? The Privacy Foundation's September 22, 2000, advisory about the :CueCat and :CRQ software indicates that each :CueCat user is assigned a unique tracking number (also called a Global User ID or GUID) that is stored on the computer and is transmitted back to Digital:Convergence along with what the user scanned during each :CueCat session and encoded information identifying the serial number of the CueCat scanner used. The details are available online at `http://privacyfoundation.org/advisories/advCueCat1.html`.

The potential for tracking personal information beyond the aggregate marketing information that is the announced goal of Digital:Convergence is truly sobering, especially when combined with the TV/Internet connection made possible by the convergence cable. The :CueCat is a clever gadget, but you should consider whether the potential loss of privacy with every bar code you scan or cue you retrieve is worth it.

Wireless Input Devices

For several years, many manufacturers have offered cordless versions of mice and keyboards. In most cases, these devices have used either infrared or short-range radio transceivers to attach to standard serial or PS/2 ports, with matching transceivers located in the mouse or keyboard. Wireless input devices are designed to be easier to use in cramped home-office environments and where a large-screen TV/monitor device is used for home entertainment and computing. Some game controllers are now available in wireless forms as well.

Radio Versus Infrared

Although some vendors still use infrared transceivers, most vendors support radio signals. Having used both kinds, I can tell you that a radio-frequency input device beats an infrared input device hands down for use at home or in a small one- or two-person office. Because infrared requires an unobstructed direct line between the transceivers, when I used an infrared keyboard/pointing stick combination at a client site, I was constantly re-aiming the keyboard at the receiver to avoid losing my signal. When I used a radio mouse, on the other hand, there were no line-of-sight issues to worry about. The only advantage to infrared is cost, but the problems of reliability in my mind outweigh any cost savings.

Major Vendors and Products

Unlike conventional mouse and keyboard producers, whose numbers are legion, the ranks of cordless input device makers are small. The major vendors include

- *Logitech.* Radio-frequency mice and keyboards
- *Intel.* Radio-frequency mice, keyboards, and game controllers
- *Microsoft.* Radio-frequency mice
- *Other vendors.* Infrared mice and keyboards (usually combination units)

Logitech

Mouse maker Logitech has recently added radio-frequency wireless keyboards to its line of radio-frequency wireless mice first developed in 1992. Because Logitech developed wireless mice for several years before developing wireless keyboards, its older wireless mouse receivers work only with mice; you must use a separate receiver for their wireless keyboards. If you want to use a wireless mouse and keyboard, you should purchase both units as a bundle; a single receiver with dual mouse and keyboard channels is usually supplied with bundled wireless keyboard/mouse sets. Check Logitech's support Web site for details about the compatibility of a particular receiver with a specified Logitech wireless mouse or keyboard.

Logitech's newest Cordless Freedom series of wireless keyboard/mouse combinations can be attached through either the PS/2 mouse/keyboard ports or the USB port, allowing them to be used with Windows 95 and Windows NT 4.0 as well as with Windows 98/Me/2000. Older wireless mice used either the PS/2 port or the serial port.

Intel

Intel, the newest major player in the cordless input device business, uses spread-spectrum radio-frequency technology and a single base station receiver for up to eight wireless devices (the Wireless Series), including keyboards, mice, and gamepads. Up to four gamepads can be supported by a single base station, enabling easy multiplayer gaming without wires. Intel's gamepads also can be used in a mouse emulation mode, allowing the user to surf the Web or select game options without changing to a different input device.

Intel's base station receiver attaches to the computer via a USB port, meaning that the Wireless Series devices can be used only with Windows 98/Me/2000. Legacy USB support should be enabled in the BIOS to allow the keyboard and mouse to work both within and outside of Windows.

Microsoft and Other Vendors

Microsoft makes only a single wireless input device at this writing; its Cordless Wheel Mouse uses a receiver that can attach to either a PS/2 mouse port or a serial port.

Infrared input devices normally combine both keyboard and mouse functions. These devices are offered by vendors such as Acer, PC Concepts, SIIG, and others and normally attach to the PS/2 mouse and keyboard ports. For improved reliability, some feature dual infrared transceivers in the keyboard or receiving unit to enable the unit to be moved around without losing the signal. Some infrared models, such as the Mind Path/Proxima WK86, have a long signal range and are designed for use in computer presentations.

Wireless Pointing Device Issues

Before you invest in wireless pointing devices for multiple computers, you should be aware of the following issues:

- *Line-of-site issues.* Infrared devices won't work if the IR beam between the pointing device and the receiver attached to the system is blocked. These units are not as suitable for casual in-the-lap use as radio-frequency units would be.

- *Radio-frequency interference.* Although early wireless mice used analog tuners that were hard to synchronize, today's wireless input devices normally use digital selectors. However, if several similar devices are used in close quarters, a receiver might actually receive data from the wrong mouse or keyboard. Also, metal desks and furniture can reduce range and cause erratic cursor movement. Check with the vendor for tips on overcoming interference issues.

- *Battery life and availability.* Early wireless devices sometimes used unusual, expensive batteries. Today's units run on common battery types, such as AAA. Battery life is usually rated at about six months. Make sure you have spare batteries for the input device to avoid failures due to running out of battery power.

- *User experience.* Different users will have different expectations of wireless input devices, but in general, the more a wireless input device acts like its wired siblings, the better. Users should "forget" the device has no wire; devices that have reliability, connection, or driver problems aren't going to be suitable.

Troubleshooting Wireless Input Devices

If your wireless input device does not work, check the following:

- *Battery failure.* The transceivers attached to the computer are powered by the computer, but the input devices themselves are battery-powered. Check the battery life suggestions published by the vendor; if your unit isn't running as long as it should, try using a better brand of battery or turning off the device if possible.

- *Lost synchronization between device and transceiver.* Both the device and the transceiver must be using the same frequency to communicate. Depending on the device, you might be able to resynchronize the device and transceiver by pressing a button, or you might need to remove the battery, insert the battery, and wait for several minutes to reestablish contact.

- *Interference between units.* Check the tranmission range of the transceivers in your wireless units and visit the manufacturer's Web site for details on how to reduce interference. Normally, you should use different frequencies for wireless devices on adjacent computers.

- *Blocked line of sight.* If you are using infrared wireless devices, check the line of sight carefully at the computer, the space between your device and the computer, and the device itself. You might be dangling a finger or two over the infrared eye and cutting off the signal—the equivalent of putting your finger over the lens on a camera.

- *Serial port IRQ conflicts.* If the wireless mouse is connected to a serial port and it stops working after you install another add-on card, check for conflicts using the Windows Device Manager.

- *Disconnected transceiver.* If you have moved the computer around, you might have disconnected the transceiver from its keyboard, PS/2 mouse, serial, or USB port. You can plug a USB device in without shutting down the system, but the other types require you to shut down, reattach the cable, and restart to work correctly.

- *USB Legacy support not enabled.* If your wireless device uses a transceiver connected to the USB port and the device works in Windows, but not at a command prompt, make sure you have enabled USB Legacy support in the BIOS.

Running Windows Without a Mouse

Many keyboard replacements for common mouse commands can be used with both the 101-key and 104-key Enhanced keyboards. For a complete list of these keyboard shortcuts, see the CD-ROM packaged with this book.

CHAPTER 19

Internet Connectivity

Relating Internet and LAN Connectivity

Communications between computers is a major part of the PC computing industry. Thanks to the World Wide Web (WWW), no computer user is an island. Whether using a modem or broadband technology, virtually all PCs can be connected to other computers, enabling them to share files, send and receive email, and access the Internet. This chapter explores the various technologies you can use to expand the reach of your PC around the block and around the world.

It might surprise you to see discussions of protocols and networking setup in both this chapter and the LAN chapter of this book, but a modem connection is really just another form of networking. In fact, the Windows 9x, Windows Me, Windows NT, and Windows 2000 operating systems have all but blended the two services into a single entity.

The reason for this combination is that the typical target for a modem connection has changed over the years. For a long time, PC users dialed in to *bulletin board systems (BBSes)*—proprietary services that provided terminal access to other computers. Online services such as America Online and CompuServe have also been around for many years, but they traditionally used proprietary clients and protocols quite different from those found on local area networks (LANs). Today, BBSes are practically extinct, and America Online, Prodigy, and CompuServe have been reborn as gateways to the Internet.

With the explosive growth of the Internet, modem and network technologies were joined because both could use the same client software and protocols. Today, the most popular suite of networking protocols—TCP/IP—is used on both LANs and the Internet. When you dial in to an Internet service provider (ISP), you are actually connecting to a network using a modem instead of a network interface card, and when you use most broadband services, your path to the Internet typically starts with a network interface card.

Asynchronous (Analog) Modems

If you want to connect to the Internet, an analog modem can serve as your on-ramp to the rest of the computing world. Modems are standard equipment with most recent systems and continue to be popular upgrades for systems that do not have access to broadband solutions, such as two-way cable modem or DSL lines. Even with some types of broadband access (such as dial-up DirecPC and one-way cable modem), modems are still needed to send page requests and email.

The word *modem* (from modulator/demodulator) basically describes a device that converts the digital data used by computers into analog signals suitable for transmission over a telephone line and converts the analog signals back to digital data at the destination. To distinguish modems that convert analog and digital signals from other types of access devices, modems are frequently referred to as *analog modems*. The typical PC modem is an asynchronous device, meaning that it transmits data in an intermittent stream of small packets. The receiving system takes the data in the packets and reassembles it into a form the computer can use.

Note

Because it has become such a familiar term, even to inexperienced computer users, the word *modem* is frequently used to describe devices that are, strictly speaking, not modems at all. Later in this chapter, you learn about ISDN and the latest Internet-access standards, such as cable modems, DirecPC, and DSL—none of which converts digital information to analog signals. However, because these devices look similar to a standard modem and are used to connect PCs to the Internet or to other networks, they are called modems.

Asynchronous modems transmit each byte of data individually as a separate packet. One byte equals 8 bits, which, using the standard ASCII codes, is enough data to transmit a single alphanumeric character. For a modem to transmit asynchronously, it must identify the beginning and end of each byte to the receiving modem. It does this by adding a start bit before and after every byte of data, thus using 10 bits to transmit each byte (see Figure 19.1). For this reason, asynchronous communications have sometimes been referred to as *start-stop* communications. This is in contrast to synchronous communications, in which a continuous stream of data is transmitted at a steady rate.

Figure 19.1 Asynchronous modems frame each byte of data with a start bit and a stop bit, whereas synchronous communications use an uninterrupted stream of data.

Synchronous modems generally are used in leased-line environments and in conjunction with multiplexers to communicate between terminals to Unix-based servers and mainframe computers. Thus, this type of modem is outside the scope of this book.

Whenever modems are referred to in this book, I will be discussing the asynchronous, analog variety. (Synchronous modems are not found in typical computer stores and aren't included in normal computer configurations, so you might not ever see one unless you go into the data center of a corporation that uses them.)

Note

During high-speed modem communications, the start and stop bits are usually not transmitted over the telephone line. Instead, the modem's data compression algorithm eliminates them. However, these bits are part of the data packets generated by the communications software in the computer, and they exist until they reach the modem hardware. If both ends of an analog modem connection don't use the same value for start and stop bits, the connection transmits gibberish instead of usable data.

The use of a single start bit is required in all forms of asynchronous communication, but some protocols use more than one stop bit. To accommodate systems with different protocols, communications software products usually enable you to modify the format of the frame used to transmit each byte. The standard format used to describe an asynchronous communications format is parity/data bits/ stop bits. Almost all asynchronous connections today are therefore abbreviated as N-8-1 (No parity/ 8 data bits/1 stop bit). The meanings for each of these parameters and their possible variations are as follows:

■ *Parity.* Before error-correction protocols became standard modem features, a simple parity mechanism was used to provide basic error checking at the software level. Today, this is almost never used, and the value for this parameter is nearly always set to none. Other possible parity values you might see in a communications software package are odd, even, mark, and space.

- *Data Bits.* This parameter indicates how many bits are actually carried in the data portion of the packet (exclusive of the start and stop bits). PCs typically use 8 data bits, but some types of computers use a 7-bit byte, and others might call for other data lengths. Communications programs provide this option to prevent a system from confusing a stop bit with a data bit.

- *Stop Bits.* This parameter specifies how many stop bits are appended to each byte. PCs typically use 1 stop bit, but other types of protocols might call for the use of 1.5 or 2 stop bits.

In most situations, you will never have to modify these parameters manually, but the controls are almost always provided. In Windows 9x/Me/2000, for example, if you open the Modems control panel and look at the Connection page of your modem's Properties dialog box, you will see Data Bits, Parity, and Stop Bits selectors.

Unless you use the Windows HyperTerminal program to establish a direct connection to another computer via phone lines, you might never need to modify these parameters. However, if you need to call a mainframe computer to perform terminal emulation for e-banking, checking a library's catalog, or working from home, you might need to adjust these parameters. (*Terminal emulation* means using software to make your PC keyboard and screen act like a terminal, such as a DEC VT-100 and so on.) Many mainframe computers use even parity and a 7-bit word length. If your PC is set incorrectly, you'll see garbage text on your monitor instead of the other system's login or welcome screen.

Modem Standards

For two modems to communicate, they must share the same *protocol*. A protocol is a specification that determines how two entities will communicate. Just as humans must share a common language and vocabulary to speak with each other, two computers or two modems must share a common protocol. In the case of modems, the protocol determines the nature of the analog signal the device creates from the computer's digital data.

Through the years, bipartisan committees have developed most of the many standards for modem communications that found acceptance from the majority of modem manufacturers. As the hardware technology has improved, modem communications have become faster and more efficient, and new standards continue to be developed to take advantage of the hardware's capabilities, enabling modems to continue to be useful devices for computer users who cannot access or cannot afford broadband connections.

Note

The term *protocol* is also used to describe software standards that must be established between different computers to allow them to communicate, such as TCP/IP.

Bell Labs and the CCITT are two of the bodies that have set standards for modem protocols. CCITT is an acronym for Comité Consultatif International Téléphonique et Télégraphique, a French term that translates into English as the Consultative Committee on International Telephone and Telegraph. The organization was renamed the International Telecommunication Union (ITU) in the early 1990s, but the protocols developed under the old name are often referred to as such. Newly developed protocols are referred to as ITU-T standards, which refers to the Telecommunication Standardization Sector of the ITU. Bell Labs no longer sets new standards for modems, although several of its older standards are still used. Most modems built in recent years conform to the standards developed by the CCITT.

The ITU, headquartered in Geneva, Switzerland, is an international body of technical experts responsible for developing data communications standards for the world. The group falls under the organizational umbrella of the United Nations, and its members include representatives from major modem manufacturers, common carriers (such as AT&T), and governmental bodies. The ITU establishes communications standards and protocols in many areas, so one modem often adheres to many different standards, depending on its various features and capabilities. Modem standards can be grouped into the following three areas:

■ **Modulation**		■ **Error Correction**
Bell 103	ITU V.32	ITU V.42
Bell 212A	ITU V.32bis	■ **Data Compression**
CCITT V.21	ITU V.34	ITU V.42bis
ITU V.22bis	ITU V.90	ITU V.44
ITU V.29	ITU V.92	

▶▶　See "Modulation Standards," p. 1002.

Various companies (aside from Bell Labs or the ITU) have developed other standards. These are sometimes called *proprietary* standards, even though most of these companies publish the full specifications of their protocols so other manufacturers can develop modems to work with them. The following list shows some of the proprietary standards that have been popular over the years:

■ **Modulation**	■ **Error Correction**
HST	MNP 1-4
K56flex	Hayes V-series
x2	■ **Data Compression**
	MNP 5 CSP

Note

K56flex and x2 were competing, proprietary methods for reaching a maximum download speed of up to 56Kbps. K56flex was developed by modem chipset makers Rockwell and Lucent, whereas x2 was developed by U.S. Robotics. These two quasi-standards have now been replaced by the ITU V.90 standard for 56Kbps downloads, but K56flex is still supported by many ISPs, and a few still also support x2.

In the interests of backward compatibility, modem manufacturers typically add support for new standards as they are developed, leaving the support for the old standards in place. As a result, when you evaluate modems, you are likely to see long lists of the standards they support, like those just shown. In most cases, you will want to know whether a modem supports the most recent standards, so support for an archaic and seldom-used protocol should not govern your purchasing decision.

Modem manufacturers used to claim to be Hayes-compatible, a phrase that became as meaningless as IBM-compatible when referring to PCs. Today modem manufacturers instead say they support standard AT command sets, which is what being Hayes-compatible meant. AT commands are text strings sent to the modem by software to activate the modem's features. For example, the ATDT command, followed by a telephone number, causes the modem to dial that number using tone dialing mode. Applications that use modems typically generate AT commands for you, but you can control a modem directly using a communications program with a terminal mode, or even the DOS ECHO command.

Because almost every modem uses the AT (Hayes) command set, this compatibility is a given and should not really affect your purchasing decisions about modems. The basic modem commands might vary slightly from manufacturer to manufacturer, depending on a modem's special features, but the basic AT command set is all but universal.

Note

A list of the basic AT commands can be found in the "Technical Reference" on the CD included with this book. However, the best source for the commands used by your modem is the manual that came with the device.

Although most modem users will never need to review these commands, if you use MS-DOS–based communication programs or some specialized Windows programs, you might be required to enter or edit an *initialization string*, which is a series of AT commands sent to the modem before dialing. If these commands are not correct, the modem will not work with these programs.

Bits and Baud Rates

When discussing modem transmission speeds, the terms *baud rate* and *bit rate* are often confused. Baud rate (named after a Frenchman named Emile Baudot, the inventor of the asynchronous telegraph printer) is the rate at which a signal between two devices changes in one second. If a signal between two modems can change frequency or phase at a rate of 300 times per second, for example, that device is said to communicate at 300 baud.

Thus, baud is a signaling rate, not a data-transmission rate. The number of bits transmitted by each baud is used to determine the actual data-transmission rate (properly expressed as bps or Kbps).

Sometimes a single modulation change is used to carry a single bit. In that case, 300 baud also equals 300bps.

If the modem could signal two bit values for each signal change, the bps rate would be twice the baud rate, or 600bps at 300 baud. Most modems transmit several bits per baud, so the actual baud rate is much slower than the bps rate. In fact, people often use the term baud incorrectly. We normally are not interested in the raw baud rate, but in the bps rate, which is the true gauge of communications speed. As Table 19.1 shows, more recent modems can signal multiple bit values with each signal change.

Table 19.1   Signaling Versus Transmission Rates

Baud Rate	Number of Bits/Baud	Actual Modem bps
600	4	2,400
2,400	4	9,600
2,400	6	14,400
3,200	9	28,800

As before, the baud rate is multiplied by the number of bits/baud to determine the actual bps speed of the modem.

Reaching rates above 2,400 baud on normal telephone lines can be difficult, which explains why a 28.8Kbps (28,800bps) modem might not work above 19,200bps when telephone line quality is poor. As you'll see later, the so-called 56Kbps modems don't use baud as explained earlier but work in a completely different manner.

Modulation Standards

Modems start with modulation, which is the electronic signaling method used by the modem. Modulation is a variance in some aspect of the transmitted signal. By modulating the signal using a predetermined pattern, the modem encodes the computer data and sends it to another modem that demodulates (or decodes) the signal. Modems must use the same modulation method to understand each other. Each data rate uses a different modulation method, and sometimes more than one method exists for a particular rate.

Regardless of the modulation method, all modems must perform the same task: Change the digital data used inside the computer (ON-OFF, 1-0) into the analog (variable tone and volume) data used by the telephone company's circuits, which were built over a period of years and were never intended for computer use. That's the "Mo(dulate)" in modem. When the analog signal is received by the other computer, the signal is changed back from the analog waveform into digital data (see Figure 19.2). That's the "Dem(odulate)" in modem.

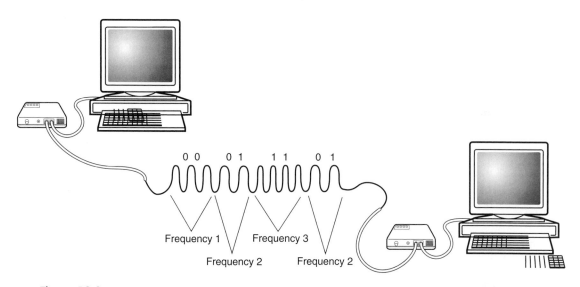

Figure 19.2   The modem at each computer changes digital (computer) signals to analog (telephone) signals when transmitting data or analog back to digital when receiving data.

The three most popular modulation methods are

- *Frequency-shift keying (FSK).* A form of frequency modulation, otherwise known as FM. By causing and monitoring frequency changes in a signal sent over the phone line, two modems can send information.

- *Phase-shift keying (PSK).* A form of phase modulation in which the timing of the carrier signal wave is altered and the frequency stays the same.

- *Quadrature amplitude modulation (QAM).* A modulation technique that combines phase changes with signal-amplitude variations, resulting in a signal that can carry more information than the other methods.

All current modem protocols (X2, K56flex, V.90, V.92, V.34, and V.34 annex) are full-duplex protocols. A *full-duplex* protocol is one in which communications can travel in both directions at the same time and at the same speed. A telephone call, for example, is full duplex because both parties can speak at the same time. In *half-duplex* mode, communications can travel in both directions, but only one side can transmit at a time. A radio call in which only one party can speak at a time is an example of half-duplex communications.

These protocols are automatically negotiated between your modem and the modem at the other end of the connection. Basically, the modems start with the fastest protocol common to both and work their way down to a speed/protocol combination that will work under the line conditions existing at the time of the call. See Table 19.2 for a listing of current modem protocols and the maximum speeds supported.

Note

To learn more about older modem protocols not listed in Table 19.2, see *Upgrading and Repairing PCs, 11th Edition*, available in electronic form on the CD-ROM packaged with this book.

Table 19.2   Current Modem Modulation Standards and Transmission Rates

Protocol	Maximum Transmission Rate (bits per second)
ITU V.34	28,800bps (28.8Kbps)
ITU V.34 annex	33,600bps (33.6Kbps)
X2	56,000bps (56Kbps)
K56flex	56,000bps (56Kbps)
ITU V.90	56,000bps (56Kbps)[1]
ITU V.92	56,000bps (56Kbps)[1]

1. *Although the ITU V.90 (successor to the proprietary 56Kflex and x2 standards) and V.92 standards allow for this speed of transmission, the U.S. FCC (Federal Communications Commission) allows only 53000bps (53Kbps) at this time.*

The ITU V.90, V.34, and V.32 family are the industry-standard protocols most commonly used today; the new V.92 modems also support V.90.

Note

For more information about older modem standards (modems with speeds of 33,600bps or below), see *Upgrading and Repairing PCs, 11th Edition*, included in electronic form on the CD-ROM that accompanies this book.

Note

The 56Kbps standards that represent the highest current increment in modem communication speed require a digital connection at one end and are therefore not purely analog. Other high-speed communication technologies such as ISDN and cable network connections eschew analog communications entirely, so they should not be called modems, strictly speaking.

V.90

V.90 is the ITU-T designation for a 56Kbps communication standard that reconciles the conflict between the U.S. Robotics (3Com) x2 and Rockwell K56flex modem specifications.

▶▶ See "56Kbps Modems," p. 1009.

V.92

V.92 is the ITU-T designation for an improved version of the V.90 standard, which provides faster negotiation of the connection, call-waiting support, and faster uploading than is possible with V.90.

▶▶ See "56Kbps Modems," p. 1009.

V.90 and V.92 are the current communication protocols supported by ISPs; any modem you want to use today should support at least the V.90 protocol.

Error-Correction Protocols

Error correction refers to the capability of some modems to identify errors during a transmission and to automatically resend data that appears to have been damaged in transit. Although you can implement error correction using software, this places an additional burden on the computer's expansion bus and processor. By performing error correction using dedicated hardware in the modem, errors are detected and corrected before any data is passed to the computer's CPU.

As with modulation, both modems must adhere to the same standard for error correction to work. Fortunately, most modem manufacturers use the same error-correction protocols.

MNP 1–4

This is a proprietary standard developed by Microcom to provide basic error correction. The Microcom Networking Protocol (MNP) levels are examined in greater detail in the "Proprietary Standards" section, later in this chapter.

MNP10, MNP10EC

MNP10 was developed to provide a better way to cope with changing line conditions. MNP10EC is an enhanced version developed to enable modems to use constantly changing cellular telephone connections.

V.42

V.42 is an error-correction protocol, with fallback to MNP 4; version 4 is an error-correction protocol as well. Because the V.42 standard includes MNP compatibility through Class 4, all MNP 4–compatible modems can establish error-controlled connections with V.42 modems.

This standard uses a protocol called LAPM (Link Access Procedure for Modems). LAPM, like MNP, copes with phone-line impairments by automatically retransmitting data corrupted during transmission, ensuring that only error-free data passes between the modems. V.42 is considered to be better than MNP 4 because it offers approximately a 20% higher transfer rate due to its more intelligent algorithms.

Data-Compression Standards

Data compression refers to a built-in capability in some modems to compress the data they're sending, thus saving time and money for modem users. Depending on the type of files the modem is sending, data can be compressed to nearly one-fourth its original size, effectively quadrupling the speed of the modem. For example, a 14,400bps modem with compression can yield transmission rates of up to 57,600bps, a 28,800bps modem can yield up to 115,200bps, and a 56,000bps modem can yield up to 224,000bps (download only)—at least in theory. This assumes that the modem has V.42bis data compression built in (true since about 1990) *and* that the data hasn't already been compressed by software. Thus, in reality, the higher throughput caused by data compression applies only to HTML and plain-text files on the Web. Graphics and Zip or EXE archives have already been compressed, as have most PDF (Adobe Acrobat Reader) files.

Can Non-56Kbps Modems Achieve Throughput Speeds Above 115,200bps?

Yes. To achieve speeds above 115,200bps, a better UART chip than the standard 16550-series chip found in modern PC serial ports and internal modems is required. 16650 UARTs have a 32-byte buffer, as opposed to the 16-byte buffer found in the standard 16550 UART. The 16650 is seldom used in PCs' built-in serial ports or as part of an internal modem, but it can be added by installing a high-speed serial port interface card (which might require you to disable your current COM ports).

Thus, to achieve the highest possible speeds, you need the following: an external modem capable of running at 230.4Kbps throughput, a 16650 UART chip in the serial (COM) port connected to the modem, and appropriate software drivers for the modem. Note that a 56Kbps-compatible modem isn't required! 230.4Kbps connections are available with anything from V.34bis to ISDN modems *if* the device is designed for that speed and you have the correct UART chip and drivers. But, as with the lower-speed throughput rates mentioned earlier, these speeds apply only to data that has not been compressed already.

External modems connected to the USB port instead of a serial port are capable of speeds above 115,200bps because of the faster throughput of the USB port. If possible, use the USB port rather than the serial port if you need to connect an external modem to your computer.

As with error correction, data compression can also be performed with software. Data can be compressed only once, so if you are transmitting files that are already in a compressed form, such as Zip archives, GIF or JPEG images, or Adobe Acrobat PDF files, there will be no palpable increase in speed from the modem's hardware compression. The transmission of plain-text files (such as HTML pages) and uncompressed bitmaps, however, is accelerated greatly by modem compression.

MNP 5

Microcom continued the development of its MNP protocols to include a compression protocol called MNP 5. This protocol is examined more fully in the section "Proprietary Standards," later in this chapter.

V.42bis

V.42bis is a CCITT data-compression standard similar to MNP Class 5, but it provides about 35% better compression. V.42bis is not actually compatible with MNP Class 5, but nearly all V.42bis modems include the MNP 5 data-compression capability as well.

This protocol can sometimes quadruple throughput, depending on the compression technique. This fact has led to some deceptive advertising; for example, a 2,400bps V.42bis modem might advertise "9,600bps throughput" by including V.42bis as well, but this would be possible in only extremely optimistic cases, such as when sending text files that are very loosely packed. V.42bis is superior to MNP 5 because it analyzes the data first and then determines whether compression would be useful. V.42bis compresses only data that needs compression. MNP 5, on the other hand, always attempts to compress the data, which slows down throughput on previously compressed files.

To negotiate a standard connection using V.42bis, V.42 also must be present. Therefore, a modem with V.42bis data compression is assumed to include V.42 error correction. When combined, these two protocols result in an error-free connection that has the maximum data compression possible.

V.44

At the same time that the V.92 protocol was introduced by the ITU in mid-2000, a companion data-compression protocol called V.44 was also introduced by the ITU. V.44 uses a new lossless LZJH compression protocol designed by Hughes Network Systems (developers of the DirecPC broadband Internet service) to achieve performance more than 25% better than that of V.42. Data throughput with V.44 can reach rates of as much as 300Kbps, compared to 150Kbps–200Kbps with V.42bis. V.42bis was developed in the late 1980s, long before the advent of the World Wide Web, so it is not optimized for Web surfing the way V.44 is. V.44 is especially designed to optimize compression of HTML text pages.

Note

V.44 is the latest compression algorithm to be based in part on the work of mathematicians Abraham Lempel and Jakob Ziv in the late 1970s. Lempel and Ziv's work also has been used in the development of LZW (Lempel-Ziv-Welch) compression for TIFF image files, GIF compressed image files, PKZIP-compatible compression, and other data compression methods.

Proprietary Standards

In addition to the industry-standard protocols for modulation, error correction, and data compression that are generally defined and approved by the ITU-T, several protocols in these areas were invented by various companies and included in their products without any official endorsement by any standards body. Some of these protocols have been quite popular at times and became pseudo-standards of their own. The only proprietary standards that continue to enjoy widespread support are the Microcom MNP standards for error correction and data compression. Others, such as 3Com's HST, CompuCom's DIS, and Hayes' V-series, are no longer popular.

Note

For more information about older proprietary protocols, see *Upgrading and Repairing PCs, 11th Edition*, included in electronic form on this book's CD-ROM.

MNP

MNP offers end-to-end error correction, meaning that the modems are capable of detecting transmission errors and requesting retransmission of corrupted data. Some levels of MNP also provide data compression.

As MNP evolved, different classes of the standard were defined, describing the extent to which a given MNP implementation supports the protocol. Most current implementations support Classes 1–5; some new PCI modems and most PC Card (PCMCIA) modems also might support Class 10 and Class 10EC. Other classes usually are unique to modems manufactured by Microcom, Inc., because they are proprietary.

MNP generally is used for its error-correction capabilities, but MNP Classes 4 and 5 also provide performance increases, with Class 5 offering real-time data compression. The lower classes of MNP are not important to today's modem user, but they are included in the following table for the sake of completeness. Efficiency ratings in Table 19.3 are compared to a non-MNP modem, with 100% equaling the performance of a non-MNP modem.

Table 19.3   MNP Classes

MNP Class	Notes
MNP Class 1 (block mode)	70% efficiency and error correction only; rarely used today
MNP Class 2 (stream mode)	84% efficiency and error correction only; rarely used today
MNP Class 3	108% efficiency and incorporates Class 2
MNP Class 4	105% overall efficiency; can rise as high as 125%–150% on some types of calls and connections
MNP Class 5	Data compression; can increase throughput to 150% of normal with text files but is actually slower with compressed files; often disabled on systems transmitting Zip and other compressed files
MNP Class 10	Error correction for impaired lines; starts with lowest data rate and goes up to fastest reliable data rate (opposite of other speed-negotiation methods); can adjust data rate up and down as line conditions change
MNP Class 10EC	Enhanced Cellular version of MNP Class 10; handles cellular hand-offs, drop-offs, echoes, and other line problems better and faster than regular MNP Class 10; works best when both ends have MNP Class 10EC support

Fax Modem Standards

Facsimile technology is a science unto itself, although it has many similarities to data communications. These similarities have led to the combination of data and fax capabilities in the same modem. Virtually all the modems on the market today support fax and data communications, although in the late 1980s, when PC fax capabilities were first developed, separate fax and modem devices were required.

Over the years, the ITU has set international standards for fax transmission. This has led to the grouping of faxes into one of four groups. Each group (I through IV) uses different technology and standards for transmitting and receiving faxes. Groups I and II are relatively slow and provide results that are unacceptable by today's standards and are therefore not discussed in detail here. Group III is the universal standard in use today by virtually all fax machines, including those combined with modems.

The Group III Fax Protocol

The Group III protocol specifies a maximum fax transmission rate of 9,600 baud and two levels of image resolution: standard (203×98 pixels) and fine (303×196 pixels). The protocol also calls for the use of a data-compression protocol defined by the CCITT (called T.4) and V.29 modulation.

Two general subdivisions exist within the Group III fax standard: Class 1 and Class 2. The difference between the two is that in Class 1 faxing, the fax software generates the images and handles the session protocol and timing with the receiving system. In Class 2, the software generates an image for each page and passes it to the fax modem, which handles the session protocol and timing. Thus, with Class 1, compatibility with other fax devices is more the responsibility of the software, whereas with Class 2, compatibility is more the responsibility of the modem. Although both classes call for additional fax-related AT commands to be recognized and acted on by the modem, the Class 2 command set is much larger, consisting of more than 40 new instructions.

The Class 1 specification was readily accepted and ratified by the CCITT in 1988, but the Class 2 document was rejected repeatedly. However, some manufacturers have designed Class 2 modems using the draft (that is, unratified) version of the standard. Today, nearly all fax modems support the

Group III, Class 1 standard, and this should be the minimum acceptable requirement for any fax modem you intend to purchase. Class 2 support is an additional benefit but by itself does not provide the almost universal compatibility of Class 1.

The Group IV Fax Protocol

Whereas Groups I through III are analog in nature (like modems) and are designed to use standard analog telephone lines, the Group IV specification calls for the digital transmission of fax images and requires an ISDN or other digital connection to the destination system. Group IV supports fax resolutions of up to 400dpi and uses a newer CCITT data compression protocol called T.6.

For a digital solution such as Group IV faxing to function, the connection between the source and the destination system must be fully digital. This means that even though your office might use a PBX-based telephone system that is digital and your telephone carrier might use digital connections, it is very likely that there is at least some analog communication involved in the circuit, such as between the PBX and the local telephone service. Until the telephone system has been converted to a fully digital network (a monumental task), Group IV fax systems will not be capable of replacing Group III systems.

56Kbps Modems

At one time, the V.34 annex speed of 33,600bps (33.6Kbps) was regarded as the absolute speed limit for asynchronous modem usage. However, starting in 1996, modem manufacturers began to produce modems that support speeds of up to 56,000bps. These so-called "56K" or "56Kbps" modems are now virtually universal, although the methods for breaking the 33.6Kbps barrier have changed several times. To understand how this additional speed was achieved, you must consider the basic principle of modem technology—that is, the digital-to-analog conversion.

As you've learned, a traditional modem converts data from digital to analog form so it can travel over the Public Switched Telephone Network (PSTN). At the destination system, another modem converts the analog data back to its digital form. This conversion from digital to analog and back causes some speed loss. Even though the phone line is physically capable of carrying data at 56Kbps or more, the effective maximum speed because of the conversions is about 33.6Kbps. A man by the name of Shannon came up with a law (Shannon's Law) stating that the maximum possible error-free data communications rate over the PSTN is approximately 35Kbps, depending on the noise present.

However, Shannon's Law assumes a fully analog connection between the two modems. That is not the case in most of the United States today. In urban areas, most circuits are digital until they reach the telephone company's central office (CO) to which your phone line is connected. The CO converts the digital signal into an analog signal before sending it to your home.

Considering the fact that the phone system is largely digital, you can—in some cases—omit the initial digital-to-analog conversion and send a purely digital signal over the PSTN to the recipient's CO (see Figure 19.3). Thus, only one digital-to-analog conversion is needed, instead of two or more. The result is that you theoretically can increase the speed of the data transmission, in one direction only, beyond the 35Kbps specified by Shannon's Law—to nearly the 56Kbps speed supported by the telephone network. Prior to the new ITU V.92 standard, the transmission in the other direction was still limited to the V.34 annex maximum of 33.6Kbps. However, both the modem and the ISP must have support for the ITU V.92 standard to overcome this limitation.

Note

See "ITU V.92 and V.44—Breaking the Upload Barrier," page 1013, this chapter, for more information on how the V.92 standard enables faster uploading.

Figure 19.3   56Kbps connections enable you to send data at standard analog modem rates (36,000bps maximum) but enable you to receive data nearly twice as fast.

56Kbps Limitations

Thus, 56Kbps modems can increase data transfer speeds beyond the limits of V.34 modems, but they are subject to certain limitations. Unlike standard modem technologies, you cannot buy two 56Kbps modems, install them on two computers, and achieve 56Kbps speeds. One side of the connection must use a special digital modem that connects directly to the PSTN without a digital-to-analog conversion.

56Kbps modems, therefore, can be used at maximum speeds only to connect to ISPs or other hosting services that have invested in the necessary infrastructure to support the connection. Because the ISP has the digital connection to the PSTN, its downstream transmissions to your computer are accelerated, whereas your communications back to the ISP are not. On a practical level, this means you can surf the Web and download files more quickly, but if you host a Web server on your PC, your users will realize no speed gain because the upstream traffic is not accelerated. If you connect to another regular modem, your connection is made at standard V.34 annex rates (33.6Kbps or less).

Also, only one digital-to-analog conversion can be in the downstream connection from the ISP to your computer. This is dictated by the nature of the physical connection to your local telephone carrier. If additional conversions are involved in your connection, 56Kbps technology will not work for you; 33.6Kbps will be your maximum possible speed. The leading Web site for line testing is the one created by U.S. Robotics, located at `http://www.3com.com/56k/need4_56k/linetest.html`.

This site provides a telephone number and a simple procedure for you to use in testing your line with your existing modem. Although 33.6Kbps and slower modems have disappeared from the market, it's still useful to know whether your telephone line supports a 56Kbps modem before you buy one.

Note

Although most advertising for 56Kbps modems refers to them as simply "56K" modems, this is inaccurate. "K" is most often used in the computer business to refer to kilobytes. If that were true, a "real" 56K modem would be downloading at 56,000 bytes per second (or 448,000 bits per second)!

Because the line test is specific to your location, test the line you'll actually be using for the modem. With the way the telephone system has had to grow to accommodate new exchanges and devices, even neighbors down the street from each other might have different results.

Caution

56Kbps modem communications are also highly susceptible to slowdowns caused by line noise. Your telephone line might be perfectly adequate for voice communications and even lower-speed modem communications, but inaudible noise easily can degrade a 56Kbps connection to the point at which there is only a marginal increase over a 33.6Kbps modem, or even no increase at all. If you do have a problem with line noise, getting a surge suppressor with noise filtration will help.

If you plan to use a modem with a notebook computer, be aware that your hotel room will soon host the world's slowest 56Kbps modem—yours! The connection quality of the separate analog phone jacks or the "data port" in the side of the typical hotel guest telephone is usually poor, and you'll be lucky to see even a 24Kbps transmission rate. The analog-digital conversions that occur between your room's telephone and the hotel's digital PBX system eliminate the possibility of using any of the 56Kbps standards the modem supports because they depend on a direct digital connection to the central switch (CS).

If you travel frequently on business and want to access the Internet more quickly without tying up your telephone line, ask the hotel staff whether they have rooms that support LAN connections, a developing option at more and more business hotels. These connections usually support 10BASE-T Ethernet, so a 10BASE-T or dual-speed 10/100 Ethernet card and cable would be a useful accessory to carry with you on the road.

56Kbps Standards

To achieve a high-speed connection, both modems and your ISP (or other hosting service to which you connect) must support the same 56Kbps technology. The first 56Kbps chipsets were introduced in late 1996:

- U.S. Robotics' X2 used Texas Instruments (TI) chipsets.
- Rockwell's K56flex was supported by Zoom and other modem makers.

These rival methods for achieving performance up to 56Kbps were incompatible with each other and were replaced in 1998 by the ITU's V.90 standard.

Note

For more information about K56flex and X2, see *Upgrading and Repairing PCs, 11th Edition*, available in electronic format on the CD-ROM supplied with this book.

Unfortunately, the 56Kbps name is rather misleading, in regards to actual transmission speeds. Although all 56Kbps modems theoretically are capable of this performance on top-quality telephone lines, the power requirements for telephone lines specified in the FCC's Part 68 regulation limit the top speed of these modems to 53Kbps. The FCC has been considering lifting this speed limitation since the fall of 1998, but it still applies to modems as of early 2001.

V.90

After more than a year of confusion and frustration for high-speed modem users, a single standard was finally created to solve the "war" between K56flex and x2. On February 5, 1998, the ITU-T approved a "determination" for a 56Kbps modem standard called V.90. The standard was ratified on September 15, 1998. Now that an official standard exists, all modem manufacturers have upgraded their current products to support V.90, and interoperability between devices supporting the two earlier standards should be possible.

Because the x2 and K56flex implementations are fundamentally similar in the hardware requirements described earlier, many existing modems of either type can be modified to support V.90 by upgrading their firmware using a flash update or a simple chip replacement. If you purchased your modem before the V.90 standard became official, see your modem vendor's Web site for information about upgrading to V.90.

Depending on your modem model, one of three outcomes is likely:

- Some users will be able to download software to "flash" their BIOS firmware to the new V.90 standard.

- Others will need to do a physical modem swap at a reduced price.

- Some will need to replace their modems outright.

Note

Need support for a Hayes-brand modem? Zoom Telephonics sells and supports Hayes-brand modems produced as of June 11, 1999 or later. Zoom also provides users of Hayes, Practical Peripherals, and Cardinal modems sold by the now-defunct Hayes Corporation the option to try firmware upgrades or replace their modems at a reduced cost through Zoom's hardware upgrade program. See the Hayes Web site at `www.hayesmicro.com` for details.

Note

Before you upgrade a K56flex modem to V.90, see the tips later in this chapter to determine whether it's really necessary; x2 owners should upgrade because x2 dial-up access is rapidly fading away. If your ISP has stopped supporting your proprietary 56Kbps standard, the best download speed you can hope for is 33.6Kbps unless you upgrade your modem to V.90 or V.92 or replace it with a V.90/V.92-compatible modem.

Since the adoption of V.90, users with x2 modems who have updated their firmware to V.90 standards have generally had good luck in connecting, often obtaining higher speeds. However, there have been a number of reports of K56flex users having problems in a V.90 world, even after updating their modems to the V.90 standard. If you have problems connecting reliably or speedily after performing a V.90 update from K56flex, try these tips.

Troubleshooting the V.90 (ex-K56flex) Modems

1. Make sure you have the latest firmware release. Even if you have just purchased your modem, your vendor might have put a firmware update on its Web site. To get there for the update, if you're having problems making the connection, dial in with your modem on a 33.6Kbps line, or pretend that your modem is an older model by installing it as a 33.6Kbps model from the same vendor.

2. See whether you can continue to use the modem as a K56flex. According to Lucent Technologies' 56K site (`http://www.k56flex.com`), many V.90-compliant sites can still support dialing in with a K56flex modem to get similar speed results compared to a user with a V.90 modem. "If it ain't broke, don't fix it!"

3. Check whether you can use both K56flex and V.90 firmware at the same time. Some modems' firmware ROM (read-only memory) chips have enough room for both K56flex and V.90 code, whereas others have space for just one or the other (Zoom Telephonics, for example, calls its

modems with provision for both standards "Dualmode"). Typically, modems with a 1MB Flash ROM chip can handle only one type of firmware, whereas modems with a 2MB Flash ROM chip have room for both. If you can't have both code types in your modem at the same time, download both K56flex and V.90 firmware to your system, try each one, and see which works better for you. As long as your ISP has a K56flex-specific modem pool or has V.90 modems that also support K56flex, you don't really need to change to V.90.

4. If your vendor has several versions of firmware available for download, try some of the earlier versions, as well as the latest version. An earlier version might actually work better for you.

5. If you are using your modem in a country other than the United States or Canada, you might need an international update. Zoom Telephonics's Web site, for example, lists separate K56flex-to-V.90 updates for Australia, Belgium, Denmark, Finland, France, Germany, Holland (the Netherlands), Italy, Portugal, Sweden, Switzerland, and the United Kingdom (Great Britain and Northern Ireland).

6. Don't forget that your operating system drivers for your modem might also need to be updated.

7. If you are using a Lucent-chipset modem, try the generic Lucent drivers as well as the drivers supplied by your modem manufacturer; Lucent-chipset drivers can generally be interchanged among various manufacturers that use the same chipset. Lucent's former Microelectronics group, which manufactures modem chipsets, was spun off during late 2000–early 2001. The new company is called Agere Systems. To locate Agere/Lucent modem drivers, go to `http://www.lucent.com/micro/K56flex/driver.html`.

Note

The problems some users have with moving from K56flex to V.90 do not apply to users who have updated their V.34 modems directly to the V.90 standard. Even if your V.34 modem was made by a company that later made K56flex modems, you don't need to worry about this unless you updated to K56flex first. Then the troubleshooting advice given earlier applies to you as well.

ITU V.92 and V.44—Breaking the Upload Barrier

56Kbps protocols, such as the early proprietary X2 and K56flex and the final ITU V.90 standard, increased the download speed from its previous maximum of 33.6Kbps to 56Kbps. However, upload speeds, which affect how quickly you can send email, page requests, and file transfers, were not affected by the development of 56Kbps technologies. Upload speeds with any of the 56Kbps technologies are limited to a maximum of 33.6Kbps. This causes severe speed lags for both pure dial-up users and those who depend on analog modems for upstream traffic, such as users of one-way broadband solutions—for example, one-way (Telco Return) cable modems, dial-up DirecPC, and one-way (Telco Return) fixed-base wireless Internet services. Other shortcomings of existing 56Kbps technology include the amount of time it takes the user's modem to negotiate its connection with the remote modem and the lack of uniform support for call-waiting features.

In mid-2000, the ITU unveiled a multifaceted solution to the problem of slow connections and uploads: the V.92 and V.44 protocols (V.92 was previously referred to as V.90 Plus).

V.92, as the name implies, is a successor to the V.90 protocol, and any modem that supports V.92 also supports V.90. V.92 doesn't increase the download speed beyond the 56Kbps barrier, but offers these major features:

■ *QuickConnect.* QuickConnect cuts the amount of time needed to make a connection by storing telephone line characteristics and using the stored information whenever the same phone line is used again. For users who connect to the Internet more than once from the same location, the amount of time the modem beeps and buzzes to make the connection will drop from as much as 27 seconds to about half that time. Bear in mind, this reduction in connection time does not come about until after the initial connection at that location is made and its characteristics are stored for future use.

■ *Modem-on-Hold*. The Modem-on-Hold feature allows the user to pick up incoming calls and talk for a longer amount of time than the few seconds allowed by current proprietary call-waiting modems. Modem-on-Hold enables the ISP to control how long you can take a voice call while online without interrupting the modem connection; the minimum amount of time supported is 10 seconds, but longer amounts of time (up to unlimited!) are supported by this feature. Modem-on-Hold also allows you to make an outgoing call without hanging up the modem connection. Modem-on-hold, similar to previous proprietary solutions, requires that you have the call-waiting feature enabled on your telephone line and also requires that your ISP support this feature of V.92.

Note

Although Modem-on-Hold is good for the Internet user with only one phone line (because it allows a single line to handle incoming as well as outgoing calls), it's not as good for ISPs because when you place your Internet connection on hold, the ISP's modem is not capable of taking other calls. ISPs that support Modem-on-Hold might need to add more modems to maintain their quality of service if this feature is enabled. More modems are needed because the ISP won't be able to count on users dropping their Internet connections to make or receive voice calls when Modem-on-Hold is available.

■ *PCM Upstream*. PCM Upstream breaks the 33.6Kbps upload barrier, boosting upload speed to a maximum of 48Kbps. Unfortunately, because of power issues, enabling PCM Upstream can reduce your downstream (download) speed by 1.3Kbps–2.7Kbps or more.

Modems that support V.92 typically also support the new V.44 data-compression standard. V.44, which replaces V.42bis, provides for compression of data at rates up to 6:1—that's more than 25% better than V.42bis. This enables V.92/V.44 modems to download pages significantly faster than V.90/V.42bis modems can at the same connection speed.

When will you be able to enjoy the benefits of V.92/V.44? Modems using these technologies have been available since late 2000 from vendors such as Zoom Telephonics, Hayes (a division of Zoom), and others, but as with the development of earlier 56Kbps standards, the ISPs must make the investment in new equipment to make V.92's benefits a reality. Although major ISP equipment vendors, such as Cisco, Lucent, and Conexant, have all announced support for V.92/V.44, some of their existing V.90-compatible terminal equipment cannot be updated to V.92/V.44 standards and needs to be replaced. Some so-called "V.92-compatible" terminal equipment support the Modem-on-Hold and QuickConnect features, but not the PCM Upstream feature—meaning that connections made through such equipment are still be limited to 33.6Kbps maximum upload speeds.

Can your existing V.90-compatible modem be upgraded to V.92/V.44? As with earlier 56Kbps modem standards, the answer is likely to be "it depends." Some Lucent LT Winmodem (Agere Systems) modem drivers for V.90 also might include V.92 commands; see Richard Gambert's V.unreliable Web site's Lucent modem section for the latest information (http://www.808news.com/56k). For modems based on other chipsets, check with your modem vendor.

As with earlier 56Kbps standards, you shouldn't worry about V.92/V.44 support until your ISP announces that it is supporting these standards. Because the V.92 standard has several components, find out which features of V.92 your ISP is planning to support before you look into a modem firmware update or modem replacement.

Modem Recommendations

A modem for a PC can take the form either of an external device with its own power supply that plugs into a PC's serial port or USB port or of an internal expansion card you insert into a bus slot inside the computer. Most manufacturers of modems have both internal and external (RS-232 serial and USB) versions of the same models.

External versions are slightly more expensive because they include a separate case and power supply and sometimes require you to buy a serial modem or USB cable. Both internal and external modems are equally functional, however, and the decision as to which type you use should typically depend on whether you have a free bus slot or serial port, whether you have USB ports and Windows 98/Me/2000, how much room you have on your desk, the capabilities of your system's internal power supply, and how comfortable you are with opening up your computer.

I often prefer external modems because of the visual feedback they provide through indicator lights. These lights let you easily see whether the modem is still connected and transmitting or receiving data. However, some communication programs today include onscreen simulations of the lights, providing the same information.

There are other situations, too, where an internal modem is preferable. In you are using an older computer whose serial ports do not have buffered UART chips, such as the 16550, many internal modems include an onboard 16550 UART. This onboard UART with the modem saves you the trouble of upgrading the UART serial port. Also, external 56Kbps modems can be hampered from achieving their full speed by the limitations of the computer's serial port. An external USB model or an internal model using the PCI slot might be preferable instead. Use Table 19.4 to see how internal and external units compare.

Table 19.4   External Versus Internal Modems

Features	External	Internal
Built-in 16550 UART or higher	No (uses computer's USB port or serial port UART).	Yes (if 14.4Kbps or faster).
Price comparison	Higher.	Lower.
Extras to buy	RS-232 Modem Interface cable or USB cable in some cases.	Nothing.
Ease of moving to another computer	Easy—unplug the cables and go! USB modems require a functioning USB port on the computer and Windows 98 or above.[1] RS-232 serial modems require you to shut down the computer first before disconnecting or reconnecting the modem; USB modems can be hot-swapped.	Difficult—must open case and remove card, open other PC's case and insert card.
Power supply	Plugs into wall ("brick" type).	None—powered by host PC.
Reset if modem hangs	Turn modem off, and then on again.	Restart computer.
Monitoring operation	Easy—External signal lights.	Difficult—unless your communication software simulates the signal lights.

Table 19.4 Continued

Features	External	Internal
Interface type	RS-232 serial or USB port; some models support both types of connections (Parallel-port modems were made a few years ago, but never proved popular and have been discontinued).	PCI or ISA; PCI is preferred for its extra speed, capability to allow mapping of COM 3 and COM 4 to unique IRQs instead of COM 1/3 and COM 2/4 sharing IRQs, and capability to work in so-called "legacy-free" systems that no longer include any ISA slots.

1 *Although late versions of Windows 95 OSR 2.x have USB support, many USB devices actually require Windows 98 or better. Use Windows 98/Me to achieve more reliable support for USB devices.*

Not all modems that function at the same speed have the same functionality. Many modem manufacturers produce modems running at the same speed but with different feature sets at different price points. The more expensive modems usually support advanced features, such as distinctive ring support, caller ID, voice and data, video teleconferencing, and call-waiting support. When purchasing a modem, be sure it supports all the features you need. You also should make sure the software you plan to use, including the operating system, has been certified for use with the modem you select.

If you live in a rural area, or in an older city neighborhood, your telephone line quality might influence your decision. Look at comparison test results carefully and pay particular attention to how well various modems perform with noisy lines. If your phone line sounds crackly during a rainstorm, that poor-quality line makes reliable modem communications difficult, too, and can limit your ability to connect at speeds above 33.6Kbps.

Another feature to consider is the modem's resistance to electrical damage. Some brands feature built-in power protection to shield against damage from digital telephone lines (higher powered and not compatible with modems) or power surges. However, every modem should be used with a surge protector that allows you to route the RJ-11 telephone cable through the unit for protection against high-voltage surges.

All modems on the market today support V.90, and even if your particular location can't support those speeds, your modem might still offer advanced features, such as voicemail or simultaneous voice and data. Keep in mind that V.90 connections seem to work better for many users if their modems also support x2. If you prefer a modem made by a vendor that also supports K56flex, try to buy a modem that contains both types of standards in its firmware (referred to by some vendors as "Dualmode" modems).

Choosing to Upgrade

If you bought your modem in 1997 or later, or if it was included in your computer, chances are good that it came with 56Kbps support or that you've upgraded it to some form of 56Kbps support. However, even though today's V.90/V.92 modems still have the same maximum speed, other changes in modem design have occurred that might make a modem upgrade desirable for you. And if you are still using a 33.6Kbps modem or even slower model, you should get a 56Kbps modem if your line quality can support it.

Table 19.5 summarizes some of the major changes in modem design and features in recent years, along with advice on who should consider these features.

Modems introduced in 1999 and beyond still run at the 53Kbps FCC maximum with the potential to run at up to 56Kbps if the FCC regulations change, but they might offer one or more of the following features:

- Call-waiting support
- PCI expansion slot for internal modems
- USB connection for external modems
- Faster performance for gaming
- MNP10 and MNP10EC
- V.92/V.44 support

Table 19.5   Modem Features and Types

Modem Feature	Benefit	Who Should Buy	Cautions
MNP10EC support	Improves performance on poor-quality phone lines by quickly adjusting line speed up and down with changing conditions.	Anyone with poor-quality lines, especially if modem at other end also has MNP10EC support; users who want to use modem with cellular phones.	Don't buy MNP10 support by mistake; MNP10EC is much better and includes MNP10. Check with ISP to see whether cellular connections are supported; speed of such connections can be 14.4Kbps or slower.
PCI bus	Works in PCI slots that dominate current systems and have replaced ISA slots. PCI modems can share IRQs with other devices and be redirected to open IRQs.	Anyone without ISA slots or who is planning to move the modem to another computer in the future and prefers internal modems.	Verify one or more PCI slots are available; look for other features listed here to make change as useful as possible; see also "Software Modem (WinModems)" later in this chapter.
USB connection	Works with USB connectors on most current and all future computers; high-speed connection and capability to connect many devices via a hub.	Anyone who wants portability and has USB connectors along with Windows 98 or above.	Although Windows 95 OSR 2.5 (Win95"C") has USB support, many devices require Win98 or better; make sure USB ports have been activated in BIOS.
Gaming-optimized modem	Faster PING and response for gaming, which is more important than data throughput.	Anyone who plays a lot of online games or wants to get started.	Game optimizations are not useful for ordinary Web surfing. These modems are more expensive than others.
Call-waiting support	Allows you to answer the phone and not lose modem connection, instead of disabling call waiting, which most modems require.	Anyone who uses call waiting and doesn't like voice callers to get busy signals; check with manufacturer to see whether your existing modem can be upgraded with a driver.	Maximum talk time might be only a few seconds; make sure you have the phone near the computer for fast "hello, I'll call you later" answers to avoid exceeding time limit.

Table 19.5   Continued

Modem Feature	Benefit	Who Should Buy	Cautions
V.92/V.44 support	Faster uploads, faster connection negotiation, Modem-on-hold, better throughput on downloads.	Anyone whose ISP supports all V.92/V.44 features.	Check with your ISP to see when V.92/V.44 support will be introduced and to see whether all features will be supported.
Voice support	Allows digitizing of received calls; computerized answering machine and faxback; inbound and outbound phone calls via computer.	Anyone who wants to use PC as a telecommunications center.	Check quality of voice recording; can use up a lot of disk space.

Software Modems (WinModems)

Software modems, sometimes referred to as *WinModems* after the pioneering U.S. Robotics version, can save you money at purchase time but can cause problems with speed and operating-system compatibility later.

For users looking for an inexpensive internal modem, a software modem using Windows instead of a UART-equipped internal or external modem looks like a great deal, often under $40. But, there is no free lunch for modem users. What can you lose with a "soft modem"?

First, you need to realize that there are actually two types of software modems: those that rely on Windows and the CPU for all operations (these modems are also called *controllerless* modems), and those that use a programmable DSP (Digital Signal Processor) chip to replace the UART. Both types of modems use less power than traditional UART-based modems, making them better for use with notebook computers. Although both are "software modems," there's an enormous difference in what you're getting.

A Windows-based modem must run under Windows because Windows provides the brains of the modem, a cost-cutting move similar to that used by some low-cost host-based printers. You should avoid this if you're planning to try Linux, move the modem to a Macintosh, or use an old MS-DOS–based communications program. If you have no drivers for your modem/operating system combination, you'll have no luck using the software modem.

Software modems that lack a DSP have a second major strike against them: They make your CPU do all the work. Although today's computers have much faster CPUs than those required for typical software modems (Pentium 133), your modem can still slow down your computer if you multitask while downloading or surfing the Web.

Most of the modems bundled with computer systems are software modems, and the major chipsets used include Lucent LT (now Agere Systems), Conexant (formerly Rockwell) HCF, U.S. Robotics WinModem, ESS Technology, Intel's Modem Silicon Operation (formerly Ambient), and PCTel.

Except for U.S. Robotics, the other companies produce chipsets that can be found in the modems made by many manufacturers.

For best results,

- Make sure your software modem uses a DSP; typically, these modems don't require a particular CPU or a particular speed of CPU.

- Consider modems built around the Lucent LT chipset; these modems have a DSP, and Lucent's firmware is frequently revised to achieve the best results in a rapidly changing telephony environment.

- Use the modem manufacturer's own drivers first, but software modems can often use any manufacturer's drivers for the same chipset with excellent results; in particular, Lucent LT chipset modems typically can use any Lucent LT driver from any modem manufacturer.

- Don't delete the old software driver when you download and install new modem software; as with UART-equipped modems, the latest firmware isn't always the best.

- Look carefully at the CPU, RAM, and operating system requirements before you buy your modem.

Tip

Many manufacturer sell both hardware-based and software modems. If you have an older system, or want the option to use MS-DOS– or Linux-based communications programs, the hardware modem with a traditional UART might cost more but be your better choice.

Finding Support for "Brand-X" Modems

Many computer users today didn't install their modems, or even purchase them as a separate unit. Their modems came bundled inside the computer and often have a bare-bones manual that makes no mention of the modem's origin or where to get help. Getting V.90 firmware updates, drivers, or even jumper settings for OEM modems such as this can be difficult.

One of the best Web sites for getting help when you don't know where to start is http://www.windrivers.com, which features a modem identification page with the following features:

- FCC ID: Enter the FCC ID number attached to the internal or external modem to determine who made it; look on the bottom of an external modem or open the case and look on the side of the internal modem to find this number

- Lookup by chipset manufacturer

- Modem throughput tests

- Links to major modem manufacturers

Squeezing Performance from Your 56Kbps Modem

Although many users of 56Kbps modems have seen significant improvements in their connect speeds and throughputs over their previous V.34-type modems, many have not or have seen only sporadic improvements. According to the research of Richard Gambert, available online at his 56k=v.Unreliable Web site (http://www.808hi.com/56k/), a combination of five factors comes into play to affect your ability to get reliable connections in the range of 45Kbps–53Kbps (the current FCC maximum):

- The modem

- The modem firmware/driver

- Your line conditions

- The ISP's modems

- The ISP's modem firmware

It's up to you to ensure that you match your modem 56Kbps type to the 56Kbps standards your ISP supports, and that you use the best (not always the latest!) modem firmware and drivers, as discussed in the previous section.

Other modem adjustments recommended at the 56k=v.Unreliable site include

■ Modifying existing modem .INF files used by Windows 9x to accurately reflect connection speed

■ Disabling 56Kbps connections (!) when playing games to minimize lag times

Note

This last suggestion might seem odd, but "fast" modems are designed to push a large amount of data through for downloads, and game play over modems actually deals with small amounts of data instead. The lag time caused by 56Kbps data handling can make a regular "fast" modem seem slow. If you want a fast modem for both downloading and game playing, see "Choosing to Upgrade," earlier in this chapter.

The site also hosts a forum area for discussing modem configuration, reliability, and performance issues.

Telco "Upgrades" and Your Modem

In addition to the well-known analog-to-digital conversion issue that prevents some phone lines from handling 56Kbps modems at anything beyond 33.6Kbps, other local telephone company (telco) practices can either prevent 56Kbps from ever working or take it away from you after you've enjoyed it for a while.

If you were getting 45Kbps or faster connections with your 56Kbps modem but can no longer get past 33.6Kbps, what happened? Some local telephone companies have been performing network "upgrades" that improve capacity for voice calls but prevent 56Kbps modems from running faster than 28Kbps. The cause seems to be the telephone companies' change from a signaling type called RBS (Robbed Bit Signaling) to SS7 (Signaling System 7), which changes how data used by the modem for high-speed access is detected.

What can you do? If you have a modem using Lucent Technologies firmware, check with your modem supplier or with Lucent (see "Software Modems (WinModems)," earlier in this chapter) for updates because Lucent has developed workarounds for this problem. You can also check with your local telephone company to see whether it can update its firmware to solve the problem. Even if your modem has different firmware, checking on an upgrade might still be useful because this problem is likely to become widespread as telephone numbers, exchanges, and area codes continue to multiply like weeds and telephone network upgrades must keep pace.

Broadband Internet Access Types

Thanks to the combination of huge multimegabyte downloads needed to update software and support hardware, dynamic Web sites with music and full-motion video, and increased demand for online services, even the fastest analog modem isn't sufficient for heavy Internet use. More and more users are taking advantage of various types of broadband Internet access solutions, including

■ ISDN

■ Cable modem

■ Fixed-base wireless

- DSL
- Satellite-based services
- Leased lines

At least one of these services might be available to you, and if you live in a large to medium-size city, you might be able to choose from two or more of these broadband solutions. The remainder of this chapter focuses on these broadband solutions and their technologies.

Note

For more information about broadband Internet access service types, installation, configuration, and troubleshooting, see Mark Edward Soper's, *The Complete Idiot's Guide to High-Speed Internet Access* published by Alpha Books (0-7897-2479-0).

High Speed = Less Freedom

Although high-speed services such as cable modems, DSL, and others all represent major improvements in speed over existing dial-up analog or 56Kbps connections, one big drawback you should consider is the loss of freedom in choosing an ISP.

With an analog or a 56Kbps modem, you can choose from a wide variety of services, including

- Local ISPs (personalized service)
- National ISPs with dial-up access across the country (great for travelers)
- Online services with customized content plus Web access (AOL and CompuServe)
- Family-friendly filtered Internet access (Mayberry USA and Lightdog)
- Business-oriented Web hosting plus Internet access plans from many vendors

The price you pay at present for faster speed is using the ISP provided with your high-speed service. Whether it's your local telephone company, a third-party vendor, or your friendly cable TV operator, their ISP is your ISP. When you evaluate a high-speed service, remember to look at the special features and services provided by the ISP and the ISP's track record for reliability and keeping customers happy. After all, the quality of the work your ISP does is reflected in the quality of your broadband connection.

Integrated Services Digital Network

To get past the speed limitations of asynchronous modems, you have to go completely digital, and Integrated Services Digital Network (ISDN) was the first step in the move to digital telecommunications. With ISDN, you can connect to the Internet at speeds of up to 128Kbps.

Even though ISDN service is now widely available, it is far from the best choice for broadband Internet access. As its telephone-company origins would suggest, ISDN primarily is designed for telephony applications, including voice, fax, and teleconferencing. Virtually any ISP can handle a normal analog modem, but only a few ISPs are capable of handling ISDN connections, which are digital for both downloading and uploading. Although some local telephone companies have de-emphasized ISDN in favor of faster broadband solutions such as DSL, ISDN doesn't require quite as good a phone line as DSL. This makes ISDN possible in areas where DSL can't work without a major upgrade of the telephone system.

What Does ISDN Really Mean for Computer Users?

Because ISDN carries three channels, it allows integrated services that can include combinations such as voice+data, data+data, voice+fax, fax+data, and so on.

The "Digital" in ISDN represents the end of the need for your venerable telecom pal, the modem. ISDN connections are digital from the origination straight to your PC—no digital-analog conversions needed. Thus, the so-called ISDN modem used to hook your PC to an ISDN line is more properly called a *terminal adapter*.

The "Network" in ISDN refers to its capability to interconnect with other ISDN devices around the world. Unlike the earlier high-speed access method for business—the leased line—ISDN isn't limited to making fast connections to a single computer. In fact, if your ISDN equipment includes support for analog services, your ISDN connection can "reach out and touch" regular telephones, fax machines, and other plain old telephone service (POTS) devices (see Figure 19.4).

Figure 19.4   This typical ISDN configuration shows how ISDN can link your advanced telecommunications devices with both the ISDN and analog worlds.

How Standard ISDN Works

On a standard ISDN connection, bandwidth is divided into bearer channels (B channels) that run at 64Kbps and a delta channel (D channel) that runs at either 16Kbps or 64Kbps, depending on the type of service. The B channels carry voice transmissions or user data, and the D channel carries control traffic. In other words, you talk, surf, or fax through the B-channel lines.

Two types of ISDN service exist: Basic Rate Interface (BRI) and Primary Rate Interface (PRI). The BRI service is intended for private and home users and consists of two B channels and one 16Kbps D channel, for a total of 144Kbps. The typical BRI service enables you to use one B channel to talk at 64Kbps and one B channel to run your computer for Web surfing at 64Kbps. Hang up the phone, and both B channels become available. If your ISDN service is configured appropriately, your Web browsing becomes supercharged because you're now running at 128Kbps.

The PRI service is oriented more toward business use, such as for PBX connections to the telephone company's central office. In North America and Japan, the PRI service consists of 23 B channels and

1 64Kbps D channel for a total of 1,536Kbps, running over a standard T-1 interface. In Europe, the PRI service is 30 B channels and 1 64Kbps D channel, totaling 1,984Kbps, corresponding to the E1 telecommunications standard. For businesses that require more bandwidth than one PRI connection provides, 1 D channel can be used to support multiple PRI channels using non-facility associated signaling (NFAS).

The BRI limit of two B channels might seem limiting to anyone other than a small office or home office user, but this is misleading. The BRI line can actually accommodate up to eight ISDN devices, each with a unique ISDN number. The D channel provides call routing and "on-hold" services, also called *multiple call signaling*, allowing all the devices to share the two B channels (see Figure 19.5).

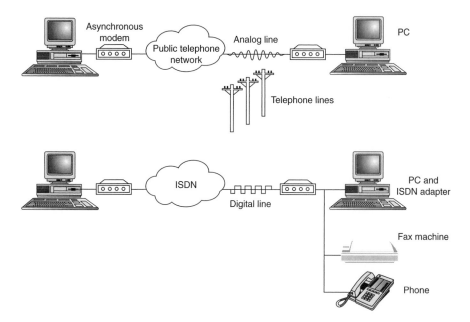

Figure 19.5 An analog modem connection connects only your PC to the Internet or other online services, whereas ISDN can connect your computer, fax, and many other devices via a single ISDN terminal adapter.

Note

When speaking of ISDN connections, 1 kilobyte equals 1,000 bytes, not 1,024 bytes as in standard computer applications.

As you saw earlier, this is also true of speed calculations for modems. Calculations that use 1,000 as a base are often referred to as *decimal* kilobytes, whereas the ones based on 1,024 are called *binary* kilobytes.

If you need a more powerful, more flexible (and more expensive) version of ISDN, use the PRI version along with a switching device, such as a PBX or server. Although PRI allows only one device per B channel, it can dynamically allocate unused channels to support high-bandwidth uses, such as video-conferencing, when a switching device is in use along with PRI.

Acquiring ISDN Service

To have an ISDN connection installed, you must be within 18,000 feet (about 3.4 miles or 5.5km) of the CO (telco central office or central switch) for the BRI service. For greater distances, expensive repeater devices are needed, and some telephone companies might not offer the service at all. Most of the existing telephone wiring in the United States is capable of supporting ISDN communications, so you usually need not pay for the installation of new telephone cable.

Prices for ISDN service vary widely depending on your location. In the United States, the initial installation fee can be in the range of from $100 to $150, depending on whether you are converting an existing line or installing a new one. The monthly charges typically range from $30 to $50, and sometimes there is a connect-time charge as well, ranging from 1 to 6 cents per minute or more, depending on the state. Keep in mind that you also must purchase an ISDN terminal adapter for your PC and possibly other hardware as well, and these charges are only for the telephone company's ISDN service. You must also pay your ISP for access to the Internet at ISDN speeds. You can easily pay $100 or more per month of ISDN service.

Because ISDN pricing plans offer many options depending on the channels you want and how you want to use them, make sure you plan out carefully how you want to use ISDN. Check the telco's Web site for pricing and package information to get a jump on the decision-making process. Even with the large multistate telcos, such as SBC or other Baby Bells, your state and location will make an enormous difference in both the pricing and availability of ISDN services. Although ISDN is unique among broadband Internet services for its capability to handle both voice and data traffic, its high cost and low speed make it a poor choice for most small-office and home-office users.

ISDN Hardware

To connect a PC to an ISDN connection, you must have a hardware component called a *terminal adapter (TA)*. The terminal adapter takes the form of an expansion board or an external device connected to a serial port, much like a modem. In fact, terminal adapters often are mistakenly referred to as ISDN modems. Actually, they are not modems at all because they do not perform analog/digital conversions.

Because an ISDN connection was originally designed to service telephony devices, most ISDN terminal adapters have connections for telephones, fax machines, and similar devices, as well as for your computer. Some terminal adapters can also be used as routers to enable multiple PCs to be networked to the ISDN connection.

Caution

To achieve the best possible performance, you should either purchase an external ISDN terminal adapter that connects to your computer's USB port or use an internal version. A terminal adapter with compression enabled easily can exceed a serial port's capability to reliably send and receive data. Consider that even a moderate 2:1 compression ratio exceeds the maximum rated speed of 232Kbps, which most high-speed COM ports support. USB ports, on the other hand, can handle signals up to 12Mbps, easily supporting even the fastest ISDN connection.

Note

For more information about ISDN hardware and configuration, see *Upgrading and Repairing PCs, 11th Edition,* available in electronic form on the CD-ROM packaged with this book.

Cable Modems and CATV Networks

For many users, cable modem service, which piggybacks on the same cable TV (CATV) service lines that bring your TV many channels, represents both a big boost in speed from that available with ISDN and a major savings in initial costs and monthly charges. Unlike ISDN, cable modem service normally is sold as an "all you can eat" unlimited-access plan with a modest installation charge (often waived) and a small monthly fee for rental of the cable modem. Some cable modem providers are now providing a low-cost (around $30) self-install kit for their existing cable TV customers, enabling customers to attach a cable modem to their computer's USB port or to a network card.

Connecting to the Internet with a "Cable Modem"

As with ISDN, the device used to connect a PC to a CATV network is somewhat inaccurately called a modem. In fact, the so-called "cable modem" (a name I will continue to use, for the sake of convenience) is actually a great deal more. The device does indeed modulate and demodulate, but it also functions as a tuner, a network bridge, an encryptor, an SNMP agent, and a hub. To connect your PC to a CATV network, you do not use a serial port as with standard modem technologies. Instead, the most typical connection used today requires that you install a standard 10BASE-T or 10/100 Ethernet network interface adapter into a bus slot. The Ethernet adapter connects to the cable modem with a crossover cable that uses the standard RJ-45 connector but has wires reversed at one end. In fact, your PC and the cable modem actually form a two-node LAN, with the modem functioning as a hub. Some older cable modem services use an internal adapter for one-way service (using the conventional modem for uploads), but the most common alternative to the Ethernet card is an external USB-based cable modem connection for two-way service.

The Cable Modem and the CATV Network

The cable modem connects to the CATV network using the same coaxial cable connection as your cable TV service (see Figure 19.6). Thus, the cable modem functions as a bridge between the tiny twisted-pair network in your home and the hybrid fiber/coax (HFC) network that connects all the cable customers in your neighborhood.

A few cable modem CATV systems have been built using the older one-way (download-only) coax cable, but this type of cable is much slower for cable modem use and is obsolete for both CATV and data communications. The industry has largely replaced coax with HFC. Before you sign up for CATV Internet service, find out which type of service is being offered. Only the two-way, HFC-based systems allow you to use the Internet independently of the telephone system; one-way cable modem service requires you to use your conventional analog modem for uploading page requests, files, and email.

Digital CATV service, which brings your TV many more channels and a clearer picture, requires the cable TV provider to upgrade to an HFC physical plant. Thus, digital CATV service is a precursor to two-way cable modem service; pure-coax CATV systems cannot be used to transmit digital service or handle two-way cable modem traffic. CATV systems that have been upgraded to digital service are able, after suitable head-end equipment is installed at the CATV central office, to provide two-way cable modem service. A good rule of thumb, therefore, is that no digital cable means that you can get either only one-way cable modem service or no cable modem service at all.

Originally, cable modems were not sold to users of CATV Internet access but were leased by the CATV companies offering Internet access to their cable modem customers. This is because each cable modem on a particular CATV network had to match the proprietary technology used by the network. In late 1998, DOCSIS-compliant cable modems began to be used by some CATV companies. DOCSIS refers to devices that meet the Data Over Cable Service Interface Specification standards. Many vendors of traditional modems and other types of communications products, such as Zoom Telephonics, 3Com, GVC, General Instruments, Philips, Motorola, Cabletron, and others, now make DOCSIS-compliant cable modems. However, because of changes in the DOCSIS standard, which can prevent free interchange of cable modems between networks, and the relatively high purchase cost of the cable modem ($200 or more versus under $50 for an analog modem), some CATV Internet providers still require you to lease their own cable modems. I recommend leasing the cable modem because the CATV operator is responsible for servicing the unit or replacing it with a newer device if necessary. Typical lease costs for the device add only about $10/month to the monthly rate of $30–$40 for cable modem service.

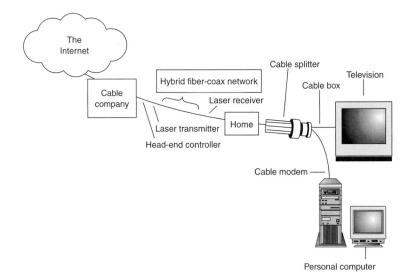

Figure 19.6   A basic cable modem connection to the Internet.

Types of Cable Modems

Cable modems come in several forms:

- *External cable modem "box"; requires an Ethernet NIC or a USB port.* Some vendors provide "bundles" that combine the external cable modem with the NIC at a lower price. This type of cable modem is designed for fast uploads as well as fast downloads and works only on newer "two-way" CATV Internet connections.

- *Internal cable modem with a 56Kbps analog modem built in.* This type of cable modem provides fast downloads but uploads at analog speeds only; this type might use either an ISA or a PCI slot.

- *Internal cable modem for use with a separate 56Kbps analog modem.* This type might use either an ISA or a PCI slot. As with the previous model, uploads are at analog speeds only.

Cable modem models that must be used with (or include) an analog modem are designed for older "one-way" CATV Internet connections; these will tie up your phone line to transmit page requests as well as to send uploads.

CATV Bandwidth

Cable TV uses what is known as a *broadband network*, meaning the bandwidth of the connection is split to carry many signals at the same time. These various signals correspond to the various channels you see on your TV. A typical HFC network provides approximately 750MHz of bandwidth, and each channel requires 6MHz. Therefore, because the television channels start at about 50MHz, you would find channel 2 in the 50MHz–56MHz range, channel 3 at 57MHz–63MHz, and continuing on up the frequency spectrum. At this rate, an HFC network can support about 110 channels.

For data networking purposes, cable systems typically allocate one channel's worth of bandwidth in the 50MHz–750MHz range for downstream traffic—that is, traffic coming into the cable modem from the CATV network. In this way, the cable modem functions as a tuner, just like your cable TV box, ensuring that your PC receives signals from the correct frequency.

Upstream traffic (data sent from your PC to the network) uses a different channel. Cable TV systems commonly reserve the bandwidth from 5MHz to 42MHz for upstream signals of various types (such as those generated by cable TV boxes that enable you to order pay-per-view programming). Depending on the bandwidth available, you might find that your CATV provider does not furnish the same high speed upstream as it does downstream. This is called an *asymmetrical network*.

Note

Because the upstream speed often does not match the downstream speed (and to minimize noise, which tends to accumulate because of the tree-and-branch nature of the network), cable TV connections usually are not practical for hosting Web servers and other Internet services. This is largely deliberate because most CATV providers are currently targeting their traditional home user market. As the technology matures, however, this type of Internet connection is likely to spread to the business world as well. There are now specialized domain name services that can be used to "point" Web surfers to your cable modem or DSL connection.

The amount of data throughput that the single 6MHz downstream channel can support depends on the type of modulation used at the head end (that is, the system to which your PC connects over the network). Using a technology called 64 QAM (quadrature amplitude modulation), the channel might be capable of carrying up to 27Mbps of downstream data. A variant called 256 QAM can boost this to 36Mbps.

You must realize, however, that you will not achieve anything even approaching this throughput on your PC. First of all, if you are using an Ethernet adapter to connect to the cable modem, you are limited to 10Mbps, but even this is well beyond the real-life results you will achieve. As with any LAN, you are sharing the available bandwidth with other users. All your neighbors who also subscribe to the service use the same 6MHz channel. As more users are added, more systems are contending for the same bandwidth, and throughput goes down.

In November 1999, ZDTV tested five brands of cable modems in typical operations and found that the overhead of CATV proved to be a major slowdown factor. The cable modems were first connected directly to the server to provide a baseline for comparisons. Some of these tests showed speeds as high as 4Mbps. However, when the CATV cable was connected and the same tests were run, the best performer dropped to just 1.1Mbps, with others running even more slowly.

Widespread reports from cable-modem users across the country indicate that rush hour–type conditions occur at certain times of the day on some systems, with big slowdowns. This rush hour is due to increasing use of cable modem systems in the late afternoon and early evening, as daytime workers get home and pull up the day's news, weather, stocks, and sports on their Internet connections. Because cable modems are shared access, this type of slowdown is inevitable and becomes exceptionally severe if the CATV Internet provider doesn't use a fast enough connection to the rest of the Internet. To minimize this problem, many CATV Internet providers use caching servers at their point of presence connections to the Internet. These servers store frequently-accessed Web pages to enable users to view pages without the delays in retrieving them from the original Web sites. By adding multiple T1 or T3 connections to the Internet backbones and using caching servers, ISPs can minimize delays during peak usage hours.

CATV Performance

The fact that you are sharing the CATV network with other users doesn't mean the performance of a cable modem isn't usually spectacular. Although the CATV network takes a big cut out of the maximum speeds, you'll still realize a throughput that hovers around 512Kbps, almost 10 times that of the fastest modem connection and four times that of ISDN. You will find the Web to be an entirely new experience at this speed. Those huge audio and video clips you avoided in the past now download in seconds, and you will soon fill your hard drives with all the free software available.

Add to this the fact that the service is typically quite reasonably priced. Remember that the CATV provider is replacing both the telephone company (if you have two-way service) and your ISP in your Internet access solution. The price can be about $40–$50 per month (including cable modem rental), which is twice that of a normal dial-up ISP account, but it is far less than ISDN, does not require a telephone line (if your provider has two-way service), and provides you with 24-hour access to the Internet. The only drawback is that the service might not be available yet in your area. In my opinion, this technology exceeds all the other Internet access solutions available today in speed, economy, convenience, and widespread availability. Its nearest rival is DSL, which is still not as widely available geographically and is plagued with poor coordination between ISPs and telephone companies. Because cable modem Internet service providers provide the physical plant, provide ISP services, and can provide equipment, you can get service installed in just days and avoid the finger-pointing common with other types of broadband Internet service.

CATV Internet Connection Security

Because your PC is sharing a network with other users in your neighborhood, and because the traffic is bidirectional on systems using two-way cable modems, the security of your PC and the network becomes an issue. In most cases, some form of encryption is involved to prevent unauthorized access to the network. As with your cable TV box, the cable modem might contain encryption circuitry necessary to access the network. Your CATV provider might also supply encryption software that uses a special protocol to log you on to the network. This protects the CATV provider from non-paying users, but it doesn't protect you. The security features vary according to which cable modem is used; the popular DOCSIS standard for cable modems features built-in encryption.

If you use an operating system such as Windows 9x/Me that has built-in peer networking capabilities, you might be able to see your neighbors' computers on the network if your provider doesn't use DOCSIS-compliant cable modems or some other form of encryption. The operating system has settings that enable you to specify whether other network users can access your drives. If these settings are configured improperly, your neighbors might be able to view, access, and even delete the files on your hard drives. Be sure the technician from the cable company installing the service addresses this problem. If you want to use a cable modem along with sharing access on your computer (for printing, file storage, and so on), I'd recommend that you use passwords for any shared drives, but you're even safer if you disable file and printer sharing on the system you connect to the cable modem.

Note

For more information on securing any type of Internet access, see "Securing Your Internet Connection," page 1045, this chapter.

Fixed-Base Wireless Broadband

If you're beyond the reach of CATV-based Internet or DSL and aren't interested in trying to install a satellite dish, you still might be able to get broadband Internet service through a fixed wireless broadband Internet provider.

Fixed wireless broadband should not be confused with text-only wireless Internet services aimed at hand-held mobile phones and PDAs. After a fixed-base wireless broadband signal reaches your computer, your Internet experience is just as rich in content and about as speedy as wired services, such as cable modem and DSL. Essentially, fixed wireless broadband Internet access is a form of cable modem service that substitutes microwave receivers or transceivers for the HFC cabling of the cable modem network. Similar to cable modems, fixed wireless broadband is an "always-on" service.

How Fixed-Base Wireless Broadband Works

Fixed-base wireless broadband is an offshoot of wireless CATV broadcasting; both use microwave towers to broadcast encrypted signals to receivers within a specified radius (35 miles or less) of the transmitter. Wireless CATV delivers the same cable TV content that conventional CATV operators provide for rural users and others who aren't served by conventional CATV services.

Similarly, fixed-base wireless broadband delivers encrypted Internet content to customers within the radius of the transmitter. If only a single transmitter/receiver site is used, the distance for two-way service can be significantly less than that available for wireless CATV users; as little as 15–20 miles. Because of the directional nature of the receiving antennas used for fixed-based wireless broadband, only some of the users in that radius might qualify for two-way service. Users who live within the radius served by the transmitter but don't qualify for two-way service might be eligible for one-way (also called Telco Return) service, which uses wireless signals for downloading only and an analog modem for uploading. Some fixed wireless broadband services offered in larger cities might use multiple transmitters, enabling all users to enjoy two-way service.

Wireless signals are similar in their bandwidth use and modulation to CATV cable modem signals; in fact, some wireless broadband routers (which serve the same function as cable modems but are used for wireless networking) can also be used in CATV cable modem service.

Figure 19.7 compares the two forms of fixed-base wireless broadband Internet service.

Figure 19.7 A two-way fixed-base wireless broadband service (1) uses wireless signals for both downloaded and uploaded data, whereas a one-way service (2) uses an analog modem and the telephone network for uploaded data and wireless signals for downloaded data only.

The Wireless Broadband Router and Other Equipment

The connection between the wireless broadband service and your computer is provided by a wireless broadband router (also referred to as a WBR or wireless cable modem). A WBR resembles an external cable modem but also includes either an RS-232 connection to an external analog phone modem or an integrated analog modem, enabling the same WBR to be used in either two-way or one-way (Telco Return) service, as shown in Figure 19.8.

One-way (Telco Return)
Wireless Broadband Configurations

RJ-45 (UTP Ethernet) crossover cable
RJ-11 telephone cable
Coaxial cable
RS-232 modem cable

From wireless receiver antenna

To telephone network

External analog modem

10BaseT or 10/100 Ethernet card

RJ-45 crossover cable

Rear of wireless broadband modem

From wireless receiver antenna

To telephone network

10BaseT or 10/100 Ethernet card

RJ-45 crossover cable

Telephone

Rear of wireless broadband modem with integrated phone modem

Figure 19.8   A typical wireless broadband router connects to coaxial cable coming from the receiver/transceiver. If the unit is used in one-way service, it can be attached to an external analog modem (top) or might include an analog modem (bottom).

The WBR is connected via the same type of coaxial cable used by CATV cable modems to various types of receivers (for one-way service) or transceivers (for two-way service) that are mounted on the roof or on a tower. The placement of the transceiver or receiver is critical, especially in systems that use only one transmitter/receiver location. A site survey performed by the provider usually is required to verify that the service is available and to select a location for the transceiver/receiver's antenna.

If a direct line of sight back to the transmission/receiving tower cannot be established, two-way service will not be possible. However, one-way service might be available if the signal can be reflected off a nearby tower or building. Devices referred to as *benders* can be mounted on nearby structures to permit receiving of the signal from the wireless broadband provider, but benders cannot be used to return data from the customer back to the provider's receiver.

Fixed Wireless Service Pricing and Availability

Generally, fixed wireless broadband Internet service is provided by either companies that also provide wireless CATV service or specialized wireless broadband companies, such as Sprint Broadband Direct. Service pricing and speeds tend to fall between typical cable modem and DSL offerings in many markets, although some fixed wireless broadband providers have pricing in the under $50/month target, which makes broadband services very attractive to many users and very competitive with cable modem service. Depending on the provider, you might be able to choose from several speeds (a provider in southern Indiana, for example, offers 128Kbps, 512Kbps, or 1.5Kbps rates) or a single speed of 512Kbps or faster.

Unlike cable modem service, though, users of fixed wireless broadband services might have to buy— and not have the option of leasing—their equipment. To get the best deals, compare the cost of month-to-month service with a longer contract. For example, in Denver, Sprint Broadband Direct charges $299 for the wireless broadband router and the transceiver if you choose month-to-month service, but the price drops to as little as $99 if you opt for a two-year contract. Some vendors charge for installation, whereas others might waive it at certain times.

To find a fixed wireless provider in your area, you can

- Contact your wireless cable TV provider
- Contact Sprint Broadband (the first national fixed wireless broadband provider) at www.sprintbroadband.com
- Check the Cable Datacom News' list of wireless broadband trials and deployments at www.cabledatacomnews.com/wireless/cmic12.html

Fixed Wireless Security Issues

All fixed wireless broadband services are encrypted, even the one-way offerings, so casual snooping by others receiving the signal isn't possible. However, you should guard against other types of Internet intrusion common to all forms of Internet access.

Note

For more information on securing any type of Internet access, see "Securing Your Internet Connection," page 1045, this chapter.

Digital Subscriber Line

The biggest rival to cable modems in the broadband Internet business is Digital Subscriber Line (DSL). DSL, like its predecessor ISDN, appeals to the telephone companies, who can use the existing POTS analog wiring to provide high-speed Internet access. Not every type of DSL is suitable for existing wiring; however, all but the fastest, most expensive types can sometimes be used with the existing POTS plant. DSL is also appealing to businesses that don't have access to cable modems but are looking for a high-performance, lower-cost alternative to the expensive ISDN services that top out at 128Kbps.

Note

Some technical discussions of DSL refer to xDSL. The x stands for the various versions of DSL being proposed and offered by local telephone companies and ISPs. DSL generally is used to refer to any type of Digital Subscriber Line service.

One advantage of DSL compared to its most popular rival—cable modems—is that cable modems are sharing common bandwidth, which means that a lot of simultaneous use by your neighbors can slow down your connection. DSL users don't have this concern; whatever bandwidth speed you paid for is yours—period.

Who Can Use DSL—and Who Can't

DSL services are slowly rolling out across the country, first to major cities and then to smaller cities and towns. As with 56Kbps modems, rural and small-town users are probably out of luck and should consider satellite-based cable modems or fixed wireless services if available for a faster-than-56Kbps experience.

Just as distance to a telephone company's central switch (CS) is an important consideration for people purchasing an ISDN connection, distance also affects who can use DSL in the markets offering it. For example, most DSL service types require that you be within about 18,000 feet (about 3 miles) *wire distance* (not a straight line!) to a telco offering DSL; some won't offer it if you're beyond 15,000 feet wire distance because the speed drops significantly at longer distances. Repeaters or a local loop that has been extended by the telco with fiber-optic line might provide longer distances. The speed of your DSL connection varies with distance: The closer you are to the telco, the faster your DSL access is. Many telcos that offer some type of DSL service provide Web sites that help you determine whether, and what type of, DSL is available to you.

If you want to locate DSL service providers in your area, compare rates, and see reviews from users of the hundreds of ISPs now providing DSL service, set your browser to `http://www.dslreports.com`. The site provides a verdict on many of the ISPs reviewed, summarizing users' experiences and ranking each ISP in six categories. An excellent FAQ can be found at `http://www.dsl.com`, which covers the many flavors of xDSL and has many links to other DSL sites. Both sites offer user forums.

Note

If you want to connect a DSL to your SOHO or office LAN, check first to see what the provider's attitude is. Some users report good cooperation, whereas others indicate they were told "we can't help you" or were told that DSL "couldn't be connected to a LAN." Again, check around for the best policies. Low-cost switch/router combinations from companies such as Linksys and Microsoft's Internet Connection Sharing provide relatively easy ways to share both DSL and other types of high-speed connections.

For "field-tested" DSL information (written originally for Pacific Bell DSL users but useful for everyone), check out `http://home.pacbell.net/golemite/`.

Major Types of DSL

Although the term *DSL* is used in advertising and popular discussions to refer to any form of DSL, there are actually many, many variations of DSL that are used in different markets and for different situations. This section discusses the most common forms of DSL and provides a table that compares the various types of DSL service. Although many types of DSL service exist, you can choose only from the service types offered by your DSL provider:

- *ADSL (Asymmetrical DSL)*. The type of DSL used most often. Asymmetrical means that downstream (download) speeds are much faster than upstream (upload) speeds. For most users, this is no problem because downloads of Web pages, graphics, and files are the major use of Internet connections. Maximum downstream speeds are up to 1.6Mbps, with up to 640Kbps upstream. Most vendors who offer ADSL provide varying levels of service at lower speeds and prices, as well. Voice calls are routed over the same wire using a small amount of bandwidth, making a single-line service that does voice and data possible. ADSL is more expensive to set up than some other forms of DSL because a splitter must be installed at the customer site, meaning that you must pay for a service call (also called a truck roll) as part of the initial setup charge.

- *CDSL (Consumer DSL)*. A slower (1Mbps upstream) form of DSL that was developed by modem chipset maker Rockwell. It doesn't require a service call because no splitter is required at the customer site.

- *G.Lite (Universal DSL, and also called DSL Lite or splitterless DSL)*. Another version that splits the line at the telco end rather than at the consumer end. Downstream speeds range from 1.544Mbps to 6.0Mbps, and upstream speeds can be from 128Kbps to 384Kbps. This is becoming one of the most popular forms of DSL because it enables consumers to use self-install kits. Note that the DSL vendor might cap the service at rates lower than those listed earlier in the chapter; check with the vendor for details.

- *SDSL (Symmetrical DSL)*. This type of DSL service provides the same speed for upstream as for downstream service. Generally, SDSL is offered to business rather than residential customers because it requires new cabling (rather than reusing existing phone lines). A long-term contract frequently is required.

Table 19.6 summarizes the various types of DSL.

Table 19.6   DSL Type Comparison

DSL Type	Description	Data Rate Downstream; Upstream	Distance Limit	Application
DSL	Digital Subscriber Line	160Kbps	18,000 feet on 24-gauge wire	Used for basic rate interface
IDSL	ISDN Digital Subscriber Line	128Kbps	18,000 feet on 24-gauge wire	Similar to the ISDN BRI service but data only (no voice on the same line)
CDSL	Consumer DSL from Rockwell	1Mbps downstream; less upstream	18,000 feet on 24-gauge wire	Splitterless home and small business service; similar to DSL Lite
DSL Lite (same as G.Lite)	Splitterless DSL without the "truck roll"	From 1.544 Mbps to 6Mbps downstream, depending on the subscribed service	18,000 feet on 24-gauge wire	The standard ADSL; sacrifices speed for not having to install a splitter at the user's home or business
HDSL	High bit-rate Digital Subscriber Line	1.544Mbps duplex on two twisted-pair lines; 2.048Mbps duplex on three twisted-pair lines	12,000 feet on 24-gauge wire	T-1/E1 service between server and phone company or within a company; WAN, LAN, server access
SDSL	Symmetric DSL (also called X-speed)	1.544Mbps duplex (U.S. and Canada); 2.048Mbps (Europe) on a single-duplex line downstream and upstream	12,000 feet on 24-gauge wire	Same as for HDSL but requiring only one line of twisted pair

Table 19.6 Continued

DSL Type	Description	Data Rate Downstream; Upstream	Distance Limit	Application
ADSL	Asymmetric Digital Subscriber Line	1.544Mbps to 8.4Mbps downstream; 16Kbps to 640Kbps upstream	1.544Mbps at 18,000 feet; 2.048Mbps at 16,000 feet; 6.312Mpbs at 12,000 feet; 8.448Mbps at 9,000 feet	Used for Internet and Web access, motion video, video on demand, and remote LAN access
RADSL	Rate-Adaptive DSL from Westell	Adapted to the line, 640Kbps to 2.2Mbps downstream; 272Kbps to 1.088Mbps upstream	Not provided	Similar to ADSL
UDSL	Unidirectional DSL proposed by a company in Europe	Not known	Not known	Similar to HDSL
VDSL	Very high Digital Subscriber Line	12.9Mbps to 52.8Mbps downstream; 1.5Mbps to 2.3Mbps upstream; 1.6Mbps to 2.3Mbps downstream	4,500 feet at 12.96Mbps; 3,000 feet at 25.82Mbps; 1,000 feet at 51.84Mbps	ATM networks; Fiber to the Neighborhood

Table copyrighted by and used with permission of whatis.com, Inc.

With any type of DSL, an external device called a DSL "modem" is attached to the computer through either

■ A crossover cable running to a 10BASE-T or 10/100 Ethernet card or port in the computer

■ A USB cable running to a USB port in the computer

An RJ-11 (standard telephone) cable is attached between the DSL "modem" and the RJ-11 port that has been set up for DSL service.f you self-install DSL, you will install small devices called microfilters to block interference from telephones, answering machines, and similar devices. These devices might fit behind the faceplate of the wall outlet used for DSL service or inline between the phone, answering machine, fax machine, and the wall outlet (see Figure 19.9).

DSL Pricing

DSL pricing varies widely, with different telephone companies offering different speeds of DSL and different rates. One thing that's true about the most commonly used flavors of DSL is that they are usually an asymmetrical service—with download speeds faster than upload speeds.

For unlimited use, typical DSL pricing ranges anywhere from $25 to $500 a month depending on the download speed, ranging from 256Kbps to 1.5Mbps.

The wide variance is partly due to the upload speeds permitted. The lower-cost plans typically use a lower upload speed (some variation on ADSL or G.Lite), but not always. Check carefully with your vendor because your traditional telephone company might not be the only DSL game in town. Some major cities might have as many as half a dozen vendors selling various flavors of DSL.

DSL Installation with In-line Microfilter

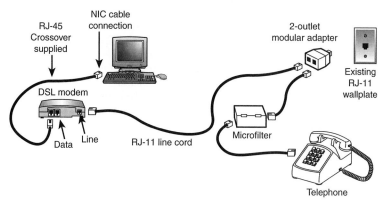

DSL Installation with Wall Outlet Microfilter

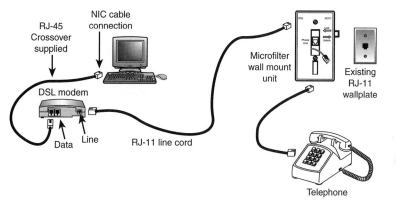

Figure 19.9   Two types of DSL self-installations; if a splitter is used to set up a separate DSL line, the microfilters shown here are not necessary.

Time Versus Access

Some so-called *Personal DSL* plans give you an interesting puzzle: time online versus data transfers.

Before the advent of unlimited Internet access, the time you spent online and the speed of your modem were the two variables used to calculate the cost per hour of services such as the original CompuServe. I remember looking for files on CIS at 2,400bps because surfing the site was cheaper that way, noting the files needed, and then hanging up and downloading them at the "blazing" speed of 9,600bps (a speed that cost you extra to use some years ago).

Some Personal DSL plans have gone back to a consumption-based pricing scheme. But with consumption-based Personal DSL plans, the speed of your connection or the time you spend are unimportant—it's the amount of data transfer you perform.

For many people, this won't be a major issue. For example, with US Family.net's Personal DSL - External IP plan (which provides a fixed IP address ideal for online gaming), 2,000MB (2GB) per month of data transfer is included at no extra charge, and users pay just $2/month for each 100MB of additional data transfer. Another provider, Roseville Telephone, has a 1GB upload/5GB download limit per month on its personal accounts; accounts exceeding this limit are changed to business accounts (which pay higher rates).

Unless you're routinely downloading massive software service packs; hosting a game, Web, or NetMeeting server; or working beyond the fringes of legality by downloading entire CDs, this limitation is more apparent than real. Even though every Web page and graphic you view on the Web counts as a file transfer, the sizes of GIF, JPG, and HTML pages are usually miniscule. Still, find out what the file-transfer limitations are before you sign up for any type of metered DSL.

DSL Security Issues

Unlike other types of broadband access, DSL is a direct one-to-one connection that isn't shared; you have no digital "neighbors" who could casually snoop on your activities. However, as with any broadband "always-on" connection, intrusion from the Internet to your computer is a very real possibility.

Note

For more information on securing any type of Internet access, see "Securing Your Internet Connection," page 1045, this chapter.

Technical Problems with DSL

Telecommunications has always had its share of difficulties, starting with the incredibly slow and tempermental 300bps modems used on early PCs, but as speed increases, so do problems. DSL connections are often very difficult to get working correctly because DSL, as you've seen, combines the problems of adding high-speed data access to the telephone line with network configuration using TCP/IP (the most powerful and most complex network protocol in widespread use; see Chapter 20, "Local Area Networking," for details).

A review of comments from DSL users in various forums, such as DSLReports.com and others, shows that the most common problems include

- *Poor coordination between the DSL sales department of the telco or third-party provider and the installers.* This can lead to broken or very late appointments; if possible, contact the installer company to verify the appointment.

- *Installers who install the hardware and software and then leave without verifying it works properly.* Ask whether the installer carries a notebook computer that can test the line; don't let the installer leave until the line is working.

- *Poor technical support before and after installation.* Record the IP address and other information used during the installation; read reviews and tips from sources listed earlier in the chapter to help you find better DSL providers and solutions you can apply yourself or ask your telco or provider to perform.

- *Lower speeds than anticipated.* This can be due to a poor-quality connection to the telco from your home or business or problems at the central switch; ask the installer to test the line for you during initial installation and tell you the top DSL speed the line can reach. On a healthy line, the problem is often traceable to a very low value for the Windows Registry key called RWIN (receive window), which should be adjusted from its default of 8192 (8KB) to a value as high as 32768 (32KB) or even 65535 (64KB). If your system previously was used with a dial-up modem, the value for RWIN can be as low as 2144; low values force your DSL connection to receive data at rates hardly faster than those for a dial-up analog modem connection. For interactive tests that will help you find the best value to use for RWIN or other Registry options, find line problems, and adjust your configuration, go to http://www.dslreports.com and follow the Tools link from the home page.

Because of the problems with trying to retrofit an aging voice-oriented telephone network with high-speed Internet service, many pure DSL companies are having financial problems, leading to service cancellations in some cases. Before you sign up for DSL service, be sure to read the "Deathwatch" page of DSLReports.com for the latest financial news on DSL companies. Before you sign a long-term contract for DSL service, you also should determine what your options are if your telco, DSL line provider, or ISP drops DSL service.

Internet Connectivity via Satellite with DirecPC or Starband

If you're in an area where cable TV doesn't exist, or you already have a DirecTV or DISH Network satellite dish, take a look at the southern sky from your home, condo, or apartment building. If you have a good, clear 45° window view to the southern sky and you want fast downloads of big files, a satellite-based service such as DirecPC or StarBand might be the high-speed choice for you.

Tip

If you want both high-speed Internet access and satellite TV with a single dish, the DirecDuo dish can connect you with both DirecPC and DirecTV services. The StarBand dish works with both DISH Network (TV) and StarBand (Internet) services.

In the discussion that follows, "DirecPC" refers to both DirecPC and DirecDuo products.

DirecPC

DirecPC, developed by Hughes Network Systems, has been available for a number of years and until early 2001 was strictly a hybrid system, meaning that incoming and outgoing data streams and other operations are actually routed two different ways:

- Downloading uses the 400Kbps (peak speed) satellite connection.
- Uploads and Web page requests require the use of a conventional analog modem.

Note

The two-way version of DirecPC is referred to as Satellite Return DirecPC and is discussed later in this chapter. See "Two-Way Satellite Internet Services," page 1040.

I refer to the original version of DirecPC as Dial-Up DirecPC in the remainder of this chapter.

The hybrid nature of Dial-Up DirecPC makes it a great choice for download junkies but not the best choice for researchers, Web surfers with an impatient mouse-clicker finger, or users looking to free up the phone line for voice calls. Although ISDN offers up to 128Kbps in both directions, DirecPC downloads are typically as much as three times faster. Dial-Up DirecPC works as shown in Figure 19.10.

Dial-Up DirecPC Requirements

Dial-Up DirecPC requires a small satellite dish, similar but not compatible to those used for DirecTV and USSB satellite services (DirecDuo combines DirecPC and DirecTV into a single service, using the same type of dish as Dial-Up DirecPC). The dish is connected to a so-called satellite modem, which is a PCI card or USB device used for data receiving. You use a conventional modem for sending out page requests or uploading data. Although all services beyond 33.6Kbps are asymmetrical—faster for downloading than uploading—except ISDN, the only other fast-download Internet service with a similarly poky speed for uploads is the 56Kbps V.90 modem and its proprietary predecessors (x2 and K56flex).

Direct PC satellite

Satellite dish

Your PC sends
a request

DirecPC
Noc

Web server

Your ISP

To the
modem

Figure 19.10   Dial-Up DirecPC routes your request for Web pages, graphics, and files using a modem. The speed advantage comes when you receive your data, with a download speed of 400Kbps, thanks to a satellite link.

You can use DirecPC's PCI card version with Windows 9x or Windows NT 4.0, but you must use Windows 98, Windows 98 SE, Windows Me, or Windows 2000 if you want to use the USB version. You must use the DirecPC client version 3.x for Windows Me and Windows 2000; this version of the client software also supports Windows 95 and Windows NT 4.0.

Installing Dial-Up DirecPC

A Dial-Up DirecPC installation combines the dangers of satellite-TV installation with the usual issues involved in connecting a network-style device to your computer. You'll need an unobstructed 45° clear line of sight to the south and room for the 21" satellite dish.

The DirecPC "Getting Started" guide (available online from http://www.direcpc.com as a PDF file) strongly suggests that Dial-Up DirecPC installers have experience with normal satellite dishes or TV antennas because issues such as running coaxial cable, proper electrical grounding to code, and other challenges await. Detailed installation instructions for the antenna and other DirecPC components are found on the CD-ROM that comes with the self-installation kit for DirecPC and also on the Web site at http://www.direcpc.com/selfhelp/. Consider professional installation for a carefree, reliable, and safe setup at a reasonable price if you're not familiar with working with satellite dish or cable TV hookups.

When you install DirecPC on a system that already has a PCI-based Ethernet card, you can choose to have both DirecPC and your existing network use the card, or use the card just with DirecPC. This choice affects the TCP/IP bindings configuration.

Be sure you have your IP addresses handy; you'll need them to complete the installation.

With the introduction of DirecPC 3.0 client software, the recommended system configuration is now

- Pentium II 333MHz or greater CPU
- PCI or AGP video adapter (can be built in or card based)
- 1,024×768 display

- Mouse
- 56K modem (hardware based)
- 20MB of free hard drive space
- CD-ROM drive
- 128MB RAM

CPUs as slow as 200MHz can be used, as can lower-resolution screens, slower modems, and less RAM (as little as 32MB), but performance will suffer. Your system should meet or exceed the requirements listed previously for satisfactory performance.

Purchasing Dial-Up DirecPC

Compared to early versions of DirecPC, which offered complex price structures, Dial-Up DirecPC now offers just two simple service pricing plans: a 25 hour/month plan (the Executive Surfer), and an unlimited hour plan (the Family Surfer Unlimited). The Family Surfer Unlimited plan is $49.99 per month including ISP charges; provide your own ISP and save $10.00 per month. The Executive Surfer plan is $29.99 per month including ISP charges, but going over the limit will cost you $1.99 per hour if DirecPC is your ISP. Pricing does not include equipment.

The typical cost of Dial-Up DirecPC hardware and software is under $200, not including installation.

Dial-Up DirecPC's FAP—Brakes on High-Speed Downloading?

A big concern for those wanting to exploit the high-speed download feature is Dial-Up DirecPC's Fair Access Policy (FAP), which was introduced long after the service was started. FAP uses unpublished guidelines to determine who is "abusing" the service with large downloads. Abusers have their download bandwidths reduced by about 50% or more until their behavior changes. A class-action lawsuit was filed in July 1998 by DirecPC users who objected to this policy. Users said that Hughes Network Systems, Inc., the developer of DirecPC, was simultaneously selling the system on the basis of very fast download times, and then punishing those who wanted to use it in the way DirecPC had sold to the public.

As a result of the class-action lawsuit, the DirecPC Web site now offers usage guidelines that are supposed to help you avoid being "FAPped," although many DirecPC users who have commented on the `alt.satellite.direcpc` newsgroup (also available via `groups.google.com`) complain that the guidelines are misleading.

DirecPC recommends that to avoid being FAPped, users should take advantage of the Turbo Newsgroups and Turbo Webcasts feature, which "pushes" newsgroup and selected Web site content to subscribers' systems without the traffic being counted for FAP calculation purposes.

Note

I'm concerned about FAP limitations when it's time to download the increasingly bulky service packs for operating systems, Web browsers, and office suites. Some users have reported their service speed dropping by 50% or more after downloading 40MB of files. At a time when a single service pack can be about 40MB by itself, this isn't good news. Because DirecPC refuses to release details of its FAP-calculating algorithm and their public guidelines are misleading, it seems to make sense to avoid downloading a lot of large files in sequence if you want to avoid being FAPped.

Dial-Up DirecPC is now available from AOL as AOL Plus Powered by DirecPC. It uses satellites different from the normal DirecPC service, and early indications are that FAPping is not an issue. For comments on the speed comparison as well as other tips on DirecPC, see the DirecPC Uncensored! Web site at **www.copperhead.cc**.

Real-World Performance

Benchmark addicts will find that Dial-Up DirecPC performs poorly on ping tests because the complex pathway your data must travel (ground to space and back again) means that pings take at least 400ms–600ms. Interactive benchmarks are also disappointing. The hybrid architecture makes Dial-Up DirecPC a very poor choice for Internet gaming, teleconferencing, and Internet telephony because these applications require fast connections in both directions. However, real-world speeds in excess of 225Kbps can be reached when downloading big files.

Dial-Up DirecPC has been a controversial choice for fast Internet access because of the confusing pricing of the original version, concerns about FAP, and its unusual hybrid architecture. However, it performs well for downloads up to 50MB–70MB at a time. (Many users report that FAP limitations often drastically cut speeds on downloads larger than this.) If you can't get cable-modem or DSL Internet access, consider DirecPC or the TV/PC combo called DirecDuo. Just remember that Dial-Up DirecPC still requires you to use your phone line for page requests and uploading. If you want to get more user-oriented information about DirecPC, join the DirecPC newsgroup at alt.satellite.direcpc, search newsgroups at www.deja.com, or see the DirecPC forum available at www.copperhead.cc.

DirecPC from AOL and Others

DirecPC is now available from several partners, including AOL (AOL Plus Powered by DirecPC), Pegasus Communications (Pegasus Express Powered by DirecPC), Earthlink (Earthlink Satellite Service Powered by DirecPC), and others. AOL Plus is based on Dial-Up DirecPC. Pegasus and Earthlink's offerings are based on Satellite Return DirecPC (see "Two-Way Satellite Internet Services," page 1040, this chapter for details).

Pricing and other service details of these versions of DirecPC might vary from standard Dial-Up and Satellite Return DirecPC packages offered by Hughes Network Systems. You should compare "pure"Dial-Up and Satellite Return DirecPC to the co-labeled versions to determine which version of DirecPC will be the best for you.

Two-Way Satellite Internet Services

During 2001, DirecPC and its partners began to introduce a new two-way (Satellite Return) version of DirecPC. This version resembles Dish Network's StarBand service, which was introduced in late 2000. Both products have the following features:

- An external USB device and satellite dish transceiver are used to provide two-way service.
- The same dish supports both satellite TV and satellite Internet service.

StarBand is also bundled with a specially configured Compaq computer and MSN service offering sold by Radio Shack retail stores. This version uses two PCI cards: one to receive and one to send satellite Internet signals. StarBand works as shown in Figure 19.11.

StarBand provides download speeds ranging from 150Kbps to 500Kbps and upload speeds ranging from 50Kbps to 150Kbps. Satellite Return DirecPC downloads at the same speed as Dial-Up DirecPC (400Kbps), with uploads at up to 128Kbps. Upgrades for existing Dial-Up DirecPC users are available; contact DirecPC for details. Professional installation is required for both StarBand and Satellite Return DirecPC.

Although two-way satellite Internet connections will be far more satisfactory to users than one-way connections because of faster uploading and no telephone-line tie-ups, gamers will still not be satisfied because the time required to send and receive signals from the satellite (22,500 miles above the equator) will still be much slower than for terrestrially based broadband services.

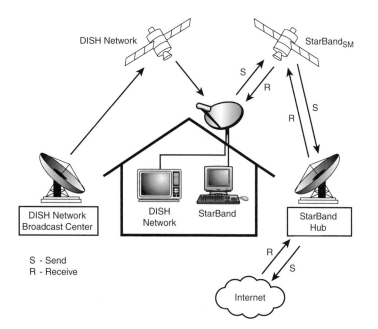

Figure 19.11 The StarBand service can receive both DISH Network TV programs (left) and StarBand Internet traffic (right) with its single 24"×36" satellite dish. The Satellite Return DirecPC service also supports both TV and Internet on its single dish and works in a similar fashion.

Comparing High-Speed Internet Access

One way of making sense out of the confusing morass of plans available from cable modem, DSL, and DirecPC vendors is to calculate the average cost per Kbps of data downloaded ($Kbps). You can calculate this figure yourself by dividing the service cost (SC) per month by the rated or average speed of the service (SPD):

SC / SPD = $Kbps

For example, a typical cable modem service costs $50/month, including cable modem lease, and has an average (not peak) speed of 500Kbps. Divide $50 by 500Kbps, and the cost per Kbps equals 10 cents.

Use this formula with any broadband or dial-up service to find the best values. Don't forget to calculate the cost of required equipment (as in the example). If you must pay for equipment or installation upfront, divide the upfront cost by the number of months you plan to keep the service and add the result to the monthly service charge to get an accurate figure.

How does a typical 56Kbps modem compare, assuming 50Kbps download speeds? Using Juno Web ($14.95/month) and assuming no charge for an analog modem, the cost per Kbps is 29.9 cents per Kbps—almost 3 times as much for service that is at least 10 times slower.

Generally, the services stack up as shown in Table 19.7, from slowest to fastest when download speeds are compared.

Table 19.7   Comparing Typical Speeds for Various Types of Internet Connections

Connection Type	Speed
V.34 annex analog modem	33.6Kbps
V.90/V.92 analog modem	53Kbps (due to FCC regulations)
ISDN (1BRI)	64Kbps
ISDN (2BRI)	128Kbps
ADSL	384Kbps[1]
DirecPC (one-way)	400Kbps
DirecPC (two-way)	400Kbps
Cable modem or fixed wireless	512Kbps[2]
ADSL	512Kbps[1]
ADSL	1GB[1]
Cable modem or fixed wireless	1.5Gbps[2]

1. *DSL bandwidth depends on the package you select; higher bandwidth packages carry higher monthly fees.*
2. *Cable modem/wireless bandwidth can depend on the package you select; higher bandwidth packages carry higher monthly fees, or speeds can vary with network traffic; ask vendor for details.*

If you're looking for a close to real-time benchmark of large-file download times, check out Bill Faust's Comparison of Cable Modem Download Speeds Web site at `http://pobox.com/~faust/soapbox/speed/speed.html`.

This site provides instructions for how to download a large (11MB) file and send the results of the download time, equipment used, Internet provider, and so on back for inclusion in the growing database of results, which can be viewed in either ASCII or as a table.

Because the connection and location are listed, stop by the site and see whether your current or possible future "fast" ISP is listed to see how well (or how badly) it's doing. Another way to compare Internet connection types is by feature, as in Table 19.8.

Table 19.8   Comparing High-Speed Internet Access by Feature

Service	Always On?	Shared with Other Users?	Ties Up Phone Line?	Reliability Affected By?	Connect Type
Cable modem (two-way)	Yes	Yes	No	Cable outages	Ethernet or USB
Cable modem (one way)	No	Yes	Yes	Cable outages; phone line outages	Ethernet or USB; might need external analog modem
Fixed wireless (two-way)	Yes	Yes	No	Transmitter outages	Ethernet
Fixed wireless (one-way)	No	Yes	Yes	Transmitter outages; phone line outages	Ethernet; might need external analog modem
DirecPC (Dial-Up)	No	No	Yes	Satellite outages; phone line outages	PCI slot or USB

Table 19.8   Continued

Service	Always On?	Shared with Other Users?	Ties Up Phone Line?	Reliability Affected By?	Connect Type
DirecPC (Satellite Return)	Yes	Yes	No	Satellite outages	USB
DSL	Yes	No	No	Phone line outages; telco network changes	Ethernet or USB

Having a Backup Plan in Case of Service Interruptions

Because no high-speed connection is immune to service interruptions, you should consider having some sort of backup plan in place in case of a significant service outage.

If your high-speed Internet access uses an ISP that can also accept 56Kbps connections, you might still be able to use your regular modem for emergencies; this might require an extra charge in some cases, though. You could also consider using a free trial subscription to an ISP that uses a conventional modem. If you temporarily switch to a different ISP, especially one that uses its own client, such as AOL, be sure to back up your current Internet configuration information before you install the client software. Your best bet is to use an Internet-only ISP whose dial-up connection can be configured manually with the Dial-Up Networking connection wizard. Then, you can construct a new connection without destroying your existing configuration.

Note

Each type of Internet connection uses a particular combination of TCP/IP settings. TCP/IP is the protocol (software rules) used by all computers on the Internet. TCP/IP is covered in Chapter 20, but for now keep in mind that different TCP/IP settings are required for modem access and access through a NIC or USB port device (cable modem, DSL, and DirecPC). Modems usually have an IP address provided dynamically by the ISP when the modem connects with the ISP. The other types of Internet access devices normally have static IP addresses that don't change. IP addresses are just one of the network settings that, if changed, will prevent you from getting on the Internet.

Leased Lines

For users with high bandwidth requirements (and deep pockets), dedicated leased lines provide digital service between two locations at speeds that can far exceed ISDN and are as fast or faster than DSL or cable modem. A *leased line* is a permanent 24-hour connection to a particular location that can be changed only by the telephone company. Businesses use leased lines to connect LANs in remote locations or to connect to the Internet through a service provider. Leased lines are available at various speeds, as described in the following sections.

T-1 and T-3 Connections

To connect networks in distant locations, networks that must support a large number of Internet users, or especially organizations that will be hosting their own Internet services, a T-1 connection might be the wise investment. A *T-1* is a digital connection running at 1.55Mbps. This is more than 10 times faster than an ISDN link. A T-1 can be split (or fractioned), depending on how it is to be used. It can be split into 24 individual 64Kbps lines or left as a single high-capacity pipeline. Some ISPs allow you to lease any portion of a T-1 connection that you want (in 64Kbps increments). Ameritech, for example, offers a flexible T-1 service it calls DS1, available at full bandwidth or in various fractional sizes. Figure 19.12 shows how a T-1 line is fractioned.

Figure 19.12   Full T-1 service uses all 24 lines (each one is 64Kbps) as a single pipeline; a fractional T-1 service of 256Kbps could use slots 1–4 only, for example.

An individual user of the Internet interacts with a T-1 line only indirectly. No matter how you're accessing the Internet (dial-up modem, ISDN, DSL, cable modem, DirecPC, Starband, or fixed-base wireless), your ISP typically will have a connection to one or more T-1 and T-3 lines, which represent the backbone of the Internet. This connection to the backbone is sometimes referred to as a *point of presence (PoP)*. When you make your connection to the Internet, your ISP shares a small chunk of that T-1 pipe with you. Depending on how many other users are accessing the Internet at your ISP or elsewhere, you might experience very fast to slow throughput, even if your modem connection speed remains constant. It's a bit like splitting up a pizza into smaller and smaller slices to accommodate more people at a party: The more users of a high-speed connection, the slower each individual part of it will be. To keep user connections fast while growing, ISPs add full or fractional T-1 lines to their points of presence. Or, they might switch from a T-1 connection to the even faster T-3 if available.

Note

Equivalent in throughput to approximately 28 T-1 lines, a T-3 connection runs at 45Mbps and is suitable for use by very large networks and university campuses. Pricing information falls into the "if-you-have-to-ask-you-can't-afford-it" category.

If your Internet connection is on a corporate LAN or your office is located in a downtown building, your relationship to a T-1 line might be much closer. If your building or office is connected directly to a T-1, you're sharing the capacity of that line with just a relatively few other users rather than with the hundreds or thousands of dial-up users a normal ISP is hosting at one time. Full or fractional T-1 lines are being added to more and more apartments and office buildings in major cities to allow residents and workers faster Internet access. In these cases, a LAN connection to the T-1 is usually provided, so your Internet access device is a network card, rather than a modem or ISDN terminal adapter.

With the rise of the Internet and the demand for high-speed data access for networks, the price of T-1 links in the United States has fallen drastically. T-1 service can be acquired from either your local telco or third-party firms. Typical pricing runs around $1,000–$1,200 per month. Fractional T-1 or burstable T-1 (which allows you to have differing levels of bandwidth up to the entire T1 1.5Mbps depending on demand) cost less. For a large organization that requires a lot of bandwidth, the lower cost of T-1 services today make it more economical than ever to install a higher-capacity service and grow into it, rather than constantly upgrading the link. Although the speed of T-1 links resembles the maximum rates available with DSL or cable modem service, most types of T-1 service provide constant bandwidth (unlike cable modems) and bypass the potentially severe problems of trying to retrofit old phone lines with digital service (unlike DSL).

Comparing Conventional High-Speed Services

Some telcos who formerly posted pricing for ISDN, T-1, or other high-end telecommunications services now have a "call us" button on their Web sites because pricing is complicated by many factors, including

- Location (state and locality because telephone companies are regulated public utilities)
- Fixed and variable costs
- Installation costs
- Your needs

Be sure to consider hardware and usage costs when you price services, and—for items such as ISDN terminal adapters and network cards—compare the official offerings with products available elsewhere. If you decide to provide some of the equipment yourself, find out whose responsibility repairs become. Some companies provide lower-cost "value" pricing for services in which you agree to configure the hardware yourself and maintain it. If you have knowledgeable staffers who can handle routers and other network configuration, you can save money every month, but if not, go with the full-service option.

Securing Your Internet Connection

Because any Internet connection must use TCP/IP, which uses built-in logical ports numbered 0–65,535 to service different types of activity, any user of the Internet can be vulnerable to various types of Internet attacks, even if precautions such as turning off drive and folder sharing have been followed. Steve Gibson of Gibson Research Corporation (makers of the classic SpinRite disk maintenance program) has established a free Web-based service called Shields Up that you should try with *any* Internet-connected PC to see how safe or vulnerable you are.

The Shields Up portion of the Gibson Research Corporation Web site (http://www.grc.com) probes your system's Internet connection security and Internet service ports, as shown in Figure 19.13.

Figure 19.13 Steve Gibson's Port Probe test looks for open, closed, and stealth Internet service ports on your system. The site also provides recommendations for firewall software to secure your system.

After testing your system, Shields Up provides reviews and recommendations for proxy server and firewall software (such as Zone Alarm, Norton Internet Security, and BlackIce Defender) that you can use to help secure your system.

With the increasing importance of the Internet and the multiple vulnerabilities we saw in 2000 and early 2001 to Internet-borne viruses, Trojan horses, and denial-of-service attacks, Shields Up provides a valuable service for *any* Internet user.

Note

Proxy servers and firewalls are subjects that go far beyond the scope of this book. If you want to learn more, I suggest you pick up a copy of *Upgrading and Repairing Networks, 3rd Edition*, also published by Que.

Sharing Your Internet Connection

Whether you have a 56Kbps dial-up modem or a broadband connection, one connection is often not enough for a home or small-office setting. A proxy server or gateway program plus a small network enables you to share a single Internet connection among two or more computers.

Gateways Versus Proxy Servers

To the typical user, it won't matter whether a gateway or proxy server is used to provide shared Internet access. Traditional gateway programs use a method of shared access called NAT (Network Address Translation), which enables sharing by converting network addresses into Internet-compatible addresses during the file request and download process. This process requires little client PC configuration but doesn't permit page caching, content filtration, firewalls, or other useful services that can be provided by a proxy server. Proxy servers traditionally required tricky configuration, sometimes at an individual application level. However, many of the products on the market today, such as WinProxy, SyGate, and WinGate, combine the ease of configuration of a gateway with the extra features of a proxy server.

Proxy server programs often are provided with SOHO-oriented Ethernet and phone line–based networks for Internet sharing, and Microsoft's ICS (Internet Connection Sharing) is a gateway program using NAT.

Windows 98 SE, Windows Me, Windows 2000, and ICS

Windows 98 Second Edition, Windows Me, and Windows 2000 feature a built-in gateway program called ICS (Internet Connection Sharing), which allows users to share a single Internet connection—either dial-up or broadband. Windows 98 SE, Windows Me, and Windows 2000 can be purchased as upgrades to older versions of Windows, and users of the original version of Windows 98 can purchase a CD-ROM from Microsoft that will upgrade the original version to the Second Edition.

Because ICS is a gateway and clients use TCP/IP networking to use the gateway, only the gateway computer needs to use Windows 98 SE, Windows Me, or Windows 2000. Any computer using TCP/IP with the option to set up a gateway can be used as a client, including computers using older versions of Windows 9x and other operating systems.

Requirements for ICS

ICS requires a network interface card (NIC) to be installed in the host computer and a network connection to each guest computer to share the host's Internet connection.

If the Internet connection is made through a NIC (as is the case with DSL, two-way cable modem, or fixed wireless broadband connections), two NICs are required: one for the Internet connection and one for sharing the connection.

ICS requires special configurations for use with one-way services that use a separate analog modem (such as some cable modem, fixed wireless, or DirecPC versions) because these devices use a separate connection for downloading and uploading.

Overview of the ICS Configuration Process

The configuration process has two parts:

- Installing ICS on the gateway computer
- Configuring the clients to use the ICS gateway to reach the Internet

Configuring ICS on the Gateway Computer

If ICS was not installed when Windows was installed, install it by selecting Start, Settings, Add/Remove Programs, Windows Setup. Select ICS from the Internet Tools category; Windows Me includes ICS as part of its Home Networking Wizard.

Next, specify whether you are using a dial-up connection (modem or ISDN) or a high-speed connection (LAN, including cable modem or DSL).

If you select dial-up, choose the dial-up connection (which must be set up already) you'll be sharing, followed by the NIC that connects you with the client PCs that will share the connection. Windows creates a client configuration floppy and prompts you to reboot the computer.

When you view the Network Configuration in the Control Panel after rebooting, you should see the following:

- Three adapters (your actual NIC, the dial-up adapter, and a new one called Internet Connection Sharing)
- Three Internet Connection Sharing protocol entries, listing the adapters mentioned earlier in the chapter
- Three TCP/IP protocol entries, listing the adapters mentioned earlier in the chapter

The TCP/IP protocol entry for Home must point to the NIC that connects the clients to the host PC; the TCP/IP protocol entry called Shared must point to Dial-Up Networking; and the remaining TCP/IP protocol entry must point to Internet Connection Sharing.

Also, check the TCP/IP configuration for Home (the NIC) and verify the IP address; it should be 192.168.0.1. This IP address might need to be provided to the computers that will share the Internet connection. If the settings aren't correct, remove ICS and start over. Start an Internet connection on the gateway (host) computer before continuing.

Configuring ICS on the Client Computers

Although the ICS configuration process on the gateway (host) computer created a disk that can be used for setting up the ICS connection on client computers, most non-Microsoft sources advocate using manual configuration instead if you are configuring ICS with Windows 98 SE or Windows 2000. The configuration disk created by the Windows Me Home Networking Wizard should be used. The following steps are required to configure ICS:

- Install the TCP/IP protocol on each client.
- Ensure that the following values are set up in the TCP/IP protocol for each client PC:

    IP address: automatically obtained

    WINS Resolution: disabled

Gateway: None

DNS: disabled

Each client will be assigned an IP address by the ICS server.

- Restart each client after performing the previous steps.

- Use a Web browser on each guest to verify the connection is working; Internet Explorer should not have any dial-up settings configured for it and should have no LAN settings enabled; the ICS client disk incorrectly selects Use a Proxy Server here. Netscape Navigator/Communicator should be set to Direct Connection to the Internet.

- Some versions of Netscape Navigator might not work unless you create a Dial-Up Networking adapter on the guest and set its gateway, as explained earlier in the chapter.

If you are using Windows 9x or Me, reboot before you test the connection.

Note

Useful Web sites that cover this process in more detail include

`http://www.practicallynetworked.com`

`http://www.duxcw.com/digest/Howto/network/win98se/`

The Practically Networked Web site also provides useful tips for sharing one-way broadband services.

The following Microsoft Web page answers common questions about Windows 98 SE:

`http://support.microsoft.com/support/windows/faq/win98se/w98seics.asp`

If you want the additional benefits of a proxy server, check out products such as WinProxy (`http://www.winproxy.com`), WinGate (`http://www.wingate.deerfield.com`), and Sybergen SyGate (`http://www.sybergen.com`). Many home-oriented networks and modems are bundled with these or similar products, so if you're in the market for a new modem or are building a small network, ask whether a proxy server program for Internet sharing is included.

Internet Troubleshooting

This section deals with hardware problems that can cause Internet problems. Software problems usually are caused by incorrect configuration of the TCP/IP protocol required by all types of Internet connections. For more information about TCP/IP or other software problems, see Chapter 20, "Local Area Networking."

Analog Modem Fails to Dial

1. Check line and phone jacks on modem. Use the line jack to attach the modem to the telephone line. The phone jack takes the same RJ-11 silver cord cable, but it's designed to let you daisy-chain a telephone to your modem, so you need only a single line for modem and telephone use. If you've reversed these cables, you'll get no dial tone.

2. If the cables are attached properly, check the cable for cuts or breaks. The shielding used on RJ-11 telephone cables is minimal. If the cable looks bad, replace it.

3. If the modem is external, make sure the RS-232 modem cable is running from the modem to a working serial port on your computer and that it is switched on. Signal lights on the front of the modem can be used to determine whether the modem is on and whether it is responding to dialing commands.

4. If the modem is a PC Card (PCMCIA card), make sure it is fully plugged into the PCMCIA/PC slot. With Windows 9x/Me/2000, you should see a small PCMCIA/PC Card icon on the toolbar. Double-click it to view the cards that are currently connected (see Figure 19.14). If your modem is properly attached, it should be visible. Otherwise, remove it, reinsert it into the PCMCIA/PC Card slot, and see whether the computer detects it.

Figure 19.14 This notebook computer has a network card properly installed in its PCMCIA slots but not a modem. If the modem isn't pushed into the slot firmly, it will appear to be missing.

Connecting a PC Card Modem via a Dongle

Most PC Card modems do not use a standard RJ-11 cable because the card is too thin. Instead, they use a connection called a *dongle*, which runs from the PC Card to the telephone. If this proprietary cable is damaged, your modem is use-less. You should purchase a spare from the modem vendor and carry it with you. And if you find the dongle is too short to reach the data jacks in a hotel room, buy a coupler from your local Radio Shack or telephone-parts department and attach a standard RJ-11 cable to your dongle via the coupler. Dongles are also used with most PC Card network cards for the same reason; the RJ-45 twisted-pair cable connector is too wide to attach to many PC Cards.

5. Make sure your modem has been properly configured by your OS. With Windows 9x/Me/2000, use the Modems control panel to view and test your modem configuration. Select your modem and click the Diagnostics tab. This displays the COM (serial) ports in your computer. Select the COM port used by the modem, and click the More Info tab. This sends test signals to your modem. A properly working modem responds with information about the port and the modem (see Figure 19.15).

6. If you get a `Couldn't Open Port` error message, your modem isn't connected properly. It might be in use already, or there might be an IRQ or I/O port address conflict with another card in your computer. Whether you have a modem installed, every COM port that is working will dis-play its IRQ, I/O port address, and UART chip type when you run Diagnostic. The UART type should be 16550 or above for use with any modern modem.

Note

You can also test your modem response by setting up a HyperTerminal session (discussed earlier) to send the modem com-mands. If the modem fails to respond, this is another indication of a problem with the modem-PC connection.

Figure 19.15   The U.S. Robotics 56000 PnP modem was configured to a nonstandard IRQ of 5 when it was installed. It contains an up-to-date 16550 UART chip.

Computer Locks Up After Installing or Using Internal Modem, Terminal Adapter, or Network Card

The usual cause of lockups after you install an internal card is an IRQ conflict. Internal analog modems that use ISA slots typically cause the "curse of the shared IRQ."

COM 3 shares IRQ 4 with COM 1, and COM 4 shares IRQ 3 with COM 2 by default. The problem is that IRQ sharing for ISA devices (such as your COM ports) works when only one device at a time is using the IRQ. The most likely cause for your problem is that your mouse is connected to COM 1, your internal modem is using COM 3, and both COM ports are using the default IRQ of 4. There is no problem as long as the mouse has IRQ 4 all to itself, but the moment you try to use the modem, the computer cannot handle two devices trying to use IRQ 4 and locks up. The only solution is to get the internal modem and mouse working on *separate*, non-conflicting IRQs. You have two options: Move the mouse to another port, or disable COM 2 in your computer to make room for an internal modem on COM 2.

ISA network cards and internal ISDN terminal adapters also can cause conflicts with either serial ports or other devices using IRQs.

You can minimize or eliminate IRQ conflicts by using PCI modems, network cards, and terminal adapters or by using external USB versions when available. With Windows 95 OSR 2.x, Windows 98, Windows Me, and Windows 2000, IRQ steering features supported by most newer Pentium-class chipsets allow multiple PCI-based devices to use the same IRQ without any problems.

Move the Mouse to Another Port

If you're still using a serial mouse, you should consider switching to a PS/2 mouse (which uses IRQ 12) or a USB mouse to avoid serial port conflicts with analog modems. If your system has no PS/2 mouse port or USB port, consider using the mouse on COM 2 instead of COM 1 and installing an analog modem as COM 1.

Any mouse that can work on COM 1 can also work on COM 2, usually without any software changes. If both COM 1 and COM 2 are the typical AT-style 9-pin ports, turn off the computer, unplug the mouse from COM 1, plug it back into COM 2, and restart the computer. You should be able to use your mouse and modem at the same time if the modem is installed as COM 1 or COM 3.

If your modem is using COM 4 and your mouse is using COM 2, move the mouse to COM 1 instead. With Windows 9x/Me/2000, use the System Properties Device Manager tab to determine which devices are using which IRQs.

On a few computers, the COM 2 port might be a 25-pin connector. If your mouse didn't ship with an adapter, any computer store will have one. (The 9-pin and 25-pin COM ports are both RS-232, and the adapter will make a device wired for one type of port work with the other.)

If your Pentium-class PC doesn't have a visible PS/2 mouse port, check your system/motherboard instruction manual to see whether the motherboard has provision for a PS/2 mouse port header cable. Most Pentium-class baby-AT motherboards have the connector, but some companies don't provide the header cable unless you think to request it (and pay extra!). Check with your system vendor.

If your system uses Windows 98/Me/2000 but doesn't have a USB port, you can add a PCI card with USB ports for less than $30, enabling you to connect a USB mouse or other USB peripherals.

Disable COM 2

COM 2, the second serial port, is found on the motherboard of most Pentium-class PCs. If you are using an ISA modem, you should disable COM 2 on the motherboard to allow the modem to use COM 2.

To disable it, go into your computer's BIOS setup program, look for the screen that controls built-in ports (such as Onboard Peripherals), and disable the port. Save the changes and exit the setup program, and the system reboots. To see whether COM 2 is disabled, use the Windows 9x/Me/2000 System Properties sheet Device Manager. Then set your modem for COM 2, IRQ 3, and install it.

Computer Can't Detect External Modem

1. Make sure the modem has been connected to the computer with the correct type of cable.

For external modems that use an RS-232 serial port, you might need a separate RS-232 modem cable, which has a 9-pin connector on one end (to connect to the computer) and a 25-pin connector on the other end (to connect to the modem). Some external modems have an integrated modem cable. Because RS-232 is a very flexible standard encompassing many pinouts, be sure the cable is constructed according to the following diagram:

PC (9-pin COM port - male)		Modem (25-pin port - female)
3	TX data	2
2	RX data	3
7	RTS	4
8	CTS	5
6	DSR	6
5	SIG GND	7
1	CXR	8
4	DTR	20
9	RI	22

If you purchase an RS-232 modem cable prebuilt at a store, you'll have a cable that works with your PC and your modem. However, you can use the preceding chart to build your own cable or, by using a cable tester, determine whether an existing RS-232 cable in your office is actually made for modems or some other device.

2. Make sure the COM (serial) port or USB port the modem is connected to is working.

   The Windows 9x/Me/2000 diagnostics test listed earlier can be useful in testing the serial port, but third-party testing programs—such as Touchstone Software's CheckIt, AMIDIAG, and many others—have more thorough methods for testing the system's COM ports. These programs can use loopback plugs to test the serial ports. The loopback plug loops signals that would be sent to the modem or other serial device back to the serial port. These programs normally work best when run from the MS-DOS prompt.

   Touchstone Software's CheckIt PRO software uses a loopback plug to test serial ports. You can build the loopback plug yourself or buy it from the vendor. Loopback plugs will vary in design depending on the vendor.

   To ensure that the USB port is working, check the Device Manager in Windows; a working USB port is listed as a USB Root hub and a PCI to USB Universal Host Controller in the Universal Serial Bus device category. Any external USB hubs also are listed in the same category. If this category is not listed and the ports are physically present on the computer, make sure you are using Windows 98/Me/2000 (only a few late versions of Windows 95 have USB support). If you are, be sure the USB ports are enabled in the system BIOS.

3. Check the power cord and power switch.

Using Your Modem Sound to Diagnose Your Modem

If you listen to your modem when it makes a connection, you might have realized that different types of modems make a distinctive connection sound and that different connection speeds also make distinctive sounds.

The various types of 56Kbps modems have distinctly different handshakes of tones, buzzes, and warbles as they negotiate speeds with the ISP's modem. Learning what your modem sounds like when it makes a 56Kbps connection and when it settles for a V.34-speed connection can help you determine when you should hang up and try to connect at a faster speed.

The 56k=v.Unreliable Web site's troubleshooting section has a number of sound samples of various modems you can play back with RealAudio:

`http://www.808hi.com/56k/`

Compare these sound samples to your own modem; be sure you adjust the speaker volume for your modem so you can hear it during the call.

Diagnosing Problems with a Shared Internet Connection

Although each Internet-sharing product has individual configuration issues, the following tips provide general guidelines useful for solving problems with all of them.

Check Your Host Configuration

If your host isn't set up correctly, it can't share its connection with clients. Check the bindings for TCP/IP or other protocols used to create the shared connection. If you are using Microsoft's ICS and two Ethernet cards, you will see entries in the Network configuration on the host computer for each Ethernet card and for the ICS software itself.

Check Your Client Configuration

Make sure your clients have correct TCP/IP, DHCP, and other protocol settings for the host. Setting up a gateway product such as Windows 98 SE/Me/Windows 2000 ICS as if it were a proxy server won't work. The ping command can be used to check the Internet connection; try pinging a Web site by opening a Windows command prompt and typing a command, such as ping www.selectsystems.com. If you have a working Internet connection, you should see the IP address for the Web site you specify and the round-trip time (or ping rate) for four signals sent to the Web site. If you get no response or see an error message, you might have a configuration problem with your TCP/IP configuration.

Note

Because pinging can also be used for denial of service (DoS) attacks by hackers on Web sites, some Web sites don't respond to pings. Use ping when your system is working properly to find a Web site that will respond to ping and use that site for troubleshooting as described previously.

Verify that the host has a working Internet connection that's active before you try to share it. Check the sharing program's documentation to see how guests can dial the host's modem to start a connection if necessary.

Speed Will Drop with Multiple Users

It's normal for the speed of an Internet connection to drop with multiple users, but if you're concerned about the degree of decline, check with the sharing-software provider for Registry tweaks and other options to improve performance.

Diagnosing Connection Problems with Signal Lights

Signal lights are found on most external broadband devices, such as cable modems, wireless broadband routers, and DSL modems. The signal lights indicate whether the unit is receiving signals from the computer, sending data to the network, or receiving data from the network, and whether the unit can "see" the network—even if no data is currently flowing through the unit.

On many units, the power light also is used to indicate problems. If the light is normally green, for example, a red light might indicate the unit has failed. Other lights flash when data is being sent or received. On cable modem or wireless broadband routers, look for a signal lock light; this light will flash if the unit is trying to lock onto a signal from the cable network or wireless transmitter.

Learn the meaning of the lights on your broadband device to help you diagnose problems; the user manual or vendor's Web site will provide the troubleshooting information you need for the particular broadband device you use.

CHAPTER 20

Local Area Networking

What Is a Network?

A *network* is a group of two or more computers that are intelligently sharing hardware or software devices with each other. A network can be as small and simple as two computers that share the printer and CD-ROM drive attached to one of them or as large as the world's largest network: the Internet.

Intelligently sharing means that each computer that shares resources with another computer or computers maintains control of that resource. Thus, a switchbox for sharing a single printer between two computers doesn't qualify as a network device; because the switchbox, not the computers, handles the print jobs, neither computer knows when the other one needs to print, and print jobs can interfere with each other.

A shared printer, on the other hand, can be controlled remotely and can store print jobs from different computers on the print server's hard disk. Users can change the sequence of print jobs, hold them, or cancel them. And, sharing of the device can be controlled through passwords, further differentiating it from a switchbox.

Shared Hardware Components

Virtually any storage or output device can be shared over a network, but the most common devices include

- Printers
- Disk drives
- CD-ROM and optical drives
- Modems
- Fax
- Tape backup units
- Scanners

Entire drives, selected folders, or individual files can be shared with other users via the network.

Benefits of Sharing Information via Networks

In addition to reducing hardware costs by sharing expensive printers and other peripherals among multiple users, networks provide additional benefits to users:

- Multiple users can share access to software and data files.
- Electronic mail (email) can be sent and received.
- Multiple users can contribute to a single document using collaboration features.
- Remote-control programs can be used to troubleshoot problems or show new users how to perform a task.
- A single Internet connection can be shared among multiple computers.

Focus of This Chapter

This chapter concentrates on how to build and use a peer-to-peer network, the lowest-cost network that is still highly useful to small business and home-office users. This type of network can be created by adding network hardware to any recent version of Windows, from Windows 9x and NT through Windows Me and 2000. As you'll see, most peer-to-peer networks can be "grown" into client/server networks at a later point by adding a dedicated server and the appropriate software to the server and client PCs.

Thus, this chapter provides the hands-on and practical information you need to create a small-office, workgroup, or home-office network. If you are managing a corporate network using Linux, Unix, Windows NT Server, Windows 2000 Server, or Novell NetWare, you will also be concerned with matters such as security, user profiles, SIDs, and other factors beyond the scope of this book.

Note

Networking is an enormous topic. For more information about client/server networking, wide-area networking, the Internet, and corporate networking, I recommend *Upgrading and Repairing Networks, Third Edition*, from Que.

Types of Networks

Several types of networks exist, from small, two-station arrangements to networks that interconnect offices in many cities:

- *Local Area Networks.* The smallest office network is referred to as a local area network (LAN). A LAN is formed from computers and components in a single office or single building. A LAN can also be built at home from the same components used in office networking, but, as you'll see later, special home-networking components now exist to allow the creation of what can be called a home area network (HAN).

- *Wide Area Networks.* LANs in different locations can be connected together by high-speed fiber-optic, satellite, or leased phone lines to form a wide area network (WAN).

- *The Internet.* The World Wide Web is the most visible part of the world's largest network, the Internet. Although many users of the Internet still use modems over a dial-up connection rather than a LAN or WAN connection, any user of the Internet is a network user. The Internet is really a network of networks, all of which are connected to each other through the TCP/IP protocol. Programs such as Web browsers, File Transfer Protocol (FTP) clients, and newsreaders are some of the most common ways users work with the Internet.

- *Intranets.* Intranets use the same Web browsers and other software and the same TCP/IP protocol as the public Internet, but intranets exist as a portion of a company's private network. Typically, intranets comprise one or more LANs that are connected to other company networks, but, unlike the Internet, the content is restricted to authorized company users only. Essentially, an intranet is a private Internet.

- *Extranets.* Intranets that share a portion of their content with customers, suppliers, or other businesses, but not with the general public, are called extranets. As with intranets, the same Web browsers and other software are used to access the content.

Note

Both intranets and extranets rely on firewalls and other security tools and procedures to keep their private contents private. If you want to learn more about firewalls and security, I recommend picking up copies of

- *Practical Firewalls*, ISBN: 0-7897-2416-2
- *Upgrading and Repairing Networks, Third Edition*, ISBN: 0-7897-2557-6

Client/Server Versus Peer Networks

Although every computer on a LAN is connected to every other computer, they do not necessarily all communicate with each other. There are two basic types of LANs, based on the communication patterns between the machines, called client/server networks and peer-to-peer networks.

Client/Server Networks

On a *client/server* network, every computer has a distinct role, that of either a client or a server. A *server* is designed to share its resources among the client computers on the network. Typically, servers are located in secured areas, such as locked closets and data centers because they hold the organization's most valuable data and do not have to be accessed by operators on a continuous basis. The rest of the computers on the network function as *clients* (see Figure 20.1).

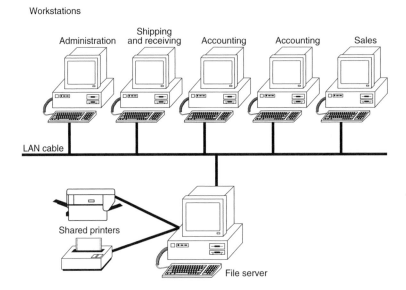

Figure 20.1 The components of a client/server LAN.

Servers

A dedicated server computer typically has a faster processor, more memory, and more storage space than a client because it might have to service dozens or even hundreds of users at the same time. High-performance servers also might use two or more processors, use the 64-bit version of the PCI expansion slot for server-optimized network interface cards, and have redundant power supplies. The server runs a special network operating system—such as Windows NT Server, Windows 2000 Server or Advanced Server, or Novell NetWare—that is designed solely to facilitate the sharing of its resources. These resources can reside on a single server or on a group of servers. When more than one server is used, each server can "specialize" in a particular task (file server, print server, fax server, email server, and so on) or provide redundancy (duplicate servers) in case of server failure. For very demanding computing tasks, several servers can act as a single unit through the use of parallel processing.

Clients

A client computer communicates only with servers, not with other clients. A client system is a standard PC that is running an operating system such as DOS or Windows. The only difference is the addition of a client software package that enables the computer to access the resources that servers share.

Peer-to-Peer Network

By contrast, on a peer-to-peer network, every computer is equal and can communicate with any other computer on the network to which it has been granted access rights (see Figure 20.2). Essentially, every computer on a peer-to-peer network can function as both a server and a client; any computer on a peer-to-peer network is considered a server if it shares a printer, a folder, a drive, or some other resource with the rest of the network. This is why you might hear about client and server activities, even when the discussion is about a peer-to-peer network. Peer-to-peer networks can be as small as two computers or as large as hundreds of systems. Although there is no theoretical limit to the size of a peer-to-peer network, performance drops significantly and security becomes a major headache on peer-based networks with more than 10 computers. Also, Microsoft imposes a 10-station limit on computers running Windows 2000 Professional that are sharing resources with other systems. For these reasons, I recommend that you switch to a client/server network when your network climbs above about 10 stations.

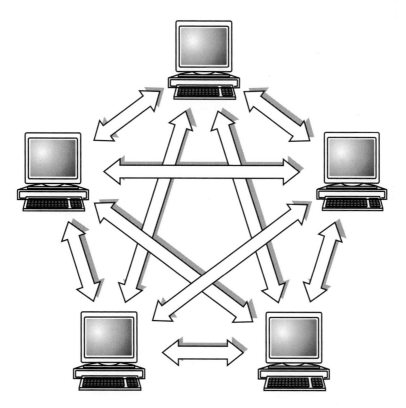

Figure 20.2   The logical architecture of a typical peer-to-peer network.

Peer-to-peer networks are more common in small offices or within a single department of a larger organization. The advantage of a peer-to-peer network is that you don't have to dedicate a computer to function as a file server. Instead, every computer can share its resources with any other. The potential disadvantages to a peer-to-peer network are that there is typically less security and less control because users normally administer their own systems, whereas client/server networks have the advantage of centralized administration.

Comparing Client/Server and Peer-to-Peer Networks

Client/server LANs offer enhanced security for shared resources, greater performance, increased backup efficiency for network-based data, and the potential for use of redundant power supplies and RAID drive arrays. Client/server LANs also have a much greater cost to purchase and maintain. Table 20.1 compares client/server and peer-to-peer server networking.

Table 20.1 Comparing Client/Server and Peer-to-Peer Networking

Item	Client/Server	Peer-to-Peer
Access control	Via user/group lists of permissions; single password provides user access to only the resources on his list; users can be given several different levels of access.	Via password lists by resource; each resource requires a separate password; all-or-nothing access; no centralized user list.
Security	High because access is controlled by user or by group identity.	Low because knowing the password gives anybody access to a shared resource.
Performance	High because the server doesn't waste time or resources handling workstation tasks.	Low because servers often act as workstations.
Hardware Cost	High, due to specialized design of server, high-performance nature of hardware, and redundancy features.	Low because any workstation can become a server by sharing resources.
Software Cost	License fees per workstation user are part of the cost of the Network Operating System server software (Windows NT and Windows 2000 Server, Novell NetWare).	Free; all client software is included with any release of Windows 9x, Windows NT Workstation, Windows 2000 Professional, and Windows Me.
Backup	Centralized when data is stored on server; enables use of high-speed, high-capacity tape backups with advanced cataloging.	Left to user decision; usually mixture of backup devices and practices at each workstation.
Redundancy	Duplicate power supplies, hot-swappable drive arrays, and even redundant servers are common; network OS normally capable of using redundant devices automatically.	No true redundancy among either peer "servers" or clients; failures require manual intervention to correct with high possibility of data loss.

Windows 9x, Windows Me, Windows NT, and Windows 2000 have peer-to-peer networking capabilities built into them. Because Windows, from version 95 forward, uses Plug-and-Play technology, installing network interface cards in a collection of these systems is relatively easy. Simply connect them with the correct kind of cable, and build your own peer-to-peer network.

Requirements for a Network

Unless the computers that are connected know they are connected and agree on a common means of communication and what resources are to be shared, they cannot work together. Networking software is just as important as networking hardware because it establishes the logical connections that make the physical connections work.

At a minimum, each network requires the following:

■ Physical (cable) or wireless (infrared [IRDA] or radio-frequency) connections between computers

■ A common set of communications rules, known as a *network protocol*

■ Software that enables resources to be shared with other PCs and controls access to shared resources, known as a *network operating system*

- Resources that can be shared, such as printers, disk drives, and CD-ROMs
- Software that enables computers to access other computers with shared resources, known as a *network client*

These rules apply to the simplest and most powerful networks, and all the ones in between, regardless of their nature. The details of the hardware and software you need are discussed in detail later in this chapter.

Ethernet Versus Token-Ring

The protocol you choose to run is the single most important decision you make when setting up a local area network. This protocol defines the speed of the network, the medium access control mechanism it uses, the types of cables you can use, the network interface adapters you must buy, and the adapter drivers you install in the network client software.

The Institute of Electrical and Electronic Engineers (IEEE) has defined and documented a set of standards for the physical characteristics of both collision-detection and token-passing networks. These standards are known as IEEE 802.3 (Ethernet) and IEEE 802.5 (Token-Ring). IEEE 802.11b defines a wireless version of Ethernet.

Note

Be aware, however, that the colloquial names Ethernet and Token-Ring actually refer to earlier versions of these protocols, on which the IEEE standards were based. Minor differences exist between the frame definitions for true Ethernet and true IEEE 802.3. In terms of the standards, IBM's 16Mbps Token-Ring products are an extension of the IEEE 802.5 standard. There is also an older data-link protocol called ARCnet that is now rarely used.

The two major choices today are Ethernet and Token-Ring, but the other major network data-link protocols you might also encounter are summarized in Table 20.2. The abbreviations used for the cable types are explained in the following sections.

Table 20.2   Wired LAN Protocol Summary

Network Type	Speed	Maximum Number of Stations	Cable Types	Notes
ARCnet	2.5Mbps	255 stations	RG-62 coax UTP/Type 1 STP	Obsolete for new installations; was used to replace IBM 3270 terminals (which used the same coax cable)
Ethernet	10Mbps	Per segment: 10BASE-T-2 10BASE-2-30 10BASE-5-100 10BASE-FL-2	UTP Cat 3 (10BASE-T), Thicknet (coax; 10BASE-5), Thinnet (RG-58 coax; 10BASE-2), fiber-optic (10BASE-F)	Being replaced by Fast Ethernet; can be interconnected with Fast Ethernet by use of dual-speed hubs and switches; use switches and routers to overcome "5-4-3" rule in building very large networks

Table 20.2   Continued

Network Type	Speed	Maximum Number of Stations	Cable Types	Notes
Fast Ethernet	100Mbps	Per segment: 2	Cat 5 UTP	Fast Ethernet can be interconnected with standard Ethernet through use of dual-speed hubs, switches, and routers; most common variety is 100BASE-TX; alternative 100BASE-T4 is not widely supported
Gigabit Ethernet	1,000Mbps	Per segment: 2	Cat 5 UTP	Gigabit Ethernet can be interconnected with Fast or standard Ethernet through use of dual-speed hubs, switches, and routers
Token-Ring	4Mbps or 16Mbps	72 on UTP, 250-260 on type 1 STP	UTP, Type 1 STP, and Fiber Optic	High price for NICs and MAUs to interconnect clients; primarily used with IBM mid-size and mainframe systems

▶▶   Wireless protocols, such as Wireless Ethernet IEEE 802.11b and others, are discussed later in this chapter. See "Wireless Network Standards," p. 1083.

A few years ago, the choice between Token-Ring or Ethernet wasn't easy. Ethernet has become the leading data link layer protocol in the world, but the original versions of standard Ethernet (10BASE-5 "Thick Ethernet" and 10BASE-2 "Thin Ethernet") used hard-to-install coaxial cable and were expensive to build beyond a certain point because of the technical limitations expressed by the "5-4-3" rule (see the following).

Token-Ring's 16Mbps version was substantially faster than 10BASE versions of Ethernet and had larger limits on the numbers of workstations permitted per segment. However, as the twenty-first century begins, the popularity and low cost of Fast Ethernet; the use of easy-to-install twisted-pair cabling for standard, 100Mbps Fast, and even 1000Mbps Gigabit Ethernet; and the use of hubs and switches to overcome classic Ethernet station limitations have made Fast Ethernet the preferred choice for workgroup-size networks and a competitor to Token-Ring for larger networks. A properly designed Fast Ethernet network can be upgraded to Gigabit Ethernet in the future.

Ethernet

With tens of millions of computers connected by Ethernet cards and cables, Ethernet is the most widely used data link layer protocol in the world. Ethernet-based LANs enable you to interconnect a wide variety of equipment, including Unix and Linux workstations, Apple computers, printers, and PCs. You can buy Ethernet adapters from dozens of competing manufacturers, supporting all three of the cable types defined in the standard: Thinnet, Thicknet, and Unshielded Twisted Pair (UTP). Traditional Ethernet operates at a speed of 10Mbps, but the more recent (and most popular of the Ethernet flavors) Fast Ethernet standards push this speed to 100Mbps. The latest version of Ethernet, Gigabit Ethernet, reaches speeds of 1000Mbps, or 100 times the speed of original Ethernet.

Fast Ethernet

Fast Ethernet requires adapters, hubs, and UTP or fiber-optic cables designed to support the higher speed, but you can buy combination devices that run at both 10Mbps and 100Mbps, enabling you to gradually upgrade your network by installing new NICs and hubs over an extended period of time.

Both the most popular form of Fast Ethernet (100BASE-TX) and 10BASE-T standard Ethernet use two of the four wire pairs found in UTP Category 5 cable. An alternative Fast Ethernet standard called 100BASE-T4 uses all four wire pairs in UTP Category 5 cable, but this Fast Ethernet standard was never popular and is seldom seen today.

Gigabit Ethernet

Gigabit Ethernet also requires special adapters, hubs, and cables. Most users of Gigabit Ethernet use fiber-optic cables, but you can run Gigabit Ethernet over the same Category 5 UTP cabling that Fast Ethernet and newer installations of standard Ethernet use.

Unlike Fast Ethernet and standard Ethernet over UTP, Gigabit Ethernet uses all four wire pairs. Thus, Gigabit Ethernet requires dedicated Ethernet cabling; you can't "borrow" two wire pairs for telephone or other data signaling with Gigabit Ethernet as you can with the slower versions.

Neither Fast Ethernet nor Gigabit Ethernet support the use of thin or thick coaxial cable originally used with traditional Ethernet, although you can interconnect coaxial-cable–based and UTP-based Ethernet networks by using media converters or specially designed hubs and switches.

Note

For more information about Ethernet, Fast Ethernet, Token-Ring, and other network data-link standards, see *Upgrading and Repairing PCs, 11th Edition*, available in electronic form on the CD-ROM provided with this book. Also see *Upgrading and Repairing Networks, Third Edition*, published by Que.

Hardware Elements of Your Network

Your network requires hardware and software components. After you have selected a data-link protocol, you can select appropriate hardware, including network interface cards, cables, and hubs or switches.

Network Interface Cards

On most computers, the network interface adapter takes the form of a network interface card (NIC) that fits into a PCI, an ISA, or an EISA slot in each computer. Some systems incorporate the network interface adapter onto the motherboard, but this practice is more commonly found in workstations and rarely in servers because most network administrators prefer to select their own NIC.

Ethernet and Token-Ring adapters have unique hardware addresses coded into their firmware. The data link layer protocol uses these addresses to identify the other systems on the network. A packet gets to the correct destination because its data link layer protocol header contains the hardware addresses of both the sending and receiving systems.

Network adapters range in price from under $30 for client adapters to as much as $300 or more for server-optimized adapters. Network adapters are built in all the popular interface-card types and are also optimized for either workstation or server use. For first-time network users, so-called network-in-a-box kits are available that contain two 10/100 Fast Ethernet NICs, a small hub or switch, and pre-built UTP cables for around $100. When combined with the built-in networking software in Windows, these kits make networking very inexpensive.

Recommended Features for Client Workstation NICs

For client workstations (including peer servers on peer-to-peer networks), here are my recommendations on the features you need.

Speed

Your NIC should run at the maximum speed you want your network to support. For a Fast Ethernet network, for example, you should purchase Ethernet cards that support 100BASE-TX's 100Mbps speed. Most Fast Ethernet cards also support standard Ethernet's 10Mbps speed, allowing the same card to be used on both older and newer portions of the network.

Your NIC should support both half-duplex and full-duplex operation:

- *Half-duplex* means that the network card can send or receive in a single operation.

- *Full-duplex* means that the network card can receive and send simultaneously. Full-duplex options boost network speed if switches are used in place of hubs.

Switches, which provide a dedicated path between two computers, offer faster performance than hubs. Although, at one time, switches were hard to justify on a workgroup peer-to-peer LAN because of their extra cost, switches are now available for little more than the price of hubs with a similar number of ports and are recommended for LANs of any size.

Bus Type

If you are networking desktop computers built from 1995 to the present, you should consider only PCI-based NICs (these computers typically have three or more PCI slots). Although many computers still have at least one ISA or combo ISA/PCI expansion slot, the superior data bus width and data transfer rate of PCI make it the only logical choice for networks of all types.

Table 20.3 summarizes differences between these expansion slot types.

Table 20.3 Bus Choices for Client PC NICs

Slot Type	Speed	Bus Width
PCI	33MHz[1]	32-bit[2]
ISA	8.33MHz[3]	16-bit[4]

1. *PCI speed of 33MHz assumes a motherboard (frontside bus) speed of 66MHz, 100MHz, or 133MHz; other motherboard speeds could cause this to vary.*

2. *Some PCI host adapters made for network servers are 64-bit or can operate in either 64-bit or 32-bit PCI slots.*

3. *An ISA speed of 8.33MHz assumes default of PCI clock speed/4; variations in motherboard speed or PCI clock divisor could cause this to vary.*

4. *Some ISA slots are only 8-bit design.*

Although ISA-based NICs are still on the market, their slow speed and narrow bus width severely restrict their performance. Most ISA-based Ethernet cards can't support speeds above 10Mbps and thus don't support Fast Ethernet or Gigabit Ethernet. A few vendors make 10/100 Ethernet cards for the ISA slot, but their performance is substantially lower than PCI cards.

Network Adapter Connectors

Ethernet adapters typically have a connector that looks like a large telephone jack called an RJ-45 (for 10BASE-T and Fast Ethernet twisted-pair cables), a single BNC connector (for Thinnet coaxial cables), or a D-shaped 15-pin connector called a DB15 (for Thicknet coaxial cables). A few older 10Mbps adapters have a combination of two or all three of these connector types; adapters with two or more connectors are referred to as *combo* adapters. Token-Ring adapters can have a 9-pin connector called a DB9 or sometimes an RJ-45 jack. Figure 20.3 shows all three of the Ethernet connectors.

Figure 20.3   Three Ethernet connectors on two NICs: RJ-45 connector (left), DB-15 connector (top right), and BNC coaxial connector (bottom right).

The following figures provide profile views of the most common types of NIC connections. Figure 20.4 shows a 10BASE-2 NIC configured to be at the end of a network; the T-adapter connected to the BNC connector has a Thinnet (RG-58) cable attached to one side and a 50-ohm terminator at the other end.

Figure 20.5 shows a 10BASE-T NIC with its UTP cable attached, whereas Figure 20.6 shows the two cables side by side.

Figure 20.4   An Ethernet 10BASE-2 NIC configured as the last station in a Thin Ethernet network.

Figure 20.5   An Ethernet 10BASE-T NIC with a UTP cable attached.

Virtually all standard and Fast Ethernet NICs made for client-PC use on the market today are designed to support twisted-pair cable exclusively. If you are adding a client PC to an existing network that uses some form of coaxial cable, you have three options:

- Purchase a combo NIC that supports coaxial cable as well as RJ-45 twisted-pair cabling.
- Purchase a media converter that can be attached to the coaxial cable to allow the newer UTP-based NICs to connect to the existing network.
- Use a switch or hub that has both coaxial cable and RJ-45 ports. A dual-speed (10/100) device is needed if you are adding one or more Fast Ethernet clients.

Network Cables

For maximum economy, NICs and network cables must match, although media converters can be used to interconnect networks based on the same standard, but using different cable.

Thick and Thin Ethernet Coaxial Cable

The first versions of Ethernet were based on coaxial cable. The original form of Ethernet, 10BASE-5, used a thick coaxial cable (called Thicknet) that was not directly attached to the NIC. A device called an attachment unit interface (AUI) ran from a DB15 connector on the rear of the NIC to the cable. The cable had a hole drilled into it to allow the "vampire tap" to be connected to the cable. NICs designed for use with thick Ethernet cable are almost impossible to find as new hardware today.

10BASE-2 Ethernet cards use a BNC (Bayonet-Neill-Concilman) connector on the rear of the NIC. Although the thin coaxial cable (called Thinnet or RG-58) used with 10BASE-2 Ethernet has a bayonet connector that can physically attach to the BNC connector on the card, this configuration is incorrect and won't work. Instead, a BNC T-connector attaches to the rear of the card, allowing a thin Ethernet cable to be connected to either both ends of the T (for a computer in the middle of the network) or to one end only (for a computer at the end of the network). A 50 ohm terminator is connected to the other arm of the T to indicate the end of the network and prevent erroneous signals from being sent to other clients on the network. Combo cards with both BNC and RJ-45 connectors are still available but can run at only standard Ethernet speeds.

Figure 20.6 shows an Ethernet BNC coaxial T-connector, and Figure 20.7 illustrates the design of coaxial cable.

Figure 20.6   An Ethernet coaxial cable T-connector.

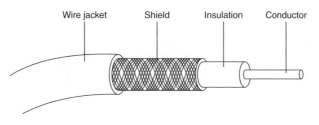

Figure 20.7   Coaxial cable.

Twisted-Pair Cable

Twisted-pair cable is just what its name implies: insulated wires within a protective casing with a specified number of twists per foot. Twisting the wires reduces the effect of electromagnetic interference (that can be generated by nearby cables, electric motors, and fluorescent lighting) on the signals being transmitted. Shielded twisted pair (STP) refers to the amount of insulation around the cluster of wires and therefore its immunity to noise. You are probably familiar with unshielded twisted-pair (UTP) cable; it is often used for telephone wiring. Figure 20.8 shows unshielded twisted-pair cable; Figure 20.9 illustrates shielded twisted-pair cable.

Figure 20.8 An unshielded twisted-pair (UTP) cable.

Figure 20.9 A shielded twisted-pair (STP) cable.

Shielded Versus Unshielded Twisted Pair

When cabling was being developed for use with computers, it was first thought that shielding the cable from external interference was the best way to reduce interference and provide for greater transmission speeds. However, it was discovered that twisting the pairs of wires is a more effective way to prevent interference from disrupting transmissions. As a result, earlier cabling scenarios relied on shielded cables rather than the unshielded cables more commonly in use today.

Shielded cables also have some special grounding concerns because one, and only one, end of a shielded cable should be connected to an earth ground; issues arose when people inadvertently caused grounding loops to occur by connecting both ends or caused the shield to act as an antenna because it wasn't grounded.

Grounding loops are situations in which two different grounds are tied together. This is a bad situation because each ground can have a slightly different potential, resulting in a circuit that has very low voltage but infinite amperage. This causes undue stress on electrical components and can be a fire hazard.

Most Ethernet and Fast Ethernet installations that use twisted-pair cabling use UTP because the physical flexibility and small size of the cable and connectors makes routing it very easy. However, its lack of electrical insulation can make interference from fluorescent lighting, elevators, and alarm systems (among other devices) a major problem. If you use UTP in installations where interference can be a problem, you need to route the cable away from the interference, use an external shield, or substitute STP for UTP near interference sources.

Network Topologies

Each computer on the network is connected to the other computers with cable (or some other medium). The physical arrangement of the cables connecting computers on a network is called the network *topology*.

These different topologies are often mixed, forming what is called a *hybrid network*. For example, you can link the hubs of several star networks together with a bus, forming a star-bus network. Rings can be connected in the same way.

Table 20.4 summarizes the relationships between network types and topologies.

Table 20.4   Network Cable Types and Topologies

Network Type	Standard	Cable Type	Topology
Ethernet	10BASE-2	Thick coaxial	Bus
	10BASE-5	Thin (RG-58) coaxial	Bus
	10BASE-T	Cat 3 or Cat 5 UTP	Star
Fast Ethernet	100BASE-TX	Cat 5 UTP	Star
Gigabit Ethernet	1000BASE-TX	Cat 5 UTP	Star
Token-Ring	(all)	STP or coaxial	Logical Ring

The bus, star, and ring topologies are discussed in the following sections.

Bus Topology

Sometimes a single piece of cable winds from station to station, visiting all the network's computers along the way. This cabling arrangement is called a *bus topology*, as shown in Figure 20.10. The potential disadvantage to this type of wiring is that if one computer or cable connection malfunctions, it can cause all the stations beyond it on the bus to lose their network connections. Thin and thick Ethernet coaxial cables are typically installed using a bus topology.

Figure 20.10   The linear bus topology, attaching all network devices to a common cable.

Star Topology

The most popular type of topology in use today has separate cables to connect each computer to a central wiring nexus, often called a hub or a concentrator; a switch can also be used in place of a hub. Figure 20.11 shows this arrangement, which is called a *star topology*. Because each computer uses a separate cable, the failure of a network connection affects only the single machine involved. The other computers can continue to function normally. Bus cabling schemes use less cable than the star but are harder to diagnose or bypass when problems occur. At this time, Fast Ethernet in a star topology is the most commonly implemented type of LAN; this is the type of network you build with most preconfigured network kits (see the following). 10BASE-T Ethernet also uses the star topology; 10BASE-T can use either Category 3 or Category 5 UTP, whereas Fast Ethernet and faster networks require Category 5 UTP.

Figure 20.11 The star topology, linking the LAN's computers and devices to one or more central hubs, or access units.

Ring Topology

The other topology often listed in discussions of this type is a *ring*, in which each workstation is connected to the next, and the last workstation is connected to the first again (essentially a bus topology with the two ends connected). Two major network types use the ring topology:

- FDDI, which uses a physical ring topology
- Token-Ring, which uses a logical ring topology

A Token-Ring network resembles an Ethernet network at first glance because both networks use a central connecting device and a physical star topology. Where is the "Ring" in Token-Ring?

The ring exists only within the device that connects the computers, which is called a multistation access unit, or MSAU, on a Token-Ring network (see Figure 20.12).

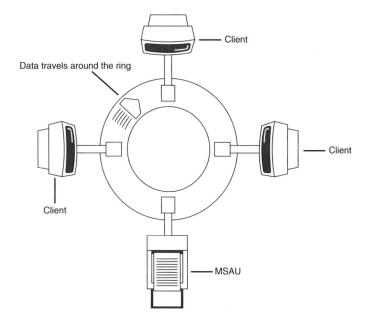

Figure 20.12 All computers and printers are connected to the same circuit, creating a loop.

Signals generated from one computer travel to the MSAU, are sent out to the next computer, and then go back to the MSAU again. The data is then passed to each system in turn until it arrives back at the computer that originated it, where it is removed from the network. Therefore, although the physical wiring topology is a star, the data path is theoretically a ring. This is called a *logical ring*.

A logical ring that Token-Ring networks use is preferable to a physical ring network topology because it affords a greater degree of fault tolerance. As on a bus network, a cable break anywhere in a physical ring network topology, such as FDDI, would affect the entire network. By contrast, on a Token-Ring network, the MSAU can effectively remove a malfunctioning computer from the logical ring, enabling the rest of the network to function normally.

Hubs for Ethernet Networks

As you have seen, modern Ethernet workgroup networks are based on UTP cable with workstations arranged in a star topology. The center of the star traditionally has been a hub, although a switch (see the section "Ethernet Switches," later in this chapter) can also be used.

All Ethernet hubs have the following features:

- Multiple RJ-45 UTP connectors
- Diagnostic and activity lights
- A power supply

The two types of Ethernet hubs are managed and unmanaged. Workgroup and home-office networks use unmanaged hubs, whereas corporate networks often use managed hubs, which are controlled with software.

Note

The now-obsolete ARCnet network used its own types of hubs: passive hubs, which were unpowered, and active hubs, which used a power supply. Neither type of hub is compatible with Ethernet.

The connection between each workstation and the hub or switch is the UTP cable running from the RJ-45 jack on the rear of the NIC to the RJ-45 jack on the rear of the hub or switch.

Signal lights on the front of the hub or switch indicate which connections are in use by computers; switches also indicate whether a full-duplex connection is in use. Dual-speed hubs and switches also indicate which connection speed is in use on each port. Your hub or switch needs to have at least one RJ-45 UTP connector for each computer you want to connect to it. Figure 20.13 shows a typical five-port hub suitable for small networks at home or a small business.

Figure 20.13 A typical 10BASE-T five-port workgroup hub. Connectors 1 and 4 are connected to computers (as shown by the lights at the front of the hub [bottom of the picture]). The light at right indicates the hub is receiving power from a AC/DC transformer "brick."

In Figure 20.13, the left cable goes to the power supply. The middle cable is a prebuilt cable that has an anti-snag design for easier threading through walls. The right cable was built from bulk cable and connectors and was assembled in the field.

How Hubs Work

A computer on an Ethernet network broadcasts (sends) a request for network information or programs from a specific computer through the cable to the hub, which broadcasts the request to all computers connected to it. When the destination computer receives the message, it sends the requested information back to the hub, which broadcasts it again to all computers, although only the requesting computer acts on the information. Thus, a hub acts similar to a radio transmitter and receiver that sends a signal to all radios, but only the radios set for the correct station can send or receive the information.

Additional Hub Features You Might Need

The least-expensive hubs are those that run at only a single speed and have only a few RJ-45 connectors. Depending on your needs, you might find the following options useful:

- *Dual-speed hubs.* If you are adding Fast Ethernet (100BASE-TX) clients to an existing 10BASE-T network, you need a dual-speed hub to connect the various types of Ethernet together.

  Even if you are building a brand-new Fast Ethernet network, a dual-speed hub is useful for occasionally hosting a "guest" PC that has only a standard 10BASE-T Ethernet NIC onboard. Many dual-speed hubs for smaller networks are only a bit more expensive than Fast Ethernet–only hubs, but the extra versatility can be worthwhile.

- *"Extra" ports beyond your current requirements.* If you are connecting four computers together into a small network, you need a four-port hub (the smallest available). But, if you buy a hub with only four ports and you want to add another client PC to the network, you must replace the hub.

  Instead, plan for the future by buying a hub that can handle your projected network growth over the next year. If you plan to add two workstations, buy at least a six-port hub (the cost per connection drops as you buy hubs with more connections). To prepare for even more growth, buy a hub that's stackable.

- *Stackable hub with an uplink port.* A *stackable* hub is one that can be connected to another hub, enabling you to add computers to your network without replacing your hub every time it runs out of connections. Most hubs on the market today are stackable, but very small hubs and some older models might lack this feature. You can use this feature to add 10/100 features to an older 10BASE-T–only network; connect a dual-speed hub (or switch) to the uplink port on your 10BASE-T hub.

To determine whether a hub is stackable, look for an uplink port. This port looks like an ordinary RJ-45 UTP port, but it is wired differently, enabling you to use a standard-pinout RJ-45 UTP cable to connect it to another hub. Without the uplink port, you'd have to use a specially wired crossover cable.

Typically, hubs with an uplink port allow you to use the port along with all but one of the normal ports on the hub (see Figure 20.14). My office uses a five-port hub made by Linksys with an uplink port. I use the uplink port to connect my network with a larger LAN for Internet access and the other four available ports for my office network. I can use all five ports if my hub is used in isolation, but if I use the uplink port to attach another hub, only the first four ports are usable. The uplink port and port #5 can't be used at the same time.

The uplink port connects
this hub to another hub.

Up to five devices (computers and
printers) can be connected to this hub.

Figure 20.14   The connectors on a typical five-port workgroup hub with an uplink port (at left) for connecting this hub to another hub (stacking the hubs). Either port #5 or the uplink port can be used, but not both.

Hub Placement

Although large networks have a wiring closet near the server, the workgroup-size LANs you'll be building don't need a wiring closet. However, the location of the hub is important.

Ethernet hubs require electrical power, whether they are small units that use a power "brick" or larger units that have an internal power supply and a standard three-prong AC cord.

In addition to electrical power, consider placing the hub where its signal lights will be easy to view for diagnostic purposes and where its RJ-45 connectors can be reached easily when it's time to add another user or two. In my office, the hub sits on the tower case of my PC, enabling me to see network problems just by looking down at the hub. The corner of an out-of-the way desk can also work for small hubs.

Except for the 328' (100 meter) limit for 100BASE-TX Fast Ethernet, distances between each computer on the network and the hub aren't critical, so put the hub wherever you can supply power and gain easy access.

Tip

Decide where you plan to put your hub before you buy prebuilt UTP wiring or make your own; if you move the hub, some of your wiring will no longer be the correct length. Although excess lengths of UTP cable can be coiled and secured with cable ties, cables that are too short should be replaced. You can buy RJ-45 connectors to create one long cable from two short cables, but you must ensure they are Category 5 if you are running Fast Ethernet. You're really better off replacing the too-short cable with the correct length.

Ethernet Switches

Switches, similar to hubs, connect computers on a UTP-based Ethernet network to each other and physically resemble hubs (see Figure 20.15).

Figure 20.15 Front (top) and rear (bottom) of a typical five-port 10/100 Ethernet switch. Photos courtesy Linksys.

But, compared to hubs, switches have several additional features that can boost the performance of even a small workgroup network, as shown in Table 20.5.

Table 20.5   Ethernet Hub and Switch Comparison

Feature	Hub	Switch
Bandwidth	Divided by total number of ports in use	Dedicated to each port in use
Data Transmission Type	Broadcast to all connected computers	Direct connection between transmitting and receiving computers
Duplex Support	Half-duplex only (receive or transmit)	Half- or full-duplex (receive and transmit) when used with full-duplex NICs; doubles effective bandwidth of the network

How Switches Work

Instead of broadcasting data to all computers on the network as hubs do, a switch uses a feature called address storing, which checks the destination for each data packet and sends it directly to the computer it's intended for. Thus, a switch can be compared to a telephone exchange, making direct connections between the originator of a call and the receiver.

Because switches establish a direct connection between the originating and receiving PC, they also provide the full bandwidth of the network to each port. Hubs, by contrast, must subdivide the network's bandwidth by the number of active connections on the network, meaning that bandwidth rises and falls depending on network activity.

For example, assume you have a four-station network workgroup using 10/100 NICs and a Fast Ethernet hub. The total bandwidth of the network is 100Mbps. However, if two stations are active, the effective bandwidth available to each station drops to 50Mbps (100Mbps divided by 2). If all four stations are active, the effective bandwidth drops to just 25Mbps (100Mbps divided by 4)! Add more active users, and the effective bandwidth continues to drop.

By replacing the hub with a switch, the effective bandwidth for each station remains 100Mbps because the switch doesn't broadcast data to all stations.

Most 10/100 NICs and Fast Ethernet or 10/100 switches also support full-duplex (simultaneous transmit and receive), enabling actual bandwidth to be double the nominal 100Mbps rating: 200Mbps.

As you can see, using a switch instead of a hub greatly increases the effective speed of a network, even if all other components remain the same.

Desirable Switch Features

Because hubs and switches perform similar tasks, it's not surprising that the list of desirable features is also similar; it includes

- *Dual network card speeds.* This enables you to freely mix and match 10BASE-T and Fast Ethernet or 10/100 NICs and derive full speed from all devices.

- *Additional ports for future expansion.* Because the cost per port drops on larger switches, just as on larger hubs, it's cheaper to buy "excess" capacity at the start than to replace your switch or add a switch later.

- *An uplink port, making the switch stackable.* A stackable switch enables you to add another switch (or hub) without replacing the original unit.

Network Cable Installations

If you have to run cables (of any type) through existing walls and ceilings, the cable installation can be the most expensive part of setting up a LAN. At every branching point, special fittings connect the intersecting wires. Sometimes, you also need various additional components along the way, such as hubs, repeaters, or MSAUs.

Note

As an alternative to wired networks, more and more companies and home users are exploring wireless networks using radio waves and other technologies. Although these networks are not yet as fast as wired solutions such as Fast Ethernet, they are useful for solutions in which wiring isn't feasible. See the section "Wireless Network Standards," later in this chapter for details.

With the development of easy-to-build (or prebuilt) Category 5 twisted-pair cabling, high-speed and low-cost NICs and hubs, and built-in basic networking in current versions of Windows, installing and setting up a network today is far easier than ever before. For small cubicle/office networking in which no wire must be routed through walls and in which Windows peer networking software will be used, you should be able to set up the network yourself if you're comfortable with the technical information in this book.

If your wiring must go through walls, be run through dropped ceilings, be piggybacked on air ducts, or be run between floors, you might want to have professional network-cable specialists install the cable. A good company knows the following:

- When UTP (unshielded twisted pair) cabling is adequate
- Where STP (shielded twisted pair) cabling might be necessary to avoid excessive cable runs and interference
- How to route cable between rooms, floors, and nonadjacent offices
- How to use wall panels to make cable attachments look better and more professional
- When you must use fireproof Plenum cable
- How to deal with sources of electrical interference, such as elevator motors, transmitters, alarm systems, and even florescent office lighting, by using fiber-optic or shielded cable

Building Your Own Twisted-Pair Cables

You should build your own twisted-pair cables if you

- Plan to perform a lot of networking
- Need cable lengths longer than the 25-foot maximum cable length you can buy preassembled at typical computer departments
- Want to create both standard and crossover cables
- Want to choose your own cable color
- Want maximum control over cable length
- Want to save money
- Have the time necessary to build cables

Selecting the Proper Cable

A network is only as fast as its slowest component; to achieve the maximum speeds of the network, all its components, including cables, must meet the standards. Two standard types of twisted pair cabling exist:

- *Category 3 Cable.* The original type of UTP cable used for Ethernet networks was also the same as that used for business telephone wiring. This is known as Category 3, or voice-grade UTP cable, and is measured according to a scale that quantifies the cable's data-transmission capabilities. The cable itself is 24 AWG (American Wire Gauge, a standard for measuring the diameter of a wire), copper-tinned with solid conductors, 100–105 ohm characteristic impedance, and a minimum of two twists per foot. Category 3 cable is adequate for networks running at up to 16Mbps. This cable usually looks like "silver" telephone cable, but with the larger RJ-45 connector. Category 3 cabling is obsolete because it doesn't support Fast Ethernet or greater network speeds.

- *Category 5 Cable.* The Newer, faster network types require greater performance levels. Fast Ethernet (100BASE-TX) uses the same two wire pairs as 10BASE-T, but Fast Ethernet needs a greater resistance to signal crosstalk and attenuation. Therefore, the use of Category 5 UTP cabling is essential with 100BASE-TX Fast Ethernet. Although the 100BASE-T4 version of Fast Ethernet can use all four wire pairs of Category 3 cable, this flavor of Fast Ethernet is not widely supported and has practically vanished from the marketplace. Thus, for practical purposes, if you mix Category 3 and Category 5 cables, you should use only 10BASE-T (10Mbps) Ethernet hubs; if you try to run Fast Ethernet 100BASE-TX over Category 3 cable, you will have a slow and unreliable network.

You should use existing Category 3 cable for your LAN only if you are content with the 10Mbps speeds of 10BASE-T and if the cable is in good condition. The silver exterior on Category 3 cabling can become brittle and deteriorate, leading to frequent network failures. If you are installing brand-new wiring for a new network, or replacing deteriorated Category 3 cable, Category 5 cabling should be used. It's widely available in either prebuilt assemblies or in bulk.

Caution

If you choose to install Category 5 UTP cable, be sure that all the connectors, wall plates, and other hardware components involved are also Category 5.

If you are trying to connect prebuilt Category 5 cabling together on a Fast Ethernet network, use Category 5–grade connectors; otherwise, you'll create a substandard section that might fail in your network.

Choosing the correct type of Category 5 cable is also important. Use solid PVC cable for network cables that represent a permanent installation. However, the slightly more expensive stranded cables are a better choice for a notebook computer or for temporary wiring of no more than 10-foot lengths (from a computer to a wall socket, for example) because it is more flexible and is thus capable of withstanding frequent movement.

If you plan to use air ducts or suspended ceilings for cable runs, you should use Plenum cable, which doesn't emit harmful fumes in a fire. It is much more expensive, but the safety issue is a worthwhile reason to use it (and it is required by some localities).

TP Wiring Standards

If you want to create twisted pair (TP) cables yourself, be sure your cable pairs match the color-coding of any existing cable or the color-coding of any prebuilt cabling you want to add to your new network. Because there are eight wires in TP cables, many incorrect combinations are possible. Several standards exist for UTP cabling.

Tip

The key is to be consistent and use the same scheme for all your cables and to be sure that anyone else working on your network understands the scheme used in your network.

One common standard is the AT&T 258A configuration (also called EIA 568B). Table 20.6 lists the wire pairing and placement within the standard RJ-45 connector.

Table 20.6   RJ-45 Connector Wire Pairing and Placement for AT&T 258A/EIA 568B Standard

Wire Pairing	Wire Connected to Pin #	Pair Used For
White/blue and blue	White/blue - #5; Blue - #4	Not used[1]
White/orange and orange	White/orange - #1; Orange - #2	Transmit
White/green and green	White/green - #3; Green - #6	Receive
White/brown and brown	White/brown - #7; Brown - #8	Not used[1]

1 This pair is not used with 10BASE-T or Fast Ethernet 100BASE-TX, but all four pairs are used with Fast Ethernet 100BASE-T4 and Gigabit Ethernet 1000BASE-TX standards.

Another common standard is the EIA 568B standard. In Figure 20.16 you can see a RJ-45 cable connector wired to this standard.

Pin 1 (white/orange)

Pin 8 (brown)

Figure 20.16   *An AT&T 258A/EIA 568B standard compliant FJ-45 connector.*

Note

You also might encounter the similar EIA 568A standard. It reverses the position of the orange and green pairs listed previously.

Crossover UTP Cables

Crossover cables are used in two situations:

- Connecting two, and only two, computers together when no hub is available
- Connecting a hub that lacks an uplink (stacking) port to another hub

The pinout for a crossover cable is shown in Table 20.7. This pinout is for one end of the cable only; the other end of the cable should correspond to the standard TIA 568B pinout, as shown previously in Figure 20.16.

Table 20.7   RJ-45 Connector Wire Pairing and Placement for Crossover Variation on EIA 568B Standard

Wire	Pin #
White/blue	5
Blue	4
White/green	1
Green	2
White/orange	3
Orange	6
White/brown	7
Brown	8

Note

It should be noted that other wiring schemes exist, such as IEEE and USOC. All told, at least eight agreed-on standards exist for connecting UTP cables and RJ-45 connectors. The ones listed in this chapter are the most common.

Making Your Own UTP Cables

You will need the following tools and supplies to build your own Ethernet cables (see Figure 20.17):

- UTP cable (Category 5 or better)
- RJ-45 connectors
- Wire stripper
- RJ-45 crimping tool

You can buy all of the previously listed items for a single price from many network-products vendors.

Before you make a "real" cable of any length, you should practice on a short length of cable. RJ-45 connectors and bulk cable are cheap; network failures are not.

Follow these steps for creating your own twisted-pair cables:

1. Determine how long your UTP cable should be. You should allow adequate slack for moving the computer and for avoiding strong interference sources. Keep the maximum distances for UTP cables listed later in this chapter in mind.

2. Roll out the appropriate length of cable.

3. Cut the cable cleanly from the box of wire.

4. Use the wire stripper to strip the insulation jacket off the cable to expose the TP wires (see Figure 20.18); you'll need to rotate the wire about 1 1/4 turns to strip away all the jacket. If you turn it too far, you'll damage the wires inside the cable.

Figure 20.17 You'll need wire strippers, a crimping tool, UTP cable, and RJ-45 connectors to make your own 10BASE-T (100BASE-T) cables.

Figure 20.18 Carefully strip the cable jacket away to expose the four wire pairs.

Caution

Don't strip the UTP wires themselves, just the jacket!

5. Check the outer jacket and inner TP wires for nicks; adjust the stripper tool and repeat steps 3 and 4 if you see damage.

6. Arrange the wires according to the EIA 568B standard listed earlier in the section "TP Wiring Standards" (see Figure 20.19).

Figure 20.19 Arrange the wire pairs for insertion into the RJ-45 connector according to your chosen scheme (EIA for instance).

7. Trim the wire edges so the eight wires are even with one another and are slightly less than 1/2 inch past the end of the jacket. If the wires are too long, crosstalk (wire-to-wire interference) can result; if the wires are too short, they can't make a good connection with the RJ-45 plug.

8. With the clip side of the RJ-45 plug facing away from you, push the cable into place (see Figure 20.20). Verify that the wires are arranged according to the EIA/TIA 568B standard *before* you crimp the plug onto the wires (see Figure 20.16, earlier in this chapter). Adjust the connection as necessary.

9. Use the crimping tool to squeeze the RJ-45 plug onto the cable (see Figure 20.21). The end of the cable should be tight enough to resist being removed by hand.

10. Repeat steps 4–9 for the other end of the cable. Recut the end of the cable if necessary before stripping it.

11. Label each cable with the following information:

- Wiring standard
- Length
- End with crossover (if any)
- _____ (blank) for computer ID

Figure 20.20   Push the RJ-45 connector into place, ensuring the cable pairs are ordered properly.

Figure 20.21   Firmly squeeze the crimping tool to attach the connector to the cable.

Note

The cables should be labeled at both ends to make matching the cable with the correct computer easy and to facilitate troubleshooting at the hub. Check with your cable supplier for suitable labeling stock or tags you can attach to each cable.

An excellent online source for this process is http://www.duxcw.com/digest/Howto/network/cable/.

Cable Distance Limitations

The people who design computer systems love to find ways to circumvent limitations. Manufacturers of Ethernet products have made it possible to build networks in star, branch, and tree designs that overcome the basic limitations already mentioned. You can have thousands of computers on a complex Ethernet network.

LANs are local because the network adapters and other hardware components typically can't send LAN messages more than a few hundred feet. Table 20.8 lists the distance limitations of various types of LAN cable. In addition to the limitations shown in the table, keep the following points in mind:

- You can't connect more than 30 computers on a single Thinnet Ethernet segment.

- You can't connect more than 100 computers on a Thicknet Ethernet segment.

- You can't connect more than 72 computers on a UTP Token-Ring cable.

- You can't connect more than 260 computers on an STP Token-Ring cable.

Table 20.8   Network Distance Limitations

Network Adapter	Cable Type	Maximum	Minimum
Ethernet	Thin[1]	607 ft.	20 in.
	Thick (drop cable)[1]	164 ft.	8 ft.
	Thick (backbone)[1]	1,640 ft.	8 ft.
100BASE-TX	UTP	328 ft.	8 ft.
10BASE-T	UTP	994 ft.	8 ft.
Token-Ring	STP	328 ft.	8 ft.
	UTP	148 ft.	8 ft.
ARCnet[1] (passive hub)		393 ft.	Depends on cable
ARCnet[1] (active hub)		1,988 ft.	Depends on cable

1. Indicates obsolete for new installations; may be found in existing installations.

Note that 10BASE-T (Ethernet on UTP) can have a maximum cable length three times longer than 100BASE-TX. If you plan to change a 10BASE-T-wired Ethernet network to Fast Ethernet 100BASE-TX, you should check the wiring distances in use. If you have a station wired with Category 5 cable that is over 328 feet (100 meters) from a hub, you must use a repeater if you want it to use Fast Ethernet, as well as replace all the NICs and hubs with Fast Ethernet–compatible hardware. If you have two or more stations beyond the 328-ft. limit for Fast Ethernet, connect them to a hub or switch that is less than 328 ft. away from the primary hub or switch, and connect the new hub or switch to the primary hub or switch via its uplink port. Because hubs and switches can act as repeaters, this feature enables you to extend the effective length of your network (see Figure 20.22).

Even if you are still installing a 10BASE-T–only network, use Category 5 cables and keep each client PC within 328 feet of the hub to enable upgrading to 100BASE-TX Fast Ethernet in the future.

Wireless Network Standards

Various forms of wireless networks using either radio or IR (infrared) have been developed over the years, but until recently, the benefits of a wireless network (no wires to pull or holes to drill) were outweighed by the lack of standards and relatively slow speed. In conventional Ethernet networks, you can use various brands of NICs, hubs, and switches without any problems, as long as each device corresponds to the same Ethernet standard.

Wi-Fi, the IEEE 802.11b Wireless Ethernet Standard

Wi-Fi (Wireless Fidelity) is the new name for IEEE 802.11b-compliant hardware that has passed the compatibility and interoperability tests of the trade group known as the Wireless Ethernet Compatibility Alliance (WECA); see their Web site at www.wi-fi.org.

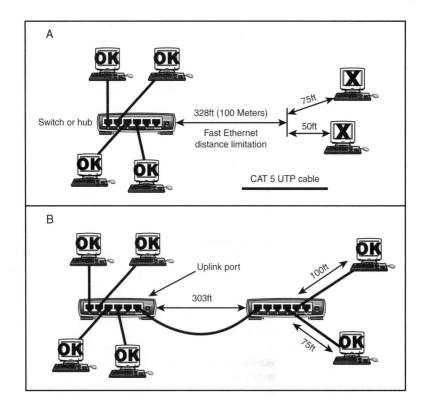

Figure 20.22 In case A (top), the workstations at right are too far away from the hub to connect to a Fast Ethernet network. In case B (bottom), an additional hub or switch is used to allow the workstations to be added to the network.

Wi-Fi–compliant wireless networks run at a maximum speed of 11Mbps, about the same as 10BASE-T Ethernet (the original version of IEEE 802.11 supported data rates up to 2Mbps only). Other data rates Wi-Fi networks support include 1Mbps, 2Mbps, and 5.5Mbps. Wi-Fi networks can connect to conventional Ethernet networks or independent networks, similar to other wireless networks. The major advantage of Wi-Fi networks is their interoperability; just as you can mix and match conventional Ethernet hardware, you can mix and match Wi-Fi–compliant hardware on the same network.

Wi-Fi Technologies

Wireless networks running Wi-Fi hardware use the same 2.4GHz spectrum used by many portable phones, wireless speakers, security devices, microwave ovens, and the now-emerging Bluetooth short-range networking products. Although the increasing use of these noncomputer products is a potential source of interference, the short range of wireless networks (indoor ranges up to 300 feet and outdoor ranges up to 1,500 feet, varying by product) minimizes the practical risks, at least for the present.

Note

To provide better performance and avoid interference, a new wireless networking standard called IEEE 802.11a has been proposed by American vendors. This protocol would use the 5GHz frequency and support data rates of 22Mbps initially, with eventual speeds up to 54Mbps.

A rival European standard called HIPERLAN/2 would also use the 5GHz frequency but doesn't use the standard Ethernet "listen before transmit" method of operation that IEEE 802.11a uses. The 5GHz Wireless LAN Industry Advisory Group is trying to bring interoperability to these two proposed standards.

Wi-Fi networks use two types of devices to connect via the 2.4GHz band:

- *Access Points.* An access point is a bookend-size device that uses an RJ-45 port to attach to a 10BASE-T or 10/100 Ethernet network (if desired) and contains a radio transceiver, encryption, and communications software. It translates conventional Ethernet signals into wireless Ethernet signals it broadcasts to wireless NICs on the network and performs the same role in reverse to transfer signals from wireless NICs to the conventional Ethernet network.

  For coverage of a large area, purchase two or more access points and connect them to an Ethernet switch or hub. This enables users to "roam" inside a building without losing contact with the network. Some access points can communicate directly with each other via radio waves, enabling you to create a wireless backbone that can cover a wide area, such as a warehouse, without the need to run any network cabling.

- *NICs equipped with radio transceivers.* NICs equipped for wireless Ethernet communications have a fixed or detachable radio antenna in place of the usual coaxial or RJ-45 port or dongle. Because a major market for wireless Ethernet use is notebook computer users, some vendors sell only PC Cards in their wireless Ethernet product lines, but most vendors support PCI cards for desktop computers. Several of these vendors now support the popular USB port. Because you can mix and match products, you can incorporate any mix of desktop and notebook computers into your wireless network.

  Client systems lock on to the strongest signal from access points and automatically roam (switch) to another access point when the signal strength is stronger and the error level is lower than the current connection.

Security and Other Features

Because wireless networks could, in theory, be accessed by anyone with a compatible NIC, most models of NICs and access points provide for encryption options. Some devices with this feature enable you to set a security code known as an ESSID on the wireless devices on your network. This seven-digit code prevents unauthorized users from sneaking onto your network and acts as an additional layer of security along with your normal network authentication methods, such as user passwords. Others use a list of authorized MAC numbers (each NIC has a unique MAC) to limit access to authorized devices only. All Wi-Fi products support at least 40-bit encryption through the wired equivalent privacy (WEP) specification, but many vendors offer 128-bit encryption products. However, the stronger encryption feature is more common among enterprise products than small-office/home-office–oriented products. You should match the encryption level used on both the access points and the NICs for best security.

Some products' access points can be managed via a Web browser and provide diagnostic and monitoring tools to help you optimize the positioning of access points.

Many products feature support for Dynamic Host Configuration Protocol (DHCP), allowing a user to move from one subnet to another without difficulties.

Figure 20.23 illustrates a typical IEEE 802.11b wireless network.

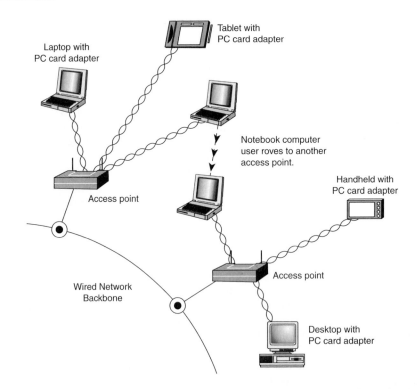

Tablet with
PC card adapter

Laptop with
PC card adapter

Notebook computer
user roves to another
access point.

Handheld with
PC card adapter

Access point

Wired Network
Backbone

Access point

Desktop with
PC card adapter

Figure 20.23   A typical wireless network with multiple access points. As users with wireless NICs move from one office to another, the roaming feature of the NIC automatically switches from one access point to another, permitting seamless network connectivity without wires or logging off the network and reconnecting.

Users per Access Point

The number of users per access point varies with the product; a recent (March 2001) review of Wi-Fi access points listed models that can support anywhere from 15 to as many as 254 users. You should contact the vendor of your preferred Wi-Fi access point device for details.

Cost per User

Although workgroup network-in-a-box solutions that use 10/100 Ethernet (wired) technology can connect two PCs for around $80 ($40 per user), and additional network cards are available for under $20, Wi-Fi networking is far more expensive because of the high cost of access points and wireless NICs. For example, the Lucent Orinoco AP-1000 Enterprise-oriented product line features a cost of $995 for its access point (which can handle up to 60 simultaneous users), with wireless PCI cards for $69 each, wireless PC Cards for notebook computers for $179 each, and wireless USB devices for $199 each. The small-office–oriented D-Link SWL-1000AP's access unit runs $349—its PCI cards are $119 each, its PC Cards are $99 each, and its USB devices are $129 each.

To determine the cost per user of a basic wireless network, use the following worksheet:

Cost per Device	Number of Devices	Extended Cost
Cost Per Access Point	Number of Access Points	
_____ ×	_____ =	_____
Cost Per PCI Card	Number of PCI cards needed	
_____ ×	_____ =	_____
Cost Per PC Card	Number of PC Cards	
_____ ×	_____ =	_____
Cost Per USB Port Device	Number of USB Port Devices	
_____ ×	_____ =	_____
Total Cost of Network Hardware (TC)		_____
Total Number of PCI, PC Card, USB Devices (TN)	/	_____
Cost per User (divide TC by TN)	=	_____

Typically, you can expect the cost per user of even the lowest-cost Wi-Fi LAN to average between $200 and $500 (based on one access point, two PC card adapters, one PCI adapter, and one USB adapter). Thus, the capability to roam with a notebook and avoid wiring problems must be very critical to make up for the much higher cost of wireless Ethernet networking when compared to basic (and obsolescent) 10BASE-T Ethernet networks (which have comparable performance to Wi-Fi).

Because IEEE 802.11b/Wi-Fi is a true standard, you can mix and match access point and wireless NIC hardware to meet your desired price, performance, and feature requirements for your wireless network, just as you can for conventional Ethernet networks.

Notebook Computers with Integrated Wi-Fi Adapters

Major notebook computer makers, including Dell, IBM, and Toshiba, are now integrating built-in Wi-Fi wireless adapters and antennas into some of their notebook computers. Although computers with built-in Wi-Fi hardware are a little more expensive than comparable models lacking Wireless Ethernet support, building the adapter and antenna into notebook computers provides for a more durable and less cumbersome way to equip portable systems than the normal PC Card and external antenna arrangement that must be fitted to ordinary notebook computers.

Notebook computers with Wi-Fi hardware onboard use the mini-PCI interface for the wireless adapter and place the antenna inside the screen housing. This enables computers with built-in Wi-Fi hardware to have one more open PC Card slot than computers that must use an external PC Card adapter and antenna.

Alternatives to the IEEE 802.11b Standard

The RadioLAN Wireless MobilLINK uses the same access point plus wireless NIC design used by the IEEE 802.11b networks discussed earlier. RadioLAN uses the 5.8GHz radio frequency, providing faster speed than IEEE 802.11b–based networks, but preventing interconnection with them (because they use the 2.4GHz radio band). However, RadioLAN products can be interconnected with conventional 10BASE-T LANs through the use of its BackboneLINK bridge, and RadioLAN also offers wireless bridges between 10BASE-T Ethernet networks up to one mile apart.

Other solutions can be regarded as industry standards because multiple companies support them. These include

- *Bluetooth.* This low-speed (up to 400Kbps), low-power standard is designed to interconnect notebook computers, PDAs, cell phones, and pagers for data synchronization and user authentication in public areas, such as airports, hotels, rental car pickups, and sporting events.

  Bluetooth-compliant devices began to arrive on the market in the second half of 2000. A list of Bluetooth products and announcements is available at the Bluetooth products page of the palowireless.com Web site.

  Bluetooth devices also use the same 2.4GHz frequency range Wi-Fi/IEEE 802.11b devices use. However, to avoid interference with Wi-Fi, Bluetooth uses a signaling method called frequency hopping spread spectrum, which switches the exact frequency used during a Bluetooth session 1,600 times per second over the 79 channels that Bluetooth uses.

  Unlike Wi-Fi, which is designed to allow a device to be part of a network at all times, Bluetooth is designed for ad hoc temporary networks in which two devices connect only long enough to transfer data and then break the connection.

- *HomeRF.* The HomeRF Consortium, headed by Proxim, has developed wireless products designed for home networking, using the Shared Wireless Access Protocol (SWAP).

  Current products run at a leisurely 1.6Mbps, but the HomeRF standard is designed to support speeds up to 10Mbps. HomeRF products can be interconnected with conventional Ethernet networks through the use of a cordless Ethernet bridge.

  HomeRF-based products are available from Proxim (Symphony), Intel (AnyPoint Wireless), Motorola (AL 200 Wireless Cable Modem), Compaq (iPAQ Connection Point), and Cayman (3220-H-W Wireless Solution). Because HomeRF is based on the SWAP standard, you can mix and match products from different vendors. HomeRF products include

  - *Cordless Ethernet bridges.* These are available from Symphony.
  - *Wireless NICs for ISA and PCI slots.* These are available from Symphony.
  - *Wireless NICs for PC Card slots.* These are available from Intel, Symphony, and Compaq.
  - *Wireless NICs for USB ports.* These are available from Intel and Compaq.
  - *Specialized devices.* These are devices such as the multiple-network–compatible iPAQ Connection Point (supports 10/100 Ethernet, HomeRF, Phoneline HomePNA 2.0, and 56Kbps modems), Cayman's 3220-H-W DSL gateway, and Motorola's AL 200 Wireless Cable Modem.

Although the 1.6Mbps performance of Symphony is far lower than that of IEEE 802.11b–based products, the cost for one or two users is much smaller because HomeRF-based products connect directly with each other.

For example, Symphony's wireless NICs for PCI and ISA slots are under $120 each, and PC Card slots are under $130 each. Symphony's cordless Ethernet bridge retails for under $400. HomeRF products also use the same 2.4GHz frequency used by IEEE 802.11b and Bluetooth wireless products, which can cause interference between devices, although these products are typically used in different environments.

Wireless Network Logical Topologies

Wireless networks use two logical topologies:

- *Star.* The star topology, used by Wi-Fi/IEEE 802.11b–based products and RadioLAN, resembles the topology used by 10BASE-T and faster versions of Ethernet that use a hub. The access point takes the place of the hub because stations connect via the access point, rather than directly with each other. This method is much more expensive per unit but permits performance near 10BASE-T Ethernet speeds and easier management.

■ *Point-to-Point.* HomeRF and Bluetooth products use the point-to-point topology. These devices connect directly with each other and require no access point or other hub-like device to communicate with each other. This method is much less expensive per unit but is suited to very small, simple networks only and is currently much slower than 10BASE-T networks.

Table 20.9 compares the major wireless network standards in current use.

Table 20.9   Comparison of Current Wireless Networks

Network	Rated Speed	Logical Topology	Connects with 10BASE-T Ethernet via	Maximum Number of PCs per Access Point	Average Cost per User[6]
IEEE 802.11b Wi-Fi	11Mbps	Logical Star (requires access point)	Access point	Varies by brand and model; up to 256 or more	$516[1, 3]; $186[2, 3]
RadioLAN	10Mbps[4]	Logical Star (requires access point)	Wireless BackboneLINK (access point)	128	$564[3]
HomeRF[5]	1.6Mbps	Point-to-Point	Symphony Cordless Ethernet Bridge	10	$134

1. *Average price of enterprise-level products from Cisco (Aironet 350) and Lucent (Orinoco AP-1000) as of 1Q2001.*

2. *Average price of small-office–level products from Linksys (Instant Wireless WAP-11) and D-Link (DWL-1000AP) as of 1Q2001.*

3. *Price includes access point (required).*

4. *The actual throughput of RadioLAN compared to average of IEEE 802.11b products is about 25% faster because of higher radio frequency used.*

5. *Figures for Proxim Symphony, first HomeRF product available.*

6. *Average cost per user based on a four-station network with two PCI desktop and two notebook PCs and one access point if needed.*

Network Protocols

The second-most important choice you must make when you create your network is which network protocol you use. The network protocol, another part of the OSI Reference model, affects with which types of computers your network can connect.

The three major network protocols are TCP/IP, IPX/SPX, and NetBEUI. Unlike data-link protocols, though, network protocols are not tied to particular hardware (NIC or cable) choices. Network protocols are software and can be installed or removed to any computer on the network at any time as necessary.

Table 20.10 summarizes the differences between these protocols.

Table 20.10 Overview of Network Protocols and Suites

Protocol	Included in Protocol Suite	Best Used for	Notes
IP	TCP/IP	Internet and large networks	Also used for dial-up Internet access; native protocol suite of Windows 2000 and Novell NetWare 5.x
IPX	IPX/SPX	Networks with Novell 4.x and earlier servers	Used by NetWare 5. for certain special features only
NetBEUI	N/A	Windows 9x, 2000, or Windows for Workgroups peer networks	Can't be routed between networks; simplest network protocol; also used with Direct Cable Connection NIC-less "networking"

All the computers on any given network must use the same network protocol or protocol suite to communicate with each other.

IP and TCP/IP

IP stands for Internet Protocol; it is the network layer of the collection of protocols (or protocol suite) developed for use on the Internet and commonly known as TCP/IP (Transmission Control Protocol/Internet Protocol).

Later, the TCP/IP protocols were adopted by the Unix operating systems, and they have now become the most commonly used protocol suite on PC LANs. Virtually every operating system with networking capabilities supports TCP/IP, and it is well on its way to displacing all the other competing protocols. Novell NetWare 5 and Windows 2000 both use TCP/IP as their native protocol for most services.

TCP/IP—LAN and Dial-Up Networks

TCP/IP, unlike the other network protocols listed in the previous section, is also a protocol people use who have never seen a NIC. People who access the Internet via modems (with what Windows 9x calls Dial-Up Networking) use TCP/IP just as those whose Web access is done with their existing LANs. Although the same protocol is used in both cases, the settings vary a great deal.

Table 20.10 summarizes the differences you're likely to encounter. If you access the Internet with both modems and a LAN, you must ensure that the TCP/IP properties for modems and LANs are set correctly. You also might need to adjust your browser settings to indicate which connection type you are using. Table 20.11 provides general guidelines; your ISP or network administrator can give you the specific details.

Table 20.11 TCP/IP Properties by Connection Type—Overview

TCP/IP Property Tab	Setting	Modem Access (Dial-Up Adapter)	LAN Access (Network Card)
IP Address	IP Address	Automatically assigned by ISP	Specified (get value from network administrator)
WINS Configuration	Enable/Disable WINS Resolution	Disabled	Indicate server or enable DHCP to allow NetBIOS over TCP/IP
Gateway	Add Gateway/ List of Gateways	None (PPP is used to connect modem to Internet)	IP address of gateway used to connect LAN to Internet
DNS Configuration	Enable/Disable Host Domain	Usually disabled, unless proxy server used by ISP	Enabled, with host and domain specified (get value from network administrator)

As you can see from Table 20.11, correct settings for LAN access to the Internet and dial-up networking (modem) settings are almost always completely different. In general, the best way to get your dial-up networking connection working correctly is to use your ISP's automatic setup software. This is usually supplied as part of your ISP's signup software kit. After the setup is working, view the properties and record them for future troubleshooting use.

Note

In Windows 98 and Me, Microsoft suggests that TCP/IP properties be viewed through the Dial-Up Networking icon for the connection, rather than through the Network icon in the control panel.

IPX

The IPX protocol suite (often referred to as IPX/SPX) is the collective term for the proprietary protocols created by Novell for their NetWare operating system. Although based loosely on some of the TCP/IP protocols, Novell privately holds the IPX protocol standards. However, this has not prevented Microsoft from creating its own IPX-compatible protocol for the Windows operating systems.

IPX (Internetwork Packet Exchange) itself is a network layer protocol that is equivalent in function to IP. The suite's equivalent to TCP is the Sequenced Packet Exchange (SPX) protocol, which provides connection-oriented, reliable service at the transport layer.

The IPX protocols typically are used today only on networks with NetWare servers and often are installed along with another protocol suite, such as TCP/IP. Even NetWare, however, is phasing out its use of IPX and making the move over to TCP/IP—along with the rest of the networking industry. NetWare 5 uses IPX/SPX only for specialized operations. Most of the product uses TCP/IP.

NetBEUI

NetBIOS Extended User Interface (NetBEUI) is a protocol used primarily on small Windows NT networks, as well as on peer networks based on Windows for Workgroups and Windows 9x. It was the default protocol in Windows NT 3.1, the first version of that operating system. Later versions, however, use the TCP/IP protocols as their defaults.

NetBEUI is a simple protocol that lacks many of the features that enable protocol suites such as TCP/IP to support networks of almost any size. NetBEUI is not routable, so it can't be used on large internetworks. It is suitable for small peer-to-peer networks, but any serious Windows NT network installation should use TCP/IP.

NetBEUI is still useful for creating "instant networks" with the Direct Cable Connection (see the following), and it is the minimum protocol required for use in a Windows 9x peer-to-peer network.

Choosing What You Need

In this section, you receive a detailed checklist of the hardware and software you need to build your network.

First, start with the number of computers you plan to network together. You need the items discussed in the following section to set up your network.

NIC

You need a NIC for every computer on the network. To simplify technical support, buy the same model of NIC for each computer in your network. If you are creating a Windows NT/2000 or Novell NetWare network with a dedicated server, you should buy server-optimized NICs for the server and less-expensive client NICs for the client PCs. However, you should still purchase the same brand to simplify support issues. Some vendors use the same driver for both their server and client NICs, further simplifying your support issue.

You should record the brand name and model number of the NIC(s) you are using, as well as the driver version or source. Use Table 20.12 as a template for creating your own record.

Table 20.12   NIC Location and Information Worksheet

NIC Location & Computer ID	Brand Name	Model #	Cable Type(s)	Speed	Driver Source or Version
_____	_____	_____	_____	_____	_____

UTP Cable

You need one cable long enough to reach comfortably between the computer's NIC and the hub for each computer. Use Table 20.13 as a guide for recording necessary information regarding your cabling.

Table 20.13   UTP Cable Worksheet

Computer ID	Cable Length	Wiring Standard
_____	_____	_____

Hub/Switch

Buy a hub or switch of the correct speed with at least enough RJ-45 ports for each computer on the network. Use the worksheet shown in Table 20.14 as a guide for recording information about your hub or switch.

Table 20.14   Hub/Switch Worksheet

Hub #	Brand	Model#	# of Ports	Uplink?	Speed(s)
_____	_____	_____	_____	_____	_____

Other Home Networking Solutions

If you are working at home or in a small office, you have an alternative to hole-drilling; pulling specialized network cabling; and learning how to configure TCP/IP, IPX, or NetBEUI protocols.

So-called "home" networking is designed to minimize the complexities of cabling and protocol configuration by providing users with a sort of instant network that requires no additional wiring and configures with little technical understanding.

HomePNA

Other than using Ethernet, the most popular form of home networking involves adapting existing telephone wiring to networking by running network signals at frequencies above those used by the telephone system. Other, less popular forms of home networking piggyback on household or office electrical wiring or are wireless, taking advantage of previously unused parts of the electromagnetic spectrum.

Because it is the most developed and most broadly supported type of home networking, this discussion focuses on the HomePNA standards that the Home Phoneline Networking Alliance (http://www.homepna.org) has created. This alliance has most of the major computer hardware and telecommunications vendors among its founding and active membership.

A companion Web site focusing on products that use HomePNA standards is http://www.homepna.com.

The Home Phoneline Networking Alliance has developed two versions of its HomePNA standard. Both versions are designed to work over existing telephone lines, but they have big differences in speed and hardware usage.

HomePNA 1.0

The original HomePNA standard, introduced in 1998, was designed to make home networking as much of a no-brainer as possible. HomePNA 1.0 has a speed of just 1Mbps, which is just 1/10 the speed of 10BASE-T or other forms of standard Ethernet. HomePNA 1.0 was designed for ease of use— rather than performance—and used parallel ports, USB ports, and PCI cards for use with desktop computers, and PC Card (PCMCIA) devices for use with notebook computers. HomePNA 1.0 is now obsolete, having been replaced by HomePNA 2.0; HomePNA 1.0 products can be used on the same network as HomePNA 2.0 products.

HomePNA 2.0

HomePNA 2.0–compatible products began to appear in late 1999. HomePNA 2.0 runs up to 10Mbps, making it comparable to standard Ethernet speeds, and is implemented through 32-bit PCI network cards for desktop computers and PC Card devices for use with notebook computers. The newest HomePNA 2.0–compatible devices include broadband modems, Internet appliances, and broadband gateways. Some home-office computers include HomePNA 2.0 interface cards.

HomePNA 2.0–compatible products are fast enough to make Internet connection sharing a workable reality and are backward-compatible with HomePNA 1.0 products.

Powerline Networking

Although many studies suggest that home networking via power lines will be even better than telephone-line networking, until recently no widely adopted standard existed for power-line network ing. The HomePlug Powerline Alliance is an industry trade group that is developing a multi-vendor standard for Ethernet-speed (10Mbps) home networking using power lines, based on technology developed by a company called Intellon. Field tests took place in 500 households early in 2001, followed by development of certification standards for compliant products. See the www.homeplug.org Web site for the latest information.

The longtime leader in the powerline networking field, Intelogis, which sold the Passport parallel-port powerline networking device, changed its name to Inari in early 2000. Inari has focused on developing its proprietary powerline networking technology (PNT) for use by various vendors, including RCA. Products available in early 2001 use the 2Mbps IPL0201 chipset, but Inari is also developing a 12Mbps chipset for future products. Inari's products are not compatible with the HomePlug Powerline Alliance standards.

At this point, I don't recommend powerline networks because of their slow performance and lack of a mature standard.Home Networking Compared to Ethernet UTP Solutions

The pricing of home networks is comparable to Ethernet UTP solutions, but which one is best for you? Use Table 20.15 to help you determine which way to go in networking your small office or home office. Networks are listed in order of speed, from slowest to fastest.

Table 20.15   Comparing Home Networking to Ethernet UTP Networking—Hardware

Network Type	Cable Type	USB?	PCI Card?	ISA Card?	Notebook PC Card?	Speed
Ethernet 10BASE-T	UTP	Yes	Yes	Yes	Yes	10Mbps
HomePNA 2.0	Phone	Yes	Yes	No	Yes	10Mbps
Fast Ethernet 100BASE-TX	UTP	Yes	Yes	No	Yes	100Mbps

In addition to speed and cable types, consider the issue of interconnecting a HomePNA network to a standard Ethernet network. You'll need a special PC Card or a HomePNA/Ethernet hub to interconnect the two networks, and many products of this type support only HomePNA 1.0 1Mbps speeds. You can't simply install HomePNA networking software onto a system that already has standard networking software installed; they aren't designed to coexist.

I recommend HomePNA 2.0–compatible networking for use only in a home-office environment in which technical expertise is scant and installing UTP wiring is out of the question. With the current rock-bottom pricing of Fast Ethernet 100BASE-TX NICs and hubs, Fast Ethernet is very close to the pricing of HomePNA 2.0 products, offers 10 times the speed, and has compatibility with a broad range of network protocols.

Putting Your Network Together

You've bought or built your cables. bought your NICs and your hub. and located your Windows 9x/Me or Windows NT/2000 CD-ROM. Now it's time to make your network a reality!

Installing a NIC

First, you must install your NICs into each computer. Install the NIC just like you would any other PCI or ISA device as explained here:

1. Open the case and locate an open expansion slot that matches the type of NIC you purchased (preferably PCI).
2. Using a screwdriver, remove the screw securing the slot cover at the rear of the case.
3. Insert the card gently, ensuring that the edge connector is seated solidly in the slot.
4. Fasten down the card with the same screw that held the slot cover.

Tip

If you are a realist like me, you might not want to close the case until you are certain the NIC is working (see the section "Testing Your Connections" later in the chapter).

A NIC uses the same hardware configuration settings most other expansion cards use:

- An IRQ
- An I/O port address range

Note

Some older network cards might require an upper memory block range for RAM buffers. Cards used on diskless workstations use a boot ROM, which also requires an upper memory block range. See your network card's documentation to find
out whether this issue applies to you.

If you are using Windows 9x, Me, or 2000 with a PnP (Plug and Play) BIOS and a PnP NIC, the computer and Windows configure your card for you in most cases. In a few cases, you might need to
adjust PnP settings in the BIOS, and in a rare case you might even need to remove your other PnP
cards and put the NIC in first if your system doesn't recognize it after you restart the system.

Even if you are installing a standard Ethernet 10BASE-T system, use PCI NICs whenever possible
(you'll need to use PCI NICs for faster versions of Ethernet on desktop computers). As you saw earlier,
PCI is faster than ISA by a wide margin.

If you install the card in a non-PnP system or under Windows NT, be sure the card comes with configuration software or manual switch settings for hardware configuration. A pure PnP card can't be
installed on a system that lacks PnP support.

Testing Your Connections

The configuration software disk or CD-ROM usually features diagnostic software. Some diagnostics
should be performed before the card is connected to the network and should be run from an MS-DOS
prompt.

After the NIC passes these tests, connect the network cable from the card to the hub, turn on the
computer and the hub, and watch for signal lights to light up on the NIC's back bracket (if so
equipped) and on the hub. Many hubs use green LEDs to indicate the presence of a computer on a
particular RJ-45 port. Connect a second computer with NIC installed to the hub. Then, run the diagnostics program on both computers to send and receive data.

Installing Networking Software

To access network resources with a PC—whether it is connected to a client/server or a peer-to-peer
network—you must install network client software on the computer. The network client can be part
of the operating system or a separate product, but it is this software that enables the system to use the
network interface adapter to communicate with other machines.

On a properly configured network workstation, accessing network resources is no different from
accessing local ones (except that they might be slightly slower). You can open a file on a network
drive just as you would open the same file on your local hard disk. This is because the network client
software is completely integrated into every level of the computer's operating system.

In most cases, the network client software is part of the operating system. Windows 9x, NT, and 2000,
for example, include all the software you need to participate in a peer-to-peer Windows network or to
connect to Windows NT, Windows 2000, and Novell NetWare servers. To connect to a network using
DOS or Windows 3.1, however, you must install a separate client software package.

When you install a NIC under Windows 95 or Windows 98, the following network protocols are
installed by default:

- NetBEUI
- TCP/IP
- IPX/SPX

Windows Me and Windows 2000 use TCP/IP by default. If you need to install particular protocols or other network components, use the Networks icon in the Windows Control Panel or right-click the Network Neighborhood (Windows 9x) or My Network Places (Windows Me/2000) icon on the Windows desktop and select Properties.

Configuring Your Network Software

You might have a few problems installing your NICs. Your NICs might pass their diagnostics flawlessly, but until each station on your network can speak the same language, has correct client or server software setups, and uses the same protocols, your network will not function properly.

Table 20.16 shows the minimum network software configuration you must install for Windows 9x/Me, Windows NT, and Windows 2000 peer-to-peer networking.

Table 20.16   Minimum Network Software for Peer-to-Peer Networking

Item	Workstation	Server
Windows Network client	Yes	No
NetBEUI protocol	Yes	Yes
File and print sharing for Microsoft Networks	No	Yes
NIC installed and bound to protocols and services above	Yes	Yes
Workgroup identification (same for all PCs in workgroup)	Yes	Yes
Computer name (each PC needs a unique name)	Yes	Yes

Depending on how you plan to use the computer, one or both of the following must be done:

■ If the computer will access a Novell NetWare client/server network, the IPX/SPX protocol must also be installed.

■ If the computer will be used to access the Internet or any other TCP/IP-based network, the TCP/IP protocol must also be installed.

Use the Network icon in the Windows Control Panel to select your network settings. You'll need the following software to set up the network:

■ Operating system CDs, disks, or hard-disk image files

■ NIC drivers

(Workgroup hubs and switches require no software.)

To install a network component, follow this procedure with Windows 9x:

1. Open the Network icon in the Control Panel.

2. The Configuration tab is displayed; select Add.

3. Select from the following:

 • *Client.* Select if you want to install the Microsoft or other network clients for your network. Every PC on a peer-to-peer network needs the Client for Microsoft Networks.

 • *Adapter.* This should already be installed, but you can use this to install a new adapter.

 • *Protocol.* For a simple, non-Internet network, install NetBEUI. If you want to use Internet Connection Sharing along with networking, install both TCP/IP and NetBEUI.

 • *Service.* Install File and Printer Sharing for Microsoft Networks on any computer that will be used as a server.

4. Click the Identification tab. Enter a unique name for each computer on the network; use the same workgroup name for all computers on the network.

5. Click OK. Supply the Windows CD-ROM or other media as necessary to install the network components you requested.

6. You are prompted to insert a CD or disk or browse to the appropriate files during the installation procedure, if they're not available on the Windows 9x CD-ROM or on your hard disk in the default location.

You must reboot your PC to complete the process. After this is completed, you'll be ready to share resources.

Configuring Users, Groups, and Resources

Depending on the network operating system software you choose, you can control access in a variety of ways.

Peer-to-Peer Access Control

Peer-to-peer Windows 9x–style networking (which can also be used by Windows for Workgroups, Windows NT, Windows Me, and Windows 2000 Professional) provides access control on a resource-by-resource basis, if desired, through the use of passwords. Passwords are optional.

Caution

If no password is used, anyone who accesses the network has full control over the shared resource.

Windows 2000 Professional and Windows NT will allow you to manage connections by user if you desire.

Client/Server Access Control

Client/server-based networks, such as Windows NT, Windows 2000 Server, and Novell NetWare, control resources on a user-permission or group-permission basis.

Caution

If the user is not listed as a permitted user or is not part of a permitted group, the user *cannot* access the shared resource.

Comparing Peer-to-Peer and Client/Server Access Control

The following example demonstrates the differences in these approaches:

- Users 1, 2, 3, and 4 need to access a CD-ROM drive, two network hard drives, a laser printer, and an inkjet printer.

- Users 1 and 4 need read/write/create access to the \Msoffice folder on hard disk #1 and access to the laser printer. User 4 also needs read-only access to the \Photoshop folder on hard disk #2 and access to the inkjet printer.

- User 3 needs read-only access to the \Msoffice folder on hard disk #1, read/write/create access to the \Photoshop folder on hard disk #2, and access to the inkjet printer.

- User 2 needs access to the laser printer only.

To limit usage, passwords *must* be used; otherwise, all users on the network can access any resource.

With a peer-to-peer network, the security settings that would be required to secure the resources are shown in Table 20.17.

Table 20.17   Peer-to-Peer Security Settings

Resource	Passwords	Reason for Second Password
CD-ROM	One	
\Msoffice	Two	One password for full access; one password for read-only access
\Photoshop	Two	One password for full access; one password for read-only access
Laser printer	One	
Inkjet printer	One	

This means that there are a total of seven passwords on the system. The number of passwords needed by each user would be as follows:

- *User 1.* Two passwords needed
- *User 2.* One password needed
- *User 3.* Three passwords needed
- *User 4.* Four passwords needed

This simple example demonstrates the not-so-simple problem of trying to control network resources. The Windows 9x–type peer-to-peer network has no way to create user lists or group permissions and therefore must assign a password to every resource. Even if all the users can remember their passwords (or store them in a password list), the challenge isn't over. Suppose the passwords are revealed to others who shouldn't have access. The authorized users must memorize up to four additional (new) passwords after the passwords are changed, assuming that the unauthorized users don't take over the system first.

In addition to the limitations of what Microsoft calls share-level access control, another flaw in the peer-to-peer network scheme is that nobody is really in charge of the network. There is no administrator or "superuser" who can set up and change passwords for all resources. Instead, the user of the computer with the shared resource can add, change, or delete shared resource settings unless user profiles are set up on each machine that eliminate access to the Windows Explorer and Printers folder for the normal user(s) of that computer.

With a client/server network, a network administrator assigns a single password to each user. These users can be divided into groups based on similar access needs. Using the previous example, this scenario would create security settings that look like the ones in Tables 20.18 and 20.19.

Table 20.18   Client/Server Network Sample Groups

User	Groups Belonged To
User 1	OfficeCreate, Laserprinter
User 2	Laserprinter
User 3	OfficeRead, PhotoCreate, Inkjet
User 4	OfficeCreate, Laserprinter, PhotoRead, Inkjet

Table 20.19   Client/Server Network Sample Security

Group	Rights	Members
Laserprinter	Use	User 2, User 1, User 4
Inkjet	Use	User 4, User 3

Table 20.19   Continued

Group	Rights	Members
OfficeCreate	Read, write, create	User 1, User 4
OfficeRead	Read	User 3
PhotoCreate	Read, write, create	User 3
PhotoRead	Read	User 4
Administrator	Full network control	

Although the client/server network looks more complex at first glance, it's actually an easier and more secure network to control. It's easier to control because each user has a single password, regardless of the number of resources she will access. It's easier to administer because rights can be changed for an entire group or for any member(s) of a group. It's more secure because a full-time network administrator is able to set up and control all user and group rights to access all network devices. It's also more secure because access rights can be controlled more precisely than with a peer-to-peer network's full access, read-only access, or no access options. Because users can have read/write/create but not delete access to a specified resource, a program can be used without the possibility of its being deleted by the user.

This discussion is not designed to minimize the benefits of peer-to-peer networking. Fast, easy to set up, and flexible, peer-to-peer networking should be used in situations in which low cost is an important factor and security is a relatively unimportant concern; many small networks use it successfully. If security and performance are important, though, use a client/server network instead.

Note

To learn more about client/server networking, see *Upgrading and Repairing Networks, 3rd Edition*, published by Que.

Tips and Tricks

Use this section to help you find faster, easier, and better ways to set up and use your network.

Installation

■ If you are setting up several systems with identical hardware, NICs, and software, consider making an image file of the first system after you complete its installation with a program such as Drive Image Professional and then connecting the other computers and "cloning" the first computer's hard disk to each additional system. Check with the imaging software vendor for details.

■ Don't click OK in the Windows Networks properties sheet until you have made all the changes you want to make (see the previous list). Whenever you click OK, you are prompted to reboot the system to apply the changes.

■ If you're salvaging old 10BASE-T Ethernet cards for a network, use Category 5 UTP and dual-speed hubs to make switching to Fast Ethernet in the future easier.

Sharing Resources

■ If you want to have network drives or folders show up as part of My Computer so you can search them and see them easily in Windows Explorer, map a drive letter to each one.

■ To make keeping drive mappings straight easier, I use the drive letter I plan to use for mapping on other workstations as the name of the shared resource on my peer server. In other words, if I want to map the D: drive on my peer server as "P:", I name it "P" when I set its sharing properties. Then, as I view the folder from another computer, I know from its name that I should map it as "P:". This enables multiple PCs to easily map the same resource as the same drive letter on different systems, which makes it easier if people in your office play musical computers.

Setting Up Security

- If you're building a peer-to-peer network, keep in mind that passwords are the only way to keep unwanted users out of your system.

Sharing Internet Connections

- If you are planning to share an Internet connection, *don't* set up File and Printer Sharing on the computer that does the sharing (the proxy server). See Chapter 19, "Internet Connectivity," for software you can add to your computer to keep your computer safe on the Internet.

Direct Cable Connections

Direct Cable Connection is a technology that enables you to connect two PCs together via their serial, parallel, or IR ports to make an instant network. Windows 9x , Me, and 2000 all include Direct Connect client and server software, but special parallel (preferred) or serial cables are required. See *Upgrading and Repairing PCs, 12th Edition*, included on this book's CD-ROM, for details.

Troubleshooting a Network

The following sections list a series of common networking problems along with solutions that can usually set things right again.

Network Software Setup

Problem

Duplicate computer IDs.

Solution

Make sure that every computer on the network has a unique ID (use Control Panel, Network, Identification to view this information). Otherwise, you'll get an error message when you reboot the workstations with networking cables attached.

Problem

Different workgroup names.

Solution

Make sure every computer that's supposed to be working together has the same workgroup name. The Windows 9x/NT Network Neighborhood displays computers by workgroup name. Different workgroup names actually create different workgroups, and you'd need to access them by browsing via Entire Network. This wastes time.

Problem

Shared resources not available.

Solution

Make sure that shared resources have been set for any servers on your network (including peer servers on Windows 9x). If you can't share a resource through Windows Explorer on the peer server, ensure that File and Printer Sharing has been installed.

Problem

Network doesn't work after making changes.

Solution

Did you reboot? Any change in the Network icon in Windows 9x/Me Control Panel requires a system reboot!

Did you log in? Any network resources can't be accessed unless you log in when prompted. You can use Start, Shutdown, and Close All Programs and Logon as a New User to recover quickly from a failure to log on.

Networks in Use

Problem

A user can't access any shared resources (but others can).

Solution

First, have user use Start, Close All Programs and Logon as a New User. Pressing Cancel or Esc instead of logging in would keep a user off the network.

Next, check cable connections at the server and workstation. Loose terminators or BNC T-connectors can cause trouble for all workstations on a Thinnet cable segment. A loose or disconnected RJ-45 cable affects only the computer (or hub) using it.

Problem

Wrong access level.

Solution

If you save your passwords in a password cache, entering the read-only password instead of the full-access password limits your access with peer servers. Try unsharing the resource and try to reshare it, or have the user of that peer server set up new full-access and read-only passwords. Alternatively, don't use password caching by unchecking the Save Password box when you log on to a shared resource. With a client/server network with user lists and rights, check with your network administrator because she will need to change the rights for you.

TCP/IP

Problem

Incorrect settings in Network Properties.

Solution

Get the correct TCP/IP settings from the administrator and enter them; restart the PC.

Problem

Can't keep connection running in Dial-Up Networking.

Solution

You might have the wrong version of PPP running (classic CompuServe uses CISPPP instead of normal PPP); change the server type in Properties under Dial-Up Networking, not Networks.

Problem

Message about duplicate IP addresses—can't connect to anything.

Solution

Duplicate IP addresses disable both TCP/IP and NetBEUI networking. If you're trying to share your Internet connection, use software such as Artisoft's Ishare, or check with your networking hardware vendor for recommendations. If your LAN uses a proxy server for connection, some sharing products might not work. A proxy server serves as a middle ground between your Internet client and the Internet. Any requests for data on the Internet are routed to the proxy server, which then fetches the data from the Internet. When your station receives the data, it's actually coming from the proxy server. Proxy servers are used by corporate networks along with security software to prevent outside access to the corporate network, as well as by filtered Internet services such as Integrity Online.

CHAPTER 21

Power Supply and Chassis/Case

Considering the Importance of the Power Supply

The power supply is not only one of the most important parts in a PC, but it is unfortunately also the most overlooked. In the words of a famous comedian, the power supply gets no respect! People spend hours discussing their processor speeds, memory capacity, disk storage capacity and speed, video adapter performance, monitor size, and so forth, but rarely even mention or consider their power supply. When a system is put together to meet the lowest possible price point, what component do you think the manufacturer will skimp on? Yes, the power supply. To most people, the power supply is a rather nondescript, unglamorous metal box that sits inside their systems, something to which they pay virtually no attention at all. The few who do pay any mind seem concerned only with how many watts of power it is rated to put out (even though no practical way exists to verify those ratings), without regard as to whether the power being produced is clean and stable, or whether it is full of noise, spikes, and surges.

I have always placed great emphasis on selecting a power supply for my systems. I consider the power supply the core of the system and am willing to spend more to get a better unit. The power supply function is critical because it supplies electrical power to every other component in the system. In my experience, the power supply is also one of the most failure-prone components in any computer system, especially due to the fact that so many system assemblers use the cheapest ones they can find. A malfunctioning power supply can not only cause other components in the system to malfunction, but it also can damage the other components in your computer by delivering an improper or erratic voltage. Because of its importance to proper and reliable system operation, you should understand both the function and limitations of a power supply, as well as its potential problems and their solutions.

This chapter covers the power supply in detail. I focus on the electrical functions of the supply and the mechanical form factors and physical designs that have been used in PC systems in the past, as well as today. Because the physical shape (form factor) of the power supply relates to the case, some of this information also relates to the type of chassis or case you have.

Primary Function and Operation

The basic function of the power supply is to convert the type of electrical power available at the wall socket to the type the computer circuitry can use. The power supply in a conventional desktop system is designed to convert either 115-volt (nominal) 60Hz AC (alternating current) or 230V (nominal) 50Hz AC power into +3.3V, +5V, and +12V DC (direct current) power. Some power supplies require you to switch between the two input ranges, whereas others auto-switch.

Positive DC Voltages

Usually, the digital electronic components and circuits in the system (motherboard, adapter cards, and disk drive logic boards) use the +3.3V or +5V power, and the motors (disk drive motors and any fans) use the +12V power. Table 21.1 lists these devices and their power consumptions.

Table 21.1 Power Consumption Ratings for PC Devices

Voltage	Devices Powered
+3.3V	Chipsets, DIMMs, PCI/AGP cards, miscellaneous chips
+5V	Disk drive logic, SIMMs, PCI/AGP cards, ISA cards, voltage regulators, miscellaneous chips
+12V	Motors, voltage regulators (high output)

The power supply must deliver a good, steady supply of DC power so that the system can operate properly. Devices that run on voltages other than these must be powered by onboard voltage regulators. For example, RIMMs run on 2.5V that is supplied by an onboard regulator, and processors are supplied by a voltage regulator module (VRM) that normally is built into the motherboard as well.

Note

When Intel began releasing processors that required a +3.3V power source, power supplies that supplied the additional output voltage were not yet available. As a result, motherboard manufacturers began adding voltage regulators to their boards, which converted +5V current to +3.3V for the processor. When other chips began using 3.3V as well, Intel created the ATX power supply specification, which supplied 3.3V to the motherboard. DIMMs (Dual In-line Memory Modules) also run on +3.3V as supplied by the power supply. You would think that having 3.3V direct from the power supply would have eliminated the need for onboard voltage regulators, but by that time, processors began running on a wide variety of voltages lower than 3.3V. Motherboard manufacturers then included adaptable regulator circuits called Voltage Regulator Modules (VRMs) to accommodate the widely varying processor voltage requirements.

◄◄ See "CPU Operating Voltages," p. 97.

Negative DC Voltages

If you look at a specification sheet for a typical PC power supply, you can see that the supply generates not only +3.3V, +5V, and +12V, but also –5V and –12V. The positive voltages seemingly power everything in the system (logic and motors), so what are the negative voltages used for? The answer is, not much! Some of the power supply designs, such as the SFX (Small form factor) design, no longer include the –5V output for that reason. The only reason it has remained in most power supply designs is that –5V is required on the Industry Standard Architecture (ISA) bus for full backward-compatibility.

Although –5V and –12V are supplied to the motherboard via the power supply connectors, the motherboard normally uses only the +3.3V, +5V, and +12V. The –5V is simply routed to the ISA bus on pin B5 so any ISA cards can use it. Today, though, not many do. However, as an example, the analog data separator circuits found in older floppy controllers do use –5V.

The motherboard logic normally doesn't use –12V either; however, it might be used in some board designs for serial port or LAN circuits.

Note

The load placed on the −12V output by an integrated LAN adapter is very small. For example, the integrated 10/100 Ethernet adapter in the Intel D815EEAL motherboard uses only 10mA of +12V and 10mA of −12V (0.01 amps each) to operate.

Although older serial port circuits used +/–12V outputs, today most run on only +3.3V or +5V.

The main function of the +12V power is to run disk drive motors as well as the higher-output processor voltage regulators in some of the newer boards. Usually, a large amount of +12V current is available from the power supply, especially in those designed for systems with a large number of drive bays (such as in a tower configuration). Besides disk drive motors and newer CPU voltage regulators, the +12V supply is used by any cooling fans in the system—which, of course, should always be running. A single cooling fan can draw between 100mA and 250mA (0.1–0.25 amps); however, most newer fans use the lower 100mA figure. Note that although most fans in desktop systems run on +12V, portable systems can use fans that run on +5V, or even +3.3V.

Most systems with newer motherboard form factors, such as the ATX, micro-ATX, or NLX, include another special signal. This feature, called PS_ON, can be used to turn the power supply (and thus the system) on or off via software. It is sometimes known as the *soft-power feature*. PS_ON is most evident when you use it with an operating system, such as Windows 9x, that supports the Advanced Power Management (APM) or Advanced Configuration and Power Interface (ACPI) specification. When you select the Shut Down the Computer option from the Start menu, Windows automatically turns off the computer after it completes the OS shutdown sequence. A system without this feature only displays a message that it's safe to shut down the computer.

The Power_Good Signal

In addition to supplying electrical power to run the system, the power supply also ensures that the system does not run unless the power supplied is sufficient to operate the system properly. In other words, the power supply actually prevents the computer from starting up or operating until all the power supply voltages are within the proper ranges.

The power supply completes internal checks and tests before allowing the system to start. If the tests are successful, the power supply sends a special signal to the motherboard, called Power_Good. This signal must be continuously present for the system to run. Therefore, when the AC voltage dips and the power supply cannot maintain outputs within regulation tolerance, the Power_Good signal is withdrawn (goes low) and forces the system to reset. The system will not restart until the Power_Good signal returns.

The Power_Good signal (sometimes called Power_OK or PWR_OK) is a +5V (nominal) active high signal (with variation from +2.4V through +6.0V generally being considered acceptable) that is supplied to the motherboard when the power supply has passed its internal self tests and the output voltages have stabilized. This normally takes place anywhere from 100ms to 500ms (0.1–0.5 seconds) after you turn on the power supply switch. The power supply then sends the Power_Good signal to the motherboard, where the processor timer chip that controls the reset line to the processor receives it.

In the absence of Power_Good, the timer chip holds the reset line on the processor, which prevents the system from running under bad or unstable power conditions. When the timer chip receives the Power_Good signal, it releases the reset, and the processor begins executing whatever code is at address FFFF:0000 (usually the ROM BIOS).

If the power supply cannot maintain proper outputs (such as when a brownout occurs), the Power_Good signal is withdrawn, and the processor is automatically reset. When the power output returns to its proper levels, the power supply regenerates the Power_Good signal and the system again begins operation (as if you had just powered on). By withdrawing Power_Good before the output voltages fall out of regulation, the system never sees the bad power because it is stopped quickly (reset) rather than being allowed to operate using unstable or improper power levels, which can cause memory parity errors and other problems.

Note

You can use the Power_Good feature as a method of implementing a reset switch for the PC. The Power_Good line is wired to the clock generator circuit, which controls the clock and reset lines to the microprocessor. When you ground the Power_Good line with a switch, the timer chip and related circuitry reset the processor. The result is a full hardware reset of the system. *Upgrading and Repairing PCs, 6th Edition*, which is located on this book's CD, contains instructions for making and installing a reset switch.

◄◄ See "Parity and ECC," p. 443.

On pre-ATX systems, the Power_Good connection is made via connector P8-1 (P8 Pin 1) from the power supply to the motherboard. ATX and later systems use pin 8 of the 20-pin connector, which is normally a gray wire.

A well-designed power supply delays the arrival of the Power_Good signal until all the voltages stabilize after you turn on the system. Badly designed power supplies, which are found in many low-cost systems, often do not delay the Power_Good signal properly and enable the processor to start too soon. (The normal Power_Good delay is 0.1–0.5 seconds.) Improper Power_Good timing also causes CMOS memory corruption in some systems.

Note

If you find that a system consistently fails to boot up properly the first time you turn on the switch, but that it subsequently boots up if you press the reset or Ctrl+Alt+Delete warm boot command, you likely have a problem with the Power_Good timing. You should install a new, higher-quality power supply and see whether that solves the problem.

Some cheaper power supplies do not have proper Power_Good circuitry and might just tie any +5V line to that signal. Some motherboards are more sensitive to an improperly designed or improperly functioning Power_Good signal than others. Intermittent startup problems are often the result of improper Power_Good signal timing. A common example is when you replace a motherboard in a system and then find that the system intermittently fails to start properly when you turn on the power. This can be very difficult to diagnose, especially for the inexperienced technician, because the problem appears to be caused by the new motherboard. Although it seems as though the new motherboard is defective, it usually turns out that the power supply is poorly designed. It either cannot produce stable enough power to properly operate the new board or has an improperly wired or timed Power_Good signal (which is more likely). In these situations, replacing the supply with a higher-quality unit, in addition to the new motherboard, is the proper solution.

Power Supply Form Factors

The shape and general physical layout of a component is called the *form factor*. Items that share a form factor are generally interchangeable, at least as far as their sizes and fits are concerned. When designing a PC, the engineers can choose to use one of the popular standard PSU (power supply unit) form factors, or they can elect to build their own. Choosing the former means that a virtually inexhaustible supply of inexpensive replacement parts will be available in a variety of quality and power output levels. Going the custom route means additional time and expense for development. In addition, the power supply is unique to the system and available only from the original manufacturer.

If you can't tell already, I am a fan of the industry-standard form factors! Having standards and then following them allows us to upgrade and repair our systems by easily replacing physically (and electrically) interchangeable components. Having interchangeable parts means that we have a better range of choices for replacement items, and the competition makes for better pricing, too.

In the PC market, IBM originally defined the standards, and everybody else copied them. This included power supplies. All the popular PC power supply form factors up through 1995 were based on one of three IBM models, including the PC/XT, AT, and PS/2 Model 30. The interesting thing is that these three power supply definitions all had the same motherboard connectors and pinouts; where they differed was mainly in shape, maximum power output, the number of peripheral power connectors, and switch mounting. PC systems using knock-offs of one of those three designs were popular through 1996 and beyond, and some systems still use them today.

Intel gave the power supply a new definition in 1995 with the introduction of the ATX form factor. ATX became popular in 1996 and started a shift away from the previous IBM-based standards. ATX and the related standards that followed have different connectors with additional voltages and signals that allow systems with greater power consumption and additional features that would otherwise not be possible with the AT style supplies.

Technically, the power supply in your PC is described as a *constant voltage half-bridge forward converting switching power supply*:

- *Constant voltage* means that the power supply puts out the same voltage to the computer's internal components, no matter what the voltage of AC current running it or the capacity (wattage) of the power supply.

- *Half-bridge forward converting switching* refers to the design and power regulation technique used by most suppliers. This design is commonly referred to as a *switching supply*. Compared to other types of power supplies, this design provides an efficient and inexpensive power source and generates a minimum amount of heat. It also maintains a small size and a low price.

Note

Although two power supplies can share the same basic design and form factor, they can differ greatly in quality and efficiency. Later in this chapter, you'll learn about some of the features and specifications to look for when evaluating PC power supplies.

Seven main power supply physical form factors have existed that can be called industry standard. Five of these are based on IBM designs, whereas two are based on Intel designs. Of these, only three are used in most modern systems; the others are pretty much obsolete.

Note that although the names of the power supply form factors seem to be the same as those of motherboard form factors, the power supply form factor is more related to the system chassis (case) than the motherboard. That is because all the form factors use one of only two types of connector designs, either AT or ATX.

For example, all PC/XT, AT, and LPX form factor supplies use the same pair of six-pin connectors to plug into the motherboard and will therefore power any board having the same type of power connections. Plugging into the motherboard is one thing, but for the power supply to physically work in the system, it must fit the case. The bottom line is that it is up to you to make sure the power supply you purchase not only plugs into your motherboard but also fits into the chassis or case you plan to use.

Table 21.2 shows these power supply form factors, their connection types, and associated motherboards.

Table 21.2   Power Supply Connector Types and Form Factors

Obsolete PS Form Factors	Originated From	Connector Type	Associated MB Form Factors
PC/XT style	IBM PC, PC-XT (1981/1983)	AT	PC/XT, Baby-AT
AT/Desk style	IBM PC-AT (1984)	AT	Fullsize AT, Baby-AT
AT/Tower style	IBM PC-AT (1984)	AT	Fullsize AT, Baby-AT
Baby-AT style	IBM PC-AT (1984)	AT	Fullsize AT, Baby-AT
Modern PS Form Factors	**Originated From**	**Connector Type**	**Associated MB Form Factors**
LPX style*	IBM PS/2 Model 30 (1987)	AT	Baby-AT, Mini-AT, LPX
ATX style	Intel ATX, ATX12V (1985/2000)	ATX	ATX, NLX, Micro-ATX
SFX style	Intel SFX (1997)	ATX	Flex-ATX, Micro-ATX

Note: LPX is also sometimes called Slimline or PS/2.

Each of these power supply form factors is available in numerous configurations and power output levels. The LPX form factor supply had been the standard used on most systems from the late 1980s to mid-1996, when the ATX form factor started to gain in popularity. Since then, ATX has become by far the dominant form factor for power supplies, with the new SFX style being added as an ATX derivative for use in very compact systems that mainly use Flex-ATX–sized boards. The earlier IBM-derived form factors have been largely obsolete for some time now.

◄◄ See "Motherboard Form Factors," p. 194.

IBM's PC and XT systems (circa 1981 and 1983, respectively) used the same power supply form factor; the only difference was that the XT supply had more than double the power output capability. Because they were identical in external appearance and the type of connectors they used, you easily could install the higher output XT supply as an upgrade for a PC system; thus, the idea of upgrading the power supply was born. The tremendous popularity of the original PC and XT systems led a number of manufacturers to begin building systems that mimicked their shapes and layouts. These clones—or compatibles—as they have been called, could interchange virtually all components with the IBM systems, including the power supply. Numerous manufacturers then began producing components that followed the form factor of these systems. The PC/XT power supply and connectors are shown in Figure 21.1. This form factor, however, is not used in modern systems today.

Figure 21.1   PC/XT form factor power supply.

AT/Desk Style

The AT desktop system introduced by IBM in August 1984, had a larger power supply and a form factor different from the original PC/XT. This system was rapidly cloned by other manufacturers and represented the basis for many subsequent IBM-compatible designs. The power supply used in these systems was called the AT/Desktop-style power supply (see Figure 21.2). Hundreds of manufacturers began making motherboards, power supplies, cases, and other components that were physically interchangeable with the original IBM AT. This form factor is no longer used today.

Figure 21.2   AT/Desktop form factor power supply.

AT/Tower Style

The AT/Tower configuration was basically a full-sized, AT-style desktop system running on its side. The tower configuration was not new; in fact, even IBM's original AT had a specially mounted logo that could be rotated when you ran the system on its side in the tower configuration.

The type of power supply used in most of the AT tower systems was identical to that used in a desktop system, except for the location of the power switch. On the original AT/Desktop systems, the power switch was built into the side of the power supply (usually in the form of a large toggle switch). AT/Tower systems instead used an external switch attached to the power supply through a four-wire cable. A full-sized AT power supply with a remote switch is called an AT/Tower form factor power supply and is identical to the AT/Desktop supply in size and dimensions. The only difference is the use of an external switch (see Figure 21.3). This form factor is still used today in large server chassis that run AT form factor motherboards.

Baby-AT Style

Another type of AT-based form factor is the so-called Baby-AT, which is a shortened version of the full-sized AT form factor. The power supply in these systems is shortened in one dimension but matches the AT design in all other respects. Baby-AT–style power supplies could fit in place of the larger AT/Desktop style supply; however, the full-sized AT/Tower supply would not fit in the Baby-AT chassis (see Figure 21.4). Because the Baby-AT PSU performed the same functions as the AT-style power supply but was in a smaller package, it became a common form factor until it was overtaken by later designs. This form factor is rarely used today.

LPX Style

The next power supply form factor to gain popularity was the LPX style, also called the PS/2 type, Slimline, or slim style (see Figure 21.5). The LPX-style power supply has the exact same motherboard and disk drive connectors as the previous standard power supply form factors; it differs mainly in the shape. LPX systems were designed to have a smaller footprint and a lower height than AT-sized systems. These computers used a different motherboard configuration that mounts the expansion bus slots on a "riser" card that plugs into the motherboard. The expansion cards plug into this riser and are mounted sideways in the system, parallel to the motherboard. Because of its smaller case, an LPX system needed a smaller power supply. The power supply designed for LPX systems is smaller than the Baby-AT style in every dimension and takes up less than half the space of its predecessor.

Figure 21.3 AT/Tower form factor power supply.

Figure 21.4 Baby-AT form factor power supply.

Note

IBM used this type of power supply in some of its PS/2 systems in the late 1980s; hence it is sometimes called a PS/2-type supply.

5.9"x5.5"x3.4"

Figure 21.5 LPX form factor power supply.

As with the Baby-AT design in its time, the LPX power supply does the same job as its predecessor but comes in a smaller package. The LPX power supply quickly found its way into many manufacturers' systems, soon becoming a de facto standard. This style of power supply became the staple of the industry for many years, coming in everything from low-profile systems using actual LPX mother-boards to full-size towers using Baby-AT or even full-size AT motherboards. It still is used in some PCs produced today; however, since 1996 the popularity of LPX has been overshadowed by the increasing popularity of the ATX design.

ATX Style

One of the newer standards in the industry today is the ATX form factor (see Figure 21.6). The ATX specification, now in version 2.03, defines a new motherboard shape, as well as a new case and power supply form factor.

The shape of the ATX power supply is based on the LPX design, but some important differences are worth noting.

One difference is that the ATX specification originally called for the fan to be mounted along the inner side of the supply, where it could draw air in from the rear of the chassis and blow it inside across the motherboard. This kind of airflow runs in the opposite direction as most standard supplies, which exhaust air out the back of the supply through a hole in the case where the fan protrudes. The idea was that the reverse flow design could cool the system more efficiently with only a single fan, eliminating the need for a fan (active) heatsink on the CPU.

Another benefit of the reverse-flow cooling is that the system would run cleaner, more free from dust and dirt. The case would be pressurized, so air would be continuously forced out of the cracks in the case—the opposite of what happens with a negative pressure design. For this reason, the reverse-flow cooling design is often referred to as a positive-pressure-ventilation design. On an ATX system with reverse-flow cooling, the air would be blown out away from the drive because the only air intake would be the single fan vent on the power supply at the rear. For systems that operate in extremely harsh environments, you can add a filter to the fan intake vent to further ensure that all the air entering the system is clean and free of dust.

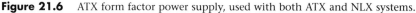

Figure 21.6 ATX form factor power supply, used with both ATX and NLX systems.

Although this sounds like a good way to ventilate a system, the positive-pressure design needs to use a more powerful fan to pull the required amount of air through a filter and to pressurize the case. Also, if a filter is used, it must be serviced on a periodic basis—depending on operating conditions, it can need changing or cleaning as often as every week. In addition, the heat load from the power supply on a fully loaded system heats up the air being ingested, blowing warm air over the CPU, reducing overall cooling capability. As newer CPUs create more and more heat, the cooling capability of the system becomes more critical. In common practice, it was found that using a standard negative-pressure system with an exhaust fan on the power supply and an additional high-quality cooling fan blowing cool air right on the CPU is the best solution. For this reason, the ATX power supply specification has been amended to allow for either positive- or negative-pressure ventilation.

Because a standard negative-pressure system offers the most cooling capacity for a given fan airspeed and flow, most of the newer ATX-style power supplies use the negative-pressure cooling system.

The ATX specification was first released by Intel in 1995. In 1996, it became increasingly popular in Pentium and Pentium Pro–based PCs, capturing 18% of the motherboard market. Since 1996, ATX has become the dominant motherboard form factor, displacing the previously popular Baby-AT. ATX and its derivatives are likely to remain the most popular form factor for several years to come.

The ATX form factor addressed several problems with the power supplies used with Baby-AT and mini-AT form factors. One is that the power supplies used with Baby-AT boards have two connectors that plug into the motherboard. If you insert these connectors backward or out of their normal sequence, you will fry the motherboard! Most responsible system manufacturers "key" the motherboard and power supply connectors so that you cannot install them backward or out of sequence. However, some vendors of cheaper systems do not feature this keying on the boards or supplies they use. The ATX form factor includes different power plugs for the motherboard to prevent users from plugging in their power supplies incorrectly. The ATX design features up to three motherboard power connectors that are definitively keyed, making plugging them in backward virtually impossible. The new ATX connectors also supply +3.3V, reducing the need for voltage regulators on the motherboard to power the chipset, DIMMs, and other +3.3V circuits.

Besides the new +3.3V outputs, another set of outputs is furnished by an ATX power supply that is not normally seen on standard power supplies. The set consists of the Power_On (PS_ON) and 5V_Standby (5VSB) outputs mentioned earlier, known collectively as *Soft Power*. This enables features to be implemented, such as Wake on Ring or Wake on LAN, in which a signal from a modem or network adapter can actually cause a PC to wake up and power on. Many such systems also have the option of setting a wake-up time, at which the PC can automatically turn itself on to perform scheduled tasks. These signals also can enable the optional use of the keyboard to power the system on—exactly like Apple systems. Users can enable these features because the 5V Standby power is always active, giving the motherboard a limited source of power even when off. Check your BIOS Setup for control over these features.

NLX Style

The NLX specification, also developed by Intel, defines a low-profile case and motherboard design with many of the same attributes as the ATX. In fact, for interchangeability, NLX systems were designed to use ATX power supplies, even though the case and motherboard dimensions are different.

As in previous LPX systems, the NLX motherboard uses a riser board for the expansion bus slots. Where NLX differs is that it is a true (and not proprietary) standard. See Chapter 4, "Motherboards and Buses," for more information on the NLX form factor.

For the purposes of this discussion, NLX systems use ATX power supplies. The only real difference is that the supply plugs into the riser card and not the motherboard, enabling NLX motherboards to be more quickly and easily removed from their chassis for service.

SFX Style

Intel released the smaller Micro-ATX motherboard form factor in December of 1997, and at the same time also released a new smaller SFX (Small form factor) power supply design to go with it (see Figure 21.7). Even so, most Micro-ATX chassis used the standard ATX power supply instead. Then in March of 1999, Intel released the Flex-ATX addendum to the Micro-ATX specification, which was a very small board designed for low-end PCs or PC-based appliances. At this point, the SFX supply has found use in many new compact system designs.

Figure 21.7 SFX style power supply (with 90mm top-mounted cooling fan).

The SFX power supply is specifically designed for use in small systems containing a limited amount of hardware and limited upgradability. Most SFX supplies can provide 90 watts of continuous power (135 watts at its peak) in four voltages (+5, +12, –12, and +3.3V). This amount of power has proved to be sufficient for a small system with a processor, an AGP interface, up to four expansion slots, and three peripheral devices—such as hard drives and CD-ROMs.

Although Intel designed the SFX power supply specification with the Micro-ATX and Flex-ATX motherboard form factors in mind, SFX is a wholly separate standard that is compliant with other motherboards as well. SFX power supplies use the same 20-pin connector defined in the ATX standard and include both the Power_On and 5V_Standby outputs. Whether you will use an ATX or SFX power supply in a given system is dependent more on the case or chassis than the motherboard. Each has the same basic electrical connectors; the main difference is which type of power supply the case is physically designed to accept.

One limiting factor on the SFX design is that it lacks the –5V and so shouldn't be used with motherboards that have ISA slots (most Micro-ATX and Flex-ATX boards do NOT have ISA slots). SFX power supplies also won't have the Auxiliary (3.3V and 5V) or ATX12V power connectors, and therefore shouldn't be used with full-size ATX boards that require those connections.

On a standard model SFX power supply, a 60mm diameter cooling fan is located on the surface of the housing, facing the inside of the computer's case. The fan draws the air into the power supply housing from the system cavity and expels it through a port at the rear of the system. Internalizing the fan in this way reduces system noise and results in a standard negative-pressure design. In many cases, additional fans might be needed in the system to cool the processor (see Figure 21.8).

Figure 21.8   SFX form factor power supply dimensions with a standard internal 60mm fan.

For systems that require more cooling capability, a version that allows for a larger 90mm top-mounted cooling fan also is available. The larger fan provides more cooling capability and airflow for systems that need it (see Figure 21.9).

Figure 21.9 SFX form factor power supply dimensions with an internal 90mm top-mounted fan.

Motherboard Power Connectors

Every PC power supply has special connectors that attach to the motherboard, giving power to the system processor, memory, and all slotted add-on boards (ISA, PCI, AGP). Attaching these connectors improperly can have a devastating effect on your PC, including burning up both your power supply and motherboard. The following sections detail the motherboard power connectors used by various power supplies.

AT Power Supply Connectors

Industry standard PC, XT, AT, Baby-AT, and LPX motherboards all use the same type of main power supply connectors. These supplies feature two main power connectors (P8 and P9), each with 6 pins that attach the power supply to the motherboard. Those two connectors are shown in Figure 21.10.

LPX/AT Main Power Connectors

Figure 21.10   AT/LPX main P8/P9 (sometimes also called P1/P2) power connectors.

All standard PC power supplies that use the P8 and P9 connectors have them installed end to end so that the two black wires (ground connections) on both power cables are next to each other. Note the designations P8 and P9 are not fully standardized, although most use those designations because that is what IBM used on the originals. Some power supplies have them labeled as P1/P2 instead. Because these connectors usually have a clasp that prevents them from being inserted backward on the pins on the motherboards, the major concern is getting the two connectors in the correct orientation side by side and also not missing a pin offset on either side. Following the black-to-black rule keeps you safe. You must take care, however, to make sure that no remaining unconnected motherboard pins exist between or on either side of the two connectors after you install them. A properly installed connector connects to and covers every motherboard power pin. If any power pins are showing on either side of the connectors, the entire connector assembly is installed incorrectly, which can result in catastrophic failure for the motherboard and everything plugged into it at the time of power-up. Figure 21.11 shows the P8 and P9 connectors (sometimes also called P1/P2) in their proper orientation when connecting.

Table 21.3 shows typical AT and LPX power supply connections.

Figure 21.11   The P8/P9 power connectors (sometimes also called P1/P2) that connect an AT/LPX power supply to the motherboard.

Table 21.3   AT/LPX Power Supply Connectors

Connector	Pin	Signal	Color	Connector	Pin	Signal	Color
P8 (or P1)	1	Power_Good (+5V)	Orange	P9 (or P2)	1	Ground	Black
	2	+5V*	Red		2	Ground	Black
	3	+12V	Yellow		3	–5V	White
	4	–12V	Blue		4	+5V	Red
	5	Ground	Black		5	+5V	Red
	6	Ground	Black		6	+5V	Red

Older PC/XT motherboards and power supplies did not use this output (P8 pin 2).

Color codes can vary from manufacturer to manufacturer;, the ones shown here are typical.

Tip

Although older PC/XT power supplies do not have any connection at connector P8 pin 2, you still can use them on AT-type motherboards, or vice versa. The presence or absence of the +5V on that pin has little or no effect on system operation because the remaining +5V wires usually can carry the load.

Note that all the power supplies from the AT/Desk through the Baby-AT and LPX power supplies use the same pin configuration.

ATX Main Power Connector

The industry standard ATX power-supply–to–motherboard main connector is the Molex 39-29-9202 (or equivalent) 20-pin ATX style connector (see Figure 21.12). First used in the ATX form factor power supply, it also is used in the SFX form factor or any other ATX-based variations. This is a 20-pin keyed connector with pins configured as shown in Table 21.4. The colors for the wires listed are those recommended by the ATX standard; however, they are not required for compliance to the specification, so they could vary from manufacturer to manufacturer. Note that I like to show these connector pinouts in a wire side view, which shows how the pins are arranged looking at the back of the connector (from the wire and not terminal side). This is because it shows how they would be oriented if you were back-probing the connector with the connector plugged in.

Figure 21.12   ATX style 20-pin motherboard main power connector, perspective view.

Figure 21.13 shows a view of the connector as if you were looking at it facing the terminal side.

Pin 1				Pin 11	
(Orange)	+3.3V			+3.3V	(Orange)
(Orange)	+3.3V			−12V	(Blue)
(Black)	GND			GND	(Black)
(Red)	+5V			PS_ON#	(Green)
(Black)	GND			GND	(Black)
(Red)	+5V			GND	(Black)
(Black)	GND			GND	(Black)
(Gray)	PWR_OK			−5V	(White)
(Purple)	+5VSB			+5V	(Red)
(Yellow)	+12V			+5V	(Red)
Pin 10				Pin 20	

ATX/NLX Main Power Connector

Figure 21.13   ATX/NLX 20-pin main power connector, terminal side view.

Table 21.4   ATX Main Power Supply Connector Pinout (Wire Side View)

Color	Signal	Pin	Pin	Signal	Color
Orange*	+3.3V	11	1	+3.3V	Orange
Blue	–12V	12	2	+3.3V	Orange
Black	GND	13	3	GND	Black
Green	PS_On	14	4	+5V	Red
Black	GND	15	5	GND	Black
Black	GND	16	6	+5V	Red
Black	GND	17	7	GND	Black
White	–5V	18	8	Power_Good	Gray
Red	+5V	19	9	+5VSB (Standby)	Purple
Red	+5V	20	10	+12V	Yellow

Might have a second orange or brown wire, used for +3.3V sense feedback—used by the power supply to monitor 3.3V regulation.

Note

The ATX supply features several voltages and signals not seen before, such as the +3.3V, PS_On, and +5V_Standby. Therefore, adapting a standard LPX form factor supply to make it work properly in an ATX system, is difficult—if not impossible—even though the shapes of the power supplies themselves are virtually identical.

However, because ATX is a superset of the older AT standard, you can use an adapter to allow an ATX power supply to connect to an older Baby-AT style motherboard. PC Power and Cooling (see the vendor list) sells this type of adapter.

ATX Auxiliary Power Connector

As motherboards and processors evolved, the need for power became greater. In particular, chipsets and DIMMs were designed to run on 3.3V, increasing the current demand at that voltage. In addition, most boards included CPU voltage regulators designed to convert +5V power into the unique voltage levels required by the processors the board supported. Eventually, the high current demands on the +3.3V and +5V outputs were proving too much for the number and gauge of the wires used. Melted connectors were becoming more and more common as these wires overheated under these loads.

Finally, Intel modified the ATX specification to add a second power connector for ATX motherboards and supplies. The criteria was that if the motherboard needed more than 18A of +3.3V power, or more than 24A of +5V power, an auxiliary connector would be defined to carry the additional load. These higher levels of power are normally necessary in systems using 250-watt to 300-watt or greater supplies.

The auxiliary connector (shown in Figure 21.14) is a 6-pin Molex-type connector, similar to one of the motherboard power connectors used on AT/LPX supplies. It is keyed to prevent misconnection.

The pinouts of the auxiliary connector are shown in Table 21.5.

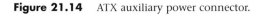

	Pin 1	GND	(Black)	
		GND	(Black)	
		GND	(Black)	
		+3.3V	(Orange)	
	Pin 6	+3.3V	(Orange)	
		+5V	(Red)	

ATX Auxiliary Power Connector

Figure 21.14   ATX auxiliary power connector.

Table 21.5   ATX Auxiliary Power Connector Pinout

Pin	Signal	Color	Pin	Signal	Color
1	Gnd	Black	4	+3.3V	Orange
2	Gnd	Black	5	+3.3V	Orange
3	Gnd	Black	6	+5V	Red

If your motherboard does not feature a mating auxiliary connector, it probably wasn't designed to consume a large amount of power, and the auxiliary connector from the power supply can be left unconnected. If your power supply is rated at 250 watts or larger, you should ensure that it has this connector and that your motherboard is capable of accepting it. This eases the load on the main power connector.

ATX12V Connector

Power for the processor comes from a device called the voltage regulator module (VRM), which is built into most modern motherboards. This device senses the CPU voltage requirements (usually via sense pins on the processor) and calibrates itself to provide the proper voltage to run the CPU. The design of a VRM enables it to run on either 5V or 12V for input power. Most have used 5V over the years, but many are now converting to 12V because of the lower current requirements at that voltage. In addition, the 5V already might be loaded by other devices, whereas, typically, only drive motors use the 12V. Whether the VRM on your board uses 5V or 12V depends on the particular motherboard or regulator design. Many modern voltage regulator ICs are designed to run on anything from a 4V to a 36V input, so it is up to the motherboard designer as to how they will be configured.

For example, I studied a system using an FIC (First International Computer) SD-11 motherboard, which used a Semtech SC1144ABCSW voltage regulator. This board design uses the +5V to convert to the lower voltage needed by the CPU. Most motherboards use voltage regulator circuits controlled by chips from Semtech (http://www.semtech.com) or Linear Technology (http://www.linear.com). You can visit their sites for more data on these chips.

That motherboard accepts an Athlon 1GHz Cartridge version (Model 2), which according to AMD has a maximum power draw of 65W and a nominal voltage requirement of 1.8V. 65W at 1.8V would equate to 36.1A of current at that voltage (volts×amps = watts). If the voltage regulator used +5V as a feed, 65W would equate to only 13A at +5V. That would assume 100% efficiency in the regulator, which is impossible. Therefore, assuming 75% efficiency (it might be better, but I like to think conservatively), there would be about 17A actual draw on the +5V due to the regulator and processor combined.

When you consider that the motherboard itself also uses some +5V power—plus ISA or PCI cards are drawing power as well—you can see how easy it is to overload the +5V lines from the supply to the motherboard.

Although most motherboard VRM designs up through the Pentium III and Athlon/Duron use 5V-based regulators, a transition is underway to use 12V-powered regulators. This is because the higher voltage will significantly reduce the current draw. As an example, using the same 65W AMD Athlon 1GHz CPU, you end up with the levels of draw at the various voltages shown in Table 21.6.

Table 21.6   Levels of Draw at Various Voltages

Watts	Volts	Amps	Amps at 75% Regulator Efficiency
65	1.8	36.1	—
65	3.3	19.7	26.3
65	5.0	13.0	17.3
65	12.0	5.4	7.2

As you can see, using 12V to power the chip results in only 5.4A of draw, or 7.2A assuming 75% efficiency on the part of the regulator.

So, modifying the motherboard VRM circuit to use the +12V power feed would seem simple. Unfortunately, the standard ATX 2.03 power supply design has only a single +12V lead in the main power connector. The auxiliary connector has no +12V leads at all, so that is no help. Pulling up to 8A more through a single 18ga. wire supplying +12V power to the motherboard is a recipe for a melted connector.

To augment the supply of +12V power to the motherboard, Intel created a new ATX12V power supply specification. This adds a third power connector, called the ATX12V connector, specifically to supply additional +12V power to the board. This connector is shown in Figure 21.15.

ATX12V Power Connector

Figure 21.15   An ATX12V power connector.

The pinout of the +12V power connector is shown in Table 21.7.

Table 21.7   ATX +12V Power Connector Pinout (Wire Side View)

Color	Signal	Pin	Pin	Signal	Color
Yellow	+12V	3	1	Gnd	Black
Yellow	+12V	4	2	Gnd	Black

If you are replacing your motherboard with a new one that requires the ATX12V connection for the CPU voltage regulator, and yet your existing power supply doesn't have that connector, an easy solution is available. Merely convert one of the peripheral power connectors to an ATX12V type.

PC Power and Cooling has released just such an adapter that can instantly make any standard ATX power supply into one with an ATX12V connector. The issue is not whether the power supply can generate the necessary 12V—that has always been available via the peripheral connectors. The ATX12V adapter shown in Figure 21.16 solves the connector problem quite nicely.

Figure 21.16 ATX12V adapter from PC Power and Cooling.

ATX Optional Connector

The ATX specification also defines an optional six-pin connector. This connector has two rows of three pins each to provide the signals and voltages. The computer can use these signals to monitor and control the cooling fan, monitor the +3.3V power to the motherboard, and provide power and grounding to IEEE 1394 (FireWire) devices.

This connector has gone through several revisions in pinout since first being published, and I have yet to see any motherboards or power supplies on the market that actually support it. In fact, the latest *ATX/ATX12V Power Supply Design Guide* published by Intel states "Details of the 2x3 'Optional Power Connector' mentioned in the ATX 2.03 Specification are omitted from this design guide until such time as the signals on that connector are more rigidly defined."

Table 21.8 lists the pinout of the optional connector as defined in the ATX 2.03 Specification.

Table 21.8   ATX Optional Power Supply Connections

Color	Signal	Pin	Pin	Signal	Color
White/Black Stripe	1394R	4	1	FanM	White
White/Red Stripe	1394V	5	2	FanC	White/Blue Stripe
	Reserved	6	3	+3.3V sense	White/Brown Stripe

The FanM signal enables the operating system to monitor the status of the power supply's cooling fan so that it can take appropriate actions, such as shutting down the system if the fan fails.

The motherboard (under operating system control) can use the FanC signal with variable voltages to control the operation of the power supply's fan, shifting it into a low power state or shutting it off completely when the system is in sleep or standby mode. The ATX standard specifies that a voltage of +1V or less indicates that the fan is to shut down, whereas +10.5V or more instructs the fan to operate at full speed. The system designer can define intermediate voltages to operate variable-speed fans at various levels. If the power supply does not include a variable-speed fan circuit, any voltage level higher than +1V on the FanC signal is interpreted as a command to run the fan at its full (and only) speed.

The 1394 connectors are for powering an optional IEEE1394 (FireWire or iLink) bus on a motherboard. The 1394V pin provides voltages from 8 to 40V to run FireWire peripherals off the bus, and the 1394R pin is a return or ground line for this power circuit. This separate power rail keeps the 1394 bus power separate from the system main power to prevent interference.

Note

The SFX specification also defines the use of a six-pin control connector, but uses it only to provide a fan control signal on one pin. The other five pins are all reserved for future use.

Dell Proprietary (Nonstandard) ATX Design

If you currently own or are considering purchasing a desktop system from Dell, you will definitely want to pay attention to this section. A potential booby trap is waiting to nail the unsuspecting Dell owner who decides to upgrade either the motherboard or power supply in his system. This hidden trap can cause the destruction of the motherboard, power supply, or both! OK, now that I have your attention, read on....

As those of you who have attended my seminars or read previous editions of this book will know, I have long been a promoter of industry-standard PCs and components and wouldn't think of purchasing a desktop PC that didn't have what I consider an industry-standard form factor motherboard, power supply, and chassis (ATX, for example). I've been down the proprietary road before with systems from Packard Bell, Compaq, IBM, and other companies that used custom, unique, or proprietary components. For example, during a momentary lapse of reason in the early '90s, I purchased a Packard Bell system. I quickly outgrew the capabilities of the system, so I thought I'd upgrade it with a new motherboard and a faster processor. It was then to my horror that I discovered that LPX systems were nonstandard. Additionally, because of riser card differences, virtually no interchangeability of motherboards, riser cards, chassis, and power supplies existed. I had what I now refer to as a "disposable PC"—the kind you can't upgrade but have to throw away instead. Suddenly, the money I thought I had saved when initially purchasing the system paled in comparison to what I'd now have to spend to completely replace it. Lesson learned.

In a similar experience, I remember paying more than $950 to IBM for a replacement 114W power supply to fit my PS/2 P75 luggable that had a power supply failure out of warranty. The supply had a totally unique shape and a weird connector I had never seen before, and no alternative choices were available from any other companies. The system wasn't even worth that much at the time, but I was using it for work and had no choice but to pay the price to get it replaced. And, of course, the replacement was the same relatively low-output 114W unit because there were simply no other versions available that would fit. Another lesson learned.

After several upgrade and repair experiences like that, I decided *never again* would I be trapped by systems using proprietary or nonstandard components. By purchasing only systems built from industry-standard parts, I could easily and inexpensively upgrade, maintain, or repair the system for many years into the future. I have been preaching the gospel of industry-standard components in my seminars and in this book ever since.

Of course, building your own system from scratch is one way to avoid proprietary components, but often that route is more costly in both time and money than purchasing a prebuilt system. And what systems should I recommend for people who want an inexpensive prebuilt system but one that uses industry-standard parts so it can be inexpensively upgraded and repaired later? Although many system vendors and assemblers exist, I've settled on companies such as Gateway, Micron, and Dell. In fact, those are really the three largest system vendors that deal direct, and they sell mostly systems that use industry-standard ATX form factor components in all their main desktop system product lines. Or so I thought.

It seems that starting after September of 1998, Dell defected from the cause of industry standardization and began using specially modified Intel-supplied ATX motherboards with custom-wired power connectors. Inevitably, they also had custom power supplies made that duplicated the nonstandard pinout of the motherboard power connectors.

An even bigger crime than simply using nonstandard power connectors is that only the pinout is nonstandard; the connectors look like and are keyed the same as is dictated by true ATX. Therefore, nothing prevents you from plugging the Dell nonstandard power supply into a new industry-standard ATX motherboard you installed in your Dell case as an upgrade, or even plugging a new upgraded industry-standard ATX power supply into your existing Dell motherboard. But mixing either a new ATX board with the Dell supply or a new ATX supply with the existing Dell board is a recipe for silicon toast. How do you like your fried chips: medium or well-done?

Frankly I'm amazed I haven't heard more about this because Dell is second only to Compaq in worldwide PC sales. I can only imagine that it is because they started using these nonstandard boards and power supplies in late 1998, and most of those systems haven't yet come due for motherboard upgrades. However, they are now passing 2 years old, which is about the time that many people consider motherboard upgrades. That is why, after discovering this information, I wanted to make it well known. I figure by getting this information out as soon as possible, I can save thousands of innocent motherboards and power supplies from instant death upon installation.

If you've already fallen victim to this nasty circumstance, believe me, I feel your pain. I discovered this the hard way as well—by frying parts. At first, I thought the upgraded power supply I installed in one of my Dell systems was bad, especially considering the dramatic way it smoked when I turned on the system: I actually saw fire through the vents! Good thing I decided to check the color codes on the connectors and verify the pinout on another Dell system by using a voltmeter before I installed and fried a second supply. I was lucky in that the smoked supply didn't take the motherboard with it; I can only surmise that the supply fried so quickly it sacrificed itself and saved the motherboard. You might not be so lucky, and in most cases I'd expect you'd fry the board and supply together.

Call me a fool, but I didn't think I'd have to check the color-coding or get out my voltmeter to verify the Dell "pseudo-ATX" power connector pinouts before I installed a new ATX supply or motherboard. You'll also find that motherboard and power supply manufacturers don't like to replace these items under warranty when they are fried in this manner due to nonstandard connector wiring.

I spoke with one of the engineers at a major power supply manufacturer and asked whether a valid technical reason (maybe some problem in the ATX specification) exists that would require Dell to use unique connector pinouts. Of course, the answer was that, no, the only reason he could imagine they did this is to lock people into purchasing replacement motherboards or power supplies from Dell. In fact, what makes this worse is that Dell uses virtually all Intel boards in their systems. One system I have uses an Intel D815EEA motherboard, which is the same board used by many of the other major system builders, including Gateway, Micron, and others. It's the same except for the power connectors, that is. The difference is that Dell has Intel custom make the boards for Dell with the nonstandard connectors. Everybody else gets virtually the same Intel boards, but with industry-standard connectors.

Tables 21.9 and 21.10 show the nonstandard Dell main and auxiliary power supply connections. This nonstandard wiring is used on Dell systems dating from after September 1998 to the present.

Table 21.9   Dell Proprietary (Nonstandard) ATX Main Power Connector Pinout (Wire Side View)

Color	Signal	Pin	Pin	Signal	Color
Gray	PS_On	11	1	+5V	Red
Black	Gnd	12	2	Gnd	Black
Black	Gnd	13	3	+5V	Red
Black	Gnd	14	4	Gnd	Black
White	−5V	15	5	Power_Good	Orange
Red	+5V	16	6	+5VSB (standby)	Purple
Red	+5V	17	7	+12V	Yellow
Red	+5V	18	8	−12V	Blue
KEY (blank)	—	19	9	Gnd	Black
Red	+5V	20	10	Gnd	Black

Table 21.10   Dell Proprietary (Nonstandard) ATX Auxiliary Power Connector Pinout

Pin	Signal	Color	Pin	Signal	Color
1	Gnd	Black	4	+3.3	Blue/White
2	Gnd	Black	5	+3.3	Blue/White
3	Gnd	Black	6	+3.3	Blue/White

At first I thought that if all they did was switch some of the terminals around, I could use a terminal pick to remove the terminals from the connectors (with the wires attached) and merely reinsert them into the proper connector positions, enabling me to use the Dell power supply with an upgraded ATX motherboard in the future. Unfortunately, if you study the Dell main and auxiliary connector pinouts I've listed here and compare them to the industry-standard ATX pinouts listed earlier, you'll see that not only are the voltage and signal positions changed, but the number of terminals carrying specific voltages and grounds has changed as well. You could modify a Dell supply to work with a standard ATX board or modify a standard ATX supply to work with a Dell board, but you'd have to do some cutting and splicing in addition to swapping some terminals around. Usually, it isn't worth the time and effort.

If you do decide to upgrade the motherboard in your Dell system (purchased on or after 09/98), a simple solution is available—just make sure you replace both the motherboard AND power supply with industry-standard ATX components at the same time. That way nothing gets fried, and you'll be back to having a true industry-standard ATX system. If you want to replace just the Dell motherboard, you're out of luck unless you get your replacement board from Dell. On the other hand, if you want to replace just the power supply, you do have one alternative. PC Power and Cooling now makes a version of its high-performance 300W ATX power supply with the modified Dell wiring for about $110. Note that the internals are identical to their industry-standard, high-performance 300W ATX supply (approximately $84), only the number and arrangement of wires has changed.

For the time being, I'm suspending any Dell purchase recommendations until Dell moves back into the fold of true industry standardization. Fortunately, others, such as Gateway and Micron, have remained true to the industry standard.

Power Switch Connectors

Three main types of power switches are used on PCs. They can be described as follows:

- Integral Power Supply AC switch
- Front Panel Power Supply AC switch
- Front Panel Motherboard Controlled switch

The earliest systems had power switches integrated or built directly into the power supply, which turned the main AC power to the system on and off. This was a simple design, but because the power supply was mounted to the rear or side of the system, it required reaching around to the back to actuate the switch. Also, switching the AC power directly meant the system couldn't be remotely started without special hardware.

Starting in the late '80s systems began using remote front panel switches. These were essentially the same power supply design as the first type. The only difference is that the AC switch was now mounted remotely (usually on the front panel of the chassis), rather than integrated in the power supply unit, and connected to the power supply via a four-wire cable. The ends of the cable are fitted with spade connector lugs, which plug onto the spade connectors on the power switch. The cable from the power supply to the switch in the case contains four color-coded wires. In addition, a fifth wire supplying a ground connection to the case might be included. The switch was usually included with the power supply and heavily shrink-wrapped or insulated where the connector lugs attached to prevent electric shock.

This solved the ergonomic problem of reaching the switch, but it still didn't enable remote or automated system power-up without special hardware. Plus, you now had a 120V AC switch mounted in the chassis, with wires carrying dangerous voltage through the system. Some of these wires are hot anytime the system is plugged in (all are hot with the system turned on), creating a dangerous environment for the average person when messing around inside her system.

Caution

At least two of the remote power switch leads to a remote mounted AC power switch in an AT/LPX supply are energized with 115V AC current at all times. You could be electrocuted if you touch the ends of these wires with the power supply plugged in, even if the unit is turned off! For this reason, always make sure the power supply is unplugged before connecting or disconnecting the remote power switch or touching any of the wires connected to it.

The four or five wires are color-coded as follows:

- *Brown and blue.* These wires are the live and neutral feed wires from the 110V power cord to the power supply. These are always hot when the power supply is plugged in.
- *Black and white.* These wires carry the AC feed from the switch back to the power supply. These leads should be hot only when the power supply is plugged in and the switch is turned on.
- *Green or green with a yellow stripe.* This is the ground lead. It should be connected to the PC case and should help ground the power supply to the case.

On the switch, the tabs for the leads are usually color-coded; if not, you'll find that most switches have two parallel tabs and two angled tabs. If no color-coding is on the switch, plug the blue and brown wires onto the tabs that are parallel to each other and the black and white wires to the tabs that are angled away from each other. If none of the tabs are angled, simply make sure the blue and brown wires are plugged into the most closely spaced tabs on one side of the switch and the black and white wires on the most closely spaced tabs on the other side.

See Figure 21.17 as a guide.

Blue wire connector

White wire connector

Brown wire connector

Black wire connector

Figure 21.17 Power supply remote push button switch connections.

Caution

Although these wire color-codings and parallel/angled tabs are used on most power supplies, they are not necessarily 100% universal. I have encountered power supplies that did not use the same coloring or tab placement scheme described here. One thing is sure: Two of the wires will be hot with AC wall current anytime the power supply is plugged in. No matter what, always disconnect the power supply from the wall socket before handling any of these wires. Be sure to insulate the connections with electrical tape or heat shrink tubing so you won't be able to touch the wires when working inside the case in the future.

As long as the blue and brown wires are on the one set of tabs and the black and white leads are on the other, the switch and supply will work properly. If you incorrectly mix the leads, you will likely blow the circuit breaker for the wall socket because mixing them can create a direct short circuit.

All ATX and subsequent power supplies that employ the 20-pin motherboard connector use the PS_ON signal to power up the system. As a result, the remote switch does not physically control the power supply's access to the 110V AC power, as in the older-style power supplies. Instead, the power supply's on or off status is toggled by a PS_ON signal received on pin 14 of the ATX connector.

The PS_ON signal can be generated physically by the computer's power switch or electronically by the operating system. PS_ON is an active low signal, meaning that the power supply voltage outputs are disabled (the system is off) when the PS_ON is high (greater than or equal to 2.0V). This excludes the +5VSB (standby) on pin 9, which is active whenever the power supply is connected to an AC power source. The PS_ON signal is maintained by the power supply at either 3.3V or 5V. This signal is then routed through the motherboard to the remote switch on the front of the case. When the switch is pressed, the PS_ON signal is grounded. When the power supply sees the PS_ON signal drop to 0.8V or less, the power supply (and system) is turned on. Thus, the remote switch in an ATX-style system (which includes NLX and SFX systems as well) carries up to only +5V of DC power, rather than the full 115–230V AC current like that of the older AT/LPX form factors.

Caution

The continuous presence of the +5VSB signal on pin 9 of the ATX connector means that the motherboard always is receiving standby power from the power supply when connected to an AC source, even when the computer is turned off. As a result, it is even more crucial to unplug an ATX system from the power source before working inside the case than it is on an earlier model system.

Peripheral Power Connectors

In addition to the motherboard power connectors, power supplies include a variety of peripheral power connectors for everything from floppy and hard drives to internal case fans. The following sections discuss the various types of connectors you're likely to find in your PC.

Peripheral and Floppy Drive Power Connectors

The disk drive connectors on power supplies are fairly universal with regard to pin configuration and even wire color. Figure 21.18 shows the peripheral and floppy power connectors.

Peripheral and Floppy Power Connectors

Figure 21.18   Peripheral and floppy power connectors.

Table 21.11 shows the standard disk drive power connector pinout and wire colors, whereas Table 21.12 shows the pinouts for the smaller floppy drive power connector.

Table 21.11   Peripheral Power Connector Pinout (Large Drive Power Connector)

Pin	Signal	Color	Pin	Signal	Color
1	+12V	Yellow	3	Gnd	Black
2	Gnd	Black	4	+5V	Red

Table 21.12   3 1/2-Inch Floppy Power Connector Pinout (Small Drive Power Connector)

Pin	Signal	Color	Pin	Signal	Color
1	+5V	Red	3	Gnd	Black
2	Gnd	Black	4	+12V	Yellow

Note that the pin numbering and voltage designations are reversed on the two connectors. Be careful if you are making or using an adapter cable from one type of connector to another. Reversing the red and yellow wires will fry the drive or device you plug into.

To determine the location of pin 1, look at the connector carefully. It is usually embossed in the plastic connector body; however, it is often tiny and difficult to read. Fortunately, these connectors are keyed and therefore difficult to insert incorrectly. Figure 21.19 shows the keying with respect to pin numbers on the larger drive power connector.

(+12V) Yellow

(Gnd) Black

(Gnd) Black

(+5V) Red

4 3 2 1

Figure 21.19   A peripheral female power supply connector.

Note

Some drive connectors might supply only two wires—usually the +5V and a single ground (pins 3 and 4)—because the floppy drives in most newer systems run on only +5V and do not use the +12V at all.

Early power supplies featured only two large style drive connectors, normally called peripheral connectors today. Later power supplies featured four or more of the larger peripheral (drive) connectors, and one or two of the smaller 3 1/2-inch floppy drive connectors. Depending on their power ratings and intended uses, some supplies have as many as eight peripheral/drive connectors.

If you are adding drives and need additional disk drive power connectors, Y splitter cables (see Figure 21.20), as well as large to small drive power connector adapters (see Figure 21.21), are available from many electronics supply houses (including Radio Shack). These cables can adapt a single power connector to service two drives or enable you to convert the large peripheral power connector to a smaller floppy drive power connector. If you are using several Y-adapters, make sure that your total power supply output is capable of supplying the additional power.

Physical Connector Part Numbers

The physical connectors used in industry-standard PC power supplies were originally specified by IBM for the supplies used in the original PC/XT/AT systems. They used a specific type of connector between the power supply and the motherboard (the P8 and P9 connectors) and specific connectors for the disk drives. The motherboard connectors used in all the industry-standard power supplies were unchanged from 1981 (when the IBM PC appeared) until 1995 (when Intel released the ATX standard). The original PC's four-pin disk drive connector was augmented by a smaller (also four-pin) power connector when 3 1/2-inch floppy drives appeared in 1986. Table 21.13 lists the standard connectors used for motherboard and disk drive power.

Figure 21.20   A common Y-adapter power cable.

Figure 21.21   A peripheral–to–floppy-drive power adapter cable.

Table 21.13   Physical Power Connectors

Connector Description	Female (on Power Cable)	Male (on Component)
ATX/NLX/SFX (20-pin)	Molex 39-29-9202	Molex 39-01-2200
ATX Optional (6-pin)	Molex 39-01-2960	Molex 39-30-1060
PC/AT/LPX Motherboard P8/P9	Burndy GTC6P-1	Burndy GTC 6RI
Disk drive (large style)	AMP 1-480424-0	AMP 1-480426-0
Floppy drive (small style)	AMP 171822-4	AMP 171826-4

You can get these raw connectors through the electronics supply houses (Allied, Newark, and Digi-Key, for example) found in the Vendor List on the CD. You also can get complete cable assemblies, including drive adapters that convert the large connectors into small connectors; disk drive Y splitter cables; and motherboard power extension cables from a number of the cable and miscellaneous supply houses, such as Ci Design and Key Power, as well as PC Power and Cooling.

Caution

Before you install additional connectors to your power supply using Y splitters or any other type of connector, be sure your power supply is capable of delivering sufficient power for all your internal peripherals. Overloading the power supply can cause damage to electrical components and stored data.

▶▶   See "Power Supply Ratings," p. 1134.

Power Factor Correction

Recently, the power line efficiency and harmonic distortion generation of PC power supplies has come under examination. This generally falls under the topic of what is called the power factor of the supply. Interest in power factor is not only due to an improvement in power efficiency, but also a reduction in the generation of harmonics back on the power line. In particular, new standards are now mandatory in many European Union (EU) countries that require harmonics be reduced below a specific amount. The circuitry required to do this is generally called power factor correction (PFC).

Power factor measures how effectively electrical power is being used, and it is expressed as a number between 0 and 1. A high power factor means that electrical power is being used effectively, whereas a low power factor indicates poor utilization of electrical power. To understand power factor, you need to understand how power is used.

Generally, two kinds of loads are placed on AC power lines:

- *Resistive.* Power converted into heat, light, motion, or work.

- *Inductive.* Sustains an electromagnetic field, such as in a transformer or motor.

A resistive load is often called *working power* and is measured in kilowatts (KW). An inductive load, on the other hand, is often called *reactive power* and is measured in kilovolt-amperes-reactive (KVAR). Working power and reactive power together make up *apparent power*. Apparent power is measured in kilovolt-amperes (KVA). The power factor is measured as the ratio of working power to apparent power, or working power / apparent power (KW/KVA). The ideal power factor is 1, where the working power and apparent power are the same.

The concept of a resistive load or working power is fairly easy to understand. A light bulb, for example, that consumes 100W of power generates 100W worth of heat and light. That is a pure resistive load. An inductive load, on the other hand, is a little harder to understand. Think about a transformer, which has coil windings to generate an electromagnetic field, and then induce current in another set of windings. A certain amount of power is required to saturate the windings and generate the magnetic field, even though no work is being done. A power transformer that is not connected to anything is a perfect example of a pure inductive load. There would be an apparent power draw to generate the fields but no working power because no actual work is being done.

When the transformer is connected to a load, it would use both working power and reactive power. In other words, power would be consumed to do work (for example, say the transformer is powering a light bulb), and apparent power would be used to maintain the electromagnetic field in the transformer windings. What can happen in an AC (alternating current) circuit is that these loads can become out of sync or phase, meaning they don't peak at the same time, which can generate harmonic distortions back down the power line. I've seen examples where electric motors caused distortions in television sets plugged into the same power circuit.

Power factor correction (PFC) usually involves adding capacitance to the circuit to be able to maintain the inductive load without drawing additional power from the line. This makes the working power and apparent power the same, which results in a power factor of 1. It usually isn't just as simple as adding some capacitors to a circuit, although that can be done and is called *passive* power factor correction. *Active* power factor correction involves a more intelligent circuit designed to match the resistive and inductive loads so they are seen as the same by the electrical outlet.

A power supply with active power factor correction draws low distortion current from the AC source and has a power factor rating of 0.9 or greater. A nonpower factor corrected supply draws highly distorted current and is sometimes referred to as a *nonlinear* load. The power factor of a noncorrected supply is normally 0.6–0.8. This means that only 60% of the apparent power consumed is actually doing real work!

Having a power supply with active PFC might or might not improve your electric bill (it depends on how your power is measured), but it will definitely reduce the load on the building wiring. With PFC, all the power going into the supply will be converted into actual work, and the wiring will be less overworked. For example, if you ran a number of computers on a single breaker-controlled circuit and found that you were blowing the breaker every so often, by switching to systems with active PFC power supplies, you'd reduce the load on the wiring by up to 40%, meaning you would be less likely to blow the breaker.

The International Electrical Committee (IEC) has released standards dealing with the low frequency public supply system. Initial standards were 555.2 (Harmonics) and 555.3 (Flicker), which have since been refined and are now available as IEC 1000-3-2 and IEC 1000-3-3, respectively. As governed by the EMC directive, most electrical devices sold within the member countries of the European Union (EU) must meet the IEC standards. The IEC1000-3-2/3 standards became mandatory in 1997 and 1998.

Even if you don't live in a country where PFC is required, I highly recommend specifying PC power supplies with active PFC. The main benefits of PFC supplies is that they do not overheat building wiring or distort the AC source waveform, causing less interference on the line for other devices.

Power Supply Loading

PC power supplies are of a *switching* rather than a *linear* design. The switching type of design uses a high-speed oscillator circuit to convert the higher wall-socket AC voltage to the much lower DC voltage used to power the PC and PC components. Switching type power supplies are noted for being very efficient in size, weight, and energy in comparison to the linear design, which uses a large internal transformer to generate various outputs. This type of transformer-based design is inefficient in at least three ways. First, the output voltage of the transformer linearly follows the input voltage (hence the name *linear*), so any fluctuations in the AC power going into the system can cause problems with the output. Second, the high current-level (power) requirements of a PC system require the use of heavy wiring in the transformer. Third, the 60Hz (hertz) frequency of the AC power supplied from your building is difficult to filter out inside the power supply, requiring large and expensive filter capacitors and rectifiers.

The switching supply, on the other hand, uses a switching circuit that chops up the incoming power at a relatively high frequency. This enables the use of high-frequency transformers that are much smaller and lighter. Also, the higher frequency is much easier and cheaper to filter out at the output, and the input voltage can vary widely. Input ranging from 90 volts to 135 volts still produces the proper output levels, and many switching supplies can automatically adjust to 220V input.

One characteristic of all switching-type power supplies is that they do not run without a *load*. This means that you must have the supply plugged into something drawing power for the supply to work. If you simply have the power supply on a bench with nothing plugged into it, either the supply burns up or its protection circuitry shuts it down. Most power supplies are protected from no-load operation and shut down automatically. Some of the cheap clone supplies, however, lack the protection circuit and relay. They are destroyed after a few seconds of no-load operation. A few power supplies have their own built-in load resistors, so they can run even though no normal load is plugged in.

According to IBM specifications for the standard 192-watt power supply used in the original AT, a minimum load of 7.0 amps was required at +5V and a minimum of 2.5 amps was required at +12V for the supply to work properly.

Because floppy drives present no +12V load unless they are spinning, systems without a hard disk drive often do not operate properly. Some power supplies have a minimum load requirement for both the +5V and +12V sides. If you fail to meet this minimum load, the supply shuts down.

Because of this characteristic, when IBM used to ship the original AT systems without a hard disk, they plugged the hard disk drive power cable into a large 5-ohm, 50-watt sandbar resistor, which was mounted in a little metal cage assembly where the drive would have been. The AT case had screw holes on top of where the hard disk would go, specifically designed to mount this resistor cage.

Note

Several computer stores I knew of in the mid-1980s would order the diskless AT and install their own 20MB or 30MB drives, which they could get more cheaply from other sources than from IBM. They were throwing away the load resistors by the hundreds! I managed to grab a couple at the time, which is how I know the type of resistor they used.

This resistor would be connected between pin 1 (+12V) and pin 2 (Ground) on the hard disk power connector. This would place a 2.4-amp load on the supply's +12V output, drawing 28.8 watts of power (it would get hot!) and thus enabling the supply to operate normally. Note that the cooling fan in most power supplies draws approximately 0.1–0.25 amps, bringing the total load to 2.5 amps or more. If the load resistor were missing, the system would intermittently fail to start up or operate properly. The motherboard would draw +5V at all times, but +12V would normally be used only by motors, and the floppy drive motors would be off most of the time.

Most of the power supplies in use today do not require as much of a load as the original IBM AT power supply. In most cases, a minimum load of 0–0.3 amps at +3.3V, 2.0–4.0 amps at +5V, and 0.5–1.0 amps at +12V is considered acceptable. Most motherboards easily draw the minimum +5V current by themselves. The standard power supply cooling fan draws only 0.1–0.25 amps, so the +12V minimum load might still be a problem for a diskless workstation. Generally, the higher the rating on the supply, the more minimum load required; however, exceptions do exist, so this is a specification you want to check when evaluating power supplies.

Some high-quality switching power supplies have built-in load resistors and can run under a no-load situation because the supply loads. Other high-quality power supplies, such as those from PC Power and Cooling, have no internal load resistors. They require only a small load on the +5V line to operate properly. Many of the cheaper clone supplies, which often do not have built-in load resistors, might require +3.3V, +5V, and +12V loads to work.

If you want to bench test a power supply, make sure you place loads on at least one but preferably all of the positive voltage outputs. This is one reason you should test the supply while it is installed in the system, instead of testing it separately on the bench. For impromptu bench testing, you can use a spare motherboard and hard disk drive to load the outputs.

Power Supply Ratings

A system manufacturer should be able to provide you the technical specifications of the power supplies it uses in its systems. This type of information can be found in the system's technical-reference manual, as well as on stickers attached directly to the power supply. Power supply manufacturers can also supply this data, which is preferable if you can identify the manufacturer and contact them directly or via the Web.

The input specifications are listed as voltages, and the output specifications are listed as amps at several voltage levels. IBM reports output wattage level as "specified output wattage." If your manufacturer does not list the total wattage, you can convert amperage to wattage by using the following simple formula:

$$watts = volts \times amps$$

For example, if a motherboard is listed as drawing 6 amps of +5V current, that would be 30 watts of power, according to the formula.

By multiplying the voltage by the amperage available at each output and then adding the results, you can calculate the total capable output wattage of the supply.

Table 21.14 shows the standard power supply output levels available in industry-standard form factors. Most manufacturers offer supplies with ratings from 100 watts to 450 watts or more. Table 21.15 shows the rated outputs at each of the voltage levels for supplies with different manufacturer-specified output ratings. To compile the table, I referred to the specification sheets for supplies from Astec Standard Power and PC Power and Cooling. Although most of the ratings are accurate, they are somewhat misleading for the higher wattage units.

Table 21.14   Typical Non-ATX Power Supply Output Ratings

Rated Output (Watts)	100W	150W	200W	250W	300W	375W	450W
Output current (amps):							
+5V	10.0	15.0	20.0	25.0	32.0	35.0	45.0
+12V	3.5	5.5	8.0	10.0	10.0	13.0	15.0
–5V	0.3	0.3	0.3	0.5	1.0	0.5	0.5
–12V	0.3	0.3	0.3	0.5	1.0	0.5	1.0
Calc. output (watts)	97.1	146.1	201.1	253.5	297.0	339.5	419.5

Adding a +3.3V output to the power supply modifies the equation significantly. Table 21.15 contains data for various ATX power supplies from PC Power and Cooling that include a +3.3V output.

Table 21.15   PC Power and Cooling ATX Power Supply Output Ratings

Rated Output	235W	275W	300W	350W	400W	425W
Output current (amps):						
+5V	22.0	30.0	30.0	32.0	30.0	50.0
+3.3V	14.0	14.0	14.0	28.0	28.0	40.0
Max watts +5V and +3.3V:	125W	150W	150W	215W	215W	300W
+12V	8.0	10.0	12.0	10.0	14.0	15.0
–5V	0.5	0.5	0.5	0.3	1.0	0.3
–12V	1.0	1.0	1.0	0.8	1.0	1.0

If you compute the total output using the formula described earlier, these power supplies seem to produce an output that is much higher than their ratings. The 300W model, for example, comes out at 354.7 watts. However, notice that the supply also has a maximum combined output for the +3.3V and +5V of 150 watts. This means you cannot draw the maximum rating on both the 5V and 3.3V lines simultaneously, but must keep the total combined draw between them at 150W. This brings the total output to a more logical 308.5 watts.

Most PC power supplies have ratings between 150 and 300 watts. Although lesser ratings are not usually desirable, you can purchase heavy-duty power supplies for most systems that have outputs as high as 600 watts or more.

The 300-watt and larger units are recommended for fully optioned desktops or tower systems. These supplies run any combination of motherboard and expansion card, as well as a large number of disk drives and other peripherals. In most cases, you cannot exceed the ratings on these power supplies—the system will be out of room for additional items first!

Most power supplies are considered to be universal, or worldwide. That is, they also can run on the 220V, 50-cycle current used in Europe and many other parts of the world. Many power supplies that can switch from 110V to 220V input do so automatically, but a few require you to set a switch on the back of the power supply to indicate which type of power you will access.

Caution

If your supply does not switch input voltages automatically, make sure the voltage setting is correct. If you plug the power supply into a 110V outlet while it's set in the 220V setting, no damage will result, but the supply won't operate properly until you correct the setting. On the other hand, if you are in a foreign country with a 220V outlet and have the switch set for 110V, you might cause damage.

Power Supply Specifications

In addition to power output, many other specifications and features go into making a high-quality power supply. I have had many systems over the years. My experience has been that if a brownout occurs in a room with several systems running, the systems with higher-quality power supplies and higher output ratings are far more likely to make it through the power disturbances unscathed, whereas others choke.

High-quality power supplies also help protect your systems. A power supply from a vendor such as Astec or PC Power and Cooling will not be damaged if any of the following conditions occur:

- A 100% power outage of any duration
- A brownout of any kind
- A spike of up to 2,500V applied directly to the AC input (for example, a lightning strike or a lightning simulation test)

Decent power supplies have an extremely low current leakage to ground of less than 500 microamps. This safety feature is important if your outlet has a missing or an improperly wired ground line.

As you can see, these specifications are fairly tough and are certainly representative of a high-quality power supply. Make sure that your supply can meet these specifications.

You can also use many other criteria to evaluate a power supply. The power supply is a component many users ignore when shopping for a PC, and it is therefore one that some system vendors might choose to skimp on. After all, a dealer is far more likely to be able to increase the price of a computer by spending money on additional memory or a larger hard drive than by installing a better power supply.

When buying a computer (or a replacement power supply), you always should learn as much as possible about the power supply. However, many consumers are intimidated by the vocabulary and statistics found in a typical power supply specification. Here are some of the most common parameters found on power supply specification sheets, along with their meanings:

- *Mean Time Between Failures (MTBF) or Mean Time To Failure (MTTF).* The (calculated) average interval, in hours, that the power supply is expected to operate before failing. Power supplies typically have MTBF ratings (such as 100,000 hours or more) that are clearly not the result of real-time empirical testing. In fact, manufacturers use published standards to calculate the results, based on the failure rates of the power supply's individual components. MTBF figures for power supplies often include the load to which the power supply was subjected (in the form of a percentage) and the temperature of the environment in which the tests were performed.

- *Input Range (or Operating Range).* The range of voltages that the power supply is prepared to accept from the AC power source. For 110V AC current, an input range of 90V–135V is common; for 220V current, a 180V–270V range is typical.

- *Peak Inrush Current.* The greatest amount of current drawn by the power supply at a given moment immediately after it is turned on, expressed in terms of amps at a particular voltage. The lower the current, the less thermal shock the system experiences.

- *Hold-Up Time.* The amount of time (in milliseconds) that a power supply can maintain output within the specified voltage ranges after a loss of input power. This enables your PC to continue running without resetting or rebooting if a brief interruption in AC power occurs. Values of 15–30 milliseconds are common for today's power supplies, and the higher (longer), the better. The ATX12V specification calls for a minimum of 17ms hold-up time.

- *Transient Response.* The amount of time (in microseconds) a power supply takes to bring its output back to the specified voltage ranges after a steep change in the output current. In other words, the amount of time it takes for the output power levels to stabilize after a device in the system starts or stops drawing power. Power supplies sample the current being used by the computer at regular intervals. When a device stops drawing power during one of these intervals (such as when a floppy drive stops spinning), the power supply might supply too high a voltage to the output for a brief time. This excess voltage is called *overshoot*, and the transient response is the time that it takes for the voltage to return to the specified level. This is seen as a spike in voltage by the system and can cause glitches and lockups. Once a major problem that came with switching power supplies, overshoot has been greatly reduced in recent years. Transient response values are sometimes expressed in time intervals, and at other times they are expressed in terms of a particular output change, such as "power output levels stay within regulation during output changes of up to 20%."

- *Overvoltage Protection.* Defines the trip points for each output at which the power supply shuts down or squelches that output. Values can be expressed as a percentage (for example, 120% for +3.3 and +5V) or as raw voltages (for example, +4.6V for the +3.3V output and +7.0V for the +5V output).

- *Maximum Load Current.* The largest amount of current (in amps) that safely can be delivered through a particular output. Values are expressed as individual amperages for each output voltage. With these figures, you can calculate not only the total amount of power the power supply can supply, but also how many devices using those various voltages it can support.

- *Minimum Load Current.* The smallest amount of current (in amps) that must be drawn from a particular output for that output to function. If the current drawn from an output falls below the minimum, the power supply could be damaged or automatically shut down.

- *Load Regulation (or Voltage Load Regulation).* When the current drawn from a particular output increases or decreases, the voltage changes slightly as well, usually increasing as the current rises. Load regulation is the change in the voltage for a particular output as it transitions from its minimum load to its maximum load (or vice versa). Values, expressed in terms of a +/– percentage, typically range from +/–1% to +/–5% for the +3.3, +5, and +12V outputs.

- *Line Regulation.* The change in output voltage as the AC input voltage transitions from the lowest to the highest value of the input range. A power supply should be capable of handling any AC voltage in its input range with a change in its output of 1% or less.

- *Efficiency.* The ratio of power input to power output, expressed in terms of a percentage. Values of 65%–85% are common for power supplies today. The remaining 15%–35% of the power input is converted to heat during the AC/DC conversion process. Although greater efficiency means less heat inside the computer (always a good thing) and lower electric bills, it should not be emphasized at the expense of precision, stability, and durability, as evidenced in the supply's load regulation and other parameters.

■ *Ripple (or Ripple and Noise, or AC Ripple, or PARD [Periodic and Random Deviation]).* The average voltage of all AC effects on the power supply outputs, normally measured in millivolts peak-to-peak or as a percentage of the nominal output voltage. The lower this figure, the better. Higher-quality units normally are rated at 1% ripple (or less), which if expressed in volts would be 1% of the output. Consequently, for +5V that would be 0.05V or 50mV (millivolts). Ripple can be caused by internal switching transients, feed through of the rectified line frequency, and other random noise.

Power Supply Certifications

Many agencies around the world list electric and electronic components for safety and quality. The most commonly known agency in the United States is Underwriters Laboratories, Inc. (UL). UL standard #1950—the *Standard for Safety of Information Technology Equipment, Including Electrical Business Equipment, Third Edition*—covers power supplies and other PC components. You always should purchase power supplies and other devices that are UL-listed. It has often been said that, although not every good product is UL-listed, no bad products are.

In Canada, electric and electronic products are listed by the Canadian Standards Agency (CSA). The German equivalents are TÜV Rheinland and VDE, and NEMKO operates in Norway. These agencies are responsible for certification of products throughout Europe. Power supply manufacturers that sell to an international market should have products that are listed at least by UL, the CSA, and TÜV—if not by all the agencies listed, and more.

Apart from UL-type certifications, many power supply manufacturers, even the most reputable ones, claim that their products have a Class B certification from the Federal Communications Commission, meaning that they meet FCC standards for electromagnetic and radio frequency interference (EMI/RFI). This is a contentious point, however, because the FCC does not list power supplies as individual components. Title 47 of the Code of Federal Regulations, Part 15, Section 15.101(c) states as follows:

"The FCC does NOT currently authorize motherboards, cases, and internal power supplies. Vendor claims that they are selling 'FCC-certified cases,' 'FCC-certified motherboards,' or 'FCC-certified internal power supplies' are false."

In fact, an FCC certification can be issued collectively only to a base unit consisting of a computer case, motherboard, and power supply. Thus, a power supply purported to be FCC-listed was actually listed along with a particular case and motherboard—not necessarily the same case and motherboard you are using in your system. This does not mean, however, that the manufacturer is being deceitful or that the power supply is inferior. If anything, this means that when evaluating power supplies, you should place less weight on the FCC certification than on other factors, such as UL certification.

Power-Use Calculations

When expanding or upgrading your PC, you should ensure that your power supply is capable of providing sufficient current to power all the system's internal devices. One way to see whether your system is capable of expansion is to calculate the levels of power drain in the various system components and deduct the total from the maximum power supplied by the power supply. This calculation can help you decide whether you must upgrade the power supply to a more capable unit. Unfortunately, these calculations can be difficult to make because many manufacturers do not publish power consumption data for their products.

In addition, getting power-consumption data for many +5V devices, including motherboards and adapter cards, can be difficult. Motherboards can consume different power levels, depending on numerous factors. Most motherboards consume about 5 amps or so, but try to get information on the one you are using. For adapter cards, if you can find the actual specifications for the card, use those figures. To be on the conservative side, however, I usually go by the maximum available power levels set forth in the respective bus standards.

For example, consider the power-consumption figures for components in a modern PC, such as a desktop or Slimline system with a 200-watt power supply rated for 20 amps at +5V and 8 amps at +12V. The ISA specification calls for a maximum of 2.0 amps of +5V power and 0.175 amps of +12V power for each slot in the system. Most systems have eight slots, and you can assume that four are filled for the purposes of calculating power draw. The calculation shown in Table 21.16 shows what happens when you subtract the amount of power necessary to run the various system components.

Table 21.16   Power Consumption Calculation

	Available 5V Power (Amps):	20.0A		Available 12V Power (Amps):	8.0A
Less:	Motherboard	−5.0A	Less:	4 slots filled at 0.175 each	−0.7A
	4 slots filled at 2.0 each	−8.0A		3 1/2-inch hard disk drive motor	−1.0A
	3 1/2-inch floppy drive logic	−0.5A		3 1/2-inch floppy drive motor	−1.0A
	3 1/2-inch hard disk drive logic	−0.5A		Cooling fan motor	−0.1A
	CD-ROM/DVD drive logic	−1.0A		CD-ROM/DVD drive motor	−1.0A
	Remaining Power (amps):	5.0A		Remaining Power (amps):	4.2A

In the preceding example, everything seems all right for the present. With half the slots filled, a floppy drive, and one hard disk, the system still has room for more. Problems with the power supply could come up, however, if this system were expanded to the extreme. With every slot filled and two or more hard disks, problems with the +5V current definitely would occur. However, the +12V does seem to have room to spare. You could add a CD-ROM drive or a second hard disk without worrying too much about the +12V power, but the +5V power would be strained.

If you anticipate loading up a system to the extreme—as in a high-end multimedia system, for example—you might want to invest in the insurance of a higher-output power supply. For example, a 250-watt supply usually has 25 amps of +5V current and 10 amps of +12V current, whereas a 300-watt unit usually has 32 amps of +5V current available. These supplies enable you to fully load the system and are likely to be found in full-sized desktop or tower case configurations in which this type of expansion is expected.

Motherboards can draw anywhere from 4 to 15 amps or more of +5V power to run. In fact, a single Pentium 66MHz CPU draws up to 3.2 amps of +5V power all by itself. A 200MHz Pentium Pro CPU or 400MHz Pentium II consumes up to 15 amps. Considering that systems with two or more processors are now becoming common, you could have 30 amps or more drawn by the processors alone. A motherboard such as this—with two CPUs and 128MB or more of RAM for each CPU—might draw more than 40 amps all by itself. Very few "no-name" power supplies can supply this kind of current. For these applications, you should consider only high-quality, high-capacity power supplies from a reputable manufacturer, such as PC Power and Cooling.

In these calculations, bus slots are allotted maximum power in amps, as shown in Table 21.17.

Table 21.17   Maximum Power Consumption in Amps per Bus Slot

Bus Type	+5V Power	+12V Power	+3.3V Power
ISA	2.0	0.175	n/a
EISA	4.5	1.5	n/a
VL-bus	2.0	n/a	n/a
16-bit MCA	1.6	0.175	n/a
32-bit MCA	2.0	0.175	n/a
PCI	5	0.5	7.6

As you can see from the table, ISA slots are allotted 2.0 amps of +5V and 0.175 amps of +12V power. Note that these are maximum figures; not all cards draw this much power. If the slot has a VL-bus extension connector, an additional 2.0 amps of +5V power are allowed for the VL-bus.

Floppy drives can vary in power consumption, but most of the newer 3 1/2-inch drives have motors that run on +5V current in addition to the logic circuits. These drives usually draw 1.0 amps of +5V power and use no +12V at all. 5 1/4-inch drives use standard +12V motors that draw about 1.0 amps. These drives also require about 0.5 amps of +5V for the logic circuits. Most cooling fans draw about 0.1 amps of +12V power, which is negligible.

Typical 3 1/2-inch hard disks today draw about 1 amp of +12V power to run the motors and only about 0.5 amps of +5V power for the logic. 5 1/4-inch hard disks, especially those that are full-height, draw much more power. A typical full-height hard drive draws 2.0 amps of +12V power and 1.0 amp of +5V power.

Another problem with hard disks is that they require much more power during the spinup phase of operation than during normal operation. In most cases, the drive draws double the +12V power during spinup, which can be 4.0 amps or more for the full-height drives. This tapers off to a normal level after the drive is spinning.

The figures that most manufacturers report for maximum power supply output are full duty-cycle figures. The power supply can supply these levels of power continuously. You usually can expect a unit that continuously supplies a given level of power to be capable of exceeding this level for some non-continuous amount of time. A supply usually can offer 50% greater output than the continuous figure indicates for as long as one minute. Systems often use this cushion to supply the necessary power to spin up a hard disk drive. After the drive has spun to full speed, the power draw drops to a value within the system's continuous supply capabilities. Drawing anything over the rated continuous figure for any extended length of time causes the power supply to run hot and fail early, and it can also create nasty symptoms in the system.

Tip

If you are using internal SCSI hard drives, you can ease the startup load on your power supply. The key is to enable the SCSI drive's Remote Start option, which causes the drive to start spinning only when it receives a startup command over the SCSI bus. The effect is that the drive remains stationary (drawing very little power) until the very end of the POST and spins up right when the SCSI portion of the POST is begun.

If you have multiple SCSI drives, they all spin up sequentially based on their SCSI ID settings. This is designed so that only one drive is spinning up at any one time and so that no drives start spinning until the rest of the system has had time to start. This greatly eases the load on the power supply when you first power the system on.

In most cases, you enable Remote Start through your SCSI host adapter's setup program. This program might be supplied with the adapter on separate media, or it might be integrated into the adapter's BIOS and activated with a specific key combination at boot time.

The biggest cause of power supply overload problems has historically been filling up the expansion slots and adding more drives. Multiple hard drives, CD-ROM drives, and floppy drives can create quite a drain on the system power supply. Make sure that you have enough +12V power to run all the drives you plan to install. Tower systems can be especially problematic because they have so many drive bays. Just because the case has room for the devices doesn't mean the power supply can support them. Be sure you have enough +5V power to run all your expansion cards, especially PCI cards. It pays to be conservative, but remember that most cards draw less than the maximum allowed. Today's newest processors can have very high current requirements for the +5- or +3.3-volt supplies. When selecting a power supply for your system, be sure to take into account any future processor upgrades.

Many people wait until an existing component fails to replace it with an upgraded version. If you are on a tight budget, this "if it ain't broke, don't fix it" attitude might be necessary. Power supplies, however, often do not fail completely all at once; they can fail in an intermittent fashion or allow fluctuating power levels to reach the system, which results in unstable operation. You might be blaming system lockups on software bugs when the culprit is an overloaded power supply. If you have been running your original power supply for a long time and have upgraded your system in other ways, you should expect some problems.

Although there is certainly an appropriate place for the exacting power-consumption calculations you've read about in this section, a great many experienced PC users prefer the "don't worry about it" power calculation method. This technique consists of buying or building a system with a good-quality 300-watt or higher power supply (or upgrading to such a supply in an existing system) and then upgrading the system freely, without concern for power consumption.

Tip

My preference is the 425W supply from PC Power and Cooling, which is probably overkill for most people, but for those who keep a system for a long time and put it through a number of upgrades, it is an excellent choice.

Unless you plan to build a system with arrays of SCSI drives and a dozen other peripherals, you will probably not exceed the capabilities of the power supply, and this method certainly requires far less effort.

Power Off When Not in Use

Should you turn off a system when it is not in use? To answer this frequent question, you should understand some facts about electrical components and what makes them fail. Combine this knowledge with information on power consumption, cost, and safety to come to your own conclusion. Because circumstances can vary, the best answer for your own situation might be different from the answer for others, depending on your particular needs and applications.

Frequently, powering a system on and off does cause deterioration and damage to the components. This seems logical, but the simple reason is not obvious to most people. Many believe that flipping system power on and off frequently is harmful because it electrically "shocks" the system. The real problem, however, is temperature or thermal shock. As the system warms up, the components expand; as it cools off, the components contract. In addition, various materials in the system have different thermal expansion coefficients, which means that they expand and contract at different rates. Over time, thermal shock causes deterioration in many areas of a system.

From a pure system-reliability viewpoint, you should insulate the system from thermal shock as much as possible. When a system is turned on, the components go from ambient (room) temperature to as high as 185° F (85° C) within 30 minutes or less. When you turn off the system, the same thing happens in reverse, and the components cool back to ambient temperature in a short period of time.

Thermal expansion and contraction remains the single largest cause of component failure. Chip cases can split, allowing moisture to enter and contaminate them. Delicate internal wires and contacts can break, and circuit boards can develop stress cracks. Surface-mounted components expand and contract at rates different from the circuit board they are mounted on, which causes enormous stress at the solder joints. Solder joints can fail due to the metal hardening from the repeated stress, resulting in cracks in the joint. Components that use heatsinks, such as processors, transistors, or voltage regulators, can overheat and fail because the thermal cycling causes heatsink adhesives to deteriorate and break the thermally conductive bond between the device and the heatsink. Thermal cycling also causes socketed devices and connections to loosen or *creep*, which can cause a variety of intermittent contact failures.

◀◀   See "SIMMs, DIMMs, and RIMMs," p. 421.

Thermal expansion and contraction affect not only chips and circuit boards, but also things such as hard disk drives. Most hard drives today have sophisticated thermal compensation routines that make adjustments in head position relative to the expanding and contracting platters. Most drives perform this thermal compensation routine once every 5 minutes for the first 30 minutes the drive is running, and then every 30 minutes thereafter. In many drives, this procedure can be heard as a rapid "tick-tick-tick-tick" sound. In essence, anything you can do to keep the system at a constant temperature prolongs the life of the system, and the best way to accomplish this is to leave the system either permanently on or permanently off. Of course, if the system is never turned on in the first place, it should last a long time indeed!

Now, I am not saying that you should leave all systems on 24 hours a day. A system powered on and left unattended can be a fire hazard (I have had monitors spontaneously catch fire—luckily, I was there at the time), is a data security risk (from cleaning crews and other nocturnal visitors), can be easily damaged if moved while running, and wastes electrical energy.

I currently pay 11 cents for a kilowatt-hour of electricity. A typical desktop-style PC with display consumes at least 300 watts (0.3 kilowatt) of electricity (and that is a conservative estimate). This means it would cost 3.3 cents to run my typical PC for an hour. Multiplying by 168 hours in a week means that it would cost $5.54 per week to run this PC continuously. If the PC were turned on at 9 a.m. and off at 5 p.m., it would be on only 40 hours per week and would cost only $1.32—a savings of $4.22 per week! Multiply this savings by 100 systems, and you are saving $422 per week. Multiply this by 1,000 systems, and you are saving $4,220 per week! Using systems listed under the EPA Energy Star program (so-called green PCs) would account for an additional savings of around $1 per system per week—or $1,000 per week for 1,000 systems. The great thing about Energy Star systems is that the savings are even greater if the systems are left on for long periods of time because the power management routines are automatic.

Based on these facts, my recommendations are that you power on the systems at the beginning of the workday and off at the end of the workday. Do not power the systems off for lunch, breaks, or any other short periods of time. If you are a home user, leave your computer on if you are going to be using it later in the day or if instant access is important. I'd normally recommend home users turn off the system when leaving the house or when sleeping. Servers, of course, should be left on continuously. This seems to be the best compromise of system longevity with pure economics. No matter what, these are just guidelines; if it works better for you to leave your system on 24 hours a day, seven days a week, make it so.

Power Management

As the standard PC configuration has grown to include capabilities formerly considered options, the power requirements of the system have increased steadily. Larger displays, CD-ROM drives, and audio adapters all need more power to run, and the cost of operating a PC rises steadily. To address these concerns, several programs and standards are now being developed that are intended to reduce the power needed to run a PC as much as possible.

For standard desktop systems, power management is a matter of economy and convenience. By turning off specific components of the PC when they are not in use, you can reduce the electric bill and avoid having to power the computer up and down manually.

For portable systems, power management is far more important. Adding CD-ROMs, speakers, and other components to a laptop or notebook computer reduces even further what is in many cases a short battery life. By adding new power management technology, a portable system can supply power only to the components it actually needs to run, thus extending the life of the battery charge.

Energy Star Systems

The EPA has started a certification program for energy-efficient PCs and peripherals. To be a member of this program, the PC or display must drop to a power draw at the outlet of 30 watts or less during periods of inactivity. Systems that conform to this specification get to wear the Energy Star logo. This is a voluntary program; however, many PC manufacturers are finding that it helps them sell their systems if they can advertise these systems as energy efficient.

One problem with this type of system is that the motherboard and disk drives can go to sleep, which means they can enter a standby mode in which they draw very little power. This causes havoc with some of the older power supplies because the low power draw does not provide enough of a load for them to function properly. Most of the newer supplies on the market, which are designed to work with these systems, have a very low minimum-load specification. I suggest you ensure that the minimum load will be provided by the equipment in your system if you buy a power supply upgrade. Otherwise, when the PC goes to sleep, it might take a power switch cycle to wake it up again. This problem would be most noticeable if you invested in a very high-output supply and used it in a system that draws very little power to begin with.

Advanced Power Management

Advanced Power Management (APM) is a specification jointly developed by Intel and Microsoft that defines a series of interfaces between power management–capable hardware and a computer's operating system. When it is fully activated, APM can automatically switch a computer between five states, depending on the system's current activity. Each state represents a further reduction in power use, accomplished by placing unused components into a low-power mode. The five system states are as follows:

- *Full On.* The system is completely operational, with no power management occurring.
- *APM Enabled.* The system is operational, with some devices being power managed. Unused devices can be powered down and the CPU clock slowed or stopped.
- *APM Standby.* The system is not operational, with most devices in a low-power state. The CPU clock can be slowed or stopped, but operational parameters are retained in memory. When triggered by a specific user or system activities, the system can return to the APM Enabled state almost instantaneously.
- *APM Suspend.* The system is not operational, with most devices unpowered. The CPU clock is stopped and operational parameters are saved to disk for later restoration. When triggered by a wakeup event, the system returns to the APM Enabled state relatively slowly.
- *Off.* The system is not operational. The power supply is off.

APM requires support from both hardware and software to function. In this chapter, you've already seen how ATX-style power supplies can be controlled by software commands using the Power_On signal and the six-pin optional power connector. Manufacturers are also integrating the same sort of control features into other system components, such as motherboards, monitors, and disk drives.

Operating systems that support APM, such as Windows 9x, trigger power management events by monitoring the activities performed by the computer user and the applications running on the system. However, the OS does not directly address the power management capabilities of the hardware.

A system can have many hardware devices and many software functions participating in APM functions, which makes communication difficult. To address this problem, both the operating system and the hardware have an abstraction layer that facilitates communication between the various elements of the APM architecture.

The operating system runs an APM driver that communicates with the various applications and software functions that trigger power management activities, while the system's APM-capable hardware devices all communicate with the system BIOS. The APM driver and the BIOS communicate directly, completing the link between the OS and the hardware.

Thus, for APM to function, support for the standard must be built into the system's individual hardware devices, the system BIOS, and the operating system (which includes the APM driver). Without all these components, APM activities cannot occur.

Advanced Configuration and Power Interface

Advanced Configuration and Power Interface (ACPI) is a newer power management and system configuration standard supported by newer system BIOS software running Windows 98 and later operating systems. If your BIOS and operating system support ACPI, full power management control is now done by the operating system, rather than by the BIOS. ACPI is intended to offer a single place for power management and system configuration control; in the past, with APM you would often be able to make power management settings in the BIOS setup as well as the operating system that often overlapped or could have conflicting settings. ACPI is supported in newer systems in lieu of APM.

Tip

If, for any reason, you find that power management activities cause problems on your system, such as operating system freeze-ups or hardware malfunctions, the easiest way to disable APM is through the system BIOS. Most BIOSes that support APM include an option to disable it. This breaks the chain of communication between the operating system and the hardware, causing all power management activities to cease. Although you also can achieve the same end by removing the APM driver from the operating system, Windows 9x's Plug-and-Play (PnP) feature detects the system's APM capabilities whenever you restart the computer and attempts to reinstall the APM driver.

If you have a newer system with ACPI, you can disable the power management settings via the Power Management icon in the Windows control panel.

Power Supply Troubleshooting

Troubleshooting the power supply basically means isolating the supply as the cause of problems within a system and, if necessary, replacing it.

Caution

It is rarely recommended that an inexperienced user open a power supply to make repairs because of the dangerous high voltages present. Even when unplugged, power supplies can retain dangerous voltage and must be discharged (like a monitor) before service. Such internal repairs are beyond the scope of this book and are specifically not recommended unless the technician knows what he or she is doing.

Many symptoms lead me to suspect that the power supply in a system is failing. This can sometimes be difficult for an inexperienced technician to see because, at times little connection seems to exist between the symptom and the cause—the power supply.

For example, in many cases a parity check error message can indicate a problem with the power supply. This might seem strange because the parity check message specifically refers to memory that has failed. The connection is that the power supply powers the memory, and memory with inadequate power fails.

It takes some experience to know when this type of failure is power related and not caused by the memory. One clue is the repeatability of the problem. If the parity check message (or other problem) appears frequently and identifies the same memory location each time, I would suspect that defective memory is the problem. However, if the problem seems random, or if the memory location the error message cites as having failed seems random, I would suspect improper power as the culprit. The following is a list of PC problems that often are related to the power supply:

- Any power-on or system startup failures or lockups.
- Spontaneous rebooting or intermittent lockups during normal operation.
- Intermittent parity check or other memory-type errors.
- Hard disk and fan simultaneously failing to spin (no +12V).
- Overheating due to fan failure.
- Small brownouts cause the system to reset.
- Electric shocks felt on the system case or connectors.
- Slight static discharges disrupt system operation.

In fact, just about any intermittent system problem can be caused by the power supply. I always suspect the supply when flaky system operation is a symptom. Of course, the following fairly obvious symptoms point right to the power supply as a possible cause:

- System is completely dead (no fan, no cursor)
- Smoke
- Blown circuit breakers

If you suspect a power supply problem, some of the simple measurements and the more sophisticated tests outlined in this section can help you determine whether the power supply is at fault. Because these measurements might not detect some intermittent failures, you might have to use a spare power supply for a long-term evaluation. If the symptoms and problems disappear when a known good spare unit is installed, you have found the source of your problem.

Following is a simple flowchart to help you zero in on common power supply–related problems:

1. Check AC power input. Make sure the cord is firmly seated in the wall socket and in the power supply socket. Try a different cord.

2. Check DC power connections. Make sure the motherboard and disk drive power connectors are firmly seated and making good contact. Check for loose screws.

3. Check DC power output. Use a digital multimeter to check for proper voltages. If it's below spec, replace the power supply.

4. Check installed peripherals. Remove all boards and drives and retest the system. If it works, add back in items one at a time until the system fails again. The last item added before the failure returns is likely defective.

Many types of symptoms can indicate problems with the power supply. Because the power supply literally powers everything else in the system, everything from disk drive problems to memory problems to motherboard problems can often be traced back to the power supply as the root cause.

Overloaded Power Supplies

A weak or inadequate power supply can put a damper on your ideas for system expansion. Some systems are designed with beefy power supplies, as if to anticipate a great deal of system add-ons and expansion components. Most desktop or tower systems are built in this manner. Some systems have inadequate power supplies from the start, however, and cannot adequately service the power-hungry options you might want to add.

The wattage rating can sometimes be very misleading. Not all 300-watt supplies are created the same. People familiar with high-end audio systems know that some watts are better than others. This goes for power supplies, too. Cheap power supplies might in fact put out the rated power, but what about noise and distortion? Some of the supplies are under-engineered to just barely meet their specifications, whereas others might greatly exceed their specifications. Many of the cheaper supplies provide noisy or unstable power, which can cause numerous problems with the system. Another problem with under-engineered power supplies is that they can run hot and force the system to do so as well. The repeated heating and cooling of solid-state components eventually causes a computer system to fail, and engineering principles dictate that the hotter a PC's temperature, the shorter its life. Many people recommend replacing the original supply in a system with a heavier-duty model, which solves the problem. Because power supplies come in common form factors, finding a heavy-duty replacement for most systems is easy, as is the installation process.

Inadequate Cooling

Some of the available replacement power supplies have higher-capacity cooling fans than the originals, which can greatly prolong system life and minimize overheating problems—especially for the newer, hotter-running processors. If system noise is a problem, models with special fans can run more quietly than the standard models. These power supplies often use larger-diameter fans that spin more slowly, so they run more quietly but move the same amount of air as the smaller fans. PC Power and Cooling specializes in heavy-duty and quiet supplies; Astec has several heavy-duty models as well.

Ventilation in a system is also important. You must ensure adequate airflow to cool the hotter items in the system. Many processors today use passive heatsinks that require a steady stream of air to cool the chip. If the processor heatsink has its own fan, this is not much of a concern. If you have free expansion slots, you should space out the boards in your system to permit airflow between them. Place the hottest running boards nearest the fan or the ventilation holes in the system. Make sure that adequate airflow exists around the hard disk drive, especially for those that spin at high rates of speed. Some hard disks can generate quite a bit of heat during operation. If the hard disks overheat, data can be lost.

Always make sure you run your computer with the case cover on, especially if you have a loaded system. Removing the cover can actually cause a system to overheat. With the cover off, the power supply fan no longer draws air through the system. Instead, the fan ends up cooling the supply only, and the rest of the system must be cooled by simple convection. Although most systems do not immediately overheat for this reason, several of my own systems, especially those that are fully expanded, have overheated within 15–30 minutes when run with the case cover off.

In addition, be sure that any empty slot positions have the filler brackets installed. If you leave these brackets off after removing a card, the resultant hole in the case disrupts the internal airflow and can cause higher internal temperatures.

If you experience intermittent problems that you suspect are related to overheating, a higher-capacity replacement power supply is usually the best cure. Specially designed supplies with additional cooling fan capacity also can help. At least one company sells a device called a fan card, but I am not convinced these are a good idea. Unless the fan is positioned to draw air to or from outside the case, all it does is blow hot air around inside the system and provide a spot cooling effect for anything it is blowing on. In fact, adding fans in this manner contributes to the overall heat inside the system because the fan consumes power and generates heat.

CPU-mounted fans are an exception because they are designed only for spot cooling of the CPU. Many newer processors run so much hotter than the other components in the system that a conventional, finned aluminum heatsink cannot do the job. In this case, a small fan placed directly over the processor provides a spot cooling effect that keeps the processor temperatures down. One drawback to these active processor cooling fans is that the processor overheats instantly and can be damaged if they fail. Whenever possible, try to use the biggest passive (finned aluminum) heatsink you can find and purchase a CPU fan from a reputable vendor.

Using Digital Multimeters

One simple test you can perform on a power supply is to check the output voltages. This shows whether a power supply is operating correctly and whether the output voltages are within the correct tolerance range. Note that you must measure all voltages with the power supply connected to a proper load, which usually means testing while the power supply is still installed in the system and connected to the motherboard and peripheral devices.

Selecting a Meter

You need a simple Digital Multimeter (DMM) or Digital Volt-Ohm Meter (DVOM) to perform voltage and resistance checks on electronic circuits (see Figure 21.22). You should use only a DMM instead of the older needle-type multimeters because the older meters work by injecting 9V into the circuit when measuring resistance, which damages most computer circuits.

Figure 21.22 A typical DMM.

A DMM uses a much smaller voltage (usually 1.5V) when making resistance measurements, which is safe for electronic equipment. You can get a good DMM with many features from several sources. I prefer the small, pocket-size meters for computer work because they are easy to carry around.

Some features to look for in a good DMM are as follows:

■ *Pocket size.* This is self-explanatory, but small meters are available that have many, if not all, of the features of larger ones. The elaborate features found on some of the larger meters are not really necessary for computer work.

■ *Overload protection.* This means that if you plug the meter into a voltage or current beyond the meter's capability to measure, the meter protects itself from damage. Cheaper meters lack this protection and can be easily damaged by reading current or voltage values that are too high.

■ *Autoranging.* This means that the meter automatically selects the proper voltage or resistance range when making measurements. This is preferable to the manual range selection; however, really good meters offer both autoranging capability and a manual range override.

■ *Detachable probe leads.* The leads easily can be damaged, and sometimes a variety of differently shaped probes are required for different tests. Cheaper meters have the leads permanently attached, which means you cannot easily replace them. Look for a meter with detachable leads that plug into the meter.

■ *Audible continuity test.* Although you can use the ohm scale for testing continuity (0 ohms indicates continuity), a continuity test function causes the meter to produce a beep noise when continuity exists between the meter test leads. By using the sound, you quickly can test cable assemblies and other items for continuity. After you use this feature, you will never want to use the ohms display for this purpose again.

■ *Automatic power off.* These meters run on batteries, and the batteries can easily be worn down if the meter is accidentally left on. Good meters have an automatic shutoff that turns off the unit when it senses no readings for a predetermined period of time.

■ *Automatic display hold.* This feature enables you to hold the last stable reading on the display even after the reading is taken. This is especially useful if you are trying to work in a difficult-to-reach area single-handedly.

■ *Minimum and maximum trap.* This feature enables the meter to trap the lowest and highest readings in memory and hold them for later display, which is especially useful if you have readings that are fluctuating too quickly to see on the display.

Although you can get a basic pocket DMM for as little as $20, one with all these features is priced in the $100–$200 range. Radio Shack carries some nice inexpensive units, and you can purchase the high-end models from electronics supply houses, such as Newark or Digi-Key.

Measuring Voltage

To measure voltages on a system that is operating, you must use a technique called *back probing* on the connectors (see Figure 21.23). You cannot disconnect any of the connectors while the system is running, so you must measure with everything connected. Nearly all the connectors you need to probe have openings in the back where the wires enter the connector. The meter probes are narrow enough to fit into the connector alongside the wire and make contact with the metal terminal inside. The technique is called back probing because you are probing the connector from the back. You must use this back-probing technique to perform virtually all the following measurements.

To test a power supply for proper output, check the voltage at the Power_Good pin (P8-1 on AT, Baby-AT, and LPX supplies; pin 8 on the ATX-type connector) for +3V to +6V of power. If the measurement is not within this range, the system never sees the Power_Good signal and therefore does not start or run properly. In most cases, the power supply is bad and must be replaced.

Figure 21.23 Back probing the power supply connectors.

Continue by measuring the voltage ranges of the pins on the motherboard and drive power connectors. If you are measuring voltages for testing purposes, any reading within 10% of the specified voltage is considered acceptable, although most manufacturers of high-quality power supplies specify a tighter 5% tolerance. For ATX power supplies, the specification requires that voltages must be within 5% of the rating, except for the 3.3V current, which must be within 4%. The following table shows the voltage ranges within these tolerances.

Desired Voltage	Min. (-10%)	Loose Tolerance Max. (+8%)	Min. (-5%)	Tight Tolerance Max. (+5%)
+3.3V	2.97V	3.63V	3.135	3.465
+/−5.0V	4.5V	5.4V	4.75	5.25
+/−12.0V	10.8V	12.9V	11.4	12.6

The Power_Good signal has tolerances that are different from the other voltages, although it is nominally +5V in most systems. The trigger point for Power_Good is about +2.4V, but most systems require the signal voltage to be within the tolerances listed here:

Signal	Minimum	Maximum
Power_Good (+5V)	3.0V	6.0V

Replace the power supply if the voltages you measure are out of these ranges. Again, it is worth noting that any and all power supply tests and measurements must be made with the power supply properly loaded, which usually means it must be installed in a system and the system must be running.

Specialized Test Equipment

You can use several types of specialized test gear to test power supplies more effectively. Because the power supply is one of the most failure-prone items in PCs today, you should have these specialized items if you service many PC systems.

Digital Infrared Thermometer

One of the greatest additions to my toolbox is a digital infrared thermometer. They also are called noncontact thermometers because they measure by sensing infrared energy without having to touch the item they are reading. This enables me to make instant spot checks of the temperature of a chip, a board, or the system chassis. They are available from companies such as Raytek (http://www.raytek.com) for under $100. To use these handheld items, you point at an object and then pull the trigger. Within seconds, the display shows a temperature readout. These devices are invaluable in checking to ensure your system is adequately cooled.

Variable Voltage Transformer

When testing power supplies, it is sometimes desirable to simulate different AC voltage conditions at the wall socket to observe how the supply reacts. A variable voltage transformer is a useful test device for checking power supplies because it enables you to exercise control over the AC line voltage used as input for the power supply (see Figure 21.24). This device consists of a large transformer mounted in a housing with a dial indicator that controls the output voltage. You plug the line cord from the transformer into the wall socket and plug the PC power cord into the socket provided on the transformer. The knob on the transformer can be used to adjust the AC line voltage received by the PC.

Most variable transformers can adjust their AC outputs from 0V to 140V, no matter what the AC input (wall socket) voltage is. Some can cover a range from 0V to 280V, as well. You can use the transformer to simulate brownout conditions, enabling you to observe the PC's response. Thus, you can check a power supply for proper Power_Good signal operation, among other things.

Figure 21.24   A variable voltage transformer.

By running the PC and dropping the voltage until the PC shuts down, you can see how much reserve is in the power supply for handling a brownout or other voltage fluctuations. If your transformer can output voltages in the 200V range, you can test the capability of the power supply to run on foreign voltage levels. A properly functioning supply should operate between 90V and 135V but should shut down cleanly if the voltage is outside that range.

One indication of a problem is seeing parity check-type error messages when you drop the voltage to 80V. This indicates that the Power_Good signal is not being withdrawn before the power supply output to the PC fails. The PC should simply stop operating as the Power_Good signal is withdrawn, causing the system to enter a continuous reset loop.

Variable voltage transformers are sold by a number of electronic parts supply houses, such as Newark and Digi-Key. You should expect to pay anywhere from $100 to $300 for this device.

Repairing the Power Supply

Hardly anyone actually repairs power supplies anymore, primarily because simply replacing the supply with a new one is usually cheaper. Even high-quality power supplies are not that expensive when compared to the labor required to repair them.

A defective power supply usually is discarded unless it happens to be one of the higher-quality or more expensive units. In that case, it is usually wise to send the supply out to a company that specializes in repairing power supplies and other components. These companies usually provide what is called depot repair, which means you send the supply to them, and they repair it and return it to you. If time is of the essence, most of the depot repair companies immediately send you a functional equivalent to your defective supply and take yours in as a core charge. Depot repair is the recommended way to service many PC components, such as power supplies, monitors, and printers. If you take your PC in to a conventional service outlet, they often determine which component has the problem and send it out to be depot repaired. You can do that yourself and save the markup the repair shop normally charges in such cases.

For those with experience around high voltages, you might be able to repair a failing supply with two relatively simple operations; however, these require opening the supply. I do not recommend doing so, but I mention it only as an alternative to replacement in some cases.

Most manufacturers try to prevent you from entering the supply by sealing it with special tamper-proof Torx screws. These screws use the familiar Torx star driver but also have a tamper-prevention pin in the center that prevents a standard driver from working. Most tool companies, such as Jensen or Specialized, sell sets of TT (tamperproof Torx) bits, which remove the tamper-resistant screws. Other manufacturers rivet the power supply case shut, which means you must drill out the rivets to gain access.

Caution

The manufacturers place these obstacles there for a reason—to prevent entry by those who are inexperienced with high voltage. Consider yourself warned!

Obtaining Replacement Units

Most of the time, it is simply easier, safer, or less expensive (considering the time and materials involved) to replace the power supply rather than to repair it. As mentioned earlier, replacement power supplies are available from many manufacturers. Before you can shop for a supplier, however, you should consider other purchasing factors.

Deciding on a Power Supply

When you are shopping for a new power supply, you should take several factors into account. First, consider the power supply's shape, or form factor. For example, the power supply used in an AT-style system differs in size from the one used in a Slimline computer. The larger AT form factor power supplies simply will not fit into a Slimline case designed for an LPX supply. ATX supplies are consistent in size, so any ATX supply should fit any ATX chassis.

Apart from electrical considerations, power supply form factors can differ physically in their sizes, shapes, screw-hole positions, connector types, number of connectors, fan locations, and switch positions. However, systems that use the same form factor can easily interchange power supplies. When ordering a replacement supply, you need to know which form factor your system requires.

Some systems use proprietary power supply designs, which makes replacement more difficult. If a system uses one of the common form factor power supplies, replacement units are available from hundreds of vendors. An unfortunate user of a system with a nonstandard form factor supply does not have this kind of choice and must get a replacement from the original manufacturer of the system—and usually pay through the nose for the unit. Although you can find standard form factor supplies for under $100, the proprietary units from some manufacturers run as high as $400 or more. PC buyers often overlook this and discover too late the consequences of having nonstandard components in a system.

▶▶ See "Power Supply Form Factors," p. 1107.

Cheaper retail-store systems are notorious for using proprietary form factor power supplies. Even Dell has been using proprietary supplies in many of their systems. Be sure you consider this if you intend to own these types of systems out of warranty. Personally, I always insist on systems that use industry-standard power supplies, such as the ATX form factor supply found in many systems today.

Sources for Replacement Power Supplies

Because one of the most failure-prone items in PC systems is the power supply, I am often asked to recommend a replacement. Literally hundreds of companies manufacture PC power supplies, and I certainly have not tested them all. I can, however, recommend some companies whose products I have come to know and trust.

Although other high-quality manufacturers are out there, at this time I recommend power supplies from either Astec Standard Power or PC Power and Cooling.

Astec makes the power supplies used in most of the high-end systems by IBM, Hewlett-Packard, Apple, and many other name-brand systems. They have power supplies available in a number of standard form factors (AT/Tower, Baby-AT, LPX, and ATX) and a variety of output levels. They have power supplies with ratings of up to 450 watts and power supplies especially designed for Green PCs, which meet the EPA Energy Star requirements for low-power consumption. Their Green power supplies are specifically designed to achieve high efficiency at low-load conditions. Be aware that high-output supplies from other manufacturers might have problems with very low loads. Astec also makes a number of power supplies for laptop and notebook PC systems and has numerous nonPC type supplies.

PC Power and Cooling has a complete line of power supplies for PC systems. They make supplies in all the standard PC form factors used today. Versions are available in a variety of quality and output levels, from inexpensive replacements to very high-quality, high-output models with ratings of up to 600–850 watts. They even have versions with built-in battery backup and redundant power systems, and a series of special models with high-volume, low-speed (quiet) fan assemblies. Their quiet models are especially welcome to people who work in quiet homes or offices and are annoyed by the fan noise that some power supplies emanate. My favorite is their 425W ATX supply, which has specs that put most others to shame.

PC Power and Cooling also has units available that fit some of Compaq's proprietary designs. This can be a real boon if you have to service or repair Compaq systems because the PC Power and Cooling units are available in higher output ratings than Compaq's. These units cost much less than Compaq's and bolt in as direct replacements.

Tip

PC Power and Cooling also have SFX style supplies that can be used to upgrade systems with Flex-ATX boards and chassis, including E-machines and other low-cost systems. If you have one of these systems and need a high-quality replacement supply to support your upgrades, PC Power and Cooling can help.

The support offered by PC Power and Cooling is excellent as well, and they have been in business a long time, which is rare in this industry. Besides power supplies, they also have an excellent line of cases.

A high-quality power supply from either of these vendors can be one of the best cures for intermittent system problems and can go a long way toward ensuring trouble-free operation in the future.

Custom Cases

Several companies make specialized cases for unique systems. These cases offer features such as multiple drive bays, unique appearance, and specialized cooling.

Perhaps the most unique cases on the market are those by Kryotech. They market a case with a built-in refrigeration unit in the base, connected directly to a thermal plate that mounts on the CPU. The plate runs at +80° F (+27° C) and can maintain a CPU temperature in the 90°–100° F range with processors generating up to 45W. These cases also feature an LCD temperature display on the front for monitoring the temperature. A safety system shutdown is designed to trip if the processor overheats. They have models available for Socket 7, Socket 370, Slot 1, or Slot A processors.

The only drawback to these cases is the expense; they cost about $400 each. They also do not include a power supply, which would cost another $100–$200 for something 300W or greater to go with it.

Note that Kryotech does make a specialized cooling system that cools the CPU down to –40° F (–40° C), but these are only sold complete with motherboards and processors because of their specialized natures.

Another company offering special cases is PC Power and Cooling. They have a line of heavy-duty, solid steel cases with multiple drive bays for serious expansion and server use. For those who want something that's different and sure to evoke stares from all that see it, they also offer a tower case with a chrome-plated front bezel and black cover.

Using Power-Protection Systems

Power-protection systems do just what the name implies: They protect your equipment from the effects of power surges and power failures. In particular, power surges and spikes can damage computer equipment, and a loss of power can result in lost data. In this section, you learn about the four primary types of power-protection devices available and when you should use them.

Before considering any further levels of power protection, you should know that a quality power supply already affords you a substantial amount of protection. High-end power supplies from the vendors I recommend are designed to provide protection from higher-than-normal voltages and currents, and they provide a limited amount of power-line noise filtering. Some of the inexpensive aftermarket power supplies probably do not have this sort of protection. If you have an inexpensive computer, further protecting your system might be wise.

Caution

All the power-protection features in this chapter and the protection features in the power supply inside your computer require that the computer's AC power cable be connected to a ground.

Many older homes do not have three-prong (grounded) outlets to accommodate grounded devices.

Do not use a three-pronged adapter (that bypasses the three-prong requirement and enables you to connect to a two-prong socket) to plug in a surge suppressor, computer, or UPS into a two-pronged outlet. They often don't provide a good ground and can inhibit the capabilities of your power-protection devices.

You also should test your power sockets to ensure they are grounded. Sometimes outlets, despite having three-prong sockets, are not connected to a ground wire; an inexpensive socket tester (available at most hardware stores) can detect this condition.

Of course, the easiest form of protection is to turn off and unplug your computer equipment (including your modem) when a thunderstorm is imminent. When this is not possible, however, other alternatives are available.

Power supplies should stay within operating specifications and continue to run a system even if any of these power line disturbances occur:

- Voltage drop to 80V for up to 2 seconds
- Voltage drop to 70V for up to .5 seconds
- Voltage surge of up to 143V for up to 1 second

Neither most high-quality power supplies nor systems will be damaged by the following occurrences:

- Full power outage
- Any voltage drop (brownout)
- A spike of up to 2,500V

Because of their internal protection, many computer manufacturers that use high-quality power supplies state in their documentation that external surge suppressors are not needed with their systems.

To verify the levels of protection built into the existing power supply in a computer system, an independent laboratory subjected several unprotected PC systems to various spikes and surges of up to 6,000V—considered the maximum level of surge that can be transmitted to a system through an electrical outlet. Any higher voltage would cause the power to arc to the ground within the outlet. None of the systems sustained permanent damage in these tests. The worst thing that happened was that some of the systems rebooted or shut down when the surge was more than 2,000V. Each system restarted when the power switch was toggled after a shutdown.

I do not use any real form of power protection on my systems, and they have survived near-direct lightning strikes and powerful surges. The most recent incident, only 50 feet from my office, was a direct lightning strike to a brick chimney that blew the top of the chimney apart. None of my systems (which were running at the time) were damaged in any way from this incident; they just shut themselves down. I was able to restart each system by toggling the power switches. An alarm system located in the same office, however, was destroyed by this strike. I am not saying that lightning strikes or even much milder spikes and surges cannot damage computer systems—another nearby lightning strike did destroy a modem and serial adapter installed in one of my systems. I was just lucky that the destruction did not include the motherboard.

This discussion points out an important oversight in some power-protection strategies: Do not forget to provide protection from spikes and surges on the phone line.

The automatic shutdown of a computer during power disturbances is a built-in function of most high-quality power supplies. You can reset the power supply by flipping the power switch from on to off and back on again. Some power supplies even have an auto-restart function. This type of power supply acts the same as others in a massive surge or spike situation: It shuts down the system. The difference is that after normal power resumes, the power supply waits for a specified delay of 3–6 seconds and then resets itself and powers the system back up. Because no manual switch resetting is required, this feature might be desirable in systems functioning as network servers or in those found in other unattended locations.

The first time I witnessed a large surge cause an immediate shutdown of all my systems, I was extremely surprised. All the systems were silent, but the monitor and modem lights were still on. My first thought was that everything was blown, but a simple toggle of each system-unit power switch caused the power supplies to reset, and the units powered up with no problem. Since that first time, this type of shutdown has happened to me several times, always without further problems.

The following types of power-protection devices are explained in the sections that follow:

- Surge suppressors
- Phone-line surge protectors
- Line conditioners
- Standby power supplies (SPS)
- Uninterruptible power supplies (UPS)

Surge Suppressors (Protectors)

The simplest form of power protection is any one of the commercially available surge protectors—that is, devices inserted between the system and the power line. These devices, which cost between $20 and $200, can absorb the high-voltage transients produced by nearby lightning strikes and power equipment. Some surge protectors can be effective for certain types of power problems, but they offer only very limited protection.

Surge protectors use several devices, usually metal-oxide varistors (MOVs), that can clamp and shunt away all voltages above a certain level. MOVs are designed to accept voltages as high as 6,000V and divert any power above 200V to ground. MOVs can handle normal surges, but powerful surges such as a direct lightning strike can blow right through them. MOVs are not designed to handle a very high level of power and self-destruct while shunting a large surge. These devices therefore cease to function after either a single large surge or a series of smaller ones. The real problem is that you cannot easily tell when they no longer are functional. The only way to test them is to subject the MOVs to a surge, which destroys them. Therefore, you never really know whether your so-called surge protector is protecting your system.

Some surge protectors have status lights that let you know when a surge large enough to blow the MOVs has occurred. A surge suppressor without this status indicator light is useless because you never know when it has stopped protecting.

Underwriters Laboratories has produced an excellent standard that governs surge suppressors, called UL 1449. Any surge suppressor that meets this standard is a very good one and definitely offers a line of protection beyond what the power supply in your PC already offers. The only types of surge suppressors worth buying, therefore, should have two features:

- Conformance to the UL 1449 standard
- A status light indicating when the MOVs are blown

Units that meet the UL 1449 specification say so on the packaging or directly on the unit. If this standard is not mentioned, it does not conform. Therefore, you should avoid it.

Another good feature to have in a surge suppressor is a built-in circuit breaker that can be manually reset rather than a fuse. The breaker protects your system if it or a peripheral develops a short. These better surge suppressors usually cost about $40.

Phone Line Surge Protectors

In addition to protecting the power lines, it is critical to provide protection to your systems from any connected phone lines. If you are using a modem or fax board that is plugged into the phone system, any surges or spikes that travel through the phone line can damage your system. In many areas, the phone lines are especially susceptible to lightning strikes, which are the leading cause of fried modems and damage to the computer equipment attached to them.

Several companies manufacture or sell simple surge protectors that plug in between your modem and the phone line. These inexpensive devices can be purchased from most electronics supply houses. Most of the cable and communication products vendors listed in the Vendor List sell these phone line surge protectors. Some of the standard power line surge protectors include connectors for phone line protection as well.

Line Conditioners

In addition to high-voltage and current conditions, other problems can occur with incoming power. The voltage might dip below the level needed to run the system, resulting in a brownout. Forms of electrical noise other than simple voltage surges or spikes might travel through the power line, such as radio-frequency interference or electrical noise caused by motors or other inductive loads.

Remember two things when you wire together digital devices (such as computers and their peripherals):

■ Any wire can act as an antenna and have voltage induced in it by nearby electromagnetic fields, which can come from other wires, telephones, CRTs, motors, fluorescent fixtures, static discharge, and, of course, radio transmitters.

■ Digital circuitry responds with surprising efficiency to noise of even a volt or two, making those induced voltages particularly troublesome. The electrical wiring in your building can act as an antenna, picking up all kinds of noise and disturbances.

A line conditioner can handle many of these types of problems. A line conditioner is designed to remedy a variety of problems. It filters the power, bridges brownouts, suppresses high-voltage and current conditions, and generally acts as a buffer between the power line and the system. A line conditioner does the job of a surge suppressor, and much more. It is more of an active device, functioning continuously, rather than a passive device that activates only when a surge is present. A line conditioner provides true power conditioning and can handle myriad problems. It contains transformers, capacitors, and other circuitry that can temporarily bridge a brownout or low-voltage situation. These units usually cost $100–$300, depending on the power-handling capacity of the unit.

Backup Power

The next level of power protection includes backup power-protection devices. These units can provide power in case of a complete blackout, thereby providing the time necessary for an orderly system shutdown. Two types are available: the standby power supply (SPS) and the uninterruptible power supply (UPS). The UPS is a special device because it does much more than just provide backup power: It is also the best kind of line conditioner you can buy.

Standby Power Supplies

A standby power supply is known as an offline device: It functions only when normal power is disrupted. An SPS system uses a special circuit that can sense the AC line current. If the sensor detects a loss of power on the line, the system quickly switches over to a standby battery and power inverter. The power inverter converts the battery power to 110V AC power, which is then supplied to the system.

SPS systems do work, but sometimes a problem occurs during the switch to battery power. If the switch is not fast enough, the computer system shuts down or reboots anyway, which defeats the purpose of having the backup power supply. A truly outstanding SPS adds to the circuit a ferroresonant transformer, a large transformer with the capability to store a small amount of power and deliver it during the switch time. This device functions as a buffer on the power line, giving the SPS almost uninterruptible capability.

SPS units also might have internal line conditioning of their own. Under normal circumstances, most cheaper units place your system directly on the regular power line and offer no conditioning. The addition of a ferroresonant transformer to an SPS gives it additional regulation and protection capabilities because of the buffer effect of the transformer. SPS devices without the ferroresonant transformer still require the use of a line conditioner for full protection. SPS systems usually cost from a couple hundred to several thousand dollars, depending on the quality and power-output capacity.

Uninterruptible Power Supplies

Perhaps the best overall solution to any power problem is to provide a power source that is conditioned and that cannot be interrupted—which is the definition of an uninterruptible power supply. UPSes are known as online systems because they continuously function and supply power to your computer systems. Because some companies advertise ferroresonant SPS devices as though they were UPS devices, many now use the term *true UPS* to describe a truly online system. A true UPS system is constructed in much the same way as an SPS system; however, because the computer is always operating from the battery, there is no switching circuit.

In a true UPS, your system always operates from the battery. A voltage inverter converts from 12V DC to 110V AC. You essentially have your own private power system that generates power independently of the AC line. A battery charger connected to the line or wall current keeps the battery charged at a rate equal to or greater than the rate at which power is consumed.

When the AC current supplying the battery charger fails, a true UPS continues functioning undisturbed because the battery-charging function is all that is lost. Because the computer was already running off the battery, no switch takes place, and no power disruption is possible. The battery begins discharging at a rate dictated by the amount of load your system places on the unit, which (based on the size of the battery) gives you plenty of time to execute an orderly system shutdown. Based on an appropriately scaled storage battery, the UPS functions continuously, generating power and preventing unpleasant surprises. When the line power returns, the battery charger begins recharging the battery, again with no interruption.

Note

Occasionally, a UPS can accumulate too much storage and not enough discharge. When this occurs, the UPS emits a loud alarm, alerting you that it's full. Simply unplugging the unit from the AC power source for a while can discharge the excess storage (as it powers your computer) and drain the UPS of the excess.

Many SPS systems are advertised as though they are true UPS systems. The giveaway is the unit's switch time. If a specification for switch time exists, the unit cannot be a true UPS because UPS units never switch. However, a good SPS with a ferroresonant transformer can virtually equal the performance of a true UPS at a lower cost.

Note

Many UPSes today come equipped with a cable and software that enables the protected computer to shut down in an orderly manner on receipt of a signal from the UPS. This way, the system can shut down properly even if the computer is unattended. Some operating systems, such as Windows NT/2000, contain their own UPS software components.

UPS cost is a direct function of both the length of time it can continue to provide power after a line current failure and how much power it can provide. You therefore should purchase a UPS that provides enough power to run your system and peripherals and enough time to close files and provide an orderly shutdown. Remember, however, to manually perform a system shutdown procedure during a power outage. You will probably need your monitor plugged into the UPS and the computer. Be sure the UPS you purchase can provide sufficient power for all the devices you must connect to it.

Because of a true UPS's almost total isolation from the line current, it is unmatched as a line conditioner and surge suppressor. The best UPS systems add a ferroresonant transformer for even greater power conditioning and protection capability. This type of UPS is the best form of power protection available. The price, however, can be high. To find out just how much power your computer system requires, look at the UL sticker on the back of the unit. This sticker lists the maximum power draw in watts, or sometimes in just volts and amperes. If only voltage and amperage are listed, multiply the two figures to calculate the wattage.

As an example, if the documentation for a system indicates that the computer can require as much as 110V at a maximum current draw of 5 amps, the maximum power the system can draw is about 550 watts. This wattage is for a system with every slot full, two hard disks, and one floppy—in other words, a system at the maximum possible level of expansion. The system should never draw any more power than that; if it does, a 5-amp fuse in the power supply will blow. This type of system normally draws an average of 300 watts; to be safe when you make calculations for UPS capacity, however, be conservative. Use the 550-watt figure. Adding a monitor that draws 100 watts brings the total to 650 watts or more. Therefore, to run two fully loaded systems, you'll need a 1,100-watt UPS. Don't forget two monitors, each drawing 100 watts. Therefore, the total is 1,300 watts. A UPS of that capacity or greater will cost approximately $500–$700. Unfortunately, that is what the best level of protection costs. Most companies can justify this type of expense only for critical-use PCs, such as network servers.

Note

The highest-capacity UPS sold for use with a conventional 15-amp outlet is about 1,400 watts. If it's any higher, you risk tripping a 15-amp circuit when the battery is charging heavily and the inverter is drawing maximum current.

In addition to the total available output power (wattage), several other factors can distinguish one UPS from another. The addition of a ferroresonant transformer improves a unit's power conditioning and buffering capabilities. Good units also have an inverter that produces a true sine wave output; the cheaper ones might generate a square wave. A square wave is an approximation of a sine wave with abrupt up-and-down voltage transitions. The abrupt transitions of a square wave are not compatible with some computer equipment power supplies. Be sure that the UPS you purchase produces power that is compatible with your computer equipment. Every unit has a specification for how long it can sustain output at the rated level. If your systems draw less than the rated level, you have some additional time.

Caution

Be careful! Most UPS systems are not designed for you to sit and compute for hours through an electrical blackout. They are designed to provide power only to essential components and to remain operating long enough to allow for an orderly shutdown. You pay a large amount for units that provide power for more than 15 minutes or so. At some point, it becomes more cost effective to buy a generator than to keep investing in extended life for a UPS.

Some of the many sources of power protection equipment include American Power Conversion (APC), Tripp Lite, and Best Power. These companies sell a variety of UPS, SPS, line, and surge protector products.

Caution

Don't connect a laser printer to a backed-up socket in any SPS or UPS unit. Such printers are electrically noisy and have widely varying current draws. This can be hard on the inverter in an SPS or a UPS, frequently causing the inverter to fail or detect an overload and shut down. Either case means that your system will lose power, too.

Printers are normally noncritical because whatever is being printed can be reprinted. Don't connect them to a UPS unless there's a good business need to do so.

Some UPSes and SPSes have sockets that are conditioned but not backed up—that is, they do not draw power from the battery. In cases such as this, you can safely plug printers and other peripherals into these sockets.

RTC/NVRAM Batteries (CMOS Chips)

All 16-bit and higher systems have a special type of chip in them that combines a real-time clock (RTC) with at least 64 bytes (including the clock data) of Non-Volatile RAM (NVRAM) memory. This chip is officially called the RTC/NVRAM chip but is often referred to as the CMOS chip or CMOS RAM because the type of chip used is produced using a CMOS (Complementary Metal-Oxide Semiconductor) process. CMOS design chips are known for very low power consumption. This special RTC/NVRAM chip is designed to run off a battery for several years.

The original chip of this type used in the IBM AT was the Motorola 146818 chip. Although the chips used today have different manufacturers and part numbers, they all are designed to be compatible with this original Motorola part.

These chips include a real-time clock. Its function should be obvious: The clock enables software to read the date and time and preserves the date and time data even when the system is powered off or unplugged.

The NVRAM portion of the chip has another function. It is designed to store basic system configuration, including the amount of memory installed, types of floppy and hard disk drives, and other information. Some of the more modern motherboards use extended NVRAM chips with as much as 2KB or more of space to hold this configuration information. This is especially true for Plug-and-Play systems, which store not only the motherboard configuration but also the configuration of adapter cards. This system can then read this information every time you power on the system.

These chips normally are powered by some type of battery while the system is off. This battery preserves the information in the NVRAM and powers the clock. Most systems use a lithium-type battery because they have a very long life, especially at the low power draw from the typical RTC/NVRAM chip.

Some systems have a chip that has the battery embedded within it. These are made by several companies—including Dallas Semiconductor and Benchmarq. These chips are notable for their long lives. Under normal conditions, the battery will last for 10 years—which is, of course, longer than the useful life of the system. If your system uses one of the Dallas or Benchmarq modules, the battery and chip must be replaced as a unit because they are integrated. Most of the time, these chip/battery combinations are installed in a socket on the motherboard just in case a problem requires an early replacement. You can get new modules direct from the manufacturers for $18 or less, which is often less than the cost of the older separate battery alone.

Some systems do not use a battery at all. Hewlett-Packard, for example, includes a special capacitor in some of their systems that is automatically recharged anytime the system is plugged in. Note that the system does not have to be running for the capacitor to charge; it only has to be plugged in. If the system is unplugged, the capacitor will power the RTC/NVRAM chip for up to a week or more. If the system remains unplugged for a duration longer than that, the NVRAM information is lost. In that case, these systems can reload the NVRAM from a backup kept in a special flash ROM chip contained on the motherboard. The only pieces of information that will actually be missing when you repower the system will be the date and time, which will have to be reentered. By using the capacitor combined with an NVRAM backup in flash ROM, these systems have a very reliable solution that will last indefinitely.

Many systems use only a conventional battery, which can be either directly soldered into the motherboard or plugged in via a battery connector. For those systems with the battery soldered in, normally a spare battery connector exists on the motherboard where you can insert a conventional plug-in battery, should the original ever fail. In most cases, you would never have to replace the motherboard battery, even if it were completely dead.

Conventional batteries come in many forms. The best are of a lithium design because they will last from two to five years or more. I have seen systems with conventional alkaline batteries mounted in a holder; these are much less desirable because they fail more frequently and do not last as long. Also, they can be prone to leak, and if a battery leaks on the motherboard, the motherboard can be severely damaged. By far, the most commonly used battery for motherboards today is the 2032 lithium coin battery, which is about the size of a quarter and is readily available.

Besides the various battery types, the chip can require any one of several voltages. The batteries in PCs are normally 3.0V, 3.6V, 4.5V, or 6V. If you are replacing the battery, be sure your replacement is the same voltage as the one you removed from the system. Some motherboards can use batteries of several voltages. Use a jumper or switch to select the various settings. If you suspect your motherboard has this capability, consult the documentation for instructions on changing the settings. Of course, the easiest thing to do is to replace the existing battery with another of the same type.

Symptoms that indicate that the battery is about to fail include having to reset the clock on your PC every time you shut down the system (especially after moving it) and problems during the system's POST, such as drive-detection difficulties. If you experience problems such as these, you should make note of your system's CMOS settings and replace the battery as soon as possible.

Caution

When you replace a PC battery, be sure you get the polarity correct; otherwise, you will damage the RTC/NVRAM (CMOS) chip. Because the chip is soldered onto most motherboards, this can be an expensive mistake! The battery connector on the motherboard and the battery normally are keyed to prevent a backward connection. The pinout of this connector is on the CD, but it should also be listed in your system documentation.

When you replace a battery, in most cases the existing data stored in the NVRAM is lost. Sometimes, however, the data remains intact for several minutes (I have observed NVRAM retain information with no power for an hour or more), so if you make the battery swap quickly, the information in the NVRAM might be retained. Just to be sure, I recommend that you record all the system configuration settings stored in the NVRAM by your system Setup program. In most cases, you would want to run the BIOS Setup program and copy or print out all the screens showing the various settings. Some Setup programs offer the capability to save the NVRAM data to a file for later restoration if necessary.

Tip

If your system BIOS is password protected and you forget the password, one possible way to bypass the block is to remove the battery for a few minutes and then replace it. This will reset the BIOS to its default settings, removing the password protection.

After replacing a battery, power up the system and use the Setup program to check the date and time setting and any other data that was stored in the NVRAM.

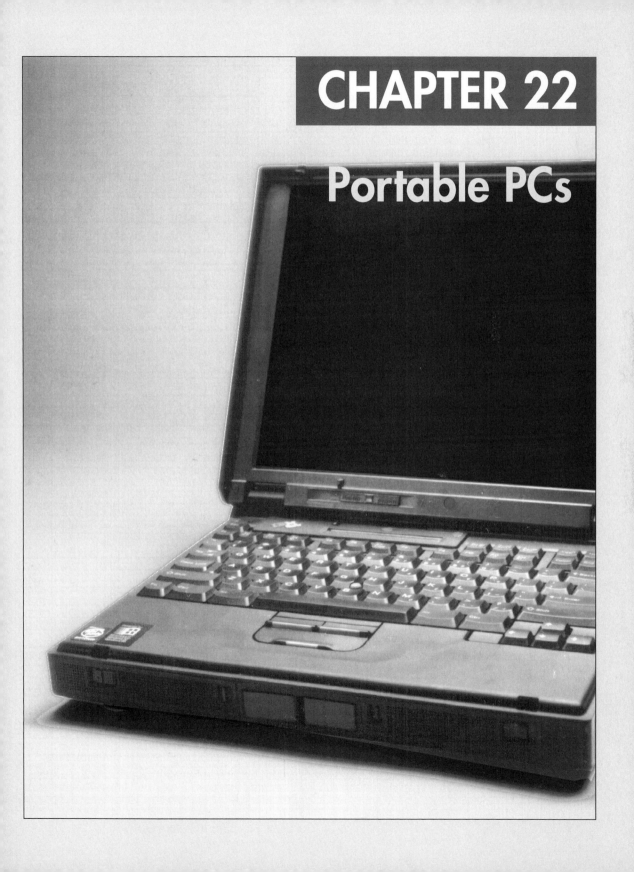

CHAPTER 22

Portable PCs

Types and Classes of Portable Computers

Three basic form factors describe most of the PC-compatible portable computers on the market today: laptops, notebooks, and subnotebooks. A fourth type, hand-held/palmtops, is not currently being distributed outside of Japan, but these are still useful if you can purchase a used model. The definitions of the first three types are fluid, with the options available on some systems causing particular models to ride the cusp of two categories. The categories are based primarily on size and weight, but these factors have a natural relationship to the capabilities of the system because a larger case obviously can fit more into it. These form factors are described in the following sections. Note that these designations are somewhat vague, and the marketing departments in most companies like to come up with their own terms for what they think a particular system might conform to. So don't be surprised if you see a system I might refer to as a *laptop* be called a *notebook*, or vice versa, by the manufacturer.

Laptops

As the original name coined for the clamshell-type portable computer, the laptop is the largest of the three major form factors. Typically, a laptop system weighs 7 pounds or more and is approximately 9×12×2 inches in size, although the larger screens now arriving on the market are causing all portable system sizes to increase. Originally the smallest possible size for a computer, laptops today have become the high-end machines, offering features and performance comparable to a desktop system.

Indeed, many laptops are being positioned in the market either as desktop replacements or as multimedia systems suitable for delivering presentations on the road. Because of their greater weight, laptops typically are used by salespeople and other travelers who require the features they provide. However, many high-performance laptops are now being issued to users as their sole computer, even if they travel only from the office to the home. Large active-matrix displays, 64MB–256MB of RAM, and hard drives of up to 20GB or more in size are all but ubiquitous, with virtually all systems now carrying fast CD-ROM or DVD drives; onboard speakers; and connectivity options that enable the use of external display, storage, and sound systems. Some models even include combo DVD-CD/RW drives and wireless Wi-Fi network capabilities.

To use them as a desktop replacement, you can equip many laptops with a docking station (or a less expensive port replicator) that functions as the user's "home base," enabling connection to a network and the use of a full-size monitor and keyboard. For someone who travels frequently, this arrangement often works better than separate desktop and portable systems, on which data must continually be kept in sync. Naturally, you pay a premium for all this functionality. Cutting-edge laptop systems can now cost as much as $2,500–$4,500 or more—at least twice the price of a comparable desktop.

Notebooks

A notebook system is designed to be somewhat smaller than a laptop in nearly every way: size, weight, features, and price. The dividing line between what we might call a notebook or laptop system is somewhat fuzzy. You'll find that these categorizations are somewhat flexible. Weighing 5–7 pounds, notebooks typically have smaller and less-capable displays and lack the high-end multimedia functions of laptops, but they need not be stripped-down machines. Many notebooks have hard drive and memory configurations comparable to laptops, and virtually all are equipped with CD-ROM or DVD drives and sound capabilities.

Designed to function as an adjunct to a desktop system rather than a replacement, a notebook can actually be used as a primary desktop replacement for all but the most power-hungry users. Notebooks typically have a wide array of options because they are targeted at a wider audience, from the power user who can't quite afford (or who doesn't want the size and weight of) the top-of-the-line laptop to the bargain hunter who requires only basic services. Prices can range from under $1,000 to more than $2,500.

Subnotebooks

Subnotebooks are substantially smaller than both notebooks and laptops and are intended for users who must enter and work with data on the road, as well as connect to the office network. Weighing 4–5 pounds, and often less than an inch thick, the subnotebook is intended for the traveler who feels overburdened by the larger machines and doesn't need their high-end capabilities.

Usually, the first component omitted in a subnotebook design is the internal floppy drive, although some include external units. You also will not find CD-ROM drives and other bulky hardware components built in, although some machines, such as IBM's ThinkPad X21, use a detachable module (or "slice") that fits under the main system to carry CD-ROM or DVD drives and floppy drives. However, many subnotebooks do include large, high-quality displays, plenty of hard drive space, and a full-size keyboard (by portable standards).

As is common in the electronics world, devices become more inexpensive as they get smaller, but only up to a certain point at which small size becomes a commodity and prices begin to go up. Some subnotebooks are intended (and priced) for the high-end market, such as for the executive who uses the system for little else but email and scheduling but who wants a lightweight, elegant, and impressive-looking system. Subnotebooks range in price from under $2,000 to around $4,000, depending on features.

Palmtop (Handheld Mini-Notebooks)

The rarest category (at least outside of Japan these days) is the palmtop PC. Not to be confused with the PDAs (such as the Palm or Handspring series) or the PocketPC, these handheld mini-notebook computers run Windows 9x and use standard applications and external accessories. Palmtop computers are typified by the Libretto series from Toshiba (now discontinued outside of Japan but still available on the used market in North America). Librettos weigh about 2 pounds, feature a built-in hard disk, have screens of 8 inches or less in size, and offer a tiny keyboard with an integral TrackPoint device. These systems don't offer the faster or more power-hungry Pentium II/III/Celeron processors but are fully functional PCs that run normal Windows and normal applications using various Pentium-class CPUs. Some of the newest Japan-market Librettos use the Transmeta Crusoe processor, which can emulate Pentium and similar x86 CPUs. If you can find a palmtop on the used or refurbished market, this type of system is ideal as a secondary system for somebody who travels and demands the smallest and lightest, yet fully functional, PC.

Palmtops such as the Libretto offer a standard layout of keys, but with the keys spaced much more closely together than with a standard keyboard. As such, this class of system is very difficult to use for extensive typing, but for simple field work, email, or Internet access—or anything that doesn't require a lot of data entry—they are incredibly useful.

Evolution of the Portable Computer

Portables, like their desktop counterparts, have evolved a great deal since the days when the word *portable* could refer to a desktop-sized case with a handle on it. Today, portable systems can rival the performance of their desktop counterparts in nearly every way. Many systems are now being marketed as "desktop replacements," which companies are providing to traveling employees as their primary systems. This chapter examines the types of portable computers available and the technologies designed specifically for use in mobile systems.

Portables started out as suitcase-sized systems that differed from desktops mainly in that all the components, including the monitor, were installed into a single case. Compaq was among the first to market portable computers such as these in the 1980s, and although their size, weight, and appearance were almost laughable when compared to today's portables, they were cutting-edge technology for the time. The components themselves were not very different from those in standard computers.

Most portable systems are now approximately the size of the notebook they are often named for and are built using the clamshell design that has become an industry standard, with nearly every component developed specifically for use in mobile systems. Portables are not the same as PDAs, however. Portable computers use the same operating systems and applications as desktop computers and use memory, CPU, and drive technologies that are similar to desktop PCs. On the other hand, PDAs, such as the Palm series, Handspring, and PocketPC systems, use different operating systems, applications, and hardware compared to either desktop or portable PCs and thus fall outside the scope of this book. This chapter focuses on notebook-style portable computers.

All my professional life I have been on the road teaching PC hardware and software. Because I am almost never home or at a single desk, I have had to rely on portable systems, usually as my primary, if not only, system. In fact, I have used portable systems even before there were PCs. I had some experience with the original Osborne portable, as well as several different Kaypro systems. These were sewing machine–sized portables that ran CP/M, the most popular operating system before DOS existed.

My first DOS portable was the original Compaq sewing machine–sized portable, and from there I graduated to an IBM Portable PC (also sewing machine–sized) and then to a succession of briefcase-sized portables. I had to use these larger AC-powered systems in lieu of laptop or notebook systems because I needed a system with desktop power, performance, and storage. In 1995, laptop and notebook systems reached parity with desktop systems in power and storage, and I was able to graduate to laptop/notebook systems, which I have been using ever since.

Every version of this book, starting with my first self-published manuscripts in 1985, has been written on a portable system of one type or another. With the processing power of modern notebook systems all but equaling that of desktop systems, I look forward to carrying even smaller, lighter, and more powerful systems in the future.

Portable computers have settled into a number of distinct roles that now determine the size and capabilities of the systems available. Traveling users have specific requirements of portable computers, and the added weight and expense incurred by additional features make it less likely for a user to carry a system more powerful than is necessary.

Portable System Designs

Obviously, portable systems are designed to be smaller and lighter than desktops, and much of the development work that has been done on desktop components has certainly contributed to this end. The 2 1/2-inch hard drives typically used in portables today are a direct extension of the size reductions that have occurred in all hard drives over the past few years. However, two other issues have created a need for the development of new technologies specifically for portable systems; those issues are power and heat.

Environmental concerns are leading to the development of more efficient power-management technologies, but, obviously, operating a computer from a battery imposes system limitations that designers of desktop systems never had to consider before the advent of portable systems. What's more, the demand for additional features, such as DVD and CD-RW drives, larger displays, and ever faster processors, has enormously increased the power drain on the typical system. The problem of conserving power and increasing the system's battery life is typically addressed in three ways:

- *Low-power components.* Nearly all the components in today's portable systems, from CPUs to memory to displays and drives, are specifically designed to use less power than their desktop counterparts.

- *Increased battery efficiency.* Newer battery technologies, such as lithium ion, are making batteries and power supplies more consistent and reliable and allowing for longer battery life on a single charge.

■ *Power management.* Operating systems and utilities that turn off specific system components, such as disk drives, when they are not in use can greatly increase battery life.

Perhaps a more serious problem than battery life in portable systems is heat. The moving parts in a computer, such as disk drives, generate heat through friction, which must somehow be dissipated. In desktop systems, this is accomplished by using fans to continuously ventilate the empty spaces inside the system. Portable systems must be designed to run fan-free most of the time, using innovative systems for moving and dissipating heat.

The worst culprit, as far as heat is concerned, is the system processor. When they were first released, the amount of heat generated by Intel's 486 and Pentium processors was a problem even in desktop systems. Heatsinks and tiny fans mounted on top of the CPU became standard components in most systems. Modern Pentium III, Celeron, Pentium 4, and Mobile Athlon systems benefit from newer processor technology featuring lower voltages, smaller die sizes, integrated L2 cache, and in general lower power consumption than their predecessors.

Because many portable systems are now being designed as replacements for desktops, users are not willing to compromise on processing power. Even the newest and fastest processors designed for desktop systems, such as the AMD Athlon and Intel Pentium III, are quickly adapted for use in mobile systems. However, for reasons of power consumption, noise, and space, fans in portable computers must be much smaller or omitted entirely, and there is very little empty space within the case for ventilation.

To address this problem, Intel and AMD have created special methods for packaging mobile processors that are designed to keep heat output to a minimum. Mobile processors also reduce heat through the use of extra-low voltage designs (dual voltage in some cases) and by integrating the Level 2 cache directly on the processor die. Other components also are designed to withstand the heat within a portable computer, which is usually greater than that of a desktop.

Upgrading and Repairing Portables

The portable systems manufactured today are less upgradable or repairable in general than desktop systems, mainly because of the lack of standard form factors for cases, motherboards, keyboards, displays, and even batteries. Even so, in some ways a portable can be easier to upgrade than a desktop because portable systems typically use modular components with snap-in connectors that eliminate the need for ribbon cables, mounting rails, and separate electrical connections. Thus, common upgrades such as adding memory and swapping out a hard drive (on models with modular drive bays) can often be accomplished in seconds.

The problem with replacing components in portables is that the hardware tends to be much less generic than it is in desktops. The exceptions are for PC Cards (which are interchangeable by definition), memory (on newer systems), and in some cases, hard drives. Purchasing a component that is not specifically intended for use in your exact system model can be risky.

In some cases, these compatibility problems are a matter of simple logistics. Portable system manufacturers jam a great deal of machinery into a very small case, and sometimes a new device just will not fit in the space left by the old one. This is particularly true of devices that must be accessible from the outside of the case, such as CD-ROM and floppy drives. Keyboards and monitors, the most easily replaceable of desktop components, are so completely integrated into the case of a portable system that they might not be practically removed at all.

In other cases, your upgrade path might be deliberately limited by the options available in the system BIOS. For example, depending on the BIOS date or revision, you might be limited in drive capacity the same as desktop systems. Fortunately, most use a flash ROM BIOS that can easily be updated—that is, if the system manufacturer makes such updates available. When shopping for a portable system, you should check with the manufacturer to see whether it has a support Web site with BIOS updates, drivers, and any accessory or utility programs necessary to support and maintain the system. A lack of BIOS or driver updates can prevent you from moving to a newer operating system in the future, or at least make such a move difficult.

◄◄   See "Upgrading the BIOS," p. 362.

Most of the time, components for portable systems are sold by referencing the system model number, even when third parties are involved. If you look through a catalog for desktop memory, for example, you see parts listed generically by attributes such as chip speed, form factor, and parity or non-parity. The memory listings for portable systems, on the other hand, most likely consist of a series of systems manufacturers' names and model numbers, plus the amount of memory in the module.

There are always exceptions to the rule, of course. However, purchasing compatible components that fit together properly is certainly more of a challenge than it is for a desktop system. Table 22.1 explains which portable PC components can be upgraded.

Note

Generally speaking, purchasing a preassembled portable system from a reputable manufacturer is strongly recommended, as is purchasing only replacement components that are advertised as being specifically designed for your system.

Table 22.1   Upgradable Portable System Components

Component	Upgradable	Sources	Notes
CPU	No[1]	n/a	Adoption of newer Intel/AMD CPU/chipset packaging enables designers to more easily incorporate new CPUs into existing system designs, but this is not intended for upgrades.
Memory	Yes	OEM vendor and third parties	Modules are often not interchangeable among many models; only one or two upgrade sockets in most systems.
Hard disk	Varies	OEM vendor and third parties	For systems that lack a modular bay, upgrade requires partial disassembly of system; older systems might not have BIOS support for largest drives; several drive form factors (thicknesses) can limit choices for some systems.
Video adapter/ chipset	No	n/a	Get fastest video circuitry with 4MB or more memory if true-color display needed; some systems offer MPEG2 hardware decoder upgrades for DVD video.
Video display	No	n/a	Get highest resolution; active-matrix if available.
Removable-media drives	Varies	n/a	For systems that lack modular bays, use PC Card or CardBus-interface adapter for highest performance peripherals (CD-RW, tape backup, SCSI devices, and so on); lower-performance devices can use USB connection (LS-120, Zip, Jaz, CD-ROM, and so on).

1. *Note that a few companies can upgrade the processor in your portable. When you send the system to them, they desolder or remove the original processor and solder or plug in a replacement. Most of the time these upgrades are limited in nature and costly to perform, and the result might include overheating or battery life problems in the future.*

Most portable systems, especially the smaller laptop or notebook designs, are difficult to disassemble. They have many more screws than desktop systems, and these screws often are hidden under stickers or covers. The case covers often feature thin plastic parts that interlock and can be tricky to separate without damage. Unlike desktops, once you've taken one portable apart, they are not all alike, so it really helps to have specific documentation on disassembly from your manufacturer.

Figure 22.1 shows the components that make up a typical laptop or notebook system, such as the IBM ThinkPad 770.

1 LCD display
2 Indicator panel
3 Keyboard
4 Standby battery
5 Upper case shield
6 Cooling fan
7 Video card
8 Modem card
9 PC card slot assembly
10 Motherboard
11 Floppy/CD-ROM/DVD-ROM drive
12 DIMM cover
13 Base cover
14 Stereo speaker assembly
15 CMOS/clock battery
16 Bay eject lever
17 Microphone
18 Lower case shield
19 DVD/enhanced video adapter (MPEG2 decoder)
20 Li-ion battery pack
21 LED card
22 CPU card (Intel mobile module)
23 Heat sink
24 DC-DC card
25 Eject lever holder assembly
26 Hard disk
27 Keyboard bezel
28 Center cover
29 Hinge cap

Figure 22.1 The components found in a typical laptop or notebook system are shown here. *Illustration courtesy of IBM Corporation.*

One reason I like the IBM ThinkPad series so much is that IBM makes the service/repair and technical reference manuals available free on its Web site. These documents include complete disassembly and reassembly instructions and a complete parts list, including detailed exploded diagrams and part numbers.

Toshiba also has detailed service and technical reference manuals, although you must purchase them through a dealer. With systems from other manufacturers, you'll have to check to see whether such documentation is available. I personally avoid any systems where I can't get this type of information from the manufacturer. I make it a point to get the service and technical reference manuals for any portable system I own. Obtaining these manuals makes future repairs and upgrades much easier.

Caution

Many if not most portable systems from even well-known vendors are actually built by OEM vendors in the Pacific Rim. If you don't know the actual manufacturer of your system and the vendor doesn't provide support, you could have a lot of difficulty in tracking down repairs and spare parts.

Portable System Hardware

From a technical standpoint, some of the components used in portable systems are similar to those in desktop computers, whereas others are completely different. The following sections examine the various subsystems found in portable computers and how they differ from their desktop counterparts.

Displays

Perhaps the most obvious difference between a portable system and a desktop is the display screen. Gone is the box with an emitter bombarding a concave glass tube with electrons. In its place is a flat screen, which is less than half an inch thick. This is called an *LCD*, or *liquid crystal display*. All the screens in portable systems today are color, although monochrome displays were at one point the industry standard, just as in standard monitors.

An LCD consists of two sheets of a flexible, polarizing material with a layer of liquid crystal solution between them. If you press gently on an LCD screen while it is lit, you can see how it gives slightly, displacing the liquid inside. When an electric current is passed through the liquid, the crystals align and become semipermeable to light.

◄◄   See "LCD Displays," p. 817.

Historically, the display has been the single most expensive component in a portable system. In fact, if the system is out of warranty, it is sometimes more economical to replace the entire computer rather than have a broken display replaced. In the first laptops with color screens, the display was a poor replacement for a standard VGA monitor. Today's portable screens are much improved, with some high-end displays even rivaling the quality of a good monitor and providing excellent performance, suitable even for graphic-intensive applications such as bitmap editing and videoconferencing. LCD displays are now becoming a popular peripheral for desktop systems as well.

The LCD display in a portable system is designed to operate at a specific resolution. This is because the size of the pixels on an LCD panel can't be changed. On a desktop system, the signal output from the video adapter can change the resolution on the monitor, thus changing the number of pixels created on the screen. Obviously, as you switch from a resolution of 640×480 to 800×600, the pixels must be smaller to fit into the same space. Systems can adjust the apparent resolution by scaling the image, but results aren't as good as with panels running at the reduced resolution by design. Systems are currently available with the following resolutions:

- ■ VGA   640×480
- ■ SVGA   800×600
- ■ XGA   1,024×768

- ■ SXGA   1,280×1,024
- ■ SXGA+   1,400×1,050
- ■ UXGA   1,600×1,200

Besides the issue of resolution, there is the issue of size. Be careful when selecting notebooks or laptops with SXGA or higher resolution displays because the higher resolution often results in much smaller text and icons than the typical desktop user is accustomed to. You can change the font size in Windows to compensate, but this often causes problems with different applications. Changing the resolution settings in the operating systems usually doesn't help either. One difference between LCD and normal analog displays is that the relative resolution of an LCD is fixed; that is, it normally can't be scaled. On a monitor, each pixel (picture element) is not tied to the individual phosphor dots, whereas on an LCD, pixels are tied to the individual LCD transistor display elements. For example, if you change from 1,024×768 to 800×600 on a standard monitor, the image still fills the screen because each pixel is now larger. On the other hand, when you do that on a portable LCD screen, the image becomes smaller, with a dark band of unused space surrounding the image in the center. An icon displayed in either resolution will be the same size on an LCD, which is not the case on a normal monitor.

To gauge the size of displayed items on an LCD, it is common to express the resolution of the screen in pixels per inch, which is a fixed value for a given screen. Table 22.2 shows the relative pixels per inch and other statistics for typical color screens available on portable systems over the years.

Table 22.2   LCD Display Dimensions and Pixel Sizes

Display	Dimension	Pixels	Aspect Ratio	Length (in)	Pixels per Inch
8.4" **VGA**	across	640	1.33	6.72	95
	down	480		5.04	
	diagonal	800		8.40	
9.5" **VGA**	across	640	1.33	7.60	84
	down	480		5.70	
	diagonal	800		9.50	
10.4" **VGA**	across	640	1.33	8.32	77
	down	480		6.24	
	diagonal	800		10.40	
10.4" **SVGA**	across	800	1.33	8.32	96
	down	600		6.24	
	diagonal	1000		10.40	
11.3" **SVGA**	across	800	1.33	9.04	88
	down	600		6.78	
	diagonal	1000		11.30	
12.1" **SVGA**	across	800	1.33	9.68	83
	down	600		7.26	
	diagonal	1000		12.10	
12.1" **XGA**	across	1024	1.33	9.68	106
	down	768		7.26	
	diagonal	1280		12.10	
13.3" **XGA**	across	1024	1.33	10.64	96
	down	768		7.98	
	diagonal	1280		13.30	

Table 22.2   Continued

Display	Dimension	Pixels	Aspect Ratio	Length (in)	Pixels per Inch
13.7"	across	1280	1.25	10.70	120
SXGA	down	1024		8.56	
	diagonal	1639		13.70	
14.1"	across	1024	1.33	11.28	91
XGA	down	768		8.46	
	diagonal	1280		14.10	
15.0"	across	1024	1.33	12.00	85
XGA	down	768		9.00	
	diagonal	1280		15.00	
15.0"	across	1400	1.33	12.00	117
SXGA+	down	1050		9.00	
	diagonal	1750		15.00	
15.4"	across	1280	1.25	12.03	106
SXGA	down	1024		9.62	
	diagonal	1639		15.40	

From this table you can see that most LCD display resolutions are under 100 pixels per inch, whereas some of the newer high-resolution displays are higher than that. Usually, anything under 100 pixels per inch is considered fairly loose, meaning that individual icons, text, and other display items are large enough for most people to easily see. Regardless of the actual resolution, any two displays having the same number of pixels per inch will display text, icons, and other elements on the screen at the same sizing. For example, both the 12.1-inch XGA display and the 15.4-inch SXGA display have the same pixel size (106 per inch), so if an object is 106 pixels wide, it is an inch wide on either display. If you have the SXGA display and change settings to display only XGA resolution, you'll see a 12.1-inch active display area centered inside the 15.4-inch screen.

After you go over 100 pixels per inch, the icons, text, and other items on the display become smaller and, for some, possibly difficult to see. In the more extreme cases, you might have to change display settings to use large fonts to make onscreen text easier to read. In my experience, I consider 120 pixels per inch the maximum that you can run Windows without absolutely requiring adjustments in font sizes, icon sizes and spacing, and so on, but this is something that depends on your vision—especially close up. If you are considering a system with more than 100 pixels per inch in the display, be sure you preview it first to ensure that the level of screen density is acceptable. The amount of desktop visible and number of open windows you can have make these high-resolution displays very appealing for desktop replacement systems.

Even with their tinier text and icons, the LCD screens are much sharper and clearer than an analog desktop monitor. So, even though they are smaller, they are often more readable with less eye strain.

An LCD panel can be thought of as a grid ruled off to a specified resolution, with transistors controlling the color displayed by each individual pixel. The arrangement of the transistors defines the two major types of LCD displays used in portable systems today: dual scan and active matrix. Although dual-scan displays ruled the notebook/laptop market for a long time, recent price drops in active-matrix displays have made them the display of choice for all except the most price-conscious shopper. Many manufacturers are now making only active-matrix systems because the costs have come down and the technology is superior.

Even though the prices for these displays have come down, they are still one of the most expensive parts of a portable system. They are also fragile. If you drop your laptop or notebook (something a standard warranty does not cover), you will likely fracture the display, which means it must be replaced. As mentioned earlier, replacements are usually close to the same cost as purchasing a new system unless you have purchased extra-cost breakage insurance (which I recommend). Another common way people damage their screens is to close the system with a pen, pencil, or other item on or above the keyboard. Make sure this area is clear before closing the system.

Caution

If you work on airplanes a lot, especially in coach, watch out for a tired traveler reclining the seat in front of you. Your notebook screen can be easily cracked by the top of the seat squeezing down on the top of your screen.

Dual-Scan (Passive-Matrix) Displays

The dual-scan display, sometimes called a passive-matrix display, has an array of transistors running down the x- and y-axes of two sides of the screen. The number of transistors determines the screen's resolution. For example, a dual-scan display with 640 transistors along the x-axis and 480 along the y-axis creates a grid similar to the horizontal and vertical lines on a piece of graph paper. Each pixel on the screen is controlled by the two transistors representing its coordinates on the x- and y-axes.

If a transistor in a dual-scan display should fail, a whole line of pixels is disabled, causing a black line across the screen (either horizontally or vertically). There is no solution for this problem other than to replace the display or just live with it. The term *dual scan* comes from the fact that the processor redraws half of the screen at a time, which marginally speeds up the refresh process.

Dual-scan displays are generally inferior to active-matrix screens. Dual-scan displays tend to be dimmer because the pixels work by modifying the properties of reflected light (either room light or, more likely, a white light source behind the screen), rather than generating their own. Dual-scan panels also are prone to ghost images and difficult to view from an angle, making it hard for two or more people to view the same screen.

However, newer passive-matrix technologies, such as color super-twist nematic (CSTN), double-layer super-twist nematic (DSTN), and especially high-performance addressing (HPA) screens, have come a long way in making passive-matrix displays a viable, lower-cost alternative to active-matrix technology. These newer displays offer better response rates and contrast—problems that plagued many of the earlier display types—but they are still not as sharp or as fast as an active-matrix screen.

◄◄ See "LCD Displays," p. 817.

For everyday use, the drawbacks of a passive-matrix display are most noticeable during video-intensive applications, such as presentations, full-color graphics, video, and fast-moving games, or under bright lighting conditions, such as in a window seat on an airplane, outdoors, or in offices with a lot of window lighting. For indoor computing tasks, such as word processing and email that consist largely of reading words onscreen, the passive-matrix display is quite serviceable, even for long periods of time.

The standard size for a dual-scan display has been 10 1/2 inches (measured diagonally), running at 640×480, but most newer systems have 12.1-inch or 13.3-inch displays that run at 800×600 or 1,024×768 resolution. If you are familiar with the dual-scan display of an older portable, you will find that today's models are greatly improved.

Dual-scan displays are becoming obsolete, thanks to improvements in the yield and reductions in the price of active-matrix LCD screens. In many cases, the difference between comparable dual-scan and active-matrix portable computers is as little as $100. Also, owners of portable computers with active-matrix screens no longer pay a price premium for breakage insurance compared to users of computers with dual-scan displays. Thus, in most cases today, dual-scan is preferable only for the most cost-conscious portable user.

Active-Matrix Displays

An active-matrix display differs from a dual scan in that it contains three transistors for every pixel onscreen (color displays), rather than just at the edges. The transistors are arranged on a grid of conductive material, with each connected to a horizontal and a vertical member. Selected voltages are applied by electrodes at the perimeter of the grid to address each pixel individually. Thus, an active-matrix screen is comparable to a sheet of graph paper that has a dot (representing a transistor) at each intersection of horizontal and vertical lines.

Most active-matrix displays use a thin film transistor (TFT) array. TFT is a method for packaging from one (monochrome) to three (RGB color) transistors per pixel within a flexible material that is the same size and shape as the display. Therefore, the transistors for each pixel lie directly behind the liquid crystal cells they control.

Two TFT manufacturing processes account for most of the active-matrix displays on the market today: hydrogenated amorphous silicon (a-Si) and low-temperature polysilicon (p-Si). These processes differ primarily in their costs. At first, most TFT displays were manufactured using the a-Si process because it required lower temperatures (less than 400°C) than the p-Si process of the time. Now, lower-temperature p-Si manufacturing processes are making this method an economically viable alternative to a-Si.

Although a TFT display has a great many transistors—4,410,000 for a color 1400×1050 display—each pixel does not have its own separate signal connection. Instead, voltages are applied through connections for each row and column, much like the transistors in a passive-matrix display.

Because every pixel is individually powered, each one generates its own light of the appropriate color, creating a display that is much brighter and more vivid than a dual-scan panel. The viewing angle is also greater, enabling multiple viewers to gather around the screen, and refreshes are faster and crisper, without the fuzziness of the dual scans, even in the case of games or full-motion video.

On the downside, it should be no surprise that with more transistors, an active-matrix display requires a lot more power than a dual scan. It drains batteries more quickly, but recent improvements in yield and manufacturing costs have reduced the once-sizeable price difference between active-matrix and dual-scan displays to virtually nothing. With all these transistors, it is not uncommon for failures to occur, resulting in displays with one or more "dead pixels," due to malfunctioning transistors. Actually we are talking about subpixels, the individual RGB triad transistor elements that make up each pixel. Subpixels can fail in either the off or on state, with failure in the on state more common. In particular, those that fail when on are very noticeable on a dark background as bright red, green, or blue dots. Most manufacturers have standards for the number of defective pixels that are allowed on their displays. It is considered acceptable to have a few, although they can be annoying. Most companies have policies allowing up to 21 dead or illuminated subpixels per display, but in practice I've never seen even close to that amount on a given display. It is normal to see perhaps one to five, and in many cases I've seen perfect displays. If you feel the number or placement of dead pixels is unworkable in your specific situation, contact your manufacturer for a possible replacement.

Because all the transistors of a TFT display are integrated into a single component, no way exists to remedy a dead pixel except by replacing the entire transistor array. Because this is one of the most expensive components in a portable system, many portable computer manufacturers refuse to accept returns of systems for less than a set number of bad pixels (this amount varies by vendor). The location or clustering of the bad pixels can also affect this policy. For example, if several bad pixels are grouped together in the middle of the display, the manufacturer is more likely to offer a replacement than if they are scattered around the edge. This is another part of the vendor's purchasing policy that you should check before ordering a system with an active-matrix display.

Although there is no normal way to repair bad pixels, there might be a simple fix that can help. I have actually repaired bad pixels by gently tapping on the screen at the pixel location. This seems to work in many cases, especially in cases in which the pixel is always illuminated instead of dead (dark). Because I find a constantly lit pixel to be more irritating than one that is constantly dark, this fix has saved me a lot of aggravation.

The 13.3-inch (diagonal) and 14.1-inch active-matrix screens are the most common on many portable systems, running at a resolution of 1,024×768; some lower-cost models run at 800×600. High-end systems now include TFT screens as large as 15 inches or more at up to 1,600×1,200 resolution. Higher resolutions and sizes are possible, but I question whether anything larger than a 15-inch display is workable for a portable system. In addition, increasing the resolution without increasing the size makes text and icons difficult to see. Many portable systems now also include AGP bus video adapters with up to 16MB of RAM, providing extra speed, even at 16- or 24-bit color depths. Toshiba now offers a gaming-oriented notebook computer: the Satellite 2805-S402, which features the nVidia GeForce2 Go AGP 4x graphics chip, 16MB of dedicated high-speed SGRAM, a 15-inch active-matrix screen running at 1,024×768, and even a subwoofer speaker. A good TFT display and integrated AGP adapter rival the quality and performance of a quality monitor and video adapter in a desktop system. In fact, a 15-inch TFT display (which, unlike most conventional monitors, describes the actual diagonal size of the image) generally has better picture quality and usability than a similarly sized CRT-type display.

Note

Another flat-screen technology, called the gas-plasma display, has been used in large display screens and a few portables. Plasma displays provide a CRT-quality picture on a thin flat screen using two glass panes filled with a neon/xenon gas mixture. Unfortunately, the displays require far more power than LCDs and have never become a practical alternative for the portable computer market.

Screen Resolution

The screen resolution of a portable system's display can be an important factor in your purchasing decision. If you are accustomed to working on desktop systems running at 1,024×768 pixels or more, you will find a 800×600 laptop screen to be very restrictive. Remember that an LCD screen's resolution is determined as much by the screen hardware as by the drivers and the amount of video memory installed in the system.

◄◄ See "Monitor Resolution," p. 825.

Some portables can use a virtual screen arrangement to provide a larger display on a smaller screen. The larger display is maintained in video memory while the actual screen displays only the portion that fits into the window provided by the native LCD resolution (see Figure 22.2). When you move the cursor to the edge of the screen, the image pans, moving the smaller window around within the larger virtual display. The effect is difficult to get used to, rather like a pan-and-scan videotape of a widescreen movie. The most serious problem with this arrangement is that some manufacturers have advertised it as a higher-resolution display, without being more clear about its actual nature. Be sure that when you evaluate a portable system's display that you look at the native or internal resolution of the LCD display.

Color depth is affected by the amount of video memory in the system, just as in a desktop system. To operate any LCD screen in 16- or 24-bit color mode, you must have sufficient video memory available. Virtually all portables have the video adapter hardware permanently installed on the motherboard, leaving little hope for a video memory upgrade, so be sure you get a system that can handle your video needs; some high-end systems, such as the Toshiba Tecra, enable you to select from a variety of display subsystems at initial purchase. Also check to ensure that the LCD natively supports the color depth you require.

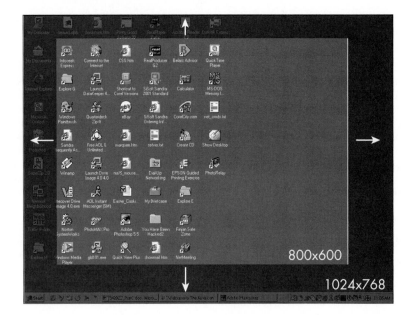

Figure 22.2 A virtual screen lets you use a small display to view a portion of a larger screen.

Tip

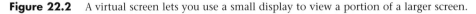

If you plan to use an external LCD projector with your portable computer, be sure you match the resolution of the projector and your computer's LCD display. If both use the same resolution, you can normally operate in simultaneous-display mode, enabling you to see onscreen what the audience is seeing. If your projector has a different resolution from the LCD display, you won't be able to use the internal display, which means you'll either need a separate monitor or have to turn around frequently to see what's being projected.

Processors

As with desktop systems, the majority of portables use Intel multiprocessors, and the creation of chips designed specifically for portable systems is a major part of the company's development effort. Intel has a complete line of processors optimized for mobile or portable use. Intel has focused on mobile processors since the 386SL and has dramatically expanded mobile processor technology and features with the Pentium, Pentium II/III, and Celeron. As with most portable system components, the main concerns with the mobile processors are reducing their sizes, power requirements, and heat generation.

Most portable systems sold today contain a mobile version of the Pentium III, Celeron, or mobile Pentium 4 processor. (There were no mobile versions of the Pentium Pro.) AMD's first major mobile processors were versions of the K6-2 and K6-III. In May 2001, AMD announced a line of mobile Athlon and Duron CPUs; the mobile Athlon is called the Athlon 4. The mobile versions of these processors have features and architecture that are similar to full-size models; they differ mainly in their packaging and power consumption. The processor's packaging defines the type of casing used to enclose and protect the internal circuitry of the chip, as well as the type of connector that provides the processor's interface with the motherboard.

Note

For more information about the Mobile Pentium CPUs, see *Upgrading and Repairing PCs, 12th Edition*, available in electronic form on the CD packaged with this book.

Mobile Pentium II and III

In April 1998, Intel announced the first mobile Pentium II processors. Running at 233MHz and 266MHz, these processors are also manufactured using the same 0.25 micron process used by the Mobile Pentium MMX. With a core voltage of 1.7v and an I/O buffer voltage of 1.8v, they run at even lower voltage levels than their Pentium MMX counterparts. Although at 8.6 watts, a 266MHz Pentium II consumes more power overall than a Pentium MMX running at the same speed, you must take into account that the Pentium II includes an integrated L2 cache, whereas the Pentium MMX, at 4.5 watts, does not.

To reduce power consumption and heat buildup while preserving speed, Intel redesigned the mobile Pentium II in late 1998 to use a different method for accessing L2 cache. The original mobile Pentium II used a 512KB L2 cache running at half CPU speed, just like the desktop Pentium II processor, but the revised design changed to an integrated on-die L2 cache of just 256KB, but running at the same speed as the CPU. By manufacturing this cache directly on the processor die, it runs at the same speed as the processor core and uses less power than slower external cache.

The Intel Mobile Pentium III is an improved version of the Mobile Pentium II, also using an on-die 256KB L2 cache, but with several design improvements, including the use of the .18 micron architecture, core voltages ranging from 1.7V (for the 1GHz and 900MHz versions) to as low as 1.1V (for the 500MHz versions), and SpeedStep power-saving technology. To reduce size, most versions of the Mobile Pentium III use the BGA-2 and Micro-PGA2 packaging. The Mobile Pentium III also supports seven clock states for a wider range of power-saving modes than on earlier mobile processors.

◀◀ See "Pentium II Processors," p. 147.

◀◀ See "Pentium III," p. 162.

Table 22.3 lists the speed, manufacturing process, and voltage specifications for the Mobile Pentium II, III, and Mobile Celeron CPUs manufactured by Intel.

Note

For more details about Mobile Pentium/MMX and Pentium II CPUs, see *Upgrading and Repairing PCs, 12th Edition*, available in electronic format on the CD packaged with this book.

Table 22.3 Current Intel Mobile Processor Specifications

Processor Voltage	Core Speed	Bus Speed	Mfg. Process	Core Voltage	I/O Buffer
Pentium II	233MHz	66MHz	0.25 micron	1.7V	1.8V
Pentium II	266MHz	66MHz	0.25 micron	1.7V	1.8V
Pentium II	300MHz	66MHz	0.25 micron	1.6V	1.8V
Pentium II	333MHz	66MHz	0.25 micron	1.6V	1.8V
Pentium II	366MHz	66MHz	0.25 micron	1.6V	1.8V
Pentium II	400MHz	66MHz	0.25 micron	1.6V	1.8V

Table 22.3   Continued

Processor Voltage	Core Speed	Bus Speed	Mfg. Process	Core Voltage	I/O Buffer
Celeron	266MHz-LV	66MHz	0.25 micron	1.5V	1.8V
Celeron	266MHz	66MHz	0.25 micron	1.6V	1.8V
Celeron	300MHz	66MHz	0.25 micron	1.6V	1.8V
Celeron	333MHz	66MHz	0.25 micron	1.6V	1.8V
Celeron	366MHz	66MHz	0.25 micron	1.6V	1.8V
Celeron	400MHz	66MHz	0.25 micron	1.6V	1.8V
Celeron	433MHz	66MHz	0.25 micron	1.9V	1.8V
Celeron	466MHz	66MHz	0.25 micron	1.9V	1.8V
Celeron	400MHz-LV	100MHz	0.18 micron	1.35V	1.5V
Celeron	450MHz	100MHz	0.18 micron	1.6V	1.5V
Celeron	500MHz-LV	100MHz	0.18 micron	1.35V	1.5V
Celeron	500MHz	100MHz	0.18 micron	1.6V	1.5V
Celeron	550MHz	100MHz	0.18 micron	1.6V	1.5V
Celeron	600MHz	100MHz	0.18 micron	1.6V	1.5V
Celeron	650MHz	100MHz	0.18 micron	1.6V	1.5V
Celeron	700MHz	100MHz	0.18 micron	1.6V	1.5V
Celeron	750MHz	100MHz	0.18 micron	1.6V	1.5V
Pentium III	400MHz	100MHz	0.18 micron	1.35V	1.5V
Pentium III	450MHz	100MHz	0.18 micron	1.6V	1.5V
Pentium III	500MHz	100MHz	0.18 micron	1.6V	1.5V
Pentium III	500MHz-ULV	100MHz	0.18 micron	1.1/0.975V[1]	1.5V
Pentium III	600MHz-LV	100MHz	0.18 micron	1.35/1.1V[1]	1.5V
Pentium III	600MHz	100MHz	0.18 micron	1.6/1.35V[1]	1.5V
Pentium III	650MHz	100MHz	0.18 micron	1.6/1.35V[1]	1.5V
Pentium III	700MHz	100MHz	0.18 micron	1.6/1.35V[1]	1.5V
Pentium III	700MHz-LV	100MHz	0.18 micron	1.35/1.1V[1]	1.5V
Pentium III	750MHz	100MHz	0.18 micron	1.6/1.35V[1]	1.5V
Pentium III	800MHz	100MHz	0.18 micron	1.6/1.35V[1]	1.5V
Pentium III	850MHz	100MHz	0.18 micron	1.6/1.35V[1]	1.5V
Pentium III	900MHz	100MHz	0.18 micron	1.7/1.35V[1]	1.5V
Pentium III	1GHz	100MHz	0.18 micron	1.7/1.35V[1]	1.5V

1. Uses Intel SpeedStep technology, optionally switching to lower speed and voltage to conserve battery life.

LV = Low Voltage

ULV = Ultra Low Voltage

SpeedStep and PowerNow! Technology

The Mobile Pentium III/Celeron, Pentium 4, AMD K6-2P, AMD K6-IIIP, AMD K6-III+, AMD Mobile Athlon 4, and AMD Mobile Duron processors all feature new technology to allow for longer battery life in mobile operation. Intel calls this technology SpeedStep (originally codenamed Geyserville), whereas AMD calls it PowerNow! This technology enables the processors to optionally reduce both speed and voltage when running on batteries. Prior processors could reduce speed, but by also reducing voltage, power consumption is significantly reduced, as is heat production.

This technology is designed to work when the notebook is running on battery power. When the notebook computer is connected to the AC outlet, CPU speed and voltage are at their maximums. When powered by a battery, the processor drops to a lower frequency (by changing ratios, the bus frequency remains constant) and voltage, thus conserving battery life while still maintaining a relatively high level of performance. In most cases the actual power consumption drops by half, which means about double the battery life as compared to full power, while reducing speed only a small amount. For example, a 750MHz Pentium III consumes up to 24.6 watts at full power (750MHz and 1.6V), whereas in SpeedStep mode the power consumption drops to only 14.4 watts (600MHz and 1.35V). This means that although power consumption drops by more than 41%, the speed drops by only about 20%.

If you don't want any performance drop when running under battery power a manual override is available as well.

When the system is powered up, the processor starts in the lower of its two speeds; in other words it starts in the Battery Optimized mode. BIOS or operating system instructions can rapidly switch the processor from mode to mode.

The requirements for this technology to work are

- A processor that supports the SpeedStep or PowerNow! technology
- A supporting motherboard (chipset, BIOS, and voltage regulator)
- An operating system and driver support
- An operating system that supports SpeedStep/PowerNow! technology (Win9x/Me, WinNT/2000/XP)
- SpeedStep/PowerNow! drivers

Contact your portable system manufacturer to see whether your system supports SpeedStep or PowerNow! Technology.

Most of the mobile processors include a built-in thermal diode that can be used to monitor CPU temperature. The notebook systems use this to control fan operation. Utilities also are available that can use this sensor to display the processor temperature information onscreen.

Intel Mobile Pentium Processor Steppings

As with Intel's desktop processor, the chips of the mobile processor line undergo continual development and are modified in the form of steppings that incorporate corrections and refinements into the hardware manufacturing process.

Note

The Mobile Pentium, Mobile Pentium MMX, and Mobile Pentium II processors are no longer being produced, but you might still encounter them in the field. For details about the Pentium and Mobile Pentium MMX versions and steppings, see *Upgrading and Repairing PCs, 12th Edition*, available in electronic form on the CD packaged with this book.

Table 22.4 lists the steppings for mobile Pentium II processors in the mobile module, mobile mini-cartridge, and other forms.

Table 22.4   Mobile Pentium II Processor Steppings

Family	Model	Core Stepping	L2 Cache Size (KB)	L2 Cache Speed	S-spec	Core/Bus	Notes
6	5	mdA0	512	1/2 core	SL2KH	233/66	MC,1.7v
6	5	mdA0	512	1/2 core	SL2KJ	266/66	MC,1.7v
6	5	mmdA0	512	1/2 core	PMD233	233/66	MMO,1.7v
6	5	mmdA0	512	1/2 core	PMD266	266/66	MMO,1.7v
6	5	mdB0	512	1/2 core	SL2RS	300/66	MC,1.6v1
6	5	mdB0	512	1/2 core	SL2RR	266/66	MC,1.6v1
6	5	mdB0	512	1/2 core	SL2RQ	233/66	MC,1.6v1
6	5	mdxA0	256	core	SL32M	266/66	MC,1.6v1
6	5	mdxA0	256	core	SL32N	300/66	MC,1.6v1
6	5	mdxA0	256	core	SL32P	333/66	MC,1.6v1
6	5	mdxA0	256	core	SL36Z	366/66	MC, 1.6v1
6	5	mdbA0	256	core	SL32Q	266/66	BG,1.6v2
6	5	mdbA0	256	core	SL32R	300/66	BG,1.6v2
6	5	mdbA0	256	core	SL32S	333/66	BG,1.6v2
6	5	mdbA0	256	core	SL3AG	366/66	BG,1.6v2
6	5	mdbA0	256	core	SL3DR	266/66	BG,1.5v
6	5	mdbA0	256	core	SL3HH	266/66	PG,1.6v2
6	5	mdbA0	256	core	SL3HJ	300/66	PG,1.6v2
6	5	mdbA0	256	core	SL3HK	333/66	PG,1.6v2
6	5	mdbA0	256	core	SL3HL	366/66	PG,1.6v2

1.7v = Core processor voltage is 1.7v for these mobile Pentium processors.

1.6v1 = Core processor voltage is 1.6v +/- 120mV for these processors.

1.6v2 = Core processor voltage is 1.6v +/- 135mV for these processors.

1.5v = Core processor voltage is 1.6v +/- 135mV for this processor.

MC = Mobile Pentium II processor mounted in a minicartridge.

MMO = Mobile Pentium II processor mounted in a mobile module including the 440BX North Bridge.

BG = Mobile Pentium II processor in BGA packaging for low-profile surface mounting.

PG = Mobile Pentium II processor in a (υ—μ) PGA1 package.

◄◄   See "Pentium Processor Models and Steppings," p. 139.

Mobile Pentium III Processors and Steppings

The Mobile Pentium III has also been available in a number of models and steppings, which can be distinguished by their specification numbers and other details (see Table 22.5).

Table 22.5   Mobile Pentium III Processor Models and Revisions

Speed Speed (MHz)	Speed Step (MHz)	S-spec	Stepping	CPUID	L2 Cache	Power (W)	Speed Step (W)	Voltage	Form Factor
400	-	SL3DU	BA2	0681	256K	10.1	-	1.35V	BGA2
400	-	SL43K	BB0	0683	256K	10.1	-	1.35V	BGA2
400	-	SL4JN	BC0	0686	256K	10.1	-	1.35V	BGA2
450	-	SL3KX	PA2	0681	256K	15.5	-	1.6V	BGA2
450	-	SL43L	BB0	0683	256K	15.5	-	1.6V	BGA2
450	-	SL4JA	BC0	0686	256K	15.5	-	1.6V	BGA2
450	-	SL4JQ	PC0	0686	256K	15.5	-	1.6V	PGA2
450	-	SL3RF	PA2	0681	256K	15.5	-	1.6V	PGA2
450	-	SL3LG	PA2	0681	256K	15.5	-	1.6V	PGA2
450	-	SL43N	PB0	0683	256K	15.5	-	1.6V	PGA2
450	-	PML45 00200 1AA	MA2	0681	256K	14.1	-	1.6/ 1.35V	MMC-2
450	-	PML45 00210 1AB	MB0	0683	256K	14.1	-	1.6/ 1.35V	MMC-2
450	-	PML45 00220 1AC	MC0	0686	256K	14.1	-	1.6V	MMC-2
500	-	SL3DT	BA2	0681	256K	16.8	-	1.6V	BGA2
500	-	SL43M	BB0	0683	256K	16.8	-	1.6V	BGA2
500	-	SL3PK	BA2	0681	256K	10.1	-	1.35V	BGA2
500	-	SL43Z	BB0	0683	256K	10.1	-	1.35V	BGA2
500	-	SL4JB	BC0	0686	256K	15.5	-	1.6V	BGA2
500	-	SL4JP	BC0	0686	256K	10.1	-	1.35V	BGA2
500	300	SL4ZH	BC0	0686	256K	8.1	4.5	1.1/ 0.975V	BGA2
500	-	SL4JR	PC0	0686	256K	16.8	-	1.6V	PGA2
500	-	SL3RG	PA2	0681	256K	16.8	-	1.6V	PGA2
500	-	SL3DW	PA2	0681	256K	16.8	-	1.6V	PGA2
500	-	SL43P	PB0	0683	256K	16.8	-	1.6V	PGA2
500	-	PML50 00200 1AA	MA2	0681	256K	15.0	-	1.6V	MMC-2
500	-	PML50 00210 1AB	MB0	0683	256K	15.0	-	1.6V	MMC-2

Table 22.5   Continued

Speed Speed (MHz)	Speed Step (MHz)	S-spec	Stepping	CPUID	L2 Cache	Power (W)	Speed Step (W)	Voltage	Form Factor
500	-	PML50 00220 1AC	MC0	0686	256K	15.0	-	1.6V	MMC-2
600	500	SL3PM	PA2	0681	256K	20.0	12.2	1.6/ 1.35V	BGA2
600	500	SL43Y	BA2	0683	256K	20.0	12.2	1.6/ 1.35V	BGA2
600	500	SL4GH	BB0	0683	256K	14.4	8.1	1.35/ 1.1V	BGA2
600	500	SL4JH	BC0	0686	256K	15.8	8.7	1.6/ 1.35V	BGA2
600	500	SL4JM	BC0	0686	256K	14.4	8.1	1.35/ 1.1V	BGA2
600	500	SL4JX	PC0	0686	256K	20.0	12.2	1.6/ 1.35V	PGA2
600	500	SL3TP	PA2	0681	256K	20.0	12.2	1.6/ 1.35V	PGA2
600	500	SL3PM	PA2	0681	256K	20.0	12.2	1.6/	PGA2 1.35V
600	500	SL443	PB0	0683	256K	20.0	12.2	1.6/ 1.35V	PGA2
600	500	PML60 00200 1AA	MA2	0681	256K	16.6	12.2	1.6/ 1.35V	MMC-2
600	500	PML60 00210 1AB	MB0	0683	256K	16.6	12.2	1.6/ 1.35V	MMC-2
600	500	PMM60 00220 1AC	MC0	0686	256K	16.6	12.2	1.6/ 1.35V	MMC-2
650	500	SL3PG	BA2	0681	256K	21.5	12.2	1.6/ 1.35V	BGA2
650	500	SL43X	BB0	0683	256K	21.5	12.2	1.6/ 1.35V	BGA2
650	500	SL4JJ	BC0	0686	256K	21.5	12.2	1.6/ 1.35V	BGA2
650	500	SL4JY	PC0	0686	256K	21.5	12.2	1.6/ 1.35V	PGA2
650	500	SL3TQ	PA2	0681	256K	21.5	12.2	1.6/ 1.35V	PGA2
650	500	SL3PL	PA2	0681	256K	21.5	12.2	1.6/ 1.35V	PGA2

Table 22.5   Continued

Speed Speed (MHz)	Speed Step (MHz)	S-spec	Stepping	CPUID	L2 Cache	Power (W)	Speed Step (W)	Voltage	Form Factor
650	500	SL442	PB0	0683	256K	21.5	12.2	1.6/ 1.35V	PGA2
650	500	PML65 00200 1AA	MA2	0681	256K	17.8	12.2	1.6/ 1.35V	MMC-2
650	500	PMM65 00210 1AB	MB0	0683	256K	17.8	12.2	1.6/ 1.35V	MMC-2
650	500	PMM65 00210 1AC	MC0	0686	256K	17.8	12.2	1.6/ 1.35V	MMC-2
700	500	SL56R	BC0	0686	256K	16.1	8.1	1.35/ 1.1V	BGA2
700	550	SL3Z7	BB0	0683	256K	22.0	13.2	1.6/ 1.35V	BGA2
700	550	SL4JK	BC0	0686	256K	22.0	13.2	1.6/ 1.35V	BGA2
700	550	SL4JZ	PC0	0683	256K	22.0	13.2	1.6/ 1.35V	PGA2
700	550	SL4DL	PB0	0683	256K	22.0	13.4	1.6/ 1.35V	PGA2
700	550	SL3Z8	PB0	0683	256K	22.0	13.4	1.6/ 1.35V	PGA2
700	550	PMM70 00210 1AA	MB0	0683	256K	19.1	13.4	1.6/ 1.35V	MMC-2
700	550	PMM70 00220 1AB	MC0	0686	256K	19.1	13.4	1.6/ 1.35V	MMC-2
750	600	SL4JL	BC0	0686	256K	24.6	14.4	1.6/ 1.35V	BGA2
750	600	SL54A	BD0	068A	256K	24.6	14.4	1.6/ 1.35V	BGA2
750	600	SL4K2	PC0	0686	256K	24.6	14.4	1.6/ 1.35V	PGA2
750	600	SL53P	PD0	068A	256K	24.6	14.4	1.6/ 1.35V	PGA2
750	600	SL4DM	MB0	0683	256K	24.6	14.4	1.6/ 1.35V	PGA2
750	600	SL44T	MB0	0683	256K	24.6	14.4	1.6/ 1.35V	PGA2
750	600	SL4AS	MB0	0683	256K	24.6	14.4	1.6/ 1.35V	BGA2

Table 22.5   Continued

Speed Speed (MHz)	Speed Step (MHz)	S-spec	Stepping	CPUID	L2 Cache	Power (W)	Speed Step (W)	Voltage	Form Factor
750	600	PMM75 00210 1AB	MB0	0683	256K	24.6	14.4	1.6/ 1.35V	MMC-2
750	600	PMM75 00210 1AA	MB0	0683	256K	24.6	14.4	1.6/ 1.35V	MMC-2
750	600	PMM75 00220 1AB	MC0	0686	256K	24.6	14.4	1.6/ 1.35V	MMC-2
800	650	SL4AK	BC0	0686	256K	25.9	15.1	1.6/ 1.35V	BGA2
800	650	SL548	BD0	068A	256K	25.9	15.1	1.6/ 1.35V	BGA2
800	650	SL4GT	PC0	0686	256K	25.9	15.1	1.6/ 1.35V	PGA2
800	650	SL53M	PD0	068A	256K	25.9	15.1	1.6/ 1.35V	PGA2
800	650	PMM80 00220 1AA	MC0	0686	256K	24.6	14.4	1.6/ 1.35V	MMC-2
850	700	SL4AG	BC0	0686	256K	27.5	16.1	1.6/ 1.35V	BGA2
850	700	SL547	BD0	068A	256K	27.5	16.1	1.6/ 1.35V	BGA2
850	700	SL4AH	PC0	0686	256K	27.5	16.1	1.6/ 1.35V	PGA2
850	700	SL53L	PD0	068A	256K	27.5	16.1	1.6/ 1.35V	PGA2
850	700	PMM85 00220 1AA	MC0	0686	256K	24.6	14.4	1.6/ 1.35V	MMC-2
900	700	SL59H	BC0	0686	256K	30.7	16.1	1.6/ 1.35V	BGA2
900	700	SL59J	PC0	0686	256K	30.7	16.1	1.7/ 1.35V	BGA2
1000	700	SL54F	BD0	068A	256K	34.0	16.1	1.7/ 1.35V	BGA2
1000	700	SL53S	PD0	068A	256K	34.0	16.1	1.7/ 1.35V	PGA2

PGA2 = 495-pin Micro-PGA2 (Pin Grid Array 2) form factor

BGA2 = 495-pin BGA2 (Ball Grid Array 2) form factor

MMC-2 = Mobile Module Connector-2 form factor

SpeedStep = Technology that optionally runs the processor at a lower speed and voltage in a battery-optimized mode

Mobile Celeron Processors and Steppings

Intel's entry into low-cost processors, the Celeron, is also available in a mobile form, featuring reduced voltages, PGA or BGA (ball grid array) packaging, and the MMC-1 and MMC-2 minicartridge modules also used by the Mobile Pentium III.

Table 22.6 lists the steppings for Mobile Celeron processors in BGA and PGA packaging.

Table 22.6   Mobile Celeron Processor Steppings

Family	Model	Core Stepping	L2 Cache (KB)	S-spec	Speed Core/Bus	Notes
6	6	mcbA0	128	SL23X	266/66	B,1
6	6	mcbA0	128	SL23Y	266/66	B,1
6	6	mcbA0	128	SL3AH	300/66	B,1
6	6	mcbA0	128	SL3C8	333/66	B,1
6	6	mcbA0	128	SL3C7	366/66	B,1
6	6	mcbA0	128	SL3DQ	266/66	B,2
6	6	mcbA0	128	SL3GQ	400/66	B,1
6	6	mcbA0	128	SL3KA	433/66	P,1
6	6	mcbA0	128	SL3KC	466/66	P,1
6	6	mcpA0	128	SL3HM	266/66	P,1
6	6	mcpA0	128	SL3HN	300/66	P,1
6	6	mcpA0	128	SL3HP	333/66	P,1
6	6	mcpA0	128	SL3HQ	366/66	P,1
6	6	mcpA0	128	SL3GR	400/66	P,1
6	6	mcpA0	128	SL3KB	433/66	P,1
6	6	mcpA0	128	SL3KD	466/66	P,1

B = In a BGA package   1 = Runs at a core voltage of 1.6v
P = In a (υ—μ) PGA package   2 = Runs at a core voltage of 1.5v

Table 22.7 lists the steppings for Mobile Celeron processors in MMC-1 and MMC-2 minicartridge packaging. All Mobile Celerons in MMC-1 and MMC-2 packaging also feature a 128KB L1 cache.

Table 22.7   Mobile Celeron Minicartridge Steppings

Speed Core/Bus	Product Stepping	CPUID	PTC	Package
266/66	cmmA0	066A	PMH26601001AA	MMC-1
266/66	cmmA0	066A	PMH26601001AA	MMC-1
300/66	cmmA0	066A	PMH30001001AA	MMC-1
333/66	cmmA0	066A	PMH33301001AA	MMC-1
366/66	cmmA0	066A	PMH36601001AA	MMC-1
400/66	cmmA0	066A	PMH40001001AA	MMC-1
433/66	cmmA0	066A	PMH43301001AA	MMC-1

Table 22.7   Continued

Speed Core/Bus	Product Stepping	CPUID	PTC	Package
466/66	cmmA0	066A	PMH46601001AA	MMC-1
266/66	cmmA0	066A	PMI26601001AA	MMC-2
300/66	cmmA0	066A	PMI30001001AA	MMC-2
333/66	cmmA0	066A	PMI33301001AA	MMC-2
366/66	cmmA0	066A	PMI36601001AA	MMC-2
400/66	cmmA0	066A	PMI40001001AA	MMC-2
433/66	cmmA0	066A	PMI43301001AA	MMC-2
466/66	cmmA0	066A	PMI46601001AA	MMC-2

The latest Mobile Celeron processors are built on the same .18 micron process and the same BGA-2 and micro PGA-2 packaging used by the Pentium III processor and feature a core (FSB) speed of 100MHz, which is faster than previous Mobile Celeron CPUs. Table 22.8 lists the steppings for .18 Micron Mobile Celeron processors in BGA-2 or Micro PGA-2 (mPGA-2) packaging.

Table 22.8   Mobile Celeron Processor (.18 Micron) Steppings

Speed (MHz) Core/Bus	S-spec	Product Stepping	CPUID	L2 Cache Size	Package
400/100	SL3UL	BA2	0681	128KB	BGA2
400/100	SL43W	BB0	0683	128KB	BGA2
400/100	SL4J8	BC0	0686	128KB	BGA2
450/100	SL3PD	BA2	0681	128KB	BGA2
450/100	SL43T	BB0	0683	128KB	BGA2
450/100	SL4JC	BC0	0686	128KB	BGA2
450/100	SL3PF	PA2	0681	128KB	mPGA2
450/100	SL43U	PB0	0683	128KB	mPGA2
450/100	SL4JS	PC0	0686	128KB	mPGA2
500/100	SL45A	BB0	0683	128KB	BGA2
500/100	SL3PC	BA2	0681	128KB	BGA2
500/100	SL43Q	BB0	0683	128KB	BGA2
500/100	SL4JD	BC0	0686	128KB	BGA2
500/100	SL4J9	BC0	0686	128KB	BGA2
500/100	SL4ZR	BC0	0686	128KB	BGA2
500/100	SL5DR	BD0	068A	128KB	BGA2
500/100	SL3PE	PA2	0681	128KB	mPGA2
500/100	SL43R	PB0	0683	128KB	mPGA2
500/100	SL4JT	PC0	0686	128KB	mPGA2
550/100	SL3ZE	BB0	0683	128KB	BGA2
550/100	SL4JE	BC0	0686	128KB	BGA2

Table 22.8   Continued

Speed (MHz) Core/Bus	S-spec	Product Stepping	CPUID	L2 Cache Size	Package
550/100	SL3ZF	PB0	0683	128KB	mPGA2
550/100	SL4JU	PC0	0686	128KB	mPGA2
600/100	SL4AR	BB0	0683	128KB	BGA2
600/100	SL4JF	BC0	0686	128KB	BGA2
600/100	SL5DS	BD0	068A	128KB	BGA2
600/100	SL582	BD0	068A	128KB	BGA2
600/100	SL4AP	PB0	0683	128KB	mPGA2
600/100	SL4JV	PC0	0686	128KB	mPGA2
650/100	SL4AD	BB0	0683	128KB	BGA2
650/100	SL4JG	BC0	0686	128KB	BGA2
650/100	SL4AE	PB0	0683	128KB	mPGA2
650/100	SL4JW	PC0	0686	128KB	mPGA2
700/100	SL4GU	BC0	0686	128KB	BGA2
700/100	SL53V	BD0	068A	128KB	BGA2
700/100	SL4GX	PC0	0686	128KB	mPGA2
700/100	SL53D	PD0	068A	128KB	mPGA2
750/100	SL56P	BC0	0686	128KB	BGA2
750/100	SL53U	BD0	068A	128KB	BGA2
750/100	SL56Q	PC0	0686	128KB	mPGA2
750/100	SL53C	PD0	068A	128KB	mPGA2
800/100	SL57X	BD0	068A	128KB	BGA2
800/100	SL584	PD0	068A	128KB	mPGA2

AMD K6-Series Mobile Processors

AMD's K6 series of processors have become very popular among cost-conscious personal and corporate computer buyers, and they have dominated the under-$1,000 computer market since the late 1990s. Starting in the fall of 1998, AMD began to develop this Socket 7–compatible series of processors for mobile use.

◄◄   See "AMD-K6 Series," p. 173.

◄◄   See "Socket 7 (and Super7)," p. 89.

All mobile versions of the AMD K6 family share some common characteristics, including low-voltage operation, MMX technology, and a choice of either ceramic pin grid array (CPGA) or the more compact ceramic ball grid array (CBGA) packaging. Mobile K6 processors, like their desktop siblings, also have a large 64KB L1 memory cache.

The newest versions of the Mobile K6 are called the K6-2+ and K6-III+. These new processors are both made on a 0.18 micron technology process, enabling reduced die size and voltage. They also both incorporate on-die L2 cache running at full processor speed and PowerNow! technology, which is AMD's version of Intel's SpeedStep technology. This allows for lower speed and voltage operation while on battery power to conserve battery life. The only difference between the K6-2+ and K6-III+ is the sizes of their on-die L2 caches. They both incorporate 64KB of L1 on-die: The K6-2+ adds a further 128KB of on-die L2 cache, whereas the L2 size is increased to 256KB in the K6-3+.

AMD offers the Mobile K6 family processors shown in Table 22.9.

Table 22.9   Mobile AMD K6 Family Processors

CPU Model	Core Voltage	Clock Speeds	Notes
Mobile K6*	2.1v	233, 266	66
Mobile K6*	2.2v	300	66
Mobile K6-2*	1.7–1.9v	266, 300, 333, 350, 366, 380,	100, 3DN
Mobile K6-2	2.0–2.2v	450, 500,	100, 3DN
	1.9–2.1v	475	100, 3DN
Mobile K6-III*	2.2v	350, 366, 380	100, 256KL2, 3DN
Mobile K6-2P*	2.2V	400, 433, 450, 475	100, 3DN
Mobile K6-III+#	1.9–2.1V	450, 475, 500	100, 256KL2, 3DN
Mobile K6-2+#	1.9–2.1V	450, 475 500, 533, 550	100, 128KL2, 3DN

66 = Has a 66MHz bus speed
100 = Has a 100MHz bus speed
256KL2 = Contains a 256KB integrated L2 cache running at full processor speed and supports L3 cache on the motherboard

3DN = Supports 3Dnow! multimedia enhancements
* = Built with the .25 micron process
 # = Built with the .18 micron process

AMD's Mobile Athlon 4 and Mobile Duron

Even though the K6 family of processors offer very good performance in their class, they are not fast enough to compete with the 600MHz and higher Mobile Pentium III and Mobile Celeron processors from Intel. In May 2001, AMD introduced its Mobile Athlon, known as the Athlon 4, and its Mobile Duron processors which, similar to their desktop siblings, directly compete with the Intel Pentium III and Celeron processors.

The Athlon 4 features 256KB of on-die L2 cache and support for either PC-133 or DDR SDRAM. The Athlon 4 uses 1.4V of power at full speed and 1.2V in battery-saving mode.

The Mobile Duron features 64KB of on-die L2 cache and uses the standard 200MHz FSB introduced by the original Athlon CPU. The Mobile Duron uses 1.5V at full speed and 1.2V in battery-saving mode.

Both the Mobile Athlon 4 and Mobile Duron use the .18 micron process, use a modified version of the 462-pin Socket A used by desktop Athlon and Duron processors, and feature 128KB of Level 1 cache and an improved version of AMD's PowerNow! battery-saving technology.

Table 22.10 lists the AMD Mobile Athlon 4 and Mobile Duron processors initially offered by AMD.

Table 22.10   AMD Mobile Duron and Mobile Athlon 4 CPUs

CPU Type	Core Speed	L1 Cache	L2 Cache	Power Usage
Mobile Duron	800	128KB	64KB	1.2–1.5V
Mobile Duron	850	128KB	64KB	1.2–1.5V
Mobile Athlon 4	850	128KB	256KB	1.2–1.4V
Mobile Athlon 4	900	128KB	256KB	1.2–1.4V
Mobile Athlon 4	950	128KB	256KB	1.2–1.4V
Mobile Athlon 4	1000 (1.0GHz)	128KB	256KB	1.2–1.4V

Mobile Processor Packaging

The heat generated by Pentium processors has been a concern since the first chips were released. In desktop systems, the heat problem is addressed, to a great extent, by computer case manufacturers. The use of multiple cooling fans and better internal layout designs can keep air flowing through the system to cool the processor, which is usually equipped with its own fan and heatsink.

For developers of portable systems, however, not as much can be accomplished with the case arrangement. So it was up to the chip manufacturers to address the problem in the packaging of the chip. At the same time, users became increasingly unwilling to compromise on the clock speed of the processors in portable systems. Running a Pentium at 133MHz or 166MHz requires more power and generates even more heat than the 75MHz Pentiums originally designed for mobile use.

Tape Carrier Packaging

An early solution to the size and heat problems for Pentium processors was the tape carrier package (TCP), a method of packaging processors for use in portable systems that reduces the size, power consumed, and heat generated by the chip. A Pentium mounted onto a motherboard using TCP is much smaller and lighter than the standard SPGA (staggered pin grid array) Pentiums used in desktop systems. The 49mm square of the SPGA is reduced to 29mm in the TCP processor, the thickness to approximately 1mm, and the weight from 55 grams to under 1 gram.

◀◀ See "PGA Chip Packaging," p. 79.

Instead of metal pins inserted into a socket on the motherboard, a TCP processor is essentially a raw die encased in an oversized piece of polyamide film. The film is similar to photographic film. The die is attached to the film using a process called tape automated bonding (TAB)—the same process used to connect electrical connections to LCD panels. The film, called the tape, is laminated with copper foil that is etched to form the leads that connect the processor to the motherboard (see Figure 22.3). This is similar to the way electrical connections are photographically etched onto a printed circuit board.

Figure 22.3 A processor mounted using the tape carrier package is attached to a piece of copper-laminated film that replaces the pins used in standard desktop processors.

After the leads are formed, they are plated with gold to allow bonding to a gold bump on the silicon die and to guard against corrosion. Next, they are bonded to the processor chip itself, and then the whole package is coated with a protective polyamide siloxane resin and mounted on a filmstrip reel for machine assembly. To get a feel for the small size of this processor, look at Figure 22.4, where it is shown next to a standard-size push-pin for comparison.

After testing, the processor ships to the motherboard manufacturer in this form. The reels of TCP chips are loaded into special machines that stamp-solder them directly to the portable system's motherboard. As such, the installation is permanent; a TCP processor can never be removed from the board for repair or upgrade. Because no heatsink or physical container is directly attached to the processor, the motherboard itself becomes the conduit to a heatsink mounted underneath it, thus using the portable system's chassis to pull heat away. Some faster portable systems include thermostatically controlled fans to further aid in heat removal.

Mounting the TCP to the system circuit board requires specific tooling available from all major board assembly equipment vendors. A special tool cuts the tape containing the processor to the proper size and folds the ends containing the leads into a modified gull-wing shape that contacts the circuit board, leaving the processor suspended just above the board (see Figure 22.5). Another tool dispenses a thermally conductive paste to the circuit board prior to placement of the tape containing the processor. This is done so that the heat can be dissipated through a sink on the underside of the motherboard while it is kept away from the soldered connections.

Figure 22.4   Pentium MMX processor in TCP Mobile Package. *Photograph used by permission of Intel Corporation.*

Figure 22.5   The tape keeps the processor's connections to the motherboard away from the chip and enables the underside of the processor to be thermally bonded to the motherboard.

Finally, a hot bar soldering tool connects the leads on the tape to the circuit board (see Figure 22.6). The completed TCP assembly forms an efficient thermal contact directly from the die to the motherboard, enabling the processor to run within its temperature limits even in such a raw state. By eliminating the package and essentially bonding the die directly to the motherboard, a significant amount of size and weight is saved.

Note

Some manufacturers of portable systems use standard desktop PGA processors, sometimes accompanied by fans. Apart from a greatly diminished battery life, systems such as these can sometimes be too hot to touch comfortably. For this reason, you should determine the exact model processor used in a system that you intend to purchase, and not just the speed.

Figure 22.6 Intel mobile Pentium tape carrier package pinout.

Mobile Module

Portable system manufacturers can purchase Pentium processors in raw TCP form and mount the processors to their motherboards themselves. Intel later introduced another form of processor packaging called the mobile module, or MMO (see Figure 22.7).

The mobile module consists of a Pentium or Pentium II processor in its TCP form, mounted on a small daughterboard along with the power supply for the processor's unique voltage requirements, the system's Level 2 cache memory, and the North Bridge part of the motherboard chipset. This is the core logic that connects the processor to standard system buses containing the South Bridge part of the chipset, as shown in the block diagram in Figure 22.8. North Bridge and South Bridge describe what has come to be an accepted method for dividing the functionality of the chipset into halves that are mounted on separate modules. In a typical portable system design, the manufacturer purchases the mobile module (complete with the North Bridge) from Intel and uses a motherboard designed by another company that contains the South Bridge.

Figure 22.7   Mobile Pentium processors in mobile module or raw tape carrier package form. *Photograph used by permission of Intel Corporation.*

A newer version of the MMO is called the MMC, which stands for Mobile Module Connector and is available in MMC-1 and MMC-2 versions. The Celeron and Pentium II were available in MMC-1 and MMC-2 versions, whereas the Pentium III is available in the MMC-2 version only. The Pentium II and III MMC-2 feature the Intel 440BX chipset's 82443BX host bridge, which connects to the PIIX4E/M PCI/ISA bridge built into the portable computer's motherboard.

In many ways, the MMO/MMC is similar to the Pentium II Single Edge Cartridge (SEC) design.

◀◀   See "Intel Chipsets," p. 228.

The module interfaces electrically to its host system via a 3.3v PCI bus, a 3.3v memory bus, and Intel chipset control signals bridging the half of the chipset on the module to the other half of the chipset on the system motherboard. The Intel mobile module also incorporates a single thermal connection that carries all the module's thermal output to the mobile PC's main cooling mechanisms.

The MMO is mounted with screws and alignment guides to secure the module against the typical shock and vibration associated with mobile PC usage. The MMO (shown in Figure 22.9) is 4 inches (101.6mm) long by 2.5 inches (63.5mm) wide by 0.315 inch (8mm) high (0.39 inch or 10mm high at connector).

Pentium® Processor with MMX™ Technology

Figure 22.8 Intel Pentium mobile module block diagram.

Figure 22.9 Intel Pentium MMX mobile module, including the processor, chipset, and L2 cache. *Photograph used by permission of Intel Corporation.*

The mobile module greatly simplifies the process of installing a Pentium III processor into a portable system, permits manufacturers to build more standardization into their portable computer designs, and eliminates the need for manufacturers to invest in the special tools needed to mount TCP processors on circuit boards themselves. The module also provides a viable processor upgrade path that was unavailable with a TCP processor permanently soldered to the motherboard. Portable systems that offer a range of processor options use mobile modules because it enables the vendor to use the same motherboard.

Minicartridge

The mobile versions of the Pentium II and Pentium III processor are available in the mobile module package, with the North Bridge portion of the Intel 440BX AGP chipset. However, Intel also has introduced another package for the Pentium II, called the minicartridge. The minicartridge is designed especially for use in ultralight portable computers in which the height or bulk of the mobile module would interfere with the system design. It contains only the processor core and 512KB of L2 cache memory in a stainless steel case that exposes the connector and processor die.

◀◀ See "Intel 440BX," p. 253.

The minicartridge is approximately 51mm×47mm in size and 4.5mm in height. Overall, the package is about one-fourth the weight, is one-sixth the size, and consumes two-thirds of the power of a desktop Pentium II processor using the SEC. To connect to the socket on the motherboard, the minicartridge has a 240-pin connector at one end of the bottom side, with the pins arranged in an 8×30 ball grid array, as shown in Figure 22.10.

BGA packaging uses solder balls on the bottom of the device, which means that after it is soldered in, there are no visible pins. The unique features of BGA packaging makes it one of the smallest physical packages, and the soldered-in design is thermally more stable than most others. It also enables better heat transfer from the device to the board.

Figure 22.10 Bottom side of the Pentium II minicartridge package.

◀◀ To learn more about BGA packaging, see "Pentium II Processors," p. 147.

The BGA packaging is also used in some versions of AMD's mobile K6 family.

BGA and PGA

The newest packaging for mobile processors is called micro-BGA or PGA. The PGA is basically just a BGA chip mounted on an interposer card with pins that plug into a slot. Usually, the BGA versions are permanently soldered in, whereas the PGA versions are socketed. The BGA form factor is currently the smallest, thinnest, and lightest packaging for mobile processors. Both Intel and AMD are using BGA and PGA form factors for their newest mobile processors.

Chipsets

As in the desktop market, Intel has come to dominate the mobile chipset industry by creating products that support the advanced features of each new processor it releases. The mobile Pentium II processor releases were accompanied by the introduction of the mobile 440BX AGPset, which provides support for the accelerated graphics port, 100MHz memory and system buses and processor power-management capabilities designed to extend battery life. Mobile Pentium III and the latest Mobile Celeron processors also use this chipset.

A similar chipset, but optimized for the older Mobile Celeron processors and their 66MHz system bus, is the 440ZX-66M AGPset.

◀◀ See "Sixth-Generation (P6 Pentium Pro/II/III Class) and Seventh-Generation (Pentium 4) Chipsets," p. 246.

Intel's440BX AGPset accommodates the mobile module package for the Pentium II/III processors. In this design, the chipset's two halves, called the North Bridge and South Bridge, are located on the mobile module and the system motherboard, respectively.

In the 440BX AGPset, for example, the host bridge system controller consists of two VLSI devices. The first of these, the 443BX host bridge (the North Bridge) is part of the mobile module. The other device is the PIIX4 PCI/ISA bridge, which the system manufacturer must incorporate into the motherboard design for the portable computer. This forms the South Bridge. The mobile module connects to the motherboard through a 3.3v PCI bus, a 3.3v memory bus, and some 443BX host bridge control signals. It is these signals that combine the North Bridge and the South Bridge into a single functional chipset.

The new 440MX chipset, designed for mobile Celeron systems, brings chipset integration to a new level, because it combines both North Bridge and South Bridge functions into a single chip. In addition to reducing the chip count at the chipset level, the 440MX provides audio and modem support at a performance level comparable to PCI-based hardware modems and sound cards, with just slightly higher CPU utilization rates.

Clearly, innovations such as the mobile module accentuate the association between a computer's processor and its motherboard chipset. Now that the development cycles for new processors tend to be measured in months, not years, it is rapidly becoming a foregone conclusion that to get the most out of the latest Intel processor, you must use an Intel chipset as well. As when shopping for a desktop system, you should be aware of what chipset is used in the portable computer you plan to buy and whether it fully supports the capabilities of the processor and the system's other components.

Memory

Adding memory is one of the most common upgrades performed on computers, and portables are no exception. However, most portable systems are exceptional in the design of their memory chips. Unlike desktop systems, in which only a few basic types of slots are available for additional RAM, literally dozens of different memory chip configurations have been designed to shoehorn RAM upgrades into the tightly packed cases of portable systems.

Most recent portables use a type of DIMM called a Small Outline DIMM (SO-DIMM), which is physically smaller but similar electrically to the standard DIMMs used in desktop systems. SO-DIMMs typically are available in extended data out (EDO) or synchronous DRAM (SDRAM) form, with various speeds and voltages available. Some of the latest portables use small outline rambus inline memory modules (SO-RIMMs) similar to the RIMMs used in desktop systems, but again physically smaller. Some systems in the past used proprietary memory cartridges that look like PC Cards but which plug into a dedicated integrated circuit (IC) memory socket. However, this isn't common anymore. In any case, appearance is not a reliable measure of compatibility; be sure the memory you are purchasing will work with your system or that you can get a refund or replacement if it doesn't. It is strongly recommended that you install only memory modules that have been designed for your system, in the configurations specified by the manufacturer.

◀◀ See "SIMMs, DIMMs, and RIMMs," p. 421.

This recommendation does not necessarily limit you to purchasing memory upgrades only from the manufacturer. Many companies now manufacture memory upgrade modules for dozens of portable systems by reverse-engineering the original vendor's products. This adds a measure of competition to the market, usually making third-party modules much cheaper than those of a manufacturer that is far more interested in selling new computers for several thousands of dollars rather than memory chips for a few hundred.

Note

Some companies have developed memory modules that exceed the original specifications of the system manufacturer, enabling you to install more memory than you could with the maker's own modules. Some manufacturers, such as IBM, have certification programs to signify their approval of these products. Otherwise, an element of risk is involved in extending the system's capabilities in this way.

Inside the memory modules, the components are not very different from those of desktop systems. Portables use the same types of DRAM and SRAM as desktops, including memory technologies such as EDO, SDRAM, and rambus DRAM (RDRAM). At one time, portable systems tended not to have memory caches because the SRAM chips typically used for this purpose generate a lot of heat. Advances in thermal management and the development of on-die L2 cache enable all portable computers to feature cache sizes and speeds comparable to desktop computers. The best philosophy to take when adding RAM to a notebook or laptop computer is "fill 'er up!" Because even the latest SO-DIMM memory modules can't be interchanged as freely as desktop memory modules (and older systems) use proprietary (non-reusable) memory modules, and because adding memory speeds up operations and extends battery life (due to less use of the hard drive for virtual memory swapping), you should bring a notebook up to at least 64MB of RAM or higher, depending on the chipset and processor. I don't recommend installing more than 64MB in Pentium systems, though, because the chipsets do not support caching for any memory over 64MB. Pentium II/III or Celeron systems can cache 512MB or 4GB, so in those systems you can install as much memory as you can afford.

Caution

If your portable computer uses Windows 9x or Windows Me, don't exceed 512MB of RAM because the VCACHE disk cache built into these versions of Windows can't support the memory addresses needed for this amount of RAM along with the memory addresses required by AGP video. If you want to use more RAM, use Windows 2000 or Windows XP.

Keep in mind that more memory means more power consumption and shorter battery life, so exceeding your needs by a wide margin won't help performance but will drain the battery more quickly. Because many notebook/laptop computers have only a single RAM connector, you need to keep that in mind when you upgrade because any future upgrades will not add to what you already have but replace it instead.

Hard Disk Drives

Hard disk drive technology is also largely unchanged in portable systems, except for the size of the disks and their packaging. Enhanced IDE drives are all but universal in portable computers. Internal hard drives typically use 2 1/2-inch platters and are available in varying heights or thicknesses. IDE drives made for portable computers also use a single cable for both data and power, rather than the two cables used by desktop varieties of the drive.

As with memory modules, systems manufacturers have various ways of mounting hard drives in the system, which can cause upgrade compatibility problems. Some systems use a caddy to hold the drive and make the electrical and data connections to the system. This makes the physical part of an upgrade as easy as inserting a new drive into the caddy and then mounting it in the system. You can purchase the drive with the caddy already installed, you can get a bare drive and swap it into your existing caddy, or you can get a bare drive and a new caddy. Usually it is much less expensive to get the bare drive—whether you also add the caddy or not—than it is to get one with the caddy pre-installed.

In many mid-range and high-end portables, replacing a hard drive is much simpler than in a desktop system. Quite a few manufacturers now design their portable systems with external bays that let you easily swap out hard drives without opening the case, as long as the drives are preinstalled in the appropriate caddies. Multiple users can share a single machine by snapping in their own hard drives, or you can use the same technique to load different operating systems on the same computer.

The most important aspect of hard drive upgrades that you must be aware of is the drive support provided by the system's BIOS. The BIOS in some systems, and particularly older ones, might offer limited hard drive size options. This is particularly true if your system was manufactured before 1995, when EIDE hard drives came into standard use. BIOSes made before this time support a maximum drive size of 528MB. In some cases, flash BIOS upgrades, which provide support for additional drives, might be available for your system.

◄◄ See "Motherboard BIOS," p. 349.

After BIOS support, you need to be concerned about the physical mounting. Whether you are going to use your existing caddy or get a new one (if required), you must be concerned about the height of the drive. 2.5-inch drives have been manufactured in various thicknesses over the years, and many notebook or laptop systems are restricted as to how thick a drive they will support. The common thicknesses that have been sold are

- 8.4mm
- 9.5mm
- 12.5mm
- 12.7mm
- 17.0mm

The popular ones are the 9.5 through 12.7mm, although some of the thicker 17mm drives are still being used. If your notebook currently has a 9.5mm–high unit, you might not be able to install a taller 12.5, 12.7, or 17mm unit in its place. Normally, though, you can always install a shorter drive in place of a taller one.

Many manufacturers have adapted the compact 2 1/2-inch hard drives on the market for aftermarket use in older notebooks, many of which have drives under 2GB in size. The kits usually start at about 3GB and can be as large as 32GB in size. You'll typically pay about two to three times per megabyte what you would for a desktop hard drive.

To make your upgrade of these systems as easy as possible, be sure you buy a data-transfer kit with the drive. These kits should come with a high-speed PC Card (PCMCIA) connector for the new drive and data-transfer/drive preparation software to automate the switchover. Some of these kits can then be used to make the old hard drive a portable model you can use through a connection via the PC Card slot.

Another option for extending hard drive space is PC Card hard drives. These are devices that fit into a type II or Type III PC Card slot and can provide as much as 2GB of disk space in a remarkably tiny package (usually with a high price per MB, although larger drives are cheaper per MB than smaller drives). You also can connect external drives to a portable PC, using a PC Card SCSI host adapter, USB port, or specialized parallel port drive interface. This frees you from the size limitations imposed by the system's case, and you can use any size drive you want, without concern for BIOS limitations.

Removable Media

Apart from hard disk drives, portable systems are now being equipped with other types of storage media that can provide access to larger amounts of data. CD-ROM are standard in laptop and notebook systems, with many of the newest mid-range and high-end systems offering DVD and even CD-RW or combo DVD/CD-RW drives. Some systems also offer removable cartridge drives, such as Iomega's Zip drive. This has been made possible by the enhanced IDE specifications that let other types of devices share the same interface as the hard drive.

Another important issue is that of the floppy drive. Smaller systems (those under 5 pounds) often omit the floppy drive to save space, sometimes including an external unit. Some other systems enable you to substitute a second hard drive or battery for the floppy drive. For certain types of users, the lack of a floppy drive might or might not be an acceptable inconvenience. Many users of portables, especially those who frequently connect to networks, have little use for a floppy drive. This is now true even for the installation of applications because virtually all software now ships on CD-ROMs.

One of the features that is becoming increasingly common in notebook systems is swappable drive bays you can use to hold any one of several types of components. This arrangement lets you customize the configuration of your system to suit your immediate needs. For example, when traveling you might remove the floppy drive and replace it with an extra battery or install a second hard drive when your storage needs increase. Notebook vendors and magazine reviews might refer to the number of spindles when discussing the number of drives a notebook can have installed simultaneously. For example, a computer that can use a floppy drive, CD-ROM, and hard drive simultaneously is a three-spindle system. If a system has two spindles, the most common configuration is a hard drive along with a bay into and out of which you can swap a floppy drive, CD-ROM drive, battery, or second hard drive. When evaluating your notebook needs and hardware, be sure to determine which devices included with a model can be used simultaneously and which require removing another device. If lightweight travel is a concern, determine which parts you don't need for travel that can be swapped out. Swappable bays should come with a cover or faceplate for the open bay to prevent dirt and foreign objects from entering when the bay is empty. If they don't include a blank cover, perhaps one is sold or available as an option.

If you aren't satisfied with the removable media drives your current notebook offers, the PC Card slot is again your gateway to virtually unlimited choices. All the popular desktop choices, such as Zip, Jaz, LS-120 SuperDrive, CD-R, and CD-RW can be attached via a dedicated PC Card version of the drive or by using a SCSI PC Card with a SCSI version of the drive.

For drives such as the Zip and LS-120 SuperDisk, you'll find that parallel port or USB interfacing is also suitable. Although parallel-port drives are also popular, you'll normally suffer a big speed drop for large file transfers, especially if you don't use the high-speed EPP/ECP IEEE-1284 LPT port modes. Instead of the parallel port, you should consider using your system's USB ports. Special cables work with some of the file transfer programs that enable direct USB-to-USB connections between different systems, even though that is not officially supported by the USB Forum. LPT.com, the originator of the Direct Cable Connection program provided with Windows 9x, Me, and 2000, is a popular source for these cables and setup help.

Tip

Frequently, each drive included in a portable computer is referred to as a *spindle*; a *three-spindle* portable computer has three drives on board (typically a floppy drive; hard drive; and CD-ROM, DVD, CD-RW, or combo DVD/CD-RW drive). If a particular portable computer is described as a *dual-spindle* or *one-spindle* computer, you should determine which drive(s) has been omitted and decide whether it's acceptable to use an external drive as a substitute. Many dual-spindle systems use a bay swappable drive, which can be inconvenient—for example, if you have to use both the optical and floppy drives during a procedure, you must swap them back and forth in mid-stream.

◀◀ See "Universal Serial Bus," p. 940.

PC Cards

In an effort to give notebook computers the kind of expandability users have grown used to in desktop systems, the Personal Computer Memory Card International Association (PCMCIA) has established several standards for credit card–size expansion boards that fit into a small slot on laptops and notebooks. The development of the PC Card interface is one of the few successful feats of hardware standardization in a market full of proprietary designs.

The PC Card standards, which were developed by a consortium of more than 300 manufacturers (including IBM, Toshiba, and Apple), have been touted as being a revolutionary advancement in mobile computing. PC Card laptop and notebook slots enable you to add memory expansion cards, fax/modems, SCSI adapters, network interface adapters, and many other types of devices to your system. If your computer has PC Card slots that conform to the standard developed by the PCMCIA, you can insert any type of PC Card (built to the same standard) into your machine and expect it to be recognized and usable.

The promise of PC Card technology is enormous. Not only are PC Card memory expansion cards, tiny hard drives, and wireless modems available, but also available are ISDN adapters, MPEG decoders, network interface adapters, sound cards, CD-ROM controllers, and even GPS systems, which use global positioning satellites to help you find your way by locating your exact position on Earth.

Note

Besides having use in nautical and aircraft environments, many newer automobiles include in-dash GPS systems that not only pinpoint your exact location, but give you directions to anywhere you want to go. If your car is not equipped with a factory-installed GPS system, you can use a notebook or laptop with a GPS receiver and mapping software to provide the same function.

Originally designed as a standard interface for memory cards, the PCMCIA document defines both the PC Card hardware and the software support architecture used to run it. The PC Cards defined in version 1 of the standard, called Type I, are credit-card size (3.4×2.1 inches) and 3.3mm thick. The standard has since been revised to support cards with many other functions. The third version, called "PC Card Specification–February 1995," defines three types of cards, with the only physical difference being their thickness. This was done to support the hardware for different card functions.

Most of the PC Cards on the market today, such as modems and network interface adapters, are 5mm-thick Type II devices. Type III cards are 10.5mm thick and have been used for PC Card hard drives, although the latest PC Card hard drives are now Type II compatible. All the card types are backward compatible; you can insert a Type I card into a Type II or III slot. The standard PC Card slot configuration for portable computers is two Type II slots, with one on top of the other. This way, you can also insert a single Type III card, taking up both slots but using only one of the connectors.

Note

In addition, a Type IV PC card, thicker still than the Type III, was designed for higher-capacity hard drives. This card type is not recognized by the PCMCIA, however, and is not included in the standard document. There is, therefore, no guarantee of compatibility between Type IV slots and devices, and they should generally be avoided.

The latest version of the standard, published in March 1997, includes many features designed to increase the speed and efficiency of the interface, such as

- DMA (direct memory access) support.
- 3.3v operation.

- Support for APM (Advanced Power Management).

- Plug and Play support.

- The PC card ATA standard, which lets manufacturers use the AT Attachment protocols to implement PC Card hard disk drives.

- Support for multiple functions on a single card (such as a modem and a network adapter).

- The Zoomed Video (ZV) interface, a direct video bus connection between the PC card adapter and the system's VGA controller, allowing high-speed video displays for videoconferencing applications and MPEG decoders.

- A thermal ratings system that can be used to warn users of excessive heat conditions.

- CardBus, a 32-bit interface that runs at 33MHz and provides 32-bit data paths to the computer's I/O and memory systems, as well as a new shielded connector that prevents CardBus devices from being inserted into slots that do not support the latest version of the standard. This is a vast improvement over the 8- or 16-bit bus width and 8MHz speed of the original PC card-16 interface. If you connect your portable computer to a 100Mbps network, CardBus can provide the high-speed interface that, in a desktop system, would be provided by PCI.

◄◄ See "DMA Channels," p. 323.

◄◄ See "Plug and Play BIOS," p. 396.

◄◄ See "ATA IDE," p. 480.

The PC Card usually has a sturdy metal case, and is sealed except for the interface to the PCMCIA adapter in the computer at one end, which consists of 68 tiny pinholes. The other end of the card might contain a connector for a cable leading to a telephone line, a network, or some other external device. Type I, Type II, and Type III PC Cards are compared to each other in Figure 22.11.

The pinouts for the PC Card interface are shown in Table 22.11.

Table 22.11   Pinouts for a PC Card (PCMCIA Card)

Pin	Signal Name	Pin	Signal Name	Pin	Signal Name
1	Ground	24	Address 5	47	Address 18
2	Data 3	25	Address 4	48	Address 19
3	Data 4	26	Address 3	49	Address 20
4	Data 5	27	Address 2	50	Address 21
5	Data 6	28	Address 1	51	+5V
6	Data 7	29	Address 0	52	Vpp2
7	-Card Enable 1	30	Data 0	53	Address 22
8	Address 10	31	Data 1	54	Address 23
9	-Output Enable	32	Data 2	55	Address 24
10	Address 11	33	Write Protect (-IOIS16)	56	Address 25
11	Address 9	34	Ground	57	RFU
12	Address 8	35	Ground	58	RESET
13	Address 13	36	-Card Detect 1	59	-WAIT
14	Address 14	37	Data 11	60	RFU (-INPACK)
15	-Write Enable/-Program	38	Data 12	61	-Register Select

Table 22.11   Continued

Pin	Signal Name	Pin	Signal Name	Pin	Signal Name
16	Ready/-Busy (IREQ)	39	Data 13	62	Batt V 2 (-SPKR)
17	+5V	40	Data 14	63	Batt V 1 (-STSCHG)
18	Vpp1	41	Data 15	64	Data 8
19	Address 16	42	-Card Enable 2	65	Data 9
20	Address 15	43	Refresh	66	Data 10
21	Address 12	44	RFU (-IOR)	67	-Card Detect 2
22	Address 7	45	RFU (-IOW)	68	Ground
23	Address 6	46	Address 17		

Figure 22.11   The Type I PC Card (upper left) is rare. Two Type I or Type II PC Cards (upper center) can be inserted into a typical notebook computer (center), but only one Type III PC Card (upper right) can be used at a time (lower center).

PC Card Software Support

PC Cards are by definition *hot-swappable*, meaning that with the proper software support you can remove a card from a slot and replace it with a different one without having to reboot the system.

If your PC card devices and operating system conform to the Plug and Play standard, inserting a new card into the slot causes the appropriate drivers for the device to be loaded and configured automatically.

To make this possible, two separate software layers are needed on the computer that provide the interface between the PCMCIA adapter (which controls the card slots) and the applications that use the services of the PC Card devices (see Figure 22.12). These two layers are called Socket Services and Card Services. A third module, called an enabler, actually configures the settings of the PC cards.

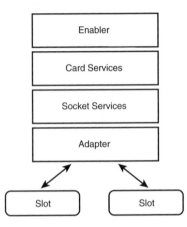

Figure 22.12   The Card and Socket Services enable an operating system to recognize the PC Card inserted into a slot and configure the appropriate system hardware resources for the device.

Socket Services

The PCMCIA adapter that provides the interface between the card slots and the rest of the computer is one of the only parts of the PCMCIA architecture not standardized. Many different adapters are available to portable systems manufacturers and, as a result, an application or operating system can't address the slot hardware directly, as it can a parallel or serial port.

Instead, a software layer called Socket Services is designed to address a specific make of PCMCIA adapter hardware. The Socket Services software layer isolates the proprietary aspects of the adapter from all the software operating above it. The communications between the driver and the adapter might be unique, but the other interface, between the Socket Services driver and the Card Services software, is defined by the PCMCIA standard.

Socket Services can take the form of a device driver, a TSR program run from the DOS prompt (or the AUTOEXEC.BAT file), or a service running on an operating system such as Windows 9x/Me or Windows NT/2000/XP. A computer can have PC card slots with different adapters, as in the case of a docking station that provides extra slots in addition to those in the portable computer itself. In this case, the computer can run multiple Socket Services drivers, which all communicate with the same Card Services program.

Card Services

The Card Services software communicates with Socket Services and is responsible for assigning the appropriate hardware resources to PC Cards. PC Cards are no different from other types of bus expansion cards, in that they require access to specific hardware resources to communicate with the computer's processor and memory subsystems. If you have ever inserted an ISA network interface card into a desktop system, you know that you must specify a hardware interrupt, and maybe an I/O port or memory address, for the card to operate.

A PC Card network adapter requires the same hardware resources, but you don't manually configure the device using jumpers or a software utility as you would an ISA card. The problem is also complicated by the fact that the PCMCIA standard requires that the computer be capable of assigning hardware resources to different devices as they are inserted into a slot. Card Services addresses this problem by maintaining a collection of various hardware resources that it allots to devices as necessary and reclaims as the devices are removed.

If, for example, you have a system with two PC Card slots, the Card Services software might be configured to use two hardware interrupts, two I/O ports, and two memory addresses, regardless of whether any cards are in the slots at boot time. No other devices in the computer can use those interrupts. When cards are inserted, Card Services assigns configuration values for the settings requested by the devices, ensuring that the settings allotted to each card are unique.

Card Services is not the equivalent of Plug and Play, although the two might seem similar. In fact, in Windows 9x/Me/2000/XP, Card Services obtains the hardware resources it assigns to PC Cards using Plug and Play. For other operating systems, the resources can be allotted to the Card Services program using a text file or command-line switches. In a non–Plug and Play system, you must configure the hardware resources assigned to Card Services with the same care you would configure an ISA board. Although Card Services won't allow two PC Cards to be assigned the same interrupt, nothing in the PCMCIA architecture prevents conflicts between the resources assigned to Card Services and those of other devices in the system.

You can have multiple Socket Services drivers loaded on one system, but there can be only one Card Services program. Socket Services must always be loaded before Card Services.

Enablers

One of the oldest rules of PC configuration is that the software configuration must match that of the hardware. For example, if you configure a network interface card to use interrupt 10, you must also configure the network driver to use the same interrupt, so it can address the device. Today, this can be confusing because most hardware is configured not by physically manipulating jumpers or DIP switches but by running a hardware configuration utility.

In spite of their other capabilities, neither Socket Services nor Card Services is capable of actually configuring the hardware settings of PC Cards. This job is left to a software module called an *enabler*. The enabler receives the configuration settings assigned by Card Services and actually communicates with the PC Card hardware itself to set the appropriate values.

Similar to Socket Services, the enabler must be designed to address the specific PC Card that is present in the slot. In most cases, a PCMCIA software implementation includes a generic enabler—that is, one that can address many types of PC Cards. This, in most cases, lets you insert a completely new card into a slot and have it be recognized and configured by the software.

The problem with a generic enabler, and with the PCMCIA software architecture in general, is it requires a significant amount of memory to run. Because it must support many different cards, a generic enabler can require 50KB of RAM or more, plus another 50KB for the Card and Socket Services. For systems running DOS (with or without Windows 3.1), this is a great deal of conventional memory just to activate one or two devices. Once installed and configured, the PC Card devices also might require additional memory for network, SCSI, or other device drivers.

Note

Windows 9x/Me or Windows 2000/XP are the preferred operating systems for running PC card devices. The combination of their advanced memory management, Plug and Play capabilities, and the integration of the Card and Socket Services into the operating system makes the process of installing a PC Card (usually) as easy as inserting it into the slot.

With Windows NT 4.0, for example, you must shut down the system and reboot to change the PC Card in a slot. What's more, it can be difficult to find Windows NT drivers for many of the PC Cards on the market.

When memory is scarce, there can be an alternative to the generic enabler. A specific enabler is designed to address only a single specific PC Card and uses much less memory for that reason. Some PC Cards ship with specific enablers that you can use in place of a generic enabler. However, you also can use a specific enabler when you have a PC Card that is not recognized by your generic enabler. You can load the specific enabler to address the unrecognized card, along with the generic enabler to address any other cards that you might use. This practice, of course, increases the memory requirements of the software.

Finally, you can avoid the overhead of generic enablers and the Card and Socket Services entirely by using what is known as a point enabler. A *point enabler* is a software module included with some PC Cards (or it can be downloaded from the vendor's Web site) that addresses the hardware directly, eliminating the need for Card and Socket Services. As a result, the point enabler removes the capability to hot-swap PC Cards and have the system automatically recognize and configure them. If, however, you intend to use the same PC Cards all the time and have no need for hot-swapping, point enablers can save you a tremendous amount of conventional memory.

Keyboards

Unlike desktop systems, portables have keyboards integrated into the one-piece unit. This makes them difficult to repair or replace. The keyboard should also be an important element of your system purchasing decision because manufacturers are forced to modify the standard 101-key desktop keyboard layout to fit in a smaller case.

The numeric keypad is always the first to go in a portable system's keyboard. Usually, its functionality is embedded into the alphanumeric keyboard and activated by a Function key combination. The Function (or Fn) key is an additional control key used on many systems to activate special features, such as the use of an alternative display or keyboard.

Most portable systems today have keyboards that approach the size and usability of desktop models. This is a vast improvement over some older designs in which the keys were reduced to a point at which you could not comfortably touch-type with both hands. Standard conventions such as the "inverted T" cursor keys also were modified, causing extreme user displeasure.

Some systems still have half-size function keys, but one of the by-products of the larger screens found in many of today's portable systems is more room for the keyboard. Thus, many manufacturers are taking advantage of the extra space.

If you plan to perform a lot of numeric data entry with your portable computer, look for numeric keypads that plug into your system and override the embedded keypad on the right side of your keyboard, or use a standard 101-key keyboard if you're at your desk.

Standard keyboards are covered in depth in Chapter 18, "Input Devices."

Pointing Devices

As with the layout and feel of the keyboard, pointing devices are a matter of performance and personal taste. Most portable systems have pointing devices that conform to one of the three following types:

- *Trackball.* A small ball (usually about 1/2-inch) partially embedded in the keyboard below the spacebar, which is rolled by the user. While serviceable and accurate, trackballs have become unpopular, primarily due to their tendency to gather dust and dirt in the well that holds the ball, causing degraded performance.

- *TrackPoint.* Developed by IBM and licensed by many other manufacturers (especially Toshiba, which calls their version the AccuPoint), the TrackPoint is a small (about 1/4-inch) rubberized button located between the G, H, and B keys of the keyboard. It looks like a pencil eraser and can be nudged in any direction with your index finger to move the cursor around the screen. The TrackPoint button doesn't actually move, instead it uses a pressure transducer to sense pressure and direction, allowing full control over the pointer. The TrackPoint is convenient because you can manipulate it without taking your hands off the keyboard home row. On some earlier models, the rubber cover tended to wear off after heavy use. Newer versions are made of sturdier materials with a grippy sandpaper surface similar to a cat's tongue.

  The TrackPoint is considered by many people, including this author, to be the best pointing device for portable systems—certainly for those who touch type. It is the most efficient, accurate, consistent, easiest to use (for most people), and by far the most reliable. If you use a portable system extensively and are a touch-typist, I'd recommend only systems with a TrackPoint. Personally I won't even consider a laptop or notebook system without one.

- *Trackpad.* The trackpad or touchpad is an electromagnetically sensitive pad, usually about 1×2 inches, that responds to the movement of a finger across its surface. Mouse clicks can be simulated by tapping the pad. Trackpads have great potential but tend to be overly sensitive to accidental touches, causing undesired cursor movements and especially unwanted mouse clicks. Trackpads are also notoriously imprecise and sensitive to humidity and moist fingers, resulting in unpredictable performance.

◄◄ For more information on the TrackPoint and Trackpad, see Chapter 18, "Input Devices," p. 953.

Some systems allow users a choice by providing both a TrackPoint and a trackpad; however, some allow only one or the other to operate, whereas others allow both to be active at the same time.

Note

If you want to use an external mouse with your portable, don't assume that the internal pointing device can be used simultaneously with the external device. Some systems have a BIOS setup option that allows you to activate both internal and external devices simultaneously, or use either one or the other. Regardless of whether you use a PS/2, USB, or serial mouse, it might be necessary on some systems to go into the portable's BIOS Setup program and disable the trackpad to avoid accidental cursor movement.

Another important part of the pointer arrangement is the location of the primary and secondary buttons. Some systems locate the buttons in peculiar configurations that require unnatural contortions to perform a click-and-drag operation. Pointing devices are definitely a feature of a portable system that you should test drive before you make a purchase. As an alternative, remember that nearly all portables have a serial port, PS/2 port, or USB port you can use to attach an external mouse or other pointing device to the system, when your workspace permits.

Batteries

Battery life is one of the biggest complaints users have about portable systems. A great deal has been done to improve the power-management capabilities and efficiency of today's portable computers, and better battery technologies such as lithium-ion have also been adopted on many systems. However, the larger power requirements of faster CPUs, more RAM, larger drives, and near-universal adoption of active-matrix displays have left the battery life of a typical portable system approximately the same as it was several years ago.

The goal sought by many mobile users has been the same for many years: a full-featured portable system that can run on a single battery for the entire duration of a transcontinental U.S. airplane flight. Some airlines are now providing 12V automotive-type power connectors under the seat for use with automotive power adapters; in this case, battery life on a plane is no longer an issue. For those who are relegated to using batteries, you still typically must carry two or more battery packs for a six-hour flight. While mobile power technologies are improving, so are the demands of today's systems. However, although typical battery life has remained in the two- to four-hour range for most reputable manufacturers, the new notebooks have the advantage of having larger hard drives, bigger and brighter screens, more RAM, faster processors, integrated speakers, and CD-ROM drives. Based on the increasing popularity of these notebook systems, the buying consumer has clearly voiced that a more powerful notebook with continuing average battery life is more important and useful than a system that would run for 6–10 hours but sacrifice features she has grown used to using.

For users who simply must have a system that can run for 6–10 hours, check for airlines that are adding at-seat power connections designed for notebook computers.

An interesting fact that many don't seem to know is that three different batteries are used in most portable systems. One is the main battery used to power the system; the next is a rechargeable standby battery that powers the RAM to maintain data when in suspend mode or when changing main batteries; and the third is the CMOS RAM/clock battery. Of these three batteries, only the CMOS/clock battery requires replacement (every two to five years depending on the design); the others are rechargeable. The standby battery in particular normally lasts the life of the system and recharges automatically anytime the system is powered on. Refer to Figure 22.1 for the locations of these batteries in a typical system.

Battery Types

The battery technology also plays a major role in the portable power issue, of course. Most portable systems today use one of four battery types for their main power batteries:

- *Nickel Cadmium (NiCad).* As the oldest of the four technologies, nickel cadmium batteries are rarely used in portable systems today as main power (some use NiCad for standby batteries) because of their shorter life and sensitivity to improper charging and discharging. The life of the battery's charge can be shortened by as much as 40% if the battery is not fully discharged before recharging or if it is overcharged. Permanent damage to the cell can be prevented by periodically discharging it to 1 volt or less. Despite this "memory" effect, however, NiCad batteries hold a charge well when not in use, losing 10% of their capacity in the first 24 hours and approximately 10% per month after that, and they can be recharged 1,500 times or more.

- *Nickel Metal-Hydride (NiMH).* More expensive than NiCads, NiMH batteries have approximately a 30% longer life than NiCads, are less sensitive to the memory effect caused by improper charging and discharging, and do not use the environmentally dangerous substances found in NiCads. They have a recommended discharge current that is lower than that of a NiCad battery (one-fifth to one-half of the rated capacity) and a self-discharge rate that is 1 1/2 times to twice that of a NiCad, and they can be recharged as many as 500 times. NiMH batteries also require nearly twice as long to recharge as NiCads. Although they are still used in many portable systems, NiMH batteries are now found mostly in computers at the lower end of the price range.

- *Lithium-Ion (Li-ion).* As the current industry standard, Li-ion batteries are longer-lived than either NiCad or NiMH technologies, can't be overcharged, and hold a charge well when not in use. Batteries that use lithium—one of the lightest of all metals, with the greatest electrochemical potential, and providing the largest energy content—have been manufactured since the 1970s. However, lithium is also an unstable substance, and some battery explosions resulted in a large number of battery recalls in the early 1990s. Subsequent models were manufactured using lithium ions from chemicals such as lithium-cobalt dioxide ($LiCoO_2$). Despite a slightly lower energy density, Li-ion batteries are much safer than the lithium designs. Various types of Li-ion batteries use different active materials for their negative electrodes; coke versions and two graphite versions have slightly different voltage characteristics. Li-ion batteries also can support the heavy-duty power requirements of today's high-end systems, and modern versions can be recharged up to 1,000 times or more. They also recharge more quickly than most of the other types. Unlike NiCad and NiMH batteries, which can be used in the same system without modification to the circuitry, Li-ion batteries can be used only in systems specifically designed for them. Inserting a Li-ion battery into a system designed for a NiCad or NiMH can result in a fire. Although the most expensive of the four technologies, Li-ion batteries have come to be used in all but the very low end of the portable system market.

- *Lithium-Ion Polymer (LIP or Li-Poly).* This is a fourth battery type that has been in development for several years, but which only recently appeared on the market. Lithium-ion polymer batteries are manufactured using a lithium ion and cobalt oxide cell with a proprietary polymer electrolyte and can be formed into flat sheets as small as 1mm thick and of almost any size. Thus, a thin battery panel can be fitted into a portable computer behind the LCD panel. Lithium-ion polymer batteries provide an energy density that is four times better than a NiCad and a charge life that is 40% longer than a Li-ion battery, at one-fifth the weight. This battery technology provides up to 500 charges and is immune to the memory effect that can prevent NiCad and NiMH batteries from recharging fully. Li-Poly batteries are now being sold as replacement batteries for portable phones but are not yet being used in PCs. After they are manufactured in sufficient quantities, lithium-ion polymer batteries could replace the bulky battery packs used today in portable systems.

Note

All the battery types in use today function best when they are completely discharged before being recharged. In fact, batteries that have gone unused for several months should be conditioned by putting them through three full discharge/recharge cycles. You can do this by leaving the system on until it automatically suspends or shuts down; additionally, battery-conditioning utilities are available that can manage this process for you. One indication that you need to discharge cycle your batteries is if charging stops before the charge indicator reaches 100%. Cycling the battery a few times usually corrects this situation and allows for proper charge indication. Lithium-ion batteries are affected the least by incomplete discharging and have a higher discharge cut-off point (2.5v–3v versus 1v for NiCads), but the effect on the life of future charges is still noticeable.

Unfortunately, buying a portable computer with a more efficient battery does not necessarily mean that you will realize a longer charge life. Power consumption depends on the components installed in the system, the power-management capabilities provided by the system software, and the size of the battery itself. Some manufacturers, for example, when moving from NiMH to Li-ion batteries, see this as an opportunity to save some space inside the computer. They decide that because they are using a more efficient power storage technology, they can make the battery smaller and still deliver the same performance.

Battery technology trails behind nearly all the other subsystems found in a portable computer, as far as the development of new innovations is concerned. Because of the continuing trend of adding more features and components to mobile computers, their power consumption has risen enormously in recent years, and power systems have barely been capable of keeping up. On a high-end laptop system, a battery life of three hours is very good, even with all the system's power-management features activated.

One other way manufacturers are addressing the battery life problem is by designing systems capable of carrying two batteries. The inclusion of multipurpose bays within the system's case on some computers enables users to replace the floppy or CD-ROM drive with a second battery pack, effectively doubling the computer's charge life.

Power Management

Various components in a computer do not need to run continuously while the system is turned on. Mobile systems often conserve battery power by shutting down these components based on the activities of the user. If, for example, you open a text file in an editor and the entire file is read into memory, there is no need for the hard drive to spin while you are working on the file.

After a certain period of inactivity, a power-management system can park the hard drive heads and stop the platters from spinning until you save the file to disk or issue any other command that requires drive access. Other components, such as floppy and CD-ROM drives and PC cards, can also be powered down when not in use, resulting in a significant reduction of the power needed to run the system.

Most portables also have systemic power saver modes that suspend the operation of the entire system when it is not in use. The names assigned to these modes can differ, but there are usually two system states that differ in that one continues to power the system's RAM while the other does not. Typically, a "suspend" mode shuts down virtually the entire system after a preset period of inactivity except for the memory. This requires only a small amount of power and allows the system to be reawakened in a few seconds, rather than having to go through the complete boot process. When in this standby mode, the memory is maintained by the main battery, or the standby battery if the main battery is dead or you are changing the main battery. The standby battery usually powers the RAM for a few minutes to a few hours or more in some models. For this reason, it is important to save any work before suspending the system.

Portable systems usually have a "hibernate" mode, as well, which writes the current contents of the system's memory to a special file on the hard disk and then shuts down the system, erasing memory as well. The hibernate mode does not require any power from either the main or standby batteries, so a system can theoretically hibernate indefinitely. When the computer is reactivated (powered up), it reads the contents of the hibernation file back into memory, restoring the system to exactly the condition it was in when hibernation started, and work can continue. The reactivation process takes a bit longer than a normal resume from suspend mode, but the system conserves more power by shutting down the memory array. Either mode is much faster than cold-booting the system.

Note

The memory swap file used for hibernate mode might, in some machines, be located in a special partition on the hard drive dedicated to this purpose. If you inadvertently destroy this partition, you might need a special utility from the system manufacturer to re-create the file. Newer operating systems such as Windows Me and 2000 create their own hibernation files.

In most cases, these functions are defined by the APM standard, a document developed jointly by Intel and Microsoft that defines an interface between an operating system power-management policy driver and the hardware-specific software that addresses devices with power-management capabilities. This interface is usually implemented in the system BIOS.

◀◀ See "Advanced Power Management," p. 1143.

However, as power-management techniques continue to develop, maintaining the complex information states necessary to implement more advanced functions becomes increasingly difficult for the BIOS. Therefore, another standard has been developed by Intel, Microsoft, and Toshiba called Advanced Configuration and Power Interface (ACPI), which is designed to implement power-management functions in the operating system. Microsoft Windows 98, Me, 2000, and XP automatically use ACPI if ACPI functions are found in the system BIOS when these operating systems are first installed. The need to update system BIOSes for ACPI support is one reason many computer vendors have recommended performing a BIOS update before installing Windows 98, Me, 2000, or XP.

◀◀ See "Power Management Menu," p. 389.

Placing power management under the control of the OS enables a greater interaction with applications. For example, a program can indicate to the operating system which of its activities are crucial, forcing an immediate activation of the hard drive, and which can be delayed until the next time the drive is activated for some other reason.

Peripherals

A great many add-on devices are available for use with portable systems, providing functions that can't practically or economically be included inside the system itself. Many of the most common uses for portable systems might require additional hardware, either because of the computer's location or the requirements of the function. The following sections discuss some of the most common peripherals used with portable systems.

External Displays

High-end laptop systems often are used to host presentations to audiences that can range in size from the boardroom to an auditorium. For all but the smallest groups of viewers, some means of enlarging the computer display is necessary. Most portable systems are equipped with a standard VGA jack that allows the connection of an external monitor.

Systems typically enable the user to choose whether the display should be sent to the internal, the external, or both displays, as controlled by a keystroke combination or the system BIOS. Depending on the capabilities of the video display adapter in the computer, you might be able to use a greater display resolution on an external monitor than you would on the LCD panel. However, if you want to use simultaneous display, you must use an external monitor or projector that uses the same native resolution as your internal display.

For environments in which the display of a standard monitor is not large enough, several alternatives exist, including standard CRT and LCD displays, LCD panels for use with overhead projectors, and self-contained LCD projectors.

◀◀ See "LCD Displays," p. 817.

Overhead LCD Display Panels

An LCD display panel is similar to the LCD screen in your computer except that there is no back on it, making the display transparent. The display technologies and screen resolution options are the same as those for the LCD displays in portable systems, although most of the products on the market use active-matrix displays. Most vendors of overhead LCD display panels have discontinued these products, although many AV houses might still have them available for rental.

Note

To learn more about these products, see *Upgrading and Repairing PCs, 12th Edition*, available in electronic form on the CD packaged with this book.

LCD Projectors

An LCD projector is a self-contained unit that is a combination of a transparent display panel and a projector. The unit connects to the VGA video output connector on the system, just like a regular monitor, and frequently includes speakers that connect with a separate cable as well. Not all LCD projectors are portable; some are intended for permanent installations. The portable models vary in weight, display technologies, and the brightness of the lamp, which is measured in ANSI lumens. Typical portable projectors have ANSI lumen outputs ranging from 500 to 3,000 or higher, with prices ranging from under $2,000 to well over $10,000. Less expensive projectors are typically SVGA (800×600) resolution, whereas more expensive models are typically XGA (1,024×768) or higher resolution.

For best results, match the resolution of your projector to the native resolution of your notebook computer. If your notebook computer has a 1024×768 resolution screen, make sure your projector offers this same resolution without resorting to tricks such as scaling or compression. Having the projector and your built-in screen match enables most systems to use simultaneous display—a great benefit for presenters.

TV-Out

One of the simplest display solutions is a feature that is being incorporated into many of the high-end laptop systems on the market today. It enables you to connect the computer to a standard television set. Called TV-out, various systems provide support for the North American NTSC television standard, the European PAL standard, or both. Once connected, a software program lets you calibrate the picture on the TV screen. If your portable computer doesn't have TV out, add-on adapter boxes are available to provide this feature. These products convert the VGA signal to a form that is compatible with the NTSC or PAL TV standards.

Obviously, TV-out is an extremely convenient solution because it provides an image size that is limited only by the type of television available, costs virtually nothing, and adds no extra weight to the presenter's load when a TV is available. However, the display resolution of a television set does not approach that of a computer monitor, and the picture quality suffers as a result. It is recommended that you test the output carefully with various size television screens before using TV-out in a presentation environment. Use simple sans-serif fonts, such as Arial or Helvetica, in presentations and limit the amount of text on any given screen to achieve best results with TV-out devices.

Docking Stations

Now that more and more portable systems are being sold as replacements for standard desktop computers, docking stations are becoming increasingly popular. A *docking station* is a desktop unit to which you attach (or dock) your portable system when you are at your home or office. At the very least, a docking station provides an AC power connection, a full-size keyboard, a standard desktop mouse, a complete set of input and output ports, and a VGA jack for a standard external monitor.

Once docked, the keyboard and display in the portable system are deactivated, but the other components—particularly the processor, memory, and hard drive—remain active. You are essentially running the same computer but using a standard full-size desktop interface. Docking stations also can contain a wide array of other features, such as a network interface adapter, external speakers, additional hard disk or CD-ROM drives, additional PC card slots, and a spare battery charger.

An operating system such as Windows 9x, Me, 2000, or XP can maintain multiple hardware profiles for a single machine. A *hardware profile* is a collection of configuration settings for the devices accessible to the system. To use a docking station, you create one profile for the portable system in its undocked state and another that adds support for the additional hardware available while docked.

The use of a docking station eliminates much of the tedium involved in maintaining separate desktop and portable systems. With two machines, you must install your applications twice and continually keep the data between the two systems synchronized. This is traditionally done using a network connection or the venerable null modem cable (a crossover cable used to transfer files between systems by connecting their parallel or serial ports). With a docking station and a suitably equipped portable, you can achieve the best of both worlds.

Docking stations are highly proprietary items designed for use with specific computer models. Prices vary widely depending on the additional hardware provided, but because a docking station lacks a CPU, memory—and a display—the cost is usually not excessive.

For systems that lack the docking station option or for those that seem too expensive, consider the less expensive port replicator. Although it lacks drive bays and might not feature a network interface card, even the simplest ones offer connectors for video, printer, serial, and keyboard/mouse, which enables you to use more comfortable devices. Because a port replicator is simpler, you might not even need to use the multiple hardware profiles in Windows.

One economic concern for both docking stations and port replicators is that any given model works with just a few computer models at most. If you plan to change computers frequently and are also looking to increase the number of printer and serial ports you have, consider the Universal Port Replicators available from Mobility Electronics. These units feature serial, parallel, PS/2 mouse, and PS/2 keyboard connectors, as well as a PC card slot. Mobility also offers model-specific port replicators for most popular notebook computer models.

Connectivity

One of the primary uses for portable computers is to keep in touch with the home office while traveling by using a modem. Because of this, many hotels and airports are starting to provide telephone jacks for use with modems, but many places still exist where finding a place to plug into a phone line can be difficult. Products are now on the market, however, that can help you overcome these problems, even if you are traveling overseas.

Line Testers

Many hotels use digital PBXs for their telephone systems, which typically carry more current than standard analog lines. This power is needed to operate additional features on the telephone, such as message lights and LCD displays. This additional current can permanently damage your modem without warning, and unfortunately, the jacks used by these systems are the same standard RJ-11 connectors used by traditional telephones.

To avoid this problem, you can purchase a line-testing device—usually called a Modem-Saver—for about $30 that plugs into a wall jack and measures the amount of current on the circuit. It then informs you whether it is safe to plug in your modem.

Acoustic Couplers

On those occasions when you can't plug your modem into the phone jack, or when no jack is available (such as at a pay phone), the last resort is an acoustic coupler. The *acoustic coupler* is an ancient telecommunications device that predates the system of modular jacks used to connect telephones today; you might have seen a very young Matthew Broderick use an acoustic coupler in the 1980s movie *War Games*. To connect to a telephone line, the coupler plugs into your modem's RJ-11 jack at one end and clamps to a telephone handset at the other end. A speaker at the mouthpiece and a microphone at the earpiece allow the audible signals generated by the modem and the phone system to interact.

The acoustic coupler can be an annoying bit of extra baggage to have to carry with you, but it is the one foolproof method for connecting to any telephone line without having to worry about international standards, line current, or wiring.

Cellular Modems

If you want to get online with no wires, one of the easiest and least expensive ways is via a cellular modem and your existing cell phone. Most business people today carry a portable cell phone, which in most cases can now be used for online communications with your laptop. The only missing items are a cellular modem compatible with your particular brand of phone and the cable that goes from the modem to the phone.

Most laptops include built-in modems these days, but unfortunately most of them are not cellular capable, in which case you must purchase a PC card–based cellular capable modem to use. 3Com and others make modems that work with most of the popular cell phones on the market using AMPS or GSM service. For example, I use a Nokia 6100 series phone, which is supported by the 3Com CXM756 (56K Data/Fax/Cell) modem. To use this, I need a cable, which 3Com also sells. Most of these modems use the Microcom MNP10EC protocol, which is designed to handle signal changes and hand-offs common in cellular operation.

After installing the modem and driver and plugging in the cable between the modem and phone, dialing out then works just as previously. You can dial your ISP using whatever numbers it provides for normal modem access; the only caveat is that connections through the cell phone run at up to 9600bps maximum, and in some cases less than that due to interference. The modem puts the cell phone into analog mode for communications, even if the phone is a digital type. No additional ISP or other service charges are necessary, and you use your normal dial-up software to log on.

Using the proper modem and cable, you can turn your ordinary cell phone into a direct wireless email and Internet connection.

◀◀ See "MNP 1–4," p. 1005.

The Traveler's Survival Kit

For successful computing on the road, have these with you at all times:

- Your operating system installation files (on CD-ROM or on your hard drive)
- A 56Kbps V.90 modem and 10BASE-T or dual-speed Ethernet card (can be combo)
- Replacement "dongle" connectors for the modem and network card(s)
- Portable surge protector with RJ-11 phone-line protection
- RJ-11 Line couplers that enable you to extend your modem and network card "dongles" with standard RJ-11 and RJ-45 cables

- RJ-11 line splitter or 2-into-1 connector
- "Modem Saver" RJ-11 line tester to check for dangerous high-voltage PBX systems
- Lightweight extension cord (like that you'd use to plug in your Christmas tree lights) for powering your notebook computer, if it uses ungrounded polarized line cord
- 2-to-3–prong outlet adapter
- 12V power adapter or 12V-to-120V car adapter for automotive or aircraft operation and recharging
- Spare battery
- List of local dial-up numbers for your national ISP (America Online, CompuServe, CompuServe 2000, and so on)
- Spare media for your disk, Zip, or LS-120 drive
- Tech-support Web sites and phone numbers

Portable Security

There is a growing concern for security and safety with portables because their small sizes and weights makes them easy targets for thieves. A prime target is the traveler at the airport: In that environment, you should always be sure you keep tight control over your computer; otherwise, it can easily be stolen.

A common scam involves two people at the X-ray scanner. They both stand in front of you in line; one goes through and the other waits until you put your system on the conveyer belt before holding up the line fumbling with change and other items in his pocket. This serves to detain you while the companion grabs your notebook and runs. By the time you get through, your system is gone. Moral of the story: Don't set your computer on the conveyer belt until there is nobody between you and the metal detector portal.

Various alarms are sold that can shriek if your system is stolen, but these are a fairly extreme solution.

System manufacturers offer protection for their systems in several ways. One is to offer a latch on the system to which a security lock cable can be bolted. This is ideal if you are working with your system on a desk and want to lock it to the desk. Companies such as Kensington Microware sell steel cables with a key lock that goes through the latch in the system case, and which can then be wrapped around a secure object. The latch in the case is made as a part of the frame and not the flimsy plastic exterior casing.

A second method for protection involves passwords. Most notebook systems offer several levels of password protection, but the most secure are the Administrator password and the Hard-disk password. Both of those, if lost, can't be reset or deleted, so losing them renders the motherboard or hard disk useless. Be careful if you set these passwords—don't forget them! Of course, the idea is that if thieves steal your portable, they won't be able to access any of the data on it, even if they move the hard disk to another machine.

IBM and other manufacturers also often include a Personalization Editor, which enables you to place information such as your name, address, phone number, company information, and even logo directly into the BIOS such that they will appear when the system is started. This easily identifies the proper owner of the system if it falls into the wrong hands. It can also be useful for identifying individual computers in a company where everybody is issued the same system.

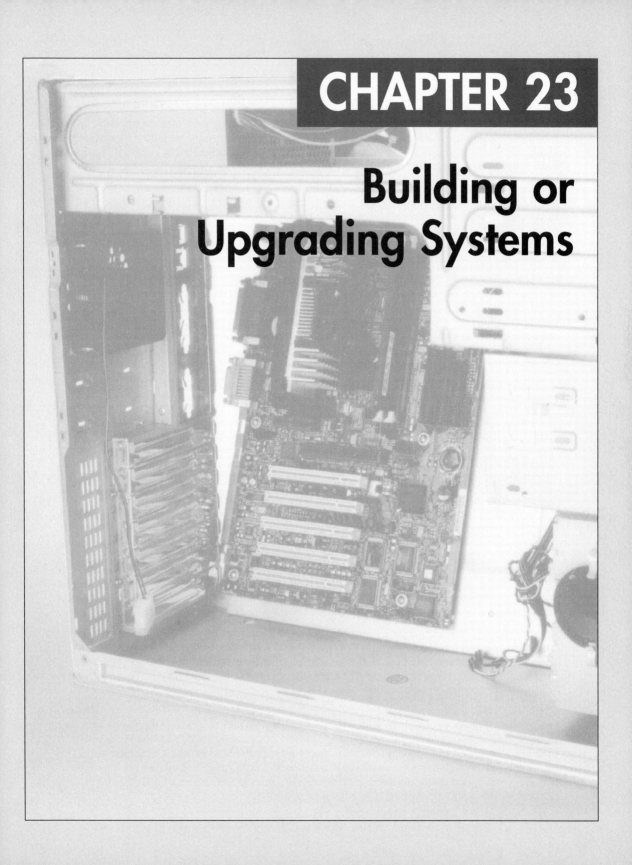

CHAPTER 23

Building or Upgrading Systems

System Components

In these days of commodity parts and component pricing, building your own system from scratch is no longer the daunting process it once was. Every component necessary to build a PC system is available off the shelf at competitive pricing. In many cases, the system you build can use the same or even better components than the top name-brand systems.

There are, however, some cautions to heed. The main thing to note is that you rarely save money when building your own system; purchasing a complete system from a mail-order vendor or mass merchandiser is almost always less expensive. The reason for this is simple: Most system vendors who build systems to order use many, if not all, of the same components you can use when building your own system. The difference is that they buy these components in quantity and receive a much larger discount than you can by purchasing only one of a particular item.

In addition, you pay only one shipping and handling charge when you purchase a complete system instead of the multiple shipping charges you pay when you purchase separate components. In fact, the shipping, handling, and phone charges from ordering all the separate parts needed to build a PC through the mail often add up to $100 or more. This cost rises if you encounter problems with any of the components and have to make additional calls or send improper or malfunctioning parts back for replacement. Many companies charge restocking fees if you purchase something and then determine you don't need it or can't use it.

If you purchase parts locally, you typically must pay the additional state sales tax, as well as the higher prices usually associated with retail store sales.

Then there is the included software. Although I can sometimes come close in price to a commercial system when building my own from scratch, the software really clinches it for the commercial system. A new copy of Windows (98 or Me) runs $100 or more, and most commercial systems also include Microsoft Office or other applications as well. I'd value the software included with most systems at $250–$500 depending on what you get.

It is clear that the reasons for building a system from scratch often have less to do with saving money and more to do with the experience you gain and the results you achieve. In the end, you have a custom system that contains the exact components and features you have selected. Most of the time when you buy a preconfigured system, you have to compromise in some way. For example, you might get the video adapter you want, but you would prefer a different make or model of motherboard. By building your own system, you can select the exact components you want and build the ultimate system for your needs. The experience is also very rewarding. You know exactly how your system is constructed and configured because you have done it yourself. This makes future support and installation of additional accessories much easier.

Another benefit of building your own system is that you are guaranteed a nonproprietary system that will be easily upgradable in the future. Of course, if you have been reading the book up to this point, you already know everything you need to ensure any preassembled systems you purchase would be nonproprietary and, therefore, upgradable and repairable in the future.

You might be able to save some money using components from your current system when building your new system. You might have recently upgraded your hard drive and memory in an attempt to extend the life of your current computer. In most cases, you can take those components with you to the new system if you plan appropriately. For example, if you bought PC133 SDRAM memory for your old system, you can move it to any motherboard that also uses PC133 SDRAM memory. This memory is fast enough to support any Pentium III or AMD Athlon CPU currently on the market. However, boards that use newer memory technologies, such as DDR SDRAM (PC1600 and PC2100) or RDRAM RIMMs, aren't designed to use older memory types.

The good news is that your monitor, keyboard, mouse, and storage devices—as well as most AGP video cards and all PCI-based add-on cards—from your old system will work in your new system.

So, if you are interested in a rewarding experience, want a customized and fully upgradable system that is not exactly the same as that offered by any vendor, are able to take on all system repair and troubleshooting tasks, want to save some money by reusing some of the components from your current system, and are not in a hurry, building your own PC might be the way to go. On the other hand, if you are interested in getting a PC with the most value for the best price, want one-stop support for in-warranty repairs and technical problems, and need an operational system quickly, building your own system should definitely be avoided.

This chapter details the components necessary to assemble your own system, explains the assembly procedures, and lists some recommendations for components and their sources.

The components used in building a typical PC are

- Case and power supply
- Motherboard
- Processor with heatsink
- Memory
- Floppy drive
- Hard disk drive
- CD-ROM/DVD drive
- CD-R/RW or Recordable DVD (such as DVD+RW)
- Keyboard
- Pointing device (mouse)
- Video card and display
- Sound card and speakers
- Modem or LAN card (Internet/email access)
- Cooling fans and heatsinks
- Cables
- Hardware (nuts, bolts, screws, and brackets)
- Operating system software (on CD-ROM)

Each of these components is discussed in the following sections.

Case and Power Supply

The case and power supply usually are sold as a unit, although some vendors do sell them separately. There are a multitude of designs from which to choose, usually dependent on the motherboard form factor you want to use, the number of drive bays available, and whether the system is desktop or floor mounted. There are cases with extra fans for cooling (recommended), air filters on the air inlets to keep down the dust, removable side panels, or motherboard trays; cases that require no tools for assembly, rack-mounted versions, and more. For most custom-built systems, an ATX mid-tower case and power supply is the recommended choice. Cases designed for the older Baby-AT motherboard form factor are still available, but the ATX architecture offers considerable improvements. The size and shape of the case, power supply, and even the motherboard are called the *form factor*. The most popular case form factors are

- Full-tower
- Mini-tower
- Desktop
- Low-profile (also called Slimline)

Cases that take ATX boards are found mostly in the full-tower, mini-tower, and desktop form factors. When deciding which type of case to purchase, you should consider where you will place your computer. Will it be on a desk? Or is it more feasible to put the system on the floor and just have the monitor, keyboard, and mouse on the desk? The amount of space you have available for the computer can affect other purchasing decisions, such as the length of the monitor, keyboard, and mouse cables.

Of the choices listed, it is recommended that you avoid the low-profile systems. Designed primarily for use in business environments, these Slimline systems have a smaller footprint, meaning that they take up less space on your desk than the typical desktop computer and usually are not designed with expansion in mind. These cases require a special type of motherboard called a Low Profile or LPX board. The low-profile version of the ATX form factor is called the NLX. LPX and NLX motherboards often have virtually everything built in, including video, sound, and even network adapters.

LPX and NLX motherboards do not have any normal adapter slots. Instead, all the expansion slots are mounted on an adapter board called a *riser card*, which plugs into a special slot on the motherboard. Standard PCI or ISA adapter cards then plug sideways into the riser card (parallel to the motherboard), making expansion difficult and somewhat limited. In addition, the small size of the case makes working inside the machine difficult. Some designs force you to remove some components to gain access to others, making system maintenance inconvenient.

◄◄ See "Motherboard Form Factors," p. 194.

Most newer cases accept ATX-style boards, which have become the standard for Athlon and Pentium III/4–based systems. If you are interested in the most flexible type of case and power supply that will support the widest variety of future upgrades, I recommend sticking with the ATX-style cases and power supplies.

Note

Generally, any ATX case, motherboard, and power supply of sufficient wattage for your equipment can be put together to form the basis of a new system. However, there are two major exceptions you need to know about:

- *Dell motherboards and power supplies built on or after September 1998 use the standard ATX power supply physical connector but have changed the pinout and voltage levels.* If you mix a Dell motherboard and a standard power supply, or a standard motherboard and a Dell power supply, you will destroy the power supply and possibly your motherboard as well! If you want to upgrade newer Dell systems, you must either buy Dell-compatible power supplies for use with the Dell motherboard or replace both Dell components with standard ATX components. See Chapter 21, "Power Supply and Chassis/Case," for more details.

- *Intel's Pentium 4 CPU requires a heavy heatsink and fan for cooling.* To prevent motherboard damage, Intel specifies a modified ATX case design that uses the case, rather than the motherboard, to support the weight of the heatsink and fan. Some Pentium 4 motherboards come with a special baseplate designed to support the heatsink in standard ATX cases. The Pentium 4 also requires a different type of auxiliary power connector to supply the additional power needed by the CPU. Pentium 4–ready power supplies are available, or you can add an adapter to your existing high-output power supplies to provide adequate power for the Pentium 4.

Whether you choose a desktop or one of the tower cases is really a matter of personal preference and system location. Most people feel that the tower systems are roomier and easier to work on, and the full-sized tower cases have lots of bays for various storage devices. Tower cases typically have enough bays to hold floppy drives, multiple hard disk drives, CD-ROM drives, tape drives, and anything else you might want to install. However, some of the desktop cases can have as much room as the towers, particularly the mini- or mid-tower models. In fact, a tower case is sometimes considered to be a desktop case turned sideways or vice versa. Some cases are convertible—that is, they can be used in either a desktop or tower orientation.

Tip

Mini-tower or micro-tower systems are an exception to the roomy tower case rule. These systems normally use the Micro-ATX motherboard and might have only two or three drive bays. These systems are almost as difficult to work on as a Slimline system.

When it comes to the power supply, the most important consideration is how many devices you plan to install in the system and how much power they require. Chapter 21 describes the process for calculating the power your system hardware requires and selecting an appropriate power supply for your needs.

◀◀ See "Power-Use Calculations," p. 1138.

When you build your own system, you should always keep upgradability in mind. A properly designed custom PC should last you far longer than an off-the-shelf model because you can more easily add and substitute new components. When choosing a case and power supply, leave yourself some room for expansion, on the assumption that you will eventually need another hard drive or that some new device will appear on the market that you won't be able to live without. To be specific, be sure you have at least two empty drive bays for internal drives and choose a larger power supply than you need for your current onboard equipment.

Motherboard

Several compatible form factors are used for motherboards. The form factor refers to the physical dimensions and size of the board and dictates into which type of case the board will fit. The types of compatible industry-standard motherboard form factors generally available for system builders are as follows:

Obsolete form factors	Modern form factors	All others
■ Baby-AT	■ ATX	■ Proprietary designs (some Compaq, Dell Optiplex, Hewlett-Packard, note-book/portable systems, and so on); Dell Dimension from September 1998–present uses ATX form factors, but with different electrical pinouts
■ Full-size AT	■ Micro-ATX	
■ LPX (semiproprietary)	■ Flex-ATX	
	■ NLX	

The ATX motherboard design is far and away the most popular and the best motherboard design for most people building their own systems today. ATX is an open architecture that improves on the older Baby-AT design in many ways that affect other components of the computer, such as the case and the power supply. An ATX motherboard has the same basic dimensions as a Baby-AT; however, it is rotated 90° in the case from the standard Baby-AT orientation. This places the expansion slots parallel to the short side of the board, allowing more space for other components without interfering with expansion boards.

Components that produce large amounts of heat, such as the CPU and memory, are located next to the power supply for better cooling and easier access to the processor and memory sockets. ATX motherboards feature a high degree of port integration, but unlike Baby-AT motherboards, all ATX external ports are built into the motherboard and are mounted to one side of the expansion slots. You won't need to use the clumsy and easily damaged or disconnected ribbon cables used by Baby-AT motherboards to carry mouse, serial, parallel, or USB ports to the rear of the system.

The ATX-style power supply features a redesigned, single-keyed (foolproof!) connector that can't be plugged in backward or off-center. Plugging power supply connectors backward or off-center by a pin is easy to do in the Baby-AT design, and the result is catastrophic: The motherboard will be destroyed the moment the power is turned on. This is impossible with the shrouded and keyed ATX power connector. This power supply provides the motherboard with the 3.3v current used by many of the newer CPUs and other components. ATX power supplies are also designed to support the advanced power-management features now found in system BIOS and operating systems.

The micro-ATX form factor is a further development of the ATX design, intended for use in lower-cost systems. The micro-ATX architecture is backward compatible with ATX and specifies a motherboard that is physically smaller, as the name implies. These smaller motherboards can be installed in standard ATX cases or in smaller cases specifically designed for the micro-ATX boards.

Other form factors used in motherboards today are the LPX and NLX form factors. These form factors require the use of a low-profile case and usually are not recommended when building your own system. This is because of the number of variations on case and riser-card designs, the limited expandability imposed by the motherboard and case architecture, and the difficulty of working in such a small space. Some LPX motherboards use a vertical riser card to mount expansion slots parallel to the motherboard, whereas others use a T-shaped riser card that lifts the expansion slots above the motherboard.

Because of the differences among systems with LPX motherboards, upgrading the motherboard on a system that uses an LPX motherboard is very difficult. The NLX form factor is another open standard Intel developed, with features comparable to the ATX but defining a Slimline-style case and motherboard arrangement. Systems based on the NLX standard should not experience the compatibility problems of LPX-based systems, but the inherent problems of the Low-Profile design remain. These types of form factors are popular with corporate clients and novice consumers because of the systems' small footprint and the "everything-on-the-motherboard" design. However, replacement NLX motherboards are relatively scarce compared to the abundance of ATX and micro-ATX motherboards on the market.

Note

For more information on all the motherboard form factors, see Chapter 4, "Motherboards and Buses." You can also find the reference standard documents detailing the modern form factors at the Desktop Form Factors Web site: http://www.formfactors.org.

In addition to the form factor, you should consider several other features when selecting a motherboard. The following sections examine each feature.

Processor

In some cases, your motherboard comes with the processor already installed. Some of the motherboard vendors like to install the processor and warranty the board and processor as a unit. This is not always the case, especially with slot-type processors because they are easier to ship with the processor removed. Most companies that sell motherboards like to sell you the processor at the same time and will give you some type of discount when you buy both. In some cases, you will get an extended warranty on the CPU and motherboard only if they are assembled and tested by the vendor. Even so, you can purchase the motherboard and processor separately if you want.

The motherboards you consider should have one of the following processor sockets or slots:

- *Socket 370 (also called PGA370).* Supports the socketed versions of the Intel Pentium III and Celeron processor
- *Socket A.* Supports the AMD Duron processor and PGA package Athlon processors
- *Socket 423.* Supports the initial versions of the Intel Pentium 4 processor
- *Slot 2 (also called SC-330).* Supports the Intel Pentium III Xeon and Pentium II Xeon processors

The following slot and socket types also can be purchased but are not being supported by the latest CPU models and will limit your future processor upgrade options:

- *Slot 1 (also called SC-242).* Supports the slot versions of the Intel Pentium III, Celeron, and Pentium II processors.
- *Socket 7 (also called Super7 if faster than 66MHz).* Supports the Intel Pentium; Pentium MMX; AMD K5, K6, K6-2, and K6-3; Cyrix 6x86 and 6x86MX; and MII processors
- *Slot A.* Supports the original AMD Athlon processors

Because the motherboard you choose dictates or limits your choice in processor, you should choose your processor first. These days the choice in processors runs the gamut from the AMD Duron series and Intel Celeron on the low end, to the AMD Athlon and Intel Pentium 4 for the midrange, to the Pentium III Xeon on the high end. For more information on these and all other processors, see Chapter 3, "Microprocessors Types and Specifications."

◄◄ See "Processor Sockets and Slots," p. 82.

◄◄ See "Intel P6 (686) Sixth-Generation Processors," p. 140, and "Other Sixth-Generation Processors," p. 172.

Depending on the type of motherboard you select, there might be jumpers on the motherboard to set. It also might have jumpers to control the voltage supplied to the processor. Typically, Socket 7 or Super7 boards have jumpers for motherboard bus speed, CPU multiplier, and CPU voltage settings. If you purchase this type of board, be sure you get these settings correct; otherwise, the system won't run properly. In a worst-case situation, you can damage the processor with too high a voltage setting, for example.

Socket 370 and 423, Slot 1, Slot 2, Socket A, and Slot A boards handle all these settings automatically, so there is little danger of incorrect settings. Even so, several boards have overrides for the automatic settings, which can be useful for those intending on hotrodding or overclocking their processors. Most of these boards use the BIOS Setup to control these overrides, so no jumpers or switches need to be set.

Chipsets

Aside from the processor, the main component on a motherboard is called the *chipset*. This usually is a set of one to five chips that contains the main motherboard circuits. These chipsets replace the 150 or more distinct components that were used in the original IBM AT systems and enable a motherboard designer to easily create a functional system from just a few parts. The chipset contains all the motherboard circuitry except the processor and memory in most systems.

Because the chipset really *is* the motherboard, the chipset used in a given motherboard has a profound effect on the performance of the board. It dictates all the performance parameters and limitations of the board, such as memory size and speed, processor types and speeds, supported buses and their speeds, and more. If you plan to incorporate technologies such as the Accelerated Graphics Port (AGP) or the Universal Serial Bus (USB) into your system, you must ensure that your motherboard has a chipset that supports these features.

Because chipsets are constantly being introduced and improved over time, I can't list all of them and their functions; however, you will find a detailed description of many of them in Chapter 4. Several popular high-performance chipsets are on the market today. The best of these offer support for Synchronous DRAM (SDRAM), Double Data Rate SDRAM (DDR SDRAM), or Rambus DRAM (RDRAM) memory; PCI and AGP 4x or faster buses; Advanced Configuration and Power Interface (ACPI); and Ultra-DMA ATA (IDE) support.

Intel is by far the most popular manufacturer of chipsets in the world, which is not surprising because the development of new chipsets parallels the introduction of new processors. Other chipset manufacturers exist, but because Intel releases new processor models at an ever-increasing rate, other developers have a difficult time keeping up. In most cases, you can use pin-compatible non-Intel processors (for example, the AMD K6 series, Cyrix MII, Cyrix III, and VIA C3) with motherboards containing Intel chipsets. However, the latest AMD CPUs (Athlon and Duron) use their own slot and socket designs and thus require their own chipsets.

◀◀ See "Chipsets," p. 225.

◀◀ See "Knowing What to Look For (Selection Criteria)," p. 340.

Clearly, the selection of a chipset must be based largely on the processor you choose and the additional components you intend to install in the computer.

However, no matter which chipset you look for, I recommend checking for the following supported features:

- 100/133MHz or faster CPU bus support
- SDRAM, DDR SDRAM, or RDRAM (main memory) support
- Error Correcting Code (ECC) memory support
- Advanced Configuration and Power Interface (ACPI) energy-saving functions
- AGP 4x or faster
- Dual Ultra-ATA/100 or Serial ATA ATA interfaces
- USB 2.0 (high-speed USB) support

Most of the better chipsets on the market today should have these features and more. If you are intent on building the ultimate PC (at least by this week's standards), you also should consider the fastest processors available. Be sure not to waste your investment on the most capable processor by using a chipset that doesn't fully exploit its capabilities.

When you are designing your system, carefully consider the number and type of expansion cards you intend to install. Then, ensure that the motherboard you select has the correct number of slots and that they are of the correct bus type for your peripherals (ISA, PCI, and AGP). Because many newer boards don't have ISA slots, it might be time to get rid of any ISA boards you have and replace them with more capable PCI versions.

When you buy a motherboard, I highly recommend you contact the chipset manufacturer and obtain the documentation (usually called the *data book*) for your particular chipset. This explains how the memory and cache controllers, as well as many other devices in the system, operate. This documentation should also describe the Advanced Chipset Setup functions in your system's Setup program. With this information, you might be able to fine-tune the motherboard configuration by altering the chipset features. Because chipsets are frequently discontinued and replaced with newer models, don't wait too long to get the chipset documentation because most manufacturers make it available only for chips currently in production.

Note

One interesting fact about chipsets is that in the volume that the motherboard manufacturers purchase them, the chipsets usually cost about $40 each. If you have an older motherboard that needs repair, you usually can't purchase the chipsets because they usually aren't stocked by the manufacturer after they are discontinued. Not to mention that most chipsets feature surface mounting with ball grid array (BGA) packages that are extremely difficult to remove manually and replace. The low-cost chipset is one of the reasons motherboards have become disposable items that are rarely, if ever, repaired.

BIOS

Another important feature on the motherboard is the BIOS (basic input/output system). This is also called the ROM BIOS because the code is stored in a read-only memory (ROM) chip. There are several things to look for here. One is that the BIOS is supplied by one of the major BIOS manufacturers, such as AMI (American Megatrends International), Phoenix, Award, or Microid Research. Also, be sure that the BIOS is contained in a special type of reprogrammable chip called a Flash ROM or EEPROM (electrically erasable programmable read-only memory). This enables you to download BIOS updates from the manufacturer and, using a program they supply, easily update the code in your BIOS. If you do not have the Flash ROM or EEPROM type, you must physically replace the chip if an update is required.

◀◀ See "Upgrading the BIOS," p. 362.

Virtually all motherboards built in the last few years include a BIOS with support for the Plug and Play (PnP) specification. This makes installing new cards, especially PnP cards, much easier. PnP automates the installation and uses special software built into the BIOS and the operating system (such as Windows 9x/Me and Windows 2000) to automatically configure adapter cards and resolve adapter resource conflicts.

Note

See "See Plug and Play BIOS," in Chapter 5, "BIOS." Also, an exhaustive listing of PnP device IDs can be found in the Technical Reference section of the CD included with this book.

Memory

Older systems had L2 cache memory on the motherboard, but for almost all newer systems, this cache is now a part of the processor. The few remaining Socket 7 or Super7 motherboards do still include cache onboard, and it is normally soldered in and not removable or upgradable.

◀◀ See "Cache Memory: SRAM," p. 408.

Most Super7 motherboards support at least 1MB–2MB of cache memory.

For Pentium II/III/4, Celeron systems, and AMD's Athlon and Duron systems, no additional L2 memory is necessary because the processors have the cache memory integrated into the processor package, although some Athlon motherboards also have additional cache onboard, which they call L3.

Main memory typically is installed in the form of Single Inline Memory Modules (SIMMs), Dual Inline Memory Modules (DIMMs), or Rambus Inline Memory Modules (RIMMs). Four physical types of main memory modules are used in PC systems today, with several variations of each. The four main types are as follows:

- 72-pin SIMMs (EDO RAM)
- 168-pin DIMMs (SDRAM)
- 184-pin DIMMs (DDR SDRAM)
- 184-pin RIMMs (RDRAM)

The 168-pin SDRAM DIMMs are common in lower-end systems today; however, just a few years ago, most systems came with 72-pin EDO SIMMs. Most systems use the DIMMs because they are 64 bits wide and can be used as a single bank on a Pentium or higher-class processor that has a 64-bit external data bus. Some of the newest and fastest systems using the Pentium 4 processor use the RDRAM RIMMs, which offer significant performance gains over standard SDRAM.

Double Data Rate (DDR) SDRAM memory is a new design of standard SDRAM in which data is transferred twice as quickly. DDR support is found in newer Athlon/Duron systems, as well as the newest server chipsets from Intel and others. Note that although both DDR SDRAM DIMMs and RDRAM RIMMs use 184-pin connectors, their memory architectures are completely different and the memory is **not** interchangeable.

◄◄ See "Physical RAM Capacity and Organization," p. 436.

◄◄ See "DDR SDRAM," p. 418.

A 64-bit Pentium class system requires two 72-pin SIMMs (32 bits wide each) or a single 168-pin DIMM (64 bits wide) to make a single bank.

Memory modules can include an extra bit for each eight for parity checking or ECC use. If ECC is important to you, be sure your chipset (and motherboard) supports ECC before purchasing the more expensive ECC modules.

◄◄ See "Parity and ECC," p. 443.

Another thing to watch out for is the type of metal on the memory module contacts, especially on motherboards using SIMMs. They are available with either tin- or gold-plated contacts. Although it might seem that gold-plated contacts are better (they are), you should not use them in all systems. You should instead always match the type of plating on the module contacts to what is also used on the socket contacts. In other words, if the motherboard SIMM, DIMM, or RIMM sockets have tin-plated contacts, you must use modules with tin-plated contacts. Most motherboards with SIMM sockets used tin-plated ones, requiring tin-plated SIMMs, whereas most DIMM and RIMM sockets are gold-plated, requiring gold-plated DIMMs and RIMMs.

If you mix dissimilar metals (tin with gold), corrosion on the tin side is rapidly accelerated, and tiny electrical currents are generated. The combination of the corrosion and tiny currents causes havoc, and all types of memory problems and errors can occur. In some systems, I have observed that everything seems fine for about a year, during which the corrosion develops. After that, random memory errors result. Removing and cleaning the memory module and socket contacts postpones the problem for another year, and then the problems return again. How would you like this problem if you have 100 or more systems to support? Of course, you can avoid these problems if you insist on using SIMMs with contacts whose metal matches the metal found in the sockets in which they will be installed.

◄◄ See "Gold Versus Tin," p. 440.

For more information on PC memory of all types, see Chapter 6, "Memory."

I/O Ports

Most motherboards today have built-in I/O ports. If these ports are not built in, they must be supplied via a plug-in expansion board that, unfortunately, wastes an expansion slot. The following ports may be included in any new system you assemble:

- Keyboard connector (mini-DIN type)
- Mouse port (mini-DIN type)
- One or two serial ports (16550A buffered UART type)
- Parallel port (EPP/ECP type)
- Two or four USB ports
- Optional display connector (integrated video)
- Optional audio/game connectors (MIDI/joystick, speaker, and microphone)
- Two local bus enhanced IDE ports (primary and secondary); UDMA 66 or faster preferred
- Floppy controller

Some motherboards lack the serial, parallel, keyboard, and mouse ports (referred to as legacy ports), instead relying on USB for those connections. You might want to avoid "legacy-free" motherboards if you still use peripherals with those types of connections. Many motherboards feature the optional integrated video and sound interfaces, especially micro-ATX motherboards.

All the integrated ports are supported either directly by the motherboard chipset or by an additional Super I/O chip and additional interface components. Adding the optional video and sound interfaces directly to the motherboard saves both money and the use of an expansion slot, especially important in the less expensive systems sold today.

If these devices are not present on the motherboard, various Super I/O or multi-I/O boards that implement all these ports are available. Again, most of the newer versions of these boards use a single-chip implementation because it is cheaper and more reliable.

◄◄ See "Super I/O Chips," p. 283.

It has become an increasingly popular practice in recent years (especially in Slimline-style systems) to integrate other standard computer functions into the motherboard design, such as video, sound, and even network adapters. The advantages of this practice include freeing up expansion slots that would normally be occupied by separate adapter cards and saving money. The price difference between a motherboard with integrated video and sound and one without would be far less than the cost of good-quality sound and video cards.

The drawback, of course, is that you have little or no choice about the features or quality of the integrated adapters. Integrated components such as these are nearly always of serviceable quality, but they certainly do not push the performance envelope of higher-end expansion cards. Most people who decide to build a system themselves do so because they want optimum performance from every component, which you do not get from integrated video and sound.

Buying a motherboard with integrated adapters, however, does not preclude you from adding expansion devices of the same type. You usually can install a video or sound card into a system with an integrated sound adapter without major problems, except that the additional cost of the integrated component is wasted. You also might encounter difficulties with the automated hardware detection routines in operating systems, such as Windows 9x/Me, detecting the wrong adapter in your system, but you can remedy this by manually identifying the expansion card to the OS.

If four or more USB ports exist, they often are split among two buses, with one set of connections on the back of the board and another set as a pin-header connector on the motherboard. A cable then plugs into this connector, enabling you to route the second USB bus port to the front of the PC case. Most newer cases have provisions for front-mounted USB ports in this manner, which makes temporarily connecting devices such as digital cameras or MP3 players for transferring files easier.

Note that if your motherboard has integrated devices such as video and sound, you must go into the BIOS Setup to disable these devices if you want to add a card-based replacement device. Check your BIOS Setup menus for an Enable/Disable setting for any integrated devices.

A trend with some newer low-cost systems is the complete elimination of the Super I/O chip and all the integrated ports contained within. These are called legacy-free PCs and lack any serial ports, parallel ports, and standard keyboard and mouse connections. All external expansion must be done via the USB ports. This means your keyboard, mouse, printer, external modem, and so on must be of the USB type.

Floppy Disk and Removable Drives

Since the advent of the CD-RW, the floppy disk drive has largely been relegated to a minor role as an alternative system boot device. Usually, today's systems are equipped with a 1.44MB 3 1/2-inch drive. All systems today are capable of booting from CD, making CD-R or especially CD-RW discs a useful high-capacity replacement for floppy or Zip drives.

For additional removable storage, I recommend a CD-RW (CD-rewritable) drive over the Zip or even LS-120 formats. These are now relatively inexpensive, and the media is low priced as well. A CD-RW drive can also write on even more inexpensive CD-R media. This provides an easy way to back up or archive up to 700MB of data (74-minute CDs hold 682MB, whereas 80-minute CDs hold 737MB).

Hard Disk Drive

Your system also needs at least one hard disk drive. In most cases, a drive with a minimum capacity of 20GB is recommended, although in some cases you can get away with less for a low-end configuration. High-end systems should have drives of 40GB or higher. One of the cardinal rules of computer shopping is that you can never have too much storage. Buy as much as you can afford, and you'll almost certainly end up filling it anyway.

Tip

If you are an Internet user, one informal method of estimating how much disk space you will need is to go by the speed of your Internet connection. If you have a high-speed link, such as that provided by an ISDN connection, a cable modem, or a LAN, you will find that the ease of downloading large amounts of data fills disk drives amazingly quickly. I would recommend at least a 40GB hard drive in these cases. In addition, a removable storage system with a large capacity, such as a CD-RW drive, is also a good idea.

Note that Windows 95 does not support any drives larger than 32GB. You should upgrade to Windows 98, Windows Me, Windows 2000, or Windows XP before installing a hard drive larger than 32GB.

The most popular hard drive interface for desktop systems is ATA (IDE), although SCSI is preferable for use with multitasking OSes. ATA generally offers greater performance for single-drive installations, but SCSI is better for use with two or more drives or with multitasking operating systems, such as Windows 95/98/Me and NT/2000/XP. This is because of the greater intelligence in the SCSI interface, which removes some of the I/O processing burden from the system's CPU. This is especially important if you are using Windows NT or Windows 2000 in a server role, where it is supporting multiple users and much heavier file access. The SCSI interface is also more versatile than ATA; it can handle either 7 or 15 devices, including scanners, tape drives, optical drives, hard drives, and removable-media drives.

Some of the newest motherboards now feature RAID-compatible ATA interfaces. These enable you to install two identical IDE drives (a pair of 30GB drives, for example) and treat them as a single very large and very fast 60GB hard drive.

◀◀ See "ATA RAID," p. 509.

Note

In most cases, a system's ATA adapter is integrated into the motherboard. With SCSI, this is much less common. Although you sometimes can purchase a motherboard with an integrated SCSI adapter, you are more likely to have to purchase a separate SCSI host adapter and install it into one of your system's expansion slots. It is recommended that you select an SCSI adapter that uses the fastest expansion bus your system supports, which in most cases today is PCI. Good-quality SCSI host adapters are considerably more complex than are ATA adapters and are therefore more expensive. Be sure to consider this additional expense and the need for an additional slot when deciding on a hard drive interface for your system.

◀◀ See "How to Reliably Record CDs," p. 756.

◀◀ See "SCSI Versus IDE," p. 540.

Several brands of high-quality hard disk drives are available from which to choose, and most of them offer similar performance within their price and capacity categories. In fact, you might notice that the capacities and specifications of the various ATA and SCSI drives certain manufacturers offer are remarkably similar. This is because a single drive assembly is manufactured for use with both interfaces. The same ATA drive, for example, with the addition of a SCSI interface chip on the logic board, becomes a SCSI drive, often at a substantially higher price.

Serial ATA is rapidly replacing the standard parallel ATA in newer systems, so that is something you might want to look for as well. See Chapter 7, "The IDE Interface," to learn more about Serial ATA.

CD/DVD-ROM Drive

A CD or DVD-ROM drive should be considered a mandatory item in any PC you construct these days. This is because virtually all software is now being distributed on CD-ROM, and many newer titles are on DVD. DVD drives can read CD-ROMs as well as DVD-ROMs, so they are more flexible. Systems can now even boot from CD-ROM drives as long as the system BIOS provides the proper support.

DVD-ROM is a high-density data storage format that uses a CD-sized disc to store a great deal more data than a CD-ROM—from 4.7GB–17GB, depending on the format. These drives can read standard CD-ROMs and audio CDs, as well as the higher-capacity DVD data and video discs.

◀◀ See "DVD," p. 718.

There are several types of CD-ROM or DVD drives to consider these days, but I generally recommend a minimum of a 32x CD-ROM or an 8x DVD-ROM drive connected using the integrated ATA interface found on all modern motherboards. This results in the best possible performance with the minimum amount of hassle. If you plan on using SCSI for your hard drives, however, you might want to select a SCSI CD- or DVD-ROM drive; you'll improve your multitasking performance.

You also might consider purchasing a rewritable CD-ROM drive, generally known as a CD-RW drive (as discussed in the next section). If you do, I recommend you get this in addition to your existing CD-ROM or DVD-ROM drive—that way you easily can copy existing data and music CDs. This is also a good idea because the recordable drives usually are slower than the ROM-only versions. Another reason to install both a CD-RW and a CD-ROM/DVD drive is to make backing up an existing CD-ROM easy without copying the contents to the hard drive first.

CD-R/RW

Burning your own CDs can be a convenient and relatively inexpensive data storage method. Drives advertised as CD-RW handle both CD-RW (rewritable) and CD-R (record once) media. Note, though, that many older CD-ROM drives can't read CD-RW media (drives labeled as MultiRead can read CD-RW media), whereas virtually all drives can read CD-R discs.

Tip

For the highest reliability when using CD-RW drives, be sure your drive incorporates one of the forms of buffer underrun protection, such as BURN-proof, JustLink, or Waste-Proof. This prevents you from making coasters (unusable discs) when burning CDs.

Keyboard and Pointing Device (Mouse)

Obviously, your system needs a keyboard and some type of pointing device, such as a mouse. Different people prefer different types of keyboards, and the "feel" of one type can vary considerably from other types. If possible, I suggest you try a variety of keyboards until you find the type that suits you best. I prefer a stiff action with tactile feedback myself, but others prefer a lighter, quieter touch.

Because two types of keyboard connectors are found in systems today, be sure that the keyboard you purchase matches the connector on your motherboard. The original 5-pin DIN and newer 6-pin mini-DIN keyboard connectors are electrically compatible, enabling you to adapt either type of keyboard connector to either type of keyboard. The newest keyboard interface is USB, driven by the widespread availability of the USB connector and the rise of legacy-free PCs that have only USB ports.

As with any USB device, you must have support in the operating system for USB, and in the case of USB keyboards, your system BIOS must support a function called Legacy USB or USB Keyboard and Mouse if you want to use the USB keyboard outside the Windows graphical user interface. Most recent BIOSes have this feature. However, to enable you to use your USB keyboard on both new and older systems, I recommend you look for a model that also supports the traditional keyboard ports.

◀◀   See "Keyboards," p. 954.

◀◀   See "Keyboard Technology," p. 960.

The same selection concept also applies to mice or other pointing devices; a number of choices are available that suit different individuals. Try several before deciding on the type you want. If your motherboard includes a built-in mouse port, be sure you get a mouse designed for that interface. This mouse is often called a PS/2 type mouse because the IBM PS/2 systems introduced this type of mouse port. Many older systems use a serial mouse connected to a serial port, but a motherboard-integrated mouse port is preferable because it leaves both serial ports free for other devices. Some USB mice work with the PS/2 port, but others are made strictly for the USB port. I recommend dual-mode mice that work with either type of system. In addition, you can even choose from cordless versions as well.

Tip

You might be tempted to skimp on your keyboard and mouse to save a few dollars. Don't! You do all your interacting with your new PC through these devices, and cheap ones make their presence known every time you use your system. I insist on high-quality mechanical switch–type keyboards on all my systems.

◀◀   See "USB Keyboards," p. 957.

Video Card and Display

You need a video adapter and a monitor or display to complete your system. Numerous choices are available in this area, but the most important piece of advice I have to give is to choose a good monitor. The display is your main interface to the system and can be the cause of many hours of either pain or pleasure, depending on what monitor you choose.

I usually recommend a minimum of a 17-inch display these days. Anything smaller can't acceptably display a 1,024×768 pixel resolution. If you opt for a 15-inch or smaller display, you might find that the maximum tolerable resolution is 800×600. This might be confusing because many 15-inch monitors are capable of displaying 1,024×768 resolution or even higher, but the characters and features are so small onscreen at that resolution that excessive eyestrain and headaches are often the result; the display often is blurry when a monitor is run at its maximum resolution. If you spend a lot of time in front of your system and want to work in the higher screen resolutions, a 17-inch display should be considered mandatory. If you can afford it, I recommend a 19-inch display; they work even better at the higher resolutions and have come down in price considerably from previous years. Look for CRT displays with lower dot-pitch (0.28dpi or less), which indicates the size and spacing of dots in the CRT mask. Lower means higher resolution and a clearer picture.

If your desk space is limited and you can afford it, consider the wide variety of flat-screen LCD panels now available (a 15-inch LCD panel is about equal in viewable area to a 17-inch CRT). In most cases, they attach to the normal VGA analog port, but the newest models work with the DVI connector available on some of the newest video cards. LCD panels are an excellent choice if you always use the native resolution (usually 1,024×768), but if you need to change resolutions (for previewing Web page designs or game playing), CRTs are better.

Your video card and monitor should be compatible in terms of refresh rate. The minimum refresh rate for a solid, nonflickering display is 70Hz–72Hz—the higher, the better. If your new video card can display 16 million colors at a resolution of 1,024×768 and a refresh rate of 76Hz, but your monitor's maximum refresh rate at 1,024×768 is 56Hz, you can't use the video card to its maximum potential. Configuring a video adapter to deliver signals the monitor can't support is one of the few software configuration processes that can physically damage the system hardware. Pushing a monitor beyond its capabilities can cause it irreparable harm.

Video adapters in recent years have become standardized on the accelerated graphics port (AGP) interface, although many older systems used PCI-based video cards. You might need to use a PCI video card if you are adding a secondary video adapter to your system to run a second monitor. Windows 98, Me, and 2000 support this feature, and it can be very useful for some applications. To save a slot in your system, you can also use a dual-display card in your AGP slot, although their 3D performance isn't as high as the best 3D accelerators now on the market.

If you are into gaming, you will want one of the high-performance 3D video cards on the market. Modern games are very video-intensive, so be sure to check with the game software companies as to which cards they would recommend. Although early 3D cards connected to the standard 2D graphics card, this design is now obsolete. High-performance 3D cards based on chipsets such as nVidia's GeForce 2 or GeForce 3 series or the ATI Radeon provide both fast 2D graphics and excellent 3D performance.

◄◄ See "Accelerated Graphics Port," p. 313.

◄◄ See "3D Graphics Accelerators," p. 863.

Sound Card and Speakers

You need a sound card and a set of external speakers for any system that you want to be multimedia capable. Although the sound card should be compatible with the Creative Labs Sound Blaster cards, which set the early standards for DOS audio, it is now more important to purchase a sound card that is compatible with Windows-based sound APIs, such as DirectX. For best performance, I recommend you get a PCI-based sound card instead of an older ISA bus design. There can be some problems with support for older DOS-based games with some of the new cards, but most of these issues have been addressed by special drivers for the newer cards.

Speakers designed for use with PCs range from tiny, underpowered devices to large audiophile systems. Many of the top manufacturers of stereo speakers are now producing speaker systems for PCs. Some include subwoofers or even a full Dolby 5.1 surround sound implementation. Let your budget be your guide.

USB Peripherals

The Universal Serial Bus (USB) promises to render the standard I/O ports on the PC obsolete. Essentially, USB brings PnP support to external peripherals by enabling you to plug up to 127 devices into a single port supporting data transfer rates up to 12Mbps. Typically, you plug in a USB hub to a port integrated into the motherboard, and then plug other devices into that. Virtually all current motherboards support USB.

◄◄ See "USB and IEEE-1394 (i.Link and FireWire)—Serial and Parallel Port Replacements," p. 940.

There are virtually no limits to the types of devices available for USB. Modems, keyboards, mice, CD-ROM drives, speakers, joysticks, tape and floppy drives, scanners, cameras, MP3 players, and printers are just some of the devices available. However, before you start buying all USB peripherals for your new system, be aware that performance problems can occur with some devices if used on a single bus, and sometimes compatibility problems can occur as well. USB 2.0 (also called high-speed USB) solves these problems, so you should be sure that any new systems you buy or build include USB 2.0 ports.

Accessories

Apart from the major components, you need a number of other accessories to complete your system. These are the small parts that can make the assembly process a pleasure or a chore. If you are purchasing your system components from mail-order sources, you should make a complete list of all the parts you need, right down to the last cable and screw, and be sure you have everything before you begin the assembly process. It is excruciating to have to wait several days with a half-assembled system for the delivery of a forgotten part.

Heatsinks/Cooling Fans

Most of today's faster processors produce a lot of heat, and this heat has to be dissipated so your system doesn't operate intermittently or even fail completely. Heatsinks are available in two main types: passive and active.

Passive heatsinks are simply finned chunks of metal (usually aluminum) that are clipped or glued to the top of the processor. They act as a radiator and, in effect, give the processor more surface area to dissipate the heat. *Active* heatsinks are required by many processors today because of their higher capacity and smaller space requirements. Often you will have no control over which heatsink you use because it comes already attached to the processor. If you have to attach it yourself, you should use a thermal transfer grease or sticky tape to fill any air gaps between the heatsink and the processor. This allows for maximum heat transfer and the best efficiency.

An active heatsink includes a built-in fan. These can offer greater cooling capacity than the passive types, and some processors—especially "boxed" processors from Intel and AMD—are sold with the heatsink and fan included. OEM processors don't include a heatsink from the processor manufacturer, but most vendors who sell them add an aftermarket heatsink and fan to the package. Note that all modern heatsinks require a thermal interface material (usually grease or paste) be applied to the base of the heatsink before installation.

Note

The ATX form factor motherboards and chassis are designed to improve system cooling. These systems move the processor and memory near the power supply for better cooling. They often feature secondary case-mounted cooling fans for extra insurance. Note that many processors today come with the heatsink integrated as a part of the unit, often an active type with a high-quality ball-bearing cooling fan built in.

Another consideration for cooling is with the case. The fan in the power supply and optionally one on the CPU heatsink often are not enough for a modern high-performance system. I recommend you get a case that includes at least one additional cooling fan. This usually is mounted in the front of the chassis, taking air in from the front and directing it over the motherboard; it often is hidden behind the card support slots used for full-length expansion cards. Some cases include extra fans near the drive bays for cooling the drives as well.

If you are upgrading an existing system, several companies make fan assemblies that insert into a drive bay for additional cooling. They take the place of a 5 1/4-inch drive and take air in through the front bezel, directing it back into the case. Bay-mounted fans are an especially good idea if you are using the 10,000rpm or faster SCSI drives on the market because they run extremely hot. There are even fan assemblies mounted on cards that blow air out the rear of the case. Keep in mind that it is best to keep the interior of the PC below 100° F; anything over 110° dramatically reduces component life and leads to stability problems.

Cables

PC systems need a number of different cables to hook up everything. These can include power cables or adapters, disk drive cables, internal or external CD-ROM cables, and many others. Most of the time, the motherboard includes the cables for any of the internal ports, such as floppy or hard drives. Other external devices you purchase come with included cables, but in some cases, they aren't supplied. The Vendor List on the CD contains contact information for several cable and small parts suppliers that can get you the cables or other parts you need to complete your system.

Another advantage of the ATX motherboard form factor is that these boards feature externally accessible I/O connectors directly mounted to the rear of the board. This eliminates the rat's nest of cables found in the common Baby-AT form factor systems and also makes the ATX system a little cheaper and more reliable.

If you build your system using all OEM (what the industry calls *white box*) components, be aware that these sometimes don't include the accessories such as cables and additional documentation that you would get with a normal boxed-retail version of the same component.

Hardware

You will need screws, standoffs, mounting rails (if your case requires them), and other miscellaneous hardware to assemble your system. Most of these parts are included with the case or your other system components. This is especially true of any card or disk drive brackets or screws. When you purchase a component such as a hard drive, some vendors offer you the option of purchasing the bare drive or a kit containing the required cables and mounting hardware for the device. Most of the time bare drives don't include any additional hardware, but you might not need it anyway if the mounting hardware comes with your case. Even so, spending the few additional dollars for the complete drive kit is rarely a waste of money. Even if you're left with some extra bits and pieces after assembling your system, they will probably come in handy someday.

In situations in which you need other hardware not included with your system components, you can consult the Vendor List for suppliers of small parts and hardware necessary to get your system operational.

Hardware and Software Resources

When you are planning to build a system, it is important to consider how all your selected components will work together and how the software you run must support them. It is not enough to be sure that you have sufficient slots on the motherboard for all your expansion cards and enough bays in the case for all your drives. You must also consider the resources required for all the components.

If you are planning to use ISA cards, for example, you need to know whether your new motherboard has any ISA slots and whether it has enough slots for your cards. Interrupt (IRQ) conflicts used to be a major problem, but if you use Windows 95 OSR 2.x (95B/95C) or newer versions with any recent chipset and have PCI cards, IRQ routing and sharing minimizes this concern. You should still be aware of IRQ use if you will be installing one or more ISA cards in your system because ISA cards can't share IRQs. Essentially, you should completely configure the system before you begin ordering any parts. Planning a system to this level of detail can be a lot of work, which is one reason the vast majority of PCs are prebuilt.

Another consideration is the operating system and other software you will need. Prebuilt systems nearly always arrive with the operating system installed, but when you build your own, you must be prepared with a copy of your selected operating system—including a system disk so that you can boot the system the first time. Because nearly any operating system in use today is distributed on CD-ROM, you must get your computer to recognize the CD-ROM drive before you can install an operating system. To make this process simpler, you should create a bootable CD. Note that the OEM versions of Windows 98 and later are bootable, but not the retail upgrade versions.

◀◀ See "Making a Bootable CD for Emergencies," p. 773.

The operating system you select for your new computer is another important decision. You must be certain that the OS supports all the hardware you've selected, which can occasionally be a difficult task. For example, you will require Windows 98 or later to properly support USB devices in your system.

Windows 98 and later come on bootable CD-ROMs if you get what is called the OEM version of the operating system. The so-called retail or upgrade editions often are restricted, aren't bootable, and might also search for preexisting files or operating systems before they will load. Because Microsoft doesn't allow OEM versions of its operating systems to be sold separately, be sure you get an OEM edition of whatever operating system you will be running with your motherboard or hard disk. The terms of the Microsoft dealer (or system builder) agreement allows dealers to sell the OS only with a PC, and the terms of the agreement state that a motherboard or hard disk qualifies as enough of a PC to allow an operating system bundle. No matter what, make sure you get the original OEM version on CD-ROM.

Tip

If you don't have the OEM version of your OS, or the system you are assembling does not support booting from CD (called El Torito support after the Phoenix-created standard), you must create a boot floppy with CD-ROM drivers. Windows 98 and later include a disk with a set of universal CD-ROM drivers that work for most systems; for Windows 95 and older operating systems, you must either borrow a Windows 98 or later startup disk or create your own bootable floppy with the correct drivers.

I'll cover this in more detail when we get to the OS load section of the building process.

Drivers for specific hardware components might also be a problem. It is a good idea to gather all the latest driver revisions for your hardware, as well as BIOS flashes, firmware updates, and other software components, and have them available when you begin the assembly process. Floppy disks are preferable for this because your CD-ROM drive and connectivity hardware might not yet be operative.

System Assembly and Disassembly

Actually assembling the system is easy after you have lined up all the components. In fact, you will find the parts procurement phase the most lengthy and trying of the entire experience. Completing the system is basically a matter of screwing everything together, plugging in all the cables and connectors, and configuring everything to operate properly together.

In short order, you will find out whether your system operates as you had planned or whether some incompatibilities exist between some of the components. Be careful and pay attention to how you install all your components. It is rare that a newly assembled system operates perfectly the first time, even for people who are somewhat experienced. It is very easy to forget a jumper, switch, or cable connection that later causes problems in system operation. Most people's first reaction when problems occur is to blame defective hardware, but that is usually not the source. Usually, the problem can be traced to some missed step or error made in the assembly process.

Above all, the most crucial rule of assembling your own system is to save every piece of documentation and software that comes with every component in your system. This material can be indispensable in troubleshooting problems you encounter during the assembly process or later. You should also retain all the packing materials used to ship mail-order components to you until you are certain they will not have to be returned.

Assembly Preparation

The process of physically assembling a PC requires only a few basic tools: a 1/4-inch nut driver or Phillips-head screwdriver for the external screws that hold the cover in place and a 3/16-inch nut driver or Phillips-head screwdriver for all the other screws. Needle-nose pliers can also help in removing motherboard standoffs, jumpers, and stubborn cable connectors. Because of marketplace standardization, only a couple types and sizes of screws (with a few exceptions) are used to hold a system together. Also, the physical arrangement of the major components is similar even among different manufacturers. Figure 23.1 shows the components that go into a typical system, and Figure 23.2 shows the system with those components assembled. Note that the components shown here are for a standard PC. Your final component list might vary.

You'll find more information on tools used to work on PCs in Chapter 24, "PC Diagnostics, Testing, and Maintenance."

Other tools you'll need are software related. You'll need the master operating system CD-ROM, and if your particular CD-ROM version isn't bootable, or your system is older and doesn't support booting from CD, you'll also need an operating system startup floppy disk with CD-ROM drivers installed. This way, your system will recognize the CD-ROM drive and enable you to install the operating system from it. Newer operating systems often come on bootable CDs, but normally only the OEM (and not retail) versions of the OS are configured that way.

The Windows 98 and later versions' startup floppies include generic ATAPI and SCSI CD-ROM drivers on them, enabling virtually all CD-ROMs to be recognized after booting from them. If you are installing Windows 95 or some other operating system that does not include a startup disk with CD-ROM drivers already installed, you can either use a Win98 or later startup disk or take your existing startup disk and install the CD-ROM drivers that came with your drive. That procedure is covered later in this chapter.

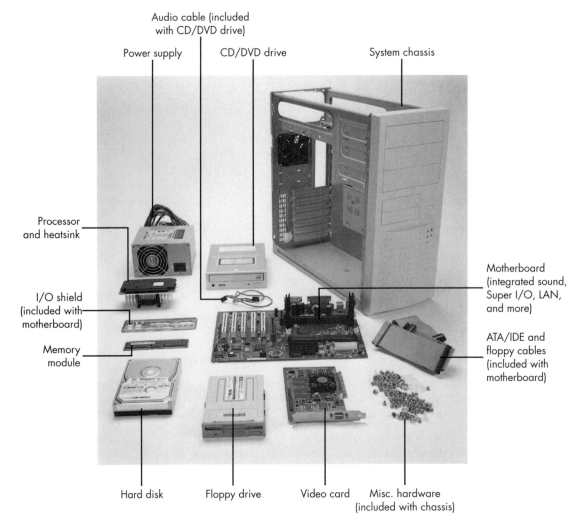

Figure 23.1   Components used in building a typical PC. *Case and power supply courtesy of PC Power & Cooling, Inc. Motherboard and processor courtesy of Intel Corporation. Other components supplied by Micro X-Press (www.microx-press.com) and Creative Labs, Inc.*

The following sections cover the assembly and disassembly procedure:

- Case or cover assembly
- Power supply
- Adapter boards
- Motherboard
- Disk drives

Figure 23.2 The completed system using all components shown in Figure 23.1. *Case and power supply courtesy of PC Power & Cooling, Inc. Motherboard and processor courtesy of Intel Corporation. Other components supplied by Micro X-Press (*www.microx-press.com*).*

Later, you learn how to install and remove these components for several types of systems. With regard to assembly and disassembly, it is best to consider each system by the type of case that it uses. All systems that have AT-type cases, for example, are assembled and disassembled in much the same manner. Tower cases are basically AT-type cases turned sideways, so the same basic instructions apply. Most Slimline and XT-style cases are similar; these systems are assembled and disassembled in much the same way.

The following section lists assembly and disassembly instructions for several case types.

ESD Protection

One issue you must be aware of is electrostatic discharge (ESD) protection. Another is recording the configuration of the system, with regard to the physical aspects of the system (such as jumper or switch settings and cable orientations) and to the logical configuration of the system (especially in terms of elements such as CMOS settings).

When you are working on the internal components of a computer, you must take the necessary precautions to prevent accidental static discharges to the components. At any time, your body can hold a large static voltage charge that can easily damage components of your system. Before I ever put my hands into an open system, I first touch a grounded portion of the chassis, such as the power supply case. This action serves to equalize the electrical charges the device and your body might be carrying. Be sure the power supply is unplugged during all phases of the assembly process. Some will claim that you should leave the system plugged in to provide an earth ground through the power cord and outlet, but that is unnecessary. If you leave the system plugged in, you open yourself up to other problems, such as accidentally turning it on or leaving it on when installing a board or device, which can damage the motherboard or other devices.

Caution

Also note that ATX power supplies used in many systems today deliver a +5v current to the motherboard continuously—that is, whenever they are plugged in. Bottom line: Be sure any system you are working on is completely unplugged from the wall outlet.

High-end workbenches at repair facilities have the entire bench grounded, so it's not as big of a problem; however, you need something to be a good ground source to prevent a current from building up in you.

A more sophisticated way to equalize the charges between you and any of the system components is to use an ESD protection kit. These kits consist of a wrist strap and mat, with ground wires for attachment to the system chassis. When you are going to work on a system, you place the mat next to or partially below the system unit. Next, you clip the ground wire to both the mat and the system's chassis, tying the grounds together. You then put on the wrist strap and attach that wire to a ground. Because the mat and system chassis are already wired together, you can attach the wrist-strap wire to the system chassis or to the mat. If you are using a wrist strap without a mat, clip the wrist-strap wire to the system chassis. When clipping these wires to the chassis, be sure to use an area that is free of paint so a good ground contact can be achieved. This setup ensures that any electrical charges are carried equally by you and any of the components in the system, preventing the sudden flow of static electricity that can damage the circuits.

As you install or remove disk drives; adapter cards; and especially delicate items such as the entire motherboard, SIMMs, or processors, you should place these components on the static mat. Sometimes people put the system unit on top of the mat, but the unit should be alongside the mat so you have room to lay out all the components as you work with them. If you are going to remove the motherboard from a system, be sure you leave enough room for it on the mat.

If you do not have such a mat, place the removed circuits and devices on a clean desk or table. Always pick up a loose adapter card by the metal bracket used to secure the card to the system. This bracket is tied into the ground circuitry of the card, so by touching the bracket first, you prevent a discharge from damaging the components of the card. If the circuit board has no metal bracket (a motherboard, for example), handle the board carefully by the edges, and try not to touch any of the connectors or components. If you don't have proper ESD equipment such as a wrist strap or mat, be sure to periodically touch the chassis while working inside the system to equalize any charge you might have built up.

Caution

Some people recommend placing loose circuit boards and chips on sheets of aluminum foil. I absolutely *do not recommend* this procedure because it can actually result in an explosion! Many motherboards, adapter cards, and other circuit boards today have built-in lithium or NiCad batteries. These batteries react violently when they are shorted out, which is exactly what you would be doing by placing such a board on a piece of aluminum foil. The batteries will quickly overheat and possibly explode like a large firecracker (with dangerous shrapnel). Because you will not always be able to tell whether a board has a battery built into it somewhere, the safest practice is to never place any board on any conductive metal surface.

Recording Physical Configuration

While you are assembling a system, you should record all the physical settings and configurations of each component, including jumper and switch settings, cable orientations and placement, ground-wire locations, and even adapter board placement. Keep a notebook handy for recording these items, and write down all the settings. See Chapter 4 for more information on motherboard connector, jumper, and other component locations. Figure 23.3 shows a typical motherboard jumper.

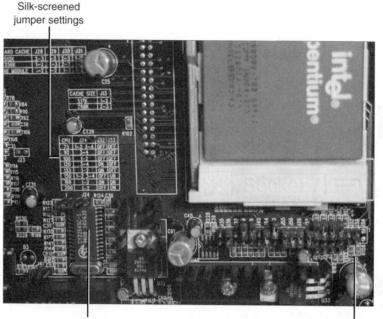

Figure 23.3 Motherboard jumpers often are silk-screened on the motherboard, as shown here; the jumper position shown here is used to configure the motherboard for a Pentium processor.

It is especially important to record all the jumper and switch settings on the motherboard, as well as those on any card you install in the system (cards seldom use jumpers or switches today, but many motherboards still do). If you accidentally disturb these jumpers or switches, you will know how they were originally set. This knowledge is very important if you do not have all the documentation for the system handy. Even if you do, undocumented jumpers and switches often do not appear in the manuals but must be set a certain way for the item to function. Also, record all cable orientations. Most name-brand systems use cables and connectors that are keyed so that they cannot be plugged in backward, but some generic PCs do not have this added feature. In addition, you can mix up hard disk and floppy cables. You should mark or record what each cable was plugged into and its proper orientation. Ribbon cables usually have an odd-colored (red, green, blue, or black) wire at one end that indicates pin 1. There might also be a mark on the connector, such as a triangle or even the number 1. The devices the cables are plugged into are also marked in some way to indicate the orientation of pin 1. Often, a dot appears next to the pin 1 side of the connector, or a 1 or other mark might appear.

Although cable orientation and placement seem to be very simple, we rarely get through the entire course of my PC troubleshooting seminars without at least one group of people having cable-connection problems. Fortunately, in most cases (except power cables), plugging any of the ribbon cables inside the system backward rarely causes any permanent damage.

Power and battery connections on pre-ATX systems are exceptions; plugging them in backward in most cases causes damage. In fact, plugging the motherboard power connectors in backward or in the wrong plug location puts 12v where only 5v should be—a situation that can cause components of the board to violently explode. I know of several people who have facial scars caused by shrapnel from exploding components caused by improper power supply connections! As a precaution, I always turn my face away from the system when I power it on for the first time. If you are using an ATX board and power supply, there is little chance of this happening because of the superior type of power connector used **unless** you mix a September 1998 or newer Dell power supply or motherboard with a standard motherboard or power supply.

Plugging in the CMOS battery backward can damage the CMOS chip, which usually is soldered into the motherboard; in such a case, the motherboard must be replaced.

Finally, you should record miscellaneous items such as the placement of any ground wires, adapter cards, and anything else that you might have difficulty remembering later. Some configurations and setups might be particular about the slots in which the adapter cards are located; it usually is a good idea to put everything back exactly the way it was originally.

Motherboard Installation

When you are installing your system's motherboard, unpack the motherboard and check to ensure you have everything that should be included. If you purchase a new board, you typically get at least the motherboard, some I/O cables, and a manual. If you ordered the motherboard with a processor or memory, it normally is installed on the board for you but might also be included separately. Some board kits include an antistatic wrist strap to help prevent damage due to static electricity when installing the board.

Prepare the New Motherboard

Before your new motherboard is installed, you should install the processor and memory. This usually is much easier to do before the board is installed in the chassis. Some motherboards have jumpers that control both the CPU speed and the voltage supplied to it. If these are set incorrectly, the system might not operate at all, might operate erratically, or might possibly even damage the CPU. If you have any questions about the proper settings, contact the vendor who sold you the board before making any jumper changes.

◀◀ See "CPU Operating Voltages," p. 97.

Most processors today run hot enough to require some form of heatsink to dissipate heat from the processor. To install the processor and heatsink, use the following procedure:

1. Take the new motherboard out of the antistatic bag it was supplied in, and set it on the bag or the antistatic mat, if you have one.

2. Install the processor. There are two procedures—one for socketed processors and the other for slot-based processors. Follow the appropriate instructions for the type you are installing:

    - *For socketed processors, the procedure is as follows:* Find pin 1 on the processor; it usually is denoted by a corner of the chip that is marked by a dot or bevel. Next, find the corresponding pin 1 of the ZIF socket for the CPU on the motherboard; it also is usually marked on the board, or there might be a bevel in one corner of the socket. Be sure the pins on the processor are straight and not bent; if they are bent, the chip won't insert properly into the socket. If necessary, use small needle-nose pliers or a hemostat to carefully straighten any pins. Don't bend them too much—they might break off, ruining the chip. Insert the CPU into the ZIF socket by lifting the release lever until it is vertical. Then, align the pins on the processor with the holes in the socket and drop it down into place. If the processor does not seem to want to drop in all the way, remove it to check for proper alignment and any possibly bent pins. When the processor is fully seated in the socket, push the locking lever on the socket down until it latches to secure the processor (see Figure 23.4).

Lever locks the CPU into the socket

Notch denotes pin 1

Figure 23.4   The lever on a ZIF socket locks the processor into the socket when lowered. Note the notch on the corner of the processor, denoting pin 1.

- *For slot-based processors, the procedure is different.* You need the processor, the universal retention mechanism brackets with included fasteners, and the heatsink supports. Most slot-based processors come with either an active or a passive heatsink already installed. Start by positioning the two universal retention mechanism brackets on either side of the processor slot so that the holes in the brackets line up with the holes in the motherboard (see Figure 23.5). Push the included fasteners through the mounting holes in the retention bracket and the motherboard until you feel them snap into place. Insert the fastener retainer pins through the holes in the fastener to lock them into place. Then, slide the processor/heatsink down between the brackets until it is firmly seated in the slot. The latches on the top sides of the processor lock into place when the processor is fully seated. Install the heatsink supports into the holes provided in the motherboard and processor.

| 1 | Retention bracket | 3 | Fastener retainer pins |
| 2 | Press-fit fasteners | 4 | 242-contact connector (Slot-1) |

Figure 23.5   Universal retention mechanism for slot-based processors. *Illustration used by permission of Intel Corporation.*

If the CPU does not already have a heatsink attached to it, attach it now. Most heatsinks clip either directly to the CPU or to the socket with one or more retainer clips (see Figure 23.6). Be careful when attaching the clip to the socket; you don't want it to scrape against the motherboard, which can damage circuit traces or components. In most cases, you should put a dab of heatsink thermal transfer compound (normally a white-colored grease) on the CPU before installing the heatsink. This prevents any air gaps and enables the heatsink to work more efficiently. If the CPU has an active heatsink (with a fan), plug the fan power connector into one of the fan connectors supplied on the motherboard (see Figure 23.7). Optionally, some heatsinks use a disk drive power connector for fan power.

3. Refer to the motherboard manufacturer's manual to set the jumpers, if any, to match the CPU you are going to install. Look for the diagram of the motherboard to find the jumper location, and look for the tables for the correct settings for your CPU. If the CPU was supplied already installed on the motherboard, the jumpers should already be correctly set for you, but it is still a good idea to check them.

SECC form factor
processor and heatsink

Universal
processor-retention
mechanism
(included with
motherboard)

Figure 23.6   Installing a slot-based (single edge contact cartridge or SECC) processor and attaching the heatsink fan power connector. *Motherboard and processor courtesy of Intel Corporation.*

Active heatsink with integral fan

Installing CPU
heatsink fan
connector

Figure 23.7 Attaching the heatsink fan power connector. *Motherboard and processor courtesy of Intel Corporation.*

Install Memory Modules

In order to function, the motherboard must have memory installed on it. Modern motherboards use either DIMMs or RIMMs. Depending on the module type, it will have a specific method of sliding into and clipping to the sockets. Usually, you install modules in the lowest-numbered sockets or banks first. Note that some boards require modules to be installed in pairs; this is most common with boards that use dual-channel RDRAM. Consult the motherboard documentation for more information on which sockets to use first and in what order and how to install the specific modules the board uses.

◄◄ See "Memory Banks," p. 438.

Memory modules frequently are keyed to the sockets by a notch on the side or on the bottom, so they go in only one way. Figure 23.8 shows how to install a DIMM or RIMM; Figure 23.9 shows how to install a SIMM. More detailed instructions for installing DIMMs, RIMMs, and SIMMs can be found in Chapter 6.

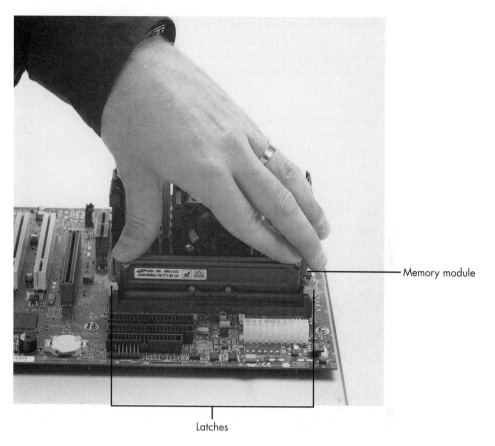

Memory module

Latches

Figure 23.8 Installing the memory modules. *Motherboard courtesy of Intel Corporation.*

Figure 23.9 Insert SIMMs into the socket at an angle; then press forward to engage the retaining clips.

Caution

Be careful not to damage the connector. If you damage the motherboard memory connector, you could be facing an expensive repair. Never force the module; it should come out easily. If it doesn't, you are doing something wrong.

Mount the New Motherboard in the Case

The motherboard attaches to the case with one or more screws and often several plastic standoffs. If you are using a new case, you might have to attach one or more metal spacers or plastic standoffs in the proper holes before you can install the motherboard. Use the following procedure to install the new motherboard in the case:

1. Find the holes in the new motherboard for the metal spacers and plastic standoffs. You should use metal spacers wherever there is a ring of solder around the hole. Use plastic standoffs where there is no ring of solder (see Figure 23.10). Screw any metal spacers into the new case in the proper positions to align with the screw holes in the motherboard.

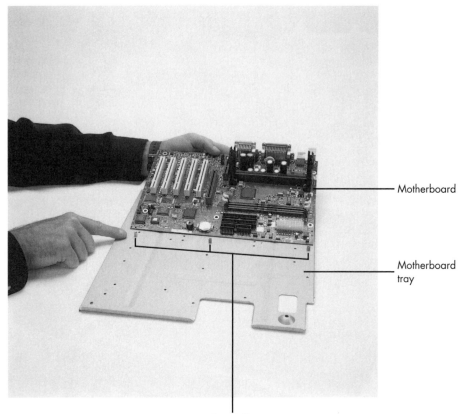

Standoffs

Figure 23.10   Make sure the standoffs align with the holes in the motherboard. *Motherboard courtesy of Intel Corporation.*

2. Most motherboards today attach directly to the chassis or to a removable motherboard tray with screws that thread into brass standoffs attached to the chassis or tray. Figure 23.11 shows three types of standoffs, including two brass types and one plastic. One screws directly to the chassis or tray, whereas the others attach to the motherboard and then slide into notches in the case or tray.

Figure 23.11   Various types of motherboard standoffs, used to support the board when installed in the chassis or motherboard tray.

If the board uses the type of standoff that fits into slots in the chassis or tray, rather than screwing directly in, insert the standoffs directly into the new motherboard from underneath until they snap into place (see Figure 23.12). Or attach them to the board with a screw if necessary. Figure 23.13 shows a typical ATX-style motherboard with arrows indicating the typical location of the screw holes for mounting the motherboard to the case (see your motherboard manual for the exact location of these screw holes).

Mounting slots

Standoffs

(Side View)

Figure 23.12   Insert standoffs into their mounting slots.

Figure 23.13 Mounting screw holes in a typical ATX motherboard. The arrows mark the screw holes for mounting the motherboard to the case.

After you have inserted the standoffs and lined up the standoffs with the screw holes on the motherboard, carefully attach the screws to secure the motherboard to the motherboard tray or case (depending on your chassis design). See Figure 23.14 Note the use of the thumb and forefinger to stabilize the screwdriver tip. This prevents accidental slippage of the screwdriver tip off of the screw, which is one of the biggest causes of new board failures.

Figure 23.14 Attaching the motherboard to the motherboard tray. *Motherboard courtesy of Intel Corporation.*

3. Install the I/O shield (if used) into the chassis by snapping it into place (see Figure 23.15).

I/O shield

Figure 23.15   Snapping the I/O shield into place in the chassis. *Case courtesy of PC Power & Cooling, Inc.*

4. Install the new motherboard into the case or motherboard tray. Either screw it directly to the standoffs or slide the standoffs already attached to the board by sliding the entire board into position. Be sure you align the I/O shield with the case or the ports on the back of the board with the I/O shield already in the case. Often, you will have to set the board into the case and slide it sideways to engage the standoffs into the slots in the case. When the board is in the proper position, the screw holes in the board should be aligned with all the metal spacers or screw holes in the case. Figure 23.16 shows a motherboard attached to a motherboard tray being installed in the chassis.

Some cases and boards, particularly ATX types, don't use any plastic spacers. Instead they use up to seven screws into metal standoffs that are installed in the case (refer to Figure 23.10). These are somewhat easier to install because the board drops into place and doesn't require that it be moved to the side to engage any standoffs.

5. Take the screws and any plastic washers that were supplied with the new motherboard and screw the board into the case (see Figure 23.17).

Figure 23.16 Installing the motherboard and tray into the chassis. *Case courtesy of PC Power & Cooling, Inc. Motherboard courtesy of Intel Corporation.*

Figure 23.17 Installing the screws that hold the motherboard tray to the chassis. *Case courtesy of PC Power & Cooling, Inc.*

Connect the Power Supply

The power supply is very easy to install, and it usually attaches to the chassis with four screws. Figures 23.18 and 23.19 show installing the power supply into the chassis and tightening the screws.

Power supply

Chassis

Figure 23.18   Installing the power supply into the chassis. *Case and power supply courtesy of PC Power & Cooling, Inc.*

Power supply mounting screws

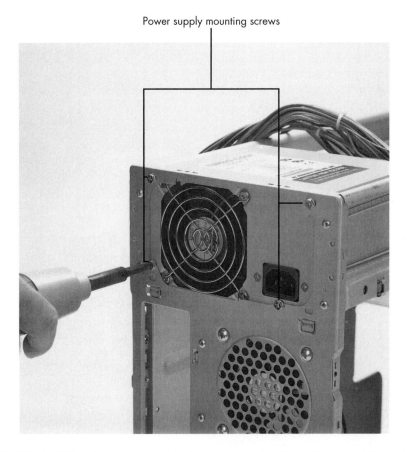

Figure 23.19   Installing the screws to retain the power supply. *Case and power supply courtesy of PC Power & Cooling, Inc.*

ATX-style motherboards have a single power connector that can go on only one way and an optional secondary connector that is also keyed (see Figure 23.20). Baby-AT and other style board designs usually have two separate six-wire power connectors from the power supply to the board, which might not be keyed and therefore might be interchangeable. See Chapter 21 for important information on proper installation of Baby-AT power supplies. Even though you might be able to insert them several ways, only one way is correct! These power leads usually are labeled P8 and P9 in most systems. The order in which you connect them to the board is crucial; if you install them backward, you can damage the motherboard when you power it up. Many systems use a CPU cooling fan, which should also be connected. To attach the power connectors from the power supply to the motherboard, do the following:

1. If the system uses a single ATX-style power connector, plug it in; it can go on only one way. If two separate six-wire connectors are used, the two black ground wires on the ends of the connectors must meet in the middle. Align the power connectors such that the black ground wires are adjacent to each other and plug in the connectors. Consult the documentation with your board to ensure that the power supply connection is correct. Incorrectly connecting the power connectors can destroy the motherboard.

2. Plug in the power lead for the CPU fan if one is used. The fan will either connect to the power supply via a disk drive power connector or connect directly to a fan power connector on the motherboard.

Figure 23.20   Attaching an ATX motherboard power connector.

◀◀   See "Motherboard Power Connectors," p. 1116.

Note

See Chapter 21 of this book for detailed coverage of the various types of power supply connectors, including new connectors used with the Intel Pentium 4.

Connect I/O and Other Cables to the Motherboard

Several connections must be made between a motherboard and the case. These include LEDs for the hard disk and power, an internal speaker connection, a reset button, and a power button. Most modern motherboards also have several built-in I/O ports that have to be connected. This includes dual IDE host adapters, a floppy controller, dual serial ports, and a parallel port. Some boards also include additional items such as built-in video, sound, or SCSI adapters.

If the board is an ATX type, the connectors for all the external I/O ports are already built into the rear of the board. If you are using a legacy Baby-AT–type board, you might have to install cables and brackets to run the serial, parallel, and other external I/O ports to the rear of the case (see Figures 23.21 and 23.22).

Figure 23.21   This parallel port header cable provides an external DB-25F parallel port connector for a typical Baby-AT motherboard.

Ribbon cable between DB-9M
connector and header pins
on motherboard

Screw to secure
bracket with serial
port connectors to case

Ribbon cable between DB-25M
connector and header pins
on motherboard

DB-9M serial port
connector for COM 1

Connectors to serial ports'
header pins on motherboard

DB-25M serial port
connector for COM 2

Empty space
for bracket

Slot covers

COM 1 serial port header pins
on motherboard (two rows of five pins)

COM 2 serial port header pins
on motherboard (two rows of five pins)

Figure 23.22   This serial port header cable provides two external serial port connections (a DB-9M and a DB-25M) for a typical Baby-AT motherboard.

If your motherboard has onboard I/O (nearly all PCs today use onboard I/O), use the following procedures to connect the cables:

1. Connect the floppy cable between the floppy drives and the 34-pin floppy controller connector on the motherboard.

2. Connect the IDE cables between the hard disk, IDE CD-ROM, and the 40-pin primary and secondary IDE connectors on the motherboard (see Figure 23.23). Typically, you will use the primary IDE channel connector for hard disks only and the secondary IDE channel connector to attach an IDE CD-ROM or other device, such as a tape drive.

ATA/IDE drive connector

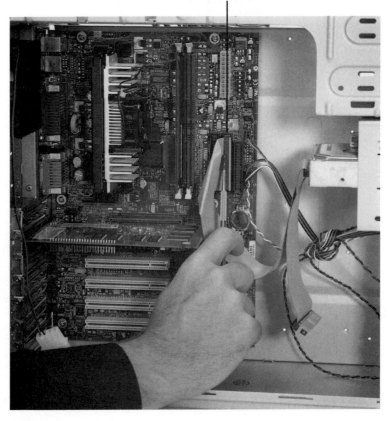

Figure 23.23 ATA drive connectors. *Motherboard courtesy of Intel Corporation.*

3. On non-ATX boards, a 25-pin female cable port bracket is used for the parallel port. Usually two serial ports exist: a 9-pin and either another 9-pin or a 25-pin male connector port. Align pin 1 on the serial and parallel port cables with pin 1 on the motherboard connector, and plug them in.

4. If the ports don't have card slot-type brackets or if you need all your expansion slots, the back of the case might have port knockouts that you can use instead. Find ones that fit the ports, and push them out, removing the metal piece covering the hole. Unscrew the hex nuts on each side of the port connector, and position the connector in the hole. Install the hex nuts back in through the case to hold the port connector in place.

5. Most newer motherboards also include a built-in mouse port. If the connector for this port is not built into the back of the motherboard (usually next to the keyboard connector), you will probably have a card bracket type connector to install. In that case, plug the cable into the motherboard mouse connector and then attach the external mouse connector bracket to the case.

6. Attach the front-panel switch, LED, and internal speaker wires from the case front panel to the motherboard. If they are not marked on the board, check where each one is on the diagram in the motherboard manual. Figure 23.24 shows the front-panel connectors.

Figure 23.24 Motherboard front-panel connectors (speaker, power switch, LEDs, and so on). *Motherboard courtesy of Intel Corporation.*

Install the Drives

At this point you should install your hard drive, floppy drive, CD-ROM or DVD drive, and optionally your CD-RW drive. This is covered in detail in Chapter 14, "Physical Drive Installation and Configuration."

The basic process for mounting CD, hard drives, and floppy drives is as follows:

1. Remove the drive bay plates (if needed). Simply bend or knock the plate out of the way.

2. To install a CD drive, simply slide the drive into a the chassis. Note that it is easier to connect the IDE cable to the rear of the drive and make jumper selections before mounting the drive. See Chapters 7 and 14 for more about IDE jumpers and drive installation. Note that some cases come with rails that must be added to 5 1/4-inch wide drives, such as the CD. In such cases, use the screws from step 3 for the drive rails.

3. After the drive is in the bay, line up the drive mounting screw holes on the drive with the holes in the case chassis. Secure the drive with four screws, using the ones that came with your case or the drive you are installing (see Figure 23.25). If the drive uses rails, the rails hold the drive in place.

4. Connect the other end of the IDE cable to your motherboard's IDE connector or to the back of another IDE device if you are chaining drives.

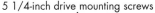

5 1/4-inch drive mounting screws

Figure 23.25 Secure the drive to the chassis using four screws. *Chassis courtesy of PC Power & Cooling, Inc. CD drive supplied by Micro X-Press.*

   5. To install floppy and hard drives, remove the drive cage (if your case has a removable drive cage). Slide your drives into the drive cage and secure them with the screws that came with your case or with the drive you are installing (see Figure 23.26). As with the CD drive, it's easier to connect the floppy and IDE cables to the rear of the drives and make any jumper selections prior to placing the drives or the drive cage into the chassis.

Note

If your chassis does not include a removable drive cage, you'll simply have to mount the drives in the chassis. This is a little more difficult because there's not much working room inside a PC.

3 1/2-inch drive mounting screws

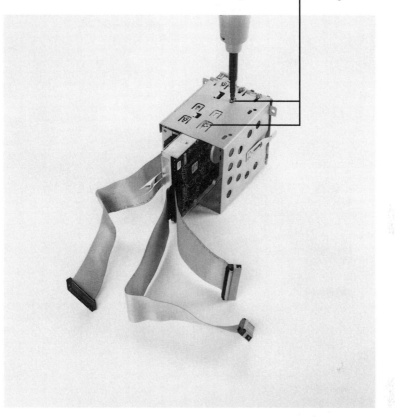

Figure 23.26 Use four screws to secure each drive to the drive cage. *Chassis courtesy of PC Power & Cooling, Inc. Hard drive supplied by Micro X-Press.*

6. Slide the drive cage back into the PC and secure it to the chassis using the screws provided with your case (see Figure 23.27).

7. Connect the drive cables to the appropriate locations on your motherboard. See Chapters 7 and 14 for more about jumper setting and cable connections for hard drives and floppy drives.

3 1/2-inch drive cage

Figure 23.27   Use four screws to secure each drive to the drive cage. *Chassis courtesy of PC Power & Cooling, Inc. Hard drive supplied by Micro X-Press.*

Install Bus Expansion Cards

Most systems use expansion cards for video, network interface, Internet connection (modem), sound, and SCSI adapters. These cards are plugged into the bus slots present on the motherboard. To install these cards, follow these steps:

1. Insert each card by holding it carefully by the edges, being sure not to touch the chips and circuitry. Put the bottom-edge finger connector into a slot that fits. Firmly press down on the top of the card, exerting even pressure, until it snaps into place (see Figure 23.28).

2. Secure each card bracket with a screw (see Figure 23.29).

3. Attach any internal cables you might have removed earlier from the cards.

Figure 23.28   This photo shows a video adapter being inserted into the slot. *Motherboard courtesy of Intel Corporation.*

Figure 23.29 Installing the screw to retain the card. *Motherboard courtesy of Intel Corporation.*

Replace the Cover and Connect External Cables

Now the system should be nearly assembled. All that remains is installing the cover assembly and connecting any external devices that are cabled to the system. I usually don't like to install the case cover screws until I have tested the system and I am sure everything is working properly. Often, I will find that a cable has been connected improperly, or some jumper setting is not correct, requiring that I remove the cover to repair the problem. Use the following procedure to complete the assembly:

1. Slide the cover onto the case.

2. Before powering up the system, connect any external cables. Most of the connectors are D-shaped and go in only one way.

3. Plug the 15-pin monitor cable into the video card female connector.

4. Attach the phone cord to the modem, if any.

5. Plug the round keyboard cable into the keyboard connector, and plug the mouse into the mouse port or serial port (if you are using a serial mouse).

6. If you have any other external cabling, such as joystick or audio jacks to a sound card, attach them now.

Run the Motherboard BIOS Setup Program (CMOS Setup)

Now that everything is connected, you can power up the system and run the BIOS Setup program. This enables you to configure the motherboard to access the installed devices and set the system date and time. The system also tests itself to determine whether any problems exists. Do the following:

1. Power on the monitor first and then the system unit. Observe the operation via the screen and listen for any beeps from the system speaker.

2. The system should automatically go through a power on self test (POST) consisting of video BIOS checking, RAM test, and usually an installed component report. If a fatal error occurs during the POST, you might not see anything onscreen and the system might beep several times, indicating a specific problem. Check the motherboard or BIOS documentation to determine what the beep codes mean.

3. If there are no fatal errors, you should see the POST display onscreen. Depending on the type of motherboard BIOS, such as Phoenix, AMI, Award, or others, you must press a key or series of keys to interrupt the normal boot sequence and get to the Setup program screens that enable you to enter important system information. Normally, the system indicates via the onscreen display which key to press to activate the BIOS setup program during the POST, but if not, check the motherboard manual for the key(s) to press to enter the BIOS setup. Common keys used to enter BIOS Setup are F1, F2, F10, Esc, Ins, and Del.

4. After the Setup program is running, use the Setup program menus to enter the current date and time, your hard drive settings, floppy drive types, video cards, keyboard settings, and so on. Most newer motherboard BIOSes can autodetect the hard drive, so you should not have to manually enter any parameters for it.

5. Entering the hard drive information is the most critical when building a new system. Most modern BIOSes feature an autodetect or auto-type setting for the drive; I recommend you choose that if it is available. This causes the BIOS to read the parameters directly from the drive, which eliminates a chance for errors—especially if the builder is less experienced. These parameters include CHS (Cylinder Head Sector) specifications and transfer speed and translation settings. Most systems also let you set a *user-definable type*, which means that the cylinder, head, and sector counts for this type were entered manually and are not constant. If you set a user-definable type (not normally recommended unless you don't have "auto" as a choice), it is especially important to write down the exact settings you use because this information might be very difficult to figure out if it is ever lost.

   Modern ATA drives also have additional configuration items that you should record. These include the translation mode and transfer speed setting. With drives larger than 528MB, you should record the translation mode, which is expressed differently in different BIOS versions. Look for settings such as CHS, ECHS (Extended CHS), Large (which equals ECHS), or LBA (Logical Block Addressing). Typically, you set LBA or Large for any drive over 528MB. Whatever you set, it should be recorded because changing this setting after the drive has been formatted can cause problems.

6. After you have checked over all the settings in the BIOS Setup, follow the instructions on the screen or in the motherboard manual to save the settings and exit the Setup menu.

◄◄ See "Running or Accessing the CMOS Setup Program," p. 373.

Troubleshooting New Installations

At this point, the system should reset and attempt to boot normally from either a floppy disk or hard disk. With the operating system startup disk in drive A:, the system should boot and either reach an installation menu or an A: prompt. If any problems exist, here are some basic items to check:

- *If the system won't power up at all, check the power cord.* If the cord is plugged into a power strip, make sure the strip is switched on. Usually, a power switch can be found on the front of the case, but some power supplies have a switch on the back as well.

- *Check to see whether the power switch is connected properly inside the case.* There is a connection from the switch to the motherboard; check both ends to ensure that they are connected properly.

- *Check the main power connector from the supply to the board.* Make sure the connectors are seated fully, and if the board is a Baby-AT type, ensure that they are plugged in with the correct orientation and sequence.

- *If the system appears to be running but you don't see anything on the display, check the monitor to ensure that it is plugged in, turned on, and properly and securely connected to the video card.*

- *Check the video card to ensure it is fully seated in the motherboard slot.* Remove and reseat the video card, and possibly try a different slot if it is a PCI card.

- *If the system beeps more than once, the BIOS is reporting a fatal error of some type.* See the BIOS Error code listings in Chapter 5 and on the CD accompanying this book for more information on what these codes mean because they depend on the type and version of BIOS you have. Also, consult your motherboard documentation—look in the BIOS section for a table of beep codes.

- *If the LED on your floppy drive, hard drive, or CD/DVD-ROM drive stays on continuously, the data cable is probably installed backward or is off by some pins.* Check that the stripe on the cable is properly oriented toward pin 1 on both the drive and board connector ends. Also, check the drive jumpers for proper master/slave relationships.

When you are sure the system is up and running successfully, power it off and screw the chassis cover securely to the case. Now your new system should be ready for the operating system installation.

Installing the Operating System

If you are starting with a new drive, you must install the operating system. If you are using a non-Windows operating system, follow the documentation for the installation procedures.

On a newer system in which you are installing an OEM version of Windows 98 or later (which comes on a bootable CD), there isn't really anything you need to do, other than simply boot from the CD (you might have to enable the CD-ROM as a boot device in your BIOS Setup) and follow the prompts to install the OS. Windows 98 or later versions automatically recognize that the drive needs to be partitioned and the partitions formatted before the installation can proceed. Additionally, Windows 98 or later versions execute these functions for you, with prompts guiding you along the way. This is the method I recommend for most people because it is relatively simple and straightforward.

If you want to do the partitioning and formatting manually (prior to installing the OS), follow the guidelines in the next few sections.

Partitioning the Drive

From the A:> prompt, with the startup disk inserted in the floppy drive, type the following command:

FDISK

This command is used to partition your drive. Follow the menus to create either a single partition for the entire drive or multiple partitions. Usually, the first partition must also be made active, which means it will be bootable. I recommend you answer Yes to the prompt Do you wish to enable large disk support (Y/N)? This enables the partition to be created using the FAT32 or NTFS file system. Then, you can continue accepting default entries for all the prompts to partition the drive as a single bootable partition that covers the entire drive.

Next, exit FDISK; this causes the system to restart.

Note

Using FDISK is covered extensively in Chapter 14.

Formatting the Drive

After rebooting on the startup floppy, you need to format each partition you've created. The first partition is formatted using the FORMAT command as follows:

FORMAT C:

All other partitions are formatted in the same manner: Merely run the command, changing the drive letter for each partition that needs to be formatted.

After the FORMAT command completes on all the drives, you should reboot again from the startup floppy. Now you are ready to install Windows.

Note

Drive formatting is covered extensively in Chapter 10, "Hard Disk Storage." See Chapter 14 for more details on installing and setting up a hard drive.

Loading the CD-ROM Driver

If your system supports booting from the CD and you are installing an OEM version of Windows 98 or later (which comes on a bootable CD), you can disregard this section because the CD-ROM drivers automatically are loaded as you boot from the CD. You can then either proceed with the installation from the CD or copy the OS files from the CD to the hard drive and install from the hard drive instead.

If you must first boot from a floppy (because your system can't boot from a CD or your version of Windows isn't bootable), you must make sure your startup floppy disk is properly configured to support the CD/DVD drive in your system. This requires that real-mode (DOS-based) drivers be installed on the disk that is compatible with your drive. The easiest solution is to use a Windows 98 or later startup floppy disk because it is already prepared with the proper drivers for 99% of all systems on the market. Even if you are installing Windows 95, you can still use the Windows 98 or later startup disk to start the process.

If you are using a Windows 95 startup disk and you don't have the CD-ROM drivers on it, you should look for a CD-ROM driver disk that normally comes with your drive. It should have a driver installation batch file on it, which if, run will copy the drivers to your startup disk and create the appropriate

CONFIG.SYS and AUTOEXEC.BAT files to enable CD-ROM support. If the driver is called CDROM.SYS, that file, along with the following line (or something similar) should be added to the CONFIG.SYS file on your Windows 95 startup disk:

```
device=CDROM.SYS /D:oemcd001
```

This causes the CDROM.SYS driver to be loaded and assigns it an in-memory driver designation of oemcd001. Any designation can be used here, but it should be eight characters or fewer and must match a similar designation in the next step.

Next, you must load the Microsoft CD-ROM extensions driver in your AUTOEXEC.BAT file. This driver is called MSCDEX.EXE and is already included on the Windows 95 startup disk. If you used the designation I listed in the previous step, add the following line to the AUTOEXEC.BAT file on the Windows 95 startup disk:

```
LH MSCDEX.EXE /D:oemcd001
```

This loads the MSCDEX.EXE driver (in upper memory via the LH or LoadHigh command if possible) and looks to attach to the CD-ROM driver loaded earlier via the driver designation oemcd001 in this case.

After these statements are added to the CONFIG.SYS and AUTOEXEC.BAT files, you should reboot on the startup floppy. Now you also should be able to access your CD-ROM drive. It will appear one drive letter after your last drive partition. If your hard disk partitions are C: and D:, the CD-ROM drive will be E:.

Note that these procedures require that you find your CD-ROM driver and copy it onto the startup disk. If you can't find the driver or have a SCSI hard disk (which uses different types of drivers), I recommend you borrow a copy of a Windows 98 or later version startup disk. These startup disks already include a series of drivers that work with virtually any CD-ROM drive on the market, even SCSI versions.

After you have successfully created a startup disk with the CD-ROM drivers (or have the Win98 startup disk), install the Windows CD-ROM in your CD/DVD drive. After booting from the startup floppy, change to the CD/DVD drive letter. Then, at that prompt run the SETUP command. This starts the Windows installation program. From here, you can follow the prompts to install Windows as you see fit. This procedure can be somewhat lengthy, so be prepared to spend some time. You will be installing not only Windows, but also the drivers for any hardware detected during the installation process.

Whether you are booting from floppy or CD, I recommend copying the Windows files to your hard disk and actually running the installation from the hard disk and not the CD. This is helpful in the future should you want to reinstall or install any additional parts of Windows because it will then work directly from the hard disk and you won't be asked to insert the CD.

To do this, first check the CD for the directory containing the *.CAB files and copy them to the hard disk. For example, using Windows 98 it would go something like this:

```
copy E:\WIN98\*.* C:\WIN98 /S
```

This copies all the files from the WIN98 directory on the CD-ROM (E: drive in this example) to the hard disk and places them in a directory called WIN98. Then, you can remove the CD (it is no longer needed) and run the installation directly from the hard disk by entering the following commands:

```
C:
CD\
C:\WIN98\SETUP
```

These commands change you to drive C:, place you in the root directory, and then run the Windows SETUP program to start the installation. From there, the menu-driven Windows installation routines guide you. If you are using a different version of Windows, merely change the directories used in the previous example to the appropriate directories for your version of Windows.

Note

If you want to create a bootable CD containing your Windows installation files, see Chapter 13, "Optical Storage." For more information about installing CD/DVD drives, see Chapter 14.

After Windows is installed, you can install any additional drivers or application programs you want. At this point, your system should be fully operational.

Installing Important Drivers

After installing the operating system, the first thing you need to do is to install drivers for devices where drivers were not found on the Windows CD. This often includes things such as chipset drivers for your motherboard, drivers for newer video cards, USB 2.0 drivers, and more. Of these, the motherboard chipset drivers are the most critical and should be installed first. A CD containing these drivers should have been included with your motherboard; insert this disc and follow the prompts to install the chipset drivers. Then install other drivers, such as video, network, modem, and so on.

Disassembly/Upgrading Preparation

After you've built your system, you probably will have to open it up again sometime to perform a repair or an upgrade. Before you power off the system for the last time and begin to open the case, you should learn and record several things about your computer. Often, when working on a system, you intentionally or accidentally wipe out the CMOS Setup information. Most systems use a special battery-powered CMOS clock and a data chip that is used to store the system's configuration information. If the battery is disconnected, or if certain pins are accidentally shorted, you can discharge the CMOS memory and lose the setup. The CMOS memory in most systems is used to store simple things such as how many and what type of floppy drives are connected, how much memory is in the system, and the date and time.

A critical piece of information is the hard disk–type settings. Most modern BIOS have an autodetect feature that reads the type information directly from the drive. I recommend you set the drive type to Auto, which automatically sets all the necessary parameters for you. With older BIOS you must explicitly tell the system the parameters of the attached hard disk. Therefore, you need to know the current settings for cylinders, heads, and sectors per track.

If you do not enter the correct hard disk–type information in the CMOS Setup program, you will not be able to access the data on the hard disk. I know of several people who lost some or all of their data because they did not enter the correct type information when they reconfigured their systems. If this information is incorrect, the usual results are a missing operating system error message when the systems starts and the inability to access the C: drive.

Some people think that it's possible to figure out the parameters by looking up the particular hard disk in a table. (I have included a table of popular hard disk drive parameters in the Technical Reference on the CD-ROM. This table has proven to be useful to me time and time again.) Unfortunately, this method works only if the person who set up the system originally entered the correct parameters. I have encountered a large number of systems in which the hard disk parameters were not entered correctly; the only way to regain access to the data is to determine, and then use, the same incorrect parameters that were used originally. As you can see, no matter what, you should record the hard disk information from your setup program.

Most systems have the setup program built right into the ROM BIOS software. These built-in setup programs are activated by a key sequence usually entered during the POST. Most systems show a prompt on the screen during the POST indicating which key to press to enter the BIOS Setup.

The major vendors have standardized on these following keystrokes to enter the BIOS Setup:

- *AMI BIOS.* Press Del during POST.
- *Phoenix BIOS.* Press F2 during POST.
- *Award BIOS.* Press Del or Ctrl+Alt+Esc during POST.
- *Microid Research BIOS.* Press Esc during POST.

If your system does not respond to one of these common keystroke settings, you might have to contact the manufacturer or read the system documentation to find the correct keystrokes to enter setup.

Some unique ones I have encountered are as follows:

- *IBM Aptiva/Valuepoint.* Press F1 during POST.
- *Older Phoenix BIOS.* Boot to a safe mode DOS command prompt, and then press Ctrl+Alt+Esc or Ctrl+Alt+S.
- *Compaq.* Press F10 during POST.

◄◄ See "Running or Accessing the CMOS Setup Program," p. 373.

After you're in the BIOS Setup main screen, you'll usually find a main menu allowing access to other menus and submenus offering various sections or screens. When you get the setup program running, record all the settings. The easiest way to do this is to print it. If a printer is connected, press Shift+Print Screen; a copy of the screen display will be sent to the printer. Some setup programs have several pages of information, so you should record the information on each page.

Many setup programs allow for specialized control of the particular chipset used in the motherboard. These complicated settings can take up to several screens of information—all should be recorded. Most systems return these settings to a BIOS default if the CMOS battery is removed, and you lose any customized settings you might have changed. See Chapter 5 for more information on the BIOS settings.

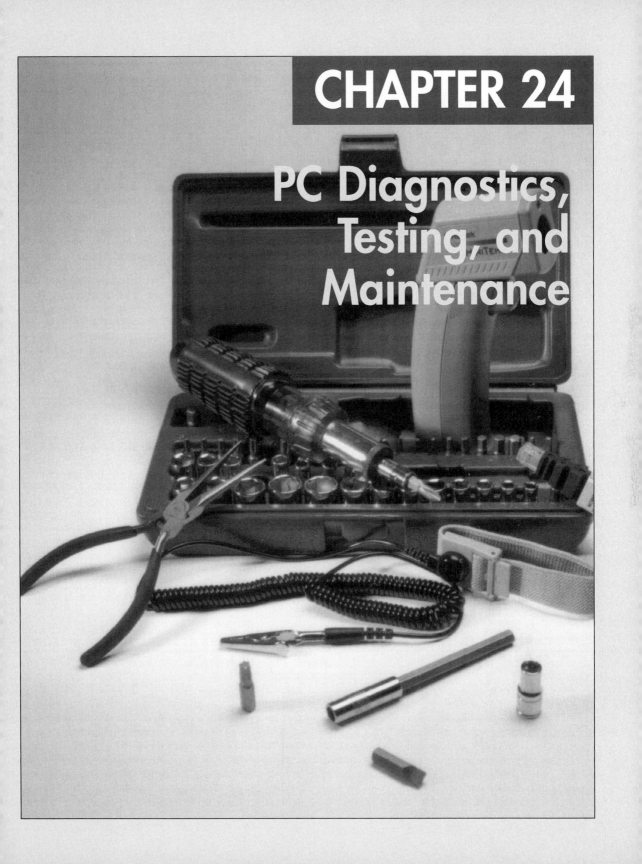

CHAPTER 24

PC Diagnostics, Testing, and Maintenance

PC Diagnostics

No matter how well built your PC is and how well written its software, something is eventually going to go wrong, and you might not always have a support system available to resolve the problem. Diagnostic software, the kind that comes with your computer, as well as that available from third parties, can be vitally important to you any time your computer malfunctions or you begin the process of upgrading a system component or adding a new device. This chapter examines the types of software available, and particularly those you might already own because they are included with common operating systems and hardware products.

You also might find that your system problems are caused by a hardware malfunction and that you must open up the computer case to perform repairs. This chapter also examines the tools and testers used to upgrade and repair PCs—both the basic items every user should own and some of the more advanced devices.

Of course, the best way to deal with a problem is to prevent it from occurring in the first place. The preventive maintenance sections of this chapter describe the procedures you should perform on a regular basis to keep your system in good working order.

This chapter describes three levels of diagnostic software (POST, system, and advanced) included with your computer or available from your computer manufacturer. The chapter describes how you can get the most from this software. It also details IBM's audio codes and error codes, which are similar to the error codes used by most computer manufacturers, and examines aftermarket diagnostics and public-domain diagnostic software.

Diagnostics Software

Several types of diagnostic software are available for PCs. Some diagnostic functions are integrated into the PC hardware or into peripheral devices, such as expansion cards, whereas others take the form of operating system utilities or separate software products. This software, some of which is included with the system when purchased, assists users in identifying many problems that can occur with a computer's components. In many cases, these programs can do most of the work in determining which PC component is defective or malfunctioning. The types of diagnostic software are as follows:

- *POST.* The power on self test operates whenever any PC is powered up (switched on).

- *Manufacturer supplied diagnostics software.* Many of the larger manufacturers—especially high-end, name-brand manufacturers such as IBM, Compaq, Hewlett-Packard, Dell, and others—make special diagnostics software expressly designed for their systems. This manufacturer-specific software normally consists of a suite of tests that thoroughly examines the system. In some cases, you can download these diagnostics from the manufacturer's online services; otherwise, you might have to purchase them. Many vendors such as Gateway include a limited version of one of the aftermarket packages that has been customized for use with their systems. In some older IBM and Compaq systems, the diagnostic software is installed on a special partition on the hard drive and can be accessed during startup. This was a convenient way for those system manufacturers to ensure that users always had diagnostics available.

- *Peripheral diagnostics software.* Many hardware devices ship with specialized diagnostics software designed to test their particular functions. Adaptec SCSI host adapters, for example, include diagnostic functions in the card's BIOS that you can access with a keystroke (Ctrl+A) at boot time. Sound cards normally include a diagnostic program on a disk along with the driver, which tests and verifies all the card's functions. Network adapters usually include a diagnostic specific to that adapter on a disk, normally with the drivers. Other devices or adapters also might provide a diagnostic program or disk, usually included with the drivers for the device.

- *Operating system diagnostics software.* Operating systems, such as Windows 9x and Windows NT/2000, include a variety of diagnostic software designed to identify and monitor the performance of various components in the computer.

- *Aftermarket diagnostics software.* A number of manufacturers make general-purpose diagnostics software for PCs. This type of software is often bundled with other system maintenance and repair utilities to form a general PC software toolkit.

The Power On Self Test

When IBM first began shipping the original PC in 1981, it included safety features that had never been seen in a personal computer. These features were the power on self test (POST) and parity-checked memory. Although parity-checked memory is being phased out on many systems, every PC still executes a POST when you turn it on. The following sections provide more detail on the POST, a series of program routines buried in the motherboard ROM-BIOS chip that tests all the main system components at power-on time. This series of routines is partially responsible for the delay when you turn on your PC; the computer executes the POST before loading the operating system.

What Is Tested?

Whenever you start up your computer, it automatically performs a series of tests that checks the primary components in your system, such as the CPU, ROM, motherboard support circuitry, memory, and major peripherals such as the expansion chassis. These tests are brief and are designed to catch hard (not intermittent) errors. The POST procedures are not very thorough compared with available disk-based diagnostics. The POST process provides error or warning messages whenever it encounters a faulty component.

Although the diagnostics performed by the system POST are not very thorough, they are the first line of defense, especially when it comes to detecting severe motherboard problems. If the POST encounters a problem severe enough to keep the system from operating properly, it halts the system boot process and generates an error message that often identifies the cause of the problem. These POST-detected problems are sometimes called *fatal errors* because they prevent the system from booting. The POST tests normally provide three types of output messages: audio codes, onscreen text messages, and hexadecimal numeric codes that are sent to an I/O port address.

POST Audio Error Codes

POST audio error codes take the form of a series of beeps that identify the faulty component. When your computer is functioning normally, you should hear one short beep when the system starts up at the completion of the POST, although some systems (such as Compaq's) beep twice at the end of a normal POST. If a problem is detected, a different number of beeps sounds, sometimes in a combination of short and long tones. These BIOS-dependent codes can vary among BIOS manufacturers and even among different BIOSes from the same manufacturer. You should consult your motherboard manufacturer for the codes specific to your board and BIOS. If that fails, the BIOS manufacturer might have this information.

The following sections detail the beep codes of the AMI, Award, Phoenix, and IBM BIOS. Others, such as Microid Research, can be found in the Technical Reference section on the CD.

AMI BIOS Beep Codes

Note

AMI BIOS beep codes used by permission of American Megatrends, Inc.

Table 24.1   AMI BIOS Beep Codes

Beeps	Error Message	Description
1	DRAM Refresh Failure	The memory refresh circuitry on the motherboard is faulty.
2	Parity Error	A parity error occurred in system memory.
3	Base 64K (First Bank) Memory Failure	A memory failure occurred in the first bank of memory.
4	System Timer Failure	A memory failure occurred in the first bank of memory, or Timer 1 on the motherboard is not functioning.
5	Processor Error	The processor on the motherboard generated an error.
6	Keyboard Controller Gate A20 Failure	The keyboard controller might be bad. The BIOS cannot switch to protected mode.
7	Virtual Mode Processor Exception Interrupt Error	The processor generated an exception interrupt.
8	Display Memory Read/Write Error	Either the system video adapter is missing or its memory is faulty.
9	ROM Checksum Error	The ROM checksum value does not match the value encoded in BIOS.
10	CMOS Shutdown Register Read/Write Error	The shutdown register for CMOS RAM failed.
11	Cache Error/L2 Cache Bad	The L2 cache is faulty.
1 long, 3 short	Conventional/Extended Memory Failure	The motherboard memory is faulty.
1 long, 8 short	Display/Retrace Test Failed	The video card is faulty; try reseating or moving to a different slot.

Award BIOS Beep Codes

Currently, only one beep code exists in the Award BIOS. A single long beep followed by two short beeps indicates that a video error has occurred and that the BIOS cannot initialize the video screen to display any additional information.

Phoenix BIOS Beep Codes

The following beep codes are for the current version of Phoenix BIOS, version 4.0, release 6. Other versions have somewhat different beeps and Port 80h codes. To view the Port 80h codes, you need a POST diagnostics card with a two-digit LED readout, available from many sources for diagnostic tools (see the Vendor List on the accompanying CD for sources). I recommend a PCI-based POST card because ISA slots are becoming obsolete.

Note

Phoenix BIOS beep codes used by permission of Phoenix Technologies, Ltd.

Table 24.2   Phoenix BIOS Beep Codes

Beeps	Port 80h Code	Explanation
1-2-2-3	16h	BIOS ROM checksum
1-3-1-1	20h	Test DRAM refresh

Table 24.2   Continued

Beeps	Port 80h Code	Explanation
1-3-1-3	22h	Test keyboard controller
1-3-3-1	28h	Autosize DRAM
1-3-3-2	29h	Initialize POST memory manager
1-3-3-3	2Ah	Clear 512KB base RAM
1-3-4-1	2Ch	RAM failure on address line xxxx
1-3-4-3	2Eh	RAM failure on data bits xxxx of low byte of memory bus
1-4-1-1	30h	RAM failure on data bits xxxx of high byte of memory bus
2-1-2-2	45h	POST device initialization
2-1-2-3	46h	Check ROM copyright notice
2-2-3-1	58h	Test for unexpected interrupts
2-2-4-1	5Ch	Test RAM between 512KB and 640KB
1-2	98h	Search for option ROMs; one long, two short beeps on checksum failure
1	B4h	One short beep before boot

IBM BIOS Beep and Alphanumeric Error Codes

After completing the power on self test, an audio code indicates either a normal condition or that one of several errors has occurred.

Note

IBM BIOS beep and Alphanumeric error codes used by permission of IBM.

Table 24.3   IBM BIOS Beep Codes

Audio Code	Sound Graph	Description
1 short beep	•	Normal POST—system okay
2 short beeps	••	POST error—error code on display
No beep		Power supply, system board
Continuous beep	————	Power supply, system board
Repeating short beeps	•••• ••	Power supply, system board
1 long, 1 short beep	-•	System board
1 long, 2 short beeps	-••	Video adapter (MDA/CGA)
1 long, 3 short beeps	-•••	Video adapter (EGA/VGA)
3 long beeps	- - -	3270 keyboard card

POST Visual Error Codes

On most PCs, the POST also displays the results of its system memory test on the monitor. The last number displayed is the amount of memory that tested successfully. For example, a system might display the following message:

```
32768 KB OK
```

The number displayed by the memory test should agree with the total amount of memory installed on the system motherboard. Some older systems display a slightly lower total because they deduct part or all of the 384KB of UMA (upper memory area) from the count. On old systems that use expanded memory cards, the memory on the card is not tested by the POST and does not count in the numbers reported. Also, this memory test is performed before any system software loads, so many memory managers or device drivers you might have installed do not affect the results of the test. If the POST memory test stops short of the expected total, the number displayed can indicate how far into the system memory array a memory error lies. This number can help you identify the exact module that is at fault and can be a valuable troubleshooting aid in itself.

If an error is detected during the POST procedures, an error message might be displayed onscreen. These messages usually are in the form of a numeric code several digits long—for example, 1790-Disk 0 Error. You should check the documentation for your motherboard or system BIOS for information about these errors. The major BIOS manufacturers also maintain Web sites where this information should be available.

Note

I've also included BIOS error messages for AMI Award, Phoenix, Microid Research (MR BIOS), and IBM on the CD, in the Technical Reference section. You should print the codes for your BIOS and keep them in a safe place in case you need them.

I/O Port POST Codes

A lesser-known feature of the POST is that at the beginning of each POST, the BIOS sends test codes to a special I/O port address. These POST codes can be read by only a special adapter card plugged in to one of the system slots. These cards originally were designed to be used by system manufacturers for burn-in testing of the motherboard, to prevent the need for a video display adapter and display. Several companies now make these cards available to technicians. Micro 2000, JDR Microdevices, Data Depot, Ultra-X, and Trinitech are just a few manufacturers that market these POST cards.

When you plug one of these POST cards into a slot, during the POST you see two-digit hexadecimal numbers flash on the card's display. If the system stops unexpectedly or hangs, you can identify the test in progress during the hang from the two-digit code. This step usually identifies the malfunctioning component.

Most of the system BIOSes on the market output the POST codes to I/O port address 80h.

Most POST cards plug in to the 8-bit connector that is a part of the ISA or EISA bus. Because most systems—even those with PCI slots—still have ISA connectors, those cards are adequate. Some PCs have no ISA slots at all, so obviously an ISA POST card won't work. Micro 2000 has a card called the Post-Probe, which has both ISA and PCI connectors on the same board. The Post-Probe also includes a MicroChannel (MCA) bus adapter, making it one of the most flexible POST cards available. Data Depot also offers slot adapters that enable its existing ISA bus cards to work in MCA bus systems. I recommend looking for POST cards designed to work in PCI slots. These will certainly become more prevalent as more PCI-only systems (no ISA slots) come on the market. Another ISA/PCI card is the POSTPlus from ForeFront Direct.

Note

A listing of POST I/O port error codes for various BIOSes (including AMI Award, Phoenix, Microid Research, and IBM) can be found in the Technical Reference section of the CD. Also, see Chapter 5, "BIOS," to learn more about working with your BIOS. Remember to consult your motherboard documentation for codes specific to your BIOS version. Also, the documentation included with the various POST cards covers most older as well as newer BIOS versions.

Hardware Diagnostics

Many types of diagnostic software are used with specific hardware products. This software can be integrated into the hardware, included with the hardware purchase, or sold as a separate product. The following sections examine several types of hardware-specific diagnostics.

Note

IBM included specialized diagnostic software for its older PS/2 systems. For more information on this software, see the sixth edition of *Upgrading and Repairing PCs* on the CD-ROM included with this book.

SCSI Diagnostics

Unlike the IDE drive support that is built into the system BIOS of virtually every PC, SCSI is an add-on technology, and most SCSI host adapters contain their own BIOS that enables you to boot the system from a SCSI hard drive. In some cases, the SCSI BIOS also contains configuration software for the adapter's various features, and diagnostics software as well.

The most popular manufacturer of SCSI host adapters is Adaptec, and most of its host adapters contain these features. An Adaptec SCSI adapter normally includes a BIOS that can be enabled or disabled. When the BIOS is activated, you see a message on the monitor as the system boots, identifying the model of the adapter and the revision number of the BIOS. The message also instructs you to press Ctrl+A to access what Adaptec calls its SCSISelect utility.

The SCSISelect utility identifies the Adaptec host adapters installed in the system and, if more than one exists, enables you to choose the adapter you want to work with by selecting its port address. After you do this, you are presented with a menu of the functions built into the adapter's BIOS. Every adapter BIOS contains a configuration program and a SCSI Disk Utilities feature that scans the SCSI bus, identifying the devices connected to it. For each hard disk drive connected to the bus, you can perform a low-level disk format or scan the disk for defects, remapping any bad blocks that are found.

For SCSI adapters that use direct memory access (DMA), a Host Adapter Diagnostics feature is also available, which tests the communication between the adapter and the main system memory array by performing a series of DMA transfers. If this test fails, you are instructed how to configure the adapter to use a lower DMA transfer rate.

Network Interface Diagnostics

As with SCSI adapters, many network interface adapters are equipped with their own diagnostics, designed to test their own specialized functions. The EZSTART program included with all SMC network interface cards, for example, contains two adapter test modes. The Basic mode performs the following internal tests on the SMC8000 adapter:

- Bus Interface Controller test
- LAN Address ROM test
- Network Interface Controller test
- RAM test
- ROM test
- Interrupt Generation
- Loopback test

The Two Node test sequence requires that you have another node installed on the same network with an SMC adapter. By running the EZSTART software on both computers, you can configure one adapter as the Responder and the other as the Initiator. The Initiator transmits test messages to the Responder, which echoes the same messages back again. If the adapters and network are functioning properly, the messages should return to the Initiator system in exactly the same form as they were transmitted.

Other network adapters have similar testing capabilities, although the names of the tests might not be exactly the same. The software for the 3Com 3C509B adapter, for example, performs the following tests:

- Register Access test
- EEPROM Vital Data test
- EEPROM Configurable Data test
- FIFO Loopback test
- Interrupt test
- Ethernet Core Loopback test
- Encoder/Decoder Loopback test
- Echo Exchange test (requires two adapters on the same network)

Both the SMC and 3Com diagnostics programs are integrated into the software you use to configure the hardware resources used by the adapters and their other features. The software is not integrated into the hardware; it takes the form of a separate program that ships with the devices and that you also can download free of charge from the manufacturers' respective Web sites.

General-Purpose Diagnostics Programs

A large number of third-party diagnostics programs are available for PC systems. In addition, specific programs are available to test memory, floppy drives, hard disks, video adapters, and most other areas of the system. Although some of these utility packages should be considered essential in any toolkit, many fall short of the level needed by professional-level troubleshooters.

Tip

Before trying a commercial diagnostic program to solve your problem, look in your operating system. Most operating systems today provide at least some of the diagnostic functions that diagnostic programs do. You might be able to save some time and money.

Unfortunately, no clear leader exists in the area of diagnostic software. Each program has unique advantages, and as a result, no program is universally better than another. When deciding which diagnostic programs, if any, to include in your arsenal, look for the features you need.

Note

The CD included with this book contains a breakdown of some of the PC diagnostics software available today. See the Technical Reference section of the CD.

Operating System Diagnostics

In many cases, it might not be necessary to purchase third-party diagnostic software because your operating system has all the diagnostic tools you need. Windows 9x/Me and NT/2000 include a large selection of programs that enable you to view, monitor, and troubleshoot the hardware in your system.

Note

The CD included with this book contains a breakdown of some of the operating-system–diagnostics software available today. See the Technical Reference section of the CD.

The Hardware Boot Process

The term *boot* comes from the word bootstrap and describes the method by which the PC becomes operational. Just as you pull on a large boot by the small strap attached to the back, a PC loads a large operating system by first loading a small program that can then pull the operating system into memory. The chain of events begins with the application of power, and finally results in a fully functional computer system with software loaded and running. Each event is triggered by the event before it and initiates the event after it.

Tracing the system boot process might help you find the location of a problem if you examine the error messages the system displays when the problem occurs. If you see an error message that is displayed by only a particular program, you can be sure the program in question was at least loaded and partially running. Combine this information with the knowledge of the boot sequence, and you can at least tell how far the system's startup procedure had progressed before the problem occurred. You usually want to look at whichever files or disk areas were being accessed during the failure in the boot process. Error messages displayed during the boot process and those displayed during normal system operation can be hard to decipher. However, the first step in decoding an error message is knowing where the message came from—which program actually generated or displayed it. The following programs are capable of displaying error messages during the boot process:

OS Independent:

- Motherboard ROM BIOS
- Adapter card ROM BIOS extensions
- Master (partition) boot record
- Volume boot record

OS Dependent:

- System files (`IO.SYS`/`IBMBIO.COM` and `MSDOS.SYS`/`IBMDOS.COM`)
- Device drivers (loaded through `CONFIG.SYS` or the Win 9x Registry `SYSTEM.DAT`)
- Shell program (`COMMAND.COM` in DOS)
- Programs run by `AUTOEXEC.BAT`, the Windows Startup group, and the Registry
- Windows (`WIN.COM`)

The first portion of the startup sequence is *operating system independent*, which means these steps are the same for all PCs no matter which operating system is installed. The latter portion of the boot sequence is *operating system dependent*, which means those steps can vary depending on which operating system is installed or being loaded. The following section examines the operating-system–independent startup sequence and provides a detailed account of many of the error messages that might occur during this process.

The Boot Process: Operating System Independent

If you have a problem with your system during startup and you can determine where in this sequence of events your system has stalled, you know which events have occurred and you probably can eliminate each of them as a cause of the problem. The following steps occur in a typical system startup regardless of which operating system you are loading:

1. You switch on electrical power to the system.

2. The power supply performs a self-test (known as the POST—power on self test). When all voltages and current levels are acceptable, the supply indicates that the power is stable and sends the Power_Good signal to the motherboard. The time from switch-on to Power_Good is normally between .1 and .5 seconds.

3. The microprocessor timer chip receives the Power_Good signal, which causes it to stop generating a reset signal to the microprocessor.

◄◄   See "The Power_Good Signal," p. 1106.

4. The microprocessor begins executing the ROM BIOS code, starting at memory address FFFF:0000. Because this location is only 16 bytes from the very end of the available ROM space, it contains a JMP (jump) instruction to the actual ROM BIOS starting address.

◄◄   See "Motherboard BIOS," p. 349.

5. The ROM BIOS performs a test of the central hardware to verify basic system functionality. Any errors that occur are indicated by audio "beep" codes because the video system has not yet been initialized. If the BIOS is Plug and Play (PnP), the following steps are executed; if not, skip to step 10.

6. The Plug and Play BIOS checks nonvolatile random access memory (RAM) for input/output (I/O) port addresses, interrupt request lines (IRQs), direct memory access (DMA) channels, and other settings necessary to configure PnP devices on the computer.

7. All Plug and Play devices found by the Plug and Play BIOS are disabled.

8. A map of used and unused resources is created.

9. The Plug and Play devices are configured and re-enabled, one at a time. If your computer does not have a Plug and Play BIOS, PnP devices are initialized using their default settings. These devices may be reconfigured dynamically when Windows 9x starts. At that point, the Windows 9x Configuration Manager queries the Plug and Play BIOS for device information, and then queries each Plug and Play device for its configuration.

10. The BIOS performs a video ROM scan of memory locations C000:0000 through C780:0000, looking for video adapter ROM BIOS programs contained on a video adapter found either on a card plugged into a slot or integrated into the motherboard. If the scan locates a video ROM BIOS, it is tested by a checksum procedure. If the video BIOS passes the checksum test, the ROM is executed; the video ROM code initializes the video adapter and a cursor appears onscreen. If the checksum test fails, the following message appears:

    `C000 ROM Error`

11. If the BIOS finds no video adapter ROM, it uses the motherboard ROM video drivers to initialize the video display hardware, and a cursor appears onscreen.

12. The motherboard ROM BIOS scans memory locations C800:0000 through DF80:0000 in 2KB increments for any other ROMs located on any other adapter cards (such as SCSI adapters). If any ROMs are found, they are checksum-tested and executed. These adapter ROMs can alter existing BIOS routines and establish new ones.

13. Failure of a checksum test for any of these ROM modules causes this message to appear:

    `XXXX ROM Error`

    where the address *XXXX* indicates the segment address of the failed ROM module.

14. The ROM BIOS checks the word value at memory location 0000:0472 to see whether this start is a cold start or a warm start. A word value of 1234h in this location is a flag that indicates a warm start, which causes the BIOS to skip the memory test portion of the POST. Any other word value in this location indicates a cold start and the BIOS performs the full POST procedure. Some system BIOSes let you control various aspects of the POST procedure, making it possible to skip the memory test, for example, which can be lengthy on a system with a lot of RAM.

15. If this is a cold start, the full POST executes; if this is a warm start, a mini-POST executes, minus the RAM test. Any errors found during the POST are reported by a combination of audio and displayed error messages. Successful completion of the POST is indicated by a single beep (with the exception of some Compaq computers, which beep twice).

16. The ROM BIOS searches for a boot record at cylinder 0, head 0, sector 1 (the very first sector) on the default boot drive. At one time, the default boot drive was always the first floppy disk, or A: drive. However, the BIOSes on today's systems often enable you to select the default boot device and the order in which the BIOS will look for other devices to boot from if needed, using a floppy disk, hard disk, or even a CD-ROM drive in any order you choose. This sector is loaded into memory at 0000:7C00 and tested.

If a disk is in the drive but the sector cannot be read, or if no disk is present, the BIOS continues with step 19.

Tip

If you do want to boot from a CD-ROM, make sure the CD-ROM drive is specified first in the boot devices menu in your BIOS setup. To ensure that you can boot from an emergency disk, set your floppy drive as the second device in the boot order. A hard disk containing your operating system should be the third drive in the boot order. This allows you to always be ready for an emergency. So long as you do not boot with a CD or floppy loaded, the BIOS will bypass both the CD and floppy disk drives and boot from the hard drive.

Note that not all operating system CDs are bootable. The Windows 95 CD is not bootable; however, starting with Windows 98, Microsoft made the operating system CD bootable, but only for OEM (original equipment manufacturer) versions. The retail Windows CDs were not bootable. Windows NT 4.0 and later, including Windows 2000, are shipped on bootable CDs. See Chapter 13, "Optical Storage," for information on how to make a bootable CD.

17. If you are booting from a floppy disk and the first byte of the volume boot record is less than 06h, or if the first byte is greater than or equal to 06h and the first nine words contain the same data pattern, this error message appears and the system stops:

```
602-Diskette Boot Record Error
```

18. If the volume boot record cannot find or load the system files, or if a problem was encountered loading them, one of the following messages appears:

```
Non-System disk or disk error
Replace and strike any key when ready
```

```
Non-System disk or disk error
Replace and press any key when ready
```

```
Invalid system disk_
Replace the disk, and then press any key
```

```
Disk Boot failure
```

```
Disk I/O Error
```

All these messages originate in the volume boot record (VBR) and relate to VBR or system file problems.

19. If no boot record can be read from drive A: (such as when no disk is in the drive), the BIOS then looks for a master boot record (MBR) at cylinder 0, head 0, sector 1 (the very first sector) of the first hard disk. If this sector is found, it is loaded into memory address 0000:7C00 and tested for a signature.

20. If the last two (signature) bytes of the MBR are not equal to 55AAh, software interrupt 18h (Int 18h) is invoked on most systems.

This causes the BIOS to display an error message that can vary for different BIOS manufacturers, but which is often something like one of the following messages, depending on which BIOS you have:

IBM BIOS:

```
The IBM Personal Computer Basic_
Version C1.10 Copyright IBM Corp 1981
62940 Bytes free_
Ok_
```

Most IBM computers since 1987 display a strange character graphic picture depicting the front of a floppy drive, a 3 1/2-inch disk, and arrows prompting you to insert a disk in the drive and press the F1 key to proceed.

AMI BIOS:

```
NO ROM BASIC - SYSTEM HALTED
```

Compaq BIOS:

```
Non-System disk or disk error
replace and strike any key when ready
```

Award BIOS:

```
DISK BOOT FAILURE, INSERT SYSTEM DISK AND PRESS ENTER
```

Phoenix BIOS:

```
No boot device available -
strike F1 to retry boot, F2 for setup utility
```

or

```
No boot sector on fixed disk -
strike F1 to retry boot, F2 for setup utility
```

Although the messages vary from BIOS to BIOS, the cause for each relates to specific bytes in the MBR, which is the first sector of a hard disk at the physical location cylinder 0, head 0, sector 1.

The problem involves a disk that either has never been partitioned or has had the Master Boot Sector corrupted. During the boot process, the BIOS checks the last two bytes in the MBR (first sector of the drive) for a signature value of 55AAh. If the last two bytes are not 55AAh, an Interrupt 18h is invoked, which calls the subroutine that displays one of the error messages just shown, which basically instruct the user to insert a bootable floppy to proceed.

The MBR (including the signature bytes) is written to the hard disk by the DOS FDISK program. Immediately after a hard disk is low-level formatted, all the sectors are initialized with a pattern of bytes, and the first sector does not contain the 55AAh signature. In other words, these ROM error messages are exactly what you see if you attempt to boot from a hard disk that has been freshly low-level formatted, but has not yet been partitioned.

21. The MBR program searches its partition table for an entry with a system indicator byte designating an extended partition. If the program finds such an entry, it loads the extended partition boot sector at the location indicated. The extended partition boot sector also has a table that is searched for another extended partition indicating logical drives. If another extended partition entry is found, that extended partition boot sector is loaded from the location indicated. The search continues until either no more logical drives are indicated or the maximum number of 24 total logical drives (including C:) has been reached.

22. The MBR searches its built-in partition table entries for a boot indicator byte marking an active partition entry.

23. If none of the partitions are marked active (bootable), the BIOS displays a disk error message.

24. If any boot indicator byte in the MBR partition table is invalid or if more than one indicates an active partition, the following message is displayed and the system stops:

```
Invalid partition table
```

25. If an active partition is found in the MBR, the partition boot record from the active partition is loaded and tested.

26. If the partition boot record cannot be read successfully from the active partition within five retries because of read errors, this message appears and the system stops:

```
Error loading operating system
```

27. The hard disk's partition boot record is tested for a signature. If it does not contain a valid signature of 55AAh as the last two bytes in the sector, this message appears and the system stops:

```
Missing operating system
```

28. The volume boot record is executed as a program. This program looks for and loads the operating system kernel or system files. If the volume boot record cannot find or load the system files, or if a problem was encountered loading them, one of the following messages appears:

```
Non-System disk or disk error
Replace and strike any key when ready

Non-System disk or disk error
Replace and press any key when ready

Invalid system disk_
Replace the disk, and then press any key

Disk Boot failure

Disk I/O Error
```

All these messages originate in the volume boot record (VBR) and relate to VBR or system file problems.

From this point forward, what happens depends on which operating system you have. The operating-system–dependent boot procedures are discussed in the next several sections.

The DOS Boot Process

1. The initial system file (called IO.SYS or IBMBIO.COM) is executed.

2. The initialization code in IO.SYS/IBMBIO.COM copies itself into the highest region of contiguous DOS memory and transfers control to the copy. The initialization code copy then relocates MSDOS.SYS over the portion of IO.SYS in low memory that contains the initialization code, because the initialization code no longer needs to be in that location. Windows 9x's IO.SYS combines the functions of DOS's IO.SYS and MSDOS.SYS.

3. The initialization code executes MSDOS.SYS (or IBMDOS.COM), which initializes the base device drivers, determines equipment status, resets the disk system, resets and initializes attached devices, and sets the system default parameters.

4. The full DOS file system is active, and control is returned to the IO.SYS initialization code.

5. The IO.SYS initialization code reads the CONFIG.SYS file multiple times. In Windows 9x, IO.SYS also looks for the SYSTEM.DAT Registry file.

6. When loading CONFIG.SYS, the DEVICE statements are first processed in the order in which they appear. Any device driver files named in those DEVICE statements are loaded and executed. Then, any INSTALL statements are processed in the order in which they appear; the programs named are loaded and executed. The SHELL statement is processed and loads the specified command processor with the specified parameters. If the CONFIG.SYS file contains no SHELL statement, the default \COMMAND.COM processor is loaded with default parameters. Loading the command processor overwrites the initialization code in memory (because the job of the initialization code is finished).

During the final reads of CONFIG.SYS, all the remaining statements are read and processed in a predetermined order. Thus, the order of appearance for statements other than DEVICE, INSTALL, and SHELL in CONFIG.SYS is of no significance.

7. If AUTOEXEC.BAT is present, COMMAND.COM loads and runs AUTOEXEC.BAT. After the commands in AUTOEXEC.BAT have been executed, the DOS prompt appears (unless AUTOEXEC.BAT calls an application program or shell of some kind, in which case the user might operate the system without ever seeing a DOS prompt).

8. If no AUTOEXEC.BAT file is present, COMMAND.COM executes the internal DATE and TIME commands, displays a copyright message, and displays the DOS prompt.

In Windows 9x, IO.SYS automatically loads HIMEM.SYS, IFSHLP.SYS, and SETVER.EXE. Finally, it loads WIN.COM and Windows 9x is officially started. For more information on how Windows 9x loads, see the section "The Windows 9x/Me Boot Process" later in this chapter.

Some minor variations from this scenario are possible, such as those introduced by other ROM programs in the various adapters that might be plugged into an expansion slot. Also, depending on the exact ROM BIOS programs involved, some of the error messages and sequences can vary. Generally, however, a computer follows this chain of events while "coming to life."

You can modify the system startup procedures by altering the CONFIG.SYS and AUTOEXEC.BAT files or the Windows 9x Registry or Startup folder. These files control the configuration of DOS or Windows 9x and allow special startup programs to be executed every time the system starts.

The Windows 9x/Me Boot Process

Knowing exactly how Windows 9x and Millennium Edition (Me) load and start can be helpful when troubleshooting startup problems. The Windows 9x boot process can be broken into three phases:

- The IO.SYS file is loaded and run.
- Real-mode configuration takes place.
- The WIN.COM file is loaded and run.

Phase 1—Loading and Running the IO.SYS File

1. The initialization code initializes the base device drivers, determines equipment status, resets the disk system, resets and initializes attached devices, and sets the system default parameters.

2. The file system is activated, and control is returned to the IO.SYS initialization code.

3. The Starting Windows message is displayed for <*n*> seconds, or until you press a Windows function key. The amount of time the message is displayed is determined by the BootDelay=<*n*> line in the MSDOS.SYS file; the default is two seconds.

4. The IO.SYS initialization code reads the MSDOS.SYS configuration file. If you have multiple hardware profiles, you receive the following message and must choose a hardware configuration to use:

Windows cannot determine what configuration your computer is in.

5. The LOGO.SYS file is loaded and displays a startup image onscreen.

6. If the DRVSPACE.INI or DBLSPACE.INI file exists, it is loaded into memory. IO.SYS also automatically loads HIMEM.SYS, IFSHLP.SYS, and SETVER.EXE.

7. The IO.SYS file checks the system Registry files (SYSTEM.DAT and USER.DAT) for valid data.

8. IO.SYS opens the SYSTEM.DAT file. If the SYSTEM.DAT file is not found, the SYSTEM.DA0 file is used for startup. If Windows 9x starts successfully, the SYSTEM.DA0 file is copied to the SYSTEM.DAT file.

9. The DBLBUFF.SYS file is loaded if the DoubleBuffer=1 is in the MSDOS.SYS file or if double buffering is enabled under the following Registry key:

HKLM\System\CurrentControlSet\Control\WinBoot\DoubleBuffer

Note

Windows 9x Setup automatically enables double buffering if it detects that it is required.

10. If you have multiple hardware profiles, the hardware profile you chose is loaded from the Registry.

11. In Windows 9x/Me, the system looks in the Registry's Hkey_Local_Machine\System\CurrentControlSet key to load the device drivers and other parameters specified there before executing the CONFIG.SYS file.

Phase 2—Real-Mode Configuration

Some older hardware devices and programs require that drivers or files be loaded in real mode (16-bit mode) for them to work properly. To ensure backward compatibility, Windows 9x processes the CONFIG.SYS and AUTOEXEC.BAT files if they exist.

1. The CONFIG.SYS file is read if it exists, and the statements within are processed, including the loading of drivers into memory. If the CONFIG.SYS file does not exist, the IO.SYS file loads the following required drivers:

IFSHLP.SYS

HIMEM.SYS

SETVER.EXE

IO.SYS obtains the location of these files from the WinBootDir= line of the MSDOS.SYS file and must be on the hard disk.

2. Windows reserves all global upper memory blocks (UMBs) for Windows 9x operating system use or for expanded memory support (EMS).

3. The AUTOEXEC.BAT file is processed if present, and any terminate-and-stay resident (TSR) programs listed within are loaded into memory.

Phase 3—Loading and Running the WIN.COM File

1. WIN.COM is loaded and run.

2. The WIN.COM file accesses the VMM32.VXD file. If enough RAM is available, the VMM32.VXD file loads into memory; otherwise, it is accessed from the hard disk (resulting in a slower startup time).

3. The real-mode virtual device driver loader checks for duplicate virtual device drivers (VxDs) in the WINDOWS\SYSTEM\VMM32 folder and the VMM32.VXD file. If a VxD exists in both the WINDOWS\SYSTEM\VMM32 folder and the VMM32.VXD file, the duplicate VxD is "marked" in the VMM32.VXD file so that it is not loaded.

4. VxDs not already loaded by the VMM32.VXD file are loaded from the [386 Enh] section of the WINDOWS\SYSTEM.INI file.

Required VxDs

Some VxDs are required for Windows to run properly. These required VxDs are loaded automatically and do not require a Registry entry. The following VxDs are required by Windows 9x:

*BIOSXLAT	*CONFIGMG	*DYNAPAGE
*DOSMGR	*EBIOS	*IFSMGR
*INT13	*IOS	*PAGESWAP
*SHELL	*V86MMGR	*VCD
*VCACHE	*VCOMM	*VCOND
*VDD	*VDMAD	*VFAT
*VKD	*VMCPD	*VPICD
*VTD	*VTDAPI	*VWIN32
*VXDLDR		

5. The real-mode virtual device driver loader checks that all required VxDs loaded successfully. If not, it attempts to load the drivers again.

6. After the real-mode virtual device driver loading is logged, driver initialization occurs. If any VxDs require real-mode initialization, they begin their process in real mode.

7. VMM32 switches the computer's processor from real mode to protected mode.

8. A three-phase VxD initialization process occurs in which the drivers are loaded according to their InitDevice instead of the order in which they are loaded into memory.

9. After all the VxDs are loaded, the KRNL32.DLL, GDI.EXE, USER.EXE, and EXPLORER.EXE (the default Windows 9x GUI shell) files are loaded.

10. If a network is specified, load the network environment and multiuser profiles. The user is prompted to log on to the network installed. Windows 9x/Me enables multiple users to save their custom desktop settings. When a user logs on to Windows, his or her desktop settings are loaded from the Registry. If the user does not log on, the desktop configuration uses a default desktop.

11. Programs in the StartUp group and the RunOnce Registry key are run during the last phase of the startup process. After each program in the RunOnce Registry key is started, the program is removed from the key.

Windows NT and Windows 2000 Startup

When you start a Windows NT or Windows 2000 system, the boot process is identical to that of a DOS or Windows 9.x/Me system, up until the time when the system reads the partition boot record from the active partition. Instead of the IO.SYS and MSDOS.SYS files, Windows NT and 2000 use an OS loader program called NTLDR that begins the hardware detection process and enables you to select the operating system to load. If, for example, you have installed Windows NT or Windows 2000 on a system already running another OS, you have the option of booting either operating system. The boot options are stored in a file called BOOT.INI.

After you elect to load Windows NT or Windows 2000, a file called NTDETECT.COM loads and detects the hardware in the computer. Then, the Windows NT Kernel (NTOSKRNL.EXE) and the hardware abstraction layer (HAL.DLL) are loaded into memory. The kernel is responsible for initializing most of the operating system, including the device drivers, Windows NT subsystems and services, and memory paging file. It isn't until you press the Ctrl+Alt+Delete key combination and log on to the system that the startup process is considered to be complete.

PC Maintenance Tools

To troubleshoot and repair PC systems properly, you need a few basic tools. If you intend to troubleshoot and repair PCs professionally, there are many more specialized tools you will want to purchase. These advanced tools enable you to more accurately diagnose problems and make jobs easier and faster. The basic tools that should be in every troubleshooter's toolbox are

- Simple hand tools for basic disassembly and reassembly procedures, including a flat blade and Phillips screwdrivers (both medium and small sizes), tweezers, an IC extraction tool, and a parts grabber or hemostat. Most of these items are included in $10–$20 starter toolkits found at most computer stores.

- Diagnostics software and hardware for testing components in a system.

- A multimeter that provides accurate measurements of voltage and resistance, as well as a continuity checker for testing cables and switches.

- Chemicals, such as contact cleaners, component freeze sprays, and compressed air for cleaning the system.

- Foam swabs, or lint-free cotton swabs if foam isn't available.

- Small nylon wire ties for "dressing" or organizing wires.

Some environments also might have the resources to purchase the following devices, although they're not required for most work:

- Memory-testing machines, used to evaluate the operation of SIMMs (single inline memory modules), DIMMs (dual inline memory modules), DIP (dual inline pin) chips, and other memory modules

- Serial and parallel loopback (or wrap) plugs to test serial and parallel ports

- A network cable scanner (if you work with networked PCs)

- A serial breakout box (if you use systems that operate over serial cables, such as UNIX dumb terminals)

In addition, an experienced troubleshooter will probably want to have soldering and desoldering tools to fix bad serial cables. These tools are discussed in more detail in the following sections.

Hand Tools

When you work with PC systems, the tools required for nearly all service operations are simple and inexpensive. You can carry most of the required tools in a small pouch. Even a top-of-the-line "master mechanics" set fits inside a briefcase-sized container. The cost of these toolkits ranges from about $20 for a small service kit to $500 for one of the briefcase-sized deluxe kits. Compare these costs with what might be necessary for an automotive technician. An automotive service technician would have to spend $5,000–$10,000 or more for a complete set of tools. Not only are PC tools much less expensive, but I can tell you from experience that you don't get nearly as dirty working on computers as you do working on cars.

In this section, you learn about the tools required to assemble a kit that is capable of performing basic, board-level service on PC systems. One of the best ways to start such a set of tools is to purchase a small kit sold especially for servicing PCs.

Figure 24.1 shows some of the basic tools you can find in one of the small PC toolkits that sell for about $20 (and a few that you'll need to purchase separately).

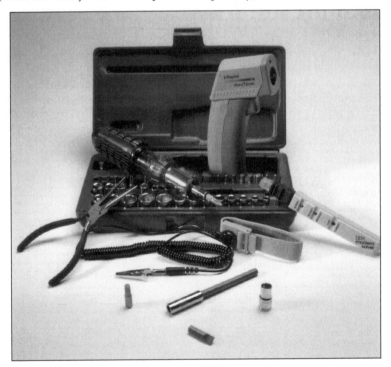

Figure 24.1 A variety of tools that you should have handy when you go to work on your PC.

The following list mentions some specific tools anyone should have if they intend to get inside their PC:

- 3/16-inch nut driver
- 1/4-inch nut driver
- Small Phillips screwdriver
- Small flat-blade screwdriver

- Medium Phillips screwdriver
- Medium flat-blade screwdriver
- Chip extractor
- Chip inserter
- Tweezers
- Claw-type parts grabber
- T10 and T15 Torx drivers

Note

Some tools aren't recommended because they are of limited use. However, they normally come with these types of kits.

You use nut drivers to remove the hexagonal-headed screws that secure the system-unit covers, adapter boards, disk drives, and power supplies in most systems. The nut drivers work much better than conventional screwdrivers.

Because some manufacturers have substituted slotted or Phillips-head screws for the more standard hexagonal-head screws, standard screwdrivers can be used for those systems.

Caution

When working in a cramped environment such as the inside of a computer case, screwdrivers with magnetic tips can be a real convenience, especially for retrieving that screw you dropped into the case. However, although I have used these types of screwdrivers many times with no problems, you must be aware of the damage a magnetic field can cause to memory chips and magnetic storage devices such as hard drives and floppy disks. Laying the screwdriver down on or near a floppy or working too close to a hard drive can damage the data on the disk.

Chip-extraction and insertion tools are rarely needed these days because memory chips are mounted on SIMMs or DIMMs and processors use zero insertion force (ZIF) sockets or other user-friendly connectors. The ZIF socket has a lever that, when raised, releases the grip on the pins of the chip, enabling you to easily lift it out with your fingers.

However, if you work with older systems, you must use a chip extractor (see Figure 24.2) to install or remove memory chips (or other smaller chips) without bending any pins on the chip. Usually, you pry out larger chips, such as microprocessors or ROMs, with the small screwdriver. Larger processors require a chip extractor if they are mounted in the older low insertion force (LIF) socket. These chips have so many pins on them that a large amount of force is required to remove them, despite the fact that they call the socket "low insertion force." If you use a screwdriver on a large physical-size chip such as a 486, you risk cracking the case of the chip and permanently damaging it. The chip extractor tool for removing these chips has a very wide end with tines that fit between the pins on the chip to distribute the force evenly along the chip's underside. This minimizes the likelihood of breakage. Most of these types of extraction tools must be purchased specially for the chip you're trying to remove.

Tip

The older-style chip extractor shown on the left in Figure 24.2 does have another use as a keycap extractor. In fact, for this role it works quite well. By placing the tool over a keycap on a keyboard and squeezing the tool so the hooks grab under the keycap on opposite sides, you can cleanly and effectively remove the keycap from the keyboard without damage. This works much better than trying to pry the caps off with a screwdriver, which often results in damaging them or sending them flying across the room.

Figure 24.2 The chip extractor (left) is used to remove an individual RAM or ROM chip from a socket, but it would not be useful for a larger processor chip. Use an extractor such as the one on the right for extracting socketed processors—if the processor does not use a ZIF socket.

The tweezers and parts grabber can be used to hold any small screws or jumper blocks that are difficult to hold in your hand. The parts grabber (see Figure 24.3) is especially useful when you drop a small part into the interior of a system; usually, you can remove the part without completely disassembling the system.

Figure 24.3 The parts grabber has three small metal prongs that can be extended to grab a part.

Finally, the Torx driver is a star-shaped driver that matches the special screws found in most Compaq systems and in many other systems as well (see Figure 24.4). You also can purchase tamperproof Torx drivers that can remove Torx screws with the tamper-resistant pin in the center of the screw. A tamperproof Torx driver has a hole drilled in it to allow clearance for the pin.

Figure 24.4   A Torx driver and bit.

Although this basic set is useful, you should supplement it with some other small hand tools, such as

- Needle-nose pliers
- Vise or clamp
- Hemostat
- File
- Wire cutter or wire stripper
- Small flashlight

Pliers are useful for straightening pins on chips, applying or removing jumpers, crimping cables, or grabbing small parts.

Hemostats are especially useful for grabbing small components, such as jumpers.

The wire cutter or stripper, obviously, is useful for making or repairing cables or wiring. For example, you'd need these (along with a crimping tool) to make 10BASE-T Ethernet cables using UTP cable and RJ45 connectors (see Chapter 20, "Local Area Networking").

You can use a vise to install connectors on cables, crimp cables to the shape you want, and hold parts during delicate operations. In addition to the vise, Radio Shack sells a nifty "extra hands" device that has two movable arms with alligator clips on the end. This type of device is very useful for making cables or for other delicate operations during which an extra set of hands to hold something might be useful.

You can use the file to smooth rough metal edges on cases and chassis and to trim the faceplates on disk drives for a perfect fit.

You might often need a flashlight to illuminate system interiors, especially when the system is cramped and the room lighting is poor, or when you are working on a system underneath a user's desk. I consider this tool to be essential.

ESD Protection Tools

Another consideration for your toolkit is an electrostatic discharge (ESD) protection kit. This kit consists of a wrist strap with a ground wire and a specially conductive mat with its own ground wire. Using a kit like this when working on a system helps ensure that you never accidentally damage any of the components with a static discharge. You also can get just the wrist strap or the antistatic mat separately. A wrist strap is shown in Figure 24.5.

Note

It is possible (but not recommended) to work without an ESD protection kit if you're disciplined and careful about working on systems. If you don't have an ESD kit available, you should discharge yourself by touching some metallic part of the case while the computer is still plugged into the AC power source; then unplug the computer. Many systems today continue to feed power to the motherboard through the soft off connection whenever the computer is plugged in, even when the power switch is turned off. It can be very dangerous to work inside a PC that is still connected to a power source.

The ESD kits, as well as all the other tools and much more, are available from a variety of tool vendors. Specialized Products Company and Jensen Tools are two of the most popular vendors of computer and electronic tools and service equipment. Their catalogs show an extensive selection of very high-quality tools. (These companies and several others are listed in the Vendor List on the CD.) With a simple set of hand tools, you will be equipped for nearly every PC repair or installation situation. The total cost of these tools should be less than $150, which is not much considering the capabilities they provide.

A Word About Hardware

This section discusses some problems you might encounter with the hardware (screws, nuts, bolts, and so on) used in assembling a system.

Figure 24.5 A typical ESD wrist strap clipped to a nonpainted surface in the case chassis.

Types of Hardware

One of the biggest aggravations you encounter in dealing with various systems is the different hardware types and designs that hold the units together.

For example, most systems use screws that fit 1/4-inch or 3/16-inch hexagonal nut drivers. IBM used these screws in all its original PC, XT, and AT systems, and most other system manufacturers use this standard hardware as well. Some manufacturers use different hardware, however. Compaq, for example, uses Torx screws extensively in many of its systems. A Torx screw has a star-shaped hole driven by the correct-size Torx driver. These drivers carry size designations such as T-8, T-9, T-10, T-15, T-20, T-25, T-30, and T-40.

A variation on the Torx screw is the tamperproof Torx screw found in power supplies, monitors, hard drives, and other assemblies. These screws are identical to the regular Torx screws, except that a pin sticks up from the middle of the star-shape hole in the screw. This pin prevents the standard Torx driver from entering the hole to grip the screw; a special tamperproof driver with a corresponding hole for the pin is required. An alternative is to use a small chisel to knock out the pin in the screw. Usually, a device sealed with these types of screws is considered to be a replaceable unit that rarely, if ever, needs to be opened.

Caution

Note that devices sealed with these types of screws generally have high voltages or other dangers waiting inside, so being able to bypass these screws doesn't mean it's always a good idea. Be sure you know what you are doing before disassembling devices such as monitors and power supplies.

Many manufacturers also use the more standard slotted-head and Phillips-head screws. Using tools on these screws is relatively easy, but tools do not grip these fasteners as well as hexagonal head or Torx screws do. In addition, the heads can be stripped more easily than the other types. Extremely cheap versions tend to lose bits of metal as they're turned with a driver, and the metal bits can fall onto the motherboard. Stay away from cheap fasteners whenever possible; the headaches of dealing with stripped screws aren't worth it.

Some system manufacturers now use cases that snap together or use thumb screws. These are usually advertised as "no-tool" cases because you literally do not need any tools to remove the cover and access the major assemblies.

A company called Curtis sells special nylon plastic thumb screws that fit most normal cases and can be used to replace the existing screws to make opening the case a no-tool proposition. However, you still should always use metal screws to install internal components, such as adapter cards, disk drives, power supplies, and the motherboard, because the metal screws provide a ground point for these devices.

English Versus Metric

Another area of aggravation with hardware is the fact that two types of thread systems exist: English and metric. IBM used mostly English-threaded fasteners in its original line of systems, but many other manufacturers used metric-threaded fasteners.

The difference between the two becomes especially apparent with disk drives. American-manufactured drives typically use English fasteners, whereas drives made in Japan and Taiwan usually use metric. Whenever you replace a floppy drive in an older PC, you encounter this problem. Try to buy the correct screws and any other hardware, such as brackets, with the drive because they might be difficult to find as separate items. Many drive manufacturers offer retail drive kits that include all the required mounting components. The OEM's drive manual lists the correct data about a specific drive's hole locations and thread size.

Hard disks can use either English or metric fasteners; check your particular drive to see which type it uses. Most drives today use metric hardware.

Caution

Some screws in a system can be length-critical, especially screws used to retain hard disk drives. You can destroy some hard disks by using a mounting screw that's too long; the screw can puncture or dent the sealed disk chamber when you install the drive and fully tighten the screw. When you install a new drive in a system, always make a trial fit of the hardware to see how far the screws can be inserted into the drive before they interfere with its internal components. When in doubt, the drive manufacturer's OEM documentation will tell you precisely which screws are required and how long they should be.

Soldering and Desoldering Tools

In certain situations—such as repairing a broken wire, making cables, reattaching a component to a circuit board, removing and installing chips that are not in a socket, and adding jumper wires or pins to a board—you must use a soldering iron to make the repair.

Although virtually all repairs these days are done by simply replacing the entire failed board and many PC technicians never touch a soldering iron, you might find one useful in some situations. The most common case is when physical damage to a system has occurred, such as when someone rips the keyboard connector off a motherboard by pulling on the cable improperly. Simple soldering skills can save the motherboard in this case.

Most motherboards these days include I/O components, such as serial and parallel ports. Many of these ports are fuse-protected on the board; however, the fuse is usually a small soldered-in component. These fuses are designed to protect the motherboard circuits from being damaged by an external source. If a short circuit or static charge from an external device blows these fuses, the motherboard can be saved if you can replace them.

To perform minor repairs such as these, you need a low-wattage soldering iron—usually about 25 watts. More than 30 watts generates too much heat and can damage the components on the board. Even with a low-wattage unit, you must limit the amount of heat to which you subject the board and its components. You can do this with quick and efficient use of the soldering iron and with the use of heatsinking devices clipped to the leads of the device being soldered. A *heatsink* is a small metal clip-on device designed to absorb excessive heat before it reaches the component the heatsink is protecting. In some cases, you can use a pair of hemostats as an effective heatsink when you solder a component.

To remove components soldered into place on a printed circuit board, you can use a soldering iron with a solder sucker. This device normally takes the form of a small tube with an air chamber and a plunger-and-spring arrangement. (I do not recommend the squeeze-bulb type of solder sucker.) The unit is "cocked" when you press the spring-loaded plunger into the air chamber. When you want to remove a device from a board, you use the soldering iron from the underside of the board and heat the point at which one of the component leads joins the circuit board until the solder melts. As soon as melting occurs, move the solder-sucker nozzle into position and press the actuator. When the plunger retracts, it creates a momentary suction that draws the liquid solder away from the connection and leaves the component lead dry in the hole.

Always perform the heating and suctioning from the underside of a board, not from the component side. Repeat this action for every component lead joined to the circuit board. When you master this technique, you can remove a small component in a minute or two with only a small likelihood of damage to the board or other components. Larger chips that have many pins can be more difficult to remove and resolder without damaging other components or the circuit board.

Tip

These procedures are intended for "through-hole" devices only. These are components whose pins extend all the way through holes in the board to the underside. Surface-mounted devices are removed with a completely different procedure, using much more expensive tools. Working on surface-mounted components is beyond the capabilities of all but the most well-equipped shops.

If you intend to add soldering and desoldering skills to your arsenal of abilities, you should practice. Take a useless circuit board and practice removing various components from the board; then, reinstall the components. Try to remove the components from the board by using the least amount of heat possible. Also, perform the solder-melting operations as quickly as possible, limiting the time the iron is applied to the joint. Before you install any components, clean out the holes through which the leads must project and mount the component in place. Then, apply the solder from the underside of the board, using as little heat and solder as possible.

Attempt to produce joints as clean as the joints the board manufacturer produced by machine. Soldered joints that do not look clean can keep the component from making a good connection with the rest of the circuit. This "cold-solder joint" is normally created because you have not used enough heat. Remember that you should not practice your new soldering skills on the motherboard of a system you are attempting to repair! Don't attempt to work on real boards until you are sure of your skills. I always keep a few junk boards around for soldering practice and experimentation.

Tip

When first learning to solder, you might be tempted to set the iron on the solder and leave it there until the solder melts. If the solder doesn't melt immediately when you apply the iron to it, you're not transferring the heat from the iron to the solder efficiently. This means that either the iron is dirty or there is debris between it and the solder. To clean the iron, take a wet sponge and drag it across the tip of the iron.

If after cleaning the iron, there's still some resistance, try to scratch the solder with the iron when it's hot. Generally, this removes any barriers to heat flow and instantly melts the solder.

No matter how good you get at soldering and desoldering, some jobs are best left to professionals. Components that are surface-mounted to a circuit board, for example, require special tools for soldering and desoldering, as do other components that have high pin densities.

Test Equipment

In some cases, you must use specialized devices to test a system board or component. This test equipment is not expensive or difficult to use, but it can add much to your troubleshooting abilities.

Electrical Testing Equipment

I consider a voltmeter to be required gear for proper system testing. A multimeter can serve many purposes, including checking for voltage signals at various points in a system, testing the output of the power supply, and checking for continuity in a circuit or cable. An outlet tester is an invaluable accessory that can check the electrical outlet for proper wiring. This capability is useful if you believe the problem lies outside the computer system.

Loopback Connectors (Wrap Plugs)

For diagnosing serial- and parallel-port problems, you need loopback connectors (also called wrap plugs), which are used to circulate, or wrap, signals (see Figure 24.6). The plugs enable the serial or parallel port to send data to itself for diagnostic purposes.

Male and female, 25-pin parallel
and serial loopback connectors

9-pin serial
loopback connectors

Figure 24.6   Typical wrap plugs including 25-pin and 9-pin serial and 25-pin parallel versions.

Various types of loopback connectors are available. To accommodate all the ports you might encounter, you need one for the 25-pin serial port, one for the 9-pin serial port, and one for the 25-pin parallel port. Many companies, including IBM, sell the plugs separately, but be aware that you also need diagnostic software that can use them. Some diagnostic software products, such as Micro 2000's Micro-Scope, include loopback connectors with the product, or you can purchase them as an option for about $30 a set.

IBM sells a special combination plug that includes all three connector types in one compact unit. The device costs about the same as a normal set of wrap plugs. If you're handy, you can even make your own wrap plugs for testing. I include wiring diagrams for the three types of wrap plugs in Chapter 17, "I/O Interfaces from Serial and Parallel to IEEE-1394 and USB." In that chapter, you also will find a detailed discussion of serial and parallel ports.

Besides simple loopback connectors, you also might want to have a breakout box for your toolkit. A breakout box is a DB25 connector device that enables you to make custom temporary cables or even to monitor signals on a cable. For most PC troubleshooting uses, a "mini" breakout box works well and is inexpensive.

Meters

Some troubleshooting procedures require that you measure voltage and resistance. You take these measurements by using a handheld Digital Multi-Meter (DMM). The meter can be an analog device (using an actual meter) or a digital-readout device. The DMM has a pair of wires called test leads or probes. The test leads make the connections so that you can take readings. Depending on the meter's setting, the probes measure electrical resistance, direct-current (DC) voltage, or alternating-current (AC) voltage.

Usually, each system-unit measurement setting has several ranges of operation. DC voltage, for example, usually can be read in several scales, to a maximum of 200 millivolts (mv), 2v, 20v, 200v, and 1,000v. Because computers use both +5v and +12v for various operations, you should use the 20v maximum scale for making your measurements. Making these measurements on the 200mv or 2v scale could "peg the meter" and possibly damage it because the voltage would be much higher than expected. Using the 200v or 1,000v scale works, but the readings at 5v and 12v are so small in proportion to the maximum that accuracy is low.

If you are taking a measurement and are unsure of the actual voltage, start at the highest scale and work your way down. Most of the better meters have autoranging capability—the meter automatically selects the best range for any measurement. This type of meter is much easier to operate. You simply set the meter to the type of reading you want, such as DC volts, and attach the probes to the signal source. The meter selects the correct voltage range and displays the value. Because of their design, these types of meters always have a digital display rather than a meter needle.

Caution

Whenever you are using a multimeter to test any voltage that could potentially be 110v or above, always use one hand to do the testing, not two. Either clip one lead to one of the sources and probe with the other or hold both leads in one hand.

If you hold a lead in each hand and accidentally slip, you can very easily become a circuit, allowing power to conduct or flow through you. When power flows from arm to arm, the path of the current is directly across the heart. Hearts tend to quit working when subjected to high voltages. They're funny that way.

I prefer the small digital meters; you can buy them for only slightly more than the analog style, and they're extremely accurate and much safer for digital circuits. Some of these meters are not much bigger than a cassette tape; they fit in a shirt pocket. Radio Shack sells a good unit (made for Radio Shack by Beckman) in the $25 price range; the meter is a half-inch thick, weighs 3 1/2 ounces, and is digital and autoranging, as well. This type of meter works well for most, if not all, PC troubleshooting and test uses.

Caution

You should be aware that many analog meters can be dangerous to digital circuits. These meters use a 9v battery to power the meter for resistance measurements. If you use this type of meter to measure resistance on some digital circuits, you can damage the electronics because you essentially are injecting 9v into the circuit. The digital meters universally run on 3v–5v or less.

Logic Probes and Logic Pulsers

A logic probe can be useful for diagnosing problems in digital circuits (see Figure 24.7). In a digital circuit, a signal is represented as either high (+5v) or low (0v). Because these signals are present for only a short time (measured in millionths of a second) or oscillate (switch on and off) rapidly, a simple voltmeter is useless. A logic probe is designed to display these signal conditions easily.

TTL/LS-CMOS

Normal/Pulse

Pulse
Low
High

Positive   Negative
   (+)   (—)

Figure 24.7   A typical logic probe.

Logic probes are especially useful for troubleshooting a dead system. By using the probe, you can determine whether the basic clock circuitry is operating and whether other signals necessary for system operation are present. In some cases, a probe can help you cross-check the signals at each pin on an integrated circuit chip. You can compare the signals present at each pin with the signals a known-good chip of the same type would show—a comparison that is helpful in isolating a failed component. Logic probes also can be useful for troubleshooting some disk drive problems by enabling you to test the signals present on the interface cable or drive-logic board.

A companion tool to the probe is the logic pulser. A *pulser* is designed to test circuit reaction by delivering a logical high (+5v) pulse into a circuit, usually lasting from 1 1/2 to 10 millionths of a second. Compare the reaction with that of a known-functional circuit. This type of device normally is used much less frequently than a logic probe, but in some cases it can be helpful for testing a circuit.

Outlet Testers

Outlet testers are very useful test tools. These simple, inexpensive devices, sold in hardware stores, test electrical outlets. You simply plug in the device, and three LEDs light up in various combinations, indicating whether the outlet is wired correctly.

Although you might think that badly wired outlets would be a rare problem, I have seen a large number of installations in which the outlets were wired incorrectly. Most of the time, the problem is in the ground wire. An improperly wired outlet can result in unstable system operation, such as random parity checks and lockups. With an improper ground circuit, currents can begin flowing on the electrical ground circuits in the system. Because the system uses the voltage on the ground circuits as a comparative signal to determine whether bits are 0 or 1, a floating ground can cause data errors in the system.

Caution

Even if you use a surge protector, it will not protect your system from an improperly wired outlet. Therefore, you still should use an outlet tester to ensure your outlet is computer friendly.

Once, while running one of my PC troubleshooting seminars, I used a system that I literally could not approach without locking it up. Whenever I walked past the system, the electrostatic field generated by my body interfered with the system and the PC locked up, displaying a parity-check error message. The problem was that the hotel at which I was giving the seminar was very old and had no grounded outlets in the room. The only way I could prevent the system from locking up was to run the class in my stocking feet because my leather-soled shoes were generating the static charge.

Other symptoms of bad ground wiring in electrical outlets are continual electrical shocks when you touch the case or chassis of the system. These shocks indicate that voltages are flowing where they should not be. This problem also can be caused by bad or improper grounds within the system. By using the simple outlet tester, you can quickly determine whether the outlet is at fault.

If you just walk up to a system and receive an initial shock, it's probably only static electricity. Touch the chassis again without moving your feet. If you receive another shock, something is very wrong. In this case, the ground wire actually has voltage applied to it. You should have a professional electrician check the outlet immediately.

If you don't like being a human rat in an electrical experiment, you can test the outlets with your multimeter. First, remember to hold both leads in one hand. Test from one blade hole to another. This should read between 110v and 125v, depending on the electrical service in the area. Then, check from each blade to the ground (the round hole). One blade hole, the smaller one, should show a voltage almost identical to the one you got from the blade-hole–to–blade-hole test. The larger blade hole when measured to ground should show less than 0.5v.

Because ground and neutral are supposed to be tied together at the electrical panel, a large difference in these readings indicates that they are not tied together. However, small differences can be accounted for by current from other outlets down the line flowing on the neutral, when there isn't any on the ground.

If you don't get the results you expect, call an electrician to test the outlets for you. More weird computer problems are caused by improper grounding and other power problems than people like to believe.

Memory Testers

I now consider a memory test machine an all-but-mandatory piece of equipment for anyone serious about performing PC troubleshooting and repair as a profession. The tester is a small device designed to evaluate SIMMs, DIMMs, RIMMs, and other types of memory modules, including individual chips such as those used as cache memory. These testers can be somewhat expensive, costing upward of $1,000–$2,500 or more, but these machines are the only truly accurate way to test memory.

Without one of these testers, you are reduced to testing memory by running a diagnostic program on the PC and testing the memory as it is installed. This can be very problematic because the memory diagnostic program can do only two things to the memory: write and read. A SIMM/DIMM/RIMM tester can do many things a memory diagnostic running in a PC cannot do, such as

- Identify the type of memory
- Identify the memory speed
- Identify whether the memory has parity or is using bogus parity emulation
- Vary the refresh timing and access speed timing
- Locate single bit failures
- Detect power- and noise-related failures
- Detect solder opens and shorts
- Isolate timing-related failures
- Detect data retention errors

No conventional memory diagnostic software can do these things because it must rely on the fixed access parameters set up by the memory controller hardware in the motherboard chipset. This prevents the software from being capable of altering the timing and methods used to access the memory. You might have memory that fails in one system and works in another when the chips are actually bad. This type of intermittent problem is almost impossible to detect with diagnostic software.

The bottom line is that there is no way you can test memory with true accuracy while it is installed in a PC; a memory tester is required for comprehensive and accurate testing. The price of a memory tester can be justified very easily in a shop environment where a lot of PCs are tested because many software and hardware upgrades today require the addition of new memory. With the large increases in the amount of memory in today's systems and the stricter timing requirements of newer motherboard designs, it has become even more important to be able to identify or rule out memory as a cause of system failure. One company manufacturing memory testers I recommend is Tanisys Technologies; its Darkhorse Systems line of memory testers can handle virtually every type of memory on the market. See the Vendor List on the CD for more information. Also, see Chapter 6, "Memory," for more information on memory in general.

Special Tools for the Enthusiast

All the tools described so far are commonly used by most technicians. However, a few additional tools do exist that a true PC enthusiast might want to have.

Electric Screwdriver

Perhaps the most useful tool I use is an electric screwdriver. It enables me to disassemble and reassemble a PC in record time and makes the job not only faster but easier as well. I like the type with a clutch you can use to set how tight it will make the screws before slipping; such a clutch makes it even faster to use. If you use the driver frequently, it makes sense to use the type with replaceable, rechargeable batteries, so when one battery dies you can quickly replace it with a fresh one.

Caution

Note that using an electric screwdriver when installing a motherboard can be dangerous because the bit can easily slip off the screw and damage the board. A telltale series of swirling scratches near the screw holes on the board can be the result, for which most manufacturers rightfully deny a warranty claim. Be especially careful if your motherboard is retained with Phillips-head screws because they are extremely easy for the bit to slip out of. Normally, I recommend using only Torx-head or hex-head screws to retain the motherboard because they are far more resistant to having the bit slip out and cause damage.

With the electric screwdriver, I recommend getting a complete set of English and metric nut driver tips as well as various sizes of Torx, flat-head, and Phillips-head screwdriver tips.

Tamperproof Torx Bits

As mentioned earlier, many devices such as power supplies and monitors are held together with tamperproof Torx screws. Tamperproof Torx driver sets are available from any good electronics tool supplier.

Temperature Probe

Determining the interior temperature of a PC is often useful when diagnosing whether heat-related issues are causing problems. This requires some way of measuring the temperature inside the PC, as well as the ambient temperature outside the system. The simplest and best tool for the job I've found is the digital thermometers sold at most auto parts stores for automobile use. They are designed to read the temperature inside and outside the car and normally come with an internal sensor, as well as one at the end of a length of wire.

With this type of probe, you can run the wired sensor inside the case (if it is metal, make sure it does not directly touch the motherboard or other exposed circuits where it might cause a short) with the wires slipped through a crack in the case or out one of the drive bays. Then, with the system running you can take the internal temperature as well as read the room's ambient temperature. Normally, the maximum limit for internal temperature should be 110° F (43° C) or less. If your system is running near or above that temperature, problems can be expected. You also can position the probe in the system to be near any heat producing devices, such as the processor, video card, and so on, to see the effect of the device. Probing the temperature with a device such as this enables you to determine whether additional cooling is necessary (that is, adding more cooling fans to the case) and enables you to check to see whether the added fans are helping.

Large Claw-Type Parts Grabber

One of the more useful tools in my toolbox is a large claw-type parts grabber, normally sold in stores that carry automotive tools. Having one of these around has saved many hours of frustration digging back into a system or behind a desk for a loose or dropped screw.

These grabbers are very similar to the small claw-type grabber included with most PC toolkits, except they are much larger—normally two feet or so in length. They can be useful if you drop a screw down inside a tower case, or even on the floor under or behind a desk or cabinet. Although magnetic parts grabbers are also available, I normally recommend the claw-type because using a powerful magnet near a computer can cause problems with any disk storage media you have about, or even the hard disk or CRT-type display.

Preventive Maintenance

Preventive maintenance is the key to obtaining years of trouble-free service from your computer system. A properly administered preventive maintenance program pays for itself by reducing problem behavior, data loss, and component failure and by ensuring a long life for your system. In several cases, I have "repaired" an ailing system with nothing more than a preventive maintenance session. Preventive maintenance also can increase your system's resale value because it will look and run better.

Developing a preventive maintenance program is important to everyone who uses or manages personal computer systems. The two types of preventive maintenance procedures are active and passive.

An *active* preventive maintenance program includes procedures that promote a longer, trouble-free life for your PC. This type of preventive maintenance primarily involves the periodic cleaning of the system and its components. The following sections describe several active preventive maintenance procedures, including cleaning and lubricating all major components, reseating chips and connectors, and reformatting hard disks.

Passive preventive maintenance includes steps you can take to protect a system from the environment, such as using power-protection devices; ensuring a clean, temperature-controlled environment; and preventing excessive vibration. In other words, passive preventive maintenance means treating your system well.

Active Preventive Maintenance Procedures

How often you should perform active preventive maintenance procedures depends on the system's environment and the quality of the system's components. If your system is in a dirty environment, such as a machine shop floor or a gas station service area, you might need to clean your system every three months or less. For normal office environments, cleaning a system every one to two years is usually fine. However, if you open your system after one year and find dust bunnies inside, you should probably shorten the cleaning interval.

Other hard disk preventive maintenance procedures include making periodic backups of your data and critical areas, such as boot sectors, file allocation tables (FATs), and directory structures on the disk. Also, you should defragment hard disks periodically to maintain disk efficiency and speed.

System Backups

One of the most important preventive maintenance procedures is the performance of regular system backups. A sad reality in the computer repair and servicing world is that hardware can always be repaired or replaced, but data cannot. Many hard disk troubleshooting and service procedures, for example, require that you repartition or reformat the disk, which overwrites all existing data.

The hard disk drive capacity in a typical PC has grown far beyond the point at which floppy disks are a viable backup solution. Backup solutions that employ floppy disk drives, such as DOS backup software, are insufficient and too costly for hard disk backups in today's systems. It would take 2,867 1.44MB floppy disks, for example, to back up the 4GB hard disk in my portable system! That would cost more than $1,000 in disks, not to mention the time involved.

The best form of backup has traditionally been magnetic tape. The two main standards are Travan and DAT (digital audio tape). Travan drives are generally slower and hold less than DAT drives, but both are available in relatively competitive versions. The latest Travan NS (Network series) tape drives store 10GB/20GB (raw/compressed) on a single tape, whereas DAT DDS3 (digital data storage) drives store 12GB/24GB per tape, and newer DAT DDS4 drives store 20GB/40GB per tape. These tapes typically cost less than $30.

Tape is generally the fastest and safest form of backup, especially considering you can make multiple backups to different tapes, and even move some of the backups offsite in case of theft or fire. Still, the initial cost of the drive has been an impediment to many. The increasing popularity of writable CD-RW drives presents an alternative, although backing up an entire drive requires multiple CDs.

Although a tape drive can cost up to $500 or more, the media costs are really far more significant than the cost of the drive. If you perform responsible backups, you should have at least three sets of media for each system you are backing up. You should use each media set on a rotating basis, and store one of them offsite at all times, in case of fire or theft. You also should introduce new media to the rotation after approximately a year to prevent excessive wear. If you are backing up multiple systems, these media costs can add up quickly.

In addition, you should factor in the cost of your time. If a backup requires manual intervention to change the media during the job, I don't recommend it. A backup system should be capable of fitting a complete backup on a single tape so you can schedule the job to run unattended. If someone has to hang around to switch tapes every so often, backups become a real chore and are more likely to be overlooked. Also, every time a media change occurs, the likelihood of errors and problems you might not see until you attempt to perform a restore operation substantially increases. Backups are far more important than most people realize, and spending a little more on a quality piece of hardware such as a Travan or DAT drive will pay off in the long run with greater reliability, lower media costs, higher performance, and unattended backups that contain the entire system file structure.

With the increasing popularity of removable bulk storage media such as cartridge drives, including Iomega's Zip and Jaz drives, and rewritable CDs (CD-RWs), many people are using these devices to perform system backups. In most cases, however, although these drives are excellent for storing backup copies of selected data, they are impractical solutions for regular system backups. This can be due to both the capacity of the media in relation to today's hard disk drives and the cost of the media.

Although the media for a CD-RW drive are quite inexpensive, it would take several discs to back up a multigigabyte hard drive, adding a measure of inconvenience to the backup process that makes it far less likely to be performed on a regular basis. Even the Iomega Jaz drive that can store up to 2GB on a single cartridge can require several media changes to complete a single system backup. Add this to the fact that the Jaz cartridges can cost $150 or more each, and you have a backup solution that is both inconvenient and expensive.

Another alternative for backup is to install a second hard drive of equal (or larger) capacity and simply copy from one drive to another. With the low cost of drives these days, this is an economical, fast, and efficient method; however, if a disaster occurs, such as theft or fire, you'll still lose everything. Also, with only one backup, if your backup goes bad when you depend on it, you'll be without any other alternatives.

What I like to do is use a second hard disk to make complete backups of my entire drive weekly, followed by monthly backups to tape. This enables me to not only back up quickly and efficiently, but I also can easily swap my backup slave drive for a failed master and be up and running again in minutes. The tape backup then becomes more of an insurance policy.

Tip

No matter which backup solution you use, the entire exercise is pointless if you cannot restore your data from the storage medium. You should test your backup system by performing random file restores at regular intervals to ensure the viability of your data.

Cleaning a System

One of the most important operations in a good preventive maintenance program is regular and thorough cleaning of the system. Dust buildup on the internal components can lead to several problems. One is that the dust acts as a thermal insulator, which prevents proper system cooling. Excessive heat shortens the life of system components and adds to the thermal stress problem caused by greater temperature changes between the system's power-on and power-off states. Additionally, the dust can contain conductive elements that can cause partial short circuits in a system. Other elements in dust and dirt can accelerate corrosion of electrical contacts, resulting in improper connections. In all, the regular removal of any layer of dust and debris from within a computer system benefits that system in the long run.

Tip

Cigarette smoke contains chemicals that can conduct electricity and cause corrosion of computer parts. The smoke residue can infiltrate the entire system, causing corrosion and contamination of electrical contacts and sensitive components, such as floppy drive read/write heads and optical drive lens assemblies. You should avoid smoking near computer equipment and encourage your company to develop and enforce a similar policy.

Floppy disk drives are particularly vulnerable to the effects of dirt and dust. A floppy drive is essentially a large "hole" in the system case through which air continuously flows. Therefore, these drives accumulate a large amount of dust and chemical buildup within a short time. Hard disk drives, on the other hand, do not present quite the same problem. Because the head disk assembly (HDA) in a hard disk is a sealed unit with a single barometric vent, no dust or dirt can enter without passing through the barometric vent filter. This filter ensures that contaminating dust and particles cannot enter the interior of the HDA. Thus, cleaning a hard disk requires blowing off the dust and dirt from outside the drive. No internal cleaning is required.

Disassembly and Cleaning Tools

Properly cleaning the system and all the boards inside requires certain supplies and tools. In addition to the tools required to disassemble the unit, you should have these items:

- Contact cleaning solution
- Canned air
- A small brush
- Lint-free foam cleaning swabs
- Antistatic wrist-grounding strap

You also might want to acquire these optional items:

- Foam tape
- Low-volatile room-temperature vulcanizing (RTV) sealer
- Silicone-type lubricant
- Computer vacuum cleaner

These simple cleaning tools and chemical solutions enable you to perform most common preventive maintenance tasks.

Chemicals

Chemicals can be used to help clean, troubleshoot, and even repair a system. You can use several types of cleaning solutions with computers and electronic assemblies. Most fall into the following categories:

- Standard cleaners
- Contact cleaner/lubricants
- Dusters

Tip

The makeup of many of the chemicals used for cleaning electronic components has been changing because many of the chemicals originally used are now considered environmentally unsafe. They have been attributed to damaging the earth's ozone layer. Chlorine atoms from chlorofluorocarbons (CFCs) and chlorinated solvents attach themselves to ozone molecules and destroy them. Many of these chemicals are now strictly regulated by federal and international agencies in an effort to preserve the ozone layer. Most of the companies that produce chemicals used for system cleaning and maintenance have had to introduce environmentally safe replacements. The only drawback is that many of these safer chemicals cost more and usually do not work as well as those they've replaced.

Standard Cleaners

For the most basic function—cleaning components, electrical connectors, and contacts—one of the most useful chemicals is 1,1,1 trichloroethane. This substance is an effective cleaner that was at one time used to clean electrical contacts and components because it does not damage most plastics and board materials. In fact, trichloroethane is very useful for cleaning stains on the system case and keyboard as well. Unfortunately, trichloroethane is now being regulated as a chlorinated solvent, along with CFCs (chlorofluorocarbons) such as Freon, but electronic chemical-supply companies are offering several replacements.

Alternative cleaning solutions are available in a variety of types and configurations. You can use pure isopropyl alcohol, acetone, Freon, trichloroethane, or a variety of other chemicals. Most board manufacturers and service shops are now leaning toward alcohol, acetone, or other chemicals that do not cause ozone depletion and comply with government regulations and environmental safety.

Recently, new biodegradable cleaners described as "citrus-based cleaners" have become popular in the industry, and in many cases are more effective and more economical for circuit board and contact cleaning. These cleaners are commonly known as d-limonene or citrus terpenes and are derived from orange peels, which gives them a strong (but pleasant) citric odor. Another type of terpene is called a-pinene, and is derived from pine trees. You must exercise care when using these cleaners, however, because they can cause swelling of some plastics, especially silicone rubber and PVC.

You should make sure your cleaning solution is designed to clean computers or electronic assemblies. In most cases, this means that the solution should be chemically pure and free from contaminants or other unwanted substances. You should not, for example, use drugstore rubbing alcohol for cleaning electronic parts or contacts because it is not pure and could contain water or perfumes. The material must be moisture-free and residue-free. The solutions should be in liquid form, not a spray. Sprays can be wasteful, and you almost never spray the solution directly on components. Instead, wet a foam or chamois swab used for wiping the component. These electronic-component cleaning solutions are available at any good electronics parts store.

Contact Cleaner/Lubricants

These chemicals are similar to the standard cleaners but include a lubricating component. The lubricant eases the force required when plugging and unplugging cables and connectors, reducing strain on the devices. The lubricant coating also acts as a conductive protectant that insulates the contacts from corrosion. These chemicals can greatly prolong the life of a system by preventing intermittent contacts in the future.

A unique type of contact enhancer and lubricant called Stabilant 22 is currently on the market. This chemical, which you apply to electrical contacts, greatly enhances the connection and lubricates the contact point; it is much more effective than conventional contact cleaners or lubricants.

Stabilant 22 is a liquid-polymer semiconductor; it behaves like liquid metal and conducts electricity in the presence of an electric current. The substance also fills the air gaps between the mating surfaces of two items that are in contact, making the surface area of the contact larger and also keeping out oxygen and other contaminants that can corrode the contact point.

This chemical is available in several forms. Stabilant 22 is the concentrated version, whereas Stabilant 22a is a version diluted with isopropanol in a 4:1 ratio. An even more diluted 8:1-ratio version is sold in many high-end stereo and audio shops under the name Tweek. Just 15ml of Stabilant 22a sells for about $40; a liter of the concentrate costs about $4,000!

As you can plainly see, Stabilant 22 is fairly expensive, but little is required in an application, and nothing else has been found to be as effective in preserving electrical contacts. (NASA uses the chemical on spacecraft electronics.) An application of Stabilant can provide protection for up to 16 years, according to its manufacturer, D.W. Electrochemicals. You will find the company's address and phone number in the Vendor List on the CD.

Stabilant is especially effective on I/O slot connectors, adapter-card edge and pin connectors, disk drive connectors, power-supply connectors, and virtually any connector in the PC. In addition to enhancing the contact and preventing corrosion, an application of Stabilant lubricates the contacts, making insertion and removal of the connector easier.

Dusters

Compressed gas often is used as an aid in system cleaning. You use the compressed gas as a blower to remove dust and debris from a system or component. Originally, these dusters used CFCs (chlorofluorocarbons) such as Freon, whereas modern dusters use either HFCs (hydrofluorocarbons such as difluoroethane) or carbon dioxide, neither of which is known to damage the ozone layer. Be careful when you use these devices because some of them can generate a static charge when the compressed gas leaves the nozzle of the can. Be sure you are using the type approved for cleaning or dusting off computer equipment, and consider wearing a static grounding strap as a precaution. The type of compressed-air cans used for cleaning camera equipment can sometimes differ from the type used for cleaning static-sensitive computer components.

When using these compressed air products, be sure you hold the can upright so that only gas is ejected from the nozzle. If you tip the can, the raw propellant will come out as a cold liquid, which not only is wasteful but can damage or discolor plastics. You should use compressed gas only on equipment that is powered off, to minimize any chance of damage through short circuits.

Closely related to compressed-air products are chemical-freeze sprays. These sprays are used to quickly cool down a suspected failing component, which often temporarily restores it to normal operation. These substances are not used to repair a device, but to confirm that you have found a failed device. Often, a component's failure is heat-related, and cooling it temporarily restores it to normal operation. If the circuit begins operating normally, the device you are cooling is the suspect device.

Vacuum Cleaners

Some people prefer to use a vacuum cleaner instead of canned gas dusters for cleaning a system. Canned gas is usually better for cleaning in small areas. A vacuum cleaner is more useful when you are cleaning a system loaded with dust and dirt. You can use the vacuum cleaner to suck out the dust and debris instead of simply blowing it around on the other components, which sometimes happens with canned air. For onsite servicing (when you are going to the location of the equipment instead of the equipment coming to you), canned air is easier to carry in a toolkit than a small vacuum cleaner. Tiny vacuum cleaners also are available for system cleaning. These small units are easy to carry and can serve as an alternative to compressed air cans.

Some special vacuum cleaners are specifically designed for use on and around electronic components; they are designed to minimize electrostatic discharge (ESD) while in use. If you are using a regular vacuum cleaner and not one specifically designed with ESD protection, you should take precautions, such as wearing a grounding wrist strap. Also, if the cleaner has a metal nozzle, be careful not to touch it to the circuit boards or components you are cleaning.

Brushes and Swabs

You can use a small makeup, photographic, or paint brush to carefully loosen the accumulated dirt and dust inside a PC before spraying it with canned air or using the vacuum cleaner. Be careful about generating static electricity, however. In most cases, you should not use a brush directly on circuit boards, but only on the case interior and other parts, such as fan blades, air vents, and keyboards. Wear a grounded wrist strap if you are brushing on or near any circuit boards, and brush slowly and lightly to prevent static discharges from occurring.

Use cleaning swabs to wipe off electrical contacts and connectors, disk drive heads, and other sensitive areas. The swabs should be made of foam or synthetic chamois material that does not leave lint or dust residue. Unfortunately, proper foam or chamois cleaning swabs are more expensive than typical cotton swabs. Do not use cotton swabs because they leave cotton fibers on everything they touch. Cotton fibers are conductive in some situations and can remain on drive heads, which can scratch disks. Foam or chamois swabs can be purchased at most electronics supply stores.

Caution

One item to avoid is an eraser for cleaning contacts. Many people (including me) have recommended using a soft pencil-type eraser for cleaning circuit-board contacts. Testing has proven this to be bad advice for several reasons. One reason is that any such abrasive wiping on electrical contacts generates friction and an ESD. This ESD can be damaging to boards and components, especially the newer low-voltage devices. These devices are especially static sensitive, and cleaning the contacts without a proper liquid solution is not recommended. Also, the eraser will wear off the gold coating on many contacts, exposing the tin contact underneath, which rapidly corrodes when exposed to air.

Some companies sell pre-moistened contact cleaning pads soaked in a proper contact cleaner and lubricant. These pads are safe to wipe on conductors and contacts with no likelihood of ESD damage or abrasion of the gold plating.

Silicone Lubricants

You can use a silicone lubricant such as WD-40 to lubricate the door mechanisms on floppy disk drives and any other part of the system that might require clean, non-oily lubrication. Other items you can lubricate are the disk-drive–head slider rails and even printer-head slider rails, to provide smoother operation.

Using silicone instead of conventional oils is important because silicone does not gum up and collect dust and other debris. Always use the silicone sparingly. Do not spray it anywhere near the equipment because it tends to migrate and will end up where it doesn't belong (such as on drive heads). Instead, apply a small amount to a toothpick or foam swab and dab the silicone lubricant on the components where needed. You can use a lint-free cleaning stick soaked in silicone to lubricate the metal print-head rails in a printer.

Obtaining Required Tools and Accessories

You can obtain most of the cleaning chemicals and tools discussed in this chapter from an electronics supply house, or even your local Radio Shack. A company called Chemtronics specializes in chemicals for the computer and electronics industry. These and other companies that supply tools, chemicals, and other computer and electronic cleaning supplies are listed in the Vendor List on the CD. With all these items on hand, you should be equipped for most preventive maintenance operations.

Disassembling and Cleaning Procedures

To properly clean your system, you must at least partially disassemble it. Some people go as far as to remove the motherboard. Removing the motherboard results in the best possible access to other areas of the system; but in the interest of saving time, you probably need to disassemble the system only to the point at which the motherboard is completely visible.

To do this, remove all the system's plug-in adapter cards and the disk drives. Complete system disassembly and reassembly procedures are listed in Chapter 23, "Building or Upgrading Systems." Although you can clean the heads of a floppy drive with a cleaning disk without opening the system unit's cover, you probably will want to do more thorough cleaning. In addition to the drive heads, you should clean and lubricate the door mechanism and clean any logic boards and connectors on the drive. This procedure usually requires removing the drive.

Next, do the same thing with the hard disk drives: Clean the logic boards and connectors, and lubricate the grounding strap. To do this, you must remove the hard disk assembly. As a precaution, be sure your data is backed up first.

Reseating Socketed Chips

Another primary preventive maintenance function is to undo the effects of chip creep. As your system heats and cools, it expands and contracts, and the physical expansion and contraction can cause components that are plugged in to sockets to gradually work their way out of those sockets. This process is called *chip creep*. To correct its effects, you must find all socketed components in the system and ensure that they are properly reseated.

In most of today's systems, the memory chips are installed in socketed SIMMs or DIMMs. SIMM/DIMM devices are retained securely in their sockets by a positive latching mechanism and cannot creep out. The memory single inline pin package (SIPP) devices (SIMMs with pins rather than contacts) used in older systems are not retained by a latching mechanism, however, and therefore can creep out of their sockets. Standard socketed memory chips are prime candidates for chip creep; most other logic components are soldered in. On an older system, you also might find the ROM chips, a math coprocessor, and even the main system processor in sockets. Newer systems place the CPU in a ZIF socket, which has a lever that releases the grip of the socket on the chip. In most cases, very little creep occurs with a ZIF socket. However, sometimes a connection oxidizes and simply removing and re-inserting the processor wipes the contact clean and restores normal operation. In most current systems, the memory (in SIMMs or DIMMs) and the processor are the only components you find in sockets; all others are soldered in.

Exceptions, however, can exist. A socketed component in one system might not be socketed in another—even if both are from the same manufacturer. Sometimes this difference results from a parts-availability problem when the boards are manufactured. Rather than halt the assembly line when a part is not available, the manufacturer adds a socket instead of the component. When the component becomes available, it is plugged in and the board is finished.

To ensure that all components are fully seated in their sockets, place your hand on the underside of the board and then apply downward pressure with the thumb of your other hand (from the top) on the chip to be seated. For larger chips, seat the chip carefully in the socket, and press separately on each end of the chip with your thumb to make sure the chip is fully seated. (The processor and math coprocessor chips can usually be seated in this manner.) In most cases, you should hear a crunching sound as the chip makes its way back into the socket. Because of the great force that is sometimes required to reseat the chips, this operation is difficult if you do not remove the board.

For motherboards, forcibly seating chips can be dangerous if you do not directly support the board from the underside with your hand. Too much pressure on the board can cause it to bow or bend in the chassis, and the pressure can crack it before the chip is fully seated. The plastic standoffs that hold the board up off the metal chassis are spaced too far apart to properly support the board under this kind of stress. Try this operation only if you can remove and support the board adequately from underneath.

You might be surprised to know that, even if you fully seat a chip, it might need reseating again within a year. The creep usually is noticeable within a year or less.

Cleaning Boards

After reseating any socketed devices that might have crept out of their sockets, the next step is to clean the boards and all connectors in the system. For this step, use the cleaning solutions and the lint-free swabs mentioned earlier.

First, clean the dust and debris off the board and then clean any connectors on the board. To clean the boards, using a vacuum cleaner designed for electronic assemblies and circuit boards or a duster can of compressed gas is usually best. The dusters are especially effective at blasting any dust and dirt off the boards.

Also, blow any dust out of the power supply, especially around the fan intake and exhaust areas. You do not need to disassemble the power supply to do this; simply use a duster can and blast the compressed air into the supply through the fan exhaust port. This will blow the dust out of the supply and clean off the fan blades and grill, which will help with system airflow.

Caution

Be careful with ESD, which can cause damage when you are cleaning electronic components. Take extra precautions in the dead of winter or in extremely dry, high-static environments. You can apply antistatic sprays and treatments to the work area to reduce the likelihood of ESD damage.

An antistatic wrist-grounding strap is recommended (refer to Figure 24.5 earlier in this chapter). This should be connected to a ground on the card or board you are wiping. This strap ensures that no electrical discharge occurs between you and the board. An alternative method is to keep a finger or thumb on the ground of the motherboard or card as you wipe it off.

Cleaning Connectors and Contacts

Cleaning the connectors and contacts in a system promotes reliable connections between devices. On a motherboard, you should clean the slot connectors, power supply connectors, keyboard and mouse connectors, and speaker connector. For most plug-in cards, you should clean the edge connectors that plug in to slots on the motherboard and any other connectors, such as external ones mounted on the card bracket.

Submerge the lint-free swabs in the liquid cleaning solution. If you are using the spray, hold the swab away from the system and spray a small amount on the foam end until the solution starts to drip.

Then, use the soaked foam swab to wipe the connectors on the boards. Presoaked wipes are the easiest to use—simply wipe them along the contacts to remove any accumulated dirt and leave a protective coating behind.

On the motherboard, pay special attention to the slot connectors. Be liberal with the liquid; resoak the foam swab repeatedly, and vigorously clean the connectors. Don't worry if some of the liquid drips on the surface of the motherboard. These solutions are entirely safe for the whole board and will not damage the components.

Use the solution to wash the dirt off the gold contacts in the slot connectors, and then clean any other connectors on the board. Clean the keyboard and mouse connectors, the grounding positions where screws ground the board to the system chassis, the power-supply connectors, the speaker connectors, and the battery connectors.

If you are cleaning a plug-in board, pay special attention to the edge connector that mates with the slot connector on the motherboard. When people handle plug-in cards, they often touch the gold contacts on these connectors. Touching the gold contacts coats them with oils and debris, which prevents proper contact with the slot connector when the board is installed. Make sure these gold contacts are free of all finger oils and residue. It is a good idea to use one of the contact cleaners that has a conductive lubricant, which makes it easier to push the adapter into the slot and also protects the contacts from corrosion.

You also should use the swab and solution to clean the ends of ribbon cables or other types of cables or connectors in a system. Clean the floppy drive cables and connectors, the hard disk cables and connectors, and any others you find. Don't forget to clean the edge connectors that are on the disk drive logic boards, as well as the power connectors to the drives.

Cleaning the Keyboard and Mouse

Keyboards and mice are notorious for picking up dirt and garbage. If you ever open up an older keyboard, you will be amazed at the junk you find in there.

To prevent problems, you should periodically clean the keyboard with a vacuum cleaner. An alternative method is to turn the keyboard upside down and shoot it with a can of compressed air. This blows out the dirt and debris that has accumulated inside the keyboard and possibly prevents future problems with sticking keys or dirty keyswitches.

If a particular key is stuck or making intermittent contact, you can soak or spray that switch with contact cleaner. The best way to do this is to first remove the keycap and then spray the cleaner into the switch. This usually does not require complete disassembly of the keyboard. Periodic vacuuming or compressed gas cleaning prevents more serious problems with sticking keys and keyswitches.

Most mice are easy to clean. In most cases, a twist-off locking retainer keeps the mouse ball retained in the body of the mouse. By removing the retainer, the ball drops out. After removing the ball, you should clean it with one of the electronic cleaners. I recommend a pure cleaner instead of a contact cleaner with lubricant because you do not want any lubricant on the mouse ball. Then, wipe off the rollers in the body of the mouse with the cleaner and some swabs.

Periodic cleaning of a mouse in this manner eliminates or prevents skipping or erratic movement. I also recommend a mouse pad for most ball-type mice because the pad prevents the mouse ball from picking up debris from your desk.

Other pointing devices requiring little or no maintenance are the IBM-designed TrackPoint and similar systems introduced by other manufacturers, such as the Glidepoint by Alps. These devices are totally sealed and use pressure transducers to control pointer movement. Optical mice that don't use a ball or roller mechanism also require little or no maintenance. Because they are sealed, cleaning need only be performed externally and is as simple as wiping the device off with a mild cleaning solution to remove oils and other deposits that have accumulated from handling them.

Hard Disk Maintenance

Certain preventive maintenance procedures protect your data and ensure that your hard disk works efficiently. Some of these procedures actually minimize wear and tear on your drive, which prolongs its life. Additionally, a high level of data protection can be implemented by performing some simple commands periodically. These commands provide methods for backing up (and possibly later restoring) critical areas of the hard disk that, if damaged, would disable access to all your files.

Defragmenting Files

Over time, as you delete and save files to a hard disk, the files become fragmented. This means they are split into many noncontiguous areas on the disk. One of the best ways to protect both your hard disk and the data on it is to periodically defragment the files on the disk. This serves two purposes. One is that by ensuring that all the files are stored in contiguous sectors on the disk, head movement and drive wear and tear is minimized. This has the added benefit of improving the speed at which the drive retrieves files by reducing the head thrashing that occurs every time it accesses a fragmented file.

The second major benefit, and in my estimation the more important of the two, is that in the case of a disaster in which the FATs and root directory are severely damaged, the data on the drive can usually be recovered easily if the files are contiguous. On the other hand, if the files are split up in many pieces across the drive, figuring out which pieces belong to which files is virtually impossible without an intact FAT and directory system. For the purposes of data integrity and protection, I recommend defragmenting your hard disk drives on a monthly basis.

The three main functions in most defragmentation programs are as follows:

- File defragmentation
- File packing (free space consolidation)
- File sorting

Defragmentation is the basic function, but most other programs also add file packing. Packing the files is optional on some programs because it usually takes additional time to perform. This function packs the files at the beginning of the disk so all free space is consolidated at the end of the disk. This feature minimizes future file fragmentation by eliminating any empty holes on the disk. Because all free space is consolidated into one large area, any new files written to the disk are capable of being written in a contiguous manner with no fragmentation.

The last function, file sorting (sometimes called disk optimizing), is not usually necessary and is performed as an option by many defragmenting programs. This function adds a tremendous amount of time to the operation and has little or no effect on the speed at which information is accessed. It can be somewhat beneficial for disaster recovery purposes because you will have an idea of which files came before or after other files if a disaster occurs. Not all defragmenting programs offer file sorting, and the extra time it takes is probably not worth any benefits you will receive. Other programs can sort the order that files are listed in directories, which is a quick and easy operation compared to sorting the file ordering the disk.

Windows 9x/Me/2000 include a disk defragmentation program with the operating system, which you can use on any file system the OS supports. For older DOS, Windows 3.x, and some versions of NT, you must purchase a third-party defragmentation program. Norton Utilities includes a disk defragmenter, as do many other utility packages. If you elect to use a third-party product on a Windows 9x/Me/2000 system, be certain that it supports the file system you use on your drives. Running a FAT16 defragmentation program on a FAT32 drive can cause severe problems. An excellent third-party defrag program that works on all systems is VOPT by Golden Bow. See the Vendor List on the CD for more information on these programs.

Before you defragment your disks, you should run a disk repair program, such as Windows 9x's ScanDisk or Norton Disk Doctor, even if you are not experiencing any problems. This ensures that your drives are in good working order before you begin the defragmentation process.

Windows 98/Millennium Maintenance Wizard

Windows 98 and Millennium include a Task Scheduler program that enables you to schedule programs for automatic execution at specified times. The Maintenance Wizard walks you through the steps of scheduling regular disk defragmentations, disk error scans, and deletions of unnecessary files. You can schedule these processes to execute during non-working hours, so regular system activities are not disturbed.

Virus Checking

Viruses are a danger to any system, and making scans with an antivirus program a regular part of your preventive maintenance program is a good idea. Although both Microsoft and IBM provide antivirus software in MS- and PC-DOS, respectively, if you run Windows 9x or Windows NT, you must obtain a third-party program to scan your system. Many aftermarket utility packages are available that scan for and remove viruses. No matter which of these programs you use, you should perform a scan for virus programs periodically, especially before making hard disk backups. This helps ensure that you catch any potential virus problem before it spreads and becomes a major catastrophe. In addition, selecting an antivirus product from a vendor that provides regular updates to the program's virus signatures is important. The signatures determine which viruses the software can detect and cure, and because new viruses are constantly being introduced, these updates are essential.

Passive Preventive Maintenance Procedures

Passive preventive maintenance involves taking care of the system by providing the best possible environment—both physical and electrical—for the system. Physical concerns are conditions such as ambient temperature, thermal stress from power cycling, dust and smoke contamination, and disturbances such as shock and vibration. Electrical concerns are items such as ESD, power-line noise, and radio-frequency interference. Each of these environmental concerns is discussed in the following sections.

Examining the Operating Environment

Oddly enough, one of the most overlooked aspects of microcomputer preventive maintenance is protecting the hardware—and the sizable financial investment it represents—from environmental abuse. Computers are relatively forgiving, and they are generally safe in an environment that is comfortable for people. Computers, however, are often treated with no more respect than desktop calculators. The result of this type of abuse is many system failures.

Before you set up a new PC, prepare a proper location for it that is free of airborne contaminants such as smoke or other pollution. Do not place your system in front of a window; the computer should not be exposed to direct sunlight or temperature variations. The environmental temperature should be as constant as possible. Power should be provided through properly grounded outlets and should be stable and free from electrical noise and interference. Keep your system away from radio transmitters or other sources of radio frequency energy.

Note

I also don't recommend using computer desks that place the system unit in a sealed cabinet; this is a good way to promote overheating.

Heating and Cooling

Thermal expansion and contraction from ambient temperature changes place stress on a computer system. Therefore, keeping the temperature in your office or room relatively constant is important to the successful operation of your computer system.

Temperature variations can lead to serious problems. You might encounter excessive chip creep, for example. If extreme variations occur over a short period, signal traces on circuit boards can crack and separate, solder joints can break, and contacts in the system can undergo accelerated corrosion. Solid-state components such as chips can be damaged also, and a host of other problems can develop.

Temperature variations can wreak havoc with hard disk drives, too. On some drives, writing to a disk at different ambient temperatures can cause data to be written at different locations relative to the track centers. This can cause read and write problems at a later time.

To ensure that your system operates in the correct ambient temperature, you must first determine your system's specified functional range. Most manufacturers provide data about the correct operating temperature range for their systems. Two temperature specifications might be available, one indicating allowable temperatures during operation and another indicating allowable temperatures under non-operating conditions. IBM, for example, indicates the following temperature ranges as acceptable for most of its systems:

> System on: 60–90° Fahrenheit
>
> System off: 50–110° Fahrenheit

For the safety of the disk and the data it contains, avoid rapid changes in ambient temperatures. If rapid temperature changes occur—for example, when a new drive is shipped to a location during the winter and then brought indoors—let the drive acclimate to room temperature before turning it on. In extreme cases, condensation can form on the platters inside the drive head-disk assembly (HDA), which is disastrous for the drive if you turn it on before the condensation has a chance to evaporate. Most drive manufacturers specify a timetable to use as a guide in acclimating a drive to room temperature before operating it. You usually must wait several hours to a day before a drive is ready to use after it has been shipped or stored in a cold environment. Manufacturers normally advise that you leave the drive in its packing until it is acclimated. Removing the drive from a shipping carton when extremely cold increases the likelihood of condensation forming as the drive warms up.

Most office environments provide a stable temperature in which to operate a computer system, but some do not. Be sure to give some consideration to the placement of your equipment.

Power Cycling (On/Off)

As you have just learned, the temperature variations a system encounters greatly stress the system's physical components. The largest temperature variations a system encounters, however, are those that occur during the warmup period right after you turn on the computer. Powering on a cold system subjects it to the greatest possible internal temperature variations. If you want a system to have the longest and most trouble-free life possible, you should limit the temperature variations in its environment. You can limit the extreme temperature cycling in two simple ways during a cold startup: Leave the system off all the time or leave it on all the time. Of these two possibilities, of course, you probably will want to choose the latter option. Leaving the power on is the best way I know to promote system reliability. If your only concern is system longevity, the simple recommendation is to keep the system unit powered on (or off!) continuously. In the real world, however, there are more variables to consider, such as the cost of electricity, the potential fire hazard of unattended running equipment, and other concerns, as well.

If you think about the way light bulbs typically fail, you can begin to understand how thermal cycling can be dangerous. Light bulbs burn out most often when you first turn them on because the filament must endure incredible thermal stress as it changes temperature, in less than one second, from ambient to several thousands of degrees. A bulb that remains on continuously lasts longer than one that is turned on and off repeatedly.

The place where problems are most likely to occur immediately at power-on is in the power supply. The startup current draw for the system during the first few seconds of operation is very high compared to the normal operating-current draw. Because the current must come from the power supply, the supply has an extremely demanding load to carry for the first few seconds of operation, especially if several disk drives must be started. Motors have an extremely high power-on current draw. This demand often overloads a marginal circuit or component in the supply and causes it to burn or break with a "snap." I have seen several power supplies die the instant a system was powered up. To enable your equipment to have the longest possible life, try to keep the temperature of solid-state components relatively constant, and limit the number of startups on the power supply. The only way I know to do this is to leave the system on.

Although it sounds like I am telling you to leave all your computer equipment on 24 hours a day, 7 days a week, I no longer recommend this type of operation. A couple of concerns have tempered my urge to leave everything running continuously. One is that an unattended system that is powered on represents a fire hazard. I have seen monitors catch fire after internally shorting and systems whose cooling fans have frozen, causing the power supply and the entire system to overheat. I do not leave any system running in an unattended building. Another problem is wasted electrical power. Many companies have adopted austerity programs that involve turning off lights and other items when not in use. The power consumption of some of today's high-powered systems and accessories is not trivial. Also, an unattended operating system is more of a security risk than one that is powered off and locked.

Realities—such as the fire hazard of unattended systems running during night or weekend hours, security problems, and power-consumption issues—might prevent you from leaving your system on all the time. Therefore, you must compromise. Power on the system only one time daily. Don't power the system on and off several times every day. This good advice is often ignored, especially when several users share systems. Each user powers on the system to perform work on the PC and then powers off the system. These systems tend to have many more problems with component failures.

If you are in a building with a programmable thermostat, you have another reason to be concerned about temperatures and disk drives. Some buildings have thermostats programmed to turn off the heat overnight or over the weekend. These thermostats are programmed also to quickly raise the temperature just before business hours every day. In Chicago, for example, outside temperatures in the winter can dip to –20° (excluding the windchill factor). An office building's interior temperature can drop to as low as 50° during the weekend. When you arrive Monday morning, the heat has been on for only an hour or so, but the hard disk platters might not yet have reached even 60° when you turn on the system. During the first 20 minutes of operation, the disk platters rapidly rise in temperature to 120° or more. If you have an inexpensive stepper motor hard disk and begin writing to the disk at these low temperatures, you are setting yourself up for trouble.

Tip

If you do not leave a system on continuously, at least give it 15 minutes or more to warm up after a cold start before writing to the hard disk. This practice does wonders for the reliability of the data on your disk.

If you do leave your system on for long periods of time, make sure the screen is blank or displays a random image if the system is not in use. The phosphor on the picture tube can burn if a stationary image is left onscreen continuously. Higher-persistence phosphor monochrome screens are most susceptible, and the color displays with low-persistence phosphors are the least susceptible. Most of the monitors used with today's PCs will not show the effect of a screen burn. If you ever have seen a monochrome display with the image of some program permanently burned in—even with the display off—you know what I mean. Look at the monitors that display flight information at the airport; they usually show some of the effects of phosphor burn.

Most modern displays that have power-saving features can automatically enter a standby mode on command by the system. If your system has these power-saving functions, enable them because they help reduce energy costs and preserve the monitor.

Static Electricity

Static electricity or electro-static discharge (ESD) can cause numerous problems within a system. The problems usually appear during the winter months when humidity is low or in extremely dry climates where the humidity is low year-round. In these cases, you might need to take special precautions to ensure that your PC is not damaged. See the section, "ESD Protection Tools," earlier in this chapter, as well as Chapter 21, "Power Supply and Chassis/Case," and Chapter 23, "Building or Upgrading Systems," for more information on ESD.

Static discharges outside a system-unit chassis are rarely a source of permanent problems within the system. Usually, the worst possible effect of a static discharge to the case, keyboard, or even a location near the computer is a parity check (memory) error or a system lockup. In some cases, I have been able to cause parity checks or system lockups by simply walking past a PC. Most static-sensitivity problems are caused by improper grounding of the system power. Be sure you always use a three-prong, grounded power cord plugged in to a properly grounded outlet. If you are unsure about the outlet, you can buy an outlet tester, such as those described earlier in this chapter, at most electronics supply or hardware stores for only a few dollars.

Whenever you open a system unit or handle circuits removed from the system, you must be much more careful with static. You can permanently damage a component with a static discharge if the charge is not routed to a ground. I usually recommend handling boards and adapters first by a grounding point such as the bracket to minimize the potential for static damage.

An easy way to prevent static problems is with good power-line grounding, which is extremely important for computer equipment. A poorly designed power-line grounding system is one of the primary causes of poor computer design. The best way to prevent static damage is to prevent the static charge from getting into the computer in the first place. The chassis ground in a properly designed system serves as a static guard for the computer and redirects the static charge safely to the ground. For this ground to be complete, therefore, the system must be plugged in to a properly grounded three-wire outlet.

If the static problem is extreme, you can resort to other measures. One is to use a grounded static mat underneath the computer. Touch the mat first before you touch the computer to ensure that any static charges are routed to ground and away from the system unit's internal parts. If problems still persist, you might want to check out the building's electrical ground. I have seen installations that had three-wire outlets that were rendered useless by the building's ungrounded electrical service.

Power-Line Noise

To run properly, a computer system requires a steady supply of clean, noise-free power. In some installations, however, the power line serving the computer also serves heavy equipment, and the voltage variations resulting from the on/off cycling of this equipment can cause problems for the computer. Certain types of equipment on the same power line also can cause voltage spikes—short, transient signals of sometimes 1,000v or more—that can physically damage a computer. Although these spikes are rare, they can be crippling. Even a dedicated electrical circuit used by only a single computer can experience spikes and transients, depending on the quality of the power supplied to the building or circuit.

During the site-preparation phase of a system installation, you should be aware of these factors to ensure a steady supply of clean power:

- If possible, the computer system should be on its own circuit with its own circuit breaker. This setup does not guarantee freedom from interference, but it helps.

- The circuit should be checked for a good, low-resistance ground, proper line voltage, freedom from interference, and freedom from brownouts (voltage dips).

- A three-wire circuit is a must, but some people substitute grounding-plug adapters to adapt a grounded plug to a two-wire socket. This setup is not recommended; the ground is there for a reason.

- Power-line noise problems increase with the resistance of the circuit, which is a function of wire size and length. So, to decrease resistance, avoid extension cords unless absolutely necessary, and then use only heavy-duty extension cords.

- Inevitably, you will want to plug in other equipment later. Plan ahead to avoid the temptation to connect too many items to a single outlet. If possible, provide a separate power circuit for non–computer-related devices.

Air conditioners, coffee makers, copy machines, laser printers, space heaters, vacuum cleaners, and power tools are some of the worst corrupters of a PC system's power. Any of these items can draw an excessive amount of current and wreak havoc with a PC system on the same electrical circuit. I've seen offices in which all the computers begin to crash at about 9:05 a.m. daily, which is when all the coffee makers are turned on!

Also, try to ensure that copy machines and laser printers do not share a circuit with other computer equipment. These devices draw a large amount of power.

Another major problem in some companies is partitioned offices. Many of these partitions are prewired with their own electrical outlets and are plugged in to one another in a sort of power-line daisy-chain, similar to chaining power strips together. I pity the person in the cubicle at the end of the electrical daisy-chain, who is likely to have very erratic power!

As a real-world example of too many devices sharing a single circuit, I can describe several instances in which a personal computer had a repeating parity check problem. All efforts to repair the system had been unsuccessful. The reported error locations from the parity-check message were inconsistent, which normally indicates a problem with power. The problem could have been the power supply in the system unit or the external power supplied from the wall outlet. This problem was solved one day as I stood watching the system. The parity check message was displayed at the same instant that someone two cubicles away turned on a copy machine. Placing the computers on a separate line solved the problem.

By following the guidelines in this section, you can create the proper power environment for your systems and help ensure trouble-free operation.

Radio-Frequency Interference

Radio-frequency interference (RFI) is easily overlooked as a problem factor. The interference is caused by any source of radio transmissions near a computer system. Living next door to a 50,000-watt commercial radio station is one sure way to get RFI problems, but less-powerful transmitters can cause problems, too. I know of many instances in which cordless telephones have caused sporadic random keystrokes to appear, as though an invisible entity were typing on the keyboard. I also have seen RFI cause a system to lock up. Solutions to RFI problems are more difficult to state because every case must be handled differently. Sometimes, simply moving the system eliminates the problem because radio signals can be directional in nature. At other times, you must invest in specially shielded cables for external devices, such as the keyboard and the monitor.

One type of solution to an RFI noise problem with cables is to pass the cable through a toroidal iron core, a doughnut-shaped piece of iron placed around a cable to suppress both the reception and transmission of electromagnetic interference (EMI). Many monitors include a toroid on the cable that connects to the computer. If you can isolate an RFI noise problem in a particular cable, you often can solve the problem by passing the cable through a toroidal core. Because the cable must pass through the center hole of the core, it often is difficult, if not impossible, to add a toroid to a cable that already has end connectors installed.

Radio Shack sells a special snap-together toroid designed specifically to be added to cables already in use. This toroid looks like a thick-walled tube that has been sliced in half. You simply lay the cable in the center of one of the halves, and snap the other half over the first. This type of construction makes adding the noise-suppression features of a toroid to virtually any existing cable easy.

The best, if not the easiest, way to eliminate an RFI problem is to correct it at the source. It is unlikely that you'll be able to convince the commercial radio station near your office to shut down, but if you are dealing with a small radio transmitter that is generating RFI, sometimes you can add a filter to the transmitter that suppresses spurious emissions. Unfortunately, problems sometimes persist until the transmitter is either switched off or moved some distance away from the affected computer.

Dust and Pollutants

Dirt, smoke, dust, and other pollutants are bad for your system. The power-supply fan carries airborne particles through your system, and they collect inside. If your system is used in an extremely harsh environment, you might want to investigate some of the industrial systems on the market designed for harsh conditions.

Many companies make special hardened versions of their systems for harsh environments. Industrial systems usually use a different cooling system from the one used in regular PCs. A large cooling fan is used to pressurize the case rather than depressurize it. The air pumped into the case passes through a filter unit that must be cleaned and changed periodically. The system is pressurized so that no contaminated air can flow into it; air flows only outward. The only way air can enter is through the fan and filter system.

These systems also might have special keyboards impervious to liquids and dirt. Some flat-membrane keyboards are difficult to type on, but are extremely rugged; others resemble the standard types of keyboards but have a thin, plastic membrane that covers all the keys. You can add this membrane to normal types of keyboards to seal them from the environment.

A new breed of humidifier can cause problems with computer equipment. This type of humidifier uses ultrasonics to generate a mist of water sprayed into the air. The extra humidity helps cure problems with static electricity resulting from a dry climate, but the airborne water contaminants can cause many problems. If you use one of these systems, you might notice a white, ash-like deposit forming on components. The deposit is the result of abrasive and corrosive minerals suspended in the vaporized water. If these deposits collect on the system components, they can cause all kinds of problems. The only safe way to run one of these ultrasonic humidifiers is to use distilled water. If you use a humidifier, be sure it does not generate these deposits.

If you do your best to keep the environment for your computer equipment clean, your system will run better and last longer. Also, you will not have to open up your unit as often for complete preventive maintenance cleaning.

Basic Troubleshooting Guidelines

This section lists basic and general system troubleshooting procedures and guidelines. For specific procedures for troubleshooting a component in the system, see the chapter or section dedicated to that part of the PC. Use Table 24.4 as a quick reference.

Table 24.4   Troubleshooting Your PC

Topic	Found on...
Processor diagnostics	p. 191
Resource conflicts	p. 328
BIOS error messages	p. 398
Memory errors	p. 455
SCSI configuration	p. 539
Floppy drives	p. 631
Tape drives	p. 684
Optical drives (DVD, CD-RW, and so on)	p. 776
Hard disk drives	p. 802
Monitor and video card	p. 875
Audio	p. 913
Serial ports	p. 931
Parallel ports	p. 939
Keyboards	p. 972
Mice	p. 981
Modems	p. 1048
Networks	p. 1100
Power supplies	p. 1144
Printers	Printers chapter on the CD

Before starting any system troubleshooting, a few basic steps should be performed to ensure a consistent starting point and to enable isolating the failed component:

1. Turn off the system and any peripheral devices. Disconnect all external peripherals from the system, except for the keyboard and video display.

2. Make sure the system is plugged in to a properly grounded power outlet.

3. Make sure the keyboard and video displays are connected to the system. Turn on the video display, and turn up the brightness and contrast controls to at least two-thirds of the maximum. Some displays have onscreen controls that might not be intuitive. Consult the display

documentation for more information on how to adjust these settings. If you can't get any video display but the system seems to be working, try moving the card to a different slot (not possible with AGP adapters) or try a different video card or monitor.

4. To enable the system to boot from a hard disk, make sure no floppy disk is in the floppy drive. Or put a known good bootable floppy with DOS or diagnostics on it in the floppy drive for testing.

5. Turn on the system. Observe the power supply, chassis fans (if any), and lights on either the system front panel or power supply. If the fans don't spin and the lights don't light, the power supply or motherboard might be defective.

6. Observe the power on self test (POST). If no errors are detected, the system beeps once and boots up. Errors that display onscreen (*nonfatal* errors) and that do not lock up the system display a text message that varies according to BIOS type and version. Record any errors that occur and refer to the CD accompanying this book for a list of BIOS error codes for more information on any specific codes you see. Errors that lock up the system (*fatal* errors) are indicated by a series of audible beeps. Refer to the CD for a list of beep error codes.

7. Confirm that the operating system loads successfully.

Note

The CD accompanying this book contains an exhaustive listing of BIOS error codes, error messages, and beep codes for BIOSes from Phoenix, AMI, Award, Microid Research, and IBM.

Problems During the POST

Problems that occur during the POST are usually caused by incorrect hardware configuration or installation. Actual hardware failure is a far less-frequent cause. If you have a POST error, check the following:

1. Are all cables correctly connected and secured?

2. Are the configuration settings correct in Setup for the devices you have installed? In particular, ensure the processor, memory, and hard drive settings are correct.

3. Are all drivers properly installed?

4. Are switches and jumpers on the baseboard correct, if changed from the default settings?

5. Are all resource settings on add-in boards and peripheral devices set so that no conflicts exist—for example, two add-in boards sharing the same interrupt?

6. Is the power supply set to the proper input voltage (110/220v)?

7. Are adapter boards and disk drives installed correctly?

8. Is a keyboard attached?

9. Is a bootable hard disk (properly partitioned and formatted) installed?

10. Does the BIOS support the drive you have installed, and if so, are the parameters entered correctly?

11. Is a bootable floppy disk installed in drive A:?

12. Are all memory SIMMs or DIMMs installed correctly? Try reseating them.

13. Is the operating system properly installed?

Hardware Problems After Booting

If problems occur after the system has been running, and without having made any hardware or software changes, a hardware fault possibly has occurred. Here is a list of items to check in that case:

1. Try reinstalling the software that has crashed or refuses to run.

2. Try clearing CMOS RAM and running Setup.

3. Check for loose cables, a marginal power supply, or other random component failures.

4. A transient voltage spike, power outage, or brownout might have occurred. Symptoms of voltage spikes include a flickering video display, unexpected system reboots, and the system not responding to user commands. Reload the software and try again.

5. Try reseating the memory modules (SIMMs, DIMMs, or RIMMs).

Problems Running Software

Problems running application software (especially new software) are usually caused by or related to the software itself, or are due to the fact that the software is incompatible with the system. Here is a list of items to check in that case:

1. Does the system meet the minimum hardware requirements for the software? Check the software documentation to be sure.

2. Check to see that the software is correctly installed. Reinstall if necessary.

3. Check to see that the latest drivers are installed.

4. Scan the system for viruses using the latest antivirus software.

Problems with Adapter Cards

Problems related to add-in boards are usually related to improper board installation or resource (interrupt, DMA, or I/O address) conflicts. Chapter 4, "Motherboards and Buses," has a detailed discussion of these system resources, what they are, how to configure them, and how to troubleshoot them. Also be sure to check drivers for the latest versions and ensure that the card is compatible with your system and the operating system version you are using.

Sometimes adapter cards can be picky about which slot they are running in. Despite the fact that, technically, a PCI or ISA adapter should be able to run in any of the slots, minor timing or signal variations sometimes occur from slot to slot. I have found on numerous occasions that simply moving a card from one slot to another can make a failing card begin to work properly. Sometimes moving a card works just by the inadvertent cleaning (wiping) of the contacts that takes place when removing and reinstalling the card, but in other cases I can duplicate the problem by inserting the card back into its original slot. When all else fails, try moving the cards around!

Caution

Note that PCI cards become slot specific after their drivers are installed. By this I mean that if you move the card to another slot, the plug-and-play resource manager sees it as if you have removed one card and installed a new one. You therefore must install the drivers all over again for that card. Don't move a PCI card to a different slot unless you are prepared with all the drivers at hand to perform the driver installation. ISA cards don't share this quirk because the system is not aware of which slot an ISA card is in.

One common problem I've seen cropping up lately is with people installing newer PCI video cards in older systems with PCI slots. The PCI bus has gone through several revisions; most older slots are "2.0" type, and most newer cards need "2.1" or later PCI slots. The version of PCI your system has is dictated by the motherboard chipset. If you install a newer video or other PCI card that requires 2.1 slots in a system with 2.0 slots, often the system won't boot up or operate at all.

If you check the chipset reference information in Chapter 4, you might be able to determine which revision of PCI slots your motherboard has by knowing which chipset it has. If this is your problem, the only solution is to change either the card or motherboard so that they are both compatible.

CHAPTER 25

File Systems and Data Recovery

FAT Disk Structures

Physically, it is the hard disks and other media that provide the basic technology for storing data. Logically, however, it is the file system that provides the hierarchical structure of volumes and directories in which you store individual files and the organizational model that enables the system to locate data anywhere on a given disk or drive. File systems typically are an integrated part of an operating system (OS), and many of the newer OSes provide support for several file systems from which you can choose.

The most commonly used file systems today are based on a file allocation table (FAT), which keeps track of the data stored in each cluster on a disk. Several varieties of the FAT system exist, called FAT12, FAT16, and FAT32—all of which are differentiated by the number of digits used in the allocation table numbers. In other words, FAT16 uses 16-bit numbers to keep track of data clusters; FAT32 uses 32-bit numbers, and so on. The various FAT systems are used as follows:

- *FAT12.* Used on all volumes smaller than 16MB (for example, floppies)
- *FAT16.* Used on volumes from 16MB through 2GB by MS-DOS and most versions of Windows; Windows NT, Windows 2000, and Windows XP support FAT16 volumes as large as 4GB
- *FAT32.* Optionally used on volumes from 512MB through 2TB

FAT12 and FAT16 are the file systems originally used by DOS and Windows and are supported by virtually every other PC operating system in use today.

FAT32 is supported by Windows 95B and later versions, including 95C, 98, Me, Windows 2000, and Windows XP (Windows 2000 and Windows XP also support NTFS). Although all PC operating systems I am aware of support at least FAT12 and FAT16, some have support for non-FAT file systems as well. Windows NT introduced the NT File System (NTFS), which is unique to NT-based operating systems, including Windows 2000 and Windows XP, and is not supported by Windows 9x/Me. OS/2 1.2 introduced the High Performance File System (HPFS), which is unique to OS/2, although NT versions 3.x also supported it. Most PC drives or volumes today are formatted under one of the FAT file systems.

This chapter examines these file systems in more detail. Because of the popularity of the FAT file systems, they are emphasized, although the additional capabilities provided by HPFS or NTFS are also discussed.

To manage files on a disk and enable all applications to see a consistent interface to the file system no matter what type of storage hardware is being used, the operating system creates several structures on the disk. These structures are the same for any OS that supports the FAT file system, including Windows 9x, Windows NT, and Windows 2000. The following list shows all the structures and areas FAT uses to manage a disk, in roughly the same order in which they appear on the media:

- Master and extended partition boot records (sectors)
- Volume boot record
- Root directory
- File allocation tables
- Clusters (allocation units in the data area)
- Diagnostic read-and-write cylinder

All these structures are detailed later in this section. A hard disk has all these disk-management structures, and a floppy disk has all but the master and extended partition boot records and diagnostic cylinder. The volume boot record through data area structures are repeated for each partition or volume on a drive. These structures are created on hard disk drives or other high-capacity media by the

FDISK program included with all operating systems. You can't use FDISK on a floppy disk because floppy disks can't be partitioned. Figure 25.1 is a simple diagram showing the relative locations of these FAT disk-management structures on a 2111MB Western Digital hard disk.

Note

Some removable cartridge drives, such as the SuperDisk (LS-120) and Iomega Zip drive, function like high-capacity floppy disk drives. They lack a master boot record (MBR) and diagnostic cylinder and can't be partitioned like hard disk drives. Other higher-capacity removable drives, such as the Iomega Jaz, can be partitioned like a hard disk drive.

Figure 25.1 shows the placement and arrangement of the file-management structures on a typical drive. This particular example uses a Western Digital Caviar AC12100, but all PC hard drives using the FAT file system would be similar except for the number of cylinders.

Figure 25.1 FAT file-management structures on a typical drive.

Each disk area has a purpose and function. If one of these special areas is damaged, serious consequences can result. Damage to one of these sensitive structures usually causes a domino effect, limiting access to other areas of the disk or causing further problems in using the disk. For example, the OS can't normally access a drive at all if the MBR is corrupted. Therefore, you should understand these data structures well enough to be able to repair them when necessary. Rebuilding these special tables and areas of the disk is essential to the art of data recovery.

Master Partition Boot Record

The first PC OS to support hard disks, DOS 2.0 released in 1983, was also the first to introduce the 16-bit FAT and the capability to partition a drive. *Partitioning* is basically dividing the drive into multiple volumes. One concept easily misunderstood is that all drives that *can* be partitioned *must* be partitioned; that is, you have to partition the drive even if you are going to set it up with only one partition. Another name for a partition is a *logical volume* because the partition shows up as an additional drive letter or volume to the OS.

Although the primary use for partitioning today is to divide a single drive into multiple volumes for use by the same OS, originally it was intended to allow multiple different OSes, each with different file systems, to coexist on a single drive. This multi-OS capability still exists today; however, additional aftermarket utilities often are required to manage and boot from multiple OSes on a single machine.

To use a hard disk with different operating systems, you can create partitions to logically divide the disk. You can, for example, use FDISK to create one or more FAT partitions for use with DOS or Windows 9x and leave the rest of the disk storage area for use by another OS's file system, such as NTFS or Linux. Each of the FAT partitions will appear to the OS as a separate drive letter. The unused or non-FAT partitions will be listed as such in Windows 9x/Me or DOS FDISK and will be ignored by the disk management and other tools in these operating systems.

Note

For more information about creating and formatting partitions, see Chapter 14, "Physical Drive Installation and Configuration."

Information about each of the partitions on the disk is stored in a partition (or volume) boot record at the beginning of each partition. Additionally, a main table lists the partitions embedded in the master partition boot record.

The master partition boot record (or master boot sector) always is located in the first sector of the entire disk (cylinder 0, head 0, sector 1) and consists of the following structures:

- *Master partition table.* Contains a list of the partitions on the disk and the locations of their volume boot records. This table is very small and can contain only four entries at the most. Therefore, to accommodate more partitions, operating systems such as DOS can divide a single extended partition into multiple logical volumes.

- *Master boot code.* A small program that is executed by the system BIOS, the main function of which is to pass control of the system to the partition that has been designated as active (or bootable).

Primary and Extended FAT Partitions

Most OSes are designed to support up to 24 partitions on a single hard disk drive (represented by the drive letters C: through Z:), but the partition table in the master partition boot record can have a maximum of only four entries. To resolve this discrepancy, the FDISK program enables you to create two types of FAT partitions: a primary partition and an extended partition. The first FAT partition you create on a disk should be the *primary*, which is listed in the master partition table and appears to the operating system as a single drive letter.

An *extended* partition is listed in the master partition table like the primary, but it differs in that you can use its disk space to create multiple logical partitions, or volumes. You can create only one extended partition on a single drive, meaning that typically there will never be more than two entries in the master partition table devoted to FAT volumes.

The logical volumes you create in the extended partition appear as separate drive letters to the operating system, but they are not listed in the master partition table. Logical volumes can't be active partitions and are therefore not bootable. You can create up to 23 volumes out of a single extended partition (assuming that you already have created a primary FAT partition, which brings the total to 24).

Each of the logical partitions (or volumes) in an extended partition includes an extended partition table that contains information about that volume. The master partition table's entry for the extended partition contains a reference to the first volume's extended partition table. This table in turn contains a reference detailing the location of the second volume's table. This chain of references continues, linking all the volumes in the extended partition to the master partition table.

Of course, few people have any reason to create 24 FAT partitions on a single disk drive, but the extended partition makes it possible to exceed the four-entry limitation of the master partition table.

Because the master boot record contains the first program the system executes when you boot a PC, it is frequently a target for creators of computer viruses. A virus that infects or destroys the master boot record can make it impossible for the BIOS to find the active partition, thus preventing the operating system from loading. Because the master boot record contains the first program executed by the system, a virus stored there loads before any antivirus code can detect it. To remove a master boot record virus, you must first boot the system from a clean, uninfected disk, such as a floppy disk, bootable CD-ROM, or high-capacity disk, and then run an antivirus program.

Each partition on a disk contains a volume boot record as its first sector, which is listed in the master partition table. With the FDISK utility, you can designate a single partition as active (or bootable). The master partition boot record causes the active partition's volume boot record to receive control whenever the system is started or reset. You can also create additional disk partitions for Novell NetWare, Windows NT/2000's NTFS, OS/2's HPFS, AIX (Unix), XENIX, or other file systems, using disk utilities provided with the operating systems that support them. These partitions are listed in the master partition table, even though they might use different structures within the partition. If you install multiple operating systems on a single system, a boot manager program (which might be included with the operating systems or installed separately) is needed to allow you to select which partition to make active each time you boot the system.

However, you can't access the data stored on these foreign operating system partitions with DOS. In some cases, you can't access FAT partitions using other operating systems either, although OS/2 and Windows NT/2000/XP do support FAT in addition to their own file systems, HPFS (OS/2) and NTFS (NT/2000/XP). You must create at least one partition on a hard disk for it to be accessible by an operating system. Creating a partition adds an entry to the master partition table.

Table 25.1 shows the format of the master boot record and its partition tables. The table lists the fields in each of the master partition table's four entries, the location on the disk where each field begins (the offset), and its length. Some of the fields are stored as *dwords*—four bytes read in reverse order—because of the internal structure of the Intel processors.

Table 25.1   Master Boot Record (Partition Tables)

		Master Partition Table Entry #1
Offset	**Length**	**Description**
1BEh 446	1 byte	Boot indicator byte (80h = active, else 00h)
1BFh 447	1 byte	Starting head (or side) of partition
1C0h 448	16 bits	Starting cylinder (10 bits) and sector (6 bits)
1C2h 450	1 byte	System indicator byte (see Table 25.2)

Table 25.1   Continued

Offset	Length	Description
		Master Partition Table Entry #1
1C3h 451	1 byte	Ending head (or side) of partition
1C4h 452	16 bits	Ending cylinder (10 bits) and sector (6 bits)
1C6h 454	1 dword	Relative sector offset of partition
1CAh 458	1 dword	Total number of sectors in partition
		Partition Table Entry #2
1CEh 462	1 byte	Boot indicator byte (80h = active, else 00h)
1CFh 463	1 byte	Starting head (or side) of partition
1D0h 464	16 bits	Starting cylinder (10 bits) and sector (6 bits)
1D2h 466	1 byte	System indicator byte (see Table 25.2)
1D3h 467	1 byte	Ending head (or side) of partition
1D4h 468	16 bits	Ending cylinder (10 bits) and sector (6 bits)
1D6h 470	1 dword	Relative sector offset of partition
1DAh 474	1 dword	Total number of sectors in partition
		Partition Table Entry #3
1DEh 478	1 byte	Boot indicator byte (80h = active, else 00h)
1DFh 479	1 byte	Starting head (or side) of partition
1E0h 480	16 bits	Starting cylinder (10 bits) and sector (6 bits)
1E2h 482	1 byte	System indicator byte (see Table 25.2)
1E3h 483	1 byte	Ending head (or side) of partition
1E4h 484	16 bits	Ending cylinder (10 bits) and sector (6 bits)
1E6h 486	1 dword	Relative sector offset of partition
1EAh 490	1 dword	Total number of sectors in partition
		Partition Table Entry #4
1EEh 494	1 byte	Boot indicator byte (80h = active, else 00h)
1EFh 495	1 byte	Starting head (or side) of partition
1F0h 496	16 bits	Starting cylinder (10 bits) and sector (6 bits)
1F2h 498	1 byte	System indicator byte (see Table 25.2)
1F3h 499	1 byte	Ending head (or side) of partition
1F4h 500	16 bits	Ending cylinder (10 bits) and sector (6 bits)
1F6h 502	1 dword	Relative sector offset of partition
1FAh 506	1 dword	Total number of sectors in partition
		Signature Bytes
1FEh 510	2 bytes	Boot sector signature (55AAh)

A word equals 2 bytes read in reverse order, and a dword equals two words read in reverse order.

The data in the partition table entries tells the system where each partition starts and ends on the drive, how big it is, whether it is bootable, and which type of file system is contained in the partition. Each entry in the master partition table contains a system indicator byte that identifies the file system type used in the partition referenced by that entry. Table 25.2 shows the standard values and meanings of the system indicator bytes, whereas Table 25.3 lists the nonstandard values.

Table 25.2   Standard System Indicator Byte Values

Value	Partition Type	Translation Mode	Partition Size
00h	None	—	—
01h	Primary FAT12	CHS	0–15MB
04h	Primary FAT16	CHS	16MB–32MB
05h	Extended	CHS	16MB–32MB
06h	Primary FAT16 (also called BigDOS)	CHS	32MB–2GB
07h	NTFS/HPFS/QNX (also Advanced Unix)	All	All
0Ah	OS/2 Bootmanager	All	All
0Bh	Primary FAT32	LBA	512MB–2TB
0Ch	Primary FAT32	LBA	512MB–2TB
0Eh	Primary FAT16	LBA	32MB–2GB
0Fh	Extended	LBA	32MB–2GB

CHS = Cylinder head sector   *LBA = Logical block address*

Table 25.3   Nonstandard System Indicator Byte Values

Value	Partition Type	Value	Partition Type
02h	MS-XENIX Root	75h	IBM PC/IX
03h	MS-XENIX usr	80h	Minix v.1.1–v1.4a
08h	AIX File System Boot	81h	Minix v1.4b-up or Linux
09h	AIX Data	82h	Linux swap file
12h	Compaq diagnostics	83h	Linux native file system
40h	ENIX 80286	93h	Amoeba file system
50h	Ontrack Disk Manager read-only DOS	94h	Amoeba bad block table
51h	Ontrack Disk Manager read/write DOS	B7h	BSDI file system (secondary swap)
52h	CP/M or Microport System V/386	B8h	BSDI file system (secondary file system)
54h	Ontrack Disk Manager non-DOS	DBh	DR Concurrent DOS/CPM-86/CTOS
55h	Micro House EZ-Drive non-DOS	E1h	SpeedStor 12-bit FAT extended
56h	Golden Bow Vfeature Deluxe	E4h	SpeedStor 16-bit FAT extended
61h	Storage Dimensions SpeedStor	F2h	DOS 3.3+secondary
63h	IBM 386/ix or Unix System V/386	F4h	SpeedStor primary
64h	Novell NetWare 286	FEh	LANstep
65h	Novell NetWare 386	FFh	Unix/Xenix Bad Block Table Partition

These values can be useful for somebody trying to manually repair a partition table using a disk editor such as the Diskedit program included with Norton Utilities.

Undocumented FDISK

FDISK is a very powerful program. In DOS 5 and later versions, including Windows 9x/Me, it gained some additional capabilities (Windows NT/2000/XP use the Disk Administrator to perform the functions of FDISK and FORMAT). Unfortunately, these capabilities were never documented in any of the Microsoft documentation for Windows or DOS. The most important undocumented parameter in FDISK is the /MBR (master boot record) parameter, which causes FDISK to rewrite the master boot record code area, leaving the partition table area intact.

The /MBR parameter is tailor-made for eliminating boot-sector virus programs that infect the master partition boot record (cylinder 0, head 0, sector 1) of a hard disk. To use this feature, enter the following:

FDISK /MBR

FDISK then rewrites the boot record code, leaving the partition tables intact. This should not cause any problems on a normally functioning system, but just in case, I recommend backing up the partition table information to floppy disk before trying it. You can do this by using a third-party product such as Norton Utilities.

Be aware that using FDISK with the /MBR switch overwrites the partition tables if the two signature bytes at the end of the sector (55AAh) are damaged. This situation is highly unlikely, however. In fact, if these signature bytes were damaged, you would know; the system would not boot and would act as though there were no partitions at all. If you are unable to access your hard disk after booting from a clean floppy or removable-media drive, your system might be infected with a boot sector virus. You should scan for viruses with an up-to-date antivirus program and use it to guide repair.

Caution

Also note that **FDISK/MBR** should be used **only** on systems using the normal master boot record structure. If a disk-management program such as Disk Manager, EZ-Drive, MaxBlast, Data Lifeguard Tools, or similar is being used to allow your system to access the drive's full capacity, do **not** use **FDISK/MBR** because these programs use a modified MBR for disk access. Using **FDISK/MBR** will wipe out the changes they made to your drive and could make your data inaccessible.

The equivalent Windows NT/2000 Recovery Console feature to DOS/Windows 9x/Me's FDISK/MBR is called FIXMBR. The Recovery Console equivalent to FDISK is DISKPART. For details on the use of these commands, type **HELP** after loading the Recovery Console.

Volume Boot Records

The volume boot record is the first sector on any area of a drive addressed as a partition or volume (or logical DOS disk). On a floppy disk or removable cartridge (such as a Zip disk), for example, this sector is the first one on the disk because DOS recognizes the disk as a volume without the need for partitioning. On a hard disk, the volume boot record or sectors are located as the first sector within any disk area allocated as a nonextended partition, or any area recognizable as a logical volume. Refer to Figure 25.1 for an idea of the physical relationship between this volume boot record and the other data structures on a disk. The volume boot record resembles the master partition boot record in that it contains two elements, which are as follows:

- *Disk parameter block.* Sometimes called the media parameter block, the disk parameter block contains specific information about the volume, such as its size, the number of disk sectors it uses, the size of its clusters, and the volume label name.

■ *Volume boot code.* The program that begins the process of loading the operating system. For DOS and Windows 9x/Me systems, this is the IO.SYS file.

Either the system ROM BIOS for floppy disks or the master partition boot record on a hard disk loads the volume boot record of the active partition on a disk. The program code in the volume boot record is given control of the system; it performs some tests and then attempts to load the first system file (in DOS/Windows this is IO.SYS). The volume boot record, like the master boot record, is transparent to the running system; it is outside the data area of the disk on which files are stored.

Note

Many of the systems today are capable of booting from drives other than standard floppy disk and hard disk drives. In these cases, the system BIOS must specifically support the boot drive. For example, some BIOS products enable you to select an ATAPI CD-ROM as a boot device, in addition to the floppy and hard disk drives.

Other types of removable media, such as Zip cartridges and LS-120 disks, can also be made bootable. When the BIOS properly supports it, an LS-120 drive can replace the existing floppy disk drive as drive A:. Some of the latest systems even support booting from USB drives.

On a FAT partition, you create a volume boot record with the FORMAT command (high-level format) included with DOS and Windows 9x. Hard disks on FAT systems have a volume boot record at the beginning of every DOS logical drive area allocated on the disk, in both the primary and extended partitions. Although all the logical drives contain the program area as well as a data table area, only the program code from the volume boot record in the active partition on a hard disk is executed. The others are read by the operating system files during bootup to obtain their data tables and determine the volume parameters.

The volume boot record contains program code and data. The single data table in this sector is called the media parameter block or disk parameter block. The operating system needs the information this table contains to verify the capacity of the disk volume as well as the location of important structures, such as the FAT. The format of this data is very specific.

Table 25.4 shows the format and layout of the DOS boot record (DBR), including the location of each field within the record (the offset) in both hexadecimal and decimal notation and the length of each field.

Table 25.4   DOS Boot Record Format Offset

Hex	Dec	Field Length	Description
00h	0	3 bytes	Jump instruction to boot program code
03h	3	8 bytes	OEM name and DOS version (IBM 5.0)
0Bh	11	1 word	Bytes/sector (usually 512)
0Dh	13	1 byte	Sectors/cluster (must be a power of 2)
0Eh	14	1 word	Reserved sectors (boot sectors, usually 1)
10h	16	1 byte	FAT copies (usually 2)
11h	17	1 word	Maximum root directory entries (usually 512)
13h	19	1 word	Total sectors (if partition <= 32MB, else 0)
15h	21	1 byte	Media descriptor byte (F8h for hard disks)
16h	22	1 word	Sectors/FAT
18h	24	1 word	Sectors/track

Table 25.4   Continued

Hex	Dec	Field Length	Description
1Ah	26	1 word	Number of heads
1Ch	28	1 dword	Hidden sectors (if partition <= 32MB, 1 word only)
			For DOS 4.0 or Higher Only, Else 00h
20h	32	1 dword	Total sectors (if partition > 32MB, else 0)
24h	36	1 byte	Physical drive no. (00h=floppy, 80h=hard disk)
25h	37	1 byte	Reserved (00h)
26h	38	1 byte	Extended boot record signature (29h)
27h	39	1 dword	Volume serial number (32-bit random number)
2Bh	43	11 bytes	Volume label (NO NAME stored if no label)
36h	54	8 bytes	File system ID (FAT12 or FAT16)
			For All Versions of DOS
3Eh	62	448 bytes	Boot program code
1FEh	510	2 bytes	Signature bytes (55AAh)

A word is 2 bytes read in reverse order, and a dword is two words read in reverse order.

Root Directory

A *directory* is a simple database containing information about the files stored on a FAT partition. Each record in this database is 32 bytes long, with no delimiters or separating characters between the fields or records. A directory stores almost all the information that the operating system knows about a file, including the following:

- *Filename and extension.* The eight-character name and three-character extension of the file. The dot between the name and the extension is implied, but not included in the entry.

Note

To see how Windows 9x/Me extends filenames to allow 255 characters within the 8.3 directory structure, see "VFAT and Long Filenames," later in this chapter.

- *File attribute byte.* The byte containing the flags representing the standard DOS file attributes, using the format shown in Table 25.6.
- *Date/Time of last change.* The date and time that the file was created or last modified.
- *File size.* The size of the file, in bytes.
- *Link to start cluster.* The number of the cluster in the partition where the beginning of the file is stored. To learn more about clusters, see the section "Clusters (Allocation Units)," later in this chapter.

Information does exist that a directory does not contain about a file. This includes where the rest of its clusters in the partition are located and whether the file is contiguous or fragmented. This information is contained in the FAT.

Two basic types of directories exist: the root directory (also called the root folder) and subdirectories (also called folders). Any given volume can have only one root directory. The root directory is always stored on a disk in a fixed location immediately following the two copies of the FAT. Root directories vary in size because of the different types and capacities of disks, but the root directory of a given disk is fixed. Using the FORMAT command creates a root directory that has a fixed length and can't be extended to hold more entries. The root directory entry limits are shown in Table 25.5. Subdirectories are stored as files in the data area of the disk and can grow in size dynamically; therefore, they have no fixed length limits.

Table 25.5   Root Directory Entry Limits

Drive Type	Maximum Root Directory Entries
Hard disk	512
1.44MB floppy disk	224
2.88MB floppy disk	448
Jaz and Zip	512
LS-120	512

Note

One advantage of the FAT32 file system is that the root directory can be located anywhere on the disk, and it can have an unlimited number of entries. FAT32 is discussed in more detail later in this chapter.

Every directory, whether it is the root directory or a subdirectory, is organized in the same way. Entries in the directory database store important information about individual files and how files are named on the disk. The directory information is linked to the FAT by the starting cluster entry. In fact, if no file on a disk were longer than one single cluster, the FAT would be unnecessary. The directory stores all the information needed by DOS to manage the file, with the exception of the list of clusters the file occupies other than the first one. The FAT stores the remaining information about the other clusters the file occupies.

To trace a file on a disk, use a disk editor, such as the DISKEDIT program that comes with the Norton Utilities. Start by looking up the directory entry to get the information about the starting cluster of the file and its size. Then, using the appropriate editor commands, go to the FAT where you can follow the chain of clusters the file occupies until you reach the end of the file. By using the directory and FAT in this manner, you can visit all the clusters on the disk that are occupied by the file. This type of technique can be useful when these entries are corrupted and when you are trying to find missing parts of a file.

FAT directory entries are 32 bytes long and are in the format shown in Table 25.6, which shows the location (or offset) of each field within the entry (in both hexadecimal and decimal form) and the length of each field.

Table 25.6   FAT Directory Format

Offset (Hex)	Offset (Dec)	Field Length	Description
00h	0	8 bytes	Filename
08h	8	3 bytes	File extension
0Bh	11	1 byte	File attributes
0Ch	12	10 bytes	Reserved (00h)
16h	22	1 word	Time of creation

Table 25.6   Continued

Offset (Hex)	Offset (Dec)	Field Length	Description
18h	24	1 word	Date of creation
1Ah	26	1 word	Starting cluster
1Ch	28	1 dword	Size in bytes

Filenames and extensions are left-justified and padded with spaces, (which are represented as ASCII 32h bytes). In other words, if your filename is "AL", it is really stored as "AL------", where the hyphens are spaces. The first byte of the filename indicates the file status for that directory entry, shown in Table 25.7.

Table 25.7   Directory Entry Status Byte (First Byte)

Hex	File Status
00h	Entry never used; entries past this point not searched.
05h	Indicates that the first character of the filename is actually E5h.
E5h	s (lowercase sigma). Indicates that the file has been erased.
2Eh	. (period). Indicates that this entry is a directory. If the second byte is also 2Eh, the cluster field contains the cluster number of the parent directory (0000h, if the parent is the root).

A word is 2 bytes read in reverse order, and a dword is two words read in reverse order.

Table 25.8 describes the FAT directory file attribute byte. Attributes are 1-bit flags that control specific properties of a file, such as whether it is hidden or designated as read-only. Each flag is individually activated (1) or deactivated (0) by changing the bit value. The combination of the eight bit values can be expressed as a single hexadecimal byte value; for example, 07h translates to 00000111, and the 1 bits in positions 3, 2, and 1 indicate the file is system, hidden, and read-only.

Table 25.8   FAT Directory File Attribute Byte

Bit Positions 7 6 5 4 3 2 1 0	Hex Value	Description
0 0 0 0 0 0 0 1	01h	Read-only file
0 0 0 0 0 0 1 0	02h	Hidden file
0 0 0 0 0 1 0 0	04h	System file
0 0 0 0 1 0 0 0	08h	Volume label
0 0 0 1 0 0 0 0	10h	Subdirectory
0 0 1 0 0 0 0 0	20h	Archive (updated since backup)
0 1 0 0 0 0 0 0	40h	Reserved
1 0 0 0 0 0 0 0	80h	Reserved
Examples		
0 0 0 0 0 1 1 1	07h	System, hidden, read-only
0 0 1 0 0 0 0 1	21h	Read-only, archive
0 0 1 1 0 0 1 0	32h	Hidden, subdirectory, archive
0 0 1 0 0 1 1 1	27h	Read-only, hidden, system, archive

File Allocation Tables

The file allocation table (FAT) is a list of numerical entries describing how each cluster in the partition is allocated. The data area of the partition has a single entry in the table for each of its clusters. Sectors in the nondata area of the partition are outside the range of the disk controlled by the FAT. Thus, the sectors that comprise the boot records, FATs, and the root directory are outside the range of sectors controlled by the FAT.

▶▶   See "The Data Area," p. 1331.

The FAT does not manage every data sector specifically, but rather allocates space in groups of sectors called *clusters* or *allocation units*. A cluster is a unit of storage consisting of one or more sectors. The FDISK program determines the size of a cluster during the creation of the partition, based on the partition's size. The smallest space a file can occupy in a partition is one cluster; all files use space in integer (whole) cluster units. If a file is one byte larger than one cluster, two whole clusters are used.

You can think of the FAT as a type of spreadsheet that tracks the allocation of the disk's clusters. Each cell in the spreadsheet corresponds to a single cluster on the disk. The number stored in that cell is a code indicating whether a file uses the cluster, if so, where the next cluster of the file is located. Thus, to determine which clusters a particular file is using, you would start by looking at the first FAT reference in the file's directory entry. When you look up the referenced cluster in the FAT, the table contains a reference to the file's next cluster. Each FAT reference, therefore, points to the next cluster in what is called a FAT *chain*, until you reach the cluster containing the end of the file. Numbers stored in the FAT are hexadecimal numbers that are either 12 or 16 bits long. The 16-bit FAT numbers are easy to follow in a disk sector editor because they take an even 2 bytes of space. The 12-bit numbers are 1 1/2 bytes long, which presents a problem because most disk sector editors show data in byte units. To edit a 12-bit FAT, you must do some hex/binary math to convert the displayed byte units to FAT numbers. Fortunately (unless you are using the DOS DEBUG program), most of the available tools and utility programs have a FAT-editing mode that automatically converts the numbers for you. Most of them also show the FAT numbers in decimal form, which most people find easier to handle. Table 25.9 shows the relationship between the directory and FAT for a given file (assuming that the file is not fragmented).

Table 25.9   Directory and FAT Relationship (File Not Fragmented)

	Directory	
Name	**Starting Cluster**	**Size**
USCONST.TXT	1000	4

	FAT16 File Allocation Table	
FAT Cluster #	**Value**	**Meaning**
00002	0	First cluster available
...	...	...
00999	0	Cluster available
01000	1001	In use, points to next cluster
01001	1002	In use, points to next cluster
01002	1003	In use, points to next cluster
01003	FFFFh	End of file
01004	0	Cluster available

Table 25.9   Continued

	FAT16 File Allocation Table	
FAT Cluster #	**Value**	**Meaning**
01005	0	Cluster available
...	...	...
65526	0	Last cluster available

In this example, the directory entry states that the file starts in cluster number 1000. In the FAT, that cluster has a nonzero value, which indicates it is in use; the specific value indicates where the file using it would continue. In this case, the entry for cluster 1000 is 1001, which means the file continues in cluster 1001. The entry in 1001 points to 1002, and from 1002 the entry points to 1003. The entry for 1003 is FFFFh, which is an indication that the cluster is in use but that the file ends here and uses no additional clusters.

The use of the FAT becomes clearer when you see that files can be fragmented. Let's say that before the USCONST.TXT file was written, another file already occupied clusters 1002 and 1003. If USCONST.TXT was written starting at 1000, it would not have been capable of being completely written before running into the other file. As such, the operating system would skip over the used clusters and continue the file in the next available cluster. The end result is shown in Table 25.10.

Table 25.10   Directory and FAT Relationship (Fragmented File)

	Directory	
Name	**Starting Cluster**	**Size**
PLEDGE.TXT	1002	2
USCONST.TXT	1000	4

	FAT16 File Allocation Table	
FAT Cluster #	**Value**	**Meaning**
00002	0	First cluster available
...	...	...
00999	0	Cluster available
01000	1001	In use, points to next cluster
01001	1004	In use, points to next cluster
01002	1003	In use, points to next cluster
01003	FFFFh	End of file
01004	1005	In use, points to next cluster
01005	FFFFh	End of file
...	...	...
65526	0	Last cluster available

In this example, the PLEDGE.TXT file that was previously written interrupted USCONST.TXT, so those clusters are skipped over, and the pointers in the FAT reflect that. Note that the defrag programs included with DOS and Windows take an example like this and move the files so they are contiguous, one after the other, and update the FAT to indicate the change in cluster use.

The first two entries in the FAT are reserved and contain information about the table itself. All remaining entries correspond to specific clusters on the disk. Most FAT entries consist of a reference to another cluster containing the next part of a particular file. However, some FAT entries contain hexadecimal values with special meanings, as follows:

- *0000h.* Indicates that the cluster is not in use by a file.

- *FFF7h.* Indicates that at least one sector in the cluster is damaged and that it should not be used to store data.

- *FFFF8h–FFFFh.* Indicates that the cluster contains the end of a file and that no reference to another cluster is necessary.

The FDISK program determines whether a 12-bit,16-bit, or 32-bit FAT is placed on a disk, even though the FAT isn't written until you perform a high-level format (using the FORMAT utility). On today's systems, usually only floppy disks use 12-bit FATs, but FDISK also creates a 12-bit FAT if you create a hard disk volume that is smaller than 16MB (32,756 sectors). On hard disk volumes of more than 16MB, FDISK creates a 16-bit FAT. On drives larger than 512MB, the FDISK program included in Windows 95 OSR2, Windows 98, and Windows Me enables you to create 32-bit FATs when you answer Yes to the question Enable Large Disk Support? when you start FDISK. You can also select FAT32 when you prepare a drive with the Windows 2000 or Windows XP Disk Administrator program.

FDISK creates two copies of the FAT. Each one occupies contiguous sectors on the disk, and the second FAT copy immediately follows the first. Unfortunately, the operating system uses the second FAT copy only if sectors in the first FAT copy become unreadable. If the first FAT copy is corrupted, which is a much more common problem, the operating system does not use the second FAT copy. Even the CHKDSK command does not check or verify the second FAT copy. Moreover, whenever the OS updates the first FAT, it automatically copies large portions of the first FAT to the second FAT. If the first copy was corrupted and subsequently updated by the OS, a large portion of the first FAT would be copied over to the second FAT copy, damaging it in the process. After the update, the second copy is usually a mirror image of the first one, complete with any corruption. Two FATs rarely stay out of sync for very long. When they are out of sync and the OS writes to the disk, it updates the first FAT and also overwrites the second FAT with the first. This is why disk repair and recovery utilities warn you to stop working as soon as you detect a FAT problem. Programs such as Norton Disk Doctor use the second copy of the FAT as a reference to repair the first one, but if the OS has already updated the second FAT, repair might be impossible.

Clusters (Allocation Units)

The term *cluster* was changed to *allocation unit* in DOS 4.0 (although many people continue to use the old term). *Allocation unit* is appropriate because a single cluster is the smallest unit of the disk that the operating system can handle when it writes or reads a file. A cluster is equal to one or more 512-byte sectors, in a power of two. Although a cluster can be a single disk sector, it is usually more than one. Having more than one sector per cluster reduces the size and processing overhead of the FAT and enables the operating system to run faster because it has fewer individual units to manage. The tradeoff is in wasted disk space. Because operating systems manage space only in full-cluster units, every file consumes space on the disk in increments of one cluster.

Table 25.11 shows the default cluster (or allocation unit) sizes for the various floppy disk formats used over the years.

Table 25.11   Default Floppy Disk Cluster (Allocation Unit) Sizes

Drive Type	Cluster (Allocation Unit) Size	Density
5 1/4-inch 360KB	2 sectors (1,024 bytes)	Low
5 1/4-inch 1.2MB	1 sector (512 bytes)	High
3 1/2-inch 720KB	2 sectors (1,024 bytes)	Low
3 1/2-inch 1.44MB	1 sector (512 bytes)	High
3 1/2-inch 2.88MB	2 sectors (1,024 bytes)	Extra

It seems strange that the high-density disks, which have many more individual sectors than low-density disks, sometimes have smaller cluster sizes. The larger the FAT, the more entries the operating system must manage, and the slower it seems to function. This sluggishness is due to the excessive overhead required to manage all the individual clusters; the more clusters to be managed, the slower things become. The trade-off is in the minimum cluster size. High-density floppy disk drives are faster than their low-density counterparts, so perhaps IBM and Microsoft determined that the decrease in cluster size balances the drive's faster operation and offsets the use of a larger FAT.

Because the operating system can allocate only whole clusters, inevitably a certain amount of wasted storage space results. File sizes rarely fall on cluster boundaries, so the last cluster allocated to a particular file is rarely filled completely. The extra space left over between the actual end of the file and the end of the cluster is called *slack*. A partition with large clusters has more slack space, whereas smaller clusters generate less slack.

For hard disks, the cluster size varies greatly among various partition sizes and file systems. With FAT16, the field in the disk parameter block that specifies the cluster size is 2 bytes long, so its maximum possible value is 65,535. Thus, the largest possible cluster is 32KB because a 64KB cluster would require a value of 65,536 in this field. Table 25.12 shows the cluster sizes FDISK selects for a particular volume size when FAT16 is the file system used.

Table 25.12   Default Hard Disk Cluster (Allocation Unit) Sizes for FAT16

Hard Disk Volume Size	Cluster (Allocation Unit) Size	FAT Type
0MB to less than 16MB	8 sectors or 4,096 bytes	12-bit
16MB–128MB	4 sectors or 2,048 bytes	16-bit
More than 128MB–256MB	8 sectors or 4,096 bytes	16-bit
More than 256BMB–512MB	16 sectors or 8,192 bytes	16-bit
More than 512MB–1,024MB	32 sectors or 16,384 bytes	16-bit
More than 1,024MB–2,048MB	64 sectors or 32,768 bytes	16-bit

The effect of larger cluster sizes on disk utilization can be substantial. A 2GB partition containing about 5,000 files, with average slack of one-half of the last 32KB cluster used for each file, wastes more than 78MB [5000×(.5×32)KB] of file space. When files under 32KB in size are stored on a drive with a 32KB allocation unit, waste (slack) factors can approach 40% of the drive's capacity.

The cluster size, in combination with the structure of the FAT, also dictates the maximum possible FAT partition size. Because the FAT uses 16-byte entries to reference the clusters in the partition, there can be a maximum of only 65,536 (2^{16}) clusters. At 32KB per cluster, the largest possible FAT16 partition is 2,096,832KB or 2,047.6875MB in size with MS-DOS and Windows 9x/Me. Even if the 2-byte cluster size field could contain the value indicating 64KB clusters, the maximum partition size would still be constrained. The maximum partition size would be limited by the field in the disk parameter block that specifies the number of sectors per cluster. This field is only 1 byte long, and its value must be a power of 2. This makes its highest possible value 128 sectors, which equates to a maximum cluster size of 64KB. 65,536 clusters at 64KB each equals a maximum partition size of 4GB.

Note

Windows NT/2000/XP support the use of 64KB clusters on FAT16 partitions, enabling you to create partitions up to 4GB in size. However, the huge amount of slack that generally results from clusters this large makes this practice undesirable. Also note that no other operating systems with FAT16 support are capable of accessing a FAT16 partition larger than 2GB.

The Data Area

The data area of a partition is the place where the actual files are stored. It is located following the boot record, file allocation tables, and root directory. This is the area of the disk that is divided into clusters and managed by the FAT and root directory.

Diagnostic Read-and-Write Cylinder

The FDISK partitioning program always reserves the last cylinder of a hard disk for use as a special diagnostic read-and-write test cylinder. Because this cylinder is reserved, FDISK always reports fewer total cylinders than the drive manufacturer states are available. Operating systems do not use this cylinder for any normal purpose because it lies outside the partitioned area of the disk.

◄◄ See "Disk Formatting," p. 577.

On systems with IDE or SCSI disk interfaces, the drive and controller also might allocate an additional area past the logical end of the drive for a bad-track table and spare sectors. This situation can account for additional discrepancies between the FDISK and the drive manufacturer's reported sizes.

The diagnostics area enables software such as a manufacturer-supplied diagnostics disk to perform read-and-write tests on a hard disk without corrupting any user data. Many of these programs also swap spare cylinders for damaged cylinders if damaged cylinders are detected during testing.

VFAT and Long Filenames

The original Windows 95 release uses what is essentially the same FAT file system as DOS, except for a few important enhancements. Like much of the rest of Windows 95, the operating system support for the FAT file system was rewritten using 32-bit code and called *VFAT* (virtual file allocation table). VFAT works in combination with the 32-bit protected mode VCACHE (which replaces the 16-bit real mode SMARTDrive cache used in DOS and Windows 3.1) to provide better file system performance. However, the most obvious improvement in VFAT is its support for long filenames. DOS and Windows 3.1 had been encumbered by the standard 8.3 filenaming convention for many years, and adding long filename support was a high priority in Windows 95—particularly in light of the fact that Macintosh and OS/2 users had long enjoyed this capability.

The problem for the Windows 95 designers, as is often the case in the PC industry, was backward compatibility. It is no great feat to make long filenames possible when you are designing a new file system from scratch, as Microsoft did years before with Windows NT's NTFS. However, the Windows 95 developers wanted to add long filenames to the existing FAT file system and still make it possible to store those names on existing DOS volumes and for previous versions of DOS and Windows to access the files.

VFAT provides the capability to assign file and directory names that are up to 255 characters in length (including the length of the path). The three-character extension is maintained because, like previous Windows versions, Windows 95 relies on the extensions to associate file types with specific applications. VFAT's long filenames can also include spaces, as well as the following characters, which standard DOS 8.3 names can't: +,;=[].

The first problem when implementing the long filenames was how to make them usable to previous versions of DOS and 16-bit Windows applications that support only 8.3 names. The resolution to this problem was to give each file two names: a long filename and an alias that uses the traditional 8.3 naming convention. When you create a file with a long filename in Windows 9x, VFAT uses the following process to create an equivalent 8.3 alias name:

1. The first three characters after the last dot in the long filename become the extension of the alias.

2. The first six characters of the long filename (excluding spaces, which are ignored) are converted into uppercase and become the first six characters of the alias filename. If any of these six characters are illegal under the standard 8.3 naming rules (that is, +,;=[]), VFAT converts those characters into underscores.

3. VFAT adds the two characters ~1 as the seventh and eighth characters of the alias filename, unless this will result in a name conflict, in which case it uses ~2, ~3, and so on, as necessary.

Aliasing in Windows NT/2000/XP

Note that Windows NT/2000/XP creates aliases differently than Windows 9x (as shown later).

NT/2000/XP begins by taking the first six legal characters in the LFN and following them with a tilde and number. If the first six characters are unique, a number 1 follows the tilde.

If the first six characters aren't unique, a number 2 is added. NT/2000/XP uses the first three legal characters following the last period in the LFN for a file extension.

At the fifth iteration of this process, NT/2000/XP takes only the first two legal characters, performs a hash on the filename to produce four hexadecimal characters, places the four hex characters after the first two legal characters, and appends a ~5. The ~5 remains for all subsequent aliases; only the hex numbers change.

Tip

You can modify the behavior of the VFAT filename truncation mechanism to make it use the first eight characters of the long filename instead of the first six characters plus ~1. To do this, you must add a new binary value to the `HKEY_LOCAL_MACHINE\System\CurrentControlSet\control\FileSystem` Registry key called `NameNumericTail`, with a value of `0`. Changing the value to `1` returns the truncation process to its original state.

Although this Registry change creates "friendly" alias names, it causes many programs working with alias names to fail and is not recommended.

VFAT stores this alias filename in the standard name field of the file's directory entry. Any version of DOS or 16-bit Windows can therefore access the file using the alias name. The big problem that still remains, however, is where to store the long filenames. Clearly, storing a 255-character filename in a 32-byte directory entry is impossible (because each character requires 1 byte). However, modifying the structure of the directory entry would make the files unusable by previous DOS versions.

The developers of VFAT resolved this problem by using additional directory entries to store the long filenames. Each of the directory entries is still 32 bytes long, so up to eight might be required for each long name, depending on its length. To ensure that these additional directory entries are not mis-interpreted by earlier DOS versions, VFAT flags them with a combination of attributes that is not possible for a normal file: read-only, hidden, system, and volume label. These attributes cause DOS to ignore the long filename entries, while preventing them from being mistakenly overwritten.

Caution

When using long filenames on a standard FAT12 or FAT16 partition, you should avoid storing them in the root directory. Files with long names that take up multiple directory entries can more easily use up the limited number of entries allotted to the root directory than files with 8.3 names. On FAT32 drives, this is not a problem because the root directory has an unlimited number of entries.

In an experiment, I created a small (1KB) text file on a floppy disk and gave it a 135-character long filename using Windows 98. I copied the file and pasted it repeatedly into the root directory of a floppy disk using Windows Explorer. Before I could make 20 copies of the file, the system displayed a `File copying` error. The disk could not accept any more files because the extremely long filename had used up all the root directory entries.

This solution for implementing backward-compatible long filenames in Windows 9x is ingenious, but it is not without its problems. Most of these problems stem from the use of applications that can access only the 8.3 alias names assigned to files. In some cases, if you open a file with a long name using one of these programs and save it again, the connection to the additional directory entries containing the long name is severed and the long name is lost.

This is especially true for older versions of disk utilities, such as Norton Disk Doctor for MS-DOS, that are not designed to support VFAT. Most older applications ignore the additional directory entries because of the combination of attributes assigned to them, but disk repair utilities usually are designed to detect and "correct" discrepancies of this type. The result is that running an old version of Norton Disk Doctor on a partition with long filenames results in the loss of all the long names. In the same way, backup utilities not designed for use with VFAT can strip off the long filenames from a partition.

Note

When using VFAT's long filename capabilities, you definitely should use disk and backup utilities that are intended to support VFAT. Windows 9x includes VFAT-compatible disk repair, defragmentation, and backup programs. If, however, you are for some reason inclined to use an older program that does not support VFAT, Windows 9x includes a clumsy, but effective, solution.

A program is included on the Windows 9x CD-ROM called LFNBK.EXE. It doesn't install with the operating system, but you can use it to strip the long filenames from a VFAT volume and store them in a text file called **LFNBK.DAT**. You can then work with the files on the volume as though they were standard 8.3 FAT files. Afterward, you can use LFNBK.EXE to restore the long filenames to their original places (assuming the file and directory structure has not changed). This is not a convenient solution, nor is it recommended for use in anything but extraordinary circumstances, but the capability is there if needed. Some backup programs designed for disaster recovery (which enable you to reconstruct the contents of the hard drive without reloading Windows first) have used this feature to enable restoration of a Windows drive with long filenames from a DOS prompt (where only 8.3 alias names usually are supported).

Another problem with VFAT's long filenames involves the process by which the file system creates the 8.3 alias names. VFAT creates a new alias every time you create or copy a file into a new directory; therefore, the alias can change. For example, you might have a file called `Expenses-January98.doc` stored in a directory with the alias `EXPENS~1.DOC`. If you use Windows 9x Explorer to copy this file to a directory that already contains a file called `Expenses-December97.doc`, you are likely to find that this existing file is already using the alias `EXPENS~1.DOC`. In this case, VFAT assigns `EXPENS~2.DOC` as the alias of the newly copied file, with no warning to the user. This is not a problem for applications that support VFAT because the long filenames are unchanged, but a user running an older application might open the `EXPENS~1.DOC` file expecting to find the list of January 1998 expenses and see the December 1997 expenses list instead.

FAT32

When the FAT file system was being developed, 2GB hard disk drives were a fantasy, and no one expected the partition size limitation imposed by the combination of 16-bit FAT entries and 32KB cluster sizes to be a problem. Today, however, even low-end PCs come equipped with hard drives holding at least 10GB, and 20GB and 30GB drives are common. When you use the standard FAT file system with these larger drives, you must create several partitions, each no larger than approximately 2GB. To many users, having multiple drive letters representing a single disk is confusing, making organizing and locating files difficult.

To address this problem, Microsoft released an enhanced version of the FAT file system, called FAT32. FAT32 works just like the standard FAT; the only difference is that it uses numbers with more digits, so it can manage more clusters on a disk. Unlike VFAT, which is a Windows 9x innovation that uses existing file system structures, FAT32 is an enhancement of the FAT file system itself. In other words, whereas VFAT is implemented as part of the Windows 9x Virtual Machine Manager (Vmm.vxd), FAT32 is implemented by the FDISK program before the Windows GUI is even loaded. FAT32 was first included in the Windows 95 OEM Service Release 2 (OSR2) and is also part of Windows 98/Me, Windows 2000, and Windows XP operating systems.

Note

Because the FDISK utility can implement the FAT32 file system when you partition the drive, you can't use FAT32 on a floppy disk or any removable cartridge that does not use a partition table. However, any medium that you can partition with FDISK, such as an Iomega Jaz cartridge, can use FAT32.

The most obvious improvement in FAT32 is that by using 32-bit values for FAT entries instead of 16-bit ones, the maximum number of clusters allowed in a single partition jumps from 65,536 (2^{16}) to 268,435,456. This value is equivalent to 2^{28}, not 2^{32}, because 4 bits out of the 32 are reserved for other uses. FAT32 also uses 32-bit values for the low-level operating system calls used to retrieve a specific disk sector.

These expanded values blow the top off the 2GB limit on partition sizes; FAT32 partitions can theoretically be up to 2TB in size (1TB = 1,024GB). This figure is derived from a new maximum of 4,294,967,296 (2^{32}) possible 512-byte sectors. Individual files can be up to 4GB in size and are limited by the size field in the directory entry, which is 4 bytes long. Because the clusters are numbered using 32-bit values instead of 16-bit ones, the format of the directory entries on a FAT32 partition must be changed slightly. The 2-byte Link to Start Cluster field is increased to 4 bytes, using 2 of the 10 bytes (bytes 12–21) in the directory entry that were reserved for future use. In reality, limitations in the design of Windows 9x and the current ATA-5 version of the IDE specification restrict maximum disk size to a still-impressive 128GB. Windows 2000 and Windows XP can format a FAT32 partition of 32GB or less but can read larger FAT32 partitions.

Another important difference in FAT32 partitions is the nature of the root directory. In a FAT32 partition, the root directory does not occupy a fixed position on the disk as in a FAT16 partition. Instead, it can be located anywhere in the partition and expand to any size. This eliminates the preset limit on root directory entries and provides the infrastructure necessary to make FAT32 partitions dynamically resizable. Microsoft has not yet implemented this feature in Windows 9x/Me, but third-party products such as PowerQuest's PartitionMagic take advantage of this capability.

The primary drawback of FAT32 is that it is not compatible with previous versions of DOS and Windows 95. You can't boot to a previous version of DOS or (pre-OSR2) Windows 95 from a FAT32 drive, nor can a system started with an old DOS or Windows 95 boot disk see FAT32 partitions. Apart from Windows 95 OSR2, Windows 98/Me, and Windows 2000/XP, the only operating system that natively supports FAT32 is Linux. Most recent distributions of Linux now support FAT32, but older ones might require a patch. Check your distribution's documentation for details.

FAT32 Cluster Sizes

Because FAT32 partitions can have so many more clusters than FAT16 partitions, the clusters themselves can be smaller. Using smaller clusters reduces the wasted disk space caused by slack. For example, the same 2GB partition with 5,000 files on it mentioned earlier would use 4KB clusters with FAT32 instead of 32KB clusters with FAT16. Assuming the same amount of slack for each file, the smaller cluster size reduces the average amount of wasted space on that partition from more than 78MB to less than 10MB.

To compare FAT16 and FAT32, you can look at how a file would be stored on each. For FAT16, I'll use the same example as before. With FAT16 the cluster numbers are stored as 16-bit entries, from 0000h to FFFFh. The largest value possible is FFFFh, which corresponds to 65,535 in decimal, but several numbers at the beginning and end are reserved for special use. The actual cluster numbers allowed in a FAT16 system range from 0002h to FFF6h, which is 2–65,526 in decimal. All files must be stored in cluster numbers within that range. That leaves only 65,524 valid clusters to use for storing files (cluster numbers below 2 and above 65,526 are reserved), meaning a partition must be broken up into that many clusters or less. A typical file entry under FAT16 might look like Table 25.13.

Table 25.13   FAT16 File Entries

		Directory
Name	**Starting Cluster**	**Size**
USCONST.TXT	1000	4

		FAT16 File Allocation Table
FAT Cluster #	**Value**	**Meaning**
00002	0	First cluster available
...	...	...
00999	0	Cluster available
01000	1001	In use, points to next cluster
01001	1002	In use, points to next cluster
01002	1003	In use, points to next cluster
01003	FFFFh	End of file
01004	0	Cluster available
...	...	...
65526	0	Last cluster available

With FAT32, the cluster numbers range from 00000000h to FFFFFFFFh, which is 0–4,294,967,295 in decimal. Again some values at the low and high ends are reserved, and only values from between 00000002h and FFFFFFF6h are valid, which means values 2–4,294,967,286 are valid. This leaves 4,294,967,284 valid entries, so the drive must be split into that many clusters or less. Because a drive can be split into so many more clusters, they can be smaller, which conserves disk space. The same file as shown earlier could be stored on a FAT32 system as shown in Table 25.14.

Table 25.14   FAT32 File Entries

		Directory
Name	**Starting Cluster**	**Size**
USCONST.TXT	1000	8

		FAT32 File Allocation Table
FAT Cluster #	**Value**	**Meaning**
0000000002	0	First cluster available
...	...	...
0000000999	0	Cluster available
0000001000	1001	In use, points to next cluster
0000001001	1002	In use, points to next cluster
0000001002	1003	In use, points to next cluster
0000001003	1004	In use, points to next cluster
0000001004	1005	In use, points to next cluster
0000001005	1006	In use, points to next cluster
0000001006	1007	In use, points to next cluster
0000001007	FFFFFFFFh	End of file
0000001008	0	Cluster available
...	...	...
4,294,967,286	0	Last cluster available

Because the FAT32 system enables many more clusters to be allocated, the cluster size is usually smaller. So, although files overall use more individual clusters, less wasted space results because the last cluster is, on average, only half filled.

Note

PC Magazine has released a free DOS utility called CHKDRV that calculates the slack on a FAT16 or FAT32 partition. You can download this program from `ftp://ftp.zdnet.com/pcmag/1995/0627/chkdrv.zip`.

Table 25.15 lists the cluster sizes for various FAT32 partition sizes.

Table 25.15   FAT32 Cluster Sizes

Partition Size	Cluster Size
0MB to less than 260MB	512 bytes
260MB–8GB	4,096 bytes
6GB–16GB	8,192 bytes
16GB–32GB	16,384 bytes
32GB–2TB	32,768 bytes

Of course, using smaller clusters means there must be many more of them and more entries in the FAT as well. A 2GB partition using FAT32 requires 524,288 FAT entries, whereas the same drive needs only 65,536 entries using FAT16. Thus, the size of one copy of the FAT16 table is 128KB (65,536 entries × 16 bits = 1,048,576 bits/8 = 131,072 bytes/1,024 = 128KB), whereas the FAT32 table is 2MB in size.

The size of the FAT has a definite impact on the performance of the file system. Windows 9x/Me uses VCACHE to try to keep the FAT in memory at all times to improve file system performance. The use of 4KB clusters for drives up to 8GB in size is, therefore, a reasonable compromise for the average PC's memory capacity. If the file system were to use clusters that are equal to one disk sector (1 sector = 512KB) in an attempt to minimize slack as much as possible, the FAT table for a 2GB drive would contain 4,194,304 entries and be 16MB in size.

This would monopolize a substantial portion of the memory in the average system, probably resulting in noticeably degraded performance. Although at first it might seem as though even a 2MB FAT is quite large when compared to 128KB, keep in mind that hard disk drives are a great deal faster now than they were when the FAT file system was originally designed. In practice, implementing FAT32 on a Windows 9x system typically results in a minor (less than 5%) improvement in file system performance. However, systems that perform a great many sequential disk writes might see an equally minor degradation in performance.

FAT Mirroring

FAT32 also takes greater advantage of the two copies of the FAT stored on a disk partition. On a FAT16 partition, the first copy of the FAT is always the primary copy and replicates its data to the secondary FAT, sometimes corrupting it in the process. On a FAT32 partition, when the system detects a problem with the primary copy of the FAT, it can switch to the other copy, which then becomes the primary. The system can also disable the FAT mirroring process to prevent the viable FAT from being corrupted by the other copy. This provides a greater degree of fault tolerance to FAT32 partitions, often enabling you to repair a damaged FAT without an immediate system interruption or a loss of table data.

Creating FAT32 Partitions

Despite the substantial changes FAT32 provides, the new file system does have a large effect on the procedures you use to create and manage partitions. You create new FAT32 partitions in Windows 9x using the FDISK utility from the command prompt, just like you would create FAT16 partitions. When you launch FDISK, the program examines your hard disk drives and, if they have a capacity greater than 512MB, presents the following message:

```
Your computer has a disk larger than 512 MB. This version of Windows
includes improved support for large disks, resulting in more efficient
use of disk space on large drives, and allowing disks over 2 GB to be
formatted as a single drive.
```

```
IMPORTANT: If you enable large disk support and create any new drives on this
disk, you will not be able to access the new drive(s) using other operating
systems, including some versions of Windows 95 and Windows NT, as well as
earlier versions of Windows and MS-DOS. In addition, disk utilities that
were not designed explicitly for the FAT32 file system will not be able
to work with this disk. If you need to access this disk with other operating
systems or older disk utilities, do not enable large drive support.

Do you wish to enable large disk support (Y/N)...........? [N]
```

If you answer Yes to this question, any partitions you create that are larger than 512MB will be FAT32 partitions. If you want to create partitions larger than 2GB, you must use FAT32. Otherwise, you can choose which file system you prefer. All the screens following this one are the same as those in previous versions of FDISK.

Normally, the FDISK utility determines the cluster size used when you format the partition, based on the partition's size and the file system used. However, you can override FDISK using an undocumented switch for the FORMAT utility. If you use the command

```
FORMAT /Z:n
```

where *n* multiplied by 512 equals the desired cluster size in bytes, you can create a partition that uses cluster sizes that are larger or smaller than the defaults for the file system.

Caution

The /Z switch does not override the 65,536-cluster limit on FAT16 partitions, so it is recommended that you use it only with FAT32. In addition, you should not use this switch on a production system without extensive testing first. Modifying the cluster size can increase or decrease the amount of slack on the partition, but it also can have a pronounced effect on the performance of the drive. Some disk utilities might not work with nonstandard cluster sizes.

Converting FAT16 to FAT32

The Windows 95 OSR2 release can create FAT32 partitions only out of empty disk space. If you want to convert an existing FAT16 partition to FAT32, you must back up the data, destroy the FAT16 partition, create a new FAT32 partition, and then restore the data. Windows 98/Me, on the other hand, includes a FAT32 Conversion Wizard that enables you to migrate existing partitions in place.

The wizard gathers the information needed to perform the conversion, informs you of the consequences of implementing FAT32, and attempts to prevent data loss and other problems. After you have selected the drive you want to convert, the wizard performs a scan for applications (such as disk utilities) that might not function properly on the converted partition. The wizard gives you the opportunity to remove these and warns you to back up the data on the partition before proceeding with the conversion. Even if you don't use the Microsoft Backup utility the wizard offers, backing up your data is a strongly recommended precaution.

After you answer all the wizard's prompts and confirm that you want to continue with the conversion, the system reboots to a DOS prompt. The actual conversion is a DOS process, making it possible to convert even the partition on which Windows 98/Me is installed. Because the conversion must deal with the existing partition data in addition to creating new volume boot record information, FATs, and clusters, the process can take far longer than partitioning and formatting an empty drive. Depending on the amount of data involved and the new cluster size, the conversion can take several hours to complete.

After you convert a FAT16 partition to FAT32, you can't convert it back with Windows 98 or Me's tools, except by destroying the partition and using FDISK to create a new one. Therefore, be sure to carefully consider your actions before proceeding. You also should take other precautions before beginning the conversion process, such as connecting the system to a UPS. A power failure during the conversion could result in a loss of data.

FAT32 and PartitionMagic

Windows 95 OSR2 and Windows 98/Me include only basic tools for creating FAT32 partitions, but a product called PartitionMagic (from PowerQuest) provides many other partition manipulation features. PartitionMagic can convert FAT16 partitions to FAT32 in place, as the Windows 98/Me FAT32 Conversion Wizard can. However, unlike Windows 98/Me, it can also convert FAT32 partitions back to FAT16.

Among many other things, this product also can resize FAT16 and FAT32 partitions without destroying the data they contain, shrink and expand FAT clusters, and tell you how much disk space you will save as the result of changing the cluster size. PartitionMagic takes advantage of the inherent capabilities of the FAT16 and FAT32 file systems to provide features that probably will be added to Windows at some future time.

FAT File System Errors

File system errors can, of course, occur because of hardware problems, but you are more likely to see them result from software crashes and improper system handling. Turning off a system without shutting down Windows properly, for example, can result in errors that cause clusters to be incorrectly listed as in use when they are not. Some of the most common file system errors that occur on FAT partitions are described in the following sections.

Lost Clusters

Probably the most common file system error, lost clusters are clusters the FAT designates as being in use when they actually are not. Most often caused by an interruption of a file system process due to an application crash or a system shutdown, for example, the FAT entry of a lost cluster might contain a reference to a subsequent cluster. However, the FAT chain stemming from the directory entry has been broken somewhere along the line.

Lost clusters would appear in the file structure as shown in Table 25.16.

Table 25.16   Lost Clusters in a File Structure

Directory		
Name	**Starting Cluster**	**Size**
(no entry)	0	0

FAT16 File Allocation Table		
FAT Cluster #	**Value**	**Meaning**
00002	0	First cluster available
...	...	...
00999	0	Cluster available
01000	1001	In use, points to next cluster
01001	1002	In use, points to next cluster

Table 25.16   Continued

	FAT16 File Allocation Table	
FAT Cluster #	**Value**	**Meaning**
01002	1003	In use, points to next cluster
01003	FFFFh	End of file
01004	0	Cluster available
…	…	…
65526	0	Last cluster available

The operating system sees a valid chain of clusters in the FAT but no corresponding directory entry to back it up. Programs that are terminated before they can close their open files typically cause this. The operating system usually modifies the FAT chain as the file is written, and the final step when closing is to create a matching directory entry. If the system is interrupted before the file is closed (such as by shutting down the system improperly), lost clusters are the result. Disk repair programs check for lost clusters by tracing the FAT chain for each file and subdirectory in the partition and building a facsimile of the FAT in memory. After compiling a list of all the FAT entries that indicate properly allocated clusters, the program compares this facsimile with the actual FAT. Any entries denoting allocated clusters in the real FAT that do not appear in the facsimile are lost clusters because they are not part of a valid FAT chain.

The utility typically gives you the opportunity to save the data in the lost clusters as a file before it changes the FAT entries to show them as unallocated clusters. If your system crashed or lost power while you were working with a word processor data file, for example, you might be able to retrieve text from the lost clusters in this way. When left unrepaired, lost clusters are unavailable for use by the system, reducing the storage capacity of your drive.

The typical choices you have for correcting lost clusters are to assign them a made-up name or zero out the FAT entries. If you assign them a name, you can at least look at the entries as a valid file and then delete the file if you find it useless. The CHKDSK and SCANDISK programs are designed to fix lost clusters by assigning them names starting with FILE0001.CHK. If more than one lost chain exists, sequential numbers following the first one are used. The lost clusters shown earlier could be corrected by CHKDSK or SCANDISK, as shown in Table 25.17.

Table 25.17   Finding Lost Clusters

	Directory	
Name	**Starting Cluster**	**Size**
FILE0001.CHK	1000	4

	FAT16 File Allocation Table	
FAT Cluster #	**Value**	**Meaning**
00002	0	First cluster available
…	…	…
00999	0	Cluster available
01000	1001	In use, points to next cluster
01001	1002	In use, points to next cluster
01002	1003	In use, points to next cluster

Table 25.17   Continued

	FAT16 File Allocation Table	
FAT Cluster #	**Value**	**Meaning**
01003	FFFFh	End of file
01004	0	Cluster available
...	...	...
65526	0	Last cluster available

As you can see, a new entry was created to match the FAT entries. The name is made up because there is no way for the repair utility to know what the original name of the file might have been.

Cross-Linked Files

Cross-linked files occur when two directory entries improperly reference the same cluster in their Link to Start Cluster fields. The result is that each file uses the same FAT chain. Because the clusters can store data from only one file, working with one of the two files can inadvertently overwrite the other file's data.

Cross-linked files would appear in the file structure as shown in Table 25.18.

Table 25.18   Cross-Linked Files

	Directory	
Name	**Starting Cluster**	**Size**
USCONST.TXT	1000	4
PLEDGE.TXT	1002	2

	FAT16 File Allocation Table	
FAT Cluster #	**Value**	**Meaning**
00002	0	First cluster available
...	...	...
00999	0	Cluster available
01000	1001	In use, points to next cluster
01001	1002	In use, points to next cluster
01002	1003	In use, points to next cluster
01003	FFFFh	End of file
01004	0	Cluster available
...	...	...
65526	0	Last cluster available

In this case, two files claim ownership of clusters 1002 and 1003. These files are said to be cross-linked on 1002. When a situation such as this arises, one of the files typically is valid and the other is corrupt, being that only one actual given set of data can occupy a given cluster. The normal repair is to copy both files involved to new names, which duplicates their data separately in another area of the disk, and then delete *all* the files that are cross-linked. Deleting them all is important because by deleting only one of them, the FAT chain is zeroed, which further damages the other entries. Then, you can examine the files you copied to determine which one is good and which is corrupt.

Detecting cross-linked files is a relatively easy task for a disk repair utility because it must examine only the partition's directory entries and not the file clusters themselves. However, by the time the utility detects the error, the data from one of the two files is probably already lost—although you might be able to recover parts of it from lost clusters.

Invalid Files or Directories

Sometimes the information in a directory entry for a file or subdirectory can be corrupted to the point at which the entry is not just erroneous (as in cross-linked files) but invalid. The entry might have a cluster or date reference that is invalid, or it might violate the rules for the entry format in some other way. In most cases, disk repair software can correct these problems, permitting access to the file.

FAT Errors

As discussed earlier, accessing its duplicate copy can sometimes repair a corrupted FAT. Disk repair utilities typically rely on this technique to restore a damaged FAT to its original state, as long as the mirroring process has not corrupted the copy. FAT32 tables are more likely to be repairable because their more advanced mirroring capabilities make the copy less likely to be corrupted.

An example of a damaged FAT might appear to the operating system as shown in Table 25.19.

Table 25.19   Damaged FAT

Directory		
Name	**Starting Cluster**	**Size**
USCONST.TXT	1000	4

FAT16 File Allocation Table		
FAT Cluster #	**Value**	**Meaning**
00002	0	First cluster available
...	...	...
00999	0	Cluster available
01000	1001	In use, points to next cluster
01001	0	Cluster available
01002	1003	In use, points to next cluster
01003	FFFFh	End of file
01004	0	Cluster available
...	...	...
65526	0	Last cluster available

This single error would cause multiple problems to appear. The file USCONST.TXT would now come up as having an *allocation error*—in which the size in the directory no longer matches the number of clusters in the FAT chain. The file would end after cluster 1001 in this example, and the rest of the data would be missing if one loaded this file for viewing. Also, two lost clusters would exist; that is, 1002 and 1003 appear to have no directory entry that owns them. When multiple problems such as these appear, a single incident of damage is often the cause. The repair in this case could involve copying the data from the backup FAT back to the primary FAT, but in most cases, the backup is similarly damaged. Normal utilities would truncate the file and create an entry for a second file out of the lost clusters. You would have to figure out yourself that they really belong together. This is where having knowledge in data recovery can help over using automated utilities that can't think for themselves.

FAT File System Utilities

The CHKDSK, RECOVER, and SCANDISK commands are the DOS damaged-disk recovery team. These commands are crude, and their actions sometimes are drastic, but at times they are all that is available or necessary. RECOVER is best known for its function as a data recovery program, and CHKDSK typically is used for inspection of the file structure. Many users are unaware that CHKDSK can implement repairs to a damaged file structure. DEBUG, a crude, manually controlled program, can help in the case of a disk disaster, if you know exactly what you are doing.

SCANDISK is a safer, more automated, more powerful replacement for CHKDSK and RECOVER. It should be used in their places if you are running Windows 95 or newer or DOS 6.

If you are using MS-DOS 5.0 or older, the only disk testing utilities supplied with your version of MS-DOS are CHKDSK and RECOVER. To learn more about how CHKDSK works, see *Upgrading and Repairing PCs, 11th Edition*, included in electronic form on the CD packaged with this book.

The *RECOVER* Command

The DOS RECOVER command is designed to mark clusters as bad in the FAT when the clusters can't be read properly. When the system can't read a file because of a problem with a sector on the disk going bad, the RECOVER command can mark the FAT so another file does not use those clusters. When used improperly, this program is highly dangerous. The RECOVER utility has not been included in DOS since version 5 and is not supplied in Windows 9x because its functionality has been replaced by SCANDISK.

Caution

Be very careful when you use **RECOVER**. Used improperly, it can do severe damage to your files and the FAT. If you enter the **RECOVER** command without a filename for it to work on, the program assumes you want every file on the disk recovered and operates on every file and subdirectory on the disk. It converts all subdirectories to files, places all filenames in the root directory, and gives them new names (**FILE0000.REC**, **FILE0001.REC**, and so on). This process essentially wipes out the file system on the entire disk. Do not use **RECOVER** without providing a filename for it to work on. This program should be considered as dangerous as the **FORMAT** command. **RECOVER** is so notorious for this behavior that older versions of the Norton Utilities had a "recover from DOS RECOVER" option that could sometimes undo the damage caused by improper use of **RECOVER**.

SCANDISK

You should check your FAT partitions regularly for the problems discussed in this chapter and any other difficulties that might arise. By far an easier and more effective solution for disk diagnosis and repair than CHKDSK and RECOVER is the SCANDISK utility, included with DOS 6 and higher versions, as well as with Windows 9x. This program is more thorough and comprehensive than CHKDSK or RECOVER and can perform the functions of both of them—and a great deal more. Windows 95 OSR2 and Windows 98 include SCANDISK versions that support FAT32 partitions.

Note

The equivalent of **SCANDISK** in Windows NT 4.0, Windows 2000, and Windows XP is called **CHKDSK**, but it is far more powerful than the old MS-DOS **CHKDSK** program. For more information on the old MS-DOS **CHKDSK** program, see *Upgrading and Repairing PCs, 12th Edition*, included in its entirety on the CD accompanying this book.

SCANDISK is similar to a scaled-down version of third-party disk repair programs such as Norton Disk Doctor, and it can verify both file structure and disk sector integrity. If SCANDISK finds problems, it can repair directories and FATs. If the program finds bad sectors in the middle of a file, it marks the clusters (allocation units) containing the bad sectors as bad in the FAT and attempts to read the file data by rerouting around the defect.

Windows 9x includes both DOS and Windows versions of SCANDISK, which are named SCANDISK.EXE and SCANDSKW.EXE, respectively. Windows 9x scans your drives at the beginning of the operating system installation process and automatically loads the DOS version of SCANDISK whenever you restart your system after turning it off without completing the proper shutdown procedure. You can also launch SCANDISK.EXE from a DOS prompt or from a batch file using the following syntax:

```
Scandisk x: [/a] [/n] [/p] [dblspace.nnn/drvspace.nnn]
x: - designator of the drive that you want to scan
/a - scans all local fixed hard disks
/n - noninteractive mode; requires no user input
/p - scans only, without correcting errors
/custom - runs Scandisk with the options configured in the
➥[CUSTOM] section of the Scandisk.ini file
dblspace.nnn or drvspace.nnn - scans a compressed volume file,
➥where nnn is replaced by the file extension (such as 001)
```

The SCANDISK.INI file, located in the C:\WINDOWS\COMMAND directory on a Windows 9x system by default, contains extensive and well-documented parameters you can use to control the behavior of SCANDISK.EXE. Note that the options in the SCANDISK.INI file are applied only to the DOS version of the utility and have no effect on the Windows GUI version.

You also can run the GUI version of the utility by opening the Start menu and selecting Programs, Accessories, System Tools. Both versions scan and repair the FAT and the directory and file structures, repair problems with long filenames, and scan volumes that have been compressed with DriveSpace or DoubleSpace.

SCANDISK provides two basic testing options: Standard and Thorough. The difference between the two is that the Thorough option causes the program to scan the entire surface of the disk for errors in addition to the items just mentioned. You also can select whether to run the program interactively or let it automatically repair any errors it finds.

The DOS and Windows 9x versions of SCANDISK also test the FAT in different ways. The DOS version scans and, if necessary, repairs the primary copy of the file allocation table. After this, it copies the repaired version of the primary to the backup copy. The Windows version, however, scans both copies of the FAT. If the program finds discrepancies between the two copies, it uses the data from the copy that it judges to be correct and reassembles the primary FAT using the best data from both copies. If the FAT information is not reconstructed correctly, some or all of your data might become inaccessible.

SCANDISK also has an Advanced Options dialog box that enables you to set the following parameters:

- Whether the program should display a summary of its findings
- Whether the program should log its findings
- How the program should repair cross-linked files (two directory entries pointing to the same cluster)
- How the program should repair lost file fragments
- Whether to check files for invalid names, dates, and times

Although SCANDISK is good, and is certainly a vast improvement over CHKDSK, I recommend using one of the commercial packages, such as the Norton Utilities or Norton System Works, for any major disk problems. These utilities go far beyond what is included in DOS or Windows 9x.

Disk Defragmentation

The entire premise of the FAT file systems is based on the storage of data in clusters that can be located anywhere on the disk. This enables the computer to store a file of nearly any size at any time. The process of following a FAT chain to locate all the clusters holding the data for a particular file can force the hard disk drive to access many locations on the disk. Because of the physical work involved in moving the disk drive heads, reading a file that is heavily fragmented in this way is slower than reading one that is stored on consecutive clusters.

As you regularly add, move, and delete files on a disk over a period of time, the files become increasingly fragmented, which can slow down disk performance. You can relieve this problem by periodically running a disk defragmentation utility on your drives, such as the one included with Windows 9x. When you run Disk Defragmenter, the program reads each of the files in the disk, using the FAT table to access its clusters, wherever they might be located.

The program then writes the file to a series of contiguous clusters and deletes the original. By progressively reading, erasing, and writing files, the program eventually leaves the disk in a state where all its files exist on contiguous clusters. As a result, the drive is capable of reading any file on the disk with a minimum of head movement, thus providing what is often a noticeable performance increase.

The Windows 95 Disk Defragmentation utility provides this basic defragmenting function. It also enables you to select whether you want to arrange the files on the disk to consolidate the empty clusters into one contiguous free space (which takes longer). The Windows 98/Me version adds a feature that examines the files on the disk and arranges them with the most frequently used program files grouped together at the front of the disk, which can make programs load more quickly.

To show how defragmenting works, see the example of a fragmented file shown in Table 25.20.

Table 25.20   Fragmented File

	Directory	
Name	**Starting Cluster**	**Size**
PLEDGE.TXT	1002	2
USCONST.TXT	1000	4

	FAT16 File Allocation Table	
FAT Cluster #	**Value**	**Meaning**
00002	0	First cluster available
...	...	...
00999	0	Cluster available
01000	1001	In use, points to next cluster
01001	1004	In use, points to next cluster
01002	1003	In use, points to next cluster
01003	FFFFh	End of file
01004	1005	In use, points to next cluster
01005	FFFFh	End of file
...	...	...
65526	0	Last cluster available

In the preceding example, the file USCONST.TXT is fragmented in two pieces. If you ran a defragmenting program, the files would be read off the disk and rewritten in a contiguous fashion. One possible outcome is shown in Table 25.21.

Table 25.21   Defragmented File

	Directory	
Name	**Starting Cluster**	**Size**
PLEDGE.TXT	1004	2
USCONST.TXT	1000	4

	FAT16 File Allocation Table	
FAT Cluster #	**Value**	**Meaning**
00002	0	First cluster available
...	...	...
00999	0	Cluster available
01000	1001	In use, points to next cluster
01001	1002	In use, points to next cluster
01002	1003	In use, points to next cluster
01003	FFFFh	End of file
01004	1005	In use, points to next cluster
01005	FFFFh	End of file
...	...	...
65526	0	Last cluster available

Although it doesn't look like much was changed, you can see that now both files are in one piece, stored one right after the other. Because defragmenting involves reading and rewriting a possibly large number of files on your drive, it can take a long time, especially if you have a large drive with a lot of fragmented files and not very much free working space on the drive.

Third-party defragmentation utilities, such as the Speed Disk program included in the Norton Utilities, provide additional features, such as the capability to select specific files that should be moved to the front of the disk. Speed Disk also can defragment the Windows 9x swap file and files that are flagged with the system and hidden attributes, which Disk Defragmenter will not touch.

Caution

Although the disk-defragmentation utilities included with Windows 9x and third-party products are usually quite safe, you should always be aware that defragmenting a disk is an inherently dangerous procedure. The program reads, erases, and rewrites every file on the disk and has the potential to cause damage to your data when interrupted improperly. Although I have never seen a problem result from the process, an unforeseen event—such as a power failure—during a defragmentation procedure can conceivably be disastrous. I strongly recommend that you always run a disk-repair utility, such as SCANDISK, on your drives before defragmenting them and have a current backup ready.

Windows NT 4.0 did not include a defragmentation utility, but Windows 2000 and Windows XP do include such a utility.

Third-Party Programs

When you get a `Sector not found` error reading drive C:, the best course of action is to use one of the third-party disk-repair utilities on the market, rather than DOS's `RECOVER` or even `SCANDISK`. The Norton Utilities by Symantec (also included in Norton System Works) stands as perhaps the premier data recovery package on the market today. This package is comprehensive and automatically repairs most types of disk problems.

Norton Utilities and Norton System Works

Programs such as Norton Disk Doctor can perform much more detailed repairs with a greater amount of safety. Disk Doctor preserves as much of the data in the file as possible and can mark the FAT so the bad sectors or clusters of the disk are not used again. These programs also save Undo information, enabling you to reverse any data recovery operation.

Disk Doctor is part of Symantec's Norton Utilities package, which includes a great many other useful tools. For example, Norton Utilities has an excellent sector editor that enables you to view and edit any part of a disk, including the master and volume boot records, FATs, and other areas that fall outside the disk's normal data area. Currently, no other program is as comprehensive or as capable of editing disks at the sector level. The disk editor included with Norton Utilities can give the professional PC troubleshooter or repairperson the ability to work directly with any sector on the disk, but this does require extensive knowledge of sector formats and disk structures. The documentation with the package is excellent and can be very helpful if you are learning data recovery on your own.

Note

Data recovery is a lucrative service the more advanced technician can provide. People are willing to pay much more to get their data back than to replace a hard drive.

You also can identify and test your hardware with Norton Diagnostics, create a rescue disk for restarting your system and testing the drive in case of emergencies, unerase accidentally deleted files (even if the Recycle Bin was bypassed), and unformat accidentally formatted drives.

Norton Utilities is now available in version 2001 as a standalone product or as a component in Norton System Works 2001 (for Windows 95 OSR 2.x, Windows 98, Windows Me, Windows NT, and Windows 2000). System Works 2001 also includes Norton Anti-Virus and Norton CleanSweep uninstaller; the Professional version also includes Norton Ghost disk imaging, WinFax Basic, and Web Services. Some of the programs provided with Norton Utilities are designed to be run from the command line or from a DOS prompt, such as

- Norton Disk Doctor (`NDD.EXE`)
- Disk Editor (`DISKEDIT.EXE`)
- UnErase (`UNERASE.EXE`)
- UnFormat (`UNFORMAT.EXE`)
- Rescue Restore (`RESCUE.EXE`)

However, most Norton Utilities programs in version 2001 are designed to be run from within the Windows GUI.

You should not use older versions of Norton Utilities, such as version 8.0 (designed for Windows 3.1 and MS-DOS), with 32-bit versions of Windows because of the possibility of data loss due to a lack of support for long filenames and large drives.

SpinRite 5

The Calibrate pattern-testing program that was part of older versions of the Norton Utilities is no longer present in Norton Utilities 2001. However, the SpinRite 5 program from Gibson Research (http://grc.com) provides a similar form of deep-pattern testing of both IDE and SCSI hard drives as well as removable-media drives of all sizes that have FAT-type file systems, including FAT32. During testing, SpinRite 5 uses its Dynastat Data Recovery feature to statistically analyze hard-to-read disk sectors to determine their original contents; it then moves the data to a properly working area of the disk. This process takes longer than with a program such as DiskDoctor, but for heavily damaged disks and drives for which no backup is available, this process is unbeatable at recovering data. Another handy feature of SpinRite 5 is its capability to query your drive's partition table to determine the disk geometry originally used to set up the disk. This enables you to access data on a disk even if the factory disk geometry values were not used to prepare the disk with FDISK and were not written down for future use.

The most important consideration when you purchase third-party disk utilities is to choose products that support your file system. For example, Norton Utilities 2001 supports both FAT (including FAT32) and NTFS files systems, whereas older versions supported only FAT16 file systems. SpinRite 5 supports all FAT file systems, but not NTFS. Never use a disk utility not designed for your file system. And, never use an out-of-date disk utility (designed for an earlier operating system) on your disk. In both cases, you could cause irreparable damage to the data on your drive.

NTFS

NTFS is the native file system of Windows NT, Windows 2000, and Windows XP. Windows 2000 and Windows XP use an enhanced version of NTFS called NTFS 5 or NTFS 2000; Windows NT 4.0 must have Service Pack 4 or above installed to be capable of accessing an NTFS 5/NTFS 2000 disk. Although NT/2000/XP support FAT partitions (and Windows 2000/XP even support FAT32), NTFS provides many advantages over FAT, including long filenames, support for larger files and partitions, extended attributes, and increased security. NTFS, like all of Windows NT, was newly designed from the ground up. Backward compatibility with previous Microsoft operating systems was not a concern because the developers were intent on creating an entirely new 32-bit platform. As a result, no operating systems other than Windows NT and Windows 2000/XP, which are based on Windows NT, can read NTFS partitions.

This is an important consideration. All the other Windows operating systems are fundamentally based on DOS and leave you the alternative of booting to a DOS prompt in special situations. Whether you have to run a special DOS utility to configure a piece of hardware or perform an emergency disk repair, the DOS option is always there.

Windows NT/2000/XP are not DOS based. You can open a window that provides a DOS-like command prompt in Windows NT/2000/XP, but this is actually a DOS emulation—not a true shell. You can't boot the system to a command prompt, avoiding the GUI, as you can with Windows 9x unless you install the Windows 2000 or Windows XP Recovery Console. As the name implies, the Recovery Console is designed for system repair and maintenance procedures, not for routine use. You can, of course, bypass NT/2000/XP entirely by starting the system with a DOS boot disk, but if you have NTFS partitions on your drives, you can't access them from the DOS prompt.

NTFS supports filenames of up to 255 characters, using spaces, multiple periods, and any other standard characters except the following: *?/\;<>|. Because NTFS file offsets are 64 bits long, files and partitions can be truly enormous: up to 16EB (exabytes) in size (1EB = 2^{64} bytes = 17,179,869,184TB)! To give you an idea of just how much data this is, it is estimated that all the words ever spoken by humans throughout history would occupy 5EB of storage.

Since Windows NT 3.51, NTFS has also supported compression on a file-by-file basis through each file's properties sheet. No third-party program, such as WinZip or PKZip, is needed to compress or decompress files stored on an NTFS drive.

NTFS Architecture

Although NTFS partitions are very different from FAT partitions internally, they do comply with the extra-partitional disk structures described earlier in this chapter. NTFS partitions are listed in the master partition table of a disk drive's master boot record, just like FAT partitions, and they have a volume boot record as well, although it is formatted somewhat differently.

When a volume is formatted with NTFS, system files are created in the root directory of the NTFS volume. These system files can be stored at any physical location on the NTFS volume. This means that damage to any specific location on the disk will probably not render the entire partition inaccessible.

Typically, 10 NTFS system files are created when you format an NTFS volume. Table 25.22 shows the names and descriptions for these files.

Table 25.22   NTFS System Files

Filename	Meaning	Description
$mft	Master file table (MFT)	Contains a record for every file on the NTFS volume in its Data attribute
$mftmirr	Master file table2 (MFT2)	Mirror of the MFT used for recoverability purposes
$badclus	Bad cluster file	Contains all the bad clusters on the volume
$bitmap	Cluster allocation bitmap	Contains the bitmap for the entire volume, showing which clusters are used
$boot	Boot file	Contains the volume's bootstrap if the volume is bootable
$attrdef	Attribute definitions table	Contains the definition of all system- and user-defined attributes on the volume
$logfile	Log file	Logs file transactions, used for recoverability purposes
$quota	Quota table	Table used to indicate disk quota usage for each user on a volume, used in NTFS 5
$upcase	Upcase table	Table used for converting uppercase and lowercase characters to the matching uppercase Unicode characters
$volume	Volume	Contains volume information, such as volume name and version

An NTFS partition is based on a structure called the master file table (MFT). The MFT concept expands on that of the FAT. Instead of using a table of cluster references, the MFT contains much more detailed information about the files and directories in the partition. In some cases, it even contains the files and directories themselves.

The first record in the MFT is called the descriptor, which contains information about the MFT itself. The volume boot record for an NTFS partition contains a reference that points to the location of this descriptor record. The second record in the MFT is a mirror copy of the descriptor, which provides fault tolerance, should the first copy be damaged.

The third record is the log file record. All NTFS transactions are logged to a file that can be used to restore data in the event of a disk problem. The bulk of the MFT consists of records for the files and directories stored on the partition. NTFS files take the form of objects that have both user- and system-defined attributes. Attributes on NTFS partitions are more comprehensive than the few simple flags used on FAT partitions. All the information on an NTFS file is stored as attributes of that file. In fact, even the file data itself is an attribute. Unlike FAT files, the attributes of NTFS files are part of the file itself; they are not listed separately in a directory entry. Directories exist as MFT records as well, but they consist mainly of indexes listing the files in the directory; they do not contain the size, date, time, and other information about the individual files.

Thus, an NTFS drive's MFT is much more than a cluster list, like a FAT; it is actually the primary data storage structure on the partition. If a file or directory is relatively small (less than approximately 1,500 bytes), the entire file or directory might even be stored in the MFT. For larger amounts of storage, the MFT record for a file or directory contains pointers to external clusters in the partition. These external clusters are called *extents*. All the records in the MFT, including the descriptors and the log file, are capable of using extents for storage of additional attributes. The attributes of a file that are part of the MFT record are called *resident* attributes. Those stored in extents are called *nonresident* attributes.

NTFS 5 (NTFS 2000)

Along with Windows 2000 came a new variation of NTFS called NTFS 5 (also called NTFS 2000); NTFS 5 is also used by Windows XP. This update of the NT file system includes several new features that are exploited and even required by Windows 2000. Because of this, when you install Windows 2000, any existing NTFS volumes automatically are upgraded to NTFS 5 (there is no way to override). If you also run Windows NT versions earlier than Windows NT 4 Service Pack 4 (SP4), NT 4 is no longer capable of accessing the NTFS 5 volumes. If you want to run both NT 4 and Windows 2000 on the same system (as in a dual-boot configuration), you must upgrade NT 4 by installing Service Pack 4 or later. An updated NTFS.SYS driver in Service Pack 4 enables NT 4 to read from and write to NTFS 5 volumes.

New features of the NTFS 5 file system include

- *Disk quotas.* System administrators can limit the amount of disk space users can consume on a per-volume basis. The three quota levels are Off, Tracking, and Enforced.

- *Encryption.* NTFS 5 can automatically encrypt and decrypt files as they are read from and written to the disk.

- *Reparse points.* Programs can trap open operations against objects in the file system and run their own code before returning file data. This can be used to extend file system features such as mount points, which you can use to redirect data read and written from a folder to another volume or physical disk.

- *Sparse files.* This feature enables programs to create very large files as placeholders but to consume disk space by adding to the files only as necessary.

- *USN (Update Sequence Number) Journal.* Provides a log of all changes made to files on the volume.

Because these features—especially the USN Journal—are required for Windows 2000 to run, a Win2000 domain controller must use an NTFS 5 partition as the system volume.

NTFS Compatibility

Although NTFS partitions are not directly accessible by DOS and other operating systems, Windows NT/2000 is designed for network use, so other operating systems are expected to be capable of accessing NTFS files via the network. For this reason, NTFS continues to support the standard DOS file attributes and the 8.3 FAT naming convention.

One of the main reasons for using NTFS is the security it provides for its files and directories. NTFS security attributes are called *permissions* and are designed to enable system administrators to control access to files and directories by granting specific rights to users and groups. This is a much more granular approach than the FAT file system attributes, which apply to all users.

However, you can still set the FAT-style attributes on NTFS files using the standard Windows NT/2000 file management tools, including Windows NT/2000 Explorer and even the command-prompt ATTRIB command. When you copy FAT files to an NTFS drive over the network, the FAT-style attributes remain in place until you explicitly remove them. This can be an important consideration because the FAT-style attributes take precedence over the NTFS permissions. A file on an NTFS drive that is flagged with the FAT read-only attribute, for example, can't be deleted by a Windows NT/2000 user, even if that user has NTFS permissions that grant her full access.

To enable DOS and 16-bit Windows systems to access files on NTFS partitions over a network, the file system maintains an 8.3 alias name for every file and directory on the partition. The algorithm for deriving the alias from the long filename is the same as that used by Windows 95's VFAT. Windows NT/2000 also provides its FAT partitions with the same type of long filename support used by VFAT, allocating additional directory entries to store the long filenames as needed.

Creating NTFS Drives

NTFS is for use on hard disk drives. You can't create an NTFS floppy disk (although you can format removable media, such as Iomega Zip and Jaz cartridges to use NTFS). Three basic ways to create an NTFS disk partition are as follows:

- Create a new NTFS volume out of unpartitioned disk space during the Windows NT/2000 installation process or after the installation with the Disk Administrator utility.

- Format an existing partition to NTFS (destroying its data in the process), using the Windows NT Format dialog box (accessible from Windows NT Explorer or Disk Administrator) or the FORMAT command (with the /fs:ntfs switch) from the command prompt.

- Convert an existing FAT partition to NTFS (preserving its data) during the Windows NT/2000 installation process or after the installation with the command-line CONVERT utility.

NTFS Tools

Because it uses a fundamentally different architecture, virtually none of the troubleshooting techniques outlined earlier in this chapter are applicable when dealing with NTFS partitions, nor can the disk utilities intended for use on FAT partitions address them. Windows NT has a rudimentary capability to check a disk for file system errors and bad sectors with its own version of CHKDSK, but apart from that, the operating system contains no other disk repair or defragmentation utilities. Windows 2000 and Windows XP include a commmand-line and GUI version of CHKDSK and also include a defragmenting tool that is run from the Windows Explorer GUI.

The NTFS file system, however, does have its own automatic disk repair capabilities. In addition to Windows NT/2000/XP's fault-tolerance features, such as disk mirroring (maintaining the same data on two separate drives) and disk striping with parity (splitting data across several drives with parity information for data reconstruction), the OS also uses a disk error recovery technique called *cluster remapping*.

With cluster remapping, when Windows (NT/2000/XP) detects a bad sector on an NTFS partition, it automatically remaps the data in that cluster to another cluster. If the drive is part of a fault-tolerant drive array, any lost data is reconstructed from the duplicate data on the other drives.

Despite these features, however, there is still a real need for disk repair and defragmentation utilities for Windows NT/2000/XP. They have been a long time in coming, but finally third-party utilities now are available that can repair and defragment NTFS drives. One I recommend is Norton Utilities 2001 by Symantec, which works with Windows 98, Windows Me, Windows NT 4.0, and Windows 2000. An updated version is necessary for Windows XP.

Common Drive Error Messages and Solutions

Several common error messages are associated with problems in the file system or drives. This section covers the common ones, listing their causes and possible solutions.

Some of the most common file system errors are as follows:

- `Missing Operating System`
- `NO ROM BASIC - SYSTEM HALTED`
- `Boot error Press F1 to retry`
- `Invalid drive specification`
- `Invalid Media Type`
- `Hard Disk Controller Failure`

These normally occur when booting the system or when trying to log in to or access a drive. The following sections describe each of these errors and offer possible solutions.

Missing Operating System

This error indicates problems in the master boot record or partition table entries. The partition table entries might be pointing to a sector that is not the actual beginning of a partition. This can also be caused by invalid BIOS settings, in some cases resulting from a dead or dying battery. In fact, in my experience, corrupt or improper BIOS settings—such as incorrect geometry (cylinder/head/sector) or LBA mode settings—are the number-one cause of this problem. Another cause can be virus damage to the MBR. This error also can occur if no active partition is defined in the partition table.

The normal solution is to correct the invalid BIOS settings. The BIOS settings for drive parameters and LBA translation must be set to the same values as when the drive was partitioned and formatted to read the drive correctly. If the MBR is damaged or virus infected, you can try `FDISK/MBR` to repair it. Other types of damage require more sophisticated use of a disk editor utility or repartitioning and reformatting the drive to start over.

NO ROM BASIC - SYSTEM HALTED

This error is generated by the AMI BIOS when the boot sector or master boot record of the boot drive is damaged or missing. This error also can occur if the boot device has been improperly configured or is not configured at all in the BIOS. In this case, data in the partition might be valid and undamaged, but no bootable partition exists.

IBM systems in this situation used to drop into a built-in BIOS version of BASIC, but most non-IBM BIOS manufacturers did not license this code from Microsoft. So, instead of dropping into BASIC, they would display this cryptic message. Because the most common cause of this type of error is a failure to set at least one partition as active (bootable), the normal solution is to run FDISK and set the primary partition as active. If this is not the problem, the solution is to repair the damaged MBR or correct the improper BIOS settings.

Other possible problems include corrupted or missing drive parameters in the BIOS Setup.

Boot Error Press F1 to Retry

This error is generated by the Phoenix BIOS when the hard disk is missing a master boot record or boot sector or when there is a problem accessing the boot drive. This has the same meaning as `NO ROM BASIC` does on an AMI BIOS. The most common cause of this message is having no partitions defined as active (bootable). See the section on `NO ROM BASIC` earlier in the chapter for more information.

Invalid Drive Specification

This error occurs when you attempt to log in to a drive that has not been partitioned or for which the partition table entry has been damaged or is incorrect. Use FDISK to partition the drive or to check out the existing partitions. If they are damaged, you probably should use a data recovery utility such as the Norton Utilities to correct the problem. Such correction might require manual editing of the partition table with the DISKEDIT program included with the Norton Utilities. Another solution is to repartition the drive from scratch, but this causes any existing data on the drive to be overwritten.

Invalid Media Type

This indicates the partition table is valid, but the volume boot sector, directory, or file allocation tables are corrupt, damaged, or not yet initialized. For example, this is the standard error you would receive if you tried to access a drive that had been partitioned but not yet formatted. The FORMAT command is what creates the volume boot record (VBR), file allocation tables, and directories on the disk.

The repair usually involves using a data recovery utility, such as the Norton Utilities Disk Doctor, or redoing the high-level format on the drive. Because high-level formatting does not actually destroy the data, one technique to recover is to high-level format (OS Format) the volume and then immediately unformat it using the unformat utility included with the Norton Utilities.

Hard Disk Controller Failure

This message indicates the hard disk controller has failed, the hard disk controller is not set up properly in the BIOS, or the controller can't communicate with the attached drives, such as with cable problems.

The solution is to check out the drive installation and ensure that the cables to the drive are properly installed, the drive is receiving power, it is spinning, and the BIOS Setup definitions are correct. If all these are correct, the drive, cable, or controller might be physically damaged. Replace them with known-good spares one at a time until the problem is solved.

General File System Troubleshooting for MS-DOS, Windows 9x, and Windows Me

Here are some general procedures to follow for troubleshooting drive access, file system, or boot problems:

1. Start the system using a Windows startup disk, or any bootable MS-DOS disk that contains FDISK.EXE, FORMAT.COM, SYS.COM, and SCANDISK.EXE (Windows 95B or later versions preferred).

2. If your system can't boot from the floppy, you might have more serious problems with your hardware. Check the floppy drive and the motherboard for proper installation and configuration. On some systems, the BIOS configuration doesn't list the floppy as a boot device or puts it after the hard disk. Reset the BIOS configuration to make the floppy disk the first boot device if necessary and restart your computer.

3. Run FDISK from the Windows startup disk. Select option 4 (Display partition information).

4. If the partitions are listed, make sure that the bootable partition (normally the primary partition) is defined as active (look for an uppercase *A* in the Status column).

5. If no partitions are listed and you do not want to recover any of the data existing on the drive now, use FDISK to create new partitions, and then use FORMAT to format the partitions. This overwrites any previously existing data on the drive.

6. If you want to recover the data on the drive and no partitions are being shown, you must use a data recovery program, such as the Norton Utilities by Symantec or Lost and Found by PowerQuest, to recover the data.

7. If all the partitions appear in FDISK.EXE and one is defined as active, run the SYS command as follows to restore the system files to the hard disk:

   SYS C:

8. For this to work properly, it is important that the disk you boot from be a startup disk from the same operating system (or version of Windows) you have on your hard disk.

9. You should receive the message System Transferred if the command works properly. Remove the disk from drive A:, and restart the system. If you still have the same error as before after you restart your computer, your drive might be improperly configured or damaged.

10. Run SCANDISK from the Windows startup disk or an aftermarket data-recovery utility, such as the Norton Utilities, to check for problems with the hard disk.

11. Using SCANDISK, perform a surface scan. If SCANDISK reports any physically damaged sectors on the hard disk, the drive might need to be replaced.

General File System Troubleshooting for Windows 2000/XP

The process for file system troubleshooting with Windows 2000/XP is similar to that used for Windows 9x. The major difference is the use of the Windows 2000/XP Recovery Console, which is clarified here:

- If the Recovery Console was added to the boot menu, start the system normally, log in as Administrator if prompted, and select the Recovery Console.

- If the Recovery Console was not previously added to the boot menu, start the system using the Windows CD-ROM or the Windows Setup disks. Select Repair from the Welcome to Setup menu, and then press C to start the Recovery Console when prompted.

If your system can't boot from CD-ROM or the floppy, you might have more serious problems with your hardware. Check your drives, your BIOS configuration, and the motherboard for proper installation and configuration. Set the floppy disk as the first boot device and the CD-ROM as the second boot device and restart the system.

After you start the Recovery Console do the following:

1. Type **HELP** for a list of Recovery Console commands and assistance.

2. Run DISKPART to examine your disk partitions.

3. If the partitions are listed, make sure that the bootable partition (normally the primary partition) is defined as active.

4. If no partitions are listed and you do not want to recover any of the data existing on the drive now, use FDISK to create new partitions, and then use FORMAT to format the partitions. This overwrites any previously existing data on the drive.

5. If you want to recover the data on the drive and no partitions are being shown, you must use a data recovery program, such as the Norton Utilities by Symantec or Lost and Found by PowerQuest, to recover the data.

6. If all the partitions appear in DISKPART and one is defined as active, run the FIXBOOT command as follows to restore the system files to the hard disk:

   FIXBOOT

7. Type **EXIT** to restart your system. Remove the disk from drive A: or the Windows 2000 CD-ROM from the CD-ROM drive.

8. If you still have the same error as before after you restart your computer, your drive might be improperly configured or damaged.

9. Restart the Recovery Console and run CHKDSK to check for problems with the hard disk.

Glossary

This glossary contains computer and electronics terms that are applicable to the subject matter in this book. The glossary is meant to be as comprehensive as possible on the subject of upgrading and repairing PCs. Many terms correspond to the latest technology in disk interfaces, modems, video and display equipment, and standards that govern the PC industry. Although a glossary is a resource not designed to be read from beginning to end, you should find that scanning through this one is interesting, if not enlightening, with respect to some of the newer PC technology.

The computer industry is filled with abbreviations used as shorthand for a number of terms. This glossary defines many abbreviations, as well as the term on which the abbreviation is based. The definition of an abbreviation usually is included under the acronym. For example, *video graphics array* is defined under the abbreviation *VGA* rather than under *video graphics array*. This organization makes it easier to look up a term—*IDE*, for example—even if you do not know in advance what it stands for (*integrated drive electronics*).

For additional reference, *Que's Computer Dictionary* (ISBN: 0-7897-1670-4) is a comprehensive dictionary of computer terminology.

These Web sites can also help you with terms not included in this glossary:

    http://coverage.cnet.com/Resources/Info/Glossary/

    http://www.webopedia.com

10BASE-2   IEEE standard for baseband Ethernet at 10Mbps over RG-58 coaxial cable to a maximum distance of 185 meters. Also known as Thin Ethernet (Thinnet) or IEEE 802.3.

10BASE-5   IEEE standard for baseband Ethernet at 10Mbps over thick coaxial cable to a maximum distance of 500 meters. Also known as Thick Ethernet or Thicknet.

10BASE-T   A 10Mbps CSMA/CD Ethernet LAN that works on Category 3 or better twisted-pair wiring, which is very similar to standard telephone cabling. 10BASE-T Ethernet LANs work on a "star" configuration, in which the wire from each workstation routes directly to a 10BASE-T hub. Hubs can be joined together.

56K   The generic term for modems that can receive data at 56Kbps. See also *V.90*, *X2*, *KFlex*.

100BASE-T   A 100Mbps CSMA/CD Ethernet local area network (LAN) that works on Category 5 twisted-pair wiring. 100BASE-T Ethernet LANs work on a "star" configuration in which the wire from each workstation routes directly to a central 100BASE-T hub. This is the new standard for 100Mbps Ethernet.

100BASE-VG   The joint Hewlett-Packard–AT&T proposal for Fast Ethernet running at 100Mbps. It uses four pairs of Category 5 cable using the 10BASE-T twisted-pair wiring scheme to transmit or receive. 100BASE-VG splits the signal across the four wire pairs at 25MHz each. This standard has not found favor with corporations and has been almost totally replaced by 100BASE-T.

286   See *80286*.

386   See *80386DX*.

486   See *80486DX*.

586   A generic term used to refer to fifth-generation processors similar to the Intel Pentium.

640KB barrier   The limit imposed by the PC-compatible memory model using DOS mode. DOS programs can address only 1MB total memory, and PC-compatibility generally requires the top 384KB to be reserved for the system, leaving only the lower 640KB for DOS or other real-mode applications.

80286   An Intel microprocessor with 16-bit registers, a 16-bit data bus, and a 24-bit address bus. It can operate in both real and protected virtual modes.

80287   An Intel math coprocessor designed to perform floating-point math with much greater speed and precision than the main CPU. The 80287 can be installed in most 286- and some 386DX-based systems, and it adds more than 50 new instructions to what is available in the primary CPU alone.

80386   See *80386DX*.

80386DX   An Intel microprocessor with 32-bit registers, a 32-bit data bus, and a 32-bit address bus. This processor can operate in real, protected virtual, and virtual real modes.

80386SX   An Intel microprocessor with 32-bit registers, a 16-bit data bus, and a 24-bit address bus. This processor, designed as a low-cost version of the 386DX, can operate in real, protected virtual, and virtual real modes.

80387   An Intel math coprocessor designed to perform floating-point math with much greater speed and precision than the main CPU. The 80387 can be installed in most 386DX-based systems and adds more than 50 new instructions to those available in the primary CPU alone.

80486   See *80486DX*.

80486DX   An Intel microprocessor with 32-bit registers, a 32-bit data bus, and a 32-bit address bus. The 486DX has a built-in cache controller with 8KB of cache memory as well as a built-in math coprocessor equivalent to a 387DX. The 486DX can operate in real, protected virtual, and virtual real modes.

80486DX2   A version of the 486DX with an internal clock-doubling circuit that causes the chip to run at twice the motherboard clock speed. If the motherboard clock is 33MHz, the DX2 chip will run at 66MHz. The DX2 designation applies to chips sold through the OEM market, whereas a retail version of the DX2 is sold as an overdrive processor.

80486DX4   A version of the 486DX with an internal clock-tripling circuit that causes the chip to run at three times the motherboard clock speed. If the motherboard clock is 33.33MHz, the DX4 chip will run at 100MHz.

80486SX   An Intel microprocessor with 32-bit registers, a 32-bit data bus, and a 32-bit address bus. The 486SX is the same as the 486DX, except that it lacks the built-in math coprocessor function and was designed as a low-cost version of the 486DX. The 486SX can operate in real, protected virtual, and virtual real modes.

8086   An Intel microprocessor with 16-bit registers, a 16-bit data bus, and a 20-bit address bus. This processor can operate only in real mode.

8087   An Intel math coprocessor designed to perform floating-point math with much greater speed and precision than the main CPU. The 8087 can be installed in most 8086- and 8088-based systems and adds more than 50 new instructions to those available in the primary CPU alone.

8088   An Intel microprocessor with 16-bit registers, an 8-bit data bus, and a 20-bit address bus. This processor can operate only in real mode and was designed as a low-cost version of the 8086.

8514/A   An analog video display adapter from IBM for the PS/2 line of personal computers. Compared to previous display adapters, such as EGA and VGA, it provides a high resolution of 1,024×768 pixels with as many as 256 colors or 64 shades of gray. It provides a video coprocessor that performs two-dimensional graphics functions internally, thus relieving the CPU of graphics tasks. It uses an interlaced monitor; it scans every other line every time the screen is refreshed.

abend   Short for *abnormal end*. A condition occurring when the execution of a program or task is terminated unexpectedly because of a bug or crash.

absolute address   An explicit identification of a memory location, device, or location within a device.

AC (alternating current)   The frequency is measured in cycles per seconds (cps) or hertz (Hz). The standard value running through the wall outlet is 120 volts at 60Hz, through a fuse or circuit breaker that usually can handle about 15 or 20 amps.

accelerator board   An add-in board replacing the computer's CPU with circuitry that enables the system to run more quickly. See *graphics accelerator*.

access light   The LED on the front of a drive or other device (or on the front panel of the system) that indicates the computer is reading or writing data on the device.

access mechanism   See *actuator*.

access time   The time that elapses from the instant information is requested to the point that delivery is completed. It's usually described in nanoseconds (ns) for memory chips and in milliseconds (ms) for disk drives. Most manufacturers rate average access time on a hard disk as the time required for a seek across one-third of the total number of cylinders plus one-half the time for a single revolution of the disk platters (latency).

accumulator   A register (temporary storage) in which the result of an operation is formed.

acoustic coupler   A device used to connect a computer modem to a phone line by connecting to the handset of a standard AT&T-style phone. The audible sounds to and from the modem are transmitted to the handset through the coupler while the handset is resting in the coupler. Although often thought of as obsolete, an acoustic coupler can be used to ensure the availability of a modem connection when traveling and access to an RJ-11 jack is unavailable.

ACPI (Advanced Configuration and Power Interface)   A standard developed by Intel, Microsoft, and Toshiba that is designed to implement power management functions in the operating system. ACPI is a replacement for APM. See also *APM*.

active high   Designates a digital signal that must go to a high value to be true. Synonymous with positive.

active low   Designates a digital signal that must go to a low value to be true. Synonymous with negative.

active matrix   A type of LCD screen that contains at least one transistor for every pixel on the screen. Color active-matrix screens use three transistors for each pixel—one each for the red, green, and blue dots. The transistors are arranged on a grid of conductive material, with each connected to a horizontal and a vertical member. See also *TFT*.

active partition   Any partition marked as bootable in the partition table.

actuator   The device that moves a disk drive's read/write heads across the platter surfaces. Also known as an access mechanism.

adapter   The device that serves as an interface between the system unit and the devices attached to it. It's often synonymous with circuit board, circuit card, or card, but also can refer to a connector or cable adapter, which changes one type of connector to another.

adapter description files (ADF)   Refers to the setup and configuration files and drivers necessary to install an adapter card, such as a network adapter card. Primarily used with Micro Channel Architecture bus cards.

add-in board   See *expansion card*.

address   Refers to where a particular piece of data or other information is found in the computer. Also can refer to the location of a set of instructions.

address bus   One or more electrical conductors used to carry the binary-coded address from the microprocessor throughout the rest of the system.

ADSL (asymmetric digital subscriber line)   A high-speed transmission technology originally developed by Bellcore and now standardized by ANSI as T1.413. ADSL uses existing UTP copper wires to communicate digitally at high speed between the telephone company central office (CO) and the subscriber. ADSL sends information asymmetrically, meaning it is faster one way than the other. The original ADSL speed was T-1 (1.536Mbps) downstream from the carrier to the subscriber's premises

and 16Kbps upstream. However, ADSL is available in a variety of configurations and speeds. See *DSL*.

AGP (accelerated graphics port)
Developed by Intel, a fast, dedicated interface between the video adapter or chipset and the motherboard chipset North Bridge. AGP is 32 bits wide; runs at 66MHz base speed; and can transfer 1, 2, or 4 bits per cycle (1x, 2x, or 4x modes) for a throughput of up to 1,066Mbytes/sec.

aliasing   Undesirable visual effects (sometimes called artifacts) in computer-generated images, caused by inadequate sampling techniques. The most common effect is jagged edges along diagonal or curved object boundaries. See also *antialiasing*.

allocation unit   See *cluster*.

alphanumeric characters   A character set that contains only letters (A–Z) and digits (0–9). Other characters, such as punctuation marks, also might be allowed.

ampere   The basic unit for measuring electrical current. Also called amp.

analog loopback   A modem self-test in which data from the keyboard is sent to the modem's transmitter, modulated into analog form, looped back to the receiver, demodulated into digital form, and returned to the screen for verification.

analog signals   Continuously variable signals. Analog circuits are more subject to distortion and noise than are digital circuits but are capable of handling complex signals with relatively simple circuitry. See also *digital signals*.

analog   The representation of numerical values by physical variables such as voltage, current, and so on; continuously variable quantities whose values correspond to the quantitative magnitude of the variables.

analog-to-digital converter   An electronic device that converts analog signals to digital form.

AND   A logic operator having the property that if P is a statement, Q is a statement, R is a statement…, then the AND of P, Q, R… is true if all statements are true and is false if any statement is false.

AND gate A logic gate in which the output is 1 only if all inputs are 1.

animation The process of displaying a sequential series of still images to achieve a motion effect.

ANSI (American National Standards Institute) A nongovernmental organization founded in 1918 to propose, modify, approve, and publish data processing standards for voluntary use in the United States. It's also the U.S. representative to the International Standards Organization (ISO) in Paris and the International Electrotechnical Commission (IEC). For more information, see the Vendor List on the CD. Contact ANSI, 1430 Broadway, New York, NY 10018.

answer mode A state in which the modem transmits at the predefined high frequency of the communications channel and receives at the low frequency. The transmit/receive frequencies are the reverse of the calling modem, which is in originate mode. See also *originate mode*.

antialiasing Software adjustment to make diagonal or curved lines appear smooth and continuous in computer-generated images. See also *aliasing*.

antistatic mat A pad placed next to a computer upon which components are placed while servicing the system to prevent static damage. Also can refer to a larger-sized mat below an entire computer desk and chair to discharge static from a user before he touches the computer.

antivirus Software that prevents files containing viruses from running on a computer or software that detects, repairs, cleans, or removes virus-infected files.

APA (all points addressable) A mode in which all points of a displayable image can be controlled by the user or a program.

aperture grille A type of shadow mask used in CRTs. The most common is used in Sony's Trinitron monitors, which use vertical phosphor stripes and vertical slots in the mask, compared to the traditional shadow mask that uses phosphor dots and round holes in the mask. See also *shadow mask*.

API (Application Program Interface) A system call (routine) that gives programmers access to the services provided by the operating system. In IBM-compatible systems, the ROM BIOS and DOS together present an API that a programmer can use to control the system hardware.

APM (Advanced Power Management) A specification sponsored by Intel and Microsoft originally proposed to extend the life of batteries in battery-powered computers. It is now used in desktop computers, as well. APM enables application programs, the system BIOS, and the hardware to work together to reduce power consumption. An APM-compliant BIOS provides built-in power-management services to the operating system. The application software communicates power-saving data via predefined APM interfaces. Replaced in newer systems by ACPI. See also *ACPI*.

application End-user–oriented software, such as a word processor, spreadsheet, database, graphics editor, game, or Web browser.

Application Layer See *OSI*.

arbitration A method by which multiple devices attached to a single bus can bid or arbitrate to get control of that bus.

archive bit The bit in a file's attribute byte that sets the archive attribute. Tells whether the file has been changed since it last was backed up.

archive medium A storage medium (floppy disk, tape cartridge, or removable cartridge) to hold files that need not be accessible instantly.

ARCnet (Attached Resource Computer Network) A baseband, token-passing LAN technology offering a flexible bus/star topology for connecting personal computers. Operating at 2.5Mbit/sec, it is one of the oldest LAN systems and was popular in low-cost networks. Was originally developed by John Murphy of Datapoint Corporation, although ARCnet interface cards are available from a variety of vendors.

areal density   A calculation of the bit density (bits per inch, or BPI) multiplied by the track density (tracks per inch, or TPI), which results in a figure indicating how many bits per square inch are present on the disk surface.

ARQ (automatic repeat request)   A general term for error-control protocols that feature error detection and automatic retransmission of defective blocks of data.

ASCII (American Standard Code for Information Interchange)   A standard 7-bit code created in 1965 by Robert W. Bemer to achieve compatibility among various types of data processing equipment. The standard ASCII character set consists of 128 decimal numbers ranging from 0 to 127, which are assigned to letters, numbers, punctuation marks, and the most common special characters. In 1981, IBM introduced the extended ASCII character set with the IBM PC, extending the code to 8 bits and adding characters from 128 to 255 to represent additional special mathematical, graphics, and foreign characters.

ASCII character   A 1-byte character from the ASCII character set, including alphabetic and numeric characters, punctuation symbols, and various graphics characters.

ASME (American Society of Mechanical Engineers) (http://www.asme.org/)   ASME International has nearly 600 codes and standards in print, and its many committees involve more than 3,000 individuals, mostly engineers but not necessarily members of the society. The standards are used in more than 90 countries throughout the world.

aspect ratio   The measurement of a film or television viewing area in terms of relative height and width. The aspect ratio of most modern motion pictures varies from 3:5 to as large as 3:7, which creates a problem when a wide-format motion picture is transferred to the more square-shaped television screen, with its aspect ratio of 3:4.

assemble   The act of translating a program expressed in an assembler language into a computer machine language.

assembler language   A computer-oriented language whose instructions are usually in one-to-one correspondence with machine language instructions.

asymmetrical modulation   A duplex transmission technique that splits the communications channel into one high-speed channel and one slower channel. During a call under asymmetrical modulation, the modem with the greater amount of data to transmit is allocated the high-speed channel. The modem with less data is allocated the slow, or back, channel. The modems dynamically reverse the channels during a call if the volume of data transfer changes.

asynchronous communication   Data transmission in which the length of time between transmitted characters can vary. Timing depends on the actual time for the transfer to take place, as opposed to synchronous communication, which is timed rigidly by an external clock signal. Because the receiving modem must be signaled about when the data bits of a character begin and end, start and stop bits are added to each character. See also *synchronous communication*.

asynchronous memory   Memory that runs using a timing or clock rate different from (usually slower than) the motherboard speed.

AT clock   Refers to the Motorola 146818 real-time clock (RTC) and CMOS RAM chip, which first debuted in the IBM AT and whose function has been present in all PC-compatible systems since. Keeps track of the time of day and makes this data available to the operating system or other software.

ATA (AT Attachment Interface)   An IDE disk interface standard introduced in March 1989 that defines a compatible register set and a 40-pin connector and its associated signals. See also *IDE*.

ATA-2   The second generation AT Attachment Interface specification. This version defines faster transfer modes and logical block addressing schemes to allow high-performance, large-capacity drives. Also called Fast ATA, Fast ATA-2, and enhanced IDE (EIDE).

ATAPI (AT Attachment Packet Interface)   A specification that defines device-side characteristics for an IDE-connected peripheral, such as a CD-ROM or tape drive. ATAPI is essentially an adaptation of the SCSI command set to the IDE interface.

Athlon   An AMD sixth-generation processor roughly comparable to the Intel Pentium II or III. Later models (code named Thunderbird) include on-die L2 cache running at full core speed. Includes MMX and AMD 3DNow! instructions for multimedia performance. Originally available in a Slot-A cartridge package, all Athlons are now available only in the Socket-A (462-pin) package.

ATM (asynchronous transfer mode)   A high-bandwidth, low-delay, packet-like switching and multiplexing technique. Usable capacity is segmented into fixed-size cells consisting of header and information fields, allocated to services on demand.

attribute byte   A byte of information, held in the directory entry of any file, that describes various attributes of the file, such as whether it is read-only or has been backed up since it last was changed. Attributes can be set by the DOS ATTRIB command.

ATX   A motherboard and power supply form factor standard designed by Intel and introduced in 1995. It is characterized by a double row of rear external I/O connectors on the motherboard, a single keyed power supply connector, memory and processor locations that are designed not to interfere with the installation of adapter cards, and an improved cooling flow.

audio   A signal that can be heard, such as through the speaker of the PC. Many PC diagnostics tests use both visual (onscreen) codes and audio signals.

audio frequencies   Frequencies that can be heard by the human ear (approximately 20–20,000Hz).

auto-answer   A setting in modems enabling them to answer incoming calls over the phone lines automatically.

auto-dial   A feature in modems enabling them to dial phone numbers without human intervention.

auto-disconnect   A modem feature that enables a modem to hang up the telephone line when the modem at the other end hangs up.

AUTOEXEC.BAT   A special batch file DOS executes at startup. Contains any number of DOS commands that are executed automatically, including the capability to start programs at startup. See also *batch file*.

automatic head parking   Disk drive head parking performed whenever the drive is powered off. Found in all modern hard disk drives with a voice-coil actuator.

auto-redial   A modem or software feature that automatically redials the last number dialed if the number is busy or does not answer.

available memory   Memory currently not in use by the operating system, drivers, or applications, which can be used to load additional software.

average access time   The average time it takes a disk drive to begin reading any data placed anywhere on the drive. This includes the average seek time, which is when the heads are moved, as well as the latency, which is the average amount of time required for any given data sector to pass underneath the heads. Together, these factors make up the average access time. See also *average seek time* and *latency*.

average latency   The average time required for any byte of data stored on a disk to rotate under the disk drive's read/write head. Equal to one-half the time required for a single rotation of a platter.

average seek time   The average amount of time it takes to move the heads from one random cylinder location to another, usually including any head settling time. In many cases, the average seek time is defined as the seek time across one-third of the total number of cylinders.

AVI (audio video interleave)   A storage technique developed by Microsoft for its Video for Windows product that combines audio and video into a single frame or track, saving valuable disk space and keeping audio in synchronization with the corresponding video.

Bézier curve   A mathematical method for describing a curve, often used in illustration and CAD programs to draw complex shapes.

backbone   The portion of the Internet or wide area network (WAN) transmission wiring that connects the main Internet/WAN servers and routers and is responsible for carrying the bulk of the Internet/WAN data.

backplane   A rarely used motherboard design in which the components normally found on a motherboard are located instead on an expansion adapter card plugged into a slot. In these systems, the board with the slots is the backplane.

backup   The process of duplicating a file or library onto a separate piece of media. It's good insurance against the loss of an original.

backup disk   Contains information copied from another disk. Used to ensure that original information is not destroyed or altered.

backward compatibility   The design of software and hardware to work with previous versions of the same software or hardware.

bad sector   A disk sector that cannot hold data reliably because of a media flaw or damaged format markings.

bad track table   A label affixed to the casing of a hard disk drive that tells which tracks are flawed and cannot hold data. The listing is entered into the low-level formatting program.

balanced signal   Refers to signals consisting of equal currents moving in opposite directions. When balanced or nearly balanced signals pass through twisted-pair lines, the electromagnetic interference effects, such as crosstalk caused by the two opposite currents, largely cancel each other out. Differential signaling is a method that uses balanced signals.

balun   Short for balanced/unbalanced. A type of transformer that enables balanced cables to be joined with unbalanced cables.

Twisted-pair (balanced) cables, for example, can be joined with coaxial (unbalanced) cables if the proper balun transformer is used.

bandwidth   1) Generally, the measure of the range of frequencies within a radiation band required to transmit a particular signal. The difference between the lowest and highest signal frequencies. The bandwidth of a computer monitor is a measure of the rate at which a monitor can handle information from the display adapter. The wider the bandwidth, the more information the monitor can carry and the greater the resolution. 2) Used to describe the data-carrying capacity of a given communications circuit or pathway. The bandwidth of a circuit is a measure of the rate at which information can be passed.

bank   The collection of memory chips or modules that make up a block of memory readable or writable by the processor in a single cycle. This block, therefore, must be as large as the data bus of the particular microprocessor. In PC systems, the processor data bus (and therefore the bank size) is usually 8, 16, 32, or 64 bits wide. Optionally, some systems also incorporate an additional parity or ECC bit for each 8 data bits, resulting in a total of 9, 18, 36, or 72 bits (respectively) for each bank. Memory in a PC always must be added or removed in full-bank increments.

bar code   The code used on consumer products and inventory parts for identification purposes. Consists of bars of varying thickness that represent characters and numerals that are read with an optical reader. The most common version is called the Universal Product Code (UPC).

base address   Starting location for a consecutive string of memory or I/O addresses/ports.

base memory   The amount of memory available to the operating system or application programs within the first megabyte, accessible in the processor's real mode.

base-2   Refers to the computer numbering system that consists of two numerals: 0 and 1. Also called binary.

baseband transmission   The transmission of digital signals over a limited distance. ARCnet and Ethernet local area networks use baseband signaling. Contrasts with broadband transmission, which refers to the transmission of analog signals over a greater distance.

BASIC (Beginner's All-purpose Symbolic Instruction Code) A popular computer programming language. Originally developed by John Kemeny and Thomas Kurtz in the mid-1960s at Dartmouth College. Normally, an interpretive language, meaning that each statement is translated and executed as it is encountered, but can be a compiled language, in which all the program statements are compiled before execution.

batch file A set of commands stored in a disk file for execution by the operating system. A special batch file called AUTOEXEC.BAT is executed by DOS each time the system is started. All DOS batch files have a .BAT file extension.

baud A unit of signaling speed denoting the number of discrete signal elements that can be transmitted per second. The word baud is derived from the name of J.M.E. Baudot (1845–1903), a French pioneer in the field of printing telegraphy and the inventor of Baudot code. Although technically inaccurate, baud rate commonly is used to mean bit rate. Because each signal element or baud can translate into many individual bits, bits per second (bps) normally differs from baud rate. A rate of 2,400 baud means that 2,400 frequency or signal changes per second are being sent, but each frequency change can signal several bits of information. For example, 33.6Kbps modems actually transmit at only 2,400 baud.

Baudot code A 5-bit code used in many types of data communications, including teletype (TTY), radio teletype (RTTY), and telecommunications devices for the deaf (TDD). Baudot code has been revised and extended several times. See also *baud*.

bay An opening in a computer case or chassis that holds disk drives.

BBS (bulletin board system) A computer that operates with a program and a modem to enable other computers with modems to communicate with it, often on a round-the-clock basis. Thousands of PC IBM- and Apple-related BBSes offer a wealth of information and public-domain software that can be downloaded.

B-channel The two bearer channels in ISDN that run at 64Kbps each and that carry the data.

benchmark A test or set of tests designed to compare the performance of hardware or software. A popular set of benchmarks for PC hardware are the Ziff Davis Media benchmarks you can download from http://www.zdnet.com.

bezel A cosmetic panel that covers the face of a drive or some other device.

bidirectional 1) Refers to lines over which data can move in two directions, such as a data bus or telephone line. 2) Refers to the capability of a printer to print from right to left and from left to right alternately.

binary See *base-2*.

BIOS (basic input/output system) The part of an operating system that handles the communications between the computer and its peripherals. Often burned into read-only memory (ROM) chips or rewritable flash (EEP-ROM) memory chips.

bipolar A category of semiconductor circuit design, which was used to create the first transistor and the first integrated circuit. Bipolar and CMOS are the two major transistor technologies. Almost all personal computers use CMOS technology chips. CMOS uses far less energy than bipolar.

bisynchronous (binary synchronous control) An earlier protocol developed by IBM for software applications and communicating devices operating in synchronous environments. The protocol defines operations at the link level of communications—for example, the format of data frames exchanged between modems over a phone line.

bit binary digit Represented logically by 0 or 1 and electrically by 0 volts and (typically) 5 volts. Other methods are used to represent binary digits physically (tones, different voltages, lights, and so on), but the logic is always the same.

bit density Expressed as bits per inch (BPI). Defines how many bits can be written onto one linear inch of a track. Sometimes also called linear density.

bit depth　The number of bits used to describe the color of each pixel on a computer display. For example, a bit depth of two means that the monitor can display only black and white pixels; a bit depth of four means the monitor can display 16 different colors; a bit depth of eight allows for 256 colors; and so on.

bitmap　A method of storing graphics information in memory, in which a bit devoted to each pixel (picture element) onscreen indicates whether that pixel is on or off. A bitmap contains a bit for each point or dot on a video display screen and enables fine resolution because any point or pixel onscreen can be addressed. A greater number of bits can be used to describe each pixel's color, intensity, and other display characteristics.

blank or blanking interval　A period in which no video signal is received by a monitor, while the videodisc or digital video player searches for the next video segment or frame to display.

block　A string of records, words, or characters formed for technical or logic reasons and to be treated as an entity.

block diagram　The logical structure or layout of a system in graphics form. Does not necessarily match the physical layout and does not specify all the components and their interconnections.

BMP　A Windows graphics format that can be device dependent or independent. Device-independent BMP files (DIB) are coded for translation to a wide variety of displays and printers.

BNC (Bayonet-Neill-Concelman)　Also known as British-Naval-Connector, Baby-N-Connector, or Bayonet-Nut-Coupler; nobody seems to be quite sure what the actual name is. This bayonet-locking connector is noted for its excellent shielding and impedance-matching characteristics, resulting in low noise and minimal signal loss at any frequency up to 4GHz. It is used in Ethernet 10BASE-2 networks (also known as IEEE 802.3, or Thinnet) to terminate coaxial cables. It is also used for some high-end video monitors.

bonding　In ISDN, joining two 64Kbps B-channels to achieve 128Kbps speed.

Boolean operation　Any operation in which each of the operands and the result take one of two values.

boot　To load a program into the computer. The term comes from the phrase "pulling a boot on by the bootstrap."

boot record　The first sector on a disk or partition that contains disk parameter information for the BIOS and operating system as well as bootstrap loader code that instructs the system how to load the operating system files into memory, thus beginning the initial boot sequence to boot the machine.

boot sector　See *boot record*.

boot sector virus　A virus designed to occupy the boot sector of a disk. Any attempt to start or boot a system from this disk transfers the virus to the hard disk, after which it subsequently is loaded every time the system is started. Most PC viruses are boot sector viruses.

bootstrap　A technique or device designed to bring itself into a desired state by means of its own action. The term is used to describe the process by which a device such as a PC goes from its initial power-on condition to a running condition without human intervention. See also *boot*.

boule　Purified, cylindrical silicon crystals from which semiconducting electronic chips, including microprocessors, memory, and other chips, in a PC are manufactured. Also called an ingot.

bps (bits per second)　The number of binary digits, or bits, transmitted per second. Sometimes confused with baud.

branch prediction　A feature of fifth-generation (Pentium and higher) processors that attempts to predict whether a program branch will be taken and then fetches the appropriate following instructions.

bridge　In local area networks, an interconnection between two similar networks. Also the hardware equipment used to establish such an interconnection.

broadband transmission   A term used to describe analog transmission. Requires modems for connecting terminals and computers to the network. Using frequency division multiplexing, many signals or sets of data can be transmitted simultaneously. The alternative transmission scheme is baseband, or digital, transmission.

brownout   An AC supply voltage drop in which the power does not shut off entirely but continues to be supplied at lower than normal levels.

bubble memory   A special type of non-volatile read/write memory introduced by Intel in which magnetic regions are suspended in crystal film and data is maintained when the power is off. A typical bubble memory chip contains about 512KB, or more than four million bubbles. Bubble memory failed to catch on because of slow access times measured in several milliseconds. It has, however, found a niche use as solid-state "disk" emulators in environments in which conventional drives are unacceptable, such as in military or factory use.

buffer   A block of memory used as a holding tank to store data temporarily. Often positioned between a slower peripheral device and the faster computer. All data moving between the peripheral and the computer passes through the buffer. A buffer enables the data to be read from or written to the peripheral in larger chunks, which improves performance. A buffer that is *x* bytes in size usually holds the last *x* bytes of data that moved between the peripheral and CPU. This method contrasts with that of a cache, which adds intelligence to the buffer so that the most often accessed data, rather than the last accessed data, remains in the buffer (cache). A cache can improve performance greatly over a plain buffer.

bug   An error or defect in a program.

burn-in   The operation of a circuit or equipment to establish that its components are stable and to screen out defective ports or assemblies.

burst mode   A memory-cycling technology that takes advantage of the fact that most memory accesses are consecutive in nature. After setting up the row and column addresses for a given access, using burst mode can then access the next three adjacent addresses with no additional latency.

Burst Static RAMs (BSRAMs)   Short for Pipeline Burst SRAM, BSRAMs are a common type of static RAM chip used for memory caches where access to subsequent memory locations after the first byte is accessed takes fewer machine cycles.

bus   A linear electrical signal pathway over which power, data, and other signals travel. It is capable of connecting to three or more attachments. A bus is generally considered to be distinct from radial or point-to-point signal connections. The term comes from the Latin *omnibus*, meaning "for all." When used to describe a topology, bus always implies a linear structure.

bus mouse   An obsolete type of mouse used in the 1980s that plugs into a special mouse expansion board instead of a serial port or motherboard mouse port. The bus mouse connector looks similar to a motherboard mouse (sometimes called PS/2 mouse) connector, but the pin configurations are different and not compatible.

busmaster   An intelligent device that, when attached to the Micro Channel, EISA, VLB, or PCI bus, can bid for and gain control of the bus to perform its specific task without processor intervention.

byte   A collection of bits that makes up a character or other designation. Generally, a byte is 8 data bits. When referring to system RAM, an additional parity (error-checking) bit is also stored (see *parity*), making the total 9 bits.

C   A high-level computer programming language. A programming language frequently used on mainframes, minis, and PC computer systems. C++ is a popular variant.

cache   An intelligent buffer. By using an intelligent algorithm, a cache contains the data accessed most often between a slower peripheral device and the faster CPU. See also *L1 cache, L2 cache*, and *disk cache*.

caddy   A cartridge designed to hold a CD or DVD disc. Some CD drives use caddies, particularly in harsh or industrial environments. DVD-RAM drives also use a caddy to protect the disc.

CAM (Common Access Method)   A committee formed in 1988 that consists of a number of computer peripheral suppliers and is dedicated to developing standards for a common software interface between SCSI peripherals and host adapters.

capacitor   A device consisting of two plates separated by insulating material and designed to store an electrical charge.

card   A printed circuit board containing electronic components that form an entire circuit, usually designed to plug into a connector or slot. Sometimes also called an adapter.

card edge connector   See *edge connector*.

CardBus   A PC card specification for a 32-bit interface that runs at 33MHz and provides 32-bit data paths to the computer's I/O and memory systems, as well as a new shielded connector that prevents CardBus devices from being inserted into slots that do not support the latest version of the PC card standard.

carpal tunnel syndrome   A painful hand injury that gets its name from the narrow tunnel in the wrist that connects ligament and bone. When undue pressure is put on the tendons, they can swell and compress the median nerve, which carries impulses from the brain to the hand, causing numbness, weakness, tingling, and burning in the fingers and hands. Computer users get carpal tunnel syndrome primarily from improper keyboard ergonomics that result in undue strain on the wrist and hand.

carrier   A continuous frequency signal capable of being either modulated or impressed with another information-carrying signal. The reference signal used for the transmission or reception of data. The most common use of this signal with computers involves modem communications over phone lines. The carrier is used as a signal on which the information is superimposed.

carrier detect signal   A modem interface signal that indicates to the attached data terminal equipment (DTE) that it is receiving a signal from the distant modem. Defined in the RS-232 specification. Same as the received line-signal detector.

cathode ray tube (CRT)   A device that contains electrodes surrounded by a glass sphere or cylinder and displays information by creating a beam of electrons that strike a phosphor coating inside the display unit. This device is most commonly used in computer monitors and terminals.

CAV (constant angular velocity)   An optical disk recording format in which the data is recorded on the disk in concentric circles. CAV disks are rotated at a constant speed. This is similar to the recording technique used on floppy disk drives. CAV limits the total recorded capacity compared to CLV (constant linear velocity), which also is used in optical recording.

CCITT   An acronym for the Comité Consultatif International de Télégraphique et Téléphonique (in English, the International Telegraph and Telephone Consultative Committee or the Consultative Committee for International Telegraph and Telephone). Renamed ITU (International Telecommunications Union). See *ITU*.

CCS (common command set)   A set of SCSI commands specified in the ANSI SCSI-1 Standard X3.131-1986 Addendum 4.B. All SCSI devices must be capable of using the CCS to be fully compatible with the ANSI SCSI-1 standard.

CD (compact disc or compact audio disc)   A 4.75-inch (12cm) optical disc that contains information encoded digitally in the constant linear velocity (CLV) format. This popular format for high-fidelity music offers 90 decibels signal/noise ratio, 74 minutes of digital sound, and no degradation of quality from playback. The standards for this format (developed by NV Philips and Sony Corporation) are known as the Red Book. The official (and rarely used) designation for the audio-only format is CD-DA (compact disc-digital audio). The simple audio format is also known as CD-A (compact disc-audio). A smaller (3-inch) version of the CD is known as CD-3.

CD Video   A CD format introduced in 1987 that combined 20 minutes of digital audio and 6 minutes of analog video on a standard 4.75-inch CD. Upon introduction, many firms renamed 8-inch and 12-inch videodiscs as CDV, in an attempt to capitalize on the consumer popularity of the audio CD. The term fell out of use in 1990 and was replaced in some part by laser disc and, more recently, DVD.

CD+G (Compact Disc-Graphics)   A CD format that includes extended graphics capabilities as written into the original CD-ROM specifications. Includes limited video graphics encoded into the CD subcode area. Developed and marketed by Warner New Media.

CD+MIDI (Compact Disc-Musical Instrument Digital Interface)   A CD format that adds to the CD+G format digital audio, graphics information, and musical instrument digital interface (MIDI) specifications and capabilities. Developed and marketed by Warner New Media.

CD-I (Compact Disc-Interactive)   A compact disc format released in October 1991 that provides audio, digital data, still graphics, and motion video. The standards for this format (developed by NV Philips and Sony Corporation) are known as the Green Book. CD-I did not catch on with consumers and is now considered obsolete.

CD-R (Compact Disc-Recordable, sometimes called CD-writable)   CD-R discs are compact discs that can be recorded and read as many times as desired. CD-R is part of the Orange Book standard defined by ISO. CD-R technology is used for mass production of multimedia applications. CD-R discs can be compatible with CD-ROM, CD-ROM XA, and CD audio. Orange Book specifies multisession capabilities, which enable data recording on the disc at various times in several recording sessions. Kodak's Photo CD is an example of CD-R technology and fits up to 100 digital photographs on a single CD. Multisession capability enables several rolls of 35mm film to be added to a single disc on different occasions.

CD-ROM (compact disc-read-only memory)   A 4.75-inch laser-encoded optical memory storage medium with the same constant linear velocity (CLV) spiral format as audio CDs and some videodiscs. CD-ROMs can hold about 650MB of data and require more error-correction information than the standard prerecorded compact audio disc. The standards for this format (developed by NV Philips and Sony Corporation) are known as the Yellow Book. See also *CD-ROM XA*.

CD-ROM drive   A device that retrieves data from a CD-ROM disc; it differs from a standard audio CD player by the incorporation of additional error-correction circuitry. CD-ROM drives usually can also play music from audio CDs.

CD-ROM XA (compact disc-read-only memory extended architecture)   The XA standard was developed jointly by Sony, Philips, and Microsoft in 1988 and is now part of the Yellow Book standard. XA is a built-in feature of newer CD-ROM drives and supports simultaneous sound playback with data transfer. Non-XA drives support either sound playback or data transfer, but not both simultaneously. XA also enables data compression right on the disk, which also can increase data transfer rates.

CD-RW (compact disc-rewritable)   A type of rewritable CD-ROM technology defined in Part III of the Orange Book standard that uses a different type of disc, which the drive can rewrite at least 1,000 times. CD-RW drives also can be used to write CD-R discs, and they can read CD-ROMs. CD-RWs have a lower reflectivity than standard CD-ROMs, and CD-ROM drives must be of the newer multiread variety to read them. CD-RW was initially known as CD-E (for CD-erasable).

CD-WO (compact disc-write once)   A variant on CD-ROM that can be written to once and read many times; developed by NV Philips and Sony Corporation. Also known as CD-WORM (CD-write once/read many), CD-recordable, or CD-writable. Standards for this format are known as the Orange Book.

CD-WORM   See *CD-WO*.

Celeron   A low-cost version of the Pentium II or Pentium III processor with less L2 cache.

Centronics connector   Refers to one of two types of cable connectors used with either parallel or SCSI devices.

ceramic substrate   A thin, flat, fired-ceramic part used to hold an IC chip (usually made of beryllium oxide or aluminum oxide).

CERN (Conseil Européen pour la Recherche Nucléaire; The European Laboratory for Particle Physics)   The site in Geneva where the World Wide Web was created in 1989.

CGA (color graphics adapter)   A type of PC video display adapter introduced by IBM on August 12, 1981, which supports text and graphics. Text is supported at a maximum resolution of 80×25 characters in 16 colors with a character box of 8×8 pixels. Graphics are supported at a maximum resolution of 320×200 pixels in 16 colors or 640×200 pixels in two colors. The CGA outputs a TTL (digital) signal with a horizontal scanning frequency of 15.75KHz and supports TTL color or NTSC composite displays.

channel   1) Any path along which signals can be sent. 2) In ISDN, data bandwidth is divided into two B-channels that bear data and one D-channel that carries information about the call.

character   A representation—coded in binary digits—of a letter, number, or other symbol.

character set   All the letters, numbers, and characters a computer can use to represent data. The ASCII standard has 256 characters, each represented by a binary number from 1 to 256. The ASCII set includes all the letters in the alphabet, numbers, most punctuation marks, some mathematical symbols, and other characters.

charge coupled device   A light-sensing and storage device used in scanners and digital cameras to capture the pixels.

check bit   See *parity*.

checksum   Short for *summation check*, a technique for determining whether a package of data is valid. The package, a string of binary digits, is added up and compared with the expected number.

chip   Another name for an IC, or integrated circuit. Housed in a plastic or ceramic carrier device with pins for making electrical connections.

chip carrier   A ceramic or plastic package that carries an integrated circuit.

chipset   A single chip or pair of chips that integrates into it the clock generator, bus controller, system timer, interrupt controller, DMA controller, CMOS RAM/clock, and keyboard controller. See also *North Bridge* and *South Bridge*.

CHS (cylinder head sector)   The term used to describe the nontranslating scheme used by the BIOS to access IDE drives that are less than or equal to 528MB in capacity. See *LBA*.

CIF (common image format)   The standard sample structure that represents the picture information of a single frame in digital HDTV, independent of frame rate and sync/blank structure. The uncompressed bit rate for transmitting CIF at 29.97 frames/sec is 36.45Mbps.

circuit   A complete electronic path.

circuit board   The collection of circuits gathered on a sheet of plastic, usually with all contacts made through a strip of pins. The circuit board usually is made by chemically etching metal-coated plastic.

CISC (complex instruction set computer)   Refers to traditional computers that operate with large sets of processor instructions. Most modern computers, including the Intel 80xxx processors, are in this category. CISC processors have expanded instruction sets that are complex in nature and require several to many execution cycles to complete. This structure contrasts with RISC (reduced instruction set computer) processors, which have far fewer instructions that execute quickly.

clean room 1) A dust-free room in which certain electronic components (such as chips or hard disk drives) must be manufactured and serviced to prevent contamination. Rooms are rated by Class numbers. A Class 100 clean room must have fewer than 100 particles larger than 0.5 microns per cubic foot of space. 2) A legal approach to copying software or hardware in which one team analyzes the product and writes a detailed description, followed by a second team who reads the description written by the first and then develops a compatible version of the product. When done correctly, such a design methodology will survive a legal attack.

client/server A type of network in which every computer is either a server with a defined role of sharing resources with clients or a client that can access the resources on the server.

clock The source of a computer's timing signals. It synchronizes every operation of the CPU.

clock multiplier A processor feature where the internal core runs at a higher speed than the motherboard or processor bus. See also *overclocking.*

clock speed A measurement of the rate at which the clock signal for a device oscillates, usually expressed in millions of cycles per second (MHz).

clone Originally referred to an IBM-compatible computer system that physically as well as electrically emulates the design of one of IBM's personal computer systems. More currently, it refers to any PC system running an Intel or compatible processor in the 80x86 family.

cluster Also called *allocation unit.* A group of one or more sectors on a disk that forms a fundamental unit of storage to the operating system. Cluster, or allocation unit, size is determined by the operating system when the disk is formatted. Larger clusters generally offer faster system performance but waste disk space.

CLV (constant linear velocity) An optical recording format in which the spacing of data is consistent throughout the disk and the rotational speed of the disk varies depending on which track is being read. Additionally, more sectors of data are placed on the outer tracks compared to the inner tracks of the disk, which is similar to zone recording on hard drives. CLV drives adjust the rotational speed to maintain a constant track velocity as the diameter of the track changes. CLV drives also rotate more quickly near the center of the disk and more slowly toward the edge. Rotational adjustment maximizes the amount of data that can be stored on a disk. CD audio and CD-ROM use CLV recording.

CMOS (complementary metal-oxide semiconductor) A type of chip design that requires little power to operate. In PCs, a battery-powered CMOS memory and clock chip is used to store and maintain the clock setting and system configuration information.

CMYK (cyan magenta yellow black) The standard four-color model used for printing.

coated media Hard disk platters coated with a reddish iron-oxide medium on which data is recorded.

coaxial cable Also called *coax cable.* A data-transmission medium noted for its wide bandwidth, immunity to interference, and high cost compared to other types of cable. Signals are transmitted inside a fully shielded environment, in which an inner conductor is surrounded by a solid insulating material and then an outer conductor or shield. Used in many local area network systems, such as Ethernet and ARCnet.

COBOL (Common Business-Oriented Language) A high-level computer programming language used primarily by some larger companies. It has never achieved popularity on personal and small business computers.

code page A table used in DOS 3.3 and later that sets up the keyboard and display characters for various foreign languages.

code page switching A DOS feature in versions 3.3 and later that changes the characters displayed onscreen or printed on an output device. Primarily used to support foreign-language characters. Requires an EGA or better video system and an IBM-compatible graphics printer.

CODEC (coder-decoder)   A device that converts voice signals from their analog form to digital signals acceptable to more modern digital PBXs and digital transmission systems. It then converts those digital signals back to analog so you can hear and understand what the other party is saying.

coercivity   A measurement in units of oersteds of the amount of magnetic energy to switch or "coerce" the flux change in the magnetic recording media. High-coercivity disk media require a stronger write current.

cold boot   The act of starting or restarting a computer from a powered-off state. If the system is on, this requires cycling the power off and then back on. A cold boot causes all RAM to be forcibly cleared. See also *warm boot*.

collision   In a LAN, if two computers transmit a packet of data at the same time on the network, the data can become garbled, which is known as a collision.

collision detection/avoidance   A process used on a LAN to prevent data packets from interfering with each other and to determine whether data packets have encountered a collision and initiate a resend of the affected packets.

color graphics adapter   See *CGA*.

color palette   The colors available to a graphics adapter for display.

COM port   A serial port on a PC that conforms to the RS-232 standard. See also *RS-232*.

COMDEX   The largest international computer trade show and conference in the world. COMDEX/Fall is held in Las Vegas during October, and COMDEX/Spring usually is held in Chicago or Atlanta during April.

command   An instruction that tells the computer to start, stop, or continue an operation.

command interpreter   The operating system program that controls a computer's shell or user interface. The command interpreter for

MS-DOS is COMMAND.COM. The command interpreter for Windows is WIN.COM.

COMMAND.COM   An operating system file that is loaded last when the computer is booted. The command interpreter or user interface and program-loader portion of DOS.

common   The ground or return path for an electrical signal. If it's a wire, it usually is colored black.

common mode noise   Noise or electrical disturbances that can be measured between a current- or signal-carrying line and its associated ground. Common mode noise is frequently introduced to signals between separate computer equipment components through the power distribution circuits. It can be a problem when single-ended signals are used to connect different equipment or components that are powered by different circuits.

CompactFlash   An ATA flash memory card physical format approximately one third the size of a standard PC card. Often abbreviated CF, CompactFlash cards are identical in function to standard ATA Flash PC cards but use 50 pin connectors instead of 68. ATA flash cards contain built-in disk controller circuitry to enable the card to function as a solid-state disk drive. CF cards can plug into a CompactFlash socket or with an adapter into a standard Type I or II PC-card slot.

compatible   1) In the early days of the PC industry when IBM dominated the market, a term used to refer to computers from other manufacturers that had the same features as a given IBM model. 2) In general, software or hardware that conforms to industry standards or other de facto standards so that it can be used in conjunction with or in lieu of other versions of software or hardware from other vendors in a like manner.

compiler   A program that translates a program written in a high-level language into its equivalent machine language. The output from a compiler is called an object program.

complete backup   A backup of all information on a hard disk, including the directory tree structure.

composite video Television picture information and sync pulses combined. The complete wave form of the color video signal composed of chrominance and luminance picture information; blanking pedestal; field, line, and color-sync pulses; and field-equalizing pulses. Some video cards have an RCA jack that outputs a composite video signal. See also *RGB*.

compressed file A file that has been reduced in size via one or more compression techniques.

computer Device capable of accepting data, applying prescribed processes to this data, and displaying the results or information produced.

computer-based training (CBT) The use of a computer to deliver instruction or training; also known as computer-aided (or assisted) instruction (CAI), computer-aided learning (CAL), computer-based instruction (CBI), and computer-based learning (CBL).

CONFIG.SYS A file that can be created to tell DOS how to configure itself when the machine starts up. It can load device drivers, set the number of DOS buffers, and so on.

configuration file A file kept by application software to record various aspects of the software's configuration, such as the printer it uses.

console The unit, such as a terminal or a keyboard, in your system with which you communicate with the computer.

contiguous Touching or joined at the edge or boundary, in one piece.

continuity In electronics, an unbroken pathway. Testing for continuity normally means testing to determine whether a wire or other conductor is complete and unbroken (by measuring 0 ohms). A broken wire shows infinite resistance (or infinite ohms).

control cable The wider of the two cables that connect an ST-506/412 or ESDI hard disk drive to a controller card. A 34-pin cable that carries commands and acknowledgments between the drive and controller.

controller The electronics that control a device, such as a hard disk drive, and intermediate the passage of data between the device and the computer.

controller card An adapter holding the control electronics for one or more devices, such as hard disks. Ordinarily occupies one of the computer's slots.

conventional memory The first megabyte or first 640KB of system memory accessible by an Intel processor in real mode. Sometimes called base memory.

convergence Describes the capability of a color monitor to focus the three colored electron beams on a single point. Poor convergence causes the characters onscreen to appear fuzzy and can cause headaches and eyestrain.

coprocessor An additional computer processing unit designed to handle specific tasks in conjunction with the main or central processing unit.

copy protection A hardware or software scheme to prohibit making illegal copies of a program.

core An old-fashioned term for computer memory.

core speed The internal speed of a processor. With all modern processors, this speed is faster than the system bus speed, and that speed relationship is regulated by the clock multiplier in the processor.

CP/M (Control Program for Microcomputers, originally Control Program/Monitor) An operating system created by Gary Kildall, the founder of Digital Research. Created for the old 8-bit microcomputers that used the 8080, 8085, and Z-80 microprocessors. It was the dominant operating system in the late 1970s and early 1980s for small computers used in business environments.

cps (characters per second) A data transfer rate generally estimated from the bit rate and the character length. At 2,400bps, for example, 8-bit characters with start and stop bits (for a total of 10 bits per character) are transmitted at a rate of approximately 240cps.

Some protocols, such as V.42 and MNP, employ advanced techniques such as longer transmission frames and data compression to increase characters per second.

CPU (central processing unit) The computer's microprocessor chip; the brains of the outfit. Typically, an IC using VLSI (very-large-scale integration) technology to pack several functions into a tiny area. The most common electronic device in the CPU is the transistor, of which several thousand to several million or more are found.

crash A malfunction that brings work to a halt. A system crash usually is caused by a software malfunction, and ordinarily you can restart the system by rebooting the machine. A head crash, however, entails physical damage to a disk and probable data loss.

CRC (cyclic redundancy checking) An error-detection technique consisting of a cyclic algorithm performed on each block or frame of data by both sending and receiving modems. The sending modem inserts the results of its computation in each data block in the form of a CRC code. The receiving modem compares its results with the received CRC code and responds with either a positive or negative acknowledgment. In the ARQ protocol implemented in high-speed modems, the receiving modem accepts no more data until a defective block is received correctly.

crosstalk The electromagnetic coupling of a signal on one line with another nearby signal line. Crosstalk is caused by electromagnetic induction, where a signal traveling through a wire creates a magnetic field that induces a current in other nearby wires.

CRT (cathode-ray tube) A term used to describe a television or monitor screen tube.

current The flow of electrons, measured in amperes, or amps.

cursor The small flashing hyphen that appears onscreen to indicate the point at which any input from the keyboard will be placed.

cycle Time for a signal to transition from one leading edge to the next leading edge.

cyclic redundancy checking See *CRC*.

cylinder The set of tracks on a disk that are on each side of all the disk platters in a stack and are the same distance from the center of the disk. The total number of tracks that can be read without moving the heads. A floppy drive with two heads usually has 160 tracks, which are accessible as 80 cylinders. A typical 4GB hard disk has 10 platters with 20 heads (19 for data and 1 servo head) and 4,000 cylinders, in which each cylinder is composed of 19 tracks.

D/A converter (DAC) A device that converts digital signals to analog form.

daisy-chain Stringing up components in such a manner that the signals move serially from one to the other. Most microcomputer multiple disk drive systems are daisy-chained. The SCSI bus system is a daisy-chain arrangement, in which the signals move from computer to disk drives to tape units, and so on.

daisywheel printer An impact printer that prints fully formed characters one at a time by rotating a circular print element composed of a series of individual spokes, each containing two characters that radiate from a center hub. Produces letter-quality output.

DAT (digital audio tape) A small cassette containing 4mm-wide tape used for storing large amounts of digital information. DAT technology emerged in Europe and Japan in 1986 as a way to produce high-quality, digital audio recordings and was modified in 1988 to conform to the digital data storage (DDS) standard for storing computer data. Raw/compressed capacities for a single tape are 2/4GB for DDS, 4/8GB for DDS-2, 12/24GB for DDS-3, and 20/40GB for DDS-4.

data 1) Groups of facts processed into information. A graphic or textural representation of facts, concepts, numbers, letters, symbols, or instructions used for communication or processing. 2) An android from the twenty-fourth century with a processing speed of 60 trillion operations per second and a storage capacity of 800 quadrillion bits, and who serves on the USS Enterprise NCC-1701-D with the rank of lieutenant commander.

data bus The connection that transmits data between the processor and the rest of the system. The width of the data bus defines the number of data bits that can be moved into or out of the processor in one cycle.

data cable   Generically, a cable that carries data. Specific to HD connections, the narrower (20-pin) of two cables that connects an ST-506/412 or ESDI hard disk drive to a controller card.

data communications   A type of communication in which computers and terminals can exchange data over an electronic medium.

data compression   A technique in which mathematical algorithms are applied to the data in a file to eliminate redundancies and therefore reduce the size of the file. See also *lossless compression* and *lossy compression*.

Data Link Layer   In networking, the layer of the OSI reference model that controls how the electrical impulses enter or leave the network cable. Ethernet and Token-Ring are the two most common examples of Data Link Layer protocols. See *OSI*.

data separator   A device that separates data and clock signals from a single encoded signal pattern. Usually, the same device performs both data separation and combination and is sometimes called an endec, or encoder/decoder.

data transfer rate   The maximum rate at which data can be transferred from one device to another.

daughterboard   Add-on board to increase functionality and/or memory. Attaches to the existing board.

DB-9   9-pin D-shell connector, primarily used for PC serial ports.

DB-25   25-pin D-shell connector, primarily used for PC parallel ports.

DC   Direct current, such as that provided by a power supply or batteries.

DC-600 (Data Cartridge 600)   A data-storage medium invented by 3M in 1971 that uses a quarter-inch–wide tape 600 feet in length.

DCE (data communications equipment)   The hardware that performs communication—usually a dialup modem that establishes and

controls the data link through the telephone network. See also *DTE*.

D-channel   In ISDN, a 16Kbps channel used to transmit control data about a connection.

DDE (dynamic data exchange)   A form of interprocess communications used by Microsoft Windows to support the exchange of commands and data between two applications running simultaneously. This capability has been enhanced further with object linking and embedding (OLE).

de facto standard   A software or hardware technology not officially made a standard by any recognized standards organization but that is used as a reference for consumers and vendors because of its dominance in the marketplace.

DEBUG   The name of a utility program included with DOS and used for specialized purposes, such as altering memory locations, tracing program execution, patching programs and disk sectors, and performing other low-level tasks.

decibel (dB)   A logarithmic measure of the ratio between two powers, voltages, currents, sound intensities, and so on. Signal-to-noise ratios are expressed in decibels.

dedicated line   A user-installed telephone line that connects a specified number of computers or terminals within a limited area, such as a single building. The line is a cable rather than a public-access telephone line. The communications channel also can be referred to as nonswitched because calls do not go through telephone company switching equipment.

dedicated servo surface   In voice-coil-actuated hard disk drives, one side of one platter given over to servo data that is used to guide and position the read/write heads.

default   Any setting assumed at startup or reset by the computer's software and attached devices and operational until changed by the user. An assumption the computer makes when no other parameters are specified. When you type DIR without specifying the drive to search, for example, the computer assumes you want it to search the default drive. The term is used in software to describe any action the computer or program takes on its own with embedded values.

defect map A list of unusable sectors and tracks coded onto a drive during the low-level format process.

defragmentation The process of rearranging disk sectors so files are stored on consecutive sectors in adjacent tracks.

degauss 1) To remove magnetic charges, or to erase magnetic images. Normal applications include monitors and disks or tapes. Most monitors incorporate a degaussing coil, which surrounds the CRT, and automatically energize this coil for a few seconds when powered up to remove color or image distorting magnetic fields from the metal mask inside the tube. Some monitors include a button or control that can be used for additional applications of this coil to remove more stubborn magnetic traces. 2) Also the act of erasing or demagnetizing a magnetic disk or tape using a special tool called a degaussing coil.

density The amount of data that can be packed into a certain area on a specific storage media.

desktop A personal computer that sits on a desk.

device driver A memory-resident program loaded by CONFIG.SYS that controls an unusual device, such as an expanded memory board.

DHCP (Dynamic Host Configuration Protocol) A protocol for assigning dynamic IP addresses to devices on a network. With dynamic addressing, a device can have a different IP address every time it connects to the network.

Dhrystone A benchmark program used as a standard figure of merit indicating aspects of a computer system's performance in areas other than floating-point math performance. Because the program does not use any floating-point operations, performs no I/O, and makes no operating system calls, it is most useful for measuring the processor performance of a system. The original Dhrystone program was developed in 1984 and was written in Ada, although the C and Pascal versions became more popular by 1989.

diagnostics Programs used to check the operation of a computer system. These programs enable the operator to check the entire system for any problems and to indicate in which area the problems lie.

dial-up adapter In Windows 9x, a software program that uses a modem to emulate a network interface card for networking. Most commonly used to connect to an Internet service provider or a dial-up server for remote access to a LAN.

die An individual chip (processor, RAM, or other integrated circuit) cut from a finished silicon chip wafer and built into the physical package that connects it to the rest of the PC or a circuit board.

differential An electrical signaling method in which a pair of lines are used for each signal in "push-pull" fashion. In most cases, differential signals are balanced so that the same current flows on each line in opposite directions. This is unlike single-ended signals, which use only one line per signal referenced to a single ground. Differential signals have a large tolerance for common-mode noise and little crosstalk when used with twisted-pair wires even in long cables. Differential signaling is expensive because two pins are required for each signal.

digital loopback A test that checks the modem's RS-232 interface and the cable that connects the terminal or computer and the modem. The modem receives data (in the form of digital signals) from the computer or terminal and immediately returns the data to the screen for verification.

digital signals Discrete, uniform signals. In this book, the term refers to the binary digits 0 and 1.

digital-to-analog converter (DAC) A device for converting digital signals to analog signals. VGA-based displays are analog, so video cards that connect to them include a DAC to convert the signals to analog to drive the display.

digitize To transform an analog wave to a digital signal a computer can store. Conversion to digital data and back is performed by a D/A converter (DAC), often a single-chip device.

How closely a digitized sample represents an analog wave depends on the number of times the amplitude of a wave is measured and recorded (the rate of digitization), as well as the number of levels that can be specified at each instance. The number of possible signal levels is dictated by the resolution in bits.

DIMM (dual inline memory module)   A 64-bit wide, 168-pin memory module used in Pentium and newer PCs. They are available in several versions, including 5v or 3v, buffered or unbuffered, with FPM/EDO or SDRAM memory, and in 64-bit (non-ECC/parity) or 72-bit (ECC/parity) form. Most Pentium and newer PCs require 3.3v unbuffered SDRAM DIMMs in either non-ECC or ECC versions (ECC recommended).

DIP (dual inline package)   A family of rectangular, integrated-circuit flat packages that have leads on the two longer sides. Package material is plastic or ceramic.

DIP switch   A tiny switch (or group of switches) on a circuit board. Named for the form factor of the carrier device in which the switch is housed.

direct memory access (DMA)   A process by which data moves between a disk drive (or other device) and system memory without direct control of the central processing unit, thus freeing it up for other tasks.

Direct Rambus DRAM   See *RDRAM*.

directory   An area of a disk that stores the titles given to the files saved on the disk and serves as a table of contents for those files. Contains data that identifies the name of a file, the size, the attributes (system, hidden, read-only, and so on), the date and time of creation, and a pointer to the location of the file. Each entry in a directory is 32 bytes long.

DirectX   A set of graphics related drivers and APIs that translates generic hardware commands into specific commands for particular pieces of hardware. DirectX lets graphical or multimedia applications take advantage of specific features supported by various graphics accelerators.

disc   Flat, circular, rotating medium that can store various types of information, both analog

and digital. Disc is often used in reference to optical storage media, whereas disk refers to magnetic storage media. Disc is often used as a short form for videodisc or compact audio disc (CD).

disk   Alternative spelling for disc that generally refers to magnetic storage medium on which information can be accessed at random. Floppy disks and hard disks are examples.

disk access time   See *access time*.

disk cache   A portion of memory on the PC motherboard or on a drive interface card or controller used to store frequently accessed information from the drive (such as the file allocation table [FAT] or directory structure) to speed up disk access. With a larger disk cache, additional data from the data portion of a drive can be cached as well. See also *cache, L1 cache*, and *L2 cache*.

disk partition   See *partition*.

display   A device used for viewing information generated by a computer.

display adapter   The interface between the computer and the monitor that transmits the signals which appear as images on the display. This can take the form of an expansion card or a chip built into the motherboard.

dithering   The process of creating more colors and shades from a given color palette. In monochrome displays or printers, dithering varies the black-and-white dot patterns to simulate shades of gray. Grayscale dithering is used to produce different shades of gray when the device can produce only limited levels of black or white outputs. Color screens or printers use dithering to create additional colors by mixing and varying the dot sizing and spacing. For example, when converting from 24-bit color to 8-bit color (an 8-bit palette has only 256 colors compared to the 24-bit palette's millions), dithering adds pixels of different colors to simulate the original color. Dithering is also known as error diffusion.

DLC (Data Link Control)   Refers to the Data Link layer in the OSI model. Every network interface card (NIC) has a unique DLC address or DLC identifier (DLCI) that identifies the node on the network. For Ethernet networks, the DLC address is usually called the Media Access Control (MAC) address.

DLL (Dynamic Link Library)　An executable driver program module for Microsoft Windows that can be loaded on demand and linked in at runtime and subsequently unloaded when the driver is no longer needed.

DMA　See *direct memory access*.

DMI (Desktop Management Interface) DMI is an operating-system– and protocol-independent standard developed by the Desktop Management Task Force (DMTF) for managing desktop systems and servers. DMI provides a bidirectional path to interrogate all the hardware and software components within a PC, enabling hardware and software configurations to be monitored from a central station in a network.

DNS (Domain Name System or Service) An Internet service that translates domain names into numeric IP addresses. Every time you use a domain name, a DNS server must translate the name into the corresponding IP address.

docking station　Equipment that enables a laptop or notebook computer to use peripherals and accessories normally associated with desktop systems.

doping　Adding chemical impurities to silicon (which is naturally a nonconductor), creating a material with semiconductor properties that is then used in the manufacturing of electronic chips.

DOS (Disk Operating System)　A collection of programs stored on the DOS disk that contain routines enabling the system and user to manage information and the hardware resources of the computer. DOS must be loaded into the computer before other programs can be started.

dot pitch　A measurement of the width of the dots that make up a pixel. The smaller the dot pitch, the sharper the image.

dot-matrix printer　An impact printer that prints characters composed of dots. Characters are printed one at a time by pressing the ends of selected wires against an inked ribbon and paper.

double density (DD)　An indication of the storage capacity of a floppy drive or disk in which eight or nine sectors per track are recorded using MFM encoding. See also *MFM encoding*.

downtime　Operating time lost because of a computer malfunction.

DPMI (DOS Protected Mode Interface) An industry-standard interface that allows DOS applications to execute program code in the protected mode of the 286 or later Intel processor. The DPMI specification is available from Intel.

DPMS (Display Power Management Signaling)　A VESA standard for signaling a monitor or display to switch into energy conservation modes. DPMS provides for two low-energy modes: standby and suspend.

DRAM (dynamic random access memory)　The most common type of computer memory, DRAM can be manufactured very inexpensively compared to other types of memory. DRAM chips are small and inexpensive because they normally require only one transistor and a capacitor to represent each bit. The capacitors must be energized every 15ms or so (hundreds of times per second) to maintain their charges. DRAM is volatile, meaning it loses data with no power or without regular refresh cycles.

drive　A mechanical device that manipulates data storage media.

driver　A program designed to interface a particular piece of hardware to an operating system or other standard software.

drum　The cylindrical photoreceptor in a laser printer that receives the document image from the laser and applies it to the page as it slowly rotates.

DSL (digital subscriber line)　A high-speed digital modem technology. DSL is either symmetric or asymmetric. Asymmetric provides faster downstream speeds, which is suited for Internet usage and video on demand. Symmetric provides the same rate coming and going. See also *ADSL*.

DSM (digital storage media)　A digital storage or transmission device or system.

DSP (digital signal processor) Dedicated, limited-function processor often found in modems, sound cards, cellular phones, and so on.

DTE (data terminal [or terminating] equipment) The device, usually a computer or terminal, that generates or is the final destination of data. See also *DCE*.

dual cavity pin grid array Chip packaging designed by Intel for use with the Pentium Pro processor that houses the processor die in one cavity of the package and the L2 cache memory in a second cavity within the same package.

dual independent bus (DIB) architecture A processor technology with the existence of two independent buses on the processor—the L2 cache bus and the processor-to-main-memory system bus. The processor can use both buses simultaneously, thus getting as much as two times more data into and out of the processor than a single bus architecture processor. The Intel Pentium Pro, Pentium II, and newer processors have DIB architecture.

dual scan display A lower-quality but economical type of LCD color display that has an array of transistors running down the x and y axes of two sides of the screen. The number of transistors determines the screen's resolution.

dumb terminal A screen and keyboard device with no inherent processing power connected to a computer that is usually remotely located.

duplex Indicates a communications channel capable of carrying signals in both directions.

Duron A low-cost version of the Athlon processor with less L2 cache. Available in the Socket A (462-pin) chip package.

DVD (digital versatile disc) Originally called digital video disc. A new type of high-capacity CD-ROM disc and drive format with up to 28 times the capacity of a standard CD-ROM. The disc is the same diameter as a CD-ROM but can be recorded on both sides and on two layers for each side. Each side holds 4.7GB on a single layer disc, whereas dual-layer versions hold 8.5GB per side, for a maximum of 17GB total if both sides and both layers are used, which is the equivalent of 28 CD-ROMs. DVD drives can read standard audio CDs and CD-ROMs.

DVI (Digital Video Interactive) A standard that was originally developed at RCA Laboratories and sold to Intel in 1988. DVI integrates digital motion, still video, sound, graphics, and special effects in a compressed format. DVI is a highly sophisticated hardware compression technique used in interactive multimedia applications.

Dvorak keyboard A keyboard design by August Dvorak that was patented in 1936 and approved by ANSI in 1982. Provides increased speed and comfort and reduces the rate of errors by placing the most frequently used letters in the center for use by the strongest fingers. Finger motions and awkward strokes are reduced by more than 90% in comparison with the familiar QWERTY keyboard. The Dvorak keyboard has the five vowel keys, AOEUI, together under the left hand in the center row and the five most frequently used consonants, DHTNS, under the fingers of the right hand.

dynamic execution A processing technique that enables the processor to dynamically predict the order of instructions and execute them out of order internally if necessary for an improvement in speed. Uses these three techniques: Multiple Branch Prediction, Data Flow Analysis, and Speculative Execution.

EBCDIC (Extended Binary Coded Decimal Interchange Code) An IBM-developed, 8-bit code for the representation of characters. It allows 256 possible character combinations within a single byte. EBCDIC is the standard code on IBM minicomputers and mainframes, but not on the IBM microcomputers, where ASCII is used instead.

ECC (error correcting code) A type of system memory or cache that is capable of detecting and correcting some types of memory errors without interrupting processing.

ECP (enhanced capabilities port) A type of high-speed parallel port jointly developed by Microsoft and Hewlett-Packard that offers improved performance for the parallel port and requires special hardware logic.

edge connector The part of a circuit board containing a series of printed contacts that is inserted into an expansion slot or connector.

EDO (extended data out) RAM A type of RAM chips that enable a timing overlap between successive accesses, thus improving memory cycle time.

EEPROM (electrically erasable programmable read-only memory) A type of non-volatile memory chip used to store semipermanent information in a computer, such as the BIOS. An EEPROM can be erased and reprogrammed directly in the host system without special equipment. This is used so manufacturers can upgrade the ROM code in a system by supplying a special program that erases and reprograms the EEPROM chip with the new code. Also called flash ROM.

EGA (enhanced graphics adapter) A type of PC video display adapter first introduced by IBM on September 10, 1984, that supports text and graphics. Text is supported at a maximum resolution of 80×25 characters in 16 colors with a character box of 8×14 pixels. Graphics is supported at a maximum resolution of 640×350 pixels in 16 (from a palette of 64) colors. The EGA outputs a TTL (digital) signal with a horizontal scanning frequency of 15.75KHz, 18.432KHz, or 21.85KHz, and supports TTL color or TTL monochrome displays.

EIA (Electronic Industries Association) An organization that defines electronic standards in the United States.

EIDE (Enhanced Integrated Drive Electronics) A specific Western Digital implementation of the ATA-2 specification. See also *ATA-2*.

EISA (Extended Industry Standard Architecture) An extension of the Industry Standard Architecture (ISA) bus developed by IBM for the AT. The EISA design was led by Compaq Corporation. Later, eight other manufacturers (AST, Epson, Hewlett-Packard, NEC, Olivetti, Tandy, Wyse, and Zenith) joined Compaq in a consortium founded September 13, 1988. This group became known as the "gang of nine." The EISA design was patterned largely after IBM's Micro Channel Architecture (MCA) in the PS/2 systems, but unlike MCA, EISA enables backward compatibility with older plug-in adapters.

electronic mail (email) A method of transferring messages from one computer to another.

electrostatic discharge (ESD) The grounding of static electricity. A sudden flow of electricity between two objects at different electrical potentials. ESD is a primary cause of integrated circuit damage or failure.

ELF (extremely low frequency) A very low-frequency electromagnetic radiation generated by common electrical appliances, including computer monitors. The Swedish MPR II standard governs this and other emissions. Also called VLF (very low frequency).

embedded controller In disk drives, a controller built into the same physical unit that houses the drive rather than on a separate adapter card. IDE and SCSI drives both use embedded controllers.

embedded servo data Magnetic markings embedded between or inside tracks on disk drives that use voice-coil actuators. These markings enable the actuator to fine-tune the position of the read/write heads.

EMM (expanded memory manager) A driver that provides a software interface to expanded memory. EMMs were originally created for expanded memory boards, but also can use the memory management capabilities of the 386 or later processors to emulate an expanded memory board. EMM386.EXE is an example of an EMM that comes with DOS.

EMS (Expanded Memory Specification) Sometimes also called the LIM spec because it was developed by Lotus, Intel, and Microsoft. Provides a way for microcomputers running under DOS to access additional memory. EMS memory management provides access to a maximum of 32MB of expanded memory through a small (usually 64KB) window in conventional memory. EMS is a cumbersome access scheme designed primarily for pre-286 systems that could not access extended memory.

emulator A piece of test apparatus that emulates or imitates the function of a particular chip.

encoding   The protocol by which data is carried or stored by a medium.

encryption   The translation of data into unreadable codes to maintain security.

endec (encoder/decoder)   A device that takes data and clock signals and combines or encodes them using a particular encoding scheme into a single signal for transmission or storage. The same device also later separates or decodes the data and clock signals during a receive or read operation. Sometimes called a data separator.

Energy Star   A certification program started by the Environmental Protection Agency. Energy Star–certified computers and peripherals are designed to draw less than 30 watts of electrical energy from a standard 110-volt AC outlet during periods of inactivity. Also called Green PCs.

enhanced graphics adapter   See *EGA*.

enhanced small device interface   See *ESDI*.

EPP (enhanced parallel port)   A type of parallel port developed by Intel, Xircom, and Zenith Data Systems that operates at almost ISA bus speed and offers a tenfold increase in the raw throughput capability over a conventional parallel port. EPP is especially designed for parallel port peripherals, such as LAN adapters, disk drives, and tape backups.

EPROM (erasable programmable read-only memory)   A type of read-only memory (ROM) in which the data pattern can be erased to allow a new pattern. EPROM usually is erased by ultraviolet light and recorded by a higher-than-normal voltage programming signal.

equalization   A compensation circuit designed into modems to counteract certain distortions introduced by the telephone channel. Two types are used: fixed (compromise) equalizers and those that adapt to channel conditions (adaptive). Good-quality modems use adaptive equalization.

error control   Various techniques that check the reliability of characters (parity) or blocks of data. V.42, MNP, and HST

error-control protocols use error detection (CRC) and retransmission of error frames (ARQ).

error message   A word or combination of words to indicate to the user that an error has occurred somewhere in the program.

ESCD (extended system configuration data)   Area in CMOS or Flash/NVRAM where plug-and-play information is stored.

ESDI (Enhanced Small Device Interface)   A hardware standard developed by Maxtor and standardized by a consortium of 22 disk drive manufacturers on January 26, 1983. A group of 27 manufacturers formed the ESDI steering committee on September 15, 1986, to enhance and improve the specification. A high-performance interface used primarily with hard disks, ESDI enables a maximum data transfer rate to and from a hard disk of between 10Mbit/sec and 24Mbit/sec.

Ethernet   A type of network protocol developed in the late 1970s by Bob Metcalf at Xerox Corporation and endorsed by the IEEE. One of the oldest LAN communications protocols in the personal computing industry, Ethernet networks use a collision-detection protocol to manage contention.

expanded memory   Otherwise known as EMS memory, it's memory that conforms to the EMS specification. Requires a special device driver and conforms to a standard developed by Lotus, Intel, and Microsoft.

expansion card   An integrated circuit card that plugs into an expansion slot on a motherboard to provide access to additional peripherals or features not built into the motherboard. Also referred to as an add-in board.

expansion slot   A slot on the motherboard that physically and electrically connects an expansion card to the motherboard and the system buses.

extended graphics array   See *XGA*.

extended memory   Direct processor-addressable memory addressed by an Intel (or compatible) 286, 386, or 486 processor in the region beyond the first megabyte. Addressable only in the processor's protected mode of operation.

extended partition A nonbootable DOS partition containing DOS volumes. Starting with DOS v3.3, the DOS FDISK program can create two partitions that serve DOS: an ordinary, bootable partition (called the primary partition) and an extended partition, which can contain as many as 23 volumes from D: to Z:.

external device A peripheral installed outside the system case.

extra-high density (ED) An indication of the storage capacity of a floppy drive or disk in which 36 sectors per track are recorded using a vertical recording technique with MFM encoding.

FAQ (frequently asked questions) Name for a list of popular questions and answers covering any particular subject.

Fast Page Mode RAM A type of RAM that improves on standard DRAM speed by enabling faster access to all the data within a given row of memory by keeping the row address the same and changing only the column.

fast-ATA (fast AT attachment interface) Also called fast ATA-2, these are specific Seagate and Quantum implementations of the ATA-2 interface. See also *ATA-2*.

FAT (file allocation table) A table held near the outer edge of a disk that tells which sectors are allocated to each file and in what order.

FAT32 A disk file allocation system from Microsoft that uses 32-bit values for FAT entries instead of the 16-bit values used by the original FAT system, enabling partition sizes up to 2TB (terabytes). FAT32 first appeared in Windows 95B and is also found in Windows 98 and Windows NT 5.0.

fault tolerance The capability of a computer to withstand a failure. Many levels of fault tolerance exist, and fault tolerance can be applied to several components or systems within the computer. For example, ECC (error correcting code) memory is considered fault tolerant because it is normally capable of automatically identifying and correcting single bit errors.

fax/modem A peripheral that integrates the capabilities of a fax machine and a modem in one expansion card or external unit.

FCPGA (flip-chip pin grid array) A type of chip packaging first used in the Socket PGA370 version of the Pentium III where the raw processor die has bumped contacts spaced on the face of the die and is mounted face-down to a pin grid array carrier. The heatsink is then directly attached to the back of the raw silicon die surface.

FDISK The name of the disk-partitioning program under several operating systems to create the master boot record and allocate partitions for the operating system's use.

feature connector On a video adapter, a connector that enables an additional video feature card, such as a separate 3D accelerator, video capture card, or MPEG decoder, to be connected to the main video adapter and display.

fiber optic A type of cable or connection using strands or threads of glass to guide a beam of modulated light. Allows for very high-speed signaling and multiplexing as well as the combining of many data streams along a single cable.

FIFO (first-in, first-out) A method of storing and retrieving items from a list, table, or stack so that the first element stored is the first one retrieved.

file A collection of information kept somewhere other than in random-access memory.

file attribute Information held in the attribute byte of a file's directory entry.

file compression See *compressed file*.

filename The name given to the disk file. For DOS, it must be one to eight characters long and can be followed by a filename extension, which can be one to three characters long. Windows 95 eases these constraints by allowing filenames of up to 255 characters.

firewall A hardware or software system designed to prevent unauthorized access to or from a private network.

FireWire Also called IEEE 1394. A serial I/O interface standard that is extremely fast, with data transfer rates up to 400MB/sec, 800MB/sec, or 3.2GB/sec, depending on the version of standard used.

firmware   Software contained in a read-only memory (ROM) device. A cross between hardware and software.

fixed disk   Also called a hard disk, it's a disk that cannot be removed from its controlling hardware or housing. Made of rigid material with a magnetic coating and used for the mass storage and retrieval of data.

flash ROM   A type of EEPROM developed by Intel that can be erased and reprogrammed in the host system. See also *EEPROM*.

flicker   A monitor condition caused by refresh rates that are too low, in which the display flashes visibly. This can cause eyestrain or more severe physical problems.

floating-point unit (FPU)   Sometimes called the math coprocessor; handles the more complex calculations of the processing cycle.

floppy disk   A removable disk using flexible magnetic media enclosed in a semirigid or rigid plastic case.

floppy disk controller   The logic and interface that connects a floppy disk drive to the system.

floppy tape   A tape standard that uses drives connecting to an ordinary floppy disk controller.

floptical drive   A special type of high-capacity removable disk drive that uses an optical mechanism to properly position the drive read/write heads over the data tracks on the disk, allowing for more precise control of the read/write positioning and therefore narrower track spacing and more data packed into a smaller area than traditional floppy disks.

flow control   A mechanism that compensates for differences in the flow of data input to and output from a modem or other device.

FM encoding   Frequency modulation encoding. An outdated method of encoding data on the disk surface that uses up half the disk space with timing signals.

FM synthesis   An audio technology that uses one sine wave operator to modify another and create an artificial sound that mimics an instrument.

folder   In a graphical user interface, a simulated file folder that holds documents (text, data, or graphics), applications, and other folders. A folder is similar to a DOS subdirectory.

footprint   Describes the shape of something. See *form factor*.

form factor   The physical dimensions of a device. Two devices with the same form factor are physically interchangeable. The IBM PC, XT, and XT Model 286, for example, all use power supplies that are internally different but have exactly the same form factor.

FORMAT   The DOS format program that performs both low- and high-level formatting on floppy disks but only high-level formatting on hard disks.

formatted capacity   The total number of bytes of data that can fit on a formatted disk. The unformatted capacity is higher because space is lost defining the boundaries between sectors.

formatting   Preparing a disk so the computer can read or write to it. Checks the disk for defects and constructs an organizational system to manage information on the disk.

FORTRAN (formula translator)   A high-level programming language developed in 1954 by John Backus at IBM, primarily for programs dealing with mathematical formulas and expressions similar to algebra and used primarily in scientific and technical applications.

fragmentation   The state of having a file scattered around a disk in pieces rather than existing in one contiguous area of the disk. Fragmented files are slower to read than files stored in contiguous areas and can be more difficult to recover if the FAT or a directory becomes damaged.

frame   1) A data communications term for a block of data with header and trailer information attached. The added information usually includes a frame number, block size data, error-check codes, and start/end indicators. 2) Also a single, complete picture in a video or film recording. A video frame consists of two interlaced fields of either 525 lines (NTSC) or 625 lines (PAL/SECAM), running at 30 frames per second (NTSC) or 25 frames per second (PAL/SECAM).

frame buffer A memory device that stores, pixel by pixel, the contents of an image. Frame buffers are used to refresh a raster image. Sometimes they incorporate local processing capability. The "depth" of the frame buffer is the number of bits per pixel, which determines the number of colors or intensities that can be displayed.

frame rate The speed at which video frames are scanned or displayed: 30 frames per second for NTSC and 25 frames a second for PAL/SECAM.

FTP (File Transfer Protocol) A method of transferring files over the Internet. FTP can be used to transfer files between two machines on which the user has accounts. Anonymous FTP can be used by a user to retrieve a file from a server without having an account on that server.

full duplex Signal flow in both directions at the same time. In microcomputer communications, it also can refer to the suppression of the online local echo.

full-height drive A drive unit that is 3 1/4 inches high, 5 3/4 inches wide, and 8 inches deep.

full-motion video A video sequence displayed at full television standard resolutions and frame rates. In the U.S., this equates to NTSC video at 30 frames per second.

function keys Special-purpose keys that can be programmed to perform various operations. They serve many functions, depending on the program being used.

gas-plasma display Commonly used in portable systems, a type of display that operates by exciting a gas, usually neon or an argon-neon mixture, through the application of a voltage. When sufficient voltage is applied at the intersection of two electrodes, the gas glows an orange-red. Because gas-plasma displays generate light, they require no backlighting.

gateway Officially, an application-to-application conversion program or system. For example, an email gateway converts from SMTP (Internet) email format to MHS (Novell) email format. The term gateway is also used as a slang term for router. See also *router*.

gender When describing connectors for PCs, connectors are described as male if they have pins or female if they have receptacles designed to accept the pins of a male connector.

genlocking The process of aligning the data rate of a video image with that of a digital device to digitize the image and enter it into computer memory. The machine that performs this function is known as a genlock.

GIF (Graphics Interchange Format) A popular raster graphics file format developed by CompuServe that handles 8-bit color (256 colors) and uses the LZW method to achieve compression ratios of approximately 1.5:1 to 2:1.

giga A multiplier indicating one billion (1,000,000,000) of some unit. Abbreviated as g or G. When used to indicate a number of bytes of memory storage, the multiplier definition changes to 1,073,741,824. One gigabit, for example, equals 1,000,000,000 bits, and one gigabyte equals 1,073,741,824 bytes.

gigabyte (GB) A unit of information storage equal to 1,073,741,824 bytes.

graphics accelerator A video processor or chipset specially designed to speed the display and rendering of graphical objects onscreen.

graphics adapter See *video adapter*.

Green Book The standard for Compact Disc-Interactive (CD-I). Philips developed CD-I technology for the consumer market, to be connected to a television instead of a computer monitor. CD-I is not a computer system but a consumer device that made a small splash in the market and disappeared. CD-I discs require special code and are not compatible with standard CD-ROMs. A CD-ROM cannot be played on the CD-I machine, but Red Book audio can be played on CD-I devices.

GUI (graphical user interface)   A type of program interface that enables users to choose commands and functions by pointing to a graphical icon using either a keyboard or pointing device, such as a mouse. Windows and OS/2 are the most popular GUIs available for PC systems.

half duplex   Signal flow in both directions but only one way at a time. In microcomputer communications, half duplex can refer to activation of the online local echo, which causes the modem to send a copy of the transmitted data to the screen of the sending computer.

half-height drive   A drive unit that is 1.625 inches high and either 5.75 or 4 inches wide and 4 or 8 inches deep.

halftoning   A process that uses dithering to simulate a continuous tone image, such as a photograph or shaded drawing, using various sizes of dots. Newspapers, magazines, and many books use halftoning. The human eye merges the dots to give the impression of gray shades.

hard disk   A high-capacity disk storage unit characterized by a normally nonremovable rigid substrate medium. The platters in a hard disk normally are constructed of aluminum or glass/ceramic. Also sometimes called a fixed disk.

hard error   An error in reading or writing data caused by damaged hardware.

hard reset   Resetting a system via the hardware, usually by pressing a dedicated reset button wired to the motherboard/processor reset circuitry. Does not clear memory like a cold boot. See *cold boot.*

hardware   Physical components that make up a microcomputer, monitor, printer, and so on.

HDLC (High-Level Data Link Control)
A standard protocol developed by the ISO for software applications and communicating devices operating in synchronous environments. Defines operations at the link level of communications—for example, the format of data frames exchanged between modems over a phone line.

head   A small electromagnetic device inside a drive that reads, records, and erases data on the media.

head actuator   The device that moves read/write heads across a disk drive's platters. Most drives use a stepper-motor or a voice-coil actuator.

head crash   A (usually) rare occurrence in which a read/write head strikes a platter surface with sufficient force to damage the magnetic medium.

head parking   A procedure in which a disk drive's read/write heads are moved to an unused track so they will not damage data in the event of a head crash or other failure.

head seek   The movement of a drive's read/write heads to a particular track.

heatsink   A mass of metal attached to a chip carrier or socket for the purpose of dissipating heat.

helical scan   A type of recording technology that has vastly increased the capacity of tape drives. Invented for use in broadcast systems and now used in VCRs. Conventional longitudinal recording records a track of data straight across the width of a single-track tape. Helical scan recording packs more data on the tape by positioning the tape at an angle to the recording heads. The heads spin to record diagonal stripes of information on the tape.

hexadecimal number   A number encoded in base-16, such that digits include the letters A–F and the numerals 0–9 (for example, 8BF3, which equals 35,827 in base-10).

hidden file   A file not displayed in DOS directory listings because the file's attribute byte holds a special setting.

high density (HD)   An indication of the storage capacity of a floppy drive or disk, in which 15 or 18 sectors per track are recorded using MFM encoding.

high sierra format   A standard format for placing files and directories on CD-ROMs, proposed by an ad hoc committee of computer vendors, software developers, and CD-ROM system integrators. (Work on the format proposal began at the High Sierra Hotel in Lake Tahoe, Nevada.) A revised version of the format was adopted by the ISO as ISO 9660.

high-definition television (HDTV) Video formats offering greater visual accuracy (or resolution) than current NTSC, PAL, or SECAM broadcast standards. HDTV formats generally range in resolution from 655 to 2,125 scanning lines, having an aspect ratio of 5:3 (or 1.67:1) and a video bandwidth of 30–50MHz (5+ times greater than the NTSC standard). Digital HDTV has a bandwidth of 300MHz. HDTV is subjectively comparable to 35mm film.

high-level formatting Formatting performed by the DOS FORMAT program. Among other things, it creates the root directory and FATs.

history file A file created by utility software to keep track of earlier use of the software. Many backup programs, for example, keep history files describing earlier backup sessions.

hit ratio In describing the efficiency of a disk or memory cache, the hit ratio is the ratio of the number of times the data is found in the cache to the total number of data requests. 1:1 is a perfect hit ratio, meaning that every data request was found in the cache. The closer to 1:1 the ratio is, the more efficient the cache.

HMA (high memory area) The first 64KB of extended memory, which typically is controlled by the HIMEM.SYS device driver. Real-mode programs can be loaded into the HMA to conserve conventional memory. Normally, DOS 5.0 and later use the HMA exclusively to reduce the DOS conventional memory footprint.

horizontal scan rate In monitors, the speed at which the electron beam moves laterally across the screen. It's normally expressed as a frequency; typical monitors range from 31.5KHz to 90KHz, with the higher frequencies being more desirable.

host The main device when two or more devices are connected. When two or more

systems are connected, the system that contains the data is typically called the host, whereas the other is called the guest or user.

HPT (high-pressure tin) A PLCC socket that promotes high forces between socket contacts and PLCC contacts for a good connection.

HST (High-Speed Technology) The U.S. Robotics proprietary high-speed modem-signaling scheme, developed as an interim protocol until the V.32 protocol could be implemented in a cost-effective manner.

HTML (Hypertext Markup Language) A language used to describe and format plain-text files on the Web. HTML is based on pairs of tags that enable the user to mix graphics with text, change the appearance of text, and create hypertext documents with links to other documents.

HTTP (Hypertext Transfer Protocol) The protocol that describes the rules a browser and server use to communicate over the World Wide Web. HTTP allows a Web browser to request HTML documents from a Web server. See also *hypertext*.

hub A common connection point for multiple devices in a network. A hub contains a number of ports to connect several segments of a LAN together. When a packet arrives at one of the ports on the hub, it is copied to all the other ports so all the segments of the LAN can see all the packets. A hub can be passive, intelligent (allowing remote management, including traffic monitoring and port configuration), or switching. A switching hub is also called a switch. See *switch*.

Huffman coding A technique that minimizes the average number of bytes required to represent the characters in a text. Huffman coding works for a given character distribution by assigning short codes to frequently occurring characters and longer codes to infrequently occurring characters.

hypertext A technology that enables quick and easy navigation between and within large documents. Hypertext links are pointers to other sections within the same document; other documents; or other resources, such as FTP sites, images, or sounds.

Hz An abbreviation for hertz—a frequency measurement unit used internationally to indicate one cycle per second.

I/O (input/output) A circuit path that enables independent communication between the processor and external devices.

I/O port (input/output port) Used to communicate to and from another device, such as a printer or disk.

IBMBIO.COM One of the DOS system files required to boot the machine. The first file loaded from disk during the boot, it contains extensions to the ROM BIOS.

IBMDOS.COM One of the DOS system files required to boot the machine. Contains the primary DOS routines. Loaded by IBMBIO.COM, it in turn loads COMMAND.COM.

IC (integrated circuit) A complete electronic circuit contained on a single chip. It can consist of only a few or thousands of transistors, capacitors, diodes, or resistors, and it generally is classified according to the complexity of the circuitry and the approximate number of circuits on the chip. SSI (small-scale integration) equals 2–10 circuits; MSI (medium-scale integration) equals 10–100 circuits. LSI (large-scale integration) equals 100–1,000 circuits, and VLSI (very-large-scale integration) equals 1,000–10,000 circuits. Finally, ULSI (ultra-large-scale integration) equals more than 10,000 circuits.

IDE (Integrated Drive Electronics) Describes a hard disk with the disk controller circuitry integrated within it. The first IDE drives commonly were called hard cards. Also refers to the ATA interface standard—the standard for attaching hard disk drives to ISA bus IBM-compatible computers. IDE drives typically operate as though they were standard ST-506/412 drives. See also *ATA*.

IEEE 802.3 See *10BASE-2*.

IEEE 1394 See *FireWire*.

impedance The total opposition a circuit offers to the flow of alternating current, measured in ohms.

incremental backup A backup of all the files that have changed since the last backup.

inductive A property in which energy can be transferred from one device to another via the magnetic field generated by the device, even though no direct electrical connection is established between the two.

.INF file A Windows driver and device information file used to install new drivers or services.

ingot See *boule*.

initiator A device attached to the SCSI bus that sends a command to another device (the target) on the SCSI bus. The SCSI host adapter plugged into the system bus is an example of a SCSI initiator.

inkjet printer A type of printer that sprays one or more colors of ink on the paper; can produce output with quality approaching that of a laser printer at a lower cost.

input Data sent to the computer from the keyboard, the telephone, a video camera, another computer, paddles, joysticks, and so on.

instruction Program step that tells the computer what to do for a single operation.

integrated circuit See *IC*.

interface A communications device or protocol that enables one device to communicate with another. Matches the output of one device to the input of the other device.

interlacing A method of scanning alternate lines of pixels on a display screen. The odd lines are scanned first from top to bottom and left to right. The electron gun goes back to the top and makes a second pass, scanning the even lines. Interlacing requires two scan passes to construct a single image. Because of this additional scanning, interlaced screens often seem to flicker unless a long-persistence phosphor is used in the display.

interleave ratio The number of sectors that pass beneath the read/write heads before the "next" numbered sector arrives. When the interleave ratio is 3:1, for example, a sector is read, two pass by, and then the next is read. A proper interleave ratio, laid down during low-level formatting, enables the disk to transfer information without excessive revolutions due to missed sectors.

interleaved memory   The process of alternating access between two banks of memory to overlap accesses, thus speeding up data retrieval.

internal command   In DOS, a command contained in COMMAND.COM so that no other file must be loaded to perform the command. DIR and COPY are two examples of internal commands.

internal device   A peripheral device installed inside the main system case in either an expansion slot or a drive bay.

internal drive   A disk or tape drive mounted inside one of a computer's disk drive bays (or a hard disk card, which is installed in one of the computer's slots).

Internet   A computer network that joins many government, university, and private computers together over phone lines. The Internet traces its origins to a network set up in 1969 by the Department of Defense. You can connect to the Internet through many online services, such as CompuServe and America Online, or you can connect through local Internet service providers (ISPs). Internet computers use the TCP/IP communications protocol. Several million hosts exist on the Internet; a host is a mainframe, mini, or workstation that directly supports the Internet protocol (the IP in TCP/IP).

interpreter   A program for a high-level language that translates and executes the program at the same time. The program statements that are interpreted remain in their original source language, the way the programmer wrote them—that is, the program does not need to be compiled before execution. Interpreted programs run more slowly than compiled programs and always must be run with the interpreter loaded in memory.

interrupt   A suspension of a process, such as the execution of a computer program, caused by an event external to that process and performed in such a way that the process can be resumed. An interrupt can be caused by internal or external conditions, such as a signal indicating that a device or program has completed a transfer of data.

interrupt vector   A pointer in a table that gives the location of a set of instructions the computer should execute when a particular interrupt occurs.

IO.SYS   One of the DOS system files required to boot the machine. The first file loaded from disk during the boot, it contains extensions to the ROM BIOS.

IP address   An identifier for a computer or device on a TCP/IP network. The format of an IP address is a 32-bit numeric address written as four numbers separated by periods, in which each number can be 0–255. The TCP/IP protocol routes messages based on the IP address of the destination.

IPX (internetwork packet exchange) Novell NetWare's native LAN communications protocol used to move data between server and/or workstation programs running on different network nodes. IPX packets are encapsulated and carried by the packets used in Ethernet and the similar frames used in Token-Ring networks.

IRQ (interrupt request)   Physical connections between external hardware devices and the interrupt controllers. When a device such as a floppy controller or a printer needs the attention of the CPU, an IRQ line is used to get the attention of the system to perform a task. On PC and XT IBM-compatible systems, eight IRQ lines are included, numbered IRQ0–IRQ7. On the AT and PS/2 systems, 16 IRQ lines are numbered IRQ0–IRQ15. IRQ lines must be used by only a single adapter in the ISA bus systems, but Micro Channel Architecture (MCA) adapters can share interrupts.

ISA (Industry Standard Architecture) The bus architecture introduced as an 8-bit bus with the original IBM PC in 1981 and later expanded to 16 bits with the IBM PC/AT in 1984. ISA slots are still found in PC systems today.

ISA bus clock   Clock that normally operates the ISA bus at 8.33MHz.

ISDN (Integrated Services Digital Network) An international telecommunications standard that enables a communications channel to carry digital data simultaneously with voice and video information.

ISO (International Standards Organization) The ISO, based in Paris, develops standards for international and national data communications. The U.S. representative to the ISO is the American National Standards Institute (ANSI). See also *high sierra format.*

ISO 9660 An international standard that defines file systems for CD-ROM discs, independent of the operating system. ISO (International Standards Organization) 9660 has two levels. Level one provides for DOS file system compatibility, whereas level two allows filenames of up to 32 characters. See also *high sierra format.*

Itanium An Intel eighth-generation processor, codenamed Merced, it will be the first 64-bit instruction PC processor from Intel. It features a new Explicitly Parallel Instruction Computing (EPIC) architecture for more performance when running optimized code. Also, it features internal L1/L2 and L3 error correcting code (ECC) caches to improve throughput and reliability. It was designed initially for the server or high-end workstation market.

ITU (International Telecommunications Union) Formerly called CCITT. An international committee organized by the United Nations to set international communications recommendations—which frequently are adopted as standards—and to develop interface, modem, and data network recommendations. The Bell 212A standard for 1,200bps communication in North America, for example, is observed internationally as CCITT V.22. For 2,400bps communication, most U.S. manufacturers observe V.22bis, whereas V.32, V.32bis, V34, and V34+ are standards for 9,600bps, 14,400bps, 28,800bps, and 33,600bps, respectively. The V.90 standard recently was defined for 56Kbps modems.

J-lead J-shaped leads on chip carriers, which can be surface-mounted on a PC board or plugged into a socket that then is mounted on a PC board, usually on .050-inch centers.

Java An object-oriented programming language and environment similar to C or C++. Java was developed by Sun Microsystems and is used to create network-based applications.

Jaz drive A proprietary type of removable media drive with a magnetic hard disk platter in a rigid plastic case. Developed by Iomega and currently available in 1GB and 2GB sizes.

JEDEC (Joint Electronic Devices Engineering Council) A group that establishes standards for the electronics industry.

joystick An input device generally used for game software usually consisting of a central upright stick that controls horizontal and vertical motion and one or more buttons to control discrete events, such as firing guns. More complex models can resemble flight yokes and steering wheels or incorporate tactile feedback.

JPEG (Joint Photographic Experts Group) The international consortium of hardware, software, and publishing interests which—under the auspices of the ISO—has defined a universal standard for digital compression and decompression of still images for use in computer systems. JPEG compresses at about a 20:1 ratio before visible image degradation occurs. A lossy data compression standard that was originally designed for still images but also can compress real-time video (30 frames per second) and animation. Lossy compression permanently discards unnecessary data, resulting in some loss of precision.

jukebox A type of CD-ROM drive that enables several CD-ROM discs to be in the drive at the same time. The drive itself determines which disc is needed by the system and loads the discs into the reading mechanism as needed.

jumper A small, plastic-covered metal clip that slips over two pins protruding from a circuit board. Sometimes also called a shunt. When in place, the jumper connects the pins electrically and closes the circuit. By doing so, it connects the two terminals of a switch, turning it "on."

Kermit A protocol designed for transferring files between microcomputers and mainframes. Developed by Frank DaCruz and Bill Catchings at Columbia University (and named after the talking frog on *The Muppet Show*), Kermit is widely accepted in the academic world.

kernel   Operating system core component.

key disk   In software copy protection, a distribution floppy disk that must be present in a floppy disk drive for an application program to run.

keyboard   The primary input device for most computers, consisting of keys with letters of the alphabet, digits, punctuation, and function control keys.

keyboard macro   A series of keystrokes automatically input when a single key is pressed.

keylock   Physical locking mechanism to prevent internal access to the system unit or peripherals.

KFlex   A proprietary standard for 56Kbps modem transmissions developed by Rockwell and implemented in modems from a variety of vendors. Superseded by the official V.90 standard for 56Kbps modems. See also *X2* and *V.90*.

kilo   A multiplier indicating one thousand (1,000) of some unit. Abbreviated as k or K. When used to indicate a number of bytes of memory storage, the multiplier definition changes to 1,024. One kilobit, for example, equals 1,000 bits, whereas one kilobyte equals 1,024 bytes.

kilobyte (KB)   A unit of information storage equal to 1,024 bytes.

L1 cache (level one)   A memory cache built into the CPU core of 486 and later generation processors. See also *cache* and *disk cache*.

L2 cache (level two)   A second-level memory cache external to the processor core, usually larger and slower than L1. Normally found on the motherboard of 386, 486, and Pentium systems and inside the processor package or module in Pentium Pro and Pentium II systems. Moving the L2 cache onto the processor in the Pentium Pro and Pentium II allows it to run at speeds up to full processor speed rather than motherboard speed. See also *SEC*, *cache*, and *disk cache*.

landing zone   An unused track on a disk surface on which the read/write heads can land when power is shut off. The place a parking program or a drive with an autopark mechanism parks the heads.

LAPM (link-access procedure for modems)   An error-control protocol incorporated in CCITT Recommendation V.42. Similar to the MNP and HST protocols, it uses cyclic redundancy checking (CRC) and retransmission of corrupted data (ARQ) to ensure data reliability.

laptop computer   A computer system smaller than a briefcase but larger than a notebook that usually has a clamshell design in which the keyboard and display are on separate halves of the system, which are hinged together. These systems normally run on battery power.

large mode   Another name for the LBA translation scheme used by IDE drives to translate the cylinder, head, and sector specifications of the drive to those usable by an enhanced BIOS.

large-scale integration   See *IC*.

laser printer   A type of printer that is a combination of an electrostatic copying machine and a computer printer. The output data from the computer is converted by an interface into a raster feed, similar to the impulses a TV picture tube receives. The impulses cause the laser beam to scan a small drum that carries a positive electrical charge. Where the laser hits, the drum is discharged. A toner, which also carries a positive charge, is then applied to the drum. This toner, a fine, black powder, sticks to only the areas of the drum that have been discharged electrically. As it rotates, the drum deposits the toner on a negatively charged sheet of paper. Another roller then heats and bonds the toner to the page.

latency   1) The amount of time required for a disk drive to rotate half of a revolution. Represents the average amount of time to locate a specific sector after the heads have arrived at a specific track. Latency is part of the average access time for a drive. 2) The initial setup time required for a memory transfer in DRAM to select the row and column addresses for the memory to be read/written.

LBA (logical block addressing) A method used with SCSI and IDE drives to translate the cylinder, head, and sector specifications of the drive to those usable by an enhanced BIOS. LBA is used with drives that are larger than 528MB and causes the BIOS to translate the drive's logical parameters to those usable by the system BIOS.

LCC (leadless chip carrier) A type of integrated circuit package that has input and output pads rather than leads on its perimeter.

LCD (liquid crystal display) A display that uses liquid crystal sealed between two pieces of polarized glass. The polarity of the liquid crystal is changed by an electric current to vary the amount of light that can pass through. Because LCD displays do not generate light, they depend on either the reflection of ambient light or backlighting the screen. The best type of LCD, the active-matrix or thin-film transistor (TFT) LCD, offers fast screen updates and true color capability.

LED (light-emitting diode) A semiconductor diode that emits light when a current is passed through it.

LIF (low insertion force) A type of socket that requires only a minimum of force to insert a chip carrier.

light pen A handheld input device with a light-sensitive probe or stylus connected to the computer's graphics adapter board by a cable. Used for writing or sketching onscreen or as a pointing device for making selections. Unlike mice, it's not widely supported by software applications.

line voltage The AC voltage available at a standard wall outlet, nominally 110–120v.

lithium ion A portable system battery type that is longer-lived than either NiCad or NiMH technologies, cannot be overcharged, and holds a charge well when not in use. Lithium ion batteries are also lighter weight than the NiCad and NiMH technologies. Because of these superior features, Li-ion batteries have come to be used in all but the very low end of the portable system market.

local area network (LAN) The connection of two or more computers, usually via a network adapter card or NIC.

local bus A generic term used to describe a bus directly attached to a processor and that operates at the processor's speed and data-transfer width.

local echo A modem feature that enables the modem to send copies of keyboard commands and transmitted data to the screen. When the modem is in command mode (not online to another system), the local echo normally is invoked through an ATE1 command, which causes the modem to display the user's typed commands. When the modem is online to another system, the local echo is invoked by an ATF0 command, which causes the modem to display the data it transmits to the remote system.

logical drive A drive as named by a DOS drive specifier, such as C: or D:. Under DOS 3.3 or later, a single physical drive can act as several logical drives, each with its own specifier.

logical unit number See *LUN*.

lossless compression A compression technique that preserves all the original information in an image or other data structures.

lossy compression A compression technique that achieves optimal data reduction by discarding redundant and unnecessary information in an image.

lost clusters Clusters that have been marked accidentally as "unavailable" in the FAT even though they don't belong to any file listed in a directory. See also *cluster*.

low-level formatting Formatting that divides tracks into sectors on the platter surfaces. Places sector-identifying information before and after each sector and fills each sector with null data (usually hex F6). Specifies the sector interleave and marks defective tracks by placing invalid checksum figures in each sector on a defective track.

LPT port Line printer port, a common system abbreviation for a parallel printer port.

LPX A semiproprietary motherboard design used in many Low Profile or Slimline case systems. Because no formal standard exists, these typically are not interchangeable between vendors and are often difficult to find replacement parts for or upgrade.

luminance   Measure of brightness usually used in specifying monitor brightness.

LUN (logical unit number)   A number given to a device (a logical unit) attached to a SCSI physical unit and not directly to the SCSI bus. Although as many as eight logical units can be attached to a single physical unit, normally a single logical unit is a built-in part of a single physical unit. A SCSI hard disk, for example, has a built-in SCSI bus adapter that is assigned a physical unit number or SCSI ID, and the controller and drive portions of the hard disk are assigned a LUN (usually 0). See also *PUN*.

LZH (Lempel Zev Welch)   A compression scheme used in the GIF graphic format.

machine address   A hexadecimal (hex) location in memory.

machine language   Hexadecimal program code a computer can understand and execute. It can be output from the assembler or compiler.

magnetic domain   A tiny segment of a track just large enough to hold one of the magnetic flux reversals that encode data on a disk surface.

magneto-optical recording   An erasable optical disk recording technique that uses a laser beam to heat pits on the disk surface to the point at which a magnet can make flux changes.

magneto-resistive   A technology originally developed by IBM and commonly used for the read element of a read/write head on a high-density magnetic disk. Based on the principle that the resistance to electricity changes in a material when brought into contact with a magnetic field, in this case, the read element material and the magnetic bit. Such drives use a magneto-resistive read sensor for reading and a standard inductive element for writing. A magneto-resistive read head is more sensitive to magnetic fields than inductive read heads.

mainframe   A somewhat vague distinction that identifies any large computer system normally capable of supporting many users and programs simultaneously.

mask   A photographic map of the circuits for a particular layer of a semiconductor chip used in manufacturing the chip.

master boot record (MBR)   On hard disks, a one-sector long record that contains the master boot program as well as the master partition table containing up to four partition entries. The master boot program reads the master partition table to determine which of the four entries is active (bootable), and then loads the first sector of that partition, called the volume boot record. The master boot program tests the volume boot record for a 55AAh signature at offset 510; if it's present, program execution is transferred to the volume boot sector, which normally contains a program designed to load the operating system files. The MBR is always the first physical sector of the disk, at Cylinder 0, Head 0, Sector 1. Also called master boot sector.

math coprocessor   A processing chip designed to quickly handle complex arithmetic computations involving floating-point arithmetic, offloading these from the main processor. Originally contained in a separate coprocessor chip, starting with the 486 family of processors. Intel now has incorporated the math coprocessor into the main processors in what is called the floating-point unit.

MCA (Micro Channel Architecture)   Developed by IBM for the PS/2 line of computers and introduced on April 2, 1987. Features include a 16- or 32-bit bus width and multiple master control. By allowing several processors to arbitrate for resources on a single bus, the MCA is optimized for multitasking, multiprocessor systems. Offers switchless configuration of adapters, which eliminates one of the biggest headaches of installing older adapters.

MCGA (multicolor graphics array)   A type of PC video display circuit introduced by IBM on April 2, 1987, which supports text and graphics. Text is supported at a maximum resolution of 80×25 characters in 16 colors with a character box of 8×16 pixels. Graphics is supported at a maximum resolution of 320×200 pixels in 256 (from a palette of 262,144) colors or 640×480 pixels in two colors. The MCGA outputs an analog signal with a horizontal scanning frequency of 31.5KHz and supports analog color or analog monochrome displays.

MCI (media control interface) A device-independent specification for controlling multimedia devices and files. MCI is a part of the multimedia extensions and offers a standard interface set of device control commands. MCI commands are used for audio recording and playback and animation playback. Device types include CD audio, digital audio tape players, scanners, MIDI sequencers, videotape players or recorders, and audio devices that play digitized waveform files.

MDA (monochrome display adapter; also, MGA—mono graphics adapter) A type of PC video display adapter introduced by IBM on August 12, 1981, that supports text only. Text is supported at a maximum resolution of 80×25 characters in four colors with a character box of 9×14 pixels. Colors, in this case, indicate black, white, bright white, and underlined. Graphics modes are not supported. The MDA outputs a digital signal with a horizontal scanning frequency of 18.432KHz and supports TTL monochrome displays. The IBM MDA also includes a parallel printer port.

mean time between failure See *MTBF*.

mean time to repair See *MTTR*.

medium The magnetic coating or plating that covers a disk or tape.

mega A multiplier indicating one million (1,000,000) of some unit. Abbreviated as m or M. When used to indicate a number of bytes of memory storage, the multiplier definition changes to 1,048,576. For example, one megabit equals 1,000,000 bits, and one megabyte equals 1,048,576 bytes.

megabyte (MB) A unit of information storage equal to 1,048,576 bytes.

memory Any component in a computer system that stores information for future use.

memory caching A service provided by extremely fast memory chips that keeps copies of the most recent memory accesses. When the CPU makes a subsequent access, the value is supplied by the fast memory rather than by the relatively slow system memory.

memory-resident program A program that remains in memory after it has been loaded, consuming memory that otherwise might be used by application software.

menu software Utility software that makes a computer easier to use by replacing DOS commands with a series of menu selections.

MFM encoding (modified frequency modulation encoding) A method of encoding data on the surface of a disk. The coding of a bit of data varies by the coding of the preceding bit to preserve clocking information.

MHz An abbreviation for megahertz, a unit of measurement indicating the frequency of one million cycles per second. One hertz (Hz) is equal to one cycle per second. Named after Heinrich R. Hertz, a German physicist who first detected electromagnetic waves in 1883.

MI/MIC (mode indicate/mode indicate common) Also called forced or manual originate. Provided for installations in which equipment other than the modem does the dialing. In such installations, the modem operates in dumb mode (no auto-dial capability), yet must go off-hook in originate mode to connect with answering modems.

micro (μ) A prefix indicating one millionth (1/1,000,000 or .000001) of some unit.

micron A unit of measurement equaling one millionth of a meter. Often used in measuring the size of circuits in chip manufacturing processes. Current state-of-the-art chip fabrication builds chips with 0.25-micron circuits.

microprocessor A solid-state central processing unit much like a computer on a chip. An integrated circuit that accepts coded instructions for execution.

microsecond (μs) A unit of time equal to one millionth (1/1,000,000 or .000001) of a second.

MIDI (musical instrument digital interface) An interface and file format standard for connecting a musical instrument to a microcomputer and storing musical instrument data. Multiple musical instruments can be daisy-chained and played simultaneously with the help of the computer and related software. The various operations of the instruments can be captured, saved, edited, and played back. A MIDI file contains note information, timing (how long a note is held), volume, and instrument type for as many as 16 channels. Sequencer programs are used to control MIDI functions such as recording, playback, and editing. MIDI files store only note instructions and not actual sound data.

milli (m) A prefix indicating one thousandth (1/1,000 or .001) of some unit.

millisecond (ms) A unit of time equal to one thousandth (1/1,000 or .001) of a second.

minitower A type of PC system case that is shorter than a full- or mid-sized tower.

MIPS (million instructions per second) Refers to the average number of machine-language instructions a computer can perform or execute in one second. Because various processors can perform different functions in a single instruction, MIPS should be used only as a general measure of performance among various types of computers.

MMX An Intel processor enhancement that adds 57 new instructions designed to improve multimedia performance. MMX also implies a doubling of the internal L1 processor cache.

mnemonic An abbreviated name for something used in a manner similar to an acronym. Computer processor instructions are often abbreviated with a mnemonic, such as JMP (jump), CLR (clear), STO (store), and INIT (initialize). A mnemonic name for an instruction or an operation makes it easy to remember and convenient to use.

MNP (Microcom Networking Protocol) Asynchronous error-control and data-compression protocols developed by Microcom, Inc., and now in the public domain. They ensure error-free transmission through error detection (CRC) and retransmission of erred frames.

MNP Levels 1–4 cover error control and have been incorporated into CCITT Recommendation V.42. MNP Level 5 includes data compression but is eclipsed in superiority by V.42bis—an international standard that is more efficient. Most high-speed modems connect with MNP Level 5 if V.42bis is unavailable.

MO (magneto-optical) MO drives use both magnetic and optical storage properties. MO technology is erasable and recordable, as opposed to CD-ROM (read-only) and WORM (write-once) drives. MO uses laser and magnetic field technology to record and erase data.

mobile module (MMO) A type of processor packing from Intel for mobile computers consisting of a Pentium or newer processor mounted on a small daughterboard along with the processor voltage regulator, the system's L2 cache memory, and the North Bridge part of the motherboard chipset.

modem (modulator/demodulator) A device that converts electrical signals from a computer into an audio form transmittable over telephone lines, or vice versa. It modulates, or transforms, digital signals from a computer into the analog form that can be carried successfully on a phone line; also demodulates signals received from the phone line back to digital signals before passing them to the receiving computer.

modulation The process of modifying some characteristic of a carrier wave or signal so that it varies in step with the changes of another signal, thus carrying the information of the other signal.

module An assembly that contains a complete circuit or subcircuit.

monitor See *display*.

monochrome display adapter See *MDA*.

MOS (metal-oxide semiconductor) Refers to the three layers used in forming the gate structure of a field-effect transistor (FET). MOS circuits offer low-power dissipation and enable transistors to be jammed close together before a critical heat problem arises. PMOS, the oldest type of MOS circuit, is a silicon-gate P-channel MOS process that uses currents made up of positive charges. NMOS is a sili-con-gate N-channel MOS process that uses currents made up of negative charges and is at least twice as fast as PMOS. CMOS, complementary MOS, is nearly immune to noise, runs off almost any power supply, and is an extremely low-power circuit technique.

motherboard   The main circuit board in the computer. Also called planar, system board, or backplane.

mouse   An input device invented by Douglas Engelbart of Stanford Research Center in 1963 and popularized by Xerox in the 1970s. A mouse consists of a roller ball and a tracking mechanism on the underside that relays the mouse's horizontal and vertical position to the computer, allowing precise control of the pointer location onscreen. The top side features two or three buttons and possibly a small wheel used to select or click items onscreen.

MPC   A trademarked abbreviation for Multimedia Personal Computer. The original MPC specification was developed by Tandy Corporation and Microsoft as the minimum platform capable of running multimedia software. In the summer of 1995, the MPC Marketing Council introduced an upgraded MPC 3 standard. The MPC 1 Specification defines the following minimum standard requirements: a 386SX or 486 CPU; 2MB RAM; 30MB hard disk; VGA video display; 8-bit digital audio subsystem; CD-ROM drive; and systems software compatible with the applications programming interfaces (APIs) of Microsoft Windows version 3.1 or later. The MPC 2 specification defines the following minimum standard requirements: 25MHz 486SX with 4MB RAM; 160MB hard disk; 16-bit sound card; 65,536 color video display; double-speed CD-ROM drive; and systems software compatible with the applications programming interfaces (APIs) of Microsoft Windows version 3.1 or later. The MPC 3 Specification defines the following minimum standard requirements: 75MHz Pentium with 8MB RAM; 540MB hard disk; 16-bit sound card; 65,536 color video display; quad-speed CD-ROM drive; OM-1–compliant MPEG-1 video, and systems software compatible with the applications programming interfaces (APIs) of

Microsoft Windows version 3.1 and DOS 6.0 or later.

MPEG (Motion Picture Experts Group)
A working ISO committee that has defined standards for lossy digital compression and decompression of motion video/audio for use in computer systems. The MPEG-1 standard delivers decompression data at 1.2MB/sec–1.5MB/sec, enabling CD players to play full-motion color movies at 30 frames per second. MPEG-1 compresses at about a 50:1 ratio before image degradation occurs, but compression ratios as high as 200:1 are attainable. MPEG-2 extends to the higher data rates (2Mbps–15Mbps) necessary for signals delivered from remote sources (such as broadcast, cable, or satellite). MPEG-2 is designed to support a range of picture aspect ratios, including 4:3 and 16:9. MPEG compression produces about a 50% volume reduction in file size. See also *lossy compression.*

MPR   The Swedish government standard for maximum video terminal radiation. The current version is called MPR II.

MSDOS.SYS   One of the DOS system files required to boot the machine. Contains the primary DOS routines. Loaded by IO.SYS, it in turn loads COMMAND.COM.

MTBF (mean time between failure)   A statistically derived measure of the probable time a device will continue to operate before a hardware failure occurs, usually given in hours. Because no standard technique exists for measuring MTBF, a device from one manufacturer can be significantly more or significantly less reliable than a device with the same MTBF rating from another manufacturer.

MTTR (mean time to repair)   A measure of the probable time it will take a technician to service or repair a specific device, usually given in hours.

multicolor graphics array   See *MCGA.*

multimedia   The integration of sound, graphic images, animation, motion video, and text in one environment on a computer. It is a set of hardware and software technologies that are rapidly changing and enhancing the computing environment.

multisession   A term used in CD-ROM recording to describe a recording event. Multisession capabilities allow data recording on the disk at various times in several recording sessions. Kodak's Photo CD is an example of CD-R technology. See also *session* (single or multisession).

multitask   To run several programs simultaneously.

multithread   To concurrently process more than one message by an application program. OS/2, Windows 95, and Windows NT are examples of multithreaded operating systems. Each program can start two or more threads, which carry out various interrelated tasks with less overhead than two separate programs would require.

multiuser system   A system in which several computer terminals share the same central processing unit (CPU).

nano (n)   A prefix indicating one billionth (1/1,000,000,000 or .000000001) of some unit.

nanosecond (ns)   A unit of time equal to one billionth (1/1,000,000,000 or .000000001) of a second.

NetBEUI (NetBIOS Extended User Interface)   A network protocol used primarily by Windows NT and most suitable for small peer-to-peer networks.

NetBIOS (Network Basic Input/Output System)   A commonly used network protocol originally developed by IBM and Sytek for PC local area networks. NetBIOS provides session and transport services (Layers 4 and 5 of the OSI model).

network   A system in which a number of independent computers are linked to share data and peripherals, such as hard disks and printers.

network interface card (NIC)   An adapter that connects a PC to a network.

Network Layer   In the OSI reference model, the layer that switches and routes the packets as necessary to get them to their destinations. This layer is responsible for addressing and delivering message packets. See also *OSI*.

NiCad   The oldest of the three battery technologies used in portable systems, nickel cadmium batteries are rarely used in portable systems today because of their shorter life and sensitivity to improper charging and discharging. See also *NiMH* and *lithium ion*.

NiMH   A battery technology used in portable systems. Nickel metal-hydride batteries have approximately a 30-percent longer life than NiCads, are less sensitive to the memory effect caused by improper charging and discharging, and do not use the environmentally dangerous substances found in NiCads. Newer lithium ion (Li-ion) batteries are far superior.

NLX   A new low-profile motherboard form factor standard that is basically an improved version of the semiproprietary LPX design. It's designed to accommodate larger processor and memory form factors and incorporate newer bus technologies, such as AGP and USB. Besides design improvements, it is fully standardized, which means you should be able to replace one NLX board with another from a different manufacturer—something that was not normally possible with LPX.

node   A device on a network. Also any junction point at which two or more items meet.

noise   Any unwanted disturbance in an electrical or mechanical system.

noninterlaced monitor   A desirable monitor design in which the electron beam sweeps the screen in lines from top to bottom, one line after the other, completing the entire screen in one pass.

nonvolatile memory (NVRAM)   Random-access memory whose data is retained when power is turned off. ROM/EPROM/EEPROM (flash) memory are examples of nonvolatile memory. Sometimes NVRAM is retained without any power whatsoever, as in EEPROM or flash memory devices. In other cases, the memory is maintained by a small battery. NVRAM that is battery maintained is sometimes also called CMOS memory (although CMOS RAM technically is volatile). CMOS NVRAM is used in IBM-compatible systems to store configuration information. True NVRAM often is used in intelligent modems to store a user-defined default configuration loaded into normal modem RAM at power-up.

nonvolatile RAM disk   A RAM disk powered by a battery supply so that it continues to hold its data during a power outage.

North Bridge   The Intel term for the main portion of the motherboard chipset that incorporates the interface between the processor and the rest of the motherboard. The North Bridge contains the cache, main memory, and AGP controllers, as well as the interface between the high-speed (normally 66MHz or 100MHz) processor bus and the 33MHz PCI (peripheral component interconnect) or 66MHz AGP (accelerated graphics port) buses. See also *chipset* and *South Bridge*.

notebook computer   A very small personal computer approximately the size of a notebook.

NTSC   The National Television Standards Committee, which governs the standard for television and video playback and recording in the United States. The NTSC was originally organized in 1941 when TV broadcasting first began on a wide scale in black and white, and the format was revised in 1953 for color. The NTSC format has 525 scan lines, a field frequency of 60Hz, a broadcast bandwidth of 4MHz, a line frequency of 15.75KHz, a frame frequency of 1/30 of a second, and a color subcarrier frequency of 3.58MHz. It is an interlaced signal, which means it scans every other line each time the screen is refreshed. The signal is generated as a composite of red, green, and blue signals for color and includes an FM frequency for audio and a signal for stereo. See also *PAL* and *SECAM*, which are incompatible systems used in Europe. NTSC is also called composite video.

null modem   A serial cable wired so that two data terminal equipment (DTE) devices, such as personal computers, or two data communication equipment (DCE) devices, such as modems or mice, can be connected. Also sometimes called a modem-eliminator or a LapLink cable. To make a null-modem cable with DB-25 connectors, you wire these pins together: 1-1, 2-3, 3-2, 4-5, 5-4, 6-8-20, 20-8-6, and 7-7.

numeric coprocessor   See *math coprocessor*.

NVRAM (nonvolatile random access memory)   Memory that retains data without power. Flash memory and battery-backed CMOS RAM are examples of NVRAM.

object hierarchy   Occurs in a graphical program when two or more objects are linked and one object's movement is dependent on the other object. This is known as a parent-child hierarchy. In an example using a human figure, the fingers would be child objects to the hand, which is a child object to the arm, which is a child to the shoulder, and so on. Object hierarchy provides much control for an animator in moving complex figures.

OCR (optical character recognition)   An information-processing technology that converts human-readable text into computer data. Usually a scanner is used to read the text on a page, and OCR software converts the images to characters.

ODI (Open Data-link Interface)   A device driver standard from Novell that enables multiple protocols to run on the same network adapter card. ODI adds functionality to Novell's NetWare and network computing environments by supporting multiple protocols and drivers.

OEM (original equipment manufacturer)   Any manufacturer who sells its product to a reseller. Usually refers to the original manufacturer of a particular device or component. Most Compaq hard disks, for example, are made by Conner Peripherals, who is considered the OEM.

OLE (object linking and embedding)   An enhancement to the original Dynamic Data Exchange (DDE) protocol that enables the user to embed or link data created in one application to a document created in another application and subsequently edit that data directly from the final document.

online fallback   A feature that enables high-speed error-control modems to monitor line quality and fall back to the next lower speed if line quality degrades. Some modems fall forward as line quality improves.

open architecture   A system design in which the specifications are made public to encourage third-party vendors to develop add-on products. The PC is a true open architecture system, but the Macintosh is proprietary.

operating system (OS)   A collection of programs for operating the computer. Operating systems perform housekeeping tasks, such as input and output between the computer and peripherals and accepting and interpreting information from the keyboard. DOS and OS/2 are examples of popular OSes.

optical disk   A disk that encodes data as a series of reflective pits that are read (and sometimes written) by a laser beam.

Orange Book   The standard for recordable compact discs (similar to CD-ROMs, but recordable instead of read-only). Recordable compact discs are called CD-R and are becoming popular with the widespread use of multimedia. Part of the Orange Book standard defines rewritable magneto-optical disks, and another section defines optical write-once, read-many (WORM) discs.

originate mode   A state in which the modem transmits at the predefined low frequency of the communications channel and receives at the high frequency. The transmit/receive frequencies are the reverse of the called modem, which is in answer mode. See also *answer mode*.

OS/2   An operating system originally developed through a joint effort by IBM and Microsoft Corporation and later by IBM alone. Originally released in 1987, OS/2 is a 32-bit operating system designed to run on computers using the Intel 386 or later microprocessors. The OS/2 Workplace Shell, an integral part of the system, is a graphical interface similar to Microsoft Windows and the Apple Macintosh system.

OSI (Open Systems Interconnection)   Reference model developed by the International Organization for Standardization (ISO) in the 1980s, the OSI model splits a computer's networking stack into seven discrete layers. Each layer provides specific services to the layers above and below it. From the top down, the Application Layer is responsible for program-to-program communication; the Presentation Layer manages data representation conversions. Next, the Session Layer is responsible for establishing and maintaining communications channels, and the Transport Layer is responsible for the integrity of data transmission. The Network Layer routes data from one node to another. The Data Link Layer is responsible for physically passing data from one node to another, and finally, the Physical Layer is responsible for moving data on and off the network media.

output   Information processed by the computer, or the act of sending that information to a mass storage device, such as a video display, printer, or modem.

overclocking   The process of running a processor at a speed faster than the officially marked speed by using a higher clock multiplier or faster bus speed. Not recommended or endorsed by processor manufacturers. See also *clock multiplier*.

OverDrive   An Intel trademark name for its line of upgrade processors.

overlay   Part of a program loaded into memory only when it is required.

overrun   A situation in which data moves from one device more quickly than a second device can accept it.

overscanning   A technique used in consumer display products that extends the deflection of a CRT's electron beam beyond the physical boundaries of the screen to ensure that images always fill the display area.

overwrite   To write data on top of existing data, thus erasing the existing data.

package   A device that includes a chip mounted on a carrier and sealed.

packet   A message sent over a network that contains data and a destination address.

pairing   Combining processor instructions for optimal execution on superscalar processors.

PAL   1) Phase Alternating Line system. Invented in 1961, a system of TV broadcasting used in England and other European countries (except France). PAL's image format is 4:3, 625 lines, 50Hz, and 4MHz video bandwidth with a total 8MHz of video channel width. With its 625-line picture delivered at 25 frames per second, PAL provides a better image and an improved color transmission over the NTSC system used in North America. 2) Programmable array logic, a type of chip that has logic gates specified by a device programmer.

palmtop computer   A computer system smaller than a notebook that is designed so it can be held in one hand while being operated by the other. Many are now called PDAs or personal digital assistants.

parallel   A method of transferring data characters in which the bits travel down parallel electrical paths simultaneously—for example, eight paths for 8-bit characters. Data is stored in computers in parallel form but can be converted to serial form for certain operations.

parity   A method of error checking in which an extra bit is sent to the receiving device to indicate whether an even or odd number of binary 1 bits was transmitted. The receiving unit compares the received information with this bit and can obtain a reasonable judgment about the validity of the character. The same type of parity (even or odd) must be used by two communicating computers, or both may omit parity. When parity is used, a parity bit is added to each transmitted character. The bit's value is 0 or 1, to make the total number of 1s in the character even or odd, depending on which type of parity is used.

park program   A program that executes a seek to the highest cylinder or just past the highest cylinder of a drive so the potential of data loss is minimized if the drive is moved.

partition   A section of a hard disk devoted to a particular operating system. Most hard disks have only one partition, devoted to DOS. A hard disk can have as many as four partitions, each occupied by a different operating system. DOS v3.3 or later can occupy two of these four partitions.

Pascal   A high-level programming language named for the French mathematician Blaise Pascal (1623–1662). Developed in the early

1970s by Niklaus Wirth for teaching programming and designed to support the concepts of structured programming.

passive matrix   Another name for dual-scan, display-type LCDs.

PC card (PCMCIA—Personal Computer Memory Card International Association) A credit card–sized expansion adapter for notebook and laptop PCs. PC card is the official PCMCIA trademark; however, both PC card and PCMCIA card are used to refer to these standards. PCMCIA cards are removable modules that can hold numerous types of devices, including memory, modems, fax/modems, radio transceivers, network adapters, solid state disks, and hard disks.

PCI (Peripheral Component Interconnect)   A standard bus specification initially developed by Intel that bypasses the standard ISA I/O bus and uses the system bus to increase the bus clock speed and take full advantage of the CPU's data path.

PCL (Printer Control Language) Developed by Hewlett-Packard in 1984 as a language for the HP LaserJet printer. PCL is now the de facto industry standard for PC printing. PCL defines a standard set of commands, enabling applications to communicate with HP or HP-compatible printers and is supported by virtually all printer manufacturers.

PCM (pulse code modulation)   A technique for digitizing analog signals by sampling the signal and converting each sample into a binary number. Also stands for powertrain control module, which is what the computer in most modern automobiles is called.

peer-to-peer   A type of network in which any computer can act as both a server (by providing access to its resources to other computers) and a client (by accessing shared resources from other computers).

pel   See *pixel*.

Pentium   An Intel microprocessor with 32-bit registers, a 64-bit data bus, and a 32-bit address bus. The Pentium has a built-in L1 cache segmented into a separate 8KB cache for code and another 8KB cache for data. The

Pentium includes an FPU or math coprocessor. It is backward compatible with the 486 and can operate in real, protected virtual, and virtual real modes.

Pentium 4 The first Intel seventh-generation processor, based on a new 32-bit micro-architecture that operates at higher clock speeds due to hyper pipelined technology, a rapid execution engine, a 400MHz system bus, and an execution trace cache. The 400MHz system bus is a quad-pumped bus running off a 100MHz system clock, making 3.2GB/sec data transfer rates possible. The advanced transfer cache is a 256KB, on-die level 2 cache with increased bandwidth over previous micro-architectures. The floating-point and multimedia units have been improved by making the registers 128 bits wide and adding a separate register for data movement. Finally, SSE2 adds 144 new instructions for double-precision floating-point, SIMD integer, and memory management. Codenamed Willamette.

Pentium II An Intel sixth-generation processor similar to the Pentium Pro, but with MMX capabilities and SEC cartridge packaging technology. Includes L2 cache running at half-core speed.

Pentium III An Intel sixth-generation processor similar to the Pentium II, but with SSE (Streaming SIMD Extensions) added. Later PIII models (codenamed Coppermine) included on-die L2 cache running at full core speed. Available in both cartridge and chip package versions.

Pentium Pro An Intel sixth-generation (P6) processor with 32-bit registers, a 64-bit data bus, and a 36-bit address bus. The Pentium Pro has the same segmented Level 1 cache as the Pentium but also includes a 256KB, 512KB, or 1MB of L2 cache on a separate die inside the processor package. The Pentium Pro includes a FPU or math coprocessor. It is backward compatible with the Pentium and can operate in real, protected, and virtual real modes.

peripheral Any piece of equipment used in computer systems that is an attachment to the computer. Disk drives, terminals, and printers are all examples of peripherals.

persistence In a monitor, the quality of the phosphor chemical that indicates how long the glow caused by the electrons striking the phosphor will remain onscreen.

PGA 1) Pin grid array. A chip package that has a large number of pins on the bottom designed for socket mounting. 2) Professional graphics adapter. A limited-production, high-resolution graphics card for XT and AT systems from IBM.

phosphor A layer of electroluminescent material applied to the inside face of a CRT (cathode-ray tube). When bombarded by electrons the material fluoresces, and after the bombardment stops it phosphoresces.

phosphorescence The emission of light from a substance after the source of excitation has been removed.

Photo CD A technology developed by Eastman Kodak and Philips that stores photographic images on a CD-R recordable compact disc. Images stored on the Photo CD can have resolutions as high as 2,048×3,072 pixels. Up to 100 true-color images (24-bit color) can be stored on one disc. Photo CD images are created by scanning film and digitally recording the images on compact discs. The digitized images are indexed (given a 4-digit code), and thumbnails of each image on the disc are shown on the front of the case along with its index number. Multisession capability enables several rolls of film to be added to a single disc on different occasions.

photolithography The photographic process used in electronic chip manufacturing that creates transistors and circuit and signal pathways in semiconductors by depositing different layers of various materials on the chip.

photoresist A chemical used to coat a silicon wafer in the semiconductor manufacturing process that makes the silicon sensitive to light for photolithography.

physical drive A single disk drive. DOS defines logical drives, which are given a specifier, such as C: or D:. A single physical drive can be divided into multiple logical drives. Conversely, special software can span a single logical drive across two physical drives.

Physical Layer   See *OSI*.

physical unit number   See *PUN*.

PIF (program information file)   A file that contains information about a non-Windows application specifying optimum settings for running the program under Windows 3.x. These are called property sheets in Windows 95.

pin   1) The lead on a connector, chip, module, or device. 2) Personal identification number. A personal password used for identification purposes.

pin compatible   Chips having the same pinout functions.

pinout   A listing of which pins have which functions on a chip, socket, slot, or other connector.

PIO mode (programmed input/output mode)   The standard data transfer modes used by IDE drives that use the processor's registers for data transfer. This is in contrast with DMA modes, which transfer data directly between main memory and the device. The slowest PIO mode is 0, and the fastest current mode is mode 4.

pipeline   A path for instructions or data to follow.

pixel   A mnemonic term meaning picture element. Any of the tiny elements that form a picture on a video display screen. Also called a pel.

planar board   A term equivalent to motherboard, used by IBM in some of its literature.

plated media   Hard disk platters plated with a form of thin metal film medium on which data is recorded.

platter   A disk contained in a hard disk drive. Most drives have two or more platters, each with data recorded on both sides.

PLCC (plastic leaded-chip carrier)   A popular chip-carrier package with J-leads around the perimeter of the package.

Plug and Play (PnP)   A hardware and software specification developed by Intel that enables a PnP system and PnP adapter cards to automatically configure themselves. PnP cards are free from switches and jumpers and are configured via the PnP BIOS in the host system, or via supplied programs for non-PnP systems.

polling   A communications technique that determines when a device is ready to send data. The system continually interrogates polled devices in a round-robin sequence. If a device has data to send, it sends back an acknowledgment and the transmission begins. Contrasts with interrupt-driven communications, in which the device generates a signal to interrupt the system when it has data to send.

port   Plug or socket that enables an external device, such as a printer, to be attached to the adapter card in the computer. Also a logical address used by a microprocessor for communication between it and various devices.

port address   One of a system of addresses used by the computer to access devices such as disk drives or printer ports. You might need to specify an unused port address when installing any adapter boards in a system unit.

port replicator   For mobile computers, a device that plugs into the laptop and provides all the ports for connecting external devices. The advantage of using a port replicator is that the external devices can be left connected to the replicator and the mobile computer connected to them all at once by connecting to the replicator, rather than connecting to each individual device. A port replicator differs from a docking station in that the latter can provide additional drive bays and expansion slots not found in port replicators.

portable computer   A computer system smaller than a transportable system but larger than a laptop system. Most portable systems conform to the lunchbox style popularized by Compaq or the briefcase style popularized by IBM, each with a fold-down (removable) keyboard and built-in display. These systems characteristically run on AC power and not on batteries, include several expansion slots, and can be as powerful as full desktop systems.

POS (Programmable Option Select) The Micro Channel Architecture's POS eliminates switches and jumpers from the system board and adapters by replacing them with programmable registers. Automatic configuration routines store the POS data in a battery-powered CMOS memory for system configuration and operations. The configuration utilities rely on adapter description files (ADF) that contain the setup data for each card.

POST (power on self test) A series of tests run by the computer at power-on. Most computers scan and test many of their circuits and sound a beep from the internal speaker if this initial test indicates proper system performance.

PostScript A page-description language developed primarily by John Warnock of Adobe Systems for converting and moving data to the laser-printed page. Instead of using the standard method of transmitting graphics or character information to a printer and telling it where to place dots one by one on a page, PostScript provides a way for the laser printer to interpret mathematically a full page of shapes and curves.

POTS (Plain Old Telephone Service) Standard analog telephone service.

power management Systems used initially in mobile computers (and now also used in desktop systems) to decrease power consumption by turning off or slowing down devices during periods of inactivity. See also *APM*.

power supply An electrical/electronic circuit that supplies all operating voltage and current to the computer system.

PPGA (plastic pin grid array) A chip-packaging form factor used by Intel as an alternative to traditional ceramic packaging.

PPP (Point-to-Point Protocol) A protocol that enables a computer to use the Internet with a standard telephone line and high-speed modem. PPP is a new standard that replaces SLIP. PPP is less common than SLIP; however, it is increasing in popularity.

precompensation A data write modification required by some older drives on the inner cylinders to compensate for the higher density of data on the (smaller) inner cylinders.

Presentation Layer See *OSI*.

primary partition An ordinary, single-volume bootable partition. See also *extended partition*.

printer A device that records information visually on paper or other material.

processor See *microprocessor*.

processor speed The clock rate at which a microprocessor processes data. A typical Pentium PC, for example, operates at 200MHz (200 million cycles per second).

program A set of instructions or steps telling the computer how to handle a problem or task.

PROM (programmable read-only memory) A type of memory chip that can be programmed to store information permanently—information that cannot be erased. Also referred to as OTP for one-time programmable.

proprietary Anything invented by one company and that uses components available from only that one company. Especially applies to cases in which the inventing company goes to lengths to hide the specifications of the new invention or to prevent other manufacturers from making similar or compatible items. The opposite of standard or open architecture. Computers with nonstandard components that are available from only the original manufacturer, such as Apple Macintosh systems, are known as proprietary.

protected mode A mode available in all Intel and compatible processors except the first-generation 8086 and 8088. In this mode, memory addressing is extended beyond the 1MB limits of the 8088 and real mode, and restricted protection levels can be set to trap software crashes and control the system.

protocol A system of rules and procedures governing communications between two or more devices. Protocols vary, but communicating devices must follow the same protocol to exchange data. The data format, readiness to receive or send, error detection, and error correction are some of the operations that can be defined in protocols.

PS/2 mouse   A mouse designed to plug into a dedicated mouse port (a round, 6-pin DIN connector) on the motherboard, rather than plugging into a serial port. The name comes from the fact that this port was first introduced on the IBM PS/2 systems.

PUN (physical unit number)   A term used to describe a device attached directly to the SCSI bus. Also known as a SCSI ID. As many as eight SCSI devices can be attached to a single SCSI bus, and each must have a unique PUN or ID assigned from 7 to 0. Normally, the SCSI host adapter is assigned the highest-priority ID, which is 7. A bootable hard disk is assigned an ID of 0, and other nonbootable drives are assigned higher priorities.

QAM (quadrature amplitude modulation)   A modulation technique used by high-speed modems that combines both phase and amplitude modulation. This technique enables multiple bits to be encoded in a single time interval.

QIC (Quarter-Inch Committee)   An industry association that sets hardware and software standards for tape-backup units that use quarter-inch–wide tapes.

QWERTY keyboard   The standard typewriter or computer keyboard, with the characters Q, W, E, R, T, and Y on the top row of alpha keys. Because of the haphazard placement of characters, this keyboard can hinder fast typing.

RAID (redundant array of independent or inexpensive disks)   A storage unit that employs two or more drives in combination for fault tolerance and greater performance, used mostly in file server applications.

rails   Plastic strips attached to the sides of disk drives mounted in IBM ATs and compatibles so that the drives can slide into place. These rails fit into channels in the side of each disk drive bay position.

RAM (random-access memory)   All memory accessible at any instant (randomly) by a microprocessor.

RAM disk   A "phantom disk drive" in which a section of system memory (RAM) is set aside to hold data, just as though it were a number of disk sectors. To DOS, a RAM disk looks and functions like any other drive.

RAMBUS Dynamic RAM   See *RDRAM*.

random-access file   A file in which all data elements (or records) are of equal length and written in the file end to end, without delimiting characters between. Any element (or record) in the file can be found directly by calculating the record's offset in the file.

random-access memory   See *RAM*.

raster   A pattern of horizontal scanning lines normally on a computer monitor. An electromagnetic field causes the beam of the monitor's tube to illuminate the correct dots to produce the required characters.

raster graphics   A technique for representing a picture image as a matrix of dots. It is the digital counterpart of the analog method used in TV. Several raster graphics standards exist.

RCA jack   Also called a phono connector. A plug and socket for a two-wire coaxial cable used to connect audio and video components. The plug is a 1/8-inch thick prong that sticks out 5/16-inch from the middle of a cylinder.

RDRAM (Rambus DRAM)   A high-speed dynamic RAM technology developed by Rambus, Inc., which is supported by Intel's 1999 and later motherboard chipsets. RDRAM transfers data at 1GB/sec or faster, which is significantly faster than SDRAM and other technologies and which will be capable of keeping up with future-generation high-speed processors. Memory modules with RDRAM chips are called RIMMs (Rambus inline memory modules). Rambus licenses its technology to other semiconductor companies, who manufacture the chips and RIMMs.

read/write head   A tiny magnet that reads and writes data on a disk track.

read-only file   A file whose attribute setting in the file's directory entry tells DOS not to allow software to write into or over the file.

read-only memory   See *ROM*.

real mode A mode available in all Intel 8086-compatible processors that enables compatibility with the original 8086. In this mode, memory addressing is limited to 1MB.

real time The actual time in which a program or event takes place. In computing, real time refers to an operating mode under which data is received and processed and the results returned so quickly that the process appears instantaneous to the user. The term also is used to describe the process of simultaneous digitization and compression of audio and video information.

reboot The process of restarting a computer and reloading the operating system.

Red Book More commonly known as Compact Disc-Digital Audio (CD-DA), one of four compact disc standards. Red Book got its name from the color of the manual used to describe the CD-Audio specifications. The Red Book audio standard requires that digital audio be sampled at a 44.1KHz sample rate using 16 bits for each sample. This is the standard used by audio CDs and many CD-ROMs.

refresh cycle A cycle in which the computer accesses all memory locations stored by DRAM chips so that the information remains intact. DRAM chips must be accessed several times a second; otherwise, the information fades.

refresh rate Another term for the vertical scan frequency of monitors.

register Storage area in memory having a specified storage capacity—such as a bit, byte, or computer word—and intended for a special purpose.

Registry The system configuration files used by Windows 9x and Windows NT to store settings about installed hardware and drivers, user preferences, installed software, and other settings required to keep Windows running properly. Replaces the WIN.INI and SYSTEM.INI files from Windows 3.x.

remote digital loopback A test that checks the phone link and a remote modem's transmitter and receiver. Data entered from the keyboard is transmitted from the initiating modem, received by the remote modem's receiver, looped through its transmitter, and returned to the local screen for verification.

remote echo A copy of the data received by the remote system, returned to the sending system, and displayed onscreen. A function of the remote system.

rendering Generating a 3-D image that incorporates the simulation of lighting effects, such as shadows and reflection.

resolution 1) A reference to the size of the pixels used in graphics. In medium-resolution graphics, pixels are large. In high-resolution graphics, pixels are small. 2) A measure of the number of horizontal and vertical pixels that can be displayed by a video adapter and monitor.

reverse engineering The act of duplicating a hardware or software component by studying the functions of the component and designing a different one that has the same functions.

RFI (radio frequency interference) A high-frequency signal radiated by improperly shielded conductors, particularly when signal path lengths are comparable to or longer than the signal wavelengths. The FCC now regulates RFI in computer equipment sold in the U.S. under FCC Regulations, Part 15, Subpart J.

RGB (red green blue) A type of computer color display output signal comprised of separately controllable red, green, and blue signals; as opposed to composite video, in which signals are combined prior to output. RGB monitors typically offer higher resolution than composite monitors.

ribbon cable Flat cable with wires running in parallel, such as those used for internal IDE or SCSI.

RIMM (Rambus inline memory module) A type of memory module made using RDRAM chips. See also *RDRAM*.

RISC (reduced instruction set computer) Differentiated from CISC, the complex instruction set computer. RISC processors have simple instruction sets requiring only one or a few execution cycles. These simple instructions can be used more effectively than CISC systems with appropriately designed software, resulting in faster operations. See also *CISC*.

RJ-11 The standard two-wire connector type used for single-line telephone connections.

RJ-14 The standard four-wire connector type used for two-line telephone connections.

RJ-45 A standard connector type used in networking with twisted-pair cabling. Resembles an RJ-11/14 telephone jack, but RJ-45 is larger with more wires.

RLL (run-length limited) A type of encoding that derives its name from the fact that the techniques used limit the distance (run length) between magnetic flux reversals on the disk platter. Several types of RLL encoding techniques exist, although only two are commonly used. (1,7) RLL encoding increases storage capacity by about 30% over MFM encoding and is most popular in the very highest capacity drives due to a better window margin, whereas (2,7) RLL encoding increases storage capacity by 50% over MFM encoding and is used in the majority of RLL implementations. Most IDE, ESDI, and SCSI hard disks use one of these forms of RLL encoding.

RMA number (return-merchandise authorization number) A number given to you by a vendor when you arrange to return an item for repairs. Used to track the item and the repair.

ROM (read-only memory) A type of memory that has values permanently or semi-permanently burned in. These locations are used to hold important programs or data that must be available to the computer when the power initially is turned on.

ROM BIOS (read-only memory basic input/output system) A BIOS encoded in a form of read-only memory for protection. It's often applied to important startup programs that must be present in a system for it to operate.

root directory The main directory of any hard or floppy disk. It has a fixed size and location for a particular disk volume and cannot be resized dynamically the way subdirectories can.

router A router is a device that is used to connect various networks, intelligently routing information between them. It is used to inter-network similar and dissimilar networks and can select the most expedient route based on traffic load, line speeds, costs, and network failures. Routers use forwarding tables to determine which packets should be forwarded between the connected networks. A cable or DSL modem is an example of a simple router that connects the Internet to your own network. Many routers include firewall capability to block suspect packets from being transmitted between networks.

routine Set of frequently used instructions. It can be considered as a subdivision of a program with two or more instructions that are related functionally.

RS-232 An interface introduced in August 1969 by the Electronic Industries Association. The RS-232 interface standard provides an electrical description for connecting peripheral devices to computers.

scan codes The hexadecimal codes actually sent by the keyboard to the motherboard when a key is pressed.

scan lines The parallel lines across a video screen, along which the scanning spot travels in painting the video information that makes up a monitor picture. NTSC systems use 525 scan lines to a screen; PAL systems use 625.

scanner A device that reads an image and converts it into computer data.

scanning frequency A monitor measurement that specifies how often the image is refreshed. See also *vertical scan frequency*.

scratch disk A disk that contains no useful information and can be used as a test disk. IBM has a routine on the Advanced Diagnostics disks that creates a specially formatted scratch disk to be used for testing floppy drives.

SCSI (small computer system interface) A standard originally developed by Shugart Associates (then called SASI for Shugart Associates System Interface) and later approved by ANSI in 1986. SCSI-2 was approved in 1994, and SCSI-3 is currently in the development process. It normally uses a 50-pin connector and permits multiple devices (up to eight including the host) to be connected in daisy-chain fashion.

SDLC (Synchronous Data Link Control) A protocol developed by IBM for software applications and communicating devices operation in IBM's Systems Network Architecture (SNA). Defines operations at the link level of communications—for example, the format of data frames exchanged between modems over a phone line.

SDRAM (synchronous DRAM) RAM that runs at the same speed as the main system bus.

SEC (single edge contact) An Intel processor packaging design in which the processor and optional L2 cache chips are mounted on a small circuit board (much like an oversized memory SIMM), which might be sealed in a metal and plastic cartridge. The cartridge is then plugged into the motherboard through an edge connector called Slot 1 or Slot 2, which looks similar to an adapter card slot. Several variations to the SEC cartridge form factor exist: The single edge contact cartridge (SECC) has a cover and a thermal plate; the single edge contact cartridge 2 (SECC2) has a cover, but no thermal plate; and the single edge processor package (SEPP) has no cover or thermal plate. In implementations with no thermal plate, the heatsink is attached directly to the processor package or die.

SECAM Sequential Couleur A Mémoire (sequential color with memory), the French color TV system also adopted in Russia. The basis of operation is the sequential recording of primary colors in alternate lines. The image format is 4:3, 625 lines, 50Hz, and 6MHz video bandwidth with a total 8MHz of video channel width.

SECC (single edge contact cartridge) See *SEC*.

SECC2 (single edge contact cartridge 2) See *SEC*.

sector A section of one track defined with identification markings and an identification number. Most sectors hold 512 bytes of data.

security software Utility software that uses a system of passwords and other devices to restrict an individual's access to subdirectories and files.

seek time The amount of time required for a disk drive to move the heads across one third of the total number of cylinders. Represents the average time it takes to move the heads from one cylinder to another randomly selected cylinder. Seek time is a part of the average access time for a drive.

semiconductor A substance, such as germanium or silicon, whose conductivity is poor at low temperatures but is improved by minute additions of certain substances or by the application of heat, light, or voltage. Depending on the temperature and pressure, a semiconductor can control a flow of electricity. Semiconductors are the basis of modern electronic-circuit technology.

SEPP (single edge processor package) See *SEC*.

sequencer A software program that controls MIDI file messages and keeps track of music timing. Because MIDI files store note instructions instead of actual sounds, a sequencer is needed to play, record, and edit MIDI sounds. Sequencer programs enable recording and playback of MIDI files by storing the instrument, note pitch (frequency), duration (in real time) that each note is held, and loudness (amplitude) of each musical or sound-effect note.

sequential file A file in which varying-length data elements are recorded end to end, with delimiting characters placed between each element. To find a particular element, you must read the whole file up to that element.

serial The transfer of data characters one bit at a time, sequentially, using a single electrical path.

serial mouse A mouse designed to connect to a computer's serial port.

serial port An I/O connector used to connect to serial devices.

server A computer in a network that enables resources such as files and printers to be shared by multiple users.

servo The mechanism in a drive that enables the head positioner to adjust continuously so that it is precisely placed above a given cylinder in the drive.

servo data Magnetic markings written on disk platters to guide the read/write heads in drives that use voice-coil actuators.

session (single or multisession) A term used in CD-ROM recording to describe a recording event. In a single session, data is recorded on a CD-ROM and an index is created. If additional space is left on the disc, another session can be used to record additional files along with another index. Some older CD-ROM drives do not expect additional recording sessions and therefore are unable to read the additional session data on the disc. The advent of Kodak's Photo CD propelled the desire for multisession CD-ROM XA (extended architecture) drives.

Session Layer See *OSI*.

settling time The time required for read/write heads to stop vibrating after they have been moved to a new track.

shadow mask A thin screen full of holes that adheres to the inside of a color CRT. The electron beam is aimed through the holes in the mask onto the phosphor dots. See also *aperture grille*.

shadow ROM A copy of a system's slower-access ROM BIOS placed in faster-access RAM, usually during the startup or boot procedure. This setup enables the system to access BIOS code without the penalty of additional wait states required by the slower ROM chips. Also called shadow RAM.

shell The generic name of any user interface software. COMMAND.COM is the standard shell for DOS. OS/2 comes with three shells: a DOS command shell, an OS/2 command shell, and the OS/2 Presentation Manager (a graphical shell).

shielded twisted-pair (STP) Unshielded twisted-pair (UTP) network cabling with a metal sheath or braid around it to reduce interference, usually used in Token-Ring networks.

shock rating A rating (usually expressed in G force units) of how much shock a disk drive can sustain without damage. Usually two specifications exist for a drive powered on or off.

signal-to-noise (S/N) ratio The strength of a video or audio signal in relation to interference (noise). The higher the S/N ratio, the better the quality of the signal.

silicon The base material for computer chips. An element, silicon (symbol Si) is contained in the majority of rock and sand on earth and is the second most abundant element on the planet next to oxygen.

SIMD (single instruction multiple data) The term used to describe the MMX and SSE instructions added to the Intel processors. These instructions can process matrixes consisting of multiple data elements with only a single instruction, enabling more efficient processing of graphics and sound data.

SIMM (single inline memory module) An array of memory chips on a small PC board with a single row of I/O contacts.

single-ended An electrical signaling method in which a single line is referenced by a ground path common to other signals. In a single-ended bus intended for moderately long distances, commonly one ground line exists between groups of signal lines to provide some resistance to signal crosstalk. Single-ended signals require only one driver or receiver pin per signal, plus one ground pin per group of signals. Single-ended signals are vulnerable to common mode noise and crosstalk but are much less expensive than differential signaling methods.

SIP (single inline package) A DIP-like package with only one row of leads.

skinny dip Twenty-four– and twenty-eight–position DIP devices with .300-inch row-to-row centerlines.

sleep See *suspend*.

SLIP (Serial Line Internet Protocol) An Internet protocol that is used to run the

Internet Protocol (IP) over serial lines, such as telephone circuits. IP enables a packet to traverse multiple networks on the way to its final destination.

slot A physical connector on a motherboard to hold an expansion card, SIMMs and DIMMs, or a processor card in place and make contact with the electrical connections.

Slot 1 The motherboard connector designed by Intel to accept its SEC cartridge processor design used by the Pentium II.

Slot 2 A motherboard connector for Pentium II Xeon processors intended mainly for file server applications. Slot 2 systems support up to four-way symmetric multiprocessing.

SMBIOS A BIOS that incorporates system management functions and reporting compatible with the Desktop Management Interface (DMI).

SMPTE time code An 80-bit standardized edit time code adopted by SMPTE, the Society of Motion Picture and Television Engineers. The SMPTE time code is a standard used to identify individual video frames in the video-editing process. SMPTE time code controls such functions as play, record, rewind, and forward of video tapes. SMPTE time code displays video in terms of hours, minutes, seconds, and frames for accurate video editing.

snow A flurry of bright dots that can appear anywhere onscreen on a monitor.

socket A receptacle, usually on a motherboard although sometimes also found on expansion cards, into which processors or chips can be plugged.

Socket 1–8 The Intel specifications for eight different sockets to accept various Intel processors in the 486, Pentium, and Pentium Pro families.

SODIMM (small outline dual inline memory module) An industry-standard 144-pin memory module designed for use primarily in laptop and portable computers.

soft error An error in reading or writing data that occurs sporadically, usually because

of a transient problem, such as a power fluctuation.

software A series of instructions loaded in the computer's memory that instructs the computer in how to accomplish a problem or task.

SO-J (small outline J-lead) A small DIP package with J-shaped leads for surface mounting or socketing.

sound card An adapter card with sound generating capabilities.

South Bridge The Intel term for the lower-speed component in the chipset that has always been a single individual chip. Also called the PIIX (PCI, ISA, IDE excelerator), the South Bridge connects to the 33MHz PCI bus and contains the IDE interface ports and the interface to the 8MHz ISA bus. It also normally contains the USB interface and even the CMOS RAM and real-time clock functions. The South Bridge contains all the components that make up the ISA bus, including the interrupt and DMA controllers. See also *chipset* and *North Bridge*.

spindle The central post on which a disk drive's platters are mounted.

spindle count In notebook and laptop computers with interchangeable drives, spindle count refers to how many drives can be installed and used at the same time.

SRAM (static random access memory) A form of high-speed memory. SRAM chips do not require a refresh cycle like DRAM chips and can be made to operate at very high-access speeds. SRAM chips are very expensive because they normally require six transistors per bit. This also makes the chip larger than conventional DRAM chips. SRAM is volatile, meaning it will lose data with no power.

SSE (streaming SIMD extensions) The name given by Intel for the 70 new MMX-type instructions added to the Pentium III processor when it was introduced. See *SIMD* and *MMX*.

ST-506/412 A hard disk interface invented by Seagate Technology and introduced in 1980 with the ST-506 5MB hard drive.

stack   An area of memory storage for temporary values that normally are read in the reverse order from which they are written. Also called last-in, first-out (LIFO).

stair-stepping   Jagged raster representation of diagonals or curves; corrected by anti-aliasing.

standby   Defines an optional operating state of minimal power reduction with the shortest recovery time.

standby power supply   A backup power supply that quickly switches into operation during a power outage.

standoffs   In a motherboard and case design, small nonconductive spacers (usually plastic or nylon) used to keep the underside of the motherboard from contacting the metallic case, therefore preventing short circuits of the motherboard.

start/stop bits   The signaling bits attached to a character before and after the character is transmitted during asynchronous transmission.

starting cluster   The number of the first cluster occupied by a file. Listed in the directory entry of every file.

stepper motor actuator   An assembly that moves disk drive read/write heads across platters by a sequence of small partial turns of a stepper motor.

stepping   The code used to identify the revision of a processor. New masks are introduced to build each successive stepping, incorporating any changes necessary to fix known bugs in prior steppings.

storage   Device or medium on or in which data can be entered or held and retrieved at a later time. Synonymous with memory.

streaming   In tape backup, a condition in which data is transferred from the hard disk as quickly as the tape drive can record the data so the drive does not start and stop or waste tape.

string   A sequence of characters.

subdirectory   A directory listed in another directory. Subdirectories themselves exist as files.

subroutine   A segment of a program that can be executed by a single call. Also called program module.

superscalar execution   The capability of a processor to execute more than one instruction at a time.

surface mount   Chip carriers and sockets designed to mount to the surface of a PC board.

surge protector   A device in the power line that feeds the computer and provides protection against voltage spikes and other transients.

suspend   Refers to a level of power management in which substantial power reduction is achieved by the display or other components. The components can have a longer recovery time from this state than from the standby state.

SVGA (Super VGA)   Refers to a video adapter or monitor capable of 800×600 resolution.

S-Video (Y/C)   Type of video signal used in the Hi8 and S-VHS videotape formats in which the luminance and chrominance (Y/C) components are kept separate, providing greater control and quality of each image. S-video transmits luminance and color portions separately, thus avoiding the NTSC encoding process and its inevitable loss of picture quality.

SWEDAC (Swedish Board for Technical Accreditation)   Regulatory agency establishing standards such as MPR1 and MPR2, which specify maximum values for both alternating electric fields and magnetic fields and provide monitor manufacturers with guidelines in creating low-emission monitors.

switch   Also called a switching hub, it's a type of hub that reads the destination address of each packet and then forwards the packet to only the correct port, minimizing traffic on other parts of the network. Unlike a regular hub that wastes network bandwidth by copying packets to all ports, a switch forwards packets to only their intended recipients, immediately reducing network traffic jams and improving overall efficiency for the entire network. See also *hub*.

SXGA (Super XGA)   Refers to a video adapter or monitor capable of 1,280×1,024 or greater resolution.

synchronous communication   A form of communication in which blocks of data are sent at strictly timed intervals. Because the timing is uniform, no start or stop bits are required. Compare with asynchronous communication. Some mainframes support only synchronous communication unless a synchronous adapter and appropriate software have been installed. See also *asynchronous communication.*

system crash   A situation in which the computer freezes up and refuses to proceed without rebooting. Usually caused by faulty software, it's unlike a hard disk crash—no permanent physical damage occurs.

system files   Files with the system attribute. Normally, the hidden files that are used to boot the operating system. The MS-DOS and Windows 9x system files include IO.SYS and MSDOS.SYS; the IBM DOS system files are IBMBIO.COM and IBMDOS.COM.

System Management Mode (SMM)   Circuitry integrated into Intel processors that operates independently to control the processor's power use based on its activity level. It enables the user to specify time intervals after which the CPU will be powered down partially or fully and also supports the suspend/resume feature that enables instant power-on and power-off.

tape drive   Any data storage drive that uses tape as the storage medium.

target   A device attached to a SCSI bus that receives and processes commands sent from another device (the initiator) on the SCSI bus. A SCSI hard disk is an example of a target.

TCM (Trellis-coded modulation)   An error-detection and correction technique employed by high-speed modems to enable higher-speed transmissions that are more resistant to line impairments.

TCO   1) Refers to the Swedish Confederation of Professional Employees, which has set stringent standards for devices that emit radiation. See also *MPR.* 2) Total cost of ownership. The

cost of using a computer. It includes the cost of the hardware, software, and upgrades as well as the cost of the in-house staff and consultants who provide training and technical support.

TCP (tape carrier package)   A method of packaging processors for use in portable systems that reduces the size, power consumed, and heat generated by the chip. A processor in the TCP form factor is essentially a raw die encased in an oversized piece of polyamide film. The film is laminated with copper foil that is etched to form the leads that will connect the processor to the motherboard.

TCP/IP (Transmission Control Protocol/Internet Protocol)   A set of protocols developed by the U.S. Department of Defense (DoD) to link dissimilar computers across many types of networks. This is the primary protocol used by the Internet.

temporary backup   A second copy of a work file, usually having the extension BAK. Created by application software so you easily can return to a previous version of your work.

temporary file   A file temporarily (and usually invisibly) created by a program for its own use.

tera   A multiplier indicating one trillion (1,000,000,000,000) of some unit. Abbreviated as t or T. When used to indicate a number of bytes of memory storage, the multiplier definition changes to 1,099,511,627,776. One terabit, for example, equals 1,000,000,000,000 bits, whereas one terabyte equals 1,099,511,627,776 bytes.

terabyte (TB)   A unit of information storage equal to 1,099,511,627,776 bytes.

terminal   A device whose keyboard and display are used for sending and receiving data over a communications link. Differs from a microcomputer in that it has no internal processing capabilities. Used to enter data into or retrieve processed data from a system or network.

terminal mode   An operational mode required for microcomputers to transmit data. In terminal mode, the computer acts as though it were a standard terminal, such as a teletypewriter, rather than a data processor. Keyboard entries go directly to the modem, whether the entry is a modem command or data to be transmitted over the phone lines. Received data is output directly to the screen. The more popular communications software products control terminal mode and enable more complex operations, including file transmission and saving received files.

terminator   Hardware or circuits that must be attached to or enabled at both ends of an electrical bus. Functions to prevent the reflection or echoing of signals that reach the ends of the bus and to ensure that the correct impedance load is placed on the driver circuits on the bus. Most commonly used with the SCSI bus.

TFT (thin film transistor)   The highest quality and brightest LCD color display type. A method for packaging one–four transistors per pixel within a flexible material that is the same size and shape as the LCD display, which enables the transistors for each pixel to lie directly behind the liquid crystal cells they control.

thick Ethernet   See *10BASE-5*.

thin Ethernet   See *10BASE-2*.

thin-film media   Hard disk platters that have a thin film (usually three-millionths of an inch) of medium deposited on the aluminum substrate through a sputtering or plating process.

Thinnet   See *10BASE-2*.

through-hole   Chip carriers and sockets equipped with leads that extend through holes in a PC board.

throughput   The amount of user data transmitted per second without the overhead of protocol information, such as start and stop bits or frame headers and trailers.

TIFF (tagged image file format)   A way of storing and exchanging digital image data. Developed by Aldus Corporation, Microsoft Corporation, and major scanner vendors to help link scanned images with the popular desktop publishing applications. Supports

three main types of image data: black-and-white data, halftones or dithered data, and grayscale data.

time code   A frame-by-frame address code time reference recorded on the spare track of a videotape or inserted in the vertical blanking interval. The time code is an eight-digit number encoding time in hours, minutes, seconds, and video frames.

Token-Ring   A type of local area network in which the workstations relay a packet of data called a token in a logical ring configuration. When a station wants to transmit, it takes possession of the token, attaches its data, and then frees the token after the data has made a complete circuit of the electrical ring. Transmits at speeds of 16Mbps. Because of the token-passing scheme, access to the network is controlled, unlike the slower 10BASE-X Ethernet system in which collisions of data can occur, which wastes time. The Token-Ring network uses shielded twisted-pair wiring, which is cheaper than the coaxial cable used by 10BASE-2 and 10BASE-5 Ethernet and ARCnet.

toner   The ultrafine colored plastic powder used in laser printers and photocopiers to produce the image on paper.

tower   A personal computer that normally sits on the floor and is mounted vertically rather than horizontally.

TPI (tracks per inch)   Used as a measurement of magnetic track density. Standard 5 1/4-inch 360KB floppy disks have a density of 48TPI, and the 1.2MB disks have a 96TPI density. All 3 1/2-inch disks have a 135.4667TPI density, and hard disks can have densities greater than 3,000TPI.

track   One of the many concentric circles that holds data on a disk surface. Consists of a single line of magnetic flux changes and is divided into some number of 512-byte sectors.

track density   Expressed as tracks per inch (TPI); defines how many tracks are recorded in one inch of space measured radially from the center of the disk. Sometimes also called radial density.

track-to-track seek time The time required for read/write heads to move between adjacent tracks.

transistor A semiconductor device invented in 1947 at Bell Labs (released in 1948) that is used to amplify a signal or open and close a circuit. In digital computers, it functions as an electronic switch. It is reduced to microscopic size in modern digital integrated circuits containing 100 million or more individual transistors.

Transport Layer In the OSI reference model, when more than one packet is in process at any time, such as when a large file must be split into multiple packets for transmission, this is the layer that controls the sequencing of the message components and regulates inbound traffic flow. See also *OSI*.

transportable computer A computer system larger than a portable system and similar in size and shape to a portable sewing machine. Most transportables conform to a design similar to the original Compaq portable, with a built-in CRT display. These systems are characteristically very heavy and run on only AC power. Because of advances primarily in LCD and plasma-display technology, these systems are largely obsolete and have been replaced by portable systems.

troubleshooting The task of determining the cause of a problem.

true-color images Also called 24-bit color images because each pixel is represented by 24 bits of data, allowing for 16.7 million colors. The number of colors possible is based on the number of bits used to represent the color. If 8 bits are used, 256 possible color values (2^8) exist. To obtain 16.7 million colors, each of the primary colors (red, green, and blue) is represented by 8 bits per pixel, which enables 256 possible shades for each of the primary red, green, and blue colors or $256 \times 256 \times 256 = 16.7$ million total colors.

TSR (terminate-and-stay-resident) A program that remains in memory after being loaded. Because they remain in memory, TSR programs can be reactivated by a predefined keystroke sequence or other operation while another program is active. Usually called resident programs.

TTL (transistor-to-transistor logic) Digital signals often are called TTL signals. A TTL display is a monitor that accepts digital input at standardized signal voltage levels.

twisted pair A type of wire in which two small, insulated copper wires are wrapped or twisted around each other to minimize interference from other wires in the cable. Two types of twisted-pair cables are available: unshielded and shielded. Unshielded twisted-pair (UTP) wiring commonly is used in telephone cables and provides little protection against interference. Shielded twisted-pair (STP) wiring is used in some networks or any application in which immunity from electrical interference is more important. Twisted-pair wire is much easier to work with than coaxial cable and is cheaper as well.

typematic The keyboard repeatedly sending the keypress code to the motherboard for a key that is held down. The delay before the code begins to repeat and the speed at which it repeats are user adjustable.

UART (Universal Asynchronous Receiver Transmitter) A chip device that controls the RS-232 serial port in a PC-compatible system. Originally developed by National Semiconductor, several UART versions are in PC-compatible systems: The 8250B is used in PC- and XT-class systems, and the 16450 and 16550A are used in AT-class systems.

UltraDMA A protocol for transferring data to an ATA interface hard drive. The Ultra DMA/33 protocol transfers data in burst mode at a rate of 33Mbytes/sec, whereas the even faster Ultra DMA/66 protocol transfers at 66Mbytes/sec. Ultra DMA/66 also requires the use of a special 80-conductor cable for signal integrity. This cable also is recommended for Ultra DMA/33 and is backward compatible with standard ATA/IDE cables.

UMB (upper memory block) A block of unused memory in the upper memory area (UMA), which is the 384KB region between 640KB and 1MB of memory space in the PC.

unformatted capacity The total number of bytes of data that can fit on a disk. The formatted capacity is lower because space is lost defining the boundaries between sectors.

uninterruptible power supply (UPS)   A device that supplies power to the computer from batteries so power will not stop, even momentarily, during a power outage. The batteries are recharged constantly from a wall socket.

Universal Asynchronous Receiver Transmitter   See *UART*.

UPC (universal product code)   A 10-digit computer-readable bar code used in labeling retail products. The code in the form of vertical bars includes a five-digit manufacturer identification number and a five-digit product code number.

update   To modify information already contained in a file or program with current information.

upper memory area (UMA)   The 384KB of memory between 640KB and 1MB.

URL (uniform resource locator)   The primary naming scheme used to identify a particular site or file on the World Wide Web. URLs combine information about the protocol being used, the address of the site where the resource is located, the subdirectory location at the site, and the name of the particular file (or page) in question.

USB (universal serial bus)   A 12Mbit/sec (1.5MB/sec) interface over a simple four-wire connection. The bus supports up to 127 devices and uses a tiered star topology built on expansion hubs that can reside in the PC, any USB peripheral, or even standalone hub boxes.

utility   Programs that carry out routine procedures to make computer use easier.

UTP (unshielded twisted pair)   A type of wire often used indoors to connect telephones or computer devices. Comes with two or four wires twisted inside a flexible plastic sheath or conduit and uses modular plugs and phone jacks.

V.21   An ITU standard for modem communications at 300bps. Modems made in the U.S. or Canada follow the Bell 103 standard but can be set to answer V.21 calls from overseas. The actual transmission rate is 300 baud and employs FSK (frequency shift keying) modulation, which encodes a single bit per baud.

V.22   An ITU standard for modem communications at 1,200bps, with an optional fallback to 600bps. V.22 is partially compatible with the Bell 212A standard observed in the U.S. and Canada. The actual transmission rate is 600 baud, using DPSK (differential-phase shift keying) to encode as much as two bits per baud.

V.22bis   An ITU standard for modem communications at 2,400bps. Includes an automatic link-negotiation fallback to 1,200bps and compatibility with Bell 212A/V.22 modems. The actual transmission rate is 600 baud, using QAM (quadrature amplitude modulation) to encode as much as four bits per baud.

V.23   An ITU standard for modem communications at 1,200 or 600bps with a 75bps back channel. Used in the United Kingdom for some videotext systems.

V.25   An ITU standard for modem communications that specifies an answer tone different from the Bell answer tone used in the U.S. and Canada. Most intelligent modems can be set with an ATB0 command so they use the V.25 2,100Hz tone when answering overseas calls.

V.32   An ITU standard for modem communications at 9,600bps and 4,800bps. V.32 modems fall back to 4,800bps when line quality is impaired and fall forward again to 9,600bps when line quality improves. The actual transmission rate is 2,400 baud using QAM (quadrature amplitude modulation) and optional TCM (trellis-coded modulation) to encode as much as four data bits per baud.

V.32bis   An ITU standard that extends the standard V.32 connection range and supports 4,800bps; 7,200bps; 9,600bps; 12,000bps; and 14,400bps transmission rates. V.32bis modems fall back to the next lower speed when line quality is impaired, fall back further as necessary, and fall forward to the next higher speed when line quality improves. The actual transmission rate is 2,400 baud using QAM (quadrature amplitude modulation) and TCM (trellis-coded modulation) to encode as much as six data bits per baud.

V.32terbo   A proprietary standard proposed by several modem manufacturers that will be cheaper to implement than the standard V.32 fast protocol but that will support only transmission speeds of up to 18,800bps. Because it is not an industry standard, it is not likely to have widespread industry support.

V.34 An ITU standard that extends the standard V.32bis connection range, supporting 28,800bps transmission rates as well as all the functions and rates of V.32bis. This was called V.32fast or V.fast while under development.

V.34+ An ITU standard that extends the standard V.34 connection range, supporting 33,600bps transmission rates as well as all the functions and rates of V.34.

V.42 An ITU standard for modem communications that defines a two-stage process of detection and negotiation for LAPM error control. Also supports MNP error-control protocol, Levels 1–4.

V.42bis An extension of CCITT V.42 that defines a specific data-compression scheme for use with V.42 and MNP error control.

V.90 ITU-T designation for defining the standard for 56Kbps communication. Supersedes the proprietary X2 schemes from U.S. Robotics (3Com) and K56Flex from Rockwell.

vaccine A type of program used to locate and eradicate virus code from infected programs or systems.

VCPI (virtual control program interface) A 386 and later processor memory management standard created by Phar Lap software in conjunction with other software developers. VCPI provides an interface between applications using DOS extenders and 386 memory managers.

vertical blanking interval (VBI) The top and bottom lines in the video field, in which frame numbers, picture stops, chapter stops, white flags, closed captions, and more may be encoded. These lines do not appear on the display screen but maintain image stability and enhance image access.

vertical scan frequency The rate at which the electron gun in a monitor scans or refreshes the entire screen each second.

very large scale integration See *IC*.

VESA (Video Electronics Standards Association) Founded in the late 1980s by NEC Home Electronics and eight other leading video board manufacturers with the main goal to standardize the electrical, timing, and programming issues surrounding 800×600 resolution video displays, commonly known as Super VGA. VESA has also developed the Video Local Bus (VL-Bus) standard for connecting high-speed adapters directly to the local processor bus.

VFAT (virtual file allocation table) A file system used in Windows for Workgroups and Windows 95/98. VFAT provides 32-bit protected mode access for file manipulation and supports long filenames (LFNs)—up to 255 characters in Windows 95 and later. VFAT compatible with the standard DOS 16-bit FAT. VFAT was called 32-bit file access in Windows for Workgroups. VFAT is not the same as FAT32.

VGA (video graphics array) A type of PC video display circuit (and adapter) first introduced by IBM on April 2, 1987, which supports text and graphics. Text is supported at a maximum resolution of 80×25 characters in 16 colors with a character box of 9×16 pixels. Graphics is supported at a maximum resolution of 320×200 pixels in 256 (from a palette of 262,144) colors or 640×480 pixels in 16 colors. The VGA outputs an analog signal with a horizontal scanning frequency of 31.5KHz and supports analog color or analog monochrome displays. Also refers generically to any adapter or display capable of 640×480 resolution.

VHS (Video Home System) A popular consumer videotape format developed by Matsushita and JVC.

Video 8 or 8mm Video Video format based on the 8mm videotapes popularized by Sony for camcorders.

video A system of recording and transmitting primarily visual information by translating moving or still images into electrical signals. The term video properly refers to only the picture, but as a generic term, video usually embraces audio and other signals that are part of a complete program. Video now includes not only broadcast television but many nonbroadcast applications, such as corporate communications, marketing, home entertainment, games, teletext, security, and even the visual display units of computer-based technology.

video adapter   An expansion card or chipset built into a motherboard that provides the capability to display text and graphics onscreen. If the adapter is part of an expansion card, it also includes the physical connector for the monitor cable. If the chipset is on the motherboard, the video connector is on the motherboard as well.

video graphics array   See *VGA*.

video-on-CD or video CD   A full-motion digital video format using MPEG video compression and incorporating a variety of VCR-like control capabilities. See also *White Book*.

virtual disk   A RAM disk or "phantom disk drive" in which a section of system memory (usually RAM) is set aside to hold data, just as though it were a number of disk sectors. To DOS, a virtual disk looks and functions like any other "real" drive.

virtual memory   A technique by which operating systems (including OS/2) load more programs and data into memory than they can hold. Parts of the programs and data are kept on disk and constantly swapped back and forth into system memory. The applications' software programs are unaware of this setup and act as though a large amount of memory is available.

virtual real mode   A mode available in all Intel 80386-compatible processors. In this mode, memory addressing is limited to 4,096MB, restricted protection levels can be set to trap software crashes and control the system, and individual real-mode compatible sessions can be set up and maintained separately from one another.

virus   A type of resident program designed to replicate itself. Usually at some later time when the virus is running, it causes an undesirable action to take place.

VL-Bus (VESA Local Bus)   A standard 32-bit expansion slot bus specification used in 486 PCs. Now replaced by PCI bus.

VMM (Virtual Memory Manager)   A facility in Windows enhanced mode that manages the task of swapping data in and out of 386 and later processor virtual real-mode memory space for multiple non-Windows applications running in virtual real mode.

voice-coil actuator   A device that moves read/write heads across hard disk platters by magnetic interaction between coils of wire and a magnet. Functions somewhat like an audio speaker, from which the name originated.

volatile memory   Memory that does not hold data without power. Both Dynamic RAM (the main RAM in a computer) and Static RAM (used for cache memory) are considered volatile memory. See *nonvolatile memory*.

voltage reduction technology   An Intel processor technology that enables a processor to draw the standard voltage from the motherboard but run the internal processor core at a lower voltage.

voltage regulator   A device that smoothes out voltage irregularities in the power fed to the computer.

volume   A portion of a disk signified by a single drive specifier. Under DOS v3.3 and later, a single hard disk can be partitioned into several volumes, each with its own logical drive specifier (C:, D:, E:, and so on).

volume label   An identifier or name of up to 11 characters that names a disk.

VPN (virtual private network)   A private network operated within a public network. To maintain privacy, VPNs use access control and encryption.

VRAM (video random-access memory) VRAM chips are modified DRAMs on video boards that enable simultaneous access by the host system's processor and the processor on the video board. A large amount of information therefore can be transferred quickly between the video board and system processor. Sometimes also called dual-ported RAM.

VxD (virtual device driver)   A special type of Windows driver. VxDs run at the most privileged CPU mode (ring 0) and enable low-level interaction with the hardware and internal Windows functions.

wafer   A thin, circular piece of silicon either 8" (200mm) or 12" (300mm) in diameter from which processors, memory, and other semiconductor electronics are manufactured.

wait states   One or more pause cycles added during certain system operations that require the processor to wait until memory or some other system component can respond. Adding wait states enables a high-speed processor to synchronize with lower-cost, slower components. A system that runs with "zero wait states" requires none of these cycles because of the use of faster memory or other components in the system.

warm boot   Rebooting a system by means of a software command rather than turning the power off and back on. See also *cold boot*.

wave table synthesis   A method of creating synthetic sound on a sound card that uses actual musical instrument sounds sampled and stored on ROM (or RAM) on the sound card. The sound card then modifies this sample to create any note needed for that instrument. Produces much better sound quality than FM synthesis.

Whetstone   A benchmark program developed in 1976 and designed to simulate arithmetic-intensive programs used in scientific computing. Remains completely CPU-bound and performs no I/O or system calls. Originally written in ALGOL, although the C and Pascal versions became more popular by the late 1980s. The speed at which a system performs floating-point operations often is measured in units of Whetstones.

White Book   A standard specification developed by Philips and JVC in 1993 for storing MPEG standard video on CDs. An extension of the Red Book standard for digital audio, Yellow Book standard for CD-ROM, Green Book standard for CD-I, and Orange Book standard for CD write-once.

Whitney technology   A term referring to a magnetic disk design that usually has oxide or thin film media, thin film read/write heads, low floating-height sliders, and low-mass actuator arms that together allow higher bit densities than the older Winchester technology. Whitney technology first was introduced with the IBM 3370 disk drive, circa 1979.

wide area network (WAN)   A LAN that extends beyond the boundaries of a single building.

Winchester drive   Any ordinary, nonremovable (or fixed) hard disk drive. The name originates from a particular IBM drive in the 1960s that had 30MB of fixed and 30MB of removable storage. This 30-30 drive matched the caliber figure for a popular series of rifles made by Winchester, so the slang term Winchester was applied to any fixed-platter hard disk.

Winchester technology   The term Winchester is loosely applied to mean any disk with a fixed or nonremovable recording medium. More precisely, the term applies to a ferrite read/write head and slider design with oxide media that was first employed in the IBM 3340 disk drive, circa 1973. Most drives today actually use Whitney technology.

Wintel   The common name given to computers running Microsoft Windows using Intel processors. A slang term for the PC standard.

wire frames   The most common technique used to construct a 3D object for animation. A wire frame is given coordinates of length, height, and width. Wire frames are then filled with textures, colors, and movement. Transforming a wire frame into a textured object is called rendering.

word length   The number of bits in a data character without parity, start, or stop bits.

workstation   A somewhat vague term describing any high-performance, single-user computer that usually has been adapted for specialized graphics, computer-aided design, computer-aided engineering, or scientific applications.

World Wide Web (WWW)   Also called the Web. A graphical information system based on hypertext that enables a user to easily access documents located on the Internet.

WORM (write-once, read-many or multiple)   An optical mass-storage device capable of storing many megabytes of information but that can be written to only once on any given area of the disk. A WORM disk typically holds more than 200MB of data. Because a WORM drive cannot write over an old version of a file, new copies of files are made and stored on other parts of the disk whenever a file is revised. WORM disks are used to store information when a history of older versions must be maintained. Recording on a WORM disk is performed by a laser writer that burns pits in a thin metallic film (usually tellurium) embedded in the disk. This burning process is called ablation. WORM drives are frequently used for archiving data.

write precompensation   A modification applied to write data by a controller to alleviate partially the problem of bit shift, which causes adjacent 1s written on magnetic media to read as though they were farther apart. When adjacent 1s are sensed by the controller, precompensation is used to write them closer together on the disk, thus enabling them to be read in the proper bit cell window. Drives with built-in controllers normally handle precompensation automatically. Precompensation usually is required for the inner cylinders of oxide media drives.

write protect   Preventing a removable disk from being overwritten by means of covering a notch or repositioning a sliding switch, depending on the type of media.

X2   A proprietary modem standard developed by U.S. Robotics (since acquired by 3Com) that enables modems to receive data at up to 56Kbps. This has been superseded by the V.90 standard. See also *V.90*.

x86   A generic term referring to Intel and Intel-compatible PC microprocessors. Although the Pentium, Pentium Pro, and Pentium II do not have a numeric designation because of trademark law, they are later generations of this family.

XGA (extended graphics array)   A type of PC video display circuit (and adapter) first introduced by IBM on October 30, 1990, that supports text and graphics. Text is supported at a maximum resolution of 132×60 characters in 16 colors with a character box of 8×6 pixels. Graphics is supported at a maximum resolution of 1,024×768 pixels in 256 (from a palette of 262,144) colors or 640×480 pixels in 65,536 colors. The XGA outputs an analog signal with a horizontal scanning frequency of 31.5KHz or

35.52KHz and supports analog color or analog monochrome displays. Also used to refer generically to any adapter or display capable of 1,024×768 resolution.

XMM (extended memory manager)   A driver that controls access to extended memory on 286 and later processor systems. HIMEM.SYS is an example of an XMM that comes with DOS.

Xmodem   A file-transfer protocol—with error checking—developed by Ward Christensen in the mid-1970s and placed in the public domain. Designed to transfer files between machines running the CP/M operating system and using 300bps or 1,200bps modems. Until the late 1980s, because of its simplicity and public-domain status, Xmodem remained the most widely used microcomputer file-transfer protocol. In standard Xmodem, the transmitted blocks are 128 bytes. 1KB-Xmodem is an extension to Xmodem that increases the block size to 1,024 bytes. Many newer file-transfer protocols that are much faster and more accurate than Xmodem have been developed, such as Ymodem and Zmodem.

XMS (extended memory specification)   A Microsoft-developed standard that provides a way for real-mode applications to access extended memory in a controlled fashion. The XMS standard is available from Microsoft.

XON/XOFF   Standard ASCII control characters used to tell an intelligent device to stop or resume transmitting data. In most systems, pressing Ctrl+S sends the XOFF character. Most devices understand Ctrl+Q as XON; others interpret the pressing of any key after Ctrl+S as XON.

Y-connector   A Y-shaped splitter cable that divides a source input into two output signals.

Yellow Book   The standard used by CD-ROM. Multimedia applications most commonly use the Yellow Book standard, which specifies how digital information is to be stored on the CD-ROM and read by a computer. Extended architecture (XA) is currently an extension of the Yellow Book that enables the combination of various data types (audio and video, for example) onto one track in a

CD-ROM. Without XA, a CD-ROM can access only one data type at a time. Many CD-ROM drives are now XA capable.

Yellow Book standards See *CD-ROM*.

Ymodem A file-transfer protocol first released as part of Chuck Forsberg's YAM (yet another modem) program. An extension to Xmodem designed to overcome some of the limitations of the original. Enables information about the transmitted file, such as the filename and length, to be sent along with the file data and increases the size of a block from 128 bytes to 1,024 bytes. Ymodem-batch adds the capability to transmit "batches" or groups of files without operator interruption. YmodemG is a variation that sends the entire file before waiting for an acknowledgment. If the receiving side detects an error in mid-stream, the transfer is aborted. YmodemG is designed for use with modems that have built-in error-correcting capabilities.

zero wait states See *wait states*.

ZIF (zero insertion force) Sockets that require no force for the insertion of a chip carrier. Usually accomplished through movable contacts and uses primarily 486, Pentium, and Pentium Pro processor systems.

ZIP (zigzag inline package) A DIP package that has all leads on one edge in a zigzag pattern and mounts in a vertical plane.

Zip drive An external drive manufactured by Iomega that supports 100MB magnetic media on a 3 1/2-inch removable drive.

Zmodem A file-transfer protocol commissioned by Telenet and placed in the public domain. Like Ymodem, it was designed by Chuck Forsberg and developed as an extension to Xmodem to overcome the inherent latency when using Send/Ack-based protocols, such as XModem and YModem. It is a streaming, sliding-window protocol.

zoned recording In hard drives, one way to increase the capacity of a hard drive is to format more sectors on the outer cylinders than on the inner ones. Zoned recording splits the cylinders into groups called zones, with each successive zone having more and more sectors per track, moving out from the inner radius of the disk. All the cylinders in a particular zone have the same number of sectors per track.

zoomed video A direct video bus connection between the PC-card adapter and a mobile system's VGA controller, enabling high-speed video displays for videoconferencing applications and MPEG decoders.

Key Vendor Contact Information

Use this vendor quick reference chart to locate primary contact information for vendors mentioned in this book. Be sure to refer to the vendor database included on the CD accompanying this book. This database contains detailed contact information and descriptions of services and is keyword searchable.

Company	Phone Number	Email	Web Site
3Com Corp.	(800)638-3266		www.3com.com
3D Labs	(408)530-4700	info@3dlabs.com	www.3dlabs.com
3Dfx Interactive	(888)367-3339	info@3dfx.com	www.3dfx.com
ABIT Computer	(510)623-0500	sales@abit-usa.com	www.abit-usa.com
Acer America	(800)733-2237		www.acer.com/aac/index.htm
Adaptec	(408)945-8600		www.adaptec.com
Amazon.com	(206)266-1000		www.amazon.com
AMD	(800)538-8450	hw.support@amd.com	www.amd.com
America Online	(800)827-6434		www.aol.com/corp
American Megatrends	(800)828-9264	support@ami.com	www.ami.com
American Power Conversion	(800)800-4272		www.apcc.com
Apple Computer, Inc.	(800)538-9696		www.apple.com
Asus Computer	(510)739-3777		www.asus.com
ATI Technologies Inc.	(905)882-2600		www.atitech.com
Belden Wire and Cable	(800)235-3361	info@belden.com	www.belden.com
Best Power	(800)356-5794	contact@bestpower.com	www.bestpower.com
Black Box Corporation	(877)877-2269	info@blackbox.com	www.blackbox.com
Byte Runner Technologies	(800)274-7897	sdudley@byterunner.com	www.byterunner.com
Cables to Go	(800)506-9607	expert@cablestogo.com	www.cablestogo.com
Canon USA, Inc.	(516)488-6700		www.usa.canon.com
Centon Electronics, Inc.	(800)923-6866		www.centon.com
CMD Technology, Inc.	(800)426-3832		www.cmd.com
Compaq	(800)231-0900		www.compaq.com
CompUSA, Inc.	(800)266-7872		www.compusa.com
CompuServe	(800)848-8990		www.compuserve.com
Computer Discount Warehouse	(800)835-4239		www.cdw.com

Company	Phone Number	Email	Web Site
Corel Systems, Inc.	(613)728-8200		www.corel.com linux.corel.com
Creative Labs, Inc.	(800)544-6146		www.creative.com
CTX International, Inc.	(909)610-2520		www.ctxintl.com
D.W. Electrochemicals	(905)508-7500	dwel@stabilant.com	www.stabilant.com
Dell Computer Corp.	(800)999-3355		www.dell.com
DiagSoft, Inc.	(800)867-9537		www.diagsoft.com
DTK Computer, Inc.	(626)810-0098		www.dtkcomputer.com
Duracell, Inc.	(800)551-2355		www.duracell.com
EarthWeb, Inc.	(800)926-8299		www.supportsource.com
Elitegroup Computer Systems	(800)829-8890	info@ecsusa.com	www.ecsusa.com
Epson America, Inc.	(562)981-3840		www.epson.com
Exabyte Corporation	(800)774-7172		www.exabyte.com
Fedco Electronics, Inc.	(800)542-9761		www.fedcoelectronics.com
FIC (First International Computer of America)	(510)252-7777	sales@fica.com	www.fica.com
Gateway, Inc.	(800)846-4208		www.gateway.com
Giga-Byte Technology	(626)854-9338		www.giga-byte.com
Hewlett-Packard			www.hp.com
Hitachi America Ltd.	(650)589-8300		www.hitachi.com
HP Information Management	(970)635-1500		www.hp.com/storage
IBM OEM Division	(914)288-3000		www.ibm.com
IBM Parts Order Center	(800)338-7080		

Company	Phone Number	Email	Web Site
IBM PC Direct	(800)772-2227		www.pc.ibm.com
Imation Enterprises Corp.	(888)466-3456	info@imation.com	www.imation.com
Inprise/Borland	(800)632-2864		www.inprise.com
Intel Corp.	(408)765-8080		www.intel.com
Iomega Corp.	(801)778-1000		www.iomega.com
Jameco Computer Products	(800)831-4242		www.jameco.com
JDR Microdevices	(800)538-5000		www.jdr.com
Jensen Tools, Inc.	(800)426-1194		www.jensentools.com
JVC Information Products	(714)816-6500		www.jvc.net/ds2
Key Tronic Corp.	(800)262-6006	info@keytronic.com	www.keytronic.com
Kingston Technology	(877)KINGSTON	tech_support@kingston.com	www.kingston.com
Labtec Enterprises, Inc.	(360)896-2000		www.labtec.com
Lexmark	(800)539-6275		www.lexmark.com
LG Electronics (Goldstar)	(201)816-2127		www.lgeus.com
Linksys	(800)546-5797	support@linksys.com	www.linksys.com
Logitech	(800)231-7717		www.logitech.com
MAG InnoVision	(800)827-3998	tech@maginnovision.com	www.maginnovision.com
Matrox Graphics	(800)361-1408		www.matrox.com/mga
Maxi Switch, Inc.	(520)294-5450		www.maxiswitch.com
Maxtor Corp.	(800)262-9867		www.maxtor.com
McAfee.com	(408)572-1500		www.mcafee.com
Micron Technologies	(800)964-2766		www.micron.com
Microsoft Corp.	(800)426-9400		www.microsoft.com
Mitsumi Electronics Corp.	(972)550-7300		www.mitsumi.com
MSI Computer Corp.	(510)623-8818		www.msicomputer.com
NEC Computer Systems	(800)524-0819	tech-support@neccsd.com	www.nec-computers.com
NEC Technologies, Inc.	(800)632-4636		www.nectech.com
nVidia	(408)615-2500	info@nvidia.com	www.nvidia.com

Company	Phone Number	Email	Web Site
Ontrack Data International	(800)645-3649		www.ontrack.com
PC Power and Cooling, Inc.	(800)722-6555	PCPower@ix.netcom.com	www.pcpowercooling.com
Philips Electronics	(212)536-0500		www.philipsusa.com
Plextor	(800)886-3935	support@plextor.com	www.plextor.com
PowerQuest Corporation	(800)379-2566	support@powerquest.com	www.powerquest.com
Quantum Corp.	(800)624-5545		www.quantum.com
Seagate Technology	(800)732-4283		www.seagate.com
SONICblue	(408)588-8000		www.sonicblue.com
Sony Electronics	(800)326-9551		www.sel.sony.com
SOYO Tek, Inc.	(510)226-7696	support@soyousa.com	www.soyousa.com
StorageSoft, Inc.	(303)381-2680		www.storagesoft.com
Supermicro Computer, Inc.	(408)895-2000	support@supermicro.com	www.supermicro.com
Symantec	(800)441-7234		www.symantec.com
Tecmar Technologies, Inc.	(800)422-2587		www.tecmar.com
Tekram Technologies	(512)833-6550	support@tekram.com	www.tekram.com
Toshiba America, Inc.	(800)TOSHIBA		www.csd.toshiba.com
Tripp Lite Manufacturing	(773)869-1111	techsupport@ tripplite.com	www.tripplite.com
Tyan Computer Corporation	(510)651-8868	techsupport@tyan.com	www.tyan.com
Ultra-X, Inc.	(800)722-3789		www.uxd.com
Veritas Software	(800)327-2232		www.veritas.com
VIA Technologies, Inc.	(510)683-3300	support@via.com.tw	www.viatech.com
Western Digital Corporation	(800)832-4778		www.westerndigital.com
Xircom	(800)438-4562		www.xircom.com
Zoom Telephonics	(800)666-6191	support@zoom.com	www.zoomtel.com

Troubleshooting Index

This special index is designed to help you find solutions to problems—*fast*. Whether your system is beeping at startup, you're getting the dreaded blue screen of death, or you can't hear your rocket launcher blasts in your latest Unreal Tournament Deathmatch, this index will help you find solutions, quickly and relatively painlessly.

	Problem		Details About Solution	
Technology	**Symptom**	**Cause**	**Solution**	**Page**
Audio	Your sound card doesn't sound quite right.	Hardware resource conflict.	Use Windows Device Manager to find conflicts and resolve them.	328
Audio	Sound card can't be detected.	Settings already in use by other cards.	Install sound card first.	335
Audio	Can hear music and sounds in Windows but not DOS.	Incorrect settings for Sound Blaster compatibility.	Install emulation settings or run DOS emulation program.	881
Audio	DOS game can't detect sound card correctly.	Inadequate Sound Blaster compliance or missing DOS drivers.	Verify DOS drivers are installed and manually select best emulation.	890
Audio	Game port on sound card conflicts with other game port in system.	Game port can uses only a single I/O address range.	Disable sound card's game port or remove other game port from system.	914
Audio	System reboots repeatedly during installation of a sound card.	Sound cards are multifunction devices, and Windows defaults to requesting a reboot as each device is set up.	Skip rebooting until all devices are detected.	910
Audio	Can't hear any sounds at all.	Various causes, including incorrect connections, mixer setup, power, and so on.	See checklist.	916

	Problem		Details About Solution	
Technology	**Symptom**	**Cause**	**Solution**	**Page**
Audio	Can hear sound through just one speaker.	Various causes, including incorrect or defective speaker jack/plug, mixer controls, and others.	See checklist.	917
Audio	Volume is low.	Various causes, including mixer controls, volume controls on speakers or sound card.	See checklist.	917
Audio	Scratchy sound.	Various causes, including interference, ISA sound card, wrong expansion slot.	See checklist.	917
Audio	Computer won't start after installing sound card.	Card might not be installed in slot properly, or Windows IOS might be corrupted.	See checklist.	918
Audio	Speaker or microphone won't work.	Incorrect jacks.	Use correct jack for each device.	922
Audio	Can't use onboard audio.	Audio might be disabled in BIOS.	Enable audio.	380
Battery for CMOS/RTC	System can't maintain correct time when turned off.	Battery is about to fail.	Replace battery.	1159
BIOS	Calendar-related and leap-year bugs.	BIOS is out-of-date.	Upgrade Flash BIOS.	362

	Problem		Details About Solution	
Technology	**Symptom**	**Cause**	**Solution**	**Page**
BIOS	Can't install Flash BIOS update.	BIOS is write-protected.	Disable write-protection.	365
BIOS	BIOS update fails.	BIOS is corrupted.	Enable Flash Recovery feature and restart update process.	368
CD-ROM	Can't boot from CD-ROM drive.	BIOS is out-of-date.	Upgrade Flash BIOS.	362
DirecPC	Download speeds drop drastically after downloading one or two large files.	DirecPC has enabled FAP (Fair Access Policy) slowdowns on your service.	Download less at one time; take breaks between big downloads, or switch to another service.	1040
DSL	Can't use DSL service after self-install.	Service might not be set up by provider; microfilter might not be installed as needed.	Make sure provider has activated DSL service; make sure all conventional phones and telephony equipment has a microfilter.	1032
File transfer	Can't connect two computers with standard parallel cable.	Standard parallel is designed for PC-to-device, not PC-to-PC connections.	Use a LapLink-compatible parallel cable.	938
Floppy disk	Can't write data to floppy disk; data can be read.	Floppy disk write protection is enabled in BIOS.	Disable floppy disk write protection.	385
Floppy disk	`File Copying Error` message when copying files with long filenames to disk.	Long filenames might use multiple directory entries, depending on length of filename.	Create subfolder on floppy disk and store files with long filenames in folder.	1331

	Problem		Details About Solution	
Technology	**Symptom**	**Cause**	**Solution**	**Page**
Floppy drive	Disk left in floppy drive prevents system bootup.	Floppy drive has higher boot priority than hard drive.	Adjust boot priority in system BIOS.	392
Floppy drive	Contents of all floppy disks viewed appear to be duplicates of the first disk, although the contents of each disk are different.	Changeline support (which detects disk changes) has failed; this problem is also called the "phantom directory."	Verify BIOS setup for drive is correct and that DC jumper (if any) has been set.	621
Floppy drive	Disks placed on top of a TV or monitor have data errors when read.	Magnetic fields generated by the picture tube can corrupt data.	Store disks away from magnetic fields.	629
Floppy drive	Dead drive— the drive does not spin and the LED never comes on.	Drive or controller not properly configured in BIOS setup.	Verify floppy controller is enabled and correct drive type selected.	631
Floppy drive	Dead drive— the drive does not spin and the LED never comes on.	Bad power supply or bad cable.	Use voltmeter to check power going to drive.	631
Floppy drive	Dead drive— the drive does not spin and the LED never comes on.	Defective data cable.	Make sure cable is connected properly; replace.	631
Floppy drive	Dead drive— the drive does not spin and the LED never comes on.	Defective drive.	Replace and retest.	631
Floppy drive	Dead drive— the drive does not spin and the LED never comes on.	Defective floppy controller.	Try drive/cable on another system; if they work there, replace motherboard or card containing controller.	631

	Problem		Details About Solution	
Technology	**Symptom**	**Cause**	**Solution**	**Page**
Floppy drive	Drive LED remains on continuously.	Data cable attached backwards.	Remove and reattach cable correctly.	631
Floppy drive	Drive LED remains on continuously.	Data cable attached offset to pins.	Remove and reattach cable correctly.	631
Floppy drive	Invalid Media or Track Zero Bad, Disk Unusable error.	Incorrect disk-type parameters might have been used during format process.	Use correct disk-type parameters when formatting the disk.	631
Floppy drive	Invalid Media or Track Zero Bad, Disk Unusable error message.	Drive heads might be dirty.	Use floppy disk head cleaner and retry.	631
Floppy drive	Invalid Media or Track Zero Bad, Disk Unusable error message.	Defective or damaged floppy disk.	Use a different disk and retry.	631
Floppy drive	CRC Error or Disk Error 23 error message.	Data read from disk does not match data written.	Clean disk heads and retry; use Norton Disk Doctor.	631
Floppy drive	General Failure Reading Drive A; Abort, Retry, Fail; or Disk Error 31 error message.	Disk isn't formatted or was formatted for a different operating system (such as a Macintosh).	Format the disk and retry.	631
Floppy drive	General Failure Reading Drive A; Abort, Retry, Fail; or Disk Error 31 error message.	Disk surface damaged.	Use Norton Disk Doctor to retrieve any readable data.	631
Floppy drive	Access Denied error.	Disk is write-protected.	Remove disk, write-enable disk, and retry write operation.	631

Problem			Details About Solution	
Technology	**Symptom**	**Cause**	**Solution**	**Page**
Floppy drive	`Access Denied` error.	File has read-only attributes set.	Remove read-only attributes with Windows Explorer or DOS Attrib and retry write or delete operation.	631
Floppy drive	`Insufficient Disk Space or Disk Full` error.	Disk has insufficient space overall or in root directory for new files.	Use a different disk, or delete files.	631
Floppy drive	`xxx bytes in bad sectors` error.	Displayed when `ScanDisk`, `CHKDSK`, or `Format` is run on disks with bad sectors.	Move data on disk to other storage and reformat.	631
Floppy drive	`Disk Type Incompatible`, `Drive Types Incompatible` or `Bad` error.	Displayed when trying to use `DISKCOPY` on disks with different sizes.	Use `XCOPY` instead; use `DISKCOPY` only for disks with same size and capacity.	631
Floppy drive	Disk access light stays on continuously after system is started.	One end of floppy cable is reversed.	Change reversed end of floppy cable, verifying pin 1 to pin 1.	811
Hard disk	Can't access full capacity of hard drive over 8.4GB.	BIOS is out-of-date.	Upgrade Flash BIOS.	362
Hard disk	Can't use UDMA drives at full speed.	BIOS is out-of-date.	Upgrade Flash BIOS.	362
Hard disk	`IDE drive not ready` errors during startup.	Drive not spinning up fast enough at startup.	Enable or increase hard disk predelay time.	382
Hard disk	Can't use drive capacity beyond 528MB.	LBA mode not enabled in BIOS.	Enable LBA mode.	382

	Problem		Details About Solution	
Technology	**Symptom**	**Cause**	**Solution**	**Page**
Hard disk	Boot section corrupted.	Boot sector virus or other problem.	Use FDISK/MBR (DOS, Windows 9x/Me) or FIXMBR (Windows NT/2000) to restore.	1322
Hard disk	Storing small file uses up a large amount of space on drive.	Files smaller than an allocation unit (cluster) still use an entire allocation unit.	Convert drive to FAT32 or NTFS to be more efficient if possible; remove outdated files from system to save space.	1329
Hard disk	Your 40GB hard disk can't be formatted by Windows 2000 or Windows XP as a single drive with FAT32.	These versions can format up to 32GB only, but can read larger drives.	Prepare drive with third-party utility such as PartitionMagic or use NTFS.	1334
Hard disk	Large numbers of files ending in .CHK are found in root directory of drive.	.CHK files are created by SCANDISK or CHKDSK from lost allocation units.	Shut down system properly to avoid lost allocation units; test drive if problem persists; delete files to free up space.	1339
Hard drive	UDMA/66 or UDMA/100 drive runs at UDMA/33 on systems that support UDMA/66 or UDMA/100.	Incorrect cable might be in use.	Use 80-wire UDMA cable in place of normal 40-wire IDE cable.	484
Hard drive	System won't boot after installing new IDE drive.	Cable might be reversed.	Make sure pin 1 on both ends of cable is connected to interfaces' pin 1.	486
Hard drive	Can't set IDE drives as master or slave when 80-wire cable is used.	80-wire cable supports cable select, not master/slave.	Install drives at correct locations on cable, and jumper both as Cable Select.	484

Problem			Details About Solution	
Technology	**Symptom**	**Cause**	**Solution**	**Page**
Hard drive	Can't read contents of IDE drive over 528MB after moving it to a new system.	Drive geometry or translation not set correctly on new system.	Set correct Cyl-Hd-Sectors setting for drive and LBA or Ext CHS translation.	495
Hard drive	BIOS recognizes full capacity of drive over 8.4GB, but operating system will not.	Some operating systems aren't designed to use drives over 8.4GB.	Upgrade or patch your operating system to achieve compliance.	501
Hard drive	Can't boot from SCSI hard drive.	SCSI BIOS might not be enabled; system BIOS might not be set properly.	Enable SCSI BIOS and disable booting from IDE drives in system BIOS.	539
Hard drive	Immediately back up your data and replace your hard disk drive. A failure may be imminent. error message is seen.	The drive uses S.M.A.R.T. to predict failures, and the S.M.A.R.T. system has detected a serious problem with the drive.	Follow the onscreen instructions to back up your drive.	599
Hard drive	Hard drive letters above C: are pushed higher when second drive is installed.	New drive was prepared with a primary partition, which takes precedence over drive letters in the first drive's extended partition.	Prepare additional drives with an extended partition.	793
Hard drive	Invalid Drive Specification error.	Drive has not been partitioned or high-level formatted, or wrong OS being used to view drive.	Verify drive is empty with recent Windows versions before running FDISK and FORMAT.	802

	Problem		Details About Solution	
Technology	**Symptom**	**Cause**	**Solution**	**Page**
Hard drive	`Invalid Media Type` error.	Drive has not been FDISKed, or drive's format is corrupt.	View drive with FDISK's #4 option, and create new partitions as necessary.	802
IDE drives	Can't detect drive with BIOS setup program.	Power cable might be loose or missing.	Reattach power cable.	787
IDE drives	Can't detect drive with BIOS setup program.	Missing or reversed IDE data cable.	Rettach IDE data cable and verify pin 1 to pin 1 at both ends of cable.	787
IDE drives	Can't detect either drive on cable with BIOS setup program.	Both drives might be cabled as master or slave.	Change one drive to master and the other drive to slave.	781
Internet	Can't share Internet connection.	Problems with host or client configuration.	See checklist.	1052
IRQ	Conflicts between PCI devices.	PCI IRQ steering not enabled.	Enable PCI IRQ steering.	320
IRQ	Conflicts between COM ports.	IRQs shared between COM 1 and 3; between COM 2 and 4.	Disable unused COM port or change IRQ if possible.	323
ISA cards	ISA cards have hardware conflicts with PCI cards.	Resources not reserved for ISA cards.	Reserve resources for ISA cards.	386
Keyboard	Num Lock stays off when starting. system.	Num Lock shut off in BIOS.	Turn on Num Lock in BIOS.	378
Keyboard	Intermittent keyboard failures.	Keyboard cable or keyboard jack might be defective.	Test keyboard cable or jack with digital multimeter.	972

	Problem		Details About Solution	
Technology	**Symptom**	**Cause**	**Solution**	**Page**
Keyboard	Keys are sticking.	Keyboard might have spilled drink or trapped debris under keys.	Remove keytops and clean under keys, or wash out keyboard.	973
LAN	Can't use onboard LAN.	LAN might be disabled in BIOS.	Enable audio.	380
Modem	Internal modem locks up system when trying to make a connection.	Modem might be set to same IRQ as the serial port the mouse is attached to.	Disable the unused COM port on the system, and set the modem to use that COM port number.	932
Modem	Modem works correctly with Internet access, but computer-to-computer terminal emulation produces garbage screens.	Incorrect bps, word length, stop bit, or terminal emulation settings compared to remote system's requirements.	Determine correct values for remote system and set up HyperTerminal or other connection program accordingly.	998
Modem	56Kbps modem connects at 33.6Kbps or less.	Some telephone lines can't provide greater than 33.6Kbps service.	Switch to a broadband service, or use modem bonding to achieve higher speeds.	1010
Modem	K56flex modem connects at lower speeds after update to V.90.	K56flex might work better than V.90 for some users with certain modems and ISPs.	See checklist.	1012
Modem	Modem drops calls unexpectedly.	You might have call-waiting enabled, which interrupts the modem carrier signal.	Disable call-waiting (ask phone company for details), or upgrade to modems with call-waiting support.	1016

	Problem		Details About Solution	
Technology	**Symptom**	**Cause**	**Solution**	**Page**
Modem	Can't dial with analog modem.	Various causes.	See checklist.	1048
Modem	System locks up after installing internal modem.	IRQ conflicts with other ports or devices.	See checklist.	1050
Modem	Computer can't detect external modem.	Wrong cable, port problems, or power problems.	Check cable, port setup, and power.	1051
Motherboard	Damage to motherboard from heatsink clips on socketed processors.	Clips slip and scratch motherboard surface.	Attach plastic tape on motherboard before installing heatsink.	99
Mouse	Mouse doesn't work.	Hardware resource conflict.	Use Windows Device Manager to find conflicts and resolve them.	328
Mouse	Can't use PS/2 mouse.	PS/2 mouse port might be disabled.	Enable PS/2 mouse port.	394
Mouse	Mouse doesn't work when attached via adapter to a different port type.	Mouse might not be hybrid type (designed for various ports).	Use adapters only with hybrid mice; use adapter packaged with mouse.	980
Mouse	Mouse pointer jerks onscreen.	Mouse ball or rollers are dirty.	Clean mouse mechanism.	981
Mouse	Mouse works for basic operations, but extra buttons or scroll doesn't work.	Incorrect or outdated mouse driver is being used.	Download and install correct mouse driver from vendor site.	976
Mouse	Mouse works in Windows, but not when booted to DOS.	DOS driver must be loaded from `AUTOEXEC.BAT` or `CONFIG.SYS`.	Install DOS mouse driver, and reference it in startup file(s).	983

Problem			Details About Solution	
Technology	**Symptom**	**Cause**	**Solution**	**Page**
Network	System locks up after installing network card.	IRQ conflicts with other ports or devices.	See checklist.	1050
Network	Can't connect to other computers on network after installing a new custom-built cable.	Cable might not match prevailing wiring standard on network.	Check wiring of other cables to see which wiring standard is used; build new cable to match.	1077
Network	Distant computer works with 10BASE-T network but not with Fast Ethernet.	Computer might be too far from hub or switch because Fast Ethernet has shorter maximum distance.	Install repeater, or use new switch/hub as repeater.	1082
Network	Can't connect to other users on network, although card diagnostics check out.	Might not have correct network software components installed.	See checklist.	1096
Network	Duplicate computer ID error.	More than one computer has the same name or IP address on the network.	Adjust computer name or IP address with the Network properties sheet.	1100
Network	Users can't see all the computers on the network.	Multiple workgroup names are in use.	Adjust workgroup name (must match for all on network) with Network properties.	1100
Network	Users can't share printers or folders with others.	File/Print sharing might not be installed; folders or printers might not be set to shared.	Install File/Print sharing, and then set shared folders and printers.	1100

	Problem		Details About Solution	
Technology	**Symptom**	**Cause**	**Solution**	**Page**
Network	Network changes made, but don't work.	Most Windows systems must be rebooted to put network changes into effect.	Reboot system and then try network operations.	1100
Network	One user can't access network, but others can.	User might not have logged on to network.	Log off system and log on; provide name and password when prompted.	1101
Network	One user can't access network, but others can.	Loose cables at computer, hub, switch, or wiring closet.	Check all cable connections.	1101
Network	One user can't access network, but others can.	Password cache might be corrupt or have outdated passwords.	Log on to resources again and give new password when prompted.	1101
Network	Can't access Internet or other TCP/IP-based resources.	Wrong TCP/IP settings.	Open Network properties sheet and adjust TCP/IP settings as needed for your network.	1101
Network	IP Address Conflict error.	Duplicate IP addresses on two or more machines.	Open Network properties sheet and enter correct, unique IP addresses for each system.	1101
Optical drives	Drive letters above C: are pushed higher when new hard drives are installed.	Hard drives take precedence over optical drives.	Set optical drives to reserved drive letters above those needed by hard drives.	655
Optical drives	Drive slows down when reading CD with a small paper label attached to the label side.	Drive can't run at full speed due to uneven weight distribution and must slow down.	Use full-size labels that cover the entire CD's top surface, or use a marker instead of small labels.	701

	Problem		Details About Solution	
Technology	Symptom	Cause	Solution	Page
Optical drives	CD-ROM drive can't read multiple-session disc.	Drive is not compatible with Orange Book multisession standard (XA standard).	Replace drive with new CD-ROM, CD-RW, or DVD drive.	710
Optical drives	Can't read CD-R or CD-RW disc on a CD-ROM drive, but only on a CD-R/CD-RW drive.	CD probably was created with packet-writing software and not closed before being removed.	Return CD-R or CD-RW disc to original system and close session.	711
Optical drives	CD-ROM disc can be read by 32-bit Windows but not by DOS.	CD was created using the UDF (packet-writing) standard.	Use standard mastering software instead of DirectCD to create CDs for use with DOS.	717
Optical drives	Drive runs very slowly or has read errors.	CD lens might be dirty or dusty.	Use a CD lens cleaner, or install a drive with a self-cleaning lens.	746, 776
Optical drives	Can't read CD-RW media on an older drive.	Drives that aren't MultiRead compliant can't read CD-RW media (usually slower than 24x speed).	Replace drive with a MultiRead-compatible CD-ROM or DVD drive or a CD-RW drive.	754
Optical drives	Can't write to a 10x CD-RW disc in a 4x CD-RW drive.	10x media meets the High-Speed ReWritable standard, not supported by 2x and 4x CD-RW drives.	Use 2x or 4x media for interchange between 10x and 2x/4x CD-RW drives.	753
Optical drives	Can't read CD-RW media in a DVD.	Drives that aren't MultiRead2 compliant can't read CD-RW or DVD-RAM media.	Replace drive with a MultiRead2 drive.	754

	Problem		Details About Solution	
Technology	**Symptom**	**Cause**	**Solution**	**Page**
Optical drives	Can't burn a CD-R disc while performing other tasks.	Multitasking operations are causing buffer underruns.	Run only CD-mastering software, slow down burn speed, or upgrade to a drive with buffer underrun protection.	756
Optical drives	CD-ROM has a different drive letter when command-prompt/DOS is run than in Windows.	CD-ROM has been assigned a specific drive letter in Windows, but defaults to the next available drive letter in DOS.	Use the /L:x option with MSCDEX in DOS to assign the drive letter used in Windows to the drive; replace x with the drive letter.	770
Optical drives	Can boot from bootable CD, but can't read contents of CD.	Bootable CD must have CD-ROM driver files and `CONFIG.SYS` and `AUTOEXEC.BAT` references to them.	Make sure bootable disk used for creating bootable CD can access CD-ROM.	777
Optical drives	Can't read CD or CD-R discs in a CD-ROM or DVD drive.	Media might not be compatible.	Try different-colored media.	776
Optical drives	ATAPI drive runs very slowly, but no read errors.	Wrong cache size.	Adjust cache size in Performance tab of System Properties.	776
Optical drives	ATAPI drive runs very slowly, but no read errors.	CD-ROM drive on same cable as hard drive.	Move CD-ROM drive to secondary cable.	776
Optical drives	ATAPI drive runs very slowly, but no read errors.	UDMA or busmastering drivers might not be installed or enabled.	Install and enable latest UDMA or busmastering drivers.	776

	Problem		Details About Solution	
Technology	**Symptom**	**Cause**	**Solution**	**Page**
Optical drives	ATAPI drive runs very slowly, but no read errors.	Drive might be using MS-DOS Compatibility Mode (BIOS-based) access.	Reinstall drive to use 32-bit Windows drivers.	776
Optical drives	Can't boot from bootable CD.	System might not support bootable CD.	Verify CD-ROM listed as bootable device and listed first in boot.	777
Optical drives	Can't boot from bootable CD.	Wrong disc format (Joliet or other).	Must use ISO 9660 CD format.	777
Optical drives	Can't boot from bootable CD.	SCSI drive and host adapter might not be configured as bootable.	Enable BIOS on SCSI adapter and disable IDE boot devices in system BIOS.	777
Optical drives	Can't hear music through sound card speakers.	Analog or digital audio cables aren't connected between drive and audio jacks on sound card or motherboard with integrated sound.	Reattach cables to drive and sound card or motherboard; check mixer settings.	804
Parallel port	Can't use onboard parallel port.	Port might be disabled in BIOS.	Enable port.	380
Parallel port	Conflict between onboard parallel port and other device.	IRQ or I/O port address conflicts with other device.	Adjust IRQ or I/O port address in use, or disable port.	380
Parallel port	Can't use ECP mode.	DMA channel conflicts with another device.	Use alternate DMA channel, or use EPP mode instead.	380

	Problem		Details About Solution	
Technology	**Symptom**	**Cause**	**Solution**	**Page**
Password	Can't access setup or start system because system prompts for password.	Setup and/or power-on passwords are enabled in BIOS.	Clear password settings.	374
Password	Can't access setup or start system because system prompts for password.	Setup and/or power-on passwords are enabled in BIOS.	Clear password settings.	388
Password	Can't access setup or start system because system prompts for password.	Setup and/or power-on passwords are enabled in BIOS.	Clear CMOS if password settings can't be cleared separately.	388
PCI	IRQ conflicts between PCI cards.	IRQs might be shared between slots.	Move conflicting cards to another PCI slot.	378
PCI	IRQ conflicts between PCI cards.	Auto PCI IRQ Priority might not work for all cards.	Set PCI IRQ priority manually.	378
PnP	Can't install new PnP cards.	PnP/PCI configuration data might be corrupted.	Clear PnP/PCI configuration data and restart system.	378
PnP	Problems with PnP cards and configuration.	BIOS is out-of-date.	Upgrade Flash BIOS.	362
Portable system	Can't run LCD projector and internal screen at same time.	LCD projector must use same resolution as internal screen's native resolution to allow simultaneous display.	Use LCD project with matching resolution, or forego simultaneous displays.	1207
Portable system	Battery won't charge completely.	Battery needs conditioning.	Recondition battery with three discharge/ recharge cycles.	1204

	Problem		Details About Solution	
Technology	**Symptom**	**Cause**	**Solution**	**Page**
Power management	System can't use power management features.	Power management disabled.	Enable power management.	389
Power management	Can't control power management through Windows.	ACPI power management disabled.	Enable ACPI power management.	389
Power management	Can't use ACPI power management.	BIOS is out-of-date.	Upgrade Flash BIOS.	362
Power management	System locks up or hardware malfunctions when power management is used.	Some older peripherals are not compatible with power management.	Disable APM power management in the system BIOS; disable ACPI power management with Windows' Power properties sheet.	1144
Power supply	System reboots (cold boots with memory check) spontaneously.	Power Good voltage level out of limits.	Check power supply with DMM; replace power supply if defective.	1148
Power supply	Dell power supply fails and replacement has different-colored wires for connectors.	Dell changed to a nonstandard version of ATX for systems built September 1998–present; standard power supplies will not work and will fry!	Buy a Dell-brand or Dell-compatible power supply, or replace motherboard and power supply with standard models.	1124
Power supply	System won't start; power is going to system.	Voltage slider on power supply might be set to wrong voltage.	Set power supply to correct voltage level for local current.	1134

	Problem		Details About Solution	
Technology	**Symptom**	**Cause**	**Solution**	**Page**
Power supply	Power supply fails after additional components are added to system.	New components require more 5V power than old power supply can provide.	Replace failed unit with a 300-watt or larger unit.	1138
Power supply	Hard disk or fan won't turn.	Defective or overloaded power supply.	Replace failed unit with a 300-watt or larger unit.	1144
Power supply	Electrical shocks on case.	Defective or overloaded power supply.	Replace failed unit with a 300-watt or larger unit.	1144
Printer	Parallel printer prints very slowly.	Printer might be attached to non-EEE or non-ECP parallel port.	Set port to use mode recommended for printer and switch to IEEE-1284 cable if necessary.	934
Printer	Your printer prints gibberish.	Hardware resource conflict.	Use Windows Device Manager to find conflicts and resolve them.	328
Processor	Can't overclock multiplier.	Multiplier locked on recent AMD, Intel CPUs.	Adjust bus speed instead.	74
Processor	Can't use FC-PGA processor in PGA-370 socket.	Change in voltages and pinout.	Upgrade motherboard or use third-party PGA/FC-PGA adapter.	91
Processor	Can't use PGA or FC-PGA processor in Slot 1.	Wrong form factor.	Use slot-key adapter.	91
Processor	Poor heat transfer from processor to heatsink.	Gaps between processor and heatsink faceplate.	Attach thermal interface pad or grease to processor before attaching heatsink.	99

	Problem		**Details About Solution**	
Technology	**Symptom**	**Cause**	**Solution**	**Page**
Processor	Pentium miscalculates floating-point math.	Errata 23 in Pentium processor.	Have Intel replace affected Pentium or use updated processor.	136
Processor	Improper CPU identification during POST.	Old BIOS.	Update BIOS from manufacturer.	191
Processor	Improper CPU identification during POST.	Board is not configured properly.	Check manual, and set board accordingly to proper bus and multiplier settings.	191
Processor	Can't install newer processors.	BIOS is out-of-date.	Upgrade Flash BIOS.	362
RAM	RAM test not detecting any problems and is finishing too quickly.	L1 and L2 memory caches might be enabled.	Disable memory caches before testing memory.	394
RAM	Soft (random) errors occur after adjusting memory timing in BIOS setup.	Refresh rate set incorrectly in BIOS.	Autoconfigure memory timing in BIOS.	378
RAM	Can't use standard 30-pin or 72-pin SIMMs in some IBM, Compaq, or HP systems.	These systems support nonstandard presence detect pins in the SIMMs.	Use SIMMs made especially for the computer model.	426
RAM	Can't insert 168-pin DIMM into the motherboard.	DIMM might be wrong voltage or type for motherboard.	PCs use unbuffered 3.3v DIMMs; others will not fit.	429
RAM	RIMM-based system won't boot up with some RIMM sockets empty.	All RIMM sockets must have memory or continuity module installed.	Install continuity modules into a RIMM socket without memory.	432

	Problem		Details About Solution	
Technology	**Symptom**	**Cause**	**Solution**	**Page**
RAM	Can't determine speed or type of memory module.	Some memory modules aren't labeled.	Look up memory chip characteristics to determine module speed and type.	436
RAM	Single 72-pin SIMM not recognized on P5-class system.	Memory must be added in banks of 64 bits on P5-class systems; 72-pin SIMM has 32 bits.	Add pair of identical SIMMs as supported by motherboard.	438
RAM	System won't boot after installing new memory.	Memory might be too slow for system.	Install new memory as fast or faster than previous memory.	440
RAM	System locks up; mixed metals (gold/tin) used in sockets and modules.	Corroded memory sockets result from mixing tin sockets/gold memory or vice versa.	Remove memory, clean sockets, and use memory with same metal as sockets.	440
RAM	Soft (random) memory errors.	Power glitches or noise on the line.	Replace power supply if it tests out-of-spec, or install power conditioning equipment.	443
RAM	Soft (random) memory errors.	Incorrect type or speed.	Use memory that matches recommended type and meets or exceeds recommended speed.	443
RAM	Soft (random) memory errors.	RF (Radio Frequency) interference.	Move causes of RF away from system.	443
RAM	Soft (random) memory errors.	ESD (electrostatic discharge).	Use antistatic spray on screen and keyboard and install antistatic mats near system.	452

Problem			Details About Solution	
Technology	**Symptom**	**Cause**	**Solution**	**Page**
RAM	Memory parity interrupt error message.	Parity checking has detected an error in RAM.	Shut down the system and restart it; remove and reinstall memory.	445
RAM	Out of memory error after upgrading system with AGP card beyond 512MB of RAM.	Windows 9x/Me can't handle memory addresses beyond 512MB along with AGP aperture addresses.	Use no more than 512MB of RAM with Windows 9x/Me and AGP video.	851
Removable media	Can't boot from SuperDisk LS-120 drive.	BIOS is out-of-date.	Upgrade Flash BIOS.	362
Removable media	Iomega Zip drive makes clicking noises and won't read media.	Drive or media has "click of death" problem.	Check media for damage; run TIP testing program on disk; use Iomega diagnostics on drive.	644
Removable media	Iomega Jaz drive makes clicking noises and won't read media.	Drive or media has "click of death" problem.	Check media for damage; run TIP testing program on disk; use Iomega diagnostics on drive.	640
Removable media	Castlewood Orb drives can't read media.	Drivers might be clashing with Iomega drivers.	Remove Iomega drivers, reinstall Orb drivers; then download and install new Iomega drivers.	652
Removable media	Castlewood Orb drives can't read media.	Orb drivers might be out-of-date.	Download and install latest drivers and firmware from Castlewood's Web site.	652

	Problem		Details About Solution	
Technology	**Symptom**	**Cause**	**Solution**	**Page**
Removable media	Castlewood Orb drives can't read media.	Drive might not be spinning up completely before being read.	Allow drive to spin up completely before accessing it.	652
Removable media	Drive letters above C: are pushed higher when new hard drives are installed.	Hard drives take precedence over removable-media drives.	Set removable-media drives to reserved drive letters above those needed by hard drives.	655
Removable-media drive	Can't boot from LS-120 SuperDisk or Zip drive.	ARMD-FDD (ATAPI Removable Device—Floppy), Zip, or LS-120 drive listed after hard drive in boot order.	Adjust boot priority in system BIOS.	392
SCSI	Data or signaling errors at higher speeds.	Passive termination not suitable for use in faster SCSI versions.	Use other types of terminators at both ends of SCSI daisy-chain.	531
SCSI	Can't use external SCSI device.	External device might have been turned on after system startup.	Turn on external devices first; then boot system.	539
SCSI	Can't detect new SCSI device.	Device might be using a duplicate device ID.	Ensure that each device and the host adapter use a unique device ID.	539
SCSI	PCI SCSI card doesn't work properly.	PCI SCSI cards require a busmastering PCI slot.	Move card to a slot that supports busmastering.	539
Serial port	Can't use onboard serial port.	Port might be disabled in BIOS.	Enable port.	380

	Problem		Details About Solution	
Technology	**Symptom**	**Cause**	**Solution**	**Page**
Serial port	Conflict between onboard serial port and other device.	IRQ or I/O port address conflicts with other device.	Adjust IRQ or I/O port address in use, or disable port.	380
Serial port	COM 3 and above work in Windows, but not DOS.	DOS can use only COM 1 and COM 2 due to BIOS limitations.	Use only COM 1 or COM 2 for DOS applications.	930
Startup	System won't start; no error messages onscreen.	Various fatal errors.	Install POST card; restart system to determine error codes and diagnose problem.	398
Startup	System won't start; various error messages indicating system can't boot.	Hard disk might not be connected to system, partitioned, formatted, or set up correctly in BIOS.	Check drive cabling, drive partitions, and BIOS configuration.	399
Startup	Problems during POST.	Various causes.	Use checklist.	1312
Startup	System beeps several times when turned on; doesn't start properly.	Serious or fatal hardware errors.	Count beeps and pattern; determine BIOS used and look up beep code to determine problem.	1267
Startup	System displays error message when turned on; doesn't start properly.	Serious hardware error.	Look up error code in Technical Reference on CD.	1269
Startup	System doesn't start properly; might not beep or display error codes.	Serious or fatal hardware errors.	Install POST diagnostics card and restart system; look up I/O port POST codes.	1270

	Problem		Details About Solution	
Technology	**Symptom**	**Cause**	**Solution**	**Page**
Startup	System can't boot from hard drive.	Configuration problem with system or drive.	See checklist.	1273
Startup	Missing Operating System error.	Incorrect drive geometry settings, bad CMOS battery, no active partition, bad MBR.	Use checklist.	1352
Startup	NO ROM BASIC - SYSTEM HALTED error.	Incorrect drive geometry settings, bad CMOS battery, no active partition, bad MBR.	Use checklist.	1352
Startup	Boot error Press F1 to retry error.	Incorrect drive geometry settings, bad CMOS battery, no active partition, bad MBR.	Use checklist.	1352
Startup	Invalid drive specification error.	No partition on disk.	Use FDISK or equivalent to partition drive.	1353
Startup	Invalid Media Type error.	No valid format on drive.	Use FORMAT or Norton Disk Doctor.	1353
Startup	Hard Disk Controller Failure error.	Incorrect cabling between drive and host adapter or failed host adapter.	Check cables; then check host adapter.	1353
System	Problems with adapter cards.	Various causes.	Use checklist.	1313

	Problem		Details About Solution	
Technology	**Symptom**	**Cause**	**Solution**	**Page**
System	System unstable when overclocking.	Incorrect voltage to processor.	Use motherboard that allows fine adjustments to processor voltage.	50
System	System is dead, no beeps, no cursor, no fan.	Power cord failure.	Plug in or replace power cord.	191
System	System is dead, no beeps, no cursor, no fan.	Power supply failure.	Replace power supply with known-good one.	191
System	System is dead, no beeps, no cursor, no fan.	Motherboard failure.	Replace motherboard with known-good one.	191
System	System is dead, no beeps, no cursor, no fan.	Memory failure.	Remove all memory except bank 1 and retest; swap bank 1 if no boot.	191
System	System is dead, no beeps, or locks up before POST begins.	All components either not installed or incorrectly installed.	Check all peripherals, especially memory and graphics adapter. Reseat all boards and socketed components.	191
System	System beeps on startup, fan is running, no cursor onscreen. Locks up during or shortly after POST.	Improperly seated or failing graphics adapter.	Reseat or replace graphics adapter. Use known-good spare for testing.	191

	Problem		Details About Solution	
Technology	**Symptom**	**Cause**	**Solution**	**Page**
System	System beeps on startup, fan is running, no cursor onscreen. Locks up during or shortly after POST.	Poor heat dissipation.	Check CPU heatsink/fan; replace if necessary; use one with higher capacity.	191
System	System beeps on startup, fan is running, no cursor onscreen. Locks up during or shortly after POST.	Improper voltage settings.	Set motherboard for proper core processor voltage.	191
System	System beeps on startup, fan is running, no cursor onscreen. Locks up during or shortly after POST.	Wrong motherboard bus speed.	Set motherboard for proper speed.	191
System	System beeps on startup, fan is running, no cursor onscreen. Locks up during or shortly after POST.	Wrong CPU clock multiplier.	Jumper motherboard for proper clock multiplier.	191
System	Device transfers data inaccurately.	Hardware resource conflict.	Use Windows Device Manager to find conflicts and resolve them.	328
System	System frequently locks up.	Hardware resource conflict.	Use Windows Device Manager to find conflicts and resolve them.	328
System	Hardware and software bugs.	BIOS is out-of-date.	Upgrade Flash BIOS.	362

| | **Problem** | | **Details About Solution** | |
Technology	**Symptom**	**Cause**	**Solution**	**Page**
System	Slow system performance.	System BIOS might not be cached.	Enable caching of system BIOS.	378
System	Memory address conflict between devices.	Two devices are using the same upper memory block.	Move one device to a nonconflicting UMB address.	473
System	Intermittent lockups, memory and drive glitches.	Improperly wired outlets might be providing bad power.	Use an outlet tester to check ground and polarity.	1292
System	Intermittent lockups, memory and drive glitches.	Other devices on circuit could be causing problems, such as AC units, coffee makers, and so on.	Move computers to their own circuit.	1308
System	Problems after system startup with hardware.	Various causes.	Use checklist.	1313
Tape drives	Tape drive can't write to older tape but can read contents of same tape type.	Most drives have limited write compatibility, but can read a wider variety of tapes.	Use correct tape type for new backups; check for write-protect setting on cartridge.	671
Tape drives	Can't run tape backup or restore; bad block errors during restore.	Defective tape cartridge, dirty heads, defective cabling, or incorrect software settings.	Replace cartridge, clean heads, check cabling, and rerun confidence test with blank cartridge.	684
USB	Can't use USB ports on system.	USB ports might be disabled, or your system has the wrong Windows version.	Enable USB ports in BIOS, and verify you are using Windows 98, Me, 2000, or XP.	945

Problem			Details About Solution	
Technology	**Symptom**	**Cause**	**Solution**	**Page**
USB	USB ports available in BIOS but not visible on system.	USB header cables not installed on motherboard.	Install USB header cables.	945
USB	USB game controller doesn't work with some older games.	USB game controller might not perfectly emulate gameport-based controllers.	Check with software vendor for patches or workarounds.	991
USB	Can't use USB keyboard and mouse outside of Windows.	USB Legacy support is disabled in BIOS.	Enable USB Legacy support.	380
USB	Can't use USB devices.	USB is disabled or not assigned an IRQ.	Enable USB; assign IRQ to USB.	386
Video	Onscreen icons too small at high resolutions.	High resolutions use more dots onscreen, so each dot takes less screen area and fixed-size icons are smaller.	If you use Windows 98 or 2000, enable Large Icons.	823
Video	Slow video performance with any card type.	Video BIOS might not be cached.	Enable caching of video BIOS.	378
Video	Garbage appears on your video screen for no apparent reason.	Hardware resource conflict.	Use Windows Device Manager to find conflicts and resolve them.	328
Video	Can't use AGP card as primary video.	PCI video is set as primary video.	Switch primary video to AGP card.	386

	Problem		Details About Solution	
Technology	Symptom	Cause	Solution	Page
Video	Color depth drops below desired setting when resolution is increased.	Video card doesn't have enough RAM to display the resolution at the same color depth.	Upgrade to a video card with more RAM, or decide whether high resolution or higher color depth is more important.	846
Video	Display is steady at lower resolutions but flickers at higher resolutions.	Higher refresh rates are needed at higher resolutions to avoid flicker.	Adjust display adapter properties to higher refresh rate if supported by monitor.	831
Video	Monitor picture is distorted.	Incorrect geometry adjustments; can vary with resolution.	Use digital picture controls to lock in desired picture quality.	834
Video	Windows can't display more than 256 colors.	Windows might have incorrectly identified the video card chipset.	Manually select the correct chipset with the Advanced option on the Display properties' Adapter section.	846
Video	Mouse pointer problems are visible onscreen.	Buggy video or mouse driver.	Upgrade video and mouse driver software; adjust acceleration one notch down.	853
Video	Frequent screen lockups or invalid page fault errors.	Buggy video driver.	Upgrade video driver or adjust acceleration to None.	
Video	System chooses wrong adapter as primary in a multiple-monitor configuration.	BIOS controls which PCI slot (or AGP) is for primary video.	Adjust BIOS options for primary video, or change slots if both adapters are PCI.	857

Problem			Details About Solution	
Technology	**Symptom**	**Cause**	**Solution**	**Page**
Video	Problems with video capture devices.	Various causes.	See checklist.	863
Video	Monitor picture too dull, bright, or dark, out of focus.	Monitor controls need to be adjusted.	Adjust front, side, or rear controls as needed; focus controls might require a long screwdriver.	875
Video	No picture.	Monitor might be in power-saving mode (flashing or yellow LED), have incorrect contrast or brightness settings (green LED), receiving no picture data; or be disconnected from power.	Activate system; adjust contrast and brightness; check data and power cables.	876
Video	Jittery picture quality (LCD).	Display not correctly adjusted, or cables might be loose.	Use display-adjustment software to correct problem; check cables.	876
Video	Jittery picture quality (CRT).	Might be caused by incorrect refresh rate settings, loose cable, interference, or bad power supply.	Adjust refresh rate lower, check cables, eliminate sources of interference; tap on monitor (temporary fix only).	876
Video	Picture displayed in DOS, not Windows.	Wrong video driver or overclocked video card.	Start system in Safe mode, verify correct video driver or use default setup for video card clock speed.	877

	Problem		Details About Solution	
Technology	**Symptom**	**Cause**	**Solution**	**Page**
Video	Can't replace built-in video card with add-on PCI video card.	Card might be in wrong slot or not compatible with system, or system might require manual disabling or onboard video.	Check manual for correct procedure for disabling built-in video, or try a different slot.	877
Windows	System running Windows NT 4.0 can't access a drive prepared with Windows 2000 or Windows XP.	If drive is running NTFS 5, Windows NT needs Service Pack 4 or above.	Install Service Pack 4 or above to be compatible with NTFS 5; third-party add-ons must be used for compatibility with FAT32.	1348
Windows	Virus warning triggered when trying to upgrade Windows.	Virus warning feature enabled in system BIOS.	Disable virus warning or boot sector write-protect feature.	394
Windows	Operating system will not boot.	Poor heat dissipation.	Check CPU fan; replace if necessary; might need higher-capacity heatsink.	191
Windows	Operating system will not boot.	Improper voltage settings.	Set motherboard for proper core processor voltage.	191
Windows	Operating system will not boot.	Wrong motherboard bus speed.	Set motherboard for proper speed.	191
Windows	Operating system will not boot.	Wrong CPU clock multiplier.	Jumper motherboard for proper clock multiplier.	191

	Problem		Details About Solution	
Technology	**Symptom**	**Cause**	**Solution**	**Page**
Windows	Operating system will not boot.	Applications will not install or run.	Improper drivers or incompatible hardware; update drivers and check for compatibility issues.	191
Windows	The PC starts in Safe mode (Windows 9x).	Hardware resource conflict.	Use Windows Device Manager to find conflicts and resolve them.	328
Windows	Problems with operating system or applications.	Various causes.	Use checklist.	1313
Windows	File system problems with Windows 9x/Me or DOS.	Various causes.	See checklist.	1353
Windows	File system problems with Windows 2000/XP.	Various causes.	See checklist.	1354
Wireless input	IR-based wireless mouse or keyboard isn't working.	Direct line-of-sight access to IR receiver might be blocked; batteries might have failed.	Check line-of-sight and move obstacles away from receiver; check and replace batteries as needed.	994
Wireless input	RF-based wireless mouse or keyboard isn't working.	Batteries might have failed, or interference from other devices might be present.	Check and replace batteries if needed; use different frequencies for nearby RF-based devices.	994

List of Acronyms

Symbols

305 RAMAC (Random Access Method of Accounting)
82C836 SCAT (Single Chip AT)

A

ACPI (Advanced Configuration and Power Interface)
ADC (analog-to-digital converter)
ADPCM (Adaptive Differential Pulse Code Modulation)
ADSL (Asymmetrical DSL)
AGC (Automatic Gain Control)
AGP (Accelerated Graphics Port)
AHRA (Audio Home Recording Act)
AMD (Advanced Micro Devices)
AMR (anisotropic magneto-resistive)
ANSI (American National Standards Institute)
API (Application Program Interface)
APIC (Advanced Programmable Interrupt Controller)
APM (Advanced Power Management)
APS (Analog Protection System)
ARLL (Advanced Run Length Limited)
ASPI (Advanced SCSI Programming Interface)
ATA (AT Attachment)
ATAPI (AT Attachment Packet Interface)

B

BASIC (Beginners All-Purpose Symbolic Instruction)
BBS (bulletin board system)
BEDO (Burst Extended-Data-Out)
BF (bus frequency)
BGA (Ball Grid Array)
BiCMOS (bipolar Complementary Metal Oxide Semiconductor)
BIOS (Basic Input Output System)
BRI (Basic Rate Interface)
BSRAM (Burst Static RAM)
BTB (Branch Target Buffer)

C

CAD (Computer Aided Drafting)
CAM (Common Access Method)
CAM ATA (Common Access Method AT Attachment)
CAV (Constant Angular Velocity)
CCITT (Consultative Committee on International Telephone and Telegraph)
CD-DA (CD-Digital Audio)
CD-i (CD-interactive)
CD-R (CD-Recordable)
CD-ROM (compact disc read-only memory)
CD-RW (CD-Rewritable)
CDSL (Consumer DSL)
CFC (chlorofluorocarbon)
CIRC (Cross-Interleave Reed-Solomon Code)
CISC (Complex Instruction Set Computer)
CLKMUL (Clock Multiplier)
CLV (Constant Linear Velocity)
CMOS (Complementary Metal-Oxide Semiconductor)
CP/M (Control Program for Microprocessors)
CPU (Central Processing Unit)
CRC (cyclical redundancy checking)
CRT (cathode ray tube)
CSA (Canadian Standards Agency)
CSEL (Cable Select)
CSN (Card Select Number)
CSS (Content Scramble System)
CSTN (color super-twist nematic)

D

DAC (Digital to Analog Converter)
DAE (Digital Audio Extraction)

DAO (Disc-at-Once)
DASP (Drive Action/Slave Present)
db (decibel)
DBB (dynamic bass boost)
DBR (DOS Boot Record)
DDR (Double Data Rate)
DDR SDRAM (Double-Data-Rate SDRAM)
DDWG (Digital Display Work Group)
DFP (Digital Flat Panel)
DIB (device-independent bitmap)
DIB (Dual Independent Bus)
DIME (DIrect Memory Execute)
DIMM (Dual Inline Memory Module)
DIN (Deutsche Industrie Norm)
DIP (Dual Inline Package)
DMA (Direct Memory Access)
DMM (Digital Multi-Meter)
DOS (Disk Operating System)
DPMI (DOS protected mode interface)
DPMS (Display Power-Management Signaling)
DRAM (Dynamic RAM)
DSL (Digital Subscriber Line)
DSP (digital signal processor)
DSTN (double-layer super-twist nematic)
DTV (Desktop Video)
DV (digital video)
DVD (Digital Versatile Disc)
DVI (Digital Visual Interface)
DVOM (Digital Volt-Ohm Meter)

E

EAX (Environmental Audio Extensions)
ECC (Error Correcting Code)
ECM (Electronic Control Module)
ECP (Enhanced Capabilities Port)
EDD (Enhanced Disk Drive)
EDO RAM (Extended Data Out RAM)
EEPROM (Electrically Erasable Programmable Read-Only Memory)
EFM (Eight to Fourteen Modulation)
EFM+ (Eight to Sixteen Modulation)
EISA (Extended Industry Standard Architecture)
ELF (extremely low frequency)
EMI (electromagnetic interference)
EMS (expanded memory support)
EPIC (Explicitly Parallel Instruction Computing)
EPP (Enhanced Parallel Port)
EPROM (Erasable Programmable Read-Only Memory)

ESD (electrostatic discharge)
ESDI (Enhanced Small Device Interface)

F

FAP (Fair Access Policy)
FAT (file allocation table)
FCC (Federal Communications Commission)
FDIV (Floating Point Divide)
FIFO (First In First Out)
FIT (Failures in Time)
FM (Frequency Modulation)
FPM (Fast Page Mode)
FPM DRAM (Fast Page Mode DRAM)
FPU (floating-point unit)
FSB (front-side bus)
FSK (frequency-shift keying)
FWH (Firmware Hub)

G-H

GMCH (Graphics Memory Controller Hub)
GMR (giant magneto-resistive)
GUI (graphical user interface)

HDA (Head Disk Assembly)
HERS (hard error rates)
HFC (hybrid fiber/coax)
HFC (hydrofluorocarbon)
HFS (Hierarchical File System)
HLF (High-Level Formatting)
HPA (high performance addressing)
HPFS (High Performance File System)
HRTF (Head Related Transfer Function)
HUD (Heads Up Display)
HVD (High Voltage Differential)
Hz (Hertz)

I

IC (integrated circuit)
ICH (Integrated Controller Hub)
iCOMP (Intel Comparative Microprocessor Performance)
IDE (Integrated Drive Electronics)
IML (Initial Microcode Load)
IPL (Initial Program Load)
IrDA (Infrared Data)
IRQ (Interrupt Request)
ISA (Industry Standard Architecture)
ISDN (Integrated Services Digital Network)
ITU (International Telecommunications Union)

J-K-L

JEDEC (Joint Electronic Devices Engineering Council)

JPEG (Joint Photographic Experts Group)

LAPM (Link Access Procedure for Modems)

LBA (Logical Block Addressing)

LCD (liquid crystal display)

Li-ion (lithium-ion)

LIF (Low Insertion Force)

LIM (Lotus Intel Microsoft)

LLF (Low-Level Formatting)

LVD (Low Voltage Differential)

M

MBR (master boot record)

MCA (Micro Channel Architecture)

MCM (Multi-Chip Module)

MDRAM (Multibank DRAM)

MFM (Modified Frequency Modulation)

MFT (Master File Table)

MIC (Memory Interface Controller)

MIDI (Musical Instrument Digital Interface)

MIG (Metal-In-Gap)

MMO (mobile module)

MMU (memory management unit)

MMX (Multi-Media eXtensions)

MNP (Microcom Networking Protocol)

modem (modulator/demodulator)

MOV (metal-oxide varistor)

MPEG (Motion Pictures Expert Group)

MPS (Multi-Processor Specification)

MSCDEX (Microsoft CD-ROM Extension)

MTBF (Mean Time Between Failures)

MTTF (Mean Time To Failure)

N

NC (network computer)

NCITS (National Committee on Information Technology Standards)

NDP (numeric data processor)

NEAT (New Enhanced AT)

NFAS (Non-Facility Associated Signaling)

NIC (Network Interface Card)

NiCad (nickel cadmium)

NiMH (nickel metal-hydride)

NMI (non-maskable interrupt)

NTSC (National Television System Committee)

NVRAM (Nonvolatile RAM)

O

OEM (original equipment manufacturer)

OLE (object linking and embedding)

OLGA (Organic Land Grid Array)

OTP (one time programmable)

P

P-CAV (Partial Constant Angular Velocity)

PAC (Pin Array Cartridge)

PARD (Periodic and Random Deviation)

PCA (Power Calibration Area)

PCI (Peripheral Component Interconnect)

PCMCIA (Personal Computer Memory Card International Association)

PFA (Predictive Failure Analysis)

PFC (power factor correction)

PGA (Pin Grid Array)

PIIX (PCI ISA IDE Xcelerator)

PLGA (Plastic Land Grid Array)

PMA (Program Memory Area)

PnP (Plug and Play)

POST (power on self test)

PPGA (Plastic Pin Grid Array)

PPI (Programmable Peripheral Interface)

PQFP (Plastic Quad Flat Pack)

PRI (Primary Rate Interface)

PRML (Partial-Response, Maximum-Likelihood)

PSK (phase-shift keying)

PSTN (Public Switched Telephone Network)

PSU (power supply unit)

PTP (Parallel Track Path)

Q-R

QAM (quadrature-amplitude modulation)

QFP (Quad Flat Pack)

QIC (Quarter Inch Committee)

RAB (RAID Advisory Board)

RAID (Redundant Array of Independent Disks)

RAM (Random Access Memory)

RAMDAC (Random Access Memory Digital-to-Analog Converter)

RFI (radio-frequency interference)

RIMM (Rambus Inline Memory Module)

RISC (Reduced Instruction Set Computer)

RLL (Run Length Limited)

RNG (Random Number Generator)

ROM (Read-Only Memory)

RPC (Regional Playback Control)

RRIP (Rock Ridge Interchange Protocol)
RTC (Real-Time Clock)
RTC/NVRAM (Real-Time Clock/Nonvolatile Memory)

S

S.M.A.R.T. (Self-Monitoring, Analysis, and Reporting Technology)
SAM (SCSI Architectural Model)
SASI (Shugart Associates System Interface)
SATA (Serial ATA)
SBIC (SCSI Bus Adapter Chip)
SCMS (Serial Copy Management System)
SCSI (Small Computer System Interface)
SDRAM (Synchronous DRAM)
SDSL (Symmetrical DSL)
SEC (Single Edge Contact)
SEC-DED (Single-Bit Error Correction—Double-Bit Error Detection)
SECC2 (Single Edge Contact Cartridge 2)
SEP (Single Edge Processor)
SERS (soft error rates)
SEU (single event upset)
SGRAM (Synchronous Graphics RAM)
SIMD (Single Instruction, Multiple Data)
SIMM (Single Inline Memory Module)
SIR (Serial Infrared)
SMI (System Management Interrupt)
SMM (System Management Mode)
SO-DIMM (Small Outline DIMM)
SO-RIMM (Small Outline RIMM)
SPD (Serial Presence Detect)
SPGA (Staggered Pin Grid Array)
SPP (Standard Parallel Port)
SPS (Standby Power Supply)
SPSYNC (Spindle Synchronization)
SSE (Streaming SIMD Extensions)
STP (shielded twisted pair)
SVGA (Super VGA)

T

TAB (tape automated bonding)
TAO (Track-at-Once)
TF (Thin Film)

TFT (thin film transistor)
THD (Total Harmonic Distortion)
TIP (Trouble in Paradise)
TLB (Translation Lookaside Buffer)
TSOP (Thin Small Outline Package)

U

UART (Universal Asynchronous Receiver/Transmitter)
UDF (Universal Disk Format)
UL (Underwriters Laboratories)
UMA (Upper Memory Area)
UMB (Upper Memory Block)
UPI (Universal Peripheral Interface)
UPS (Uninterruptible Power Supply)
USB (Universal Serial Bus)
UTP (unshielded twisted pair)
UVGA (Ultra VGA)

V

VESA (Video Electronics Standards Association)
VESA VIP (VESA Video Interface Port)
VFAT (virtual file allocation table)
VGA (Video Graphics Array)
VID (Voltage Identification)
VLF (very low frequency)
VLSI (very large scale integration)
VRAM (Video RAM)
VRM (Voltage Regulator Module)
VRT (Voltage Reduction Technology)
VxD (virtual device driver)

W

WORM (write-once, read many)
WRAM (Window RAM)
WYSIWYG (what you see is what you get)

X-Y-Z

XGA (eXtended Graphics Array)
XMS (extended memory specification)

ZIF (Zero Insertion Force)
ZV (Zoomed Video)

Symbols

Other Related Titles

Upgrading and Repairing PCs: Technicians Portable Reference, Third Edition
by Scott Mueller and Mark E. Soper
ISBN 0-7897-2694-7
$19.99 USA/
$29.95 CAN

How Computers Work, Sixth Edition
by Ron White
ISBN 0-7897-2549-5
$34.95 USA/$52.95 CAN

Special Edition Using Windows, XP Professional
by Bob Cowart and Brian Knittel
ISBN 0-7897-2628-9
$49.99 USA/$74.95 CAN

Special Edition Using DOS 6.22, Third Edition
by Jim Cooper
ISBN 0-7897-2573-8
$49.99 USA/$74.95 CAN

Special Edition Using Microsoft Office XP
by Ed Bott and Woody Leonhard
ISBN 0-7897-2513-4
$39.99 USA/$59.95 CAN

How Wireless Works
by Preston Gralla
ISBN 0-7897-2487-1
$29.99 USA/$44.95 CAN

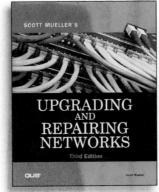

Upgrading and Repairing Networks, Third Edition
by Terry W. Ogletree
ISBN 0-7897-2557-6
$59.99 USA/
$89.95 CAN

Upgrading and Repairing PCs: A+ Certification Study Guide, Second Edition
by Scott Mueller and Mark E. Soper
ISBN 0-7897-2453-7
$34.99 USA/
$49.95 CAN

www.quecorp.com

All prices are subject to change.

Upgrading and Repairing PCs, 13th Edition

Scott Mueller

Thank you for making *Upgrading and Repairing PCs* by Scott Mueller the best-selling PC hardware repair book of all time. Please help us tailor the content of the next edition to best fit your needs by taking a few minutes to answer these questions and returning this self-addressed form. Your opinion counts!

1. Does your job involve upgrading, repairing, building, or troubleshooting PCs on a regular basis?
   - ❏ Yes   ❏ No

2. Did you buy this book for personal or professional use?
   - ❏ Professional use   ❏ Personal use   ❏ Both

3. Have you purchased previous versions of this book?
   - ❏ Yes (list versions) _____   ❏ No

4. If you are new to Scott's Upgrading and Repairing PCs, how did you first hear about it?
   - ❏ Friend   ❏ Web advertisement (list site) _____
   - ❏ Colleague   ❏ Bookstore (list book store) _____
   - ❏ School   ❏ TV (list program) _____
   - ❏ Other (specify) _____

5. Where did you buy this book?
   - ❏ Bookstore   ❏ Office club   ❏ Computer store
   - ❏ Warehouse club   ❏ Internet site (name of Web site) _____
   - ❏ Consumer electronics store   ❏ Other _____

6. Which of the following certifications have you earned or do you plan to earn in the next 6 months?
   - A+:   ❏ Have   ❏ Plan to have
   - MCSE: ❏ Have   ❏ Plan to have
   - Network+:   ❏ Have   ❏ Plan to have
   - Cisco (any)   ❏ Have   ❏ Plan to have
   - Other _____   ❏ Have   ❏ Plan to have

7. What types of processors are in the computers that you currently use, upgrade, repair, build, or troubleshoot?
   - ❏ Pentium 4   ❏ Pentium Pro   ❏ AMD K6 II
   - ❏ Pentium III   ❏ Pentium/Pentium MMX   ❏ AMD K6
   - ❏ Pentium II   ❏ Mobile Pentium   ❏ AMD K5
   - ❏ Celeron   ❏ 486   ❏ Cyrix Media GX
   - ❏ Xeon   ❏ 386   ❏ Cyrix 6x86/6x86MX
   - ❏ Itanium   ❏ AMD Athlon   ❏ Other _____
   - ❏ Mobile Pentium II   ❏ AMD Duron

8. Which of the following processor architectures do you prefer or recommend in your systems?:
   - ❏ Slot 1/Slot 2   ❏ Socket 370   ❏ Slot A
   - ❏ Socket 7   ❏ Socket 423   ❏ Socket A
   - ❏ No Preference

9. What type of bus slots are in use in the systems that you currently use, upgrade, repair, build, or troubleshoot?
   - ❏ AGP   ❏ EISA   ❏ 16-bit ISA
   - ❏ PCI   ❏ MCA   ❏ 8-bit ISA
   - ❏ VL-Bus

10. What types of removable magnetic media drives are currently in use in the systems that you use, upgrade, repair, build, or troubleshoot?
    - ❏ 1.44M 3-1/2" floppy   ❏ LS-120 (120M) SuperDisk   ❏ Syquest or other optical
    - ❏ 2.88M floppy   ❏ Zip   ❏ Sparq
    - ❏ 21M floptical   ❏ Jaz   ❏ DAT
    - ❏ Other _____

11. What type of hard drive interfaces are currently in use in the systems that you use, upgrade, repair, build, or troubleshoot?
    - ❏ IDE (ATA/33)   ❏ IDE (ATA/100)   ❏ SCSI (Any type)
    - ❏ IDE (ATA/66)

12. What operating systems are currently in use in the systems that you use, upgrade, repair, build, or troubleshoot?

- ❏ MS DOS 5 or earlier DOS versions
- ❏ MS DOS 6.x
- ❏ Windows 95
- ❏ Windows 98
- ❏ Windows Millennium Edition (Me)
- ❏ Windows NT 3.5x
- ❏ Windows NT 4
- ❏ Windows 2000 Professional
- ❏ Windows 2000 Server
- ❏ Windows XP Professional
- ❏ Windows XP Home
- ❏ Linux
- ❏ Other_____

13. What troubleshooting, diagnostic, or configuration software do you use to upgrade, repair, build, or troubleshoot PCs?

- ❏ PartitionMagic
- ❏ DriveImage
- ❏ Disk Manager
- ❏ Norton Utilities
- ❏ Checkit
- ❏ MicroScope
- ❏ Windows 98 System Information
- ❏ Other _____

14. Please list the chapter numbers of the 3 chapters in this book that you find most useful:

- ❏ Most useful _____
- ❏ 2nd most useful _____
- ❏ 3rd most useful _____

15. Please list the chapter numbers of the 3 chapters in this book that you find least useful:

- ❏ Least useful _____
- ❏ 2nd least useful _____
- ❏ 3rd least useful _____

16. Please list any other upgrading, repairing, troubleshooting, or hardware configuration topics that are not covered in this book that you would like to see covered or that are covered that you would like to see covered in more detail:

17. What other books in the Scott Mueller Library do you plan on purchasing in the next 6 months?

- ❏ *Upgrading and Repairing Networks Third Edition*
- ❏ *Upgrading and Repairing PCs: Technician's Portable Reference, Third Edition*
- ❏ *Upgrading and Repairing PCs: A+ Certification Study Guide, Second Edition*

18. Have you visited Scott Mueller's Web site at www.upgradingandrepairingpcs.com?

- ❏ Yes
- ❏ No

19. What portions of the site do you find most useful or interesting?

- ❏ Videos
- ❏ Frequently Asked Questions
- ❏ Monthly Technology Articles
- ❏ Ask Scott
- ❏ Press releases and information about Scott's books

If you would agree to be contacted for follow-up surveys or questions regarding this book or other Que books, please list fill in the following information. Otherwise, you can leave this blank:

Name _____

Address _____

City_____ State _____ ZIP code _____

Phone number _____ Email address _____

- -

Scottsdale, AZ 85267
Dept 20070
P.O. Box 15809
Upgrading and Repairing PCs 13th Edition

||۱|۱۰۰|۱۰|۱۱|۱۱|۱۱|۱۱|۱۱|۱۱

CD Installation Instructions

Installation Instructions for Windows 95, 98, Millennium Edition, NT 4, 2000, and XP

1. Insert the CD-ROM into your CD-ROM drive.
2. From the Windows desktop, double-click the My Computer icon.
3. Double-click the icon representing your CD-ROM drive (Windows XP users can skip the next step).
4. Double-click the icon titled START.EXE to run the Que Interface application.

Note

If Windows is installed on your computer, and you have the AutoPlay feature enabled, the SETUP.EXE program starts automatically whenever you insert the disc into your CD-ROM drive. Also, if the interface will not run on your machine, you should read the README.TXT in the root directory of the CD to navigate the disc via Explorer.

Note

This CD-ROM uses long and mixed-case filenames requiring the use of a protected-mode CD-ROM driver.

Installation Instructions for Windows NT 3.5.1

1. Insert the CD-ROM into your CD-ROM drive.
2. From the File Manager, select the drive letter assigned to your CD-ROM drive.
3. Open the Readme.txt file to view the contents of the CD-ROM.

MS-DOS and Other OSes

Look in the individual directories for software and associated documentation. A README file in standard text format is available in the root directory of the CD-ROM for program descriptions.